Routledge
Encyclopedia of
PHILOSOPHY

General Editor
EDWARD CRAIG

London and New York

First published 1998
by Routledge
New Fetter Lane, London EC4P 4EE
Simultaneously published in the USA and Canada
by Routledge
29 West 35th Street, New York, NY 10001

©1998 Routledge

Typeset in Monotype Times New Roman by
Routledge

Printed in England by
T J International Ltd, Padstow, Cornwall, England

Printed on acid-free paper which conforms to ANS1.Z39, 48-1992 and ISO 9706 standards

British Library Cataloguing-in-Publication Data
A catalogue record for this book is available from the British Library

The Library of Congress Cataloguing-in-Publication data is given in volume 10.

ISBN: 0415-07310-3 (10-volume set)
ISBN: 0415-18706-0 (volume 1)
ISBN: 0415-18707-9 (volume 2)
ISBN: 0415-18708-7 (volume 3)
ISBN: 0415-18709-5 (volume 4)
ISBN: 0415-18710-9 (volume 5)
ISBN: 0415-18711-7 (volume 6)
ISBN: 0415-18712-5 (volume 7)
ISBN: 0415-18713-3 (volume 8)
ISBN: 0415-18714-1 (volume 9)
ISBN: 0415-18715-X (volume 10)

ISBN: 0415-16916-X (CD-ROM)
ISBN: 0415-16917-8 (10-volume set and CD-ROM)

Contents

Using the *Encyclopedia*

List of entries

Using the *Encyclopedia*

The *Routledge Encyclopedia of Philosophy* is designed for ease of use. The following notes outline its organization and editorial approach and explain the ways of locating material. This will help readers make the most of the *Encyclopedia*.

SEQUENCE OF ENTRIES

The *Encyclopedia* contains 2,054 entries (from 500 to 19,000 words in length) arranged in nine volumes with a tenth volume for the index. Volumes 1–9 are arranged in a single alphabetical sequence, as follows:

Volume 1: A posteriori *to* Bradwardine, Thomas

Volume 2: Brahman *to* Derrida, Jacques

Volume 3: Descartes, René *to* Gender and science

Volume 4: Genealogy *to* Iqbal, Muhammad

Volume 5: Irigaray, Luce *to* Lushi chunqiu

Volume 6: Luther, Martin *to* Nifo, Agostino

Volume 7: Nihilism *to* Quantum mechanics, interpretation of

Volume 8: Questions *to* Sociobiology

Volume 9: Sociology of knowledge *to* Zoroastrianism

Alphabetical order

Entries are listed in alphabetical order by word rather than by letter with all words including *and*, *in*, *of* and *the* being given equal status. The exceptions to this rule are as follows:

- biographies: where the forenames and surname of a philosopher are inverted, the entry takes priority in the sequence, for example:

  Alexander, Samuel (1859–1938)
  Alexander of Aphrodisias (*c.* AD 200)
  Alexander of Hales (*c.* 1185–1245)

- names with prefixes, which follow conventional alphabetical placing (see Transliteration and naming conventions below).

A complete alphabetical list of entries is given in each of the Volumes 1 to 9.

Inverted titles

Titles of entries consisting of more than one word are often inverted so that the key term (in a thematic or signpost entry) or the surname (in a biographical entry) determines the place of the entry in the alphabetical sequence, for example:

  Law, philosophy of *or*
  Market, ethics of the *or*
  Hart, Herbert Lionel Adolphus (1907–93)

Conceptual organization

Several concerns have had a bearing on the sequence of entries where there is more than one key term.

In deciding on the sequence of entries we have tried, wherever possible, to integrate philosophy as it is known and studied in the USA and Europe with philosophy from around the world. This means that the reader will frequently find entries from different philosophical traditions or approaches to the same topic close to each other, for example, in the sequence:

  Political philosophy [signpost entry]
  Political philosophy, history of
  Political philosophy in classical Islam
  Political philosophy, Indian

Similarly, in entries where a philosophical tradition or approach is surveyed we have tried, whenever appropriate, to keep philosophical traditions from different countries together. An example is the sequence:

  Confucian philosophy, Chinese
  Confucian philosophy, Japanese
  Confucian philosophy, Korean
  Confucius (551–479 BC)

Finally, historical entries are usually placed with contemporary entries under the topic rather than the historical period. For example, in the sequence:

  Language, ancient philosophy of
  Language and gender
  Language, conventionality of
  Language, early modern philosophy of
  Language, Indian theories of
  Language, innateness of

DUMMY TITLES

The *Encyclopedia* has been extensively cross-referenced in order to help the reader locate their topic of interest. Dummy titles are placed throughout the alphabetical sequence of entries to direct the reader to the actual title of the entry where a topic is discussed. This may be under a different entry title, a synonym or as part of a larger entry. Wherever useful we have included the numbers of the sections (§§) in which a particular topic or subject is discussed. Examples of this type of cross-reference are:

AFRICAN AESTHETICS *see*
AESTHETICS, AFRICAN

CANGUILHEM, GEORGES *see*
FRENCH PHILOSOPHY OF SCIENCE §§3–4

TAO *see* DAO

GLOSSARY OF LOGICAL AND MATHEMATICAL TERMS

A glossary of logical and mathematical terms is provided to help users with terms from formal logic and mathematics. 'See also' cross-references to the glossary are provided at the end of entries where the user might benefit from help with unfamiliar terms. The glossary can be found in Volume 5 under L (LOGICAL AND MATHEMATICAL TERMS, GLOSSARY OF).

THE INDEX VOLUME

Volume 10 is devoted to a comprehensive index of key terms, concepts and names covered in Volumes 1–9, allowing readers to reap maximum benefit from the *Encyclopedia*. A guide to the index can be found at the beginning of the index. The index volume includes a full listing of contributors, their affiliations and the entries they have written. It also includes permission acknowledgements, listed in publisher order.

STRUCTURE OF ENTRIES

The *Routledge Encyclopedia of Philosophy* contains three types of entry:

- 'signpost' entries, for example, METAPHYSICS; SCIENCE, PHILOSOPHY OF; EAST ASIAN PHILOSOPHY. These entries provide an accessible overview of the sub-disciplines or regional coverage within the *Encyclopedia*; they provide a 'map' which directs the reader towards and around the many entries relating to each topic;
- thematic entries, ranging from general entries such as KNOWLEDGE, CONCEPT OF, to specialized topics such as VIRTUE EPISTEMOLOGY;
- biographical entries, devoted to individual philosophers, emphasizing the work rather than the life of the subject and with a list of the subject's major works.

Overview

All thematic and biographical entries begin with an overview which provides a concise and accessible summary of the topic or subject. This can be referred to on its own if the reader does not require the depth and detail of the main part of the entry.

Table of contents

All thematic and biographical entries over 1000 words in length are divided into sections and have a numbered table of contents following the overview. This gives the headings of each of the sections of the entry, enabling the reader to see the scope and structure of the entry at a glance. For example, the table of contents in the entry on HERACLITUS:

1 Life and work
2 Methodology
3 Unity of opposites and perspectivism
4 Cosmology
5 Psychology, ethics and religion
6 Influence

Cross-references within an entry

Entries in the *Encyclopedia* have been extensively cross-referenced in order to indicate other entries that may be of interest to the reader. There are two types of cross-reference in the *Encyclopedia*:

1. 'See' cross-references

Cross-references within the text of an entry direct the reader to other entries on or closely related to the topic under discussion. For example, a reader may be directed from a conceptual entry to a biography of the philosopher whose work is under discussion or vice versa. These internal cross-references appear in small capital letters, either in parentheses, for example:

> Opponents of naturalism before and since Wittgenstein have been animated by the notion that the aims of social science are not causal explanation and improving prediction, but uncovering rules that make social life intelligible to its participants (see EXPLANATION IN HISTORY AND SOCIAL SCIENCE).

or sometimes, when the reference is to a person who

has a biographical entry, as small capitals in the text itself, for example:

> Thomas NAGEL emphasizes the discrepancy between the objective insignificance of our lives and projects and the seriousness and energy we devote to them.

For entries over 1,000 words in length we have included the numbers of the sections (§) in which a topic is discussed, wherever useful, for example:

> In *Nicomachean Ethics*, Aristotle criticizes Plato's account for not telling us anything about particular kinds of goodness (see ARISTOTLE §§ 21–6).

2. 'See also' cross-references

At the end of the text of each entry, 'See also' cross-references guide the reader to other entries of related interest, such as more specialized entries, biographical entries, historical entries, geographical entries and so on. These cross-references appear in small capitals in alphabetical order.

References

References in the text are given in the Harvard style, for example, Kant (1788), Rawls (1971). Exceptions to this rule are made when presenting works with established conventions, for example, with some major works in ancient philosophy. Full bibliographical details are given in the 'List of works' and 'References and further reading'.

Bibliography

List of works

Biographical entries are followed by a list of works which gives full bibliographical details of the major works of the philosopher. This is in chronological order and includes items cited in the text, significant editions, dates of composition for pre-modern works (where known), preferred English-language translations and English translations for the titles of untranslated foreign-language works.

References and further reading

Both biographical and thematic entries have a list of references and further reading. Items are listed alphabetically by author's name. (Publications with joint authors are listed under the name of the first author and after any individual publications by that author). References cited in the text are preceded by an asterisk (*). Further reading which the reader may find particularly useful is also included.

The authors and editors have attempted to provide the fullest possible bibliographical information for every item.

Annotations

Publications in the 'List of works' and the 'References and further reading' have been annotated with a brief description of the content so that their relevance to readers' interests can be quickly assessed.

EDITORIAL STYLE

Spelling and punctuation in the *Encyclopedia* have been standardized to follow British English usage.

Transliteration and naming conventions

All names and terms from non-roman alphabets have been romanized in the *Encyclopedia*. Foreign names have been given according to the conventions within the particular language.

Arabic

Arabic has been transliterated in a simplified form, that is, without macrons or subscripts. Names of philosophers are given in their Arabic form rather than their Latinate form, for example, IBN RUSHD rather than AVERROES. Arabic names beginning with the prefix 'al-' are alphabetized under the substantive part of the name and not the prefix, for example:

> KILWARDBY, ROBERT (d. 1279)
> AL-KINDI, ABU YUSUF YAQUB IBN ISHAQ (d. *c*.866–73)
> KNOWLEDGE AND JUSTIFICATION, COHERENCE THEORY OF

Arabic names beginning with the prefix 'Ibn' are alphabetized under 'I'.

Chinese, Korean and Japanese

Chinese has been transliterated using the Pinyin system. Dummy titles in the older Wade–Giles system are given for names and key terms; these direct the reader to the Pinyin titles.

Japanese has been transliterated using a modified version of the Hepburn system.

Chinese, Japanese and Korean names are given in Asian form, that is, surname preceding forenames, for example:

> WANG FUZHI
> NISHITANI KEIJI

The exception is where an author has chosen to present their own name in conventional Western form.

Hebrew

Hebrew has been transliterated in a simplified form, that is, without macrons or subscripts.

Russian

Cyrillic characters have been transliterated using the Library of Congress system. Russian names are usually given with their patronymic, for example, BAKUNIN, MIKHAIL ALEKSANDROVICH.

Sanskrit

A guide to the pronunciation of Sanskrit can be found in the INDIAN AND TIBETAN PHILOSOPHY signpost entry.

Tibetan

Tibetan has been transliterated using the Wylie system. Dummy titles in the Virginia system are given for names and key terms. A guide to Tibetan pronunciation can be found in the INDIAN AND TIBETAN PHILOSOPHY signpost entry.

European names

Names beginning with the prefixes 'de', 'von' or 'van' are usually alphabetized under the substantive part of the name. For example:

BEAUVOIR, SIMONE DE
HUMBOLDT, WILHELM VON

The exception to this rule is when the person is either a national of or has spent some time living or working in an English-speaking country. For example:

DE MORGAN, AUGUSTUS
VON WRIGHT, GEORG HENRIK

Names beginning with the prefix 'de la' or 'le' are alphabetized under the prefix 'la' or 'le'. For example:

LA FORGE, LOUIS DE
LE DOEUFF, MICHÈLE

Names beginning with 'Mc' or 'Mac' are treated as 'Mac' and appear before Ma.

Historical names

Medieval and Renaissance names where a person is not usually known by a surname are alphabetized under the forename, for example:

GILES OF ROME
JOHN OF SALISBURY

List of entries

Below is a complete list of entries in the order in which they appear in the *Routledge Encyclopedia of Philosophy.*

An alphabetical list of contributors, their affiliations and the entries they have written can be found in the index volume (Volume 10).

SOCIOLOGY OF KNOWLEDGE

Sociologists of knowledge contribute to the enterprise of generating a naturalistic account of knowledge by describing and explaining the observed characteristics of shared cultures. They assume that knowledge can be treated as an object of empirical investigation (rather than mere celebration or condemnation). Because science is understandably taken as our best example of knowledge, the sociology of scientific knowledge plays a pivotal role in the field. It is argued that our natural reasoning capacities, and our sense experience, are necessary but not sufficient conditions for scientific knowledge. Sociologists looking for the causes of its content and style focus on the contribution of conventions and institutions.

The aim of sociologists of knowledge, is to identify such features as (1) the general character of the processes by which new cultural members are 'socialized', that is, trained and educated; (2) the specific institutions and authorities charged with this task in particular cases; (3) the mechanisms by which a body of culture is kept relatively stable and hence available for use; (4) the precise circumstances and purposes associated with its employment on particular occasions; (5) the processes by which change is managed and its locus and extent negotiated; (6) the distribution of taken-for-granted beliefs according to status and membership criteria, for example, professional or amateur, male or female, doctor and patient, scientist or technician.

Sociologists emphasize that accepted systems of belief cannot be adequately accounted for by the reasonableness of our individual cognitive faculties, or our sensory experience of the environment. Reason and experience are vital parts of the story of knowledge (social learning and cultural transmission would be unintelligible without them), but they are necessary, not sufficient, conditions. There is always the need to introduce further elements such as the traditional background of practices on which experience impinges, and the highly consequential fact that individuals must make allowances in their calculations for the calculations of others. Individual reason operates in a social context. Furthermore, our individual conclusions and reactions must be coordinated and collectively assessed before they count as knowledge rather than subjective belief, idiosyncrasy or error.

These empirical features are conspicuously visible in scientific culture, hence the central role played by the sociology of scientific knowledge within the

general field. This also explains why, wittingly or unwittingly, philosophers of science have done much of the theoretical groundwork for the discipline. In particular they have emphasized that scientific conclusions are under-determined by observational or experimental input, and by the canons of formal logic or the powers of individual reason. Whether it be Duhem's insight that hypotheses cannot meet the test of experience in isolation, Popper's insistence on the conjectural character of all knowledge claims, Carnap's discovery of an infinity of inductive strategies, Kuhn's highlighting the role of dogmatically accepted paradigms, or Hesse's (1974) development of a Bayesian approach with its dependence on a negotiable network of shared classifications and prior probabilities, the conclusions all point in the same direction. Scientific knowledge – our best example of knowledge – depends for its structure, stability, content and dynamics on phenomena best identified, and investigated, as social institutions (see DUHEM, P.M.M. §4; CARNAP, R.; POPPER, K.R.; KUHN, T.S. §2).

Not all philosophical work is relevant in this way. Some gives every appearance of being deliberately fashioned to inhibit naturalistic inquiry. There are philosophers who effectively define 'rationality' in terms of its supposed opposition to causality, and particularly social causality. They assume social considerations can only illuminate the general conditions encouraging or discouraging the progress of knowledge, and explain distortions, or deviations from the demands of the scientific method. The task of the sociologist is then confined to explaining, say, the deleterious effect of totalitarian state interference with the freedom of science. This limited agenda may be called the 'weak programme' in the sociology of knowledge, in contrast to the 'strong programme' suggested by under-determination, which seeks the social dimension to be found in all bodies of knowledge however they are currently evaluated.

Some of the best work in the sociology of knowledge, concentrating on the hardest cases, has been done by historians of science. Ignoring the proscriptions of philosophers who would restrict them to the weak programme, they have provided an abundance of high-quality studies, readable as contributions to the strong programme. These exhibit the problematic, contextual character of the interpretation of experimental findings and, in many cases, press the argument further and identify plausible causes for the preferences and opinions of the actors involved, for example, contingent commitments to a theory or research method, or the utility the result had for a range of goals and purposes, some of them narrowly professional, others broader and even overtly political. These studies often identify an interest at work. It is important to realize that interests can be generated internally, within the workings of the social system of science itself. The sociology of knowledge carries no prior commitment to what is sometimes called 'externalism', rather than 'internalism', in its methods. The richness of this empirical material precludes summary here, but it spans early Royal Society work on the air pump, the attractions of the corpuscular philosophy, nineteenth-century anatomy and evolutionary theory, cellular biology, geological controversies, non-Euclidean geometry, astronomical discoveries, statistical techniques, genetic theory, and modern particle physics.

Sadly, many of the critical discussions of the sociology of knowledge are blighted by ill-informed and hostile stereotypes. These sustain a number of oft-repeated arguments that are widely taken to discredit the enterprise. For example, the sociology of knowledge is said to be 'self-refuting'. The charge begs the question, because it simply takes for granted the premises of the weak programme: that causal determination equals error or distortion. Again, a distinction is often drawn between the 'context of discovery' and the 'context of justification'. Is not the sociologist concerned with the origin of beliefs, and is that not irrelevant to their epistemological status? In fact, sociologists have little to offer on the origin of ideas, but much to say about their evaluation and subsequent elaboration; so the criticism gets things the wrong way round. Nor, as is often alleged, need the sociology of knowledge derive from, or issue in, a negative stance towards the beliefs under study, as if the only purpose were to 'unmask'. To exhibit, the social construction of science is no more to criticize it than studying the physiology of the eye is to criticize vision.

See also: FEMINIST EPISTEMOLOGY; FOUCAULT, M.; NATURALISM IN SOCIAL SCIENCE

References and further reading

Barnes, B. (1982) *T.S. Kuhn and Social Science*, London: Macmillan. (Provides an excellent sociological reading of Kuhn, and brings out the connection with Hesse's work.)

Bloor, D. (1991) *Knowledge and Social Imagery*, Chicago, IL: University of Chicago Press. (A defence of the strong programme with a discussion of some of the main philosophical objections.)

Brown, J.R. (1984) *Scientific Rationality: The Sociological Turn*, Dordrecht: Reidel. (A selection of papers both by those for and those against the sociology of knowledge in its strong form.)

Collins, H. (1992) *Changing Order*, Chicago, IL: University of Chicago Press. (Valuable study centring on the dispute over gravity wave detection and the problematic character of replication.)

Desmond, A. (1989) *The Politics of Evolution*, Chicago, IL: University of Chicago Press. (Fascinating analysis of the social basis of the scientific elite's fears about 'materialistic' and (pre-Darwinian) evolutionary ideas.)

Fleck, L. (1935) *Genesis and Development of a Scientific Fact*, Chicago, IL: University of Chicago Press, 1979. (Outstanding and pioneering work in the sociology of knowledge. It was mentioned in passing by Reichenbach, and then forgotten until it acted as a source of inspiration for Kuhn.)

Harwood, J. (1994) *Styles of Scientific Thought*, Chicago, IL: University of Chicago Press. (A study of the German genetics community between 1900 and 1933, describes and explains the stylistic and substantial differences between German and US genetics, and differences within the German community.)

* Hesse, M. (1974) *The Structure of Scientific Inference*, London: Macmillan. (Sophisticated Bayesian model of knowledge, particularly useful to the sociologist because of its 'network' model of a classificatory system.)

Hollis, M. and Lukes, S. (1982) *Rationality and Relativism*, Oxford: Blackwell. (Arguments for and against a 'relativist' account of knowledge of the kind associated with the sociology of knowledge.)

Pickering, A. (1984) *Constructing Quarks*, Edinburgh: Edinburgh University Press. (A detailed history of elementary particle physics.)

Shapin, S. (1982) 'History of Science and its Sociological Reconstructions', *History of Science* 20: 157–211. (Though now dated, it still provides the best introduction to the literature on the sociology of knowledge. Contains a bibliography of 149 items.)

Shapin, S. and Schaffer, S. (1985) *Leviathan and the Air-Pump*, Princeton, NJ: Princeton University Press. (An account of the disputes between Hobbes and Boyle over the interpretation of the air-pump experiments, emphasizing the unity of the problem of natural order and social order.)

DAVID BLOOR

SOCIOLOGY, THEORIES OF

Throughout the history of sociology, three types of theorizing have co-existed, sometimes uneasily. 'The-

ories of' provide abstract models of empirical processes; they function both as guides for sociological research and as sources for covering laws whose falsification or validation is intended to provide the basis for a cumulative science. 'Presuppositional studies' abstract away from particular empirical processes, seeking instead to articulate the fundamental properties of social action and order; meta-methodological warrants for the scientific investigation of societies; and normative foundations for moral evaluations of contemporary social life. 'Hermeneutical theory' addresses these basic sociological questions more indirectly, by interpreting the meanings and intentions of classical texts.

The relation between these three forms of theorizing varies historically. In the post-war period, under the institutional and intellectual influence of US sociologists like Parsons and Merton, presuppositional and hermeneutical issues seemed to be settled; 'theories of' proliferated and prospects seemed bright for a cumulative, theoretically-organized science of society. Subsequent social and intellectual developments undermined this brief period of relative consensus. In the midst of the crises of the 1960s and 1970s, presuppositional and hermeneutical studies gained much greater importance, and became increasingly disarticulated from empirical 'theories of'. Confronting the prospect of growing fragmentation, in the late 1970s and early 1980s there appeared a series of ambitious, synthetical works that sought to reground the discipline by providing coherent examples of how the different forms of sociological theory could once again be intertwined. While widely read inside and outside the discipline, these efforts failed in their foundational ambitions.

As a result of this failure, over the last decade sociological theory has had diminishing influence both inside the discipline and without. Inside social science, economic and anthropological theories have been much more influential. In the broader intellectual arena, the most important presuppositional and hermeneutical debates have occurred in philosophy and literary studies. Sociological theorists are now participating in these extra-disciplinary debates even as they have returned to the task of developing 'theories of' particular institutional domains. The future of specifically sociological theory depends on reviving coherent relationships between these different theoretical domains.

1   The forms of sociological theory

Theories of. Following what is taken to be the natural science approach, theorists have produced sets of highly general causal or descriptive propositions aimed at modelling empirical processes (Stinchcombe 1968). These models have had a dual purpose. On the one hand, they are guides to more specific empirical studies of particular social processes. On the other hand, they are designed to produce putative covering laws which such particular empirical studies will falsify or validate.

Max Weber's famous essay on bureaucracy can be viewed as providing a classic example of theorizing along these lines. Weber presented a series of propositions about the structure and processes of bureaucratic authority that has provided the central reference for empirical studies, complementary elaborations, and competing general models in the sociological study of organizations over the last fifty years. In an effort to test the model's insistence on rationality, formal rules and hierarchical command, for example studies emerged that emphasized informal organization and decentralized, problem-oriented decision making; the limited, primarily short-term rationality of bureaucratic action; and even the ceremonial, merely ritualistic qualities of bureaucratic processes. Yet, because Weber's original essay has been accepted as an empirically grounded 'theory of', the field of organizational studies has organized and conceptualized itself as being guided by an accumulative, increasingly elaborated, essentially progressive theoretical model.

While few theoretical models have exercised comparable hegemony, in many empirical sub-fields of sociology one can find 'theories of' that have played similar roles for more limited periods of time.

Presuppositional studies. Rather than developing empirical generalizations to guide studies or provide covering laws, another kind of theoretical effort generalizes away from particular empirical realms to consider fundamental issues that are held to undergird them (Alexander 1982).

Some of these theoretical efforts discuss issues like action and order: is social action practical and goal-oriented or is it normatively guided and oriented by aesthetic, emotional, or moral concerns? Does the patterned nature of social activity derive from controls exercised over individuals by institutions, whether coercive or moral, or does it emerge from pragmatic negotiations between actors as they spontaneously confront the unpredictable contingencies of everyday life?

Some presuppositional studies address more meta-methodological issues: should sociology be modelled after the nomological sciences that aim at producing covering laws and abstract away from the particular and idiographic, or should it be more hermeneutical and aim at producing rich ethnographic interpretations of particular institutions and events?

Other presuppositional studies take the form of critical ideological and moral inquiry: is capitalism an oppressive social system? Is modernity healthy? What are the social obligations of scientists when they are faced with injustice or abuse?

If we consider the relationship of presuppositional studies to the earlier example of bureaucracy, we find an illuminating point of contrast with the 'theories of' approach. Rather than arguing on the basis of empirical studies that informal ties exist alongside formal rules, presuppositional theorists have argued that, because emotion is central to action and cooperation basic to order, bureaucratic institutions simply cannot be conceived or explained in the way Weber proposed. Arguing that Weber was, in fact, generalizing from only distinctively Prussian authority structures rather than from bureaucratic organizations as such, other presuppositional theorists have pushed for a case-study approach to organizations in different countries and different historical milieu. Others, focusing on the moral dimension, have condemned both the idea and the practice of bureaucratic organization for ignoring the possibility of democratic self-regulation.

Hermeneutical. 'Theories of' and presuppositional studies are highly abstract enterprises, each broaching the question 'what is society?' in a direct way. By contrast, the third form of sociological theorizing is not abstracting but idiographic and concrete. Hermeneutical theory seeks to explain human society by explicating, through interpretive argument, the meaning of sociological texts whose consequentiality has given them a classical status (Levine 1995).

These textual efforts are neither historical nor literary. Rather than being primarily directed to questions of intellectual and social context or to questions of genre and aesthetic form, they engage the hermeneutical method to investigate the traditional questions of sociology, albeit in an indirect and idiographic rather than direct and abstracting manner. By reinterpreting canonical texts, hermeneutical readings challenge extant theories and empirical studies that derive their authority from the covering laws or the presuppositions espoused by these classics. By producing new and authoritative versions of canonical texts, the hermeneutical ambition is to re-orient theoretical and empirical practice.

Once again, Weber's organizational studies provide an illustration. Arguing that Parsons' translation of Weber's term, *Herrschaft*, as 'imperative coordination'

implied that Weber intended a consensual rather than coercive model of authority, hermeneutical theorists have suggested that 'domination' is closer to the meaning Weber intended (Roth 1968). This translation challenge has, in fact, been part of the broader theoretical debate between functionalist and conflict-oriented 'theories of' various institutional realms (see FUNCTIONALISM IN SOCIAL SCIENCE). Within the specific field of organizational studies, hermeneutical students of Weber's corpus have argued that he envisaged his essay on bureaucracy primarily as a historical and comparative explanation of the development of Western authority structures over time rather than as an effort to model the processes involved in contemporary organizations as such. Making connections to the emphases on charisma and morality in Weber's other historical studies, these hermeneutical theorists have, indirectly, tried to reframe his original bureaucracy model as one that can incorporate without contradiction the informal, emotional, and normative elements of organizational life.

Very similar kinds of hermeneutical arguments have been made in regard to the classical writings of Marx, Durkheim, and Parsons. Through translations and explications of his earlier writings, Marx has been reinterpreted as being more concerned with the qualitative, cultural, and psychological problems of capitalism than with the quantitative and economic. By exposing the increasing influence of religion in Durkheim's later and posthumously published work, Durkheim has been reinterpreted as aiming to produce a symbolic rather than morphological sociology. By emphasizing the disjuncture between the early and the later Parsons, hermeneutical theorists have indirectly argued against systems theory and in support of more pragmatic presuppositions about action and order (see SYSTEMS THEORY IN SOCIAL SCIENCE §§1–2).

While these three forms of theoretical activity in sociology represent distinct and long-standing traditions, each of them has been the object of polemical challenges from champions of the other types. In practice, however, the three types have often interpenetrated one another. Thus, rather than taking as data only empirical studies, 'theories of' particular institutions have often justified their abstract models by making textual interpretations, challenging or elaborating classical works that earlier sought to explain the same institution. Presuppositional studies, for their part, are often deeply implicated in evaluative statements about the moral worth of different approaches to action and order. Similarly, ideological debates are replete with explanatory claims about the empirical causes and effects of particular institutions.

The classical example of such a blurred genre is Talcott Parsons' *The Structure of Social Action* (1937), perhaps the single most influential theoretical work of post-war sociology. Parsons presented the work primarily as a hermeneutical one, describing it as an investigation of the writings of a group of important European social thinkers, Pareto, Marshall, Durkheim, and Weber. In the lengthy first section of his work, however, Parsons developed a series of highly abstract presuppositional arguments; while ostensibly provided to facilitate his subsequent textual interpretation, this discussion became a fundamental, *sui generis* theoretical argument in itself. Throughout his subsequent exegetical discussions, Parsons also produced pointedly polemical 'theories of', using his textual interpretations to challenge existing empirical models of various institutions.

2 Sociological theory in the post-war world

While the three forms of sociological theorizing have, indeed, always interpenetrated in significant ways, over time there have been remarkable shifts in the relative importance of each genre in the theoretical field. These changes are caused not only by intellectual developments within sociology but also by developments outside of it, by shifts in the intellectual life of society and in the institutions of society itself. These shifts have had significant effects on the relation of sociological theory to theory in other social scientific disciplines and to theoretical efforts in philosophy and aesthetics.

Despite the fundamental and continuing role of theories produced by classical sociological theorists – Marx, Weber, Durkheim, Simmel and Mead – the story line of 'modern' sociological theory begins in 1937 with the publication of Parsons' *The Structure of Social Action*. Despite its intrinsic intellectual power, this blurred genre made virtually no impact at the time. Under the impact of the Great Depression and massive social movements on the Left and Right, US and European sociology was highly fragmented. No single institutional or intellectual centre dominated, and within each sociological community radically divergent theories struggled for recognition. In the wake of the world-historical realignment that followed the Second World War, the social and intellectual situation was fundamentally changed. While European theorizing retained its distinctive forms and practices, the social stability, institutional power, and ideological hegemony of the USA allowed it to emerge as the arbiter of sociology in its professionalized, disciplinary form.

In this new context, Parsons emerged as the dominant theorist of his time. A new generation of sociologists came to consider his (1937) work as having established the canonical foundations of a distinctively modern sociological theory. While this theory was termed 'structural-functionalism', it might more accurately be considered a version of Kantianism (Munch 1981). Rather than using biological models to establish an organicist model of society, Parsons actually devoted his efforts to describing the institutional, psychological, and cultural foundations of differentiated and pluralistic societies that could process economic, political, religious, and ethnic conflicts in democratic, fundamentally cooperative ways (Turner and Holton 1986). Within this Parsonian framework, during the 1950s and early 1960s 'theories of' dominated other types of theoretical practice, and sociology increasingly was viewed as a maturing and cumulative science of society. This optimistic scientism was encouraged by the impression that the post-war explosion of large scale quantitative empirical studies were conducted within the rubric of functionalist thought, an illusion encouraged by the institutionally-oriented, 'middle level' functionalist models of Parsons' discipline (Merton 1967).

Because of its high degree of internal consensus, its cumulative character, and its high degree of intellectual creativity, in the post-war period US sociological theory achieved a high level of influence, both inside the discipline of sociology and outside. Historians, political scientists, and anthropologists, for example, drew heavily upon the premises of modernization theory, which was the historical foundation of Kantian functionalism. Literary critics drew upon sociological theory to investigate the origins of modern genres. While philosophy remained largely in the analytical mode, more historical and socially-oriented philosophical efforts also drew upon these sociological ideas.

The social and intellectual upheavals that rocked Western societies between the mid 1960s and the 1970s had the effect of displacing not only Kantian functionalism but the approach that emphasized 'theories of'. Pragmatic, phenomenological, and behaviouristic traditions re-emerged as 'micro-sociological theories', powerfully challenging Parsonian theory in various domains (Homans 1961; Garfinkel 1967). Conflict theories and Marxism became increasingly influential, constituting 'macro' challenges to functionalism's optimistic and relatively consensual social models (Collins 1975). As both the models and the canon established by Parsons were put to the test, sociological theorists became increasingly involved in presuppositional and hermeneutical studies (see PRAGMATISM; BEHAVIOURISM IN THE SOCIAL SCIENCES).

By the end of the 1970s, Parsons' challengers had triumphed. Sociology was proclaimed a 'multi-paradigmatic' field which, once again, was devoid of either an institutional or theoretical centre. Paradoxically, even as this dramatic sea change reached its climax, the historical context facilitating it dramatically changed. The waves of anti-Establishment protests subsided, backlash movements against them asserted increasing strength, and Western societies began to experience conservative retrenchments. During the same period, state-communist societies began to crumble under their own weight.

These shifts placed sociological theory in a precarious position, even when its prestige was at its greatest height. Responding to the de-centred situation of sociology and to the broader sense of imminent transition in the intellectual and social world at large, the most influential theoretical works that emerged at this time were marked by their refusal to endorse the notion of pluralistic and relativistic social science. To the contrary, these highly ambitious theoretical efforts stepped outside their respective traditions and created grand syntheses (Bourdieu 1977; Giddens 1984; Habermas 1984; Alexander 1982; Collins 1975). Despite marked differences, they had a common aim: to found a new era of intellectual cooperation and social progress in a post-positivistic frame. Indeed, with their combination of hermeneutical, presuppositional, and explanatory ambitions, these efforts closely resembled Parsons' earlier effort to overcome intellectual and social fragmentation in 1937.

But the post-war world that had allowed Parsons' earlier effort to succeed had been dramatically and fundamentally changed. Despite the fact that these ambitiously synthetical works were widely read and admired both inside and outside the discipline of sociology, they turned out to have brought the curtain down on an era rather than ushering in a new one. In a *fin-de-siècle* world torn between deeply pessimistic moods of fragmentation and decline and wildly optimistic hopes of utopian rebirth, none of these synthetic efforts to recreate a new version of Neo-Kantian sociological theory succeeded in gaining hegemony or even in creating traditions that could convincingly establish coherent new lines of theoretical and empirical work.

3 Sociological theory today

The failure of these synthetic efforts, and the continuing impact of the social and intellectual conditions that gave rise to them, has given rise to developments that have had significant repercussions for sociological theory.

Self-identified 'sociological theorists' have been increasingly less able to exert influence over the explanatory models and canonical texts inside the discipline of sociology. Instead, sociological theory is now increasingly viewed merely as one sub-field among many, one devoted to hermeneutical reconstructions of the origins of classical texts, on the one hand, and to 'meta-theoretical' commentaries and arguments about presuppositions, on the other (Ritzer 1992). With the exception of the work of BOURDIEU, whose influence, while substantial, remains relatively limited, there exists at present no over-arching general theory that combines hermeneutical and presuppositional arguments with sociological 'theories of' various institutional spheres. While empirical sub-fields continue to be organized theoretically, and the three different types of sociological theorizing flourish within each, these discussions are hermetically cut off from the more generalized theoretical debates in the discipline at large.

Distinctively sociological theories have lost their influence *vis-à-vis* theorizing in other social scientific disciplines. This is demonstrated by two contradictory developments. The model of society as based upon exchanges between rational actors, derived from economics, has become an international cross-disciplinary tradition that already exercises a deep influence in political science and, increasingly, in sociology (Coleman 1990). At the same time, cultural models of symbolic action and ritual order, which emerged in anthropology (Geertz 1973), have had far-reaching theoretical and empirical effects in history and sociology.

The most influential presuppositional and hermeneutical studies, and even some of the most important theoretical discussions about the nature of contemporary societies (that is, 'theories of'), now occur outside the social sciences in philosophy and literary studies. Under the influence of Michel FOUCAULT and Jacques DERRIDA, deconstructionism and postmodernism have established an anti-universalist position that has had widespread repercussions throughout Western intellectual life, including the social sciences (Bauman 1995; Seidman 1991). In opposition to this position, Neo-Kantian theorizing about the possibilities for universalism and democracy has been rejuvenated under the influence of John RAWLS and Jürgen HABERMAS (§1) (Cohen and Arato 1992). Between these two poles there have emerged arguments for new forms of pluralistic, identity-based democratic associations, arguments derived from Aristotle, Hegel, and US pragmatism and associated most significantly with the writings of Charles TAYLOR (§5), Richard RORTY, and Michael Walzer (Boltanski and Thevenot 1991; Warnke 1992).

4 Prospects

In considering the future development of sociological theory, it is important to observe two apparently contradictory developments within the work of those who participated in the creation of synthetic general theories in the 1980s. Leading sociological theorists are now participating in the broader philosophical, political, and literary debates outside of the discipline itself (Calhoun 1992). At the same time, they have also turned towards empirically-focused topics and are developing 'theories of' particular institutional spheres. Only if and when these very different kinds of practices can be brought back together (Mouzelis 1995) will sociological theory regain the coherence, vitality, and intellectual power that allowed it to exercise such wide influence in an earlier day.

References and further reading

* Alexander, J. (1982) 'Positivism, presuppositions, and current controversies', in *Theoretical Logic in Sociology*, London: Routledge & Kegan Paul, vol. l.
—— (1995) *Fin-de-Siècle Social Theory: Relativism, Reduction, and the Problem of Reason*, London: Verso. (Criticizes the alarming growth of relativism in recent social theory.)
* Bauman, Z. (1995) *Life in Fragments: Essays in Postmodern Morality*, Oxford: Blackwell. (Argues that our new era may yet prove to represent a dawning, rather than a twilight, for ethics, emancipated from the false consciousness entailed by modernity.)
* Boltanski, L. and Thevenot, L. (1991) *De la justification: Les economies de la grandeur*, Paris: Gallimard.
* Bourdieu, P. (1972) *Esquisse d'une théorie de la pratique: précédée de trois études d'ethnologie kabyle*, Geneva: Droz; trans. R. Nice, *Outline of a Theory of Practice*, Cambridge: Cambridge University Press, 1977. (Bourdieu discusses the main outline of his social theory. Complex. The English version differs substantially from the original *Esquisse*.)
* Calhoun, C. (ed.) (1992) *Habermas and the Public Sphere*, Cambridge, MA: MIT Press. (An important example of how contemporary discussions reach well beyond, but still include, sociological theory.)

* Cohen, J.L. and Arato, A. (1992) *Civil Society and Political Theory*, Cambridge, MA: MIT Press. (Looks at how Neo-Kantian theorizing about the possibilities for universalism and democracy has been rejuvenated under the influence of Rawls and Habermas.)
* Coleman, J. (1990) *Foundations of Social Theory*, Cambridge, MA: Harvard University Press.
* Collins, R. (1975) *Conflict Sociology*, New York: Academic Press.
* Garfinkel, H. (1967) *Studies in Ethnomethodology*, Englewood Cliffs, NJ: Prentice Hall.
* Geertz, C. (1973) *The Interpretation of Cultures*, New York: Basic Books. (Collection of essays forwarding a view of what culture is, what role it plays in social life and how it ought to be properly studied.)
* Giddens, A. (1984) *The Constitution of Society*, London: Blackwell.
* Habermas, J. (1981) *Theorie des kommunikativen Handelns*, Frankfurt: Suhrkamp; trans. T. McCarthy, *The Theory of Communicative Action*, Boston: Beacon Press, 1984/1987. (His two-volume *magnum opus*, a systematic treatise on the foundations of social theory and one-sided process of rationalization in modern societies.)
* Homans, G.C. (1961) *Social Behavior: Its Elementary Forms*, New York: Harcourt, Brace, and World.
* Levine, D.N. (1995) *Visions of the Sociological Imagination*, Chicago, IL: University of Chicago Press.
* Merton, R.K. (1967) *On Theoretical Sociology*, New York: Free Press.
* Mouzelis, N. (1995) *Sociological Theory: What Went Wrong? Diagnoses and Remedies*, London: Routledge. (Analysis of the central problems of sociological theory and the means to resolve them.)
* Munch, R. (1981) 'Talcott Parsons and the theory of action, I: the structure of the Kantian core', *American Journal of Sociology* 86: 709–39.
* —— (1987) *Theory of Action*, London: Routledge & Kegan Paul.
* Parsons, T. (1937) *The Structure of Social Action*, New York: Free Press.
* Ritzer, G. (ed.) (1992) *Metatheorizing*, Los Angeles, CA and London: Sage.
* Roth, G. (1968) 'Introduction', in *Max Weber, Economy and Society*, New York: Bedminster Press, xxxii-cx. (Examines the translation of the term *Herrschaft* and Weber's intended meaning.)
* Seidman, S. (1991) 'The End of Sociological Theory: the Postmodern Hope', *Sociological Theory* 8 (Fall).
* Stinchcombe, A.L. (1968) *Constructing Social Theories*, New York: Harcourt Brace.

Sztompka, P. (1979) *Sociological Dilemmas: Toward a Dialectical Paradigm*, New York: Academic Press.

* Turner, B.S. and Holton, R.J. (1986) 'Against Nostalgia: Talcott Parsons and a Sociology for the Modern World', in *Talcott Parsons on Economy and Society*, London: Routledge, 207–34.

* Warnke, G. (1992) *Justice and Interpretation*, Cambridge, MA: MIT Press. (An illuminating discussion of major currents within the new 'interpretive' philosophy by a scholar who remains committed to a more Neo-Kantian project.)

* Weber, M. (1968) 'Bureaucracy', in *Economy and Society*, New York: Bedminster Press, 956–1005. (Detailed examination of the basic concepts of social and economics, as applied to history.)

JEFFREY C. ALEXANDER

SOCRATES (469–399 BC)

*Socrates, an Athenian Greek of the second half of the fifth century BC, wrote no philosophical works but was uniquely influential in the later history of philosophy. His philosophical interests were restricted to ethics and the conduct of life, topics which thereafter became central to philosophy. He discussed these in public places in Athens, sometimes with other prominent intellectuals or political leaders, sometimes with young men, who gathered round him in large numbers, and other admirers. Among these young men was Plato. Socrates' philosophical ideas and – equally important for his philosophical influence – his personality and methods as a 'teacher' were handed on to posterity in the 'dialogues' that several of his friends wrote after his death, depicting such discussions. Only those of Xenophon (*Memorabilia, Apology, Symposium*) and the early dialogues of Plato survive (for example* Euthyphro, Apology, Crito*). Later Platonic dialogues such as* Phaedo, Symposium *and* Republic *do not present the historical Socrates' ideas; the 'Socrates' appearing in them is a spokesman for Plato's own ideas.*

Socrates' discussions took the form of face-to-face interrogations of another person. Most often they concerned the nature of some moral virtue, such as courage or justice. Socrates asked what the respondent thought these qualities of mind and character amounted to, what their value was, how they were acquired. He would then test their ideas for logical consistency with other highly plausible general views about morality and goodness that the respondent also agreed to accept, once Socrates presented them. He succeeded in showing, to his satisfaction and that of the respondent and any bystanders, that the respondent's ideas were not consistent. By this practice of 'elenchus' or refutation he was able to prove that politicians and others who claimed to have 'wisdom' about human affairs in fact lacked it, and to draw attention to at least apparent errors in their thinking. He wanted to encourage them and others to think harder and to improve their ideas about the virtues and about how to conduct a good human life. He never argued directly for ideas of his own, but always questioned those of others. None the less, one can infer, from the questions he asks and his attitudes to the answers he receives, something about his own views.

Socrates was convinced that our souls – where virtues and vices are found – are vastly more important for our lives than our bodies or external circumstances. The quality of our souls determines the character of our lives, for better or for worse, much more than whether we are healthy or sick, or rich or poor. If we are to live well and happily, as he assumed we all want to do more than we want anything else, we must place the highest priority on the care of our souls. That means we must above all want to acquire the virtues, since they perfect our souls and enable them to direct our lives for the better. If only we could know what each of the virtues is we could then make an effort to obtain them. As to the nature of the virtues, Socrates seems to have held quite strict and, from the popular point of view, paradoxical views. Each virtue consists entirely in knowledge, of how it is best to act in some area of life, and why: additional 'emotional' aspects, such as the disciplining of our feelings and desires, he dismissed as of no importance. Weakness of will is not psychologically possible: if you act wrongly or badly, that is due to your ignorance of how you ought to act and why. He thought each of the apparently separate virtues amounts to the same single body of knowledge: the comprehensive knowledge of what is and is not good for a human being. Thus his quest was to acquire this single wisdom: all the particular virtues would follow automatically.

At the age of 70 Socrates was charged before an Athenian popular court with 'impiety' – with not believing in the Olympian gods and corrupting young men through his constant questioning of everything. He was found guilty and condemned to death. Plato's Apology, where Socrates gives a passionate defence of his life and philosophy, is one of the classics of Western literature. For different groups of later Greek philosophers he was the model both of a sceptical inquirer who never claims to know the truth, and of a 'sage' who knows the whole truth about human life and the human good. Among modern philosophers, the interpretations of his innermost meaning given by Montaigne, Hegel, Kierkegaard, and Nietzsche are especially notable.

1   Life and sources

Socrates, an Athenian citizen proud of his devotion to Athens, lived his adult life there engaging in open philosophical discussion and debate on fundamental questions of ethics, politics, religion and education. Going against the grain of the traditional education, he insisted that personal investigation and reasoned argument, rather than ancestral custom, or appeal to the authority of HOMER, HESIOD and other respected poets, was the only proper basis for answering these questions. His emphasis on argument and logic and his opposition to unquestioning acceptance of tradition allied him with such Sophists of a generation earlier as PROTAGORAS, GORGIAS and PRODICUS, none of whom was an Athenian, but all of whom spent time lecturing and teaching at Athens (see SOPHISTS). Unlike these Sophists Socrates did not formally offer himself or accept pay as a teacher. But many upper-class young Athenian men gathered round him to hear and engage in his discussions, and he had an inspirational and educational effect upon them, heightening their powers of critical thought and encouraging them to take seriously their individual responsibility to think through and decide how to conduct their lives. Many of his contemporaries perceived this education as morally and socially destructive – it certainly involved subverting accepted beliefs – and he was tried in 399 BC before an Athenian popular court and condemned to death on a charge of 'impiety': that he did not believe in the Olympian gods, but in new ones instead, and corrupted the young. Scholars sometimes mention specifically political motives of revenge, based on guilt by association: a number of prominent Athenians who were with Socrates as young men or were close friends did turn against the Athenian democracy and collaborated with the Spartans in their victory over Athens in the Peloponnesian war. But an amnesty passed by the restored democracy in 403 BC prohibited prosecution for political offences before that date. The rhetorician Polycrates included Socrates' responsibility for these political crimes in his *Accusation of Socrates* (see Xenophon, *Memorabilia* I 2.12), a rhetorical exercise written at least five years after Socrates' death. But there is no evidence that, in contravention of the amnesty, Socrates' actual accu-sers covertly attacked him, or his jurors condemned him, on that ground. The defences PLATO and XENOPHON constructed for Socrates, each in his respective *Apology*, imply that it was his own questioning mind and what was perceived as the bad moral influence he had on his young men that led to his trial and condemnation.

Socrates left no philosophical works, and apparently wrote none. His philosophy and personality were made known to later generations through the dialogues that several of his associates wrote with him as principal speaker (see SOCRATIC DIALOGUES). Only fragments survive of those by Aeschines of Sphettus and ANTISTHENES, both Athenians, and Phaedo of Elis (after whom Plato's dialogue *Phaedo* is named). Our own knowledge of Socrates depends primarily on the dialogues of Plato and the Socratic works of the military leader and historian Xenophon. Plato was a young associate of Socrates' during perhaps the last ten years of his life, and Xenophon knew him during that same period, though he was absent from Athens at the time of Socrates' death and for several years before and many years after.

We also have secondary evidence from the comic playwright Aristophanes and from Aristotle. Aristotle, although born fifteen years after Socrates' death, had access through Plato and others to first-hand information about the man and his philosophy. Aristophanes knew Socrates personally; his *Clouds* (first produced c.423 BC) pillories the 'new' education offered by Sophists and philosophers by showing Socrates at work in a 'thinkery', propounding outlandish physical theories and teaching young men how to argue cleverly in defence of their improper behaviour. It is significant that in 423, when Socrates was about 45 years old, he could plausibly be taken as a leading representative in Athens of the 'new' education. But one cannot expect a comic play making fun of a whole intellectual movement to contain an authentic account of Socrates' specific philosophical commitments.

However, the literary genre to which Plato's and Xenophon's Socratic works belong (along with the other, lost dialogues) also permits the author much latitude; in his *Poetics* Aristotle counts such works as fictions of a certain kind, alongside epic poems and tragedies. They are by no means records of actual discussions (despite the fact that Xenophon explicitly so represents his). Each author was free to develop his own ideas behind the mask of Socrates, at least within the limits of what his personal experience had led him to believe was Socrates' basic philosophical and moral outlook. Especially in view of the many inconsistencies between Plato's and Xenophon's portraits (see §7 below), it is a difficult question for historical–

philosophical interpretation whether the philosophical and moral views the character Socrates puts forward in any of these dialogues can legitimately be attributed to the historical philosopher. The problem of interpretation is made more difficult by the fact that Socrates appears in many of Plato's dialogues – ones belonging to his middle and later periods (see PLATO §§10–16) – discussing and expounding views that we have good reason to believe resulted from Plato's own philosophical investigations into questions of metaphysics and epistemology, questions that were not entered into at all by the historical Socrates. To resolve this problem – what scholars call the 'Socratic problem' – most agree in preferring Plato to Xenophon as a witness. Xenophon is not thought to have been philosopher enough to have understood Socrates well or to have captured the depth of his views and his personality. As for Plato, most scholars accept only the philosophical interests and procedures, and the moral and philosophical views, of the Socrates of the early dialogues, and, more guardedly, the Socrates of 'transitional' ones such as *Meno* and *Gorgias*, as legitimate representations of the historical personage. These dialogues are the ones that predate the emergence of the metaphysical and epistemological inquiries just referred to. However, even Plato's early dialogues are philosophical works written to further Plato's own philosophical interests. That could produce distortions, also; and Xenophon's relative philosophical innocence could make his portrait in some respects more reliable. Moreover, it is possible, even probable, that in his efforts to help his young men improve themselves Socrates spoke differently to the philosophically more promising ones among them – including Plato – from the way he spoke to others, for example Xenophon. Both portraits could be true, but partial and needing to be combined (see §7). The account of Socrates' philosophy given below follows Plato, with caution, while giving independent weight also to Xenophon and to Aristotle.

2 Life and sources (cont.)

Xenophon's *Apology* of Socrates, *Symposium* and *Memorabilia* (or *Memoirs*) may well reflect knowledge of Plato's own *Apology* and some of his early and middle period dialogues, as well as lost dialogues of Antisthenes and others. Xenophon composed the *Memorabilia* over many years, beginning only some ten years after Socrates' death, avowedly in order to defend Socrates' reputation as a good man, a true Athenian gentleman, and a good influence upon his young men. The same intention motivated his *Apology* and *Symposium*. Anything these works contain about Socrates' philosophical opinions and procedures is ancillary to that apologetic purpose. Plato's *Apology*, of course, is similarly apologetic, but it and his other early dialogues are carefully constructed discussions, strongly focused upon questions of philosophical substance. Plato evidently thought Socrates' philosophical ideas and methods were central to his life and to his mission. Xenophon's and Plato's testimony are agreed that Socrates' discussions consistently concerned the *aretai*, the recognized 'virtues' or excellences of character (see ARETĒ), such as justice, piety, self-control or moderation (*sōphrosynē*), courage and wisdom; what these individual characteristics consist in and require of a person, what their value is, and how they are acquired, whether by teaching or in some other way. In his *Apology* and elsewhere Plato has Socrates insist that these discussions were always inquiries, efforts made to engage his fellow-discussants in coming jointly to an adequate understanding of the matters inquired into. He does not himself know, and therefore cannot teach anyone else – whether by means of these discussions or in some other way – either how to be virtuous or what virtue in general or any particular virtue is. Furthermore, given his general characterization of virtue (see §§4–5), Plato's Socrates makes a point of suggesting the impossibility in principle of teaching virtue at all, by contrast with the Sophists who declared they could teach it. Virtue was not a matter of information about living or rote techniques of some sort to be handed on from teacher to pupil, but required an open-ended personal understanding that individuals could only come to for themselves. Xenophon, too, reports that Socrates denied he was a teacher of *aretē*, but he pays no attention to such issues of philosophical principle. He does not hesitate to show Socrates speaking of himself as a teacher (see *Apology* 26, *Memorabilia* I 6.13–14), and describes him as accepting young men from their fathers as his pupils (but not for a fee), and teaching them the virtues by displaying his own virtues to them for emulation, as well as through conversation and precepts. Perhaps Socrates did not insist on holding to strict philosophical principles in dealing with people on whom their point would have been lost.

In his *Apology* Plato's Socrates traces his practice of spending his days discussing and inquiring about virtue to an oracle delivered at the shrine of Apollo at Delphi. Xenophon also mentions this oracle in his *Apology*. A friend of Socrates', Chaerephon, had asked the god whether anyone was wiser than Socrates; the priestess answered that no one was. Because he was sure he was not wise at all – only the gods, he suspected, could actually *know* how a human life ought to be led – Socrates cross-examined others at Athens with reputations for that kind of wisdom. He wanted to show that there were people wiser than he and thus discover the true meaning of the oracle – Apollo was known to speak in riddles requiring interpretation to reach their deeper meaning. In the event, it turned out that the people he examined were not wise, since they could not even give a self-consistent set of answers to his questions: obviously, true knowledge requires at least that one think and speak consistently on the subjects one professes to know. So he concluded that the priestess's reply had meant that of all those with reputations for wisdom only he came close to deserving it; he wisely did not profess to know these things that only gods can know, and that was wisdom enough for a human being. Because only he knew that he did *not* know, only he was ready earnestly to inquire into virtue and the other ingredients of the human good, in an effort to learn. He understood therefore that Apollo's true intention in the oracle had been to encourage him to continue his inquiries, to help others to realize that it is beyond human powers actually to *know* how to live – that is the prerogative of the gods – and to do his best to understand as far as a human being can how one ought to live. The life of philosophy, as led by him, was therefore something he was effectively ordered by Apollo to undertake.

We must remember that Socrates was on trial on a charge of 'impiety'. In tracing his philosophical vocation back to Apollo's oracle, and linking it to a humble recognition of human weakness and divine perfection, he was constructing a powerful rebuttal of the charges brought against him. But it cannot be literally true – if that is what he intended to say – that Socrates began his inquiries about virtue only after hearing of the oracle. Chaerephon's question to Apollo shows he had established a reputation in Athens for wisdom before that. That reputation cannot have rested on philosophical inquiries of another sort. In Plato's *Phaedo* Socrates says he had been interested as a young man in philosophical speculations about the structure and causes of the natural world, but he plainly did not take those interests very far; and in any event, his reputation was not for that kind of wisdom, but wisdom about how to lead a human life. In fact we do not hear of the duty to Apollo in Xenophon, or in other dialogues of Plato, where we might expect to find it if from the beginning Socrates thought Apollo had commanded his life of philosophizing. However, we need not think Socrates was false to the essential spirit of philosophy as he practised it if in looking back on his life under threat of condemnation for impiety he chose, inaccurately, to see it as initially imposed on him by Apollo's oracle.

Despite its impressiveness, Socrates' speech failed to convince his jury of 501 male fellow citizens, and he died in the state prison by drinking hemlock as required by law. His speech evidently offended the majority of the jurors by its disdain for the charges and the proceedings; Xenophon explains his lofty behaviour, which he thinks would otherwise have been lunatic – and damaging to his reputation – by reporting that he had told friends in advance that as a 70-year-old still in possession of his health and faculties it was time for him to die anyhow, before senility set in. Furthermore, his 'divine sign' – the 'voice' he sometimes heard warning him for his own good against a contemplated course of action – had prevented him from spending time crafting a defence speech. (This voice seems to have been the basis for the charge of introducing 'new' gods.) So he would do nothing to soften his manner in order to win his freedom. Even if this story is true, Plato could be right that Socrates put on a spirited, deeply serious defence of his life and beliefs – one that he thought should have convinced the jurors of his innocence, if only they had judged him intelligently and fairly.

3 Socratic elenchus, or refutation

In cross-examining those with reputations for wisdom about human affairs and showing their lack of it, Socrates employed a special method of dialectical argument that he himself had perfected, the method of 'elenchus' – Greek for 'putting to the test' or 'refutation'. He gives an example at his trial when he cross-examines Meletus, one of his accusers (Plato, *Apology* 24d–27e). The respondent states a thesis, as something he *knows* to be true because he is wise about the matter in question. Socrates then asks questions, eliciting clarifications, qualifications and extensions of the thesis, and seeking further opinions of the respondent on related matters. He then argues, and the respondent sees no way not to grant, that the original thesis is logically inconsistent with something affirmed in these further responses. For Socrates, it follows at once that the respondent did not know what he was talking about in stating his original thesis: true knowledge would prevent one from such self-contradiction. So the respondent suffers a personal set-back; *he* is refuted – revealed as incompetent. Meletus, for example, does not have consistent ideas about the gods or what would show someone not to believe in them, and he does not have consistent ideas about who corrupts the young, and how; so he does not know what he is talking about, and no one should take *his* word for it that Socrates disbelieves in the gods or has corrupted his young men. In many of his early dialogues Plato shows Socrates using this method to examine the opinions of persons who claim to be wise in some matter: the religious expert Euthyphro on piety (*Euthyphro*), the generals Laches and Nicias on courage (*Laches*), the Sophist Protagoras on the distinctions among the virtues and whether virtue can be taught (*Protagoras*), the rhapsodist Ion on what is involved in knowing poetry (*Ion*), the budding politician Alcibiades on justice and other political values (*Alcibiades*), the Sophist Hippias on which was the better man, Odysseus or Achilles (*Lesser Hippias*), and on the nature of moral and aesthetic beauty (*Greater Hippias*). They are all refuted – shown to have mutually inconsistent ideas on the subject discussed (see PLATO §§4, 6, 8–9).

But Socrates is not content merely to demonstrate his interlocutor's lack of wisdom or knowledge. That might humiliate him into inquiring further or seeking by some other means the knowledge he has been shown to lack, instead of remaining puffed up with self-conceit. That would be a good thing. But Socrates often also indicates clearly that his cross-examination justifies him and the interlocutor in rejecting as false the interlocutor's original thesis. Logically, that is obviously wrong: if the interlocutor contradicts himself, at least one of the things he has said must be false (indeed, all of them could be), but the fact alone of self-contradiction does not show where the falsehood resides. For example, when Socrates leads Euthyphro to accept ideas that contradict his own definition of the pious as whatever pleases all the gods, Socrates concludes that that definition has been shown to be false (*Euthyphro* 10d–11a), and asks Euthyphro to come up with another one. He does not usually seem to consider that perhaps on further thought the additional ideas would seem faulty and so merit rejection instead.

Socrates uses his elenctic method also in discussion with persons who are not puffed up with false pride, and are quite willing to admit their ignorance and to reason out the truth about these important matters. Examples are his discussions with his long-time friend Crito on whether he should escape prison and set aside the court's death sentence (Plato, *Crito*), and with the young men Charmides, on self-control (*Charmides*), and Lysis and Menexenus, on the nature of friendship (*Lysis*). Socrates examines Crito's proposal that he escape on the basis of principles that he presents to him for his approval, and he, together with Crito (however half-heartedly), rejects it when it fails to be consistent with them. And he examines the young men's successive ideas about these virtues, rejecting some of them and refining others, by relying on their own acceptance of further ideas that he puts to them. Again, he is confident that the inconsistencies brought to light in their ideas indicate

the inadequacy of their successive proposals as to the nature of the moral virtue in question.

In many of his discussions, both with young men and the allegedly wise, Socrates seeks to know what some morally valuable property is – for example, piety, courage, self-control or friendship (see §5). Rejecting the idea that one could learn this simply from attending to examples, he insisted on an articulated 'definition' of the item in question – some *single* account that would capture all at once the presumed common feature that would entitle anything to count as a legitimate instance. Such a definition, providing the essence of the thing defined, would give us a 'model' or 'paradigm' to use in judging whether or not some proposed action or person possesses the moral value so defined (*Euthyphro* 6d–e). Aristotle says (in *Metaphysics* I, 6) that Socrates was the first to interest himself in such 'universal definitions', and traces to his interest in them Plato's first impetus towards a theory of Forms, or 'separated' universals (see PLATO §10).

In none of his discussions in Plato's early works does Socrates profess to think an adequate final result has actually been established – about the nature of friendship, or self-control, or piety, or any of the other matters he inquires about. Indeed, on the contrary, these works regularly end with professions of profound ignorance about the matter under investigation. Knowledge is never attained, and further questions always remain to be considered. But Socrates does plainly think that progress towards reaching final understanding has taken place (even if only a god, and no human being, could ever actually attain it). Not only has one discovered some things that are definitely wrong to say; one has also achieved some positive insights that are worth holding onto in seeking further systematic understanding. Given that Socrates' method of discussion is elenctic throughout, what does he think justifies this optimism?

On balance, our evidence suggests that Socrates had worked out no elaborate theory to support him here. The ideas he was stimulated to propound in an elenctic examination which went against some initial thesis seemed to him, and usually also to the others present, so plausible, and so supportable by further considerations, that he and they felt content to reject the initial thesis. Until someone came up with arguments to neutralize their force, it seemed the thesis was doomed, as contrary to reason itself. Occasionally Socrates expresses himself in just those terms: however unpalatable the option might seem, it remains open to someone to challenge the grounds on which his conclusions rest (see *Euthyphro* 15c, *Gorgias* 461d–462a, 509a, *Crito* 54d). But until they do, he is satisfied to treat his and his interlocutor's agreement as a firm basis for thought and action. Later, when Plato himself became interested in questions of philosophical methodology in his *Meno*, this came to seem a philosophically unsatisfactory position; Plato's demand for justification for one's beliefs independent of what seemed on reflection most plausible led him to epistemological and metaphysical inquiries that went well beyond the self-imposed restriction of Socratic philosophy to ethical thought in the broadest sense. But Socrates did not raise these questions. In this respect more bound by traditional views than Plato, he had great implicit confidence in his and his interlocutors' capacity, after disciplined dialectical examination of the issues, to reach firm ground for constructing positive ideas about the virtues and about how best to lead a human life – even if these ideas never received the sort of final validation that a god, understanding fully the truth about human life, could give them.

4   Elenchus and moral progress

The topics Socrates discussed were always ethical, and never included questions of physical theory or metaphysics or other branches of philosophical study. Moreover, he always conducted his discussions not as theoretical inquiries but as profoundly personal moral tests. Questioner and interlocutor were equally putting their ways of life to what Socrates thought was the most important test of all – their capacity to stand up to scrutiny in rational argument about how one ought to live. In speaking about human life, he wanted his respondents to indicate what they truly believed, and as questioner he was prepared to do the same, at least at crucial junctures. Those beliefs were assumed to express not theoretical ideas, but the very ones on which they themselves were conducting their lives. In losing an argument with Socrates you did not merely show yourself logically or argumentatively deficient, but also put into question the very basis on which you were living. Your way of life might ultimately prove defensible, but if you cannot now defend it successfully, you are not leading it *with* any such justification. In that case, according to Socrates' views, your way of life is morally deficient. Thus if Menexenus, Lysis and Socrates profess to value friendship among the most important things in life and profess to be one another's friends, but cannot satisfactorily explain under pressure of elenctic investigation what a friend is, that casts serious doubt on the quality of any 'friendship' they might form (Plato, *Lysis* 212a, 223b). Moral consistency and personal integrity, and not mere delight in argument and logical thought, should therefore lead you to repeated elenctic examination of your views, in an effort to render them coherent and at the same time defensible on all sides through appeal to plausible arguments. Or, if some of your views have been shown false, by conflicting with extremely plausible general principles, it behoves you to drop them – and so to cease living in a way that depends upon accepting them. In this way, philosophical inquiry via the elenchus is fundamentally a personal moral quest. It is a quest not just to understand adequately the basis on which one is actually living, and the personal and moral commitments that this contains. It is also a quest to change the way one lives as the results of argument show one ought to, so that, at the logical limit of inquiry, one's way of life would be completely vindicated. Accordingly, Socrates in Plato's dialogues regularly insists on the individual and personal character of his discussions. He wants to hear the views of the one person with whom he is speaking. He dismisses as of no interest what outsiders or most people may think – provided that is not what his discussant is personally convinced is true. The views of 'the many' may well not rest on thought or argument at all. Socrates insists that his discussant shoulder the responsibility to explain and defend rationally the views he holds, and follow the argument – reason – wherever it may lead.

We learn a good deal about Socrates' own principles from both Plato and Xenophon. Those were ones that had stood up well over a lifetime of frequent elenctic discussions and had, as he thought, a wealth of plausible arguments in their favour. Foremost is his conviction that the virtues – self-control, courage, justice, piety, wisdom and related qualities of mind and soul – are essential if anyone is to lead a good and happy life. They are good in themselves for a human being, and they guarantee a happy life, *eudaimonia* – something that he thought all human beings always wanted, and wanted more than anything else. The virtues belong to the soul – they are the condition of a soul that has been properly cared for and brought to its best state. The soul is vastly more important for happiness than are health and strength of the body or social and political power, wealth and other external circumstances of life; the goods of the soul, and preeminently the virtues, are worth far more than any quantity of bodily or external goods. Socrates seems to have thought these other goods *are* truly good, but they only *do* people good, and thereby contribute to their happiness, under the condition that they are chosen and used in accordance with virtues indwelling in their souls (see Plato, *Apology* 30b, *Euthydemus* 280d–282d, *Meno* 87d–89a).

More specific principles followed. Doing injustice is worse for oneself than being subjected to it (*Gorgias* 469c–522e): by acting unjustly you make your soul worse, and that affects for the worse the whole of your life, whereas one who treats you unjustly at most harms your body or your possessions but leaves your soul unaffected. On the same ground Socrates firmly rejected the deeply entrenched Greek precept to aid one's friends and harm one's enemies, and the accompanying principle of retaliation, which he equated with returning wrongs for wrongs done to oneself and one's friends (*Crito* 49a–d). Socrates' daily life gave witness to his principles. He was poor, shabbily dressed and unshod, and made do with whatever ordinary food came his way: such things matter little. Wealth, finery and delicacies for the palate are not worth panting after and exerting oneself to enjoy. However, Socrates was fully capable of relishing both refined and plain enjoyments as occasion warranted (see §7).

5   The unity of virtue

The Greeks recognized a series of specially prized qualities of mind and character as *aretai* or virtues. Each was regarded as a distinct, separate quality: justice was one thing, concerned with treating other people fairly, courage quite another, showing itself in vigorous, correct behaviour in circumstances that normally cause people to be afraid; and self-control or moderation, piety and wisdom were yet others. Each of these ensured that its possessor would act in some specific ways, regularly and reliably over their lifetime, having the justified conviction that those are ways one *ought* to act – *agathon* (good) and *kalon* (fine, noble, admirable or beautiful) ways of acting. But each type of virtuous person acts rightly and well not only in regularly recurring, but also in unusual and unheralded, circumstances; the virtue involves always getting something right about how to live a good human life. Socrates thought these virtues were essential if one was to live happily (see §4). But what exactly were they? What was it about someone that made them just, or courageous, or wise? If you did not know that, you would not know what to do in order to acquire those qualities. Furthermore, supposing you did possess a virtue, you would have to be able to explain and defend by argument the consequent ways in which you lived – otherwise your conviction that those are ways one *ought* to act would be shallow and unjustified. And in order to do that you would have to know what state of mind the virtue was, since that is essential to them (see Plato, *Charmides* 158e–159a). Consequently, in his discussions Socrates constantly asked for 'definitions' of various virtues: what is courage (*Laches*); what is self-control or moderation (*Charmides*), what is friendship (*Lysis*) and what is piety (*Euthyphro*). As this context

shows, he was asking not for a 'dictionary definition', an account of the accepted linguistic understanding of a term, but for an ethically defensible account of an actual condition of mind or character to which the word in common use would be correctly applied. In later terminology, he was seeking a 'real' rather than a 'nominal' definition (see DEFINITION; PLATO §§6–9).

Socrates objected to definitions that make a virtue some external aspect of a virtuous action (such as the manner in which it is done – for example its 'quiet' or measured quality in the case of moderation, *Charmides* 160b–d), or simply the doing of specific types of action, described in terms of their external circumstances (such as, for courage, standing one's ground in battle; *Laches* 190e–191d). He also objected to more psychological definitions that located a virtue in some non-rational and non-cognitive aspect of the soul (for example, in the case of courage, the soul's endurance or strength of resistance) (*Laches* 192d–193e). For his own part, he regularly shows himself ready to accept only definitions that identify a virtue with some sort of knowledge or wisdom about what is valuable for a human being. That 'intellectualist' expectation about the nature of virtue, although never worked out to his satisfaction in any Platonic dialogue, is central to Socrates' philosophy.

Given that in his discussions he is always the questioner, probing the opinions of his respondent and not arguing for views of his own, we never find Socrates stating clearly what led him to this intellectualism. Probably, however, it was considerations drawn from the generally agreed premise that each virtue is a condition motivating certain voluntary actions, chosen because they are good and fine or noble. He took it that what lies behind and produces any voluntary action is the idea under which it is done, the conception of the action in the agent's mind that makes it seem the thing to do just then. If so, each virtue must be some state of the mind, the possessor of which constantly has certain distinctive general ideas about how one ought to behave. Furthermore, since virtues get this *right*, these are true ideas. And since a virtuous person acts well and correctly in a *perfectly reliable* way, they must be seated so deeply in the mind as to be ineradicable and unwaveringly present. The only state of mind that meets these conditions is knowledge: to know a subject is not just to be thoroughly convinced, but to have a deep, fully articulated understanding, being ready with explanations to fend off objections and apparent difficulties and to extend old principles into new situations, and being prepared to show with the full weight of reason precisely why each thing falling under it is and must be so. Each virtue, then, must be knowledge about how one ought to behave in some area of life, and why – a knowledge so deep and rationally secure that those who have it can be counted upon never to change their minds, never to be argued out of or otherwise persuaded away from, or to waver in, their conviction about how to act.

In Plato's *Protagoras* Socrates goes beyond this, and identifies himself with the position, rejected by Protagoras in their discussion, that the apparently separate virtues of justice, piety, self-control, courage and wisdom are somehow one and the same thing – some single knowledge (361a–b). Xenophon too confirms that Socrates held this view (*Memorabilia* III 9.5). Protagoras defends the position that each of the virtues is not only a distinct thing from each of the others, but so different in kind that a person could possess one of them without possessing the others (329d–e). In opposing him, Socrates sometimes speaks plainly of two allegedly distinct virtues being 'one' (333b). Given this unity of the virtues, it would follow that a person could not possess one without having them all. And in speaking of justice and piety in particular, Socrates seems to go further, to imply that every action produced by virtue is equally an instance of *all* the standardly recognized virtues: pious as well as just, wise and self-controlled and courageous also. Among his early dialogues, however, Plato's own philosophical interests show themselves particularly heavily in the *Protagoras*, so it is doubtful how far the details of his arguments are to be attributed to the historical Socrates. The issues raised by Socrates in the *Protagoras* were, none the less, vigorously pursued by subsequent 'Socratic' philosophers (as Plutarch's report in *On Moral Virtue* 2 demonstrates). And the positions apparently adopted by Plato's Socrates were taken up and ingeniously defended by the Stoic philosopher Chrysippus (see STOICISM §16). As usual, because of his questioner's role, it is difficult to work out Socrates' grounds for holding to the unity of virtue; and it is difficult to tell whether, and if so how, he allowed that despite this unity there were some real differences between, say, justice and self-control, or courage and piety. Apparently he thought the same body of knowledge – knowledge of the whole of what is and is not good for human beings, and why it is so or not – must at least underlie the allegedly separate virtues. If you did not have that vast, comprehensive knowledge you could not be in the state of mind which is justice or in that which is courage, and so on; and if you did have it you would necessarily be in those states of mind. It seems doubtful whether Socrates himself progressed beyond that point. Efforts to do that were made by Chrysippus and the other philosophers referred to above. And despite denying that all virtues consist in knowledge, Plato in the *Republic* and Aristotle in

Nicomachean Ethics VI follow Socrates to the extent of holding, in different ways, that you need to have all the virtues in order to have any one.

6 Weakness of will denied

In Plato's *Protagoras* Socrates also denies the possibility of weakness of will – being 'mastered' by some desire so as to act voluntarily in a way one knows is wrong or bad (see also Xenophon, *Memorabilia* III 9.4, IV 5.6.) All voluntary wrongdoing or bad action is due to ignorance of how one ought to act and why, and to nothing else. This would be easy to understand if Socrates were using 'knowing' quite strictly, to refer to the elevated and demanding sort of knowledge described in §5 (sometimes called 'Socratic knowledge'). Someone could know an action was wrong or bad, with full 'Socratic knowledge', only if they were not just thoroughly convinced, but had a deep, fully articulated understanding, being ready with explanations to fend off objections and apparent difficulties, and prepared to show precisely *why* it was so. That would mean that these ideas were seated so deeply in the mind as to be ineradicable and unwaveringly present. Accordingly, a person with 'Socratic knowledge' could not come to hold even momentarily that the action in question would be the thing to do, and so they could never do it voluntarily.

However, Plato's Socrates goes further. He explains his denial of weak-willed action by saying that a person cannot voluntarily do actions which, in doing them, they even *believe* to be a wrong or bad thing to do (*Protagoras* 358c–e). He gives a much-discussed, elaborate argument to establish this stronger conclusion, starting from assumptions identifying that which is pleasant with that which is good (352a–357e). These assumptions, however, he attributes only to ordinary people, the ones who say they believe in the possibility of weak-willed action; he makes it clear to the careful reader, if not to Protagoras, that his own view is simply that pleasure is a good thing, not 'the' good (351c–e; see 354b–d). Although some scholars have thought otherwise, Socrates himself does not adopt a hedonist analysis of the good in the *Protagoras* or elsewhere either in Plato or Xenophon; indeed, he speaks elsewhere against hedonist views (see HEDONISM). The fundamental principle underlying his argument – a principle he thinks ordinary people will accept – is that voluntary action is always 'subjectively' rational, in the sense that an agent who acts to achieve some particular sort of value always acts with the idea that what they are doing achieves *more* of that value than alternatives then thought by them to be available would achieve. If someone performs an overall bad action because of some (lesser) good they think they will get from it, they cannot do it while *believing* it is bad overall. That would mean they thought they could have got *more* good by refraining, and their action would violate the principle just stated. Instead, at the time they acted (despite what they may have thought before or after acting), they believed (wrongly and ignorantly) that the action would be good overall for them to do. Thus ignorance, and only ignorance, is responsible for voluntary error. Weakness of will – knowingly pursuing the worse outcome – is psychologically impossible: 'No one does wrong willingly'.

The details of this argument may not represent explicit commitments of the historical Socrates. None the less, his denial of weakness of will, understood as presented in Plato's *Protagoras*, was the centre of a protracted debate in later times. First Plato himself, in *Republic* IV, then Aristotle in *Nicomachean Ethics* VII, argued against Socrates' conclusion, on the ground that he had overlooked the fact that human beings have other sources of motivation that can produce voluntary actions, besides their ideas about what is good or bad, or right or wrong to do. 'Appetites' and 'spirited desires' exist also, which can lead a person to act in fulfilment of them without having to adopt the idea, in their beliefs about what is best to do, that so acting would be a good thing (see PLATO §14; ARISTOTLE §20, 22–23). The Stoics, however, and especially Chrysippus, argued vigorously and ingeniously in defence of Socrates' analysis and against the Platonic–Aristotelian assumption of alternative sources of motivation that produce voluntary action on their own (see STOICISM §19). In fact, during Hellenistic times it was the Socratic, 'unitary' psychology of action that carried the day; the Platonic–Aristotelian alternative, dominant in the 'common sense' and the philosophy of modern times, was a minority view. The issues Socrates raised about weakness of will continue to be debated today.

7 Socrates' personality

Socrates drew to himself many of the brightest and most prominent people in Athens, securing their fascinated attention and their passionate friendship and support. His effectiveness as a philosopher, and the Socratic 'legend' itself, depended as much on the strength and interest of his personality as on the power of his mind. Plato's and Xenophon's portraits of Socrates as a person differ significantly, however. Plato's Socrates is aloof and often speaks ironically, although also with unusual and deeply held moral convictions; paradoxically, the depth and clarity of his convictions, maintained alongside the firm disclaimer

to know what was true, could seem all the stronger testimony to their truth, and made them felt the more strongly as a rebuke to the superficiality of one's own way of living. In Xenophon, Socrates is also sometimes ironical and playful, especially in the *Symposium*, but his conversation is usually direct, even didactic, and often chummy in tone; his attitudes are for the most part conventional though earnest; and there is nothing to unsettle anyone or make them suspect hidden depths. It is much easier to believe that the Socrates of Plato's dialogues could have had such profound effects on the lives of the brightest of his contemporaries than did the character in Xenophon. That is one reason given for trusting Plato's more than Xenophon's portrait of the historical personage. But perhaps Socrates used the more kindly and genial manner and conventional approach depicted by Xenophon to draw out the best in some of his young men and his friends – ones who would have been put off by the Platonic subtleties. The historical Socrates may have been a more complex person than even Plato presents.

Plato and Xenophon both represent Socrates as strongly attracted to good-looking young men in the 'bloom' of their middle to late teens, just the period when they were also coming of age morally and intellectually. In both he speaks of himself as unusually 'erotic' by temperament and constantly 'in love'. But he explains his 'erotic' attachments in terms of his desire to converse with bright and serious young men, to question them about virtue and how best to live a human life, and to draw out what was best in their minds and characters. In Xenophon he describes his love as love for their souls, not their bodies, and he vigorously condemns sexual relations with any young man: using him that way disgraces him and harms him by encouraging a loose attitude as regards physical pleasures (*Symposium* 8). The overheated sexuality of Plato's own accounts (*Symposium* and *Phaedrus*) of *erōs*, sexual love, for a young man's beauty as motivating an adult male to pursue philosophical truth into an eternal realm of Forms (see PLATO §12) is to be distinguished sharply from Socrates' ideas, as we can gather them from Xenophon and from Plato's own early dialogues.

Xenophon emphasizes Socrates' freedom from the strong appetites for food, drink, sex and physical comfort that dominate other people; his *enkrateia* or self-mastery is the first of the virtues that Xenophon claims for him (*Memorabilia* I 2.1). He was notorious for going barefoot even in winter and dressing always in a simple cloak. Socrates' self-mastery was at the centre of Antisthenes' portrayal, and is reflected also in several incidents reported in Plato, such as his serene dismissal of the young Alcibiades' efforts to seduce him sexually (Plato, *Symposium* 217b–219e), or, perhaps when engrossed in a philosophical problem, his standing in the open (during a break in the action while on military service) from morning to night, totally indifferent to everything around him (*Symposium* 220c–d). This 'ascetic' Socrates, especially as presented by Antisthenes – rejecting conventional comforts and conventional behaviour – became an inspiration for the 'Cynics' of later centuries (see CYNICS).

8 Socrates in the history of philosophy

Looking back on the early history of philosophy, later philosophers traced to Socrates a major turn in its development. As Cicero puts it: 'Socrates was the first to call philosophy down from the heavens... and compel it to ask questions about life and morality' (*Tusculan Disputations* V 10–11). Previously it had been concerned with the origins and nature of the physical world and the explanation of celestial and other natural phenomena. Modern scholarship follows the ancients' lead in referring standardly to philosophers before Socrates collectively as 'Presocratics' (see PRESOCRATIC PHILOSOPHY). This includes DEMOCRITUS, in fact a slightly younger contemporary of Socrates; Cicero's verdict needs adjustment, in that Democritus, independently of Socrates, also investigated questions about ethics and morality. With the sole exception of Epicureanism, which developed separately out of Democritean origins, all the major movements of Greek philosophy after Socrates had roots in his teaching and example. This obviously applies to Plato, whose philosophical development began with a thorough reworking and assimilation of Socratic moral inquiry, and through him to Aristotle and his fellow members of Plato's Academy, Speusippus and Xenocrates and others, as well as to later Platonists. Among Socrates' inner circle were also Aristippus of Cyrene, who founded the hedonist Cyrenaic school (see ARISTIPPUS THE ELDER; CYRENAICS), and Antisthenes, an older rival of Plato's and major teacher in Athens of philosophical dialectic. Both of these figure in Xenophon's *Memorabilia* (Antisthenes also in his *Symposium*), where they are vividly characterized in conversation with Socrates. Another Socratic, Euclides, founded the Megarian school (see MEGARIAN SCHOOL). These 'Socratic schools' developed different themes already prominent in Socrates' own investigations, and competed in the claim to be his true philosophical heirs (see SOCRATIC SCHOOLS; DIALECTICAL SCHOOL).

In the third to first centuries BC, both the Stoics and their rivals the Academic sceptics claimed to be carrying forward the Socratic tradition. In both cases this was based upon a reading of Plato's dialogues and perhaps other eye-witness reconstructions of Socrates' philosophy. The Academic ARCESILAUS interpreted the Platonic Socrates as a sceptical inquirer, avidly searching but never satisfied that the truth on any disputed question had been finally uncovered. He could point to much about Plato's Socrates in support: his modest but firm denial that he possessed any knowledge, and his constant practice of inquiring into the truth by examining others' opinions on the basis of ideas which they themselves accepted, without formally committing himself to these ideas even when he was the one to first suggest them. Arcesilaus, however, applied his sceptical Socratic dialectic to more than the questions of ethics and human life about which Socrates himself had argued, making it cover the whole range of philosophical topics being investigated in his day. The Stoics read the dialogues (especially the *Euthydemus* and *Protagoras*) quite differently. They found Socrates espousing a complete doctrine of ethics and the psychology of human action. He posed his questions on the basis of this doctrine, leaving the respondent (and the reader) to recover for themselves the philosophical considerations underlying it. They thus emphasized the conceptions of virtue as knowledge, of virtue as unified in wisdom, and of voluntary action as motivated always by an agent's beliefs about what is best to do, that emerged through Socrates' examination of Protagoras (see §§6–7). They thought these constituted a positive, Socratic moral philosophy, and in their own moral theory they set out to revive and strengthen it with systematic arguments and with added metaphysical and physical speculations of their own. Later Stoics regularly referred to Socrates as a genuine wise man or 'sage', perhaps the only one who ever lived. He had brought to final, systematic perfection his knowledge, along Stoic lines, of what is good and bad for human beings, and what is not, and therefore possessed all the virtues and no vices, and lived unwaveringly the best, happy life, free from emotion and all other errors about human life. It is a tribute to the complexity and enigmatic character of Socrates that he could stand simultaneously as a paragon both of sceptical, non-committal inquiry and life led on that uncommitted basis, and of dogmatic knowledge of the final truth about all things human.

The figure of Socrates has continued to fascinate and to inspire ever-new interpretations of his innermost meaning. For MONTAIGNE, he proved that human beings can convincingly and attractively order their own lives from their own resources of mind, without direction from God or religion or tradition. In the nineteenth century KIERKEGAARD and NIETZSCHE offered extensive interpretations of him,

SOCRATES

both heavily dependent upon Hegel's absolute-idealist analysis. HEGEL interpreted Socrates as a quintessentially negative thinker, aiming at making people vacillate in their superficial moral beliefs and endorse none of them wholeheartedly, thus hinting that the truth, although universal and objective, lies deep within the freedom of their own subjectivity. For Kierkegaard he represents, on the contrary, the possibility of living wholeheartedly by occupying an unarticulated position somehow beyond the negative rejection but expressed through it: 'infinite absolute negativity'. In *Die Geburt der Tragödie* (*The Birth of Tragedy*) Nietzsche treats Socrates principally as having poisoned the 'tragic' attitude that made possible the great achievements of classical culture, by insisting that life should be grounded in rational understanding and justified by 'knowledge'; but his fascinated regard for Socrates led him to return to him repeatedly in his writings. Socrates was paradigmatically a philosopher whose thought, however taken up with logic and abstract argument, is inseparable from the search for self-understanding and from a deeply felt attachment to the concerns of human life. His power to fascinate and inspire is surely not exhausted.

References and further reading

* Aristophanes (*c*.423 BC) *Clouds*, ed. K.J. Dover, *Aristophanes' Clouds*, Oxford: Clarendon Press, 1968; trans. A.H. Sommerstein, Warminster: Aris & Phillips, 1982; trans. A.H. Sommerstein, *Aristophanes: Lysistrata, The Acharnians, The Clouds*, Harmondsworth: Penguin, 1973. (Classic comic portrayal of Socrates. Dover is an edition of the Greek text with explanatory notes; Sommerstein's 1982 translation also includes the Greek text and explanatory notes.)
* Aristotle (*c*. mid 4th century BC) *Metaphysics* I 6, XIII 4, *Nicomachean Ethics* VII 2–3, *Sophistical Refutations* 34, *Magna Moralia* I 1, *Poetics* 1, in J. Barnes (ed.) *The Complete Works of Aristotle*, revised Oxford Translation, Princeton, NJ: Princeton University Press, 1984, 2 vols. (Important testimony on Socrates. The *Magna Moralia* is possibly by a follower of Aristotle, and is of uncertain date.)
Benson, H.H. (ed.) (1992) *Essays on the Philosophy of Socrates*, New York: Oxford University Press. (Reprints fifteen of the best journal articles of the 1970s and 1980s on Socrates and Socratic philosophy; broad coverage of topics, full bibliography.)
* Cicero, M.T. (late 45 BC) *Tusculan Disputations*, trans. J.E. King, Loeb Classical Library, Cambridge, MA: Harvard University Press and London:

Heinemann, 1927. (Parallel Latin text and English translation.)
Giannantoni, G. (1990) *Socratis et Socraticorum Reliquiae* (The Fragments of Socrates and the Socratics), Naples: Bibliopolis, 4 vols. (Volumes 1 and 2 contain the surviving Greek and Latin testimonia of Socrates – other than in Plato and Xenophon – and of Antisthenes, Aeschines, Aristippus and other 'minor' Socratics; volume 4 has notes in Italian.)
Grote, G. (1875) *Plato and the Other Companions of Socrates*, London: Murray, 3 vols. (Judicious, perceptive older account of Socrates in Plato's works and of the other Socratics; still valuable.)
* Hegel, G.W.F. (1833–6) *Lectures on the History of Philosophy*, trans. E.S. Haldane and F.H. Simpson, London: Routledge & Kegan Paul, 1892. (Volume 1, pages 384–487 concern Socrates and the 'minor' Socratics.)
* Kierkegaard, S. (1840–1) *Om Begrebet Iron*, trans. L.M. Capel, *The Concept of Irony*, London: Collins, 1965. (Subtitled 'with constant reference to Socrates'.)
Maier, H. (1913) *Sokrates*, Tübingen: Mohr. (Authoritative German treatment of the 'Socratic problem', arguing for the reliability of Plato's testimony as against that of Xenophon.)
* Nietzsche, F. (1872) *Die Geburt der Tragödie*, trans. W. Kaufmann, *The Birth of Tragedy*, New York: Vintage Books, 1967. (Sections 7–13 especially concern Socrates.)
* Plato (*c*.390s–380s BC) *Apology, Euthyphro, Crito, Charmides, Laches, Lysis, Ion, Lesser Hippias, Protagoras, Greater Hippias*, in *Plato: Complete Works*, ed. J.M. Cooper, Indianapolis, IN: Hackett, 1997. (These are the works of Plato usually categorized as 'early' or 'Socratic' dialogues.)
* —— (*c*.380s–365 BC) *Meno, Gorgias, Phaedo, Symposium, Republic* I, *Phaedrus, Euthydemus, Theaetetus*, in *Plato: Complete Works*, ed. J.M. Cooper, Indianapolis, IN: Hackett, 1997. (The philosophical ideas in these dialogues cannot in general be assumed to be those of the historical Socrates; but they do contain biographical information and characteristic portrayals of his philosophical personality and manner.)
Reeve, C.D.C. (1989) *Socrates in the Apology*, Indianapolis, IN: Hackett. (Commentary on Plato's *Apology* in the light of Socrates' general philosophy; accessible to the general reader.)
Vlastos, G. (ed.) (1971) *The Philosophy of Socrates*, Garden City, NY: Doubleday. (Collection of essays: see especially G. Vlastos, 'The Paradox of Socrates', A.R. Lacey, 'Our Knowledge of Socrates', and M.F. Burnyeat, 'Virtues in Action'.)

18

—— (1991) *Socrates, Ironist and Moral Philosopher*, Ithaca, NY: Cornell University Press. (Comprehensive account based on a lifetime's engagement with Socrates' philosophy; good bibliography.)

* Xenophon (*c.*385 BC) *Apology of Socrates to the Jury*, trans. O.J. Todd, *Socrates' Defence to the Jury (Apology)*, Loeb Classical Library, Cambridge, MA: Harvard University Press and London: Heinemann, 1922. (Parallel Greek text and English translation.)

* —— (*c.*370s BC) *Symposium*, trans. O.J. Todd, *The Banquet*, Loeb Classical Library, Cambridge, MA: Harvard University Press and London: Heinemann, 1922. (Parallel Greek text and English translation.)

* —— (*c.*360s BC) *Memorabilia*, trans. E.C. Marchant, *Memoirs*, Loeb Classical Library, Cambridge, MA: Harvard University Press and London: Heinemann, 1923. (Parallel Greek text and English translation.)

Zeller, E. (1875) *Die Philosophie der Griechen*, 2. Teil, 1. Abteilung, *Sokrates und die Sokratiker*, trans. O.J. Reichel, *Socrates and the Socratic Schools*, London: Longmans, Green, 1885. (Exhaustive scholarly discussion and interpretation, which is still useful; part 2, section 1 concerns Socrates.)

JOHN M. COOPER

SOCRATIC DIALOGUES

After Socrates' death in 399 BC, a number of his followers composed imaginary dialogues between Socrates and various persons, usually historical. In addition to the dialogues of Plato there were works by Antisthenes, Aeschines, Phaedo, Euclides and, somewhat later, Xenophon. Only the writings of Plato and Xenophon have survived intact. The portrayal of Socrates varied from author to author, but the charismatic personality and skilful questioner is recognizable in each version. The connection between love and Socratic philosophy was frequently illustrated in Socrates' relationship to Alcibiades. The erotic theme was also represented in the role played by Aspasia, Pericles' mistress, in at least four authors, including Plato. Historical fact and even chronological possibility were regularly disregarded. This was essentially a genre of fiction.

1   The dialogue as a fictional genre
2   Literary interaction and common themes
3   The historical Socrates?
4   External form

1   The dialogue as a fictional genre

Socratic dialogues or 'Conversations with Socrates' (*Sōkratikoi logoi*) are recognized as a literary genre by Aristotle (*Poetics* 1), who is reported to have named a certain Alexamenos of Teos as the first author of such works. We know nothing further of Alexamenos, but we have remains from dialogues by Antisthenes, Aeschines, Phaedo and Euclides, in addition to the extant works of Plato and Xenophon. There must have been others, but the titles listed by the biographer Diogenes Laertius (II 12–16), of works by Crito, Simon the shoemaker, Glaucon, Simmias and Cebes, are probably all spurious.

The conversations are fictitious. Socrates' interlocutors are typically historical, but even here there are exceptions. The unwashed Pythagorean Telauges, after whom one of Aeschines' dialogues is named, is likely to be an imaginary stereotype. And in PLATO, Ion as typical rhapsode and CALLICLES as the unscrupulous politician, ideologically 'liberated' by the Enlightenment, may well be fictitious characters. The contrast with history is clearest in the case of XENOPHON, who wrote historical works as well as Socratic dialogues. When Xenophon in the *Memorabilia* or the *Oeconomicus* says 'I was there when Socrates said . . . ,' no one is expected to believe him. He begins his *Symposium* with the remark that he was present at the occasion. But the fictive date is set in 421 BC, when Xenophon would have been a child, and Xenophon is in fact not mentioned again in the dialogue. His claim to have been present seems to be only a device for introducing the narrative form without specifying a narrator.

In Aeschines' *Aspasia*, the occasion itself is fantastic. When asked by Callias to recommend a moral tutor for his son, Socrates proposes Aspasia, Pericles' mistress and a symbol of loose living in Attic comedy. The episodes are all chronologically dubious. Thus Aspasia is represented as interrogating Xenophon and his wife, although Aspasia must have been long dead before Xenophon was old enough to get married. In Aeschines' *Alcibiades* we find Alcibiades bursting into tears and laying his head on Socrates' knees, which is no more likely to be historical than the bedroom scene reported by Alcibiades in Plato's *Symposium*. In Phaedo's dialogue *Zopyrus*, an oriental sage of that name arrives in Athens and offers to read Socrates' character from his appearance. The diagnosis is surprising: Socrates is described as a sensualist. Both the episode and Zopyrus himself seem to have been invented by Phaedo in order to permit Socrates to respond: 'Such are my native tendencies, but they have been overcome by philosophy.'

Plato is probably unique in creating the illusion of historical reality for his dialogues (although Xenophon has tried to imitate this in his own *Symposium*). Historians have been misled therefore into dating Parmenides and Zeno by their trip to Athens, imagined by Plato in the *Parmenides*. Here again it seems clear that the occasion was invented for dramatic and philosophical reasons, since in Plato's eyes only Parmenides deserved the honour of refuting Socrates and criticizing the doctrine of Forms. The fictional character of the genre is even more obvious in Plato's *Menexenus*. There Socrates delivers a funeral oration which alludes to events of 386 BC (thirteen years after his own death), but the speech is attributed to Aspasia, who made it 'from the scraps left over from the funeral oration she composed for Pericles in 431 BC' (*Menexenus* 236b).

2 Literary interaction and common themes

By introducing Aspasia as author of funeral orations, Plato is developing a motif from Aeschines' *Aspasia*, where Aspasia is said to have taught rhetoric to Pericles and sharpened his tongue on the whetstone of Gorgias (fr. 22 Dittmar, A65 Giannantoni). We can trace this literary contact between Aeschines and Plato in several dialogues, and in both directions. Literary interaction on a larger scale is found in the erotic themes that are common to all the known Socratic authors. Thus dialogues named *Alcibiades* and *Aspasia* were composed both by Antisthenes and by Aeschines. Euclides is also credited with an *Alcibiades*, and with an *Eroticus* as well (unless these are two names for the same work). And, as we have seen, Phaedo's *Zopyrus* dealt explicitly with Socrates' erotic temperament. As generally with Socrates, we cannot know just what historical reality underlies this well-defined Socratic literary theme. What we can see is that Plato's treatment of love (*erōs*) in the *Lysis* and *Symposium*, and the erotic allusions to Alcibiades in the *Gorgias* and *Protagoras*, are firmly rooted in the Socratic literary tradition. Diotima in the *Symposium* seems to be Plato's answer to Aeschines' Aspasia, who gives a Socratic lesson on virtue to Xenophon and his wife.

There are many examples of Platonic influence on Xenophon, who seems also to have absorbed material from Antisthenes and Aeschines. There is no trace of Xenophon's Socratic writings in Plato.

3 The historical Socrates?

Parallels between different Socratic authors may allow us to catch a glimpse of the historical Socrates. Thus there is an interesting parallel to the Platonic Socrates' avowal of ignorance in Aeschines' *Alcibiades*, where Socrates insists that it was not by any art (*technē*) or knowledge (*mathēma*) that he thought he could help Alcibiades in his quest for virtue, but only by love (fr. 11 Dittmar, A53 Giannantoni). The same dialogue depicts an elenchus, in which Socrates succeeds in bringing Alcibiades to a consciousness of his own ignorance and need for improvement – not by a systematic argument, however, but by presenting him with the model of Themistocles, in comparison to which Alcibiades feels immensely inferior. This confirms the suggestion given in several Platonic passages (for example, *Apology* 24–7 and *Laches* 187e–188b), that the original elenchus was more a testing of persons than of propositions.

4 External form

The earliest Socratic dialogues are likely to have been in simple mime form (without narration or dramatic proem) as in Plato's *Crito*, *Ion*, and *Hippias Minor*. Aeschines' *Alcibiades* is more complex: it is narrated by Socrates and located in a gymnasium, like Plato's *Charmides* and *Lysis*. Antisthenes may have introduced himself into the dialogue as narrator or interlocutor, as Xenophon does (and later Cicero); whereas Plato and (as far as we know) Aeschines never appear in their own works. From the literary point of view, Aeschines was probably the most gifted Socratic author after Plato. But this was originally a minor genre, comprising short works like the *Ion* and *Hippias Minor*. With large compositions like the *Gorgias* and *Protagoras* Plato transformed the Socratic dialogue into a major art form, the vehicle for his own philosophy.

Writing after Plato, Xenophon composed the *Memorabilia* as a large work by putting together many mini-dialogues. In form, Xenophon's *Symposium* is loosely modelled after Plato's work of that name, although the content is altogether different.

See also: ANTISTHENES §1; SOCRATES §§1–2

References and further reading

For the Socratic dialogues of Plato and Xenophon, see 'List of works' under Plato and Xenophon.

* Aeschines (420–380 BC) Fragments in *Aischines von Sphettos*, ed. H. Dittmar, Berlin: Weidmann, 1912. (The basic study of Aeschines, with a full collection of his fragments, as known in 1912.)

Ehlers, B. (1966) *Eine vorplatonische Deutung des sokratischen Eros: Der Dialog Aspasia des Sokratikers Aischines* (A pre-Platonic Interpretation of

Socratic Love: The Dialogue *Aspasia* by Aeschines Socraticus), Munich: C.H. Beck'sche Verlagsbuchhandlung. (Convincing reconstruction of Aeschines' *Aspasia* and *Alcibiades*, in German.)

* Giannantoni, G. (1991) *Socratis et Socraticorum Reliquiae* (The Fragments of Socrates and the Socratics), Naples: Bibliopolis, 4 vols. (Volumes 1–2 include the fragments, in Greek or Latin, of the lost dialogues of the Socratics.)

Kahn, C.H. (1996) *Plato and the Socratic Dialogue*, Cambridge: Cambridge University Press. (Chapter 1 discusses Plato's relationship to the Socratic literary genre.)

Momigliano, A. (1971) *The Development of Greek Biography*, Cambridge, MA: Harvard University Press. (Best discussion in English of the non-historical character of the Socratic literature.)

Rossetti, L. (1980) 'Ricerche sui dialoghi socratici di Fedone e di Euclide' (Research on the Socratic Dialogues of Phaedrus and Euclides), *Hermes* 108: 183–200. (The fullest collection of evidence for the dialogues of Phaedo.)

C.H. KAHN

SOCRATIC SCHOOLS

*For approximately one and a half centuries after Socrates' death in 399 BC, several Greek philosophical schools and sects each claimed to be the true intellectual heirs of Socrates. Later doxographers emphasized the Socratic pedigree of each of these schools by establishing an uninterrupted succession (*diadochē*) between its alleged founder, who was invariably a member of Socrates' own entourage, and the philosophers who succeeded him as leaders of the school.*

Leaving aside Plato, the founder of the Academy, the members of the Socratic circle who left a succession behind them are Antisthenes, Aristippus of Cyrene, Euclides of Megara, and Phaedo of Elis, considered respectively the founders of Cynicism, and of the Cyrenaic, Megarian and Elian schools. It is these groupings, plus several of their offshoots, that are conventionally known as the 'Socratic schools'. All can be seen as, in their own ways, developing Socrates' ethical outlook, and several were concerned with exploring the logical and metaphysical implications of his dialectical principles.

1   **Cynics, Cyrenaics, Megarians and Dialecticians**
2   **The Elian and the Eretrian schools**
3   **How Socratic are the Socratic schools?**

1   Cynics, Cyrenaics, Megarians and Dialecticians

The Cynic movement appears intermittently for a period of about ten centuries, from the fourth century BC to the sixth century AD. Its archetypal figure was DIOGENES OF SINOPE, whose bohemian lifestyle and beggarly appearance exemplified the unity of principle and practice governing early Cynicism. Although ANTISTHENES (§1) was looked back on as the founder of Cynicism, his connection with the movement is problematic. Lacking any institutional structure, it could not, in any formal sense, have a founder. Nor can he be considered the forerunner of the kind of philosophical instruction practised by the Cynics, since unlike Antisthenes they undermined curricular education, preferred practical example to philosophical argumentation and adopted informal means of instruction (see CYNICS §1).

However, there is a sense in which the claims that Antisthenes is the predecessor of the movement and that the Cynics as a Socratic school are legitimate. Antisthenes is often considered the closest associate of Socrates, as reflected in both his logic and his ethical doctrine. In ethics, he shared the intellectualism of the Platonic Socrates, in that he considered virtue an understanding which, once acquired, amounts to wisdom and cannot be lost. But he also stressed the importance of physical and mental exercise, and the strength of character by which one overcomes one's weaknesses and achieves virtue. This moderated version of Socratic intellectualism provides a substantial common ground between the doctrine of Antisthenes and those of various Cynics.

The Cyrenaic school clearly counted as Socratic because founded by an associate of Socrates, Aristippus of Cyrene, whose own descendants succeeded him as the leaders of the school. Philosophically however, its doctrines have often been considered un-Socratic. For in ethics the Cyrenaics held various versions of hedonism, and several of them maintained that the bodily pleasure experienced at the present moment is the moral end. Again, in epistemology they developed a radical scepticism regarding our knowledge of the properties of external objects, whereas much of the evidence for Socrates suggests that, at least in the period in which Aristippus would have known him, he was concerned primarily with ethics. None the less, there were ways in which the Cyrenaics could reasonably claim that they remained faithful to the spirit of Socratic philosophy (see CYRENAICS §5; ARISTIPPUS THE ELDER).

The Socratic pedigree of the Megarian school is secured through Socrates' friend Euclides, who founded the school in his native Megara, although it is widely held to have been influenced also by the

Eleatic philosopher PARMENIDES. Its doctrines were ethical and metaphysical, and also concerned philosophical methodology and logic. Euclides taught an ethical monism related to the doctrine of the unity of virtue held by the Platonic Socrates and, perhaps, to the belief of Xenophon's Socrates in a providential universe that, presumably, is wholly good (see MEGARIAN SCHOOL).

The Megarians overlapped for about fifty years with the rival school of the Dialecticians, linked with Socrates via its founder, Clinomachus of Thurii, himself a pupil of Euclides. Although this school's speciality was apparently the development of dialectical skills for their own sake, it was classified as one of the ten ethical sects which developed the ethical part of philosophy that originated with Socrates (see DIALECTICAL SCHOOL).

2 The Elian and Eretrian schools

The Elian school was founded by Socrates' associate, Phaedo of Elis, soon after Socrates' death. Its founder is recorded as the author of several Socratic dialogues, of which only the *Zopyrus* and *Simon* were certainly his own works (see SOCRATIC DIALOGUES §1). The evidence suggests that both dialogues explored ethical subjects. The *Zopyrus*, named after a fifth-century physiognomist, probably aimed to modify the principle that there is an intrinsic relation between natural disposition and bodily form by arguing that the first can be entirely transformed – as in Socrates' own life – by the power of philosophy. *Simon* may have discussed various conceptions of virtue and its relation to pleasure, and perhaps defended a position according to which certain joys or pleasures are compatible with virtue. The themes linking the two works and securing a Socratic pedigree for Phaedo are the healing and reformative power of philosophy, its appropriateness for every person in every condition, the gradual and imperceptible effects of good and evil habits, and the importance of spiritual freedom with regard to external circumstances.

Phaedo's immediate successor was Plestanus of Elis, otherwise unknown. Anchipylus and Moschus, also from Elis, are listed as members of the Elian school, although Cynic features are attributed to them as well. But the most important philosophical heir of Phaedo was Menedemus of Eretria, after whom the school was relabelled the 'Eretrian school'. His criticisms of Plato, of Xenocrates, of the Cyrenaic Paraebates, of the Megarian Alexinus and of Aeschines suggest that he too was bidding for the mantle of Socrates. Even the testimony that he wrote nothing and did not adhere firmly to any doctrine may point to deliberate imitation of Socrates. However, a number of logical, metaphysical and ethical tenets are attributed to him. Reportedly, he accepted affirmative propositions and simple propositions but disallowed negative, complex or conditional statements. Although the point of this position is unclear, it may have been related to his beliefs that each thing can only be called by its own name, and that nothing must be at once one and many. These led him to remove the verb 'to be' from sentences such as 'that man is pale' and to remodel them with a periphrasis involving no use of the copula. In these respects, as well as in the commendation of tautologies, Menedemus' doctrine approaches Antisthenes' logic (see ANTISTHENES §4). Although he argued with great keenness and occasionally used paradoxes, he rejected Megarian eristics; on this account too Menedemus could claim to be faithful to the spirit of Socrates.

In ethics, Menedemus maintained that virtue is one thing called by many names, and probably implied that names which conventionally designate the different virtues are in fact synonyms – a point on which the Platonic Socrates is notoriously ambiguous. He espoused Euclides' position concerning the unity of the good (see §1) and he probably identified the good with virtue. He shared the intellectualism of other Socratics in that he placed the supreme moral good in the soul and believed that it can be achieved only by means of philosophical education which, therefore, is the single most important activity. But his bodily habits indicate that, like Antisthenes and the Cynics (see §1), he attributed moral importance to physical training as well. His proneness to superstition may suggest that he believed in a providential universe and, perhaps, in a divine creator. If so, his beliefs are comparable to those of Xenophon's Socrates and of Euclides. He took an active part in politics (a fact much resented by the Cynics), but similarly to many Socratics he kept his dignity, frankness and spiritual independence in the face of the powerful men of his day. His end, sadly, is reminiscent of Socrates' own: he was unjustly denounced for treason but, unlike Socrates, he left Eretria and died in exile by his own hand.

3 How Socratic are the Socratic schools?

Apart from the fact that the Socratic schools are founded by the entourage of Socrates, one should perhaps not attempt to find one single common thread unifying them. The links between them consist rather in family resemblances, between Socratics of the same generation or of different generations, many of them attributable with greater or lesser plausibility to Socrates himself. For example: Antisthenes and Aristippus stressed the importance of self-mastery and self-control regarding pleasure; Antisthenes and Phaedo considered some pleasures entirely compatible with virtue; Aristippus and the Cynics adopted the political attitudes of cosmopolitanism and of detachment from obligations to any particular city; Menedemus veered towards the ethics of the Cynics, and also held similar positions to Antisthenes in logic; the Megarians and the Dialecticians also worked on similar logical topics, such as modality, although their inquiries differed in scope and depth; Antisthenes, Stilpo, Menedemus and, perhaps the Dialecticians, subscribed to various forms of the doctrine that each thing has only one essence and that there is only one *logos* describing it (see LOGOS §1).

Some of the schools appear more formally organized than others. Aristippus and Phaedo probably ran proper schools, Antisthenes had a steady number of followers identified as 'the Antisthenians'; the Cynics and the later Cyrenaic sects were dispersed; and Menedemus was entirely informal in his teaching. Nevertheless, the label 'Socratic' is to a certain extent justified. The doctrinal links both with each other and with the views attributed to the historical Socrates are symptomatic of the competition, widespread in the fourth century BC and after, to recover and expound Socrates' authentic teachings.

See also: PLATO; SOCRATES §8; XENOPHON

References and further reading

Diogenes Laertius (*c.* early 3rd century AD) *Lives of the Philosophers*, trans. R.D. Hicks, *Diogenes Laertius Lives of Eminent Philosophers*, Loeb Classical Library, Cambridge, MA: Harvard University Press, 1925, 2 vols. (Greek text with English translation; see especially book II on the Socratics and book VI on Antisthenes and the Cynics.)

Giannantoni, G. (1990) *Socratis et Socraticorum Reliquiae* (The Fragments of Socrates and the Socratics), Naples: Bibliopolis. (The standard collection of Greek and Latin testimonies on the Socratic schools.)

Vander Waerdt, P. (1994) *The Socratic Movement*, Ithaca, NY: Cornell University Press. (Collection of essays.)

Zeller, E. (1869–82) *Die Philosophie der Griechen* (The Philosophy of the Greeks), 3rd edn, Leipzig: Reisland; relevant part available in English trans. by O.J. Reichel, *Socrates and the Socratic Schools*, Leipzig: Fues' Verlag (Reisland), 3rd edn, 1988. (Still in most ways the best overall account.)

VOULA TSOUNA

SOHRAVARDI
see AL-SUHRAWARDI, SHIHAB AL-DIN YAHYA

SOKRATIKOI LOGOI
see SOCRATIC DIALOGUES

SOLIDARITY

Solidarity exists among a group of people when they are committed to abiding by the outcome of some process of collective decision-making, or to promoting the wellbeing of other members of the group, perhaps at significant cost to themselves. Many regard solidarity as an important political ideal on the grounds that it is related to community and fraternity, and conducive to social cohesion and stability. Some individualists, however, believe that it is incompatible with autonomy on the grounds that full autonomy requires one always to take the final decision oneself about what one should do.

Solidarity is generally seen in two ways. First, as a commitment to other members of a group to abide by the outcome of their collective decision-making. Second, as a concern for other members of a group, which may require an unwillingness to receive a benefit unless the others do, or an unwillingness to receive a benefit when this will harm them. This commitment to the wellbeing of others is sometimes conceived in terms of the recognition of special obligations between the members of a group, which exist in virtue of their being members of it.

Solidarity has been of interest to social theorists concerned with the issue of what bonds unite people together in societies (see, for example, Durkheim 1983) (see DURKHEIM, É. §3). An understanding of the causes of solidarity can provide an insight into what makes societies stable, and what leads them to disintegrate. Because of its potential contribution to social stability and cohesiveness, solidarity has been regarded as instrumentally valuable.

Many political philosophers, particularly communitarians, have supposed that solidarity is also intrinsically valuable, believing that there is a conceptual connection between it and community or fraternity (see COMMUNITY AND COMMUNITARIANISM). For some communitarians, part of what it is to be a member of a community is to be in a reciprocal relationship of solidarity with the other members.

Socialist theorists have had special reasons for valuing solidarity because they have regarded it as a weapon against exploitation by capitalists, both in the struggle for better wages and conditions within the capitalist system, and in the fight against that system (see SOCIALISM). Reformist socialists have thought that strikes are likely to be effective only if there is solidarity among the workers. Some revolutionary socialists have thought that capitalism will be overthrown only if there is solidarity among the working class in general.

The existence of solidarity can provide a way of out situations which have the structure of a 'prisoner's dilemma' (see RATIONAL CHOICE THEORY §2). In the original prisoner's dilemma, two prisoners who have committed a certain crime are interviewed separately and offered a deal. If only one confesses, that prisoner alone will be released, whereas the other will receive a harsh sentence. If both confess, each will receive an intermediate sentence. If both refuse to confess, they will get a milder sentence for some different crime which can be proved independently of either confessing. If each prisoner is concerned solely with their own interest, it is rational for them to confess, even though if neither confesses the outcome will be better for each. But if each is unwilling to receive a benefit when this will harm the other, then each will refuse to confess, and both will be better off.

Solidarity will not, however, provide a way out of every such situation, because in many-person cases, it is often the case that one's own actions, even when motivated by a consideration of the good of others, will make no appreciable difference to the overall outcome. Consider, for example, the question of whether I should modify my car to reduce emissions from it. In such cases, it is not clear that solidarity will or should make any difference to my reasoning, except in the special case in which my community can be understood to have made some collective decision, perhaps to reduce emissions from cars, and solidarity is understood as a commitment to abide by such decisions. This kind of problem apparently besets Marxist analyses of how the revolution against capitalism will occur. One person's contribution will make no difference to whether the revolution will occur, so what reason does any individual have to expend energy in attempting to bring it about, even if they have a sense of solidarity with other working-class people?

Not everyone values solidarity, however, and even those who do value it may disagree about when it is valuable. It might be argued that solidarity is valuable only when channelled in pursuit of morally permissible or worthwhile goals. More fundamentally, someone might doubt whether solidarity is ever valuable because they believe that it is incompatible with personal autonomy (see AUTONOMY, ETHICAL). R.P. Wolff (1970), for example, argues that being autonomous always involves taking the final decision about what one should do, and that it is incompatible with any form of commitment requiring that one should act in accordance with the outcome of collective decision-making. First, however, not all conceptions of autonomy require that one should always retain the final decision about how to act. Second, even if autonomy is valuable and is incompatible with solidarity, this does not show that solidarity has no value, for perhaps there can be genuine values that are incompatible with one another (see MORAL PLURALISM). Third, a commitment to act in accordance with the outcome of a process of collective decision-making need not mean that one accepts that outcome uncritically. One might, for example, simply give the fact that it is such an outcome considerable weight in making the final decision about what one should do.

There are also disputes about the sort of relationships in which solidarity can be realized. Some maintain that solidarity is feasible only for small groups, whereas others believe that it is realizable among large groups. A society in which everyone willingly accepted and acted from what John Rawls (1971) has termed 'the difference principle' might be thought to embody solidarity (see RAWLS, J. §§1–2). The difference principle holds that inequalities in a society are permissible only if they benefit (or at least, do not harm) the worst-off. If the best-off were willing to forego benefits when by accepting them they would harm the worst-off, then solidarity would exist between them. Richard Rorty (1989) has argued that it makes sense to aim at solidarity even at the global level (see RORTY, R. §3). In his view solidarity would require not a belief in a shared human essence, but rather an ability to see traditional differences (for instance, those between tribes, nations, religions and races) as unimportant compared to our shared capacity to experience pain and humiliation.

See also: FAMILY, ETHICS AND THE; FRIENDSHIP; HONOUR

References and further reading

Benn, S.I. (1988) *A Theory of Freedom*, Cambridge: Cambridge University Press, ch. 12. (Traces the connections between notions such as comradeship, mutual concern, community and autonomy, and raises the question in what sort of relationships each of these can be realized.)

* Durkheim, É. (1983) *De la division du travail social,*

trans. W.D. Halls, *The Division of Labour in Society*, London: Macmillan. (Distinguishes different kinds of solidarity and examines their causes.)

Dworkin, G. (1988) *The Theory and Practice of Autonomy*, Cambridge: Cambridge University Press, ch. 1. (Criticizes conceptions of autonomy which are logically incompatible with commitment.)

Elster, J. (1985) *Making Sense of Marx*, Cambridge: Cambridge University Press, 6.2. (Raises the issue of how Marxists are to explain the emergence of revolutionary motivation.)

* Rawls, J. (1971) *A Theory of Justice*, Oxford: Clarendon Press, 60–65, 76–80, 105–6. (Defends the 'difference principle' as an interpretation of fraternity.)

* Rorty, R. (1989) *Contingency, Irony, and Solidarity*, Cambridge: Cambridge University Press, ch. 9. (Offers an account of how solidarity should be understood at the global level.)

* Wolff, R.P. (1970) *In Defence of Anarchism*, New York: Harper & Row. (Defends the idea that full autonomy is incompatible with a commitment to abiding by collective decision-making.)

ANDREW MASON

SOLIPSISM

'Solipsism' (from the Latin solus ipse *– oneself alone) is the doctrine that only oneself exists. This formulation covers two doctrines, each of which has been called solipsism, namely (1) that one is the only self, the only centre of consciousness, and, more radically, (2) that nothing at all exists apart from one's own mind and mental states. These are not always distinguished from corresponding epistemic forms: for all we know, (1) or (2) might be true.*

A more recent coinage is 'methodological solipsism', which has a quite different meaning: that the content of an individual's thoughts is fully determined by facts about them, and is independent of facts about their environment.

Philosophical interest in solipsism does not arise from the fact that some significant philosopher has advocated it, for none has done so. Rather, solipsism has played dialectical roles, as for instance when philosophers try to argue that their opponents' positions, consistently pursued, lead to solipsism – and are thereby shown to be harbouring an absurdity. It plays another such role when philosophers ask whether there are any rational considerations capable of refuting it. More extreme forms of scepticism are sometimes treated in the same way – unsurprisingly, since the epistemic versions of solipsism are themselves extreme forms of scepticism.

That one is, for all one knows, the only centre of consciousness, is precisely the traditional problem of other minds (see OTHER MINDS). It can be based on the thoughts that one has no direct awareness of the mental states of others, and that to infer that they must have mental states because of the outward resemblance between their bodily behaviour and one's own is to make an inference based on one case only – not normally regarded as sound inductive procedure. Another, more radical, argument is that one is unable even to form any concept of a state of consciousness that is not one's own. This approach is discussed by Wittgenstein – who was not, however, recommending that we should accept its conclusion, but rather that we should abandon the natural, though mistaken, conception of a state of consciousness which leads us into it. On a right understanding of the matter, ascriptions of mental states to ourselves and to others are co-ordinate achievements. Solipsists wrongly think they can ascribe such states to themselves and *then* consider the question whether other human bodies have associated mental states as well (see CRITERIA; PRIVATE LANGUAGE ARGUMENT).

The second type of solipsism, which finds problematic not just the existence of other minds but of *everything* other than one's own mind and mental states, is a very close relation of scepticism about the existence of the external world (see SCEPTICISM). Although closely related, it is not the same thing, since a number of philosophers from widely varying traditions have denied the existence – or at least the independent existence – of a material world, while showing no tendency to assert that theirs was the only mind. BERKELEY is a prime example, and DHARMAKĪRTI, having portrayed the material world as illusory, wrote a treatise explaining why solipsism was not an inevitable consequence.

The expression 'methodological solipsism' is a recent coinage popularized by, in particular, Hilary PUTNAM and Jerry FODOR. This phrase refers to the view that the content of an individual's thoughts is fully determined by intrinsic, non-relational facts about that individual, hence is not affected by the nature of the objects that form their environment (see CONTENT: WIDE AND NARROW; METHODOLOGICAL INDIVIDUALISM).

References and further reading

Dharmakīrti (mid 7th century) *Samtānāntarasiddhi* (Proof of other continua); English trans. in Kitagawa, Hidenori, *Indo koten ronrigaku no kenkyū:*

Jinna (Dignāga) no taikei, Tokyo: Suzuki Gaku-jutsu Zaidan, 2nd edn, 1973, Appendix A. (Dharmakirti's defence against the threat of solipsism. The 'continuum' of the Sanskrit title is a Buddhist word for mind in the sense of a continuous series of mental events.)

Russell, B. (1948) *Human Knowledge: its Scope and its Limits*, London: George Allen & Unwin. (Part III Chapter 2, 'Solipsism', introduces a radical version of solipsism and considers reasons against it.)

Wittgenstein, L. (1953) *Philosophical Investigations*, Oxford: Blackwell. (Contains an extended discussion of the idea that mental states are inner objects, awareness of which gives us our primary understanding of the mental – see approximately Sections 243–317; suggestive, but difficult.)

EDWARD CRAIG

SOLOMON IBN GABIROL

see IBN GABIROL, SOLOMON

SOLOVEITCHIK, JOSEPH B. (1903–93)

Joseph B. Soloveitchik was a Jewish philosopher in the fullest sense. For such thinkers, the task of building intellectual and spiritual bridges between their particular traditions and other cultures permeates and shapes all their philosophic commitments and endeavours.

Medieval philosophers sought to integrate the competing knowledge claims of natural reason and authoritative revelation. Soloveitchik, by contrast, ignored metaphysics and epistemology, focusing instead on refuting the alleged incompatibility between Judaism and the active, human-centred ethos of modernity. His major concern was not the truth of religion but the relevance and significance of religious human types and ideals in modern Western culture.

1 *Halakhic* man as religious hero
2 'The Lonely Man of Faith'

1 *Halakhic* man as religious hero

Unlike BUBER, who introduced traditional Judaism to modern Western culture by focusing on such universal themes as religious existentialism, pietism and mysticism, Soloveitchik introduced a new human archetype into the philosophic discussion: the *talmid hakham*, the Talmudic scholar, the hero of the eastern European (especially Lithuanian) Jewish intellectual tradition. Although such a figure seems *prima facie* to be the very obverse of the modern, triumphant man of action, Soloveitchik set out to reveal the implicit modern human spirit of the Talmudic scholar. The culture of Talmudic learning, Soloveitchik showed, was unique in its conceptual methodology and distinctive in its consuming devotion to study. Its values of intellectual rigour, integrity, boldness and creativity cultivated a human type that personified a special variety of human independence, autonomy and self-worth – the principal characteristics of the hero of modern Western culture.

Soloveitchik's methodology, which he pursues in later writings, consists in constructing contrasting human types, in this case cognitive man versus *homo religiosus*. The former is an archetype of the modern scientist – this-worldly, action-oriented, confident, triumphant, at home in the world. *Homo religiosus*, on the other hand, is guilt-driven and grace-oriented, a spiritual manic-depressive who oscillates between a disgust for this imperfect world and a longing for the transcendent perfection of the divine reality.

Unlike his countertype, the man of natural religion, who is torn between self-negation and self-glorification, *halakhic* man possesses an objective normative way of life which fortifies him against the wild fluctuations of subjectivity, giving him a permanent sense of legitimacy and self-worth. The performance of *mitzvot* (commandments) entails a sense of covenantal responsibility which confirms the doer, as God's, that is, the covenantal partner – with dignity and legitimacy.

In Soloveitchik's conceptual scheme, not only law and the Sinaitic covenant but also the biblical narrative of creation itself constitutes a mandate enjoining human autonomy and dignity. Soloveitchik makes a bold exegetical move by extending the idea of *imitatio Dei* (which is applied to ethical attributes in rabbinic literature to include the attribute of God as creator). Creative human behaviour becomes metaphysically similar to divine creativity.

SPINOZA had claimed that the Judaic legal tradition fostered a slave morality that inhibited the development of personal moral responsibility. Soloveitchik countered both this and Kant's critique of Judaism for holding to what he deemed a heteronomous ethics by arguing that *halakhic* man appropriates the heteronomous, revealed norm as an autonomous, self-created norm (see KANT, I.). Soloveitchik himself creatively showed how modern existentialist typologies could find roots in *halakhah*.

2 'The Lonely Man of Faith'

In later works, Soloveitchik's protagonist changes from the heroic *halakhic* man (in many ways a counterpart to the archetypal ideal of American Pragmatism) into a more dialectical, existentialist figure: the lonely man of faith. The empathy of Soloveitchik's prose shift from the active, outward-directed virtues of creativity and autonomy, to the more introspective, radically personal experiences of loneliness, crisis and defeat.

The essay 'The Lonely Man of Faith' (1965) discusses two human types derived from the two creation stories in Genesis: 'Adam the first' is created in the image of God, together with Eve, and ordered by God to 'fill the earth and master it' (Genesis 1: 28); 'Adam the second' is fashioned alone from the dust of the earth by God, who responds to his existential predicament ('It is not good for man to be alone' (Genesis 2: 18)) by creating another human being.

While this typological structure resembles the dichotomy between the cognitive-man and *homo-religiosus* of *Ish ha-Halakhah* (Halakhic Man) (1944), the superior human synthesis, now called covenantal man, is less weighted in favour of assertiveness and adequacy. Here we find the strong countervailing influence of existential loneliness and defeat.

Adam the first fulfils the mandate of the impersonal God of Being by pursuing science and technology and by gaining dominion over an impersonal nature. Adam the second responds to an inner, existential need by seeking relationship with another individual or indeed, with a personal God (Adonai, the Lord, the God who is named by the Tetragrammaton).

Soloveitchik argues that *halakhic* culture addressed the second Adam's existential quest through the covenant and the *mitzvot*. The individual can transcend temporality and personal death through participation in the normative history of the Jewish people. The existential need for relationship can be met by encountering a God who addresses one as thou and with whom one can share in a relationship of covenantal mutuality. The fundamental point of the covenantal faith community of Adam the second is that it seeks redemption through sacrifice, even in defeat and retreat. The underlying crisis calling for redemption is loneliness rather than sin or inadequacy.

The man of faith is far more complex than his heroic predecessor, *halakhic* man. Like the latter, he knows that achieving and expressing individual dignity and adequacy are integral constituents of the total faith gesture. Human majesty and creativity are forms of *imitatio Dei*. Faith thus requires that the man of faith be creative, free and assertive, as well as

obedient, subservient and sacrificial. The God who commands the former also commands the latter (see FAITH).

See also: HALAKHAH; JEWISH PHILOSOPHY, CONTEMPORARY

List of works

Soloveitchik, J. (1944) *Ish ha-Halakhah*, trans. L. Kaplan, *Halakhic Man*, Philadelphia, PA: Jewish Publications Society, 1983. (His early analysis of the notion of the *halakhic* individual as hero.)
—— (1944) *Ish ha-Halakhah Gahu ve-nistar*, trans. L. Kaplan, *The Halakhic Mind: An Essay on Jewish Tradition and Modern Thought*, New York: Free Press, 1986. (Analysis of the nature of Jewish law with its implications for human action.)
—— (1964) 'Confrontation', *Tradition* 6 (2): 5–29. (Discussion of modernity versus tradition.)
—— (1965) 'The Lonely Man of Faith', *Tradition* 7 (2): 5–67. (Crucial essay of his later period stressing existentialist strategies.)
—— (1979) *Reflections of the Rav*, ed. A.R. Besdin, Jerusalem: World Zionist Organization. (Collection of his papers.)
—— (1989) *Man of Faith in the Modern World: Reflections Of The Rav, II*, ed. A.R. Besdin, Hoboken, NJ: Ktav. (Adaptation and translation of lectures.)

References and further reading

Fox, M. (1989) 'The Unity and Structure of Rabbi Joseph B. Soloveitchik's Thought', *Tradition* 24 (2): 44–65. (An interesting but forced attempt at unifying all of Soloveitchik's thought.)
Hartman, D. (1985) *A Living Covenant*, New York: Free Press, 60–109, 150–60. (A critique of Soloveitchik's *halakhic* anthropology.)
Leaman, O. (1996) 'Jewish Existentialism: Rosenzweig, Buber and Soloveitchik', in D. Frank and O. Leaman (eds) *History of Jewish Philosophy*, London: Routledge, 799–819. (Examination of the links between Soloveitchik and other Jewish existentialists.)
Singer, D. and Sokol, M. (1982) 'Joseph Soloveitchik: Lonely Man of Faith', *Modern Judaism* 2: 227–72. (A psychological analysis of the inner tensions in Soloveitchik's thought.)
Spero, S. (1996) 'Rabbi Joseph Dov Soloveitchik and the Philosophy of Halakha', *Tradition* 30 (2): 41–64.

(A critique of Soloveitchik's understanding of the relationship of nature and *halakhah*.)

D. HARTMAN

SOLOV'ËV, VLADIMIR SERGEEVICH (1853–1900)

It has been widely acknowledged that Vladimir Solov'ëv is the greatest Russian philosopher of the nineteenth century; his significance for Russian philosophy is often compared to the significance of Aleksandr Pushkin for Russian poetry. His first works marked the beginning of the revolt against positivism in Russian thought, followed by a revival of metaphysical idealism and culminating in the so-called Religious-Philosophical Renaissance of the early twentieth century.

Unlike the Russian idealists of the Romantic epoch, Solov'ëv was a professional, systematic philosopher. He created the first all-round philosophical system in Russia and thus inaugurated the transition to the construction of systems in Russian philosophical thought. At the same time he remained faithful to the Russian intellectual tradition of reluctance to engage in purely theoretical problems; his ideal of 'integrality' postulated that theoretical philosophy be organically linked to religion and social practice. He saw himself not as an academic philosopher, but rather as a prophet, discovering the way to universal regeneration.

One of the main themes of Solov'ëv's philosophy of history was Russia's mission in universal history. Owing to this he was interested in the ideas of the Slavophiles and, in the first period of his intellectual evolution, established close relations with the Slavophile and Pan-Slavic circle of Ivan Aksakov. He was close also to Dostoevskii, on whom he made a very deep impression. At the beginning of the 1880s he began to dissociate himself from the epigones of Slavophilism; his final break with them came in 1883, when he became a contributor to the liberal and Westernizing Vestnik Evropy *(European Messenger). The main reason for this was the pro-Catholic tendency of his thought, which led him to believe that Russia had to acknowledge the primacy of the Pope. In his view, this was a necessary condition of fulfilling Russia's universal mission, defined as the unification of the Christian Churches and the establishment of a theocratic Kingdom of God on earth.*

In the early 1890s Solov'ëv abandoned this utopian vision and concentrated on working out an autonomous ethic and a liberal philosophy of law. This reflected his optimistic faith in liberal progress and his confidence that even the secularization of ethics was essentially a part of the divine–human process of salvation. In the last year of his life, however, historiosophical optimism gave way to a pessimistic apocalypticism, as expressed in his philosophical dialogue Tri razgovora *(Three Conversations) (1900), and especially the 'Tale of the Antichrist' appended to it.*

1 **The philosophy of All-Unity**
2 **Godmanhood and Sophia**
3 **Theocratic utopia**
4 **Ethics, philosophy of law and theory of knowledge**
5 **Solov'ëv's continuators**

1 The philosophy of All-Unity

Vladimir Solov'ëv was the son of Sergei Solov'ëv, a leading Westernizing historian and professor at Moscow University. After the brilliant defence of his master's thesis, *Krizis zapadnoi filosofii: protiv pozitivistov* (The Crisis of Western Philosophy: Against the Positivists) (1874), he began lecturing at St Petersburg University. His academic career, however, proved to be short-lived. The assassination of Alexander II (March 1881) prompted him to give a public lecture in which, while condemning the revolutionary terrorists, he appealed to the new tsar to spare their lives. As a result he was forbidden to lecture in public and shortly afterwards resigned from the university.

The general outline of Solov'ëv's philosophy follows the Neoplatonic scheme of self-enriching alienation. Conceiving the world as the divine absolute in the process of becoming, he distinguished in it three moments, corresponding to the three persons of the Holy Trinity: the moment of a static, undifferentiated unity, the moment of individuation and differentiation and, finally, the highest moment of a free, differentiated unity. In his *Filosofskie nachala tselnogo znaniya* (*Philosophical Principles of Integral Knowledge*) (1877) and in his doctoral dissertation, *Kritika otvlechënnych nachal* (*The Critique of Abstract Principles*) (1880), Solov'ëv applied this scheme to human history and knowledge. In the evolution of humankind, he argued, the first phase (substantial monism) was represented by the Eastern world (including nineteenth-century Islam), and the second phase (atomism) by Western European civilization. During the first phase the three spheres of human activity – creativity, knowledge and social practice – were entirely subordinated to religion. In the sphere of creativity, technology (the material grade) was fused with art (the formal grade) and mysticism (the highest, absolute grade) in a mystical *theurgy*. In the sphere of knowledge, positive science (the material grade) was fused with abstract philosophy (the formal

28

grade) in an undifferentiated *theosophy*. In the sphere of social practice, the economic self-government or *zemstvo* (the material grade) was fused with the state (the formal grade) and the Church (the absolute grade) in a homogeneous *theocracy*. In the second evolutionary phase the different grades within each sphere strove for absolute autonomy and mastery over one another. In the resulting struggle matter conquered spirit: the final outcome of Western civilization was materialistic socialism (the true scion of capitalism) in the social sphere, positivism in the sphere of knowledge, and utilitarian realism in the sphere of creativity. Now the time had come for the third phase – that of *free unity* – in which the separate spheres and grades of human creativity, knowledge and social practice would once more be united, but without losing their distinctiveness: as a free theurgy, a free theosophy and a free theocracy. The mission of inaugurating this universal regeneration and reintegration of human life was to be fulfilled by the Russians.

In the sphere of knowledge Solov'ëv distinguished three types of philosophy – naturalism (empiricism), rationalism and mysticism. Empiricism and rationalism took different paths to arrive at the same result – the denial of the substantial reality of both the external world and the knower himself. Following the elderly Schelling and the Slavophiles, Solov'ëv saw Hegelianism as the last word in rationalism (see SCHELLING, F.W.J.; SLAVOPHILISM). He accused Hegel of creating a merely 'negative' philosophy, dealing only with empty concepts, and, like Schelling, set against this a programmatically 'positive' philosophy, rehabilitating 'the given'. It involved a rehabilitation of nature, as a manifestation of the divine absolute, and, above all, a philosophical interpretation of the Christian revelation.

The central idea in Solov'ëv's system was that of positive 'All-Unity'. He also used Kireevskii's concept of 'integral wholeness' (see SLAVOPHILISM §1) but interpreted it differently, stressing that free unity presupposes the differentiation of the original wholeness and autonomization of different spheres of life and knowledge. Therefore, Western civilization, including Western philosophy, was for him not a 'wrong path' (as it was for the Slavophiles), but a necessary phase of human development.

2 Godmanhood and Sophia

Solov'ëv's reinterpretation of Christianity revolves around the concept of Godmanhood, developed by him in a series of extremely successful lectures in St Petersburg *Chteniia o bogochelovechestve* (*Lectures on Godmanhood*) (1877–81). The concept of 'God made

man', Solov'ëv asserted, does not assume either a dualistic belief in the transcendence of God, or a pantheistic belief in his immanence in the world. God is both immanent and transcendent, and the mediating principle that allows the world to become transfused by the divine spirit is Man. The ultimate purpose of the universe is to achieve the stage of a free, innerly differentiated All-Unity. The cosmic history began with a dramatic event: the soul of the world, or Sophia, had once fallen away from the divine Logos, plunging the world into a chaotic struggle of hostile elements. The second act of the cosmic drama was the appearance of man. Since then Sophia, having identified itself with 'ideal humanity', began to ascend to a renewed unity with God in Godmanhood. The union of Logos with Sophia, of God with man, was accomplished in Jesus Christ. The incarnation of God in Jesus was thus the central event in the entire cosmic process. Even this, however, was only the beginning of the soteriological process. To finish the work of salvation, that is, to achieve the universal regeneration and transfiguration of the world, it was necessary to pass through all stages of human history and to realize the destiny of man in the Kingdom of God on earth.

The concept of Sophia in Solov'ëv's philosophy is somewhat ambiguous and subject to different interpretations. In some of his writings Solov'ëv defined Sophia, or the Wisdom of God, as 'the substance of the Holy Ghost', the passive, female element in God, 'external Womanhood'. In the autobiographical poem 'Three Meetings' he identified Sophia with the mysterious feminine being which visited him in his mystic visions. He was thoroughly acquainted with a vast mystical and theosophical literature on Sophia: in the Bible (Solomon's Proverbs), in the Kabbalah (where Sophia is presented as a woman) (see KABBALAH), in the writings of the gnostics (where it is 'divine matter' and the 'feminine aeon') (see GNOSTICISM §4), in Jakob Boehme (who identified it with 'eternal virginity'), in Emanuel Swedenborg and Louis-Claude Saint-Martin. He thought that the idea of Sophia was particularly close to the traditions of Eastern Christianity, and saw a proof of this in an old icon with the image of Sophia in the cathedral of Novgorod. In the most general terms it may be said that he needed the concept of Sophia to define divinity within the world, unity in the creation, and the link between the world and the transcendent God.

As 'the feminine principle in God' Sophia was bound up with Solov'ëv's theory of sexual love, expounded in *Smysl liubvi* (*The Meaning of Love*) (1892–4). It claimed that the real significance of love consists not in procreation, which is merely the absurd multiplication of mortal beings, but in the human striving for the likeness of God in a restored androgynous unity.

Solov'ëv's vision of universal reintegration can also be found in his aesthetics. As a motto for his essay 'Beauty in Nature' (1889) Solov'ëv chose Dostoevskii's words 'Beauty will save the world'. Natural beauty, he maintained, is a manifestation of the concrete operations of the Absolute in the material world; by 'transilluminating' and spiritualizing matter, beauty helps to raise the fallen World Soul and to introduce an element of the divine into reality. In the essay 'The Overall Meaning of Art' (1890) Solov'ëv applied this conception to artistic beauty: art, he argued, is an instrument of reintegration, a theurgic force capable of 'transilluminating' and transforming the human world.

3 Theocratic utopia

Russia's mission in universal history was defined by Solov'ëv as the realization of a 'free theocracy' – a social system based upon Christian principles and thus establishing the Kingdom of God on earth. Solov'ëv's Slavophile friends warmly sympathized with this vision but remained sceptical about his ecumenical ideas. When Solov'ëv arrived at the conclusion that Russia, in order to fulfil her mission, should recognize the authority of the Pope, his break with the Slavophile circles became unavoidable.

To avoid censorship, Solov'ëv's vision of 'free theocracy' had to be expounded in books published abroad, such as *Istoriia i budushchnost' teokratii* (The History and the Future of Theocracy) (Zagreb, 1887), *L'Idée Russe* (The Russian Idea) (Paris, 1888) and *La Russie et l'Église Universelle* (*Russia and the Universal Church*) (London 1889). In Russia these books were received as Roman Catholic propaganda and consequently often aroused hostility. This was not just a misunderstanding; in 1886 Solov'ëv recognized the Pope as supreme judge in matters of religion, and three years later, in *Russia and the Universal Church*, publicly defended this view. It was known, as well, that his vision was supported by the influential Croatian bishop, Josip Strossmayer (who commended Solov'ëv's ideas to Pope Leo XIII). On the other hand, however, it needs to be stressed that the French Jesuits ceased to support his project on the grounds of its heterodox ideas (especially in the theosophical part of his views).

Solov'ëv's conception of 'free theocracy' rested on his view that the structure of legitimate authority had to be triune, corresponding to the three persons of the Holy Trinity. The Kingdom of God on earth, he argued, will be established when humanity becomes unified under the authority of one high priest (representing God the Father) and one emperor (representing the Son), and when genuine prophets, 'the free breath of the Holy Ghost', appear constantly among the common people to mediate between the temporal and spiritual authorities. This vision was to materialize in the unification of the human race under the spiritual rule of the Pope and the secular rule of the Russian tsar. In this way Russia would take up the old idea of a Christian Empire, formulated by Constantine the Great, Charlemagne and the greatest Catholic writer, Dante Alighieri. In the realization of this task Russia would be supported by the two 'theocratic nations' which shared in her historical fate: the Jews and the Poles.

Solov'ëv did not proclaim that members of the Orthodox Churches should simply convert to Roman Catholicism. On the contrary: he combined sharp criticism of religious particularism (or even the nationalism of the Greek and Russian clergy), with an emphasis on the unique spiritual values of Eastern Christianity. The Roman Pope was, in his view, the legitimate head of the Universal Church, but this did not mean equating the Universal Church with the Roman Catholic Church. The Universal Church was a broader notion, embracing both Western and Eastern Christianity. Solov'ëv concluded from this that the recognition of the authority of the Pope would liberate the Orthodox Church from humiliating dependence on the imperial power without entailing any danger for the existence of the distinctively Eastern religious culture.

Solov'ëv saw no contradiction between his theocratic ideal and his growing sympathy with liberal political ideas. He stressed that his theocracy was to be 'free', hence liberal and universalist, and thus incompatible with nationalism (which he distinguished from patriotism). In a series of articles published in the liberal *Vestnik Evropy* (European Messenger) and reprinted in the book entitled *Natsional'nyi vopros Rossii* (The Problem of Nationalities in Russia) (two volumes, 1891), he firmly condemned all forms of persecution and discrimination against national and religious minorities.

At the beginning of the 1890s Solov'ëv became disillusioned with theocratic utopianism and as a result drew even closer to the liberals. But he remained faithful to the view that, in order to resist the evils of national egoism, Russia should embrace liberal principles without abandoning her imperial calling.

4 Ethics, philosophy of law and theory of knowledge

The de-utopianization of Solov'ëv's thought brought about a marked secularization of his views on ethics.

His comprehensive treatise *Opravdanie dobra* (*The Justification of the Good*) (1897) was to be a system of independent ethics, in the sense of the independence of ethical conduct from metaphysical theories and religious dogmas. It is divided into three parts: (1) The Good in Human Nature, (2) The Good from God and (3) The Good in the History of Humankind. In Part I Solov'ëv tried to give his ethic empirical foundations by deriving it from feelings of shame, compassion, and religious adoration; he stressed, however, that empirical ethics must be supplemented by rational ethics whose highest principle is the categorical imperative of Kant (see KANT, I. §9). In Part II he dealt with moral progress, explaining it as the development of man's divine features, or the realization of the idea of Godmanhood. The two parts of this process were (1) the realization of Godmanhood in an individual, and (2) the realization of Godmanhood in the collective life of humankind.

With this conclusion Solov'ëv passed to Part III of his ethical system – to 'objective ethics', or the institutionalized forms of the historical education of humanity, as opposed to 'subjective ethics', concentrating on purely individual perfection and salvation. The emphasis on objective ethics, embodied in the institutions of the state, was also an essential feature of his theocratic ideal. But the difference was profound: according to Solov'ëv's objective ethics Church and state were to be formally separated and the task of securing the moral character of social and political life was to be fulfilled not by a theocratic government, but by an impersonal system of legal rules. In this way the realization of the idea of Godmanhood in history was made dependent on man's maturity, on his full moral autonomy, incompatible with any form of tutelage in the spiritual sphere.

This Kantian reinterpretation of the idea of Godmanhood found expression in Solov'ëv's philosophy of law, elaborated in the relevant chapters of *The Justification of the Good* and in a separate booklet *Law and Morality* (1897). This legal philosophy, defining law as the compulsory and enforceable minimum morality, was the earliest Russian variant of a 'new liberalism' concerned not only with negative freedom, but with positive freedom as well. In Solov'ëv's conception, the modern rule-of-law state was given a new function: that of ensuring for everyone a minimum of positive freedom and justice, that is equal opportunity and the minimum of welfare necessary for a 'dignified existence'. Solov'ëv saw 'dignified existence' as a new human right, as something legally claimable, and interpreted it very broadly. In his view, 'the right to a dignified existence' included not only rights to employment, to proper working conditions and proper earnings, but also to rest and free time. He anticipated modern ecological movements by postulating that enterprising individuals should not be given a free hand in conquering and exploiting nature, because the preservation of the natural environment is a necessary condition of a worthwhile existence.

Solov'ëv made it clear that even the best realization of this ideal would not have amounted to the millenarian Kingdom of God. He stressed that he did not want to legislate absolute morality but only to give legal backing to a moral minimum.

Another consequence of the de-utopianization of Solov'ëv's views was his increased willingness to treat interest in theoretical questions as autonomous, independent of social and religious concerns. This shift in his thought is shown in his three epistemological articles under the title *Osnovy teoreticheskoi filosofii* (Foundations of Theoretical Philosophy) (1897–9). His reflections on epistemological issues led Solov'ëv to reject the Cartesian tradition of 'spiritualist dogmatism' that assumed the substantiality of the knower. He also substantially modified his conception of 'integral knowledge' by de-emphasizing its mystical character and stressing instead 'purposeful cognition', or a 'vital act of decision' that directs the consciousness towards absolute truth and transforms immediate sense impressions into the material of the complex process of active cognition. To some extent the concept of 'purposeful cognition' recalls the phenomenological notion of 'intention' and the 'intentional act'. Unfortunately, further elaboration of these ideas was prevented by Solov'ëv's premature death.

5 Solov'ëv's continuators

During his lifetime Solov'ëv won recognition in the milieu of professional philosophers grouped around the periodical *Problems of Philosophy and Psychology*. He had also two direct and very talented disciples, brothers Sergei and Evgenii Trubetskoi. His influence, however, only became widespread, reaching far beyond professional philosophers, in the first decade of the twentieth century, due to the powerful revival of the interest in religious ideas in Russian thought. It is no exaggeration to say that an entire generation of Russian idealist philosophers and religious thinkers was schooled in his philosophy. Sergei BULGAKOV, Semën FRANK, Father Pavel FLORENSKII and Lev Karsavin based their work on Solov'ëv's metaphysics of All-Unity and developed different variants of 'Sophiology'. Prince Sergei Trubetskoi made use of Solov'ëv's ideas in his polemics against 'epistemological individualism', in which he referred to the concept of a supra-individual consciousness identified by him with Sophia. The intuitivist Nicholas LOSSKY tried to use Solov'ëv's ideas in a different way, combining his notion of All-Unity with a monadistic pluralism. Messianic and eschatological motifs in Solov'ëv's thought exercised a strong, formative influence on Nikolai BERDIAEV and on the critic and novelist Dmitrii Merezhkovskii who formulated the ideas of a 'new religious consciousness' (see RUSSIAN RELIGIOUS-PHILOSOPHICAL RENAISSANCE §3). Solov'ëv's seminal influence can also be traced in the work of the Russian symbolist poets – Viacheslav Ivanov, Andrei Belyi, and Aleksandr Blok (see RUSSIAN RELIGIOUS-PHILOSOPHICAL RENAISSANCE §4). Solov'ëv's conception of the 'right to a dignified existence' was taken up and developed by Pavel Novgorodtsev, the leading representative of the neo-idealist current in Russian philosophy of law, closely bound up with Russian liberalism (see LIBERALISM, RUSSIAN §3). Another philosopher of Russian 'new liberalism', Sergei HESSEN, elaborated a Neo-Kantian reinterpretation of Solov'ëv's philosophy of All-Unity, stressing the idea of the autonomy of different spheres of culture and setting it against utopian motifs in Solov'ëv's thought.

In the Soviet Union interest in Solov'ëv was deliberately suppressed. The first Soviet edition of Solov'ëv's selected works appeared only under Gorbachev's *perestroika*, in 1988. In the West interest in Solov'ëv is still limited but constantly growing. He is best known in Germany, where his selected works were first published in 1914–17 (Jena, three volumes) and 1921–2 (Stuttgart, four volumes), paving the way for the ambitious undertaking of a German edition of his collected works, started in 1953. In France Solov'ëv is known mostly in Catholic circles interested in ecumenical ideas. At the end of 1991 a transnational 'Vladimir Solovyov Society' (with offices in Norwich, Vermont, and in Moscow) was called into being at a meeting in Moscow between American and Russian scholars.

List of works

Solov'ëv, V.S. (1966–70) *Sobranie sochinenii* (Collected Works), phototype edn, Brussels, 12 vols. (Solov'ëv's collected works in Russian.)
—— [Solowjew. W.S.] (1977–9) *Deutsche Gesamtausgabe der Werke von Wladimir Solowjew* (German edn of Solov'ëv's Collected Works), ed. W. Szylkarski, W. Lettenbauer and L. Müller, Munich: E. Wewel, 8 vols.
—— (1877–81) *Chteniia o bogochelovechestve*; trans. P. Zouboff, *Lectures on Godmanhood*, London: Dennis Dobson, 1948.

—— (1889) *La Russie et l'Église Universelle*, Paris, trans. H. Rees, *Russia and the Universal Church*, London: The Centenary Press, 1948.
—— (1892–4) *Smysl lyubvi*; revised trans. T.R. Beyer (ed.), *The Meaning of Love*, West Stockbridge, MA: Lindisfarne Press, 1985.
—— (1897) *Opravdanie dobra: Nravstvennaya Filosofiya*, Moscow; trans. N. Duddington, *The Justification of the Good: An Essay in Moral Philosophy*, London: Constable, 1918.
—— (1937) *God, Man and the Church: The Spiritual Foundations of Life*, trans. D. Attwater, Greenwood, SC: Attic Press, 1974.
—— (1978) *La Sophia et les autres écrits Français* (Sophia and Other Works in French), Lausanne: Editions l'Age d'Homme. (Solov'ëv's works in French published by Father F. Rouleau.)
—— (1988) *Sochinenia* (Works), Moscow: Mys'l, 2 vols. (Soviet edition selected from his collected works (1966–70), with the introduction by A.V. Gulyga.)

References and further reading

Dahm, H. (1975) *Vladimir Solovyev and Max Scheller: Attempt at a Comparative Interpretation*, Dordrecht and Boston, MA: Reidel. (A good example of the German contribution to Solov'ëv scholarship. Contains a bibliography.)
Losev, A. (1990) *Vladimir Solov'ëv i ego vremia* (Vladimir Solov'ëv and his Times), Moscow: Progress. (The best work on Solov'ëv produced in the Soviet Union.)
Mochulsky, K. (1951) *Vladimir Solov'ëv: Zhizn' i uchenie* (Vladimir Solov'ëv: Life and Teaching), Paris: YMCA-Press. (A standard monograph of Solov'ëv by a Russian émigré scholar.)
Solov'ëv, S.M. (1977) *Zhizn' i tvorcheskaia evoliutsiia Vladimira Solov'ëva* (Life and Intellectual Evolution of Vladimir Solov'ëv), Brussels: Foyer Oriental Chretien. (A presentation of Solov'ëv's religious philosophy from a Catholic standpoint. The work of his nephew who had converted to Catholicism and became a priest.)
Stremoukhoff, D. (1979) *Vladimir Soloviev and His Messianic work*, Belmont: Nordland. (Translated from the French edition of 1935, this is the most comprehensive monograph in English.)
Trubetskoi, E.N. (1913) *Mirosozertsanie Vl. S. Solov'ëva* (The Worldview of V.S. Solov'ëv), Moscow: Put', 2 vols; new edn, Moscow: Medium, 1995. (The classic and most comprehensive work on Solov'ëv.)
Walicki, A. (1987) *Legal Philosophies of Russian*

Liberalism, Oxford: Clarendon Press. (Solov'ëv's philosophy of law is analysed in detail in ch. 3.)

Zenkovsky, V.V. (1948–50) *Istoriia russkoi filosofii*, Paris: YMCA-Press, vol. 2; 2nd edn 1989; trans. G.L. Kline, *A History of Russian Philosophy*, London: Routledge & Kegan Paul and New York: Columbia University Press, 1953, vol. 2, chs 16 and 17. (A thoughtful discussion of Solov' ëv's philosophy from an Orthodox Christian point of view.)

ANDRZEJ WALICKI

SOPHISTS

The Sophists were itinerant educators, the first professors of higher learning, who appeared in Greece in the middle and later fifth century BC. The earliest seems to have been Protagoras, who was personally associated with the statesman Pericles. The next most eminent was Gorgias, an influential author and prose stylist. The Sophists succeeded in earning very large sums for their instruction. They lectured on many subjects, including the new natural philosophy, but their most important teaching was in rhetoric, the art of influencing political assemblies and law courts by persuasive speech. In conservative circles their great influence was regarded with hostility, as corrupting the young.

The term *sophistēs* is an agent noun from the Greek verb *sophizesthai*, 'to be skilful' (*sophos*). So a *sophistēs* was originally an expert in any form of wisdom or skill (*sophia*). The term was thus applied to poets, philosophers and sages of all sorts. But by the late fifth century BC it had received a special application to a new class of men: the professional educators, known to Plato and posterity as the 'Sophists'.

According to Plato, PROTAGORAS (§2) was the first to identify himself as a Sophist and to offer training in public affairs for a fee. He professed to teach men 'to manage their households well and to administer the business of the city' (*Protagoras* 318e). For this, Protagoras and the other Sophists could expect to be paid handsomely. Their instruction was particularly attractive to ambitious young men in pursuit of a political career. Skill in public speaking was of supreme importance, above all in Athens, where political decisions were made in public assemblies and in very large law courts. Some Sophists, such as Gorgias, claimed only to teach rhetoric, that is, skill in public speaking. Typically, however, the goal of Sophistic training was conceived in terms of civic virtue or excellence (see ARETĒ). Hence the urgency of

the question, much debated in the dialogues of PLATO (§11), whether virtue can be taught.

The Sophists were travelling professors who founded no permanent schools. They came from all parts of Greece but were frequently active in Athens, the richest and most powerful Greek city of the time. They were often public figures: GORGIAS, HIPPIAS and PRODICUS came to Athens as political representatives of their native cities, and Protagoras wrote the lawcode for the Periclean colony of Thurii. Their closest Athenian colleague was Socrates, who was popularly regarded as a Sophist, although he insisted that he was not a teacher and took no fees. But Socrates belonged to the same intellectual circles and was believed to exercise a similar influence on the young (see SOCRATES §1,2,7).

The content of Sophistic education was very diverse. Although the principal subject was political eloquence, training also included the study of Homer and the other poets as presenting traditional paradigms of excellence. Rhetoric was taught by example, and by memorizing and imitating such display pieces as the *Encomium of Helen of Troy* and the *Defence of Palamedes* by Gorgias, and the 'Choice of Heracles' by Prodicus. Some Sophists also taught mathematics, astronomy and natural philosophy. All of them were acquainted with, and served to propagate and popularize, the new naturalistic worldview that had begun to replace traditional religious and mythopoetic ways of thought. The new outlook had begun in sixth-century Miletus and been developed by Xenophanes, Heraclitus and Parmenides, as well as by fifth-century cosmologists such as Anaxagoras and Empedocles. This is the world view of the fifth-century Enlightenment, whose influence can be seen in Euripides, Thucydides and many of the Hippocratic treatises (see HIPPOCRATIC MEDICINE).

The Sophists played a key role not only in the transmission but also in the development of this new rationalism in the second half of the fifth century. The theological scepticism and epistemological relativism expressed in Protagoras' thesis that 'man is the measure of all things' mark a radical break with the traditional Greek worldview centred on the gods. And the psychological cynicism displayed in Gorgias' defence of Helen of Troy implies a similar alienation from traditional Greek morality. All this lies behind Aristophanes' hostile caricature of the new education in his comedy the *Clouds*, in the figure of the Unjust Argument who defends adultery and self-indulgence as 'necessities of nature' and urges his auditor to 'follow nature, frolic, laugh, consider nothing shameful' (*Clouds* 1075–8).

Aristophanes is alluding here not only to Gorgias' amoral defence of Helen's adultery, but more generally to the antithesis between nature and convention (*physis* and *nomos*) that was made popular in Sophistic rhetoric and used by some of the Sophists to undermine the authority of the traditional moral code, treated now as a mere human convention (see ANTIPHON; CALLICLES; PHYSIS AND NOMOS). So in Aristophanes' *Clouds* the pupil of the Unjust Argument will learn 'to despise the established norms (*nomoi*)' and to treat the rule against father-beating as a matter of convention that can be changed by persuasive speech. All of this is presented by Aristophanes as the fruit of the Sophistic enterprise of making the weaker argument the stronger.

Aristophanes is a representative of the popular, conservative reaction against the new rationalism, which was seen as a threat to traditional values. In this regard Socrates and the Sophists were tarred with the same brush, and in the *Clouds* Socrates is in fact presented as the principal Sophist. It was Plato who succeeded in distinguishing the philosophers from the Sophists and thus separating Socrates from the professional educators, despite the fact that both belonged to the new Enlightenment tradition. For Plato, the sophist is a false image or imitation of the philosopher. For Aristotle, the sophist is a specialist in invalid but persuasive argument. It is this Platonic–Aristotelian conception of sophistry that has been transmitted to the present day.

Since the Sophists founded no schools, their influence extended beyond their own lifetime only through their writings and the work of their pupils, notably the rhetoricians Isocrates and Alcidamas, who had studied with Gorgias. Among the followers of Socrates, ANTISTHENES §1 was also heavily influenced by Sophistic modes of thought, and he too is alleged to have been a pupil of Gorgias, presumably before he attached himself to Socrates.

See also: DISSOI LOGOI

References and further reading

* Aristophanes (*c.*455–386 BC) *Clouds*, trans. W. Arrowsmith, Ann Arbor, MI: University of Michigan Press, 1962. (Comic presentation of Socrates as a typical Sophist, headmaster of a Thinking-School.)
Classen, C.J. (ed.) (1976) *Sophistik*, Darmstadt: Wissenschaftliche Buchgesellschaft. (An anthology of scholarly articles, some in English; includes extensive bibliography.)
Diels, H. and Kranz, W. (1952) *Die Fragmente der Vorsokratiker* (Fragments of the Presocratics), Berlin: Weidemann, 6th edn, vol. 2, 252–416. (The standard collection of the ancient sources; includes Greek texts with translations in German.)
Dodds, E.R. (1956) 'Rationalism and Reaction in the Classical Age', in *The Greeks and the Irrational*, Berkeley and Los Angeles, CA: University of California Press, ch. 6. (A brilliant study of the moral and cultural context of the Sophistic movement.)
Guthrie, W.K.C. (1969) *A History of Greek Philosophy*, vol. 3, Cambridge: Cambridge University Press; part of vol. 3 repr. as *The Sophists*, Cambridge: Cambridge University Press, 1971. (A full, scholarly account.)
Kerferd, G.B. (1981) *The Sophistic Movement*, Cambridge: Cambridge University Press. (A briefer, more personal interpretation than Guthrie (1969).)
Sprague, R.K. (ed.) (1972) *The Older Sophists*, Columbia, SC: University of South Carolina Press. (Full English translation of the fragments and testimonia from Diels and Kranz (1954).)

C.H. KAHN

SOREL, GEORGES (1847–1922)

The French social theorist Georges Sorel is best known for his controversial work Réflexions sur la violence *(*Reflections on Violence*), first published in 1908. He here argued that the world could be saved from 'barbarism' through acts of proletarian violence, most notably the general strike. This, he believed, would not only establish an ethic of the producers but would also serve to secure the economic foundations of socialism. Moreover the inspiration for these heroic deeds would be derived from a series of 'myths' that encapsulated the highest aspirations of the working class. More broadly Sorel should be seen as an innovator in Marxist theory and the methodology of the social sciences.*

Born in Cherbourg, Sorel was educated at the prestigious *École Polytechnique* in Paris before gaining employment as a government engineer. Remaining in this position until 1893, it was not until the late 1880s that Sorel's writings began to appear. Upon retirement he took up residence in the Paris suburb of Boulogne-sur-Seine and thence became a central figure in the intellectual world of the Parisian Left Bank. Associated with the intriguing figure of Charles Péguy, Sorel quickly established a wide range of international correspondents (for example, Benedetto Croce and Antonio Labriola) and over a period of thirty years was intimately associated with an extensive series of reviews that did much to introduce new ideas into France.

Fascinated by what he termed the 'ethics of

socialism', it was during a period of intense trade union strike activity and government repression that Sorel published *Réflexions sur la violence* (*Reflections on Violence*) (1908a). Heavily influenced by VICO, NIETZSCHE and BERGSON (as well as by MARX), Sorel here argued that it would be through acts of violence that the proletariat would establish the economic foundations of socialism while simultaneously engendering a new morality of the producers. If the working class, and more narrowly the revolutionary syndicalist movement, was to be the vehicle of this radical transformation of society, its inspiration was to be a series of 'myths' associated principally with what was characterized as the proletarian epic of the general strike. Arguing against what he termed 'the intellectualist philosophy' Sorel's point was that 'people who are living in the world of "myths" are secure from all refutation' and therefore are capable of heroic deeds. It was such heroism on an almost Homeric scale that was required if the 'total ruin of institutions and of morals' was to be reversed.

To understand why Sorel adopted this stance it is necessary to be familiar with at least two dimensions of his thought. First, an intense moralism characterizes his writings throughout and underpins and explains his frequent changes in political position. Sorel was convinced that he lived in a world of moral decline and decadence and this he came increasingly to associate with the Western bourgeoisie. Sorel's own preference was for what was, in effect, a Catholic and Proudhon-inspired morality of extreme severity, leading him to argue (for example) that the 'world becomes more just to the extent that it becomes more chaste'. Always a pessimist, he saw the image of the Wandering Jew, 'condemned to march forever without knowing rest', as the symbol of man's highest aspirations. What mattered was that the working class should not be contaminated by this decadence.

Second, if Sorel was one of the people most responsible for the introduction of the ideas of Marx into France during the 1890s, then he also engaged in the process of an extensive reformulation and reinterpretation of what he took to be the central tenets of Marxist philosophy. Quickly abandoning the idea that Marx had discovered the laws that 'determined' the development of capitalism, he first redefined Marx's key notions (for example, the theory of value) as metaphysics, then as 'social poetry', before finally hitting upon the idea that they were best seen as 'myths' capable of inspiring action in the proletariat. In political terms this initially meant support for social democracy (and agreement with Eduard Bernstein), but the outcome of the Dreyfus Affair convinced Sorel that the 'revolutionary idea' was indispensable for Marxism. Crucially, however, the revolution (if it ever occurred) was not to take the form of the collapse of capitalism but of the transvaluation of all values (a term he borrowed from Nietzsche to denote his rejection of orthodox Marxism and its emphasis upon economics).

By 1909 Sorel had lost faith in the capacity of the French working class to effect the social transformation he so desired. There followed a brief association with intellectuals on the extreme Right, opposition to the First World War and the plutocratic civilization it represented, before a final enthusiasm for Lenin's Bolshevik Revolution and the hope that this might bring the end of 'the arrogant bourgeois democracies, today shamelessly triumphant'.

Yet beneath this lay a deeper interest in the philosophical issues of the day. Educated in the positivist tradition of COMTE, Sorel repeatedly sought to defend science as a progressive, experimental activity while refuting the universalistic claims of the scientism he associated with the positivism he had imbibed in his youth. His extensive writings on both religion and science reveal a thinker determined to defend the validity of our different forms of knowledge, embracing a methodological and epistemological pluralism that would itself avoid the perils of subjectivism. In this he drew inspiration not just from Vico's notion of *verum ipsum factum*, that we can only have knowledge of what we have made ourselves, but in turn from the conventionalism of POINCARÉ, the intuitivism of Bergson and the pragmatism of William JAMES.

See also: REVOLUTION; SOCIALISM

List of works

Sorel, G. (1889) *Le Procès de Socrate* (The Trial of Socrates), Paris: Alcan. (An early statement of Sorel's moral position.)

—— (1906) *Le Système historique de Renan* (The Historical System of Renan), Paris: Jacques. (Sorel's most extensive discussion of historical methodology and religion.)

—— (1908a) *Réflexions sur la Violence*, Paris: Pages libres; trans. T.E. Hulme, *Reflections on Violence*, New York: Collier Books, 1972. (Sorel's standard work.)

—— (1908b) *La Décomposition du Marxisme* (The Decomposition of Marxism), Paris: Rivière. (Sorel's most succinct analysis of Marxism.)

—— (1908c) *Les Illusions du progrès*, Paris: Rivière; trans. J.L. Stanley, *Illusions of Progress*, Berkeley and Los Angeles, CA: University of California Press, 1969. (A full-blooded attack on the Enlightenment as bourgeois ideology.)

—— (1921) *De l'utilité du pragmatisme* (The Utility of Pragmatism), Paris: Rivière. (Sorel's final philosophical statement.)

—— (1976) *From Georges Sorel: Essays in Socialism and Philosophy*, ed. J.L. Stanley, New York: Oxford University Press. (An excellent selection of Sorel's writings.)

References and further reading

Andreu, P. (1982) *Georges Sorel: entre le noir et le rouge* (Georges Sorel: Between the Black and the Red), Paris: Syros. (Published originally in 1953, this remains a standard work of reference.)

Jennings, J. (1985) *Georges Sorel; The Character and Development of his Thought*, London: Macmillan. (An account of the full range of Sorel's ideas from the 1880s until his death.)

Sand, S. (1985) *L'illusion du politique: Georges Sorel et le débat intellectuel 1900* (The Illusion of Politics: Georges Sorel and intellectual debate around 1900), Paris: La Découverte. (Brilliant exegesis of Sorel's encounter with Marxism.)

Stanley, J. (1981) *The Sociology of Virtue: The Political and Social Theories of Georges Sorel*, Los Angeles, CA: University of California Press. (A challenging interpretation of Sorel's thought.)

JEREMY JENNINGS

SORITES ARGUMENTS

see VAGUENESS

SÔSAN HYUJÔNG (1520–1604)

Sôsan was a Korean Sôn Buddhist monk who sought to establish the equality of various ideas and systems. His philosophical perspective conferred equality on Confucianism, Daoism and Buddhism alike, and within Buddhism he denied there was any inherent conflict between the Kyo and Sôn schools. However, he viewed Sôn (meditation) as being the most advanced form of practice.

Sôsan Hyujông, popularly known as 'Sôsan,' was a Korean Sôn (Zen, in Japanese) Buddhist monk of the Chosôn Dynasty (1393–1910) who espoused 'liberal' views. Why were Sôsan's views so liberal? The answer may lie in the fact that he was an extremely pure Sôn monk. True to the spirit of Sôn, he perceived all things and all beings as equal. Perhaps we can clarify this point through the well-known Buddhist simile of an ink-seal, used to stamp three different elements: clay, water and air. In both clay and water, traces of the seal remain, but in air the seal makes no imprint whatsoever. Sôsan was like the air: whatever happened to him, he was not influenced by it but remained the same. This was perhaps his most valuable asset, as it afforded him much flexibility in both thought and action.

Sôsan is important in the history of Korean Buddhism for three reasons. First, during the Japanese invasion of Korea in 1592, he organized an army of Buddhist monks to participate in the country's defence. Though this force helped to repel the invaders, he was later criticized for breaking the Buddhist precept against killing. While believing that his actions had been necessary, Sôsan himself allegedly felt a certain amount of remorse. After the war, King Sônjo recognized his contribution with an award, and the two men subsequently developed a friendship.

Second, Sôsan pioneered an overarching philosophical perspective which stressed the essential equality of all three of the religious systems then active in Korea: Confucianism, Daoism and Buddhism. One commentator has explained Sôsan's view of the relationship of the three religions in terms of rice farming: while the practice of Confucianism is akin to planting the seeds, and that of Daoism is akin to nourishing them, the practice of Buddhism is akin to uprooting sick shoots and replacing them with healthy ones. Sôsan thus viewed all three thought systems as cooperative and complementary, and believed that each should be allowed to perform its own special function free of interference from the others. Due to his influence, communication was greatly expanded among the leading thinkers of his day.

Third, Sôsan espoused a similar doctrine of non-interference within Buddhism itself, particularly in regard to the longstanding antagonism between the scriptural (Kyo) and meditational (Sôn) schools. Denying the view that there was an inherent conflict between these schools, Sôsan instead forged a conceptual link between them by equating Kyo with the Buddha's words and Sôn with his mind. How can they be contradictory, he asked, since both originate from the same source? He did feel, however, that once a practitioner had achieved a firm grasp of scripture he should continue on to the next stage, which was meditational practice. Thus Sôsan still viewed Sôn, or meditation, as the more advanced form of practice. In this sense he deserves to be called a typical Chan master, in the tradition of the Linji school.

See also: BUDDHIST PHILOSOPHY, KOREAN

List of works

Han'guk pulgyo chônsô (The Collected Works of Korean Buddhism), Seoul: Dongguk University press, 1979, vol. 7, 616–751; trans. in P.H. Lee (ed.) *Source Book of Korean Civilization*, vol. 1, *From Early Times to the Sixteenth Century*, New York: Columbia University Press, 1993. (Lee's translation is not entirely complete, but does include all the important intellectual works. Lee's work is a well-written, comprehensive anthology of Korean civilization.)

References and further reading

The Korean Buddhist Research Institute (ed.) (1994) *Buddhist Thought in Korea*, Seoul: Dongguk University Press. (A collection of articles by various authors on various aspects of Korean Buddhist thought.)

Kim Young-tae (1975) *Sôsan Daesa ûi Saeng'ae wa Sasang* (Venerable Sôsan's Life and Thought), Seoul: Pagyongsa. (A biography of Sôsan, including a discussion of his thought.)

SUNG BAE PARK

SOTO, DOMINGO DE (1494–1560)

The sixteenth-century Spanish Dominican, Domingo de Soto, was a mainstay of the Thomistic revival begun at Salamanca by Vitoria. After study at Paris (where he was taught by the nominalist John Major) and Alcalá, Soto taught both philosophy and theology. He was influential within the Dominican Order and the Catholic Church; he served as Emperor Charles V's theologian at the Council of Trent and played an active role in the development of the Council of Trent's teaching on original sin. Besides his theological writings, Soto composed philosophical works chiefly in logic, natural philosophy and juridical theory. In logic, he authored an exposition of the Summulae *of Peter of Spain and a commentary, by way of questions, on three of Aristotle's works. His natural philosophy anticipated later scientific approaches, while in his philosophy of law Soto presented a basically Thomistic doctrine updated to confront sixteenth-century issues.*

1   Life and works
2   Logic
3   Natural philosophy
4   Philosophy of law

1   Life and works

Born in 1494 at Segovia in Spain, Domingo de Soto studied at the University of Alcalá between 1512 and 1516. In 1517 he received a master of arts degree at the University of Paris, where he came under nominalist influence. Between 1517 and 1519, while teaching philosophy at Paris, he studied theology there, principally under the Scottish master, John MAJOR. At this time he may have attended lectures by Francisco de VITORIA at the Dominican house of St Jacques in Paris. Returning to Spain, he continued the study of theology, as well as teaching philosophy, at Alcalá, where in 1525 he received his doctorate in theology. That same year he joined the Order of Preachers, the Dominicans. From 1525 to 1532 he was teaching philosophy and theology in the Dominican convent of San Esteban at Salamanca. In 1529 he published at Burgos the first edition of his *Summulae*. This work, which he would revise extensively in 1539, was a logic textbook partly based upon the famous *Summulae logicales* of PETER OF SPAIN. In 1532 he assumed the 'Chair of Vespers' in theology at the University of Salamanca, which office he held until 1549. During this period he served two terms as prior of San Esteban.

Soto was chosen by Charles V to be an imperial theologian at the first sessions of the Council of Trent; between 1545 and 1547 he played an active role in the development of the Council's teaching on original sin. He also wrote an important treatise, *De natura et gratia, libri tres* (Three Books on Nature and Grace), published at Venice in 1547. From 1548 to 1550 he was confessor to Charles V in Germany. At this time Charles offered him the bishopric of his native Segovia, which Soto respectfully but firmly refused. Back in Spain, the following year he presided over the Junta de Vallodolid, made up of fourteen theologians selected to judge the matter of the Spanish conquest of the Indians of the New World. The principal business before the Junta was a debate between the humanist Gino de Sepúlveda, the defender of the Spanish role, and its most severe critic, Bartolomé de las Casas, Bishop of Chiapa in Mexico (see LATIN AMERICA, COLONIAL THOUGHT IN §1). Soto composed an objective summary of the debate which presented both positions fairly but did not take sides.

In 1552, Soto succeeded Melchior Cano in the 'Chair of Prime' in theology at Salamanca, a chair earlier occupied by Vitoria. In this position, he continued Vitoria's renewal of Thomism and its development to meet new problems presented by the Reformation, the discovery of America, and the rise of a free-market system in Spain. In 1554 Soto published a third edition of his *Summulae*, in 1555–6 a commentary on the fourth book of the *Sentences* of Peter LOMBARD, and in 1553–4 his famous *De justitia et jure, libri decem* (Ten Books on Justice and Law). Retiring from his chair in 1556, he once more became prior of San Esteban, in which office he died on 15 November 1560.

Soto's philosophical work is in three main parts: logic, natural philosophy, and juridical theory or philosophy of law. In addition, his theological writings touch on diverse philosophical issues. For example, in his treatise on nature and grace, he dealt at length with the nature of human beings, the soul's relation to the body, the intellect's need for the senses, and the freedom of the human will *vis-à-vis* the causality of God. At different points in his commentary on the fourth book of the *Sentences*, which is mainly concerned with sacramental theology, he discussed signs and things signified, conditions required for a definition, the existence of accidents in material substances, the possibility of accidents existing without a subject in which they inhere, the transcendental and non-generic character of being as shared between substance and accidents, the immortality of the human soul, as well as the communication of temporal authority by God first to the people and then to the sovereigns they choose.

2 Logic

In logic, Soto's revised *Summulae* of 1539 and 1554 comprises five books, plus two treatises on insolubles and obligations. Book 1 is on terms, which PETER OF SPAIN defined as 'words which are by convention significative'. This occasions for Soto, in Lecture 1 of Chapter 2, an extended treatment of signification and signs. The latter are divided into natural, conventional and customary. Natural signs in turn are divided into formal and instrumental. Book 2 is on propositions. Here he deals with nouns and verbs as they compose propositions. He then treats of definition, division and argumentation. Chapters 5 to 8 of Book 2 treat of categorical and hypothetical propositions, while further chapters cover supposition, relatives, induction, ampliation and appellation. Book 3 concerns the opposition, equipollence and conversion of propositions. Book 4 treats exponible propositions and their species such as exclusives, exceptives, reduplicatives and so on. Book 5 examines the syllogism, its figures and moods, its essential conditions and defects.

In the first volume of his work *In Dialecticam Aristotelis* (On the Logic of Aristotle) (1543), Soto begins with questions about the scientific character and subject matter of logic. Following this he comments on the *Isagōgē* of PORPHYRY and treats the notions of genus, species, difference, property and

accident. In a second volume, he deals with *antepredicamenta* (which are the definitions of equivocal, univocal and analogical terms, the division of terms into simple and complex, and so on), the ten categories of substance and accidents, as well as *postpredicamenta* (for example, opposition and its species). In the same volume, he comments on twenty-seven chapters of Book 1 of the *Posterior Analytics*, raising special questions with regard to science and demonstration. Then more briefly he explains eighteen chapters of Book 2 of the *Posterior Analytics*, without raising any special questions (see LANGUAGE, RENAISSANCE PHILOSOPHY OF §1; LOGIC, RENAISSANCE §2; ARISTOTELIANISM, RENAISSANCE).

3 Natural philosophy

In his work *Super VIII libros Physicorum Aristotelis* (On the Eight Books of Aristotle's *Physics*) (1545), Soto was concerned, according to Marcial Solana (1940), not so much to know what Aristotle thought as to know the truth with respect to nature, its principles and causes, movement, place, time, infinity, continuity, and so on. In at least one passage, Soto has, in the estimate of Pierre Duhem (1913), anticipated GALILEO (§1) on the free fall of bodies. The core of this passage reads: 'When a body falls from a height through a uniform medium, it is moved with more velocity at the end of its fall than at the beginning. But the motion of projectiles is slower at the end than at the beginning. And in this way the first [motion] "gets faster with uniform acceleration" (*uniformiter difformiter intenditur*) while the second "declines with uniform deceleration" (*uniformiter difformiter remittitur*)' (*Super VIII libros Physicorum*, VII q.3). However, Soto did not anticipate the careful experimentation and the mathematics on which the fame of Galileo rests.

4 Philosophy of law

Soto's *De justitia et jure, libri decem* presents a basically Thomistic doctrine updated to confront sixteenth-century issues. In Book 1 he explicates the notion of *jus*, which first means 'law', but also means 'right' in the sense of what is right or just. In this latter sense, *jus* is the object of the virtue of justice. Law is defined as 'an ordinance of reason promulgated for the common good by one who has charge of the republic'. Law is divided into eternal, natural and positive (divine and human). Eternal law is the divine reason which from eternity has ordered all things to their respective ends. Natural law is an impression of the eternal law upon human beings to guide them in ordering their actions to the end for which they were created (see NATURAL LAW §1). The natural law is made up of precepts which are immediately evident and unchangeable and precepts inferred from these as conclusions which are subject to change by addition or by changing circumstances (*mutatio materiae*). Divine positive law comprises prescriptions and proscriptions of the Old and New Testaments. Human positive law is either civil or canon law, plus the law of nations (*jus gentium*). The law of nations is positive law which human beings inasmuch as they are rational have everywhere established for themselves. For this establishment, unlike that of civil law, there was no need of a general assembly or an explicit enactment. Instead, by reason alone, human beings everywhere are in substantial agreement on the main facts of dominion, private property, exchanges, buying and selling, war and peace, slavery in some instances, keeping faith even with enemies, the immunity and protection of ambassadors, and so on. After treating distributive justice in Book 3, Soto deals in Book 4 with commutative justice. Here he looks at ownership and its transfer. In Book 5, he treats injustice of various kinds and its punishment. Here he supports the right of the state to exact the death penalty and to wage a just war. In the remaining books, Soto deals in more detail with property rights and their transfer, partnerships, sales contracts, just prices, deposits, loans, interest and usury. On numerous occasions he discusses the rights of individuals *vis-à-vis* those of the community (see LAW, PHILOSOPHY OF; POLITICAL PHILOSOPHY, HISTORY OF §8).

See also: ARISTOTELIANISM, RENAISSANCE §§2–3, 7; LAW, PHILOSOPHY OF; LOGIC, RENAISSANCE

List of works

Soto, D. de (1529) *Summulae*, Burgos; 2nd edn, Salamanca: Andreas de Portonariis, 1539; 3rd edn, 1554; repr. Hildesheim: Olms, 1980. (A logic textbook partly based on the *Summulae logicales* of Peter of Spain and extensively revised in 1539.)

—— (1543) *In Dialecticam Aristotelis Commentarii* (Commentary on the Logic of Aristotle), Salamanca: Juan de Junta; Venice, 1587; repr. Frankfurt: Minerva, 1967. (Soto's commentary on Porphyry's *Isagōgē*, and Aristotle's *Categories* and *Posterior Analytics*.)

—— (1545) *Super VIII libros Physicorum Aristotelis commentaria* (Commentary on the Eight Books of Aristotle's *Physics*), Salamanca, 1st complete edn, 1551. (An independent commentary, by way of questions.)

—— (1553–4) *De Justitia et jure, libri decem* (Ten Books on Justice and Law), Salamanca, 2nd edn,

1559; Spanish trans. M. González Ordóñez, *De justitia et jure. De la justicia y del derecho*, Madrid: Instituto de Estudios Politicos, 1967–8, 5 vols. (Soto's main work of jurisprudence; the Madrid edition provides Latin text with Spanish translation, and an introduction by V.D. Carro.)

References and further reading

Ashworth, E.J. (1974) *Language and Logic in the Post-Medieval Period*, Dordrecht and Boston, MA: Reidel. (A general study which includes extensive discussion of Soto's logical doctrine.)

—— (1990) 'Domingo de Soto (1494–1560) and the Doctrine of Signs', in G.L. Bursill-Hall, S. Ebbesen and K. Koerner (eds) *De Ortu Grammaticae: Studies in Medieval Grammar and Linguistic Theory in Memory of Jan Pinborg*, Amsterdam: John Benjamins, 35–48. (Soto's semiotic theory discussed.)

—— (1988) 'Changes in Logic Textbooks from 1500 to 1650: The New Aristotelianism', in E. Kessler, C.H. Lohr and W. Sparn (eds) *Aristotelismus und Renaissance: In memoriam Charles B. Schmitt*, Wiesbaden: Harrassowitz, 75–87. (Discusses the change between Soto's *Summulae* of 1529 and 1539 on pages 80–1.)

Barrientos García, J. (1985) *Un siglo de moral económica en Salamanca (1526–1629): I, Francisco de Vitoria y Domingo Soto* (A Century of Economic Morality in Salamanca), Salamanca: Ediciones Universidad de Salamanca. (Contains extensive discussion of the economic philosophy of Soto.)

Beuchot, M. (1988) 'Un libro de texto para la Nueva España: La Lógica de Domingo de Soto' (A Textbook for New Spain: the Logic of Domingo de Soto), *Revista de Filosofia de la Universidad Ibero-Americana* 21: 62, 152–67. (Treats the influence of Soto's logic in sixteenth-century Mexico.)

Carro, V.D. (1943) *Domingo de Soto y su doctrina jurídica* (Domingo de Soto: His Juridical Doctrine), Salamanca: Hijos E. Minuesa. (Treatment of Soto's legal theory.)

* Duhem, P.M.M. (1913) 'Les précurseurs parisiens de Galilée: Dominique Soto et la scolastique parisienne' (Galileo's Parisian Forebears: Domingo de Soto and Scholasticism in Paris), in *Études sur Léonard de Vinci*, chap. 3, 261–583. (Referred to in §3; Soto as anticipating Galileo.)

Hamilton, B. (1963) *Political thought in sixteenth-century Spain: A Study of the Political Ideas of Vitoria, Soto, Suarez and Molina*, Oxford: Clarendon Press. (Soto's political theory treated in the course of a wider study.)

Lohr, C.H. (1987) *Latin Aristotle Commentaries: II*

Renaissance Authors, Florence: Olschki, 430–1. (Contains biographical and bibliographical information on Soto.)

Muñoz Delgado, V. (1964) *Lógica formal y filosofía en Domingo de Soto (1494–1560)* (Formal Logic and Philosophy in Domingo de Soto), Madrid: Edita Revista Estudios. (A good treatment of Soto's logic.)

Risse, W. (1964) *Die Logik der Neuzeit. I Band. 1500–1640* (The Logic of the Modern Period), Stuttgart and Bad Cannstatt: Frommann, vol. 1, 329–36. (Soto's logic treated within its historical context.)

* Solana, M. (1940) *Historia de la filosofía española: Época del renacimiento (siglo XVI)* (History of Spanish Philosophy. The Time of the Renaissance (16th Century)), Madrid: Asociación Española para el Progreso de las Ciencias, vol. 3, 91–130. (Referred to in §3. A good introduction to Soto.)

Wallace, W.A. (1981) *Prelude to Galileo: Essays on Medieval and Sixteenth-Century Sources of Galileo's Thought*, Dordrecht and Boston, MA: Reidel, esp. 99–109. (Discussion of Soto's adumbration of Galileo on the free fall of bodies.)

JOHN P. DOYLE

SOUL IN ISLAMIC PHILOSOPHY

The discussion of the human soul, its existence, nature, ultimate objective and eternity, occupies a highly important position in Islamic philosophy and forms its main focus. For the most part Muslim philosophers agreed, as did their Greek predecessors, that the soul consists of non-rational and rational parts. The non-rational part they divided into the plant and animal souls, the rational part into the practical and the theoretical intellects. All believed that the non-rational part is linked essentially to the body, but some considered the rational part as separate from the body by nature and others that all the parts of the soul are by nature material. The philosophers agreed that, while the soul is in the body, its non-rational part is to manage the body, its practical intellect is to manage worldly affairs, including those of the body, and its theoretical intellect is to know the eternal aspects of the universe. They thought that the ultimate end or happiness of the soul depends on its ability to separate itself from the demands of the body and to focus on grasping the eternal aspects of the universe. All believed that the non-rational soul comes into being and unavoidably perishes. Some, like al-Farabi, believed that the rational soul may or may not survive eternally; others, like Ibn Sina, believed that it has no beginning and no end; still others, such as Ibn Rushd, believed that the soul with all its individual parts comes into existence and is eventually destroyed.

1 **The existence of the soul**
2 **The nature of the soul**
3 **The rational soul**
4 **The ultimate objective of the soul**
5 **Eternity of the soul**

1 The existence of the soul

All Muslim philosophers concerned themselves with the subject of the soul. The most detailed and most important works on this subject are those of al-Kindi, al-Farabi, Ibn Sina and Ibn Rushd. Muslim philosophers recognized that the first issue that confronts the human mind with regard to the soul is its existence. That is why, at the very beginning of his inquiry about the soul in *al-Shifa'* (Healing), Ibn Sina (§6) asserts that we infer the existence of the soul from the fact that we observe bodies that perform certain acts with some degree of will. These acts are exemplified in taking nourishment, growing, reproducing, moving and perceiving. Since these acts do not belong to the nature of bodies, for this nature is devoid of will, they must belong to a principle they have other than bodies. This principle is what is called 'soul'.

This argument is intended to prove the existence of the animal soul, which includes the plant soul. The soul is the source of acts performed by the will, not inasmuch as it is 'a substance' (an independent entity), but inasmuch as it is 'the principle of such acts'. The rational soul, on the other hand, need not look outside itself to infer its existence. It is aware of its existence with immediacy, that is, without any instruments. Ibn Sina's example of the suspended man is intended to prove that the rational soul is aware of itself apart from any body. His argument boils down to the view that, even if the adult rational soul is not aware of anything material, not even its body, it remains aware of its own existence.

2 The nature of the soul

While Islam made it incumbent on Muslim philosophers to occupy themselves extensively with the study of the soul and to make certain statements that in some cases appear consistent with Islamic beliefs, Greek philosophy had the upper hand in forming the real convictions of Muslim philosophers with regard to the nature of the soul. Unless otherwise specified, reference to the soul here is limited to the terrestrial soul to the exclusion of the celestial one, since Muslim philosophers concerned themselves primarily with the former. It must be pointed out at the outset that 'soul' (*nafs*) was used in more than one sense in Islamic philosophy; the term was used to refer to the plant or vegetative part of a living being, the animal or sensitive part, the rational part and finally the totality of all three parts. The first two are the non-rational soul and the totality is the human soul. To add to the confusion, 'human soul' is used only in the sense of this fourth type of soul. The plant, animal and rational souls are also called powers or parts of the soul. Only from the context can one understand whether a Muslim philosopher was using 'soul' in the broad sense to mean the human soul (the totality of the parts of the soul), or in the narrow sense to mean a specific part of the human soul.

Inasmuch as it has a certain relation to a body, the soul is a form for that body, that is, the perfection of that body. It is a form because a natural body is composed of matter and form, which in the case of animals are body and soul. Since it has been shown that the soul is the source of will and therefore is not matter, it remains a form. Perfection is of two types, primary and secondary. A primary perfection is what makes a thing actually a species, as shape does for the sword, or a genus, as sensation and movement do for animals. A secondary perfection is an act necessitated by the nature of the species or genus, such as cutting for the sword and touching for animal. The soul is a primary perfection of a natural body capable of performing the secondary perfections necessitated by this primary perfection. Together with its body, the soul constitutes a material substance. This substance can be the subject of plant, animal or human life.

The soul is a perfection inasmuch as it makes a natural body into a plant, an animal or a rational being. However, to define the soul as a perfection does not give us a clue as to what the soul is in itself, but only inasmuch as it has a relation to the body. The body is, therefore, an essential element in the definition of the soul. Without relating to a body, the thing we call 'soul' is not a soul and does not require the body as an essential part of its definition. Note, however, that in spite of this assertion, perhaps for the lack of any better term, Muslim philosophers use 'soul' also to refer to the rational soul after it separates from the body and reaches a complete state of purity from matter.

In its first or lowest stages of relating to the body, the soul is the plant soul, which is a primary perfection for an organic natural body inasmuch as this body can take nourishment, grow and reproduce. The plant soul is the power human beings and other animals share with plants. If the body with a soul is an animal, the soul develops into the animal soul, which is a primary perfection for an organic natural body inasmuch as this body has sensation and movement through will. While this soul includes the plant soul, it has also a sensitive power and a locomotive one. The sensitive power has both external and internal senses. The external senses are, in priority of existence, touch, taste, smell, hearing and sight. The first three are said to be necessary for survival and the last two for well being. In *Talkhis kitab an-nafs* (Middle Commentary on Aristotle's *On the Soul*), IBN RUSHD (§3) asserts that the five external senses may be in potentiality, as in infancy and sleep, or in actuality, as in daily seeing or hearing. He also argues that there cannot be any external sense other than these five because there would be no function for it, since there is no external sensation other than the objects of the five senses mentioned above. Most Muslim philosophers mention three types of internal senses: common sense, imagination and memory. IBN SINA (§3) enumerates five internal senses: common sense, representational power, imagination, estimative power and memory. On the whole, the philosophers agree on the function of the common sense, imagination and memory; the function that Ibn Sina limits to the representational and estimative powers, other Muslim philosophers allocate to the imagination.

The common sense is an internal power in which all the objects of the external senses are collected. Contrary to the external senses, which can grasp only one type of sensation, as sight grasps light and hearing grasps sound, the common sense can grasp all external sensations, such as that honey is of such and such a colour, texture and smell. The representational power preserves the sensations of the common sense even after sensible things disappear. The imagination selects at will to combine some of the objects of the representational power with each other and to separate the rest. It makes its judgment about external things, but in the absence of these things. That is why it functions best when the external senses, which represent external things, are not at work, as in sleep. Ibn Rushd points out that animals such as worms and flies that do not act except in the presence of sensible things are devoid of imagination. The imagination is called such inasmuch as it is an animal instrument; it is called cognitive inasmuch as it is a rational instrument. The estimative power grasps non-sensible notions of sensible things, such as the sheep's notion that the wolf is to be avoided. This notion is about a sensible thing but is not grasped through the external senses, as is the colour or shape of a wolf. Memory preserves the notions of the estimative power. The imagination acts on the objects of memory in the same way it acts on those of the representational powers. Like the objects of the external senses, those of the internal senses are particular and material. The difference is that they can be experienced in the absence of external things and are to some degree abstracted from matter.

The locomotive power branches into that which causes movement and that which actually moves. The former, the desiderative power, subdivides into the appetitive and the irascible. The appetitive causes movement toward what is imagined to be necessary or beneficial in the pursuit of pleasure. The irascible causes avoidance of what is imagined to be harmful or an impediment in the pursuit of dominance. The power that actually moves uses the nerves to relax the muscles at the demands of the appetitive power or tighten them at the demands of the irascible one.

3 The rational soul

The rational soul, which is defined as a primary perfection for an organic natural body inasmuch as this body can act by rational choice and grasp the universals, is divided into the practical and the theoretical intellects. The practical intellect seeks knowledge in order to act in accordance with the good in its individual body, its family and its state. It must, therefore, know the principles for properly managing the body, the family and the state, that is, ethics, home management and politics. The practical intellect is the rational soul turning its face downward. The function of the theoretical intellect is to know just for the sake of having the universals (the realities or natures of things). Some of these natures, such as God and the intellect, cannot attach to movement; knowledge of them is metaphysics. Other natures, such as unity, can attach to movement but do not; knowledge of them is mathematics. Still other natures, such as humanity and squareness, can attach to movement either in reality and thought, such as humanity, or in reality but not in thought, such as squareness. Knowledge of these is physics.

The theoretical intellect is the rational soul with its face upward. The practical intellect looks up to the theoretical one and moves its body accordingly. In this, the practical intellect is similar to the celestial soul that looks up to the intellect of its sphere and moves its sphere accordingly. Thus, like the celestial soul, the practical intellect is the link between intellect as such and matter.

On the whole, Muslim philosophers followed al-Kindi's division of the theoretical intellect into the material intellect (*al-'aql al-hayulani*), the habitual intellect (*al-'aql bil-malaka*), the actual intellect (*al-'aql bi'l-fi'l*) and the acquired intellect (*al-'aql al-mustafad*). The material intellect is a blank slate with the potentiality for grasping the intelligible forms or universals. Ibn Sina points out that it is referred to as material, not because it is actually material but because it resembles matter in accepting the form. The habitual intellect grasps the universals, as one acquires the skill to write; in other words, this intellect has the ability to use the universals but does not always do so. The actual intellect grasps the universals in actuality and is always ready to use them. While Muslim philosophers differed slightly with regard to their accounts of the acquired intellect, their general view is that it is the highest human state, the point of contact with the divine, the agent intellect (the intelligence of the moon, the lowest celestial intellect), which makes it possible for the theoretical intellect to acquire the universals in the purest form (see EPISTEMOLOGY IN ISLAMIC PHILOSOPHY §4).

4 The ultimate objective of the soul

AL-FARABI asserts that even though the soul is of different parts, it is a unity with all its parts working for one final end, happiness. While the plant soul, for example, serves a specific function, it also serves the powers that are higher than it in rank, the animal powers. Without nourishment, growth and reproduction, the animal powers cannot perform their necessary functions. Similarly, while the function of the animal powers is to have sensation and movement, by performing this function they also promote the functions of the powers above them, the rational ones. The operations of the animal powers, especially those of the senses, are particularly important for the attainment of the final end. The external senses strip the forms from material objects and convey them to the internal senses. The more they are transferred internally, the less mixed with matter do they become. Since the innermost sense they reach is the imagination, they are there in their purest material existence (see IMAGINATION).

The role of the objects of the imagination is not always clearly defined in Islamic philosophy. Occasionally it is said by somebody like Ibn Sina to be one of preparation for the theoretical intellect to receive the universals from the agent intellect. At other times Ibn Sina, like other Aristotelians such as Ibn Rushd, takes these objects to be the ingredients out of which the universals are made after the last process of purification (see EPISTEMOLOGY IN ISLAMIC PHILOSOPHY). It seems, however, that in either case the light of the agent intellect is needed to complete the process. In the former case, this light gives the intelligible forms to the theoretical intellect when this intellect is prepared. In the latter case, it sheds itself on the objects of the imagination, which are then reflected on the theoretical intellect without their matter. Since the theoretical intellect is in its first stages in potentiality, it cannot act on the objects of the imagination directly; hence the need for the agent intellect, which is pure actuality. The role of the practical intellect in all this is to put order into the body. This sets free the theoretical intellect from preoccupation with the body and helps the powers whose function is necessary for theoretical knowledge to function unhampered.

Muslim philosophers adhered to the view that the acquired intellect is one with its objects, for they thought the knower and the known are one, as did their Greek predecessors. This means that the highest human state is one in which unity with the universals or the eternal aspects of the universe is reached. This state is described as happiness because in it eternity, an aspect of the objects of the acquired intellect, is attained.

5 Eternity of the soul

When Muslim philosophers assert that the soul comes into existence simultaneously with the coming into existence of the body, some, such as Ibn Sina (§6), who believe that the rational soul is in essence non-material, are thinking only of the non-rational soul. Others, such as Ibn Rushd (§3), who believe that the rational soul is originally not separate from matter, contend that the whole human soul comes into existence. The latter believe that since the rational soul grasps the universals from particular sensibles, and since such sensibles are material and have a temporal beginning, this soul must also be material and must have a temporal beginning. Those who attribute non-materiality to the essence of the rational soul, such as AL-KINDI and Ibn Sina, assert that this soul pre-exists the body. While all of them agree that the non-rational soul is destroyed after the destruction of the body, they differ with regard to the end of the rational soul.

Al-Kindi and Ibn Sina, for example, strongly adhere to the view that all rational souls are indestructible because by nature they are simple. AL-FARABI reminds us that the reason for eternal existence is the rational soul's knowledge of the eternal aspects of the universe. From this he draws the conclusion, as did ALEXANDER OF APHRODISIAS before him, that only those rational souls that have this knowledge at their separation from the body are indestructible. Other rational souls are eventually destroyed. Ibn Sina finds in the grasping of the universals the grounds for happiness, not the eternity of the soul. Ibn Rushd seems to hold that only the acquired intellect can be indestructible; but the

acquired intellect, he argues (as does his teacher IBN BAJJA), is divine and numerically one in all. Ibn Rushd was attacked for this view because it denies eternal existence of individual souls (see AVERROISM; SOUL, NATURE AND IMMORTALITY OF THE).

See also: ARISTOTELIANISM IN ISLAMIC PHILOSOPHY; EPISTEMOLOGY IN ISLAMIC PHILOSOPHY; ETHICS IN ISLAMIC PHILOSOPHY; IBN RUSHD §3; IBN SINA §6; MYSTICAL PHILOSOPHY IN ISLAM; SOUL, NATURE AND IMMORTALITY OF THE

References and further reading

al-Farabi (*c.*870–950) *al-Madina al-fadila* (The Virtuous City), trans. R. Walzer, *Al-Farabi on the Perfect State: Abu Nasr al-Farabi's Mabadi' Ara' Ahl al-Madina al-Fadila*, Oxford: Clarendon Press, 1985. (English and Arabic of the most comprehensive and best known philosophical work of al-Farabi.)

Ibn Rushd (1180) *Tahafut al-tahafut* (The Incoherence of the Incoherence), trans. S. Van Den Bergh, London: Luzac, 1954. (A response to a number of issues raised by al-Ghazali against philosophers. One of the three most important of these issues is that of the soul and its fate.)

* —— (*c.*1174) *Talkhis kitab an-nafs* (Middle Commentary on Aristotle's *On the Soul*), ed. A.F. al-Ahwani, Cairo: Maktabat an-Nahda, 1950. (Includes also four other essays: Ibn Bajja's *Risalat al-ittisal* (Essay on Conjunction), Ishaq Ibn Hunayn's *Kitab fi an-nafs* (Book on the Soul), Ibn Rushd's *Risalat al-ittisal* (Essay on Conjunction) and al-Kindi's *Risalat al-'aql* (Essay on Intellect).)

* Ibn Sina (980–1037) *an-Nafs* (The Soul), ed. F. Rahman, *Avicenna's de Anima*, London: Oxford University Press, 1959. (The most important and detailed philosophical treatise on the soul in Islamic philosophy, the sixth part of the *Physics* of *al-Shifa'*. An Arabic edition of the text is included.)

—— (980–1037) *Ahwal an-nafs* (The States of the Soul), ed. A.F. al-Ahwani, Cairo: Dar Ihya' al-Kutub al-'Arabiyya, 1952. (Includes *Risala fi an-nafs wa-baqa'ha wa-ma'adiha* (Essay on the Soul, Its Permanence and Its Second Life), *Mabhath 'an al-qiwa an-nafsaniyya* (Inquiry about Psychic Powers), *Risala fi ma'rifat an-nafs an-natiqa* (Essay on Knowing the Rational Soul) and *Risala fi al-kalam 'ala an-nafs an-natiqa* (Essay on an Inquiry Concerning the Rational Soul).)

—— (980–1037) *an-Najat* (Deliverance), ed. F. Rahman, *Avicenna's Psychology*, London: Oxford University Press, 1952. (The psychology of *an-Najat* is an abridgement by Ibn Sina of his encyclopedic work *al-Shifa'* (Healing).)

—— (980–1037) *Rasa'il ash-shaykh ar-ra'is fi asrar al-hikma al-mashriqiyya* (Essays of the Master of the Head on the Secrets of Oriental Wisdom), ed. M. Mehren, *Traités mystiques d'Avicenna*, Leiden: Brill, 1889–99. (Ibn Sina's 'oriental philosophy'.)

Inati, S.C. (1996) *A Study of Ibn Sina's Mysticism*, London: Kegan Paul International. (Includes a detailed analysis of Ibn Sina's notion of the soul and a translation of the fourth part of *al-Isharat wa-'l-tanbihat* (Remarks and Admonitions).)

al-Kindi (before 873) *Rasa'il al-Kindi al-falsafiyya* (Al-Kindi's Philosophical Treatises), ed. M. Abu Rida, Cairo: Dar al-Fikr al-'Arabi, 1953. (Includes al-Kindi's most relevant works on the subject of the soul, *al-Qawl fi an-nafs* (Discourse on the Soul), *Fi an-nafs* (On the Soul) and *Fi mahiyyat an-nawm war-ru'ya* (On the Essence of Sleep and Internal Vision).)

SHAMS C. INATI

SOUL, NATURE AND IMMORTALITY OF THE

For the Greeks, the soul is what gives life to the body. Plato thought of it as a thing separate from the body. A human living on earth consists of two parts, soul and body. The soul is the essential part of the human – what makes me me. It is the part to which the mental life of humans pertains – it is the soul which thinks and feels and chooses. Soul and body interact. Bodily states often cause soul states, and soul states often cause bodily states. This view is known as substance dualism. It normally includes the view that the soul is simple, that it does not have parts. If an object has parts, then one of those parts can have properties which another part does not. But for any experience that I have, an auditory or visual sensation or thought, it happens to the whole me. Plato also held that at death, soul and body are separated; the body decays while the soul departs to live another life. Aristotle, by contrast, thought of the soul simply as a 'form', that is, as a way of behaving and thinking; a human having a soul just is the human behaving (by moving parts of the body) and thinking in certain characteristic human ways. And just as there cannot be a dance without people dancing, so there cannot be ways of behaving without embodied humans to behave in those ways. Hence, for Aristotle, the soul does not exist without the body.

Christian theology, believing in life after death, found it natural to take over Plato's conception of the soul.

But in the thirteenth century, St Thomas Aquinas sought to develop an Aristotelian conception modified to accommodate Christian doctrine. The soul, Aquinas taught, was indeed a form, but a special kind of form, one which could temporarily exist without the body to which it was naturally fitted. It has always been difficult to articulate this view in a coherent way which makes it distinct from Plato's. Descartes restated Plato's view. In more modern times, the view that humans have souls has always been understood as the view that humans have an essential part, separable from the body, as depicted by Plato and Aquinas. The pure Aristotelian view has more normally been expressed as the view that humans do not have souls; humans consist of matter alone, though it may be organized in a very complicated way and have properties that inanimate things do not have. In other words, Aristotelianism is a kind of materialism.

If, however, one thinks of the soul as a thing separable from the body, it could still cease to exist at death, when the body ceases to function. Plato had a number of arguments designed to show that the soul is naturally immortal; in virtue of its own nature, because of what it is, it will continue to exist forever. Later philosophers have developed some of these arguments and produced others. Even if these arguments do not show it (and most philosophers think that they do not), the soul may still be naturally immortal; or it may be immortal because God or some other force keeps it in being forever, either by itself or joined to a new body. If there is an omnipotent God, he could keep it in existence forever; and he might have revealed to us that he is going to do so.

1 The existence and nature of the soul
2 The immortality of the soul

1 The existence and nature of the soul

The form of a thing is its shape, appearance, pattern of reaction, and (in the case of a living thing) its way of changing over time and acting, in fact, all the properties that make it the kind of thing it is. The form of a living thing is, for ARISTOTLE, its soul. Plants have 'vegetative' souls, animals have 'sensitive' souls and humans have rational or intellectual souls; a human soul is not just a way of behaving publicly, but also a way of thinking. Forms for Aristotle are universals, in the sense that the same form can be instantiated in many different things. The form of a table, for example, can be instantiated in many different tables. What individuates, what makes the particular table the one it is, is the matter of which it is made. So too, claims Aristotle, what makes a particular human the one they are is the matter of which they are made. No form, he claims, can exist apart from the thing (a particular substance) in which it is instantiated. So a human soul cannot be separated from its body. At least, a whole soul cannot be separated, for Aristotle considers that a soul has parts, and he adds (*On the Soul* 413a) that some parts of the soul may be separable. He may have in mind the part or parts responsible for thought.

AQUINAS (§10–11) claimed that the soul does not need any bodily organ for thinking, and that is a main reason why he supposes that the whole soul can continue to exist without a body. In accord with the normal articulation of the Christian doctrine of life after death, Aquinas holds that the soul does continue to exist on the destruction of the body until it is reunited with it in the general resurrection. But what survives, claims Aquinas, is not the whole human being, but that essential part of it with limited functions, whose nature it is to be united with the body, and make it live and have its normal human operations of thought, perception and bodily action. Yet what makes such a separated soul my soul as opposed to yours? This question cannot be answered within a pure Aristotelian scheme. For Aristotelian forms are universals. There is just the form of humanity, which can be instantiated in many different individuals, and the separated soul is not united with matter. Aquinas says that each form has an 'inclination', is 'fitted', to be reunited with a certain body, the one from which it has been separated. Duns Scotus objected to this answer on the ground that there cannot be a bare inclination; an inclination has to be grounded in some actually existing feature of the soul. To take a modern analogy, if some substance has an inclination to liquefy at a certain temperature, that must be grounded in its chemical constitution. Hence Scotus holds that souls are not mere universals, but individual forms or essences, that is, that there is an essence of Socrates as well as of humanity. Anyone who holds that souls can exist separately from bodies must give an account of what makes a soul this particular soul, and the same soul as that of some earlier person. For Plato and for Descartes, this is something ultimate, just as perhaps what makes this chunk of matter different from that chunk of matter is something not analysable further. So too for Scotus, even though he thinks of souls as forms of bodies (*Ordinatio* II, d.3).

If Aquinas' view is to be spelled out coherently, it must be done in the same way. What did happen to a soul in the past, namely that it was united to a certain body, and will happen to it in future cannot make it the soul it is now. That must be something internal to it now. Religious believers who believe that humans can exist without their bodies, even if only tempora-

rily, must hold that. So too must any believer who holds that there is life after death, even if souls do not exist separately from bodies. For if I come to live again, the question arises as to what makes some subsequent human me, for my body will be largely if not entirely destroyed. If the answer is given that (most of) the atoms of my original body will be reassembled into bodily form, there are two problems. First, many of the atoms may no longer exist; they may have been transmuted into energy. And second, what proportion of the atoms do we need? Sixty per cent, seventy per cent, or what? If it is mere atoms which make some body mine and so some living human me, then no body will be fully mine unless it has all my atoms. Yet some of my atoms, even if not destroyed, will have come to form other human bodies. It will be a matter of degree whether a human survives, unless what makes a human the individual human they are is something other than the body, namely the soul (see RESURRECTION).

But why suppose that there is a separate soul? DESCARTES (§§5, 8), in his *Meditations*, gave a famous argument which must be the basis of any justification of substance dualism. He argues that I know infallibly that I exist as a thinking thing, but I do not know infallibly that I have a body; maybe that is all a dream. Hence the body is a separate thing from what is essential to me, namely my soul. A traditional criticism of this argument is that the mere fact that I do not know infallibly that my body exists does not show that it is separable from me; maybe I do not know what is involved in my present existence. After all, the argument has the same form as this clearly invalid argument: I know infallibly that I am Bloggs; I do not know infallibly that I am the son of John and Mary; hence the son of John and Mary is not the same thing as Bloggs. The argument can, however, be rephrased to meet this objection, not as an argument from knowledge and ignorance, but as one from logical possibility and impossibility. Descartes, in writing of what is 'imaginable', is often near to phrasing the argument in this way. Here is a rephrased version:

(1) I exist as a thinking thing now.
(2) It is logically possible that I go on thinking and so existing, even if my body is suddenly destroyed (and this remains logically possible, whatever else might be the case now inside or outside my body compatible with my existing now as a thinking thing).
(3) It is not logically possible that any thing continue to exist unless some part of it continue to exist.

Hence I must already have another part beside my body, namely my soul. (For a more detailed presentation of this version of Descartes' argument, see Swinburne [1986] 1997: 145–60, 322–32.)

Most objectors to the argument in this form will deny (2) (see, for example, Shoemaker and Swinburne 1984: 141–8). They would claim that it is not logically possible that I survive without my body. It certainly seems logically possible. Our only grounds for supposing something to be logically possible are that we can make sense of it; we can spell out what it would be like for it to be true. Our only grounds for supposing something to be logically impossible are that we can derive a contradiction from it. It does look as if each of us can tell a coherent story of losing our body and yet continuing to think, and it does not look as if there is an obvious contradiction involved. So to some philosophers it looks as if the conclusion is sound.

Some claim that the causal interaction which substance dualism postulates between the soul and the body is unintelligible unless we can have some grasp of a mechanism through which brain states cause soul states and vice versa. A defender of substance dualism will respond that we often know very well that certain states cause others without having the least idea how this could occur. Before the theory of electromagnetism was developed, people knew that the motion of a magnetic charge caused an electric current, but had no idea how these very diverse states could influence each other.

2 The immortality of the soul

Even if the soul is simple and separable from the body, it does not follow that it will continue to exist after death, let alone exist forever with a mental life, with thoughts, feelings and sensations. It might instead exist in the way that our souls exist while we have a dreamless sleep. There have been a large number of arguments for the natural immortality of the soul, purporting to show that it is the nature of the soul to be immortal; it will naturally go on forever, without God or any external agency needing to intervene to give it special powers to continue in existence. Most of these are arguments which try to show that the soul has such a peculiar nature that the normal forces which cause things to cease to exist would not affect it.

One well-known argument is that given by PLATO (§§10–11, 13) (*Phaedo* 78b) and repeated by, among others, BERKELEY (§8) (1710, section 141) and Joseph BUTLER (§6) (1736 I, ch. 1), from the simplicity of the soul. It runs as follows. We only know of things ceasing to exist when they have parts; and they cease to exist only when the parts are separated from each other. A house ceases to exist when the bricks are

taken away from each other. But the soul has no parts, and so we know of nothing which in the normal course of things would cause it to cease to exist, barring divine intervention. So it is reasonable to suppose that it is naturally immortal. But this argument is weak. We do know of things ceasing to exist without any parts being separated from each other. An atom ceases to exist when it is turned into energy. Further, it does look as if the functioning of the soul, its having a mental life, depends on the functioning of the brain. (Does not damage to the brain render a person un-conscious?) We need more positive argument to show that the soul could function without the brain sustaining it. And if it turns out that the soul is incapable of functioning without the brain, why suppose that it even exists?

Plato gives several other arguments for the natural immortality of the soul. They include the argument (*Phaedo* 73a–78a; *Meno* 81b–86b) that humans know many things and have many concepts which they have not learned or acquired on earth. In the *Meno*, Plato describes a slave-boy being led by Socrates to assert various truths of mathematics which no one has taught him. Hence, Plato argues, he must have learned them in a previous existence. But if souls exist before birth and through a life of embodiment on earth, it is natural to suppose that they will continue to exist after death. An objector, however, may reasonably argue that the slave-boy did not know the truths in question until Socrates helped him to become aware of them. The argument from pre-existence did not appeal to Christian philosophers, for Christians have normally held that souls come into existence at conception or birth, though they continue to exist after death. Aquinas appealed to the fact that humans naturally desire to exist forever and that 'it is impossible that natural appetite should be in vain' (*Summa contra gentiles* II, 79.6). Yet it is far from obvious why that is impossible. He also appealed to the ability of the soul to 'apprehend incompatible things', that is, to understand the eternal truths of mathematics and to have contact with God, as showing that the soul's own nature is 'incorruptible', or naturally immortal (*Summa contra gentiles* II, 79.5). But it is in no way obvious that the finite cannot understand the infinite or that the mortal cannot understand the immortal.

Arguments to the *natural* immortality of the soul are very unappealing today. Some philosophers find arguments to show that the world is such that something external to the soul will guarantee its immortality more persuasive. An argument of KANT captures much more ordinary thinking. It is not strictly speaking, Kant claims, a theoretical argument which proves that the soul is immortal, but a 'practical argument' to this effect: we are obliged to act morally, and it only makes sense to do so if we suppose that we, and so our souls, will continue to live forever. Kant regards the various moral obligations under which we stand as different aspects of the obligation to realize the supremely good state of affairs, the *summum bonum*. The *summum bonum* involves our own moral perfection, something towards which we make only slow progress in this life and need endless duration finally to achieve. For moral actions to make sense, we must regard the *summum bonum* as attainable and so regard ourselves as having an endless life. Kant backs up his argument with the further consideration that the *summum bonum* requires that happiness be in proportion to good moral behaviour, both for ourselves and others. But in this world the good are not always happy. So again for the *summum bonum* to be attainable we need another world in which 'the greatest happiness is... combined... with the highest degree of moral perfection' (Kant 1788, bk 2, ch. 2, section 5). This, Kant claims, requires the operation of God, who alone can bring about such coincidence. Now Kant has a very high conception of the status of moral obligation. Others may not regard its claims so highly. Yet even if we conceive of it as Kant did, it is in no way obvious that to make sense of our doing some moral action, we need to think of it as a step towards our own moral perfection which will eventually be achieved. When conscious of an obligation to help the starving, I give money to a charity; the point of my action is achieved by my giving the money, independently of whether it improves my character. Likewise its purpose is achieved whether or not I am the happier for achieving it. Holiness of will combined with supreme happiness may be good, but acting morally seems to have its own point quite apart from whether all that results from it. Moral actions are in general fully worth doing for totally mundane reasons, even if there are also reasons connected with an after-life for doing them.

Kant's argument has very considerable similarity to the argument of Eastern religions from the law of karma, which they affirm to be a basic principle governing the universe, that all actions get their proper reward (see KARMA AND REBIRTH, INDIAN CONCEPTIONS OF; REINCARNATION). Good actions lead to happiness, and bad actions to unhappiness. Since so often this does not happen to a soul during a given earthly life, it must have another life in which morality and reward can be evened out. Although karma does not require another life on this earth, Eastern religions believe that we are normally reincarnated on earth. The good are reincarnated in more desirable states; the good poor man has a more

wealthy next life, and the bad poor man may be reincarnated as a mere animal. But Eastern religions do not all hold that this necessarily goes on forever. Buddhism claims that our supreme goal should be to break the cycle of death and rebirth, by living such holy lives that after death we are not reincarnated at all, but depart to *nirvāṇa* (nothingness). It is disputable whether this means 'annihilation' or, on the contrary, a totally blissful state (see NIRVĀṆA). However, before we could accept this argument, we would need good grounds for believing that the law of karma operates.

If the soul is not naturally immortal, then the action of some supernatural law (karma) or agent (God) is required to make it immortal. Much Christian tradition affirms that the free action of God is required for this purpose and that he is under no obligation so to act. In that case, in order to have grounds to believe in immortality, we will need his assurance that he will so act. At this point Christian tradition normally produces, not a Kantian argument, but the claim that it is an item of revelation. God has told us that he will so act, that he will bring the dead to life again – the good dead to an everlasting good life, and the bad dead to an everlasting bad life. (There are, however, differences within Christian tradition about what will happen to the bad, and to those who die before they become clearly good or bad (see HEAVEN; HELL; LIMBO; PURGATORY; REVELATION §§2–3).)

As well as such very general arguments for life after death, there are some empirical arguments. Eastern religions occasionally produce children who claim to be able to recall events of a previous life, events which they could not have known to have happened by any normal means, but which subsequent investigation reveals to have happened. Some child describes the house at some place where 'he' lived in his previous life, and then such a house is found. But there are doubts about the worth of such evidence. Relatively few children make such claims; the story which they tell about the previous life can be vague; and there are doubts about whether ordinary means of their having obtained the information about that life have really been excluded. Then there are arguments from what mediums declare is told to them, while they are in a trance, by persons already dead. The evidence that those persons give is supposed to be the knowledge that mediums acquire of details of those persons' past lives, which, it is claimed, they could not have acquired by any normal means. But there are similar doubts about the worth of evidence of this kind. The knowledge acquired may be vague and might have been obtained by some normal route. Even if these doubts could be satisfactorily resolved, a hypothesis of some abnormal way of acquiring information about the past might seem less radical than a hypothesis of the present existence of persons who have died. Finally, and most interestingly, there has been the discovery of 'after-death experiences'. Some ten to fifteen per cent of subjects resuscitated after being clinically as good as dead report having had 'transcendental experiences' during the period in which they were virtually dead. These experiences consist of a very vivid awareness of approaching a border or frontier and seeing into a strange, normally immensely pleasing world and then being called back. This coincidence of kinds of experience among people of various backgrounds is interesting; but the experiences have relatively little common detail, so as hardly to provide by themselves very strong evidence that what was observed was really there. These observations would require support from other considerations. In any case, none of the empirical evidence by itself gives any reason at all for supposing the subsequent existence to be everlasting.

See also: ALEXANDER OF APHRODISIAS §2; ESCHATOLOGY; MENDELSSOHN, M.; PSYCHĒ; SALVATION; SOUL IN ISLAMIC PHILOSOPHY

References and further reading

* Aquinas, T. (1259–65) *Summa contra gentiles* II, trans. J.F. Anderson, *On the Truth of the Catholic Faith*, Garden City, NY: Doubleday., 1956. (Aquinas' account of the nature of 'intellectual substances', that is, souls, and defence of the view that they can be united to human bodies as their forms; see chapters 46–89. Fairly difficult for those unfamiliar with Greek or medieval philosophy.)
* Aristotle (*c.* mid 4th century BC) *On the Soul* (*De Anima*) 412a–418a; bks 2–3 trans. and notes by D.W. Hamlyn, Oxford: Clarendon Press, 1968. (Aristotle's account of the nature and attributes of the soul. Fairly difficult for those unfamiliar with Greek philosophy.)
* Berkeley, G. (1710) *The Principles of Human Knowledge*, London: J.M. Dent & Sons, 1975. (Section 141 gives Berkeley's argument for the immortality of the soul.)
* Butler, J. (1736) *The Analogy of Religion*, London: George Bell & Sons, 1902. (Butler's argument for the reasonableness of belief in life after death; see part 1, chapter 1, 'Of a Future Life'.)
Churchland, P.M. (1984) *Matter and Consciousness*, Cambridge, MA: MIT Press. (Simple and fair introduction to the mind–body problem by a firm materialist.)
* Descartes, R. (1641) *Meditations on First Philosophy*, in E.S. Haldane and G.R.T. Ross, *The Philosophical Works of Descartes*, Cambridge: Cambridge University Press, 1972, vol. 1. (Descartes' easy-to-read argument for substance dualism; see particularly meditations 2 and 6.)
* Duns Scotus, J. (*c.*1305) *Ordinatio* II d.3, vol. 7 of *Omnia opera*, Vatican City: Scotistic Commission, 1950–. (Scotus' account of the nature of the soul. There is no available English translation.)
Edwards, P. (ed.) (1992) *Immortality*, New York: Macmillan. (A large collection of short excerpts from various writers from Plato onwards.)
* Kant, I. (1788) *Critique of Practical Reason*, trans. T.K. Abbott, London: Longmans, Green & Co., 1909. (Kant's argument that we can only make sense of morality if we suppose the soul to be immortal; see book 2, chapter 2, sections 4–5.)
* Plato (*c.*386–380 BC) *Meno*, trans. W.K.C. Guthrie, *Protagoras and Meno*, Harmondsworth: Penguin, 1956. (Includes the 'slave-boy' argument.)
* —— (*c.*386–380 BC) *Phaedo*, trans. with notes by D. Gallop, Oxford: Clarendon Press, 1975. (Socrates justifies his view that his soul will continue to live after the death of his body.)
* Shoemaker S. and Swinburne R. (1984) *Personal Identity*, Oxford: Blackwell. (A debate between a materialist and a dualist about personal identity.)
* Swinburne, R. (1986) *The Evolution of the Soul*, Oxford: Clarendon Press; revised edn, 1997. (A full modern statement of the dualist position.)

RICHARD SWINBURNE

SOUTH AMERICA, PHILOSOPHY IN *see* LATIN AMERICA, PHILOSOPHY IN

SOUTH SLAVS, PHILOSOPHY OF

Philosophy as a distinct intellectual activity emerged in the coastal towns of the Adriatic during the Renaissance. Philosophers from this area wrote in Latin and taught philosophy in Italy, Germany and Austria. The first popular philosophical works in the vernacular did not appear until late in the eighteenth century, and it was almost one hundred years later that the first chairs in logic and philosophy were founded in the universities. Academic philosophy, usually derived from German or British models, was thus brought into the intellectual life of South Slavs. Local academic philosophers, mostly educated in Germany, brought home a variety of philosophical approaches, and by the early twentieth century many schools of thought flourished: Neo-Kantianism flourished in Beograd, while Neo-Thomism was particularly strong in Ljubljana and Zagreb (until 1941 the Meinongian phenomenological approach also flourished in Ljubljana). In their quest for originality, local philosophers constructed various eclectic philosophical systems.

The Soviet Marxism-Leninism, imposed in all Yugoslav universities after 1945, was replaced in the late 1950s by a Neo-Marxist approach based on the concept of praxis. This was a concept of a purposeful human activity which, among other things, results in social change (for example, the development of socialism). These Neo-Marxists engaged in vigorous debates on the nature of truth and knowledge, on human freedom, alienation, socialism and humanism as well as on social and political issues. Their work reached an international audience through the international journal Praxis, *published in Zagreb, and through their international summer school of philosophy at Korčula. As their support for the Yugoslav communist regime turned into open criticism, the regime halted the publication of* Praxis *and in 1974 forced the Beograd Neo-Marxists from their teaching posts.*

The Neo-Marxist interest in non-Marxist philosophy facilitated the reception of various non-Marxist approaches. From the early 1960s, existentialism, structuralism, hermeneutics and phenomenology – in particular the philosophy of Heidegger – exerted considerable influence on Neo-Marxists as well as on philosophers who had gradually abandoned this approach. In the early 1970s, a younger generation of thinkers in Beograd, Zagreb, Ljubljana and Zadar developed an interest in analytic philosophy. Since that time no approach or trend in philosophy has emerged as the dominant one in any of the academic centres in the countries which were formerly part of Yugoslavia.

1   **Philosophy in Latin**
2   **Non-academic philosophy in the vernacular**
3   **Academic philosophy before the Second World War**
4   **Philosophy after 1945**

1   Philosophy in Latin

Until the Renaissance, philosophy among the South Slavs (on the territory of the former Yugoslavia) was practised only within the theological framework of Roman Catholicism and Eastern Orthodoxy. In the fifteenth century, the Ottoman conquest and the resulting intermittent warfare had greatly impeded intellectual activity. At the same time Renaissance humanism penetrated the coastal towns of the Adriatic (which were not exposed to the Ottoman onslaught). In the Republic of Ragusa (Dubrovnik) especially, an indigenous literature flourished in the local Serbo-Croat dialect, as well as in Italian and Latin. The growth of interest in philosophy nurtured philosophers of South Slav origin who subsequently taught philosophy and published their philosophical works in Latin in various countries of Europe, principally in Italy, Austria and Germany.

Among the first of the South Slav humanist philosophers was Juraj Dragišić (Georgius Benignus de Salviatis), born in Bosnia in 1450 and educated in Dubrovnik, Paris, Oxford and Florence. A Franciscan monk, he was a courtier to Lorenzo di Medici and later a professor of philosophy at the University of Pisa. Philosophically, he was inclined towards Platonism, and in his polemical works he defended PICO DELLA MIRANDOLA as well as Savanarola. His main works were in logic (*Artis dialecticae praecepta vetera ac nova* 1520) and metaphysics (*De natura caelestium spirituum* 1499). The humanist Matija Hvale, born in what is now Slovenia, was active at the University of Vienna in the early sixteenth century.

Matija Vlačić (Mattias Flacius Illyricus) born in Labin in Istria, was educated in Germany where he became one of the leading Lutheran theologians and polemicists of the sixteenth century, firmly opposed to any compromise with Roman Catholicism. In his theological treatise *Clavis Scripturae Sacrae* (A Key to the Holy Scriptures) he not only offered a systematic linguistic exegesis of the Bible, but expounded a succinct philosophy of language and of translation. Language is a sign or image of things, that is, 'glasses, as it were, through which we look at things'. The meaning of words is determined by the historical context in which they are used, and is thus subject to change. This contextual view of meaning guides Vlačić's own Biblical exegesis, which Wilhelm DILTHEY considered the forerunner of modern hermeneutics (1914–90 (5): 325).

Also in the sixteenth century, Franjo Petrić (Franciscus Patricius) was born in Cres, Dalmatia, educated in Germany and Italy and taught philosophy at the Universities in Ferrara and Rome. His youthful *La cità felice* (The happy city) belongs to the tradition of Renaissance utopianism exemplified by Campanella's *City of the Sun*. His philosophical system, expounded in his *Nova de universis philosophia* (The new universal philosophy), is an attempt to synthesize Catholicism and Platonism: the light, as a spiritual force, is the first cause, the source of all movement and life in the universe; the spiritual thus permeates the whole universe and in this the human microcosm reflects the universe's macrocosmic order.

In this, as in his earlier works, he rejected Aristotle's philosophy as false and godless, which resulted in his work being briefly placed on the Roman Catholic Index of prohibited books.

Rudjer Josip Bošković, (Roger Joseph Boscovich), a native of Dubrovnik who joined the Jesuit order, was educated and taught philosophy in Rome. A scientist and mathematician, he is today best known for his theory of non-extended atoms or *puncta*. In Article 164 of his *Theoria philosophiae naturalis* (A Theory of Natural Philosophy) (1763), he claims that 'Matter is composed of perfectly indivisible, non-extended, discrete points'. Having no mass, these points do not exert force in the Newtonian sense but still interact with each other. They repel each other at very small distances, reaching an equilibrium, beyond which the points attract and then again repel each other. This process is governed by Bošković's law of oscillation. Within the framework of their spatial relations, pairs of oscillating points form minute composite particles. Assemblies of these first-order particles form larger particles which, in turn, form seemingly hard bodies. The collision of impenetrable atoms, he observed, would introduce non-continuous or sudden change in their velocity (Art. 18). In order to avoid this violation of the law of continuity, he conceived atoms as non-extended and impenetrable; in contrast, observable, hard bodies are held to be extended and penetrable. Thus Bošković attempted to uphold the law of continuity which he derived from Leibniz and held to be an axiom. As L.L. Whyte (1961) shows, his deductive kinematic theory of non-extended atoms was highly influential until experimental research on the composition of atoms began early in the twentieth century.

2 Non-academic philosophy in the vernacular

At the end of the eighteenth century, the first philosophical works began to appear in as yet unstandardized South Slav vernaculars. These were works of non-academic philosophy, either popularizing philosophical ideas or presenting them in verse form. Dositej Obradović, a defrocked Serbian Orthodox monk who had attended philosophy lectures at the universities of Halle and Leipzig, was one of the first to popularize the ideas of Enlightenment. But the most original work in the vernacular was a philosophical epic in six cantos, *Luča Mikrokosma* (The Ray of Microcosm) (1845), by Petar Petrović Njegoš, Bishop-Prince of Montenegro. The epic presents a thoroughly dualistic metaphysics and a rather unorthodox cosmogony. To the duality of matter and spirit corresponds the duality of good and evil (although the source of evil is not located exclusively in the matter). The world of light borders on the world of darkness – Hades – which as a sun has its own globe of darkness. God created the heavens, the realm of light, by a stroke of shining light which destroyed the reigning realm of darkness. Satan, a duke of angels, rejected this view of the creation and rebelled against God in the name of the equality of all spirits. Upon his defeat, he was thrown into Hades while Adam (who repented of his association with Satan) and his progeny were settled on Earth, a halfway house between the heavens and Hades. Caged in the body, the human soul is governed by the conflicting laws of good and evil, and is thus condemned to the realm of tears and suffering. Both in its epic style and its pessimistic dualism, this metaphysical poem is unique in South Slav literature and philosophy.

Throughout the nineteenth century, liberal political ideas were disseminated through political pamphlets and popular encyclopedias such as Vladimir Jovanović's incomplete *Politički rečnik* (Political dictionary) published in Novi Sad, then in Austro-Hungary. Svetozar Marković, a socialist journalist, popularized socialist political ideas (mainly drawn from the works of Chernyshevski and Pisarev) through his newspapers and pamphlets published in Serbia. The future king of Serbia, Petar Karađorđević, while still in exile, published his (now standard) translation of Mill's *On Liberty*.

Božidar Knežević, a poor secondary school teacher, was educated at Beograd, where in 1898 he published his visionary treatise *Principi istorije* (Principles of history). Since everything that exists, he argued, exists only in history, history takes over the fields of other sciences and offers the highest human understanding. In addition, history binds all peoples and leads to their reconciliation and overall harmony. Knežević's optimism and belief in the progress of the human mind is tempered with his belief that the total quantity of time available to the living is limited: human civilization and even human life is thus bound to disappear. Proportion, he boldly states, is the telos of history. As both nature and humans strive after this ideal, proportion is used to explain the nature of truth, reason, good, progress, beauty, justice and freedom. Once elements achieve proportion and balance with each other, 'they live simultaneously' in a great organic whole in which one can ultimately arrive at 'complete morality, freedom, justice and truth'. Whereas academic philosophers repudiated this system as incoherent, many Serb avant garde poets and writers found in it a congenial vision of the universe in which everything, including poetry and beauty, had its own rightful place in a world striving after proportion.

3 Academic philosophy before the Second World War

From their inception, the first South Slav institutions of higher learning have established chairs of philosophy or logic: in 1863, the Beograd Great School (since 1905 the University of Beograd), in 1874 the University of Zagreb, and in 1919 the University of Ljubljana. These, as well as the universities which were founded later, have remained centres of academic philosophy.

The first professor of logic in Beograd, Konstantin Branković, based his handbooks dealing with philosophy and logic on the works of the German academic W.T. Krug. His successor, Alimpije Vasiljević, used J.S. MILL's *Logic* for the same purpose. The first philosophy professor at Zagreb, Franjo Marković (a pupil of Herbart) called for the study of Croatian philosophy, arguing that 'only the people to have acquired a homeland of thought have firmly come to own their real homeland'.

Albert Bazala, Marković's successor, was the author of *Povjest filozofije* (A history of philosophy) (1906), one of the first original works in history of philosophy in Serbo-Croat, in which Kant's work is presented as the highest achievement of modern philosophy. He continued Marković's research in the history of South Slav as well as Croatian philosophy. In his *Metalogički korjen filozofije* (The metalogical root of philosophy) Bazala argued that the human mind is not a static faculty but 'a dynamic-teleological activity'. As a dynamic activity, cognition requires that its object be sustained in time and organically related to a whole; therefore, there are no singular truths about discrete objects. In opposition to this, Bazala's colleague Pavao Vuk-Pavlović expounded a dualist theory in his *Spoznaja i spoznajna teorija* (Knowledge and theory of knowledge) (1926), where the truth-value of cognition is found in 'an experience of the logically evident' which may constitute singular truths. The relation between cognition and its objects is a subject-matter not of science but of a meta-empirical or metaphysical investigation. In defending his philosophical humanism, Vuk-Pavlović argued against Bazala's determinism and emphasized the autonomy and creativity of each human being.

France Veber (Franz Weber), the first professor of philosophy at the University of Ljubljana, was also the first academic philosopher to write in Slovene. A pupil of MEINONG, his *Sistem filozofije* (A system of philosophy) developed a theory of mental presentation and of objects. The presentations (*Vorstellungen*) are the basic ingredients of all experiences, including the sensory ones. Each sensory experience can be evaluated in terms of its function either of 'attainment' or 'presentation'. The attainment is primary in sensory experiences of touch; in consequence, such experiences are closer to 'encountering reality' than any others. In visual experiences, presentation is primary, and thus reality is represented, not 'encountered'. From 1930 onwards, Veber developed a philosophical anthropology and a philosophy of God as well as a new dynamic ontology, eschewing his earlier dichotomy of object–mental presentation. Several of his students developed his earlier theory of presentation, but as the communist regime removed him from his chair in 1945, his work was ignored in Slovenia until 1987.

Branislav Petronijević from Beograd was educated in Germany and inspired by the writings of LOTZE and VON HARTMANN. In his principal work *Prinzipien der Metaphysik* (Principles of metaphysics) (1904), he argued that being consists of simple, discrete qualitative points which are mutually related in various ways to form a unity. His metaphysical system was thus conceived as a synthesis of the metaphysics of Spinoza and Leibniz into 'mono-pluralism'. Our immediate experience not only presents reality as is but is also the source of basic logical and metaphysical axioms (for example, the laws of identity, of contradiction and of excluded middle): all are derived from the data of immediate experience. His eclectic 'empirio-rationalist' epistemology was thus based on a rather complex derivation of logical laws from immediate experience.

Ksenija Atanasijević from Beograd was the first recognized woman philosopher among South Slavs and a leader of Beograd's women's movement. Educated in Paris, she wrote in French and German, producing studies on the philosophy of Epicurus and of Giordano Bruno as well as on the history of South Slav philosophy. Her principal work *Filosofski fragmenti* (Philosophical fragments) (1929), attempted to reconcile her metaphysical belief in the inevitability of evil with a justification of her activist, humanist stance.

Until the outbreak of war in 1941, philosophers at Zagreb, Ljubljana and Beograd pursued a wide variety of philosophical interests. In Ljubljana, the Neo-Thomist approach had been developed since the 1860s. Additionally, philosophers in Zagreb had interest in logical positivism, in Marxism and in the contemporary philosophy of education. In Beograd, philosophers had developed interests in Neo-Kantianism, pragmatism and Bergson's philosophy, as well as in Eastern Orthodox philosophical traditions. Toma Živanović and Đorđe Tasić, Beograd professors of law, wrote in German, French and Italian on the relation of morality and law and on the fundamental grounds of law. Their colleague Slobodan Jovanović critically examined the political philosophy of Plato,

51

Machiavelli, Burke and Marx; his essays, published in the 1930s, are minor classics of Serbian prose. Partly due to this divergence of interests, there was almost no contact or dialogue between these three academic centres during this period.

4 Philosophy after 1945

With the communist takeover in 1945, Soviet Marxism-Leninism became the official philosophy in Yugoslavia. Non-Marxist academic philosophers were faced with conversion to the official philosophy or dismissal. After the expulsion of the Yugoslav Communist Party from the Soviet-dominated international communist organization in 1948, Yugoslav Marxists were called upon to revise the official philosophy. Responding to this call, the post-war generation of Yugoslav philosophers developed a Neo-Marxist approach based on Marx's concept of praxis (mentioned in his early writings) and inspired by the writings of the Frankfurt School members as well as French existentialists (see EXISTENTIALISM; FRANKFURT SCHOOL). The concept of praxis was chosen partly because it symbolized the Marxist commitment to bringing about social change through purposeful action.

By 1960 the orthodox historical and dialectical materialism was replaced at all Yugoslav universities by this less rigid approach. From then until the early 1980s, Yugoslav philosophers vigorously debated the nature and scope of praxis, of knowledge and truth, of freedom, alienation, socialism and humanism as well as a variety of social and political issues. These debates were carried out not only in the newly founded philosophical journals (*Filozofija* in Beograd, *Pregled* in Sarajevo, *Perspektive* in Ljubljana) but also in the mass media. During these debates the concept of praxis came to be interpreted in the following distinct but ultimately compatible ways: (1) as a free and creative activity which defines a specifically human existence – this primarily anthropological interpretation was first advocated by Gajo Petrović in Zagreb; (2) as an object-directed activity firmly anchored in human history, providing an ontological ground not only for the human universe but also for the world of nature (Milan Kangrga, Zagreb); (3) as a source and criterion of human knowledge from which one could further derive the concepts of a subject and an object (Mihailo Marković, Beograd); (4) as a social activity, aiming at abolishing and transcending the limitations of the present social reality (this axiological interpretation was advocated both by Marković and Petrović).

Yugoslav Neo-Marxists organized an international summer school of philosophy on the island of Korčula

and, from 1964, published the international journal *Praxis* in Zagreb. By the late 1960s, they had changed from ardent supporters to open critics of the Yugoslav communist regime; as a result, *Praxis* was forced to cease publication and Beograd Neo-Marxists were forced out of their teaching posts in 1975. This ended the Neo-Marxist domination of Yugoslav philosophy. The dialogue which they had initiated between Yugoslav philosophers from different academic centres – the first such sustained dialogue – ended in 1983 with a quarrel between Neo-Marxists from Zagreb and Beograd concerning the publication abroad of *Praxis International* (this journal ceased in 1994).

As Praxis-Neo-Marxists cultivated interests and contacts outside Marxist philosophy, Yugoslav academic philosophers became acquainted with various non-Marxist approaches to philosophy. Among the first to promote Heidegger's approach to philosophy was Vanja Sutlić from Zagreb. In his principal work *Bit i suvremenost* (Essence and contemporaneity) (1967) he endeavoured to reinterpret the concept of praxis in Heideggerian terms: praxis was presented as the production of *Sein* from *Dasein* (see HEIDEGGER, M. §4). Abdulah Šarčević from Sarajevo engaged in a multifaceted critique of bourgeois society and of modernity. His *De Homine* (1986) rejected the domination of Western technology-laden thought over non-Western (such as Islamic) approaches to philosophy, and pointed out how, with its own narrow boundaries, scientific and technological progress has failed to humanize our society and has failed to humanize nature. Ivan Foht from Sarajevo developed an aesthetics in which our understanding as well as the ontological status of a work of art depends primarily on its form and not on its content. Art, he argued in his *Savremena estetika muzike* (Contemporary aesthetics of music) (1980) is a highly autonomous human activity; music, in particular, has an atemporal validity. Foht's search for an ontological definition of art, inspired in part by INGARDEN, is unique in post-1945 Yugoslav philosophy.

Equally unique is the philosophical development of Mihailo Đurić from Beograd. His work in philosophy started in the early 1950s with studies in Ancient Greek philosophy and the early Wittgenstein. In the 1960s he published in Serbo-Croat a selection of Max WEBER's writings, which was highly influential. In the 1970s he repudiated attempts to develop Marxist sociology or economics, arguing that Marx was neither a philosopher nor a scientist but a visionary and a critic of the inhumanity of bourgeois society. About the same time he developed an interest in Heidegger and his thesis on the crisis and the end of European metaphysics. Since the 1980s he has concentrated on the contemporary relevance of

Nietzsche's philosophy: as an open workshop of thought, Nietzsche's philosophy points the way out of the crisis of metaphysics and of Western philosophy in general (see NIETZSCHE, F.).

In the late 1970s, Slavoj Žižek from Ljubljana developed a unique Lacanian psychoanalytic critique of totalitarian ideology and thought (see LACAN, J.). In his later writings, published in French and English, he applied this Lacanian approach to other ideologies, including the liberal-democratic one, and to popular culture and film. In his *Looking Awry* (1991) he advocated the maxim of psychoanalytic ethic 'avoid as much as possible any violation of the fantasy space of the other', and argued that nationalism is the way subjects of a given nation organize their collective enjoyment through national myths.

Interest in logical positivism and the analytic approach to philosophy developed in the 1920s in Zagreb and in Beograd. Zvonko Richtman and Rikard Podhorski from Zagreb defended a logical positivist approach to science (see ANALYTICAL PHILOSOPHY; LOGICAL POSITIVISM). In Beograd, Dragiša M. Đurić developed a highly reductive phenomenalism (which reduced the concept of time to the phenomenon of now), while Kajica Milanov discussed Frege's and the logical positivists' analyses of meaning (see PHENOMENALISM). In the early 1960s, Yugoslav Neo-Marxists revived interest in the analytic philosophy of meaning and meta-ethics within their Neo-Marxist framework, while Jovan Ćulum from Beograd in his *Filozofske beleške* (Philosophical notes) (1967) used analytic techniques to criticize the Hegelian and Marxist approach to philosophy. At the same time, Svetlana Knjazev-Adamović and Staniša Novaković wrote about analytic philosophy of knowledge and of science, while Aleksandar Kron started his work in symbolic logic outside any Marxist framework. In his later *Hipoteze i znanje* (Hypotheses and knowledge) (1984) Novaković argued against the view that the acceptance or rejection of hypotheses in modern science is based exclusively on empirical evidence.

In the early 1970s, analytic philosophers in Beograd engaged in a polemic concerning the analysis of moral terms. Igor Primorac forcefully defended a deontological theory. His arguments, appealing to our moral intuitions and ordinary usage of moral terms, were criticized by Knjazev-Adamović and others. In the early 1990s, she and Jovan Babić extended the debate in the journal *Theoria* to issues in normative ethics, including that of pacifism in times of war. A similar debate concerning scepticism and knowledge was sparked in 1974 by a series of articles by Neven Sesardić from Zagreb. Sesardić rejected both the argument from the evil demon and from illusion as invalid. In response, Aleksandar Pavković in his *Razlozi za sumnju* (Reasons for doubt) (1988) argued that, suitably reconstructed, these sceptical arguments could be rendered valid (see PERCEPTION, EPISTEMIC ISSUES IN). Živan Lazović from Beograd argued for the contextualism of principles in *O prirodi epistemičkog opravdanja* (On the nature of epistemic justification), an alternative to both foundationalism and coherentism which emphasizes the constitutive role of the established epistemic principles, techniques and procedures (see JUSTIFICATION, EPISTEMIC).

In his *Fizikalizam* (Physicalism) (1984), the first examination of contemporary materialism in Serbo-Croat, Sesardić defended the mind–body identity thesis, arguing that the replacement of intentional terms by descriptions of behavioural dispositions will facilitate scientific discovery of the relations between behavioural dispositions and structural states of the brain (see MIND, IDENTITY THEORY OF). In contrast, in his *Materija, svest, saznanje* (Matter, mind and knowledge) (1990) Nikola Grahek from Beograd argued that a materialist view of the mind such as Sesardić's, faces serious problems in explaining introspection of the subject's own mental states. The debate concerning materialism and functionalism, which started in 1980s in the philosophical journals in Beograd, Zagreb and Ljubljana, appears to be continuing (see MATERIALISM IN THE PHILOSOPHY OF MIND).

Writing on the philosophy of language, Nenad Miščević (formerly from Zadar, now at Maribor) shares Sesardić's scientific naturalism. Cognitive science and linguistics, he argued in his 1987 work *Od misli do jezika* (From thought to language), would provide the best basis for a comprehensive theory of language. Matijaž Potrč from Ljubljana has also extensively discussed current analytic approaches to the philosophy of language. Miloš Arsenijević, in his unique treatment of Zeno's paradoxes and contemporary philosophy of space and time, *Prostor, vreme, Zenon* (Space, time, Zeno) (1986), has attempted to solve the paradoxes by arguing that Zeno's premises are tenable each on their own but are not cotenable.

The break-up of Yugoslavia in 1991 has, perhaps temporarily, put an end to the debates among philosophers from Zagreb, Beograd, Ljubljana and Sarajevo. Many of them, however, continue to participate in philosophical debate outside their newly established states.

See also: MARX, K.; MARXIST PHILOSOPHY, RUSSIAN AND SOVIET

References and further reading

* Arsenijević, M. (1986) *Prostor, vreme, Zenon* (Space, time, Zeno), Beograd and Zagreb: Filozofsko Društvo Srbije & Liber. (A systematic examination of various attempts to solve Zeno's paradoxes, arguing, at the end, that Zeno's premises are not cotenable.)

—— (1989) 'How many physically distinguished parts can a limited body contain', *Analysis* 1 (49): 36–42. (An exercise in a metaphysical speculation over divisibility of bodies.)

—— (1993–4) 'Mathematics, Infinity and the Physical World', *Dialektik* 89–107. (A new approach to the ancient question of the relation of mathematics to reality.)

Atanasijević, K. (1923) *The Metaphysical and Geometrical Doctrine of Bruno as Given in His work 'De Triplici Minimo'*, trans. and intro. G.V. Tomashevich, St Louis, MO: Warren H. Green, 1972. (Attempt at a modern interpretation of Bruno's work.)

* —— (1929) *Filosofski fragmenti* (Philosophical fragments), Beograd: Geca Kon. (A humanist approach to various questions of normative ethics.)

* Babić, J. (1992) 'Primenjena etika I' (Applied ethics I), *Theoria* 34 (1): 97–105. (The debates on this topic, continued in the following issue.)

* Bazala, A. (1906) *Povjest filozofije* (A history of philosophy), Zagreb: Liber, 1989, 2nd edn. (A Kantian exposition of the history of philosophy with Kant's philosophy presented as the highest achievement of Western Philosophy.)

* Boscovich (Bošković), R.J. (1763) *Theoria philosophiae naturalis: A Theory of Natural Philosophy*, trans. J.M. Child (1921), London: MIT Press, 1966. (Contains a useful introduction by the translator.)

* Campanella, T. (1602) *La Città del Sole: Dialogo Poetico* (The City of the Sun: A Poetical Dialogue), trans. with notes by D.J. Donno, Berkeley and Los Angeles, CA, and London: University of California Press, 1981. (A scientifically ordered utopia presided over by metaphysicians and scientists.)

* Ćulum, J. (1967) *Filozofske beleške* (Philosophical notes), Beograd: Nolit. (Elegant essays in analytic philosophy, arguing for the untenability of Hegelian metaphysics and its Marxist derivatives.)

* Dilthey, W. (1914–90) *Gesammelte Schriften* (Collected Works), Göttingen: Vandenhoeck & Ruprecht, 20 vols. (The standard complete works.)

* Dragišić, J. (Salviatis, Georgius Benignus de) (1499) *De natura caelestium spirituum* (On the nature of celestial spirits), Florence: Bartolommeo di Libri. (A Neoplatonist treatise of metaphysics. His 1520 work *Artis dialecticae praecepta vetera ac nova* (Principles old and new of the dialectic art) was a discourse on logic and rhetoric.)

Đurić, M. (1985) *Nietzsche und die Metaphysik* (Nietzsche and metaphysics), Berlin and New York: de Gruyter. (Holds that Nietzsche's philosophy points the way out of the crisis in contemporary Western metaphysics.)

Đurić, M. and Žunjić, S. (eds) (1993) *Die Serbische Philosophie Heute* (Serb philosophy today), Munich: Slavica Verlag Dr Anton Kovač. (A collection of essays by eleven Serb philosophers, with a detailed historical introduction.)

* Foht, I. (1980) *Savremena estetika muzike* (Contemporary aesthetics of music), Beograd: Nolit. (A collection of essays on the main trends in contemporary aesthetics of music written from a phenomenological point of view.)

* Grahek, N. (1990) *Materija, svest, saznanje* (Matter, mind and knowledge), Beograd: Filozofsko društvo Srbije. (A systematic refutation of various contemporary materialists' arguments, presenting an argument for the irreducibility of the mental.)

—— (1995) 'The Sensory Dimension of Pain', *Philosophical Studies* 79: 167–81. (An argument for the irreducibility of the sensory content of pain feelings.)

Kangrga, M. (1966) *Etika i sloboda* (Ethics and freedom), Zagreb: Naprijed. (An influential Neo-Marxist approach to ethics.)

* Knežević, B. (1898) *Principi istorije* (The Principles of History), Beograd: B. Knežević, 2 vols. (A highly speculative attempt at the formulation of the most general laws of history.)

—— (1921) *History, the Anatomy of Time; the Final Phase of Sunlight*, trans. and intro. G.V. Tomashevich, New York: The Philosophical Library, 1980. (Translations from his *Dva zakona* first published in 1921.)

* Lazović, Ž. (1994) *O prirodi epistemičkog opravdanja* (On the nature of epistemic justification), Beograd: Filozofsko društvo Srbije. (A defence of a contextualist theory of epistemic justification.)

* Marković, F. (1881) 'Filosofijske struke pisci hrvatskog roda s onkraj Velebita u stelječih XV. do XVIII' (The philosophical writers of Croatian birth from the other side of Velebit from the fifteenth to the eighteenth century) in *Izvještaj Sveučilišta u Zagrebu* (The Annual Report of the University of Zagreb), Zagreb: Sveučilište u Zagrebu, 1882 (reprinted in *Prilozi za istraživanje hrvatske filozofske baštine* (Contributions to the study of the Croatian philosophical heritage), 1 (1–2, 1975): 255–81. (Marković's speech as Rector of the University of Zagreb in 1881, with a short history of philosophy of the Adriatic littoral.)

Marković, M. and Cohen, R.S. (1975) *Yugoslavia: The Rise and Fall of Socialist Humanism. A History of the Praxis Group*, Nottingham: Bertrand Russell Peace Foundation. (A polemical account of the Praxis group, co-authored by one of its members.)

* Miščević, N. (1987) *Od misli do jezika* (From thought to language), Rijeka: Dometi. (An examination of contemporary analytic theories in the philosophy of language.)

—— (1996) 'Computation, Content and Cause', *Philosophical Studies* 2 (82): 241–63. (A discussion of intentionality and causation.)

* Njegoš, P.P. (1845) *Luča Mikrokozma – The Ray of Microcosm*, trans. A. Savić-Rebac, Beograd: Vajat, 1989. (This translation and foreword were originally published in *Harvard Slavic Studies* 3 (1957).)

* Novaković, S. (1984) *Hipoteze i saznanje* (Hypotheses and knowledge), Beograd: Nolit. (Scientific hypotheses, it argues, are not rejected or accepted on the basis of empirical evidence alone.)

* Pavković, A. (1988) *Razlozi za sumnju* (Reasons for doubt), Beograd: Istraživačko-izdavački centar SSO. (A reconstruction of arguments from illusion, from dreams and from the evil daemon.)

—— (ed.) (1988) *Contemporary Yugoslav Philosophy: The Analytic Approach*, Dordrecht and New York: Kluwer. (Seventeen essays by Yugoslav analytic philosophers; includes a short historical introduction and a select bibliography.)

—— (1990) 'Two Thaws in Yugoslav Philosophy', in M. Pavlyshyn (ed.) *Glasnost in Context*, Oxford: Berg. (A short outline of post-1945 Yugoslav philosophy in its political context.)

* Petrić, F. (Patricius, Franciscus) (1593) *Nova de universis philosophia* (The new universal philosophy), Venice: NP. (A synthesis of Catholicism and Platonism. *La citá felice*, by the same author, described a utopia in the tradition of Campanella's *City of the Sun*.)

* Petronijević, B. (1904) *Prinzipien der Metaphysik* (Principles of metaphysics), Heidelberg: C. Winter. (Holds that the universe consists of simple, discrete qualitative points and our immediate experience is the source of basic logical and metaphysical axioms.)

Petrović, G. (1967) *Marx in the Mid-Twentieth Century*, Garden City, NY: Anchor Books. (An unorthodox interpretation of Marx by a prominent Praxis philosopher from Zagreb.)

Petrović, G. and Marković, M. (eds) (1979) *Praxis: Yugoslav Essays in the Philosophy and Methodology of the Social Sciences*, Dordrecht: Reidel. (A selection of Neo-Marxist papers from the journal *Praxis* dealing with the philosophy of social sciences.)

Potrč, M. (1992) 'The Sensory Basis of Content in Veber', *Slovene Studies* 13 (1): 71–90. (A systematic examination of Veber's theory of representation.)

Primorac, I. (1978) *Kazna i prestup* (Punishment and offence), Beograd: Mladost. (A defence of a deontological and retributivist theory of punishment.)

* Šarčević, A. (1986) *De Homine: Mišljenje i moderni mit o čovjeku* (On man: thought and the modern myth about man), Sarajevo: Veselin Masleša. (A critique of Western philosophy, science and technology and its failure to humanize society.)

* Sesardić, N. (1984) *Fizikalizam* (Physicalism), Beograd: Istraživačko-izdavački centar SSO. (The first defence of the mind-body identity thesis in Serbo-Croat.)

—— (1993) 'Heritability and Causality', *Philosophy of Science* 3 (60): 396–418. (A discussion of recent theories of heritability and causality.)

Stojanović, S. (1973) *Between Ideals and Reality: A Critique of Socialism and its Future*, New York: Oxford University Press. (A prominent Beograd Praxis philosopher presents his vision of socialism.)

* Sutlić, V. (1967) *Bit i suvremenost* (Essence and contemporaneity), Sarajevo: Veselin Masleša. (An early Heideggerian interpretation of Marxist concept of praxis.)

Urbančič, I. (1993) 'Philosophy with the Slovenes', *Nationalities Papers* 21 (1): 127–137. (Thorough post-communist account of the Slovene philosophy.)

* Vlačić, M. (Flacius Illyricus, Matthias) (1567) *Clavis Scripturae Sacrae* (A Key to the Holy Scriptures), Basel: Per Iaonnem Oporinum et Eusebium Episcopium. (A systematic exegesis of the Bible based on a philosophy of language anticipating modern hermeneutics.)

* Vuk-Pavlović, P. (1926) Spoznaja i spoznajna teorija (Knowledge and theory of knowledge) in *Duševnost i umjetnost*, Zagreb: Liber, 1989. (A call for a meta-empirical or metaphysical investigation of the relation of cognition and its objects.)

* Weber (Veber) F. (1921) *Sistem filozofije* (A system of philosophy) Ljubljana: K&B. (A system of philosophy based on a complex theory of mental presentation of objects.)

—— (1987) 'Empfindungsgrundlagen der Gegenstandstheorie' (The experiental grounds of the theory of objects), *Conceptus* 21: 75–87. (A lecture on the Meinongian theory of objects presented in Graz in 1954.)

* Whyte, L.L. (ed.) (1961) *Roger Joseph Boscovich, S.J., F.R.S., 1711–1787*, London: Allen & Unwin. (Very good essays on his philosophical and scientific contributions; comprehensive bibliography.)

* Žižek, S. (1991) *Looking Awry: An Introduction to Jacques Lacan through Popular Culture*, London: MIT Press. (A humorous and Lacanian examination of various manifestations of popular culture, including film.)

ŽIVAN LAZOVIĆ
ALEKSANDAR PAVKOVIĆ

SOVEREIGNTY

In legal and political philosophy sovereignty is the attribute by which a person or institution exercises ultimate authority over every other person or institution in its domain. Traditionally, the existence of a final arbiter or legislator is said to be essential if people are to live together in peace and security. The example brought most readily to mind by the word 'sovereign' is the individual monarch, and the theory of sovereignty was at one time closely linked with the defence of monarchy. But leading theorists of sovereignty, like Jean Bodin and Thomas Hobbes, recognize that authority can be exercised by sovereign bodies of people; and later writers, like Rousseau and Austin, locate sovereignty in the people, to whom the officials of more democratic institutions are ultimately accountable.

Traditionally, too, it is deduced from the nature of the state or law that the sovereign's authority must be absolute, not limited by conditions; perpetual, not merely delegated for a time; and indivisible, not distributed between different persons or institutions. It is further deduced that the sovereign must be independent from external domination as well as internally supreme. All these inferences have been subjected to criticism, not least because they can be difficult to reconcile with the actual practice of states and legal systems.

1   Sovereignty and utility
2   Sovereignty and logic
3   Sovereignty and republicanism
4   Sovereignty and independence

1   Sovereignty and utility

It seems to have been no coincidence that the two foundation texts of the modern theory of sovereignty were both published in conditions of civil conflict, Jean Bodin's *Six livres de la république* (1576) at the height of the French wars of religion, Thomas Hobbes' *Leviathan* (1651) in the immediate aftermath of the English Civil War (see BODIN, J. §2; HOBBES,

T.). For the early appeal of the concept delineated in these works lay largely in its apparent solution to the problem of anarchy. Hobbes' treatment is particularly illuminating in this respect. He begins by arguing that given certain features of human nature the life of people outside the commonwealth is bound to be, as he famously put it, solitary, poor, nasty, brutish and short. To live in peace and security people have to submit to a power that is able to compel them to fulfil their obligations.

To begin with people live in small family units, but their existence at this stage is characterized by internecine feuds, not by peace and security. The emergence of more powerful groupings of individuals or families may achieve a greater measure of stability, but Hobbes maintains that however large and powerful these groups may be they cannot ultimately enable people to live peacefully and securely. The balance of power may shift through regrouping, and within each group people will continue to pursue their individual interests. The appearance of a common enemy may draw them together, but only temporarily, and even then they will argue about the best use of their resources. In short, the collective life of people will of itself be no different from the solitary life.

To live in peace and security people need to establish a commonwealth, and for Hobbes that means submitting to a 'Soveraigne Power'. Each subject individual must surrender their personal power to do what they think best for their own preservation and accept the determination of another, until one person alone is left with the authority to decide what should be done. That person, whether an individual or an assembly of individuals, will then have the sovereign power necessary to coerce the rest of the people into fulfilling their obligations. The person may in fact have been the head of a family or larger grouping, but their judgment will now be final and decisive, and their exercise of power will not be limited to the duration of an emergency. Their sovereignty will continue for as long as they are able to protect their people, and the people will have peace and security for as long as they have a sovereign.

2   Sovereignty and logic

If it was this sort of argument for the expediency of submitting to a final arbiter that first attracted exponents of sovereignty, and if this sense of the practical necessity of an ultimate authority has remained important throughout the history of the concept, a more prominent feature of its presentation has been an emphasis on logical analysis. Hobbes himself was committed to a mode of exposition that starts with the definition of a term, then proceeds to explore its implications. So from the definition of sovereignty it may be deduced that it must be absolute and indivisible. It must be absolute because conditions could only be meaningfully imposed on a sovereign's exercise of power if there were some other person with authority to determine when they were being violated, in which case the sovereign would not be the final arbiter. Similarly sovereignty must be indivisible because otherwise there might be disagreements between the different bearers of authority, in which case there would again be no final arbiter.

For Hobbes the definition of the sovereign's authority is effectively the definition of the state. So too for Bodin the concept of absolute and indivisible sovereignty is logically entailed by the very idea of the state, which he defines as the just government, with sovereign power, of several families and their belongings. Bodin claims to have broken new ground by providing a clear analysis of the sovereign authority that must be inherent in any genuine state. He identifies two aspects in particular. First, sovereignty must be perpetual and not the kind of power that is entrusted to someone for a time by people who may take it back again. There cannot be a state where authority is merely delegated to the ruler, and where there is a state it is the fact that lesser magistrates have only delegated authority that distinguishes them most clearly from the sovereign. Second, Bodin goes to greater length in stressing that sovereignty must be absolute and not the kind of power that is hedged in with obligations and conditions. In essence, he concludes, sovereignty is the power to lay down laws that will bind the subjects in a commonwealth but not the sovereign themselves. The sovereign must be able to legislate without their subjects' consent, and cannot be bound by the laws of predecessors, still less by their own laws. It would be logical nonsense to say that a sovereign legislator was bound by the laws of a sovereign.

Bodin declares that law is nothing else than the command of the sovereign in the exercise of sovereign power, a view maintained more recently by analytical jurists in an effort to anatomize law properly so called (see LEGAL POSITIVISM §§1–2). In *The Province of Jurisprudence Determined* (1832) John Austin defines the positive laws of men as the general commands of sovereigns backed up by the threat of sanctions (see AUSTIN, J.). Laws emanate from a sovereign power whenever the majority of the people in a reasonably populous society are in the habit of obeying the legislator, and the legislator in turn is not in the habit of obeying anyone else. Expressed like this the concept of sovereignty has purely analytical significance, and Austin makes no attempt in his legal theory to explain why or when a legislator should be obeyed. He is content to specify that there must be a 'habit' of obedience on the part of the 'bulk' of the people to a superior who is both 'determinate' and 'common' to them all.

Austin also reinforces the point that the legislator must not themselves be in the habit of obeying anyone else. This standard assertion made in one form or another that sovereignty is logically illimitable has attracted widespread criticism. It can seem contradictory for Bodin to write as he does of the sovereign being bound to legislate in accordance with divine and natural laws. If one response is to agree with Austin that this type of requirement imposes moral, not legal, constraints, the same cannot so easily be said with respect to Bodin's claim that the sovereign should also legislate in accordance with the fundamental laws of the state, or to Hobbes' concession that the subject need not obey a sovereign intent on his destruction. It may instead be replied that the legislator is sovereign only so long as they act like a sovereign. But who must decide when they do not, and on what basis? Must it then be said that the state and the law have ceased to exist? To many critics it seems more plausible to recognize that legislators in theory may and in practice often do operate under constitutional constraints which are both fundamental and properly legal.

3 Sovereignty and republicanism

Another standard assertion that has been widely criticized is that sovereignty is logically indivisible. Initially the assertion was made in opposition to the republican ideal of a blend of monarchic, aristocratic and democratic modes of government (see REPUBLICANISM). While Bodin and Hobbes do not exclude the possibility of genuinely sovereign rule by popular assemblies, instead merely exhibiting a preference for monarchy, they consider it absurd to talk of a mixed constitution. Restated in the juridical language of sovereignty the republican theory of balanced interests does seem rather less coherent. Yet it is equally apparent that the theory of sovereignty is difficult to apply to the practice of states in which legislative authority is distributed among distinct institutions, particularly where the structure of the state is federal.

The author who did most to reconcile the languages of sovereignty and republicanism was Jean-Jacques ROUSSEAU, writing in the century between Hobbes and Austin. Although Rousseau does not entirely agree with Hobbes' pessimistic account of the nature of human beings, he does accept that discord is an inevitable consequence of the human condition and that the solution lies in the establishment of civil societies. Indeed, for Rousseau, people do not surrender their freedom on entering into civil society but find there the possibility of fulfilment in a life of virtue and genuine liberty. In his *Du contrat social* (1762) Rousseau makes the famous observation that people are born free but are everywhere in chains, before going on to show how that bondage might be avoided in a properly constituted republic. The crucial requirement is that people must not transfer their sovereignty to the ruler but must retain it for themselves. By adopting the paradoxical position that the people as sovereign legislate for themselves as subjects, Rousseau is able to argue that laws will never be oppressive when enacted by the general will.

In most respects the concept of sovereignty deployed here remains traditional. In particular, sovereign power is still conceived to be absolute. Though Rousseau admits that it must be exercised in keeping with natural law (see NATURAL LAW §4) and for the common good, both concessions are consistent with the usual qualifications. In the first case, Rousseau denies that there can be any judge of the conformity of legislation with natural law other than the general will itself. In the second case, he takes the failure to legislate for the common good to show not so much that a sovereign people has exceeded the limits of its authority as that the law is not the enactment of a sovereign people after all. For the general will is not to be equated with the will of the majority, nor even with the will of all. The general will consists in an interpretation of the common good of the society, not in an amalgamation of individual interests.

Sovereignty thus remains unlimited in the usual sense, and Rousseau also understands it to be indivisible. However, now that legislative sovereignty remains with the people the concept no longer excludes the possibility of mixed government. While the people must assent to legislation for the common good, they can be governed by separate agencies which may take any form, though some forms of government will be less likely to engender corruption than others. A good ruler will frame sound laws to introduce for the people's assent, and by enforcing sound laws will help to shape and preserve a virtuous people capable of exercising the general will. The good ruler will not attempt to encroach on the people's sovereignty, though Rousseau accepts that in practice this will be likely to happen.

Accordingly, if the problem with Rousseau's version of sovereignty is that it will seldom exist in reality, it does have the advantage that it could in principle be discovered in any state, including one with a mixed constitution or federal structure. Moreover, the problem can be avoided and the advantage retained if the notion of the general will is abandoned. Austin, for example, is able to identify undivided sovereigns in complex states by focusing on the electors of representative assemblies rather than on the assemblies themselves. Yet the difficulty that still remains is the need to regard the same persons as both rulers and ruled. On this analysis, sovereignty ceases to be an attribute of those who appear to legislate and rule and becomes instead an abstract quality of those who appear to obey and be ruled but who are in fact the ultimate source of authority. As such, the concept of sovereignty must compete with other attempts to explain what it is that gives unity and integrity to states or legal systems.

4 Sovereignty and independence

On the sovereignty model the unity and integrity of states or legal systems is taken to depend not only on the absence of an internal or domestic rival to the unity and superiority of the sovereign, but also on the absence of an external or foreign rival. Where external independence is regarded as a further facet of the internal superiority of the sovereign, the constraints of international law can no more be considered properly legal than the constraints of natural law, and international institutions can at best be considered to have delegated authority. With corollaries like these, the connection between sovereignty and independence has understandably been questioned, especially in an era like the present in which the legitimacy of state activity is increasingly assessed according to the standards of wider communities. Keeping the two aspects of sovereignty distinct is therefore urged as an essential means of avoiding confusion, yet what can scarcely be denied is that sovereignty has historically been associated with the idea of the independent state.

Historians have found the earliest expression of the concept in the observations of the Roman jurist Ulpian, that the *imperium* of the Roman people was transferred to the emperor, that the emperor was not bound by the laws, and that what pleased the emperor had the force of law. But although these statements were not unknown in medieval Europe, it was not until the sixteenth century that the theory of sovereignty was fully developed. Consequently it may be said that the notion of absolute, perpetual and indivisible sovereignty made its first appearance under a monolithic empire and reappeared only with the emergence of the modern nation state. If this is correct, it may well transpire that the concept has had its day. If the idea of the nation state continues to decline as a focus for legal and political identity, the concept of sovereignty seems likely to decline with it.

See also: ABSOLUTISM; AUTHORITY; CONSTITUTIONALISM; DE; GENERAL WILL; LAW, PHILOSOPHY OF; RULE OF LAW (RECHTSSTAAT); SHINTŌ §5; SHŌTOKU CONSTITUTION; STATE, THE

References and further reading

* Austin, J. (1832) *The Province of Jurisprudence Determined*, H.L.A. Hart (ed.), London: Weidenfeld & Nicolson, 1954. (Deals with sovereignty especially in Lecture VI.)
* Bodin, J. (1576) *Six livres de la république* (*Six Books of a Commonweal*), trans. R. Knolles, 1606; K.D. McRae (ed.), Cambridge, MA: Harvard University Press, 1962. (Deals with sovereignty especially in Book I, chapters 8–10.)
  Hinsley, F.H. (1986) *Sovereignty*, 2nd edn, Cambridge: Cambridge University Press. (Surveys the history of the concept while presenting a historical thesis about the conditions for its emergence; also contains a useful bibliography.)
* Hobbes, T. (1651) *Leviathan*, R. Tuck (ed.), Cambridge: Cambridge University Press, 1991. (Deals with sovereignty especially in Part II.)
  Jouvenel, B. de (1957) *Sovereignty*, Cambridge: Cambridge University Press. (Develops a philosophical thesis about the place of sovereignty in political science, providing historical observations along the way.)
  King, P. (1974) *The Ideology of Order*, London: Allen & Unwin. (Like most monographs on the leading authors referred to, comments on their conception of sovereignty; this study of Bodin and Hobbes pays special attention to the theme.)
  Merriam, C.E. (1900) *History of the Theory of Sovereignty since Rousseau*, New York: Columbia University Press. (Provides a more detailed survey than Hinsley of the history of the theory in the nineteenth century.)
* Rousseau, J.-J. (1762) *Du contrat social* (*The Social Contract*), trans. M. Cranston, Harmondsworth: Penguin, 1968. (Reflects on sovereignty.)

JOHN D. FORD

SOZIALTHEOLOGIE
see THEOLOGY, POLITICAL

SPACE

In some of its uses, the word 'space' designates an empty or potentially empty expanse among things, for example, when a driver finds a space in a crowded parking lot, or when a typesetter increases the space between words on a page. In other uses, 'space' is meant to stand for a boundless extension which supposedly contains everything, or every thing of a certain sort. The former sense is well-grounded in ordinary experience and can be traced back to the etymology of the word (from the Latin word spatium, *meaning 'race-track', or generally 'distance', 'interval', 'terrain'). The latter sense originated in scholarly circles – possibly as late as the fourteenth century – by a bold extrapolation of the former; it does not refer to anything that can be exhibited in sense-perception; and yet, through the influence of Newtonian science on Euro-American common sense, it has become so entrenched in ordinary usage that it is normally viewed as the primary meaning of 'space', from which all others are derived.*

According to Cornford, the 'invention of space' as a boundless, all-encompassing container happened in the fifth century BC. *However, it is more likely to have occurred in the late Middle Ages. At any rate, the idea was rampant in Cambridge in the 1660s, when Newton made it a fundamental ingredient in his framework for the description of the phenomena of motion. In a posthumous paper, Newton stressed that space evades the traditional classification of entities into substances and attributes, and has 'its own manner of existence'. Until the publication of this paper in 1962, philosophers took Newtonian space for a substance, and most of them thought this to be utterly absurd. In view of the role of all-encompassing space in Newtonian physics, Kant opted for regarding it as a precondition of human knowledge, contributed once and for all by the human mind. Newton had written that the points of space owe their individual identity to the relational system in which they are set. Nineteenth-century mathematicians vastly extended this concept of space by conceiving many such relational systems. They thus made it possible for relativity theory to substitute four-dimensional spacetime for Newtonian space and time, and for current string theory to countenance a ten-dimensional physical space. These developments confirm the productivity, but not the fixity, of the knowing mind.*

1　**The emergence of space**
2　**Newtonian space**
3　**Philosophies of space**
4　**General spaces**

1 The emergence of space

The invention of space as a boundless, all-encompassing expanse was traced back by Cornford (1936) to the fifth century BC. He argued that Greek geometry, which developed at that time, presupposed such an expanse, and that this was identical with the void postulated by the atomist philosophers. However, the atomists' void, though boundless, is not an expanse that *contains* everything, but rather the nothingness *outside* all things. The relation between space in this sense and Greek geometry is less straightforward. The Greeks conceived of geometry as a study of figures, their properties and relations, not as the science of space. Greek geometrical discourse involved the tacit assumption – eventually expressed in Euclid's postulate – that any two coplanar straight lines meet at a point unless they are both perpendicular to a third straight line. Obviously, if two coplanar straights are almost perpendicular to a third one, their intersection can be enormously far away, and an infinite expanse is needed to make room for all such intersections. However, Aristotle did not see this requirement as a constraint on physical reality; he argued that such an infinite expanse is inconceivable and shrewdly remarked that any construction involved in the solution of a geometrical problem can be made to fit – by rescaling – within the finite expanse beneath the firmament (inasmuch as 'any magnitude whatsoever can be divided in the same ratio as the greatest magnitude' (*Physica* 207b31–2)).

In the late Middle Ages, the idea of space springs up in several writers in connection with God's omnipotence. Catholic authorities condemned the proposition that 'God cannot move the firmament in a straight line'. Yet most theologians were loath to admit the existence of a void beyond the firmament. Thomas BRADWARDINE came up with the idea of an 'infinite imaginary vacuum' which God can make real (in part), should he decide to move the world. Nicole ORESME also speaks of an 'imaginary infinite and motionless space outside the world' (c.1375: 368), but he asserts its actual existence: 'Outside the firmament there is a bodyless empty space in a manner that differs from that of any full and corporeal space' (c.1375: 176). According to Oresme, the speed of moving bodies 'is measured in regard to' the said 'motionless imaginary space' (c.1375: 372).

By 1600, space had become a familiar ingredient of natural philosophy. In Bruno's words:

Space is a continuous three-dimensional natural quantity, in which the magnitude of bodies is contained, which is prior by nature to all bodies and subsists without them but indifferently receives them all and is free from the conditions of action and passion, unmixable, impenetrable, unshapeable, non-locatable, outside all bodies yet encompassing and incomprehensibly containing them all.
(1591: 1.8)

2 Newtonian space

Newton's idea of space stems from this tradition, but it also benefited from the conversion of geometry into a science of space by Descartes. Geometrical figures were henceforth conceived as sets of spatial points meeting specific conditions, each point being identified by its coordinates, that is, its (oriented) distances from three pairwise intersecting infinite planes. By bestowing on the class of oriented lengths on a straight line the structure of an algebraic field (actually indistinguishable from our real number field $\mathbb{R}$), Descartes managed to express geometrical properties and relations by systems of algebraic equations. He maintained that bodies are really nothing but their extension, because their geometrical properties and relations are the only ones that we can grasp clearly and distinctly (see DESCARTES, R. §5). But geometry was still too weak to meet the demands of a total geometrization of physics, and Newton began his career as a physicist by 'doing away' with Descartes' 'fictions' (1962: 92). He neatly distinguished bodies from the infinite space in which God created them, which is a repository of points that satisfy the theorems of Euclidean (that is, Cartesian) geometry.

Newton sought to ascertain the forces of nature by studying the motions of bodies in space. The motion of a body can be accurately described by means of the varying coordinates of some suitably chosen points in it. The set of three planes from which such coordinates are measured defines a reference frame. Newton was aware that any usable reference frame must be anchored to a rigid body. But a description of motions referred to such a frame cannot exhibit real forces unless that body rests in space or is known to move in it in a definite way. Newton acknowledges two sorts of force: the force of inertia inherent in each body causes it to move in space with constant velocity in a straight line; and the impressed forces acting on a body cause a change – an acceleration – in its state of motion. An inertial frame is a reference frame anchored to a body free from impressed forces. Newton assumes that every impressed force issues from a body and that if a body A acts upon a body B with a force $\mathbf{f}$, A is simultaneously acted upon by a force issuing from B, opposite to $\mathbf{f}$ but equally strong. In principle, this assumption should enable one to pick out the inertial frames. The very geometry of space makes it impossible to identify an inertial frame as being at rest, but this has no effect on the study of impressed forces, for the acceleration they cause on a given body displays the same magnitude and direction in every inertial frame, regardless of its state of motion (see MECHANICS, CLASSICAL §2; NEWTON, I. §3).

3 Philosophies of space

What *is* space? The successes of Newtonian physics forced philosophers to face this question, although it proved impossible to bring space under one of the traditional metaphysical categories. Much needless discussion might have been forestalled had Newton's manuscript 'De gravitatione et aequipondio fluidorum' (On the Gravity and Equilibrium of Liquids) not remained unpublished until 1962. In it he boldly asserts that space is neither a substance nor an attribute of a substance, but has 'its own manner of existence' (1962: 99, 132). There follows a characterization which is reminiscent of Bruno, but which includes an unprecedented feature: according to Newton, each point of space is the particular point it is by virtue of the relations it has to the other points, and the only source of its individuality (*individuationis principium*) is the post it holds in the system of such relations. Thus, Newton's concept of space provides the prototype for what is now known as a (categoric) mathematical structure, which can be roughly described as a collection of objects fully specified by a list of mutual relations.

A conception of space as a purely relational system or mathematical structure was also put forward by Leibniz in his polemic against the view of space as a substance, which he imputes to Newton. Leibniz characterizes space as the abstract order of coexisting things. If we forget the peculiarities of each thing and retain only its '*situation* or distance' to the other things we obtain the notion of the thing's place, which may be taken by anything. 'And that which comprehends all those places, is called *Space*' (Leibniz 1716: §47). But Leibniz abides by the traditional view (rooted in the medieval notion that God must be capable of annihilating any particular creature without essentially affecting the others) according to which everything that exists is either a substance or an attribute of a substance. Since space is neither, he maintains that it is no more than a well-grounded phenomenon, lacking genuine reality (see LEIBNIZ, G.W. §11). From then on, the debate raged between Leibnizian relationalists and 'Newtonian' substantialists, the former insisting that space must be based on and can only be known through the relations among bodies, the latter pointing out that the one scientifi-

cally effective description of bodies and their motions – namely, Newton's – required a logically and ontologically independent space. In particular, Berkeley maintained that space without bodies, 'infinite, immoveable, indivisible, insensible, without relation and without distinction', was 'mere nothing' (Berkeley 1721: §53). On the other hand, Euler (1748), though opposed to Newtonian action-at-a-distance, argued for absolute space as a condition of scientific dynamics.

The tension between relationalism and substantialism is clearly visible in Kant's philosophical development. In his first book he ventured a Leibnizian view based on Newtonian physics: space has three dimensions because bodies attract each other with a force proportional to the inverse square of their distances; if matter had different dynamical properties, space would sport 'other properties and dimensions'; the 'highest geometry' would deal with 'all these possible kinds of space' (Kant 1746: §10). But in 1768 Kant alighted on an idea which, he thought, implied the ontological priority of space over bodies. Take two bodies which are exact mirror images of each other (say, a right and a left shoe, or two molecules of, respectively, laevorotary and dextrorotary glucose). An exhaustive description of the mutual distances between all the component parts of one such body would be identical to a similar description of the other. Therefore, the intrinsic difference between them must depend on the relation of each to space. Thus, space is involved in the constitution of each body. Yet space does not meet the traditional requirements of thinghood: its actual existence would require the 'complete synthesis' of infinitely many parts – an impossible task. Moreover, each part of space is infinitely divisible into further parts, so when all relational bonds are removed no substantive foundation remains on which they might rest. Kant solved this philosophical difficulty – and many others – by conceiving space as a 'form of sensibility': 'not something objective and real, not a substance, nor an attribute, nor a relation, but a subjective and ideal sort of scheme for mutually coordinating all external sensations in every way, which issues from the nature of the mind according to a stable law' (Kant 1770: §15D). Since bodies depend on space for their very being, they do not exist in and of themselves, apart from the mind, which is the source of spatial order; they are mere appearances of an underlying reality, which eludes our senses. In the *Critik der reinen Vernunft* (Critique of Pure Reason) (1781, 1787), Kant acknowledges that such underlying reality, though undeniable, is also inaccessible to our intellect, which can only be guaranteed to work within the bounds of sense experience. Space is now described with greater precision as a 'form of appearance', a condition imposed by the mind on sense impressions which *allows* them to be ordered in certain relations by the understanding and thereby to be grasped as presentations of objects. This provides a welcome explanation of the purported fact – which Kant took for granted – that all bodies comply with the truths of geometry and that these truths can be known a priori, ahead of experience. For, as Kant saw, geometric theorems do not simply flow from definitions and the truths of logic (they are 'synthetic', not 'analytic', statements) (see KANT, I. §§4–5).

Although Kant was the most influential philosopher of modern times, his doctrine of space was not adopted by any major thinker except Schopenhauer. Thanks to Kant's critique, the rigid substance–attribute ontology carried no weight in the nineteenth century. Therefore, the primacy of space over bodies no longer appeared to threaten reason and even morality, as it had in the eyes of Leibniz, Berkeley and Kant. But the formulation of new geometries that contradicted the Euclidean canon (see §4 below) undermined Kant's view of geometry as a nonempirical science providing the descriptive framework required for empirical research. Kant's view is not endangered by the existence of consistent axiomatic theories about points, lines and planes containing the negation of some of Euclid's theorems. Indeed, Kant's claim that geometric theorems are synthetic a priori statements entails that there must be such theories. But after several alternative geometries became known, most researchers felt it was only fair that experience should be called upon to decide between them.

In his youth, Russell (1897) proposed a curious compromise on this issue. He retained the classical affine structure of space – supporting the notion of 'constant direction', and hence of straight line – as an apanage of reason, while leaving to experience the choice between three distinct metric structures – supporting alternative concepts of distance and size – which Klein had proved to be compatible with the said affine structure, namely, the Euclidean, in which the three internal angles of a plane triangle are always equal to two right angles or 180°, and two non-Euclidean ones, in which the said three angles always add up to, respectively, less than or more than 180°. Later Russell called this arrangement 'somewhat foolish' because it excludes the Riemannian geometries of variable curvature employed in Einstein's gravitational theory (see RELATIVITY THEORY, PHILOSOPHICAL SIGNIFICANCE OF §4; SPACETIME §3).

In an unpublished fragment written in about 1893, C.S. Peirce emphasized the utter unlikelihood that, among the infinitely many values in any neighbourhood of 180°, the sum of the three internal angles of a triangle should always settle exactly at 180° (Peirce 1931–58: §1.130). Similar reflections may have inspired, in part, Poincaré's innovative thesis on the conventionality of geometry. For him, any consistent geometry can be used in physics, provided it is comfortable. Euclidean geometry meets this requirement because the motions of ordinary solids agree fairly well with the translations and rotations of rigid figures in Euclidean three-dimensional space. Thus, Euclidean geometry, in which all triangles have internal angles adding up to precisely 180°, constitutes a useful idealization of experience, but it would be ridiculous to claim truth for it (see POINCARÉ, H.J. §3).

In Newtonian physics, the geometry of space plays a dynamical role through the law of inertia: a force-free particle moves along a straight line, traversing equal distances in equal times. Thus, we may say that space fixes the norm of default dynamical behaviour. Why does matter comply with it? The very idea that uniform, inert space can thus be 'read' at each point by bodies as an infinitely rich but perfectly definite network of routes seems, at first blush, nonsensical. Mach (1883) proposed that inertial behaviour was caused by the presence of very distant masses. From this standpoint he criticized the water-bucket experiment devised by Newton to show the difference between relative motion and 'true' motion in absolute space. In this experiment, a bucket filled with water is made to rotate. Initially the rotation of the bucket is not communicated to the water; the latter therefore rotates relative to its container; its surface remains flat. But as soon as the water acquires the bucket's rotation, that is, as soon as it is again at rest relative to its container and moves with it in space, the surface takes a concave shape. Mach notes that 'moving in space' is here just Newton's idiom for 'moving relatively to the bulk of matter'. He wrily comments that the outcome of the experiment might be quite different if the bucket had lead walls that were one mile thick. Mach did not provide a viable alternative to Newtonian dynamics, but his view of inertia deeply influenced Einstein's quest for a relativistic theory of gravitation (see RELATIVITY THEORY, PHILOSOPHICAL SIGNIFICANCE OF §6; EINSTEIN, A. §3). Einstein, indeed, worked with two ideas that Mach never dreamed of using: he substituted spacetime for space-plus-time as the arena of nature, and Riemannian for Euclidean geometry. This was made possible by the mathematical developments sketched below.

4 General spaces

Bourbaki defined the mathematical concept of 'structure' for the sake of ordering and classifying the rich and intricate concept jungle generated by mathematicians since 1800 (Bourbaki 1970). As noted above, space – as understood by Newton in the wake of Descartes (and Euclid) – furnished a prototype for that concept. However, not every structure is called a 'space' by mathematicians. They reserve the word for structures which somehow resemble Newtonian space because they involve a notion of distance ('metric' spaces), of straightness ('affine' and 'projective' spaces), or of neighbourhood and continuity ('topological' spaces). The conception of such general spaces owes much to Grassmann's *Die lineale Ausdehnungslehre* (The Theory of Linear Extension) (1844), Riemann's lecture 'Über die Hypothesen, welche der Geometrie zugrunde liegen' (On the Hypotheses which lie at the Foundations of Geometry) (1854) and Klein's so-called Erlangen Programme (1872). We shall briefly comment on the latter two (for applications, see SPACETIME).

New geometries flourished in the nineteenth century. Most famous outside mathematics is Lobachevskii's non-Euclidean geometry, which took over all the explicit and tacit assumptions of Euclidean geometry except Euclid's postulate, which was replaced by its denial. Much more influential, however, was the projective geometry of Poncelet (1822), which added a 'point at infinity' to each Euclidean straight. This point is the intersection of a family of parallels and can be reached by travelling along any of them in either direction. Because of this last feature, the neighbourhood systems – the topology – of projective and Euclidean space are drastically different. The power and elegance of projective geometry led nineteenth-century geometers to view ordinary geometry as the theory of a truncated projective space. Klein proposed to bring all past and future geometries under a single unifying standpoint. This was supplied by the notion of a transformation group acting on a space. Let S be the set of all points in Euclidean space. A transformation of S is a bijection of S onto itself, that is, a mapping f which assigns to every $p \in S$ an exclusive 'value' $f(p) \in S$ so that every $q \in S$ is thus assigned to some $p \in S$. It is clear that (1) the identity mapping i that assigns each point $p \in S$ to itself is a transformation of S; (2) if f and g are transformations, the composite mapping gf which assigns to each $p \in S$ the value assigned by g to $f(p)$ is also a transformation; (3) for every transformation f there is an inverse transformation f' such that $f'f = ff' = i$. Conditions (1)–(3) entail that the set of all transformations of S constitutes a group in the standard algebraic sense. Call it T_S. Let $f \in T_S$ and let R be an n-ary relation on S. We say that f preserves R and that R is invariant under f if whenever R holds between $p_1, \ldots, p_n \in S$ it also holds between $f(p_1), \ldots, f(p_n)$. If every transfor-

mation of a group G preserves R we say that R is an invariant of G. Though no significant geometrical relation is an invariant of T_S, distinct sets of geometrical relations turn out to be the invariants of different subgroups of T_S (a subgroup is a subset of a group which is a group in its own right). Thus, a short reflection will show that all transformations which map continuous paths onto continuous paths form a group; that collinearity of points and the mutual intersection between straights are invariants of a subgroup of that group; and that congruence of segments and angles are invariants of a subgroup of the latter. The invariants of a group determine a structure which is studied by a geometry. Different groups acting on the same arbitrary set of points will organize them into very different structures. In particular, Klein showed that Euclidean and Lobachevskian geometry study the invariants of different subgroups of the projective group. Poincaré concluded that the choice between them is conventional, for 'the existence of one group is not incompatible with that of another' (1887: 90).

While Klein sought to reorganize geometry as a branch of pure mathematics, Riemann's chief aim was to make it more responsive to the needs of physical research, to replace the Euclidean-Newtonian straitjacket with something much more pliable. Physicists write nature's laws as differential equations involving time and three spatial coordinates. It may seem that they thereby assume that physical space is homeomorphic (topologically equivalent) to $\mathbb{R}^3$, the structured set of ordered triples of real numbers. However, the stated assumption is unnecessarily strong. Physicists need only coordinatize a finite region surrounding the objects under study. They must therefore assume that each point of space has a *neighbourhood* homeomorphic to $\mathbb{R}^3$. But such neighbourhoods may be pieced together in a global structure that is very different from $\mathbb{R}^3$, just as the patches mapped by cartographers onto the *flat* pages of an atlas jointly form the surface of the earth, which is homeomorphic to a *sphere*. Physical space should therefore be regarded as a threefold instance of what Riemann called 'n-fold extended quantities'. A good explication of this notion is supplied by our current concept of a 'real n-dimensional differentiable manifold', that is, a topological space M, every point of which has a neighbourhood homeomorphic with $\mathbb{R}^n$ which is mapped bijectively and bicontinuously onto an open region of $\mathbb{R}^n$, so that (1) every point of M lies in the domain of one of these mappings or 'coordinate systems', and (2) if two such coordinate systems, g and h, have overlapping domains, the 'coordinate transformations' gh^{-1} and hg^{-1} are differentiable. (Here h^{-1} designates the inverse of h, that is, the mapping that assigns to each real number n-tuple in the range of h the point $p \in M$ such that the said n-tuple is $h(p)$; differentiability is required in order to write laws as differential equations.) A particle's trajectory in M can be described by a mapping f of a time interval into M. The mapping f must be differentiable in the following sense: if its range lies within the domain of a coordinate system g, the composite mapping gf (which yields the g-coordinates of successive positions of the particle) is differentiable. The quantitative description of motion requires that such trajectories have definite lengths. Riemann thought that the length of a real trajectory depends on the interplay of forces acting on and about it. The success of the standard definition of lengths expressed in Pythagoras' theorem betokens its approximate validity on the human scale. But it could well break down on a larger or smaller scale. Physicists should therefore wield a more flexible definition, enabling them to give – whenever experience makes it advisable – a more accurate description of motions. This is secured by Riemann's concept of a 'metric' on the manifold M. Roughly, a metric is a rule for measuring, at each $p \in M$, the velocity of every conceivable trajectory through p in such a way that the velocity varies smoothly, if at all, along the trajectory. Along a trajectory of velocity 1, the integral of the velocities measures the length of the trajectory. Since a metric based on Pythagoras' theorem had until then proved suitable, Riemann thought that for the time being one ought only to allow metrics that agree to first order with the Pythagorean metric on a neighbourhood of each point. Such metrics are called 'Riemannian'.

See also: COSMOLOGY AND COSMOGONY, INDIAN THEORIES OF; GEOMETRY, PHILOSOPHICAL ISSUES IN

References and further reading

* Aristotle (*c.* mid-4th century BC) *Physica*, ed. and with notes by W.D. Ross, Oxford: Clarendon Press, 1956. (Aristotle's lectures on the principles of natural philosophy; regarded as the fundamental treatise on the subject at the time Galileo and Descartes went to school.)
* Berkeley, G. (1721) *De motu* (On Motion), London: Tonson. (A spirited defence of the relativity of motion, against Newton and the Newtonians.)
  Boi, L. (1995) *Le problème mathématique de l'espace: Une quête de l'intelligible* (The Mathematical Problem of Space: A Quest For Intelligibility), Berlin: Springer. (A careful and intelligent exposition of the subject touched on in §4, rich in mathematical detail and philosophical insights.)
* Bourbaki, N. (1970) *Théorie des ensembles* (Set Theory), Paris: Hermann. (Lays the groundwork for Bourbaki's systematic ordering of mid-twentieth-century mathematical lore around the concept of structure.)
* Bruno, G. (1591) *De immenso et innumerabilibus* (On the Immense and the Uncountables), in *Opera Latina Conscripta*, Naples: Morano, 1879, vol. 1, 1. (Expanded Latin version of Bruno's great Italian dialogues *De l'infinito, universo e mondi* (On the Infinite, the Universe and the Worlds) (1584), which argued for the existence of an infinite number of worlds; cited here for its description of space.)
  Buroker, J.V. (1981) *Space and Incongruence: The Origin of Kant's Idealism*, Dordrecht: Reidel. (Stresses the significance of the philosophical problem of space in the development of Kant's critical philosophy; an original and very illuminating study.)
* Cornford, F.M. (1936) 'The Invention of Space', in *Essays in Honour of Gilbert Murray*, London: Allen & Unwin, 215–35; repr. in M. Capek (ed.) *The Concepts of Space and Time*, Dordrecht: Reidel, 1976, 3–16. (According to Cornford, boundless all-encompassing space was invented in Greece during the fifth century BC.)
  Earman, J. (1989) *World-Enough and Space-Time: Absolute versus Relational Theories of Space and Time*, Cambridge, MA: MIT Press. (Twentieth-century perspectives on the classical debate between Leibniz and Clarke.)
* Euler, L. (1748) 'Réflexions sur l'espace et le tems' (Reflections on Space and Time), *Mémoires de l'Académie des Sciences de Berlin* 4; repr. in *Leonhardi Euleri Opera omnia*, series 3, vol. 2, 376–83. (Space and time are indispensable presuppositions of mechanics, required by the law of inertia.)
  Grant, E. (1981) *Much Ado About Nothing: Theories of Space and the Vacuum from the Middle Ages to the Scientific Revolution*, Cambridge: Cambridge University Press. (Very learned and instructive; no mathematics at all.)
* Grassmann, H. (1844) *Die lineale Ausdehnungslehre, ein neuer Zweig der Mathematik* (The Linear Theory of Extension: A New Branch of Mathematics), Leipzig: Otto Wigand; 2nd edn, 1862. (The first, very difficult version of the author's theory of extension; it develops n-dimensional vector algebra as part of a much more comprehensive, ambitious and original system of geometric algebra.)
  Hall, A.R. (1980) *Philosophers at War: The Quarrel Between Newton and Leibniz*, Cambridge: Cam-

bridge University Press. (Good historical narrative of the various aspects of this regrettable dispute.)

* Kant, I. (1746) *Gedanken von der wahren Schätzung der lebendingen Kräfte* (Thoughts on the True Measure of Live Forces), Königsberg: Dorn. (Kant's MA thesis, on the question, disputed between Cartesians and Leibnizians, whether the 'live force' of bodies in motion equals mass times speed or mass times squared speed.)

* —— (1768) 'Von dem ersten Grunde des Unterschiedes der Gegenden im Raume' (On the Foundation of the Difference between Regions in Space), *Wochentliche Königsbergsche Frag- und Anzeigungs-Nachrichten* 6–8. (In this short paper published in an obscure local journal, Kant made the turnabout in the philosophy of space which eventually led to his critique of reason; in it he argues that the difference between incongruent bodies which are exact mirror images of each other can only be grasped in terms of the relation of each body to absolute space.)

* —— (1770) *De mundi sensibilis atque intelligibilis forma et principiis* (On the Form and Principles of the Sensible and the Intelligible World), Regiomonti: Kanter. (Kant's inaugural dissertation on taking the chair of metaphysics in Königsberg; argues for the thesis that real things, as such, are neither spatial nor temporal.)

* —— (1781) *Critik der reinen Vernunft* (Critique of Pure Reason), Riga: Hartknoch. (This enormously influential book brought about Kant's 'Copernican revolution' in philosophy; this first edition is often denoted by the letter A.)

* —— (1787) *Critik der reinen Vernunft, Zweyte hin und wieder verbesserte Auflage* (Critique of Pure Reason, Second Improved Edition), Riga: Hartknoch. (Edition B of Kant's book; emphasizes more strongly than A the productive role of the human intellect in the constitution of human knowledge.)

* Klein, F. (1872) *Vergleichende Betrachtungen über neuere geometrische Forschungen* (Comparative Reflections about Modern Geometrical Inquiries), Erlangen: A. Düchert. (A programme for unifying the newly developed forms of geometry from the point of view of transformation groups and group invariants.)

Koyré, A. (1957) *From the Closed World to the Infinite Universe*, Baltimore, MD: Johns Hopkins University Press. (A lively narrative of the emergence of space.)

* Leibniz, G.W. (1716) 'Mr. Leibnitz's Fifth Paper, being an Answer to Dr Clarke's Fourth Reply', in *The Leibniz–Clarke Correspondence*, ed. with intro. and notes by H.G. Alexander, Manchester: Manchester University Press, 1956. (Part of a polemical correspondence, on the nature of space and time and related subjects, between Leibniz and Newton's spokesman Samuel Clarke.)

* Mach, E. (1883) *Die Mechanik in ihrer Entwicklung historisch-kritisch dargestellt* (The Development of Mechanics: A Historico-Critical Exposition), Leipzig: Brockhaus; trans. T. McCormack, *The Science of Mechanics*, 1893; La Salle, IL: Open Court, 1974. (A critical history of mechanics from Galileo to Hamilton and Jacobi, somewhat weak in its appreciation of the power of mathematical ideas; Mach's criticism of Newton's allegedly needless 'metaphysics', especially in the matter of space and time, had some influence on Einstein.)

* Newton, I. (1962) 'De gravitatione et aequipondio fluidorum' (On the Gravity and Equilibrium of Liquids), ed. and trans. A.R. Hall and M.B. Hall, in *Unpublished Scientific Papers of Isaac Newton*, Cambridge: Cambridge University Press, 89–121; trans. 121–56. (A long paper, posthumously edited, containing much criticism of Descartes and elucidations of the fundamental concepts of mechanics.)

* Oresme, N. (*c.*1375) *Le Livre du ciel et du monde* (The Book of Heaven and the World), ed. A.D. Menut and A.J. Denomy, Madison, WI: University of Wisconsin Press, 1968. (Late medieval treatise of cosmology. Contains a facing English translation by A.D. Menut.)

* Peirce, C.S. (1931–58) *Collected Papers*, ed. C. Hartshorne, P. Weiss and A.W. Burks, Cambridge, MA: Belknap Press, 8 vols. (A selection of papers and excerpts from manuscripts, organized thematically; though not altogether reliable, this edition is still probably more useful for the new reader than *The Writings of Charles S. Peirce: A Chronological Edition*, ed. M. Fisch *et al.*, Bloomington, IN: Indiana University Press, 1982–, which will eventually supersede it.)

* Poincaré, H. (1887) 'Sur les hipothèses fondamentales de la géométrie' (On the Fundamental Hypotheses of Geometry), *Bulletin de la Société mathématique de France* 15: 203–16; repr. in *Oeuvres*, Paris: Gauthier-Villars, 1916–56, vol. 11, 79–91. (Poincaré's attempt to state without redundancy all the necessary assumptions of plane geometry; provides important cues for understanding Poincaré's conventionalist philosophy of geometry.)

* Poncelet, J.V. (1822) *Traité des propriétés projectives des figures* (Treatise on the Projective Properties of Figures), Paris: Bachelier. (First systematic treatise of projective geometry.)

* Riemann, B. (1854) 'Über die Hypothesen, welche der Geometrie zugrunde liegen' (On the Hypotheses which lie at the Foundations of Geometry),

Abhandlungen der Kgl. Gesellschaft der Wissenschaften zu Göttingen 13: 133–52; trans. with mathematical commentary in M. Spivak, *A Comprehensive Introduction to Differential Geometry*, Berkeley, CA: Publish or Perish, 1979, vol. 2, 135–. (A lecture, on the occasion of Riemann's habilitation as *Privatdozent*; the starting point of modern physical geometry.)

Rosenfeld, B.A. (1988) *A History of Non-Euclidean Geometry: Evolution of the Concept of a Geometric Space*, trans. A. Shenitzer, New York: Springer. (Excellent, moderately technical exposition.)

* Russell, B.A.W. (1897) *An Essay on the Foundations of Geometry*, Cambridge: Cambridge University Press. (Russell's youthful attempt at solving all the main philosophical problems of geometry; ingenious and befuddled.)

Schutz, B.F. (1980) *Geometrical Methods of Mathematical Physics*, Cambridge: Cambridge University Press. (A very readable, suitably technical but not overwhelmingly rigorous introduction to Riemannian methods and ideas.)

ROBERTO TORRETTI

SPACETIME

Spacetime is the four-dimensional manifold proposed by current physics as the arena for Nature's show. Although Newtonian physics can very well be reformulated in a spacetime setting, the idea of spacetime was not developed until the twentieth century, in connection with Einstein's theories of special and general relativity. Due to the success of special relativity in microphysics and of general relativity in astronomy and cosmology, every advanced physical theory is now a spacetime theory. Spacetime *is undoubtedly an artificial concept, which our hominid ancestors did not possess, but the same is true of Newtonian* space *and* time.

1 **A world of events**
2 **Minkowski spacetime**
3 **Curved relativistic spacetimes**
4 **A wealth of worlds**

1 A world of events

Newtonian physics conceives the course of nature as the motion and change in time of bodies located in space (see MECHANICS, CLASSICAL §1; SPACE §2). Einstein's special theory of relativity implies that the shape of bodies and the order of succession of their changes varies with – 'is relative to' – the reference frame adopted for describing them (see RELATIVITY THEORY, PHILOSOPHICAL SIGNIFICANCE OF §2). Hermann Minkowski (1909, 1915) showed that a unique – 'absolute' – description of natural phenomena consonant with Einstein's theory can be achieved by analysing them into instantaneous events-at-a-point. Such events typically constitute the history of ordinary lumps of matter but they may also occur – in the guise, say, of oscillations of the electromagnetic field – in a perfect vacuum. *Spacetime* is our name for the four-dimensional continuum of such events (Minkowski called it *the world*). It can be regarded – in infinitely many alternative ways – as compounded of one-dimensional time and three-dimensional space. Indeed, each one of the inertial reference frames privileged by classical physics and special relativity defines a distinct way of splitting spacetime into time and space. No wonder, then, that the spatial groupings ('bodies'), and the time series into which events coalesce relatively to each such reference frame differ, from one frame to another. At first Einstein viewed Minkowski's approach somewhat disparagingly, as a 'formalism' which made calculations easier but contributed no genuine insight. However, Einstein's subsequent development of a theory of gravity ('general relativity') is inconceivable without Minkowski's achievement (see EINSTEIN, A. §3).

2 Minkowski spacetime

Should we decide to regard all natural phenomena as embedded in some sort of continuum, a four-dimensional spacetime is a much more obvious choice than a three-dimensional space lasting through time. Imagine a butterfly flying: one may eventually succeed – after much work – in *analysing* this phenomenon into a succession of infinitely many instantaneous postures, but it is originally *given* as a single coherent spacetime flow. Nevertheless, Minkowski's conception of spacetime does not stem from this intuitive idea, but rather from reflecting about the numerical representation of phenomena in the new kinematics proposed by Einstein (1905). Let P_1 and P_2 be two points marked on a rigid rod R at rest in an inertially moving laboratory L. Let E_1 and E_2 be events at P_1 and P_2, respectively. Let L be furnished with a time coordinate t, defined by Einstein's radar method, and a Cartesian system of space coordinates x, y, z. Let (x_1, y_1, z_1) and (x_2, y_2, z_2) be the coordinates assigned in this system to P_1 and P_2, and let t_1 and t_2 be the times of occurrence of E_1 and E_2. Then, the lapse of time between E_1 and E_2 is given by $\tau = |t_1 - t_2|$, and the distance λ between P_1 and P_2 is given at all times by the positive square root of $(x_1 - x_2)^2 + (y_1 - y_2)^2 + (z_1 - z_2)^2$. Consider now a laboratory L' furnished with a time coordinate t' and a Cartesian system x', y', z', based on the same measurement units as the unprimed coordinates of L. For simplicity's sake, we assume that

(i)   at some instant, the origin of the primed and the unprimed Cartesian systems coincide;
(ii)   at that instant the axes of the unprimed system are aligned with the homonymous axes of the primed system;
(iii) this coincidence occurs at time $t = t' = 0$.

Suppose that L moves relatively to L' in the direction of the x'-axis, with constant speed v. Let (x_1', y_1', z_1') and (x_2', y_2', z_2') be the coordinates assigned in the primed Cartesian system to two simultaneous positions of P_1 and P_2 in L. The distance λ' between these two positions is equal to the positive square root of $(x_1' - x_2')^2 + (y_1' - y_2')^2 + (z_1' - z_2')^2$. However, unless $v = 0$, $\lambda' < \lambda$ ('length contraction'), for $\lambda' = \lambda\sqrt{1 - (v/c)^2}$ (where c denotes the constant speed of light *in vacuo*, expressed in the units employed in the definition of our coordinate systems). Relative to L', the time lapse τ' between E_1 and E_2 is equal to $|t_1' - t_2'|$. Unless $v = 0$, $\tau' > \tau$ ('time dilation'), for $\tau' = \tau/\sqrt{(1 - v/c)^2}$. Thus the two fundamental kinematic quantities of length and duration turn out to be relative to the inertial frame of reference chosen. On the other hand, as Minkowski observed, the following equation holds always, even if we lift the simplifying restrictions (i)–(iii) and we allow L to move in L' with constant speed in *any* fixed direction:

$$(x_1 - x_2)^2 + (y_1 - y_2)^2 + (z_1 - z_2)^2 - c^2(t_1 - t_2)^2$$
$$= (x_1' - x_2')^2 + (y_1' - y_2')^2 + (z_1' - z_2')^2 - c^2(t_1' - t_2')^2$$
$$= \sigma_{12}$$

The invariant quantity σ_{12} is the *spacetime interval* between events E_1 and E_2. If $\sigma_{12} < 0$, the last term must be larger than the sum of the other three, in which case σ_{12} is *timelike*. Likewise, σ is *spacelike* if $\sigma_{12} > 0$. Finally, σ_{12} is said to be *lightlike* if $\sigma_{12} = 0$, for only in this case can one of the events be the emission and the other the reception of a light signal that travels *in vacuo*. The kinematics of Einstein (1905) can therefore be conceived as the geometry of a four-dimensional continuum, a locus of events – Minkowski's 'world' or spacetime – characterized by the display equation. Since the change of the primed into the unprimed coordinates can be effected by any transformation of the Poincaré–Lorentz group (see RELATIVITY THEORY, PHILOSOPHICAL SIGNIFICANCE OF §1), the said geometry can be characterized, from Klein's standpoint, (see SPACE §4), by the action of the Poincaré–Lorentz group on a manifold homeomorphic to $\mathbb{R}^4$. It can also be characterized, from

Riemann's standpoint (see SPACE §4), by conferring on such a manifold a Riemannian metric η that can be – inelegantly but accurately – described as follows:

(a) if E_1 and E_2 are simultaneous in a given inertial lab L, then σ_{12} is the squared length assigned by the metric η to a straight line joining the locations of E_1 and E_2 in the relative space of L;
(b) if E_1 and E_2 are events in the history of an inertial particle p, then σ_{12} is the squared length assigned by the metric η to the spacetime trajectory – the 'world-line' – of p between E_1 and E_2.

Because spacetime intervals can be negative or zero, the said metric η is not a standard Riemannian metric and is sometimes described as *semi*-Riemannian. In a manifold endowed with a Riemannian metric, one can discriminate between curves with or without a steady direction. The former are called *geodesics*. Thus, on a plane the geodesics are straight lines, on a sphere they are great circles. In Minkowski spacetime, the world-lines of inertial particles and light-signals *in vacuo* are geodesics. At each point of the manifold the metric determines a quantity called the *curvature scalar*, which is constant $= 0$ on a plane, $= 1/r$ on a sphere of radius r. In Minkowski spacetime the curvature scalar is 0 everywhere, so we say that it is *flat*. (It is perhaps worth noting that the flatness or deviation from flatness of a Riemannian manifold $\mathcal{M}$ is measured by the so-called *curvature tensor*, whose value at each point p of $\mathcal{M}$ is expressed – relative to a coordinate system defined on a neighbourhood of p – by an *array* of real numbers. The curvature scalar generally conveys less information than the curvature tensor, on which it depends. However, if every term of the array equals 0 everywhere, the curvature scalar is also constant and equal to 0; and if $\mathcal{M}$ is two-dimensional the said array has only one term, equal to the curvature scalar.)

3   Curved relativistic spacetimes

Prompted by the radical incompatibility between special relativity and Newtonian gravity, Einstein worked from 1907 on a theory of gravitation. He was guided by the assumption – known as the *equivalence principle* – that an observer in a closed laboratory has no way of telling whether the lab moves inertially, or falls freely in a uniform gravitational field. If the world were filled by a uniform gravitational field it could therefore be regarded as a Minkowski spacetime in which freely falling particles are constrained by gravitational forces to stick to geodesics. But real gravitational fields are not uniform, and the equivalence of free fall and inertial motion holds only approximately. This suggested to Einstein the following bold analogy: just as the Riemannian metric of a sphere is approximated on a small neighbourhood of each point by the Pythagorean metric of the Euclidian plane (see SPACE §4), so the (semi-)Riemannian metric of real spacetime is approximated on a small neighbourhood of each event by the flat Minkowski metric η. But the actual metric is not flat: it deviates more or less from flatness according to the presence or absence of matter. Freely falling particles follow geodesic world-lines as determined by this metric. Thus, gravitational phenomena depend, *through the geometry*, on the distribution of matter. The theory finally attained by Einstein (1915, 1916), known as 'general relativity', roughly fits this scheme (although its equations admit solutions in which the density of matter is equal to 0 everywhere and the law of geodesic free fall generally holds only for uncharged spinless particles). Celebrated until *c.*1950 chiefly for its beauty, it has since then enjoyed a spectacular run of experimental successes which place it far ahead of other available theories of gravity (on the other hand, it is incompatible with the currently accepted quantum theories of non-gravitational forces). The theory turns on a system of differential equations, the *Einstein field equations* (EFE), in which the spacetime metric is the unknown and a particular distribution of matter is assumed. Under different assumptions, the equations yield diverse solutions, which is why one usually speaks, in the plural, of relativistic spacetimes.

4 A wealth of worlds

Philosophers have been greatly exercised by the many surprising alternative ways of conceiving the overall structure of spacetime offered by general relativity. Assuming that the density of matter ρ is always and everywhere roughly the same, Einstein (1917) obtained the first cosmological solution of the EFE: a spacetime that can be decomposed into a succession of geometrically identical slices of simultaneous events, homeomorphic to the three-dimensional sphere S^3. This was hailed as a solution of Kant's antinomy concerning the world's size, for Einstein's spherical space is finite and yet, being boundless, it poses no questions about what lies beyond it. But Einstein's world clashes with the redshift noticeable in radiation from extragalactic sources, which would indicate that ρ is decreasing. It is, moreover, an unstable limiting case of a family of solutions found by Friedmann (1922, 1924), under the less stringent assumption that ρ is spatially uniform but may vary with time. A generic Friedmann world will either

(i)   contract indefinitely,

(ii) expand indefinitely,

(iii) expand for a finite time and then contract.

Cases (ii) and (iii) could agree, to a first approximation, with the world as we see it. They share this feature: ρ increases beyond all bounds within a finite time as we go back into the past along any world-line of matter. Since the metric is undefined unless ρ is finite, spacetime cannot contain a point at which $\rho = \infty$. Hence at present only a finite time T has elapsed along each world-line of matter. Friedmann called T 'the time since the creation of the world' (1922: 384), and some writers believe that his work lends scientific support to Genesis 1: 1. Be that as it may, one should bear in mind that *every* given moment in a Friedmann world is preceded by *some* time, no matter how short, Thus, his cosmology solves Kant's antinomy concerning the world's duration, for Friedmann time is finite and yet, having no beginning, it raises no questions about what was the case before it.

Less realistic but no less exciting is a family of solutions of the EFE discovered by Gödel (1949a), characterized by the presence of closed (potential) world-lines. If one of these happens to be the world-line of a conscious particle, it will re-experience its past infinitely many times as it lives on into the future (see TIME TRAVEL). Opinions on this matter are divided between those who believe with Gödel (1949b) that the mere conceivability of such relativistic worlds should affect our understanding of time, and those who think that those features of an abstract mathematical structure which in a realistic model constitute a plausible representation of time may well not have any significant analogy with time in other models (see TIME §3).

Earman (1995) surveys the whole range of such relativistic 'monsters'. Particularly interesting for the philosopher are the 'observationally indistinguishable spacetimes' discovered by Glymour (1972, 1977). Let us say, with Malament (1977), that two solutions of the EFE, $\mathcal{W}_1$ and $\mathcal{W}_2$, are *weakly observationally indistinguishable* if for every event x_1 in $\mathcal{W}_1$ there is an event x_2 in $\mathcal{W}_2$ such that the spacetime region $\mathcal{I}^-(x_1) \subset \mathcal{W}_1$ from which slower-than-light signals can reach x_1 is isometric with the region $\mathcal{I}^-(x_2) \subset \mathcal{W}_2$ from which slower-than-light signals can reach x_2. This entails that observers in $\mathcal{W}_1$ cannot learn from experience whether they live in $\mathcal{W}_1$ or in $\mathcal{W}_2$, although it may occur that $\mathcal{W}_1$ and $\mathcal{W}_2$ do not share some very important global properties (for example, the existence of closed world-lines).

References and further reading

Ciufolini, I. and Wheeler, J.A. (1995) *Gravitation and*

Inertia, Princeton, NJ: Princeton University Press. (A recent, quick-paced exposition of general relativity, with all the brilliance and keen sense of essentials which are normal in books coauthored by Wheeler.)

Earman, J. (1989) *World-Enough and Space-Time; Absolute versus Relational Theories of Space and Time*, Cambridge, MA: MIT Press. (Discusses absolutism and relationalism in both the Newtonian and the relativistic setting.)

* —— (1995) *Bangs, Crunches, Whimpers, and Shrieks: Singularities and Acausalities in Relativistic Spacetimes*, New York and Oxford: Oxford University Press. (A critical survey of spacetime singularities – naked and clothed – supertasks, horizons, time travel, and so on, by a distinguished philosopher well-versed in physics and mathematics.)

* Einstein, A. (1905) 'Zur Elektrodynamik bewegter Körper' (On the Electrodynamics of Moving Bodies), *Annalen der Physik* 17: 891–921. (Einstein's first – and principal – paper on special relativity.)

* —— (1915) 'Die Feldgleichungen der Gravitation' (The Field Equations of Gravitation), *K. Preußische Akademie der Wissenschaften. Sitzungsberichte*, 844–7. (First publication of the Einstein field equations.)

* —— (1916) 'Die Grundlage der allgemeinen Relativitätstheorie' (The Foundation of the General Theory of Relativity), *Annalen der Physik* 49: 769–822. (Einstein's detailed presentation of his theory of gravity.)

* —— (1917) 'Kosmologische Betrachtungen zur allgemeinen Relativitätstheorie' (Cosmological Considerations on the General Theory of Relativity), *K. Preußische Akademie der Wissenschaften; math.-phys. Cl. Sitzungsberichte*, 142–52. (In this trailblazing paper Albert Einstein founded modern cosmology.)

Ellis, G.F.R. and Williams, R.M. (1988) *Flat and Curved Space-Times*, Cambridge: Cambridge University Press. (Outstanding introduction to the mathematics of relativistic spacetime; requires high-school geometry and algebra but no higher mathematics; an excellent reading list directs the student to more advanced books.)

* Friedmann, A. (1922) 'Über die Krümmung des Raumes' (On the Curvature of Space), *Zeitschrift für Physik* 10: 377–86. (Alexander Friedmann's first paper on relativistic cosmology.)

* —— (1924) 'Über die Möglichkeit einer Welt mit konstanter negativer Krümmung des Raumes' (On the Possibility of a World with Constant Negative Curvature of Space), *Zeitschrift für Physik* 21:

326–32. (Alexander Friedmann's second paper on relativistic cosmology.)

Friedman, M. (1983) *Foundations of Space-Time Theories: Relativistic Physics and Philosophy of Science*, Princeton, NJ: Princeton University Press. (Currently, the standard philosophical treatment of spacetime theories.)

* Glymour, C. (1972) 'Topology, Cosmology and Convention', *Synthèse* 24: 195–218. (The possibility of indistinguishable spacetimes was first announced here.)

* —— (1977) 'Indistinguishable Space-times and the Fundamental Group', *Minnesota Studies in the Philosophy of Science* 8: 50–60. (Glymour's principal publication on the subject.)

* Gödel, K. (1949a) 'An Example of a New Type of Cosmological Solution of Einstein's Field Equations of Gravitation', *Reviews of Modern Physics* 21: 447–50. (Gödel's cosmological solution of the Einstein field equations, which allows closed timelike curves.)

* —— (1949b) 'A Remark about the Relationship Between Relativity Theory and Idealistic Philosophy', in P.A. Schilpp (ed.) *Albert Einstein, Philosopher-Scientist*, Evanston, IL: Northwestern University, 555–62. (Gödel's philosophical comments on his cosmological solution of the Einstein field equations.)

* Grünbaum, A. (1973) *Philosophical Problems of Space and Time*, Dordrecht: Reidel, 2nd edn enlarged. (Detailed coverage of philosophical debate until the date of publication.)

* —— (1991) 'Creation as Pseudo-explanation in Current Physical Cosmology', *Erkenntnis* 35: 233–54. (Discusses creationism in connexion with relativistic cosmology.)

* Malament, D. (1977) 'Observationally Indistinguishable Space-times', *Minnesota Studies in the Philosophy of Science* 8: 61–80. (A very clear presentation of the subject, which in some ways improves on Glymour's original work, listed above.)

* Minkowski, H. (1909) 'Raum und Zeit' (Space and Time), *Physikalische Zeitschrift* 10: 104–11. (Minkowski's classical lecture of 1908, in which he presented his conception of spacetime to a broad scientific audience.)

* —— (1915) 'Das Relativitätsprinzip' (The Principle of Relativity), *Jahresbericht der Deutschen Mathematiker-Vereinigung* 24: 372–82. (Posthumously published text of the first public lecture on Minkowski's formulation of special relativity theory, delivered in Göttingen in 1907.)

Stein, H. (1967) 'Newtonian Spacetime', *Texas Quarterly* 10: 174–200. (This remarkable essay, written for non-mathematicians, shows how much more natural it is to formulate Newtonian dynamics in a spacetime setting, rather than in the traditional space-and-time setting.)

Torretti, R. (1983) *Relativity and Geometry*, Oxford: Pergamon Press; repr. New York: Dover, 1996. (An essay on spacetime geometry by the author of this article.)

ROBERTO TORRETTI

SPAIN, PHILOSOPHY IN

Historians have argued about precisely when to date the commencement of Spanish history proper, rendering dubious any reference to Spain as such in the period prior to the official constitution of nationality. If this is the case, one can not really speak of philosophy in Spain before 1474, although it remains a fact that philosophy had been practised on the Iberian Peninsula from the earliest times. During the period of the Roman Empire, distinguished philosophical figures included Lucius Annqeus Seneca; under Visigothic rule, Saint Isidore of Seville came to the fore; and the Islamic Empire featured some of the most eminent philosophers of the Arabic and Judaic traditions, such as Ibn Hazm, Averroes, Ibn Gabirol, Yehuda Ha-Levi and Maimonides. There is no doubt that the centre of philosophical activity within the peninsula during the Middle Ages was the so-called School of Translators of Toledo, where numerous thinkers from many countries gathered. Together with Spanish scholars such as Domingo Gundisalvo and Juan Hispano, they collaborated in making Greek philosophy available to the countries of Europe; instrumental in this process were Gerard of Cremona, Daniel of Morlay, Alexander Neckham and Michael Scot.

After Spanish nationality was constituted under the Catholic Monarchs (1474–1516) on the basis of a single, unified faith, philosophy was destined to become closely linked with religion. During the sixteenth century, this gave rise to a burgeoning of philosophy of the very highest order, which followed two separate paths: that of the Erasmian-style Renaissance, featuring Luis Vives, which developed in line with the vanguard of the European Renaissance; and that of Spanish Scholasticism, which was fuelled by the thrust of the Counter-Reformation on the one hand, and by the discovery of America on the other. After the reigns of Charles I and Philip II (the chief protagonists in the creation of the empire 'in which the sun never set'), the seventeenth, eighteenth and nineteenth centuries witnessed a relentless decline which, towards the beginning

of the twentieth, seemed to come to an end. The Generation of 1898, with its revolutionary secular theories, provided the catalyst for a philosophical recovery whose greatest protagonists were Miguel de Unamuno, José Ortega y Gasset and Xavier Zubir. These thinkers were succeeded by the philosophers who went into exile after the Civil War of 1936–9: José Ferrater Mora, José Gaos, María Zambrano, Joaquín Xirau, and Juan David García Bacca.

1   **The Middle Ages**
2   **The Renaissance**
3   **The Golden Age**
4   **Decline and the seeds of recovery**
5   **The Generation of 1898**
6   **The School of Madrid**
7   **Philosophy in exile**
8   **Independent thinkers**
9   **From dictatorship to democracy**

1   The Middle Ages

One cannot speak of a strictly Spanish philosophy until after the founding of the Spanish State in 1474. Nevertheless, one cannot dismiss the importance of Hispano-Arabic and Hispano-Judaic philosophy prior to that date, as well as certain figures from within the Christian community who attained great prominence during Medieval times. An outstanding figure of this period was Ramón Llull, Mallorcan by birth, who developed a complicated combinatory logic – called the 'Ars Luliana' – which offered an ingenious foretaste of our current axiomatized logics. He was the author of an immense and highly diverse series of works, which sparked off a long tradition of Lullism that has continued to the present. His thought contains the seeds of the *mathesis universalis*, which served as the basis for European Rationalism as developed later by Descartes and Leibniz. The study of Llull has continued to the present day in the journal *Estudios Lulianos*, and at the Ramundus Llullus Institute in Fribourg-am-Brisgovia. Llull was the first European philosopher to write in a Romance language, since part of his work is in Catalan, although most is in Latin and some even in Arabic (see LLULL, R.).

2   The Renaissance

The founding of the Spanish State brought about by the marriage of Ferdinand V of Aragon and Isabel I of Castile – the so-called Catholic Monarchs – took place during a time of crisis for Christianity, the effects of which were felt most acutely in the Catholic countries. In Spain, this was expressed initially in the widespread diffusion of the doctrines of Erasmus of Rotterdam which took on a novel and highly radical form, propounded by men as renowned as Juan and Alfonso de Valdés and Andrés Laguna. From a philosophical point of view, the single most important figure was Luis VIVES who lived the greater part of his life in Bruges, although he also spent some time in Oxford after being appointed private tutor to princess Mary Tudor and reader to queen Catherine of Aragon during her marriage to Henry VIII. Vives was one of the most eminent representatives of the Renaissance spirit: his critique of Scholasticism, his rehabilitation of the classics, the attention he devoted to anthropological problems and his practical vision of philosophy were unparalleled. Perhaps his most important book is *De anima et vita* (On the soul and on life) (1538), a precursor to differential psychology and vocational guidance, since he recognizes the need to observe and distinguish the differences in aptitude and disposition between individuals with a view to choosing their office or profession. Vives also developed an original theory of the passions very much along the modern lines which Descartes was later to pursue. All in all, Vives was a cosmopolitan and universal spirit who showed himself to have advanced beyond European thinking in his *De concordia et discordia in humano genere* (On harmony and discord in humankind) (1529), as well as in his social attitudes regarding aid and protection for the needy classes, as he revealed in *De subventione pauperum* (On poor relief) (1526). Generally speaking, Erasmianism was also a form of Europeanism which endorsed the notion of the Carlist Empire as a 'universitas christiana', not an 'imperium mundi' as it was conceived of by the pagan emperors. One important representative of this Europeanism was Andrés Laguna, doctor to king Charles V and author of *Discurso de Europa* (Discourse on Europe) (1542), in which he argued for a coalition of the Christian monarchs to form a unified force designed to counter the threat of the Ottoman Empire.

3 The Golden Age

The Spanish Renaissance, which began as a reaction to the crisis faced by European Christianity, gradually changed in character during the seventeenth century when Protestantism consolidated its advance throughout the Germanic and Anglo-Saxon countries, and also as the possibilities opened up by the discovery and colonization of America were exploited. As a result, two key philosophical fronts emerged. The first, whose common denominator was the Roman Catholic Counter-Reformation, was to give rise to the movement known as Spanish scholasticism. The greatest practitioners of this scholasticism were two religious orders, the Dominicans and the Jesuits. The main centre of activity for the Dominicans was the University of Salamanca, aided by their nearby monastery of St. Stephen, and among the main representatives were Melchor Cano, Domingo de SOTO and Francisco de VITORIA. Cano's most important work is *De Locis teologicis* (On theological standpoints) (1563), while Soto's famous treatise is entitled *De iustitia et de iure* (On justice and law) (1553). Both helped to prepare the ground which formed the bedrock for the Council of Trent (1545–63), where the fundamentals of Catholic doctrine for the next four centuries were formulated.

As for Francisco de Vitoria, he was chiefly occupied with problems stemming from the conquest and colonization of America, concerns which he voiced in his books *De indis prior* (The question of the Indies) (1539), *De iure belli* (The law of war) (1539) and *De potestate civili* (On civil power) (1528). In these works he developed his theory of the 'just war', as well as that of Spain's legal rights to the conquest and colonization of America, implementing a doctrine which would later form the basis of future international law. Here Vitoria introduced the concept of a 'world community' to which all people belong as a consequence of their fundamentally social nature which exists above and beyond their division into nation states. This world community was governed by natural law (*ius naturale*) and, in those matters beyond its sphere, by the law of peoples (*ius gentium*) which functioned in accordance with various principles concerning international cohabitation. According to Vitoria:

> There can be no doubt that the whole world, which is, in a certain sense, a republic, has the right to dictate just and profitable laws to all of its members, similar to those laid down in the law of peoples.... From this it follows that whoever breaks the law of peoples, whether in peacetime or in war, is committing a mortal sin, and that in matters of import, such as that concerning the immunity of ambassadors, it is forbidden for any republic to refuse to comply with the law of peoples.... Just as the majority in a republic has the right to appoint a king, so too the majority of Christians, whether or not the minority be in agreement, has the right to name a sovereign leader, who must be obeyed by all.
>
> (Vitoria 1557: Ch. 8)

Even if they only appear in embryonic form, the rubrics of a future 'society of nations' are clearly and succinctly mapped out in this passage, providing an ingenious antecedent to what would only be put into practice some four centuries later, as a consequence of which Vitoria might be viewed as the founder of international law.

The impact of the discovery of America on the price of goods, and even on the value of currency, completely disrupted economic relations within the Iberian Peninsula, most severely in the city ports such as Seville. This led some theologians to speculate on the laws of supply and demand, as well as on the nature and conditions regarding the borrowing and lending of money, and eventually led them to state for the first time the 'theoretical principles of quantitative analysis' (Vilar 1974; Grice-Hutchison 1952). Martín de Azpilcueta and Tomás de Mercado developed their work along these lines in the sixteenth century; the former wrote the famous *Comentario resolutorio de cambios* (A resolutory commentary on exchange) (1556) while the latter was author of the equally famous *Suma de tratos y contratos* (Summa of deals and contracts) (1569).

Juan de Mairena was an outstanding Jesuit, an advocate of highly advanced social doctrines such as the common ownership of goods, and of theories such as that of regicide which he set out in *De rege et de regis institutione* (On the king and his training) (1599) – this work was banned in France, because it was thought to have played a part in the assassinations of kings Henry III and IV. Worth mentioning within the context of the Jesuits is the polemic known as 'de auxiliis' which took place between Luis de MOLINA and Domingo BÁÑEZ (the latter was a Dominican). This was sparked off by Molina's work *Concordia liberi arbitrii cum gratiae donis, divina praescientia, providentia, praedestinatione* (The harmonious concordance of free will with the gifts of grace, divine prescience, providence and predestination) (1588) in which he posed the question of the difficulty of reconciling divine grace and the provident omniscience of God with human liberty. Molina's doctrine availed itself of the traditional scholastic notion known as 'simultaneous concurrence', but Báñez's counter-argument in his *De vera et legitima concordia liberi arbitrii cum auxiliis gratiae Dei* (On the true and legitimate concordance of free will with the aid of God's grace) (1595) led Molina to formulate the theory of the 'middle science', the theoretical core of which were the so-called 'futuribles' (conditional futures which, despite never having occurred, can be freely determined by man and known as such by God). Báñez restricted himself to re-formulating his own theory of 'physical premonition', incorporating subtle new disquisitions such as those known as the 'science of vision' and the 'science of simple understanding'.

However, from a philosophical point of view, the most important Jesuit philosopher was Francisco SUÁREZ, whose major works include *Disputationes metaphysicae* (Debates on metaphysics) (1597) and *De legibus ac de Deo legislatore* (On laws and on God as legislator) (1612). The first of these (although belonging to Thomist scholasticism, deviated from it significantly to the point of constituting an independent doctrine which became known as *Suarism*), takes original standpoints on issues such as the formal distinction between essence and existence, the uniqueness of the principle of individuation, and the consideration of 'real being' as the starting point for metaphysics. In his work he examined the transcendental properties of being and its grounding principles, which he then applied to the two fundamental classes of being: the infinite or uncreated (God) and the finite or created (humans). In so doing, he abandoned the medieval style of the 'commentary' and adopted instead a form of argument which proceeded according to its own intrinsic necessities, giving his work an unmistakable air of 'modernity'. This is most evident in his construction of a systematic metaphysical corpus which existed independently of Aristotelian-style scholastic commentary. It resulted in the book appearing in a host of editions as soon as it was published, and it even found its way onto the syllabus in numerous Protestant universities throughout Europe. Its influence on modern authors – Descartes, Spinoza, Leibniz, Vico – cannot be disputed.

4 Decline and the seeds of recovery

The pinnacle of Spanish Scholasticism which was reached with Suárez marked the end of a glorious epoch. The next two centuries were centuries of decline; in the seventeenth, eighteenth, and a significant portion of the nineteenth centuries, philosophical Spain lost its nerve, but a faint intellectual flame was kept alight by a few minority groups who thus saved the tradition. In the eighteenth century the *Novatores* (renovators) movement, headed by Andrés Piquer, gradually laid the foundations for a future renaissance which never materialized. A few enlightened thinkers such as B.J. Feijoo, G.M. de Jovellanos and Francisco Cabarrús helped to check the landslide, but the French invasion under Napoleon Bonaparte put an end to everything. The subsequent civil wars – the so-called 'Carlist Wars' – left an intellectual wasteland behind them. It was only in the middle of the nineteenth century that Julián Sanz del Río managed to turn the tide: his trip to Germany in 1843 and his contact with the few remaining disciples of Christian KRAUSE in Heidelberg, allowed him to take back a few seeds of Krausist idealism to his

Iberian homestead where they blossomed into a movement of spiritual and cultural renewal. This had its most important centre of diffusion at the famous Institución Libre de Enseñanza (Institute of Free Education), founded in 1876 by Francisco Giner de los Ríos and other Krausist teachers, among whom Nicolás Salmerón and Gumersindo de Azcárate were the most distinguished.

The philosophy of Giner de los Ríos was the result of the fruitful marriage of Krausist idealism and the positivism which dominated the epoch, a strikingly original movement known in the history of Spanish philosophy as 'Krauso-positivism'. The tangible gains of this philosophy were most apparent in the sphere of education. From the Institución Libre de Enseñanza, which was dedicated to primary and secondary education, emerged organizations such as the Junta para Ampliación de Estudios e Investigaciones Científicas (Group for the broadening of scientific studies and research) in 1907, of which Santiago Ramón y Cajal, winner of the Nobel Prize for Medicine in 1906, and José Castillejo, an eminent Romanist, were the principals. After its foundation in 1910, the Residencia de Estudiantes was run by Alberto Jiménez Fraud, whose pioneering spirit and aesthetic sensibility made it the cradle of modernism and the avant garde. Among others, Juan Ramón Jiménez, Frederico García Lorca, Rafael Alberti and Luis Buñuel studied there. Following in the wake of this great wave of renewal, mention should also be made of the foundation of the Instituto-Escuela (1918), the Residencia de Señoritas (1915) and the Misiones Pedagógicas (1931), organized and run by Manuel Bartolomé Cossío, the successor to Giner de los Ríos.

5   The Generation of 1898

The stimulus towards recovery provided by Krausism and institutionism eventually came to fruition in a powerful regenerative movement which was to bear its first great literary and philosophical fruits with the so-called Generation of 1898. From a philosophical perspective, the most eminent of this group is Miguel de UNAMUNO, a precursor of existentialism who made the contradiction between reason and life the crux of a philosophical conception of the world marked by anguish (*Congoja*) in the face of death. This led to his most famous work – *Del sentimiento trágico de la vida* (The tragic sense of life and peoples) (1912) – where he describes the struggle to attain personal immortality in the face of the uncertainties of reason. That struggle takes the form of an agonistic interplay between life and death in its religious version, represented by him in his book *La agonía del*

cristianismo (The agony of Christianity) (1925). As with the French existentialists, this nexus of problems was to be carried over into a literary oeuvre which consisted of a variety of novels, poetry and theatrical works (see EXISTENTIALISM).

6   The School of Madrid

The secularizing philosophical theories of the Generation of 1898 broke with the philosophical tradition marked by its links with Catholicism, and this opened up the way for an important transformation of the entire discipline. Within this rebuilding process the so-called Generation of 1914 played a role of utmost importance. Most prominent here was José ORTEGA Y GASSET who, after his education at the Neo-Kantian school of Marburg, reacted against its teachings to found a philosophy of his own. This doctrine is to be found in works such as *Meditaciones del Quijote* (Meditations on Quixote) (1914) and *El tema del nuestro tiempo* (The modern theme) (1923), among others. Ortega suggested the following maxim as the key to his philosophy: 'I am myself and my circumstances, and if I cannot come to terms with these, then I can never come to terms with myself' ([1914] 1983 (1): 322).

The framework consisting of the self and its circumstances was specifically *life as radical reality*, by means of which Ortega attempted to overcome every form of rationalism. 'Reason cannot, and need not aspire to supplant life', he said in 1914; this approach to the matter was fully developed in *El tema de nuestro tiempo*, in which he proposed that culture be replaced by life, since it was the latter that constituted primary reality. By life Ortega here meant individual human life:

> This radical reality on the basis of the strict observation of which we must ultimately establish and secure all of our knowledge of anything, is our life, human life. Human life as radical reality is only the life of every individual, it is only my own life. For the sake of linguistic convenience I will sometimes call it 'our life', but it must always be understood that with this expression I am referring to the life of every individual and not to that of others nor to an assumed plural and collective life. What we call 'other people's lives', the life of our friend, of the one we love, is already an added element which encroaches on the scene which is my life. By calling it 'radical reality' I do not mean that it is the only, nor even the highest, most respectable, sublime or supreme reality, but simply that it is the root – hence the term radical – of all of the others, in the sense that the latter, of whatever

nature, must, for us to experience them as reality, somehow make themselves present or, at least, announce themselves by causing the boundaries of our own life to tremble. Therefore this radical reality – my life – is so little ego-oriented, so utterly non-solipsistic, that it is, quintessentially, the space or scene which is offered to me and opened up so that any other reality can manifest itself therein. Hence no knowledge of anything is sufficient, that is to say sufficiently profound or radical, if it does not begin by pinpointing the place and specifying the way, within the sphere that is our life, wherein and whereby that something appears, shows itself, bursts forth or rises up, in short, exists.

(Ortega [1923] 1983 (7): 99–101)

As one of the finest commentators on Ortega's philosophy has said, what we are witnessing here is a metaphysical revolution characterized by the 'real correlation of self and world, of thought and its object, of love and what is loved: (that is) it is exactly what we call life. Living is feeling things, thinking things; it is the coexistence of self and world. Life is the primary, fundamental fact, absolutely present and evident, upon which all philosophy must base itself. Life, on a deeper and more essential plane, is the 'cogito' of the new philosophy' (García Morente 1987: 67).

This discovery of life as metaphysical reality, demanded a method through which it could be rendered accessible: the method was that of 'vital reason', which was conceived of as the same thing as living since 'reason is only a form and function of life'. What we have here is a new conception of reason that goes beyond the rationalism of 'pure reason', as an expression of modernity. According to this new formulation, reason 'is nothing more than a tiny island floating on the sea of primary vitality; far from supplanting the latter, it must depend on it for support and sustenance, just as each one of the members of the body is given life by the body as a whole' (Ortega [1923] 1983 (3): 177–8).

We are faced with a philosophical programme which implies a reversal of the tenets of traditional Western culture – as opposed to a culture which un-houses life, a culture which gains sustenance from it, injecting it with new values; as opposed to the old irony of Socrates, the irony of Don Juan, who reaffirms spontaneity, sincerity and joyousness. This was the *modern theme* which consisted in 'making reason bow before vitality, placing it within the sphere of the purely biological, subordinating it to spontaneity'; a programme which, in its philosophical essence, might be formulated thus: 'pure reason must abdicate in favour of vital reason' (Ortega [1923] 1983 (3): 178).

The vitalism so described did not imply any form of irrationalism, but constituted a new mode of understanding which Ortega named 'ratio-vitalist', within which there took shape a new theory of knowledge, essential to which was the concept of 'perspective'. Ratio-vitalism was, then, a form of perspectivism.

Ortega's philosophical theories were to attract some important philosophical figures, such as Manuel García Morente, José Gaos María de Maetzu, Xavier Zubiri, María Zambrano, Luis Recasens Siches and Lorenzo Luzuriaga who, in 1933, would give rise to what can be referred to as the School of Madrid, even if the brevity of its existence (a result of the civil war) prevented it from producing what seemed destined to be a wealth of fine philosophy.

Although he belonged in principle to the School of Madrid, Xavier Zubiri was to follow his own highly original philosophy. His starting point was one of his own theories, according to which the human is a 'reality animal' characterized by what Zubiri called 'sentient intelligence' – that is to say, a sensuous intellection and an intellectual sensing – by means of which he is able carry out his most proper function, which consists in the 'actualization of the real in so far as it is real'. This theory, which had already appeared in embryonic form in his first work, *Naturaleza, Historia, Dios* (Nature, history, God) (1944), was to be consistently developed and elaborated in his later works *Sobre la esencia* (On essence) (1962) and, above all, in his trilogy on *Sentient Intelligence* (1980).

7 Philosophy in exile

Despite the fact that the civil war (1936–9) destroyed what ought to have been the natural continuity of the School of Madrid, its members (the majority of whom went into exile) proceeded to produce a magnificent body of philosophical work in the different countries which granted them asylum. Examples include José Gaos, who formulated his own particular theory which he described as 'a philosophy of philosophy', and which has had an obvious impact on the history of Hispanic thinking; María Zambrano, who expounded and developed her method of 'poetic reasoning'; Luis Recasens Siches, who made use of Ortega's vital reason in order to produce a highly individual philosophy of law; Manuel Granell, who carried out similar work in the field of logic; José Ferrater Mora, author of a famous dictionary of philosophy, among other publications; and finally, Eduardo Nicol, an original and independent thinker who developed a meditation on the nature and future of philosophy.

Probably the most original thinker of all of those

exiled from Spain was Juan David García Bacca, author of a multifaceted and highly varied oeuvre which revolved principally around a metaphysical meditation on the artificial world created by man, while within the sphere of Marxist socialism and related fields particularly significant is Fernando de los Ríos who later went on to write more historical studies, although his leanings were always towards social and political philosophy. His *Mi Viaje a la Rusia Soviética* (My journey to Soviet Russia) (1921) was decisive in keeping the Spanish Socialist Party away from the Third International. Within the tradition of more rigorously orthodox Marxist thought, mention should be made of the then young thinker Adolfo Sánchez Vásquez whose philosophical reflections have been directed at its more practical aspects, especially those relating to art and aesthetics, although his most important work continues to be *Filosofía de la praxis* (The philosophy of praxis) (1967).

8 Independent thinkers

From the end of the nineteenth and during the first half of the twentieth century, a number of independent figures – difficult to categorize in terms of any one school or movement – appeared in Spain. The most striking of these was Jorge Ruiz de Santayana, better known as George SANTAYANA, the name with which he signed his writings, since they all appeared in English in the USA, where he was professor at Harvard. After 1912 he lived in various European countries – England, Spain, Italy – before finally settling down in Rome where he remained until his death in 1952. He was the author of a highly diverse body of work, without doubt the most important of which was *The Realms of Being* (1942). His philosophy is best categorized as a form of sceptical materialism marked by a heightened aesthetic sensibility. Although an atheist, he placed a great deal of importance on religion from a symbolic point of view (in fact he lived and died in a monastery) which has led people to speak of an aesthetic naturalism.

A second independent thinker was the priest Angel Amor Ruibal, author of the dense and colossal work *Los problemas fundamentales de la filosofía y el dogma* (The fundamental problems of philosophy and dogma) most of which remained unedited during the author's lifetime, but which has been gradually published since his death in 1930. It has now been shown that these writings contain an original philosophical system which might be termed correlationism or transcendental relativism, since it is not a pure and simple relativism, but rather a universal atomism in which the value of the individual is retained. It sees the universe as being composed of a series of interrelated fundamental systems, in which beings constitute 'links' which subordinate one another until they interconnect – like a vertically structured chain running from the lowest being to the highest – in a continuous universal interaction which is monistic in nature, since the parts acquire meaning only through their relation to the whole.

A third thinker of importance is Eugenio d'Ors who, at the start of his career, was noted for his close links with the Catalonian Government and in his later years for those he established with General Franco's dictatorship, but who led a solitary existence during the greater part of his life. Within his varied output he developed a sort of 'figurative thinking' upon which he constructed certain 'figures of intelligence', the object of which was to arrive at a 'harmonious reason', which he located precisely half way between life and pure reason. This in turn provides the basis for what he called a 'Keplerian reform of philosophy', in which the principle of contradiction was replaced by the principle of participation, and that of sufficient reason by that of required function. All of this gave rise to an understanding of the universe as a syntactical structure.

9 From dictatorship to democracy

Franco's victory in the civil war of 1936–9 determined the subsequent course taken by philosophy in Spain. First, it forced the majority of thinkers and teachers of philosophy into exile; second, it imposed on secondary and university education a sort of 'official philosophy', the basis of which was the most antiquated scholasticism. It should be stressed, however, that the later peaceful transition from the dictatorship period to democracy owed much to those philosophers who managed to retain an independent sense of judgment, by adhering to their liberal principles as far as the regime would allow. Among these is José Luis Aranguren who, starting out from a Roman Catholic standpoint, allowed his thinking to open out onto increasingly broad perspectives, incorporating the latest ideas to emerge from existentialism, from Anglo-Saxon thought and from the dialectical strains of Marxism. Another is Pedro Laín Entralgo who was deeply involved in work as a historian of medicine, which gradually opened up the way for him to formulate a philosophy of hope and a medical anthropology in which the reality of the 'other' is always present. Also of importance is Enrique Tierno Galván, a committed socialist who played an active role in politics – he became Mayor of Madrid – which did not prevent him from producing an important body of philosophical work, to which his book *Razón mecánica y razón dialéctica* (Mechanical reason and dialectical reason) (1969) is testimony.

Among those who kept the sacred torch of Ortega's philosophy burning in Spain are Paulino Garagorri, an important exegete and compiler of Ortega's work, and Julián Marías, perhaps the most faithful disciple of the master whose philosophy he has systematized in his magnum opus *Ortega* (1962, 1983). It was this group of thinkers who made it possible for the first sparks of rebellion against Franco's regime to flare up in 1956.

See also: Collegium Conimbricense; Molinism

References and further reading

Abellán, J.L. (1967) *Filosofía Española en América 1936–1966* (Spanish Philosophy in America), Madrid: Ediciones Guadarrama. (Currently the only existing work on the Spanish philosophical exile resulting from the Spanish Civil War.)
—— (1978) *Panorama de la Filosofía Española Actual* (A survey on the Current Spanish Philosophy), Madrid: Espasa-Calpe. (A panoramic and critical view of the Spanish philosophy after the 1936–9 Civil War.)
—— (1979–92) *Historia Crítica del Pensamiento Español* (A Critical History of Spanish Thought), Madrid: Espasa-Calpe, 7 vols. (Spanish philosophy from the Middle Ages up to the present, from the perspective of the history of ideas.)
* Amor Ruibal, A. (1914–36) *Los Problemas Fundamentales de la Filosofía y el Dogma* (Fundamental Problems of Philosophy and Dogma), Madrid: Victoriano Suárez, 10 vols. (A historical-critical presentation of the author's philosophical system.)
* Azpilcueta, M. de (1556) *Comentario Resolutorio de Cambios* (A Resolutary Commentary on Exchange), Salamanca: Andrea de Pontinariis. (Develops a theory of money as a starting point for the moral regulation of the economics between individuals and nations.)
* Bañez, D. (1595) *De Vera et Legitima Concordia Liberi Arbitrii cum Auxiliis Gratiae Dei* (On the True and Legitimate Concordance of Free Will with the Aid of God's Grace), unedited manuscript, Inquisition Section at the National Historical Archive, Madrid: File 4.437. (A fundamental text for understanding the position of the Dominican Order regarding the controversial 'de auxiliis' about divine grace.)
* Cano, M. (1563) *De Locis Teologicis* (On Theological Standpoints), Salamanca: Matías Gast. (A basic text about the different locations in the Holy Scriptures where the revealed truths abide, which served as the doctrine of the Counter-Reformation.)
* *Estudios Lulianos* (Lullian Studies) (1957–), Palma de Mallorca. (A journal dedicated to the study and research on Ramón Llul – essential work for researching this author.)
* García Morente, M. (1987) *Escritos Desconocidos e Inéditos* (Unknown and Unedited Writings), Madrid: BAC. (A posthumous publication with some of the author's most important philosophical writings.)
Guy, A. (1983) *Histoire de la Philosophie Espagnole* (A History of Spanish Philosophy), Toulouse: Université de Toulouse-Le Mirail. (A complete history of Spanish Philosophy from the Middle Ages to the present; it gives priority to the twentieth century, to which half the volume is dedicated.)
* Grice-Hutchinson, M. (1952) *The School of Salamanca. Readings in Spanish Monetary Theory*, Oxford: Clarendon Press. (Serious studies and investigations of the monetary discoveries of sixteenth-century Spanish theologians.)
* Laguna, A. (1542) *Discurso de Europa* (Discourse of Europe), Colonia: Lupum Ioannes Aquensis. (Fundamental text for knowing the Europeanism characteristic of the Erasmists who became ideological speakers during the reign of Charles V.)
* Mairena, J. de (1599) *De Rege et de Regis Institutione* (On the King and his Training), Petrum Rodericum: Toledo. (An important work on the political philosophy which defends the legitimity of regicide and provoked great controversies in its time.)
* Marías, J. (1962) *Ortega. I. Circunstancia y vocación* (Ortega. I. Circumstances and Vocation), Madrid: Revista de Occidente. (The first systematic treatment of Ortega's philosophy.)
—— (1970) *Antropología Filosófica* (Philosophical Anthropology), Madrid: Revista de Occidente. (The most complete presentation of what the author calls the 'empirical structure of human life', the central point of his philosophical ideology.)
* —— (1983) *Ortega. II. Las Trayectorias* (Ortega. II. The Trajectories), Madrid: Alianza Editorial. (In this volume, the author culminates and resolves the dilemmas that arise in the first volume.)
* Mercado, T. de (1569) *Suma de tratos y Contratos* (Summa of Deals and Contracts), Salamanca: Matías Gast. (Observance of marine commercial transactions in Seville resulted in the author's formulation of the first laws on economic and financial exchange, as well as his moral ideology.)
Molina, L. de (1588) *Concordia Liberi Arbitrii cum Donis, Divina Praesciencial, Providentia, Praedestinatione* (The Harmonious Concordance of Free Will with the Gifts of Grace, Divine Prescience,

Providence and Predestination), Lisbon: Antonio Ribeiro. (Molina's formulation of his doctrine on 'middle knowledge', intended to make human freedom compatible with divine omnipresence.)

* Ortega y Gasset, J. (1914) *Meditaciones del Quijote* (Meditations on Quixote), Madrid: Residencia de Estudiantes. (Ortega's first book, essential for understanding his philosophy.)

* —— (1923) *El Tema de Nuestro Tiempo* (The Modern Theme), Madrid: Calpe. (Presentation of Ortegan 'ratiovitalism', central to his doctrine on 'vital reason'.)

* —— (1983) *Obras Completas* (Complete Works), Madrid: Alianza Editorial. (The works of this twentieth-century philosopher can serve as a point of reference for the whole of this entry.)

* Ríos, F. de los (1921) *Mi Viaje a la Rusia Soviética* (My Journey to Soviet Russia), Madrid: Caro Raggio. (Describes the difference that separates the Spanish socialism from the Third International.)

* Sánchez Vázquez, A. (1967) *Filosofía de la Praxis* (The Philosophy of Praxis), Mexico: Grijalbo. (An interpretation of Marxism in relation to practical questions, especially about the concept of 'praxis' as a central category.)

* Santayana, G. (1942) *The Realms of Being*, New York: Scribner. (Defines and describes the four reigns of the being which Santayana considers fundamental: matter, essence, truth and spirit.)

* Soto, D. de (1553) *De Iustitia et Iure* (On Justice and Law), Salamanca: Ioannis Aute. (A theological text fundamental for understanding the differences that developed over the centuries between eternal law, natural law and positive law resulting in the foundations of the philosophy of law.)

* Suárez, F. (1597) *Disputaciones Metaphisicae* (Debates on Metaphysics), Salamanca: Juan y Andrés Renaut. (A combination of Spanish Reinassance scholastics and modern philosophical thought in Europe.)

* —— (1612) *De Legibus ac de Deo Legislatore* (On Laws and on God as Legislator), Coimbra: Diego Gómez Loureyro. (The practical aspects of Suárez's metaphysical work are addressed in this great theological-political treaty, elaborated in ten books.)

* Tierno Galván, E. (1969) *Razón Mecánica y Razón Dialéctica* (Mechanical Reason and Dialectical Reason), Madrid: Tecnos. (A discussion from the Marxist viewpoint of the relations between scientific determinism and dialectics, as well as of its practical consequences.)

* Unamuno, M. de (1912) *Del Sentimiento Trágico de la Vida* (The Tragic Sense of Life and Peoples), Madrid: Renacimiento. (A major work of Unamu-

no's philosophical ideology, in which he explains the irreductible opposition between 'reason' and 'life'.)

* —— (1925) *La Agonía del Cristianismo* (The Agony of Christianity), Madrid: Renacimiento. (The religious version of the 'tragic feeling' achieves its highest dramatism in this book.)

* Vilar, P. (1974) 'Los Primitivos Españoles del Pensamiento Económico. "Cuantitativismo y Bullonismo"' (The Primitive Spaniards of Economical Thought: Cuantitativism and Bullonism) in *Crecimiento y Desarrollo* (Growth and Development), Barcelona: Crítica, 135–62. (A lucid presentation of 'Cuantitativism', developed by Spanish thinkers of the sixteenth century.)

* Vitoria, F. de (1557) *Relectiones Theologicae* (Theological Reflections), Lyon: Jacobo Boyer. (All the texts that constitute this work, which includes the three mentioned in §3 above, form the first scientific proposal about the philosophy of law and international law.)

* Vives, J.L. (1526) *De Subventione Pauperum* (On Poor Relief), Brujas: Hubert de Crook. (One of the first formulations of doctrines of social welfare found in European thought.)

* —— (1529) *De Concordia et Discordia in Humano Genere* (On Harmony and Discord in Humankind), Amberes: Michele & Hillenium. (The author's pacifism reaches a maximum radical level in this work.)

* —— (1538) *De Anima et Vita* (On the Soul and on Life), Basilea: Robert Winter. (This text is one of the first foundations of scientific psychology.)

Zubiri, X. (1944) *Naturaleza, Historia, Dios* (Nature, History, God), Madrid: Editorial Nacional. (The first presentation, albeit in an embryonic form, of Zubiri's idea of man as an 'animal of realities'.)

* —— (1962) *Sobre la Esencia* (On Essence), Madrid: Sociedad de Estudios y Publicaciones. (Develops the fundamental concepts of Zubiri's philosophical system – a key work to understand this author.)

* —— (1980) *Inteligencia Sentiente* (Sentient Intelligence), Madrid: Alianza Editorial, 3 vols. (In this trilogy the author's philosophy and his development of what he calls 'feeling intelligence' reach their apex.)

Translated by Dominic Moran and
Gemma Belmonte Talero

JOSÉ LUIS ABELLÁN

77

SPEAKER'S INTENTION

see COMMUNICATION AND INTENTION

SPECIES

The diversity of life is not seamless but comes in relatively discrete packages, species. Is that packaging real, or an artefact of our limited temporal perspective on the history of life? If all living forms are descended from one or a few ancestors, there may be no real distinction between living and ancestral forms, or between closely related living animals.

Received wisdom holds that species are the 'units of evolution', for it is they that evolve. They are the upshot *of evolutionary processes, but, if species and not just their component organisms compete with one another, they are also important* agents *in the evolutionary process. If so, species are real units in nature, not arbitrary segmentations of seamless variation.*

The 'species problem' has been approached from two angles. One focus has been on specific taxa of the tree of life. What would settle whether some arbitrarily chosen organism is a member of homo sapiens *or* canis familiaris*? This is sometimes known as the 'species taxon' problem. An alternate way of approaching diversity has been to ask what all species have in common. What do all the populations we think of as species share? This is the 'species category' problem.*

One idea is to group organisms into species by appealing to the overall similarity. This 'phenetic' conception is in retreat. Most contemporary species definitions are relational, the animals that compose pan troglodytes *are a species, not because they are all very similar (they are very like the pygmy chimps as well) but because of their relations amongst themselves and with their ancestors. The most famous relational definition is the 'biological species concept', according to which conspecific organisms are organisms that can interbreed, however different they look.*

Relational species definitions aim to define a category of theoretical and explanatory interest to evolutionary and ecological theory. Given that there are many explanatory interests, one problem in evaluating these accounts is to determine whether they are genuinely rivals.

1 **Species as historical entities**
2 **The biological species concept**
3 **Phylogenetic species concepts**

1 Species as historical entities

There have been three main views of the species category. So-called 'phenetic' species concepts define species membership and difference by appeal to some measure of overall morphological, genetic or behavioural similarity. This view has slid from favour. First, there are many measures of similarity at any one time. These give different results and choice between them is arbitrary. Second, the similarity conception of species entails that the segmentation of the tree of life is arbitrary. As the population gradually changes there are many ways of dividing up the twig, many different similarity groupings, on the tree of life leading to us. The distinction between *homo sapiens* and *homo erectus* emerges as nothing but a curator's convenience. Third, the collections of organisms so recognized would be of no particular evolutionary significance. If species are just collections of similar organisms, measured by one of the many different similarity measures, the species category is not a natural kind.

The alternatives accept some version of the Ghiselin (1974) and Hull (1978) proposal that particular species are defined by their histories. 'Platypus' names a segment of the tree of life. Species come into existence, change, and go extinct. Whereas any appropriately latticed arrangement of carbon atoms is a diamond, a *rattus rattus* lookalike produced through convergent evolution near Alpha Centauri is not a member of the rat species. But to say that species are historical kinds is one thing, to say what historical kinds, another. Why do we regard *canis familiaris* as a single species rather than as a group of sister species? What do we need to find out to determine whether the Neanderthals were a separate species of *homo*, or a mere subspecies of *homo sapiens*?

The biological species concept offers one answer to this question: a species is a population of actually or potentially interbreeding organisms. Coexisting with the biological species concept are a plethora of *phylogenetic species concepts*. These all identify species with segments of lineages of ancestral/descendent populations. Species are segments of a phylogenetic tree. Which segments? Proponents of phylogenetic definitions differ in their proposals for specifying the depth of the lineage in time, and its cross-section at a time.

One of our problems is to determine the extent to which the biological species concept genuinely competes with the variants of the phylogenetic concept. I, like many, think the phylogenetic and biological species concepts divide the labour between them. Species are chunks of the genealogical nexus between speciation events. The biological species concept gives us an account of speciation events, that is, the process through which a single ancestral species becomes two or more descendent species.

2   The biological species concept

The biological species concept takes the reproductive community to be central to the role of species as evolutionary units. Adaptation and speciation require some isolating mechanism so that an incipient species, a small population in a new selective regime, can preserve in its gene pool the evolutionary innovations that develop within it. An unprotected gene pool will be diluted by migration. The special genetic information will disappear if there is substantial flow between it and the parent population. There can be no special suite of adaptations without some form of isolation; no protection of that suite of adaptations without entrenching that isolation which erects permanent barriers between old and descendant populations. The biological species concept identifies a category of populations – reproductively isolated populations – that can evolve distinctive adaptations.

This proposal faces problems important enough to show that the biological species concept is at best an incomplete account of the nature of species.

First, the notion of a reproductively isolated community is an idealisation, and we can legitimately choose different idealisations. We have to bear in mind two problems. Lineages can be genuinely separate despite some gene flow. There are occasional 'freak' crossings. Major Mitchell cockatoos occasionally hybridise with galahs, but these two lineages are distinct. Lineage-crossing is common amongst plants, amongst whom gene flow across species boundaries is common. There are more problematic cases. As a consequence of human modification of river ecologies in New Zealand, black stilts now hybridise with pied stilts sufficiently often to threaten the survival of the black stilt lineage – if it is a lineage. But we are faced not just with freak crossings but pseudo-division. Groups which merely happen to breed only amongst themselves do not constitute a new lineage. Royal families are members of *homo sapiens* however unsullied their blood lines. So the reproductive criterion yields no unique segmentation of organisms into species. The notion of 'potentially interbreeding' neither is nor can be made fully precise (Kitcher 1989; O'Hara 1993). There is no unique count of protected genetic pools. Gene flow really does come in degrees.

Second, the limitation of gene flow is just one factor that make a lineage 'cohesive'. A buffered gene pool is not all that matters in explaining the distinctness and common fate of a group of popula-tions. Both phylogeny, shared environment, and exposure to a common selective regime must equally be part of the cohesiveness of a species. Ehrlich and Raven (1969) show that in many species gene flow is very limited between local populations ('demes'). So we can have cohesiveness with little flow.

A third problem concerns time. The biological species concept seems to give no good way of segmenting a lineage over time that recognizes that the *Erectus/Sapiens* distinction is a real division in a continuous lineage. It gives no good way of deciding whether organisms living at different times are members of the same species. Perhaps we might suppose that an organism ceases to be conspecific with a member of a later generation if it would not recognize that changed organism as a potential mate. But then, in a gradually evolving lineage the segmentation into species would depend on the choice of baseline. The biological species concept needs supplementation. The interbreeding criterion should not be applied to organisms at different times. If Abe and Adolf are members of different generations they are in the same species, if Adolf has descended from organisms conspecific with Abe by the interbreeding criterion and no speciation event has intervened in the genealogical tree.

Finally, the biological species concept is mute in the face of obligatorily asexual organisms. These are not so rare or unimportant that they can be fudged away as a minor exception.

3   Phylogenetic species concepts

The basic idea of phylogenetic species concepts is to identify a species with a segment of a phylogenetic tree between two speciation events, or between speciation and extinction. Two organisms are members of the same species if they are part of the same lineage, and no speciation event has separated them. On this view, two conspecific organisms could be morphologically very different from one another, so long as the lineage of which they are part has not split in the course of its evolutionary transformation. Phylogenetic species definitions therefore owe us an account of speciation, extinction, and a method for counting lineages. Granted satisfactory solutions to these problems, phylogenetic accounts have clear attractions. They may apply to both sexual and asexual species. If a suitable way of individuating lineages can be developed, a phylogenetic account might be noncommittal on the causes of 'cohesion'. There is some advantage to that if in different lineages, gene flow, stabilising selection and phyloge-netic inertia have different weights in establishing cohesion. The idea is that the phylogenetic species concept is founded in the objective branching *pattern* of nature rather than in a theory of evolutionary *process*. Humans are not conspecific with protists even though we descend from them because there exist punctuations of the tree in which lineages split into descendent lineages.

But it is not clear that this potential advantage is actual. Consider a minor evolutionary pattern: the fissuring or pseudo-fissuring of the lineage of the Australian brushtail possum into many Australian populations and assorted populations in the New Zealand archipelago. Which of these populations are new species? The phylogenetic species concept – in some incarnations – gives the crazy result that most are. Some proposals for counting lineages rely on the idea of a population having a separate historical fate or entering a new adaptive zone (Van Valen 1976; Wiley 1978). If that were right, the New Zealand possum population would be a separate species, as their adaptive zone and fate is distinct from the Australian population. So would be tiny populations that persisted for a few generations on small islands or isolated fragments of bushland. Phylogenetic identification of independent lineages seem to either count too finely, be excessively vague, or to tacitly depend on the biological species concept, and thus to inherit its problems with asexual species.

So the most obvious way of delimiting chunks of a tree is through appeal to reproductive isolation. Yet this ignores asexual species. Even if asexuality were rare, the problem would be serious. Reproductive isolation is alleged to be constitutive of being a species, not merely a good symptom of it (Kitcher 1989). A heroic solution would be to deny that asexual organisms are in species. This is heroic, for we would then have to explain just why 'pseudo-populations' of, for example, some whiptail lizards seem to be species. Moreover, and more seriously the distinction between asexuality and sexuality is not sharp. Rather, asexuality is the endpoint of a continuum of degrees of gene flow whose other point is the promiscuity of plant hybridisation (Templeton 1989).

An ideal response would be to find a genuine equivalent in asexual organisms of reproductive isolation amongst sexual ones. We could try to find string to bundle the clones together, and an equivalent of the attainment of isolation to underwrite the segmentation of the bundles into two. Some version of Templeton's 'cohesion' species concept may do the job: Templeton argues that in most species 'cohesion' – the clumping in the space of possible organisms which allows us to recognize species in the first place – is produced by ecology and selection, not just gene flow. Asexual species might be cohesive just in virtue

of these other forces, though it remains unclear what the asexual equivalent of speciation would be.

Kitcher (1989) urges on us a more radical moral: multiply species concepts. He thinks it plain that asexual organisms clump into species. The phenetic concept of morphological distinctness is *constitutive* of the species category for asexual organisms. Why then not say that it is constitutive of at least *a species category* for sexual organisms? If Kitcher is right about asexual organisms, the same conclusion is not forced elsewhere. In both sexual and asexual lineages, clumped diversity is a residue of a historical process. But with sexual species that historical process is one in which gene exchange and a protected gene pool played a central role. That process is important enough to mark by regarding sexual organisms as clumped into species in a different sense than are asexual organisms. It is not at all obvious that a group of similar asexual clones form an evolutionary unit; the sexually reproducing population does.

We might have good reasons to consider organisms grouped by their intrinsic similarities of morphology, physiology or behaviour. It is perfectly appropriate to formulate hypotheses about the molecular mechanisms of, say, the retroviruses whether or not they all spring from the same stock, a hypothesis about the mechanism of reverse transcription could still be true and their distinctive adaptation might have a single molecular basis. Not all biology is historical biology. Even so, the validity of physiological groups in functional biology does not show that there is a notion of species defined by appeal to a shared physiology.

What emerges from all this? The most plausible account of species seems to be an evolutionary account: species are lineages between speciation events. The biological species concept re-emerges as an account of the process by which a lineage divides into two. Lineages split when their components become reproductive isolated, one from another. Lineages converge when two formerly isolated lineages become a reproductive community through, for example, hybridisation. Two central problems remain to be solved. First, the inherent roughness of the notion of reproductive isolation means that the identification of species is in principle, not just in practice less sharp than some have claimed. Second, the status of asexuality remains problematic.

See also: EVOLUTION, THEORY OF; TAXONOMY

References and further reading

* Ehrlich, P. and Raven, P. (1969) 'The Differentiation of Populations', *Science* 165: 1228–32. (A classic

statement of a problem for the biological species concept: many species seem to preserve their distinctive suite of morphological, physiological and behavioural traits – their cohesion – with very little gene flow within them.)

Ereshevsky, M. (ed.) (1992) *The Units of Evolution: Essays on the Nature of Species*, Cambridge, MA: MIT Press. (An excellent collection of most of the central papers on the species problem.)

* Ghiselin, M. (1974) 'A Radical Solution to the Species Problem', *Systematic Zoology* 23: 535–44. (The first clear statement of the idea that species are individuals not sets, an idea developed further in Hull 1978.)

* Hull, D. (1978) 'A Matter of Individuality', *Philosophy of Science* 45: 335–60. (One of the two classic defences of the idea that a species' essential property is its history. This idea was originally formulated as the claim that a species is not a set of organisms but is instead, like the British Empire, a single thing though one scattered in space and time. It is now widely agreed that this is not the best formulation of that insight. Species may be kinds or sets, but if so the membership condition is historical.)

* Kitcher, P. (1989) 'Some Puzzles about Species', in M. Ruse (ed.) *What the Philosophy of Biology Is*, Dordrecht: Kluwer, 183–208. (A defence of the idea that the notion of species is equivocal. We have many good species concepts, and we should not suppose that one is the 'right' concept.)

Mayr, E. (1988) *Towards a New Philosophy of Biology*, Cambridge, MA: Harvard University Press. (Mayr is the most famous defender of the biological species concept. Parts VI and VII defends his views on species and speciation against all comers.)

* O'Hara, R.J. (1993) 'Systematic Generalization, Historical Fate and The Species Problem', *Systematic Biology* 42: 231–46. (A very clear demonstration of the inherent imprecision of the notion of reproductive isolation, and of the consequences of that imprecision for the notion of species.)

Ridley, M. (1989) 'The Cladistic Solution to the Species Problem', *Biology and Philosophy* 4: 1–16. (Defends the simplest possible version of a phylogenetic species definition.)

* Templeton, A. (1989) 'The Meaning of Species and Speciation: A Genetic Perspective' in D. Otte and J. Endler (eds) *Speciation and Its Consequences*, Sunderland, MA: Sinauer, 3–27. (Following on from Ehrlich and Raven 1969 in arguing that species must be defined by appeal to all the factors that make species cohesive, not just gene flow.)

* Van Valen, L. (1976) 'Ecological Species, Multispecies and Oaks', *Taxon* 25: 233–9. (Defends a version of the phylogenetic species definition in which ecological factors play the central role in counting lineages.)

* Wiley, E. (1978) 'The Evolutionary Species Concept Reconsidered', *Systematic Zoology* 27: 17–26. (Wiley defends a version of the phylogenetic species definition in which the notion of a shared historical fate plays the central role in counting lineages.)

KIM STERELNY

SPEECH ACTS

Making a statement may be the paradigmatic use of language, but there are all sorts of other things we can do with words. We can make requests, ask questions, give orders, make promises, give thanks, offer apologies and so on. Moreover, almost any speech act is really the performance of several acts at once, distinguished by different aspects of the speaker's intention; there is the act of saying something, what one does in saying it, such as requesting or promising, and how one is trying to affect one's audience.

The theory of speech acts is partly taxonomic and partly explanatory. It must systematically classify types of speech acts and the ways in which they can succeed or fail. It must reckon with the fact that the relationship between the words being used and the force of their utterance is often oblique. For example, the sentence 'This is a pig sty' might be used nonliterally to state that a certain room is messy, and further to demand indirectly that it be tidied up. Even when this sentence is used literally and directly, say to describe a certain area of a farmyard, the content of its utterance is not fully determined by its linguistic meaning – in particular, the meaning of the word 'this' does not determine which area is being referred to. A major task for the theory of speech acts is to account for how speakers can succeed in what they do despite the various ways in which linguistic meaning underdetermines use.

In general, speech acts are acts of communication. To communicate is to express a certain attitude, and the type of speech act being performed corresponds to the type of attitude being expressed. For example, a statement expresses a belief, a request expresses a desire, and an apology expresses a regret. As an act of communication, a speech act succeeds if the audience identifies, in accordance with the speaker's intention, the attitude being expressed.

Some speech acts, however, are not primarily acts of communication and have the function not of communicating but of affecting institutional states of affairs. They can do so in either of two ways. Some officially judge something to be the case, and others actually make something the case. Those of the first kind include judges' rulings, referees' decisions and assessors' appraisals, and the latter include sentencing, bequeathing and appointing. Acts of both kinds can be performed only in certain ways under certain circumstances by those in certain institutional or social positions.

1 **Levels of speech acts**
2 **Communicative and conventional speech acts**
3 **Types of speech acts**
4 **Direct, indirect and nonliteral speech acts**
5 **Philosophical importance of speech act theory**

1 Levels of speech acts

How language represents the world has long been, and still is, a major concern of philosophers of language. Many thinkers, such as Leibniz, Frege, Russell, the early Wittgenstein and Carnap, have thought that understanding the structure of language could illuminate the nature of reality. However noble their concerns, such philosophers have implicitly assumed, as J.L. AUSTIN complains at the beginning of *How to Do Things with Words* (1962), that 'the business of a (sentence) can only be to "describe" some state of affairs, or to "state some fact", which it must do either truly or falsely'. Austin reminds us that we perform all sorts of 'speech acts' besides making statements, and that there are other ways for them to go wrong or be 'infelicitous' besides not being true. The later Wittgenstein also came to think of language not primarily as a system of representation but as a vehicle for all sorts of social activity. 'Don't ask for the meaning', he admonished, 'ask for the use'. But it was Austin who presented the first systematic account of the use of language. And whereas Wittgenstein could be charged with conflating meaning and use, Austin was careful to separate the two. He distinguished the meaning (and reference) of the words used from the speech acts performed by the speaker using them.

Austin's attention was first attracted to what he called 'explicit performative utterances', in which one uses sentences like 'I nominate', 'You're fired', 'The meeting is adjourned' and 'You are hereby sentenced...' to perform acts of the very sort named by the verb, such as nominating, firing, adjourning, or sentencing (see PERFORMATIVES). Austin held that performatives are neither true nor false, unlike what he called 'constatives'. However, he came to realize that constatives work just like performatives. Just as a suggestion or an apology can be made by uttering 'I suggest...' or 'I apologize...', so an assertion or a prediction can be made by uttering 'I assert...' or 'I

predict...'. Accordingly, the distinction between constative and performative utterances is, in AUSTIN's general theory of speech acts, superseded by that between saying something and what one does in saying it. This broader distinction applies to both statements and other sorts of speech acts, and takes into account the fact that one does not have to say 'I suggest...' to make a suggestion, 'I apologize...' to make an apology, or 'I assert...' to make an assertion.

The theory of speech acts aims to do justice to the fact that even though words (phrases, sentences) encode information, people do more things with words than convey information, and that when people do convey information, they often convey more than their words encode. Although the focus of speech act theory has been on utterances, especially those made in conversational and other face-to-face situations, the phrase 'speech act' should be taken as a generic term for any sort of language use, oral or otherwise. Speech acts, whatever the medium of their performance, fall under the broad category of intentional action, with which they share certain general features (see ACTION; INTENTION §5). An especially pertinent feature is that when one acts intentionally, generally one has a set of nested intentions. For instance, having arrived home without one's keys, one might push a button with the intention not just of pushing the button but of ringing a bell, rousing one's spouse and, ultimately, getting into one's house. The single bodily movement involved in pushing the button comprises a multiplicity of actions, each corresponding to a different one of the nested intentions. Similarly, speech acts are not just acts of producing certain sounds.

Austin identifies three distinct levels of action beyond the act of utterance itself. He distinguished the act *of* saying something, what one does *in* saying it, and what one does *by* saying it, and dubs these the 'locutionary', the 'illocutionary' and the 'perlocutionary' act, respectively. Suppose, for example, that a bartender utters the words, 'The bar will be closed in five minutes.' He is thereby performing the locutionary act of saying that the bar (that is, the one he is tending) will be closed in five minutes (from the time of utterance). Notice that what the bartender is saying, the content of his locutionary act, is not fully determined by the words he is using, for they do not specify the bar in question or the time of the utterance. In saying this, the bartender is performing the illocutionary act of informing the patrons of the bar's imminent closing and perhaps also the act of urging them to order a last drink. Whereas the upshot of these illocutionary acts is understanding on the part of the audience, perlocutionary acts are performed with the intention of producing a further effect. The bartender intends to be performing the perlocutionary acts of causing the patrons to believe that the bar is about to close and of getting them to order one last drink. He is performing all these speech acts, at all three levels, just by uttering certain words.

There seems to be a straightforward relationship in this example between the words uttered ('The bar will be closed in five minutes'), what is thereby said, and the act of informing the patrons that the bar will close in five minutes. Less direct is the connection between the utterance and the act of urging the patrons to order one last drink. Clearly there is no linguistic connection here, for the words make no mention of drinks or of ordering. This indirect connection is inferential. The patrons must infer that the bartender intends to be urging them to leave and, indeed, it seems that the reason his utterance counts as an act of that sort is that he is speaking with this intention. There is a similarly indirect connection when an utterance of 'It's getting cold in here' is made not merely as a statement about the temperature but as a request to close the window or as a proposal to go somewhere warmer. Whether it is intended (and is taken) as a request or as a proposal depends on contextual information that the speaker relies on the audience to rely on. This is true even when the connection between word and deed is more direct than in the above example, for the form of the sentence uttered may fail to determine just which sort of illocutionary act is being performed. Consider, by analogy, the fact that in shaking hands we can, depending on the circumstances, do any one of several different things: introduce ourselves, greet each other, seal a deal, or bid farewell. Similarly, a given sentence can be used in a variety of ways, so that, for example, 'I will call a lawyer' could be used as a prediction, a promise, or a warning. How one intends it determines the sort of act it is.

2 Communicative and conventional speech acts

The examples considered thus far suggest that performing a speech act, in particular an illocutionary act, is a matter of having a certain communicative intention in uttering certain words. Such an act succeeds, and the intention with which it is performed is fulfilled, if the audience recognizes that intention. Not by magic, of course – one must choose one's words in such a way that their utterance makes one's intention recognizable under the circumstances. However, as illustrated above, the utterance need not encode one's intention. So, in general, understanding an utterance is not merely a matter of decoding it.

A specifically communicative intention is a reflex-ive intention, of the sort characterized by H.P. Grice (1989) (see COMMUNICATION AND INTENTION). This is an intention part of whose content is that it be recognized, indeed be recognized partly on the basis that this is intended. Accordingly, it is an intention whose fulfilment consists in its recognition. This feature distinguishes acts of communication from most sorts of acts, whose success does not depend on anyone's recognizing the intention with which they are performed. One cannot succeed in running a marathon just by virtue of someone's recognizing one's intention to do so, but one can succeed in stating something, requesting something, and so on, by virtue of one's addressee recognizing that one is stating it, requesting it, or whatever. This is success at the illocutionary level. It is a further matter, a condition on the success of the perlocutionary act, whether the addressee believes what one states or does what one requests.

Now Austin did not take into account the central role of speakers' intentions and hearers' inferences. He supposed that the successful performance of an illocutionary act is a matter of convention, not intention. Indeed, he held that the use of a sentence with a certain illocutionary force is conventional in the peculiar sense that this force can be 'made explicit by the performative formula'. P.F. Strawson (1964) argues that in making this claim Austin was overly impressed by the special case of utterances that affect institutional states of affairs, and should have not taken them as a model of illocutionary acts in general. Austin was especially struck by the character of explicit performative utterances, in which one uses a verb that names the very type of act one is performing. For them he developed an account of what it takes for such acts to be performed success-fully and felicitously, classifying the various things that can go wrong as 'flaws', 'hitches' and other sorts of 'infelicities'. It is only in certain conventionally designated circumstances and by people in certain positions that certain utterances can have the force they do. For example, only in certain circumstances does a jury foreman's pronouncement of 'Guilty' or 'Not guilty' count as a verdict, a legislator's 'Aye' or 'Nay' as a vote, and a baseball umpire's cry of 'Y'er out' as calling a runner out. In these cases it is only by conforming to a convention that an utterance of a certain form counts as the performance of an act of a certain sort. However, as Strawson argues, most illocutionary acts succeed not by conformity to convention but by recognition of intention. They are not conventional except in the irrelevant sense that the words and sentences being used have their linguistic meanings by virtue of convention (see LANGUAGE, CONVENTIONALITY OF).

Strawson's argument raises a serious problem for theories inspired by Austin's view. Consider, for example, the theory advanced by John Searle (1969), who proposes to explain illocutionary forces by means of 'constitutive rules' (conventions) for using 'force-indicating' devices, such as performative verbs and sentential moods. The problem is that the same sorts of illocutionary acts that can be performed by means of such devices can be performed without them. For example, one does not have to use a performative, as in 'I demand that you be quiet', or the imperative mood, as in 'Be quiet!', to demand that someone be quiet. Clearly a theory that relies on rules for using such devices is not equipped to explain the illocutionary forces of utterances lacking such devices. No such difficulty arises for a theory according to which most illocutionary acts are performed not with an intention to conform to a convention but with a communicative intention.

3 Types of speech acts

Pre-theoretically, we think of an act of communication, linguistic or otherwise, as an act of expressing oneself. This rather vague idea can be made more precise if we get more specific about what is being expressed. Take the case of an apology. If you utter '(I'm) sorry I didn't call back' and intend this as an apology, you are expressing regret for not returning a phone call. An apology just *is* the act of (verbally) expressing regret for, and thereby acknowledging, something one did that might have harmed the hearer. An apology is communicative because it is intended to be taken as expressing a certain attitude, in this case regret. It succeeds as such if it is so taken. In general, an act of communication succeeds if it is taken as intended. That is, it must be understood or, in Austin's words, 'produce uptake'. With an apology, this is a matter of the addressee recognizing the speaker's intention to be expressing regret for some deed or omission. Using a special device such as the performative 'I apologize' may of course facilitate understanding (understanding is correlative with communicating), but in general this is unnecessary. Communicative success is achieved if the speaker chooses their words in such a way that the hearer will, under the circumstances of utterance, recognize their communicative intention. So, for example, if you spill some beer on someone and say 'Oops' in the right way, your utterance will be taken as an apology.

In saying something one generally intends more than just to communicate – getting oneself understood is intended to produce some effect on the listener. However, our speech act vocabulary can obscure this fact. When one apologizes, for example, one may intend not merely to express regret but also to seek forgiveness. Seeking forgiveness is, strictly speaking, distinct from apologizing, even though one utterance is the performance of an act of both types. As an apology, the utterance succeeds if taken as expressing regret for the deed in question: as an act of seeking forgiveness, it succeeds if forgiveness is thereby obtained. Speech acts, being perlocutionary as well as illocutionary, generally have some ulterior purpose, but they are distinguished primarily by their illocutionary type, such as asserting, requesting, promising and apologizing, which in turn is distinguished by the type of attitude expressed. The perlocutionary act is a matter of trying to get the hearer to form some correlative attitude and in some cases to act in a certain way. For example, a statement expresses a belief and normally has the further purpose of getting the addressee to form the same belief. A request expresses a desire for the addressee to do a certain thing and normally aims for the addressee to intend to and, indeed, actually do that thing. A promise expresses the speaker's firm intention to do something, together with the belief that by their utterance they are obliged to do it, and normally aims further for the addressee to expect, and to feel entitled to expect, them to do it.

Statements, requests, promises and apologies are examples of the four major categories of communicative illocutionary acts: *constatives*, *directives*, *commissives* and *acknowledgements*. This is the nomenclature used by Bach and Harnish (1979) who develop a detailed taxonomy in which each type of illocutionary act is individuated by the type of attitude expressed (in some cases there are constraints on the content as well). There is no generally accepted terminology here, and Bach and Harnish borrow the terms 'constative' and 'commissive' from Austin and 'directive' from Searle. They adopt the term 'acknowledgement', over Austin's 'behabitive' and Searle's 'expressive', for apologies, greetings, congratulations, and so on, which express an attitude regarding the hearer occasioned by some event that is thereby being acknowledged, often in satisfaction of a social expectation. Here are assorted examples of each type:

Constatives. Affirming, alleging, announcing, answering, attributing, claiming, classifying, concurring, confirming, conjecturing, denying, disagreeing, disclosing, disputing, identifying, informing, insisting, predicting, ranking, reporting, stating, stipulating.

Directives. Advising, admonishing, asking, begging, dismissing, excusing, forbidding, instructing, ordering, permitting, requesting, requiring, suggesting, urging, warning.

Commissives. Agreeing, guaranteeing, inviting, offering, promising, swearing, volunteering.

Acknowledgements. Apologizing, condoling, congratulating, greeting, thanking, accepting (acknowledging an acknowledgement).

Bach and Harnish spell out the correlation between type of illocutionary act and type of expressed attitude. In many cases, such as answering, disputing, excusing and agreeing, as well as all types of acknowledgement, the act and the attitude it expresses presuppose a specific conversational or other social circumstance.

For types of acts that are distinguished by the type of attitude expressed, there is no need to invoke the notion of convention to explain how it can succeed. The act can succeed if the hearer recognizes the attitude being expressed, such as a belief in the case of a statement and a desire in the case of a request. Any further effect it has on the hearer, such as being believed or being complied with, or just being taken as sincere, is not essential to its being a statement or a request. Thus an utterance can succeed as an act of communication even if the speaker does not possess the attitude they are expressing: communication is one thing, sincerity another. Communicating is as it were just putting an attitude on the table; sincerity is actually possessing the attitude one is expressing. Correlatively, the hearer can understand the utterance without regarding it as sincere – for example, take it as an apology, as expressing regret for something, without believing that the speaker regrets having done the deed in question. Getting one's audience to believe that one actually possesses the attitude one is expressing is not an illocutionary but a perlocutionary act.

4 Direct, indirect and nonliteral speech acts

As Austin observed, the content of a locutionary act (what is said) is not always determined by what is meant by the sentence being uttered. Ambiguous words or phrases need to be disambiguated (see AMBIGUITY) and the references of indexical and other context-sensitive expressions need to be fixed in order for what is said to be determined fully (see DEMONSTRATIVES AND INDEXICALS). Moreover, what is said does not determine the illocutionary act(s) being performed. We can perform a speech act (1) directly or indirectly, by way of performing another speech act, (2) literally or nonliterally, depending on how we are using our words, and (3) explicitly or inexplicitly, depending on whether we fully spell out what we mean.

These three contrasts are distinct and should not be confused. The first two concern the relation between the utterance and the speech act(s) thereby performed. In indirection a single utterance is the performance of one illocutionary act by way of performing another. For example, we can make a request or give permission by way of making a statement, say by uttering 'I am getting thirsty' or 'It doesn't matter to me', and we can make a statement or give an order by way of asking a question, such as 'Will the sun rise tomorrow?' or 'Can you clean up your room?' When an illocutionary act is performed indirectly, it is performed by way of performing some other one directly. In the case of nonliteral utterances, we do not mean what our words mean but something else instead. With nonliterality the illocutionary act we are performing is not the one that would be predicted just from the meanings of the words being used, as with likely utterances of 'My mind got derailed' or 'You can stick that in your ear'. Occasionally utterances are both nonliteral and indirect. For example, you might utter 'I love the sound of your voice' to tell someone nonliterally (ironically) that you cannot stand the sound of their voice and thereby indirectly to ask them to stop singing.

Nonliterality and indirection are the two main ways in which the semantic content of a sentence can fail to determine the full force and content of the illocutionary act being performed in using the sentence. They rely on the same sorts of processes that Grice discovered in connection with what he called 'conversational implicature' (see IMPLICATURE), which, as is clear from Grice's examples, is nothing more than the special case of nonliteral or indirect constatives made with the use of indicative sentences. A few of Grice's examples illustrate nonliterality, such as 'He was a little intoxicated', used to explain why a man smashed some furniture, but most of them are indirect statements, such as 'There is a garage around the corner', used to tell someone where to get petrol, and 'Mr X's command of English is excellent, and his attendance has been regular', giving the high points in a letter of recommendation. These are all examples in which what is meant is not determined by what is said. However, Grice overlooks a different kind of case, marked by contrast (3) listed above.

There are many sentences whose standard uses are not strictly determined by their meanings but are not implicatures or figurative uses either. For example, if one's spouse says 'I will be home later', they are likely to mean that they will be home later that night, not merely some time in the future. In such cases what one means is an *expansion* of what one says, in that adding more words ('tonight', in the example) would have made what was meant fully explicit. In other cases, such as 'Jack is ready' and 'Jill is late', the sentence does not express a complete proposition. There must be something which Jack is being claimed to be ready for and something which Jill is being claimed to be late for. In these cases what one means is a *completion* of what one says. In neither sort of case is a particular word or phrase being used nonliterally and there is no indirection. They both exemplify what may be called 'impliciture', since part of what is meant is communicated not explicitly but implicitly, by way of expansion or completion.

5 Philosophical importance of speech act theory

The theory of speech acts has applications to philosophy in general, but these can only be illustrated here. In ethics, for example, it has been supposed that sentences containing words like 'good' and 'right' are used not to describe but to commend, hence that such sentences are not used to make statements and that questions of value and morals are not matters of fact. This line of argument is fallacious. Sentences used for ethical evaluation, such as 'Loyalty is good' and 'Abortion is wrong', are no different in form from other indicative sentences. Whatever the status of their contents, they are standardly used to make statements. This leaves open the possibility that there is something fundamentally problematic about their contents. Perhaps such statements are factually defective and, despite syntactic appearances, are neither true nor false. However, this is a metaphysical issue about the status of the properties to which ethical predicates purport to refer. It is not the business of the philosophy of language to determine whether or not there are such properties as goodness or rightness and whether or not the goodness of loyalty and the rightness of abortion are matters of fact. The above argument is but one illustration of what Searle calls the 'speech act fallacy'. He also identifies examples of the 'assertion fallacy', whereby conditions of making an assertion are confused with what is asserted. For example, one might fallaciously argue, on the grounds that because one would not assert that one believes something if one was prepared to assert that one knows it, that knowing does not entail believing. Grice identifies the same fallacy in a parallel argument, according to which seeming to have a certain feature entails not actually having that feature (see ORDINARY LANGUAGE PHILOSOPHY).

For philosophy of language in particular, the theory of speech acts underscores the importance of the distinction between language use and linguistic meaning (see PRAGMATICS; SEMANTICS). This distinction sharpens the formulation of questions about the nature of linguistic knowledge, by separating questions about capacities exercised in linguistic interaction from those specific to knowledge of language itself. A parallel distinction, between speaker reference and linguistic reference (see REFERENCE), provokes the question of to what extent linguistic expressions refer independently of speakers' use of them to refer. It is common, for example, for philosophers to describe expressions like 'the car', 'Robert Jones' and 'they' as having different references in different contexts, but it is arguable that this is merely a misleading way of saying that speakers use such expressions to refer to different things in different contexts.

See also: GRICE, H.P.; LANGUAGE, PHILOSOPHY OF; PRAGMATICS; SEMANTICS

References and further reading

* Austin, J.L. (1962) *How to Do Things with Words*, Cambridge, MA: Harvard University Press. (Develops the distinction between performative and constative utterances into the first systematic account of speech acts.)

Bach, K. (1994) 'Conversational Implicature', *Mind and Language* 9: 124–62. (Identifies the middle ground between explicit utterances and Gricean implicatures.)

* Bach, K. and Harnish, R.M. (1979) *Linguistic Communication and Speech Acts*, Cambridge, MA: MIT Press. (Combines elements of Austin's taxonomy and Grice's theory of conversation into a systematic account of the roles of the speaker's communicative intention and the hearer's inference in literal, nonliteral and indirect uses of sentences to perform speech acts.)

* Grice, H.P. (1989) *Studies in the Way of Words*, Cambridge, MA: Harvard University Press. (The essays on meaning and conversational implicature provide a framework for distinguishing speaker meaning from linguistic meaning and for explaining their relationship.)

* Searle, J.R. (1969) *Speech Acts: An Essay in the Philosophy of Language*, Cambridge: Cambridge University Press. (Presents a theory of speech acts relying on the notion of constitutive rules.)

* Strawson, P.F. (1964) 'Intention and Convention in Speech Acts', *Philosophical Review* 73: 439–60. (Applies Grice's account of meaning to support the claim that most speech acts are communicative rather than conventional, as Austin had suggested.)

Tsohatzidis, S.L. (ed.) (1994) *Foundations of Speech Act Theory: Philosophical and Linguistic Perspectives*, London: Routledge. (Collection of original essays on outstanding problems in the field, with useful bibliography.)

KENT BACH

SPEECH, FREEDOM OF

see FREEDOM OF SPEECH

SPENCER, HERBERT (1820–1903)

Herbert Spencer is chiefly remembered for his classical liberalism and his evolutionary theory. His fame was considerable during the mid- to late-nineteenth century, especially in the USA, which he visited in 1882 to be lionized by New York society as the prophetic philosopher of capitalism. In Britain, however, Spencer's reputation suffered two fatal blows towards the end of his life. First, collectivist legislation was introduced to protect citizens from the ravages of the industrial revolution, and Spencer's spirited defence of economic laissez-faire *became discredited. Second, his evolutionary theory, which was based largely on the Lamarckian principle of the inheritance of organic modifications produced by use and disuse, was superseded by Darwin's theory of natural selection. Nearly a century after his death, however, there is renewed interest in his ideas, partly because the world has become more sympathetic to market philosophies, and partly because the application of evolutionary principles to human society has become fashionable once more.*

Spencer was born into a Nonconformist family in Derby, England, and never lost the individualistic temperament conferred by his upbringing. Trained as a civil engineer working for a railway company during the boom years of railway expansion, Spencer's fertile mind soon spread to social and economic issues, and he joined the *Economist* as a sub-editor in 1848. In 1851 the publication of his first book, *Social Statics*, established his reputation as a thinker of extraordinary power and originality. In it he deduced the features of a civilized society from the central principle of justice – the law of equal freedom – that 'every person has freedom to do all that he wills, provided he infringes not the equal freedom of any other man' (1851: 103). This principle of equal freedom, which has been regarded ever since as the cornerstone of classical liberalism, led Spencer to insist on a very narrow role for the state (see LIBERALISM; STATE, THE §§1–2). The state was at best a necessary evil to prevent one person from violating the rights of another – that is, to defend natural rights. *Social Statics* is the definitive text of the minimal or 'nightwatchman' theory of the state.

Spencer subsequently embarked upon an ambitious task of creating a wholly new understanding of philosophy, at the heart of which was the theory of evolution. In *Social Statics* an idea of the evolutionary progress of humanity had been implicitly assumed but not developed. Spencer explicitly applied evolutionary theory in his essay 'The Development Hypothesis' ([1890] 1852). He rejected the religious notion of 'special creation' – that each of the 10 million species had been individually created by God – arguing instead, like Lamarck, that new species emerged as a result of modifications in existing species, brought about by exposure to new conditions. Spencer elaborated this evolutionary theory in his essay 'Progress: its Law and Cause' ([1890] 1857) where he introduced the word 'evolution'. Following Von Baer, Spencer claimed that progress was defined in terms of a change from the homogenous to the heterogeneous. His originality lay in the fact that he saw this 'law' at work across the whole range of natural and human phenomena. The ten volumes of Spencer's *magnum opus*, the 'Synthetic Philosophy', traced the operation of evolutionary principles successively in psychology, metaphysics, biology, sociology and ethics.

In his *Principles of Psychology* (1855), Spencer put forward a Lamarckian explanation of mental development. For example, intelligence was a faculty developed as a result of cumulative modifications of the mind in successive generations of organisms responding to their environment. In *First Principles* (1862), he addressed the vexed question for his Victorian readership of the relation between science and religion. For Spencer, science entailed the deduction of general laws, such as the conservation of energy, which were not empirical generalizations, but necessary truths about empirical phenomena. But these truths could never be completely grasped. We could never know, for example, *why* energy was conserved. Such ultimate questions about the nature of reality formed what Spencer called 'the Unknowable'. Religion yielded similarly unanswerable questions about fundamental issues – such as 'does God exist, and if so, how did He come into existence?' These issues were also part of the Unknowable; Spencer was an agnostic, not an atheist – he rejected anti-evolutionary religious doctrines, but God's existence was not incompatible with his theory of evolution.

In his *Principles of Biology* (1864, 1867) Spencer

acknowledged the centrality of Darwinian natural selection, but insisted that Lamarckian modifications played their part in the evolution of organisms from simple to complex structures. In *Principles of Sociology* (1876–96) he explained how, as humanity advanced, a process of differentiation of functions occurred, and society was gradually transformed from the 'militant' type, which was characterized by authoritarianism, uniformity and status, to the 'industrial' type, which was characterized by liberty, diversity and contract. He made use of the organic analogy (likening society to an organism) to sustain his *laissez-faire* theory, by interpreting organisms as made up of individualistic parts. Finally, in *Principles of Ethics* (1879–93) he gave the law of equal freedom an evolutionary dimension by linking it to the principle that each person ought to experience the full consequences of their actions, both good and bad – a principle which entailed that the fittest survived.

Spencer has left two enduring contributions to philosophy. The first is a highly cogent analysis of the philosophical foundations of classical liberalism. *Social Statics* is a masterpiece of argumentation, not far short of the stature of a Hobbesian or Lockeian text. The second is the evolutionary idea: it was Spencer, not Darwin, who was the founder of the philosophy later known as Social Darwinism, and who coined the term 'the survival of the fittest'. Although Spencer failed to answer many questions raised by his theory of evolution, it cannot be denied that his evolutionary vision marks an important stage in our understanding of social development.

See also: DARWIN, C.R.; EVOLUTION, THEORY OF; EVOLUTIONARY THEORY AND SOCIAL SCIENCE; FREEDOM AND LIBERTY; HOLISM AND INDIVIDUALISM IN HISTORY AND SOCIAL SCIENCE; RELIGION AND SCIENCE; SOCIAL SCIENCE, HISTORY OF PHILOSOPHY OF §10

List of works

Spencer, H. (1851) *Social Statics: or the Conditions Essential to Human Happiness and the First of them Developed*, London: Chapman. (Spencer's best work on political philosophy; hard but rewarding.)
—— (1855) *Principles of Psychology*, London: Williams & Norgate; 4th edn, 1899. (A comprehensive account of mind, intelligence, the nervous system, feelings, perceptions, memory, reasoning, sympathy and realism; very dense.)
—— (1861) *Education, Intellectual, Moral and Physical*, London: Everyman's Library, 1961. (Four very readable, instructive and popular essays extolling the value of natural methods in education.)

—— (1862) *First Principles*, London: Williams & Norgate; 6th edn, 1900. (A work in two parts: 'The Unknowable', which shows how all science led ultimately (like all religion) to a belief in an Absolute that transcended human understanding; and 'Laws of the Knowable' – a statement of the fundamental scientific principles governing the world.)
—— (1864, 1867) *Principles of Biology*, London: Williams & Norgate, 2 vols; 2nd edn, 1898, 1899. (A comprehensive and highly technical account of morphology, physiology, reproduction, growth, development, heredity, variation and evolution.)
—— (1873) *The Study of Sociology*, Ann Arbor, MI: Ann Arbor Paperback, 1961. (A pioneering work of popularization for the discipline of sociology, providing an easy-to-read explanation of the nature and importance of the sociological method; still a standard text.)
—— (1876–96) *Principles of Sociology*, London: Williams & Norgate, vol. 1, 1876; 3rd edn, 1885; vol. 2, part 4, 1879; part 5, 1882; vol. 3, part 6, 1885; parts 7 and 8, 1896. (At 2,300 pages, a massive but very readable study of anthropology, social structure, the family and ceremonial, political, religious, professional and industrial institutions.)
—— (1879–93) *Principles of Ethics*, London: Williams & Norgate, vol. 1, part 1, 1879; parts 2 and 3, 1892; vol. 2, part 4, 1891; parts 5 and 6, 1893. (An evolutionary approach to moral philosophy, in which justice and beneficence are dissected for their social value; readable but much less impressive than *Social Statics*.)
—— (1884) *The Man Versus The State*, repr. with abridged edn of *Social Statics*, London: Williams & Norgate, 1892. (Four highly polemical essays in which Spencer denounces the increasing collectivism of governmental policy in late nineteenth-century Britain; entertaining and thought-provoking.)
—— (1890) *Essays: Scientific, Political and Speculative*, London: Williams & Norgate, 3 vols, revised edition. (A collection of highly accessible articles published by Spencer in leading Victorian periodicals, ranging over science, philosophy, aesthetics, ethics, psychology and politics. Contains 'The Development Hypothesis' (1852) and 'Progress: its Law and Cause' (1857) in vol. 1.)

References and further reading

Gray, J.N. (1982) 'Spencer on the Ethics of Liberty and the Limits of State Interference', *History of Political Thought* 3 (3): 456–81. (Gray argues that Spencer was an 'indirect utilitarian', justifying the law of equal freedom on grounds that it would lead to happiness.)

Gray, T.S. (1988) 'Is Herbert Spencer's Law of Equal Freedom a Utilitarian or a Rights-Based Theory of Justice?', *Journal of the History of Philosophy* 26 (2): 259–78. (Argues that Spencer's law of equal freedom drew its authority neither from utility nor from rights, but from the moral sense.)

—— (1996) *Herbert Spencer's Political Philosophy: Individualism and Organicism*, Hampshire: Avebury. (A comprehensive rebuttal of the repeated charge that Spencer was contradictory in yoking together political individualism and social organicism.)

Hodgson, G. (1993) *Economics and Evolution*, Cambridge: Polity Press. (An authoritative book containing an impressive chapter on Spencer.)

Peel, J.D.Y. (1971) *Herbert Spencer, The Evolution of a Sociologist*, London: Heinemann. (This scholarly book is by far the best critical study of Spencer's ideas. Peel sets these ideas in their historical and intellectual context, and shows their enduring influence.)

Steiner, H. (1982) 'Land, Liberty and the Early Herbert Spencer', *History of Political Thought* 3 (3): 515–33. (Steiner argues that Spencer presents his law of equal freedom as a basic moral axiom – an intrinsic principle of right.)

Taylor, M. (1992) *Men Versus the State – Herbert Spencer and Late Victorian Individualism*, Oxford: Clarendon Press. (A major study of Spencer in relation to other individualists in Britain at the end of the nineteenth century.)

TIM S. GRAY

SPEUSIPPUS (*c.*410–339 BC)

The Greek philosopher Speusippus was the second head of the Platonic Academy. Succeeding his uncle Plato on the latter's death, he developed his thought in interesting directions. He pursued further the tendency in the Academy to mathematicize reality that so annoyed Aristotle, postulating a complicated metaphysics, which started from a 'One' superior to being and all other qualities, and a material principle, 'multiplicity', from the union of which arose, first number, then geometrical entities, and then soul and the material world. In his hands, Plato's doctrines of first principles, of Forms, and of the union of Forms with matter, suffered transformations of which we have only imperfect reports. His later influence was greater on Neo-Pythagoreanism than on 'orthodox' Platonism, until Plotinus.

1 Life and works
2 Metaphysics
3 Ethics and logic

1 Life and works

Speusippus was the son of Plato's sister. He became the second head of the ACADEMY upon his uncle's death in 347 BC, and continued as head till his own death, when he was himself succeeded by Xenocrates. He may have gained the headship for family reasons, but he was a considerable philosopher in his own right, even if his original contributions have been much obscured by the loss of all his writings, and by the hostile criticisms of Aristotle. Other details of his life are hard to come by, since the surviving biography by Diogenes Laertius is most unreliable. Diogenes gives a list of thirty works by Speusippus. Most important, perhaps, were those *On Pleasure, On Philosophy, On the Gods, On the Soul*, and *On Pythagorean Numbers* and a treatise *On Congeners* (*homoia*) in ten volumes, which seems to have exercised the technique of division (*diaeresis*) on most of the species of the natural world. Speusippus apparently also pioneered the linking of Plato's philosophy with that of Pythagoras, which gave an impetus to the later 'Pythagoreanizing' of Platonism (see NEO-PYTHAGOREANISM; PLATONISM, EARLY AND MIDDLE §1).

2 Metaphysics

Speusippus' concern was to carry on the work of Plato, but he developed Platonic doctrine in various interesting ways, which, although legitimate, seem to have found no other partisans in official Platonist circles before Plotinus (although certain Neo-Pythagorean speculations may perhaps be traced to his inspiration). Speusippus accepted the doctrine of two opposite principles, but modified it by laying particular emphasis on their status as 'seeds' or 'potencies' of all things. He argued that what is itself the cause of some quality in other things cannot have that quality itself in the same way, so that if the One is the cause of goodness and being for all other things, it cannot itself properly be termed good or even existent (fr. 42). The One is not even properly a creative principle – the Indefinite Dyad, or 'multiplicity', being credited with that role, as being the cause of all differentiation and individuation. The latter in turn should not be taken as 'evil', any more than the One is 'good' (fr. 44). Good and evil only arise at the level of actualized being, and perhaps only at the level of soul.

Aristotle condemns Speusippus for propounding an 'episodic' universe, with different first principles for every level of being (fr. 30). This is a satirical misrepresentation of the complexity of his position, however, which was based on the argument that a simple and unitary first principle working on an absolutely formless substratum could only produce one thing (for example, numbers), and that this could not account for the multifariousness of the actual cosmos. We must therefore postulate a process by which the product of a higher or more basic union becomes, somehow, the first principle of the next level of being, by uniting, once again, with the material principle.

This may all be less than convincing, but it is much less foolish than unquestioning reliance on Aristotle's testimony would make out. It depends, unfortunately, on accepting as evidence a passage from a work of Iamblichus, *Common Mathematical Theory* (ch. 4), which, although probably, is not indisputably Speusippan. Even Aristotle, however, if his evidence is properly understood, testifies to Speusippus' positing a first principle which is 'not yet existent' (fr. 43).

Exactly how Speusippus modified the Platonic theory of Forms is not clear, but Aristotle claims that he abandoned them in favour of numbers or 'mathematicals' (frs 31, 34). He is probably here only developing the tendency of the late Plato to mathematicize the Forms, while tidying up the confusion between the non-addible 'forms' of numbers, and 'mathematicals' or numbers in the ususal sense (see PLATONISM, EARLY AND MIDDLE §3). The Forms proper, as mathematical (or perhaps rather geometrical) entities, are closely allied with the soul, defined as 'the [F]orm of the omnidimensionally extended' (fr. 54). The soul receives both number and geometrical extension from above, and these, synthesized, become its formal principle, which then combines once again with the material principle to form the physical world.

3 Ethics and logic

In ethics we have various reports of Speusippus' views. He defined happiness (*eudaimonia*) as 'the state of perfection in things natural' (fr. 77), which seems to prefigure the Stoic principle of 'living in accordance with nature' (see STOICISM §17). The ideal to be aimed at is 'freedom from disturbance' (*aochlēsia*) – an anticipation of the Epicurean ideal (see EPICUREANISM §10). This fits his attested belief that pleasure and pain are alike evils (fr. 80), the ideal being a state median between them.

In the sphere of logic, he was, as noted above, primarily an adherent of Platonic division (*diairesis*), but he developed certain distinctive theories. He held that in order to define anything adequately one must know all the differentiae of that thing in respect of

everything with which it is not identical. This would logically involve knowledge of all the relations of the thing in question, however remote, with everything else in the world (fr. 63). This did not lead him to scepticism, however, but rather to a mighty effort to classify, by means of *diairesis*, as much of reality as he could, the results of which are attested in the remains of his *On Congeners*. Apart from this, his distinction between homonyms and synonyms (fr. 68) seems to have provoked Aristotle to his slightly different classification; and in the field of epistemology he seems to anticipate Aristotle in holding that first principles must be apprehended immediately if there is to be any knowledge at all (fr. 73) (see ARISTOTLE §§4, 6).

Finally, mention may be made of Speusippus' work *On Pythagorean Numbers*, a report of whose contents and a longish extract (on the Decad) are preserved in the pseudo-Iamblichean *Theology of Arithmetic* (fr. 28). In the first half of this work Speusippus, depending heavily on the writings of the Pythagorean Philolaus, discussed the 'linear, polygonal, plane and solid numbers', and also the five cosmic figures (of Plato's *Timaeus*). The second half of the work he devoted entirely to the Decad, declaring it to be the most 'natural' and perfect of numbers, and a model for the creator god in his creation of the world. Speusippus would seem thus to identify the 'paradigm' of the *Timaeus* with the Decad, while the creator or 'demiurge' is probably to be identified with the first principle of number. One can see here Speusippus' 'Pythagoreanism' coming out very strongly, as well as that mathematicization of reality to which Aristotle so strongly objected.

References and further reading

Cherniss, H. (1945) *The Riddle of the Early Academy*, Berkeley and Los Angeles, CA: University of California Press. (A useful discussion of Form-numbers and other mysteries can be found in chapter 2, although from a somewhat perverse perspective.)

Dancy, R.M. (1989) 'Ancient Non-Beings: Speusippus and Others', *Ancient Philosophy* 9: 207–44. (A good discussion of Speusippus' metaphysics.)

Dillon, J. (1977) *The Middle Platonists*, London: Duckworth. (Introductory account of Speusippus is given at pages 11–22.)

—— (1984) 'Speusippus in Iamblichus', *Phronesis* 29: 325–32. (Critique of Tarán's *Speusippus of Athens*.)

Iamblichus (early 4th century AD) *Common Mathematical Theory*, ed. N. Festa, *Iamblichi de communi mathematica scientia*, Leipzig: Teubner, 1891; repr. Stuttgart, 1975. (Greek text.)

Merlan, P. (1960) *From Platonism to Neoplatonism*, The Hague: Martinus Nijhoff, 2nd edn. (Speusippus can be found at pages 96–140.)

* Speusippus (*c*.410–339 BC) Fragments, in L. Tarán, *Speusippus of Athens*, Leiden: Brill, 1981. (Collection of fragments, with copious introduction, commentary and bibliography, but somewhat too credulous of Aristotle. Includes *On Congeners*.)

J.M. DILLON

SPINOZA, BENEDICT DE (1632–77)

A Dutch philosopher of Jewish origin, Spinoza was born Baruch de Spinoza in Amsterdam. Initially given a traditional Talmudic education, he was encouraged by some of his teachers to study secular subjects as well, including Latin and modern philosophy. Perhaps as a result of this study, he abandoned Jewish practices and beliefs and, after receiving stern warnings, he was excommunicated from the synagogue in 1656. Alone and without means of support, he Latinized his name and took up the trade of lens grinder with the intention of devoting his life to philosophy. He remained in Amsterdam until 1660, lived for the next decade in nearby villages, and in The Hague from 1670 until his death from consumption in 1677. During these years he worked continuously on his philosophy and discussed it with a small circle of friends and correspondents. His masterpiece, Ethica Ordine Geometrico Demonstrata (Ethics Demonstrated in a Geometrical Manner), was completed in 1675; but because of its radical doctrines, it was only published after his death.

The full scope of Spinoza's Ethics *is not indicated by its title. It begins with a highly abstract account of the nature of substance, which is identified with God, and culminates in an analysis of human beings, their nature and place in the universe, and the conditions of their true happiness. Written in a geometrical form modelled after Euclid, each of its five parts contains a set of definitions, axioms and propositions which are followed by their demonstrations and frequently by explanatory scholia.*

The defining feature of Spinoza's thought is its uncompromising rationalism. Like other philosophers of the time, Spinoza is a rationalist in at least three distinct senses: metaphysical, epistemological and ethical. That is to say, he maintains that the universe embodies a necessary rational order; that, in principle, this order is knowable by the human mind; and that the true good for human beings consists in the knowledge of this order and a life governed by this knowledge. What is distinctive of Spinoza's brand of rationalism, however, is that it allows no place for an inscrutable creator-God distinct from his creation, who acts according to hidden purposes. Instead, Spinoza boldly identifies God with nature, albeit with nature regarded as this necessary rational order rather than as the sum-total of particular things.

In its identification of God with nature, Spinoza's philosophy is also thoroughly naturalistic and deterministic. Since nature (as infinite and eternal) is all-inclusive and all-powerful, it follows that nothing can be or even be conceived apart from it: this means that everything, including human actions and emotions, must be explicable in terms of nature's universal and necessary laws. Moreover, given this identification, it also follows that knowledge of the order of nature specified through these laws is equivalent to the knowledge of God. Thus, in sharp opposition to the entire Judaeo-Christian tradition, Spinoza claims that the human mind is capable of adequate knowledge of God.

The attainment of such knowledge is, however, dependent on the use of the correct method. In agreement with Descartes and Thomas Hobbes (the two modern philosophers who exerted the greatest influence on his thought) and thoroughly in the spirit of the scientific revolution, Spinoza held that the key to this method lies in mathematics. This conviction is obviously reflected in the geometrical form of the Ethics; *but it actually runs much deeper, determining what for Spinoza counts as genuine knowledge as opposed to spurious belief. More precisely, it means that an adequate understanding of anything consists in seeing it as the logical consequence of its cause, just as the properties of a geometrical figure are understood by seeing them as the logical consequence of its definition. This, in turn, leads directly to the complete rejection of final causes, that is, the idea that things in nature (or nature as a whole) serve or have an end, and that understanding them involves understanding their end. Not only did Spinoza reject final causes as unscientific, a view which he shared with most proponents of the new science, he also regarded it as the source of superstition and a major obstacle to the attainment of genuine knowledge.*

The same spirit underlies Spinoza's practical philosophy, which is marked by his clinical, dispassionate analysis of human nature and behaviour. In contrast to traditional moralists (both religious and secular), he rejects any appeal to a set of absolute values that are independent of human desire. Since the basic desire of every being is self-preservation, virtue is identified with the capacity to preserve one's being, the good with what is truly useful in this regard and the bad with what is truly harmful. In the case of human beings, however, what is truly useful is knowledge; so virtue consists essentially in knowledge. This is because knowledge is both the major weapon against the passions (which are the chief sources of human misery) and, in so far as it is directed to God or the necessary order of nature, the source of the highest satisfaction.

Apart from the Ethics, *Spinoza is best known for his contributions to the development of an historical approach to the Bible and to liberal political theory. The former is contained in the* Tractatus Theologico-politicus *(Theological-Political Treatise), which he published anonymously in 1670 as a plea for religious toleration and freedom of thought. The latter is contained both in that work and in the unfinished* Tractatus Politicus *(Political Treatise) of 1677, in which Spinoza attempts to extend his scientific approach to questions in political philosophy.*

1   The geometrical method

Although Spinoza uses the geometrical method in the *Ethica Ordine Geometrico Demonstrata* (*Ethics Demonstrated in a Geometrical Manner*) (1677a), he does not attempt to justify or even explain it. This has led many readers to view its argument as an intricate and fascinating chain of reasoning from arbitrary premises, which, as such, never touches reality. Nevertheless, Spinoza was very much aware of this problem and dealt with it both in an important early and unfinished work on method, *Tractatus de Intellectus Emendatione* (*Treatise on the Emendation of the Intellect*) (1677b) and in some of his correspondence.

At the heart of the problem is the nature of the definitions (and to a lesser extent the axioms) on the basis of which Spinoza attempts to demonstrate the propositions of the *Ethics*. In a 1663 letter to a young friend, Simon De Vries, who queried him about this very problem, Spinoza offers his version of the traditional distinction between nominal and real definitions. The former kind stipulates what is meant by a word or thought in a concept. Such a definition can be conceivable or inconceivable, clear or obscure; but, as arbitrarily invented, it cannot, strictly speaking, be either true or false. By contrast, the real

definition, which supposedly 'explains a thing as it exists outside of the understanding', defines a thing rather than a term (Leibniz 1966 letter 9: 106–7). Consequently, it can be either true or false.

Since the definitions of the *Ethics* are typically introduced by expressions such as 'by... I mean that', or 'a thing is called', it would seem that they are of the nominal type, which gives rise to the charge of arbitrariness. It is clear from their use, however, that Spinoza regards them as real definitions. Like the definitions of geometrical figures in Euclid, they are intended to express not merely the names used, but the objects named.

The question, then, is how can one know that one has arrived at a true definition. Spinoza's answer reveals the depth of his commitment to the geometrical way of thinking, especially to the method of analytic geometry developed by DESCARTES. He appeals to the example of the mathematician, who knows that one has a real definition of a figure when one is able to construct it. The definition of a figure is thus a rule for its construction, what is usually called a 'genetic definition'. Spinoza develops this point in *On the Emendation of the Intellect* ([1677b] 1985 vol.1: 39–40) by contrasting the nominal definition of a circle as 'a figure in which the lines drawn from the centre to the circumference are equal' with the genetic definition as 'the figure that is described by any line of which one end is fixed and the other movable'. The point is that the latter definition, but not the former, tells us how such a figure can be constructed and from this rule of construction we can deduce all its essential properties.

Spinoza's claim, then, is that the principles that apply to mathematical objects and perhaps other abstract entities also apply to reality as such. Thus, we have a real definition, an adequate, true or clear and distinct idea of a thing (all of these terms being more or less interchangeable) in so far as we know its 'proximate cause' and can see how its properties necessarily follow from this cause.

But if knowledge of a thing reduces to knowledge of its proximate cause, then either we find ourselves involved in an infinite regress, which would lead to a hopeless scepticism, or the chain of reasoning must be grounded in a single first principle. Furthermore, this first principle must have a unique status: if it is to provide the ultimate ground in terms of which everything else is to be explained, it must somehow be self-grounded or have the reason for its existence in itself. In the scholastic terminology which Spinoza adopts, it must be *causa sui* (self-caused). Thus, Spinoza's rationalist method leads necessarily to the concept of God, which he defines as 'a being absolutely infinite, i.e., a substance consisting of an infinity of attributes, of which each one expresses an eternal and infinite essence' (*Ethics*: I, def. 6).

Given this concept, together with other essential concepts such as substance, attribute and mode (which are treated in the definitions of part one), the argument of the *Ethics* proceeds in a deductive manner. Its goal is to enable us to understand reality as a whole in light of this concept in just the same way that the mathematician can understand all the essential properties of a geometrical figure in terms of its concept or genetic definition. At least this is the project of part one of the *Ethics* (On God). The remainder of the work is devoted to the demonstration of the most important consequences of this result in so far as they concern the human condition.

2 Substance-monism

The first fourteen propositions of the *Ethics* contain an argument intended to show that 'Except God, no substance can be or be conceived' (*Ethics*: I, prop. 14). Since it follows from an analysis of the concept of substance that whatever is not itself substance must be a modification thereof, Spinoza concludes in the next proposition that 'Whatever is, is in God, and nothing can be or be conceived without God'. Together they express Spinoza's substance-monism, which can be defined as the complex thesis that there is only one substance in the universe; that this substance is to be identified with God; and that all things, as modes of this one substance are, in some sense 'in God'.

The argument for this thesis is based largely on the analysis of the concept of substance, defined as 'what is in itself and is conceived through itself, i.e., that whose concept does not require the concept of another thing, from which it must be formed' (*Ethics*: I, def. 3). This definition is quite close to Descartes who likewise made a capacity for independent existence the criterion of substance; but the two philosophers drew diametrically opposed conclusions from their similar definitions. Although Descartes held that God is substance in a pre-eminent sense, he also maintained that there are two kinds of created substance – thinking things or minds, and extended things, both of which depend for their existence on God but not on each other. For Spinoza, by contrast, there is only the one substance – God – and thought and extension are among its attributes.

Spinoza argues indirectly for his monism by criticizing the two major alternatives that a substance-based metaphysics can provide: that there is a plurality of substances of the same nature or attribute and that there is a plurality of substances with different natures or attributes. Since Descartes is committed to both forms of pluralism, both parts of the argument cut against his views. In considering Spinoza's position, however, it should be kept in mind that his target is not merely Descartes, but an entire philosophical and theological tradition which conceived of the universe as composed of a number of finite substances created by God (see MEDIEVAL PHILOSOPHY). In spite of his radical critique of scholastic ways of thinking and his appeal to mathematics as the ideal of knowledge, Descartes remained in many ways a part of that tradition.

The argument against the first form of pluralism turns on the claim that 'In nature there cannot be two or more substances of the same nature or kind' (*Ethics*: I, prop. 5). This is at once one of the most important and controversial propositions in the *Ethics*. It is important because of its pivotal role in the overall argument for monism, controversial because of the demonstration offered in its support which is based on a consideration of the grounds on which two or more substances might be distinguished. This could be done either on the basis of their attributes, if they are substances of different types (for example, Descartes' thinking and extended substances), or on the basis of their modifications, if they are distinct substances of the same kind (for example, particular minds or bodies). The claim is that neither procedure can distinguish two or more substances of the same kind; and since these are the only possible ways of distinguishing substances, it follows that such substances could not be distinguished from one another.

The unsuitability of the first alternative seems obvious and would be recognized as such by Descartes. Since a substance-type for Descartes is defined in terms of its attribute, it follows that two or more substances of the same kind could not be distinguished on the basis of their attributes. As obvious as this seems, however, it was criticized by Leibniz on the grounds that two substances might have some attributes in common and others that were distinct. For example, substance *A* might have attributes *x* and *y*, and substance *B* attributes *y* and *z*. Although a Cartesian would reject this analysis on the grounds that a substance cannot have more than one attribute, Spinoza (for whom God is a substance with infinite attributes) could hardly accept this Cartesian principle. Moreover, we shall see that it is essential to the overall argument for monism to eliminate the possibility suggested by Leibniz (see LEIBNIZ, G.W. §§4–7).

Various strategies for dealing with this problem have been suggested in the literature, perhaps the most plausible of which turns on the principle that if two or more substances were to share a single attribute, they would have to share all, and would, therefore, be numerically identical. Although Spinoza never argues explicitly in this way, it seems a reasonable inference from his conception of attribute as 'what the intellect perceives of a substance as constituting its essence' (*Ethics*: I, def. 4). This entails that attribute *y* of substance *A* is identical to attribute *y* of substance *B* just in case they express the same nature or essence – that is, are descriptions of the same kind of thing. But if they are things of the same kind, then any attribute *A* has will be possessed by *B* as well.

Against the second alternative Spinoza argues that, since by definition substance is prior to its modifications, if we consider substance as it is in itself then we cannot distinguish one substance from another. Although the claim is surely correct, the suggestion that we set the modifications aside seems to beg the question against Descartes. After all, two Cartesian thinking substances share the same nature or attribute and are distinguished precisely by their different modifications (thoughts).

Spinoza's reasoning at this point is unclear, but one could respond that, on the hypothesis under consideration, the substances must be assumed to be indistinguishable prior to the assignment of modifications. Moreover, it follows from this that the assignment of modifications could not serve to distinguish otherwise indistinguishable substances unless it is already assumed that they are numerically distinct. In other words, while we can distinguish two Cartesian substances by means of their modifications, we can only do so by presupposing that the distinct modifications belong to numerically distinct substances. But it is just this assumption to which the Cartesian is not entitled.

3 Substance-monism (cont.)

This, however, is only the first step in the argument for monism. It is also necessary to rule out the possibility of a plurality of substances of different kinds. Essential to this project is the demonstration that substance is infinite not merely 'in its own kind', that is, unlimited by anything of the same kind, but 'absolutely infinite', that is, all-inclusive or possessing all reality, which, for Spinoza, means infinite attributes. For example, Descartes' extended substance is infinite in the first sense because it is not limited or determined by anything outside itself (for example, empty space); but it is not infinite in the second and decisive sense because it does not constitute all reality. Moreover, this is precisely why the first sense of infinity is not sufficient to preclude a plurality of substances.

The basis of the argument for the absolute infinity of substance is the claim that 'The more reality or being each thing has the more attributes belong to it' (*Ethics*: I, prop. 9). This is a direct challenge to the Cartesian conception of substance as defined in terms of a single attribute, resting on the dual assumption that some things can possess more reality than others and that this superior degree of reality is manifested in a greater number of attributes. Unfortunately, in defence of this claim Spinoza merely refers to the definition of attribute as 'what the intellect perceives of a substance as constituting its essence' (*Ethics*: I, def. 4). Nevertheless, it does seem possible to understand Spinoza's point if we interpret attributes as something like distinct descriptions under which substance or reality can be taken. Consider, for example, a simple human action such as raising an arm. Although it may be possible to give a complete neurophysiological account of such an action in terms of impulses sent to the brain, the contraction of muscles and the like, one could still argue that no such account, no matter how detailed, is adequate to understanding it as an action. This requires reference to psychological factors such as the beliefs and intentions of an agent, which in Spinoza's metaphysics belong to the attribute of thought. Thus, we might say both that there is 'more reality' to an action than is given in a purely neurophysiological account and that this 'greater reality' can be understood as the possession of a greater number of attributes.

It follows from this that a being possessing all reality – that is, God, or the *ens realissimum* (most real being) of the tradition – may be described as possessing infinite attributes. It also follows that the Cartesian must either accept the possibility of a substance with infinite attributes or deny the possibility of God. And since the orthodox Cartesian could hardly do the latter, the former must be admitted.

Even granting this, however, at least two problems remain. One is how to understand the infinity of attributes. This might mean either that substance possesses infinitely many attributes, of which the human mind knows only two (thought and extension), or that it possesses all possible attributes, which is compatible with there being only two. Although scholars are divided on the point and there are indications from Spinoza's correspondence that he held the former view, it is important to realize that the argument for monism requires only the latter. This argument turns on the claim that God is a substance that possesses all the attributes there are and, therefore, that there are none left for any other conceivable substance. Combining this with the proposition that two substances cannot share an attribute, it follows that there can be no substance apart from God.

The second problem is that the argument up to this

point is completely hypothetical. It shows that *if* we assume the existence of God, defined as a substance possessing infinite attributes, then it follows that no substance apart from God is possible; but it has not yet established the existence of substance so conceived. Spinoza had, however, laid the foundation for this claim in *Ethics* (I, prop. 7) with the demonstration that existence pertains to the nature of substance; so it remains merely to apply this result to God. This is the task of proposition eleven, which contains Spinoza's arguments for the existence of God. Spinoza offers three separate proofs, the major one being his version of the ontological argument, which was first developed by Anselm and later reformulated by Descartes (see ANSELM §4; DESCARTES, R. §6). Like his predecessors, Spinoza attempts to derive God's existence from the mere concept; but unlike them he makes no reference to God's perfection. Instead he appeals merely to the definition of God as a substance, from which it follows (by proposition seven) that God necessarily exists.

The nerve of the overall argument is, therefore, the proposition that existence pertains to the nature of substance or, equivalently, that its essence necessarily involves existence. Moreover, Spinoza's argument for this claim reveals the extent of his rationalism. From the premise that substance cannot be produced by anything external to itself (since such a cause would have to be another substance of the same nature, which has already been ruled out), he concludes that it must be the cause of itself, which is just to say that existence necessarily follows from its essence. Underlying this reasoning is what, at least since Leibniz, is usually termed the principle of sufficient reason, that is, the principle that everything must have a ground, reason or cause (these terms often being used interchangeably) why it is so and not otherwise. Although followers of Leibniz such as Christian Wolff attempted to demonstrate this principle, Spinoza, like most rationalists before Kant (including Leibniz), seems to have regarded it as self-evident (see WOLFF, C. §6).

This characterization of substance as self-caused or self-sufficient being anticipates its identification with God. Quite apart from the question of its validity, however, perhaps the most interesting feature of Spinoza's argument for the necessary existence of his God-substance is that it is at the same time an argument for the non-existence of God the creator. Nevertheless, it should not be inferred from this that the result is purely negative or that Spinoza is concerned to deny the existence of God in every sense. On the contrary, his real concern in the opening propositions of the *Ethics* is to show that necessary existence and, therefore, the property of being a self-contained, self-explicated reality, is to be predicated of the order of nature as a whole rather than of some distinct and inscrutable ground of this order. And this also expresses the deepest meaning of his monism.

4 God and the world

Spinoza's monism does not, however, mean the end of all dualities. In fact, the identification of God with nature leads immediately to the distinction between two aspects of nature, which he terms *natura naturans* (active or generating nature), and *natura naturata* (passive or generated nature). The former refers to God as conceived through himself, that is, substance with infinite attributes, and the latter to the modal system conceived through these attributes (which includes, but is not identical to, the totality of particular things). Consequently, the task is to explain the connection between these two aspects of nature, a task which is the Spinozistic analogue to the traditional problem of explaining the relationship between God and creation.

Like the theologians, whose procedure he adopts even while subverting their claims, Spinoza divides his analysis into two parts: a consideration of the divine causality as it is in itself (or as *natura naturans*) and a consideration of it as expressed in the modal system (or as *natura naturata*). Given what we have already seen, the former holds few surprises. The basic claim is that 'From the necessity of the divine nature there must follow infinitely many things in infinitely many ways, (i.e., everything which can fall under an infinite intellect)' (*Ethics*: I, prop. 16). Spinoza here characterizes both the nature and extent of the divine causality or power. By locating this power in the 'necessity of the divine nature' rather than creative will and by identifying its extent with 'everything which can fall under an infinite intellect', that is, everything conceivable, Spinoza might seem to be denying freedom to God. Certainly he is denying anything like freedom of choice. To object on these grounds, however, is to ignore the conception of freedom which Spinoza does affirm and to appeal to the very anthropomorphic conception of the deity against which his whole analysis is directed. To be free for Spinoza is not to be undetermined but to be self-determined (*Ethics*: I, def. 7); and God, precisely because he acts from the necessity of his own nature, is completely self-determined and, therefore, completely free.

The question of the relationship between God, so construed, and the 'infinitely many things' or modes that supposedly follow from God in 'infinitely many ways', which is perhaps the central question in Spinoza's metaphysics, is greatly complicated by the fact that Spinoza distinguishes between two radically distinct types of modes. As modifications of the one substance, both types are dependent on and in a sense 'follow from' God, but they do so in quite different ways.

First, there are those modes that either follow directly from an attribute of substance or follow from one that does directly follow. These are termed respectively 'immediate' and 'mediate eternal and infinite modes'. They are eternal and infinite because they follow (logically) from an attribute of substance, but they are not eternal and infinite in the same manner as substance and its attributes. Although Spinoza tells us very little about these modes in the *Ethics*, we know from his correspondence and the *Short Treatise on God, Man, and his Well-Being* (*c.*1660–5)) which contains the earliest statement of his system, that he regarded 'motion' or 'motion and rest', and 'intellect' or 'infinite intellect', as immediate eternal and infinite modes in the attributes of extension and thought respectively. As an example of a mediate eternal and infinite mode, he mentions only the 'face of the whole universe' (*facies totius universi*) which pertains to extension.

Given the highly schematic and fragmentary nature of the surviving accounts of these eternal and infinite modes, any interpretation is hazardous. Nevertheless, both their systematic function as mediators between God or substance and the particular things in nature (finite modes), and the names chosen for the modes of extension, suggest that the latter are best construed as the fundamental laws of physics. In fact, Spinoza's characterization of motion and rest as an eternal and infinite mode may be seen as his attempt to overcome a basic difficulty in Cartesian physics. Having identified matter with extension, Descartes could not account for either motion or the division of matter into distinct bodies without appealing to divine intervention. On Spinoza's view, however, this is not necessary, since extended substance has its principle within itself. Otherwise expressed, matter is inherently dynamical, a property which cannot be explained in terms of Descartes' purely geometrical physics.

The 'face of the whole universe', which is identified with corporeal nature as a whole, may be understood in a similar fashion. By claiming that this is a mediate eternal and infinite mode of extension following directly from motion and rest, Spinoza is implying that the proportion of motion and rest in corporeal nature as a whole remains constant, even though it may be in continual flux in any given region. Moreover, this is equivalent to affirming the principle of the conservation of motion, which is a basic principle of Cartesian physics.

Viewing Spinoza's account in the light of seven-teenth-century physics also helps to understand his doctrine of finite modes, or the series of particular things, which is usually regarded as one of the more problematic aspects of his metaphysics. The problem is how to conceive the relationship between the series of these modes and God. If one assumes that, like the mediate eternal and infinite modes, they follow mediately from the attributes of God, then they too become eternal and infinite; but this is absurd, since it is of the essence of such modes to be transitory. If, however, one denies that they follow from God at all, then the dependence of all things on God, and with it Spinoza's monism, is negated. Accordingly, it must be explained how, in spite of their finitude, particular things and occurrences depend on God and partici-pate in the divine necessity.

Spinoza's solution to this dilemma consists in claiming that the series of finite modes constitutes an infinite causal chain, wherein each finite mode is both cause and effect of others, *ad infinitum*, while the entire series (viewed as a totality) is dependent on the attributes of God and the eternal and infinite modes. Expressed in scientific terms, this means that every occurrence in nature is to be understood in terms of two intersecting lines of explanation. On the one hand, there is a set of general laws which for Spinoza are logically necessary (since they follow from the divine attributes); on the other hand, there must be a set of antecedent conditions. Both are required to explain a given phenomenon, say a clap of thunder. Clearly, no such explanation is possible without appealing to the relevant physical laws; but of themselves these laws are not sufficient to explain anything. It is also necessary to refer to the relevant antecedent conditions: in this case the state of the atmosphere. But, given these laws and the atmo-spheric state at t_1, it is possible to deduce the occurrence of thunder at t_2. And this means that nature is to be conceived as a thoroughly determinis-tic system.

Spinoza concludes from this that 'In nature there is nothing contingent, but all things have been deter-mined from the necessity of the divine nature to exist and to produce an effect in a certain way' (*Ethics*: I, prop. 29). But because of this denial of contingency, he is sometimes accused of conflating determinism with the stronger thesis (usually termed 'necessitar-ianism') according to which the entire order of nature, that is, the infinite series of finite modes, could not have been different. The point is that determinism entails merely that, given the laws of nature and the set of appropriate antecedent conditions, any parti-cular occurrence is necessary; but this leaves room for contingency, since it leaves open the possibility of a different set of antecedent conditions.

In response, one might distinguish between a consideration of finite modes, or a subset thereof, taken individually and a consideration of the series of such modes as a whole. The former fails to eliminate contingency, since any particular mode or subset of modes, viewed in abstraction from the whole, can easily be thought (or imagined) to be different. But the same cannot be said of the series taken as a whole. Since this series (considered as a totality) depends on God, it could not be different without God being different (which is impossible). The problem here is with the idea that the set of modes as a whole requires an explanation or grounding distinct from that of its constituent elements. Such a move is usually dismissed as a 'category mistake' (treating a collection as if it were a higher-order individual). But if it is a mistake, it is one to which Spinoza is prone in virtue of his rationalism; for nothing could be less Spinozistic than the idea that while particular events may be intelligible, the order of nature as a whole is not. And since for Spinoza making something intelligible involves demonstrating its necessity, this commits him to necessitarianism.

5   The human mind

Just as the target of part one of the *Ethics* is the dualism of God and created nature, so that of part two is the dualism of mind and body. Rather than holding with Descartes that the mind and the body are two distinct substances that somehow come together to constitute a human being, Spinoza maintains that they constitute a single individual expressed in the attributes of thought and extension. Since the fundamental modifications of thought are ideas (other modifications, such as desires and volitions, presuppose an idea of their object), while those of extension are bodies, this means that the human mind is an idea of a rather complex sort and that together with its correlate or object in extension (the body), it constitutes a single thing or individual. The great attractiveness of this view, particularly when contrasted with both Descartes' dualism and Hobbes' reductive materialism, is that it allows for the conception of persons as unified beings with correlative and irreducible mental and physical aspects (see Hobbes, T.). Unfortunately, this attractiveness is diminished considerably by its inherent obscurity. How can the mind be identified with an idea (even a very complex one)? And how can such an idea constitute a single thing with its object?

The place to begin a consideration of these questions is with Spinoza's elusive conception of an idea, which he defines as 'a conception of the mind that the mind forms because it is a thinking being' (*Ethics*: II, def. 3). As he makes clear in his explication of this definition through the distinction between conception and perception, the emphasis falls on the activity of thought. To say that the mind has the idea of x is to say that it is engaged in the activity of conceiving x, not merely passively perceiving its mental image. Indeed, in one sense of the term, an idea for Spinoza just is the act of thinking. Moreover, this helps to remove at least some of the mystery in the identification of the mind with an idea. On the Spinozistic view, this means that the mind is identified with its characteristic activity, thinking; that its unity is the unity of this activity.

As acts of thinking, ideas may be identified with beliefs or 'believings'; but this reflects only one dimension of Spinoza's conception of an idea. For beliefs have propositional content and this, too, is an essential aspect of every idea. In short, ideas have both psychological and logical (or epistemological) properties. Moreover, although Spinoza is often charged with conflating these, he was well aware of the difference and of the importance of keeping them apart. This is evident from his appeal to the scholastic distinction, also invoked by Descartes, between the 'formal' and the 'objective reality' of ideas. The former refers to the psychological side of ideas as acts of thinking or mental events, the latter to their logical side or propositional content. Construed in the former way, ideas have causes which, in view of the self-contained nature of each attribute, are always other ideas. Construed in the latter way, they have rational grounds which likewise are always other ideas.

Spinoza differs from Descartes, however, in his understanding of the objective reality of ideas. For Descartes, talk about the objective reality of an idea as it exists in someone's mind refers to that idea *qua* intentional object to which a 'real' (extra-mental) object may or may not correspond. For Spinoza, by contrast, the idea viewed objectively just is its object (a corresponding mode of extension) as it exists in thought. This is a direct consequence of Spinoza's mind-body monism and we shall see that it has important implications for his epistemology.

6   The human mind (cont.)

Our immediate concern, however, is with the implications of this conception of ideas for Spinoza's account of the mind–body relationship. Unquestionably, the key feature in this account is the principle that 'The order and connection of ideas is the same as the order and connection of things' (*Ethics*: II, prop. 7). Taken by itself, this might be viewed as the assertion of a parallelism or isomorphism between the two orders, thereby leaving open the possibility that the elements contained in these orders might be ontologically distinct, as, for example, in Leibniz's pre-established harmony (see LEIBNIZ, G.W. §§4–7). In the scholium attached to this proposition, however, Spinoza indicates that he takes it to entail something more. Thus, he explains that just as thinking and extended substance are 'one and the same substance, comprehended now under this attribute and now under that. So also a mode of extension and the idea of that mode are one and the same thing, but expressed in two ways' (*Ethics*: II, prop. 7). In other words, rather than there being two series, one of extended things and the other of ideas, there is only a single series of finite modes, which may be regarded from two points of view, or taken under two descriptions. This also defines the sense in which Spinoza affirms an identity between mind and body. In claiming that mind and body constitute the same thing, he is not asserting that ultimately there is only one set of properties (which would make him a reductionist like Hobbes); rather, he is denying that the two sets of properties or, better, the two descriptions, can be assigned to two ontologically distinct things (as they are for Descartes).

Although the proposition makes a completely general claim about the relationship between the attributes of thought and extension, and their respective modifications, it also provides the metaphysical foundation for Spinoza's descent from the attribute of thought to its most interesting finite modification – the human mind. The descent is somewhat circuitous, however, since in subsequent propositions Spinoza stops to dwell on some topics that do not seem directly germane, such as the status of ideas of non-existent things; but the main line of the argument is clear enough. As a finite mode of thought, the essence of the mind must be constituted by an idea. Since the mind itself is something actual (an actual power of thinking), it must be the idea of an actually existing thing. And since this actually existing thing can only be a corresponding modification of extension, that is, a body, Spinoza concludes that 'The object of the idea constituting the human mind is the body, or a certain mode of extension which actually exists, and nothing else' (*Ethics*: II, prop 13).

Even if one accepts Spinoza's premises and the chain of reasoning leading to the conclusion, this 'deduction' of the human mind as the idea of the body raises at least two major questions. One is how to reconcile the identification of the body as the unique object of the mind with the capacity of the mind to know and, therefore, presumably, to have ideas of things quite distinct from the body with which it is identified. This will be discussed in the next section in connection with Spinoza's epistemology. The other question concerns how this enables us to understand what is distinctive about the human mind. As Spinoza himself remarks in the scholium to proposition thirteen, this result is perfectly general, applying no more to human beings than to other individuals. And, by way of accentuating the point, he adds that these other individuals are 'all animate [*animata*], albeit in different degrees'. Now, given the principles of Spinoza's metaphysics, it certainly follows that there must be 'in God' an idea corresponding to every mode of extension in the same way as an idea of a human body corresponds to that body. Thus, the claim that the human mind is the idea of the body may serve to determine its ontological status, but it does not enable us to understand its specific nature and activity. But unless Spinoza's deduction of the mind can accomplish this result, it cannot be judged a success, even on his own terms. Moreover, by suggesting that all individuals in nature are to some extent *animata*, he introduces a fresh element of paradox into his discussion. Indeed, this is particularly so if we take Spinoza to be claiming that something like a soul, or a rudimentary mind, must be attributed to all individuals.

Since the Latin '*animatus*' is cognate with the English 'animate', the sense of paradox can be lessened somewhat if we take the claim to be merely that all individuals are alive. Although this itself might seem bizarre, it becomes more plausible when one considers Spinoza's conception of life which, in the appendix to his early work *Descartes's 'Principles of Philosophy'*, he defines as 'the force through which things persevere in their being'. Since, as we shall see, Spinoza's conatus doctrine consists in the claim that each thing, in so far as it can, strives to preserve its being, it follows that every thing is in this sense 'alive'. And from this it is perhaps not too large a step to the conclusion that every thing has a 'soul' in the sense of an animating principle. But, of course, it does not follow from this that everything has a mental life that is even remotely analogous to that enjoyed by the human mind.

This makes it incumbent on Spinoza to account for the different degrees of animation and to explain thereby the superiority of the human mind to the 'minds' of other things in the order of nature. And he proceeds to do so by focusing on the nature of body. In essence, Spinoza's view is that 'mindedness' is a function of organic complexity; so the greater the capacity of a body (that is, brain and central nervous system) to interact with its environment, the greater the capacity of the mind to comprehend it. Thus, in a kind of speculative biophysics, Spinoza attempts to demonstrate that the human body is, indeed, a highly complex individual, which stands in a complex and reciprocal relationship with its environment. Although this account is extremely cryptic, it is also highly suggestive and points in the direction of an analysis of the phenomenon of life that goes far beyond the crude mechanism of the Cartesians (for whom the body is merely a machine). Perhaps more to the point, it also provides a theoretical basis for locating conscious awareness and rational insight on a continuum of mental powers, all of which are strictly correlated with physical capacities, rather than viewing them with Descartes as unique properties of a distinct mental substance.

7 Theory of knowledge

Although Spinoza does not assign to epistemological questions the priority given them by Descartes and the British empiricists, he certainly does not neglect them. In fact, his analysis of human knowledge, which follows directly upon his account of the mind, may be viewed as an attempt to show how the human mind, so conceived, is capable of the kind of knowledge presupposed by the geometrical method of the *Ethics*. In Spinoza's own terms, this means that what must be shown is nothing less than that the human mind is capable of adequate knowledge of the eternal and infinite essence of God.

Since adequate knowledge rests on adequate ideas, Spinoza must demonstrate that the human mind possesses such ideas. He defines an adequate idea as one which 'considered in itself, without relation to an object, has all the properties or intrinsic denominations of a true idea' (*Ethics*: II, def. 4). The term 'intrinsic' functions to rule out the extrinsic feature of a true idea: namely, agreement with its object. Thus, Spinoza's view is that truth and adequacy are reciprocal concepts: all adequate ideas are true (agree with their object) and all true ideas are adequate. Moreover, this enables him to dismiss the radical doubt regarding even our most evident conceptions envisaged by Descartes, which is supposedly overcome only by the manifestly circular appeal to God as the guarantor of truth. Since adequacy is an intrinsic feature of all true ideas, it serves as the criterion of truth. Consequently, someone who has a true idea immediately recognizes it as such and there is no longer room for Cartesian doubt. As Spinoza puts it with uncharacteristic elegance: 'As the light makes both itself and the darkness plain, so truth is the standard both of itself and of the false' (*Ethics*: II, prop. 43, scholium).

The intrinsic property through which truth manifests itself is explanatory completeness. An idea of *x* is adequate and, therefore, true just in case it suffices for the determination of all of the essential properties of *x*. For example, the mathematician's idea of a triangle is adequate because all of the mathematically relevant properties of the figure can be deduced from it. Conversely, the conception of a triangle by someone ignorant of mathematics is inadequate because it is incapable of yielding any such consequences.

It does not follow from this, however, that inadequate ideas are simply false. On the contrary, since every idea agrees with its object, every idea must in some sense be true. Specifically, 'All ideas, insofar as they are related to God, are true' (*Ethics*: II, prop. 32). Error or falsity arises because not every idea possessed by the human intellect is related by that intellect to God, that is, viewed as a determinate member of the total system of ideas. In other words, error or falsity is a function of incomplete comprehension, of partial truth being taken as complete. Spinoza illustrates the point by an example also used by Descartes: the imaginative, non-scientific idea of the sun as a disk in the sky located a few hundred feet above the earth. This idea is 'true' in so far as it is taken as an accurate representation of how the sun appears to us under certain conditions; but since it is not understood in this way by someone ignorant of optics and astronomy, such a person's idea is false in the sense of being inadequate or incomplete. It is not, however, 'materially false' in the Cartesian sense that there is nothing in the realm of extension corresponding to it.

Correlative with the distinction between inadequate and adequate ideas is a contrast between two mutually exclusive ways in which ideas can be connected in the mind: either according to the 'common order of nature' or the 'order of the intellect'. The former refers to the order in which the human mind receives its ideas in sense perception or through imaginative association. Since these correspond exactly to the order in which the body is affected by the objects of these ideas, it reflects the condition of the body in its interaction with its environment rather than the true nature of an independent reality. And from this Spinoza concludes that all such ideas are inadequate. In fact, he argues that, in so far as its ideas reflect this order or, equivalently, are based on sense perception or imagination, the mind is incapable of adequate knowledge of either external objects in nature, its own body or even of itself. Spinoza also contends, however, that adequate knowledge of all three is possible in so far as the mind conceives things according to the order of the intellect, that is, the true order of logical and causal dependence, which, once again, is precisely why the correct method is so essential.

8   Theory of knowledge (cont.)

The central problem of Spinozistic epistemology is thus to explain how conception according to the order of the intellect is possible for the human mind. This is a problem because the possibility of such conception seems to be ruled out by the ontological status of the mind as the idea of the body. For how could a mind, so conceived, have any ideas that do not reflect the condition of its body? The gist of Spinoza's answer is that there are certain ideas that the human mind possesses completely and hence can conceive adequately because, unlike ideas derived from sense perception or imagination, they do not 'involve', or logically depend on, ideas of particular modifications of the body.

Spinoza's doctrine is particularly obscure at this point; but it is perhaps best approached by comparing it to the doctrine of innate ideas, which was appealed to by Descartes and later Leibniz to deal with a similar problem. Like Spinoza, they held that sensory experience cannot account for the possibility of knowledge of necessary and universal truth. Instead, they claimed that the source of such knowledge must lie in the mind and reflect its very structure. This was not understood in a naïve psychological sense, however, as if an infant were born with knowledge of the basic principles of mathematics. Rather, innate ideas were viewed more as dispositions that pertain essentially to the human mind, but of which individuals are not necessarily conscious (see INNATE KNOWLEDGE).

Although Spinoza's account of the mind as the idea of the body precludes the distinction drawn by Descartes between innate and adventitious ideas (that is, those that come from the mind and those that come from sensory experience), it does allow for an analogous distinction, which leads to much the same result. This is the distinction between ideas that are correlated with specific features of particular bodies and those whose correlates are common to all bodies or a large proportion thereof. The latter fall into two classes, corresponding to two levels of generality, which Spinoza terms respectively 'common notions' and 'adequate ideas of the common properties of things'. Their distinctive feature is that they do not arise in connection with an encounter with any particular kind of thing; and this enables Spinoza to claim that the mind possesses them in their totality and comprehends them adequately. Unfortunately, he does not provide examples of either class of these adequate ideas; but it seems reasonable to assume that the common notions include the axioms of geometry and first principles of physics (which are common to all bodies). Correlatively, since the adequate ideas of

common properties of things correspond to properties that are common and peculiar to the human body and to other bodies by which it is affected (*Ethics*: II, prop. 39), it is likely that Spinoza was here referring to the basic principles of biology (or perhaps physiology). In any event, the crucial point is that the commonality of these ideas enables the human mind to grasp them completely, which is what is required for adequate knowledge.

The epistemological teaching of the *Ethics* culminates in the distinction between three kinds of knowledge (*Ethics*: II, prop. 40, scholium 2). The first is an experientially determined knowledge, which can be based either on the perception of particular things or on signs, which for Spinoza includes both sensory and memory images. The second is knowledge through reason, which is based on common notions and ideas of the common properties of things. Since the former mode of knowledge involves inadequate ideas and the latter adequate ones, this is just the contrast one would expect. At this point, however, Spinoza unexpectedly introduces a third kind of knowledge, termed 'intuitive knowledge' (*scientia intuitiva*), which supposedly 'proceeds from an adequate idea of the formal essence of certain attributes of God to the adequate knowledge of the essence of things'. He also attempts to clarify the difference between all three by comparing their respective treatments of the problem of finding a fourth proportional. Someone with the first kind of knowledge proceeds by rule of thumb, multiplying the second by the third and dividing the product by the first, thereby arriving at the correct answer without really understanding the principle at work. Someone with the second kind understands the principle and is, therefore, able to derive the result from the common property of proportionals as established by Euclid. Someone who possesses the third kind of knowledge, however, immediately grasps the result, without applying a rule or relying on a process of ratiocination.

Although both reason and intuition are sources of adequate knowledge, Spinoza recognizes two senses in which intuition is superior. First, whereas the province of reason concerns general truths based on common notions and consequently is abstract and general, that of intuition concerns the individual case and consequently is concrete and particular. This difference is not directly germane to Spinoza's epistemology, but it plays a significant role in his practical philosophy. Second, and of more immediate relevance, knowledge from general principles alone remains ultimately ungrounded. Accordingly, as in Spinoza's example, while the conclusion is inferred correctly from the principle, the status of the principle itself remains in question. Within the framework of Spinoza's metaphysics, this question can be resolved only by grounding the principle in the nature of God, which is supposedly what is accomplished by intuitive knowledge.

But grounding our knowledge of things in the eternal and infinite essence of God obviously presupposes a knowledge of that essence; and even for a rationalist such as Descartes, this far transcends the capacity of the human intellect. This is not the case for Spinoza, however, given his unique conception of God. Since 'it is of the nature of reason to regard things as necessary, not as contingent' (*Ethics*: II, prop. 44), and since to conceive things in this way is to conceive them in relation to God, Spinoza in effect concludes that in so far as the mind has an adequate idea of anything at all, it must have an adequate idea of God. Moreover, since it presumably has been established that the human mind knows some things (has some adequate ideas), it follows that the mind has an adequate idea of God. Although initially this seems paradoxical in the extreme, it becomes much less so if one keeps in mind the nature of Spinoza's God.

9 The emotions

Nowhere is Spinoza's unique combination of rationalism and naturalism more evident than in his doctrine of the emotions, the topic of the third part of the *Ethics*. Appealing to the conception of the mind as the idea of the body, he defines the emotions or affects (*affectiones*) as 'affections of the body by which the body's power of acting is increased or diminished, aided or restrained, and at the same time, the ideas of these affections' (*Ethics*: III, def. 3). Emotions are, therefore, directly related to the body's capacity for action or level of vitality and have both a physiological and a psychological side. Moreover, given mind-body identity, these are seen as distinct expressions of the same thing. Thus, a conscious desire for some object and a corresponding bodily appetite are the same state considered under the attributes of thought and extension respectively.

Among other things, Spinoza's conception of mind precludes the assumption of a distinct power of will through which the mind can exert control over the bodily appetites. Strictly speaking, there is nothing pertaining to the mind but ideas, that is, acts of thinking; but these ideas have a conative or volitional and affective as well as a cognitive dimension. In other words, to have an idea of *x* is to have not only a belief or propositional attitude with respect to *x*, but also some sort of evaluative attitude (pro or con). Moreover, this enables Spinoza to avoid concluding

from his denial of will that the mind is powerless, condemned to being the passive observer of the bodily appetites. The mind, for Spinoza, is active in so far as it is the 'adequate', that is sufficient, cause of its states; and it is such in so far as it possesses adequate ideas, that is, in so far as its desires and hence its 'decisions,' are grounded in rational considerations – for example, when it desires a particular food because of the knowledge (adequate idea) that it is nutritious. Conversely, it is passive when its desires reflect inadequate ideas connected with sense perception and imagination.

But regardless of whether it is active or passive, the mind's evaluative attitude is always an expression of its conatus, which is identified with the endeavour of each thing to persist in its own being. This endeavour pertains to the nature of every finite mode; but in human beings, who are conscious of this endeavour, it becomes the desire for self-preservation. Spinoza thus agrees with Hobbes in regarding this desire as the basic motivating force in human behaviour. But rather than inferring this from observation, he deduces it from the ontological status of human beings as finite modes. This allows him to affirm not merely that this desire is, as a matter of fact, basic to human beings, but that it constitutes their very essence. Accordingly, one can no more help striving to preserve one's being than a stone can help falling when it is dropped.

Perhaps under the influence of Hobbes, Spinoza also identifies this endeavour to preserve one's being with a striving for greater perfection, understood as an increased power of action. Just as Hobbes insisted that individuals continually desire to increase their power because there can never be any assurance that it is sufficient for self-preservation, so Spinoza maintains that the endeavour of an organism to preserve its existence is identical to its effort to increase its power of acting or level of vitality. This is because anything that lessens an organism's power, lessens its ability to preserve its being, while anything that increases this power enhances that ability.

The so-called primary emotions (pleasure, pain and desire) are correlated with the transition from one state of perfection or level of vitality to another. Thus, pleasure or joy (*laetitia*) is defined as the emotion whereby the mind passes to a greater state of perfection, and pain or sorrow (*tristitia*) is that by which it passes to a lesser state. Both reflect changes brought about in the organism through interaction with its environment. Although particular desires are directly related to pleasures, desire is none the less a distinct primary emotion because a desire for a particular object viewed as a source of pleasure is distinct from that pleasure.

The great bulk of part three of the *Ethics* is devoted to showing how the other emotions can be derived from the primary ones by means of combination and association with other ideas. Central to this project is the thesis that pleasure, pain and desire relate to present objects, which cause the affections of the body to which these emotions (as ideas) correspond. Accordingly, the derivative emotions are all species or combinations of pleasure, pain or desire, which are directed in various ways either to objects that do not presently affect the body or to those that are not themselves directly the cause of these affections. For example, love and hatred are defined respectively as pleasure and pain accompanied by the idea of an external cause. Similarly, hope and fear are understood as pleasures and pains that arise under conditions of uncertainty, when the image of some past or future thing is connected with an outcome that is in doubt. This analysis is extended with considerable subtlety, showing, among other things, how ambivalence is possible; and how, through various forms of association, the mind can come to feel love, hatred, hope or fear towards things with regard to which it has no direct desire or aversion. The key point, however, is that, like everything else in nature, these emotions do not arise capriciously, but in accordance with universal and necessary laws.

But these laws concern the mind only in so far as it is passive, that is, in so far as its ideas are inadequate and it is, therefore, only the partial or inadequate cause of its affections. Accordingly, at the end of his lengthy account of the passive emotions or passions, Spinoza turns briefly to the active emotions, which are connected with adequate ideas. Of the three primary emotions, only desire and pleasure have active forms, because only they can be grounded in adequate ideas. Active desire has already been described; it is simply rational desire. Active pleasure is a concomitant of all adequate cognition; for when the mind cognizes anything adequately it is necessarily aware of this and, therefore, of its own power or activity. And it is the awareness of its activity, not the nature of the object known, that is the source of pleasure. Finally, since pain or sorrow reflects a diminution of the mind's power of activity (adequate ideas), Spinoza concludes that it can never be the result of this activity, but must always result from the mind's inadequate knowledge and determination by external forces.

10 Moral theory

Spinoza's moral theory is based on his analysis of the emotions and is formulated with the same clinical detachment as the remainder of the *Ethics*. In sharp contrast to Judaeo-Christian moralists and their secular counterparts, he proposes neither a set of obligations nor a list of actions, the performance of which make one morally 'good', and their omission or neglect morally 'evil': all such moral systems and concepts are based on inadequate ideas, particularly the ideas of free will and final causes. Instead, he is concerned to determine the means through which and the extent to which human beings, as finite modes, are capable of attaining freedom, understood as the capacity to act rather than to be governed by the passions. Morality in the traditional sense is, therefore, replaced by a kind of therapy, which is one reason why Spinoza is frequently compared with FREUD. The concept of virtue is retained; but it is given its original meaning as power, which is itself understood in light of the conatus doctrine as the power to preserve one's being. In the same spirit, the good is identified with what is truly useful in this regard and the bad with what is truly harmful.

In spite of his amoralism, Spinoza does not equate virtue with the ability to survive or the good with what is in one's self-interest, narrowly conceived. What matters is not mere living, but living well; and this means being active – that is, being, to the fullest extent possible, the adequate cause of one's condition. And since being an adequate cause is a function of adequate ideas, virtue is directly correlated with knowledge. Knowledge, however, has a dual role in the Spinozistic scheme. It is the major weapon in the struggle against the passions, since it is through understanding our passions and their causes that we are able to gain some measure of control over them. But it is also itself constitutive of the good life, since our freedom is manifested essentially in the exercise of reason.

Nevertheless, Spinoza was under no illusions about the extent of the power of reason. Human virtue or perfection is merely relative and its attainment a rare and difficult feat. Thus, the first eighteen propositions of part four of the *Ethics*, which is significantly entitled 'On Human Bondage, or the Powers of the Affects', are concerned with the limits of the power of reason in its conflict with the passions. The basic point is that, as finite modes, the force through which human beings endeavour to preserve their being is infinitely surpassed by other forces in nature and, therefore, to some extent at least, they will always be subject to the passions. Moreover, knowledge itself has no motivating power simply *qua* knowledge, but only in so far as it is also an affect. Now knowledge is, indeed, an affect for Spinoza, since all ideas have an affective component, that is, possess a certain motivational force. But, as he attempts to demonstrate by means of an elaborate psychodynamics, the affective component of even an adequate idea is strictly limited and can easily be overcome by other (inadequate) ideas, which is why rational desires, based on a knowledge of what is truly beneficial, all too frequently give way to irrational urges.

After his analysis of human weakness, Spinoza turns to the question of what reason, limited as its power may be, prescribes. The basic answer, of course, is knowledge and, given Spinoza's metaphysics and epistemology, this ultimately means knowledge of God. Thus, he concludes that 'Knowledge of God is the mind's greatest good; its greatest virtue is to know God' (*Ethics*: IV, prop. 28). At this point, however, the discussion takes a surprising turn, one which indicates both the complexity of, and the inherent tensions in, Spinoza's thought. For while this austere intellectualism suggests the picture of the isolated, asocial thinker, devoted exclusively to the life of the mind, what is affirmed instead is the essentially social character of human existence. For Spinoza, as for Aristotle, human beings are social animals; and the life lived under the guidance of reason is, at least to some extent, a social life (see ARISTOTLE §22). This is not because human beings are intrinsically altruistic, but rather because, as relatively limited and weak finite modes, they are ineluctably interdependent. Thus, Spinoza argues that those who live under the guidance of reason desire nothing for themselves that they do not also desire for others (*Ethics*: IV, prop. 37). This reflects his undoubtedly idealized portrait of those devoted to the life of the mind. In so far as this devotion is pure (which it can never be completely), such individuals will not come into conflict because the good which they all seek, knowledge, can be held in common. In fact, not only will genuine seekers after truth not compete, they will cooperate; for in helping others acquire knowledge and the control of the passions that goes with it, one is also helping oneself. Moreover, although only the few capable (to some extent) of living under the guidance of reason may be able to grasp adequately and, therefore, internalize this truth, the need for cooperation applies to all; for all are members of the same human community of interdependent beings.

11 Moral theory (cont.)

Spinoza's account of the specific virtues reflect his general principles. These virtues are identified with certain affects or emotional states and their value is regarded as a function of their capacity to promote an individual's conatus. For this purpose the affects are divided into three classes: those that are intrinsically good and can never become excessive (the virtues); those that are intrinsically bad; and a large group that

are good in moderation but bad if they become excessive. In identifying the virtues with affects that can never become excessive, Spinoza differs from Aristotle for whom virtues are regarded as means between two extremes.

Paramount in the group of virtuous affects is pleasure or joy. Since it reflects in the attribute of thought an increase in the body's power of activity, it can never be harmful. This gives Spinoza's thought a strongly anti-ascetic tone which stands in sharp contrast to the Calvinistic austerity of many of his countryman. Nevertheless, it is crucial to distinguish between genuine pleasure, which reflects the wellbeing of the organism as a whole, and titillation (*titillatio*) or localized pleasure, which merely reflects that of a part. Although the latter can be good, it can also be quite harmful. Other affects in this mixed category include cheerfulness and self-esteem. In the latter case, the crucial factor is whether or not the affect is grounded in reason. Pride, or self-esteem, without any rational basis is obviously harmful and is to be avoided at all costs. But, in so far as self-approval arises from an adequate idea of one's power, it is the highest thing we can hope for, since it is simply the consciousness of one's virtue. Perhaps even more than his anti-asceticism, this indicates how much closer Spinoza is to the classical ideal of the virtuous life than he is to traditional religious morality.

In addition to pain, Spinoza assigns first place among the intrinsically harmful affects to hate. Closely associated with hate, and rejected in similarly unqualified terms, are affects such as envy, derision, contempt, anger and revenge. These might be termed the social vices, since they serve to alienate human beings from one another. It is also noteworthy that Spinoza here locates many of the traditional religious virtues: hope, fear, humility, repentance and pity. Since they all reflect ignorance and lack of power, they cannot be regarded as beneficial, or assigned any place in the life of reason. Nevertheless, in a concession to human frailty, Spinoza does acknowledge that because human beings rarely live in this manner, these affects have a certain pragmatic value as checks on our more aggressive tendencies.

The affects that can be either good or bad include – besides titillation – desire and love. If directed towards an object that stimulates or gratifies a part of the organism or one of its appetites at the expense of the whole, they can become excessive and hence harmful. And this is precisely what occurs in pathological states such as avarice, ambition, gluttony and above all, lust. In spite of his generally anti-ascetic attitude, Spinoza tended to regard sexual desire as an unmitigated evil. In sharp contrast to it stands the one kind of love that can never become excessive: the love of God.

12 The love of God and human blessedness

Although it does not enter into the account of virtue, the love of God plays a central role in the final part of the *Ethics*. The situation is complicated, however, by the fact that this part deals with two distinct topics, which may be characterized as mental health and blessedness; and the love of God is crucial to both. The question of health is the subject of the first twenty propositions, which are concerned with reason's unremitting struggle with the passions. Here Spinoza functions explicitly as therapist, providing his alternative not only to the religious tradition, but also to the training of the will advocated by the Stoics and Descartes (see STOICISM). Since what is crucial is that, as far as possible, one be moved by pleasurable thoughts (rather than reactive, negative affects), Spinoza's account amounts to an essay on the power of positive thinking. Moreover, since the ultimate positive thought is the love of God, this love serves as the chief remedy against the passions.

In spite of the religious language in which it is expressed, this claim is readily understandable in Spinozistic terms. Since by 'love' is meant simply pleasure accompanied by the idea of its cause, any pleasure accompanied by God as its cause counts as the love of God. But all adequate cognition is both inherently pleasurable, since it expresses the activity of the mind, and involves the idea of God as cause, since it consists in an idea of the object as following from God (the third kind of knowledge). Thus, the adequate knowledge of anything involves the love of God as its affective dimension. Moreover, since, in principle at least, it is possible to acquire an adequate idea of any modification of substance, it follows that this love can be occasioned by virtually anything. Consequently, it is its potential ubiquity, together with its superior affective force as expression of pure activity, that qualifies this love-knowledge of God as the supreme remedy against the passions.

In the second half of part five, the love of God is now explicitly characterized as 'intellectual' and paradoxically identified with the love with which God loves himself. And if this were not puzzling enough, Spinoza introduces the new discussion by proclaiming: 'With this I have completed everything which concerns this present life . . . so it is now time to pass to those things which pertain to the mind's duration without relation to the body' (*Ethics*: V, prop. 20, scholium). This sets the agenda for the final propositions, the basic concern of which is to show that 'The human mind cannot be absolutely destroyed with the body, but something of it remains which is eternal' (*Ethics*: V, prop. 23). It is within this context that Spinoza refers to the intellectual love of God.

Because of their apparent incompatibility with the central teachings of the *Ethics*, these final propositions remain a source of perplexity. Nevertheless, it does seem possible to make sense of Spinoza's thought here, if we see it in the context of a shift of focus from the concern with reason (including the love of God) in its struggle with the passions, to a concern with the life of reason as the highest condition of which human beings are capable and, therefore, as constitutive of human blessedness. So construed, the abrupt change of tone is simply Spinoza's way of marking that shift rather than an indication of a lapse into a mysticism that is totally at variance with the spirit of his philosophy. Such a reading leads to an essentially epistemological rather than a metaphysical reading of the doctrine of the eternity of the mind. According to this reading, the human mind is 'eternal' to the extent to which it is capable of grasping eternal truth and ultimately of understanding itself by the third kind of knowledge, which, in turn, leads to the intellectual love of God. To be sure, this is not the eternal life promised by religion; but it is a state of blessedness or perfection in the sense that it involves the full realization of our capacities. Moreover, it is precisely the mode of life to which the *Ethics* as a whole points the way.

Such a reading is also supported by the final proposition in which Spinoza returns to the theme of virtue and links it with both health and blessedness. As he there puts it, 'Blessedness is not the reward of virtue, but virtue itself; nor do we enjoy it because we restrain our lusts; on the contrary, because we enjoy it, we are able to constrain them' (*Ethics*: V, prop. 41). There is not a trace of mysticism here, but merely the familiar Spinozistic emphasis on the connection between blessedness and knowledge on the one hand, and knowledge and power on the other. Accordingly, the point is that we do not acquire this knowledge by first controlling our lusts, but that we have the power to control them (virtue) only to the extent to which we already possess adequate knowledge. And it is in this knowledge, also characterized as peace of mind, that blessedness consists.

13 Politics

Spinoza's concern with political theory has its philosophical roots in his conception of human beings as social animals, which entails the necessity of living in a state under a system of laws; but it was also triggered by the political situation in his own time. In the Netherlands, the monarchist party was intent on overthrowing the republican form of government, and their allies, the Reformed clergy, desired to establish a state church. In spite of his commitment to a life of philosophical contemplation, Spinoza was keenly aware of this situation and the dangers it posed to freedom of thought and expression, which he regarded as essential. His philosophical response to this threat, as well as the statement of his own views about the nature and function of the state, are to be found in the *Tractatus Theologico-politicus* (*Theological-Political Treatise*) and the *Tractatus Politicus* (*Political Treatise*). The former is a polemical work, intended, at least in part, as a response to the Reformed clergy, while the latter is a dispassionate essay in political science. But despite this difference in tone and some disagreement on substantive matters, both works argue for freedom as the supreme political value and both investigate the conditions under which it can be realized and preserved.

Spinoza's political thought is best approached by way of a comparison with Hobbes. Both thinkers view human beings as thoroughly determined parts of nature and as driven by the desire for self-preservation; both are amoralists in the sense that they hold that everyone has a 'natural right' to do whatever is deemed necessary for self-preservation; as a direct consequence of this view of natural right, both view the state of nature (the pre-political condition) as one of unavoidable conflict and insecurity; and, finally, both maintain that peace and security can be attained only if everyone surrenders all of their natural right to a sovereign power (which takes the form of a social contract). But whereas Hobbes concludes from his account the necessity of an absolute sovereign power, preferably in the form of a monarchy, Spinoza infers from substantially the same premises that the true end of the state is freedom, and, at least in the *Theological-Political Treatise*, that democracy is 'the most natural form of state'.

To some extent, these differences can be understood in terms of the different social and political conditions under which the two thinkers lived. There are also important philosophical differences, however, one of which is their respective conceptions of human reason. For Hobbes, reason has a merely instrumental value as a means to the attainment of ends dictated by desire. We have seen, however, that for Spinoza the goal is to transform desire through reason, which naturally leads him to focus on the conditions under which the life of reason can best be lived. Moreover, Spinoza seems to have arrived at his conclusions through a kind of internal critique of Hobbes. As he informed a correspondent in 1674:

> With regard to politics, the difference between Hobbes and me... consists in this, that I ever preserve the natural right intact so that the

supreme power in a state has no more right over a subject than is proportionate to the power by which it is superior to the subject. This is what always takes place in the state of nature.
>
> (Spinoza 1966 letter 50: 269)

By suggesting that Hobbes did not keep natural right intact, Spinoza is implying that he did not consistently equate right with power. This is indeed true; but it does not explain how the identification of might with right enables Spinoza to arrive at his conclusions. The gist of the answer, as suggested by this passage, is that the identification applies also to sovereign power. In other words, rather than gaining absolute right over its subjects through the social contract, as Hobbes maintained, the sovereign's right is limited by its power; and since this power is inevitably limited, so too are the things that a sovereign may 'legitimately' demand of its subjects.

Among the things that a sovereign cannot require are acts so contrary to human nature that no threat or promise could lead a person to perform them. These include things such as forcing people to testify against themselves or to make no effort to avoid death. But Spinoza does not stop at such obvious cases. He also emphasizes the limitation of legislative power with respect to private morality; and he finds an argument for freedom of thought in the fact that a government is powerless to prevent it. More importantly, he points out that there are some things which a government can do by brute force, but in doing so inevitably undermines its own authority. And since a government cannot do these things with impunity, it does not have the 'right' to do them at all. Thus, he argues on entirely pragmatic grounds for the limitation of governmental power through the power of public opinion.

Spinoza's main concern as political theorist, however, is not to determine what the state cannot do, but rather what it should do in order to realize the end for which it was established. Moreover, while verbally agreeing with Hobbes in construing this end as peace and security, Spinoza understands these in a much broader sense. Accordingly, peace is not merely an absence of war or the threat thereof, but a positive condition in which people can exercise their virtue. Thus, the goal of the state is to create this condition, which is also the social condition necessary for the life of reason as depicted in the *Ethics*.

But the life of reason is only for the few, and political arrangements must concern the many. Moreover, since it is the many who determine the public opinion to which the government must pay heed if it is to rule effectively, it follows that there can be valid laws, approved at least tacitly by a majority, which are none the less inimical to true virtue. Spinoza was keenly aware of this problem; but his way of dealing with it indicates the tension between his democratic tendencies and his elitism that runs throughout his theory. Thus on the one hand he insists on the right of free expression, including the right to protest against laws deemed unjust, while on the other hand he emphasizes the necessity of total obedience to the existing law, no matter how contrary to reason it may be. The reason for this conservative turn, which is also reflected in the complete rejection of revolution as a political remedy, lies in his profound sense of the irrationality of the multitude. Given this irrationality, which poses a constant threat to the power of reason, Spinoza concludes with Hobbes that even under a tyrannical regime, obedience to the established authority is the lesser evil.

14 Scripture

Spinoza's revolutionary treatment of the Bible in the *Theological-Political Treatise* must also be understood within the framework of his political thought. In line with his concern to secure the freedom to philosophize, he launches a systematic attack on the authority of Scripture: its claim to be the revealed word of God. But rather than offering an external philosophical critique in the manner of the *Ethics*, he attempts, in a somewhat paradoxical fashion, to show from Scripture itself that it makes no such claim to authority. This strategy, in turn, rests on a new method of Biblical exegesis, one based on the Cartesian principle that nothing should be attributed to the text that is not clearly and distinctly perceived to be contained in it. In light of this principle, he rejects both the Calvinist doctrine that a supernatural faculty is required for interpreting the Bible and the older Jewish rationalism of Maimonides, which held that if the literal reading of a passage conflicts with reason, it must be interpreted in some metaphorical sense (see MAIMONIDES, M.). Both of these approaches he regards as not only useless for interpreting the Bible, but as dangerous politically, since they lead to the establishment of spiritual authorities.

Applying his method, Spinoza argues that neither prophecy nor miracles, the twin pillars of biblical authority, are able to support the orthodox claims. The prophets are shown to differ from other individuals in their superior imaginations, not in their intellects. Similarly, biblical miracles are treated as natural occurrences, which only appeared mysterious to the biblical authors because of their limited understandings and, as such, have no probative value. More generally, the Bible is viewed as a document which reflects the limited understandings of a crude

people rather than the dictates of an omniscient deity. And by analysing Scripture in this way, Spinoza laid the foundation for the subsequent historical study of the Bible ('higher criticism'), which endeavours to interpret it by the same methods applicable to any other ancient text.

Spinoza's critique of the Bible is, however, largely directed against its speculative content and claim to be a source of theoretical truth. Thus, he affirms that in moral matters the Bible has a consistent and true teaching, which reduces essentially to the requirement to love one's neighbour. Moreover, precisely because it appeals to the imagination rather than the intellect, it has the great virtue of presenting morality in a form which the multitude can grasp. Such a view of religion as morality for the masses is hardly original to Spinoza. It had already been expressed in the twelfth century by Averroes (see IBN RUSHD §4), and it found expression in many subsequent politically minded thinkers, including Machiavelli (see MACHIAVELLI, N. §6). But, if not original to Spinoza, it is still an integral part of his political thought, since it enables him to 'save' religion while also protecting the autonomy of philosophy. And the latter is, of course, necessary for the life of reason as depicted in the *Ethics*.

See also: ARETĒ; EUDAIMONIA; GOD, CONCEPTS OF; MONISM; SUBSTANCE; WILL

List of works

Spinoza, B. de (1925) *Spinoza Opera*, ed. C. Gebhardt, 4 vols, Heidelberg: Carl Winter. (The standard edition of Spinoza's writings.)

—— (c.1660–5) *Korte Verhandelung van God, de Mensch, en Deszelfs Welstand* (Short Treatise on God, Man, and his Well-Being), ed. and trans. A. Wolf, New York: Russell & Russell, 1963. (Written in Dutch, this is the earliest systematic statement of Spinoza's philosophy, dating from the early 1660s but not published until 1862. The Wolf translation also has an introduction, commentary and life of Spinoza.

—— (1663) *Renati Des Cartes Principiorum Philosphiae* (Descartes' 'Principles of Philosophy'), in *The Collected Works of Spinoza*, vol. 1, ed. and trans. E. Curley, Princeton, NJ: Princeton University Press, 1985. (An early work in which Spinoza expounds part of Descartes' *Principles* for a student.)

—— (1670) *Tractatus Theologico-politicus* (Theological-Political Treatise), in *The Chief Works of Benedict de Spinoza*, vol. 1, trans. R.H.M. Elwes, New York: Dover, 1951. (A polemical work, which makes a major contribution to both political theory and interpretation of the Bible.)

—— (1677a) *Ethica Ordine Geometrico Demonstrata* (Ethics Demonstrated in a Geometrical Manner), in *The Collected Works of Spinoza*, vol. 1, ed. and trans. E. Curley, Princeton, NJ: Princeton University Press, 1985. (Spinoza's major systematic work.)

—— (1677b) *Tractatus de Intellectus Emendatione* (Treatise on the Emendation of the Intellect), in *The Collected Works of Spinoza*, vol. 1, ed. and trans. E. Curley, Princeton, NJ: Princeton University Press, 1985. (An early fragment which contains an important account of Spinoza's philosophical method.)

—— (1677c) *Tractatus Politicus* (Political Treatise), in *Benedict de Spinoza: The Political Works*, ed. and trans. A.G. Wernham, Oxford: Clarendon Press, 1958. (Although unfinished, it contains the most systematic statement of Spinoza's political philosophy.)

—— (1966) *The Correspondence of Spinoza*, trans. A. Wolf, London: Frank Cass. (Contains all the extant letters to and from Spinoza of philosophical significance.)

References and further reading

Allison, H.E. (1987) *Benedict de Spinoza: An Introduction*, New Haven, CT, and London: Yale University Press. (The contributor's own general introduction to Spinoza.)

Bennett, J. (1984) *A Study of Spinoza's Ethics*, Indianapolis, IN: Hackett Publishing Company. (A very challenging and controversial discussion of the central topics in the *Ethics*.)

Curley, E.M. (1988) *Behind the Geometrical Method, A Reading of Spinoza's Ethics*, Princeton, NJ: Princeton University Press. (Clearly written, useful introduction to the *Ethics*, emphasizing the connections between Spinoza and Hobbes).

Delahunty, R.J. (1985) *Spinoza*, London: Routledge & Kegan Paul. (Contains a useful discussion of some of the major interpretive issues in the secondary literature.)

Donagan, A. (1989) *Spinoza*, Chicago, IL: University of Chicago Press. (Good, scholarly introduction to Spinoza's thought.)

Gueroult, M. (1968) *Spinoza I, Dieu (Ethique, I)*, Paris: Aubier. (Probably the richest and most detailed study available in any language of the first part of the *Ethics*.)

—— (1974) *Spinoza II, L'Ame (Ethique, II)*, Hildesheim: Olms. (The most detailed study of the second part of the *Ethics* available in any language.)

Hampshire, S. (1951) *Spinoza*, London: Faber. (A clearly written and still useful overview of Spinoza's thought).

Joachim, H.H. (1901) *A Study of the Ethics of Spinoza*, London: Oxford University Press; repr. New York: Russell & Russell, 1964. (One of the classic commentaries on the *Ethics*.)

Wolfson, H.A. (1958) *The Philosophy of Spinoza*, New York: Meridian Books, 2 vols. (The major study of the historical origins of Spinoza's thought; emphasizes the Medieval connections).

HENRY E. ALLISON

SPLIT BRAINS

Severing the direct neural connections between the two cerebral hemispheres produces a 'split brain'. Does it also multiply minds? The most extensive tests of the psychological results of this operation were conducted by Roger Sperry and his colleagues. He concluded that split-brain patients have 'Two separate spheres of conscious awareness, two separate conscious entities or minds, running in parallel in the same cranium, each with its own sensations, cognitive processes, learning processes, memories and so on'. Sperry's view faces both conservative and radical challenges. The conservative challenge is that the results of the tests do not imply that split-brain patients have two minds and are two persons. The radical challenge is that the operation does not multiply minds but, instead, reveals a startling fact: human beings with intact commissures already have two spheres of consciousness, house two minds, and are two persons.

For the purposes of this entry, a split-brain patient is one who has had a *complete* forebrain commissurotomy. In this operation (which has been replaced by less radical procedures), the *corpus callosum* and the other neural links ('commissures') between the two cerebral hemispheres were completely severed.

Patients underwent the operation for the relief of otherwise uncontrollable epilepsy, and it was considered a therapeutic success. Epileptic attacks disappeared, became less frequent or were confined to one hemisphere. Once the patients recovered from the operation, they were able to resume their normal lives; people who knew these patients before the operation would not notice any dramatic changes in their personality, intellect or everyday behaviour.

Observation under controlled conditions discloses a different picture. When input is limited to one cerebral hemisphere and response demanded of it, the behaviour of split-brain patients is decidedly abnor-

107

mal, as the following simple example illustrates. 'Key ring' is flashed on a screen for a tenth of a second so that 'key' appears in the left visual field and 'ring' in the right. If split-brain subjects are asked to *say* what they saw, they respond that they saw 'ring' and show no sign of seeing 'key'. But, if they are asked, instead, to *retrieve* with their left hands the object named on the screen from an array of items concealed from sight, they will pick out a key while rejecting a ring. Asked to point with the left hand to the object named on the screen, they point to a key or a picture of a key and not to a ring or a picture of a ring. If they are allowed to use both hands to pick out the object named from an array of items hidden from sight, their left and right hands work independently, the right settling on a ring while rejecting a key and the left doing the opposite. Someone seems to have seen 'key'. Someone else seems to have seen 'ring'. No one seems to have seen 'key ring'. With suitable controls, input from the other sensory modalities, except taste, can also be confined exclusively to one hemisphere. When a response depends upon it, split-brain patients behave in similar abnormal ways.

The standard explanation of such behaviour is roughly as follows. The structure of the visual system assures that the left half of the field of vision is conveyed to the right hemisphere and vice versa. Normally, information about the contralateral visual field is supplied to each hemisphere by neural communication across the commissures and by subsequent eye movement. Since the commissures of split-brain patients are severed and the short exposure time serves as a control for eye movement, their right hemispheres see only the word 'key' and their left only the word 'ring'. In most people, speech production is localized in the left hemisphere; and so the oral response to the question reports only what the left hemisphere saw: the word 'ring'. The left hand is primarily controlled by the right hemisphere; so it retrieves the object the right hemisphere saw named – a key – and points to a key or a picture of a key. (Notice that this explanation presupposes speech comprehension in the mute right hemisphere.) Similarly, the right hand is primarily controlled by the left hemisphere, thus accounting for the independent search of items concealed from sight. The failure to elicit any response suggesting that 'key ring' was seen is that the contents of the visual field available to each hemisphere are not the same and, because of the severing of the commissures and the experimental controls, not communicated to the opposite hemisphere.

Behaviour of the sort illustrated in the 'key ring' example and its explanation fuel a natural, tantalizing line of inference.

(1) *The behaviour shows that the split-brain patient sometimes has a disunified consciousness.* No one has doubted that the behaviour associated with the left hemisphere in the 'key ring' example indicates that the subject consciously saw 'ring'. The behaviour associated with the right hemisphere seems to be equally clear and prototypical evidence that the subject has a conscious experience of seeing 'key'; in fact, it is difficult to see how this can be denied short of a general scepticism about the consciousness of human beings who can comprehend, but not produce, language. So, in the example, the patient has simultaneous conscious experiences of seeing 'key' and of seeing 'ring', but none of seeing both.

(2) *This disunity of consciousness is a standing condition.* The cause of the disunity of consciousness, behaviourally evident in the 'key ring' example, is the severing of the neural connections between the two cerebral hemispheres. These remain severed and their neural functions unduplicated whatever the behaviour of split-brain patients. In the absence of controls to prevent it, the separate spheres of consciousness associated with the left and right hemispheres have highly similar contents. This overlap of content and other factors explain why the split-brain patient's everyday behaviour does not dramatically display two separate spheres of consciousness.

(3) *Split-brain patients have two minds and are two persons.* Despite the significant differences between the two hemispheres, each sustains a range and complexity of psychological functions, including self-awareness, that is characteristically human. Examinations of hemispherectomy patients and their near functional kin – patients with severe strokes in a single hemisphere – confirm the observations of split-brain patients. Neither hemisphere has any better access to the conscious contents of the other than we do to those of other people; each has as direct access to its own experiences as we do to ours. So split-brain patients have two minds. If an embodied mind of characteristic human complexity is a person, then the split-brain patient is two persons since the patient embodies two of them.

(4) *If split-brain patients have two minds and are two persons, so do human beings with intact commissures.* Even with commissures intact, each hemisphere receives a separate neural representation of 'key' and 'ring' in conditions like the 'key ring' example. Why, then, do we not see the behaviour of a split-brain patient? The usual answer is that neural communication between the hemispheres ensures that the right hemisphere is made aware that the left is seeing 'ring' and, perhaps, brought to have such an experience itself and vice versa for the right hemisphere. But, then, we have a duplicate of the split-

brain case. Communication between the two hemi-spheres provides a behavioural mask of two independent streams of consciousness – two minds – and two persons just as the duplication of content in everyday circumstances does in the split-brain patients. So, starting from incontestable neurological and behavioural facts about split-brain patients, one apparently arrives at the paradoxical conclusion that we are small collectives of two minds and two persons (see MIND, BUNDLE THEORY OF; PERSONAL IDENTITY).

The line of inference just sketched can be used to define philosophical positions on split brains. For a variety of reasons, conservative challenges to Sperry (see above) hold that it should stop short of its third step. Eccles (1970) once claimed that there are no conscious mental phenomena known to be associated with the nonverbal right hemisphere and, later, that whatever conscious processes might be associated with it are subhuman in character. Others have argued that the disunity in consciousness split-brain patients sometimes exhibit is not a standing condition and does not imply two minds; yet others that, although split-brain patients have two minds, they constitute a single person because a single control structure governs both. Sperry (1968) has consistently held the middle ground, endorsing the line of inference as far as its third step. He has refused to join Bogen (1985) and Puccetti (1973) in taking the radical fourth step because, he claims, intact cerebral commissures are the physical basis of unity of consciousness and mind. Many other positions have been taken besides those mentioned. Thomas Nagel's is particularly striking. He claims that there is no answer to the question of how many minds or persons split-brain patients contain, and that this shows that our ordinary concept of the unity of a person 'may resist the sort of coordination with the understanding of humans as physical systems, that would be necessary to anything describable as an understanding of the physical basis of mind' (1971).

The wide diversity of opinion has several sources. The data are unexpected and sometimes messy. Any attempt to deal with them faces a special version of the mind–body problem. One must decide, on some principled grounds, the relation of various anatomic, neurological and behavioural data to mentalistic descriptions; and the proper account of the mentalistic notions of prime concern – consciousness, mind and person – is, to put it mildly, controversial. We also still lack a detailed understanding of how brain structures are responsible for the psychological distinctions involved, for example, what specific role the *corpus callosum* plays, what a control structure is, and how to count centres of consciousness.

Besides raising the philosophical issues discussed above, research on split brains has provided much insight into problems of deep physiological and psychological interest, for example, hemispheric specialization, which are not immediately tied to them. It has also provided a launching pad for a variety of 'thought experiments' in philosophical discussions of personal identity.

See also: MIND, BUNDLE THEORY OF; CONSCIOUSNESS; PERSONAL IDENTITY

References and further reading

With the single exception noted, the individual works listed are understandable without any esoteric technical knowledge.

Benson, D.F. and Zaidel, E. (eds) (1985) *The Dual Brain: Hemispheric Specialization in Humans*, New York: Guilford. (A representative sample of the psychological and neuroscientific work inspired, in part, by the split-brain phenomena; some of the articles require some advanced technical knowledge.)

* Bogen, J.E. (1985) 'The Dual Brain: Some Historical and Methodological Aspects', in D.F. Benson and E. Zaidel (eds) *The Dual Brain: Hemispheric Specialization in Humans*, New York: Guilford, 27–43. (History of thought on the two cerebral hemispheres and partial defence of his 'two persons' account of uncommissurotomized human beings; good bibliography. Some technical knowledge necessary.)

* Eccles, J.C. (1970) 'The Brain and the Unity of Conscious Experience', in *Facing Reality: Philosophical Adventures of a Brain Scientist*, New York: Springer, 63–84. (Argument that right hemisphere processes are not conscious.)

Gillett, G. (1986) 'Brain Bisection and Personal Identity', *Mind* 95: 224–9. (Doubts about whether the right hemisphere is a conscious rational thinker.)

McKay, D.M. (1966) 'Cerebral Organization and the Conscious Control of Actions', in J.C. Eccles (ed.) *Brain and Conscious Experience*, Heidelberg: Springer, 422–44. (Argument that there is a single control structure for the operations of the disconnected hemispheres.)

Marks, C.E. (1981) *Commissurotomy, Consciousness, and Unity of Mind*, Cambridge, MA: MIT Press. (Defence of a conservative interpretation of the split-brain phenomena; extensive bibliography.)

* Nagel, T. (1971) 'Brain Bisection and the Unity of Consciousness', *Synthèse* 22: 396–413; repr. in *Mortal Questions*, Cambridge: Cambridge Univer-

sity Press, 1979, 147–64. (Argument that the split-brain data present an obstacle to understanding the physical basis of mind.)

* Puccetti, R. (1973) 'Brain Bisection and Personal Identity', *British Journal for the Philosophy of Science* 42: 339–55. (Argument that the split-brain data lead to the view that uncommissurotomized human beings have two streams of consciousness and are two persons.)

—— (1981) 'The Case for Mental Duality: Evidence from Split-Brain Data and Other Considerations', *Behavioral and Brain Sciences* 4: 93–123. (Amplification of the viewpoint of Puccetti (1973); with extensive commentary, the author's responses and a large bibliography.)

* Sperry, R.W. (1968) 'Hemisphere Deconnection and Unity in Conscious Awareness', *American Psychologist* 23: 723–33. (Early presentation of the view that split-brain patients, but not those with unsplit brains, have two spheres of consciousness and two minds. Good non-technical introduction to the empirical data by the leading researcher.)

—— (1977a) 'Consciousness, Personal Identity, and the Divided Brain', repr. with editorial updating of references, in D.F. Benson and E. Zaidel (eds) *The Dual Brain: Hemispheric Specialization in Humans*, New York: Guildford, 1985, 11–26. (Amplification and defence of the viewpoint of the previous article; excellent bibliography. Good introduction to empirical research.)

—— (1977b) 'Forebrain Commissurotomy and Conscious Awareness', repr. in C. Travarthen (ed.) *Brain Circuits and Functions of the Mind: Essays in Honor of Roger W. Sperry*, Cambridge: Cambridge University Press, 1990, 371–88. (Also an amplification and defence of the viewpoint of Sperry's 1968 article, including his most careful consideration of rival views; excellent bibliography.)

Travarthen, C. (ed.) (1990) *Brain Circuits and Functions of the Mind: Essays in Honor of Roger W. Sperry*, Cambridge: Cambridge University Press. (A representative sample of the psychological and neuroscientific work inspired, in part, by the split-brain phenomena; some of the articles require some advanced technical knowledge.)

Wilkes, K.V. (1988) *Real People: Personal Identity without Thought Experiments*, Oxford: Oxford University Press, 132–67. (Expanded version of her earlier conservative assessment of the split-brain phenomena.)

CHARLES MARKS

SPORT AND ETHICS

Ethical controversies have formed some of the liveliest debate in the philosophy of sport. Some of the issues arise out of the very nature of sport as a rule-governed activity, especially since the breaking of those rules often presents opportunities for competitive advantage. Other debates concern over-emphasis on winning, which can lead to various forms of cheating. The 'problem of winning' is clearly related to the larger problem of competition itself, which has led to lively dialogue over whether competition in athletics inevitably causes alienation. Finally, one of the most provocative controversies has been over the question of performance-enhancing drugs and whether they should be banned.

1 **Sport as rule-governed activity**
2 **The problem of winning**
3 **Competition**
4 **Performance-enhancing drugs**

1 Sport as rule-governed activity

The French writer, Albert Camus, once wrote that it was from his youthful involvement in sport that he 'learned everything he knew about ethics'. Whatever Camus meant by this cryptic remark, it is clear that ethical issues in sport have become one of the central concerns of the philosophy of sport. In part, this may be because in sport our ethical commitments are not merely articulated in speech; we *see* an athlete's ethical standards exhibited in the way they play.

Although some sporting activities such as jogging or recreational skiing, would seem to have few explicit rules, most are rule-governed to one extent or another. Adherence to these rules becomes an immediate ethical issue, especially since often an apparent advantage can be gained by cheating. Many sport philosophers have argued that since playing a given game can virtually be defined as adhering to its rules ('playing basketball' means conforming to the rules of basketball), someone who breaks those rules is not really playing that game at all.

This is complicated by the fact that in many sports certain instances of breaking the rules are so common that they are regarded as 'part of the game'. Consider personal fouls in basketball, offsides in football or soccer, or hitting a batter in baseball. Would we want to say that a soccer player who moves offside is not playing the game? This raises the yet further issue of certain strategies that involve unconcealed breaking of the rules. Consider, for example, 'taking a foul' in basketball when an opposing player has an easy shot. Is this cheating or smart strategy? If cheating, is the fouler still playing basketball? These and related issues are given perhaps the most thorough discussion in Warren Fraleigh (1984).

2 The problem of winning

Since all competitive sports entail that one person or team will win, the other lose, how could there be a 'problem' with winning? The obvious but troublesome answer is that the competitive drive to win has led many to take illicit steps in that pursuit. The 'overemphasis on winning' has been cited as the cause of everything from cheating within the game to unfair or even illicit steps to prepare for winning, such as recruiting violations, accepting unqualified athletes into college and the use of performance-enhancing drugs.

Public debate on this issue has tended towards two simplistic responses, encapsulated in the well-known maxims, 'Winning isn't everything, it's the only thing', and its contrary, 'It's not whether you win or lose but how you play the game'. The first assumes that there are no values or goals in competitive sport other than winning, which is clearly false. Though winning is *a* goal of every game, so also are such things as getting a good workout, having fun, and developing a sense of teamwork. On the other hand, no committed athlete will be satisfied with the second maxim, which implies that winning simply does not matter. Of course it does; every athlete feels exhilaration at victory and disappointment at defeat. The real issue is to recognize winning as *one* of the values in sport, but one among others, and to put it in proper perspective alongside the other legitimate values of participation. How to do that, of course, is a complicated issue.

3 Competition

The overemphasis on winning discussed above is evidently a function of the competitive nature of sport and the abuses competition can generate. Not surprisingly, there has been much criticism of competitive sport on these grounds, deriving often from Marxian criticisms of competition in capitalism. A central contention here is that competition, whether in the economic sphere or in sport, *causes* alienation in its various guises (see MARKET, ETHICS OF §3). No one can deny that too often in sport the competitive situation devolves into alienation. Every athlete has experienced alienation in sport, and it is an easy inference that such alienation is a function of the competition central to sporting games. On the other hand, not all competitive sporting events involve alienation; indeed, the vast majority of athletic games occur among friends and are occasions of friendship.

So if many or even most athletic contests are friendly, it is hardly obvious that competition *per se* causes alienation.

Part of the problem may be that we tend to think of the paradigms of sport in terms of *professional* sport, where the aspirations of the players are complicated (some would say polluted) by financial factors. Although it is neither the case that all amateur sporting events are friendly, nor all professional ones alienated, it is nevertheless plausible – and compatible with the Marxian analysis – that once sport becomes an economic issue the likelihood of alienation is increased.

One way to think about this is to consider a teleological account of competitive sport. What is sport like when it 'really works', when it is the best that it can be? It has been argued that, at its best, sport is indeed an occasion of friendship, that competitive sport can offer a particularly intense encounter among friendly participants who wish to challenge each other to be the best that they can be. On this view, when competitive events do degenerate into alienation, that should be construed as a defective mode of sport, certainly not as 'the way competition is' or the way sport has to be. That should lead in turn to efforts to determine what causes competitive sport to devolve into alienation and how to avoid those conditions.

4 Performance-enhancing drugs

One of the major ethical controversies in sport philosophy involves the use by athletes of so-called performance-enhancing drugs, the best known of which are probably anabolic steroids. The claim and the belief of many athletes is that high doses of these drugs coupled with strenuous training will build significant muscle mass and therefore enhance the athlete's abilities. There is some evidence, however, that such drugs, particularly in the doses employed by some athletes, are harmful to one's physical and mental health, resulting in everything from acne and danger of cancer to pathological aggressiveness. This has led most sports organizations to ban the use of performance-enhancing drugs.

But should they be banned? This has become the subject of considerable controversy. Most writers have argued that they ought to be banned on several grounds. The main objections to their use have been danger to health, the issue of fairness, and the problem of coercion.

The danger-to-health argument hinges on the validity of the data suggesting that these drugs are indeed dangerous to health, and a certain commitment to paternalism, arguing that since such drugs are dangerous, athletes should be 'protected from them-selves' by having the drugs banned (see PATERNAL-ISM). The fairness argument turns on the clear sense that those athletes who do choose to use performance-enhancers, even at the risk of their health, will have an unfair advantage over those presumably more pru-dent athletes who choose not to use them. This leads in turn to the third argument, that athletes who wish to excel will be unfairly coerced into using the drugs if they want to compete with drug users.

All these arguments have been contested in a set of important and provocative articles by W.M. Brown (1980, 1984). Brown begins by pointing out the difficulty of determining nonarbitrarily just what a performance-enhancing drug is. What about aspirin for pains before a game? What about caffeine for stimulation? Do they not enhance performance? With regard to the presumed danger to health, Brown argues that even if it is shown conclusively that, say, anabolic steroids do constitute a health danger (in fact a disputed point), the very activities of most sports involve dangers to health much more severe than the putative dangers of performance-enhancers: various injuries and even, as in the case of sports such as rock climbing or automobile racing, risk of death. If 'danger to health' is a criterion for banning, it appears most sports should be banned.

Turning to the fairness argument, Brown rejoins that there are all sorts of unfairness inherent in most sports. Is it not 'unfair' to me as a normal sized male if my opponent in basketball is seven feet tall? Is it not 'unfair' if my cross-country ski opponent grew up in snowy Vermont while I grew up in Florida? Is it not 'unfair' of my opponent to practice for long hours or lift weights to gain an advantage when I do not? How, in short, do we separate nonarbitrarily the unfairness of performance-enhancing drugs from the myriad other unfairnesses that competitive sport entails?

Regarding the coercion argument, Brown retorts that the use of the term 'coercion' here is overblown. 'No one forces athletes to seek Olympic gold,' he says; the pressures on athletes to take performance-enhan-cing drugs are no different in principle from all the other pressures – and difficult decisions – that top level athletes face all the time. The debate continues.

See also: SPORT, PHILOSOPHY OF

References and further reading

* Brown, W.M. (1980) 'Ethics, Drugs, and Sport', *Journal of the Philosophy of Sport* 7: 15–23. (The provocative article that began the controversy over performance-enhancing drugs, arguing that the decision should be the individual athlete's.)
* —— (1984) 'Paternalism, Drugs, and the Nature of Sports', *Journal of the Philosophy of Sport* 11: 14–22. (A follow-up article in which Brown answers his critics and modifies his position slightly.)
* Fraleigh, W. (1984) *Right Actions in Sport: Ethics for Contestants*, Champaign, IL: Human Kinetics Publishers. (A comprehensive look at problems in sport ethics)
Hyland, D. (1990) 'Ethical Issues in Sport', in *Philosophy of Sport*, New York: Paragon House, ch. 2. (Treats the issues discussed above in greater detail, including the problem of winning, competi-tion and alienation, and the debate over perfor-mance-enhancing drugs.)
Various, *Journal of the Philosophy of Sport*. (The leading journal in the field, containing most of the important articles in sport ethics. See especially volume 11 for a symposium on performance-enhancing drugs.)

DREW A. HYLAND

SPORT, PHILOSOPHY OF

The philosophy of sport as a separate area of philosophy is largely a phenomenon of the second half of the twentieth century, although previous philoso-phers, back to the ancient Greeks, occasionally made reference to sport or used it as an example in a larger point. Within the philosophy of sport, a number of sub-areas have emerged as important: sport and ethics, questions concerning sport and society, the issue of self-knowledge in sport, the mind–body problem as it relates to sport, sport and art, and the controversy over the possibility of defining certain key terms within sport, such as sport, game, play and athletics.

Within the area of sport and society, several major debates have arisen. The first is about whether sport teaches values and, if so, whether the values taught are desirable or not. Second, considerable attention has been paid to how certain societal problems, such as sexism and racism, have manifested themselves in sport, and how they might be addressed within sport. Third, attention has been directed to the phenomenon of the athlete as cultural hero.

The relevance to sport of the age-old philosophical issue of self-knowledge is manifest, with a number of different construals of what counts as self-knowledge emerging as important. Attention has been paid to self-knowledge in the psychological sense, self-knowledge as manifested in Zen thought and self-knowledge in the Socratic sense, among others. The mind–body problem, also an old philosophic issue, has clear relevance within the domain of sport. Dualism, physicalism and phenomenological accounts have all been represented, the latter being the most dominant and persuasive so far.

1 **Introduction: historical background**
2 **Sport and society**
3 **Sport and self-knowledge**
4 **Mind and body in sport**

1 Introduction: historical background

The history of the philosophic interest in sport in one sense goes back to the ancient Greeks, but in another sense is a phenomenon of the middle and late twentieth century. Greek culture in general placed great emphasis on what they called *gymnastikē*, the training of the body, making it, along with education in the arts (*mousikē*), one of the two foundations of education. Plato, in Books III–V of his *Republic*, reflects this interest by making education in gymnastics a core aspect of the education of those who will become the famous 'philosopher-rulers', and in his *Laws* (803c), the Athenian Stranger praises play as the very highest of human activities. In addition, Aristotle sometimes uses examples from athletics to make important points. Nevertheless, no Platonic dialogue, Aristotelian treatise or other philosophic work in ancient Greece focused explicitly on sport as a topic worthy of philosophic reflection in its own right.

This situation remained almost until the middle of the twentieth century. Indeed, for long periods of time, there was very little mention of sport or athletics by philosophers at all. In the late eighteenth and the nineteenth centuries, philosophers such as Schiller and Nietzsche praised play as a high human activity, and Nietzsche made it a guiding metaphor for his notion of the purposeless 'happening' of the will to power. Following him in the twentieth century, continental thinkers such as Heidegger, Gadamer, Foucault and Derrida used play as a metaphor for their guiding notions, and Wittgenstein used the concept of 'language games' as a core notion in his philosophy, but none of them treat sport as a philosophical theme in itself.

In 1938, however, the historian Johan Huizinga published his book *Homo Ludens: A Study of the Play Element in Culture* in which he argued the thesis that 'civilization arises and unfolds as play'. Part of the importance of this book was that it legitimized play and sport as respectable topics for intellectual reflection and research. A few decades later, the US philosopher Paul Weiss published his *Sport: A Philosophic Inquiry* (1969), after which sport became

a legitimate and identifiable area of philosophic investigation.

We shall discuss a number of the most important topics and issues in the philosophy of sport. Some of the most important topics not treated below at least deserve mention. We shall not here address the crucial connection between sport and ethics (see SPORT AND ETHICS). There is also a lively discussion in the philosophical literature concerning the definition of key terms in philosophy of sport. Can terms such as game, play, sport and athletics be defined? Or, in a Wittgensteinian mode, can we at best find a number of 'family resemblances' in and among these terms? Probably the most important single contribution to this debate has been Bernard Suits' 1978 work *The Grasshopper: Games, Life, and Utopia*, a book-length study devoted to the thesis that 'game' can indeed be defined. There is also an active discussion regarding the connection of sport and art, ranging from thinkers who virtually identify the two to those whose interest focuses on the aesthetic element in sport.

2 Sport and society

Huizinga established beyond doubt that sport is essentially a cultural phenomenon. Not surprisingly, many striking philosophical issues concerning sport centre upon the relation between sport and society. One crucial issue of controversy concerns the relation of sport and the teaching or inculcating of 'values'. Nearly everyone, from the most fanatical devotees of sport to its harshest critics, agrees that sport teaches values. The disagreement is over what values sport teaches. The litany that the partisans of sport offer is well known: sport teaches such virtues as self-discipline, teamwork, being a gracious winner and a fair loser, fair play and courage. The critics of sport are no less sure that sport teaches values: mindless obedience to authority, the desire to hurt or humiliate others, dog-eat-dog competitiveness, cheating and a willingness to ruin one's body in the name of winning a game.

A look at the empirical evidence attests that both are sometimes right. Depending on the situation, on the coaches and the players involved, sport can probably help inculcate the most desirable or the most deplorable qualities. The issue, much more complex, is how to structure our athletic situations so that the desirable qualities are encouraged and the deplorable ones resisted.

It is usually assumed that the values inculcated, whether positive or negative, derive originally from society. This raises the subsidiary and subtle question of whether there are any values or qualities genuinely peculiar to sport that could be productively redirected into the larger culture. Nevertheless, most of the values, it is assumed, come from society into sport. Two of the most problematic in this regard are racism and sexism, about which there is a lively literature in sport philosophy.

No one argues that sport is inherently racist. The racism that has long infected sport, it is plausibly assumed, is a reflection of the racism in society where it originates. And indeed, the history of racism in sport has closely paralleled that of society, from formal segregation early on, to the introduction of 'token' numbers of blacks in college and professional sports teams, to various 'quotas', explicit or implicit. In recent years, as blacks have come to dominate many of the most popular US sports, the issue of racism has taken on a different form. One of the early 'justifications' often offered for the segregation of blacks into their own leagues was that it was 'for their own good', that they were naturally inferior athletes who would only be humiliated by a direct comparison in competition with whites. As blacks were gradually integrated into sporting life, and especially as they began to be remarkably successful, the argument quickly reversed itself, but ironically, in order to serve the same racist ends. Blacks, it was suggested, are 'naturally superior athletes', only a few generations away from the primitive conditions of the jungle. The easy inference drawn from this claim is that because blacks' superior athletic ability is 'natural', it is not a consequence of the hard work, discipline, and perseverance attributed to whites who exhibit athletic ability. Whites get good by exhibiting hard work and other virtues. Blacks just do it 'naturally'. A second consequence often drawn was that the natural physical superiority of black athletes was matched by a corresponding intellectual superiority of whites. White players are 'smart', 'heady', 'know the game'. Blacks, by implication, lack the intelligence of white athletes.

Still, something calls for explanation here. Blacks have been enormously successful at athletics in proportion to their representation in society at large. Two basic explanations have been offered, one much more controversial than the other. The first, less controversial one emphasizes environmental factors. Perhaps the generally greater poverty of blacks has made them tend to be more competitive. Perhaps their exclusion from more common pursuits (business careers, law, medicine and so on) leads the most talented of them to focus their youthful energies on athletics. All such explanations make the athletic success of blacks not a function of inherent or natural differences but of social environment. And social environment can be changed.

The second, more controversial explanation argues

that there are genetic or at least physiological differences between blacks and whites that explain blacks' athletic prowess. Claims have been made that blacks tend to have more fast-twitch muscles, that their muscle-to-fat ratio is superior to that of whites, or that their physiology tends towards longer limbs that enhance athletic ability. These claims are controversial on two grounds. First, the empirical evidence is highly disputed. Many of the 'experiments' conducted are replete with uncontrolled variables that make the results highly suspect. It is even doubted by many biologists whether the very concept of 'race' is a viable biological category. Second, claims regarding 'natural' differences are controversial in that claims of just this sort have long been used in the service of racism; blacks are 'just different', we have long been told, and 'different' too often implies 'inferior' (see RACE, THEORIES OF).

The case of women's participation in sport has in some ways paralleled the case of blacks. For all too long, women were virtually excluded from participation. Gradually, especially with the passage in the 1970s in the US of Title IX legislation demanding equal opportunity in sports for women, they began to have more opportunities to play sports and, accordingly, began to play in much greater numbers. Still, the perception remains widespread that because of physiological differences affecting speed, size and strength, women are inevitably inferior athletes to men.

Again the 'nature versus nurture' argument becomes germane. Is the gap both in participation and relative abilities largely explicable by appeal to the greater opportunities given to young male athletes and the greater encouragement given to them to compete athletically? Or do the physiological differences remain fundamental, and is the statistically significant extent to which men are stronger, faster and bigger than women a function of natural physiological differences?

Even if the latter argument is accepted, an important qualification must be admitted. The physiological differences may be natural, but the sports are invented. And most sports have been invented by men, in ways that highlight precisely those qualities – speed, size, strength – typically characteristic of male physiology. Suppose we used other criteria, perhaps balance and grace, as the criteria for determining athletic superiority. Suppose, for example, we used as a test of athletic ability one of the very few sports designed explicitly to highlight qualities exhibited paradigmatically by women: the balance beam in gymnastics. If we did, we would discover that women were by far superior 'natural athletes' to men (see FEMINISM §5).

A final issue regarding sports and society that has caused considerable controversy concerns the widespread tendency in contemporary culture to raise outstanding athletes to the status of cultural heroes. A culture's heroes are often informative of the culture's needs and values. What does the widespread elevation of athletes to the status of cultural heroes suggest about contemporary culture? It might suggest a nostalgia for the past. Physical prowess such as that exhibited by athletes, after all, is increasingly unnecessary in a culture dominated by technological developments that render physical strength, speed or size largely irrelevant. Or, to put a different slant on the same point, is our worship of athletes as heroes part of an effort to preserve the value of a set of characteristics – physical abilities exhibited by athletes – that we recognize are in danger of being lost? Or, finally, is the phenomenon of athletes as heroes an indication of a higher culture, one that raises to high status a set of activities of relatively little practical worth precisely because they are not merely practical? In any case, the elevation to hero status of athletes, especially since those outstanding athletes do not always exhibit the personal and moral qualities we desire, remains a controversial question in the philosophy of sport.

3   Sport and self-knowledge

'Know thyself' has been a core goal of philosophy since before Socrates. A claim is often made that athletic involvement, at least of the right kind, can lead to genuine self-knowledge. But what kind of self-knowledge? Several different senses of self-knowledge have received attention in the philosophy of sport. First is self-knowledge in a roughly psychoanalytic sense. The psychiatrist Arnold Beisser, in his book *The Madness in Sports* (1977), analyses troubled athletes and relates their choice of sport or their mode of involvement in sports to their respective pathologies. But implicit in his analysis is the inference that any athlete, pathologically troubled or not, can gain this sort of self-knowledge through reflection on their involvement in sport. A number of psychological categories come quickly to mind as clearly applicable.

Consider, for example, the social significance of one's choice of sport. Suppose one is from an impoverished social background, and one's favourite sports are golf, polo and squash. Does that suggest a desperate attempt to deny one's social status, or a healthy refusal to be limited by it? Or suppose one is from a wealthy background and one chooses the same sports. Does that suggest an inability to escape from the social expectations of one's class or a healthy acceptance of it? Note in each case that the issue itself does not supply the answer. Rather, it enables one to formulate the potentially fruitful question, which must be answered in each case individually.

There are numerous other categories of analysis that might prove fruitful. Consider the issue of team sports versus individual sports. What does it suggest about oneself if one's preference is predominantly for one or the other? Or again, take the difference between competitive and non-competitive sports. Many people love to jog, swim or ski, but would never consider doing so competitively. Others get bored unless the activity can be transformed into a competitive game. Either way, reflection on one's choices might be psychologically revealing. Other sets of contrasts can be no less revealing: contact or non-contact sports; coeducational or single-sex sports; spectator sports or non-spectator sports and so on.

One's mode of involvement in sports can also be psychologically revealing. Certain people are notoriously poor losers or gracious winners, who 'come through in the clutch' or, to the contrary, 'fold' in key situations. Others are peculiarly injury-prone, or play well only when alienated from the opposition. All such phenomena can be occasions for self-knowledge.

But self-knowledge in the psychological sense is hardly the only sense of self-knowledge available in sport. A second construal that has gained considerable popularity in sport philosophy involves a convergence of the notion of 'peak experiences' popularized by Irving Mazlow and certain aspects of Zen Buddhist theory. The notion of a peak experience, originally conceived in terms of certain profound experiences such as love, friendship, or religious revelation, found a receptive audience among talented athletes. After long periods of preparation, these occasionally experience moments when a technically difficult activity, say shooting a basketball, hitting a baseball or skiing a steep slope, seems suddenly to happen easily, smoothly and without effort or analytic thought. Such experiences seem related to aspects of Zen Buddhist experience, especially as that has been applied to athletic activity. The key figure in the popularization of this notion is Eugen Herrigel, whose book, *Zen in the Art of Archery* (1953), set the stage for a host of other books applying the themes of Zen Buddhism to other sports. The key notion here seems to be that the 'self' in the sense of the ego or egoistic self must be 'let go', left behind in favour of a more profound experience of immersion that no longer separates the egoistic self from the experience in which it is involved.

Finally, considerable attention has been paid to self-knowledge in roughly the Socratic sense of 'knowing what I know and what I do not know'. In the sporting domain, this has been translated into something like 'knowing what I can do and cannot do', and this in turn has two dimensions. First, this sense of self-knowledge entails recognizing one's limits and staying within them, 'playing within oneself', as coaches sometimes exhort. But second, it also entails taking oneself to the limits of one's ability, doing everything that one can do. To the extent that an athlete fulfils both of these goals implicit in the Socratic sense of self-knowledge, they will be likely to attain the peak of athletic prowess.

4 Mind and body in sport

Most sporting activity is a consummate example of the conjoining of mental and physical activity. As such, it is a rich testing ground for one of the oldest of philosophical problems, the connection of physical and mental activity or, as it is sometimes expressed, 'the mind–body problem'. Three basic views have received some attention in the philosophy of sport literature. The first is the age-old position of the so-called dualism of mind and body. This view has mostly been criticized in philosophy of sport, often because the notion of somehow being two substantial entities (soul and body or mind and body) that mysteriously interact together is so far from the actual experience of most athletes. Second is the materialist or physicalist view, which has also received relatively little support among philosophers of sport, in part because of the standard reductionist criticisms, but probably more because it does not succeed, at least so far, in taking adequate account of the many experiential factors in sport. For this reason, the dominant and most well-received view has been the phenomenological approach that attempts to give an adequate description of the structures of the athletic experience *as experienced*, which is the main interest of most athletes and sport philosophers.

References and further reading

* Beisser, A. (1977) *The Madness in Sports*, Bowie, MD: Charles Press. (Referred to in §3. A psychiatrist relates his patients' pathologies to their sport involvement in ways that can be extended beyond the specific cases.)
* Herrigel, E. (1953) *Zen in the Art of Archery*, New York: Vintage Books. (Referred to in §3. This is the first and best of those books that relate Zen teachings to sport experience.)
* Huizinga, J. (1938) *Homo Ludens: A Study of the Play Element in Culture*, Boston, MA: Beacon Press, 1950. (Referred to in §1. The pioneering book that

established the study of sport as a legitimate and important intellectual enterprise.)
Hyland, D. (1990) *Philosophy of Sport*, New York: Paragon House. (An introduction to the main issues. Chapter 5 outlines the debate about sport and aesthetics, not discussed above.)
Journal of the Philosophy of Sport, Champaign, IL: Human Kinetics Publishers. (The leading journal in the field, and an invaluable source of major articles on all aspects of the philosophy of sport.)
Morgan, W. and Meier, K.V. (1988) *Philosophic Inquiry in Sport*, Champaign, IL: Human Kinetics Publishers. (A large compendium of some of the best-known articles on all aspects of the philosophy of sport.)
* Suits, B. (1978) *The Grasshopper: Games, Life and Utopia*, Toronto, Ont.: University of Toronto Press. (Referred to in §1. The main book in the controversy over whether key terms such as 'game' can be defined – he argues in the affirmative.)
* Weiss, P. (1969) *Sport: A Philosophic Inquiry*, Carbondale, IL: Southern Illinois University Press. (Referred to in §1. The first book by a major philosopher devoted explicitly to the philosophy of sport. Both widely praised and criticized, the book did much to get philosophy of sport established as a discipline.)

DREW A. HYLAND

SRI AUROBINDO *see* AUROBINDO GHOSE

STAËL, MADAME DE *see* STAËL-HOLSTEIN, ANNE-LOUISE-GERMAINE MME DE

STAËL-HOLSTEIN, ANNE-LOUISE-GERMAINE, MME DE (1766–1817)

Staël was a French woman of letters, whose corpus includes novels, plays, memoirs, criticism and works of historical and sociological observation. As a novelist and critic, Staël is perhaps best known as a forerunner of the Romantic movement in French literature, and for her typology of European culture. However, her extensive body of work also included a perfectibilist philosophy of history; an account of German character and literature containing an influential survey of contemporary philosophy; and a liberal defence of the French Revolution, in which Staël had been an active participant.

Staël was born in Paris on 22 April 1766, the daughter of Jacques Necker, the Genevan chief minister of Louis XVI. She supplemented an emotionally unrewarding marriage to Baron de Staël-Holstein, the Swedish ambassador in Paris, with a number of (often distinguished) lovers, and, in 1816, secretly married a Genevan soldier, John Rocca. Her salon became an important centre of intellectual and political activity, and her extensive entourage included the liberal writer and politician, Benjamin Constant; the economist and historian, Sismonde de Sismondi; and the scholar and translator, August Wilhelm von Schlegel. She welcomed the French Revolution, despite feelings of loyalty to the fallen monarchy and an attachment to a tradition of aristocratic liberty. A moderate republican emphasizing respect for the rule of law, Staël retreated to Coppet (the family château on Lake Geneva) ahead of the September massacres (1792). She travelled to England, returning to France in 1795. She supported the Directory and initially welcomed the Consulate, as instruments of social and political stability. However, her growing opposition to Napoleon eventually resulted in exile. From Coppet, she visited Germany and Italy, before, in 1812, fleeing Napoleonic Europe and making her way (through Austria, Russia, Finland and Sweden) to England. After the Bourbon Restoration, to which she became reconciled, Staël, ravaged by opium, returned to Paris, where she died on 14 July 1817.

Staël's nonfiction writings include studies of Rousseau, suicide, and the role of the passions, but her most important works are *De la littérature considérée dans ses rapports avec les institutions sociales* (On Literature Considered in its Relation to Social Institutions) (1800), *De l'Allemagne* (On Germany) (1810) and *Considérations sur les principaux événments de la Révolution* (Considerations on the Principal Events of the French Revolution) (1818).

In *De la littérature*, Staël propounded the claim that literature (expansively defined) reflects the historical influence of social institutions, laws and mores. The book includes digressions on a range of political and philosophical topics, as well as tracing the development of literature from the ancient world to the present. Staël advanced a perfectibilist view of historical development as exemplifying the progressive development of human faculties (promoting the medieval over the ancient world), and suggestively

contrasted two 'completely distinct' European cultures, the light and elegant literature of the 'South' and the meditative and melancholy literature of the 'North'. This distinction was later identified with that between the 'classical' and 'romantic' (associated with France and Germany respectively), terms also connoting 'two eras in world history' (before and after the establishment of Christianity).

De l'Allemagne was banned by Napoleon and only properly published (in revised form and in England) in 1813. Surveying geography, customs, literature and religion, *De l'Allemagne* sought to introduce and interpret a foreign culture to a French audience, and undermine complacency about French cultural superiority. As part of this portrait 'of the German character and the distinctive spirit of their literature', Staël offered 'a simple and popular notion of their philosophical systems'. Staël provides synopses of Leibniz, Jacobi, Fichte, Friedrich Schlegel and Schelling, as part of a narrative largely structured around her account of the work of KANT. There are also thumbnail sketches of the state of, and connections between, French and English philosophy, and a general attempt to discredit sensationalism for undermining the possibility of morality. Although highly readable, doubts remain about the plausibility of Staël's picture of Germany as the paradigmatically contemplative nation, about the coherence of her Romantic enthusiasms, and about the accuracy and derivativeness of her account of German philosophy.

Considérations is a defence of the French Revolution, which established a tradition of liberal historiography. Staël sought to subvert the conservative myth of the Revolution as a rupture with fourteen centuries of unbroken order, by insisting that it was part of a continuing process (the latest episode in a thousand-year struggle for liberty). Moreover, she attempted to identify the liberal current that she represented with part of the Revolution (the Constituent Assembly), and thereby deny responsibility for, or sympathy with, its other aspects (such as the Terror). *Considérations* also illustrates Staël's lifelong and determined defence of her father's reputation, and her Anglophilia. For Staël, England provided an enviable example of an enlightened nobility, working within the constitutional framework of bicameralism and the protection of individual rights, sharing political responsibility with a moderate bourgeoisie. England was also a Protestant country, and Staël, who considered Christianity indispensable to modern society, saw liberalism and Protestantism (which she sought to establish as the state religion of France) as linked by the shared assumption of moral equality.

Staël's political thought defended the value of privacy and of the liberty of the moderns (who prefer 'to fulfil their destiny apart from public affairs'). She challenged the identity of virtue and citizenship that underpinned republican models of freedom, arguing that 'liberty in modern times consists of whatever guarantees the independence of citizens from the power of the state', and rejected conceptions of sovereignty as unlimited and indivisible, insisting that political power should be limited and shared among different authorities.

Staël's literary success was considerable, and her intellectual and political importance was widely proclaimed. But although still acknowledged as an important precursor of the Romantic movement in French literature, and notwithstanding some recent feminist interest in her fiction, Staël has fallen into comparative neglect. It remains difficult to claim great philosophical significance for her work, but her accounts of historical development and of German philosophy are not without interest, and her political theory still merits attention.

See also: GERMAN IDEALISM; HISTORY, PHILOSOPHY OF

List of works

Staël-Holstein, A.-L.-G., Mme de (1820–1) *Oeuvres complètes* (Complete Works), ed. A. de Staël, Paris: Treuttel & Würtz, 17 vols. (First collected edition of Staël's work, reprinted Geneva, Slatkine Reprints, 1967.)
—— (1800) *De la littérature considérée dans ses rapports avec les institutions sociales* (On Literature Considered in its Relation to Social Institutions), ed. P. van Tieghem, Geneva: Droz, 1959. (A good modern edition of Staël's text.)
—— (1810) *De l'Allemagne* (On Germany), ed. J. de Pange and S. Balayé, Paris: Hachette, 5 vols, 1958–60. (A good modern edition of Staël's text.)
—— (1818) *Considerations sur le Révolution française* (Considerations on the French Revolution), ed. J. Godechot, Paris: Tallandier, 1983. (A good modern edition of Staël's text.)
—— (1960–93) *Correspondance générale* (Collected Correspondence), ed. B. Jasinski, Paris: Pauvert, 6 vols; Hachette, 1982–5; Klincksieck, 1993. (The most complete edition of Staël's correspondence.)
—— (1987) *Major Writings of Madame de Staël*, trans. and with intro. by V. Folkenflik, New York: Columbia University Press. (Translated excerpts from a wide variety of Staël's works.)

References and further reading

Balayé, S. (1979) *Madame de Staël: Lumières et liberté*

(Madame de Staël: Enlightenment and Liberty), Paris: Klincksieck. (An important work by an eminent Staël scholar.)
—— (1996) *Madame de Staël et les Français*, the Zaharoff Lecture for 1994–5, Oxford: Clarendon Press. (An engaging account of aspects of Staël's relation to France and French society.)
Besser, G.R. (1994) *Germaine de Staël Revisited*, New York: Twayne. (An introductory account of Staël's major works.)
Gutwirth, M. (1978) *Madame de Staël, Novelist*, Urbana, IL: University of Illinois Press. (A feminist study of Staël's fiction.)
Gwynne, G.E. (1969) *Madame de Staël et la Revolution française: Politique, philosophie, littérature* (Madame de Staël and the French Revolution: Politics, Philosophy, Literature), Paris: Nizet. (An account of Staël's political thought.)
Herold, J.C. (1959) *Mistress to an Age. A Life of Madame de Staël*, London: Hamish Hamilton. (A biographical introduction.)
Isbell, J.C. (1994) *The Birth of European Romanticism. Truth and Propaganda in Staël's 'De l'Allemagne'*, Cambridge: Cambridge University Press. (A study of Romantic themes in *De l'Allemagne*.)

DAVID LEOPOLD

STAIR, JAMES DALRYMPLE, VISCOUNT (1619–95)

An outstanding lawyer, senior judge, politician, and the founding father of modern Scots Law, Stair is also an interesting, if minor, philosopher of law of the seventeenth century. Stair believed that law is an inherently rational discipline and that its content can be derived from the principles of natural law which are self-evident to all humans. Stair led an active life at the heart of public affairs in seventeenth-century Scotland, finishing up as the chief judge of the supreme civil court. Born in Ayrshire, Scotland, he became a teacher at Glasgow University in 1641, was called to the Bar in 1648, became Judge in the Scots Cromwellian Court 1657, Vice President of the Court of Session 1660, Lord President of the Court of Session (Scotland's most senior judge) 1671, exiled to Holland 1682, and reappointed Lord President in 1689 subsequent to the 'Glorious Revolution'.

Stair was a philosopher and a devout Calvinist as well as politician and judge. His thought reflected all these elements, stressing the role of God as the upholder of the natural law and the need for order in human affairs as expressed through contemporary positive law. Stair never published a purely philosophical work. Instead his legal theory is expounded within the *Institutions of the Law of Scotland* (1681), a book expounding the national law of Scotland, and which presupposes that there is a divine and rational basis for that law, and indeed all man-made law. The *Institutions* continues to be a work of high authority within the modern Scots legal system. Stair rejects the notion, widely held even in the seventeenth century, that human laws lack any inherently rational basis, being rather based on the arbitrary will of humans as expressed through custom, court decisions and legislation. This apparent lack of rationality in the law extended according to its exponents both to the content of the law and to its organization.

Stair took it for granted that God was the ultimate source of human values and law, and his thought is very much in the line of classical natural law thought in Europe as derived from Aquinas (see AQUINAS, T. §13) through to that of his near contemporary Hugo Grotius (see GROTIUS, H.), whose *De iure belli ac pacis* (The Law of War and Peace) (1625) seems to have been a major influence on Stair (see NATURAL LAW §1). The *Institutions* differs from the work of Grotius in two completely opposite ways: in its greater emphasis on God as the ultimate source of law and in its concentration on the actual positive law. The structure of Stair's thought has a definite Aristotelian flavour, derived from the strongly Aristotelian syllabus he both studied and taught at Glasgow University, and is organized according to Aristotle's doctrine of causes: formal, efficient and final. Stair argues that the formal cause of law is reason, its efficient cause the actions of God and man, its final cause the promotion of human welfare. This is seen in his definition of law, which is similar to that of Grotius, as 'the dictate of reason determining every rational being to that which is congruous and convenient for the nature and condition thereof' (1681: I.1.1).

Stair is ambiguous as to how we know the natural law, an ambiguity also found in earlier natural law thinkers, in asserting that humans have both the inclination or instinct to follow the natural law and are also led to follow the natural law by the light of reason. This contradiction, also found in earlier natural law theories, Stair seems to have made no effort to resolve or even to be aware of. To the obvious objection that, if this is so, then what need have humans of positive human law, Stair answers that there is no conflict: 'the principles of equity are the efficient cause of rights and laws' (1681: I.1.17) (Stair understands the term equity to be synonymous with the natural law, particularly its role as the measure of positive law; see JUSTICE, EQUITY AND LAW). The three principles of equity are obedience to God, that man is free to act except as specifically limited by God's commands, and the obligation to fulfil one's engagements (contracts). The principles of positive law derived from these principles of natural law are society, property and commerce, a concise trinity of proto-bourgeois values reflective of the developing mercantile economy of the seventeenth century. From these principles in turn are derived the three different types of human rights: *liberty*, the right to life and to personal integrity; *dominium*, the right of ownership of possessions; and *obligation*, the right to freely make contracts and the duty to fulfil those contracts. Stair stresses that it is these three types of rights which are 'the formal and proper object of law'; this is perhaps his most original insight and anticipates one of the central principles of the later legal positivists.

Stair's notion that positive legal rights are the proper object of the law becomes his organizing principle, enabling him to reject the hallowed practice of the civilian tradition, derived from Justinian's *Institutes*, of dividing the law according to the categories of persons, things and actions (see ROMAN LAW §4; GAIUS; JUSTINIAN). Instead, the *Institutions* deals first with the constitution and nature of rights, second the conveyance of rights and third the enforcement of rights. The thesis that law can be a 'rational discipline' is interestingly tested in this work.

See also: LAW, PHILOSOPHY OF

List of works

Stair, J.D. (1681) *Institutions of the Law of Scotland*, 2nd edn, substantially revised, 1693; ed. D.M. Walker, Edinburgh: Edinburgh University Press, 1981. (D.M. Walker's standard modern edition based on the 1693 edition, not on later revisions by eighteenth- and nineteenth-century editors.)

References and further reading

Campbell, A.H. (1954) *The Structure of Stair's Institutions*, David Murray Lecture, no. 98, Glasgow: Glasgow University Publications. (Influence of Aristotle and Pufendorf in Stair's thought.)

MacCormick, D.N. (1981) 'Stair As An Analytical Jurist', in *Stair Tercentenary Studies*, Edinburgh: The Stair Society, 187–99. (Analytical concepts in Stair.)

—— (1982) 'Law, Obligation, and Consent: Reflections on Stair and Locke', in *Legal Right and Social Democracy*, Oxford: Oxford University Press, 60–83. (Contrasts and compares Stair with Locke.)

Stein, P.G. (1981) 'Stair's General Concepts', in *Stair Tercentenary Studies*, Edinburgh: The Stair Society, 187–99. (Intellectual influences on Stair.)

SCOTT C. STYLES

STATE, THE

States are inescapable, powerful and fundamentally important in the modern world. They spend a substantial portion of their members' wealth; they tax, confiscate or compulsorily purchase private property; conscript; impose punishments, including capital punishment; defend their members from aggression and protect their rights; and provide educational, health and other essential social services.

States are also central to modern political philosophy, and figure in its main topics. For instance, the various theories of social justice concern which principle or principles of justice should be followed by states. Again, discussions of the rights of individuals, or of groups, presuppose states to make the preferred rights effective. The answers to traditional questions, such as whether one is morally obliged to obey the laws of a state, or whether freedom is reduced by the state or made possible by it, must depend in part on what a state is taken to be.

The principal features of the modern state are basically agreed upon (population, territory, effective and legitimate government, independence). But there are underlying assumptions needing notice, and many questions about the state, especially concerning its proper activities, are controversial and disputed. Moreover, the value of the state can be challenged, and its future doubted, especially in the light of increasing economic and political globalization and moral cosmopolitanism.

1 **Main features of the state**
2 **Controversial issues**
3 **The future of the state**

1 Main features of the state

'State' is sometimes used in the broad sense to mean any independent political organization, sometimes in the narrow sense, to mean one particular type of political organization – the modern state. The latter is the usage considered here. The modern state emerged gradually as European political institutions changed. The date of its initial recognition by political philosophers is much discussed. Some put it in the sixteenth century (Skinner 1989), others several

centuries earlier (Black 1992). Machiavelli, Bodin and Hobbes were prominent among early theorists of the state.

The modern state has been defined in different ways by anthropologists, sociologists, political scientists, historians and lawyers, as well as by philosophers. There is much overlap between the definitions and broad agreement on the main features which a political organization must exhibit in order to belong to the class 'the state' (Green 1988: ch. 3; MacCallum 1987: chaps 3 and 5; Vincent 1987: ch. 1). (1) There is a population which reproduces itself and whose members are socially related. (2) There is territory. (3) There is a single government, which: (a) is a distinct body of rule, supported by a judicial, administrative and military machine; (b) is the ultimate prescriber and enforcer of law for all those within its jurisdiction; (c) claims exclusive control of the use of force within the territory and has preponderant control of its use; (d) claims authority for its existence and actions and is generally accepted as authoritative. (4) The state is legally and politically independent from other states, and recognized by other states as an independent or sovereign state (see SOVEREIGNTY §4).

These features are necessary conditions and together are sufficient. A state without a population is inconceivable, for example; as is one without a territory, except possibly in the short term. However there is considerable vagueness about what counts as meeting the conditions, and much variation in the degree to which they are met. Moreover, probably no state fully realizes all the characteristics ascribed to the abstraction 'the state'. For example, there is no agreement on what size the population or territory must be, how effective the government must be in enforcing its decisions, how coherent and consistent the legal system must be, how many inhabitants may reject the government's or the state's authority even to the extent of active resistance, or by how many other states recognition is required.

It should be noted that the state cannot be the same as its government. The government is the state's administrative organ, and acts in its name; it may be constrained in what it does by a formal constitution (see CONSTITUTIONALISM). The state persists through changes of government and through changes in the form of constitution. Again, the state is not the same as its society, being only the political aspect of it, only one social institution among the many that constitute society (for example, religious, economic and family groups); states vary however in the amount of independence they permit to the other social institutions (this is part of what distinguishes liberal from totalitarian states). Although it is often urged that a state should be a nation, and every nation a state, seldom if ever do states coincide with nations (if 'nation' means anything more than the body of those who are fellow nationals of a state), and being a nation is not a condition of being a state (see NATION AND NATIONALISM §1). Nor need a state rest on any particular principle of legitimacy, or take a particular constitutional form, although there is now an expectation that it should be in some sense democratic (see LEGITIMACY §4).

2 Controversial issues

It is important to appreciate that, given the historical specificity of the modern state and of the philosophical discussion of it, the terms in which the modern state has been and still is conceived include values which are neither permanent nor universal, but derive from the political, cultural, religious and economic assumptions of their times. For example, the early states were thoroughly patriarchal, and in their accounts of them philosophers took for granted that the members of the state were male heads of households (Pateman 1988). More generally, early theorists operated with a particular view of what an 'individual' is, which affected their understanding of what the state is (Siedentop 1983). Contemporary theorists need to examine their own assumptions to check that they are not treating ephemeral values as if they were those of human beings as such. For instance, a philosopher in the Anglo-American tradition may unconsciously take a more sceptical view of the state and what it is capable of than one in the continental European tradition, and a Western philosopher implicitly may make numerous assumptions about the place of religion in politics or the nature of the individual which are not held universally.

The value component of the idea of the state becomes even more obvious when one asks what the proper role of the state is. There is no agreement on the purpose or purposes of the state. Empirically, a huge range of tasks, not all compatible, has been given to – and sometimes taken away from – the state (see LAW, LIMITS OF). Theoretically, there have been great divergences. For example, some have allowed very limited scope to the state, claiming that if it has greater powers it infringes the rights of individuals, particularly with regard to liberty and property (for example, see NOZICK, R. §2). Others contend that the state must act extensively to enable individuals to enjoy their rights, which otherwise remain formal and empty, or in order to to achieve other desirable goals such as social justice (see RAWLS, J.). Again, some view the state instrumentally as the means of

protecting the material interests of its members; whereas others think it is intrinsically good because its citizens can exercise public virtue by participating in its affairs (see REPUBLICANISM).

Given the controversy over the role of the state, it seems hopeless to stipulate as a necessary feature of the state any particular function beyond protection of basic rights against force and fraud, resolution or control of dispute and conflict, and maintenance of its own ability to enforce its own decisions and to remain independent internationally. These would be regarded as realistic and morally acceptable by all except anarchists (Wolff 1970). But even when the state is defined minimally, its future may still be in doubt.

3 The future of the state

The state's role, whether limited or extensive, is difficult, and there is always dissatisfaction with its performance. The world system of states also is found inadequate because it is disfigured by war. Inevitably it is asked whether the purposes assigned to the state could be achieved better by other means; either without any political organization as the anarchist contends, or by a different political organization.

State theorists judge the state far preferable to anarchy, especially in modern political circumstances. The proposal to abolish it overlooks the problems, especially in complex societies, of social life without central authority, and ignores the substantial benefits which states do provide. Of course having a state involves risks (such as oppression by the government), but the appropriate response is to minimize the risks and maximize the benefits (as liberal democracy seeks to do). The anarchist 'solution' forgoes the best means to achieve that. Furthermore, there is one moral benefit which would be impossible under anarchy: the personal self-education and development which comes from participating in law making and taking responsibility for important public decisions and their enforcement (see ANARCHISM §3).

The main political alternative to the state is a cosmopolitan organization which strictly could not be a state, there being no other equal body, but which had the attributes of a state (making it unacceptable to anarchism). Its population would be humanity and its territory the world, and it would be superior in law and power to every other political body. States would lose their sovereignty and necessarily cease to be states (see INTERNATIONAL RELATIONS, PHILOSOPHY OF §4).

This idea has been seriously discussed since the eighteenth century, and involves no impossibility. It is claimed that the political problems of the present system are so great it must give way. The cosmopolis could achieve the aims of states as well as or better than states. In addition it could achieve material and moral goals which states are incapable of – eliminating war, protecting the environment and eradicating world poverty. In particular, if justice is to be achieved on an international scale it cannot be left to states: states make exclusive claims to resources and territory, on behalf of their own members, which conflict with the distribution required by principles of international justice (Baldwin 1992) (see JUSTICE, INTERNATIONAL §4). Since the ultimate moral criterion is the equality of claims of all human beings, the final political unit should reflect this.

There are two issues here. First, should a cosmopolitan morality be given priority over the moralities of individual states? A major reservation is that the principles and content of the universal cosmopolitan morality are not agreed among philosophers let alone accepted by all states. There is also an objection: if the cosmopolitan morality conflicts with the state's morality, why should the former take precedence in all cases? May not a state's values, rooted in its own culture, have independent and greater moral importance?

Second, even if the case for cosmopolitan morality were conceded, why should states be replaced by a cosmopolitan 'state'? It is uncertain that the cosmopolis would perform its functions adequately; or effectively continue what states had done (whatever that was thought to be); or enable its citizens to participate adequately. If it fell short, there could be no political body to correct or control it.

However, it is not necessary to abolish states in order for cosmopolitan morality to be practised. The latter could be combined with legal and political statism. Each state could accept that it had obligations to human beings other than its own members; although it would be left to the state itself to decide what the obligation amounted to and what action was required. Legally, states could continue as sovereign: morally, they would subject themselves to global standards and recognize and act on wider obligations and responsibilities.

Beginning from a world of states, the way forward is through states, whether this be via a system of cooperation between states or their replacement by a single global political organization. In either case, questions about the nature, purpose and best form of the state remain important.

References and further reading

* Baldwin, T. (1992) 'The Territorial State', in H. Gross and R. Harrison (eds) *Jurisprudence: Cambridge Essays*, Oxford: Clarendon Press, 207–30. (Examines the basis for the legitimacy of the territorial claims states make; suggests some principles.)

Barry, B. (1983) 'Self-government Revisited', in D. Miller and L. Siedentop (eds) *The Nature of Political Theory*, Oxford: Clarendon Press, 121–54; repr. in B. Barry, *Democracy, Power and Justice*, Oxford: Clarendon Press, 1989, 156–86. (Illuminating and analytically sharp discussion of 'nation' and 'nation-state'.)

Beitz, C.R. (1991) 'Sovereignty and Morality in International Affairs', in D. Held (ed.) *Political Theory Today*, Cambridge: Polity Press, 236–54. (Introductory survey.)

* Black, A. (1992) *Political Thought in Europe 1250–1450*, Cambridge: Cambridge University Press. (An introductory history.)

* Dunn, J. (1994) *Contemporary Crisis of the Nation State?*, Political Studies series, special issue no. 42, Oxford: Blackwell. (Includes contemporary and historical perspectives, and considers the theoretical implications.)

d'Entréves, A.P. (1967, 1969) *The Notion of the State: An Introduction to Political Theory*, Oxford: Clarendon Press. (Useful systematic survey of the basic ideas and issues, set in the perspective of the history of political thought.)

Fain, H. (1972) 'The Idea of the State', *Nous* 6 (1): 15–26. (Hostile view of the rights states assign one another.)

* Green, L. (1988) *The Authority of the State*, Oxford: Clarendon Press, ch. 3. (Careful and accessible investigation of the distinctive features of the state, with robust responses to doubts about 'state' as a theoretical concept.)

Hoffman, J. (1995) *Beyond the State: An Introductory Critique*, Cambridge: Polity Press. (Valuably sceptical discussion of the worth of and need for states, investigating alternatives 'beyond' them.)

Linklater, A. (1982, 1990) *Men and Citizens in the Theory of International Relations*, London: Macmillan. (Philosophical and historical exploration of the tensions between moral obligations as a human being and rights and duties as a member of a state.)

* MacCallum, G.C. (1987) *Political Philosophy*, Englewood Cliffs, NJ: Prentice Hall. (Introductory level analyses, although compressed, of the main terms, including state, nation, government, authority and sovereignty; also includes a discussion of the main issues.)

Miller, D. (1995) *On Nationality*, Oxford: Clarendon Press. (Stresses the connection between state and nationality, and the consequent limit on cosmopolitanism.)

* Pateman, C. (1988) *The Sexual Contract*, Cambridge:

Polity Press. (Exposes the patriarchalism in the social contract and in modern forms of contract.)

* Siedentop, L. (1983) 'Political Theory and Ideology: The Case of the State', in D. Miller and L. Siedentop (eds) *The Nature of Political Theory*, Oxford: Clarendon Press, 53–73. (Analyses 'state' in conjunction with 'individual' and claims both are historically specific to the modern Western idea of the state.)

* Skinner, Q. (1989) 'The State', in T. Ball, J. Farr and R.L. Hanson (eds) *Political Innovation and Conceptual Change*, Cambridge: Cambridge University Press, 90–131. (Historical sketch of the emergence of the term 'state'.)

Thompson, J. (1992) *Justice and World Order: A Philosophical Enquiry*, London and New York: Routledge. (Clear, politically informed and judicious introductory level examination of the moral issues concerning the role of states in achieving a just world.)

* Vincent, A. (1987) *Theories of the State*, Oxford: Blackwell. (Introductory survey of the main theories, with a helpful general chapter.)

* Wolff, R.P. (1970, 1976) *In Defense of Anarchism*, New York: Harper & Row. (Spirited statement of philosophical anarchism, denying there can be any theoretical justification for the authority of the state.)

PETER P. NICHOLSON

STATEMENTS *see* PROPOSITIONS, SENTENCES AND STATEMENTS; SPEECH ACTS

STATISTICS

The discipline of statistics encompasses an extremely broad and heterogeneous set of problems and techniques. We deal here with the problems of statistical inference, which have to do with inferring from a body of sample data (for example, the observed results of tossing a coin or of drawing a number of balls at random from an urn containing balls of different colours) to some feature of the underlying distribution from which the sample is drawn (for example, the probability of heads when the coin is tossed, or the relative proportion of red balls in the urn).

There are two conflicting approaches to the foundations of statistical inference. The classical tradition derives from ideas of Ronald Fisher, Jerzy Neyman and Egon Pearson and embodies the standard treatments of hypothesis testing, confidence intervals and estimation found in many statistics textbooks. Classicists adopt a relative-frequency conception of probability and, except in special circumstances, eschew the assignment of probabilities to hypotheses, seeking instead a rationale for statistical inference in facts about the error characteristics of testing procedures. By contrast, the Bayesian tradition, so-called because of the central role it assigns to Bayes' theorem, adopts a subjective or degree-of-belief conception of probability and represents the upshot of a statistical inference as a claim about how probable a statistical hypothesis is in the light of the evidence.

1 **The classical tradition**
2 **The Bayesian tradition**
3 **Criticisms of the classical tradition**
4 **Criticisms of the Bayesian tradition**

1 The classical tradition

Because classicists adopt a frequentist conception of probability (see PROBABILITY, INTERPRETATIONS OF §3), the upshot of statistical inference within the classical framework is not, as it is within the Bayesian approach, the assignment of a probability to a hypothesis which measures how well the hypothesis is supported by the evidence. Instead, the classical approach focuses on finding rules or policies to guide the investigator's behaviour with respect to hypotheses – where the rationale for adopting such rules has to do with how often we can expect to make various sorts of mistake in the long run if we follow them. In this respect, the classical approach is similar in spirit to reliabilist programmes in epistemology (see RELIABILISM).

Thus, for example, in classical significance tests the investigator proceeds by choosing a significance level (for example, 0.05) that corresponds to what they regard as an acceptable probability that they will mistakenly reject the hypothesis under test (the null hypothesis) even though it is true. The investigator then constructs a rejection region – a set of actions that would lead to rejection of the hypothesis – in such a way that the probability of rejecting the hypothesis even though it is true is less than or equal to the significance level. Intuitively, the rejection region will consist of outcomes that are unfavourable to the null hypothesis grouped together with the other possible outcomes that are even more 'extreme' or unfavourable to the null hypothesis. To illustrate, suppose that the investigator wishes to test the hypothesis that a coin is fair by flipping it twenty times and observing the number of heads, and there is no particular reason to think that, if the coin is biased, it will be biased towards heads rather than tails. The total probability of obtaining fifteen or more heads or five or fewer heads when flipping a fair coin twenty times is just under 0.05 and the observation of one of these outcomes will lead to rejection of the hypothesis that the coin is fair at a 0.05 significance level.

Within a classical framework, when we reject a hypothesis at the 0.05 level of significance, we are *not* entitled to infer that the hypothesis has at least a 0.95 probability of being false or at most a 0.05 probability of being true. Instead, the classical justification for the adoption of the above test is that, if it were repeated a large number of times, the characteristics of the test are such that we may expect to make a certain kind of mistake – rejecting the null hypothesis even though it is true – roughly 5 per cent of the time. According to classicists, this is a probability that has a perfectly straightforward frequency interpretation. It should also be understood that nothing in the formal theory of significance testing requires the particular choice of significance level adopted in this example. While 0.05 is a common choice, particularly within the social and behavioural sciences, investigators in many areas of science may and often do choose different significance levels. In general, this choice will correspond to the cost the researcher attaches to the error of rejecting the null hypothesis even though it is true. Presumably this cost will often vary from context to context – depending, for example, on the use to which the test result is to be put. This introduces what many critics regard as a subjective or arbitrary element: an outcome which would lead to the rejection of a hypothesis at one significance level might not lead one to reject that hypothesis at some different (lower) significance level.

Suppose that one carries out a significance test and observes an outcome that does not fall within the rejection region. Properly speaking, an investigator can conclude in this case only that one has 'failed to reject' the null. The theory of hypothesis testing developed by Neyman and Pearson (1928) is motivated in part by the desire to construct an account of testing that permits decisions to 'accept' hypotheses as well as decisions to reject. Given that acceptance is a possibility, it is easy to see that significance testing focuses on only one of two possible errors one can make in testing a hypothesis. In addition to the possibility of mistakenly rejecting a true hypothesis (a so-called type I error), there is also the possibility of mistakenly accepting the hypothesis under test even though it is false (a so-called type II error). To specify the latter probability we must make reference to some

alternative hypothesis against which the null is being tested. Thus, one of the distinctive features of the Neyman–Pearson account is that one tests a hypothesis by comparing it with some competing, rival hypothesis or set of such hypotheses (see CONFIRMATION THEORY; CRUCIAL EXPERIMENTS). Ideally a good test would minimize the probability of both a type I and a type II error, but unfortunately these two desiderata conflict, for reducing the former probability will in general increase the latter probability, and vice versa. The reader should consult the references for the solution to this difficulty recommended by Neyman and Pearson, but the fundamental point to appreciate is that, again, the basic rationale for adopting a test within this framework has to do with the frequencies with which one may expect to make various kinds of mistake if that testing procedure were to be repeatedly followed.

A similar rationale in terms of the error characteristics of repeated procedures underlies other forms of classical statistical inference. For example, a *confidence interval* is an interval constructed in such a way that it has a high probability (for example, 95 per cent) of containing some unknown parameter θ such as the bias of a coin. Since, for a classicist, θ is a parameter with a fixed value rather than a random variable, we cannot say in this case that the probability that θ falls within the constructed interval is 95 per cent. Instead, it is the confidence interval itself which is thought of as a random variable to which a probability attaches. The idea is that, if we were repeatedly to follow the same rule in constructing confidence intervals for θ, in the long run the intervals would contain θ about 95 per cent of the time.

2 The Bayesian tradition

The basic result on which the Bayesian approach relies is Bayes' theorem, a simple form of which is

$$P(H \mid E) = \frac{P(E \mid H) \cdot P(H)}{P(E)} \qquad (1)$$

Bayesians interpret this theorem as telling us that the probability of a hypothesis H given evidence E – often called the posterior probability – is a function of the prior probabilities $P(H)$ and $P(E)$ (so called because they are the probabilities the investigator assigns to H and E prior to the collection of evidence) and the conditional probability or likelihood term $P(E \mid H)$ (see PROBABILITY, INTERPRETATIONS OF §5). In many statistical applications it will be more appropriate to use instead a continuous form of Bayes' theorem rather than the discrete form (1), but the basic structure of the inference will be the same. To illustrate, suppose that we are interested in estimating the unknown mean μ of some random variable which is normally distributed with known variance σ^2. Suppose that our prior probability regarding μ can itself be represented by a variable X ranging over different possible values of μ where X also follows a normal distribution with mean μ' and variance σ'^2, and that we draw a sample of size n and that the sample mean is $\bar{y}$. When one combines these priors with the sample information, in accord with Bayes' theorem, the result is a posterior distribution for μ which is also normal and the mean μ'' and variance σ''^2 of which are given by

$$\mu'' = \frac{\frac{1}{\sigma'^2}\mu' + \frac{1}{\sigma^2/n}\bar{y}}{\frac{1}{\sigma'^2} + \frac{1}{\sigma^2/n}}, \qquad \sigma''^2 = \frac{1}{\frac{1}{\sigma'^2} + \frac{1}{\sigma^2/n}} \qquad (2)$$

Here, unlike the classical approach, the result of the inference is the assignment of a probability distribution to μ'' and σ'' themselves. For example, we can use (2) to calculate the probability that μ falls within an interval centred around $\bar{y}$ while no such interpretation of a classical confidence interval is legitimate.

3 Criticisms of the classical tradition

One prominent Bayesian criticism focuses on the fact that, within classical approaches, the significance of evidence seems to depend on the test procedure or stopping rule by which the evidence is produced. For example, a significance test like that described above, in which we flip a coin a fixed number of times (for example, twenty) and observe the number of heads which result, will have different error characteristics from a significance test in which we flip the coin until a fixed, predetermined number of heads are observed (for example, six) even though it may be the case that the observed result in both cases is six heads in twenty tosses. Indeed, the hypothesis that the coin is fair will be rejected at the 0.05 level if the observed outcome of six heads and fourteen tails is the result of a test conducted according to the second rule, but not if this outcome is the result of a test conducted according to the first rule.

Many Bayesians find it counterintuitive that the 'same' evidence should lead to different decisions about whether to reject depending upon which testing procedure is followed. If one is willing to assume, as many Bayesians are, that features of the stopping rule employed should not affect the likelihood term in a Bayesian analysis, then that approach will yield the result in the above example that the observed outcome of six heads, fourteen tails has the same evidential significance for the hypothesis that the coin

is fair, regardless of which of the above rules was followed. Classicists respond by arguing, with considerable plausibility, that in many cases the testing procedure followed does seem relevant to the evidential import of the data it generates and that it is a defect in standard Bayesian analyses that they tend to ignore this.

Bayesians also argue that the classical notions of acceptance or rejection lack a clear meaning. Within a classical framework, to accept (reject) a hypothesis is not to regard it as true (false) beyond all reasonable doubt nor to assign it a high (low) probability. Bayesians argue that their picture, in which an investigator can have any degree of belief between zero and one and will continually change this as additional evidence accumulates, better fits the range of epistemic attitudes one finds in science and in ordinary life. Yet another Bayesian criticism focuses on what Bayesians regard as unacceptably subjective or arbitrary factors within the classical framework – for example, the choice of significance level. As we have emphasized, many of these features derive from the role that judgments about epistemic costs or values play within the classical framework.

While it is not possible to discuss these criticisms in detail, several further observations seem in order. The first is that, while the notions of acceptance and rejection may seem unclear, it is also by no means obvious that the Bayesian framework, with its demand for precise point-valued degrees of belief conforming to the probability calculus, adequately represents the structure of opinions and epistemic attitudes present in real life or in scientific investigation. The second point is that Bayesian strictures about acceptance and rejection within statistical contexts connect up with a more general debate within philosophy of science about whether scientists in fact ever accept hypotheses (or which may or may not be the same thing, believe them simpliciter) as opposed to assigning them degrees of belief strictly between zero and one and, if so, what such acceptance involves and whether, as a normative matter, it is ever rationally defensible (see SCIENTIFIC REALISM AND ANTIREALISM). Many writers – including some Bayesians – have argued that acceptance and rejection are ineliminable parts of scientific practice. The debate over the role that classicists assign to costs and benefits within hypothesis testing also echoes a more general debate within epistemology and philosophy of science over whether the stringency of standards for knowledge, justifiable belief and acceptance vary from context to context depending on, among other things, what is at stake in making various sorts of mistake and the investigator's conception of the goals of inquiry (see SCIENTIFIC METHOD).

125

4 Criticisms of the Bayesian tradition

The fundamental classical objection to Bayesian approaches is the apparent subjectivity introduced by the choice of a prior distribution. One Bayesian response to this criticism, as noted above, is that subjectivity also enters into the classical programme at a number of points. Bayesians claim that their programme systematizes and makes explicit aspects of statistical inference that are unavoidably subjective, while avoiding certain objectionable kinds of subjectivity which are present in the classical programme, but often in an *ad hoc* and concealed form. The second Bayesian reply is that, as more and more data accumulates, the effects of different choices of prior distribution on one's posterior distribution will often become less and less important. We can see this in the case of formula (2) – as sample size n grows, the sample data become more influential and the prior distribution less influential in determining the shape of the posterior distribution. Moreover, Bayesians point out that, when the choice of prior distribution does make a difference, the investigator can always produce a kind of robustness or sensitivity analysis, showing how (and to what extent) different choices of priors will lead to a different posterior distribution, and leaving it up to other investigators to decide which priors to adopt.

See also: INDUCTION, EPISTEMIC ISSUES; INDUCTIVE INFERENCE; PROBABILITY THEORY AND EPISTEMOLOGY; STATISTICS AND SOCIAL SCIENCE

References and further reading

Cramér, H. (1971) *Mathematical Methods of Statistics*, Princeton, NJ: Princeton University Press. (An authoritative text at an advanced level in the classical tradition.)

Fisher, R.A. (1925) *Statistical Methods for Research Workers*, Edinburgh: Oliver & Boyd, 14th edn. (see 1947)

—— (1947) *The Design of Experiments*, New York: Hafner, 4th edn. (Along with 1925, provides a classic exposition of the basic ideas of significance testing and experimental design.)

Giere, R. (1977) 'Testing Versus Information Models of Statistical Inference', in *Logic, Laws and Life: Some Philosophical Complications*, Pittsburgh, PA: University of Pittsburgh. (Giere defends the classical approach, and this paper, as well as the 1973, contains responses to the criticisms of the classical approach discussed in §3 above.)

—— (1973) 'Empirical Probability, Objective Statistical Methods and Scientific Inquiry', in W.L. Harper and C.A. Hooker (eds) *Foundations of Probability Theory, Statistical Inference and Statistical Theories of Science*, vol. II, *Foundations and Philosophy of Statistical Inference*, 63–93. (A systematic philosophical defence of the Neyman–Pearson tradition.)

Hacking, I. (1965) *The Logic of Statistical Inference*, Cambridge: Cambridge University Press. (Discusses numerous criticisms of the classical approach. Highly recommended.)

Hodges, J.L. and Lehmann, E.L. (1970) *Basic Concepts of Probability and Statistics*, San Francisco, CA: Holden-Day. (Well-known textbook at a relatively elementary level which describes basic ideas in probability theory and statistical inference from a classical perspective.)

Howson, C. and Urbach, P. (1993) *Scientific Reasoning: The Bayesian Approach*, Chicago, IL: Open Court, 2nd edn. (Contains a lucid exposition of classical and Bayesian approaches to statistical inference, along with extensive criticism of the classical approach from a Bayesian perspective.)

Kyburg, H. (1974) *The Logical Foundation of Statistical Inference*, Dordrecht: Reidel. (Discusses many of the difficulties with the classical approach described in §3 and offers an account of statistical inference which is neither classical nor conventionally Bayesian.)

Lehmann, E.L. (1959) *Testing Statistical Hypothesis*, New York: John Wiley & Sons. (Well-known text in the classical tradition. Somewhat more technically sophisticated and demanding than Hodges and Lehmann 1970.)

Lindley, D.V. (1956) *Introduction to Probability and Statistics from a Bayesian Viewpoint*, Cambridge: Cambridge University Press. (Systematic exposition of the Bayesian approach by one of its best-known defenders.)

Maher, P. (1993) 'Acceptance in Bayesian Philosophy of Science', in D. Hull, M. Forbes and K. Okruhlik (eds) *PSA 1992*, vol. 2, East Lansing, MI: Philosophy of Science Association. (Argues that acceptance of hypotheses plays an important role in science and that Bayesians should recognize this. See §3.)

Mayo, D. (1979) 'Testing Statistical Testing', in J. Pitt (ed.) *Philosophy in Economics*, Dordrecht: Reidel, 175–203. (A defence of the classical theory of hypothesis testing which explicitly addresses the Bayesian criticisms regarding stopping rules discussed in §3 above.)

—— (1996) *Error and Growth in Experimental Knowledge*, Chicago, IL: University of Chicago Press. (Extensive discussion of foundational issues in statistics and their relation to general philosophy of science. Defends classical and criticizes Bayesian approaches.)

* Neyman, J. and Pearson, E.S. (1928) 'On the Use and Interpretation of Certain Test Criteria for the Purposes of Statistical Inference', *Biometrika* 20: 175–240, 263–94. (Basic ideas of the Neyman–Pearson theory of hypothesis testing.)

Nozick, R. (1993) *The Nature of Rationality*, Princeton, NJ: Princeton University Press. (Although not explicitly concerned with problems of statistical inference, contains relevant material on the role of costs and epistemic values in justification and acceptance. See especially pages 65–106.)

Rosenkrantz, R. (1977) *Inference, Method and Decision: Toward a Bayesian Philosophy of Science*, Dordrecht: Reidel. (A general defence of an 'objective' Bayesian approach to inductive inference, but pages 177–223 contain an interesting discussion of problems of statistical inference, including an argument from within a Bayesian framework that in the coin-tossing example the evidential import of data is affected by the stopping rule employed. See §3.)

Seidenfeld, T. (1979) *Philosophical Problems of Statistical Inference: Learning from R.A. Fisher*, Dordrecht: Reidel. (Extensive, technically informed discussion of foundational problems of statistical inference from a Bayesian perspective.)

JAMES WOODWARD

STATISTICS AND SOCIAL SCIENCE

There are a number of distinct uses for statistics in the social sciences. One use is simply to provide a summary description of complicated features in a population.

A second use of statistics is to predict (some) features of a unit or group in a population, given other features of the unit or group. For example, a company may charge lower health insurance rates for people who do not smoke, because smokers have a lower risk of lung cancer. Some companies could also charge lower health insurance rates for people who do not have a heavy cough, because the probability of having lung cancer is lower for such people. Predictions can be made by developing a probabilistic model of the joint distribution of incidence of smoking, lung cancer, and incidence of heavy coughs in the population.

A third use of statistics is to help predict the probable effects of adopting different policies. For example, the government may consider a number of alternative policies for reducing the rate of lung cancer. One policy would ban smoking. Another policy would make every-one who coughs take cough medicine. Both smoking and coughing are predictors of lung cancer. But because smoking is a cause of lung cancer, while coughing is an effect of lung cancer, the first policy seems as if it might achieve the desired effect, while the second does not. In order to answer policy questions we need to know not only how the variables are distributed in the actual population, but also how they are causally related. A causal model specifies the causal relations between features in a population, as well as specifying a probability distribution of the features. Statistical information together with causal information can be used to predict the effects of adopting a certain policy.

A fourth use of statistics is in helping decide which policies should be adopted in order to achieve specific goals. Such decisions are based not only on the probable effects of each policy, but also on assigning different utilities to each possible outcome. This use of statistics is a branch of decision theory.

1 **Summary statistics**
2 **Probabilistic models**
3 **Causal models**

1 Summary statistics

Consider a purely hypothetical example. Suppose a random sample of fifty units is taken from a population, and for each unit the values of three random variables (properties) are measured: *NCIG*, how heavy a smoker a person has been (on a scale from 0 to 7), *LC*, the presence of lung cancer, and *HC*, the presence of a heavy cough (on a scale from 0 to 7 of severity). (For this example, the sample was pseudo-randomly generated on a computer from an arbitrarily chosen population distribution.)

When the data are presented in the form of a table, the sheer volume of the information makes it uninformative, and it would be even less informative if the sample size were larger or the values of more random variables had been measured. For that reason, it is often useful to provide statistics which summarize important features of the sample. A number of summary statistics for the sample are shown in Table 1.

Table 1. Summary statistics

	NCIG	*LC*	*HC*
Minimum	0	0	0
Maximum	7	1	7
Median	3	0	3
Mean	2.84	0.42	3.04
Variance	4.30	0.25	5.63

A more informative visual presentation of the sample information about an individual variable such as *NCIG* is the histogram shown in Figure 1. The histogram shows the number of people in each category.

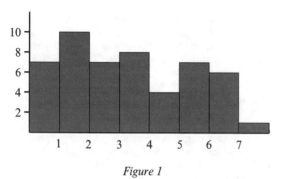

Figure 1

A histogram is useful for summarizing the distribution of a single variable, but it does not show the relationships between variables. One way of showing the relationship between a pair of multinomial variables is a contingency table, such as the one shown in Table 2. For each pair of values of *NCIG* and *LC* there is a box, and the number in the box represents the number of units in the population with that pair of values.

Table 2

					NCIG				
		0	1	2	3	4	5	6	7
LC	0	6	9	3	0	0	2	3	7
	1	2	5	5	1	1	2	0	4

Devising visually informative displays of relationships between three or more variables is much more difficult than for two variables.

2 Probabilistic models

If *LC* is a variable that is difficult or expensive to measure, and *NCIG* and *HC* are relatively easy to measure, then given a new unit from the population, a doctor may wish to predict the value of *LC* for that unit from the more easily measured values of *NCIG* and *HC* for that unit. One simple method for predicting the value of *LC* for a new unit, given the values of $NCIG = x$ and $HC = z$ for that unit involves the following two steps:

First, use the sample to 'estimate' a population joint probability distribution P. (Strictly speaking, as explained below, statisticians usually speak of estimating the parameters of a family of distributions which may single out a unique probability distribution P, rather than of estimating P itself.)

Second, choose the value of *LC* for which

$$P(LC \mid NCIG = x, HC = z)$$

is the highest (using an arbitrary rule to break ties).

One often attempts to 'estimate' a joint probability distribution from a sample by first choosing a family of probability distributions, and then progressively narrowing down the family until one probability distribution is left. Deciding which family of distributions to start from, and which choices to make in the course of narrowing down the family of distributions is usually more of an art than a science. Let us now consider how the sample data might be used to obtain a joint probability distribution for *NCIG*, *LC*, and *HC* in the following way. First choose a family of distributions that is believed to contain the population distribution. This may be done by looking at the data, using background knowledge, or both. While the data may suggest a family of distributions, it does not generally single out a unique one. In the very simple example, *NCIG* and *HC* take on any of eight different values, and *LC* takes on one of two different values in the sample. In this case, it follows from the way that we have measured the variables that the distribution is a multinomial.

Having selected the family of distributions, a sample can be used to 'estimate' a unique distribution from the family of distributions. One way to do this uses the following formula, which is true of any multinomial probability distribution:

$$P(NCIG = x, LC = y, HC = z)$$
$$= P(NCIG = x) \times P(LC = y \mid NCIG = x)$$
$$\times P(HC = z \mid NCIG = x, LC = y) \qquad (1)$$

Let H_1 be the family of distributions that can be represented in the form of equation (1). It is possible to pick out a unique multinomial distribution from the family of multinomial distributions by specifying $P(NCIG)$, $P(LC \mid NCIG)$, and $P(HC \mid NCIG, LC)$. The quantities to be specified in order to select a unique distribution from a family of distributions are the parameters of the distribution family. The values of parameters can be fixed in one of two ways. A parameter can simply be assumed to have a value, perhaps on the basis of background knowledge. For example, the value of $P(NCIG = 2)$ could be fixed at 0.2; in that case $P(NCIG = 2)$ is a fixed parameter. If the value of a parameter is not fixed, but is instead estimated from the sample data, then the parameter is a free parameter. A free parameter is typically estimated by some formula that uses the values of the measured random variables in the sample. For example, an estimate of $P(NCIG = 2)$ in the population is given by the number of units in the sample with $NCIG = 2$ divided by the number of units in the sample, and the other parameters can be calculated in an analogous way. Suppose that the free parameters are estimated in this way from the sample; let the resulting distribution be called P_1.

The same population parameter can be estimated by a number of different estimators. How should an estimator be chosen? One desirable property is that it be practically certain that the estimator can be made as close to the true value of the parameter as desired, as long as the sample is made large enough; such an estimator is 'consistent'. A second desirable feature of an estimator is that the expected value of the estimator equal the population value of the parameter; such an estimator is 'unbiased'. A third desirable property is that the probability of large differences between the value of the estimator on different samples of the same size is small; such an estimator has 'low variance'. Typically, the variance of an estimator decreases with increasing sample size. An estimator of a parameter which makes the sample data as likely as possible, given the constraints of the model is called a 'maximum likelihood' estimator; under a wide variety of conditions maximum likelihood estimators are unbiased and consistent. For a discrete distribution, the number of units in the sample with $NCIG = x$ divided by the number of units in the sample is a maximum likelihood estimator.

How well does P_1 do in predicting the value of LC? In order to show how well P_1 predicts on a number of different samples, ten different samples of size fifty were pseudo-randomly generated on a computer from the same population probability distribution (the first sample was used to 'estimate' P_1). The number of errors in each sample made by P_1 in predicting the value of LC given the measured values of HC and $NCIG$ is shown in Table 3.

Table 3

Sample	1	2	3	4	5	6	7	8	9	10
Number wrong	3	7	13	14	17	11	13	12	12	9

H_1 is a very flexible family of distributions, and can reproduce any multinomial distribution exactly. A disadvantage of this is that it makes the 'estimate' of the population distribution vary a lot from sample to sample. That is why the number of wrong predictions of LC is relatively small in the sample which we used

to 'estimate' (sample 1) but much larger on the other samples. Another way of looking at this is that the family of distributions chosen has a large number of free parameters that have to be estimated with relatively few data points. This means that estimates from different samples vary quite widely. This in turn can lead to variations in the prediction of the value of LC, given the same values of $NCIG$ and HC.

One way to reduce the variation in parameter estimates is to choose initially a family of models that has fewer free parameters. For example, let H_2 be the family of distributions that can be represented by the following formula:

$$\begin{aligned} P(NCIG = x, LC = y, HC = z) \\ = P(NCIG = x) \times P(LC = y \mid NCIG = x) \\ \times P(HC = z \mid NCIG = x) \end{aligned} \qquad (2)$$

H_2 consists of those multinomial distributions in which

$$\begin{aligned} P(HC = z \mid NCIG = x, LC = y) \\ = P(HC = z \mid NCIG = x), \end{aligned}$$

that is, HC is independent of LC conditional on $NCIG$. H_2 is properly contained in H_1. The free parameters of H_2 can be estimated using this formula and the sample by substituting the conditional frequencies in the sample for the corresponding conditional probabilities in the equation; call the resulting probability distribution P_2. Unlike H_1, not every multinomial distribution is contained in H_2. If the population distribution falls within H_2 (as it did in this example) then in general the predictions of LC from P_2 will be more accurate than the predictions of LC from P_1, because the number of parameters that need to be estimated has been reduced, and the estimates of the parameters tend to vary less from sample to sample. In the first sample, there are four units with $NCIG = 4$, where three of those four have $LC = 1$ and one has $LC = 0$. These four points are used to estimate fourteen parameters of P_1 (that is, $P_1(HC \mid NCIG = 4, LC = 0)$ and $P_1(HC \mid NCIG = 4, LC = 1)$) but only seven parameters of P_2 (that is, $P_2(HC \mid NCIG = 4)$). Moreover, the predictions of LC are in general more accurate when the estimates of the population distributions are made using P_2 rather than P_1. Calculating the number of errors made in predicting LC from HC and $NCIG$ on the same ten samples used before, the number of errors made by P_2 is shown in Table 4.

Note that the number of errors made in sample 1 is larger for P_2 than for P_1. This is partially because sample 1 is the sample that was used to estimate the parameters of H_1 and H_2, and H_2 cannot reproduce

Table 4

Sample	1	2	3	4	5	6	7	8	9	10
Number wrong	5	11	12	10	17	7	10	8	9	14

the sample distribution exactly, while H_1 can. However, on all of the other samples, except samples 2 and 10, the prediction of *LC* from P_2 is at least as accurate as the prediction of *LC* from P_1.

While there are advantages to assuming that the population distribution lies in H_2, there are also possible disadvantages. If the assumption is false, the predictions of *LC* from P_2 may be worse than the predictions of *LC* made from P_1, because the parameter estimates could be biased. However, even if the population distribution does not lie in H_2, but it is close to a distribution that lies in H_2, the prediction of *LC* from P_2 may be better than the prediction made from H_1. Whether or not this is the case depends upon how close the population distribution is to a distribution that lies in H_2, and how much the variance of the estimator is reduced by assuming the distribution is in H_2. One way of judging whether the population distribution is a member of H_2 is by performing a significance test.

The simplest form of a significance test compares two hypotheses: in our case that the population distribution equals P_2 or that the population distribution equals P_1. The procedure either rejects P_2 or accepts P_2. There are two kinds of errors that can be made: rejecting P_2 when it is true, and accepting P_2 when it is false. In this context, the hypothesis that P_2 is true is called the 'null hypothesis', the first kind of error is called a 'type I error', and the second kind of error is called a 'type II error'. The power of the test is 1 – P(type II error). The goal is to minimize type I and type II errors. Unfortunately, these two goals usually conflict, so the actual procedure is to choose an acceptable probability of type I error, and then attempt to minimize the probability of type II error. An adaptation of the procedure can be used to test a given hypothesis against more than one alternative hypothesis. In that case, given a fixed acceptable probability of type I error, the goal is to find a test that minimizes the probability of type II error against each of the alternative hypotheses. Although this procedure is widely employed in the social sciences to test probabilistic hypotheses, it has also come under severe criticism. The answer that one gets depends upon a number of free choices: the choice of which hypothesis is the null hypothesis, the choice of the alternative hypothesis, the choice of a

test statistic, and the choice of a significance level. Moreover, given many parameters and small sample size, the probability of a type II error can be quite high.

The Bayesian approach to 'estimating' $P(LC \mid NCIG, HC)$ is different from the procedure described above. First, choose some family of distributions, such as H_1. Let Θ represent the space of the set of parameters for the family of distributions. Next, for each θ in Θ, let $f(\theta)$ be the value of a prior density function based on background knowledge. In the absence of specific background knowledge some variant of a 'non-informative prior' is often placed over Θ. Then the following equation can be used to calculate $P(LC \mid NCIG, HC)$:

$$P(LC \mid NCIG, HC)$$
$$= \int_{\Theta} P(LC \mid NCIG, HC, \theta) f(\theta \mid NCIG, HC) d\theta$$

3 Causal models

Consider the following questions: what would the distribution of *LC* be if *NCIG* was forced to have the value 0 for each member of the population? What would the distribution of *LC* be if *HC* was forced to be 0 for each unit in the population?

These are questions about hypothetical populations, which may never exist. If P(*NCIG*, *LC*, *HC*) is the probability distribution in the actual population, let $P_{\text{Man}(NCIG=0)}(NCIG, LC, HC)$ and $P_{\text{Man}(HC=0)}(NCIG, LC, HC)$ be the probability distributions in the hypothetical population where *NCIG* has been forced to be zero, and the hypothetical population where *HC* has been forced to be zero, respectively.

How can $P_{\text{Man}(NCIG=0)}(LC)$ and $P_{\text{Man}(HC=0)}(LC)$ be inferred from P(*NCIG*, *LC*, *HC*)? Suppose hypothetically, that *NCIG* is a direct cause of *LC*, and *LC* is a direct cause of *HC*, but *NCIG* causes *HC* only via *LC*, and that these causal facts are known. This causal information can be represented in a directed acyclic graph of the following form:

$$NCIG \rightarrow LC \rightarrow HC$$

Figure 2

Here the arrow from *NCIG* to *LC* means that *NCIG* is a direct cause of *LC*, the arrow from *LC* to *HC* means that *LC* is a direct cause of *HC*, and the lack of an arrow from *NCIG* to *HC* means that *NCIG* is not a direct cause of *HC*.

Suppose that with each causal structure represented by a directed acyclic graph there is an associated set of probability distributions that are compatible with that causal structure. In the case of discrete distributions the rule can be stated very simply. If G is a directed acyclic graph representing a given causal structure, and every common cause of a pair of variables in G is also represented in G, assume that every probability distribution in a population with causal graph G can be factored in the following way:

$$P(\mathbf{V}) = \prod_{V \in \mathbf{V}} P(V \mid \mathbf{Parents}(V, G))$$

where $\mathbf{V}$ is the set of variables in G, and $\mathbf{Parents}(V,G)$ is the set of variables in G at the tail of a directed edge into V, for example, if $A \rightarrow B$ in G then A is a parent of B in G. If a distribution P can be factored according to this formula for directed acyclic graph G, then the distribution is said to satisfy the local directed Markov condition for G. In the case of Figure 2, the formula entails that

$$P(NCIG, LC, HC) = P(NCIG)$$
$$\times P(LC \mid NCIG) \times P(HC \mid LC).$$

The local directed Markov condition is often, if not always explicitly, assumed in social science research. However, it is not universally true. In particular, if a directed graph is used to represent feedback, or if the properties of one unit affect the properties of another unit (via second-hand smoke, for example) the Markov condition may be false.

The following formula states a general rule for inferring the effects of forcing an 'ideal intervention' on variable X in a directed graph G, where an 'ideal intervention' forces some probability distribution $\mathrm{Man}(X)$ upon X, and has no other effect upon the system than through changing X.

$$P_{\mathrm{Man}(X)}(\mathbf{V}) = P_{\mathrm{Man}(X)}(X)$$
$$\times \prod_{V \in \mathbf{V} \setminus \{X\}} P(V \mid \mathbf{Parents}(V, G))$$

where $\mathbf{V} \setminus \{X\}$ is the set of all variables in $\mathbf{V}$ except X. Applying this equation to Figure 2, it follows that

$$P_{\mathrm{Man}(NCIG)}(NCIG, LC, HC)$$
$$= P_{\mathrm{Man}(NCIG)}(NCIG)$$
$$\times P(LC \mid NCIG) \times P(HC \mid LC),$$

so with a little arithmetic

$$P_{\mathrm{Man}(NCIG)}(LC) = P(LC \mid NCIG).$$

Similarly,

$$P_{\mathrm{Man}(HC)}(NCIG, LC, HC) = P(NCIG)$$
$$\times P(LC \mid NCIG)$$
$$\times P_{\mathrm{Man}(HC)}(HC),$$

so with a little arithmetic $P_{\mathrm{Man}(HC)}(LC) = P(LC)$. This accords with our intuition that manipulating a cause of LC changes the distribution of LC, but manipulating an effect of LC does not. (Formulation of this theorem in the form presented here is found in Spirtes, Glymour and Scheines 1993; and is stated in a form that does not use directed acyclic graphs in Robins 1986; and Wold and Strotz 1971.)

If the causal structure is not known, how can it be discovered? One approach would be to do a randomized experiment. A random sample could be taken from the actual population, and using some random device people could be assigned to a control group, who are forced to smoke a given number of cigarettes, or a treatment group, who are forced not to smoke. These two samples are just like samples from a hypothetical population in which everyone is forced to smoke a given number of cigarettes, and a hypothetical population in which everyone is forced not to smoke. This reduces the problem of determining the effect of $NCIG$ on LC to a problem of inference about a population distribution from a sample distribution, which is the same question considered in §2.

In many cases, a randomized experiment cannot be performed, either for practical or for ethical reasons. The local directed Markov condition associates a given causal structure with a set of population probability distributions. If it is inferred from a sample that the population distribution does not lie in the set of distributions compatible with a given causal structure G, it could be concluded that G is false. This strategy obviously suffers all the problems of inferences about a population probability distribution from a sample distribution that were discussed in §2, but there are other problems in addition. If it is inferred from a sample that the population distribution does lie in the set of distributions compatible with a given causal structure G, it cannot be concluded that G is true, because the population distribution might also lie in the set of distributions compatible with other causal structures. For example, in the discrete case, every distribution that is compatible with any of the following three causal structures, is also compatible with the other two. Background information, such as time order, may be able to eliminate some of the alternatives, but if the background information is not available, using only the statistical data it is not possible reliably to decide between the three alternatives.

$NCIG{\rightarrow}LC{\rightarrow}HC$ $NCIG{\leftarrow}LC{\rightarrow}HC$ $NCIG{\leftarrow}LC{\leftarrow}HC$

(i)   (ii)   (iii)

Figure 3

When the possibility of unmeasured common causes is considered, then the problem is even worse. For example, any distribution compatible with the causal models of Figure 3 is also compatible with either of the models depicted in Figure 4, as well as many others, where the 'T' variables are unmeasured.

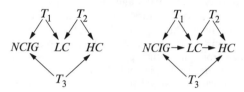

Figure 4

Again, strong background knowledge to the effect that there are no unmeasured common causes would eliminate the causal models in Figure 4 as a possibility. Another way to eliminate models such as those in Figure 4 is to make the (controversial) assumption that if the population distribution satisfies a given factorization, then it is entailed to satisfy that factorization for all parameterizations of the graph by the local directed Markov condition; call this the 'faithfulness' condition. Thus while there exist some parameterizations of the graphs in Figure 4 that can be factored according to equation 2, applying the local directed Markov condition to either of the graphs in Figure 4 does not entail that all parameterizations of these graphs can be factored according to equation 2. Given the assumption that a probability distribution is the marginal of a distribution that satisfies the local directed Markov condition and the faithfulness condition for the causal graph G that generated it, it is possible in some cases to narrow the set of graphs compatible with a given population distribution sufficiently to determine that X is a cause of Y, without knowing which occurred first. There is active research into devising algorithms for the automatic generation of causal models from sample statistics, background knowledge, and principles like the Markov condition, the faithfulness condition, and weaker assumptions.

For example, suppose that the causal structure G shown in Figure 5 generated a probability distribution P that satisfied the local directed Markov condition and the faithfulness condition for G, and that one knew P, but not G. If one admits the possibility of unmeasured common causes of variables, then P satisfies the local directed Markov condition and the faithfulness condition for an infinite number of different acyclic causal structures; however, all of those causal structures contain a directed path from Z to W, so it can be concluded from the local directed Markov condition, the faithfulness condition, and P, that Z is a cause of W. But in practice, one has knowledge of a sample distribution rather than the population distribution P, which makes the inference more difficult.

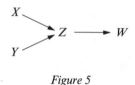

Figure 5

See also: STATISTICS

References and further reading

Bentler, P. (1989) *EQS: Structural Equations Program Manual*, Los Angeles, CA: BMDP Statistical Software Inc. (The user's manual for a statistical programme widely used in the social sciences, with a number of examples.)

Blalock, H.M. (1969) *Theory Construction: From Verbal to Mathematical Formulations*, Englewood Cliffs, NJ: Prentice Hall. (An elementary introduction to formulation social science models.)

Blalock, H.M. (ed.) (1971) *Causal Models in the Social Sciences*, Chicago, IL: Aldine-Atheston. (Collection of articles on problems of causal inference in the social sciences.)

Bollen, K. (1989) *Structural Equations with Latent Variables*, New York: Wiley. (Advanced undergraduate text describing construction, estimation, and testing of structural equation models.)

Freudenthal, H. (1965) *Probability and Statistics*, New York: Elsevier Publishing Co. (Undergraduate level introduction to statistics and probability.)

Fisher, R. (1990) *Statistical Methods, Experimental Design, and Scientific Inference*, Oxford: Oxford University Press. (A collection of classic works on experimental design.)

Lindley, D. (1985) *Making Decisions*, New York: Wiley. (Elementary introduction to Bayesian decision theory.)

Pearl, J. (1988) *Probabilistic Reasoning in Intelligent Systems*, San Mateo, CA: Morgan and Kaufman. (Explains recent advances in using Bayesian techniques in expert systems.)

* Robins, J. (1986) 'A New Approach to Causal Inference in Mortality Studies with Sustained Exposure Periods – Application to Control of the Healthy Worker Survivor Effect', *Mathematical Modeling* 7: 1393–512. (Contains a non-graphical version of the manipulation theorem.)
* Spirtes, P., Glymour, C. and Scheines, P. (1993) *Causation, Prediction, and Search*, New York: Springer Verlag Lecture Notes in Statistics, 81. (Graduate level text on causal inference from statistical data.)
* Wold, H. and Strotz, J. (1971) 'Recursive versus Nonrecursive Systems: An Attempt at a Synthesis', in H. Blalock (ed.), *Causal Models in the Social Sciences*, Chicago, IL: Aldine-Atheston. (Contains a version of the manipulation theorem for linear systems.)

PETER SPIRTES

STATUS AND ETHICS

see MORAL RELATIVISM

STEINER, RUDOLF (1861–1925)

Rudolf Steiner held that humanity has passed through an astral and an etheric stage and has possessed intuitive and clairvoyant modes of consciousness. People, he held, once enjoyed psychic powers and existed in forms of matter more rarefied than those that characterize their current successors. Nevertheless, people still exist on four levels, the physical, the etheric, the astral and the spiritual, and earlier psychic skills are retrievable. Steiner, who called this theory 'anthroposophy', was particularly influenced by Goethe and theosophy.

Born on February 27, 1861, Rudolf Steiner studied from 1890 to 1897 at the Goethe-Archiv in Weimar, and from 1897–1900 was the editor of *Magazin: Monatschrift für Literatur* (Magazine: Monthly Writings on Literature). In 1902, Steiner became general secretary of the new German section of the Theosophical Society (see THEOSOPHY §2). He came to disagree with Annie Besant and Madame Blavatsky over attempts to build a 'spiritual science' on Eastern mysticism and over the promotion of Jiddu Krishnamurti as a messiah. In 1913, he founded the Anthroposophical Society. He died in 1925.

Steiner was initiated into an occult tradition by an adept whom he called 'The Master', and at the age of forty he began to speak publicly about what he believed to be clairvoyant experiences that had occurred to him since he was eight. He accepted the doctrines of reincarnation and karma, and the Hermetic teaching that humankind is the microscomic clue to the macrocosm, so that discovering the true nature of humanity would also lead to a knowledge of the secrets of the universe. In 1896, he wrote his major work *Die Philosophie der Freiheit: Grundzuge einer modernen Weltanschauung* (The Philosophy of Freedom: Essentials of a Modern Outlook), which contends that mechanistic science gives us only an abstract knowledge of natural uniformities. His model for a fuller human knowledge than that provided by mechanistic science was that of Goethe's 'primal plant', a self-evolving, self-developing organism (see GOETHE, J.W. VON §3). He claimed to have access to the Akashic records, which theosophists hold to be master records of all that has occurred since the beginning of the universe. These records allegedly exist in the form of impressions in the astral plane. Here, Steiner reported, he learned that humanity once possessed supranormal capacities that have since been lost.

Steiner taught that Christ came at the low point of the human descent into materialism and provided the opportunity for reascent. Uniting (South Asian) Indian and theosophical ideas with his interpretation of Christianity and the contents of his clairvoyant experiences, he constructed what he conceived of as a correct combination of modern science and religion. He reported perceiving nonhuman intelligences who affect human consciousness, some promoting spiritual advancement and some acting on behalf of human belief in a mechanistic materialism.

Steiner held that human nature has four levels: the physical body, the etheric body, the astral or soul body, and the spirit. The notion of an etheric body is connected with the notion of the aura, thought of as an envelope of vital energy that radiates from everything in nature and possesses a magnetic field. The etheric body is regarded as part of the aura, which is accessible only clairvoyantly. The notion of the astral body also links up with the notion of the aura, astral bodies also being said to be parts of auras. The astral body is viewed as the seat of emotions and as the carrier of consciousness in out-of-body and near-death experiences.

To each level of human nature, Steiner taught, there corresponds a level of human cognition: to the physical body corresponds perception; to the ethereal body, imaginative knowledge; to the astral body, inspirational knowledge; to the spirit, intuitive knowledge. He alleged that there are etheric forces at work among minerals and plants, and that awareness of these forces – through imaginative knowledge – provides the basis for a new science of 'biodynamic forming'. Inspirational knowledge is understood as knowledge of one's astral body, thought of as capable of existing independently of one's physical body and as what makes thought, memory and a sense of personal identity possible. Having intuitive knowledge involves experiencing one's entire life backwards, and, he held, includes encountering beings of higher intelligence.

List of works

Steiner, R. (1896) *Die Philosophie der Freiheit: Grundzüge einer modernen Weltanschauung* (The Philosophy of Freedom: Essentials of a Modern Outlook), Dornach: Philosophisch-Antroposophischer Verlag Goetheanum; trans. R. Stebbing and ed. P.M. Allen, *The Philosophy of Spiritual Activity*, West Nyack: Rudolph Steiner Publications, 1963. (Originally published in English in 1916; argues that mechanistic science gives only formal knowledge and needs supplementation by Goethean epistemology.)
—— (1925) *Mein Lebensgand*, Dornach: Schweitz; *The Course of My Life*, Blauvelt: Rudolph Steiner Publications, 1977. (Steiner's autobiography.)
—— (1950) *Anthroposophische Grundlagen für die Arzneikunst* (Foundations of Anthroposophy for the Art of Medicine), Dornach: Schweiz; *Anthroposophy: An Introduction*, London: Rudolph Steiner Press, 1983. (Four lectures given in Stuttgart in October 1922, forming an introduction to Steiner's adaptation of theosophy.)
—— (1984) *The Essential Steiner*, ed. R.A. McDermott, San Francisco, CA: Harper & Row. (Steiner's publication list contains over two hundred and fifty items; this selection offers a manageable starting point and information as to how to proceed in following up various topics on which he wrote.)

References and further reading

Davy, J. (ed.) (1975) *Works Arising from the Life of Rudolph Steiner*, London: Rudolph Steiner Press. (Articles published to mark the fiftieth anniversary of Steiner's death.)

KEITH E. YANDELL

STEVENSON, CHARLES LESLIE (1908–79)

Stevenson's major contribution to philosophy was his development of emotivism, a theory of ethical language according to which moral judgments do not state any sort of fact, but rather express the moral emotions of the speaker and attempt to influence others.

What do we mean when we say that something is good or bad? On the face of it, we are describing, attributing to the thing some property, goodness or badness. What could these properties be? How do we find out about them? Much of philosophical moral theory explores various answers to these questions. Stevenson thought that questions about the nature of moral properties were misplaced. Our moral judgments do not, at least primarily, describe at all. Uttering moral sentences has a different function: to express emotions, and to influence or invite others to share them. All of his main contributions appeared in *Ethics and Language* (1944) and a collection of papers, *Facts and Values* (1963).

If I say 'Ann Arbor is in Michigan', I express my belief that Ann Arbor is in Michigan, but I do not say that I believe such a thing. For what makes what I said true? Not that I really do believe that Ann Arbor is in Michigan; only the fact that Ann Arbor really is in Michigan. Stevenson's theory of ethical language, in a nutshell, was that when I say 'Inequality is bad', I have expressed a certain negative moral attitude towards inequality, though I have not said that I have it.

Stevenson's main argument for his theory was that '[a] person who recognizes X to be "good" must ipso facto acquire a stronger tendency to act in its favor than he otherwise would have had' (1963: 13). Following Hume, Stevenson thought this showed that the 'belief' that something is good must really be no belief at all, but an emotive attitude, since beliefs do not of themselves give us any tendency to act (see HUME, D. §§3–4).

Besides expressing the speaker's attitude, Stevenson said, moral statements also 'create an influence', they invite the audience to share in the emotion expressed. Thus, 'x is good' is akin to 'Let us approve of x'. And, in context, ethical statements can come to have secondary descriptive content; in Victorian England, for example, calling a woman 'virtuous' implied that she was chaste.

Stevenson's theory was enormously influential. Taking its cue from Ayer's brief remarks on ethics in *Language, Truth and Logic* (1936), Stevenson's theory added sophistication and subtlety (see AYER,

A.J.). His view has important affinities both with the work of R.M. HARE and with some later theories, all of which share the central tenet that moral judgments express not beliefs but conative attitudes (see PRESCRIPTIVISM). Stevenson in particular stressed that his work did not include any substantive moral judgments, but rather comprised 'analytic ethics', or what is now commonly called 'meta-ethics', the branch of moral theory that is *about* ethics and ethical language (see ANALYTIC ETHICS). For by claiming that moral judgments serve to express emotions, he had not expressed his own moral emotions at all.

See also: EMOTIVISM; EMOTIVE MEANING; MORAL JUDGMENT; MORAL SCEPTICISM; MORALITY AND EMOTIONS

List of works

Stevenson, C.L. (1944) *Ethics and Language*, New Haven, CT: Yale University Press. (Stevenson's only published monograph.)

—— (1963) *Facts and Values: Studies in Ethical Analysis*, New Haven, CT: Yale University Press. (A collection of papers. Essay 2 is especially useful as an introduction; essay 11 contains the most mature version of the theory.)

References and further reading

* Ayer, A.J. (1936) *Language, Truth and Logic*, London: Gollancz; 2nd edn, 1946, ch. 6. (Contains the germ of emotivism, which Stevenson developed into a full and sophisticated theory.)

Blackburn, S. (1984) *Spreading the Word*, Oxford: Oxford University Press, esp. ch. 6. (Develops a variation on emotivism designed to address prominent objections.)

Geach, P.T. (1960) 'Ascriptivism', *Philosophical Review* 69 (2): 221–5. (An influential, but somewhat technical, objection to emotivism.)

Goldman, A. and Kim, J. (eds) (1978) *Values and Morals: Essays in Honor of William Frankena, Charles Stevenson, and Richard Brandt*, Dordrecht and Boston, MA: D. Reidel. (A collection of critical essays; those on Stevenson's work are quite accessible. Contains a comprehensive bibliography of Stevenson's writing.)

Hare, R.M. (1952) *The Language of Morals*, Oxford: Oxford University Press. (A work contemporary with Stevenson's, with important similarities and contrasts.)

JAMES DREIER

STEWART, DUGALD (1753–1828)

Dugald Stewart was, after Thomas Reid, the most influential figure in the Common Sense School; he was a major influence on Victor Cousin and Théodore Jouffroy in France and on most academic philosophers in the United States. Along with Reid and Cousin, Stewart made the Scottish tradition the dominant philosophy in America for half a century. His Elements of the Philosophy of the Human Mind *and* Philosophy of the Active and Moral Powers of Man *were his most important works and went through a number of printings. The abridged edition of his* Active and Moral Powers *was reprinted ten times from 1849 to 1868.*

Stewart followed Reid in claiming that any philosophy which contravenes the principles of common sense must be false, and the problem is to discover and eliminate the premise which yields such results. He added the requirement that philosophical propositions must not change the meanings of concepts in ordinary life, and he also added a new dimension to Reid's agency theory. More than any other writer he emphasized correctly the epistemic similarities between Reid and Immanuel Kant, but he followed Reid in avoiding Kant's distinction between phenomena and noumena.

Stewart disagreed with Reid in avoiding the phrase 'principles of common sense' as misleading, rejected his mentor's realistic interpretation of universals and provided his own nominalistic alternative. He also modified to some extent, though quite cautiously, Reid's rigid inductivism and made some concessions to a realistic interpretation of scientific hypotheses. Stewart was equipped to discuss issues in the philosophy of science since he was well versed in mathematics and physics, having been professor of mathematics at Edinburgh for ten years before being named professor of moral philosophy. Stewart was arguably the first and finest philosopher of science in the Scottish tradition.

1 Background
2 Reid's common-sense view
3 Stewart's contributions to this tradition
4 Stewart's deviations from this tradition

1 Background

Dugald Stewart was educated at the University of Edinburgh and in 1771 went to Glasgow, primarily to attend the lectures of Thomas REID. He became, first, professor of mathematics and, ten years later, professor of moral philosophy at Edinburgh; his philosophical work, published in eleven volumes by

Sir William HAMILTON, shows him to have been no carbon copy of Reid, but a philosopher who added important new dimensions to the Scottish tradition and occasionally criticized and departed from it.

2 Reid's common-sense view

Thomas Reid formulated a number of what he called principles of common sense, including such judgments as that objects are perceived as in space, and events are perceived as in time. Space and time are not concepts learned from experience, since 'object' presupposes 'space' and 'event' presupposes 'time'. Thus space and time constitute nativistic epistemic input possessed by perceivers themselves. Other examples of nativistic input include intuitions to the effect that every event has a cause, qualities are directly perceived as properties of objects, objects exist independently of being known, and agents in some cases act freely. Principles of common sense can be identified (not proven) because they are universally held and are unavoidable in the sense that denying them is pointless because in so doing one never gets rid of them. The philosopher who momentarily denies them reaffirms them in the marketplace or even while denying them acts upon them unwittingly. That David HUME pointed out this state of affairs was, for Reid, a very honest if self-defeating thing for a sceptic to do. Because the knowledge incorporated in the principles is nativistic (though activated by appropriate experiences) and because the principles are universal and unavoidable, they always take precedence over any discursive argument which contravenes them. When philosophy comes into conflict with common-sense principles, so much the worse for philosophy. Any philosophy which contravenes the principles must contain a fallacy and should be rejected.

Reid rejected scepticism because it violated the principles of common sense, not only claiming that their truth-values are not reliable but that even if they were one could not know it to be the case. Absolute idealism would have presented Reid with an even more standard example of the rejection of his principles. Absolute idealists undermine the truth-values of ordinary propositions with the concept of internal relations. They do not deny the ordinary meanings of 'physical object', 'space' and 'time', but insist that such entities are never exemplified except as misleading appearances. Since everything is internally related there are no separate entities, and since ordinary statements imply the existence of such entities such statements cannot be true of reality, only of appearances. As with the sceptic, the problem for the idealist, Reid thought, is to discover the premise that leads to such absurdities and reject it.

3 Stewart's contributions to this tradition

Stewart wholly agreed with Reid's Common Sense metaphilosophy, according to which sceptics and absolute idealists who violate the truth-values of ordinary statements are *ipso facto* mistaken. However he did not think that Reid succeeded in showing that George BERKELEY rejected the truths of common-sense principles and he felt that a new dimension needed to be added to Reid's metaphilosophy. Stewart was impressed with Berkeley's insistence that his views squared completely with common sense. 'The cup is on the table' remains true, if true to begin with, whether the cup and table are construed as independently existing objects or as clusters of sensations. Or, again, Kepler's laws of planetary motion remain what they are if the planets are interpreted as independent objects or clusters of sensations in God's mind. Stewart concluded that Berkeley had escaped Reid's net, though he thought the good bishop contravened common sense by violating the meaning of ordinary terms. What we need, he believed, is an accurate analysis of the meaning of the word existence,

> which analysis would have at once shown, not only that we are irresistibly led to ascribe to the material world all the independent reality which this word expresses, but that it is from the material world that our first and most satisfactory notions of *existence* are drawn.
>
> ([1854–60] 1877, vol.3: 54)

Hence both the meaning-value and the truth-value of ordinary propositions are inviolable and cannot be contravened by philosophical analysis.

Stewart's remarks on Berkeley seem well taken and yield a supplementary ingredient to Reid's metaphilosophy, namely that it is just as illegitimate for a philosophical position to violate the *meanings* of ordinary propositions as it is to contravene their truth-value. He formulated this supplementary criterion very clearly and distinctly but unfortunately did not consistently apply it in his subsequent discussion of the meaning of 'causality' and Hume's denial of natural necessity. Even though he did not consistently maintain the meaning-inviolability of common sense principles, he succeeded in making the point in an admirably clear and telling way. With the exception of Asa Mahan at Oberlin College and some others, subsequent members of the tradition omitted to take account of Stewart's criterion. Indeed, even G.E. MOORE, much later, failed entirely where Stewart had succeeded, by formulating only the Reidian truth-inviolability criterion. Moreover, it must be kept in mind that Stewart indicated that philosophical positions often result from semantical misadventures, and that philosophers often argue from misleading analogies, and that such claims are essentially related to, and reflect, his meaning-inviolability criterion. The fact remains that Stewart, above all others in the Scottish tradition, stressed the importance of meaning analysis, and was outdone in this respect only in the twentieth century, by various strands of analytic philosophy.

Stewart contributed to the Common Sense tradition in still another way. He saw more clearly than most others the striking similarity of Kant's transcendental aesthetic to Reid's views on space and time. Kant and Reid had the same goals, namely to show the inadequacy of John Locke's empirical construal of space and time (or the inadequacy of any empirical construal), and to attribute the experience of objects in space and time to laws or forms inherent in the structure of the human intellect itself (see KANT, I. §§3–7; LOCKE, J. §§2–6). These fundamental laws or forms, of course, are not independent of experience, since they are awakened into their proper functioning only by the occurrence of a contingent relevant sensation. Stewart concluded:

> This is precisely the ground on which Reid has made his stand...and I leave it to my readers to judge whether it was not more philosophical to state...the *fact*, in simple and perspicuous terms, as a demonstration of the imperfection of Locke's theory, than to have reared upon it a superstructure of technical mystery, similar to what is exhibited in the system of the German metaphysicians.
> ([1854–60] 1877, vol. 5: 118)

Unless, like Stewart, one sees the epistemic similarities of Reid and Kant (discounting their very great metaphysical dissimilarities), one will not be able to understand the American philosophical movement called transcendentalism, with Ralph Waldo EMERSON and Theodore Parker sharing nativistic epistemic points of departure but developing totally different metaphysical views. From the initial intuitionistic framework, Emerson went towards absolute idealism, while Parker embraced the Scottish realist tradition of Reid and Stewart. The two Americans did not disagree on the importance of intuitive truth; they simply had incompatible intuitions. Stewart would have thought Emerson's intuitions unacceptable because they were not universal and unavoidable.

A further contribution made by Stewart to the Scottish tradition was in the area of agency theory. He argued that the concept of cause is not applicable to human actions: in general people act from motives which explain the point of what they do but do not cause them to do it. Agents are the causes of their own actions, guided by motives. Stewart accepted that all actions have motives, but stressed that 'motive' is a metaphorical way of referring to agents' intentions or purposes in performing acts and not to substantive factors that necessarily cause their actions. His important contribution, however, was to reject any need for criteria to distinguish between cause–effect and motive–act explanations. He rejected James Gregory's proposal that causal relations hold universally whereas motive–act relations cannot be universalized. In addition, he rejected the criterion that causes and effects can be described independently of each other while motives and acts cannot since they are logically or conceptually connected. As for his general argument against the need for any criterion whatever, Stewart looked upon a criterion as a sign that something else is the case and thought a criterion unnecessary since agent-causality is *directly attested to* by consciousness. Consciousness attests to the *fact* (Stewart's emphasis) that people can decide among contending motives, can initiate an act, and could have done other than they did; and such agent causality is obviously not applicable to the physical world.

Stewart's claim that the concept of causality is not applicable to human agency (though it may be applicable to abnormal behaviour) has the great merit of clarity and succinctness as well as philosophical insight. Moreover, his rejection of criteria for distinguishing causal and motive-model explanations seems a praiseworthy addition to the tradition. Why should it be necessary to provide a *criterion* for what is *evident*?

4 Stewart's deviations from this tradition

Stewart was critical of Reid's use of the phrase 'principles of common sense'. The use of this phrase, he felt, is easily misunderstood. 'Common sense' is a phrase that already has a fixed meaning in ordinary parlance which is different from Reid's, and the result is constant misrepresentation. In ordinary language, 'common sense' ordinarily denotes a type of wisdom different from what can be acquired through education. To claim, then, as Reid did, that a philosophical analysis which contravenes the principles of common sense is thereby nullified, is to suggest, unfortunately, that learned philosophers are to be governed by the voice of the general population. As Stewart pointed out, Reid did not of course intend this outcome, but his use of 'common sense' encouraged it. Surely there must be some more appropriate name for the fundamental laws of human belief?

Stewart's criticism of Reid's use of 'common sense' seems plausible and, in any case, influenced the later Scottish realists. His criticism amounts to saying that

Reid gave a technical definition of the expression 'common sense' and one that, in fact, violates its ordinary meaning. Subsequent figures in the Scottish tradition, among them Victor COUSIN, Henry Tappan, Asa Mahan, and James McCosh, apparently agreed with Stewart's criticism, since they all used different locutions for Reid's fundamental principles – common consciousness, basic intuitions, and fundamental laws of human belief.

Stewart was also critical of Reid's realistic interpretation of universals. Philosophers of distinction, Stewart wrote, have managed to reject the messenger theory of perception, but unwittingly cling to Locke's theory of ideas in other operations of the mind. When Richard PRICE and Reid abstracted from particulars certain properties shared in common and then generalized such abstractions into classes, they were committing themselves to universals which either exist as entities of some sort or exist as images in the minds of those who use propositions containing such universals. Stewart was unimpressed because people are no more introspectively aware of the existence of universals apart from particulars than they are aware of impressions apart from the object perceived. He had an elaborate analysis to show that there is no reason to believe in the existence of anything in the mind distinct from the operations of the mind itself. The correct view, he maintained, is the nominalistic one, according to which general terms refer wholly to sets of particulars which exemplify them – any one of which in a given set can be given as an example or paradigm of the general term being used. Stewart put forward a nominalistic analysis that depended upon signs and language. Universals, he thought, refer to general signs wholly linguistic in nature, and thus require no ontological or psychological entities as referents. Reasoning involving universals is sign-reasoning, in which general terms have no other existence than the linguistic one shared with all other parts of a well-constructed language.

Stewart's discussion of the nature of universals is a felicitous attack on Locke's theory of ideas; and Stewart's nominalism, phrased in terms of linguistic signs, is not an unsophisticated viewpoint – particularly his notion that the significance of a general term conceived as a sign consists in its successful use as a memory device that conserves experiences individually learned (and can always be checked, upon demand, by paradigm instances of its denotation). Certainly such a view eliminates any necessity of referring general terms to images in the mind, as did Reid. However, Reid apparently did not think that images in the mind were substantive entities like Locke's ideas or Hume's impressions. If not, was Reid's view that just as we should substitute 'sensing' for 'sensation', we should substitute 'imaging' for 'image'? Stewart was not sure, and wiped the board clean by giving a linguistic analysis of universals.

A further way in which Stewart departed from Reid and enriched the Scottish tradition was to weaken, albeit hesitantly, Reid's rigid inductivism. Reid interpreted Newton's 'hypotheses non fingo' literally, and, indeed, found most of the mistakes in physics and philosophy to be based on unfortunate hypotheses, such as Descartes' vortices and Locke's intervening messengers. But according to Stewart, we must not, after all, take Newton's 'hypotheses non fingo' too literally. Did not NEWTON himself suggest numerous hypotheses in his *Optics* and assume that his readers would understand that his 'Queries' had experimental consequences and thus could be scientifically tested? They are quite unlike Descartes' vortices, which are defended wholly on a priori grounds (see DESCARTES §11). It is likely that Newton, in damning the use of hypotheses, referred only to those like Descartes' vortices that are immune to falsification. He approvingly quoted Boscovich's view that hypotheses or theories are necessary anticipations of solid scientific advances since there can be no relevant observation without hypotheses as a guide for where to look and what to look for.

Notwithstanding the aforesaid, Stewart makes it clear that he is not endorsing the use of hypotheses in science in any way except as heuristic devices. Principles of science are not established until they have been fairly inferred from undoubted facts and not from the uninterrupted confirmation of the consequences of hypotheses. Stewart's reservation about giving a realistic interpretation to scientific hypotheses was simply the familiar criticism that the confirmation of hypotheses commits the fallacy of affirming the consequent (see FALLACIES). This issue was the key one among anti-Copernican astronomers during the Renaissance. They wanted to interpret all astronomical hypotheses as mathematical fictions. Nicolas Reymer Baer in 1597 publicly defended a nonrealistic theory of astronomical hypotheses. Reymer had expounded the nonrealistic theory in its most extreme form: not only were astronomical hypotheses merely mathematical fictions, they would not be hypotheses if they were true! In his monumental work *Apologia Tychonis contra Nicolaum Ursum*, Kepler rejected this view, claiming that a logical fallacy is not a scientific mistake and that the available confirmation overwhelmingly allows a realistic interpretation of the Copernican hypothesis. And Galileo emphatically agreed with Kepler. Stewart could not set himself against such scientific and methodological stalwarts and agreed that the evidence in Galileo's day already justified his realistic claim, which science in the future continued to support even in more direct ways. But even at this point Stewart claimed that it was not only that Copernicus correctly predicted all the facts that made the acceptance of his hypothesis legitimate even in his own day, but that there were various analogies between sources of illumination that also made the hypothesis acceptable. But of course Stewart could not deny that analogies themselves are a form of hypothesis.

Stewart's dependence upon Boscovich further confirms the attraction that hypotheses held for him. Boscovich himself argued against an inductive view of science, since his own physical theory had concepts that referred to unobservable events. Since Stewart accepted Boscovich's methodology he again committed himself by implication to the legitimacy of hypotheses with unobservables as long as they had testable consequences. Stewart was drawn to Boscovich's physical theory of point centres. He was also drawn to Boscovich's argument that corpuscularian theory is incoherent, because compressible bodies can interact by contact since they do not instantaneously acquire a common velocity but by mutual compression are enabled to slow down or accelerate in a finite time; however, this concept of interaction cannot be applied to the ultimate corpuscles because they are absolutely incompressible. Hence there can be no transfer of motion between ultimate particles. Stewart was reassured by this argument because it undercut the atomistic materialism of David HARTLEY and Joseph PRIESTLEY. However, such reassurance makes no sense unless Stewart acknowledged the existential import of the corpuscularian hypothesis. It would be absurd to accept, as Stewart did, Boscovich's theory of point centres of mutual influence and the corpuscularian theory as legitimate competitors and yet deny on the methodological level that a system with reference to unobservables is ever justified.

Stewart was perfectly aware of the tensions in his own thinking. On the one hand, he was a thorough inductivist in philosophy and psychology and respected Bacon's methodological dicta. On the other hand, he was sensitive to the realistic interpretations of Kepler and Galileo, who saw that hypotheses were not simply instrumental devices. He was pulled both ways, and his work emerges as a significant connecting link between the naïve inductivism of Reid and the later technical views on scientific theory and causality held by James McCosh (see McCosh 1867), the last first-rate figure in the Scottish tradition.

See also: AMERICAN PHILOSOPHY IN THE 18TH AND 19TH CENTURIES; COMMON SENSE SCHOOL; COMMONSENSISM; THEORIES, SCIENTIFIC

List of works

Stewart, D. (1854–60) *Collected Works*, ed. W. Hamilton, Edinburgh: Constable; ed. W. Hamilton, Edinburgh: Clark, 1877. (Of the eleven volumes in the *Collected Works*, the best known are *Elements of the Philosophy of the Human Mind* (3 vols), and *Philosophy of the Active and Moral Powers of Man* (2 vols).)

—— (1803) *Account of the Life and Writings of Thomas Reid*, Edinburgh: Creech.

—— (1841) *Esquisser de philosophie morale* (Sketch of Moral Philosophy), Paris: Johanneau.

—— (1868) *Philosophy of the Active and Moral Powers of Man*, ed. J. Walker, Boston, MA: Phillips Sampson. (Walker, of Harvard, abridged Stewart's book and improved it pedagogically by placing the long appendix on agency theory appropriately in volume 1, book. 2.)

References and further reading

Griffin-Collart, E. (1980) *La Philosophie écossaise du sense commun: Thomas Reid et Dugald Stewart* (The Scottish Philosophy of Common Sense: Thomas Reid and Dugald Stewart), Bruxelles: Palais des Académies.

Madden, E.H. (1968) *Civil Disobedience and Moral Law*, Seattle, WA: University of Washington Press. (Portrays the dominance of Reid, Stewart, and Cousin in nineteenth-century American philosophy.)

—— (1981) 'Asa Mahan's Analysis of Synthetic Apriori Judgments', *Transactions of the C.S. Peirce Society* 17: 297–318. (Shows the similarities and differences between the Scottish tradition and Kant in a way that makes Stewart's efforts in this direction understandable.)

—— (1986) 'Stewart's Enrichment of the Common-sense Tradition', *History of Philosophy Quarterly* 3 (1): 45–63. (Considers in greater detail aspects discussed in §§2–3, giving a modified account.)

McCosh, J. (1867) *Intuitions of the Mind*, New York: Carter. (Provides the realistic interpretation of science for which Stewart was groping.)

—— (1875) *The Scottish Philosophy, from Hutcheson to Hamilton*, New York: Carter. (Contains a rewarding chapter on Stewart.)

Meyer, D.H. (1974) *The Instructed Conscience*, Philadelphia, PA: University of Pennsylvania Press. (Portrays Stewart as 'the great systematizer' and shows the impact of the Scottish tradition in shaping the American national ethic.)

Olson, R. (1975) *Scottish Philosophy and British Physics, 1750–1880*, Princeton, NJ: Princeton University Press. (Argues that Stewart saw geometry as more basic than algebra and hence influenced British physicists such as James Clerk Maxwell and William M. Rankine.)

Robinson, D. N. (1989) 'Thomas Reid's Critique of Dugald Stewart', *Journal of the History of Philosophy* 27: 405–22. (An examination of Reid's critique of a pre-publication draft of Stewart's *Elements of the Philosophy of the Human Mind*.)

E.H. MADDEN

STILLINGFLEET, E

see CAMBRIDGE PLATONISM; LATITUDINARIANISM; LOCKE, JOHN

STILPO OF MEGARA

see MEGARIAN SCHOOL

STIRNER, MAX (1806–56)

Max Stirner is the author of Der Einzige und sein Eigentum *(The Ego and Its Own), first published in Germany in 1844 and best known for its idiosyncrasies of argument and idiom. Stirner condemns modernity as entrenched in religious modes of thought and envisages a positive egoistic future in which individuals are liberated from the tyranny of those ideas and social arrangements which restrict autonomy.* The Ego and Its Own *was an impulse to the decline of the Hegelian left as a coherent intellectual movement, and played an important role in the genesis of Marxism; Stirner has also been variously portrayed as a precursor of Nietzsche, an individualist anarchist and a forerunner of existentialism.*

Stirner (born Johann Caspar Schmidt on 25 October 1806 in Bayreuth, Germany) had a largely unpropitious start to adult life, passing through university without distinction, before becoming a teacher at a respectable private girls' school in Berlin. However, in his spare time he became increasingly involved with 'the free' (a group of left Hegelians led by Bruno BAUER), before leaving his teaching post in 1844 and publishing *Der Einzige und sein Eigentum* (The Ego and Its Own), his most important and influential work. Following a brief period of unremunerative notoriety, Stirner settled into a somewhat indigent and solitary lifestyle. Hack journalism, translation

work and (before she left him) his second wife's dwindling inheritance failed to avert two brief spells in a debtors' prison. Stirner contracted a fever after an insect bite on his neck, and died on 25 June 1856.

Insisting on the relativity of rationality, truth and language, Stirner rejects traditional forms of expression and modes of exposition. The consequent employment of aphorism and metaphor, neologisms, relentless paronomasia and juxtaposition of words with formal similarities or related meanings to present his views makes *The Ego and Its Own* a stylistically striking, if idiosyncratic, text. The only limitation which Stirner places upon use of language and mode of argument is that it should serve our individual ends.

The Ego and Its Own is structured around a tripartite division of human experience into categories of 'realism' (where individuals are dominated by external forces), 'idealism' (where individuals are dominated by ideas), and 'egoism' (where individuals escape domination by dealing with things and ideas as they wish, setting their personal satisfaction above all else). This tripartite division is elaborated and exemplified in accounts of individual development (in which childhood, youth and adulthood correspond to stages of realism, idealism and egoism), of human history (in which the ancient, Christian and future worlds are portrayed as epochs of realism, idealism and egoism respectively) and in a racial (and racist) analogue of that historical account (in which the Caucasian race passes through the realist stage of 'Negroidity' and the idealist stage of 'Mongolism' before reaching the 'truly Caucasian' future in which the race is liberated from the hegemony of natural forces and ideas).

Part One aims to demonstrate that modernity, the epoch of idealism, fails to escape from that which it claims to have outgrown, namely religious modes of thought. Thus Stirner rejects the contemporary consensus that Ludwig FEUERBACH (§2), the leading figure of the Hegelian left, had completed the critique of religion (see HEGELIANISM §2). For Stirner, the errors of religion are not overcome by a rejection of God as transcendent subject, but by opposing the subordination of the individual to 'spirit' in any form. Feuerbach's anthropological reduction had not revealed human nature as it was, but rather deified an abstract and prescriptive account of what being human involved, thus leaving the 'real kernel' of religion, the positing of an 'essence over me', intact. This continued immurement within religious thinking is portrayed as paradigmatic of modernity. Liberals, socialists (including the young Karl MARX) and contemporary critics of all kinds are convicted of separating individuals from their real natures and positing some fictitious essence as their goal. In contrast, Stirner seeks to rehabilitate the concrete and diverse 'un-man' (*unmensch*) in each of us, to whom this 'foolish mania to be something else' is completely alien.

Part Two elaborates Stirner's conception of egoism by relating it to 'ownness' (*Eigenheit*), a form of substantive individual autonomy valued above all else. 'Ownness' is violated by any desire or action which involves waiving or suspending individual judgment, and thus conflicts with any conception, however grounded, of obligation or duty. Even the legitimacy of self-assumed obligations, incurred, for example, by the act of promising, is denied. Perhaps most importantly (not least in establishing his anarchist credentials), Stirner maintains that a relationship of absolute hostility exists between the individual and the state, based on the incompatibility of 'ownness' and any obligation to obey the law. The notorious adjunct is that crime is applauded as an assertion of 'ownness' against its chief usurper, weakening the 'cement' (respect for law) which holds the state together.

Morality, defined by its positing of duties on the individual, is also sacrificed to 'ownness'. For those (including Stirner) who dispute the idea of an exclusive opposition between morality and immorality, it does not follow that the egoist is immoral. Nor is Stirner inconsistent in stressing the evaluative superiority of egoism over other modes of experience and action. Stirner's rejection of morality is grounded in an affirmation of the nonmoral good of egoism and not in a repudiation of values: that is, he allows a realm of actions and desires, which although not moral (because they involve no obligations to others) are still to be assessed positively. Stirner's conception of morality is in this sense a narrow one, and his rejection of its claims is not coextensive with a denial of the validity of all evaluative judgment.

The escape from social relations which conflict with 'ownness' is not the end of all contact between persons, only the end of binding rules for resolving conflicts between competing interests, and the end of constraints, other than 'ownness', upon the pursuit of individual enjoyment. Stirner consistently characterizes the resulting relationship between egoists and their objects (including other individuals) in proprietorial terms, although, in contrast to traditional juridical conceptions of ownership, 'egoistic property' largely collapses into a notion of instrumental treatment. The 'union of egoists' is established as the only form of association which does not violate 'ownness' and so can constitute a suitable vehicle for advancing individual interests. In the historical maturity of egoism, community survives only in the form of this constantly shifting alliance which enables

egoists to unite without loss of sovereignty, a purely instrumental combination whose good is solely the advantages which individuals derive from the pursuit of their interests – there are no final ends and association is not valued in itself.

See also: ANARCHISM; EGOISM AND ALTRUISM

List of works

Stirner, M. (1842–7) *Kleinere Schriften* (Short Works), ed. J.H. Mackay, Berlin: Bernhard Zack, 1914. (An interesting miscellany of Stirner's articles.)

—— (1844) *Der Einzige und sein Eigentum*, trans. S.T. Byington, *The Ego and Its Own*, ed. D. Leopold, Cambridge: Cambridge University Press, 1994. (This excellent edition contains a translation of Stirner's most important work, extensive annotations and a most substantial annotation.)

—— (1852) *Geschichte der Reaktion* (A History of Reaction), Berlin: Allgemeine Deutsche Verlags-Anstalt, 2 vols. (An incomplete work largely compiled from the writings of others, including Burke, Comte, Hengstenberg and Florencourt.)

References and further reading

Clark, J.P. (1976) *Max Stirner's Egoism*, London: Freedom Press. (A short but useful critical discussion of *The Ego and Its Own*.)

Helms, H.G. (1966) *Die Ideologie der anonymen Gesellschaft* (The Ideology of the Anonymous Society), Cologne: DuMont Schauberg. (A rather idiosyncratic interpretation of Stirner but contains an outstanding bibliography.)

Mackay, J.H. (1977) *Max Stirner: sein Leben und sein Werk* (Max Stirner: His Life and Work), Berlin: Mackay Gesellschaft. (First published in 1898 this remains the standard biography of Stirner.)

Paterson, R.W.K. (1971) *The Nihilistic Egoist: Max Stirner*, Oxford: Oxford University Press. (An introductory study, especially helpful on the relation between Stirner and later thinkers.)

DAVID LEOPOLD

STOICISM

Stoicism is the Greek philosophical system founded by Zeno of Citium c.300 BC and developed by him and his successors into the most influential philosophy of the Hellenistic age. It views the world as permeated by rationality and divinely planned as the best possible organization of matter. Moral goodness and happiness are achieved, if at all, by replicating that perfect rationality in oneself, and by finding out and enacting one's own assigned role in the cosmic scheme of things.

The leading figures in classical, or early, Stoicism are the school's first three heads: Zeno of Citium, Cleanthes and Chrysippus. It is above all the brilliant and indefatigable Chrysippus who can be credited with building Stoicism up into a truly comprehensive system. 'Early Stoicism' – the main topic of this entry – is in effect largely identical with his philosophy.

No formal philosophical writings of the early Stoics survives intact. We are mainly dependent on isolated quotations and secondary reports, many of them hostile. Nevertheless, the system has been reconstructed in great detail, and, despite gaps and uncertainties, it does live up to its own self-description as a unified whole. It is divided into three main parts: physics, logic and ethics.

The world is an ideally good organism, whose own rational soul governs it for the best. Any impression of imperfection arises from misleadingly viewing its parts (including ourselves) in isolation, as if one were to consider the interests of the foot in isolation from the needs of the whole body. The entire sequence of cosmic events is pre-ordained in every detail. Being the best possible sequence, it is repeated identically from one world phase to the next, with each phase ending in a conflagration followed by cosmic renewal. The causal nexus of 'fate' does not, however, pre-empt our individual responsibility for our actions. These remain 'in our power', because we, rather than external circumstances, are their principal causes, and in some appropriate sense it is 'possible' for us to do otherwise, even though it is predetermined that we will not.

At the lowest level of physical analysis, the world and its contents consist of two coextensive principles: passive 'matter' and active 'god'. At the lowest observable level, however, these are already constituted into the four elements earth, water, air and fire. Air and fire form an active and pervasive life force called pneuma or 'breath', which constitutes the qualities of all bodies and, in an especially rarefied form, serves as the souls of living things.

'Being' is a property of bodies alone, but most things are analysed as bodies – even moral qualities, sounds, seasons and so forth – since only bodies can causally interact. For example, justice is the soul in a certain condition, the soul itself being pneuma and hence a body. A scheme of four ontological categories is used to aid this kind of analysis. In addition, four incorporeals are acknowledged: place, void, time and the lekton (roughly, the expressed content of a sentence or predicate). Universals are sidelined as fictional thought constructs, albeit rather useful ones.

The world is a physical continuum, infinitely divisible and unpunctuated by any void, although surrounded by an infinite void. Its perfect rationality, and hence the existence of an immanent god, are defended by various versions of the Argument from Design, with apparent imperfections explained away, for example, as blessings in disguise or unavoidable concomitants of the best possible structure.

'Logic' includes not only dialectic, which is the science of argument and hence logic in its modern sense, but also theory of knowledge, as well as primarily linguistic disciplines like rhetoric and grammar. Stoic inferential logic takes as its basic units not individual terms, as in Aristotelian logic, but whole propositions. Simple propositions are classified into types, and organized into complex propositions (for example, conditionals) and complete arguments. All arguments conform to, or are reducible to, five basic 'indemonstrable' argument formats. The study of logical puzzles is another central area of Stoic research.

The Stoics doggedly defended, against attacks from the sceptical Academy, the conviction that cognitive certainty is achieved through ordinary sensory encounters, provided an entirely clear impression (phantasia) is attained. This, the 'cognitive impression' (phantasia katalēptikē), is one of such a nature that the information it conveys could not be false. These self-certifying impressions, along with the natural 'preconceptions' (prolēpseis) which constitute human reason, are criteria of truth, on which fully scientific knowledge (epistēmē) – possessed only by the wise – can eventually be built.

Stoic ethics starts from oikeiōsis, our natural 'appropriation' first of ourselves and later of those around us, which makes other-concern integral to human nature. Certain conventionally prized items, like honour and health, are commended by nature and should be sought, but not for their own sake. They are instrumentally preferable, because learning to choose rationally between them is a step towards the eventual goal of 'living in agreement with nature'. It is the coherence of one's choices, not the attainment of their objects, that matters. The patterns of action which promote such a life were systematically codified as kathēkonta, 'proper functions'.

Virtue and vice are intellectual states. Vice is founded on 'passions': these are at root false value judgments, in which we lose rational control by overvaluing things which are in fact indifferent. Virtue, a set of sciences governing moral choice, is the one thing of intrinsic worth and therefore genuinely 'good'. The wise are not only the sole possessors of virtue and happiness, but also, paradoxically, of the things people conventionally value – beauty, freedom, power, and so on. However geographically scattered, the wise form a true community or 'city', governed by natural law.

The school's later phases are the 'middle Stoicism' of Panaetius and Posidonius (second to first century BC) and the 'Roman' period (first to second century AD) represented for us by the predominantly ethical writings of Seneca, Epictetus and Marcus Aurelius.

1   School history, sources

The name 'Stoic' originates from the Stoa Poikile or 'Painted Colonnade' at Athens, where at least the school's first generation used to meet. At first called 'Zenonians', they came in time to be known as the 'Stoa people', or 'Stoics'. The founder ZENO OF CITIUM and his successor as school head, CLEANTHES, forged the system in large measure. But it was the third head, CHRYSIPPUS, at the end of the third century BC, who developed it into a truly global philosophical creed.

Stoicism was in many ways a technically updated version of Socrates' century-old philosophy. Its debt to earlier thinkers like Heraclitus and Plato is also manifest. How far it took account of Aristotle's work, on the other hand, is disputed. Contemporary negative influences included Epicureanism, to which it was diametrically opposed on most issues, and the sceptical critiques of Stoic positions launched from the New Academy.

Chrysippus is the main voice of Early Stoicism. His successors Diogenes of Babylon and Antipater made their own contributions and modifications, but are seen as continuing the same tradition. In the late second and early first century BC, there was some softening of positions and a renewed interest in the writings of Plato. This has led many scholars to classify PANAETIUS and POSIDONIUS as leading a separate phase, known as 'Middle Stoicism'. Finally, 'Roman' Stoicism designates that of the early Roman Empire, whose main spokesmen for us are the Latin essayist SENECA and the Greek writers EPICTETUS and MARCUS AURELIUS. The great bulk of their interests lies in moral philosophy.

The chart is a guide to entries on individual Stoics (listed in capitals).

We possess little evidence about the school's institutional base, in Athens or elsewhere, and it is not even clear whether it ever occupied its own premises. Its cohesion was, at any rate, primarily

ZENO OF CITIUM ARISTON OF CHIOS CLEANTHES CHRYSIPPUS	Early Stoicism *c.*300–129 BC
PANAETIUS POSIDONIUS	Middle Stoicism 129–*c.*50 BC
SENECA MUSONIUS RUFUS EPICTETUS CLEOMEDES MARCUS AURELIUS	Roman Stoicism *c.* AD 30–180

doctrinal. There was extensive agreement between individual Stoics, alongside a good deal of in-school quarrelling over specific issues. The most publicized dispute occurred in the first generation, between Zeno and the independent-minded ARISTON OF CHIOS. After his death, Zeno was revered by most Stoics, who would not openly criticize him. Rather, their philosophical disagreements often took the outward form of disputes as to what Zeno had really meant.

No early Stoic text survives, apart from Cleanthes' short *Hymn to Zeus*. But modern scholarship has managed to reconstruct most of the system in considerable detail from secondary sources, which incorporate numerous verbatim quotations. Book VII of Diogenes Laertius' *Lives of the Philosophers* is a major source, as is the doxographer Arius Didymus. Cicero's philosophical treatises contain first-rate presentations of various parts of the system. And invaluable evidence is available even from entrenched critics of the Stoics, such as the Platonist Plutarch, the Pyrrhonist Sceptic Sextus Empiricus and the doctor Galen.

2 The parts of philosophy

The Stoics formally sanctioned what was to become thereafter the canonical division of philosophy into three parts: physics, logic and ethics. Stoicism is arguably the first fully and self-consciously *systematic* philosophy. In the next three paragraphs correspondences will be noted between these three main areas of philosophy and the individual topics covered in the following sections. However, some of these topics (especially those in §§6–9, 14, 20) may not fit quite as neatly into any one of the three areas as the schematization implies.

Logic (§§10–13), the science of rationality (derived from *logos*, 'reason'), included not only inferential logic in the modern sense (more correctly called 'dialectic' by the Stoics), but also theory of knowledge, in which generation after generation of Stoics defended the existence of cognitive certainty against sceptical attacks. All Stoics, with the exception of Ariston of Chios, regarded logic as a fundamental part of philosophy.

Physics (§§3–9) – the study of nature (*physis*) – was a largely speculative or theoretical discipline, concerned with understanding the world's rational structure, and therefore embracing such diverse disciplines as biology, psychology and theology within its scope. It drew on the findings of contemporary scientists, but was not itself any kind of empirical science. Indeed, opponents accused it of wilful blindness to inconvenient new scientific discoveries, such as the demonstration by Alexandrian doctors

that the rational mind is in the head, not the chest. Physics presupposed logic, at least to the extent that its findings were largely developed in strings of syllogisms.

Ethics (§§14–19), the authentically Socratic core of Stoic philosophy, was the discipline which described how happiness could be achieved. It presupposed physics, which supplied an understanding of the world's rational structure and goodness and of the individual's place in it.

There was less agreement about how the three parts related to each other. One favoured model compared philosophy to an orchard in which logic was the protective outer wall, physics the soil and trees, and ethics the fruit. Posidonius favoured the analogy to a living animal, in which logic was the bones and sinews, physics the flesh and ethics the soul. These and other analogies probably agreed in making ethics the ultimate aim and crowning achievement of philosophy. The value of physics and logic was in a way instrumental – to acquire the understanding which would make a happy life possible. But that understanding, a perfected rationality, was itself so integral to the Stoic conception of happiness that to call it instrumental may be to underestimate the true unity of Stoic philosophy.

Most leading Stoics put the three parts of philosophy into the sequence logic–physics–ethics, but some favoured other orders. Here they are likely to have been specifying nothing more than the best order in which to teach it, with no implications which might threaten its conceptual unity.

3 The foundations of physics

Physics is the study of nature (*physis*), and to understand the true nature of the world it is necessary to start at the very lowest level of physical analysis. The world and its contents consist of passive 'matter' (*hylē*) and active 'god' (*theos*). These two 'principles' (*archai*) totally interpenetrate each other, and their interaction underlies all change. The active principle is quite literally god, a divine causal force which imbues the entire world with rationality.

Why is the second principle, matter, added? Not in order to make the world corporeal, since god (as well as matter) is already corporeal. It is a fundamental Stoic principle that only bodies are capable of causal interaction, and god could not shape the world if he lacked causal powers. Rather, matter is added because god is an entirely active causal power, and there must therefore be something passive on which he acts. Matter is thus a purely theoretical construct, with no properties of its own to contribute beyond its mere passivity.

Matter and god, then, are conceptual rather than empirical items. At the lowest *observable* level, at which cosmic processes of change can actually be studied, matter and god are already by their interaction constituted into the traditional four 'elements' – earth, water, air and fire. Of these, air and fire form an active and pervasive life force called *pneuma* or 'breath', which by its presence in things constitutes their qualities (see PNEUMA §2). Earth and water, on the other hand, are essentially passive elements, which serve a primarily material role: it is only the pervasive presence of *pneuma* in them that shapes them into complex items, including living things. Thus at the lowest phenomenal level earth and water take over the role which pure matter had held at the lowest theoretical level, while air and fire, paired as *pneuma*, take over a role analogous to that of the second principle, god.

Pneuma, as the combination of warmth and breathed air that is fundamental to animal life, had already earned a central place in medical theory, to which Stoic physics was heavily indebted. The distinctive contribution of Stoicism, at any rate by the time of Chrysippus, was to extend the explanatory role of *pneuma* beyond individual animal life, and to make it the vital power of the world as a whole. Since the Stoic world (following Plato among others) is itself a living creature, this extension was not as surprising as it may at first seem. *Pneuma* is the vehicle of the divine 'reason' (*logos*) which pervades and governs the entire world (see LOGOS §1).

Pneuma is all-pervasive, but varies in its properties according to its degree of tension. In its most highly attuned form, a portion of it may serve as the soul (*psychē*) of an animal (see PSYCHĒ). Many Stoics held that the human soul, at least, survives the death of the body (although it must of course eventually perish in the conflagration, see §5). A lesser grade of it is called 'nature' (*physis*), in a special sense in which the vegetative life force of a plant may be called its 'nature'. Finally, a still less refined form of *pneuma* is present in any discrete object, even a stone or a cup, being what endows it with its cohesion as a single object: as such, it is called the thing's 'tenor' or 'state' (*hexis*).

Both the primary 'principles' and *pneuma* play a key role in securing one of the most characteristic of Stoic tenets, the identification of 'being' with corporeality. At *Sophist* 246–7 Plato had launched a devastating attack on crude materialists who restrict being to bodies. Since they can neither deny that there *is* (for example) justice, nor equate justice with some body, Plato suggests, they must abandon their position in favour of a new existential criterion, namely that to be is to have the power to interact.

Stoicism sets out to defend the materialist position from Plato's attack: the two criteria considered by Plato are in reality one and the same, since the only things that have the power to interact *are* bodies. Hence to be is, after all, to be a body.

Virtually everything in the Stoic world is a body (for the few exceptions, see §7–8). This should not be misunderstood as reductive materialism. At the lowest level, 'god' is a body, but not a *mere* body: life and intelligence are his irreducible properties. God has corporeality in addition to these vital properties simply because only thus can he have any causal role in moving and shaping matter. Once this link of corporeality to causality is accepted, it is extended to the vast majority of items traditionally thought incorporeal. Justice, for example, must have causal powers if it is to do any good. It must sometimes make the limbs and voice move in ways in which they would otherwise not have moved. Therefore justice is a body. This apparently paradoxical outcome is defused once we learn *what* body it is. Justice is simply the soul in a certain condition; and the soul is a body, being an individual portion of *pneuma* pervading the organism and therefore able to govern its movements. Similarly, (spoken) words are bodies because they are vibrating portions of air, and that is how they can affect the thoughts of a listener.

Stoic corporealism was much derided by ancient critics, but it has the considerable merit of explanatory economy.

4 The continuum

Matter is permeated by god, and the passive elements by the active ones which constitute *pneuma* (see §3). What is this permeation? Mere juxtaposition of particles, such as atomism posits, could never constitute the intimate causal link between god and the matter which makes the Stoic world an inherently and ideally intelligent being. The active body must permeate the passive body 'through and through'. Stoic theory distinguishes three grades of mixture. 'Juxtaposition', for example of mixed grains, conforms to the atomist model. 'Fusion' (*synchysis*) is a kind of interpenetration in which the ingredients irreversibly lose their distinctive properties and a single new stuff is generated. In between these lies 'blending' (*krasis*), which also involves total interpenetration, but with the ingredients retaining their own distinctive properties. A helpful Stoic example, the fire which is seen to permeate a red-hot piece of iron, may clarify how the two ingredients can be seen as literally coextensive, rather than alternating as in 'juxtapostion'. It is 'blending' that describes the relation of *pneuma* to the material substrate.

145

'Division is to infinity, or "infinite" according to Chrysippus (for there is not some infinity which the division reaches, it is just unceasing). And blendings, also, are through and through' (Diogenes Laertius, VII 150–1). The doctrine of total interpenetration depends on the infinite divisibility of body, because if each of the blended stuffs consisted of indivisibly small particles these could only be juxtaposed, and not further blended. Hence the Stoics are, like Aristotle, committed defenders of the infinite division, on both mathematical and physical grounds.

For example, critics of the continuum had argued that if a finite body is infinitely divisible it will consist of infinitely many equal parts, and hence, impossibly, be infinite in size. Chrysippus replied that a finite object does not consist of any particular number of ultimate parts, finite or infinite. On an old puzzle of Democritus', whether the two circular planes yielded by horizontally slicing a cone are equal (in which case why isn't it a cylinder?) or unequal, Chrysippus replied that they are 'neither equal nor unequal'. Unfortunately our sources are so depleted as to permit little more than speculation about his defence of this claim. The same applies to the traces of a Stoic solution to the celebrated paradox according to which motion through an infinitely divisible continuum is impossible because it would consist of an infinite, and therefore uncompletable, series of sub-motions (see ZENO OF ELEA §5). They replied that the moving object may complete a distance in a single undivided (though divisible) motion – possibly on the ground that divisions are thought constructs, of which only a finite number can be actually imposed on a distance.

5 Cosmology and theology

The Stoic world is a living creature with a fixed life cycle, ending in a total 'conflagration' (ekpyrōsis). Being the best possible world, it will then be succeeded by another identical world, since any variation on the formula would have to be for the worse. Thus the Stoics arrive at the astonishing conception of an endless series of identical worlds – the doctrine of cyclical recurrence, according to which history repeats itself in every minute detail. (For the leading Stoic dissenter on this, see PANAETIUS §1.)

Although a conflagration terminates each world phase, this is not its collapse into ruin but its achievement of perfection. That is because 'creative fire' (pyr technikon) is the purest, the most divine and the most creative form of divine pneuma, to be associated more with the light and warmth that promote growth than with flame. In our present world phase, the strongest concentration of creative fire is the sun, which some Stoics identified as the world's divine 'commanding-faculty' (hēgemonikon). During the conflagration what exists is in effect pure intelligence, which plans the next world phase in every detail. There follows a process by which the fiery stuff differentiates and stratifies itself into the four elements. It already at this stage contains the 'seminal principles' (spermatikoi logoi), which may be viewed as blueprints for the individual organisms and other entities which will eventually emerge. Both the dominant role assigned to fire and its association with divine 'reason' (logos) owed much to the influence of Heraclitus (see HERACLITUS §4; LOGOS §1).

By 'god' the Stoics meant, primarily, the immanent principle governing the world, variously also identified with 'creative fire', with 'nature' or with 'fate' (on which see §20). Second, the world itself was also called 'god'. But – characteristically of Greek religious thought – this apparent monotheism did not exclude polytheism. Individual cosmic masses were identified with individual gods: for example the sea and the air were linked with Poseidon and Hera respectively, and the remaining traditional gods were likewise assigned specific cosmic functions. By means of allegorical rationalization, Stoic theology incorporated and interpreted traditional religion, rather than replacing it. Etymology (sometimes highly fanciful) was one tool used in this process. For example, two common forms of the name Zeus were 'Zēn' and 'Dia', which could also mean respectively 'Life' and 'Because of': this made it easy to interpret the traditional head of the pagan pantheon as symbolizing the Stoic primary deity, who was the world's life-force and causal principle.

The world, then, is itself divine, and is from first to last providentially planned and governed by an immanent intelligence. This thoroughgoing teleology owed much to Plato's Timaeus, but also to his Phaedo, where (96–9) Socrates had been portrayed as advocating a teleological physics, while admitting his own incapacity to develop one. We can here glimpse one of the many ways in which Stoicism sees itself as working out in full technical detail what was already implicit in the thought and life of Socrates.

Since the world is god, in his most manifest form, there is no distinction in Stoicism between proving the existence of god and proving the perfect rationality of the world. These proofs, most of which are variants on the Argument from Design, generated massive controversy between the Stoics and their critics (see especially Cicero, On the Nature of the Gods II–III). They include the following lines of argument. First, the world (especially the heaven) is like a giant mechanism, vastly superior to the most elaborate human invention. If must therefore, a fortiori, have an intelligent designer. Second, the creation of such a world by mere accident (for which see EPICUREANISM §8) is as unlikely as producing a literary masterpiece by shaking out letters randomly onto the ground. Third, the world is full of beneficial structures which cannot have been invented by its inhabitants: for example, the cycle of seasons, the temporal uniformity of the heavenly rotations, symbiotic relationships between species, and the food chain – including that miraculous foodstore the pig, created as a living being purely in order to keep the meat fresh. Fourth, the world is supremely beautiful, and therefore the work of a consummate artist. And fifth, any imperfections are either merely apparent (for example, wild beasts, which encourage the virtue of courage in us), or inevitable concomitants of the best possible structure (for instance, an example borrowed from Plato, the fragility of the human head). Sometimes localized sufferings are justified by the greater good they serve, even if it is not always evident what that good is. Chrysippus remarked, 'If I knew that I was fated to be ill now, I would set out to be ill. So too the foot, if it could think, would set out to get muddy'.

The syllogisms used to further this theology contained some highly controversial premises, for example: if there is anything which human beings cannot create, whoever did create it is superhuman. Or again: if a thing has rational parts (as the world does – namely us), then the whole must be rational too.

6 The 'categories'

Aristotle developed a complex ontological scheme, his ten 'categories' (see ARISTOTLE §7; CATEGORIES). The Stoics, following not Aristotle but the early Academy, recognized just two categories: that is, they divided all existing things into absolute or *per se* items, and relative items. For example, a house or dog is something absolute, whereas to be a slave, or sweet, is relative: being a dog does not, as such, involve standing in any relation, but to be a slave is to be somebody's slave, and to be sweet is to taste sweet to one or more percipients.

However, the Stoics also developed a more original, fourfold ontological classification, commonly known to modern interpreters as the Stoic 'categories', although it is unlikely that they used this term for it, and it is safer to call them 'genera'. It is disputed what the origins and purpose of this scheme were, but its most interesting recorded uses are to account for individual identity over time, and to amplify the thesis described in §3 that 'being' belongs only to bodies.

According to this classification, any given item may be seen as: (1) a mere 'substrate' (*hypokeimenon*); (2) something 'qualified' (*poion*); (3) something 'disposed in a certain way' (*pōs echon*); and (4) something 'disposed in a certain relation' (*pros ti pōs echon*).

To start with the first pair. To pick out a thing as (1), a 'substrate', is merely to individuate it as a (temporary) lump of matter, for example, by pointing at it. To mark it as (2), something 'qualified', is to distinguish it by one or more qualities which it possesses. Here the Stoics have a precise physical analysis of what a quality is: a portion of *pneuma* imbuing the thing, whether as its soul or as some other inherent property, for example, its colour or its weight. There is a further subdivision of the 'qualified' into (a), what is 'commonly qualified', for example, dog, human, wise, green, and (b), what is 'peculiarly qualified', for example, Fido, Socrates. These correspond, roughly, to what is signified by (a) common nouns and adjectives, and (b) proper names.

It is the first pair that is invoked to explain diachronic identity. Such identity had been challenged by the growing argument (*auxanomenos logos*), a puzzle much favoured by the Stoics' sceptical opponents in the New Academy. This argument objected that any 'growth', however slight, must generate a new individual, since a body with even one new particle added is not the same body as before; therefore there can be no enduring subject of growth; and hence no growth. The Stoic answer is that what endures as the subject of growth is not the material substrate (or 'substance', *ousia*), but the 'peculiarly qualified individual'. *Qua* 'substrate' Dion (to use the Stoics' favourite stock name) has little if any endurance, but *qua* 'peculiarly qualified individual' (*idiōs poios*), that is, *qua* Dion, he endures throughout his life. Although Dion's matter constantly changes, the individuating quality that makes him Dion with him, unchanged, from birth to death. That there is such a lifelong peculiar quality is a thesis of Stoic physics (there is no evidence what they thought it consisted in; the uniqueness of fingerprints is a modern discovery), but the need to solve the growing argument elevates it to the status of a metaphysical necessity. It also plays a part in Stoic epistemology (see §12).

As well as being (1) a lump of matter, and (2) both (a) human, wise and so on and (b) Dion, he is also at all times (3) in some disposition or other, for example, sitting, and (4) in some relation, for example, the person on my right. Here (3) and (4) represent the final two genera. The third genus, 'disposed in a certain way', is widely used to analyse as corporeal items commonly believed to be incorporeal (see §3). For example, knowledge is analysed as 'the commanding-faculty of the soul disposed in a certain way' – where the soul itself is corporeal, being *pneuma*. The fourth genus has similar analytic uses.

147

What is special about it as a mode of being is that it picks out, not all relative items, but those whose being what they are is wholly parasitic on that relation, so that they could cease to exist merely because their external correlate changes or perishes. Suppose Dion is Theon's accomplice. *Qua* Dion he may continue to exist despite Theon's desertion or death; but *qua* accomplice he cannot. Hence 'accomplice' is a fourth genus item, while 'Dion' is not. For an important debate about the status of virtue, using this fourth genus, see §16.

7 Space and time

After their heroic defence of corporealism (see §3), it may come as a disappointment that the Stoics do nevertheless admit four kinds of incorporeal: place, void, time and the *lekton* or 'sayable'. These do not have actual being, because none of them possesses any causal powers to act or be acted upon. Nevertheless, an account of the world is incomplete without them, and they are therefore proper subjects of discourse. This entitles them to be described, with a lesser label, as having 'subsistence'.

A thing's 'place' is conceived by the Stoics as a portion of three-dimensional (geometrical) space, coextensive with its own occupant. This is given in the Stoic definition of place as 'that which (i) is able to be occupied by what-is and (ii) is occupied throughout, (iii) whether by some thing or by some things'. Here (i) gives place its genus – roughly, space; (ii) adds its differentia, namely that its capacity to be occupied must be being exercised; (iii) specifies that the 'being', that is, body, which occupies it may be comprised of one or more discrete individuals. Put non-technically, a place is a fully occupied portion of space, whether occupied by a single entity or by a collection of entities.

When on the other hand some space's capacity to be occupied is not being exercised, it is called 'void' (or 'vacuum'). Void is defined as 'that which is able to be occupied by what-is, but which is not occupied'. As a matter of fact, this failure to be occupied is held to be a possibility only for the infinite space surrounding the world, since the world itself is an absolute plenum, containing no vacuum at all. The extra-cosmic void comes to be occupied – at least, some of it does – only during the 'conflagration' (see §5), when the world in its pure fiery state is said to expand into it.

The whole universe, called the 'all' in the sense of 'sum total', consists of the world body plus the infinite surrounding void. But of this combination, it is only the world body which is called the 'whole'. A whole, to qualify as such, must have a single unifying *pneuma* (see §3), something with which the void, being altogether empty, could not possibly be imbued. Thus the terminological distinction captures the Stoic thesis that the void is not any interacting part of the cosmic organism. It provides the conditions for one special kind of cosmic change, but it is not itself a participant in any change.

Since void is undeniably an incorporeal, and since void and place are both generically the same, it is hardly imaginable that the Stoics could have found a way of re-analysing place as a body. In any case, an adequate account of place must make sense of motion, that is, of a place being entered or vacated by a body. If the place were itself identified with the occupying body, no such account would be feasible.

The third incorporeal on the Stoic list is 'time'. Yet, curiously, in our sources individual parts of time are often analysed, in typical Stoic fashion, as corporeal. For instance, days and nights are simply the world's atmosphere in such and such a condition, and hence both they and the longer periods of time composed of them are said to be bodies. And reasonably so, one may think, since these temporal items could easily be deemed to have active or passive causal powers – for example, to be caused by the movement of the sun, and in turn to cause the progression of life cycles, and so on.

It seems to be only time as a whole which is conceded to be an incorporeal. Why so? Time (in this sense) is defined as 'the dimension of the world's motion'. Probably then the idea is as follows. The regularity of a body's motion – including the rotation of the heaven, which paradigmatically displays the progress of time – presupposes fixed spatial and temporal intervals through which it takes place. If either of those intervals were (in the usual Stoic corporealizing fashion) identified with the moving body itself, its motion would be left altogether without objective coordinates. This consideration may be what motivates the thesis that not only the spatial interval – 'place' – but also the temporal interval – 'time' – subsists independently of the moving bodies which pass through it.

8 The *lekton*

The fourth incorporeal on the list, the *lekton* (plural *lekta*), 'sayable', is a key term in Stoicism. Plato in the *Sophist* (261–2) distinguishes two linguistic tasks: naming, which is to pick out a subject, and 'saying' (*legein*), which is, roughly, to attach a predicate to that subject. This is probably the background to the Stoic *lekton*, which seems to have originally meant, as distinct from a subject, the sort of thing that you can say about a subject. As in Plato, it is typically expressed by a verb like 'walks' or 'to walk'. The actual action, walking, is itself a body: it is analysed as the commanding faculty of the soul (itself *pneuma*, and therefore a body) functioning in a certain way. But in certain contexts the predicate expressed by the verb 'to walk' is not properly identified with some body. The Stoics noted at least two cases – wishing, and causation. (1) When we say 'I *want* to walk', the soul which wishes is a body, but what it wishes for is not either itself, or for some further body to be added to it: it is for some predicate to become true of it. (2) When, for example, fire *causes* wood to be burnt, the effect generated is not some new body, burnt wood, since the wood already exists: it is that some new predicate becomes true of the wood. Thus, both the objects of wishes and the effects of causes are incorporeal predicates, technically called *lekta*.

The most prominent role of the *lekton* is in logic. Stoic logic (see §§10–11) is less interested in predicates as such – what they call 'incomplete *lekta*' – than in the complete propositions containing them, the primary bearers of truth. Normally speaking the predicate expressed by a verb, for example, '... walks', serves a full linguistic function only when it has a subject term supplied by a noun, for example, when someone says 'Dion walks'. The notion of a 'complete *lekton*' is used to distinguish such cases. Most commonly, a complete *lekton* is the proposition expressed by a complete declarative sentence, as in the example given, although other complete *lekta* include questions ('Is Dion walking?'), commands ('Walk, Dion') and so on.

A complete *lekton* is said to be produced by attaching a predicate to a 'nominative case (*ptōsis*)'. This generates an interpretative puzzle. A *lekton* is well attested to be an incorporeal, yet a nominative case, being a grammatical form, ought to be a word and hence a body (a spoken word being vibrating air; a written word probably ink). Can a complete *lekton* be incorporeal and yet have one part which is corporeal? It may be that the subject term, by being expressed, makes the *lekton* complete without actually becoming part of it. Or it may be that the Stoics posited, in addition to the predicate expressed by the verb, a further incorporeal incomplete *lekton*, namely the subject of the complete *lekton*, expressed by the subjective nominative noun of the corresponding uttered sentence. Both suggestions (which do not exhaust those available) are problematic, and neither gains unequivocal support from the surviving evidence.

Nor is it easy to find a link between the incorporeality of the *lekton* and that of place, void and time (see §7). These latter three have some sort of mind-independent reality. Can the same be said for *lekta*? This is controversial, but the causal role of *lekta* must lend them some degree of objectivity, since causal processes presumably go on in the same way whether or not anyone is there to observe or analyse them. The *lekton* is defined as 'that which subsists in correspondence with a rational impression' (that is, roughly, with a human thought (see §12). This could be taken to make it parasitic on the thought processes of rational beings. But it may alternatively mean no more than that a *lekton* is a formal structure onto which rational thoughts, like the sentences into which they can be translated, must be mapped. This latter possibility bears some comparison to space and time, which, although defined by reference to their potential or actual occupants, are the objective dimensions onto which the positions and motions of those occupants are to be mapped, and are not altogether parasitic on them for their reality. The analogy must not be pushed too far, since the *lekton* differs from the other three incorporeals in not being any kind of mathematically analysable extension. But rationality is as much an intrinsic feature of the Stoic world as dimensionality, and it would be entirely Stoic to hold that there are objective parameters onto which its rational structures can be mapped

9 Particular and universal

There seems to be no room for universals in a Stoic world, where to exist is to be a body and hence, it seems, a particular. The highest ontological class recognized by Stoicism is that of 'something' (*ti*, plural *tina*), a class so broad as to include both bodies and incorporeals. Yet even this class excludes certain 'not-somethings' (*outina*), which Stoics identify with universals. That a universal is a 'not-something' they demonstrate by the following syllogism, diagnosed as being invalid precisely because in the minor premise it illegitimately substitutes a universal, 'man', for 'someone' (*tis*, the masculine form corresponding to the neuter *ti*) in the major premise: 'If someone is in Athens, they are not in Megara; but man is in Athens; therefore man is not in Megara'. So universals are apparently metaphysical outlaws, intractable even to basic logical laws.

On the other hand, universals have a fundamental place in the job of the dialectician. In the tradition bequeathed by Plato, the Stoics regard the science of dialectic (see §10) as largely concerned with the activities of division and definition: dividing genera into species and defining individual terms. And the things divided and defined are, of course, universals – as Plato had already indicated by equating them with Forms.

Hence a dilemma: universals are essential to dialectic, and yet are logically incoherent items with no place in a Stoic ontology. Their resolution of the dilemma comes in two parts, one logical, the other epistemological. Logically, the dialectician's use of universals is justified by a re-analysis. A dialectician's definition, for example, 'Man is a rational mortal animal', actually means 'If something (*ti*) is a man, it is a rational mortal animal'. A similar analysis was offered for statements of division. Thus dialectical pronouncements which appear to have universals as subjects are legitimate only because they are disguised conditional statements about particulars ('somethings'). (A partial analogy can be found in modern attempts to re-analyse as logically coherent 'The average man has 2.4 children'.)

The epistemological side of the resolution is required because Plato had maintained that universals are, as such, proper objects of thought. This time the conditional re-analysis offers little help in formulating a Stoic response. Rather, their reply is that universals are indeed objects of thought, or 'concepts' (*ennoē-mata*), but that far from being objective parts of the world's furniture they are nothing more than thought constructs. The thoughts themselves are real enough: being 'conceptions' (*ennoiai*), they are simply our mental *pneuma* in a certain condition, and hence bodies; but the 'concepts' which constitute the intentional objects of those conceptions are not themselves bodies, or indeed anything at all. This position makes it appropriate to call the Stoic doctrine of universals an early variety of 'conceptualism' (see NOMINALISM §1).

10 Dialectic

Dialectic is the main branch of what the Stoics called 'logic', and amounts, roughly, to the science of argument. Although dialectic was both theorized and applied in innumerable treatises, the Stoics never lost sight of the Platonic conception of it as a fundamentally two-person activity, involving the interrogation of an interlocutor. 'Dialectic' actually means 'the science of dialogue'. The science of rhetoric differed from dialectic precisely in being the science of producing a good monologue, and was treated as a separate branch of logic. There was no uniform Stoic view as to whether theory of knowledge (see §§12–13) counted as part of dialectic, or as a third branch of logic.

In so far as it is concerned with argument, dialectic has distinct parts dealing with (1) signifiers and (2) significates. The former are words (and hence bodies; see §8), and Stoic dialectic's concern with language as such led it, among other things, to develop the first real grammatical theory in Western thought. It became the basis of all subsequent work on grammar in antiquity and far beyond.

The latter term, 'significates', designates *lekta* (see §8), the incorporeal meanings which in their complete form are expressed only by whole sentences. Stoic logic (to use the word now in its modern sense) concentrates on one species of *lekta*, the declarative ones, called *axiōmata*. This term, literally 'judgments', is more familiarly translated as 'propositions'. Stoic logic is indeed the first fully developed propositional or sentential logic. In this it differs radically from Aristotelian logic, which is a logic of terms (see LOGIC, ANCIENT). The origins of Stoic logic probably lie less in Aristotle than in the work of the Dialectical school (see DIALECTICAL SCHOOL; DIODORUS CRONUS; PHILO THE DIALECTICIAN).

11 Inferential logic

Propositions are the bearers of truth and falsity, and simple propositions are the atomic units of Stoic logic. One symptom of the latter is that in syllogistic the negation sign 'Not...' is properly prefixed to the entire proposition, rather than (as in Aristotle's logic) to its predicate. On the other hand, propositions are classified partly according to the subject terms which they contain: 'This individual is walking' (ideally accompanied by pointing) is a 'definite' proposition; 'Someone is walking' is 'indefinite'; and propositions expressed with a noun in the subject position, for example, 'A human being is walking', 'Dion is walking', are 'intermediate'. This triple distinction, like most aspects of Stoic logic, is adopted ultimately for the sake of validating the arguments in which these simple propositions feature. Indefinite propositions are verified by the corresponding intermediate or definite ones, but not vice versa. Hence in a syllogism whose major premise begins 'If x is walking...' and whose minor premise has the form 'But y is walking...', validity will normally be preserved if 'x is walking' is indefinite, but neither if it is definite while 'y is walking' is indefinite or intermediate, nor if it is intermediate while 'y is walking' is indefinite.

Complex propositions are those compounded of two or more simple propositions with the help of connectives like 'and' or 'if'. Here again, they are selected for their role in syllogistic theory. Thus they comprise: conjunctive propositions, for example, 'It is day and it is light', which are important mainly in negated conjunctions, for example, 'Not: it is day and it is dark'; disjunctive propositions, for example, 'Either it is day or it is night'; and conditionals, for example, 'If it is day, it is light'.

Simple and complex propositions are the basic components of syllogisms. These are held either to have, or to be reducible to by four rules of analysis known as the *themata* (see LOGIC, ANCIENT §6), one of the following five forms: (1) 'If the first, the second; but the first; therefore the second'; (2) 'If the first, the second; but not the second; therefore not the first'; (3) 'Not: the first and the second'; but the first; therefore not the second; (4) 'Either the first or the second; but the first; therefore not the second'; (5) 'Either the first or the second; but not the second; therefore the first'. These are considered irreducibly primitive argument forms, hence called the five 'indemonstrables'.

A great deal of work went into the diagnosis of argument validity (see LOGIC, ANCIENT §5). Both formal rigour and inferential cogency were demanded. A valid argument, according to Stoic logic, is one in which the conclusion follows from the conjunction of the premises in just the way in which in a true conditional the consequent follows from the antecedent. Hence the notion of 'following' became a focal point of debate. Some Stoics adopted a truthfunctional analysis of a true conditional: the second proposition follows from the first just if 'Not (the first and not the second)' is true (see PHILO THE DIALECTICIAN for the background to this). But Chrysippus adopted a much stronger criterion, called *synartēsis* or 'cohesion': 'If the first, the second' is true just if the negation of the second is incompatible with the first. This restricts 'following' to a strongly conceptual kind of implication.

The restriction in turn led Chrysippus to the view that many ordinary-language uses of 'if' do not represent real conditionals, and should properly be expressed by the negated conjunction: not 'If the first, the second', but 'Not both: the first and not the second'. He applied this, for example, to the rules of empirical sciences such as divination (see §20); and analogous doubts led at least some Stoics to deny the validity of inductive inference. It was also applied, importantly, to the individual steps of the Little-by-little argument or Sorites (see VAGUENESS §2). The Academic sceptics plagued the Stoics with this puzzle, aimed at challenging important philosophical distinctions by asking to be told the exact cut-off point. The archetypal Sorites is 'If two grains are not a heap, three aren't; if three aren't, four aren't; . . .' – and so on to the conclusion that if two grains are not a heap then 10,000 are not. Chrysippus, who wrote extensively on this problem, advised that at some point in the procedure there will be premises of this form which it is proper neither to affirm nor to deny. But he also seems to have authorized the Stoic practice of insisting that the individual steps be formulated not as conditionals, as above, but as negated conjunctions: for example, 'Not both: seven grains are not a heap and eight grains are a heap'. Part of the point is clearly that, whatever the grounds for asserting such a premise may be, there is no actual incompatibility between 'Seven grains are not a heap' and 'Eight grains are a heap', so that assent to the premise must remain optional.

A wide range of other logical puzzles exercised Chrysippus and other Stoics. Some turned on ambiguities, and they developed a sophisticated classification of ambiguity types. The most persistent thorn in their flesh, however, was the liar paradox: 'I am lying' is, if false, true, and, if true, false (see SEMANTIC PARADOXES AND THEORIES OF TRUTH §1). This, along with the Sorites, was wielded by the Academics as a potentially lethal weapon against Stoic logic. It appeared to undermine the most basic tenet – that every proposition is either true or false. Chrysippus wrote many books in refutation of the liar paradox, but if he had his own favoured solution it is impossible now to recover it from our sources.

Inferential logic is ubiquitously employed in Stoic texts on physics and ethics. These regularly purport to demonstrate their tenets, and a demonstration is itself defined as an argument in which evident premises serve to reveal a non-evident conclusion.

12 Cognitive certainty

The main Stoic epistemological theorist was Zeno of Citium, who developed his ideas in response to a series of challenges from the Academic sceptic Arcesilaus (see ARCESILAUS §2). His key term is *katalēpsis* – 'apprehension' or 'cognition' – the infallible grasping of some truth, usually by use of the senses. Arcesilaus systematically questioned the grounding of this notion, and argued instead for *akatalēpsia*, 'inapprehensibility', or 'the impossibility of cognition'.

The starting notion is *phantasia*, literally 'appearance' but commonly translated as 'impression' or 'presentation'. To have an impression is simply for things to strike you as being a certain way. Whether or not you take the impression to be true depends on a further cognitive act, assent (*synkatathesis*), which you may give or withhold at will. Since mature human beings are rational, their impressions are called 'rational impressions', meaning that their content can be expressed in language. Strictly speaking it is the proposition associated with it that we are taking to be true when we assent to an impression.

Zeno symbolized an impression by spreading the fingers of one hand, and assent by pulling them together. The next stage, represented by a fist, was *katalēpsis*, literally 'grasping', that is, infallibly recognizing the truth. This is not so much successive to assent as an ideally successful *way* of assenting, based on a sufficiently lucid impression. If instead someone assents to an unreliable impression, that will not count as cognition, but as mere fallible 'opinion' (*doxa*).

One final stage in the hand simile is *epistēmē*, 'knowledge' – not everyday knowing (which is better identified with *katalēpsis*) but absolute, scientific knowledge, such as is possessed only by the wise. Zeno symbolized *epistēmē* by bringing the other hand over to grasp his fist firmly. The point is as follows. *Katalēpsis* is infallible, in that it successfully applies a simple guaranteed cognitive mechanism shared by virtually all human beings: the truth stares you in the face, and you assent to it without the slightest possibility of being wrong. However, although on this very ordinary model of knowing all of us know lots of things, only the genuinely wise know that they know. This is because the wise, having a complete set of mutually supporting cognitions, could never be argued into disbelieving one of them. The unwise, that is, most people, could be argued out of their assent to genuine cognitions, because they are likely to have also a number of false beliefs, adopted as if they were genuine cognitions. You may, for example, plainly witness a miracle but disbelieve it because, being an Epicurean sympathizer, you falsely believe that the gods do not intervene.

The interest of the Stoic–Academic debate lies largely in its concentration, not on the wise, but on the infallible cognition attributed to ordinary people. The Stoics remained convinced, perhaps like most of us, that in everyday encounters where the truth stares you in the face you cannot be wrong and would be insane to withhold assent. But this common-sense position proved extraordinarily vulnerable to Academic criticism.

Debate centred on the kind of impression to which assent might be fully justified. Zeno called this the *phantasia katalēptikē*, 'cognitive impression', and initially defined it as one which is '(i) from something real (*apo hyparchontos*), and (ii) moulded and impressed according to that real thing itself'. Here (i) is likely to mean, not 'caused by something real' (no impression, however delusory, could be either caused by something unreal or totally uncaused), but 'representing something actual' – where it is indifferent whether the thing represented is an object or a fact. What (ii) adds is that the impression depicts this thing in full graphic detail. Arcesilaus' complaint was that such an impression would still not be unmistakably true, since an identical but false impression could occur. This led Zeno to add a third clause, '(iii) such as could not be from something unreal', which we can take to mean 'such as could not represent some non-actual object or fact'.

The problem now was whether there could be such

an impression. The ensuing debate focused partly on the nature of external objects, with the Stoics asserting that each object – even an identical twin – has some unique feature (see §6 for the metaphysical justification of this), and the Academics asking in reply how we could ever be sure that the relevant feature was currently evident. The Stoics also tried to describe the phenomenological features of these cognitive impressions, suggesting that as a species of impression they somehow carried their own badge of identity 'just as horned snakes differ from other snakes'. The Academic reply, now through the mouth of Carneades, included appeal to cases where false impressions are so graphic that they lead to action, exactly as allegedly cognitive ones do: can the latter then have any intrinsic features to differentiate them from the former?

The final word belongs to a group reported simply as the 'later Stoics' (Sextus Empiricus, *Against the Professors* VII 253–60), probably including Antipater, a contemporary of Carneades. They point out that in all but the most special circumstances we simply have no choice whether to assent to a cognitive impression. Once you have such an impression, you do believe it, and that is that. What is in our own hands is not whether, once we are in a position where the truth is unmistakable, we accept it, but whether we take the trouble to get ourselves into such a position in the first place (moving closer, turning on the light, and so on).

This is quite an effective reply to those, like the Academics, who recommend suspending assent. But it leaves the question why the irresistibility of certain impressions should imply their truth. The Stoics here had recourse to a teleological argument: we would not have been given this superb cognitive equipment for any other purpose than to learn the truth. But of course the Academics could easily question the empirical premises on which that teleology was founded, bringing the debate full circle.

13 Criteria of truth

To identify the 'criterion (or criteria) of truth' was a standard requirement of Hellenistic philosophers (see HELLENISTIC PHILOSOPHY). The Greek word *kritērion* is literally a 'discriminator', and a common equivalent was *kanōn*, 'yardstick'. A criterion of truth was expected to be something naturally available to every mature human being as a basis for distinguishing true from false. Since it was that which made progress towards philosophical understanding possible, its availability and use could not be restricted to those who were already philosophers. When it came to naming the criterion of truth, the Stoics differed among themselves, but in some form or other they all identified it primarily with the 'cognitive impression' (see §12), the concept on which the Academic attack on the criterion likewise focused.

A second criterion, widely used in Stoicism and formally named as a criterion at least by Chrysippus, was *prolēpsis*, inadequately translated as 'preconception'. A *prolēpsis*, literally 'prior grasp', is any naturally acquired generic 'conception' (*ennoia*) of a thing. Two other terms which are in most contexts interchangeable with it are *koinē ennoia*, 'common conception' (that is, common to all human beings) and *physikē ennoia*, 'natural conception'. These descriptions distinguish *prolēpsis* from artificially acquired conceptions, usually culture-dependent ones, most of which are not directly given in experience but depend on a synthetic mental process. A centaur, for example, is arrived at by combining natural conceptions, a giant by enlarging them, and so on. Some artificial conceptions are liable to be misleading, but others are an integral part of scientific understanding, for example, one's conception of the centre of the earth, acquired 'by analogy with smaller spheres'. Human reason is itself simply an ample stock of conceptions, some but not all of them natural ones.

What makes a *prolēpsis* a reliable guide to truth is precisely the fact that the natural conception has not been tampered with. But where does the *prolēpsis* itself come from? The Stoics sometimes sound like hard-line empiricists, as when they compare the mind of a new-born infant to a blank sheet of paper which will in due course have its stock of natural conceptions written on it by repeated sense impressions, classified and stored as 'experience'. Here a *prolēpsis* is 'natural' in the sense of being mechanically imprinted on us, and hence unmediated by fallible reasoning. However, some texts indicate that at least basic moral notions are called natural for the quite different reason that they are dispositionally innate in us.

Many Stoic arguments proceeded from appeals to some *prolēpsis* or 'common conception'. This was their version of the widespread philosophical practice of citing what are alleged to be 'our intuitions'. It ran into the difficulty that such a practice always faces: separating genuinely natural conceptions from those infected by one's culture or other beliefs becomes the new bone of contention. For example, both Stoics and Epicureans appealed to the *prolēpsis* of 'god', but while the Stoics regarded providence as an integral part of this *prolēpsis*, the Epicureans argued that god's providentiality was a cultural imposition on the basic *prolēpsis*, motivated by human bafflement at the world's workings (see EPICUREANISM §9). A very similar dispute launches Stoic ethics.

14 *Oikeiōsis*

Epicurus proposed a method for identifying the genuinely natural human value: consult a new-born baby. Inarticulate infants, and for that matter irrational animals, cannot possibly have been infected yet with the norms of society, and their actions tell us, louder than any words, that their sole motivation is the acquisition of pleasure and the avoidance of pain. Stoic ethics responds by adopting the same starting point but questioning the Epicurean analysis of infant behaviour.

The highly influential concept which the Stoics introduced to facilitate their own analysis is *oikeiōsis*, variously translated as 'appropriation', 'familiarization', 'affiliation' or 'affinity'. Literally, this is the process of 'making something one's own'. An animal's *oikeiōsis* is its natural impulse or inclination towards something which it regards as belonging to it.

A creature's first *oikeiōsis*, Stoics argue, is towards itself and its own constitution, a priority which it displays by making self-preservation its dominant goal. Far from pursuing pleasure, it courts pain in order to preserve and develop its natural constitution, as when we see a toddler repeatedly fall in striving to walk, and an overturned tortoise struggling to regain its upright position. As the human child develops, its *oikeiōsis* is extended beyond itself: it treats its parents and siblings as belonging to it, and cares for them accordingly, in much the same way in which it already cares for itself. In due course this same other-concern is extended to cover a wider range of people, albeit in increasingly diluted measure. At an extreme it takes in the entire human race. (For a graphic Stoic elaboration of this idea, see HIEROCLES.)

Oikeiōsis is a continuum, stretching from the instinctive self-preservation of the new-born infant to the other-regarding conduct which is equally natural in rational adults. Where most ancient ethical systems struggled to explain altruism as an extended form of self-interest, there is no such tension in Stoicism, where others already fall within the ambit of our natural affection in much the same way as we ourselves do. This rationally extended sense of what belongs to us does not yet amount to moral goodness, but it is its indispensable basis. Goodness lies in our understanding and collaborating with the ideally rational world plan. It is no wonder that our natural *oikeiōsis* towards the rest of the human race should be what grounds the project of completely integrating ourselves into that plan.

Oikeiōsis is an affinity founded on the shared rationality of the entire human race. The doctrine thus helped to foster Stoic cosmopolitanism and other widely admired humanitarian stances (see §18).

SENECA (§1), for example, reminded his readers of their moral obligations even to their slaves. Conversely, however, the *oikeiōsis* doctrine also encouraged a hardening of attitudes to non-rational animals, with which humans were judged to stand in no moral relation at all.

15 The indifferents

Perhaps the most characteristic doctrine of Stoic ethics is that virtue alone is good, vice alone bad. Everything else traditionally assigned a positive or negative value – health or illness, wealth or poverty, sight or blindness, even life or death – is 'indifferent'. By making this move, the Stoics authorized the use of the word 'good' in a distinctly moral sense – a usage which is still with us, although they themselves bought it at the high price of simply denying that the word, properly understood, has any other sense.

The inspiration of this doctrine is undoubtedly Socratic. In various Platonic dialogues (see especially *Euthydemus* 278–81, *Meno* 86–9), Socrates argued that most things traditionally called good – typified with largely the same examples as the Stoic 'indifferents' – are in their own nature intermediate between good and bad. If used wisely, they become good, if unwisely, bad. Hence wisdom is the only intrinsically or underivatively good thing (see SOCRATES §§4–6).

This Socratic argument encouraged the Cynic idea that only wisdom – or more generally, virtue – is good, and that such coveted possessions as reputation, health and physical comfort are literally irrelevant to the goodness, and hence the happiness, of one's life (see CYNICS). The Cynics acted on this by adopting a bohemian lifestyle, disdaining the values of society. And Zeno, the founder of Stoicism, had his first philosophical training from a Cynic. Zeno's independent-minded colleague Ariston stuck close to the Cynic thesis (see ARISTON OF CHIOS §2). Zeno, on the other hand, modified it in a way which does more than anything else to account for the widespread success of Stoicism; Zeno's subtly revised position leaves wealth, fame, and so on morally indifferent, while explaining why we are nevertheless fully justified in pursuing them.

Although being healthy does not make you happy, Zeno maintains, the natural thing to do in ordinary circumstances is nevertheless to stay healthy and avoid illness. We should not try to suppress this natural instinct, because to be happy – the ultimate goal to which we all aspire – is to be totally in tune with nature. Therefore the proper way to start out is to respect the preferences which nature dictates, opting where possible for affluence, high civic status, family values and other 'natural' desiderata. As you

progress, you will learn when to vary the formula. It may be that in special circumstance the right way for you to fit in with nature's plan is to be poor, or sick, or even to die. If you understand why one of these is the rational and natural thing for you, you will embrace it willingly, and thus further rather than hinder your project of perfect conformity with nature. But barring such special circumstances, the natural values to adopt coincide on the whole with the ordinary values of society.

This leads, in typical Stoic fashion, to a terminological jungle of epithets for the 'indifferents'. The 'things which accord with nature' (*ta kata physin*), such as health, have a positive, albeit non-moral, 'value' (*axia*), and are therefore labelled 'preferred' (*proēgmena*), which means that in normal circumstances we should opt for them, they are 'to be taken' (*lēpta*). The 'things which are contrary to nature' (*ta para physin*), such as illness, earn a contrary set of technical terms: 'disvalue' (*apaxia*), 'dispreferred' (*apoproēgmena*), 'not to be taken' (*alēpta*).

The linchpin of Stoic ethics is the way in which it legitimizes a familiar scale of personal and social values, while denying them any intrinsic worth. Their value is purely instrumental, because they are the subject matter of the choices by means of which we progress towards true moral understanding. We might compare the relative 'values' of, say, illness, fame and eyesight, in Stoic eyes to the relative values of cards in a card game. Learning how to choose between these, and even to sacrifice cards of higher value when the circumstances dictate, is an essential part of becoming a skilled player. But these choices matter only instrumentally: it would be absurd to compare the value of an ace to the value of being a good card-player. In Stoic eyes it is an equally grave error – although unfortunately one of which most people are guilty – to rank wealth or power along with moral goodness on one and the same scale.

The things which are naturally 'preferred' can be encapsulated in rules: honour your parents, take care of your health, cultivate friends, and so on. From the start – although again with the dissent of Ariston of Chios – the Stoics attached importance to rules or 'precepts' as the basis of moral progress. What a precept prescribes is a *kathēkon* (plural *kathēkonta*), a 'proper function' or 'duty', and many Stoic treatises were devoted to working out detailed lists of *kathēkonta*. A *kathēkon* is defined as 'that which, when done, has a reasonable justification': for a rational adult, what is reasonable and what is natural should coincide.

There are two main types of *kathēkonta*: circumstantial and non-circumstantial. Circumstantial *kathēkonta*, that is, those prescribed only in very special circumstances, include such abnormal acts as self-mutilation, giving away your property, and even suicide (something of a Stoic obsession, inspired by Socrates' willing death). Non-circumstantial *kathēkonta* are, despite their name, not prescribed in literally all circumstances, since to each non-circumstantial *kathēkon* (for example, looking after one's health), there is opposed a circumstantial one, (for example, in very unusual circumstances, getting ill). Rather, they are 'non-circumstantial' because they are what, other things being equal, you should do as a matter of course, and not as a response to your present circumstances.

16 Goodness

Kathēkonta are 'intermediate' patterns of behaviour – that is, available to everybody, wise and non-wise alike. Yet in advertizing them the Stoics regularly referred to the conduct of the 'sage', the idealized wise person whom they always held up as a model, despite admitting that the criteria for this status were so tough that few people, if any, ever attained them. What was possible for everybody, they insisted, was progress (*prokopē*) towards this state of wisdom, and that is why they stressed the continuity between the proper conduct of the non-wise and the ideally good conduct of the wise. When you actually become wise and virtuous, what are outwardly the very same kind of *kathēkonta* which you were already habitually performing are suddenly transformed by your new state of understanding, earning themselves the name *katorthōmata* or 'right actions'.

Alongside this continuity in moral progress, there is also the sharpest possible discontinuity. One of the most notorious Stoic paradoxes was that all sins are equal. If you are not virtuous and wise, you are totally bad and foolish. The wise are totally happy, the foolish totally unhappy. Whatever strides you may have made towards virtue, you are no happier till you get there. They compared what it is like to be drowning: whether you are yards from the surface or only inches from it, you are still just as effectively drowning.

The motivation of this depressing thesis is not entirely clear. Stoic concern with the paradox of the Sorites (see §11) may have contributed to it, but the main driving force seems to be the conviction that actual goodness, if achieved, differs not in degree, but in kind, from the scale of natural values. At a certain point of moral development, you notice an emerging agreement or harmony between your individual choices and acts. It is, thereafter, not the choices and acts or their objects that matter any longer, but harmony for its own sake. Only from that point on do you have a conception of what goodness is: it is located in a perfect 'agreement' both within the individual and between that individual and cosmic nature.

What does this agreement consist in? Despite the Stoics' extensive cataloguing and classification of the *kathēkonta* which the sage will perform, ultimately the wise are characterized, not by the actual success of their actions – which may not always be in their control – but by the morally perfect frame of mind with which they act – in other words, by virtue (see ARETĒ). Socrates had propounded that paradox that virtue is knowledge: all there is to being good is to *know* the right things. The Stoics develop this Socratic idea to the full. The word for knowledge – *epistēmē* – can also more specifically mean 'science', and they regard each virtue as a genuine science, complete with its own constituent theorems. The skill of living in harmony is a skill analogous to, although vastly more difficult than, any branch of mathematics or medicine.

Plato had given four virtues canonical status: justice, wisdom, temperance or self-control (*sōphrosynē*), and courage. The Stoics adopt this list, and treat all other virtues as subordinate species, or perhaps branches, of the four. Are these, then, four entirely distinct sciences? No. Among Socrates' most enduringly influential doctrines was that of the Unity of the Virtues. On one widely accepted version, adopted by some early Stoics (see ARISTON OF CHIOS §3; CLEANTHES), Socrates' thesis meant that the four virtues are all simply one and the same state of mind, albeit going under different names in different external circumstances. Others took the view that the unity of the virtues consists rather in their inseparability. For example, you could hardly count as just if you were not brave and temperate too, or else you might be deflected from just behaviour through intimidation or bribery. It is perhaps this thought that led Chrysippus to the following view: the four virtues are four separate sciences, each with its own defining set of theorems; but each virtue incorporates and uses the theorems of the other three as subsidiary theorems. The thesis that the virtues are distinct sciences was put by Chrysippus, in the technical language of Stoic metaphysics (see §6), by saying that they belong to the second category, 'quality', and not the fourth category, 'relative disposition'. That is, they differ from each other as distinct qualities or states of mind, not simply as one state of mind differentiated by the varying external situations with which it is confronted.

17 The goal

The 'goal' or 'end' (*telos*) is defined as 'that for the sake of which everything is done, while it is not itself done for the sake of any further thing'. This is identified with happiness (*eudaimonia*), or 'living well'. Both are commonplace to the Greek philosophical tradition. The partisan content arises when philosophers offer their formulas for what this end actually consists in. Zeno's formula was 'living in agreement' (*homologoumenōs zēn*). The history of Stoic ethics over the next two centuries is largely a history of successive attempts to work out what Zeno must have meant.

Zeno's vagueness was probably deliberate. The 'agreement' comprises both the perfect internal coherence and rationality (the '-*log*-' part of *homologoumenōs* means 'reason') of the good life – 'living in accordance with one concordant reason' – and its conformity with nature, the 'nature' in question being itself equated with both one's own individual nature and the nature of the world. Happiness is also identified as a 'smooth flow of life', and Zeno's real point was that only those with complete understanding of cosmic rationality can make their own aims and choices entirely one with those of nature, and thus never come into conflict with either their own or the world's rationality.

Pressure for clarification led either Zeno himself or Cleanthes to make the first addition to the formula, which now became 'living in agreement *with nature*'. Chrysippus substituted 'living in accordance with experience of what happens by nature'. What became clearer, as these and other formulations competed, was that the ideal life was defined in terms of things which were themselves morally indifferent – the 'things which accord with nature' (see §15). The challenge which the Stoics faced from their opponents in the Academy was how moral good could depend on a set of aims whose attainment was morally indifferent. The answer – compare §15 – was as follows. What matters is not necessarily *achieving* natural advantages like health, which cannot be guaranteed in all circumstances, and which in any case do not bring happiness. What matters is making the right rational choices – doing everything that lies in your power towards achieving what nature recommends. It is the consistency of those *efforts*, not of their results, that may ultimately become perfect agreement with nature, that is, happiness. Formulas for the goal designed to capture this emphasis included (Diogenes of Babylon) 'reasoning well in the selection and disselection of things which accord with nature', and (Antipater) 'to live continuously selecting things which accord with nature

and disselecting things contrary to nature'. Zeno's original formulation had more to recommend it.

18 The cosmic city

Everybody without exception strives for a good and happy life, but only the wise achieve it. Most people in fact misapply the very words 'good' and 'happiness', which they mistakenly associate with morally indifferent states like wealth and honour. This simple point came to be extended by the Stoics to all the other things which are conventionally prized. Everybody wants to be rich, free, powerful, beautiful, loveable, and so on, but, paradoxically, only the wise achieve these goals. Everyone else is, whatever they may think, actually poor, enslaved, powerless, ugly and unloveable. This is because real wealth is to have something of genuine worth (that is, virtue), or to lack nothing that you need; real freedom is to be in full control of your life (including the knowledge of when to accept death rather than ever be forced to do what you do not truly want to do); real power is to be able to achieve everything you want; real beauty is a quality of the soul not the body; and only the genuinely beautiful are genuinely loveable. These Stoic 'paradoxes' are of Socratic inspiration.

A primary motif of Stoic political thought is the extension of such paradoxes into the civic realm. Conventional political ambitions belong to the realm of the indifferent just as much as wealth and health do. Thus, while Stoicism actively promotes conventional political activity as a way of following human nature, it at the same time downgrades it in relation to true moral goodness. Everybody wants to have power, and would like if they could to be a king; but only the wise have power (only they can achieve everything they want) and kingship (defined as 'rule which is accountable to no one'). These Socratic redefinitions were extended even to humbler civic aims: only the wise are generals, orators, magistrates, lawyers, and so on.

An upshot of this was a corresponding downgrading of the civic institution within which such offices operated. A city, in the conventional sense of a human cohabitation with geographical boundaries, a legal code and so on, is an artificial construct. A city in the most correct sense is not constrained in these ways: in fact the world itself is the ultimate city, being a habitation common to humans and gods, united by their shared rationality.

The idea was of Cynic inspiration. The Cynics had already coined the expression 'citizen of the world', *kosmou politēs*, which the Stoics took over. In a way every human being is a citizen of the world, and this generous version of Stoic cosmopolitanism was to become enormously influential on the ideology of the Roman Empire, as well as leading some Stoics to challenge entrenched gender and class barriers. But on a narrower criterion – influenced by Zeno's early utopian work the *Republic* (see ZENO OF CITIUM) – it is not all human beings, but only the wise, who participate in the real cosmic city. The cosmic city has its own law, a natural moral law defined as 'right reason (*orthos logos*) which commands what should be done and forbids what should not'. This notion of a cosmic moral law which transcends local legal codes exerted a powerful influence on later theories of natural law.

Although the Stoics encouraged political involvement in conventional cities, and were themselves prepared to act as advisors to monarchs, there is little reason to think that any Stoic before the late second century BC (see PANAETIUS §2) made a serious contribution to non-utopian political theory.

19 Passions

Everyone who has not achieved virtue is in a state of vice or moral badness. Most commonly – for example, in the work of Plato and Aristotle – vice was viewed as a state in which reason is dominated and deflected by strong irrational emotions, or 'passions' (*pathē*, singular *pathos*). But Socrates had established an enduring intellectualist alternative, according to which the soul has no irrational parts, and virtue is knowledge, so that its lack, vice, is simply ignorance: 'No one does wrong willingly.' The Stoics are fully committed to developing Socrates' position, in particular the thesis that passions are really value judgments.

A passion is commonly thought of as disobedient to reason. Reason says that you should face some danger, but fear disobeys. Reason chooses to abstain from embezzlement, but greed wins out. This suggests that an emotion can hardly itself be a rational state. The Stoics accept the description of emotions as 'disobedient to reason', but redescribe what this amounts to.

An emotion is primarily a judgment – a false one. A fear may be the false judgment that some impending thing, say injury, is bad for you. The falsity lies in the fact that physical injury is actually not bad, just a 'dispreferred indifferent' (see §15) and therefore strictly irrelevant to happiness. Your belief that it is bad takes the form of an 'excessive impulse' to avoid it, and that impulse, as well as being a judgment, is like any intellectual state also a physical modification (in this case called a 'contraction') of the *pneuma* that constitutes the commanding-faculty of your soul. The new overtensioned and perturbed state of your mental *pneuma* is one that you cannot instantly snap out of. Were you to entertain the correct judgment that you should not shrink from the danger, your *pneuma* would not be able to respond. That is what makes the passionate state of fear 'disobedient to reason' – a status it can have while itself also being a piece of faulty reasoning. Chrysippus compared it to a runner who is going too fast and therefore cannot stop at will. (For a later Stoic's disagreement with Chrysippus on this issue, see POSIDONIUS §5.)

The four main kinds of emotion are appetite, fear, pleasure and distress. Appetite and fear are faulty evaluations of future things as good and bad respectively. Pleasure and distress are corresponding mis-evaluations of things already present. Each has a variety of sub-species, and one of particular importance in Stoic discussions (see Seneca, *On Anger*) is anger, identified as a species of desire, namely the desire for revenge. Calling pleasure a passion and a vice may sound harsh, but the kind of pleasure envisaged here is one involving conscious evaluative attitudes, such that its sub-species include gloating and self-gratification. ('Pleasure' understood as that sensation of wellbeing which automatically accompanies certain states and activities is not a vice but an 'indifferent'. It is the view that pleasure – in this latter sense – and pain are indifferent that has given 'stoical' its most familiar modern meaning.)

It should not be inferred that a Stoic sage is feelingless. The wise lack the 'passions', which are overevaluations, but they do instead have the correct affective states, which the Stoics call *eupatheiai*, or 'good feelings'. Thus the sage has no 'appetites', but does have 'wishes', whose species include kindness, generosity, warmth and affection. Similarly, instead of 'fear' the wise have 'watchfulness', and so on.

The Stoics' conviction that emotional states, far from being mere irrational drives, are primarily specified by their cognitive content is one of their most valuable contributions to moral philosophy. Its most important implication in their eyes is that philosophical understanding is the best and perhaps the only remedy for emotional disquiet. In the short term strong emotions are disobedient to correct reasoning, but in the long term rational therapy can restructure the intellect and dispel all passions (see EMOTIONS, NATURE OF).

20 Fate

Socrates had been a firm believer in the powers of divination and in divine providence. Stoicism took over this outlook and developed it into a doctrine of 'fate' (*heimarmenē*), which by the time of Chrysippus had become a full-scale thesis of determinism.

That everything that happens is predetermined is a thesis which flows easily from all three branches of Stoic philosophy. Ethics locates human happiness in willing conformity to a pre-ordained plan (§17), and treats the use of divination as a legitimate means towards this goal. Physics provides the theory of the world's divinely planned cyclical recurrence, unvarying in order to maintain its own perfection (§5).

Physics also supplies a fundamental principle, regarded as conceptually self-evident, that nothing happens without a cause. This quickly leads to the conclusion that the world's entire history is an unbroken causal network. 'Fate is a natural everlasting ordering of the whole: one set of things follows on and succeeds another, and the interconnection is inviolable.' 'The passage of time is like the unwinding of a rope, bringing about nothing new and unrolling each stage in its turn.' A modern analogy might be the continual rerunning of a film.

Finally, logic offers the principle of bivalence: every proposition, including those about the future, is either true or false. Therefore, Chrysippus argued, it is true *now* of any given future event either that it will happen or that it will not happen. What does that present truth consist in? It can only lie in the causes now present, sufficient either to bring the event about or to prevent its happening. Therefore all events are predetermined by antecedent causes sufficient to bring them about and to prevent all alternatives from occurring. (Compare ARISTOTLE §20 and EPICUREANISM §12, for escape routes from this argument.)

21 Responsibility

The greatest interest of this determinist position lies in the Stoics' attempts to meet the challenge it poses to moral responsibility (see FREE WILL). They implicitly accept that a person is responsible for an action only if they could have done otherwise. But how could this latter be true in a Stoic world, where the actual action performed is causally determined and even predictable in advance? Chrysippus was the author of the main Stoic answers to this challenge. His task (see Cicero, *On Fate*) was to show that even in such a world 'could have done otherwise' makes sense: an action which I did not in the event perform may nevertheless have been *possible* for me, that is, my failure to perform it was not *necessary*. The strategy for securing this result included the following lines of argument.

(1) A 'possible' proposition is defined in Stoic sources as 'one which (i) admits of being true, and (ii) is not prevented by external circumstances from being true'. Suppose that you have failed to pay a bill despite having the cash. Paying the bill was 'possible' for you. (i) It 'admits of being true': there is such a thing as paying a bill, unlike for example, being in two places at once. (ii) Nothing external to you prevented you: you did not lack the funds, you were not forcibly detained, and so forth. This account of possibility does allow that something *internal* to you may (indeed must) have prevented you from paying: for example, your meanness, forgetfulness or laziness. Still, it was possible for you to pay, in the sense that you had the *opportunity* to pay. Chrysippus seems to maintain that the 'could have done otherwise' notion of responsibility holds in his world, because alternative actions are 'possible' in just this sense: we regularly have the opportunity to do otherwise, and therefore have only ourselves to blame for what we actually do.

Stoicism resists the alternative that 'could have done otherwise' might entail our being actually *capable* of acting otherwise: surely the good, in order to claim credit for their conduct, do not have to be capable of wrongdoing, nor need the bad, if they are to be blamed, be capable of acting well.

(2) Much this same point was also expressed in terms of a causal distinction (one among many: the Stoics were accused of introducing a 'swarm of causes'). When a cylinder is pushed and rolls, the 'principal' cause of the rolling is its shape, the push being just the triggering or 'proximate' cause. From our point of view as agents, Chrysippus argues, fate functions as a series of mere triggering causes – the openings, provocations and so on with which the world presents us. Given our respective states of character, we are bound to respond to these prompts in just the ways we do. But the principal cause lies in our character. And that makes us, not fate, responsible for our actions.

Importantly, the Greek word for a cause, *aition*, literally means the 'thing responsible'. However, the Stoics' technical term for moral responsibility is *eph' hēmin*: our actions are 'within our power'. This is not a thesis of free will. What matters to them is not to posit an open future, but to establish the moral accountability of human action even within a rigid causal nexus.

(3) Divination might be thought to make the future necessary. Take an astrological law: if you were born at the rising of the dog star, you will not die at sea. Suppose you *were* born at the rising of the dog star. This is an unalterable fact about the past, and therefore, Chrysippus accepts, necessary. There is also a widely accepted law of logic that if the antecedent of a conditional is necessary so is its consequent. Therefore 'You will not die at sea' also becomes a

necessary truth. One of Chrysippus' replies was that divinatory laws do not express conceptually indubitable truths, and are therefore not properly expressed as conditionals, but rather as negated conjunctions (see §11), in which this transmission of necessity does not occur.

(4) One remaining challenge was the Lazy Argument. Why, its proponents asked, should we bother to make decisions if the outcome is already fixed? Why call the doctor, if whether you will die or recover from your illness is already fated? Chrysippus' answer is that such sequences of events as calling the doctor and recovering are 'co-fated'. In most cases the outcome is fated *via* the means, not regardless of them.

Some landmark events, however, such as the day of your death, may be fated regardless of the means. Your character will cause you to decline numerous alternative actions to those you will choose, but even if, counterfactually, you were going to choose one of those alternatives, it would still be going to lead to your death on that same day. For example Socrates (in Plato's *Crito*) knew through a prophetic dream that he would die in three days' time, and his reasoned decision to stay and accept execution was willing cooperation with the rational world plan, where a bad person would have resisted by escaping but still died on that same fated day. Zeno and Chrysippus compared a human being to a dog tied to a cart: it can follow willingly, or be dragged.

In this way, morality is not simply argued to be compatible with determinism, but to require it. Only within a framework of rational predestination can moral choices have their true significance. There remains, however, the question why, in a world where it was pre-ordained that we would be precisely the kind of people we are, our choices should have any moral significance at all. The answer is that goodness belongs primarily to the world as a whole (identifiable with god). It is from this that moral qualities filter down to individuals and their actions, as a measure of their cooperation with or obstruction of the rational world plan.

22 Later fortunes

Stoicism's success ran high in the first century AD. It was perceived by writers like Seneca and Lucan as embodying the traditional Roman virtues whose decline was so widely lamented. Roman Stoics formed the main resistance to the emperor's rule, and, following the earlier model of the Stoic Cato, made the principled act of suicide into a virtual art form.

In a way Stoicism's crowning achievement was in AD 161, when its adherent MARCUS AURELIUS became

Roman emperor. Here at last was a genuine philosopher-ruler. When Marcus established chairs of philosophy at Athens, these included one of Stoic philosophy. Nevertheless, Stoicism was already on the decline in the late second century, eclipsed by the revived philosophies of Plato and Aristotle. By then, however, it had entered the intellectual bloodstream of the ancient world, where its concepts remained pervasive in such diverse disciplines as grammar, rhetoric and law, as well as strongly influencing the thought of Platonist philosophers like Porphyry, and Church Fathers such as Clement of Alexandria.

Through the writings of Cicero (whose philosophical works, although not Stoic, embody much Stoicism) and Seneca, Stoic moral and political thought exercised a pivotal influence throughout the Renaissance (see RENAISSANCE PHILOSOPHY). Early modern philosophers who incorporated substantial Stoic ethical ideas include SPINOZA and KANT. The recovery of Stoic physics, epistemology and logic, however, has been largely an achievement of the nineteenth and twentieth centuries.

See also: CLEOMEDES; EPICTETUS; MUSONUS RUFUS

References and further reading

Arnim, H. von (1903–5) *Stoicorum Veterum Fragmenta* (Fragments of the Early Stoics), Leipzig: Teubner, with vol. 4, indexes, by M. Adler, 1924. (The standard collection of early Stoic fragments, in Greek and Latin, commonly abbreviated as *SVF*.)

Atherton, C. (1993) *The Stoics on Ambiguity*, Cambridge: Cambridge University Press. (Outstanding rediscovery of a sophisticated theory; technically demanding.)

Brunschwig, J. (ed.) (1978) *Les Stoïciens et leur logique* (The Stoics and their Logic), Paris: Vrin. (Important collection of papers.)

Burnyeat, M.F. (1982) 'Gods and Heaps', in *Language and Logos*, ed. M. Schofield and M. Nussbaum, Cambridge: Cambridge University Press, 315–38. (Classic study of Stoic treatment of the Sorites; see §11.)

Cicero, M.T. (46 BC) *Stoic Paradoxes*, in *On Stoic Good and Evil: 'De finibus' 3 and 'Paradoxa Stoicorum'*, trans. M.R. Wright, Warminster: Aris & Phillips, 1991. (Latin text with English translation and notes; short declamations defending six Stoic moral paradoxes.)

—— (45 BC) *On Ends*, book III, in *On Stoic Good and Evil: 'De finibus' 3 and 'Paradoxa Stoicorum'*, trans. M.R. Wright, Warminster: Aris & Phillips, 1991. (Latin text with English translation and notes; an outstandingly lucid defence of Stoic ethics.)

* —— (45 BC) *On the Nature of the Gods*, trans. H. Rackham, Loeb Classical Library, Cambridge, MA: Harvard University Press and London: Heinemann, 1933. (Latin text with English translation; books II–III are a report and critique of Stoic theology.)

—— (early 44 BC) *On Divination*, trans. W.A. Falconer, Loeb Classical Library, Cambridge, MA: Harvard University Press and London: Heinemann, 1923. (Latin text with English translation; defence, followed by a critique, of Stoic belief in divination.)

* —— (mid 44 BC) *On Fate*, trans. R.W. Sharples, Warminster: Aris & Phillips, 1991. (Latin text with English translation; includes much of our best information on the Stoic doctrine of fate, see also §§20–1.)

Colish, M.L. (1985) *The Stoic Tradition from Antiquity to the Early Middle Ages. I, Stoicism in Classical Latin Literature* Leiden: Brill. (A very thorough survey of Stoic influence.)

* Diogenes Laertius (*c.* early 3rd century AD) *Lives of the Philosophers*, trans. R.D. Hicks, *Diogenes Laertius Lives of Eminent Philosophers*, Loeb Classical Library, Cambridge, MA: Harvard University Press, 1925, 2 vols. (Greek text with English translation; book VII, in volume 2, contains the lives of the leading Stoics, along with much doxographical and other information.)

Dragona-Monachou, M. (1976) *The Stoic Arguments for the Existence and Providence of the Gods*, Athens: National University Press. (Valuable study of Stoic theological arguments.)

Epp, R.H. (ed.) (1985) *Spindel Conference 1984: Recovering the Stoics*, suppl. vol. 23, *Southern Journal of Philosophy*. (Collection of articles on Stoicism, together with a comprehensive bibliography.)

Erskine, A. (1990) *The Hellenistic Stoa*, London: Duckworth. (A challenging reinterpretation of Stoic political thought and practice.)

Frede, M. (1974) *Die stoische Logik* (Stoic Logic), Göttingen: Vandenhoeck & Ruprecht. (The best study of Stoic logic.)

Hülser, K. (1987) *Die Fragmente zur Dialektik der Stoiker* (The Fragments on the Dialectic of the Stoics), Stuttgart and Bad Cannstatt: Frommann-Holzboog, 4 vols. (State-of-the-art collection, with German translation and commentary, of the texts bearing on Stoic dialectic; abbreviated as *FDS*.)

Inwood, B. (1985) *Ethics and Human Action in Early Stoicism*, Oxford: Oxford University Press. (Among the most valuable studies of Stoic ethics.)

Inwood, B. and Gerson, L.P. (1988) *Hellenistic Philosophy, Introductory Readings*, Indianapolis, IN: Hackett. (Includes a large body of primary texts on Stoicism, in translation.)

Kneale, W. and Kneale, M. (1962) *The Development of Logic*, Oxford: Oxford University Press. (Contains what is still among the best evaluations of Stoic logic.)

Long, A.A. (ed.) (1971) *Problems in Stoicism*, London: Athlone. (Collection of articles, some seminal.)

—— (1974) *Hellenistic Philosophy*, London: Duckworth. (Includes what in most ways is still the best introductory study of Stoicism; very accessible.)

—— (1996) *Stoic Studies*, Cambridge: Cambridge University Press. (Almost complete collection of articles by the leading post-war specialist in Stoicism.)

Long, A.A. and Sedley, D.N. (1987) *The Hellenistic Philosophers*, Cambridge: Cambridge University Press. (Volume 1 contains Stoic sources in translation with commentary; volume 2 has the original texts.)

Mates, B. (1961) *Stoic Logic* (2nd edn; 1st edn 1953), Berkeley, CA: University of California Press. (Largely superseded by Frede (1974), but still an exceptionally lucid and helpful introduction.)

Nussbaum, M. (1994) *The Therapy of Desire*, Princeton, NJ: Princeton University Press. (An eloquent defence of the Stoic intellectualist treatment of emotions, see also §19.)

Pohlenz, M. (1959) *Die Stoa*, Göttingen: Vandenhoeck & Ruprecht, 2nd edn, 2 vols; 1st edn, 1948. (The classic study of the school, still not fully superseded; later editions do not alter the main text.)

Rist, J.M. (ed.) (1978) *The Stoics*, Berkeley, CA: University of California Press. (First-rate collection of papers; includes valuable introductory accounts of Stoic cosmology and logic.)

Sambursky, S. (1959) *Physics of the Stoics*, New York: Macmillan. (A classic attempt to link Stoic to modern physics.)

Sandbach, F.H. (1975) *The Stoics*, London: Chatto & Windus. (An outstandingly accessible introduction.)

—— (1985) *Aristotle and the Stoics*, Cambridge: Cambridge Philological Society. (Seminal but controversial critique of the view that Stoicism was indebted to Aristotle.)

Sedley, D. (1982) 'The Stoic Criterion of Identity', *Phronesis* 27: 255–75. (On the Growing Argument and the 'categories'; see also §6.)

* Sextus Empiricus (2nd century AD) *Against the Professors*, books VII–XI, trans. R.G. Bury, Loeb Classical Library, Cambridge, MA: Harvard University Press and London: Heinemann, 1935–6.

(Greek text with English translation; contains extensive reports of Stoic doctrine and argument.)

DAVID SEDLEY

STRATO (d. *c.*269 BC)

The third head of Aristotle's school, from c.287 to c.269 BC, Strato has been regarded as substituting materialism for Aristotelian metaphysics, mechanism for teleology, atheism for theology and empiricism for intuition; and he has been blamed for the decline of Aristotle's school, or (less often) praised for his adoption of a more scientific outlook, especially in psychology. However, on some issues at least it may be more a matter of a selective emphasis of certain parts of Aristotle's teachings than of conscious and deliberate anti-Aristotelianism. None of Strato's writings survives.

1 **General**
2 **Mechanism**
3 **Microvoid and *horror vacui***
4 **Time, place, motion**
5 **Soul**
6 **Scientific method**

1 General

Strato, whose date of birth is unknown, was the third head of the Lyceum, the school founded by ARISTOTLE. After teaching the future king Ptolemy II Philadelphus in Alexandria, he succeeded THEOPHRASTUS (§1) as head of the school on the latter's death *c.*287 BC and remained in office until his own death eighteen years later. In some respects the most innovative and original member of the school after Aristotle, he has been held responsible for its subsequent decline, on the grounds that he abandoned certain Aristotelian doctrines; but there is room for debate both about Strato's actual views – given our complete dependence on second-hand reports – and about their relation to Aristotle's (see PERIPATETICS).

Where logic and ethics are concerned we know little of the contents of Strato's works, as opposed to their titles, and according to Cicero his interest in ethics was slight (frs12–13, Wehrli 1969); these reports must be read in the context of the perspective on the history of philosophy which Cicero derived from ANTIOCHUS, but may still be accurate enough as to the actual facts. Indeed Strato was often referred to by ancient sources as 'Strato the natural philosopher' (*ho physikos*).

2 Mechanism

Strato has often been interpreted both as a materialist and mechanist; in the eighteenth century 'Stratonist' was applied to those who denied divine influence on processes in the natural world. Purpose and form are connected in Aristotle, and Strato was supposed to differ from him on both issues. Certainly Strato (like Theophrastus before him, as far as our evidence goes) shows little interest in the role of the formal cause or in such issues as the status of universals, and is more concerned with the interactions of the elements than the division into matter and form. He regarded heat and cold as the fundamental principles of physical change (frs 42–8, Wehrli 1969), following Aristotle (*Generation and Corruption* II.2). The influence of Strato's approach can be seen in works attributed to Aristotle but in fact written in the third century, such as the *Problems*, the *Mechanics* and *On Things Heard* (*De audibilibus*).

That Strato rejected teleological explanations as a matter of principle, however, is less certain. Cicero reports him as saying that things are created by natural weights and movements, not by god (fr. 32, Wehrli) and as placing in nature a divine power which causes coming-to-be, growth and decay but lacks consciousness and form or shape – Latin *sensus* and *figura* – which in the context probably means, as Repici (1988) has argued, that it is not an anthropomorphic divinity (fr. 33, Wehrli 1969, see also frs 34, 36, 37). None of this sounds un-Aristotelian; Aristotle himself does not hold that things are created by god rather than by natural processes, does not regard nature as a conscious force, and shows in his zoological works how purpose and necessity work together for the most part but not always. Plutarch attributes to Strato (fr. 35, Wehrli 1969) the view not only that the world is not a living creature (where Aristotle, again, would agree; *On the Heaven* II.2, sometimes appealed to for the contrary view, is in fact concerned with the heaven, not the whole world), but also that chance (or 'the spontaneous': *to automaton*) is primary, nature secondary; this has been explained by scholars as a distortion resulting from Plutarch's desire, in the context, to stress Strato's disagreement with Platonism, or as indicating that, while processes in the world are brought about by nature, there is no further source or explanation of the existence of movement in the world as a whole, such as the Unmoved Mover provides in Aristotle's theory.

We have, indeed, no instances of Strato's actually using teleological explanations of nature; but our evidence is scanty in any case. It may be appropriate to speak, not of a rejection of Aristotelian positions by Strato, but of a selective emphasis on certain aspects of Aristotle's teaching rather than others. Strato almost certainly rejected Aristotle's doctrine of the Unmoved Mover, which Theophrastus had questioned and which Aristotle had not held throughout his career. He also (fr. 84, Wehrli 1969) rejected the fifth element, the incorruptible *aithēr* of which Aristotle held the heavens were made.

3 Microvoid and *horror vacui*

In the physics of the sublunary world Strato's greatest innovation was his readiness to allow the temporary existence of imperceptibly small and completely empty void spaces – 'microvoids' – within material bodies (frs 54–67, Wehrli 1969), using this to explain the compressibility of bodies and penetration, such as that of light through water. The idea that penetration of one body by another is to be explained in terms of 'pores' or passages is already present in Theophrastus and in book IV of Aristotle's *Meteorology* (which some have, questionably, attributed to Strato himself or to Theophrastus, rather than to Aristotle), but here the pores seem not to be void but to be filled with a substance different from that surrounding them. (Gatzemeier's (1970) view that no more than such a theory of *potential* void was to be attributed to Strato has been refuted by Furley (1985).) Where Aristotle had held that light was propagated as a change in a medium, Strato regarded light-rays as material.

There is no direct evidence for Strato's use of the principle of 'nature abhorring a vacuum' (henceforth *horror vacui*); fr. 5 (Gottschalk (1965)), from Theophrastus' *Meteorology* on the motion of the winds, is claimed for Strato rather than Theophrastus by Gottschalk, but the attribution has subsequently been challenged. The doctrines of *horror vacui* and of microvoids are logically distinct; but it seems likely that Strato combined them, by relating *horror vacui* only to a 'massed' or 'perceptible' vacuum. Such a connection was made by the Alexandrian physician Erasistratus, who had been a pupil of Theophrastus – like Strato – and used *horror vacui* to explain physiological processes (see HELLLENISTIC MEDICAL EPISTEMOLOGY §1); it also appears in the *Pneumatics* of the first-century AD technological writer Hero of Alexandria, where the influence of Strato is present though its extent is uncertain. But Strato's theory is in any case far removed from the atomist conception of discrete particles of matter moving within an otherwise empty space, and of indivisible minima of extension (see EPICUREANISM §§2–3; (ATOMISM, ANCIENT).

4 Time, place, motion

Strato rejected Aristotle's view of time as the numbered aspect of motion, arguing that motion and time are continuous whereas number is discrete; the disagreement with Aristotle concerns the implications of 'numbered' rather than the actual continuity of time. Similarly, in defining time as quantity or measure both in motion and in rest, Strato may be differing from Aristotle more in the formulation than in the underlying doctrine (see also frs 75–9, Wehrli 1969). Strato rejected Aristotle's view of place as 'the first unmoved boundary of what surrounds', and defined it instead as the interval or extension delimited by the outermost surface of what is contained or the innermost surface of what contains it – which amounts to saying that the place of a thing is, not as for Aristotle what bounds it, but the space that it occupies (see also frs 55, 59–60, Wehrli 1969; Gottschalk 1965: 169). Unlike Aristotle, but like the Stoics, Strato held that all four elements, earth, air, fire and water, naturally move to the centre of the universe (frs 50–2, Wehrli 1969). He agreed with Aristotle that falling heavy bodies accelerate, and demonstrated this, in a notable combination of reasoning and empirical observation, from the facts that water which falls as a continuous stream breaks into separate droplets further down, and that a body dropped from a height makes an impression in the earth which it does not if dropped from a short distance (fr. 73, Wehrli 1969).

5 Soul

Strato emphasized the role of *pneuma*, 'breath' or 'spirit' (see PNEUMA), in the functioning of the soul (see PSYCHĒ). Aristotle and Theophrastus had used *pneuma* to explain bodily processes, but it is debated how far they had identified specific channels through which it functioned. For Strato (frs 119–20, Wehrli 1969) soul-activities were explained by *pneuma* extending throughout the body; the 'ruling part' *(hēgemonikon)* he located (perhaps not under that name, which is Stoic) not in the chest, as in Epicureanism and Stoicism, but in the head, more precisely in the space between the eyebrows. Tertullian illustrates Strato's theory with the analogy of air in a musical pipe (Strato fr. 108, Wehrli 1969), the point in the context being that the same air can function in different ways; but he attributes the analogy also to Heraclitus and Aenesidemus. Strato may have been influenced in his theory of *pneuma* by developments in contemporary medicine and anatomy; Erasistratus investigated the function of the nerves by dissection and argued that they contained 'psychic' *pneuma* extending from the brain. But there is no explicit evidence that Strato himself linked *pneuma* with the nerves. Sensation was actually felt, he argued, in the ruling part of the soul, rather than in the bodily extremities (frs 110–11, Wehrli 1969).

For Strato, all sensation involved thought (fr. 112, Wehrli 1969, noting what happens if our attention wanders while reading). Conversely, there is no thought not derived from sensation (fr.74, Wehrli 1969). SEXTUS EMPIRICUS goes further and says that for Strato sensation and thought (*dianoia*) were identical (fr.109, Wehrli 1969), but this is an oversimplification; for Strato thought is *based on* sensation (and for Aristotle too it depends on images; *On the Soul* 432a13–14). Epiphanius' claim that for Strato (fr. 48, Wehrli 1969) every living creature was capable of thought may be as unreliable as many of his other statements. Plutarch too cites the claim that all sensation involves thought (fr. 112, Wehrli 1969) in the context of animal intelligence, though there is nothing in the report itself to suggest this. Strato's emphasis on *pneuma* as the means through which soul functions is a development, not a rejection, of Aristotle's own (arguably functionalist) view of soul as form. There is no place in Strato's theory of soul for the individual soul conceived as form separable, at least in part, from the body; but this is not the only possible interpretation of Aristotle's own position, even if many have adopted it for Platonizing, theological or anti-materialist reasons of their own. Strato brought some highly pertinent criticisms (frs 122–7, Wehrli 1969) against Plato's arguments for immortality in the *Phaedo*, pointing out for example that the fact that a soul cannot be dead does not show that the soul is everlasting.

6 Scientific method

In criticizing Plato's arguments for immortality Strato contrasted demonstrative argument with the Platonic theory of recollection (see PLATO §§11, 13) to the disadvantage of the latter (frs 125–6, Wehrli 1969; fr. 14b, Gottschalk 1965). Isnardi Parente (1991) connects this with Strato's use of experimental method and with Hero's reporting that microvoid is shown to exist by 'demonstration from sense-perception' (*aisthētikē apodeixis*, Strato fr.1a p.112.13, Gottschalk 1965). Although the connection of the latter passage with Strato is not certain, this reconstruction of a Stratonian epistemology which based demonstrative argument on empiricist foundations, and which was influential for Hellenistic science (see HELLENISTIC MEDICAL EPISTEMOLOGY), is plausible enough. However, the contrast often drawn in this respect between Aristotle himself and Strato

depends on the questionable attribution to the former of a belief in intuition as a mode of cognition independent of the senses (see ARISTOTLE §6).

See also: ARISTOTELIANISM, MEDIEVAL

References and further reading

None of Strato's own writings survives except for fragments cited by other authors.

Annas, J.E. (1992) *Hellenistic Philosophy of Mind*, Berkeley, CA: University of California Press. (Discusses Strato's doctrine of soul and *pneuma*.)

* Aristotle (*c.* mid 4th century BC) *The Complete Works of Aristotle*, ed. J. Barnes, Princeton, NJ: Princeton University Press, 1984. (Includes the works falsely attributed to Aristotle in the ancient tradition.)

* Furley, D.J. (1985) 'Strato's Theory of the Void', in D.J. Furley, *Cosmic Problems*, Cambridge: Cambridge University Press, 1989: 149–60. (A comprehensive account of the evidence for Strato's microvoid theory.)

* Gatzemeier, M. (1970) *Die Naturphilosophie des Straton von Lampsakos* (The Natural Philosophy of Strato of Lampsacus), Meisenheim an Glan: Anton Hain. (Detailed study of Strato's treatment of motion in various aspects of his philosophy; includes a full survey of earlier literature, and a listing of passages other than those in Wehrli which have been connected with Strato.)

* Gottschalk, H.B. (1965) 'Strato of Lampsacus: Some Texts', *Proceedings of the Leeds Philosophical and Literary Society, Literary and Historical Section* 11 (6): 95–182. (Texts additional to those in Wehrli, not all explicitly attributed to Strato, with English commentary.)

Hackforth, R. (1955) *Plato's Phaedo*, Cambridge: Cambridge University Press. (Translation of Strato's criticisms of the *Phaedo*, pages 195–8.)

* Isnardi Parente, M. (1991) *Filosofia e scienza nel pensiero ellenistico* (Philosophy and Science in Hellenistic Thought), Naples: Morano. (On Strato's epistemology and scientific method, see pages 123–48.)

* Repici, L. (1988) *La natura e l'anima: saggi su Stratone di Lampsaco* (Nature and the Soul: Essays on Strato of Lampsacus), Torino: Tirrenia. (Detailed discussion of ancient reports of Strato's theory of soul, his physiology and his theory of nature; argues forcefully against false contrasts between Strato's views and Aristotle's.)

Sorabji, R. (1983) *Time, Creation and the Continuum*, London: Duckworth. (On Strato's theory of time, see pages 82, 377–9.)

* Wehrli, F. (1969) *Die Schule des Aristoteles*, vol.5 *Straton von Lampsakos* (The School of Aristotle: vol 5 Strato of Lampsacus), 2nd edn, Basle: Schwabe. (The standard collection of fragments and testimonia, with German commentary.)

R.W. SHARPLES

STRAUSS, DAVID FRIEDRICH (1808–74)

The Christian faith rests upon two major beliefs: the existence of a God who created the universe, and the claim that in the historical person of Jesus of Nazareth this God in a unique way entered into world history. Like the two foci of an ellipse, these beliefs, which may be designated the metaphysical and the historical, constitute the fundamental foundation of the Christian faith. Strauss was the first major theological figure to openly challenge this foundation. The revolutionary Das Leben Jesu *(Life of Jesus), which appeared in 1835, was Strauss's attempt to disprove these two fundamental beliefs from a point of view which no longer accepted the old orthodox dogmas. As an alternative explanation to a divine Christ, Strauss posited a mythological Jesus; in his lifelong search to find a substitute for theism, Strauss moved through a philosophy of nature to Hegelianism, atheism and finally Darwinism.*

1 **Life of Jesus**
2 **Later works**

1 Life of Jesus

David Friedrich Strauss was born in the town of Ludwigsburg, a few miles north of Stuttgart, in the province of Württemberg, on 27 January 1808. He studied theology at the University of Tübingen (one of his teachers being Ferdinand Christian Baur), and also devoted considerable time to philosophy. He found Kant too involved and difficult to understand. Romanticism was the ruling sentiment of the day, and Strauss enthusiastically embraced the works of GOETHE, SCHILLER and other Romantics of the age. But the leading philosopher of Romanticism at that time was Schelling, whose pantheistic philosophy of nature Strauss eagerly absorbed (see SCHELLING, F.W.J. §1). In doing so he rejected the idea of a God who was both transcendent and personal. 'I have still not been able to convince myself of the personality of God, as it is found in theism', he wrote to a friend. 'In that teaching God is a personal, self-conscious God; the consciousness, however, is nothing other than the

expression of a particular life of the Spirit which develops *in time*' (1851 (Harris 1973: 11)).

It was in 1828 that Strauss first began a serious study of Hegel's *Phenomenology*. What drew him most of all to Hegel was the alternative explanation which Hegel provided for the creating source behind the universe – a God who was not the three-person Creator of the Bible, but an unconscious Spirit which in a threefold process enters into history, becomes conscious, and returns to itself as the Absolute Spirit (see HEGEL, G.W.F. §8). In 1831 Strauss travelled to Berlin, hoping to attend lectures from Hegel himself. He did indeed meet the Master, but after attending two lectures was informed by Schleiermacher that Hegel had died of cholera on the previous day. Strauss decided to remain in Berlin, and it was at this time he conceived his plan for a 'Life of Jesus' in which the Gospels would be interpreted from a new philosophical viewpoint.

In his investigation of the New Testament, Strauss's primary concern was to evaluate the Gospels as *historical* documents, going behind the supernatural elements to arrive at the historical truth lying behind the sources. Here he had first to make the determining assumption that everything supernatural was *ipso facto* unhistorical and unauthentic. For he perceived that to allow even one supernatural element to remain would vitiate the philosophical framework he envisaged. Therefore, the interpretation was above all 'a-theistic', meaning that a supernatural God (if existent) was excluded from the reckoning, without there being any explicit *denial* that such a God existed (the atheistic interpretation). This a-theistic or purely historical viewpoint, later also espoused by Baur (who after 1835 became the leading Hegelian theologian), may be called the Tübingen theological perspective. Strauss was the first to apply this a-theistic viewpoint openly and consistently to the whole of the New Testament, and not just piecemeal to certain isolated passages. From this point, Strauss abandoned the supernatural element completely in favour of the philosophical principle that in history only the rational is real and the real rational.

Strauss was not the first to interpret the Biblical narratives in this way. The rationalists, pre-eminent among them H.E.G. Paulus, had sought to explain miracles without recourse to the supernatural. But what was new in Strauss was a completely different method of interpreting the historical element. The rationalists had explained each miracle by a variety of natural causes; H.S. Reimarus had accused the Biblical authors of conscious fabrication. But Strauss was the first to interpret the Gospel narratives as a whole neither by rationalism nor by fraud, but by a new explanation called the 'mythological' interpretation, in which he claimed that the Biblical writers *unconsciously* presupposed miraculous events in the life of Christ on the ground of supposed prophecies in the Old Testament. Thus, according to Strauss, the accounts of miracles in the Gospels were simply creations in the minds of the Gospel writers, who reasoned that since such miracles and events were predicted in the Old Testament, then they must have happened, and accordingly represented them as having so happened.

These were the interpretive principles which Strauss used, and they were thus far quite independent of his Hegelian views. But when it came to explaining positively what had actually happened – for Strauss did not deny that there was a historical person called Jesus – he employed his Hegelian philosophical viewpoint. Jesus was the God-man, not in the old traditional sense of an actual unity between the divine Son of God (the second person of the Trinity) and the human body which he adopted through the virgin birth, but in the sense that the man Jesus was simply the representation of what every man actually was, the unity of the divine and human in every personality. 'The infinite Spirit is real only when it discloses itself in finite spirits, just as the finite spirit is true only when it merges itself in the infinite. The true and real existence of the Spirit, therefore, is neither God by himself, nor man by himself, but the God-man' ([1835–6] 1972: 777). As such everyone is a God-man, and Jesus is simply on a higher level with other men of genius, such as Napoleon, Goethe, Raphael and Mozart, with the distinction that the religious genius occupies a higher place, since the divine Spirit is present in this form of consciousness directly, and not merely indirectly.

These, then, were essentially the views which in 1835 caused an uproar in the theological circles of Germany. 'The book stood there', wrote the Hegelian Karl Schwarz, 'with the hard indifference of fate; it was the final account drawn up in the criticism of the Gospel history, and the inventory read: Bankrupt! For this reason the effect of the work was enormous. An electric shock ripped through the whole of German theology' (1869: 97). In Britain the book was translated into English by the young Mary Ann Evans, later to achieve fame as the novelist George ELIOT.

Reaction was not long in following. Strauss was dismissed from his position as tutor in the Tübingen Seminary. For a time he taught classical languages in the school at Ludwigsburg. An attempt by the new democratic government at Zurich to appoint him professor of theology aroused such strong opposition throughout the Canton that he had to be pensioned off without having set foot in the city; the pension,

however, secured his financial independence. Marriage to a famous singer, Agnese Schebest, in 1842, brought him only temporary happiness, a divorce being agreed five years later. In 1848, following the revolution, Strauss was appointed to the Württemberg Parliament as the liberal candidate for Ludwigsburg, but he could not agree with the radical majority and after a few months handed in his resignation.

2 Later works

For some years Strauss devoted his time to literary works, producing biographies and sketches of lesser known historical figures. A new version of the *Life of Jesus* was published in 1864, *Das Leben Jesu für das deutsche Volk bearbeitet* (A New Life of Jesus), in which Strauss followed the same a-theistic approach, but abandoned his Hegelian reconstruction of the person of Jesus. In 1872 his final work was published, *Der alte und der neue Glaube* (The Old and the New Faith), in which he espoused the new evolutionary views of Charles DARWIN – the first theologian to do so. Thirty-seven years had passed since he had written his first *Life of Jesus* and his philosophical views had undergone a great change; no longer did he hold the Hegelian ideas he had endorsed in his youth. In the 1840s the Hegelian bubble had burst (see HEGELIANISM §2). Baur's pupils, Strauss, Eduard Zeller, Albrecht Ritschl and others, had all slowly abandoned the Hegelian rhetoric. Ludwig FEUERBACH (§2) drove the final nail into the Hegelian coffin, declaring that such metaphysical ideas were simply so much verbiage; finally Baur himself discarded his former Hegelian convictions. Feuerbach had convincingly demonstrated that there was no absolute, infinite Spirit; such ideas were just the projection of man's mind into space. The secret of theology was nothing but anthropology; the knowledge of God nothing more than the knowledge of man! All Hegel's metaphysical ponderings were in the end just grandiose illusions. What remained was nothing but man himself.

But where had the universe come from? Where had humankind come from? Strauss's examination of the various possibilities began with Schopenhauer's unconscious primeval Will, which evolved through consciousness and intelligence, through the plant and animal world, to humankind itself as the highest manifestation of that Will (see SCHOPENHAUER, A. §§3–4). Eduard von HARTMANN developed these ideas further, and asserted that everything must have originated from the Unconscious, for if God was conscious and aware of what he was doing when he created the world, then his creation would be an enormous and inexpiable crime. Strauss was fascinated by these solutions, and though he did not accept all of Schopenhauer's ideas and was extremely critical of Hartmann, he saw in the evolutionary process the key for which he was looking in order to unlock the riddle of the universe. In Darwin's natural selection he found the confirmation he was seeking. In that direction lay the way the train of scientific thinking would go.

In espousing evolution and Darwin, Strauss was criticized by many of his supporters, but his keen sense of logic and consistency have certainly been vindicated by the twentieth-century acceptance of the evolutionary viewpoint. In adopting this viewpoint Strauss was, as always, ahead of the radical thinking of his time. The book went through six large editions in a year, a success which had never before attended any theological or philosophical work in Germany. Even Nietzsche's vituperative and rude attack in the following year (Nietzsche looked upon Strauss as a representative of a decrepit, bourgeois culture and morality) could not significantly detract from the enormous popularity the book had enjoyed (see NIETZSCHE, F.).

Strauss died two years later on 8 February 1874, having expressly forbidden a Christian funeral. His first *Life of Jesus* set in motion the whole 'quest' for the historical Jesus, which sought to discover the true Jesus of history stripped of his supernatural features. Strauss's criticism of the Gospel sources also provided the foundation on which Baur built up the historical criticism of the New Testament, with other scholars working on parallel lines in the Old Testament. Rudolf Bultmann's later demythologization of the New Testament, where everything supernatural is regarded as mythical, is simply a modern extension of Strauss's work (see BULTMANN, R.). Strauss has no 'followers' as such today, but his a-theistic principles and views in various ways have permeated and influenced almost every area of theological scholarship.

See also: ATHEISM

List of works

Strauss, D.F. (1876–8) *Gesammelte Schriften*, Bonn: Emil Strauss, 12 vols. (The collected works of Strauss containing most of his major writings, apart from the *Life of Jesus*, the *Streitschriften* and the *Christliche Glaubenslehre* (The Doctrine of Christian Faith). A complete list is contained in H. Harris, *David Friedrich Strauss and his Theology*, below.)
—— (1835–6) *Das Leben Jesu*, Tübingen: Osiander; trans. M.A. Evans (George Eliot, 1846), *Life of Jesus*, Philadelphia, PA: Fortress, 1972. (The work which made Strauss famous and initiated the 'quest' for the historical Jesus. Translation reprinted 1892, 1898 and 1972, the last with an introduction by Peter C. Hodgson.)
—— (1837) *Streitschriften zur Verteidigung meiner Schrift über das Leben Jesu* (Writings in Defence of my Book about the Life of Jesus), Tübingen: Osiander. (A section of these 'Writings' dealing with the Hegelians was translated and introduced by M.C. Massey, *In Defense of my Life of Jesus against the Hegelians*, Hamden, CT, Archon Books, 1983.)
—— (1864) *Das Leben Jesu für das deutsche Volk bearbeitet*, Leipzig: Brockhaus; trans. *A New Life of Jesus*, London: Williams & Norgate, 1865. (A revision of the 1835 *Life of Jesus*, but no longer from the Hegelian perspective that Strauss had long previously abandoned.)
—— (1865) *Der Christus des Glaubens und der Jesus der Geschichte. Eine Kritik des Schleiermacher'schen Lebens Jesu*, Berlin; trans. and with intro. by L.C. Keck, *The Christ of Faith and the Jesus of History*, Philadelphia, PA: Fortress, 1977. (Strauss's view of Schleiermacher's understanding of Jesus and of Schleiermacher's theology in general.)
—— (1872) *Der alte und der neue Glaube*, Leipzig: Hirzel; trans. M. Blind, *The Old and the New Faith*, London: Asher, 1873. (Strauss's final major work comprising an examination of the validity of the Christian religion and the origin and purpose of the universe.)

References and further reading

Cromwell, R.S. (1974) *David Friedrich Strauss and his Place in Modern Thought*, Fairlawn, NJ: Burdick. (A well-written account of Strauss's life and historical background.)
Graf, F.W. (1982) *Kritik und Pseudo-Spekulation* (Criticism and Pseudo-Speculation), Munich: Kaiser. (A massive account of Strauss's theology in the Hegelian period. Easily the best German work in modern times, with a full bibliography.)
* Harris, H. (1973) *David Friedrich Strauss and his Theology*, Cambridge: Cambridge University Press. (This contains the most comprehensive theological assessment in English of Strauss's life and theology.)
—— (1975) *The Tübingen School*, Oxford: Oxford University Press; 2nd edn, Grand Rapids, MI: Baker Book House, 1990. (A comprehensive survey of the Tübingen School, which also includes a discussion of the influence of Schleiermacher and Hegel.)

Lawler, E.G. (1986) *David Friedrich Strauss and his Critics*, New York: P. Lang. (Surveys early criticisms of Strauss.)

Sandberger, J. (1972) *David Friedrich Strauss als theologischer Hegelianer* (David Strauss as a theological Hegelian), Göttingen: Vandenhoeck & Ruprecht. (Discusses Strauss's Hegelian period.)

* Schwarz, K. (1869) *Zur Geschichte der neuesten Theologie* (The History of Recent Philosophy), Leipzig, 4th edn; quotation in §1 trans. H. Harris, in Harris, 1973, 66–7. (A review of philosophy and theology in the first half of the nineteenth century from a Hegelian perspective.)

HORTON HARRIS

STRAUSS, LEO (1899–1973)

Leo Strauss was a German-Jewish émigré political philosopher and historian of political thought, who wrote some fifteen books and eighty articles on the history of political thought from Socrates to Nietzsche. Strauss was no ordinary historian of ideas; he used the history of thought as a vehicle for expressing his own ideas. In his writings, he contrasted the wisdom of ancient philosophers such as Plato and Aristotle with the foolhardiness of modern philosophers such as Hobbes and Locke. He thought that the loss of ancient wisdom was the reason for the 'crisis of the West' – an expression that was in part a reference to the barbarities of the Holocaust. He therefore sought to recover the lost wisdom. He studied the classics and was a great devotee of Plato and Aristotle. However, he developed unusual interpretations of classical texts.

Strauss was born in Kirchhain, Hessen, Germany. He studied at the Universities of Marburg and Hamburg where he came into contact with Edmund Husserl and the young Martin Heidegger. He left Germany in 1932 and eventually settled in the USA where from 1949 to 1968 he was professor of political science at the University of Chicago. He amassed a sizeable following of devoted students, who have played a significant role in US academic life and government.

According to Strauss, the fundamental issue that divides ancient and modern thinkers is the relative importance of reason and revelation in human life. Modern philosophers such as Hobbes (§§6–7) and Locke (§10), exalt reason and believe that a political order can be founded on purely rational and secular principles. But Strauss believed that this modern liberal project was doomed to failure. He thought that reason cannot provide the requisite support for moral and political life; what is needed is belief in a transcendent God who punishes the wicked and rewards the righteous. Strauss thought that ancient philosophers understood this very well and that modern philosophers were seriously misguided in thinking that rational self-interest was a sufficient ground of social life. In Strauss' view, the modern faith in reason is at the heart of the 'crisis of the West'. Reason has destroyed faith and in so doing has opened the door to barbarism. Ancient philosophers understood that reason and philosophy have a corrosive effect on the 'city', as Strauss called the state. By the same token, Strauss was committed to philosophy and had no intention of denouncing it out of hand. He therefore argued that philosophy must be kept hidden or secret, not simply to permit philosophers to avoid persecution, but for the sake of the people and the for wellbeing of the city.

In *Persecution and the Art of Writing* (1952), a paradigmatic work, Strauss argued that all the great philosophers of the past understood the dangers involved in their own philosophical activity. Accordingly, they peppered their work with riddles, hints, clues, allusions, confusing language, intentional contradictions and other forms of subterfuge designed to conceal their true thoughts. Strauss argued that every great book contained a dual teaching: an exoteric or public teaching and an esoteric or private message. The former was a salutary teaching or noble lie intended for the consumption of the many while the latter was the dangerous truth intended only for the few.

Strauss' discovery of esotericism led him to advance unusual interpretations of classic texts. For example, Strauss argued that Plato (§4) wrote dialogues in order to conceal his true thinking. And contrary to popular belief, Strauss denied that Socrates was Plato's mouthpiece. He thought that in *Republic* Thrasymachus, not Socrates, was Plato's true spokesman (Strauss 1964: 77). According to Strauss, the argument made by Socrates was simply Plato's exoteric teaching. In arguing that justice leads to happiness, Socrates was displaying his sophistic skill – that is to say, his ability to make the weaker argument appear the better. Strauss thought that the Socratic argument in favour of justice could not succeed. He was certain that Plato was wise enough to realize that Thrasymachus was right – that justice is a function of power, and that in acting justly one serves the interest of others and not oneself. Strauss surmised that Socrates must have taken Thrasymachus aside and explained to him that his views were true, but too dangerous to express publicly. In this way, Socrates managed to silence Thrasymachus without refuting him. For Strauss, the truth is a luxury meant only for the few who hunger for the reality behind the necessary myths and illusions of the city.

Strauss insists that although the truth is dark, even 'sordid', it is still the erotic object of the philosopher's quest. However, it would seem that if we accept Nietzsche's premises, we must also accept his conclusion – if the truth is dark, then we must renounce it and live according to the humanizing illusions, the life-giving myths we create for ourselves. By accepting Nietzsche's premises and rejecting his conclusion, Strauss cultivates an elite that is more vulgar than wise (see NIETZSCHE, F.).

The devotion of Strauss' followers, coupled with his esotericism, has made him a figure of some controversy. But one thing is clear, Strauss' followers regard US liberalism as the embodiment of the legacy of modernity and its attendant dangers, and their aim is to rescue the USA from such modernity. Strauss taught them that this would be possible if they could win the ear of the powerful, hence their interest in government and public policy. Some find Strauss' elitism disconcerting. An elite that is radical, secretive and duplicitous, an elite that exempts itself from the moral principles it deems applicable to the rest of humanity, cannot be trusted with political power.

List of works

Strauss, L. (1952) *Persecution and the Art of Writing*, Chicago, IL: University of Chicago Press. (His best account of the esoteric/exoteric thesis.)
—— (1953) *Natural Right and History*, Chicago, IL: University of Chicago Press. (His best account of the difference between ancient and modern thinkers.)
—— (1959) *What is Political Philosophy?*, New York: Free Press. (Collection of well-known essays.)
—— (1964) *The City and Man*, Chicago, IL: University of Chicago Press. (Discussion of Plato, Aristotle and Thucydides.)
—— (1968) *On Tyranny*, Ithaca, NY: Cornell University Press. (A commentary on Xenephon's *Hiero* on *Tyrannicus*.)

References and further reading

Bloom, A. (1987) *The Closing of the American Mind*, New York: Simon & Schuster. (This best-selling book is a popularization of Strauss' thought by one of his students.)
Burnyeat, M.F. (1985) 'Sphinx Without a Secret', *New York Review of Books*, 32 (9): 30–6. (A criticism of Strauss' understanding of classical philosophy, especially Plato.)
Drury, S.B. (1988) *The Political Ideas of Leo Strauss*, New York: St Martin's Press. (Argues that Strauss' ideas are largely inspired by Nietzsche. Contains a comprehensive bibliography.)
New York Review of Books (1985) 'The Studies of Leo Strauss: An Exchange', 32 (15). (Responses from Strauss' admirers to Burnyeat.)

SHADIA B. DRURY

STRAWSON, PETER FREDERICK (1919–)

Strawson taught at the University of Oxford from 1947, becoming Waynflete Professor of Metaphysical Philosophy in 1968, and retiring in 1987. A sequence of influential books and articles established him as one of the leading philosophers in Oxford during that period. He had a crucial role in the transition there from the dominance of Austin and linguistic philosophy in the 1950s to the more liberal and metaphysical approaches in the 1960s and later. The principal topics about which he has written are the philosophy of language, metaphysics, epistemology and the history of philosophy.

Strawson became famous with 'On Referring' (1950), in which he criticized Russell for misconstruing our ordinary use of definite descriptions. Strawson endorses the slogan 'ordinary language has no exact logic', a viewpoint which is explored in Introduction to Logical Theory *(1952). He argues that the utility of formal logic in its application to ordinary speech does not imply that the meaning of ordinary language is captured by the semantics of standard formal systems.*

In Individuals *(1959), Strawson's most discussed work, his task is descriptive metaphysics. He attempts to describe the referentially basic subject matter of our thought. They are relatively enduring, perceptible and reidentifiable bodies. The other element in the basic framework is what Strawson calls persons, enduring entities with both material and psychological features. In* The Bounds of Sense *(1966), Strawson continued the development of his metaphysical and epistemological ideas, by combining a critical study of Kant's* Critique of Pure Reason, *with the defence of some transcendental claims similar to Kant's. To think of oneself as an enduring subject of experience requires that one recognize objects which are independent of oneself. So the major epistemological problem in the empiricist tradition, of building up to the external world from private experiences, cannot arise.*

Skepticism and Naturalism; Some Varieties (1985a) studies the conflicts between fundamental opinions which are natural to us, such as that we know things, and philosophical viewpoints claiming that these opinions are mistaken. Strawson argues that scepticism about these natural views can and should be resisted. Throughout his career, Strawson has tried to describe the basic content of our thoughts and experiences, to counter scepticism about or revisions of such thoughts, to illuminate them by making analytical connections between their basic elements, as well as investigating language, our vehicle for expressing these thoughts. He has linked his explorations to the insights of philosophers of the past, while engaging in critical debate with the period's other leading philosophers, such as Austin, Quine, Davidson and Dummett.

1 Life

Peter Frederick Strawson was born in London in 1919. He was educated at St John's College, Oxford, and, in 1948, became a Fellow at University College, Oxford, until, in 1968, he succeeded Gilbert Ryle as Waynflete Professor of Metaphysical Philosophy. He was knighted in 1977 and retired in 1987.

2 'On Referring'

The theory of reference has been central to the philosophy of language. Strawson initiated the debate about definite descriptions and has made a developing contribution to that debate and to one about proper names.

'On Referring' (1950) is one of Strawson's most discussed and influential articles. The target is Russell's theory of definite descriptions (see RUSSELL, B.A.W. §9). According to it, a sentence of the form 'The F is G' (which I shall call 'S') is equivalent to 'there is an F, and only one F, and it is G' (which I shall call S*). Strawson argues that S is importantly different from S*. Thus, if there is no F then S* is false; whereas for S, in these circumstances, the question of its truth or falsity does not arise. Further, S* says that there only one F, whereas utterances of S do not claim that there is only one F, since it is quite possible to say 'The car won't start', despite there

being lots of cars. Strawson suggests that a sentence like S has a context-independent meaning, but when used in the right context, 'The F' is used referentially, being somewhat similar to 'That F'.

The paper inspired an enormous debate. It was disputed (1) whether there are truth-value gaps, that is whether uses of S where there is no F are neither true nor false, and (2) whether Strawson's proposal fits many sentences containing 'the'. Strawson subsequently introduced the important concept of 'identifying reference' ('Identifying Reference and Truth Values' in *Logico-Linguistic Papers*). Roughly, hearers have knowledge of many objects around them. Speakers employ definite descriptions (at least sometimes), in identifying reference, when they exploit this knowledge to enable the hearer to know which object is being spoken of. According to Strawson, Russell's fundamental mistake is to deny this role to definite descriptions. Strawson also separates the issue of the validity of the notion of identifying reference from the issue of truth-value gaps, by allowing that whether there is a gap is influenced by other aspects of a speech situation (see DESCRIPTIONS) (Neale 1990).

3 Logic and language

Introduction to Logical Theory (1952) is Strawson's first book. It aims, first, to explain standard formal logic. Second, it aims to give philosophical elucidations to some notions which logicians employ, crucially inconsistency. Third, and most originally, it aims to determine the relation between formal logic and ordinary language.

Strawson argues that logical appraisal applies to statements (singly or in groups) and not to sentences, because in different contexts individual sentences make different claims. He takes the notion of inconsistency as basic, one in terms of which to explain others, such as entailment. Inconsistency is itself explained by 'our own determination of the limits of application of words' (1952: 9). Strawson therefore adopts, and tries to elucidate, the view that entailments are, in some sense, linguistically grounded.

The most original aspect of the work is its discussion of logical constants and other elements of ordinary language. I shall mention two points. First, in Chapter 6, he introduces the notion of 'presupposition', to be distinguished from entailment. Roughly, S presupposes S* if the truth of S* is a necessary condition of the truth or falsity of S, whereas S entails S* if the truth of S* is a necessary condition for only the truth of S. This notion enables Strawson to claim, that 'The F is G' presupposes but does not entail 'The F exists'. Presupposition is a notion which has been utilized more extensively by grammarians than by philosophers (see PRESUPPOSITION).

The second aspect is Strawson's account of the meaning of the logical constants. He argues that it is a mistake to equate the meaning of the formal logical constant with the meaning of the natural language expressions with which logicians pair them. The case most extensively argued for is the pair '→' and 'if . . . then . . .'.

Strawson's view is that natural language expressions have a meaning because their use is governed by various context-relative and imprecise rules, some relating to entailment, others to reference in a context. The formal logician has devised a system to track various general entailments, but this system gives neither an exhaustive nor totally accurate account of the complexities of natural language (see FORMAL AND INFORMAL LOGIC).

4 Truth and meaning

Strawson published a series of articles about truth, most of them collected in *Logico-Linguistic Papers* (1971). The central idea is that Ramsey's redundancy theory is correct (according to which roughly 'S is true' is equivalent to 'S'), but that it can be supplemented by noting that the presence of the truth-predicate enables us to perform various distinctive speech acts. For example, we can use it to concede ('It is true that p, but . . .'). Initially Strawson was close to, and was taken to be, endorsing a 'performative theory' of truth. Strawson defended these ideas against Austin's version of the correspondence theory of truth. Austin endorsed a formula claiming, roughly, that a statement is true if the state of affairs with which it is demonstratively correlated (to which it refers) is of the type with which the statement is descriptively correlated (see AUSTIN, J.L.; TRUTH, CORRESPONDENCE THEORY OF; TRUTH, DEFLATIONARY THEORIES OF).

Strawson offers many criticisms. Among the crucial problems he alleges are the following: (1) the formula can apply to only a limited class of descriptive sentences; it can hardly fit, for example, generalizations; (2) talk of a sentence being correlated with a state of affairs is vague; (3) even if, contrary to fact, it captures what must hold for a sentence to be true, when we say 'it is true that p' we are not *reporting* the fulfilment of that condition.

The prolonged debate about truth between Strawson and Austin was the most important discussion of truth in the period until Dummett and Davidson, in their different ways, significantly altered its direction. Strawson has contributed to both the subsequent debates about antirealism and about the truth-conditional theory of meaning, with its attendant idea of specifying the logical form of natural language sentences. About the former, Strawson (1976) argues that antirealism is a plain distortion of our thought, for example, about other minds. It is a distortion, and it is needless, answering to no legitimate demands (see REALISM AND ANTIREALISM). Strawson's attitude to Davidson is more extensively presented. In 'Meaning and Truth' (1971) Strawson argues that the notion of truth is secondary to that of saying, and that saying itself involves the idea of belief expression, and concludes that truth-theoretic accounts of meaning are unsuccessful and a better elucidation of meaning would analyse it in terms of the expression of basic psychological states, along the lines sketched by H.P. Grice (see COMMUNICATION AND INTENTION; MEANING AND TRUTH).

Strawson has also repeatedly criticized the views of QUINE. In an article written with H.P. Grice, 'In Defence of a Dogma' (1956), it is argued that Quine's criticisms of the analytic/synthetic distinction rest on an illegitimate demand that semantic notions should be reducible to non-semantic ones, and that the agreement observed in applying the distinction indicates that it corresponds to something real. In other articles (for example, Strawson 1985) Strawson has argued that some of the categories which Quine himself applies to language presuppose the application of other semantic notions which Quine rejects, and he has also argued that we cannot engage with language in the way we do and at the same time be sceptical about the application of the notions which Quine rejects, for example, determinacy of meaning (see ANALYTICITY; RADICAL TRANSLATION AND RADICAL INTERPRETATION).

5 Subject and predicate

Strawson has written on a number of occasions about the distinction between subject and predicate. His constant aim has been to explain the linguistic features of the distinction in terms of the ontological differences between the items that different parts of language introduce. Both his discussion of this problem in part 2 of *Individuals* (1959) and in *Subject and Predicate in Logic and Grammar* (1974b) exemplify this. In the latter he begins by listing various suggested differences between subjects and predicates, including Geach's proposal that negation and compounding attach to predicates, and Quine's that subject expressions alone yield places for quantification, but argues that, even if they are not dubious, they cannot be regarded as fundamental, precisely because they are in need of explanation. Strawson suggests that the explanation is that a basic type of judgment, central to human thought, in which it is judged that a spatiotemporal particular possesses a general character, are expressed by subject/predicate sentences, and the role of subject expressions is to indicate the particular and one of the roles of the predicate is to indicate the general characteristic. (Predicates also have an assigning role, of representing that the general characteristic is being assigned to the particular.) Strawson suggests that the initial marks of the subject/predicate distinction can be derived from this fundamental characterization once the contrasting nature of empirical particulars and general characteristics is described. Thus, if C is a feature then lacking C is also a feature, whereas, if X is a particular object there is no such object as the other-than-X. This is why negation goes with predicates, and not with subject expressions (see PREDICATION; REFERENCE).

6 *Individuals*

Strawson's project in *Individuals* is 'descriptive metaphysics', as opposed, on the one side, to 'revisionary metaphysics', and on the other, to ordinary philosophical analysis. It differs from the latter by aiming to lay bare the fundamental and most general features of our conceptual scheme, from the former by aiming only to describe the structure of our thought and not revise it. In *Individuals*, and in more recent writings, Strawson has opposed attempts to revise the fundamentals of our conceptual scheme, and part of the point of the division is to show that fundamental investigations need not be motivated by a revisionary purpose.

Strawson starts with the idea that a hearer can know of which object a speaker is speaking. He talks of the hearer *identifying* the particular, and of the speaker making an identifying reference (see §2 above). It may be that some types of particulars are identifiable only on the basis of prior identification of another type of particular. The latter are then described as more basic in our scheme of thought. His picture is that identification by demonstration is possible for sensibly present particulars, and that other particulars can be identified by their relation to such sensibly present items. But we can have a grasp of this spatiotemporal framework only if we can *re*identify particulars over time. An epistemological conclusion follows; no one can think that all our criteria for reidentification are mistaken or dubious, since this claim undermines the intelligibility of our thought of the framework in terms of which the doubt is expressed. Strawson argues that within this framework bodies are, in the sense explained earlier, the basic particulars. They are observable, enduring, and

form a relatively stable framework. They are to be contrasted with what Strawson calls 'private particulars', such as P's pain, which can be identified only via their possessors; theoretical unobservables; and events, some of which are perceptually observable but which, as a type of thing, do not form a sufficiently stable framework. Finally, the reidentifiable entities necessary for our grasp of the spatiotemporal framework are bodies, and reidentifying events rests on reidentifying the bodies involved in them.

This complex leading argument in *Individuals* has inspired considerable debate, both about the truth of some of the claims, for example, whether events are secondary to bodies, and whether the framework of events is so irregular, and about the status of Strawson's claims, for example, how far the argument rests on contingencies of the human environment and how far is it supposed to be necessary (see Campbell 1994).

In Chapter 2, Strawson considers this last question by attempting to find a place for the concepts of an unperceived and reidentifiable particular, and of oneself, in the thought of an imagined creature whose experiences are restricted to a world of sound. Sounds are not intrinsically spatial, and so considering such a world illuminates the degree to which space is fundamental to our thought. Strawson argues that some ground is needed to distinguish between hearing the same sort of sound on different occasions and hearing the same individual sound. He employs a master-sound-sequence, which is constantly heard and which varies in regular ways, to substitute for spatial location, and thereby grounds a distinction analogous to the one required. It is conceded to be incomplete, and, moreover, it is problematic that there is a ground in this world for the experiencer to think of itself, for, as Strawson puts it, a 'non-solipsistic consciousness'. The purpose of this brilliant chapter is to promote understanding of the character of our own scheme, rather than to make the sound world genuinely intelligible (see Evans 1980).

7 Persons

Strawson begins Chapter 3 of *Individuals* with two questions. Why do we ascribe states of consciousness to anything? Why do we ascribe them to the same thing to which we ascribe physical predicates? Two theories would not accept this characterization of our concepts: according to the no-ownership theory consciousness is not really ascribed to any object at all, and according to Cartesian dualism we ascribe the two characteristics to two separate entities: egos and bodies (see DUALISM). However, the no-ownership

171

account is incoherent because it needs to explain how conscious states are associated with bodies, and it can do that only by picking out a range of experiences as being someone's. Against dualism Strawson brings a fundamental principle: it is a necessary condition of ascribing states of consciousness to oneself that one does, or is prepared to, ascribe them to others. To be available for identification, other subjects must have non-mental, that is physical, characteristics. Another subject cannot be picked out as the ego standing in that same relation to that body as I stand to mine, because this makes reference to others secondary to self-reference, contrary to Strawson's fundamental principle. Further, by what right is it assumed there is only one such ego per body? Strawson also stresses in 'Mind, Body and Soul' (1974a) that it is hard to understand the notion of non-spatial particulars; the way that we have of understanding the possibility of numerically distinct but qualitatively identical particulars of a spatial kind, namely that they occupy different *places* in a spatial framework, is not available for egos.

Rejecting these characterizations, Strawson suggests that the concept of a person is 'a primitive concept' (1959: 101), by which he means that it is a primitive practice to recognize oneself and others as objects with both physical and psychological characteristics. From this he draws the epistemological consequence that at least for some psychological properties the ways of telling 'that they apply to others must constitute logically adequate kinds of criteria' (1959: 105). Strawson is suggesting that there cannot be a genuine problem of other minds. Nothing so far says how the material and the psychological relate. In Chapter 3 of *Skepticism and Naturalism* (1985a) Strawson claims that it is more satisfactory to regard psychological and neural events as causally related, rather than as identical.

Strawson's claims have been widely discussed. In particular, his fundamental principle and his epistemological claim about logically adequate criteria have been questioned (see Ayer 1964). Whatever the resolution of these questions, Strawson has undoubtedly articulated some fundamental aspects of our thought about ourselves and others (see PERSONS).

8   The Bounds of Sense

The Bounds of Sense (1966) is an exposition and criticism of Kant's *Critique of Pure Reason* and a defence of certain claims about the necessary structure of our experience, which resemble those advanced by KANT.

Strawson rejects Kant's transcendental idealism.

He provides a careful interpretation of it but argues that its incoherence is particularly clear in relation to the self, the location of which oscillates between the phenomenal world and the noumenal world. Strawson is, however, highly sympathetic to many others among Kant's positive and negative claims. In particular, he suggests that from Kant's arguments in the Transcendental Deduction a strong case can be reconstructed for saying that it is unintelligible to suppose that there is a self-conscious subject unless some of the experiences of the subject are of, and are taken to be of, independent objects other than itself. From Kant's arguments in the Analogies support can also be extracted for the claim that the subject's experience must allow the application of concepts of persisting and re-encounterable objects in a spatial framework, and of causal properties and powers.

Strawson defends the first necessity, that unity of experiences in a single subject requires experience of objects, by arguing that there is no point in ascribing a succession of experiences to a single subject unless for some of its experiences a distinction exists between the way, in that experience, it seems to the subject and the way the experienced item actually is. Then the notion of experience, as something distinct from but related to reality, has a point, and with it, the notion of the possessor of the experience, the subject. If, *per impossibile*, we had a subject none of whose experiences permit this distinction to be applied, then we have lost the idea that there is experience at all, and we have lost the idea of a subject. If Strawson's modified Kantian claims are correct, there is no genuine problem corresponding to that which gripped the empiricists, of showing that there is an external world on the basis of the character of private experiences. Indeed, part of the point of Strawson's enquiry is to outlaw that problem.

Strawson's brilliant treatment of Kant has been widely discussed. Two areas of debate may be singled out. One is that the force and soundness of transcendental arguments, as a style of philosophical argument, is disputable (see §9 below). The other is whether Strawson, despite his sympathetic approach, has provided the best account of the significance of Kant's idealism (see TRANSCENDENTAL ARGUMENTS) (Walker 1978).

9   Epistemology

In *Individuals* and *The Bounds of Sense* Strawson developed a response to different types of scepticism by defending transcendental arguments. These are of two sorts. In *Individuals*, especially Chapter 3, which deals with other minds, he claims that in order to employ psychological concepts at all – which, of course, the sceptics themselves do – one must acknowledge the adequacy of our basic ways of telling that they apply to others. In *The Bounds of Sense* the transcendental claim is that the conceptual applications which the sceptic is prepared to make (roughly about themselves and their experience) require the application of the concepts about the application of which they are sceptical.

Against such arguments it has been objected that we cannot be confident that the intelligibility of the concepts requires what is claimed. There is the permanent fear of an overlooked possibility. It has also been disputed what the force of the final requirement is. Is it merely that the concepts are applied or is it that they are veridically applied (see Stroud 1968)? Finally, what other things, if any, need to be said in response to the sceptic, even if the transcendental claims are accepted?

In *Skepticism and Naturalism*, Strawson, developing themes in Hume and Wittgenstein, argues that it is simply natural for us to believe in bodies, and this psychological fact renders any chance of sceptical arguments generating real doubt impossible, which means that such arguments need not be taken seriously. As Strawson says, 'Arguments on both sides are idle' (1985a: 29). Strawson's new viewpoint seems to be sustained by doubts, of the kind mentioned, about the anti-sceptical value of transcendental arguments. The proposal has been much debated, the chief issue being whether the idleness of the sceptical arguments is itself ground for ignoring them (see SCEPTICISM).

10 Philosophy

There are certain general and recurring themes in his philosophical writings (particularly his later writings) which need to be described. Although Strawson does not share Wittgenstein's conception of philosophy, regarding philosophy as a rational and theoretical (and not primarily therapeutic) activity, he has evident sympathy with the conceptual conservatism implicit in the slogan that philosophy 'leaves everything as it is'. There is no ground in philosophy to criticize our fundamental opinions. An example is Strawson's treatment of the supposed conflict between moral responsibility and determinism in 'Freedom and Resentment' (1962). His basic claim is that our view of ourselves as responsible is an ingredient in a network of emotional responses which cannot be abandoned and which do not rest on any general conviction that might be refuted. Philosophy is, in this way, full of false forced choices. They have their sources in multifarious misconceptions. One misconception is scientism, the idea that science is the arbiter

of all empirical truth. Another is a tendency to misinterpret common convictions: for instance, our tendency to refer to abstract objects seems problematic because all objects are regarded as necessarily material or quasi-material. Another is the failure to appreciate that there can be autonomous conceptual levels, evidenced in philosophical demands that all truths be reducible to some favoured base, say, the language of science, or a neutral sense-datum language. Strawson's idea here is that either the favoured language is itself a development of, and hence secondary to, the prior language (as in the case of science), or is mythical (sense-datum language). A central task of philosophy is to describe, and in the best way we can, explain the irrevocable fundamentals of human thought. The explanation consists in linking elements in the structure of concepts and experience, for example by displaying how our thought of ourselves links with our conception of the nature of experience. This structure of philosophical convictions has been enormously influential, for example, on and through the work of Gareth EVANS, David Wiggins and John McDowell.

List of works

Strawson, P.F. (1950) 'On Referring', *Mind* 59: 320–44: repr. in *Logico-Linguistic Papers*, London: Methuen, 1971. (Strawson's first, and very famous, discussion of definite descriptions and Russell's treatment of them.)
—— (1952) *Introduction to Logical Theory*, London: Methuen. (Strawson's account of the fundamental notions of formal logic, and of the relation between formal logic and natural language. Chapter 9 is Strawson's influential attempt to 'dissolve' the problem of induction.)
Strawson, P.F. and Grice, H.P. (1956) 'In Defence of a Dogma', *Philosophical Review* 65: 141–58. (A jointly written reply to Quine's criticisms of the analytic–synthetic distinction.)
Strawson, P.F. (1959) *Individuals: An Essay in Descriptive Metaphysics*, London: Methuen. (Strawson's highly original essay in descriptive metaphysics. Part 1 tries to determine the role of bodies and of persons in our thought, and Part 2 links the subject–prediacte distinction to these roles.)
—— (1966) *The Bounds of Sense*, London: Methuen. (Strawson's magisterial study of Kant's first Critique.)
—— (1971) *Logico-Linguistic Papers*, London: Methuen. (Contains, among others, 'Identifying Reference and Truth Values' (1964) and 'Meaning and Truth' (1969).)

—— (1974a) *Freedom and Resentment and Other Essays*, London: Methuen. (Contains 'Mind, Body and Soul' (1966) and 'Freedom and Resentment' (1962).)

—— (1974b) *Subject and Predicate in Logic and Grammar*, London: Methuen. (A further discussion of the subject–predicate distinction, and of other aspects of natural language.)

—— (1976) 'Scruton and Wright on Anti-Realism etc.', in *Proceedings of the Aristotelian Society* 77: 15–21. (A brief presentation of Strawson's views on antirealism.)

—— (1979) 'Perception and Its Objects', *Perception and Identity*, ed. J. MacDonald, London: Macmillan. (A characteristic treatment of philosophical problems to do with perception.)

—— (1985a) *Skepticism and Naturalism: Some Varieties*, London: Methuen. (Strawson's widely discussed study and rejection of philosophical revisions of ordinary thought.)

—— (1985b) *Analyse et Metaphysique*, Paris: Vrin. (An account, in French, of Strawson's approach to philosophy.)

—— (1992) *Analysis and Metaphysics*, Oxford: Oxford University Press. (Strawson's description of philosophy, overlapping with (1985b), but containing further topics.)

References and further reading

* Ayer, A.J. (1964) *The Concept of a Person*, London: Macmillan. (Contains Ayer's famous and readable discussion of Strawson on persons.)
* Campbell, J. (1994) *Past, Space and Self*, Cambridge, MA; MIT Press. (The first (difficult) chapter links with the first chapter of *Individuals*.)
* Evans, G. (1980) 'Things Without the Mind', in Z. Van Straaten (ed.) Philosophical Subjects, Oxford: Clarendon Press. (A brilliant critical discussion of the 'sound worlds' of *Individuals*, Chapter 2.)

Neale, S. (1990) *Descriptions*, Cambridge, MA: MIT Press. (A difficult discussion of descriptions, including Strawson's views.)

Sen, P.B. and Verma, R.R. (eds) (1995) *The Philosophy of P.F. Strawson*, New Delhi: Indian Council of Philosophical Research. (A collection of articles on Strawson by, among others, Putnam, Dummett, Platts and Cassam, with replies by Strawson.)

* Stroud, B. (1968) 'Transcendental Arguments', *Journal of Philosophy* 65: 241–56. (A critical examination of the claims made for transcendental arguments.)

Van Straaten, Z. (ed.) (1980) *Philosophical Subjects*, Oxford: Clarendon Press. (A book containing excellent but difficult articles on Strawson by

Evans, McDowell, Ishiguro, Wiggins and others, with replies by Strawson.)

* Walker, R.C.S. (1978) *Kant*, London: Routledge. (A readable book on Kant which discusses some of Strawson's interpretations and arguments).

Special journal issue (1981) *Philosophia* 10: 141–328. (A collection of articles on many of Strawson's views, with a long reply by Strawson himself.)

PAUL F. SNOWDON

STRUCTURALISM

The term 'structuralism' can be applied to any analysis that emphasizes structures and relations, but it usually designates a twentieth-century European (especially French) school of thought that applies the methods of structural linguistics to the study of social and cultural phenomena. Starting from the insight that social and cultural phenomena are not physical objects and events but objects and events with meaning, and that their signification must therefore be a focus of analysis, structuralists reject causal analysis and any attempt to explain social and cultural phenomena one-by-one. Rather, they focus on the internal structure of cultural objects and, more importantly, the underlying structures that make them possible. To investigate neckties, for instance, structuralism would attempt to reconstruct (1) the internal structure of neckties (the oppositions – wide/narrow, loud/subdued – that enable different sorts of neckties to bear different meanings for members of a culture) and (2) the underlying 'vestimentary' structures or system of a given culture (how do neckties relate to other items of clothing and the wearing of neckties to other socially-coded actions).

Ferdinand de Saussure, the founder of structural linguistics, insists that to study language, analysts must describe a linguistic system, which consists of structures, not substance. The physical sound of a word or sign is irrelevant to its linguistic function: what counts are the relations, the contrasts, that differentiate signs. Thus in Morse code a beginner's dot may be longer than an expert's dash: the structural relation, the distinction, between dot and dash is what matters.

For structuralism, the crucial point is that the object of analysis is not the corpus of utterances linguists might collect, that which Saussure identifies as parole *(speech), but the underlying system (*la langue*), a set of formal elements defined in relation to each other and which can be variously combined to form sentences. Arguing that the analysis of systems of relation is the appropriate way to study human phenomena, that our world consists not of things but of relations, structur-*

alists often claim to provide a new paradigm for the human sciences. In France, structuralism displaced existentialism in the 1960s as a public philosophical movement. Philosophically, proponents of structuralism have been concerned to distinguish it from phenomenology.

1 **Development and domain**
2 **Shared principles**

1 Development and domain

Structural linguistics was developed by the Swiss linguist Ferdinand de SAUSSURE in lectures published as the *Cours de linguistique générale* (1916), but the term 'structuralism' was coined by the Russian linguist and literary theorist Roman Jakobson in 1929. Jakobson was a member of the Prague Linguistic Circle which, between 1926 and 1938, drew upon Saussurian linguistics, Russian Formalist literary criticism, Husserl's phenomenology and Gestalt psychology to develop Prague Structuralism. Structuralism was opposed to atomism and was presented as a general method for the humanities and social sciences, although most of the circle's work focused on language, literature and art. A literary work is a structural whole; to study it is to analyse its internal relations (it is a hierarchically ordered system of structures of different kinds) and its place in the systems of a language and a culture, especially the system of literary genres and conventions.

Jakobson himself provided a link between Prague Structuralism and the structuralism which developed in post-Second World War France, first in anthropology (Claude LÉVI-STRAUSS), then in literary and cultural studies (Jakobson, Roland BARTHES, Algirdas Greimas, Gérard Genette), psychoanalysis (Jacques LACAN), intellectual history (Michel FOUCAULT) and political theory (Louis ALTHUSSER). Although these thinkers never formed a school as such, it was under the heading of 'structuralism' that their work was exported and read in the UK, the USA and elsewhere in the late 1960s and 1970s, where it was influential first in anthropology and literary studies, and later in historical and cultural analysis.

In anthropology, structuralism insists on the reconstruction of underlying systems (of kinship, of totemic and mythic thought) through which a culture orders the world. Within the field of the history of thought it seeks to identify the system of possibilities or formation rules that permit the emergence, in a particular era, of certain disciplines and theoretical objects. In literary studies it promotes a poetics interested in the conventions that make literary works possible, and it seeks not to produce new interpretations of works but to understand how they can have the meanings and effects that they do. In cultural studies generally it encourages attempts to make explicit the rules and signifying procedures that govern fashion or other cultural practices.

According to structuralist theory, the identity of structuralism should come from contrasts within the system of modern thought, from the differences shared by a range of thinkers, rather than from a historical filiation. In fact, the term 'structuralism' is generally used to designate work that marks its debts to structural linguistics and deploys a Saussurian vocabulary, including *sign*, *signifier* and *signified*, *syntagmatic* and *paradigmatic*. There are many writings, from Aristotle to Chomsky, that share the structuralist propensity to analyse objects as the products of a combination of structural elements within a system, but if they do not display a Saussurian ancestry, they are often not deemed structuralist, whatever their affinities with the writings so designated.

Once structuralism came to be defined as a movement or theoretical stance based on a set of principles, some theorists began to distance themselves from it. Readers who could see that works by some 'structuralists' did not fit certain accounts of structuralism began to regard some of these thinkers (particularly Barthes, Lacan, and Foucault) as post-structuralists, going beyond a structuralism defined as a project aiming at mastery of objective structures (see POST-STRUCTURALISM). In fact, many of the views associated with post-structuralism – such as the difficulty for any metalanguage to escape entanglement in the phenomena it purports to describe, the possibility for texts to create meaning by violating the conventions that structural analysis seeks to delineate, or the inappropriateness of positing a complete system because systems are always changing – are manifest even in the early work of such thinkers as Barthes, Foucault and Lacan who were at the time regarded as structuralists. Post-structuralism involves not so much the demonstration of the inadequacies or errors of structuralism as a turning away from the project of working out what makes cultural phenomena possible and intelligible, and a return to interpreting and narrating (sometimes called 'historicizing').

It is difficult to distinguish, in a principled way, structuralism from semiotics, the science of signs, which traces its lineage to Saussure and Charles Sanders Peirce. However semiotics is an international movement that has sought to adopt a scientific model and to cultivate links with, for example, zoology, while mostly eschewing the philosophical speculation and cultural critique that has marked structuralism in its French and related versions (see SEMIOTICS).

2 Shared principles

Structuralism takes many different forms, but there are some general principles that could be identified as structuralist. Most of these are best stated differentially, as contrasts. Structuralism has defined itself against historicism, atomism, mechanism, behaviourism, psychologism, and humanism.

Structuralism is not hermeneutics (see HERMENEUTICS). Structural analysis seeks to understand the conditions of meaning, and in that sense it takes the cultural meaning of objects and events as a point of departure, as what requires explanation. Hermeneutics characteristically seeks to discover the meanings of a text or cultural phenomenon. Linguistic analysis does not try to tell us what sentences mean but to explain how these sequences are constructed and how they can have the meaning they do for speakers of a language. The linguistic model enjoins a concentration on poetics rather than interpretation (Culler 1975).

Structuralism is not phenomenology (see PHENOMENOLOGICAL MOVEMENT). Although the intuitions of subjects about the meaning or at least the well-formedness or deviance of cultural phenomena are often its point of departure, structuralism seeks explanation at the level not of structures of consciousness but of unconscious infrastructures, systems of relation that operate through subjects and work to constitute subjects but are not necessarily accessible to them. In *Le Visible et l'invisible* (1964), Maurice Merleau-Ponty imagined the possibility of linking a phenomenological critique of the distinction between subject and object (both subject and object are a posteriori constructs, notions derived from a unitary experience rather than experiential givens) to a structuralist account of the differential nature of meaning. Most theorists, however, have insisted on the fundamental difference in focus and approach between phenomenology and structuralism (Ricoeur 1969).

Cultural phenomena have a relational identity. They are defined by their differences from one another, not by any essential features. This basic principle of Saussurian linguistics has wide applicability.

The object of analysis is not the phenomena themselves but the underlying system which makes them possible or intelligible. Analysts cannot examine all the texts, artefacts or acts related to a given system, for the system, like a language, may have the capacity to produce an infinite set of objects or events. The goal is to identify the set of contrastive elements which combine, according to rules to be discovered, to produce the cultural forms.

Structure, which is not form alone but the formal organization of content, plays a determining role in human affairs. One writer speaks of 'superstructuralism' to indicate that, in contrast with Marxism which treats language and culture as a superstructure determined by a material base, structuralism and post-structuralism share the conviction that the structures of language and meaning generally are not direct reflections of economic relations but themselves determine the parameters within which human beings live and act (Harland 1987).

The priority of synchronic over diachronic analysis. Saussure distinguishes the study of language as a system (synchronic analysis) from the study of changes in languages over time (diachronic) and argues that describing systems is a condition of understanding changes from one state or system to another. Generally, structuralism has maintained that culture should be studied as a series of synchronic systems, that much 'historical' analysis should be seen as synchronic analysis of moments in the past, and that the analysis of change requires prior understanding of the systems that change.

Structuralism does not narrate. In place of explanation which proceeds narratively, by linking a phenomenon to origins and ends, structural analysis explores conditions of possibility. The critique of structuralism known as post-structuralism often entails, in effect, a return to narrative as a mode of knowledge, but with no confidence in its authority, perhaps because the principled structuralist rejection of narrative explanation has been ignored rather than refuted.

For structuralism, the subject or self is a construct that needs to be explained, not a principle of explanation. It is not that the subject 'man' and human beings do not exist but that what counts as man or what counts as the subject depends upon a cultural system that requires analysis.

Some structuralists (for example, Lévi-Strauss and Lacan) claim to analyse the 'laws of thought' but most are agnostic on the question of whether the categories and rules of one system might be universals. Unlike transformational-generative grammar, which posits a rich universal grammar (a human language faculty that strongly constrains the properties of possible human languages), structural linguistics assumes that one language (linguistic system) may differ radically from the next. Nevertheless, most structural analyses treat meaning as the product of hierarchically-ordered sets of binary oppositions and thus, in effect, posit some universal principles of signification (see CHOMSKY, N.).

See also: STRUCTURALISM IN LINGUISTICS; STRUCTURALISM IN LITERARY THEORY; STRUCTURALISM IN SOCIAL SCIENCE

References and further reading

Caws, P. (1988) *Structuralism: The Art of the Intelligible*, Atlantic Highlands, NJ: Humanities Press. (An account of the foundations of structuralism, with specific reflection on structuralism as philosophy. Clear and disinterested.)
* Culler, J. (1975) *Structuralist Poetics: Structuralism, Linguistics, and the Study of Literature*, London: Routledge. (Discussion of the linguistic model and its applicability to literary and other domains. Presumes no prior knowledge of linguistics or philosophy.)
* Harland, R. (1987) *Superstructuralism: The Philosophy of Structuralism and Post-Structuralism*, London: Methuen. (A broad and lively introductory survey.)
* Merleau-Ponty, M. (1964) *Le Visible et l'invisible*, ed. C. Lefort, Paris: Gallimard; *The Visible and the Invisible*, trans. A. Lingis, Evanston, IL: Northwestern University Press, 1968. (Unfinished philosophical reflections exploring the possibility of deploying a structuralist perspective within phenomenology.)
* Ricoeur, P. (1969) 'Structure et hermeneutique', in *Le Conflit des interpretations*, Paris: Seuil; *The Conflict of Interpretations*, trans. D. Ihde, Evanston, IL: Northwestern University Press, 1974. (One of several essays in this volume which seeks to distinguish structuralism from other approaches.)
* Saussure, F. de (1916) *Cours de linguistique générale*, ed. T. de Mauro, Paris: Payot, 1973; *Course in General Linguistics*, trans. R. Harris, London: Duckworth, 1983. (The foundations of structural linguistics, structuralism, and semiotics.)
Wahl, F., Sperber, D., Ducrot, O., Todorov, T. and Safouan, M. (1968) *Qu'est-ce que le structuralisme?* (What is structuralism?), Paris: Seuil. (Essays on structuralism in anthropology (Sperber), linguistics (Ducrot), literary criticism (Todorov), philosophy (Wahl) and psychoanalysis (Safouan), produced at the height of the movement.)

JONATHAN CULLER

STRUCTURALISM IN LINGUISTICS

The term structural linguistics can be used to refer to two movements which developed independently of each other. The first is European and can be characterized as post-Saussurean, since Saussure is generally regarded as its inspiration. The central claim of this movement is that terms of a language of all kinds (sounds, words, meanings) present themselves in Saussure's phrase 'as a system', and can only be identified by describing their relations to other terms of the same language; one cannot first identify the terms of a language and then ask which system they belong to. Moreover, because a language is a system of signs, one cannot identify expression-elements (sounds, words) independently of the content-elements (meanings), so that a study of language cannot be divorced from one of meaning. The second movement is an American one, which developed from the work of Leonard Bloomfield and dominated American linguistics in the 1940s and 1950s. It attached great importance to methodological rigour and, influenced by behaviourist psychology, was hostile to mentalism (any theory which posits an independent category of mental events and processes). As a result, unlike the first movement, it excluded the study of meaning from that of grammar, and tried to develop a methodology to describe any corpus in terms of the distribution of its expression-elements relative to each other. Whereas the first movement provided a model for structuralist thought in general, and had a significant impact on such thinkers as Barthes, Lacan and Lévi-Strauss, the second made a major contribution to the development of formal models of language, however inadequate they may seem now in the light of Chomsky's criticisms.

1 The concept of structural linguistics
2 The Prague School and functionalism
3 The Copenhagen School and glossematics
4 Post-Bloomfieldian linguistics and distributional relations

1 The concept of structural linguistics

Though a wide range of linguistic studies raise issues which are in some sense structural, we shall focus on two uses of the term *structural linguistics* which refer to separate movements, each of which advanced strong hypotheses about the nature of language and the methodology of linguistics. However, though each of the movements attaches great importance to structural analysis, their reasons for doing so differ profoundly; hence, the need to distinguish them.

The origin of the first movement is to be found in the work of Ferdinand de SAUSSURE, the fundamental contention of which is that, since linguistic items of all kinds (sounds, words, meanings) present themselves as a system, they can only be identified in terms of the relations in which they stand to other elements within the system (Lyons 1973: 6). An acceptance of this thesis, together with one, sometimes qualified, of the following three Saussurean theses, defines post-Saussurean structuralism: it is necessary to distinguish *la langue* from *la parole*, and a synchronic study from a diachronic one; the fundamental linguistic study is a synchronic one of *la langue*; and, finally, a study of expression-elements (sounds and words) cannot be divorced from one of meanings. Of course, within this framework much is underdetermined, leaving scope for different emphases and developments, two of which are considered in §§2 and 3 below.

The origins of the second movement are to be found in the work of the American linguist Leonard Bloomfield, and, in particular, in his book *Language* (1933). Strongly influenced by behaviourist psychology (see BEHAVIOURISM, METHODOLOGICAL AND SCIENTIFIC), Bloomfield proposed an analysis of a speech act in terms of the notions of a *stimulus* and a *response*. In response to a feeling of hunger (a stimulus) one thing I might do is reach for an apple; but if I have mastered a language, another thing that I can do is to utter 'Pass me the apple', which is itself not only a response to my hunger but also a stimulus designed to get you to respond by passing the apple. So language increases the range of responses enormously by bridging the gap between different nervous systems. A problem with this analysis, as Bloomfield concedes, is that in most cases we seem unable to identify independently either the stimulus or the response. Since he defines the meaning of an utterance as a function of the situation in which it is uttered and the response called forth, it is hardly surprising that he concludes that the study of meaning largely evades our grasp. What can be studied nevertheless are the utterances themselves but, to avoid a lapse into a discredited mentalism, or an appeal to a theory which is not available to us, sound methodology requires that the study of language does not appeal to meaning. The study of language becomes, therefore, a study of a set of utterances, or of a corpus – indeed, Bloomfield once defined a language as the set of utterances uttered by its speakers. Such a study concentrates on the formal relations between constituents of utterances. It argues that for each constituent there is a limited range of environments in which it can occur; for instance, 'cat' can occur in the environment 'The —— jumped', but not in 'John —— Jill'. So if an item's distribution is

defined as the ranges of environments in which it can occur nondeviantly, there seem to be promising ways of defining its type in terms of its distribution, and of making generalizations about the relations between types. More and more sophisticated approaches to the analysis of a corpus in terms of the distributional relations holding between its constituents were developed in America in the 1940s and 1950s, culminating in the work of Z.S. Harris which will be discussed in §4. So three main features of post-Bloomfieldian structuralism are: it was corpus based; an appeal to meaning was rigorously excluded from the methodology adopted; and the object of analysis was the identification of the constituents of the utterances in a corpus, and the construction of a compact description of the distributional relations holding between them. Paradoxically, whilst it is clear why both movements should be regarded as structuralist, each from the point of view of the other is radically misconceived. Arguably the first movement is the more interesting from a philosophical point of view because of its impact on structuralist thought in general; but the second movement undoubtedly developed much more detailed formal models than the first.

2 The Prague School and functionalism

The central thesis of post-Saussurean structuralism is that the terms of a language present themselves as a system; but precisely what kind of a system do they belong to? A group of linguists whose work was strongly associated with Prague and who became known as the Prague School developed a distinctive answer to this question. For them a language is a dynamic system with many subsystems which interact with each other; one of these concerns the structure of its functional sounds (phonology), another the structure of its words (morphology), another the structure of its sentences (syntax), and so on. Each of these has a stable core, surrounded by a less stable periphery, and is striving for a state of equilibrium which it never quite attains, since a change which stabilizes one part of the system can adversely affect another. The Russian linguist Jakobson, who played a major part in the development of this conception, likened the attempt to restore equilibrium to the moves made in a chess game after the loss of a piece, which may strengthen one part of a defence at the expense of another. The Prague School's dynamic conception of a language as a system of subsystems striving to reach equilibrium led it in turn to adopt a different conception of diachrony from that held by Saussure, for all that it agreed with him that a synchronic perspective is logically prior. Since a language is a dynamic system, the School argued that the force for change in many cases is a state of the system itself, whereas Saussure had argued that change is brought about by factors external to the system which never affect it directly.

An important area in which the School made a major contribution to our understanding of what the system involved was phonology, the study of the functional sound units of a language. It seems clear that all languages utilize a relatively small number of such units (called phonemes), so that 'cat', for instance, contains /c/, /a/ and /t/; but how are they to be characterized, and in what way do they form a system? Saussure was prevented from answering this question in part because he assumed that phonemes were not complex, and that oppositions arise from differences. However, Trubetzkoy and Jakobson questioned both of these assumptions. They argued that phonemes can be analysed in terms of so called distinctive features, which are the ways in which phonemes belonging to the same language are opposed to each other, and that the differences between them arise from these oppositions. For instance, one way in which /m/ differs from /n/ is that the lips are closed when pronouncing it, so that there is a feature (labial) present in one case which is absent in the other. Features of this kind the School called 'distinctive features', claiming that each phoneme can be described in terms of the presence or absence of a small number of such features. Moreover, since what is being described is a set of ways in which the phonemes of a language can be opposed to each other, differences rest on oppositions. This theory was to have a major impact on structuralist thinkers; for example, Lévi-Strauss asked whether there are other kinds of oppositions which give rise to different kinds of structures in domains such as kinship and myth (see STRUCTURALISM IN SOCIAL SCIENCE).

Another novel feature of the Prague School was its attempt to combine a functionalist conception of language with its structuralist conception. The central idea is that a study of a language cannot be divorced from its uses: 'language is not a self-contained whole, hermetically separated from the extra-lingual reality, but in fact its main function is to react to and to refer to this reality' (Vahek 1966: 7). Just as one cannot understand chess fully unless one understands what it is players are trying to achieve, so one cannot understand a language if one does not understand its uses. Moreover, various aspects of use have specific linguistic means of expression; for example, it is natural if one wants someone to do something to use an imperative, if one wants information to use an interrogative, and so forth. Whether functionalism is ultimately consistent with the strong form of the principle of the arbitrariness of the sign embraced by Saussure is questionable. However, by recognizing the diverse uses of language, the Prague School greatly extended the range of domains open to structural analyses. For instance, if an utterance may have an expressive function as well as a descriptive one, may we not, as a limiting case, have a text which is purely expressive but which can nevertheless be analysed structurally – a poem for instance?

3 The Copenhagen School and glossematics

Arguably, the Prague School's theory of oppositions, which positively characterizes one item in an opposition, is incompatible with the Saussurean theses that in language there are only differences without positive terms, and that language is a form not a substance. The work of the Danish linguist Hjelmslev, which takes these theses as its cornerstone, is in this respect a more faithful development of the Saussurean conception of a system.

The fact that a given domain is structured in different ways by different languages shows, Hjelmslev argues, that a language is a form not a substance, with its own autonomous principles of organization. In the domain of colour, for instance, we find that 'Welsh lacks the English boundary between *blue* and *grey*, and likewise the English boundary between *grey* and *brown*' (Hjelmslev 1943: 53); other examples of this phenomenon are systems of tense and pronouns. But how can an autonomous system be described without characterizing some elements positively, and so appealing to something external to it? This can be done, Hjelmslev argues, by characterizing the elements *only* in terms of the relations they can stand in to other items, so that it matters not at all what the elements are, provided that *they are different from each other*.

The resulting description is a linguistic algebra which Hjelmslev called a *linguistic schema*; whilst the result of interpreting a schema, that is of applying it to a domain, he called a *linguistic usage*. The difference between schema and usage corresponds to a more and a less abstract conception of *la langue*; and for Hjelmslev the primary object of linguistics is the schema. The proper way of studying this is to develop a deductive system and to define its entities relationally. For example, an item of a given kind *A* is said to presuppose an item *B* in a context *C* if *A* cannot occur without *B*, but *B* can occur without *A*; for instance, an indefinite article requires a count-noun in a noun-phrase, but not vice versa. Another relation distinguished by Hjelmslev is that of inter-dependence, that is, of mutual presupposition, which is a relation holding, for instance, between vowels and consonants, or mood and tense. Finally, there is a relation called 'solidarity' which obtains when *A*, though compatible with *B*, can occur without it, and vice versa; for instance, this relationship holds between *accusative* and *plural* within a case system. By appeal to such relationships one can, Hjelmslev argued, characterize a linguistic-schema in purely formal terms without recourse to phonetic, phenomenological or ontological premises. Moreover, he argued that such an abstract study underlines the theory of meaning as well as that of expression-elements. For just as in phonetics 'cat' can be further analysed into /c/, /a/, /t/, so the content of 'ram' can be analysed as 'he-sheep', that of 'horse' as 'he-horse', and so on; so that in formal terms we can ask what is the set of minimal constituents and operations on them which will enable us to describe the structure of the content of the words of a language. To distinguish his conception of linguistics as the study of form, that is of a science which 'would be an algebra of language, operating with unnamed entities' (1943: 79), Hjelmselv coined the term 'glossematics'. Whether so abstract a study could be the fundamental study of a natural language, and indeed whether Saussure thought it could be, seems doubtful. But Hjelmslev's work is important because his development of the Saussurean claim that language is a form led to a formal conception of linguistics, and encouraged the comparison of the structure of natural languages with other formal structures in a number of fruitful ways.

4 Post-Bloomfieldian linguistics and distributional relations

Post-Bloomfieldian linguistics developed sophisticated methodologies for the analysis of a linguistic corpus, and, as an example, we shall concentrate on one of those developed by Z.S. Harris. This methodology did not have to be used when framing hypotheses, Harris argued, but it is needed to check the validity of claims made; and though there is no uniquely correct methodology, 'what is essential is the restriction to distribution as determining the relevance of the inquiry' (Harris 1951: 6). Since distributional relations are ones of co-occurrence or of mutual substitutability, the restriction is tantamount to the Saussurean one of the study of syntagmatic and paradigmatic relations. So that, though a corpus-based study like Harris' has no use for the conception of *la langue*, it does restrict the field of inquiry in one important respect in an analogous way to that in which Saussure did.

A distributional analysis must proceed at two levels, phonemic and morphologic. At each of these levels it must first identify the relevant units, before going on to describe the distributional relations holding between them. To analyse *This is my house* on the morphemic level we must identify its morphemic segments. What shows, for instance, that *house* is such a segment is the fact that it is replaceable by many other *prima facie* segments, such as *car*, *hat* and *dog*, all of which can occur in other environments, such as *She has a* ——, *big* ——, and so forth. Having identified the morphemic segments in a corpus, then to give as compact a description of the corpus as possible it is necessary to group the segments into morphemic classes, and these in turn into more inclusive classes. For instance, segments occurring in the environments *The* —— and ——*s* are classed as *N*; whilst those which occur in ——*ed-past* are classed as *V*, within which class we could, for instance, distinguish segments occurring before *N* (*V-trans*) from those which do not (*V-intrans*). The need for more inclusive classes is shown by the fact that $N + S$ can occur whenever *N* occurs except when *N* itself is $N + S$ – we have both *the dog* and *the dogs* but not *the dogss* – so it is necessary to distinguish $N + S$ from *N* as an N^2. More inclusive classes can be defined in analogous ways, making very compact descriptions of a sentence's constituents (its 'phrase structure') possible. *The boys run*, for instance, consists of a higher order *N* followed by a *V-intrans*; whilst the higher order *N* (an *NP* in more familiar terminology) consists of a determiner and an N^2 which in turn consists of an $N + S$.

The great achievement of the post-Bloomfieldian linguistics was to propose many detailed analyses of sentences in terms of their phrase structure. This made the development of a theory of syntax possible, which is something that Saussure had notoriously failed to do. It also enabled the formulation of a strong hypothesis about *all* theories of structural linguistics, namely that because of the restriction to distributional relations, the most powerful syntactic description of a sentence available to it is of that sentence's phrase structure. Whether the kind of methodology proposed by Harris is capable of yielding such descriptions is another matter. Because of the refusal to appeal to meaning it is fatally flawed from a Saussurean perspective. And whether or not that is so, it seems that to apply his methodology Harris would often have to assume he knew something which at that stage had still to be established; it is hard to see, for instance, how on his account one could identify any morphemic segment unless one had already identified some others. But though the methodology is flawed, the crucial objection – due to Chomsky – is that the linguistic descriptions proposed are inadequate; a phrase structure analysis cannot distinguish *John is eager to please* from *John is easy to please*, for all that in the first *John* is the agent, but not in the second. So despite its many insights and achievements, structural linguistics has inherent limitations.

See also: MOSCOW-TARTU SCHOOL; RUSSIAN LITERARY FORMALISM; STRUCTURALISM; STRUCTURALISM IN LITERARY THEORY; SYNTAX

References and further reading

* Bloomfield, L. (1933) *Language*, New York: Holt. (A classic text which proposes a behaviourist approach to linguistics modelled on contemporary psychology, and sets the agenda for American structuralism.)

Caws, P. (1988) *Structuralism: The Art of the Intelligible*, Atlantic Highlands, NJ: Humanities Press. (Part IB is an excellent introduction to the linguistic basis of structuralism.)

Ducrot, O. and Todorov, T. (1972) *Dictionnaire encyclopédique des sciences du langage*, trans. C. Porter, *Encyclopaedic Dictionary of the Sciences of Language*, Oxford: Blackwell, 1981. (Contains helpful essays on functionalism, glossematics and distributionalism.)

* Harris, Z.S. (1951) *Structural Linguistics*, Chicago, IL: University of Chicago Press. (A classic; Chapter 2 on methodology is an important statement.)

* Hjelmslev, L. (1943) *Omkring sprogteoriens grundloeggelse*, trans. F.J. Whitfield, *Prolegomena to a Theory of Language*, Madison, WI: University of Wisconsin Press, 1961. (The best introduction to Hjelmslev's thinking.)

Joos, M. (ed.) (1958) *Reading in Linguistics: The Development of Descriptive Linguistics in America since 1925*, New York: American Council of Learned Societies. (Amongst other papers in this classic collection, Bloomfield (1926), Harris (1946) and Wells (1947) provide a good introduction to American structural linguistics.)

* Lyons, J. (1973) 'Structuralism and Linguistics', in D. Robey (ed.) *Structuralism, An Introduction*, Oxford: Clarendon Press, 1973, 5–19. (A brilliant introductory essay.)

* Vahek, J. (1966) *The Linguistic School of Prague: An Introduction to its Theory and Practice*, Bloomington, IN, and London: Indiana University Press. (An impressive introduction by a member of the School, with a detailed bibliography.)

D. HOLDCROFT

STRUCTURALISM IN LITERARY THEORY

'Structuralism' is a term embracing a family of theories that between them address all phenomena of the human world – notably language, literature, cookery, kinship relations, dress, human self-perception. In all these domains, structuralists claim, the observable, apparently separate elements are rightly understood only when seen as positions in a structure or system of relations.

The linguist Ferdinand de Saussure is generally recognized as the founder of the structuralist movement. For him semiology – the science of the meaning of natural languages – consists in determining the formal place of any signe *within the inclusive system of signs that is language (*langue*), that is, to see it as a 'difference' among the system of inseparably linked 'differences'. Literary significance is treated in a similar way. But both in linguistic and literary studies the existence of a complete and closed system has been largely anticipated, presupposed rather than confirmed, where no more than fragments of the supposed system could ever really be collected.*

This itself is a point of serious contention: for one thing, the meaning of any fragment of a would-be system seems, on the structuralist view, not to be defined if the full system is not accessible; for another, there is no way to approximate to the inclusive system to which apparent fragments belong. But if that is so, it is asked, then can structuralism – whether applied to literature or to language in general – be a science at all?

1 **Historical overview**
2 **General features of structuralism**
3 **Treatment of literature**

1 Historical overview

The earliest structuralist practitioners include Saussure, the Russian linguist and theorist T.S. Trubetzkoy, and Roman Jakobson. The movement expanded rapidly to encompass a remarkably diverse company, of which the best-known (though not theoretically uniform) contributors include the anthropologist Claude Lévi-Strauss, the psychoanalyst Jacques Lacan, the narratologist Gérard Genette, the early Roland Barthes, the literary critic Michael Riffaterre, the theoretical linguist Louis Hjelmslev, the analyst of narrative and social structure A.J. Greimas, and the folklorist V. Propp. To list such a diverse group is to confirm structuralism's cross-breeding tendencies. This was already apparent in the strong Slavophone branch of the movement, which linked Russian

Formalism with structuralism and saw the flowering of Prague linguistics and literary studies in the second and third decades of the twentieth century. Remarkably, Roman Jakobson was prominent in both Slavic movements and appears to have introduced Lévi-Strauss to structuralism.

Once it became clear that the fixed system of *langue* or literature was unlikely to be determined and the seminal idea of an underlying network of internally linked significative *relata* became more and more generously construed, it became commonplace to recognize conceptual homologues of the structuralist orientation: for instance, in the works of Louis Althusser, Michel Foucault, Mikhail Bakhtin, Northrop Frye, Noam Chomsky, Lucien Goldmann, René Wellek, Jean Piaget, Bourbaki, Pierre Bourdieu, and even Ernst Cassirer. In any case, the general eclipse of the movement's core (that is, the eclipse of the model of a science of 'differences' or *relata* functioning within a closed system of *relata*) has ensured the permanent presence of the structuralist theme itself – among the human studies (for instance, various literary, linguistic and cultural studies). For there is no commanding alternative model of description and explanation among these studies that has been able to displace the semiological (significative, symbolic, syntactive, self-referential or interpretable) dimension of the human world, or to account for it in a way that does not to some extent suggest a system of differentiated *relata* construed as a holist model of rationality (a closed system factored by constituent *relata*).

2   General features of structuralism

Structuralism is traced as a distinct movement largely through the genealogy of its originating theories. For example, it is often claimed that Northop Frye's *Anatomy of Criticism* (1957) contributed to English-language literary structuralism. But Frye is explicitly an Aristotelian; his theory of determinate literary genres is largely based on Aristotle's conception of a biological species applied to forms such as tragedy and related genres that Frye believes fit the same scientific analogy. Frye's 'structuralism' cannot reasonably be traced back to Saussure or Jakobson or to any intermediary figures, and so it is rightly thought not to be structuralist in the original sense of the term, though it bears a remote resemblance to structuralism. A similar argument may be mounted to show that Noam Chomsky is not a structuralist. There is little to be gained from such disputes.

Structuralism was originally motivated by a repugnance for those fields of the human studies that could not reasonably claim the status of a bona fide science – that is, could not address what is distinctive about the human world and at the same time be capable of supporting a methodological rigour comparable to that of the natural sciences. Without ever proving it, the structuralists (notably, Lévi-Strauss) believed that the 'laws of thought' (which supposedly determined the system underlying the phenomena of the human world) were ultimately the same as the laws of physical nature. In fact, they could not provide a sustained account of how the underlying structure could be confirmably abstracted from or imposed a priori on the pertinent phenomena.

The difficulty is deeper than it first appears. Consider that distinctly human phenomena are formed, entrenched and made legible to the apt members of a human society through practices that enable new cohorts both to share those practices and to discern their significance. The aggregated body of such practices is plainly collective, in the sense that no single participating human can master all of them. Oddly, on the one hand the structuralists tend *not* to theorize about the causative conditions under which system-like structures may be deemed to regularize the variable phenomena of cultural life; on the other, there are many theories that admit something like the structuralist thesis but are palpably not structuralist in the relevant sense. Almost any account of societal life – Hegelian, Marxist, Durkheimian, Weberian, Diltheyan, phenomenological, neo-Kantian, hermeneutic, Frankfurt Critical, Wittgensteinian and possibly even Aristotelian – will bear some resemblance to the structuralist emphasis; but that hardly warrants marking them down as structuralists, in all but an unacceptably vacuous sense. It is currently well-nigh impossible to distinguish sharply between structuralist or semiological analyses of literary materials and, for instance, hermeneutic accounts – except for differences in their theoretical lineage.

In this sense, both Barthes (1977) and Bloom (1973) favour the imposition of interpretive codes on canonical texts and canonical readings – codes that claim no canonical validity of their own beyond the power of their sheer plausibility and fresh force; and yet, Barthes, but not Bloom, will be recognized as a kind of structuralist despite his (welcome) liberties. In fact, Jakobson and Lévi-Strauss' analysis of Baudelaire's *Les Chats* (1962), which many claim to be the very paradigm of a structuralist analysis of poetry, has been seriously (and reasonably) challenged – not so much for the details of its analysis as for the mistaken picture of structuralist analysis it affords (Riffaterre 1970).

3   Treatment of literature

To speak of a structuralist account of literature – chiefly poetry and narrative prose – is to emphasize, however informally, one or more of the following themes:

(1) the underlying and invariant laws of mental activity, unconscious at the level of linguistic and other cultural phenomena (Lévi-Strauss' central theme (1967));

(2) a dominant binarism of Saussure's kind (*signif- iant/signifié*), applied congruently with Jakobson's analysis of metaphor and metonomy (1956);

(3) a formal system of interpretive analytic codes said to constitute the underlying structure of the domain in question (notably, in V. Propp (1928) and A.J. Greimas (1987));

(4) any combination of (1)–(3), strictly or loosely.

Any interpretive critic or theorist meeting conditions (1)–(4), exhibiting a relevant lineage, may reasonably be said to be a structuralist. In this sense, Barthes (here, the 'later' Barthes, author of *S/Z*) and Foucault *are* structuralists, in spite of the fact – though possibly because of it – that they are also poststructuralists, that is, critics of the extreme presumption of the canonical structuralists; they are themselves interpretive critics who attack the sense of closure, apodictic certainty, a priori necessity or the fixities of canonical structuralism.

Barthes and Riffaterre provide an interesting contrast in their development; for both may be said to exhibit the general marks of structuralist lineage: in *The Elements of Semiology* (1964), for instance, Barthes accepts a relatively straightforward Saussurean theory; but, in *S/Z* (1970), in 'From Work to Text' (1977) and in other places, he overthrows strict structuralism in a decidedly florid poststructuralist manner. Riffaterre begins early on as a critic of Jakobson's poetic model, but then adheres quite strictly to the closure and relative isolation of the poetic domain itself (1984). Tacitly, Barthes' model calls Riffaterre's closure into question; and Riffaterre's would deny the coherence of Barthes' practice. Yet both are structuralist. Without giving a detailed comparison of their critical methods, it needs to be said that the underlying dispute that their opposed practices implicate is the one that animates Lévi-Strauss' criticism of Jean-Paul Sartre (*Tristes Tropiques* 1955). Lévi-Strauss challenges the putatively superficial history of phenomenal change, favouring instead the 'diachronic' articulation of an underlying 'synchronic' system – and this yields a sense of history deeper than empirical history could ever afford. This is what Lévi-Strauss means by 'anthropology' and its

justified displacement of 'history'. The difference between Barthes and Riffaterre is the difference between Lévi-Strauss' and Sartre's conceptions – within the space of structuralism.

Riffaterre's isolation of the poetic world from the intrusions of contingent history (developed through his theory of reference) justifies in his eyes the rejection of historical hermeneutics, historical genre studies, associative and impressionistic literary criticism and the like. Riffaterre falls back on the implicit codes of interpretation (sets of formal homologues, he believes) rightly applied to the images of particular poems. Barthes, by contrast, invents new interpretive 'codes' *ad hoc* from the 'infinite' resources of our enveloping culture; here, the undeniable ingenuity of his interpretation (in *S/Z*) threatens (implicitly) to confound Riffaterre's exclusiveness. On the historicist side (ultimately, Foucault's theme), the pretence of constructing a fixed, unconscious system is itself no more than an artefact of a contingent *episteme* (a regime of reason or knowledge) that, in time, will also be superseded. On the 'anthropological' side (which Riffaterre advocates), there can be no methodological rigour in a practice of analysis that is entirely open to the vagaries of phenomenal history.

The formalism of the structuralist approach to literature is possibly more the result of Jakobson's conviction and influence than that of any other early structuralist. Jakobson himself theorized more about poetry than narrative prose. But his single most important contribution to a structuralist analysis of literature, abstracted in a relatively late summary (1960), marks the distinction of poetry but also accords implicitly with Propp's influential study on the narrative structure of the folktale, originally published in 1928. Both Barthes (on narrative) and Riffaterre (on poetry) derive from Jakobson, although Barthes is certainly no formalist and Riffaterre expressly objects to Jakobson's theoretical model. The line of narrative analysis (which extends to psychoanalysis and film) may be fruitfully traced to Greimas, Genette, Todorov, Eco and Kristeva. Regarding the analysis of poetry, there is hardly any figure who compares favourably with Riffaterre (1978).

Jakobson's formula (1960) is both famous and arresting: 'The poetic function projects the principle of equivalence from the axis of selection into the axis of combination.' With this, Jakobson means to distinguish between metaphor (vertical equivalences of meaning drawn from a suitable fund: 'selection') and metonomy (horizontal equivalences affected by contiguities of sentential structure: 'combination'); and to indicate the executive direction of poetry *from* the 'associative' equivalences of an imaginative play with images and meanings *to* the 'syntagmatic' equivalences of structural role, stress and the like in sentential contexts. Ironically, Barthes' treatment of *S/Z* may resemble Jakobson's model of poetry more than Riffaterre's treatment of poetry itself.

See also: ALTHUSSER, L.; BAKHTIN, M.; BARTHES, R.; BOURDIEU, P.; CASSIRER, E.; CHOMSKY, N.; FOUCAULT, M.; KRISTEVA, J.; LACAN, J.; LÉVI-STRAUSS, C. §2; PIAGET, J.; SARTRE, J.-P.; STRUCTURALISM; STRUCTURALISM IN LINGUISTICS

References and further reading

* Barthes, R. (1964) *Elements of Semiology*, trans. A. Lavers and C. Smith, London: Jonathan Cape, 1967. (Mentioned in §3. Barthes' view of Saussurean semiology.)

* —— (1970) *S/Z*, trans. R. Miller, New York: Farrar, Straus & Giroux, 1974. (Mentioned in §3. Barthes' freewheeling quasi-structuralist reading of Balzac's *Sarrasine*.)

* —— (1977) 'From Work to Text', in S. Heath (trans.) *Image, Music, Text*, New York: Wang & Hill. (Mentioned in §§2, 3. Perhaps the best-known of Barthes' short statements on reading literature, as a poststructuralist.)

* Bloom, H. (1973) *The Anxiety of Influence*, London: Oxford University Press. (Mentioned in §2. Possibly the best-known American poststructuralist manifesto of critical reading.)

  Caws, P. (1988) *Structuralism: The Art of the Intelligible*, Atlantic Highlands, NJ: Humanities Press International. (A reliable overview of the entire movement.)

* Frye, N. (1957) *Anatomy of Criticism: Four Essays*, Princeton, NJ: Princeton University Press. (Mentioned in §2. Frye's Aristotelian model applied to literature.)

* Greimas, A.J. (1987) *On Meaning*, trans. P. Perron and F.H. Collins, Minneapolis, MN: University of Minnesota Press. (A selection of Greimas' writings, taken from various volumes.)

* Jakobson, R. and Halle, M. (1956) *Fundamentals of Language*, The Hague: Mouton. (Mentioned in §3. Contains Jakobson's discussion of metaphor and metonymy.)

* Jakobson, R. (1960) 'Closing Statement: Linguistics and Poetics', in A. Sebeok (ed.) *Style in Language*, Cambridge, MA: MIT Press, esp. 350–77. (Mentioned in §3. Possibly the most succinct and accessible of Jakobson's statements on poetics.)

* Jakobson, R. and Lévi-Strauss, C. (1962) '"Les Chats" de Charles Baudelaire', *L'Homme* 2 (1): 5–21. (The text of Jakobson and Lévi-Strauss' famous analysis.)

* Lévi-Strauss, C. (1955) *Tristes Tropiques*, trans. J. and D. Weightman, London: Jonathan Cape, 1973. (Mentioned in §3. Autobiographical approach to Lévi-Strauss' reflections on the development of his method.)

* —— (1967) *The Elementary Structures of Kinship*, trans. J.H. Bell, J.R. von Sturmer and R. Needham, Boston, MA: Beacon Press, 1969. (Mentioned in §3. Affords a sense of Lévi-Strauss' view on the laws of the human mind.)

* Propp, V. (1928) *Morphology of the Folktale*, trans. L. Scott, revised L.A. Wagner, Austin, TX: University of Texas Press, 1968, 2nd edn. (Mentioned in §3. The famous structuralist analysis of the folktale.)

* Riffaterre, M. (1970) 'Describing Poetic Structures: Two Approaches to Baudelaire's *Les Chats*', in J. Ehrmann (ed.) *Structuralism*, Garden City, NY: Anchor Books, esp. 188–230. (Mentioned in §2. Riffaterre's well-known criticism of Jakobson and Lévi-Strauss' reading of Baudelaire's poem.)

* —— (1978) *Semiotics of Poetry*, Bloomington, IN: Indiana University Press. (A good introduction to Riffaterre's critical practice.)

* —— (1984) 'Intertextual Representation: On Mimesis as Interpretive Discourse', *Critical Inquiry* 11 (1): 141–62. (Mentioned in §3. A clear summary of Riffaterre's theory of critical reading.)

* Saussure, F. de (1983) *Course in General Linguistics*, trans. R. Harris, La Salle, IL: Open Court. (The essential source of structuralism.)

JOSEPH MARGOLIS

STRUCTURALISM IN SOCIAL SCIENCE

Any school of thought in the social sciences that stresses the priority of order over action is 'structural'. In the twentieth century, however, 'structuralism' has been used to denote a European, largely French language, school of thought that applied methods and conceptions of order developed in structural linguistics to a wide variety of cultural and social phenomena. Structuralism aspired to be a scientific approach to language and social phenomena that, in conceiving of them as governed by autonomous law-governed structures, minimized consideration of social-historical context and individual as well as collective action. Structural linguistics was developed in the early part of the twentieth century primarily by the Swiss linguist, Ferdinand de Saussure. After the Second World War, it fostered roughly three phases of structural approaches to social phenomena. Under the lead of above all the French anthropologist Claude Lévi-Strauss, classical structuralism applied structural linguistic conceptions of structure with relatively little transformation to such social phenomena as kinship structures, myths, cooking practices, religion and ideology. At the same time, the French psychoanalyst Jacques Lacan appropriated Saussure's conceptual apparatus to retheorize the Freudian unconscious. In the 1960s, a second phase of structural thought, neo-structuralism, extended structural linguistic notions of order to a fuller spectrum of social phenomena, including knowledge, politics and society as a whole. Many of Saussure's trademark conceptions were abandoned, however, during this phase. Since the 1970s, a third phase of structuralism has advanced general theories of social life that centre on how structures govern action. In so refocusing structural theory, however, the new structuralists have broken with the conception of structure that heretofore reigned in structural thought.

1 **Social structure**
2 **Structural linguistics**
3 **Classical structuralism**
4 **Neo-structuralism**
5 **The new structuralists**

1 Social structure

The idea of social structure articulates the intuition and experience that social existence is ordered and not merely random and chaotic. Roughly four conceptions of social structure dominate in the social disciplines. At one extreme lies voluntarism, which combines the thesis that all there is to social phenomena are individuals' actions (and mental states) with the idea that with every action individuals wilfully recreate whatever order exists in social life. On this view, there are no real social structures. A second position, considerably more popular than voluntarism, is empiricism, the view that social structures are patterns in actions and practices. These patterns are usually not thought of as determinants of human activity. Rather, they are by-products of actions and practices and the mental states responsible for these. A third conception, grammaticism, assimilates structure to grammatical rules conceived of as nonconscious principles governing speech. On this view, social structures are the sets of rules and principles that govern activities in the different domains of social life. These rules do not determine action, but structure its possibilities, and do so by being embedded in actors' practical understandings or cognitive processes. A final conception, determinism,

construes structures as abstract systems that determine action and social phenomena without working through practical or cognitive understanding. These systems are highly counterintuitive, for they are composed of elements, relations and principles known to social scientists alone. Structuralism typically works with structures of this fourth kind.

2 Structural linguistics

The notions of structure and order applied by later structuralists to cultural and social phenomena were introduced first in linguistics by Ferdinand de Saussure in his *Cours de linguistique générale* (1916). Above all two Saussurian ideas influenced structural thought after the Second World War. The first was that language is an autonomous structure distinct from the world. Saussure conceived of language as a system of signs and of a sign as a combination of signifier and signified. A signifier is a material entity – a sound, image, pencil mark – with meaning. Its meaning is the signified associated with it. Saussure argued that the signifiers and signifieds that together constitute signs are defined solely through their differences with other signifiers and signifieds, respectively. This thesis draws signifiers, signifieds and thereby signs into closed, discrete systems. Language is an autonomous structure of elements defined internally through differences, which can be studied in isolation from the world to which it refers and the activities in which it is used (see SAUSSURE, F. DE).

Saussure's second telling idea was that abstract structures govern spatial-temporal events. The autonomous system of elements that constitutes language (*langue*) is an abstract (or 'synchronic') entity lying outside space and time that governs spatial–temporal (or 'diachronic') acts of speaking and writing (*parole*). This famous distinction between *langue* and *parole*, between abstract and concrete linguistic entities, lines up with at least two further oppositions, namely, depth/surface and essential/accidental. Concrete speech acts are accidental and variable phenomena in comparison to the underlying, abstract and essential structure of language.

Saussure thus detached language from social–historical context as well as from the understandings and practices of actual speakers and writers. In studying language, consequently, both history and people can be bracketed (except for comparative purposes).

3 Classical structuralism

After the Second World War, structuralism broke out of the domain of language (and poetry as well as folklore) to focus upon cultural and social phenomena more generally. Its initial phase was marked by wholesale application of the Saussurian apparatus to social affairs and by the resulting assimilation of these affairs to language. Among the social sciences, classical structuralism enjoyed greatest impact in social anthropology, undoubtedly because of the brilliance of that theorist who, more than any other, epitomizes structural social investigation: Claude LÉVI-STRAUSS.

Heralding structural linguistics as the long awaited breakthrough that set the human studies for the first time firmly on the road to scientific knowledge, Lévi-Strauss proposed to extend the field's methods and conceptions of order to encompass communication, or symbolic, systems generally. He wielded, moreover, an expansive notion of a communication system, one that embraced not only myths, religion, and ideology, but kinship structures and social organization as well.

Lévi-Strauss took from Saussure the idea that communication systems are closed, discrete systems that can be studied in isolation from both socio-historical context and the consciousness of actors. Each communication system and type thereof, moreover, possesses an underlying synchronic structure that governs spatial-temporal practices and contents even though it is unknown to the actors involved. Lévi-Strauss further retained the idea that differences and relations, especially binary oppositions, play a crucial role in defining structural elements.

Structures, for Lévi-Strauss, are scientifically constructed matrices of possible combinations of relations (between elements). In the case of a particular kinship system, for instance, an anthropologist might construct a matrix along whose horizontal axis lie 'warm' (friendly) and 'cold' (distant) brother–sister and husband–wife relations, and along whose vertical axis lie warm and cold father–son and mother's brother–sister's son relations. The kinship structure involved would then consist in the possible combinations of warm and cold relations that can characterize the kinship system. According to Lévi-Strauss, which combinations of relations are possible is determined by a rule of transformation (a law), which thus specifies the range of combinations of warm and cold kin relations possible in the system. In this way, autonomous and internally defined structures lying outside space and time govern spatial-temporal states of affairs encompassing individuals.

Most provocatively, Lévi-Strauss maintained not only that all communication systems of a given type (for example, kinship systems) share certain structures, but that the different communication systems found both in a given society and across societies generally are governed by homologous structures. The

reason for this homology, he hypothesized, was that all communication (symbolic) systems are ultimately grounded in the logical properties of cognitive brain processes.

The grandeur and scope of Lévi-Strauss' vision captivated a generation of anthropologists and other social scientists, especially in France and the UK, and secured for him acclaim as one of the leading twentieth-century theoreticians of social life.

As Lévi-Strauss was extending Saussurian analysis to cultural phenomena, Jacques LACAN was focusing Saussure's signifier–signified model of the sign inward upon the Freudian unconscious. Although Lacan transcended Saussure's conceptions in important ways, and for this reason is labelled a 'post-structuralist' by some commentators, his theories of child development represent one of the most consequent applications of the Saussurian model of the sign to human beings. Like Lévi-Strauss, moreover, Lacan believed that to apply Saussurian conceptions to phenomena other than language is to analyse these phenomena as if they were language. This attitude, it should be noted, also characterizes those 'semiotic' analyses that, in applying Saussure's conception of the sign to social and cultural phenomena, treat those phenomena as systems of signs, for example, some of Roland Barthes' work (see BARTHES, R. §2; SEMIOTICS).

Lacan's account postulated an initial pre-Oedipal, or 'imaginary', phase of development in which the identity of the child is bound up with its mother's body. The subsequent Oedipal, or 'symbolic', phase is inaugurated when the father (the law) divides the child from the mother's body and drives its desire for her underground, thus forming the unconscious. The child's identity now derives from difference (rejection as the mother's lover, absence of the mother's body); and possession of the mother can occur only in the realm of language. So the child's desire for its mother, severed forever from real possession, can only reverberate within the system of language, moving anchorlessly from signifier to signifier. Dreams offer an especially fertile realm of signifiers for the articulation of desire. In this realm, the movement of desire among signifiers, which Freud had referred to as 'dreamwork', is effected by the substitution and association of signifiers. Dreams are series of signifiers, and the unconscious generally a movement of signifiers, whose signifieds are not immediately obvious. Lacan's theory is summed up in his famous epigram, that the unconscious is structured like a language.

Lacan's controversial Saussurian theories of child development and the unconscious have had greater influence in literary studies than in the human sciences. They have also found greater resonance in movements such as academic feminism and post-structuralism that became prominent after structuralism proper. This reflects how Lacan undermines the structural notion of determinate associations between signifiers and signifieds by fracturing desire among a plurality of signifiers to which stable signifieds cannot be attached. It also bespeaks how Lacan, in following Freud and making other people crucial to children's identity and development, opens the door to acknowledging of the crucial impact of society and history upon systems of signifiers and signifieds.

4 Neo-structuralism

During the 1960s, a wide variety of thinkers adopted an array of theses forcefully promoted by classical structuralism: de-emphasis of history, opposition to basing social life in individual subjects, belief in abstract structures and postulation of a governing stratum that underlies the surface appearances of social life. These thinkers were not, however, in a strict sense structuralists. They did not (1) emphasize the role of difference and opposition in the constitution of abstract, underlying structures; (2) employ Saussure's terminology of signifier and signified; or (3) work with a clear distinction between synchrony and diachrony. These changes meant that, although neo-structuralists retained classical structuralism's notion of internally-defined governing structures, they no longer assimilated the social phenomena governed by these structures to language. These changes also facilitated their attempt to extend the scope of governing structures beyond Lévi-Strauss' communications systems to embrace political systems, the organization of knowledge, and societies as wholes. Accordingly, neo-structuralism exploded classical structuralism's confinement primarily to social anthropology and spread structural ways of thinking to political theory, history and sociology.

Perhaps the most prominent branch of neo-structuralism was so-called 'structural Marxism'. Led by the French thinker Louis ALTHUSSER, this school theorized society as a set of political, economic, cultural, educational and other structures. The structures comprising a given society were thought to form a total state of interrelatedness, moreover, to which Althusser gave the name 'mode of production'. For the structural Marxists, all social change is a matter of either the recalibration of the different structures constituting a given society (piecemeal change), or the lining up of these structures in a 'structural conjunction' that enables wholesale transformation of the mode of production (revolution). All social causality and change is thus rooted in the realm of interlocking structures. Individuals, as mere occupants of positions established by structures, are powerless to effect change. Significantly, Althusser abandoned Marx's claim that the economy determined all other social sectors, arguing instead that the economic structure determined the remainder of social life only 'in the last instance'. Although this represented a welcome loosening of economic determinism, Althusser's extreme structural determinism made his position unpalatable to most.

A second especially fertile ground for the broadening of structural thinking was the organization of human knowledge. Jean PIAGET and Michel FOUCAULT proposed that human knowledge forms systems governed by abstract principles. Piaget elaborated an account of the genetic stages though which children's knowledge of the world progresses, on each level of which a different set of principles structures knowledge. Foucault, meanwhile, espied three large-scale *epistemes* in Western history since the Middle Ages, in each of which different rules governed the formulation and certification of knowledge of living beings, language and wealth. During each such period, in his view, knowledge of these matters formed systems governed by rules that were unknown to the individual thinkers and researchers who complied with them. But while Foucault retained the structural marginalization of the individual subject, he like Lacan contravened the structural slighting of history. The rules governing knowledge are 'historical a prioris' that change over time. His work thus broke down the distinction between synchrony and diachrony, and in this and other ways marked a shift into post-structuralism.

5 The new structuralists

Classical and neo-structuralism's de-emphasis of history and agency worked against them in the 1970s and 1980s. Social theorists increasingly found it implausible to isolate communication and sign systems, and social phenomena more broadly, from either speakers/writers/actors or the social-historical contexts of speech, script and action. This, together with (1) the post-structural assault on the differences and binary oppositions wielded by classical structuralists, (2) the earlier mentioned (§3) break-up of determinate associations between signifiers, signifieds and referents, (3) the inability of structuralists to theorize satisfactorily the connections between abstract structures and action-practices, and (4) the spreading European reaction against unself-critical scientistic approaches in the social sciences, dampened enthusiasm for both flavours of structural thought.

Remnants of these movements remain however. Cultural studies in the 1980s and 1990s still widely employed Saussure's figure of signifier–signified. The idea of abstract, underlying structures that govern social phenomena similarly persisted in the social sciences. That these structures are composed of relations also persevered as an influential notion.

Revisions of the latter two ideas formed the heart of a third phase of structural thinking. The 'new structuralists' – the French anthropologist Pierre BOURDIEU, the English sociologist Anthony Giddens and the English philosopher Roy Bhaskar (see CRITICAL REALISM) – prolonged structuralism's emphasis on governing structures. In constructing theories of social life in general, moreover, they perpetuated the structural Marxist attempt to theorize all of social life as governed by structures. Their pursuit of this aim, however, granted action unprecedented prominence: structures relate to social phenomena only by way of governing the actions that constitute these phenomena.

This move underlay the profoundest difference between new structuralism and the two prior phases of structural thought. Structures are not autonomous systems outside space and time whose relations to social phenomena and spatial-temporal doings are an unresolved enigma. Structures instead govern action in being the contents of the practical knowledge on the basis of which people act and interact. The new structuralists thus abandoned the hitherto reigning 'deterministic' conception of structure in favour of a 'grammatical' one (see §1). Indeed, on their view, not only does structure govern action, but structure exists and is able to govern action only because action draws on and thus renews structure. Structure is both the medium and result of action. This circular dependency was accompanied by retheorization of how structures 'govern' action. In Giddens, for example, structures accomplish this by opening and closing possibilities of action.

At the same time, the new structuralists reached back to classical structuralism in depicting the structures embedded in practical understanding as centrally composed of relations and differences. Giddens, for instance, theorized structures as sets of interrelated rules (of meaning and normativity) and resources (arising from commands over persons and objects). These sets are linked by relations of interconvertibility, and thereby form 'structural sets'; redolent of Lévi-Strauss' matrices, that govern systems of action and practice. Bourdieu, meanwhile, exhibited greatest continuity with classical structuralism, construing the structures that govern action and practice as systems of oppositions (such as those between up/down, hot/cold and wet/dry). He com-

bated the hypostatization of abstract structure pervasive in the two earlier phases of structuralism, however, by basing the system of oppositions on opposed movements of the human body and on the biological difference between male and female.

Despite their abandonment of the deterministic notion of structure, the new structuralists perpetuated Saussurian thinking in their accounts of grammatical structure. The future of structural thinking presumably rests on the possibility of further novel transformations of traditional structural themes.

See also: POST-STRUCTURALISM IN THE SOCIAL SCIENCES §1

References and further reading

Althusser, L. (1965) *Pour Marx*, Paris: Librairie François Maspero S.A.; trans. B. Brewster, *For Marx*, London: Allen Lane, 1969. (A difficult but rewarding entry into structural Marxism.)

Barthes, R. (1957) *Mythologies*, Paris: Éditions du Seuil; trans. A. Lavers, New York: Hill & Wang, 1972. (An entertaining work illustrating the influence of structuralism on semiotics.)

Bourdieu, P. (1980) *Le sens pratique*, Paris: Éditions de Minuit; trans. R. Nice, *The Logic of Practice*, Stanford, CA: Stanford University Press, 1990. (A masterful but difficult theory of the relations between practice and structure combining a structural emphasis on oppositions with a strong practical sensibility.)

Foucault, M. (1966) *Les Mots et les choses*, Paris: Éditions Gallimard; trans. A. Sheridan, *The Order of Things*, London: Tavistock, 1970. (Foucault's analysis of the three *epistemes* of modernity and their limits.)

Giddens, A. (1979) *Central Problems in Social Theory*, Berkeley, CA: University of California Press. (A comprehensive work that surveys central questions while constructing answers through an innovative theory of action-structure.)

Lacan, J. (1966) *Écrits*, Paris: Éditions du Seuil; trans. A. Sheridan, *Écrits: A Selection*, London: Tavistock, 1977. (An extremely difficult collection of essays setting forth Lacan's account of child development and the unconscious.)

Lévi-Strauss, C. (1958) *Anthropologie structurale*, Paris: Librairie Plon; trans. C. Jacobson and B.G. Schoepf, *Structural Anthropology*, New York: Basic Books, 1963. (An accessible and recommended introduction to the dimensions and concerns of classical structuralism.)

—— (1962) *La Pensée sauvage*, Paris: Librairie Plon; *The Savage Mind*, Chicago, IL: University of

Chicago Press, 1966. (A somewhat more difficult and synoptic presentation of classical structuralism.)

Piaget, J. (1970) *Genetic Epistemology*, trans. Eleanor Duckworth, New York: Columbia University Press. (A succinct introduction to structural epistemology.)

Robey, D. (ed.) (1973) *Structuralism: An Introduction*, Oxford: Clarendon Press. (A useful multidisciplinary overview of the subject.)

* Saussure, F. de (1916) *Cours de linguistique générale*, C. Bally, A. Sechechaye and A. Riedlinger (eds), Paris: Payot; trans. W. Baskin, *Course in General Linguistics*, New York: Philosophical Library, 1959. (The original formulation of structural linguistics that underlies all subsequent structuralism, semiotics, and post-structuralism.)

THEODORE R. SCHATZKI

SUÁREZ, FRANCISCO (1548–1617)

Francisco Suárez was the main channel through which medieval philosophy flowed into the modern world. He was educated first in law and, after his entry into the Jesuits, in philosophy and theology. He wrote on all three subjects. His philosophical writing was principally in the areas of metaphysics, psychology and philosophy of law, but in both his philosophical and theological works he treated many related epistemological, cosmological and ethical issues. While his basic outlook is that of a very independent Thomist, his metaphysics follows along a line earlier drawn by Avicenna (980–1037) and Duns Scotus (1266–1308) to treat as its subject 'being in so far as it is real being'. By the addition of the word 'real' to Aristotle's formula, Suárez emphasized Aristotle's division of being into categorial being and 'being as true', as well as Aristotle's exclusion of the latter from the object of metaphysics. Divided into a general part dealing with the concept of being as such, its properties and causes, and a second part which considers particular beings (God and creatures) in addition to the categories of being, Suárez's metaphysics ends with a notable treatment of mind-dependent beings, or 'beings of reason'. These last encompass negations, privations and relations of reason, but Suárez's treatment centres on those negations which are 'impossible' or self-contradictory. Inasmuch as such beings of reason cannot exist outside the mind, they are excluded from the object of metaphysics and relegated to the status of 'being as true'. In philosophy of law he was a proponent of natural law and of a theory of government in which power comes from God through the people. He was important for the early development of modern international law and the doctrine of just war. While his brand of Thomism was opposed in his own time and after by some scholastics, especially Dominicans, he had great authority among his fellow Jesuits, as well as other Catholic and Protestant authors. Outside scholasticism, he has influenced a variety of modern thinkers.

1 Life and works
2 Metaphysics
3 Philosophical psychology
4 Philosophy of law and society
5 Influence

1 Life and works

Francisco Suárez was born at Granada in Spain. After preparatory studies, in 1561 he enrolled at the University of Salamanca, where he studied law until on 16 June 1564 he entered the Society of Jesus (the Jesuits). Three months later he began the study of philosophy. In October 1566, still at Salamanca, he went on to theological studies. Chief among his mentors in these was the Dominican, Juan Mancio (1497–1576), himself a successor of Francisco de VITORIA (*c.*1486–1546) in Salamanca's principal chair of theology.

Following his theological studies, Suárez began to teach philosophy in 1570, initially at Salamanca and then at Segovia. Ordained a priest in 1572, he continued to lecture in philosophy until, in 1574, at the Jesuit College, Valladolid, he began his main life's work as a theology teacher. Later he taught theology at Avila (1575), Segovia (1575), Valladolid again (1576), Rome (1580), Alcalá (1585) and Salamanca (1593). In 1597, he assumed the principal chair of theology at the University of Coimbra, in which he remained until his retirement in 1615.

Besides teaching, Suárez took part in theological and political disputes. The most famous of these was the debate *De auxiliis* (On the Helps [for Salvation]), between sixteenth-century Jesuits and Dominicans. The controversy concerned God's foreknowledge and causality, grace and human freedom. In this debate Suárez, along with fellow Jesuits, Robert Bellarmine (1542–1621) and Luis de MOLINA (1535–1600), allowed for divine prerogatives but championed human free will. On the core question of conditional future contingents (*futuribilia*), Suárez adopts Molina's doctrine of a 'middle knowledge' that falls between God's knowledge of merely possible things and God's knowledge of things other than himself that are, were, or will be actual. However, he modifies Molina's view that God knows all things other than himself by a 'super-comprehension' of them in his own essence, substituting for this a view that God knows these things immediately in themselves as they exist in a purely intentional or objective way. More political was a quarrel between the republic of Venice and the papacy about the limits of papal jurisdiction. In defence of the papal position, Suárez in 1607 composed a treatise, *De immunitate ecclesiastica a Venetis violata* (On the Ecclesiastical Immunity Violated by the Venetians). Commending his effort, Pope Paul V stated that the work revealed its author to be 'an eminent and pious theologian'. From this came the honorific title with which Suárez passed into history – *Doctor eximius ac pius* (Eminent and Pious Teacher).

The majority of Suárez's writings are theological, often corresponding to specific parts of the *Summa theologiae* of Thomas AQUINAS (§6), but there is also the extremely influential *De legibus seu de Deo legislatore* (On Laws or on God the Legislator), the fruit of Suárez's teaching between 1601 and 1603, published at Coimbra in 1612. Outside the Thomistic framework are the work on ecclesiastical immunity mentioned above and, at Coimbra in 1613, the *Defensio fidei catholicae adversus anglicanae sectae errores, cum responsione ad apologiam pro juramento fidelitatis et praefationem monitoriam serenissimi Jacobi Angliae Regis* (Defence of the Catholic Faith against the Errors of the Anglican Sect, with a Reply to the 'Apology' for the 'Oath of Fidelity' and the 'Warning Preface' of James, the Most Serene King of England). Upon its publication, this work, which details Suárez's political philosophy, was condemned by James I and publicly burned in London, because in it Suárez had opposed the absolute right of kings and defended the indirect power of the papacy over temporal rulers, as well as the right of the citizens to resist a tyrannical monarch. Suárez even defended tyrannicide in the case of a monarch deposed for heresy by the pope.

2 Metaphysics

Also outside the Thomistic framework are the two volumes of Suárez's most important work, the *Disputationes metaphysicae* (Metaphysical Disputations), which first appeared at Salamanca in 1597. A résumé of his own and previous thought on myriad questions, it is arranged in the form of fifty-four 'Disputations' dealing systematically with metaphysics. In this format, Suárez's volumes mark a radical departure from previous metaphysical treatises, which usually had been either short works, such as Aquinas'

De ente et essentia (On Being and Essence), or commentaries on the text of Aristotle.

The *Disputationes metaphysicae* is a feat of learning. After stating each problem, Suárez has searched the history of philosophy and theology for solutions offered to it. Every conceivable Greek, Arabic, patristic and especially scholastic writer seems to have been cited at least once. As many as twenty-two opinions have been cited in connection with a single question. The historian J. Iturrioz (see Martín, Ceñal, Hellin *et al.* 1948) has compiled a list of 7,709 of these citations, which refer to 245 different authors. Of these, ARISTOTLE was mentioned most often (a total of 1,735 times), and AQUINAS the next most (cited 1,008 times). No mere compiler of opinions, Suárez was an independent thinker who, as he reported positions and gave due regard even to those he opposed, was intent on presenting his own metaphysics.

The disputations begin with Suárez telling us that the object of metaphysics is 'being in so far as it is real being' (*Disputationes metaphysicae* 1). To explain this, he employs two distinctions, already familiar among scholastic authors. The first of these is between the 'formal concept' as an act of the mind, and the 'objective concept' as what that act immediately intends as its object. This latter may be some individual thing or some common or universal character (*ratio*). Again, it may be something actual, possible or merely objective. The second distinction falls between 'being (*ens*) taken as a participle' (which refers to an actual existent), rather than 'being taken as a noun' (which refers to whatever is not a mere fiction but is true in itself and apt really to exist). The object of metaphysics is then more exactly identified with the 'common objective concept of being as a noun' (*Disputationes* 2). This object, which reflects Avicenna's interpretation of Aristotle's *Metaphysics*, prescinds from existence and, precisely as common, transcends all genera, species and differences to encompass everything real, from extrinsic denominations (such as 'being right', 'being left', 'being known' or 'being willed'), through mere possibles (which at their core reduce to non-contradiction), to actual created substances and accidents, to the subsistent, purely actual and necessary reality of God. Over the range of such beings, the common concept of being is analogous with 'an analogy of intrinsic attribution'. In this analogy, a unified concept is shared in an ordered way by different beings (God and creatures, substance and accidents) inasmuch as the being of what is posterior depends upon the being of what is prior (see LANGUAGE, RENAISSANCE PHILOSOPHY OF §4).

After a general treatment (*Disputationes* 3) of the transcendental properties of every being as it is a being – namely, unity, truth and goodness – questions are raised under unity about individuation, universal natures, and various kinds of distinction (*Disputationes* 5–7). Rejecting the Aristotelian and Thomistic account of individuation in terms of 'quantified matter', as well as Scotistic 'thisness', Suárez comes close to nominalism and says that every thing is individual by its very entity. On universals, he again leans towards nominalism and denies any real common nature independent of individuals, yet he insists that the universalizing activity of the mind has a foundation in the likenesses of things. Restricting distinctions to real, rational and modal, he rejects the formal distinction, which Duns Scotus asserted to be present between 'formalities' prior to any operation of the intellect. In following disputations, discussion of truth, which centres on the conformity of formal with objective concepts, is balanced by discussion of falsity (*Disputationes* 8–9); and discussion of goodness is balanced by that of evil, which in standard scholastic fashion is regarded as a privation of good (*Disputationes* 10–1). The twelfth disputation generally treats causes, while 13–25 deal specifically with material, formal, efficient and final causes. Concluding this first part is a consideration of causes in comparison with their effects and in relation one to another (*Disputationes* 26–7).

The second part opens with the main division and principal analogy of being between infinite and finite (*Disputationes* 28). The existence of God is then causally demonstrated in an expressly metaphysical way which, again reflecting Avicenna, employs the principle, 'Everything which comes to be, comes to be by another' (*Disputationes* 29) and follows the analogous common concept of being from lesser and lower being to a First Being. In the same disputation, Suárez rejects any physical demonstration, like that of Aristotle, adopted by Averroes and Aquinas, which would employ the principle, 'Everything which is moved is moved by another', to pass from motion to a First Mover. Suárez goes on to investigate the perfection, simplicity, immensity, immutability, wisdom and omnipotence of God (*Disputationes* 30). Disputation 31 begins treatment of finite being with a denial of the Thomistic distinction in creatures between essence and existence, which Suárez understands as falling between two 'things' (*res*). Rejecting Scotistic formal or modal distinctions, Suárez says that the only distinction here is one of reason with a foundation in reality. Disputation 32 considers substance and accidents in general, plus the analogy of being between created substances and accidents. Substance is treated in detail through the next four disputations while the different categories of accident are the subject matter of Disputations 37–53.

Of particular interest is Disputation 47, where Suárez treats real relations, which divide into transcendental and predicamental. Transcendental relations – such as those between matter and form, accidents and substance, creatures and God – transcend the lines of categories, whereas predicamental relations are restricted to the accidental category of relation. Every such relation (for example, one of likeness) involves a real subject (one person), a real terminus (another person), and a real foundation (brown hair), but Suárez maintains in nominalist fashion that a predicamental relation is ultimately identical with its foundation, as this exists in both the subject and the terminus. The work concludes with a discussion of 'beings of reason', which divide into negations (including impossible objects), privations and reason-dependent relations – all of which fall outside real being, the object of metaphysics (*Disputationes* 54).

3 Philosophical psychology

While Suárez treated topics like abstraction, universal knowledge and personhood also within metaphysics, he regarded philosophical psychology as properly a part of physics (that is, the Aristotelian philosophy of nature). His work *De anima* (On the Soul), which he was revising at the time of his death and which was again a systematic presentation rather than itself a commentary, returned to the medieval tradition of commentary on Aristotle's *On the Soul*. Divided into six books, it dealt successively with the nature, attributes, faculties, operations and ultimate status of the rational soul, which in the human composite is related to the body as form to matter.

The only substantial form of a human being, the rational soul is principle for a variety of vegetative, sensitive and intellectual activities (*De anima* I). The distinction among such activities indicates specifically distinct powers (vegetative, sensitive and intellectual) from which they immediately stem, as well as a real distinction between such powers and the soul itself (II c.1–2). Differing from the whole scholastic tradition, Suárez unites the common sense, imagination, memory and estimative sense in one internal sense power (III c.30). At the intellectual level, he distinguishes between the adequate object of the intellect as such (that is, being as being, which embraces all intelligible items), and the object proportionate to the human intellect in its present state (that is, sensible or material things). He also allows for a direct and immediate knowledge of the singular (IV c.1–2). The excellence of its intellectual operations indicates the intrinsic spirituality and the transcendence of the soul over the body (I c.9).

For the immortality of the soul, Suárez offers two

main arguments (*De anima* I c.10). First, inasmuch as the human intellective power is incorporeal and spiritual it is also substantially simple. Therefore, of its nature it is incorruptible and thus immortal. Second, under the justice of God evil persons should be punished and good persons rewarded. However, that often does not happen in this life. Therefore, there must be another life in which it can happen and this can only be if the soul is immortal.

Both in this life and in any afterlife the soul alone without the body would be less than a full human being. To designate it as such, Suárez accepts the bold word of CAJETAN (§3–4): the soul by itself is a 'semi-person' (*De anima* VI c.1). This incomplete character of the soul alone may suggest a philosophical suasion for the resurrection of the body (VI c.9) (see ARIS-TOTELIANISM, RENAISSANCE §§4–5).

4 Philosophy of law and society

For Suárez all law stems from the 'eternal law', which is 'a free decree of the will of God establishing the order to be observed either generally by all parts of the universe in relation to the common good... or especially to be observed by intellectual creatures in their free operations' (*De legibus* II c.3). In so emphasizing God's will, Suárez has distinguished himself from Aquinas who identified the eternal law with divine reason as it governs the created universe.

Immediately derived from the eternal law is the natural law which resides in human minds and enables human beings to discern moral good and evil (see NATURAL LAW). Suárez (*De legibus* II c.7) tells us that natural law first embraces general moral principles like: 'Good must be done and evil avoided' and 'Do not do to anyone else what you would not want done to you'. Next come principles more particular but still evident from their terms, such as: 'Justice should be observed', 'God should be worshipped', 'One should live with self-control', and so on. From these principles come conclusions more or less easily and broadly known, for example, that such things as adultery and theft are wrong. Requiring more reasoning and not easily known to all are conclusions like: fornication is intrinsically evil, usury is unjust, or lying is never justified.

While it may be affected extrinsically because of changed circumstances, no true principle of natural law can be diminished or dispensed from by any human law or power (*De legibus* II c.14 n.5). Rejecting both the opinion of WILLIAM OF OCKHAM, that God can dispense from the entire Decalogue and could indeed abrogate the whole natural law, and the opinion of Duns Scotus, that God can dispense from the precepts in the second table of the Decalogue

(which regard human beings or other creatures), Suárez maintains that the whole Decalogue is indispensible even by the absolute power of God (c.15 n.16). Thus, even though it is rooted in the divine will, law is not arbitrary either for men or for God.

Close on natural law, the 'law of nations' (*jus gentium*) has the general character of positive law but differs from the civil law of particular states. Unwritten, it has been established not by a single state but by the customs of almost all nations (*De legibus* II c.19 n.7). It thus originates in human consensus and it can in principle, though not with ease, be changed.

In one sense, the *jus gentium* is 'the law of nations among themselves (*inter se*)' – a law which different nations are obliged to observe *vis-à-vis* one another. Such items as the immunity of ambassadors and free commerce, as well as the 'right of war' (*jus belli*), belong to the *jus gentium* understood in this way. In a second way, it is 'the law of nations within themselves (*intra se*).' This is the law which individual states commonly observe within their own borders. Items such as the division of goods or possessions, private property, buying and selling, and the use of money, belong to the *jus gentium* taken in this second way. The first way, which is effectively an international law, is most properly called 'the law of nations' (*De legibus* II c.19 n.10).

Like other Catholic thinkers of his day, Suárez did not regard war as intrinsically evil (see WAR AND PEACE, PHILOSOPHY OF §2). Although it was deplorable and should be avoided wherever possible, at times war was the only option open for the preservation of the republic, which has a right and even an obligation to defend itself (*De legibus* II c.18 n.5). That any war be 'just', proper authority (legitimate, public and supreme) was required to declare it. Again, a just cause of sufficient gravity was needed. Furthermore, right conduct should be the rule at the beginning of the war, in its prosecution and in victory afterwards. As regards authority to declare and wage it, war may be based upon one state's right to punish or avenge an injury done to it by another. Each state, 'supreme in its own order' – that is, the temporal order – with no tribunal beyond, has the authority forcibly to redress injuries against itself (c.19 n.8).

Because civil power as such is not greater in Christian than in pagan princes, Christians can have no more reason than pagans for a just war. Neither can Christians make war against pagans solely because these lack faith. By Suárez's time, questions raised by the evangelization of the Native Americans were largely settled for Catholic thinkers. From Vitoria on, it was commonly held that they were human beings, masters of their own lives and possessions, and that it was not lawful without just cause to subjugate and despoil them – even in order to Christianize them. This was also Suárez's position, which he took, however, on an abstract level, almost without mention of the Native Americans. Against a possible application to them of Aristotle's division of human beings into those fitted by nature to rule and those who were by nature 'slaves' (*Politics* 1.5.1254a18–1255a2), Suárez's view was simple and direct. It is incredible to say that all the people in any region or province have been born 'monstrous and in a way that contradicts the natural disposition' of human beings to be free (*De justitia* q.6). In fact, all persons, as made in the image of God, are equally capable of dominion over themselves and their possessions (*Defence of the Catholic Faith* III c.1).

At its origin, the state is natural; but it is also voluntary (see STATE, THE). Free persons, naturally inclined to political association, must still agree to it. Hence, the state itself arises out of a contract, or 'a consensus', explicit or tacit, freely entered into by the community (*De legibus* III c.3). People are not forced by nature to choose any particular form of state and in fact different forms exist, with a natural equality among them all. In practice, the best kind of government is some form of monarchy (c.4). But what form a monarchy takes and how much power any monarch has will depend upon the terms of the initial grant of the people (*Defensio fidei catholicae* III c.2). Thus, civil authority or power, in any form, is ultimately from nature, and the God of nature, but immediately from the people.

Even though each state is 'supreme in its own order', the power and laws of one end where those of another begin. Again, while the state has power to enact laws from which there is no appeal to any other earthly tribunal, the power of any state, even within its own territory, is not absolute. Though ordinarily their gift of power is irrevocable, in principle the people retain authority over their government. Accordingly, as the common good demands, political power, even that of a monarch, may in different circumstances be changed or limited (*Defensio fidei catholicae* III c.3).

Other restrictions on state power occur inasmuch as it stops short at the private zone of families and individuals. For these are by nature prior to the state. In addition, human beings are not just citizens of this world. And while he admits a legitimate concern by the republic for its members' morality, Suárez tells us that, even at a natural level, each person aims at a final happiness which transcends the reach of civil law and power (*De legibus* III c.11).

While temporal power is ultimately from God, immediately its origin is natural and human; in contrast, ecclesiastical power is directly of divine origin, 'from the special promise and grant of Christ' (*Defensio fidei catholicae* III c.6 n.17). Although church and state are each 'supreme in [their] own order', the basic relation between the two is hierarchical, comparable to that between the soul and the body (*De legibus* IV c.9 n.3). The power of the many states of this world is directly and exclusively within the temporal order, aiming at a common temporal good of 'political happiness' (I c.13). The power of the one Christian church, pointed towards the eternal salvation of its members, is directly within the spiritual order. Indirectly, however, that church has power over a Christian state even in temporal matters (III c.6). Conversely, civil power, at least in Christian states, is indirectly dependent upon and should be at the service of the higher goal of the church (*Defensio fidei catholicae* III c.5). Suárez acknowledged in this a certain inequality between Christian and infidel princes, but he counts it a plus for Christian states and sovereigns that their power is raised to a new height in its subordination to the church (c.30) (see POLITICAL PHILOSOPHY, HISTORY OF §8).

5 Influence

Suárez exercised wide and deep influence on post-Renaissance Catholic scholasticism. Also, largely through the growth and agency of the Jesuit Order, Suarezian metaphysics spread from the Catholic schools of Iberia to various northern European locales. It penetrated the Lutheran universities of Germany where the *Disputationes metaphysicae* (of which seventeen editions appeared between 1597 and 1636) was pondered especially by those who preferred Melanchthon's attitude towards philosophy to Luther's. Indeed, in a number of seventeenth-century Lutheran universities it served as a textbook in philosophy. In much the same way, Suárez had major influence in the Reformed tradition of German and Dutch schools for both metaphysics and law, including international law. To sense Suárez's importance here for the provenance of modern international law, it is enough to recall that, for the famous Dutch jurisprudent, Hugo GROTIUS, the Jesuit doctor was a philosopher and theologian of such penetration 'that he hardly had an equal' (*Epistola* CLIV; quoted in Scorraille 1912–3, vol. 2: 437).

As Martin HEIDEGGER later saw it, Suárez was the main source through which Greek ontology passed from the Middle Ages to usher in the metaphysics and the transcendental philosophy of modern times. Most likely, Suarezian metaphysics was that first learned by DESCARTES from his Jesuit teachers at La Flèche. On at least one occasion he refers to the *Disputationes*, of which he is believed to have owned a copy. LEIBNIZ boasted that while yet a youth he had read Suárez 'like a novel'. SCHOPENHAUER, in his chief work, *Die Welt als Wille und Vorstellung* (The World as Will and Representation), displays much acquaintance with the *Disputationes*, which he values as 'an authentic compendium of the whole scholastic tradition' (quoted in Grabmann 1926: 535). Similarly, Franz BRENTANO, in his 1862 work on the manifold meaning of being according to Aristotle (*Von der mannigfachen Bedeutung des Seienden nach Aristoteles*), has recommended the *Disputationes metaphysicae* to anyone who wants to learn of the diversity of medieval views on Aristotle. But perhaps most strikingly, for Christian von Wolff (whose *Ontologia* Immanuel Kant thought practically coterminous with pre-critical metaphysics) it was 'Francisco Suárez, of the Society of Jesus, who among scholastics pondered metaphysical questions with particular penetration' (*Philosophia prima sive ontologia* I.2.3 n.169; quoted in Gilson 1952: 117).

See also: AQUINAS, T.; ARISTOTELIANISM, RENAISSANCE; COLLEGIUM CONIMBRICENSE; INTERNATIONAL RELATIONS, PHILOSOPHY OF; MOLINA, L. DE; NATURAL LAW; WAR AND PEACE, PHILOSOPHY OF

List of works

Suárez, F. (1590–1617) *Opera omnia* (Complete Works), Paris: Louis Vivès, 1856–66, 26 vols; two supplementary volumes of indices, 1878. (This is the latest and most accessible edition of Suárez's complete works.)

—— (1584) *De justitia et jure* (On Justice and Law), ed. J. Giers, in *Die Gerechtigkeitslehre des jungen Suárez: Edition und Untersuchung seiner Römischen Vorlesungen 'De Iustitia et Iure'*, Freiburg im Breisgau, 1958. (Suárez's early lectures at Rome on justice and law; cited in §4.)

—— (1597a) *Disputationes metaphysicae* (Metaphysical Disputations), in F. Suárez, *Opera omnia*, vols 25–6, Paris: Louis Vivès, 1856–66; repr. Hildesheim: Olms, 1965. (Suárez's systematic presentation of metaphysics.)

—— (1597b) *Disputatio V: Individual Unity and its Principle*, trans. J.J.E. Gracia, in *Suárez on Individuation*, Milwaukee, WI: Marquette University Press, 1982. (In addition to its own intrinsic worth, this disputation is important for its possible influence on the young Leibniz.)

—— (1597c) *On Formal and Universal Unity (Disputatio VI)*, trans. J.F. Ross, Milwaukee, WI:

Marquette University Press, 1964. (This disputation contains Suárez's teaching on the problem of the universals which situates him between medieval nominalism and realism.)

—— (1597d) *On the Various Kinds of Distinctions (Disputatio VII)*, trans. C. Vollert, Milwaukee, WI: Marquette University Press, 1947. (In connection with Suárez's own theory, this disputation presents an overview of medieval doctrines of distinction.)

—— (1597e) *The Metaphysics of Good and Evil according to Suárez: Metaphysical Disputations X and XI and Selected Passages from Disputation XXII and Other Works*, trans. J.J.E. Gracia and D. Davis, München: Philosophia, 1989. (These disputations contain Suárez's basic metaphysical optimism, and the translation contains a good introduction plus a very useful glossary.)

—— (1597f) *On Efficient Causality: Metaphysical Disputations 17, 18, and 19*, trans. A.J. Freddoso, New Haven, CT: Yale University Press, 1994. (These disputations give an excellent overview of the medieval Aristotelian tradition as well as Suárez's own teaching on efficient causality.)

—— (1597g) *On the Essence of Finite Being as Such, on the Existence of that Essence and their Distinction (Disputatio XXXI)*, trans. and intro. N.J. Wells, Milwaukee, WI: Marquette University Press, 1983. (Contains Suárez's famed denial of the real distinction of essence and existence in creatures.)

—— (1597h) *On Beings of Reason (De Entibus Rationis): Metaphysical Disputation LIV*, trans. and intro. J.P. Doyle, Milwaukee, WI: Marquette University Press, 1995. (This disputation was very influential for the development of late scholastic intentionality theory.)

—— (1607) *De immunitate ecclesiastica a Venetis violata* (On the Ecclesiastical Immunity Violated by the Venetians), in J.B. Malou (ed.) *Opuscula sex inedita*, Brussels and Paris: Greuse, 1859. (Treatise on the superiority of papal authority over that of the Venetian republic.)

—— (1612) *De legibus seu de Deo legislatore* (On Laws or on God the Legislator), in L. Pereña *et al.* (eds) *Corpus Hispanorum de Pace*, vols 11–7, 21–2, Madrid: Consejo Superior de Investigaciones Cientificas, 1971–81. (A Latin–Spanish edition of *De legibus*, with good commentary and excellent footnotes.)

—— (1612–21) *Selections from Three Works of Francisco Suárez, S.J.*, trans. G.L. Williams *et al.*, in J.B. Scott (ed.) *Classics of International Law* 20, Oxford: Clarendon Press, 1944, 2 vols. (Translates passages from the *De legibus*, *Defensio fidei*, and a section from the treatise 'On Charity' which contains Suárez's teaching on war.)

—— (1613) *Defensio fidei catholicae adversus anglicanae sectae errores, cum responsione ad apologiam pro juramento fidelitatis et praefationem monitoriam serenissimi Jacobi Angliae Regis* (Defence of the Catholic Faith against the Errors of the Anglican Sect, with a Reply to the 'Apology' for the 'Oath of Fidelity' and the 'Warning Preface' of James, the Most Serene King of England), Coimbra; in F. Suárez, *Opera omnia*, vol. 24, Paris: Louis Vivès, 1856–66. (Outlines Suárez's political philosophy; the work's opposition to absolute monarchy lead to its public condemnation in England.)

—— (1614) *Defensio fidei III. Principatus politicus o la soberania popular* (Defence of Faith III: the Political Supremacy of Popular Sovereignty), trans. and ed. E. Elorduy and L. Pereña, Madrid: Consejo Superior de Investigaciones Cientificas, 1965. (A Latin and Spanish edition of part of the *Defensio fidei*, with good introduction and notes.)

—— (1614) *De juramento fidelitatis* (On the Oath of Fidelity), trans. and ed. L. Pereña, V. Abril and C. Baciero, with A. Garcia and C. Villanueva, in *Corpus Hispanorum de Pace*, vol. 19, Madrid: Consejo Superior de Investigaciones Cientificas, 1978. (A Latin and Spanish critical edition of part of the *Defensio fidei*, with notes, bibliography and indices.)

—— (1620–1) *De anima* (On the Soul), ed. and intro. S. Castellote, foreword by X. Zubiri, trans. into Spanish by C. Baciero and L. Baciero, vols 1–3, Madrid: Sociedad de Estudios y Publicaciones, 1978–91. (A critical Latin edition, with Spanish translation, of Suárez's *De anima* which incorporates the manuscript changes left by Suárez himself.)

References and further reading

Alejandro, J.M. (1948) *La gnoseología del Doctor Eximio y la acusación nominalista* (The Epistemology of the 'Eminent Doctor' and the Accusation of Nominalism), Comillas: Pontificia Universitas Comillensis. (A defence of Suárez's epistemology against the accusation of nominalism.)

* Aristotle (1995) *Politics*, trans. T.J. Saunders, Oxford: Clarendon Press. (Referred to in §4. This edition gives a translation of the first two books of Aristotle's *Politics* and a commentary.)

Courtine, J.-F. (1990) *Suárez et le système de la métaphysique* (Suárez and the Plan of Metaphysics), Paris: Presses Universitaires de France. (Situates 'the Suarezian moment' in the history of metaphysics as the point from which an Aristotelian doctrine of transcendental being passes to a modern concern for pure objectivity.)

Cronin, T. (1966) *Objective Being in Descartes and in Suarez*, Rome: Gregorian University Press. (Suárez's doctrine of objective being is treated in relation to its scholastic sources and for its influence on Descartes.)

Davitt, T. (1960) *The Nature of Law*, St. Louis, MO: Herder, 1960, 86–108. (Presents Suárez's doctrine of law as voluntaristic.)

Doyle, J.P. (1967) 'Suárez on the Reality of the Possibles', *The Modern Schoolman* 44: 29–40. (Highlights the 'double negative' – that is, noncontradictory – character of possible being according to Suárez.)

—— (1969) 'Suárez on the Analogy of Being', *The Modern Schoolman* 46: 219–49, 323–41. (Treats Suarezian analogy of being as it presupposes the common objective concept of being as a noun.)

—— (1972) 'Heidegger and Scholastic Metaphysics', *The Modern Schoolman* 49: 201–20. (Contrasts Suarezian and Thomistic metaphysics in view of Heidegger's 'the forgetfulness of being' charge against medieval metaphysics.)

—— (1982) 'The Suarezian Proof for God's Existence', in L.J. Thro (ed.) *History of Philosophy in the Making: A Symposium of Essays to Honor Professor James D. Collins on his 65th Birthday*, Washington, DC: University Press of America, 105–17. (Treats the Suarezian metaphysical proof for God's existence as it presupposes the common objective concept of being as a noun.)

—— (1984) 'Prolegomena to a Study of Extrinsic Denomination in the Work of Francis Suárez, S.J.', *Vivarium* 22 (2): 121–60. (An introductory study of the minimal being falling under the common objective concept of being as a noun.)

—— (1987–8) 'Suárez on Beings of Reason and Truth', *Vivarium* 25 (1): 47–75, 26 (1): 51–72. (Treats Suárez's doctrine of truth with regard to beings of reason, especially impossible objects.)

—— (1992) 'Francisco Suárez: On Preaching the Gospel to People like the American Indians', *Fordham International Law Journal* 15 (4): 879–951. (Treats Suárez's legal and political theory, including his just war doctrine, within the context of the Spanish discovery and conquest of the New World.)

* Gilson, E. (1952) *Being and Some Philosophers*, Toronto, Ont.: Pontifical Institute of Mediaeval Studies, 2nd edn, 96–107. (Presents Suárez as developing the 'essentialism' which he inherited from the metaphysics of Avicenna and Duns Scotus. Referred to in §5.)

* Grabmann, M. (1926) 'Die Disputationes Metaphysicae des Franz Suárez in ihrer methodischen Eigenart und Fortwirkung' (The *Disputationes*

Metaphysicae of Francis Suárez: its Methodical Character and Influence), in *Mittelalterliches Geistesleben: Abhandlungen zur Geschichte der Scholastik und Mystik*, Munich: Max Hueber, vol. 1, 525–60. (This work treats the context, the character and the division of the *Metaphysical Disputations*, as well as its influence from the date of its appearance up to the 20th century. Referred to in §5.)

Gracia, J.J.E. (ed.) (1991) 'Francisco Suárez', special issue of *American Catholic Philosophical Quarterly* 65 (3). (Contains articles on various aspects of Suárez's work.)

Hoeres, W. (1965) 'Francis Suárez and the Teaching of John Duns Scotus on *Univocatio entis*', in J.K. Ryan and B.M. Bonansea (eds) *John Duns Scotus (1265–1965)*, Washington, DC: Catholic University Press, 263–90. (Compares and contrasts the doctrines of Suárez and Scotus on the concept of being.)

Iriarte, J. (1948) 'La proyección sobre Europa de una gran metafísica, o Suárez en la filosofía de los días del barroco' (The spread over Europe of a great metaphysics...), *Razón y fe* 138: 229–65. (Treats the spread of Suarezian metaphysics through Europe in the seventeenth century.)

* Martín, J.I., Ceñal, R., Hellin, J., Elorduy, E., Iturrioz, J., Rommen, H. *et al.* (1948) 'Suárez en el cuarto centenario de su nacimiento (1548–1617)' (Suárez on the Fourth Centenary of His Birth), special issue of *Pensamiento* 4. (An important collection of articles on Suárez commemorating the four-hundredth anniversary of his birth, with a laudatory introduction by the then Spanish minister of education, José Ibañez Martín. Referred to in §2.)

Robinet, A. (1980) 'Suárez dans l'oeuvre de Leibniz' (Suárez in the Work of Leibniz), *Cuadernos Salmantinos de Filosofía* 7: 269–84. (A cautious consideration of the possible influence of Suárez on Leibniz.)

Rommen, H. (1926) *Die Staatslehre des Franz Suárez, S.J.* (The Political Doctrine of Francisco Suárez), München-Gladbach: Volksverein-Verlag. (An exposition of Suárez's views on political society including the relation between church and state.)

Ruiz Moreno, I. (1949) 'El derecho internacional y Francisco Suárez' (International Law and Francisco Suárez), in *Actas del IV Centenario del Nacimiento de Francisco Suárez (1548–1948)*, Burgos, 1949, vol. 2, 331–63. (Treats the role of Suárez in the development of international law.)

* Scorraille, R. de (1912–3) *François Suárez de la Compagnie de Jésus* (Francisco Suárez of the Society of Jesus), Paris: Lethielleux, 2 vols. (The definitive biography of Suárez. Referred to in §5.)

Wells, N.J. (1962) 'Suárez, Historian and Critic of the Modal Distinction between Essential Being and Existential Being', *The New Scholasticism* 36: 419–44. (An exposition and criticism of Suárez's view of one proposed distinction between essence and existence in creatures.)

—— (1980–1) 'Suárez on the Eternal Truths, I and II', *The Modern Schoolman* 58: 73–104, 159–74. (Critical presentation of Suárez's understanding of the eternal status of necessary truths.)

—— (1984) 'Material Falsity in Descartes, Arnauld, and Suárez', *Journal of the History of Philosophy* 22: 25–50. (Treats a particular doctrine as it passed into modern philosophy from Suárez through Descartes.)

Wundt, M. (1939) *Die deutsche Schulmetaphysik des 17 Jahrhunderts* (The German 'School-metaphysics' of the 17th Century), Tübingen: Mohr. (Treats the influence of Suárez on seventeenth-century Lutheran and Calvinist thinkers in Germany and Holland.)

JOHN P. DOYLE

SUBJECT see Persons; Subject, postmodern critique of

SUBJECT/PREDICATE
see Predication

SUBJECT, POSTMODERN CRITIQUE OF THE

The critique of the subject in late twentieth-century continental philosophy is associated primarily with the work of Foucault, Derrida, Lacan and Deleuze. Driven by philosophical, political and therapeutic concerns, these thinkers question the subject's ability to declare itself self-evidently independent of the external conditions of its own possibility, such as the language in which it expresses clear and distinct ideas, the body whose deceptions it fears, and the historical or cultural conditions in which it perceives reason or tyranny. Moreover, they fear that the ethical price of such insistence upon absolute self-possession is the exclusion and oppression of social groups whose supposed irrationality or savagery represent the self's own rejected possibilities for change and discovery. Their work draws upon Marxist, Freudian and Nietzschean insights concerning the dependence of consciousness upon its material conditions, unconscious roots, or constituting 'outside'. However, their use of these influences is guided by a common fidelity to Kant's search for the 'conditions of possibility' underlying subjective experience, as well as his scepticism regarding our capacity to know the self and its motivations as objects 'in themselves'.

1   **Intellectual and historical context**
2   **Thinkers and themes**
3   **Debates**

1   Intellectual and historical context

The work of Foucault, Derrida, Lacan and Deleuze, the thinkers primarily associated with the critique of the subject in late twentieth-century philosophy, reflects the intellectual and the political milieu of 1950s and 1960s France, but it also challenges important currents of thought regarding the relation of philosophical reason to historical change or progress. The critique of the subject is simultaneously an attack upon the idea of a universal humanist subject whose reason is reflected in the thought of all 'civilized' cultures, and an attack upon traditional philosophical dichotomies such as reason/madness, consciousness/embodiment or civilization/savagery. To a certain extent, therefore, the critique of the subject is an attempt to renegotiate the conceptual relation between history and philosophy, questioning whether the philosophical or scientific subject is necessarily the primary factor in the intelligibility of historical events. It is both an event in the history of ideas and a challenge to the way in which events (including intellectual events) have been conceptualized by philosophical reason. Traditionally, the self-present, freely acting subject has been considered the pivot linking historicist and transcendental accounts of Western political and psychological experience. A philosophical perspective which questions the plausibility of such a subject reopens the question of how philosophers can make sense of their own historical and psychological experience.

Anti-subjectivist approaches to philosophy arose in reaction to Sartrean existentialism and the extreme capacity for freedom, self-creation and historical agency with which Sartre credited the conscious ego (see SARTRE, J.-P.). But Hegel was an equally prominent ghost on the intellectual horizon of this time, due to Kojève's influential lectures and translation of the *Phenomenology of Spirit* (see HEGEL, G.W.F. §5; KOJÈVE, A.). Where for Kant the self

remained ignorant of its own nature and motivations as thing-in-itself, Hegel argued that the self *was* capable of thorough self-knowledge and conscious freedom to the extent that it recognized social and historical structures as mediating the relation between itself as consciousness and as thing-in-itself. Anti-subjectivist thinkers focused on the role played by mediating social structures in the formation of self-consciousness while retaining Kant's suspicion that such self-knowledge could never be complete. Unlike Kant, however, they placed higher ethical and political significance upon the recognition of this *blind spot* in the constitution of human freedom than upon the belief in human autonomy made possible by such scepticism.

Both Hegel and Sartre believed that historical struggles for freedom constituted the objective basis for the increasing rationality and self-knowledge of the subject. Western political culture, liberal or Marxist respectively, represented for these thinkers the highest form of this self-consciousness to date. It is significant, therefore, that the anti-subjectivist reaction against Hegel and Sartre took place amid upheavals in the world-historical role of the French state. Well before the student uprisings and general strike of May 1968, anti-colonial revolutions in Southeast Asia and Africa explicitly challenged the traditional equation of universal human subjectivity with the political consciousness specific to Western 'man'. The Nazi Holocaust and the legacy of Western imperialism had made it increasingly difficult to perceive the subject described by Western philosophy as the unquestionable vanguard of humankind's march toward historically embodied reason and freedom. Indeed, it became clear how much of the West's material progress and cultural self-sufficiency were built upon the oppression and exclusion of ethnic populations elsewhere in the world.

Ironically, considering his personal history of Nazi involvement, one of the single most important influences upon postmodern critiques of the subject was Martin Heidegger's lifelong investigation into the nature of the subject's *subjectivity* – into what makes it a 'subject' and makes it possible for us to speak of 'subjectivity' as such. For Heidegger, the subject's autonomy and capacity for knowledge do not precede its interaction with objects and other humans but arise amid a pre-given world of involvements, projects, moods and historically given meanings. Heidegger insists that human 'being-there' (*Dasein*) can only be understood from *within* those involvements, through an investigation of the *Being* of both subject and object. Language indicates the various ways in which Being occurs in the world of human involvements. Both the etymology and the ordinary usage of 'being' offer archaeological evidence of the ways in which humans have historically understood the relation between their self-conception as subjects and the way in which both subjects and objects come to *be* (see HEIDEGGER, M. §§2–4).

2 Thinkers and themes

Heidegger's effort to illuminate suppressed or latent philosophical alternatives to the structures through which subjects and objects currently appear to one another served as a starting point for Foucault's investigation into the relationship between history and traditional philosophical conceptions of the self-knowing subject (see FOUCAULT, M.). The Foucauldian critique of the subject explores the historical conditions making possible various conceptions of subjectivity, agency and truth. In his most anti-Sartrean work, *L'Archéologie du savoir* (1969) (*The Archaeology of Knowledge*, 1972), Foucault questions whether historical events are best understood as expressions of human agency, especially the sort of agency thought to define the Western political subject. Like Derrida, Foucault also questions the ontological unity of the philosophical and literary author, exploring the way in which the agency and consciousness attributed by readers to a philosophical or literary author depend upon social and academic conventions regarding the relation between types of texts. In doing so, he draws attention to the different ways in which the concept of truth has established criteria for the assignment of agency and consciousness to particular actors, writers and processes at different points in history. Like Derrida and Deleuze, Foucault attempts to develop the broader philosophical implications of Nietzsche's inquiry (known as genealogy; see GENEALOGY) into the historical or political origins of central metaphysical concepts such as truth or the good. His goal is less to embed these structures and criteria in a more accurate and complete history than to emphasize their contingency and possible malleability.

Foucault is best known, however, for philosophical histories which describe the production of modern individualized self-consciousness through the everyday social impact of institutions such as the school, prison, hospital, social welfare apparatus, and psychiatric and psychoanalytic discourses concerning sexuality. His work considers the human body as a plastic medium which expresses the biological and productive power of a population insofar as it observes and controls itself under the direction of specific social institutions. Foucault locates modern 'subjectivity' at the nexus of these techniques of control and surveillance, which affect bodies in their most everyday existence and may become the sites of resistance to such institutions.

Analysis of the subject of desire and sexuality forms a major point of contact and contestation among Foucault, Lacan and Deleuze, in addition to 'French' feminists such as Irigaray and Kristeva. In questioning the nature of the subject's relation to history, and in examining the conditions which allow us to perceive reason in both subjectivity and historicity, anti-subjectivist thinkers were also forced to reconsider the nature of the psychological experience in which the relation between reason and madness is expressed. The debt which this philosophical conversation owes to psychoanalysis is enormous. At the turn of the century, Freud's clinical discoveries had undermined the concept of a pure rationality or transparent subjectivity and drawn attention to the complexity of distinctions between the normal and the abnormal or the intellectual and the sexual. Yet by the 1950s the psychoanalytic establishment had downplayed the potentially revolutionary implications of Freudian theory in favour of a practical emphasis on therapeutic techniques designed to *adapt* patients to a social reality considered given and unquestionable. Foucault's early work on the distinction between madness and sanity, and his later accounts of the changing concept of 'sexuality', argued for a historical understanding of the conditions of the possibility of the desiring subject. Yet, despite Freud's contribution to philosophical critiques of the transparent and ahistorical subject, Foucault regarded psychoanalysis as one in a long series of institutions for the identification, study and eventual normalization of those who either would not or could not apprehend themselves as subjects.

Rather than investigate the historical conditions of the possibility of subjective experience and sexual desire, radical psychoanalyst Jacques LACAN remained interested in the structural and logical conditions making such experience possible and recognizable at *any* point in history. In an effort to restore the critical implications of psychoanalytic theory, Lacan stressed the structural and logical conditions underlying the individual personality as subject of language and desire. His major innovation in Freudian theory is to have interpreted psychoanalysis as a linguistic account of self-formation, and thus to have conceptualized sexual identification and desire as the result of inclusion in a speaking community. In contrast to Anglo-American efforts to think of the psychoanalytic subject as a self-contained (and more or less 'normal') manipulator of words, the Lacanian school expressed deep suspicion regarding the extent of the ego's self-control. For Lacan, neurosis *results* from the ego's refusal to acknowledge its dependence upon a (conflicted) social and linguistic field in order to maintain an imaginary bodily integrity. Lacan's theory describes an inevitably *split* subject, whose activity is largely unconscious; a subject formed in the child's struggle to be represented by language as a speaker. The sexual specificity and desire of the resulting subject are irrevocable marks of this split or insufficiency. Because Lacan considers sexual difference to be a transcendental condition of the possibility of psychological experience as such, his work was both influential upon and ultimately reworked by feminist thinkers who shared his scepticism regarding the existence of transparent (and sexually neuter) subjects (see FEMINISM AND PSYCHO-ANALYSIS).

Many of the thinkers under consideration here share a general conviction that the terms of dichotomies such as reason/madness, thought/embodiment, freedom/power, or self/other ultimately depend upon one another and are only maintained *as dichotomies* through an inescapable act of exclusion, intellectual or political. This principle has been most explicitly developed in the work of Jacques DERRIDA. Like Foucault and Lacan, Derrida was greatly influenced by Heidegger, but unlike the other two he engages directly with Heideggerian texts and problems. Derrida is best known for his critique of the philosophical subject as self-present in the language of its thought. Derrida argues that the history of philosophy has regarded thinking as a sort of transparent awareness of present meaning, comparable to the testimony of a spoken confession rather than the (potentially misunderstood or forged) evidence of a written signature. In fact, he contends, thought always bears witness to ambiguities, to metaphoric constructions, and to prior texts and social contexts which render it partially opaque even to thinkers themselves. 'Deconstruction', the name given to Derrida's technique for the analysis of authoritative philosophical texts, disrupts apparent hierarchies and identities within texts and cultural phenomena by demonstrating the dependence of a superior or independent term upon a constituting exterior or Other. Deconstruction attempts to show that political, ethical, and philosophical subjectivity bears traces of production by a prior social or conceptual field – one traditionally considered to be the subject's textual *product*, subordinate to him or her.

The 'French' feminist critique of the subject as embodied and sexually differentiated expands upon the critique of universal subjectivity offered by psychoanalysis and deconstruction. Yet, because of its links to an evolving international political movement, it also attempts to explore the positive aspects of certain non-traditional accounts of subjectivity and community, especially those which give a central role to embodiment or the act of writing rather than the self-presence of consciousness. 'French' feminism is usually identified with the work of Luce IRIGARAY, Hélène CIXOUS and Julia KRISTEVA, despite great differences in their individual philosophical projects and the spread of 'continental' feminism well beyond the borders of France. This philosophical genre is unique for its critique of the supposed sexual neutrality (and therefore *de facto masculinity*) of the universal philosophical subject. Continental-style feminist philosophy seeks to undo the apparent simplicity and givenness of the notion of sex, and to investigate the manner in which culture and language shape the sexed individual's opportunities for pleasure, political agency and philosophical activity. Like critics of colonialism, continental feminists are particularly concerned to undermine the association of subjectivity with particular dichotomies such as masculine/feminine or Western/non-Western.

Finally, the work of Gilles DELEUZE combines a Derridean emphasis on difference and differentiation, a Foucauldian conception of power and the social field, and the psychoanalytic notion of desire (thought of as productive, rather than split) to create a resolutely Nietzschean understanding of the subject as a multiplicity of forces. In fact, subjectivity is for Deleuze only *one* aspect or face of multiplicity. He regards neither the traditional, transparent subject nor the split psychoanalytic subject as the healthiest or most liberating vehicles for productive, desiring multiplication. His collaboration with radical psychoanalyst Félix Guattari produced a major theoretical study of the way in which psychoanalysis itself perpetuates a form of subjectivity appropriate to capitalist production. *Anti-Oedipus* hoped to find in schizophrenia's noted inaccessibility to analysis the resources for a way of thinking about history, desire and subjectivity which resists capitalist culture itself. Deleuze's other works on cinema, literature and historical figures such as Nietzsche, Hume, Spinoza and Bergson offer concepts with which the philosopher may actively *think* of him or herself as multiple without falling into despair at his or her failure to live up to the Oedipalized subject, whether supposedly self-present or self-absent.

3 Debates

This field of continental philosophy is characterized by several key debates. Many of the critical positions described above are designed to undo traditional political and conceptual hierarchies which limit the political agency of the oppressed, as well as the political imagination of theorists. The question remains, however, whether critiques of the subject do not undermine the very idea of an 'agent' capable of political contestation, thus perpetuating the hierarchies they were meant to subvert. Similarly, do theoretical accounts of 'constructed' subjects (those of Lacan and Foucault) attribute so much power to social structures that it no longer seems possible to imagine subjects exercising the power which capitalist and disciplinary institutions have invested in their bodily activity and self-policing? Critiques of the humanist subject and of the subject of scientific certainty have raised the spectre of cultural incommensurability which provokes many of the arguments between French-influenced continental philosophers and descendants of the Frankfurt School such as Jürgen Habermas. Another heated debate concerns the purported 'valorization' of schizophrenia, hysteria and madness in the works of Foucault, Deleuze and the 'French' feminists. In attempting to scrutinize the theoretical and political context in which distinctions are made between the sane and the insane, do they romanticize or inappropriately universalize their conception of mental illness?

Finally, it must be noted that the concept of 'postmodernism' itself is controversial (see POST-MODERNISM). The term and its possible relevance or meaningfulness depend upon our ability to conceptualize continuity, progress or clear breaks between historical periods. Jean-François LYOTARD uses the term 'postmodern' to indicate the historical condition making possible various aspects of *modernity*, including the distrust of totalizing historical narratives which has characterized much of late twentieth-century thought. Both Lyotard and the American literary critic and Marxist Fredric Jameson emphasize the difference between post-structuralism, a philosophical movement which questions the ahistoricism and rigidity of structuralist accounts of subjectivity and culture, and postmodernism, a sociological or historical characterization of the culture of late capitalist societies (primarily in the First World). Jameson is critical of the supposed distinction between 'modern' and 'postmodern' periods, but does acknowledge that the decentralization of productive forces and communications networks, not to mention the saturation of everyday life with advertising, have fragmented social consciousness in a new and potentially problematic way. Whether one regards the critique of the subject and the advent of late capitalism as the results of transcendental structures or historical events, the difficult concept of the 'postmodern' calls attention to the uneasy relation between historical frameworks of analysis and the philosophical frameworks which have traditionally made sense of history by relying upon the agency of a supposedly self-present subject.

See also: ALTERITY AND IDENTITY, POSTMODERN THEORIES OF; DELEUZE, G.; FOUCAULT, M.; HEIDEGGER, M.; LACAN, J.; POSTMODERNISM

References and further reading

Butler, J. (1987) *Subjects of Desire: Hegelian Reflections in Twentieth Century France*, New York: Columbia University Press. (Considers desire as a major Hegelian theme adapted into twentieth-century French thought by Kojève and Sartre and radically transformed by Lacan, Deleuze and Foucault.)

Deleuze, G. (1962) *Nietzsche et la philosophie*, trans. H. Tomlinson, *Nietzsche and Philosophy*, New York: Columbia University Press, 1983. (Creative, influential interpretation of Nietzsche according to an ontology of active and reactive forces rather than subjects, intentions and objects.)

* Deleuze, G. and Guattari, F. (1972) *L'Anti-Oedipe*, trans. R. Hurley. M. Seem and H. Lane, *Capitalism and Schizophrenia*, vol. 1, *Anti-Oedipus*, New York: Viking, 1977. (Major anti-psychoanalytic work linking capitalism, psychoanalytic ideology concerning the family and the sane or 'analysable' subject.)

Derrida, J. (1967) 'La Structure, le signe et le jeu dans le discours des sciences humaines', trans. A. Bass, 'Structure, Sign, and Play in the Discourse of the Human Sciences', in *Writing and Difference*, Chicago, IL: University of Chicago Press, 1978. (Excellent introduction to basic concepts and techniques of deconstruction in the context of Lévi-Strauss's analysis of myths as 'centred structures'.)

—— (1972a) 'The Ends of Man', in *Marges de la philosophie*, trans. A. Bass, *Margins of Philosophy*, Chicago, IL: University of Chicago Press, 1982. (Explores the Eurocentric presuppositions of Western humanism and opposes deconstruction to humanist themes in phenomenology and existentialism.)

—— (1972b) 'Signature Event Context', in *Marges de la philosophie*, trans. A. Bass, *Margins of Philosophy*, Chicago, IL: University of Chicago Press, 1982. (Difficult but crucial argument to the effect that iterability, the ability of signs and performances to be transplanted from one context to another, is a necessary condition of their ability to guarantee the authenticity of their use in any given context; first article in a long-running debate between Derrida and the proponents of speech act theory.)

* Foucault, M. (1969a) *L'Archéologie du savoir*, trans. A. Sheridan Smith, *The Archaeology of Knowledge and the Discourse on Language*, London: Tavistock Publications, 1972. (Suggests a (non-Marxist) materialist framework for conceptualizing historical change without reference to the agency of individual or collective subjects.)

—— (1969b) 'Qu'est-ce qu'un auteur?', trans. D. Bouchard and S. Simon, 'What is an Author?', in *Language, Counter-Memory, Practice: Selected Essays and Interviews*, ed. D. Bouchard, Ithaca, NY: Cornell University Press, 1977. (Proposes that the idea of 'authorship' is a complex effect of conventions linking texts and institutions.)

—— (1976) *La Volonté de savoir*, trans. R. Hurley, *The History of Sexuality*, vol. 1, *An Introduction*, New York: Random House, 1978. (Extremely influential and accessible account of the social construction of sexuality through discourses linking social power to the individual's quest for self-knowledge and authenticity.)

Fraser, N. (1989) *Unruly Practices: Power, Discourse and Gender in Contemporary Social Theory*, Minneapolis, MN: University of Minnesota Press. (Presents debates regarding possible political implications of philosophical critiques of the subject).

Irigaray, L. (1984) *Éthique de la différence sexuelle*, trans. C. Burke and G. Gill, *An Ethics of Sexual Difference*, Ithaca, NY: Cornell University Press, 1993. (Attempts to conceptualize a respectful relation between the sexed philosophical subject and his or her 'other', with special attention paid to the imaginative frameworks employed by major figures in the history of philosophy.)

* Jameson, F. (1991) *Postmodernism, or, The Cultural Logic of Late Capitalism*, Durham, NC: Duke University Press. (Influential cultural study placing 'postmodernism' as a phenomenon of architectural, artistic, literary and philosophical style in the context of worldwide social and economic changes.)

* Kojève, A. (1947) *Introduction à la lecture de Hegel*, assem. R. Queneau, trans. J. Nichols, Jr, *Introduction to the Reading of Hegel*, ed. A. Bloom, Ithaca, NY: Cornell University Press, 1980. (Series of lectures which greatly influenced French reception of Hegel, focusing on individual subjectivity as the locus of historical agency and emphasizing the relationship between the beginning sections of *The Phenomenology of Spirit* and the early Marx.)

Lacan, J. (1966) *Écrits*, trans. A. Sheridan, *Écrits: A Selection*, New York: W.W. Norton, 1977. (Selected articles from the French edition; see especially 'The Mirror Stage as Formative of the Function of the I').

* Lyotard, J.-F. (1979) *La Condition postmoderne: rapport sur le savoir*, trans. G. Bennington and B. Massumi, *The Postmodern Condition: A Report on Knowledge*, Minneapolis, MN: University of Minnesota Press, Theory and History of Literature Series vol. 10, 1984. (Explores the declining legitimacy of 'grand narratives' of liberation and scientific progress and its impact on late twentieth-century ideas concerning the role of knowledge in technological societies.)

Megill, A. (1985) *Prophets of Extremity: Nietzsche, Heidegger, Foucault, Derrida*, Berkeley, CA: University of California Press. (Clear, accessible exposition of major themes linking these four authors developmentally.)

Turkle, S. (1978) *Psychoanalytic Politics: Jacques Lacan and Freud's French Revolution*, London: Guilford Press, revised and updated 1992. (Sociological account of Lacanian intellectual scene.)

Whitford, M. (1991) *Luce Irigaray: Philosophy in the Feminine*, London: Routledge. (Detailed and influential account introducing psychoanalytic and philosophical issues in the work of one 'French' feminist philosopher.)

Young, R. (1990) *White Mythologies: Writing History and the West*, London: Routledge. (Places the critique of the subject in the context of post-Second World War anti-colonialist and structuralist thought.)

LAURA HENGEHOLD

SUBJECTIVISM/ SUBJECTIVITY *see* OBJECTIVITY

SUBJUNCTIVE CONDITIONALS

see COUNTERFACTUAL CONDITIONALS

SUBLIME, THE

The origin of the term 'the sublime' is found in ancient philosophy, where, for example, Longinus linked it with a lofty and elevated use of literary language. In the eighteenth century, the term came into much broader use, when it was applied not only to literature but also to the experience of nature, whereafter it became one of the most hotly debated subjects in the cultural discourse of that age.

The theories of Addison, Burke and Kant are especially significant. Addison developed and extended the Longinian view of the sublime as a mode of elevated self-transcendence, while Burke extended John Dennis's insight concerning sublimity's connection with terror and a sense of self-preservation. While Addison and Burke encompassed both art and nature in their approaches, Kant confined the experience of the sublime to our encounters with nature. In his theory, the sublime is defined as a pleasure in the way that nature's capacity to overwhelm our powers of perception and imagination is contained by and serves to vivify our powers of rational comprehension. It is a distinctive aesthetic experience.

In the 1980s and 1990s Kant's and (to a much lesser extent) Burke's theories of the sublime became the objects of a massive revival of interest, in the immediate context of a more general discussion of postmodern society. Kant's theory, for example, has been used by J.-F. Lyotard and others to explain the sensibility – orientated towards the enjoyment of complexity, rapid change and a breakdown of categories – that seems to characterize that society.

1　**Origins**
2　**Nature**
3　**Kant**
4　**Postmodern revival**

1　Origins

Boileau's translation of Longinus' treatise *Peri Hupsous* (first published in 1674) was probably the single most important factor in the establishment of the sublime as a critical and aesthetic concept. For Longinus, the sublime consists essentially in a loftiness and excellence of language which, rather than engaging reason, serves to transport the reader to a higher plane. Indeed, to express and even exceed the vastness of nature through lofty thought and literature is the ultimate human vocation. It is to transcend the baseness and ignobility intrinsic to merely finite being. This is why Longinus goes on to suggest that those who achieve the sublime in literature are more than mortal; they lift us towards the Deity.

Before considering the influence of Longinus' 'self-transcendent' notion of the sublime on the theorists of the eighteenth century, we must first look at a second fundamental source of the concept. It is to be found in the literary criticism of John Dennis, and especially in his *The Grounds of Criticism in Poetry* (1704). In this work, we are told that the sublime consists of great thoughts that move the reader to 'Enthusiasm'. For Dennis, loftiness (that is, great

thought) is a necessary, but not (as it is for Longinus) sufficient condition of the sublime. We require in addition that the great thought should transport the soul by means of 'passion'. This leads to a crucial step. Dennis first suggests that ideas producing terror are especially suited to the sublime. In this respect, he distinguishes between terror *per se* and 'Enthusiastic Terror' – terror that is experienced from a position of safety and is consequently attended by joy. (The paradigm here, one presumes, would be terrible events encountered as the subject matter in literature.) Second, the reason for our pleasure in the sublime is shifted on to a reflective awareness of our present immunity from the terrible events under consideration. Self-preservation rather than self-transcendence provides the ground of our response, and while this emphasis on self-preservation is only an aspect of Dennis's theory of the sublime, it is one which he originates and which marks the logical opposite of Longinus' notion. Together, however, the themes of self-preservation and self-transcendence constitute the seed from which eighteenth-century theories of the sublime grew. I shall now consider this in the context of possibly the most influential pre-Kantian theorists: Addison and Burke.

2　Nature

Addison's major discussion of the sublime is to be found in his famous *Spectator* articles on the pleasures of the imagination. In article 412, the subject is introduced by a way of threefold distinction between the great, the uncommon and the beautiful. For Addison, the 'Great' consists not in mere bulk, but in the largeness of a whole view – such as the scenes of an open country, mountains or wide expanses of water. We will remember that, for Longinus, the state of sublime self-transcendence is achieved through the creation of and response to 'lofty' thought and literature – literature that expresses and exceeds nature's greatness. Addison, by contrast, argues that a similar state of self-transcendence can come about when we encounter nature's greatness *by visual perception alone*. Nature provides us with a kind of image of liberty, which takes us beyond the confines of the immediate. The mediation of literature or lofty thoughts is not a prerequisite for the sublime in this context.

While Addison extends Longinus' self-transcendent approach to the sublime, Burke develops Dennis' notion of self-preservation (see BURKE, E.). He bases his argument on the idea that pleasure and pain are logically independent of one another; pleasure is not simply the absence or diminution of pain, and vice versa. The reasoning behind this is as follows. Most of the time, we are in a state of 'indifference' (or 'tranquillity') where neither pleasure nor pain preponderates. Given this, it is clearly possible to move from a state of indifference to a state of pleasure without the mediation of pain, and vice versa. These unmediated states Burke terms 'positive pleasure' and 'positive pain' respectively. Having established this logical independence, Burke suggests that while the diminution or removal of pain and danger does not yield positive pleasure, it can be characterized as an agreeable state of 'delight'. Hence, when terrible things excite ideas of pain or – from a position of safety – danger in our minds, the terror we feel is moderated into a state of delight. A similar state can be occasioned in us, indeed, when we behold vast or obscure items, which test or strain our perceptual faculties without pushing us over the threshold of conscious pain.

Interestingly, Burke explains both these routes to the sublime in terms of a common causal structure. Just as labour is necessary to keep the 'grosser' parts of the body healthy, so stimulation is required for the 'finer' parts upon which the mental powers act. Indeed, it is on the very occasions that we experience moderated terror or pre-conscious pain that the finer parts receive healthy stimulation – thus diminishing the possible danger that inactivity poses to the system. Burke's causal argument is far from compelling, however, and towards the end of the eighteenth century Kant offered a more convincing account – an explanation orientated towards the cognitive.

3   Kant

Kant's most thorough treatment of the sublime is found in his *The Critique of Judgment* (1790). It unites the self-transcendent and self-preservatory approaches in the context of a much broader and more complex theory concerning our ultimate human vocation as rational human beings (see KANT, I.). He distinguishes two fundamental varieties or modes of the sublime. First, the 'mathematical' mode arises through our perceptual engagements with vast objects. While his exposition of this is notoriously intricate and often obscure, his basic strategy can be described as follows. As rational beings, when we are presented with some perceptually overwhelming object, we strive to comprehend it – to find some measure whereby we can make its overwhelming aspect intelligible. The use of mathematical rules is the most obvious means to this end. (A towering mountain in the distance, for example, does not perhaps seem quite as towering if we can define it as 'no more than x metres in height'.) However, all rules of measure presuppose units of measurement, and

these are, in the final analysis, 'aesthetic estimates', that is, based on what we can grasp 'by the eye alone' in direct perception. It is at this point that Kant's reasoning becomes particularly difficult. He seems to hold that, when faced with particularly impressive and vast objects, our search for an appropriate measure leads us towards the idea of infinity itself. We cannot, however, comprehend this notion in perceptual and imaginative terms. It defeats all our attempts to form an aesthetic estimate. The vast object therefore serves a mediating function. In our struggle to find a measure for it, the sense of being perceptually or imaginatively overwhelmed by the infinite illuminates the extraordinary scope of our rational powers. For we can, despite our sensible limitations, at least comprehend the infinite *as an idea*. The experience of the mathematical sublime therefore involves a 'mental movement' from privation to exhilaration at the superiority of our rational being over all sensible limitations.

The second mode of the sublime – the 'dynamical' – involves a similar mental movement, in this case instigated by our experience of mighty or dangerous objects or phenomena (from a position of safety). Again, Kant's presentation of the argument is often awkward, but in contrast to the account of the mathematical sublime its logical structure is more straightforward. When beholding a mighty object or phenomenon, we know that in relation to our puny natural being the mighty item has absolute physical authority. It could destroy us many times over. However, as rational beings, we know that we are more than simply entities of physical nature. Life, destruction and death are not blind mechanistic forces; they are given meaning in the context of our rational endeavours. Hence while the mighty object indeed makes us fearful, we can, as rational beings, nevertheless evince a kind of moral resistance to it. In comprehending and articulating the danger, we are elevated above it. Thus the object serves a mediating role. It provokes an awareness of our sensible limitations, which in turn vivifies the extraordinary scope of our rational being.

The importance of Kant's theory is that it coherently articulates the sublime as an aesthetic experience of 'the containment of excess'. In both the mathematical and dynamical modes an overwhelming item in the natural world is contained by our rational comprehension of it. The fact that this involves a direct interplay between our receptive sensible capacities and rational insight (rather than intellectual comprehension alone) is what gives it aesthetic character. By characterizing it in these terms, Kant is also able to link it (albeit problematically) to general criteria of aesthetic judgment involving, fundamentally, disinterestedness and universality.

4 Postmodern revival

The 1980s and 1990s saw the development of a widespread discussion of contemporary society in relation to the term 'postmodernism'. One of the most remarkable aspects of this development was a massive concomitant revival of interest in the concept of the sublime. J.-F. LYOTARD, for example, has not only published a closely detailed account of Kant's position (1994) but also more speculative articles applying the theory. These extremely influential works centre on a modified concept of the Kantian sublime that is analysed in terms of two varieties or modes – on the one hand, a nostalgic, backward-looking mode, which yearns for the lost metaphysical absolutes of Romanticism, and, on the other, a forward-looking mode ('novatio') associated fundamentally with avant-garde art.

In this latter variety the difficulty or *outré* character of the particular work serves to represent the infinite developmental possibilities of artistic creativity. This suggestion of infinite potential is congruent with the ever-accelerating surge of technological transformation – a surge which seems especially manifest in the societal changes brought about by new information technologies. This congruence is taken by Lyotard to indicate an important continuity between avant-garde modern culture and new postmodern sensibility.

Lyotard's application of Kant is at best oracular, and at worst obscure. He seems to focus in particular on the idea that the sublime hinges on a 'mental movement' from a negative to a positive state. But what are the criteria for the ascription of such states? On this point, Lyotard takes us no further than Kant himself. An alternative approach is the one proposed by the author of this entry – again, in a detailed study of Kant and in a number of papers applying a Kantian-type theory. The basic strategy is to eliminate all talk of 'mental movement' and to recentre the theory on logical presuppositions. No matter how overwhelming or excessive an object may be in relation to our powers of perception or imagination, it is, *qua* phenomenal item, of *finite* extent and power. This means that it can be comprehended or contained in rational terms. The sublime object is one whose presence makes this intellectual insight emotionally vivid.

The sublime, then, has become fashionable once again. Raw nature was once the major source of this experience, but now the accelerating complexity and instability of society itself is also acknowledged as a basis of the spectacle. This broadening scope is further reflected in a burgeoning quantity of writing on the relation between sublimity, psychoanalysis, politics and literature. Slavoj Žižek (1988), for example, has considered the sublime in almost all these contexts (and more besides), and reads the experience on the basis of Lacanian psychoanalysis. Thomas Weiskel (1976) has attempted to reconstruct the Kantian approach in relation to the reading and content of texts, on the basis of both Freudian theory and structural linguistics (see STRUCTURALISM IN LINGUISTICS). There is much in philosophical terms that is obscure and/or problematic about all these psychoanalytic strategies. However, it is significant that they draw on Kant's theory to greater or lesser degrees. His approach – suitably modified – seems to offer the best philosophical tool for understanding the basic experiential structure of sublimity that underlies its many historical and cultural changes of emphasis and context.

See also: NATURE, AESTHETIC APPRECIATION OF §1

References and further reading

* Addison J. (1712) *Critical Essays from The Spectator*, ed. D.F. Bond, Oxford: Clarendon Press, 1970. (Highly readable; see especially essays 409 and 411–21.)
* Burke E. (1757) *A Philosophical Inquiry to the Origin of Our Ideas of the Sublime and the Beautiful*, Oxford: Blackwell, 1987. (A basic and straightforward text.)
  Crowther P. (1989) *The Kantian Sublime: From Morality to Art*, Oxford: Clarendon Press. (A close but accessible account of Kant's theory in the context of his general aesthetics and moral philosophy.)
* —— (1993) *Critical Aesthetics and Postmodernism*, Oxford: Clarendon Press. (Part 2 offers clear critical discussions of Burke, Kant and Lyotard.)
* Dennis, J. (1704) *The Grounds of Criticism in Poetry*, London. (A basic, historically significant text.)
* Kant, I. (1790) *The Critique of Judgment*, trans. J.C. Meredith, Oxford: Clarendon Press, 1973. (The essential text, albeit one of great interpretative complexity.)
* Longinus (1st century AD) *On the Sublime*, trans. A.O. Pritchard, in *Criticism: The Rational Statement*, ed. Charles Kaplan, New York: St Martin's Press, 1975. (A clear and important text, addressing the sublime primarily in relation to literature.)
* Lyotard J.-F. (1994) *Lessons on the Analytic of the Sublime*, trans. E. Rottenberg, Stanford, CA: Stanford University Press. (A clear, sophisticated

and extremely close reading of Kant's position in *The Critique of Judgment*.)

—— (1984) *The Postmodern Condition: A Report on Knowledge*, trans. G. Bennington and B. Massumi, Manchester: Manchester University Press. (The appendix is a difficult, speculative piece linking the sublime to questions of postmodernism.)

* Weiskel T. (1976) *The Romantic Sublime: Studies in the Structure and Psychology of Transcendence*, Baltimore, MD: Johns Hopkins University Press. (A reasonably accessible discussion of the sublime in relation to literature.)

* Žižek, S. (1988) *The Sublime Object of Ideology*, London: Verso. (An influential but difficult psychoanalytic exposition of the sublime.)

PAUL CROWTHER

SUBSTANCE

For Aristotle, 'substances' are the things which exist in their own right, both the logically ultimate subjects of predication and the ultimate objects of scientific inquiry. They are the unified material objects, as well as the natural stuffs, identifiable in sense-experience, each taken to be a member of a natural species with its 'form' and functional essence. Entities in other categories – qualities, actions, relations and so forth – are treated as dependent on, if not just abstracted aspects of, these independent realities.

With the rise of mechanistic physics in the seventeenth century, the Aristotelian multiplicity of substances was reduced to universal matter mechanically differentiated. This move sharpened the issue of the relation of mind to the physical world. The consequent variety of ways in which the notion of substance was manipulated by materialists, dualists, immaterialists and anti-dogmatists encouraged later scepticism about the distinction between independent realities and human abstractions, and so idealism.

Twentieth-century conceptualism, like some earlier versions of idealism, rejects the distinction altogether, commonly ascribing the logical priority of material things in natural language to the utility of a folk physics, as if they were the theoretical entities of everyday life. As such, their identity and existence are determined only through applications of a theory outdated by modern science. Yet this 'top-down', holistic philosophy of language is belied by the detailed insights of traditional logic, which point clearly to a 'bottom-up' account of classification and identity, that is an account which recognizes the possibility of perceptually picking out material objects prior to

knowledge of their kind or nature, and of subsequently classifying them. The idea that material things are theoretical entities, and that their individuation is accordingly kind-dependent, is a hangover from an atomistic approach to perception which calls on theory to tie sensory information together. A more accurate understanding of sensation as the already integrated presentation of bodies in spatial relations to one another and to the perceiver is consonant with the possibility denied by the idealist– namely, that, with respect to its primitive referents, language and thought are shaped around reality itself, the independent objects given in active sense-experience. That the coherence or discrete unity of material objects has a physical explanation does not mean that physics explains it away.

1 **The canonical concept of substance**
2 **Early-modern heretical concepts of substance**
3 **A new role for substance: realism versus conceptualism**

1 The canonical concept of substance

The definitive concept of substance is Aristotle's, but it arose within an existing debate about what fundamentally 'is' in the world – meaning thereby not only what ultimately *exists*, but also what ultimately *is* such or such, as the subject of predication. The term employed, *ousia* (being), was later translated in Aristotle's use of it as *substantia*, substance. Another Aristotelian term applicable to substance, *hpokeimenon*, was more usually translated *substratum*, substrate.

ARISTOTLE (see *Metaphysics* I) identifies two extremes. The first, typified by atomism, takes matter to be 'that of which all things that are consist, and from which they come, and into which they are finally resolved'. For atomism, all change occurs through the motion and rearrangement of immutable material atoms (see ATOMISM, ANCIENT). PLATO (see *Republic* V–VII), on the other hand, held the sensible world, because in perpetual flux, to be less real than the eternal universal characteristics or Forms fleetingly manifested in that world. It is the Forms which, as the subject-matter of enduring knowledge, are in the strong sense. Aristotle's middle way (see *Metaphysics* VI) takes unitary 'bodies', both living things and homogeneous stuffs, to be the fundamental objects of knowledge and subjects of predication. Such substances comprise two elements, particularizing matter and universal form. An individual horse is the specific form of a horse embodied in *this* matter. Forms are the objects of universal science – teleological principles of activity and change within what is material and individual.

The Aristotelian theory has two aspects, as it figures in logic on the one hand, and in the theory of scientific knowledge and explanation on the other. In the former role, substance is the first of the 'categories' or 'things said' (see *Categories*). Substances, falling under such predicates as 'horse' or 'wood', *are* in the primary and most fundamental sense. Other 'things said', sometimes called 'accidents', are somewhat arbitrarily listed under nine or ten heads. Such entities as a horse's shape, colour, location or neigh *are* in a derivative sense. They can be subjects of predication, but are themselves 'said of' and exist 'in' something else (in this case, the horse), whereas substances are neither 'said of' nor exist 'in' anything else. The brownness or neigh of a horse exists just in so far as the horse is brown or neighing, but the primitive noun-predicate 'horse' simply names the given individual, the horse itself. The horse is thus a logically independent entity, whereas its neighing or brownness is dependent on a subject or substrate. Aristotle called the individual horse the 'primary substance', which cannot be 'said of' anything, while the specific 'secondary substance' *horse* can be 'said of' (but does not exist 'in') the individual, and the generic secondary substance *animal* can be 'said of' both the individual and the species.

Only substances can be the subjects of contraries, that is endure through change, change explicable in terms of their natures or essences. Aristotle's schema for scientific definition by *genus* and *difference*, later called the Doctrine of Predicables, applies primarily to substances. Non-substantial entities have definable essences in a sense, but Aristotle held, with reason, that only substances fall into natural species with genuine essences. *Properties* are attributes necessarily connected to essence, while *accidents* in the strict sense are those attributes of a substance which neither figure in, nor flow from, its definition. The Doctrine of Categories and the Doctrine of Predicables both encourage a question to which Scholastic Aristotelians gave a variety of answers: what is it for accidents to exist in a substance? The variety reflected the extent to which different philosophers were prepared to treat accidents as 'real' (that is, really distinct, if naturally dependent) entities, as opposed to taking the view, which EPICURUS had held, that they are merely conceptually distinct aspects of independent bodies. WILLIAM OF OCKHAM and Francisco SUAREZ wrote famous contributions to this debate (see ARISTOTLE §§12–14; EPICUREANISM §§2–3; PLATO §§2, 3, 8).

2 Early-modern heretical concepts of substance.

Modern European philosophy began with a prolifera-tion of variant conceptions of substance in an extended attempt to replace the dominant Aristotelian metaphysics and science with a new authoritative system. Later scepticism about the notion of substance arose with the rejection of this dogmatic enterprise. The very multiplicity of conceptions of substance may suggest that substance-based metaphysics was arbitrary and confused. Yet the various directions taken all fall within an intelligible framework of argument. The crucially productive move was the expulsion of teleological explanations from science through a reversion to something like the ancient atomists' conception of matter as a substance possessing mechanical properties sufficient to explain all physical phenomena (see TELEOLOGY). Materialists such as Thomas Hobbes (1651) concluded that matter or body, determinately modified, is all there is (see HOBBES, T. §3). The variety of sensible qualities by which we distinguish things is a mere 'diversity of seeming' consequent on differences in structure and motion. The activity of substances is simply the motion of bodies in accordance with necessary laws. Sensation and thought are themselves species of motion. More popular than materialism, however, in that religious age, was René Descartes' dualism (see Descartes 1641), which postulated incorporeal thinking substance in addition to extended substance (see DESCARTES §18). A respectable philosophical motive for dualism was that it by-passed the insoluble problem of explaining consciousness, including 'seeming' itself, in mechanical terms.

This new physics might seem far from the theory of predication, but mechanists saw themselves as explaining the logical relation between substance and accidents: accidents are simply the various and changing sizes, shapes and motions of bodies, limits or determinations of extension rather than Suárez's distinct real entities mysteriously inherent in a subject. Descartes (1644) took it that, analogously, particular modes of thought are determinations of thought in general, and that the formal idea of a *subject* of extension or thought refers to nothing over and above these attributes. The connection with predication also figured in the system of Spinoza (1677), whose monism constitutes not only a holistic, deterministic philosophy of nature, but also a logical model according to which the ultimate subject of predication is the universe as a whole, of which individuals are modes or aspects (see SPINOZA, B. DE §§2–3). Leibniz (1686 and 1714), too, in arguing for his anti-materialist monadism, associated two principles: the claim that our awareness of ourselves thinking gives us our only intelligible paradigm of variety within a unitary, active substance, and the logical principle that in every true proposition the predicate is conceptually contained in the subject (see LEIBNIZ, G.W. §§4–5). Partly by means of the latter principle he attempted to explain the identity and diversity of immaterial substances in a non-spatial, non-material world, and his failure supplies an invaluable philosophical lesson. There is, as Aristotle supposed, a demonstrable tie between concrete substantial existence and existence in space.

Logical theory and philosophy of science were differently linked by John Locke (1689), who rejected all claims to know essences and so to understand the substance – accident relation. Substances, including matter and mind, are known to us only through a plurality of disparate observable qualities and powers, which we take to flow from some common cause. Hence we define the primitive noun-predicates which are the names of substances in terms which include a place-marker for that unknown essence: 'When we speak of any sort of substance, we say it is a *thing* having such or such qualities, as body is a *thing* that is extended, figured, and capable of motion' (1689, II. xxiii, 3). 'Substance' is just a name for the unknown. Modes, on the other hand, such as a *triangle*, *democracy* or a *triumph* are not mind-independent unknowns, but constructs reflecting human interests and containing nothing more than the features by which they are defined (see LOCKE, J. §§4–5). Locke was not denigrating the notion of substance, but attacking the pretensions of dogmatic theories. Scepticism was taken further by David Hume(1739–40), however, for whom the philosophical conception of substance was deconstructed as a product of deranged imagination (see HUME, D. §2). After Hume, Immanuel Kant attempted to reinstate the notion on a new basis, advancing the 'transcendental' argument that, for objective experience to be possible, it must be experience of a substance (that is, matter) undergoing change in accordance with law. The very ineluctability of the category, however, he took as proof that it does not correspond to anything in independent reality, but is generated by the interplay of sense and intellect, the forms of judgment and the forms of sensibility (see KANT, I. §§5, 6).

3 A new role for substance: realism versus conceptualism.

Humean empiricism revived in the twentieth century. For A.J. Ayer, for example, the philosophical notion of substance reflects only a 'primitive superstition' about names, since nothing is independently there to be named except sense-data, the equivalent of Hume's impressions (see Ayer 1936). But much present-day philosophy, although influenced by both Hume and

Kant, in general denies both that there is anything ineluctable about the way we think about the world, and that anything is simply there to be named. W.V. Quine (1953) expresses this denial in the terms of Russellian logic holding that to be is to be the value of a bound variable. For Quine, ontology is a matter of deciding which types of entity to postulate and quantify over – material objects, events, properties, 'stages', 'fusions', 'sense-data' or what you will – a decision that is not determined for us by reality. The difference between types of entity is a difference between criteria of identity – between what we count as the same individual again (1960). Here a rational decision is simply a pragmatic one (see QUINE, W.V. §5; ONTOLOGICAL COMMITMENT). Material objects may fill the fundamental place in evolved natural language, but that is a matter of practical convenience or utility. Indeed, the folk-physics embodied in natural language has been supplanted, unless for everyday purposes, by a physics with no room for the 'bodies' canonically assigned to the category of substance.

Is the traditional notion of substance therefore dispensable, the manifestation of an illusion engendered by contingent features of natural, everyday language? To suppose so would arguably be to set aside a storehouse of philosophical insight capable of suggesting to us just what can most cogently be brought against a conceptualism like Quine's. Conceptualism is a 'top-down' philosophy, taking the structure of our thought and language to be the structure of an imposed theory of interpretation of sensory input such that (contrary to Humean empiricism) even input itself must be conceived of in terms of the theory. Concepts are holistically inter-related, slicing out entities as theoretical postulates of the whole scheme. There are no independently given individuals. Not all conceptualists approve the analogy between natural language and scientific theory. Wittgenstein (1953), for example, invites us to see the structure of language as a product of its employment in, above all, social interaction. But all conceptualists have agreed, since the first modern idealists, that we cannot compare our scheme of notions or beliefs directly with reality. An equally old, still popular conclusion is that we can therefore only aim for coherence, and the total scheme that best anticipates experience.

The stiffest opposition to this aspect of pragmatism has come largely from two directions. Drawing on Kant, Peter Strawson (1958) has constructed a transcendental argument aimed at demonstrating that the distinction between experience of independent objects and merely subjective experience – in effect the distinction between oneself and other things which even the sceptic takes for granted – presupposes that both the individual objects and the individual subject of experience exist, endure, are mobile, and interact in space (see STRAWSON, P.F. §8; TRANSCENDENTAL ARGUMENTS). Whether or not this argument rebuts scepticism (would it not be enough for these distinctions that the subject should seem to itself to be so related to bodies in space?), it does offer an explanation of the primacy of the category of substance in natural language, and of the unreality of the suggestion that, but for utility, entities of a different category – events, thing-stages, sense-data or whatever, might have played the basic role. Yet although Strawson disavows an idealism like Kant's, and presents a powerful alternative to Quine's relativism, he does not clearly depart from a 'top-down', conceptualist picture. Indeed he has talked of his thesis as if it concerned the necessary structure of any conceptual scheme that could be the vehicle of objective experience – the general scheme or order which sensory input must fit, as it were, for there to be experience of objects. Individual substances are necessarily basic, but are picked out only by means of sortal concepts applied to input.

A different line of argument, pioneered by Saul KRIPKE (1980) and Hilary PUTNAM (1975), might be taken to refute the idea that our conceptual scheme structures the world for us, rather than being structured by the world. This proposes that, like proper names, names of natural kinds owe their meaning not to some concept in our heads but to their naming what they name. Consequently, 'gold' on the lips of a present-day physical chemist means the same as an ancient Chinese character, whatever differences exist between the users' conceptions of, or theories about, the natural kind of stuff that both name. That their words mean the same could not be determined by an inspection of their 'ideas' or definitions, but would depend on the identity, that is the actual (and, for at least one of them, unknown) common nature, of what each names (see REFERENCE §3). Yet even if this point is taken to undermine the analogy between language and theory, and to demonstrate the possibility of a pre-theoretical naming of things, it does not speak directly to the question of the distinction between what is naturally, and what is only conceptually distinct. For it could be made almost as readily about the general names of natural events, processes or properties as about the names of substances. The term 'freezing' has the same pre-theoretical grip on a natural kind of process as 'horse' has on a natural kind of substance, yet the freezing of some water in a glass is not a naturally discrete whole in the way that a horse or, for that matter, a glass is. Although no process is properly freezing unless it shares the

common nature of freezing, unknown to most of us, yet a particular instance of freezing is individuated and bounded by the concept, not by nature. Every event or process is part of indefinitely many wider events or processes, and there are no natural, only conceptual, parts and wholes. But a horse is a natural whole, and its hooves and tail are natural parts. Because it has nothing directly to say about boundaries, unity, individuation and identity, the Kripke–Putnam thesis is compatible with conceptualism, as Putnam himself has claimed. David Wiggins (1980) has presented a 'conceptualist-realist' theory of the identity of substances drawing on Kripke's insights, but remains firmly within the conceptualist fold.

To rebut conceptualism, therefore, more is needed than a Kantian transcendental argument or the recognition of natural kinds in the Kripke–Putnam sense. It must be shown that reality itself contributes to the way we take the world to be articulated or divided, and this contribution must be distinguished from the contribution of the mind as receptor or interpreter or speculator – from the contingencies of sense-experience, language or theory. The canonical doctrine of substance took it that primitive logical subjects are apprehended as naturally unitary, naturally whole, naturally enduring individuals, prior to their classification by us. Such 'bodies' are standardly contrasted with merely notionally distinct and unitary individuals in other categories. Any philosophy of experience, identity and classification must either endorse such a distinction or rule it out: that is, must be either realist or conceptualist.

What reasons are there for adopting a realist, 'bottom-up' theory of identity and classification? A non-substantial entity such as an event is not determinately individuated except in virtue of some general concept, commonly a correspondent to nominalized predicate, adjectival or verbal. If standard conceptualist theories of identity were correct, the same would apply to substances. Only in virtue of a quasi-theoretical concept of an *insect*, or insect of a certain type, would it be possible to single out the individual which is in turn egg, larva, pupa and imago. Yet it seems evident that a material object can be picked out without our knowing what kind of thing it is, and that we can then learn from observation what metamorphoses such an object will normally undergo, or can survive. The possibility of refined classification comes with sustained observation of previously identified individuals. To classify substances is to group given individuals. Genera are groups of these groups. There is therefore no question of the individuals of the genus being different from the individuals of the species. This peculiarity of substances lies behind the Aristotelian principle that there are no ultimate species or individuals except in the category of substance. If a class of non-substances, say, *public assemblies*, is divided for some purpose into peaceful ones and violent ones so as to include, say, *demonstrations* and *riots*, then the class of riots is as good a species as the class of assemblies, and the individuals of these classes have different principles of individuation. An assembly exists while people are assembled, but a riot exists only as long as they riot. If an assembly is composed of a demonstration followed by a riot, the assembly, the demonstration and the riot are three distinct individuals. With substances, however, species can be divided without creating new species or individuals, as the species of human beings is divided almost indefinitely by natural languages. Bakers, adolescents, albinos, diabetics and rioters constitute neither distinct species nor individuals distinct from human beings. Rioters do not cease to exist when they cease to riot, nor children when they grow up. This is not an accidental feature of natural language, modifiable by stipulation. To stipulate identity-conditions for an entity, (say) a *bakens*, such that a *bakens* exists just as long as a baker is a baker, is only to individuate a non-substantial entity such as a baker's practice of baking. The notion of a temporal part or 'stage' has played a central role in twentieth-century conceptualist theories of identity, but what comes to an end when a kitten becomes adult is its kittenhood, a part or stage of its life, not a temporal part of a cat – there is no such thing. 'Kitten' is a compound predicate satisfied by naturally unitary individuals whose identity through time consists in their continuing so united, not in their satisfaction of that or any other predicate. Things which satisfy primitive noun-predicates such as 'cat' do so throughout their existence, but that is because these predicates mark membership of more or less natural groups by origin, morphology and structure. The individuality of the members of the kind is prior to such classification. The unity upon which their continuity depends is the natural discreteness and coherence of a material object: materiality and the possibility of such natural unity go together. In contrast, individual non-substances are notional unities sliced out by general terms; which is why modification of the terms in question breeds new individuals, and new species.

Other considerations relating to identity confirm the contrast between the category of substance and other categories of entity. For example, just as we can literally place a material object in new circumstances, so we can consider what would have happened to it if circumstances had been different. The very same individual might have had very different attributes – that is implicit in our ordinary understanding of a material thing as possessing indefinitely many potentialities. An event or state of affairs or action could not in this way be supposed qualitatively different and yet numerically identical: a possible Battle of Hastings won by the Saxons cannot be the same event as the battle actually won by the Normans.

Realism's strength lies not only in its philosophy of language but in an epistemology which explains how substantial individuals can be 'given' prior to conceptualization. It has traditionally been supposed that the deliverances of the different senses present only qualities which have somehow to be tied together conceptually or theoretically in order that we should conceive of the things or substances that possess them. In the Second Mediation Descartes saw this process as the intellect's employing an innate idea of extended substance in order to think the reality behind appearances, but idealists and some empiricists have seen it as an act of quasi-theoretical construction (see KANT, I. §3; PHENOMENALISM). Yet the model itself is wrong. That we have several senses does not mean that they are not integrated in their operation, presenting a unified field of bodies in space oriented in relation to our own perceived and perceiving body (that is, ourselves). Indeed, the briefest reflection on the phenomenology of perception supplies instances of such integration not only of sense with sense, but of sense with action. That we can hear a sound close to our ear does not mean that we hear our ear, or infer a relation to our ear from a quality of the sound, but that hearing is integrated with bodily awareness. That prismatic spectacles can invert all the objects in the visual field equally demonstrates that the way we feel our body to be, which includes our feeling it to be upright, can frame the deliverances of another sense. Eye and hand are coordinated in normal subjects because sight, bodily awareness and touch present a single sense-field integrated with the field of action. Here the philosophy and empirical psychology of perception converge, allowing us to understand the possibility of our pre-theoretical, pre-conceptual apprehension of just those natural individuals, traditional 'substances' that are logically fundamental in natural language. Although such objects are not also, as Aristotle supposed, fundamental in natural science, their unity and structure are there for physics to explain. It is false, then, that the world as we experience it, conceive of it and act within it in ordinary life owes its articulation to the structure of language, theory or 'conceptual scheme'. Rather, thought is shaped by the experienced world, and language owes the possibility of its deepest features, reference and predication, to the senses' grasp of really discrete individuals. That is a lesson that traditional theory of substance can still help to teach us.

See also: BEING; CONTINUANTS; IDENTITY; MATTER; MATTER, INDIAN CONCEPTIONS OF; ONTOLOGY; PHENOMENOLOGICAL MOVEMENT; REALISM AND ANTIREALISM; SCIENTIFIC REALISM AND ANTIREALISM; THEORIES, SCIENTIFIC

References and Further Reading

* Aristotle (*c*. mid 4th century BC) Categories, in *The Complete Works of Aristotle, (Revised Oxford Translation)*, ed. J. Barnes, Princeton, NJ: Princeton University Press, vol. 1, 1984. (Sets out the logical doctrine of substance.)
* —— (*c*. mid 4th century BC) *Metaphysics*, in *The Complete Works of Aristotle (Revised Oxford Translation)*, vol. 2, ed. J. Barnes, Princeton, NJ: Princeton University Press, 1984. (Explores ways in which substance is fundamental. Book I (A) considers earlier views, and VII (Z) argues that unitary bodies, that is individual living things, are substances.)
* Ayer, A.J. (1936) *Language, Truth and Logic*, London: Victor Gollancz. (Chapter 1, 'The Elimination of Metaphysics', argues that theories of substance are confusions due to language.)
  Ayers, M.R. (1991) *Locke*, London: Routledge. (Volume 1, Part 3 contains a theory of integrated perception of objects. Volume 2, Part 1 finds insights in Locke's and other theories of substance; Part 3 expounds a realist theory of identity.)
* Descartes, R. (1641) Meditations on First Philosophy, in *The Philosophical Writings of Descartes* vol. 2, trans. J. Cottingham, R. Stoothoff and D. Murdoch, Cambridge: Cambridge University Press, 1985. (Classic argument for mind–body dualism.)
* —— (1644) *Principles of Philosophy*, Part 1, §§ 51–65, in *The Philosophical Writings of Descartes*, vol. 1, trans. J. Cottingham, R. Stoothoff and D. Murdoch, Cambridge: Cambridge University Press, 1985. (Descartes' account of substances and their relation to their principle attributes and modes.)
* Epicurus (*c*.305 BC) Letter to Herodotus (from Diogenes Laertius, Lives of the Philosophers) in *Epicurus: The Extant Remains*, ed. C. Bailey, Oxford: Oxford University Press, 1926. (Argues that bodies, in particular atoms, are substances, and that accidents are not distinct entities.)
* Hobbes, T. (1651) *Leviathan*, ed. R. Tuck, Cambridge: Cambridge University Press, 1991. (Chapter 34 sets out Hobbes' materialist conception of substance and accident.)
* Hume, D. (1739–40) *A Treatise of Human Nature*, ed. L.A. Selby Bigge, revised P.H. Nidditch, Oxford: Oxford University Press, 1978. (Book I, part 1, § 7;

part 4, §§ 3 and 5 criticize the traditional concept of substance, and the substance-mode relation.)
* Kant, I. (1781) *Critique of Pure Reason*, trans. N. Kemp Smith, London: Macmillan, 1963. (Argues that substance is an ineluctable category of judgment, imposed by the mind on what is given to sensibility.)
* Kripke, S.A. (1980) *Naming and Necessity*, Oxford: Oxford University Press, 1980. (Rejects accounts of proper names which assign them sense or treat them as abbreviated descriptions, and extends a causal theory of meaning from this to other areas of language; revolutionary.)
* Leibniz, G. W. (1686) *Discourse on Metaphysics, in Philosophical Essays*, trans. and ed. R. Ariew and D. Garber, Indianapolis, IN: Hackett Publishing Company, 1989. (Expounds a notion of individual substances, whose concepts contain all their predicates.)
* —— (1714) *The Principles of Philosophy, or, the Monadology*, in *Philosophical Essays*, trans. and ed. R. Ariew and D. Garber, Indianapolis, IN: Hackett Publishing Company, 1989. (Identifies 'monads', simple immaterial individuals, as the only substances.)
* Locke, J. (1689) *Essay concerning Human Understanding*, ed. P.H. Nidditch, Oxford: Oxford University Press, 1975. (See Book II, chapter 23, Book III, chapter 6, and following, for an interpretation of the idea of substance as place-marker for unknown essences or natures.)
* Plato (*c*.380–367 BC) *The Republic*, in *The Dialogues of Plato*, ed. B. Jowett, Oxford: Oxford University Press, 1892. (Books V–VIII give an account of what is.)
* Putnam, H. (1975) *Mind, Language and Reality*, in *Philosophical Papers*, vol. 2, Cambridge: Cambridge University Press. (Contains a series of papers arguing that the meaning of natural-kind names lies in their reference to reality, not in definitions 'in the head'; revolutionary.)
* Quine, W.V. (1953) 'On what there is', in *From a Logical Point of View*, New York: Harper & Row. (An early statement of Quine's view that ontological commitment is expressed through qualification.)
* —— (1960) *Word and Object*, Cambridge, MA: MIT Press. (Classic exposition of contemporary pragmatist conceptualism, arguing that ontology is relative to language or conceptual scheme.)
* Rorty, R. (1980) *Philosophy and the Mirror of Nature*, Oxford: Blackwell. (An extreme version of relativistic conceptualism, with sympathetic interpretations of many modern exponents; widely read and influential.)

* Spinoza, B. de (1677) *Ethics*, in *The Collected Works of Spinoza*, vol. 1, ed. E. Curley, Princeton, NJ: Princeton University Press, 1985. (Makes thought and extension attributes of the one substance, of which all individual minds and bodies are modes.)
* Strawson, P.F. (1958) *Individuals*, London: Methuen. (Argues that objective experience would be impossible without material things such as are basic objects of reference in natural language.)
* Suárez, F. (1597) *Metaphysical Disputations*, Book VII, trans. C. Vollert, *On the Various Kinds of Distinction*, Milwaukee, WI: Marquette University Press, 1947. (Holds that accidents are 'modally distinct' and, although naturally dependent, in principle separable from substances in which they inhere.)
* Wiggins, D. (1980) *Sameness and Substance*, Oxford: Blackwell. (Advances a theory of identity consonant with Kripke's insights, which attempts to combine conceptualism and realism.)
* William of Ockham (1322–7) *Summa Logica*, Part 1, trans. M.J. Loux, *Ockham's Theory of Terms*, Notre Dame, IN: University of Notre Dame Press, 1974. (Chapters 19–62 consider which categories of abstract terms stand for really distinct particular beings. Not many do.)
* Wittgenstein, L. (1953) *Philosophical Investigations*, Oxford: Blackwell. (Wittgenstein's late masterpiece, identifying the source of philosophical theories in misunderstandings of language and its structures, and the source of those structures in the roles of language in life.)

M.R. AYERS

SUBSTITUTIONAL INTERPRETATION OF QUANTIFIERS *see* QUANTIFIERS, SUBSTITUTIONAL AND OBJECTUAL

SUCHON, GABRIELLE (1631–1703)

Seventeenth-century rationalist feminist philosopher and author of two books dealing with many moral, social and political issues, Suchon advocated liberty, knowledge, authority and the possibility of an unmarried life for women. In this she did not employ any ready-made philosophy but created her own. Freedom and knowledge are everyone's natural rights, understood as rights that get their strength from themselves only and are to be observed everywhere alike.

Self-taught philosopher, author of a *Traité de la morale et de la politique* (Treatise on morals and politics) (1693) and *Du Célibat volontaire* (Of voluntary single life) (1700), Gabrielle Suchon was born at Semur in Burgundy, France. Forced into a convent, she later went to Rome and got a Papal writ releasing her from her vows. Her family took her to court and the Dijon Parliament ruled that she had to go back to her convent. Evading the sentence she spent the rest of her life reading and writing, 'abandoned of all creatures, but not of my Creator, who gave me the grace not to abandon myself' (1693: XV).

Suchon's *Traité* on morality and politics is valuable as a work of metaphysics, epistemology and theology. Advocating 'liberty, knowledge and authority' for women, the book provides inventive theories about, among other things, 'privation' (described as being productive of effects), natural rights, original sin and constraint. Suchon is not a relativist. Her method implies that looking at women's position with respect to knowledge, liberty, marriage and the like, provides a deeper insight into what those things are in themselves and helps better to judge of their exact values.

Like many others, Suchon was scandalized that schools and universities were closed to women while male 'idiots' had access to them. Yet she considered that personal reflection and use of the seeds of light given by God were most important of all, learning acquired by reading being second. As for knowledge derived from tutors, it is an enjoyable luxury but no more. Furthermore, the original sin was not the transgression of an interdict against knowledge of good and evil: God wanted humankind to know, and Suchon seems not to acknowledge any ban on curiosity. But Adam and Eve should have sought wisdom through their own intellectual effort, rather than seeking a ready-made answer by the facile method of eating an apple. Women can acquire a valuable understanding of moral, political and metaphysical questions by thinking for themselves. Reason is the name of that which enables us to be self-taught people. Although this applies to men and women alike, it can be best demonstrated by first considering women's position and then drawing from this an indication of how things stand in themselves, and so incidentally for men as well.

Knowledge and freedom are everyone's natural rights, natural right being a 'right that holds its strength from itself only and is to be observed everywhere alike' (1693: 23). It is not contingent upon laws or capricious custom. Knowledge and freedom both come into being by being exerted, but there is an interaction between the two. And knowledge is 'beatitude commenced'.

It is a knowledge of values that Suchon ultimately seeks. Why is freedom so good? What different kinds of liberties are most important? What is marriage but an oppression and a burden only a saint's sister could bear? Bad enough in itself, submission becomes so insufferable when one is forced to obey a person with no sense that it requires a special grace to endure the miseries involved. Again Suchon writes this with women's marital duties in mind. But in this second work, *Of voluntary single life*, she considers, as she did in her first treatise, that what is true for women must also to some extent be true for men. After all, male authors have harped on the many vexations of married life.

Suchon makes the female the universal, and her strategy is supported by a linguistic feature in French. The word 'person', which refers to men, women and components of the Holy Trinity alike, is grammatically feminine. It is therefore quite easy for her to have a universal 'she' and constantly to shift from statements concerning women to statements concerning 'persons' and vice versa. Her work is dedicated to the Trinity, again a feminine word in French and, obviously enough, a female power under Suchon's pen.

Nothing is known yet about how Suchon managed to educate herself. Through the authors she quotes, one may surmise what books she had access to: ancient philosophers, (though not all), countless Church Fathers, perhaps the Scriptures themselves (not obviously a possession for a lay person in Louis XIV's France), some modern authors such as Petrarch, Pascal and Poulain de la Barre (a Cartesian who had published *De l'égalité des deux sexes* (On Equality of Both Sexes) in 1673). Her convent's library may well have been decently furnished, and she did make a point about using whatever little money one has to buy books. The reception of her work is not much known either. Perhaps it was not too bad. Her two books were reviewed in *Le Journal des Savants* in 1694 and 1700, the second one also in *Nouvelles de la République des Lettres*. Long after her death, an entry 'Gabrielle Suchon' appeared in Papillon's *Bibliothèque des auteurs de Bourgogne* (1745).

List of works

Suchon, G. (1693) *Traité de la morale et de la politique* (Treatise on morals and politics), Lyon: B. Vignieu; selections of part I, ed. S. Auffret, repr. Paris: Des Femmes, 1988. (Although now deprived of freedom, knowledge and authority, women have a natural capacity for and claim to them. Originally published under the pen name of G.S. Aristophile.)

—— (1700) *Du Célibat volontaire ou la vie sans engagement* (Of voluntary single life), Paris: J.&M. Guignard, 2 vols; selected chaps, ed. S. Auffret, repr. Paris: Indigo & Côté-femmes, 1994. (There are now two positions only for a woman, namely matrimony or the cloister. There should be a third one, lay single life, for women who do not want to submit to a husband's authority nor to a monastic rule. Containing sharp criticisms of matrimony and the way families trade their daughters away to the cloister, the book provides a utopian vision of single women's lives.)

References and further reading

Albistur, M. and Armogathe, D. (1977) *Histoire du Féminisme Français* (A history of French Feminism), vol. 1, Paris: Des Femmes. (A very brief survey of Suchon's life and work.)

Barre, P. de la (1673) *De l'égalité des deux sexes*, Paris: Fayard, 1984; trans. A.L. as *The Woman as good as the man, or, the Equality of both sexes*, London, 1677; repr. ed. G.M. McLean, Detroit, MI: Wayne State University Press, 1988. (When considered independently of custom, both sexes are utterly equal; the matter, disregarding great men's authority, must be discussed from the point of view of reason and common sense only.)

Bertolini, S. (1977) *Gabrielle Suchon: une Écrivaine engagée pour une vie sans engagement* (A writer committed to a life without commitment), unpublished dissertation, Geneva, Faculté des Lettres. (A scholarly essay on Suchon's *Of voluntary single life*, containing findings about her life and family background.)

Geffriaud-Rosso, J. (1988) 'Gabrielle Suchon: une troisième voie pour la femme?', in Döring, U. (ed.) *Ouverture et Dialogue*, Tübingen: Gunther Narr Verlag, 669–78. (Appraisal of Suchon's views on single life.)

Hoffman, P. (1978) 'Le Féminisme spirituel de Gabrielle Suchon', *XVIIe Siècle* 121: 269–76. (Suchon regarded as a masochist follower of Poulain de la Barre.)

Papillon (1745) *Bibliothèque des auteurs de Bourgogne* (Library of Bourgogne authors), Dijon: F. Desventes; repr. Geneva: Slatline, 1970. (Papillon, who had met Suchon, is a main source about her life. Entry contains some remarks about the reception of her books.)

Ronzeaud, P. (1975) 'La femme au pouvoir ou le

monde à l'envers', *XVIIe Siècle* 108: 9–33. (Views
Suchon's way of thinking as not theoretical but as a
spiritual quest for a feminine identity.)

MICHÈLE LE DOEUFF

SUFFERING

*Although sometimes identified with pain, suffering is
better understood as a highly unpleasant emotional
state associated with considerable pain or distress.
Whether and how much one suffers can vary in
accordance with any meaning attached to the associated
pain or distress, or with expectations regarding the
future. Because suffering can be affected by thoughts of
meaning or of the future, some have focused on this
dimension of suffering and asserted that only humans
can suffer. But there is a very strong empirical case that
many nonhuman animals suffer. The fact of suffering
provokes moral concern, especially when suffering is
caused unnecessarily, and raises ethical questions,
mainly regarding the nature and extent of our obligations to those who suffer. Suffering is also an important
source of personal or religious meaning in many
people's lives.*

1   Concept
2   Subjects of suffering
3   Ethical importance
4   Personal and religious meaning

1   Concept

What is suffering? Casual usage sometimes suggests
that suffering is identical to *pain*, but surely the pain
caused by an ordinary pinch on the arm is too mild to
count as suffering. Moreover, pain, but not suffering,
can be located in specific body parts. While pain and
suffering differ, it is possible to overstate their
differences. On the *sensation model*, pain is simply a
kind of sensation, which varies in intensity, duration,
location, and features that permit classifying it as a
particular kind of pain (such as an ache or twinge).
On this model, pain need not be at all unpleasant: we
may or may not suffer even when we are in great pain,
since pain does not necessarily involve an affective
dimension. On the *attitude model*, however, pain is
any sensation (or perhaps any feeling) we dislike for
its own felt qualities, suggesting less conceptual
distance between pain and suffering. Each model of
pain faces certain theoretical challenges. It seems safe
to say, however, that pain is at least typically (whether
or not intrinsically) unpleasant, in which case at least

most painful experiences involve some degree of affect
– a feature shared with suffering, as we will see (see
BODILY SENSATIONS).

Suffering also bears a close relationship to *distress*
but cannot be identified with it. The mild distress of a
professor who is late to class need not involve
suffering, even if someone having an anxiety attack
(a kind of distress) clearly does suffer. Very roughly,
distress is an emotional state that can be caused by, or
take the form of, various more specific mental states
such as fear, anxiety and discomfort.

While any precise analysis of 'suffering' will be
controversial, suffering may be understood roughly as
*a highly unpleasant emotional state associated with
considerable pain or distress*. The words 'associated
with' bypass the issue of whether considerable pain or
distress *causes* suffering or *is a form of* (or conceptually overlaps with) suffering. Perhaps terror is a
form of suffering, not a mere cause. Perhaps
excruciating pain in its affective dimension (as
opposed to its bodily location) is suffering. One's
judgments here will depend on one's specific analyses
of these mental states.

Whether and how much one suffers can vary in
accordance with attitudes or expectations about the
associated pain or distress or about the context in
which it occurs. Even the mild pain of a common
headache can lead to great distress and suffering if the
pain endures with no end in sight, or if the subject
believes the headache is a sign of impending physical
deterioration. On the other hand, soldiers have
sometimes received major injuries yet apparently not
suffered much, due, for instance, to the relief of
expecting removal from combat, or to positive
attitudes to the heroic context of their injury. Long-
distance runners who experience pain and discomfort
in a race may or may not suffer, or may suffer more or
less, depending on such psychological factors as how
they evaluate their efforts, and whether they are
relaxed or fearful in their attitudes regarding the
remainder of the course. Thus any meaning one
attaches to one's situation, as well as one's expectations for the future, are important factors in whether
and how much one suffers.

2   Subjects of suffering

Who can suffer? Because meaning and expectations
for the future are important factors in human
suffering, and because nonhuman animals are often
thought incapable of assigning meaning and anticipating the future, it is sometimes asserted that only
humans can suffer (see MORAL STANDING §2).

This assertion is highly doubtful, however. First, to
say that meaning and expectations for the future are

important factors in human suffering is not to say either is a necessary condition of suffering. It seems plausible that pouring scalding water on a human baby would cause suffering, even if the baby could assign no more meaning to the event than a dog could. And even if expectations for the future were necessary for suffering, the thesis that only humans can suffer would depend on the premise that animals have no sense of the future. But it is highly questionable whether the behaviour of 'higher' animals, as studied in cognitive ethology, can be adequately understood without attributing at least minimal awareness of time to them.

Because suffering is an emotional state, only sentient beings can possibly suffer. Behavioural evidence, physiological data, and evolutionary considerations together make a strong case that many animals – possibly including most or all vertebrates – are sentient. But there may be sentient animals who cannot suffer, either because they can experience only minimal pain and distress or because they are incapable of highly unpleasant emotional states.

3 Ethical importance

It is generally agreed that suffering tends to make one less well off, due to its intrinsic aversiveness and its instrumental disvalue, the way it interferes with our doing and getting things we want. Suffering is a harm.

Suffering therefore provokes moral concern and raises ethical issues. It often isolates the subject, posing special challenges, for example, to medical professionals and families dealing with infirm elderly persons. When suffering results from human action, it clearly becomes an ethical matter, and virtually every ethical theory or tradition includes some injunction against unnecessary causing of suffering (see EVIL). But whose suffering counts? While humans uncontroversially fall under the scope of such an injunction, it is increasingly believed that sentient animals do as well (see ANIMALS AND ETHICS).

Points of controversy include the following. First, when is it 'necessary' – that is, justified – to cause suffering? For example, do the products of factory farming justify the suffering caused to the animals? Second, do we have positive obligations to those who suffer and, if so, to what extent? What are our obligations, if any, to famine victims, politically persecuted individuals, and women sold into spousal slavery? Third, what affective capacities and moral virtues are required for appropriate responses to suffering? Can one respond well to a grieving associate without vividly grasping their experience? Could an appropriate response be described without mentioning virtues, such as compassion and sensitivity?

4 Personal and religious meaning

Although a harm, suffering is for many people a source of personal or religious meaning. Those who have suffered extensively often report that their experience has enabled them to appreciate what is truly important in life as opposed to what is superficial and fleeting. Someone who has endured cancer may say that they are now less concerned with personal accolades and more involved in their children's lives. The experience of suffering sometimes increases one's sensitivity to others' suffering. Someone evicted unexpectedly from their apartment and rendered temporarily homeless may better understand and care about the plight of the chronically homeless. It is also often asserted that suffering builds character. A confident individual for whom things always came easily may be devastated by a spouse's death but, in the aftermath, begin to cultivate courage, perseverance, and humility. Moreover, when suffering provokes a compassionate response from others, this may strengthen the subject's faith in their fellows. (Sometimes such positive experiences of meaning help to alleviate present suffering (see §1).)

Religious individuals often understand suffering to have a positive aspect or some other important meaning. Priests and monks of various religions may embrace self-denial, the suffering that comes with it, and the virtues such suffering encourages. Christians understand suffering to permit greater identification with Jesus, who is believed to have suffered for the benefit of all, providing a model of virtuous sacrifice. According to Buddhism, suffering results from desire or craving – whether for sensual pleasure, wealth, or even personal ideals – and all desire involves the idea of oneself as separate from other things. Suffering is eliminated by extinguishing desire, through right living, meditation, and the eventual achievement of *nirvāna*, a state of peace and insight in which one abandons the notion of a separate self (see ASCETICISM).

See also: EVIL, PROBLEM OF; GOOD, THEORIES OF THE; HEDONISM; PLEASURE; SUFFERING, BUDDHIST VIEWS OF ORIGINATION OF; VULNERABILITY AND FINITUDE

References and further reading

Cassell, E. (1991) *The Nature of Suffering and the Goals of Medicine*, New York: Oxford University Press. (An insightful and well-informed discussion of suffering and its relation to the goals of medicine.)

DeGrazia, D. (1996) *Taking Animals Seriously:*

Mental Life and Moral Status, Cambridge: Cambridge University Press. (A philosophical examination of the mental life of nonhuman animals, including their suffering, and of basic ethical issues regarding animals.)

Melzack, R. and Wall, P.D. (1983) *The Challenge of Pain*, New York: Basic Books. (A thoughtful scientific investigation of the physiology, psychology and control of pain.)

Pitcher, G. (1970) 'The Awfulness of Pain', *Journal of Philosophy* 68: 481–92. (An excellent examination of the strengths and weaknesses of different models of pain.)

Rahula, W. (1959) *What the Buddha Taught*, New York: Grove Press; revised edns, 1974, 1987. (A relatively clear, though not philosophically precise, introduction to the essential ideas of Buddhism, including the Buddhist understanding of suffering.)

Rose, M. and Adams, D. (1989) 'Evidence for Pain and Suffering in Other Animals', in G. Langley (ed.) *Animal Experimentation: The Consensus Changes*, 42–71, New York: Chapman and Hall. (An excellent summary of empirical evidence for pain and suffering in nonhuman animals.)

Sumner, W.L. (1992) 'Welfare, Happiness, and Pleasure', *Utilitas* 4: 199–223. (An exceptionally clear examination of competing models of some mental states of interest to utilitarianism, including pain and suffering.)

DAVID DeGRAZIA

SUFFERING, BUDDHIST VIEWS OF ORIGINATION OF

The Sanskrit term pratītyasamutpāda *(Pāli,* paṭiccasamuppāda*) literally translates as 'arising [of a thing] after encountering [its causes and conditions]'. This term, conventionally translated as 'dependent origination', 'conditioned co-arising' or 'interdependent arising', signifies the Buddhist doctrine of causality. This doctrine is usually applied to explain the origin of suffering (*duḥkha*) as well as the means of liberation from it. According to the Buddhist tradition, the Buddha discovered the law of dependent origination during his meditation on the night he attained his awakening. According to traditional accounts, he saw all his former lives and the lives of all other beings, understood the principle governing transmigration, and found the way of liberation. He then formulated the so-called Four Noble Truths, the Eightfold Noble Path and the Law of Dependent Origination. The twelve elements of the chain of dependent origination were designed to explain the mechanism of entanglement of a sentient being in a wheel of consecutive lives, and, at the same time, to explain how this entanglement is possible without admitting the concept of a permanent principle, like 'self', 'ego', and the like. These twelve members are: (1) ignorance, (2) formations (volitional dispositions), (3) consciousness, (4) name and form, (5) six bases of cognition, (6) contact, (7) feeling, (8) desire, (9) attachment, (10) existence, (11) rebirth, (12) ageing and death. In addition to the twelvefold formula, there is also the so-called 'general formula' of dependent origination, which goes 'when this is, that arises; when this is not, that does not arise.'*

1 **Canonical accounts**
2 **Scholastic interpretations**
3 **Mādhyamika and Yogācāra**

1 Canonical accounts

The Buddhist tradition has it that Prince Siddhārtha Gautama, after a prolonged meditation under the bodhi tree, attained enlightenment or awakening (*bodhi*), the ultimate understanding of the Four Noble Truths: (1) there is suffering, (2) there is a cause of the arising of suffering, (3) there is an extinction of suffering, and (4) there is a means to come to the end of suffering. The means is to follow the so-called middle path between the extremes of self-indulgence and self-mortification. This fundamental teaching was expounded in the Buddha's first sermon, the so-called 'Sermon of the Turning of the Wheel of the Law' (*Dhammacakkapavattana Sutta*) (see BUDDHA).

The second of the Noble Truths, the Noble Truth of the Arising of Suffering, is often explained in terms of the twelvefold law of dependent origination. The twelve members of the chain of dependent origination are: (1) ignorance, (2) formations (volitional dispositions), (3) consciousness, (4) name and form (body and mentality), (5) six bases of cognition (sense faculties), (6) contact (of sense faculty with sensible object), (7) (physical and mental) feeling, (8) desire, (9) attachment, (10) existence, (11) birth, (12) old age and death. Each member of this sequence is conditioned by what precedes it. The doctrine is commonly regarded as the fundamental teaching of the Buddha, together with his teaching on the Four Noble Truths and the Eightfold Noble Path. An often-quoted canonical passage says that 'He who sees dependent origination sees the Doctrine (*Dharma*; Pāli, *Dhamma*); he who sees the Doctrine sees dependent origination' (*Majjhima Nikāya* 1.190–1). Elsewhere it is said that one who sees the Doctrine sees the Buddha. Thus, to see the principle of dependent origination is equivalent to seeing the Buddha. From the very beginning, this doctrine was regarded as the most profound and difficult teaching of the Buddha.

Some traditional texts declare that the law of dependent origination exists independently of whether Tathāgatas, those who know the truth, appear in the world to discover it. According to these texts, the law of dependent origination is rediscovered each time by the present *buddha*, as an old deserted city hidden in the jungle is discovered by a traveller. Sāriputra, one the most prominent disciples of the Buddha, was converted to his teachings by means of a single stanza uttered by Aśvajit (Assaji), one of the five first disciples: 'All things are born of causes, and of these the Tathāgata has proclaimed the cause, and their extinction too: thus does the Great Ascetic speak' (see Takasaki 1987: 72). This stanza summarizes the law of dependent origination, the very core of the Buddha's teaching on the causal character of the phenomena of existence. It later became regarded as a kind of Buddhist credo.

Research by Lamotte (1980) has shown that the Buddhist sources are not unanimous as to the moment of the discovery of dependent origination by the Buddha and its place within his doctrine. According to some texts, the Buddha acquired a full comprehension of the twelve-membered chain of dependent origination before the attainment of enlightenment, while other texts place the event during or after the enlightenment.

The notion of suffering (*duḥkha*) has in Buddhism an existential dimension and extends over all aspects of human life in this world. Everything existing is produced from causes, is momentary and devoid of a 'self' (that is, of any permanent unchangeable principle), and therefore is painful. Since the Buddhist doctrine denies any permanent principle like a soul, self or ego that transmigrates by virtue of previously committed actions from one life to another, it is admitted that a 'human being', a 'person' is but a conventional designation of a conglomerate of various factors, which appear in a stream of five groups of psychical and physical existential phenomena, and which are mutually conditioned and regulated by the law of dependent origination. A full insight into the twelve members of the chain of dependent origination, and into the extinction of consecutive members, brings realization of the ultimate goal of Buddhism, attainment of buddhahood.

According to Frauwallner's hypothesis, it is possible to demonstrate that the chain of dependent origination has a composite character; the twelvefold chain could have been compiled by the Buddha himself from two shorter causal chains. Also, the so-called *Pratītyasamutpādasūtra*, a fundamental canonical exposition of the doctrine, is to be regarded as a later compilation (Frauwallner 1956). This text was the object of a lengthy commentary by the fifth-century Buddhist philosopher VASUBANDHU.

One can also show that beside the twelvefold chain of dependent origination there existed in the canonical texts other causal sequences, in which are clearly visible the components known to us from the former sequence. The final formulation of the doctrine seems to have been completed only after a long process of compilation which may have lasted until the great schism within the Buddhist order, perhaps shortly before Aśoka (middle of the third century BC).

2 Scholastic interpretations

The doctrine of dependent origination has been variously modified and interpreted within the schools of Buddhism. Usually it is applied to explain an individual human life in three time periods: past, present and future. Vasubandhu's *Abhidharmakośa* (Treasury of the Doctrine) (3.20–) presents several classifications of the twelve members of dependent origination (see §1). Vasubandhu distributes the twelve items into three periods of time: (1) and (2) belong to the past, (3) to (10) to the present, and (11) and (12) to the future. Alternatively, there is a twofold division of the members, whereby (1) to (7) belong to past existence, and the remainder to future existence. From the point of view of karma, (1), (8) and (9) are regarded as defilements that predispose one to karma, (2) and (10) are regarded as actions (karma itself), and the remaining seven members are regarded as supports of the defilements and actions.

The Pāli canonical *Mahātaṇhāsaṅkhayasutta* (Great Discourse on Destruction of Desire) juxtaposes the theory of dependent origination and another explication of entanglement in the painful world, namely the theory of *gandhabba* (Sanskrit, *gandharva*), an immaterial being that acts as a bridge for human beings from one incarnation to another. The text describes the consecutive stages of conception, embryonic development, birth, growing up and sensual contact with the outer world, which result in origination of the whole mass of suffering. Conception takes place when mother and father are sexually united, when the mother is ovulating and when a *gandhabba* is present. When the child is born, its senses mature, and it amuses itself with the pleasures of the senses. It becomes attached to pleasant experiences and vexed by unpleasant ones. This delight in feelings is attachment; conditioned by attachment, there is desire for further becoming; conditioning by this desire, there is birth; conditioned by birth, there is old age and death, and also sorrow, lamentation, pain, grief and despair. Such is the origin of this whole aggregate of suffering, without any permanent 'soul' or 'self' or any other unchangeable principle.

The fusion of the theory of an intermediate immaterial being and the theory of the twelve links of dependent origination is mentioned in Vasubandhu's *Abhidharmakośa* (ad 3.15a–b; 3.19). His *Abhidharmakośa* (ad 3.28ab) contains the Sarvāstivāda interpretation of dependent origination, which is outlined in as follows. A fool who does not comprehend that the world is nothing more than a collection of mutually dependent phenomena develops a false notion of a self. He performs bodily, vocal and intellectual actions with the intention of experiencing pleasure. He performs beneficial deeds in the hopes of securing a better future life. He may perform harmful deeds in order to secure short-term gains. In this way he accumulates karma conditioned by ignorance. His stream of consciousness, forced by his previous karma, goes from one destiny to another in the same way that a flame 'moves'; in reality there is no motion, but merely the arising of contiguous moments, each caused by its predecessors. At death of the body, the predisposition to survive continues, so the stream of consciousness seeks out a new body in which to dwell. In this way karma gives rise to new consciousness. When it finds a new body, consciousness conditions the acquisition of body and mentality. When these mature, sense faculties arise. These come into contact with sensible objects, giving rise to pleasant or unpleasant feelings. From these feelings there arises craving. Pleasant experiences give rise to a craving for pleasure to continue, while unpleasant experiences give rise to a craving for discomfort to end. These cravings are the condition for the development of clinging to false views and belief in (or hope for) an enduring self. This clinging conditions desires for future existence, as a result of which there is birth. From birth there inevitably follows ageing and death (see Mejor 1991: 96–7).

3 Mādhyamika and Yogācāra

With NĀGĀRJUNA (second century), the founder of the Mādhyamika school, the theorem of dependent origination acquired a central position. The full comprehension of dependent origination is tantamount to comprehension of the Four Noble Truths: 'Whoever comprehends dependent origination also comprehends suffering, its arising, its ceasing and the path' (*Mūlamadhyamakakārikā* (Fundamental Treatise on the Middle Path) 24.40). The ultimate elements of being arise from causes. They are mutually conditioned, are dependent on others, and thus, devoid of any kind of self-nature, they have no real

existence of their own. Whatever exists that has originated dependently is said to be empty (*śūnya*). Therefore, dependent origination is tantamount to emptiness (*śūnyatā*) (see BUDDHIST CONCEPT OF EMPTINESS). All names are but conventional designations, for ultimately they refer to no real existents. Discrimination of the two truths, conventional and ultimate, shows the equality of the emptiness and dependent origination of the elements of being. Nāgārjuna says: 'We say that dependent origination is emptiness. That is dependence upon convention. That itself is the middle path' (*Mūlamadhyamakakārikā* 24.18).

In the Yogācāra school, the functioning of twelvefold dependent origination is applied to the transformation of consciousness. According to Vasubandhu's exposition of the doctrine of 'ideation-only' (*vijñaptimātra*), all distinctions between subject and object are due to the threefold transformation of consciousness, which itself depends on various causes. Thus, the transformation of consciousness is but an ideation, a false imagining of subject and object, and all this is a mere representation of consciousness. As the sixth-century Yogācārin philosopher Sthiramati states in his commentary on Vasubandhu's *Triṃśikā* (Thirty Stanzas):

No cognizable object exists in reality, because it is in its nature wrongly imagined. Further, consciousness does not exist substantially, because it is dependently originated. So it is assumed. Further, the dependent origination of consciousness is known under the term 'transformation'.

> (commentary on stanza 1;
> see Vasubandhu, ed. Levi 1925)

In other words, the process whereby the elements of being arise and accumulate is a process of obscuration or defilement of thought. And this is dependent origination in its ascending order; that is, beginning with consideration of ignorance, one realizes that it conditions volitions, and so forth through the cycle of conditions to birth and its inevitable consequences of ageing and death. The reverse process of purification of thought is dependent origination in descending order, leading to final liberation; that is, realizing that there would be no ageing and death without birth, no birth without the desire to continue being, and ultimately none of this without ignorance, one knows that one must eliminate the ignorance that takes the form of imposing a distinction between subject and object upon experience as a whole (see La Vallée Poussin 1913: 65).

In the Perfection of Wisdom (*Prajñāpāramitā*) literature, the contemplation of dependent origination is included in the practice of a *bodhisattva* who aspires to perfection of wisdom. In this literature, it said, for example, that the *bodhisattva* should aspire to realize that no phenomenon whatsoever is produced without a cause. On seeing this, the *bodhisattva* will know that nothing is permanent, and nothing is spared eventual extinction. On seeing this in turn, he will see no item of experience as a self, a being, a soul, a creature, a human being, a person, a youth, a personality, an agent, one with feelings, one who knows or one who sees. If the *bodhisattva* does not see experience in these terms, he will not see experience as either permanent or impermanent, as pleasant or unpleasant, or as 'self' or 'other' (see Conze 1984: 491).

See also: BUDDHISM, MĀDHYAMIKA: INDIA AND TIBET; BUDDHISM, YOGĀCĀRA SCHOOL OF; BUDDHIST PHILOSOPHY, INDIAN; BUDDHIST PHILOSOPHY, CHINESE §13; NIRVĀṆA

References and further reading

Bernhard, F. (1969) 'Zur Interpretation der *Pratītya-samutpāda*-Formel' (On the Interpretation of the *Pratītyasamutpāda* Formula), *Wiener Zeitschrift für die Kunde Südasiens* 12/13: 53–63. (Supports with textual evidence Frauwallner's hypothesis on the original form of the formula of dependent origination.)

* Conze, E. (1984) *The Large Sutra on Perfect Wisdom with the Divisions of the Abhisamayālaṅkāra*, Berkeley, CA: University of California Press. (English translation of a Mahāyāna text.)

De Jong, J.W. (1974) 'A propos de Nidānasaṃyukta', in *Mélanges de Sinologie offerts à Monsieur Paul Demiéville*, Paris, vol. 2: 137–49; repr. in De Jong, J.W., *Buddhist Studies*, ed. G. Schopen, Berkeley, CA: University of California Press, 1979. (An important survey of Buddhist texts dealing with the *pratītyasamutpāda*.)

* Frauwallner, E. (trans.) (1956) *Die Philosophie des Buddhismus*, ed. W. Ruben, Berlin: Akademie-Verlag, 4th edn, 1994. (An anthology of Buddhist philosophical texts, translated and presented by one of the best scholars of the subject.)

Gupta, R. (1977) '"Twelve-Membered Dependent Origination": An Attempted Reappraisal', *Journal of Indian Philosophy* 5: 163–86. (An attempt towards interpretation of the meaning of the twelve-membered formula of dependent origination.)

Kalupahana, D.J. (1975) *Causality: The Central Philosophy of Buddhism*, Honolulu, HI: University Press of Hawaii. (A thorough study of the Buddhist concept of causality in the context of non-Buddhist doctrines, with a chapter devoted to the exposition of dependent origination based mostly on Pāli sources.)

—— (1987) 'Pratītya-samutpāda', in M. Eliade (ed.) *Encyclopedia of Religion*, New York and London: Macmillan, vol. 11, 484–8. (The author singles out the *Kātyāyana-avavāda* from the Pāli *Saṃyutta Nikāya* (2.16–17) as a text 'which serves as the *locus classicus* of all subsequent interpretations of the Buddha's "middle path".'.)

Kochumuttom, T.A. (1982) *A Buddhist Doctrine of Experience: A New Translation and Interpretation of the Works of Vasubandhu the Yogācārin*, Delhi: Motilal Banarsidass. (A study of Vasubandhu's works representing the 'ideation-only' doctrine; contains discussions and translations of numerous fragments.)

* La Vallée Poussin, L. de (1913) *Théorie des douze causes*, Receuil de travaux publiés par la Faculté de Philosophies et Lettres de l'Université de Gand, fasc. 40, Gand: Librairie Scientifique E. Van Goethem. (A classical study by one of the greatest masters of Buddhist studies. Contains original texts in Sanskrit and Tibetan.)

* Lamotte, E. (1980) 'Conditioned Co-production and Supreme Enlightenment', in S. Balasooriya, A. Bareau, R. Gombrich, S. Gunasingha, U. Mallawarachchi and E. Perry (eds) *Buddhist Studies in Honour of Walpola Rahula*, London: Gordon Fraser, 118–32. (An attempt to classify Buddhist records on the Buddha's discovery of the law of dependent origination.)

Law, B.C. (1937) 'Formulation of *Pratītyasamutpāda*', *Journal of the Royal Asiatic Society* (April): 287–92. (Somewhat dated but still useful paper introducing the formula of dependent origination from Pāli sources.)

* Mejor, M. (1991) *Vasubandhu's Abhidharmakośa and the Commentaries Preserved in the Tanjur*, Alt- und Neu-Indische Studien 42, Stuttgart: Franz Steiner Verlag. (Contains useful information on Vasubandhu and his works, and a comparative description of the commentaries in the Tanjur, with special reference to the formula of dependent origination.)

Muroji, Y. (1993) *Vasubandhus Interpretation des Pratītyasamutpāda. Eine kritische Bearbeitung der Pratītyasamutpādavyākhyā (Saṃskāra- und Vijñānavibhaṅga)*, Alt- und Neu-Indische Studien 43, Stuttgart: Franz Steiner Verlag. (Two chapters from Vasubanhu's commentary on the basic text of *pratītyasamutpāda* doctrine.)

Murti, T.R.V. (1955) *The Central Philosophy of Buddhism: A Study of the Mādhyamika System*, London: Unwin, 2nd edn, 1980. (A classic study of the Madhyamaka system of thought; contains discussion of the interpretation of the *pratītyasa-mutpāda* doctrine.)

* Nāgārjuna (*c.* AD 150–200) *Mūlamadhyamakakārikā* (Fundamental Treatise on the Middle Path), trans. D.J. Kalupahana, *Mūlamadhyamakakārikā of Nā-gārjuna. The Philosophy of the Middle Way. Introduction, Sanskrit Text, English Translation and Annotations*, Delhi: Motilal Banarsidass, 1991. (Useful volume, although some of the translator's interpretations are questionable.)

Schlingloff, D. (1988) 'The Buddhist Wheel of Existence', in *Studies in the Ajanta Paintings: Identifications and Interpretations*, Delhi: Ajanta Publications, 167–74, 383–4. (New interpretation of a famous Ajanta painting in cave 17, which represents the twelve members of the law of dependent origination.)

* Takasaki, J. (1987) *An Introduction to Buddhism*, trans. R.W. Geibel, Tokyo: The Tōhō Gakkai. (An excellent, lucid exposition of Buddhist doctrine, based mostly on Vasubandhu's *Abhidharmakośa*.)

Tucci, G. (1930) 'A Fragment from the *Pratītya-samutpāda-vyàāhyā* of Vasubandhu', *Journal of the Royal Asiatic Society* 611–23; repr. in *Opera Minora*, Rome, 1971, Part 1, 239–48. (Sanskrit fragments of Vasubandhu's commentary from a Nepalese manuscript.)

* Vasubandhu (5th century) *Abhidharmakośa* (Treasury of the Doctrine), ed. and trans. L. de la Vallée Poussin, *L'Abhidharmakośa de Vasubandhu, trad. et annoté*, Paris/Louvain: Paul Geuthner, 1923–31, 6 vols; new edn ed. É. Lamotte, Mélanges chinois et bouddhiques 16, Brussels: Institut belge des hautes études chinoises, 1980, 6 vols. (This 'Treasury of Doctrine' by Vasubandhu, one of the most important thinkers in the the history of Indo-Buddhist thought, is a fundamental exposition of Buddhist philosophy; a masterpiece of scholar-ship.)

* —— (5th century) *Triṃśikā*, ed. S. Lévi, in *Vijñapti-mātratāsiddhi*, Bibliothèque de l'École des Hautes Études 245, Paris: Libraire Ancienne Honoré Champion, 1925; trans. S. Lévi, *Matériaux pour l'étude du système vijñaptimātratā*, Bibliothèque de l'École des Hautes Études 260, Paris: Libraire Ancienne Honoré Champion, 1932. (The 1925 edition also contains the Sanskrit text of Vasubandhu's *Viṃśatikā* (Twenty Stanzas), to-gether with commentaries; the 1932 edition is a French translation of the two works by Vasu-bandhu, with a useful index of terms.)

Wayman, A. (1971) 'Buddhist Dependent Origination', *History of Religions* 10: 185–203. (An attempt to show a historical evolution of the

doctrine of dependent origination from Pāli, Sanskrit and Tibetan sources.)

MAREK MEJOR

SUFISM *see* AL-GHAZALI, ABU HAMID; IBN MASSARA, MUHAMMAD IBN 'ABD ALLAH; IBN SAB'IN, MUHAMMAD IBN 'ABD AL-HAQQ; MYSTICAL PHILOSOPHY IN ISLAM

AL-SUHRAWARDI, SHIHAB AL-DIN YAHYA (1154–91)

*Al-Suhrawardi, whose life spanned a period of less than forty years in the middle of the twelfth century AD, produced a series of highly assured works which established him as the founder of a new school of philosophy in the Muslim world, the school of Illuminationist philosophy (*hikmat al-ishraq*). Although arising out of the peripatetic philosophy developed by Ibn Sina, al-Suhrawardi's Illuminationist philosophy is critical of several of the positions taken by Ibn Sina, and radically departs from the latter through the creation of a symbolic language to give expression to his metaphysics and cosmology, his 'science of lights'. The fundamental constituent of reality for al-Suhrawardi is pure, immaterial light, than which nothing is more manifest, and which unfolds from the Light of Lights in emanationist fashion through a descending order of lights of ever diminishing intensity; through complex interactions, these in turn give rise to horizontal arrays of lights, similar in concept to the Platonic Forms, which govern the species of mundane reality. Al-Suhrawardi also elaborated the idea of an independent, intermediary world, the imaginal world (*alam al-mithal*). His views have exerted a powerful influence down to this day, particularly through Mulla Sadra's adaptation of his concept of intensity and gradation to existence, wherein he combined Peripatetic and Illuminationist descriptions of reality.*

1 Al-Suhrawardi and the philosophy of *ishraq*
2 Epistemology
3 Logic, physics, metaphysics and cosmology
4 The language of *ishraq*

1 Al-Suhrawardi and the philosophy of *ishraq*

Shihab al-Din Yahya ibn Habash ibn Amirak Abu 'l-Futuh al-Suhrawardi, known as al-Maqtul (the Slain) in reference to his execution, and usually referred to as Shaykh al-Ishraq after the Illuminationist philosophy (*hikmat al-ishraq*) which he espoused, was born in AH 549/AD 1154 in the village of Suhraward in northwest Iran. After studying in Maraghah (with Majd al-Din al-Jili, who also taught Fakhr al-Din AL-RAZI) and Isfahan, he passed several years in southwest Anatolia, associating with Seljuq rulers and princes, before moving to Aleppo in AH 579/AD 1183. Here he taught and became a friend of the governor, al-Malik al-Zahir al-Ghazi (son of the Ayyubid Salah al-Din, famous in European literature as Saladin), who later also befriended IBN AL-'ARABI. However, he fell foul of the religious authorities, and was executed in AH 587/AD 1191 on the orders of Salah al-Din, in circumstances which remain unclear but which involved charges of corrupting the religion and allegations of claims to prophecy, and may also have had a political dimension.

Al-Suhrawardi clearly intended his philosophy to make a distinctive break with the previous peripatetic tradition of IBN SINA, but the significance of this break has been interpreted in a number of ways. For subsequent Islamic philosophy, he was above all the conceiver and main proponent of the theory of the primacy of quiddity. While the predominant trend in Western scholarship has been to depict him as the originator of a distinctive mystical and esoteric philosophy, recent Western scholarship has emphasized his critique of peripatetic logic and epistemology and his own theories in these fields (see for example Ziai 1990).

Ibn Sina famously tackled the question of mystical knowledge in the last section of his *Kitab al-Isharat wa-'l-tanbihat* (Remarks and Admonitions), thus assuring a place for this area of knowledge within the domain of *hikma* (wisdom). It was al-Suhrawardi, however, who turned mystical and intuitive knowledge into a paradigm of knowledge in general. This epistemology then served as a basis on which to construct both a critique of peripatetic philosophy and an original philosophy of lights, or Illumination (*ishraq*). Yet, however important it was for al-Suhrawardi to stress his radical departure from peripatetic philosophy, he also emphasized the necessity for those who would follow his method to study the peripatetic method closely.

Al-Suhrawardi's writings fall into several categories. First, there are his four major philosophical works, written in Arabic: *Kitab al-talwihat* (The Intimations), *Kitab al-muqawamat* (The Oppositions), *Kitab al-mashari' wa-'l-mutarahat* (The Paths and Heavens) and *Kitab hikmat al-ishraq* (The Philosophy of Illumination). These were apparently intended by al-Suhrawardi to be studied in this order, and roughly follow a progression from a more or less conventionally peripatetic style to one in which the 'science of lights' is expressed through its own technical vocabulary and method, a progression described by al-Suhrawardi as a movement from a discursive philosophy (*hikma bahthiyya*) to an intuitive philosophy (*hikma dhawqiyya*). The second group of works contains a set of symbolic narratives, mostly in Persian but a few in Arabic, expounding the journey of the soul through the stages of self-realization and offering striking images of some of the notions of Illuminationism while seeking to cultivate the kind of intuitive vision at its heart. The remaining works consist of a number of shorter treatises in Arabic, such as the *Hayakil al-nur* (The Temples of Light), and others in Persian expounding Illuminationist philosophy in a simpler form, a collection of prayers and invocations, and some miscellaneous translations (or versions) and commentaries.

2 Epistemology

By basing his philosophy on light, al-Suhrawardi was able to introduce two important notions which may be thought of as the seeds of the entire system: that of intensity and gradation, and that of presence and self-manifestation. It is possible to see his philosophy as experiential, although his notion of experience was not confined to that obtained through the senses but embraced other forms including that of mystical experience. Ibn Sina's explanation of knowledge is based on the inhering of the form of the thing known in the mind of the knower, but for al-Suhrawardi such knowledge only guarantees certainty and the correspondence of knowledge with reality, because there exists a more fundamental kind of knowledge that does not depend on form and which is, like the experience of pain, unmediated and undeniable. The prime mode of this presential knowledge (*al-'ilm al-huduri*) is self-awareness, and every being existing in itself which is capable of self-awareness is a pure and simple light, as evinced by the pellucid clarity with which it is manifest to itself. In fact, being a pure and simple light is precisely the same as having self-awareness, and this is true of all self-aware entities up to and including God, the Light of Lights, the intensity of whose illumination and self-awareness encompasses everything else. The main constituent of reality is the hierarchies of such pure lights, differing solely in the intensity of their Illumination, and thus of self-awareness (see ILLUMINATIONIST PHILO-SOPHY).

How then is the philosopher to realize this self-awareness? The prospective Illuminationist must engage in a variety of recommended ascetic practices (including forty-day retreats and abstaining from meat) to detach himself from the darknesses of this world and prepare himself for the experiences of the world of lights. The heightened pleasure afforded by this latter kind of experience is emphasized. Having spiritually purified himself, the philosopher is ready to receive the Divine Light and is rewarded with visions of 'apocalyptic' lights which form the basis for real knowledge. At this point the Illuminationist must employ discursive philosophy to analyse the experience and systematize it, in the same way as with sensory experience.

The relation between this direct intuitive knowledge and the philosophy of Illumination is compared to that between observation of the heavens and astronomy. The major portion of al-Suhrawardi's writings is devoted to this last stage of rational analysis and systematization, although he sometimes relates his visions. His symbolic narratives in Persian are in some sense a record of these, although in them al-Suhrawardi, the author, is never explicitly the first person. The narratives have a pedagogic function, and are guides to the kind of experiences to be encountered by the seeker and to their interpretation; indeed a central figure in these narratives is often a guide, the lord of the human species, sometimes though not exclusively identified as Gabriel.

3 Logic, physics, metaphysics and cosmology

The unfolding of reality in Illuminationism is governed by the different ways in which the pure lights interact to produce further levels of lights and darknesses, and by the subsequent interaction of all these different levels with each other, resulting eventually in a densely populated universe. The pure lights are the causes of three other categories of entities: accidental lights (actual physical light, and certain accidents of intellects and souls), dark modes (accidental categories in bodies excluding accidental lights) and intermediary isthmuses (*barzakhs*) or boundaries (bodies). The luminous properties of these degrees are also properties of self-awareness; thus for example, an accidental light subsists in something other than itself, and is also in need of something else to be aware of itself.

Existence as such does not perform much more than an explanatory role in Illuminationism, quite different from the central position it occupied in peripatetic philosophy, a major question for which

was the nature of the relationship between existence and quiddity. However, it is important to notice that light does not merely act as a substitute for existence: existence, and its explanatory function, is rendered totally redundant. The lights (and darknesses and *barzakhs* caused by lights) in al-Suhrawardi's system are discrete entities whose interactions in turn bring about other lights. There is thus a primacy of the entity, and al-Suhrawardi regards existence as such to be no more than a mental abstraction having no external reality. Furthermore, although lights differ in intensity, there is nothing in this system to correspond with Ibn al-'Arabi's *wahdat al-wujud* (unity of being) (see IBN AL-'ARABI); al-Suhrawardi would not have said that all reality is light, but that it is lights. It is for these reasons that he was subsequently held responsible for the idea of the primacy of quiddity (*asalat al-mahiya*), although he did not use this expression himself. It was MULLA SADRA who, four centuries later, built upon the insight that reality was in effect a continuum of graded intensities, but a continuum of existence, not of light. He was thus able to fuse al-Suhrawardi's system with those of the peripatetics and Ibn al- 'Arabi into a metaphysical theory in which reality was nothing more than existence itself, and to turn quiddity into the purely mental abstraction which existence was for al-Suhrawardi.

His insight concerning presential knowledge (which al-Suhrawardi himself declared was vouchsafed to him by Aristotle in a dream) suggested solutions to weaknesses which al-Suhrawardi had detected in Ibn Sina's philosophical system. The most important of these concerned the theory of definition, and the problem of definition as the basis of scientific knowledge. First, he objects that it is impossible to give a complete definition, for a complete definition should contain all the constituents of the definiendum, and such an enumeration is impossible. Second, the peripatetics held that definition is a means of proceeding from the known to the unknown; but the essential constituents, al-Suhrawardi asserts, are just as unknown as the definiendum, so this cannot be so. Contained within this is also an objection against induction: how can one know if the collection of essential elements of a thing is complete merely by enumerating them? His conclusion is that prior knowledge is always necessary and presupposed.

Another area of disagreement with peripatetic philosophy was the categories, which were treated by al-Suhrawardi not in his logic, but in his physics. He reduces the accidental categories to four (quality, quantity, relation and motion), and holds intensity to be a property of substances as well as of accidents. With change in intensity, there is no change in the essence of an accident (a colour, for example) or a substance (such as cause and effect); the only difference is the degree of perfection.

As is to be expected, al-Suhrawardi's physics also contained a new theory of vision. He not only rejected the idea that the forms of objects were imprinted in the eye, but also the other current theory that light was emitted from the eye and fell onto the object. Vision is only possible, according to al-Suhrawardi, when the soul is illuminated by the light, substantial or accidental, of the object, and thus he brings vision within the compass of his illuminative theory of knowledge.

The physical or elemental world as depicted by al-Suhrawardi rejects the peripatetic division of matter and form, and substitutes for it a world of bodies composed of varying mixtures of light and darkness, which permit the passage of light to different degrees. Above the physical world the lights are arranged in a vertical array, corresponding to the emanationist scheme of Ibn Sina. However, these pure, immaterial lights are not restricted to ten as are the intellects of the peripatetic scheme. Al-Suhrawardi says only that they are limited to the number of stars in the fixed heavens; thus they are indefinite in number, but not infinite. Moreover, these vertically arrayed 'triumphal' (*qahira*) lights interact with each other to produce a horizontal array of similarly immaterial, 'regent' (*mudabbira*) lights. Each of these horizontally arrayed lights is the lord of a species, analogous to the Platonic Forms, but with the important difference that they are lights which 'govern' the species under them rather than universals. The species are depicted as 'idols' (*asnam*) of their archetypes. It is the interactions of both the vertical and the horizontal lights which give rise to the bodies of the lower world, which are also classified into degrees depending on the extent to which they receive and transmit light, each being a boundary (*barzakh*) between light and darkness. Al-Suhrawardi also elaborated the idea of the immaterial imaginal world (*'alam al-mithal*), situated between the physical world and the world of the lords of species. This is the locus for the kinds of veridical experiences recounted in his symbolic narratives, an unmediated account of which can only be given in this way and not through discursive reason. Al-Suhrawardi's cosmology is a good deal more complicated than this survey has suggested, employing a detailed terminology for the divisions of lights which classifies them in a variety of different ways.

4 The language of *ishraq*

The integrity of al-Suhrawardi's complex philosophy is achieved in no small measure by the elegance and refinement of his means of expression. His original Illuminationist vocabulary – the Islamic roots of which are sometimes overlooked – is one aspect of this. AL-GHAZALI had set a precedent with his *Mishkat al-anwar* (The Niche of the Lights), which commented on the Light verse in the Qur'an (24: 35). However, al-Suhrawardi also uses a number of other devices to stretch the reader's conceptual boundaries and to convey further dimensions of his total vision of reality. All the lights are related to each other in a downward sense by their being 'triumphal' or 'exalted', but cohesion is further maintained by the 'desire' or 'love' which the lower degrees feel for the upper, and by the explanation which this affords of such things as the joy we experience in the presence of the sun and our fear in the presence of darkness, and the delight which we take in certain minerals such as gold and rubies.

Al-Suhrawardi also chose to describe the horizontal lights as angels, using names of the *Anshaspands* of Zoroastrian mythology to denote them (Khordad, Murdad, Urdibihisht and so on), and he taps the vocabulary of Pahlawi for further terms. In various places in his works he also traces a genealogy for the transmission of illuminationist wisdom which goes back simultaneously through a Greek/Western line (including PYTHAGORAS and PLATO) and an Iranian/Eastern line including Zoroaster (see ZORO-ASTRIANISM) to Hermes Trismegistus, and asserts that there have been illuminationists (*ishraqiyyun*) throughout time. All of this raises the question of precedents for, and influences on, al-Suhrawardi's thought, a subject which has caused some controversy in the Western literature on this subject. It is not necessary to go into the details of Corbin's largely phenomenological argument for the existence of a Persian *ishraqi* philosophical tradition independent from the peripatetic (Corbin 1971); it is sufficient to point out the paucity of historical evidence for such a thesis, and indeed the paucity of textual evidence for any specific conclusions about influences on al-Suhrawardi. The more economical approach is to regard his use of ancient Persian mythology and his genealogy as a means of expressing his overwhelming conviction that he had restored the original foundation of philosophy in the certainty of intuitive experience, a foundation which he believed had been undermined by the excessive discursiveness of such philosophers as Ibn Sina. He saw the traces of this foundation in the writings of Plato and Aristotle (who in the Islamic tradition was also the author of the famous *Theology*), in the remnants of the Zoroastrian religion which he encountered, and in the utterances and writings attributed to certain Sufis.

The influence of al-Suhrawardi on Mulla Sadra has

been mentioned above, but there is in addition a long and lively tradition of commentaries on several of his texts. In the philosophical tradition which continued after the Mongol period in Iran and further east in India, al-Suhrawardi stands second only to Ibn Sina. Perhaps the greatest testimony to his lasting importance is the fact that to this day in Iran philosophers are still informally classified as either *mashsha'i* (peripatetic) or *ishraqi*, depending on their leaning towards rationality or mysticism.

See also: IBN SINA; ILLUMINATIONIST PHILOSOPHY; MULLA SADRA; MYSTICAL PHILOSOPHY IN ISLAM; NEOPLATONISM IN ISLAMIC PHILOSOPHY; PLATONISM IN ISLAMIC PHILOSOPHY

List of works

al-Suhrawardi [Sohravardi, Shihaboddin Yahya] (1180?–91) *Œuvres philosophiques et mystiques*, vol. I: *La métaphysique: I. Kitab al-talwihat. 2. Kitab al-moqawamat. 3. Kitab al-mashari' wa'l-motarahat*, Arabic texts edited with introduction in French by H. Corbin, Tehran: Imperial Iranian Academy of Philosophy, and Paris: Adrien Maisonneuve, 1976; vol II: *I. Le Livre de la Théosophie oriental (Kitab Hikmat al-ishraq). 2. Le Symbole de foi des philosophes. 3. Le Récit de l'Exil occidental*, Arabic texts edited with introduction in French by H. Corbin, Tehran: Imperial Iranian Academy of Philosophy, and Paris: Adrien Maisonneuve, 1977; vol III: *Oeuvres en persan*, Persian texts edited with introduction in Persian by S.H. Nasr, introduction in French by H. Corbin, Tehran: Imperial Iranian Academy of Philosophy, and Paris: Adrien Maisonneuve, 1977. (Only the metaphysics of the three texts in Vol. I were published. Vol. III contains a Persian version of the *Hayakil al-nur*, ed. and trans. H. Corbin, *L'Archange empourpré: quinze traités et récits mystiques*, Paris: Fayard, 1976, contains translations of most of the texts in vol. III of *Œuvres philosophiques et mystiques*, plus four others. Corbin provides introductions to each treatise, and includes several extracts from commentaries on the texts. W.M. Thackston, Jr, *The mystical and visionary treatises of Shihabuddin Yahya Suhrawardi*, London: Octagon Press, 1982, provides an English translation of most of the treatises in vol. III of *Œuvres philosophiques et mystiques*, which eschews all but the most basic annotation; it is therefore less useful than Corbin's translation from a philosophical point of view.)

—— (1154–91) *Hayakil al-nur* (The Temples of Light), ed. M.A. Abu Rayyan, Cairo: al-Maktaba al-Tijariyyah al-Kubra, 1957. (The Persian version appears in *Œuvres* vol. III.)

—— (1180?–91) *Mantiq al-talwihat*, ed. A.A. Fayyaz, Tehran: Tehran University Press, 1955. (The logic of the *Kitab al-talwihat* (The Intimations).)

—— (1186–91) *Kitab hikmat al-ishraq* (The Philosophy of Illumination), trans H. Corbin, ed. and intro. C. Jambet, *Le livre de la sagesse orientale: Kitab Hikmat al-Ishraq*, Lagrasse: Verdier, 1986. (Corbin's translation of the Prologue and the Second Part (The Divine Lights), together with the introduction of Shams al-Din al-Shahrazuri and liberal extracts from the commentaries of Qutb al-Din al-Shirazi and Mulla Sadra. Published after Corbin's death, this copiously annotated translation gives to the reader without Arabic immediate access to al-Suhrawardi's illuminationist method and language.)

References and further reading

Amin Razavi, M. (1997) *Suhrawardi and the School of Illumination*, Richmond: Curzon. (Clear and intelligent account of the main principles of his thought.)

* Corbin, H. (1971) *En Islam iranien: aspects spirituels et philosophiques*, vol. II: *Sohrawardi et les Platoniciens de Perse*, Paris: Gallimard. (Corbin devoted more of his time to the study of al-Suhrawardi than to any other figure, and this volume represents the essence of his research.)

Ha'iri Yazdi, M. (1992) *The Principles of Epistemology in Islamic Philosophy: Knowledge by Presence*, Albany, NY: State University of New York Press. (An original work on epistemology by a contemporary Iranian philosopher drawing critical comparisons between certain Islamic and Western philosophers; incorporates the best exposition in a Western language of al-Suhrawardi's theory of knowledge.)

Nasr, S.H. (1983) 'Shihab al-Din Suhrawardi Maqtul', in M.M. Sharif (ed.) *A History of Muslim Philosophy*, vol. I, Wiesbaden: Otto Harrassowitz, 1963; repr. Karachi, no date. (Still one of the best short introductions to al-Suhrawardi, particularly useful on the cosmology.)

al-Shahrazuri, Shams al-Din (c.1288) *Sharh hikmat al-ishraq* (Commentary on the Philosophy of Illumination), ed. H. Ziai, Tehran: Institute for Cultural Studies and Research, 1993. (Critical edition of the thirteenth-century original; Arabic text only, but a useful short introduction in English.)

Walbridge, J. (1992) *The Science of Mystic Lights: Qutb al-Din Shirazi and the Illuminationist Tradition* in *Islamic Philosophy*, Cambridge, MA: Harvard University Press, for the Centre for Middle Eastern Studies of Harvard University. (A study of one of al-Suhrawardi's principal commentators, with a useful introduction on the philosophy of illumination.)

* Ziai, H. (1990) *Knowledge and Illumination: a Study of Suhrawardi's Hikmat al-ishraq*, Atlanta, GA: Scholars Press. (A pioneering study of al-Suhrawardi's logic and epistemology, particularly his criticism of the peripatetic theory of definition; unfortunately this work suffers from sloppy production.)

—— (1996a) 'Shihab al-Din Suhrawardi: Founder of the Illuminationist School', in S.H. Nasr and O. Leaman (eds) *History of Islamic Philosophy*, London: Routledge, 434–64. (Biography of al-Suhrawardi.)

—— (1996b) 'The Illuminationist Tradition', in S.H. Nasr and O. Leaman (eds) *History of Islamic Philosophy*, London: Routledge, 465–96. (General description of the Illuminationist tradition.)

JOHN COOPER

SUICIDE, ETHICS OF

Suicide has been condemned as necessarily immoral by most Western religions and also by many philosophers. It is argued that suicide defies the will of God, that it is socially harmful and that it is opposed to 'nature'. According to Kant, those who commit suicide 'degrade' humanity by treating themselves as things rather than as persons; furthermore, since they are the subject of moral acts, they 'root out' morality by removing themselves from the scene.

In opposition to this tradition the Stoics and the philosophers of the Enlightenment maintained that there is nothing necessarily immoral about suicide. It is sometimes unwise, causing needless suffering, but it is frequently entirely rational and occasionally even heroic. Judging by the reforms in laws against suicide and the reactions to the suicides of prominent persons in recent decades, it appears that the Enlightenment position is becoming very generally accepted.

1   **The horror of suicide**
2   **Humans as God's property**
3   **Adverse effects on survivors**
4   **An offence against nature**
5   **Kant's arguments**
6   **The legal punishment of suicide**

1   The horror of suicide

The word 'suicide' is used here in the sense defined by Emile Durkheim (1897), the leading sociological writer on the subject. He refers to 'all cases of death resulting directly or indirectly from a positive or negative act of the victim himself, which he knows will produce this result' (see DURKHEIM, E. §3). The question of whether suicide can ever be morally justified has been extensively discussed both by secular philosophers and by religious moralists. According to Plato, Aristotle, St Augustine, St Thomas Aquinas, Kant and Hegel suicide is always morally wrong, although Plato inconsistently allowed some exceptions. According to another tradition which goes back to Epicurus and the Stoic philosophers, suicide is not only frequently justified but on occasions highly admirable. 'Against all the injuries of life', wrote Seneca, 'I always have the refuge of death'. The Stoic view was revived in the sixteenth century by Montaigne and it had the support of all the leading figures of the French Enlightenment, notably Montesquieu, Holbach, Diderot, Rousseau and Voltaire. David Hume's 'On Suicide', which could not be published during his lifetime, may be regarded as the classic statement of the Enlightenment viewpoint. In Germany in the nineteenth century the Enlightenment position was championed by Schopenhauer and also by Nietzsche, who even went so far as to suggest that chronically sick people should be encouraged to commit suicide. 'In a certain state', Nietzsche wrote in *Twilight of the Idols* (1888: §36), 'it is indecent to live longer – to go on vegetating in cowardly dependence on physicians and medications, after the meaning of life... has been lost, ought to prompt a profound contempt in society'.

In the past, the anti-suicide viewpoint was frequently stated with extreme ferocity. Entirely typical of sermons in the eighteenth and nineteenth centuries is *The Guilt, Folly and Sources of Suicide* by Samuel Miller D.D., delivered and published in New York City in 1805. According to Miller suicide is 'repugnant to every genuine feeling of human nature'. It is 'as degrading as it is criminal'. It is a crime of 'complicated malignity' against which 'man, depraved, afflicted, and covered with evil, requires to be guarded by restraints'. The person who commits suicide 'is as great a monster in morals as an atheist in religion, or as the most hideous assemblage of deformities in animal nature'. Writing in 1908, the English poet and novelist G.K. Chesterton (1874–1935) declared suicide to be the worst of all crimes. 'Not only is suicide a sin', according to Chesterton, 'it is *the* sin. It is the ultimate and absolute evil.... The man who kills a man, kills a man. The man who kills himself, kills all men; as far as he is concerned he wipes out the world'. It is of some interest to note that the Talmud contains a similar idea. We are told that 'there is none more wicked than one who has committed suicide'. This is so because the world was created 'for the sake of one individual' and 'thus he who destroys one's soul is considered as though he had destroyed the whole world' (see BIOETHICS, JEWISH §3).

If we take Chesterton literally, then Cato, Brutus, Cassius, Thomas Chatterton, Samuel Romilly, Heinrich von Kleist, Gerard de Nerval, Ludwig Boltzmann, Vladimir Maiakovskii, Wilhelm Stekel, Stefan Zweig, Ernest Hemingway, Percy Bridgman, Sylvia Plath, Paul Celan, Marilyn Monroe and Arthur Koestler, to mention just a few, were criminals; and indeed far worse criminals than mass murderers. Hitler's extermination of millions of innocent men and women was a lesser crime than his own eventual suicide. Chesterton did not at all deplore the 'weird harshness' that Christianity has shown to the suicide: 'The suicide is ignoble...he is a mere destroyer; spiritually, he destroys the universe'. We are assured that there is much rational and philosophic truth in the practice of driving stakes through the bodies of suicides and burying them at crossroads. The suicide 'was so bad that his bones would pollute his brethren' (Kant [1775/80] 1930: 151).

Miller and Chesterton may be dismissed as religious fanatics and marginal figures. Immanuel Kant was not a religious fanatic and can hardly be dismissed as a marginal figure, but his denunciations of suicide are just as furious. According to Kant 'suicide is in *no* circumstances permissible'. The man who commits suicide 'sinks lower than the beasts'. We 'shrink from him in horror'. 'Nothing more terrible can be imagined'. 'We look upon the suicide as carrion'. If a man attempts suicide and survives, he has in effect 'discarded his humanity' and we are entitled to 'treat him as a beast, as a thing, and to use him for our sport as we do a horse or a dog'.

None of these writers showed the slightest compassion for a person who committed suicide, and their ravings were directed even against philosophers who did show such compassion and who denied that suicide was necessarily wrong or criminal. Hume in particular was denounced by clerical enthusiasts. G. Clayton, author of *The Dreadful Sin of Suicide* (1812: 48n), called Hume's essay a 'source of incalculable evil', and in a huge treatise, *A Full Inquiry into the Subject of Suicide* (1790 vol. 2: 54), Charles Moore denounced Hume as 'a more pernicious and destructive member of society than even the profligate and abandoned liver'.

2 Humans as God's property

According to Sir William Blackstone (1723–80), the influential English jurist, the suicide is guilty of a double offence. The first of these is 'spiritual' and consists in 'evading the prerogative of the Almighty, and rushing into his immediate presence' (Blackstone 1765–9 IV: 189). We evade God's prerogative, according to some theologians, because we are God's property and he alone has the right to terminate our lives. This argument is found in Plato's *Phaedo* (61c) where Socrates remarks that humans are 'the possession of the deity' and ought not to kill themselves before the deity lays them under a necessity of doing so: 'if one of your slaves were to kill himself, without your having intimated that you wished him to die, should you not be angry with him, and should you not punish him if you could?' This argument is repeated, almost verbatim, by Aquinas and also by Kant.

Kant relies primarily on purely secular arguments, but at the end of his most extended discussion of suicide he also appeals to the Divine ownership of man. 'We have been placed in this world', he writes, 'under certain conditions and for specific purposes. But a suicide opposes the purpose of his Creator; he arrives in the other world as one who has deserted his post; he must be looked upon as a rebel against God'. Human beings 'are sentinels on earth and may not leave their posts until relieved by another beneficent hand' (Kant [1775/80] 1930: 154). This notion had already been put forward in Locke's *Second Treatise on Civil Government*. We are there told that all are the 'servants of one sovereign Master...they are His property' and must not 'quit their station wilfully' (Locke 1690: §6).

The views just quoted are frequently accompanied by pronouncements that God created human beings primarily for his glory. Zachary Pearce (1690–1774), Bishop of Rochester, may be taken as a typical representative of this position. In his 'Sermon on Self-Murder' (1736), he declares that God had two ends in view when he created humans. These 'could have been no other than... the promoting of His own Glory and Service, and of our true and real happiness'. We promote God's glory 'by the practice of every virtue'. Patience and submission to the Divine Will are virtues that are 'chiefly exercised in a state of adversity'. From all of this it clearly follows that suicide is impermissible. 'The greater the adversity, the more conspicuous these virtues appear', and it follows 'very plainly' that 'the most afflicted man is capable of advancing the honour and interests of his Maker'.

All these arguments are open to a number of serious objections, even if one allows that the universe was created by God. In the first place, the fact that God created human beings does not mean that they are his property. My parents created me, but I am not their property. Similarly, the assertion that God presented me with the gift of life does not imply that I may not dispose of it in any way I please. A donor surely has no right to dictate to the recipient what they are to do with the gift. It might also be observed that human beings did not request the gift of life. Schopenhauer in one place remarks that many a human being 'would have declined such a gift if he could have seen it and tested it beforehand' ([1818] 1883, vol. 3: 390).

Another objection relates to God's perfect goodness and wisdom. It is not easy to see why such a being would be so concerned about his own glory, gripped by what Hume called 'one of the lowest of human passions, a restless appetite for applause' ([1777] 1965: 300). Nor is it at all obvious that a human being in a state of extreme physical or mental agony, especially with no relief or improvement in sight, would be promoting God's glory by continuing to live. Moreover, if God is good and kind he will hardly wish human beings to suffer for *his* sake.

Furthermore, although it is, according to Kant, 'God's intention to preserve life', this is apparently consistent with human life being destroyed by all manner of causes other than by suicidal acts. Why is it not equally consistent with the latter? Kant remarks that 'human beings are sentinels on earth and may not leave their posts until relieved by another beneficent hand' (Kant [1775/80] 1930: 154). Why cannot the desire to die on the part of a person whose 'patience', in Hume's words, has been 'overcome by pain and sorrow' qualify as one of the manifestations of such a 'beneficent hand'? In such a situation, Hume adds, 'I may conclude that I am recalled from my station in the clearest and most express terms' ([1777] 1965: 301). If it is remembered that 'relief by the beneficent hand' may take such forms as cancer or murder at times when the person very much *wishes to live*, it is not easy to see that committing suicide when the individual does not wish to live will not also qualify as relief by the same hand.

3 Adverse effects on survivors

As mentioned above, Sir William Blackstone condemned suicide as a 'double offence'. The first, the 'spiritual' offence, was discussed in the previous section. The second offence is 'temporal, against the king, who hath an interest in the preservation of all his subjects'. This argument is found in Aristotle's *Ethics*, and stated more fully by Aquinas who writes:

It is altogether unlawful to kill oneself, because every part, as such, belongs to the whole. Now every man is part of the community, and so, as such, he belongs to the community. Hence by killing himself he injures the community.

(*Summa theologiae* IIaIIae.64.5)

Some writers have been less concerned with harm to the community than with the grief and suffering that a suicide may bring to friends and family. 'It is not wisdom but barbarity', in the words of the great Italian poet-philosopher Giacomo Leopardi ([1827] 1893: 225), 'to reckon as nothing the grief and anguish of the home circle, the intimate friends and companions'.

A little reflection shows that such considerations fail to establish the conclusion that suicide is always wrong. The most they show is that a responsible individual would carefully take into account the effects on others before taking such a drastic step. One need not deny that an individual has obligations to society or to family and friends. However, apart from the fact that some people have neither family nor friends and that some people are justly aggrieved against the society in which they live, there are two objections to all arguments of this kind. In the first place, in any number of situations, a person's welfare may rightly take precedence over obligations to others. If by suffering a little, a person can avoid a great deal of suffering on the part of friends and family or the whole of society, his suffering is justified. If, on the other hand, the continuation of the person's life involves terrible pain, far exceeding the sufferings which their suicide would produce on other people, the person is not obliged to go on living. Hume discussed this topic at some length. Allowing for the sake of argument, he writes, 'that our obligations to do good (to society) were perpetual, they certainly have some bounds; I am not obliged to do a small good to society at the expense of a great harm to myself' (Hume [1777] 1965: 304). In a great many cases, furthermore, a person who commits suicide acts, at least in the long run, for the *benefit* of others. Although death may produce grief it also produces relief. 'Suppose that it is no longer in my power to promote the interest of society', Hume writes, 'suppose that I am a burden to it; suppose that my life hinders some person from being much more useful to society; in such cases, my resignation of life must not only be innocent, but laudable'. Since we are here dealing with utilitarian considerations it may not be amiss to observe that the suicide of a malevolent tyrant may bring great joy to large numbers, and not only to those he has harmed. Millions of people were happy to hear of Hitler's death, but the fact that he committed suicide gave greater satisfaction than if he had died of cancer or heart disease: it was, in effect, an admission of defeat.

4 An offence against nature

One of the most widely used arguments against suicide is that it is opposed to 'nature'. Thus, in a much-quoted judgment, Mr Justice Brown in 1562 declared suicide to be a crime on the ground that it is 'an offence against nature: because to destroy oneself is contrary to nature, and a thing most horrible'. In Aquinas the appeal to nature is the first of his three reasons for condemning suicide. Suicide, he tells us, 'is contrary to the inclination of nature and to the charity whereby every man should love himself' (*Summa theologiae* IIaIIae.64.5). It follows from this that suicide is 'always a mortal sin'. The argument is also found in numerous Protestant tracts of the eighteenth and nineteenth centuries. Samuel Miller employs his usual hell-fire rhetoric. 'Suicide is repugnant to every genuine feeling of human nature,' he tells us. 'It is an outrage on the dignity of those faculties with which the Author of Nature has endowed us'. Although most writers who used this argument were believers in God and also employed theological arguments, the appeal to nature is meant to be of a purely secular character. Leopardi, a total atheist, expressed himself in similar language. 'Nature itself', he wrote, 'unmistakeably teaches that it is not permitted to quit this world by our mere will and our own act'. It is implied that if humans were to cut off their arms or pluck out their eyes, this would be horrendously unnatural. Such acts, however, are not nearly as unnatural as to extinguish one's very life. Such an act is 'the one most opposed to nature which a person can commit' (Leopardi [1827] 1893: 215).

The sufficient answer to this argument is that the suppression of an instinctive urge is not necessarily wrong. A surgeon who gets extremely hungry in the course of an operation can surely not be blamed for suppressing a passionate desire for a roast beef sandwich. Furthermore, instinctive desires may and frequently do conflict with one another, and then the right action, whatever it is, will have to frustrate our instincts. It may be granted that our desire to continue life is natural, but it is just as natural to avoid intolerable pain with no relief in sight. In such a situation suicide may be no less 'in accord with nature' than continuing to live. The best comment on the arbitrariness of the orthodox position has come from Henry Romilly Fedden in *Suicide – A Social and Historical Study* (1938). 'A monk', Fedden writes, 'denies sex, the suicide disregards self preservation:

both should be equally guilty, yet one is a saint and the other a sinner' ([1938] 1972: 282).

5 Kant's arguments

Kant appeals not only to the alleged fact that man is God's property for his blanket rejection of suicide. He also offers a number of purely secular arguments. Two of these deserve some discussion. According to one of these, people who commit suicide are 'abasing' and 'degrading' their humanity by treating themselves as no more than things:

> Man can only dispose of things; beasts are things in this sense; but man is not a thing, not a beast. If he disposes of himself, he treats his value as that of a beast. He who so behaves, who has no respect for human nature makes a thing of himself.
> (Kant [1775/80] 1930: 151)

Kant is surely wildly wrong here. I am treating people as things and debasing their humanity if I try to dominate them so that they will, under the force of my superior will, automatically do what *I* want. Setting aside the notion of treating somebody as a thing, it is unquestionable that people frequently debase other human beings. I am debasing people if I humiliate them, if I get them to the point at which, to preserve their jobs which I control, they have to fawn and beg for mercy or to confess to wrongs they never committed. In such circumstances I have no regard for the others' feelings, especially for their pride and dignity. In reply to Kant it must be emphasized that a great many cases in which people committed or attempted to commit suicide do not at all resemble debasements of this kind. If I commit suicide I am not necessarily the victim of the stronger will of somebody else. I am not indifferent to my own feelings or dignity, but on the contrary I may *compassionately* decide to terminate what I regard as my pointless (perhaps even degrading) suffering. I have not become a thing and I have not at all debased myself.

Kant's other argument is based on the undeniable fact that if people commit suicide they can no longer perform any moral acts. 'It cannot be moral', he says, 'to root out the existence of morality itself from the world'. The suicide 'robs himself of his person. This is contrary to the highest duty we have towards ourselves, for it annuls the condition of all other duties' (Kant [1775/80] 1930: 152). To this it must be replied that people who commit suicide do *not* root out the existence of morality itself from the world. They do not do so any more than when they die a natural death or are killed in battle. They 'root out' any new moral acts on their part, but presumably there will be other people left. They would root out 'morality itself' only if they wiped out the human race.

Kant's argument involves a confusion between: (1) I ought to do my duty as long as I am alive, and (2) It is my duty to go on living as long as possible. Kant's basic value judgment that doing one's duty is the highest good implies (1), but it does not imply (2); and only (2) could serve as a basis for condemning suicide.

It should be noted that Kant himself in various places rejects statement (2). In one place he remarks 'there is much in the world far more important than life' and that 'it is better to sacrifice one's life than one's morality'. Furthermore, it is entirely permissible and even laudable 'to risk one's life against one's enemies, and even to sacrifice it, in order to observe one's duties towards oneself'. Kant also fully endorses the right of 'the sovereign' to 'call his subjects to fight to the death for their country'. Those who die in battle, Kant goes on, are not suicides but 'victims of fate'. They are to be admired as 'noble and high-minded' in contrast with soldiers who run away to save their lives. Yet the deaths of the noble 'victims of fate' root out the existence of 'morality itself' from the world just as much as the deaths of people who commit suicide, while cowardly soldiers who saves their own lives thereby preserve the condition for further moral action. Hence the mere fact of not preserving the presupposition of future moral action cannot be a sufficient reason for condemning suicide.

6 The legal punishment of suicide

Until relatively recently suicide was regarded as a capital crime in the legal statutes of most Western countries. Unfortunately from the point of view of the punishers, it is not possible to carry out a death sentence in the case of successful suicides. This does not mean, however, that nothing has been done by the state or church to show their extreme disapproval. The suicide was declared a felon and their property confiscated. Regular burials were strictly forbidden and Christian rites denied. The body was usually taken to the crossroads, a stake driven through it and a stone placed over the face. The Prussian Code published in 1788 and confirmed in 1794 declares that 'the corpse of a suicide shall be duly executed, if, in the opinion of the judge, the act would operate as a deterrent'. Such laws are perhaps not as absurd as they appear at first. Most people, almost regardless of their philosophical or religious views, are concerned about the disposition of their body and repelled by the notion of its mutilation.

In the case of suicides whose attempts fail, the authorities were in a position to carry out the execution of the 'murderer'. It is not known how often this was actually done but we have an appallingly gruesome description of one such case that took place in England in 1860 (Carr 1981: 336).

Laws against suicide were abolished in France in 1790 largely as a result of the influence of Beccaria, Montesquieu, Diderot and Voltaire. Other European countries and several US states followed the lead, but in Britain people were prosecuted as recently as 1955. Several of these cases are described in Glanville Williams (1958). The 'criminality' of attempted suicide was finally abolished in Britain in 1961 following a recommendation (1959) by a commission appointed by the Archbishop of Canterbury. Much of the report repeats, in very strong language, some of the older Christian condemnations, but in the end, after quoting extensively from the writings of Hastings Rashdall, Dean Inge and Canon Peter Green, it is grudgingly admitted that, in certain situations, suicide is not immoral.

Assisting suicide remains a crime in thirty-two US states but, as is generally known, such prohibitions are commonly disregarded by humane physicians. Dr Jack Kevorkian, a Michigan pathologist, has openly defied this law. He has been tried several times and acquitted on each occasion. In two (April and May 1996), one in New York City, the other in San Francisco, Courts of Appeal found statutes forbidding physician-assisted suicide to be unconstitutional. Both cases are under appeal at the time of writing, but there is every indication that, before long, physical-assisted suicide will be regarded as a constitutional right.

See also: BIOETHICS; DEATH; LIFE AND DEATH; MEDICAL ETHICS

References and further reading

Alvarez, A. (1971) *The Savage God: A Study of Suicide*, London: Weidenfeld & Nicholson. (Historical account of religious and secular attitudes towards suicide, as well as a survey of theories about the causation of suicide.)

* Aquinas, T. (1266–73) *Summa theologiae* (Synopsis of Theology), trans. the English Dominican Fathers as *The Summa Theologica*, London, 1912–36, 22 vols. (Aquinas discusses suicide in IIaIIae.64.5.)

* Aristotle (*c.* mid 4th century BC) *Nicomachean Ethics*, trans. J.A.K. Thompson, London: George Allen & Unwin, 1953; trans. T.H. Irwin, Indianapolis, IN: Hackett Publishing Company, 1985. (See 1138a6–14 for Aristotle's argument that the suicide acts unjustly towards the state.)

Battin, M.P. (1982) *Ethical Issues in Suicide*, Englewood Cliffs, NJ: Prentice Hall. (Critical survey of all major religious and secular arguments against the justifiability of suicide.)

Battin, M.P. and Mayo, D.J. (eds) (1980) *Suicide: The Philosophical Issues*, New York: St Martin's Press. (Full discussion of all philosophical and psychological questions about suicide by writers from different fields.)

Beauchamp, T.L. and Perlin, S. (eds) (1978) *Ethical Issues of Death and Dying*, Englewood Cliffs, NJ: Prentice Hall. (Contains sections on suicide, euthanasia and the meaning of life and death; religious and secular positions are both represented.)

* Blackstone, W. (1765–9) *Commentaries on the Laws of England*, London, 4 vols; 1st edn repr. Chicago, IL: Chicago University Press, 1979. (The first comprehensive description of the principles of English law.)

* Carr, E.H. (1981) *The Romantic Exiles: A Nineteenth-Century Portrait Gallery*, Cambridge, MA: MIT Press. (Illustrates the lengths to which authorities were prepared to go in pursuance of the law against suicide.)

* Chesterton, G.K. (1908) *Orthodoxy*, London: John Lane; repr. New York: Doubleday, 1991. (Condemnation of suicide based on the view that 'cosmic patriots' have taken an 'oath of loyalty to life'. A person who commits suicide denies the 'primary sacredness' of the universe.)

* Clayton, G. (1812) *The Dreadful Sin of Suicide*, London: Black, Parry & Kingsbury. (Sermon denouncing suicide delivered in London in 1812.)

* Committee Appointed by the Archbishop of Canterbury (1959) *Ought Suicide to be a Crime?*, Report of a Committee Appointed by the Archbishop of Canterbury, London: Church Information Office. (Statement of the Anglican position on suicide, allowing that on some occasions suicide is not morally blameworthy.)

Donnelly, G. (ed.) (1990) *Suicide – Rights or Wrong?*, Buffalo, NY: Prometheus Books. (Anthology representing all major viewpoints on the morality of suicide.)

* Durkheim, E. (1897) *Suicide: A Study in Sociology*, trans. J.A. Spaulding and G. Simpson, Glencoe, IL: Free Press, 1951. (Pioneer study of different types of suicide and of their causation, based on the statistical data available at the end of the nineteenth century. The main thesis is that the frequency of suicide varies inversely with the degree of integration of the social group to which the individual belongs.)

Dworkin, R. *et al.* (1997) 'Assisted Suicide: The Philosophers' Brief', *New York Review of Books* 27

March 1997. (Submission to the US Supreme Court in connection with recent cases of assisted suicide.)

* Fedden, H.R. (1938) *Suicide – A Social and Historical Study*, New York: Benjamin Blom, 1972. (Covers much the same ground as Alvarez, with greater emphasis on the irrational attitudes of Christian theologians.)

* Hume, D. (1777) 'On Suicide', in A. MacIntyre (ed.) *Hume's Ethical Writings*, New York: Macmillan, 1965. (The classic statement of the view that suicide is not necessarily wicked or even unwise.)

* —— (1779) *Dialogues concerning Natural Religion*, ed. N.K. Smith, London: Thomas Nelson, 1935. (Classic statement of the main objections to the teleological and cosmological arguments for the existence of God.)

* Kant, I. (1775/80) *Lectures on Ethics*, trans. L. Infield, London: Methuen, 1930. (A little-known volume containing Kant's lectures on ethics, as recorded by his students.)

Lecky, W.E.H. (1869) *History of European Morals from Augustine to Charlemagne*, London, 2 vols. (Contains amusing titbits about Roman philosophers who preached that death was better than life, resulting in suicide epidemics.)

* Leopardi, G. (1827) *Essays, Dialogues and Thoughts*, trans. P. Maxwell, London: Walter Scott, 1893. (In the 'Dialogue between Plotinus and Porphyrius', the former character argues that we must 'accommodate ourselves to the inevitable conditions of our existence' and 'self-destruction is an atrocious and inhuman act'.)

* Locke, J. (1690) *Second Treatise on Civil Government*, in *Locke's Two Treatises of Government*, ed. P. Laslett, Cambridge: Cambridge University Press, 1970. (Classic work of political philosophy. For Locke's comments on suicide see §§6, 23 and 135.)

* Miller, S. (1805) *The Guilt, Folly and Sources of Suicide*, New York. (Sermon delivered in New York city in 1805.)

* Moore, C. (1790) *A Full Inquiry into the Subject of Suicide*, London, 2 vols. (Detailed critique of defenders of suicide such as Donne and Hume, conducted in extremely immoderate language.)

* Nietzsche, F. (1888) *The Twilight of the Idols*, trans. R.J. Hollingdale, Harmondsworth: Penguin, 1969. (The quotation in §1 above comes from the section entitled 'Expeditions of an Untimely Man'.)

* Pearce, Z. (1736) 'Sermon on Self-Murder', London. (Pamphlet arguing that 'it is our duty to receive evil, as well as good, at the hand of God'.)

Perlin, S. (ed.) (1975) *A Handbook for the Study of Suicide*, New York: Oxford University Press. (Cross-disciplinary volume including articles by philosophers, biologists and psychiatrists.)

* Plato (*c*386–380 BC) *Phaedo*, trans. with notes D. Gallop, *Plato Phaedo*, Oxford and New York: Oxford University Press, 1993. (Dialogue concerning the immortality of the soul.)

Rosen, G. (1975) 'History', in S. Perlin (ed.) *A Handbook for the Study of Suicide*, New York: Oxford University Press. (Contains much fascinating material on the nineteenth-century literature in England and France.)

Russell, B. (1932) 'Illegal?', in *Mortals and Others – American Essays 1931–1935*, ed. H. Ruja, London, Routledge & Kegan Paul, 1975. (Excellent article outlining Russell's views on suicide.)

* Schopenhauer, A. (1818) *The World As Will and Idea*, trans. R.B. Haldane and J. Kemp, London: George Routledge & Sons, 1883. (Section 69 of Volume 1 outlines his attitude to suicide, which is also discussed in his specific essay on the topic.)

—— (1891) 'Of Suicide', in *Studies in Pessimism*, trans. T.B. Saunders, London; repr. New York: Wiley & Sons, 1992. (Endorses Hume's arguments against the Christian view of suicide as sin, but also argues that it is only an apparent and not a real release from the sufferings of life.)

* Seneca (*c*. AD early 60s) *Seneca's Letters to Lucilius*, trans. E.P. Barker, Oxford: Clarendon Press, 1932, 2 vols. (Classical statement of the view of the Stoic philosophers that we are permitted to escape the ills of the world by ending our lives. Seneca himself committed suicide.)

Sprott, S.E. (1961) *The English Debate on Suicide from Donne to Hume*, La Salle, IL: Open Court. (Detailed account of many seventeenth- and eighteenth-century publications defending the traditional Christian viewpoint.)

Voltaire, F.-M. de (1764–9) *Philosophical Dictionary*, London: J. & H.L. Hunt, 1824, 6 vols. (Huge, misleadingly entitled collection of mostly short pieces, many in dialogue form, on a great variety of topics.)

Westermarck, E.A. (1906–8) *The Origin and Development of the Moral Ideas*, London and New York: Macmillan, 2 vols. (History of major moral ideas written from a relativistic viewpoint.)

* Williams, G. (1958) *The Sanctity of Life and the Criminal Law*, London: Faber & Faber. (Contains a highly informative chapter on the history of the laws concerning suicide. This work cannot be sufficiently praised for its humanity.)

PAUL EDWARDS

SUN BIN/SUN PIN/SUN TZU/ SUN WU *see* SUNZI

ŚŪNYATĀ *see* BUDDHIST CONCEPT OF EMPTINESS

SUNZI

Sunzi: The Art of Warfare *(or Sunzi bingfa), a text traditionally ascribed to Sun Wu, a contemporary of Confucius, is the most widely read military classic in human history. Although it provides counsel on military strategy and tactics, it is fundamentally a philosophical text, reflecting a way of thinking and living that is distinctively Chinese. The received text has thirteen 'core' chapters, but in 1972 an additional six chapters of the original eighty-two-chapter text was recovered from a Han dynasty tomb. In the same tomb, a text called* Sun Bin *(or* Sun Bin bingfa*), ascribed to a later descendent of Sun Wu, was also recovered. This work elaborates on the substance of the* Sunzi's *military philosophy.*

In the centuries leading up to the founding of the Chinese empire in 221 BC, death had become a way of life and military texts were among the most widely circulating documents. The *Sunzi* and *Sun Bin* date from what is aptly called the Warring States period (403–221 BC), a period in which the heat and ferocity of warfare among independent nation-states, caught up in the frenzy of zero-sum politics, was rising exponentially. Historical records report that, between 350 and 250 BC, the approximate dates for the *Sunzi* and *Sun Bin* respectively, average battle casualties rose from 30,000–40,000 to ten times that number.

Many factors contributed to the carnage, including widespread use of the crossbow, siege engines to attack increasingly important population centres, advances in metallurgy and the introduction of cavalry. But in the final analysis, the revolution was intellectual. During this period, loosely organized militia gave way to the use of fixed formations, creating unrelenting killing machines similar in concept to the Roman phalanx, the revival of which in modern Europe made the Napoleonic armies so formidable.

The key and defining idea in the *Sunzi* is *shi* (pronounced like the affirmative, 'sure!'), translated variously as 'circumstances', 'situation', 'power', 'strategic advantage' and 'military or political purchase'. *Shi* entails manipulating circumstances to create a strategic advantage. It separates the skilful manipulation of a situation from brute force, and military wisdom from mere physical prowess.

An exploration of *shi* provides a contrast between an agent-centred model of order which tends to emphasize linear efficient cause, and the more situationally-defined alternative. When *shi* is translated as 'strategic advantage', many readers move immediately to assign it to one side of the conflict or the other. *Shi*, however, refers to the synergistic relationship that obtains among all of the factors on both sides of the conflict (numbers, terrain, logistics, morale, weaponry and so on) as they converge on the battlefield to give one side the advantage over the other. It is the tension generated in the contest between surplus and deficiency that becomes the 'force of circumstances'. *Shi* is both the shape and the momentum that the encounter assumes: it is the tide of battle. It is the purchase and the leverage that gives troops the will to join the battle and to win it.

Shi is thus not a given; it must be created and carefully cultivated. A failure to cultivate *shi* will surely give the upper hand to the enemy, and even the best soldiers under the worst circumstances will turn and flee. What makes cultivation of a situation possible are the indeterminate elements. At the same time, these ever-present fluid factors make each battlefield unique, and render any formulaic or mechanical application of even a proven military stratagem ultimately unreliable. Indeed, each new situation that develops in the field brings with it the necessity for reconsideration, and a flexibility that must constantly be ready to take account of any eventuality. It is this indeterminacy that makes the range of available strategies limitless.

The capacity of the small, incipient and seemingly incidental to control the large by virtue of its pivotal position is an enduring theme in classical Chinese philosophy, and underlies the notion of getting the most from a situation while minimizing loss. The commander must search the circumstances to identify a 'trigger' that can alter the propensity of battle. In this sense of order, this initially indeterminate aspect, while relatively small, can become a motivating force for reorganization and renewal, thus constituting a critical turning point. Because uncertainty can provide the occasion for transformation, it can offer either 'danger' or 'opportunity', depending upon whether or not the commander is able to capitalize on the moment and make the most of it. In fact, in modern Chinese, the combination of 'danger' and 'opportunity' – *weiji* – means 'critical point'.

In the *Sunzi*, the prosecution of warfare must imitate nature, and nature is too complex to be linear and scale-invariant. Reconfiguration can take place on the battlefield in the same way that renewal can occur in nature because both situations are fluid, and rich in disorder and surprise. Small, pointed alterations can have precipitous and cascading consequences. Rather than separating what orders from what is ordered, this dynamic sense of order locates the energy of change within the situation itself by assuming order to be richly vague, ever-changing and always unique. When understood in this way, order is reflexive: it is self-organizing and self-renewing. While the stabilizing regularity of a specific event anticipates the way in which it will continue to unfold, the chaotic aspect within the event itself defeats any notion of necessity or absolute predictability. The combination of pattern and uncertainty in nature and on the field of battle undermines the possibility of universalizable claims and renders precarious any globalizing generalizations. All the commander can depend upon is the *relative* stability of site-specific and emerging patterns of order, and enough knowledge of the situation to identify and act upon the positive uncertainties that present themselves. He must constantly weigh the stochastic variables at every level of the battle and be prepared to parlay them into large scale advantages.

In the sequel text of the same lineage, the *Sun Bin*, the meaning of *shi*, a rather complex idea, was subcontracted out to other technical terms, a cluster of images which became evocative in both communicating and stimulating military insights. Among the most important were *quan* (weighing up with the lever scales or steelyard), *zhen* (battle formation and display), *bian* (adaptability) and *zhi* (foreknowledge based upon information gathering). These two texts belong to a lineage of military philosophy which, in modern times, has attracted a cult following with their ideas being extended from the battlefield to all other forms of competition, notably diplomacy, the marketplace and the field of play.

See also: CHINESE PHILOSOPHY; POLITICAL PHILOSOPHY, HISTORY OF; WAR AND PEACE, PHILOSOPHY OF

References and further reading

Ames, R.T. (1993) *Sun-tzu: The Art of Warfare*, New York: Ballantine. (A translation and philosophical introduction to this classic based upon a 1972 archaeological find, including the lost six chapters and encyclopedic references.)

Lau, D.C. and Ames, R.T. (1996) *Sun Pin: The Art of Warfare*, New York: Ballantine. (A translation and philosophical introduction to the newly recovered classic based upon a 1972 archaeological find, including encyclopedic references.)

ROGER T. AMES

SUPEREROGATION

Supererogatory actions are usually characterized as 'actions above and beyond the call of duty'. Historically, Catholic thinkers defended the doctrine of supererogation by distinguishing what God commands from what he merely prefers, while Reformation thinkers claimed that all actions willed by God are obligatory. In contemporary philosophy, it is often argued that if morality is to permit us to pursue our own personal interests, it must recognize that many self-sacrificing altruistic acts are supererogatory rather than obligatory. The need for some category of the supererogatory is particularly urgent if moral obligations are thought of as rationally overriding. There are three main contemporary approaches to defining the supererogatory. The first locates the obligatory/supererogatory distinction within positive social morality, holding that the former are actions we are blameworthy for failing to perform, while the latter are actions we may refrain from performing without blame. The second holds that obligatory actions are supported by morally conclusive reasons, while supererogatory actions are not. On this approach the personal sacrifice sometimes involved in acting altruistically counts against it from the moral point of view, making some altruistic actions supererogatory rather than obligatory. The third approach appeals to virtue and vice, holding that obligatory actions are those failure to perform which reveals some defect in the agent's character, while supererogatory actions are those that may be omitted without vice.

1   **Historical antecedents**
2   **The contemporary argument for supererogation**
3   **Supererogation and positive social morality**
4   **Supererogatory acts as morally optional**
5   **Supererogation, virtue, and vice**
6   **Supererogation and praiseworthiness**

1   Historical antecedents

Early Christian writers like Ambrose and TERTULLIAN often distinguished those things that God willed through commandments or precepts, and those things that he willed only through counsels. They held that we are obliged only to obey God's precepts, and that we are permitted to disregard God's counsels if we so choose, although following them is always better than disregarding them. Actions in conformity with the counsels are called 'supererogatory'. The 'Evangelical Counsels', as they were first called, are poverty, chastity, and obedience (Tertullian, *Exhortation to Chastity*, section 3). It was held that in giving permission, for example, to live a life of less than complete chastity, God exercises his will 'in a spirit of indulgence', as a concession to the weakness of human character.

Scholastic thinkers typically offered a rather different account, sometimes side by side with this more traditional one. Aquinas, for example, held that only the conduct required by the precepts is necessary for salvation (see AQUINAS, T. §13). Conduct recommended by the counsels is either advice about the most efficient way to gain salvation (*Summa theologiae*), or advice about the way to go beyond what is required for salvation, in order to attain perfection (*Summa contra gentiles*). On Aquinas' teleological view of moral necessity, conformity to the precepts is thus obligatory, or morally necessary, because it is necessary for salvation. Conformity to the counsels is morally optional because it is optional (though perhaps useful) with respect to that same end.

According to Catholic doctrine, God chooses to reward acts of supererogation with the gift of greater merit than the agent requires for salvation. This surplus merit is stored in the 'Treasury of the Saints', owned by the Church, and available to be drawn on by others. This notion of 'congruent merit' or freely-given and transferable reward provided the theological underpinnings for, among other things, the practice of granting indulgences, or the cancelling of another's punishment for some or all of their sins (Heyd 1982: 26).

The Reformers, particularly LUTHER and CALVIN, vehemently criticized the doctrine of supererogation; but much of the criticism that was focused specifically on this doctrine was directed less to the Thomistic position than to the older view formulated by Tertullian (Calvin 1536; see Mellema 1991; Heyd 1982: 26–9).

2   The contemporary argument for supererogation

The Reformation disputations over the coherence and the legitimacy of the notion of supererogation are echoed in contemporary secular debates. It is often argued that if one were always obliged to promote wellbeing, then the demands of morality would be far too strenuous. Our own personal projects would never get off the ground; and even once launched they would constantly be held hostage to the needs of others (Wolf 1982). On the other hand, it is said, if morality recognized a category of supererogatory action and assigned many of the more personally demanding acts of beneficence to this category, then we would have some opportunity to pursue our own interests without moral penalty (see HELP AND BENEFICENCE).

This argument assumes, first, that there are two distinct and competing perspectives: the moral point of view and the self-interested point of view; and that these can recommend conflicting courses of action in the same circumstances (see EGOISM AND ALTRUISM). Second, the argument locates the cause of the conflict in a too-narrow, tripartite conception of the moral realm. This conception recognizes only three categories of action: the forbidden, the required, and the morally indifferent (morally permissible) (Urmson 1958). After all, the reasoning goes, since presumably acts of beneficence are never morally indifferent, on the tripartite conception (unless they are forbidden) they will be obligatory. Hence the conflict with self-interest.

But does the mere prospect of such conflict, however extensive, really require the introduction of some notion of the supererogatory? Why not just accept that such conflicts can occur? Alternatively, why not take the possibility of such widespread conflict with personal concerns to de-legitimize the very conception of the moral on which that possibility turns?

These questions show that our two assumptions do not force the introduction of a category of the supererogatory. However, if we are willing to set aside the option of rejecting our working conception of the moral, we can introduce a third assumption that makes the need for a category of the supererogatory more urgent. This is the assumption that moral reasons are rationally overriding. Suppose that moral reasons always outweigh reasons of self-interest, and that beneficent action is (nearly always) obligatory. It follows that to the extent that beneficence and self-interest are in frequent and fundamental conflict our pursuit of personal projects will be contrary to reason. This conclusion seems entirely unacceptable. To see whether admitting the idea of supererogatory action will avoid this conclusion, however, we must understand how supererogation is to be defined.

3 Supererogation and positive social morality

Assuming that supererogatory action and obligatory action can both be supported by moral reasons, how are we to distinguish them? There are at least three possible approaches. The first is John Stuart Mill's proposal to restrict the operation of the distinction to the realm of social morality. On this proposal (1861), both supererogatory actions and obligatory actions

are actions that maximize utility, and hence actions that one ought to perform. The difference lies only in whether various external and internalized sanctions like blame and guilt are appropriate (useful) given failure to perform. Here Mill echoes Tertullian's idea that it is God's willingness to punish failure to perform that distinguishes obligation from supererogation. To avoid the unacceptable conclusion described in the previous section, this approach must hold that to say moral reasons are overriding is only a way of making the point that they are strongly reinforced by negative social sanctions. It will then follow that only obligation-making reasons will be 'overriding'.

4 Supererogatory acts as morally optional

The second approach focuses attention not on social morality but on the character of the reasons that support beneficent acts. Suppose we accept the following as partial definitions of obligation and supererogation: an act is obligatory only if its omission is morally impermissible; and an act is supererogatory only if its omission is morally permissible. Suppose we further posit that it is morally permissible to act against some set of moral considerations if and only if those considerations are not morally conclusive. We then have a criterion for distinguishing obligatory action from supererogatory action: any action supported by morally conclusive reasons will be obligatory; any action supported by reasons that are less than morally conclusive, will be supererogatory (Dancy 1993).

We can complete this approach by adding an account of overridingness: moral considerations are rationally overriding (if and) only if they are morally conclusive. This approach thus allows for the rational pursuit of self-interest whenever considerations of personal cost (represented within morality) are powerful enough to render the balance of moral reasons inconclusive. Conversely, only when morality regards certain considerations as conclusive must reason do so as well. Hence one is rationally required only to do one's duty (see DUTY §3).

5 Supererogation, virtue, and vice

The third approach accepts the partial definitions of obligatory action and supererogatory action with which the previous approach began. But it proposes that we regard both obligatory action and supererogatory action as supported by morally conclusive reasons. This proposal is backed by the suggestion that considerations about personal inconvenience are not really full-blown moral considerations, on a par

233

with considerations about human wellbeing, fairness, loyalty, honesty, and so forth. Thus helping others can be 'the moral thing to do', this approach says, regardless of whether it happens to require self-sacrifice.

Here is the puzzle for this third approach: whenever an action is supererogatory, it must be morally permissible to refrain from acting altruistically. But how can it ever be morally permissible to act against morally conclusive reasons?

We might solve this puzzle by making a distinction between first- and second-order moral judgments. Think of first-order judgments as being about agents' actions, while second-order judgments are about the motivation or perhaps the character agents display in their choice of actions. Judgments about the moral conclusiveness of the considerations at stake are first-order judgments. Now in some cases, when the cost to the agent is negligible and the human value at stake is great, to disregard morally conclusive considerations would be to show a degree of callousness, indifference, or smallness of spirit so great that it could only be called a vice (see VIRTUES AND VICES §§4–5). This is why refraining from acting in accordance with the first-order reasons is impermissible in this case, and why acting in accordance with those reasons is therefore obligatory.

In other cases, for instance when the cost to the agent is substantial, although to disregard the first-order moral considerations would be to display a less-than-ideal level of motivation, it would hardly be to sink so low as to warrant the imputation of vice. This is why it is permissible to refrain from acting in accordance with the first-order reasons in this case, and why acting in accordance with them is therefore supererogatory (see Trianosky 1986).

Finally, we can add to this third approach a more nuanced account of overridingness. On this account, morally conclusive first-order considerations will be rationally overriding if and only if to disregard them is to display some vice (and hence to do what is morally impermissible). Thus this third approach makes room for the rational pursuit of personal concerns just to the extent that morality is lenient in its judgments about virtue and vice.

6 Supererogation and praiseworthiness

By providing various accounts of overridingness, all three approaches offer some way to interpret the attractive idea that in doing what is supererogatory one acts freely, while in doing what is required, one is bound. It is often thought that this freedom is the ground of the special merit or praiseworthiness that is characteristic of supererogatory action (Heyd 1988).

But are all supererogatory acts necessarily praiseworthy? After all, whichever one of these three approaches one takes, the definition of the supererogatory will remain a purely *deontic* one, on a par with the definitions of the obligatory, the permissible, and the forbidden. This means that an agent can perform supererogatory acts from any one of a variety of motives, some morally admirable and some not. (Even the third approach says nothing about the motives of those who do what is supererogatory. It evaluates only the motives of those who refrain. Compare Brandt's discussion of obligation (1969).) In some ways this consequence seems intuitively plausible, since people can and sometimes do go 'beyond duty' for the most self-serving of reasons.

Even on a deontic analysis of supererogation there remains a certain conceptual link between supererogatory action and praiseworthy motivation: to go beyond duty, not for ulterior, self-interested reasons but for the sake of the moral concerns that are at stake, is necessarily praiseworthy. Here we have a notion of acting from *non*-obligatory moral considerations that is a strict analogue of Kant's notion of acting from duty. In the case of obligation, action from this praiseworthy motivation is what Kant calls 'dutiful' action. In the case of supererogation, it is what Mill (1843) calls 'noble' action. But not all actions in accordance with duty are dutiful; and not all actions beyond duty are noble (Mellema 1991: 3).

References and further reading

* Aquinas, T. (c.1259–65) *Summa contra gentiles* (Synopsis [of Christian Doctrine] Directed Against Unbelievers), trans. V.J. Bourke, Notre Dame, IN: University of Notre Dame Press, 1975. (Defends the claim that the counsels recommend conduct required for perfection, but not for salvation.)
* —— (1266–73) *Summa theologiae* (Synopsis of Theology), trans. Fathers of the English Dominican Province, Westminster, MD: Christian Classics, 1981. (Defends the claim that the counsels recommend more efficient ways of attaining salvation.)
* Brandt, R.B. (1969) 'A Utilitarian Theory of Excuses', *Philosophical Review* 78: 337–61. (Contains a discussion of obligation that is seminal for the approach to supererogation which holds that morally conclusive first-order considerations will be rationally overriding if and only if to disregard them is to display some vice – and hence to do what is morally impermissible.)
* Calvin, J. (1536) *Institutes of the Christian Religion*, trans. F.L. Battles, Grand Rapids, MI: W.B. Eerdmans, revised edn, 1986, esp. 2.8.51, 56–7. (Central

Reformation critique of the concept of super-erogation.)

* Dancy, J. (1993) *Moral Reasons*, Oxford: Blackwell, ch. 8. (Contains the seminal presentation of the view that any action supported by morally conclusive reasons will be obligatory, while any action supported by reasons that are less than morally conclusive will be supererogatory; somewhat technical.)

* Heyd, D. (1982) *Supererogation: Its Status in Ethical Theory*, London: Cambridge University Press. (A very useful and accessible survey of historical and philosophical issues concerning supererogation.)

* —— (1988) 'Moral Subjects, Freedom, and Idiosyncrasy', in J. Dancy, J.M.E. Moravscik and C.C.W. Taylor (eds) *Human Agency, Language, Duty, and Value: Philosophical Essays in Honor of J.O. Urmson*, Stanford, CA: Stanford University Press. (A discussion of the idea that supererogatory action are performed freely in a way that obligatory action cannot be.)

* Mellema, G. (1991) *Supererogation, Obligation, and Offence*, Albany, NY: State University of New York Press. (Clearly written, accessible, and theologically informed discussion of historical and philosophical questions about supererogation. Ch. 3 deals with Luther and Calvin's criticism of the doctrine.)

* Mill, J.S. (1843) *A System of Logic*, selections repr. in *Utilitarianism and Other Essays*, ed. A. Ryan, Harmondsworth: Penguin, 1987. (6.12.7 provides a discussion of the pursuit of noble character.)

* —— (1861) *Utilitarianism*, repr. in *Utilitarianism and Other Essays*, ed. A. Ryan, Harmondsworth: Penguin, 1987, ch. 5. (The *locus classicus* for the approach which suggests that while both supererogatory actions and obligatory actions are actions that maximize utility, and hence actions that one ought to perform, only obligation-making reasons are 'overriding'.)

* Tertullian, Quintus Septimus Florens (*c.*AD 160–*c.*AD 220) *Exhortation to Chastity*, in *Treatises on Marriage and Remarriage: Ancient Christian Writers, The Works of the Fathers in Translation*, vol. 13, trans. W.P. Le Saint, Westminster, MD: The Newman Press, 1951. (Seminal early discussion of the counsels/precepts distinction.)

* Trianosky, G. (1986) 'Supererogation, Wrongdoing, and Vice', *Journal of Philosophy* 83: 26–40. (Elaboration of the distinction between deontic judgments and judgments of virtue and vice (aretaic judgments).)

* Urmson, J.O. (1958) 'Saints and Heroes', in A.I. Melden (ed.) *Essays in Moral Philosophy*, Seattle, WA: University of Washington Press. (Seminal contemporary discussion of the need for a category of supererogation.)

* Wolf, S. (1982) 'Moral Saints', *Journal of Philosophy* 79: 419–39. (Influential and engagingly written discussion of the conflict between morality and self-interest. Wolf concludes with suggestive remarks about the role of supererogation in resolving the conflict.)

GREGORY VELAZCO Y TRIANOSKY

SUPERVENIENCE

Supervenience is used of the relationship between two kinds of properties that things may have. It refers to the way in which one kind of property may only be present in virtue of the presence of some other kind: a thing can only possess a property of the first, supervening kind because it has properties of the underlying kind, but once the underlying kind is fixed, then the properties of the first kind are fixed as well. The supervening features exist only because of the underlying, or 'subjacent' properties, and these are sufficient to determine how the supervening features come out. For example, a person can only be good in virtue of being kind, or generous, or possessing some other personal qualities, and an animal can only be alive in virtue of possessing some kind of advanced physical organization. Equally, a painting can only represent a subject in virtue of the geometrical arrangement of light-reflecting surfaces, and its representational powers supervene on this arrangement. A melody supervenes on a sequence of notes, and the dispositions and powers of a thing may supervene on its physical constitution.

Although the word supervenience first appears in twentieth-century philosophy, the concept had previously appeared in discussion of the 'emergence' of life from underlying physical complexity. The central philosophical problem lies in understanding the relationship between the two levels. We do not want the relationship to be entirely mysterious, as if it is just a metaphysical accident that properties of the upper level arise when things are suitably organized at the lower level. On the other hand, if the relationship becomes too close so that, for instance, it is a logical truth that once the lower-level properties are in place the upper-level ones emerge, the idea that there are two genuinely distinct levels becomes problematic: perhaps the upper-level properties are really nothing but lower-level ones differently described.

If this problem is dealt with, there may still remain difficulties in thinking about the upper-level properties. For example, can they be said to cause things, or explain things, or must these notions be reserved for the lower-level properties? Supposing that only lower-level properties really do any work leads to epiphenomenal- ism – the idea that the upper-level properties really play no role in determining the course of events. This seems to clash with common-sense belief in the causal powers of various properties that undoubtedly supervene on others, and also leads to a difficult search for some conception of the final, basic or lowest level of fact on which all else supervenes.

1 **Varieties of supervenience**
2 **The promises and problems of supervenience**

1 **Varieties of supervenience**

The basic instinct behind a supervenience claim is that although we talk in terms of two levels of fact, one of them is fundamental in that once it is fixed then so is the other. It is as if God had only to decide how the basic level is arranged and the other follows on automatically, just as a composer need only decide on the notes and the tempo and then the melody emerges without anything further being done. In this kind of case the relationship is simply one of composition, and there is perhaps nothing mysterious in the way that the melody supervenes upon the notes and tempo, any more than there is anything mysterious in a house supervening on an arrangement of bricks and mortar. But in other cases we are not talking of the supervenience of one thing upon other things, but of one kind of fact upon other kinds of fact, and the relationship seems not to be so simple. In the philosophy of mind, for example, physicalists will certainly want to say that the fact that a creature is alive or conscious supervenes upon complex neuro- physiological facts. God needs only to create beings of sufficient neurophysiological complexity and thereby will have created living or conscious beings; no further act of breathing life into the being is necessary.

But it seems only metaphorical to say that life is 'composed' of neurophysiological complexity. The relationship is not simply that of a building to its building blocks. Similarly, one might think that the fact that a computer is running a particular pro- gramme supervenes upon microphysical facts about its components, yet it is hard to make sense of the idea that its running the programme is literally composed of some arrangement of hardware. The term 'super- venience' was itself originally applied to the way ethical properties relate to natural ones, and in this case too it is hard to see how a person's virtue can literally be composed out of their natural dispositions, although here it may be more appropriate to think in analogous terms, since at least their virtue may be said

to have components, such as charity or honesty. In any event, a general definition is needed.

If the root idea is that once the basic level is fixed, nothing more need be done to fix the upper level, then at least it should be true that if two things are identical in respect of their basic properties, then they must also be identical in respect of the upper-level properties. The other way round this is not necessarily so, for two things may be identical in the upper-level respect without being identical all the way down. For example, two computers might be running the same programme but with rather different configurations of hardware, or two people may be equally virtuous but because of somewhat different characters. This is frequently referred to as the 'variable realization' of the upper-level properties, and is compatible with their supervenience on the lower level. Returning to the root idea, we can now frame it as an impossibility claim:

(S) It is not possible that two things should be identical in respect of their lower-level properties without also being identical in respect of their upper-level properties.

Various questions arise. First, and most obviously, any such claim only makes sense given a background distinction between the two levels of property. If we cannot genuinely separate the basic or subjacent (sometimes called subvenient) level from the upper or supervening level, then no such claim can be formulated. And in interesting cases, such as the supervenience of the ethical on the natural, there will be philosophers who deny that such a separation can be achieved, seeing it as dependent on a doubtful fact–value distinction.

Similarly, there may be disputes about priority: some philosophers may hold that the semantic elements of a language supervene upon the intentions with which its speakers use its elements; others hold that the content of peoples' intentions supervene upon the semantics of the language in which they would be disposed to express them (this kind of dispute also generates the battle between methodo- logical individualism and various kinds of holism). There may also be disputes about the extent of the basic class. Thus, to some philosophers it is important that the present content of someone's sayings should supervene only on their present brain states; to others it is important that it supervene upon the nature of the historically extended entire social and physical environment in which they live.

A second range of problems arises because we might worry about the strength of impossibility in any particular case. Is it a matter of logical impossibility, or metaphysical impossibility, or is it simply a question of the laws of nature? One might need to advance claims in different strengths, such as:

(E) It is not possible, as a conceptual matter, that two things should be identical in respect of their natural properties without being identical in respect of their ethical properties.

(M) It is not possible, as a metaphysical matter, that two things should be identical in respect of their physical properties without being identical in respect of their mental properties.

(P) It is not possible, given the laws of physics as they are, that two things should be identical in respect of their microphysical properties without being identical in respect of their macro-physical properties (such as weight or tensile strength).

Such formulations probably do not exhaust the intended significance of supervenience claims. For example, they do not capture the asymmetrical dependency, whereby the upper arises 'in virtue of' the lower (after all, denying variable realization, someone might think it impossible that two things should be identical mentally without being identical physically, but this would not mean that the physical supervenes on the mental). Nevertheless, they form the essential core.

The third kind of claim is perhaps the easiest to understand: it only demands that the laws of physics, as they actually obtain, connect the two levels in such a way that identity in one respect delivers identity in the other. In different possible worlds obeying different physical laws, the connection may be severed, with the weight or tensile strength of objects depending on other factors also (in fact weight, in our world, actually depends on other factors, such as the distribution of matter around the universe). The only problem with this kind of supervenience claim is that it inherits the difficulties surrounding the concept of a law of nature.

A claim such as (M) raises the stakes. Here we want to say that there is a more intimate connection between the physical and the mental. It is not just in the world as we have it that mental properties emerge out of physical properties. Rather, in any world we can properly describe, the mental must emerge out of the physical. There is simply no metaphysical possibility of a 'ghost stuff' or separate source or underlying basis of mentality. It has to occur in creatures of particular kinds of physical complexity. It offends against metaphysics, not just physics as we have it, to postulate two physically identical creatures, one of whom is conscious, the other a zombie. Anybody denying this would be thinking in terms of a dualism of some metaphysically improper stamp. Notice that

although many philosophers will subscribe to this thought, it is not altogether easy to formulate it. One distinction frequently made is between 'strong' supervenience, whereby the claim applies to any two things in any possible worlds, and 'weak' supervenience, whereby it only governs things within the same world. The difference is that across worlds we might imagine different laws of nature, and perhaps different constituent elements of nature, whereas one world must be governed by one set of laws and contain only whatever elements it has.

Finally according to (E) anyone denying the supervenience is in conceptual error, betraying some kind of incompetence with the concepts involved. This goes further than (M), unless we think that metaphysics is no more than a display of what is implicit in the concepts with which we think. It is, at least, clear that someone disposed to value two things differently, although admitting that they are identical in every other respect, is somehow confused or out of line, or ignoring the entire purpose of the notion of valuing a thing, compared with someone who denies (M), perhaps because of lingering Cartesian dualism (see DUALISM).

2   The promises and problems of supervenience

Once a supervenience claim is properly formulated and its strength suitably identified, it offers the seductive promise of a path between full-scale reduction of upper-level to lower-level properties, and an uncomfortable dualism. Full-scale reduction is here the attempt to show that there is really nothing but the underlying level, and that talk in upper-level terms merely makes disguised reference to this one kind of reality. It is prompted by metaphysical unease but it is expensive, since it usually turns out that the requisite reductions distort what we mean or what we are referring to. For example, it is highly unnatural to say that when we describe a computer by saying which programme it is running we either mean anything about its electronics or are referring to its engineering configuration. We are doing something different altogether, yet we ought to be able to make software descriptions metaphysically innocuous even if we think that all that is fundamentally going on is captured by the full story about the machine's hardware. Allowing that the software characterization supervenes on the hardware may fulfil this promise. Supervenience promises the relief from metaphysical anxiety, but without the costs of reduction.

To fulfil this promise it is clear that we must understand why the impossibilities in question arise. Without such an understanding, the upper-level properties may still seem to be unexplained 'danglers' or unexplained arrivals on the scene (reduction at least promises this explanation, by collapsing the two levels into one). This in turn may be a useful constraint on philosophies of various areas: for example, understanding why (E) is true may be easier on some accounts of ethical commitment than others. But without such extra commentary, and in particular in the philosophy of mind and the philosophy of language, supervenience claims may easily be part of the problem rather than part of the solution (see REDUCTIONISM IN THE PHILOSOPHY OF MIND).

See also: CAUSATION; SUPERVENIENCE OF THE MENTAL

References and further reading

Blackburn, S. (1973) 'Moral Realism' and 'Supervenience Revisited', in *Essays in Quasi-Realism*, New York: Oxford University Press, 1993. (Both papers stress the importance of an exact definition of the supervenience of the ethical on the natural, and the difficulty of explaining the fact on various views of ethics.)

Grimes, T.R. (1988) 'The Myth of Supervenience', *Pacific Philosophical Quarterly* 69: 152–60. (A critical look at proposed attempts to explicate the concept.)

Hare, R.M. (1952) *The Language of Morals*, Oxford: Oxford University Press. (The standard introduction of the notion of supervenience into modern debate.)

Hellman, G. and Thompson, F. (1975) 'Physicalism: Ontology, Determinism and Reduction', *Journal of Philosophy* 72 (17): 551–64. (A classic investigation of the metaphysics of supervenience.)

Kim, J. (1984) 'Concepts of Supervenience', *Philosophy and Phenomenological Research* 45: 153–76. (The classic paper defining and separating various concepts of supervenience.)

—— (1990) 'Supervenience as a Philosophical Concept', *Metaphilosophy* 21: 3–27. (A somewhat more pessimistic revisitation of the concept.)

Klagge, J.C. (1984) 'An Alleged Difficulty Concerning Moral Properties', *Mind* 93: 370–80. (An attempted rebuttal of Blackburn's argument.)

Morgen, C.L. (1923) *Emergent Evolution*, London: Williams & Norgate; repr. New York: AMS Press, 1977. ('Emergence' especially of life from chemical and physical complex systems, labelled the phenomenon of supervenience for an older generation of philosophers of mind and of biological science.)

SIMON BLACKBURN

SUPERVENIENCE OF THE MENTAL

Phenomena of one kind 'supervene on' phenomena of another kind just in case differences with respect to the first kind require differences with respect to the second. G.E. Moore claimed that beauty supervenes on non-aesthetic properties: if one painting is beautiful and another is not, there must be some relevant non-aesthetic difference between them. Supervenience seems to offer the possibility that a property may depend on other properties, without being explicable in terms of them. Contemporary philosophers of mind have employed the idea to capture the relation that appears to obtain between mental and physical properties.

Various supervenience relations have figured in recent discussions in philosophy of mind, of which the most important is 'strong property' supervenience characterized as follows:

> Q strongly supervenes on $\{P_1, P_2, \ldots\}$ if and only if any individuals x and y, in any nomologically possible worlds, that differ with respect to Q also differ with respect to some of the Ps.

Thus, beauty supervenes on physical properties if and only if any two things in any two nomologically possible worlds (worlds compatible with the laws of physics) that differ in their beauty also differ physically.

Supervenience has been claimed to capture two ideas. One is that individuals that agree on all their P properties also agree with respect to Q. The other is that the possession of Q *depends* on the possession of P properties. Besides capturing the relation that plausibly obtains between evaluative and non-evaluative properties (see SUPERVENIENCE), it has recently seemed apt for capturing views about the relations between the mental and the non-mental.

One important doctrine concerning the relationship between mental and physical properties that has been formulated in terms of supervenience is 'externalism'. This is the *denial* of the claim that intentional mental properties (for example, the property of thinking that water is wet) strongly supervene on neurophysiological properties: two people may be exactly alike with respect to their neurophysiological properties, but differ with respect to their intentional ones. This is not surprising in the case of certain, obviously *relational* intentional properties, such as *knowing* that France has no king: two people could be neurophysiological duplicates, but one might live in a world in which France had no king, but another in a world in which it did. Since knowledge entails the truth of what is known, the first person would, but the second would not *know* that France had no king.

More controversially, Hilary PUTNAM argued for externalism by proposing a thought experiment in which two individuals are exactly alike neurophysiologically but live in different environments, the first in one like ours containing *water*, that is, H_2O, and the other in one containing a superficially similar but *different* substance, XYZ. He concluded that in this scenario the two individuals would be *thinking about* different substances when they assert 'water is wet' (see CONTENT: WIDE AND NARROW; METHODOLOGICAL INDIVIDUALISM).

Supervenience figures in a more positive way in formulating another important doctrine in contemporary philosophy of mind, 'non-reductive physicalism'. Many philosophers (for example, Davidson 1980) think there are good reasons for supposing that mental properties, such as thinking about water, could not be *identified* or 'reduced to' (for example, defined in terms of) any physical properties, but that, nevertheless, the exemplifications of the mental properties depend on the exemplifications of physical ones. For example, although the property of thinking about water may not be reducible to physical properties, the occurrence of thoughts about water depend on the occurrence of physical events and states (see ANOMALOUS MONISM; PROPERTY THEORY; REDUCTIONISM IN THE PHILOSOPHY OF MIND). (Note that non-reductive physicalism is compatible with externalism since the properties on which intentional mental properties are said to depend – the 'supervenience base' – may include properties other than neurophysiological ones, for example, actual causal interactions with H_2O.)

This strong supervenience of mental properties on physical properties does not entail that mental properties are physical properties, or even that the instantiation of physical properties can provide an illuminating *explanation* of the instantiation of mental ones. Thus, supervenience appears not to entail the reducibility of the mental to the physical (see REDUCTIONISM IN THE PHILOSOPHY OF MIND). But it is unclear whether it actually captures the physicalist idea that mental properties *depend* on physical ones. As formulated above, supervenience is compatible with there being irreducible laws that link mental with physical properties; if so, then there might be different irreducible mental-physical laws in worlds that were otherwise physically identical. One can get closer to the spirit of physicalism by requiring in the above definition that all the laws involved in characterizing nomologically possible worlds include *only* physical laws.

Two significant philosophical questions about supervenience arise. (1) Why should we believe that mental properties supervene on physical properties? (2) What, if anything, explains why mental properties supervene on physical properties? Loewer (1994) suggests that supervenience follows from two reasonable assumptions: that mental properties are causally connected with physical properties, and that physics is causally closed and complete. The latter means that every physical change, if it can be explained at all, can be explained in terms of prior physical events. If mental properties failed to supervene on physical properties then there could be two nomologically possible worlds exactly alike physically, but in one, mental property M is instantiated while in the other, M is not instantiated. Since physical events in these worlds are fully accounted for by prior events the presence/absence of M is, contrary to our assumption, causally irrelevant (see MENTAL CAUSATION).

Although the preceding argument may provide reason to believe that the mental supervenes on the physical, it does not provide any explanation of the supervenience relation itself. Without such an explanation, supervenience may seem to be a mysterious brute fact. The explanations that have been suggested are that mental properties are identical to physical properties, or that they are functional properties that are realized by physical properties (see FUNCTIONALISM; MIND, IDENTITY THEORY OF). While these accounts do explain supervenience, they may be stronger than some advocates of non-reductive physicalism have in mind when they claim that mental properties cannot be reduced to or explained in terms of physical properties. These philosophers may have to accept supervenience as unexplained.

References and further reading

Blackburn, S. (1993) 'Supervenience Revisited', in *Essays in Quasi-Realism*, Oxford: Oxford University Press. (Discusses an argument that some forms of supervenience suggest non-realism of the supervening properties, and that strong supervenience suggests reduction of the supervening properties.)

* Davidson, D. (1980) 'Mental Events', in *Essays on Actions and Events*, New York: Oxford University Press. (Davidson introduces the notion of supervenience into philosophy of mind to formulate his version of non-reductive physicalism.)

Kim, J. (1993) *Supervenience and Mind*, Cambridge: Cambridge University Press. (The most comprehensive treatments of the use of supervenience to formulate non-reductive physicalism.)

* Loewer, B. (1994) 'An Argument for Strong Supervenience', in E. Savellos (ed.) *New Essays on*

Supervenience, Cambridge: Cambridge University Press. (Argues that the causal completeness of physics and the causal relevance of the mental implies that the mental supervenes on the physical.)

* Moore, G.E. (1922) 'The Conception of Intrinsic Value', in *Philosophical Studies*, London: Routledge & Kegan Paul. (First expresses the idea that evaluative properties supervene on natural properties.)

B. LOEWER

SURPRISE EXAMINATION PARADOX *see* PARADOXES, EPISTEMIC

SUSO, HENRY (*c.*1295–1366)

Suso was a Dominican friar and mystic and, with his friend John Tauler, a student of Master Eckhart. The three form the nucleus of the Rhineland school of mysticism. As a lyric poet and troubadour of divine wisdom, Suso explored with psychological intensity the spiritual truths of Eckhart's mystical philosophy. His devotional works were extremely popular in the later Middle Ages.

A native of Swabia, centre of the *Minnesang* and chivalry, Suso became a Dominican novice at thirteen and experienced a radical conversion at eighteen. There followed a decade of intense contemplation, accompanied by severe asceticism and self-torture. During his theological studies at Cologne (1324–8), a centre for Christian Neoplatonism since ALBERT THE GREAT, he met John TAULER and may have studied under MEISTER ECKHART. Returning to Constance, he served as lector, then prior at the friary school until 1348, after which he lived in Ulm until his death in 1366. These last decades involved preaching and pastoral care in Dominican convents and in the Beghard and Beguine communities.

Suso's disciple Elsbeth Stagel, a nun at Töss, compiled anecdotes from his life which became the nucleus for *Das Buch von dem Diener* (The Life of the Servant) (1362), the first autobiography in German literature. Suso presents himself as a spiritual knight in pursuit of divine Wisdom. Parts of the *Life* echo Eckhartian themes, but its focus on love and interior experience places this and his other works squarely in the Augustinian tradition of spirituality of the sort found in the writings of Bernard of Clairvaux. Traditional aspects of monastic spirituality, like intense prayer and penance, are blended with features more typical of fourteenth-century hagiography such as raptures, visions and a general emphasis on personal experiences.

His first work, *Das Büchlein der Wahrheit* (The Little Book of Truth) (1328), is an introduction to Eckhart's speculative mysticism and scholastic theology in the form of a dialogue between the disciple (Suso) and Eternal Truth. This didactic use of dialogue as a literary device, the first in German literature, recalls Boethius' *De consolatione philosophiae*. Suso defends Eckhart's views, particularly concerning the absorption of the soul into God, against charges of heresy and explores the spiritual ideal of detachment (*Gelassenheit*). The goal of the spiritual life is to lose oneself in God, but Suso differs from Eckhart in holding that mystical union preserves the distinction between Creator and creature. Moreover, Suso adapts key aspects of Eckhart's Neoplatonic mystical theology to his more devotional spirituality. All things are nothing before the transcendence of the divine being. The effective means to attain God is to transcend all thought and self-will. God as the divine ground of being (*Grund*) is pure simplicity, an 'interior fortress'. Human nature is 'poured out' and God pours in, culminating in the 'breakthrough' (*Durchbruch*) to the divine ground through the Son. Suso connects the soul to God through Eckhart's likening the nothingness of creatures to the abyss of the divine ground, that is, the Godhead beyond God. The remarkable fifth chapter speaks of Suso's own mystical raptures and ecstasies, while the seventh and final chapter explores *Gelassenheit*, the detachment and resignation necessary to attain the highest spiritual state.

His second work, *Das Büchlein der ewigen Weisheit* (The Little Book of Eternal Wisdom) (1327–34), abandons theological speculation completely. In its expanded Latin version, the *Horologium sapientiae* (Clock of Wisdom), it became the most popular devotional book in the late Middle Ages. This lyrical dialogue, which owes a great deal to the *Song of Songs*, embodies practical devotion in the form of meditations on the Passion of Christ and on the spiritual value of suffering. The uniqueness of the work derives from its combination of chivalrous imagery with mystical symbolism. The Wisdom pursued by the spiritual knight is also the incomprehensible Good which is utterly inexpressible in language: all creatures 'are swept away into the Good, from whom they emanated'.

Das Briefbüchlein (The Little Book of Letters) (1362), condensed from the larger Das grosse Briefbuch (The Great Book of Letters) (*c.*1360), is a devotional manual in the form of pastoral epistles, similar in tone to Seneca's *Moral Epistles* (see SENECA). Suso's poetic gifts transform natural images into spiritual allegories. Suso acts as spiritual guide, offering practical advice to his disciples amid life's tribulations. Here and throughout his writings Suso's psychological insight and poetic subtlety aim at furthering progress on the spiritual path to the ultimate goal.

See also: MEISTER ECKHART; MYSTICISM, HISTORY OF; NEOPLATONISM; PLATONISM, MEDIEVAL

List of works

Suso, Henry (*c.*1295–1366) Works, ed. K. Bihlmeyer, *Heinrich Seuse. Deutsche Schriften*, 1907; trans. F. Tobin, *The Exemplar, with Two German Sermons*, New York: Paulist Press, 1989. (Bihlmeyer is the standard edition of Suso's works in Middle High German. Tobin's translation is accurate, highly readable, and the only complete English translation of the vernacular works from medieval German, with excellent introduction and detailed notes.)

—— (1328) *Das Büchlein der Wahrheit* (The Little Book of Truth), ed. K. Bihlmeyer, *Heinrich Seuse. Deutsche Schriften*, 1907; trans. F. Tobin, *The Exemplar, with Two German Sermons*, New York: Paulist Press, 1989. (Suso's first work, an introduction to Meister Eckhart's mysticism and speculative theology.)

—— (1327–34) *Das Büchlein der ewigen Weisheit* (The Little Book of Eternal Wisdom), ed. K. Bihlmeyer, *Heinrich Seuse. Deutsche Schriften*, 1907; trans. F. Tobin, *The Exemplar, with Two German Sermons*, New York: Paulist Press, 1989. (Devotional work.)

—— (1327–34) *Horologium sapientiae* (Clock of Wisdom), ed. P. Künzle, *Heinrich Seuses Horologium sapientiae*, Freiburg: Universitatsverlag, 1977. (The Latin version of *Das Büchlein der ewigen Weisheit*.)

—— (1362) *Das Briefbüchlein* (The Little Book of Letters), ed. K. Bihlmeyer, *Heinrich Seuse. Deutsche Schriften*, 1907; trans. F. Tobin, *The Exemplar, with Two German Sermons*, New York: Paulist Press, 1989. (Condensed from *Das grosse Briefbuch*, devotional manual in the form of pastoral epistles.)

—— (1362) *Das Buch von dem Diener* (The Life of the Servant), ed. K. Bihlmeyer, *Heinrich Seuse. Deutsche Schriften*, 1907; trans. F. Tobin, *The Exemplar, with Two German Sermons*, New York: Paulist Press, 1989. (Suso's autobiography.)

References and further reading

Haas, A. (1971) *Nim din selbes war. Studien zur Lehre von der Selbsterkenntnis bei Meister Eckhart, Johannes Tauler und Heinrich Seuse*, Freiburg: Universitatsverlag. (Excellent account of the theme of self-knowledge in the Rhineland mystics.)

Kieckhefer, R. (1984) *Unquiet Souls: Fourteenth-Century Saints and Their Religious Milieu*, Chicago, IL: University of Chicago Press. (Excellent discussion of Suso's devotional spirituality and personal mysticism within the context of late medieval spirituality.)

Filthaut, E.M. (ed.) (1966) *Seuse-Studien: Heinrich Seuse. Studien zum 600. Todestag, 1366–1966*, Cologne: Albertus Magnus Verlag. (Excellent collection of scholarly articles on spiritual, textual and literary aspects of Suso's works.)

JOHN BUSSANICH

ŚVETĀMBARA JAINISM
see JAINA PHILOSOPHY

SWEDEN, PHILOSOPHY IN
see SCANDINAVIA, PHILOSOPHY IN

SWEDENBORG, EMANUEL (1688–1772)

Swedenborg was an eighteenth-century Swedish dignitary of considerable learning who believed that he had the power to communicate with spirits and angels and that these beings would help him fulfil the task allotted to him by God, namely to reveal the hidden meaning of Scripture and to usher in the new Church. His thought attracted the critical attention of no less a figure than Immanuel Kant.

Swedenborg was born in Stockholm to a prominent Lutheran cleric. At the age of eleven, he entered the University of Upsala, where he developed a keen interest in mathematics and natural philosophy. He was to pursue scholarly interests for the rest of his life. In 1716, Charles XII made him an honorary appointment to the Swedish Board of Mines. Swedenborg rose to the salaried position of Assessor Ordinary. Under this title, Swedenborg served the

King with distinction in many different capacities, including that of statesman, engineer and geologist.

Swedenborg retired from the Board in 1747 to devote himself to biblical exegesis. He believed that God had given him the power to communicate with angels and spirits so that he could reveal the hidden meaning of Scripture. In 1756, he published anonymously the *Arcana coelestia*, a massive line-by-line commentary on Genesis and Exodus.

Stories about Swedenborg's prophetic gift began to spread throughout Europe at this time. In 1756, during a dinner party in Gotenborg, Swedenborg claimed to see a fire spreading in Stockholm fifty miles away. He described the catastrophe in such minute detail that his vision could be checked against reports from the stricken capital which arrived in Gotenborg shortly thereafter. These reports apparently confirmed Swedenborg's vision on every point. Swedenborg had now made his name as a visionary. More stories added to his fame and excited interest in the *Arcana coelestia*, which was now known to be his work.

The problem is what to make of Swedenborg. Was he a prophet, a lunatic, or a man with questions too difficult to answer by the usual methods of scientific enquiry? Whatever else we might think, it is important to understand that Swedenborg saw himself as a Church reformer. He believed that the Church had lost sight of a fundamental truth, namely that God is one and operates through all of creation. The Nicene Council was the first indication of spiritual myopia, because it ruled that there have been three distinct divine persons from eternity. According to Swedenborg, this was to make three different gods out of the Father, Son and Holy Spirit (see TRINITY). Worse, it encouraged us to represent the Trinity as a council of human dignitaries, or even as a gang of thugs such as the Triumvirate at Rome. The polytheism of the Nicene Council and its attendant heresies were transmitted to the Roman Catholic Church, and from that Church to all the reformed Churches of Swedenborg's day. Swedenborg's mission was to right such wrong thinking and to prepare us for salvation in the new Church. His strategy was simple: he had only to describe his encounters with angels and spirits. Thus he reported how angels set him on the right path and how the spirits of churchmen revealed themselves in an otherworldly burlesque show as the buffoons they had been all along. Swedenborg found followers, not least the young William Blake. The Swedenborgian church is alive to this day.

Swedenborg thought that philosophers had as little spiritual insight as churchmen. Since they could not see spiritual things, as Swedenborg did, they could never formulate a true metaphysics of immaterial substances. So Swedenborg complained that metaphysics is all conjecture. He illustrated his complaint with reports of his discussions with the spirits of metaphysicians. Once, he said, they discussed the mind–body union. Swedenborg watched as the spirits divided into three camps representing the three hypotheses of the day: occasionalism, pre-established harmony and real interaction. When the discussion became acrimonious, a neutral spirit arrived to settle things. He invited a representative from each camp to write his favourite hypothesis on a slip of paper. The three slips of paper were put in a hat, and the spirits drew lots. Not surprisingly, Swedenborg's way of understanding things won the day. The lot chosen from the hat was 'spiritual influx', which Swedenborg interpreted as his own view that all life and wisdom flows from God into the human soul and from the human soul into the body.

Swedenborg was right at least about rational psychology. Champions of the different systems of mind–body union claimed to offer nothing more than hypotheses. The only way to make progress in the debate was to discredit the rival systems, and one might have concluded that too many opposing metaphysicians had done too good a job of that. Swedenborg was frustrated by the apparent futility of the debate. He assumed that metaphysicians themselves would lose patience, if they had not done so already, and succumb to temptation – namely to simplify things by denying the existence of anything immaterial (including the rational soul) and to think that material nature operates under its own steam. They would come to think that God and nature are one. Swedenborg apparently believed that Spinozism results when human reason applies itself to metaphysics (see SPINOZA, B. DE). In this, he was to anticipate JACOBI.

Swedenborg himself believed that everything in material nature flows out of the thoughts of angels and spirits and that the power of thought in angels and spirits flows ultimately from God. This is the basis of his 'correspondence' theory. Accordingly, every material thing 'corresponds' to the spiritual thing of which it is an effect. Thus cows correspond to angels thinking about the affections of nature-bound minds; sheep correspond to angels thinking about spiritually uplifted minds, and so on. The correspondence theory is in turn the basis of Swedenborg's biblical exegesis. Swedenborg believed that every word in Scripture expresses a correspondence.

Swedenborg had a wide influence. His ideas were of interest to EMERSON, JASPERS and KANT (§2). Kant became convinced in the mid-1760s that Swedenborg's visions were somehow emblematic of fundamental errors in Kant's own metaphysics. In 1766 he published a devastating self-critique in the guise of a satirical review of Swedenborg's *Arcana coelestia*. The title of Kant's review was *Dreams of a Spirit-Seer*. The writing of this review was to move Kant by 1770 to treat our representations of space and time as subjective forms of sensibility – an important step in the direction of his considered views in the *Critique of Pure Reason* (1781).

See also: DUALISM; MYSTICISM, HISTORY OF; SOUL, NATURE AND IMMORTALITY OF THE

List of works

Swedenborg, E. (1756) *Arcana coelestia*, trans. J.F. Potts, *Heavenly Secrets*, New York: The Swedenborg Foundation, 1978, 12 vols. (Commentary on Genesis and Exodus.)

—— (1758) *De coelo et ejus mirabilibus et de inferno*, trans. G.F. Dole, *Heaven and Hell*, New York: The Swedenborg Foundation, 1979. (Swedenborg's visions of heaven and hell.)

—— (1768a) *De Amore conjugiali*, trans. W.F. Wunsch, *Marital Love*, New York: The Swedenborg Foundation, 1975. (On the nature of love.)

—— (1768b) *Apocalypsis revalata*, trans. J. Whitehead, *Apocalypse Revealed*, New York: The Swedenborg Foundation, 1975, 2 vols. (The meaning of Apocalypse revealed.)

—— (1771a) *Vera Christiana religio*, trans. J.C. Ager, *True Christian Religion*, New York: The Swedenborg Foundation, 1980, 2 vols. (The theology of the new Church.)

References and further reading

Emerson, R.W. (1875) *Representative Men*, Boston, MA: Houghton Mifflin. (Includes an interesting and sympathetic study of Swedenborg and his claim that spiritual things lie behind every material thing.)

Kant, I. (1766) *Träume eines Geistersehers, erläutert durch Träume der Metaphysik* (Dreams of a Spirit-Seer, explained through dreams of Metaphysics), Königsberg: Johann Jacob Kanter. (A scathing, satirical review of the *Arcana coelestia*, important for later developments in Kant's *Inaugural Dissertation* of 1770. See Volume 2 of the Academy Edition of Kant's works.)

Laywine, A. (1993) *Kant's Early Metaphysics and the Origins of the Critical Philosophy*, Atascadero, CA: Ridgeview Press. (A study of the development of Kant's early metaphysics with an extended discussion of Swedenborg's significance for Kant.)

Toksvig, S. (1948) *Emanuel Swedenborg*, New Haven, CT: Yale University Press. (An informative and sympathetic intellectual and spiritual biography.)

A. LAYWINE

SWINESHEAD, RICHARD
see OXFORD CALCULATORS

SYLVESTER, FRANCIS, OF FERRARA *see* SILVESTRI, FRANCESCO

SYMBOLIC INTERACTIONISM

Symbolic interactionism is in the main a US sociological and social psychological perspective that has focused on the reciprocal relationship between language, identity and society. Philosophically it has largely been associated with pragmatists such as James (1907), Mead (1934), Dewey (1922) and Pierce (1958), although in the European context it has affinities with hermeneutics and phenomenology. In addition, it has links with various 'dramaturgical' approaches to communication that emphasize the interactive processes underpinning the construction, negotiation, presentation and affirmation of the self. In brief, symbolic interactionism is premised on the supposition that human beings are 'active' and not 'reactive'.

Although it is not easy to spell out the central propositions of Symbolic Interactionism in a systematic way, nevertheless, most of its proponents are committed to an interactive view of self and society, that is, they take issue with those views that see the social world as a seamless unity that completely encapsulates and determines individual conduct.

1 **The language matrix**
2 **Reflexivity: the self and language**
3 **The self as social**
4 **Motives, intentions and identities as social constructions**
5 **Society**

1 The language matrix

Very simply, this assumption suggests that the mind,

self and society cannot be explained as separate phenomena. Their existence depends upon the way in which persons talk, interact, and communicate. Language, spoken or otherwise, is the medium through which men and women come to know themselves as individuals and members of social groups. In other words, the distinction between subjectivity and objectivity is always a matter of convention and historical situation. A person can only bear witness to their inner states and experiences in a shared symbolic context.

2 Reflexivity: the self and language

A critical thing about language for symbolic interactionism is its reflexivity, that is, its self-referring properties. Language allows a person to see themselves from the point of view of others, but simultaneously, it opens up the possibility of internal dialogue and debate. Hence, thinking is not a solitary activity, but is of necessity social. 'I think' because others around me talk to me. Accordingly, even the most private aspect of a person's inner life is somehow framed and performed as a conversation between social actors. Thought processes, in this view, replicate the dynamics of everyday communication. It could be said, although very circumspectly, that for symbolic interactionists, there is no distinction to be made between private and public language.

For symbolic interactionists, like Blumer (1969), it is reflexivity that makes it possible for people to overcome the limits set by social and physiological forces. Language, in this sense, is both liberating and imprisoning. It is liberating because it enables a person to envisage and construct alternative futures and pasts, and it is imprisoning because it often seems to coerce our sense of self.

3 The self as social

Perhaps more than anything else it is the symbolic interactionist view of the self as a social process that distinguishes it from other approaches. Against those versions of self that see it in terms of some underlying agency, symbolic interactionism highlights the tentativeness of all claims about the self. Nothing can be asserted about the self that does not meet the test of the situation or context. Put differently, this means that every social encounter may involve a different kind of self activity. So instead of a unitary self, the typical self in symbolic interactionist literature is multiple and episodic. Logically this means that there are as many selves as there are situations – perhaps an absurd proposition.

However, the apparent situatedness of the self is premised on some kind of notion of biographical continuity. Who I claim to be now, depends to a large extent on my past history. Even though each new interpersonal encounter may evoke a new way of 'presenting' myself, I am none the less not detached from earlier encounters. I have not invented my gender, class and ethnic affiliations, nor have I acquired my ability to speak and write my language in a random haphazard way. What this means therefore, is that biography always enters into interaction episodes, but simultaneously, biography is modified and challenged in interpersonal situations. In short, the self is constituted in the dialogue between the contingencies of everyday life, and the consequences of past interactions with significant others like parents, teachers, siblings and peers.

4 Motives, intentions and identities as social constructions

In positing a social origin and deployment of the self, the symbolic interactionist takes issue with theories of behaviour that assume that human action is governed by drive-like motives. Motivation can only be understood in terms of the accounts, intentions, excuses, rationalizations of persons who live in a definite cultural milieu. In other words, motives are the meanings attributed to subjective states by persons participating in social encounters. At the same time, although motives are social, from the point of view of the individual, they are 'real'. The agent's 'definition of the situation' is thus a crucial aspect of any ongoing interaction episode.

Motives, then, are meanings that we give to our actions, and in the final analysis, these meanings are only significant if they are validated socially. They can be understood solely within the rubric of what people do and say as members of a society. For example, it makes no sense to talk of ambition in a context in which competition or achievement are not part and parcel of everyday activity. On the other hand, in most mundane situations, motives are taken for granted. We impute motives as a normal feature of our relationship with others.

For symbolic interactionists, the question of motives is also a question of identity. Who I believe myself to be is connected with what I believe I desire or want. The identity that I value also may be the reason for my actions. Be that as it may, both motives and identities are fashioned in social interaction.

5 Society

The symbolic interactionist view of society does not give it some overarching explanatory power. Society is what people do when they interact with each other in a multiplicity of situations. What we call society consists of literally countless encounters between people who talk, agree, argue and negotiate meanings and identities. In general, all interaction is sustained by implicit understandings of 'what is the case'. Each new encounter is gained by some kind of background knowledge about the manner in which interactions work. We know what to do when we greet a friend, because in the past we have found occasion to learn what is meant by 'friend' and the requirements of a 'greeting'.

Basically what this entails is seeing society as a communicative network in which participants are engaged in a ceaseless interpretive exercise to maintain some sense of order and identity. In this respect, society is never at rest – it is always in the process of being produced in interaction. At any one time the members of groups, collectivities, or institutions create and produce the conditions of their membership. Even a most rigidly structured bureaucratic institution, such as the army, depends on the reciprocal interaction of soldiers, officers and other ranks who interpret and monitor each others' behaviour.

This does not mean that social order is simply a matter of *ad hoc* negotiation. What is negotiated is constrained by what has been negotiated in the past. While symbolic interactionists believe that individuals 'make' history, they also argue that what is 'made' has consequences for future interaction. Thus we have a picture of society as a set of flowing and volatile self-other processes intermeshing with an already interpreted history that profoundly influences the alternatives perceived as being possible in the present (see SOCIETY, CONCEPT OF §§1, 3).

There are a number of objections that may be raised in conceiving of society in this way. First, there are situations in which negotiation appears to be irrelevant. How do concentration camp inmates negotiate with the functionaries who torture and incinerate them? There is not much scope here for the construction of new identities and meanings. Second, it may be that the symbolic interactionist picture of society is far too optimistic, and that it operates with an over-romanticized conception of human potentiality, a conception that gives the 'underdog', the 'rebel', and the 'deviant' almost superhuman status. Third, in its eagerness to demonstrate how selves and motives are socially constructed, it relies too heavily on the reflexive fecundity of language.

It could be argued that these objections are not only applicable to Symbolic Interactionism, but also to most social constructionist positions that give explanatory primacy to language. On the other hand,

some of these criticisms may be misconceived because they have not taken into account the fact that Symbolic Interactionism is not a codified theoretical position, but is rather an orientation that questions the reifications of mainstream social science, as well as mocking and even subverting the myths and pretensions of policy makers and cultural ideologues.

See also: MEAD, G.H.

References and further reading

* Blumer, H. (1969) *Symbolic Interaction*, Englewood Cliffs, NJ: Prentice Hall. (A key text.)

Burke, K. (1962) *A Grammar of Motives and a Rhetoric of Motives*, Cleveland, OH: World Publishing. (A seminal discussion of dramatism and its relationship to motivation.)

Denzen, N.K. (1992) *Symbolic Interactionism and Cultural Studies*, Oxford: Blackwell. (A contemporary attempt to integrate symbolic interactionism and postmodernism.)

* Dewey, J. (1922) *Human Nature and Conduct*, New York: Holt. (An attempt to explain human behaviour as a function of communicative and social process.)

Goffman, E. (1969) *The Presentation of Self in Everyday Life*, Garden City, NY: Doubleday. (A first statement of Goffman's dramaturgical perspective.)

* James, W. (1907) *Pragmatism*, New York: Longmans, Green and Co. (A clear statement of the central philosophical influence on symbolic interactionism.)

* Mead, G.H. (1934) *Mind, Self and Society: From the Standpoint of a Social Behaviourist*, Chicago, IL: University of Chicago Press. (Perhaps the most important text in the symbolic interactionist canon.)

* Pierce, C.S. (1958) *Selected Writings*, Chicago, IL: University of Chicago Press. (Important discussions about language and the self and the development of US semiotics.)

Perinbanayagam, R.S. (1985) *Signifying Acts: Structure and Meaning in Everyday Life*, Carbondale and Edwardsville, IL: Southern Illinois University Press. (An important contribution to the construction of symbolic interactionist theory.)

Rock, P. (1979) *The Making of Symbolic Interactionism*, London: Macmillan. (A clear historical analysis.)

ARTHUR BRITTAN

SYMBOLIST MOVEMENT

see NIETZSCHE, IMPACT ON
RUSSIAN THOUGHT (§1); RUSSIAN
RELIGIOUS-PHILOSOPHICAL
RENAISSANCE (§4)

SYNTAX

Syntax (more loosely, 'grammar') is the study of the properties of expressions that distinguish them as members of different linguistic categories, and 'well-formedness', that is, the ways in which expressions belonging to these categories may be combined to form larger units. Typical syntactic categories include noun, verb and sentence. Syntactic properties have played an important role not only in the study of 'natural' languages (such as English or Urdu) but also in the study of logic and computation. For example, in symbolic logic, classes of well-formed formulas are specified without mentioning what formulas (or their parts) mean, or whether they are true or false; similarly, the operations of a computer can be fruitfully specified using only syntactic properties, a fact that has a bearing on the viability of computational theories of mind.

The study of the syntax of natural language has taken on significance for philosophy in the twentieth century, partly because of the suspicion, voiced by Russell, Wittgenstein and the logical positivists, that philosophical problems often turned on misunderstandings of syntax (or the closely related notion of 'logical form'). Moreover, an idea that has been fruitfully developed since the pioneering work of Frege is that a proper understanding of syntax offers an important basis for any understanding of semantics, since the meaning of a complex expression is compositional, that is, built up from the meanings of its parts as determined by syntax.

In the mid-twentieth century, philosophical interest in the systematic study of the syntax of natural language was heightened by Noam Chomsky's work on the nature of syntactic rules and on the innateness of mental structures specific to the acquisition (or growth) of grammatical knowledge. This work formalized traditional work on grammatical categories within an approach to the theory of computability, and also revived proposals of traditional philosophical rationalists that many twentieth-century empiricists had regarded as bankrupt. Chomskian theories of grammar have become the focus of most contemporary work on syntax.

1 The need for structure
2 Syntactic categories and constituent structure
3 Phrase structure grammars
4 Recursion and sentential verbs
5 Scope
6 Ambiguities of scope

1 The need for structure

One central aim of *semantics* is to explain how the meaning of a sentence (or any other complex expression) is a function of the meanings of its parts (see COMPOSITIONALITY), a project that presupposes an understanding of how the parts are put together, that is, an understanding of its *syntax*.

Let us call any sequence of words a 'string'. The following strings can be put together from the list of words 'Bill', 'slept', 'soundly', 'last' and 'night':

(1) (a) Bill slept soundly last night

   (b) last night Bill slept soundly

   (c) *last soundly Bill slept night

   (d) *night Bill soundly last slept.

There is a clear difference between, on the one hand, (1a) and (1b) and, on the other, (1c) and (1d). In ordinary talk, the former are *sentences*; the latter are not. (Asterisks indicate non-sentences.) In order for a string of words to be a sentence (in this ordinary sense) the words must be put together in a certain way. Syntax is, in part, the study of the rules (or conditions) that determine the way that sentences are structured. The order of words in a string does more than determine whether or not a string is a sentence; it also plays a role in determining meaning. Compare (2a) and (2b):

(2) (a) The dog chased the cat.

   (b) The cat chased the dog.

The fact that (2a) and (2b) differ in meaning cannot be a consequence of their containing words with different meanings, since they contain precisely the same words. The difference in meaning is attributable to a difference in *word order*. In the terminology of traditional grammar, in English we understand a noun phrase preceding a verb (in the active voice) as the subject, and the noun phrase following that verb as its direct object. Not all languages mark the subject–object distinction in this way. Thus, for example Latin marks it by inflection and this allows for the possibility of much freer word order.

Initially, the following generalizations might seem reasonable: (a) sentence meaning is the product of word meaning and word order; (b) a difference in word order results in a difference in sentence meaning. But in fact neither is accurate. Although a change in word order frequently results in a change in meaning, sentences (1a) and (1b) above show that this is not always the case, so (b) is incorrect. To see that (a) is incorrect consider

(3)   Mary said Bill left voluntarily.

This admits of two distinct interpretations (or readings), which can be paraphrased as (a) 'Mary said that Bill left and she said this voluntarily' and (b) 'Mary said that Bill left and that he did so voluntarily'. It is as if the word 'voluntarily' can be understood in connection with either the saying or the leaving. Sentence meaning, then, is the product of more than word meaning and word order; it is the product of word meaning and sentence structure, and there is more to the sentence structure than the linear order in which its words appear: the way in which the words are grouped is crucial. One way of cashing out this idea might be to say that 'voluntarily' can be understood as an attachment either to the sentence 'Mary said Bill left' or to the smaller sentence 'Bill left'. Using square brackets to group parts of the sentence, we can represent the two different interpretations of (3) as follows:

(4)   (a) [Mary said [Bill left]] voluntarily.

      (b) Mary said [[Bill left] voluntarily].

In a sense that we can make precise, the moral of an example such as (3) is that the *hierarchical* organization (grouping) of the words in a sentence is just as important as their *linear* organization. (In terms explained in §5 below, the *scope* of 'voluntarily' is different in (4a) and (4b).)

2   Syntactic categories and constituent structure

The use of syntactic theory in projects such as compositional semantics requires that the theory have some systematic way of describing the syntax of sentences. The ways in which grammatical theories can describe linguistic structure are varied, but the following exposition will illustrate the most common. Since we are not here concerned with the internal structure of words (their morphology), let us say that words are the 'ultimate constituents' of sentences. The two parts of the sentence 'Odysseus returned' correspond to the traditional distinction between subject and predicate. Of course, both subject and predicate expressions can be more complex. If we replace the subject expression 'Odysseus' in 'Odysseus returned' by 'the hero', 'no hero' or 'a hero as great as godlike Achilles', in each case the result is another sentence. Since all of these expressions are built upon

nouns, they are said to belong to the category of noun phrase (NP).

If we replace the verb 'returned' in the sentence 'Odysseus returned' by 'loves Penelope', or 'shaves another customer', in each case the result is another sentence. Since expressions in predicate position are (typically) based on verbs, they are said to belong to the linguistic category of verb phrase (VP). Using 'S' for 'sentence', we can represent the syntactic structure of the sentence 'Odysseus returned' using a 'phrase structure tree' (or 'phrase marker') as follows:

(5)

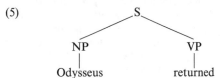

Alternatively, we can represent exactly the same syntactic information using a 'labelled bracketing':

(6) $[_S[_{NP}Odysseus][_{VP}returned]]$.

(5) and (6) are notational variants of one another, they are equivalent descriptions of the same structure – 'structural descriptions' – that is, tree notation and bracket notation are two informationally equivalent ways of specifying syntactic structure.

We can begin to characterize a set of sentences by formulating a rule to the effect that an NP followed by a VP forms a sentence, S. The standard way of doing this is to use a 'phrase structure rule' (or 'rewrite rule'):

(7) $S \Rightarrow NP + VP$.

This is read as 'S goes to NP VP'. All (7) says is that a sentence, or S, may be composed of an NP followed by a VP.

Let us turn now to the internal structures of NPs and VPs. Many NPs appear to be composed of words belonging to the traditional grammatical categories of article (for example, 'the', 'a') and noun (for example, 'cat', 'man'). Rather than using the category of article, let us use the broader category of *determiner* that includes not just 'the' and 'a', but also, for example, 'every', 'some', 'no', 'neither' and 'one'. We can represent the fact that an NP may be composed of a determiner (D) and a noun (N) using the following phrase structure rule:

(8) $NP \Rightarrow D + N$.

Now we can provide a phrase structure tree for 'The hero returned' using the rules in (7) and (8):

(9)

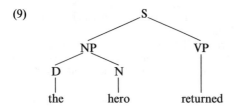

Or we can use a labelled bracketing:

(10) $[_S[_{NP}[_D\text{the}][_N\text{hero}]][_{VP}\text{returned}]]$.

Some VPs may contain NPs as parts, for example, 'loves Penelope', and 'shaves another customer' (see above). Unlike verbs such as 'return' and 'snore', verbs like 'see' and 'respect' are *transitive*: they take NPs as direct objects. We have, then, at least two types of VPs to examine: those 'headed by' (that is, built around) intransitive verbs (V_is), such as 'return' and 'snore', and those headed by transitive verbs (V_ts), such as 'respect' and 'like'. Consequently, we need at least two phrase structure rules for VPs:

(11) $\text{VP} \Rightarrow V_i$

(12) $\text{VP} \Rightarrow V_t + \text{NP}$.

The syntax of 'The hero returned' can now be spelled out in more detail:

(13)

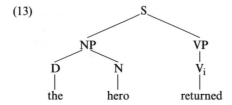

The syntax of 'The hero loved the goddess' is given by

(14)

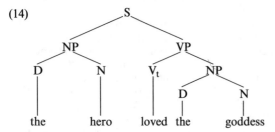

3 Phrase structure grammars

Not only do philosophical applications of syntactic theory require a set vocabulary for describing linguistic structure, they require linguistic theories to specify well-formed linguistic structures in a finite

way. Contemporary syntactic theory offers just such resources.

One aim of what CHOMSKY has called 'generative grammar' is to articulate a finitely statable theory that generates all and only the phrase markers of a given language. With the resources made available in the previous section, we can construct a generative grammar for a fragment of English. For purposes of illustration, we can do this by articulating a 'phrase structure grammar'. Such a grammar can be viewed as a formal system consisting of two parts: a 'lexicon' (a list of words together with a specification of the grammatical category of each word), and a set of phrase structure rules specifying how words from these categories may be put together to form sentences. In effect, then, a grammar is a theory, and like any other theory its usefulness lies in its predictive power. For any string of English words, the theory must say whether or not that string is a sentence. The following is a simple generative grammar:

Lexicon

$$\text{PN} = \{\text{Fred, Mary, Bill}\}$$
$$\text{D} = \{\text{a, every, the}\}$$
$$\text{N} = \{\text{man, woman}\}$$
$$V_i = \{\text{left, returned}\}$$
$$V_t = \{\text{likes, respects}\}$$

Phrase structure rules

$$S \Rightarrow \text{NP} + \text{VP}$$
$$\text{NP} \Rightarrow \text{PN} \ (\text{'proper name'})$$
$$\text{NP} \Rightarrow \text{D} + \text{N} >$$
$$\text{VP} \Rightarrow V_i$$
$$\text{VP} \Rightarrow V_t + \text{NP}$$

Notice that each of the phrase structure rules has the following form:

(15) $\alpha \Rightarrow \beta_1 + \ldots + \beta_n$.

The important feature here is that in each rule of this type exactly one symbol α appears on the left-hand side of '$\Rightarrow$'. Such rules are called 'context-free' phrase structure rules, the idea behind the terminology being that they are blind to whatever symbols may appear on either side of α, that is, they are blind to the syntactic 'context' in which α appears. The systematic use of a set of context-free rules is a way of formalizing traditional work on grammatical categories within an elegant approach to the theory of computability (or recursive functions); a context-free phrase structure grammar is equivalent to a categorial grammar in the sense of Ajdukiewicz (1935; see Ajdukiewicz, K. §5).

In a sense to be defined, the grammar just given generates the following phrase structure tree:

(16)

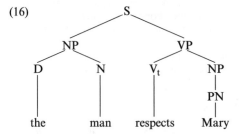

There is a specialized vocabulary in formal language theory (mathematical linguistics) for describing the parts of phrase structure trees and the relationships that obtain between the parts. We can tailor some of this vocabulary, rather informally, to suit our concerns:

(i) Each position in a tree is a *node*. A line connecting two nodes is a *branch*.

So, for example, in (1) there are twelve distinct nodes: S, NP, VP, D, N, V_t, PN, 'the', 'man', 'respects' and 'Mary'. Branches connect D and 'the', NP and D, and NP and N.

(ii) The S node at the 'top' of a tree is the *root node* of that tree. The words at the 'bottom' of a tree are its *leaf nodes* (or *terminal nodes*).

We are concerned with (a fragment of) English, so every leaf node will be a word of English.

(iii) A sequence of branches that connects two nodes is a *path*. Node β is *properly dominated* by node α if and only if the path from β back to the root node passes through α. The set of nodes properly dominated by node α is the *proper domain* of α.

Example: in (16) there is a path between D and 'the', and a path between S and D. Indeed, there is a path between any two distinct nodes. Additionally, D properly dominates 'the', NP properly dominates D, N, 'the' and 'man', and S properly dominates every node in the tree (apart from itself). (It dominates but does not properly dominate itself, just as a set is a subset but not a proper subset of itself.)

(iv) Each node in a tree corresponds to a *constituent* of the sentence in question.

So, for example, in (16) the NP node corresponds to the constituent 'the man'; and the VP node corresponds to the constituent 'respects Mary'. So whereas 'the', 'the man', 'respects' and 'respects Mary' are

constituents of (16), 'man respects', 'man respects Mary' and 'the man respects' are not.

(v) If Γ is a phrase structure grammar and τ is a tree, then Γ *generates* τ if and only if

(a) the root node of τ is S;

(b) every terminal node of τ is in the lexicon for Γ; and

(c) every step from the root node to the string of terminal nodes is licensed by one of the phrase structure rules of Γ.

(vi) A *string* of Γ is a linear sequence of words taken from the lexicon for Γ. Γ *generates a string* Σ if and only if Γ generates a tree for Σ.

(vii) The set of strings generated by a grammar Γ is the *language* L_Γ of Γ, that is, the set of *sentences* of L_Γ.

An interesting feature of (vii) is that it appropriates the English words 'language' and 'sentence' and assigns them technical meanings. Later, the theoretical use of these words will be specified precisely to satisfy theoretical demands that arise when syntax and semantics come together.

The picture just presented is deliberately simplified. Nevertheless, it is widely held that context-free grammars of this form are inadequate to describe natural languages. In addition to context-free rules of the type we have just discussed, Chomsky (1957, 1965) posited 'transformational' rules that operated on the trees generated by context-free phrase structure grammars to produce trees that could not be produced in any satisfactory way by phrase structure rules alone. For example, Chomsky wanted to explain the syntactic and semantic relationships between the active and passive voice and accomplished this by postulating a transformational rule that derived a phrase structure tree for a passive sentence from the tree for its corresponding active. Much work by generative linguists in the 1970s sought to impose a rigorous set of constraints on possible transformational rules. Beginning with Chomsky (1981), generative linguists began to explore alternative ways of generating sentences using methods that depart from those of traditional phrase structure grammars.

4 Recursion and sentential verbs

The grammar above was finite, as was the language that it generated (it consists of a finite number of sentences). There are, however, finite grammars that generate infinite languages. This can be seen easily enough in connection with philosophically interesting verbs such as 'believe', 'know', 'prove', 'remember' and 'say', which can be used in ways that preclude classifying them as either V_is or V_ts. Consider the following sentences:

(17) Mary believes (that) Fred left.

(18) Mary said (that) Fred left voluntarily.

The VPs in these sentences seem to consist of a verb combined with a whole sentence. Since they seem to take whole sentences as their complements, these can be called 'sentential verbs' (V_s). Let us now add some V_ss to our lexicon:

> $V_s = \{$believe, know, doubt, say, suggest, realize, remember, prove$\}$.

(Some V_ss are also known as *psychological* verbs' or 'verbs of propositional attitude', a label due to Russell – see PROPOSITIONAL ATTITUDE STATEMENTS; §5 below.) We can now add the following phrase structure rule to produce a new grammar:

(19) $VP \Rightarrow V_s + S$.

The resulting grammar generates the following phrase marker:

(20)

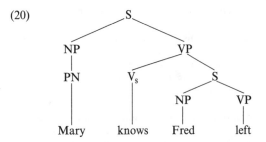

As this tree diagram reveals, the rules '$S \Rightarrow NP + VP$' and '$VP \Rightarrow V_s + S$' taken together give our grammar the capacity to generate trees in which S nodes are properly dominated by other S nodes. More precisely, our grammar generates trees in which an S node properly dominates a VP node that properly dominates another S node that properly dominates another VP node that.... So, for example, the grammar generates trees for both of the following:

(21) Bill knows Mary thinks Fred left.

(22) Mary doubts Fred knows Bill said Mary left.

Clearly, there is no end to the list of sentences generated: if our grammar generates a sentence ϕ, it also generates every sentence of the form

> $[_S[_{NP}...][_{VP}[_V s...]\phi]]$.

Despite containing a finite set of rules, it generates an infinite set of sentences (the language generated is

infinite). A structure such as (20) in which a node of category X properly dominates a distinct node also of category X is a *recursive* structure. We now say that our grammar *recursively generates* an infinite set of sentences. The recursive nature of natural language is further revealed once connectives such as 'and', 'or' and 'but' are introduced. A primary function of connectives is to join two sentences – they may also be used to connect, for example, NPs and VPs – in such a way that the result is a larger sentence, as in

(23) Bill left and Mary returned.

(24) Bill snores or Mary snores.

The following phrase structure rule can therefore be postulated:

(25) $S \Rightarrow S$ CONN S,

where CONN is the category 'connective'. This rule exploits the possibility of having three symbols on the right-hand side of '$\Rightarrow$', but it is still a context-free phrase structure rule of the form given in (15). Recursive structures are also found in (for example) NPs containing relative clauses such as 'the man who loves the woman who found the child who...'.

5 Scope

There are a number of semantic issues of independent philosophical importance that can be illuminated by appealing to syntactic structure. The nature of scope in natural language is an instructive case study (see SCOPE). The following strings are all ambiguous:

(26) (a) everyone strives for some good

    (b) if I know that p then necessarily p

    (c) the number of planets is necessarily greater than seven

    (d) Bill returned or Fred returned and Mary left

    (e) George thought the King wasn't the King

    (f) Mary said Bill left voluntarily.

For example, someone uttering (26a) might be understood as saying that there is some particular good such that everyone strives for it or merely that everyone strives for some good or other. All of these examples involve ambiguities of scope that can be explicated within sophisticated syntactic theories. For present concerns, we restrict ourselves to a simple case mentioned earlier involving the scope of the adverb 'voluntarily' as it occurs in a string such as (26f), which is ambiguous between readings corresponding to the syntactic structures given earlier by (4a) and (4b). To provide a general characterization of scope in terms of phrase structure is straightforward once we introduce some new notions. First,

(viii) Node β is *immediately dominated* by node α if and only if β is properly dominated by α and there is no intervening node γ, that is, no node γ such that α properly dominates γ and γ properly dominates β.

In the following diagram, A properly dominates every other node; in addition it immediately dominates B and C, but not D, E, F or G:

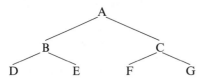

(ix) If distinct nodes β and γ are immediately dominated by node α, then α is a *branching node*.

A, B and C are branching nodes; D, E, F and G are not. We can now define 'scope' in a phrase structure tree:

(x) The *scope* of node α is (the constituent corresponding to) the first branching node properly dominating α. Node β is *within the scope* of node α if and only if the first branching node properly dominating α properly dominates β.

So in (20), the scope of 'Mary' is the entire sentence, whereas the scope of 'Fred' is the smaller sentence 'Fred left'.

(xi) If node β is within the scope of node α and node α is not within the scope of node β, then α has larger scope than β (and β has smaller scope than α).

Thus 'Mary' has larger scope than 'Fred' in (20). The scope of 'knows' in this phrase marker is the VP 'knows Fred left'. Thus the name 'Fred' occurs within the scope of 'knows', but the name 'Mary' does not. This is widely held to have important logical consequences. If Mary is Elizabeth – that is, if 'Mary' and 'Elizabeth' are two names of the same person – then the truth of (21) guarantees the truth of

(27) Elizabeth thinks Fred left.

Now suppose that Fred is Bert. Does the truth of (21) guarantee the truth of (28)?

(28) Mary thinks Bert left.

Following FREGE, many philosophers believe it does not. (Mary may not know that Fred is Bert.) If this is

correct, then we can describe the situation syntactically: the fact that 'Fred' appears within the scope of a 'psychological' verb (in this case, 'think') means there is no guarantee that 'Fred' can be replaced by a coreferring name to produce a sentence with the same truth-value as the original. A name occupying such a position is said to occur in a context that is 'referentially opaque' (see PROPOSITIONAL ATTITUDE STATEMENTS §§1–2).

6 Ambiguities of scope

We turn now to an example involving what is usually called a 'structural ambiguity' or an 'ambiguity of scope'. The latter label (due to Russell) is more dominant in philosophy, logic, and mathematics. As Russell pointed out, much bad philosophy has resulted from inattention to scope ambiguities. Indeed, uncovering and avoiding them are skills all philosophers must acquire. Davidson has emphasized the importance of an understanding of the semantics of adverbs to a number of philosophical questions involving actions and events. Earlier, the fact that the following string is ambiguous was used to call attention to the grouping of words within a sentence:

(3) Mary said Bill left voluntarily.

It was suggested that the ambiguity in question was structural in that the words can legitimately be grouped in two different ways:

(4) (a) [Mary said [Bill left]] voluntarily.

(b) Mary said [[Bill left] voluntarily].

We can implement this suggestion by providing distinct phrase markers corresponding to (4a) and (4b). We will consider two rival ways of doing this. The word 'voluntarily' belongs to the category of adverb, so let us add to our lexicon the following:

(29) ADV = {voluntarily, hastily, discreetly}.

In line with the informal account of the ambiguity suggested earlier, the first attempt to characterize the syntax of adverbs involves positing the following phrase structure rule:

(30) $S \Rightarrow S + ADV$.

The resulting grammar generates the following distinct phrase markers for (3):

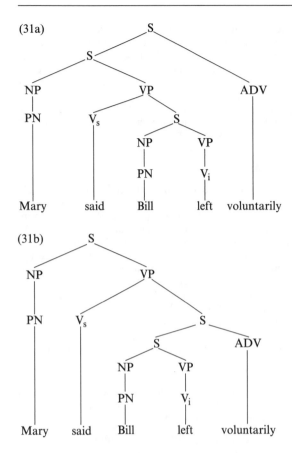

(31a)

Mary said Bill left voluntarily

(31b)

Mary said Bill left voluntarily

In (31a) the scope – as defined above – of 'voluntarily' is the entire sentence. Thus the verb 'said' is within its scope. By contrast, in (31b) the scope of 'voluntarily' is just the smaller sentence 'Bill left voluntarily'. Thus the verb 'said' is not within its scope, but the verb 'left' is. On the assumption that, as the etymology suggests, an adverb modifies a verb in some way, the verb it modifies is the main verb of the sentence to which it is attached. Thus (31a) corresponds to the reading of (3) that might be loosely paraphrased as 'Of her own volition, Mary said that Bill left' and (31b) corresponds to the reading that might be paraphrased as 'Mary said that Bill left as a matter of his own volition'. (Of course, until an account is provided of how syntactic structure contributes to meaning, the pairing of distinct phrase markers with distinct readings of a string is largely intuitive.)

We now make two observations about our definition of scope. First, by the definition provided, every constituent has a scope; but there are only certain types of constituents whose scopes will interest us (usually, connectives, quantifiers, verbs and adverbs).

Second, notice that it is not always the case that for two constituents one is within the scope of the other.

It is worth asking whether this is the best way of characterizing the syntax of sentences containing adverbs. An alternative account emerges if we take the etymology of 'adverb' more seriously and view ADVs as attaching to VP nodes rather than S nodes. Only detailed empirical and logical work will tell which of these analyses is better. The best theory may tell us that there are two distinct types of ADV: one sort that attaches to an S node, another that attaches to VP. There is no need for us to settle this difficult matter here. Suffice to say, that if we find that claims about the semantic properties of adverbs are doing some philosophical work, we will have to look carefully at their syntax.

More than a few philosophical muddles have been due to confusions over the scope of operators in natural language sentences. Utilizing the resources of syntactic theory, it becomes possible for us to study scope relations in a more rigorous fashion, and to marshal arguments for and against certain proposals about the logical form of natural language. Indeed, whenever we encounter philosophical claims which rely upon the semantic properties of quantifiers, adverbs and so on, we will want to look carefully at their syntactic properties. This specific point is just an instance of a quite general principle concerning the relationship between the philosophy of language and theoretical syntax: the former cannot properly proceed independently of the latter.

See also: ANALYTICAL PHILOSOPHY; CHOMSKY, N.; LANGUAGE OF THOUGHT; LOGICAL FORM; MIND, COMPUTATIONAL THEORIES OF; SCOPE

References and further reading

* Ajdukiewicz, K. (1935) 'Die Syntaktische Konnexität', *Studia Philosophica* 1: 1–27; trans. 'Syntactic Connexion', in S. McCall (ed.) *Polish Logic*, Oxford: Clarendon Press, 1967. (A full statement of the theory of categorial grammar.)

* Chomsky, N. (1957) *Syntactic Structures*, The Hague: Mouton. (Early statement of the formal limitations of various approaches to syntax, mathematical properties of different types of grammars, and the theory of transformational grammar. Very readable.)

* —— (1965) *Aspects of the Theory of Syntax*, Cambridge, MA: MIT Press. (Detailed statement of Chomskian methodology, and Chomsky's 'Standard Theory'.)

* —— (1981) *Lectures on Government and Binding*, Dordrecht: Foris. (Detailed statement of major

components of Chomsky's 'principles and para-meters' approach to syntax that moves well beyond the transformational approach of his earlier work. Hard going.)

—— (1986) *Knowledge of Language*, New York: Praeger. (Very readable account of the philosophical and technical details of the 'principles and parameters' approach.)

Davidson, D. (1980) 'The Logical Form of Action Sentences', in *Essays on Actions and Events*, Oxford: Clarendon Press. (A proposal about the logical form of sentences involving action verbs.)

Lewis, D.K. (1983) 'General Semantics', in *Philosophical Papers*, vol. 1, Oxford: Oxford University Press. (Accessible exposition of a categorial grammar for a part of English and a corresponding compositional semantics.)

May, R. (1985) *Logical Form: Its Structure and Derivation*, Cambridge, MA: MIT Press. (First sustained attempt to connect work in Chomsky (1981) with traditional philosophical work on 'logical form'.)

Neale, S. (1994) 'Logical Form and LF', in C. Otero (ed.) *Noam Chomsky: Critical Assessments*, London: Routledge & Kegan Paul. (An attempt to connect Chomsky's syntactic programme to work on meaning, reference and logical form.)

Russell, B.A.W. (1905) 'On Denoting', *Mind* 14: 479–93; repr. in *Logic and Knowledge: Essays 1901–1950*, ed. R.C. Marsh, London: Allen & Unwin, 1956, 41–56. (The classic theory of definite descriptions that provided a paradigm for analysis of logical form.)

Sells, P. (1985) *Lectures on Contemporary Syntactic Theories*, Stanford, CA: Center for the Study of Language and Information, Stanford University. (Accessible overview and exposition of competing approaches to generative grammar.)

Wittgenstein, L. (1922) *Tractatus Logico-Philosophicus*, trans. D. Pears and B. McGuinness, London: Routledge & Kegan Paul, 1961. (An early, philosophically ambitious theory of logical form.)

STEPHEN NEALE

SYSTEMS THEORY IN SOCIAL SCIENCE

'Systems theory' is a label for two very different approaches to social analysis. The first was a post-1945 successor to traditional organicist theories of society that for some twenty years dominated US sociology and political science. It was never very popular outside the USA, and is now of largely historical interest; social scientists who aspire to develop a positive science of social interaction have for the past two decades rested their hopes on the individualist analyses provided by rational choice theory.

Systems theory in the first sense of the term flourished in US sociology and political science from the late 1940s to the late 1960s, and is especially associated with the names of Talcott Parsons in sociology and David Easton and Gabriel Almond in political science. A systems approach to social analysis was commonly, though not universally, associated with some form of functionalism, especially in the work of Parsons, the leading structural-functionalist of his day. It fell into disrepute along with functionalism, a victim of the changed political climate of the 1960s as much as of its purely intellectual weaknesses.

The second form of systems theory is associated especially with the name of Niklas Luhmann, and its leading critic is Jürgen Habermas. The second form is in vigorous life, but not well known in the USA.

1   The organicist background
2   The modern revival
3   Niklas Luhmann's systems theory

1   The organicist background

Systems theory in this sense inherited the assumptions of traditional organicist theories of society. The belief that social analysis must be grounded in a distinctively holistic and organic approach to its subject matter was characteristic of conservative critics of eighteenth-century rationalism such as Edmund BURKE; its philosophical defence was one of those few of Hegel's achievements that Marx unhesitatingly applauded (see HEGEL, G.W.F.). In part, this was a way of staking out a terrain for sociology distinct from the terrain of economic analysis. The conservative implications of these ideas as understood by writers such as Burke and Hegel were not intrinsic to an emphasis on the organic character of society. Few thinkers were more conscious of the depth of social and economic conflict than Karl Marx, and his belief that social and economic relations formed a system of exploitation was one of the things that persuaded him that revolution rather than reformist tinkering was demanded.

At the end of the nineteenth century, liberals, too, rested their hopes on a new, more organic conception of society than they thought their predecessors – particularly the British utilitarians – had attained. In France, Émile DURKHEIM (§2) defended an extreme holism as to sociological method. So widely felt was the wish to ground ethics in sociology and to rescue liberal politics from exaggerated individualism that one might think it part of the *fin de siècle* spirit of the age (see HOLISM AND INDIVIDUALISM IN HISTORY AND SOCIAL SCIENCE).

This conception of the social organism fell into (something like) disrepute after the First World War; the obvious dissimilarities between a society and organisms such as fish, sheep or human beings had, of course, never been denied by nineteenth-century social thinkers, but they had perhaps not appeared to be worth mentioning in the course of arguments intended to emphasize that, whatever else they might be, societies were not established by freely contracting, independently formed, self-sustaining and autonomous individuals. Turn of the century liberal organicists had no such conservative purposes as, say, Burke had had, but the association of organicism with authoritarianism and irrationalism, however, was subsequently sufficient to damn it in the eyes of most interwar liberal thinkers.

2 The modern revival

Not every work that stresses the idea of system rests on such a form of systems theory. Kenneth Waltz's *The Theory of International Politics* (1979), is perhaps the most famous work in the field in the past two decades; it strongly emphasizes the opportunities and constraints that membership of an international system of states offers to and imposes on each state in the international system. It is, for all that, concerned with the international system as a balance of opposed forces, not with its quasi-organic qualities as something self-maintaining, self-reinforcing, and self-repairing. It is systems theory in this latter sense that was briefly popular, and so harshly criticized.

Several representative samples will stand for many. Talcott Parsons (1950) provided a framework for social analysis that saw the social system as a system of interaction, or, as he put it an 'action-system'. The system as a whole was made up of four sub-systems: in effect, the economic, cultural, political and psychological aspects of a social order. It is important to emphasize that these 'sub-systems' were defined in terms of function, not concretely in terms of institutions. These functions included such things as socializing individuals into an acceptance of the local norms of sexual identity and moral conviction, or organizing their efforts at producing and distributing the means of life. Understanding how this was achieved was equally a matter of asking how social norms affected the orientation of individuals towards interactions with others: for instance, whether we treat each other instrumentally or in terms of some non-instrumental moral norm.

Much the same controversy beset systems theorists in political science, although none of them produced the elaborate categorical system that Parsons had produced; nor did they arouse the same intensity of discipleship and opposition. David Easton (1953) represented the political system as an input-output device as it were embedded in the wider social system; from the social system there flowed demands on the one hand and support on the other, and from the political system there flowed 'authoritatively allocated' values. Critics tended to complain not only that this was only a way of redescribing what everyone knew already, but that it misrepresented the nature of politics. Only in advanced modern societies was there a formal distinction between the realm of the political and that of the economic or the cultural, so this was not a picture of all forms of politics. Again, in some societies the political system is active rather than reactive, trying to mould the society rather than waiting to receive 'inputs'.

Almond's functional analyses of the political system were not entirely similar. In his account (*The Politics of the Developing Areas*, with James S. Coleman; *Comparative Politics Today*, with G. Bingham Powell) the political system must perform three output functions of 'rule-making, rule-enforcing and rule-adjudication', categories that bear perhaps too clear a resemblance to the three powers of the US legislature, executive and judiciary. Similarly, the 'input functions' of 'interest articulation' and 'interest aggregation' were sometimes derided as ornate synonyms for the work done by pressure groups and political parties in the USA. Enthusiasts for the approach responded by applying it to the then Soviet Union (David S. Lane, *Politics and Society in the USSR*) and employing it as a basis for the general theories of revolution (Chalmers Johnson, *Revolutionary Change*); unappeased critics continued to claim that such efforts showed that it was possible to restate the conventional wisdom in the new terminology, but not that there were new insights to be gained from its use.

What turned out to be intellectually unsatisfying and politically implausible were the unintended but hard to escape implications of the systems approach; that societies were 'naturally' orderly, that order was properly maintained by norms that integrated individuals into the social system, the selfishness required of economic actors would readily be held in check by altruistic and family-oriented norms, and more views of the same sort.

Systems theory was always criticized for its political deficiencies as much as its intellectual shortcomings. Among the complaints levelled at it, the best known were that it endorsed the US *status quo* by emphasizing the forces that made for social 'integration' and overlooking social conflict, that its adherents defined social and political development as a society's similarity to the USA, and that they removed the critical bite from democratic theory by elevating 'democratic stability' to the highest place among political values, at the expense of justice and equality. In general, it was widely argued the conflicts of interest and disparities of power were either ignored or made light of in the perspective so concerned to associate normality with stability.

3 Niklas Luhmann's systems theory

Just as the influence of Parsons' structural-functionalism began to wane in the USA, the German sociologist Niklas Luhmann emerged as the leading proponent of a new version of systems theory. Luhmann thought that the previous attempts to use systems theory in the social sciences applied cybernetic concepts too directly and suffered from the residual normative orientations of Durkheim and Parsons, which he, like structuralists and post-structuralists, denounced as so much 'old European humanism'. To be rigorous and consistent, systems theory had to drop all reference to actors and their self-interpretations, which were nothing but 'psychical systems' that form part of the environment for other systems. In this way, systems theory could replace the functionalist account of social integration through norms with the anonymous integration of interdependent parts and wholes and be generally applicable to every level of social analysis (Luhmann 1976).

Such a general and radical systems theory recognizes the fundamental fact of the large scale and complex forms of social organization in modern societies, such as global markets and enormous bureaucracies, that work 'behind the backs' of social actors. Rather than being the product of intentional actions, such order is described in terms of functionally differentiated, yet interdependent, parts, whereby the internal operations of each maintain the system as a whole. Luhmann's theoretical innovation was to emphasize how such social systems arise. Much like living organisms, social systems emerge through 'autopoiesis', that is, they are generated and maintained 'exclusively' by their own internal operations, and yet remain open to their environments. For Luhmann, systems are like Leibnizian monads, equipped with windows; 'meaning' is but one internal operation whose function is to reduce complexity, while 'norms' serve to restrict the possible operations of the system. Modern society can thus best be explained as a series of systems that have other systems as their environments, including law, the economy, organizations, science (including systems theory itself). Their internal complexity requires that they are externally related and do not form an overarching system.

According to Luhmann, systems may be formally defined in terms of their complexity. Although systems are always less complex than their environments, they must also constantly heighten their own complexity in order to adapt and remain stable. Once the inner–outer boundary is maintained and stabilized, a system becomes 'operationally closed', that is, it registers events in its environment only to the extent that they can be translated into its code and programming. This conception of 'operational closure' marks the most important difference between the theories of Luhmann and Parsons. Luhmann denies that modern societies are integrated in Parsons' functionalist sense: there is no central or organizing system, whether state or society, but only the interdependencies between systems. In *Social Systems* (1984), Luhmann calls modern, highly complex and functionally differentiated societies 'polycentric', with no integrating centre or apex of power. As opposed to Parsons' optimistic liberalism (1971), Luhmann sees democratic participation and control as an illusion in the face of overwhelming complexity and necessarily latent functional imperatives.

Luhmann does not limit his analysis to large scale social phenomena, but rather applies his systems theory to all levels of analysis, even to intimate relationships such as love. It is the lack of any restriction on the scope of such explanations that opens the theory to criticism, most thoroughly by Jürgen Habermas in his debate with Luhmann (1971). Luhmann's analysis, according to Habermas, cannot recognize the coordinating effects of ordinary language communication within modern institutions. Such communication requires that actors are allowed back into social theory (Habermas 1970).

Habermas criticizes Luhmann's systems theory on several levels. Theoretically, Habermas criticizes Luhmann for ignoring the continuing role of institutions, and thus of social integration, in 'anchoring' systemic mechanisms in the cultural life-worlds of their members. Because of the interaction of social and systemic integration, systemic mechanisms can have perverse effects, disrupting and 'colonizing' the domain of cultural reproduction. Methodologically, Habermas argues that action descriptions from the agents' point of view remain a necessary condition for any social explanation. Normatively, Luhmann's 'methodological anti-humanism' blinds the theory from the start to the possible influence of a society-wide and critical public sphere on complex, institutional processes.

See also: FUNCTIONALISM IN SOCIAL SCIENCE; STRUCTURALISM IN SOCIAL SCIENCE

References and further reading

Alexander, J., Giesen, B., Münch, R. and Smelser, N. (1987) *The Macro-Micro Link*, Berkeley, CA: University of California Press. (Useful collection of essays on anti-reductionism, or linking individualist and collectivist explanation.)

Almond, G.A. and Coleman, J. (1960) *The Politics of Developing Areas*, Princeton, NJ: Princeton University Press. (Explanation of developing areas as input–output systems.)

* Almond, G.A. and Powell, G.B. (1988) *Comparative Politics Today: A World View*, London: Harper-Collins, 4th edn. (A study of comparative politics.)

Bohman, J. (1991) *New Philosophy of Social Science: Problems of Indeterminacy*, Oxford and Cambridge, MA: Polity/MIT Press. (Includes introduction to issues concerning collective explanations in the social sciences, including systems theory, with examples.)

* Easton, D. (1953) *The Political System: A Systems Theory of Political Life*, New York: Alfred A. Knopf. (An early attempt by a political scientist to get some mileage of the idea of a 'system'.)

* Habermas, J. (1970) *The Logic of the Social Sciences*, trans. S. Nicholsen, Cambridge, MA: MIT Press, 1988. (Most complete statement of Habermas' view of social science, including criticisms of Parsons, systems theory and functionalism.)

* Habermas, J. and Luhmann, N. (1971) *Theorie der Gesellschaft oder Sozialtechnologie: Was leistet die Sozialforschung?* (Theory of Society or Social Technology: What is the Purpose of Social Research?), Frankfurt: Suhrkamp Verlag. (Extensive debate between Habermas and Luhmann on social theory.)

* Johnson, C. (1982) *Revolutionary Change*, Cambridge: Cambridge University Press, 2nd edn. (General theories of revolution.)

* Lane, D.S. (1971) *Politics and Society in the USSR*, New York: Random House. (Uses systems theory as the basis for a general account of revolutions.)

* Luhmann, N. (1976) *The Differentiation of Society*, trans. S. Holmes and C. Larmore, New York: Columbia University Press, 1982. (Best available collection of Luhmann's essays, covering a variety of topics from law to science.)

* —— (1984) *Soziale Systeme* (Social Systems), Frankfurt: Suhrkamp Verlag. (Luhmann's most systematic theoretical work, written in an intricate technical vocabulary.)

McCarthy, T. (1978) *The Critical Theory of Jürgen Habermas*, Cambridge, MA: MIT Press. (Includes an accessible summary of the Habermas/Luhmann debate and extensive bibliography.)

* Parsons, T. (1950) *The Social System*, London: Routledge, 1991. (The classical statement of Parsonian systems theory; new edition with introduction by Brian Turner.)

—— (1966) *Societies: Evolutionary and Comparative Perspectives*, Englewood Cliffs, NJ: Prentice Hall. (A short introductory treatment of its topic, markedly different from the above (Parsons 1950).)

—— (1968) 'Social Systems and Subsystems', in *Encyclopedia of the Social Sciences*, New York: Macmillan and Free Press. (Less 'Parsonian' than many of its author's accounts of the topic.)

* —— (1971) *The System of Modern Societies*, Englewood Cliffs, NJ: Prentice Hall. (Best introduction to Parsons' use of systems theory.)

* Waltz, K. (1979) *The Theory of International Politics*, New York: McGraw-Hill. (An analysis of international relations as a staff-maintaining system.)

ALAN RYAN
JAMES BOHMAN

T

TABLEAU SYSTEMS

TACIT KNOWLEDGE

TAGORE, RABINDRANATH (1886–1941)

In the flurry of intellectual activity in nineteenth- and twentieth-century Bengal, Rabindranath Tagore became one of the best-known playwrights, poets, novelists, educators and philosophers, winning the Nobel Prize for literature in 1913. His thought drew on the English Romantics as well as Sanskrit and Bengali writers and movements.

Tagore was not a systematic philosopher. He termed his position 'a poet's religion' which valued imagination above reason. He moved between the personal warmth of human relationships to a theistic Divine and belief in an Absolute as a unifying principle. He advocated a thoughtful but active life, criticizing asceticism and ritualism.

Nineteenth- and twentieth-century Bengal witnessed a renewed flurry of intellectual activity as a response to the new Western presence in India. As a member of the 'Bengal renaissance', Rabindranath Tagore was both a prolific writer and an active educator. He left school aged fourteen, finding traditional education 'stifling', and in 1901 he founded a 'forest retreat' academy called Santiniketan which emphasized the arts and nature. In 1918 he founded Visvabharati, an international university promoting international understanding as well as Indian culture.

Tagore was brought up in a cosmopolitan home dominated by his father, Debendranath, who led a monotheistic and iconoclastic reform movement known as the Brahmo Samaj, founded in 1828 (see BRAHMO SAMAJ). Debendranath was a religious and social reformer open to the ideas of the West. At home Rabindranath studied English, Sanskrit and Bengali literature and came to love the English Romantics Keats and Shelley, the classical Sanskrit writer Kālidāsa and the poetry of love for the Divine of the Bengali devotees of Kṛṣṇa, particularly the songs of the wandering singers known as the Bauls.

Although Tagore's writings reveal consistent themes and concerns, Tagore was not a systematic, philosophical thinker. He is best known for his plays, poetry, songs, essays and novels. He wrote his first poem at the age of eight. A collection of his devotional poems entitled *Gitanjali* (Song Offerings), which he translated into English himself, brought him the Nobel Prize for literature in 1913. In four major religious-philosophical works, *Sādhanā: The Realization of Life* (1913), *Personality* (1917b), *Creative Unity* (1922) and *The Religion of Man* (1931), Tagore set forth his thought more fully. However, these are collections of essays and speeches: they are not solidly argued systematic treatises.

Tagore called his position 'a poet's religion', affirming that reality is best known through experience and emotion and that imagination is more important than reason (SENSE PERCEPTION, INDIAN VIEWS OF). Reality is understood through recognition of the Absolute One behind the multiplicity, which is a 'creative principle of unity'. This means not only that the Divine is immanent in creation but that creation itself is a manifestation of the Divine. The world and its particulars are real because they are the Divine in playful manifestation. The underlying harmony and the inner interrelationship of each of the parts to the others is experienced as the expression of Divine joy and love. This affirmation of unity in Tagore's thought enabled contemporary Indian monists to read Tagore as a modern follower of ŚAṄKARA.

Tagore, however, rarely used the term 'Absolute' as he did not merely affirm an impersonal consciousness as the highest reality. Thus, early Western interpreters spoke of a Christian influence on Tagore. Besides the personal sense of the Divine he inherited through his father's Brahmo Samaj, his discovery at the age of fifteen of the love poems of the Bengali devotional movements, which sang of Kṛṣṇa and his loving relationship with his followers, was enough to redirect his understanding (see GAUḌĪYA VAIṢṆAVISM). These poems provided inspiration both for Tagore's emphasis on the personal as the key to the universe and his philosophy of Divine joy and love. Ultimate reality, he believed, could not be divorced from personality; the Absolute is the supreme personality in intimate, personal and interdependent relationship with human beings. The Divine is not aloof, but involved with humanity. Their relationship of mutual love involves God's loving service for human wellbeing and the human response of realizing the infinite in the finite and becoming increasingly more united to the Divine.

The fullest expression of the Divine is in the human being. However, this does not mean that the individual does not exist as a separate entity, or that union with the Divine means absorption of the individual so as to lose its distinctive existence. Like the traditional philosophical position called *bhedābheda*, identity in difference, Tagore saw the human being as both identical with and different from the Divine. From what he describes as his first religious experience at the age of eighteen, a vision lasting four days, he saw the personal as the central fact of the Divine–human–world relationship.

For Tagore, the poet, not the abstract philosopher, is the true seer. The poet reveals the Divine through song, paradox and aesthetic awareness. All art is the response of the soul to the Divine for it reveals beauty which is truth. Tagore defines beauty as the revelation of the harmony of the universe; conflict and chaos are the result of a limited vision which does not penetrate into the harmonious relationship of the whole but settles for usefulness and efficiency. Reason is limited to space and time, but the creative imagination found in all artistic endeavour connects humanity to the all and results in a response of active participation. Tagore, therefore, persistently criticizes the ascetic who flees from life as an escapist separated from the world. He also chides the religious devotee who is lost to the world in emotionalism. The traditional ascetic ideal, Tagore believed, would not further India's progress nor that of humanity. The active individual who transcends the egoistic desire for gain in the love of the Divine and its creation lives the good life. The poet stirs one to involvement in the world. The path to the realization of the Divine, *sādhanā*, includes all creative activity, which for Tagore was his writing, painting, composing and educating. 'Expression', he once wrote to a friend, 'is my religion'.

See also: HINDU PHILOSOPHY; MONISM, INDIAN; VEDĀNTA

List of works

Tagore, R. (1912) *Gitanjali* (Song Offerings), London: The India Society. (Collection of devotional poetry Tagore himself translated from his original Bengali poems.)

—— (1913) *Sādhanā: The Realization of Life*, London: Macmillan. (Nontechnical, collected papers which discuss major themes in Tagore's thought.)

—— (1917a) *Nationalism*, London: Macmillan. (Lectures given in the USA and Japan on Tagore's political philosophy.)

—— (1917b) *Personality*, London: Macmillan. (Collection of lectures delivered in the USA.)

—— (1922) *Creative Unity*, London: Macmillan. (Philosophical essays addressing the concepts of the human being, religion and art.)

—— (1931) *The Religion of Man*, London: Allen & Unwin. (The Hibbert lectures delivered at Manchester University which survey the full range of Tagore's thought.)

References and further reading

Atkinson, D. (1989) *Gandhi and Tagore: Visionaries of Modern India*, Hong Kong: Asian Research Services. (An insightful introduction to Tagore's thought.)

Naravane, V. (1977) *An Introduction to Rabindranath Tagore*, Delhi: Macmillan. (A standard introduction to Tagore from the perspective of a monist philosopher.)

O'Connell, J. (1989) *Tagore's Heritage*, Toronto: Rabindranath Tagore Foundation. (A useful collection of essays analysing Tagore's thought and influence.)

ROBERT N. MINOR

TAI CHEN *see* DAI ZHEN

TAINE, HIPPOLYTE-ADOLPHE (1828–93)

Hippolyte Taine dominated the intellectual life of France in the second half of the nineteenth century. He was seen as the leader of the positivist, empiricist, anti-clerical forces in a period characterized by dramatic advances in science and technology and inspired by the hope that scientific method could be applied to human affairs. Yet at the heart of his life and work was the rationalist, essentialist imperative of Spinoza and of Hegel: to demonstrate the world as system, as necessity, to 'banish contingency'. The story of his life is the story of the abandonment of this project: it is a long, painful learning experience ending in the acceptance of loss; his richly varied works can be seen as the products of this philosophical journey.

Taine (born in Vouziers in the Ardennes) was the Sartre of his time. As with Sartre, philosophy (more specifically, metaphysics) was the mainspring of all his work; but (again like Sartre) this work was variegated and popular and quite different from that of the philosophers – Spinoza, Hegel, J.S. Mill – who were his models. Most of Taine's writing was first published in newspapers and periodicals, such as *Le Journal des Débats* or *La Revue des Deux-Mondes*, before being revised, collected and published in book form.

He produced literary criticism (the various collections of essays and *La Fontaine et ses fables* (La Fontaine and his fables) (1861)); literary history (one of the first histories of English literature in any language); books of travel and social observation (the *Voyages* (Travels) and *Notes sur Paris* (1867)); and a monumental political and intellectual history of France, *Les Origines de la France contemporaine* (*The Origins of Contemporary France*) (1875–93). He also wrote an iconoclastic account of the *spiritualiste* philosophers of the preceding generation – Victor Cousin, Maine de Biran, Théodore Jouffroy – and published an influential work of psychological philosophy, *De l'Intelligence* (On Intelligence) (1870). The *Vie et Correspondance* (Life and Letters) (1902–7) is one of the great collections of the century and contains, besides remarkable letters, a great deal of crucial unpublished early material.

The published works give an appearance of dispersion and fail to reveal how fundamental the quest for philosophical unity was for him. There are two main reasons for this. First, like most thinkers of his time he was deeply attached to scientific observation, empirical reality, inductive method, experience – to what he called 'facts'. Throughout, he starts from the concrete – specific works of art or literature, historical records, psychological phenomena – the range is great but the underlying motivation is always philosophical in the sense of an urge towards the general and the abstract. The key is always the preface or the conclusion. Whether he acknowledges it or not, his aim is always a philosophy of art or literature, a philosophy of history, a philosophy of mind and, ultimately, a metaphysics. His aspiration, like Hegel's, is enyclopedic, and the apparently disparate parts of his investigation are aspects of an envisaged totality.

In modern terms, Taine is a critical theorist and not a literary critic.

The second reason involves the process of reception, the way in which, during their lifetime and subsequently, writers are constructed, by themselves and others so as to be non-contradictory. In his twenties, as a consequence of his loss of religious faith, Taine was deeply concerned with metaphysics. A remarkable unpublished text, written in 1848, called 'De la Destinée humaine' (On Human Destiny) describes his loss of religious faith, his systematic doubt, and his salvation through Spinoza and pantheism. Soon after, he learned German to read Hegel (then untranslated). His voluminous writings of this period remained unpublished during his lifetime and he himself progressively attenuated the expression of his metaphysical ambitions. Thus, by the end of his life, he was seen as a positivist and a pluralist. Only the publication of the *Life and Letters* and subsequent studies of unpublished material and variants revealed the underlying idealism, the persistent urge to refute Kant, Hume and Mill, and the need to 'banish contingency'. For some critics he then became a sort of closet idealist; for many he was just confused and 'flawed'. Only recently has his work been seen as a dramatic struggle between competing forces.

Taine is representative not only because he was the public spokesman for the positivist, deterministic, anti-clerical, anti-Romantic aspects of his society, but because he lived the tensions and contradictions of that period and left a precise record. His writings can be read as a succession of attempts to square the circle, to demonstrate the world as system, as necessary, not accidental, or to show, as he put it, 'that philosophy was possible'. 'De la Destinée humaine' is full of youthful optimism. But the sceptic grows stronger: Spinoza, he complains, 'destroys the world' and ignores Time. Hegel, whom Taine in many ways resembles, seemed to offer salvation: he writes in the *Philosophes français*, 'I read Hegel every day for a whole year. I will probably never again experience sensations like those he gave me' (1857: 126; author's translation). But Taine (who had not read the *Phenomenology of Spirit*) concludes by finding Hegel 'abstract', positing order a priori, but not proving it. He too 'destroys the world'.

Thereafter Taine's life is a series of attempts to succeed where Hegel failed; each time the goal seems less attainable; each effort is followed by a period of illness and depression. This rhythm continues even after he has renounced philosophy and become a historian: every re-edition of *On Intelligence* has a modified ending. By the final (4th) edition of 1883, Hegel's name has disappeared and Taine seems resigned to the loss of the Absolute. Sartre saw that the book was not an 'empiricism' as people had thought, but was in fact 'a realist metaphysics *manqué*'.

Taine does not have a 'philosophy'. His achievement is to have struggled throughout his life to reconcile an inherited rationalist desire for system with a scrupulous respect for concrete experience, to reconcile Spinoza and Hegel with Kant, Hume and Mill. The attempt ended in failure. The *Derniers essais* (1894) are suffused with a sense of wasted potential. But the story of this painful and honest coming to terms with loss over a lifetime's philosophical effort is dramatic and moving. It is also modern – and more characteristic of the lives of philosophers than is usually acknowledged.

See also: HEGELIANISM §4

List of works

Taine H.-A. (1857) *Les Philosophes français du XIXe siècle* (French Philosophers of the Nineteenth Century), Paris: Hachette. (Iconoclastic account of previous generation of French philosophers.)
—— (1858) *Essais de critique et d'histoire* (Critical and Historical Essays), Paris: Hachette. (The preface of this work is especially interesting.)
—— (1861) *La Fontaine et ses fables* (La Fontaine and His Fables), Paris: Hachette. (Taine's doctoral thesis, written when a projected work on Hegel was declared unacceptable to the University.)
—— (1864) *Histoire de la littérature anglaise*, Paris: Hachette; trans H. Van Laun, *History of English Literature*, New York, Holt, 1872. (The introduction and the chapter on J.S. Mill are especially interesting.)
—— (1865a) *Philosophie de l'art*, Paris: Hachette; trans. J. Durand, *Lectures on Art*, New York, Holt, 1896. (A version of his lectures at the École des Beaux Arts, where he was Professor.)
—— (1865b) *Nouveaux essais de critique et d'histoire* (New Critical and Historical Essays), Paris: Hachette. (Contains essays on Balzac, Marcus Aurelius and Racine.)
—— (1866) *Voyage en Italie*, Paris: Hachette; trans. J. Durand, *Italy*, 1870, 1871, New York, Holt. (Travel descriptions and personal responses to works of art.)
—— (1867) *Notes sur Paris, vie et opinions de M. Frédéric-Thomas Graindorge*, Paris: Hachette; trans. J.A. Stevens, *Notes on Paris*, New York, Holt, 1879. (In this work, Graindorge is a fictional American visitor to Paris.)
—— (1870) *De l'Intelligence*, Paris: Hachette; trans. T.D. Haye, *On Intelligence*, New York, Holt, 1899.

(Taine revised each edition, changing especially the ending, to make the work less Hegelian.)
—— (1872) *Notes sur l'Angleterre*, Paris: Hachette; trans. W.F. Rae, *Notes on England*, New York, Holt. (Lively, detailed response to England and English society.)
—— (1875–93) *Les Origines de la France contemporaine*; trans J. Durand, *The Origins of Contemporary France*, New York, Holt, 1885–94. (Taine's highly controversial history of France, designed as a 'medical consultation'.)
—— (1894) *Derniers essais de critique et d'histoire* (Last Critical and Historical Essays), Paris: Hachette. (Contains moving, elegiac and confessional accounts of minor writers. The theme is '*Ubi sunt*'.)
—— (1902–7) *H. Taine, sa vie et sa correspondance*, Paris: Hachette, 4 vols; trans. R.L. Devonshire (vols 1 and 2) and E. Sparvel-Bayly (vol. 3. abridged), *Life and letters of H. Taine*, New York, Holt, 1902–8. (One of the great collections of the century. The editors made certain omissions, however, and the correspondence with Camille Selden was destroyed – see F. Léger below. Volume 1 contains extracts from 'De la Destinée humaine'.)

References and further reading

Charlton, D.G. (1959) *Positivist thought in France during the Second Empire*, Oxford: Oxford University Press. (Contains chapters on all the so-called positivist thinkers of the period, showing how there was always a tension with idealism.)
Evans, C. (1975) *Taine, essai de biographie intérieure*, Paris: Nizet, esp. 173–308. (Very long and detailed *doctorat d'état* thesis, adopting extreme diachronic approach; uses unpublished material; full bibliography.)
—— (1978) 'Taine and his fate', *Nineteenth-century French Studies* 6 (1–2): 118–28. (An account of Taine's critical reception.)
Léger, F. (1980) *La Jeunesse d'Hippolyte Taine*, Paris: Albatros. (A biography of Taine's life until the age of thirty.)
—— (1993) *Monsieur Taine*, Paris: Critérion. (A less academic account, but covers the whole life.)
Sartre, J.-P. (1936) *L'Imagination*, Paris: Presses Universitaires de France. (Offers a perceptive account of Taine's psychology: see chapter 2, 'The Problem of the Image'.)
Weinstein, L. (1972) *Hippolyte Taine*, New York: Twayne. (The best full treatment of Taine's thought in English.)

COLIN EVANS

TANABE HAJIME (1885–1962)

Tanabe Hajime was a central figure of the so-called Kyoto School, and is generally acknowledged to be one of the most important philosophers of modern Japan. He held Kant in high esteem, and used a Neo-Kantian critical methodology in his early studies in epistemology. In the 1920s he was chiefly influenced by Nishida Kitarō's original cosmological system. He adapted Nishida's idea of 'absolute nothingness' to political situations and, in so doing, contributed much to establishing the foundations of what became the most influential philosophical school in Japan up until the end of the Second World War.

In 1919, Tanabe was appointed associate professor under NISHIDA KITARŌ at Kyoto University. In 1927 he was promoted to full professor, replacing Nishida soon after. In 1945 he retired to Kitakaruizawa, Gunma-ken, and dedicated his later life to meditation and writing.

Under the influence of Nishida, Tanabe wished to develop his own cosmological system. This desire grew stronger during his stay in Germany from 1922 to 1924, where he studied under Edmund HUSSERL at Freiburg University and became friends with Martin HEIDEGGER. Although he did not accept much of their phenomenological method, he was stimulated by Heidegger's intention to remodel phenomenology into a cosmology by assimilating existentialism. Returning to Japan, he began to turn his interpretation of Kantian philosophy into a systematic cosmology. The fruit of these efforts was his work *Kanto no Mokutekiron* (Kant's Teleology), published in 1924, in which he characterized Kantian reflective judgement as the faculty of a comprehensive teleological world view (see KANT, I.).

Tanabe's attention then turned to dialectics. He held Hegelian dialectics to be just the logical method that could give concrete shape to a teleological comprehension of the world (see HEGEL, G.W.F.). According to him, the formula 'thesis–antithesis–synthesis' represents the process through which teleologically driven objects gradually realize themselves. The final aim of the process indicates the teleological perfection of the world. To this he applied the term 'absolute nothingness', chiefly on the grounds that this term describes the activity of dialectical negation. Thus 'absolute nothingness' took on an active meaning in his understanding, where it had been originally used by Nishida in a meditative, introspective way. Tanabe described his steps to a thorough acceptance of dialectics in his work *Hegerutetsugaku to Benshoho* (Hegel's Philosophy and Dialectics) in 1932.

In 1934 Tanabe introduced a new notion, 'the logic of species', the novelty of which earned him a reputation as an original thinker. As he understood it, the triad of genus–species–individual was simply a variant of the triad of propositional logic, universal–particular–singular, as it is applied to human existence. In his logic of species, therefore, Tanabe was concerned with giving a new priority to the particular in human experience.

In its methodological structure, the logic of species was an attempt to apply dialectics to the real world. The individual is determined decisively by the species; conversely, the former seeks of its own free will to determine the latter. The two face each other as opposites in tension. Each is irrational and selfish in that each immediately affirms its own being, but through mutual interpenetration they can be purified of their irrational qualities and raised to the level of rationality. The resultant synthesis is the genus. Thus the individual and the species are synthesized in the genus; that is, a particular society is 'generalized'. Tanabe lumped together these results in the notion of the 'state'. The state as the realization of the universal had an important position in his thought. It was only natural for him to take the next steps towards a theory of the state, identifying the dialectical process with the perpetual self-renewal of the polity. Among his articles during this period, great importance can be attached to the one entitled 'Kokkatekisonzai no Ronri' (The Logic of National Existence), which appeared in 1939.

Tanabe's theory of the state was in its basic structure an admittedly rationalistic one. Pivoting on a dynamic in which ethnic unity is 'generalized' into rationality through the activity of free individuals, it offered the ideal of the nation-state. It was Tanabe's intention to give the Japanese state a rational, democratic basis; in this way, he set himself to check the irrationalistic, warlike modes of thinking. Obviously his efforts failed, chiefly due to the confusion of the ideal state with the real Japanese state. Tanabe watched as his own words were twisted by the nationalists into a justification for military aggression and, with pangs of conscience at this turn of events, his thinking came to a standstill.

After December 1941, Tanabe was no longer able to publish any philosophical work. It was only at the end of the war, with *Zangedo toshiteno Tetsugaku* (Philosophy as Metanoetics), that his struggles bore fruit and released his thinking from its predicament. This work is often characterized as Tanabe's 'Confessions', for he described in it his experience of personal salvation. In despair over his philosophy up to that time, he had abandoned all attempts at realization under his own power and repented his errors. At this point he came to the awareness of returning to life by the grace of a transcendent Other-power. Since the new form of his philosophy was based on this experience, he named it 'metanoetics'. Thereafter he concentrated on religious thinking.

Tanabe then tried to reorganize his logic of species in light of the experience of metanoetic salvation. The particular society is 'generalized' through human action deriving ultimately from Other-power. This time, the resulting society is called not the state, but the religious community in its universal character. From here, Tanabe developed his interest in sociological research into the history of religions. In his notable work *Kirisutokyo no Bensho* (Dialectic of Christianity), published in 1948, he explicated the development of primitive Christianity as typical of the way in which a religious community is founded. In his last years, he theorized on the bodhisattva-way of Mahāyāna Buddhism from the perspective of sociological philosophy of religion.

See also: JAPANESE PHILOSOPHY; KYOTO SCHOOL; LOGIC IN JAPAN

List of works

Tanabe Hajime (1910–61) *Tanabe Hajime zenshū* (The Complete Works of Tanabe Hajime), ed. Y. Takeuchi *et al.*, Tokyo: Chikuma Shobo, 1963–4, 15 vols. (Edition of Tanabe's complete works.)

—— (1924) *Kanto no Mokutekiron* (Kant's Teleology), in *Tanabe Hajime zenshū* (The Complete Works of Tanabe Hajime), Tokyo: Chikuma Shobo, 1963–4. (On Kant's reflective judgment.)

—— (1932) *Hegerutetsugaku to Benshoho* (Hegel's Philosophy and Dialectics), in *Tanabe Hajime zenshū* (The Complete Works of Tanabe Hajime), Tokyo: Chikuma Shobo, 1963–4. (Tanabe's view of Hegelian dialectics.)

—— (1939) 'Kokkatekisonzai no Ronri' (The Logic of National Existence), in *Tanabe Hajime zenshū* (The Complete Works of Tanabe Hajime), Tokyo: Chikuma Shobo, 1963–4. (Identifies Tanabe's dialectical process with a theory of the state.)

—— (1946) *Zangedo toshiteno Tetsugaku* (Philosophy as Metanoetics), trans. Y. Takeuchi and J.W. Heisig, Los Angeles, CA: University of California Press, 1986. (Tanabe's 'Confessions', as the start of his late philosophy.)

—— (1947) 'The Logic of the Species as Dialectics', trans. D.A. Dilworth, *Monumenta Nipponica* 1969, 24 (3): 273–88. (An attempt to reorganize the logic of species in the light of the metanoetic experience.)

—— (1948) *Kirisutokyo no Bensho* (Dialectic of Christianity), in *Tanabe Hajime zenshū* (The Complete Works of Tanabe Hajime), Tokyo: Chikuma Shobo, 1963–4. (Tanabe's study of the development of Christianity.)

—— (1959) 'Memento Mori', trans. V.H. Viglielmo, *Philosophical Studies of Japan* I, Compiled by the National Commission for UNESCO: 1–12. (Summary of Tanabe's meditation on death in his late days.)

References and further reading

Himi Kiyoshi (1990) *Tanabetetsugaku Kenkyu – Shukyotetsugaku no Kanten kara* (Studies in the Thought of Tanabe: A Perspective from the Philosophy of Religion), Tokyo: Hokuju Shuppan. (Pursuit of the development of Tanabe's thought, laying great emphasis on his late religious philosophy.)

Laube, J. (1984) *Dialektik der absoluten Vermittlung* (Dialectic of the Absolute Mediation), Freiburg: Verlag Herder. (Critical researches on Tanabe's dialectical philosophy.)

Unno Taitetsu and Heisig, J.W. (eds) (1990) *The Religious Philosophy of Tanabe Hajime: The Metanoetic Imperative*, Berkeley, CA: Asian Humanities Press. (Record of the International Symposium on Tanabe's Metanoetics held in Massachusetts, 1989.)

HIMI KIYOSHI

TANAKH *see* BIBLE, HEBREW

TAO *see* DAO

TAO TE CHING *see* DAODEJING

TAOIST PHILOSOPHY
see DAOIST PHILOSOPHY

TARSKI, ALFRED (1901–83)

Alfred Tarski was a Polish mathematician and logician. He worked in metamathematics and semantics, set theory, algebra and the foundations of geometry. Some of his logical works, in particular his definition of truth, were also significant contributions to philosophy. He was a successful teacher and a master of writing simply and with great clarity about complicated matters.

Tarski was born Alfred Tajtelbaum in Warsaw. (The family name was changed in 1924.) Between 1918 and 1924 Tarski studied at the University of Warsaw where he received his doctorate in mathematics under the direction of S. Leśniewski. In 1926 he was appointed as a lecturer. In 1939 Tarski set out for a lecture tour of the USA and was prevented from returning to Poland by the outbreak of the Second World War. He then briefly held positions at Harvard University, the City College of New York and the Institute for Advanced Study at Princeton. In 1942 he was appointed to the mathematics department of the University of California at Berkeley, where he remained until his retirement in 1968.

Tarski's best known logical achievements, being also of philosophical significance, are certainly his definitions of satisfaction and truth and his work on logical consequence (see TARSKI'S DEFINITION OF TRUTH; CONSEQUENCE, CONCEPTIONS OF). All Tarski's logical investigations were determined by his interests in the methodology of the deductive sciences, which he termed metamathematics. In fact, general metamathematics was one of his chief areas of activity. He distinguished three main types of deductive systems and studied their metamathematical properties – in particular, their axiomatizability, the independence of their axioms, and their consistency and completeness. Gradually, his metamathematical investigations took on an algebraic character, as reflected in his increasing emphasis on semantics. This approach led to the algebraic treatment of logic and the development of model theory, of which he was a founder and the author of various fundamental results.

Tarski's interest in model theory was connected to his studies on decidability. Here too his approach was fundamentally semantical and connected to matters of definability in theories. The key notion was that of interpretability, and Tarski developed general methods of proving (essential) undecidability of various theories (in particular, various algebraic and geometrical theories) by considering their interpretability in certain other theories. Another method used by Tarski in connection with the study of definability was that of quantifier elimination. It was also applied by Tarski to prove decidability of various theories (for example, of the theory of real closed fields).

Tarski used logical methods to study the foundations of various mathematical theories, in particular of geometry. Being interested mainly in Euclidean and general affine geometry he proposed various axiom systems for them and studied their metamathematical properties. Particularly prominent in Tarski's geometrical work was the problem of determining and selecting primitive notions. Connected with his work in geometry and set theory is the Banach–Tarski theorem, which is a remarkable consequence of the axiom of choice. It asserts that any sphere can be decomposed into a finite number of subsets which can be reassembled by rigid motions to form two spheres each having the same volume as the original. Tarski also proved that several statements of the arithmetic of the infinite cardinals are equivalent to the axiom of choice.

Tarski left few philosophical papers. Nevertheless, various parts of his logical work and, in particular, those concerned chiefly with the methodology of the deductive sciences and the nature of truth and consequence, are of considerable philosophical interest. He described himself as 'a mathematician (as well as a logician, perhaps a philosopher of a sort)'. It is difficult to characterize his philosophical views. He did, however, indicate that he believed logical and mathematical research ought not to be restricted by any general philosophical viewpoint.

List of works

Tarski's bibliography comprises 109 papers, 94 abstracts and 20 monographs (some of them translated into several languages). Listed here are some of his works with the most importance for logic and philosophy.

Tarski, A. (1981) *The Collected Works of Alfred Tarski*, ed. S.R. Givant and R.N. McKenzie, Berkeley, CA: University of California Press, 4 vols. (Includes all Tarski's published works.)

Tarski, A. and Banach, S. (1924) 'Sur la décomposition des ensembles de points en parties respectivement congruentes' (On the Decomposition of Point-Sets into Mutually Congruent Parts), *Fundamenta Mathematicae* 6: 244–77. (Includes the Banach–Tarski theorem on the decomposition of the sphere.)

Tarski, A. (1930) 'Fundamentale Begriffe der Methodologie der deduktiven Wissenschaften I', *Monatshefte für Mathematik und Physik* 37: 361–404; trans. J.H. Woodger (1956), 'Fundamental Concepts of the Methodology of Deductive Sciences', in *Logic, Semantics, Metamathematics: Papers from 1923 to 1938*, ed. J. Corcoran, Indianapolis, IN: Hackett Publishing Company, 2nd edn, 1983, 60–109. (Introduces and investigates fundamental notions of the methodology of deductive sciences.)

—— (1933) *Pojęcie prawdy w językach nauk dedukcyjnych*, Warsaw; trans. J.H. Woodger (1956), 'The Concept of Truth in Formalized Languages', in *Logic, Semantics, Metamathematics: Papers from 1923 to 1938*, ed. J. Corcoran,

Indianapolis, IN: Hackett Publishing Company, 2nd edn, 1983, 152–278. (One of the most fundamental of Tarski's works, including his famous definition of truth.)

—— (1935) *O logice matematycznej i metodzie dedukcyjnej*, Lwów; trans. *Introduction to Logic and to the Methodology of Deductive Sciences*, Oxford and New York: Oxford University Press, 1941. (This book gives a general introduction, and shows how logic can be applied in the construction of mathematical theories.)

—— (1944) 'The Semantic Conception of Truth and the Foundations of Semantics', *Philosophy and Phenomenological Research* 4: 341–75; repr. in L. Linsky (ed.) *Semantics and the Philosophy of Language*, Urbana, IL: University of Illinois Press, 1952. (Tarski's definition of satisfaction and truth.)

—— (1948) *A Decision Method for Elementary Algebra and Geometry*, prepared for publication by J.C.C. McKinsey, Santa Monica, CA: Rand. (One of the most important of Tarski's results in decidability theory, namely the proof of decidability of the theory of reals.)

—— (1949) *Cardinal Algebras*, Oxford and New York: Oxford University Press. (A monograph devoted to the algebra of cardinal numbers.)

Tarski, A., Mostowski, A. and Robinson, R.M. (1953) *Undecidable Theories*, Amsterdam: North Holland. (Includes three papers devoted to general methods of proving undecidability of theories, of various systems of arithmetic and of group theory.)

—— (1956) *Logic, Semantics, Metamathematics: Papers from 1923 to 1938*, trans. and ed. J.H. Woodger, Oxford: Clarendon Press; repr. and ed. J. Corcoran, Indianapolis, IN: Hackett Publishing Company, 2nd edn, 1983. (Includes English translations of Tarski's main logical papers from 1923 to 1938.)

—— (1967) *The Completeness of Elementary Algebra and Geometry*, Paris: Institut Blaise Pascal. (The proof of the decidability of the theory of reals and of geometry.)

Tarski, A., Henkin, L. and Monk, J.D. (1971, 1985) *Cylindric Algebras*, Amsterdam: North Holland, 2 vols. (A monograph devoted to cylindric algebras.)

Tarski, A., Doner, J. and Mostowski, A. (1978) 'The Elementary Theory of Well-Ordering – A Metamathematical Study', in A. MacIntyre *et al.* (eds) *Logic Colloquium 77*, Amsterdam: North Holland, 1–54. (The proof of the decidability of the elementary theory of well-ordering.)

Tarski, A., Schwabhäuser, W. and Szmielew, W. (1983) *Metamathematische Methoden in der Geometrie*, Berlin and New York: Springer. (The development and metamathematical investigation of absolute and Euclidean geometry on the basis of a system of axioms introduced by Tarski.)

Tarski, A. and Givant, S. (1987) *A Formalization of Set Theory Without Variables*, Providence, RI: American Mathematical Society. (A demonstration that set theory and number theory can be developed within the framework of a new, different and simple equational formalism, closely related to the formalism of the theory of relational algebras.)

References and further reading

Blok, W.J. and Pigozzi, D. (1988) 'Alfred Tarski's Work on General Metamathematics', *Journal of Symbolic Logic* 53: 36–50. (A discussion of Tarski's work on the methodology of the deductive sciences.)

Doner, J. and Hodges, W. (1988) 'Alfred Tarski and Decidable Theories', *Journal of Symbolic Logic* 53: 20–35. (Discusses Tarski's work on the decidability of theories.)

Dries, L. van den (1988) 'Alfred Tarski's Elimination Theory for Real Closed Fields', *Journal of Symbolic Logic* 53: 7–19. (Discusses Tarski's theorem on quantifier elimination for the theory of reals, and its influence on mathematics and logic.)

Etchemendy, J. (1988) 'Tarski on Truth and Logical Consequence', *Journal of Symbolic Logic* 53: 51–79. (Discusses Tarski's writings on the concept of truth and logical consequence.)

Givant, S. (1986) 'Bibliography of Alfred Tarski', *Journal of Symbolic Logic* 51: 913–41. (With a complete bibliography, including information on translations.)

Jønsson, B. (1986) 'The Contributions of Alfred Tarski to General Algebra', *Journal of Symbolic Logic* 51: 883–9. (A discussion of Tarski's writings on general algebra.)

Levy, A. (1988) 'Alfred Tarski's Work in Set Theory', *Journal of Symbolic Logic* 53: 2–6. (Considers Tarski's contribution to set theory.)

Monk, J.D. (1986) 'The Contribution of Alfred Tarski to Algebraic Logic', *Journal of Symbolic Logic* 51: 899–906. (Studies the meaning of Tarski's writings on algebraic logic.)

McNulty, G.F. (1986) 'Alfred Tarski and Undecidable Theories', *Journal of Symbolic Logic* 51: 890–8. (Discusses Tarski's methods of proving undecidability of theories, as well as their applications.)

Suppes, P. (1988) 'Philosophical Implications of Tarski's Work', *Journal of Symbolic Logic* 53: 80–91. (Discusses the implications for philosophy of Tarski's work.)

Szczerba, L.W. (1986) 'Tarski and Geometry', *Journal of Symbolic Logic* 51: 907–12. (Considers Tarski's work in the field of foundations of geometry.)

Vaught, R.L. (1986) 'Alfred Tarski's Work in Model Theory', *Journal of Symbolic Logic* 51: 869–82. (Studies Tarski's contribution to the development of model theory.)

ROMAN MURAWSKI

TARSKI'S DEFINITION OF TRUTH

Alfred Tarski's definition of truth is unlike any that philosophers have given in their long struggle to understand the concept of truth. Tarski's definition is more clear and precise than any previous definition, but it is also unusual in character and more restricted in scope. Tarski does not provide a general definition of truth. He provides instead a method of constructing, for a range of formalized languages L, definitions of the notions 'true sentence of L'. A remarkable feature of Tarski's work on truth is his 'Criterion T', which lays down a general condition that any definition of 'true sentence of L' must satisfy. Tarski's ideas have exercised an enormous influence in philosophy. They have played an important role in the formulation and defence of a range of views in logic, semantics and metaphysics.

1   **Formal correctness and material adequacy**
2   **The liar paradox**
3   **Examples of Tarskian truth definitions**
4   **Philosophical influence**

1   Formal correctness and material adequacy

Any definition that aims to elucidate some aspect of a concept must satisfy two sets of requirements: the definition must be, in Tarski's terminology, 'formally correct' and 'materially adequate'. Under formal correctness fall requirements concerning the form of the definition and the vocabulary that the definition may use. Concerning these requirements, let us note only that a definition of 'true' of the form

x is true iff ___ x ___

is bound to be formally correct provided that the right-hand side of the equivalence contains only 'admissible' vocabulary, that is, vocabulary that may legitimately be used in defining 'true'. For example, the definition

x is true iff x corresponds to reality

fails to satisfy the requirement of formal correctness, because the terms 'corresponds' and 'reality' are much too unclear to be considered admissible. On the other hand, no doubts should arise about the formal correctness of the definition

x is true iff x is identical to x.

The definition is, of course, unsatisfactory. But that is because it is materially inadequate: it fails to conform to our ordinary notion of truth.

The most remarkable feature of Tarski's work on truth (1936, 1944) is his formulation, known as 'Criterion T', of the requirement of material adequacy. It is this Criterion that is responsible for the special characteristics, both positive and negative, of Tarski's definition. On the positive side, it enables Tarski to give a precise definition of truth and to prove its material adequacy. On the negative side, it is the source of the unusual and, from the philosophical point of view, strange character of Tarski's definition.

Criterion T lays down two conditions that a materially adequate definition of truth must meet. The second, and less important, condition is that the definition should imply that only sentences are true. Tarski imposes this condition because he takes truth to be a predicate of sentences. The first, and more important, condition is that the definition should imply all the 'T-biconditionals', that is, all sentences of the form

(T)   '___' is a true sentence (of English) iff ___.

Thus, Criterion T requires that a definition of truth (for English) should imply, for example, the famous T-biconditional,

'Snow is white' is a true sentence (of English) iff snow is white.

Note that any definition that implies this biconditional is bound to define a concept that agrees with truth over the sentence 'Snow is white': the sentence will fall under the concept if and only if it falls under truth. Hence, any definition that implies *all* the T-biconditionals is bound to define a concept C that agrees with truth over all the sentences: the concept defined is bound to be coextensive with truth (assuming that truth and C agree over non-sentences). Furthermore, since this argument uses no special contingent assumptions, the claim of coextensiveness holds irrespective of the contingent facts. In one sense of 'intension', then, the concept defined is bound to have the same intension as truth.

The equivalence of the two sides of the T-biconditionals has been noted by many philosophers and logicians, including Aristotle, Gottlob Frege and Frank Ramsey. Tarski is the first, however, to have used the equivalence to formulate a material adequacy condition on a definition of truth. The simplicity of Tarski's formulation should not obscure the important and surprising claim that it contains. Definitions of virtually all of our concepts can be assessed for material adequacy only in a piecemeal way, namely, by comparing their consequences with the ordinary uses of the concepts defined. No general conditions of material adequacy can be laid down. One would have expected the same of truth. But Criterion T puts forward a general and a priori condition of material adequacy on a definition of truth – a condition that, surprisingly, is highly plausible. Criterion T embodies Tarski's key philosophical claim. If it is granted then there can be no denying that it marks an important philosophical advance.

The formulation of Criterion T given above, it must be acknowledged, is unsatisfactory in several respects. First, it is formulated only for a definition of truth *for* English *in* English. What is wanted – and what Tarski's works provide – is a more general criterion that also applies to other languages. Second, the criterion as formulated is plausible only for sentences that are free of ambiguity, indexicals, tenses and other context-dependent elements. Tarski himself never attempted to overcome this limitation – his primary interest was in formalized languages for which these problems do not arise – but other philosophers have attempted to do so. Third, and most important, the criterion as formulated requires the definition of truth to be inconsistent. This inconsistency is a consequence of the liar paradox.

2 The liar paradox

Suppose, following Saul Kripke, that we introduce a name 'Jack' into English with the understanding that it names the sentence 'Jack is not a true sentence (of English)'. Suppressing the parenthetical relativization, the T-biconditional for Jack is

'Jack is not a true sentence' is a true sentence iff Jack is not a true sentence.

Our stipulation ensures that

Jack = 'Jack is not a true sentence'.

Hence, by the principle of substitutivity of identicals, the T-biconditional for Jack implies

Jack is a true sentence iff Jack is not a true sentence.

This in turn yields a contradiction by the rules of propositional logic. Note that the difficulty cannot be overcome by stipulating away names such as 'Jack'. Self-referential 'liar' sentences, which yield an incon-

sistency, can be constructed without the aid of such names.

Tarski makes constructive use of the argument of the liar paradox. He uses it to prove (a version of) the indefinability theorem named after him: arithmetical truth is not arithmetical. More precisely, no formula of Peano arithmetic (PA) is true precisely of (the codes of) the true sentences of PA (see GÖDEL'S THEOREMS). The theorem has a more general version: no classical language L_1 that is rich in syntactic resources can contain its own notion of truth. L_1 can be extended to a new language L_2 by the addition of a predicate that represents 'true in L_1'. But, by Tarski's theorem, L_2 will not contain its own truth predicate. As before, L_2 can be extended to yet another language L_3; this will contain a truth predicate for L_2, but again not for L_3. By repeating this procedure, we obtain a Tarskian hierarchy of languages, $L_1, L_2, \ldots, L_n, \ldots$, in which truth for a language of level n is contained in the language at level $n+1$. 'Tarski's indefinability theorem' motivates a way of getting around the difficulty that the paradoxes pose for Criterion T: (1) Draw a distinction between the language *in* which the definition of truth is given (the 'metalanguage') and the language *for* which the definition is given (the 'object language'); and (2) require that the object language not contain its own notion of truth. This manoeuvre ensures that no liar sentences occur in the object language. Consequently, the threat of inconsistency is removed from the T-biconditionals, and we regain Criterion T as a plausible material adequacy condition.

The manoeuvre allows us to proceed with the definition of truth for certain kinds of languages. But it does not help us to understand the behaviour of truth in languages (such as English) that contain paradoxical sentences. Tarski's response to this problem was an impatient one: he dismissed all such languages as inconsistent. In the past twenty-five years or so, however, Tarskian ideas have been used to develop a better, and certainly less impatient, response to the problem. The response that is most Tarskian in spirit is the 'hierarchy theory' of Charles Parsons and Tyler Burge. This theory sees our ordinary notion of truth as implicitly hierarchical. Each occurrence of 'true', according to the theory, corresponds to a truth predicate at a certain level in Tarski's hierarchy – with different occurrences corresponding to predicates at possibly different levels. So, for example, in the sentence

'"Snow is white" is true' is true.

the first occurrence of 'true' might correspond to the truth predicate at the first level of the hierarchy, and the second occurrence to that at the second level. The substantial burden on a hierarchy theory is to give a systematic explanation of the levels of the occurrences of 'true'. There are other approaches to the paradoxes that build on Tarski's ideas. The principal ones are the 'fixed-point theory' (see SEMANTIC PARADOXES AND THEORIES OF TRUTH §4) and the 'revision theory' (see DEFINITION §4).

Tarski showed how to construct definitions of truth that meet Criterion T. The next section contains some examples of Tarskian truth definitions. But before turning to these, let us note some general features of Tarski's method. First, this method does not yield a definition of the relational notion 'true in L', with variable L; its primary application is to the definition of 'true in L' for particular L. Second, the method enables us to give truth definitions only for formalized languages, not for natural languages. Third, it yields a definition in a metalanguage ML that is distinct from the object language L. If ML is a classical language then the distinction is forced by Tarski's indefinability theorem.

3 Examples of Tarskian truth definitions

This section gives three examples of Tarskian truth definitions. Two of these are very simple; only the third begins to approach the complexity of Tarski's actual definition.

Example A. Suppose that L is a fragment of English that contains only a finite number of sentences (say, a million). Suppose that the sentences of L contain no occurrence of 'true' or of any other term whose use is inadmissible in a definition of truth. Further, let 'S_1', 'S_2',..., 'S_{10^6}' be abbreviations of the sentences of L. A definition of 'true sentence of L' may now be given as follows:

x is a true sentence of L iff S_1 and x is 'S_1', or S_2 and x is 'S_2', or..., or S_{10^6} and x is 'S_{10^6}'.

The definition is evidently formally correct. Apart from the vocabulary of $S_1, S_2, ..., S_{10^6}$, which is stipulated to be admissible, it uses only the logical notions 'or' and 'is' (identity) and the quotation names for the sentences of L. The definition is also materially adequate since, under the assumption of such simple syntactic facts as 'S_1' is not 'S_2', it implies all instances of the form (T).

Example B. Let us now construct a definition of truth for a language L' that has an infinite number of sentences. Suppose that L' has two sentential connectives, '$\sim$' (negation: 'it is not the case that') and '&' (conjunction: 'and'). Suppose further that L' has a finite number of atomic sentences, that is, sentences that are not built using the connectives '$\sim$' and '&'. Now truth for atomic sentences can be defined as in example A. Over compound sentences, truth can be defined recursively: the negation of a sentence A is true iff A is not true; a conjunction is true iff both its conjuncts are true. Putting these elements together we can construct an explicit definition of 'true sentence of L'' in the following way. First let us define an intermediary notion, that of a 'closed' set; this will enable us to give a more compact definition of truth. A set Z is 'closed' iff (1) Z contains all true, and only true, atomic sentences of L'; (2) Z contains the negation of a sentence A iff it does not contain A; and (3) Z contains the conjunction of sentences A and B iff it contains the conjuncts A and B.

x is a true sentence of L' iff x belongs to every closed set.

Assuming that the atomic sentences of L' do not contain any terms that are inadmissible, our definition is formally correct. Further, it is materially adequate, since it implies all the T-biconditionals of L'. Note that the implication requires some syntactic facts about L' and some low-level set-theoretic facts.

Example C. Finally, let us see how to construct a definition of truth for a quantificational language L''. Such a language has an infinite number of sentences, so the definition of truth cannot proceed in the list-like way of example A; it relies instead on a recursion. However, in these languages compound sentences may have immediate components that are not themselves sentences. For example, the quantificational compound '$(\forall v)Red(v)$' ('Everything is red') has as its immediate component '$Red(v)$', which is not a sentence. Consequently, in these languages, the truth of compounds cannot in general be explained recursively in terms of the truth of their components. To solve the problem Tarski first defines recursively a more general notion, namely, 'satisfaction', and then he defines truth using satisfaction.

Satisfaction is a relation that holds between 'assignments' (of values to variables) and formulas. We can think of assignments as functions from variables into objects. So, if s is an assignment and v is a variable then $s(v)$ is the value s assigns to v. Intuitively, an assignment s satisfies a formula A iff A is true when the free variables in it are interpreted as naming the values that s assigns them. The notion of satisfaction is easy to define for atomic formulas: any assignment that assigns a red object to the variable v satisfies the formula '$Red(v)$'. Similarly, any assignment s such that $s(v)$ is larger than $s(w)$ satisfies the formula '$Larger(v,w)$'. The clauses for n-ary predications are analogous. Satisfaction for complex formulas is defined recursively in terms of the satisfaction of the components:

267

An assignment s satisfies the negation of a formula A iff s does not satisfy A.

An assignment s satisfies the conjunction of B and C iff s satisfies B and s satisfies C.

An assignment s satisfies the universal quantification of A with respect to the variable v iff A is satisfied by all assignments s' such that for all variables v' distinct from v, $s'(v') = s(v')$.

This recursive explanation can be converted to an explicit definition of satisfaction (see example B). It is easy to show that the satisfaction of a formula A by an assignment s depends only on the values that s assigns to the free variables of A. Consequently, a sentence is satisfied either by all assignments or by none. This motivates the following definition of truth:

x is a true sentence of L'' iff x is a sentence of L'' that is satisfied by all assignments.

The reader will find a more leisurely presentation of this example in W.V. Quine's *Philosophy of Logic* (1970).

4   Philosophical influence

Tarski's avowed aim in constructing a definition of truth was to lay down the foundations of a scientific semantics, and it is here that his work has been most influential. Tarski's work provides the foundations for a semantic study of logic – a study that has been vigorously pursued in the twentieth century and to which Tarski made important contributions. Two key notions in this study – 'model' and 'truth in a model' – are generalizations of the notions of 'assignment' and 'satisfaction' introduced in example C. An assignment specifies the values of the variables; a model specifies the domain of quantification and the 'values' of all the nonlogical constants in the language. Furthermore, just as satisfaction tells us what formulas are true under what assignments, similarly 'truth in a model' tells us what formulas are true when the quantifiers and the nonlogical constants are interpreted as specified in the model. The notions 'model' and 'truth in a model' enable a semantic explanation of the various logical notions. For example, an argument is 'valid' if and only if its conclusion is true in all models in which all the premises are true. The semantic analysis of logical concepts has yielded valuable insights into logic (see MODEL THEORY).

Tarski's definition of truth is also of importance in natural-language semantics. Here it has inspired two different kinds of approaches: the Davidsonian approach and the model-theoretic approach. The Davidsonian approach takes the goal of a semantic theory for a language L to be the construction of a theory of truth for it: a finite theory that implies all the T-biconditionals of L. (This is only a rough characterization; see MEANING AND TRUTH.) Davidson has argued that such a theory must proceed recursively, explaining semantic properties of compounds in terms of the semantic properties of the components. As a result, the theory will reveal the logical structure of language. The model-theoretic approach, developed by Richard Montague and others, takes the goal of the semantic theory to be the definition of the notion 'truth in a model'. This requires the characterization of the notion of model and it, in turn, requires an analysis of the logical structure of language. Davidson's work has been highly influential in philosophy, but less so in linguistics. The model-theoretic approach has, however, gained many adherents in linguistics.

Tarski gave his definition in a philosophical climate that was sceptical of the notion of truth. Some logical positivists suggested, for example, that the notion was unanalysable in empirical terms and, hence, unacceptable in a scientific philosophy. Tarski's definition provided a decisive refutation of their suggestion. Let L be the positivists' language – purified of all elements that the positivists judge to be unempirical and meaningless. The notion 'true in L', Tarski showed, can be rigorously defined using only resources that the positivists would accept: the definition uses only some syntactic and logical concepts and those that are expressed in L. Tarski's results were accepted by the positivists and significantly influenced their philosophical work (especially that of Rudolf Carnap).

Tarski's definition has also been influential in more recent philosophy. Some philosophers (for example, Hartry Field (1972) and Michael Devitt) have sought to construct a correspondence theory of truth on its basis. These philosophers accept the recursive parts of Tarski's definition. But they argue that the definition does not provide a substantial account of the semantic properties of the simplest elements of the language. It does not explain, for example, when a name denotes an object or when an object falls under a predicate. To obtain a fully fledged correspondence theory, they suggest, Tarski's recursive explanation of truth should be supplemented with a substantial account of the semantics of the simples. Some philosophers have seen in this kind of theory a way of vindicating realism. But others have questioned both the feasibility of the theory and its links to the realism issue.

It is ironic that while Tarski put forward his definition to show that the concept of truth is useful for certain logical and philosophical purposes, his ideas have also been used in defence of 'deflationism' – the view that the concept has no substantive role to play in logic and philosophy. The thought here is that something like Tarski's definition explains completely the meaning of 'true', and that this makes truth a philosophically lightweight concept. Hence, it is claimed, the concept can play no substantive role in, for example, the explanation of validity or the realism debate. Consider, for instance, the explanation of validity – say, of the argument *P*, therefore *Q* – in terms of truth: the argument is valid iff it is impossible that *P* be true but *Q* false. The T-biconditionals, the deflationists argue, reduce this explanation to the nearly vacuous claim that the argument is valid iff it is impossible that *P* and not *Q*. Neither the explanation nor the concept of truth seem to be doing any substantive work.

The role of the concept of truth in philosophy continues to be a topic of intense debate. In this debate, Tarski's definition and Tarski's ideas occupy centre stage.

See also: CONSEQUENCE, CONCEPTIONS OF §5; LOGICAL AND MATHEMATICAL TERMS, GLOSSARY OF; SEMANTICS

References and further reading

Etchemendy, J. (1988) 'Tarski on Truth and Logical Consequence', *Journal of Symbolic Logic* 53: 51–79. (Nontechnical; makes useful critical points.)

* Field, H. (1972) 'Tarski's Theory of Truth', *Journal of Philosophy* 69: 347–75; repr. in M. Platts (ed.) *Reference, Truth and Reality*, London: Routledge & Kegan Paul, 1980. (Referred to in §4; argues for a transformation of Tarski's definition into a correspondence theory of truth.)

Gupta, A. and Belnap, N.D. (1993) *The Revision Theory of Truth*, Cambridge, MA: MIT Press. (Chapters 1 and 4 are nontechnical and discuss Criterion T and the liar paradox; the rest of the book is quite technical.)

Horwich, P. (1990) *Truth*, Oxford: Blackwell. (A clear defence of deflationism.)

* Quine, W.V. (1970) *Philosophy of Logic*, Englewood Cliffs, NJ: Prentice-Hall. (Referred to in §3; presents a Tarskian truth definition in detail.)

* Tarski, A. (1936) 'Der Wahrheitsbegriff in den formalisierten Sprachen', *Studia Philosophica* 1: 261–405; trans. J.H. Woodger, 'The Concept of Truth in Formalized Languages', in *Logic, Semantics, Metamathematics: Papers from 1923 to 1938*, Oxford: Clarendon Press, 1956; ed. J. Corcoran, Indianapolis, IN: Hackett Publishing Company, 2nd edn, 1983, 152–278. (*The* classic paper on the subject;

the introduction and the first section of the paper are nontechnical and are highly recommended.)

* —— (1944) 'The Semantic Conception of Truth and the Foundations of Semantics', *Philosophy and Phenomenological Research* 4: 341–76; repr. in L. Linsky (ed.) *Semantics and the Philosophy of Language*, Urbana, IL: University of Illinois Press, 1952. (Nontechnical; includes valuable philosophical material.)

—— (1969) 'Truth and Proof', *Scientific American* 220 (6): 63–77; repr. in R.I.G. Hughes (ed.) *A Philosophical Companion to First-Order Logic*, Indianapolis, IN: Hackett Publishing Company, 1993. (A particularly good popular exposition of the main ideas.)

ANIL GUPTA

TARTU SCHOOL *see* MOSCOW-TARTU SCHOOL

TASAN *see* CHÔNG YAGYONG

TASTE, ARTISTIC *see* ARTISTIC TASTE

TAULER, JOHN (*c.*1300–1361)

Tauler was a Dominican preacher and mystic, the author of seventy-nine vernacular sermons which presented the Neoplatonic speculative mysticism of his teacher Eckhart in more personal and concrete terms. Tauler greatly influenced late medieval mendicant spirituality, Luther, and the German pietists and romantics. His primary aims were to inculcate the spiritual virtues and devotion to God.

Tauler, his friend Henry SUSO and MEISTER ECKHART are the central figures in the Rhineland school of mysticism. Tauler enrolled in the Dominican *studium generale* in Cologne in 1324, together with Suso, but little is known of a life devoted to preaching and spiritual direction in the Dominican nunneries and Beguines around Strasbourg and Basel. Among Tauler's spiritual contacts were Suso, who was like Tauler also a leader of and moderating influence on the Friends of God who were inclined to antinomian spirituality, the influential mystical Dominican nun

Margareta Ebner and the famous Rhenish mystic John Ruusbroec.

The social situation during Tauler's maturity was chaotic. The Strasbourg Dominicans were exiled in Basel (1339–43) during the time the anti-papal civic authorities supported Emperor Louis. The ensuing civil war and the Black Death strained conventional morality, creating a challenge for a preacher calling lay people to the spiritual life. These conditions may have contributed to the ferocity and intense gloom of some of the sermons. In any case, Tauler's sermons are more personal and emotional than Eckhart's but generally more moderate and balanced than Suso's. At his death Tauler had published nothing; the sermons were written down in the Middle High German vernacular by listeners who were most often Dominican nuns.

Tauler's sermons combine biblical commentary with German mystical themes, supplemented by distinctions drawn from scholastic thinkers, especially Peter LOMBARD and Thomas AQUINAS. They orient pastoral concern towards spiritual transformation, and combine various strands of medieval Christian mysticism: practical monastic spirituality, Dominican intellectualist mysticism, and beatitude and divinisation. Philosophically, Tauler was most influenced by the Neoplatonised Aristotelianism of ALBERT THE GREAT and the stronger Neoplatonism of PSEUDO-DIONYSIUS and Meister Eckhart. Notably absent from the sermons is the love imagery prominent in medieval exponents of *Song of Songs* mysticism. Tauler is deeply versed in Eckhart's teachings; thus, he regularly employs the themes and concepts of Dominican mystical psychology, though his language is usually more concrete. Fundamental are the notions of 'the ground', 'summit' or 'spark' of the soul, the mysterious essence of human nature that can touch the ineffable divine nature, the 'imageless Image' which is the Trinity. Paradoxically, however, the soul returns to God by returning to itself: 'This spark flies up to the summits where its true place is, even beyond this world, where intelligence cannot follow it, for it does not rest until it returns to that centre from which it originates and where it used to be in its uncreated state' (Sermons 64, 2). Clearly, Tauler suscribes to the 'breakthrough' (*Durchbruch*) of the soul into eternity, but unlike Eckhart, he favours an account of divinization consistent with the orthodox distinction between God and creature. This and other departures from his teacher's extreme views should be understood in part as precautions against the ecclesiastical pressures increased by Eckhart's condemnation in 1328.

Negative theology becomes a supple psychological instrument in Tauler's hands (see NEGATIVE THEOL-OGY). Instead of emphasising Eckhart's heterodox notion of the soul's birth as the Son, Tauler counsels humility, self-denial and detachment (*Gelassenheit*) – also Eckhartian themes. Meditative concentration on the humanity of Christ entails for Tauler the negation of overly abstract theological concepts and the abandonment of free will, external goods and attachments, as in Matthew 19: 29: 'whoever leaves father and mother and all possessions for my sake shall receive a hundredfold and eternal life'. Tauler's own words serve well as the motto of this more homely, devotional spirituality: 'The lower the descent, the higher the ascent'. Like Suso, Tauler is more inclined than Eckhart to explain human error and sin and their overcoming through ascetic exercises and the sacraments. Unlike his friend, however, Tauler does not speak explicitly of his own spiritual experiences. Paradigmatic stages of the spiritual life are explored via scriptural exegesis. Instead of Suso's imaginative flights Tauler employs vivid imagery drawn from common life, crafts and popular examples to convey abstract points. His overall aim is to strike a balance between the aridity of scholastic theology and the excesses of pseudo-mystical enthusiasm, with its widespread dangers of mistaking inner spiritual freedom with libertinism.

See also: MEISTER ECKHART; MYSTICISM, HISTORY OF; NEOPLATONISM; PLATONISM, MEDIEVAL

List of works

Tauler, John (*c.*1300–61) Sermons, ed. F. Vetter, *Die Predigten Taulers*, Frankfurt: Weidmann, 1910; 2nd edn, 1968. (A good English translation of selected sermons is E. Colledge and Sister M. Jane (ed. and trans.) *Spiritual Conferences by John Tauler*, Rockford, IL: Tan Books, 1978. *Johannes Tauler: Sermons*, trans. M. Shrady, New York: Paulist Press, 1985, is a fine collection of twenty-three sermons in a good English translation, accompanied by a useful preface by A. Haas and an excellent introduction by J. Schmidt.)

References and further reading

de Gandillac, M. (1956) *Valeur du temps dans la pédagogie spirituelle de Jean Tauler*, Montreal, Que.: Institut d'études medievales. (A fine assessment of Tauler's spirituality.)

Haas, A. (1971) *Nim din selbes war. Studien zur Lehre von der Selbsterkenntnis bei Meister Eckhart, Johannes Tauler und Heinrich Seuse*, Freiburg: Universtätsverlag. (Excellent account of the theme of self-knowledge in the Rhineland mystics.)

Ozment, S.E. (1969) *Homo Spiritualis: A Comparative Study of the Anthropology of Johannes Tauler, Jean Gerson and Martin Luther (1509–16)*, Leiden: Brill. (Valuable exploration of Tauler's mysticism and its influence.)

JOHN BUSSANICH

AL-TAWHIDI, ABU HAYYAN (*c.*930–1023)

Al-Tawhidi was an Arabic litterateur and philosopher, probably of Persian origin, and author of numerous books which reflect all the main themes of debate and reflection in the cultivated circles of his time. His basic outlook could be defined as a kind of simplified and vulgarized Neoplatonism, influenced by Gnostic elements, with four hypostases: God, Intellect, Soul and Nature. He also has a strong interest in moral questions on both the individual and social level.

'Ali ibn Muhammad Abu Hayyan al-Tawhidi was probably of Persian origin. However, Arabic is the only language he is known to have used, and most of his life was spent in Baghdad and in Rayy (Tehran) at the court of the Buyid princes and their ministers, in particular the famous Ibn Sa'dan. It is in the latter's presence that the discussions recorded in *al-Imta' wa'-mu'anasa* (Enjoyment and Conviviality) took place. His last years were spent in Shiraz, where he died in AH 414/AD 1023.

Al-Tawhidi is a representative of Arabic belles-lettres (*adab*) rather than a philosopher in the strict sense. However, some of his main works report discussions devoted to philosophical themes and shed interesting sidelights on questions dealt with in a more systematic fashion by the great Arab philosophers. It goes with the genre adopted by al-Tawhidi that he rarely expresses his own opinions; his main authority is his master, Abu Sulayman AL-SIJISTANI. He also appears to make extensive use of the *Rasa'il Ikhwan al-Safa'* (Epistles of the Brethren of Purity), although their name is rarely cited (see IKHWAN AL-SAFA'). Another source of inspiration is the ethical thinker IBN MISKAWAYH, with whom he exchanged a philosophical correspondence, *al-Hawamil wal-shawa-mil* (Rambling and Comprehensive Questions). Among Greek philosophers, ARISTOTLE is by far the most commonly invoked authority.

Al-Tawhidi's main philosophical work is *al-Muqa-basat* (Borrowed Lights). *Al-Imta' wa'-mu'anasa* also contains some philosophical material, besides some which is predominantly literary or grammatical. In

metaphysics, he follows the basic Neoplatonic scheme of emanation (see NEOPLATONISM IN ISLAMIC PHILOSOPHY). The First, frequently called the Creator, is the source of the world of nature which emanates continuously from him; God is thus also characterized by his generosity. Intellect, Soul and Nature are the three main levels of being, or hypostases, emanating from the First. The process is sometimes expressed in terms of illumination; the Intellect receives its light from the First, the Soul from the Intellect and Nature from the Soul. Elsewhere, the soul is considered as being pure light. Conversely, the First is said to encompass the Intellect, which in turn encompasses the Soul and so forth.

Many paragraphs are devoted to the human soul, concerning which al-Tawhidi takes up positions that can be defined as Platonic. The soul subsists by itself and is not tied down to the body; on the contrary, it uses the body as an instrument. The soul does not arise from the mixture of the elements; thus the Galenic theory is implicitly rejected, although it is ascribed in one passage to Zeno (probably meaning the Stoic) (see GALEN; ZENO OF CITIUM). The union with the body is described as a kind of fall in a way which has clear antecedents in some soteriological conceptions of Gnosticism and Neoplatonism (see GNOSTICISM; NEOPLATONISM). In the course of the soul's descent from the heavenly realm it became covered in scales or veils, which it will cast off after physical death, that is, when it relinquishes the body. The soul becomes like a rusty mirror; just as the latter is no longer capable of reflecting external objects, the soul forgot what it knew in the intelligible world. Its true nature is also more fully active in sleep. In our ordinary waking life, we do not remember the world where our soul originated because we have been overcome by matter. These two states of the soul, incarnate and immaterial, correspond to the two realms of intellection and sense-perception. Intellection is an immediate form of apprehension, devoid of reflection and deliberation, whereas sense-perception is linked to discursive and inductive modes of thought, such as syllogism.

Humanity is thus in an intermediate position between the world of intellect and the world of nature. The latter is integrated into the emanationist scheme more neatly than is the case in Greek Neoplatonism; nature is a life force which emanates from the First Principle and penetrates all bodies, giving them their forms and linking them together. The Aristotelian definition of nature as principle of motion and rest is also quoted more than once.

Al-Tawhidi evinces a keen interest in linguistic questions. He predictably maintains the superiority of Arabic over other languages, but also discusses such topics as the respective place and function of prose and verse (see AESTHETICS IN ISLAMIC PHILOSOPHY). It is thanks to him that we have a report of the controversy between the partisans of logic and Greek culture and those of traditional Arabic grammar. Another discussion tackles the sensitive problem of the relationship between philosophy and religion. Among the current themes of his time, that of the characters and respective merits of the nations is taken up on several occasions. In the field of ethics, he devoted an entire epistle to friendship, and this is one of his more personal and interesting works.

See also: IBN MISKAWAYH; NEOPLATONISM IN ISLAMIC PHILOSOPHY; AL-SIJISTANI

List of works

al-Tawhidi (*c.*977–82) *al-Hawamil wa'-shawamil* (Rambling and Comprehensive Questions), ed. A. Amin and A. Saqr, Cairo, 1951. (A correspondence with Ibn Miskawayh on a variety of topics.)

—— (*c.*983–5) *al-Imta' wa'-mu'anasa* (Enjoyment and Conviviality), ed. A. Amin and A. al-Zayn, Cairo, 1953. (A collection of forty 'nights' or gatherings devoted to the discussion of literary, philosophical, religious, grammatical and other subjects.)

—— (*c.*996) *al-Muqabasat* (Borrowed Lights), ed. M.T. Husayn, Baghdad, 1970. (A collection of 106 discussions, mainly theological and philosophical.)

—— (*c.*1010) *al-Sadaqa wa'-sadiq* (Friendship and Friend), ed. I. Keilani, Damascus, 1964. (A short personal essay on friendship.)

References and further reading

Berge, M. (1979) *Pour un humanisme vécu: Abu Hayyan al-Tawhidi* (Towards a Living Humanism: Abu Hayyan al-Tawhidi), Damascus: Institut Français de Damas, 1979. (A general study of Tawhidi's life, works and thought, the only such in a European language.)

Leaman, O. (1996) 'Islamic Humanism in the Fourth/ Tenth Century', in S.H. Nasr and O. Leaman (eds) *History of Islamic Philosophy*, London: Routledge, ch. 10, 155–64. (Analysis of the nature of this important period of Islamic philosophy, concentrating on the ethical thought of the period.)

Rowson, E.K. (1990) 'The Philosopher as Littérateur: al-Tawhidi and his Predecessors', *Zeitschrift für Geschichte der Arabisch-Islamischen Wissenschaften* 6: 50–92. (Short study of al-Tawhidi in English.)

CHARLES GENEQUAND

TAXONOMY

The fundamental elements of any classification are its theoretical commitments, basic units and the criteria for ordering these basic units into a classification. Two fundamentally different sorts of classification are those that reflect structural organization and those that are systematically related to historical development.

In biological classification, evolution supplies the theoretical orientation. The goal is to make the basic units of classification (taxonomic species) identical to the basic units of biological evolution (evolutionary species). The principle of order is supplied by phylogeny. Species splitting successively through time produce a phylogenetic tree. The primary goal of taxonomy since Darwin has been to reflect these successive splittings in a hierarchical classification made up of species, genera, families, and so on.

The major point of contention in taxonomy is epistemological. A recurrent complaint against classifications that attempt to reflect phylogeny is that phylogeny cannot be 'known' with certainty sufficient to warrant using it as the object of classification. Instead, small but persistent groups of taxonomists have insisted that classifications be more 'operational'. Instead of attempting to reflect something as difficult to infer as phylogeny, advocates of this position contend that systematists should stick more closely to observational reality.

1   The goals of taxonomy
2   The basic units of classification
3   Homology and monophyly
4   Taxonomic hierarchies
5   Epistemology and the goals of classification

1   The goals of taxonomy

Any set of entities can be classified in indefinitely many ways. Books can be classified according to author, title, subject matter, and so on. Although these various classifications can be integrated into a single reference system so that any book can be retrieved on a variety of different counts, books as physical objects can be arrayed on library shelves in only one order. Even here, contingent problems arise. For example, very large books may have to be shelved out of order, and expensive first editions may be locked away in separate collections.

More stringent requirements apply to scientific classifications. The ultimate goal for scientific classifications is to group entities so that these classes function in, or facilitate the formation of, scientific laws (see LAWS, NATURAL §1). Aristotle divided motion into super- and sub-lunar as well as forced and natural (see MECHANICS, ARISTOTELIAN). The primary justification of his classification was the system of laws that he was able to generate using it. When Newton introduced his quite different system, his classification replaced Aristotle's because Newton's system of laws was more powerful, accurate and inclusive. In general, systems of scientific classification are intimately connected to scientific theories and cannot be evaluated independently of them. Different sorts of theories require different classifications.

One major difference is between structural and historical classifications. The periodic table of physical elements is structural. The elements are individuated and ordered linearly according to their atomic number. Hydrogen comes first, then helium, lithium, and so on. These elements in turn can be arranged hierarchically as metals, rare earths, and so on. Some of these arrangements are perfectly nested; others are not. A more contemporary classification would include reference to subatomic particles and their relations (see CHEMISTRY, PHILOSOPHICAL ASPECTS OF §4). In general, structural hierarchies do not include very many levels. They are not very deep. Although cosmology is a legitimate area of physics, no one has suggested a historical classification of the physical elements; for example, classifying them in the order in which they appeared after the Big Bang.

Historical classifications are more prominent in other areas of scientific investigation. For example, linguists produce both structural and historical classifications of languages. Phonemes are the basic units of the structural classifications. Historical linguists also reconstruct the history of languages, indicating which evolved from which and how various sounds changed through time. One sign that a classification is historical rather than structural is the number of levels it exhibits. Historical classifications tend to be much deeper than structural classifications.

The logical structure of structural classifications is quite intuitive. Geometric figures can be divided into those that have three, four, five, and more sides. Three-sided figures in turn can be divided into triangles that have three, two and no sides of equal length. The logical structure of historical classifications also appears to be intuitively clear. It is anything but. Appearances notwithstanding, historical relations, especially those that form genealogical trees, are not easily represented in hierarchical classifications. Because these issues have been worked out most extensively with respect to classifications of living creatures, and because biological classifications are among the most familiar, the rest of this discussion concentrates on biological classifications.

2 The basic units of classification

The organisms with which people are most familiar seem to fall naturally into discrete kinds. No one has any trouble telling apart cats, dogs, elephants and whales. However, this ease stems from limitation of perspective. If a particular species is followed across its range, problems frequently arise as the traits that characterize the species change geographically. Populations of a species in one locale frequently differ statistically from populations at other locales. If biological species are traced through successive geological strata, the same sort of variation occurs. In addition, not all organisms seem to form species of the same sort. For example, organisms that reproduce sexually may well form species that are significantly different from the species formed by organisms that reproduce asexually. Plant species may differ systematically from animal or protist species. For example, hybrid species are rare among animals but common among plants.

Most systematists are willing to put up with these difficulties in order to produce classifications that reflect the evolutionary process. Others, however, have suggested subdividing organisms into basic units of the sort that can be recognized with greater ease and reliability. For example, the basic units of classification might reflect some one measure of overall similarity. One of the problems with this suggestion is deciding on the measure. Another is that, no matter the measure, many of the resulting 'species' are exceedingly nonstandard; for example, males and females of the same evolutionary species may be placed in separate 'species'. Still other systematists have proposed to define species so that males, females and their immediate descendants are included in the same species, but thereafter all that is required is one or more diagnostic characters. Species can be defined in numerous different ways for different purposes, but systematists must settle on a single way for their classifications (see SPECIES §1).

3 Homology and monophyly

For centuries systematists attempted to produce structural classifications of living creatures. At times, they thought that they had found criteria that promised to group organisms into something like the periodic table, but insuperable problems always arose. Living creatures seemed to embody two different kinds of similarity. As much as sharks, boney fishes and whales look alike on the basis of some characteristics, they are fundamentally different on other sets. With the introduction of Darwin's theory of evolution, systematists realized why they were having such a difficult time. Biological kinds (taxa) are characterized by both structural and historical relations, and no one classification can represent both (see DARWIN, C.R.; EVOLUTION, THEORY OF).

Nothing requires systematists to accept descent as the relation that they represent in their classifications. If some other principle of order had proven feasible and productive, it might have been adopted. But once systematists accepted the task of constructing classifications that reflect genealogy, they had to rework their basic conceptual system from the ground up, redefining terms that had no genealogical component so that they did. For example, the terms 'homology' and 'analogy' originally implied nothing about descent but concerned differences in structural patterns. Evolutionists redefined these terms to indicate descent. Apes, fish and amphibians all have eyes, and these eyes are homologies because they evolved as eyes in a common ancestor. They are vertebrate eyes. Cephelapods also have eyes, but these 'eyes' cannot count as the same character as vertebrate eyes because they evolved independently. Similarly, snakes belong to Tetrapoda even though they have lost their legs. Having lost a character is importantly different from never having possessed it in the first place.

According to evolutionary systematists, all taxa must be monophyletic. However, some systematists are satisfied with a weak notion of monophyly, while others insist on a much stronger notion. On the weak definition, all species that make up a monophyletic taxon must arise from a single immediately ancestral stem species. Willi Hennig and his intellectual descendants (termed 'cladists') are convinced that a much stronger notion of monophyly is required. Not only must all species included in a monophyletic taxon be descended from a single stem species, but also all the species descended from a single stem species must be included in a single higher taxon. One problem with this stronger definition of 'monophyly' is that it obliterates numerous time-honoured taxa. For example, Reptilia has been part of biological classifications for centuries. However, Reptilia is not monophyletic in this stronger sense because some organisms that share an immediate common ancestor with reptiles are nevertheless not included in Reptilia, for example, birds.

4 Taxonomic hierarchies

Because phylogenetic trees consist of successive branches and hierarchical classifications consist of successively less inclusive taxa, systematists were led for a long time into thinking that the relationship

between the two systems is quite straightforward. It is not. The source of this mistake can be seen in Figure 1(A), which represents a typical phylogeny. The intuitive classification of this phylogeny is presented in Figure 1(B). A moment's reflection should reveal that something is wrong with this classification. The phylogenetic tree is made up of five species, while the classification lists only two species. The taxon listed as Tribe *a* is not a Tribe but a species.

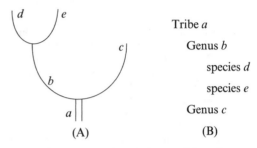

Figure 1. A representative phylogeny (A) and an intuitive but mistaken way of classifying it (B)

A more appropriate classification of the phylogeny depicted in Figure 1(A) is presented in Figure 2(A). The way in which this classification groups species into higher taxa is represented in Figure 2(B). In this classification, the five species are at least listed as species. However, problems remain. All the taxa in this classification are monophyletic in the weak sense. Each stems from a single ancestral species. But not all of these taxa are monophyletic in the stronger sense. The source of the problem is, surprisingly, the presence of common ancestors. No collection of species that includes one or more species that are ancestral to the others can be classified monophyletically in the strong sense. If species *a* in Figure 1(A) is classified with species *b*, then species *c* is left out. Conversely, if species *a* is classified with species *c*, then species *b* is left out. As a result, no classification that includes common ancestors can be monophyletic in the strong sense.

Parallel problems arise at the level of characters. If the list of species to be classified happens to include a common ancestor, then no single set of nested characters can be found to define the relevant higher taxa. Some characters will imply that species *a* should be classed with species *b*; other characters will imply that species *a* should be classed with species *c*. Every time an ancestral species is included in a taxonomic study, the result will be conflicting character distributions. In fact, one hint that a set of species under investigation includes common ancestors is continued conflict in character distributions as the study progresses.

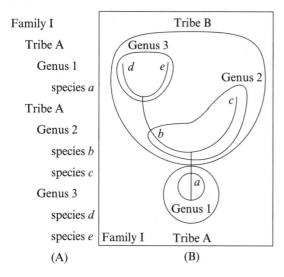

Family I

Tribe A

 Genus 1

  species *a*

Tribe A

 Genus 2

  species *b*

  species *c*

 Genus 3

  species *d*

  species *e*

(A)

Figure 2. Classification (A) of a phylogeny and that same classification indicated on that phylogeny (B)

The source of the preceding problem is not nature but the structure of the Linnaean hierarchy. The Linnaean hierarchy was developed for structural classifications (see LINNAEUS, C. VON). When the goal of systematics was changed to have classifications reflect genealogy, no one noticed the deep problems posed by any attempt to translate a historically connected tree into nested sets of taxa. The traditional Linnaean hierarchy is not up to the task. It cannot represent splitting. Nor can it represent the symmetrical relation – merger. Species of hybrid origin are no easier to represent than are common ancestors.

5 Epistemology and the goals of classification

Throughout the history of biological systematics, conflicts have arisen over the kind and degree of certainty that is required in science. At one extreme, some systematists are satisfied to produce classifications based on a host of tacit evaluations and patchy evidence. For them, classification is mainly an art. At the other extreme, are those systematists who insist that intuitive guesses must be replaced by strict quantitative techniques. These systematists also view scientific theories with suspicion. Two sorts of 'theory' have come under special scrutiny – phylogeny reconstruction and evolutionary theory itself. Systematists have rediscovered a problem long familiar to philosophers. How can one know that a particular chunk of metal is gold unless one knows what gold is, and how can one know what gold is without inspecting some samples of gold? But if one does not know what gold is, one cannot decide what to inspect . . . .

The appropriate response to the preceding question is not all that satisfying. On the basis of very little knowledge mixed with lots of error, one develops a conception of gold. On the basis of this imperfect conception, additional investigations are performed, and these investigations uncover past errors, which increase our ability to discern gold, and so on. On the basis of sketchy data and an imperfect understanding of how evolution occurs, one attempts to reconstruct phylogeny. From these imperfect reconstructions, evolutionary theory is improved, which permits better phylogenetic reconstructions, and so on (see SCIENTIFIC METHOD §2).

Although character covariations are the primary evidence in phylogeny reconstruction, they are not the sole evidence. Two sessile species that have equally sessile propagules cannot possibly be closely related phylogenetically if the one lives in Mexico and the other in Ethiopia. The goal of making scientific method as simple, straightforward and reliable as possible is justified, but such methodological injunctions should not be made so rigorous that the progress of science is stopped in its tracks. In the last analysis, classifications succeed or fail on the basis of the use that scientists can make of them.

See also: THEORIES, SCIENTIFIC

References and further reading

Ereshefsky, M. (ed.) (1992) *The Units of Evolution: Essays on the Nature of Species*, Cambridge, MA: MIT Press. (A collection of classic papers on the species' problem.)

Mayr, E. and Ashlock, P.D. (1991) *Principles of Systematic Zoology*, New York: McGraw-Hill, 2nd edn. (A discussion of the principles of traditional evolutionary taxonomy.)

Ridley, M. (1986) *Evolution and Classification: The Reformation of Cladism*, London and New York: Longman. (A philosophical critique of cladistic analysis.)

Sneath, P.H.A. (1995) 'Thirty Years of Numerical Taxonomy', *Systematic Biology* 44: 281–98. (An evaluation of numerical taxonomy by one of its founders.)

Sober, E. (1988) *Reconstructing the Past: Parsimony, Evolution, Inference*, Cambridge, MA: MIT Press.

(A philosophical evaluation of cladistic methods for reconstructing the past.)

Sokal, R.R. (1986) 'Phenetic Taxonomy: Theory and Methods', *Annual Review of Ecology and Systematics* 17: 423–42. (A summary of the principles of phenetic taxonomy by one of its founders.)

Wiley, E.O., Siegel-Causey, D., Brooks, D.R. and Funk, V.A. (1991) *The Complete Cladist: A Primer of Phylogenetic Systematics*, Lawrence, KS: Special Publication, Museum of Natural History. (A discussion of the principles of cladistic analysis.)

DAVID L. HULL

TAYLOR, CHARLES (1931–)

Among the most influential of late twentieth-century philosophers, Taylor has written on human agency, identity and the self; language; the limits of epistemology; interpretation and explanation in social science; ethics; and democratic politics. His work is distinctive because of his innovative treatments of long-standing philosophical problems, especially those deriving from applications of Enlightenment epistemology to theories of language, the self and political action, and his unusually thorough integration of 'analytic' and 'continental' philosophical concerns and approaches.

Taylor's work is shaped by the view that adequate understanding of philosophical arguments requires an appreciation of their origins, changing contexts and transformed meanings. Thus it often takes the form of historical reconstructions that seek to identify the paths by which particular theories and languages of understanding or evaluation have been developed. This reflects both Taylor's sustained engagement with Hegel's philosophy and his resistance to epistemological dichotomies such as 'truth' and 'falsehood' in favour of a notion of 'epistemic gain' influenced by H.G. Gadamer.

1 **Explanation and interpretation**
2 **Hegel**
3 **Language**
4 **Strong evaluation and the self**
5 **Communitarianism and multiculturalism**

1 Explanation and interpretation

In his most prominent early publications, Taylor addressed the status of explanation in psychology and the social sciences. *The Explanation of Behaviour* (1967) challenged the adequacy of behaviourism in psychology, principally by arguing that accounting for

intentional action entails a teleological understanding of the ends of action that cannot be achieved within purely causal theories. 'Interpretation and the Sciences of Man' (1971) extended this argument to politics and social analysis, showing that attempts at explanation in terms of external approaches to 'brute facts' not only fail to satisfy those who seek more meaningful understandings of human agency, but are also incoherent or incomplete on their own terms. These studies are all parts of a more general argument against the epistemology that both inspired and drew strength from the scientific revolutions of the seventeenth century and after. Taylor holds that this epistemological tradition both relied on an atomistic account of putatively undifferentiated nature (including human nature) and erected a perniciously sharp distinction between knower and object of knowledge, with the result that it drastically distorted and narrowed the scope of understanding of human life (see BEHAVIOURISM, METHODOLOGICAL AND SCIENTIFIC §1).

2 Hegel

The same issues motivate much of Taylor's engagement with HEGEL. Hegel too challenged the reigning epistemological tradition and especially its atomistic inattention to the necessary relatedness of all subjects and objects, and to the internal differentiation of both subjects and objects. He argued that any adequate account of the human subject must rely on an understanding of persons as existing only in interaction, as becoming individuals only through participation in an intersubjective reality. Taylor argues that this richer account of the person requires an understanding of language as not merely neutrally picking out objects of attention or reflecting pre-given inner states, but as helping to constitute phenomena and our understanding of external phenomena. Following Johann Herder (see HERDER, J. §2), Taylor places these positions on bases significantly different from Hegel's.

This is necessary because Taylor holds that Hegel ultimately failed to achieve the rational certainty about the absolute that he sought. Hegel's arguments reveal an interpretive vision of power and insight, but not a system of determinate necessity. Building then on the critical foundation he shares in large part with Hegel, but rejecting the more extreme claims of Hegel's *Logic* and related elements of his substantive philosophical anthropology and social theory, Taylor has sought to advance an understanding of the nature and activities of and relations among human subjects and of the kind of science that can grasp these subjects, their relations and activities. This entails moving 'beyond epistemology', but not following Hegel in the attempt to ground all argument in ontology.

3 Language

Dualist epistemology is predicated on a rigid separation of subject and object that makes us unable to grasp distinctive features of human life and activity as distinct from the behaviour of physical objects and natural systems. Taylor moves beyond this by developing 'expressivist' or 'constitutive' theories of language, inaugurated by Herder and important to the Romantic tradition, but often left inadequately grounded in an appeal to immediate self-knowledge. These theories help Taylor to show the human agent to be understandable only as a participant in a linguistic community. Correspondingly, language itself cannot be understood entirely as a matter of reference and predication; instead, Taylor suggests that linguistic activity also involves constructing objects by making identifications of significance that cannot adequately be rendered in truth-conditional form, and that agents are never in a purely external relationship to language, nor indeed to the rest of their worlds in so far as these are constituted through language.

4 Strong evaluation and the self

In a similar fashion, Taylor argues that human agents necessarily engage in different orders of cognition and evaluation. We engage in practical reason always against a background of 'strong evaluations'. These are simultaneously intellectual and moral commitments that constitute us as knowers and judgers, and that make possible our more specific and immediate knowledge and judgments. Such commitments may vary, but are necessary to the constitution of the self.

Modern moral philosophy has tended to focus on what it is right to do rather than on what it is good to be, and on defining the content of obligation rather than the nature of the good life. In this, it reflects the reliance on the notion of a disembodied, decontextualized and disengaged subject pioneered by post-seventeenth-century science and the epistemology to which it helped give rise. Accordingly, it is a philosophical priority to reconstruct both the dominant modern understandings of the self and alternative interpretations of human agents. Taylor takes on this task in *Sources of the Self* (1989). A key feature of human agency, he shows, is that it is constituted only within frameworks of strong evaluation – whether these are traditional notions of the primacy of honour, Platonic accounts of the virtues of reason

and self-mastery, modern understandings of the expressive power of inner selves or the virtues of counting everyone's interests equally. The historical story of the changing character of the modern self is thus inextricably an account of the transformation of more capacities, because these are rooted in changing constructions of agency. Changes in the idea of self, moreover, were often driven directly by attempts to resolve moral or religious problems, though their long-term results were sometimes to undermine the theological or other commitments that give rise to the new conceptions. A crucial moment in this process was the transformation in evaluation of ordinary life, the movement of the world of work and family from the margins of morality to the centre of the modern agent's moral commitments. This helped to make possible new positive understandings of the self as a physical, including sexual being, and contributed both to utilitarianism, with its reckonings of all manner of satisfactions without reference to the hierarchy that had previously denigrated those of ordinary life, and to Romanticism, with its understanding of the primacy of individual expression (see SUBJECT, POSTMODERN CRITIQUE OF THE §1).

5 Communitarianism and multiculturalism

Although these modern transformations of the self lead to new capacities for individuation and fulfilment in interpersonal relationships, these new capacities give rise to new ethical and political challenges. Increased attention to intersubjective community is therefore important not only for philosophical accuracy but for moral life and personal satisfaction. Taylor is thus part of the diverse philosophical and political movement termed 'communitarianism'. In addition to his enduring emphases on the constitutive role of language and the intersubjective nature of agency, in his work of the 1990s Taylor focused attention on the sociological dimensions of community, including especially the nature of nationalism and the irreducibly social nature of some human goods.

Drawing on his analysis of the modern self, Taylor shows in *The Ethics of Authenticity* (1991) how the search for authentic self-fulfilment can become incoherent and self-defeating when it is tied to atomistic individualism, the overvaluation of instrumental reason and an alienation from public life. At the same time, he argues against pessimism, suggesting that the other elements of our philosophical and cultural traditions give us resources for confronting our current crisis – including the recognition that our wants are necessarily qualitatively distinguishable (so that, among other things, we can want to have better wants), that our individuality is grounded in sociality (so that we can conceive of freedom in ways other than absence of external constraint), and that frameworks of strong evaluation are inescapable (so that the attribution of significance is not simply a matter of immediate subjective choice).

Among the most important themes in this work is a renewed link to Hegel. In many different versions of the fragmentation of political life, Taylor sees a common theme of competing demands for recognition of the legitimacy or value of different identities. This 'politics of recognition', appearing in nationalism, ethnic politics, feminism and multiculturalism, is an outgrowth of the modern valuation of self and ordinary life. Claims often assert the rightness and value of differences among people, in contradiction to earlier politics that stressed universal dignity by recommending blindness to differences. Many are incoherent, however, in demanding a recognition of equal worth that can only be met by a 'soft relativism', since it is demanded in advance of genuine evaluative engagement. There is no resolution to this dilemma in pure individualistic liberalism because of its homogenizing conception of the person and consequent incapacity to provide a sense of significant differentiation so that partial communities can be centres of value within larger politics in ways that connect members to the whole. A presumption of mutual respect is a useful beginning, but also a 'mere ought', unless linked to a notion of the self as, first, necessarily socially engaged rather than merely observing from an external vantage point; second, limited in its capacity for understanding by the very cultural frameworks that make its individuality and understanding possible; and, third, open to change through communicative interaction. Such a notion of the self fits with the aspiration to combine full moral autonomy with the recovery of community both expressive of the common life of its members and constitutive of their individuality (see COMMUNITY AND COMMUNITARIANISM §§2–3).

List of works

Taylor, C. (1967) *The Explanation of Behaviour*, London: Routledge. (A critique of psychological behaviourism, emphasizing the limits of purely causal theories and the need for teleological accounts of the ends of action.)

——(1971) 'Interpretation and the Sciences of Man', *The Review of Metaphysics* 25 (1): 3–51. (A classic essay on the inevitability of interpretation to the human sciences, and the conseqeunt impossibility of pure objectivist behaviourism.)

——(1975) *Hegel*, Cambridge: Cambridge University Press. (A sustained inquiry into Hegel's philosophy, establishing the unity of his thought, the embeddedness of his project in the problems of its historical epoch, the reasons for the ultimate failure of that project, and the insights it none the less offers for philosophy and social thought.)

——(1977) *Hegel and Modern Society*, Cambridge: Cambridge University Press. (A consideration of Hegel's contribution to grasping the distinct nature of modern society and its enduring problems.)

—— (1985a) *Philosphical Papers, vol. 1: Human Agency and Language*, Cambridge: Cambridge University Press. (Taylor's major early papers addressing themes of agency, language and the intersubjective constitution of the person.)

—— (1985b) *Philosophical Papers, vol. 2: Philosophy and the Human Sciences*, Cambridge: Cambridge University Press. (Taylor's major early papers on the social and behavioural sciences, including Taylor (1971).)

——(1989) *Sources of the Self*, Cambridge, MA: Harvard University Press. (Taylor's investigation of the genesis of modern Western constructions of the self, emphasizing that agency is only constituted within frameworks of 'strong evaluation', and studying how these change with attempts to resolve moral and religious problems.)

——(1991) *The Malaises of Modernity*, Toronto, Ont.: Anansi; also publ. as *The Ethics of Authenticity*, Cambridge, MA: Harvard University Press. (A series of lectures examining the challenges posed to the modern era by tying the search for self-fulfilment to atomistic individualism, an overvaluation of instrumental reason, and alienation from public life, and arguing for the inadequacy of 'soft relativism' when faced with significant cultural and interpersonal differences.)

——(1995) *Philosophical Arguments*, Cambridge, MA: Harvard University Press. (A collection of Taylor's major recent papers on themes ranging from moral obligation to public goods and the self to nationalism, including the widely debated 'The Politics of Recognition'.)

References and further reading

Calhoun, C. (1991) 'Morality, Identity and Historical Explanation: Charles Taylor on the Sources of the Self', *Sociological Theory* 9 (2): 232–63. (An analysis of Taylor's account of transitions in self and moral reasoning.)

Gutmann, A. (ed.) (1994) *Multiculturalism and the Politics of Recognition*, Princeton, NJ: Princeton University Press. (A collection of responses to one of Taylor's key arguments by Anthony Appiah, Jürgen Habermas, Michael Walzer and others).

Phillips, D. (1993) *Looking Backward: A Critical Appraisal of Communitarian Thought*, Princeton, NJ: Princeton University Press. (An unsympathetic but wide-ranging critique of Taylor and other communitarians in favour of a version of liberalism.)

Tully, J. (ed.) (1994) *Philosophy in an Age of Pluralism*, Cambridge: Cambridge University Press. (A collection of papers, mainly concerning *The Sources of the Self*, with a reply by Taylor.)

CRAIG CALHOUN

TAYLOR, HARRIET (1807–58)

Harriet Taylor was John Stuart Mill's intellectual collaborator and great love. Married to John Taylor in 1826, Harriet met Mill in 1830 and they began a brazenly unconventional intimacy which lasted throughout her life. Her thoughts on poetry, equality, liberty and individuality shaped Mill's work on these topics.

Harriet Taylor, *née* Hardy, was born and raised in Walworth, England, where she married John Taylor in 1826. She was introduced to John Stuart MILL in 1830. At the time, she was a restless young wife and mother, deeply involved in a coterie of unitarian radicals whose liberal politics, feminism, and literary and philosophical activities suited her exactly. She had hoped to become a writer, but put aside this aspiration in order to become Mill's intellectual partner. Her amiable and generous husband acquiesced in the peculiar arrangement for her sake. In 1851, two years after Taylor's death, Taylor married Mill, and the couple lived and worked together until her death in 1858. In 1859, Mill began publishing the work of their marital collaboration, extravagantly dedicating everything to her.

Their first collaborative work was the chapter on the labouring classes in Mill's *Principles of Political Economy* (which, published in 1848, prompted an overblown dedication from Mill, discreetly pasted into a few gift copies). Taylor also directed his work on the writings later published as *Three Essays on Religion* (1874). In 1851, she wrote 'The Enfranchisement of Women', which argued for full equality between the sexes with special emphasis on educational reform and equal access to employment. Taylor's greatest claim to lasting importance stems from her role in the writing of *On Liberty* (1859), which Mill later called 'more directly and literally our

joint production than anything else which bears my name' (Mill 1873: 249).

Unfortunately, Mill's sober record of Taylor's contributions has been rendered suspect by the hallucinatory lavishness of his praise of her powers. The questions surrounding their collaboration, however, do not concern Taylor's personal attributes, but the extent and nature of her contribution to Mill's work. Her own writing does not settle those questions definitively.

Most of the relevant letters, essays and notes in Taylor's solitary corpus are allusive supplements to ongoing dialogue with Mill. Some of this writing supports Mill's account of her work. Taylor's paragraphs on marriage (*c.*1832, Hayek 1951) are echoed in 'The Subjection of Women' (1869) and the distinctive themes in *On Liberty* first appear in her essay on toleration (*c.*1832, Hayek 1951). There she treats social conformity as a great evil which breeds injustice, stifles individuality and discourages character development. She charges that the indolent acceptance of popular opinion leaves people with baseless conviction and neither the patience nor skills needed to acquire genuine knowledge. She complains that independent thinkers must contend with ignorant majorities. Her arguments are weak, but her whole mode of thought on these topics informs *On Liberty*.

Mill's corpus sometimes seems to split irreconcilably in two, and Taylor's influence may have caused the apparent fissure. Perhaps the author of *On Liberty*, 'The Subjection of Women' and various writings on art and society was the offspring of their intimacy, conceived and nurtured in their conversations.

See also: FEMINIST POLITICAL PHILOSOPHY §2

List of works

Hayek, F.A. (ed.) (1951) *John Stuart Mill and Harriet Taylor: Their Friendship and Subsequent Marriage*, Chicago, IL: University of Chicago Press. (The standard collection of their correspondence, which includes Harriet's poems and early essays on marriage and toleration, sometimes catalogued with 'J.S. Mill' listed as author.)

Rossi, A. (ed.) (1970) *Essays on Sex Equality*, Chicago, IL: University of Chicago Press. (Contains Taylor's essays on marriage, 'The Enfranchisement of Women' (1851) and 'The Subjection of Women' (1869) with an excellent critical preface by Alice Rossi.)

References and further reading

Bain, A. (1882) *John Stuart Mill: A Criticism with Personal Recollections*, London: Longman, Green. (In the final chapter, 'Character and Influence', Bain takes up the question of Mill's relationship with Harriet, notes 'Mill's hallucination about his wife's genius', but supports Mill's detailed, precise account of Harriet's contributions.)

Himmelfarb, G. (1974) *On Liberty and Liberalism: The Case of John Stuart Mill*, New York: Alfred A. Knopf. (A lively, detailed examination of Mill's conflicting accounts of liberty, hostile to Harriet Taylor and supportive of Mill's claim that *On Liberty* was a joint production.)

* Mill, J.S. (1848) *Principles of Political Economy*, in *Collected Works of John Stuart Mill*, Toronto, Ont.: University of Toronto Press, vols 2–3. (Mill's work on empirical and theoretical economics as a social science.)

* —— (1859) *On Liberty*, in *Collected Works of John Stuart Mill*, Toronto, Ont.: University of Toronto Press, vol. 18: 213–310. (Mill's powerful defence of extensive civil liberties, probably co-authored by Harriet Taylor.)

* —— (1873) *Autobiography*, in *Collected Works of John Stuart Mill*, Toronto, Ont.: University of Toronto Press, vol. 1: 1–290. (Mill's oddly impersonal account of his own life, containing the sober record of Taylor's contribution to his work; the same volume of the *Collected Works* contains literary essays which betray her influence.)

* —— (1874) *Three Essays on Religion*, in *Collected Works of John Stuart Mill*, Toronto, Ont.: University of Toronto Press, vol. 10: 369–489. (Essays on religion and nature for which Taylor set topics and about which they corresponded.)

Packe, M. (1954) *The Life of John Stuart Mill*, New York: Macmillan. (An excellent biography with a superb account of Harriet Taylor's relationship with Mill.)

CANDACE A. VOGLER

TE *see* DE

TECHNOLOGY AND ETHICS

Only within the modern period have philosophers made a direct and sustained study of ethics and technology. Their work follows two philosophical traditions, each marked by distinct styles: the Continental or phenomenological tradition, and the Anglo-American or analytical tradition.

Hans Jonas (1979) articulated one of the basic premises of Continental approaches when he argued for technology as a special subject of ethics: because technology has fundamentally transformed the human condition, generating problems of global magnitude extending into the indefinite future, it calls for a new approach to ethics. Jonas' basic premise is expressed variously in the works of Karl Marx, Max Scheler, José Ortega y Gasset, Martin Heidegger and others.

Work within the Anglo-American tradition tends not to deal with technology as a whole but to be organized around particular technologies, such as computing, engineering, and medical and biological sciences. It draws on concepts and principles of traditional ethical theory at least as a starting point for analyses. Although each of the technologies has a unique set of problems, certain themes, such as responsibility, risk, equity and autonomy, are common to almost all.

Social scientists have also raised important issues for the field of ethics and technology. Their work has yielded two dominant schools of thought: technological determinism and social constructivism.

1 **Attitudes to technology**
2 **Continental discussions**
3 **Anglo-American discussions**
4 **Other approaches to ethics and technology**

1 Attitudes to technology

The history of philosophy contains two broad moral appraisals of technology. The first, implicitly present in most normative theories prior to the Renaissance, is that technological change is socially destabilizing and therefore should be delimited carefully. Without social stability, it was argued, people die even under conditions where nature is abundant, and technological change easily undermines such stability. The second, characteristic of modern ethics, is that technological change is inherently beneficial because it enhances human welfare and autonomy. Here the argument is that people suffer more from the elements than from other human beings, and that they should therefore work together to conquer nature through technological progress. These two broad ethical views further reflect opposed ideals of human life: on the one hand, an ideal of social community subordinate to nature; on the other, human autonomy and freedom from natural constraint (see TECHNOLOGY, PHILOSOPHY OF).

Only within the modern period have questions of ethics and technology been examined in detail, with two approaches emerging. One grows out of the

Continental or phenomenological tradition in philosophy, the other out of the Anglo-American analytical tradition (see ANALYTICAL PHILOSOPHY; PHENOMENOLOGICAL MOVEMENT). Continental philosophers seek to evaluate technology as a whole while Anglo-American philosophers are oriented towards piecemeal assessments of particular technologies. Continental philosophers also commonly argue that traditional ethical theories are inadequate to the moral issues presented by modern technology, whereas Anglo-American philosophers have been more comfortable adapting existing utilitarian or deontological ethical frameworks (see DEONTOLOGICAL ETHICS; UTILITARIANISM).

2 Continental discussions

Within Continental discussions, Hans Jonas has made the most sustained argument for technology as a special subject of ethics. For Jonas, ethics in premodern times could reasonably allow technology to remain in the background because technology itself had no high moral purpose. Unlike politics or religion, for instance, technology was treated as a marginal aspect of human life, one limited in both power and effect. By contrast, during the modern period technology entered the foreground of human experience. According to Francis Bacon (1620), for instance, the inventions of printing, gunpowder and the compass have done more to benefit humanity than all politics and religion. Jonas believes that because of the Baconian evaluation of technology, 'modern technology has introduced actions of such novel scale, objects, and consequences that the framework of former ethics can no longer contain them' (1984: 6). According to Jonas, 'no previous ethics had to consider the global condition of human life and the far-off future, even existence of the race. These now being an issue demands... a new conception of duties and rights, for which previous ethics... provided not even the principles' (1984: 8).

The exact way in which technology engenders an epochal transformation of the human condition is, however, open to dispute within Continental discussions. Philosophers as diverse as Karl Marx, Max Scheler, José Ortega y Gasset, and Martin Heidegger all claim that modern technology has transformed the human condition and undermined traditional moralities. But about the particular ways in which technology has altered the human lifeworld there are major disagreements. With regard to appropriate moral responses there are still further disputes.

According to Marx (1867), for instance, 'the modern science of technology' undermines traditional skills and the satisfactions of craft production, placing workers under the control of large-scale, capitalist-owned factories in which labour functions have become equal and interchangeable. The new system of production destroys a traditional social ecology in which the 'species essence' of making things benefited all social classes. Under capitalism material production unequally benefits the upper classes. This disequilibrium can be corrected only by means of a social revolution in ownership of the new technologies. The Marxist ethical assessment of industrial technology thus points up the inadequacy of the modern economic order as a means for the social control of technology, because of the way participation in that order has been restructured by technological change (see MARX, K. §4).

According to Scheler (1915), the technological transformation of the lifeworld is more than an economic phenomenon; it is also the rise and dominance of a new 'ethos of industrialism' even among technical workers themselves. Such an ethos exalts utility and instrumental values such as efficiency over vital and organic ones such as love. This is an axiological disorder that calls for cultural reformation.

For Ortega (1939), however, inherent within the modern science of technology and the ethos of industrialization there arises a moral problem that cannot be addressed by means of either Marx's social revolution or Scheler's cultural reform. Modern scientific technology, in contrast with traditional crafts, radically increases what can be done without any corresponding enhancement of ideals about what should be done. In Ortega's own formulation of the issue: in the pre-modern period, human beings acquired only very specific technical abilities, tightly coupled to particular uses, such as pottery for making pots. They never possessed any generalized technological powers. Now, however, human beings do possess technology in general without any clear idea of particular uses. To address this problem Ortega suggested a need to cultivate what he called 'techniques of the soul' such as yoga.

Undoubtedly the most influential European philosopher to address the issue of ethics and technology, even though he explicitly rejects the discipline of ethics as such, is Heidegger. Heidegger undercuts the distinction between science and technology, and argues that modern scientific technology or technoscience is not so much an ethos as a form of truth. This truth or knowledge reduces the world to *Bestand* or resources available for manipulation by a world-configuring, nihilistic destiny he calls *Gestell*. Heidegger seems at once to make ethical reflection more necessary than ever before and to destroy its very possibility (see HEIDEGGER, M. §6).

One of Heidegger's less controversial theses is the notion that science and technology are interpenetrating practices: the science of nuclear physics is as much the applied technology of cyclotrons and reactors as the technology of nuclear engineering is applied nuclear physics. To the extent that this is the case, the ethics of science tends to merge with the ethics of technology (see HEIDEGGERIAN PHILOSOPHY OF SCIENCE).

3 Anglo-American discussions

In contrast to the Continental approach, philosophers following an Anglo-American analytical tradition organize ethical discussions around particular technologies. For example, biomedical ethics includes the study of ethical implications of the use and development of advanced medical technologies (see BIOETHICS; MEDICAL ETHICS); information technology ethics (also known as computer ethics) examines social and ethical ramifications of computers and high-speed digital networks (see INFORMATION TECHNOLOGY AND ETHICS); engineering ethics studies the professional responsibilities of engineers (see ENGINEERING AND ETHICS); and environmental ethics evaluates the effects of various technologies on the natural environment (see ENVIRONMENTAL ETHICS). Work in these areas applies concepts and modes of analysis drawn from analytical moral philosophy and political theory even though, at times, the special problems of new technologies demand an extension of these concepts and methodology beyond their traditional usage.

Each sub-area of ethics and technology is marked by a distinctive community of discourse and unique set of issues. Nevertheless, a number of common themes cut across these specialized domains. Prominent among them are: equity or justice; the problem of risk; responsibility for technology; and the effect of technology on liberty and autonomy.

Historically, issues of social justice, related to the distribution of technological goods and services, were first to become a focus of moral concern. This set of issues played a major role in the nineteenth-century rise of the labour movement, socialism, and the state regulation of technology. More recently, equity issues have re-emerged in acute form in relation to biomedicine, environmental pollution and computers. On what basis should scarce medical resources such as donated or artificial organs be allocated? To what extent does protection of an environmental commons legitimately limit private ownership? How should access to information technologies be facilitated under democratic capitalist structures?

A different dimension of the problem of just distribution of technological benefits is the problem of the equitable distribution of technological costs and risks. The general problem of risk due to technology, however, goes beyond equity concerns, and is part of the more general effort of technology assessment. Technologies often have unintended consequences which, if known in advance, might have altered decisions about their adoption. These consequences may include an increase in risk. Two scholars who have especially influenced work in this area are David Collingridge (1980) and Kristin Shrader-Frechette (1991). Collingridge is well-known for his dilemma of technological (and risk) assessment: in the early development of a technology, when it is relatively easy to control its direction, we inevitably lack the knowledge to exercise reasonable control; yet by the time we have more experience and, along with it, a better understanding of the risks, control has become difficult, if not impossible. Shrader-Frechette argues that persons should not be subjected to technological risk until they have clearly understood the risk and have granted their consent without being unduly constrained by economic or other external pressures. She contends that the concept of free and informed consent as applied in the field of medicine is applicable to technology in general and ought to be a part of what guides morally grounded public policy (see RISK; RISK ASSESSMENT).

The issue of responsibility for the effects of technology involves two dominant lines of inquiry. One is concerned with the special responsibilities of technical professionals (see PROFESSIONAL ETHICS). Paul Durbin (1992), for instance, argues that engineers have an obligation to go outside their technical communities to lobby public policy, as when physicists during the 1950s and early 1960s lobbied for a worldwide ban on the atmospheric testing of nuclear weapons or when computer scientists in the United States opposed funding of the Strategic Defense Initiative (the 'Star Wars' project) in the 1980s. The second line of inquiry focuses on questions of blameworthiness and accountability when technological innovations or products cause individual or societal harms (see RESPONSIBILITY; RESPONSIBILITIES OF SCIENTISTS AND INTELLECTUALS §3).

Finally, invention and utilization of advanced technologies may be evaluated in terms of liberty and autonomy. In biomedicine, for example, in the name of liberty and autonomy, there have been numerous efforts to work out the exact parameters of free and informed consent, and then to propose ways to institutionalize them (see CONSENT). In the area of information technology, liberty and autonomy are a key to explaining normative dimensions of privacy as well as prescribing the extent of freedom of speech over the digital networks (see PRIVACY §2). Langdon Winner (1986) has discussed, in more general terms, the relationship of technology with control and autonomy by looking at ways in which the technological design process and large technical systems, such as roads, restrict human agency, affect political and personal autonomy and delimit the exercise of democratic citizenship.

4 Other approaches to ethics and technology

Political, economic, and social science studies of technology also often have ethical dimensions. For example, political science studies of the governmental regulation of technology and of law-technology relations have obvious implications for ethics. Not only public policy efforts at technology assessment, but attempts to develop scientific techniques of policy analysis ultimately reflect and influence ethical decision-making. The same is true for efforts to manage more effectively social investments in innovation at both the state and corporate levels, and even for welfare economics.

The ethical implications of social science approaches to technology centre around the issue of technological determinism, that is, the idea that technology is the primary determinant of social life, developing in an almost independent or autonomous manner. During the 1950s and 1960s, critics often opposed popular optimism about the unqualified benefits of technological progress with theories of technological determinism. Ironically, these theories almost immediately galvanized moral protest against technology. This protest was subsequently provided with theoretical justification by new studies that developed a social constructivist understanding of technological change, in which numerous agents and influences could be seen to exercise a series of micro-influences often invisible at the macro level (see TECHNOLOGY, PHILOSOPHY OF §4). Determinist and social constructivist interpretations, although apparently opposed, have quite similar moral implications. Both effectively highlight the continuing need for ethical examination of technology in a highly technological world.

References and further reading

* Bacon, F. (1620) *Novum organum* (The New Method), trans. P. Urbach and J. Gibson, La Salle, IL: Open Court, 1994, esp. book I, ch. 129. (Argues that the goal of science is not simply knowledge but technological power.)

Bijker, W.E., Hughes, T.P. and Pinch, T.J. (eds) (1987) *The Social Construction of Technological Systems,* Cambridge, MA: MIT Press. (A standard presentation of the social constructivist theory of technology.)

* Collingridge, D. (1980) *The Social Control of Technology,* New York: St Martin's Press. (Outlines the dilemma in assessing technology: by the time we know enough about a technology to want to control it, the technology has often developed so much social momentum that it is almost impossible to do so.)

* Durbin, P.T. (1992) *Social Responsibility in Science, Technology, and Medicine,* Bethlehem, PA: Lehigh University Press. (On obligations of engineers and others.)

Ellul, J. (1954) *La Technique ou L'Enjeu du Siècle,* trans. J. Wilkinson, *The Technological Society,* New York: Alfred A. Knopf, 1964. (The classic presentation of technological determinism.)

* Heidegger, M. (1954) 'Die Frage nach der Technik', in *Vorträge und Aufsätze,* Pfullingen: Neske; trans. W. Lovitt, 'The Question Concerning Technology', in *The Question Concerning Technology and Other Essays,* New York: Harper & Row, 1977. (Argues that technology is not just a neutral or instrumental means but a way of revealing the world that influences the whole life of all who are involved with it.)

Illich, I. (1973) *Tools for Conviviality,* New York: Pantheon. (Representative of the moral protest against determinism.)

Jasanoff, S. (1990) *The Fifth Branch: Science Advisers as Policymakers,* Cambridge, MA: Harvard University Press. (Examines how science and technology are regulated in an advanced industrial state.)

Jaspers, K. (1931) *Die geistige Situation der Zeit,* trans. E. Paul and C. Paul, *Man in the Modern Age,* London: Routledge, 1933. (Representative of the classical Continental attitude.)

* Jonas, H. (1979) *The Imperative of Responsibility: In Search of an Ethics for the Technological Age,* trans. H. Jonas and D. Herr, Chicago, IL: University of Chicago Press, 1984. (Enlargements of human power through technology carry with them expansions of human moral responsibility.)

Marcuse, H. (1964) *One-Dimensional Man: Studies in the Ideology of Advanced Industrial Society,* Boston, MA: Beacon Press. (Important Marxist presentation of technological determinism and moral protest.)

* Marx, K. (1867) *Das Kapital: Kritik der Politischen Ökonomie,* trans. D. Fernbach, *Capital: A Critique of Political Economy,* New York: Penguin, 3 vols, 1992, book I, ch. 13. (Critique of technology under capitalism. Includes an analysis of technology as a

new force that, along with capitalist ownership, has transformed economic life.)

* Ortega y Gasset, José (1939) *Meditación de la técnica*, Buenos Aires: Escalpe; repr. in *Obras Completas*, vol. 5, Madrid: Revista de Occidente, 2nd edn, 1950/1; trans. H. Weyl and E. Williams, 'Thoughts on Technology', in C. Mitcham and R. Mackey (eds) *Philosophy and Technology: Readings in the Philosophical Problems of Technology*, New York: Free Press, 1972. (On modernity and technology. Argues that human beings are essentially technological and that history is transformed by changes in technology.)

* Scheler, M. (1915) *Das Ressentiment im Aufbau der Moralen*, trans. W.W. Holdheim, *Ressentiment*, Milwaukee, WI: Marquette University Press, 1994, ch. 5. (Discusses 'ethos of industrialism', suggesting that the modern world is characterized by an egalitarian resentment of aristocratic achievement that also supports technology.)

* Shrader-Frechette, K.S. (1991) *Risk and Rationality: Philosophical Foundations for Populist Reforms*, Berkeley, CA: University of California Press. (The subjection of human beings to technological risks is morally legitimate only to the extent people have given their free and informed consent.)

* Winner, L. (1986) *The Whale and the Reactor: A Search for Limits in an Age of High Technology*, Chicago, IL: University of Chicago Press. (Technologies are like political constitutions in that they set up ways of life, and as such ought to be created on a democratic basis.)

CARL MITCHAM
HELEN NISSENBAUM

TECHNOLOGY, INFORMATION *see* INFORMATION TECHNOLOGY AND ETHICS

TECHNOLOGY, PHILOSOPHY OF

The philosophy of technology deals with the nature of technology and its effects on human life and society. The increasing influence of modern technology on human existence has triggered a growing interest in a philosophical analysis of technology. Nevertheless, the philosophy of technology as a coherent field of research does not yet exist. The subject covers studies from almost every branch of thinking in philosophy and deals with a great variety of topics because of a lack of consensus about the primary meaning of the term 'technology', which may, among others, refer to a collection of artifacts, a form of human action, a form of knowledge or a social process.

Among the most fundamental issues are two demarcation problems directly related to the definition of technology. The first concerns the distinction between technological (artificial) and natural objects. It involves the relation between man, nature and culture. The second pertains to the distinction between science and technology as types of knowledge. The science–technology relationship has become of central importance because of the widespread assumption that the distinguishing feature of modern technology, as compared to traditional forms of technology, is that it is science-based. Another much discussed issue is the autonomy of technology. It deals with the question of whether technology follows its own inevitable course of development, irrespective of its social, political, economic and cultural context.

1 **Philosophy and technology**
2 **Technology and artifacts**
3 **Technology as knowledge**
4 **The dynamics of technological change**

1 Philosophy and technology

The following enumeration of approaches is intended to convey an impression of the strongly fragmented field of study that goes by the name of philosophy of technology.

What is (the essence of) technology? In philosophical-anthropological studies, the starting point for answering this question is the human being and its place in and relation to nature. The human being is considered to be a defective animal that is dependent on technology for its survival; technology becomes the substitute for biological shortcomings and is therefore determined to a large degree by the nature of these shortcomings. For Heidegger (1977) such a characterization of the essence of technology is not sufficient; an answer at the metaphysical level is also needed. For him the essence of technology is not that it is a means to some end: technology brings to the fore what was hidden and does not by itself present itself (see HEIDEGGER, M. §6; HEIDEGGERIAN PHILOSOPHY OF SCIENCE). In Dessauer's (1927) metaphysical approach, invention is the essence of technology and the ontological conditions that make invention possible are explored.

The social philosophy of technology focuses on the relations between (specific forms of) technology and social, economic and political structures. It analyses technological development as a social process and addresses the problem of how to control its development. One of the key problems in this field is whether technological development is primarily determined by its context (social shaping of technology), or whether technology determines the social context including its systems of norms and values (a position often attributed to Marx). In the latter case, the idea of a technocratic society emerges in which technological rationality imposes itself on all domains of social life (technology as an ideology (Habermas 1968); see HABERMAS, J. §1).

Ethical studies take a prominent place in the philosophy of technology. New technological possibilities for human intervention create new moral problems. Do these require new ethical principles? Arguments in favour are based mostly on the idea that modern, science-based technology is essentially different from earlier forms of technology (the crafts), and that its impact on man and nature is of a different order (for example, the consequences of applying modern technology are no longer limited in space and time (Jonas 1984)). Another issue in this field concerns the claim that technology itself, as a system of means, is ethically neutral. Arguments against the neutrality thesis attempt to show that the conception of technology as a mere system of means is inadequate, because its impact on human life stretches much further: it replaces the natural with an artificial environment (see TECHNOLOGY AND ETHICS).

The so-called 'analytical philosophy of technology' (Rapp 1974) shows a strong focus on epistemological and methodological problems of technology, particularly of the engineering sciences. These problems have long been neglected, because of the widespread idea that technology is applied science. A specific feature of this approach is that it takes into account the various types and stages of technology and its concrete historical form of appearance. Key topics are the nature of technological knowledge, the nature of engineering design, design methodology and the relation between science and technology. Its main disciplinary sources are, besides philosophy, technology itself and the history of technology.

2 Technology and artifacts

The usual conception of technology is that it is the transformation or manipulation of nature (the existing physical (material) and biological environments) to satisfy human needs and goals. Technology is thus conceived to be a specific form of purposeful (teleological) action, that may result in a 'technological artefact': a human-made object or state of affairs that fulfils a utilitarian or practical function. The transformation of nature may or may not itself be mediated by artifacts, which are then called tools (see TELEOLOGY).

This conception of technology raises many questions. On the one hand, it appears too restrictive, for it does not fit certain domains which are considered to belong to modern technology, such as software engineering which deals with the transformation of something immaterial (information). On the other hand, it is too broad, since it makes any object or state of affairs which satisfies a practical need, and is the result of intentional human intervention in nature, a technological artefact (for example, a wild tree planted deliberately at a certain place to provide shadow, or an organism with a slightly modified genetic structure).

The demarcation problem – what kind of action constitutes a technological action and what kind of objects or states of affairs are technological artifacts? – remains an open issue. Not only is the distinction between the technological and the artificial problematic, but also that between the artificial and the natural. The latter raises fundamental philosophical issues about the relation between the human race and nature. The distinction makes sense only if the human race is considered in some respect not to be part of nature. As an integral part of nature (and as a result of natural evolution), a human being cannot interfere with nature. The distinction between the natural and the artificial is commonly taken to be identical to the distinction between the spontaneous and the intentional; these notions themselves, however, raise all kinds of philosophical problems (see ENVIRONMENTAL ETHICS §4).

Similar questions arise when technological artifacts are characterized as objects that perform practical functions on the basis of *human designs*. In technology a design is taken to be a pattern or scheme that describes the structure and mode of operation of a system and shows how a given practical aim or function may be realized. The notion of design stresses the inherently intentional/teleological nature of technological artifacts. The distinctive feature of technological artifacts as compared to objects from nature remains problematic, however. Is the difference primarily a genetic one (produced by humans or by nature), or is it more fundamental in the sense that the attribution of a design to objects of nature is meaningless (as in the modern scientific conception of nature)? These questions inevitably lead to issues in the philosophy of nature.

3 Technology as knowledge

For Aristotle science and technology belonged to two different spheres of human experience (contemplation versus productive action) and constituted two different forms of knowledge (theoretical versus practical knowledge). Scientific knowledge was, moreover, not inherently relevant for solving technological problems (see ARISTOTLE §6). Modern technology and science, however, have merged to such a degree that even the demarcation between them has become problematic. Modern technology is science-based (and modern science, technology-based) and alongside the traditional natural sciences engineering sciences have established themselves. The so-called 'scientification of technology' is generally considered to be the characteristic feature of modern technology that is directly related to its prominent role in society. This has directed attention to the problem of the relation between science and technology and how science has altered the nature of technology. From a cognitive point of view, the nature of technological knowledge and its relation to scientific knowledge is at issue.

One of the most influential models for the science–technology relationship has been the technology-is-applied-science model. It stresses that technology, in contrast to the traditional crafts, is as theory-laden as science and that it applies scientific theories to systems which are of practical use. It considers technological knowledge to be a derivative kind of scientific knowledge. This model has been criticized severely. It is historically inadequate because it makes technological progress wholly dependent on scientific development. From a cognitive point of view it is highly problematic because it assumes that there is a logically deductive path from scientific knowledge (theories) to technological designs.

A generally accepted alternative for the technology-is-applied-science model is, however, still missing. A strong case could be made for considering technological knowledge, with respect to scientific knowledge, to be a form of knowledge *sui generis*, which deals with the design and production of artifacts. One of the considerations in favour of such a view concerns the fact that the criteria for evaluating cognitive claims are fundamentally different in the two domains.

In its most basic form technological knowledge is prescriptive; it consists of procedures (rules) which describe actions that have to be performed in order to achieve practical ends. Often, an adequate performance of these actions requires practical skills; these also constitute a form of technological knowledge, which, however, cannot be expressed in terms of prescriptions in language. The first criterion for evaluating a procedure that purports to solve a technological problem is its *effectiveness*: does the procedure bring about the desired state of affairs? The second criterion for assessing a solution is its degree of *efficiency*: is it possible to bring about the desired state of affairs in a better way, that is, with less effort or costs. (In general, measures of efficiency are based on quantitative comparisons of input and output of technological systems.) In modern technology, the notion of efficiency plays a dominant role, and the evaluation of the efficiency of artifacts is often carried out with theoretical means; at this point scientific theories about the operative principles of an artefact turn out to be of great value.

While efficiency, effectiveness, and other criteria like durability, costs, manufacturability, safety and utility, are key notions in the structure of thinking in technology, they play almost no role in science, because scientific knowledge is primarily descriptive and explanatory. Among its principal evaluative criteria we find truth, empirical adequacy and explanatory power. This difference in basic concepts for interpreting and evaluating knowledge claims strongly supports the idea that two different forms of knowledge (and of rationality) are involved in science and technology. Further insight into the characteristic features of technological knowledge, that is, in the epistemology of technology, has to come from detailed case studies (Vincenti 1990).

4 The dynamics of technological change

A recurrent theme in the philosophy of technology is the autonomy of technological development relative to its social embedding. It concerns the dynamics of technological change. This is an extremely complex topic since technological innovation, in its various stages from design, development, production and diffusion, is influenced by very heterogeneous factors (cognitive, economic, social, political, military, geographic, cultural, and so on). Views on the dynamics of technological change tend to show strong reductionistic tenets by taking one of these factors as the prime mover of technological change. Well-known illustrations are 'technological determinism' and 'social constructivist interpretations of technology'. According to technological determinism technology itself is the prime mover; this view maintains that technology follows its own intrinsic course of evolution to which society has to adapt; it is self-determinative with increase of efficiency as one of its main dynamical principles. So there is no room for alternative forms of technology. Social constructivist interpretations of technology, on the other hand, claim that technology is to a large degree, or even completely, socially determined (see CONSTRUCTIVISM).

In order to uncover some of the basic assumptions underlying these ideas we will briefly examine the shaping of artifacts in the design phase. The final form of an artifact is schematically determined by two kinds of constraint. On the one hand, there is the list of specifications which describes all kinds of requirements the artefact should fulfil. This heterogeneous list may contain, among others, constraints derived from the primary technological function of the artefact, the conditions under which this function has to be performed in practice (for instance, safety regulations), the conditions under which the artifact has to be produced (for example, mass production), its price, standards and norms. The defining feature of this list is that it is the outcome of a process of negotiation between all parties with some interest in the artefact; it contains social or contextual constraints, which are imposed by convention. On the other hand, there is a list of technological constraints, constraints due to what is, as a matter of fact, physically and technically possible (this list may, of course, change over time). The desired artefact should satisfy both lists of constraints, but because of conflicts this is often not possible in practice. Such conflicts can be resolved, again schematically, by adapting the list of specifications or by creating new technological possibilities.

According to this conception of the design process, the driving force behind technological change is the tension between two lists of constraints which are different in nature (one describing what is desirable, the other what is possible) and in principle independent of each other. Defenders of the autonomy of technology reject this independence; they assume that the list of specifications is determined primarily by technological constraints ('what can be done, will be done'). The decisions leading up to the list of specifications are supposed to be dictated by technological imperatives (technological rationality). Social constructivists, on their part, tend to deny any difference in nature between the two types of constraint: they assume that physical and technological constraints are socially constructed in ways similar to the constraints contained in the list of specifications.

These assumptions may be criticized on philosophical grounds, but much more important for the assessment of these views is that the issue of the autonomy of technology is not to be settled by philosophical arguments alone. Models for the dynamics of technological change (with their underlying philosophical assumptions) must prove their value in empirical research, particularly in the history of technology. Generally speaking, a 'historical-empirical turn' in the philosophy of technology might prove to be fruitful for developing more adequate conceptual schemes for interpreting technology and its development.

See also: FUNCTIONAL EXPLANATION; GENDER AND SCIENCE §5; MARXIST PHILOSOPHY OF SCIENCE; RISK ASSESSMENT

References and further reading

The following list contains works on philosophy of technology at a general level and at a more advanced level.

Bijker, W.E., Hughes, T.P. and Pinch, T.J. (eds) (1989) *The Social Construction of Technological Systems*, Cambridge, MA: MIT Press. (Contains contributions which interpret technology from a social constructivist point of view. See §4.)

* Dessauer, F. (1927) *Philosophie der Technik* (Philosophy of Technology), Bonn: Cohen. (Metaphysical analysis of invention as the core activity of technology. See §1.)

* Habermas, J. (1968) *Technik und Wissenschaft als 'Ideologie'* (Technology and Science as 'Ideology'), Frankfurt: Suhrkamp. (Analysis of the ideological character of technology and science. See §1.)

* Heidegger, M. (1977) *The Question Concerning Technology and other Essays*, trans. W. Lovitt, New York: Harper & Row. (Generally considered to be the most outstanding metaphysical analysis of technology. See §1.)

* Jonas, H. (1984) *The Imperative of Responsibility: In Search of an Ethics for the Technological Age*, Chicago, IL: University of Chicago Press. (Argues that modern technology requires a new ethics based on the notion of responsibility. See §1.)

Philosophy and Technology (1983–93) Society for Philosophy of Technology, 10 vols. (Official publication of the society for philosophy of technology; vols 6 and 7 discuss various interpretations and approaches in the philosophy of technology.)

* Rapp, F. (ed.) (1974) *Contributions to a Philosophy of Technology*, Dordrecht: Reidel. (This anthology marks the beginning of the analytical philosophy of technology and addresses mainly methodological and epistemological issues. See §1.)

Research in Philosophy and Technology (1978–93) Greenwich, CT: JAI Press, vols 1–13. (For a long time the only regular publication in the field; its content illustrates the diversity of approaches and of topics addressed in the philosophy of technology.

Several volumes contain extensive bibliographies on various topics in the philosophy of technology.)

Staudenmaier, J.M. (1985) *Technology's Storytellers*, Cambridge, MA: MIT Press. (Contains an extensive discussion of attempts by historians and philosophers of science and technology to analyse the relationship between science and technology and of the debate over technological determinism. See §5.)

* Vincenti, W.G. (1990) *What Engineers Know and How They Know It: Analytical Studies from Aeronautical History*, Baltimore, MD: Johns Hopkins University Press. (Contains detailed studies of the nature of technological knowledge and its use and generation by engineers. See §3.)

PETER KROES

TEILHARD DE CHARDIN, PIERRE (1881–1955)

Pierre Teilhard de Chardin taught that the evolutionary process is governed by a 'law of complexification' which dictates that inorganic matter will reach ever more complex forms, resulting in inorganic matter being followed by organic matter and organic matter being followed by conscious life forms. Viewed by observers, humans are material systems within a larger physical system. Viewed introspectively, a human being is a self-conscious creature possessed of freedom and rationality, with the capacity for action and inquiry. Each element in the world has some form of this dual 'exterior' aspect and 'interior' aspect, though consciousness arises only late in the evolutionary history. Teilhard de Chardin saw neither reason to doubt that matter can give rise to mind, nor any basis for reducing mind to matter. The prospects for humanity are gratifying, as evolution, following the law of complexification with the cooperation of human choice, moves to an Omega point at which Christ's fullness will include as his 'body' a unified humanity that is at peace.

Scientific critics of Teilhard de Chardin's theory have charged that his optimism involves extrapolation far beyond what the present evidence warrants. Theological critics have argued that he does not sufficiently consider the degree of evil in the world; optimism can only be justified if we assume that evil can be redeemed by transcendent divine action, because immanent evolutionary processes may not suffice.

1 Life
2 Priest and scientist
3 Optimism and evolution
4 Beginning and goal
5 Criticisms

1 Life

Pierre Teilhard de Chardin, the fourth of eleven children, received his secondary education at the Collège Notre-Dame at Mongré, and, at eighteen, entered the Society of Jesus. He read Bergson's writings, and an association with Eduard Le Roy, a Bergsonian scholar, deepened the Bergsonian influence on Teilhard de Chardin's thought. While his views often sparked keen dissent within the Church, he remained a Jesuit and a loyal Catholic. Repeated requests to the Church for permission to publish his best-known work, *Le Phénomène humaine* (1953), were refused, and it was published only posthumously. He sought a way to unite his 'love for God' and his 'love for the world'. The product was not merely a view which sanctions the dignity of scientific endeavour, but a complex worldview in which cosmic evolution is the process by which God brings into being a 'fullness of Christ' that includes a morally and spiritually mature humanity and a fully developed natural environment.

Teilhard de Chardin taught in the Jesuit College in Cairo (1906–8), served in the First World War, and taught at the Catholic Institute in Paris; when he was fired from this post, he travelled to China. He was a distinguished geologist and palaeontologist, especially concerned with human prehistory, and in China participated in the palaeontological researches surrounding the discovery of Peking Man. He was associated with many expeditions and became director of the research office of the Centre National de la Recherche Scientifique in Paris. After the Second World War, he was offered a chair at the Collège de France, but instead went to New York, where he was made permanent assistant at the Wenner-Gren Foundation for Anthropological Research. He was an Honorary Fellow of the Royal Anthropological Society of Great Britain, and an honorary member of the Academy of Sciences of New York, as well as a member of the French Academy of Sciences and the American Association for Geology.

2 Priest and scientist

It was Teilhard de Chardin's goal to find for himself, and then share with others, a worldview that unified his theological beliefs as a Catholic and professional beliefs as a scientist. He thus developed a synthesis of Catholic theology and evolutionary theory which he claimed was satisfactorily founded in evidence and reason. In it, he rightly remarked, the traditional juridical and political terms in which much of Catholic thought had come to be classically expressed were replaced by terms derived from the natural sciences, although he extended them beyond their native home in scientific theory. It would seem that he thought these terms received much less stretching at his hands than many of his readers, both scientists and theologians, suppose.

It seems clear as well that while Teilhard de Chardin had apologetic interests – he wanted to argue for his faith – and communication interests – he wanted his faith to be intelligible to modern readers – he had a more basic motivation. He thought that his newly crafted worldview was a natural and appropriate convergence of the picture of the world presented descriptively by evolutionary science, and the doctrines of an orthodox (if nontraditionally stated) Catholicism; his main reason for presenting his worldview was that he thought it was true.

Teilhard de Chardin described his intellectual project as providing a phenomenology of the physical universe – a description of the universe that arises from and is justified by what the natural sciences have discovered the world to be. The resulting account of things has a surprising consequence. Included in his notion of a phenomenology is that it should say what the functions of the phenomena are and give an account of the purposiveness that phenomena actually exhibit. His account of the function and purpose of the evolutionary process is, of course, controversial. He contends, for example, that since the evolutionary process has plainly produced human beings, and we see no new species on the horizon to replace them, it is in humanity that we find the best clue to understanding the process. This in effect involves him in thinking in terms of final as well as efficient causes (to put the matter in traditional language), and in viewing this as part of what is properly included in a phenomenology that is scientifically based.

Teilhard de Chardin viewed the universe in both theistic and evolutionary terms; the world owes its existence and structure to God, and God is immanent in it. The universe is an immense organic whole which is driven by its inner energies toward greater and greater order and complexity. His notion of evolution is cosmic, not simply biological; within the framework of his evolutionary theory there appear not only mutating forms of life but also inorganic matter and, ultimately, social and cultural systems.

3 Optimism and evolution

Much has been written about the medieval view of an orderly universe, quite limited in scope, created for human habitation, and centred on our earth, whose plants and animals served human ends. Earth was a rather manageable habitation which served its resident landlords rather well as a temporary home until their real home was reached in the afterlife. Then astronomers revealed the vastness of the universe, physicists discovered that the same laws applied beyond the moon as applied below it and that the universe is a vast machine, biologists found a minuscule universe of a vastness comparable to the macrocosm, Darwin robbed humanity of its uniqueness, and Freud stole from humanity its fundamental rationality. The result is a universe in which human beings live a precarious unfree existence in a natural environment that is at best neutral, while beset with inner forces that threaten what sanity they possess as they wait for entropy to wind things down.

Without considering how accurate all this is, either as regards medieval or modern thought, perhaps the broad strokes of the preceding paragraph give some sense of what Teilhard de Chardin was fighting. He insisted that the very evolutionary theory that played a significant role in questioning the uniqueness and hence special worth of human beings, when properly understood and articulated, restored that very uniqueness and worth. He denied that the universe was machinelike, static, deterministic, neutral or unfriendly to human existence, or doomed to an inelegant ending. He held that humanity is an entirely natural denizen of the world without thinking that the existence of human beings is to be naturalistically explained – not, at any rate, if 'being naturalistically explained' denies either human rational and volitional transcendence of determining conditions or theological explanation of the evolutionary process.

Teilhard de Chardin suggested that the earth's history has three phases. First, there is the cooling of the earth's crust and the presence of inorganic matter. In the second stage, organic matter arises as life emerges and diversifies. The third stage begins with the appearance of mind. Geosphere is succeeded by biosphere, biosphere is followed by noosphere. While the first stage leads naturally to the second, and the second to the third, both later stages none the less contain something qualitatively new. In the third stage, there is a qualitative shift in the nature of the evolutionary process itself as the products of evolution become capable of contributing to, and potentially directing, the future of the process.

Humanity, Teilhard de Chardin held, is 'separated [from the other elements of the evolutionary process] by a chasm – or a threshold – which it cannot cross. Because we are reflective we are not only different but quite other. It is not a matter of change of degree, but a change of nature, resulting from a change of state'

([1953] 1959: 165–6). Thus the evolutionary process exhibits discontinuity within continuity in an ascent from less to more organized forms of matter. Material synthesis and complexity are viewed as one aspect of the same stuff that, in its highly complex versions, has intellectual and spiritual capacity as another aspect.

4 Beginning and goal

Teilhard de Chardin saw human beings as both the end or goal of the evolutionary process and as a new evolutionary beginning, not to be replaced by a new species. Evolution now and in future is a process under new rules; humans act freely in the context of natural laws, rather than one nonintelligent event following another. Without supposing that detailed projections are possible, he took the future to be the key to the past and believed that science justifies an optimistic forecast of the future of humanity. It is likely that this optimism, grounded at least in intent in a rationally developed worldview, is part of the explanation for the enthusiasm Teilhard de Chardin's views often elicit.

Currently, humanity experiences diverse cultures and forms of intellectual life; it is an often warring, significantly immature species. None the less, humanity's capacity for self-conscious thought and action provides a new layer or sphere on the surface of the earth – a 'noosphere' that is the unique environment of human beings, shared not even with the highest nonhuman animals. This sphere too is subject to the law of complexification, and thus there will be a cultural unification in which humans learn to live in love and peace. When this 'Omega point' is reached, a united humanity will serve as the body of Christ, and Christ will have achieved the fullness that it has been the point of evolution to produce.

It follows from Teilhard de Chardin's views that it is important to understand the world in terms of theistic cosmic evolution. While there are powerful tendencies to 'complexification' in nature, once human beings arrive on the scene there is in principle the possibility of their acting sufficiently unwisely or wickedly as to postpone, diminish or even prevent the arrival of the Omega point. After all, according to Teilhard de Chardin's view (though this is certainly not unique to his perspective), the course of evolution is now significantly in human hands; none the less, it is plainly his view that optimism is justified concerning the prospects of the Omega point actually being reached. The later chapters of the book of evolution seem sure to be happy ones.

For Teilhard de Chardin, Christ himself is primarily the Cosmic Goal of the evolutionary process ('Christ' here is intended to refer to both the Second Person of the Christian trinity and his 'body' of collective mature humanity). The redemption that Christ provides according to the Christian message is seen in cosmic as well as individual terms, and for Teilhard de Chardin, these cosmic terms are seen along the lines of a gradual and predictable change for the better, and are conceived more in terms of immanence than transcendence.

5 Criticisms

Teilhard de Chardin's scientific critics, even those who agree that the course of evolution is now partly under human management, find in rising population, environmental pollution and decreasing resources significant grounds for being dubious about evolutionary optimism. They worry that entropy in the long run will end human life and that increasing specialization will diminish the quality of life. Most fundamentally, they find in Teilhard de Chardin's perspective an extrapolation that goes far beyond anything they discover in actual science, and are unconvinced that anyone who follows his lead will thereby be walking in the overall direction (if any) suggested by scientific conclusions. Thus they see little or no justification in actual scientific theory for Teilhard de Chardin's Christian cosmic evolutionism.

Theological critics (for example, Smulders 1967 and Thielicke 1964) have worried that the 'in principle' possibility of human evil, manifested individually and institutionally, might not be too deep for real confidence in any immanent process leading to a cosmic kingdom of God. They view Teilhard de Chardin as taking altogether insufficient account of the depth of evil in the human heart and in the institutions that we have created. It seems to them all too likely that the outcome will be at least no better than what we currently experience unless there is special divine intervention of a sort not really in the spirit of his theory.

Teilhard de Chardin sees sin as an inevitable feature of the evolutionary process, which is to be overcome as the law of complexification works in concert with right human choices and actions. This seems to his critics to involve a sort of self-healing theory of the universe in which they have no great confidence. Much of the Christian tradition has insisted on a significantly greater role for transcendent divine action than seems evident in, or consistent with, Teilhard de Chardin's conception of things. For most of that tradition, the Fall is neither a fall 'up' towards maturity, nor an inevitable part of a process that leads upward. It has thought in terms of people, and often also of nature, as needing regeneration, not merely time to develop. Its optimism rests more on faith and hope in the activities of a transcendent Saviour than on faith in the progressive unfolding of immanent principles built by the Creator into the creation. Thus Teilhard de Chardin's Christian critics stress that the problem that Christ came to deal with was our sin, which includes not only individual wrong actions knowingly performed, but a commitment to a style of life centred on our own apparent advantage in disregard to the will of God and the good of others. Christ is thus the Saviour who dies for our sins and rises again for our justification, the Judge who condemns both sin and the unrepentant sinner who clings to sinfulness and rejects forgiveness and grace, and the Lord of all Creation. The Christian critics argue that Teilhard de Chardin subordinates the roles of Saviour and Judge to that of Lord of Nature in a way that trims the sails of Christian doctrine to fit the masts of evolutionary optimism.

At times asserting that his views arose naturally and with considerable evidential support from the data of science, Teilhard de Chardin at other times emphasized the tentative and partial nature of his perspective. At the least, he coherently placed a massive amount of scientific data within a theological perspective that most of his colleagues had dismissed or ignored, and (perhaps not altogether intentionally) illustrated the fact that scientific data, as philosophers of science say, 'underdetermine' the world views based on them.

See also: RELIGION AND SCIENCE §§4–5

List of works

Teilhard de Chardin, P. (1955) *Le Phénomène humaine*, Paris: Éditions de Seuil; trans. B. Wall, *The Phenomenon of Man*, London: Collins, 1959. (This is Teilhard de Chardin's *magnum opus*, in which he endeavours to unify the data of science and the data of the Christian revelation.)
—— (1956) *L'Apparition de l'homme*, Paris: Éditions de Seuil; trans. J.M. Cohen, *The Appearance of Man*, London: Collins, 1965. (Teilhard de Chardin here offers his views on the evolutionary rise of humanity.)
—— (1959) *L'Avenir de l'homme*, Paris: Éditions de Seuil; trans. N. Denny, *The Future of Man*, London: Collins, 1964. (Teilhard de Chardin's vision of the future of humanity and the world.)

References and further reading

Cuenot, C. (1965) *Teilhard de Chardin*, London and Baltimore, MD: Burns, Oates & Helicon. (A substantial biography.)

Lubac, H. de (1962) *La Pensée religieuse du Père Teilhard de Chardin*, Paris: Éditions Montaigne; trans. R. Hague, *The Religion of Teilhard de Chardin*, London: Collins, 1967. (Includes an appendix of letters by Teilhard de Chardin.)
Smulders, P. (1967) *The Design of Teilhard de Chardin*, Westminster, MD: Newman Press. (Examines the theological implications of Teilhard de Chardin's views.)
Thielicke, H. (1964) *Mensch Sein – Mensch Werden*, Munich: R. Piper Verlag; *Being Human... Becoming Human*, Garden City, NY: Doubleday, 1976. (Contains a theological critique of Teilhard de Chardin, and reviews a scientific critique.)
Wilders, N.M. (1963) *Teilhard de Chardin: Eeninleiding in zijn denken*, Antwerp and Amsterdam: N.V. Standaard-Boekhandel Uitgeversmaatschappij; trans. H. Hoskins, *An Introduction to Teilhard de Chardin*, New York: Harper & Row, 1963. (An accessible, sympathetic discussion of Teilhard de Chardin's perspective.)
—— (1966) *Teilhard de Chardin and the Mystery of Christ*, London: Collins. (Endeavours to exhibit Teilhard's thought as a single system.)

KEITH E. YANDELL

TEL QUEL SCHOOL

Tel Quel was a review published in Paris from 1960 to 1982. Under the direction of Philippe Sollers, it became a key source of avant-garde work in literature and critical theory. Concerned with the relations between art and politics, the Tel Quel group drew on semiotics, psychoanalysis and Marxism as the bases for an overall theory that would establish writing – écriture – as having its own specific and necessary revolutionary force. Influential in its emphasis on literary practices seen as breaking with the given social ordering of 'reality' and 'subject' (the 'limit-texts' of writers such as Sade or Artaud), the review emphasized textuality, the condition of all fields of knowledge as textual productions. Less a coherent school of thought than a site of shifting theoretical-political interventions and new explorations in writing, Tel Quel was at its most powerful in the late 1960s and early 1970s.

1 History
2 Theory

1 History

Founded in 1960 by a handful of young writers under

291

the auspices of the French publishing house *Editions du Seuil*, *Tel Quel* was a review appearing quarterly until 1982. Purely literary concerns quickly gave way to attempts to define a specific role for literature as a factor in social change and to explore possible alliances with existing political formations. In the late 1960s, while elaborating a revolutionary cultural theory of writing and its practice, the review drew close to the French Communist Party (*PCF*), espousing many of its positions. In 1969 there was a shift to criticism of the Party's 'revisionism', with *Tel Quel* asserting a Marxism-Leninism of which Maoism and the Chinese Cultural Revolution were regarded as the authentic contemporary manifestation. The final break with the *PCF* came in 1971, with some members of the review's board forming the *Mouvement de Juin 1971* which briefly issued *Tel Quel Informations*, a bulletin devoted to violent criticism of the *PCF* and unbridled celebration of the People's Republic. A *Tel Quel* delegation visited China in 1974 but the visit coincided with, and contributed to, a disaffection with Communism that led in 1976 to dissociation from the Chinese model and the 'Marxist church'. Communism and the 'myths' of the left now became the object of the review's combat, with dissidence valued as the epitome of literature's purpose. *Tel Quel* ended in 1982, only to be resurrected as *L'Infini*.

The core members of the editorial board were Philippe Sollers, Marcelin Pleynet and Julia Kristeva. Jacques Derrida was a decisive contributor in the 1960s and Roland Barthes a major one throughout. A series of books – the '*Collection Tel Quel*' – was linked with the review, which also instigated various cultural events.

2 Theory

Tel Quel's initial orientation was determinedly literary, in opposition to Sartrean existentialism and the demand for *littérature engagée* (literature as an instrument of social commitment). Stating its aim to be a clear understanding of 'the powers of writing', the review began with a vaguely romantic declaration of literature's value and a determination to free it from moral and political imperatives: literature was to be taken on its own necessary terms as the mode of discovery of the world as sensory whole. Surrealism was acknowledged as a significant historical precedent but also as a movement in relation to which the review sought to make its own distinct advance.

Consideration of writing's powers and of the nature of its realization of the world 'as is' (the sense of the review's title) was undertaken both through an analysis of literary forms and through an engagement with bodies of writing that questioned given conventions. An immediate reference was to the critique of the traditional terms of the novel represented by the *nouveau roman* and notably to the work of Alain Robbe-Grillet, itself critical of Sartre's instrumentalization of literature and self-reflexively involved in the showing up of conventional fictional structures. The nouveau roman, however, was soon repudiated as complicit with old assumptions, as once more referring literature to the representation of a reality projected as external to its writing, whether physical ('realism') or mental ('psychologism'). Hence the contrary importance of 'limit-texts' that disturb the homogeneity of reality in its accepted forms, subverting representational coherence, subject unity and the notion of a truth outside linguistic constructions: Sade and Artaud, Lautréamont and BATAILLE were read as inscribing within the Western tradition a permanent refusal of the comforts of any such 'truth'. The force of literature was defined as exactly that refusal, its practice as a radical knowledge of the tissue of fictions in which we and our world are 'made up'.

To take literature in this way was to break with ideas of it as the expression of universal ('human') meanings and values, and to assign to it a fundamental role for change. Literature and politics were seen as interdependent, not in terms of the former's subordination to the latter (submission to imperatives again), but in as much as literature – in *Tel Quel*'s avant-garde version of its excessive practice – was understood as a condition of political transformation: no economic and social revolution without symbolic revolution. Surrealism's weakness was identified precisely as its failure scientifically to make the link between revolution and writing – it lacked the textual theory that from the mid-1960s to the mid-1970s became *Tel Quel*'s purpose to provide.

The beginnings of the theory were in structuralism and semiotics: the analysis of the underlying structures of cultural phenomena grasped as systems of signs seemed to offer a possible science of literature rid of any idea of the latter as externally derived (works as originating in a reality they represent or an author they express). Confronted, however, with the experience of writing realized in the limit-texts, as in the *Tel Quel* group's own novels and poetry, structuralism appeared as based on a static conception of structure which, while effectively serving to remove the subject as consciousness from any central and founding position, ended in an ahistorical 'objectivity'. If everything is only signs, structuralism's metalinguistic certainty of structures to be perceived through the agency of its analyses is itself in question. The recognition semiotics should provoke is that there can be no mastery of language since language includes – is constitutive of – the subject assuming such mastery. A science of literature must work with just this recognition which is, indeed, literature's own troubling power and so its challenge to any science or knowledge classically conceived (in terms of a closure of textual production, of the elimination precisely of all 'literariness' of language).

Crucial here was the work of Jacques Derrida with its development of an idea of writing – tracing of differences – as the structuring condition of presence (see DERRIDA, J. §2). There is nothing without writing, no 'outside-text' in the sense of some instance to which a text could be referred that would not itself be textual. Derrida's critique of the Western conception of the sign as underpinning a continual denial of writing (the signified received as having an identity distinct from the signifier) could be given an explicit political thrust when carried over to the understanding of ideologies as systems masking textuality and the production of posited 'grounds' of meaning. The struggle against what *Tel Quel* called 'the hypostasized result of a genesis effaced' and the retrieval of the materiality of the signifying process determined the ambition of the group's textual theory: 'a kind of permanent writing' that would break down the discursive orders of social intelligibility and accede to 'the figured truth of the world'. The *semanalysis* of J. KRISTEVA reformulated semiotics in these terms, pushing it beyond the study of sign systems into that of signifying practices, demanding an attention each time to the production of meaning and subject involved.

Tel Quel was thus characterized by a militant critique of representation for its containment of textual productivity but this critique was characterized in turn by the resolve not to be caught thereby in the position of accounting language the only reality. Against such idealism, *Tel Quel* proposed a 'semantic materialism': a text – any representation, discourse, piece of literature, philosophy or whatever – is never derived or justified from a point outside of textuality *and* there is a heterogeneous material reality inscribed in the subject's production in and through textuality that is at once social and psycho-sexual. The review thus took as its necessary task the articulation of historical materialism (using the work of Louis ALTHUSSER) and psychoanalysis (using that of Jacques LACAN) within a general theory of this textual process of the production together of subject-history-desire.

By 1977, belated disillusionment with existing Communist societies had shifted the review into distrust of any political vision of the world and the conviction of the impossibility of revolution. With Freud's pessimism concerning the human psyche defeating Marx's optimism regarding social transformation, the limit-texts were again important, read as engaging the impasses of sexuality and subjectivity, as exploding the dangerously deluded Enlightenment ideas of reason and progress to which political projects like Marxism refer. To these texts were now added the literary testimonies of the modern dissidents (Alexander Solzhenitsyn in particular). *Tel Quel*'s conception of writing was discharged of political terms and returned to an insistence on literature's value in itself as the fundamental site of freedom, dissidently marginal to all establishments of meaning.

Throughout the changes and reversals in the review's positions, what remained constant was the will to propose literature as a vital and vitally specific force. *Tel Quel*'s significance lies in its extreme theoretical and practical exploration of the political possibilities and contradictions of such a proposition.

See also: SEMIOTICS; STRUCTURALISM

References and further reading

Forrest, P. (1995) *Histoire de Tel Quel*, Paris: Editions du Seuil. (A detailed, sympathetic account of *Tel Quel*'s intellectual history.)

Kauppi, N. (1990) *The Making of an Avant-Garde: Tel Quel*, trans. A.R Epstein, Berlin and New York: Mouton de Gruyter, 1994. (A critical examination of the socio-cultural conditions of the review's appearance, development and importance.)

Kristeva, J. (1969) Σημειωτική: *Recherches pour une sémanalyse*, Paris: Editions du Seuil, Collection *Tel Quel*. (The collection of essays in which Kristeva first defined and elaborated semanalysis.)

Sollers, P. (1968) *Logiques*, Paris: Editions du Seuil, Collection *Tel Quel*. (Readings of limit-texts as the approach to a theory of writing.)

Sollers, P. and Hayman, D. (1981) *Visionà New York*, Paris: Grasset. (In a series of interviews Sollers describes and explains the evolution of *Tel Quel* in the 1960s and 1970s.)

Suleiman, S. R. (1989) 'As is', in D. Hollier (ed.) *A New History of French Literature*, Cambridge, MA: Harvard University Press. (A succinct presentation of the review and its context.)

* *Tel Quel* (1962–82) Paris: Editions du Seuil. (The original quarterly review.)

Tel Quel (1968) *Théorie d'ensemble*, Paris: Editions du Seuil, Collection *Tel Quel*. (The fundamental collective statement, in a series of essays by members of the board, of the review's theoretical project at the moment of its greatest influence.)

STEPHEN HEATH

TELEOLOGICAL ARGUMENT
see GOD, ARGUMENTS FOR THE
EXISTENCE OF

TELEOLOGICAL ETHICS

The Greek telos *means final purpose; a teleological ethical theory explains and justifies ethical values by reference to some final purpose or good. Two different types of ethical theory have been called teleological, however. Ancient Greek theories are 'teleological' because they identify virtue with the perfection of human nature. Modern utilitarianism is 'teleological' because it defines right conduct as that which promotes the best consequences.*

Twentieth-century philosophers have distinguished ethical theories as 'teleological' or 'deontological', placing classical Greek and Roman theories alongside utilitarianism in the first category, and Kant's ethical theory together with rational intuitionism in the second. As the distinction is usually drawn, a teleologist explains the rightness or virtue of action in terms of the good realized by means of it, while a deontologist treats rightness as an independent value, and argues that we may be required to do what is right at the expense of realizing the good (see GOOD, THEORIES OF THE; RIGHT AND GOOD).

This distinction, however, obscures the difference between two different types of theories that have been called 'teleological'. Classical philosophers like PLATO and ARISTOTLE, and modern Idealists like BRADLEY and GREEN, are 'teleologists' because they believe that human nature is fully realized or perfected through the practice of virtue (see PERFECTIONISM). Virtue, according to these philosophers, is not a means to human perfection: instead, virtue is itself the perfection of human nature – in the way that intelligence is the perfection of thought, or beauty of appearance. In these theories there is no general distinction between 'the right' and 'the good': as expressions of the virtues, virtuous actions are good in themselves.

Modern 'teleologists', by contrast, assign virtuous or right action only an instrumental value (see CONSEQUENTIALISM). In this respect, modern 'deon-

tologists', who see the rightness or virtue of an action as a kind of value that is intrinsic to it, are closer to the classical teleologists (see DEONTOLOGICAL ETHICS). What distinguishes modern deontologists from classical thinkers is that they recognize forms of 'natural' or nonethical goodness which are independent of, and can conflict with, ethical values. For instance, many modern deontologists identify happiness with nonethical goods like pleasure, the pursuit of which can conflict with the right (see HAPPINESS). By contrast, Plato and Aristotle argued that *eudaimonia*, happiness or flourishing, essentially involves virtue (see EUDAIMONIA). In treating happiness as an independent or nonethical value, modern deontologists resemble the modern 'teleologists', who believe that right action is simply that which promotes an independently identifiable good.

Thus although both classical and modern teleologists believe that the good is realized through virtuous action, it is in different senses. Classical teleologists argue that virtue is identical with the best state of a human being, while modern ones argue that virtue promotes an independent, nonethical good. Philosophers in the late twentieth century have begun to mark this distinction by referring to those who believe that rightness consists in the production of nonethical good as 'consequentialists' rather than 'teleologists'.

See also: INTUITIONISM IN ETHICS; KANTIAN ETHICS; STOICISM; UTILITARIANISM; VALUES

References and further reading

Frankena, W. (1963) *Ethics*, Foundations of Philosophy Series, Englewood Cliffs, NJ: Prentice Hall. (A very influential introduction to ethics, in which the teleological/deontological distinction is made, and various theories categorized, very much as they are in the opening paragraphs of this entry.)

Herman, B. (1993) 'Leaving Deontology Behind', in *The Practice of Moral Judgment*, Cambridge, MA: Harvard University Press. (An attack on the idea that Kant is a deontologist, as well as on the idea of deontology, and with it, the deontological/teleological distinction.)

Korsgaard, C.M. (1996) 'From Duty and for the Sake of the Noble: Kant and Aristotle on Morally Good Action', in S. Engstrom and J. Whiting (eds) Aristotle, Kant, and the Stoics: Rethinking Happiness and Duty, New York: Cambridge University Press. (A comparison of Kant's and Aristotle's views on the value of actions, defending the claim that Kant inherits the classical view that there is a special kind of value intrinsic to actions.)

Mill, J.S. (1861) *Utilitarianism*, ed. G. Sher, Indiana-polis, IN: Hackett Publishing Company, 1979. (Mill claimed an alliance between utilitarians and ancient Greek moralists, and he opposed this approach to that of the intuitionists and Kant. His influence helped to popularize this way of categorizing theories.)

Muirhead, J.H. (1932) *Rule and End in Morals*, Oxford: Oxford University Press. (Muirhead was the first to divide ethical theories into the categories 'teleological' and 'deontological'. In this book he discusses the debate between the two types of theories, and urges the one-sidedness of both positions.)

CHRISTINE M. KORSGAARD

TELEOLOGICAL SEMANTICS

see SEMANTICS, TELEOLOGICAL

TELEOLOGY

Teleology is the study of purposes, goals, ends and functions. Intrinsic or immanent teleology is concerned with cases of aiming or striving towards goals; extrinsic teleology covers cases where an object, event or characteristic serves a function for something.

Teleological explanations attempt to explain X by saying that X exists or occurs for the sake of Y. Since the question 'For what purpose...?' may be construed either intrinsically or extrinsically, such explanations split into two broad types: those that cite goals of an agent, and those that cite functions.

The history of Western philosophy and science has been characterized by major debates about the logic, legitimacy and proper domains of these types of explanation. They still raise problems in contemporary biology and psychology. The modern debates have progressed considerably from the earlier ones, although continuities do exist.

1 Goals
2 Functions

1 Goals

Aristotle's views about the domain of striving that is present in nature were challenged during the Renaissance. Aristotle held that goals were 'final causes', that inanimate things seek natural places or states which are proper to their kind, and that growth and development in living things is directed towards the attainment of maturity.

The term 'final cause' misled some commentators, who assumed that a final cause is an efficient cause that comes after its effect. This could not have been Aristotle's view. Aristotle believed that trees grow leaves in order to protect their fruit (*Physics*: 199a 26–9), but he recognized that the fruit is not always successfully protected. If birds eat the fruit, and hence the final cause fails to come about, this fact in no way undermines the teleological explanation. If he had meant that fruit-protection was an efficient cause working backwards in time, the failure to come about would undercut the efficient causal explanation. A final cause, for Aristotle, is a 'that for the sake of which' (see ARISTOTLE §9).

Still, there were other objections to his explaining the movements of inorganic bodies by ascribing goals to them. Francis BACON, Galileo and Newton eschewed such explanations on the grounds that they were entirely speculative and otiose. First, the alleged striving could not be identified independently of the changes that actually occurred to the body, nor could its goal be identified – the hypothesis was untestable. Second, the hypothesis was unnecessary, at least in the fields of mechanics and dynamics, since a complete explanation could be provided in terms of antecedent causes and the laws of motion. As Bacon (1623 III: ch. 5) put it, 'Inquiry into final causes is sterile, and, like a virgin consecrated to God, produces nothing'.

Modern science does not sanction the ascription of goals or strivings to inanimate objects, except possibly to such artefacts as guided missiles, autonomous robots, and mechanical searching devices, which were first designed in the 1940s. But here the goal-talk is perhaps only 'as if' (Woodfield 1976: ch. 11).

In the life sciences, however, it is accepted that human beings and animals *do* strive after goals. The conviction that we are intentional agents is central to our self-image and to society. Moreover, animal and human goals can be identified in advance of the behaviour that they explain. The hypothesis that an animal is striving for food, for example, can be tested experimentally. So it is not true that goal-explanations are *in principle* vacuous.

Whether plants strive is, perhaps, unclear. Although we speak as if they did ('The flower turned in order to face the sun' and so on), such locutions may be merely a hangover from an Aristotelian tradition. They survive because we find them pictur-esque or convenient. In late-twentieth-century biology, vitalistic teleological theories of growth and development are not thought to be respectable, even though such processes cannot quite be explained in wholly physico-chemical terms (see VITALISM).

Are goal-explanations restricted, then, to the domain of intentional behaviour performed by intelligent organisms? The central case is surely that of the animate agent, conscious of what it wants, sensitive to information about its environment and able to represent alternative plans to itself. If goals always involve desires, beliefs and other mental states, then intrinsic teleological explanations are a species of mentalistic explanation. The main problem that arises next is to provide a satisfactory account of intentionality (see INTENTIONALITY).

Several philosophers in the twentieth century have tried to make room for a distinctive form of goal-explanation which is not necessarily mentalistic (Braithwaite 1953; Nagel 1961; Taylor 1964; Wright 1976). Such theories may be viewed as broadly Aristotelian in the sense that they locate striving in activity which exhibits a distinctive pattern or causal structure.

2 Functions

Aristotle maintained that if an item X is a part of a system S in which X performs a characteristic activity that benefits S, then X exists and acts for the sake of S. S might be a living organism or something bigger, such as a bee-colony, an ecosystem or even the world as a whole. The fact that X serves a function for S is supposed to explain why X is present in S. Aristotle's doctrine was naturalistic in the sense that it did not postulate a supernatural designer, but it was not wholly naturalistic, since it employed the notion of *benefiting*. The main problem with extrinsic teleological explanations in biology is to see precisely how they work.

Even supposing that it is a 'fact' that X does good to a bigger system S, that fact alone is insufficient to account for X's existence. Some additional premise or principle seems to be required. For example, if nature had been designed and created by a benevolent and omnipotent God, the existence of X in S would be explicable in terms of God's wishes, beliefs and creative acts. This form of functional explanation has a familiar logic: we use such explanations when giving the reasoning that leads human beings to design and produce useful artefacts. By supplementing the explanation in this way, we present extrinsic teleology as being derivative upon the intrinsic teleology of the designer (see GOD, ARGUMENTS FOR THE EXISTENCE OF §4). This solution is unsatisfactory, however, since neither biologists nor laypeople feel that the validity of 'natural function' explanations is dependent upon any theological assumptions. Either the explanations have some other form, then, or they are not genuine explanations at all.

In 1859, Darwin's theory of evolution by natural selection showed how harmonious systems could have arisen naturally, without the need for a designer. Darwin's theory explains the existence of X in S as the outcome of a gradual process. Ancestors of S who possessed parts similar to X survived and reproduced more successfully than their relatives who lacked parts similar to X, and these ancestors reproduced true to form (their offspring had organs like X, including S who has X).

Darwin made the designer-hypothesis redundant. Was his theory anti-teleological? Darwin took it as a datum that biological parts and characteristics which have survived the selection process are normally useful for their owners; his theory asserted that they persisted *because* they were useful. This looks like a vindication of Aristotelian extrinsic teleology. Upon further reflection, however, it hardly amounts to a ringing endorsement since Darwin's theory can be stated without employing the term 'function' or any teleological language at all (see DARWIN, C.R.; EVOLUTION, THEORY OF).

Contemporary philosophers separate into two camps on the question of the logic of functional explanations in biology. The 'naturalistic revisionists' *redefine* the concept of function in terms of the causal-historical Darwinian selection hypothesis. They keep the old teleological language but sanitize it (Wright 1976; Millikan 1984).The other camp consists of 'semantic conservationists' who maintain that natural functionality cannot be *defined* in terms of Darwin's theory (Woodfield 1976). On the latter view, talk of natural functions is committed to assumptions about benefit and harmony and goodness that are extraneous to science and probably perspective-dependent. This view implies that functional explanations are still potentially problematic.

It is possible to maintain that functional explanations of undesigned phenomena have some scientific merit even if they are not wholly objective. Kant (1790) argues that the attribution of natural functions to organs is heuristic: it helps to systematize our knowledge of organisms and generates further 'how?' questions. Kant's sophisticated defence does not license the unbridled attribution of good consequences to everything in nature – a tendency ridiculed earlier by Voltaire (1758) (See KANT, I. §13).

In the 1980s, naturalistic revisionists, notably Millikan (1984), began to exploit the Darwinian account of functionality as a tool for solving the problem of intentionality. The key insight is that desires, intentions and other mental states with intentional contents can themselves be seen as biologically adaptive states or as the products of mechanisms that are adaptive. The hope is to provide a naturalistic reduction of intentionality. This ambitious research-programme would make extrinsic teleology more fundamental than intrinsic teleology.

After more than two millennia of debates since Aristotle, teleology continues to provoke lively controversy among analytic philosophers.

See also: FUNCTIONAL EXPLANATION

References and further reading

* Aristotle (*c.* mid 4th century BC) *Physica*, trans. R.P. Hardie and R.K. Gaye in *The Works of Aristotle*, ed. W.D. Ross and J.A. Smith, vol. 2, Oxford: Oxford University Press, 1930. (The classic account of teleology.)
* Bacon, F. (1623) *De Augmentis Scientiarum*, in *Works of Sir Francis Bacon*, vol. 7, London: W. Baynes & Son, 1824. (Renaissance classic, emphasizing observation and induction as the royal route to knowledge.)
* Braithwaite, R.B. (1953) *Scientific Explanation*, Cambridge: Cambridge University Press. (Textbook in analytic philosophy of science, still rewarding after nearly half a century.)
* Darwin, C. (1859) *The Origin of Species*, London: John Murray. (Classic. The source of modern evolutionary theory.)
* Kant, I. (1790) *Critique of Teleological Judgement*, trans. J.C. Meredith, Oxford: Oxford University Press, 1928. (Complement to Kant's Critiques of Pure Reason and Practical Reason.)
* Millikan, R. (1984) *Language, Thought, and Other Biological Categories*, Cambridge, MA: MIT Press. (Original defence of a biological theory of representation.)
* Nagel, E. (1961) *The Structure of Science*, London: Routledge & Kegan Paul. (Logical empiricist textbook in the philosophy of science.)
* Taylor, C. (1964) *The Explanation of Behaviour*, London: Routledge & Kegan Paul. (Defines a kind of non-mentalistic explanation that has a distinctive teleological form.)
* Voltaire, F.-M. de (1758) *Candide*, trans. J. Butt, Harmondsworth: Penguin, 1947. (Satire directed against unthinking optimism.)
* Woodfield, A. (1976) *Teleology*, Cambridge: Cambridge University Press. (Monograph defending a unified analysis of teleological language.)
* Wright, L. (1976) *Teleological Explanations*, Berkeley, CA: University of California Press. (Monograph arguing that such explanations are a special kind of causal explanation.)

ANDREW WOODFIELD

TELESIO, BERNARDINO (1509–88)

Bernardino Telesio was a philosopher from southern Italy. He was one of the Renaissance philosophers who developed a new philosophy of nature: his most important book was called De rerum natura iuxta propria principia *(On the Nature of Things According to Their Own Principles). Telesio approached natural philosophy empirically, and regarded it as a separate field of study from theology and metaphysics. He believed that all natural beings were animate; and, by arguing that the two general principles of heat and cold affected the whole universe, he resisted the Aristotelian division between the corruptible earth and the eternal heavens. However, despite his apparent anti-Aristotelianism and his sympathy for the Presocratics, Telesio owed much to Aristotle, and tried to transform rather than destroy Aristotle's work. Telesio became the head of a Calabrian school, and was influential and widely discussed in his own time. Francesco Patrizi criticized him, but with respect; Tommaso Campanella followed him in his early works; and Thomas Hobbes drew inspiration from him.*

1 Life
2 Approach to nature
3 The principles and structure of the universe
4 The soul
5 The immortal intellect of human beings

1 Life

Not much is known about the circumstances of Telesio's life, the 'man of one book' who was entirely devoted to the development of a new philosophy of nature and who died when he had completed his task. He was born at Cosenza in southern Italy, the first of eight children in a poor but noble family. At an early age he followed his uncle and teacher Antonio Telesio to the north, where his uncle taught Latin and Greek (first in Milan and then in Venice). He attended the University of Padua, which was well known throughout Europe, studying mathematics with Federico Delfino and philosophy with the Aristotelian Vincenzo Maggi (or Madius). He probably received his doctorate in 1535, after which he returned to his native province and retired to a monastery to work on his own philosophical projects. In 1552 he married a noble widow, who died eight years later. In 1565 Pope Pius IV offered Telesio the archbishopric of Cosenza, but he refused, and in 1576 he also refused Pope Gregory XIII's invitation to teach his philosophy in Rome. Despite his reluctance to enter public life, from

1547 on he made it known that he was working on a philosophy which would destroy the tyranny of Aristotle. In 1563 he travelled to Brescia, to discuss his ideas with his old friend and teacher, Maggi. With Maggi's approval, he published the first version of his natural philosophy, *De natura iuxta propria principia* (On Nature According to Its Own Principles) in 1565. Five years later, he published a revised second version with the definitive title *De rerum natura iuxta propria principia* (On the Nature of Things According to their Own Principles), as well as three minor treatises, containing additional material. These works met with the critical approval of Francesco Patrizi, who was to develop his own views in his *Nova de universis philosophia* (New Philosophy of Universes) (1591). In 1586 Telesio published the final version of his treatise, now enlarged from two books to nine. He founded the *Accademia Cosentina* in Cosenza in order to promote the study of nature according to Telesio's principles, and it was in Cosenza that he died in 1588.

2 Approach to nature

Telesio's initial claim is of fundamental importance for his new philosophy of nature. He said that, in contrast to his predecessors, he would not rely on abstract principles invented by human reason, but would content himself with those concrete aspects of nature which are given in sense perception, and with what can be inferred from their similitudes. He did not wish to make the false claim that he was the first to deal with nature in an empirical manner, nor, contrary to Patrizi's accusation, did he pretend to be able to philosophize on the basis of mere sense perception. As he makes clear in the ninth and tenth chapters of the first book, he meant that he would refuse to explain what is perceived in nature in terms of what lies beyond the world of sensible experience, and hence is properly a metaphysical concern. Thus from the very beginning he postulated that natural philosophy should be developed as an autonomous science, independent of metaphysics and theology, and that nature itself should be considered as an autonomous structure, rationally designed to preserve itself eternally according to its own principles (*iuxta propria principia*).

3 The principles and structure of the universe

When Telesio began to determine the first principles of nature itself, he simply said that it is obvious to the senses that heat and cold are the most active general principles which constitute all natural beings, and offered no other justifications for this opinion. PATRIZI and many scholars after him objected that

these were the principles of PARMENIDES, so Telesio was not original, nor were his principles based on sense perception. However, one should not forget that for Aristotle natural beings (in so far as they are sensible bodies) are constituted by the most basic sensible, that is tangible, qualities (hot, cold, wet and dry). Of these primary qualities, heat and cold are defined as the active ones. Thus in the basically Aristotelian world of sixteenth-century thought, Telesio's identification of the first sensible active principles with heat and cold seemed quite natural.

Telesio's originality lies in his use of the two principles. He did not regard them as being primary qualities or forms of prime matter, but as incorporeal substances which are received by the third passive principle, the corporeal mass (*moles*) on which they operate through condensation and rarefaction. Heat, since it is white, bright, extremely rarefied and in rapid continuous motion, is concentrated in the sun and the heavens. Cold, on the other hand, since it is black, dark, dense and totally unmoved, is concentrated in the earth. Since both are endowed with the capacity to regenerate and multiply themselves, to spread out in all directions, and to occupy and transform the whole mass according to their own nature, they fight each other. In so doing, they constitute the whole variety of natural beings through a continuous process of self-organization.

This general model of the universe has some interesting consequences from the perspective of the modern concept of nature. By locating the centre of one of the active principles, heat, in the sun and the heavens, Telesio identifies elementary heat, present in fire, with heavenly warmth, operating through the sun. In the Aristotelian tradition these were regarded as being different, and nature, which for centuries had been divided into the corruptible earthly sphere and the eternal heavenly natures, was thus unified by Telesio. Moreover, since it would obviously be difficult to derive space and time from his principles of nature, Telesio taught that time was not identical with the motion of bodies, and that space was not identical with the place (*locus*) formed by the surface of bodies. Rather, both are absolute entities, presupposed by the operations of the active principles. As a result, there is no doubt that a vacuum is possible, even though bodies, thanks to a certain delight in contact with one another, try to avoid it (see COSMOLOGY §1).

4 The soul

When the active principles operate, they do so in order to overthrow their opposite and to preserve themselves. In order to be able to do this, they need the capacity to perceive both favourable and unfavourable operations, and to discriminate between them. Thus sense perception is as basic as the active principles themselves, for without it the whole process of interaction and self-organization would not work. If sense perception is linked to having a soul, as in the Aristotelian tradition, the active principles must be animate, and as a result all natural beings that are constituted by these principles and that are active in self-preservation must also be animate.

Thanks to the general animation of natural beings in so far as they are natural, even the lowest natural entities are raised to the dignity of sense perception and discrimination; and indeed the whole cosmos seems to be regarded as a living being. The capacities of sense perception and discrimination come to be seen as the most basic and most common natural qualities, which provide the general conditions for any natural process as such, even the most simple and mechanical ones such as rarefaction and condensation through heat and cold. However, when we arrive at more sophisticated organizations in the hierarchy of natural beings, such as those of plants, animals and human beings, it is only natural that their powers of perception and discrimination are also more sophisticated. Sense perception, cognition and judgment as found in human beings differ from the faculties of the souls of other natural beings only in their higher perfection, and it is tempting to suggest that for Telesio the very development of a philosophy of nature is just the natural operation of the most perfect natural being in its striving for self-preservation (see SOUL, NATURE AND IMMORTALITY OF THE).

5   The immortal intellect of human beings

The soul which enables human beings, the most perfect of natural beings, to fulfil their specific operations, is diffused through their bodies in the form of spirits (*spiritus*) or highly rarefied matter, and since human spirits differ from animal spirits only in the degree of rarefaction, the perfection of human beings is based on this difference alone. As a result it seems puzzling that in his eighth book, Telesio introduces a second type of intellect which is immaterial and immortal. This intellect is created by God and infused into human beings so that they can contemplate and know divine and eternal objects in addition to sense objects, and so that they can strive for the preservation of their supernatural, incorporeal self. It has been supposed that this divine intellect, which seems inconsistent with Telesio's pure natural philosophy, was merely a prudent sign of submission to the church, or else a proof that Telesio was conscious of the indispensability of metaphysics.

However, before the general separation of physics and metaphysics developed in sixteenth-century Aristotelianism, the autonomy of natural philosophy was not thought to be affected by the admission of such metaphysical notions as an intellect that enters the body from outside (the so-called *nous thyrathen*) or of a second end for human beings (as discussed in Aristotelian ethics) beyond the purely natural one of self-preservation. Telesio may well have placed himself in this tradition.

See also: ARISTOTELIANISM, RENAISSANCE

List of works

Telesio, B. (1565) *De natura iuxta propria principia liber primus et secundus* (On Nature According to Its Own Principles), Rome: Antonius Bladus Impressor Cameralis. (The first version of Telesio's natural philosophy.)

—— (1570) *De rerum natura iuxta propria principia liber primus et secundus, denuo editi* (On the Nature of Things According to their Own Principles), Naples: Josephus Cacchius; repr. Naples: Istituto Suor Orsola Benincasa, 1989. (The revised second edition of Telesio's work on natural philosophy, in two books. The 1989 reprint includes Telesio's own notes.)

—— (1586) *De rerum natura iuxta propria principia libri IX* (On the Nature of Things According to their Own Principles), Naples: Horatius Salvianus; repr. Hildesheim: Olms, 1971; ed. with Italian trans. L. De Franco, vols 1–2, Cosenza: Casa del libro, vol. 3, Florence: La Nuova Italia, 1965–76. (The final version of Telesio's work on natural philosophy, enlarged to nine books from the original two. The 1971 reprint has a preface by C. Vasoli.)

—— (1590) *Varii de naturalibus rebus libelli* (Diverse Short Works on Natural Things), ed. A. Persius, Venice: Felix Valgrisius; repr. Hildesheim: Olms, 1971; ed. L. De Franco, Florence: La Nuova Italia, 1981. (Several treatises, written by Telesio while he was preparing his natural philosophy. The 1971 reprint has a preface by C. Vasoli; De Franco's 1981 edition includes Patrizi's objections to Telesio's philosophy on pages 463–74.)

References and further reading

De Franco, L. (1989) *Bernardino Telesio. La vita e l'opera* (His Life and Works), Cosenza: Edizioni Periferia. (Collection of essays on the life and work of Telesio by one of the most competent scholars in the field.)

—— (ed.) (1991) *Atti del convegno internazionale su*

Bernardino Telesio Cosenza 12–13 Maggio 1989 (Proceedings of the International Convention on Bernardino Telesio...), Cosenza: Edizioni Periferia. (Various contributions on the life, works, and fortunes of Telesio.)

Kessler, E. (1992) 'Selbstorganisation in der Naturphilosophie der Renaissance' (Self-organization in Renaissance Natural Philosophy), *Selbstorganisation. Jahrbuch für Komplexität in den Natur-, Sozial- und Geisteswissenschaften* 3: 15–29. (Analysis of Telesio's universe as a self-organized system.)

Kristeller, P.O. (1964) 'Telesio', in *Eight Philosophers of the Italian Renaissance*, Stanford, CA: Stanford University Press, 91–109. (Short but reliable overview.)

Schuhmann, K. (1988) 'Hobbes and Telesio', *Hobbes Studies* 1: 109–33. (Shows that Hobbes was inspired by Telesio.)

Van Deusen, N.C. (1932) *Telesio: The first of the moderns*, New York: Columbia University Press. (On the life, cosmology, psychology, theology and fortunes of Telesio.)

ECKHARD KESSLER

TEMPLE, WILLIAM (1881–1944)

William Temple was concerned to unite personal Christian religion and social action, finding in the doctrine of the incarnation of God in Jesus Christ the basis for human dignity. He held that while the universe long existed without finite minds, and finite thought has its origin in the functioning of physical organisms, thought transcends its origins, creating ideas not occasioned by or referring to its physical environment, and purposively affecting that environment. Our capacities to seek truth, appreciate beauty and recognize duty are best explained by a purposive creative Mind using physical creation to bring other minds into existence. Created minds continually depend for their existence on God's continuing to sustain them.

Born in 1881, the son of an Archbishop of Canterbury, William Temple entered the Church of England and rose to the positions of Bishop of Manchester and then Archbishop of York before himself becoming Archbishop of Canterbury in 1942, at the height of the Second World War. He died in 1944.

An Anglican Platonist, Temple was concerned with overcoming the problems of evil and embracing good within a Christian context, and sought to reconcile the existence of evil and the existence of God. While it is the nature of evil to be against the will of God, monotheism, in order to retain plausibility, must be able not merely to show that the propositions 'God exists' and 'There is evil' are logically consistent, but to explain how God can use evil to further a providential plan. A basic theme in Temple's *Nature, Man, and God* (1934) is that what is wanted is some ground for the belief that the occurrence of evil is an element in the total good. Temple endeavoured to provide this by arguing that human beings are so created as to act in terms of what they believe their good to be. Creatures such as ourselves, in whom thought is rooted in a physiological organism, naturally tend to find their apparent good in what brings gratification, comfort and security. While not strictly necessary, that such creatures should sin is 'too probable not to happen'. Thus if thought is to arise from material conditions, it is natural (that is, easily explicable and to be expected) that those in whom it arises should have a bent towards self-concern and selfishness. This leads us to identify as our good conditions that are not our true good; we tend to a self-concern unwise even as regards our own interests. From this oversized self-concern arise individual and social evils.

Perhaps, Temple suggested, the conditions that involve the suffering of nonhuman animals are those which in humans give opportunity for forbearance, fortitude, courage, compassion and the like, presaging human moral life in the way that nonhuman animal consciousness prepares the way for human thought. In any case, since our actual good includes our coming to recognize a worth in our neighbours equal to that which we find in ourselves, our bent to selfishness precludes our identifying and successfully embracing our real good. We are unable on our own to correct this situation. While the successes of our searches for truth, beauty and goodness may not be ignored or repudiated, we can embrace our own good only by help from resources beyond our own. We find that self-centredness is sometimes temporarily and partially overcome by unselfish love.

If it is to be sufficiently conquered for us firmly to identify and seek our genuine good, we must ourselves be objects of an unselfish love that enables us to make others the object of an unselfish love of our own. Philosophical reflection and our knowledge of ourselves can make clear what is needed, but cannot say whether it is available to us. Temple endeavoured, then, to develop a defensible monotheism which would explain human thought and leave as little of the puzzle of human existence philosophically unilluminated as possible. He contended that when this is done, there remains a missing piece whose shape exactly corresponds to that of the Christian gospel, which proclaims that God became incarnate in Jesus Christ, whose exemplary life, atoning death, and resurrection from the dead for our justification manifested a costly unselfish love on the part of a God who can empower us to achieve our actual good. Temple claimed that this position is not refuted by the existence of evil, quoting as expressing his own position a passage from Bosanquet's *The Principle of Individuality and Value*:

> For a Christianity which has the courage of its opinions the idea of victory involves the idea of the Fall, and the answer [to the question of whether a world with both sin and divine atonement is better than one without sin] would be that the scheme of salvation, involving finiteness and sin, seem essential to the nature of God and the perfection of the universe.
>
> (Bosanquet 1912: 425)

Temple was important in Anglican Christianity's effort to relate its worldview to increasing scientific knowledge and contemporary social problems without abandoning its distinctive traditional content.

See also: EVIL, PROBLEM OF

List of works

Temple, W. (1911) *The Nature of Personality*, London: Macmillan. (An account of personality developed in terms of Trinitarian doctrine.)
—— (1917) *Mens Creatrix* (The Creative Mind), London: Macmillan. (Philosophical companion to *Christus Veritas* that argues that a correct philosophical perspective leads to the doctrine of the incarnation of God in Jesus Christ.)
—— (1923) *The Universality of Christ*, London: SCM Press. (Discussion of criteria for, and of Christianity as, a universal religion.)
—— (1924) *Christus Veritas* (The True Christ), London: Macmillan. (Theological companion to *Mens Creatrix* that finds the clue to the meaning of history in the doctrine of the Incarnation.)
—— (1934) *Nature, Man, and God*, London: Macmillan. (Gifford Lectures that present a monotheistic and Christian understanding of the development of human beings and the fact of evil.)

References and further reading

* Bosanquet, B. (1912) *The Principle of Individuality and Value: The Gifford Lectures for 1911*, London: Macmillan. (Outlines Bosanquet's idealist metaphysics.)

Elliot-Binns, J.E. (1956) *English Thought 1860–1900: The Theological Aspect*, London: Longmans, Green & Co. (Discusses the historical, philosophical, theological and social setting of English theology in the indicated period.)
Horton, W.M. *Contemporary English Theology*, London: SCM Press. (Treats pre- and post-First-World-War English theology from a perceptive American perspective.)
Iremonger, F. (1948) *William Temple, Archbishop of Canterbury*, London: Oxford University Press. (The standard biography.)
Langford, T. (1969) *In Search of Foundations: English Theology 1900–1920*, Nashville, TN: Abington Press. (Presentation of English theological thought in its cultural and philosophical context; good bibliography.)
Mozley, J.K. (1951) *Some Tendencies in British Theology*, London: SPCK. (Discussion of British theology from *Lux mundi* (1889) to the thought of Oman.)
Thomas, O.C. (1961) *William Temple's Philosophy of Religion*, London: SPCK. (General philosophical assessment of Temple's views.)

KEITH E. YANDELL

TEMPORAL LOGIC *see* TENSE AND TEMPORAL LOGIC

TENNANT, FREDERICK ROBERT (1866–1957)

A prolific writer on religion and philosophical theology, Tennant produced book-length studies of topics as diverse as the philosophy of science and the origin of sin. He is best known by philosophers for his two-volume Philosophical Theology *(1928, 1930), which offered the most sophisticated version then available of the argument from design for the existence of God. Tennant's philosophical legacy consists primarily in the influence his methodology has exerted on later philosophical theologians.*

F.R. Tennant received his graduate education at Cambridge University and spent his academic career there, as a fellow of Trinity College and, eventually, as a university lecturer in philosophy of religion. His specifically theological works include three studies of the concepts of sin and the Fall. His philosophical works include monographs on the concept of miracles and the nature of belief.

Tennant's most influential contribution to philosophy, the richly detailed *Philosophical Theology* (1928, 1930), employs his thinking on topics in the philosophy of empirical science to produce an intricate version of the argument from design for the existence of God (see GOD, ARGUMENTS FOR THE EXISTENCE OF §§4–5). Recognizing the force of Hume's attack on traditional forms of the argument (see HUME, D. §6), Tennant proposes a deliberately weakened conclusion: 'The attributes to be ascribed to God will be such as empirical facts and their sufficient explanation indicate or require' (1930: 78), a list of attributes that, he concedes, may fall well short of the elaborate list theists have traditionally ascribed to God.

Like previous versions of the design argument, Tennant's version claims only to render its conclusion probable, where the probability in question is inductive, rather than statistical or logical. Inductive probability, the sort of probability that empirical evidence is supposed to lend to a scientific hypothesis, forms the basis, according to Tennant, of empirical reasoning in both science and everyday life. The 'multitude of interwoven adaptations by which the world is constituted a theatre of life, intelligence, and morality', he argues, makes inductively probable the existence of a purposive, intelligent creator (1930: 121).

Tennant concedes that naturalistic accounts such as evolutionary theory may explain each of the individual adaptations he cites, but he insists that in this case the whole exceeds the sum of its parts: naturalism can explain each adaptation but not their totality. Here Tennant anticipates the kind of 'cumulative case' arguments for theism offered by Basil Mitchell (1973) and others: while no single piece of evidence rationally compels belief in God, the pieces are said to reinforce one another in such a way that theism becomes inductively probable. Critics have insisted on focusing on the cogency of each piece of theistic evidence – reminding us that, in the end, ten leaky buckets hold no more water than one.

Tennant's design argument has encountered other, more specific objections. Some critics, such as John Hick (1966) and D.H. Mellor (1968), have objected to Tennant's particular use of probability theory and have challenged the relevance of any kind of probabilistic reasoning to theistic belief. They give Tennant credit for recognizing that statistical and logical probability apply only dubiously to the question of how likely it is that the entire universe arose by chance. But they charge him with appealing to a notion of inductive probability that he fails to explain rigorously and with using even inductive probability in a fallacious way. Others, including D.L. Scudder (1940), have faulted Tennant for failing to treat religious experiences either as a fundamental basis for religious belief or as further data in support of the theistic hypothesis.

These objections have since been addressed by a number of philosophers who, because of Tennant's apparent influence on them, may be counted among his successors, including Mitchell, George Schlesinger and especially Richard Swinburne. Like Tennant, they have treated theism as in some sense a scientific hypothesis to be tested by the usual inductive methods. Swinburne's contributions to philosophical theology have sought to apply more sophisticated versions of probability theory to the question of God's existence, a methodological improvement on Tennant's work but squarely in the same spirit. Swinburne has also tried to meet another objection to Tennant's argument by making the widespread existence of religious experiences an explicit part of the case for theism (see RELIGIOUS EXPERIENCE §2). Although cited less frequently with each generation, Tennant's writings stand at the head of a steady stream of probabilistic arguments from design.

List of works

Tennant, F.R. (1902) *The Origin and Propagation of Sin*, Cambridge: Cambridge University Press. (Four very clear lectures on original sin, with a long preface responding to criticism.)

—— (1903) *The Sources of the Doctrines of the Fall and Original Sin*, Cambridge: Cambridge University Press. (A companion to the previous volume, containing a thorough survey of the historical origins of the doctrine.)

—— (1912) *The Concept of Sin*, Cambridge: Cambridge University Press. (A clear and precise conceptual clarification of the connotation of 'sin'.)

—— (1925) *Miracle and Its Philosophical Presuppositions*, Cambridge: Cambridge University Press. (Three very short and lucid lectures on miracle, law and supernatural causation, credibility and actuality.)

—— (1928, 1930) *Philosophical Theology*, Cambridge: Cambridge University Press, 2 vols. (Immensely detailed and fairly technical but still readable philosophy of self and soul, of religious experience and knowledge, and the idea of God.)

—— (1932) *Philosophy of the Sciences*, Cambridge: Cambridge University Press. (Another short, lucid lecture series, placing science and theology with respect to the 'psychology of knowledge'.)

—— (1943) *The Nature of Belief*, London: Centenary

Press. (A slightly longer and more complex work on the nature and justification of faith.)

References and further reading

* Hick, J. (1966) *Faith and Knowledge*, Ithaca, NY: Cornell University Press, 2nd edn. (Questions the applicability of probability theory to religious belief.)

* Mellor, D.H. (1968) 'God and Probability', *Religious Studies* 5: 223–34. (Criticizes Tennant's use of probability theory and questions the applicability of probabilistic reasoning to religious belief.)

* Mitchell, B. (1973) *The Justification of Religious Belief*, London: Macmillan. (Explores the prospects for a probabilistic, 'cumulative case' argument for theism.)

Schlesinger, G. (1977) *Religion and Scientific Method*, Dordrecht: Reidel. (Assimilates reasoning about God to scientific reasoning; useful discussions of confirmation theory.)

* Scudder, D.L. (1940) *Tennant's Philosophical Theology*, New Haven, CT: Yale University Press. (Detailed critique of Tennant's major work, focusing on Tennant's allegedly inadequate treatment of religious experiences.)

Swinburne, R. (1979) *The Existence of God*, Oxford: Clarendon Press. (Detailed and influential argument, in the spirit of Tennant, for the conclusion that, more probably than not, God exists.)

STEPHEN MAITZEN

TENSE AND TEMPORAL LOGIC

A special kind of logic is needed to represent the valid kinds of arguments involving tensed sentences. The first significant presentation of a tense logic appeared in Prior (1957). Sentential tense logic, in its simplest form, adds to classical sentential logic two tense operators, P and F. The basic idea is to analyse past and future tenses in terms of prefixes 'It was true that' and 'It will be true that', attached to present-tensed sentences. (Present-tensed sentences do not need present tense operators, since 'It is true that Jane is walking' is equivalent to 'Jane is walking'.) Translating the symbols into English is merely a preliminary to a semantics for tense logic; we may translate 'P' as 'it was true that' but we still have the question of the meaning of 'it was true that'. There are at least two versions of the tensed theory of time – the minimalist version and the maximalist version – that can be used for the interpretation of the tense logic symbols.

The minimalist version implies that there are no past or future particulars, and thus no things or events that have properties of pastness or futurity. What exists are the things, with their properties and relations, that can be mentioned in certain present-tensed sentences. If 'Jane is walking' is true, then there is a thing, Jane, which possesses the property of walking. 'Socrates was discoursing', even if true, does not contain a name that refers to a past thing, Socrates, since there are no past things. The ontological commitments of past and future tensed sentences are merely to propositions, which are sentence-like abstract objects that are the meanings or senses of sentences. 'Socrates was discoursing' merely commits us to the proposition expressed by the sentence 'It was true that Socrates is discoursing'.

The maximalist tensed theory of time, by contrast, implies that there are past, present and future things and events; that past items possess the property of pastness, present items possess the property of presentness, and future items possess the property of being future. 'Socrates was discoursing' involves a reference to a past thing, Socrates, and implies that the event of Socrates discoursing has the property of being past.

1   *De dicto* and *de re* occurrences of tenses
2   **Quantified tense logic**
3   **A paradox for the minimalist theory**
4   **Do *de dicto* occurrences imply *de re* occurrences?**
5   **Past and future existents**

1   *De dicto* and *de re* occurrences of tenses

If a tense occurs *de dicto*, then the tensed expression ascribes a temporal property to a 'dictum' (proposition). 'It will be true that the sun is exploding' involves a *de dicto* occurrence of 'will be': the property 'having future truth' is ascribed to the proposition expressed by 'The sun is exploding'. If a tense occurs *de re*, then the tensed expression ascribes a property to a thing or event. The sentence 'The sun will explode' involves a *de re* use of 'will' since the tensed expression 'will explode' ascribes the temporal property 'exploding in the future' to the sun (see DE RE/DE DICTO).

The tense logic favoured by minimalists is based on the idea that all occurrences of past and future tenses are *de dicto* (even though some might appear to be *de re*) and therefore can be represented by sentential operators, such as 'it was true that'. According to this theory, the sentence 'The sun will explode' only appears to ascribe a temporal property to the sun; in reality it ascribes a temporal property to a proposition. 'The sun will explode' means the same as 'It will be true that the sun is exploding'.

2 Quantified tense logic

The *de re/de dicto* distinction also appears in the different approaches of the maximalist and minimalist theorists to the syntax of quantified tense logic. Quantified tense logic may be formulated in at least two ways. One way is based on the idea that quantifiers ('any', 'some') occur only within the scope of tense operators. In the sentence 'Some thing will fly to Mars', the quantifier 'some' does not occur within the scope of a tense operator. But it does in 'It will be true that some thing flies to Mars'.

The minimalist theory implies that quantification over past or future particulars should occur only in the scope of tense operators. Consider the sentence 'Some person did exist who wrote *The Republic*'. The minimalist will take this to express the same proposition as 'It was true that some person is writing *The Republic*', which has the symbolic form $P(\exists x)Gx$. The quantified expression 'some person' occurs within the scope of 'it was true that'; this implies that 'some person' does not now refer to anything (there are no past people for it to refer to), but used to refer to something; to a person that existed at the time the proposition was true.

The minimalist assumption that temporal properties should be ascribed only to propositions also appears in the treatment of quantification over present particulars. The sentence 'Some person is presently writing a book' is not interpreted as ascribing the temporal property 'presently writing a book' to a person. Rather, it is taken to mean 'It is true that some person is writing a book', which would involve a present tense operator. This sentence ascribes the property of being presently true to the proposition 'Some person is writing a book'. This minimalist interpretation of quantification is exemplified in A.N. Prior's remark in *Past, Present and Future*: 'a quantifier preceding any such operator [any tense operator] is naturally taken to be governed by the "It is the case that-", which is prefixable to anything we say, and therefore to range over what *now* exists' (1967: 144; emphasis added).

The maximalist tensed theory of time, by contrast, allows quantification over past, present or future particulars to occur outside the scope of tense operators. The expression 'some person' in the sentence 'Some person existed who wrote *The Republic*' quantifies over all past, present and future persons. This reflects the assumption that some people exemplify pastness, some, presentness and some, futurity.

The maximalist theory implies a *de re* use of the symbols P and F. Traditional tense logic (following Prior) uses P and F only in a *de dicto* manner, to mean 'it was true that' or 'it will be true that'. But in an expression of the form $(\exists x)Px$, 'P' does not mean 'it was true that' but stands for a property of x; the property of pastness. The expression translates as 'Something is past'. Since 'P' here is not used as a sentential operator, but as a predicate, this should be marked in our symbolic notation. We may put an asterisk after P to mark the use of this symbol as a predicate. Thus we should say $(\exists x)P^*x$.

The symbol P is also used in a *de re* manner in $(\exists x)[PG]x$. Here the symbol P operates on the predicate G to form a more complex predicate. This translates as 'Something exemplifies past G-ness' or, equivalently, 'Something's exemplification of G has pastness'. To mark this distinctive use of P as a predicate operator, we can underline P, so that we say $(\exists x)[\underline{P}G]x$.

According to the maximalist tensed theory of time, an adequate quantified tense logic must include P (a sentential operator), P^* (a predicate) *and* $\underline{P}$ (a predicate operator). Given these symbolic distinctions, maximalists can allow that P is used only *de dicto*.

The distinction between *de dicto* and *de re* occurrences of tense logic symbols is partly analogous to the same distinction in modal logic. The box is used *de dicto* in $\Box A$, which means 'It is necessarily true that A', where A is some proposition. The box is used *de re* in $(\exists x)\Box Fx$, which means that some thing is necessarily F.

3 A paradox for the minimalist theory

The minimalist tensed theory of time is false if there is a true sentence which a minimalist interpretation turns into a logical contradiction. The maximalist may claim there are such sentences. For example, the maximalist may claim that 10 billion years ago, before any intelligent organisms evolved, there was no language and thus no truths or falsehoods. Consider the sentence 'It is logically possible that there was a time t at which there were no truths'. If 'there was' and 'there were' are *de dicto* occurrences of tense, then this sentence says the same as 'It is logically possible that it was true at time t that there are no truths', which is a logical contradiction. The sentence must instead be taken to mean that it is logically possible that some time t exemplifies both pastness and having contained no truths.

The minimalist may counter that Platonic realism is true and thus that it is necessary that there be truths at all times. The maximalist may respond that the truth of Platonic realism and the falsity of nominalism are determined by metaphysics, not by formal logic. 'Platonic realism is true' is not a logical theorem and 'There were no truths 10 billion years ago' is not a logical contradiction. Thus a formal logic that implies these sentences are logical truths or falsehoods is not in fact valid.

The minimalist may have a second response, namely that the sentence 'It is logically possible that it was true at time t that there are no truths' does not imply the existence of a truth at time t. The tense operator 'it was true at time t that' does not imply that the proposition 'There are no truths' *existed* at time t. Rather, it implies merely that the time at which the (present tense) proposition should be evaluated for truth or falsity is the past time t, and that the proposition possesses truth at this time. The maximalist will say that this response depends on the intelligibility of the thesis that the proposition 'There are no truths' possesses at time t the property of being true and yet does not exist at this time. How can a nonexistent (at time t) proposition possess a property (at time t)? It is debatable whether the maximalist can derive a contradiction from the minimalist theory that some propositions do not exist at some of the times at which they exemplify the property of being true.

A.N. Prior, who presented the first significant tense logic (1957), defends a minimalist tensed theory of time (1967) and is the most influential opponent of the maximalist theory and *de re* occurrences of tenses. Prior's critical stance is analogous to Quine's position regarding quantified modal logic. Prior found problematic *de re* occurrences of 'was' and 'will be', objecting to the realism about properties of pastness, futurity and presentness associated with constructions of the form $(\exists x)P^*x$ (something exemplifies 'being past'). (Similarly, Quine found problematic *de re* occurrences of 'must be', and objected to the realism about essential properties associated with constructions of the form $(\exists x)\Box Fx$ (something exemplifies 'being necessarily F').)

In Prior's case, the rejection of the realist position is in part due to his categorization of pastness, presentness and futurity as *activities*. Prior suggests that these temporal properties of events (if there were such properties) belong in the same ontological category as activities done by things. He denies that there are *events* 'momentarily doing something called "being present" and then doing something else called "being past" for much longer' (1967: 18). Prior may be interpreted as suggesting that it is a mistake to categorize presentness and pastness along with such activities as running or talking, and then say that presentness and pastness (if there are such properties) are activities performed not by things, but by events.

The realist may grant this point, but argue that presentness and pastness need not be categorized as activities performed by events. 'Events possess tem-poral properties of being present or being past or being future' does not entail 'Presentness, pastness and futurity are activities done by events'. These temporal properties, like such properties as existence or self-identity, are unusual kinds of properties and should be placed in an ontological category by themselves.

4 Do *de dicto* occurrences imply *de re* occurrences?

The idea that all occurrences of tenses are *de dicto* leads to a minimalist semantic interpretation of such present-tensed sentences as 'The moon is bright'. According to this interpretation, this sentence does not report that an event, the moon's exemplification of brightness, has presentness. There is no first-order property of presentness and no event; there is only the thing, the moon, exemplifying brightness. The maximalist may argue that problems with this interpretation arise as soon as we ask *when* the moon exemplifies brightness. If 'exemplify' is tenseless, then there is no answer, and the analysis is faulty, since the present tense sentence 'The moon is bright' implies the moon is now exemplifying brightness. But if 'exemplify' is present-tensed, then we must ask what the semantic content of the present-tensed aspect of this verb is. The present tense must have some semantic content or meaning, since it conveys temporal information and is not a meaningless syntactic device such as 'It' in 'It is raining'. Further, to what ontological category does this temporal information belong?

According to the minimalist *de dicto* theory of tenses, the semantic category of the present tense is 'sentential operator' (the present tense has the same semantic content as 'it is true that') and the relevant ontological category is 'second-order property'; the present tense ascribes the property of 'being presently true' to a proposition. This theory implies that if the sentence 'The moon is bright' is true, we are ontologically committed to (1) the proposition, 'The moon is bright', (2) the proposition's exemplification of the property, 'being presently true', (3) the thing, the moon, and (4) this thing's exemplifying the property of brightness. The maximalist may object that 'exemplifying' in (4) is present-tensed, reflecting the fact that the thing presently exemplifies a property of brightness. According to the maximalist, the thing's *present* exemplification of brightness (rather than a timeless, past or future exemplification of brightness) is the ground for the proposition's being presently true.

5 Past and future existents

According to the minimalist theory, the ontological commitments of the sentence 'Plato had been alive' are merely the proposition 'Plato is alive' and the proposition's property of having been true. The maximalist may grant that these are the only ontological commitments if we accept the coherentist or eliminativist theory of truth. But the maximalist accepts the correspondence theory of truth and argues that this theory requires further ontological commitments. 'Plato had been alive' commits us to a past thing, namely, Plato, and a past event or state, namely, Plato's being alive. 'Correspondence' is a symmetrical property. (It is a dyadic property and thus a relation.) If the proposition 'Plato is alive' had been true in the past, then this proposition exemplifies past correspondence to Plato's being alive. Since correspondence is a symmetrical relation, this implies that some event, Plato's being alive, exemplifies past correspondence to the proposition 'Plato is alive'. The reason this event exemplifies past correspondence is that the event exemplifies pastness. Since Plato is a part of this past event, Plato exemplifies pastness. It follows, the maximalist concludes, that some events and things are past.

This maximalist conclusion implies that the temporal property 'pastness' is *de re*, since it is a property of a thing, Plato, and of an event, Plato's being alive. There was something, Plato, over which we can now quantify; it is the case that $(\exists x)P^*x$. The same results hold for propositions that will correspond to something exemplifying some property.

One concern that minimalists have about the maximalist interpretation of tense logic pertains to the maximalists' thesis that past or future things or events *presently* possess properties. Consider the formula $(\exists x)P^*x$. Does not $(\exists x)$ in this formula convey that there presently exists an x? And does not P^*x mean that this x is not presently existing but is past? If so (the minimalist may argue), the symbolic representation of *de re* occurrences of tenses turns true sentences into contradictions.

But the maximalist may respond that $(\exists x)$ has at least three different meanings in an adequate quantified tense logic, corresponding to three different senses of 'exists'. If 'exists' is present-tensed, it can have one of two senses. In one sense, it is logically equivalent to 'has the property of presentness', so that 'Mount Everest exists' is logically equivalent to 'Mount Everest has the property of presentness'. In the second sense, it can be equivalent to 'presently possesses some property'. Something that is past or future exists in this present-tensed sense, since if something is now past, it presently possesses the property of pastness. If 'exists' is tenseless, it is in effect disjunctively tensed; that is, it is equivalent to 'has existed, exists or will exist', where the middle 'exists' is equivalent to 'has the property of present-ness'. If we say 'Socrates exists', we mean that Socrates either has existed or exists (presently) or will exist.

The maximalist argues that this threefold distinction shows that there is no logical difficulty in the idea that some past or future item presently possesses a property. The maximalist may note that 'Some past thing presently has the polyadic property of being remembered' is not a logical contradiction. Nor can it be turned into a logical contradiction by substitution of synonyms. Indeed, the maximalist continues, an analysis of the concept expressed by 'remembering' implies that the minimalist theory is false. Remembering is not a relation between a present person and a present image. If it were such a relation, it would follow that what is being remembered is in every case an image that exists simultaneously with the act of remembering. But this is an analytic contradiction, since it is a part of the logic of 'remembers' that what is remembered exists earlier than the act of remembering. Remembering a thing is a three-termed relation: a person remembers a past thing by forming a present image of that past thing. The 'of' expresses the relation in which the present image stands to the past thing.

The maximalist may elaborate that there will appear to be a difficulty about non-present items presently possessing properties if one is mistaken about the sorts of properties a past or future item can possess. Since Plato does not now exist, Plato cannot now possess the properties of walking, breathing, writing, thinking and so on. These properties can only be possessed by Plato when he is present. But Plato now possesses the properties of being past, of being referred to by the name 'Plato', of being thought about, of being earlier in time than Descartes, and so on. Further, Plato now possesses the properties of having walked, having written *The Republic*, having been alive, having been human, and so on, all of which can be expressed in a symbolic notation of the form $(\exists x)[\underline{PG}]x$, where $(\exists x)$ can be taken as tenseless or as present-tensed in the second sense distinguished by the maximalist.

See also: ADVERBS; CONTINUANTS §2; DEMONSTRATIVES AND INDEXICALS §1; INTENSIONAL LOGICS; MODAL LOGIC; LOGICAL AND MATHEMATICAL TERMS, GLOSSARY OF; MODAL OPERATORS; TIME

References and further reading

Burgess, J. (1984) 'Basic Tense Logic', in D. Gabbay and F. Guenthner, *Handbook of Philosophical Logic*, vol. 2, Dordrecht: Reidel. (A technical account of sentential tense logic.)

Cocchiarella, N. (1984) 'Philosophical Perspectives on Quantification in Tense and Modal Logic', in D. Gabbay and F. Guenthner, *Handbook of Philosophical Logic*, vol. 2, Dordrecht: Reidel. (A presentation, with technical detail, of issues in quantified tense logic.)

Craig, W.L. (1996a) 'Tense and the New B-Theory of Language', *Philosophy* 71: 5–26. (Presents a defence of the tensed theory of time against the new tenseless theory (the B-theory) of time.)

—— (1996b) 'The New B-Theory's *tu quoque* Argument', *Synthese* 105: 1–21. (Shows how recent work on indexicals, such as Kaplan's and Perry's, supports the tensed theory of time.)

Forbes, G. (1984) *The Metaphysics of Modality*, Oxford: Clarendon Press. (Includes a clear discussion of tense logic and its relation to modal logic.)

Gale, R. (1968) *The Language of Time*, New York: Humanities Press. (An influential book that includes a classic defence of the maximalist tensed theory of time.)

Haack, S. (1978) *Philosophy of Logics*, Cambridge: Cambridge University Press. (Chapter 9 of this book includes one of the most accessible introductions to tense logic.)

Kamp, J.A.W. (1971) 'Formal Properties of "Now"', *Theoria* 37: 227–73. (An influential technical account.)

Le Poidevin, R. (1991) *Change, Cause and Contradiction: A Defence of the Tenseless Theory of Time*, New York: St. Martin's Press. (Includes an accessible defence of the thesis that the tensed theory of time is false.)

—— (ed.) (1998) *Question of Time and Tense*, Oxford: Clarendon Press. (A collection of essays by Le Poidevin, Craig, Nerlich, Oaklander, Dyke, Smith and others about the tensed theory of time.)

Oaklander, L.N. (1984) *Temporal Relations and Temporal Becoming*, Lantham, MD: University of America Press. (Presents a sustained criticism of the tensed theory of time.)

Oaklander, L.N. and Smith, Q. (eds) (1994) *The New Theory of Time*, New Haven, CT: Yale University Press. (Essays by Kaplan, Oaklander, Mellor, Schlesinger, C. Williams, Smith and others on the tensed theory of time versus the new tenseless theory of time.)

* Prior, A.N. (1957) *Time and Modality*, Oxford: Clarendon Press. (This classic is the primary source for modern tense logic.)

* —— (1967) *Past, Present and Future*, Oxford: Clarendon Press. (A collection of papers on time and tense logic, some of which articulate and defend the minimalist tensed theory of time.)

—— (1968) *Papers on Time and Tense*, Oxford: Clarendon Press. (Papers relevant to tense logic and the minimalist tensed theory of time.)

Smith, Q. (1993) *Language and Time*, New York: Oxford University Press. (An explication and defence of the maximalist tensed theory of time, and criticism of the minimalist tensed theory and the tenseless theory of time.)

Smith, Q and Oaklander, L.N. (1995) *Time, Change and Freedom*, London: Routledge. (An introductory discussion of the tensed and tenseless theories of time and their relation to other topics in metaphysics.)

QUENTIN SMITH

TERMS, LOGICAL *see* LOGICAL CONSTANTS

TERTULLIAN, QUINTUS SEPTIMUS FLORENS (*c.* AD 160–*c.* AD 220)

Tertullian was the first Christian theological author to write in Latin, and is responsible for initiating the Latin vocabulary of Christian theology, including such important terms as persona *(person) and* substantia *(substance). His early works, including the* Apologeticum, *refute pagan misconceptions about Christianity and argue on philosophical and juridical grounds for religious freedom. His later theological treatises, such as* De anima *(On the Soul) and* Adversus Marcionem *(Against Marcion) reflect Tertullian's adherence, in about AD 205–6, to Montanism, a Christian sect which emphasized asceticism, apocalypticism and prophecy. These lengthy works represent an effort to oppose those forms of Christianity that sought to ally themselves with Platonism, such as Gnosticism. After these defences of apocalyptic Christianity, Tertullian fades from historical view around AD 220, leaving a legacy of charismatic truculence.*

Tertullian was born about AD 160 in Carthage. His family was pagan and his early education included rhetoric and law, together with some philosophy. Tertullian practised law at Rome until his conversion to Christianity around AD 193, after which he returned to Africa where he devoted himself to propagating his new faith and producing apologetical literature on its behalf.

Tertullian's lasting impact on the history of Western thought is a result of the brilliance of his rhetoric. His writings are highly individualistic: intense, pungent and paradoxical. They are full of striking aphorisms that have become famous in Western culture. Of the relationship of Christianity to reason and philosophy, he maintained 'What does Athens have to do with Jerusalem? What agreement is there between the Academy and the Church, between heretics and Christians?' (*De praescriptione haereticorum* 7) and of the incarnation: 'it is certain because impossible' (*De carne Christi* 5).

Tertullian was strongly opposed to the transcendentalism of earlier Christian apologists and Platonists (Justin Martyr, Theophilus, Irenaeus) and of the Gnostics (Marcion, Hermogenes, Valentinus). His ontology is Stoic in its origins. His major philosophical treatise is *De anima* (On the Soul), an attempt to disprove the Platonic conception of a naturally immortal soul. For Tertullian, the soul is corporeal, a product of a 'soul-seed' transmitted at conception. According to Tertullian, the soul is a free material being whose continued existence depends upon its redemption by Christ and whose spiritual hope rests in its resurrection (see SOUL, NATURE AND IMMORTALITY OF THE). By adopting this materialist psychology, Tertullian sought to associate Christianity with opponents of psychic pre-existence and transmigration. This was an act of deliberate philosophical positioning, setting the nascent Christian movement into alliance with Stoic and medical writers whose outlook on theology was materialistic.

Yet it is difficult to assess Tertullian's theological materialism. He insists that everything which exists is corporeal (*De carne Christi* 11) and that God is corporeal, albeit a 'spiritual' body (*Adversus Praxean* 7). This conflation of *spiritus* and *corpus* in God signals his unique character, since God alone is a perfect corporeal being, not produced by any other. However, God remains a substance distinct from other material entities, which are his products. His existence is known through them (*De resurrectione* 2–3). God is, however, understood by Tertullian to be at the extremity or outer surface of the cosmos, so that he is literally greater than all other things (*Adversus Praxean* 16). Thus, Tertullian draws on the Stoics for his attenuated materialist theology, but his precludes the Stoic tendency to assimilate God to the world. In insisting that God is *corpus*, Tertullian is

unique among Patristic authors. His early treatise on Gnosticism, *Adversus Hermogenem* (Against Hermogenes), attacks the common ancient theory that matter is eternal, and with it the 'demiurgic' view of God as the fashioner of order from disordered matter. Tertullian maintains instead that God, while himself a material spirit, is free from any constraint imposed by pre-existent matter, creating *ex nihilo* by his free will.

Finally, Tertullian contributed importantly to the Latin Christian definition of God as a 'trinity'; he is the first Latin author to employ the term *trinitas* in a technical sense (see TRINITY). His formulation 'one substance, three persons' (*una substantia, tres personae*) became fixed in subsequent Latin theology. It was meant to capture the original unity of his material God, who is conceived as 'shooting forth' the Logos and the Spirit in a temporal process. The Logos is understood to exist before this act of generation within the Father's mind as a *ratio*, but to emerge subsequently as a distinct *persona* with the beginning of the cosmos. While Nicene orthodoxy would later reject these materialist and temporal implications, his innovative terminology would be adopted by Christian orthodoxy.

Tertullian is thus an outrider in early Christian thought, a radical opponent of its developing Platonic mainstream. As such, he helps to show how different Christian theology might have been had its scriptural deposit been read through a materialist philosophical prism.

See also: GNOSTICISM; GOD, CONCEPTS OF; NEOPLATONISM; PATRISTIC PHILOSOPHY; STOICISM; TRINITY

List of works

Tertullian, Quintus Septimus Florens (*c.* AD 197–*c.* AD 220) *Opera* (Works), ed. J.G.P. Borleffs, E. Dekkers *et al.*, *Quinti Septimi Tertulliani Opera*, The Hague: Brepols, 1953–4, 2 vols; Corpus Scriptorum Ecclesiasticorum Latinorum vol. 20, ed. A. Reifferscheid and G. Wissowa, Vienna: F. Tempsky, 1890; vol. 47, ed. A. Kroymann, Vienna: F. Tempsky, 1906; vol. 69, ed. H. Hoppe, Vienna: F. Tempsky, 1939; vol. 70, ed. A. Kroymann, Vienna: F. Tempsky, 1942.

—— (AD 197) *De testimonio animae* (The Testimony of the Soul), Corpus Scriptorum Ecclesiasticorum Latinorum vol. 20, ed. A. Reifferscheid and G. Wissowa, Vienna: F. Tempsky, 1890. (A short treatise on the soul, closely related to the *Apologeticum*.)

—— (*c.* AD 197) *Apologeticum*, Corpus Scriptorum Ecclesiasticorum Latinorum vol. 69, ed. H. Hoppe,

Vienna: F. Tempsky, 1939. (An important legal and cultural defence of Christianity.)

—— (before *c.* AD 200) *De praescriptione haereticorum* (The Prescription of Heretics), Corpus Scriptorum Ecclesiasticorum Latinorum vol. 70, ed. A. Kroymann, Vienna: F. Tempsky, 1942. (A debate between orthodox Christianity and its heretical opponents, written during Tertullian's Catholic phase.)

—— (after AD 200) *Adversus Hermogenem* (Against Hermogenes), Corpus Scriptorum Ecclesiasticorum Latinorum vol. 47, ed. A. Kroymann, Vienna: F. Tempsky, 1906. (An attack on the Gnostic Hermogenes of Carthage.)

—— (*c.* AD 202–10) *Adversus Valentinianos* (Against the Valentinians), Corpus Scriptorum Ecclesiasticorum Latinorum vol. 47, ed. A. Kroymann, Vienna: F. Tempsky, 1906. (On the tenets of the Valentinians, a Gnostic group. A good source for the developing polemical traditions within Christianity.)

—— (*c.* AD 205) *De carne Christi* (On the Flesh of Christ), Corpus Scriptorum Ecclesiasticorum Latinorum vol. 70, ed. A. Kroymann, Vienna: F. Tempsky, 1942. (An initial treatment of Christ's bodily resurrection, closely related to *De resurrectione carnis.*)

—— (*c.* AD 205–7) *De resurrectione carnis* (The Resurrection of the Flesh), Corpus Scriptorum Ecclesiasticorum Latinorum vol. 47, ed. A. Kroymann, Vienna: F. Tempsky, 1906; ed. and trans. E. Evans, Treatise on the Resurrection, London: SPCK, 1960. (A defense of the Christian concept of the resurrection of the body.)

—— (*c.* AD 207–12) *Adversus Marcionem* (Against Marcion), Corpus Scriptorum Ecclesiasticorum Latinorum vol. 47, ed. A. Kroymann, Vienna: F. Tempsky, 1906; ed. and trans E. Evans, *Adversus Marcionem*, Oxford: Clarendon Press, 1972, 2 vols. (A lengthy refutation of the Gnostic heresy of Marcion.)

—— (*c.* AD 210–13) *De anima* (On the Soul), Corpus Scriptorum Ecclesiasticorum Latinorum vol. 20, ed. A. Reifferscheid and G. Wissowa, Vienna: F. Tempsky, 1890. (One of Tertullian's longest and most important philosophical treatises. Written during Tertullian's later Montanist period.)

—— (*c.* AD 213) *Adversus Praxean* (Against Praxeas), Corpus Scriptorum Ecclesiasticorum Latinorum vol. 47, ed. A. Kroymann, Vienna: F. Tempsky, 1906; ed. and trans. E. Evans, *Treatise Against Praxeas*, London: SPCK, 1948. (Directed against Praxeas, the work articulates Tertullian's mature Trinitarian theology.)

References and further reading

Koch, H. (1934) 'Tertullianus', in A. Pauly and G. Wissowa (eds) *Real-Encyclopädie der classischen Altertumswissenschaft*, cols. 822–44. (An old but still significant study.)

Sider, R.D. (1971) *Ancient Rhetoric and the Art of Tertullian*, London: Oxford University Press. (Tertullian and ancient rhetorical traditions.)

Spanneut, M. (1957) *Le stoïcisme des pères de l'église* (The Stoicism of the Church Fathers), Paris: Éditions du Seuil. (Study locating Tertullian in the history of ancient thought.)

—— (1969) *Tertullien et les premiers moralistes africains* (Tertullian and the First African Moralists), Gembloux: J. Duculot. (Study locating Tertullian in the history of ancient thought.)

JOHN PETER KENNEY

TESTIMONY

Philosophical treatment of the problems posed by the concept of knowledge has been curiously blind to the role played by testimony in the accumulation and validation of knowledge or, for that matter, justified belief. This is all the more surprising, given that an enormous amount of what any individual can plausibly claim to know, whether in everyday affairs or in theoretical pursuits, is dependent in various ways upon what others have to say. The idea that someone can only really attain knowledge if they get it entirely by the use of their own resources provides a seductive ideal of autonomous knowledge that may help explain the way epistemologists have averted their gaze from the topic of testimony. But, unless they are prepared to limit the scope of knowledge dramatically, theorists who support this individualist ideal of autonomy need to explain how our wide-ranging reliance upon what we are told is consistent with it. Characteristically, those who consider the matter acknowledge the reliance, but seek to show that the individual cognizer can 'justify' dependence upon testimony by sole resort to the individual's resources of observation, memory and inference. Testimony is thus viewed as a second-order source of knowledge. But this reductionist project is subject to major difficulties, as can be seen in David Hume's version. It has problems with the way the proposed justification is structured, with its assumptions about language and with the way the individual's epistemic resources are already enmeshed with testimony. The success or failure of the reductionist project has significant implications for other areas of inquiry.

1   The epistemological background

Philosophy in the Western tradition, and beyond, has long enshrined a particular picture of the starting point and the task of epistemology. The task has principally been seen as trying to understand what sort of thing or goal knowledge is and thereby to distinguish it from counterfeit, inferior or merely different items such as superstition, opinion or belief. In pursuit of this, it became necessary to further contrast or identify knowledge with such notions as justified or reliable belief. Often the task was propelled by worries about (or enthusiasm for) scepticism, either total or partial. But equally, philosophers uninterested in the sceptical problem have attempted to distinguish knowledge from various pretenders to its title and to chart the interrelations of the various areas, types or sources of knowledge (see EPISTEMOLOGY, HISTORY OF; RYLE, G.).

In all of this thinking about the nature and value of knowledge, however, the picture has persisted (except in the speculations of a handful of thinkers) of the subject doing the investigation as initially positioned in a state of cognitive isolation. This picture has endured in spite of the fact that the data to be accommodated and explained seem ill at ease with it. Such data include the fact that these cognizers unhesitatingly claim to know many things that surely transcend the power of the individual resources they bring to the epistemic task. To be sure, individual cognizers know about the existence and disposition of middle-sized objects and their surroundings in the more or less immediate vicinity, but they also know facts well beyond their immediate ken, such as numerous everyday facts of geography and history. They also know how conceptually to identify and linguistically to label these objects and surroundings in terms intelligible to others. Beyond this array of relatively ordinary convictions, there are a host of more recondite things many such individuals know – such as the population of the USA, the day-to-day temperature of the environment, the non-existence of a largest prime number, the military practices of ancient peoples, the chemical composition of water or of various medicines, certain facts about the workings of engines and about the workings of institutions.

It is, I think, perfectly clear that the isolated individual imagined as the hero of so much episte-mological writing is not equal to the task of amassing such knowledge from purely individual resources of perception, experiment, memory and inference. Some theorists, it is true, heroically deny that anything that involves accepting the word of others can really deserve the name of knowledge. But they have either failed to appreciate the enormity of this denial, in terms of the massive amount and quality of information thus excluded and its often intimate connection with much else that is included, or they have so construed knowledge as to make its attainment a rare privilege for the elite (as in Plato who banishes not only testimony but also perception from the realm of knowledge, and then imagines that a purified 'science' will emerge from contemplation of the unchanging Forms). Short of such heroic, but either myopic or puritan, responses we have no option but to recognize the need for a pooling of resources so that knowledge requires some reliance upon one's fellow cognizers. But the individualist picture dies hard. So the idea emerges that the necessary reliance upon the word of others in the enterprise of knowledge is itself something for which the isolated individual discovers the need and provides (from individual resources alone) the justification.

2   Autonomy and reduction

This individualist idea is essentially reductionist, in the sense that it attempts to show that, at the significant core of the epistemological enterprise, we have no need of any basic or primitive reliance upon the word of others. At this level, we need only the individual resources of perception, memory and inference. We rely extensively on the reports of others, of course, in the final development of knowledge, but this reliance is itself established by and dependent upon the primary operations of those individual resources. The idea that this must be so has great appeal because of the influence of a certain ideal of intellectual 'autonomy'. This ideal is well captured at the beginning of modern philosophy in Descartes' philosophy. There we find an outlook on knowledge that remains immensely influential today even among those who reject, and even denounce, most of Descartes' specific conclusions and many of his assumptions. Descartes makes it clear that the task he sets himself is precisely that of finding out whether it is possible to have fully autonomous knowledge, knowledge that you have rationally guaranteed entirely by and for yourself. As he puts it in the *Discourse on Method*:

> So, too, I reflected that we were all children before being men and had to be governed for some time

by our appetites and our teachers, which were often opposed to each other and neither of which, perhaps, always gave us the best advice; hence I thought it virtually impossible that our judgments should be as unclouded and firm as they would have been if we had had the full use of our reason from the moment of our birth, *and if we had always been guided by it alone.*

(Descartes [1637] 1985: 117, emphasis added)

Although Descartes then tries to establish how he is entitled to trust himself in the proper exercise of his own isolated cognitive powers, he never addresses the question of how solitary cognizers can employ their reason to validate in an 'unclouded' fashion their inevitable reliance upon others. Later theorists, however, occasionally try to deal with this problem. From an ideal of entirely 'autonomous' knowledge there is born the correlative portrait of the autonomous knower who extends and enriches knowledge by relying upon others only by licensing their word to be reliable by unaided epistemic efforts. Different theorists have different stories to tell about how the autonomous knower brings off this remarkable feat. One of the most vivid presentations of the picture, and one of the most influential accounts of how the feat is to be done, may be found in David Hume, though there are also different attempts in a similar reductive spirit by other philosophers such as F.H. Bradley and Bertrand Russell.

3 Hume and the reductionist project

Hume's idea is that the 'autonomous knower' does indeed rely, and rely quite extensively, on the testimony of others, but does so because of constant conjunctions discovered by personal checking on their reliability in a testimony-free way. So Hume says of reliance upon testimony:

> our assurance in any argument of this kind is derived from no other principle than our observation of the veracity of human testimony, and of the usual conformity of facts to the reports of witnesses. It being a general maxim, that no objects have any discoverable connexion together, and that all the inferences, which we can draw from one to another, are founded merely on our experience of their constant and regular conjunction; it is evident that we ought not to make an exception to this maxim in favour of human testimony, whose connexion with any other event seems, in itself, as little necessary as any other.
>
> (Hume [1748] 1975: 111)

The idea turns out to be methodologically ambigu-

ous: do the autonomous knowers accept testimony in an entirely piecemeal fashion because they have independently ascertained the reliability of this or that particular witness, or do they proceed by determining the reliability of the various classes of cognitive agents to which witnesses belong, or is it merely that they know they can do one or other of these checks if needs be? Given the scope and depth of our dependence on what others tell us, the first suggestion opens up our cognitive landscape to interminable investigative travelling that would make a nonsense of inquiry itself. The third asserts a mere possibility and hardly seems a move in the justificatory game. The second, which is more plausibly Hume's idea, reduces the labour somewhat, but still requires an immense amount of checking, and more significantly owes us a non question-begging account of what counts as a class of witnesses. This is much harder to provide than it seems.

When Hume discusses the task of justifying reliance upon testimony, he talks at one point of its being 'founded on past experience' and varying in probity 'according as the conjunction between any particular kind of report and any kind of object has been found to be constant or variable' (Hume [1748] 1975: 112). But it is unclear whether 'kinds of report' are to be individuated by reference to type of speaker or type of content. If the former, then we are really checking upon expertise: we are seeking to find whether there is a high correlation between expert reports and the sorts of situations that experts report upon. But, even if we allow a broad interpretation of expertise (as we must if we are to include enough testimony for the project's ambitions), we cannot detect expertise as we might detect colour or smell. That someone is an expert on the geography of Southeast Asia is either itself known in ways that rely directly or indirectly on the testimony of others, or it must be determined by observing personally some very high correlation between their reports and the state of the world. If the former, then we are no further advanced on the reductionist programme since the same problem arises over and over again; if the latter, then not only does the notion of an expert no longer provide us with a specification of a kind of report, but we would usually have to be experts ourselves to be in a position to determine whether the particular correlations obtain. On the other hand, if we interpret 'kinds of report' as 'reports of kinds of situation' we face other intractable problems. For instance, a problem arises immediately about the degree of specificity to be attached to the classification of kinds of situation. For the purpose of checking do we classify the utterance 'This is a car that is in perfect working order' as an existence report, a motor vehicle report, a mechanical report or an evaluation? There seems no intrinsic reason to proceed one way or another here, and yet it seems to be of the first importance how we go.

4 Vulnerable assumptions

Another problem for any reductionist project concerns the fact that the plausibility of supposing that testimony-free verifications of reliability are usually available seems covertly to depend upon accepting testimony-laden checks, observations and falsifications. We have seen this problem arise in the particular case of checking for expertise, but its significance is wider than that since all sorts of apparently personal verifications will turn out to be dependent upon unchecked testimony. If I become suspicious of a job applicant's claim to have a Ph.D., for instance, I can seek to check personally on the claim (in the sense of conducting the investigation on my own behalf) but this endeavour will invariably involve accepting the word of some people or institutions that the degree was or was not awarded. Moreover, the reliability of these people or institutions will often be either taken for granted or accepted on the basis of reputation, which is itself a complex form of hearsay, as are the documents and certificates the institutions may offer as evidence. Such often-ignored facts account for the way Hume and others persistently and unconsciously conflate individual and social readings of the term 'observation', a conflation that makes Hume's project seem more manageable than it really is. When he refers to the need to base 'our' (that is, the sum of individual cognizers') reliance upon testimony on 'no other principle than our observation of the veracity of human testimony' ([1748] 1975: 111), Hume is sliding between the two senses of 'observation'. 'We' can observe the veracity of human testimony only if we already trust each other's testimony sufficiently for the project to be no longer that of the autonomous knower.

Hume's problems are symptomatic of the fact that the reductionist picture in which the autonomous knower figures so centrally is flawed at heart since the existence of a common language in which reports are made and accepted or rejected already carries with it a commitment to some degree of unmediated acceptance of testimony. The reductionist strategy necessarily supposes that we can fully understand what we are told in a public language and then independently investigate its truth or correctness, but the connections between linguistic comprehension and truth (or at least correct assertibility) are much closer than this picture allows. The reductionist project must concede

that the autonomous knower might consistently understand correctly all that they were told but none the less find every report mistaken or deceitful. But any such 'discovery' would rather serve to refute the initial supposition that the reports had been correctly understood. Public languages are, after all, learnt and their use is subject to correction, so reports on usage and on some facts embodying that usage must have a degree of success that the reductionist ignores. Fixity of meaning depends upon some degree of successful reporting, though just what degree is a further question (Coady 1992: Ch. 9).

5 Further issues

Foundationalist theories of knowledge have recently been subjected to much scorn and criticism, a good deal of it deserved, but one thing that seems right about the foundationalist emphasis is the idea that individual perception, memory and inference deserve a particular respect as sources of information in a way that speculation, guessing and suggestion (whatever their other cognitive value) do not (see FOUNDATIONALISM). The challenge posed by testimony is that it seems to deserve a similar respect to perception, memory and inference, indeed, the respect we owe them may require us to accord it parallel honour. This is because testimony puts us in touch with the perceptions, memories and inferences of others, and a certain coherence between individual and communal resources underpins the individual's reliance on their own epistemic skills and achievements. It is precisely this status that the ideal of autonomous knowledge rejects.

Abandonment of the reductionist project does not mean that our general attitude to testimony should be one of gullibility. A comparison with memory makes the situation clearer: we cannot reduce our reliance upon memory to inferences from present perceptions but we also learn not to trust our memories blindly in all circumstances. The question of *how* trustworthy memories or testimonies are cannot be addressed by initially allowing that they might not be trustworthy at all, but this still allows that there are contexts and circumstances in which we should be wary of them. It also allows that there is room for serious investigation of the reliability of the testimonies of certain groups whose dependability is often questioned in legal and other contexts (for example, very young children, the seriously mentally ill, parties to an issue for adjudication), and the more general question of how reliable testimony might be in any given culture or context.

Throughout the above I have, in accordance with philosophical tradition, used 'testimony' as a broad term for certain sorts of telling, but it is an interesting and difficult task to give a serviceable definition of what these sorts are. The term is most at home in legal settings, but clearly a wider notion than that is required. One strategy is to define it as a type of speech act, but to allow extensions from the speech-act model for such things as maps, signposts and documentary records. There remain problems about whether to include competency and sincerity conditions in the definition and whether there is a sense of 'evidence' in which testimony by definition falls into the category of evidence. Some would see the former move as too demanding and the latter as question-begging.

Finally, the neglect of the topic by philosophers has left many important questions of law, history, psychology and religion to be debated without the benefit of concentrated philosophical input. These include such matters as the status of children's testimony at law, the problems posed by expert evidence, psychological claims about the unreliability of eye-witness identifications, and certain aspects of historical methodology, including the 'higher' biblical criticism.

See also: SOCIAL EPISTEMOLOGY; TESTIMONY IN INDIAN PHILOSOPHY

References and further reading

Anscombe, G.E.M. (1981) 'Hume and Julius Caesar', in *The Collected Philosophical Papers of G.E.M. Anscombe*, vol. 1, Oxford: Blackwell. (Strong criticism of Hume's views on the transmission of historical knowledge.)

Aquinas, T. (1257–9) *Commentary on Boethius's De Trinitate*, Toronto, Ont.: Pontifical Institute of Medieval Studies, 1958. (Aquinas has interesting reflections on testimony as a kind of natural faith, occupying a position midway between knowledge and opinion.)

Augustine (386–429) *The Works of Aurelius Augustinus*, ed. M. Dods, Edinburgh: T.&T. Clark, 1871–6. (Of all the philosophers of the ancient world, Augustine has the surest appreciation of the extent of our dependence upon the word of others and makes an interesting attempt to fit it into a Platonist epistemological framework. See especially, *De Trinitate, De Magistro, De Utilitate Credendi, Retractiones.*)

Bradley, F.H. (1935a) 'The Presuppositions of Critical History', in *Collected Essays*, vol. 1, Oxford: Oxford University Press. (Bradley's first publication, this is an essay on historical method which supports the new German school of historical criticism of the Bible, and seeks to undermine the credibility of historical testimony to what is 'non-analogous' to present experience.)

—— (1935b) 'The Evidences of Spiritualism', in *Collected Essays*, vol. 2, Oxford: Oxford University Press. (After Hume, Bradley is one of the most significant writers on testimony. Here he tries to accommodate the importance of testimony by giving a reductive treatment of its epistemic significance, and attempting to show the limits of its value to 'critical' history. His attack on spiritualism extends his treatment in interesting ways.)

Burnyeat, M.F. (1980) 'Socrates and the Jury: Paradoxes in Plato's Distinction between Knowledge and True Belief', *Proceedings of the Aristotelian Society* supplementary vol. 54: 173–91. (An important discussion of Plato's epistemology, which includes an analysis of Plato's approach to epistemology.)

—— (1987) 'Wittgenstein and Augustine De Magistro', *Proceedings of the Aristotelian Society* supplementary vol. 61: 1–24. (Augustine's views on teaching are explored and compared to Wittgenstein's epistemological outlook. The discussion illuminates the significance of testimony for the theory of knowledge.)

Coady, C.A.J. (1992) *Testimony: A Philosophical Study*, Oxford: Oxford University Press. (Extended treatment of the topic that defends a non-reductionist approach to the epistemology of testimony.)

—— (1994) 'Speaking of Ghosts', in F.F. Schmitt (ed.) *Socializing Epistemology*, Lanham, MD and London: Rowman & Littlefield. (Discusses what seems to be a challenge to some of the methodology and conclusions of Coady's 1992 work.)

* Descartes, R. (1637) *Discourse on Method*, in *The Philosophical Works of Descartes*, vol. 1, trans. J. Cottingham, R. Stoothoff and D. Murdoch, Cambridge, Cambridge University Press, 1985. (Formative work on the theory of knowledge by one of the great figures of modern philosophy. Does not discuss testimony, but his outlook embodies the individualism that significantly influenced later theorists.)

Dummett, M.A.E. (1994) 'Memory and Testimony', in B.K. Matilal and A. Chakrabarti (eds) *Knowing from Words*, Dordrecht: Kluwer. (Exploration of the deep links between the epistemological status of testimony and of memory. Argues for an anti-reductionist stance on testimony.)

Fricker, E. (1987) 'The Epistemology of Testimony', *Proceedings of the Aristotelian Society* supplementary vol. 61: 57–83. (Argues for the superiority of justificationist over reliabilist accounts of the status of testimony, and treats testimony as a 'secondary' epistemic link compared with such 'primary' links as seeing.)

—— (1995) 'Telling and Trusting: Reductionism and Anti-Reductionism in the Epistemology of Testimony: Critical Notice of C.A.J. Coady: *Testimony: A Philosophical Study*', *Mind*, 104: 393–411. (Seeks to distinguish the merits of different kinds of reductionism and opposition to them in this area.)

Hardwig, J. (1985) 'Epistemic Dependence', *Journal of Philosophy* 82 (7): 335–49. (Argues that appeal to epistemic authority is an essential ingredient in much knowledge and that, because of this, rationality sometimes consists in refusing to think for oneself.)

—— (1991) 'The Role of Trust in Knowledge', *Journal of Philosophy* 88 (12): 693–708. (Emphasizes the significance of trust for the project of knowledge, and the related importance of ethics for epistemology.)

* Hume, D. (1748) *An Enquiry Concerning Human Understanding*, in *Enquiries*, ed. P.H. Nidditch and L.A. Selby-Bigge, Oxford: Oxford University Press, 1975. (Although Hume does not have an extended treatment of testimony, his discussions of its epistemic status in the essay 'On Miracles' represent an acknowledgement of its practical importance combined with an influential attempt to make it theoretically derivative from more fundamental sources of information.)

Locke, J. (1689) *An Essay Concerning Human Understanding*, ed. P.H. Nidditch, Oxford: Oxford University Press, 1975. (Locke discusses problems about the assessment of particular testimonies and the apparent decay of the reliability of testimony through transmission chains in book 4, chapter 16.)

Mackie, J.L. (1969–70) 'The Possibility of Innate Knowledge', *Proceedings of the Aristotelian Society* 70: 245–57. (Discusses the problem of testimony and coins the phrase 'autonomous knowledge' to describe the ideal driving the reductionist about testimony.)

Matilal, B.K. and Chakrabarti, A. (1994) *Knowing from Words: Western and Indian Philosophical Analysis of Understanding and Testimony*, Dordrecht: Kluwer. (Collection of papers discussing issues about testimony from Western and Indian perspectives. In addition to the essays by Dummett and Strawson listed separately here, there are, among others, chapters by Coady, Fricker, Lehrer, Sosa and Welbourne.)

Plato (4th century BC) *Theaetetus* and *Meno*, in *The Dialogues of Plato*, trans. and intro. B. Jowett, Oxford, Oxford University Press, 1953. (*Theaetetus* 201 and *Meno* 97a–b insist that testimony would not provide knowledge even if perception did.)

Popper, K. (1968) *Conjectures and Refutations: the Growth of Scientific Knowledge*, 2nd. edn, New York: Harper & Row. (Notable for viewing our reliance upon testimony as a reason for being opposed to foundationalism.)

Price, H.H. (1969) *Belief*, Lecture 5, New York: Humanities Press. (Interesting modern discussion of testimony that is fully sensitive to many of the central problems.)

Reid, T. (1983) *Philosophical Works*, with notes by Sir W. Hamilton, ed. H. Bracken, Hildesheim: George Olms Verlag. (Reid treats our regard for testimony as epistemologically basic because it stems from first principles of common sense.)

Ross, J.F. (1975) 'Testimonial Evidence', in *Analysis and Metaphysics: Essays in Honor of R.M. Chisholm*, ed. K. Lehrer, Dordrecht: Reidel. (Perceptive treatment, in the mode of Chisholm, of what it is to know on the basis of testimony.)

Russell, B. (1948) *Human Knowledge: Its Scope and Limits*, New York: Allen & Unwin. (Here and elsewhere Russell shows awareness of the complexities of our dependence upon testimony, and he offers an analogical argument to deal with them.)

Schmitt, F.F. (1987) 'Justification, Sociality and Autonomy', *Synthèse* 73: 43–86. (Argues against the individualism implicit in traditional epistemologies and criticizes their treatment of testimony. Rejects the 'extreme' theory of Locke and the 'milder' theory of Hume, and explores an alternative view of intellectual autonomy to that inherent in the tradition.)

—— (1994) 'Socializing Epistemology: An Introduction through Two Sample Issues', in *Socializing Epistemology: the Social Dimensions of Knowledge*, Lanham, MD and London: Rowman & Littlefield. (Schmitt uses testimony as one example of the need for a new, social approach to epistemology.)

Strawson, P.F. (1994) 'Knowing from Words', in B.K. Matilal and A. Chakrabarti (eds) *Knowing from Words*, Dordrecht: Kluwer. (A brief critique of reductionist approaches to testimony.)

Welbourne, M. (1986) *The Community of Knowledge*, Aberdeen: Aberdeen University Press. (Short but interesting book that argues for a conception of knowledge as 'commonable' and is strongly anti-reductionist about testimony. Also argues that knowledge is conceptually prior to belief and cannot be defined in terms of it.)

C.A.J. COADY

TESTIMONY IN INDIAN PHILOSOPHY

A prominent topic in Indian epistemology is śābdapra-bdapramāṇa, *knowledge derived from linguistic utterance or testimony. The classical material is extensive and varied, initially concerned with providing grounds for accepting the wisdom of* śruti *or 'the heard word', that is, the canonical scriptures. The Buddhists, however, saw no need for* śābdajñāna (*information gained through words*) *as an independent source of knowledge, because any utterance (including the Buddha's) that has not been tested in one's own experience cannot be relied upon; and in any case, the operation of such knowledge can be accounted for in terms of inference and perception.*

The Nyāya, following the Mīmāṃsā, developed sophisticated analyses and a spirited defence of the viability and autonomy of testimony. The problem is recast thus: is śābdapramāṇa *linguistic knowledge eo ipso, or does verbal understanding amount to knowledge only when certain specifiable conditions, in addition to the generating conditions, are satisfied? The more usual answer is that where the speaker is reliable and sincere, and there is no evidence to the contrary, the generating semantic and phenomenological conditions suffice to deliver valid knowledge. If doubt arises, then other resources can be utilized for checking the truth or falsity of the understanding, or the reliability of the author (or nonpersonal source), and for overcoming the defects.*

1   The problem of *śabda*

Ever since some traditional philosophers made the intriguing claim that the Vedas (canonical Brahmanical texts) are an inviolable authority on all manner of things, debate has raged in Indian thought over whether *śabda*, or information derived from words, can rightfully be accepted as an autonomous mode of knowing. In other words, how can hearing a sentence under appropriate conditions serve as a means of acquiring knowledge? Philosophers in the tradition recognized that a theory is needed that gives an account of both the instrumental conditions by which words or linguistic utterances convey appropriate understanding and the epistemological grounds for adjudicating the validity of the understanding or cognition so derived. Indian schools of philosophy have responded in differing ways to this challenge.

In the general accounts of knowledge developed in India, a properly accredited source of knowledge (*pramāṇa*) is thought to be fundamental to the production of knowledge (see KNOWLEDGE, INDIAN VIEWS OF). What could such a source be in the case of *śābdapramāṇa*? Obviously, but nontrivially, words themselves. This response indicates a remarkable recognition of the deep connection between words and knowledge, beyond the usual preoccupations with words and objects, names and things, and even knowing words. It does not take much argument to point out that a vast body of knowledge and beliefs is derived from sources other than perception and inference, namely, from the words of others, notably through hearing (direct conversation, rumour, radio and television) or reading (books, newspapers, documents, lexicons, inscriptions), not to mention the role of testimony under oath ('nothing but the truth') submitted in legal proceedings and courts of law. It should be noted that this account is not committed to suggesting that words exhaust or constitute the sole set of conditions that deliver the knowledge, or that the delivery is unproblematic in every instance. A number of factors are involved, and words arguably happen to be the primary causal antecedent, without which the delivery would flounder. That much is uncontroversial. The extent of the input from or reliance on other *pramāṇas*, including further testimony, remains to be established; much depends on the nature of the individual inquiry and the strength of conviction expected. Seen in this light, the question of the autonomy of testimony takes on a somewhat different significance, as does that of the reductivity of *śābdapramāṇa*. We shall return to this point.

2   Sentential meaning

The primary causal antecedent of knowledge through testimony is not just any string of words but a sentence (*vākya*). (This is also the basic unit of linguistic understanding for grammarians.) A sentence is made up of words, and sentential meaning is made up of word-meanings. A word (for example, 'cow') signifies either a universal (cowness) or a particular (dewlap-thing) possessing that universal, or it denotes a general class (cows), or perhaps even names an entity (Gokula). There is much discussion as to whether it is words or their meanings, whether singly or together, or the indivisible sentential structure, that convey the meaning of a sentence (*vākyārtha*) to a hearer. And the corollary issue of whether words achieve their signification individually, or by piecemeal compounding, or only by being related to other parts in the whole context of a sentence, is equally rehearsed, with various compromise positions. However, the main issue boils down to this: what does a sentence succeed in conveying, under appropriate conditions? It is clearly the (sentential) meaning that is grasped. But 'meaning' here is not exactly what linguists and grammarians are usually concerned with; it is more than the structure of the cognitive state constructed from the grasped words. *Vākyārtha* is literally the object out there, a compound object whose components are the component word-meanings. For example, grasping the meaning of the expression 'The lotus (is) blue', regardless of whether the object spoken of is present or not, amounts to cognizing a substratum, possessing lotusness, characterized by the quality blueness (the substratum that registers in awareness is represented by an oblique 'this': the awareness that there is something, *X*, qualified by blueness). Let us for now call this special cognition *śābdabodha* (standing in for *śābdajñāna* – awareness of the linguistic components or structure – and *anvayabodha* – comprehension of sense, or linguistic understanding), and render this as 'linguistic knowing'.

But what exactly is the meaning in respect of – reference or sense, or some other kind of designation? Some writers have argued that Indian philosophy does not have a clear notion of sense (as an abstracted conceptual representation or phenomenological 'thought') either because the sense–reference distinction is altogether lacking, or because some theory of reference has been dominant and sense has been subsumed as merely a mode of presentation consistent with the theory of reference (Mohanty 1992). Thus it falls short of allowing a sentence to achieve signification of any kind other than a direct denotation of the objective state that is its referent; this is construed as a complex relational object (in Nyāya) or related designation (in Prābhākara Mīmāṃsā). K.C. Bhattacharyya (1956) put it succinctly thus: 'The word directly refers to the thing, expresses the thing, touches it in a sense... The sentence at once refers to an objective relation.' (Clearly it is neither belief nor proposition that is of concern here, for the epistemic content of the word-derived cognition is more primitive than presupposed by either of these two pervasive categories of analysis.)

What is grasped in the cognitive state – that is, in *śābdabodha* under appropriate conditions – is a structure with various qualifying items that bear direct reference to objects thereby known. It follows that if in the process of grasping an expression some object fails to be clearly registered in the cognitive state (*anubhava*) or conflicts with another item in the structure, then a *śābdabodha* properly speaking cannot arise. The epistemic significance of this rider cannot be overstated, as it is connected with the fulfilment of the often-mentioned appropriate or specified conditions (*kāraṇas*). These conditions mark the uniqueness and therefore autonomy of *śābdabodha* in a way that is not available to perception and inference.

3 The conditions of understanding

Just as a sentence is not just any string of words, so sentential meaning is not conveyed unless certain conditions obtain. These conditions pertain to the relation, connection, integration and presentation of the words and their respective meanings or senses, and provide checks against vitiating factors, thus ensuring an unhindered and 'valid' grasp of sentential meaning. There are four conditions, whose relative degrees of importance depend on the school one follows. The first is contiguity (*āsatti*), which requires that words should follow each other in contiguous or proximate relation, for too large a spatial or temporal distance between words can be a linguistic hazard. The second condition is expectancy (*ākāṅkṣā*). When a word is uttered it arouses the expectation of another word that will appropriately complete the syntactical relation. When a speaker utters the words 'the door' the hearer expects another word (or series of words), such as 'close' or 'paint', to connect a pending meaning so as to complete the *śābdabodha* set in motion. The third condition is intentionality (*tātparya*), which refers to the speaker's intention or the intended purport of the expression. This is needed especially to disambiguate petrified meanings where the speaker desires a particular meaning to be conveyed, and also to carry the meaning of an expression whose speaker is either unavailable or nonexistent beyond the didactic (or literal) meaning (as in the case of the allegedly authorless scriptures and impersonal ordinances). The fourth and probably most controversial condition is semantic compatibility (*yogyatā*).

Yogyatā or semantic 'fitness' is related to *ākāṅkṣā*, as what is to follow the anticipation aroused should be a meaning which appropriately and not simply contingently completes the objective reference. In other words, it would be a source of frustration if after hearing someone utter the words 'the door', the hearer were to be presented with the words 'fuels the sun's fire'. With respect to whole utterances, the condition of *yogyatā* would rule out *śābdabodha* from expressions such as 'He wets with fire', since 'wetting' and 'fire' are mutually incompatible. On the strict Nyāya interpretation, there is no possibility of linguistic knowing arising here because there is incompatibility between the items being conjoined. The fitness expected is as much between the things signified (related in the reference) as it is with the signifying terms. With one part of the reference left as it were 'unsaturated' the truth-value presented is incomplete. On this interpretation, a sentence '*a* is *F*' is characterized by fitness (*yogyatā*) only if *a* is *F*. It follows that if a sentence is false, it cannot generate *śābdabodha*. Only true sentences, on this interpretation, are fit and so can generate *śābdabodha*. Not only contradictory sentences such as 'The fireless hill has fire', but also syntactically consistent but semantically absurd sentences such as 'Idleness is green' and even contingently false sentences such as 'It is raining' (when it in fact is not) – all these, strictly speaking, cannot generate *śābdabodha*, for there are no objective relational referents that answer to the disparate component-meanings.

The virtue of this argument is that it restricts the scope of *śābdapramāṇa* or testimony by stipulating a criterion that raises the epistemic value of the word-derived cognition so that not every expression can present itself as a fit candidate. And this criterion is built into the linguistic operation itself. But this also implies that if a sentence is not true, it lacks fitness and will fail to generate linguistic knowing. Two questions arise: (1) Does this mean that in the case of a false sentence no linguistic understanding at all arises? (2) Is the truth of a sentence always established or given a priori when the sentence is being understood? With respect to (1), it is urged that even with a patently false sentence (such as 'The sun is a ball of golden jelly') one does understand something from it; one at least knows that it is false. Why should this be any different from erroneous perceptions, which are still admitted to be 'perceptions' even though hopelessly false? Why can there not simply be 'false linguistic cognitions'? But even to know that a sentence is false, one has to understand something about the complex content of the sentence, in a way not dissimilar to understanding the complex relational object of a true sentence.

This recognition of a further, if weaker, cognitive process requires that we make a distinction between knowing and understanding. But the line of analysis followed so far has almost precluded the admission of such a distinction. This is due in large measure to the overwhelming influence of the Nyāya approach to the whole problem of language, which, with its unstinted commitment to a naïve realist ontology, has tended to eclipse more sanguine and less rigid analyses which not only admit of such a distinction but consider the function of understanding to be indispensable and necessary to the process. Prābhākara Mīmāṃsā, the Vedānta, the Jaina and the grammarians would side with the latter position. It is generally overlooked that Mīmāṃsā begins its theory of meaning with the thesis

of language being eternal (*autpattika*), which, like Saussurean semiology, posits the inseparability of signifier (sound-form) and signified (mental/conceptual image) in a word (see MĪMĀṂSĀ §3; SAUSSURE, F. DE §2). The composite designation derived from the component meanings need refer to no object(s) in the world as such, or can be simply a mode of presentation, and so on. Often, in the transmission of teachings, the pupil may acquire very directly images or complex ideas which have no objective correlate answering to the 'related designation' (see §2), which would be therefore better rendered as 'sense'. The inquiry into duty (*dharma*), the highest good and supplementary ethical notions, injunctional precepts, performatives (involving mantras), various illocutionary and perlocutionary speech-acts, poetic and mimetic evocations, and so on, involve an endeavour to generate verbal associations of this sort; the question of their truth and falsity, and of their being knowledge, can hardly be said to arise before their full significance and purport (teleological, soteriological or transcendental) is assimilated into the larger body of one's knowledge or beliefs. If the distinction is admitted, and understanding is permitted before the question of knowing is raised, then the thesis that identifies or collapses semantic fitness with truth-value is effectively shattered. This takes us to the second question.

4   Truth and falsity

Do all sentences come ready-stamped with the mark of truth or falsity? The idea that they might is not only counterintuitive, but an opponent might well urge that one hears a sentence and then, for the sake of conjecture and adventure, proceeds to determine whether it is true or false. From the hearer's subjective position, there is no other sense in which one can speak of the sentence being true or false moments prior to it being heard, without begging the question. (The speaker being aware or believing that the sentence uttered is false is of no relevance as this information is not available to the hearer, and besides, the sentence may well turn out to be true.)

Furthermore, a hearer may defer to the reliability of a speaker, trusting that the speaker is and has always been sincere and reliable. There may be no reason to doubt the reliability of the speaker and the hearer may take the speaker's authority to be a reason for attending to the utterance in the first place. And suppose that the hearer wishes to know about certain things to which it is not possible to have access through perception and inference. Would it be an act of epistemological violence if the hearer decided to accept what they heard from the testifier, but perhaps subsequently made detailed investigations to either prove or disprove what they thus came to 'know'? When no further evidence either way is forthcoming – notably from perception and inference – one either reviews one's reliance on the authority itself, or one turns to logical and metaphysical arguments, as philosophers frequently do, to assuage growing doubts about the truth of one's forebears' utterances.

Finally, on the question of the non-reductiveness of *śābdapramāṇa*, some general points only can be noted here. The first issue is whether the requisite linguistic conditions are sufficient, in and of themselves, to mediate and deliver the kind of knowledge claimed for language. We observed earlier a resistance to collapsing semantic fitness into the requirement for truth so that it is not always possible to question whether what one understands is true or not. Even the scholastic Prābhākara Mīmāṃsā, for whom all cognitions arising from the appropriate use of the accepted *pramāṇas* are intrinsically true – that is, truth is given by virtue of the cognition being a knowing-state – will concede that errors do creep in, that one could be mistaken about what one takes to be true, especially with regard to nonperceptibles, and that such falsified knowledge has to be set aside.

Ironically for Nyāya, it is a general principle that truth is never self-evidentially given, for whether anything is a source of knowledge is a matter to be established *ab extra* (*parataḥ*), by certain 'marks of excellence' of evidence, and further corroboration that may involve pragmatic testing. One may even attempt to falsify a cognition to assess its tenacity. But if this is extended to *śābdabodha*, then it could be argued that testimony comes to depend on other resources for its validation and therefore loses its claim to be *sui generis*. Paradoxically, if such resources are not available in the case of nonperceptibles, then the risk of allowing certain linguistic understandings to stand without validation could become onerous; and deferring to further testimonies or to consensus on their reliability would only serve to perpetuate the process.

See also: LANGUAGE, INDIAN THEORIES OF; MEANING, INDIAN THEORIES OF

References and further readings

* Bhattacharyya, K.C. (1956) *Studies in Philosophy*, ed. G. Bhattacharyya, vol. 1, ch. 2, Calcutta: Progress Publishers; repr. Delhi: Motilal Banarsidass, 1983, page 83–. (Bhattacharyya pioneered a uniquely Indian genre of Neo-Kantian realism and phenomenological style in the 1920s, working out of Calcutta, where he had no contact with philosophers in the West.)

Bilimoria, P. (1988) *Śābdapramāṇa: Word and Knowledge, A Doctrine in Nyāya-Mīmāṃsā Philosophy*, Dordrecht: Reidel/Kluwer. (The first comprehensive treatment and analytical exposition in English of testimony in Indian philosophy. Based on classical material, it makes relevant connections with Western theories of knowledge and philosophy of language.)

—— (1993) '*Pramāṇa* Epistemology: Some Recent Developments', in G. Floistad (ed.) *Contemporary Philosophy: A New Survey*, Asian Philosophy 7, Dordrecht: Kluwer. (This essay surveys current developments in Indian epistemology pertaining to debates over language, knowledge and truth.)

—— (1995) 'Authorless Voice, Tradition and Authority in Mīmāṃsā', *Nagoya Studies in Indian Culture and Buddhism* 16: 137–60. (The paper analyses the locution of 'authorless texts' in Mīmāṃsā exegetical hermeneutics, via the framework of Saussurean semiology, which is also criticized here.)

Hayes, R. (1988) *Dignāga on the Interpretation of Signs*, Dordrecht: Reidel/Kluwer. (Hayes presents an elegant treatment of Dignāga's theory of signs and language, critically reviewing non-Buddhist ideas on semiology and interpretation.)

Matilal, B.K. (1990) *The Word and the World: India's Contribution to the Study of Language*, Oxford: Oxford University Press. (The last book to be published before the author succumbed to cancer in Oxford is an eclectic set of reflections on the problem of language and knowledge across Indian thought, from Nyāya–Bhartṛhari holism to Derridean deconstructionism.)

Matilal, B.K. and Chakrabarti, A. (eds) (1994) *Knowing from Words: Western and Indian Philosophical Analysis of Understanding and Testimony*, Dordrecht: Kluwer. (This is a useful collection of essays from philosophers in India and the West (including Strawson and Coady) on the variety of ways in which the question of testimony, its viability in terms of linguistic and epistemological process-content, can be approached in both the 'pure' and 'comparative' understandings.)

Matilal, B.K. and Evans, R. (eds) (1986) *Buddhist Logic and Epistemology*, Dordrecht: Reidel/Kluwer. (This is a useful collection of essays on the development of logic and its relations with the problem of knowing in Buddhist philosophy. The more difficult and technical areas of Nāgārjunian dialectic also receive lucid treatment here.)

* Mohanty, J.N. (1992) *Reason and Tradition in Indian Thought: An Essay on the Nature of Indian Philosophical Thinking*, Oxford: Clarendon Press. (This

is about the most authoritative philosophical work to date on reason, rationality and responses to the question of tradition in Indian thought, and is written in a highly accessible style combining analytical and phenomenological idiom.)

—— (1993) *Essays in Indian Philosophy Traditional and Modern*, ed. with intro. by P. Bilimoria, New Delhi/York: Oxford University Press; repr. 1995. (A collection of rare essays spanning a thirty-year period. Issues in metaphysics and social philosophy are covered, and the comparative standing of key doctrines, including testimony, in Indian and European philosophy is examined.)

Siderits, M. (1991) *Indian Philosophy of Language: Studies in Selected Issues*, Dordrecht: Kluwer. (A short, highly technical work treating the key issues in Indian philosophy of language. It picks up on recent linguistic developments and major paradigm debates in the analysis of language in modern philosophy, but focuses for its responses on Buddhist critiques of Nyāya and Mīmāṃsā theories.)

Staal, F. (1989) *Rules without Meaning: Rituals, Mantras and the Human Sciences*, New York: Peter Lang. (Staal explores a thesis of meaning which goes beyond semantic and purely linguistic components by shifting the analysis to the ritual structures and perfomative context of utterances (such as *mantras*) in highly sophisticated texts exemplified in the Vedas.)

PURUSHOTTAMA BILIMORIA

TETENS, JOHANN NICOLAUS (1736–1807)

Tetens was a German philosopher, mathematician and physicist, with a second career as a Danish government official, who was active in Northern Germany and Denmark during the second half of the eighteenth century. Together with Johann Heinrich Lambert and Moses Mendelssohn, Tetens forms the transition from the German school philosophy of Leibniz, Wolff and Crusius to the new, critical philosophy of Kant. Tetens' philosophical work reflects the combined influence of contemporary German, British and French philosophical currents. His main contribution to philosophy is a detailed descriptive account of the principal operations of the human mind that combines psychological, epistemological and metaphysical considerations. While showing a strong empiricist leaning, Tetens rejected the associationist and materialist accounts of the mind, favoured in Britain and France, and insisted on the active, spontaneous role of the mind in the formation and processing of mental contents.

1 Life
2 Metaphysics
3 Philosophical psychology

1 Life

Tetens was born in Tetenbüll (Schleswig, Northern Germany) – or, on another account, in 1738 in Tönning (Schleswig) – and died in Copenhagen. From 1755 until 1758 he studied mathematics, physics and philosophy at the universities of Copenhagen and Rostock. In 1759 he earned the degree of *magister* and began teaching at Rostock, where he defended his dissertation in 1760. From 1760 until 1776 he taught physics and philosophy at the newly founded Bützow Academy. In 1765 he also assumed the directorship of the local *Gymnasium*. From 1776 until 1789 he held a professorship at the University of Kiel, first in philosophy, and later also in mathematics. In 1789 he entered public service and had a distinguished career in the Danish Ministry of Finance.

Tetens' main philosophical works were written in the 1770s under the influence of Leibniz's posthumously published *Nouveaux Essais* (1765) and Kant's pre-critical writings. Tetens also made contributions to applied mathematics, meteorology, pedagogy and environmental engineering. With his wide range of research activities and his dual career in academia and government, Tetens was one of the few truly universal scholars in the tradition of Leibniz. His philosophical work places him among the very best in German philosophy between Leibniz and Kant. In several respects he is a direct precursor of Kant's critical philosophy.

2 Metaphysics

Tetens' philosophical work is informed by a sweeping knowledge of the main philosophical movements of his time. He was well acquainted with the Leibnizian–Wolffian school of philosophy and its pietist critics, was conversant with the Scottish Common Sense philosophers, knew the French materialist and sensualist philosophers, and was one of the few philosophers in Germany to read Locke and Hume before their works became available in translation (see WOLFF, C.; PIETISM; COMMON SENSE SCHOOL). In his eclectic stance towards those philosophical currents, Tetens resembled the position of the Berlin Academy and German *Popularphilosophie* in general. Yet unlike the main representatives of that movement, he held on to the German school-philosophical project of a 'first philosophy' or metaphysics. Like other proponents of metaphysics in eighteenth-century Germany, Tetens responded to the sceptical and materialist challenges to metaphysics with an investigation into the very possibility of metaphysical knowledge. In Tetens this methodological and epistemological reoriententation of metaphysics has a decidedly psychological character; metaphysical concepts and the principles into which they enter are traced to their origin in the general operations of the human mind.

Tetens' guiding interest in the reform of metaphysics shows most clearly in his first significant work, *Über die allgemeine speculativische Philosophie* (On General Speculative Philosophy) of 1775. He argues for a truly general and comprehensive foundational science that is indifferent to the specifics of the two principal object domains of metaphysics – spiritual and corporeal reality. The science in question would not have specific objects as its domain but only the most general concepts and principles that pertain to being as such. Tetens' term for this discipline, that transcends all knowledge of specific objects, is 'transcendent philosophy'. According to Tetens, previous metaphysics suffers from a confusion of what is genuinely transcendent with the features of either corporeal or spiritual reality.

Tetens' chief concern is to ensure that the transcendent concepts and principles are not merely figments of the mind but have reality and pertain to objects outside the mind entertaining them. According to Tetens, the validation of such metaphysical claims proceeds by appealing to psychological facts to be discovered through observation of the workings of one's own mind. Transcendent principles, such as the Principle of Sufficient Reason, are validated by the feeling of necessity that accompanies consideration of them. The reality of general concepts, including such transcendent concepts as causality and substance, is established by showing their material basis in sensations. For Tetens, there is no sceptical wedge to be inserted between our best evidence about the world and the way the world really is. Psychological necessity carries logical and ontological weight. He seeks to respond to Hume's doubt about the reality of causal connection by making a distinction between contingent mental habits and necessary manners of thinking. Yet while assuming the reality of universal forms of thinking, Tetens does not go on to draw ontological consequences from this fact, in the manner of Kant's distinction between things in themselves and appearances. Tetens came to see that before transcendent philosophy can be applied to objects outside the understanding, its concepts and principles have to be

derived through a comprehensive philosophical account of human understanding.

3 Philosophical psychology

Tetens undertook such a detailed examination of the human mind in his main philosophical work, the *Philosophische Versuche über die menschliche Natur und ihre Entwickelung* (Philosophical Essays on Human Nature and its Development), which was published in two volumes in 1777. In the first ten of the work's fourteen essays, Tetens follows Locke's descriptive method and provides a detailed classification of the mental powers and their modes of operation. The emphasis is on the power of cognition. Tetens here exceeds the confines of contemporary empirical psychology through the ontological and epistemological scope of his psychological considerations. The last four essays take up topics in rational psychology by discussing the nature of the soul with regard to its basic power, its freedom, its relation to the body and its perfectibility. The work often digresses and the relation between the various classifications of mental powers offered is not always clear. Yet the *Philosophische Versuche* contains a number of original contributions to the study of the human mind and constitutes a significant step in the prehistory of scientific psychology and cognitive science.

Tetens distinguishes three principal forces that make up the human power of cognition: feeling, representing and thinking. Feeling is the initial, merely passive stage of cognition. It consists in the mind's modificability or receptivity to sensations, but also includes the mind's passive ability of noticing its own states. Representing involves both phantasy, responsible for the associative grouping of representations, and imagination, through which new representations are formed. Thinking consists in the detection of relations among the mental contents presented through feeling and representation. The relations are articulated through concepts and judgments. Tetens provides a psychological derivation of the general relational concepts, such as identity and diversity or simultaneity and succession. He considers those general concepts and the judgments into which they enter sufficiently validated through the psychological necessity with which they present themselves in the mind.

Tetens stresses the active, spontaneous nature of representing and thinking. Even perception is said to involve mental activity beyond the reception of sensation. He considers whether there might be a fundamental principle underlying the three basic powers of cognition, but concedes the hypothetical nature of his speculations on a primitive mental force that would be both feeling and active.

When surveying the overall organization of the human mind with an eye to its most basic powers, Tetens separates the active cognitive powers from passive feeling. Representing and thinking now make up the understanding, while feeling is taken in a broader sense, encompassing the mind's affective response to its modifications through the sensations of pleasure and pain. To understanding and feeling Tetens adds volition as the third basic mental power, thus providing the immediate precedent for Kant's threefold division of the human mind into the faculty of cognition, the feeling of pleasure and displeasure, and the faculty of desire.

Tetens' inquiry into the basic force of the human mind as a whole leads him to broader considerations regarding the basic character of humanity, which he identifies as extraordinary modifiability and disposition to spontaneous activity. This double characterization combines the recognition that physical and mental development is highly susceptible to external circumstances with the recognition that human mental life develops on the basis of internal forces.

While Tetens' contributions to the reform of metaphysics were soon overshadowed by Kant's *Critique of Pure Reason*, the psychological approach to philosophical issues practised by Tetens found a number of successors in post-Kantian philosophy from FRIES and HERBART to Laas and BRENTANO. In fact, Kant's distinction between a psychological, descriptive, and a nonpsychological, justificatory, dimension of knowledge, which had been developed mainly in response to Tetens, did not achieve canonical status until the neo-Kantianism of the late nineteenth century and the advent of anti-psychologism in logic – only to be questioned again in twentieth-century efforts to naturalize epistemology and ontology (see NEO-KANTIANISM).

See also: LAMBERT, J.H.; MENDELSSOHN, M.; TRANSCENDENTAL ARGUMENTS

List of works

Tetens, J.N. (1775) *Über die allgemeine speculativische Philosophie* (On General Speculative Philosophy), Bützow and Wismar; ed. W. Uebele, Berlin: Reuther & Reichard, 1913. (The Uebele edition also reprints the *Philosophische Versuche*.)
—— (1777) *Philosophische Versuche über die menschliche Natur und ihre Entwickelung* (Philosophical Essays on Human Nature and its Development), Leipzig, 2 vols; repr. in *Die philosophischen Werke*, vols 1–2, Hildesheim: Olms, 1979; vol. 1 repr. in W.

Uebele (ed.), Berlin: Reuther & Reichard, 1913. (The Uebele edition also reprints *Über die allgemeine speculativische Philosophie*.)
—— (1971) *Sprachphilosophische Versuche* (Experiments in Philosophy of Language), ed. H. Pfannkuch, Hamburg: Felix Meiner. (Introduction by E. Heintel. This collection contains *Über die Grundsätze und den Nutzen der Etymologie* (On the Principles and Advantages of Etymology, 1765–6); *Über den Ursprung der Sprachen und der Schrift* (On the Origin of Languages and Writing, 1772); and selections from Essay 11 of the *Philosophische Versuche*. Includes a bibliography.)

References and further reading

Barnouw, J. (1979) 'The Philosophical Achievement and Historical Significance of Johann Nicolaus Tetens', *Studies in Eighteenth Century Culture* 9: 301–35. (De-emphasizes Tetens' relation to Kant.)
Baumgarten, H.-U. (1992) *Kant und Tetens. Untersuchungen zum Problem von Vorstellung und Gegenstand* (Kant and Tetens. Investigations into the Problem of Representation and Object), Stuttgart: Metzler & Poeschel. (Emphasizes Tetens' relation to Kant.)
Beck, L.W. (1969) *Early German Philosophy: Kant and his Predecessors*, Cambridge, MA: Harvard University Press, 412–25. (Contrasts Tetens with Kant.)
Ciafardone, R. (1983) *Johann Nicolaus Tetens. Saggi filosofici e scritti minori*, L'Aquila. (A comprehensive monograph on Tetens.)
Dessoir, M. (1892) 'Des Nic. Tetens Stellung in der Geschichte der Philosophie' (On Tetens' Place in the History of Philosophy), *Vierteljahresschrift für wissenschaftliche Philosophie* 16: 335–68. (A concise account of Tetens' position in the history of philosophy.)
Gelder, B. de (1975) 'Kant en Tetens', *Tijdschrift voor filosofi* 37: 226–60. (A comparison of Kant and Tetens.)
Hauser, C. (1994) *Selbstbewußtsein und personale Identität. Positionen und Aporien ihrer vorkantischen Geschichte. Locke, Leibniz, Hume und Tetens* (Self-consciousness and Personal Identity. Positions and Aporia of their Pre-Kantian History. Locke, Leibniz, Hume and Tetens), Stuttgart-Bad Cannstatt: Frommann-Holzboog, 124–51. (An account of Tetens' contributions to eighteenth-century accounts of self-consciousness and personal identity; includes bibliography.)
Kuehn, M. (1987) *Scottish Common-sense in Germany*, Kingston, NY, and Montreal: McGill University Press, 119–40. (An account of Tetens'

relation to Thomas Reid, James Oswald and James Beattie.)

Störring, G. (1901) *Die Erkenntnistheorie von Tetens* (Tetens' Epistemology), Leipzig. (An account of Tetens' theory of knowledge.)

Uebele, W. (1911) *Johann Nicolaus Tetens nach seiner Gesamtentwicklung betrachtet, mit besonderer Berücksichtigung des Verhältnisses zu Kant* (Johann Nicolaus Tetens and his Development Considered, with Special Consideration of the Relationship to Kant), Berlin: Reuther & Reichard. (Emphasises the relationship between the philosophy of Tetens and that of Kant.)

G. ZÖLLER

THALES (*fl. c.*585 BC)

Known as the first Greek philosopher, Thales initiated a way of understanding the world that was based on reason and nature rather than tradition and mythology. He held that water is in some sense the basic material, that all things are full of gods and (purportedly) that all things possess soul. He predicted an eclipse of the sun and was considered the founder of Greek astronomy and mathematics.

1 Life and legacy
2 Philosophy
3 Mathematics and astronomy

1 Life and legacy

The first Presocratic philosopher and reputed founder of Western philosophy and science, Thales lived in the early sixth century BC in Miletus, a prosperous Ionian Greek city on the seaboard of Asia Minor. At Miletus he was followed in turn by ANAXIMANDER and ANAXIMENES, the other members of the so-called Milesian School. These two refined his rational approach to the study of nature and extended its application, leaving an intellectual legacy that was decisive for later Presocratic philosophers and, through them, for Plato, Aristotle and the Hellenistic philosophical schools, and consequently for the rest of the Western cultural tradition.

It is doubtful whether Thales wrote anything. Although ancient sources ascribe several works to him, no writing of his was available to Aristotle. Our knowledge depends entirely on the reports of others, many of which are inaccurate and even fanciful, thanks to the legendary status Thales achieved. Thales was the only Presocratic philosopher numbered among the Seven Sages, and this honour is probably due to his reputation for practical advice rather than for his scientific and philosophical work. He is said to have told the Ionian cities to form a political union with a common, centrally located governing council, the better to resist Persian aggression (Herodotus, I 170, A4) and to have advised the Lydian king Croesus how to ford the Halys River (I 75, A6). He was most famous for predicting a solar eclipse that took place on 28 May 585 BC (I 74, A5).

2 Philosophy

Thales is widely believed to have held that all things are made of water. This interpretation goes back at least to Aristotle (*Metaphysics* I 3, A12), who attributes it to Thales in summarizing the views of his predecessors which he regards as pertinent to his own investigation of *aitiai* (causes or explanatory factors). Thales, like 'others who first pursued philosophy', held that 'the only principles (*archai*) of all things are principles in the form of matter'. He chose water as the unique material principle, in the sense that everything originally evolves from water and ultimately perishes into water and, more strongly, that all things are composed of water, which persists in them although its attributes change. Thus Thales is the first Ionian material monist and the founder of physical science (see ARCHĒ).

How accurately Aristotle's interpretation represents Thales' views is open to question, for it dresses Thales in Aristotelian language and concepts and presupposes that he was interested in the very problems that excited Aristotle two centuries later. Furthermore, it is possible that Aristotle's account ('Thales, the originator of this kind of philosophy, says it is water; this is why he declared that the earth rests on water' (*Metaphysics* I 3, A12)) merely records Aristotle's own inference that Thales held water to be the material principle on the basis of the view, which he confidently attributes to Thales, that the earth rests on water. This possibility, together with the weakness of the inference, makes it less likely that Thales was a material monist in Aristotle's sense.

On an alternative theory, also based on ancient evidence, Thales borrowed the belief that the world floats on water from Egyptian and/or Babylonian creation myths such as the *Enuma Elish* (see EGYPTIAN PHILOSOPHY, INFLUENCE ON ANCIENT GREEK THOUGHT §1). This view is not implausible since Thales reportedly visited Egypt and Miletus had commercial connections with Egypt and the Near East. According to these creation myths, the earth or land arose in the middle of primeval waters through the agency of one or more gods. Thales may thus have borrowed also the idea that water is the origin of the world, conceiving of it not as an Aristotelian material principle, but as the ultimate ancestor of all things. It may be significant that *archē*, Aristotle's word for 'principle', also means 'origin' or 'beginning'.

Even on this account Thales did more than borrow; he took a decisive step away from the traditional and mythological towards the philosophical and scientific by demythologizing the views he adopted. Not that he was an atheist; he and his successors believed strongly in the divine and its importance in the universe. However, they abandoned the traditional Greek tendency to explain events through the Olympian gods. Where tradition had attributed earthquakes to Poseidon, Thales explained them in terms of the motion of the water that supports the earth (Seneca, *Natural Questions* III 14, A15). This way of thinking is more apparent in the theories of later Presocratics than in what we know of Thales himself, but their agreement on this approach was doubtless one of Aristotle's reasons for calling Thales the originator of materialism and for distinguishing him from purveyors of mythological accounts of creation.

Thales' views on divinity and on soul are attested as follows. 'He said that the magnet possesses soul (*psychē*) because it moves iron' (Aristotle, *On the Soul* 405a20, A22) (see PSYCHĒ). 'Some say that soul permeates the universe. This may have been Thales' reason for thinking that all things are full of gods' (*On the Soul* 411a7, A22). These reports have led some to describe Thales' world view as panpsychism and pantheism, but such labels by themselves contribute little to understanding a philosopher's thought. In the first place, the notion of soul needs clarification. Briefly and dogmatically, on the Greek view of soul which Aristotle develops and for which he finds evidence in Thales, the presence of soul is what makes something alive; non-living things have no soul, and dead things no longer have one. Signs of life include the capacities to move and change, and to cause other things to move and change. In Thales' case we have three claims: (1) the magnet moves iron, therefore it possesses soul; (2) soul permeates the universe; and (3) all things are full of gods. Only (1) and (3) are explicitly attributed to Thales; (2) is conjectured to be his reason for holding (3), and no connection is asserted to hold between (1) and (3). Now (3) does not follow from (2) without further premises, including one that amounts to: (4) wherever there is soul, there are gods. If Thales held this view (a hypothesis that is historically plausible, if unprovable), then (1) becomes relevant, since it establishes that soul occurs in more things than people suppose, and hence provides support for (2). Even so, the argument falls short. Even granted that anything that makes other

things move is alive, we need not suppose that everything whatsoever is alive. Still, this could be how Thales reasoned, in view of the Presocratic tendency to make generalizations on the basis of slender evidence.

This reconstruction of Thales' reasoning is tentative and optimistic, for (1) and (3) are the only views ascribed to him, and he could have held them independently of one another. However, his views on the role of water in the universe support the connection of ideas suggested above. Briefly and dogmatically again, the Greeks commonly held that anything was divine that was immortal and had the power to affect things independently of human will. On the second account of water presented above, water could be considered as divine and (for reasons given above) also as possessing soul. Things made out of water, or ultimately descended from water – that is, *all* things – thus have a claim to possessing soul and being divine, although these properties are more or less obvious in different things (just as some things are wetter than others).

3 Mathematics and astronomy

As Aristotle made Thales the originator of philosophy, so Aristotle's student Eudemus, who wrote histories of geometry and astronomy, made him the first Greek mathematician and astronomer. Here too the nature of his originality and contributions is uncertain. Reportedly he brought geometry to Greece from Egypt, where it was used for practical purposes and 'attacked some [theorems] more generally and others more perceptually' (Proclus, *On the First Book of Euclid's Elements* 65.3, A11). He was the first to prove that a circle is bisected by its diameter (157.10, A20), and to know that triangles having one side and the two adjacent angles equal are congruent, 'since he must have used this theorem in his method for demonstrating the distance of ships at sea' (352.14, A20). He is also credited with discovering several other theorems. The evidence supports different interpretations, from the extreme position that Thales stated and proved certain theorems exactly as they appear in Euclid, to the other extreme that he was no mathematician at all, but that Eudemus attributed certain results to him in order to give geometry as noble an ancestry as philosophy. An intermediate view is preferable; that he made certain discoveries about spatial relations and used them to solve practical problems, but did not have a general conception of mathematical proof, let alone of a Euclidean axiomatization of geometry, and probably did not even state the propositions generally. He is explicitly credited with proving only the claim about the circle – a proposition which Euclid does not prove, but incorporates into his definition of the diameter of a circle (*Elements* I def. 17). He may have proved this result by 'superposition' – drawing a circle, cutting it along a diameter, and seeing that one piece fits exactly over the other. This is not a rigorous demonstration, but since it shows that one fact follows from another and holds generally of all circles, not only the one used in the proof, it contains the essence of the conception of mathematical proof, and would represent a decisive advance from the problem-solving and rule-oriented approach of the Egyptians and Babylonians.

In astronomy he was credited with many discoveries, but in the end his fame as an astronomer rests on his prediction of the eclipse. However, even this cannot be accepted straightforwardly. For Thales certainly lacked the knowledge needed to predict eclipses by modern methods. At most he reported a Babylonian prediction: the Babylonians had methods of predicting when eclipses might occur, and there is nothing improbable about Thales' having come into contact with such knowledge.

The central problem in assessing Thales' contribution concerns his originality and his borrowing from others: how much was there of each, and what relative value are we to assign them? The evidence is unanimous in singling him out as a great innovator, and it would be rash to deny him all claims to importance, even if much of what he professed was due to others, especially non-Greeks. Later Ionian philosophers admired him and recognized him as their predecessor, and their ideas and methods are plausibly interpreted in terms of a historical sequence that originated with his evident curiosity about the world, his polymathy and his rational approach.

See also: DOXOGRAPHY; HESIOD

References and further reading

Classen, C.J. (1965) 'Thales', in A. Pauly, G. Wissowa and W. Kroll (eds) *Realencyclopädie der Altertumswissenschaft*, Stuttgart: Druckenmueller, suppl. vol. 10, cols 930–47. (Detailed and exhaustive discussion of the evidence; German text.)

Guthrie, W.K.C. (1962–78) *A History of Greek Philosophy*, Cambridge: Cambridge University Press, 6 vols. (Volume 1 pages 45–72 offers a thorough discussion of Thales; good bibliography.)

Heath, T.L. (1921) *A History of Greek Mathematics*, Oxford: Oxford University Press. (Still the best general account of Greek mathematics; volume 1 pages 128–39 covers Thales.)

Kahn, C.H. (1960) *Anaximander and the Origins of Greek Cosmology*, New York: Columbia University Press; repr. Indianapolis, IN: Hackett, 1994. (The best book on the Milesians.)

Kirk, G.S., Raven, J.E. and Schofield, M. (1982) *The Presocratic Philosophers*, Cambridge: Cambridge University Press, 2nd edn. (Chapter 2 offers a general treatment of Thales based on texts which are given in the original and in English translation.)

McKirahan, R.D. (1994) *Philosophy before Socrates*, Indianapolis, IN: Hackett. (Translation and discussion of source materials; chapter 4 covers Thales.)

* Thales (*fl. c.*585 BC) Fragments, in H. Diels and W. Kranz (eds) *Die Fragmente der Vorsokratiker* (Fragments of the Presocratics), Berlin: Weidemann, 6th edn, 1952, vol. 1, 67– 81. (The standard collection of the ancient sources in the original languages; includes Greek texts with translations in German.)

RICHARD McKIRAHAN

THEMISTIUS
(*c.*AD 317–*c.* AD 388)

As a pagan philosopher and adviser to Christian Roman emperors, Themistius aimed at making the celebrated writings of his heroes Plato and Aristotle more accessible through explanatory paraphrase. An apostle of cultural Hellenism to his contemporaries, in the Middle Ages he was widely known as an important epitomizer of Aristotle.

Themistius was a philosopher, orator, politician and imperial adviser. In Constantinople he administered a school from AD 345 to 355, where he lectured to large audiences on classical philosophy, especially that of ARISTOTLE. Unlike most Aristotelian commentators in late antiquity, Themistius combined theoretical and practical aspects of Hellenistic thought and presented them in a rhetorically effective manner. After his official appointments in 355 to a chair of philosophy and to the new Senate at Constantinople, he served Christian emperors from Constantius II to Theodosius I, eventually attaining the high rank of City Prefect in 384. His thirty-four surviving speeches celebrate imperial occasions and, more generally, articulate an influential ideology of monarchy and ecumenical empire, where foreigners with their different religions would be welcome. As a champion of the new secular Hellenism, Themistius argued that an emperor should display the qualities of a philosopher-king, that is, be both an Alexander and a Socrates. His advocacy of religious toleration is remarkable for a fourth-century pagan intellectual; he considered Christianity valid as one of the ancient cults ordained by the highest god.

The popularizing method of teaching employed by Themistius is evident in his philosophical writings. Instead of the traditional detailed textual commentary for advanced students, Themistius composed paraphrases which were designed as explanatory recapitulations to be read in conjunction with the original texts. This type of exegesis, particularly of Aristotelian works, became extremely popular throughout the medieval period in western Europe, Islamic countries and Byzantium. Of the five surviving paraphrases of Aristotelian works, three (on the *Posterior Analytics*, on *On the Soul* and on the *Physics*) survive in Greek. Those on *On the Heavens* and *Metaphysics* XII survive in medieval Hebrew translations from Arabic. Perhaps the most noteworthy of the lost paraphrases is one on the *Topics*, which influenced BOETHIUS and early medieval logical theory (see LOGIC, MEDIEVAL). Themistius' commentaries on Plato do not survive.

Certainly the most significant and influential of the surviving works is the paraphrase of the *On the Soul*. Themistius' interpretation of Aristotle's theory of the intellect became available to thirteenth-century philosophers through Averroes' commentaries on Aristotle (see IBN RUSHD) and William of Moerbeke's Latin translation. It had considerable impact on Thomas AQUINAS and SIGER OF BRABANT, the most important representative of Latin Averroism (see AVERROISM). New translations appeared in the fifteenth and sixteenth centuries.

Inasmuch as Themistius' epitomizing writings closely follow their Aristotelian originals, attention should be focused on his original interpretation of Aristotle's notoriously obscure account of the agent intellect (*nous poêtikos*) in *De Anima* III, 5. Themistius adds a substantial excursus on this difficult chapter, which analyses it in tandem with other Aristotelian texts and passages from Plato and THEOPHRASTUS. Aristotle spoke of two intellects, one actual and productive and one potential and receptive. The agent intellect is 'separable and unaffected and unmixed, being essentially actuality.... And when separated it is just what it is, and this alone is immortal and eternal.' ALEXANDER OF APHRODISIAS, the last great Aristotelian commentator before Themistius (more than a century earlier), boldly asserted that the agent intellect was identical with Aristotle's supreme principle and cause of the universe, the unmoved mover which is a self-thinking intellect. Themistius rejected Alexander's equation on the grounds that Aristotle located the agent intellect 'in' the soul. He suggested instead that the productive

intellect might be a secondary god, a suprahuman entity which is the cause activating each human being's 'possible' intellect. Thus, as the cause of thinking Themistius identified it with the Platonic form of the good (see PLATONISM, EARLY AND MIDDLE). The agent intellect, which Aristotle compared to light, is present like a ray to each mind when it thinks. The highest part of the human self is therefore a compound formed of the transcendent agent intellect and the individual's potential intellect. Unlike Aristotle and Alexander, Themistius claimed that the possible intellect when joined to the productive intellect constitutes the immortal aspect of human nature. Some scholars argue that human access to the transcendent aspect of the intellect is evidence of the influence of the noetic theory of PLOTINUS. Others emphasize Themistius' straightforward restatements of Aristotelian views and his preference for Aristotle's less idealistic ethical and political positions as compared to those of Plato and Plotinus as evidence that his views are fundamentally Peripatetic.

See also: ARISTOTELIANISM, MEDIEVAL; ARISTOTLE COMMENTATORS; PLATONISM, EARLY AND MIDDLE

List of works

Themistius (AD 345–55) *Analyticorum posteriorum paraphrasis* (Paraphrase on *Posterior Analytics*), ed. M. Wallies, *Commentaria in Aristotelem Graeca*, vol. 5, part 1, Berlin: G. Reimeri, 1900. (Aristotelian commentary.)

—— (AD 345–55) *In libros Aristoteles De anima paraphrasis* (Paraphrase on *De anima*), ed. R. Heinze, *Commentaria in Aristotelem Graeca*, vol. 5, part 3, Berlin: G. Reimeri, 1899; trans. R. B. Todd in F. M. Schroeder and R.B. Todd (eds) *Two Greek Aristotelian Commentators on the Intellect: The De Intellectu Attributed to Alexander of Aphrodisias and Themistius's Paraphrase of Aristotle De Anima, 3.4–8*, Toronto, Ont.: Pontifical Institute of Mediaeval Studies, 1990. (An edition of the medieval Latin translation by William of Moerbeke is in G. Verbeke (ed.) *Commentaire sur le traite De l'ame d'Aristote traduction de Guillaume de Moerbeke*, Louvain: Publications universitaires de Louvain, 1957; this edition also includes an essay by Verbeke on Thomas Aquinas' use of Themistius' commentary on Aristotle.)

—— (AD 345–55) *In Aristotelis Physica paraphrasis* (Paraphrase on the *Physics*), ed. H. Schenkl, *Commentaria in Aristotelem Graeca*, vol. 5, part 2, Berlin: G. Reimeri, 1900. (Aristotelian commentary.)

—— (AD 345–55) *In libros Aristotelis De caelo paraphrasis hebraice et latine* (Paraphrase on *On the Heavens* in Hebrew and Latin), ed. S. Landauer, *Commentaria in Aristotelem Graeca*, vol. 5, part 4, Berlin: G. Reimeri, 1902. (Aristotelian commentary.)

—— (AD 345–55) *In Metaphysicorum librum a paraphrasis hebraice et latine* (Paraphrase on the *Metaphysics* in Hebrew and Latin), ed. S. Landauer, *Commentaria in Aristotelem Graeca*, vol. 5, part 5, Berlin: G. Reimeri, 1903. (Aristotelian commentary.)

—— (after AD 355) *Orationes*, ed. H. Schenkl and G. Downey, Leipzig: Teubner, 1965–74.

References and further reading

Blumenthal, H. (1990) 'Themistius, the last Peripatetic commentator on Aristotle?', in R. Sorabji (ed.) *Aristotle Transformed*, London: Duckworth, 113–23. (Argues that Themistius is straightforwardly Aristotelian in his commentaries on Aristotle, without the Neoplatonic commitments of other commentators.)

Schroeder, F.M. and Todd, R.B. (1990) *Two Greek Aristotelian Commentators on the Intellect: The De Intellectu Attributed to Alexander of Aphrodisias and Themistius' Paraphrase of Aristotle De Anima, 3.4–8*, Toronto, Ont.: Pontifical Institute of Mediaeval Studies. (Introduction, translation and commentary. In his introduction to Themistius' Paraphrase, pages 31–41, and in the commentary accompanying the translation, Todd outlines Themistius' thought and argues against Blumenthal and in favor of considerable Neoplatonic influence on Themistius.)

JOHN BUSSANICH

THEODORUS *see* CYRENAICS

THEOLOGICAL VIRTUES

The three theological virtues of faith, hope and love, referred to frequently by the apostle Paul in his letters, play an indispensable role in Christian theorizing about a person's duties with respect to God. Thomas Aquinas is responsible for the most thorough and influential philosophical theory of the theological virtues. According to him, faith, hope and love are virtues because they are dispositions whose possession enables a person to act well to achieve a good thing – in this case, the ultimate good of salvation and beatitude. Without them, people would have neither the awareness of nor the will to strive for salvation. Despite the fact that they are infused in persons by God's grace, one can wilfully and culpably fail to let them develop.

Faith for Aquinas is the voluntary assent to propositions about God that cannot be known by the evidence available to the natural capacities of humans. Other theologians, such as Martin Luther and Søren Kierkegaard, deny the assumption that faith is primarily cognitive or propositional in nature, insisting instead that it is trust in God. Kierkegaard even challenges the presupposition that faith is logically continuous with natural knowledge. There has been much debate in the second half of the twentieth century as to whether it is ever rationally permissible to believe something on the basis of insufficient evidence.

According to Aquinas, hope for one's salvation requires that one already have faith. Hope requires that one remain steadfast in the face of despair on the one hand and presumption on the other. Aquinas models the virtue of love on one strand of Aristotle's notion of friendship. Love of God entails desiring the good that God has to offer, seeking to advance God's goals, and communicating one's love to God. Love for others follows from the realization that they are also created with good natures by God.

1 Aquinas on the theological virtues in general
2 Aquinas on faith
3 Difficulties with Aquinas' view
4 Alternative conceptions of faith
5 Hope and love

1 Aquinas on the theological virtues in general

For AQUINAS (§13), a human virtue is a disposition whose operation enables its possessor to act well to achieve an end that is good for human beings. Following Aristotle, Aquinas distinguishes between intellectual and moral virtues. The intellectual virtues pertain to the human intellect in so far as it is capable of acquiring theoretical or scientific knowledge. The moral virtues help to govern human actions and emotions. The division of human virtues into intellectual and moral would be exhaustive if every end good for humans were natural. But Aquinas thinks that the ultimate end for humans is supernatural, the beatific vision of God (see HEAVEN §3). Because this end is beyond the natural order of things and because the intellectual and moral virtues are fit only for the achievement of natural ends, acts directed towards achieving the supernatural end must issue from dispositions that go beyond the natural capacities of humans, namely, the theological virtues. The theological virtues are unlike the moral virtues in two important respects: (1) the moral virtues are acquired by practice – a person becomes courageous, for example, by acting as the courageous person would act; and (2) with regard to the emotions, choices and actions appropriate to a particular moral virtue, the possessor of that virtue displays a state that is a mean, neither deficient nor excessive. Thus a courageous person's emotions, choices and actions will be neither cowardly (the deficient state) nor rash (the excessive state). In contrast to point (1), the theological virtues are 'infused', instilled in a person by an act of God's grace. The infusion need not lead to success: a person can freely and culpably fail to respond to and develop the theological virtues. Aquinas claims that even though faith, hope and love are infused simultaneously, faith and hope can develop without the development of love; we then have 'unformed' or 'dead' faith. Love, however, cannot develop without the development of faith and hope, even though the blessed in heaven retain love but no longer have any need for faith or hope. In contrast to point (2), even though the theological virtues can be enhanced or diminished, they do not conform to the doctrine of the mean in the way in which the moral virtues do: one cannot believe in, hope for or love God excessively.

2   Aquinas on faith

The theological virtues, on Aquinas' understanding of them, are complexes whose analysis reveals both cognitive and volitional components. This interplay between intellect and will makes Aquinas' account of faith distinctive and subject to criticism. The primary object of faith (*fides*) is God, in so far as he can be grasped by human intellects. Human intellects operate by considering propositions. Some true propositions about God can be known by the intellect functioning within its natural capacities. For example, Aquinas thinks that there are sound arguments, appealing only to the testimony of our senses and obvious metaphysical principles, that enable us to know the truth of the proposition that God exists. Other propositions about God and God's relation to the world cannot be ascertained by reason and experience alone. Only divine revelation can convey such truths as that the world has not existed forever but was created by God, and that God is triune in nature.

Aquinas reserves the term 'understanding' (*intellectus*) for the intellectual virtue that enables one to grasp self-evident truths. 'Knowledge' (*scientia*) can refer either to the intellectual virtue that enables one

to make correct inferences, or to the cognitive state one is in when one grasps a truth by understanding or by inference, or to the body of propositions thereby known. In contrast to the proposition that triangles have three sides, the mere understanding of which compels the intellect's assent, or the proposition that the sum of the interior angles of a triangle is equal to two right angles, which follows deductively from other propositions that are obviously true, the proposition that God is triune in nature is neither self-evident nor a demonstrable consequence of self-evident truths. Yet belief in this and similar supernatural doctrines of the Christian faith is necessary for human salvation. Faith is not identical to understanding or knowledge, because the propositions constitutive of faith are not rationally compelling. An act of will is necessary to bring the intellect to assent to the propositions of faith. The resultant mental state, belief, is not identical with any of the other cognitive states induced by the will, such as opinion, suspicion or doubt, because the latter involve, to varying degrees, an element of psychological uncertainty, whereas belief involves certainty. Aquinas appears to endorse the notion that faithful belief lies between knowledge and opinion. Belief is more like opinion and less like knowledge in so far as the evidence is insufficient to warrant psychological certainty. But because faithful belief nevertheless has no taint of psychological uncertainty, it is in that respect more like knowledge than opinion.

Aquinas believes that the possession of any virtue must be meritorious. The meritoriousness of 'formed' or 'living' faith resides in the facts that the belief is the voluntary assent to revealed divine authority, and that the assent is directed by love for the ultimate good, God. If either the voluntariness or the love for the ultimate good were lacking, faith would not be a virtue.

Aquinas' position, then, is that faith is a voluntarily induced belief whose content is a set of propositions revealed authoritatively by God and typically codified in a confessional creed. The disposition to believe is infused by God. Faith is not knowledge because the intellect is not able by natural means to acquire knowledge of the propositions to which the believer assents. Unlike other voluntarily induced cognitive states, faith entails psychological certainty. Living faith is a virtue because the relevant propositional assent is voluntary and motivated by love for the object of faith, God. Some criticisms of Aquinas' position appear to be compatible with modification and redeployment (see §3 below). Other criticisms are more radical, advocating the abandonment of Aquinas' position (see §4 below).

3 Difficulties with Aquinas' view

Aquinas insists that the virtue of faith cannot be separated from the propositions that give faith its content. Since the propositional content is revealed by an essentially truthful God, one cannot have faith in a proposition that is false. (Thus faith must be distinguished from the ordinary cognitive state of belief.) Moreover, one has faith, according to Aquinas, only if one assents to all the propositions contained in the confessional creeds. To reject some part of the creeds is to fail to regard the creeds themselves as underwritten by divine authority. Thus Aquinas' view entails that all non-Christians lack faith. It also entails that a Christian heretic, who might deny some article of faith while accepting all the others, lacks faith. If one seeks an analysis of faith that is neutral among different religions, one will either have to modify Aquinas' view or look elsewhere.

Aquinas' compartmentalization of various cognitive attitudes contributes to two difficulties for his view, one involving the difference between knowledge and belief, another involving the difference between faith and doubt. On the biblical authority of the Epistle of James, Aquinas thinks that there are demons or malignant spirits who believe various propositions about God. If the virtue of faith is simply a matter of believing those propositions, then the demons would appear to have faith, contrary to their diabolical natures. Aquinas attempts to deny merit for the demons' cognitive state by attributing to them intellectual powers superior to those of humans, appearing to suggest that the evidence is so clear for the demons as to make their assent involuntary. If Aquinas accepts this position, then he is forced to concede that the demons do not *believe*; they *know*. Since Aquinas regards knowledge and belief as two separate and incompatible cognitive states, he would then have to gainsay James, whom he acknowledges to be one source of revelation. On the other hand, if the demons' belief is voluntary, then Aquinas' account of faith would seem to confer merit on their belief.

Because faith as a virtue is a disposition that entails psychological certainty, and doubt entails lack of certainty, it is impossible for Aquinas' believer to harbour any doubts about the content of faith. Aquinas' account thus has the consequence that believers who struggle to hold on to their religious convictions in the face of lingering doubts simply do not have faith at all. In the light of this, one might seek to deny Aquinas' requirement of psychological certainty.

Aquinas' view presupposes that, to some extent, what people believe is within their voluntary control. Aquinas does not believe that all beliefs are voluntary: the verdicts of understanding and knowledge, in his technical senses of those terms, are not subject to the will. One might wonder, however, whether any beliefs can be voluntarily induced, and, in particular, whether religious beliefs can be adopted as a matter of conscious decision, as Aquinas' doctrine requires. It is unclear whether Aquinas thinks that someone infused with faith must be able to come *directly* to will to believe, or that infused faith allows for the *indirect* development of belief by the will. Consider this analogy. A person might realize that they would be happier if they did not believe that others were conspiring against them, yet be unable to eradicate the belief simply by willing it away. Nevertheless, they might be able to take small steps, such as associating cautiously but more freely with others, which would have the indirect and cumulative effect of weakening and eventually dislodging the paranoid belief. Similarly, a person might be able to embrace religious belief by associating with believers and emulating their practices. Even if no one can directly will to believe, it may be enough for an account of faith like Aquinas' that one be able to nourish infused faith by such indirect means.

4 Alternative conceptions of faith

Martin Luther's articulation of faith has been traditionally interpreted as a rejection of any view that maintains that faith is a cognitive virtue (see Luther L,M.). It would seem that if faith is a virtue, then its possessors have the power to make progress towards achieving salvation on their own. But Luther insists that personal salvation can only be attained through the recognition that one's sinful state makes one incapable of living righteously. Nor is faith primarily cognitive. A person of faith believes that various propositions about God are true, but those beliefs are subordinate to trust in God, which for Luther is the core of faith. To trust in God is to resign oneself to the will of God, a resignation that is precipitated by awareness of one's own helplessness and lack of merit. But even the resignation is not under one's voluntary control: Luther views it as a gift from God. Luther's insistence on 'justification by faith alone, not by works' epitomizes his view that faith is the only path to salvation (see Justification, religious §4).

Some observers have argued that the differences between Aquinas' and Luther's accounts of faith are not as great as they may first appear. Luther claims that love is a necessary consequence of faith, whereas Aquinas regards living faith as faith informed by love.

For both accounts, then, genuine faith entails love of God and neighbour. Even so, Aquinas and Luther appear to differ about the status of hope (see §5 below).

The implications of treating faith as absolute trust in God are pursued further in the writings of Søren KIERKEGAARD (§§4–5). Aquinas' view allows faith's cognitive content to extend beyond the content accessible to natural reason while remaining compatible with it. Many of Kierkegaard's remarks can be interpreted as an attack on such a view, on the grounds that it underestimates the radical 'leap' that religious faith requires. To conceive of faith as somehow continuous with natural knowledge is to succumb to the temptation to base faith on evidence, whether that evidence be historical (such as the testimony of miraculous events) or scientific (such as the evidence that the world is only finitely old). But the evidence will always be less than conclusive, whereas the passion of faith is infinite. Kierkegaard thinks that as long as one is guided by canons of objectivity, under conditions of incomplete or ambiguous evidence one will endlessly defer forming a religious conviction, refusing to take the 'risk'. In fact, Kierkegaard thinks that from the point of view of natural objectivity, faith can only appear absurd. Abraham's complete trust in God, manifested by his unhesitating willingness to sacrifice Isaac at God's command, is for Kierkegaard an admirable example of faith that shows how alien faith is from objective inquiry. Although the differences between Aquinas' and Kierkegaard's views are pronounced, it is not clear whether those differences preclude Kierkegaard from regarding faith as a virtue.

W.K. Clifford provides the classic statement of the opinion that faith is a vice and not a virtue. According to Clifford, 'It is wrong always, everywhere, and for any one, to believe anything upon insufficient evidence' (1877: 346). A person who subscribes to any belief, religious or otherwise, on the basis of insufficient evidence thereby exhibits the vice of credulity, which Clifford regards as both an intellectual and a moral flaw. It follows from Clifford's position that a religious believer would be free from credulity only if the content of the belief were backed by evidence, available to and entertained by the believer, that is sufficient to warrant the belief. Many contemporary philosophers have denied Clifford's position, arguing that there need be no flaw in believing some propositions more strongly than the strength of the evidence would warrant. Even if this opinion can be sustained, it would take further argument to show that religious propositions can fit into the favoured class of beliefs.

Finally, some philosophers challenge the assumption, common to thinkers as diverse as Aquinas and Kierkegaard, that faith is necessarily distinct from knowledge. The challenge takes form by maintaining that Aquinas' conception of knowledge is overly restrictive, confining knowledge to the systematic rigour exhibited in a treatise on geometry or an axiomatization of particle mechanics. Epistemological reliabilism, in contrast, claims that a true belief is a specimen of knowledge if the belief was produced in the believer in a reliable way – for example, a perceptual belief brought about by means of a perceptual faculty functioning properly in an environment in which it is fit to function. Reliabilists typically insist that it is not necessary, in order for a true belief to count as knowledge, that the believer be in a position to justify the belief. A reliabilist who agreed with Aquinas that faith is divinely infused could regard divine infusion itself as a reliable process. If so, then contrary to what Aquinas claims, the believer's infused faith is a kind of knowledge. A proponent of such a view could still agree on Aquinas' own terms that faith is a virtue: that faith turns out to be knowledge is compatible with its being both voluntary and motivated by love of God.

5 Hope and love

Like faith, hope as a theological virtue has a specific propositional content, namely, that one will survive death and final judgment to enjoy the beatific vision of God. Augustine, in *Faith, Hope and Charity*, claimed that hope (*spes*) is directed only towards good things to be had in the future by the person who hopes. This seems to preclude the possibility that one could hope for the salvation of others. If one can hope only for one's own salvation, then it is not obvious why hope should count as a virtue, conferring moral credit on its possessor.

Aquinas' opinion is that unlike wishful thinking, hope is arduous. First, hope presupposes faith: those who have no beliefs about God's plans for humankind can have no hope that they will be saved by God. Second, even though the theological virtues do not conform to the doctrine of the mean, Aquinas thinks that hope does steer a course between two opposite vices, despair and presumption. Those who despair do not have too little hope; they have utterly abandoned hope, believing that they are too sinful to be an object of God's love. Similarly, presumption is not too much hope; it is rather a rejection of hope as unnecessary, on the belief either that one can attain salvation without God's aid or that God is so merciful that his salvation will extend to those who are unrepentant.

Aquinas' conception of hope is augmented by his remarks on love. He uses the term *amor* to characterize the ordinary notion of love as a passion, reserving the term *caritas* for the kind of love that is a theological virtue. Aquinas appeals to Aristotle's remarks on friendship in the *Nicomachean Ethics* (Books VIII and IX) in order to explicate the notion of *caritas* (see ARISTOTLE §25). The sort of friendship (*amicitia*) that constitutes *caritas* involves three components. First, one must desire the good that the loved thing or person is in a position to provide. Although necessary, such a desire is not sufficient to distinguish *caritas* from *amor*, for the desire can be directed towards animals and inanimate objects, with whom one cannot enter into a relation of friendship. Second, one must wish well for the object of one's desire, seeking to further that person's own interests. Aquinas believes that one cannot literally have this type of desire towards animals, for it presupposes in the object of *caritas* something that animals do not have, namely, freedom of will concerning the disposal of interests. The satisfaction of the first two components is compatible with one's love remaining hidden or unrequited, and is therefore insufficient for an analysis of *caritas* as friendship. The third requisite component is that *caritas* be shared and communicated among those who participate in it. The first component, supplemented by the principle that one's love should be proportionate to the goodness of the object loved, undergirds Aquinas' claim that *caritas* requires that one love God more than anything else, including oneself, because God is the supreme good and source of all other goods. The second component allows Aquinas to extend *caritas* to other persons, including one's enemies, inasmuch as all persons are created with good natures. The second component thus explains how one can hope for the salvation of others: if one is united to others by *caritas*, one adopts their ultimate best interests as one's own.

Aquinas' remarks on hope and his depiction of love as involving friendship between God and person reflect a guardedly optimistic conception of the human situation with respect to God. This conception appears to be irreconcilable with views expressed by Luther in his *Lectures on Romans* (1515–16). 'Pure love' of God, which Luther regards as the highest state a person can attain in this life, entails hatred of oneself, based on an awareness of one's inability to avoid sin and of God's detestation of all sinners. Luther's notion of pure love implies that even if hope is a virtue, it is not necessary for salvation and that despair need not be a vice. Moreover, it is hard to see how love of others can be a virtue for one who has pure love of God: if one hates oneself and realizes that all other are equally detestable, then one should hate them also.

See also: FAITH; GRACE; RELIGION AND EPISTEMOLOGY; VIRTUE ETHICS; VIRTUES AND VICES

References and further reading

Adams, R.M. (1987) *The Virtue of Faith and Other Essays in Philosophical Theology*, New York: Oxford University Press. (The title essay provides some reason for thinking that faith is better than knowledge. Two other essays discuss Kierkegaard's views.)

* Aquinas, T. (*c*.1265–73) *Summa theologiae*, trans. Fathers of the English Dominican Province, London: Burns, Oates & Washbourne, 2nd edn, 1920–9; reprinted Westminster, MD: Christian Classics, 1981. (The writing style requires getting used to. Virtues and vices in general are discussed in questions 49–89 of the first part of the second part; the theological virtues and vices in questions 1–46 of the second part of the second part.)

* Aristotle (*c*. mid 4th century BC) *Nicomachean Ethics*, trans. T. Irwin, Indianapolis, IN: Hackett Publishing Company, 1985. (Perhaps the most influential book in the history of ethics, its thought is evident in the massive second part of Aquinas' *Summa theologiae*.)

* Augustine (*c*.423) *Faith, Hope and Charity*, trans. and with introduction by B.M. Peebles, The Fathers of the Church, vol. 2, Washington: Catholic University of America Press, 1947, 355–472. (Often referred to as the *Enchiridion*, this is perhaps the first sustained treatise on the theological virtues.)

* Clifford, W.K. (1877) 'The Ethics of Belief', in L. Stephen and F. Pollock (eds) *Lectures and Essays by the Late William Kingdon Clifford, F.R.S.*, London: Macmillan, 2nd edn, 1886, 339–63. (Clifford's classic attack on belief based on insufficient evidence.)

James, W. (1896) 'The Will to Believe', in *The Will to Believe and Other Essays in Popular Philosophy*, The Works of Willam James, vol. 6, ed. F.H. Burkhardt, F. Bowers and I.K. Skrupskelis, Cambridge, MA: Harvard University Press, 1979, 13–33. (A famous rejoinder to Clifford's position.)

Kenny, A. (1992) *What is Faith?*, Oxford: Oxford University Press. (Contains a series of lectures on faith and reason, endorsing parts of Plantinga's case against views like Clifford's.)

Kierkegaard, S. (1843) *Fear and Trembling*, trans. and with introduction by A. Hannay, Harmondsworth: Penguin, 1985. (Kierkegaard's meditation on Abraham's faith.)

—— (1846) *Concluding Unscientific Postscript*, trans. D.F. Swenson and W. Lowrie, Princeton, NJ: Princeton University Press, 1941. (Part II, chapter

2 contains Kierkegaard's comments on the discontinuity between faith and objectivity.)

* Luther, M. (1515–16) *Lectures on Romans*, trans. J.A.O. Preus, *Luther's Works*, vol. 25, St Louis, MO: Concordia, 1972. (Chapters 8 and 9 contain Luther's comments on pure love.)

—— (1520) 'The Freedom of a Christian', trans. W.A. Lambert, revised H.J. Grimm, *Luther's Works*, vol. 31, Philadelphia, PA: Muhlenberg, 1957, 343–77. (Luther on justification by faith alone.)

Mann, W.E. (1993) 'Hope', in E. Stump (ed.) *Reasoned Faith*, Ithaca, NY: Cornell University Press, 251–80. (A discussion of Luther's notion of pure love and Aquinas' remarks on hope.)

Penelhum, T. (1977) 'The Analysis of Faith in St Thomas Aquinas', *Religious Studies* 13 (2): 133–54. (A careful discussion of Aquinas' views that develops the criticisms about demonic belief and the incompatibility of faith with doubt.)

Pieper, J. (1986) *On Hope*, trans. M.F. McCarthy, San Francisco, CA: Ignatius Press. (An elementary presentation of Aquinas' views.)

Plantinga, A. (1982) 'Rationality and Religious Belief', in S.M. Cahn and D. Schatz (eds) *Contemporary Philosophy of Religion*, New York: Oxford University Press, 255–77. (An influential critique of Clifford that is hospitable to reliabilism.)

Swinburne, R. (1981) *Faith and Reason*, Oxford: Clarendon Press. (Chapter 4 argues that the differences between Aquinas' and Luther's conceptions are not as great as they seem.)

WILLIAM E. MANN

THEOLOGY, EXISTENTIALIST

see EXISTENTIALIST THEOLOGY

THEOLOGY, ISLAMIC

see ISLAMIC THEOLOGY

THEOLOGY OF LIBERATION

see LIBERATION THEOLOGY

THEOLOGY, POLITICAL

The concept of political theology was the subject of important controversies in European, and especially German, philosophy, social science and jurisprudence in the twentieth century. After the First World War, a debate took place between the jurist Carl Schmitt, an influential right-wing critic of parliamentary democracy in the Weimar Republic, and the theologian Erik Peterson. Another debate was occasioned by a new, leftist political interpretation of biblical texts in the years after 1960. In that context, 'political theology' designates philosophical positions influenced by neo-Marxist philosophies, such as the critical theory of the Frankfurt School. The earlier controversy between Schmitt and Peterson played a role in this later debate as well. Johann Baptist Metz is probably the most important representative of political theology in the later controversy.

In his writings on the problem of the legitimacy of the modern state and its constitution, the jurist Carl SCHMITT focused on the question of sovereignty. In his view, the sovereignty of the modern state is derived from an earlier theological tradition centred on God's existence and nature. The modern theory of the state, Schmitt held, had shifted the idea of God's omnipotence, which theologians understood as determined only by God's goodness, to the concept of the sovereignty of the people. ROUSSEAU (§3), for example, had described 'the general will' as the expression of the absolute will of a state's citizens, which could never be wrong or evil. The problem is that when reference to transcendence is abandoned, the notion of the state that remains is despotic, as, for example, in Hobbes' *Leviathan* (see HOBBES, T. §7). To describe the fundamental condition of modern politics, Schmitt introduced the notion of a situation of exemption. In a situation of exemption, radical political movements and charismatic leaders are allowed to annul laws simply by a decision to do so. Schmitt articulated a principle which helped to support both left- and right-wing political messianism: 'Authority, not truth, makes law'.

The most important opposition to Schmitt's account of the political theology of the modern state did not arise either from classical theories of natural law, in the Aristotelian or Thomistic traditions, or from a Kantian theory of law as based on arguments supported by practical reason. Instead it came from a theologian, Erik Peterson, who had converted to Catholicism from Protestantism. Peterson emphatically rejected Schmitt's understanding of the voluntary character of law as theological. He based his argument against Schmitt's position on historical as well as philosophical grounds. He pointed to the decision of the early Church to reject Arianism and to accept the doctrine of the Trinity. One of the consequences of this position was set out by Augustine, Peterson thought. In his *De civitate Dei* (City of God), Augustine rejects a version of political theology which he thinks he finds in Eusebius of Caesarea; instead, Augustine maintains that there is and must be a separation between the City of God, on the one hand, and the earthly city, or state, on the other. In Peterson's view, this Christian position effectively undermines any possibility of a political theology of the sort Schmitt propounded.

After the Second World War, the Catholic theologian Johann Baptist Metz established a new version of political theology. In the 1960s, and especially during the time of Vatican II (1962–5), the Catholic Church was engaged in a process of reform and was searching for a renewed dialogue with the society in which it found itself. Metz's political theology was part of this larger trend. Metz took a positive view of the Enlightenment and modern freedom of thought, and saw his position as a legitimate consequence (supported by biblical studies) of modern anthropology. Like his teacher Karl RAHNER, Metz was concerned to bring the work of Thomas Aquinas into contemporary philosophical discussion. In his earlier writings, Metz also followed Rahner in trying to integrate Kant's transcendental philosophy and German idealism in general with the philosophical presuppositions of systematic theology. These efforts significantly transformed the Neo-Thomist account of human nature.

Metz's political theology was also based on a critical understanding of Kant's account of human freedom and Marx's concept of history. To some extent, it was influenced also by the views of Horkheimer and Adorno, who were critical of the Enlightenment and of modern theories of rationality, and by Benjamin's view of history as 'one single catastrophe where we perceive a chain of events' (1950, Thesis IX). So understood, political theology constitutes an important theological theory of modern times. At its heart, there is the concept of an eschatological reservation with regard to all stages of progress and emancipation in history. This feature of Metz's political theology allows it to avoid the sort of mistakes for which Peterson reproached Schmitt.

See also: RELIGION AND POLITICAL PHILOSOPHY

References and further reading

Anglet, K. (1995) *Messianität und Geschichte. Walter Benjamins Konstruktion der historischen Dialektik und deren Aufhebung ins Eschatologische durch Erik Peterson* (Messianism and History. Walter Benjamin's Construction of the Historical Dialectic and their Shift into the Eschatological through the Work of Erik Peterson), Berlin: Akademie. (An important study of the relation between political theology, Critical Theory and messianism.)

* Augustine (413–27) *De civitate Dei* (The City of God), Corpus Christianorum, Series Latina, 47–8, Turnhout: Brepols, 1955–. (One of the most influential Christian views of history and politics, criticizing the ancient pagan identification of state and religion.)

Bendersky, J.W. (1983) *Carl Schmitt, Theorist for the Reich*, Princeton, NJ: Princeton University Press. (General introduction with bibliography.)

* Benjamin, W. (1950) 'Über den Begriff der Geschichte' (On the Concept of History), *Neue Rundschau* 61; trans. H. Zohn, New York: Schocken Books, 1969. (Although first published in 1950, this was written in 1940. This is the most important text of Benjamin, containing his programmatic intentions.)

Habermas, J. (1997) 'Israel oder Athen: Wem gehört die anamnestische Vernunft?' (Israel or Athens: To Whom does Anamnestic Reason Belong?), in *Vom sinnlichen Eindruck zum symbolischen Ausdruck* (From Sensible Impression to Symbolic Expression), Frankfurt: Suhrkamp. (Philosophically, one of Habermas' most important studies defining the relation between his version of Critical Theory and political theology.)

Horkheimer, M. and Adorno, T. (1947) *Dialektik der Aufklärung* (Dialectic of Enlightenment), trans. J. Cumming, New York: Continuum, 1994. (The programmatic study of earlier Critical Theory on the internal dialectic of the process of Western civilization.)

Lutz-Bachmann, M. (1980) 'Freiheitsgeschichte und Theologie' (Liberation History and Theology), in *Philosophische Rundschau* 27. (Introduction to the political theology of Metz and others.)

Maier, H. (1970) *Kritik der politischen Theologie*, Einsiedeln: Johannes. (A criticism of Metz inspired by the work of Erik Peterson.)

Metz, J.B. (1968) *Zur Theologie der Welt* (On the Theology of the World), Mainz/Munich: Grünewald. (Collected articles introducing the new concept of political theology.)

—— (1977) *Glaube in Geschichte und Gesellschaft, Studien zu einer praktischen Fundamentaltheologie* (Faith in History and Society, Studies Towards a Practical Fundamental Theology), Mainz: Grünewald. (Collected articles deepening the new concept of political theology.)

—— (1980) *Jenseits bürgerlicher Religion, Reden über die Zukunft des Christentums* (Beyond Bourgeois Religion, Lectures on the Future of Christianity), Mainz: Grünewald. (A collection of lectures and homilies, easy to understand.)

Nichtweiß, B. (1992) *Erik Peterson. Neue Sicht auf Leben und Werk* (Erik Peterson. A New View of his Life and Work), Freiburg: Herder. (An informative introduction to Peterson's work.)

Peterson, E. (1935) *Der Monotheismus als politisches Problem, ein Beitrag zur Geschichte der politischen Theologie im Imperium Romanum* (Monotheism as a Political Problem, a Contribution to the History of Political Theology in the Roman Empire), Leipzig: Jakob Hegner. (An important critique of Carl Schmitt's concept of political theology.)

—— (1994) *Ausgewählte Schriften* (Selected Writings), vol. 1, *Theologische Traktate*, ed. B. Nichtweiß, Würzburg: Echter. (First volume of the new edition of Peterson's works.)

Schmitt, C. (1922) *Politische Theologie*, Munich and Leipzig: Duncker & Humblot. (The important work in which Schmitt introduces his theory of the religious origin of the modern state.)

—— (1970) *Politische Theologie II*, Berlin: Duncker & Humblot. (An apology in which Schmitt defends his concept of political theology against his critics.)

Sölle, D. (1982) *Politische Theologie*, Stuttgart: Kreuz. (A Protestant version of modern political theology in Germany.)

MATTHIAS LUTZ-BACHMANN

THEOLOGY, RABBINIC

The Talmud, a shelf of folio volumes built up out of the expansive reflections of generations of scholar/thinkers whose discourse formed a commentary or complement (Gemara) to the ancient legal code of the Mishnah, encapsulates rabbinic sayings and discussions dating from before the first century to around 600. The monotheistic idea of God affords a key perspective on the Talmud's variegated themes: God's uniqueness and ultimacy preclude any easy direct commerce between the human and the divine. Literal contact may be endlessly deferred; yet God remains ever present and ever active in human life. Rabbinic thought, textually represented in the Talmud and in the institutions it fosters, seeks to mediate God's 'absent presence' to a community of believers in a way that renders manifest the penetration of divine concern into every cranny of human consciousness without compromising God's transcendence or explanatory uniqueness.

1 The rabbinic framework
2 Rabbinic norms
3 Action and intention
4 Progress and retrospection
5 The underdetermination of meaning by text

1 The rabbinic framework

The location of the believer *vis-à-vis* the God of Israel is elegantly captured in the Talmudic dictum: 'Everything is in the hands of Heaven except the fear of Heaven' (Babylonian Talmud (B.T.) Berakhoth 33b; Megillah 25a; Niddah 16b). Everything falls under God's sway, but only human beings can decide whether or not to hold God in awe. Whatever occurs in the world comes under the purview of the monotheistic God – except the affirmation of his role as God. The concatenated system of beliefs and practices that constitute Judaism works only through such acknowledgement of God as creator and ruler of the universe.

The unbridgeable conceptual gap between God and ourselves presupposes a critical epistemology readily capable of registering the inadequacy of our knowledge claims about God. It delineates the outermost limits of defensible human utterance and locates God beyond those limits. The pattern of argument parallels that of philosophical scepticism in urging that whole species of statements exceed the bounds of coherence. But where scepticism introjects its critique, negative theology projects it outward, onto God (see NEGATIVE THEOLOGY).

Since all descriptions of God here are irresolvably metaphoric, it is only human accetance of God's centrality that sets the religious life in motion. All discourse about God is ultimately metaphoric. Its 'cash value', the only 'hard currency' for which invocations of God can be exchanged in the end, is the act of human consent that establishes God's sovereignty in our lives, acceptance, as the Talmudic rabbis call it, of the yoke of the kingdom of Heaven (GOD, CONCEPTS OF).

For the rabbis the supreme mitzvah or divine commandment is the study of Torah – both the written law of Scripture and the oral law of the rabbinic canon itself (B.T. Shabbat 127b). The centrality of the monotheistic idea helps to explain this privileging of the intellectual in a system that is, by and large, practical, even pragmatic, in orientation: The rabbis find spiritual elevation, even rapture, in the intellectual cultivation linked with the study of Torah, its norms and intricacies. Having no tangible object of religious devotion, we pursue the Infinite through unending occupation with God's word, will and law, ceaselessly testing the limits of our rational faculties, trying again and again to transcend literalism and probe the nexus between symbol and object that is the genesis of metaphor. The outward and upward movement towards a grasp of the divine thus converges with an inward and downward movement, towards self-reflection, integrating the lessons of the limitations of reason.

2 Rabbinic norms

Rabbinic ideas of the good life reflect the metaphysical priorities evoked by the monotheistic idea. The rabbis look with sharp disapproval on a life of asceticism (see ASCETICISM). One who merely refrains from drinking wine, they observe, is deemed a sinner against the self (B.T. Nedarim 10a) – how much more so those who refrain from marriage! The Sages (as the ancient rabbis are often called) warmly echo Isaiah's words about the earth, that God 'created it not a waste, He formed it to be inhabited' (Isaiah 45: 18; B.T. Yevamot 62a): divine transcendence does not empty the world of value, since the world is God's work; but it does mean that our guidelines to human perfectibility must emerge from a sensibility informed by an enlightened understanding of our concerted interactions with one another and with our natural environment. Such guidelines are not simply vouchsafed to us – not even by revelation. Just as monotheism continually thrusts us back upon our own intellectual resources theologically, so too does it prod us persistently to refocus on the ways in which our existence in the world can be made better by greater attentiveness to the norms and limitations of the human condition. Monotheism does not urge us to abandon these norms or transcend these limitations by some lurch into an Ethical Beyond; it does not countenance notions of a transmoral imperative or teleological suspension of the ethical.

Six times in the Talmud (for example, B.T. Shabbat 63a) the prominent rabbinic Sage Samuel emphasizes that only Israel's subjection to the nations distinguishes historical time from the Messianic age. The remark is highly evocative of the rabbinic perspective: since it indicates that human success in reaching the consummation of history has no overtly miraculous emblem by which it is to be judged: monotheism does not give us the mind of God to read. There are human initiatives and reconsiderations but no end-stage within sight that can be declared to have God's full sanction, no Hegelian or Marxian final stage of history, until the parameters of history themselves have been transcended (see HISTORY, PHILOSOPHY OF).

We approach God not by theorizing but by continual mobilization of our energies and will, orienting ourselves towards what we can grasp of our canonical texts and thereby, in the course of time, improving human lives and the world. But the Judaic stress on fulfilling God's commandments goes hand in hand with affirmation of what we might call partial redemption. Judaism is deeply suspicious of human claims to have attained complete redemption. The inaccessibility of God redirects our energies towards this world – and so towards events whose outcomes, inevitably ambiguous and partial, spur us to further action, *since they are never validated supernaturally as the sufficient consummation of human effort and achievement.*

3 Action and intention

A recurring controversy in the Talmud (for example, B.T. Rosh Hashanah 28b) addresses the question whether religious obligations need to be fulfilled with deliberate intention. That such an issue could even be disputed is highly illuminating. The rabbis view with equanimity the prospect of assigning primacy to actions whose motives, in an underlying network of thoughts and feelings, are not perfectly defined. Two reflections on the monotheistic idea shed light on this rabbinic stance. First, as we have seen, the conceptual non-negotiability of the monotheistic God makes all human formulations about Him rebound into metaphoric approximations whose major point of intersection with our reality is pragmatic. If what we are comparing – and what we are comparing it to – can never be fixed as divine unreservedly, then our frame of reference in assigning content to our statements about God remains irredeemably human. For example, God is conceived by us relationally – that is, through his actions – as creator of the world, not as he is in himself. Human beings, correspondingly, are invisible to ourselves and others, and are known, if we can be known at all, only through what we do, not through what we think or feel. Second, since action is as metaphoric in relation to God as are the categories of thought and feeling (its primacy in a monotheistic vocabulary merely reflecting the impossibility of our penetrating God's interiority – God's thoughts and feelings, as it were) monotheistic 'action', when viewed as a registering of human possibilities, would be, correspondingly, much more amorphous than our traditional concepts of action would suggest. It might invoke no more specific a reality than that of power – where everything that we utter, think, feel, or do constitutes an assertion of power, but where the familiar demarcations of thought and action, expression and intention become blurred. It is perhaps for this reason that the rabbis can at times seem rather cavalier about thoughts and feelings in the performance of *mitzvot* – not because they denigrate human intentions but because intentions themselves have been absorbed in a broader ontology. Some rabbinic authorities (for example, Abraham Danzig, Hayyei Adam 68: 9), consider the mere engagement in the performance of a mitzvah a sufficient registering of intention; they see no further need for an explicit or separate mental articulation of intention.

4 Progress and retrospection

Two famous themes of rabbinic exegesis seem to point in conflicting directions. The first is the notion of 'It is not in heaven' (Deuteronomy 30: 12) as expounded in the Babylonian Talmudic tractate Baba Metzia 59b, where the biblical dictum about the accessibility of the law is taken to assign to human inquirers the power and responsibility to interpret (and elaborate) it. The other is the idea that 'Even what a conscientious student is destined to say before his teacher was stated to Moses at Sinai' (Midrash Vayikrah Rabbah 22: 1). The first statement conjures up images of irreversible forward movement, in which we are thrust upon our own resources, however paltry, to structure and organize a *halakhic* (Jewishly mandated) life. The second suggests preformation rather than evolution and an inevitable retrospection or even backward movement.

One strategy for reconciling these two texts is to say that the principle of 'It is not in heaven' does not ordain a strictly linear and irreversible development of Jewish law, but something more dialectical and more nearly akin to Hans-Georg Gadamer's hermeneutics. GADAMER argues for the contemporaneity of all texts, their essential incompleteness, subject to the fusion of horizons between an author and all subsequent generations of readers. Yosef Hayim Yerushalmi in his book *Zakhor* (1982) similarly argues eloquently for an unbridgeable tension between the ever-dynamic practice of Torah and the more positive, diachronic demands of ordinary historical writing. For historical writing, the narrative sequence moves irreversibly from past to present. The uniqueness and separateness of the past are preserved forever. But, in the perspective of the Sages, the movement, at least as momentously, is from future to past – so that time forms a seamless web with no sharp chronological divisions. Later interpretations fill in the content of the original teaching, retroactively. The past remains present as a reservoir of legitimation for the expansion of meaning; the future constitutes an inevitable resource for the extension of meaning and reference. The hermeneutical principle of the underdetermination of meaning by text becomes a cardinal rabbinic tool for balancing the authority of precedent and the demands of crisis and creativity (see HERMENEUTICS, BIBLICAL).

5 The underdetermination of meaning by text

As the few examples cited here clearly suggest, biblical and earlier rabbinic texts are often quoted out of context in the Talmud, stripped of their original significations and outfitted with wholly new connotations germane to matters at hand. By such unremitting recontextualizing, the Talmud makes texts speak to ever new issues. What is the significance of this pervasive Talmudic device based on the underdetermination of meaning by text?

From a purely practical standpoint, recognition of the underdetermination is a key factor in rabbinic innovation, allowing the application to unanticipated circumstances of ideas, methods and principles well established in Jewish law.

Hermeneutically as well, the recognition of underdetermination introduces an element of complexity into the idea and the project of historical continuity and faithfulness. A good part of what the Talmudic Sages were doing was consciously to subvert a slavishly historical approach to biblical texts and rabbinic precedents. The rabbis work and play with the texts, almost endlessly reinventing them. The Talmud thus contains an ineradicably storytelling element, even in the most austerely legal discussions. Thus, paradoxically, to give a historically faithful account of a Talmudic discussion or legal analysis, one must somehow accommodate historiography to the Talmud's own resolute anti-historicism.

A jarring theological issue emerges from the centrality of the underdetermination principle in Talmudic exegesis. For this principle points towards scepticism and seems to destabilize all interpretation. Once scepticism is unleashed with regard to the textual sources of Jewish tradition, how can it be contained with regard to the norms that those texts enunciate? The tension between the demand to conserve the Torah's norms and the pressure to decontextualize them (whether as expressed in the Torah text or in its canonical offshoots among the codes), so as to make the underlying norms relevant in transformed contexts – temporally extending the normative reach of the Torah in the broadest sense by way of skeptical strategies of underdetermination – has profound implications for the project of the rabbis as founders and exponents, and, in a sense, reinventors, of Jewish tradition.

The same underdetermination illuminates the priority assigned to speech over writing in Talmudic discourse. It was only by reference to the pressure of persecution that reduction to writing was deemed permissible (B.T. Berakhot 54a). Even then, apparently, it was expected that the writing should resemble speech as closely as possible, by remaining dialectical in structure and even in diction. Texts can engender an illusion of fixity and finality that orality continually belies. Only speech, it seems, is deemed in good faith; writing is always in bad faith. The fact of persecution and the risk of the utter loss of collective memory permits recourse to writing. But dialectical writing, with its tentativeness and recursiveness, its continually interrogatory aspects, presents itself as the mere record of living speech.

A contrast is often drawn between the Talmud's legalistic mode of argument and the methods familiar to philosophers. The Talmud is practically oriented, we are told, where philosophy is theoretical. But in the light of our present analysis, that dichotomy loses its force. The vast canon of Talmudic-legalistic argument itself insinuates a monumental philosophical project.

Articulation simultaneously constitutes erasure, effacing the very possibilities that have just been spoken. What each speaker says can always be decomposed and reconstituted along lines other than those in which the words seemed officially to be pointing. Sentences continually posit their silent others, as dialectical alternatives, and as presuppositions and implications that can always be regrouped and rearranged to yield new configurations of meaning and unsuspected, but possibly hinted, constellations of referents. The whole notion of the primacy of intention is thus reverently mocked, as dicta are made precedents or pretexts for understandings far removed from their literal or naive or historical imputations. Talmudic argument, viewed from this perspective, constitutes one of the most imposing rhetorical edifices ever erected in defence of the notion of the 'floating statement' and the endless process of decontextualization and re-contextualization.

The theological backdrop for all Talmudic argument is the fabric formed by the tenets of monotheism. The very utterance of the word 'God' initiates a process of endless displacement that finds no resting place. All we can ever do towards assigning a content or pinpointing a sense for this word is to say, without letup, that God is not literally to be construed in this way or that, not to be found in a humanly cognizable sense here or there or elsewhere. Talmudic discourse itself mimics this elusiveness; its stability and steadiness of focus through the endless process of deconstruction and reconstruction refuses to come to rest in some merely fixed and positive content. The deliteralizing of positive ascriptions to God of particular attributes is translated in the Talmud – with its continually rendering fluid of the sense and reference

of human utterances – into an implicit acknowledgement of the ultimate ungroundedness of all mere acts of language. In this negative sense, God for the Talmudic speakers and editors becomes the paradigm case of the humanly sayable.

See also: HALAKHAH; ISLAMIC THEOLOGY; KARAISM; MIDRASH

References and further reading

Botwinick, A. (1995) 'Underdetermination of Meaning by the Talmudic Text', in D.H. Frank (ed.) *Commandment and Community: New Essays in Jewish Legal and Political Philosophy*, New York: State University of New York Press. (Expands on the theme of underdetermination of meaning by text in the rabbinic sources.)

Handelman, S.A. (1982) *The Slayers of Moses*, New York: State University of New York Press. (Invokes post-structuralist and postmodernist methods and perspectives for analysing rabbinic texts.)

Heschel, A.J. (1962, 1965, 1990) *Torah Min H'Shamayim B'Asplakaria shel ha-Dorot* (Theology of Ancient Judaism), vol. 1, *Darkei Machshavah B'Tekufat ha-Tana'im* (Pathways of Thought in the Age of the Tana'im), vol. 2, *Torah M'Sinai V'Torah Min ha-Shamayim* (Torah from Sinai and Torah from Heaven), London: Soncino Press; vol. 3, *Elu V'Elu Divrei Elokim chaim* (Both these Words and Those are the Words of the Living God), Jerusalem: Jewish Theological Seminary. (Heschel builds a typological contrast between the approaches to the Torah of Rabbi Akiva and Rabbi Ishmael and their schools. He shows how the unbridgeable conceptual distance between God and human beings is compatible with normal logical-linguistic protocols in deciphering the Torah text.)

Kaddushin, M. (1972) *The Rabbinic Mind*, New York: Bloch, 3rd edn. (Focuses on 'normal mysticism' – the rabbinic theological approach that domesticates divine distance and integrates it into a fabric of daily living.)

Neusner, J. (1988) *Torah: From Scroll to Symbol in Formative Judaism*, Atlanta, GA: Scholars Press. (Shows how the Torah as finite text, a simple scroll, is transformed into an all-encompassing context that defines a way of life for individuals and for the people of Israel.)

Urbach, E.E. (1969) *Chazal: Pirkei Emunot V'Deot*, Jerusalem: The Magnes Press; trans. I. Abrahams, *The Sages – Their Concepts and Beliefs*, Jerusalem: The Magnes Press, 1975, 2 vols. (A classic reconstruction of the fundamental normative and descriptive categories of rabbinic Judaism.)

Yerushalmi, Y.H. (1982) *Zakhor: Jewish History and Jewish Memory*, Seattle, WA: University of Washington Press.

ARYEH BOTWINICK

THEOPHRASTUS
(*c*.372–*c*.287 BC)

Theophrastus, the pupil and successor of Aristotle, shared all the latter's interests, and produced a large number of works on the same topics. Some, like the extant botanical works, went far beyond Aristotle, and Theophrastus is known as the Father of Botany; others amplified and criticized what Aristotle had done. The short Metaphysics, *also extant, raises many questions about the nature and the possibility of metaphysics, but most of his work on logic, science, psychology, ethics, politics and religion survives only in fragments, some material coming from the Arabs, and some only from medieval Latin sources. His developments of modal logic and various forms of the syllogism were regarded as important, and his amplification of Aristotle's account of the human intellect was studied in the Middle Ages in the West. His little* Characters, *an entertaining set of sketches of human peculiarities, has had considerable influence on later literature, and his surveys of earlier opinions, of which his* On the Senses *survives, influenced later doxographers. He was an older contemporary of Zeno, the founder of Stoicism, but his influence on Stoicism remains uncertain, and we also know little of his relationship with Epicurus.*

1 Life and writings
2 Logic and grammar
3 Psychology
4 Metaphysics
5 Theology and religion
6 Ethics
7 Science
8 Other work

1 Life and writings

Theophrastus was born in Eresos on the island of Lesbos, but went to Athens for higher education and became the pupil and then the constant companion of ARISTOTLE, whom he succeeded as head of his school, the Peripatos, in 323 BC. He probably shared Aristotle's sojourns from 348 onwards in Assos, Lesbos and Macedonia, where Aristotle taught the future Alexander the Great, and returned with him in 335 to Athens, where most of the rest of his life was spent. He was succeeded by his pupil STRATO (died *c*.269 BC). He shared all Aristotle's interests, and wrote widely in a very careful style. Diogenes Laertius lists over 200 of his works. His two botanical works, known popularly as the *History of Plants* and the *Causes of Plants*, have survived, as well as his *Characters*, an entertaining and widely influential work, whose original purpose is uncertain: it seems to have influenced the playwright Menander, himself a pupil of Theophrastus, and may have rhetorical, ethical or theoretical purposes. It enjoyed considerable vogue in the seventeenth and eighteenth centuries, particularly in France. There survive also the short *Metaphysics*, and a number of treatises on scientific matters, but much more survives only in fragments. It is likely that he and his fellow Peripatetic Eudemus worked out their logical theories while Aristotle was alive, but other material presupposes the existence of Aristotle's works as we have them now, which suggests that it was produced after his death. A large part of it was concerned with questioning, widening and improving the works of Aristotle, and Theophrastus himself probably played a part in editing Aristotle's lectures into the form in which we now have them. It is also likely that through his pupil Demetrius of Phalerum he had some influence on the direction taken by the Library and Museum of Alexandria. His contemporary Epicurus wrote a work addressed to him (fr. 280), but we know little else about his relations with either Epicurus or the Stoics.

2 Logic and grammar

Theophrastus made a number of contributions to logic (see LOGIC, ANCIENT §4). He added a few footnotes to Aristotle's system of categorical propositions, such as a new account of the relations between the second and third figures of the syllogism and the first, and a study of the basis on which the premises of a syllogism are themselves to be accepted (fr. 94). The invention of the fourth figure of the categorical syllogism has been ascribed to him, mistakenly, but he did add a number of additional moods to those recognized by Aristotle (frs 91–6). He went much further in attacking Aristotle's unsatisfactory system of modal logic, working closely with his contemporary, Eudemus. For this, evidence from Arabic sources goes beyond what we have from the Greeks (frs 98–109). Aristotle held that in a modal syllogism, which uses the notions of 'necessary', 'actual' or 'assertoric', and 'possible' in its premises and conclusions, one of which might for example be 'All men are possibly good', the mode of the conclusion follows that of the major premise. But his pupils saw flaws in that position and suggested that the conclusion always follows the mode of the weaker premise: that is, if one premise is necessary and the other assertoric then the conclusion is always assertoric, whichever of the premises is. This also involved revised accounts of the meaning of terms such as 'necessary' and 'possible', and of the conversion of propositions. 'Some *A* is *B*' implies 'Some *B* is *A*', but if *A* possibly belongs to no *B*, does *B* possibly belong to no *A*? Aristotle argued against this, but Theophrastus and Eudemus produced a proof that it does.

Theophrastus also developed some remarks of Aristotle into a theory of prosleptic syllogisms, such as '*A* is said of all of that of all of which *B* is said' (fr. 110), and with Eudemus worked out a theory of hypothetical syllogisms (frs 111–13), such as 'If virtue is knowledge, it is teachable. But it is knowledge. Therefore it is teachable', the relation of which to Stoic logic is controversial. Finally, he revised Aristotle's system of topics, and gave some definitions of key terms such as 'topic'.

He also made advances in the theory of grammar, which Plato and Aristotle had begun by recognizing nouns and verbs. Theophrastus added 'joints and ligaments', which probably included conjunctions, prepositions and articles, and he also paid attention to aspects of style (fr. 683).

3 Psychology

For Theophrastus' psychology we have evidence from Themistius (fourth century AD) and Priscian of Lydia (sixth century AD) which provides a considerable proportion of Theophrastus' *On the Soul*, a work devoted mainly to a critique of Aristotle's own *On the Soul*. Curiously, Priscian used Theophrastus as a peg on which to hang his own Neoplatonic account of the same subject matter, sensation, imagination and thought. Theophrastus laid the ground for future work by bringing material from Aristotle's *Generation of Animals* into discussion about the origin of soul and intellect in the embryo. In the field of sensation he worried over Aristotle's claim that in sensing the sense organ becomes like its object (see ARISTOTLE §18), for it could hardly become like it in colour or taste, for example, so he fastened on Aristotle's references to form and *logos* as explanations of this process, and considered detailed aspects of sensation, such as light, colour, reflections and the transparent. Where Aristotle is obscure he can be obscure himself, as in the section on why there are only five senses. He also found difficulties in Aristotle's condensed account of intellect (see ARISTOTLE §19; NOUS), asking how intellect differed from matter, for both seemed to have no characteristics in themselves; and how intellect and

its objects, the thinker and its thoughts, could causally affect one another. He seems to have distinguished intellect from matter by saying that while matter receives individual forms intellect receives universal forms (fr. 308). He insisted again and again on the importance of using language appropriately, to avoid being misled, accepting that we have sometimes to transfer words appropriate primarily to one subject matter to another subject matter; this can be done successfully provided we are aware of what we are doing.

In his epistemology, if Sextus Empiricus (second century AD) is correct, he provided an empiricist theory of knowledge (fr. 301A) similar to that given by Aristotle at the end of his *Posterior Analytics*. He stressed the importance of self-evidence as a criterion of truth, and claimed that both sensation and thought are foundations of knowledge.

4 Metaphysics

Theophrastus' *Metaphysics*, now generally agreed to be a complete work in itself, is a critique not only of the views of Aristotle but also of those of Plato and other philosophers. In particular it deals with themes in *Metaphysics*, Aristotle's 'theological' work, and it has been argued plausibly that it was an early work of Theophrastus. Its original title is unknown: 'First Philosophy' would be appropriate. It has been seen as the classic formulation of a whole complex of problems. First he tackles some of the assumptions made by Aristotle, starting with the claim that there exist 'first things', known by reason. These must be either in mathematical objects, or in something prior to them; they are the cause of motion, but are themselves unmoved; as objects of desire they cause the rotation of the heavens. In all this he is following Aristotle, but he then asks how many they are: if there is only one, why do the heavenly bodies move differently, but if there are more than one, how is their influence harmonized? And why does love of the unmoved cause movement as an imitation? Further, if the heavenly bodies have desire, they must have soul, and the movement of soul, which is thought, is better than rotary movement.

After a criticism of Plato and his successor, SPEUSIPPUS (died 339 BC), for not carrying through their accounts of the nature of the world into a complete system, he suggests that perhaps metaphysics is only concerned with first principles. But then what are these principles? He appears to consider two kinds: the ultimate entities out of which things are made and the general laws by which all things are governed.

Turning to details, he considers various basic

notions, form and matter as conceived by Aristotle, good and evil, being, and how various kinds of being may be known. He wonders why there is so much evil in the world. On a lower level he considers cases which seem to lack final causes, such as floods and male breasts. These raise difficulties for Aristotle's claim that nothing happens without a purpose. Theophrastus suggests that perhaps these anomalies result automatically from the rotation of the heavens, or perhaps there is a limit to purposiveness and the desire for what is good. Recently discovered Arabic texts show him arguing that god is responsible only for order in the universe, and that things like thunderbolts are not sent by god.

It is possible that the later lack of interest in metaphysics in the Peripatos is due to Theophrastus' devastating criticism. Certainly his successor, Strato, was primarily interested in science.

5 Theology and religion

For Theophrastus' theological views, apart from what is mentioned above, we are dependent on later writers. Cicero (106–43 BC) says that he identified god with heaven and with mind or spirit, but his evidence is superficial. ALBERT THE GREAT (thirteenth century) says that Theophrastus argued that god had no will, giving five detailed arguments (fr. 259) which may however owe much to Arabic developments, and that the relationship between god and the intellect is like light. Denis the Carthusian (1402–71) suggests that he was the founder of negative theology (fr. 260), saying that we know better what god is not than what he is. It also seems that he wrote about *daimons*, the beings supposed to exist on a level between gods and mortals (see PLATONISM, EARLY AND MIDDLE §7). Porphyry (mid 3rd–early 4th century) gives us long excerpts from a work which may be his *On Piety*, which are largely on what types of sacrifice are appropriate to the gods, and advocate vegetarianism (frs 584–5).

6 Ethics

Much of the evidence for his ethics is trivial, but PORPHYRY gives us sections from his attack on meat eating, probably slanted to suit Porphyry's own interests, and Jerome quotes from his very funny attack on marriage, in order to support Christian views on chastity (fr. 486). We also have Theophrastus' doctrine of the natural kinship of all human beings and, more, of human beings and animals, because of their physiological and psychological similarities – sometimes known as the doctrine of *oikeiotēs* (frs 531, 584), though it is still debated whether it is related to the *oikeiōsis* of the Stoics (see

STOICISM §14); also his attack on Plato's account of false pleasure in the *Philebus* (fr. 556), where he stresses the importance of language. There is also evidence that he had new ideas about emotions (frs 438–48), in particular using the notion of 'the more and less', that is, differences in degree, to relate similar emotions such as anger and rage. He attained some notoriety among the Romans for holding a less austere view of how virtue and happiness are related than did Aristotle (and after him the Stoics), saying that a happy life does not lie in virtue alone (fr. 497). His three books on friendship had considerable influence, but little now survives (frs 532–46).

7 Science

The line between philosophy and early science is difficult to draw, and his work in botany and biology contains both empirical work based on observation and attempts at establishing theoretical foundations. The opening of his *Physics* gives an account of the fundamentals of natural science, that natural bodies are composite, and have elements and causes and principles, and he goes on to place (criticizing in detail Aristotle's odd account; frs 146–9), time (relating it, like Aristotle, to motion; frs 150–1), motion and change. His remarks on place, at least adumbrating a relativist view of space, have been given great significance by some scholars, but it is more likely that as usual he was raising more problems than he answered. Large sections of a work in which he stated and refuted in detail several arguments of his predecessors against the eternity of the universe are preserved by Philo of Alexandria (frs 184–5). He extended Aristotle's work in zoology with studies of the nature and habits of many creatures, and focused in particular on peculiar phenomena such as swarming and hibernation, trying to show that these had a natural explanation. In botany he applied to plants the principle of classification originally developed by Plato, but further developed by Aristotle. The opening of the *History of Plants*, or better, *Inquiry into Plants*, attempts to list the parts of plants, stem, root, leaf, flower and so on, and later there is a division of plants into trees, shrubs, undershrubs and herbs. In *On the Causes of Plants*, or better, *Plant Explanations*, he covers aspects of the growth of plants, such as methods of reproduction and climatic effects. He built on a mass of information gathered by others, including herbalists and agriculturalists, but also by his own observation, and provided a theoretical framework which lasted for centuries.

In addition there are several short treatises including *On Fire*, *On Stones*, *On Tiredness* and *On Sweating*, and a number of scientific works attributed to Aristotle but not thought to be by him which have by some been attributed to Theophrastus. These include *On Colours*, parts of the *History of Animals* VIII and IX, and parts of the *Mirabilia*.

8 Other work

Theophrastus has also been seen as an influential doxographer and the source of other later doxographies (see DOXOGRAPHY): his *On the Senses* has survived with its treatment of the views of the Presocratics and Plato about sensation, and we have evidence for similar work in physics (frs 224–45).

He followed Aristotle in working on politics (frs 589–665) and rhetoric (frs 666– 713), particularly on style (frs 684–704), and wrote some difficult theoretical material on music (frs 714–26).

List of works

Theophrastus (*c*.372–287 BC) Fragments, in W.W. Fortenbaugh, P.M. Huby, R.W. Sharples and D. Gutas (eds) *Theophrastus of Eresus, Sources for his Life, Writings, Thought and Influence*, Leiden: Brill, 1992. (A collection of texts and translations relating to Theophrastus until the fourteenth century, including evidence for his work in logic, science, psychology, theology, religion, ethics, political theory and rhetoric; volume 5, *Sources on Biology*, ed. R.W. Sharples appeared in 1995.)
—— (*c*.372–287 BC) *Metaphysics*, trans. W.D. Ross and F.H. Fobes, Oxford: Clarendon Press, 1929; repr. Hildesheim: Olms, 1967; trans. M. van Raalte, Leiden: Brill, 1993. (Greek and English text, with notes.)
—— (*c*.372–287 BC) *Characters*, ed. and trans. J. Rusten Loeb Classical Library, Cambridge, MA: Harvard University Press and London: Heinemann, 2nd edn, 1992. (Sketches of character weaknesses; parallel Greek text and English translations)
—— (*c*.372–287 BC) *Inquiry into Plants*, ed. and trans. A. Holt Loeb Classical Library, Cambridge, MA: Harvard University Press and London: Heinemann, 2 vols 1916–26. (Botany; parallel Greek text and English translations.)
—— (*c*.372–287 BC) *Causes of Plants*, ed. and trans. B. Einarson and G. Link Loeb Classical Library, Cambridge, MA: Harvard University Press and London: Heinemann, 3 vols, 1976–90. (Botany; parallel Greek texts and English translations.)
—— (*c*.372–287 BC) *On the Senses*, trans. in G.M. Stratton, *Theophrastus and the Greek Physiological Psychology before Aristotle*, London: Allen & Unwin, 1917; repr. Amsterdam: Grüner, 1964. (A

study of earlier theories of perception. Greek text, translation and notes by an eminent cognitive psychologist)

References and further reading

Rutgers University Studies in Classical Humanities (1983–) New Brunswick, NJ, and London: Transaction Publishers. (Includes several volumes of conference proceedings relating to Theophrastus, especially volume 2, *Theophrastus of Eresus: On His Life and Work*; volume 3, *Theophrastean Studies: On Natural Science, Physics and Metaphysics, Ethics, Religion and Rhetoric*; and volume 5, *Theophrastus: His Psychological, Doxographical and Scientific Writings*.)
Huby, P.M. (1985) 'Theophrastus in the Aristotelian Corpus, with Particular Reference to the Biological Problems', in A. Gotthelf (ed.) *Aristotle on Nature and Living Things*, Bristol: Bristol Classical Press. (Surveys suggestions about works attributed to Aristotle which might have been written by Theophrastus.)

PAMELA M. HUBY

THEORETICAL ENTITIES

see OBSERVATION; SCIENTIFIC REALISM AND ANTIREALISM; THEORIES, SCIENTIFIC

THEORETICAL (EPISTEMIC) VIRTUES

When two competing theories or hypotheses explain or accommodate just the same data (and both are unrefuted), which should be preferred? According to a classical, purely formal confirmation theory, neither – each is confirmed to the same degree, and so the two hypotheses are precisely equal in epistemic status, warrant or credibility. Yet in real life, one of the two may be preferred very strongly, for any of a number of pragmatic reasons: it may be simpler, more readily testable, more fruitful or less at odds with what we already believe. The philosophical question is whether such pragmatic virtues are of no specifically epistemic, truth-conducing value, or are instead genuine reasons for accepting a theory as more likely to be true than is a competitor that lacks them.

1 Some of the virtues
2 The spartan argument
3 Replies to the sceptic

1 Some of the virtues

The preference for simplicity in particular is illustrated by the example of experimental scientists' practice in curve-fitting on graphs: given a set of data points that lie along a straight line, any scientist will draw a straight line through them rather than any more complicated curve, and leave it that way unless further, refuting data should come in. This compelling smoothness of the linear hypothesis is a virtue of some sort, one that is not shared by the hypotheses expressed by the countlessly many more complex curves that pass through the very same data points and hence are just as well confirmed in the classical sense as is the linear theory. (The immediacy and vividness of the curve-fitting example should not be allowed to suggest that 'simplicity' is easily measured, or even that it can be given a clear general characterization – Foster and Martin 1966; Sober 1975 – see SIMPLICITY IN SCIENTIFIC THEORIES)

Other pragmatic virtues having simplicity's non-classical and doubtful epistemic character include: (1) *Testability* – other things being equal, a hypothesis H_1 will be preferred to a competitor H_2 if H_1 has more readily testable implications; (2) *Fertility* – H_1 will be preferred to H_2 if H_1 is more fruitful in suggesting further related hypotheses, or parallel hypotheses in other areas; (3) *Neatness* – H_1 will be preferred to H_2 if H_1 leaves fewer messy unanswered questions behind, and especially if H_1 does not itself raise such questions; (4) *Conservativeness* – H_1 will be preferred to H_2 if H_1 fits better with what we already believe. (If this sounds dogmatic, notice that, inescapably, we never even consider competing hypotheses that would strike us as grossly implausible; for example, no detective considers the hypothesis that the crime was committed by invisible Venusian invaders.) Also, often listed as a pragmatic virtue is 'generality' or *explanatory power*, the property of comprehending more various data than one's competitors; but we have stipulated for the sake of argument that our competing theories comprehend just the same data, and in any case it seems that power is just a wider, more global simplicity.

Every pragmatic virtue is a matter of degree. And our preference for any one of them always comes qualified by 'other things being equal', for clearly they can conflict among themselves. Perhaps the most obvious tension holds between simplicity and conservativeness, since often simplification is gained only through bold overthrowing of previously accepted

theory, as in the case of Copernican versus Ptolemaic astronomy. But because of the complexity of any detailed real-world case study, there is no generally accepted policy for weighing the various degrees of the various virtues against each other in any particular inquiry. The lack of such a policy, understandably, has led some epistemologists to scepticism or relativism concerning theory choice based on pragmatic virtues. But there is also a more fundamental issue, outlined in section two below.

2 The spartan argument

It seems we have considerations of two sorts: data or hard evidence bearing a quasi-formal probabilifying or confirming relation to each of the competing hypotheses H_1 and H_2, and the pragmatic virtues attaching differentially to H_1 and H_2. The former is expressed commonly by words like 'likely', 'probable' and 'confirms' in our narrow sense; the model for it is formal inductive logic or confirmation theory based on probability theory, conceived by the Logical Positivists as a strict analogue to deductive logic (see CONFIRMATION THEORY). Let us call this 'narrow confirmation'. Following mainstream epistemology, let us also use the words 'justified' and 'justification' respectively to mark out the class of beliefs it is epistemically rational to hold, and the relation between those beliefs and the evidence in virtue of which holding them is rational. The question then arises, 'is justification exhausted by narrow confirmation?'

The affirmative is emphatically urged by van Fraassen (1980). On that spartan view, the pragmatic virtues are merely pragmatic, a matter of what is utile or convenient and (in Ian Hacking's phrase) makes our minds feel good; the virtues contribute not at all to justification. It is the spartan view that drives van Fraassen's and others' radical scepticism about the unobservable. Unobservable entities are posited or hypothesized at best, so if hypothesis-choice requires appeal to pragmatic virtues and the virtues do not ever make for justification, no belief in unobservables can be justified. It is also the spartan view that drives evil-demon scepticism about the external world: by hypothesis, the evil-demon theory makes exactly the same observational predictions as does the realist external-world theory, so both are equally probable or well-confirmed on our evidence, so we have no reason to believe the external-world theory to the exclusion of the other. Further, the spartan view drives Nelson Goodman's famous 'Grue Paradox', for the problem is that for every well-confirmed hypothesis, say that the next emerald to be observed after a certain future time t will be green, there are innumerably many truth-functionally mocked-up competitors that are equally well confirmed, say that the next emerald will be 'grue' (either examined before *t* and green, or not examined before *t* and blue) (see INDUCTION, EPISTEMIC ISSUES IN; KNOWLEDGE, CONCEPT OF §9).

Since the spartan position gives rise to such sceptical quandaries, why not abandon it forthwith and admit the pragmatic virtues' justificatory power? But one must not simply presume the falsity of scepticism in the face of arguments that to many philosophers have seemed unanswerable. Also, there is a very attractive direct argument against taking the virtues as justificatory.

A first formulation of the argument is this: the virtues' pragmatic 'utility' is really a mixture of corner-cutting convenience – a form of intellectual laziness – and merely aesthetic appeal. We prefer the smoothest hypothesis in curve-fitting because the smooth curve is easier to draw and looks prettier. But why should anyone think that convenience and prettiness count in any way towards truth? Few philosophers would share the Grecian Urn's motto that beauty and truth are one.

The spartan argument is most compelling for the case of conservativeness. That a hypothesis fits comfortably with what we already believe makes that hypothesis pleasant and attractive to us, but hardly justifies it; for to think it does is to assume that what we already believe is justified merely by the fact of our believing it, and that idea strikes most philosophers as blatantly false – however, see Sklar (1975) and Lycan (1988). The spartan argument is memorably embellished by van Fraassen:

> Judgements of simplicity and explanatory power are the intuitive and natural vehicle for expressing our epistemic appraisal. What can an empiricist make of these... virtues which go so clearly beyond the ones he considers pre-eminent?
>
> There are specifically human concerns, a function of our interests and pleasures, which make some theories more valuable and appealing to us than others. Values of this sort, however... cannot rationally guide our epistemic attitudes and decisions. For example, if it matters more to us to have one sort of question answered rather than another, that is no reason to think that a theory which answers more of the first sort of question is more likely to be true.
>
> (van Fraassen 1980: 87)

Truth is a relation between a theory or hypothesis and the world. But the pragmatic virtues are relations between theories and our human minds, to which relations the world seems irrelevant. The virtues have to do with the roles that hypotheses play in our private cognitive economies, not with anything external to us. Making our minds feel good is hardly a warrant of truth.

Notice that, if correct, the spartan position undermines an entire theory of epistemic justification, that which in this century originated with Quine (1960) and with Sellars (1963, 1973). It is the view that what justifies some (or all) beliefs is those beliefs' felicitous explanatory relations to others, and since the goodness of an explanation is measured almost entirely by its pragmatic virtues, they are indispensable to the explanationist theory of justification (see INFERENCE TO THE BEST EXPLANATION).

3 Replies to the sceptic

Two replies may be made to the embellished spartan argument. First, it falsely assimilates the pragmatic virtues to crassly self-seeking 'reasons' for believing things (as in Pascal's Wager, or a case in which we are offered money if we can get ourselves to believe that Mrs Thatcher was Britain's greatest leader ever). The virtues are at least genuinely *cognitive* and, in one important sense, epistemic values. It is fairly easy to see that truth cannot be the only epistemic value. For suppose it were – if the idea, like Descartes', is merely to avoid falsehood, then we could reach our ultimate epistemic goal simply by confining our assent to tautologies; if instead the idea is to believe *all* truths, the goal would be radically unreachable. Fully realizing those things, the truth-centred epistemologist usually alludes to a 'favourable balance of truth over error'. But 'favourable' as regards what? Some further value or interest must be consulted to judge what is 'favourable'. Also, more specifically, it is hardly unreasonable to suppose that beliefs are *for* something, and that cognition has a function. Truth is often called 'the goal of' cognition, but we have just seen that truth cannot be the only goal of cognition; there must at least be something in the way of informativeness, however it might be measured. Since belief is a guide to action, a belief's other pragmatic virtues may also contribute to its overall cognitive goodness. And now the burden is on the spartan to say why justification is constituted by only a subcomponent of overall cognitive goodness, in the face of the sceptical quandaries expounded in §2.

Second, we should advert to the epistemology of epistemology. Epistemology is a study of norms, and (so the present reply goes) the epistemology appropriate to a normative subject is that of 'reflective equilibrium' as first proposed by Goodman (1955) and developed by Rawls (1971). Roughly, we begin with our instinctive normative intuitions and build an accordingly normative theory to systematize them.

Mutual adjustment occurs until what Rawls calls 'narrow' reflective equilibrium is reached; then factual knowledge and perhaps also other norms are admitted to the equation, resulting in further adjustment and eventual 'wide' reflective equilibrium. In epistemology, as in ethical theory and for that matter in deductive logic, the intuitions in question are normative to begin with.

On the present view, epistemology starts with the attempt at narrow reflective equilibrium. The move to wide equilibrium will involve attending to empirical cognitive science. But each is likely to respect the pragmatic virtues. For our pragmatic preferences are not merely preferences, but normative practices: we instruct our science students in the techniques of curve-fitting, epicycle elimination and the like, and science would be in a bad way if we did not.

One may or may not be persuaded by the foregoing two rebuttals of spartan scepticism. If not, and if one does not want simply to acquiesce in a radical scepticism about all of nature, one has the task of showing how a classical confirmation theory can overcome the sceptical quandaries without at least tacit appeal to the pragmatic virtues. If one is persuaded, there are three paths: to modify classical confirmation theory in order to respect the virtues; to relegate classical confirmation theory to a confined role in inquiry, granting that justification far outruns narrow confirmation; or to abandon confirmation theory entirely as a bad job.

Roughly the first path has been taken by Clark Glymour (1980). The idea is to broaden the notion of 'confirmation', so that H_1 may be counted as 'better confirmed' than H_2 even though H_1 and H_2 are still equally probabilified by the evidence base. If, however, one wants to demote or abandon confirmation theory entirely, one faces the daunting task of building a systematic account of the pragmatic virtues, their measurement and their comparative interaction – to date, no theorist has taken more than a step or two in that direction.

See also: JUSTIFICATION, EPISTEMIC; SCEPTICISM

References and further reading

Cartwright, N. (1983) *How the Laws of Physics Lie*, Oxford: Oxford University Press. (Attacks the pragmatic virtues conceived as justificatory.)

* Foster, M.H. and Martin, M.L. (1966) *Probability, Confirmation, and Simplicity*, New York: Odyssey Press. (Contains some classic papers on simplicity. R. Ackermann's 'Inductive Simplicity' in particular expresses pessimism as regards the taming of that notion.)

* Fraassen, B. van (1980) *The Scientific Image*, Oxford: Oxford University Press. (Attacks the pragmatic virtues conceived as justificatory.)

* Glymour, C. (1980) *Theory and Evidence*, Princeton, NJ: Princeton University Press. (Tries to broaden narrow confirmation in the direction of the pragmatic virtues.)

* Goodman, N. (1955) 'The New Riddle of Induction', in *Fact, Fiction, and Forecast*, Cambridge, MA: Harvard University Press. (Proposes the method of reflective equilibrium, and expounds the Grue Paradox.)

Hacking, I. (1982) 'Experimentation and Scientific Realism', *Philosophical Topics* 13 (1): 71–88. (Attacks the pragmatic virtues conceived as justificatory.)

* Lycan, W.G. (1988) *Judgement and Justification*, Cambridge: Cambridge University Press. (Part 2 defends an explanationist epistemology; chapter 7 defends the pragmatic virtues as justificatory, and chapter 8 makes the case for conservativeness in particular.)

* Quine, W.V. (1960) *Word and Object*, Cambridge, MA: MIT Press. (Seminal work in which Quine brings his own brand of empiricism to bear on epistemic issues.)

Quine, W.V. and Ullian, J.S. (1970) *The Web of Belief*, New York: Random House, 2nd edn, 1978. (Chapter 5 discusses and defends some representative pragmatic virtues.)

* Rawls, J. (1971) *A Theory of Justice*, Cambridge, MA: Harvard University Press. (Develops the theory of reflective equilibrium.)

* Sellars, W. (1963) 'Some Reflections on Language Games', in *Science, Perception and Reality*, London: Routledge & Kegan Paul. (The locus classicus of Sellars' explanationist epistemology.)

* —— (1973) 'Givenness and Explanatory Coherence', *Journal of Philosophy* 70 (18): 612–24. (Further development of Sellars' view.)

* Sklar, L. (1975) 'Methodological Conservatism', *Philosophical Review* 84 (3): 374–400. (A qualified defence of conservativeness as justificatory.)

* Sober, E. (1975) *Simplicity*, Oxford: Oxford University Press. (Standard work on the subject.)

Thagard, P. (1978) 'The Best Explanation: Criteria for Theory Choice', *Journal of Philosophy* 75 (2): 76–92. (Discusses and defends three of the pragmatic virtues.)

WILLIAM G. LYCAN

THEORIES, SCIENTIFIC

The term 'theory' is used variously in science to refer to an unproven hunch, a scientific field (as in 'electromagnetic theory'), and a conceptual device for systematically characterizing the state-transition behaviour of systems. Philosophers of science have tended to view the latter as the most fundamental, and most analyses of theories focus on it.

The Einsteinian revolution involved the rejection of the chemical ether on experimental grounds. It thus prompted philosophers and scientists to examine closely the nature of scientific theories and their connections to observation. Many sought normative analyses that precluded the introduction of 'fictitious' theoretical entities such as the ether. Such analyses amounted to criteria for demarcating scientific or cognitively significant claims from unscientific or metaphysical claims.

Logical positivism sought to develop an ideal language for science that would guarantee cognitive significance. The language was symbolic logic with the nonlogical vocabulary bifurcated into observational and theoretical subvocabularies. Observation terms directly designated observable entities and attributes, and the truth of statements using them was unproblematic. To prevent postulation of fictitious unobservable entities, theoretical terms were allowed only in the context of a theory which guaranteed the cognitive significance of theoretical assertions. Theories were required to contain correspondence rules that interpret theoretical terms by coordinating them in some way with observational conditions.

In the 1960s this 'received view' was attacked on grounds that the observational–theoretical distinction was untenable; that the correspondence rules were a heterogeneous confusion of meaning relationships, experimental design, measurement and causal relationships; that the notion of partial interpretation associated with more liberal requirements on correspondence rules was incoherent; that theories are not axiomatic systems; that symbolic logic is an inappropriate formalism; and that theories are not linguistic entities.

Alternative analyses of theories were suggested – construing theories as answers to scientific problems or as paradigms or conceptual frameworks. Gradually analyses that construe theories as extra-linguistic set-theoretic structures came to dominate post-positivistic thought. The semantic conception identifies theories with abstract theory structures like configurated state spaces that stand in mapping relations to phenomena and are the referents of linguistic theory formulations. Depending on the sort of mapping relationship required for theoretical adequacy, realist, quasi-realist or anti-realist versions are obtained. Correspondence rules are avoided and some versions eschew observational–nonobservational distinctions altogether. Development of the semantic conception has tended to focus on the mediation of theories and phenomena via observation or experiment, the relations between models and theories, confirmation of theories, their ontological commitments, and semantic relations between theories, phenomena and linguistic formulations. The structuralist approach also analyses theories set-theoretically as comprised of a theory structure and a set of intended applications, but is neopositivistic in spirit and in its reliance on a relativized theoretical–nontheoretical term distinction. It has been used to explore theoreticity, the dynamics of theories as they undergo development, and incommensurability notions.

One's analysis of theories tends to influence strongly the position one takes on issues such as such as observation, confirmation and testing, and realism versus instrumentalism versus antirealism.

1 Background

Part of the mathematically specified content of special relativity cannot be reduced to observations. Logical positivism emerged out of attempts to reconcile that feature with Mach's doctrine that observations exhaust the empirical content of a theory. Exploiting recent developments in logic and the foundations of mathematics such as *Principia mathematica*, the logical positivists concluded that mathematics was tautological and so mathematical portions of scientific theories did not add to their empirical content – a reconciliation called into question by their own later work on pure versus applied geometries.

Joining with this effort was a strongly Neo-Kantian approach to epistemology and metaphysics. Carnap 's *Aufbau* (1928) essentially reworked Kant's 'transcendental analytic': the unique categories and their principles of the metaphysical deduction were replaced by the notion of a nonunique constructional system (*Konstitutionstheorie*) and the transcendental ego, by a physical person constructed out of subjective experiences. Carnap maintained that this particular constitutional scheme was not unique, and thus that realism, idealism, and his favoured constructional scheme were just different ways of speaking. Insofar as such schemes were valid they were in agreement. The disadvantage of realist or idealist schemes was that they contained language that allowed metaphysical assertions which were not cognitively significant. The advantage of a logically ideal scheme was that only what was cognitively significant could be asserted. Therefore anything legitimate in any other scheme could be translated into a logically ideal scheme. Philosophical analysis became canonical formulation in the ideal syntactical language.

2 Syntactical approaches: the 'received view'

Syntactical approaches analyse theories as *linguistic entities* which are individuated by their syntactic characteristics. Thus alterations in the syntax of a theory (say, by changing the axioms or the language) result in a different theory.

Whitehead and Russell's *Principia mathematica* did not clearly distinguish syntax from semantics, assuming syntactical axioms had a given standard interpretation, and so early syntactical investigations were of interpreted sentences. Thus when positivists syntactically distinguished the observational and theoretical components of a scientific language, the observational portion was presumed to be interpreted; however, the problem of fictitious theoretical entities rendered problematic whether theoretical assertions genuinely referred.

Following constructions in the *Aufbau*, Rudolf CARNAP initially construed the observational sublanguage as a sense datum language. Later he switched to the more realistic 'thing' language. Observational assertions were statements about directly observable entities and their attributes. Carnap never attempted rigorous delineation of the observational–theoretical distinction because he viewed it as somewhat arbitrary and probably just a matter of language choice. In the terminology of his 'Empiricism, Semantics, and Ontology' (1950), choice of a language is an external question, but truth is an internal question that can only be raised in the context of a specific language system. Thus demarcation of the observation language from the theoretical language is an external question.

A logically ideal scientific language trifurcated its vocabulary into the logical, *observational* V_O and *theoretical* V_T. The observational sub-language consisted in sentences using just V_O augmented by the logical, and the theoretical sublanguage utilized V_T and logical terms. *Mixed sentences* contained both observational and theoretical terms. Observation language sentences were fully interpreted, whereas theoretical assertions depended on the theory for their interpretation. The laws, T, (axioms in the theoretical language) *implicitly defined* their terms by imposing relationships that restricted potential interpretations. Mixed language *correspondence rules* C infused observational meaning into the theoretical terms, so that the interpretation of theoretical assertions was a function of implicit definition and infused operational meaning. The theory consisted of the conjunction TC.

Since implicit definition restricted but did not fix referents for theoretical terms, the empirical referents of theoretical assertions depended essentially on the standard interpretation of V_O mediated via C. Initially the C were *explicit definitions* that identified the content of theoretical assertions with complex observable conditions. Existence of alternative procedures for defining the 'same' concept and problems in capturing the logic of dispositional terms using symbolic logic led to the more liberal requirement that the C be *reduction sentences* partially defining theoretical terms in the context of a particular experimental set-up as characteristic outcomes to stimuli. Difficulties in giving observational interpretations to theoretical terms such as the ψ function in quantum mechanics and real valued measures led to allowing C to be *interpretive systems* that do not individually coordinate V_T terms with observable conditions, instead requiring that their inclusion in a theory make a difference in the theory's observable predictions.

Figure 1 will help clarify the differences in these proposals. When the C were required to be explicit definitions, theoretical assertions were guaranteed to refer to observable reality within TC's scope. Once reduction sentences or interpretative systems were allowed, V_T terms could refer to observables or to nonobservables. That is to say that the models of TC included both. A general problem was that the Löwenheim–Skolem theorem implied that the models of TC included both intended models and wildly unintended ones (see MODEL THEORY). Unintended models are the source of potential counterexamples. Blocking them more concerns eliminating artifacts of the syntactical approach than it does dealing with substantive content of the analysis. Positivistic syntactical analyses of theories, confirmation and explanation persistently were plagued by problems of unintended models.

3 Instrumentalism versus realism

The arguments that prompted Carnap and C.G. HEMPEL to move from explicit definitions to reduction sentences or interpretive systems as preferred correspondence rules C are persuasive only within a realistic perspective. Those who resisted realism

345

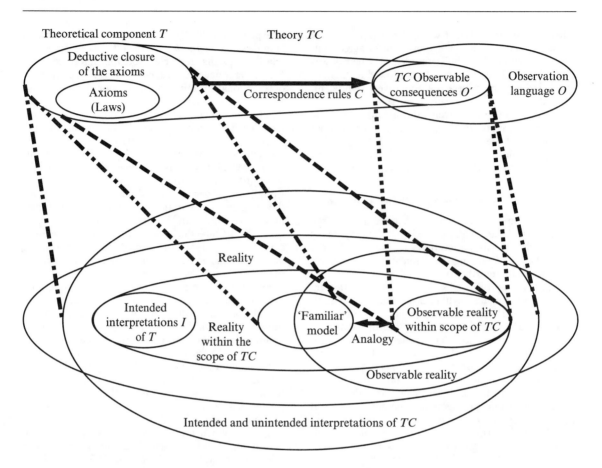

Figure 1. Semantic properties of the received view on theories under explicit and partial definition versions and when augmented by 'familiar' analogical models.

Key:

- ▪ ▪ ▪ ▪ ▪ Pre-established meanings for observation sentences cause observable consequences O' to pick out observable reality within the scope of TC.

- ▬ ▬ When correspondence rules are explicit definitions, TC and the interpretation of O' cause the theory component T to pick out observable consequences redundent of those O' pick out.

- ▬ ▪ ▬ When the correspondence rules C are reduction sentences or interpretive systems that only partially define theoretical terms in T, the allowed interpretations of T include not only the intended interpretations of T but many wildly unintended and unrealistic interpretations as well. Further the choice of the correspondence rules C that partially define T is alleged by Campbell and Hesse to be highly irrational.

- ▬ ▪ ▪ To counter this they propose that the theory T must admit of a second interpretation in terms of a 'familiar' model that stands in an analogical relationship to the observable portion of reality within the intended scope of theory TC. This analogy rationally suggests plausible candidates for correspondence rules C, but does nothing to solve the problem of wildly unintended interpretations for T.

turned to instrumentalism to accommodate the undeniable benefits of theory not reducible to observation. Ramsey proposed that theoretical content be construed as a second-order existential quantification of theoretical laws which entailed the observable consequences of the theory. This, of course, only asserts that *some* system within the intended and unintended interpretations of Figure 1 yields observational consequences O' and thus does little to avoid realism, other than being noncommittal.

Craig's theorem asserts that whenever we bifurcate the nonlogical vocabulary of a theory T into V_T and V_O there is a new theory T_O using only the subvocabulary V_O that has precisely the V_O theorems. Thus theoretical assertions are alleged to be eliminable in science. Unfortunately T_O has an infinite axiom set whereas positivists construe theories as being finitely axiomatizable, and so this theorem's relevance is suspect. With the gradual liberalization of C-rules the received view became increasingly realistic. Nevertheless there is an artificiality to the realistic versus instrumentalistic debates since they erroneously assume that either all the terms in a theory are interpreted realistically or none are.

4 Demise of the received view

Logical positivists were concerned to accommodate real science and whenever they found incompatibilities with uncontroversial scientific achievement they modified their analyses accordingly. In practice this meant that they adjusted their analyses to accommodate the best physics had to offer, but deployed them normatively in evaluation of the social sciences. Positivists, especially Carnap and Hempel, were paragons of intellectual integrity, relentlessly subjecting their own analysis to scrutiny and revelling in the discovery of defects that required modifications.

Such internal critique did not challenge the presuppositions of their enterprise, but a series of external critiques in the 1950s and 1960s did. Most fundamental were the attacks on the observational–theoretical distinction by Achinstein and Hilary PUTNAM who charged that the distinction could not be drawn in a satisfactory manner. Later Suppe (1989) showed that these arguments established only that such a distinction could not be drawn on the basis of natural language usage and that, if artificially drawn, did not mark an epistemologically significant distinction. Achinstein and Putnam also charged that the notion of 'partial interpretation' associated with more liberal C-rules was incoherent; later Suppe (1989) gave a model-theoretic construal compatible with positivism, once it was realized that not all interpretation had to be via the observation language.

Putnam and Achinstein's attacks prevailed and were joined by new historically based accounts of theorizing that semi-explicitly rejected the received view. Hanson argued that observations were theory-laden – from which it followed that the observational–theoretical distinction was untenable. P.K. FEYERABEND noted that observations and theories use the same descriptive vocabulary.

Thomas S. KUHN's *Structure of Scientific Revolutions* is the classic reworking of positivism. He rejected the positivistic observational–theoretical distinction, instead embracing a version of N.R. HANSON's claim that observation is theory-laden. He denied that the connections between theory and phenomena can be mediated by any *explicit* set of correspondence rules. Instead exemplary applications are studied as one becomes a scientist and subsequent applications are modelled on these exemplars, and both phenomena and theory use the same vocabulary. His account of how, in revolutionary episodes, science switches 'paradigms' or organizing frameworks closely resembles Carnap's views on the arbitrariness of choosing a particular language or conceptual framework. In particular, both agree that the choice cannot be assessed on the basis of truth determination.

Schaffner (1969) charged that positivist C-rules conflated meaning relations, experimental procedures and causal relations. Thus they lumped together components that were epistemically distinct. Suppes (1962) argued that the C-rules account failed to reveal what was epistemologically central to the application of theories to phenomena. Suppe (1977) argued that the inclusion of C-rules as proper parts of theories resulted in improper individuation criteria for theories since the received view required that, contra actual scientific practice, a change in experimental procedure was a change in theory. The relevance of formalist approaches was challenged by Toulmin and others including, surprisingly, Hempel (in Suppe 1977).

Increasingly positivists had become sidetracked from the development of their substantive ideas by technical problems that were mere artifacts of their strategy of modelling science via predicate calculus axiomatizations. Suppes (1967) contrasted their 'intrinsic formulation' approach to the 'extrinsic' approach wherein one directly designates an intended family of models. Although formal semantics is incapable of designating precisely the intended set of models, our ordinary linguistic resources suffice. In practice we do pick out just intended models (else there would not be a problem of unintended models), and so we can proceed directly to the specification of these models without recourse to syntactic axiomatization. What is surprising about this line of criticism is that Carnap and others were seminal developers of formal semantics, yet that work had little impact on their approach to formal analysis of theories which, to the end, was aggressively syntactical.

Under the weight of these objections the consensus emerged that the received view was fundamentally untenable.

5 The semantic conception

Questions such as whether Schrödinger's wave mechanics and Heisenberg's matrix mechanics are the same theory were resolved when von Neumann showed that they both admitted of the same canonical Hilbert space representations. That and a related paper construing theories as configured state spaces mapped onto observation spaces inspired the development of the semantic conception. The basic idea is that a theory is identified by a suitably connected family of models.

Everet Beth used set-theoretic techniques to analyse several specific theories, speculated about the potential for semantic analyses, and pioneered the semantics of amplified usage wherein the same formalism can refer variously to different set-theoretic structures.

In the early 1950s Patrick Suppes, J.C.C. McKinsey and others investigated foundational issues in physics via set-theoretic axiomatizations. Generalizing from these studies Suppes argued that theories were extra-linguistic set-theoretic structures and offered a general structural analysis. One argument for this semantic approach was that extrinsic presentation of theories avoided the problem of blocking unintended interpretations that had so diverted positivism from its philosophical agenda. Suppes (1962) explored theory structures associated with phenomena in experimental circumstances (see MEASUREMENT, THEORY OF). Drawing on his mathematical learning theory laboratory experience, he argued that the connection between theory and experiment is mediated via a hierarchy of models including the model of the experiment, models of data, experimental design, and *ceteris paribus* conditions.

Drawing on his jet-engine flight-test research experiences, Suppe (1989) argued that correspondence rule accounts bore little resemblance to how theories attached to phenomena or how theories were tested. Analysing theories as essentially describing state transitions in a 'state space', he argued that propounding a theory consisted in asserting a suitable mapping relation between the configured state space and systems within the theory's scope. Because theories ignored all but a selected finite number of variables, the relation had to be counterfactual

wherein the theory structure specified how systems within the theory's scope *would* behave *were* they isolated from influences not showing up as variables in the theory.

The counterfactual interpretation of theories has implications for how theories are confirmed by experiment. Characteristic of experimental design is control of extraneous variables so that only variables of the theory are influential. Suppe viewed the logic of confirmation as turning essentially on issues of experimental control, and offered a rigorous epistemology where the adequacy of theories under controlled circumstances licensed the generalized conclusion that the theory was counterfactually true of *all* systems within its scope. On Suppe's epistemology, observational knowledge of one carefully crafted experimental instance is sufficient to establish a scientific theory non-inductively.

Whereas Suppes and Suppe have concentrated on the experimental mediation of theory to experiment, van Fraassen's version of the semantic conception focuses on ontological issues. His investigations have focused on the semantic relations between theories, their formulations, and reality. His starting point is the supposition that not everything referred to in a theory engenders ontological commitment. The problem is to give full semantic interpretations of theoretical language without excessive ontological commitments. His solution is the theory of *semi-interpreted languages* wherein languages are interpreted as referring to 'logical spaces' which provide a full semantic interpretation for the language of theorizing. However ontological commitments are left unconstrained, being a matter of which points in the logical space one wishes to ontologically commit to. Such commitments are made via individual mapping functions (called *Loc* functions) from the real-world objects to points in logical space. For van Fraassen scientific theories are just suitably configurated logical spaces.

Figure 2 illustrates the main features of the semantic conception and relations between prominent versions. Detailed examinations of biological theory using the semantic conception have been made by Lloyd (1988) and Thompson (1989), and of quantum theory by van Fraassen (1991).

In contrasting semantic and syntactical approaches, some people refer to the latter as 'the statement view'. That is misleading since some philosophers view statements as linguistic entities having a syntax, and others do not. When theories are characterized as collections of statements construed extra-linguistically, one is presenting a semantic analysis. Proponents of the semantic conception view such statements as structurally too problematic or

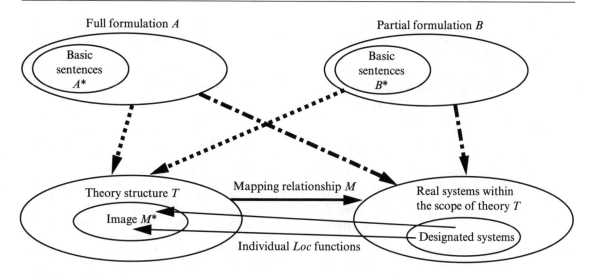

Figure 2. The semantic conceptions of theories.

Here theory structure T consists of precisely the intended interpretations of formation A. Note that no observational–theoretical interpretation of the theory formulation languages A or B are presupposed nor are there any correspondence rules as proper parts of the theory. Theory-structure T provides a full semantic interpretation ■ ■ ▶ of the formulation languages A and B which are also interpreted ▬ ■ ▶ as referring to real systems within T's scope. Theories are asserted to stand in some mapping relationship M to real systems within the scope of the theory. On a realistic version, M would be a homomorphism; on Suppe's quasi-realistic version, M would be a counterfactual relationship specifying how the real systems would behave were they isolated from influence by variables not in T; on van Fraassen's constructive empiricism the mapping M is between a designated subset of the real systems and its image M^* under individual Loc functions. When M^* is contained in T then T is said to be empirically adequate. The Loc functions specify the ontological commitments one makes in asserting the theory T. On Suppes' version, the mapping relation M is mediated by a hierarchy of models including models of the experiment and models of data. Experimental design, instrumentation and so on, are not proper parts of theories but are used to determine whether mapping M does hold.

impoverished to shed much illumination on the structure of theories.

6 Realism versus antirealism

Since theories are extra-linguistic entities, realism–instrumentalism disputes have to be recast. On the semantic conception theory, structures specify state-transitions where states are n-tuples of simultaneous values for the theory's variables or, in theories like quantum mechanics and natural selection, probability distributions over such values. Realism debates concern the nature of the mapping relationship between theory structure and the world (see Figure 2).

Realism maintains that theories give literally true accounts of reality. That means that one is ontologically commited to all the state variables. A theory is empirically true just in case the allowed state-transitions in the theory structure are identical to those which could occur in the actual world.

Van Fraassen's *antirealism* does not commit ontologically to all state variables. On his scheme a realist will have Loc functions onto every state variable, whereas he only countenances Loc functions from observables. Let W be that portion of reality to which one attaches Loc functions. Then according to van Fraassen a theory is *empirically adequate* precisely if the image M^* of W is among the models comprising the theory. Although van Fraassen resorts to an observational–nonobservational distinction to motivate his analysis, it works for any vocabulary bifurcation. The result is a general account of how language can have full semantic interpretations without generating ontological commitments to every semantically utilized entity. Van Fraassen is particularly concerned about the fact that at various junctures science is irreducibly modal, yet it seems excessive to commit ontologically to unreal possible worlds. Semi-interpreted languages provide an escape from such ontological commitment. Within the range of ontological commitment empirical adequacy is equivalent to empirical truth. His antirealism thus is just realism attenuated to the range of one's ontological commitment.

Suppe questions whether any theories meet realistic truth or antirealistic empirical adequacy requirements since the scope of a theory includes systems influenced by variables not taken into account by the theory. Real world state-transitions often diverge from those specified in theory structures – thus making the theory false or empirically inadequate. In actual practice we only test theories against systems isolated under experimental control. Suppe's *quasi-realism* consists in ontological commitment to all variables that can be detected, together with the claim that empirically true theories provided counterfactual characterizations of how systems would behave were they isolated from influences not taken into explicit account by the theory. One could develop quasi-realisms with van Fraassen-like restricted ontological commitments.

Van Fraassen's semi-interpreted languages provide a general framework for evading excessive metaphysical commitment. (Thus, Suppe who is far more realistic, utilizes van Fraassen's semi-interpreted languages in his treatment of the relations between theory structure and linguistic formations, and in the analysis of empirical probabilities and causal modalities.) It accommodates, but does not require, commitment to van Fraassen's *antirealism*.

Although van Fraassen's enterprise is antimetaphysical in a manner not unlike Carnap's 'Empiricism, Semantics, and Ontology', neither he nor the other developers intend the semantic conception to demarcate the scientific from the unscientific or the real from the metaphysical. Indeed, semi-interpreted languages show that issues of ontological commitment are independent of the structure of theories, though not of one's epistemology.

7 Models and theories

For positivists theoretical terms have no empirical referents until they receive infused meaning from correspondence rules. How does one rationally choose reduction sentences or interpretive systems if theoretical terms have no independent meaning? N.R. CAMPBELL argued that the choice was irrational unless there were some interpretation of the theory's axioms to guide you. He proposed that theoretical terms should be given an independent semantic interpretation in terms of concrete familiar models that are analogous to systems in the observable portion of the theory's scope (see Figure 1). Correspondence rules that mirror the analogy then would

be tried. Later followers like Harré and Hesse argued that such models were what made theories explanatory.

To accommodate theories like quantum mechanics, which does not admit of concrete familiar models, they allowed that the mathematical formalisms (presumably the structures not the equations) themselves could be the models. The proposal did nothing to solve the problem of unintended interpretations of the theory. Little illumination as to the nature of models resulted beyond the notion that they were analogical and hence akin to metaphors.

Suppes noted that the word 'model' variously refers to metamathematical models (set-theoretic structures used to interpret axiom systems), scientific theories, and physical or scientific models. He argued that the latter two sorts can be analysed in terms of metamathematical models. The semantic conception does so for scientific theories.

Although the philosophical literature on scientific models has focused on familiar concrete models used heuristically or along Campbell's lines, models are often vehicles of scientific knowledge, not mere analogues or metaphors. Data typically are presented as a *model of the data* into which the raw data have been embedded and structurally enhanced. Typically the model is some sort of configured hyperspace. *Simulation modelling* is increasingly an alternative source of experimental data. Simulation and other *dynamic models* are state-transition systems used to probe or model real-world systems. Thus both theories and models consist of configured mathematical spaces or structures standing in mapping relations to other systems, and so the structure of various scientific models can be studied along the lines of the semantic conception. Fair progress analysing dynamic and simulation models has been made by Burks and Suppe. As other sorts of scientific models are studied and given semantic analyses, we should come to the point where systematic comparative investigations of the scientific models and scientific theories can be given.

8 Dynamics of theories

One reason for rejecting the positivists' analysis was that theories were improperly individuated since experimental procedures were incorporated into correspondence rules. The semantic conception also is inadequate if it cannot properly individuate theories.

Theories do undergo development. Lakatos construed this as a progression of static theories within a research programme. Others maintain that theories are dynamic entities that expand their scope and undergo development. Developing a dynamic account where partial or sub-models individuate theories is central to Sneed's *structuralist* analysis which began as an application of Suppes's set-theoretic techniques to the problem of theoretical terms. Sneed noticed that determination of mass and force function values when applying classical particle mechanics must invariably utilize classical particle mechanics itself and claimed this is the characteristic mark of theoretical functions or terms. Theoretical functions threaten to make the predictive testing of a theory viciously circular unless their contribution to the empirical content of a theory is restricted.

Sneed's solution is that the empirical content of a theory varies from application to application, and so the portion of the theory used in an application to calculate theory functions is not part of the empirical content of *that* application of the theory. Yet theories have a unified content that cannot be accounted for by a conjunction of statements. More precisely: a theory consists of a theory structure T and a set I of intended applications that are physical systems. Let M_p be the possible physical systems, and let M_{pp} be the partial possible systems obtained by function r that strips the M_p of their theoretical functions. The theory's empirical content is expressed by the statement that there exists a class of extensions E of the M_{pp} obtained via the addition of suitably constrained theoretical functions, such that these extensions E all are models in T. The analysis here is a set-theoretic modification of the Ramsey sentence (§3).

It follows that theories cannot be individuated on the basis of theory structure T. Sneed generalizes the notion of the empirical content of a theory to a set-theoretic analysis of the *core* $T_C = \langle M_p, M_{pp}, r, M, C \rangle$ of the theory structure T, where M is the law of the theory and C is a set of constraints. Although I is a part of the theory $\langle T, I \rangle$, individuation of the theory only depends on a core I' of paradigmatic intended applications. Theories are individuated on the basis of T_C and I'.

Sneed's analysis of the dynamics and individuation of theories is driven by his formulation of the problem of theoretical terms, which depends crucially on the supposition that the testing of a theory requires a prediction and an independent determination of whether the prediction is correct. If, as a growing number of philosophers and historians maintain, prediction is not central to testing or confirmation, Sneed's analysis is unlikely to be compelling. More generally, although set-theoretic apparatus makes this a semantic approach, its perspective is neo-positivistic, being wedded to a hypothetico-deductive view of testing, concern over distinguishing theoretical from nontheoretical terms and modified Ramsey sentences.

In this respect it joins a number of other neo-positivistic efforts that attempt to exploit model-theoretic notions. Subsequent development of the structuralist programme has focused on applying Sneed's perspective to Kuhn's views on science and incommensurability controversies (see INCOMMEN-SURABILITY).

Despite such reservations over the structuralist programme, the idea of individuating dynamically evolving theories on the basis of a structural core or partial models is a promising one. DaCosta and French (1990) present an analysis of partial models that is not tied to neo-positivistic ideas, but they do not apply it to theory individuation issues. Another untried approach would be to analyse theory structures as adaptive systems capable of reorganizing. Before expending much effort here, better data on how developing theories are individuated should be obtained.

See also: EXPERIMENT; IDEALIZATIONS; LOGICAL POSITIVISM; MODELS; OBSERVATION; OPERATIONALISM; RELATIVITY THEORY, PHILOSOPHICAL SIGNIFICANCE OF; SCIENTIFIC REALISM AND ANTIREALISM

References and further reading

* Achinstein, P. (1968) *Concepts of Science: A Philosophical Analysis*, Baltimore, MD: Johns Hopkins University Press. (Contains reprintings of his objections to positivistic operational–theoretical distinction and partial interpretation notion.)
* Beth, E. (1949) 'Towards an Up-to-Date Philosophy of the Natural Sciences', *Methodos* 1: 178–85. (Articulates his vision of a semantic conception of theories developed in his *Natuursphilosophie*, Gorinchem: Noorduyn, 1948, that inspired van Fraassen's version of the semantic conception.)
* —— (1963) 'Carnap's Views on the Advantages of Constructed Systems Over Natural Languages in the Philosophy of Science', in P. Schilpp (ed.) *The Philosophy of Rudolf Carnap*, La Salle, IL: Open Court, 469–502. (Develops his amplified usage semantic doctrines that influenced Suppe's version of the semantic conception.)
* Birkhoff, G. and Neumann, J. von (1936) 'The Logic of Quantum Mechanics', *Annals of Mathematics* 37: 823–43; repr. in J. von Neumann, *Collected Works*, New York: Pergamon Press, 1962, vol. 4, 1–5–125. (The fundamental paper that influenced the development of the semantic conception of theories.)
Bromberger, S. (1963) 'A theory about the Theory of Theory and about the Theory of Theories', in B.

Baumrin (ed.) *Philosophy of Science: The Delaware Seminar*, New York: Interscience, vol. II, 79–106. (Proposes an erotetic logic approach to theories and distinguishes different senses of 'theory'.)

* Burks, A.W. (1975) 'Models of Deterministic Systems', *Mathematical Systems Theory* 8: 295–308. (Detailed technical analysis of modelling deterministic and indeterministic state-transition systems using the mathematics of sequence generators.)

* Campbell, N. (1920) *Physics: The Elements*, Cambridge: Cambridge University Press; repr. as *Foundations of Science*, New York: Dover, 1957. (Positivistic analysis arguing that theories must contain analogical models.)

* Carnap, R. (1928) *Der Logische Aufbau der Welt*, Berlin; 2nd edn, Berlin: Felix Meiner, 1961; trans. R. George, *The Logical Structure of The World*, Berkeley, CA: University of California Press, 1969. (Carnap's reworking of the transcendental analytic of Kant's first *Critique* which lays the basis for his later treatment of theories. The translation is of the 2nd edition.)

* —— (1936–7) 'Testability and Meaning', *Philosophy of Science* 3: 420–66, 4: 1–40. (Classic rejection of explicit definition correspondence rules in favour of reduction sentences.)

* —— (1950) 'Empiricism, Semantics, and Ontology', *Revue internationale de Philosophie* 11, 208–28; repr. in *Meaning and Necessity*, enlarged edn, Chicago, IL: University of Chicago Press, 1956. (Carnap's later semantic reworking of his *Aufbau*.)

* —— (1956) 'Methodological Character of Theoretical Concepts', in H. Feigl and M. Scriven (eds) *Minnesota Studies in the Philosophy of Science*, Minneapolis, MN: University of Minnesota Press, vol. 1, 33–76. (Carnap's most comprehensive received-view treatment of the structure of theories.)

—— (1963) 'Replies and Systematic Expositions', in P. Schilpp (ed.) *The Philosophy of Rudolf Carnap*, La Salle, IL: Open Court, 859–1013. (Contains responses to Hempel's version of the positivistic received view on theories.)

—— (1966) *Philosophical Foundations of Physics*, New York: Basic Books. (Contains Carnap's most sustained discussion of the observational–theoretical distinction.)

Cartwright, N. (1983) *How the Laws of Physics Lie*, Oxford: Clarendon Press. (Criticizes realistic construal of theories and discusses how models attach to phenomena.)

Churchland, P. and Hooker, C. (eds) (1985) *Images of Science: Essays on Realism and Empiricism, with a Reply from Bas C. van Fraassen*, Chicago, IL: University of Chicago Press. (A volume of criticisms of van Fraassen's constructive empiricism account of theory testing on his version of the semantic conception, with replies by van Fraassen.)

Coffa, A. (1991) *The Semantic Tradition from Kant to Carnap: To the Vienna Station*, ed. L. Wessels, Cambridge: Cambridge University Press. (Authoritative historical account of the positivistic programme of language reform and its precursors.)

* Craig, W. (1953) 'On Axiomatizability with a System', *Journal of Symbolic Logic* 18: 30–2. (Theorem that some sought to use to defend instrumentalism.)

* DaCosta, N.C. and French, S. (1990) 'The Model-Theoretic Approach in the Philosophy of Science', *Philosophy of Science* 57 (2): 248–65. (A partial models attempt to deal with the dynamics of theory development on the semantic conception.)

Dalla Chiara Scabia, M. and Toraldo di Franca, G. (1973) 'A Logical Analysis of Physical Theories', *Revisto del Nuovo Cimento*, 2nd series, 3: 1–20. (Neo-positivistic semantic analysis of theories.)

* Feyerabend, P. (1958) 'An Attempt at a Realistic Interpretation of Experience', *Proceedings of the Aristotelian Society*, new series, 58: 143–70. (Analysis of scientific observation wherein theory and observation use the same vocabulary.)

* Fraassen, B.C. van (1967) 'Meaning Relations Among Predicates', *Nous* 1: 161–80. (Fundamental paper on the theory of semi-interpreted languages.)

* —— (1969) 'Meaning Relations and Modalities', *Nous* 3: 155–68. (Extends theory of semi-interpreted languages to include modal operators.)

* —— (1970) 'On the Extension of Beth's Semantics of Physical Theories', *Philosophy of Science* 37: 325–39. (Develops a semantic conception of theories based upon his theory of semi-interpreted languages.)

* —— (1979) 'Foundations of Probability: A Modal Frequency Interpretation', in G. Toraldo di Francia (ed.) *Problems in the Foundations of Physics*, Amsterdam: North Holland, 343–94. (Extends the theory of semi-interpreted languages to probabilistic and relative frequency statements.)

* —— (1980) *The Scientific Image*, New York: Oxford University Press. (Develops the associated constructive empiricist epistemology for his antirealist version of the semantic conception.)

—— (1989) *Laws and Symmetry*, Oxford: Oxford University Press. (Contains his most systematic articulation of semantic approaches to the analysis of science.)

* —— (1991) *Quantum Mechanics: An Empiricist View*, New York: Oxford University Press. (Extends theory of semi-interpreted languages to modal

probabilistic systems by presenting a semantic conception analysis of quantum mechanics.)

Giere, R. (1979) *Understanding Scientific Reasoning*, New York: Holt. (Elementary textbook that presents a clear nontechnical discussion of the semantic conception of theories.)

* —— (1988) *Explaining Science: A Cognitive Approach*, Chicago, IL: University of Chicago Press. (Defends a realistic version of the semantic conception of theories.)

* Hanson, N.R. (1958) *Patterns of Discovery*, Cambridge: Cambridge University Press. (Classic work arguing that observation is theory-laden.)

* Harré, R. (1983) *An Introduction to the Logic of the Sciences*, New York: St Martin's Press, 2nd edn. (Contains a comprehensive presentation of the analogical view of models and their necessity within theories.)

* Hempel, C.G. (1952) *Fundamentals of Concept Formation in Empirical Science*, Chicago, IL: University of Chicago Press. (Argues that some legitimate theoretical concepts cannot be defined by reduction sentences and introduces interpretive sentences as the general form of correspondence rules for the positivistic received-view account.)

—— (1963) 'Implications of Carnap's Work for the Philosophy of Science', in P. Schilpp (ed.) *The Philosophy of Rudolf Carnap*, La Salle, IL: Open Court, 685–710. (Hempel's critical discussion of Carnap's version of the positivistic received view analysis of theories.)

* —— (1965) *Aspects of Scientific Explanation and Other Essays in Philosophy of Science*, New York: Free Press. (Reprints a number of his papers, including ones on cognitive significance, theories and instrumentalism versus realism.)

Henkin, L., Suppes, P. and Tarski, A. (eds) (1959) *The Axiomatic Method with Special Reference to Geometry and Physics*, Amsterdam: North Holland. (Presents a number of attempts to axiomatize theories using semantic methods.)

* Hesse, M. (1966) *Models and Analogies in Science*, Notre Dame, IN: University of Notre Dame Press. (Modern classic defence of the necessity of analogical models as components of theories.)

Hooker, C. (1975) 'On Global Theories', *Philosophy of Science* 42: 152–79. (Appendix presents a detailed cloud chamber example of the complexities of applying theory to phenomena.)

* Kuhn, T.S. (1962) *The Structure of Scientific Revolutions*, Chicago, IL: University of Chicago Press; rev. edn 1970. (The classic reform of positivist doctrines that rejects the observational-theoretical distinction and correspondence rules,

while maintaining that basic choice of theory cannot be made on the basis of testing.)

* Lakatos, I. (1970) 'Falsification and the Methodology of Scientific Research Programmes', in I. Lakatos and A. Musgrave (eds) *Criticism and the Growth of Knowledge*, Cambridge: Cambridge University Press, 149–86. (Presents an approach to dealing with the dynamics of theorizing via a 'problem shift' sequence of successor theories.)

Lambert, K. and Brittan, G.G., Jr (1987) *An Introduction to the Philosophy of Science*, Atascadero, CA: Ridgeview Publishing Co., 3rd edn. (Contains excellent elementary presentation of positivistic and semantic analyses of theories.)

Laymon, R. (1985) 'Idealization and the Testing of Theories by Experimentation', in P. Achinstein and O. Hannaway (eds) *Observation, Experiment, and Hypothesis in Modern Physical Science*, Cambridge, MA: MIT Press, 147–74. (Focuses on the role of idealization in theories and implications for theory testing.)

Leplin, J. (ed.) (1984) *Scientific Realism*, Berkeley, CA: University of California Press. (Anthology containing articles representing many main stances on scientific realism versus antirealism.)

* Lloyd, E. (1988) *The Structure and Confirmation of Evolutionary Theory*, Westport, CT: Greenwood Press. (Develops a semantic conception account of evolutionary theory.)

Moulines, C.U. (1975) 'A Logical Reconstruction of Simple Equilibrium Thermodynamics', *Erkenntnis* 9: 101–30. (An application of Sneed's structuralist analysis of theories to thermodynamics.)

—— (1976) 'Approximate Application of Empirical Theories: A General Explication', *Erkenntnis* 10: 201–27. (Concerns the application of theories to phenomena a under Sneed's structuralist account.)

* McKinsey, J.C.C., Sugar, A. and Suppes, P. (1953) 'Axiomatic Foundations of Classical Particle Mechanics', *Journal of Rational Mechanics and Analysis*, 2: 253–72. (Semantic axiomatization of a theory via Suppes' set-theoretic predicates version of the semantic conception of theories.)

* McKinsey, J.C.C. and Suppes, P. (1953) 'Transformations of Systems of Classical Particle Mechanics', *Journal of Rational Mechanics and Analysis* 2: 273–89. (Semantic axiomatization of a theory via Suppes' set-theoretic predicates version of the semantic conception of theories.)

* Neumann, J. von (1932) *Mathematische Gründlagen der Quantenmechanik*, Berlin: Springer; trans. *Mathematical Foundations of Quantum Mechanics*, Princeton, NJ: Princeton University Press, 1955. (Classical demonstration of the power of semantic approaches by showing the equivalence of wave

and matrix mechanics using a canonical Hilbert space model.)

Prezełecki, M., Szaniawski, K. and Wójcicki, R. (eds) (1976) *Formal Methods in the Methodology of Science*, Wrocław: Ossolineum. (Contains a number of semantic approaches to the analysis of theories, most of them being neo-positivistic.)

* Putnam, H. (1962) 'What Theories Are Not', in E. Nagel, P. Suppes, and A. Tarski (eds) *Logic, Methodology, and Philosophy of Science: Proceedings of the 1960 International Congress*, Stanford, CA: Stanford University Press, 240–51. (Putnam's classic attacks on the positivistic observational/theoretical distinction and partial interpretation notion; stresses problems of unintended interpretations.)

* Ramsey, F.P. (1931) 'Theories', in R.B. Braithwaite (ed.) *The Foundations of Mathematics*, London: Kegan-Paul, 212–36; repr. Paterson, NJ: Littlefield, Adams & Co., 1960. (Introduces a canonical received view formulation for theories that others attempted to transform into method for eliminating theoretical terms used in defence of instrumentalism. Sneed's structuralist account of theories and theoricity utilizes a modification of Ramsey's method.)

* Schaffner, K. (1969) 'Correspondence Rules', *Philosophy of Science* 36: 280–90. (Argues that positivistic received-view correspondence rules jumble together meaning, causal and experimental relationships that are epistemologically distinct.)

—— (1993) *Discovery and Explanation in Biology and Medicine*, Chicago, IL: University of Chicago Press. (Explores modifications of the semantic conception in the analysis of theories in molecular biology.)

Shapere, D. (1969) 'Notes Toward a Post-Positivistic Interpretation of Science', in P. Achinstein and S. Barker (eds) *The Legacy of Logical Positivism*, Baltimore, MD: Johns Hopkins University Press, 115–60. (Criticizes the assumption that all terms must be given realistic or all must be given instrumentalistic interpretations.)

* Sneed, J. (1971) *The Logical Structure of Mathematical Physics*, Dordrecht: Reidel. (Basic work presenting the structuralist analysis of theories.)

—— (1976) 'Philosophical Problems in the Empirical Science of Science: A Formal Approach', *Erkenntnis* 10: 115–46. (Further development of Sneed's structuralist account of theories.)

Stegmüller, W. (1976) *The Structure and Dynamics of Theories*, New York: Springer. (Attempts, with partial success, to make Sneed's structuralist analysis more accessible.)

* Suppe, F. (1977) *The Structure of Scientific Theories*, Urbana, IL: University of Illinois Press, 2nd edn.

(Introduction and Afterword provide a comprehensive account of the development of the positivistic received view, criticisms of it (including individuation arguments) that led to its eventual demise, and post-positivistic attempts to understand scientific theorizing including the semantic conception. The volume also contains a number of important papers on theories, including Hempel's objections to Suppes' like formalization.)

* —— (1989) *The Semantic Conception of Theories and Scientific Realism*, Urbana, IL: University of Illinois Press. (Comprehensive detailed development of a quasi-realistic version of the semantic conception of theories; also contains a history of the origins of the semantic conception, reprintings of his rejoinders to Achinstein and Putnam on positivistic partial interpretation and observational–theoretical doctrines, and a response to Schaffner's attempts to modify the semantic conception to deal with molecular biology theories.)

* —— (forthcoming) *Facts, Theories, and Scientific Observation*, vol. 1, *A Posteriori Knowledge and Truth*, vol. 2, *Scientific Knowledge*, Urbana, IL: University of Illinois Press. (Detailed development of the epistemology of observation and theory testing for the quasi-realistic version of the semantic conception. Also contains a detailed formal analysis of simulation modelling.)

Suppes, P. (1957) *Introduction to Logic*, New York: Van Nostrand. (Part II articulates the linguistic versus set-theoretic entity distinction and presents Suppes' set-theoretic predicate axiomatization approach to the semantic conception of theories. Technical but accessible.)

* —— (1961) 'A Comparison of the Meaning and Use of Models in Mathematics and the Empirical Sciences', in H. Freudenthal (ed.) *The Concept and the Role of the Model in Mathematics and Natural and Social Sciences*, Dordrecht: Reidel, 163–77. (Distinguishes theory, metamathematical and scientific model senses of 'model' and argues all can be analysed metamathematically.)

* —— (1962) 'Models of Data', in E. Nagel, P. Suppes and A. Tarski (eds) *Logic, Methodology, and Philosophy of Science: Proceedings of the 1960 International Congress*, Stanford, CA: Stanford University Press, 252–61. (Model theoretic analysis of how theories are fitted experimentally to phenomena under his version of the semantic conception of theories.)

* —— (1967) 'What is a Scientific Theory?', in S. Morgenbesser (ed.) *Philosophy of Science Today*, New York: Basic Books, 55–67. (Contains Suppes' articulation of extrinsic and intrinsic approaches to

specifying theories, arguing for the superiority of extrinsic semantic approaches.)

—— (1968) 'The Desirability of Formalization in Science', *Journal of Philosophy* 65, 651–4. (Addresses criticism of formal approaches to the analysis of science, including his vision of the semantic conception.)

* Thompson, P. (1989) *The Structure of Biological Theories*, New York: State University of New York Press. (A semantic conception analysis of biological theories.)

* Toulmin, S. (1953) *Philosophy of Science*, London: Hutchinson. (Argues against formalized analyses of theories and maintains that theories do not contain their scopes.)

* Whitehead, A.N. and Russell, B. (1910–3) *Principia mathematica*, Cambridge: Cambridge University Press. (Syntactical axiomatization of mathematics that convinces positivists that mathematics is tautological, hence does not add any empirical content to scientific theories.)

FREDERICK SUPPE

THEORY AND OBSERVATION IN SOCIAL SCIENCES

The concept of observation has received relatively little systematic attention in the social sciences, with the important exceptions of social psychology, social anthropology and some areas of sociological methodology such as 'participant observation'. In a broader sense, however, concern with the relation between theory and 'reality', 'data', 'empirical research' and so on, has been a pervasive theme in the philosophy of social science and in the methodological self-reflection of the individual social sciences.

The social sciences differ very substantially in the extent and character of their metatheoretical preoccupations. Some are still dominated by what sometimes used to be called the 'standard view' in Anglo-American philosophy of science derived from the Vienna Circle's logical empiricism and consolidated by Karl Popper in the middle decades of the twentieth century (see POSITIVISM IN THE SOCIAL SCIENCES). In this conception, theories consist essentially of law-like statements verified or, in Popper's more refined version, falsified, in a fairly direct confrontation with 'the facts'.

Both elements of this relation came under fire from the 1960s onwards. The traditional view of theory was attacked from three directions. Philosophers of

science such as Mary Hesse, Rom Harré, Norwood Russell Hanson and Michael Scriven questioned the deductivist model of scientific theory. Historians and sociologists of science, building on the pioneering work of Thomas Kuhn (1962), himself inspired by a much earlier monograph by the neurologist Ludvik Fleck (1935), noted that scientists were much more collectivistic and conservative in their theoretical affiliations than Popper's model suggested (see SOCIOLOGY OF KNOWLEDGE; KUHN, T.). And social scientists, beginning with historians and philosophers of history, pointed out that explanations by reference to general laws had little application in the social world (see EXPLANATION IN HISTORY AND SOCIAL SCIENCE §§1–2).

At the 'factual' or observational end of the relation, a convergent set of criticisms stressed the theory-dependence of observation statements in science as a whole and the additional complexities of 'understanding' social phenomena. Peter Winch (1958) developed themes of Wittgenstein's later work in directions which paralleled the traditional concerns of 'continental' hermeneutic theory. Here 'theory' builds on, and generally remains close to, the informal or common-sense understanding of a society of the kind possessed by its more reflective members. A variety of approaches, often grouped under the heading of 'social constructionism' and inspired directly or indirectly by Berger and Luckmann (1966), pursue their claim that what we call social reality is essentially the product of our own conceptualization. 'Critical' hermeneutics, combining hermeneutics with the Frankfurt School's critical theory, emphasizes, however, that these understandings can be systematically distorted by unequal power relations and the ideologies which sustain them (see CRITICAL THEORY).

All this occurred against the background of the increasing polarization of the social sciences in the late 1960s and early 1970s, a marked revival of interest in the classics of nineteenth- and early twentieth-century sociology and, to a lesser extent the other social sciences, and more broadly, what has been called 'the return of grand theory' in the human sciences (Skinner 1985). The diversity of old and new perspectives led to something of a free-for-all in the more theoretically reflective social sciences. It also suggested however that earlier conceptions of the relation between theory and observational data were perhaps more relevant and productive than those found in the standard view. In both their substantive theorizing and in their metatheoretical reflections, Marx, Weber, Durkheim and the other classics, seemed less like remote ancestors of a social scientific practice which had since become 'scientific', and more like senior contemporaries.

As a result, English-language social science re-established connections with more theoretical traditions in continental Europe, and also with the philosophy of science (see SOCIAL SCIENCE, CONTEMPORARY PHILOSOPHY OF §4). In particular, the realist philosophies of science which became influential in Britain and elsewhere in the 1970s were inspired largely by a rejection of positivistic social science (see SCIENTIFIC REALISM AND SOCIAL SCIENCE §§1–2). But whereas the interpretive or hermeneutic traditions and those of critical theory had focused mainly on the inappropriateness of positivism as a theory of social science, realists offered an explicit alternative to positivist and conventionalist theories of science as a whole, thus leaving the way open, as was noted by Russell Keat (1971), to a restatement of naturalism, the thesis that the natural and the social sciences were alike concerned with the identification of structures and explanatory mechanisms. Realists accept that observations are theory-laden but reject conventionalist conclusions, asserting instead that science is an open-ended, developing and fallible attempt to capture in our descriptions, models and theories the underlying structures of social reality. With this view, theory-choice cannot simply be based on observational adequacy or predictive success, but on a more complex and contestable assessment of explanatory power, involving bolder conjectures about the stratification of nature than one finds in the standard view, even among those like Popper, who defended a version of realism.

See also: HERMENEUTICS

References and further reading

* Berger, P. and Luckmann, T. (1966) *The Social Construction of Reality: a Treatise in the Sociology of Knowledge*, Harmondsworth: Penguin. (Despite the subtitle this book is better understood as a phenomenological theory of society.)
Bhaskar, R. (1979) *The Possibility of Naturalism*, Brighton: Harvester Press. (Brilliant extension of the model developed in his *A Realist Theory of Science* to the social sciences.)
* Fleck, L. (1935) *Genesis and Development of a Scientific Fact*, Chicago, IL and London: University of Chicago Press, 1979. (This classic monograph on theories of syphilis and the development of the Wassermann test explores the nature of scientific communities and their 'styles of thought'.)
Halfpenny, P. (1982) *Positivism and Sociology*, London: Allen & Unwin. (Outstanding brief

discussion of the multifarious relations between the two.)
* Keat, R. (1971) 'Social scientific knowledge and the problem of naturalism', *Journal for the Theory of Social Behaviour* 1 (1): 3–17. (Classic early statement of the implications of scientific realism for the philosophy of social science.)
* Kuhn, T. (1962) *The Structure of Scientific Revolutions*, Chicago, IL: University of Chicago Press. (Kuhn's account of the history of science transformed the subject, and also had a substantial impact on the philosophy of science.)
Outhwaite, W. (1987a) 'Laws and explanations in sociology', in R.J. Anderson, J.A. Hughes and W.W. Sharrock (eds), *Classic Disputes in Sociology*, London: Allen & Unwin, 157–83. (Critique of the covering-law model of explanation and its application to the social sciences.)
—— (1987b) *New Philosophies of Social Science: Realism Hermeneutics and Critical Theory*, London: Macmillan. (Argues for a convergence between the three.)
—— (1988) 'Theory', in M. Haralambos (ed.), *Developments in Sociology*, Ormskirk: Causeway Press, vol. 5, 165–86. (Survey of recent trends.)
* Skinner, Q. (ed.) (1985) *The Return of Grand Theory in the Human Sciences*, Cambridge: Cambridge University Press. (Documents the revival of 'theory' with essays on a number of influential recent philosophers and social and political thinkers.)
* Winch, P. (1958) *The Idea of a Social Science and its Relation to Philosophy*, London: Routledge, 2nd edn, 1976. (Classic application of Wittgensteinian philosophy to the understanding of societies, thus demonstrating links back to German idealist philosophy.)

WILLIAM OUTHWAITE

THEORY AND PRACTICE

Questions concerning the relation of 'theory' to 'practice' include whether there is a role for theory in the practical realm of ethics and politics; if so, how it can guide or provide justificatory reasons for practice; how reference to ethical practices might enter into the justification of theory; and whether theory can play a role in the critical appraisal of social practice. In responding to these issues, different conceptions of theory and practice need to be distinguished. Justifiable scepticism about ambitious claims for ethical theory need not rule out a more modest role for theoretical reflection on practice.

1   Theory and practice

The concepts of both 'theory' and 'practice' are used in a variety of ways. The term 'theory' is sometimes a shorthand for 'ethical theory' (see MORALITY AND ETHICS §1). Minimally it can refer to any systematic framework of general ethical principles. More elaborately it refers to those systematizations which specify some basic set of principles from which more detailed moral injunctions that guide practice can be derived or with reference to which they can be tested: Kantian and utilitarian theories provide standard examples (see KANTIAN ETHICS; UTILITARIANISM). Other properties are commonly attributed to 'ethical theory' in this style: that it specifies principles that are 'abstract', that it be justifiable from an impartial perspective, that it make a claim on any rational agent (see IMPARTIALITY; UNIVERSALISM IN ETHICS §2). In addition to this specific use, the concept of theory is also used more broadly to include social and political thought which has both explanatory and normative components: Marxian and Austrian economic theories are standard examples (see ECONOMICS, PHILOSOPHY OF §§1, 3). The concept of practice is similarly used in a variety of ways. It can refer to specific actions (such as the act of giving this drug to this patient); to a kind of act (the giving of drugs, for instance); to a group of systematically related activities pursued for some common end (such as the practice of medicine); or, more broadly still, to a set of social institutions (for example, political and economic arrangements with different distributions of rights and goods). Finally, the concept of 'moral practices' is often used in contrast to 'ethical theory' to refer to the embodiment of ethical life in the specific responses and institutions of particular communities.

2   Principle and action

How are ethical principles which appear as general statements in a theory to specify or guide particular courses of action? One possible answer, the algorithmic, is that knowledge of the principle determines all the cases that fall under it. The principle specifies a finite list of properties that can be mechanically ascertained, so that for any situation it specifies unequivocally the act to be performed. Denials of this algorithmic approach standardly invoke the need for judgment (see UNIVERSALISM IN ETHICS §3). Rules cannot specify in advance the conditions under which they apply for they require an act of judgment about particulars which cannot be itself rule-determined. This role of judgment can be understood in a strong or weak sense. In the weak sense it is confined to seeing that a particular case falls under the rule. The principle is not itself infected by the judgment. On the strong position, the act of judgment, ascertaining whether an act falls under the rule, is akin to an act of interpretation which infects our understanding of the principle itself. The application extends our understanding of the principle. Defences of such positions often invoke Wittgensteinian considerations about rule-following: every application is a new interpretation (see WITTGENSTEIN, L. §10). Consider, for example, the question of whether an act of 'date rape' should come under the principle prohibiting rape. On the algorithmic position, there should be general rules which will determine for us whether the act falls under the principle. On the weak judgmental position, a concept of rape is given and judgment is applied to ascertain whether this particular case falls under it. On the strong position, what the case does is to raise the question of how we are to understand the general principle against rape: the concept of rape itself is extended by this (and every other) new case.

The positions outlined put increasing emphasis on the importance of 'particular' as against 'universal' principles in ethical deliberation. This emphasis on the particular often takes the form of general scepticism about the very idea of ethical theory as a set of general principles that guide practice. The strong particularist rejects the whole picture of moral theory as a set of systematic general principles from which particular moral injunctions can be derived (see MORAL PARTICULARISM). Ethics is not codifiable. It is a matter of having the virtues, those dispositions of character that enable one to see and respond to a situation in a certain way, which cannot be settled in advance by the application of principles (McDowell 1979) (see VIRTUE ETHICS; VIRTUES AND VICES §3). Within the conservative tradition of politics the idea of ethical theory is taken to be a rationalist misunderstanding of the nature of moral knowledge: a theoretical approach involves a confusion of technical knowledge, which can be articulated in a set of rules and reflected upon, with practical knowledge, which is unreflective, exists only in use, and cannot be formulated in rules (Oakeshott 1962) (see CONSERVATISM §5). Scepticism about theory as a guide to practice is often allied with scepticism about the possibility of ethical theories providing justificatory reasons for a practice. There is no perspective external to ethical practices from which justification is possible. Only from within an ethical practice do we know how to go on. Correspondingly, appeals to principles of reason such as consistency or to formal features of moral language are too thin to justify any system of ethical belief (see MORAL SCEPTICISM §2).

This sceptical approach to moral and political theory may have force against a particular ambitious model of theory according to which we can have a moral theory that takes a standpoint entirely external to any particular moral practice, makes a claim on any rational agent irrespective of time and place, and offers a decision procedure for settling any practical problem by the mechanical application of a system of universal principles. Criticism of ambitious theory can be granted. However, the sceptical arguments do not rule out theory in a more modest sense of systematic reflection on our ethical beliefs, attitudes and practices, nor do they show that such reflection cannot give us reasons to change and even abandon some existing practices. An antitheoretical position that rules out even modest ethical theory renders both particular acts and social practices opaque to criticism and public judgment. Reflective equilibrium in the Rawlsian sense in which theory starts from considered ethical judgments in everyday practices, subsequently revising some in the attempt to render judgments coherent, does not require us to reason from a point of view external to our practices (Rawls 1971). Neither do the forms of radical critical social theory developed within the Marxian tradition.

3 Social theory and political practice

Critical social theory within the Marxian tradition especially as systematized in the Frankfurt School (Fay 1985) proceeds through immanent critique of social practices from the inside through theoretical reflection (see FRANKFURT SCHOOL; CRITICAL THEORY). The account runs roughly as follows. Social practices, in the widest sense of the term, are constituted and sustained by particular pre-theoretical self-understandings and norms. For example, market contract is constituted by self-understandings of the participants as independent agents with property rights which are exchanged according to certain norms; and it is sustained by the assumption that these norms are legitimate (see IDEOLOGY). Theoretical reflection on social practices will in part involve making explicit these assumptions. At the same time it may make assertions that conflict with the self-understandings of actors by claiming that they are either false or incoherent. Typical is Marx's claim that the market contract between wage worker and the owner of capital is not the free exchange between independent agents that the actors within it conceive it to be (see MARX, K. §9). The conflicts between the self-understandings of actors and the claims of social theory form the core of critical social theory, which takes as its aim the liberation of agents from those self-understandings through the changing of those practices that depend on them (Marx 1843). Within the early philosophical work of Marx this is conjoined with the more radical claim that, since many theoretical errors are the articulation of the false understandings that constitute or sustain particular practices, overcoming the theoretical errors requires changes to those practices (Marx 1845).

The extent to which critical theory can provide a purely internal criticism of any social practice is open to doubt. It presupposes contested Enlightenment norms of consistency and transparency of self-understanding. Moreover, those norms of themselves may be too thin to sustain a critique of social practices without the support of others. Hence a more general reflection on the goods of human life may be a presupposition of critical theory.

See also: APPLIED ETHICS; CASUISTRY; EXAMPLES IN ETHICS; IDEALS

References and further reading

Aristotle (*c.* mid 4th century BC) *Nicomachean Ethics*, trans. with notes by T. Irwin, Indianapolis, IN: Hackett Publishing Company, 1985, esp. books VI and X. (The classic account of the role of practical judgment about particulars in ethical deliberation.)

* Fay, B. (1985) *Critical Social Science*, Oxford: Blackwell. (An accessible statement and assessment of the central claims of critical social theory.)

Kant, I. (1793) 'On the Common Saying: "This May be True in Theory, but it does not Apply in Practice"', in H. Reiss (ed.) Political Writings, Cambridge: Cambridge University Press, 1991. (An accessible account of Kant's account of the relation of theory and practice.)

* McDowell, J. (1979) 'Virtue and Reason', *Monist* 62: 331–50. (An influential statement of a particularism in ethics.)

* Marx, K. (1843) *Zur Kritik der Hegelschen Rechtsphilosophie*, trans. R. Livingstone and G. Benton, Critique of Hegel's Philosophy of Right, in L. Colletti (ed.) Early Writings, Harmondsworth: Penguin, 1975, 57–198. (An early and influential statement of the aims of critical social theory.)

* —— (1845) 'Theses on Feuerbach', trans. R. Livingston and G. Benton, in L. Coletti (ed.) Early Writings, Harmondsworth: Penguin, 1975, 421–3. (The classic text on theory and practice in the Marxian tradition.)

* Oakeshott, M. (1962) *Rationalism in Politics*, London: Methuen. (A clearly stated conservative defence of

the primacy of practical knowledge in political and social life.)

* Rawls, J. (1971) *A Theory of Justice*, Cambridge, MA: Harvard University Press, ch. 1, section 9. (Contains the basic account of the methodology of 'reflective equilibrium'.)

Sidgwick, H. (1895) 'Theory and Practice', *Mind* (new series) 4: 370–75. (A pithy account of the relation of theory to practice from a classical utilitarian theorist.)

Williams, B. (1985) *Ethics and the Limits of Philosophy*, Cambridge, MA: Harvard University Press and London: Fontana. (An influential criticism of the ambitions of ethical theory.)

JOHN O'NEILL

THEORY OF TYPES

The theory of types was first described by Bertrand Russell in 1908. He was seeking a logical theory that could serve as a framework for mathematics, and, in particular, a theory that would avoid the so-called 'vicious-circle' antinomies, such as his own paradox of the property of those properties that are not properties of themselves – or, similarly, of the class of those classes that are not members of themselves. Such paradoxes can be thought of as resulting when logical distinctions are not made between different types of entities, and, in particular, between different types of properties and relations that might be predicated of entities, such as the distinction between concrete objects and their properties, and the properties of those properties, and so on. In 'ramified' type theory, the hierarchy of properties and relations is, as it were, two-dimensional, where properties and relations are distinguished first by their order, and then by their level within each order. In 'simple' type theory properties and relations are distinguished only by their orders.

1 Ramified type theory
2 The axiom of reducibility
3 The simple v. the ramified theory of types

1 Ramified type theory

The theory of (ramified) types was first described by Bertrand Russell (1908) as a way of avoiding vicious-circle antinomies, including the one discovered by Russell himself regarding the property that applies to all and only those properties that do not apply to themselves (see RUSSELL, B.A.W. §§7–8; PARADOXES OF SET AND PROPERTY §5). A property is said to be 'impredicable' if, and only if, it is not predicable of itself; thus, the property of being impredicable is impredicable if, and only if, it is not impredicable.

$$\text{Impred(Impred)} \equiv \neg\text{Impred(Impred)}$$

From this the contradiction follows that the property of being impredicable both is and is not impredicable. The theory of ramified types for propositional functions was developed in *Principia Mathematica* (1910–13). For Russell, such a theory was the framework of a 'logically perfect language', by which he meant a language that would show at a glance the logical structure of the facts that can be described by means of it, and in particular a language 'in which everything that we might wish to say in the way of propositions that are intelligible to us, could be said, and in which, further, structure would always be made explicit' (1959: 165). All that would be needed to add to such a theory is a vocabulary of descriptive constants that correspond to the meaningful words and phrases of the natural sciences or of natural language. The basic laws of a natural science would then be listed as nonlogical postulates of that science, and (as later proposed by Rudolf Carnap) the analytic connections between the words and phrases of natural language would be listed as meaning postulates. The constants and postulates of pure mathematics do not also need to be added, according to Russell, because they are all definable and provable in purely logical terms within the framework of type theory itself – a view known as (Russell's form of) logicism (see LOGICISM §1).

The way type theory avoids vicious-circle antinomies is by imposing logico-grammatical constraints on the logic of predicates. The basic idea is that predicates (and the propositional functions they stand for) are to be typed in a hierarchical manner so that predicates of a given type (and their corresponding propositional functions) could never meaningfully be applied to predicates (propositional functions) of the same or higher type. (Thus both Impred(Impred) and ¬Impred(Impred) are meaningless in type theory.) In 'ramified' type theory, the hierarchy is, as it were, two-dimensional, having a 'vertical' dimension consisting of a hierarchy of orders and, within each order, a 'horizontal' dimension consisting of a hierarchy of levels. That is, properties are distinguished in ramified type theory as being both of a given order (for example, first-order, second-order and so on) and of a specific level within that order. Thus, for example, where 'being shrewd', 'being courageous', 'being insightful about enemy positions' and so on are examples of first-order/first-level properties that Napoleon and other great generals shared (that is, properties of r-type (*i*)/1, as defined below, assuming

359

Napoleon and other generals to be of r-type i), Napoleon's having *all of the (first-order/first-level) properties of a great general* – that is, all of the (first-order/first-level) properties that make up what it is to be a great general – amounts to Napoleon having a first-order property of level two (that is, a property of r-type $(i)/2$, as defined below). 'Simple' type theory has only the 'vertical' hierarchy.

The description of the ramified hierarchy given by Russell was informal and relied on a use/mention confusion (see USE/MENTION DISTINCTION AND QUOTATION §3) between propositional functions (properties or relations) and the open formulas with 'apparent' (that is, 'bound' as opposed to 'free') variables taken to represent those functions. The ramified theory was not given a precise, formal description until Alonzo Church's paper of 1976, which, in accordance with contemporary terminology, uses the notion of 'order' to represent the 'vertical' hierarchy (instead of Russell's informal notion of order corresponding to the 'horizontal' hierarchy), and which uses the notion of 'level' to represent the 'horizontal' hierarchy. Church's definition of ramified types ('r-types') is as follows:

(1) There is an r-type i to which all and only individuals belong, and whose order is stipulated to be 0.

(2) If m is a non-negative integer and n is a positive integer and $\beta_1, \ldots, \beta_m$ are any given r-types, then there is an r-type $(\beta_1, \ldots, \beta_m)/n$ to which belong all and only m-ary propositional functions of level n and with arguments of r-types $\leqslant \beta_1, \ldots, \beta_m$, respectively; and the order of such a function is $N + n$, where N is the greatest of the orders corresponding to the types $\beta_1, \ldots, \beta_m$ (and $N = 0$ if $m = 0$).

Here, by an 'individual', that is, an entity of r-type i, Russell meant a concrete object (in particular, an event) as compared to the propositional functions (abstract properties and relations) that make up the entities of all other r-types. (It is not essential for all logical purposes that the entities of the basic type i be concrete, however.) The notion of the level of a propositional function ϕ of r-type $(\beta_1, \ldots, \beta_m)/n$ represents what Russell intended in speaking informally of the 'apparent' (bound) variables occurring in ϕ. If N, for example, is the greatest of the orders of $\beta_1, \ldots, \beta_m$, and k is the greatest of the orders of the 'apparent' variables occurring in ϕ (construed as a formula of r-type $(\beta_1, \ldots, \beta_m)/n)$, then $n = 1$ if $k \leqslant N$, and $n = k + 1$ if $N < k$. According to Russell, a propositional function (or formula for such) was said to be 'predicative' if 'it is of the lowest order

compatible with its having the arguments it has' (1910–13: vol. 1, 53); that is, in terms of the notion of level, ϕ is predicative if, and only if, $n = 1$.

In the simple theory of types the distinction between levels is dropped and only the distinction between orders is retained, so that in effect all propositional functions of the simple theory are predicative – although the comprehension principle of simple type theory, unlike that of ramified type theory, allows that such functions can be specified 'impredicatively', that is, in terms of a totality to which they belong.

2 The axiom of reducibility

It was Russell's view that all of traditional mathematics about numbers as abstract objects could be represented in terms of the predicative propositional functions of his theory of ramified types. He could not justify such a view, however, without assuming an 'axiom (schema) of reducibility', which stipulates that every propositional function of whatever r-type is coextensive with a predicative propositional function (having arguments of the same r-type). In symbols:

$$(\forall \phi)(\exists \psi)(x_1) \ldots (x_m)[\phi(x_1, \ldots, x_m)$$
$$\equiv \psi!(x_1, \ldots, x_m)],$$

where 'ϕ' and 'ψ' are variables for propositional functions of r-types $(\beta_1, \ldots, \beta_m)/n$ and $(\beta_1, \ldots, \beta_m)/1$, respectively, and '$x_1$', ..., '$x_m$' are variables of r-type $\beta_1, \ldots, \beta_m$, respectively. (Russell used '$\psi!$' to indicate that the propositional function represented by 'ψ' is predicative.) This axiom was criticized by a number of logicians (including L. Chwistek 1922; F. Ramsey 1931; W.V. Quine 1936) who argued that, on the assumption that type theory is an extensional system in which propositional functions of the same r-type are identical if they are coextensive (that is, true of all the same objects), the effect of the axiom of reducibility was to nullify the distinction between the different levels of propositional functions – in which case ramified type theory amounted to nothing more than a notationally complex version of simple type theory.

The extensionality assumption is dubious, however, if propositional functions are interpreted intensionally as properties and relations (as Russell originally intended). The point of the axiom of reducibility was not to identify properties and relations with their extensions, but to represent their extensions within the wider intensional framework, which is why Russell also called it 'the axiom of classes' (1910–13: vol. 1, 167). The effect of the axiom is that so-called 'impredicative' specifications of propositional functions – that is, specifications of functions in terms of a totality to which they belong – are 'annulled in extensional but not in intensional matters' (Church 1976: 758).

Ramsey emphasized a distinction between so-called logical and semantic antinomies, both of which the theory of ramified types was designed to avoid. Russell's paradox, for example, is one of the logical antinomies, as is Georg Cantor's paradox that there are classes (such as the universal class) larger than all other classes, even though, by a theorem of Cantor's, there is a class larger than any given class. These are paradoxes that, without some restrictions such as those imposed in a theory of types, simple or ramified, might occur in any system rich enough to represent properties as objects having properties, or classes as members of classes. The semantic antinomies, on the other hand, assume special semantic notions, such as truth (as in the liar paradox of a sentence that says of itself that it is false, which if true is false, and if false is true), or definability (as in G.G. Berry's paradox of 'the least integer not nameable in fewer than nineteen syllables', which is itself a name with just eighteen syllables), and other related notions of semantics. Ramsey (1931) thought of the semantic paradoxes as 'epistemological' in nature. (See PARADOXES OF SET AND PROPERTY.)

3 The simple v. the ramified theory of types

The simple theory of types suffices to avoid the logical paradoxes, but not the semantic ones, unless a distinction is made (as first proposed by A. Tarski) between the object language of simple type theory and a metalanguage in which the different semantic notions for the expressions of simple type theory can be defined or developed axiomatically (see TARSKI'S DEFINITION OF TRUTH). The ramified theory of types avoids the semantic paradoxes by incorporating an additional hierarchy of levels that (combined with the hierarchy of orders) implicitly contains a hierarchy of languages, and that in effect amounts to a special form of the metalanguage/object language distinction by which the semantic (and related intensional) paradoxes can be avoided (as noted by Church 1976: §4). Adding the axiom of reducibility does not nullify the way ramified type theory resolves or avoids the semantic (and related intensional) paradoxes. (See Church (1976: §5) and Myhill (1979) for justification of this claim.)

Different versions of the simple theory of types have been formulated by L. Chwistek (1922), F. Ramsey (1931), R. Carnap (1929), K. Gödel (1931), and A. Church (1940). The simple theory is not committed to an extensional logic, although it is often

formulated as such. R.M. Montague (1974), for example, extended Church's simple theory of types by incorporating into it operators for representing the intensions and extensions of expressions, and then used the resulting system as an intensional logic by which to provide an interpretation of a variety of intensional contexts of natural language (along lines originally described by Frege). Church (1974) has also formulated an intensional version of the simple theory by adding to it a formula operator for the Russellian notion of propositional identity. But in 1984, Church also showed that, given Russell's notion of a proposition, and hence of propositional identity, Russell's antinomy of propositions (Russell 1903: §500) can be reconstructed in simple type theory, but not in ramified type theory. According to this antinomy, there cannot be more classes of propositions than there are propositions – because every non-empty class of propositions can be associated with its 'logical product', which, by Russell's notion of propositional identity, is unique for that class; and yet, by Cantor's theorem, there must be more classes of propositions than there are propositions (see CANTOR'S THEOREM).

See also: CHURCH, A. §3; INTENSIONAL LOGIC; LOGICAL AND MATHEMATICAL TERMS, GLOSSARY OF

References and further reading

* Carnap, R. (1929) *Abriss der Logistik, mit besonderer Berücksichtigung der Relationstheorie und ihrer Anwendungen* (Outline of Logistic, with Special Consideration of the Theory of Relations and their Applications), Vienna: Springer. (This work includes an early formulation of simple type theory and its applications as a logical framework for the axiomatic method. Examples of axiomatic theories, such as set theory, Peano arithmetic, projective geometry and space-time topology are given within the simple type theory formulated. The book was later expanded and developed as Carnap (1954).)

—— (1954) *Einführung in die symbolische Logik, mit besonderer Berücksichtigung ihrer Anwendungen*, Vienna: Springer; trans. *Introduction to Symbolic Logic and its Applications*, New York: Dover, 1958. (A simple, clear description of Carnap's version of simple type theory can be found in this book, which also includes many important applications of type theory to the construction of the different kinds of numbers, the foundations of mathematics, space-time physics, anthropological kinship theories, and axiomatic biology.)

* Church, A. (1940) 'A Formulation of the Simple Theory of Types', *Journal of Symbolic Logic* 5: 56–

68. (Elegant, but somewhat difficult for students with only an introductory understanding of logic.)

* —— (1974) 'Russellian Simple Type Theory', *Proceedings and Addresses of the American Philosophical Association* 47: 21–33. (This paper includes a formulation of simple type theory with a primitive operator for propositional identity.)

* —— (1976) 'Comparison of Russell's Resolution of the Semantical Antinomies with That of Tarski', *Journal of Symbolic Logic* 41: 747–60. (An intermediate level understanding of logic should suffice to read this paper, which includes some important observations on how ramified, but not simple, type theory can avoid certain semantic and intensional paradoxes.)

* —— (1984) 'Russell's Theory of Identity of Propositions', *Philosophia Naturalis* 21 (2–4): 513–22. (Reviews Russell's antinomy about propositions (Russell 1903: §500). Church shows that this antinomy cannot be resolved in simple type theory, given Russell's view of propositional identity, but it can be resolved in ramified type theory.)

* Chwistek, L. (1922) 'Über die Antinomien der Prinzipien der Mathematik' (On the Antinomies of the Principles of Mathematics), *Mathematische Zeitschrift* 14: 236–43. (Now read mostly for historical interest.)

Cocchiarella, N.B. (1987) *Logical Studies in Early Analytic Philosophy*, Columbus, OH: Ohio State University Press. (Chapter 1 includes a detailed description of the theory of logical types in the development of Russell's views from his 1903 analysis of his paradox to the 1910–13 formulation of his ramified theory. Chapter 2 compares and reconstructs without paradox both Russell's and Frege's early versions of logicism. Chapter 5 explains how Russell's 1925 modifications to his ramified theory commit him to a system too weak for his earlier logicism.)

Copi, I. (1971) *The Theory of Logical Types*, London: Routledge & Kegan Paul. (A good, elementary introduction.)

* Gödel, K. (1931) 'Über formal unentscheidbare Sätze der *Principia Mathematica* und verwandter Systeme I', *Monatshefte für Mathematik und Physik* 38: 173–98; trans. 'On Formally Undecidable Propositions of *Principia Mathematica* and Related Systems', in J. van Heijenoort (ed.) *From Frege to Gödel: A Source Book in Mathematical Logic, 1879–1931*, Cambridge, MA: Harvard University Press, 1967, 592–617. (A classic, including Gödel's famous incompleteness theorems as applied to a type-theoretical development of arithmetic.)

* Montague, R. (1974) *Formal Philosophy: Selected Papers of Richard Montague*, ed. R.H. Thomason,

New Haven, CT: Yale University Press. (See especially the essays 'Universal Grammar' and 'The Proper Treatment of Quantification in Ordinary English', for Montague's development of Church's simple type theory as an intensional logic.)

* Myhill, J. (1979) 'A Refutation of an Unjustified Attack on the Axiom of Reducibility', in G.W. Roberts (ed.) *Bertrand Russell Memorial Volume*, London: Allen & Unwin. (Readable with an intermediate level of understanding of logic; explains how the addition of the axiom of reducibility to ramified type theory results in a system essentially different from simple type theory.)

* Quine, W.V. (1936) 'On the Axiom of Reducibility', *Mind* 45: 498–500. (One of the earliest arguments that the addition of the axiom of reducibility to ramified type theory amounts to a system only notationally different from simple type theory.)

* Ramsey, F.P. (1931) 'The Foundations of Mathematics', in *The Foundations of Mathematics and Other Logical Essays*, ed. R.B. Braithwaite, London: Routledge & Kegan Paul. (Ramsey's version of simple type theory, and his arguments why, as a foundation for mathematics, the simple theory is to be preferred to the ramified theory.)

* Russell, B.A.W. (1903) *The Principles of Mathematics*, Cambridge: Cambridge University Press; 2nd edn, London: Allen & Unwin, 1937; repr. London: Routledge, 1992, esp. chap. 10. (Russell's first extended discussion of his paradox, along with some proposals for avoiding it. His first rough ideas about a theory of types are described in appendix B, which also contains an account, in §500, of his antinomy about propositions.)

—— (1908) 'Mathematical Logic as Based on the Theory of Types', *American Journal Of Mathematics* 30: 222–62; repr. in *Logic and Knowledge, Essays 1901–1950*, ed. R.C. Marsh, London: Allen & Unwin, 1956, 59–102; repr. London: Routledge, 1992. (Accessible to readers with an intermediate-level understanding of logic.)

—— (1959) *My Philosophical Development*, London: Allen & Unwin; repr. London: Routledge, 1993. (An autobiographical account of the development of Russell's philosophical and logical views.)

* Whitehead, A.N. and Russell, B.A.W. (1910–13) *Principia Mathematica*, Cambridge: Cambridge University Press, 3 vols; 2nd edn, 1925–7. (Development of the theory of ramified types.)

NINO B. COCCHIARELLA

THEOSOPHY

Etymologically, 'theosophy' means wisdom concerning God or divine things, from the Greek 'theos' (God) and 'sophia' (wisdom). Seventeenth-century philosophers and speculative mystics used 'theosophy' to refer to a knowledge of nature based on mystical, symbolical or intuitive knowledge of the divine nature and its manifestations. It referred also to an analogical knowledge of God's nature obtained by deciphering correspondences between the macrocosm and God.

In the late nineteenth century, 'theosophy' became associated with the doctrines of Helena Petrovna Blavatsky, the founder of the popular Theosophical Society. She drew on Buddhist and Hindu philosophy and fragments from the Western esoteric tradition, especially Neoplatonism. She espoused an absolutist metaphysics in which there is a single, ultimate, eternal principle which remains unchanged and undiminished, despite manifesting itself partially in the periodic emanation and reabsorption of universes. Her cosmology included a spiritual account of the evolution of material bodies, which serve as the necessary vehicles by which individuals gradually perfect themselves through cyclic rebirth.

1   **Traditional theosophy and Western esotericism**
2   **Theosophy and the Theosophical Society**

1   Traditional theosophy and Western esotericism

Prior to the influence of the Theosophical Society, the term 'theosophy' was used to refer to any intellectual system of pagan, Jewish or Christian origin which purported to describe the secret constitution of the divine nature. Typically, this wisdom or 'gnosis' was used to achieve an understanding of the mystical relationships among the universe, humanity and God unavailable to either the empirical sciences or rational theology. Western theosophists saw themselves as heirs to a tradition of mystical and occult knowledge with roots in Pythagoreanism, Platonism, Neoplatonism, Gnosticism, Hermetism, the Jewish Kabbalah, medieval Christian mysticism and Renaissance nature philosophy.

According to Antoine Faivre (1994), the term 'theosophy' was used occasionally as a synonym for 'theology' even by some medieval philosophers, for example by Pseudo-Dionysius and Johannes Scottus Eriugena. It was used more frequently during the Renaissance, but acquired its distinctive meaning only at the beginning of the seventeenth century. At that time, alchemy, Alexandrian Hermetism and Jewish mysticism (the Kabbalah) were influencing the philosophy of nature and Rosicrucianism was gaining

adherents. The latter was a loosely knit movement associated with members of the fraternal Society of the Rose Cross. Rosicrucians followed the teachings of the legendary Christian Rosencreutz, who preached the possibility of an initiatory knowledge of a supersensible reality. In this context, some German authors began to use 'theosophy' to describe the knowledge of God's nature obtained by esoteric and mystical interpretation of sacred texts. Jakob BOEHME, for example, the German speculative mystic, described himself as a theosophist.

During the seventeenth century, 'theosophy' was closely associated with 'pansophy', a term used by Rosicrucians and Paracelsians to refer to a knowledge of divine things obtained by deciphering the 'signatures' found in the 'book of nature' (see PARACELSUS §2). For seventeenth-century theosophy, the wisdom concerning the divine nature was understood first and a gnostic comprehension of nature was derived from it, whereas for pansophy the order was reversed – decoding the 'signatures' came first and God was known by understanding the correspondences between nature and God. But from the eighteenth century onward, 'theosophy' was used to refer to hermeneutic speculations in either direction.

'Theosophy' entered the world of academic discourse largely through Jakob Brucker's chapter on theosophy in his *Historia critica philosophiae* (Critical History of Philosophy) (1741), a work which became a standard reference for the history of philosophy in the eighteenth century. According to Faivre (1994), Denis Diderot's *Encyclopédie* article on theosophers used long passages from Brucker's chapter without citation. Diderot's article introduced 'théosophie' into the French language and served as the definitive exposition of the term during the Enlightenment.

Christian theosophy was unified more by its hermeneutical method and its goal of achieving a transformative experience of divine revelation than by the specific claims made by various theosophists about nature and God's nature. Christian theosophists interpreted divine revelation by symbolically re-experiencing the events described in a sacred narrative. They relied on their imaginative responses to the text, confident that the imagination could be used as an organ of perception when divinely inspired and interiorly illuminated. Analogical principles that related the created world to God provided both an intellectual framework for, and a corrective to, the enthusiastic imagination. For example, Christian theosophists used this hermeneutical method to explain the existence of evil and the alienated spiritual condition of humanity in terms of the constitution of the Godhead.

Important figures in the Christian theosophical

tradition are MEISTER ECKHART, NICHOLAS OF CUSA (§2), AGRIPPA VON NETTESHEIM (§§1–2, 5), Robert FLUDD, Angelus Silesius, Johann Georg Gichtel, Emanuel SWEDENBORG, Friedrich Christoph Oetinger, Louis-Claude de Saint-Martin, F.W.J. von SCHELLING (§3) (especially in his later work – for example, his *Of Human Freedom*) and Franz von Baader.

In the late nineteenth century, the Theosophical Society introduced the term 'theosophy' into popular culture and widened its scope by including the theosophical doctrines of Oriental religion and philosophy.

2 Theosophy and the Theosophical Society

Helena Petrovna Blavatsky (1831–91) and the American journalist and lawyer Henry Steel Olcott founded the Theosophical Society in 1875 in New York City. Its mission was defined by three objects: first, to form a nucleus of the universal brotherhood of humanity, without distinction of race, creed, sex, caste or colour; second, to encourage the study of comparative religion, philosophy and science; and third, to investigate unexplained laws of nature and the powers latent in human beings. Blavatsky and Olcott moved to India in 1879, and in 1882 they established the Theosophical Society's headquarters at Adyar. In 1896, the American branch broke away, establishing the Theosophical Society of America.

Blavatsky's message appealed to nineteenth-century Americans because it harmonized science and religious faith, and delineated a worldview in which salvation was largely up to the individual. The publication of Darwin's *The Origin of Species* in 1859 contributed to a growing awareness that the findings of science were undermining belief in biblical texts as divine revelation. The apparent conflict between science and religion prompted some believers to look for a scientific basis for religious faith. The American ideal of self-improvement led some to question the moral acceptability of the Christian doctrines of vicarious atonement and eternal damnation. Blavatsky responded to these concerns by spiritualizing evolutionary theory and emphasizing self-reliance in the quest for moral and spiritual perfection. The Theosophical Society's influence was not confined to America, however: the Eastern ideas it popularized inspired many European artists at the beginning of the twentieth century, and its members were even influential in the revival of Buddhism in Ceylon (now Sri Lanka).

Blavatsky's theosophy has several distinctive features, some in common with the traditional theosophy of Western esotericism, and others in common with Oriental esotericism:

(1) It has an absolutist metaphysics which tends towards monism and idealism. There is an unknowable, impersonal, eternal, unitary First Principle which is the transcendent ground and source of everything (see BRAHMAN). The doctrine is monistic because the absolute is the only self-sufficient substance, and ultimately all individual minds are substances in virtue of being rooted in the absolute. They are one with the absolute and with each other. The doctrine is idealistic because intelligence and consciousness are the primary manifestations of the absolute, although these attributes cannot properly be affirmed of it, according to theosophy's negative theology.

(2) Theosophy has an emanationist cosmology: the absolute's perfection remains undiminished and unchanged, though it manifests periodically as a lesser reality, the Logos or the manifest God, from whom numberless universes gradually emanate and dissolve in a rhythmic process (see CREATION AND CONSERVATION, RELIGIOUS DOCTRINE OF §3). The absolute does not create the universe; both creation from nothing and from a pre-existing matter are ruled out. Rather, the Logos periodically differentiates itself from the absolute as an expression of the absolute's inner nature.

(3) Theosophy has a hierarchical account of reality: there are seven degrees of being which manifest different aspects of the Logos, and for each 'plane' of being there is a grade of matter appropriate for manifesting intelligence and consciousness at that level. Ultimately, however, both matter and intelligence are manifestations of the Logos, which in turn is a manifestation of the First Principle.

(4) Theosophy espouses a teleological and idealistic evolutionary theory. It is idealistic because it claims that the evolution of diversified physical forms is preceded by an involution of consciousness into matter. General species-specific characteristics first exist in the Logos, and through the process of physical evolution become more fully expressed by the functioning and capacities of biological organisms. In contrast, materialistic Darwinian theory claims that these characteristics are the result of entirely natural processes, that is, random genetic mutation and natural selection. Theosophical evolutionary theory is teleological because the evolutionary process aims at developing enlightened individuals who are conscious of the full range of their multidimensional existence and are dedicated to the project of leading others to spiritual truth. All individuals, from solar systems to human beings, gradually descend from the

highest degree of being to the lowest and then ascend again. Human beings have a sevenfold constitution which reflects the seven degrees of being, and each principle of the human microcosm enables the individual to participate in the corresponding macrocosmic principle.

(5) The evolutionary process requires that human beings actualize and balance their gnostic, affective and volitional capacities. These capacities include direct insight into the transcendent reality, imaginative and mythic grasp of truths about the correspondences between the macrocosm and microcosm, unbiased reasoning which corrects intuition and unmasks self-deception, and compassionate concern for all living things. The awakening of compassion leads to a forceful commitment to the project of reshaping one's character and overcoming all obstacles to enlightenment, first in oneself and then in others.

(6) Theosophy claims that the universe works in accordance with ethical principles which guarantee that morality coincides with self-interest; in the long term, justice prevails. The 'law of karma' holds individuals accountable for their thoughts and intentional actions via a natural causal process. Both justice and evolutionary teleology require a long series of rebirths, in which individuals slowly perfect themselves by experiencing the painful consequences of their ignorance and misguided actions (see REINCARNATION).

(7) The apparent conflict between the teachings of the various historical religions can be harmonized by understanding their esoteric and mystical core. In some cases, development or correction must be supplied from the unadulterated primeval tradition, allegedly preserved by a secret brotherhood of adepts and sages.

(8) There is an 'occult science' comprised of natural laws unknown to modern science.

See also: GNOSTICISM; HERMETISM; KABBALAH; MYSTICISM, HISTORY OF; NEOPLATONISM; PYTHAGOREANISM; STEINER, R.

References and further reading

Blavatsky, H.P. (1877) *Isis Unveiled: A Master-Key to the Mysteries of Ancient and Modern Science and Theology*, New York: J.W. Bouton; repr. Pasadena, CA: Theosophical Press, 1972. (Syncretic, wideranging and fragmentary discussions of Blavatsky's thesis that there is a secret wisdom-tradition which harmonizes spiritual truths and scientific theory.)
—— (1888) *The Secret Doctrine: The Synthesis of Science, Religion, and Philosophy*, ed. with intro. by B. de Zirkoff, London: Theosophical Publishing Company; repr. Adyar: Theosophical Publishing House, 1978. (Volume 1, 'Cosmogenesis', describes an emanationist cosmology and Volume 2, 'Anthropogenesis', describes the history of the earth and the evolution of successive human 'root races'. Difficult reading, but the 'Proem' summarizes some key points. The 1978 edition has a useful index.)
—— (1889) *The Voice of the Silence, Being Chosen Fragments from the 'Book of the Golden Precepts'*, London: Theosophical Publishing Company; repr. Wheaton, IL: Theosophical Publishing House, 1992. (Very readable – a devotional manual about the theosophical path to enlightenment.)
—— (1889) *The Key to Theosophy*, London: Theosophical Publishing Company; repr. London: Theosophical Publishing House, 1968. (An accessible introduction to the tenets of the Theosophical Society.)
* Brucker, J. (1741) *Historia critica philosophiae* (A Critical History of Philosophy), Leipzig. (No English translation available.)
Brunton, P. (1943) *The Wisdom of the Overself*, New York: E.P. Dutton. (A clear, jargon-free exposition of the central teachings of Oriental theosophy written for those who aspire to spiritual wisdom.)
—— (1984–8) *The Notebooks of Paul Brunton*, Burdett, NY: Larson, 16 vols. (A posthumously published selection from Brunton's notebooks, arranged into sixteen categories. Volumes 13–16 are especially useful for those interested in both the theory and practice of Oriental theosophy.)
Campbell, B. (1980) *Ancient Wisdom Revived: A History of the Theosophical Movement*, Berkeley, CA: University of California Press. (Accessible introduction to the history, tenets and cultural influences of Blavatsky's theosophical movement.)
* Diderot, D. (1779–82) *Encyclopédie*, in J. Assézat and M. Tourneux (eds) *Oeuvres complètes de Diderot*, Paris, 1875–7. (Volume 17 contains the article on theosophers, but no English translation of it is available.)
Ellwood, R. (1986) *Theosophy, a Modern Expression of the Wisdom of the Ages*, Wheaton, IL: Quest Books. (A sympathetic discussion of Blavatsky's theosophy by a scholar of religious studies.)
* Faivre, A. (1994) *Access to Western Esotericism*, Albany, NY: State University of New York Press. (Contains an expansion of the material of §1 of this entry on the history of the term 'theosophy', a history of Western esoteric currents, historical studies of several Christian theosophists, and an excellent bibliographical guide to research, including recent European scholarship.)
Faivre, A. and Needleman, J. (eds) (1992) *Modern*

Esoteric Spirituality, New York: Crossroad. (Studies of esoteric traditions and writers in the modern period, including Paracelsus, Rosicrucianism, Jakob Boehme and the Theosophical Society, introduced by an article on the ancient and medieval sources of modern esoteric movements.)

Godwin, J. (1989) *The Beginnings of Theosophy in France*, London: Theosophical History Centre. (A scholarly historical work.)

—— (1994) *The Theosophical Enlightenment*, Albany, NY: State University of New York Press. (Historical study of theosophy and occultism in England from the seventeenth century to the early twentieth century which argues that theosophy is indebted to both the French Enlightenment and the Hermetic tradition.)

Gomes, M. (1994) *Theosophy in the Nineteenth Century: An Annotated Bibliography*, New York: Garland Publishing. (Comprehensive bibliography of nineteenth-century works by and about H.P. Blavatsky, the Theosophical Society and other theosophists.)

Nasr, S.H. (1989) *Knowledge and the Sacred*, Albany, NY: State University of New York Press. (Based on Nasr's 1981 Gifford Lectures on esotericism and tradition. In the context of arguing that knowledge must be resacralized, he presents a historical survey of Western theosophical currents from ancient Greek thinkers to the present.)

Peuckert, W.E. (1936) *Pansophie. Ein Versuch zur Geschichte der weissen und schwarzen Magie* (Pansophy: An Essay in the History of White and Black Magic), Stuttgart: Kohlhammer. (A study of Christian theosophy and pansophy, not available in English.)

* Schelling, F.W.J. (1809) *Philosophische Untersuchungen über das Wesen der menschlichen Freiheit und die damit zusammenhängenden Gegenstände* (Philosophical Inquiries into the Nature of Human Freedom and Connected Topics), trans. J. Gutmann, *Schelling: Of Human Freedom*, Chicago, IL: Open Court, 1936. (The translator's introduction discusses Schelling's views about mysticism and theosophy in relation to philosophy.)

Weeks, A. (1993) *German Mysticism from Hildegard of Bingen to Ludwig Wittgenstein: A Literary and Intellectual History*, Albany, NY: State University of New York Press. (Accessible intellectual history of German mysticism and theosophy.)

MICHAEL B. WAKOFF

THERMODYNAMICS

Thermodynamics began as the science that elucidated the law-like order present in the behaviour of heat and in its transformations to and from mechanical work. It became of interest to philosophers of science when the nature of heat was discovered to be that of the hidden energy of motion of the microscopic constituents of matter.

Attempts at accounting for the phenomenological laws of heat that make up thermodynamics on the basis of the so-called kinetic theory of heat gave rise to the first fundamental introduction into physics of probabilistic concepts and of probabilistic explanation. This led to so-called statistical mechanics.

Some of the issues of thermodynamics with importance to philosophers are: the meaning of the probabilistic claims made in statistical mechanics; the nature of the probabilistic explanations it proffers for the observed macroscopic phenomena; the structure of the alleged reduction of thermodynamic theory to the theory of the dynamics of the underlying microscopic constituents of matter; the place of cosmological posits in explaining the behaviour of local systems; and the alleged reducibility of our very notion of the asymmetry of time to thermodynamic asymmetries of systems in time.

1 **Historical sketch**
2 **Equilibrium theory**
3 **Non-equilibrium theory**
4 **Asymmetry in time**
5 **The direction of time**

1 Historical sketch

One of the great discoveries of phenomenological thermodynamics was the joint conservation of the totality of overt mechanical energy and internal heat, a law confirmed by Joule and called the first law of thermodynamics. Another was the realization that the ability to transform the internal heat of a system into usable mechanical work required a process in which heat was introduced into the system at a higher temperature and recovered at the end of the process only at a lower temperature where it was less available for conversion into work. These insights began with the investigations of Carnot, and were brought to fruition by Clausius with his introduction of the concept of entropy and the postulation of the second law of thermodynamics.

The idea that heat was merely energy of motion of microscopic constituents of matter was already suggested by Francis Bacon and Bernoulli. These ideas were resurrected by Herepath and Waterston, but ignored by the scientific community. Finally, when once more discovered by Krönig and developed by Clausius, this theory became the dominant theory of heat.

The full-blown kinetic theory receives its greatest impetus from Maxwell's ingenious derivation of the distribution of velocities of the molecules of a system which has obtained equilibrium, and from the derivation of a law governing the path followed by a system from an initial non-equilibrium condition to equilibrium by J.C. MAXWELL and by Boltzmann. Boltzmann also provided a proof that any system not in equilibrium must move to equilibrium and then stay there, providing an underpinning at the kinetic level for the behaviour demanded by the second law.

The kinetic theory of heat was criticized by such positivistically minded philosophers as Duhem and Mach for its introduction of unobservables and its insistence on mechanistic explanations (see DUHEM, P.M.M. §2; MACH, E.). More important were the specific objections made to the theory of approach to equilibrium. The kinetic theory predicts inevitable approach to equilibrium in the future time direction. But the underlying dynamics of the molecules is time-reversal invariant. Furthermore, the dynamical theory predicts the 'almost recurrence' to its initial state by the system, a recurrence that is incompatible with a monotonic approach to stationary equilibrium.

In response to these observations Maxwell and Boltzmann introduced probabilistic considerations into the theory. Boltzmann characterized equilibrium as the 'most probable' state of a system. He also argued that his equation gave the probable evolution of a system, not its inevitable evolution. Even this interpretation of Boltzmann's equation is subject to objections, and Boltzmann finally moved to a time-symmetric interpretation of his theory: almost all the time systems are at equilibrium. Occasionally they fluctuate from it. When a system is in non-equilibrium it is usually closer to equilibrium in both future and past time, as described by Boltzmann's equation.

But why, then, do we live in a non-equilibrium world? Boltzmann suggested that our region of the universe is a local fluctuation from equilibrium, the universe as a whole being at that most probable state. The consistency of the Boltzmann account was elucidated in an important survey piece by Ehrenfest and Ehrenfest (1959).

2 Equilibrium theory

A standard method for calculating the values of quantities at equilibrium was invented by Maxwell and Boltzmann, and generalized by Gibbs. A probability distribution is placed over the set of micro-scopic conditions of the system compatible with its macroscopic constraints (such as its fixed total energy and confinement to a box of specific volume). Macroscopic quantities at equilibrium are then identified with averages, calculated using the probability distribution, of the values of functions of the possible microscopic conditions.

But what justifies choosing a specific probability distribution? And with what physical proportion or frequency in the world is it to be associated?

One proposal (by Jaynes (1983)) takes it that the distribution is justified by standard principles of inductive reasoning and that the probability in question is to receive a subjective interpretation. More common is the proposal, suggested by Maxwell and Boltzmann, that the probabilities in question are representative of proportions of time, in the limit as time goes to infinity, in which a single system has microscopic conditions of a given kind (see PROBABILITY, INTERPRETATION OF §§3, 5).

The attempt to justify this latter claim led Maxwell and Boltzmann to the ergodic hypothesis, the posit that over infinite time a system's microscopic condition would take on every possible value. This posit leads one to the conclusion that the standard probability distribution is the unique such distribution stationary in time, and that its probabilities do indeed correspond to time proportions in the infinite time limit. But the hypothesis is provably false.

The ergodic hypothesis was later replaced by the ergodic theorem, a theorem that holds for specifiable dynamical systems and from which weakened versions of the consequences of the hypothesis can be derived. The central question for the philosopher is the degree to which the results of ergodic theory provide statistical explanations of the equilibrium nature of systems. Two crucial problems are the facts that the results require idealizations concerning systems often not met by realistic systems (see IDEALIZATIONS), and that the results connect probabilities with proportions only in an infinite time limit.

3 Non-equilibrium theory

Equilibrium theory cannot explain approach to equilibrium observed experimentally in the world. For this, one needs a statistical mechanical derivation of the appropriate 'kinetic equation', the equation generalizing that found by Boltzmann for gases of low density.

The standard derivations of the kinetic equations invoke re-randomizing posits, the descendants of Boltzmann's hypothesis with regard to collision numbers and of the hypothesis of molecular chaos of the Ehrenfests. The problem is, however, that once an initial probability distribution is specified for a system, its dynamic evolution is fixed by the underlying deterministic dynamical laws governing the micro-constituents. Therefore the consistency of a re-randomization posit is always in doubt. Much of orthodox non-equilibrium theory consists in getting rid of such dubious posits.

Two important approaches to non-equilibrium theory are those of 'mixing' and of the 'rigorous derivation of the Boltzmann equation'. The former approach generalizes the results of the ergodic theorem to rationalize a model presented by Gibbs. In this approach one tries to show that for appropriately idealized systems, at least in the infinite time limit, any initial probability distribution assigned to a system and associated with its initial non-equilibrium condition will approach the probability distribution associated with equilibrium for the system in a 'coarse-grained' sense. One uses only the dynamical laws and imposes no re-randomizing. The kinetic equation is taken as having its solution curve give the sequence of 'most probable states' of a collection of systems all started in a common non-equilibrium condition, but having different initial micro-states.

The latter approach tries to show that in a different idealized circumstance (the Boltzmann–Grad limit) the kinetic equation solution can be correctly asserted to show, at least for short time intervals, the overwhelmingly probable evolution of members of a collection of systems described by a special initial probability distribution.

Important questions arise as to the nature and role of the idealizations used and the kind of probabilistic explanation of the experimentally determined nature of approach to equilibrium offered by these alternative accounts. Especially important is the observation that they offer accounts of the physical processes that are conceptually at odds with one another, although they are not contradictory to one another since they posit quite different idealizations.

4   Asymmetry in time

A core issue of non-equilibrium theory remains the attempt to find an appropriate physical explanation for the fact that macroscopic systems show asymmetry in time in their thermodynamic features, whereas the underlying laws governing the micro-constituents are taken to be time-symmetric.

A number of unorthodox approaches to the problem exist. In some the underlying dynamical laws have their time symmetry denied. In others the origin of time asymmetry of systems, systems usually taken to be energetically isolated from the world, is accounted for in terms of their ineliminable residual causal interaction with their external environments. A subjectivist approach to the second law exists as well.

In the orthodox accounts a crucial role is played by the initial probability distribution over micro-states assigned to a non-equilibrium system. In the 'rigorous derivation' approach, this initial probability assignment is necessary to derive the asymmetric Boltzmann behaviour. In the 'mixing' approach it is noted that mixing and its generalizations are all time-symmetric notions. But whereas a non-equilibrium system will coarsely approach equilibrium in both the infinite future and the infinite past, it is possible to specify an initial probability distribution that will behave asymmetrically in time for finite time intervals. Another approach, due to Prigogine (1980), focuses on singular initial probability distributions to break the time symmetry.

In order to account for the asymmetry in time of the behaviour of individual systems, resort is often made to the behaviour in time of the cosmos as a whole. In the new cosmological models one thinks of the overall universe not as in equilibrium, as Boltzmann speculated it was, but as in expansion from an initial Big Bang singularity and showing entropic increase.

Why does the entropy of the universe increase in time? Some accounts (Gold) tie the entropy increase to the expansion of the universe. The more common view is, however, that expansion by itself will not explain the entropic asymmetry of the cosmos. Rather one must assume an initial low-entropy state for the universe, not paralleled by a low-entropy final state. One important version of this approach (Penrose) takes the initial low entropy to be found in the 'smooth' initial spacetime structure (see COSMOLOGY §3). The matter of the world starts thermalized and then clumps into hot stars living in cold space, the decrease in entropy of the matter being paid for by the increased 'clumpiness' of spacetime, a change that corresponds to an increase of entropy overall.

Many profound philosophical questions arise when one speculates about what kind of an answer could be given to such questions as: 'why is the initial entropy of the universe so surprisingly low?' Here philosophical discussion is reminiscent of older arguments about the origin of order in the universe and teleological arguments for the existence of a deity.

The purpose of invoking the entropic asymmetry of the cosmos as a whole was to give a physical account of the ground of the second law of thermodynamics. But cosmic entropy increase can perform this task only if it can be shown that it can account for the parallel increase in entropy in time of the individual systems with which the second law deals. Reichenbach calls these individual systems, energetically isolated from the overall cosmos only for finite time intervals, 'branch systems' (Reichenbach 1956).

One could simply posit that branch systems show an entropy asymmetry in time parallel to one another and parallel in time to the entropic asymmetry of the cosmic system. Several proposals exist to do away with this posit, but all of them, including Reichenbach's own (positing that the collection of branch systems constitutes what he called a 'lattice of mixture'), ultimately introduce parallelism of the direction of entropy increase for the branch systems with each other and with the main system as a posit. The physical origin of the temporal asymmetry of systems remains a very controversial subject.

5   The direction of time

Suppose we accept it as a fact that branch systems do indeed show parallel increase of entropy in the same direction of time. The question remains, 'Why do systems have their entropy increase towards the future and not towards the past?' It was Boltzmann who first suggested the answer that our very conception of the past–future distinction in time is one that is itself founded upon the asymmetry in time of the entropy of systems. What counts as the future direction of time, he claimed, is just the direction of time in which systems have their entropy increasing.

In order to evaluate this claim one needs to know what it really amounts to. It is sometimes suggested that the claim amounts to the assertion that we determine which direction of time is the future by examining the entropic states of systems. Thus we can tell if a film has been put in a projector in the correct direction only by consulting the entropic features of the states it pictures. But such an understanding of Boltzmann's claim founders on the fact that we have direct, non-inferential knowledge for many pairs of states as to which member of the pair is later than the other.

A more plausible reading of the Boltzmann claim takes it that entropic facts ground our intuitive means for determining time order in much the same way that facts about gravity ground our distinction between the directions in space we take as upward and downward. From this point of view the entropic asymmetry of the world offers a full explanatory account of all the other general asymmetries of the world we intuitively take to hold. These intuitive asymmetries include our differential epistemic access to past and future (we remember the past and have records of it, but not the future); the direction of causation from past to future; our differential concern with past and future; and the alleged 'fixity' of the past but openness of the future. Although interesting arguments have been given to

back up this claim, it remains an open one   (see CAUSATION; TIME).

References and Further Reading

Brush, S. (1983) *Statistical Physics and the Atomic Theory of Matter*, Princeton, NJ: Princeton University Press. (Outline of foundational issues.)

Davies, P. (1974) *The Physics of Time Asymmetry*, Berkeley, CA: University of California Press. (Outline of physical aspects of asymmetry in time.)

Earman, J. (1974) 'An Attempt to Add a Little Direction to "The Problem of the Direction of Time"' *Philosophy of Science* 41 (1): 15–47. (Philosophical discussion of entropy asymmetry and the direction of time.)

* Ehrenfest P. and Ehrenfest, T. (1959) *The Conceptual Foundations of the Statistical Approach in Mechanics*, Ithaca, NY: Cornell University Press. (Important foundational review, originally published in 1910.)

Horwich, P. (1987) *Asymmetries in Time*, Cambridge, MA: MIT Press. (Philosophical discussion of asymmetries in time and the direction of time problem.)

Jancel, R. (1969) *Foundations of Classical and Quantum Statistical Mechanics*, Oxford: Pergamon Press. (Physics of statistical mechanics from a foundational point of view.)

* Jaynes, E. (1983) *Papers on Probability, Statistics and Statistical Physics*, Dordrecht: Reidel. (Subjectivist approach to statistical mechanics.)

* Prigogine, I. (1980) *From Being to Becoming*, San Francisco: W.H. Freeman. (Nontechnical discussion of foundational issues.)

* Reichenbach, H. (1956) *The Direction of Time*, Berkeley, CA: University of California Press. (Foundations of statistical physics with emphasis on the direction of time problem.)

Sklar, L. (1992) *Philosophy of Physics*, Boulder, CO: Westview. (Elementary survey of the issues in chapter 3.)

—— (1993) *Physics and Chance*, Cambridge: Cambridge University Press. (Comprehensive survey of the physical and philosophical issues.)

Tolman, R. (1938) *The Principles of Statistical Mechanics*, Oxford: Oxford University Press. (Clear foundational treatment of statistical mechanics at the time of its publication.)

Zeh, H.-D. (1989) *The Direction of Time*, Berlin: Springer. (Survey of time asymmetries in physics.)

LAWRENCE SKLAR

THIELICKE, HELMUT
(1908–86)

Helmut Thielicke presented a systematic Christian theology with particular reference to concrete issues and situations within the world. He held that statements about God are inevitably conditioned by the fact that God reveals himself to and through humanity; they thus always have an anthropological aspect. Similarly, while theology arises from transcendent revelation, it necessarily belongs to a particular historical context. Thielicke maintained that the notion of a 'perennial theology' is therefore mistaken. This raises the question as to whether it is a perennial truth that there is no perennial theology, and, if so, how Thielicke could, on his grounds, know this.

Born in 1908, Helmut Thielicke was a Lutheran theologian whose preaching was silenced by the Nazis in 1940. He was a professor at Heidelberg, Tübingen and, from 1954, Hamburg. He died in 1986.

Thielicke expounded a Lutheran (but also typically Christian) doctrine of justification, the doctrine of forgiveness of sins through the death and resurrection of Christ. He aimed to decline 'the doctrine of justification through all the case forms in which it appears within the grammar of our existence' ([1959] 1969: xiv). As the Latin professor teaches by putting nouns through their declensions, Thielicke presented Christian theology by weaving a Christian perspective on politics, society, economics, sexuality, law and art. He used concrete issues (for example, truthfulness at the sick bed) as models: the doctrines and principles of Christian ethics are explained in terms of specific situations and described in detail. He wrote:

> Since God discloses himself in man and seeks to be his God, any statement about God is also a statement about his relation to man. To that degree man is there in every theological utterance and thus gives it an anthropological reference... [this] book is about the relation between God and man and not about a purely transcendent God taken theistically in and for himself. I understand primarily by this relation an ontic rather than a noetic relation. Man 'is' his relation to God. He is the one created by him, in flight from him, visited by him and justified.
>
> ([1968] 1974: 15)

That each human person is created and constantly sustained by God, and that each person's good lies in trust and obedience to God, structures Thielicke's ethic.

Thielicke saw it as the nature of theology to respond to challenges. In this lies its potential for growth and continued relevance. He sought a world-view that was uncompromisingly Christian, preachable in and to the Church, and plainly of relevance to moral problems. He interacted with the best of contemporary thought without sacrificing the distinctiveness of the Christian gospel.

In *Der evangelische Glaube* (*The Evangelical Faith*), he wrote that:

> [God's] Word is historical not merely in the sense of being grounded in history [that is, in part concerning the religious significance of historical events in Israel's history and the life of Jesus] but also as it is addressed to historical situation. Both the authors and the recipients of verbal messages are subject to the process of history. The message, then, cannot be detached at either point. If an effort is made in this direction, there arises the false notion of perennial theology characterized by an abstract conceptual system. Scholasticism and seventeenth century orthodoxy are classical examples.
>
> ([1968] 1974: 23)

Theology necessarily arises from a transcendent revelation conditioned by the cultural context of, and the challenges peculiar to, a particular time. It exists in an inescapable tension, requiring faithfulness to its status as revelation and sensitivity to the historically conditioned nature of its proclamations. In effect, Thielicke wanted to retain what he saw as the best in his evangelical colleagues and his neo-orthodox predecessors (such as Karl Barth and Emil Brunner).

There remains this question: can a theology that allows only the sorts of statements about God that Thielicke permitted have any content, let alone respond to contemporary challenges? If there are no statements concerning God save those that describe God's relations to humans, then those relational statements themselves do not inform us about God's nature. But then it is hard to see what the relational statements themselves mean. If 'God loves us' does not entail 'God is by nature loving', or anything else about God's nature, it is unclear just what 'loves' means.

In addition, Thielicke's statement that theology must rest on a transcendent revelation only expressible in the terms of some particular culture is itself expressed in the terms of Thielicke's culture. Yet it is supposed to be categorically and universally true, and hence it is supposed to escape being conditioned by Thielicke's culture. But if that statement can somehow, or in some degree, escape such conditioning, is it impossible that theological claims should somehow, or in some degree, do so as well?

List of works

Thielicke, H. (1958, 1959, 1964) *Theologische Ethik*, Tübingen: Mohr (Paul Siebeck), 3 vols; ed. W.H. Lazareth, *Theological Ethics*, Philadelphia, PA: Fortress Press, vols 1–2, 1966, 1969, and Grand Rapids, MI: Baker Book House, vol. 3, 1975. (The English translation is an abridgement of the German work.)

—— (1964) *Mensch Sein – Mensch Werden*, Munich: R. Piper Verlag; *Being Human... Becoming Human*, Garden City, NY: Doubleday, 1976. (Presents Thielicke's anthropology in the context of dialogue with competing perspectives.)

—— (1968, 1973, 1978) *Der evangelische Glaube*, Tübingen: Mohr (Paul Siebeck), 3 vols; trans. and ed. G.W. Bromiley, *The Evangelical Faith*, Grand Rapids, MI: Eerdmans, vols 1–2, 1974, 1977, and Edinburgh: T. & T. Clark, vol. 3, 1982. (Relates Christian theology to modern forms of thought.)

—— (1988) *Glauben und Denken in der Neuzeit*, Tübingen: Mohr (Paul Siebeck); trans. G.W. Bromiley, *Modern Faith and Thought*, Grand Rapids, MI: Eerdmans, 1990. (Thielicke surveys and assesses contemporary theological movements.)

References and further reading

McGrath, A.E. (1994) *Christian Theology: An Introduction*, Oxford: Blackwell. (Accessible introduction to many of the issues that concerned Thielicke.)

Nygren, A. (1972) *Meaning and Method: Prolegomena to a Scientific Philosophy of Religion and a Scientific Theology*, trans. P.S. Watson, London: Epworth Press. (Authorized translation of an unpublished Swedish manuscript that presents an alternative approach to Thielicke's.)

KEITH E. YANDELL

THIERRY OF CHARTRES
(*fl. c.*1130–50)

Thierry of Chartres, who taught at Paris and Chartres in the mid-twelfth century, was a polymath and a Platonist. The Heptateuchon, *a large and ambitious collection of texts for teaching the liberal arts, testifies to the range of his interests from grammar, logic and rhetoric to mathematics and astronomy; they also stretched to theology. To Thierry is attributed an explanation of the account of creation in Genesis, after God's initial action, in physical terms. He also used arithmetical analogies to illustrate the Trinity and, drawing on a variety of Platonic and Neoplatonic sources, analysed the relationship between God and his creation.*

Thierry of Chartres was born in Brittany (he usually called himself Theodoricus Brito, Thierry the Breton). In the 1140s he was chancellor of Chartres Cathedral, before he retired in the 1150s to a monastery. He taught, almost certainly in both Paris and Chartres, from the 1130s or earlier. Among his pupils were JOHN OF SALISBURY, the grammarian Peter Helias and the scientist and translator Hermann of Carinthia, who described him as 'the soul of Plato restored to mankind from heaven'. Unfortunately, the records of his wide range of teaching are scant. His commentaries (*c.*1130–9) on the two main textbooks of rhetoric, Cicero's *On Invention* and the pseudo-Ciceronian *Rhetorica ad Herennium* survive. His logical writings have been lost, although Thierry is known to have been one of the earliest writers to teach Aristotle's *On Sophistical Refutations* (before 1132) and perhaps also the *Prior Analytics*. He also taught grammar, and the *Heptateuchon* (which includes extracts from Euclid and al-Khwarizmi's astronomical tables) shows his lively interest in the various branches of mathematics. Thierry's modern reputation as a philosopher depends mainly, however, on a short treatise *De sex dierum operibus* (On the Work of the Six Days) and on various commentaries and glosses to Boethius' theological treatises (*Opuscula sacra*). Yet these too pose considerable problems of integrity and authorship.

It was Thierry's pupil CLAREMBALD OF ARRAS who gave *De sex dierum operibus* its title and attributed it to Thierry. He added to it a further collection of remarks on Genesis, taken from Thierry's lectures. Sir Richard Southern's suggestion (Southern 1970) that the treatise itself (which circulated separately in other manuscripts) was also reworked by Clarembald is implausible; but the work is certainly unfinished in all surviving copies. As it stands, it divides into two parts. The first offers what is called a 'natural and literal' exposition of the first five verses of Genesis. Here Thierry is following a tradition going back to AUGUSTINE and the Greek Fathers of using scientific material to gloss and expand the biblical account of creation. However, he is unusually rigorous in restricting himself to naturalistic explanation, drawing on Plato's *Timaeus* and Calcidius' commentary and using a number of ideas he may have taken from WILLIAM OF CONCHES. The second section is a long (and unfinished) digression on the nature of God and his triunity. Thierry promises to use four methods of mathematical reasoning to lead us to knowledge of the creator, arithmetical, musical, geometrical and astronomical; but only the arithmetical 'proofs' are preserved. God, who is the 'form of being' for individual things, is unity. The unities from which numbers are made are participations in this divine unity. The Son is related to the Father as 'equality' to unity and, when the treatise breaks off, Thierry is about to discuss the Holy Spirit as the link (*connexio*) between unity and equality.

To Clarembald also is owed the identification of Thierry's most important philosophical work. From his remarks, it is clear that Clarembald based his own commentary on Boethius' *De trinitate* (On the Trinity) mainly on Thierry; and comparison shows that a commentary known as *Librum hunc* (written late 1140s; incipit 'Inchoantibus librum hunc', edited as the *Commentum*) is, or closely resembles, Clarembald's source. *Librum hunc*, therefore, is certainly based on Thierry's teaching, but exactly how accurately remains an open question. Two other commentaries on the *De trinitate* related to *Librum hunc* have been argued by his editor to be later works of Thierry: the *Lectiones* (Lectures: incipit 'Intentio auctoris') and the *Glosa* (Gloss: incipit 'Aggreditur propositum'). But do the doctrines they contain, often at variance with those of *Librum hunc*, all go back to the same man?

Besides developing a numerological account of the Trinity similar to that in Thierry's treatise on the creation, *Librum hunc* shows a concern to develop Boethius' somewhat disparate remarks on matter and form into a theory about God's relation to his creation. God is said to be the only true form. By contact with matter this form is determined into forms of different kinds (humanity, stone-ness and so on). These forms cannot exist apart from the individuals they inform. Were there to be, for instance, no human beings, the form humanity would lose its specific identity and return to the simplicity of the one true form, God. Both the *Lectiones* and the *Glosa* share this view of God as the single true form, but they also admit a multiplicity of pure forms as ideas in the mind of God; and the *Glosa* elaborates this plan in terms of act and potentiality. Peter Dronke has made a bold attempt to find a unity of thought in these various works by or connected with Thierry. He argues (looking to the *Lectiones* and the *Glosa*) that Thierry distinguished four modes of envisaging the universe: as 'absolute necessity' or the 'form of forms'; 'necessity of make-up' (linked to Ideas, natural law and the World Soul); absolute possibility (primordial matter); and determinate possibility (contingent reality). By using this diversity of perspectives, Thierry is able to reconcile 'an extreme Platonism – in which forms and names exist

indissolubly in the mind of God, and in which "names essentiate things" – with a far reaching naturalism' (Dronke 1988: 384).

See also: CHARTRES, SCHOOL OF; CLAREMBALD OF ARRAS

List of works

Thierry of Chartres (1130–39) Commentary on Cicero's *On Invention*, ed. K.M. Fredborg, *The Latin Rhetorical Commentaries by Thierry of Chartres*, Studies and Texts 84, Toronto, Ont.: Pontifical Institute of Mediaeval Studies, 1988. (Thierry's Ciceronian commentary.)

—— (1130–39) Commentary on *Rhetorica ad Herennium*, ed. K.M. Fredborg, *The Latin Rhetorical Commentaries by Thierry of Chartres*, Studies and Texts 84, Toronto, Ont.: Pontifical Institute of Mediaeval Studies, 1988. (Shows Thierry's work as a teacher of rhetoric.)

—— (*c.*1150) Heptateuchon. (The original manuscripts of this work from the Chartres library have been destroyed, but a microfilm exists.)

—— (*c.*1150) *De sex dierum operibus* (On the Work of Six Days), ed. N.M. Häring, *Commentaries on Boethius by Thierry of Chartres and his Sschool*, Studies and Texts 20, Toronto, Ont.: Pontifical Institute of Mediaeval Studies, 1971, 557–75. (Naturalistic account of the stages of creation.)

—— (*c.*1150) *Librum hunc (Commentum)*, ed. N.M. Häring, *Commentaries on Boethius by Thierry of Chartres and his School*, Studies and Texts 20, Toronto, Ont.: Pontifical Institute of Mediaeval Studies, 1971, 57–121. (Based on Thierry's teaching, but not certainly his work.)

—— (*c.*1150) *Lectiones* (Lectures), ed. N.M. Häring, *Commentaries on Boethius by Thierry of Chartres and his School*, Studies and Texts 20, Toronto, Ont.: Pontifical Institute of Mediaeval Studies, 1971, 125–229. (Based on Thierry's teaching, but not certainly his work.)

—— (*c.*1150) *Glosa* (Gloss), ed. N.M. Häring, *Commentaries on Boethius by Thierry of Chartres and his School*, Studies and Texts 20, Toronto, Ont.: Pontifical Institute of Mediaeval Studies, 1971, 259–300. (Based on Thierry's teaching, but not certainly his work.)

References and further reading

* Dronke, P. (1988) 'Thierry of Chartres', in P. Dronke (ed.) *A History of Twelfth-Century Western Philosophy*, Cambridge: Cambridge University Press,

358–85. (A bold reconstruction of Thierry's underlying ideas.)

Gersh, S. (1982) 'Platonism – Neoplatonism – Aristotelianism: a Twelfth-Century Metaphysical System and its Sources', in R.L. Benson and G. Constable (eds) *Renaissance and Renewal in the Twelfth Century*, Oxford: Clarendon Press, 512–34. (The *Librum hunc* and its Neoplatonic sources.)

Häring, N.M. (1965) *Life and Works of Clarembald of Arras*, Studies and Texts 10, Toronto: Pontifical Institute of Mediaeval Studies. (Arguments for attributing *Librum hunc* and related commentaries to Thierry.)

Jeauneau, E. (1973) *Lectio philosophorum*, Amsterdam: Hakkert. (Includes essays on the *Heptateuchon* and on Thierry's mathematical discussions of the Trinity.)

* Southern, R.W. (1970) 'Humanism and the school of Chartres', *Medieval Humanism and Other Studies*, Oxford: Blackwell, 61–85. (The canon of Thierry's works and its relation to twelfth-century Platonism.)

JOHN MARENBON

THOMAS À KEMPIS (1379/80–1471)

Thomas Hemerken was born in Kempen, Germany. He spent his life in foundations of the Modern Devotion (Devotio Moderna), a spiritual movement of the late fourteenth and fifteenth centuries that originated in the Low Countries and spread throughout northern Europe. In 1406 he entered the monastery of Mount Saint Agnes in Windesheim (St Agnietenberg, the Netherlands), the origin and centre of a reformed congregation of Augustinian Canons Regular, which disseminated the Modern Devotion in the Low Countries and Germany. Thomas was ordained a priest in 1413, and was the novice master in the monastery for many years. He is generally recognized as the author of De imitatione Christi *(The Imitation of Christ), perhaps the most popular work on the spiritual life ever written.*

Thomas wrote a number of spiritual and ascetic treatises, meditations on the life of Christ, lives of the leading figures of the Modern Devotion and a chronicle of his monastery. Most of these writings can be related to his duties as novice master. He is most famous as the author of *De imitatione Christi* (The Imitation of Christ). His authorship of this work, however, has always been disputed. His claim rests mainly on the tradition of his religious order. *De imitatione* comprises four treatises, composed separately. Some early copies (1420s) of the treatises attribute them to Thomas, but most are anonymous. Thomas copied the treatises more than once; one copy made by him, containing the four treatises and completed in 1441, bears corrections indicating that he worked on the manuscript for many years. The manuscript suggests that if Thomas was not the original composer of all the texts, he was their compiler and editor. However, none of the evidence is conclusive. Other evidence points to a Carthusian monk as the author, possibly as early as the end of the fourteenth century; Carthusians were closely associated with early foundations of the Modern Devotion, and through them the core texts of *De imitatione* may have circulated among the Devout (that is, the followers of the Modern Devotion).

The style of *De imitatione* complicates attribution. The Devout were accustomed to collect texts of spiritual authorities, ordering them under general topics for their meditation and personal use. The books of *De imitatione* are related to such collections, weaving together 'sentences', or moral and psychological maxims, into a continuous discourse. The 'sentences' of *De imitatione* are drawn largely from the Scriptures, but also from anonymous teachers and a few named authorities. Doubtless the author crafted his own 'sentences' as well. Such a text readily became the common property of those in the monastic life; perhaps this is why *De imitatione* was later ascribed to so many authors.

Similarly, the treatises of *De imitatione* express the common themes of the Modern Devotion. They develop the dialectic between the world and the kingdom of God, which is within. They contrast the vanity of the world, the emptiness of sensible goods, false happiness, self-love and the pride of the intellect with the inner life of the kingdom of God, which requires purification of the senses and mind, abandonment to God, obedience, patience, humility and the practice of divine charity, which directs every act to God. These virtues yield interior peace (the ordering and calming of desires and passions), interior freedom (liberation from concupiscence and regard for human esteem), and simplicity of spirit. Christ is the exemplar of the soul's dispositions; only by participation in, and responsiveness to, his divine grace can the disorder of sinful human nature be repaired and the kingdom of God within be attained. *De imitatione* seeks a practical reform of Christian life, in principle accessible to all. It avoids complex questions concerning mystical contemplation.

Although in its time the devotion of *De imitatione* was called 'new', it in fact echoes an older Christian wisdom, the chief sources of which are AUGUSTINE, Gregory the Great, John Cassian and BERNARD OF CLAIRVAUX (see PATRISTIC PHILOSOPHY). Devout authors were sceptical of theological speculation which, they thought, induced vanity and was a diversion from the evangelical life. Some historians nevertheless see the Modern Devotion as a coefficient of the religious attitude underlying the scholastic *via moderna*. This interpretation is not wholly convincing. The 'philosophic' roots of *De imitatione Christi* lie elsewhere, as its 'sententious' and 'gathering' style suggests. The letters of Seneca, which treat self-knowledge, recollection of the memory, the ordering of the passions, and the necessity of solitude, were favourite readings among the Devout and the earlier monastic writers who inspired their spiritual teaching. The author of *De imitatione* adapts Stoic psychological teaching to the narrative of Christ's life and death and to the Christian doctrines of sin, grace and redemption (see STOICISM).

See also: GRACE; MYSTICISM, HISTORY OF

List of works

Thomas à Kempis (1379/80–1471) *Opera omnia* (Complete Works), ed. M.J. Pohl, *Thomae Hemerken a Kempis Opera omnia*, 7 vols, Freiburg: Herder, 1902–22. (Reprinted Hildesheim, 1985. This is the standard critical edition of Thomas' works; *De imitatione Christi* is in vol. 2, 3–263.)
—— (1379/80–1471) *De imitatione Christi* (The Imitation of Christ), ed. L.M.J. Delaisse, *Le manuscrit autographe de Thomas à Kempis et 'L'Imitation de Jésus-Christ': Examen archéologique et édition diplomatique de Bruxellensis 5855–61*, Les Publications de Scriptorium 2, Paris: Erasme, 1956; ed. T. Lupi, *De imitatione Christi libri quatuor*, Vatican City: Libreria Editrice Vaticana, 1982. (Delaisse includes a detailed study of Thomas' 1441 copy of the treatises of *De imitatione*, with a diplomatic edition of the manuscript's Latin text; Lupi is an edition of the Latin text by one of the leading scholars of its manuscript transmission, who disputes the authorship of Thomas à Kempis. There are a number of English translations, including those of W.C. Creasy, Macon, GA: Mercer University Press, 1989 (a new reading of the 1441 Latin autograph manuscript); E. Daplyn, London: Marshall, Morgan & Scott, 1979 (from the full text of the autograph manuscript of 1441); G.F. Maine, London: Collins, 1957; and L. Sherley-Price, Hammondsworth: Penguin, 1952.)

References and further reading

Ampe, A. (1973) *L'Imitation de Jésus-Christ et son auteur: Reflexions critiques* (The Imitation of Jesus Christ and its Author: Critical Reflections), Rome: Edizioni di storia e letteratura. (A detailed study of the question of authorship, which concludes that none of the previous arguments for one author or another is decisive.)
Ampe, A. and Spaapen, B. (1971) 'Imitation de Jésus-Christ: I. Le livre et auteur. II. Doctrine' (The Imitation of Jesus Christ: I. The Book and its Author. II. Doctrine), *Dictionnaire de spiritualité ascétique et mystique, histoire et doctrine*, Paris: Beauchesne, vol. 7, 2338–68. (Ampe here outlines the evidence concerning the authorship of *De imitatione*, and Spaapen studies the work's doctrine. The article contains an ample bibliography.)
Colish, M.L. (1985) *The Stoic Tradition from Antiquity to the Early Middle Ages*, Studies in the History of Christian Thought 34–5, Leiden: Brill, 2 vols. (The second volume contains surveys of the Stoic influences on Latin fathers and early monastic writers, including the major sources of the Modern Devotion: Jerome, Augustine, Cassian and Gregory the Great.)
Geurts, A.J. *et al.* (eds) (1985) *Moderne Devotie Figuren en Facetten: Tentoonstelling ter herdenking van het sterfjaar van Geert Grote 1384–1984, Catalogus* (Figures and Facets of the Modern Devotion: An Exhibition on the Anniversary of the Death of Geert Grote, 1384–1984), Nijmegen: Katholieke Universiteit. (This exhibition catalogue is the best scholarly work on the different genres of literature produced by the Devout. For 'collection books' and *De imitatione*, see pp 152–67, 204–11.)
Post, R.R. (1968) *The Modern Devotion: Confrontation with Reformation and Humanism*, Leiden: Brill. (The most authoritative historical study of the movement, disputing the notion that it was connected with 'humanism' and was a 'precursor' of the Protestant Reformation.)
Van Dijk, R.T.M. (1990) 'Thomas Hemerken à Kempis', *Dictionnaire de spiritualité ascétique et mystique, histoire et doctrine*, Paris: Beauchesne, vol. 15, 817–26. (An introduction to the life, works and doctrine of Thomas à Kempis; the bibliography updates the article of Ampe and Spaapen.)
Van Engen, J. (1988) *Devotio Moderna: Basic Writings*, New York: Paulist Press. (Translations of typical writings by the Devout, with an excellent

introduction to the spirituality of the movement. The notes contain extensive bibliography.)

KENT EMERY, JR

THOMAS, CHRISTIAN
see THOMASIUS, CHRISTIAN

THOMAS OF YORK
(*fl. c.*1255)

A philosopher of remarkably wide reading in the works of Western and non-Western thinkers, Thomas attempted to assemble, and to some extent to synthesize, the views he had encountered. Whatever the eventual judgement on Thomas's thought, the Sapientiale *(Wisdom), a lengthy metaphysical work, certainly reflects the intellectual ferment brought about in the thirteenth century by the influx of new works by Aristotle and by Jewish and Islamic philosophers and commentators.*

A member of the Franciscan order from at least 1245, Thomas of York incepted as master of theology at Oxford in 1253. He was lecturer to the Oxford Franciscans until 1256, and to the Cambridge convent in 1256–7. He wrote a work entitled the *Manus quae contra omnipotentem* (The Hand That is Raised Against the Omnipotent), a polemic work defending voluntary poverty and mendicancy, but his most important philosophical work is the *Sapientiale* (Wisdom).

The *Sapientiale* is a summa – or it might be more properly called a compendium – of arguments addressing what Thomas labels as 'general' and 'special' metaphysics. The first five books discuss God, creation, being and causation, substance and accident, and attributes of being such as truth and falsity, while the remaining section on special metaphysics discusses the soul. The second section is incomplete: it breaks off unfinished, omitting projected discussions of the inanimate world and of plants and animals. Prominent throughout is Thomas' concern to include extensive and accurate citations from a very wide range of sources (including writers of antiquity, Jewish and Islamic philosophers and commentators, patristic writers and Thomas's predecessors at Oxford and Paris), and where possible to adjudicate between or reconcile opposed views. In addition to the difficulty of fixing Thomas' views

amid the remarkable breadth and extent of his citations – unmatched in any later Franciscan philosophical work – there is the problem that an edition of the *Sapientiale* is not yet available.

In his general metaphysics, Thomas develops an elaborate explanation of the natures of matter and form. While the complexity of his scheme may in part be attributed to his efforts to accommodate both Aristotelian and Neoplatonic systems, its intrinsic interest has yet to be evaluated. Thomas equates form and matter with act and potency, and identifies these as the two principles of created being. Not willing to admit a third principle, he classes privation as an attribute of matter. However, since not all matter is subject to privation, he must distinguish three varieties of matter: 1) matter subject to privation, and hence to generation and corruption; 2) matter having dimension and location, but not subject to privation (such as heavenly bodies); and 3) 'spiritual matter', a potentiality capable of taking on form but neither subject to privation nor having any particular location or dimension. Thomas also distinguishes a 'potential' variety of form. He attempts to reconcile those who insist that common forms or natures (such as 'man' or 'white') exist independently, separate from their realization in matter and outside the minds of those who understand them, with their opponents who deny any such separate existence to forms. He does so by proposing that common forms do exist outside the mind, for otherwise demonstrative knowledge would be impossible, but that their external existence is merely potential, awaiting realization in matter.

Thomas' special metaphysics focuses on the human soul but does not, as might be expected, discuss philosophical psychology. Instead, it is largely devoted to the metaphysics of the rational soul, arguing that the soul is not a form but rather is compounded from form and spiritual matter and related to the body as a pilot to a ship. (Thomas does not offer any solution to the potential difficulty that creatures with souls would then seem to have more than one substantial form.) Considerable attention has nonetheless been devoted to Thomas's philosophy of mind. However, granted that Thomas affirms earlier in the *Sapientiale* that some human knowledge derives 'from something higher and not from sense', and that he notes the incompleteness of Aristotle's account of the soul – the only one, he says, to assert that all knowledge stems from the senses – Thomas nonetheless devotes the bulk of his attention to explaining how the intellect apprehends though a process of abstraction from the data of sensory perception. His acceptance that some human knowledge derives from divine illumination is standard rather than controversial: AQUINAS, whom it has been suggested he opposed on this issue, also granted it a restricted role.

See also: ARISTOTELIANISM, MEDIEVAL ; MATTER

List of works

Thomas of York (*c.*1256) *Manus quae contra omnipotentem* (The Hand That is Raised Against the Omnipotent), ed. M. Bierbaum, *Franziskanische Studien* Beiheft 2, 37–168. (A polemic work defending voluntary poverty and mendicancy.)
—— (*c.*1250–60) *Sapientiale* (Wisdom). (No complete edition of this work is available. Portions edited in four University of Toronto dissertations are not yet available on microfilm. Book II, chapters 4, 5 and 6 appear in E. Longpré, 'Thomas d'York et Matthieu d'Aquasparta', *Archives d'histoire doctrinale et littéraire du Moyen Age* 1, 1926: 268–308.)

References and further reading

Emden, A.B. (1957–9) *A Biographical Register of the University of Oxford to a. d. 1500*, 3 vols, Oxford: Clarendon Press. (Gives all known details of the lives and works of Oxford scholars to 1500.)
Gilson, E. (1955) *History of Christian Philosophy in the Middle Ages*, London: Sheed & Ward, 666 n.51. (A summary of Treserra 1929, in English.)
Grabmann, M. (1913) 'Die Metaphysik des Thomas von York' (The Metaphysics of Thomas of York), Beiträge zur Geschichte der Philosophie (und Theologie) des Mittelalters Suppbd. I, Münster: Aschendorff, 181–93. (Includes an overview briefly summarizing the contents of each book of the *Sapientiale.*)
Longpré, E. (1926) 'F. Thomas d'York, O.F.M.', *Archivum Franciscanum Historium* 19: 875–930. (Includes a transcription of the table of contents to the *Sapientiale.*)
Reilly, J.P., Jr (1953) 'Thomas of York on the Efficacy of Secondary Causes', *Mediaeval Studies* 15: 225–32. (Explains Thomas' theory of secondary causation and contrasts it with his theory of knowledge. The reader should note that Thomas discusses secondary causation in animal and human reproduction rather than in activity more generally.)
Sharp, D.E. (1930) *Franciscan Philosophy at Oxford in the Thirteenth Century*, London: Oxford University Press, 49–112. (The only detailed treatment of the whole of the *Sapientiale* available in English. Unfortunately the discussion is organized under rather idiosyncratic categories applied in turn to a series of philosophers, but some parts are still useful. A full list of works cited by Thomas appears on pages 53–5.)
Treserra, F. (1929) 'De Doctrinis Metaphysicis Fratris Thomae de Eboraco OFM' (The Metaphysical Teachings of Thomas of York OFM), *Analecta Sacra Tarraconensis* 5: 33–102. (An exposition of Book III of the *Sapientiale.*)

FIONA SOMERSET

THOMASIUS (THOMAS), CHRISTIAN (1655–1728)

Christian Thomasius' stature as the 'founder' of the German Enlightenment has been the source of much debate. His many essays dealing with issues in moral enlightenment and law reform (bigamy, witchcraft, torture, heresy, adultery, the use of the vernacular and so on) certainly single him out from other seventeenth-century writers. He was the public philosopher par excellence, a suitable match for August Hermann Francke, the great public theologian. Both men spent most of their career in Halle (in Brandenburg), and it was there that Francke institutionalized pietism, just as Thomasius propagated secular natural law theory. Despite many tensions, pietism and modern natural law thereby fused into a social duty-ethics that was of the greatest importance in shaping the modern Prussian state. The basis for natural law was God's will and it was the attempt to follow this law that made humanity a moral species. Since humankind could not have any certain knowledge of the content of God's law, the natural powers of the mind would have to be relied upon, and Thomasius' thought was an investigation into the nature and social effect of these powers. His best-known result was a series of linked divisions between law and morality, between public and private spheres, between external and internal obligation, and between action and intention.

1 Life
2 Theoretical philosophy
3 Practical philosophy
4 Conclusion

1 Life

Christian Thomasius was born in Leipzig, Saxony, the son of the jurist and philosopher Jacob Thomasius. He was educated at the University of Leipzig by Valentin Alberti, one of the most prominent critics of PUFENDORF, and by his own father who some years previously had taught Leibniz. Thomasius took his law degree at the University of Frankfurt an der Oder in 1679. He spent his early career in Leipzig as an advocate, private lecturer and founder of a controversial periodical, *Monatsgespräche* (Monthly conversations), the first intellectual monthly written in German. He made it his cause to criticize Aristotelianism, orthodox Lutheranism and Roman jurisprudence, and his public doubts about the divine right of kingship eventually made it prudent for him to leave Saxony in 1690. His alternative programme of German history, natural law and German jurisprudence was, however, welcome in neighbouring Brandenburg, where Thomasius was instrumental in the foundation of the University of Halle in 1694. In 1710 he became Direktor (President) for life of this institution which had a formative influence on German Enlightenment universities. By the time of his death here in 1728, Thomasius had established himself as a towering cultural figure, with a public philosophy promoting polite sociability.

2 Theoretical philosophy

From a philosophical point of view, Thomasius' huge *oeuvre* divides into three periods. In the 1680s he worked to complete Pufendorf's project of separating natural law from theology, culminating in 1688 with *Institutiones jurisprudentiæ divinæ* (Institutions of divine jurisprudence). This was accompanied by *An Introduction to Court Philosophy* – that is to say, a theory of the centralist political culture that was necessary to maintain a state based upon the law of reason alone. Thomasius' reaction against orthodoxy broadened to a comprehensive philosophical outlook, resulting in works on reason and on moral theory in the 1690s. Strongly influenced by pietism, Thomasius pursued his doubts about the sufficiency of reason in the conduct of life, leading him to a spiritualist metaphysics in the tradition of fashionable mysticism. This prepared the way for a change after 1700 to a deterministic theory of the will and a scheme of moral, legal and political regulation based on governance of the passions.

Thomasius owed much to the long tradition of eclecticism in philosophy, but he can hardly be called an eclectic in a strict sense. His debt to eclecticism was largely methodological, not a substantive philosophical doctrine. And while he argued against the dominance of Aristotelianism and Cartesianism and other schools, he did not, in the manner of eclecticism, see his philosophy as inherently an argument for the freedom of the individual spirit from the tyranny of all 'sects'.

His epistemology was a basic empiricism inspired by Aristotle and, subsequently, reinforced by his reading of Locke's *Essay* (see EMPIRICISM). But although he maintained that all knowledge has a basis in experience, Thomasius retained the notion of ideas of reason that are merely *awoken* through experience. These have a universality and certainty missing from the merely probable knowledge that is formed inductively from experience. It never becomes clear whether the ideas of reason are a remnant of humanity's pristine nature before the Fall. In that condition, Thomasius suggests, each person, from birth, was able immediately to apprehend the very nature of things and actions. After the Fall, experience, including the sciences, has to make up for this loss of insight into the essence of life and the world by piecing together such appearances as humanity can manage. Any success in this endeavour presupposes a systematic critique of all prejudices and this is in effect an implementation of systematic doubt – not 'sceptical' Cartesian doubt which is contradictory in denying the possibility of truth and falsehood, but 'dogmatic' doubt premised on such a possibility.

The world is, for Thomasius, ultimately spiritual; each thing is a living being with a purpose. But humans stand out as the only beings not entirely determined by their purpose but prone to error through the influence of other aims. He develops a theory of the passions to account for these pervasive aberrations, while his moral theory concerns the moral rules and institutions that allow us to live in pursuit of moral aims that, ultimately, are beyond most of us in this life. The great change in Thomasius is that in the earlier work, passions and morals are vying for control of a free will; but from his 1705 work *Fundamenta juris naturae et gentium ex sensu communi deducta* (Foundations of the Law of Nature and of Nations, deduced from Common Sense) onwards, morality is an epiphenomenon in a deterministic world.

3 Practical philosophy

In practical philosophy, Thomasius' starting-point was Samuel von PUFENDORF and, in a sense, this remained the case across the otherwise dramatic developments of his ideas. The Pufendorfian-Thomasian theory is profoundly voluntarist in the sense that it sees all moral values – in fact, all values – as directly or indirectly dependent upon acts of will. No thing (such as a creature), no state of affairs (such as a relationship between creatures), and no event (such as an act of one creature towards another) has any *inherent* value. Human acts of will are in themselves nothing but natural events, and only assume a moral aspect through their relationship to the law of nature;

the law of nature is only a moral law because it is God's will.

Much intellectual energy was spent during Thomasius' generation on the obvious problem that this line of argument simply transforms the question of the foundation of morals into the question of the goodness of God, and Thomasius' early work is first of all a contribution to this debate. His answer was that it is impious to raise the question of God's goodness, for it assumes that there is enough in common between God and humans to make sense of such a question; but we can know nothing whatsoever by natural means about God – except the bare fact that we are obliged to obey his will. Even if we could know God's goodness, this would not imply *what* we should do, if it were not for the fact that God, in addition to being good, also would will us to do what his goodness implies. We here meet the common assumption that obligation arises only from a law imposed by a superior. In sum, we know that we are obliged to obey God's will but also that we do not have a sufficient notion of God from which we can derive what our actual duties are. As a consequence, we have to turn to that which God's will has left us with, namely our reason. In this way Thomasius effectively excludes theology from any role in the theory of morals, including jurisprudence.

Central to the concept of reason upon which Thomasius relies is the idea of a dialogue or conversation. Reasoning consists of the manipulation of signs, and we learn the use of signs only in dealing with other people. So, without some minimum of social living, there could be no language and no ability to reason; these functions are interdependent. They are also distinctive for humanity, and they are the means by which we alone can live under the guidance of natural law. It is through reason that we can reflect upon the fact that we would not have reason if we were not social, and that we could not be social if others were not reasoning likewise. Thomasius takes these undeniable facts as the best indication we have of what God's will for us is, namely that we should always act so as to benefit the whole of humanity considered as rational and social. This *utilitas totius humani generis* is again to be understood as *pax* or *vita tranquilla*, peace or the quiet life with others, and this can also be characterized as the essence of temporal happiness, *beatitudo*. This rational sociality (*socialitas* or *Geselligkeit*) is the basic natural law and thus the foundation for all society (*societas* or *Gesellschaft*).

In the 1688 work, the *Institutiones jurisprudentiae divinae*, Thomasius thus identified morality with a broad concept of obligation to natural law or, in other words, justice. He never indicated any room for other areas of morality nor tried to differentiate the concept of natural law to make room for such areas; in fact, he simply followed Pufendorf's traditional division according to the objects of the duties imposed by natural law, namely God, other people and oneself. However, Thomasius was certainly at work on this problem. Just four years after the Institutiones, he published a different account of morals in *Einleitung zur Sitten Lehre*. Morality is now seen as based on love rather than sociality, but the nature of love is that it cannot be enforced and this is the distinguishing characteristic of morality as opposed to justice and law. The acts that comprise justice – giving each their due, abstaining from injury and so on – may be done out of neighbourly love, but they may also be enforced, in which case they move from love to justice, from morality to law.

In the *Einleitung* Thomasius pays little attention to justice and the foundation of law; his concern is to develop a theory of morality as rational love. This is a topic which we cannot pursue here, just as we have to ignore Thomasius' prolonged despair at making sense of the way in which reason might be said to regulate the love of humanity as the basis for the moral life. He could not see how a free will could escape the storms of passion and make any moral progress merely by rational means; the only way was to lose itself in mystical identification with God.

Thomasius escaped this pietistic replacement of morality by faith through a rejection of the idea of free will. Instead, he regarded the will as determined by the good, and developed a theory of the varieties of goods in life that we may cultivate as the objects of will. This was the basis for his attempt in the late work, especially the *Fundamenta* (1705), to put together a theory that could accommodate both the theory of justice and law, and the theory of morality, and to account for their difference.

The starting point is an identification of the good with peace or quietness of life that can be either internal – peace of mind – or external – security of action. Further, the external peace can either be a purely negative matter of being left in peace, or it can be a matter of having one's welfare actively secured or promoted. This is the basis for Thomasius' famous distinction between *honestum*, *justum* and *decorum*. Actions that contribute to or are in accordance with the inner peace or balance of a person make up the *honestum*. This is the sphere of morality proper, for such actions are obligatory as part of the moral nature God has prescribed for humanity, but they are only obligatory internally, in conscience, and cannot be enforced – like acts of love, they would lose their specific moral character if enforced. Actions that simply avoid breaking the external peace make up the *justum*; they carry external obligation or obligation to action, and they are enforceable and thus suitable objects of positive legislation. Actions that actively promote the external quiet of life, finally, make up the *decorum*. They are externally obligatory but not enforceable; they thus provide a middle way between the *honestum* and the *justum*, between morality and law, and they are characterized as prudence, or politics.

4 Conclusion

Thomasius' threefold division of morals made available much clearer conceptual and linguistic means than previously for distinguishing between law and morality, and thus between public and private spheres. It also showed just how easily voluntaristic natural law could lose most of its meaning *as* natural law. The gain and the loss went hand in hand as follows: once the basic obligation to morality – or natural law – is reduced to mere obedience to the supreme divine will, all content of this law has to be derived from temporal sources, that is, from human acts of will. But the investigation of human voluntary activity invites empirical methods, and much of Thomasius' progress consisted of his erratic acceptance of this invitation, resulting in a combination of a kind of philosophical anthropology and moral, especially legal, history based upon his three spheres of *honestum*, *justum* and *decorum*. Morals and law are thus increasingly seen as historical or cultural – in the broad sense, conventional – phenomena, and it is not evident that any objectively or universally valid *natural* law is left on the basis of which they could be criticized and changed. At the same time, of course, his linked divisions between law and morality, between public and private, between external and internal obligation, between action and intention, were tools to be taken up and refined by Kant in a way that was far from Thomasius' own troubled Lutheran horizon (see KANT, I. §§9–10).

Of Thomasius' many students and disciples, the most prominent include the theologian Johann Franz Budde (Buddeus), the philosopher Nicolaus Hieronymus Gundling and the legal theorist Johann Peter von Ludewig. He was also influential in the new University of Göttingen, but more in jurisprudence than in philosophy, and especially on J.J. Schmauß and Gottfried Achenwall, whose textbook was used by Kant. But despite their numbers, the Thomasius students never formed a 'school' as did followers of WOLFF, partly because the master was difficult to get on with, partly because the Wolff-gang swept the field.

See also: ENLIGHTENMENT, CONTINENTAL; NATURAL LAW

List of works

Thomasius' works are not available in English translation.

Thomasius, C. (1995–) *Ausgewählte Werke*, Werner Schneiders, Hildesheim: Olms Verlag. (In progress – when complete, this comprehensive edition will contain all works listed below.)

—— (1688) *Institutiones jurisprudentiæ divinæ libri tres* (Institutions of divine jurisprudence in three books); repr. 7th edn (1730) Aalen: Scientia Verlag, 1963; German trans., *Drei Bücher der Göttlichen Rechtsgelahrheit*, 1709. (Thomasius' most Pufendorfian work.)

—— (1688) *Introductio ad philosophiam aulicam* (Introduction to Court Philosophy); German trans., *Einleitung zur Hof-Philosophie*, 1710. (Politico-pedagogical application of the theory of reason.)

—— (1691a) *Einleitung zu der Vernunfft-Lehre* (Introduction to the theory of reason), repr. Hildesheim: Olms Verlag, 1968. (This and the following are his main epistemological works.)

—— (1691b) *Aushbung der Vernunfft-Lehre* (Application of the theory of reason), repr. Hildesheim: Olms Verlag, 1968. (Companion volume to the preceding work.)

—— (1692) *Einleitung zu der Sitten-Lehre (Introduction to moral philosophy)*, repr. Hildesheim: Olms Verlag, 1968. (Morality based on love rather than sociality – compare this with the *Institutiones*.)

—— (1696) *Aushbung der Sitten-Lehre* (Application of moral theory), repr. Hildesheim: Olms Verlag, 1968. (Under the influence of pietism, the sufficiency of reason is in doubt.)

—— (1699) *Summarischer Entwurff derer Grundlehren, die einem Studioso Juris zu wissen… nöthig* (Sketch of basic teaching, necessary knowledge for a student of law), repr. Aalen: Scientia Verlag, 1979. (Useful jurisprudential compendium.)

—— (1699) *Versuch vom Wesen des Geistes* (Essay on the Nature of Spirit). (Pietistic mysticism.)

—— (1705) *Fundamenta juris naturae et gentium ex sensu communi deducta* (Foundations of the Law of Nature and Nations, deduced from Common Sense); repr. 4th edn (1718) Aalen: Scientia Verlag, 1970; German trans., *Grundlehren des Natur- und Völkerrechts*, 1709. (Re-writing of the practical philosophy on a deterministic basis; development of the influential theory of *honestum*, *justum* and *decorum* – morality, law and prudence.)

—— (1719) *Paulo plenior, Historia juris naturalis*, repr. Stuttgart-Bad Cannstatt: Frommann-holsboog, 1972. (Brief history of natural jurisprudence.)

References and further reading

Barnard, F.M. (1971) 'The "Practical Philosophy" of Christian Thomasius', *Journal of the History of Ideas* 32: 221–46. (General overview of Thomasius' practical philosophy.)

Haakonssen, K. (forthcoming) 'Natural Law and the German Tradition', in M. Goldie and R. Wokler (eds) *Cambridge History of Eighteenth-Century Political Thought*, Cambridge: Cambridge University Press. (Thomasius in the context of German natural law theory from Pufendorf to Kant.)

Hammerstein, N. (1972) *Jus und Historie. Ein Beitrag zur Geschichte des historischen Denkens an deutschen Universitäten im späten 17. und im 18. Jahrhundert* (Law and history. A contribution to the development of historical thought at German universities in the late seventeenth and eighteenth centuries), Göttingen: Vandenhoeck & Ruprecht. (Important, comprehensive study of Thomasius' intellectual and university milieu.)

Hinrichs, C. (1971) *Preußentum und Pietismus. Der Pietismus in Brandenburg-Preußen als religiös-soziale Reformbewegung* (Prussianism and pietism. Pietism in Brandenburg-Prussia as a socio-religious reform movement), Göttingen: Vandenhoeck & Ruprecht. (Fundamental study of pietism with much attention to Thomasius.)

Lieberwirth, R. (1955) *Christian Thomasius. Sein wissenschaftliches Lebenswerk. Eine Bibliographie* (Christian Thomasius. Bibliography of a scholarly life), Thomasiana. Arbeiten aus dem Institut für Staats- und Rechtsgeschichte bei der Martin-Luther-Universität Halle-Wittenberg. Heft 2. Weimar. (Standard bibliography.)

Rüping, H. (1968) *Die Naturrechtslehre des Christian Thomasius und ihre Fortbildung in der Thomasius-Schule* (The natural-law theory of Christian Thomasius and its development in the Thomasian school), Bonner Rechtswissenschaftliche Abhandlungen, Bd. 81. Bonn. (Comprehensive study of Thomasius' jurisprudence with emphasis on the later work.)

Schmidt, W. (1995) *Ein vergessener Rebell. Leben und Wirken des Christian Thomasius* (A forgotten rebel. The life and work of Christian Thomasius), Munich: Diedrichs. (General biography.)

Schneiders, W. (1971) *Naturrecht und Liebesethik. Zur Geschichte der praktischen Philosophie im Hinblick auf Christian Thomasius* (Natural law and the love of ethics. Christian Thomasius and the history of practical philosophy), Hildesheim and New York: Olms Verlag. (The most important philosophical analysis of Thomasius.)

—— (ed.) (1989) *Christian Thomasius, 1655–1728. Interpretationen zu Werk und Wirkung. Mit einer Bibliographie der neueren Thomasius-Literatur* (Christian Thomasius, 1655–1728. Interpretations of his work and influence. With a bibliography of modern scholarship), Hamburg: Meiner Verlag. (Valuable collection of essays covering most aspects of Thomasius' thought. Excellent bibliography of secondary literature.)

KNUD HAAKONSSEN

THOMISM

Deriving from Thomas Aquinas in the thirteenth century, Thomism is a body of philosophical and theological ideas that seeks to articulate the intellectual content of Catholic Christianity. In its nineteenth and twentieth-century revivals Thomism has often characterized itself as the 'perennial philosophy'. This description has several aspects: first, the suggestion that there is a set of central and enduring philosophical questions about reality, knowledge and value; second, that Thomism offers an ever-relevant set of answers to these; and third, that these answers constitute an integrated philosophical system.

In its general orientation Thomism is indeed preoccupied with an ancient philosophical agenda and does claim to offer a comprehensive, non-sceptical and realist response based on a synthesis of Greek thought – in particular that of Aristotle – and Judaeo-Christian religious doctrines. However, in their concern to emphasize the continuity of their tradition, Thomists have sometimes overlooked the extent to which it is reinterpretative of its earlier phases. The period from the original writings of Thomas Aquinas to late twentieth-century neo-scholastic and 'analytical' Thomism covers eight centuries and a stretch of intellectual history more varied in its composition than any other comparable period.

Not only have some self-proclaimed Thomists held positions with which Aquinas would probably have taken issue, some have advanced claims that he would not have been able to understand. Examples of the first are found in Neo-Kantian treatments of epistemology and ethics favoured by some twentieth-century Thomists. Examples of the second include attempts to reconcile Aquinas' philosophy of nature with modern physics, and his informal Aristotelian logic with quantified predicate calculus and possible world semantics.

The term 'Thomism' is sometimes used narrowly to refer to the thought of Aquinas, and to its interpretation and elaboration by sixteenth- and seventeenth-century commentators such as Cajetan, Sylvester of Ferrara, Domingo Bañez and John of St Thomas. At other times it is employed in connection with any view that takes its central ideas from Aquinas but which may depart from other of his doctrines, or which combines his ideas with those of other philosophers and philosophies. Prominent examples of Thomists in this wider sense include Francisco Suárez (1548– 1617) who also drew on the epistemology and metaphysics of another great medieval thinker Duns Scotus; and, more recently, Joseph Marechal (1878–1944) whose 'Transcendental Thomism' accepted as its starting point the Kantian assumption that experience is of phenomena and not of reality as it is in itself. An example drawn from the ranks of contemporary analytical philosophers is Peter Geach who draws in equal measure from Aquinas, Frege and Wittgenstein.

In the twentieth century there have been two major proponents of the philosophy of Aquinas, namely Jacques Maritain and Etienne Gilson, both of whom contributed significantly to the development of Neo-Thomism in North America. Interestingly, both men were French, neither had been trained in a Thomistic tradition and both were drawn into philosophy by attending lectures by Henri Bergson at the Collège de France in Paris. The Neo-Thomism they inspired declined following the Second Vatican Council (1962–5) as Catholics looked to other philosophical movements, including existentialism and phenomenology, or away from philosophy altogether. Today Thomists tend to be close followers and interpreters of the writings of Aquinas, but there is also a growing interest among mainstream English-language philosophers in some of his central ideas. While not a movement, this approach has been described as 'analytical' Thomism.

1 **Aquinas and the first Thomism: 13th–15th centuries**
2 **The second Thomism: 16th–18th centuries**
3 **Neo-Thomism: 19th and 20th centuries**
4 **Aquinas and Thomism: future prospects**

1 Aquinas and the first Thomism: 13th–15th centuries

AQUINAS was born into a religious culture in which the dominant style of thought was a form of Neoplatonist Catholic theology. The main source of this was AUGUSTINE of Hippo, mediated via later Latin thinkers such as ANSELM. Early in his life, however, Aquinas fell under the influence of the recently founded Dominican Order of which he became a member. Under the direction of ALBERT THE GREAT, the foremost of the Order's early masters, he developed an intense interest in the more naturalistic philosophy of Aristotle whom he came to refer to as 'the philosopher'. Works of Aristotle were being translated into Latin for the first time during Aquinas' life, having been rediscovered through contact with the Arab world where they had been preserved.

To Albert and Aquinas, Aristotle offered a more promising resource for the articulation of Christian doctrine than did the Augustinian Platonism current in the cathedral schools and universities. However this new synthesis met with considerable opposition since it seemed to be at odds with orthodoxy. In fact, Aquinas found himself in dispute with two groups. To one side were the Augustinians represented by the secular teachers and the Franciscans; to the other were extreme Aristotelian naturalists who held doctrines that are indeed difficult to reconcile with Christian orthodoxy. Aquinas sought to tread a middle path, directing writings against each group in turn: *De aeternitate mundi contra murmurantes* (On the eternity of the world) (1271) against BONAVENTURE and other Augustinian Franciscans, and *De unitate intellectus* (On the Unity of the Intellect) (1270) against SIGER OF BRABANT and other Latin Averroists (named after Averroes (IBN RUSHD) the Arab philosopher and interpreter of Aristotle – see AVERROISM).

Although Aquinas' Christian Aristotelianism was later to be judged the 'most perfect' reconciliation of philosophy and faith, and was made, in effect, the official system of thought of Roman Catholicism, it was initially attacked and subjected to ecclesiastical denunciation. In 1270 Bishop Tempier of Paris condemned a number of propositions associated with Aristotelianism. None directly attributable to Albert or Aquinas was included; but in 1277, three years after the death of Aquinas, Tempier issued a further condemnation and this time Thomistic claims (about the soul and the total nonmateriality of spiritual substances) were specified, although Aquinas was not named. In the same year Robert KILWARDBY, Bishop of Oxford (and, like Aquinas, a Dominican) issued a similar condemnation; the following month the Pope endorsed Tempier's decree. Two years later William de la Mare, a Franciscan, produced a work 'correcting' the error of Aquinas' ways (*Correctorium fratris Thomae*).

The general Dominican response was to defend their master against these attacks from within and without. In 1278 the Dominican general chapter appointed a committee to investigate English Dominican disloyalty, and in the meantime set about promoting the cause of Thomas as a thinker and as a saint. In 1282 William of Macclesfield responded to de la Mare countering the charges with his *Correctorium corruptorii 'Quaestione'*. Around this time John of Paris responded similarly; by 1286 study of Aquinas was made compulsory by the Parisian Dominicans and this was repeated elsewhere: in Saragossa (1309) in London (1314) and in Bologna (1315). Defence gave way to counter-attack and on 18 July 1323, within fifty years of his death, Aquinas was declared a saint by Pope John XXII. Two years later Bishop Bourret of Paris revoked Tempier's condemnation.

Ecclesiastical approval removed one obstacle to acceptance of Thomistic thought, and by stages his ideas spread and gained influence. Apart from the intrinsic merit of those ideas, an important factor in this development was the increasing number of colleges and universities. Each approved place of study (*studium generale*) had houses belonging to the main teaching orders, and by this means, through the multiplication of copies of Thomistic texts and by translation into other languages (German and Greek), the Dominicans ensured that their master's voice could be heard throughout Europe.

Early in the fifteenth century Aquinas found a powerful follower in John CAPREOLUS. In the late scholastic period, the ideas of Aquinas had to compete with those of two other medieval figures, namely DUNS SCOTUS and WILLIAM OF OCKHAM. Capreolus challenged various views of Scotus and others to such good effect that he earned the title 'foremost Thomist' (*princeps Thomistarum*). More common than dialectical defences, however, were informed commentaries on the works of Aquinas, in particular the *Summa theologiae* (1266–73). These were important in transmitting Thomist doctrines, yet in themselves they did little to combat the rising tide of Ockhamist nominalism. Also, and somewhat unjustly, they were in part associated with the formalistic scholasticism against which the Renaissance humanists rebelled.

2 The Second Thomism: 16th–18th centuries

The sixteenth century was perhaps the most troubled in the history of post-medieval Christendom. The Reformation divided Europe into Catholic and Protestant states. It would be natural – but incorrect – to suppose that Aquinas was read only by Catholics. In England, the Anglican Richard HOOKER, and in Holland the Calvinist Hugo GROTIUS were both influenced by studying his work. However, it was within Catholic countries and regions that the next phase of Thomism developed. In particular, Spain and Italy gave rise to new theologically and metaphysically oriented presentations of Thomas' thought. In England the Reformation was more a matter of politics than theology; elsewhere (including Scotland) the reformers drove their axe to the roots of Catholic belief. In response, the Church of Rome set about renewing its intellectual resources. Thus was born the Counter-Reformation.

The Council of Trent (1545–63) sought to systematize Catholic doctrine and led to the production of a definitive Catechism in 1566 (*Catechismus romanus*) on which the thought of Aquinas had a major influence. (Contrary to an often-repeated tale, however, the *Summa theologiae* was not placed on the altar alongside the Bible during meetings of the Council.) Trent encouraged the study of philosophy and theology in all Catholic colleges, seminaries and universities. This created a need for appropriate textbooks and that was met with a new style of manual setting out Thomistic thought. A further response to the reformers was the development of new religious orders. The most famous of these was the 'Jesuits', the Society of Jesus founded by Ignatius of Loyola. Ignatius explicitly encouraged the study of Aquinas and Aristotle, and expressed the hope that interpretations of their ideas adapted to the needs of the time would be forthcoming.

In saying this, Ignatius was drawing upon an earlier pre-Tridentine tradition of teaching and commenting on Aquinas. The major figures associated with this tradition were Dominicans. In the first decade of the sixteenth century Peter Crockaert, a Belgian working in Paris, had substituted the *Summa theologiae* for the *Sentences* of Peter Lombard which had previously been the standard text for theological instruction. Likewise in Italy Thomas de Vio CAJETAN was lecturing on the *Summa* and producing a major commentary which was later to be published in an edition of the complete works of Aquinas. In Spain Francisco de VITORIA also used the *Summa* as a basis of theological education and he was followed in this by his disciple Domingo de SOTO.

Early Jesuit Thomists included students of de Soto. But the full Jesuit appropriation of Aquinas came later with Luis de MOLINA and, most notably of all, with Francisco SUÁREZ. The latter's great work was the 1597 *Disputationes Metaphysicae* (Metaphysical Disputations). Starting from a recognized need to produce theology adequate to meet that of the reformers, Suárez came to the conclusion that it was not appropriate simply to invoke the philosophy of Aristotle; rather fundamental issues needed to be addressed afresh. The result was a mix of Thomistic and non-Thomistic (largely Scotist) metaphysics. In fact, Suárez anticipates much of the thinking about essence, existence, identity and modality that emerged as a result of the equally focused attention in a century of analytical metaphysicians.

The Dominicans meanwhile had stayed closer to the detail of Aquinas' philosophy, in part because they were still operating with the idea that their first duty was one of loyalty to a brother who had long been misrepresented and maligned. The need to evangelize and to educate added to the tradition of exact commentary a series of course-book texts, the most famous of which (still in use in Catholic institutions into the twentieth century) were the philosophical and theological courses (*Cursus philosophicus* and *Cursus theologicus*) of Jean Poinsot, better known as JOHN OF ST THOMAS.

In 1568 Aquinas was named a 'Doctor of the Church'. Taken from the Latin for teacher (*docens*), the first official use of the title occurred in the thirteenth century when eight saints (including Augustine) were so honoured. It is a measure of the Church's estimate that Aquinas was named its ninth *docens*, known honorifically as the 'Angelic Doctor'.

The sixteenth century ended with two main schools of Thomism. The first had its strongest base in Italy and was associated with Dominican exegetical interpretation. The second was rooted in Spain and centred around the Jesuit appropriation of Aquinas. The first was more narrowly Thomist, being closer to the historical doctrines of St Thomas, and found its natural expression in the form of close textual commentaries. The second was more broadly Thomistic and gave rise to treatises on particular philosophical themes such as existence and essence.

Inevitably there was competition between these traditions; but the most heated conflict was not methodological or interpretative but doctrinal. This occurred from around 1590 to 1610, and continued intermittently thereafter. The subject was the nature of grace, free-will and divine foreknowledge. On the one side, the Jesuit Molina argued in his 1588 *Liberi arbitrii cum gratiae donis* (A Reconciliation of Free Choice with the Gifts of Grace, Divine Foreknowledge, Providence, Predestination and Reprobation) that God's total omniscience is compatible with human liberty, because the former includes 'middle knowledge' (*scientia media*) by which God knows what each person would freely do in every possible circumstance of choice, and distributes grace accordingly. In opposition to what is certainly not a position advanced or accepted by Aquinas, the Dominicans, of whom the most prominent was Dominic BAÑEZ, contended that God knows who will be saved and who

will be damned because he has distributed fully effective grace to some but not all. The Jesuits accused the Dominicans of embracing Calvinist predestinarianism, while the Dominicans charged the Jesuits with Pelagianism (see PELAGIANISM; PREDESTINATION).

This 'heresy calling' led to papal attempts to tame the debate, if not to end it, although without much success. In the meantime the intellectual energies of Thomists had been largely distracted from the important task of developing the general system so as to take account of the rise of modern science and the new philosophies of rationalism and empiricism. The trial of Galileo and the replies to Descartes show the Thomists to have fallen behind the times. Indeed, so far as the intellectual aspect is concerned, it was their ill-preparedness to engage modern thought, rather than intrinsic weaknesses within Thomism, that led to the marginalization of the tradition in the seventeenth and eighteenth centuries.

The fate of Catholic Thomism in the eighteenth century was also a reflection of the general circumstance of the Church. As in the Reformation, the period featured many social and political disruptions and much ecclesiastical infighting. In 1772 the Jesuits were suppressed on the order of the Pope and, in the next decade, Catholicism itself was battered by the French Revolution and by the rise of secularism. The new political thinking was antitheocratic, anticlerical, broadly democratic and at best deistic, although often atheistic (see DEISM). It is hardly surprising, therefore, that a system of thought born out of medieval Catholicism did not flourish in these circumstances. The Dominicans continued to produce critical editions of Aquinas' writings but it is doubtful whether they were read outside the Dominican order. Even in Rome ecclesiastics had lost interest in Thomism.

3 Neo-Thomism: 19th and 20th centuries

As in the past, however, a process of revitalisation led in due course to a renaissance. Following the period of the French Revolution, Catholic thought in France, Belgium and Italy tended to be divided between two movements: a quasi-fideistic movement that emphasized the centrality of faith and sought to deal with the threat from rationalism by side-stepping it; and a philosophical approach which maintained, along lines first suggested by Christian Neoplatonists, and later developed by Cartesians such as MALEBRANCHE, that the intellect directly intuits God in all its acts of knowledge. These two approaches came to be known as 'traditionalism' and 'ontologism'; their main proponents being Lammenais (1782–1854) and de Maistre (1752–1821), and Gioberti (1801–52) and ROSMINI-SERBATI, respectively.

383

Elsewhere in Italy (particularly in Naples) and in Spain, the Dominicans maintained their loyalty to Aquinas. The Italian Dominican Tommaso Zigliara (1833–93) found favour with Bishop Pecci of Perugia (later to become Pope Leo III), and in 1873 was appointed Regent of Studies in the Dominican College in Rome where he was joined by Alberto Lepidi (1838–1922). Both men were critical of the traditionalists and the ontologists; and through their writings, teachings and administration they did much to encourage members of their order in Italy and France to develop Neo-Thomistic responses to these movements, as well as to the empiricism and rationalism to which they had been reactions. The revival of Thomism was much encouraged by the papacy. In 1846 Pope Pius IX argued that reason and faith are compatible and that lapses into fideism and intellectual intuitionism are both to be avoided. Versions of traditionalism and ontologism were condemned in 1855 and 1866, respectively, and a return to the scholastic approaches was openly favoured.

An important figure in this revival was Joseph Kleutgen (1811–83) a German Jesuit. In a five-volume work entitled *Die Theologie der Vorzeit*, Kleutgen identified the weaknesses in Catholic intellectual responses to modern thought. He argued that only Aristotelian metaphysics could provide a sure foundation for Catholic theology. In a second work, *Die Philosophie der Vorzeit*, he expounded his own version of neo-Aristotelianism, rejecting the epistemological method of Descartes in favour of cognitive realism, attacking Cartesian mind-body dualism. Like Aquinas, Kleutgen and his colleagues, such as Matteo Liberatore (1810–92), affirmed the unity of the human person as a psychophysical substance. Also while upholding the epistemological primacy of experience they maintained the possibility of establishing, by abstract reflection, various necessary truths about reality – principally that it is the creation of God. Although the thought of Aquinas featured here, this movement was more generally a revival of scholasticism rather than of Thomism as such. In fact neither Kleutgen nor Liberatore were Thomists in the narrow sense.

In 1878 Gioacchino Pecci was elected pope and was crowned Leo XIII. He had long supported the revivalist movement, and the following year he published the famous encyclical *Aeterni Patris* in which Aquinas is commended as providing the surest intellectual foundation for, and articulation of Catholic doctrine. Kleutgen is reputed to have contributed to the draft of the encyclical and certainly his scholastic stance was vindicated by it. Leo also appointed neo-scholastics to important posts in Rome. Once again, then, through the edict of a pope, Thomism became the orthodox system of thought for Roman Catholicism.

Neo-Thomism looked in two directions. On the one hand it was called into being to address contemporary philosophical issues; on the other hand it drew its inspiration from the distant past. These two orientations gave rise to two strands, one 'problematic' the other historical. An unquestionable beneficiary of the revival was the history of medieval philosophy. At the University of Louvain in Belgium, where once ontologism had been enthroned, a new school of scholastic scholarship developed to which important contributions were made by Cardinal Mercier (1851–1926), Maurice de Wulf (1867–1947) and Martin Grabmann (1875–1959).

The problematic strand was first developed in response to the challenges of empiricism and Kantian idealism. Traditional Thomism assumed that the mind was in direct engagement with reality through experience. According to Aquinas both perception and intellection involve the reception of the forms of external substances. After Descartes, Locke, Hume and Kant, however, this view seemed difficult to maintain – indeed some found it difficult even to make sense of. The new orthodoxy was that the starting point of all philosophy is consciousness and the appearances it offers. Somehow from this we need to argue to the existence of something independent – external reality. Like others awed by Kantianism, several Neo-Thomists maintained that no philosophy could be credible that did not accept the new starting point of immanent consciousness. Influenced by Maurice Blondel (1861–1947) and Pierre Rousselot (1878–1915), the philosopher Joseph Marechal (1878–1944), and the theologians Karl RAHNER and Bernard LONERGAN – all of whom, like Rousselot, were Jesuits – tried to show that it was possible to combine Kant's critical philosophy with the transcendental realism and theism of Aquinas. The result, known as 'Transcendental Thomism', though widespread in its influence among theologians, was never taken very seriously by philosophers.

Another example of the attempt to synthesize Thomism with a modern philosophy is represented by the 'Lublin school' founded with the establishment (in 1946) of the Catholic University of Lublin in Poland, the only independent university during the period of the Soviet bloc. Here the sources were several: Thomism was represented by French interpreters; realist phenomenology was advocated by Roman INGARDEN who had been a student of Husserl; and logic and philosophy of science in the technical style was favoured by the Lwów-Warsaw school (see POLAND, PHILOSOPHY IN §3). The leading figures were Kamiński and Krąpiec. The most famous member of the school, however, was Karol Wojtyla (1920–) who drew on the value theory of Max SCHELER, Husserlian phenomenology and the anthropology of Aquinas, to devise a form of Thomist personalism articulated in his work *The Acting Person*. Better known as John Paul II, Wojtyla was not the first, nor probably the last pope to favour Thomism. His time at Lublin was short, however, being promoted to the see of Cracow in 1958, and elected Pope in 1978. Other members of the movement moved on, were diverted into administration, or died (Kamiński in 1986). The Lublin school is now moribund (see POLAND, PHILOSOPHY IN §4).

Two of the most important twentieth-century Neo-Thomists were French laymen, Jacques Maritain and Etienne Gilson. Both were critics of transcendental Thomism and both had enormous influence in North America as well as in Europe. Maritain was raised in a comfortable, politically liberal, Protestant family. Despairing of the materialism and secularism characteristic of Paris university and intellectual life, he and his wife made a suicide pact but revoked this after attending lectures by Henri BERGSON. While Bergson's 'vitalist' philosophy lifted their despair, it was not until they converted to Roman Catholicism in 1906, and thereafter discovered the philosophy of Aquinas, that the Maritains felt they had found a wholly adequate worldview combining humanism with transcendence.

Maritain lectured and published very widely in almost all areas of philosophy, and was a dominant influence in Catholic thought from the post-First World War period to the Second Vatican Council (1962–5). He approached the thought of Aquinas somewhat ahistorically rather than as medieval revivalist, and derived from it a realist metaphysics, epistemology and value theory. In his most important work of speculative philosophy, *The Degrees of Knowledge* (1959), he argues, following Aquinas and John of St Thomas, that concepts or ideas are principles of thought but not (save in reflection) the objects of cognition. Likewise, he insists that the natural order has an objective metaphysical structure of essential kinds and that these are the proper concern of science. His theory of value is likewise keyed to external realities, but value is seen as directed towards participation in the life of God. In his social and political philosophy Maritain emphasized the irreducibility of community and of the common good. These notions featured prominently in Catholic social teaching throughout the twentieth century and Maritain is often looked to as a source of inspiration by followers of this tradition (see MARITAIN, J.).

Like Maritain, Gilson was taught by Bergson, but his own interests lay principally in the history of ideas, and in particular in the relationship between modern philosophy as represented by Descartes and pre-modern scholasticism. From 1921 he held several Parisian posts in medieval philosophy at the Sorbonne, the École Pratique des Hautes Études, and at the Collège de France. His influence on the Neo-Thomist revival was as much through his teaching and academic leadership as through his writings. He lectured in North America, and co-founded the Pontifical Institute of Medieval Studies in Toronto. This has been one of the major centres of medieval scholarship and has helped to shape the interpretation of Aquinas by insisting on the need to understand his ideas in their historical context.

Gilson deplored the subjective turn introduced by the modern doctrines of mental images and ideas. However, he believed that any attempt to invoke medieval thinking in opposition to modern philosophy must be mindful of the variety of views held during the Middle Ages and, even more importantly, of the fact that they were developed primarily in theological contexts. Whereas Maritain presented Thomism as if it were a set of timeless abstract ideas, Gilson distinguished between the teachings of Aquinas and those of late commentators who sometimes imported their own views or who sought to synthesize Thomism with approaches current in their own day. Similarly he argued that while Aquinas drew heavily on the work of Aristotle he often used Aristotelian notions for different purposes, generally to defend Christian theology, and added ideas of his own; the most important of these being the claim that God is necessary existence and the source of the existence of contingent being.

Gilson's contextualist approach has been most widely followed among the Catholic historians of the medieval period, but its indirect influence is also apparent in the philosophical account of reason as immanent within traditions of enquiry advanced by Alasdair MACINTYRE. A convert, like so many other English-speaking Catholic philosophers (including ANSCOMBE, DUMMETT and Geach), MacIntyre's understanding and use of Aquinas has been shaped not by a Thomistic education but by personal study and in response to the views of others. For some years he taught at the University of Notre Dame, Indiana, where the Medieval Institute and the Jacques Maritain Center each engage scholastic thought. The second of these has been directed by Ralph McInerny, one of the leading representatives of Neo-Thomism in North America. McInerny has published extensively on Aquinas, increasingly in a popularizing vein. He was also for many years editor of the *New Scholasticism* (now the *American Catholic Philosophi-*

cal Quarterly). Together with the *Modern Schoolman*, the *Thomist* and to a lesser extent the *Review of Metaphysics* (edited by another senior Neo-Thomist, Jude Dougherty of the Catholic University of America), this journal and its successor have been the main fora for the presentation of essays in neo-scholastic historical and problematic traditions.

4   Aquinas and Thomism: future prospects

Contemporary historical scholarship in Thomistic philosophy is of a high standard. In the Anglo-Saxon world this is a consequence of the particular efforts of Gilson and his followers in Toronto, Notre Dame and elsewhere. Aquinas and other medieval and scholastic figures have also benefited from a general rise of interest in the history of philosophy, and by no means are all who now study Christian medieval thought themselves Catholics or even theists. At the same time it is natural that those who avow a Christian worldview should look with intense interest at the work of the individual who is beyond question the greatest Christian philosopher-theologian.

Future trends are difficult to predict in any detail, but if there is a future, and if it resembles the past even in broad outline, then the tide of interest in the thought of Aquinas will rise and fall as before. To some extent this will reflect the intellectual condition of the Roman Catholic Church and that of the colleges, seminaries and universities established to serve it. As was noted, however, Aquinas and Thomism are not the preserve of Catholics only. Indeed, there is a growing interest among philosophers trained wholly or partly in analytical philosophy. Some younger writers, drawing on the example of the British philosophers Elizabeth Anscombe, Peter Geach and Anthony Kenny, are using Thomistic resources to deal with contemporary philosophical problems. Others in the English-speaking world have turned to Aquinas as an important figure in the history of philosophy to be studied as one might any other thinker from the past. This second (mainly US) group is represented principally by scholars trained at Cornell under Norman Kretzmann and at Notre Dame under Ralph McInerny. As throughout previous centuries, interest in Aquinas will continue along two broad and connecting paths: one followed by those who wish to give an accurate representation of his thought; the other taken by those who wish to mine it as a source of interesting ideas.

See also: GARRIGOU-LAGRANGE, R.; RELIGION, PHILOSOPHY OF

References and further reading

Works cited in the text not listed here can be found in the respective biographical entries of the particular author.

The following English-language journals continue to publish work in the broadly Thomistic tradition: the *American Catholic Philosophical Quarterly* edited from the University of Dallas, TX (formerly the *New Scholasticism*, edited from the University of Notre Dame); the *Modern Schoolman* (Quarterly) edited from the University of St Louis, MO; the *Review of Metaphysics* (Quarterly) edited from the Catholic University of America in Washington, DC; and the *Thomist* (Quarterly) edited from the Dominican house of studies in Washington, DC. Of these, the *ACPQ* and the *Review of Metaphysics* are the most pluralistic, and the *Thomist* is the most traditional.

Bourke, V.J. (1945) 'Thomistic Bibliography 1920–1940', *The Modern Schoolman*, supplementary vol. 21. (The first English-language bibliography of modern neo-Thomism.)

* Brezik, V.B. (1981) *One Hundred Years of Thomism*, Houston, TX: Center for Thomistic Studies. (Collection of essays on the past, present and future of modern Thomism with the text of *Aeterni Patris* 'Encyclical Letter on the Restoration of Christian Philosophy' by Pope Leo XIII.)

Chesterton, G.K. (1933) *St Thomas Aquinas*, London: Hodder & Stoughton. (Although unscholarly and somewhat idiosyncratic, this shows a strong intuitive grasp of the main realist thrust of Thomism.)

Dougherty, J. (1995) 'Analysis in Search of Wisdom', ed. T. Druart, *Reason in History, Proceedings of the American Catholic Philosophical Association* 68. (Reflections by a senior contemporary neo-Thomist on the current condition of philosophy, delivered on the occasion of his receiving the Aquinas Medal from the ACPA in 1994.)

Fitzpatrick, P.J. (1982) 'Neoscholasticism', in N. Kretzmann, A. Kenny and J. Pinborg (eds) *The Cambridge History of Later Medieval Philosophy*, Cambridge: Cambridge University Press. (The best single-volume reference work on the philosophy of the high-middle ages. It contains over forty essays by as many authors on a wide range of subjects. Also included are biographies of medieval figures, an extensive bibliography, and name and subject indexes.)

Gilson, E. (1936) *The Spirit of Medieval Philosophy*, New York: Scribner. (The text of Gilson's 1931–2 Gifford Lectures, in which he argues for the importance of seeing medieval thinkers as religious, while also recognizing the very broad range of views held by them.)

—— (1937) *The Unity of Philosophical Experience*, New York: Scribner. (A short study, much admired within and beyond neo-Thomist circles for its inspirational view of the nature of philosophical enquiry.)

—— (1952) *Being and Some Philosophers*, Toronto, Ont.: Pontifical Institute of Medieval Studies. (An advanced work in which Gilson explores the ways in which the notion of being features in the philosophy of Aquinas' predecessors and argues for the originality of Aquinas' own contribution.)

—— (1964) *The Spirit of Thomism*, New York: P.J. Kennedy & Sons. (A short account of the nature and condition of neo-Thomism in relation to the religious philosophy of Aquinas. Useful on the question of how basic Thomist principles should be applied in challenging modern philosophies.)

Haldane, J. (1994) 'MacIntyre's Thomist Revival: What Next?' in J. Horton and S. Mendus (eds) *After MacIntyre*, Cambridge: Polity Press. (A critical examination of MacIntyre's claims concerning Thomism – as developed in MacIntyre's *Whose Justice? Which Rationality?* and *Three Rival Versions of Moral Inquiry*.)

—— (1997) 'Analytical Thomism', *The Monist* 80 (4). (Collection of new articles by philosophers in the analytical tradition exploring aspects of Aquinas' thought as it bears on central philosophical problems.)

—— (1998) 'What Future has Catholic Philosophy?', ed. T. Druart, *Virtues and Virtue Theories, Proceedings of the American Catholic Philosophical Association* 71. (An examination of the current state of philosophy as practised by Catholic thinkers. It argues that neo-Thomism has suffered from isolation from the mainstream analytical tradition of English-language philosophy.)

Hudson, D.W. and Moran, D.W. (1992) *The Future of Thomism*, Mishawaka, IN: American Maritain Association. (Collection of essays presenting a wide range of sometimes conflicting interpretations of the meaning of Thomism and its place within contemporary philosophy.)

Ingardia, R. (1993) *Thomas Aquinas: International Bibliography 1977–1990*, Bowling Green, OH: Philosophy Documentation Center. (The most up-to-date guide to publications on Aquinas and Thomism in English, French, German, Italian and Spanish.)

Kennedy, L.A. (1987) *A Catalogue of Thomists, 1270–1900*, Notre Dame, IN: University of Notre Dame Press. (A scholarly listing without commentary of 2034 Thomists: from Richard Knapwell (of England) in the thirteenth century to Walsch (of unknown country) at the end of the nineteenth.)

* Kleutgen, J. (1850–3) *Die Philosophie der Vorzeit Verteidigt* (A Defence of the Philosophy of the Past), Munich: Theissings'sche Buchhandlung, 5 vols. (Influential work in the nineteenth-century revival of Thomism which argues that Western philosophy suffered a radical break in the modern period and thus can be divided into two phases: from Socrates to the medievals and the late scholastics, and from Descartes onwards.)

Knasas, J.F.X. (1994) *Thomistic Papers VI*, Houston, TX: Center for Thomistic Studies. (Set of essays by many of the same authors as in Brezik's *One Hundred Years of Thomism*, discussing the claims of McCool's *From Unity to Pluralism*.)

MacIntyre, A. (1988) *Whose Justice? Which Rationality?*, London: Duckworth. (An important statement of MacIntyre's view that all reason is immanent within traditions of inquiry.)

—— (1990) *Three Rival Versions of Moral Inquiry*, London: Duckworth. (A revised version of his 1988 Gifford Lectures, this is a further development of MacIntyre's account of reason, this time applied in relation to three contrasting perspectives, one of which – Thomism – is judged to be superior.)

Maritain, J. (1930) *Art and Scholasticism*, London: Sheed & Ward. (An influential and once widely read account of the nature of art and beauty conceived of from a Thomistic perspective.)

—— (1948) *A Preface to Metaphysics*, New York: Sheed & Ward. (A useful starting point for Maritain's Thomism, this short book consists of seven lectures and is something of a prospectus for the metaphysics he favoured.)

* —— (1959) *The Degrees of Knowledge*, New York: Charles Scribner. (The definitive presentation of Maritain's epistemology in which he draws upon the interpretation of John of St Thomas to argue for realism. An important work, though hard going for the uninitiated.)

McCool, G. (1989) *Nineteenth Century Scholasticism: The Search for a Unitary Method*, New York: Fordham University Press. (An examination of the development of Catholic theology and the impact on this of the revival of Thomism.)

—— (1992) *From Unity to Pluralism: The Internal Evolution of Thomism*, New York: Fordham University Press. (A study of the debate between traditional and largely Jesuit neo-Kantian Thomists over the question of whether there can be a diversity of philosophical approaches.)

—— (1994) *The Neo-Thomists*, Milwaukee, WI: Marquette University Press. (The best available survey of Thomism, concentrating mainly on the nineteenth and twentieth centuries).

McInerny, R. (1968) *Thomism in an Age of Renewal*, Notre Dame, IN: University of Notre Dame Press. (A study of central features of Thomistic thought in relation to developments in Catholic theology following the Second Vatican Council.)

—— (1982) *St Thomas Aquinas*, Notre Dame, IN: University of Notre Dame Press. (A short but clear and systematic account of Aquinas, indicating his reliance on the thought of his predecessors, in particular Aristotle and Boethius.)

Miethe, T.L. and Bourke, V.J. (1981) *Thomistic Bibliography 1940–1978*, London: Greenwood Press. (A further useful bibliography, this spanning the gap between the periods covered by Bourke and Ingardia.)

Phillips, R.P. (1934) *Modern Thomistic Philosophy, Volumes I and II*, London: Burns Oates & Washbourne. (Example of the seminary-manual style of systematic presentation of Thomistic philosophy – in this case philosophy of nature and metaphysics).

Roensch, F.J. (1964) *The Early Thomistic School*, Dubuque, IA: Priory Press. (A scholarly study of the range of issues and opinions disputed among medieval and neo-scholarly Thomists.)

Trentman, J.A. (1982) 'Scholasticism in the Seventeenth Century', in N. Kretzmann, A. Kenny and J. Pinborg (eds) *The Cambridge History of Later Medieval Philosophy*, Cambridge: Cambridge University Press. (Good survey – see Fitzpatrick (1982) above.)

* William de la Mare (1279) *Correctorium Corruptorii*, in P. Glorieux (ed) *Les premières polemiques thomistes* (The First Thomistic Polemics), Kain: Bibliothèque thomiste, 1927. (A scholarly collection of various writings by de la Mare advancing Augustinian positions in opposition to neo-Aristotelian ones.)

* Wojtyla, K. (Pope John Paul II) (1979) *The Acting Person*, trans. A. Potocki, Dordrecht: Reidel. (An advanced presentation of Lublin-style, Thomistic philosophical anthropology. Drawing on Aquinas and phenomenology, Wojtyla emphasizes the unity of the agent.)

JOHN HALDANE

THOREAU, HENRY DAVID (1817–62)

Thoreau was one of the founders of the new literature that emerged within the fledgling culture of the United States in the middle decades of the nineteenth century. He inherited an education in the classics and in the transcendentalism of his older friend and teacher Ralph Waldo Emerson. Thoreau forged a means of writing which was dedicated to recording particular events in all their transience but capable of rendering graphic the permanent laws of nature and conscience. His incorporation of both confidence and self-questioning into the texture of his writing forms the ground of his standpoint as an observer of human lives and other natural histories.

Thoreau's relation to philosophy goes beyond his inheritance from Plato, Kant, Emerson and Eastern thought. Above all, his quest for philosophy is evident in the ways his writing seeks its own foundations. It is in the act of writing that Thoreau locates the perspectives within which to give an account of the humanness of a life. His project is to report sincerely and unselfconsciously a life of passion and simplicity, using himself as a representative of basic human needs and projects. Influenced by Plato's Republic, *Thoreau gives an account of some basic human needs, such as food, shelter and society. But also, like Plato, he shows that the particular institutions by which human needs are met are very far from being necessary. Tracing the relationship between need and necessity is one of the primary goals of Thoreau's work.*

1   **Thoreau's vocation**
2   **Emerson and transcendentalism**
3   **Cavell's reading of Thoreau**
4   **Thoreau as inheritor of philosophy**

1   Thoreau's vocation

During two years spent at Walden Pond, a small lake near his birthplace of Concord, Massachusetts, Thoreau began the work that culminated in the book called *Walden* (1854). In that same period of time, he spent the night in jail, and this experience is the point of departure for his essay 'Resistance to Civil Government' (1849), better known under its later title 'Civil Disobedience'. Despite the efforts of scholars like Perry Miller to promote the accomplishment of Thoreau's fourteen-volume *Journal* (1906), it is for *Walden* and 'Civil Disobedience' that Thoreau is best known. As literature, *Walden* stands with the work of Melville, Dickinson and Whitman, and is one of the founding documents of the transcendentalist tradition in American philosophy.

Thoreau possessed unrivalled powers of observation, the desire for a life of independence, and a vocation as a writer that dominated his everyday existence. His powers of observation were devoted to providing an account of the natural and human events that occurred around him. He sought both to find the order in these events and to disrupt the received categories of perception, understanding and narration. Long before twentieth-century physics, he was questioning the standpoint of the observer of nature, as well as the standpoint of the observer of human affairs. He sought the laws by which we could calculate the path of the apparently irregular occurrences of observers, along with the regularities in their observations.

Thoreau's requirement that we seek solitude and independence was not a recommendation of total isolation. He focused on solitude as a condition in which human beings learn how to hear what there is to hear. He thought that the modern conditions of cities and societies place us generally in a false proximity to other human beings. This falseness makes it difficult to take any steps towards a more genuine closeness or communication. Withdrawing to a place like Walden is not the same as acquiring freedom from the false sense of companionship and society. Taking that step, however, is meant to be an acknowledgement of the difficulties involved in achieving the proper distance from human affairs. Physical distance and isolation were symbols for the kind of mental perspective he sought.

Thoreau's work shows the way he absorbed and reworked his reading of classical philosophers, especially Plato. He was one of the first thinkers in the West to avail himself of Eastern works: the *Bhagavad Gītā* and the *Laws of Manu* figure pervasively in *Walden* (see DUTY AND VIRTUE, INDIAN CONCEPTIONS OF). Thoreau does not distinguish greatly between Eastern and Western traditions; rather he is concerned to distinguish between 'easy reading' and what he calls the 'heroic books' (Thoreau [1854] 1963 ch. III: 75). The latter require our best efforts of reading, while the former suits the cheapness of contemporary literature and serves to dissipate its readers' faculties and to confirm their shallowness.

What Thoreau characterizes as 'heroic' is connected to what he sees as the need for an epistemology of human possibility. He offers us an investigation of the relation between the literary depiction of mental liberation and the natural conditions of practical freedom. The ways in which we read, as much as the newspapers and novels that constitute the bulk of our reading, are indications of our habits of attention in every sphere of human practice. Thoreau finds the dominant characteristic of these various enterprises to be a self-dissipation that undermines our ability to concentrate our powers. Reading in a 'high sense' is a primary path on which we may recover our concentration and discernment. Reading thus becomes a way to discover the conditions under which we work and act.

2 Emerson and transcendentalism

Early in his life, Thoreau experienced the power of the work and capacity for friendship of Ralph Waldo EMERSON. Paradoxically, it was Emerson's entry into life that enabled Thoreau to discover his originality. Thoreau's reputation as a thinker has suffered doubly from this situation: he is almost invariably regarded not only as a transcendentalist, but as one whose basic ideas were derived from Emerson. And Emerson's own writing is consistently characterized as lacking the rigour and methodical development of philosophical thought.

The transcendentalist movement took its name from Kant's notion of the transcendental employment of ideas. Rather than seeking to go beyond human experience, transcendental knowledge seeks the conditions under which our current human knowledge and the experience of ordinary objects is possible. Transcendentalists interpreted this Kantian problematic as requiring a reciprocal relation between the quality of daily experience and the possibility of achieving a knowledge of the conditions of that experience. Taking the state of mind in which a thing or event gets perceived to be as critical as our knowledge of the manner in which the thing or event is caused, transcendentalism combined an idealist vision of the world as created or coloured by the human spirit, with a Romantic characterization of human beings as losing interest in the world. This loss of interest is taken not merely as a mood but as an increasingly fundamental and characteristic relationship between the individual and the world. The sense of boredom and melancholy concerning the world was understood as affecting the very perception of the world. A renewal of interest in the world was regarded as necessary to the renewal both of knowledge and of the powers of creativity.

Thoreau's transcendentalism provides a critical piece of the background to his justification of resistance to unjust government. 'Civil Disobedience' is both a statement of principle and an account of the actions which led to his spending a night in jail for refusing to pay a poll tax. The work was intended as both an intellectual example and a moral provocation. Thoreau exhibits the connections of the call to conscience with his own call to a less economically dependent mode of life. As Plato's philosopher must go back into the cave, so Thoreau declares that some of his 'generative energy' must be devoted to abolishing the conditions that prevent other individuals from responding to fundamental human possibilities. His appeal to his fellow citizens to resist the tyrannies of slavery and imperialism are couched in terms that demonstrate his hopes for a national awakening and moral regeneration.

3 Cavell's reading of Thoreau

In *The Senses of Walden* (1972), the American philosopher Stanley Cavell depicts the unwillingness of readers to grant the powers of philosophy or consecutive thought to Thoreau's words. He characterizes this blankness towards Thoreau as an estrangement from a region of our own powers of thought. Cavell's project has spiralled back to a reconsideration of Emerson's work, and he propounds a vision of perfectionism in Thoreau and Emerson. This interpretation of a dimension of moral thought at least as old as Socrates' 'care of the soul' requires the shedding of false possibilities and false necessities. Only by giving up an apparent wholeness of the self can we take a step towards an integrity that is internal to the self's own constitution. Emerson and Thoreau thus stand at the core of a tradition of American thinking that has been neglected and even suppressed.

In characterizing our distance from Thoreau's writing as a form of distance from our own capacities for self-reflection, Cavell's work provides the grounds for considering Thoreau's relation to philosophy. Among the central claims of Cavell's investigation are these: (1) Thoreau's penetration of the world is made possible by his acceptance of our necessities and by the capacity to convert necessity into forms of habitation. Specifically, (2) human labour is not only one of the necessities of our lives but one of the forms in which we make contact with the necessities of the world. All forms of labour are thus expressive of one another, not only in the debased terms of economic value but as different modes of knowledge and of contact with reality (see WORK, PHILOSOPHY OF). (3) Cavell locates in *Walden* the apparent paradox according to which we must let a book provide the terms that teach us how to read the book. The immediate methodological step is that we are to relinquish our inherited images and ways of reading. (4) Cavell discerns in Thoreau the intention to compose a nation's scripture, overturning not only personal deadness to our words but a national faithlessness to its founding vision. (5) There is a corresponding project to redeem the economic terms of value and expression, and this project in turn releases a more humanly adequate conception of labour and value. (6) Cavell discovers in Thoreau a quasi-Kantian vision of the necessities of life in nature as creating the medium within which a life of freedom is found to be liveable. Thoreau's task is not so much to learn independence by living in the woods as to find out what could make his life in the woods a form of independence. From the beginning of his sojourn there, he demonstrates his awareness that he must be prepared to leave it.

4 Thoreau as inheritor of philosophy

Thoreau's work often invokes the figure of the philosopher, as when he writes that 'To a philosopher all news, as it is called, is gossip' (Thoreau [1854] 1963 ch. II: 70). Thoreau thought of newspapers as purveying what was essentially gossip, and urged philosophers to find ways of getting beyond the superficial claims of merely current events. At the same time, Thoreau characterizes gossip as one of the primary modes in which the members of modern society communicate messages to each other. What makes it gossip is not the content of what is said but the uprooted disposition of the speakers from the ground of their real concern. Thoreau understood gossip as disguising the sources of our concern and the unsettled quality of our communications.

The sense of the social as precisely constituted by a certain kind of talk is most immediately related to Emerson's depiction of the whole 'cry of voices' standing against the solitary voice of the self-reliant. Thoreau's sense of social communication also bears comparison to the fifth chapter of J.S. Mill's *On Liberty* and to the places in *Being and Time* where Heidegger attempts to specify the conditions of 'mere talk' (*Gerede*) as constitutive of our being with one another. The degeneracy of our talk and speech is linked by Thoreau ([1854] 1963 ch. XIII: 186) to the distance between our 'parlours', or places of speech, and the 'kitchens' where our the object of our needs are most immediately transformed into the possibility of satisfaction. The proximity of human words to the concerns from which the words arise is part of the accomplishment of the truer speech and deeper knowledge which is the province of the humanities.

Thoreau sees his own capacity for vision as deriving from the same sources as other philosophers, in other places and other epochs. He explicitly mentions sharing certain perceptions with the 'oldest Egyptian or Hindoo philosopher' ([1854] 1963 ch. III: 74). This mingling of identities in our capacity to apprehend our condition is not mystical. It is a precise declaration of the impersonality of that part of the mind which is capable of spectatorship and criticism. He declares his sense that:

> To be a philosopher is not just to have subtle thoughts but so to love wisdom as to live according to its dictates, a life of simplicity, magnanimity, and trust. It is to solve some of the problems of life, not only theoretically, but practically.
>
> (Thoreau [1854] 1963 ch. I: 10)

Many readers have taken such remarks to imply that Thoreau is exhorting us to bring our lives into accord not only with simplicity but with a relatively simple doctrine of life. Richardson's 1986 biography simply omits the word 'just', as if to insist that a philosopher should dispense with subtle thoughts. Thoreau associates philosophy with its classical task of searching out and heeding the dictates of a practical wisdom. This association is a valuable clue to Thoreau's conception of a philosophical life. Thoreau's search for what he called the writer's 'equable life' is also a search for the 'occasions' of writing ([1854] 1963 ch. III: 76). These occasions provide simultaneously a chance for immediate perception and a chance to secure the vantage points of his observations. The reader must remember that the search for these occasions of simplicity is not itself very simple. Thoreau scrupulously records the failures as well as the successes in his search for the conditions of writing and observation. In these moments of reflection and self-criticism, we find Thoreau's deepest engagements with the issues of philosophy. One train of Thoreau's thought about simplicity leads to the analogy that:

> Our life is like a German confederacy, made up of petty states, with its boundary forever fluctuating, so that even a German cannot tell you how it is bounded at any moment.
>
> (Thoreau [1854] 1963 ch. II: 68)

The object of this little gibe is the effort of post-Kantian German philosophers to chart in systematic prose the limits of the mind and the limits of its freedom. As *Walden* unfolds, we learn that 'simplicity' is only one face of the answer. Simplicity is as little or as much of a solution to the problem of the soul as it is in Plato's *Phaedo*. It is the smallness as well as the transience of the states composing our minds that Thoreau wants us to overcome.

Thoreau depicts the fluctuation of the boundaries of our life as containing a philosophically positive possibility. In the conclusion of *Walden* he speaks of passing beyond an 'invisible boundary'. He goes on to say that 'in view of the future or possible' we should learn to live 'quite laxly and undefined in front' ([1854] 1963 ch. XVIII: 245). He was not content to

arrive at a simple life, if that meant establishing rigid defences against the complications of society. He also suggested that the transformations of an individual's development could not be bounded by a single experience, or a single theory of such an experience. The primary example in his culture was the Christian experience of conversion and its role in the doctrine of atonement.

Thoreau's reflections on language attempt to characterize the volatile presence of words at the core of all experience. The transience of our spoken words is analogous to the disappearance of significance from a written text. Both can be instructive to those who know how to listen and to read. An appropriate mode of reading points inwards to the possibility of locating our freedom in a world of natural law. For Thoreau the act of reading thus takes on some of the functions of judgment in Kant's *Critique of Aesthetic Judgment*. As judgments of the beautiful are meant to apprise us of 'traces' of harmony between nature and the functioning of our practical reason, so the act of reading teaches us how to understand and to appropriate what is rightfully ours. For Thoreau, reading is the path on which we learn to conceive the connection between the accidents of nature and the necessities of human freedom.

See also: AMERICAN PHILOSOPHY IN THE EIGHTEENTH AND NINETEENTH CENTURIES

List of works

Thoreau, H.D. (1906) *The Writings of Henry David Thoreau*, Boston, MA: Houghton Mifflin, 20 vols; vols. 7–20, ed. B.Torrey and F. Allen repr. as *The Journal of Henry David Thoreau*, ed. W. Harding, Salt Lake City, UT: Gibbs & Smith,1984. (Volumes 1–5 were unedited reprints from earlier editions of his works; volume 6, 'Familiar Letters', was edited by F.B. Sanborn. Volumes 7–20 were the first complete edition of the 'Journal'.)

—— (1981–) *The Writings of Henry David Thoreau*, ed. E. Witherall, Princeton, NJ: Princeton University Press. (Now the standard scholarly edition.)

—— (1849a) *A Week on the Concord and Merrimack Rivers*, Boston, MA: James. (Structured as a journey, it contains early versions of Thoreau's preoccupations with nature, friendship, memory and the act of writing.)

—— (1849b) 'Resistance to Civil Government', *Aesthetic Papers*, ed. E. Peabody, Boston, MA: G.P. Putnam, 189–211. (Later re-titled 'Civil Disobedience' and often reprinted.)

—— (1854) *Walden; or Life in the Woods*, Boston, MA: Ticknor & Fields; repr. as *The Variorum*

Walden, ed. W. Harding, New York: Washington Square Press, 1963. (The subtitle was omitted after the first edition. The 1963 annotated edition contains useful accounts of sources, references and background.)

—— (1864) *Maine Woods*, Boston, MA: Ticknor & Fields. (Contains an account of climbing Mount Ktadin, a late masterpiece of Thoreau's writing.)

—— (1890) *Anti-Slavery and Reform Papers*, London: Swan Sonnenschein. (Contains 'Civil Disobedience', 'A Plea for Captain John Brown' and other political writings.)

—— (1981) *Walden and other Writings*, ed. W. Howarth, New York: Random House. (Good selection of writings including *Walden*, 'Walking', 'Civil Disobedience' and 'A Plea for Captain John Brown'.)

References and further reading

Cameron, S. (1985) *Writing Nature: Henry Thoreau's Journal*, New York: Oxford University Press. (Argues for the priority of Thoreau's Journals as the main embodiment of his literary enterprise.)

* Cavell, S. (1972) *The Senses of Walden*, Chicago, IL: University of Chicago Press; expanded edn, 1980. (An exploration of Thoreau's relation to Romanticism, Emerson, Kant and modern philosophy.)

Emerson, R.W. (1883) 'Thoreau'; repr. in *The Complete Works of Ralph Waldo Emerson*, vol. 10, ed. E.W. Emerson, Boston, MA: Houghton Mifflin,1903–4. (A revised version of Emerson's memorial address, delivered at Thoreau's funeral, containing a pertinent introduction to the man and his work.)

Gould, T. (1992) 'Henry David Thoreau', *Encyclopedia of Ethics*, New York and London: Garland Press. (Outline of Thoreau's contribution to transcendentalism, moral perfectionism and ethical action.)

Harding, W. (1966) *The Days of Henry Thoreau*, New York: Knopf. (Reconstructs the way Thoreau spent his days from the writings themselves.)

* Heidegger, M. (1927) *Being and Time*, trans. J. Macquarrie and E. Robinson, New York: Harper & Row, 1962. (Heidegger's first masterwork, containing diagnoses of inauthenticity and idle speech as intrinsic to the social constitution of the human being.)

* Kant, I. (1790) *Critique of Judgment*, trans. W. Pluhar, Indianapolis, IN: Hackett Publishing Company, 1987. (Kant's third critique cast an immense shadow on the thinkers of New England, in part through the influence of Goethe and Coleridge. See especially §42, pages 165–70.)

* Mill, J.S. (1859) *On Liberty*, in *The Philosophy of John Stuart Mill*, ed. M.Cohen, The Modern Library Edition, New York: Random House, 1961. (See pages 248–71. In addition, this collection also contains Mill's writing on poetry, originality and Coleridge as opposing conformity and custom which forms a rare contemporary point of comparison with the work of Thoreau and Emerson.)

Miller, P. (1958) *Consciousness at Concord: The Text of Thoreau's Hitherto Lost Journal (1840–1841)*, Boston, MA: Houghton Mifflin. (A polemical but still useful confrontation with Thoreau, by one of the most important historians of American literature.)

Myerson, J. (1988) *Critical Essays on Henry David Thoreau's Walden*, Boston, MA: G.K. Hall. (Contains a selection of nineteenth-century reviews, including George Eliot, Horace Greely and others, and twentieth-century essays.)

Packer, B.L. (1995) *The Transcendentalists*, in *The Cambridge History of American Literature*, ed. S. Bercovitch, Cambridge: Cambridge University Press, vol. 2, 329–604. (A consideration of Thoreau's literary projects in relation to transcendentalism and to the social and political conditions of the age.)

Paul, S. (1958) *The Shores of America: Thoreau's Inward Exploration*, Urbana, IL: University of Illinois Press. (A major critical statement about Thoreau's enterprise as a writer.)

* Richardson, R., Jr. (1986) *Henry Thoreau: A Life of the Mind*, Los Angeles, CA: University of California Press. (Intellectual biography which maps Thoreau's background of reading and some central themes of his writing against the major events of his life.)

Sattelmeyer, R. (1988) *Thoreau's Reading: A Study in Intellectual History, with Bibliographical Catalogue*, Princeton, NJ: Princeton University Press. (Extensive background, with chronological details of Thoreau's reading.)

TIMOTHY GOULD

THOUGHT EXPERIMENTS

Thought experiments are strange: they have the power to present surprising results and can profoundly change the way we view the world, all without requiring us to examine the world in the way that ordinary scientific experiments do. Philosophers who view all hypothetical reasoning as a form of thought experimentation regard the method as being as old as philosophy itself. Others maintain that truly informative thought experiments are found only in mathematics and the natural sciences. These emerged in the seventeenth century when the new experimental science of Bacon, Boyle, Galileo, Newton and others forced a distinction between the passive observation of Aristotelian mental narratives and the active interventions of real-world experiment. The new science gave rise to a philosophical puzzle: how can mere thought be so informative about the world? Rationalists argue that thought experiments are exercises in which thought apprehends laws of nature and mathematical truths directly. Empiricists argue that thought experiments are not exercises of 'mere thought' because they actually rely upon hidden empirical information – otherwise they would not count as experiments at all. More recently it has been argued that thought experiments are not mysterious because they are constructed arguments that are embedded in the world so as to combine logical and conceptual analysis with relevant features of the world.

1 **Features of thought experiments**
2 **Thought experiments in science**
3 **Thought experiments in philosophy**
4 **Further issues**

1 Features of thought experiments

As literary entities, thought experiments are more accessible, repeatable and persuasive than any real-world experiment. Thought experiments have other features, which we illustrate with an experiment by Simon Stevin. This shows that the force needed to balance a ball on an inclined plane varies inversely with the length of the plane. We know that a ball on a smooth horizontal plane is supported by the plane: no force is needed to keep it stationary. A ball against a vertical plane is not supported by the plane at all, so a force equal and opposite to its weight is needed to keep it stationary. What force is needed for the intermediate cases where the plane is inclined?

Can this question be answered just by thinking? First imagine a triangular prism positioned with its base horizontal some distance above a table. Now imagine a necklace consisting of fourteen identical, perfectly spherical-balls draped over the prism so that four rest on the left-hand longer incline and two rest on the shorter incline. The remainder of the chain forms a loop below the prism. The balls are connected at equal distances in a way that allows them to roll freely. Will the necklace move? To imagine that it moves is to suppose that perpetual motion is possible. Observe, instead, that the necklace is in equilibrium. The third step in the experiment is to imagine cutting the necklace simultaneously at two

points just beneath the prism (or more easily, perhaps, at a single point where it is closest to the table). What happens to the six balls remaining on the prism? Our knowledge of this situation suggests that they will remain in equilibrium: four balls on the left balance the two on the steeper incline on the right. This is an imaginary result. But we do not need to make a real experiment because to suppose any other outcome is to deny one or more conditions of the experiment. Now the length of each plane is given by the number of balls resting on it (here, 4:2), so the force needed to balance any ball varies inversely with the length of the plane.

This illustrates nine features shared by most thought experiments in science and by many in philosophy:

(i) Method of abstraction: the experiment presupposes a method (determine the limiting cases (force = 0, force = weight of the ball)) then constructs an idealized intermediate case in which only two outcomes are possible.

(ii) There is a situated procedure: this is conveyed as a narrative describing a sequence of operations on simple objects, which takes place in an idealized situation (Stevin's set-up is frictionless).

(iii) Causality is important: operations are connected to outcomes by causal principles and causality is governed by simple principles such as symmetry or conservation.

(iv) Intervention is important but unproblematic: the reader/observer is involved, but is perfectly competent (the cuts in the necklace must be made perfectly simultaneously, so they are).

(v) Interpretation is constrained: the scenario is interpreted according to agreed principles (impossibility of perpetual motion).

(vi) Results are unambiguous and are usually limited to just two possibilities (the balls move, or they do not). Binary outcomes are a feature through which thought experiments expose the tension between two disparate ways of thinking about the situation.

(vii) Implications are clear: the meaning of the result is unequivocal (lack of motion implies the proportionality described above). We describe other examples below in which thought experiments generate a paradox or contradiction whose resolution requires a profound change of view.

(viii) Implications are compelling: however surprising the resolution may be, the intellectual experience engendered by a thought experiment is compelling; whether the experiment could be performed in the world seems as irrelevant as whether the story-line of a good joke is actually true.

(ix) Thus, a thought experiment always works and is easy to replicate. In this respect it differs from real experiments (excepting text-book idealizations).

A thought experiment is an idealization which transcends the particularity and the accidents of worldly human activities in order to achieve the generality and rigour of a demonstrative procedure. We argue in §4 that this effectiveness owes as much to knowledge brought to bear by a reader of the narrative as it does to the ingenuity and knowledge of the experimentalist who authored it. We note in §3 that thought experiments in philosophy are typically less constrained by situational knowledge and are open to counter-interpretation; that is, they may lack features (ii), (iii) and (v) and, therefore, (vii) as well.

2 Thought experiments in science

In Aristotelian and medieval science the narration of an experiment usually supplanted actual performance. The new experimental narratives of Francis BACON, BOYLE, Galileo GALILEI, and NEWTON discredited these speculative narratives. By the end of the seventeenth century actual performance was necessary to establish a fact. Yet thought experiments are advanced as fictions. How could they assume such an important role in the new science? A Platonist explanation advanced by Koyré is that thought experiments became central to science because they use idealizations necessary for mathematical descriptions of nature. Since nature is ultimately a rational mathematical system it is to be expected that such experiments deliver truths about reality. They work because they appeal directly to intuitive knowledge rather than empirical experience. Philosophers go on to argue that the informativeness of thought experiments is evidence for the Platonist view that human knowledge is of transcendent realities. EINSTEIN, a master of thought experiments, is often enlisted in support of this rationalist view.

The power of thought experiments as seemingly independent of publicly repeatable observations led a few empiricist philosophers, such as Pierre DUHEM (1954) and Carl HEMPEL (1965), to deny that they constitute a legitimate method of scientific investigation: at best they have an heuristic role as guides to discovery. Another empiricist interpretation is that all thought experiments are deductive arguments whose empirical content is hidden as suppressed premises. In a response to Koyré's Platonist interpretation, KUHN

(1964) argued that thought experiments can work effectively only in simulated worlds to which experimenters successfully apply their own real-world knowledge and experience. We develop this important insight further in §4. It is true that most thought experiments can be reconstructed as deductions; however, this does not show that thought experimentation is deductive. Some philosophers argue that the content of an idealization may be greater than can be expressed by a set of propositions. Thought experiments are narratives from which readers construct non-propositional mental models. The persuasiveness of such experiments does not necessarily depend on logical structure. Logic is only used afterwards, to validate conclusions reached by thinking with models.

The view that thought experiments are no more than deductions can be refuted by an example, one of Galileo's best-known objections to the Aristotelian doctrine of motion applied to falling bodies. According to Aristotle (and to untutored common sense) heavy bodies fall more quickly than light ones. Imagine that two stones, L and H, are falling. Grant the common-sense belief that H falls more quickly than L. Now imagine that H becomes attached to L. Since light objects fall more slowly, L will retard the fall of H. Yet L + H weigh more than H, so the conjoined stones must fall more quickly than H. This experiment displays all the features listed in §1. There is a narrative in which a sequence of events and interventions can cause two contradictory outcomes. The experimenter must choose. In a truly efficacious thought experiment the procedures cannot be faulted (as they routinely are in real experiments). A contradiction or paradox therefore exposes a fallacious assumption rather than incompetent practices. Here the only candidate is the postulate that velocity is proportional to weight. The problem is resolved if velocity is not affected by weight:

$$V_H = V_L = V_{H+L}.$$

This means that the accelerative force is the only relevant factor. Galileo's narrative sequence may be reconstructed as a deductive argument. However the crucial move – assenting to the proposition that '$V_H = V_L = V_{H+L}$' – cannot be *deduced* from what has gone before. It is an insight, a new way of perceiving the whole sequence of events which also creates new experimental possibilities.

After a crucial insight has been accepted, another kind of thought experiment is possible, in which material impediments such as air resistance are removed (see IDEALIZATIONS). These idealizations sometimes become real experiments as technology develops. Consider an imaginary experiment in Newton's *System of the World* in which the altitude of the point from which a cannon ball is fired becomes higher and higher so that the projectile eventually goes into orbit. Incremental steps take us from plausible, familiar circumstances and consequences to one that is impossible and implausible. Newton's purpose was to demonstrate the counter-intuitive proposition that the force that pulls a projectile back to the ground is the same force that holds the moon in orbit. Here conceivability suggests the physical possibility of artificial satellites. Viewed as a deductive argument, it presents directly the impossible consequence of applying the laws of gravitational and centripetal force to projectiles. We can reconstruct this as a deductive argument, but as a self-contained argument this is no longer an experiment.

3 Thought experiments in philosophy

Thought experiments are used widely in philosophy. Some philosophers define thought experiments to include any argument that invokes a hypothetical situation (as, for example, moral dilemmas raised by a pressing need to choose between two equally unjustifiable actions). Others hold that such arguments only appear to be experiments. Plato argued Socrates' thesis that all knowledge is recollection by means of a thought experiment in the *Meno* in which Socrates responds to a dilemma about inquiry (see PLATO §11). Someone posing a question either knows the answer (so has no need to ask) or has no knowledge of the answer (so would not recognize the answer). The questioning is therefore pointless. Meno's uneducated slave boy is asked to construct a square double the size of a given square. Does his success prove that the boy remembers mathematical knowledge that he had not realized that he possessed? Not necessarily. An alternative interpretation is that in the course of eliciting an answer, Socrates' questioning educates the boy, enabling him to solve the problem. This illustrates the point made in §1 that scientific thought experiments are less open to interpretation than are philosophical ones.

Some philosophical experiments are imaginary excursions into intriguing but impossible worlds. HOBBES' refutation of the immateriality of mind involves imagining oneself shrinking until one can wander amongst the smallest corpuscular components of the brain. Could such an observer see thoughts? Not if thoughts are due to the interactions of corpuscles. The experiment works by diverting our attention from the fact that to enter this corpuscular world is to assent implicitly to a materialist metaphysics. One can always deny the presumption on which the possibility of making the experiment

depends. If, for example, we re-interpret Plato's narrative about Meno's slave as an example of instruction, then it ceases to be a demonstration that knowledge is the recollection of eternal, transcendent truths. Because of this interpretive flexibility about central features of the narrative, philosophical thought experiments are rarely as decisive as their scientific counterparts.

The argument of Searle's Chinese Room experiment is that semantic meaning is not reducible to physical symbol-manipulation. This develops a version of Turing's behavioural test of the indistinguishability of the linguistic competence of machines and humans. Searle aims to undermine Turing's criterion of equivalence by granting to a Chinese-speaking room the capacity to do whatever is necessary to pass Turing's test (that is, solve arithmetical problems, converse about preferences, tell jokes and so on). The experiment involves examining the inner workings, especially the procedures whereby an operator inside applies rules of syntax to interpret and respond to questions. Since the operator can do this without understanding any Chinese pictogram, Searle concludes that symbol manipulation does not involve semantic understanding of this or any other language (see CHINESE ROOM ARGUMENT). Are Hobbes and Searle describing experiments? Or do their narratives have only the appearance of being experimental? These exercises expound the consequences of a metaphysical position. It is difficult to see that they test it in the way that Galileo's experiment (see §2) tests Aristotle's theory of motion.

4 Further issues

A thought experiment constructed by an ill-informed experimenter may persuade, but it will also mislead if it is not constrained in the way that thought experiments in mathematics and physics are. This is why similarities between armchair experiments and scientific ones should not be pressed too far. The constraints are illustrated by an armchair refutation of Einstein's principle that no signal can travel faster than light. Imagine that a rigid rod is extended upwards from the surface of the rotating earth. The velocity of its tip will eventually exceed the speed of light. However this logical necessity has no physical relevance. Physicists deny the possibility of such an experiment, pointing to the fact that, as material from the earth is used to extend the rod, the velocity of rotation must decrease. The experiment indicates ignorance of the relevant physical laws. A further example illustrates the importance of knowing how to apply such knowledge consistently. What happens to a very small hole bored through a large metal ring when the latter is heated: does the hole get larger or smaller? A would-be experimenter needs to know both that heating causes expansion and how to apply this fact to the ring. What is needed is a combination of empirical knowledge and the ability to reason with it. This fact opens the way for an answer to our opening question about the informativeness of imaginary experiments.

Can the mysterious efficacy of thought experiments be explained? We approach this by addressing two further questions:

(1) What distinguishes this kind of mental activity as experimentation rather than hypothetical reasoning? If a thought experiment is a purely mental affair then it cannot be an experiment at all. If it is not a purely mental affair then there is no paradox. Naturalism argues that personal participation – represented by items (ii)–(iv) in §1 – is what makes a thought experiment more than a hypothetical argument. (This is why we perform experiments but do not 'perform' an argument.) A thought experiment is effective if it is both logically well-formed and empirically informed about relevant features of the world it purports to investigate. It expresses the minimum set of conditions necessary to sustain the appearance of an argument of some generality, whilst giving the appearance of the situated-ness that real experiments actually have.

(2) Does an informed thought experiment express tacit knowledge or intuitively apprehended principles? Empiricists have argued that thought experiments articulate and apply intuitions formed from human experience. Ernst MACH appealed to DARWIN's principle of natural selection to guarantee that these intuitions adequately represent the world: natural selection favours those minds which successfully imitate causal patterns in nature. This explanation embeds experiment in the world but it does not go far enough. Naturalistic explanations emphasize cognitive capacities and culturally transmitted knowledge (see NATURALIZED PHILOSOPHY OF SCIENCE). Such capacities and knowledge enable abstraction. The degree of abstraction possible in a thought experiment depends on how much both its author and its readers have participated in the culture of the experiment. In this respect thought experiments have much in common with jokes. Both are sparse, carefully crafted, narratives which include only essential details. There is a punch-line requiring an insight which changes our understanding of the story. In both cases we see the point without its being articulated as an argument. Yet philosophers do not appeal to intuition or sense experience to explain how people understand jokes. Thought experiments are powerful because they appeal to lived experience of a world which their narratives reflect, selectively, back at us.

See also: EMPIRICISM; EXPERIMENT; RATIONALISM; SCIENTIFIC METHOD

References and further reading

Brown, J.R. (1991) *The Laboratory of the Mind: Thought Experiments in the Natural Sciences*, London: Routledge. (An accessible account of influential thought experiments in physics and mathematics; defends the rationalist interpretation advanced by Koyré, described in §2.)

* Duhem, P. (1954) *The Aim and Structure of Physical Theory*, Princeton, NJ: Princeton University Press. (Originally published in the *Revue de Philosophie* 4, 1904; 5, 1904; and 6, 1905. Duhem's rejection of thought experiments for scientific investigation.)

Gooding, D. (1993) 'What Is *Experimental* about Thought Experiments?', in D. Hull, M. Forbes and K. Okruhlik (eds) *PSA 1992*, East Lansing, MI: Philosophy of Science Association, vol. 2, 280–90. (Develops a naturalistic resolution of the paradox generated by approaching thought experiments from either a rationalist or an empiricist standpoint.)

* Hempel, C.G. (1965) *Aspects of Scientific Explanation*, London: Macmillan, and New York: Free Press. (Reproduces some fifteen previously published essays, with commentary, blending and revision. The title essay is original. Hempel, like Duhem, rejects the legitimacy of thought experiments in scientific investigation.)

Horowitz, T. and Massey, G.J. (eds) (1991) *Thought Experiments in Science and Philosophy*, Savage, MD: Rowman & Littlefield. (Essays in the analytical tradition illustrating the variety of thought experiments in philosophy, logic, mathematics and various sciences.)

* Kuhn, T.S. (1964) 'A Function for Thought Experiments', in *L' aventure de la science, Mélanges Alexandre Koyré*, Paris: Hermann, vol. 2, 307–34, 2 vols; repr. in T.S. Kuhn *The Essential Tension*, Chicago, IL: University of Chicago Press, 1977, 240–65. (This influential essay argues that thought experiments bring about major changes of viewpoint by using tensions between conceptual schemes to expose anomalies; that is, inconsistencies in the way that one of the schemes relates to the world.)

Sorensen, R.A. (1992) *Thought Experiments*, Oxford: Oxford University Press. (An accessible comprehensive study, containing many examples, which develops an empiricist explanation of the efficacy of thought experiments as limiting cases of ordinary experiments.)

Tiles, J.E. (1993) 'Experiment as Intervention', *British Journal for the Philosophy of Science* 44: 463–75. (Develops the argument in §2 that the new science of Bacon and others forced a distinction between the passive observation of mental narratives and the active interventions of experimental ones, giving rise to the distinction between thought experiments and real-world experiments).

DAVID GOODING

THOUGHT, LANGUAGE OF

see LANGUAGE OF THOUGHT

THRASYMACHUS (late 5th century BC)

Thrasymachus, a Greek Sophist and orator, is known principally for his role in book 1 of Plato's Republic, in which he argues that justice is simply a social institution created by rulers to further their own interests. It is intended solely for the subjects; the rulers themselves need not practise it. Since justice thus consists in promoting another's advantage rather than one's own, injustice is far more profitable. Apart from issues of internal coherence, his claims raise many questions. What, for example, are our true interests? And what are the actual and ideal operations of power?

Very little is known of Thrasymachus' life. He was a teacher of rhetoric, of an apparently aggressive disposition, although Plato's portrait may be distorted by anti-Sophistic bias (see SOPHISTS). In the *Republic* (see PLATO §14) he makes two main speeches, and it is debated whether their claims are compatible. In the first he declares that what we call justice is simply the interest of the stronger: in every city the stronger wield political power and make the laws in their own interest, calling obedience to these laws 'justice'. Whether the government is tyrannical, aristocratic or democratic, the institution of justice is merely a cover for *force majeure*. This legalistic conception of justice, however, is modified when Thrasymachus adds that obedience to the laws will only constitute justice when the laws really are in the interests of the rulers, since the rulers may be mistaken about where their advantage lies.

In his second speech Thrasymachus extends the discussion to include private as well as political relations. What we term injustice is simply the pursuit of self-interest, and pays the individual far better than justice. He boldly suggests that injustice is positively a virtue (*aretē*), the virtue of common sense. The unjust are prudent and admirable; the just are naïve fools. Indeed, we partially admit this: although we criticize and punish petty wrongdoers, when injustice is practised on a sufficiently grand scale by, say, a tyrant, we merely call the tyrant fortunate. We would all be tyrants if we could.

These two positions may appear at odds. If justice is simply the interest of the stronger, then surely the tyrant who supremely promotes his self-interest is supremely just? Yet Thrasymachus clearly states that the tyrant is supremely *un*just. Some have argued that he is operating with two notions of justice, conventional and natural (see CALLICLES), but a simpler reading suggests that a conventional description is retained throughout. Injustice is ruthlessly promoting your own desires at the expense of others; justice is giving others their due. In theory each can be practised by both rulers and ruled (as Thrasymachus admits in his second speech); in practice, however, opportunities for injustice will chiefly be available to the rulers, whereas the ruled will generally have to accept the imposition of justice. The initial statement that justice is the interest of the stronger is therefore not to be taken as a complete definition, but as a description of how justice operates in the world of *realpolitik*.

Thrasymachus does, however, complicate his position by admitting that the practice of injustice may sometimes be an unsuccessful means of satisfying one's desires (one may get caught and imprisoned), and this leaves open the possibility that in some circumstances justice would be the more prudent course of action. His implicit ideal is the person who successfully promotes their own interests. This will often involve acting unjustly, but not necessarily always – a key consideration will be one's political status. Underlying the ideal is a notion of human flourishing seen in terms of material wealth, autonomy and power.

Thrasymachus' position thus goes deeper than its superficial cynicism might suggest. But does his ideal carry with it any notion of moral obligation? The answer depends on how one interprets (1) his use of the word 'virtue', and (2) his claim that everything normally predicated of justice should in fact be predicated of injustice. Whether he is prescribing or simply commending his ideal, however, the practical implications remain unclear. If the rulers fare so much better than the ruled, is he advocating that the ruled seize power? Or that they embark on a programme of mass disobedience? Or is he just recommending opportunism? Whatever the answer, it is plain that his doctrines could be used to endorse all these possibilities, plus tyranny and imperialism, as THUCYDIDES shows. It is because of this that Plato takes his challenge so seriously in the *Republic*.

It is also debated whether Thrasymachus actually endorses the doctrines he voices. The ambiguous tone of his responses to Socrates precludes certainty, but it is possible (and may be supported by a separate fragment) that his attitude is that of the embittered and disillusioned moralist, ironically praising injustice because justice no longer pays. His intention may be simply to expose current hypocrisies, rather than to applaud their manipulation.

See also: ANTIPHON; PHYSIS AND NOMOS

References and further reading

Chappell, T.D.J. (1993) 'The Virtues of Thrasymachus', *Phronesis* 38: 1–17. (A crisp and stimulating discussion.)

Guthrie, W.K.C. (1969) *A History of Greek Philosophy*, vol. 3, Cambridge: Cambridge University Press; part of vol. 3 repr. as *The Sophists*, Cambridge: Cambridge University Press, 1971. (Thoughtful discussions of Thrasymachus, especially pages 294–8.)

Kerferd, G.B. (1947–8) 'The Doctrine of Thrasymachus in Plato's Republic', *Durham University Journal* 40: 19–27; repr. in C.J. Classen (ed.) *Sophistik*, Darmstadt: Wissenschaftliche Buchgesellschaft, 1976, 545–63.(A classic study; lucid and exhilarating.)

— (1981) *The Sophistic Movement*, Cambridge: Cambridge University Press. (The best introductory handbook to the Sophists in general; for Thrasymachus see especially pages 120–3.)

* Plato (*c*.380–367 BC) *Republic*, trans. H.D.P. Lee, Harmondsworth: Penguin, 1955; repr. 1974. (Book I is our main source on Thrasymachus.)

Sprague, R.K. (ed.) (1972) *The Older Sophists*, Columbia, SC: University of South Carolina Press, 86–93. (Full English translation of the fragments and testimonia from Diels and Kranz (1952).)

* Thrasymachus (late 5th century BC) Fragments, in H. Diels and W. Kranz (eds) *Die Fragmente der Vorsokratiker* (Fragments of the Presocratics), Berlin: Weidemann, 6th edn, 1952, vol. 2, 319–26. (The standard collection of the ancient sources; includes Greek texts with translations in German.)

ANGELA HOBBS

THUCYDIDES (*fl. c.*400 BC)

A Greek historian with philosophical interests, Thucydides wrote about the Peloponnesian War between Athens and Sparta (431–404 BC). He elaborates on the decisions of war in brilliantly reconstructed debates and speeches, reflecting his training under various Sophists. Many of these speeches take for granted that people care less for justice than for their own narrow interests. This dark view of human nature influenced Hobbes, while the style of the debates and speeches has had an enduring effect on public rhetoric. His account of Athenian democracy in action is cautionary, and his conservative political views anticipated Aristotle's in some respects.

A wealthy Athenian, Thucydides served as general in 424 BC, but failed to prevent the Spartan capture of an important outpost and was punished by exile. He did not return to Athens until after its defeat in 404. Beginning work on his *History of the Peloponnesian War* during this exile, he brought his account up to the year 411, at which point it breaks off. The dates of his birth and death are not known, but it is likely that he was born between 460 and 455 and died early in the fourth century BC. He is said to have studied with the sophist Antiphon and the natural philosopher Anaxagoras, and it seems likely that he also learned style and argument from other Sophists such as Protagoras (see SOPHISTS). His *History* is unusual in that nearly one fourth of the text consists of speeches and debates. These are all composed in Thucydides' style and display methods of argument taught by Sophists. Pericles' funeral oration is especially well known, with its reflections on the culture and constitution of Athens. Thucydides states his own views sparingly, 'having', as Hobbes puts it, 'so clearly set before men's eyes the ways and events of good and evil counsels, that the narration itself doth secretly instruct the reader' (Schlatter 1975: 18).

On human motivation, Thucydides' views are no secret. Fear, ambition and avarice dominate his explanations of events. Expansion of the Athenian empire is due to these factors; this expansion put fear into the Spartans which drove them to start the war. Thucydides' description of the plague at Athens in 430 BC shows how badly he believes people behave when they no longer have any reason to fear the laws. He sounds a similar theme in his account of a civil war on the island of Corcyra between the parties of 'the many' and the 'few', that is, the democrats and the oligarchs. These combatants were led by avarice and ambition to commit violent acts that they justified by a reversal in their use of moral language; the results included all sorts of betrayal, revenge and the slaughter of prisoners. Human nature, Thucydides believed, will overcome the effects of law whenever a breakdown of authority gives it the opportunity.

The same principle is at work in international affairs. Neither Athens nor Sparta considers justice when deciding how to treat its neighbour states. When the Athenians decide not to slaughter the people of Mytilene, whose rebellion they have just put down, they do so from a calculation of their own advantage. Justice, the Athenians believe, is relevant only when both parties are equally subject to authority. The Athenians do in each case what they deem necessary for the survival of their empire, and go so far as to conquer the harmless island of Melos and execute its male population for this reason. Although Sparta claims to support justice, it too destroys a city and its people out of self-interest.

Thucydides' dark view of human nature explains the value he places on maintaining a stable system of law and fending off radical democracy, which, in his view, leads to lawlessness. Thucydides praises Pericles for ruling like a monarch in Athens when it was a democracy 'in name only'. Much later, when Athens blundered into war with Syracuse, it was defeated by the conservative leadership of Hermocrates, which Thucydides contrasts with the foolish partisanship of the democrat Athenagoras. Conservative democracy was the strength of Syracuse, but democracy after Pericles did not serve Athens well. The best sort of constitution, according to Thucydides, is neither democracy nor oligarchy but 'a moderate blending of the interests of the few and many', in which neither party is allowed to make gains at the expense of the other.

The methods of argument displayed in the *History* are as important as the views expressed. Historiographers are interested in the manner in which Thucydides constructs an account of prehistoric Greece using myth, poetry, archaeology, local traditions and analogies with primitive peoples of his own time. Here and in the speeches he makes use of a type of inference known as *eikos* ('probable' or 'reasonable expectation'). Thucydides' speakers often argue in favour of actions they believe it is necessary (*ananke*) for them to take in view of the outcome they think it is reasonable to expect (*eikos*). Such a speaker is frequently contradicted either by the outcome (which is often unexpected) or by another speaker making an equally powerful argument for the other side. Reasoning on such matters is what philosophers now call *defeasible*; it holds only for normal conditions and is defeated by unexpected abnormalities. Alcibiades, for example, predicts that when the Athenian army reaches Syracuse the people there will be divided, owing to their complex cultural heritage, and so more easily defeated. Such a strategy worked for Athens in cities where civil war was the norm. Syracuse, however, was exceptionally stable owing to the conservative leadership of its democracy; the city did not divide and it was not conquered. Unusual circumstances defeat arguments based on reasonable expectations, and this pattern is illustrated throughout the *History*. Thucydides' opposed pairs of speeches, as well as his frequent oppositions of speech and event, illustrate not only his theory of motivation but also kinds of reasoning, good and bad, that were current in the teaching of the sophists.

See also: PHYSIS AND NOMOS

List of works

Thucydides (*fl. c.*400 BC) *History of the Peloponnesian War*, trans. R. Crawley, London, 1876, revised by R. Feetham, Chicago, IL, 1910; trans. B. Jowett, *Thucydides, History of the Peloponnesian War*, 1881, revised by S. Hornblower, 3rd edn, 1995. (Crawley is the most admired and widely used translation; the Jowett translation reflects recent scholarship.)

References and further reading

Connor, W.R. (1984) *Thucydides*, Princeton, NJ: Princeton University Press. (The most thorough modern treatment.)

Farrar, C. (1988) *The Origins of Democratic Thinking*, Cambridge: Cambridge University Press. (Substantial discussion of Thucydides' importance to political thought.)

Hornblower, S. (1988) *Thucydides*, London: Duckworth. (Contains a useful discussion of Thucydides' views.)

Orwin, C. (1994) *The Humanity of Thucydides*, Princeton, NJ: Princeton University Press. (A discussion of Thucydides as a political thinker.)

Ostwald, M. (1988) *ANANKE in Thucydides*, American Classical Studies 18, Atlanta, GA: Scholars Press. (A brilliant study of Thucydides' views and method.)

* Schlatter, R. (1975) *Hobbes' Thucydides*, New Brunswick, NJ: Rutgers University Press. (Hobbes' famous translation of 1629, still the most vigorous in English.)

PAUL WOODRUFF

TI AND YONG

Ti *and* yong *(literally 'body' or 'substance' and 'use' or 'function') are technical terms in Chinese philosophy. Ti often is used to denote the essence or fundamental nature of a given thing, for example, 'the substance/true essence of the Way'. As a verb, it can also mean to 'embody' or 'instantiate' a given characteristic or virtue, for example 'to embody/fully realize humanity'. A thing's* yong *is its characteristic activity in accordance with its nature.*

Neo-Confucians made extensive use of the idea that the universe was – like the parts of a single individual – 'one body'. Those who realize this, both in the sense of cognitively assenting to this proposition as true as well as appreciating its moral implications, will feel an injury to another (in some cases even to inanimate objects) as an injury to their own bodies. The notion of 'one body' was also used in a related but distinct sense to describe phenomena which, while logically distinguishable, cannot actually exist apart from one another: in Chapter 15 of the *Platform Sutra*, a lighted lamp and its light are said to be 'one body' (see PLATFORM SUTRA). This recalls Aristotle's distinction between phenomena which are by definition distinct but by nature inseparable, such as concave and convex in the circumference of a circle.

The first occurrence of *ti* and *yong* as a conceptual pair occurs in Wang Bi's commentary on the thirty-eighth chapter of the *Daodejing*, where he uses it to discuss the *ti* (essence) of things and their *yong* (characteristic functions). Here, and in other passages, the *yong* of a thing is not simply what a given thing happens to be doing; there is a normative aspect to the notion. It is thus not wholly unlike Aristotle's use of the term *ergon* (see ARISTOTLE §22). It is what that thing will do according to its particular *ti* (essence) when allowed to operate freely in an environment conducive to its natural functioning. Thus, in the passage from the *Platform Sutra* quoted above, the *yong* of a lighted lamp is to emit light; or as Chen Chun says, 'That which is one whole within is the substance; its response when stimulated is the function' (Graham 1992: 40).

The pair *ti* and *yong* are used extensively by neo-Confucian thinkers in the normative sense mentioned above. Thus, in his commentary on *Analects* 1.2, ZHU XI says, 'Humanity is human nature, filial piety and brotherly respect are its *yong* "function"'. On *Analects* 1.12, he cites an earlier commentator who says, 'The *ti* "substance" of all rituals rests in reverence but in their *yong* "application" harmony is valued'.

Later Confucian thinkers tried, unsuccessfully, to deploy the two concepts to effect a synthesis or at least a symbiosis of Chinese and Western culture. The first and best-known example of such attempts was that of Zhang Zhidong (1837–1909), who coined the slogan, 'Chinese learning for *ti* "substance" and Western learning for *yong* "utility"' (Levenson 1965: 60): traditional Chinese culture was to serve as the fundamental basis for a modern Chinese society that adopted Western technology and ideas, but only for their efficacy. However, since the *ti* and *yong* of any given thing are inextricably related to one another, there was no hope of ever separating them in the way Zhang suggested.

See also: DAODEJING; NEO-CONFUCIAN PHILOSOPHY; PLATFORM SUTRA

References and further reading

* Graham, A.C. (1992) *Two Chinese Philosophers*, La Salle, IL: Open Court. (Contains very helpful discussions and illustrations of both terms; see the index under *t'i* and *yung* (substance and function).)
* Levenson, J.R. (1965) *Confucianism and Its Modern Fate*, Berkeley, CA: University of California Press. (Contains an excellent discussion of late nineteenth and early twentieth century Chinese attempts to apply the notions of *ti* and *yong* to meet the challenges posed by Western imperialism; see in particular chapter 4, pages 59–78.)

PHILIP J. IVANHOE

TIAN

Tian, *conventionally translated as 'Heaven', is both what our world is and how it is. The myriad things are not the creatures of* tian *or disciplined by a* tian *which stands independent of what is ordered; rather, they are constitutive of it.* Tian *is both creator and the field of creatures. There is no apparent distinction between the order itself and what orders it. This absence of superordination is a condition made familiar in related notions of the Daoist* dao *and the Buddhist* dharma, *which also refer to concrete phenomena and the order that obtains among them. On this basis,* tian *can be described as an inhering, emergent order negotiated out of the dispositioning of the particulars that are constitutive of it. In the human world,* tian *is the experience of meaningful context felt differently by each person in the fellowship of family and community.*

The conventional translation of *tian* as 'Heaven' (with a capital 'H') inappropriately conjures up the notion of transcendence, concealing precisely those aspects of the term most essential to a correct appreciation of its meaning. We can, however, make several observations that reinstate aspects of *tian* that tend to be concealed by this translation. First, the association between *tian* and the sky encourages proper notice of the profound temporality and historicity that attends this idea, frustrating any analogy one might want to find between '*tian*' and 'sky' on the one hand and 'Heaven' and 'the heavens' on the other. *Tian* is inextricably linked to the pervasive processes of change, and is understood often as an abbreviation of *tiandi* (heaven and earth), or 'the autogenerative and self-sustaining world'. The Judaeo-Christian God, often referred to metonymically as 'Heaven', *creates* the world, but classical Chinese *tian is* the world.

Tian further is not only 'the sky', but an articulated and patterned sky. *Tian* is thus defined as the 'day' and the 'skies' under which culture accumulates, rather than as some more disjunctive atemporal and aspatial 'Other', some ontologically different order of Being. Significantly, there is a continuity between the articulation of nature generally, and the inscription of human culture. The nature–nurture dualism familiar in Greek-based culture is not operative; instead, the natural world and human culture are both vigorous and continuous.

A corollary to this notion of an invigorated world is the absence of any final boundary between the sentient and insentient, animate and inanimate, living and lifeless. Since spirituality and life go hand in hand, spirituality, like life, pervades all things.

To say that spirituality and life are all-pervasive has two immediate implications. First, there is no value-neutral nature which can stand as encouragement for the pathetic fallacy. Humanity, instead of constituting a privileged link along a Chain of Being which discriminates on the basis of given ontological disparities, achieves its hierarchical cosmic role through its cultivation of a complex spirituality, where this spirituality is understood in terms of extension, influence, and inclusion. In fact, as is evident from the connotations of the character *shen*, conventionally translated as both 'human spirituality' and 'divinity', and also from entrenched cultural practices such as ancestor worship and the worship of cultural heroes such as Confucius, gods in the Chinese tradition are generally 'extended human beings' (see CONFUCIUS). *Tian* itself is the aggregate spirituality generated by a continuous culture.

Tian is 'self-so-ing' (*ziran*). There is no distinction between nature and its power of organization and generation. There is nothing antecedent to it; there is no beginning to it or end of it. *Tian* is also

anthropomorphic, suggesting its intimate relationship with the process of euhemerization that grounds Chinese ancestor worship. It is probably this common foundation in ancestor worship that allowed for the conflation of the Shang dynasty's *di* with the notion of *tian* imported with the Zhou tribes. There seems to be sufficient reason to assume that *tian*, like all Chinese gods, is by and large constituted by dead people. Culturally significant human beings – persons such as the Duke of Zhou and Confucius – ascend to become *tian*, and *tian* is itself made determinate in their persons. This is the meaning of the familiar notion, *tianren heyi* (the continuity of *tian* and humanity). Not only does *tian* entail anthropomorphism – gods are man-shaped – it also entails a 'theomorphism' – exemplary persons are god-shaped. Worthiness in the human world defines *tian*. As a narrative constituted by cultural heroes, *tian* thus is genealogical and biographical.

Tian is not only culturally specific, it is also geographical. The discovery of a new and sophisticated culture would anticipate the discovery of a *tian* representative of that culture. Just as there are many skies, one would expect other cultural traditions to have *tian* of their own.

Finally, *tian* does not speak but communicates effectively, although not always clearly, through oracles, perturbations in the climate and alterations in the natural conditions of the human world. *Tian* participates in a discourse shared by the human community: at least, by the most worthy among them. Given the interrelatedness and interdependency of the orders defining the Chinese world, what affects one affects all. A failure of order in the human world will automatically be reflected in the natural environment. Although *tian* is not a 'personal' deity responsive to individual needs as in the Judeo-Christian world view, as aggregate ancestor it would seem that *tian* functions impartially on behalf of its progeny to maximize the possibilities of emergent harmony at all levels.

See also: ANAXAGORAS §3; CHINESE PHILOSOPHY; CONFUCIAN PHILOSOPHY, CHINESE; CREATION AND CONSERVATION, RELIGIOUS DOCTRINE OF; DAO; DE; DAOIST PHILOSOPHY; GOD, CONCEPTS OF

References and further reading

Berthrong, J. (1994) *All Under Heaven: Transforming Paradigms in Confucian–Christian Dialogue*, Albany, NY: State University of New York Press. (A study of the critical issues which arise from the confrontation between modern interpretations of Confucian philosophy and Christian theology.)

Hall, D.L. and Ames, R.T. (1997) *Thinking From the Han: Self, Truth, and Transcendence in Chinese and Western Culture*, Albany, NY: State University of New York Press. (An exploration of several central philosophical issues that illustrate the difference between Chinese and Western assumptions.)

DAVID L. HALL
ROGER T. AMES

TIBETAN BUDDHISM

see BUDDHISM, MĀDHYAMIKA: INDIA AND TIBET

TIBETAN PHILOSOPHY

*Tibetan philosophy – if we can make a rough separation between what is predominantly argument-oriented and analytical and what is more a question of ritual, devotion or vision – is best characterized as a form of scholasticism. It exhibits marked parallels with philosophy in Western medieval contexts, including a heavy emphasis on logic, philosophy of language and metaphysics, all in the service of exegesis of religious doctrine found in root texts. Just as in Western scholasticism, there is a reliance upon scripture, but within that traditional context there is also ample room for rational analysis and synthesis of potentially disparate doctrines, as well as a considerable quantity of argumentation which is a type of 'fine tuning' of Indian issues. Tibetan thinkers explored matters which are often of genuine importance in our understanding of Indian texts. In particular, in Mādhyamika Buddhist philosophy we find an important synthesis of Indian Yogācāra ideas with a relatively natural interpretation of key ideas in the literature on the Buddha-nature (*tathāgatagarbha*); we also find important debates on the nature of the two truths, the status of means of valid cognition (*pramāṇas*), and on questions of philosophical method, such as the possibility or impossibility of Mādhyamikas holding theses and themselves defending positions. Beginning with the Great Debate of bSamyas (Samyay) in the latter part of the eighth century, we find constantly recurring reflection on questions concerning the nature of spiritual realizations and the role of conceptual and analytic thought in leading to such insights. In the logico-epistemological literature, the hotly debated issues generally centre around the problem of universals, the Indian Buddhist philosophy of language and the theory of the triply characterized*

*logical reason (*trirūpahetu*). In addition, the Tibetans developed an elaborate logic of debate, an indigenous system containing many original elements unknown in or even alien to Indian Buddhist logic.*

1   Issues in Mādhyamika philosophy
2   Subschools of Mādhyamika
3   The role of conceptual understanding in spiritual realization
4   Epistemology, logic and philosophy of language

1   Issues in Mādhyamika philosophy

Tibetan Buddhist thinkers, being generally adherents of some form of the Mādhyamika, had to provide answers to the question as to what was the correct and highest interpretation of Nāgārjuna's thought and what were the erroneous interpretations and traps into which thinkers might fall when dealing with this difficult and often maddeningly ambiguous Indian philosopher (see NĀGĀRJUNA; BUDDHISM, MĀDHYAMIKA: INDIA AND TIBET). Thus, for example, the Sa-skya-pa (Sagyaba) thinker Go ram pa bSod nams seng ge (Goramba Sönam sengge, 1429–89), in a text called *lTa ba'i shan'byed* (Differentiation of the Views), polemically described three types of Mādhyamika philosophy in Tibet: (1) those which took the extreme of permanence to be the middle way; (2) those which took the extreme of annihilation to be the middle way; (3) the Mādhyamika free from extremes. The first two views are those of mistaken interpreters, while the latter is supposedly Go ram pa's own. The dGe-lugs-pa (Gelukba) thinker 'Jam dbyangs bzhad pa (Jamyang shayba, 1648–1722), in his *Grub mtha' chen mo* (Great Systems of Tenets), speaks of three sorts of erroneous view: (1) the theory of the Chinese monk Hva-shang and certain bKa'-brgyud-pa (Gagyuba) philosophers that nothing exists (*ci yang med*); (2) the voidness-of-what-is-other (*gzhan stong*) theory of the Jo-nang-pa (Jonangba); (3) the view that the Mādhyamika does not accept means of valid cognition (*pramāṇas*), does not accept anything himself on either of the two levels of truth and does not have a system of his own (*rang lugs*).

To take the first view mentioned by Go ram pa (the second one mentioned by 'Jam dbyangs bzhad pa), much of Tibetan thought was indeed strongly influenced by an indigenous version of the Mādhyamika which attempted to integrate Nāgārjuna's thought with Yogācāra and with the principal ideas in Indian texts such as the *Ratnagotravibhāga* (Differentiation of the Lineage of the [Three] Jewels), an early fifth-century text which notoriously speaks of a permanent (*nitya*), stable (*dhruva*) and eternal (*śāśvata*) Buddha-nature present in sentient beings.

This Tibetan synthesis was initially put forward by the Jo-nang-pa school, founded by Dol bu pa Shes rab rgyal mtshan (Dolbuba Shayrap gyeltsen, 1292–1361); for reasons that will become clear, the Jo-nang-pas and their successors came to be known as gZhan-stong-pas (Shendongbas), 'those who accept voidness-of-what-is-other'. The gZhan-stong-pa position had adherents in three of the four major traditions of Tibet – namely the Sa-skya, the bKa'-brgyud and the rNying-ma (Nyingma) traditions – and was championed by such major Tibetan thinkers as gSer mdog Paṇ chen Śākya mchog ldan (Serdok Panchen Shākya chokden, 1428–1507), Tāranātha (b. 1575) and many others (see MI BSKYOD RDO RJE); in the nineteenth century, with the 'rediscovery' of the Jo-nang-pa texts, it became the philosophical under-pinning of the 'nonsectarian movement' (ris med), founded by the syncretic thinker 'Jam mgon kong sprul (Jamgön gongtrul, 1813–99). Only the dGe-lugs-pa school rejected it completely and unanimously, the Jo-nang-pas being for them a sort of bête noire both politically and philosophically, against which TSONG KHA PA BLO BZANG GRAGS PA (Dzongkaba Losang dragba, 1357–1419) and his school repeatedly directed their ire.

The Jo-nang-pas and other gZhan-stong-pas relied on an adaptation of the Yogācāra theory of voidness that one finds in the Tattvārtha chapter of Asaṅga's Bodhisattvabhūmi. This they combined with the three-nature theory found in the Saṃdhinirmocanasūtra (Discourse on the Interpretation of the [Buddha's] Thought; possibly second–fourth centuries AD), the theory that things have falsely imagined natures (parikalpitasvabhāva) invented by thought and lan-guage, causally dependent natures (paratantrasva-bhāva) and an absolute or a perfected nature (pariniṣpannasvabhāva) (see BUDDHISM, YOGĀCĀRA SCHOOL OF). The combination of Yogācāra with the Ratnagotravibhāga yields the key Tibetan distinction between 'void-of-oneself' (rang stong) and 'void-of-what-is-other' (gzhan stong) that has inspired en-ormous debates in Tibetan Mādhyamika up to the present day. In brief, the fundamental gZhan-stong-pa ideas go like this for a Jo-nang-pa: the Absolute, pariniṣpannasvabhāva, whose existence enables us to avoid the nihilistic view that everything is just a complete illusion, is only void of the imagined and dependent natures: it is void of what is other than it, but is not void of itself. The imagined and dependent natures, on the other hand, are nonexistent and are void of themselves. This key stance is then fleshed out to include most of the other major currents in Indian Mādhyamika, Yogācāra, Tathāgatagarbha and even Tantric systems: for example, Nāgārjuna's arguments in the Mūlamadhyamakakārikā show only that con-ventional truths (saṃvṛtisatya) are void of themselves; the Absolute is an existent, truly established gnosis (ye shes); as in Yogācāra thought, this gnosis admits of no distinction between subject (grāhaka) and object (grāhya) and is suchness (tathatā) and the bhūtakoṭi ('limit of the real'); it is identifiable with the Buddha-nature spoken of in the Ratnagotravibhāga; Tantric principles such as the union of voidness and bliss (bde stong zung 'jug) are said to be inexplicable without this version of voidness.

Not surprisingly, the Jo-nang-pas were often criticized, especially by the dGe-lugs-pas, but also by Sa-skya-pas such as Go ram pa, as reifying the Absolute and thus transforming Buddhism into a substantialist philosophy. This is what was behind Go ram pa's charge that this school 'took the extreme of permanence as the Middle Way'. (The Mongolian dGe-lugs-pa writer Thu'u bkwan Chos kyi nyi ma (Tugen Chögyi nyima, 1737–1802) went so far as to say that the Jo-nang-pas were in effect like partisans of a type of Brahmanism.) The Jo-nang-pas thus supposedly went badly astray from Indian Mādhya-mika by adopting positive descriptions which hypos-tasized a permanent Absolute, although, in all fairness, it has to be said that this criticism largely depends on which Indian texts one emphasizes and what literature one takes as authoritative. It can be intelligently argued in defence of the Jo-nang-pas that there were Indian Mādhyamika texts, like the hymns attributed to Nāgārjuna, which did exhibit a positive, cataphatic approach not far from that of the Ratnagotravibhāga, and that Indian Mādhyamika did not consist exclusively in the negative apophatic dialectic or the insistence upon dependent origination (pratītyasamutpāda) that one finds in Nāgārjuna's Mūlamadhyamakakārikā.

2 Subschools of Mādhyamika

Tsong kha pa and his followers, the dGa'-ldan-pa (Gandenba) and then the dGe-lugs-pa school, reject this all-encompassing syncretism, arguing that Yogā-cāra and Mādhyamika are quite distinct schools, and that Tantra and the Tathāgatagarbha theories are to be interpreted along the lines of Nāgārjuna, and especially along the lines of the branch of Mādhya-mika founded by Candrakīrti, the so-called *Prāsaṅgika or Thal-'gyur-ba (Talgyurwa) school. Whereas the *Svātantrika or Rang-rgyud-pa (Rang-gyuba) philosophy of Indian Mādhyamika, attributed by Tibetans to Śāntarakṣita, Bhāvaviveka et al., had been dominant in the earlier diffusion of Buddhism in Tibet (starting in the eighth century) and had been the philosophy of the first traditions in the beginning of the second diffusion (from the eleventh century on), Tsong kha pa came squarely down on the side of the *Prāsaṅgika Mādhyamika, a school which owes much of its influence in Tibet to Pa tshab Nyi ma grags (Batsap Nyimadrak, b. 1054/55), who was the translator of Candrakīrti's *Madhyamakāvatāra* (Introduction to the Middle Way) and other works. Note that the terms *Prāsaṅgika (*thal 'gyur ba*) and *Svātantrika (*rang rgyud pa*), although frequently used in the modern secondary literature, are not clearly attested in Indian texts. This terminology to distinguish between Mādhyamika schools is Tibetan in origin and is especially found in a genre of literature which had great importance in Tibet, the hierarchical presentation of the 'systems of tenets' (*siddhānta*; *grub mtha'*) of the four Indian Buddhist schools and their various subschools.

There were numerous theories among Tibetans of the eleventh to fifteenth centuries about what the difference between *Svātantrika and *Prāsaṅgika actually came down to – indeed, the matter took on such importance that the question of how to construe the difference became one of the key issues in Tsong kha pa's thought, just as it was a key issue for his predecessors and for many of his successors. Some Tibetans had conceived of the difference between *Svātantrika and *Prāsaṅgika solely in terms of the logical forms which the two schools employed (namely, objectively valid reasons versus mere *reductio ad absurdum*); others focused on the fact that *Prāsaṅgika rejected means of valid cognition (*pramāṇas*) while *Svātantrika did not, or on the fact that *Prāsaṅgikas did not have any theses (*pakṣa*) whatsoever of their own, not even on conventional matters. (Compare 'Jam dbyangs bzhad pa's third type of erroneous Mādhyamika.) Reacting to the views of these opponents, Tsong kha pa formulated the difference as turning, above all, on a difference in ontology, in particular on the acceptance or rejection of things being in some way established with/through their own intrinsic natures (*rang bzhin*; *svabhāva*). *Svabhāva*, a key notion that Nāgārjuna and his commentators argue against, figures throughout the Tibetan presentations of the systems of Buddhist schools in the *grub mtha'* literature, but with each school adopting an ever subtler position on the question – it is only, according to Tsong kha pa, the *Prāsaṅgika branch of the Mādhyamika school which rejects it completely and unconditionally; the *Svātantrikas still hold on to a kind of rarefied version of *svabhāva*, albeit only on the level of conventional truth. The basic argumentation for this attribution turns on the *Svātantrikas' own construal of the Yogācāra three-nature theory.

The question as to precisely what a Mādhyamika denies became a major issue in Tibet. A dominant trend in Tibetan Mādhyamika thought was that promulgated by Pa tshab's disciple Zhang Thang sag pa (Shang tangsakba), Go ram pa bSod nams seng ge and others, a position which came to be known as 'the Mādhyamika free from extremes' (*mtha' bral dbu ma*) and which was often depicted as 'the view of neither being nor nonbeing' (*yod min med min gyi lta ba*). This view advocated using Mādhyamika-style arguments to show the incoherence of any and all things that one might analyse, with the result that no predication of being, nonbeing, both being and nonbeing, or neither being nor nonbeing is rationally justified. We thus have, on this interpretation of the Mādhyamika, a literal and unqualified negation of all members of the 'tetralemma' (*catuṣkoṭi*), with the purpose of thoroughly overcoming the possibility of any conceptualizations and discursive thought. This 'Mādhyamika free from extremes', it should be remarked, is a pretty fair characterization of the usual Indian position, and corresponds quite well to the way in which certain important Western authors would characterize Indian Mādhyamika. (In this sense, S. Matsumoto (1990) is certainly right to stress just how remarkable and unique Tsong kha pa was in the history of Indo-Tibetan Mādhyamika in *opposing* the fundamental position of the 'Mādhyamika free from extremes'.)

The question does, however, arise as to whether this version of the fourfold negation leads to a deviant logic, as negating nonbeing would seem to imply being, and negating the last lemma would seem to imply being or nonbeing. Tsong kha pa and his school avoid these types of unwelcome consequences by adding the modal qualifiers 'truly' (*bden par*) and 'conventionally' (*tha snyad du*) to the tetralemma, so that, for example, the first two negations end up being that things are not truly existent and not conventionally nonexistent. The tactic obviously avoids violations of logical laws. Equally, it allows the Mādhyamikas to make a clear separation between the conventional and the ultimate, so that they can argue that a thing like a pot exists (conventionally) and is established by means of valid cognition. We can thus easily hold the thesis that the pot exists, but where the Mādhyamika philosophy comes in is to show that it does not *truly* exist. Indeed, the advocates of the 'Mādhyamika free from extremes', as well as the gZhan-stong-pas, do have serious problems in accounting for conventional truths: to say, for example, that such truths merely exist for mistaken minds (*blo 'khrul ba'i ngor yod pa*) and are not established by means of valid cognition (*pramāṇas*) comes perilously close to just falling into the trap of subjectivism, where one says that things exist or have such-and-such properties when one believes that they do. (Quite a bit more than *that* is needed to explain how we can discover new things and how we can show that things which many people believe in at some particular time do not exist and have never existed even conventionally.) The issue of the acceptance or rejection of *pramāṇas* establishing conventional truths is developed at length from the fifteenth century onwards, starting with a critique of Tsong kha pa on this and other points by the Sa-skya-pa thinker sTag tshang lō tsa ba (Daktsang lodzawa, b. 1405).

It should be stressed that the logical simplicity and lucidity of Tsong kha pa's version of Mādhyamika comes at a high exegetical and philosophical price: not only is he constrained to add words everywhere to Indian texts, but, what is perhaps more serious, he can well be accused of inventing a factitious notion, 'true existence', which he then refutes as incoherent and contradictory, leaving the ordinary world intact and even reified. This was a common criticism of Tsong kha pa. Arguably, as his critics maintained (be they advocates of the 'Mādhyamika free from extremes' or gZhan-stong-pas), Nāgārjuna and his commentators were showing the utter incoherence of ordinary things themselves, and were leaving nothing whatsoever unassailed and intact among these conventional entities.

3 The role of conceptual understanding in spiritual realization

Tibetan thought on the nature of meditation and spiritual realization seems to be divided into two camps, both stemming (in very complex ways) from the Great Debate of bSam-yas (Samyay) in the latter part of the eighth century. This debate was a (year-long?) series of exchanges which are reputed to have opposed the 'Gradualist' (*rim gyis pa*) Indian Buddhism represented by Kamalaśīla and others to the Chinese 'Subitists/Simultaneists' (*cig car ba*), who were represented by Hva-shang Mahāyāna, a monk from Dunhuang holding Chan positions. The historical details of the Great Debate (which is with few exceptions depicted in Tibetan sources as having been won by the Gradualists) cannot be developed here, except to say that it now seems clear that several 'heretical' positions of Chinese, Tibetan and even Indian origin were under attack from the Kamalaśīla side.

In fact, as D. Seyfort Ruegg (1992) has insightfully remarked, the debate became a partly dehistoricized topos in the Tibetan representation of the history of their own philosophy. The bSam-yas debate and its traces were perceived to recur constantly in the form of an opposition between two models of the Buddhist path, namely mediacy versus immediacy – the path taken as a progression, where philosophical analysis and various moral practices lead step by step to awakening versus the path which is not a series of intermediate steps, but is fundamentally identical with the fruit to be attained. This latter 'path' is one where realization comes from a mode of awareness that is characterized by no mentation (*amanasikāra*; *ci yang yid la mi byed pa*), an awareness that consists in seeing or coming face to face (*ngo 'phrod*) with the nature of the mind (*sems nyid*) without reliance upon any concepts whatsoever – this realization is all we need to become enlightened at once. To take an important example of the recurrence of this debate, the thirteenth century's greatest thinker, SA SKYA PAṆḌITA (Sagya Paṇḍita, 1182–1251), makes a rapprochement between the Hva-shang side and the Tibetan tradition of Great Perfection (*rdzogs chen*) by criticizing the 'Self-sufficient White Remedy' (*dkar po chig thub*) doctrine of the bKa'-brgyud-pa scholars sGam-po-pa (Gamboba, 1079–1153) and Zhang-Tshal-pa (Shangtselba, 1123–93) as being a revival of the 'Great Perfection of the Chinese tradition' (*rgya nag lugs kyi rdzogs chen*). (Compare 'Jam dbyangs bzhad pa's first type of erroneous Mādhyamika.) Another example: for Tsong kha pa, Hva-shang becomes an exponent of a mere blank-mindedness, a kind of stupefaction where one supposedly rests virtually unconscious. This Hva-shang-style blank-mindedness is then taken to be what will ensue if, like certain 'Mādhyamikas free from extremes' who deny 'too much', one rejects all entities and all predication whatsoever and hence fails to make the proper distinction between so-called truly established things and conventional things.

What was the issue? Did the Hva-shang position lead to nothing but voluntary stupefaction, as Tsong kha pa and even some contemporary Western writers depict it? To use Ruegg's phrase, the Great Debate involved 'lattices' of related ideas, and the lattice of ideas associated with the partly dehistoricized version of the Hva-shang position involves, very noticeably, the idea of an innate nature which is in some sense already perfect and actual. Indeed, in a twelfth-century account of the Great Debate, the *Chos 'byung me tog snying po*, and in the sixteenth-century historical work the *mKhas pa'i dga' ston* (Feast for Scholars; Minzu chubanshe edition, 1986: 389; see also Ruegg 1992: 73, 86, note 164), one of the ways in which the issue is formulated is whether sentient beings are 'Buddhas from the beginning' (*dang po nas sangs rgyas*) – Hva-shang's side supposedly advocated a kind of innate version of the Buddha-nature (*tathāgatagarbha*) existing fully *ab initio*, not just as a germ or potentiality for enlightenment, but as already accomplished. (Compare, for example, the view found in the nine sorts of Great Perfection teachings described in an early work, the *bSam gtan mig sgron* (Lamp for the Eye of Meditative Absorption) of gNubs Sangs rgyas ye shes (Nup Sanggyay yayshay, tenth century): 'The nature of the Buddha, sentient beings and their objects is to be without exception enlightened in the great state of the spontaneous *dharmatā*, which is without beginning nor end' (1974: 320; see also Karmay 1988: 114).) It is not surprising, if one holds that there is a type of innate perfected nature, that the path should consist essentially in stopping thought and seeing this nature. It is also probably not very surprising that focusing on good actions along the path should seem to Subitists such as Hva-shang and others a significant distraction. Non-mentation would not be a stupefaction, where the mind is reduced to virtual insentience, but would be more like a re-cognition or 'anagnosis' (to use the phrase of Giuseppe Tucci (1980: 13)) of what was already there.

Kamalaśīla's side and its later followers of course panned this Buddhahood *ab initio* as an utter absurdity. During the Debate, for example, Ye-shes dbang-po (Yayshay wangbo) supposedly argued: 'If you accede simultaneously [to enlightenment] then why are you still doing anything; if you are a *buddha* from the beginning (*dang po nas sangs rgyas*), what then is wrong?' (*mKhas pa'i dga' ston*, 1986: 389). And elsewhere on the same page in the *mKhas pa'i dga' ston*, he is represented as criticizing the idea of 'being enlightened without having done anything' (*ci yang ma byas par 'tshang rgya ba*). All this is a kind of Gradualist common sense, but it is also somewhat unimaginative, especially so in that a number of clear-headed Tibetan and Chan philosophers devoted a lot of deep thought to this difficult subject and seem to have been quite aware of the gross absurdities into which one should not fall.

Finally, it is hard to agree with Samten Karmay (1988: 87–8) that the Subitists and Gradualists both accepted an identical version of the 'spiritual basis' (*gzhi*), and that therefore the debate turned only on questions of method. Karmay argues this because of 'correspondences' that he sees between various key terms on each side, although these correspondences are far from clear; even when the same word is used on the Gradualist and Subitist sides (for example, *tathāgatagarbha*), it is unlikely that the concept is being taken in altogether the same way. In short, the idea of some sort of innate perfected nature is a crucial issue in the Great Debate; we are not dealing just with methods. Indeed, if there is only method involved, and no question of Buddhahood *ab initio* being re-cognized, the general Subitist position becomes an almost grotesquely unintelligent method, and the criticisms by Kamalaśīla, Tsong kha pa and

others about meditation without analysis yielding a rather useless mental *tabula rasa* become difficult to avoid.

4 Epistemology, logic and philosophy of language

The major developments by Tibetans in this area are to be found in the interaction of two currents of interpretation of Dignāga and Dharmakīrti's thought (see DIGNĀGA; DHARMAKĪRTI). The first current has its origin largely in gSang-phu Ne'u-thog monastery (Sangpu Nay-utok, founded in 1073), in the works of rNgog lo tsa ba Blo ldan shes rab (Ngok lodzawa Loden shayrap, 1059–1109), Phya pa Chos kyi seng ge (Chaba Chögyi sengge, 1109–69) and their disciples. Subsequently, Phya pa's *Tshad ma'i bsdus pa* (Summaries of Epistemology and Logic) became the groundwork for the 'Collected Topics', or *bsdus grwa* (düra) literature, which furnished so much of the epistemology of the dGe-lugs school. From what we can glean of Phya pa's thought from other works in his tradition and the works of his adversaries – his own works have not survived – he combined a creative intellect with what was probably a quite lacunary knowledge of the main texts of the Indian Buddhist epistemological school: the result is not unlike what we find in certain early Chinese Buddhists, namely numerous insightful interpretations and new ideas, and, at the same time, many notions which were no doubt invented and had no actual basis in Indian texts.

The gSang-phu positions were strongly criticized by Sa skya Paṇḍita, the Tibetan who probably came closest to faithfully representing the positions of later Indian epistemology and logic. In his *Rigs gter* (The Treasure of Reasoning), we find a repeated trenchant critique of 'Tibetans' or 'Tibetans who pride themselves on being logicians' – polemical shorthand for the gSang-phu philosophers. None the less, gSang-phu thought had a persistent appeal due to what must have been its extremely seductive appearance of subtlety and rigour – indeed, as D. Jackson (1987: 137–8) points out, Śākya mchog ldan reported that in his time, in the fifteenth century, people often felt that the 'Summaries' were subtle and proven correct, while the *Rigs gter* was 'extremely rough'.

Central to the gSang-phu-ba versus Rigs-gter-ba debates was the problem of universals (see UNIVERSALS, INDIAN THEORIES OF §3). The gSang-phu side (including the dGe-lugs) maintained a type of realism where at least some universals were thought to be real entities (*dngos po*), while Sa skya Paṇḍita himself and many of his Rigs-gter-ba followers, such as Go ram pa and Śākya mchog ldan, argued for the more usual Dharmakīrtian *apoha* theory, maintaining the unreality of all universals, indeed of all objects of conceptual thought. (The *apoha* theory of language is the Buddhist explanation of the unreality of all concepts, treating a concept of *A* as a mind-invented exclusion of non-*A* (see NOMINALISM, BUDDHIST DOCTRINE OF)). Indian Buddhism's philosophy of language was thus considerably reinterpreted by the Phya-pa school, especially by the dGe-lugs-pa. The latter would find textual sources in later writers like Śaṅkaranandana, but while certain Indian Buddhists (for example, Dharmottara, Mokṣākaragupta and perhaps Śaṅkaranandana) were probably tending towards some form of realism on the question of universals, it is very difficult to see how the Tibetans' rationale for realism had much, if anything, to do with the reasonings of these Indian Buddhists. The Phya-pa school's interpretation of the Dignāgan–Dharmakīrtian version of concepts-*qua*-exclusion (*ldog pa*; *vyāvṛtti*), which they also applied to universals, logical reasons and all other mind-invented constructs, was to say that 'exclusion itself' or 'universal itself' (*spyi kho rang*) is unreal, but not all exclusions, universals, and so on, are unreal. The point probably partly turns on certain features of the Tibetan language which make this type of explanation possible. This and closely related moves, which the dGe-lugs-pas would maintain to be at the heart of 'the difficult point of the *apoha* theory' (*gzhan sel dka' gnad*), had already been criticized by Sa skya Paṇḍita himself and would be devastatingly attacked by Śākya mchog ldan.

There were also numerous Tibetan developments in epistemology which genuinely contributed to clarifying key Dignāgan and Dharmakīrtian issues: for example, the Tibetan debates on the theory of truth in Indian Buddhism, on the notion of nonperception (*anupalabdhi*), and on the use of scriptural arguments, and Tibetan positions on the question of how to interpret Dharmakīrti's proofs of the Buddha's authority. We find gSang-phu-bas and Rigs-gter-bas offering (conflicting) explanations of Dignāga's *Hetucakra* (The Wheel of Logical Reasons), in particular of the so-called 'inconclusive reason which is too exclusive' (*asādhāraṇānaikāntikahetu*), which is by far the most difficult fallacy to understand in Dignāga's system of nine reasons. We also find the gSang-phu traditions, including the dGe-lugs, accepting many of the key elements of Ratnākaraśānti's idea of 'intrinsic entailment' (*antarvyāpti*) as presented in his *Antarvyāptisamarthana* (The Justification of Intrinsic Entailment), even though these same thinkers still did not go so far as to accept the Antarvyāptivāda position that examples are dispensable in argumentation, and are only used for dullards (*rmongs pa*). There were actually very few Tibetans who considered

themselves real Antarvyāptivādins, the major possible exception being the Sa-skya-pa thinker Nya dbon Kun dga' dpal (Nyawön Güngapel, *c.* 1300–80), who is said to have espoused this view in his now lost commentary on Dharmakīrti's *Pramāṇavārttika* (Commentary on Valid Cognition).

The Phya-pa tradition, largely independently, developed a remarkably sophisticated type of debating logic, with consequences (*thal 'gyur; prasaṅga*) replacing the usual triply-characterized reasons (*trirūpahetu*) and inferences-for-others (*parārthānumāna*) of Indian Buddhist argumentation. This logic, which one finds elaborately developed in *bsdus grwa* texts, has a unique type of quantification and employs variables. The Dharmakīrtian idea of the general entailment (*vyāpti*, literally 'pervasion') between the reason and what is to be proved had presented enormous philosophical problems in Indian logic, as it was very difficult to say precisely how one was to establish or know for certain when there was *vyāpti* – *vyāpti* had to be assured by ascertaining a necessary connection (*sambandha*) between terms (see INFERENCE, INDIAN THEORIES OF §§5–6). In this debating logic, however, the epistemological questions as to how we know that there really is *vyāpti*, or that there can be no counterexamples, are of curiously minor importance; they are, in any case, separated from the purely logical matter of the truth conditions for a universally quantified statement, that is, absence of counterexamples. This is a type of progress, freeing the logical and formal matters around *vyāpti* from the probably unsolvable epistemological issues which preoccupied the Indians. Interestingly enough, the Phya-pa school and its successors, in their classifications of various types of consequences as having twelve different types of *vyāpti*, went into considerable detail on the logical connections between statements in a way which was quite unknown in India. Moreover, we see here and elsewhere a marked turn towards a formal perspective: saying, for example, that such-and-such a consequence-statement will satisfy a certain kind of *vyāpti* if it satisfies another kind is indeed an abstraction away from content to matters of form. It is, however, difficult to argue that the rules and approach of this logic represent a propositional or term logic of the sort developed by Stoic or Aristotelian philosophers, although it is certainly not opposed to classical theorems.

See also: BUDDHIST CONCEPT OF EMPTINESS; BUDDHIST PHILOSOPHY, INDIAN; BUDDHIST PHILOSOPHY, CHINESE; mKHAS GRUB DGE LEGS DPAL BZANG PO; rGYAL TSHAB DAR MA RIN CHEN

References and further reading

Cabezón, J. (1994) *Buddhism and Language: A Study of Indo-Tibetan Scholasticism*, Albany, NY: State University of New York Press. (A relatively non-technical introduction to epistemological issues.)

* dPa' bo gtsug lag phreng ba (16th century) *mKhas pa'i dga' ston* (Feast for Scholars), ed. rDo rje rGyal po, Beijing: Minzu chubanshe, 1986. (Cited in §3; the full title is *Dam pa'i chos kyi 'khor lo bsgyur ba rnams kyi byung ba gsal bar byed pa mkhas pa'i dga' ston*.)

Dreyfus, G. (1997) *Recognizing Reality. Dharmakīrti's Philosophy and its Tibetan Interpretations*, Albany, NY: State University of New York Press. (Detailed discussion of Sa-skya-pa versus dGe-lugs-pa debates on epistemology.)

* gNubs chen Sangs rgyas ye shes (10th century) *bSam gtan mig sgron* (Lamp for the Eye of Meditative Absorption), Smanrtsis Sherig Spendzod Series 74, Leh, India: N. Topgyal, 1974. (Cited in §3; excerpts are discussed in Karmay 1988. The full title is *sGom gyi gnad gsal bar phye ba bsam gtan mig sgron*.)

Gomez, L.O. (1983) 'Indian Materials on the Doctrine of Sudden Enlightenment', in W. Lai and L.R. Lancaster (eds) *Early Ch'an in China and Tibet*, Berkeley, CA: University of California Press, 393–434. (The bSam-yas debate and the role of Indian 'Subitists' such as Vimalamitra.)

* Jackson, D.P. (1987) *The Entrance Gate for the Wise*, Vienna: Arbeitskreis für Tibetische und Buddhistische Studien. (Detailed information on Sa skya Paṇḍita and his tradition.)

—— (1994) *Enlightenment by a Single Means: Tibetan Controversies on The 'Self-Sufficient White Remedy' (dkar po chig thub)*, Vienna: Österreichischen Akademie der Wissenschaften. (Expands upon the discussion in §3 about the continuation of themes from the Great Debate into certain bKa'-brgyud-pa schools.)

* Karmay, Samten Gyaltsen (1988) *The Great Perfection: A Philosophical and Meditative Training of Tibetan Buddhism*, Leiden: Brill. (A reference work on the history and principal doctrines of the Great Perfection school and on issues concerning the Subitist school in the Great Debate.)

Kuijp, L. van der (1983) *Contributions to the Development of Tibetan Buddhist Epistemology from the Eleventh to the Thirteenth Century*, Wiesbaden: Franz Steiner. (A reference work on the subject.)

* Matsumoto, S. (1990) 'The Mādhyamika Philosophy of Tsong kha pa', *Memoirs of the Research Department of the Toyo Bunko* 48: 17–47. (A vigorous argument for the importance and unique-ness of Tsong kha pa in Indo-Tibetan Mādhyamika thought.)

Mimaki, K. (1982) *Blo gsal grub mtha': Chapitres IX (Vaibhāṣika) et XI (Yogācāra) édités et Chapitre XII (Mādhyamika) édité et traduit*, Kyoto: Zinbun Kagaku Kenkyusyo. (A reference work on Tibetan philosophies and the grub mtha' literature.)

Onoda, S. (1992) *Monastic Debate in Tibet: A Study on the History and Structures of bsDus grwa logic*, Vienna: Arbeitskreis für Tibetische und Buddhistische Studien. (A reference work on the Phya-pa tradition and its successors. See page 98– on the twelve sorts of *vyāpti* mentioned in §4.)

Ruegg, D. Seyfort (1963) 'The Jo naṅ pas: A School of Buddhist Ontologists according to the Grub mtha' śel gyi me loṅ', *Journal of the American Oriental Society* 83: 73–91. (Expands upon §1; discusses the Jo-nang-pa position and its critique by the dGe-lugs-pa.)

* —— (1992) *Buddha-nature, Mind and the Problem of Gradualism in a Comparative Perspective: On the Transmission and Reception of Buddhism in India and Tibet*, London: School of Oriental and African Studies. (An important study of the bSam-yas debate and its philosophical issues.)

* Sa skya Paṇḍita Kun dga' rgyal mtshan (1182–1251) *Rigs gter* (Treasure of Reasoning), in *Sa skya pa'i bKa' 'bum, The Complete Works of the Great Masters of the Sa skya Sect of Tibetan Buddhism*, compiled by bSod nams rgya mtsho, vol. 5, Tokyo: The Toyo Bunko, 1968. (The full title is *Tshad ma rigs pa'i gter*. The text is being edited and translated into Japanese in a series of monographs by Y. Fukuda *et al.* as *Chibetto ronrigakukenkyū* (Studies in Tibetan Logic), Tokyo: The Toyo Bunko.)

Tillemans, T. (1989) 'Formal and Semantic Aspects of Tibetan Buddhist Debate Logic', *Journal of Indian Philosophy* 17: 265–97. (Expands upon §2 and §4 of this entry.)

—— (1990) 'On Sapakṣa', *Journal of Indian Philosophy* 18: 53–79. (Expands upon §4 of this entry.)

—— (1995) 'On the So-called Difficult Point of the Apoha Theory', *Asiatische Studien–Études Asiatiques* 49(4): 853–89. (Expands upon §4 of this entry.)

* Tucci, G. (1980) *The Religions of Tibet*, trans. G. Samuel, London: Routledge. (Tucci's work remains one of the best introductions to Tibetan religions.)

Williams, P. (1992) 'Non-Conceptuality, Critical Reasoning and Religious Experience: Some Tibetan Buddhist Discussions', in M. McGhee (ed.) *Philosophy, Religion, and the Spiritual Life*, Cambridge: Cambridge University Press, 189–210. (A strong philosophical defence of the Gradualist position and of the dGe-lugs critique of Hva-shang's 'blank-minded' meditation.)

Yoshimizu, C. (1993) 'The Madhyamaka Theories Regarded as False by the Dge lugs pas', *Wiener Zeitschrift für die Kunde Südasiens* 37: 201–27. (On some of the historical issues discussed in §§1–2.)

TOM J.F. TILLEMANS

T'IEN *see* TIAN

TILLICH, PAUL (1886–1965)

Tillich was one of the most influential Christian theologians of the twentieth century. Notable for his effort to translate the language of the Western religious tradition into terms comprehensible to modernity, he drew upon various secular philosophies, including Marxism, existentialism and psychoanalysis, as well as literature and the arts. In his view, these contemporary secular expressions contain the questions which theology must address. He was sometimes criticized for losing one or another aspect of Christian orthodoxy, but more often praised for making it possible to be both Christian and modern. He fled Germany in 1933, in the early days of Nazism. As an expatriated German who became an American citizen, Tillich came to understand his life as one standing 'on the boundary'. He saw himself as an interpreter, occupying the boundary between the Old World and the New, between philosophy and theology, between religious orthodoxy and humanistic secularity, and between university and church.

Tillich was an intellectual who achieved widespread popular acclaim. Even though his lectures and publications were strewn with allusions to obscure thinkers, he gained a substantial following and was frequently quoted in the popular press. His courses were immensely popular, and his sermons – delivered mostly in college chapels – met with great public approbation.

Two of Tillich's themes stand out as most influential. First was his advocacy of a broadened category of the religious. By defining religion as a person's 'ultimate concern', he was able to maintain that virtually everyone has some religious commitment. Through this conceptualization it became possible to view such twentieth-century ideologies as Nazism and Communism – as well as Americanism – as in significant respects religious perspectives. This broadened definition of religion gained wide acceptance, with sociopolitical and even judicial implications. (The US Supreme Court's definition of conscientious objection was influenced by Tillich's formulation.) Second, Tillich's persistent claim that all language about God is symbolic had great impact. Objecting to views of religious language as merely symbolic, he contended that efforts to be literal in one's talk of God are seriously deficient. By the same token, he argued that the mythic quality of religious narratives cannot be removed without detriment. Finding much American religion strongly literalistic, Tillich persistently argued the contrary view.

1 **Life**
2 **Epistemology and ontology**
3 **Revelation and God**
4 **Anxiety and faith**
5 **The doctrine of Christ**
6 **Ethics and social philosophy**

1 Life

Paul Tillich was born in the village of Starzeddel in eastern Germany (now in Poland), the son of a minister and high official of the Evangelical Church of Prussia. After studying philosophy and theology, receiving advanced degrees at Breslau (1910) and Halle (1912), he entered the ministry and became a chaplain in the German army at the outbreak of World War I. At the conclusion of the war – which was at once traumatic and transformative for him – he began an academic career, becoming a professor of philosophy and theology, first at Berlin and subsequently at Marburg, Dresden and Frankfurt. In the late 1920s he participated in a religio-political movement called 'religious socialism', which attempted to offer an ideological alternative to traditionalistic and pro-capitalist views on the one hand and fascist and communist views on the other. Tillich's *The Socialist Decision* (1933) derives from this period and is thought to be one of the first theological essays to analyse the dangers of the Nazi movement. During this period he also argued that German Christians ought to align themselves with the Jews of Germany rather than succumbing to the prevailing anti-Semitism. With Hitler's accession to power in 1933, Tillich was dismissed from his position at the University of Frankfurt; he was among the first to be removed from his state university appointment. Soon thereafter he sought refuge in the USA.

Gradually mastering the English language, Tillich spent his American career as a professor at three influential educational institutions: Union Theological Seminary at Columbia University (1933–55), Harvard University (1955–62) and the University of Chicago (1962–5). Although his involvements were therefore predominantly academic rather than churchly or political, he became widely influential as an interpreter of American culture and its religious dimension (termed by Tillich 'the depth dimension'). The English-speaking public became familiar with his earlier cultural analyses, which were frequently informed by Marxian categories, through the translated essays collected in *The Protestant Era* (1948); during his years in the USA, he produced the essays found in *Theology of Culture* (1959). Tillich's increasing engagement with psychology, principally Freudian, and his increasing use of existentialist categories were reflected in his widely read work *The Courage To Be* (1952), while his distinctive combination of ontology and ethics was displayed in *Love, Power and Justice* (1954). The most significant of his English language publications was the three-volume *Systematic Theology* (1951, 1957, 1963), the first volume of which contains many of his most penetrating contributions to philosophy and theology.

In 1960, Tillich journeyed to Japan, where he engaged in dialogues with Zen masters and other religious leaders. The trip represented the culmination of a shift in his interests from dialogue with Western secularity to dialogue with non-Western religions, a shift reflected in the slender but important volume *Christianity and the Encounter of the World Religions* (1963), and in his last public lecture, 'The Significance of the History of Religions for the Systematic Theologian', found in the posthumous collection of essays *The Future of Religions* (1966).

2 Epistemology and ontology

Like his nineteenth-century mentors, the German idealist philosophers Fichte, Schelling and Hegel, Tillich sought to discover a new path to ontology. Following the lead of his contemporary, the existentialist philosopher Martin HEIDEGGER (§2), he concluded that 'the way to ontology passes through the doctrine of man'. Reaffirming the Renaissance notion of the human as microcosmic, Tillich asserted that the structure of being can be discovered in and through us in the polarity of the 'self–world correlation'. The structures of finitude (as well as its destructive tensions) can be analysed philosophically, but finitude is not self-sufficient. Finitude has to ask about the possibility of a self-caused ground of being, beyond finitude. Such a ground can be conceived as ultimate reality or the unconditioned, but proofs for its existence fail. Indeed, argued Tillich, existence belongs to finitude and suggests limitation. If the unconditioned is real, it lies beyond the self–world correlation and is not a being which exists as an object for us as subjects. Nevertheless, ontology shares the existential anguish: it longs for an ultimate in being and meaning.

3 Revelation and God

Tillich followed Aquinas in asserting the equivalence of the ground of being and God. The modern ontological quest replaces static with dynamic categories; power and life replace being and substance as the fundamental ontological concepts. What is sought is an unambiguous power of being, an eternal life. Revelation – the ecstasy of reason – fulfils this quest. In Tillich's view, the world's religions are based upon revelation. All revelatory religious language about God, however, is symbolic; religious terminology, always experiential and drawn from finitude, can only point beyond the finite towards the transcendent reality (see RELIGIOUS LANGUAGE §3). Taken literally, it becomes idolatrous. 'God' is a symbol for the ultimate reality. Primary among the symbols constituting the theistic God is the personal symbol. For Tillich, this is an essential symbol because it authenticates the moral relationship of divinity and humanity; moral demand suggests that human beings are separated from what they essentially are and ought to be (thus God is judge). But this symbol must be balanced by a participatory symbol: the unity of spiritual presence (thus God is reconciling love). Morality and mystical experience – interpreted broadly as experiential aspects of individualization and participation – are for Tillich the two principal avenues to knowledge of God. Notable here is the way Tillich's approach to God is compatible with both fatherly and motherly symbols.

4 Anxiety and faith

In his analysis of human existence Tillich drew much from Kierkegaard and other existentialists, though describing Tillich as an existentialist theologian is misleadingly one-sided (see EXISTENTIALIST THEOLOGY §3). Like his one-time colleagues in the Frankfurt Institute for Social Research, he drew upon a wide range of psychological, sociological and philosophical analyses of the human condition, tending, however, to use as a key coordinating concept the Hegelian/existentialist theme of estrangement. In our finite freedom we find ourselves estranged from the power of being; finitude is invariably experienced in us as anxiety. Hypothetically, any one of us could obey the injunction of Jesus to 'be not anxious'; in fact, however, without the sustenance of some faith we fall into destructive despair.

Religious faith as interpreted by Tillich is a

virtually universal phenomenon, which he analysed both as gift (or passive mystical experience) and as risky moral choice (see FAITH §2). Religion, first and foremost, is the experience of being grasped by the power of an ultimate concern. All objects of such concern possess not only ultimacy or holiness but also concreteness. To the extent that they involve being grasped by ultimate reality, all faiths offer a kind of compelling self-authentication; but true faith can nevertheless be distinguished from idolatrous faith by the extent to which the concrete symbolic object of faith is perceived as pointing beyond itself to what is truly ultimate in being and meaning. These self-authenticating aspects of faith are most fully explored in Tillich's book *Dynamics of Faith* (1957), where he shows evidence of his Lutheran heritage.

The more active, willing aspect of faith is the courage of self-affirmation and the affirmation of meaning in the face of threats to our finitude. Tillich identified the principal threats as death, guilt and meaninglessness, all of which may be subsumed under the threat of nonbeing. Both the moral/personal God of theism and the all-encompassing God of mysticism have been offered as sources of the courage to be. In the face of doubts about both of these symbols, Tillich in his most radical arguments, at the end of *The Courage To Be*, proposed absolute faith. Absolute faith may be described as affirmation of the meaningfulness of individual finite existence without the symbolic moral endorsement of the theistic God, but also without a sense of mystical fusion with the divine. Following Nietzsche, Tillich appears to arrive here at a point of the death of concrete symbols for the ultimate and a quest for new symbols.

5 The doctrine of Christ

For Tillich, Christianity's primary symbol is the sacrificial life of Jesus, or the New Testament picture of Jesus as the Christ. Jesus' life, as remembered by the early church, was a pivotal point of history, a central manifestation of Spiritual Presence. Exemplifying fully the New Being – a state beyond estrangement available fragmentarily to the believer – Jesus at the same time consistently pointed beyond himself to the ultimate reality. Consequently, his life and death became the prototypical religious symbol, in relation to which other symbols can be judged.

In this approach to religious symbols, Tillich combined what he called 'Catholic substance' and 'Protestant principle'. Symbols for God are manifold; some are more powerful than others, and around ones of uncommon power, institutions and traditions gather. These symbols and their institutional embodiments grow (and they may die) in the course of historical contingencies. Symbolic content is religious or Catholic substance in the Tillichian lexicon; without it, traditions become sterile and spiritually empty. But claims are sometimes made for religious symbols that they are, or possess significant aspects of, the reality symbolized. Then they become idolatrous and even demonic and must be criticized. Such claims fail to recognize the religious principle that only God is God; only the ultimate reality can claim ultimacy. Tillich called this the prophetic or Protestant principle. This principle of criticism must be applied against all concrete religions, including Christianity itself.

In his later lectures and publications, Tillich advocated dialogue with other religions. This was not with the intent of achieving a superficial eclectic synthesis, but rather with the hope of finding convergences by plumbing the depths of each concrete tradition.

6 Ethics and social philosophy

Tillich linked moral demand and conscience with separation and individualization; he linked love and 'transmoral' conscience (the conscience that accepts forgiveness) with reunion and participation. Indeed, he insisted that love in all its forms is the drive towards the reunion of the separated. He explicitly rejected the sharp opposition of desiring love (*eros*) and self-forgetting love (*agape*) postulated by some theologians (see NYGREN, A.). Distinctions should be made, but within a broader unity; self-forgetting love seeks the good of the other in God, but is no less than desiring love the drive towards reunion. Justice, too, is encompassed in this schematism: it preserves that which is to be reunited. Tillich's high evaluation of desiring love is unique among major twentieth-century theologians. His sensitive reflections on the intricate interweavings of body and spirit will endure as permanent contributions even if he 'failed to reconcile the power of eros with the demands of justice in his private life' (Irwin 1991: 118).

If Tillich's approach to ethics appears much indebted to German idealism, so also does his social philosophy. Early cultures are thought to be characterized by a high degree of communalism, rooted in religion (in the broad sense), and are described by Tillich as archaic 'theonomies'. Modernity brings with it trends towards autonomy, with concomitant rationalization. But modern cultures tend to become increasingly sterile and empty of meaning-giving linkages. Authoritarian heteronomies arise to counteract these threats. Only in a culture in touch with its own religious depth, yet prophetically self-critical – a new theonomy – can autonomous individualization be preserved along with meaningful participation in community. In his later work, *Systematic Theology* (Volume 3) and *Christianity and the Encounter of the World Religions*, Tillich interpreted the theme of the kingdom of God as the key Christian symbol for the goal of history. This personalistic, social symbol captures the affirmation of the essential goodness of finite existence, along with a critique of the injustices of the presently existing kingdoms of this world. Although Tillich backed away from explicit commitment to socialism in his American years, he remained a steadfast critic of capitalism and the secular culture of self-sufficient finitude. He was similarly steadfast in his criticism of all forms of utopianism, whether religious or secular; nevertheless, he sought to rehabilitate the spirit of utopia, in the process suggesting a distinction relevant to liberation theology.

List of works

Tillich, P. (1959–75) *Gesammelte Werke* (Collected Works), 14 vols, ed. R. Albrecht, Stuttgart: Evangelisches Verlagswerk. (Bibliography in volume 14; the second edition of volume 14 (Berlin and New York: de Gruyter, 1990) contains an updated bibliography.)

—— (1933) *Die Sozialistische Entscheidung*, Potsdam: Protte; trans. F. Sherman, *The Socialist Decision*, New York: Harper & Row, 1977. (An analysis of Germany in the early 1930s and a defence of religious socialism as an alternative to national socialism (Nazism).)

—— (1948) *The Protestant Era*, trans. and ed. J.L. Adams, Chicago, IL: University of Chicago Press. (A translation of a number of Tillich's German-language articles.)

—— (1951, 1957, 1963) *Systematic Theology*, vols 1, 2 and 3, Chicago, IL: University of Chicago Press. (Tillich's fullest theological statement, employing the method of correlation.)

—— (1952) *The Courage to Be*, New Haven, CT: Yale University Press. (Existentialist analysis of anxiety and faith.)

—— (1954) *Love, Power and Justice*, New York and London: Oxford University Press. (Tillich's distinctive combination of ontology and ethics.)

—— (1957) *Dynamics of Faith*, New York: Harper & Row. (Analysis of what faith is and is not; valuable as an introduction to Tillich's thought.)

—— (1959) *Theology of Culture*, ed. R.C. Kimball, New York and London: Oxford University Press. (Important essays from Tillich's later period, including discussions of existentialism and psychoanalysis.)

—— (1963) *Christianity and the Encounter of the World Religions*, New York: Columbia University Press. (Tillich in dialogue with non-Western religions, especially Buddhism.)

—— (1987–93) *Main Works/Hauptwerke*, 6 vols, gen. ed. C.H. Ratschow, Berlin and New York: Evangelisches Verlagswerk and de Gruyter. (A simultaneously published critical edition of the collected works of Tillich in the original language (German or English).)

References and further reading

Adams, J.L. (1965) *Paul Tillich's Philosophy of Culture, Science, and Religion*, New York: Harper & Row. (An authoritative interpretation by a close associate, covering Tillich's works written before 1945.)

Adams, J.L., Pauck, W. and Shinn, R.L. (eds) (1985) *The Thought of Paul Tillich*, San Francisco, CA: Harper & Row. (Essays on different aspects of Tillich's thought by recognized scholars.)

Carey, J.J. (ed.) (1984) *Theonomy and Autonomy: Studies in Paul Tillich's Engagement with Modern Culture*, Macon, GA: Mercer University Press. (A collection of essays sponsored by the North American Paul Tillich Society.)

Gilkey, L. (1990) *Gilkey on Tillich*, New York: Crossroad Publishing. (An appraisal of Tillich, including personal recollections, by a younger contemporary on the faculty at the University of Chicago, now a major theologian.)

Hopper, D. (1967) *Tillich: A Theological Portrait*, Philadelphia, PA: J.P. Lippincott. (A summary view of the man and his work for the non-specialist.)

* Irwin, A.C. (1991) *Eros Toward the World: Paul Tillich and the Theology of the Erotic*, Minneapolis, MN: Fortress. (Traces the theme of *eros* in Tillich's writings and brings Tillich into dialogue with feminist theology.)

Kegley, C.W. (ed.) (1952) *The Theology of Paul Tillich*, New York: Pilgrim, revised edn, 1982. (Contains a collection of interpretive essays, autobiographical reflections and a reply to the essays by Tillich, and a complete bibliography of Tillich's writings.)

O'Meara, T.A. and Weisser, C.D. (eds) (1964) *Paul Tillich in Catholic Thought*, Dubuque, IA: Priory. (Essays on the theme, with an afterword by Paul Tillich.)

Pasewark, K.A. (1993) *A Theology of Power: Being Beyond Domination*, Minneapolis, MN: Fortress Press, 236–336. (Detailed analysis of Tillich's approach to 'power', exploring its ontological and ethical dimensions.)

Pauck, W. and Pauck, M. (1976) *Paul Tillich: His Life*

and Thought, vol. 1, *Life*, New York: Harper & Row. (The standard biography of Tillich; volume 2 was never published.)

Rowe, W.L. (1968) *Religious Symbols and God: A Philosophical Study of Tillich's Theology*, Chicago, IL: University of Chicago Press. (A representative philosophical study of Tillich focusing on the doctrine of God and the theory of religious symbols.)

Scharlemann, R.P. (1969) *Reflection and Doubt in the Thought of Paul Tillich*, New Haven, CT: Yale University Press. (A closely reasoned exploration of theological themes such as correlation and paradox in Tillich's work.)

Stumme, J.R. (1978) *Socialism in Theological Perspective: A Study of Paul Tillich, 1918–1933*, Missoula, MT: Scholars Press. (A careful study of Tillich's religious socialism, with primary and secondary bibliography.)

Tillich, H. (1973) *From Time to Time*, New York: Stein & Day. (Memoirs and reflections by Tillich's wife, Hannah.)

GUYTON B. HAMMOND

TILLOTSON, J. *see* CAMBRIDGE PLATONISM; LATITUDINARIANISM

TIME

Time is the single most pervasive component of our experience and the most fundamental concept in our physical theories. For these reasons time has received intensive attention from philosophy. Reflection on our ordinary-tensed language of time has led many to posit a relation of metaphysical importance between time and existence. Closely connected with such intuitions are claims to the effect that time is unlike space, and in deep and important ways.

The development of physical theories from Newtonian dynamics through relativistic theories, statistical mechanics, and quantum mechanics has had a profound effect on philosophical views about time. Relativity threatens the notion of a universal, global present, and with it the alleged connections of time to existence. The connection between temporal order and causal order in relativity theories, and between the asymmetry of time and entropic asymmetry in statistical mechanics, suggest various 'reductive' accounts of temporal phenomena.

Finally, the radical differences between time as it appears in our physical theory and time as it appears in our immediate experience, show important and difficult problems concerning the relation of the time of 'theory' to the time of 'our immediate awareness'.

1 **Time and existence**
2 **Relationism and its problems**
3 **Time in relativistic theories**
4 **Time and causation**
5 **Time in experience and time in nature**

1 Time and existence

There is much philosophical debate about the degree to which the temporality of the world is like or unlike its spatiality. All agree that space and time differ in their dimensionality, and all agree, even in a relativistic context, that the temporality of the world is not a spatial dimension. Spatial and temporal aspects of the world are, for example, differentially interconnected with causal features.

One aspect that distinguishes time from space is the intuitive asymmetry of the former, unmatched by any related feature of the latter. While there is debate about what this asymmetry consists in, and how it is connected to other features of the world such as entropic asymmetry, there is not much question that it is uniquely characteristic of the temporal structure of the world (see THERMODYNAMICS §§4–5).

But that distinction alone is often thought insufficient to capture the special nature of time. Expressions such as the 'flux' or 'flow' of time are often invoked metaphorically to capture what is intended, as in Bergson's treatment of temporality (see BERGSON, H.-L. §2). McTaggart (1934) distinguished between those aspects of time that could be characterized using timeless temporal relations (such as one event being after another), called by him the B-series, and those aspects of time that were expressed in tensed discourse, called by him the A-series. It was McTaggart's contention that only the A-series captured the essence of temporality, but that since this essence was self-contradictory, time was 'unreal' (see McTAGGART, J.M.E. §2).

The core of such claims lies, perhaps, in the intuition expressed by St Augustine that while being elsewhere than here hardly reduced the reality of an object, that which was not presently existing had no genuine existence at all (see AUGUSTINE §6). Other versions of this line take it that only past and present have 'determinate reality', the future, not yet having come into being, having no genuine determinate reality at all.

An important response to such ideas argues that

there is no ultimate distinction in 'reality' between the present as contrasted with the past and future or between the present and past as contrasted with the future. This approach admits that past and future do not 'exist', of course, if 'exist' is being used in its tensed form, but finds in that only an interesting feature of natural language (having tensed-verb forms but no parallel structure for spatial location) and not anything of metaphysical importance.

McTaggart's claim that tensed expressions cannot be translated into tenseless ones, since the former have truth-values that vary with time and the latter do not, is admitted, but the proponents of the view that nothing metaphysical is represented by tense take it that this shows only that tensed discourse has an ineliminable 'token reflexive' or 'indexical' nature. To say 'x occurred' is to say 'x occurred before *now*'. 'Now' is a term whose reference varies with its use, since it refers to any moment of time at which it is uttered. Only this implicit indexicality, it is claimed, distinguishes tensed from untensed discourse, not some ability of the former but not the latter, to capture the essential metaphysical nature of time.

Those who reject this line offer several ways of trying to express what they think is missing in its account. Tense logics and models of splitting worlds (with the past as unique and the future as still offering manifold possibilities) are one approach. Others note the analogy with modal logic where the actual world is (in most accounts) metaphysically distinguished in its reality from the other possible worlds, much as the present is, allegedly, distinguished in its reality from other temporal moments of past and future (see TENSE AND TEMPORAL LOGIC §6). The analogy goes only so far, however, since each moment of time is, when it is the present, the moment of reality. Formulating a full-fledged metaphysical perspectivalism that would capture the essence of the metaphysical claims of those who think time is specially connected with existence has proven a difficult task.

2   Relationism and its problems

Just as in philosophical explorations of space, the idea that time can be considered as nothing but a structured family of relations of material events is an important one (see SPACE §3). The doctrine is, perhaps, already implicit in Aristotle's description of time as 'the measure of motion' and becomes explicit in Leibniz's full-fledged relationism for space and time (see LEIBNIZ, G.W. §11).

One question that immediately arises in a relationist perspective is whether there could be passage of time without change (see CHANGE §2). One response to this is to introduce modality into the discourse. Just as empty space can be thought of as given by unactualized possibilities of spatial relations, so one might think of time intervals without actual change as given by possible but not actual changes. Important insights are contained in Shoemaker's notion of limits to situations themselves relationally acceptable (such as the limit of a sequence of ever-larger regions of the universe that abide without change) (Shoemaker 1969).

Newton introduces novel elements into the philosophical discussion in his insistence on 'absolute time' to accompany space as reference frame for absolute inertial motions (see NEWTON, I. §3). Many relationists like to think of the time interval as being arbitrarily specified by any periodic process. Newton emphasizes the distinction between the ideal process and any actual one. More importantly his theory, with its notion of distinguished absolutely uniform motions, presupposes that uniformity of time interval is fixed by physical processes other than arbitrarily chosen periodic processes. Without an absolute notion of equality of time interval the absolute notion of uniformity of motion is incoherent.

Within contemporary relativistic theories the issue of the adequacy of a relationist account of time becomes absorbed into the more general issues concerning the opposition between relationistically and substantivally interpreted spacetime theories (see RELATIVITY THEORY, PHILOSOPHICAL SIGNIFICANCE OF §§5–7).

3   Time in relativistic theories

The introduction of the novel conceptualization of space and time forced upon us by the theories of special and general relativity once again illustrates the crucial interdependence of philosophical and physicist thought in this area.

In the special theory of relativity, the notion of simultaneity for events spatially separated from one another, and with it the time interval between any two separated non-simultaneous events, becomes relative to a chosen inertial reference frame (see RELATIVITY THEORY, PHILOSOPHICAL SIGNIFICANCE OF §2). There is no longer a global 'now' that selects one and the same set of events for all observers, no matter what their state of motion relative to one another. Such a relativization of the notion of time is not to be confused with the relationist conception of time described above. With the advent of special relativity one has the beginning of the radical divergence between our intuitive notions of time and those posited by physical theories.

It is often claimed that within the relativistic picture the doctrines that connect existence with temporality (as discussed above) are no longer viable. If what is present and what is past can vary from observer to observer, then how can one maintain that past and future (or, alternatively, future alone) have no genuine reality? A frequent claim is that relativity forces upon us the view of the timelessness of existence contrasted with the 'essentially tensed nature of existence' theories.

As is so often the case, however, such an inference from physics to philosophy is premature. One could, for example, relativize one's notion of existence, thus claiming that past and future are unreal, but that events unreal for one observer can be real for another observer itself real to the first. Alternatively, one could utilize only invariant spacetime features in the account. In one version of this approach the past remains real at a spacetime point-event, in the sense of the past light-cone at the point-event constituting the real (see RELATIVITY THEORY, PHILOSOPHICAL SIGNIFICANCE OF §1). In another version reality is collapsed even more radically than in the Augustinian view, so that what is real at a place–time is only that unextended point place–time and its features.

General relativity, with its dynamic spacetime, makes matters even more peculiar. Models of the world in this theory exist with closed timelike curves. In such a world an event can be (globally) in its own past and future (see TIME TRAVEL). Such possibilities led Kurt Gödel (1949) to assert that time was 'ideal' and that the '*t*' parameter of physics did not stand for time at all.

4 Time and causation

Various claims have been made to the effect that time 'is defined by' or 'reduces to' some other feature of the world. Causal theories date back to Leibniz, who pointed out that simultaneity for events could be characterized by their not being causally connectable. The breakdown of this association in the special theory of relativity is often taken as the key factor in claims to the effect that distant simultaneity is a matter of convention.

The issue of the extent to which temporal notions are, or are not, causally definable in relativistic theories is a complex one. In the special theory there is a relation framed in terms of causal connectability that is coextensive with simultaneity. In general relativity causal definitions of temporal metric and topological notions utilizing causal connectability alone fail in general. But one can characterize topological spatiotemporal notions in terms of the continuity of causal (timelike) paths. This suggests a reduction of the spatiotemporal notions not to causal notions *per se*, but to the epistemically accessible

topological features of the spacetime, those directly available to an observer (see RELATIVITY THEORY, PHILOSOPHICAL SIGNIFICANCE OF §3).

Both the physical connections of spatial and temporal (and spatiotemporal) features to causal features of the world, and the philosophical understanding of what these might tell us about 'what time is' in the world, remain controversial issues (see CAUSATION).

5 Time in experience and time in nature

Temporality enters our conceptual framework both as a descriptive component of our immediate experience and as a component of our theoretical description of the physical world. But how are these aspects of time related to one another? This would be a problem for philosophy even if we took the time of nature to have the features we think of time having prescientifically. Once we have been told by science that time in nature is radically unlike anything we encounter in our immediate experience, as we seem to be told in relativistic theories and as we are likely to be even more radically informed when a fully quantum mechanical account of spacetime is forthcoming, the problem of relating experienced time to the time of theory becomes even more pressing.

One tradition starts from the time of our immediate experience and suggests that the time of nature is in some way or another a construct dependent on the time of conscious awareness. A seminal version of this approach is the treatment of time in Kant (1781/7). Time is, along with space, one of the structuring principles of all experience, called by Kant, a pure intuition. As such it is a feature of the phenomenal world and not of 'things-in-themselves'. Both outer experience of physical objects and inner experience of psychological states are framed in the format of the temporal intuitive structure. Behind the temporal psychological self is the transcendental self, that which unifies all our experience with its implicit 'I think'. Non-temporal, the transcendental self is the ground of the temporal structuring of physical and psychological experience (see KANT, I. §§5–7).

The idealist tradition is continued in Husserl's phenomenological account of the ground and nature of our experience of time (1928). Here emphasis is placed on what the necessary features of such experience must be like in order that we experience things as past, present and future, and have the sense that we do of time as passage. In Heidegger's pragmatist-phenomenology, time as it functions in human activity is the ground of time altogether (see HEIDEGGER, M. §§1–2). One begins with time as it appears in our experienced world of the fixed past, the present of action and the future of projected intentions. The time of nature and science, the time of the 'present-at-hand', is only derivative from the primordial time of experience as decision and action. In these (external, transcendental) idealist accounts of time, the time of past, present and future is taken as central.

Contrasted with such approaches is that of the physicalist-naturalist, to whom the time of the physical world is basic and the time of human experience supervenient at best. In these accounts it is the timeless temporal relations of the B-series that are usually taken as fundamental. Time in experience is usually thought of in something in the vein of a secondary quality.

But even such naturalistic accounts have their problematic aspects. Any proposal to make time as experienced a mere secondary quality (such as that of Gödel noted above), and that takes the 't' of physics to be a parameter disconnected from time as we immediately encounter it, leaves little ground for understanding how physical theories can receive a realistic (as opposed to instrumentalistic) interpretation, or for theoretical realism in general (see SCIENTIFIC REALISM AND ANTIREALISM §1).

See also: CONTINUANTS §2

References and further reading

Broad, C. (1938) *Examination of McTaggart's Philosophy*, Cambridge: Cambridge University Press. (Tensed versus tenseless theories of time.)

Capek, M. (1961) *The Philosophical Impact of Contemporary Physics*, Princeton, NJ: Van Nostrand. (Relativity and the relation of time to existence.)

Davies, P. (1974) *The Physics of Time Asymmetry*, Berkeley, CA: University of California Press. (Time asymmetry and the asymmetry of physical processes in time.)

Earman, J. (1974) 'An Attempt to Add a Little Direction to "The Problem of the Direction of Time"', *Philosophy of Science* 41 (1): 15–47.

Flood, R. and Lockwood, M. (1986) *The Nature of Time*, Oxford: Blackwell. (Essays on time in physics and in philosophy.)

* Gödel, K. (1949) 'A Remark About the Relationship Between Relativity Theory and Idealistic Philosophy', in P. Schillp (ed.) *Albert Einstein: Philosopher–Scientist*, New York: Tudor. (General relativity, closed timelike lines and the distinction between the time of physics and the time of experience.)

Grünbaum, A. (1973) *Philosophical Problems of Space and Time*, Dordrecht: Reidel, 2nd edn. (Time in physics and philosophy.)

Horwich, P. (1987) *Asymmetries in Time*, Cambridge, MA: MIT Press. (Time asymmetry and the asymmetry of physical processes in time.)

* Husserl, E. (1928) *Vorlesungen zur Phänomenologie des inneren Zeitbewußtseins*; trans. J.B. Brough, *On the Phenomenology of the Consciousness of Internal Time (1893–1917)*, The Hague: Nijhoff, 1991. (Husserl's main texts on time and time-consciousness. Phenomenological treatment of time awareness.)

* Kant, I. (1781/7) *The Critique of Pure Reason*; trans. N. Kemp Smith, London: Macmillan, 1929. (Kant's theory of time as pure intuition.)

Kroes, P. (1985) *Time: Its Structure and Role in Physical Theories*, Dordrecht: Reidel. (Time and time asymmetry in physics.)

Landsberg, P. (1983) *The Enigma of Time*, Bristol: Adam Hilger. (Readings on time in physics.)

Le Poidevin, R. and MacBeath, M. (1993) *The Philosophy of Time*, Oxford: Oxford University Press. (Collection of philosophical papers on time.)

McInerney, P. (1991) *Time and Experience*, Philadelphia, PA: Temple University Press. (Survey of phenomenological approaches to time in experience.)

* McTaggart, J. (1934) *Philosophical Studies*, ed. S.V. Keeling, London: Arnold, and New York: Longmans. (McTaggart on tense and the unreality of time.)

Mellor, H. (1981) *Real Time*, Cambridge: Cambridge University Press. (Tense and indexicals.)

Newton-Smith, W. (1980) *The Structure of Time*, London: Routledge & Kegan Paul. (Philosophical issues about time.)

Prior, A. (1967) *Past, Present and Future*, Oxford: Oxford University Press. (Time, tense, reality and tense logic.)

Reichenbach, H. (1928) *Philosophie der Raum-Zeit-Lehre*, Berlin and Leipzig: de Gruyter; trans. M. Reichenbach, *The Philosophy of Space and Time*, New York: Dover, 1957. (Time in the spacetime of relativity theories.)

—— (1956) *The Direction of Time*, Berkeley, CA: University of California Press. (Asymmetry of physics in time and the direction of time problem.)

Schlesinger, G. (1980) *Aspects of Time*, Indianapolis, IN: Hackett Publishing Company. (Time and tense and other philosophical issues.)

Sherover, C. (1975) *The Human Experience of Time*, New York: New York University Press. (Historical survey of philosophical views on the place of time in human experience.)

* Shoemaker, S. (1969) 'Time Without Change', *Journal*

of Philosophy 66: 363–81. (Intelligibility of change-less time.)

Sklar, L. (1993) *Physics and Chance*, Cambridge: Cambridge University Press. (Asymmetry of systems in time and the direction of time.)

—— (1985) *Philosophy and Spacetime Physics*, Berkeley, CA: University of California Press. (Papers on time in physics and philosophy.)

—— (1974) *Space, Time and Spacetime*, Berkeley, CA: University of California Press. (Time in relativity and the direction of time.)

Smart, J. (1964) *Problems of Space and Time*, New York: Macmillan. (Readings on time in philosophy and in physics.)

Stein, H. (1991) 'On Relativity Theory and Openness of the Future', *Philosophy of Science* 58 (2): 147–67. (Time and reality in a relativistic context.)

Yourgrau, P. (1991) *The Disappearance of Time*, Cambridge: Cambridge University Press. (Time in experience and in relativity, emphasizing Gödel's views.)

Zeh, H. (1989) *The Direction of Time*, Berlin: Springer. (Physical asymmetries in time.)

LAWRENCE SKLAR

TIME TRAVEL

The prospect of a machine in which one could be transported through time is no longer mere fantasy, having become in this century the subject of serious scientific and philosophical debate. From Einstein's special theory of relativity we have learned that a form of time travel into the future may be accomplished by moving quickly, and therefore ageing slowly (exploiting the time dilation effect). And in 1949 Kurt Gödel announced his discovery of (general relativistic) space-times whose global curvature allows voyages into the past as well. Since then the study of time travel has had three main strands. First, there has been research by theoretical physicists into the character and plausibility of structures, beyond those found by Gödel, that could engender closed timelike lines and closed causal chains. These phenomena include rotating universes, black holes, traversable wormholes and infinite cosmic strings (Earman 1995). Second, there has been concern with the semantic issue of whether the terms 'cause', 'time' and 'travel' are applicable, strictly speaking, to such bizarre models, given how different they are from the contexts in which those terms are normally employed (Yourgrau 1993). However, one may be sceptical about the significance of this issue, since the questions of primary interest – focused on the nature and reality of

the Gödel-style models – seem independent of whether their description requires a shift in the meanings of those words. And, third, there has been considerable discussion within both physics and philosophy of various alleged paradoxes of time travel, and of their power to preclude the spacetime models in which time travel could occur.

1 **Paradoxes of time travel**
2 **Implications for the character of spacetime**
3 **Open questions**

1 Paradoxes of time travel

The simplest (and weakest) of the alleged paradoxes is the argument that time travel would permit 'changing the past', which would be a patent absurdity. Suppose, for example, you were *not* at the Battle of Hastings. If time travel were possible, it would seem that there would be nothing to stop you from going to the Battle, thus bringing about a contradiction with what was the case, namely, with your not having been there. However, this apparent problem is removed by recognizing that time travel would merely allow one to *influence* the past – to help make it what it was – but not to *change* it. Thus, if you were at the Battle, this fact would be a consequence of your present decision to travel back in time; and if you were not there, this would be because you now freely choose not to go, or fail to arrive for some other reason. Either way there is nothing that deserves to be called 'changing the past' and nothing contradictory.

But there are related problems, not so easily dismissed: most notoriously that time travel would appear to open the door to 'killing one's infant self'; or, more generally, to going back and doing something that one has strong present evidence was not done; or, even more generally, to producing a self-defeating causal chain – a closed string of events in which the occurrence of E at some particular space-time point has a looping sequence of effects eventuating in the absence of E at that very point. It might be argued that since: one, such chains are evidently self-contradictory, and since, two, their possibility is entailed by the possibility of time travel, it follows that time travel is impossible. But in this formulation the allegation of paradox is unpersuasive, since premise two may well be denied. For it need not be conceded that in countenancing the prospect of time travel, hence of *some* closed causal chains, we necessarily become committed, in addition, to the possibility of self-defeating logically impossible chains (Lewis 1986).

An alternative formulation of the puzzle raised by these examples focuses on certain physical anomalies

417

that would be associated with time travel, given the logical inadmissibility of self-defeating chains. For example, repeated attempts to commit autoinfanticide would have to be constantly yet inexplicably frustrated by unfavourable circumstances (such as memory lapses, gun jammings, brilliant surgeons on hand, and so on), which would add up to a peculiarly extreme coincidence; but we have empirical reason to believe that such a coincidence would never occur in our world; so we can infer that regular time travel will not take place. Not that such a thing is logically or conceptually impossible, but rather that what we see of our world (in particular, that massive coincidences do not happen) provides evidence against its occurrence (Horwich 1989).

2 Implications for the character of spacetime

Could some such argument show, in addition, that spacetime does not have the sort of structure (containing closed timelike lines) that is needed for time travel into the past? Not according to Gödel. He reasoned that the mass–energy required for such trips would be so immense (Malament 1984) that they could never become technologically feasible; and so we should not think that if we were really in a Gödelian spacetime, we ought to be encountering the kind of anomaly (massive coincidences) that we do not in fact observe.

But this reasoning has been questioned by De (1969) who considers electromagnetic energy sources that Gödel did not take into account. Moreover one might suspect that a version of the autoinfanticide argument could be developed that does not depend upon things being transported back into the past. For it would seem that the existence of closed timelike lines, and the requirement that the causal chains located on them not be self-defeating, will together imply certain constraints on the distribution of matter (on the constituents of the chains) – constraints which we might observe to be violated. The idea, again very crudely, is that of all the otherwise possible 'initial conditions', only a restricted subset would, given our dynamical laws, be capable of 'causing themselves', and thereby avoiding the production of self-defeating chains; but insofar as we observe no such restriction, it would follow that our world could not contain closed causal chains.

3 Open questions

Although suggestive, this line of thought stands in need of considerable development in various directions. For it is as yet unclear what exactly the constraints implied by closed timelike curves would

be, whether their severity is or is not substantially increased by the supposition of the special type of closed causal chains that embody human voyages into the past, and whether we do or do not have reason to believe that the constraints are violated. These are hard questions even to formulate precisely, let alone answer. Thus the topic of time travel promises to remain puzzling and vibrant for some time to come.

See also: RELATIVITY THEORY, PHILOSOPHICAL SIGNIFICANCE OF; SPACETIME; TIME

References and further reading

* De, U.K. (1969) 'Paths in Universes Having Closed Time-Like Lines', *Journal of Physics A*, series 2, 2: 427–32. (See §3.)

* Earman, J. (1995) 'Recent Work on Time Travel', S. Savitt (ed.), in *Time's Arrow Today*, Cambridge: Cambridge University Press. (Includes a comprehensive, critical review of the physics literature. See §1.)

  Gödel, K. (1949a) 'An Example of a New Type of Cosmological Solution to Einstein's Field Equations of Gravitation', *Reviews of Modern Physics* 21, 447–50. (A technical paper providing solutions to the field equations of general relativity that characterize spacetimes with closed timelike lines.)

  —— (1949b) 'A Remark about the Relationship between Relativity Theory and Idealistic Philosophy', in P.A. Schilpp (ed.) *Albert Einstein: Philosopher–Scientist*, La Salle, IL: Open Court, 1988, 557–62. (An informal discussion of the implications of Gödel's solutions, especially of their import for time travel and for the 'moving-Now' conception of time. See §2.)

* Horwich, P. (1989) *Asymmetries in Time*, Cambridge, MA: MIT Press. (Discusses the alleged paradoxes in the context of a general treatment of time-asymmetric phenomena, and argues that the autoinfanticide considerations provide empirical evidence that time travel to our local past will never be feasible. See §2.)

* Lewis, D. (1986) 'The Paradoxes of Time Travel', *Philosophical Papers*, Oxford: Oxford University Press, vol. 2, 67–80. (Defuses various alleged paradoxes and argues that time travel is a conceptual possibility. See §1.)

* Malament, D. (1984) '"Time Travel" in the Gödel Universe', in D. Hull, M. Forbes and R.M. Burian (eds) *PSA 1984*, East Lansing, MI: Philosophy of Science Association, vol. 2, 91–100. (Calculates the mass–energy required for trips into the local past. See §2.)

* Yourgrau, P. (1993) *The Disappearance of Time,*

Cambridge: Cambridge University Press. (Argues that the import of Gödel's results is the non-existence of time rather than the possibility of time travel.)

PAUL HORWICH

TIMON (*c*.315–*c*.225 BC)

Timon was a Greek philosopher-poet. The formative influence on his life was his meeting with Pyrrho, who was later hailed as the founder of Scepticism. He devoted his literary talents to eulogizing Pyrrho, and his satirical vigour to criticizing other philosophers. He, more than anyone else, carved the image of Pyrrho into what was to become its traditional form and placed it on its pedestal. In this, Timon seems to have been not only a fervent propagandist but also a major philosophical figure, exerting a decisive influence on the history and the very definition of neo-Pyrrhonian scepticism.

Timon was born in Phlius around 315 BC, dying in Athens around 225 BC (this chronology revises the traditional dating forwards by a decade, lengthening Timon's potential acquaintance with the philosophical debates of Hellenistic Athens). What evidence we have portrays him as cultivated, spiritual, a *bon vivant*, a caustic wit, absent-minded and unselfish. According to Diogenes Laertius (IX 109–16) he had a colourful life, full of ups and downs. Orphaned early, he first became a dancer, then lived at Megara, where he worked with the philosopher Stilpo (see MEGARIAN SCHOOL). His meeting with PYRRHO transformed his life and thought: he moved with his family to live close to Pyrrho, where he remained for twenty years. After Pyrrho's death, material problems flung him into an itinerant life, but his manifold talents in the end won him wealth and renown. He ended his days in Athens. There the Platonic Academy had just passed into the hands of ARCESILAUS, and it was by contrast with the type of scepticism which Arcesilaus represented that Timon set out to define Pyrrhonian scepticism (see ACADEMY).

Timon was quite unlike Pyrrho in that he was a prolific, versatile and talented writer. According to Diogenes Laertius (IX 110), 'the leisure which he snatched from philosophy he devoted to composing poetry.' He must have snatched a lot of it, because he wrote epics, dozens of tragedies and comedies, his *Silloi*, and prose works totalling 20,000 lines. The *Silloi* (that is 'Mockeries' – the original meaning of the word is disputed) are the least unknown of his works. Of these we possess sixty-six fragments (some

very short) and a synopsis. Taking up the literary genre of parody (mainly of Homer) already made familiar by Xenophanes and the Cynic Crates of Thebes (see CYNICS §3), Timon turned the mockery onto dogmatic philosophers. In the last two of the poem's three books, he portrayed himself – probably under the fictional guise of a descent to Hades – in conversation with Xenophanes, first about early philosophers, then about recent ones. The surviving fragments confirm that the style was parodic, and show the precision with which he aimed his barbs. More than thirty philosophers are mentioned, from the Presocratics down to Timon's contemporaries, each spiced with jokes of greater or lesser piquancy (and greater or lesser intelligibility to us). Only Pyrrho is unreservedly eulogized. Xenophanes, owing to his sceptical tendencies (see XENOPHANES §5), occupies a privileged place: he is an interlocutor and guide, and perhaps intercedes on behalf of some philosophers who are treated with relative leniency (the Eleatics, Democritus, Protagoras). Even so Timon, not without malice, makes him say that in his old age he ended up himself falling back into dogmatism. This gallery of philosophers and the accompanying comments certainly played a leading role in the process by which Pyrrhonism defined itself (see PYRRHONISM), establishing its own pedigree and locating itself relatively to those philosophies with which it had affinities and differences.

Beyond the primarily critical *Silloi*, Timon wrote another philosophical poem, the *Indalmoi* ('Images'), apparently the constructive part of his programme for exalting, if not deifying, the moral figure of Pyrrho. His prose works are even less well known. The most important seems to have been the *Python*, where Timon's meeting with Pyrrho was ceremonially depicted, and where the pupil, in a restrained tone, expounded the main outlines of his master's work. This last work is probably the source of a summary of Pyrrho which Aristocles attributes to Timon, and which is undoubtedly the most important text in the entire doxography of PYRRHO (§3). Treatises by Timon titled *On Sensations* and *Against the Physicist* are also cited: remains of these works show that this master of mockery could discuss technical philosophical questions with the utmost seriousness.

Timon's place in the history of Pyrrhonian scepticism gave rise to disagreements in antiquity (Diogenes Laertius, IX 115). According to some, the 'succession' of teachers and pupils continued without interruption from Timon down to the Neo-Pyrrhonism we know from the writings of SEXTUS EMPIRICUS (*c*. AD 200). Others, more plausibly, held that the line was broken after Timon and renewed later. It would be especially interesting to know whether Timon himself was merely Pyrrho's 'spokesman' (Sextus' description of him in *Against the Professors* I 53), however effective and brilliant, or whether he left his own mark on the image he projected of his master's thought. Since Pyrrho wrote nothing, and is known through testimonies which depend, directly or indirectly, mainly on Timon, the answer can only be conjectural. In the summary reported by Aristocles, some details seem to imply that Pyrrho's own aim was exclusively or primarily ethical, and that it was Timon who imposed on him a sort of epistemological distortion. That would make Timon in effect the first of the Neo-Pyrrhonians. Even if one simply reflects on Timon's location (in both time and space), interests and personality, it will seem most unlikely that he was a mere clone of Pyrrho.

References and further reading

Brochard, V. (1887) *Les Sceptiques grecs*, Paris: Alcan; repr. 1923. (A classic which has aged well.)

Brunschwig, J. (1994a) 'Once Again on Eusebius on Aristocles on Timon on Pyrrho', in *Papers in Hellenistic Philosophy*, Cambridge: Cambridge University Press, 190–211. (Defends the hypothesis that Timon added the epistemological dimension to an essentially moral philosophy taught by Pyrrho.)

—— (1994b) 'The Title of Timon's Indalmoi: From Odysseus to Pyrrho', in *Papers in Hellenistic Philosophy*, ed. J. Brunschwig, Cambridge: Cambridge University Press, 212–23. (Analysis of Timon's use of the text of Homer, based on one specific example.)

* Diogenes Laertius (*c.* early 3rd century AD) *Lives of the Philosophers*, trans. R.D. Hicks, *Diogenes Laertius Lives of Eminent Philosophers*, Loeb Classical Library, Cambridge, MA: Harvard University Press and London: Heinemann, 1925, 2 vols. (See book IX 109–16 for Timon's life, character, works and pupils.)

Hankinson, R.J. (1995) *The Sceptics*, London and New York: Routledge. (The best modern book-length study.)

* Lloyd-Jones, H. and Parsons, P. (1983) *Supplementum Hellenisticum*, Berlin and New York: de Gruyter. (Now the standard reference work for Timon's poetry.)

Long, A.A. (1978) 'Timon of Phlius: Pyrrhonist and Satirist', *Proceedings of the Cambridge Philological Society* 204: 68–91. (Pioneering work, which dramatically advanced the study of Timon.)

Long, A.A. and Sedley, D.N. (1987) *The Hellenistic Philosophers*, Cambridge: Cambridge University Press, 2 vols. (Includes Timon's main philosophical fragments, with English translation and brief but excellent commentary.)

* Pyrrho (*c.*365–*c.*275 BC) Testimonia, ed. F. Decleva Caizzi, *Pirrone – Testimonianze*, Naples: Bibliopolis, 1981. (Standard edition of the testimonies on Pyrrho; includes Italian translation and valuable commentary.)

* Timon (*c.*315–*c.*225 BC) *Silloi*, ed. M. Di Marco, *Timone di Fliunte: Silli – Introduzione, edizione critica, traduzione e commento*, Rome: Edizioni dell'Ateneo, 1989. (Authoritative scholarly edition of the *Silloi*, with in-depth literary and philosophical commentary and an extensive bibliography.)

JACQUES BRUNSCHWIG

TINDAL, MATTHEW (1657–1733)

Matthew Tindal was one of the last and most learned exponents of English deism. His most famous work is Christianity as Old as the Creation *(1730), a comprehensive apology for natural religion. In it, he argued that God's law is imprinted on the nature of all things, including the human soul, and is accessible to reason. Revealed religion merely restates this universal law – the will of God – in a different form. Religion enables us to act in accordance with this natural order, and its end is happiness. However, Tindal was scathingly critical of the clergy, and cast doubt on the reliability of the Bible. Although Tindal's work was severely criticized by William Law, it exerted a considerable influence on the English and Continental Enlightenment.*

1 Life and work
2 The religion of nature
3 Polemical deism and its opponents

1 Life and work

Born in Bere Ferrers in Devonshire, Matthew Tindal was brought up in the High-Church tradition of his father, the local parish priest. In 1673, he matriculated at Lincoln College at Oxford, where he was tutored by George Hickes, a High-Churchman. He later moved to Exeter College. He was elected a Fellow of All Souls in 1678 and was made a Doctor of Civil Law in 1685.

Tindal's England was deeply divided along political and religious lines. Theological controversies between Catholics and Protestants were further complicated by the self-confidence of reason, the claims of natural philosophy, and a rising interest in textual criticism. Like John Chillingworth and Pierre Bayle, Tindal went through a short Roman Catholic phase. But craving for freedom of thought, he returned to Protestantism in early 1688, eventually disencumbered of High-Churchism. At the time of the Glorious Revolution, Tindal rallied to William III, championed Whig opinions and discovered affinities with Low-Churchism. His early publications – *An Essay Concerning Obedience to Supreme Powers* (1693) and *An Essay Concerning the Laws of Nations, and the Rights of Soveraigns* (1694) – were concerned with legal matters. An unmitigated assault on episcopacy, *The Rights of the Christian Church Asserted*, caused a considerable stir in 1706 and established his reputation as a freethinker. In spite of a *Defence* (1707–8), the book was condemned by Parliament in 1710 and burned by the hangman. By then his offensive against the High-Church party had gathered pace with *A New Catechism, with Dr. Hickes's thirty nine Articles* (1710).

The first volume of *Christianity as Old as the Creation or, the Gospel, a Republication of the Religion of Nature* came out in 1730, ending two decades of quiet. Inspired by Cicero's *On the Nature of the Gods* and *On Divination* (see CICERO §3), Tindal's dialogue on religion, though repetitive and crammed with innumerable excerpts from Latitudinarian and rationalist divines, is typically in both argument and style the work of a mature and aged scholar. The second volume, though completed, was never published. The executor of Tindal's will was delinquent and the manuscript vanished. The first volume, Tindal's masterpiece, was a synthesis of the deist argument developed over a century by HERBERT OF CHERBURY (§§3–4), Charles Blount, John Toland, Lord SHAFTESBURY (§2), Anthony COLLINS (§1), Thomas Chubb and Thomas Woolston (see DEISM). After Tindal's death in 1733, it was hailed as the Bible of the deists, and in 1741 it was translated into German. It spurred the Enlightenment; Reimarus, Lessing and KANT (§14) are indebted to Tindal for their understanding of natural and revealed religion. In France, the *philosophes* revelled in Tindal, whom VOLTAIRE (§2) praised as the most intrepid defender of natural religion. Jacques-André Naigeon was, however, not permitted to publish an abridged translation in French before 1770.

2 The religion of nature

It was the ambition of deism to define a creed, minimalist and natural, that might provide a common basis for belief, upon which theologians and natural philosophers would agree regardless of their denomi-nation. In promoting the religion of nature on the basis of 'a Law of Nature, or Reason... a Law which is common, or natural, to all rational creatures' ([1730] 1995: 7), Tindal, a rationalist in principle, pursued a threefold objective: the reconciliation of Christian revelation with human rationality, the settlement of religious conflicts, and the establishment of religious freedom and toleration. Beyond its theological and cultural aspects, the construction of a philosophical religion responded to a social and political need of the time.

In order to solve problems that the Latitudinarians (who advocated an alliance of Christian theology with reason) were among the first to perceive, Tindal postulated the innateness of religion. A law is imprinted on the human soul by virtue of creation and can be known by reason regardless of historical and cultural circumstances. This law is the will of the supreme legislator, the creator of the universe. Borrowing a key ontological principle from Samuel CLARKE (§1), whose Boyle Lectures were emblematic of a rationalist age, Tindal enunciated the view that God's will was entrenched in 'the Nature and Reason of Things' ([1730] 1995: 56), in the immutable relations governing nature. The possibility of religion in general, and natural religion in particular, is established on a rationalist ontology.

But if true religion is a priori, natural and universal, should Christian belief not be dispensed with? The anthropomorphisms propagated by the Judaeo-Christian scriptures were as revolting to Tindal as the arbitrariness of a God who selected a miserable and ignorant tribe and demanded that human beings believe in magical phenomena and acknowledge absurd doctrines in order to receive the benefits of salvation. None the less, since Tindal aimed at bringing the Judaeo-Christian God and the God of deism into harmony, he espoused a hypothesis which has since become famous, namely that the a posteriori, revealed or historical religion was 'a Republication of the Law of Nature', 'a Restoration' or 'a Transcript of the religion of Nature' ([1730] 1995: 68, 176, 334; the first of these was originally a quote from Thomas Sherlock). This hypothesis had already gained some currency in seventeenth-century England owing to the sermons of Archbishop John Tillotson (1630–94) and Bishop Thomas Sherlock. Natural and revealed religion were 'like two Tallies... [which] exactly answer one another' ([1730] 1995: 51). It follows from this that Christianity is not a new religion, but, as the title of Tindal's book audaciously claimed, as old as creation.

Tindal's definition of true religion as 'plain, simple, and natural' ([1730] 1995: 241) is followed by six corollaries: (1) The sufficiency of natural religion.

Natural religion is perfect: it originates from 'the Author of all Perfection' ([1730] 1995: 255); it is accessible universally; it discloses the divine will exhaustively; it allows for a reasonable worship; and it grounds revealed religion. (2) The equation of morality with nature. The law of nature expresses the will of God. All natural duties are summarized in the commandment to love God and our neighbour. (3) The equation of religion with ethics. Both Confucius and Jesus taught truths that encapsulated the substance of natural religion. Whereas morality is 'acting according to the Reason and Nature of Things considered in themselves', religion is 'acting according to the same Reason of Things consider'd as the Will of God' ([1730] 1995: 270). (4) Eudaimonia constitutes the purpose of religion. 'The ultimate End of all God's Laws, and consequently, of all Religion, is human happiness' ([1730] 1995: 90). (5) The difference between natural and revealed religion is reduced to a question of form. 'Natural and Revealed Religion only differ in the Manner of their being delivered' ([1730] 1995: 114). They are identical as regards the source of their being, namely the divine will, but distinct as regards the way in which they are known. Natural religion is known rationally, revealed religion historically. (6) The distinction between true religion and superstition. True religion deals with ends and prescribes means. What is concerned with matters irrelevant to morality is called superstition.

3 Polemical deism and its opponents

In the wake of Collins' *Priestcraft in Perfection* (1709), Tindal launched a veiled attack against the clergy, the Bible and the external evidences of Christian belief. He stigmatized the power of priestcraft and the evils of religious enthusiasm by ridiculing the customs, rites and mores of heathens and Jews. The clergy is charged with bigotry, fraud and cruelty. Self-serving Christian priests teach absurdities, impose arbitrary duties and foster superstition. Subjecting the Judaeo-Christian scriptures to the critique of reason, Tindal drew attention to a collection of scriptural problems that the nascent biblical criticism was beginning to exhume (see HERMENEUTICS, BIBLICAL §2). Not only did he cast doubt on the authority and reliability of the Bible, but he also disparaged the allegorical and typological interpretations of the Anglican tradition. The refutation of the external proofs of revealed religion had been a main feature of deism since John Toland. Seeking to eliminate from Christianity teachings that were either against or beyond reason, Tindal listed miracles among those things that can only nurture superstition. 'If you look no further than the Christian World, you will find, that Ignorance, and

the Belief of daily Miracles go hand in hand; and that there's nothing too absurd for the Peoples Belief' ([1730] 1995: 192). Tindal's offensive against Christian orthodoxy anticipated d'Holbach's *Christianity Unveiled* (1756), which provided Feuerbach's and Marx's critiques of religion with their main arguments (see FEUERBACH, L.A. §2; MARX, K. §3).

Tindal's natural and ahistorical rationalism resulted in a sophisticated moral elitism which cut right across doctrinal and ecclesiastical boundaries, but at the huge cost of an unsophisticated anticlericalism, antibiblicism and anti-Judaism. There were not many replies to his polemical book. In 1731, Daniel Waterland unsuccessfully tried to vindicate the Old Testament picture of God in an anonymous *Scripture Vindicated*, while William Law more successfully exculpated the God of orthodoxy from the charge of arbitrariness in *The Case of Religion and Reason, or Natural Religion, Fairly and Fully Stated* (1731). Law further blamed Tindal for failing to see in human beings the importance of both irrationality and evil.

See also: NATURAL THEOLOGY

List of works

Tindal, M. (1693) *An Essay Concerning Obedience to Supreme Powers*, London; microfilm, Ann Arbor, MI: University Microfilms, 'Early English Books 1641–1700', 1969. (A combination of reflection on the contemporary political scene and discussion of the general duties of citizenship in times of crisis; the microfilm version is of a 1709 reprint that also includes Tindal 1694a and 1697, and another essay.)

—— (1694a) *An Essay Concerning the Laws of Nations, and the Rights of Soveraigns*, London; microfilm, Ann Arbor, MI: University Microfilms, 'Early English Books 1641–1700', 1969. (Tindal indulges in a controversy sparked by naval policy.)

—— (1694b) *A Letter to the Reverend Clergy of Both Universities, concerning the Trinity and the Athanasian Creed*, London; microfilm, Ann Arbor, MI: University Microfilms, 'Early English Books 1641–1700', 1974. (Tindal's first major religious controversy.)

—— (1697) *An Essay concerning the Power of the Magistrate, and the Rights of Mankind in Matters of Religion*, London; microfilm, Ann Arbor, MI: University Microfilms, 'Early English Books 1641–1700', 1974. (Argues, among other things, for the political rights of dissenters.)

—— (1706) *The Rights of the Christian Church Asserted*, London, Part I (no more published); microfilm, Woodbridge, CT: Research Publications, 'The Eighteenth Century', 1991. ('. . . against the

Romish, and all other priests, who claim an independent power over it' – Tindal's first major work, the source of heated controversy.)

—— (1707–8) *A Defence of the Rights of the Christian Church*, London, 2 parts. (Tindal's two vain attempts to defend his 1706 work; republished together in 1709.)

—— (1710) *A New Catechism, with Dr. Hickes's thirty nine Articles*, London; microfilm, Woodbridge, CT: Research Publications, 'The Eighteenth Century', 1986. (Against the High-Church party in the Church of England, and Tindal's old Oxford tutor, Hickes.)

—— (1718) *An Account of a Manuscript, entitul'd, Destruction the Certain Consequence of Division*, London; microfilm, Woodbridge, CT: Research Publications, 'The Eighteenth Century', 1986. (Turning to a more positive tack, Tindal makes a plea for the political unity of all Protestants.)

—— (1730) *Christianity as Old as the Creation or, the Gospel, a Republication of the Religion of Nature*, London, vol. 1 (no more published); facs. edn ed. J.V. Price, London: Thoemmes, 1995. (Tindal's most famous work, which provoked some 150 published replies in the years following.)

References and further reading

* Collins, A. (1709) *Priestcraft in Perfection*, London; microfilm, Woodbridge, CT: Research Publications, 'The Eighteenth Century', 1986. (Arguing against the power of priests, via a criticism of the Articles of the Church of England, this essay paved the way for Tindal's own attacks.)
* Conybeare, J. (1732) *A Defence of Reveal'd Religion*, Dublin. (One of the most sympathetic and insightful replies to Tindal 1730.)
Gawlick, G. (1967) 'Einleitung', in *Christianity as Old as the Creation*, Stuttgart: Cannstatt, facs. edn. (A good discussion of the famous book, with an extensive bibliography.)
* Law, W. (1731) *The Case of Religion and Reason, or Natural Religion, Fairly and Fully Stated*, London; microfilm, Woodbridge, CT: Research Publications, 'The Eighteenth Century', 1988. (The most successful attack on Tindal and on deism in general, showing that Tindal's arguments hit natural religion as much as revealed.)
Rupp, E.G. (1986) *Religion in England 1688–1791*, Oxford: Clarendon Press. (Contains a brief but clear description of the deist controversies.)
Stephen, L. (1991) *History of English Thought in the Eighteenth Century*, Bristol: Thoemmes, 2 vols. (This is a facsimile of the 1902 third edition; it is dated, but expansive and readable.)
* Waterland, D. (1731–2) *Scripture Vindicated*, London, 3 parts; microfilm, Woodbridge, CT: Research Publications, 'The Eighteenth Century', 1986. (One of the many rather hasty replies to Tindal, itself attacked by moderates for its strict literalism in interpreting the Old Testament.)

JEAN-LOUP SEBAN

TKACHËV, P. *see* RUSSIAN MATERIALISM: 'THE 1860s'

TOCQUEVILLE, ALEXIS DE (1805–59)

Tocqueville once observed that his temperament was the 'least philosophical' imaginable. He meant that his mind was governed by passionate commitment, a determination to defend civil and political liberty against threats resulting from social levelling and the growth of state power. Thus, Tocqueville's most famous work, De la démocratie en Amérique *(Democracy in America) (1835, 1840), did not spring from detached curiosity about US institutions. It was rather an attempt to draw lessons from US society and government which could be used to reform French institutions. His belief in local autonomy – he called the New England township a 'school for citizens' – led him to develop a distinctive conception of liberty that combined elements of ancient citizenship and modern autonomy. That conception also shaped his own political career and later writings. In* L'Ancien régime et la révolution *(The Old Regime and the French Revolution) (1856) Tocqueville traced bitter class conflicts in France to the destruction of local autonomy long before 1789.*

Tocqueville was the child of aristocratic parents who had nearly died on the scaffold in the Reign of Terror. His childhood was overshadowed by stories of relations who did not escape, including his famous grandfather, Lamoignon de Malesherbes – the pre-Revolutionary reformer and critic of royal despotism who became the young Tocqueville's hero. The sense of danger surrounding an aristocratic family after the Revolution left a profound mark on the boy. But that sense was strengthened by political developments in France during the Restoration (1815–30). The advent of a reactionary ultra-royalist government in the 1820s gradually convinced Tocqueville that it was not only futile but unjust to resist social change. He learned from a group of Restoration liberals called the *Doctrinaires* to consider the long-term movement from an aristocratic to a democratic social order – the 'Democratic Revolution' – as 'irresistible' and 'providential'. But that is not all he learned from the *Doctrinaires*. After completing his legal studies and becoming a junior magistrate, Tocqueville attended lectures by the historian François Guizot which deepened his understanding of two potentially dangerous consequences of the democratic social revolution in France, what the older Royer-Collard had called 'atomization' and 'centralization'.

These concepts shaped Tocqueville's intellectual development after 1828. By 'atomization' he understood the threat to association which resulted from the destruction of a corporate society, leaving a society in which individuals are equal but isolated and equally weak. The beneficiary is the state with its claim to a sovereign right which can be used to justify an indefinite concentration of power at the centre, controlling the periphery of society through a bureaucratic machine. Restoration liberals had begun to invoke a 'new federalism' to meet this threat and establish a balance between central power and local autonomy. Guizot, in particular, had criticized the concept of sovereignty passed down from Bodin and Hobbes, with its stipulation of a monopoly of authority in one agency (see SOVEREIGNTY).

Tocqueville evidently found the new liberal prescription tantalizing but vague – for would not local autonomy lead to the dissolution of the state through the emergence of competing 'sovereigns'? Such questions probably helped to direct his attention to the USA. Restoration liberals had laid emphasis on the role of class conflict between the aristocracy and middle classes in explaining why power had been centralized in France under the *ancien régime*. Tocqueville began to wonder if US political institutions might have a didactic potential because they had developed in a society which had been democratic from the outset.

The journey Tocqueville and his friend Beaumont made through America in the years 1831–2 confirmed this suspicion. US federalism embodied a balance between central power and local autonomy that enabled Tocqueville to complete the critique of the concept of sovereignty by demonstrating that political unity did not entail administrative centralization. But observation of the vibrant life of townships in New England led him beyond his initial concern with dispersing power into a new conception of liberty – what he was to call 'free *moeurs*', or the attitudes and habits of a free people. In that way Tocqueville stepped outside the confines of late eighteenth- and

early nineteenth-century liberalism, with its emphasis on constitutionalism and legal rights. Instead, social attitudes became the focus of his concern. But while seeking to analyse and defend the civic spirit or citizenship which local participation fostered in the USA, Tocqueville also sought to avoid the drawbacks of a concept like Rousseau's general will (see GENERAL WILL).

In his *Du contrat social* (*The Social Contract*) (1762) Rousseau had defined active citizenship and concern for the general welfare into a concept of real or moral freedom (the general will) which might conflict with the *de facto* wishes of individuals (see ROUSSEAU, J.-J. §3). At the outset of the Restoration, Benjamin CONSTANT (§1) had argued that Rousseau's defence of citizenship or ancient liberty had sacrificed the most important modern meaning of liberty; that is, individual autonomy protected by rights. Restoration liberals such as Constant charged Rousseau with creating a concept which could serve as a weapon of tyranny. They had in mind especially appeals to the 'will of the people' which had been used during the Reign of Terror to justify the sacrifice of individual liberty. Consequently they looked upon arguments for political participation with suspicion, if not with hostility. Tocqueville, after his journey through America, stood out against that trend. What he had observed about local autonomy persuaded him that it had a crucial moralizing potential. What is striking about the argument of *De la démocratie en Amérique* (*Democracy in America*) (1835, 1840) is that instead of tying political participation to 'correct' political decisions by definition, Tocqueville put forward a concept of free *moeurs* – the attitudes and habits of a people by self-reliance and the habit of association – which makes the moralizing process probable rather than necessary. In that way Tocqueville 'rescued' the value of citizenship by reconciling it with individual autonomy or rights in an unambiguously liberal doctrine of citizenship (see CITIZENSHIP §2).

The success of *Democracy in America* was stunning. It helped to launch Tocqueville into a political career. Yet the 1840s turned him into a sad and frustrated critic of Louis Philippe's July Monarchy, with its cynical manipulation of the limited franchise. Tocqueville's greatest political prominence came after the revolution of 1848, when he served briefly as French foreign minister. But it was a short-lived success. For Louis Napoleon's *coup d'état* (1859) and the Second Empire obliged Tocqueville to withdraw into a kind of internal exile. He would not serve a tyrant. Instead, he devoted his final years to showing how the bureaucratic French state and class hatreds had developed together in a vicious alliance. The structure of argument in *L'Ancien régime et la révolution* (*The*

Old Regime and the French Revolution) (1856) remained essentially the same as that of *Democracy in America*. Tocqueville's insistence on the importance of decentralization and political participation made him a liberal moralist of a new kind. In his view, liberalism could not safely confine itself to an interest in market relations or legal structures. Fostering the virile attitudes of a free people was all-important. Sad but unswerving in his opposition to tyranny, he died in 1859.

See also: LIBERALISM

List of works

Tocqueville, A. de (1835, 1840) *De la démocratie en Amérique* (*Democracy in America*), trans G. Lawrence, ed. J.P. Mayer and M. Lerner, London: Fontana, 1966.
—— (1856) *L'Ancien régime et la révolution* (*The Old Regime and the French Revolution*), trans. S. Gilbert, Garden City, NY: Doubleday, 1955.

References and further reading

Jardin, A. (1988) *Tocqueville*, London: Halban.
Kelly, G.A. (1992) *The Humane Comedy: Constant, Tocqueville and French Liberalism*, Cambridge: Cambridge University Press. (Uneven but imaginative.)
Lamberti, J.-C. (1983) *Tocqueville et les deux Démocraties* (*Tocqueville and the Two Democracies*), Paris: Presses Universitaires de France. (An interesting study.)
Lively, J. (1965) *The Social and Political Thought of Alexis de Tocqueville*, Oxford: Clarendon Press. (A somewhat unhistorical, topical approach to Tocqueville's thought.)
Mill, J.S. (1840) 'M. de Tocqueville on *Democracy in America*', in *Collected Works of John Stuart Mill*, vol. 17, Toronto, Ont.: University of Toronto Press, 1977, 47–90 and 153–204. (This remains a penetrating analysis.)
Pierson, G. (1938) *Tocqueville and Beaumont in America*, New York: Oxford University Press. (A magisterial account of the journey through America.)
Rousseau, J.-J. (1762) *Du contrat social*, in *The Social Contract, with Geneva Manuscript and Political Economy*, ed. R.D. Masters, New York: St Martin's Press, 1978.
Schleifer, J. (1980) *The Making of Tocqueville's Democracy in America*, Chapel Hill, NC: University of North Carolina Press.
Siedentop, L. (1979) 'Two Liberal Traditions', in *The Idea of Freedom*, ed. A. Ryan, Oxford: Oxford University Press. (A contrast between English and French liberalism.)
—— (1994) *Tocqueville*, Oxford: Oxford University Press. (An intellectual biography and survey of his thought.)
Zeitlin, I. (1971) *Liberty, Equality and Revolution in Alexis de Tocqueville*, Boston, MA: Little, Brown. (Useful.)

L.A. SIEDENTOP

TODOROV, TZVETAN (1936–)

Tzvetan Todorov is a Bulgarian thinker and literary theorist who lives and works in France. His thought is 'structuralist' in that it seeks stable abstract principles explanatory of, but not directly given in, phenomena of literature and history. His thought is not only a milestone in the history of structuralism but is 'negatively' important to the development of post-structuralist thought: the rules and oppositions conveyed by structuralist typologies such as those of Todorov constitute much of what thinkers such as Jacques Derrida seek to 'deconstruct'.

Tzvetan Todorov was born and received his early education in Sofia, Bulgaria. At the age of 24, he moved to France, where he is (1996) Director of Research at the Centre National de Recherches Scientifiques in Paris. He has also taught at the University of Paris and at several American universities, among them Columbia and Yale. In addition to broader, more 'philosophical' works, he has published important studies on Rousseau, Goethe and Bakhtin. He has also edited a number of anthologies, including the *Dictionnaire encyclopédique des sciences du langage* (1972).

Todorov's earliest works (1968, 1971, 1978b) concern the study of literature, which he divides into two parts: 'poetics', which seeks the abstract structures governing literary genres, and 'interpretation', which concerns the meaning of individual texts. Poetics, for its part, is 'objective' and 'scientific'; its central concept, that of genre, plays a role in it akin to that of species in biology. 'Interpretation' is more subjective: while some interpretations can be wrong, none is ever the only correct one.

Todorov's poetics explores three basic aspects of the literary text: semantic, syntactic and verbal. Unlike traditional semantic units (for example, sentences), the literary work is 'dialogical' or 'intertextual': it refers, not merely to non-literary states of affairs, but also to prior and posterior texts (including earlier and later stages of itself). As fictional, or 'feigned' speech, it claims, not truth, but verisimilitude: accordance with the rules of its genre and with the expectations of its readers, or 'public opinion'. Following Russian formalists such as Mikhail Bakhtin, Vladimir Propp and others (see BAKHTIN, M.; RUSSIAN LITERARY FORMALISM), Todorov argues that the 'syntactic' order of the literary text is not grammatical, but narrative: the events narrated follow each other in a logical order ('mythological' narrative) or contribute to the manifestation of a single idea ('ideological' narrative). Its 'verbal' aspect is the way in which it enables the reader to construct a fictional world and includes the text's use of time, perspective and voice. None of these aspects, of course, is limited to what we call 'literature': all are widespread in many types of discourse. Hence no structural definition of literature is possible (1978b: 11). The proper object of literary theory remains the genre.

But a literary genre differs crucially from a biological species:

> The impact of individual organisms on the evolution of the species is so slow that we can discount it in practice. ... [But] we grant a text the right to figure in a history of literature or of science only insofar as it produces a change in our notion of one activity or the other.
>
> (1970: 6)

Hence, poetics by itself is incomplete, and must be supplemented by the interpretive investigation of individual works. Todorov's most extended pursuit of such investigation can be found in *The Fantastic* (1970). His main historical account of it is in *Theories of the Symbol* (1977), which investigates the development of the modern or 'romantic' conception of the symbol, in which the work of art no longer 'imitates' reality but functions according to its own inner logic (thus making poetics itself possible). Finally, *Symbolism and Interpretation* (1978a) undertakes a general typology of interpretive strategies.

The rules which a work of literature obeys – those of its genre and of its own intertextuality – are not thought up by its author: they are beyond authorial control. Such a text is thus governed by elements which may be called foreign to it. If allowing foreign elements to dominate one's own thought and work is 'primitive', then as early as *Theories of the Symbol* Todorov is engaged in 'identifying the supposedly primitive mechanisms in our own thinking' (1977: 223). Structuralist poetics is thus from the start an enquiry into the otherness always resident in our own thought. By the time of *Literature and its Theorists* (1984), the theme of alterity has become 'the focal point of [Todorov's] work' (1984: 3). Together with this new emphasis on alterity goes a shift in interest from literature to history.

The most important document in this shift is Todorov's *The Conquest of America* (1982). In this classic work, Todorov undertakes to examine the ways in which the European conquerors of America thought about its pre-Columbian inhabitants. The book is not, then, a 'theory' of anything. Rather, it recounts an 'exemplary narrative' with ethical meaning (1982: 4). The aim is not merely to understand the practices of the *conquistadors*, but to change those aspects of contemporary culture which exhibit their vestiges: 'to become aware of the relativity (hence the arbitrariness) of any feature of our culture is already to shift it a little' (1982: 254).

But the book retains a 'typological perspective' (1982: 252); the typology in question is developed in *On Human Diversity: Nationalism, Racism, and Exoticism* (1989). There are, it argues, three main ways to handle the empirical fact of human diversity. One is ethnocentrism, which simply generalizes characteristics of one's own society into 'universal' values. A second, more respectable today, is 'scientism': the scientific examination of human beings will teach us what they should pursue and avoid. Both are dangerous: ethnocentrism inevitably arrives at the result that we should rule others, while scientism arrives at the rule of scientists. Apart from the 'indefensible' approach of complete relativism, which falls to a version of the sceptical paradox (1989: 389) (see RELATIVISM), only 'critical humanism' is left. This sees liberty – the capacity to reject any determination of one's nature – as the central feature of humanity. The universalism to which it aspires is always open to revision, but – like truth itself – always there as a goal.

See also: STRUCTURALISM IN LITERARY THEORY

List of works

Todorov, T. (1968; rev. edn 1973) *Qu'est-ce que le structuralisme: Poétique*, Paris: Éditions du Seuil, rev. edn 1973; trans. R. Howard, *Introduction to Poetics*, Minneapolis, MN: University of Minnesota Press, 1981. (An introductory handbook to structuralism, containing a key statement of its basic principles.)

—— (1970) *Introduction à la littérature fantastique*, Paris: Éditions du Seuil; trans. R. Howard, *The Fantastic: A Structural Approach to a Literary Genre*, Cleveland, OH: Case Western Reserve University Press, 1973. (Pursues the structural principles of the literary distinction between what strikes the reader as strange, but natural, and what is truly marvellous or 'fantastic'.)

—— (1971) *Poétique de la prose*, Paris: Éditions du Seuil; trans. R. Howard, *The Poetics of Prose*, Ithaca, NY: Cornell University Press, 1977. (One of Todorov's most influential works; at once an introduction to and a critical discussion of structuralist literary criticism, it also applies structuralism to texts from a variety of languages and periods.)

—— (1972) *Dictionnaire encyclopédique des sciences du langage*, Paris: éditions du Seuil.

—— (1977) *Théorie du symbole*, Paris: Éditions du Seuil; trans. C. Porter, *Theories of the Symbol*, Ithaca, NY: Cornell University Press, 1982. (A history of semiotics through one of its key concepts – that of the symbol – this work constitutes a major irruption of history into the supposedly atemporal features uncovered by structuralist analysis.)

—— (1978a) *Symbolisme et interpretation*, Paris: Éditions du Seuil; trans. C. Porter, *Symbolism and Interpretation*, Ithaca, NY: Cornell University Press, 1982. (A general typology of interpretive strategies that can be taken with respect to 'symbols'.)

—— (1978b) *Les Genres du discours*, Paris: Éditions du Seuil; trans. C. Porter, *Genres in Discourse*, Ithaca, NY: Cornell University Press, 1990. (A discussion of the types of, and principles underlying, literary genres.)

—— (1981) *Mikhail Bakhtin: le principe dialogique*, Paris: Éditions du Seuil; trans. W. Godzich, *Mikhail Bakhtin: The Dialogical Principle*, Minneapolis, MN: University of Minnesota Press, 1984. (An extremely influential systematic account of Bakhtin, showing how the polysemy of his writings is meant to engage the reader in a dialogue in which the reader must decipher (or not decipher) the various ambiguities in Bakhtin's works.)

—— (1982) *La Conquête de l'Amérique*, Paris: Éditions du Seuil; trans. R. Howard, *The Conquest of America*, New York: Harper & Row, 1984. (One of Todorov's most influential works; examines Europe's encounter with the Other (in this case, with the inhabitants of what came to be called Latin America) via an examination of the mind of the conquistadors as evidenced by contemporary accounts.)

—— (1984) *Critique de la critique*, Paris: Éditions du Seuil; trans. C. Porter, *Literature and its Theorists*, Ithaca, NY: Cornell University Press, 1987. (A personal and critical history of major developments in twentieth-century literary criticism.)

—— (1989) *Nous et les autres*, Paris: Éditions du Seuil; trans. C. Porter, *On Human Diversity: Nationalism,*

Racism, and Exoticism in French Thought, Cambridge, MA: Harvard University Press, 1993. (A critical and typological account of ways of handling human diversity; widely recognized as contributing to the French debates on decolonization.)

—— (1991a) *Face à l'extrème*, Paris: Éditions du Seuil; trans. A. Denner and A. Pollak, *Facing the Extreme*, New York: Metropolitan Books, 1996.

—— (1991b) *Les Morales de l'histoire*, Paris: Grasset & Fasquelle; trans. A. Waters, *The Morals of History*, Minneapolis, MN: University of Minnesota Press, 1995. (A discussion of the types and structures of cross-cultural encounter.)

FRANÇOISE LIONNET

T'OEGYE *see* YI HWANG

TOKEN *see* TYPE/TOKEN DISTINCTION

TOLAND, JOHN (1670–1722)

Deist, freethinker and political republican, the Irishman John Toland's reputation is closely associated with the radical attack on Christian metaphysics and institutions in the Augustan period. His philosophical achievement was to turn the more erudite thinking of Spinoza, Hobbes and Locke into a popular polemic against the shibboleths of orthodox religious belief. In Christianity Not Mysterious *(1696), burnt in Dublin by Parliamentary command in 1697, he exploited and extended the epistemology of Locke's* Essay Concerning Human Understanding *into a revision of Christian descriptions of the relationship between faith and knowledge, and a consequent defence of liberty of thought and belief.*

Toland's contribution to philosophical developments can be traced to his scholarly training in the universities of Glasgow, Edinburgh, Leiden and Oxford in the 1690s. Skilful in languages and criticism, Toland forged his contemporary reputation as a figure of learning in the Republic of Letters. Associated at different times with powerful men such as John LOCKE, Anthony Ashley, the third Earl of SHAFTESBURY and Robert Harley in English society, and Prince Eugene of Savoy and Sophia of Hanover on the continent, Toland was a conduit for the diffusion of radical ideas across Europe. Controversial since his university days, he repeatedly found himself the subject of orthodox condemnation and hostility, whether publishing studies of apocryphal literature or defences of his political philosophy. The novelty of Toland's approach was to bring together and radicalize the achievements of a number of earlier philosophical positions.

As a pamphleteer and philosopher, Toland combined political radicalism with his heterodoxy: during the 1690s he was single-handedly responsible for publishing standard editions of the republican figures of the 1640s and 1650s, adapting the political philosophy of such commonwealthsmen as James HARRINGTON to the exigencies of a monarchical constitution. Crucially, as his editorial work on the life and work of John Milton indicates, Toland made textual criticism (again adapted from the hermeneutical advances of Spinoza and the French Biblical critic Richard Simon) a tool of political and philosophical reform. Coiner of the neologism 'pantheist', Toland's private metaphysics (a combination of a Ciceronian neo-Stoicism, materialism and Spinozist ethics), disseminated in the Latin work *Pantheisticon* (1720), was a profound influence on the heterodoxy of the later French 'High' Enlightenment.

Christianity Not Mysterious (1696) was Toland's first major work. Premised on a combination of the epistemologies of Locke and Hobbes which emphasized the role of reason in the construction of knowledge, Toland argued that no Christian doctrine could be mysterious. Insisting that all theologies must be rational in order that every human being might understand them, Toland undercut the traditional Christian assertion that some doctrines (most obviously the Trinity for the Church of England) might be above the capacity of human rationality. Executing a historical examination of the meaning of the word 'mystery', Toland suggested that mysteries might be 'hidden' from human understanding rather than 'incomprehensible' to rational capacities. Toland's point, much vilified by Churchmen, was that no belief could legitimately be imposed by either Church or State on any individual. As Toland made clear in this and later works, the corrosion of the authority of clerical imposition in matters of interpretation was as much a political as a religious action.

Toland made the link between religion and politics in his series of canonical editions of commonwealth political philosophy in the 1690s. The works of Algernon Sidney, James Harrington, John Milton and Edmund Ludlow were adapted to the demands of eighteenth-century political culture in Toland's editions. Re-writing the millenarian language of Ludlow, or the puritanical idiom of John Milton, to the more civil demands of political discourse in the late seventeenth century was a skilled and long-lived

achievement: Toland's editions remained canonical into the nineteenth century. In changing republican political philosophy from a programme of institutional reform into a language more suitable for a monarchical constitution, Toland placed the development of a civic theology and religion at the heart of his revision. 'Commonwealthsmen' pursued not the execution of all monarchs, but the imperatives of civic virtue. Protecting the safety of the people and advancing the cause of civic sociability were the central planks of this political philosophy. Importantly, making the connection between religion and politics, Toland, again adapting Harringtonian suggestions, insisted that public religion was the most effective way of establishing civic virtue.

As a corollary to his insistence that religion must be tuned to establish the harmony of civic communities, Toland embarked on a lifelong polemic against the corruptions and deviancies of priestcraft. His strategy was contrived as a deliberately public attempt to undercut the apostolic claims of clerical orthodoxy by establishing all religion as the manifestation of historical circumstance. Writing with a deliberately accentuated emphasis on his learning and skill, appropriating the scholarship of more orthodox authors, Toland, in works such as *Letters to Serena* (1704), suggested that key Christian doctrines such as the immortality of the soul were derived from 'heathen' origins. Similar essays on 'prejudice', 'idolatry' and the primitive church, stressed the continuities of all false religions: priests had ever corrupted the virtuous injunctions of natural religion. Pre-empting the naturalistic accounts of later thinkers such as David HUME and the *philosophes* of the Enlightenment, Toland established – importantly for a non-learned audience – that the ceremonial, doctrinal and institutional elements of all religions were culturally specific (see ENLIGHTENMENT, CONTINENTAL).

Drawing from the relativism implicit in such historical perspectives, Toland insisted that since there were no clear divine imperatives in favour of any one religious economy, all religions were equal. Concepts of religious truth were thus displaced for Toland by assessments of religious function. Good religion was focused on facilitating the values of civic community. Corrupt religion was a system calculated for the false private advantage of priests and kings. The high point of such arguments was to be found in Toland's *Nazarenus. Or Jewish, Gentile and Mahometan Christianity* (1718), a work first composed as a private, clandestine manuscript for the purview of Prince Eugene of Savoy. In the published work, using the device of a commentary on a suppositious gnostic work, the Gospel of Barnabas, Toland surveyed the historical relationships of Judaism, Christianity and Islam, concluding that as historical manifestations of specific cultural contexts the three religions were of equal value. Such an emphasis on locating the claims of religious truth in historical context has led some commentators to suggest that in Toland's works, and in the scholarly response to them on the continent, lie the origins of a modern *Textsgeschichte* identified in the Tübingen school.

List of works

Toland, J. (1696) *Christianity not Mysterious*, London: Samuel Buckley. (The work was condemned and prosecuted in London and Dublin. There are various modern reprints.)
—— (1698) *The Life of John Milton*, Amsterdam; repr. in H. Darbishire (ed.) *The Early Lives of Milton*, London: Constable, 1932. (Controversial edition and defence of the republican poet's life and work.)
—— (1699) *Amyntor*, London: The Booksellers of London. (Critical defence of his edition of Milton; exploits textual criticism of Scripture to undercut clerical authority.)
—— (1700) *The Oceana of James Harrington and his other works*, London: The Booksellers of London (Critical edition, much reprinted in the eighteenth century.)
—— (1704) *Letters to Serena*, London: Bernard Lintot; modern edn, ed. G. Gawlick, Stuttgart: Friedrich Frommann, 1964. (Five essays on idolatry, prejudice and materialist metaphysics; sections were later translated into French by the atheistic Baron D'Holbach.)
—— (1705) *Socinianism Truly Stated*, London. (A very rare pamphlet that contains the first use of the word 'Pantheist'.)
—— (1709) *Adeisdaemon, sive Titus Livius a superstitione vindicatus* (The unsuperstitious man. A vindication of Titus Livy from the charge of superstition), The Hague: Thomas Johnson. (Radical historical reading of the life of Moses as a political legislator: poses hermeneutical doubts about the status of revelation.)
—— (1714) *Reasons for Naturalising the Jews in Great Britain and Ireland*, London: J. Roberts; modern edn, ed. H. Mainusch, Stuttgart: W. Kohlhammer, 1965. (Radical defence of toleration for Jews.)
—— (1718) *Nazarenus, or Jewish, Gentile, and Mahometan Christianity*, London: J. Roberts; critical edn, ed. J.A.I. Champion, Oxford: Voltaire Foundation, 1998. (Controversial re-reading of the historical relationships between the three great religions.)
—— (1720) *Pantheisticon*, Cosmopoli (London).

(Translated into English in 1751; a parody of Christianity and vehicle for Toland's pantheist metaphysics.)
—— (1726) *A Collection of several pieces of John Toland* London: J. Peele, 2 vols. (The posthumous works and unpublished correspondence.)

References and further reading

Brykman, G. (ed.) (1995) *John Toland (1670–1722) et la crise de conscience européene* (John Toland and the crisis of the European mind), in *Revue de synthèse*, Paris: Albin Michel. (Collection of essays that covers the diverse contexts of Toland's thought.)
Carabelli, G. (1975) *Tolandiana. Materiali bibliografici per lo studio dell'opera e della fortuna di John Toland (1670–1722)* (A bibliography for the study of the life and works of John Toland), Florence: La Nuova Italia. (Massive bibliographical study of Toland: indispensable for context and reception).
Jacob, M. (1981) *The Radical Enlightenment*, London: Allen & Unwin. (Locates Toland's thought within the radical context of republican freemasonry.)
Sullivan, R.E. (1982) *John Toland and the Deist Controversy*, Cambridge MA: Harvard University Press. (The best intellectual biography of Toland, which locates him within the broader intellectual and religious traditions.)

J.A.I. CHAMPION

TOLEDO, FRANCISCO DE
see TOLETUS, FRANCISCUS

TOLERATION

Toleration emerged as an important idea in the seventeenth century, receiving its fullest defence in John Locke's A Letter Concerning Toleration *(1689). Initially developed in the context of attempts to restore peace in a Europe convulsed by religious conflicts, in the nineteenth and twentieth centuries it came to be extended to the accommodation of disputes about racial, sexual and social differences. Toleration is widely thought to be an essential element of a free society, especially one marked by moral and cultural pluralism, and it figures particularly prominently in the political theory of liberalism.*

The paradigm example of toleration is the deliberate decision to refrain from prohibiting, hindering or otherwise coercively interfering with conduct of which one disapproves, although one has the power to do so. The principal components of the concept of toleration are: a tolerating subject and a tolerated subject (either may be an individual, group, organization or institution); an action, belief or practice which is the object of toleration; a negative attitude (dislike or moral disapproval) on the part of tolerator toward the object of toleration; and a significant degree of restraint in acting against it.

Philosophical arguments have mostly concerned: the range of toleration (what things should or should not be tolerated?); the degree of restraint required by toleration (what forms of opposition are consistent with toleration?); and, most importantly, the justification of toleration (why should some things be tolerated?).

1 Historical development
2 The concept of toleration
3 The justification of toleration

1 Historical development

While intimations of the idea of toleration have been discerned in aspects of Ancient Greek, Roman and medieval thought, it was in sixteenth-century Europe that the concept began to emerge in a distinct and recognizable form (see, for example, the work of Jean Bodin); and in the seventeenth century that it became a crucial component in theorizing about how civil peace could be restored and maintained in a Europe riven by wars of religion. Althusius, Spinoza, Milton and Bayle were all important defenders of some conception of toleration. However, it is in John Locke's *A Letter Concerning Toleration*, first published anonymously in Latin in 1689, that the formulation and defence of the idea of toleration received its fullest statement.

Locke's arguments were addressed exclusively to the religious disputes of his time. Many of his arguments were based on religious or scriptural considerations and there was little in them that was entirely new. What Locke did, however, was to organize existing arguments into a coherent, powerful and principled defence of toleration. In particular, he emphasized the irrationality of religious intolerance, arguing that the attempt to coerce people into believing what they could not conscientiously assent to was both futile and destructive of the civil order. In Locke's view the prime function of government was to maintain civil order and public security: it was not the business of the government to save souls, for which it had neither the appropriate means nor the requisite expertise. However, where religious belief, or its lack, posed a genuine threat to civil order – for example, in

the case of Catholics who owed their allegiance to a foreign power, or that of atheists who, in the absence of an effective threat of divine retribution, could not be trusted to keep their promises – intolerance was in principle entirely proper, although whether in fact it should be employed was a matter of prudential judgment (see LOCKE, J. §7).

Locke's argument for toleration was modest in its scope and cautious in its application. However, its central contention about the proper limits of government intervention in the lives of its citizens contained the seeds of a more expansive and positive conception of toleration. Both the ideas of the Enlightenment and the theory and practice of the US Constitution provided significant further support for toleration, especially for the toleration of heretical or unpopular ideas and opinions. Voltaire was a particularly influential publicist, being attributed with perhaps the most famous remark in defence of toleration: 'I disapprove of what you say, but I will defend to the death your right to say it'.

It is in J.S. Mill's *On Liberty* (1859), probably the most sustained and eloquent plea for toleration yet written, that toleration is wholeheartedly celebrated as part of a general defence of the value of liberty. Essentially, Mill argued for toleration on two grounds. First, he contended that it was a necessary condition for social improvement, intellectual progress and the growth of knowledge. Second, he claimed that it was required for the moral and spiritual development of the individual. Toleration, therefore, is an essential ingredient of a good society, being both a means to social progress and a prerequisite for the development of individuality (see MILL, J.S. §12). Mill's arguments have been enormously influential for modern liberal theorists such as Ronald DWORKIN, H.L.A. HART, Joseph Raz and, more ambiguously, John RAWLS.

Arguments for toleration have been important in removing religious disabilities, easing discrimination against minority groups and promoting a more permissive attitude towards differing life styles. Modern arguments about toleration invariably presume that some substantial element of toleration is essential to a free and democratic society and disagreement generally concerns where, and on what grounds, the limits of toleration should be drawn.

This is not to deny that any robust idea of toleration continues to have, as it always has, its opponents. The case against toleration has usually centred on the claim that it effectively condones immorality or undesirable behaviour; and that in doing so it undermines personal virtue and social cohesiveness. In relation to modern Western society, opponents claim that we have too much toleration, not too little.

2 The concept of toleration

Toleration is sometimes used loosely to mean freedom or liberty but is more accurately understood as a narrower concept. It is concerned specifically with permitting the expression of beliefs, actions or practices which the tolerator would prefer not to exist. Three components of the core concept of toleration can be identified. First, there must be some conduct about which the tolerator has a negative attitude. Second, this negative attitude must not be acted upon in ways which coercively interfere with others acting in the disapproved manner. Third, this refusal to interfere coercively must be more than mere acquiescence or resignation. Toleration is particularly important and problematic when it involves a principled refusal to prohibit conduct believed to be wrong. This gives rise to the so-called 'paradox of toleration' according to which toleration requires that it is right to permit that which is wrong.

Normally, one cannot be tolerant of something if one is either indifferent to it or approves of it. Acting tolerantly characteristically implies some sort of negative attitude or judgment on the part of the tolerator – ranging from mere dislike to intense moral disapproval – towards that which is tolerated. However, a tolerant disposition may also relate to the extent of the negative judgments. For example, to say that a person is tolerant may be to claim that they do not possess an inappropriate range or unjustified number of negative attitudes to the conduct of other people.

To describe a person or group as acting tolerantly standardly implies that they have the power to prohibit or interfere with that which they are tolerating, but choose not to do so. However, not all cases of such restraint are instances of toleration: only where the restraint is motivated by an appropriate reason is the response a distinctively tolerant one. There is some unavoidable vagueness about how restrictive 'interference' with the disapproved conduct can be while remaining consistent with toleration. At one extreme, in normal circumstances, the mere attempt to dissuade a person by reasonable argument from engaging in the disapproved conduct is entirely consistent with acting tolerantly. At the other extreme, the use of physical coercion to prevent an agent engaging in the disapproved conduct is utterly inconsistent with toleration. The key variable is the degree of coerciveness of the interference. The extent to which the imposition of costs which fall short of prohibition or prevention, such as informal social ostracism, higher taxation of disapproved conduct and other forms of disincentive, is compatible with toleration is partly a matter of circumstance and intent, and often involves judgments which allow for reasonable disagreement. In general terms, the more such disincentives incline towards coercion the less consistent they are with toleration. The paradigm of intolerance is the deliberate attempt to eliminate disapproved conduct by coercive means; in its most extreme and ruthless form, persecution. Toleration is therefore a matter of degree (see COERCION).

The moral ideal of toleration can be seen as a mean between intolerance, or the refusal to permit that which should be permitted, and indulgence or laxity, the permitting of that which should not be permitted, without lapsing into indifference, the refusal to judge that which should be judged. Much dispute about toleration has concerned its proper scope and limits. This, in turn, is usually related to differing accounts of the moral grounds or justification of toleration.

3 The justification of toleration

Many arguments for a policy of toleration with respect to particular beliefs or actions are largely prudential or pragmatic. They are couched in terms of the costs (social, economic or political) of intolerance for the intolerant themselves. Such arguments have been, and continue to be, of enormous practical importance, especially in the context of violent religious or political disputes. They are often effective where appeals to more high-minded concerns are not. Nor can such prudential considerations be separated entirely from moral arguments for toleration since they commonly invoke values such as peace, order, security and the avoidance of suffering. However, they do not involve any deeply principled defence of toleration.

The limitations of such arguments are evident in assessing utilitarian justifications of toleration. Utilitarians typically argue for toleration in terms of the maximization of happiness, welfare, preference satisfaction or whatever interpretation is given to utility. The limits of toleration should be set so as to obtain the optimum balance of benefits over harms. As with all utilitarian arguments, however, this defence of toleration is unavoidably conditional upon the truth of many controversial and disputable historically and culturally variable empirical claims. Thus utilitarianism offers a rather precarious and uncertain defence of toleration, heavily dependent upon contingent social circumstances. Moreover, in view of the difficulty of establishing the truth of many of the empirical claims, it is perhaps not surprising that while some utilitarians, such as J.S. Mill, have been uncompromising advocates of toleration, others, such as Mill's contemporary J.F. Stephen, have been considerably less enthusiastic in their support. Indeed, utilitarians are likely to have most difficulty justifying toleration precisely where it may be most needed; that is, in a society with an intensely intolerant majority (see UTILITARIANISM).

Another argument for toleration has derived from moral or religious scepticism (see MORAL SCEPTICISM). On this view, since we can have no guarantee that we possess moral or religious truth we are not justified in imposing on others our own beliefs about these matters. Toleration, therefore, is the only proper response to our fallibility or to the absence of any discernible truth with respect to moral and religious beliefs. Undoubtedly the growth of religious scepticism was an important source of increased religious toleration but the affinity between toleration and scepticism is not as straightforward as it might appear. It has also been argued that if we can never have knowledge of the truth in moral and religious matters, or if there is no truth about such matters to be discovered, then there is nothing wrong with enforcing uniformity of belief. If allowing freedom of belief promotes disunity and creates social tensions, and suppression of beliefs involves no loss of truth, why not seek to rigorously control such diversity?

What this discussion so far suggests is that neither pragmatic nor utilitarian nor sceptical arguments can provide a very secure basis for a principle of toleration. Such a principle must be underpinned by a moral theory which provides stronger support. Much recent moral and political philosophy has been concerned to articulate a defence of toleration in terms of principles or values such as autonomy, impartiality and respect for persons. What these arguments typically seek to show is that toleration is an essential element of any society in which each individual will have the possibility of living an autonomous life; or a necessary implication of the requirement that the state should be impartial between different conceptions of the good; or integral to the idea that every person is an end in themselves and therefore deserving of respect.

All of these arguments are complex and give rise to controversy, and each has been developed in interestingly different ways. In very broad and general terms, however, they are all informed by a particular conception of the person and a view about the proper limits of coercive interference, especially by the state, in people's lives. Persons are conceived as choosers, capable of forming and pursuing their own conception of the good. Each person should be able to exercise significant control over their own life, to make and act on their own choices and decisions, without being subject to coercive interference by other people or the state. The responsibility of government is to secure the conditions under which this is

possible, though it is a matter of dispute exactly what this will entail. There is, however, widespread agreement among proponents of these arguments for toleration that it is not the government's role to prohibit, or even on some views to promote, any specific conceptions of the good (see NEUTRALITY, POLITICAL §2).

In modern Western societies, disagreements about the scope and limits of toleration have centred around race, religion, gender, sexual practices and political affiliation. In particular, dispute has surrounded the permissibility of 'hate' speech, pornography and, in the UK at least, blasphemy. Many of these disputes have been further complicated by the development of multicultural societies and the need to arrive at mutually acceptable terms of accommodation for groups with deeply opposed conceptions of what constitutes a valuable life. What is particularly noteworthy is that attacks on toleration in these areas have frequently come not from the traditional opponents of toleration but from groups such as feminists, socialists and even some liberals. While the question of the extent to which the intolerant should themselves be tolerated has always proved difficult, many of these more recent disputes go well beyond this familiar problem, calling into question some of the most basic tenets of typical liberal accounts of toleration.

See also: FREEDOM OF SPEECH; LAW, LIMITS OF; LIBERALISM; MULTICULTURALISM

References and further reading

Bollinger, L. (1986) *The Tolerant Society: Freedom of Speech and Extremist Speech in America*, New York: Oxford University Press. (A thorough exploration of the justification and limits of freedom of speech in the context of the USA.)

Budziszewski, J. (1992) *True Tolerance: Liberalism and the Necessity of Judgement*, New Brunswick, NJ: Transaction Publishers. (A critique of tolerance as ethical neutrality.)

Gray, J. and Smith, G.W. (eds) (1991) *J.S. Mill: On Liberty in Focus*, London: Routledge. (Mill's *On Liberty* along with the most important modern discussions of it.)

Heyd, D. (ed.) (1996) *Toleration: An Elusive Virtue*, Princeton, NJ: Princeton University Press. (A collection of articles on the meaning, scope and justification of toleration in the modern world.)

Horton, J. (ed.) (1993) *Liberalism, Multiculturalism and Toleration*, London: Macmillan. (Essays on multiculturalism and toleration with particular reference to the 'Rushdie Affair'.)

Horton, J. and Mendus, S. (eds) (1991) *John Locke: A Letter Concerning Toleration in Focus*, London: Routledge. (Popple's translation of Locke's *Letter* with historical and philosophical discussions.)

Horton, J. and Nicholson, P.P. (eds) (1992) *Toleration: Philosophy and Practice*, Aldershot: Avebury. (A diverse collection of articles on various aspects of toleration.)

Kamen, H. (1967) *The Rise of Toleration*, London: Weidenfeld & Nicolson. (An introductory historical account of the development of toleration.)

King, P. (1976) *Toleration*, London: Allen & Unwin. (A comprehensive analysis of the concept of toleration.)

* Locke, J. (1689) *A Letter Concerning Toleration*, ed. R. Kilbansky, trans. J.W. Gough, Oxford: Clarendon Press, 1968. (An accurate modern translation of Locke's letter.)

Mendus, S. (1988) *Justifying Toleration. Conceptual and Historical Perspectives*, Cambridge: Cambridge University Press. (An excellent collection of historical and analytic discussions.)

—— (ed.) (1989) *Toleration and the Limits of Liberalism*, London: Macmillan. (A probing assessment of liberal arguments for toleration.)

* Mill, J.S. (1859) *On Liberty*, in *Collected Works of John Stuart Mill*, ed. J.M. Robson, London: Routledge, 1991, vol. 18, 213–310. (A classic liberal defence of toleration.)

Newman, J. (1982) *Foundations of Religious Tolerance*, Toronto, Ont.: University of Toronto Press. (An analysis and defence of religious tolerance.)

Rawls, J. (1993) *Political Liberalism*, New York: Columbia University Press. (The latest statement of the most influential contemporary liberal defence of toleration.)

Richards, D.J. (1986) *Toleration and the Constitution*, New York: Oxford University Press. (A magisterial discussion of the US Constitution and its interpretation of toleration.)

Tinder, G. (1975) *Tolerance: Toward a New Civility*, Amherst, MA: University of Massachusetts Press. (Develops an account of toleration on grounds which challenge some of the standard liberal argument in its defence as ethical neutrality.)

Wolff, R.P., Marcuse, H. and Moore, B. (1969) *A Critique of Pure Tolerance*, London: Jonathan Cape. (A celebrated series of radical critiques of 'liberal' tolerance.)

JOHN HORTON

TOLETUS, FRANCISCUS (1533–96)

Toletus had an independent, somewhat eclectic, but fundamentally Thomistic outlook. In philosophy his most important works were his commentaries on Aristotle in the areas of logic and natural philosophy. In these commentaries he drew upon the whole previous scholastic tradition to raise and answer questions which were debated in his time and later. In theology he commented upon the greater part of Aquinas' Summa theologiae. Here again he drew upon scholastic philosophers to raise and discuss a wide variety of metaphysical, epistemological and ethical topics. Far from being a slavish follower of Aquinas or Aristotle, he expressed his respectful disagreement with them wherever reason compelled it.

1 Life
2 Commentary on Aquinas
3 Logic
4 Physics
5 Other works

1 Life

Franciscus Toletus (Francisco de Toledo) was born at Cordoba in Spain. After receiving a master of arts at Valencia, he studied theology at Salamanca under the famous Domingo de SOTO. Ordained a priest in 1556, Toletus was already teaching philosophy at Salamanca when he entered the Society of Jesus (the Jesuits) in 1558. In the following year he was sent to Rome where he taught philosophy and then theology, bringing with him the Thomistic outlook emphasized at Salamanca by Francisco de VITORIA and his disciple, Soto. Toletus went on diplomatic missions to Germany, Poland, the Low Countries and France for the Holy See, and in 1593 became the first Jesuit cardinal. He died in Rome.

2 Commentary on Aquinas

His partial commentary on the *Summa theologiae* of Thomas AQUINAS (§6) was left in autograph at the time of his death and was published in four volumes only in the nineteenth century. It addresses issues about most of the first sixty-four questions of the First Part (Ia), the first eighty-eight questions of the second part of the Second Part (IIaIIae) and the ninety questions of the Third Part (IIIa) of the *Summa*. Written in a clear and lively style, it is not simply an exposition of the text of Aquinas. Toletus is interested in the whole of scholasticism, especially in

DUNS SCOTUS, DURANDUS OF ST POURÇAIN, WILLIAM OF OCKHAM, CAJETAN, Lychetus and others in relation to Aquinas. In discussing their concerns, he goes far beyond the text of the *Summa*. For example, in a First Part (*In Summam Theologiae* q.2 a.1) discussion of self-evident propositions he explores the historical issue of the self-denying statement, 'There is no truth.' In the same part (*In Summam Theologiae* q.2 a.3), most likely reflecting Cajetan, he says that taken by itself each of Aquinas' famous five ways proves the existence of God only imperfectly, but taken together they demonstrate a collection of attributes which can belong only to God. In a Second Part (*In Summam Theologiae* q.57 a.3) discussion Toletus separated the 'law of nations' (*jus gentium*) from the natural law and thus set the stage for later Jesuits such as SUÁREZ (§4) to do the same. Again in the Second Part, he expanded Aquinas' treatment of war in various ways. For example (*In Summam Theologiae* q.34 a.1 dub.4), he distinguished three classes of soldiers (those subject to some prince, those not subject who have accepted salaries to fight in time of war, those not subject and not salaried) and discussed their respective obligations to consider the justice of any war in which they may take part, as well as the obligations to restitution they may incur.

3 Logic

The first of Toletus' expressly philosophical works was his *Introductio in dialecticam Aristotelis* (Introduction to the Dialectic of Aristotle) which appeared at Rome in 1560. Reflecting medieval as well as Aristotelian concerns, through five books it dealt with the definition and division of dialectics; with terms (nouns and verbs) and propositions; the supposition, the ampliation, the restriction and so on, of terms; the opposition, equipollence and conversion of propositions; modal propositions and exponibles; reasoning and syllogisms (both proper and fallacious). In 1572, Toletus published at Rome a commentary together with questions on Aristotle's logic. Through seven parts, he treated questions on logic in general, on the five universals of Porphyry, as well as on the *Categories*, *Perihermeneias* and *Posterior Analytics* of Aristotle. His procedure, as he laid it out, was first to explain a question, and then to give those opinions 'which beyond the fact that they are the views of eminent men seem able to offer some reward to their hearer' ('Lectori', *Introductio in dialecticam*). Third, he showed what should be held as more certain and, finally, he refuted opposing arguments (see LOGIC, RENAISSANCE).

4 Physics

In 1573, Toletus published a commentary with questions on the eight books of Aristotle's *Physics*. In this work, disagreeing with Aquinas and a majority of scholastics, he sided with BONAVENTURE and HENRY OF GHENT to deny the possibility of an eternal creation. In support of his position, he offered twelve arguments, of which the first seven he said were demonstrative and the last five less than that. His first argument which went back beyond Bonaventure, at least to al-Ghazali, was to the effect that if the world had existed from all eternity there would have been by now an infinity of human beings. But since every human being has an immortal soul, there would at the present time exist an actual infinite number of such souls. But an actual infinite number is an impossibility. His sixth argument asks, if the world had been created from all eternity, where would the sun have been created? Would it have been created in the east or in the west, in the north or in the south? It could not have been created simultaneously in all these places. Neither could it have been created in one of these places to the exclusion of the others. Otherwise, we could obviously mark a first *terminus a quo* for the motion of the sun and thus a first moment of time. Hence the world could not have been created from eternity. His ninth argument is that if the world were eternal, by now (judging from the multiplication of the human race from Adam) there would be an actually infinite number of human beings on this earth. Again, apart from the obvious fact that this is not the case, such an actual infinite number would be impossible. His tenth argument is that if the world were eternal, the hours, days, months and years before now would all be infinite. And inasmuch as one infinity cannot be greater than another, all of these would be equal. But this would amount to saying that an hour would be equal to a day, to a year, or to a century – which is patently absurd.

It is difficult to reconcile Toletus' position here with the one he took on an actual infinite number when commenting on the First Part (Ia) of the *Summa theologiae*. In his *In Summam Theologiae* (q.7 a.4), Toletus treats the matter 'theologically', siding with Avicenna (see IBN SINA §4), AL-GHAZALI (§2), and also William of Ockham, GREGORY OF RIMINI and Gabriel BIEL (§4), to oppose Aquinas and say that most probably such a number can be realized. In support of this he claims that God can create more and more human beings without limit and that such an unlimited multitude can actually exist together from eternity in the divine knowledge. It is further probable, he thinks, that God, by his absolute power, could create such an unlimited number all at once. In an *ad hominem* argument aimed at Aquinas, Toletus says that anyone who accepts the possibility of an eternal world should admit the possibility of an actual infinite number of immortal human souls. At the same time, consistent with his commentary on the *Physics*, Toletus does allow some probability to the opposite view that an actual infinite number is impossible. Linked with this he says that 'because I do not understand, I prefer to grant to, rather than take away from, the divine power what is a mark of perfection and what I do not understand' (*In Summam Theologiae* q.7 a.4).

5 Other works

Two other philosophical works published by Toletus at Venice in 1575 were in the form of commentaries with questions, on Aristotle's *On the Soul* and *On Generation and Corruption*. In the former work (which was reprinted twenty-two times by 1625), he allowed (in opposition to Aquinas) a direct intellectual cognition of a singular material thing. And although he thinks it 'more probable' that an agent intellect is necessary, he regards it as 'probable' that there is no agent intellect or that such an intellect differs only aspectually (*ratione*) from the possible intellect. Affirming the immortality of the soul, he held it as probable (again in opposition to Aquinas) that although a phantasm was necessary for the inception of intellectual knowledge, once such knowledge was acquired the intellect could dispense with phantasms, and thus could function after death in separation from the body. He also maintained that the intelligible species is not an efficient cause of cognition, but is at best only a condition required for the causality of the possible intellect. Again, apparently reflecting Duns Scotus, Toletus sharply distinguished the apprehension of a propositional synthesis from the judgment which either assents to or dissents from it. This last was to be a much debated item in seventeenth-century scholasticism.

See also: AQUINAS, T.; ARISTOTELIANISM IN THE SEVENTEENTH CENTURY §§2–4; ARISTOTELIANISM, MEDIEVAL; ARISTOTELIANISM, RENAISSANCE; LANGUAGE, RENAISSANCE PHILOSOPHY OF; LOGIC, RENAISSANCE

List of works

Toletus, F. (1533–96) *Opera omnia philosophica* (Complete Philosophical Works), Cologne, 1615; repr. Hildesheim: Olms, 1985. (Contains Toletus' logical works from 1560 and 1572, plus his physical and psychological works from 1575.)

—— (1560) *Introductio in dialecticam Aristotelis* (Introduction to the Dialectic of Aristotle), in F. Toletus, *Opera omnia philosophica*, vol. 1, Hildesheim: Olms, 1985. (An Aristotelian introduction to the logic of terms, propositions and argumentation.)

—— (c.1563) *In Summam Theologiae S. Thomae Aquinatis Enarratio* (An Exposition of Aquinas' *Summa theologiae*), Rome, 1869, 4 vols. (Toletus' partial exposition of the *Summa*, which remained an unpublished manuscript at Toletus' death.)

References and further reading

Ashworth, E.J. (1969) 'The Doctrine of Supposition in the Sixteenth and Seventeenth Centuries', *Archiv für Geschichte der Philosophie* 51: 260–85. (A specific doctrine of Toletus is treated within a wider context.)

—— (1974) *Language and Logic in the Post-Medieval Period*, Dordrecht and Boston, MA: Reidel. (A general study which includes discussion of Toletus.)

Charron, W.C. and Doyle, J.P. (1993) 'On the Self-Refuting Statement "There is no Truth": A Medieval Treatment', *Vivarium* 31: 241–66. (Contains an exposition of Toletus' summation of and judgment on a long-standing scholastic discussion.)

Lohr, C.H. (1987) *Latin Aristotle Commentaries. II Renaissance Authors*, Florence: Olschki, 458–61. (Contains bibliographical information on Toletus.)

Risse, W. (1964) *Die Logik der Neuzeit. I Band. 1500–1640* (The Logic of the Modern Period), Stuttgart and Bad Cannstatt: Frommann, vol. 1, 382–5. (Toletus' logic treated within its historical context.)

Solana, M. (1940) *Historia de la filosofía española. Época del renacimiento (siglo XVI)* (History of Spanish Philosophy. The Time of the Renaissance (16th Century)), Madrid: Asociación Española para el Progreso de las Ciencias, vol. 3, 311–37. (An introductory overview of Toletus.)

JOHN P. DOYLE

TOLSTOI, COUNT LEV NIKOLAEVICH (1828–1910)

Tolstoi expressed philosophical ideas in his novels Voina i mir *(War and Peace) (1865–9) and* Anna Karenina *(1875–7), which are often regarded as the summit of realism, as well as in shorter fictional works, such as* Smert' Ivana Il'icha *(The Death of Ivan Il'ich) (1886), often praised as the finest novella in European literature. In addition, he wrote numerous essays and tracts on religious, moral, social, educational and aesthetic topics, most notably 'Chto takoe iskusstvo?' (What Is Art?) (1898),* Tsarstvo Bozhie vnutri vas *(*The Kingdom of God Is Within You*) (1893) and his autobiographical meditation* Ispoved' *(A Confession) (1884).*

Tolstoi apparently used his essays, letters and diaries to explore ideas by stating them in their most extreme form, while his fiction developed them with much greater subtlety. Critics have discerned a sharp break in his work: an earlier period, in which he produced the two great novels, is dominated by deep scepticism; and a later period following the existential trauma and subsequent conversion experience described in Ispoved'. *Tolstoi stressed the radical contingency of events, valued practical over theoretical reasoning, and satirized any and all overarching systems. After 1880, he assumed the role of a prophet, claiming to have found the true meaning of Christianity. He 'edited' the Gospels by keeping only those passages containing the essence of Christ's teaching and dismissed the rest as so many layers of falsification imposed by ecclesiastics. Tolstoi preached pacifism, anarchism, vegetarianism, passive resistance to evil (a doctrine that influenced Gandhi), a radical asceticism that would have banned sex even within marriage, and a theory of art that rejected most classic authors, including the plays of Shakespeare and Tolstoi's own earlier novels.*

1   **Life**
2   ***War and Peace***
3   ***Anna Karenina***
4   **Aesthetics and late writings**

1   Life

Born into a prominent aristocratic family, Tolstoi studied oriental languages and law at Kazan University, where he failed to earn a degree. He then tried to reform his estate according to philosophical principles, a topic which recurs in *Anna Karenina*, whose hero, Konstantin Levin, meditates on why such efforts almost invariably fail. A compulsive diarist, the young Tolstoi repeatedly formulated complex rules for behaviour, which he never followed, then devised rules for insuring obedience to the earlier rules, and at last reflected on the inadequacy of all rules or systems for an understanding of human behaviour, another key theme of his fiction. Enlisting in the army during the Crimean War, he wrote military stories (the Sevastopol sketches, 1855–6) concentrating on the difference between standard narratives, whether official, literary or historical, and the realities of combat. He later recalled that immediately after a battle, soldiers would narrate their experiences in a confused way and describe events as rife with contingency; but a month later, after official accounts had described a smooth series of military engagements in conventional language, the same soldiers would 'remember' events according to the received narratives. Such experiences led Tolstoi to a deep suspicion of narrative neatness, which rules out the contingency actually governing events, a theme central to *War and Peace*.

After the Crimean War, Tolstoi was hailed as a major writer but, always suspicious of the intelligentsia he deemed self-congratulatory, he joined no intellectual camp. In 1862 he married Sofia Andreevna Bers, and devoted the ensuing years to his marriage (he eventually had thirteen children) and the writing of *War and Peace*. In the 1870s he wrote *Anna Karenina* and then experienced the most significant of his many psychological crises, leading to the adoption of his own reformulated Christianity. His new ideas led to estrangement from his wife, and their marriage from this point on deteriorated and became complicated; it has been the subject of numerous, vaguely voyeuristic biographical treatments.

In addition to theological tracts and many essays, Tolstoi wrote endless diaries, which were evidently designed to be published and so resemble stage whispers. Regarded around the world as a sage, he corresponded with countless writers and thinkers, and his estate, Iasnaia Poliana, became a place of pilgrimage. His best fiction of the period deals with sexuality (in *Kreitserova sonata* (The Kreutzer Sonata) (1891)), death (*The Death of Ivan Il'ich*), and the complex psychology of sainthood (*Father Sergei* (1898)), but he also wrote one long novel, *Voskresenie* (Resurrection) (1899), usually regarded as a heavy-handed, didactic failure. Always perplexed by the contradiction between his wealthy life and the simple existence he preached, he fled Iasnaia Poliana and soon died in the course of his pilgrimage.

2   *War and Peace*

In his most lasting work, Tolstoi was deeply impressed by all those aspects of life that elude systematization or theoretical knowledge. He loved to formulate negative laws, dicta about what cannot be known or found in an unmixed state. 'Pure and absolute sorrow is as impossible as pure and absolute joy', he writes in *War and Peace*, a sentence that reflects in its very style Tolstoian habits of thought.

In Tolstoi's view, it is not primarily grand incidents, broad laws or dramatic decisions that shape individual or historical life, but the sum total of ordinary events. Life is made by 'tiny, tiny alterations' of action and consciousness, changes so small that they usually pass unnoticed, even though they are right before our eyes. What really counts is hidden in plain view, a sentiment that seems to have influenced WITTGENSTEIN, who was an admirer of Tolstoi. At each small moment of existence, contingency reigns, not in the sense that anything can happen, but in the sense that more than one thing can happen. Time branches not only at critical moments, but always, and so our smallest decisions have moral value. Apparently inconsequential events may turn out to have great impact over time. Our decisions at critical moments are shaped by the climate of our minds, which in turn depends on the sum total of our smallest thoughts at odd moments.

No algorithm can reduce these small events to laws. With withering irony, Tolstoi, who was superb at logical analysis, detects the fallacies in attempts to construct systems that aspire to eliminate contingency. Theoreticians often assume that behind the apparent chaos of the social world reigns a hidden order, which may be expressed in a few simple laws; but Tolstoi insists that all such reasoning manages to rule out inconvenient facts and at crucial moments presumes what it hopes to prove. One example he cites for this is the Hegelian assumption that certain events not fitting a central story are 'nonhistorical'. In *War and Peace*, he refers to reasoning by 'stencil work'. Tolstoi suggests that the opposite assumption is closer to lived experience: the social world is fundamentally messy and order is always the result of work. It is regularity, not contingency, that requires an explanation.

In *War and Peace*, Tolstoi develops these insights in the philosophical reflections of his characters, in the events of their lives and in embedded essays, expressed not through a narrator but directly through the voice of the author. In this work, battle becomes a metaphor for history, and the radical uncertainty of combat, which only fools think can be reduced to a science of warfare, suggests the radical unpredictability of history. Tolstoi utterly rejects the possibility of laws of history and in several writings expressed particular animus to the idea of an underlying law of progress. One of the novel's heroes, Prince Andrei, begins the novel believing in heroism, which he conceives as the ability to grasp the laws of battle and to act decisively upon them in dangerous moments. He eventually learns that battles cannot be shaped by strategy but are decided instead by 'a hundred million diverse chances, which will be decided on the instant by whether we run or they run, whether this man or that man is killed' – decided, that is, by events that are in principle unpredictable and chancy. The emphasis on what happens 'on the

instant' reflects Tolstoi's belief in the crucial importance of presentness and on the futility of assuming that only timeless principles represent the highest form of thinking. Tolstoi believed deeply in what Aristotle called *phronesis*, or practical reasoning (see ARISTOTLE §23).

'What science can there be', Prince Andrei asks, 'in a matter in which, as in every practical matter, nothing can be determined and everything depends on innumerable conditions, the significance of which becomes manifest at a particular moment, and no one can tell when that moment will come?' Thus, the most effective soldier in the novel, Nikolai Rostov, cares nothing for theories but has developed the practical ability to grasp the shifting situations of each moment and, on the basis of unformalizable experience, to take advantage of unique and short-lived opportunities. The best generals in the novel, such as the Russian commander Kutuzov, know that they can be effective not by planning battles but by inspiring soldiers with the confidence to act intelligently. Kutuzov, in fact, falls asleep during councils of war because effective action depends on alertness. He explains that the best preparation for a battle, or any especially unpredictable and rapidly changing situation, is 'a good night's sleep'.

For a variety of reasons, historical narratives smooth out the contingencies of battles and of history. They therefore misrepresent the course of events, and, when taken as empirical knowledge on which to base future actions, lead to ill-conceived plans and to overconfidence in planning itself. In large part, the regularity of historical narratives reflects the essentially aesthetic need for a good story. Genres of historical writing differ, but each reflects a particular kind of plotting, all of which understate the radical uncertainty of the world precisely by telling a neat story. Plot contains implicit philosophy, and Tolstoi relentlessly teases out the hidden and fallacious assumptions behind various narrative forms. For reasons of mental economy, memory also works by filtering out the contingent. Indeed, the fallacies of memory and narrative are present in initial acts of perception. In his novels, Tolstoi demonstrates these truths with portraits of events, their perception, their later appearance in memory and their encapsulation in the narratives characters and real historians construct.

In a series of draft introductions to *War and Peace*, Tolstoi evokes the image of a man viewing a distant hill on which only trees are visible. The man may conclude that the region in question contains nothing but trees. This conclusion would be a trick of perception, because smaller objects are simply not visible at a distance. In the same way, historians focus on unusual and big events because they are the most likely to be recorded. Part of the strategy of *War and Peace* is to contrast the picture of historians with a recreation of what events must have been like. We also commit this fallacy of perception in our individual lives, because memory does not preserve, or we cannot easily recall, small events that do not fit a pattern or story, but which may have been most effective and may even have constituted the essential quality of our lives. *War and Peace* is largely about the need to reverse some mental habits.

3 Anna Karenina

In both *War and Peace* and *Anna Karenina*, Tolstoi develops a theory of psychology. Perhaps indebted to Locke through the medium of Laurence Sterne's novel *Tristram Shandy*, Tolstoi conceives the mind as an agglomeration of mental habits, each the result of small actions taken many times. These habits do not cohere into a whole; wholeness, like moral integrity, is a project we undertake but never complete. At any given moment, the mind has many thoughts and sensations, too many for effective action if we did not have the capacity to focus our attention on one or a few of them. Numerous tiny alterations are taking place on the periphery of consciousness, much as small events are always taking place in history, and these have their effect. But we rarely notice them, precisely because by definition one cannot focus one's attention on what escapes one's attention. One can only glimpse them at moments when attention shifts, and Tolstoi illustrates this process in detail.

Tolstoi is also famous for exploring in meticulous detail the relation of the body to the mind. At the periphery of attention characters are dimly aware of bodily sensations but are usually unaware of how they affect the direction of their thoughts. Or a character may be smiling out of habit or because of a thought experienced some time earlier, with the smile simply forgotten on his face. Anyone trying to guess his current thoughts by that smile would be mistaken because the mind is never whole and because at any given moment is temporally layered. We are all palimpsests.

In both *War and Peace* and *Anna Karenina*, Tolstoi develops an approach to ethics that might be called casuistical in the root sense of the word. Theoretical reasoning, proceeding from general principles to the particular situation, tends to oversimplify events. We do better by educating an ethical sensibility through sensitive attention to particular cases as they arise throughout life and then, at each moment, trusting a well-developed ethical sensibility (see MORAL PARTICULARISM).

Anna Karenina applies these general ideas to social life and to the problem of reform. As *War and Peace* rejects the romanticized idea of great heroes directing history, *Anna Karenina* may be viewed as a polemic against the assumption that romantic love (the sort to be found in *Romeo and Juliet* and in countless works of popular culture) is the only kind. The tragedy of Anna derives from her acceptance of this myth. The wiser characters, such as Kitty, understand that love may also be prosaic and that a successful marriage must be based precisely on prosaic love, which cultivates not grand gestures but small acts of intimacy that do not make a compelling story. The novel's famous first sentence – 'All happy families resemble each other; each unhappy family is unhappy in its own way' – suggests that unhappy families each have a unique story, whereas happy family lives are composed of prosaic incidents that do not make a compelling story. Plot is an index of error and of a life lived badly.

The novel's hero, Levin, hopes to reform Russian agriculture by introducing Western machinery and applying the conclusions of social science. He discovers that successful reform never proceeds down from universal principles forced on a reluctant population, but by reasoning up from local conditions, which are always particular, and adopting measures that improve upon what already exists. We sense here Tolstoi's deep conservatism and scepticism about the abstract theorizing of intellectuals.

4 Aesthetics and late writings

For Tolstoi before his conversion, realistic novels were the supreme art form because they provide, more than any other literary or non-literary writing, a rich sense of the particularities of ordinary existence. Nevertheless, novels also mislead because they, like other forms of narrative art, offer too neat a picture. Precisely because the author knows the story in advance and plans everything to fit, novels misrepresent our temporal experience by letting a pattern of the whole dictate what happens and by ruling out contingency. Tolstoi experimented with various ways of avoiding this error, and so wrote *War and Peace* (and to a great extent *Anna Karenina*) without an advance plan, letting each serialized part develop potentials in earlier parts but with no overall end in view. In fact, *War and Peace* never really ends, it just breaks off.

In *Anna Karenina*, Tolstoi developed a general theory of art on which he expanded in *What Is Art?* and other writings. The novel's true artist, Mikhailov, paints not by applying techniques or by adhering to the tenets of any school, but by learning to see and record the particularities of experience. He is always observing small events of life and remembering them. Because everyone's experience is unique, he can be certain that his painting will convey an aspect of experience no one else has conveyed.

In *What Is Art?*, Tolstoi first offers a showcase demolition of all the received schools of aesthetics and then presents his own view. Like Mikhailov, the true artist conveys an experience so sensitively that he manages to 'infect' his audience with the feelings he himself had. But many so-called artists work quite differently, by applying a set of abstract techniques copied from other artists. Though gaudily 'interesting', their work is not true but 'counterfeit' art because it results from no particular and unique experience. True art may be divided into good and bad on moral grounds. A bad but true artist successfully infects his readers with pernicious moral feelings (see ART AND MORALITY §3). Tolstoi rejects most of the canon of Western art as either immoral (Maupassant) or counterfeit (Wagner) or both (Shakespeare). His favourite example of good, true art was the story of Joseph in the Bible.

By goodness Tolstoi came to mean the tenets of Tolstoian Christianity. He rejected all miracles, all sacraments and the divinity of Christ. Relying on the Sermon on the Mount (Matthew: 6–7), he took Christ's most important commandment to be 'non-resistance to evil', from which he derived a rejection of any institution based on force and so arrived at anarchism. He interpreted social and cultural institutions as so many curtains for concealing from ourselves our mortality (the theme of *The Death of Ivan Il'ich*) and for creating intermediaries between the practitioners of violence and ourselves, who benefit from it. He went so far as to argue that crime would cease if prisons and police were abolished. In these writings, Tolstoi seems far from the radical sceptic of his earlier years – and from occasional works of his old age, such as his novella *Father Sergei*, which reflects with evident self-irony on the distortions induced by aspirations to sainthood. Admirers of Tolstoi's thought are divided between those who think of him as the prophet of non-resistance and those who prefer his sense of the futility of all-embracing systems.

See also: GANDHI, M.K.; WAR AND PEACE, PHILOSOPHY OF §4

List of works

Tolstoi [Tolstoy], L. (1929–58) *Polnoe sobranie sochinenii*, Moscow: Khudozhestvennaia literatura, 90 vols. (The authoritative edition of Tolstoi's works in Russian.)

—— (1967) *Great Short Works*, trans. L. and A. Maude, New York: Harper & Row. (Contains *The Death of Ivan Il'ich* (1886), *The Kreutzer Sonata* (1891), *Father Sergei* (1898) and other works.)

—— (1865–9) *Voina i mir*, trans. A. Dunnigan, *War and Peace*, New York: Signet, 1968. (Discussed in detail in §2.)

—— (1875–7) *Anna Karenina*, trans. C. Garnett, ed. L. Kent and N. Berberova, New York: Modern Library, 1965. (Discussed in detail in §3.)

—— (1893) *Tsarstvo Bozhie vnutri vas*, trans. L. Weiner, *The Kingdom of God Is Within You: Or, Christianity Not As A Mystical Teaching But As A New Concept of Life*, New York: Noonday, 1961.

—— (1899) *Voskresenie*, trans. L. Maude, *Resurrection*, Oxford: Oxford University Press, 1994.

—— (1971) *A Confession, The Gospel in Brief and What I Believe*, trans. A. Maude, London: Oxford University Press. (From the original Russian texts of 'Ispoved'' (1884), 'Soedinenie i perevod chetyrekh evangelii' (1881) and 'V chem moia vera' (1884) respectively.)

—— (1961) *Recollections and Essays*, trans. A. Maude, London: Oxford University Press. (Anthology containing 'Why Do Men Stupefy Themselves?' (1890), in which Tolstoi develops his theme of 'tiny alterations'; his main critique of Shakespeare, 'Shakespeare and the Drama' (1906); 'Non-Acting' (1893); and the Gandhi letters (1910).)

—— (1969) *What Is Art? and Essays on Art*, trans. A. Maude, London: Oxford University Press. (Anthology containing *What Is Art?* (1898); 'Introduction to the Works of Guy de Maupassant' (1894); Tolstoi's 'Afterword' (1905) to Chekhov's story 'Darling'; and other essays on art.)

References and further reading

Berlin, I. (1970) *The Hedgehog and the Fox: An Essay on Tolstoy's View of History*, New York: Simon & Schuster. (Views Tolstoi as torn between scepticism and dogmatism.)

Eikhenbaum, B. (1930) *Tolstoi in the Sixties*, trans. D. White, Ann Arbor, MI: Ardis, 1982. (By a leading Russian formalist, this book also examines Tolstoi's relation to the thinkers of his time.)

Feuer, K.B. (1996) *Tolstoy and the Genesis of 'War and Peace'*, ed. R. Miller and D. Orwin, Ithaca, NY: Cornell University Press. (Considers the creation of the novel in relation to Tolstoi's evolving thought about society.)

Gustafson, R.F. (1986) *Leo Tolstoy, Resident and Stranger: A Study in Fiction and Theology*, Princeton, NJ: Princeton University Press. (Outlines

Tolstoi's theological views and reads Tolstoi's late ideas into his early fiction.)

Morson, G.S. (1987) *Hidden in Plain View: Narrative and Creative Potentials in 'War and Peace'*, Stanford, CA: Stanford University Press. (Discusses Tolstoi's views on history, historiography and psychology in relation to the forms and themes of *War and Peace*.)

GARY SAUL MORSON

TOMINAGA NAKAMOTO (1715–46)

Tominaga Nakamoto was a leading representative of what some scholars have called the eighteenth-century 'enlightenment' movement in Tokugawa thought. Nakamoto's philological critiques of the historical development of Buddhist, Confucian and Shintō doctrines are noteworthy for their modern, empiricist tendencies. His advocacy of makoto no michi, *or 'the True Way', a quotidian ethics advocating practical morality, gained no real following during Nakamoto's brief life.*

Nakamoto was the third son of Tominaga Hōshun, an Ōsaka *shōyu* (soya sauce) merchant who co-founded the Kaitokudō academy. The neo-Confucian scholar Miyake Sekian (1665–1730), directed Nakamoto's education at the Kaitokudō. However, early on Nakamoto studied *kogaku*, or 'Ancient Learning', the philologically-oriented Confucianism of ITŌ JINSAI, OGYŪ SORAI and Itō Tōgai. Those *kogaku* scholars had criticized neo-Confucians for misconstruing the original Confucian teachings. The latter, they generally agreed, conveyed a sagely wisdom worthy of faithful obedience.

Nakamoto surpassed contemporary *kogaku* schools by claiming that there was nothing sacrosanct about ancient Confucianism: it was one of several schools which appeared during an age of profuse philosophical activity in ancient China. After expounding this view in his *Setsuhei* (Philosophical Obscurantism), Nakamoto was expelled from the Kaitokudō. The *Setsuhei* is no longer extant, suggesting that contemporaries saw it as a pariah work. Its ideas were recalled, however, in Nakamoto's *Okina no fumi* (An Old Man's Notes).

In his *Shutsujō gogo* (Buddha's Post-Enlightenment Teachings), Nakamoto similarly criticized the history of Buddhism, claiming that Mahāyāna teachings were later accretions, not legitimate accounts of the historical Buddha's sermons as Mahāyāna Buddhists claimed them to be. *Shutsujō gogo* explained the cardinal principle of Nakamoto's critical philology, *kajō*, or 'transformative accretion'. It asserted that throughout the Buddhist tradition new ideas had been attributed (*ka*) to the Buddha, effectively and illegitimately transforming (*jō*) his message time and again (see BUDDHIST PHILOSOPHY, JAPANESE).

Nakamoto cautioned that language must be understood relative to three factors: the person using it, the historical period in which it is used, and the context of its use (see LANGUAGE, PHILOSOPHY OF). Nakamoto also distinguished five contexts of meaning: (1) later explication, (2) the original teaching, (3) implicit significance, (4) heated debate and (5) rebuttal. Through hermeneutics based on these contexts, one could come to understand the history of philosophical thought.

In his last work, *Okina no fumi*, Nakamoto criticized Shintō, arguing that it had been invented by medieval Japanese to compete with Confucianism and Buddhism (see SHINTŌ). Nakamoto faulted Shintō for its excessive secrecy, which contradicted his notion of *makoto no michi* (the True Way). While allowing that elements of Confucianism, Buddhism and Shintō were intrinsic to *makoto no michi*, Nakamoto suggested, contrary to his principle of *kajō*, that his 'True Way' was not just a later accretion.

Nakamoto's writings never circulated widely. Prior to the efforts of Professor Naitō Konan at Kyoto University in the 1920s, *Okina no fumi* was an obscure work even among specialists in Tokugawa thought. Nakamoto's *Shutsujō gogo* did, however, influence *kokugaku* (National Learning) scholars such as MOTOORI NORINAGA and Hirata Atsutane in their rejection of Buddhism.

See also: BUDDHIST PHILOSOPHY, JAPANESE; CONFUCIAN PHILOSOPHY, JAPANESE; SHINTŌ

List of works

Tominaga Nakamoto (1745) *Shutsujō gogo* (Buddha's Post-Enlightenment Teachings), in Mizuta Norihisa and Arisaka Takamichi (eds) *Tominaga Nakamoto/Yamagata Bantō*, Nihon shisō taikei vol. 43, Tokyo: Iwanami shoten, 1975. (Edition of *Shutsujō gogo* in Sino-Japanese along with a classical Japanese translation and copious annotations.)

—— (1746) *Okina no fumi* (An Old Man's Notes), in Nakamoto Yukihiko (ed.), *Andō Shōeki/Tominaga Nakamoto/Miura Baien/Ishida Baigan/Ninomiya Sontoku/Kaihō Seiryō*, Nihon no shisō vol. 18, Tokyo: Chikuma shobō, 1971. (Includes *Okina no fumi* in classical Japanese along with a modern translation and notes.)

References and further reading

Minamoto Ryōen (1973) *Tokugawa shisō shōshi*, Tokyo: Chūō kōronsha. (Focuses on Nakamoto's critiques of Confucianism, Buddhism and Shintō, arguing that Nakamoto's ideas relativized traditional currents of Japanese thought.)

Najita Tetsuo (1987) *Visions of Virtue in Tokugawa Japan: The Kaitokudō Merchant Academy of Osaka*, Chicago, IL: University of Chicago Press. (Examines Nakamoto in the context of the Kaitokudō academy, the *kogaku* movement and *kokugaku* thought.)

Tsunoda Ryusaku, de Bary, W.T. and Keene, D. (eds) (1964) *Sources of Japanese Tradition*, vol. 1, New York: Columbia University Press. (Discusses Nakamoto's 'historical relativism' as part of Japan's 'Eighteenth-Century Rationalism'. Includes translated excerpts of *Okina no fumi*.)

JOHN ALLEN TUCKER

TONGHAK

Tonghak is an indigenous religion in Korea. Founded by Ch'oe Cheu (1824–64), it presently flourishes under the new name of Ch'ŏndogyo. An eclectic religion, Tonghak borrowed from Confucianism, Buddhism, Daoism, Christianity, shamanism and other folk beliefs. Its central tenet is founded on the concept of In nae ch'ŏn *(Man is God). God is not a supernatural God who exists outside or beyond man, but is an immanent God who is present within every man.*

Disturbed by the unsettling political, social and economic conditions, and frustrated by his own unhappy family circumstances, the founder of Tonghak, Ch'oe Cheu (also known by his honorific name Suun), embarked on a long and tortuous search by means of meditation and study for a new way for the salvation of his fellow men. Suddenly, on the fifth day of the fourth month of 1860, he fell shivering into a trance, during which he heard a voice from Heaven. For a year thereafter, he experienced similar encounters from time to time. In 1861 he started to proselytize, based on the revelations he received. He named his teaching Tonghak (Eastern Learning) as a counter to Catholicism (known then as Sŏhak, or Western Learning), which had made significant inroads in Korea. In 1864, he was executed by the provincial government on the charge of spreading false teaching to confuse the people.

The basic doctrine as taught by Ch'oe Cheu is embodied in the *Tonggyŏng taejŏn* (Bible of the Tonghak Doctrine) and *Yongdam yusa* (Hymns from the Dragon Pool), and was further clarified and refined by the leaders who succeeded him. From the moment of conception, according to Ch'oe Cheu, man is endowed with the mind of God and God is present within every man ever after. (In referring to God, Ch'oe Cheu used both the Sino-Korean word *Ch'ŏnju* (Lord of Heaven) and the native Korean word *Hanulim* (God) interchangeably.) Thus, God said: 'My mind is your mind (*Osim chŭk yŏsim*).' Accordingly, Tonghak emphasizes the oneness of God and man, in which man is a manifestation of God. Though God is omniscient and omnipotent, he can realize his will only through men. Hence there is room for evolution in this world (see GOD, CONCEPTS OF).

Man must work, according to Ch'oe Cheu, to 'serve God (*si ch'ŏnju*)' by maintaining the upright mind and proper deportment (*susim chŏnggi*) in addition to the 'humanity, righteousness, propriety and wisdom that the former sage taught'. The essence of the Tonghak teaching, he said, lies in the three words: sincerity (*sŏng*), reverence (*kyŏng*) and faith (*sin*) (see XIN). But whereas in Confucianism, only the educated are capable of becoming 'superior men', in Tonghak all men without regard to their educational or social background can attain that status (see CONFUCIAN PHILOSOPHY, CHINESE).

Concomitant with the idea that Man is God is the concept emphasized by Ch'oe Sihyŏng (1829–98), the second leader of Tonghak, who maintained that because man is God, 'every man should be treated as a God (*sain yŏch'ŏn*)'. There can be no social distinction based on birth, education or any other factor. Ch'oe Sihyŏng said: 'Because man is God, all men are equal and there can be no discrimination. Any artificial distinction of men between high and low violates God's will.' Another concept that underlies Tonghak is the idea that 'all men evolve toward oneness' (*tonggwi ilch'e*). When people realize the truth that man and God are one, all will turn to this truth and evolve towards becoming one with God. The Tonghak teaching also contains a nationalistic element, in so far as Ch'oe Cheu called for 'protecting the nation and securing peace for the people' (*poguk anmin*) against the potential threat from Japan and the Western nations.

In addition to such theological and scholarly principles, Tonghak appealed to the uneducated masses by promising salvation via mystical experience (see MYSTICISM, NATURE OF). It promised that those who practised the true faith would have their diseases cured, and that the ritual incantations of certain sacred formulas and the possession of a prescribed talisman would give them supernatural power to ward off evil and sickness. It also assured faithful followers freedom from worldly oppression and suffering. The Tonghak founder then urged his followers to work for 'the salvation of all people' (*Kwangje ch'angsaeng*).

Attracted by its humanitarian and egalitarian teaching, many people at the grassroots level accepted Tonghak, especially peasants. In spite of harassment and persecution by the government, its strength grew rapidly and it became a powerful social and political force in Korea. In 1894, Tonghak followers played a central role in leading the great insurrection known as the Tonghak rebellion that almost brought down the Chosôn dynasty and touched off the first Sino-Japanese war. In 1905, under the leadership of Son Pyônghûi, Tonghak was reorganized, adopting the new name Ch'ôndogyo (Religion of the Heavenly Way). Throughout the Japanese colonial period, Ch'ôndogyo remained strongly nationalistic, playing a leading role in the March First movement in 1919. In addition to being a religious organization, Ch'ôndogyo has played an active role in promoting Korea's national, social and cultural causes. Today it has about 600,000 followers.

See also: CONFUCIAN PHILOSOPHY, KOREAN; RELIGION, PHILOSOPHY OF

References and further reading

Ch'ôndogyo paengnyôn yaksa (Abridged One Hundred Year History of Ch'ôndogyo) (1981), Seoul: Mirae munhwasa. (An official history compiled by a special committee of the church, to be published in two volumes.)

Hong Chang-hwa (1990) *Ch'ôndogyo kyori wa sasang* (Doctrine and Thought of Ch'ôndogyo), Seoul: Ch'ôndogyo Chungang Chongbu Ch'ulp'anbu. (An explanation of the basic doctrine of Ch'ôndogyo in simple Korean.)

Kim Yong Choon (1972) 'The Ch'ôndogyo Concept of the Origin of Man', *Philosophy East and West* 22: 373–84. (Examines the original and unique nature of its concept with a contrasting Judaeo-Christian perspective.)

—— (1973) 'The Ch'ôndogyo Concept of the Nature of Man', *International Philosophical Quarterly* 13: 209–28. (Analyses the basic concept of 'Man is God'.)

O Chiyông (1940) *Tonghak sa* (History of Tonghak), Seoul: Yôngch'ang Sôgwan. (An authoritative history by an active participant.)

Shin, S.S. (1978) 'The Tonghak Movement: From Enlightenment to Revolution', *Korean Studies Forum* 5: 1–79. (A good study of how the obscure and apolitical religion of Tonghak was transformed

to play a leading role in the nationwide uprising of 1894.)

—— (1979) 'Tonghak Thought: The Roots of Revolution', *Korea Journal* 19 (9): 11–20. (A scholarly study of the basic doctrine of Tonghak thought tracing the formulation of its founder's teachings.)

Weems, B.B. (1964) *Reform, Rebellion and the Heavenly Way*, Tucson, AZ: University of Arizona Press. (A still useful English history of Tonghak from its beginnings until 1950.)

Yi Ton-hwa (1933) *Ch'ôndogyo ch'anggôn sa* (History of Founding of Ch'ôndogyo), Seoul: Ch'ôndogyo Chungang Chongriwôn. (An instructive account of Ch'ôndogyo's early history by one of its active members).

YÔNG-HO CH'OE

TORAH *see* BIBLE, HEBREW

TOTALITARIANISM

A term adopted in the 1920s by the Italian philosopher Giovanni Gentile to describe the ideal fascist state, 'totalitarianism' quickly acquired negative connotations as it was applied to the regimes of Hitler in Germany and Stalin in the USSR. Within political science it has generally been used to refer to a distinctively modern form of dictatorship based not only on terror but also on mass support mobilized behind an ideology prescribing radical social change. Controversially, the specific content of the ideology is considered less significant than the regime's determination to form the minds of the population through control of all communications.

Totalitarianism has attracted the attention of philosophers as well as political scientists because a number of classic philosophical systems have been suspected of harbouring totalitarian aspirations, and also because the model of total power exercised through discourse has been used by critical theorists to mount an attack on modernity in general.

1   The fascist doctrine of totalitarianism
2   Ideological domination
3   Philosophy as a source of totalitarianism
4   Totalitarianism and the critique of modernity

1   The fascist doctrine of totalitarianism

The concept of totalitarianism began its career in

Italy in the 1920s as an ideal formulated for Mussolini's Fascist regime by Giovanni GENTILE (§3) (see FASCISM). Gentile, whose idealist philosophy was deeply indebted to Hegel, argued that the state is an all-embracing ethical reality, that state and individual are inseparable and that only in and through the state can individuals realize their true freedom. Fascism, to Gentile, was essentially a spirit that ought to manifest itself in every aspect of life. In 'The Doctrine of Fascism', published under Mussolini's name in 1932, he declared: 'For the Fascist all is in the state and nothing human or spiritual exists, or much less has value, outside the state. In this sense, Fascism is totalitarian' (Gregor 1969: 223). For a while the connotations of the term were favourable, sufficiently so for it to be used approvingly by the Marxist thinker Antonio Gramsci to describe the Communist Party. However, it took on different senses upon being borrowed to describe the more formidable dictatorships of Hitler and Stalin, and was developed into an ideal-type within political science.

2 Ideological domination

According to the classic theories put forward after the Second World War by Hannah Arendt in *The Origins of Totalitarianism* (1951) and by Friedrich and Brzezinski in *Totalitarian Dictatorship and Autocracy* (1967), 'totalitarianism' means a distinctively modern type of dictatorship of which Nazism and Stalinism are the most prominent examples. Power within such a state rests not only upon the control exercised by a single party over all aspects of social organization, nor even merely upon the terror wielded by the secret police. An essential aspect of totalitarian rule is ideological domination, guided by an official ideology aimed at radical transformation. Whether this ideology appears to be right-wing or left-wing is beside the point. Differences of content between the racist ideology of Nazism and Stalin's Marxism-Leninism seemed to the theorists of totalitarianism to be less significant than the structural similarities between two regimes that attempted to mould the thoughts of their subjects into conformity with official ideology. Criticism of the concept of totalitarianism has focused particularly upon this central claim that regimes whose ideologies appear to be diametrically opposite are in fact essentially similar.

Friedrich and Brzezinski regard all ideological one-party regimes as totalitarian, whereas Arendt's use of the concept is more complex and is restricted to a few particularly extreme cases. For ARENDT, the most characteristic totalitarian institution is the concentration camp, which exemplifies the pursuit of total power by dehumanizing its victims to the point where the human attributes of plurality and spontaneity have been destroyed. Totalitarian ideology is the intellectual expression of this, since it allows no room for individual thought. The key feature of these regimes for Arendt was not simply the adoption of an ideological principle (such as the claim that class struggle or race war is the key to history), but rather the relentless working out of that principle to its logical conclusion in the extermination of whole peoples or classes deemed to be 'objective enemies'. At the heart of totalitarianism, according to Arendt, was the blind pursuit of logical reasoning unrestrained by common sense. In her view, atomized individuals in modern mass societies are particularly vulnerable to the appeal of this kind of ideological reasoning.

3 Philosophy as a source of totalitarianism

If there is an affinity between totalitarianism and logic, if totalitarian regimes are distinctively ideological dictatorships, and if the concept itself began life as a philosophical ideal, does philosophy itself (or at any rate certain philosophers) bear some responsibility for the horrors of the twentieth century? This claim was advanced most notoriously by Karl POPPER (§4), who argued in *The Open Society and Its Enemies* (1945) that Plato in the ancient world and Hegel and Marx more recently had harboured the seeds of totalitarianism, opposing the 'open society' in which critical thinking, freedom and progress can flourish. Popper concentrated his attack particularly on 'historicism', or the claim that there are laws of history which can be discovered, enabling one to predict the future (see HISTORICISM §2).

As the most notable philosopher of history, HEGEL (§8) has been especially liable to be accused of being a progenitor of totalitarianism, particularly since his influence can be clearly traced both in Marxism-Leninism and in Gentile's fascism (although not in Nazism). Students of Hegel maintain that this imputation is unjust, and even that Hegel should be seen as a liberal. It should be noted, however, that Gentile was also a liberal who considered that since true freedom is to be found through the ethical state, fascism was the consummation of liberalism. Isaiah Berlin's attack in 'Two Concepts of Liberty' (1969) on 'positive' concepts of freedom was largely directed at the use made by fascists and Marxists of Hegelian ideas (see BERLIN, I.).

The notion of any *direct* connection between totalitarian atrocities and philosophic indiscretions was dismissed by Hannah Arendt, who argued that the advent of totalitarianism owed more to practices developed by imperialist regimes than to abstract theories. Nevertheless she maintained that philosophers from Plato to Marx and Heidegger (a prominent supporter of Nazism) had facilitated totalitarianism because they had failed to appreciate human plurality. She suggested that this failure to notice the political implications of plural actions and multiple points of view might be an occupational hazard of philosophic solitude.

Another political thinker prompted by bitter experience to criticize intellectual hubris was Albert CAMUS, who argued in *The Rebel* (1951) that totalitarianism was the ultimate consequence of humanism gone sour, of a metaphysical rebellion that had culminated in the attempt to deify man.

4 Totalitarianism and the critique of modernity

Although the notion of totalitarianism has been applied primarily by theorists living in comparatively 'open' societies to regimes that have been manifestly terroristic, this model of domination in and through ideas and discourse has also been turned into a stick with which to beat liberal societies themselves. In *One-Dimensional Man* (1964), Herbert MARCUSE argued that the apparent freedom of individuals in modern capitalist societies was illusory, because the desires and choices of consumers were moulded by cultural forces that served the purposes of the system of production while failing to satisfy the real needs of the population. 'Under the rule of a repressive whole, liberty can be made into a powerful instrument of domination' (Marcuse 1964: 21). From this point of view, the fact that people in the USA could be controlled without the use of terror made the USA even more effectively totalitarian than more overtly repressive regimes, and made liberation less likely.

Marcuse's Frankfurt School colleagues Max Horkheimer and Theodor Adorno had already discovered totalitarianism deeply embedded in modern civilization. In *Dialectic of Enlightenment* (1973), they claimed that the project of liberating mankind by developing instrumental reason, science and technology had given rise first to the domination of nature and then (by a dialectical process) to the enslavement of mankind. On this deeply pessimistic view, totalitarianism is the direct outcome of enlightenment (see CRITICAL THEORY §5). A generation later Michel FOUCAULT, focusing on the development during the Age of Reason of prisons and other disciplinary institutions, also discovered totalitarianism at the heart of liberal modernity, and set out to unmask the power inherent in the production of truth and the discipline exercised through scientific disciplines (Foucault 1977). As in the cases of Horkheimer and Adorno and of Marcuse, power is diffused throughout Foucault's 'disciplinary society' rather than being concentrated in the hands of the dictator. Even in Arendt's version, however, the apparently all-powerful dictators have made themselves slaves of suprahuman forces. Common to many theories of totalitarianism is a sense that the imprisoning structures and destructive processes have been created by human beings but have escaped from human control. This nightmare forms a sharp contrast to the original philosophical vision of a totally intelligible and totally harmonious society.

References and further reading

* Arendt, H. (1951) *The Origins of Totalitarianism*, New York: Harcourt Brace. (A classic text of the theory of totalitarianism.)
* Berlin, I. (1969) 'Two Concepts of Liberty', in *Four Essays on Liberty*, Oxford: Oxford University Press. (Finds totalitarian implications in 'positive' concepts of liberty.)
* Camus, A. (1951) *The Rebel*, trans. A. Bower, London: Hamish Hamilton, 1953. (Traces totalitarianism to intellectual hubris.)
* Foucault, M. (1977) *Discipline and Punish*, London: Allen Lane. (Study of the development of prisons and organizations for social control, and of the growth of disciplinary society as a whole.)
* Friedrich, C.J. and Brzezinski, Z. (1967) *Totalitarian Dictatorship and Autocracy*, New York: Praeger. (The classic text of the theory of totalitarianism as an ideal type in political science.)
* Gregor, A.J. (1969) *The Ideology of Fascism: The Rationale of Totalitarianism*, New York: Free Press. (Includes an account of the ideal of totalitarianism.)
  Harris, H.S. (1960) *The Social Philosophy of Giovanni Gentile*, Urbana, IL: University of Illinois Press. (Includes a comprehensive account of Gentile's philosophy of fascism.)
* Horkheimer, M. and Adorno, T. (1973) *Dialectic of Enlightenment*, London: Allen Lane. (Argues that the roots of totalitarianism are to be found in instrumental reason.)
* Marcuse, H. (1964) *One-Dimensional Man*, London: Routledge & Kegan Paul. (Depicts advanced capitalist societies as totalitarian.)
* Popper, K. (1945) *The Open Society and Its Enemies*, London: Routledge, 2 vols. (A denunciation of Plato, Hegel and Marx as proto-totalitarians.)

MARGARET CANOVAN

TRADITION AND TRADITIONALISM

Tradition is that body of practice and belief which is socially transmitted from the past. It is regarded as having authority in the present simply because it comes from the past, and encapsulates the wisdom and experience of the past. For some, the very idea of tradition is anathema. It is characteristic of modernity to reject the authority of the past in favour of the present deployment of reason, unencumbered by tradition or prejudice. While prior to the seventeenth century tradition was largely unquestioned as a source of insight, and in need of no defence, since the Enlightenment the notion of tradition has been defended by traditionalists such as Burke and, more recently, Hayek. Upon inspection, however, traditionalism, if not indefensibly irrational, turns out to be a demonstration of the overlooked rationality contained within traditions. Traditions often turn out upon inspection to be not so much irrational as subtle and flexible deployments of reason in particular spheres.

1   **Antitraditionalism**
2   **Burkean traditionalism**
3   **Hayek's evolutionary account of tradition**
4   **The flexibility of traditions**

1   Antitraditionalism

According to Karl Popper, a prevalent modern attitude to the past holds that 'I am not interested in tradition. I want to judge everything on its own merits... quite independently of any tradition... with my own brain, and not with the brains of other people who lived long ago' ([1949] 1963: 120–1).

Have there ever been people who thought in this way? In *The Frogs* Aristophanes depicts Euripides as wanting to teach his audiences to use their own brains, unfettered by meaningless traditions, and uncowed by authoritarian windbags who simply spout outdated myths. But we should remember that Aristophanes was hostile to Euripides. Furthermore, Euripides' plays certainly exploit old myths, and not always with new intentions.

In the eighteenth century, DIDEROT insisted that a true philosopher would 'trample underfoot prejudice, tradition, venerability' and admit nothing 'save on the testimony of his own reason and experience', possibly oblivious of the fact that that doctrine itself had by 1750 become well embedded in the philosophical tradition to which he belonged (Wilson 1972: 237). Critics of the French Revolution, such as Burke and de Maistre certainly saw the revolutionaries as

attempting to break with tradition, but again, in view of their constant invocations of ancient Roman and republican virtue, it is doubtful that the revolutionaries conceived themselves as operating independently of any tradition. In the twentieth century, Keynes, along with many others, saw traditional morality as a crippling burden. Every decade or so artistic avant-gardists have called for the need to create anew, 'burning one's path behind one' (as the Russian constructivist Malevich put it). In retrospect, of course, the reality is that antitraditionalism is always selectively antitraditional, and that, as Popper says, whether we like it or not, we always stand on the shoulders of at least some of our predecessors.

2   Burkean traditionalism

Nevertheless since the end of the eighteenth century, in face of explicit verbal attacks on traditions, attacks on respect for tradition and successful assaults on parts of actual traditions, a line of thinking has developed which defends the virtues of tradition against its critics. In this explicit defence we encounter what might be called traditionalism, an attitude of mind intended to curb the pretensions of present reason to criticize traditional beliefs, institutions and practices.

One of the first and certainly one of the most famous expositions of traditionalism is that of Burke.

> We are afraid to put men to live and trade each on his own private stock of reason; because we suspect that this stock in each man is small, and that the individuals would do better to avail themselves of the general bank and capital of nations and of ages.
> ([1790] 1967: 84)

Burke argues that old prejudices should be cherished both because they are prejudices, and because they are old. Prejudices are easily applied in emergencies, and they can also become habitual, rendering, as he says, a man's virtue his habit. He also argues that if they are examined sympathetically, they will generally be found to contain 'latent wisdom', encapsulating the wisdom of the ages and of much experience, which would be likely to elude us if we relied solely on our present stock of reason (see BURKE, E.).

In Burke's approach to tradition there is not a little hint of Adam Smith's invisible hand, transposed to the moral and political sphere; that is, reason as well as economic equilibrium can emerge through the actions and decision of individuals who have no conception of the greater order to which they contribute (see SMITH, A.). By a process resembling natural selection, fruitful lines of behaviour will be rewarded and reinforced and eventually embedded in society as a whole, although the individuals concerned may be quite unaware of this aspect of their decisions, and be taking them for reasons quite other than the evolutionary advantage they bring to the society to which they belong.

3   Hayek's evolutionary account of tradition

In the twentieth century the conception of a tradition in terms of spontaneously developing orders has been associated particularly with the work of HAYEK (§3). Hayek points out that societies with successful economies have reproduced and spread themselves more than those with unsuccessful economies. Along with economic success the rules of behaviour which underlie or accompany success have also been reproduced. In particular, in Hayek's view, the institutions of the family and private property have not just been an irrelevant accompaniment to economic success; they have been central to the market order. But in market societies, these institutions have usually been promulgated and defended for religious reasons, and as the societies have prospered, so has their religion. Conversely, societies with belief systems prejudicial to the market order have tended to die out, their belief systems dying with them (see Hayek 1988).

While Hayek's conception of tradition might help throw light on unsuspected links between a society's historical success and apparently unrelated aspects of its beliefs and practices, it is less clear how far what he says can amount to a defence of the traditional as such. He and Burke can certainly be read as counselling us against premature attempts to over-throw traditions, warning us to examine the unsuspected consequences of so doing in greater depth than would a Diderot or a Keynes. It is also true that any explicit judgment we make will always be made against a background of unspoken and largely traditionally based agreement, again to a greater extent than many rationalists might suspect. But, at the end of the day, when confronted by any explicit controversy, we still must make a decision, and the mere fact that something has always been done is a less than compelling reason for continuing to do it. For example, we need to know whether its always having been done has had good or bad consequences. The simple fact that a particular religion's morality is conducive to the market order is not, in itself, a reason for a sceptic to accept that religion, even if they were concerned to promote or promulgate the market. The sceptic would have to accept or reject the religion in the light of its credibility, and not in the light of its supposed contribution to social wellbeing.

A sceptic may even lament their inability to go along with a traditional belief or practice precisely because they are aware of its incidental benefits.

Hayek is particularly critical of modern thinkers who find market arrangements unjust, and who believe that they can improve on them by use of their own reason. He argues that experience of the comparative success of planned and unplanned economies shows that tradition is in some respects superior to conscious human reason. In reality, it demonstrates no such thing. What experience shows is that adherence to some traditions is sometimes better than attempting to improve or replace them. And if, following Hayek, we decide to defend and develop the traditions central to the market order, this will not be because of our love of tradition as such, but because we have reasoned that experience has shown one particular tradition has superiority over others. The fact that tradition suggests limits to the scope of rational planning and advances strategies for encouraging unplanned economic activity does not mean that a decision in its favour is either irrational or purely tradition-based. So while a prejudice in favour of tradition need not be irrational, particularly if associated with a Burkean attempt to reveal its latent wisdom, this hardly amounts to a full-blooded commitment to tradition as such. Traditionalism, then, is itself either irrational, or a rather sophisticated form of rationalism, a prejudice in favour of tradition, but for good reason in so far as the traditions in question can be shown to be reasonable.

4   The flexibility of traditions

Flexibility as a characteristic of traditions would not necessarily prove unacceptable to traditionalists, who usually emphasize such a flexible nature, the way in which traditions respond to circumstances of various sorts. One of the circumstances to which traditions respond is the reasoning and discussion their adherents engage in for both internal and external reasons. There can be no denying that a long-lasting tradition of belief, such as Roman Catholicism, has undergone many developments and changes of emphasis over the centuries, so much so that one might be tempted to wonder just how much there is in common between a twentieth-century bishop and one of the Apostles. It was this question among others which Cardinal Newman addressed in his 1845 *Essay on the Development of Christian Doctrine* (see NEWMAN, J.H.). Although specifically dealing with theology and the Church, Newman's essay is a profound analysis of the continuity through discontinuity present in any long-lasting tradition, with implications for any field of human endeavour which manifests creative interplay between inherited tradition, rational reflection and the wider social circumstances in which it is located. Doubtless many fields do manifest such creative interplay, although it is noteworthy that visual art has largely turned its back on its past achievements. Newman shows that the success of a tradition is related to its ability to assimilate new data, while conserving its past principles and achievements, and also to its ability to develop complex sequences of thought and practice while anticipating future development. He brings to the study of tradition a subtlety and a comparative perspective often lacking in the blanket statements of self-professed traditionalists and antitraditionalists alike.

See also: CONSERVATISM

References and further reading

* Burke, E. (1790) *Reflections on the Revolution in France*, London, Dent, 1967. (The classic statement of the argument for tradition.)
* Hayek, F.A. (1988) *The Fatal Conceit*, London, Routledge. (The source for the discussion of Hayek in §3. Gives an evolutionary account of the importance of apparently unthinking traditions.)
* Newman, J.H. (1845) *Essay on the Development of Christian Doctrine*, London: Longmans Green, 1890. (Analyses the continuity in discontinuity in a long-lasting tradition. Referred to in §4.)
  O'Hear, A. (1992) 'Criticism and Tradition in Popper, Oakeshott and Hayek', *Journal of Applied Philosophy* 9 (1): 65–75. (Explores the interplay of tradition and reason in the three cited authors.)
* Popper, K.R. (1949) 'Towards a Rational Theory of Tradition', in *Conjectures and Reflections*, London: Routledge & Kegan Paul, 1963, ch. 4. (The work referred to in §1. What its title suggests: an attempt to defend traditions against its rationalistic opponents and its conservative friends.)
  Shils, E. (1981) *Tradition*, London: Faber & Faber. (An analytical treatment of tradition, defending it against those who regard it simply as a barrier to progress.)
  Taylor, C. (1990) *Sources of the Self*, Cambridge: Cambridge University Press. (Explores the development of rationalism in the modern world.)
* Wilson, A. (1972) *Diderot*, Oxford: Oxford University Press. (Diderot gives voice to the classic Enlightenment hostility to tradition.)

ANTHONY O'HEAR

TRAGEDY

Tragedy is primarily a type of drama, though non-dramatic poetry ('lyric tragedy') and some novels (for example, Moby Dick*) have laid claim to the description. As a genre, it began in ancient Greece and forms a part of the western European tradition. Historically, it has carried prestige for playwrights and actors because it dealt with persons, generally men, of 'high' or noble birth, who, by virtue of their stature, represented the most profound sufferings and conflicts of humanity, both morally and metaphysically. The history of the genre is part of the history of how art and culture reflect views about class and gender.*

Tragic theory has concentrated primarily on how to define the genre. A persistent feature is the tragic hero, who begins by occupying a position of power or nobility, but comes to a catastrophic end through some action of his own. According to the Aristotelian tradition, the audience is supposed to experience pity and fear in response to the sufferings of the tragic hero, and perhaps pleasure from its cathartic effects. Hegel initiated a paradigm shift in tragic theory in proposing that tragic plots essentially involve conflicts of duty rather than suffering.

Greek tragedy and Shakespearean tragedy provide two different exemplars of the genre. The tradition inspired by Greek tragedy emphasized a rigidly defined genre of dramatic poetry; French neoclassic tragedy is part of this tradition. Shakespearean tragedy, on the other hand, is written partly in prose, and includes comic elements and characters who are not nobly born. Lessing and Ibsen also resisted restraints imposed on the genre in terms of its representation of social class and gender in favour of drama that was more realistic and relevant to a bourgeois audience. Twentieth-century criticism has questioned the viability of the genre for modern times.

1   **Greek tragedy to Plato**
2   **From Aristotle to Rome**
3   **Italy and France**
4   **England**
5   **Germany**
6   **The twentieth century**

1   Greek tragedy to Plato

Greek tragedy sprang from dithyrambs (choral songs to Dionysus); when dialogue was included in these, tragedy developed as a distinct genre. In about 534 BC the poet Thespis is said to have introduced dialogue between the chorus (or its representative) and a choral leader, and in about 500 BC Aeschylus introduced a second actor, thereby making dialogue independent of the chorus. Either could be seen as the originator of tragedy. Tragedy was considered to be a kind of poetry; poets, and hence tragedians, were regarded as teachers of morality and religion, and tragedies were performed at annual festivals rich with civic and religious significance. The classic tragedies of Aeschylus, Sophocles and Euripides, all written in the fifth century BC, dramatize well-known myths involving important and powerful families, sometimes in altered forms. There were no female tragedians and all roles were performed by men, including those of female characters. Tragedy arose out of ritual, and the exclusively male participation in ritual reinforced a gender-linked social hierarchy.

GORGIAS of Leontini, Sicily, held that tragedy (and other poetry) produced pleasure through deception. He also recognized the two main emotions generally associated with tragedy – pity and fear – though it remains unclear why precisely these two were singled out as characteristic of the genre. PLATO argued that poetry was imitation, not necessarily deception. Nevertheless, he argued that writing, performing and witnessing performances of poetry could have undesirable, damaging effects on our ability to reason. In his early dialogue *Ion*, he argued that one writes good poetry and performs (recites) it well by 'divine inspiration', not rational understanding. He also argued that our emotional responses to poetry are not rational.

Plato refused to allow imitative or mimetic poetry (as opposed to narrative poetry) into the Republic, his ideal state. One reason was that poetry often portrays things that are not true and describes gods doing things that are not good models for behaviour (*Republic* 387b *et passim*). Another was that most people enjoy giving vent to emotions; we do not enjoy representations of intelligent and temperate dispositions (ibid. 604e), but what we do enjoy vicariously tends to become part of ourselves (ibid. 606b). The audience's vicarious pleasure in experiencing appetites (for example, sex) and pains and pleasures 'of the soul' (anger) strengthens those appetites when they ought to be weakened and brought under the control of reason (ibid. 606d).

2   From Aristotle to Rome

Aristotle's *Poetics* is probably the single most influential work on tragedy ever written (see ARISTOTLE). In contrast to Plato, Aristotle argued that writing tragedy required an understanding of the functions of tragedy and of the principles that ensure that those functions are fulfilled. Writing good tragedy thus develops reason. He also argued that some pleasure gained from tragedy derives from

learning about the things imitated, so that responses to it are cognitively rewarding.

Aristotle's famous definition of tragedy at the beginning of chapter six of the *Poetics* differentiates it from other types of imitation (painting, music, dithyramb, epic, comedy): 'Tragedy is an imitation of an action that is serious, complete, and possessing magnitude; in embellished language; ... in the mode of action and not narrated; and effecting through pity and fear the catharsis of such emotions' (1449b24–28.) Aristotle also held that tragedy has an end or purpose (*telos*), but there is controversy about what this is. Is its purpose to produce pity and fear, a catharsis, or pleasure (through imitation, pity and fear, and/or catharsis), or is it possibly to construct a plot of the kind which produces the appropriate effect? Aristotle clearly held that only certain kinds of plots will produce the emotions appropriate to tragedy. They are complex plots, involving recognition (of the tragic implications of the action) and reversal (of fortune). Tragic characters must be presented as better people than most and as agents actively affecting the course of action through their own choices, but operating in a world beyond their control.

The suffering that elicits pity and fear comes about through the actions of an agent who makes some kind of mistake or error in judgment (*hamartia*). Even very good people can make mistakes when subjected to forces beyond their control: we thus pity them (since pity is the appropriate response to undeserved misfortune) and fear for them and for ourselves (since if it can happen to people better than ourselves it can certainly happen to us). Aristotle allowed that tragedies could even have happy endings, on the grounds that the *threat* of suffering is capable of generating the 'tragic emotions'.

Historically, catharsis has loomed large in discussions of Aristotle's conception of tragedy, though the passage quoted above contains the *Poetics'* only occurrence of *katharsis* in the relevant sense, and gives no explanation of what it means. *Katharsis* has in fact been translated as both a purging and a clarification. The 'homeopathic' account, in which emotional responses to tragedy purge us of their harmful effects, is probably the most popular. Other accounts of catharsis hold that emotions are rendered pure and clear, so that knowledge of them as psychological states is enhanced; emotions are clarified in the sense that we feel them in response to their proper objects, that is, we pity and fear the right kinds of things; and emotional responses clarify our understanding of the structure of the plot (see KATHARSIS).

Tragedies were written during Roman times, notably by the Roman Stoic politician and philosopher SENECA. He emphasized the nobility of suffering and gave little attention to action. His works were filled with rhetorical conceits, and are now generally held to be affected, sentimental and bombastic. Horace's *Ars Poetica* proposed that poetry (including tragedy) is *utile dulce*, 'delightful instruction': poetry is seen here as a form of rhetoric that is styled to give pleasure and moral instruction.

3 Italy and France

Seneca's influence was significant, especially in fifteenth- and sixteenth-century Italy and in seventeenth-century France. In Italy, the sixteenth century saw the development of 'true' tragedy, with the playwright Torquato Tasso emerging as the major figure. Though animated by religious ideals, he tried to adhere to the prescriptions of Aristotle and Horace. French tragedy of this period consisted of a great deal of declamation and little action, and is widely regarded as an insignificant precursor to the neoclassical drama of Corneille and Racine, which also showed Senecan influence.

From the time of its first Latin translation in 1498, Aristotle's *Poetics* had substantial influence. Inspired by Aristotle, Bernardino Daniello formulated the Doctrine of Fixed Forms (1536) and Lodovico Castelvetro invented the three unities of time, place and action (1576): the action must take place during a single day, in a single place, and there should be only one main plot with no subplots. Castelvetro also argued that pleasure is tragedy's proper end; if instruction were its end, it would be a utilitarian art. Other rules acquiring more limited acceptance were that the ending should be unhappy, the performance time should be the same as the time of the action, there should be five acts, and no death or violence should take place on stage. Culminating with Nicholas Boileau-Despréaux (*L'art poëtique*, 1674), French theorists entrenched the rules developed by sixteenth-century Italians as absolute and unchanging standards for the production and evaluation of tragedy, though exactly which rules and how absolute their status became issues of continuing controversy.

Corneille and Racine were rivals for the title of preeminent dramatist of their day. Racine was best known for his literary craft, but Corneille, whose most notable tragedy was *Le Cid*, also wrote essays (*Discourses*). Corneille argued that we should recognize that many tragedies are effective even though they do not obey strict Aristotelian rules. However, it was still the function of poets to please according to the rules of their art, and their art included more than the three unities: for example, the tragic hero must be noble, plays were to be entirely in verse, there were to

be no representations of violence on stage and no more than three speaking characters on stage at once. There was, moreover, more concern with general character types than the psychology of individuals. Plays were still declamatory in style, and extolled the virtues of reason or will in the face of the temptation to be ruled by passion. They were thus part of the Cartesian rationalist spirit, following up Plato's praise of reason and critiques of pleasure and emotion.

4 England

In *The Monk's Tale*, Geoffrey Chaucer provided a famous definition of tragedy as a (narrative) story of one who falls from prosperity into misery (teaching us not to trust our temporary good fortune). Sir Philip Sidney (*An Apology for Poetry*, 1598) argued that emotional responses to tragedy are morally useful because they move us to want to know and do what is good. He held that our admiration and commiseration teach us about the uncertainties of this world, but that fear is felt only by royal spectators!

The tragedies of William Shakespeare are now viewed as hallmarks of the genre. In a major break from both Greek and Roman tragedy and the morality plays of the Middle Ages, Shakespeare's plays explore the psychology and actions of individuals, rather than general character types. Writing and acting were still male preserves, and women did not act female roles in England until the Restoration.

One topic of recurrent speculation among English theorists is the so-called paradox of tragedy: how and why do we enjoy being moved by scenes of pity, fear, suffering, and distress? Thomas Hobbes, true to his psychological egoism, suggested that the pleasure is of the thank-God-it's-not-me sort: the suffering of the tragic hero makes spectators appreciate their own relative security and comfort. Thomas Rymer (1693), who developed the concept of 'poetic justice', which requires that the plot must provide a clear moral lesson, held that pleasure arises from the moral appreciation of seeing poetic justice take place.

David Hume's essay *'Of Tragedy'* (1757) attempts to explain 'the unaccountable pleasure…[we] receive from sorrow, terror, anxiety and other passions, that are in themselves disagreeable and uneasy'. He claims that there may be some value in the observation of L'Abbé Du Bos that simply being dislodged from listlessness is itself pleasurable, and in Fontenelle's idea that the sorrows of the theatre are softened by our recognizing 'it is nothing but a fiction'. He adds that the eloquence of the poet pleases us and that all imitations please in themselves, so that these new passions predominate over and 'convert' the unpleasant ones. Hume's view was not moralistic, though he asserted that conflicts between our own morality and the morality expressed in the play, and the sight of horrific violence (such as being 'besmeared all over with mingled blood and gore'), can prevent us from being pleased by the play (see HUME, D.).

5 Germany

In the mid-eighteenth century, Johann Christoph Gottsched led a movement aiming to bring a strict and pedantic version of neoclassic French tragic theory and practice, along the lines of Boileau, to Germany. Tragedy carried literary prestige, but the forms prescribed by the rules were increasingly felt to be forced and unnatural, the elevated diction to be stilted, and the practice of *éloignement* – the distancing of characters and their actions from the audience in status, time and place – to be remote from most people's experience. Gotthold Ephraim Lessing gradually acknowledged the need to change the forms. His *Miss Sara Sampson* has been called the first really 'modern' tragedy; it is written in prose, with fictional (rather than historical) characters from the lower fringe of the nobility, and has a contemporary setting. His *Hamburg Dramaturgy* (1767–8) articulated later ideas about tragedy, notably that the hero should not be admired but pitied, and that tragedy should enhance the audience's moral awareness through this pity.

Friedrich Schiller's views (see SCHILLER, J.C.F. §2) on tragedy grew out of Kantian metaphysics. The 'play impulse' unifies the phenomenal world (of determinism) with the noumenal world (of free choice). The tragic hero is not simply determined by physical forces, but challenged by suffering to choose freely what is morally right. Schiller thought that neoclassic French tragedy erred by overemphasizing reason: to be truly effective tragedy must strike a balance between reason and passion. Both Schiller and Goethe wrote so-called 'bourgeois tragedies', spurning the requirement that tragedy should portray persons of noble birth.

A precursor to Hegel, August Schlegel saw as essential to tragedy the conflict between our aspirations to know both the (noumenal) infinite and our own (phenomenal) finite existence. Our pleasure derives from the affirmation of human striving for something beyond ourselves, even though we suffer in the effort. Goethe's *Faust* could be considered tragedy on this account. Hegel himself transformed tragic theory by focusing on conflict and by de-emphasizing the role of suffering, emotion, pleasure and purgation. Conflicts arise between parents and children, or between the family and the state or ruler, because of one-sidedness: each party ignores the rights of the

other. Tragedies can end with a peaceful reconciliation, at which the tragic hero submits to a course of action that he has previously fundamentally opposed. In these resolutions, what is justified on each side is preserved. Among his examples are the *Eumenides*, where claims of contending powers are adjusted, and *Oedipus Coloneus*, where Oedipus accepts as just the exile which is his fate. Thus, Hegel's dialectical notion of tragedy looks to the (rational) reconciliation of conflicting ethical claims, in contrast with the ancient concept which saw people as victims of unpredictable, irrational forces.

Arthur SCHOPENHAUER (§§4–6) borrowed from Buddhist philosophy the idea of nirvana – the state of release from the compulsions of human will and desire. In Schopenhauer's writings, will is a blind, irrational cosmic force and its unceasing demands are responsible for all the suffering in the world. The essence of tragedy is suffering, and not action and conflict, as Hegel proposed. The greatest tragedies show the resignation and surrender of the will, including the will to live. It is not replaced by a will to die, he adds, but by disinterested pleasure in the momentary release from 'the penal servitude of willing'.

Friedrich Nietzsche's *The Birth of Tragedy* (1872) portrayed two forces at work in human nature. The Apollonian force is calm, orderly, structured, harmonious, rational. It exemplifies the glory of the individual and the wisdom of the ancient Greek maxim, 'Know thyself.' The Dionysian force is, by contrast, intoxicated, irrational, aggressive, disorderly, destructive, wilful. The tragic hero represents the Apollonian side, and the chorus – where the individual disappears – the Dionysian. The hero is annihilated, but in this destruction of the individual there exists an affirmation of (Dionysian) life in a cosmic sense. Nietzsche thus rejected Schopenhauer's resignation to fate and instead championed the joyful identification with nature, no longer limited by concerns for self (see NIETZSCHE, F.).

6 The twentieth century

Henrik Ibsen gave his 1879 play *A Doll's House* the subtitle 'A Modern Tragedy', though the heroine Nora embodies a (Hegelian) conflict of respect for authority and being true to one's own feelings. But the play is modern in its middle class, domestic, contemporary setting, its use of prose and its recognition of the rights of women. That women could be tragic figures, representing humankind and the conflicts that plague us all, was an extraordinary advance.

A.C. Bradley defended a fundamentally Hegelian

analysis of tragedy in 'Hegel's Theory of Tragedy' (1909). He agreed with Hegel's emphasis on conflict rather than suffering, but argued that some conflicts depend not only on the character of the agents but on fate, and result from warring between good and evil, rather than just conflicts between different goods.

Miguel de Unamuno (1913) proposed that tragedy was a way of looking at life, and many writings of the twentieth century emphasize a 'tragic vision' or 'tragic sense' rather than its essential properties as a literary genre. For example, Joseph Wood Krutch's impassioned essay 'The Tragic Fallacy' (1929) held it a fallacy to attribute nobility to actions themselves, as an objective property of certain actions. Rather, tragedy represents human actions *as* noble. Tragedy satisfies the 'universally human desire to find in the world some justice, some meaning, or, at the very least, some recognizable order'. He claims that Ibsen presented life as trivial and meaningless, and hence that his work lacked the tragic spirit that expressed the value of human life, rather than despair.

Several forces emerged in the twentieth century to question the viability and relevance of tragedy as a genre. Ibsen's 'democratization' of tragedy (with its own precursors in German 'bourgeois tragedy') rejected rigid class structures and gender roles. Marxist and feminist theories undermine the concept of a tragic hero as an independent agent responsible for the course of the 'tragic action'. Bertolt Brecht, himself a Marxist, encouraged a stylized form of acting which produces an intellectualized rather than emotional response. This is reminiscent of early French neoclassic tragic acting, but to an opposite end: whereas the French reaffirmed the power of an individual's rationality to guide their fate, Brecht saw the individual as alienated from the social forces that determine the course of history. The Absurdists (Ionesco, Genet, Beckett, Pinter) depicted the world as meaningless and refused to represent human actions, in Krutch's words, *as* noble. In general, the side of tragedy consisting of a positive affirmation of human life, of value, of the power and nobility of the individual, has been subdued. But forces working in the late twentieth century for the empowerment of and respect for difference among traditionally marginalized and disempowered peoples – women, people of colour, and cultural minorities of all types – create an environment in which a new set of values could provide a foundation for the affirmation of human worth which tragedy entails.

See also: COMEDY §§3–4; EMOTION IN RESPONSE TO ART §5; HEGEL, G.W.F. §8; LESSING, G.E.; MIMESIS; POETRY

References and further reading

* Aristotle (*c.* mid 4th century BC) *Poetics*, trans., with intro. and notes J. Hutton, New York: W.W. Norton, 1982. (Highly influential account of what could be called a 'science' of writing and understanding tragedy, describing its function and how it should be structured to fulfil that function. Established the paradigm of tragedy involving a tragic hero; pity, fear, and suffering; and its effect as catharsis.)

* Bradley, A.C. (1909) 'Hegel's Theory of Tragedy', in *Oxford Lectures on Poetry*, London: Macmillan. (Lucid discussion of Hegel's views, extending them to cover cases of conflict between good and evil, not just a reconciliation of various goods.)

Hegel, G.W.F. (1835–8) *The Philosophy of Fine Art*, trans. and intro. F.P.B. Osmaston, London: G. Bell & Sons, 1920, 4 vols. (A dense and difficult work in which Hegel integrates theories of tragedy and poetry with his larger metaphysical scheme. He establishes a new paradigm of tragic action as conflict and its resolution, rather than pity, fear and suffering.)

* Hume, D. (1757) 'Of Tragedy', in J.W. Lenz (ed.) *Of the Standard of Taste and Other Essays*, Indianapolis, IN: Bobbs-Merrill, 1965. (A delightful essay attempting to explain why we enjoy tragic drama.)

* Krutch, J.W. (1929) 'The Tragic Fallacy', in *The Modern Temper*, New York: Harcourt Brace. (Passionate – perhaps maddening, but certainly stirring – defence of the nobility of the desire to find meaning in the world. Condemns plays that end in despair, where the pursuit of the good is depicted as not important enough to justify the suffering.)

* Lessing, G.E. (1767–8) *Hamburg Dramaturgy*, trans. H. Zimmern, New York: Dover, 1962. (A series of essays that turns away from neoclassicism, proposing instead, for example, that the language of tragedy should be more natural and the psychology of its characters more realistic.)

* Nietzsche, F. (1872) 'The Birth of Tragedy', in W. Kaufmann (ed. and trans.) *The Birth of Tragedy and the Case of Wagner*, New York: Random House, 1967. (A dramatic and challenging account of the Apollonian and Dionysian as psychological forces at work in tragedy.)

* Plato (*c.*395–387 BC) *Ion*, trans. L. Cooper, Ithaca, NY: Cornell University Press, 1938. (Short, accessible dialogue arguing that the abilities to write, appreciate and dramatically recite poetry are not developed through reason.)

* —— (*c.*380–367 BC) *Republic*, III and X, trans. B. Jowett, *The Dialogues of Plato*, 3rd edn, London:

Oxford University Press, 1892. (A complex dialogue presenting, *inter alia*, moral, epistemic and metaphysical reasons for why tragedy and mimetic poetry do not have a useful role to play in the ideal state.)

* Rymer, T. (1693) *A Short View of Tragedy*, London: Richard Baldwin. (A dated but at times amusing critique of tragedies through the centuries, arguing that they should serve the purpose of edifying the public about justice and virtue.)

* Schopenhauer, A. (1883) *The World as Will and Idea*, vol. 3, trans. R.B. Haldane and J. Kemp, New York: Charles Scribner's Sons. (A clear and accessible discussion of how tragedy shows us that suffering results from the drive to satisfy our will, and pleasure results from surrendering the will to live.)

Steiner, G. (1961) *The Death of Tragedy*, New York: Alfred A. Knopf. (Proposes that tragedy arises in cultures that see indomitable and implacable forces as limiting and thwarting human power and reason, leading to suffering and destruction.)

* Unamuno, M. (1913) *The Tragic Sense of Life*, trans. J.E. Crawford Flitch, New York: Dover, 1954. (A passionate exploration of themes we now identify as existentialist, proposing that human tension and conflict, sorrow and anguish are 'solved', paradoxically, only by a longing for eternal life.)

Williams, R. (1966) *Modern Tragedy*, London: Chatto & Windus. (A poet and critic, he argues that our understanding of the history of tragedy and tragic theory is coloured by our own perspectives, and this helps us to resolve the conflict between what is accepted as tradition and our own ordinary notion of a tragic event.)

SUSAN L. FEAGIN

TRANSCENDENTAL ARGUMENTS

Transcendental arguments seek to answer scepticism by showing that the things doubted by a sceptic are in fact preconditions for the scepticism to make sense. Hence the scepticism is either meaningless or false. A transcendental argument works by finding the preconditions of meaningful thought or judgment. For example, scepticism about other minds suggests that only the thinker themselves might have sensations. A transcendental argument which answered this scepticism would show that a precondition for thinking oneself to have sensations is that others do so as well. Expressing the scepticism involves thinking oneself to have sensations; and the argument shows that if this thought is expressible, then it is also false.

Arguments with such powerful consequences have, unsurprisingly, been much criticized. One criticism is that it is not possible to discover the necessary conditions of judgment. Another is that transcendental arguments can only show us how we have to think, whereas defeating scepticism involves showing instead how things really are.

1   **Nature of argument**
2   **Problems**
3   **Further criticisms**

1   Nature of argument

The name 'transcendental argument' originally comes from Kant, who called the most difficult part of his most difficult work a 'transcendental deduction' (see KANT, I. §6). In the twentieth century, the name has been applied by both proponents and critics to a loosely similar set of arguments, sometimes directly inspired by Kant, sometimes not. The central figure in re-launching such arguments was P.F. Strawson in his work on metaphysics, *Individuals* (1959), and his reconstruction of Kant, *The Bounds of Sense* (1966) (see STRAWSON, P.F. §8). Subsequently the work of Davidson, Putnam and Searle on the relations between language and the world has been called 'transcendental argument' both by themselves and by others; indeed Richard Rorty calls Davidson's argument a 'transcendental argument to end all transcendental arguments' (Bieri, Horstmann and Krüger 1979: 78).

One example of a transcendental argument is Strawson's attack on scepticism about other minds. He maintains that the ability to attribute mental states to others is a precondition for attributing mental states to oneself. Therefore, if the scepticism is stated in its standard form of wondering whether anyone apart from the thinker has thoughts or feelings, it is also answerable. For the argument shows that a precondition for any such wondering is that we also attribute such states to others. Hence, if scepticism makes sense at all, it is mistaken; the sceptic is reduced to either error or silence.

This particular example is a kind of private language argument (see PRIVATE LANGUAGE ARGUMENT). Wittgenstein has retrospectively been seen as having made these kinds or arguments, as more obviously and recently has Donald DAVIDSON,

The closest analogy to them in Kant is not the *Transcendental Deduction* but, rather, the *Refutation of Idealism*, where Kant argued that knowledge of outer states is a precondition for knowledge of inner states, and hence claimed that 'the game played by idealism has been turned against itself' (1781/1787: B276). As in Strawson, the way that the sceptical position (here idealism) enters the game means that it can be defeated.

This briefly sketched family of arguments illustrates several things about modern transcendental arguments. They are arguments about the preconditions of thought or judgment. They start with a supposition about our thoughts, such as that we have thoughts of some particular kind. A necessary condition for having such thoughts is then derived, followed by a necessary condition for this necessary condition, and so on. Assuming that the first assumption is correct, all its necessary conditions will then have been found also to apply.

2 Problems

As an answer to scepticism, a transcendental argument is only as strong as its initial assumption. In the example in §1 above, the assumption is that we think ourselves to have mental states. However, a sceptic could try to meet this by claiming that we might be mistaken about the content of our thoughts. Similarly Putnam's transcendental argument that we would not even be able to think that we were seeing an apple unless this kind of state was typically caused by real apples (and hence that external-world scepticism must be false) could be met by doubting whether I correctly identify my thoughts as being of the apple variety.

If, however, the initial assumption is not about the contents of thoughts but is just that there is thought (or language), then the sceptical move can be met. For this is something which no one, and hence no sceptic, can properly think that they doubt. Hence the most robust transcendental arguments concern themselves merely with the preconditions of there being thought or language at all. Examples are (again) the Private Language Argument, or Davidson's argument that there is only one conceptual scheme. The next possible point of weakness after the initial assumption is the discovery of its necessary conditions. Obviously this must not have a purely observational basis. The argument that people could not think without brains – we think, hence we have brains, hence the external world exists – would not be an effective answer to scepticism. So the arguments have to be (at least relatively) a priori.

Some people have therefore held that transcendental arguments may only draw out the purely conceptual, or analytic, consequences of their initial assumptions. This gives them better security against scepticism but makes their chances of reaching interesting conclusions rather slim. Others have held, rather more ambitiously, that the connections do not need to be narrowly analytic: transcendental arguments show the necessary conditions for having thoughts. Therefore, if the having of one kind of thought is a necessary condition for having another kind of thought, this will be good enough, even if the contents of the thoughts themselves are not analytically connected.

3 Further criticisms

In transcendental arguments, necessary conditions are often demonstrated by discovering the unique conditions which enable some kind of thought to be had. Yet it has been claimed, most prominently by Stefan Körner (1969), that the uniqueness of a conceptual structure cannot be established. Uniqueness, he says, could only be demonstrated by the elimination of all possible rivals. Yet although we may eliminate all rivals that occur to us, there may always be a possibility that we might have overlooked or might not be able to envisage. Other people have similarly claimed that, at best, we can only describe how we currently think, or the limits of currently imaginable alternatives. However, neither of these can show how we must think; they cannot demonstrate the necessary conditions of thought.

Another criticism is that, even if it can be shown what we must think, this will not defeat scepticism. Defeating scepticism demands a demonstration that we are justified in thinking that our beliefs show how things actually are. However, showing that we must think something does not show that the thought is correct – a necessary illusion is still an illusion. The force of this criticism depends on the kinds of necessary conditions derived in transcendental arguments. If some matter of fact is shown to be a necessary condition for having thoughts, then it does not apply. However, in modern arguments, the necessary conditions derived for having one kind of thought are frequently other kinds of thought. For example in the Strawson argument discussed above in §1, it is belief in other people's pains that is the required presupposition. It can be objected that this is insufficient to answer scepticism (in this case about other minds) since the crucial point is not whether we have to believe that others have pains, but, rather, whether this belief is correct.

A version of this objection is the one which Stroud mounts against Strawson and others in his highly influential paper about transcendental arguments

(1968). This is his claim that transcendental arguments need a version of the Verification Principle in order to work (see MEANING AND VERIFICATION). However, Stroud continues, if we are entitled to presuppose the Verification Principle, then transcendental arguments are not needed, since the Verification Principle by itself will do the anti-sceptical work. The principle shows that it makes no sense to suppose that our best-verified beliefs might not be true. Analogously, it can show that it makes no sense to suppose that beliefs that we must have are not true. However it is the verificationist assumption which is doing the deadly anti-sceptical work, not the transcendental argument which gets us from belief to necessary belief. Therefore the route through necessary belief is superfluous; transcendental arguments are either redundant or invalid.

Alternatively, the transition from what we (have to) believe to how things actually are can be made by shrinking the distance between them. A supposition of idealism would do this; so that in the end we do not distinguish between the structure of thought and an independent, real world waiting to be described. In Kant, some kind of idealism was required in order to make the transcendental arguments work, and it has been suggested by Bernard Williams (1973) and others that this also applies to modern users of transcendental arguments. However, some modern users would not take this to be a criticism (see IDEALISM; REALISM AND ANTIREALISM).

See also: SCEPTICISM

References and further reading

* Bieri, P., Horstmann, R.-P. and Krüger, L. (1979) *Transcendental Arguments and Science*, Dordrecht: Reidel. (Contains papers by Bennett, Rorty, Stroud and others on transcendental arguments.)

Brueckner, A. (1983) 'Transcendental Arguments I', *Nous* 17 (4): 551–75. (Pushes Stroud's verificationist objection against modern attempts at making transcendental arguments.)

Davidson, D. (1984) *Inquiries into Truth and Interpretation*, Oxford: Oxford University Press. (Rather elliptical, at times technical, but very stimulating. Essays 11 and 13 contain examples of transcendental arguments.)

—— (1991) 'Three varieties of knowledge', in A. Phillips Griffiths (ed.) *A.J. Ayer Memorial Essays*, Cambridge: Cambridge University Press. (Succinct summary of his transcendental arguments about other minds and external world; easy to follow.)

Grayling, A.C. (1985) *The Refutation of Scepticism*, London: Duckworth. (Puts reconstructed Strawson and reconstructed Davidson together to build a transcendental argument which he thinks survives all the standard objections.)

Harrison, R. (1982) 'Transcendental arguments and idealism', in G. Vesey (ed.) *Idealism, Past and Present*, Cambridge: Cambridge University Press. (Replies to the criticism made above in §3 that transcendental arguments involve idealism.)

* Kant, I. (1781/1787) *Critique of Pure Reason*, trans. N. Kemp Smith, London: Macmillan, 1929. (Contains the passages referred to in §1.)

* Körner, S. (1969) *Fundamental Questions in Philosophy*, Harmondsworth: Allen Lane, The Penguin Press. (Chapter 12 contains the objection mentioned in §2 above; moderately difficult work.)

Peacocke, C. (1989) *Transcendental Arguments in the Theory of Content*, Oxford: Oxford University Press. (Exhibits his work on mental content as a transcendental argument; at times over-condensed.)

* Putnam, H. (1981) *Reason, Truth and History*, Cambridge: Cambridge University Press. (Chapter 1 contains the striking argument referred to above in §2; moderate difficulty, but not technical.)

Schaper, E. (1972) 'Arguing transcendentally', *Kant-Studien* 63 (1): 101–16. (Direct reply to Körner.)

Schaper, E. and Vossenkuhl, W. (1989) *Reading Kant*, Oxford: Blackwell. (In spite of its title, this collection contains papers on the modern use of transcendental arguments against scepticism as well as a good bibliography.)

* Searle, J. (1995) *The Construction of Social Reality*, Harmondsworth: Allen Lane, The Penguin Press. (The argument mentioned above in §1 appears in ch. 8; easy work.)

* Strawson, P.F. (1959) *Individuals*, London: Methuen. (Mentioned in §1 above; influential transcendental arguments in first three chapters. Very solid argument, but no technicality.)

* —— (1966) *The Bounds of Sense*, London: Methuen. (Mentioned above in §1; a reconstruction of Kantian arguments.)

* Stroud, B. (1968) 'Transcendental Arguments', *The Journal of Philosophy* 65 (9): 241–56. (Mentioned in §3 above; frequently cited article which is not particularly difficult.)

* Williams, B. (1973) *Problems of the Self*, Cambridge: Cambridge University Press. (The argument referred to in §3 above is contained in paper number 8; a fairly difficult work.)

ROSS HARRISON

TRANSLATION, RADICAL

see RADICAL TRANSLATION AND
RADICAL INTERPRETATION (§§7–10)

TRANSLATORS

Translators played a crucial role in the history of medieval philosophy. Since multilingualism was generally restricted to places in which a direct contact between different languages was possible, such as Byzantium, the Near East, southern Italy or Spain, the dissemination of knowledge into foreign cultures was mainly brought about by means of translation. In this conversion process various kinds of writings were involved, including the Bible, the Qur'an and liturgical and hagiographic works as well as literary and historiographic texts.

1 Early Greek–Latin translations
2 The science of the Arabs
3 The *Aristoteles Latinus*

1 Early Greek–Latin translations

The tradition of Greek–Latin translations of philosophical and scientific texts goes back to CICERO, whose philosophical works contain some translated fragments (for example, of Plato's *Timaeus*), but consist for the greater part of free adaptations of some contemporary Greek models. The practice of both translation and paraphrase was continued by early Christian writers such as MARIUS VICTORINUS and Ambrose (see PATRISTIC PHILOSOPHY). As for Plato's *Timaeus*, the greater part of it was known to medieval thinkers through the Latin translation and commentary of CALCIDIUS in the fourth/fifth century.

The famous debate over translation *ad verbum* (according to the verbal expression) and *ad sensum* (according to the meaning) also originated in Roman times. Jerome in the fourth century, following Cicero, was a representative of the latter method but defended literal translation when a highly authoritative text such as the Bible was at issue. BOETHIUS in the sixth century adopted the same position with respect to the works of a renowned philosopher such as Aristotle: he translated 'word for word' the *Categories*, *De interpretatione*, *Prior Analytics*, *Topics* and *Sophistici Elenchi*, as well as Porphyry's *Isagoge* (see PORPHYRY). Boethius' translation strategy was followed in the Carolingian Renaissance by Johannes Scottus ERIUGENA, who made the Neoplatonism of the Greek

Fathers accessible to Latin readers (see CAROLINGIAN RENAISSANCE).

2 The science of the Arabs

The twelfth century was an age of revival in European science and philosophy. This cultural phenomenon was, to a large extent, a consequence of the appearance of Latin translations of a number of Greek works, and also of some writings of the Arabs in which Greek science had been incorporated and developed. The initiator of this movement was Constantine the African, a monk of Monte Cassino in the second half of the eleventh century. He was a contemporary of Alfanus, archbishop of Salerno, who translated from Greek (under the title *Premnon physicon*) the treatise *On the Nature of Man* by NEMESIUS of Emesa. Constantine wrote several Latin versions of Arabic works, or of Arabic translations from Greek, on medicine, the most influential of which was the *Pantegni*, an adaptation of Haly Abbas' *Kitab al-malaki*.

An intriguing personality is Adelard of Bath, active in the first half of the twelfth century; his translations include the *Elements* of Euclid, the *Astronomical Tables* of al-Khwarizmi and the *Shorter Introduction to Astronomy* by Abu Ma'shar, and yet he does not seem to have had a profound knowledge of Arabic. Probably these versions were made with the collaboration of Adelard's teacher, the Spanish Jew Petrus Alfonsi. It was actually in Spain that most Arabic–Latin translations originated in the course of the twelfth century. Important translators were John of Seville and Hermann of Carinthia, both of whom produced Latin versions of Abu Ma'shar's *Greater Introduction* (in 1135 and 1140), and Hugh of Santalla, who shared with his contemporaries a strong interest in astronomy and astrology.

3 The *Aristoteles Latinus*

In the second half of the twelfth century, the flourishing centre of Arabic–Latin translations was Toledo. It was here that Dominicus Gundissalinus, with the help of the Jewish scholar Avendauth, translated into Latin some parts of Avicenna's *Kitab al-shifa'* (see IBN SINA). GERARD OF CREMONA, probably the most prolific of all medieval translators, also worked in Toledo. Apart from his Latin translations of scientific works in almost every field, Gerard made a substantial contribution to the *Aristoteles Latinus*, the medieval Latin version of Aristotle's works: *Posterior Analytics*, *Physics*, *On the Heavens*, *On Generation and Corruption*, *Meteora* I–III and the pseudo-Aristotelian *Liber de causis* (see

ARISTOTELIANISM, MEDIEVAL; LIBER DE CAUSIS). Meanwhile, probably before 1150, the first two of these works as well as *On the Heavens*, some of the *Parva naturalia* and *Metaphysics*, had been translated directly from Greek by James of Venice. Also known as 'Iacobus Veneticus Grecus', this translator probably lived in Byzantium for at least some time, like his contemporary Burgundio of Pisa, who produced a new version of Nemesius' *On the Nature of Man* and of several Galenic treatises (see NEMESIUS; GALEN). In addition, Burgundio was probably responsible for the oldest Greek–Latin translations of Aristotle's *On Generation and Corruption* and *Nicomachean Ethics*, while the fourth book of the *Meteora* had been translated from Greek by Henricus Aristippus, archdeacon of Catania, before 1162. To Henricus we owe also a Latin version of Plato's dialogues *Phaedo* and *Meno*.

Many twelfth-century Greek–Latin translations that have come down to us are still anonymous. Sometimes it is possible, on the basis of certain similarities of style and terminology, to ascribe two or more of these versions to one and the same unknown scholar. Thus both the so-called 'Fragmentum Vaticanum' of the *Physics* and the 'Metaphysica Media' are probably the work of one person. Likewise, the anonymous Greek–Latin translation of Euclid's *Elements* seems to go back to the translator of the oldest Latin version of Ptolemy's *Almagest*, translated from Greek in Sicily about 1160 and so preceding Gerard of Cremona's Arabic–Latin rendering by more than ten years.

Around the turn of the century, Alfred of Sareshel, who may have learned Arabic in Spain, translated the pseudo-Aristotelian *De plantis* and an extract from Avicenna's *Meteora*. One of the most influential medieval translators was Michael Scot, active in the early thirteenth century, but the real extent of his work is not well known; attested are his versions of al-Bitruji's *On the Sphere* (made at Toledo with the help of 'Abuteus levita'), Aristotle's *De animalibus* in nineteen books (probably executed at the same place), and Avicenna's *De animalibus* (which must have been done in Italy, since it is dedicated to Emperor Frederick II). We cannot be as certain of his part in the translation of the huge Averroistic corpus. He certainly or probably translated into Latin Averroes' 'great' (that is, long) commentaries on the *Physics*, *On the Heavens*, *On the Soul* and *Metaphysics*, and these versions were the starting point for intensive study of those Aristotelian treatises (see IBN RUSHD). Averroes' 'middle' commentaries on the logical works were translated about the same time by William of Luna, while those on the *Nicomachean Ethics*, *Rhetoric* and *Poetics* were translated in this period by Hermann the German.

In the field of Greek–Latin translations, it is important to mention Robert GROSSETESTE for his rendering of the *Nicomachean Ethics* with commentaries by various authors, and of a fragment of the *De caelo* with Simplicius' commentary. In the second half of the thirteenth century, a number of pseudo-Aristotelian works were translated by Bartholomew of Messina at the court of Manfred, King of Sicily, while the corpus of Greek–Latin translations of Aristotle's genuine works was revised and completed by William of Moerbeke. This prolific translator, who worked in Greece and at the papal court, was responsible for the first complete Greek–Latin versions of the *On the Heavens*, *Meteora*, *De animalibus*, *Metaphysics*, *Politics* and *Poetics*. Moreover, he produced an impressive series of Latin versions of Greek commentaries on Aristotle, including *In Meteora* and *In de sensu* by ALEXANDER OF APHRODISIAS, *In de interpretatione* by AMMONIUS, *In de anima* by PHILOPONUS, *In categorias* and *In de caelo* by SIMPLICIUS, and *In de anima* by THEMISTIUS. In addition, William translated Proclus' *Elements of Theology* (see PROCLUS), *Tria opuscula*, *In Parmenidem* and *In Timaeum*, Alexander's *De fato*, several treatises of Archimedes and Eutocius, Heron's *Catoptrica*, Ptolemy's *De analemmate* and *Quadripartitum* and Galen's *De virtute alimentorum*. The Greek–Latin Galenic corpus was added to by Peter of Abano around the turn of the century and, particularly, by Nicholas of Reggio in the early fourteenth century.

See also: ARISTOTELIANISM, MEDIEVAL; ARISTOTLE COMMENTATORS; AVERROISM; BOETHIUS, A.M.S.; CAROLINGIAN RENAISSANCE; CHARTRES, SCHOOL OF; ENCYCLOPEDISTS; GERARD OF CREMONA; GROSSETESTE, R.; ISLAMIC PHILOSOPHY: TRANSMISSION INTO WESTERN EUROPE; PATRISTIC PHILOSOPHY; PLATONISM, EARLY AND MIDDLE; PLATONISM, MEDIEVAL

References and further reading

d'Alverny, M.-T. (1982) 'Translations and Translators', in R.L. Benson, G. Constable and C.D. Lanham (eds) *Renaissance and Renewal in the Twelfth Century*, Cambridge, MA: Harvard University Press, 421–62. (Updates Haskins' work.)

Contamine, G. (ed.) (1989) *Traduction et traducteurs au moyen âge* (Translation and Translators in the Middle Ages), Paris: Éditions du CNRS. (Various kinds of translations are considered from divergent points of view, such as differences between languages, working conditions of translators and centres of translation.)

Dod, B.G. (1982) 'Aristoteles Latinus', in N. Kretzmann, A. Kenny and J. Pinborg (eds) *The Cambridge History of Later Medieval Philosophy*, Cambridge: Cambridge University Press, 45–79. (Includes useful table of medieval Latin translations of Aristotle's works and of Greek and Arabic commentaries.)

Hamesse, J. and Fattori, M. (eds) (1990) *Rencontres de cultures dans la philosophie médiévale. Traductions et traducteurs de l'antiquité tardive au XIVe siècle* (The Meeting of Cultures in Medieval Philosophy: Translations and Translators from Late Antiquity through the Fourteenth Century), Louvain: Université Catholique de Louvain, and Cassino: Università degli Studi di Cassino. (Concentrates on the methodological problems of medieval translations of philosophical and scientific texts.)

Haskins, C.H. (1924) *Studies in the History of Mediaeval Science*, Cambridge, MA: Harvard University Press. (Despite its age, still valuable as a source of information about translators of the twelfth and early thirteenth centuries.)

Lindberg, D.C. (1978) 'The Transmission of Greek and Arabic Learning to the West', in *Science in the Middle Ages*, Chicago, IL: University of Chicago Press, 52–90. (A handy survey of the data concerning the translators.)

Minio-Paluello, L. (1972) *Opuscula – The Latin Aristotle*, Amsterdam: Hakkert. (Contains almost all the articles published before 1969 by the famous specialist in medieval Latin translations of Aristotle's works.)

JOZEF BRAMS

TRAPEZOUNTIOS, GEORGE

see GEORGE OF TREBIZOND

TRINITY

The doctrine of the Holy Trinity is a central and essential element of Christian theology. The part of the doctrine that is of special concern in the present entry may be stated in these words: the Father, the Son and the Holy Spirit are each God; they are distinct from one another; and yet (in the words of the Athanasian Creed), 'they are not three Gods, but there is one God'. This is not to be explained by saying that 'the Father', 'the Son' and 'the Holy Spirit' are three names that are applied to the one God in various circumstances; nor is it to be explained by saying that the Father, the Son, and the Holy Spirit are parts or aspects of God (like the leaves of a shamrock or the faces of a cube). In the words of St Augustine:

> *Thus there are the Father, the Son, and the Holy Spirit, and each is God and at the same time all are one God; and each of them is a full substance, and at the same time all are one substance. The Father is neither the Son nor the Holy Spirit; the Son is neither the Father nor the Holy Spirit; the Holy Spirit is neither the Father nor the Son. But the Father is the Father uniquely; the Son is the Son uniquely; and the Holy Spirit is the Holy Spirit uniquely.*
>
> (De doctrina christiana I, 5, 5)

The doctrine of the Trinity seems on the face of it to be logically incoherent. It seems to imply that identity is not transitive – for the Father is identical with God, the Son is identical with God, and the Father is not identical with the Son. There have been two recent attempts by philosophers to defend the logical coherency of the doctrine. Richard Swinburne has suggested that the Father, the Son and the Holy Spirit be thought of as numerically distinct Gods, and he has argued that, properly understood, this suggestion is consistent with historical orthodoxy. Peter Geach and various others have suggested that a coherent statement of the doctrine is possible on the assumption that identity is 'always relative to a sortal term'. Swinburne's formulation of the doctrine of the Trinity is certainly free from logical incoherency, but it is debatable whether it is consistent with historical orthodoxy. As to 'relative identity' formulations of the doctrine, not all philosophers would agree that the idea that identity is always relative to a sortal term is even intelligible.

1 The logical problem of the Trinity
2 Swinburne's theory
3 Relative identity

1 The logical problem of the Trinity

The words 'the Trinity' are the English equivalent of the Latin word *Trinitas*, which was coined by the early Christian writer TERTULLIAN. The word, which, etymologically, means something like 'the tripleness', is used to refer collectively to the Father, the Son and the Holy Spirit. (Tertullian also originated the use of the word 'person' (*persona*) as a common noun that applies to the Father, the Son and the Holy Spirit.

Outside theology, the Latin word means a mask of the sort worn by characters in a classical drama, and, by extension, a *dramatis persona*, a character in a drama. What Tertullian's application of this word to the Father, the Son and the Holy Spirit was intended to suggest is disputed.) Theologians writing in Latin have generally said that, although God is a single *substantia*, there are in God three *personae*. Theologians writing in Greek have generally said that, although God is a single *ousia*, there are in God three *hypostases*. These two pairs of terms have caused some confusion, owing to the fact that *substantia* and *hypostasis* have the same literal or etymological meaning: 'that which stands under'.

The purpose of this entry is neither theological nor historical. Its purpose is rather to discuss the philosophical difficulties presented by the 'developed' doctrine (as it is to be found in the Athanasian Creed, of around AD 500). These difficulties are mainly logical. They are well stated in an anonymous seventeenth-century work that has been ascribed to the Socinian John Biddle:

> You may add yet more absurdly, that there are three persons who are *severally and each of them true God*, and yet there is but one God: this is *an Error* in counting or numbering; which, when stood in, is of all others the most brute and inexcusable, and not to discern it is not to be a Man.
>
> (quoted in Hodgson 1940)

The author of this passage is, essentially, charging that the doctrine of the Trinity implies a violation of the principle of the transitivity of identity, for it implies that the Father is identical with God, God is identical with the Son, and the Father is not identical with the Son. (For a full development of this charge, see Cartwright 1987.) The central problem that faces the doctrine of the Trinity is this: how can the doctrine be stated in a way that is orthodox, clear and does not violate the principle of the transitivity of identity?

The doctrine of the Trinity is one of the Christian mysteries, which means that it cannot be seen to be true, or even to be possible, by the use of unaided human reason. This does not mean, however, that human beings, employing only their unaided reason, cannot usefully discuss the question whether the doctrine is formally self-contradictory. (If it could be demonstrated that the doctrine of the Trinity was formally self-contradictory, that would, of course, show that it was impossible; but the converse entailment does not hold.) The task undertaken in this entry does not, therefore, rest on a failure to appreciate the fact that the doctrine is held by those who accept it to be a mystery.

This entry will consider two recent attempts to avoid the conflict with Leibniz's Law that the doctrine of the Trinity seems to face (see IDENTITY OF INDISCERNIBLES §1). One proceeds by affirming that the Father, the Son and the Holy Spirit are numerically distinct from one another, and attempting to show that this thesis is consistent with historical orthodoxy. The other proceeds by denying the ultimate reality of numerical identity – and thus by denying that Leibniz's Law has anything to apply to. The first risks falling into tritheism, the heresy that there are three Gods. The second risks incoherence if not outright unintelligibility.

2 Swinburne's theory

Richard Swinburne (1988) has argued for a Trinitarian theology according to which the Father, the Son and the Holy Spirit are numerically distinct from one another and each of them is a God – each is a necessarily existent, omnipotent, omniscient, perfectly good being who is the creator of whatever world there may be, and who has each of these attributes essentially. Swinburne's theology, moreover, represents the Father as the creator of the Son. He does not, however, freely choose to create the Son, as he freely chooses to create a physical world. He is, rather, constrained by his own nature – by his perfect goodness – to create the Son (that is, he is constrained to create that very being, as opposed to being constrained to create some being or other who has certain properties that in actuality belong to the Son). 'There being a God and there being no physical world' and 'There being a God and there being a physical world that is "very good"' are morally or ethically indifferent states of affairs, and a God's perfect goodness does not, therefore, constrain him to prefer either to the other: which of these states of affairs obtains is a matter of the exercise of divine free will. But the two states of affairs 'There being only one God' and 'There being more than one God' are not morally or ethically indifferent; the second is better than the first, and the Father is, therefore, constrained by his own perfect goodness to prefer the latter. He therefore creates – eternally, of course: not at some point in time – the Son. Although Swinburne does not explicitly say this, it would appear that the individual essence of the Son must be supposed to include the property 'being created by the Father if any divine being is created by the Father'; if this were not the case, there would be no ontological ground for the fact that the Father creates the Son and not some other divine being. The Son is therefore a necessary being: he exists in all possible worlds, for the Father exists in all possible worlds, and, in every world in which he exists, he is constrained by his essential nature to create the Son. The necessity of the Father and the necessity of the Son may, in consequence, be contrasted by using a pair of phrases that Aquinas used in respect of a different kind of necessity (imperishability): the Father has his necessity of himself, but the Son receives his necessity from another.

The state of affairs 'There being more than one God' is better than the state of affairs 'There being only one God' because it is better that there should be a plurality of Gods who form a community of love than that there should be a solitary God. Swinburne argues, moreover, that it is better for a divine community of love to contain more than two Gods than to contain only two, for it is good for two beings to cooperate to benefit a third, and such cooperation could not exist within the divine nature if there were only two Gods. Hence, the Father and the Son are constrained by their moral perfection to cooperate to create a third God, the God called the Holy Spirit. There is, however, no good that requires the existence of more than three Gods, and the 'process' of the successive creation of Gods stops at three. (The ontological priority of the Father, Swinburne argues, gives him an authority over the Son and the Spirit, with the consequence that – of necessity – they conform their wills to his in matters about which a solitary God would have a free choice. The wills of the three Gods, therefore, can never be in conflict.)

Can Swinburne plausibly contend that his account of the Trinity is orthodox? There would seem to be two points on which Swinburne might be charged with unorthodoxy. There is, first, the fact that both the Creeds of the Church and every Trinitarian theologian whose writings have not been condemned have insisted that (as the Nicene Creed puts it) the Son is 'begotten, not made' (*genitus, non factus*). And, historical orthodoxy insists, although the word 'begotten' is not used of the Holy Spirit, he too is 'not made'. Second, one might well ask Swinburne why he should not be called a tritheist: after all, he says that there are three Gods, and tritheism is the thesis that there are three Gods. As to the first point, Swinburne contends that in the vocabulary of traditional theology, 'create' (*creare*) and 'make' (*facere*) have been used to express relations that God bears to finite, contingent creatures, and that traditional theologians would have objected to the words '*Pater filium creavit*' only because they would have understood those words to imply that the Son was a finite, contingent being. If, however, the word 'create' is used in the very abstract sense of 'eternally bring about the existence of' – there being no implication that the being whose existence is brought about be contingent or finite – nothing contrary to historical

orthodoxy is implied by 'The Father created the Son'. On the second point, the charge of tritheism, Swinburne has chosen his words very carefully:

> A substance is not unnaturally understood as an individual thing which does not have parts capable of independent existence. Now the three persons are such that of logical necessity none can exist without the other.... They are therefore not unnaturally said to form one 'first substance,' and we may follow a natural tradition in calling that substance 'God'.
>
> (1988: 236)

The sense of this passage seems to be this: the Father, the Son and the Holy Spirit are parts (albeit parts that are not 'capable of independent existence') of a composite being, and it is therefore natural to apply the name 'God' (derived from the general term 'a God', whose extension is the three divine parts of the composite being) to this composite being. If this is a correct interpretation of this passage, it seems unlikely that St Augustine or the framers of the Athanasian Creed would agree that Swinburne's theory adequately captured the sense in which it is true of the Father, the Son and the Holy Spirit that 'all are one God; and each of them is a full substance, and at the same time all are one substance' (Augustine, *De doctrina christiana* I, 5, 5).

Whether or not Swinburne's theory of the Trinity can plausibly be identified with the historical doctrine of the Trinity, it is clear that it faces none of the logical difficulties that the historical doctrine seems to face, for there are, according to Swinburne, three metaphysically simple beings to which the general term 'a God' applies, and one composite being to which the name 'God' applies. None of these four beings (of course) is numerically identical with any of the others, and each has – as their non-identity allows – properties that the others lack. Swinburne's purpose was not simply to solve the logical problems that the historical doctrine seems to face, but to provide and argue for the truth of a comprehensive account of the 'internal structure' of the Trinity.

The other recent attempt to solve the logical problems raised by the doctrine of the Trinity is that and no more; the philosophers who have contributed to this attempt have been concerned only to show that the doctrine can be stated without internal logical contradiction, and they have said very little of an ontological nature about the Trinity.

3 Relative identity

The originator of this approach to the logical problems raised by the doctrine of the Trinity is Peter

Geach (1977; Geach and Anscombe 1963), who has developed a theory according to which 'identity is always relative to a sortal term', which he has applied to the problems of counting and predication that confront the doctrine of the Trinity. Geach's work has been continued by Martinich (1978) and van Inwagen (1988). The exposition that follows is a composite of things said by these three authors.

The 'theory of the relativity of identity' proceeds from the axiom that there is no such relation as numerical identity *simpliciter*: there is rather an indefinite number of relations expressed by phrases of the form 'is the same N as', where N represents the place of a count-noun. There are, for example, such relations as 'is the same horse as' and 'is the same apple as', but there is, strictly speaking, no such relation as 'is the same as *simpliciter*' or 'is numerically identical with'. Identity *simpliciter* (expressed below by '='') is defined by two characteristics: it is *universally reflexive* (everything bears identity *simpliciter* to itself) and it *forces absolute indiscernibility* (this characteristic is embodied in Leibniz's Law or the principle of the indiscernibility of identicals: if $x = y$, then anything whatever that is true of x is also true of y). Relative-identity relations, however, are not in general universally reflexive. (Socrates is not the same horse as Socrates because Socrates is not the same horse as anything; that is to say, Socrates is not a horse.) Relative-identity relations, moreover, cannot be assumed to force absolute indiscernibility – although any given such relation may have this feature. If it were assumed that every relative-identity relation forced absolute indiscernibility, then the logic of relative identities would simply be a fragment of the standard logic of identity *simpliciter*, and anything that could be said by using relative-identity predicates could be said equally well without them. (If every relative-identity relation forced absolute indiscernibility, then 'x is the same N as y' could always be replaced by 'x is an N and $x = y$'.)

The logic of relative identities is easily described. Its language is that of first-order predicate logic (without '=' and the description operator, and without singular terms), its two-place predicates being partitioned into two classes (somehow visibly differentiated), the 'ordinary' two-place predicates, and the 'relative-identity' predicates. Its rules of inference are those of ordinary predicate logic, plus two rules that state, in effect, that relative-identity predicates express symmetrical and transitive relations. Relative-identity logic must do without anything corresponding to Leibniz's Law, for the reason outlined above. It must also do without singular terms. This is because a singular term is supposed to denote exactly one object

(if it does not fail of denotation), and the concept of a singular term therefore involves the notion of identity *simpliciter*. (If a denotes x and also denotes y, it follows that $x = y$.) If, however, relative-identity logic is to have any power to represent ordinary, informal reasoning, its users must be able to employ some substitute for singular terms. This can be done through the use of an adaptation of Russell's Theory of Descriptions. For example, 'The present pope is bald' could be read as 'There is an x such that [x is at present a pope, and, for any y (if y is at present a pope, then y is the same man as x), and x is bald].' There is, of course, nothing special about the word 'man' that dictated its use in this sentence; we might as well have used 'person' or 'animal' or any of indefinitely many other count-nouns that would apply to anyone who was a pope. The sentence obtained by substituting 'person' in the above sentence is not equivalent in relative-identity logic to that sentence; to deduce either from the other, one would need a premise not endorsed by relative-identity logic. For example: 'For any x and for any y, if x is a man (that is, if x is the same man as something) and if y is a man, then x is the same person as y if and only if x is the same man as y.' No doubt most people would say that this proposition was *true*, but it is of the essence of the theory of the relativity of identities not to regard such propositions as truths of logic.

The customary term for 'what there is one of' in the Trinity is 'substance'. (But Geach and Martinich use 'God' for 'what there is one of' in the Trinity, and van Inwagen uses 'being'.) The customary terms for 'what there are three of' in the Trinity are 'person' and 'hypostasis'. (The relation between the meaning of 'person' in Trinitarian theology and 'person' in ordinary speech is a matter of dispute.)

All of the propositions of Trinitarian theology that raise logical problems can be represented using two relative-identity predicates ('is the same substance as' and 'is the same person as'), a predicate that expresses the divine nature ('is a God' or 'is divine'), and some predicates that express the relations that individuate the Father, the Son and the Holy Spirit. (The three persons or hypostases have traditionally been held to be individuated by the relations they bear to one another: the Father *begets* the Son; the Holy Spirit *proceeds from* the Father *and* – or *through* – the Son.) For example, the proposition that there are three divine persons can be expressed as 'There exist x, y and z, all of which are divine and are such that none of them is the same person as the others, and such that anything divine is the same person as one of them.' The proposition that there is one God (one divine substance) can be expressed as 'Something is divine and anything divine is the same substance as it.' These two sentences are consistent in relative-identity logic. The proposition that God is omnipotent can be expressed as 'Something is divine and anything divine is the same substance as it and it is omnipotent.' 'Reference' to the Father, the Son and the Holy Spirit can be accomplished by a device similar to the one that was used to 'refer' to God in the preceding sentence; in applying this device, use must be made of the predicates that express the relations that individuate the Father, the Son and the Spirit. Van Inwagen has shown (by constructing a model in which the interpretations of these sentences are true and in which 'is the same person as' and 'is the same substance as' express symmetrical and transitive relations) that the formal analogues of the whole set of logically problematic sentences endorsed by the doctrine of the Trinity are consistent in relative-identity logic. One striking consequence of this result is that the formal analogues of the sentences 'The Father is the same person as God', 'God is the same person as the Son' and 'The Father is not the same person as the Son' are consistent – and this despite the fact that 'is the same person as' expresses a transitive relation. (Needless to say, the formal sentences do not have the logical forms suggested by the English sentences they are held to translate.)

The main problem facing this account of the 'logic' of the Trinity would seem to be whether it is intelligible. Is it, in the final analysis, intelligible to suppose, for some x and for some y – where x and y are both substances and both persons – that x is the same substance as y, but not the same person as y? Alleged non-theological cases in which x is the same N as y, but not the same M (the statue is the same lump of clay as the vase, but not the same artefact; Dr Jekyll and Mr Hyde were the same man but not the same person; James I of England and James VI of Scotland were the same man but not the same monarch) are all susceptible of lucid and plausible philosophical analyses that do not presuppose that 'identity is always relative to a sortal term'.

See also: IDENTITY; INCARNATION AND CHRISTOLOGY; SUBSTANCE

References and further reading

* Augustine (396–426) De doctrina christiana (On Christian Doctrine), trans. E. Hill, Teaching Christianity, Hyde Park, NY: New City Press, 1996. (A good modern translation.)
Brown, D. (1985) The Divine Trinity, London: Duckworth. (A widely discussed book on the topic.)
* Cartwright, R. (1987) 'On the Logical Problem of the Trinity', in Philosophical Essays, Cambridge, MA and London: MIT Press. (A sustained, rigorous attempt to show that the logical problems faced by the doctrine of the Trinity are insoluble by any means that have so far been proposed.)
* Geach, P. (1977) The Virtues, Cambridge: Cambridge University Press. (This and the following item are Geach's most important statements of his attempt at a solution to the logical problems presented by Trinitarian theology; see especially pages 72–81.)
* Geach, P. and Anscombe, G.E.M. (1963) Three Philosophers, Oxford: Blackwell. (See previous item; see especially pages 118–20.)
Hill, E. (1985) The Mystery of the Trinity, London: Geoffrey Chapman. (A very useful exposition of Augustine and Aquinas on the Trinity.)
* Hodgson, L. (1940) The Doctrine of the Trinity, New York: Scribner. (A classic work.)
McGrath, A.E. (1994) Christian Theology: An Introduction, Oxford: Blackwell. (Recommended for readers with no background in theology or church history. Clear and reliable.)
* Martinich, A.P. (1978) 'Identity and Trinity', Journal of Religion 58: 169–81. (An attempt at a Geach-style solution to the logical problems of the Trinity. More systematic than Geach.)
* Swinburne, R. (1988) 'Could There Be More Than One God?', Faith and Philosophy 5: 225–41. (Swinburne's account of the Trinity.)
Tertullian, Q.S.F. (c.213) Adversus Praxean (Against Praxeas), trans. A. Souter, London: SPCK, 1920. (Contains Tertullian's treatment of the Trinity; this is the source of the technical terminology used in Latin Christian discussions.)
* Van Inwagen, P. (1988) 'And Yet They Are Not Three Gods but One God', in T.V. Morris (ed.) Philosophy and the Christian Faith, South Bend, IN: University of Notre Dame Press. (An attempt at a Geach-style solution to the logical problems of the Trinity. A broader range of problems than those considered by Geach and Martinich is addressed. This essay may be consulted for further references.)

PETER VAN INWAGEN

TROELTSCH, ERNST PETER WILHELM (1865–1923)

Ernst Troeltsch was a theologian, sociological historian, and philosopher of religion and history. He aimed to reconcile theology with modern scientific culture by grounding his philosophy of religion on historical analysis, and is regarded as the systematician of the

461

'history of religion school'. He is famous for his critical appraisal of the Protestant Reformation, which, he argued, had retarded the development of modern culture.

A native of Haunstetten, Bavaria, Troeltsch studied theology first at Erlangen, where the philosopher Gustav Class strove to reconcile idealism with empiricism and historicism, then at Berlin, where he attended Julius Kaftan's and Heinrich von Treitschke's lectures. Finally he went to Göttingen, where he became one of Albrecht Ritschl's (1822–89) last pupils. There he met progressive theologians who later formed the 'history of religion school', submitted his dissertation, and started work as an assistant lecturer. In 1894 he assumed the chair of systematic theology at Heidelberg, which he left in 1915 to take up a personal chair of philosophy at Berlin. The collapse of the German Empire lured him into politics and, as a committed democrat, he took an active yet unrewarding part in establishing the Weimar Republic. Politics clouded the close of his otherwise successful career.

As a theologian, Troeltsch searched for an auspicious compromise with modern secular culture. He was an apologist in disguise, who sought to moderate the shattering effect of modern science on orthodox belief. In a positivistic and historically conscious age, Christian theologians had to establish their discipline on a scientifically unassailable foundation. Neither supernatural revelation nor rational metaphysics but only history could fulfil such a function (Troeltsch 1902). A philosophy of religion drawn from analysis of the history and development of religious consciousness would, in Troeltsch's opinion, strengthen the standing of the science of religion among other sciences. In addition, it would assist the Christian strategy against materialism, naturalism, scepticism, aestheticism and pantheism. Besides, Troeltsch shared Wilhelm Herrmann's assumption that ethics provided the framework for the study of religion. An heir to both Schleiermacher's religious consciousness and Hegel's concept of development, Troeltsch unfolded an idealism of historical development, which aimed at bridging the gulf between 'scientific' (historical) and 'dogmatic' (ecclesiastical) theology. He therefore ascribed to theology a threefold task: the justification of the supremacy of Christianity on a historical and comparative religion basis; the specification of the essence of Christianity; the exposition of the Christian understanding of God, the world, the soul and redemption.

As a historian, Troeltsch interpreted Protestant and Roman Catholic Christianity, as well as contemporary intellectual culture, from a philosophical-socio-logical perspective (Troeltsch 1906a, 1915). He emphasized the cultural value of religion and derived most standards of truth and value from an analysis of history. In Dilthey's wake, he also reflected on the relation of historiography and relativism (Troeltsch 1922). As a philosopher, Troeltsch upheld a post-Kantian, eclectic idealism. Initially close to Hermann Lotze and Wilhelm Dilthey, he later shifted to the School of Baden (Windelband, Rickert). However, he opposed the neo-Kantian distinction between knowledge and faith then current, and refused to ground religious belief in value-judgments alone. In *Das Historische in Kants Religionsphilosophie* (The Historical in Kant's Philosophy of Religion, 1904), Troeltsch strove to restore a more authentic Kant, in whom he found evidences of the beginning of a modern historical consciousness.

Die Bedeutung des Protestantismus für die Entstehung der modernen Welt (*Protestantism and Progress*, 1906b) argues that early Protestantism marked a retreat to medieval theocratic civilization. By holding to the principle of authority and enforcing inward asceticism, the Protestant Reformation merely modified medieval Catholicism and thereby delayed the development of modern culture. It was the Enlightenment that fulfilled the Renaissance and produced the modern world. With regard to sociology, Troeltsch closely followed Max Weber, though he disagreed with him on some issues. His masterpiece, *Die Soziallehren der christlichen Kirchen* (*The Social Teaching of the Christian Churches*, 1912), considers whether the development of religious beliefs and movements was conditioned by external factors and whether, in turn, religion has influenced society and culture. From a detailed study of Christian social history, Troeltsch derived three types of sociological self-formation of the Christian idea: the Church, the sect and the mystic. It was Troeltsch's conclusion that the permanent quest for, and opposition to, a cultural compromise wove the fabric of the Christian ethos.

List of works

Troeltsch, E. (1912–25) *Gesammelte Schriften* (Collected Writings), Tübingen: Mohr. (Mainly published during Troeltsch's lifetime, this collection is not exhaustive.)

—— (1895–6) 'Die Selbständigkeit der Religion' (The Autonomy of Religion), in *Zeitschrift für Theologie und Kirche* 5–6. (An over-ambitious set of addresses on the origins and development of religion in the individual consciousness and in history.)

—— (1900) 'Über historische und dogmatische Methode der Theologie', in G. Sauter (ed.) *Theologie als Wissenschaft* (Theology as Science),

Munich: Chr. Kaiser Verlag, 1971; trans. W.F. Bense, 'Historical and Dogmatic Method in Theology', in J.L. Adams and W.F. Bense (eds) *Religion in History*, Edinburgh: T. & T. Clark. (Responding to criticisms of his work by F. Niebegall, Troeltsch presents his version of historical method.)

—— (1902) *Die Absolutheit des Christentums und die Religionsgeschichte*, Munich/Hamburg: Siebensten Taschenbuch Verlag, 1970 (repr. of 3rd, 1929, edn); trans. D. Reid, *The Absoluteness of Christianity and the History of Religions*, London: SCM Press, 1972. (A famous and much reprinted work, in which Troeltsch argues that judgments of the value of Christianity can only emerge from study of its historical development.)

—— (1904) *Das Historische in Kants Religionsphilosophie* (The Historical in Kant's Philosophy of Religion), Berlin: Reuther & Reichard. (Both an appropriation of Kantian themes in the philosophy of religion and an historical discussion of Enlightenment thought.)

—— (1905) *Psychologie und Erkenntnistheorie in der Religionswissenschaft* (Psychology and Epistemology in the Scientific Study of Religion), Tübingen: Mohr. (Lecture given at the World Congress of Arts and Sciences in the United States, which spread Troeltsch's fame and included his first discussion of the religious a priori.)

—— (1906a) 'Protestantisches Christentum und Kirche in der Neuzeit' (Protestant Christianity and Church in the Modern Era), in P. Hinneberg (ed.) *Die christliche Religion mit Einschluss der israelitisch-jüdischen Religion* (The Christian Religion with the Inclusion of the Israelite-Jewish Religion), Berlin/Leipzig: B.G. Teubner. (A contribution towards a history of the European mind, focusing on the Reformation and later developments springing from it, all in cultural context.)

—— (1906b) *Die Bedeutung des Protestantismus für die Entstehung der modernen Welt* (The Significance of Protestantism for the Formation of the Modern World), Munich/Berlin: Oldenbourg; trans. W. Montgomery, *Protestantism and Progress: A Historical Study of the Relation of Protestantism to the Modern World*, Boston, MA: Beacon Press, 1966. (A controversial work, claiming that early Protestantism was a retrogade step in the development of modernity.)

—— (1909) 'Zur Frage des religiösen a priori', *Gesammelte Schriften* II, Tübingen: Mohr; trans. W.F. Bense, 'On the Question of the Religious A Priori', in J.L. Adams and W.F. Bense (eds) *Religion in History*, Edinburgh: T. & T. Clark. (Clarifies Troeltsch's views on the religious a priori, in response to criticisms by P. Speiss.)

—— (1912) *Die Soziallehren der christlichen Kirchen*, *Gesammelte Schriften* I, Tübingen: Mohr; trans. O. Wyon, *The Social Teaching of the Christian Churches*, London: Allen & Unwin, 1949. (Troeltsch's favourite of his own works, in which he develops his famous typology of social forms of Christian institution.)

—— (1913a) 'Prinzip, religiöses', in F.M. Schiele and L. Zscharnack (eds) *Die Religion in Geschichte und Gegenwart* (Religion in History and the Present), Tübingen: Mohr, 5 vols, 1909–14; trans. R.A. Wilson, 'Religious Principle', in J. Pelikan (ed.) *Twentieth Century Theology in the Making*, London: Fontana, vol. 2, 1970. (A good, short introduction to Troeltsch's combination of historical method and philosophy of religion; there are several more articles by Troeltsch in the Schiele and Zscharnack volumes.)

—— (1913b) *Zur religiösen Lage, Religionsphilosophie und Ethik* (On the Religious Situation, Philosophy of Religion, and Ethics), *Gesammelte Schriften* II, Tübingen: Mohr; excerpts trans. in J.L. Adams and W.F. Bense (eds) *Religion in History*, Edinburgh: T. & T. Clark. (Collected essays in the philosophy of religion.)

—— (1915) *Augustin, die christliche Antike und das Mittelalter im Anschluß an die Schrift 'De Civitate Dei'* (Augustine, Christian Antiquity and the Middle Ages, with Reference to 'The City of God'), Aalen: Scientia Verlag, new edn, 1963. (Another philosophical and sociological investigation of the development of Christianity, this time of an earlier period.)

—— (1922) *Der Historismus und seine Probleme: Das logische Problem der Geschichtsphilosophie* (Historicism and its Problems: the Logical Problem of the Philosophy of History), *Gesammelte Schriften* III, Tübingen: Mohr. (This was to be the first of two volumes, but the second was never finished; it presents Troeltsch's mature philosophy of history at length.)

—— (1925) *Aufsätze zur Geistesgeschichte und Religionssoziologie* (Essays on Intellectual History and the Sociology of Religion), ed. H. Baron, *Gesammelte Schriften* IV, Tübingen: Mohr. (The closest we have to the unfinished second volume of *Der Historismus und seine Probleme*, containing various short essays.)

—— (1977) *Ernst Troeltsch: Writings on Theology and Religion*, ed. R. Morgan and M. Pye, London: Duckworth. (Short essays on theology in the nineteenth century, the essence of Christianity, and the historical Jesus.)

References and further reading

Clayton, J.P. (ed.) (1976) *Ernst Troeltsch and the Future of Theology*, Cambridge: Cambridge University Press. (The best collection of essays around; includes a bibliography of secondary sources and of English translations.)

Coakley, S. (1988) *Christ without Absolutes: A Study of the Christology of Ernst Troeltsch*, Oxford: Clarendon Press. (Explores how Troeltsch treated Christian claims about Jesus within his pluralist, relativist framework.)

Drescher, H.-G. (1991) *Ernst Troeltsch. Leben und Werk*, Göttingen: Vandenhoeck & Ruprecht; trans. J. Bowden, *Ernst Troeltsch, His Life and Work*, London: SCM Press, 1992. (The most detailed intellectual biography available.)

Graf, F.W. (1982) *Ernst Troeltsch Bibliographie*, Tübingen: Mohr, 4 vols. (Contains brief, mainly bibliographical comments to many entries.)

Niebuhr, H.R. (1960) 'Introduction', in Troeltsch, E., *The Social Teaching of the Christian Churches*, New York: Harper. (A prominent American theologian, who was influenced by a curious mix of Karl Barth and Ernst Troeltsch, pays tribute to the latter.)

Rubanowice, R.J. (1982) *Crisis in Consciousness: The Thought of Ernst Troeltsch*, Tallahassee, FL: University Press of Florida. (Describes Troeltsch as a representative of an early twentieth-century crisis, in which ideas of cultured civilization became problematized.)

Yamin, G.S., Jr (1993) *In the Absence of Fantasia: Troeltsch's Relation to Hegel*, Gainesville, FL: University Press of Florida. (Although Troeltsch criticised Hegel, the latter had a profound effect on him.)

JEAN-LOUP SEBAN

TROTSKY, LEON (1879–1940)

Trotsky's chief claim to attention is as the leader of the Russian Revolution who opposed the consolidation of the Stalin regime in the Soviet Union and sought to dissociate the classical Marxist tradition from that regime and its official ideology. In doing so, however, he developed a version of Marxism which sought to give proper place to the 'subjective factor' in history, and at the same time to integrate Marx's social theory into a broader, dialectical theory of nature.

Trotsky's life belongs chiefly to the principal drama of the twentieth century – the Russian Revolution of October 1917 and the emergence, in its aftermath, of the Stalinist regime which survived until the collapse of the Soviet Union in 1991. Born in Yankova, Lev Davidovich Bronstein assumed the name Leon Trotsky while escaping exile in Siberia in 1902. A revolutionary activist from his teens, he presided over the St Petersburg Soviet of Workers' Deputies during the 1905 Revolution, and held the same position when, as a leader of the Bolshevik Party, he helped organize the uprising of October 1917. As War Commissar, Trotsky played a pivotal role in securing a Bolshevik victory in the post-revolutionary Civil War. Defeated in the factional struggles which led to the dominance of Josef Stalin in Party and state, he was exiled in 1929. Trotsky spent his remaining years desperately seeking to rally socialist opposition to the Stalin regime. Isolated and persecuted, he was murdered by a Soviet agent.

Trotsky's voluminous writings reflect this life. They represent an attempt to preserve and to extend the classical Marxist tradition in opposition to Stalinism and its official ideology of Marxism-Leninism. This stance distinguishes Trotsky from Western Marxists such as ADORNO, MARCUSE and other members of the Frankfurt School, who kept their distance equally from the Soviet regime and from classical Marxism, which they tended to regard as excessively and reductively materialist (see FRANKFURT SCHOOL; CRITICAL THEORY).

Trotsky was, by contrast, an unapologetically orthodox Marxist. Thus he sought to provide an explanation of Stalinism which took as its starting point the economic circumstances of the Bolshevik regime after 1917. It was the isolation of the Revolution and the consequent prevalence of scarcity in a backward, predominantly peasant country that accounted for the rise of Stalin and the *nomenklatura*. At the same time, however, he vehemently denied that Marxism was a version of economic determinism. His theory of permanent revolution, first developed after the 1905 Revolution, sought to show how processes of 'uneven and combined development' on a world scale made possible socialist revolutions even in underdeveloped countries such as Tsarist Russia. Similarly, Trotsky's political and historical writings constantly stress that the outcomes of social and political crises are not predetermined by the economic contradictions that cause them, but depend on the 'subjective factor' – human agency in the shape of social classes, political organizations and even individual leaders.

A similar combination of orthodoxy and flexibility characterizes Trotsky's strictly philosophical writings, which are devoted to a defence of the proposition that Marxism possesses a dialectical method which sets it apart from other social theories. MARX inherited from Hegel the idea that contradictions exist in reality and developed it into a theory of social contradictions – for example, the structural conflict between capitalist relations of production and the development of the productive forces. ENGELS then extended this, most notably in *Dialectics of Nature* (1925), into a general theory of nature, in which certain dialectical laws govern both physical and social worlds.

'Dialectical materialism' thus understood became a basic element of Marxist orthodoxy (see DIALECTICAL MATERIALISM). During the 1930s, however, some of Trotsky's US followers, influenced by pragmatism, sought to separate Marxist social theory from this broader metaphysical doctrine. Trotsky responded vigorously, arguing that abandonment of the dialectic would lead sooner or later to the rejection of Marxism itself. The dialectical method was indispensable for scientific inquiry. Following Hegel, Trotsky argued that formal logic is unable to comprehend any process of change:

It wishes to content itself with motionless imprints of a reality which consists of eternal motion. Dialectical thinking gives to concepts, by means of closer approximations, corrections, concretizations, a richness of content and flexibility; I would even say a succulence which to a certain extent brings them close to living phenomena.

([1942] 1973: 50)

The more scientific discoveries reveal nature itself to be undergoing processes of historical transformation, the more important the dialectical method becomes: thus Darwin was an 'unconscious dialectician' ([1942] 1973: 51–4). But this line of argument poses the following dilemma. If Darwin could get as far as he did 'unconsciously', what need of a 'conscious' dialectic? If, on the other hand, research is held to depend on dialectical thinking, does this not license the kind of ideological terror suffered by Soviet biologists during the Lysenko era?

Trotsky, however, loosened Engels' conception of universal 'laws of the dialectic'. Only 'the conversion of quantity into quality' – the concept of qualitative transformation – is 'the fundamental law of dialectics' because 'the entire universe' is 'a product of formation and transformation' (1986: 88–9). One such 'transition from quantity to quality' is '"the autonomy" of psychological phenomena': 'the psyche, arising from matter, is "freed" from the determinism of matter, so that it can – by its own laws – influence matter'. Trotsky compared this to the interaction between base and superstructure – 'politics grows out of economics in order for it in turn to influence the base' – but admitted that the relationship between mind and body is 'incomparably more puzzling' (1986: 106–7). Nature is thus conceived as stratified – divided into distinct domains each governed by its own laws – yet forming an integrated and historically evolving totality. The dialectic is not a substitute for empirical research into these different domains, but 'it gives investigative thought elasticity, helps it to cope with ossified prejudices, arms it with invaluable analogies, and educates it in a spirit of daring, grounded in circumspection' (1986: 92). Although even many Marxists regard the idea of a dialectic of nature as an embarrassment, Trotsky would no doubt argue that it has been vindicated now that cosmologists tell us of a universe formed through a series of phase transitions producing radical changes in physical structures.

See also: MARXIST PHILOSOPHY, RUSSIAN AND SOVIET

List of works

Trotsky, L. (1909) *1905*, trans. A. Bostock, Harmondsworth: Penguin, 1973. (An account of the Russian Revolution of 1905 containing a particularly good statement of Trotsky's theory of permanent revolution.)

—— (1930) *Moia zizhn': opyt avtobiografii*, trans. as *My Life*, Harmondsworth: Penguin, 1975. (A polemical autobiography; the opening chapters, on Trotsky's early years, are of exceptional literary quality.)

—— (1931–2) *Istoriia russkoi revoliutsii*, trans. M. Eastman, *The History of the Russian Revolution*, London: Pluto Press, 1977. (A historiographic masterpiece, and Trotsky's most powerful statement of his conception of the role of human agency in the historical process.)

—— (1936) *The Revolution Betrayed*, trans. M. Eastman, New York: Pathfinder, 1972. (Trotsky's definitive account of the nature and origins of Stalinism.)

—— (1942) *In Defence of Marxism*, New York: Pathfinder, 1973. (Trotsky's last thoughts on Stalinism and the future of Marxism; also contains his most celebrated defence of the dialectic.)

—— (1969) *The Permanent Revolution and Results and Prospects*, trans. J.G. Wright and B. Pearce, New York: Pathfinder. (The two main statements of the theory of permanent revolution.)

—— (1986) *Notebooks 1933–1935*, trans. P. Pomper, New York: Columbia University Press. (A previously unpublished manuscript containing Trotsky's most sustained discussion of the dialectic.)

Trotsky, L., Dewey, J. and Novack, G. (1978) *Their Morals and Ours*, New York: Pathfinder. (A debate on revolutionary morality in which Dewey makes some shrewd points against Trotsky.)

Further reading and references

Anderson, P. (1984) 'Trotsky's Interpretation of Stalinism', in T. Ali (ed.) *The Stalinist Legacy*, Harmondsworth: Penguin, 118–28. (A sympathetic but critical assessment of *The Revolution Betrayed*.)

Beilharz, P. (1987) *Trotsky, Trotskyism and the Transition to Socialism*, Beckenham: Croom Helm. (Trotsky interpreted as a fatalist and evolutionist Marxist.)

Callinicos, A. (1990) *Trotskyism*, Milton Keynes: Open University Press. (A brief critical survey of Trotsky's thought and the traditions stemming from it.)

Cliff, T. (1955) *State Capitalism in Russia*, London: Bookmarks, 1988. (The most important single attempt to develop Trotsky's analysis of Stalinism.)

Deutscher, I. (1954–63) *The Prophet Armed: Trotsky 1879–1921*, *The Prophet Unarmed: Trotsky 1921–29* and *The Prophet Outcast: Trotsky 1929–40*, Oxford: Oxford University Press, 3 vols, 1970. (An outstanding biography.)

* Engels, F. (1925) *Dialectics of Nature*, Moscow: Progress, 1972. (The main source for the view that both physical and social reality is governed by certain universal, dialectical laws.)

Knei-Paz, B. (1978) *The Social and Political Thought of Leon Trotsky*, Oxford: Clarendon Press. (A systematic critical treatment of the theory of permanent revolution which relates it to more recent social-scientific literature on development and modernization.)

Levins, R. and Lewontin, R. (1985) *The Dialectical Biologist*, Cambridge, MA: Harvard University Press. (Two working scientists seek to show the relevance of dialectical concepts to contemporary biology.)

Löwy, M. (1981) *The Politics of Combined and Uneven Development*, London: Verso. (A historical and theoretical survey of the idea of permanent revolution.)

Novack, G. (1972) *Understanding History*, New York: Pathfinder. (Includes an influential discussion of the concept of uneven and combined development.)

Rees, J. (1990) 'Trotsky and the Dialectic of History', *International Socialism* 47: 113–35. (A discussion of Trotsky's *Notebooks*.)

ALEX CALLINICOS

TROTTER, CATHARINE

see COCKBURN, CATHARINE

TRUST

Most people writing on trust accept the following claims: trust involves risk; trusters do not constantly monitor those they trust; trust enhances the effectiveness of agency; and trust and distrust are self-confirming. Three further claims are widely accepted: trust and distrust are contraries but not contradictories; trust cannot be willed; and trust has noninstrumental value. Accounts of trust divide into three families: risk-assessment accounts, which are indifferent to the reasons why one trusts; will-based accounts, which stress the importance of the motives of those who are trusted; and affective attitude accounts, which claim that trust is a feeling as well as a judgment and a disposition to act. One of the central questions concerns when trust is justified, and, in particular, whether justified trusting can outstrip evidence for the belief that the person trusted is trustworthy. If trust can leap ahead of evidence of trustworthiness, then trust poses a problem for evidentialism, or the view that one should never believe anything without sufficient evidence. Further central questions include whether trusting is a virtue and trustworthiness morally required, while a final set of questions concerns the role of trust in politics and the connection between interpersonal trust and trust in institutions.

1   Common observations about trust
2   Accounts of trust
3   When trust is justified
4   Trust and social and political institutions

1   Common observations about trust

Trust is part of love and friendship, and vital for any cooperative task. Trust's pervasiveness can render it almost invisible; we notice how much we trust only when trust has been betrayed.

Any account of trust should aim to be compatible with and seek to explain a number of commonly accepted observations. There is a core of four such observations which are generally accepted by people writing about trust and a further three which, while not universally accepted, are frequently noted. The four core observations about trust are as follows.

(1) Trust involves risk. A person who trusts another is willing both to run the risk of letting them near things that they care about, and to rely on their words and promised actions. When trust is betrayed the truster is usually left worse off than had they refrained from trusting. (2) Those who trust are willing to forgo an immediate accounting of how or even whether the one trusted has responded to trust with trustworthiness, and to allow the one trusted

some discretion as to how to fulfil that trust. While contractual relations might involve a degree of trust, noncontractual trust relations are distinguished from contractual arrangements by their relative open-endedness. When there is trust, there is no need to specify exactly what must be done to fulfil it. The flexibility of trust relations in part explains trust's usefulness: contingency and ignorance often make us unable to specify what we are counting on the other to do; trust removes the need to do so. (3) Trust enhances the effectiveness of agency: it enables us to attempt cooperative tasks that could not rationally be attempted without trust, and, as Luhmann (1973) points out, it lets us inhabit a simpler and less threatening world, a world in which we need not plan for every contingency. (4) Trust and distrust are self-confirming, distrust even more strongly so than trust. When there is distrust, cooperative relations will be minimized and there will be little chance of getting evidence that the person is after all trustworthy. Trust and distrust also influence how we interpret the actions and behaviour of others: when there is room for a more or less favourable interpretation, we will adopt the interpretation which most fits with our view of their trustworthiness. In addition, sometimes displaying trust or distrust itself affects the behaviour of the person in question and tends to make them either trustworthy or untrustworthy.

Three additional claims enjoy wide agreement. (5) Trust and distrust are contraries but not contradictories. Just because one does not trust, it does not follow that one thereby distrusts, for there can be a neutral stance of neither trusting nor distrusting. (6) Trust cannot be willed. One cannot will oneself to trust in the acknowledged presence of substantial reasons to distrust, though one may be able to make oneself act as if one trusted. (7) The value of trust is not exhausted by its instrumental role in making possible cooperative relations. Trust, when well placed, is valuable in itself and is a constitutive part of other things valuable in themselves, such as love and friendship (see Friendship §1).

2 Accounts of trust

Accounts of trust divide into three families, depending on the degrees to which they distinguish trust from reliance, and to which they emphasize affect or feeling.

The first family of accounts view trust as a form of risk assessment (see Risk assessment). Such accounts tend to begin by considering trust in institutions and then extend the results of that reflection to cover interpersonal trust. Gambetta offers the following definition of trust:

trust (or, symmetrically, distrust) is a certain level of subjective probability with which an agent assesses that another agent or group of agents will perform a particular action, both *before* he can monitor such action (or independently of his capacity ever to be able to monitor it) *and* in a context in which it affects *his own* action

(1988: 217; original emphasis).

The definition emphasizes the way trusting makes one vulnerable, but it does not distinguish among the reasons why one might assign a sufficiently high degree of probability to agents' performing an action. One might think agents will perform that action out of fear or stupidity, or because it coincides with their own self-interest, or because they have, and wish to display, goodwill towards those who are counting on them. Gambetta includes all these alike in his definition. Proponents of such accounts are thus unlikely to accept that trust is anything other than instrumentally good, for if trust can rest on any assessment of motivation it is hard to see how it could be valuable in itself. Several writers hold that accounts which ignore motivation confuse trust with mere reliance.

Trust is distinguished from reliance in two ways. One can rely on something, or someone, simply because one has no choice but to do so: the bridge, rickety and unsafe though it might be, is the only way to escape the oncoming fire and so one is forced to rely on it and hope for the best. When one trusts, in contrast, one has the confident expectation that the one trusted will respond favourably. According to Thomas Hobbes, '[t]rust is a passion proceeding from the belief of him whom we expect or hope for good, so free from doubt that upon the same we pursue no other way' (1650).

Trust is thus distinguished from hope by confidence of expectations. But confident expectations can be grounded in all manner of psychological features. Most who clearly distinguish trust from reliance suggest that the difference is that in trust one relies on goodwill rather than on some other aspect of a person's psychology. Thus, the second family of accounts of trust, will-based accounts, tend to begin by considering interpersonal trust. Annette Baier's article, 'Trust and Anti-trust', offers an entrusting model. On this model, trusting is a three-place relation: A trusts B with valued thing C (1986: 236); and trusting is distinguished from mere reliance in so far as trust is always reliance on the goodwill (and competence) of another. We value another's goodwill towards us in itself, not merely because of its usefulness; therefore, on will-based accounts, the value of well-placed trust is not exclusively instrumental.

The first two families of accounts of trust take trust to involve both cognitive and conative aspects, both judgments about the likely actions of another and readiness to undertake risky actions on the basis of those judgments. The third family of accounts, affective attitude accounts, adds an affective aspect: trust is a feeling as well as a judgment and a disposition to act. '[Trust] has a special "feel", most easily acknowledged when it is missed, say, when one moves from a friendly, "safe" neighbourhood to a tense, insecure one' (Baier 1992: 112–3).

3   When trust is justified

If our trust in strangers can be justified, then it seems that we sometimes trust without good evidence for the belief that the one trusted is trustworthy. Thus trust, like faith, might seem to conflict with evidentialism, or the view that we should never believe anything without sufficient evidence (see FAITH). In response, we might claim that in certain social climates we have sufficient evidence that strangers will be trustworthy and that outside such climates our trust in strangers is unjustified. In this way we reconcile trust with evidentialism by requiring trust to meet the normal justification standards for belief. Alternatively, we might, following some writers on faith, reject evidentialism and claim that trust does not require the same evidence as other beliefs but can still be justified. Finally, we might stress the affective aspect of trust and claim that since evidentialism governs the adoption of beliefs and not the adoption of affective attitudes, trust falls outside the scope of the evidentialist requirement.

It might be thought that trust should be our default stance: if we distrust without solid evidence of untrustworthiness our willingness to assume ill will or unreliability shows a lack of respect for the person distrusted (see RESPECT FOR PERSONS). At least initially, everyone should be given the benefit of the doubt. On this view, willingness to trust is a virtue (see VIRTUES AND VICES §§2–3). Similarly, it might be thought that we are required to respond to trusting with trustworthiness, and so when trust is betrayed the moral fault always lies with the one who responded to trust with untrustworthiness. Both of these claims ignore how trust and trustworthiness can be used to foster exploitation, to hide abuse and to promote cooperation in the service of unworthy ends. In this respect, trust and trustworthiness are like loyalty. Loyalty can promote bad causes as well as good ones. Sometimes, one is required to respond to trust with selective untrustworthiness, and to demands for loyalty with judicious disloyalty. Just because well-placed trust has noninstrumental value,

it need not follow that poorly placed trust has such value.

What conditions are likely to give rise to trust and how is trust to be maintained and extended? Good's contribution to the Gambetta volume shows that some insight into these questions can be gained from game theory and from laboratory studies of cooperation (see DECISION AND GAME THEORY §§3, 6, 8). Trustworthy behaviour is more likely to be shown by those who are engaged in ongoing cooperative exchanges since, by being untrustworthy, they risk losing the benefits of all future cooperative exchanges. Likewise, communication facilitates trust since the more we know about persons, the more certain we can be about how they will act. Trust is more easily extended in incremental steps because we do not deliberate extensively about small extensions to previous policy; further, trust is more easily developed through small initial risks. These observations suggest strategies for those who would initiate and develop trusting relations. Baier (1992) offers a sensitive discussion of the functional virtues needed to maintain trust. Chief among them are tact and willingness to forgive breaches in trust, though judgment is indispensable in working out which breaches should be forgiven, and which not.

4   Trust and social and political institutions

Social and political institutions (such as licensing boards, marketplaces and schools) can make possible and strengthen interpersonal trust, by removing incentives to untrustworthiness and so creating a confluence of motives for trustworthiness, by helping to create stable expectations and by providing a framework for understanding communication and interpreting behaviour.

If social and political institutions can underwrite interpersonal trust, could it be possible to replace interpersonal trust with trust in well-designed institutions? Trusting in institutions rather than in individuals would eliminate the need for information about particular persons filling institutional roles. We could count on whoever happens to fill a well-designed social role. In large impersonal societies, where we must frequently interact with persons unknown to us, the advantages of shifting from interpersonal to institutional trust are obvious. The contrast between institutional and interpersonal trust is not hard and fast, and a particular instance of trust, say trust in one's physician, could involve elements of both. That the two sorts of trust can overlap suggests we need not think it possible to replace interpersonal trust with institutional trust to think it worth heading in such a direction.

One reason for being suspicious of the claim that we should trust in institutions is the concern that doing so requires that we forswear vigilance and forgo checking. Consider the claim, advanced by John Locke (1690), that the relation between citizens and government is one of trust. If trust is generally appropriate towards parents and always appropriate towards God, it might be thought just plain foolish towards governments. This objection is based, however, on a misunderstanding of the way theorists have thought that the notion of trust enters into the relation between citizens and government. According to Locke, citizens entrust the government with coercive power to act on their behalf for their benefit and for the protection of their rights. When governments fail to fulfil their trust, they lose legitimate authority (see LOCKE, J. §10). The people also retain the power to judge when a breach of trust has occurred:

> for who shall be *Judge* whether his Trustee or Deputy acts well, and according to the Trust reposed in him, but he who deputes him, and must, by having deputed him, have still a Power to discard him, when he fails in his Trust?
>
> (1690: 445; original emphasis)

That the relation between government and governed is one of trust is thus compatible with holding the government accountable, provided that we understand the relation in question to be one of entrusting. However, for societies to flourish they need political institutions that merit trust and allow citizens to be confident that power is safely entrusted to them.

How significant one finds trust to be in public life will depend in part on the account of trust that one adopts. Thus, while risk-assessment accounts encounter problems thinking about interpersonal trust, will-based accounts are less readily generalized from interpersonal relations to social and political institutions.

See also: HOPE; PROFESSIONAL ETHICS; PROMISING; RECIPROCITY; SOLIDARITY; TRUTHFULNESS; VULNERABILITY AND FINITUDE; XIN (TRUSTWORTHINESS)

References and further reading

* Baier, A. (1986) 'Trust and Anti-trust', *Ethics* 96: 231–60. (The best introduction to the topic and the single most influential article in the area.)
* —— (1992) 'The Pathologies of Trust' and 'Appropriate Trust', *Tanner Lectures on Human Values*, vol. 13, Salt Lake City, UT: University of Utah Press. (Delivered originally at Princeton University in 1991, these lectures develop the account given in 'Trust and Anti-trust'.)

Baker, J. (1987) 'Trust and Rationality', *Pacific Philosophical Quarterly* 68: 1–13. (A useful introduction to the problems of trust and evidentialism.)

Becker, L. (1996) 'Trust as Noncognitive Security About Motives', *Ethics* 107: 43–61. (Emphasizes the noncognitive aspects of trust.)

* Gambetta, D. (1988) 'Can We Trust Trust?' in D. Gambetta (ed.) *Trust: Making and Breaking Cooperative Relations*, New York: Blackwell, 1988, 213–37. (Addresses the question of whether and when it is rational to trust.).

—— (ed.) (1988) *Trust: Making and Breaking Cooperative Relations*, New York: Blackwell. (A collection of essays most of which provide risk-assessment accounts of trust. Contains articles by Patrick Bateson, Partha Dasgupta, John Dunn, Ernest Gellner, Keith Hart, Geoffrey Hawthorn, Edward Lorenz, Niklas Luhmann, Anthony Pagden and Bernard Williams. Dunn's contribution, 'Trust and Political Agency', is an especially useful discussion of the role of trust in politics.)

* Good, D. (1988) 'Individuals, Interpersonal Relations, and Trust', in D. Gambetta (ed.) *Trust: Making and Breaking Cooperative Relations*, New York: Blackwell, 1988, 31–48. (Applies game theory to the question of when to trust.)

Govier, T. (1992) 'Trust, Distrust, and Feminist Theory', *Hypatia* 7: 16–33. (A survey of feminist reflections on trust.)

Hardin, R. (1991) 'Trusting Persons, Trusting Institutions', in R. Zeckhauser (ed.) *Strategy and Choice*, Cambridge, MA: MIT Press, 185–209. (Presents a critique of will-based and affective attitude accounts of trust.)

* Hobbes, T. (1650) 'Human Nature', part I of *The Elements of Law, Natural and Politic*, Oxford: Oxford University Press, 1994, chapter IX, section 9. (Contains a brief treatment of trust in the context of a discussion of the passions.)

* Locke, J. (1690) *Two Treatises of Government*, ed. and with notes by P. Laslett, Cambridge: Cambridge University Press, 1960. (Argues that the relation between citizens and government is one of trust. The editor's introduction to this critical edition deals with Locke's use of the concept of trust.)

* Luhmann, N. (1973) 'Trust: A Mechanism for the Reduction of Social Complexity', trans. H. Davis, J. Raffman and K. Rooney, in T. Burns and G. Poggi (eds) *Trust and Power*, Chichester, NY: Wiley, 1979, 4–103. (A complex and subtle discussion of trust from a sociological perspective. Quite difficult.)

Thomas, L. (1990) 'Trust, Affirmation, and Moral Character: A Critique of Kantian Morality', in O.

Flanagan and A. Rorty (eds) *Identity, Character and Morality*, Cambridge, MA: MIT Press, 1990, 235–57. (Offers a detailed will-based account of trust and argues that trust has noninstrumental value.)

KAREN JONES

TRUTH AND MEANING
see MEANING AND TRUTH

TRUTH BY CONVENTION
see CONVENTIONALISM; NECESSARY TRUTH AND CONVENTION

TRUTH, COHERENCE THEORY OF

The term 'coherence' in the phrase 'coherence theory of truth' has never been very precisely defined. The most we can say by way of a general definition is that a set of two or more beliefs are said to cohere if they 'fit' together or 'agree' with one another. Typically, then, a coherence theory of truth would claim that the beliefs of a given individual are true to the extent that the set of all their beliefs is coherent. Such theories, thus, make truth a matter of a truth bearer's relations to other truth bearers rather than its relations to reality. This latter implication is the chief hindrance to plausibility faced by coherence theories, and most coherence theorists try to escape the problem by denying that there is any extra-mental reality.

1   **Essential elements of coherence theories**
2   **Objections to coherence theories**
3   **Scepticism and coherence theories**

1   Essential elements of coherence theories

John LOCKE voiced what might be the earliest statement of a coherence theory of truth when he said in *An Essay Concerning Human Understanding* that ideas are true if they agree with each other. But a few pages later he reverted to a correspondence theory by declaring that there were 'chimerical' truths and real truths, and what distinguishes the latter from the former is that real truths agree with reality. When the character Philonous, representing George BERKELEY

in the latter's *Three Dialogues*, is asked how his idealist doctrine can distinguish fact from fiction, reality from illusion, and waking life from dreaming, he replies that fictional ideas, illusions, and dreams are known to be such because they are disconnected from the great mass of the rest of our ideas. This can be taken as an endorsement of what would today be called a coherence theory of truth. Moreover, coherence theories were in their golden age during the nineteenth century, the heyday of ontological idealism in Western philosophy. It is not surprising that coherence theories should cohabit with anti-realist ontology. If reality itself is just a system of mental entities – thoughts – then not even the true thoughts can correspond to some *other* reality, since there is no other. So, it would be natural to suppose that the truth of a true thought must consist in its relations to other thoughts (see TRUTH, CORRESPONDENCE THEORY OF §2).

Nineteenth-century coherence theories provided a more detailed definition of coherence: a set of beliefs coheres if and only if each member of the set is consistent with any subset of the others, and if each is implied (inductively, if not deductively) by all of the others taken as premises or, according to some coherence theories, each is implied by each of the others individually.

Unfortunately, the distinction between theories of justification and theories of truth was not deployed in the nineteenth century. As a result, there are few individuals to whom one can unhesitatingly attribute a coherence theory of truth, distinct from a coherence theory of justification. One to whom we can make such an attribution is Brand Blanshard: 'coherence is the sole criterion of truth. We have now to face the question whether it also gives us the nature of truth... one may reject coherence as the definition of truth while accepting it as the test' (Blanshard 1941: 260). *Pure* truth, he says, is a fully coherent set of beliefs, and 'fully coherent knowledge would be knowledge which in every judgment entailed, and was entailed by, the rest of the system'. But even this understates the entailment relations between the members of the system: 'every proposition would be entailed by the others jointly and even singly'. Since an inconsistent subset of beliefs would trivially entail anything and everything, and since presumably Blanshard does not want that kind of entailment to be a truth-making relation, there is an implied condition of consistency on any system of beliefs before it will count as true. However, Blanshard does not want to say that two such systems, each coherent within itself but inconsistent with the other, are *both* true. A true system of beliefs would be one 'in which everything real and possible is coherently included'.

So, a purely true system would be one that gives us a complete picture of the world. This theory can be expressed in the following formula:

> For each belief, *b*, *b* is purely true if and only if *b* is a member of a consistent set of beliefs that among them give a complete picture of the world and each of which entails each of the others.

But pure truth has never been attained, so Blanshard, typically for a coherence theorist, proposes that truth comes in degrees: 'A given judgment is true in the *degree* to which its content could maintain itself in the light of a completed system of knowledge, false in the *degree* to which its appearance there would require transformation' (Blanshard 1941: 304). This is captured in the formula:

> For each belief, *b*, *b* is true to degree *n* if and only if *n* per cent of the content of *b* would be present in a purely true system of beliefs.

2 Objections to coherence theories

The most common objection to coherence theories is that the conditions they place on truth are too weak. Traditionally, this objection is expressed with the quip that on a coherence theory a well-written novel would be true, literally not figuratively. Taken at face value, such an objection is only telling against those theories which require mere mutual consistency for coherence. But there are no such coherence theories. Blanshard's, as we have seen, requires mutual entailment among the beliefs in a set if the set is to count as coherent. Nevertheless, it is certainly possible to construct two sets of consistent, mutually entailing propositions which contradict each other and which, thus, cannot both be true. Blanshard of course, following Bradley (1914), tries to eliminate this possibility by insisting that final truth is found only in a set which is not only coherent but also *complete*. Yet even this might not be a strong enough condition on truth. Could there not be two complete pictures of the universe, inconsistent with each other, but each internally coherent? Since there is not even one such complete picture, an answer to that question must remain uncertain; but it is worth noting that there are large domains of phenomena for which humankind possesses two (or more) competing theories, each of which seems to have approximately equal degrees of internal coherence. There are for example the geometries of Euclid and Riemann; and one thinks also of Western medicine, on the one hand, and the traditional medicine of China, on the other.

Since the concepts of entailment and consistency are usually defined in terms of truth, a theory which, like coherence theories, defines the latter concept in terms of entailment or consistency is uninformatively circular. One might try to eliminate the circularity by defining entailment and consistency in terms of a certain set of rules of derivation; for example '*p* entails *q* if and only if *q* can be derived from *p* via one or more of the rules in *R*', where *R* is a set of rules of inference whose members refer only to the syntactic structure of propositions, not to their truth values. One such rule might be 'from propositions of the form *p* and "if *p*, then *q*", one may derive the proposition *q*'. But suppose *R* contains 'from a proposition *p*, one may derive the proposition "not-*p*"'. Then no one would take seriously a theory claiming that a set of propositions that are mutually 'entailing' via such a set of rules is, for that reason, true. Hence, defining entailment and consistency proof-theoretically requires that the set of rules in question be restricted to those which are *truth*-preserving; and so the circularity problem arises again.

Defining the truth-value of a truth bearer in terms of its relations with other truth bearers instead of its relations with the world is initially considered implausible by most, because doing so seems to make it logically possible for 'Kendall is red-headed' to be true even if she is not in fact red-headed, and for 'Emory is handsome' to be false even if he is, in fact, handsome. The only way to make such situations impossible is to embrace an anti-realist notion of what it is to be a fact. For example, if we define a fact to be an idea in the mind of God and declare that God's ideas are a complete and perfectly coherent set, then facts and truths are not disjoint. But since the plausibility of the coherence theory depends on an anti-realist ontology, the difficulties facing such ontologies become difficulties for the coherence theory (see IDEALISM; REALISM AND ANTIREALISM).

3 Scepticism and coherence theories

Given the difficulties facing coherence theories of truth, one might wonder why some have found them attractive. There are remarkably few positive arguments for such theories in the literature, and those which can be found are nearly all variations on what might be called the argument from scepticism – that it is very hard (some would say it is impossible) ever to be justified in believing that this or that is a mind-independent fact. Our subconscious minds so thoroughly filter and modify observational input that what we take to be facts have no resemblance to any mind-independent facts. So, if we make the existence of a mind-independent fact a necessary condition for the truth of a belief (or sentence, or whatever) we would never be justified in thinking that *any* belief is

471

true. Thus, such a theory of truth would entail scepticism. Given that scepticism is wrong, so too must be any such theory of truth.

But begging the question is no more respectable when directed against scepticism than when directed against any other philosophical proposal. A sceptical thesis such as 'No belief is justified as true' (which does not say 'I am justified in believing that no belief is justified as true') is not self-contradictory and thus might well be correct. That pill will be less bitter if we remember that it need not imply that no belief is any more rational than any other; for the rationality of beliefs could be defined in terms of their possession of values, such as explanatory power, *other than* the value of being justified as true.

A second problem with the argument from scepticism for coherence theories of truth is that the latter theories do not really solve the problem of scepticism anyway. Coherence theorists of truth, in effect if not in intention, try to deal with scepticism by redefining truth so as to make it more attainable. They define it in such a way that it becomes easy to have beliefs justified as probably true. But no satisfying rebuttal to scepticism can come from this strategy, for the problem of scepticism is the concern that our beliefs may not be justified as accurate reflections of a mind-independent world. The manoeuvre under consideration tells us in the large print that we have adequate justification for most of our beliefs about the world; but, simultaneously, the small print tells us that this 'world' we believe in consists of mental constructs and may not even vaguely resemble the mind-independent world. Of course, a coherence theorist of truth believes we are mistaken in thinking there is any mind-independent world in the first place. But to say this is to surrender to scepticism, not to refute it. Davidson makes the same point thus: '[Such theories] are sceptical in the way idealism or phenomenalism are sceptical; they are sceptical not because they make reality unknowable, but because they reduce reality to so much less than we believe there is' (Davidson 1990: 298).

See also: MEANING AND TRUTH; TRUTH, DEFLATIONARY THEORIES OF; TRUTH, PRAGMATIC THEORY OF

References and further reading

* Berkeley, G. (1713) *Three Dialogues between Hylas and Philonous*, Peru, IL: Open Court, 1969. (A readable and entertaining summary of the author's philosophy.)
* Blanshard, B. (1941) *The Nature of Thought*, New York: Macmillan, vol. 2. (The author's coherence theory of truth is presented on pages 260–308.)
* Bradley, F.H. (1914) *Essays on Truth and Reality*, Oxford: Clarendon Press. (A coherence theory which unfortunately mixes together issues of justification with issues of truth.)
* Davidson, D. (1990) 'The Structure and Content of Truth', *Journal of Philosophy* 87: 279–328. (A summary of the author's mature views on truth and semantics.)
  Kirkham, R.L. (1992) *Theories of Truth: A Critical Introduction*, Cambridge, MA: MIT Press. (An introduction to theories of truth. Sects 3.5–3.6 expand on the issues in this entry.)
* Locke, J. (1690) *An Essay Concerning Human Understanding*, New York: E.P. Dutton, 1976. (Book IV, Chapter V contains the author's theory of truth.)

RICHARD L. KIRKHAM

TRUTH CONDITIONS
see MEANING AND TRUTH

TRUTH, CORRESPONDENCE THEORY OF

The two oldest theories of truth in Western philosophy, those of Plato and Aristotle, are both correspondence theories. And if the non-philosopher can be said to subscribe to a theory of truth, it would most likely be to a correspondence theory; so called because such theories are often summed up with the slogans 'truth is correspondence with the facts' or 'truth is agreement with reality'. Aristotle puts it thus: 'to say that [either] that which is is not or that which is not is, is a falsehood; and to say that that which is is and that which is not is not, is true'. In epistemology, such theories offer an analysis of that at which, supposedly, investigation aims: truth. But correspondence theories are also now thought to play important roles in philosophical semantics and in the physicalist programme, which is the task of reducing all non-physical concepts to the concepts of logic, mathematics, and physics.

1   **Two kinds of correspondence theory**
2   **The common essence of correspondence theories**
3   **Objections to correspondence theories**

1 Two kinds of correspondence theory

Correspondence theories come in two varieties – correspondence as correlation, and correspondence as congruence. The former variety asserts that every truth bearer (proposition, sentence, belief, and so on) is correlated to a possible fact. If the possible fact to which a given truth bearer is correlated actually obtains, the truth bearer is true; otherwise it is false. What the correspondence-as-correlation theory does not claim is that the truth bearer depicts, or is structurally isomorphic with, the possible fact to which it is correlated. Rather, a truth bearer as a whole is correlated to a possible fact as a whole. A correspondence-as-congruence theory does claim that truth bearers and the possible facts to which they correspond have parallel structures. Representing this second school is Bertrand Russell, who affirms that Othello's belief that Desdemona loves Cassio is a complex relation between Othello (the subject), Desdemona (an object-term), Cassio (another object-term) and loving (the object-relation) (Russell 1912). Truth requires a congruence between this four-term relation and a second, three-term relation called 'a fact' which has Desdemona, loving, and Cassio (in that order) as its terms. If such a three-term relation exists in reality, then Othello's belief is true. If there is no such fact, the belief is false (see RUSSELL, B. §10).

J.L. Austin has offered a correspondence-as-correlation theory. Truth is considered as a single, four-term relation between a statement, a sentence, a state of affairs (that is, a possible fact), and a *type* of state of affairs. For Austin, a statement is the information conveyed by a declarative sentence. So a sentence is the medium in which a statement is made. And the meaning of statements is a matter of two kinds of conventions that have evolved in our language. First, there are descriptive conventions correlating *sentences* with types of states of affairs. Second, there are demonstrative conventions correlating *statements* to particular states of affairs. Thus, 'A statement is said to be true when the historic [that is, particular] state of affairs to which it is correlated by the demonstrative conventions (the one to which it "refers") is of a type which the sentence used in making it is correlated by the descriptive conventions' (Austin [1950] 1970: 121–2). Hence, 'there is no need whatsoever for the words used in making a true statement to "mirror" in any way, however indirect, any feature whatsoever of the situation or event'. The correspondence between the truth bearer and the world is *absolutely and purely conventional*. For example, 'the cat is on the mat' would in an ordinary context refer to the present state of affairs in which speaker and hearer find themselves, along with a cat and a nearby mat. Therefore, if a cat is on a mat in the state of affairs in which the speaker is located, the statement is true because the present state of affairs is of just the type described by the sentence.

In favour of the correspondence-as-correlation view is the fact that some sentences (for example, the Latin word 'sum', which translates as 'I am') are atomic meaning units which have no internal semantic structure and thus could correlate with possible facts only whole-for-whole.

2 The common essence of correspondence theories

If we strip out of Russell's theory of truth the assumption that beliefs are four-termed relations, and strip out of Austin's theory his assumptions about meaning being a matter of conventions, we can then encapsulate the two stripped-down theories of truth in these two formulas:

Russell: A belief is true if and only if it is a belief that an object x bears relation R to another object y, and x does bear relation R to y.

Austin: A statement is true if and only if it expresses a state of affairs, and that state of affairs obtains.

If we abstract the common elements of these two theories, we get the following thesis which can be taken as expressing the common denominator of all correspondence theories of truth:

Correspondence: A truth bearer is true if and only if it corresponds to a state of affairs and that state of affairs obtains.

But it must be emphasized that the 'corresponds to' in this thesis does not express some particular relation. Rather it should be thought of as a placeholder which any given correspondence theory would replace with some particular and familiar relation. Which relation a particular correspondence theorist would cite will vary, depending on their choice of truth bearer. For beliefs, the relation would be 'is a belief that'. For linguistic entities such as sentences, 'says that' or 'means that' or 'expresses' would be more appropriate choices. If a proposition is the bearer in question, then the appropriate relation would depend on how one defines propositions. (The differences between the formula expressing Russell's theory and the schema are attributable to Russell's conviction that the belief must be isomorphic to the corresponding fact.)

Note that the 'obtains' in the correspondence schema does not require that the state of affairs should obtain mind-independently. It is perfectly possible to hold that truth consists in correspondence with facts and to hold also that facts are mind-dependent entities. McTaggart (1921) endorsed such a correspondence theory, and Kant (1781) and Wilfred Sellars (1963) can be read this way too (see KANT, I.;

McTAGGART, J.M.E.; SELLARS, W.). Thus, while most correspondence theorists have been ontological realists, the common belief that a correspondence theory is committed to realism is erroneous.

3 Objections to correspondence theories

Traditionally, three kinds of criticisms have been levelled at correspondence theories. The first concerns whatever it is the theory identifies as the truth bearer (beliefs, propositions, statements and so on): some allege that such things cannot, for various reasons, be truth bearers. Second, some allege, about whatever (facts, situations, states of affairs and so on) is identified by the theory as the correspondent of the truth bearer, that such things cannot, for various reasons, serve as the correspondents. Third, there are objections to the alleged relation between truth bearers and reality on the grounds that there is no such relation or that its nature has not been clearly explained by the theory.

The first sort of issue arises with any kind of truth theory, so nothing more will be said of it here. The third sort of objection is rarely legitimate because it aims at the sort of slogans with which correspondence theorists sum up their theories (for example, 'truth is a correspondence with the facts') and is thus irrelevant to the theories themselves, such as that of Russell and Austin, in which no such special relation makes any appearance. A closely related objection is that correspondence theories use concepts like 'belief' or 'means that' which themselves have no undisputed philosophical analysis. But such an accusation is of dubious significance precisely because it is difficult to imagine any philosophical theory against which the same objection could not be made: philosophically important topics tend to link with one another, so such an objection implicitly assumes that a theory does not solve any problem unless it solves every problem.

A correspondence theorist's description of the connection between truth bearers and facts is largely dictated by the choice of truth bearer anyway. And the latter choice, in turn, is dictated by the needs of the broader philosophical programme which has 'placed an order' for a theory of truth. Traditional epistemology is concerned with the comparative evaluation of competing theories about how our beliefs can be justified as likely to be true. But such evaluations would be impossible without first having a notion of what truth, specifically, what true *belief*, is. On the other hand, the Davidson programme aims to put a theory of truth to work in semantics and, thus, requires a theory of true *sentences* (see DAVIDSON, D. §4).

Many have rejected the very notion of a fact as some non-linguistic entity existing in the world; facts are really just reifications of true sentences. The evidence for the claim that 'fact' is just another name for 'true sentence' is supposed to be that we cannot individuate and identify any particular fact save by using the very same words that we use to individuate and identify its corresponding sentence. There are, however, good reasons for resisting this line of thought. First, it should be no surprise that we cannot specify a given fact save by means of the sentence to which the fact corresponds, because it could not possibly be otherwise. Suppose our language contained a series of nouns ('Fact1', 'Fact2' and so on) each referring uniquely to a different fact. We could then use these nouns to identify particular facts, but we could also use these terms to make statements. Any expression that could be used to identify facts could be used to make statements. Second, facts can enter into causal relations in a way that true sentences cannot: the fact that the war was lost caused the government to fall, but the true sentence 'the war was lost' cannot cause the government to fall. Third, one of the constituents of the fact that the war was lost is a certain war, but no war (distinct from the word 'war') can be a constituent of the true sentence 'the war was lost'.

Some who would accept the existence of atomic facts would still object to the correspondence theory on the grounds that there are no disjunctive, conditional or negative facts; hence, there are no facts to be the correspondents of true disjunctions, conditionals, or negations. In response to this, a correspondence theorist would rightly note that, on the ordinary sense of fact, it is perfectly correct to say 'It is a fact that either she gets here on time or I spend the night under a bridge' or 'It is a fact that if the donated liver is late, then the patient will die' or 'It is a fact that I am not going to make it'. Moreover, a correspondence theory could avoid commitment to conditional, negative or disjunctive facts by giving a recursive analysis of the truth of non-atomic truth bearers.

See also: MEANING AND TRUTH; REALISM AND ANTIREALISM; TRUTH, COHERENCE THEORY OF; TRUTH, DEFLATIONARY THEORIES OF; TRUTH, PRAGMATIC THEORY OF

References and further reading

* Aristotle (*c.* mid 4th century BC) *Metaphysics*, in R. McKeon (ed.) *Basic Works of Aristotle*, New York: Random House, 1941. (At 1011b26, the author states the earliest correspondence-as-correlation theory of truth in Western philosophy.)

* Austin, J.L. (1950) 'Truth', in J.O. Urmson and G.J. Warnock (eds) *Philosophical Papers*, Oxford: Oxford University Press, 1970. (A modern correspondence-as-correlation theory, originally published in *Proceedings of the Aristotelian Society* supplement to vol. 24: 111–28.)

Bealer, G. (1982) *Quality and Concept*, Oxford: Clarendon Press. (Pages 11 and 186–203 offer a contemporary correspondence-as-congruence theory that identifies the fundamental elements of thoughts with the fundamental elements of states of affairs.)

* Kant, I. (1781) *The Critique of Pure Reason*, trans. N. Kemp Smith, New York: St Martin's Press, 1929. (The author's words at A58 suggest a correspondence theory, which in light of the rest of his views could not be taken as implying ontological realism.)

Kirkham, R.L. (1992) *Theories of Truth: A Critical Introduction*, Cambridge, MA: MIT Press. (An introduction to theories of truth. Chapter 4 expands on the issues in this entry.)

* McTaggart, J. McT.E. (1921) *The Nature of Existence*, vol. 1. Cambridge: Cambridge University Press. (Pages 10–37 present the author's correspondence theory in the context of his ontological anti-realism.)

Pitcher, G. (ed.) (1964) *Truth*, Englewood Cliffs, NJ: Prentice Hall. (The only anthology of theories of truth in print. Somewhat dated, but still valuable.)

* Plato (*c.*366–360 BC) *Sophist*, in E. Hamilton and H. Cairns (eds) *Plato: The Collected Dialogues*, Princeton, NJ: Princeton University Press, 1961. (At 262E–263D the Stranger presents the Western world's first theory of truth.)

* Russell, B. (1912) *The Problems of Philosophy*, Oxford: Oxford University Press. (The chapter on 'Truth' is the prototypical modern correspondence-as-congruence theory.)

* Sellars, W. (1963) *Science, Perception and Reality*, New York: Humanities Press. (Another modern example of an ontological anti-realist endorsing a correspondence theory.)

RICHARD L. KIRKHAM

TRUTH, DEFLATIONARY THEORIES OF

So-called deflationary theories of truth, of which the best known are the redundancy, performative and prosentential theories, are really theories of truth ascriptions. This is because they are not theories of what truth is; rather, they are theories of what we are saying when we make utterances like '"Routledge editors are fine folks" is true'. The surface grammar of such utterances suggests that we use them to predicate a property, truth, of sentences or propositions; but the several deflationary theories all deny this. Indeed, they all endorse the Deflationary Thesis that there is no such property as truth and thus there is no need for, or sense to, a theory of truth distinct from a theory of truth ascriptions. Thus, for deflationists, the classical theories of truth, such as correspondence, coherence and pragmatic, are not wrong. They are something worse: they are wrong-headed from the start, for they are attempting to analyse something which simply is not there.

1   Problems with the Deflationary Thesis
2   Problems with the Gratuity Thesis

1   Problems with the Deflationary Thesis

What *are* we saying when we make utterances that *appear* to be ascribing truth to some truth bearer? According to the redundancy theory, whose invention is usually credited to F.P. Ramsey, we are saying nothing more or less than what is said in the statement to which we appear to be ascribing truth: '"Routledge editors are fine folks" is true' is synonymous with 'Routledge editors are fine folks' (see RAMSEY, F.P. §3). The redundancy theory, then, endorses the view that anything we can say or do with the predicate 'is true' can be said or done perfectly well without that predicate. The latter contention, which I shall call the Gratuity Thesis, is shared by the performative and prosentential theories of truth ascriptions discussed below, although these offer different accounts of what we are saying or doing when we ascribe truth. By itself, the Gratuity Thesis would be of importance only to linguists. Philosophical interest arises because redundancy theorists, and their performative and prosentential counterparts, make a breathtaking and rather cloudy inferential leap from the Gratuity Thesis to the Deflationary Thesis.

The description of the Deflationary Thesis given above seems to presuppose Platonism: that there are universal properties, and most predicates name properties. We can make it neutral with regard to Platonist–Nominalist debates by rewriting it thus: '"is true" is not a genuine predicate'.

It would be absurd to suppose that most predicates are not genuine predicates, so it would be equally absurd to take as a methodological principle that we should assume a predicate is not genuine until it is proven to be. Strangely, however, deflationists have adopted that principle, and anti-deflationists have let them get away with it. Indeed, it was not until the late 1970s and 1980s that the slow decline of ordinary language philosophy brought either contender to an awareness that linguistic analysis alone cannot settle the question (see ORDINARY LANGUAGE PHILOSOPHY §1). If indeed we do not need to postulate a property of truth (whether Platonically or Nominalistically construed) to explain what we are doing with our truth-ascribing utterances, then that is a point in favour of the Deflationary Thesis. But it is not decisive, for there may well be non-linguistic programmes which cannot be carried out without supposing that truth is some kind of property. Anti-deflationists have suggested, for example, that without such a postulation, we cannot explain why our scientific theories are so successful. To this, deflationists have responded that there is really nothing here that needs explanation: we have the theories we do just *because* they are successful. But this will not do. The fact that we would not have automobiles if they did not succeed in getting us from place to place does not preclude the need for an explanation of why they work, which would presumably be given in terms of the properties of automobiles and the forces at work in them.

Explaining the success of science is just a special case of the traditional epistemological programme of discovering the correct theory of justification. The task of the latter project is to refute scepticism by finding some property, called a 'mark' of truth, which correlates, perhaps imperfectly, with truth, and whose possession or non-possession by a given proposition is reasonably easy to detect. Coherence theories of justification (not truth) propose 'coherence with other propositions' as the mark. Foundationalists propose that it is 'self-evident (perhaps defeasibly), or inferred from self-evident premises'. One cannot judge whether a proposed mark does indeed correlate with truth unless one has some notion of what truth *is*, so this programme must postulate that truth is some kind of property. Those few deflationists who have considered this proposal respond by insisting, in effect, that we are entitled just to beg the question against scepticism, and hence there is no need for traditional epistemology in the first place. Begging the question against scepticism has been popular in contemporary philosophy, but anyone tempted to think that this is philosophically respectable should consider the following analogy: to prove the soundness and completeness theorems for classical logic is, in effect, to prove that the results of the logic's rules of inference correlate (perfectly) with truth (as defined in the logic's model theory). How seriously would we take one who claimed that such proofs (and hence the

model theory itself) are unneeded because we are entitled to assume that the inference rules of classical logic are correct? (And how would 'correct' as used here be defined without postulating a property of truth?) Even mathematical intuitionism does not want to say that there is no such thing as truth. It simply defines truth in terms of justification, that is, proof.

2 Problems with the Gratuity Thesis

The intense interest in the Deflationary Thesis in the later decades of the twentieth century should not give the impression that the Gratuity Thesis is itself beyond doubt. All existing theories of truth ascriptions face problems. In particular, at least two of the difficulties confronting the redundancy theory are worth mentioning. First, what are we to make of blind truth ascriptions such as 'What the editor says is true', which do not explicitly identify the proposition to which truth is being ascribed? Given that the speaker (and for that matter the audience) might not even know what proposition the editor has asserted, the idea that this truth ascription is just an alternative way of asserting that same proposition loses some plausibility. The two best redundancy theories, those of C.J.F. Williams (1976) and Paul Horwich (1990), handle this problem quite cleverly. But neither of them deals adequately with the fact that, as Horwich concedes, the redundancy theory cannot actually be stated. It can be *described* as the conjunction of all clauses of the form: '"p is true" is synonymous with "p"'. Obviously, one cannot state an infinitely long conjunction. Nor can one simply append the quantifier 'For all p' to the front of this schema. Such a quantifier cannot be objectual, on the one hand, because the first appearance of the 'p' in the schema stands in for a noun, while the second appearance stands in for a grammatically complete clause. On the other hand, such a quantifier cannot be substitutional, for then the redundancy theory would be saying 'all substitution instances of the schema are true' and thus the theory would be parasitic on some other antecedent notion of truth.

P. F. Strawson's (1950) performative theory of truth (ascriptions) denies that apparent truth ascriptions say *anything* in any familiar sense of 'say' (see STRAWSON, P. §4). Such utterances are more *doings* than *sayings*. They are gestures of agreement, much like nodding one's head. Hence, to utter '"Routledge editors are fine folks" is true' is to signal agreement with the notion that Routledge editors are fine folks. Utterances which do something rather than say something are called illocutionary or performative utterances (see PERFORMATIVES).

Strawson concedes that certain conditions in the

non-linguistic world must obtain before one may properly signal one's agreement, where the force of 'properly' is not 'appropriate from the standpoint of honesty or accuracy' but 'appropriate from the standpoint of correct usage'. For example, one ought not utter the words '"The dam has collapsed" is true' unless one believes it is a fact that the dam has collapsed. But if uttering an apparent truth ascription is just to signal agreement, why would the facts of the matter have any relevance? If 'is true' in no way asserts that these conditions are fulfilled, then how and why would these conditions be conditions for uttering 'is true'? One can after all *signal* agreement, dishonestly, even when one does not in fact agree. A second reason for doubting that the performative theory can establish the Gratuity Thesis is that, as H. Price (1988) has pointed out, the theory makes it a mystery why 'is true' is only applicable to indicative sentences. Why can we not use it to endorse the appropriateness of some question (for example, '"Is snow white?" is true') just as we can use it to endorse someone's assertion? And why can we not say '"Shut the door!" is true' to express our endorsement of the importance of obeying this command? It seems that any answer to these questions would have to concede that 'is true', 'is a good question', and 'ought to be obeyed' *mean* different things and this would imply that each of them *says* something.

Besides pronouns, English also contains pro-verbs, such as the 'did' in 'Mary ran quickly, so Bill did too', and pro-adjectives such as 'such' in 'The happy man was no longer such'; and pro-adverbs such as the 'so' in 'She twitched violently and, while so twitching, expired'. D. Grover, J. Camp and N. Belnap (1975), inventors of the prosentential theory of truth (ascriptions), suggest that there are also prosentences. 'So' is used this way in 'I do not believe Rachel is sick, but if so, she should stay home'. More to the immediate point, they contend that the phrases 'it is true' and 'that is true', despite their subject–predicate structure, are really one-word prosentences. And they claim that every locution in which 'is true' appears can be replaced by a locution that uses one of these prosentences. Thus, they endorse a modified version of the Gratuity Thesis: 'is true', as a separable predicate, is a gratuitous feature of the language. For example, 'Everything John says is true' is 'For every proposition, if John says that *it is true,* then *it is true*', where neither the 'it' nor the 'is true' have any separate meaning whatsoever.

The most serious objection to the prosentential theory concerns modified uses of 'is true' such as 'is not true' or 'will be true'. The prosentential theory postulates that the deep structure of English contains a number of sentential operators including 'It-will-be-

true-that' and 'It-is-not-true-that', and that all modified uses of 'is true' involve one or the other of the two prosentences within the scope of one of these operators. Thus, the deep structure of 'Everything John says will be true' is 'For all propositions, if John says that it is true, then it-will-be-true-that it is true', where, again, the 'it is true' is a prosentence. To analyse apparent predications of falsehood, they postulate the operator 'It-is-false-that'. Thus, the deep structure of 'That is false' is 'It-is-false-that that is true'. But, then, how do we account for the 'true' that appears in the sentential operators? The operators cannot themselves be given a prosentential analysis: if they could, there would have been no need to postulate them in the first place. The use of hyphens to connect the words of the operators tempts us to think of them each as a single word, in which case the 'true' in them has no independent meaning. But it is not easy to see how we could explain the meanings of these one-word operators without using a substantive notion of truth, and even if we could, our explanations of such one-word operators would miss out entirely on the common element in the meanings of, say, 'it-will-be-true-that' and 'it-was-true-that'.

See also: DŌGEN; JUSTIFICATION, EPISTEMIC; MEANING AND TRUTH; TRUTH, COHERENCE THEORY OF; TRUTH, CORRESPONDENCE THEORY OF; TRUTH, PRAGMATIC THEORY OF

References and further reading

Field, H. (1986) 'The Deflationary Conception of Truth', in G. MacDonald and C. Wright (eds) *Fact, Science and Morality*, Oxford: Blackwell. (An important attack on the Deflationary Thesis. Not for beginners.)

Geyer, D.L. (1917) 'The Relation of Truth to Tests', *Journal of Philosophy, Psychology and Scientific Methods* 13: 626–33. (Contains the earliest statement of what today would be called a redundancy theory.)

* Grover, D.L., Camp, J.L., Jr and Belnap, N.D., Jr (1975) 'A Prosentential Theory of Truth', *Philosophical Studies* 27: 73–125. (Presentation of a prosentential theory of truth by its inventors.)

* Horwich, P. (1990) *Truth*, Oxford: Blackwell. (Along with Williams – see below – one of the most thorough and best-argued defences of the redundancy theory. Horwich, however, rejects the Gratuity Thesis and endorses a milder than usual version of the Deflationary Thesis.)

Kirkham, R.L. (1992) *Theories of Truth: A Critical Introduction*, Cambridge, MA: MIT Press. (An introduction to theories of truth. Chapter 10 expands on the issues in this entry.)

Körner, S. (1955) 'Truth as a Predicate', *Analysis* 15: 106–9. (A potent, early attack on what is now called deflationism before the latter became popular.)

* Price, H. (1988) *Facts and the Function of Truth*, Oxford: Blackwell. (Presents a Darwinian theory of truth ascriptions.)

Ramsey, F.P. (1927) 'Facts and Propositions', *Proceedings of the Aristotelian Society* supplement to 7: 153–70. (The first statement of a redundancy theory to have a widespread impact.)

* Strawson, P.F. (1950) 'Truth', *Proceedings of the Aristotelian Society* supplement to 24: 129–56. (The classic statement of the performative theory of truth ascriptions.)

* Williams, C.J.F. (1976) *What is Truth?*, Cambridge: Cambridge University Press. (Along with Horwich – see above – one of the most thorough and best-argued defences of what could fairly be called a redundancy theory.)

RICHARD L. KIRKHAM

TRUTH, PRAGMATIC THEORY OF

Two distinctly different kinds of theories parade under the banner of the 'pragmatic theory of truth'. First, there is the consensus theory of C.S. Peirce, according to which a true proposition is one which would be endorsed unanimously by all persons who had had sufficient relevant experiences to judge it. Second, there is the instrumentalist theory associated with William James, John Dewey, and F.C.S. Schiller, according to which a proposition counts as true if and only if behaviour based on a belief in the proposition leads, in the long run and all things considered, to beneficial results for the believers. (Peirce renamed his theory 'pragmaticism' when his original term 'pragmatism' was appropriated by the instrumentalists.) Unless they are married to some form of ontological anti-realism, which they usually are, both theories imply that the facts of the matter are not relevant to the truth-value of the proposition.

1   Pragmaticism
2   Instrumentalism

1   Pragmaticism

C.S. Peirce believed that any two minds investigating a given question would tend eventually to arrive at the same answer, even if they used different methods and different pools of evidence: 'Let any human being have enough information and exert enough thought upon any question, and the result will be that he will arrive at a certain definite conclusion, which is the same that any other mind will reach' (Peirce 1931–58 (7): 319). Moreover, this one answer that all would reach is, by definition, the true answer: 'The opinion which is fated to be ultimately agreed to by all who investigate is what we mean by truth' (Peirce 1931–58 (5): 407). Indeed, in principle, consensus embodies the truth *no matter what method was used to bring about the consensus.* 'If a general belief can in any way be produced, though it be by the faggot and the rack, to talk of error in such belief is utterly absurd' (Peirce 1931–58 (8): 16). Although Peirce thought that in the long run the only method which could produce and sustain a consensus agreement is what he called 'abduction' (what is now called 'inference to the best explanation'), it is important to remember that he did not think propositions which would be universally accepted are true because they were arrived at by abduction; rather, he thought they are true just because they would be universally accepted (see PEIRCE, C.S. §3).

Whence Peirce's confidence that investigators would move towards a common conclusion? Ultimately, our evidence takes the form of perceptions, and these perceptions are controlled by a single fixed reality which is public to all. Since there is just one objective reality and it is driving all of us to beliefs that accurately reflect it, we are driven to agree with one another. So, in the long run, the only propositions with which everyone would agree are those that accurately reflect reality. Hence, 'is true' is equivalent to 'accurately reflects reality'. It might seem odd, then, that Peirce turns his attention away from this equivalence and focuses instead on what would otherwise seem to be an incidental equivalence between 'is true' and 'would eventually be agreed to by everyone with sufficient relevant experiences'. But for Peirce it is the former relation which is the trivial one because reality, he thought, is just a construct of the community of human minds. Specifically, what is real is just whatever we would come to agree is real: 'the real is the idea in which the community ultimately settles down' (Peirce 1931–58 (6): 610) and 'everything, therefore which will be thought to exist in the final opinion is real, and nothing else' (Peirce 1931–58 (8): 12). Peirce called this his 'social theory of reality'.

But notice now how this ontological doctrine undermines Peirce's own explanation for why all who investigate a given question would ultimately come to agreement: on a realist ontology, the notion of reality controlling our perceptions is based on common sense; but on the social theory of reality, it is an idea in the minds of those who have already reached the final opinion which is causing those who have not reached it to have certain perceptions. Indeed, matters are even stranger than this; for the very perceptions that caused those who have reached the final conclusion to reach it were forced on them, *in a reverse-chronological direction*, by the final conclusion which, at the time they had the perceptions, they had not reached. Therefore, some of the perceptions you and I are having right now are forced on us by an idea which, if we have it at all, we will only have at some future time. Peirce himself was aware of this rather fantastic implication of his views and attempted to defend it:

At first sight it seems no doubt a paradoxical statement that, 'The object of final belief which exists only in consequence of the belief, should itself produce the belief'; ... there is:

> nothing extraordinary... in saying that the existence of external realities depends upon the fact, that opinion will finally settle in the belief in them. And yet that these realities existed before the belief took rise, and were even the cause of that belief, just as the force of gravity is the cause of the falling of the inkstand – although the force of gravity consists merely in the fact that the inkstand and other objects will fall.
>
> (Peirce 1931–58 (7): 340–4)

But this will not do. On the analysis of causation which Peirce is assuming, the relation between gravity and the tendency of things to fall is one of identity, not of mutual causation. Moreover, even if we allow that gravity is in some sense a consequence of the fact that things tend to fall, neither gravity nor the tendency are events in time. Hence, to assert that the former is both a cause and a consequence of the latter is not to assert the possibility of reverse-chronological causation. But coming to believe the final conclusion, and the occurrence of the perceptions that bring about that belief, are both events in time, and they come at different times. Hence, to assert that the chronologically earlier of these is caused by the chronologically later is to assert something not at all analogous to any causal relations involving the inkstand.

The problems in Peirce's account go even deeper. Although Peirce sometimes speaks as if the final conclusion is fated or destined, on those occasions on which he self-consciously considers whether this conclusion will ever actually be reached, he is much more cautious: 'We cannot be quite sure the community will ever settle down to an unalterable conclusion upon any given question nor can we rationally presume any overwhelming *consensus* of opinion will be reached upon every question' (Peirce 1931–58 (6): 610).

> I do not say that it is infallibly true that there is any belief to which a person would come if he were to carry his inquiries far enough. I only say that that alone is what I call Truth. I cannot infallibly know that there *is* any truth.
>
> (Peirce 1966: 398)

So the causal action of the final conclusion on our present actual perceptions is not only reverse-chronological, it is also action from within a hypothetical domain to the actual domain.

2 Instrumentalism

William James always claimed to accept the definition of truth embodied in correspondence theories of truth, namely that a true belief or statement is one that 'agrees with reality' (see JAMES, W. §5). But, for James, the reality to which true ideas must agree is mind-dependent: 'By "reality" humanism [one of James's names for his philosophy] means nothing more than the other conceptual or perceptual experiences with which a given present experience may find itself in point of fact mixed up'. And, 'we are not required to seek [truth] in a relation of experience as such to anything beyond itself'. And, 'reality is an accumulation of our own intellectual inventions'. These inventions include 'the notions of one Time and of one Space as single continuous receptacles; the distinction between thoughts and things, matter and mind; between permanent subjects and changing attributes; the conception of classes with sub-classes within them; the separation of fortuitous from regularly caused connexions'. Unlike Kant, however, James does not think that these constructs are built into our minds. Rather, these constructs are inventions of our ancestors. They *made* the world this way, by so conceiving of it. Why did they choose to structure the world with these features and not some other features? James's answer is that they found it more *useful* to organize the world in this manner. The last quotation continues:

> surely all these were once definite conquests made... by our ancestors in their attempts to get the chaos of their crude individual experiences into a more shareable and manageable shape. They proved of such sovereign use as *denkmittel* [instruments of thought] that they are now a part of the very structure of our mind.
>
> (James 1909: 42)

James also wants to give the word 'agree', in the phrase 'agrees with reality', a different sense from the typical correspondence theorist. Given that reality is just useful mental constructs of the collection of past and present minds, a belief agrees with reality by proving useful to those who believe it. The examples James offers suggest that useful beliefs are those which: (1) enable us to manipulate the objects of the world; (2) allow us to communicate successfully with our fellows; (3) provide good explanations for other occurrences; and (4) lead to accurate predictions.

It should be kept in mind, if for no other reason than to forestall overly facile counterexamples, that James identifies truth with beliefs that are useful over the long run and all things considered: "*"The true"*, *to put it very briefly, is only the expedient in the way of our thinking, just as "the right" is only the expedient in the way of our behaving.* Expedient in almost any fashion; and expedient in the long run and on the whole of course; for what meets expediently all the experience in sight will not necessarily meet all farther experiences equally satisfactorily' (James 1907: 106). Still, opponents of instrumentalism would insist, it might be useful throughout a person's life for them to believe that they are better at their job than anyone else (because, for example, the increased confidence it gives them pays huge dividends.) And this can be the case even if they are not in fact better at their job than anyone else. James, however, denied that there can be any cases in which the truth and the facts are disjoint, and the reason for his denial lies in his ontology: if the facts are themselves just mental constructs which have proved useful, then there cannot be a case of a useful belief that does not agree with the facts.

So, both Peirce and James can happily accept what have been called 'T-sentences' – sentences of the form '"p is true" if and only if p'. But for both of them, this coordination of truth and reality is itself an incidental side effect which distracts from, rather than reveals, the essential nature of truth.

See also: MEANING AND TRUTH; PRAGMATISM; REALISM AND ANTIREALISM; SCHILLER, F.C.S.; TRUTH, COHERENCE THEORY OF; TRUTH, CORRESPONDENCE THEORY OF; TRUTH, DEFLATIONARY THEORIES OF

References and further reading

* James, W. (1907) *Pragmatism*, Cambridge, MA: Harvard University Press, 1975. (A superbly produced critical edition of the author's most famous work, in which he attempts to provide a survey of his philosophical views.)
* —— (1909) *The Meaning of Truth*, Cambridge, MA: Harvard University Press, 1975. (A collection of essays on truth, mainly written in the last few years before the author's death, in an excellent critical edition.)
Kirkham, R.L. (1992) *Theories of Truth: A Critical Introduction*, Cambridge, MA: MIT Press. (An introduction to theories of truth. Sects 3.2–3.4 expand on the issues in this entry.)
* Peirce, C.S. (1931–58) *Collected Papers of Charles Sanders Peirce*, Cambridge, MA: Harvard University Press, 8 vols, C. Hartshorne and P. Weiss (eds) vols 1–6, A.W. Burks (ed.) vols 7–8. (The author's views on truth are scattered throughout his works, so the reader will have to look under 'truth' in the index of this collection. References in this entry to this work have been by volume and section.)
* —— (1966) 'Letters to Lady Welby', in P.P. Wiener (ed.) *Charles S. Peirce: Selected Writings*, New York: Dover. (An interesting selection of Peirce's writings.)

RICHARD L. KIRKHAM

TRUTH, TARSKI'S DEFINITION OF *see* TARSKI'S DEFINITION OF TRUTH

TRUTH-BEARERS *see* PROPOSITIONS, SENTENCES AND STATEMENTS

TRUTH-CONDITIONAL SEMANTICS *see* MEANING AND TRUTH

TRUTHFULNESS

Humans are the only species capable of speech and thus of lies. Choices regarding truthfulness and deceit are woven into all that they say and do. From childhood on, everyone knows the experience of being deceived and of deceiving others, of doubting someone's word and of being thought a liar. Throughout life, no moral choice is more common than that of whether to speak truthfully, equivocate, or lie – whether to flatter, get out of trouble, retaliate, or gain some advantage.

All societies, as well as all major moral, religious and legal traditions have condemned forms of deceit such as bearing false witness; but many have also held that deceit can be excusable or even mandated under certain circumstances, as, for instance, to deflect enemies in war or criminals bent on doing violence to innocent victims. Opinions diverge about such cases, however, as well as about many common choices about truthfulness and deceit. How open should spouses be to one another about adultery, for example, or physicians to dying patients? These are quandaries familiar since antiquity. Others, such as those involving the backdating of computerized documents, false claims on résumés in applying for work, or misrepresenting one's HIV-positive status to sexual partners, present themselves in new garb.

Hard choices involving truthfulness and lying inevitably raise certain underlying questions. How should truthfulness be defined? Is lying ever morally justified, and if so under what conditions? How should one deal with borderline cases between truthfulness and clear-cut falsehood, and between more and less egregious forms of deceit? And how do attitudes towards truthfulness relate to personal integrity and character? The rich philosophical debate of these issues has focused on issues of definition, justification, and line-drawing, and on their relevance to practical moral choice.

1 **Truth, truthfulness, falsity and deceit**
2 **Justification**
3 **Line-drawing**

1 Truth, truthfulness, falsity and deceit

By what criteria can we distinguish between truthfulness and deceit? Should all deceptive messages, whether intended to deceive or not, whether verbal or nonverbal, count as lies so long as they end up misleading recipients? Such an all-encompassing view is unpersuasive: it is hard to claim that erroneous weather forecasts, for example, or promises people make in good faith but are later unable to honour, constitute lies.

If one limits the category of lies to intentionally false speech, however, problems arise about how to characterize the use of metaphor and other figurative speech, rhetorical flourishes, and works of fiction (see METAPHOR; FICTIONAL ENTITIES; ART AND TRUTH §2). Some thinkers have been known to hold that the very purpose of all art, including fiction, is to deceive: they may defend the practice, as Oscar Wilde does in 'The Decay of Lying' (1892), suggesting that, 'the final revelation is that Lying, the telling of beautiful untrue things, is the proper aim of Art'; or deplore it, as does Socrates in Plato's *Republic*, when he argues that poets

mislead their audiences in speaking, for instance, of the gods as undignified or immoral. Many people, rejecting the view that fiction must involve lying, prefer to limit the category of lies to spoken communication intended to mislead. They take what Samuel Coleridge called 'the willing suspension of disbelief' (1817: 6) to operate in such a way that fiction does not count as deceitful, and may regard persons who cannot distinguish between lies and fiction as obtuse. Thus John Stuart Mill pointed to Jeremy Bentham's aphorism 'All poetry is misrepresentation' as revealing his literalness and his impoverished understanding of human nature (1838: 50–1).

The failure to sort out such disagreements about the scope of definitions generates needless confusion in debates about truthfulness and deceit. In turn, this failure risks perpetuating a conceptual muddle with regard to the crucial differences between the *moral* domain of intended truthfulness and deception and the *epistemological* domain of truth and falsity. The moral question of whether you are lying or not is not *settled* by establishing the truth or falsity of what you say. In order to settle this question, we must know whether you intend your statement to mislead those to whom you address yourself. The two domains often overlap; but truth and truthfulness are not identical, any more than falsehood and falsity (see Aquinas, *Summa theologiae*). Confusing the domains of 'truth' and 'truthfulness' has especially problematic consequences for persons whose scepticism about all epistemological claims concerning truth bleeds into their attitudes with respect to the moral questions about deceit and truthfulness. They may leap from doubting that we can ever know the full truth about anything to doubting that there are differences between aiming to lie or to speak truthfully, and in turn to regarding all communication as equally unreliable. Iris Murdoch, in *Metaphysics as a Guide to Morals* (1992), discusses how structuralists make this leap with regard to history, thus blotting out 'the conception of seeking carefully for some truthful conception of the past' (198). 'Fabulation' means providing accounts in the form of fables, as did Ovid, or, more generally, to concoct and fabricate. 'Confabulation' has come into common parlance as a psychiatric term so recently that it has yet to be recorded in a major dictionary. The term, which used to carry the meaning of persons simply coming together to talk or chat, is now used to refer to the stories told by brain-damaged persons suffering from Alzheimer's disease and a variety of other psychiatric and neurological conditions. They may spin false tales about their lives with great aplomb and in utter confidence that they are correct. They cannot, therefore, be thought of as engaging in lying or any form of deceit; at the same time, because their statements depart so clearly from the truth, it is difficult to speak of truthfulness in characterizing their stories.

Such cases show that the moral dimensions of choices concerning truthfulness and deceit are not exhausted by referring to the intentions of those who make statements. There is a large category of statements where deceit is not intended but where truthful communication is far from being achieved. In exploring this category, it is important to take into account all that can help to distort communication quite apart from an intention to deceive. When people convey false information in the belief that it is true, they may be tired, mistaken, uninformed, inarticulate, intoxicated, or duped by others; but so long as they do not intend to mislead anyone, they are not acting in a manner that is in any way deceitful. Their statements may be false, but they have not knowingly uttered falsehoods. If the information is conveyed through intermediaries, as through gossip or via the media, further distortion from such causes is likely to ensue. At the receiving end of such information, likewise, similar factors and others such as deafness may operate so that people end up deceived through no fault of the person who originated the message or those who passed it along.

Allowing for these qualifications, a truthful person is someone who aims consistently to speak so as not to mislead others. A scrupulously truthful person is one who takes special care to try to counteract factors known to skew or distort communication. The trait of 'truthfulness', defined as the disposition to tell the truth, is widely regarded as a virtue. Truthfulness can take either the baseline form of avoiding all lies or the wider form of being as forthcoming and sincere as possible at all times. The fourth Buddhist Precept of Right Action spans this spectrum, in enjoining followers of Buddha 'not to lie but to practice sincerity and honesty'. And Michel de Montaigne, who took a firm stance against lying and all forms of deceit, put the difference as follows: 'We must not always say everything, for that would be folly; but what we say must be what we think; otherwise it is wickedness' (1533–92: 401).

The disposition to be truthful is generally held to be both admirable in its own right and central to the larger cluster of traits called honesty. 'Honesty' characterizes a person of integrity and trustworthiness who avoids not only lies and intentional deception, but also theft, cheating, plagiarism and other forms of duplicity and betrayal. Conversely, 'dishonesty' refers to the disposition to lie, deceive, steal, cheat and defraud more generally. 'Veracity' is often used synonymously with 'truthfulness', in the

above sense, but carries an additional stress on the accuracy of what is stated.

Just as false statements need not be deceitful, moreover, so true statements can sometimes be meant to deceive. An isolated true statement told by someone known to be a habitual liar can be intended to mislead listeners, and succeed in doing so, as much as lies by persons thought honest. Persons adept at producing 'information overload', moreover, as in lengthy, confusing sales agreements or insurance documents, can aim to deceive others without actual lies.

Withholding part of the information needed by interlocutors, finally, can be as deceptive as any lie. Sellers of medications, toys or automobiles who purposely omit information regarding dangerous defects or other risks attendant on using their products, engage in such deceit. So do investigators who enrol patients in studies of experimental drugs without asking for their fully informed consent. Persons wishing to engage in such communications while at the same time maintaining that they adhere strictly to the truth have often had recourse to the concept of a 'mental reservation'. It involves speaking only a partial but highly misleading truth with the intent to deceive, while adding in one's mind the missing words that would render the statement non-deceptive: as, for instance, when a thief responds to an inquiry about a theft the previous week by claiming that he had not stolen anything, adding silently 'today'.

2 Justification

From the Bible's Ten Commandments to the Buddhist Five Precepts for Right Action, from the Five Jaina Great Vows to the Hindu prescriptions in the *Bhagavadgītā* (see Bok 1996), from the maxims of Confucius to the dictates of the Roman Stoics, false speech, along with the resort to violence, has been rejected consistently. However much these traditions differ over questions of religious belief, asceticism or sexual conduct, they speak in unison in condemning violence and lies, the two ways by which human beings deliberately bring about injury to one another. Because no society or human relationship could survive without at least a degree of truthfulness in communication, all communities have stressed truthfulness as a trait to be fostered, at least with respect to intimates, friends and colleagues. Even the devils themselves, as Samuel Johnson said, quoting Sir Thomas Brown, do not lie to one another: truth is as necessary to their society as to all others (see HINDU PHILOSOPHY; JAINA PHILOSOPHY; CONFUCIAN PHILOSOPHY, CHINESE; STOICISM).

Even so, the world's traditions rest their preference

for truthfulness and their condemnations of deceit on widely differing forms of justification. They may claim a variety of religious reasons for condemning lying, argue that it goes against the natural order, hold that it jars with our 'moral sense', or invoke other reasons. Further differences arise within each tradition with respect to whether or not exceptions are permitted under certain circumstances, and, if so, which ones and on what grounds. Is it excusable to lie, for example, where truthfulness might endanger innocent persons, precipitate violence, or cause despair? Or possibly even justifiable?

While a degree of truthfulness has been recognized as necessary everywhere, the pull of lying has been ever-present. It offers the simplest and most tempting way of trying to generate false beliefs among listeners and thus of achieving power over them or eluding their power over oneself. But because truthfulness is uniformly seen as the norm and lies as morally problematic, the burden of proof falls on those who would defend particular categories of departures from truthfulness.

Two positions have been taken within most traditions on this score. The first, absolutist, position was held by, among others, Augustine and Immanuel Kant, who took there to be no sufficient justification for lying. According to Augustine, lies can be ranked according to their severity, with lies about God the most severe and lies by a virgin to guard against violation the most excusable. Such excusable lies, while not mortal sins unlike the former, are nevertheless forbidden by God and should be avoided. Kant (1788) also rejected all lies as unjustifiable and recognized, under the heading of 'casuistical questions', cases of seemingly more excusable lies; but he refused to rank them as Augustine had done. He insisted, instead, that truthfulness is an unconditional duty which holds in all circumstances. All persons who lie, he claimed, thereby repudiate their own human dignity and contribute to undermining the precarious trust on which human society is based.

The second position is shared by many thinkers who set forth certain types of lies as excusable or even justifiable. Some of them argue that lies to certain kinds of people – children, the dying, the mentally ill, or enemies in war – should not count as lies properly speaking, and are justifiable whenever told to deceive these persons for their own good or in self-defence. There is no need for complex moral reasoning in such cases, these writers claim. Thus Hugo Grotius (1625) held that falsehoods told to children or to the insane show no disrespect for their liberty of judgment, since they have no such liberty in the first place. Others argue that lies *by* certain persons are justified in the exercise of their professions, as in the law or policing

or medicine or, as urged by Machiavelli in *Il principe (The Prince)* (1532), governing (see MACHIAVELLI, N. §2). While they agree that high standards of honesty should be encouraged in most walks of life, these advocates maintain that there are special circumstances and pressures within their own profession that necessitate forgoing candour at times. Important goals such as the interests of one's nation or one's clients, the public welfare, the advancement of knowledge, or the uncovering of corruption, may be at stake, and may outweigh a strict commitment to veracity.

John Stuart Mill argued, on utilitarian grounds, that it is possible so to estimate the consequences of particular lies as to sort out those few lies that would be justifiable (see UTILITARIANISM; CONSEQUENTIALISM). Henry Sidgwick (1874) likewise concluded on such grounds that certain lies are justifiable – among them those told to invalids where the truth might prove too great a shock to them. W.D. Ross (1930) held that, while there is a *prima facie* duty of fidelity, which includes that of veracity, it can conflict with other *prima facie* duties such as that of 'not injuring others'. It is worth noting, however, that Mill and Sidgwick both took seriously what Kant also emphasized but Machiavelli did not: the central importance of the virtue of veracity for purposes of societal trust.

3 Line-drawing

Problems of line-drawing will always arise with respect to the interlocking distinctions having to do with truth, truthfulness, falsity, and deceit, both when it comes to definitions and forms of justification or excuse. In considering definitions, first of all, just where should the boundaries be between intentional and unintentional deception? Or between jokes understood as such by all listeners and tricks meant to mislead them? Or between mild exaggeration and outright lies? Are so-called white lies even lies in the first place? When do errors due to poor memory shade into confabulation? When does the transmission of false information – say by reporters covering public officials – shade into complicity in deceit? How easy is it even for historians to tell when they are engaged in conscious rewriting of history, let alone their readers? And in evaluating possible justifications for accepting or ruling out lying, by what means might a Kantian best distinguish intentionally and unintentionally deceptive statements? How might Grotius compare what degree of truth is owed to preadolescents? How do Ross and others weigh conflicting *prima facie* duties in marginal cases? And how should utilitarians weigh the gains or losses that will flow from comparatively similar forms of deceit?

From the earliest texts onward, the moral perplexities in trying to sort out and compare forms of deceit have been set forth: as in the account of Adam and Eve and the serpent in Genesis, the kiss of Judas in the New Testament, the false protestations of lifelong truthfulness in the Egyptian *Book of the Dead*, or the trickery of Ulysses in Homer's *Odyssey* and *Iliad*. And thinkers in the great traditions of casuistry and practical moral inquiry – among them Confucians, Stoics and commentators on Christian, Jewish, Buddhist, Hindu and Islamic ethics – have worked to weigh the difficult 'cases of conscience' in which the duty not to lie appears to conflict with such duties as that of keeping promises of secrecy or saving intended victims from murderers.

Drawing lines with respect to truthfulness and deceit often turns out differently, however, depending on whose choices are being considered. Truthfulness is a trait that people tend to prize more in others than regard as fully called for when it comes to their own choices. When they consider themselves as being on the receiving end of other people's lies, they are more suspicious of the underlying motives than when they weigh possible lies of their own. Each of these perspectives on truthfulness and deceit – that of the deceived and that of those considering engaging in deception – is incomplete, biased, and undiscriminating by itself. The perspective of those who see themselves as at the receiving end of lies is, understandably, suspicious in the extreme. As a result, they are more likely to blur the distinction between errors and lies, between the honest and the dishonest, between intended and unintended injuries. By contrast, the perspective of those who wonder whether or not to lie blurs and confuses the harm that lying does not only to those lied to but also to those who do the lying, and, most insidiously and indelibly, to trust. To persons adopting this latter perspective, lies may seem far more excusable or innocuous and the risks of discovery or of slipping into broader practices of deceit less worrisome.

It is only by examining one's choices not only as subject and agent but as recipient, sometimes victim, that a fuller perception of truthfulness and lying becomes possible, and of ways to counteract the biases present in each of the perspectives. These biases operate not only to skew line-drawing when it comes to defining truthfulness and lying, but also with respect to justifying or excusing particular choices. In this way, those considering lies of their own may give themselves far more latitude than they grant to others in declaring certain forms of duplicity such as white lies nondeceptive; and greater latitude, too, when it comes to excusing or justifying what they acknowledge as lies.

Both Kant, who characterized lying as a repudiation of one's own human dignity, and Mill, who wrote in *Utilitarianism* (1861) of the need to cultivate in oneself a 'sensitive feeling on the subject of veracity', addressed, albeit from different points of view, the importance of taking truthfulness seriously in one's own life. The role that one assigns to truthfulness, they both thought, should be central in considering what kind of person one wants to be – how one wishes to treat not only other people, but oneself. Everyone can make mistakes when it comes to truthfulness and deception and be swayed by poorly understood forces and temptations; it is another matter altogether to choose to be someone who deals with others through deceit. Such a choice is made easier by neglecting to take these forces and temptations into adequate account. Though Mill would have insisted on certain rare exceptions to what he characterized as the 'sacred rule' of veracity, he might otherwise have concurred in Kant's linking internal and external truthfulness, in the last of his books published in his lifetime, *Anthropology from a Pragmatic Point of View* (1798: 207): 'Briefly, as the highest maxim, uninhibited internal truthfulness toward oneself, as well as in the behavior toward everyone else, is the only proof of a person's having character.'

See also: SELF-DECEPTION; SELF-DECEPTION, ETHICS OF; TRUST; VIRTUES AND VICES

References and further reading

* Aquinas, T. (1266–73) *Summa theologiae* (Synopsis of Theology), trans. Fathers of the English Dominican Province, Westminster, MD: Christian Classics, 1948, IIaIIae.109–113. (Authoritative statement of the Roman Catholic Natural Law position, building on Augustine.)

Arendt, H. (1970) 'Truth and Politics', in P. Laslett, and W.G. Runciman (eds) *Philosophy, Politics, and Society*, New York: Barnes and Noble, 1967. (An analysis of the politics of lying and truthfulness in the context of the Vietnam War.)

Augustine (395) *De mendacio* (Of Lying), ed. R.J. Deferrari, in *Fathers of the Church: A New Translation*, vol. 16, New York: Catholic University of America Press, 1952, 45–110. (A subtle analysis of issues related to truthfulness and the sin of lying.)

—— (420) *Contra mendacium* (Against Lying), ed. R.J. Deferrari, in *Fathers of the Church: A New Translation*, vol. 16, New York: Catholic University of America Press, 1952, 111–79. (The second of Augustine's treatises on lying and truthfulness.)

Bok, S. (1978) *Lying: Moral Choices in Public and Private Life*, New York: Pantheon. (A contemporary treatment of the ethics of lying and truthfulness and of the traditions of debate on these subjects. Appendix has selections from Augustine, Thomas Aquinas, Grotius, Kant, Sidgwick, Ross and others.)

* —— (1996) *Common Values*, Columbia, MO: University of Missouri Press. (Includes discussion of the Buddhist Five Precepts for Right Action, the Five Jaina Great Vows, and the Hindu prescriptions in the Bhagavadgītā.)

* Coleridge, S.T. (1817) *Biographia Literaria*, in J. Engels and W. Jackson Bate (eds) *Biographia Literaria*, vol. 2, Princeton, NJ: Princeton University Press, 1984. (The finest text of philosophical and literary criticism of the romantic period.)

* Grotius, H. (1625) *De iure belli ac pacis* (On the Law of War and Peace), trans. F. Kelsey, Indianapolis, IN: Bobbs-Merrill, 1925, book III, ch. 1. (Treats of lies in the context of war and peace.)

* Kant, I. (1788) 'On a Supposed Right to Lie from Benevolent Motives', in *The Critique of Pure Practical Writings in Moral Philosophy*, trans. L.W. Beck, Chicago, IL: University of Chicago Press, 1949, 346–50. (Kant's much-discussed statement of an absolutist position on lying.)

* —— (1798) *Anthropology from a Pragmatic Point of View*, trans. V.L. Dowdell, Carbondale, IL: Southern Illinois University Press, 1996, 207. (Kant's last published book, containing the summation of decades of teaching.)

* Machiavelli, N. (1532) *Il principe*, trans. L. Ricci, The Prince, in *The Prince and The Discourses*, New York: Modern Library, 1950. (Machiavelli's advice to princes on politics and morality, with indications regarding when, how, and why to lie most advantageously.)

* Mill, J.S. (1838) *Bentham*, in M. Cohen (ed.) *The Philosophy of J.S. Mill*, New York: Modern Library, 1961, 50–1. (Mill's evaluation of Bentham's contributions.)

* —— (1861) *Utilitarianism*, in M. Cohen (ed.) *The Philosophy of J.S. Mill*, New York: Modern Library, 1961, 348. (Mill's statement of his position on ethics in general, including his views on lying.)

* Montaigne, M. de (1533–92) 'Des Menteurs', trans. D.M. Frame, 'On Liars', in *The Complete Works of Montaigne*, Stanford, CA: Stanford University Press, 1957, book I, ch. 9. (One of the most profound meditations on lying in the literature.)

* Murdoch, I. (1992) *Metaphysics as a Guide to Morals*, London: Chatto & Windus. (Includes discussion of

how structuralists, with regard to history, make the leap from doubting that we can ever know the full truth about anything to doubting that there are differences between aiming to lie or to speak truthfully, and in turn to regarding all communication as equally unreliable.)

* Plato (*c.*380–367 BC) *Republic*, trans. A. Bloom, New York: Basic Books, 1968, book III. (Plato's rejection of theatre and poetry that corrupt and mislead.)

Radhakrishnan, S. and Moore, C.A. (eds) (1957) *A Sourcebook in Indian Philosophy*, Princeton, NJ: Princeton University Press, 1957. (Index listings refer to Buddhist, Hindu, and Jain texts and to explorations of truthfulness and deceit.)

* Ross, W.D. (1930) *The Right and the Good*, Oxford: Clarendon Press. (Contains Ross' specifications of the duty not to tell lies as a *prima facie* duty of fidelity.)

* Sidgwick, H. (1874) 'Classification of Duties – Veracity', in *The Methods of Ethics*, London: Macmillan; 7th edn, 1907. (Sidgwick's uncharacteristically casual discussion of the duty of veracity and of exceptions to this duty.)

* Wilde, O. (1892) 'The Decay of Lying', in V. Holland (ed.) *The Complete Works of Oscar Wilde*, New York: Harper & Row, 1989, 970–92. (A defence of lying on aesthetic grounds.)

SISSELA BOK

TSCHIRNHAUS, EHRENFRIED WALTHER VON (1651–1708)

The natural philosopher E.W. von Tschirnhaus emphasized bodily and mental health, was a friend of Spinoza and correspondent of Leibniz. He perfected the construction of concave mirrors (used to generate extremely high temperatures) and was probably the first European to produce porcelain. Hoping to make scientific progress more predictable, Tschirnhaus devised a method of inquiry orientated to mathematics and experimentation.

Ehrenfried Walther (Walter) von Tschirnhaus was born in Kieslingswalde, east of Dresden, on the family's estate. After studying medicine and science at the University of Leiden, he went on extended educational travels. In 1682, he was elected the first German member of the Académie Royale des Sciences in Paris for his chemical experiments and innovations in making burning mirrors. Upon returning to Kieslingswalde, Tschirnhaus built a laboratory and tried to unlock the secrets of porcelain production. He died shortly after the decisive experimental breakthrough. Ludwig Böttger, his assistant and co-worker, passed himself off successfully as the sole inventor of European porcelain after Tschirnhaus' death.

The general theme of Tschirnhaus' writings is the achievement of bodily and mental health. Mental health consists in a state of wisdom, tranquillity and happiness. This state results from the striving for self-perfection through scholarly study, intellectual creativity and scientific discovery.

The *Medicina Corporis* (Medicine for the body) (1686) was Tschirnhaus' first book, comprising twelve rules for a physically healthy life. His second and main work was the *Medicina Mentis* (Medicine for the mind) (1687). It contains a methodology for a philosophy of nature based on experimentation and deduction. The oblique but nonetheless obvious references to SPINOZA in the *Medicina Mentis* prompted Christian THOMASIUS to charge Tschirnhaus with heresy and Spinozism, to which the accused replied with *Eilfertiges Bedencken* (1688). Tschirnhaus' later treatises are devoted to pedagogy: the *Gründliche Anleitung zu nützlichen Wissenschafften* (The select primer of useful sciences) (1700), on the scientific education of young people, and *Dreissig Hinweise für einen guten Hofmeister* (Thirty suggestions for a good steward) (1704, published posthumously 1727), on the general education of gentlemen and court officials. He also published a variety of mathematical papers in the *Acta Eruditorum*, founded in Leipzig in 1686. However, the errors these contained did more harm than good to Tschirnhaus' reputation.

Since mathematics is the most successful of all sciences, Tschirnhaus argued, like Descartes, that the scientific investigation of nature ought to follow the example of mathematics and adopt its deductive methods. Although mathematics is abstract, dealing solely with notional entities, it can and should be applied to the study of material entities occurring in nature. Physics is most successful when quantitative. The study of nature ought to start with the classification of evident truths about the object under investigation. Empirical features of the object should be identified by experiments that are to be performed systematically, according to rules. Ideally, a complete list of all relevant data will then be generated, containing the basic notions (*primi conceptus* or definitions) of the object under investigation. Individual definitions yield axioms, combined definitions yield theorems, and the statements so deduced constitute the exhaustive knowledge of the object.

Tschirnhaus has often been misunderstood. Christian WOLFF, who claimed to have been influenced by him, took this methodology of natural philosophy as an apology for the so-called geometric method of metaphysics. Wolff held that philosophy can imitate mathematics in style without employing it in content, and aprioristic non-quantitative deductions are permissible without experimental confirmation. Twentieth-century Marxists regarded Tschirnhaus as a spiritual forerunner, whose alleged atheism was illustrated by his Spinozist sympathies and whose putative social awareness was indicated by his interest in practical questions of engineering and manufacturing.

See also: ENLIGHTENMENT, CONTINENTAL

List of works

Tschirnhaus, E.W. von (1686) *Medicina Corporis, seu Cogitationes admodum probabile de conservanda Sanitate* (Medicine for the body, or, quite plausible thoughts on the conservation of health), Amsterdam: Albertus Magnus & Johannes Rieuwerts Jr; 2nd edn, Leipzig: Fritsch, 1695; 3rd edn, Leipzig: A. Martin, 1733; Dutch trans., Amsterdam, 1687; German trans., Frankfurt & Leipzig, 1688. (A physician's text, containing dietary recommendations and advice for a healthy lifestyle.)

—— (1687) *Medicina Mentis, sive Tentamen genuinae Logicae, in qua disseritur de Methodo detegendi incognitas veritates* (Medicine for the mind, or an essay with genuine logic, investigating the method for the discovery of unknown truths), Amsterdam: Albertus Magnus & Johannes Rieuwerts Jr; Dutch trans., Amsterdam, 1687; 2nd revised edn, *Medicina Mentis, sive Artis inveniendi Praecepta generalia* (Medicine for the mind, or, general precepts for the art of invention) Leipzig: Fritsch, 1695; repr. Hildesheim: G. Olms, 1964; German trans. J. Haussleiter, in *Acta Historica Leopoldina 1963/1*, Leipzig: Barth; 3rd edn, Leipzig: A. Martin, 1733. (Tschirnhaus' best-known work; introductory reflections on the relation of knowledge and happiness are followed by a detailed methodology for scientific discovery that involves both rational and empirical principles.)

—— (1688) *Eilfertiges Bedencken wieder die Objectiones, so im Menso Martio Schertz und Ernsthafftiger Gedancken über den Tractat Medicinae Mentis enthalten* (Zealous Misgivings about the Objections to the Tract *Medicinae Mentis* in the March Issue of the Journal *Schertz und Ernsthafftiger Gedancken*),

Halle: Salfelden. (A short pamphlet directed against Christian Thomasius' critique of the *Medicina Mentis*.)

—— (1700) *Gründliche Anleitung zu nützlichen Wissenschafften absonderlich Zu der Mathesi und Physica Wie sie anitzo von den Gelehrtesten abgehandelt werden* (The select primer of useful sciences, in particular of mathematics and physics, as they are treated by truly competent researchers), Halle; 2nd edn, Frankfurt and Leipzig: Ritscheln, 1708; 3rd edn, 1712; 4th edn, 1729; repr. Stuttgart and Bad Cannstatt: Frommann-Holzboog, 1967. (A brief sequel to the *Medicina Mentis* for students, containing methods for the efficient and systematic acquisition of knowledge.)

—— (1704) *Dreissig Hinweise für einen guten Hofmeister* (Thirty suggestions for a good steward), in W.B. von Tschirnhaus (ed.) *Getreuer Hofmeister auf Academien und Reisen* (The Loyal Steward at Academies and on Travels), Hanover: Nicolaus Förster, 1727. (A short pedagogical tract concerning manners and learning.)

References and further reading

Van Peursen, C.A. (1993) 'E.W. von Tschirnhaus and the *Ars Inveniendi*', *Journal of the History of Ideas* 54: 395–410. (A detailed exposition of Tschirnhaus' method for philosophy.)

Winter, E. (1959) 'E.W. v. Tschirnhaus (1651–1708). Ein Leben im Dienste des Akademiegedankens' (E.W. v. Tschirnhaus (1651–1708). A Life Devoted to the Project of an Academy), *Sitzungsberichte der deutschen Akademie der Wissenschaften zu Berlin* 1959/1, Berlin: Akademieverlag. (A concise account of Tschirnhaus' scientific activities.)

—— (ed.) (1960) *E.W. von Tschirnhaus und die Frühaufklärung in Mittel- und Osteuropa* (E.W. von Tschirnhaus and the Early Enlightenment in Central and Eastern Europe), Berlin: Akademieverlag. (A collection of rather ideological papers by East German, Czech, Polish and Soviet authors on the political and economic importance of Tschirnhaus' work.)

—— (1977) 'Der Freund B. Spinozas E.W. v. Tschirnhaus. Die Einheit von Theorie und Praxis' (E.W. v. Tschirnhaus as Friend of B. Spinoza: The Unity of Theory and Practice), *Akademie der Wissenschaften der DDR: Sitzungsbericht G 1977/7*, Berlin: Akademieverlag. (A study of the relation between Tschirnhaus and Spinoza.)

—— (1979) 'Ein Ketzerspiegel: Ehrenfried Walter von Tschirnhaus (1651–1708)' (Example of a Heretic: Ehrenfried Walter von Tschirnhaus (1651–1708)), *Ketzerschicksale. Christliche Denker aus 9 Jahrhun-*

derten, Berlin: Union Verlag, 164–83. (A Marxist characterization of Tschirnhaus as a revolutionary heretic.)

Wollgast, S. (1988) *Ehrenfried Walther von Tschirnhaus und die deutsche Frühaufklärung* (Ehrenfried Walther von Tschirnhaus and the Early German Enlightenment), Berlin: Akademieverlag. (Tschirnhaus' role in the early German Enlightenment, as interpreted through the Marxist categories of historical materialism.)

Wurtz, J.-P. (1988) 'Über einige offene oder strittige, die *Medicina Mentis* von Tschirnhaus betreffene Fragen' (On some Open or Disputed Questions concerning Tschirnhaus' *Medicina Mentis*), *Studia Leibnitiana* 20: 191–211. (A scholarly analysis of Tschirnhaus' response to Thomasius' charge of Spinozism, the role of experimental confirmation in Tschirnhaus' methodology, and other issues.)

Zaunick, R. (1963) 'Einführung: Ehrenfried Walther von Tschirnhaus in seinem Werden und Wirken' (Introduction: The Development and Influence of Ehrenfried Walther von Tschirnhaus), introduction to E.W. von Tschirnhaus, *Medicina mentis sive artis inveniendi praecepta generalia*, ed. and German trans. J. Hausleiter, Leipzig: Barth, 5–28. (Probably the most useful survey of Tschirnhaus' philosophical, scientific and technical work.)

MARTIN SCHÖNFELD

TSONG KHA PA BLO BZANG GRAGS PA (1357–1419)

Tsong kha pa Blo bzang grags pa (Dzongkaba Losang dragba), the founder of the dGa'-ldan-pa (Gandenba) school of Tibetan Buddhism, was born in Tsong-kha, in the extreme northeastern region of Tibet. He is often depicted as a type of reformer, putting great emphasis on moral precepts and interpreting Tantra in a way which would not create any conflict with the traditional Mahāyāna doctrines found in the sūtras and treatises. He was also an eclectic, drawing upon and synthesizing numerous different currents of Indian Buddhism – for example, he put forth a version of *Prāsaṅgika-Mādhyamika which was inextricably bound up with the logical tradition of Dignāga and Dharmakīrti. On the Tibetan side, one of his major philosophical debts was undoubtedly to the gSang-phu (Sangpu) traditions stemming from the highly original thinker Phya pa Chos kyi seng ge (Chaba Chögyi sengge, 1109–69). Finally, his dGa'-ldan-pa school subsequently became the dGe-lugs-pa (Gelukba), a predominantly monastic tradition which in time became the dominant current of

Buddhism in Tibet. Tsong kha pa thus had, in addition to his philosophical influence, a long-term impact on the Tibetan political situation, contributing to the transfer of power from the southern provinces to the Lhasa region and laying the groundwork for the peculiarly Tibetan synthesis of religion and political power which was to be embodied in the institution of the Dalai Lamas.

1 **Life and works**
2 **Elements of Tsong kha pa's Mādhyamika**
3 **Tsong kha pa on Tantra**

1 Life and works

The education of Tsong kha pa Blo bzang grags pa (Dzongkaba Losang dragba) was characterized by a series of stays at various monasteries, where he studied the principal philosophical treatises of Indian Buddhism as well as the root texts and commentaries of Tantra. His scholastic knowledge was regularly tested and refined through debate, but equally he engaged in long periods of analytic meditation and in meditative retreats devoted essentially to Tantric practices and rituals. Among the figures who played a role in Tsong kha pa's intellectual development, two are particularly prominent: Red mda' ba gZhon nu blo gros (Rendawa Shönnu lodrö, 1349–1412), who taught him, *inter alia*, Prajñāpāramitā philosophy, Abhidharma and Mādhyamika; and a certain dBu ma pa (Umaba), who seems to have been, for some time at least, the intermediary for Tsong kha pa to question the bodhisattva Mañjuśrī and thus to come to definite convictions on various matters, including the superiority of *Prāsaṅgika-Mādhyamika to all other views. While Red mda' ba is relatively well known to us, and some of his works are still extant, Lama dBu ma pa remains an obscure figure.

Tsong kha pa's *Collected Works* span eighteen Tibetan volumes (from volume *ka* to *tsha*), with about nine volumes (*ga* to *na*) devoted to Tantra, and the other volumes devoted to Mādhyamika, monastic discipline, Prajñāpāramitā topics, rituals, and miscellaneous works and letters. His most famous work is probably the voluminous *Lam rim chen mo* (The Great Work on the Stages of the Path, volume *pa*), a summa of Buddhist thought which was written as an elaborate and loose commentary on Atīsa's *Bodhipathapradīpa* (The Lamp for the Path to Enlightenment). Equally extremely important is *Drang nges legs bshad snying po* (The Essential Correct Explanation of Intentional and Definitive Meaning, volume *pha*), a later work where we find Tsong kha pa's position on the classification of scriptures as being of definitive (*nītārtha*) or inten-

tional (*neyārtha*) meaning; the work gives his stance on his use of Indian sources and was written largely as a response to Jo-nang-pa (Jonangba) hermeneutics. His major Mādhyamika works are his commentaries on Candrakīrti's *Madhyamakāvatāra* (Introduction to the Middle Way, volume *ma*) and on Nāgārjuna's *Mūlamadhyamakakārikā* (The Fundamental Treatise on the Middle Way, volume *ba*). In Tantric exegesis, besides several commentaries on the *Guhyasamājatantra*, *Cakrasaṃvara*, *Pañcakrama* (The Five Steps), and so forth, he is well known for his great compendium, the *sNgags rim chen mo* (The Great Work on the Stages of Tantra, volume *ga*). Although Tsong kha pa lectured on logic and epistemology (*tshad ma*), curiously enough he did not write any major works on these subjects; the few texts in his *Collected Works* concerning *tshad ma* are (with perhaps one exception) notes of his teachings taken down by his two closest disciples, rGYAL TSHAB DAR MA RIN CHEN (Gyeltsap Darma rinchen, 1364–1432) and mKHAS GRUB dGE LEGS DPAL BZANG PO (Kaydrup Gelek belsangbo, 1385–1438). It is, none the less, abundantly clear that his positions on the soteriological import of Dharmakīrti's *Pramāṇavārttika* (Commentary on Valid Cognition), on the nominalist theory of language and on the importance of Dharmakīrtian logic generally (even for a Mādhyamika), constitute some of the most fundamental elements of his thought (see DHARMA-KĪRTI).

2 Elements of Tsong kha pa's Mādhyamika

Tsong kha pa advocated what might be called a 'minimalist' Mādhyamika, with no place for the type of Absolute that one finds in the synthesis of Mādhyamika and Buddha-nature doctrines developed by rival Tibetan Mādhyamika schools, notably those of a gZhan-stong-pa (Shendongba) orientation. For him, contrary to gZhan-stong schools, Mādhyamika's analysis of the inconsistency of phenomena was not designed to prove the existence of an Absolute free of phenomenal qualities, but rather to lead to an understanding of the principle of dependent origination (*pratītyasamutpāda*), the thoroughly relative nature of the phenomena themselves. His *brTen 'grel bstod pa* (Praise of Dependent Origination, volume *kha*), a short text in verse, is often cited as an eloquent statement of this theme.

Undoubtedly, one of the major issues of Mādhyamika philosophy for Tsong kha pa is the question of precisely what and how much Mādhyamikas should deny if they are to avoid reification of entities, yet preserve conventional truth. How one stands on this matter – in particular, how one 'recognizes the object to be negated' (*dgag bya ngos 'dzin*) – is argued to have very wide-ranging consequences: it will, *inter alia*, significantly affect the exact formulations of the logical arguments which the Mādhyamika uses, and will even determine the importance that one attaches to analysis and conceptual thought in the quest for spiritual realization. Other important aspects of Tsong kha pa's Mādhyamika philosophy can be summarized in a series of recurring concepts known as the 'eight difficult points'. These form the subject matter of a short work, the *dKa' gnad brgyad kyi zin bris* (The Résumé of [Tsong kha pa's teaching on] the Eight Difficult Points). In the opening section he says:

> Concerning the [ontological] bases, there are the following [three points]: (1) the conventional nonacceptance of particulars and of (2) the storehouse consciousness, and (3) the acceptance of external objects. Concerning the path, there are the following [four points]: (4) the nonacceptance of autonomous reasonings as being means for understanding reality and (5) the nonacceptance of self-awareness; (6) the way in which the two obscurations exist; (7) how it is accepted that the Buddha's disciples and those who become awakened without a Buddha's help realize that things are without any own-nature. Concerning the result, there is: (8) the way in which the *buddhas* know [conventional] things in their full extent. Thus, there are four accepted theses and four unaccepted theses.
>
> (Volume *ba*–, 1b–2a; translation by
> T.J.F. Tillemans)

Some of these points are arguably quite faithful to the Indian positions, but others – such as (2), the rejection of the usual Buddhist ideas about latent karmic tendencies being transmitted from life to life via some type of medium like the 'storehouse consciousness' in favour of a mere continuum of causally efficient cessations with no medium of transmission whatsoever – are extraordinarily creative developments with fairly little or no grounding in Indian sources (see BUDDHISM, YOGĀCĀRA SCHOOL OF §§5–8). Almost needless to add, they were also very controversial in Tibet. Indeed, Tsong kha pa was savagely mocked by one of his opponents, Go ram pa bSod nams seng ge (Goramba Sönam Sennge, 1429–89), for formulating his Mādhyamika with reliance upon deceptive 'visions' of Mañjuśrī, coming to him second-hand via dBu ma pa, rather than upon actual Indian texts.

Although he was a staunch follower of NĀGĀR-JUNA and Candrakīrti, Tsong kha pa remained uncompromisingly committed to having philosophical theses and doctrinal positions, and in this respect too he was significantly different from most other Tibetan Mādhyamika philosophers. A singular feature of his approach was that while *Prāsaṅgika was the school that he professed, he remained uncomfortable with the usual Indo-Tibetan version of *prasaṅga*-method, namely a systematic *reductio ad absurdum* which was required only to refute adversaries by pointing out internal inconsistencies in their views, and did not have to establish true propositions. Repeatedly, Tsong kha pa argued that it was not possible to lead an adversary to a correct view on the basis of arguments which were not supported by some means of valid cognition (*pramāṇa*): as a result, the 'adversary-established reason' (*gzhan grags kyi gtan tshig*) could not be established *only* for the adversary; it also had to be, in some way, actually valid and established for the Mādhyamika proponent. Not surprisingly, he was also attacked by critics on this. Go ram pa, in his *lTa ba'i shan 'byed* (Differentiation of the Views, 31b–32a), accused Tsong kha pa of transforming *Prāsaṅgika methods into a logic like that of the *Svātantrikas, who maintained that reasoning had to follow the strictures of DIGNĀGA and Dharmakīrti, that is, that the terms had to be established for both parties in the debate.

3 Tsong kha pa on Tantra

Tsong kha pa's Tantric system was mainly based on the textual cycles of the divinities Guhyasamāja, Saṃvara and Vajrabhairava. Though the majority of his writings were devoted to Guhyasamāja and Saṃvara, Vajrabhairava did have a marked importance for him. Vajrabhairava was Tsong kha pa's tutelary deity (*yi dam*) from the time of his ordination as a novice monk and represented the fierce aspect of Mañjuśri, who, as we have seen, played such a recurring role in Tsong kha pa's choices of philosophical orientation. As for the Guhyasamāja cycle, which was without a doubt the main Tantric cycle to which he devoted his attention, Tsong kha pa relied here upon the Indian exegetical system known as the 'Ārya tradition', believing (as did most other Tibetan scholars) that the authors of the fundamental treatises of this tradition, namely Nāgārjuna, Āryadeva and Candrakīrti, were identical with the famous Mādhyamika philosophers of the same name. In choosing the Ārya tradition, then, Tsong kha pa seems to have sought to reinforce his basic methodological standpoint that both Tantric and non-Tantric Buddhism had to be understood according to the *Prāsaṅgika philosophy of Candrakīrti.

In many respects, however, Tsong kha pa's Tantric system owes much to syntheses with cycles other than Guhyasamāja. The instructions on the 'veins' (*nāḍī*), 'energy centres' (*cakra*) and 'inner heat' (*caṇḍālī*), all of which play an important role in Tsong kha pa's views on Tantra, are, notably, virtually absent in the fundamental Indian texts of the Ārya tradition on Guhyasamāja. Rather, we must look to the *Nāro chos drug* (Six Teachings of Nāropa), a later Indian synthesis of diverse Tantric practices, as having influenced Tsong kha pa in this regard. Indeed, it was the *Pañcakramasaṃgrahaprakāśa* (Illumination of the Summary of the Five Steps), a short treatise attributed to Nāropa (956–1040) combining the Six Teachings with the 'Five Steps' (*pañcakrama*) of the Ārya tradition, which provided Tsong kha pa with the basic ideas of his Tantric system.

See also: BUDDHISM, MĀDHYAMIKA: INDIA AND TIBET; MI BSKYOD RDO RJE; SA SKYA PAṆḌITA; TIBETAN PHILOSOPHY; WŎNCH'ŬK

List of works

Tsong kha pa (1357–1419) *Collected Works*, Gedan sungrab mi nyam gyunphel Series 79–105, Delhi: Ngawang Gelek Demo, 1975–9, 27 vols. (The volumes are ordered following the letters of the Tibetan alphabet. For an enumeration and brief description of the individual works in this edition, see the section on Tsong kha pa in Yoshimizu 1989.)

—— (1357–1419) *Drang nges legs bshad snying po*, trans. R. Thurman, *Tsong kha pa's Speech of Gold in the Essence of True Eloquence*, Princeton, NJ: Princeton University Press, 1984. (A translation usable with considerable reservations.)

—— (1357–1419) *Yid dang kun gzhi dka' ba'i gnas*, trans. G. Sparham, *Ocean of Eloquence: Tsong kha pa's Commentary on the Yogācāra Doctrine of Mind*, Albany, NY: State University of New York Press, 1993. (An excellent translation of Tsong kha pa's text on the mental faculty and the storehouse consciousness.)

References and further reading

* Go ram pa bSod nams seng ge (1429–89) *lTa ba'i shan 'byed* (Differentiation of the Views), in *Sa skya pa'i bKa' 'bum, The Complete Works of the Great Masters of the Sa skya Sect of Tibetan Buddhism*, compiled by bSod nams rgya mtsho, vol. 13, Tokyo: The Toyo Bunko, 1969. (The full title of this work is *lTa ba'i shan 'byed theg mchog gnad kyi zla zer*.)

Kaschewsky, R. (1971) *Das Leben des Lamaistischen Heiligen Tsongkhapa Blo bzang grags pa (1357–1419)* (The Life of the Lamaist Holy Man Tsong kha pa Blo bzang grags pa (1357–1419)), Wiesbaden: Harrasowitz. (An account of Tsong kha pa's life based on an eighteenth-century Tibetan biography.)

Napper, E. (1989) *Dependent-Arising and Emptiness*, London: Wisdom Publications, 1989. (An introduction to Tsong kha pa's Mādhyamika with a translation of parts of the *Lam rim chen mo*.)

Tauscher, H. (1995) *Die Lehre von den zwei Wirklichkeiten in Tsoṅ kha pas Madhyamaka-Werken* (The Two-Truth Theory in Tsong kha pa's Madhyamaka Works), Vienna: Arbeitskreis für Tibetische und Buddhistische Studien. (A thorough study of an important theme in Tsong kha pa's philosophy.)

Tillemans, T. (1992) 'Tsong kha pa *et al.* on the Bhāvaviveka–Candrakīrti Debate', in Shōren Ihara and Zuihō Yamaguchi (eds) *Tibetan Studies*, Narita: Naritasan Shinshoji, vol. 1, 316–26. (Tsong kha pa and other dGe-lugs-pas on the debate in the first chapter of Candrakīrti's *Prasannapadā*.)

Tomabechi, T. (1992). 'Nāropa no Pañcakrama chū to sono Tibetto Bukkyō ni okeru Ichi – Tsoṅ kha pa no Tachiba o Chūshin ni' (Nāropa's Commentary on the Pañcakrama, and its Place in Tibetan Buddhism – On Tsong kha pa's Standpoint), *Report of the Japanese Association for Tibetan Studies* 38: 1–9. (An investigation of Tsong kha pa's synthesis of the *Pañcakrama* of Tantric Nāgārjuna and the Six Teachings of Nāropa. We gratefully acknowledge Tomabechi's assistance in the preparation of section §3 of the present entry.)

Yoshimizu, C. (1989) *Descriptive Catalogue of the Naritasan Institute Collection of Tibetan Works*, vol. 1, Narita: Naritasan shinshoji. (Includes a list, with brief descriptions, of the works in Tsong kha pa's *Collected Works*.)

TOM J.F. TILLEMANS

TSUNG-MI *see* ZONGMI

TUCKER, ABRAHAM (1705–74)

Like many of his eighteenth-century British contemporaries, Abraham Tucker was an empiricist follower of John Locke. Tucker held that the mind begins as a blank slate and remains nothing more than a passive receptacle for 'trains' of ideas with 'a motion of their own'. In his moral philosophy Tucker proposed that the motive of all our actions is the prospect of our own satisfaction, and that the maximization of everyone's satisfaction is the ultimate moral good. (The latter view became a central tenet of the utilitarians who followed him.) According to Tucker, God ensures that our self-interested motivation will be congruent with morality, for God has arranged that we will be rewarded for good and punished for evil – either in this world or in the next. Among those most influenced by his work was the utilitarian and philosophical theologian William Paley.

1 **Life**
2 **Associationist psychology**
3 **Moral and religious philosophy**
4 **Influences**

1 Life

Abraham Tucker was born in London to wealthy parents in 1705. His father died during Abraham's infancy, and an uncle, Isaac Tillard, became his guardian. Tucker studied law at Oxford, but never practised. At 22, he purchased Betchworth Castle; at 31, he married Dorothy Barker, with whom he had two daughters.

Tucker's most significant philosophical work is *The Light of Nature Pursued*, published under the pseudonym Edward Search. A preliminary version of this work appeared in 1763 under the title *Freewill, Foreknowledge, and Fate*, but the full seven volumes of *The Light of Nature Pursued* were not published until 1777, three years after Tucker's death.

2 Associationist psychology

Like several other philosophers in the British empiricist tradition (notably David Hume), Tucker sought to explain the workings of the mind in terms of the principles of association that cause one idea to follow upon another. Among the associationists, Tucker makes explicit what some others seem to take as an unstated assumption: that if the flow of our ideas is entirely determined by certain principles of association, then the understanding has no role to play save that of a passive receptacle for ideas that flow through it according to laws of their own.

Our ideas combine with one another in either of two ways – by composition, in which several ideas 'melt together' to form a complex idea, and by association proper, in which ideas 'appear in couples strongly adhering to each other, but not blended' ([1777] 1977, vol. 1: 221). Ideas that are related through association can link together severally to form 'trains', in which a first idea couples with a second, which couples with a third, and so on.

After ideas become associated in a 'train', some of them may drop out, so that the earlier elements of the train come to associate directly with the later ones by means of 'translation'. When we first see a proof of a mathematical theorem, the theorem, the steps of the proof, and the certainty that we attach to each of these steps will associate with one another to form a train. Yet later we may recall only the theorem itself and the certainty that we once associated with the proof.

Tucker takes this process of translation to be the explanation for a variety of psychological phenomena, including (for example) our sympathy with the moods of others. As children, we soon learn to associate our own happiness with the actions of others, and to associate their actions with their moods – they may play with us when they are happy or ignore us when they are sad. Eventually, we come simply to associate our own pleasure or displeasure with their happy or unhappy moods – without any intervening link of action.

3 Moral and religious philosophy

Tucker says of the will (the active element of the mind) that 'all her motions depend upon motives, thrown upon her from external objects, or conveyed by the channels of experience, education, and example, or procured by her own cares and industry, whereto she was instigated by former motives' ([1777] 1977, vol. 4: 302). The 'active ingredient' in all our motives, however we might describe their details, is the prospect of our own satisfaction. (Tucker understood 'satisfaction' to be a more general term than pleasure, combining the presence of any desirable feelings with the avoidance of any undesirable feelings.) And 'the summum bonum...happiness...is the aggregate of satisfactions' ([1777] 1977, vol. 2: 233). Thus we are absolutely determined to seek our own happiness. But Tucker's is a soft determinism that is compatible with free will, since 'freewill needs no compulsive force to keep her steady, for she communicates, by antecedent and external causes giving birth to her motives, with the fountain [God's design] whence all the other streams derive' ([1777] 1977, vol. 4: 303).

According to Tucker, 'rectitude hath not a substantiality or distinct essence of its own, but subsists in the relation to happiness, those actions being right which upon every occasion tend most effectually to happiness' ([1777] 1977, vol. 7: 151). And in this context, Tucker understands happiness to encompass the aggregate of satisfaction for all God's creatures. Thus he anticipates the later utilitarians William PALEY and Jeremy BENTHAM not only in asserting that the greatest total happiness is the greatest good, but also in proposing a consequentialist morality in which the good is prior to the right (see UTILITARIANISM).

So we are absolutely determined to pursue our own happiness, yet moral rectitude lies in the maximal happiness of all. But according to Tucker there is no difficulty here: our self-interested motivation and moral rectitude are congruent; for God has arranged that each of us shall achieve our greatest happiness through the greatest happiness of all.

In order to establish the existence of God and gain insight into God's attributes, Tucker employs an extended argument that combines elements of the first-cause argument with elements of the argument from design (see GOD, ARGUMENTS FOR THE EX-ISTENCE OF §§1, 4–5). (At one point in this argument Tucker makes use of the clock and clockmaker analogy that William Paley would later popularize.) Tucker's God is omnipresent (existing necessarily, thus existing everywhere and for all time), omnipotent (powerful enough to be the cause of everything), and omniscient (intelligent enough to plan a universe).

Among the attributes of the creator which are most important to Tucker's moral philosophy are two manifestations of God's goodness: God's providence and God's equity. Tucker proposes that the workings of nature give evidence of the providence of a creator who aims at the happiness of everyone. Tucker also argues that because of 'the wants and weaknesses of human nature' ([1777] 1977, vol. 3: 278) we humans are partial to those from whose good opinion we think we may benefit, while God wants no benefit that any human being can provide. So God must be impartial.

Thus the creator aims at our happiness, and the creator also plays no favourites – each of us will receive an equal measure of happiness over eternity. (Tucker rejects the notion of eternal punishment for the wicked.) For that reason, if we seek to advance our own satisfaction at the expense of others, we know that any short-term advantage we may gain will ultimately be lost – either in this world or in the next. And if we choose to sacrifice our own satisfaction to promote the general good, we know that God will compensate us fully in the end.

Now it may seem that on Tucker's account, we will come out no better if we do good than if we do evil. It may not pay to do wrong, but does it pay to do right? Tucker argues that when we promote the general good, we increase the store of happiness that is available to us all, so that every benevolent act will enhance the 'profit to the common stock in partnership' ([1777] 1977, vol. 4: 502). Thus 'whoever adds to the happiness of another, adds thereby to his own' ([1777] 1977, vol. 4: 500).

4 Influences

Throughout *The Light of Nature Pursued* Tucker repeatedly acknowledges his debts to John Locke, but his other influences are hard to trace. He often mentions David HARTLEY (whose associationist psychology probably inspired Tucker's own) and George BERKELEY, but both of these thinkers are usually cited in criticism. Tucker undoubtedly owes a debt to John Gay, but never refers to him by name; perhaps Gay's influence on Tucker came chiefly through Hartley. And Tucker may have been completely ignorant of his most famous contemporary, David Hume. Even where the two thinkers' ideas seem most similar, as in their belief in soft determinism and their associationist accounts of sympathy, they diverge in their arguments and in the details of their views.

Tucker's influence on the utilitarians who followed him, particularly William Paley, is powerful and direct. In the preface to his *Principles of Moral and Political Philosophy*, Paley says:

> There is, however, one work to which I owe so much that it would be ungrateful not to confess the obligation. I mean the writings of the late Abraham Tucker.... I have found in this writer more original thinking and observation, upon the several subjects that he has taken in hand, than in any other, not to say, than in all others put together.
>
> (1785: xiii)

See also: HUME, D.; LOCKE, J.

List of works

Tucker, A. (1755) *The country gentleman's advice to his son, on his coming of age, in the year 1755, with regard to his political conduct. Shewing, amongst other things, the folly and pernicious consequences of all party clubs*, London: Owen. (A short tract advising against affiliation with political parties.)

—— (1763) *Freewill, Foreknowledge, and Fate*, London: Dodsley. (A preliminary version of what would later become *The Light of Nature Pursued*. Published under the pseudonym Edward Search.)

—— (1763) *Man in Quest of Himself: or A Defence of the Individuality of the Human Mind, or Self*, London: Dodsley; repr. in S. Parr (ed.) *Metaphysical Tracts by English Philosophers of the Eighteenth Century*, London: Lumley, 1837, 171–210. (A response to some criticisms of *Freewill, Foreknowledge, and Fate*. Originally published under the pseudonym Cuthbert Comment.)

—— (1773) *Vocal Sounds*, Menston: Scholar Press,

1969. (A curious little volume in which Tucker proposes a reformed English alphabet.)

—— (1777) *The Light of Nature Pursued*, 7 vols; 2nd edn, 1805; repr. London: Garland, 1977. (Tucker's major work, written in a discursive and painstaking style. Includes a short biography of the author. The first edition was published under the pseudonym Edward Search.)

References and further reading

Albee, E. (1902) *A History of English Utilitarianism*, Bristol: Thoemmes, 1990, 130–64. (A clear summary of Tucker's thought and its place in the context of British moral philosophy.)

* Paley, W. (1785) *Principles of Moral and Political Philosophy*, London: Faulder, xiii. (Source of the quotation that closes this entry.)

Stephen, L. (1876) *History of English Thought in the Eighteenth Century*, New York: Harcourt Brace, 1962, vol. 2, 92–104. (A short but somewhat abstruse account of Tucker's thought, including his religious philosophy.)

T. McNAIR

TULLY *see* CICERO

TUNG CHUNG-SHU *see* DONG ZHONGSHU

TURING, ALAN MATHISON (1912–54)

Alan Turing was a mathematical logician who made fundamental contributions to the theory of computation. He developed the concept of an abstract computing device (a 'Turing machine') which precisely characterizes the concept of computation, and provided the basis for the practical development of electronic digital computers beginning in the 1940s. He demonstrated both the scope and limitations of computation, proving that some mathematical functions are not computable in principle by such machines.

Turing believed that human behaviour might be understood in terms of computation, and his views inspired contemporary computational theories of mind. He proposed a comparative test for machine intelligence, the 'Turing test', in which a human interrogator tries to distinguish a computer from a human by interacting with them only over a teletypewriter. Although the validity of the Turing test is controversial, the test and modifications of it remain influential measures for evaluating artificial intelligence.

1 Life
2 Turing machines and minds
3 The Turing test

1 Life

Turing was born in London. He was educated at King's College, Cambridge, where he began work in mathematical logic, soon writing his most brilliant article 'On Computable Numbers with an Application to the *Entscheidungsproblem*'. The German '*Entscheidungsproblem*' refers to David Hilbert's question whether mathematics is *decidable*, that is, whether there is for any mathematical assertion a definite procedure which will determine whether or not the assertion is true. Turing's work, along with contemporary work of Kurt GÖDEL and Alonzo CHURCH, demonstrated the impossibility of such a general decision procedure. Moreover, his work on computable numbers and universal computing machines provided the conceptual foundation for the development of the modern computer.

During the Second World War Turing helped to design special computing equipment to decipher the German 'enigma' codes. Afterwards he led efforts to design some of the earliest computers, including the Automatic Computing Engine (ACE) in 1945 and the Manchester Automatic Digital Machine (MADAM) in 1948. Turing was prosecuted for his homosexuality in 1952. He died at the peak of his intellectual powers, an apparent suicide.

2 Turing machines and minds

Turing machines are highly idealized 'machines' (properly regarded as abstract objects that may or may not be realized in any physical material) that consist of a potentially infinite tape, divided into individual cells, on which the machine can read and write discrete symbols, and a set of state descriptions which specify what the machine is to do when, in a particular state, it reads a particular symbol: it can leave it alone, erase it, write a new symbol in its place, move one cell to the left or right, and enter a new or the same state (see TURING MACHINES). Turing showed how such machines could compute many ordinary arithmetic functions, and conjectured that anything that could be intuitively regarded as computable at all could be computed by such a machine (what has become known as the 'Church–Turing thesis'; see CHURCH'S THESIS).

A particularly important Turing machine is the universal Turing machine, which serves as the prototype of the standard 'computer': when its tape is supplied with a coded description of any Turing machine (or 'program') and some input for that machine, it computes precisely what *that* machine *would* compute when supplied with that input.

The concept of a Turing machine furnishes a theoretical foundation for much work in cognitive science and artificial intelligence, where the driving idea is that cognitive processes, and maybe all mental processes, are ultimately computational (see ARTIFICIAL INTELLIGENCE; MIND, COMPUTATIONAL THEORIES OF). Processes of perception, reasoning, and decision making, for example, are to be explained in terms of computations operating on the input to sense organs. A version of this computational approach to the mind is called 'Turing machine functionalism' (see Block 1980).

One of the philosophically most important consequences of Turing's proposal is that it provides a method of explaining overall mental activity in simple mechanical terms. It thereby meets a recurring worry about psychological theories; that they vacuously postulate an intelligent 'homunculus' to explain intelligent activity. Rather than resorting to a master homunculus to explain the mind, a hierarchy of computational systems is postulated, each of which is made up of simpler computational systems, until finally there is nothing left but simple mechanical components whose operations can be understood purely in terms of physical causation.

3 The Turing test

Turing not only provided a rigorous account of computation in terms of Turing Machines, but also proposed a classic test for examining machine mentality. His test, the Turing test, is designed to examine the ability of computers to imitate humans. In the Turing test a human interrogator or 'judge' puts questions to two unseen subjects – one a computer and the other a human. The task of the interrogator is to determine, based on teletypewriter communication with the two unseen subjects, which is the computer and which is the human. The goal of the computer is to imitate a human, including the imitation of typical human strengths and weaknesses. To use Turing's own example, when the computer subject is asked to add 34,957 and 70,764, it does not respond immediately but waits about 30 seconds and then responds with 105,621 rather than the correct answer 105,721. Although Turing does not specify, it

is reasonable to assume that the interrogator is allowed to ask many questions over an extended period of time. The computer passes the test if and only if the interrogator cannot distinguish (better than chance) between the computer and human responses.

The Turing test has a number of virtues as a scientific test. First, the test is conducted with blind impartiality. The interrogator in the test cannot judge the computer to be non-intelligent because of its appearance alone. The sophistication of the behaviour is the crucial variable, and linguistic behaviour in the test can be evaluated without subtle bias due to appearance (see BEHAVIOURISM, ANALYTIC). Second, the test is reproducible. If the computer really has intelligence, then it has a cluster of abilities that can be demonstrated over and over again.

The Turing test is, however, open to many criticisms.

(1) The *action* objection: the Turing test examines only linguistic behaviour, but intelligence and thinking must be evaluated in terms of bodily actions within real contexts, not merely through linguistic behaviour over a teletypewriter. A possible reply: actions of any kind can be *discussed* within the Turing test, and that is sufficient to establish intelligence. After all, a human who is largely paralysed but who has adequate linguistic capabilities can still demonstrate intelligence.

(2) The *jukebox* objection: because the test is finite, pre-selected answers could be entered for every possible question (see Block 1981), but surely merely accessing such a list should not be intelligence. A possible reply: this is not a practical option as the number of answers needed is astronomically high. In any remotely realistic test, the proper response at any given time depends on common knowledge of the real world which is constantly and unpredictably changing.

(3) The *syntax* objection: computers operate syntactically, not semantically, and can never understand what they produce even if the result passes the Turing test (see Searle 1980; CHINESE ROOM ARGUMENT). A possible reply: although the computer's operations are defined purely syntactically (in terms of what the cursor reads and writes), this does not preclude the possibility that they possess causally efficacious semantic properties. A computer as a whole functioning system may possess semantics and hence be capable of understanding (see LANGUAGE OF THOUGHT).

(4) The *Barnum* objection: there have been *restricted* Turing tests (subject to limits of time, topic and style of question) that have been actually staged, and which a number of computer programs have passed (see Shieber 1994 for discussion). However, as Block (1981) points out, they only show what P.T.

Barnum claimed: people are easy to fool. A possible reply: the restrictions on these tests have been too severe; it is very implausible that a computer that passed a fully *unrestricted* test, in which any topic could be discussed in any way for substantial amounts of time, could really lack intelligence.

The Turing test is often understood as providing necessary and sufficient conditions, an 'operational' definition, for computer thinking. Turing, himself, did not insist that the test be so interpreted. Indeed, on the contrary, Turing believed that a machine might fail the test, not due to a lack of intelligence, but due to a lack of the ability to imitate a human. The computer might add too quickly and give itself away. A weaker, inductive interpretation of the Turing test is more defensible. On the inductive interpretation the Turing test is not expected to provide *deductively conclusive* evidence, but merely *scientific inductive* evidence for the hypothesis that computers have intelligence similar to humans. How good the evidence is depends on how well the computer does in the test. If a computer actually passed a full Turing Test, then the proponent of the Turing test would claim that good inductive evidence would exist to infer that the computer has intelligence similar to our own.

List of works

Turing, A.M. (1992) *Collected Works of A.M. Turing*, ed. D.C. Ince, Amsterdam: Elsevier. (The standard edition of Turing's works.)
—— (1964) 'Computing, Machinery and Intelligence', repr. in A.R. Anderson (ed.) *Minds and Machines*, Englewood Cliffs, NJ: Prentice Hall. (Turing's proposal of the 'Turing test'.)

References and further reading

* Block, N. (ed.) (1980) *Readings in Philosophy of Psychology*, vol. 1, Cambridge, MA: Harvard University Press. (Part 3 has an introduction and selection of articles discussing Turing machine functionalism.)
—— (1981) 'Psychologism and Behaviorism', *Philosophical Review* 90: 5–43. (Develops the *jukebox* – or 'blockhead' – counterexample to the Turing test, claiming it could be passed by a machine consisting of a vast look-up table.)
—— (1990) 'The Computer Model of the Mind', in D. Osherson and E. Smith (eds) *An Invitation to Cognitive Science*, vol. 3, *Thinking*, Cambridge, MA: MIT Press. (A useful introduction to the topic, and some problems both with the model and with the Turing test.)

Boden, M. (ed.) (1990) *The Philosophy of Artificial Intelligence*, Oxford: Oxford University Press. (Selection of articles about the Turing test and the computer model of the mind.)
Hodges, A. (1983) *Alan Turing: The Enigma*, New York: Simon & Schuster. (Excellent biography.)
* Searle, J. (1980) 'Minds, Brains, and Programs', *Behavioral and Brain Sciences* 3: 417–24. (Gives the well-known Chinese room argument to criticize the Turing test.)
* Shieber, S. (1994) 'Lessons from a Restricted Turing Test', *Communications of the ACM* 37: 70–8. (A discussion of some actual stagings of highly restricted Turing tests, which some computers passed.)

JAMES MOOR

TURING MACHINES

Turing machines are abstract computing devices, named after Alan Mathison Turing. A Turing machine operates on a potentially infinite tape uniformly divided into squares, and is capable of entering only a finite number of distinct internal configurations. Each square may contain a symbol from a finite alphabet. The machine can scan one square at a time and perform, depending on the content of the scanned square and its own internal configuration, one of the following operations: print or erase a symbol on the scanned square or move on to scan either one of the immediately adjacent squares. These elementary operations are possibly accompanied by a change of internal configuration. Turing argued that the class of functions calculable by means of an algorithmic procedure (a mechanical, stepwise, deterministic procedure) is to be identified with the class of functions computable by Turing machines. The epistemological significance of Turing machines and related mathematical results hinges upon this identification, which later became known as Turing's thesis; an equivalent claim, Church's thesis, had been advanced independently by Alonzo Church. Most crucially, mathematical results stating that certain functions cannot be computed by any Turing machine are interpreted, by Turing's thesis, as establishing absolute limitations of computing agents.

1 **Human computors**
2 **(Universal) Turing machines**
3 **The horizon of computability (and beyond)**

1 Human computors

In his seminal article of 1937, 'On Computable Numbers, With an Application to the *Entscheidungsproblem* [decision problem]', Alan Mathison Turing argued that a function is calculable by some algorithmic procedure if and only if it is computable by a Turing machine. The main claim in Turing's argument is that the behaviour of a human being carrying out an algorithmic procedure (adopting the terminology of Gandy (1988), a 'computor') is constrained by limitations of human memory and sensory capacities. It is appropriate to review briefly these restrictive conditions, for they are reflected in the mathematical definition of a Turing machine. (For a careful analysis of Turing's argument, see Sieg (1994); an analogue of Turing's argument for parallel computations by digital computers is given by Gandy (1980).)

Turing considered a 'one-dimensional' computing space formed by a potentially infinite tape uniformly divided into squares, in each of which at most one symbol may be written. What are the possible processes which can be carried out by a computor working on this computing space?

(1) The computor can write on the tape symbols from a fixed finite list (for example, letters of the alphabet). This restriction is argued for on the ground that if one allowed an infinity of symbols, then one would have symbols differing to an arbitrarily small extent (which, presumably, could not be unambiguously recognized or written down by the computor in view of sensory and memory limitations).

(2) The computor can observe squares on the tape. Limitations of human visual apparatus seem sufficient to justify the existence of a fixed finite bound B on the number of contiguous squares observable at any one moment.

(3) The computor can remember earlier stages of the computation and bring this information to bear on future behaviour. This memory consists in what Turing calls the computor's 'states of mind'. There is a fixed finite bound on the number of 'states of mind' which need be taken into account in a mechanical calculation. If one admitted the possibility of using infinitely many states of mind, Turing observes, some of them would be arbitrarily close and would be confused by the computor.

(4) The elementary actions the computor can perform consist of a change of either (a) observed squares or (b) the contents of some squares, possibly accompanied by a change of 'state of mind'. Any other operation of the computor can be viewed as a composition of these elementary actions. Furthermore, Turing assumes that (c) each of the newly observed squares must be within a bounded distance L of an immediately previously observed square, and that nothing will be lost by supposing that only the contents of observed squares can be changed.

(5) Which elementary action the computor is to undertake at a given moment depends only on what the computor currently sees and remembers. Thus, the observed squares and the 'state of mind' at any moment uniquely determine the action to be undertaken.

These restrictive conditions ensure that the computor's behaviour is fixed by a finite list of instructions: there are only finitely many different types of observable configurations of symbols (by (1) and (2)) and finitely many 'states of mind' (by (3)); to each pair formed by a 'state of mind' and type of observable configuration is uniquely associated (by (5)) an elementary action (fixed by (4)).

2 (Universal) Turing machines

Turing claims that the behaviour of a computor satisfying the restrictive conditions above can be faithfully simulated by a machine organized as follows. The internal configurations $q_1, \ldots, q_n$ of the machine correspond to the states of mind $m_1, \ldots, m_n$ of the computor. The machine scans B squares corresponding to the B squares observed by the computor. In any of its actions, the machine can change a symbol on one of the scanned squares or shift attention to observe another configuration of symbols in such a way that condition (4)(c) is satisfied. The action undertaken at any moment by the machine, and its next internal configuration, are uniquely determined by the scanned symbols and the internal configuration at that moment. In turn, one can show that any computation of this machine can be carried out by a machine M endowed with a more elementary repertoire of actions, which provides an intuitive visualization of a Turing machine. This machine has a fixed finite number of internal configurations; it is capable of scanning only one square at a time (that is, $B = 1$); it may print or erase a symbol on the scanned square or else move on to scan either of the immediately adjacent squares (that is, $L = 1$).

To the machine M one can associate a function $f(x_1, \ldots, x_n)$ of n non-negative integers in the following way. Given an n-tuple $a_1, \ldots, a_n$, since the machine can print at least one symbol, say 1, the input $\langle a_1, \ldots, a_n \rangle$ can be represented on an otherwise blank tape by a sequence of $a_1 + 1$ consecutive 1's followed by a blank square followed by a sequence of $a_2 + 1$ consecutive 1's followed by a blank square... followed by a sequence of $a_n + 1$ consecutive 1's. The machine is to be started in a specific internal configuration, q_1, scanning the leftmost square containing a 1. The output number (if any), which is to be identified with $f(a_1, \ldots, a_n)$, is given by the number of 1's written on the tape to the right of the scanned square when (and if) the machine halts. These stipulations enable one to associate to M an n-ary *partial* (rather than total) function (that is, a function which may be undefined for some n-tuple of non-negative integers), because for some input the machine may fail to provide an output by not halting.

The initial stage of computation of M on the input $\langle a_1, \ldots, a_n \rangle$ has been described by giving (1) the tape content, (2) the machine's internal configuration, and (3) the scanned square. Each subsequent stage of the computation can be described by providing this information, which is called an 'instantaneous description' of the machine. Any computation which produces a final output can be described by a finite sequence of instantaneous descriptions.

The essential features of this type of machine can be captured by precise mathematical definitions. Let us consider the list of symbols $S_0, S_1, S_2, \ldots$, $q_1, q_2, q_3, \ldots$, R and L, and sequences of symbols from this list having one of the following forms:

(1) $q_i S_j S_k q_l$

(2) $q_i S_j R q_l$

(3) $q_i S_j L q_l$.

Sequences of this form are called 'quadruples'. Turing machines will be now defined (following Davis 1958) entirely in terms of quadruples, which can be interpreted as specifying the next action of a Turing machine when its internal configuration is q_i and the symbol it is scanning is S_j. Quadruple (1) indicates that S_j is to be replaced by S_k and the machine is to enter internal configuration q_l; quadruples (2) and (3) indicate that the machine is to shift one square to the right or to the left, respectively, and then enter internal configuration q_l. We stipulate that the symbol S_0 will serve as a blank; thus, replacing symbol S_j by S_0 amounts to erasing it.

Now a Turing machine is a finite, non-empty set of quadruples that contains no two quadruples with the same first two symbols. The latter condition guarantees the deterministic character of the machine operation, since no more than one instruction will be applicable at any given moment.

This definition identifies a Turing machine with a finite table of instructions in a certain normal form. Equally rigorous definitions can be given for the notions of instantaneous description and computation, as well as for the Turing computable functions, that is, the class of partial functions that Turing

machines can compute (see Davis 1958: ch. 1). A basic result of computability theory is the extensional equivalence between this class of functions and the partial recursive functions. Analogous results have been obtained for classes of functions defined in terms of other algorithmic processes (Markov algorithms, lambda-calculi, Post's production systems, Kleene's equational calculus, and so on; see CHURCH'S THESIS; COMPUTABILITY THEORY).

One can define an algorithmic one-one correspondence of the members of the class of Turing machines with the set of all non-negative integers. This fact entails that there is an algorithm (and, by Turing's thesis, a Turing machine) enabling one to retrieve, given any integer x, the Turing machine indexed by x and, conversely, given any Turing machine, the integer associated with it (see Rogers 1958). This mapping yields an enumeration $M_0, M_1, M_2, \ldots$ of the class of Turing machines. Correspondingly, we shall indicate by f_x the partial function computable by M_x.

Under any such enumeration, there is a number u such that for any numbers x and y, the machine M_u computes the following binary function:

$$f_u(x, y) = \begin{cases} f_x(y) & \text{if } f_x(y) \text{ is defined} \\ \text{undefined} & \text{otherwise.} \end{cases}$$

Thus, the machine M_u can be employed to compute any unary Turing computable function. Furthermore, M_u can also compute the n-ary Turing computable functions, provided one codes any n-tuple $\langle y_1, \ldots, y_n \rangle$ of input numbers by means of a non-negative integer. Again, this coding can be given by means of Turing computable functions (see Davis 1958: ch. 4). In view of these properties, M_u is called a universal Turing machine. A universal Turing machine is explicitly described in Turing (1937).

3   The horizon of computability (and beyond)

There are number-theoretic functions which cannot be computed by any Turing machine. The mere existence of such functions follows from the fact that the class of Turing computable functions is denumerable (it can be put into a one-one correspondence with the non-negative integers) whereas, by Cantor's theorem (see CANTOR, G.), there are indenumerably many number-theoretic functions.

Specific examples of non-computable functions were provided by Turing in his 1937 paper. Consider the so-called 'halting problem': is there a Turing machine capable of deciding for arbitrary x and y whether the Turing machine M_x will eventually halt after being started on input y? In other words, is the total number-theoretic function

$$h(x,y) = \begin{cases} 1 & \text{if } f_x(y) \text{ is defined} \\ 0 & \text{otherwise} \end{cases}$$

a Turing computable function? The answer to this question is negative: the function $h(x,y)$ is not Turing computable, and the halting problem is said to be unsolvable. Turing used the unsolvability of the halting problem to establish a negative solution to Hilbert's *Entscheidungsproblem* [decision problem] (see CHURCH'S THEOREM AND THE DECISION PROBLEM; HILBERT'S PROGRAMME AND FORMALISM).

The unsolvability of the halting problem implies that the behaviour of some Turing machines cannot be completely predicted by any Turing machine. An example of such 'unpredictable' machines is just the universal Turing machine M_u. The existence of a Turing machine capable of determining, for every x and y, whether the machine M_u will eventually halt when started on input $\langle x,y \rangle$ conflicts with the negative solution to the halting problem.

The import of this and other 'negative' results concerning Turing machines crucially hinges upon Turing's thesis. Indeed, if a function cannot be computed by a Turing machine then, by Turing's thesis, one can infer that there is no algorithm enabling one to calculate the values of this function. In particular, no algorithmic procedure can enable one to answer, for each x and y, all questions of the form 'Does M_x halt on y?' or, equivalently, 'Does x belong to the set K_y formed by the numbers z such that $f_z(y)$ is defined?'.

Suppose we are provided with some unspecified means – an oracle, as it were – for solving problems of the form 'Does x belong to X?', where X is a set of non-negative integers. One may then define a new class of machines, which one may call O-machines, suitably extending the definition of Turing machine so as to allow for quadruples of the form

(4) $q_i S_j q_k q_l$,

and associating to each O-machine a specific set X of non-negative integers. An O-machine in internal configuration q_i which is scanning symbol S_j may be interpreted as asking the oracle: 'Does the number x of occurrences of 1 on my tape at this moment belong to X?' If the answer is 'yes' then the O-machine changes its internal configuration to q_k; if the answer is 'no' then the O-machine changes its internal configuration to q_l (see Davis 1958: ch. 1). The function computable by an O-machine is said to be computable in the set X associated with that machine.

A class of functions computable in a set X may include functions that are not Turing computable. Furthermore, given a set X, one can prove the

existence of functions that are not computable in X, that is, functions which cannot be computed by O-machines having access to an oracle capable of deciding membership of the set X. Results of this kind are central to the theory of the degrees of unsolvability, which introduces a hierarchy of classes of unsolvable problems.

One may also distinguish between classes of solvable problems, in terms of the amount of resources a computing machine may need for their solution. Among the various, equivalent models that are available, the model of computation commonly chosen to estimate these resources is that of the Turing machine (see COMPLEXITY, COMPUTATIONAL).

The notion of (universal) Turing machine also plays a prominent role in philosophical discussions of the mind–machine problem. Theoretical limitations of (universal) Turing machines have been appealed to in arguments purporting to show that the human mind is not subject to analogous limitations. Turing (1950) employed this notion in order to circumscribe the class of devices that are admitted to compete with human beings in his test for intelligent behaviour. More recently, (universal) Turing machines have been used to isolate distinguishing features of the notion of computational explanation in cognitive science, as well as heuristic ideas underlying research programmes in artificial intelligence (see, for example, Newell and Simon 1976).

See also: LOGICAL AND MATHEMATICAL TERMS, GLOSSARY OF

References and further reading

* Davis, M. (1958) *Computability and Unsolvability*, New York: McGraw-Hill; repr. New York: Dover, 1982. (Classic introduction to Turing machines and the theory of computability. The first part of this book is accessible to readers with no special mathematical training.)

—— (ed.) (1965) *The Undecidable: Basic Papers on Undecidable Propositions, Unsolvable Problems and Computable Functions*, Hewlett, NY: Raven Press. (An anthology of fundamental papers on undecidability and unsolvability, which includes Turing (1937).)

* Gandy, R. (1980) 'Church's Thesis and Principles for Mechanisms', in J. Barwise, H.J. Keisler and K. Kunen (eds) *The Kleene Symposium*, Amsterdam: North Holland, 123–45. (Presents an analogue of Turing's argument for parallel computations by digital computers.)

* —— (1988) 'The Confluence of Ideas in 1936', in R. Herken (ed.) *The Universal Turing Machine: A*

Half-Century Survey, Oxford: Oxford University Press, 55–112. (An informative discussion of the conceptual background of Turing's analysis.)

Herken, R. (ed.) (1988) *The Universal Turing Machine: A Half-Century Survey*, Oxford: Oxford University Press. (See especially Kleene's and Gandy's articles. Feferman's article reviews the ideas leading to the notion of oracle machine.)

Kleene, S.C. (1988) 'Turing's Analysis of Computability, and Major Applications of It', in R. Herken (ed.) *The Universal Turing Machine: A Half-Century Survey*, Oxford: Oxford University Press, 17–54. (Includes a terse outline of Gödel's incompleteness theorems, highlighting their relation to Turing machines in a form accessible to non-specialists.)

* Newell, A. and Simon, H. (1976) 'Computer Science as Empirical Enquiry: Symbols and Search', *Communications of the ACM* 19: 113–26. (Formulates broad heuristic hypotheses in artificial intelligence and cognitive science by crucial appeal to universal computing machines.)

* Rogers, H. (1958) 'Gödel Numbers of Partial Recursive Functions', *Journal of Symbolic Logic* 23: 331–41. (A technical analysis of the numerical codings referred to in §2.)

* Sieg, W. (1994) 'Mechanical Procedures and Mathematical Experience', in A. George (ed.) *Mathematics and Mind*, Oxford: Oxford University Press, 71–117. (Includes a careful analysis of Turing's argument.)

* Turing, A.M. (1937) 'On Computable Numbers, With an Application to the *Entscheidungsproblem* [decision problem]', *Proceedings of the London Mathematical Society*, series 2, 42: 230–65; repr. in M. Davis (ed.) *The Undecidable*, Hewlett, NY: Raven Press, 1965. (Turing's seminal article in the theory of computability: §9 presents the major argument for Turing's thesis.)

* —— (1950) 'Computing Machinery and Intelligence', *Mind* 59: 433–60; repr. in D.C. Ince (ed.) *Collected Works of A.M. Turing*, vol. 3, *Mechanical Intelligence*, Amsterdam: North Holland, 1992. (An influential article on the mind–machine problem, presenting Turing's reflections on (universal) computing machines and intelligent behaviour.)

GUGLIELMO TAMBURRINI

TURING REDUCIBILITY AND TURING DEGREES

A reducibility is a relation of comparative computational complexity (which can be made precise in various non-equivalent ways) between mathematical objects of appropriate sorts. Much of recursion theory concerns such relations, initially between sets of natural numbers (in so-called classical recursion theory), but later between sets of other sorts (in so-called generalized recursion theory). This article considers only the classical setting. Also Turing first defined such a relation, now called Turing- (or just T-) reducibility; probably most logicians regard it as the most important such relation. Turing- (or T-) degrees are the units of computational complexity when comparative complexity is taken to be T-reducibility.

1   **Usage and notation**
2   **Informal characterization of T-reducibility**
3   **Two rigorous definitions**
4   **More definitions and facts**

1   Usage and notation

ω = the set of all natural numbers; a real is a subset of ω. For sets $A, B: A \cup B = \{x : x \in A \text{ or } x \in B\}$; $A \times B = \{ <x, y> : x \in X, y \in Y\}$; for $n \in \omega$, $n \neq 0: A^n = A \times \ldots \times A$ (taking A n-times). For a function $\varphi : \text{dom}(\varphi$ = the domain of φ; φ is a particle function on ω^n iff $\text{dom}(\varphi) \subseteq \omega^n$; such a function is total iff its domain is ω^n. In this article a partial function will be partial on ω^n for some $n \in \omega$; φ is total iff $\text{dom}(\varphi) = \omega^n$. (So a total function on ω^n is also partial – an unfortunate, but standard, usage.) For a real X, χ_X, is X's characteristic function: $\chi_X(x) = 1$ if $x \in X$; $\chi_X(x) = 0$ if $x \notin X$.

2   Informal characterization of T-reducibility

For reals X and Y: X is reducible to Y iff Y is at least as computationally complex (in a sense whose specification determines the reducibility relation) as X is, that is, given any $n \in \omega$ we could answer the question '$n \in x$?' by means that are in some sense computational except (perhaps) for using (subject to various possible constraints) answers to membership-questions about Y. For T-reducibility, we require computation to be effective and impose no restraints. A relativized algorithm consists of instructions like an 'absolute' algorithm (see COMPUTABILITY THEORY) except that they may tell one to 'ask a question of an oracle', one of the form 'what about y?', where y can be any natural number given to the oracle as a numeral; running the algorithm relative to Y, in a finite time the oracle says 'yes' if $y \in Y$, and 'no' otherwise. Suppose A is such a relativized algorithm, and we have an oracle for the real Y and infinite amount of time. Were we to apply A to a given input, we would grind along following A as we would an 'absolute' algorithm, except that from time to time A might specify a natural number (in some sort of numeral form) for us to ask the oracle about; the oracle would answer; we would grind on following A, exactly what A requires us to do being 'mechanically' determined by the answers the oracle gave to this and previous queries; eventually A might tell us to stop, delivering an output; A also might leave us computing forever. The oracle is oracular in that we do not trouble ourselves about how it comes up with its answers; going from a query of the oracle to its answer is a non-effective step in an otherwise effective computation. Now we will introduce some 'informal' definitions.

(I) A partial function φ on ω is computed by an algorithm A relative to a real Y iff for any $x \in \omega$, were we to run A on input x using an oracle for Y: if $x \in \mathrm{dom}(\varphi)$ the computation would halt giving the value $\varphi(x)$; if $x \notin \mathrm{dom}(\varphi)$ the computation would not halt. φ is computable relative to Y iff φ is computed by some such A relative to Y. X is decidable relative to Y iff χ_X is computable relative to y (that is, for some A for any $\chi \in \omega$, were we to run A on input x using an oracle for Y, the computation would eventually halt with a correct answer (1 = 'yes', 0 = 'no') to the question '$x \in X$?'. X is recursively enumerable relative to Y iff X is the range of a function that is total on ω and computable relative to Y.

3 Two rigorous definitions

One way to replace these informal definitions by rigorous definitions uses the notion of an oracle machine (that is, a relativized Turing machine (see TURING MACHINES)), credited by Rogers (1967) to M. Davis. Fix a finite set ALPH (an alphabet) whose members we will call symbols, say with $0(= \text{blank}), 1, 2 \in \text{ALPH}$; without mathematical loss, we could suppose that $\text{ALPH} = \{0, 1, 2\}$. Recall the three usual rule-schemata defining being a Turing-machine table (for a single tape infinite in both directions and with '0' meaning 'blank') relative to ALPH and to a set STATE of internal states. Add to them this fourth schema (Query): for y = the number of occurrences of 1 on the tape at the moment, if in state q then: if the oracle says 'yes' to y then change to state q'; if it says 'no' change the state q''. (By using occurrences of 2 rather than 1, the device can record and preserve results of previous steps while 'asking

the oracle a question', insulating this record from the question asked.)

Pick $L, R \notin \text{ALPH}, \text{ACT} = \text{ALPH} \cup \{L, R\}$. Represent any Turing-machine rule by a quadruple of the form $< q, s, a, q' >$ for $q \in \text{STATE}$, $s \in \text{ALPH}$, $a \in \text{ACT}$, $q' \in \text{STATE}$, with this understanding: if $a \in \text{ALPH}$ the instruction says 'Erase the cell and write a'; L and R represent 'Move the tape one cell to the left (that is, the head one cell to the right)' and 'Move the tape one cell to the right', respectively. Any rule of form (Query) can be represented by a quadruple $< q, s, a, q'q'' >$ for $q, q', q'' \in \text{STATE}$, $s \in \text{ALPH}$.

Let an oracle-machine table on $< \text{ALPH}, \text{STATE} >$ be a function from $\text{STATE} \times \text{ALPH}$ into $(\text{ACT} \cup \text{STATE}) \times \text{STATE}$. Identifying a function f with the set of ordered pairs of the form $< x, f(x) >$, and identifying an ordered pair of the form $< < a, b >, < cd >>$ with $< a, b, c, d >$, such a table is a set of quadruples coding instructions. For mathematical purposes, an oracle machine is an ordered pair $M = < T, q_0 >$ for T an oracle-machine table and $q_0 \in \text{STATE}$; q_0 is M's initial state. Given a tape with cells in any condition, a particular cell on that tape, and a real Y, if each query of the oracle is true to Y (that is, if the device is in state q reading s, y is as above, and $T(< q, s >) = < q', q'' >$, then the machine goes into state q' if $y \in Y$, and goes into state q'' otherwise), an oracle machine M carries out a uniquely determined succession of operations starting in state q_0 with its head on that chosen cell, one which may or may not terminate in a finite number of steps; this is its computation (also known as its run) relative to Y. The definition of an oracle machine does not involve a particular value for 'Y': a given oracle machine M with a given input can run with any real Y, perhaps producing different computations for different reals. Also, talk of tapes and devices is heuristic, replaceable by an austere but tedious definition of the computation M carries out input x using Y.

(II) We associate with each such M and Y a partial function φ on ω as follows: represent a natural number x as input by string of $x + 1$ consecutive occurrences of 1 on the tape with all other cells blank; adding 1 distinguishes input 0 from starting with a blank tape. Start M in state q_0 reading the leftmost cell containing a 1; as output take the total number of occurrences of 1 appearing anywhere on the tape when and if the machine stops; thus $\varphi(x) =$ that total number of 1s; $x \in \mathrm{dom}(\varphi)$ iff M eventually halts when run with input x; if M does not halt, $x \notin \mathrm{dom}(\varphi)$ and $\varphi(x)$ does not exist (as mathematicians say, '$\varphi(x)$ is undefined'). This φ is the partial function computed by M using Y. φ is T-computable from Y iff φ is computed by some oracle machine using Y. X is T-reducible to Y (in symbols $X \leq_T Y$) iff χ_X is T-computable from Y.

For ALPH $= \{0,1,2\}$, represent the possible 'actions' by natural numbers: $i \leq 2$ for 'Erase the cell and write i'; 3 for L; 4 for R; represent the internal states as natural numbers greater than 4. Represent (or better, define) a machine-table as a function from a finite subset of $\omega \times \{0,1,2\}$ into a finite subset of $\omega \times \omega$; such a function can then be represented by a single natural number. An oracle machine M can be coded by a single natural number, M's Gödel-number (see GÖDEL'S THEOREMS). For $e = M$'s Gödel-number, let φ_Y^e (alternative notation: $\{e\}^Y$) be the partial function M computes using Y.

(III) Turing himself did not use the notion of an oracle machine in his original definition of T-reducibility; rather he defined the class of partial functions (each on ω^n for any $n \in \omega$) recursive in a real Y (also known as the class of functions partial recursive in Y) to be the least class $\underline{C}$ meeting these conditions: (1) all initial functions belong to $\underline{C}$; these are successor, the function mapping each ω^n into $\{0\}$, and all projections (that is, functions of the form $f(x_1,\ldots,x_n) = x_i$ for some i, $1 \leq i \leq n$); (2) $\chi_Y \in \underline{C}$; (3) $\underline{C}$ is closed under composition, primitive recursion and minimization. A real X is recursive in Y iff χ_X is.

It is tedious but not hard to prove that this class is exactly the class of partial functions T-computable from Y. Thus X is recursive in Y iff X is T-reducible to Y. In fact, each of the various ways of defining being a recursive function extends naturally to a definition of being a function recursive in an arbitrary real Y. Some regard the coextensiveness of (II), (III), and those other definitions, as evidence that they all rigorously define what (I) informally defines, that is, as evidence for the relativized version of Church's thesis: a function is computable relative to Y iff it is T-computable relative to Y (see CHURCH'S THESIS).

4 More definitions and facts

Let $X <_T Y$ iff $X \leq_T Y$ and not $Y \leq_T X$; X and Y are T-equivalent (in symbols $X \equiv_T Y$) iff $X \leq_T Y$ and $Y \leq_T X$. As the notation suggests: $\leq_T$ is a reflexive transitive relation; $\equiv_T$ is an equivalence relation. We could prove these facts from the mathematical definition of (II) or (III); but it is easier to work informally.

Sample proof Let A and B be algorithms computing χ_X and χ_Y relative to Y and Z respectively. Consider this algorithm: given any x, run A on X; whenever A tells us to ask the oracle for Y about a y, run B on y, using the oracle for Z; eventually such a run of B halts; if it yields 1 or 0 take that as a 'yes' or

'no' respectively from an oracle for Y. A halts on an input if responses to its queries of an oracle are true to Y; a run of B using an oracle for Z does deliver the truth about Y (since it computes χ_Y); so this process halts, yielding $\chi_X(x)$, and it uses an oracle for Z (rather than Y, unless $Y = Z$). Thus $\leq T$ is transitive. (One of recursion theory's advantages is that we can almost always work in this informal way.)

For a real X let $\deg(x) = \{Y : X \equiv_T Y\}$. Let a be a T-degree iff $a = \deg(x)$ for some real X; $\mathcal{D} =$ the set of T-degrees. For $a, b \in \mathcal{D}$ let $a \leq b$ iff for some $X \in a, Y \in b, X \leq_T Y$. Note that if $a \leq b$ then for any $X \in a, Y \in b : X \leq_T Y$. The relation $\leq$ is partial ordering, that is, it is reflexive , transitive, and antisymmetric (that is, if $a \leq b$ and $b \leq a$ then $a = b$). Let $0 =$ the set of recursive reals. For X, $Y \in 0 : X \equiv_T Y$; for any real Z if $Z \leq_T X$ then $Z \in 0$; thus $0 \in \mathcal{D}$. T-degrees are sometimes called 'degrees of unsolvability', rather misleading since one of them, 0, represents solvability (= recursiveness). For any real Y and any $X \in 0, X \leq_T Y$; thus 0 is the least T-degree under this (the standard) ordering. Study of the algebraic properties of the structure $< \mathcal{D}, \leq >$ is a major component of recursion theory. One basic fact is that the partial ordering $\leq$ is very partial; for $a, b \in \mathcal{D}$, a and b are incomparable iff neither $a \leq b$ nor $b \leq a$; each T-degree is incomparable with continuum-many other T-degrees – as many as there are reals.

Let a degree be recursively enumerable (hereafter r.e.) iff it contains an r.e. real. Recursive reals are r.e.; so 0 is r.e. Let $K^X = \{x : \varphi_x^X(x)$ is defined$\}$. In 1944 E. Post gave the first example of a non-recursive r.e. set: for $K = K^{\{\}}$ for $\{\} =$ the empty set; so $\deg(K)$ is another r.e. degree. He went on to pose 'Post's problem': are there other r.e. T-degrees? In 1956 R. Friedberg and A. Muchnik independently proved that there are others; some consider this the first deep result in degree theory. (See Friedberg 1957 or any of the textbooks referred to below.) The study of r.e. degrees is a flourishing corner of recursion theory.

The jump function on the reals assigns each real X to K^X. The effective version of Cantor's diagonal argument for the unaccountability of the set of reals (see CANTOR'S THEOREM) shows that $K^X \leq_T X$; since $X \leq_T K^X, X \leq_T K^X$. If $X \equiv_T Y$ then $K^X \equiv_T K^Y$; so it makes sense to define the jump function on the T-degrees: the jump of a (usually written a') is the T-degree of K^X for some (thus any) $X \in a$. Thus $a < a'$, showing the jump for degrees is a natural uniform way of transforming a T-degree into a more complex one. Obviously jumping iterates any finite number of times, yielding degrees of increasingly complex sets; in fact, it iterates through the so-called constructibly countable ordinals (see Hodes 1980), a matter closely connected to Gödel's constructible hierarchy (see THE CONSTRUCTIBLE UNIVERSE).

A sentence in a formal language can be effectively coded as a natural number by 'Gödel numbering' (see GÖDEL'S THEOREMS); so a set of sentences, for example, a theory (in the logician's sense (see MODEL THEORY)), can be coded as a real; so its complexity can be identified with the T-degree of that real. Examples are: the theory of a dense linear ordering without endpoints has degree 0; the set of validities of first-order logic is r.e. and so has degree $0'$; ditto for the set of theorems of any axiomatizable theory in a countable language; the set of truths of first-order arithmetic has degree $= 0^\omega =$ the result of jumping 0 ω-times.

S. Simpson (1977) proved that the first-order theory of $< \mathcal{D}, \leq,' >$ (that is, the set of true first-order sentences based on a two-place predicate for $\leq$, a one-place function-constant for the jump, and 'first-order logic' with variables ranging over $\mathcal{D}$) was very complicated – of the same T-degree as the set of truths of second-order arithmetic. In 1990 B. Cooper announced a proof (still unpublished at the end of 1993) that the jump-function on $\mathcal{D}$ is first-order definable over $< \mathcal{D}, \leq >$, that is, there is a formula $F(x,y)$ with exactly free variables x and y, based on a two place predicate for $\leq$ and 'predicate logic', so that with quantifiers ranging over $\mathcal{D}$: for any $a, b \in \mathcal{D}$ $F(a,b)$ is true iff $b = a'$. With Simpson's theorem, this showed that the first-order theory of $< \mathcal{D}, \leq >$ is as complex as the truth-set of second-order arithmetic. Analysis of T-degree of the truth-set have been carried out for many other kinds of structures, including various pieces of $< \mathcal{D}, \leq >$.

See also: LOGICAL AND MATHEMATICAL TERMS, GLOSSARY OF

References and further reading

* Friedberg, R. (1957) 'Two recursively enumberable sets of incomparable degrees of unsolvability', *Proceedings of the National Academy of Science* 43: 236–8. (One of the first two answers to Post's problem.)
* Hodes, H. (1980) 'Jumping through the transfinite', *Journal of Symbolic Logic* 45: 204–20. (On iterating the jump through the constructibly countable ordinals.)
Griffor, E. ed. (forthcoming) *Handbook of Recursion Theory*, Amsterdam: North-Holland Publishing. (Survey articles that will be up-to-date as of publication.)
Lerman, M. (1983) *The Degrees of Unsolvability*, Berlin: Springer-Verlag. (For advanced students.)
Nerode, A., and Shore, R. (1980) 'Second-order logic and first-order theories of reducibility orderings' in Barwise *et al.* (eds) *Kleene Symposium*, Amsterdam: North-Holland Publishing, 181–200. (A proof of Simpson's theorem, one easier that the original proof.)
Odifreddi, P. (1989) *Classical Recursion Theory*, Amsterdam: North-Holland Publishing, Elsevier Science Publishers. (A very good introductory text, emphasising breadth, up-to-date as of 1989; the author plans to extend this with at least one further volume.)
* Rogers, H. (1967) *The Theory of Recursive Functions and Effective Computability*, New York: McGraw Hill Inc. (The original text on recursion theory, and excellent complement to Odifreddi's text, with very good exercises.)
Shoenfield, J. (1971) *Degrees of Unsolvability*, Amsterdam: North-Holland Publishing, and New York: American Elsevier. (Lecture notes, not comprehensive, but very readable.)
* Simpson, S. (1977) 'First-order theory of the degrees of recursive unsolvability', *Annals of Mathematics* 105: 212–138. (The proof in Nerode and Shore (1980) is easier.)
Soare, R. (1987) *Recursively Enumberable Sets and Degrees*, Berlin: Springer-Verlag. (For advanced students.)

HAROLD HODES

TURNBULL, GEORGE (1698–1748)

George Turnbull was an early champion of the use of empirical methods in the moral sciences. Involved in contemporary religious debate, he favoured religious toleration and the use of rational argument in defence of Christian belief. He also made contributions to educational theory and practice.

Born in Alloa, Scotland, on 11 July 1698, George Turnbull studied at the University of Edinburgh, where he was an early member of the Rankenian Club. Like his fellow Rankenians, Turnbull was interested in contemporary religious debates, and in 1718 he tried to initiate a correspondence with the deist John Toland (1670–1722) (see DEISM; TOLAND, J.). During the late 1710s he also composed a manuscript treatise on civil religion which remained unpublished because of the controversial nature of his argument in favour of religious toleration. After graduating with his MA from Edinburgh in April

1721, he became a regent at Marischal College, Aberdeen, and taught there until he resigned in 1727.

Although Turnbull had a chequered career in Aberdeen, he played a major part in the transformation of Marischal's philosophy curriculum. He helped to popularize the writings of the Third Earl of SHAFTESBURY, and he joined with other regents to promote the study of natural jurisprudence and history. Along with some of his colleagues, Turnbull expounded the political views of Old Whigs like Lord Molesworth (1656–1725), with whom he corresponded about education and religion. He also mobilized Newtonian natural philosophy in the service of religion, and developed a rational form of Christianity designed to counter the attacks of deists and atheists. But perhaps his most important contribution was his proposed methodological reformation of moral philosophy. Although he may have been indebted to his teachers at Edinburgh for the initial idea, Turnbull was the first Scottish moralist to advocate in print the use of the experimental method to investigate moral questions, and his advocacy of a scientistic approach to morals left a permanent mark on eighteenth-century Scottish philosophy, especially through the influence of his pupil Thomas REID.

After such an auspicious start, Turnbull's subsequent career was something of a prolonged anticlimax. Following his departure from Aberdeen, he worked as a tutor to young aristocrats on the Grand Tour until he settled in London in the mid-1730s. During his travels he published two tracts on the rational basis of Christian belief (1731, 1732), and he addressed this topic again in 1740 in his most substantial publication, *The Principles of Moral Philosophy*. Turnbull here reiterated his call for the use of the experimental method in the moral sciences, and elaborated upon this theme in a dissertation appended to his translation of Heineccius' work on natural law (1741). 1740 also saw the appearance of his *Treatise on Ancient Painting*, wherein he expanded upon the basic elements of Shaftesbury's aesthetics in the context of a historical review of the development of painting and sculpture among the ancients. In addition, the *Treatise* considered the role of the fine arts in education, and issues of pedagogy were the primary focus of his last significant book, the *Observations upon Liberal Education* (1742), which despite its derivativeness makes a persuasive case for the structural unity of all branches of human learning. Turnbull's feverish literary activity points to his continuing search for settled employment and, having been ordained in 1739, he sought preferment in the Anglican Church. He was eventually rewarded with a minor position in Ireland, and he died in relative obscurity in the Hague on 31 January 1748.

See also: COMMON SENSE SCHOOL; ENLIGHTENMENT, SCOTTISH; OSWALD, J.; TINDAL, M.

List of works

Turnbull, G. (1723) *De scientiae naturalis cum philosophia morali conjunctione*, Aberdeen: Nicol. (The text of this graduation thesis argues for the close connection of natural science and moral philosophy.)

—— (1726) *De pulcherrima mundi cum materialis tum rationalis constitutione* (On the Beauty of the World in its Material and Rational Constitution), Aberdeen: Nicol. (Turnbull's formulation of the argument from design in response to the deists' critique of Christianity.)

—— (1731) *A Philosophical Enquiry concerning the Connexion betwixt the Doctrines and Miracles of Jesus Christ*, London: Willock; rev. edns 1732, 1739. (Ostensibly written in 1726, this pamphlet argues that Christ's miracles provided 'experimental' proofs for the central doctrines of Christianity.)

—— (1732) *Christianity neither False nor Useless, tho' not as Old as the Creation*, London: Willock. (A defence of Samuel Clarke's Boyle Lectures against the criticisms advanced in Matthew Tindal's *Christianity as Old as the Creation* (1730).)

—— (1740a) *The Principles of Moral Philosophy*, London: Noon, 2 vols; repr. Hildesheim: Olms, 1976. (Based on Turnbull's moral philosophy lectures at Marischal College, and incorporating ideas taken from Shaftesbury, Hutcheson, Butler, Berkeley, Pope, Newton and John Clark among others.)

—— (1740b) *A Treatise on Ancient Painting*, London: Millar; repr., with intro. by V. Bevilacqua, Munich: Fink, 1971. (The reprint does not contain the lavish plates of the original, which Turnbull also published separately in 1741.)

—— (1740c) *An Impartial Enquiry into the Moral Character of Jesus Christ; Wherein he is Considered as a Philosopher. In a Letter to a Friend*, London: Roberts; 2nd edn, 1743. (Published anonymously, this pamphlet argues that Christ was a greater philosopher than Socrates, and that the purity of his morals demonstrates the truth of the essentials of Christianity.)

—— (trans.) (1741) *A Methodical System of Universal Law*, by J.G. Heineccius, London: Noon, 2 vols. (Includes Turnbull's important dissertation 'A Discourse upon the Nature and Origine of Moral and Civil Laws'.)

—— (1742) *Observations upon Liberal Education*, London: Millar. (Turnbull's most comprehensive statement of his pedagogical ideals, which blends together themes from the writings of Locke, Shaftesbury, Molesworth, Rollin, Cicero and Plato.)

References and further reading

Gibson-Wood, C. (1987) 'Painting as Philosophy: George Turnbull's *Treatise on Ancient Painting*', in J.J. Carter and J.H. Pittock (eds) *Aberdeen and the Enlightenment*, Aberdeen: Aberdeen University Press, 189–98. (Draws out the subversive implications of Turnbull's view of the didactic functions of the fine arts for neoclassical art theory.)

Mackinnon, K.A.B. (1987) 'George Turnbull's Common Sense Jurisprudence', in J.J. Carter and J.H. Pittock (eds) *Aberdeen and the Enlightenment*, Aberdeen: Aberdeen University Press, 104–10. (A brief survey of the main themes of Turnbull's science of morals.)

Norton, D.F. (1975) 'George Turnbull and the Furniture of the Mind', *Journal of the History of Ideas* 35: 701–16. (The only substantial treatment of Turnbull's epistemology.)

Stewart, M.A. (1987) 'George Turnbull and Educational Reform', in J.J. Carter and J.H. Pittock (eds) *Aberdeen and the Enlightenment*, Aberdeen: Aberdeen University Press, 95–103. (A careful reconstruction of Turnbull's career.)

Wood, P.B. (1993) *The Aberdeen Enlightenment: The Arts Curriculum in the Eighteenth Century*, Aberdeen: Aberdeen University Press. (Discusses Turnbull's teaching career at Marischal College and his impact on the Aberdeen philosophical tradition.)

PAUL WOOD

AL-TUSI, KHWAJAH NASIR (1201–74)

While philosophical activity in the Islamic west virtually ceased after Ibn Rushd at the close of the sixth century AH (twelfth century AD), it experienced renewed vigour in the east through the intellectual efforts and political involvement of Nasir al-Din al-Tusi. Although primarily a reviver of the peripatetic tradition of Ibn Sina, he was also possibly influenced by the ideas of al-Suhrawardi. He defended Ibn Sina from the criticisms levelled against him from the direction of theology, notably by Fakhr al-Din al-Razi, made a significant contribution to the acceptance of metaphysical argumentation and terminology in Twelver Shi'i theology, brought the ethical tradition of Ibn Miskawayh and the philosophers into the centre of Islamic ethical discourse, and had a lasting effect on the study of the exact sciences in Islam through both his original contributions to mathematics and astronomy and the observatory at Maraghah which the Mongol Khan Hülegü established for him.

1   **Intellectual development**
2   **Logic, metaphysics and theology**
3   **Ethics, mathematics and the natural sciences**

1   Intellectual development

Al-Tusi's intellectual development cannot be divorced from the drama of his own life, and the catastrophe of the Mongol invasion of the Islamic east. From his birth in Tus in Khurasan in northwest Iran in AH 597/ AD 1201 up to his middle or late twenties, al-Tusi lived in a Twelver Shi'i milieu, in a family whose idea of learning was, according to his own account, the study of the religious law, and whose behaviour was measured by its practice. His jurist father, however, was sufficiently broad-minded to encourage him beyond scholastic studies to the philosophical and natural sciences, and to acquaint himself with the doctrines of other schools and sects. To study philosophy, al-Tusi went to nearby Nishapur, where he was taught by a scholar whose teaching lineage went back to Ibn Sina. Early in his career, as al-Tusi himself later wrote, he was not convinced that the intellect could answer the ultimate metaphysical questions, since it would thereby be inquiring into its own origins, something of which it would be incapable. Perhaps as a way out of his perplexity, and quite possibly as the result of sectarian connections through an uncle, he turned to the Isma'ilism of his day, which had been influenced by the Neoplatonic speculations of Isma'ili thinkers in the third and fourth centuries AH (ninth and tenth centuries AD). Isma'ili doctrine turned on the concept of an infallible Imam, without whose guidance, it claimed, the unaided intellect was unable to reach the truth.

From his late twenties or early thirties, al-Tusi was in the service of the local Isma'ili leaders of northern Iran, writing a number of theological and philosophical works for them in both Persian and Arabic and beginning his contribution to a major revival of Peripatetic philosophy in eastern Islamic lands. With the Mongol invasion of Iran in the middle of the thirteenth century the Isma'ili strongholds were destroyed, and al-Tusi found himself involved in the negotiations leading to the surrender of the Grand Isma'ili Master to the invaders. His efforts were appreciated by the Mongol conqueror Hülegü, who took him on as an advisor, in which capacity he assisted at the sacking of Baghdad in AH 656/AD 1258.

Later al-Tusi was put in charge of religious endowments and affairs. Hülegü also had the great observatory and library at Maraghah built for al-Tusi, where he led a team of scientists and mathematicians from as far away as China. It is clear that immense resources were put at his disposal for this project, where the teaching and study of philosophy went on hand in hand with that of the exact sciences.

The end of his Isma'ili period also marked al-Tusi's turn (or return) to Twelver Shi'ism, and the last period of his life witnessed not only a remarkable output of scientific works but also a reformulation of Imami theology in philosophical terms which was as influential in the Shi'i world as was that of Fakhr al-Din AL-RAZI in the Sunni. Al-Tusi died in AH 672/AD 1274 in Baghdad, in the same year as Thomas Aquinas. He was buried according to his last wishes beside the shrine of the seventh Twelver Imam, Musa ibn Ja'far, in Kazimayn just outside Baghdad. Among his most remarkable students were the philosopher Qutb al-Din al-Shirazi (d. AH 710/AD 1310) and the Imami jurist and theologian, the 'Allamah al-Hilli (d. AH 726/AD 1325).

If in his early life al-Tusi believed in the need for reason to be sustained by a non-rational (or suprarational) guarantor, his move to Twelver Shi'ism, with its doctrine of the hidden, inaccessible Imam, indicates a growing strength in his convictions about the ability of the intellect. His sectarian shifts have given rise to much argument concerning his genuine doctrinal loyalties, but throughout his life there runs a consistent philosophical thread whose main characteristic was the defence, rehabilitation and elaboration of Ibn Sina's method and theories. It is through his interpretations in texts, epitomes, commentaries and refutations that subsequent generations in the Islamic east have approached their understanding of Ibn Sina. His output as an author in both Arabic and Persian was prodigious, including lasting contributions to logic, metaphysics, ethics, mathematics and astronomy.

2 Logic, metaphysics and theology

Al-Tusi's main contribution to logic is contained in his Persian *Asas al-iqtibas* (The Ground for the Acquisition of Knowledge), written during his Isma'ili period. It is divided according to the habitual ten sections of the organon of the Islamic world, and its discussion of substance has recently attracted attention (Morewedge 1975). It also stands as a testimony to al-Tusi's ability to write about technical subjects in Persian, by incorporating Arabic terminology into a fluent and graceful style. An Arabic manual of logic by al-Tusi, the *Tajrid al-mantiq*

(Abstract of Logic), was commented on by his pupil the 'Allamah al-Hilli.

However, the major text on which al-Tusi's reputation as an interpreter of Ibn Sina's philosophy rests is his commentary on the *Kitab al-Isharat* (Remarks and Admonitions), written towards the end of his stay with the Isma'ilis. Al-Tusi's work was in part, at least, intended as a response to the commentary of Fakhr al-Din AL-RAZI on the same text. This work shows one of al-Tusi's continuing complaints, that those who attack Ibn Sina are generally ill-equipped as philosophers and that analysis can reveal their weaknesses. He is not averse to the use of polemic himself, but his insistence that a philosopher be evaluated in terms of the soundness of his argumentation and not according to preconceived ideas about conclusions demonstrates his faithfulness to Ibn Sina's own method. Thus, although on the whole defending Ibn Sina's theories, he disagrees with the latter when he sees fit. In his interpretation of emanation, for example, al-Tusi is partly in agreement with AL-SUHRAWARDI concerning the nature of God's knowledge, although he does not entirely reject Ibn Sina's theory of identity of form between knower and known as being applicable to other existents (see IBN SINA). God's knowledge of the First Intellect, and consequently of the entire universe, is identical with its existence through a kind of presential knowledge, while lower entities in the emanative chain derive their knowledge through forms and representations as well as through presence. Al-Tusi's commentary is clear and systematic, and is still studied with the original text because of his lucid explanations of Ibn Sina's often difficult and dense prose.

The texts discussed so far belong to al-Tusi's Isma'ili period, but the break with this past was decisively accomplished in *Masari' al-musari'* (The Floorings of the Wrestler), a refutation of an Isma'ili Neoplatonic text by the crypto-Isma'ili al-Shahrastani (d. AH 548/AD 1153) which attacked Ibn Sina for deviating from 'prophetic theology'. Al-Tusi's vehemently anti-Isma'ili defence of Ibn Sina is unreservedly polemical, using the same tactic of accusations of weak logic and feeble-mindedness which he had employed against al-Razi. Perhaps also a rejection of al-Tusi's own past, this text marks another stage in the development of his conviction of the superiority of philosophical thinking over religious dialectics.

Al-Tusi made several contributions to the field of metaphysical theology. The first attempt in this direction was an exposition of Isma'ili *qiyama* (resurrection) theology in his *Rawdat al-taslim* (The Garden of Submission), but of more enduring consequence was his later Twelver work, the *Tajrid al-kalam* (Abstract of Theology). This has been the subject of numerous commentaries down to the present century, the most important of which is the 'Allamah al-Hilli's *Kashf al-murad* (Disclosing the Intention). After the *Tajrid*, practically all Imami theological works would be expressed in the terminology of metaphysics, with MULLA SADRA eventually achieving a comprehensive and lasting fusion.

3 Ethics, mathematics and the natural sciences

There are two main works in al-Tusi's ethical output, the *Akhlaq-i Muhtashami* (Muhtashamean Ethics) and the *Akhlaq-i Nasiri* (The Nasirean Ethics), both written in Persian. The first of these was commissioned by the Isma'ili ruler (*muhtasham*) of Quhistan, Nasir al-Din 'Abd al-Rahman, who provided the outline and approved its contents but called in al-Tusi to do the major work because of the demands of his own political duties. This is scarcely more than a manual of ethical precepts, amply illustrated with quotations from the Qur'an, the Shi'i Imams and Greek sources. The *Akhlaq-i Nasiri*, the first 'edition' of which was dedicated to the same Nasir al-Din, is arranged as a work of philosophical ethics. Its divisions into three parts – ethics (*akhlaq*), domestic economics (*tadbir-e manzil*), politics (*siyasat-e mudun*) – set the pattern for subsequent works on practical philosophy in the Islamic tradition (see AL-DAWANI).

The first part on ethics is modelled on Ibn Miskawayh's *Tahdhib al-akhlaq* (Cultivation of Morals), of which the work was initially commissioned to be merely a Persian translation (see IBN MISKAWAYH). However, al-Tusi expands on Ibn Miskawayh both in the initial section on principles, mainly a theoretical treatment of psychology (the soul), and in his subsequent treatment of character and the virtues. This first part finishes with the addition of a section on the treatment of the vices as sicknesses of the soul, and of the cures to remedy them. The sources of the second part on domestic economics are the Arabic translation of Bryson's *Oikonomikos* and a text by Ibn Sina, his *Kitab al-siyasa* (Book of Politics), while the third part, on politics, goes back to al-Farabi's *Kitab al-siyasah al-madaniyyah* (The Political Regime) and *Fusul al-madani* (Aphorisms of the Statesman) (see AL-FARABI). The last part contains an important section on the virtue of love (*mahabbah*) as the cement of societies.

After al-Tusi joined Hülegü, he changed the introduction and conclusion to this work, excusing his previous praise of the Isma'ili leadership as the product of exigency. Moreover, he added that this was strictly a work of philosophy which transcended sectarian differences and was available to all. The work made available to Persian readers the Islamic

ethical tradition taken from Greek philosophy but now incorporating Qur'anic material alongside the opinions of Plato and Aristotle. Justice explicitly comes to the fore as the supreme virtue running through all three parts of the book, implicitly linking it with Shi'i theology and the priority given in the latter to justice among the divine attributes; and philosophical ethics and the religious law are stated to be concerned with the same subject matter, thus affirming the intellect's capacity to view normative values in a way which could only have been acceptable at that time within Shi'i circles (see ETHICS IN ISLAMIC PHILOSOPHY).

Throughout his life al-Tusi was a prolific writer in mathematics and the natural sciences, and made advances in trigonometry, mathematics and astronomy. This aspect of his intellectual endeavour was eventually rewarded with the foundation of the Maraghah observatory. The result of the astronomical observations and calculations made there was the famous tables of the *Zij-e Ilkhani* (in Persian, but also translated into Arabic). Prior to Maraghah, the rational sciences had been cultivated by individuals with (or without) private patronage, the schools in Islam being devoted almost entirely to the law and dismissive of, if not actually hostile to philosophical activity. The setting up of the observatory and the institutionalization of the rational sciences created a demand for teaching materials, and al-Tusi was himself the author of a number of recensions (*tahrir*) of scientific texts as well as summaries and abridgements of theological, logical, and philosophical texts, clearly intended to supply this teaching need. Al-Tusi's lasting influence can be seen in the subsequent surge of activity in the rational sciences in the Islamic east, as well as in their gradual absorption into religious education, which in turn affected the development of theology, particularly among Shi'i scholars (see SCIENCE IN ISLAMIC PHILOSOPHY).

See also: IBN SINA; AL-RAZI, FAKHR AL-DIN; SCIENCE IN ISLAMIC PHILOSOPHY

List of works

—— (1235, 1265) *Akhlaq-i Nasiri* (The Nasirean Ethics), trans. G.M. Wickens, London: George Allen & Unwin, 1964. (An excellent, meticulous translation of the *Akhlaq-ei Nasiri*, with a brief introduction and notes.)

—— (1242) *Rawdat al-taslim* (The Garden of Submission), trans. C. Jambet, *La convocation d'Alamût: somme de philosophie ismaélienne (Radat al-taslîm: Le jardin de vraie foi)*, Lagrasse and Paris:

Éditions Verdier and Éditions UNESCO, 1996. (A work of Isma'ili theology.)

—— (1244–5) *Asas al-iqtibas* (The Ground for the Acquisition of Knowledge), ed. M. Radawi, Tehran: Tehran University Press, 1947. (Al-Tusi's major logical text, in Persian.)

—— (probably after 1246) *Sayr wa suluk* (Contemplation and Action), ed. and trans. S.J.H. Badakhchani, London: Institute for Ismaili Studies, 1997. (This is the autobiography which al-Tusi wrote during his stay with the Isma'ilis, and is untinged with the complaints which he later made of this period in his life.)

—— (before 1258) *Sharh al-Isharat* (Commentary on the *Isharat*), ed. S. Dunya in Ibn Sina, *al-Isharat wa-'l-tanbihat*, Cairo: Dar al-Ma'arif, 1957–60, 4 parts, 3 vols in 2; also in Ibn Sina, *al-Isharat wa-'l-tanbihat*, Tehran: Matba'at al-Haydari, 1957–9, 3 vols. (Both these editions contain al-Tusi's commentary as parts of Fakhr al-Din al-Razi's commentary, to which al-Tusi is responding. The Tehran edition also contains Qutb al-Din al-Razi's commentary, which sets out to adjudicate between al-Tusi and al-Razi.)

al-Tusi (probably before 1270–1) *Tajrid al-kalam* (Abstract of Theology). (The text of this, al-Tusi's major theological work (also known as *Tajrid al-'aqa'id* and *Tajrid al-i'tiqad*), can be found in the commentary by his pupil Hasan ibn Yusuf ibn al-Mutahhar al-Hilli, *Kashf al-murad fi sharh tajrid al-i'tiqad*, Qum: Jama'at al-Mudarrisin, no date.)

References and further reading

Dabashi, H. (1995) 'Khwajah Nasir al-Din al-Tusi: The Philosopher/Vizier and the Intellectual Climate of His Times', in S.H. Nasr and O. Leaman (eds) *History of Islamic Philosophy*, London: Routledge: 527–84. (Good introduction to al-Tusi, his work and his times.)

Ibn Sina (980–1037) *Kitab al-isharat wa-'l-tanbihat* (Remarks and Admonitions), trans. A.-M. Goichon, *Livre des directives et remarques*, Beirut: Commission Internationale pour la Traduction des Chefs d'Oeuvres, and Paris: Vrin, 1951. (A useful French translation of Ibn Sina's text with introduction and notes by the translator; also contains many of al-Tusi's explanations in the notes, as well as some of his criticisms of al-Razi.)

Madelung, W. (1985) 'Nasir al-Din Tusi's Ethics Between Philosophy, Shi'ism, and Sufism', in R.G. Hovannisian (ed.) *Ethics in Islam*, Malibu, CA: Undena, 85–101. (Discusses the developments of al-Tusi's ethical ideas in relation to his political involvement and religious allegiances.)

* Morewedge, P. (1975) 'The Analysis of "Substance" in Tusi's *Logic* and in the Ibn Sinian tradition', in G. Hourani (ed.) *Essays on Islamic philosophy and science*, Albany, NY: State University of New York Press. (Morewedge is one of the few scholars to have made specific studies of al-Tusi's metaphysics, and this article discusses substance in the *Asas al-iqtibas*.)

Mudarris Radawi, M.T. (1975) *Ahwal wa athar-e ... Abu Ja'far Muhammad ... al-Tusi ...* (Life and Works of ... Abu Ja'far Muhammad ... al-Tusi ...), Tehran: Bunyad-e Farhang-e Iran. (In the absence of any comprehensive work on al-Tusi in a European language, it is necessary to turn to this Persian work which contains a comprehensive inventory of al-Tusi's works.)

JOHN COOPER

TWARDOWSKI, KAZIMIERZ (1866–1938)

Twardowski, one of the most distinguished of Brentano's students, became famous for his distinction between the content and object of presentations. Twardowski, after his appointment as a professor of philosophy at the University of Lwów (Lvov), considerably limited his own philosophical research for the sake of teaching activities. He set himself an ambitious task: to create a scientific philosophy in Poland. Twardowski fully realized his aim, giving the first step towards the so-called Lvov–Warsaw School, a group of philosophers working in analytic philosophy – in particular, logic, philosophy of science, and philosophy of language. In spite of his concentration on teaching, Twardowski also made remarkable contributions to philosophy after coming to Lwów.

1 Life and teaching activity
2 The conception of philosophy
3 The content–object distinction
4 Other contributions to philosophy

1 Life and teaching activity

Kazimierz Twardowski was born in Vienna on 10 October 1866. He was educated in a famous Viennese secondary school, *Theresianum*. In 1885–9 he studied philosophy at Vienna University, mainly under Franz BRENTANO. He obtained his Ph.D. in 1892 for a thesis on the relation between ideas and perception in DESCARTES. Two years later Twardowski obtained his *Habilitation* on the basis of a dissertation on the content and object of presentations. Having *venia legendi*, Twardowski started lecturing at the University of Vienna as *Privatdozent*. In 1895 he was appointed Professor of Philosophy at the University of Lwów. Twardowski came to Lwów with the definite aim of establishing a scientific philosophical school in Poland. Indeed he subordinated all his academic activities to the realization of this goal, which he regarded as an important national duty; when Twardowski came to Lwów, Poland was still partitioned between Germany, Russia and the Austro-Hungarian Empire. Twardowski spent the rest of his life in Lwów, where he died on 11 February 1938.

The results of Twardowski's activities as a teacher were enormous. Almost all important Polish philosophers of the first half of the twentieth century were his students, in particular Kazimierz AJDUKIEWICZ, Tadeusz KOTARBIŃSKI, Stanisław LEŚNIEWSKI, Jan ŁUKASIEWICZ and, briefly, Roman INGARDEN. Twardowski's teaching activity gave rise to the Lwów–Warsaw School, the most important school in the history of Polish philosophy.

2 The conception of philosophy

Following Brentano, Twardowski embraced a conception of philosophy as a science based on descriptive psychology. For Twardowski, scientific philosophy should avoid hopeless general problems, like the question whether the world is material or spiritual, and concentrate on particular problems which might be properly analysed. Twardowski regarded most traditional philosophical questions, particularly in metaphysics, as matters of faith and worldview rather than proper science. He strongly insisted that philosophy must begin with careful and precise clarifications, because otherwise it is simply impossible to understand what is going on in philosophical questions and discussions. Thus, a clear statement of a given question is the first duty of philosophers. Twardowski's general metaphilosophical claims decisively favoured some philosophical fields, like logic, semantics (in the broad sense: that is, including syntax, semantics as a theory of reference, and pragmatics), epistemology, and philosophy of science. This is why his students undertook their basic research in those areas of philosophy.

3 The content–object distinction

Twardowski adopted the main theses of Brentano's descriptive psychology, in particular his conception of the psychic as essentially intentional and his distinction between mental acts and their objects. Twardowski's main contribution to the Brentanist philosophical tradition consists in his having added to the act–object distinction a third ingredient: the content. In his *Habilitation* dissertation Twardowski gave a detailed analysis of the content–object distinction in the case of presentations. (see INTENTIONALITY).

Twardowski offers three direct arguments for introducing contents of presentations: (a) contents and objects cannot be identical, because true negative judgments which deny the existence of objects are based on presentations; their contents exist, their objects do not; (b) contents have properties which objects lack, and conversely objects have properties which contents lack; for example, redness as a property of an object cannot be attributed to the content of this object; (c) there are non-equivalent contents of presentations which refer to the same objects; for example, 'the city located at the site of Roman Juvavum', and 'the birthplace of Mozart'.

Twardowski observed that there is a close analogy between psychology and semantics. In particular, names and presentations are parallel, because names (a) make known acts of presentation which occur in the speaker, (b) arouse mental contents in the listener (for Twardowski, mental contents are meanings of names), (c) designate objects which are presented by meanings of names. This parallelism played a significant heuristic role in Twardowski's distinction. However, perhaps its more important function was that it led Twardowski to employ semantic analysis in descriptive psychology. Thus, Twardowski noted that when we use the expression 'a presented object', the adjective 'presented' may function as a determiner or as a modifier. This ambiguity is responsible for a confusion between contents and objects, in particular for the idealistic thesis that contents are genuine objects of our presentations. This observation led Twardowski to the realistic account of intentionality: our mental acts are usually directed to ordinary objects.

Twardowski extended his psychological and semantic analysis by important ontological considerations. Contrary to BOLZANO, he defended the thesis that there are no objectless presentations. He also outlined a mereological theory of objects of presentations.

Twardowski's *Habilitation* dissertation had considerable historical significance. It influenced MEINONG, in his general theory of objects, and Husserl's theory of intentionality. However, HUSSERL criticized Twardowski for psychologism and unclarities in the nature of content. Although the objection of psychologism was fully justified and recognized by Twardowski himself, Husserl's accusation that Twardowski fell into the picture theory of content is a misunderstanding.

4 Other contributions to philosophy

As already noted, Twardowski agreed that his account in his *Habilitation* dissertation was too psychologistic. Later he proposed an important distinction between actions and products. Twardowski begins by pointing out that there are characteristic pairs in which the first word is a verb (for example, sing, command) or a gerund (singing, commanding) and the second is a related noun (song, command). The first word refers to an action and the second to the product of that action. Products may be non-durable, for example the song which terminates when singing stops, or durable, for example the painting as a product of painting. Twardowski was mainly interested in durable psychophysical products. For Twardowski, such products express mental states and become their signs. In this sense, expressed mental states may be considered as meanings of the given signs. This scheme enables us to draw a distinction between logic and psychology. Psychology is primarily interested in actions, but logic in their durable products and their formal connections. Moreover, there is an obvious linkage between both fields, because meanings are generated by actions.

Twardowski strongly defended the view that there are no relative truths: if something is true, it is absolutely true. He argued that typical arguments for the existence of relative truths are based on simple confusions. For example, if one says that 'today it is raining' is an example of a relative truth, one forgets that this phrase expresses only an incomplete proposition. Once it is made complete (by indicating spatiotemporal coordinates), it becomes absolutely true. Also empirical hypotheses do not provide examples of relative truths. Twardowski points out that if we accept hypotheses as only probable, this means only that we do not know their actual logical values. If it turns out that a given hypothesis is at variance with fact, we consider it as false from the very beginning, and not as a proposition which changes its logical value.

See also: POLAND, PHILOSOPHY IN

List of works

Twardowski, K. (1892) *Idee und Perzeption: Eine erkenntnistheoretische Untersuchung aus Descartes*, Vienna: Konegen. (Twardowski's Ph.D. dissertation.)
—— (1894) *Zur Lehre vom Inhalt und Gegenstand der Vorstellungen: Eine psychologische Untersuchung*, Vienna: Hölder; 2nd edn, Munich: Philosophia-Verlag, 1982; trans. H. Grossmann, *On the Concept and Object of Presentations*, The Hague: Nijhoff, 1976. (Twardowski's *Habilitation* dissertation.)
—— (1998) *Selected Papers*, eds J. Brandl and J. Wolenski, Amsterdam: Rodopi. (This collection contains Twardowski's most important papers.)

References and further reading

Cavallin, J. (1990) *Content and Object: Husserl, Twardowski and Psychologism*, Stockholm: Department of Philosophy, University of Stockholm. (A detailed presentation of Twardowski's content–object distinction and Husserl's criticism of it; the book contains valuable bibliographical information.)
Smith, B. (1989) 'Kasimir Twardowski: An Essay on the Borderlines of Ontology, Psychology and Logic', in K. Szaniawski (ed.) *The Vienna Circle and the Lvov–Warsaw School*, Dordrecht: Kluwer, 312–73. (An extensive treatment of Twardowski's ontological views.)
Woleński, J. (1989) *Logic and Philosophy in the Lvov–Warsaw School*, Dordrecht: Kluwer. (Chapter II is devoted to Twardowski.)

JAN WOLEŃSKI

TWO-FOLD ARGUMENTS
see DISSOI LOGOI

TYPES, THEORY OF *see* THEORY OF TYPES

TYPE/TOKEN DISTINCTION

The type/token distinction is related to that between universals and particulars. C.S. Peirce introduced the terms 'type' and 'token', and illustrated the distinction by pointing to two senses of 'word': in one, there is only one word 'the' in the English language; in the other, there are numerous words 'the' on the physical page you are now looking at. The latter are spatiotemporal objects composed of ink; they are said to be word tokens of the former, which is said to be the word type and is abstract. Phonemes, letters and sentences also come in types and tokens.

The distinction between 'type' and 'token', or something very like it, seems to be applicable beyond language to, for example, Beethoven's *Fifth Symphony* and performances of it, the grizzly bear and specimens of it, the Kentucky Derby and runnings of it, and the bubonic plague and outbreaks of it. The type/token distinction is important to linguistics, logic, aesthetics and philosophy of science. In philosophy of mind it is critical to distinguish types of events/states/processes from tokens of them, because those who identify mental events with physical events agree that every mental event token is a physical event token, but divide over whether mental event types, for example, pain, are identical to physical event types, for example, C-fibre stimulation (see MIND, IDENTITY THEORY OF). Just what types are, whether they exist, whether they are 'present in' their tokens and whether all types have tokens are matters of controversy.

To see that we often refer to types, consider the grizzly bear. At one time its US range was most of the west and it numbered 10,000 in California alone. At the end of the twentieth century its range is Montana, Wyoming and Idaho, and it numbers fewer than 1,000. But no particular flesh and blood bear numbers 1,000 or once had a range comprising most of the western USA; if anything, it is a type which does. Similarly, Old Glory had twenty-nine stars in 1846 but fifty in 1996, whether or not any particular American flag underwent such a transformation; Old Glory is also a type.

This last example points to a related notion, that of an 'occurrence'. The stars on Old Glory number fifty; but fifty star *types* or fifty star *tokens*? In fact it cannot be either: not star types, because all the stars on the flag are of the same (five-pointed) type; nor star tokens, because tokens are concrete and the flag in question is abstract and cannot contain concrete parts. Old Glory contains fifty occurrences of the (five-pointed) star. Similarly, the letter '*x*' (the very same letter type) occurs three times in the formula (type) '$(\forall x)(Fx \rightarrow Gx)$'. Thus the notion of an occurrence of '*x*' must not be confused with the notion of a token of '*x*' (although it often is so confused). The notion of 'an occurrence of *x* in *y*' involves not only *x* and *y*, but also how *x* is situated in *y*. If we think of a formula as a sequence, then the air of mystery over how the same identical thing can occur twice vanishes. Even concrete particulars can occur more than once (for example, the same person occurs twice in the sequence of New Jersey million dollar lottery winners).

Tokens are particulars. Are types universals? They are if having instances makes something a universal. But in many ordinary and theoretical contexts, terms which refer to types function not as predicates but as singular terms, in sentences that permit existential generalization. ('The grizzly bear ranged over most of

the west' entails 'Something ranged over most of the west', for example.) As values of bound first-order variables, they meet a Quinean necessary condition for existence, and thus may also be viewed as particulars (see ONTOLOGICAL COMMITMENT §1).

Do types exist? If types are universals, then the debate over whether they exist goes back at least to Plato. Still, as the preceding paragraph noted, types seem to have an existential advantage over more traditional universals. (Quine held that expression types exist, though not more traditional universals (1987).) Nominalists who deny that there are any abstract objects argue that this is an illusion; that talk about types is just shorthand for talk about tokens. The matter cannot be resolved here, but it may be useful to examine one popular nominalistic account, namely, that every reference to a type (for example, 'The grizzly bear is ferocious') can be replaced without change of information by quantification over all tokens (for example, 'Every grizzly bear is ferocious'). One problem for this account is the existence of numerous counterexamples. 'The grizzly bear ranged over most of the west', for example, cannot be analysed as 'Every grizzly bear ranged over most of the west'. (Perhaps it can be analysed in some other 'type-free' way, but the point is that the nominalistic account under consideration cannot be the systematic one needed to eliminate all the many references to types which occur in our ordinary and scientific talk.)

A second problem is created by the implication that all types have tokens. Peirce (1931–58) claimed they do, but many thinkers since have denied this. Chomsky (1957), for example, claimed that there are sentences that never have been or will be instantiated – infinitely many. A third problem arises when we try to find a replacement for even a simple true sentence about, say, the word 'one', given the myriad senses it has, and the myriad forms its tokens may take: printed in ink in any number of fonts and handwritings, raised in Braille, incised in marble, existing briefly as so many pixels of light on a computer screen, electronic strings of dots and dashes, smoke signals, hand signals, individual air disturbances produced by human vocal cords, electromagnetic pulses on phone lines, pronounced (and mispronounced) in countless ways in countless accents. Even an (appropriately surrounded) empty space can be a token of 'one'. About the only thing all and only tokens of 'one' clearly have in common is being tokens of 'one' – the type, that is; if that word (type) does not exist, then they would seem to have nothing in common and hence no appropriate quantification could even be formulated.

See also: ABSTRACT OBJECTS; LOGICAL AND
MATHEMATICAL TERMS, GLOSSARY OF; UNIVERSALS

References and further reading

Block, N. (ed.) (1980) *Readings in Philosophy of
Psychology*, Cambridge, MA: Harvard University
Press, vol.1. (Includes numerous important articles
in philosophy of mind pertinent to the debate
between token materialists and type materialists.)

Bromberger, S. (1992) 'Types and Tokens in Linguistics', in *On What We Know We Don't Know*,
Chicago, IL: University of Chicago Press. (A fine
attempt to explain the relationship between types
and tokens, in order to explain how linguistics is an
empirical science although about abstract types.)

* Chomsky, N. (1957) *Syntactic Structures*, The Hague:
Mouton. (The classic attack on structuralism which
started the Chomskian revolution in linguistics.)

Goodman, N. (1951) *The Structure of Appearance*,
Dordrecht: Reidel, 3rd edn, 1977. (Although not a
book about types, Goodman's attempt to do
without them produces many instructive passages.)

Goodman, N. and Quine, W.V. (1947) 'Steps Toward a
Constructive Nominalism', *Journal of Symbolic
Logic* 12: 105–22; repr. in *Problems and Projects*,
Indianapolis, IN: Bobbs-Merrill, 1972. (A nomin-
alist attempt at proof theory without expression
types.)

Hale, R.J. (1987) *Abstract Objects*, Oxford and New
York: Blackwell. (An excellent discussion about
abstract objects generally, including types, and our
reasons for being justified in concluding they exist.)

Hutton, C. (1990) *Abstraction and Instance: The
Type–Token Relation in Linguistic Theory*, Oxford:
Pergamon. (By means of an impressive survey of
the relevant literature, Hutton argues that linguistic
theories rely uncritically on the type/token distinction (and on related notions such as that of
langue–parole and competence–performance) and
that all such accounts are problematic.)

Katz, J.J. (1981) *Language and Other Abstract Objects*,
Totowa, NJ: Rowman & Littlefield. (A robust
defence of languages and sentences as abstract
objects.)

* Peirce, C.S. (1931–58) *Collected Papers of Charles
Sanders Peirce*, ed. C. Hartshorne and P. Weiss,
Cambridge, MA: Harvard University Press, vol. 4,
para. 537; vol. 8, para. 334; vol. 2, para. 243–6.
(The eight-volume collection of Peirce's papers.)

* Quine, W.V. (1987) *Quiddities: An Intermittently
Philosophical Dictionary*, Cambridge, MA: Harvard University Press, 216–19. (This is Quine
distilled down to eighty-three alphabetically
arranged entries, including a two-page entry on
'Type versus Token'.)

Wetzel, L. (1993) 'What Are Occurrences of
Expressions?', *Journal of Philosophical Logic* 22:
215–20. (Provides an answer to the title question.)

Wollheim, R. (1968) *Art and Its Objects*, New York:
Harper & Row. (Argues that many works of art
cannot be physical objects/events or classes thereof,
but are types that none the less are 'present in' their
tokens.)

Wolterstorff, N. (1975) 'Toward an Ontology of Art
Works', *Noûs* 9: 115–42. (Wolterstorff argues that
many works of art are types, or 'kinds', and
proposes a suitable analysis of the notion of a kind.)

LINDA WETZEL

U

UDAYANA (11th century)

*Perhaps the most important philosopher of the Nyāya school, Udayana authored several works in the eleventh century which brought to a close the long-standing debate between Nyāya and Buddhist philosophers. The realist Nyāya philosophers had argued for the existence of an enduring self (*ātman*), a thesis denied by their Buddhist opponents. Such was the importance of this disagreement that it pervaded all other areas of philosophical contention between them. In the Ātmatattvaviveka (On the Discrimination of the Reality of the Self), Udayana systematically clarified the connections between the ātman debate and many other areas of philosophical dispute, with the result that, in defending ātman, he also produced a masterly defence of Nyāya realism. Udayana is also credited with giving the definitive defence of theism in the Nyāyakusumāñjali (A Handful of Nyāya-Tree Flowers).*

Tradition has it that Udayana came from Mithila in north-east India, a centre of great learning, especially for the Nyāya school. His life is shrouded in mythical tales of his brilliance. There is no question, however, about his pre-eminent place in the evolution of Nyāya thought. Udayana was the last of the Nyāya philosophers to enjoy the stimulus of a powerful Buddhist opposition, for it was shortly after his death that Buddhism began to disappear from India. After Buddhism's demise, Nyāya thought became characterized by increasing subtlety of argument and a greater preoccupation with method than with content. Although Navya-Nyāya (New Nyāya), as the school in its later period is called, is usually said to date from the fourteenth century, the subtlety of Udayana's work is such that some critics regard him as its real source. Certainly Udayana's style and rigour look forward to Navya-Nyāya, but at the same time his work brings to fruition the arguments that traditional Nyāya philosophers had developed in their efforts to defeat the Buddhists. While no one would want to credit the demise of Buddhism in India to Udayana's polemics, the quality of the philosophical exchange between him and his Buddhist opponent, the monk Jñānaśrīmitra, represents one of the greatest achievements of Indian philosophy.

In the *Ātmatattvaviveka* (On the Discrimination of the Reality of the Self), Udayana states that there are four main theses which the Buddhists give to refute the existence of *ātman* (Self): (1) all existent things are momentary; (2) there are no objects external to our judgments; (3) there is no difference between an object and its qualities; and (4) the *ātman* is not perceived. Apart from the last thesis, it can be seen that the Buddhist denial of *ātman* is a consequence of a more general argument about the nature of reality (see MOMENTARINESS, BUDDHIST DOCTRINE OF). Udayana concentrates his arguments against these general theses rather than arguing about *ātman* in particular, and it is this that gives the work its philosophical breadth and interest.

For example, the thesis of universal momentariness not only rules out the possibility of an enduring *ātman*, but is also the antithesis of Nyāya's realist view of the world and becomes a denial of the enduring existence of everything, from the *ātman* to the kitchen pot. Thus Udayana denies any concomitance between existence and momentariness and attacks the related notion of causal efficacy. It is only when causal efficacy is understood to mean the immediate production of an effect that the concomitance between existence and momentariness is established. Jñānaśrīmitra states that an enduring entity is incapable of causal efficacy and so lacks existence. The relationship between a dormant seed in the granary and a sprouting seed in the field is the locus for this debate. For the Buddhist argument to succeed, the nature of causal efficacy must be such that it creates a difference in identity between the nonsprouting granary seed and the sprouting field seed. Udayana argues for an interpretation of causal efficacy which allows for one and the same object to be causally efficacious at one time and not at another, thus allowing for the continuity of the granary seed with the field seed. He argues that to be causally potent does not mean that a cause must produce its effect immediately, but rather that it has the potential to do so given the presence of the right accessories – in the case of the seed, such things as sunshine and water. Udayana notes that we call seeds in the granary 'seeds' precisely because of their potential to produce sprouts. He charges that the Buddhists are not even entitled to call the seeds in the granary 'seeds' if, as they claim, those seeds are not responsible for the final production of sprouts. According to Udayana, the capacity or disposition of a seed to produce a sprout ultimately depends on the universal 'seedness' inhering in each individual seed. The presence of this universal along with the necessary accessories allows a nonproductive seed to become productive. The Buddhist position represents a lapse into chaos, where sprouts can be produced without seeds, and seeds are deprived of their very nature. Udayana's detailed critique of the Buddhist understanding of causality was accepted as definitive by later Nyāya philosophers (see CAUSATION, INDIAN THEORIES OF §§5–6).

Although real universals were essential to Udayana's attack on the Buddhist account of causality, and although he was a severe critic of Buddhist nominalism, he did recognize that not all general terms represent universals that have an independent reality (see NOMINALISM, BUDDHIST DOCTRINE OF §§1–2; UNIVERSALS, INDIAN THEORIES OF §§2–3). UDDYOTAKARA had distinguished real universals, such as 'cowness', from those constructed by us, such as the property of being a cook. In the *Kiraṇāvalī* (Garland of Rays), Udayana contributed to the debate by giving a list of formal conditions which distinguish real universals (*jāti*) from those that are convenient devices of our own construction (*upādhi*). Some contemporary philosophers of language have noted an affinity between Udayana's *jāti* and what are now called 'natural kinds'.

Despite Udayana's obvious flair for rigorous philosophical debate, he did not abandon the traditional soteriological concerns of philosophy. In the *Nyāyakusumāñjali* (A Handful of Nyāya-Tree Flowers), he defends the theism of his school by developing a rational theology, using arguments that would be familiar to Western theologians. We infer the existence of God, for example, from our experience of order in the world, just as we infer the existence of a potter from the presence of a pot. For Udayana, the realism of the Nyāya school provided the most coherent support for *ātman* and, in a remarkable passage in the *Ātmatattvaviveka*, he places Nyāya at the pinnacle of philosophical thought. In accordance with the Nyāya system, he emphasizes that liberation cannot just be a matter of transcendental experience, but must incorporate correct philosophical knowledge.

See also: NYĀYA-VAIŚEṢIKA

List of works

A great deal of Udayana's work remains to be translated from the Sanskrit. His works are listed below in chronological order. These are the Sanskrit texts unless indicated otherwise.

Udayana (11th century) *Lakṣaṇāvalī* (The Garland of Definitions), ed. G. Jha, Darbhanga: Mithila Institute Series 13, 1963; trans. M. Tachikawa, in *The Structure of the World in Udayana's Realism*, Dordrecht: Reidel, 1981. (A manuscript on the categories of the Vaiśeṣika school.)

—— (11th century) *Lakṣaṇamāla* (The Wreath of Definitions), ed. G. Jha, Darbhanga: Mithila Institute Series 14, 1964. (A manual on the categories of the Nyāya school.)

—— (11th century) *Ātmatattvaviveka* (On the Discrimination of the Reality of the Self), ed. D. Sastri, Varanasi: Chowkhamba, 1940. (A comprehensive survey of the Buddhist arguments against the existence of the self or *ātman*. In countering these arguments, Udayana also gives a defence of the realism of the Nyāya school.)

—— (11th century) *Nyāyapariśiṣṭa* (The Nyāya Appendix), ed. N.C. Vedantatirtha, Calcutta: Calcutta Sanskrit Series, 1938. (A commentary on the fifth chapter of the *Nyāyasūtra*, the foundational text of the Nyāya school.)

—— (11th century) *Nyāyavārttika-tātparyaṭīkā-pariśuddhi* (An Exoneration of the *Nyāyavārttika-tātparyaṭīkā*), ed. L.S. Dravid and V.P. Dvivedin, Calcutta: Bibliotheca Indica, 1911; trans. in part in Jha, G., *The Nyāya-Sūtras of Gautama with the Bhāṣya of Vātsyāyana and the Vārtika of Uddyotakara*, Delhi: Motilal Banarsidass, 1984. (A partially extant work which continues with the tradition of building on previous subcommentaries on the *Nyāyasūtra*, in this case Vācaspati Miśra's commentary, the *Nyāyavārttika-tātparyaṭīkā*, which is itself a commentary on Uddyotakara's *Nyāyavārttika*.)

—— (11th century) *Nyāyakusumāñjali* (A Handful of Nyāya-Tree Flowers), ed. L.S. Dravid and N.C. Vedantatirtha, Calcutta: Kashi Sanskrit Series, 1912; Books 1 and 2 trans. Ravitirtha, *Adyar Library Bulletin* 5 (1941), 6 (1942), 7 (1943), 10 (1946). (Considered by some to be Udayana's greatest work, in which he gives a definitive defence of the Nyāya conception of God.)

—— (11th century) *Kiraṇāvalī* (The Garland of Rays), ed. Sivachandra Sarvabhauma and N.C. Vedantatirtha, Calcutta: Bibliotheca Indica, 1956. (A commentary on Praśastapāda's *Padārthadharmasaṇgraha*, an early, foundational work on the Vaiśeṣika system. Portions of the *Kiraṇāvalī* are translated in Tachikawa 1981.)

References and further reading

Dravid, R. (1971) *The Problem of Universals in Indian Philosophy*, Varanasi: Motilal Banarsidass. (Chapter 11 of this survey focuses on Udayana's arguments against the Buddhist theory of meaning as presented by Jñānaśrīmitra and Ratnakīrti.)

Matilal, B.K. (1977) *A History of Indian Literature*, vol. 6, *Scientific and Technical Literature*, Wiesbaden: Otto Harrassowitz. (Part 3, fasc. 2 is about Nyāya–Vaiśeṣika, and contains a translation of a small portion of the *Ātmatattvaviveka*.)

—— (1986) *Perception: An Essay on Classical Indian Theories of Knowledge*, Oxford: Clarendon Press. (In this comprehensive work describing the epistemological differences between the Nyāya realists and their Buddhist opponents there are frequent references to Udayana's contributions.)

Phillips, S.H. (1995) *Classical Indian Metaphysics*, La Salle, IL: Open Court. (Although the focus of this book is on the debate between the New Nyāya school and the Advaitin philosopher Śrīharṣa in the period immediately after Udayana, it does contain frequent references to him, and one chapter is devoted to the views of traditional Nyāya philosophers up to and including Udayana.)

Potter, K.H. (ed.) (1977) *Encyclopedia of Indian Philosophies*, vol. 2, *Nyāya Vaiśeṣika*, Delhi: Motilal Banarsidass. (A comprehensive introduction to the Nyāya–Vaiśeṣika system, containing detailed summaries of all known Nyāya-Vaiśeṣika works.)

Sastri, D.N. (1964) *The Philosophy of Nyāya-Vaiśeṣika and its Conflict with the Buddhist Dignāga School*, Delhi: Bharatiya Vidya Prakashan. (A detailed account of the defence of Nyāya realism in the face of Buddhist opposition. Although the focus is on philosophers of an earlier period, there are frequent references to Udayana and his role in this philosophical debate.)

Sharma, D. (1969) *The Differentiation Theory of Meaning in Indian Logic*, The Hague: Mouton. (Sharma introduces his translation of Ratnakīrti's *Apohasiddhi* by describing the differences separating Nyāya and Buddhist theories of meaning.)

Tachikawa, M. (1981) *The Structure of the World in Udayana's Realism*, Dordrecht: Reidel. (Contains translations of the *Lakṣaṇāvalī* and the *Kiraṇāvalī*.)

JOY LAINE

UDDYOTAKARA (6th century)

Uddyotakara, a philosopher of the Nyāya school, wrote the Nyāyavārttika, *a lengthy commentary on the* Nyāyasūtra. *His most urgent task was to re-establish the authority of the Nyāya school in the face of extensive criticism from the great Buddhist logician* Dignāga. *Dignāga had been particularly critical of the logical work of Vātsyāyana, Uddyotakara's predecessor. In response, Uddyotakara incorporated Dignāga's logical work into the Nyāya school, and added his own interpretation. He was less receptive to Dignāga's other views, especially his account of perception and its relation to language.*

Uddyotakara ('The Enlightener') was sometimes referred to as a Pāśupata teacher, indicating membership of a particular sect of devotees of Śiva. It is not therefore surprising to find in him a strong proponent of theism. Certainly since Vātsyāyana, Nyāya contained an element of theism inasmuch as God was recognized as a substantial Self distinct from other selves. Uddyotakara, however, gives a much fuller articulation of the Nyāya conception of God as creator, as omnipotent and as being beyond *dharma*. His arguments in support of such a God became an important aspect of the Nyāya tradition. Udayana's classic defence of theism, in his *Nyāyakusumāñjali* (A Handful of Nyāya-Tree Flowers), was the culmination of Uddyotakara's efforts in this vein.

Uddyotakara's importance for the Nyāya school, however, lies in his response to DIGNĀGA. A skilled logician himself, he fully appreciated Dignāga's work. Dignāga had grasped the formal character of inference and had formulated three conditions under which the reason given for a thesis would result in a correct inference. Uddyotakara's acceptance of his opponent's analysis of logical inference was mitigated by his criticisms of its details. He demonstrated that Dignāga's three conditions actually mask sixteen possible ways in which the reason could be combined with the other members of the inference. Thus a more precise analysis would be needed to demarcate correct and incorrect inferences (see INFERENCE, INDIAN THEORIES OF §§5–6).

In other areas Uddyotakara asserted his differences with Dignāga more vehemently. Unlike Nāgārjuna, Vātsyāyana's opponent, Dignāga offered a clearly articulated metaphysics in opposition to Nyāya realism. In his system there is a radical break between language and the world. The world is made up of unique momentary particulars (*svalakṣaṇas*) whose fleeting existence can be grasped only by perception. The judgments that we make about the world and express in language create a set of fictional categories, such as physical objects and universals, which are a result of our mental construction. Uddyotakara opposed this view by reaffirming and expanding Vātsyāyana's arguments for the perceptual basis of physical objects (see VĀTSYĀYANA). He also initiated the Nyāya opposition to the Buddhist theory of meaning, known as *apohavāda*, which originated with

Dignāga. Dignāga had avoided all commitment to any real basis for the terms of our language, such as universals, by proposing that words derive their meaning and usefulness on the basis of a common exclusion, rather than any set of properties held in common.

Since the *Nyāyasūtra* had given a definition of perception as being that which is not expressible, it might seem that Dignāga's separation of perception from language was in accord with them. Uddyotakara's commentary reaffirms Vātsyāyana's interpretation of this *sūtra* (1.1.4). Like Vātsyāyana, he states that the purpose of defining perception in this way is to stress that, since perception comes about as a result of contact between object and sense organ, no linguistic skills are necessary for its occurrence. This does not mean, however, that when we acquire those skills and begin to make judgments about our perceptions we are superimposing mental constructs, which have no basis in reality.

Hence for Uddyotakara physical objects are perceptual 'firsts' and he produces a dazzling array of counterarguments to defend Nyāya realism against Dignāga's offensive. As with Vātsyāyana, the recurring theme is that without the acceptance of a whole distinct from its component parts, we cannot explain how we arrive at the notion of an object such as a tree (see SENSE PERCEPTION, INDIAN VIEWS OF §5). An additional argument which Uddyotakara uses concerns the relationship between vision and touch. For the Buddhist, there is no single entity apprehended by both vision and touch, so that we do not see the very same jar that we touch. Our conception of a jar arises from grouping a particular set of perceptual qualities together. Uddyotakara therefore argues from the premise that we do in fact have a cognition of a jar, and that only the Nyāya view of a substance as separate from its qualities can explain this cognition that we all have. Udayana, in the *Ātmatattvaviveka* (On the Discrimination of the Reality of the Self), was later to argue this same point in meticulous detail. Uddyotakara also addresses the difficult question of exactly how the whole is related to its parts. In answer to the question whether the whole resides in each of its parts partially or in its entirety, Uddyotakara replies that neither alternative is applicable. He resists all attempts to pull the whole apart and compares it to other entities, such as numbers, that are indivisible yet can be present in several things.

Uddyotakara employs a very similar argument when explaining the relationship between a universal (such as 'cowness') and the individual objects in which the universal is manifested (in this case, individual cows). As in the above argument, Uddyotakara deflects the question as to whether the universal is present in the individual in its entirety or in part. Universals are simple entities not subject to partition in this way, and they are related to the appropriate individuals by the relation of 'inherence'. Despite Uddyotakara's efforts, there is no doubt that the notion of real universals remains problematic for the Nyāya system. It might seem puzzling that the Naiyāyikas clung to it, especially given Uddyotakara's recognition that in many instances we can explain our use of a common noun without invoking real universals. It would be a mistake, Uddyotakara tells us, to conjure up the notion of 'cookness' to explain how we label a variety of individuals as cooks. People are cooks in virtue of the fact that they all perform the common action of cooking, not in virtue of some universal inhering in them. Uddyotakara demonstrates a sophisticated understanding of language in his recognition that no uniform account can be given of how general terms function in a language. Many contemporary philosophers of language would agree. The role of real universals, such as 'cowness', was crucial, however, in the Nyāya account of causality (see UDAYANA) and in their attack on the Buddhist negative theory of meaning (*apohavāda*).

See also: NOMINALISM, BUDDHIST DOCTRINE OF; NYĀYA–VAIŚEṢIKA; UNIVERSALS, INDIAN THEORIES OF §§2–3

List of works

Uddyotakara (6th century) *Nyāyavārttika*, in G. Jha (trans.) *The Nyāya-Sūtras of Gautama with the Bhāṣya of Vātsyāyana and the Vārttika of Uddyotakara*, Delhi: Motilal Banarsidass, 4 vols, 1984. (This four-volume set gives a translation of Uddyotakara's *vārttika*, which can be read alongside the *sūtra* and the *bhāṣya*.)

References and further reading

Matilal, B.K. (1971) *Epistemology, Logic and Grammar in Indian Philosophical Analysis*, The Hague: Mouton. (A detailed account of the differences between the Nyāya and Buddhist schools, with particular references to theories of perception and language. Contains frequent references to Uddyotakara.)

—— (1977) *A History of Indian Literature*, vol. 6, *Scientific and Technical Literature*, Wiesbaden: Otto Harrassowitz. (Part 3, fasc. 2 deals with Nyāya-Vaiśeṣika.)

* *Nyāyasūtra* (*c*.400 AD) trans. G. Jha, *The Nyāya-Sūtras of Gautama with the Bhāṣya of Vātsyāyana and the Vārttika of Uddyotakara*, Delhi: Motilal

Banarsidass, 4 vols, 1984. (Complete translation with detailed notes.)

Phillips, S.H. (1995) *Classical Indian Metaphysics*, La Salle, IL: Open Court. (Although this study of Indian metaphysics focuses on the philosophers of a later period of the Nyāya school, there is a chapter specifically about the earlier Nyāya philosophers, including Uddyotakara.)

Potter, K.H. (ed.) (1977) *Encyclopedia of Indian Philosophies*, vol. 2, *Nyāya Vaiśeṣika*, Delhi: Motilal Banarsidass. (A comprehensive introduction to the Nyāya-Vaiśeṣika system, containing detailed summaries of all known Nyāya-Vaiśeṣika works.)

Sastri, D.N. (1964) *The Philosophy of Nyāya-Vaiśeṣika and its Conflict with the Buddhist Dignāga School*, Delhi: Bharatiya Vidya Prakashan. (A detailed account of the defence of Nyāya realism in the face of Buddhist opposition. There are frequent references to Uddyotakara and his role in this long philosophical dispute.)

JOY LAINE

ÛISANG (605–702)

Ûisang was the founder of the Korean branch of the Flower Garland (Hwaôm; in Chinese, Huayan) school of East Asian Buddhism which emerged as the main scholastic tradition within Korean Buddhism, thanks in large measure to Ûisang himself. His works emphasize the unimpeded interpenetration that Hwaôm posits to pertain between all phenomena in the universe.

Ûisang was ordained in the Silla kingdom of Korea, but soon decided to make a pilgrimage to the mecca of the Chinese mainland to study with Chinese teachers. After one unsuccessful attempt in 650, when he was repatriated to Silla on suspicion of espionage, Ûisang eventually arrived in Tang China in 661, where he became one of the principal disciples of the second patriarch of the Chinese Huayan school, Zhiyan (602–68). After his teacher's death he emerged as one of the two leaders of Zhiyan's congregation, along with FAZANG (643–712). In 670, however, Ûisang learned of an imminent Chinese invasion of Korea and promptly returned to Korea to warn his king of the danger. The invasion forestalled, Ûisang was rewarded with munificent royal support and his Flower Garland School dominated Korean Buddhist scholasticism from that point onward.

Ûisang's works, though few in number, were extremely influential throughout East Asia and contributed much to establishing the doctrinal foundations for a distinctively Korean tradition of Buddhism. His vision of Buddhism is laid out in summary form in his principal work, the *Hwaôm ilsûng pôpkyedo* (Diagram of the Flower Garland One-Vehicle Realm-of-Reality), a verse of 210 Chinese characters with accompanying autocommentary, written in 668 while he was still in China. The chart is a novel attempt to represent diagrammatically all the teachings of the *Avataṃsakasūtra* (Flower Garland Scripture). Ûisang's poem is arranged in a wavelike form, the 'Ocean seal diagram' (*sagaramudrā-maṇḍala*), which represents the Flower Garland teaching of the 'six marks': universality and particularity, identity and difference, and integration and disintegration. The totality of the diagram represents the marks of universality, identity and integration, while its sinuous curves represent particularity, difference and disintegration. The one continuous line of the chart, upon which each individual logograph of the poem is superimposed, demonstrates the cardinal Flower Garland doctrine of the unimpeded interpenetration between all independent phenomena in the universe. The meanderings of the line of verse around the diagram's fifty-four corners symbolize the pilgrimage of the lad Sudhana to spiritual teachers, as recounted in the lengthy 'Entering the Realm of Reality' (*Gaṇḍavyūha*) chapter of the *Avataṃsakasūtra*. The fact that the snaking line of verse begins and ends at the same spot on the diagram illustrates the Hwaôm doctrine of soteriological interpenetration: the initial arousing of the thought of enlightenment (*bodhicittotpāda*), the inception of spiritual practice, is the same as complete, perfect enlightenment (*anuttarasamyaksaṃbodhi*), the consummation of that practice. Ûisang's autocommentary helps to elaborate the doctrinal implications of the diagram's visual form, creating a uniquely East Asian type of philosophical document.

See also: BUDDHIST PHILOSOPHY, CHINESE; BUDDHIST PHILOSOPHY, KOREAN; FAZANG

List of works

Ûisang (625–702) Collected works, in *Han'guk Pulgyo chônsô* (Collected Works of Korean Buddhism), ed. Han'guk Pulgyo chônsô p'yônch'an wiwônhoe, Seoul: Tongguk University Press, vol. 2, 1–9. (The standard Korean edition of Ûisang's works.)

—— (668) *Hwaôm ilsûng pôpkyedo* (Diagram of the Flower Garland One-Vehicle Realm-of-Reality), trans. S. Odin in *Process Metaphysics and Hua-yen Buddhism: A Critical Study of Cumulative Penetration vs. Interpenetration*, Albany, NY: State University of New York Press, 1982. (The diagram, along with its autocommentary, is translated in the appendix, though without annotation.)

References and further reading

Odin, S. (1982) *Process Metaphysics and Hua-yen Buddhism: A Critical Study of Cumulative Penetration vs. Interpenetration*, Albany, NY: State University of New York Press. (The expository section includes a comparative treatment of Ûisang and Whitehead.)

ROBERT E. BUSWELL, JR

ULRICH OF STRASBOURG (*c.*1220/5–1277)

A Dominican theologian and philosopher and a student of Albert The Great, Ulrich was well known for a widely studied summa theologiae, De summo bono *(On the Supreme Good), which represents an advance over previous summae in plan and organization. Ulrich provides a rich synthesis of Christian Neoplatonic theology and mysticism by systematizing the Aristotelianized Neoplatonic philosophical theologies of Albert the Great, Pseudo-Dionysius'* De divinis nominibus *and the* Liber de causis. *He exercised a notable influence on the Rhineland mystics.*

Ulrich was a student of ALBERT THE GREAT at Cologne between 1248 and 1254; his fellow students included Thomas AQUINAS and Hugh of Strasbourg. Ulrich was both a popular lecturer in theology at Strasbourg and, during the last five years of his life, the influential provincial of the German province. Ulrich was an intimate friend of Albert and his regular walking companion. Their long, warm friendship is evident in extant letters.

During the thirteenth century, Albert was the great figure in the Dominican school at Cologne from which his scientific interests and philosophical theology were transmitted through his immediate students Ulrich and Hugh to later important figures such as DIETRICH OF FREIBERG and to the Rhineland mystics MEISTER ECKHART, John TAULER and Henry SUSO. The dominant philosophical influences in the school were ARISTOTLE, PROCLUS, Avicenna (see IBN SINA), AL-FARABI, AUGUSTINE, the *Liber de causis* (see LIBER DE CAUSIS) and PSEUDO-DIONYSIUS the Areopagite. Ulrich is deeply indebted to Albert's complex synthesis of the Augustinian theology of WILLIAM OF AUXERRE and WILLIAM OF AUVERGNE, which was enriched with Aristotle's precise terminol-

ogy, and the Neoplatonic ontology of Proclus and Pseudo-Dionysius.

Ulrich's works included commentaries on Aristotle's *Meteorology* and on Peter Lombard's *Sentences*. His only extant work is the summa *De summo bono* (On the Supreme Good), composed between 1262 and 1272. Probably completed in eight books, the surviving manuscripts end at Book 6 tractate 5 and fill more than 600 folios; publication of the text is still in progress. The importance of the treatise is evident from the large number of manuscripts circulating in the thirteenth and fourteenth centuries. Ulrich was widely considered one of the most important Dominican thinkers after Albert and Thomas.

The treatise is organized according to an architectonic scheme derived from Peter LOMBARD. Book 1 concerns theology as science of the highest good; Book 2 concerns the being of the highest good; Book 3 concerns the Trinity; Book 4 concerns the Father and creation; Book 5 concerns Christ; Book 6 (200 folios) concerns the Holy Spirit and its ethical workings in human psychology; Book 7 concerns the sacraments; and Book 8 concerns beatitude and the attainment of the highest good (see GOOD, THEORIES OF THE §1). The central themes of Ulrich's philosophical theology are presented in Books 1, 2 and 4.

The pervasive influence on Ulrich of the Christian Neoplatonist Pseudo-Dionysius is evident in the first two books, which comprise a loose commentary on the latter's *De divinis nominibus* (On the Divine Names). In Book 1 tractate 1, the Neoplatonic metaphysics of light lays the foundation for an account of how the mind can know God. We know that God exists and what God is by means of the light conveyed by the angelic intelligences from the divine nature itself, both of which illuminate the agent intellect, the natural image of God in us. The theory of illumination endows the mind with the capacity to understand God in three ways: first, the negation of finite and imperfect properties generates infinite perfections which are worthy of the divine nature (symbolic theology); second, God is identified as the cause and source of all perfections (positive theology); and third, all properties are transcended in God (mystical theology) (see GOD, CONCEPTS OF).

Book 1 tractate 2 argues that theology must be a supernatural science since even our natural knowledge of God's effects is not based on the dark and defective human intellect. It is faith, therefore, which presents God as the object of this science, and theology which grasps scientifically what is believed: God in himself and in his attributes, and God as both the supreme cause or first principle of creation and the supreme end or salvational goal of all. With

517

greater precision and clarity than many scholastics, Ulrich articulates first principles for theological inquiry. In an Aristotelian manner, he argues that the four absolute first principles of theology, from which all other truths can be known, are immediately self-evident, again by means of intellectual illumination: (1) God is the highest truth and the source of all truth; (2) this primary truth is infallible and warrants unconditional faith; (3) God's spokespersons must be believed; and (4) since it is inspired by God, Scripture must be true. It is only on the basis of the certain knowledge of these rules that the articles of faith, which are not evident in themselves, can be established. Book 2 expounds the divine names, divine substance and the transcendentals.

Book 4 tractate 1 examines the First Principle and its relations with created beings, and offers a compendium of Ulrich's doctrines in metaphysics, natural theology and cosmogony. His metaphysics of being derives from the *Liber de causis*: that 'being is the first among created things'. This Neoplatonic formulation holds that being is the first expression of or 'outflow' (*emanatio*) from God; it is the first form and basis of all other forms. Since being is universal it is indefinable in itself; but since being is mixed with non-being, it differs from the pure absolute being of God (see BEING). Ulrich stresses that God must be distinguished from this universal being in order to avoid pantheism. The two realities also differ fundamentally as regards unity and relations. Universal being is not absolutely simple since it stands in real relations to non-being and God, for example, whereas God's pure unity is not abrogated by the relations of created beings to him. The rest of Book 4 comprises an extensive discussion of the Aristotelian causes and categories (tractate 2) and of transcendent substances and their mode of knowledge (tractate 3).

Ulrich's neglected treatise is a rich synthesis of the Christianized version of Neoplatonic themes scattered throughout the voluminous writings of Albert the Great. These include the identity of being and form, the hierarchy of intellects (Avicenna) combined with the doctrine of angels (Pseudo-Dionysius), the emanation of beings and forms from God via the process of universal illumination, and the confluence of being and value in the supreme principle.

See also: ALBERT THE GREAT; LIBER DE CAUSIS; PSEUDO-DIONYSIUS

List of works

Ulrich of Strasbourg (1262–72) *De summo bono* (On the Supreme Good), Corpus philosophorum Teutonicum Medii Aevi, Book 1 ed. A. de Libera and B. Mojsisch, Book 2 tractates 1–4 ed. A. de Libera, Book 4 tractates 1, 2 and 7 ed. S. Pieperhoff, Hamburg: F. Meiner, 1987–9. (Earlier partial editions include Book 1, ed. J. Daguillon, *La 'Summa de bono'. Livre I*, Paris: Vrin, 1930; Book 4, tractate 1 in F.J. Lescoe, *God as First Principle in Ulrich of Strasbourg*, New York: Alba House, 1979, 145–242.)

—— (1272–7) Letters, in H. Finke (ed.) *Ungedruckte Dominikanerbriefe des 13. Jahrhunderts*, Paderborn: F. Schoningh, 1891, 78–104. (Edition of collected letters.)

References and further reading

Backes, I. (1975) *Die Christologie, Soteriologie und Mariologie des Ulrich von Strassburg: ein Beitrag zur Geistegeschichte des 13. Jahrhunderts* (The Christology, Soteriology and Mariology of Ulrich of Strasbourg: A Contribution to Thirteenth-Century Intellectual History), Trier: Paulinus-Verlag. (The most extensive study of central topics in Ulrich's theology.)

Grabmann, M. (1926) 'Studien über Ulrich von Strassburg' (Studies on Ulrich of Strasbourg), in M. Grabmann, *Mittelalterliches Geistesleben: Abhandlungen zur Geschichte der Scholastik und Mystik*, Munich: Max Hueber, vol. 1, 147–221. (A comprehensive survey of Ulrich's life, the manuscripts of his treatise and a summary of its contents.)

Lescoe, F.J. (1979) *God as First Principle in Ulrich of Strasbourg*, New York: Alba House. (As well as the edited but untranslated text of Book 4 tractate 1, Lescoe provides a comprehensive discussion of the authenticity and contents of the entire treatise, a detailed study of the central metaphysical themes in Ulrich's thought, and an extensive bibliography which is especially useful for information on the many bits and pieces of Ulrich's treatise that have been edited and studied in unpublished doctoral dissertations.)

Putnam, C. (1961) 'Ulrich of Strasbourg and the Aristotelian Causes', in J.K. Ryan (ed.) *Studies in Philosophy and the History of Philosophy* vol. I, 139–59. (Useful account of Ulrich's adaptation of Aristotelian causal theory within a Neoplatonic ontology.)

Théry, G. (1922) 'Originalité du plan de la Summa de Bono d'Ulrich de Strasbourg', *Revue Thomiste* 27: 376–97. (Demonstrates that Books 1–2 of the treatise comment on Pseudo-Dionysius' *De divinis nominibus*.)

JOHN BUSSANICH

UMASVATI *see* Jaina philosophy

UNAMUNO Y JUGO, MIGUEL DE (1864–1936)

The Spanish philosopher-poet Miguel de Unamuno upheld a heterodoxical Catholicism, resembling much nineteenth-century Liberal Protestantism, which viewed reason and faith as antagonistic. By 'reason', he understood scientific induction and deduction; by 'faith', a sentiment varying with his readings and personal experiences. Adolescent scepticism led him to reconcile science with religion by grafting Spencer's positivism onto various German idealisms, but a family tragedy brought this period of experimentation to an abrupt end. Obsessed with mortality, Unamuno achieved philosophical maturity with a blend of Liberal Protestant theology and the philosophies of James and Kierkegaard in his conception of the 'tragic sense of life' – the theme of his essays, novels, dramas, poetry and journalism. He acquired deep and intense insights into the quest for immortality. Unamuno was a professional in neither philosophy nor theology.

1 Life
2 Reason and faith
3 Chief works

1 Life

Like many Spanish intellectual reformers of the late nineteenth and early twentieth centuries, Miguel de Unamuno sought to save Spain with rationalized religiousness. He dreamed of becoming the Spanish Luther. Brought up as a strict Catholic in the liberal Basque city of Bilbao, he lost his faith in Madrid of 1880, a city awash with many different philosophical currents, and thenceforth struggled to reconcile reason with religion and to stimulate Spaniards to follow his lead. To those ends he used his Chair in Greek Philology, obtained in 1891, and his controversial rectorship at the University of Salamanca (1901–14; 1930–6).

2 Reason and faith

Unamuno transposed problems of logic to the anthropological problem of life after death. Knowing that Hegel's dialectic somehow equated being and nonbeing, the sceptical young Unamuno of 1880 dreaded nonbeing after death. Hegel's logic starts from the datum of being (the thesis), whose indeter-minacy is nonbeing (the antithesis). Thesis and antithesis rise to equality on a higher plane of discourse, the synthesis, termed by Hegel 'becoming'. By analogy, might not the negation of human being (death) imply salvation in a (higher) life eternal? Such a hope appeared in Unamuno's diaries and verses. In the 1880s he avidly read Herbert Spencer, who saw self-conscious individual existence as an incontrovertible truth, and in 1886 Unamuno began elaborating his own *'Filosofía lógica'* ('Philosophy of Logic') to unite Spencer with Hegel. Beginning with the undeniable fact of individual existence, Unamuno affirmed with Spencer the relativism of every relationship between subject and object (including mental representations of God and the soul). Unamuno called these representations 'images' in Hegel's sense of propositions or forms transcending common sense. Had the youthful Unamuno been bolder, he might have asserted endless individual existence as a matter of faith, defying common sense, yet demanded by a higher, rational dialectic; but he stopped himself making such a leap of faith.

Later he grafted Spencer onto a pre-existing system combining religion and science: Krausism, imported from Germany in 1844 (see Krause, K.C.F.). A leading Spanish Krausist, Unamuno's teacher Francisco Giner de los Ríos reinterpreted Krause to aid in the moral and intellectual reform of Spain. Younger Krausists sometimes adopted positivistic methods to buttress idealistic speculations, and styled themselves 'Krausopositivists'. Accordingly, Unamuno used Spencer to prove Krausist theories of human history in his influential 'Krausopositivistic' series of essays, En torno al casticismo (On Authentic Tradition) (1895). Here humanity is said to harmonize contraries such as reason and faith in a subrational collective heritage, the 'inner history'. However, Castilian intransigence hinders such syntheses and accounts for Spanish decadence. Unamuno's 1895 work helped writers of his literary generation of 1898 to explain Spain's defeat in her humiliatingly brief war with the United States.

Nevertheless, a personal crisis caused Unamuno to sweep aside previous intellectual accomplishments. In 1897, his son's death aroused in him nightmares of the abyss. Renouncing intellectualism, Unamuno sought to reconquer his childhood faith. He oscillated between retreating to orthodox Catholicism, converting to Liberal Protestantism, and yielding to scepticism. At the time, he was studying the prestigious Neo-Kantian school of Liberal Protestantism known as Ritschlianism, which he found compatible with Krausism. Aiming for an original philosophy of religion, he immersed himself in the history of Christian dogma as interpreted by the Ritschlian

519

theologian Adolf von Harnack. Ritschl and Harnack held that Protestants, through justification by faith, receive forgiveness for their sins and are consequently guaranteed salvation; while Catholics harbour doubts about salvation because of their indecisive theology. The troubled Unamuno uncritically accepted this Protestant opinion: hence the resemblances of his heterodoxy to conservative Ritschlianism. Yet in 1904 he valiantly tried to turn alleged Catholic uncertainty about salvation to his advantage, presenting it as a dynamic heritage he shared with all Spaniards. His concurrent readings in William James suggested the universality of the yearning for immortality.

Unamuno resolved to inculcate in his readers anxiety for their own immortality as a way to save Spain from dogmatic inertia. Spain's national Bible could be *Don Quixote*, whose hero equated the act of believing (*creer*) with creating (*crear*) its object: belief in a saving God makes the Saviour real. Just as Ritschl desired a nation of believers in forgiveness of sin, so Unamuno sought a nation of doubting believers in salvation. He modified Protestant thinkers such as Kierkegaard and Ritschl by substituting their concern about redemption with his own desire for immortality (see Ritschl 1883).

3 Chief works

Unamuno's main philosophical work, *Del sentimiento trágico dela vida en los hombres y en los pueblos* (The Tragic Sense of Life) (1911–12), contains a philosophy of religion more systematic than its doctrines allowed him to admit. Every flesh-and-blood human, Unamuno finds, desires immortality, but this desire clashes with sceptical scientific reason. If faith wins out, then God exists for human salvation; consists of Will and Personality, rather than of Reason; as Personality, is both finite and infinite, defying discursive reason; and is multifaceted and merciful enough to save every creature. Therefore the end of human history is the 'apocatastasis', the union of everything in God and the spiritualization of the universe. It is the human's moral duty to make the 'apocatastasis' a practical norm of everyday living and to deserve immortality. Structurally, Unamuno's system of ideas follows Ritschl's, which also begins with reflections on the conservation of personality, presents God as Personality and Love, and ends with an ethics of dominion over the world with devotion to vocation. Yet Unamuno substitutes considerations about life after death for Ritschl's concern with redemption here and now.

While *The Tragic Sense of Life* is Unamuno's most respected essayistic work, *La agonía del cristianismo* (The Agony of Christianity) (1931) is his most terse

and anguished. Written in 1925 while Unamuno was in exile, this booklet derives the word 'agony' from the Greek word for struggle. Christianity entails struggle between universality and personalism; between truth, social and collective, and revelation, personal by essence; between Jewish belief in resurrection of the flesh and Hellenic credence in immortality of the soul; between monkish nihilism and the immortalizing desire for parenthood; between Catholicism and Protestantism, opposites which attract. Unamuno himself 'agonizes' while writing, hoping to serve Spain best by polemicizing from afar against her dictator Primo de Rivera.

The tragic sense of life generated Unamuno's best philosophical novels, *Niebla* (Mist) (1914), *Abel Sánchez* (1917) and *San Manuel Bueno, mártir* (Saint Emmanuel the Good, Martyr) (1933). *Mist* protests against the world-plan hypothesized by William James, with God and humans unfairly competing as if in a game of chess with an invincible champion. Unamuno yearned for a relationship of saving love between deity and humankind. His protagonist Augusto Pérez, confronting his Author-God Unamuno (a caricature of the flesh-and-blood author), anguishes for independence of his tyrannical creator. *Abel Sánchez* lodges a more specific protest against the world order, seen this time as a hospital for incurables afflicted by spiritual diseases, such as hate. Unamuno's modernization of the tale of Cain and Abel recounts Cain's experience from two tragically clashing viewpoints – the orthodox and the modern. Cain's malice is comprehensible both from the traditional standpoint, as envy, a sin, a disease, and, from the perspective of Unamuno's correspondent Croce, as the fact of human passion, capable of aggrandizing the individual.

In a subtler novelistic experiment, *Saint Emmanuel the Good, Martyr*, a beloved rural priest preaches immortality, in which he secretly does not believe. Greenfield (1979) defines him as a suicidal drive with a life-promoting direction. Ethically, his selflessness towards his parishioners daily helps spiritualize the universe; psychologically, his self-destructive tendency clashes with his desire for parenthood, which is equated in *The Agony of Christianity* to a yearning for immortality; existentially, he corresponds to Kierkegaard's individual feeling himself nothing before God, not because of sinfulness as in the case of the Danish philosopher himself, but because of doubt in immortality. In conclusion, though neither a professional philosopher like the Kierkegaardian phenomenologist Heidegger, nor a professional theologian like the post-Ritschlian Barth, Unamuno expressed the tragedy of human mortality with multifaceted intensity.

See also: SPAIN, PHILOSOPHY IN

List of works

Unamuno, M. de (1886) *'Filosofía lógica'* (Philosophy of Logic), unpublished manuscript, Casa-Museo Unamuno (Unamuno Homestead Museum), Salamanca. (Early work, influenced by Hegel, superseded by *Del sentimiento*....)

—— (1895) En torno al casticismo (On Authentic Tradition), *La Revista Moderna* 7 (74–8); Madrid: Biblioteca Moderna de Ciencias Sociales, 1902; 1 essay of 5, 'El espíritu castellano', trans. J.F. Crawford-Flitch, in *Essays and Soliloquies*, New York, 1925. (Series of essays on the concept of *casticismo* and Spanish national identity, considered as important, if idiosyncratic, statement of the principles of the group of writers and thinkers known as the 'Generation of '98'.)

—— (1911–12) *Del sentimiento trágico de la vida en los hombres y en los pueblos, La España Moderna,* Madrid; Madrid: Renacimiento, 1913; trans. J.E. Crawford-Flitch, *Tragic Sense of Life,* London, 1921. (His major philosophical work, influenced by Nietzsche, pre-empting much existential thought and theologically unorthodox for Spain at the time; argues for the capacity of feeling rather than reason as the motivating force behind human creativity.)

—— (1914) *Niebla (Nivola),* Madrid: Renacimiento; trans. W. Fite, *Mist: A Tragi-Comic Novel,* New York, 1928. (The first modernist novel in Spain, constituting a playful questioning and overturning of the hierarchical author-character and author-reader relationship, in the form of a transposition onto aesthetics of his theological and philosophical thought.)

—— (1917) *Abel Sánchez. Una historia de pasión,* Madrid: Renacimiento; trans. A. Kerrigan, *Abel Sánchez and Other Stories,* Chicago, IL, 1956. (Mid-period novel, reworking of the Cain and Abel story.)

—— (1920) *Tres novelas ejemplares y un prólogo,* Madrid: Espasa-Calpe; trans. Á. Flores, *Three Exemplary Novels,* New York: Grove Press, 1956. (Novellas: the prologue constitutes a major work of literary criticism; elaborates the idea of reading as creative play or *re-creación,* and marks the beginning of his interest in the status of women within society.)

—— (1921) *La tía Tula,* Madrid: Espasa-Calpe. (A novel which attempts to reconcile and comment on the contradictory images of women within Christianity; contains some proto-feminist statements by the main character, Gertrudis.)

—— (1925) *La agonía del cristianismo,* Madrid:

Compañía Ibero Americana de Publicaciones; trans. J. Cassou, *L'Agonie du christianisme,* Paris, 1931; trans. A. Kerrigan, *The Agony of Christianity* and *Essays on Faith,* Princeton, NJ, 1974. (Written in exile, Unamuno's last major essayistic statement on theology, still playing on the concept of anguished suffering in the face of *la nada* (*le néant*) as humanity's source of creativity.)

—— (1933) *San Manuel Bueno, mártir y tres historias más,* Madrid: Espasa-Calpe; trans. A. Kerrigan, *Saint Emmanuel the Good, Martyr,* in *Abel Sánchez and Other Stories,* Chicago, IL, 1956; repr. in *The Existential Imagination,* ed. F.R. Karl and L. Hamalian, Greenwich, CT, 1963. (Short novel on the paradoxes of faith and doubt, knowledge and innocence; the last work in what Unamuno considered to be a trilogy consisting of *Del sentimiento*..., *La agonía*... and *San Manuel*....)

—— (1959–64) *Obras completas* (Complete Works), Madrid: Vergara Editorial, 16 vols; repr. Madrid: Escelicer, 1966, 9 vols. (Standard complete works, but neither complete nor carefully edited.)

References and further reading

Fernández, P.H. (1976) *Bibliografía crítica de Miguel de Unamuno,* Madrid: J. Porrúa. (The most complete bibliography on Unamuno criticism, ordered by date of publication.)

* Greenfield, S. (1979) 'La iglesia terrestre de San Manuel Bueno', *Cuadernos Hispanoamericanos* 348: 609–20. (A view of Manuel Bueno, Unamuno's best-known fictional character, as a suicidal drive which takes a socially productive direction.)

Jiménez García, A. (1985) *El krausismo y la Institución Libre de Enseñanza,* Madrid: Cincel. (A concise history of Spanish Krausism.)

Nozick, M. (1971) *Miguel de Unamuno,* New York: Twayne. (The deepest, most concise and comprehensive treatment of Unamuno's philosophy.)

Orringer, N.R. (1986–7) 'Martin Nozick's Unamuno: A Fountainhead of Future Discoveries', *Siglo XX/ 20th Century* 4 (1–2): 30–43. (Survey of convincing philosophical criticism of all Unamuno's works, with suggestions for future research.)

—— (1985) 'Unamuno y los protestantes liberales', in *Sobre las fuentes de 'Del sentimiento trágico de la vida',* Madrid: Gredos. (Contributor's analysis of Liberal Protestantism within *Tragic Sense of Life.*)

Ritschl, A. (1883) *Die christliche Lehre der Rechtfertigung und Versöhnung,* Bonn: Adolph Marcus, 2nd edn. (The Liberal-Protestant theological treatise from which Unamuno took the structure of ideas he used in *'Tragic Sense of Life'.*)

Valdés, M.J. and Elena, M. (1973) *An Unamuno*

source book: *A Catalogue of Readings and Acquisitions with an Introductory Essay on Unamuno's Dialectical Enquiry*, Toronto, Ont.: University of Toronto Press. (Indispensable list of holdings and annotations in Unamuno's personal library at the Casa-Museo Unamuno, Salamanca.)

NELSON R. ORRINGER

UNCONSCIOUS MENTAL STATES

Unconscious phenomena are those mental phenomena which their possessor cannot introspect, not only at the moment at which the phenomenon occurs, but even when prompted ('Do you think/want/...?'). There are abundant allusions to many kinds of unconscious phenomena from classical times to Freud. Most notably, Plato in his Meno *defended a doctrine of* anamnesis *according to which a priori knowledge of, for example, geometry is 'recollected' from a previous life. But the notion of a rich, unconscious mental life really takes hold in nineteenth-century writers, such as Herder, Hegel, Helmholtz and Schopenhauer. It is partly out of this latter tradition that Freud's famous postulations of unconscious, 'repressed' desires and memories emerged.*

Partly in reaction to the excesses of introspection and partly because of the rise of computational models of mental processes, twentieth-century psychology has often been tempted by Lashley's view that 'no activity of mind is ever conscious' (1956). A wide range of recent experiments do suggest that people can be unaware of a multitude of sensory cognitive factors (for example, pupillary dilation, cognitive dissonance, subliminal cues to problem-solving) that demonstrably affect their behaviour. And Weiskrantz has documented cases of 'blindsight' in which patients with damage to their visual cortex can be shown to be sensitive to visual material they sincerely claim they cannot see.

The most controversial cases of unconscious phenomena are those which the agent could not possibly introspect, even in principle. Chomsky ascribes unconscious knowledge of quite abstract principles of grammar to adults and even newborn children that only a linguist could infer.

Many philosophers have found these claims about the unconscious unconvincing, even incoherent. However, they need to show how the evidence cited above could be otherwise explained, and why appeals to the unconscious have seemed so perfectly intelligible throughout history.

1   What counts?

Some care is needed to define exactly what counts as unconscious. Not just any phenomenon that fails to be conscious is *unconscious* in the intended sense. Thus, planets do not unconsciously follow elliptical orbits; nor does one's stomach unconsciously follow rules for digesting food; nor (to take a fallacy from popular biology) do we or our genes unconsciously seek replication when we act in ways that may in the past have had that consequence. We might call these phenomena simply '*non*-conscious', distinguishing as *unconscious* only those *mental* phenomena of which the possessor could not be made aware at the time of their occurrence, even if prompted. Thus, planets, stomachs and genes are non-conscious, having no mental lives at all.

But this definition is not quite enough. Suppose it were true that someone, Seymour, unconsciously feared castration; and suppose that Seymour read in a book that all men unconsciously fear castration, and concluded *merely* from this that he, too, must have such a fear. Presumably his unconscious fear would not *thereby* have been rendered conscious. The fear remains 'unconscious' so long as he is not conscious of it in the *right*, 'introspective' sort of way. Specifying this right way may be none too easy; but this is a problem that arises with respect to other mental phenomena (for example, the relation of intentions to the intended act).

Whyte (1978) has usefully compiled allusions to unconscious processes from classical times to Freud (not always distinguishing, however, between unconscious and non-conscious). Not only did Plato posit unconscious memories (see PLATO §11), but the Greek physiologist, Galen, postulated unconscious inferences in perception and Plotinus, 'feelings without awareness'. Aquinas inferred the existence of unconscious 'processes of the soul' from the fact that he 'did not observe [his] soul apart from its acts'. Leibniz argued that ordinary perceptions must be the result of innumerable smaller perceptions occurring below a quantitative threshold (see LEIBNIZ, G.W. §8). Unconscious thoughts and desires were a common theme among eighteenth- and nineteenth-century romantic poets and philosophers, such as Herder, Novalis, Richter, Wordsworth, Hegel and SCHOPENHAUER; and, anticipating contemporary computational models of mind, the great nineteenth-century psychologist, Helmholtz, developed a fairly elaborate theory of unconscious inferential processing (see HELMHOLTZ, H. VON §2) Much of this served as the background for perhaps the most famous advocate of the unconscious, Freud.

2 Freud

Sigmund Freud postulated unconscious mental states to explain a wide variety of behaviours. His earliest evidence came from experiments involving hypnotic suggestion, experiments which, though fascinating, remain still quite controversial (see Hilgard 1977). Freud's primary argument is that parapraxes (for example, slips of the tongue), dreams, hysterical and neurotic symptoms, even 'ideas that come into our head we do not know from where' remain 'disconnected and unintelligible' if we insist that all mental states are conscious, whereas they 'fall into a demonstrable connection if we interpolate between them the unconscious acts we [psychoanalysts] have inferred' (1915: 168). Moreover, he argues, if it turns out that this interpolation enables us to 'exert an effective influence upon the course of conscious processes, this success will have given us an incontrovertible proof of the existence of what we have assumed' (1915: 168).

'Incontrovertible' seems a little strong. Certainly there *could be* plausible theories of 'the ideas that come into our head', and perhaps even of dreams and neuroses, that do not postulate unconscious mental states: especially the random flow of ideas in both dreams and daily life could have a purely physical explanation. Of course, we can imagine a standard mentalistic explanation in terms of beliefs and motives. But it is not enough to imagine the pattern; one has to provide some reason to think the pattern is genuine. For example, one has to find some critical evidence that could not be explained by any independently warranted purely physiological hypothesis. Of course, these latter explanations may not make a person's behaviour 'intelligible', if what that means is that they should be seen as part of some kind of 'rational' or 'symbolic' pattern. There is no doubt that Freud's explanations often possess an extraordinary charm in this way (Wittgenstein 1966). But then we need an argument that the charming pattern Freud seeks actually corresponds to any real processes in a person's mind. Perhaps there is no true *causal* explanation of dreams or neuroses that makes them 'intelligible' in *that* particular way.

Freud's further argument from therapeutic success is, moreover, a notorious fallacy: the history of religion and psychotherapy is full of success stories involving theories that there is no serious reason to believe. Many such effects may well be due to suggestion or well-established 'placebo' effects, whereby someone's belief merely that they have been cared for at all can actually improve their condition (Grünbaum 1984). None of this implies that Freud's postulations are *false*. The point is that the truth in this domain may be harder to ascertain than Freud recognizes.

What Freud needs, and sometimes does provide, are regularities that could not be explained except by adverting to the specific contentful states he posits. He and Breuer began to do this when they noted that hysterical patients were often 'paralysed' not at places at which normal paralyses occurred, but, rather, at places that were *popularly and mistakenly believed* to be subject to paralysis (for example, 'glove' anaesthesia). Here the only plausible explanation of such curious paralyses involves appeal to the *content* of those popular beliefs, and this it does whether or not the believer is aware of that content.

Freud's actual account of the unconscious (in what he sometimes calls 'the truly dynamic sense', and which he comes to call the 'id') is actually quite special. He thinks that unconscious or 'primary' processes are intellectually quite primitive: they have no representation of negation, degrees of certainty, time or an independent reality, and are only subject to 'the pleasure principle'. Interestingly, he denies the existence of unconscious *affect* (Freud 1933). Nevertheless, he claims, 'every psychical act begins as an unconscious one, and...may remain so or go on developing into consciousness according as it meets resistance or not' (1915: 55). It appears that the only reason he can see for material not becoming conscious is that it has been in this way censored or 'repressed'. It seems not to have occurred to him that there could be other reasons for material to remain unconscious: for example, that there may not be the right kind of causal or 'informational' path between the material and mechanisms of introspection (see PSYCHOANALYSIS, METHODOLOGICAL ISSUES IN).

3 Recent experiments

This latter possibility emerges in contemporary cognitive science. In an influential article, Nisbett and Wilson (1977) reviewed a wide range of experiments in which people can be shown to be sensitive to a variety of what would appear to be conceptualized contents, but without any awareness of them. Instead of noticing these factors, the subjects frequently 'introspect' material that can be independently shown to be irrelevant to the causation of their behaviour. Indeed, even when explicitly asked about the relevant material, they will deny that it played any role. For example, Latané and Darley (1970) showed that subjects are less likely to aid strangers in distress the greater the number of bystanders in the situation, but with no awareness of this effect. And Nisbett and Wilson (1977) asked fifty-two subjects to choose between what were (unknown to them) four *identical* pairs of nylon stockings presented in a left-to-right array: 80 per cent of them tended to choose the rightmost pair; but, when asked, virtually all subjects denied that position had any effect. Similar results obtain for cognitive dissonance, subliminal clues in problem solving and semantic disambiguation, and subtle perceptual cues, such as the dilation of pupils in a face (Hess 1975).

One of the most philosophically interesting phenomena supporting the evidence for unconscious mental states is that of 'blindsight'. This occurs in patients who have suffered damage to their visual cortex and who claim not to be able to see various stimulus materials that have been presented to them; nevertheless, they can be shown to score well above chance when they are forced to 'guess' at what they may be seeing (Weiskrantz 1986).

What exactly such data show about the *extent* of unconscious processes is still a matter of considerable controversy. Velmans (1991), supporting Lashley (1956), argues that all cognitive processes can occur unconsciously. In an important study, Ericsson and Simon (1984) try to sort out the different informational paths involved in different mental processes such as perception, long- and short-term memory retrieval, and in a person's surmises about the causation of their behaviour, arguing that some of these paths do and some do not provide a basis for genuine introspection.

4 Chomsky

All the examples considered so far are examples of cognitive contents that people would at least ordinarily *understand*. However, more theoretical cognitive scientists, influenced especially by the linguist, Noam CHOMSKY, often ascribe quite technical contents even to newborn children. Chomsky (1986) argues, for example, that the best explanation of the rapidity with which children acquire natural language is that they have innate knowledge of general principles of what he calls 'universal grammar' (see LANGUAGE, INNATENESS OF). This includes such principles, for example, as that a pronoun cannot be used to refer to something picked out by a noun in a clause subordinate to the clause in which it occurs. For example, in sentence (1), 'he' cannot be knowingly used to refer to John, although it can in (2):

(1) He hoped John would win.

(2) John hoped he would win.

The full statement of the rules for pronouns is actually quite technical, involving notions such as 'c-command' and 'phrasal head' that require a good deal of theoretical study to understand. If a newborn child is said to 'know' such a principle, it would patently be a piece of unconscious (or 'tacit') knowledge, at least in the sense that the child is entirely unable to express it, even when prompted. Indeed, there is no *introspective* route even in an adult linguist from the unconsciously known principle to any awareness of it.

Chomsky's research has stimulated an entire movement not only in linguistics, but in many other parts of psychology (for example, vision, reasoning, cognitive development), where knowledge of similarly abstract principles about material objects, biological kinds and folk physics are also attributed to adults and young children alike. In a different vein, Polanyi (1967) has stressed the role of 'tacit' knowledge in guiding creativity and scientific research (see KNOWLEDGE, TACIT; NATIVISM).

There can be no doubt that much of the evidence adduced by Chomsky and these other psychologists is impressive and cries out for explanation, which is not easy to provide. But many philosophers doubt that the explanation needs actually to claim that people *know*, *believe* or, in Chomsky's phrase, even 'cognize' (1986: 265) the relevant principles. It may be enough that they simply *obey* the principles in the way that their bodies obey the laws of gravity, without *following* them, indeed, without them being represented or otherwise part of their *mental* lives. They may explain people's knowing *how* to do certain things, without requiring that they know *that* certain principles obtain (see Ryle 1949; Devitt and Sterelny 1989).

Much here depends upon being clearer than anyone is about what is required for ascribing any mental content at all. Quite apart from issues of awareness, Davidson (1980) claims that content ascription only makes sense when many contents are ascribed as some kind of interacting rational system. If so, then many of Freud's and Chomsky's claims would appear to be in trouble: as Stich (1978) points out, if Chomsky were correct, someone could know innately some principle P, be convinced as an adult that P entailed Q, but not be the least disposed to infer Q. But then, on a Davidsonian view, that should be a reason not to ascribe P to that person in the first place.

Stich proposes thinking of Chomsky's grammatical principles as contents occurring at a different, 'subdoxastic' level of psychology, a suggestion taken up systematically by Fodor (1983) in his postulation of 'informationally encapsulated modules' of the mind (see MODULARITY OF MIND). But the question persists: why think that the principles comprise genuine *mental contents* inside a module? Peacocke (1989) suggests that it is enough that a system be 'sensitive to the information' expressed by the principle. But this seems too broad: for example, if we are to take talk of 'genetic information' seriously, DNA would seem to have contentful attitudes about the structure of amino acids.

5 Philosophical qualms

A number of philosophers have objected to the postulation of unconscious mental states. McIntyre (1958) and Searle (1992) have insisted that it is some sort of conceptual truth that mental states involve at least a disposition to have certain experiences. Searle, for example, defends what he calls the 'connection principle', according to which 'we understand the notion of an unconscious mental state only as...the *sort of thing* that...could be...conscious' (1992: 155–6). Now, of course, *any* contents – from the most abstruse Chomskean principles to the most sordid of Freudian analyses – are, for almost anyone, 'possible contents of consciousness': most people can be brought at least to *understand the words*. Reiterating the point we made early on, what Searle presumably means is that mental contents have to be *accessible* to their possessor in something like the normal introspective way, whatever way that is. But once one reflects on how very special that way may be, it is puzzling why the existence of a mental state should depend upon it.

Strawson goes further and claims that 'there are, strictly speaking, no dispositional non-experiential mental phenomena' (1994: 167), comparing a non-experiential brain to a CD recording of a Beethoven quartet that is not currently being played, and which could be used either to produce a genuine acoustical event on a CD player or a light show.

What tells against all this scepticism, however, is the explanatory usefulness of unconscious intentional states having genuine causal powers. Freud's and contemporary cognitive postulations of unconscious states are interesting because, if true, they would explain certain *content-sensitive* behaviours, such as parapraxes, neuroses, and differential willingness to come to the aid of strangers; Chomsky's, because, if true, they would explain language acquisition. Weiskrantz's postulation of 'blindsight' explains his patients' ability to perform better than chance at picking out stimuli of which they are unaware. The crucial difference between Strawson's example of the unplayed CD and the unconscious brain is that, whereas the *musical* properties of the unplayed CD are, indeed, at that time causally inert, the intentional content properties of these unconscious mental states are not. If Freud, Chomsky, Nisbett and Wilson or Weiskrantz are correct, they are responsible for a variety of observable phenomena. Someone sceptical of unconscious states needs to show how all the phenomena these figures cite can be otherwise explained.

Searle does provide a further argument against entirely unconscious states, claiming that no postulation of an attitude lacking consciousness can account for 'aspectual shape' (1992: 156–61, 169–72), or what is better known as the phenomena of (hyper-) intensionality, whereby minds are able to distinguish among even necessarily coextensive concepts, such as [water] and [H$_2$O]. Searle believes that only a conscious mind can possess such an ability (see Bealer 1984 for a similar, more formidable argument).

A full reply to this point would require setting out the various proposals of a great number of writers regarding how the problems of both intentionality and (hyper-)intensionality are to be solved. Suffice it to say that there are a number of possibilities to be considered in detail. For example, many think that a computational theory of mind involving a language of thought, endowed with both narrow and wide contents, will suffice (see LANGUAGE OF THOUGHT; CONTENT: WIDE AND NARROW). Many different sentences with different causal roles within the mind – for example, 'Water is wet', 'H$_2$O is wet' – may express the same *wide* content, and so constitute different 'aspectual shapes' of that content. Searle would in turn reject such an account, invoking his 'Chinese room argument'; however, the soundness of this argument is widely disputed (see CHINESE ROOM ARGUMENT).

In any case, the fact that so many people, from antiquity to the present, find the postulation of unconscious phenomena both intelligible and illuminating provides an at least *prima facie* case that they are not incoherent in the ways these philosophers claim. Indeed, until better explanations of the various phenomena we have discussed are presented, that postulation needs to be taken seriously.

See also: CONSCIOUSNESS; INTROSPECTION, EPISTEMOLOGY OF; INTROSPECTION, PSYCHOLOGY OF; PSYCHOANALYSIS, METHODOLOGICAL ISSUES IN

References and further reading

* Bealer, G. (1984) 'Mind and Anti-Mind', *Midwest Studies in Philosophy* 9: 283–328. (A rich presenta-

tion of an argument, derived from Quine, that the phenomenon of hyper-intensionality requires first-person conscious experience.)

Brown, D. (1995) 'Pseudo Memories: The Standard of Science and the Standard of Care in Trauma Treatment', *American Journal of Clinical Hypnosis* 37: 1–24. (Recent experimental work on 'repressed memory'.)

* Chomsky, N. (1986) *Knowledge of Language*, New York: Praeger. (A recent, relatively non-technical presentation of his views about innate knowledge of grammar.)

* Davidson, D. (1980) *Essays on Actions and Events*, Oxford: Oxford University Press. (Development of a view of the ascription of mental states as involving making rational sense of an agent overall.)

Davies, M. (1989) 'Tacit Knowledge and Sub-Doxastic States', in A. George (ed.) *Reflections on Chomsky*, Oxford: Blackwell. (Subtle discussion of whether 'modules' for language and perception can be full mental states.)

—— (forthcoming) *Tacit Knowledge*, Oxford: Blackwell. (Brings together the author's developments of his views about the kind of tacit knowledge Chomsky ascribes to language users.)

* Devitt, M. and Sterelny, K. (1989) 'Linguistics: What's Wrong with "the Right View"', in J. Tomberlin (ed.) *Philosophical Perspectives*, vol. 3, *Philosophy of Mind and Action Theory*, Atascadero, CA: Ridgeview. (A sceptical response to Chomsky's claims about the psychological reality of grammars.)

* Ericsson, K. and Simon, H. (1984) *Protocol Analysis: Verbal Reports as Data*, Cambridge, MA: MIT Press, 2nd edn, 1993. (A detailed development of a theory of reliable introspective processes, and the 'protocols' to which they give rise.)

Evans, G. (1981) 'Semantic Theory and Tacit Knowledge', in S. Holtzman and C. Leich (eds) *Wittgenstein: To Follow a Rule*, Oxford: Routledge & Kegan Paul. (Subtle discussion of whether a Chomskean appeal to tacit knowledge of rules can explain people's grasp of the *semantics*, as well as of the syntax, of their language.)

Fisher, J. (1974) 'Knowledge of Rules', *Review of Metaphysics* 28: 237–60. (Useful discussion distinguishing knowledge of a rule of grammar from knowledge about such a rule.)

* Fodor, J. (1983) *The Modularity of Mind*, Cambridge, MA: MIT Press. (Postulation of 'informationally encapsulated modules' of the mind.)

Freud, S. (1912) 'A Note on the Unconscious in Psychoanalysis', in *The Standard Edition of the Complete Psychological Works of Sigmund Freud*, vol. 12, trans. and ed. J. Strachey *et al.*, London: Hogarth Press, 1958. (Short, early anticipation of the 1915 essay.)

* —— (1915) 'The Unconscious', in *The Standard Edition of the Complete Psychological Works of Sigmund Freud*, vol. 14, trans. and ed. J. Strachey *et al.*, London: Hogarth Press, 1958. (Freud's most extended, explicit treatment of the topic.)

* —— (1933) 'New Introductory Lectures on Psychoanalysis', in *The Complete Introductory Lectures on Psychoanalysis*, trans. and ed. J. Strachey, New York: Norton, 1966. (Freud's best summaries of his own theories.)

George, A. (ed.) (1989) *Reflections on Chomsky*, Oxford: Blackwell. (Excellent collection of a number of recent articles listed here on Chomsky's claims about tacit knowledge.)

* Grünbaum, A. (1984) *The Foundations of Psychoanalysis: A Philosophical Critique*, Berkeley, CA: University of California Press. (A standard philosophical critique of Freudian theories.)

* Hess, R. (1975) 'The Role of Pupil Size in Communication', *Scientific American* 233 (5): 110–18. (Experiment in which males' preferences for female faces were shown to depend upon the size of the pupil in the depicted face, without the males noticing this fact.)

* Hilgard, E. (1977) *Divided Consciousness: Multiple Controls in Human Thought and Action*, New York: Wiley & Sons. (Interesting contemporary research on hypnosis and suggestion.)

* Lashley, K. (1956) 'Cerebral Organization and Behavior', in H. Solomon, S. Cobb and W. Penfield (eds) *The Brain and Human Behavior*, Baltimore, MD: Williams and Wilkens Press. (Classic statement of the widespread contemporary view that most – Lashley claims 'all' – important mental processes are unconscious.)

* Latané, B. and Darley, J. (1970) *The Unconscious Bystander: Why Doesn't He Help Us?*, New York: Appleton-Century-Crofts. (Experiment in which a person's readiness to come to the aid of someone in distress was reduced if there were more bystanders, without the person being aware of this fact.)

Loftus, E., Polonsky, S. and Fullilove, M.T. (1994) 'Memories of Childhood Sexual Abuse: Remembering and Repressing', *Psychology of Women Quarterly* 18: 67–84. (Recent experimental studies of 'repressed memory' of sexual abuse.)

Lyons, W. (1986) *The Disappearance of Introspection*, Cambridge, MA: MIT Press. (A discussion of the decline of introspection in our understanding of the mind.)

* McIntyre, A. (1958) *The Unconscious*, Oxford: Routledge & Kegan Paul. (Some philosophical criticism

of Freudian appeals to the unconscious, from days prior to cognitive science.)

* Nisbett, R. and Wilson, T. (1977) 'On Telling More Than We Can Know: Verbal Reports on Mental Processes', *Psychological Review* 84 (3): 231–59. (Influential and fascinating review of a wide range of experiments showing people to be sensitive to phenomena of which they are unaware.)
* Peacocke, C. (1989) 'When Is a Grammar Psychologically Real?', in A. George (ed.) *Reflections on Chomsky*, Oxford: Blackwell. (Argues that psychological reality turns on a system's sensitivity to information – irrespective of whether it is conscious.)
  Pinker, S. (1994) *The Language Instinct: How the Mind Creates Language*, New York: Harper & Row. (A superb introduction to the revolution caused by Chomsky's postulation of innate, tacit knowledge of grammar.)
* Polanyi, M. (1967) *The Tacit Dimension*, Oxford: Routledge & Kegan Paul. (Discussion of the role of unconscious knowledge in creative thought.)
  Rey, G. (1997) *Contemporary Philosophy of Mind: A Contentiously Classical Approach*, Oxford: Blackwell. (Sets out in detail the structure of contemporary computational/representational theories of mind, arguing that their success does not depend upon the postulated cognitive states' being conscious.)
* Ryle, G. (1949) *The Concept of Mind*, London: Hutcheson. (Historical source of the suggestion that much unconscious knowledge may be merely 'know how', not 'knowledge that'.)
* Searle, J. (1992) *The Rediscovery of the Mind*, Cambridge, MA: MIT Press. (A vigorous denial of the possibility of unconscious mental phenomena.)
* Stich, S. (1978) 'Beliefs and Sub-Doxastic States', *Philosophy of Science* 45: 499–518. (Proposes thinking of Chomsky's grammatical principles as contents occurring at a different, 'sub-doxastic' level of psychology.)
* Strawson, G. (1994) *Mental Reality*, Cambridge, MA: MIT Press. (An effort to argue against unconscious mental phenomena on intuitive philosophical grounds.)
* Velmans, M. (1991) 'Is Human Information Processing Conscious?', *Behavioral and Brain Sciences* 14 (4): 691–2. (Argues that consciousness is inessential to all cognitive processing.)
* Weiskrantz, L. (1986) *Blindsight: A Case Study and Implications*, Oxford: Oxford University Press. (The major study of the surprising phenomenon of blindsight.)
* Whyte, L. (1978) *The Unconscious Before Freud*, New York: St Martin's Press. (A not particularly philosophical, but very useful, survey of claims about the unconscious from classical Greece to Freud.)
* Wittgenstein, L. (1966) *Lectures and Conversations on Aesthetics, Psychology and Religious Belief*, Berkeley, CA: University of California Press. (Early philosophical criticism of Freud.)

GEORGES REY

UNDERDETERMINATION

The term underdetermination refers to a broad family of arguments about the relations between theory and evidence. All share the conclusion that evidence is more or less impotent to guide choice between rival theories or hypotheses. In one or other of its guises, underdetermination has probably been the most potent and most pervasive idea driving twentieth-century forms of scepticism and epistemological relativism. It figures prominently in the writing of diverse influential philosophers. It is a complex family of doctrines, each with a different argumentative structure. Most, however, suppose that only the logical consequences of a hypothesis are relevant to its empirical support. This supposition can be challenged.

1   Relevant terminology
2   Deductive and ampliative underdetermination
3   Holistic underdetermination (the 'D-thesis')
4   Undermining underdetermination

1   Relevant terminology

The thesis of underdetermination involves a set of specific claims about the relations between bodies of evidence or statements about that evidence, on the one hand, and theories, on the other. All forms of that thesis insist that multiple, mutually incompatible, theories can enjoy the same relation to any given body of evidence. Beyond that point of agreement, however, there are more and less ambitious versions of underdetermination. A few terminological preliminaries are in order before we proceed to examine some of them. To facilitate comparison of the various versions of underdetermination, I shall use this vocabulary: e will refer to whatever evidence is in hand; c will refer to relevant rules or criteria for choosing between hypotheses; and I shall further suppose that we are confronted by a single hypothesis h or, more commonly, by a set of rival hypotheses, $h_1, h_2, \ldots, _n$ (some of which may not have been explicitly formulated).

Now, what every version of the thesis of underdetermination shares in common is this claim: that the relevant criteria, c, and available evidence, e, will provide no rational grounds for preferring h_i to some (and perhaps not to any) of the rivals to h_i. Various versions of the thesis of underdetermination explore its plausibility under various interpretations of c, the criteria of appraisal.

2 Deductive and ampliative underdetermination

Hume argued convincingly that one cannot derive a genuinely universal statement from any finite set of its positive instances (see HUME, D. §2). This is surely correct, but what does it entail for the theory of knowledge? One thing it certainly shows is that if the only criteria of theory choice we allow are those of deductive logic, then the rational acceptance of a theory is always underdetermined by any conceivable evidence. Karl Popper explicitly drew this moral from Hume's work (see POPPER, K.R. §2). It explains why Popper resisted the idea that positive belief in a theory could ever be rational. (Belief for Popper, as for Hume, was a matter of 'animal instinct'.)

Most philosophers refuse to follow Popper in supposing that the rules of deductive logic exhaust the epistemic and methodological resources available for the appraisal of hypotheses. They believe that there are various principles of ampliative inference that come into play in the evaluation of hypotheses. The fact that deductive logic underdetermines theory choice leaves open, they insist, the possibility that these other nondeductive principles may guide theory choice unambiguously.

One plausible, if simplistic, ampliative rule of theory evaluation is what Carl Hempel called the Nicod criterion (1965). According to this idea, if some h entails a particular observation report, then the truth of that observation report counts as evidence for h; if the observation report is false, then it counts as evidence against h. About a century ago, Henri Poincaré and others stressed the significance of the fact that, through any finite number of points, indefinitely many curves could be drawn. This made clear that indefinitely many alternative hypotheses were compatible with (indeed, deductively entailed by) any given body of data. If one supposes, with the Nicod criterion, that the potential evidence for h consists simply in its observational consequences, then it is clear that indefinitely many different and conflicting hypotheses will share the *same* evidential instances. If we take the Nicod rule as a criterion for hypothesis evaluation, it follows that, whenever we are confronted with an h enjoying apparent evidential support (that is, having many true positive or entailed instances), we know that there will be indefinitely

many incompatible hypotheses possessing those same instances as 'evidence' – even if we cannot formulate them. In sum, theory choice is underdetermined by any methodology which countenances all and only the known positive (or otherwise entailed) instances of a hypothesis as confirmatory.

Nelson Goodman's new riddles of induction provided concrete illustrations of the point (1965). Consider a hypothesis like 'all emeralds are green' and a contrived rival like 'all emeralds are green before the year 2000 AD and blue thereafter'. If our observations consist entirely of green-appearing emeralds examined before 2000, then both hypotheses can claim all the same positive instances. Prior to the year 2000, the evidence, however extensive, appears impotent to guide choice between them (see GOODMAN, N. §3; INDUCTION, EPISTEMIC ISSUES IN).

It is important to note that, even if hypothesis choice is underdetermined in this specific sense, that does not entail that *every* rival to a given h will fare as well as h does. It means, rather, that *there will be* rivals which will fare as well.

3 Holistic underdetermination (the 'D-thesis')

Arguments of a very different sort undergird an even more global form of underdetermination. During the 1950s, W.V. Quine revived arguments made earlier in the century by Pierre Duhem (1906) about the inconclusiveness of falsification (see DUHEM, P.M.M.; QUINE, W.V. §3). Specifically, the Duhem thesis (D-thesis) holds that hypotheses never approach the tribunal of experience singly but only as parts of much larger webs of belief. This must be so, since auxiliary hypotheses are typically needed even to determine what a given hypothesis predicts about experience. Suppose, asks Quine, that the result predicted by a web of such hypotheses turns out to be mistaken? In that case, he maintains, all we have learned is that we have made a mistake somewhere in our body of beliefs but that blame cannot be further localized. Moreover, he insists that we can hang on to any particular hypothesis we like 'come what may', since we can always blame any empirical failures of the web on other strands. More precisely, Quine holds that *any* given h can be maintained in the face of any apparently negative evidence because (he thinks) there will always be some auxiliary that can be legitimately invoked which will bring h into line with whatever we observe. Any h can, with suitable changes elsewhere in our beliefs, be made to explain any evidence. Although Quine and others have repeatedly asserted this thesis to be true, it has never been proven that every apparently refuted hypothesis can be saved in the face of any evidence by invoking a nontrivial auxiliary hypothesis.

If, however, this is correct, then we have a much more global sort of underdetermination to contend with. Whereas previous versions of the underdetermination thesis argued that, for any apparently successful *h*, there will be at least one rival which exhibits the same success, the holistic version of the underdeterminationist thesis seems to say that, given any apparently successful *h*, *all* of its rivals can be made to fit the same evidence that supports *h*, whatever *e* is. This view appears to entail a thesis of cognitive egalitarianism, namely, that all rival hypotheses can – with sufficient ingenuity – be made to appear equally well supported by whatever evidence is in hand.

4 Undermining underdetermination

What Quine's version of the underdetermination thesis takes for granted, as do virtually all others, is the idea that a hypothesis' entailed instances are coextensive with its epistemically supporting instances. He is committed to this since he countenances two hypotheses as equally well supported by *e* provided that both hypotheses entail *e*. This idea, the Nicod criterion, undergirds the paradoxes of confirmation, the Goodman paradoxes of induction and Quinean underdetermination.

Those who are less taken with the underdetermination thesis believe that its identification of entailed consequences with evidentially supporting instances rests on a misunderstanding of how empirical support works. Specifically, it is easy to show both (a) that many entailed instances of a hypothesis lend it no empirical support and (b) that much of the support enjoyed by many hypotheses comes from outside the set of its entailed consequences. As an example of (a), consider the fact that data used to fix the parameters of a hypothesis, by virtue of being built into *h* itself, cannot then be used as reasons for accepting *h*, even though (trivially) *h* entails them. As regards (b), it is virtually a truism that hypotheses can derive evidential support from instances not entailed by those hypotheses. For instance, the information that the last 10,000 crows have been black is evidence for the hypothesis that the next crow I observe will be black, even though that latter hypothesis entails nothing about the 10,000 crows. Equally, probabilistic statements (for example, 'most humans die before the age of 100') typically do not entail any specific claim about observed relative frequencies, even though those same relative frequencies can both confirm and disconfirm statistical hypotheses. Even with respect to a nonprobabilistic hypothesis, one can often derive empirical support from evidence which *h*

does not entail but which is entailed by yet more general hypotheses that in turn entail *h*. Thus, after the Newtonian synthesis, evidence about bodies falling on the face of the earth supports Kepler's laws, even though Kepler's laws themselves entail nothing whatever about cases of terrestrial free fall.

In sum, the supporting instances for a hypothesis are not coextensive with its entailed instances nor are its undermining instances exclusively those denied by *h*. Where does this leave the thesis of underdetermination? Because all the advocates of underdetermination have operated with this mistaken notion of empirical support – which assimilates support to being a logical consequence of a hypothesis – we do not presently know whether choice of theory is underdetermined by the evidence. While we do know that rival theories may well have the same known empirical consequences, this knowledge seems to be irrelevant to questions of empirical support, since there are ample grounds for denying that empirical consequences and supporting instances amount to the same thing.

It should be noted, finally, that virtually all formulations of the thesis of underdetermination presuppose that, in judging whether the available evidence supports a given hypothesis, we must assure ourselves that there is no *possible* hypothesis which could be equally well supported. The idea that extant hypotheses are being compared (at least implicitly) with all possible rival hypotheses is probably a hyperbolic view of the theory choice situation. Scientists repeatedly point out that the problem generally facing them is finding even one hypothesis that will fit with the available evidence. The philosopher's penchant for supposing that the function of evidence is to enable one to choose, not merely between extant hypotheses, but between all possible hypotheses is a conceit that could profitably be dispensed with.

See also: CONFIRMATION THEORY; CRUCIAL EXPERIMENTS; INDUCTIVE INFERENCE; SCIENTIFIC METHOD

References and further reading

* Duhem, P. (1906) *La théorie physique. Son objet et sa structure*, Paris: Chevalier et Rivière; trans. P.P. Wiener, *The Aim and Structure of Physical Theory*, Princeton, NJ: Princeton University Press, 1954. (One of the earliest attempts to explore the implications of underdetermination for the epistemology of science.)

Glymour, C. (1980) *Theory and Evidence*, Princeton, NJ: Princeton University Press. (A detailed account of the evidence relation in science.)

* Goodman, N. (1965) *Fact, Fiction and Forecast*, Indianapolis, IN: Bobbs-Merrill. (A nominalist's formulation of new challenges to the idea of instance confirmation, discussed in §2.)

Grünbaum, A. (1974) *Philosophical Problems of Space and Time*, Dordrecht: Reidel. (The standard critique of Duhem and Quine's accounts of underdetermination.)

* Hempel, C.G. (1965) *Aspects of Explanation*, New York: Free Press. (The principal formulation and critique of the qualitative theory of confirmation.)

Laudan, L. and Leplin, J. (1991) 'Empirical Equivalence and Underdetermination', *Journal of Philosophy* 88: 449–72. (Elaboration of many of the themes discussed here.)

* Quine, W.V. (1953) *From a Logical Point of View*, Cambridge, MA: Harvard University Press. (The *locus classicus* for the 'Duhem–Quine thesis', discussed in §3.)

LARRY LAUDAN

UNDERSTANDING AND MEANING *see* MEANING AND UNDERSTANDING

UNITY OF SCIENCE

How should our scientific knowledge be organized? Is scientific knowledge unified and, if so, does it mirror a unity of the world as a whole? Or is it merely a matter of simplicity and economy of thought? Either way, what sort of unity is it? If the world can be decomposed into elementary constituents, must our knowledge be in some way reducible to, or even replaced by, the concepts and theories describing such constituents? Can economics be reduced to microphysics, as Einstein claimed? Can sociology be derived from molecular genetics? Might the sciences be unified in the sense of all following the same method, whether or not they are all ultimately reducible to physics? Considerations of the unity problem begin at least with Greek cosmology and the question of the one and the many. In the late twentieth century the increasing tendency is to argue for the disunity of science and to deny reducibility to physics.

What kinds of integration are manifested, or sought after, in the claims and practices of the different fields of inquiry we call 'sciences'? This question should be carefully distinguished from any of the different specific theses addressing it and yet it should be stressed as the linking thread of a time-honoured philosophical debate. The question belongs to a tradition of thought that can be traced back to Presocratic Greek cosmology, in particular to the preoccupation with the question of the one and the many. In what senses are the world, and thereby our knowledge of it, one? A number of representations of the world emerged in terms of its decomposition into a few simple constituents: Parmenides' static substance, Heraclitus' flux of becoming, Empedocles' four elements, Democritus' atoms, or Pythagoras' numbers, Plato's forms, Aristotle's categories.

With the advent and expansion of Christian monotheism, the organization of knowledge reflected the idea of a world governed by the laws dictated by God, creator and legislator. Encyclopaedic efforts such as the Etymologies, compiled in the sixth century by Isidore, Bishop of Seville, the works of Ramon LLULL in the Middle Ages and of Petrus RAMUS in the Renaissance emerged from this tradition. Llull introduced tree-diagrams and forest-encyclopedias organizing different disciplines (including law, medicine, theology and logic). He also introduced more abstract diagrams – not unlike some found in Kabbalistic and esoteric traditions – in an attempt to encode combinatorially the knowledge of God's creation in a universal language of symbols. Ramus introduced diagrams representing dichotomies and gave prominence to the view that the starting point of all philosophy is the classification of the arts and sciences.

The emergence of a distinctive tradition of scientific thought addressed the question of unity through science's designation of a privileged method, set of concepts and language. Francis BACON held that a unity of the sciences emerges out of our classifications of material facts in the form of a pyramid with different levels of generalities. Galileo GALILEI proclaimed that the Book of Nature was written by God in the language of mathematical symbols and geometrical truths: the story of Nature's laws is told in that language in terms of a reduced set of primary qualities – extension, quantity of matter and motion.

Descartes and Leibniz gave this tradition a rationalist twist centred on the powers of human reason. Like Llull's, their conception of unity is combinatorial, that is, determined by rules of analysis and combination. According to Descartes the science of geometry, with its demonstrative reasoning from the simplest and clearest thoughts, constitutes the paradigm for the ideal of unification of all knowledge (see DESCARTES, R. §§2–3). Descartes symbolized this unity again using the image of a tree. Unlike in the manual arts, there should be no division of labour in the sciences; they ought not to be studied separately according to their subject matter. Leibniz proposed a 'general science' in the form of a Demonstrative Encyclopaedia. This would be based on a 'catalogue of simple thoughts' and an algebraic language of symbols, 'characteristica universalis', which would render all knowledge demonstrative and allow disputes to be resolved by precise calculation (see LEIBNIZ, G.W. §10).

The notion of unity of science, along with that of the universality of rationality, was given its strongest promotion during the European Enlightenment. The most important expression of the encyclopaedic tradition came in the mid-eighteenth century from DIDEROT and D'ALEMBERT, editors of the *Encyclopédie* (1751–72). Diderot stressed in his own entry, 'Encyclopaedia', that 'the word Encyclopaedia signifies the unification of the sciences'. The function of the encyclopedia was to exhibit the unity of human knowledge. Diderot and D'Alembert, in contrast with Leibniz, made classification by subject primary, and introduced cross-references by way of logical connections.

For Kant the unity of science is not the reflection of a unity found in nature; rather, it has its foundations in the allegedly unifying nature of reason itself (see KANT, I. §7). This, however, lacks the Leibnizian form of a deductive system and combinatorial framework. Instead, Kant adopts the image of an organic architecture. Each science is a self-subsistent whole and separate buildings connect to other sciences by passages. He also held the view that biology cannot be reduced to mechanics.

Kant's ideas set the frame of reference for discussions of unification in German thought throughout the nineteenth century. He gave philosophical currency to the notion of world-picture (*Weltbild*), establishing unity of science as an intellectual ideal. Influenced by this tradition, which culminated with the work of Albert Einstein, the physicists Max PLANCK and Ernst MACH engaged in a heated debate about the precise character of the unified scientific world-picture. Mach's, more influential, view was phenomenological and Darwinian: the unification of knowledge took the form of an analysis of ideas into elementary sensations and was ultimately a matter of adaptive economy of thought. In physics the 'electromagnetic world-picture' and Planck's thermodynamical worldview constituted some of the alternatives to a long-standing mechanistic view that since Newton had affected biology as well as most branches of physics.

Kant also distinguished between several types of judgement that, in turn, characterized different intellectual disciplines. In this way he set the basis for the famous distinction between the natural sciences (*Naturwissenschaften*) and the cultural or social sciences (*Geisteswissenschaften*) introduced by Wilhelm DILTHEY. Followers of this distinction, such as Max WEBER and Heinrich Rickert (for Rickert, see NEO-KANTIANISM §7), claimed that the difference in subject matter between the two kinds of science forced a distinctive difference between their respective methods – this despite the fact that since Hume, Comte and J.S. Mill, the social sciences had relied on analogies with the natural sciences, from Newtonian and statistical mechanics and also from biology.

The logical positivists, notably the members of the Vienna Circle, introduced, under the banner of 'unity of science without metaphysics', a model of demarcation between science and metaphysics based on the unity of method and language that included all the sciences, natural and social (see DEMARCATION PROBLEM; LOGICAL POSITIVISM; VIENNA CIRCLE). Notice that a common method does not imply a more substantive unity of content involving theories and their concepts. In the stronger model especially recommended by Rudolf CARNAP, however, unity was affirmed because of the associated value of simplicity, and was characterized by axiomatic structures, reductive logical connections between concepts, and laws of the different sciences at different levels, with physics as the fundamental basis, and the possibility of empirical grounding and testability. Carnap was influenced by the empiricist tradition (especially Russell and Mach) and the ideals of simplicity and reductive logical analysis in the early works of Russell and Wittgenstein (see ANALYTICAL PHILOSOPHY §2). Otto NEURATH, by contrast, favoured a more realistic and less reductive model of unity which emphasized a unity of language and the local exchanges of scientific tools, although it was not constrained by Carnap's ideals of conceptual precision, deductive systematicity and logical rigour (Neurath spoke of a 'boat', a 'mosaic', an 'orchestration', a 'universal jargon'). In 1934 Neurath spearheaded a movement for Unity of Science that encouraged international cooperation among scientists and launched the project of an *International Encyclopedia of Unified Science*. For both Carnap and Neurath the ideal of unified science against metaphysics had deep social and political significance.

Two new ideas by logical positivists in the USA after the Second World War again placed the question of unity of science at the core of philosophy of science: Carl Hempel's deductive-nomological model of explanation and Ernest Nagel's (1961) model of reduction (see EXPLANATION; REDUCTION, PROBLEMS OF §§2–3). Hempel's model characterizes the scientific explanation of events as a subsumption under an empirically testable generalization. In the 1950s, when positivism was extending to the social sciences, the model was offered as a criterion of demarcation. Explanations in the historical sciences too must fit the model if they are to count as scientific (see POSITIVISM IN THE SOCIAL SCIENCES §2). The applicability of Hempel's model was soon contested – notably by W. Dray – and this opened a debate about the nature of the historical sciences that remains unresolved. In the process, some have claimed as historical natural sciences the like of geology and biology. It has been argued that Hempel's model, especially the requirement of empirically testable strict universal laws, is satisfied neither in the physical sciences nor the historical sciences, including biology (Cartwright 1983; Ehreshefsky 1992).

Since Nagel's influential model of reduction by derivation, most discussions of unity of science have been cast in terms of reductions between concepts and between theories. The hierarchy of levels of reduction was set by the levels of aggregation of entities all the way down to atomic particles, thus rendering microphysics the fundamental science (Oppenheim and Putnam 1958). Criticism for the rejection of Nagel's model and its emendations has occupied the last three decades of philosophical discussions of the unity of physics, and especially in psychology and biology. In the latter the availability of laws and theories and the feasibility of global reductions have been contested (see REDUCTIONISM IN THE PHILOSOPHY OF MIND). The possibility and the necessity of reductions in a number of forms have been discussed in connection with issues of explanation, realism and scientific progress (see NATURALIZED PHILOSOPHY OF SCIENCE §1). Debates on unification and reduction have taken place also within the sciences as renewed reductionistic ideals have been revived in physics, driven by the success of the unified theories of fundamental forces in the 1970s, and in biology – especially sociobiology – driven by successes in molecular genetics (see MOLECULAR BIOLOGY; SOCIOBIOLOGY).

In anti-reductionist quarters, models of unification without reduction have appeared: for instance, the notion of 'interfield theories' (Darden and Maull 1977) and, less theory-oriented, the emphasis on the plurality of kinds of unity (Hacking 1996) and the idea of science as a historical process, manifesting a historical unity with a Darwinian-like pattern of evolution (Hull 1988). A more radical departure is the more recent criticism of the methodological values of reductionism and unification in science – also as embedded in society and affecting it. This view argues for the replacement of the emphasis on global unity – including unity of method – by the emphasis on disunity, epistemological and ontological pluralism and local cooperation. The suggestion is that the notion of a science should be understood, now following the later Wittgenstein, as at best a family resemblance concept (Dupré 1993).

References and further reading

* D'Alembert, J. and Diderot, D. (eds) (1751–72) *Encyclopédie, ou dictionnaire raisonné des sciences, des arts at des metiers*, Paris: Plon. (This is the classic paradigm of encyclopedic work, with especial significance in the context of the culture of the enlightenment.)

Carnap, R., Morris, C. and Neurath, O. (eds) (1938–70) *International Encyclopedia of Unified Science*, vols 1 and 2, Foundations of the Unity of Science, Chicago, IL: University of Chicago Press. (The *Encyclopedia* was planned as a series of monographs applying the philosophy of logical empiricism to the different sciences and as a way of showing and promoting cross-bearings. Publication ended in 1970 and, ironically, it contains as one of the later pieces Kuhn's *The Structure of Scientific Revolutions*.)

* Cartwright, N. (1983) *How the Laws of Physics Lie*, Oxford: Oxford University Press. (Criticizes the application of Hempel's deductive-nomological model of explanation in physics.)

Cohen, I.B. (1995) *Interactions*, Cambridge, MA: MIT Press. (Historical examination of the different mechanistic and organistic analogies and metaphors used in the development of the social sciences.)

* Darden, L. and Maull, N. (1977) 'Interfield Theories', *Philosophy of Science* 44: 43–64. (Against standard models of theory-reduction, it proposes a model of unification, especially in biology, in which theories do not identify fields but rather bring them together.)

* Dupré, J. (1993) *The Disorder of Things. Metaphysical Foundations of the Disunity of Science*, Cambridge, MA: Harvard University Press. (Powerful criticism of reductionism and essentialism, as well as other formulations of the unity of science; a *fin-de-siècle* classic.)

* Ehreshefsky, M. (1992) 'The Historical Nature of Evolutionary Theory', in M.H. Nitecki and D.V. Nitecki (eds) *History and Evolution*, New York: State University of New York Press. (Claims that neither the physical nor the biological sciences can be adequately brought together under Hempel's model of explanation.)

Galison, P. and Stump, D. (eds) (1996) *The Disunity of Science. Boundaries, Contexts and Power*, Stanford,

CA: Stanford University Press. (A very interesting collection of articles with an emphasis on disunity and cultural contexts.)

* Hacking, I. (1996) 'The Disunities of Science', in P. Galison and D. Stump (eds) *The Disunity of Science. Boundaries, Contexts and Power*, Stanford, CA: Stanford University Press, 1996. (Points to the number of different possible kinds of unities).

* Hull, D. (1988) *Science as Progress*, Chicago, IL: University of Chicago Press. (An attempt to apply evolutionary ideas to the dynamics of scientific practice.)

McRae, R. (1961) *The Problem of the Unity of the Sciences: Bacon to Kant*, Toronto, Ont.: University of Toronto Press. (The only monograph on the issue in Bacon, Descartes, Leibniz and Kant; very general; it omits Hume and it does not address the relation between natural and social sciences.)

Mayr, E. (1982) *The Growth of Biological Thought*, Cambridge, MA: Harvard University Press. (A classic in philosophy of biology that criticizes physicists' reductionism, especially Weinberg's, and defends the concept of emergence in biology.)

* Nagel, E. (1961) *The Structure of Science*, London: Routledge. (Chapter 11 presents the author's account of reduction.)

* Oppenheim, P. and Putnam, H. (1958) 'The Unity of Science as a Working Hypothesis', in H. Feigl *et al.* (eds) *Minnesota Studies in the Philosophy of Science*, vol. 2, Minneapolis, MN: Minnesota University Press. (A standard formulation of the metaphysics of reductionism as a hierarchy of objects in the scientific domain.)

Primas, H. (1983) *Chemistry, Quantum Mechanics and Reductionism*, Berlin: Springer. (A criticism of the straightforward reducibility of chemistry to quantum mechanics.)

Schaffner, K. (1993) *Discovery and Explanation in Biology and Medicine*, Chicago, IL: University of Chicago Press. (Presents a survey of the literature and a discussion of the applicability of different notions of reductionism in the biomedical sciences, especially his own; it includes a very helpful bibliography with essential primary sources.)

JORDI CAT

UNIVERSAL GENERALIZATION

see QUANTIFICATION AND INFERENCE

UNIVERSAL LANGUAGE

Most often associated with attempts to establish an international language such as Esperanto, the idea of a universal language is rooted in the biblical claim of an original language common to all human beings. The idea received its most thorough investigation during the seventeenth century. Drawing on the example of Chinese characters, early schemes involved a system of written signs that would allow communication between speakers of different languages. Later thinkers argued for the importance of an ideal 'philosophical language' in which the structure of signs exactly mirrored the structure of reality. While such projects fell short of their authors' expectations, their influence can be discerned in the formalisms of modern logic and science.

1   **Adamic language**
2   **Artificial schemes**
3   **Leibniz**

1   Adamic language

The earliest source for the idea of a universal language is the biblical story of an original language used by Adam to name the different species of animals created by God (*Genesis* 2: 19–20). In both the Jewish and Christian traditions, it was commonly assumed that this 'Adamic' language expressed Adam's perfect knowledge of things prior to the Fall: each name of a creature exactly conveyed its essence. It was natural to suppose a corruption of this language at the Fall; however, the crucial event in the loss of a universal language is told in the story of Babel, when 'the Lord confused the language of all the earth' (*Genesis* 11: 9). Thereafter, human beings were condemned to speak a multitude of languages and to suffer the pain of mutual incomprehension.

This biblical background remained central to conceptions of a universal language well into the seventeenth century. Numerous attempts were made to identify and recover the original language of Adam. Among Jewish and Christian thinkers alike, Hebrew retained the greatest claim to this honour, although other candidates were proposed (including Latin, Chinese, Dutch and Swedish). The attempt to recover the Adamic language, and the knowledge implicit in it, was significantly influenced by the Jewish kabbalah, which assigned a mystical significance to the letters of the Hebrew alphabet and prescribed techniques for their interpretation and manipulation (see KABBALAH). Another important source was the thirteenth-century theologian Ramon

Llull, who stressed a method of achieving universal knowledge through combinations of letters signifying fundamental categories of reality (see LLULL, R. §2).

2 Artificial schemes

During the seventeenth century, there occurred an explosion of interest in universal language schemes, conceived for the first time as systems of artificial signs or 'characters' constructed by human beings as a means of overcoming the limitations of natural languages. The causes of this newfound fascination with universal languages are complex. Clearly, a role must be assigned to the growing importance of vernacular languages and the decline of Latin as a shared medium of commerce, scholarship and diplomacy. An increase in millenarian religious sentiment, particularly in England, renewed the call for a recovery of the Adamic language. Finally, and most importantly, there was a growing recognition of the significance of language as a factor in the acquisition of scientific knowledge.

One of the earliest and most influential statements on the topic was Francis Bacon's reference in *The Advancement of Learning* (1605 II: ch. 16) to languages such as Chinese, whose users 'write in characters real, which express neither letters nor words in gross, but things or notions'. To many seventeenth-century thinkers, Chinese provided a model of what a universal language might be: a single set of characters that could be pronounced differently in different languages, but which when written would offer a shared basis for understanding. Implicit in Bacon's remark, however, was a further idea that pointed toward the scientific value of such a language. In his *New Organon* (1620 I: aph. 59), Bacon complained of how words commonly obscure 'the true divisions of nature'. It was a short step from this to the idea that these 'true divisions' might be better represented in a language composed of 'real characters', which directly expressed 'things or notions' (see BACON, F. §§4–5).

Most early proponents of artificial language schemes stressed the practical value of their inventions as instruments of communication. Their works were primarily attempts to devise a system of writing, modelled variously on Chinese characters, cryptographic codes or shorthand notation, whereby synonymous words in different languages would be represented by a common sign. It was not long, however, before the more ambitious idea of a 'philosophical language' took hold. In a 1629 letter to Marin Mersenne, Descartes had already expressed scepticism concerning the usefulness of artificial languages of the first sort. However, he went on to postulate another kind of language in which ideas would be represented so clearly that errors of judgment would be 'almost impossible'. To realize such a language, all of our thoughts would first have to be given a proper order 'like the natural order of the numbers'; and this presupposes the 'true philosophy', by which the analysis and ordering of thoughts would be carried out. Although Descartes pursues the plan no further, he is optimistic that 'such a language is possible and that the knowledge on which it depends can be discovered'.

A philosophical language of the sort envisioned by Descartes is described in Mersenne's *Harmonie Universelle* (1636) and was pursued in many later works, culminating in George Dalgarno's *Ars Signorum* (1661) and John Wilkins' *An Essay Towards a Real Character and a Philosophical Language* (1668). Such schemes typically consisted of two parts: a system of categories summarizing the 'true divisions' of nature, and a set of characters suitable for representing these categories and the elements within them. Although informed by the discoveries of seventeenth-century science, the first part of the scheme was strongly indebted to the systems of categories propounded by Aristotle and medieval philosophers. In his *Essay*, Wilkins begins with forty genera (classified as transcendentals, substances, quantities, qualities, actions and relations), each of which he subdivides into its 'proper differences and species'. He then proposes two ways of representing the composition of concepts from their respective genus, difference and species: (1) a real character, or system of ideographic signs formed from combinations of vertical and horizontal lines; (2) a speakable philosophical language, consisting of novel combinations of syllables, consonants and vowels. In both cases, additional signs must be added to play the role of particles underwriting the grammatical structure of the language.

3 Leibniz

The idea of a universal language received its final significant development in the seventeenth century in the writings of Gottfried Wilhelm Leibniz. Although indebted to the efforts of Dalgarno and Wilkins, Leibniz criticizes these authors for their reliance on what he sees as an arbitrary number of basic categories. Harking back to Descartes, Leibniz locates the key to a philosophical language in an analysis by which every concept would be broken down into its simplest elements, the 'alphabet of human thoughts'. With these simples identified, and appropriate characters assigned to each, we would, in effect, possess the Adamic language: one in which the structure of every character perfectly mirrors the structure of reality.

Leibniz's plans for a universal language are among the most ambitious devised; in practice, however, they met with limited success. Early on, he recognized that an analysis of concepts into ultimate simples lies beyond the power of the human mind. What we are left with, then, are classificatory systems, like that of Wilkins, which represent our best attempts to order reality as we conceive it. Leibniz's greatest achievement in the area lies in his *specieuse générale* or 'general science of forms', a collection of calculi designed to support the formalization of reasoning in every branch of knowledge. Anticipating twentieth-century developments in logic and methodology, Leibniz's studies represent one of the enduring legacies of the universal language movement (see LEIBNIZ, G.W. §10).

See also: FORMAL LANGUAGES AND SYSTEMS

References and further reading

* Bacon, F. (1605) *The Advancement of Learning*, ed. G.W. Kitchin, London: Dent, 1976. (Bacon's discussion of 'characters real' occurs in book 2, chapter 16.)
* —— (1620) *The New Organon*, ed. F.H. Anderson, New York: Macmillan, 1960. (Bacon criticizes words as 'idols of the marketplace' in book I, aphorisms 43, 59–60.)
* Dalgarno, G. (1834) *The Works of George Dalgarno*, Edinburgh; repr. New York: AMS Press, 1971. (Contains all of Dalgarno's writings on artificial language schemes, including his 1661 *Ars Signorum*.)
* Descartes, R. (1991) *The Philosophical Writings of Descartes*, vol. 3 (The Correspondence), trans. J. Cottingham, R. Stoothoof, D. Murdoch and A. Kenny, Cambridge: Cambridge University Press. (Descartes' letter to Mersenne is dated 20 November 1629.)
  Katz, D.S. (1982) *Philo-Semitism and the Readmission of the Jews to England (1603–1655)*, Oxford: Clarendon Press. (Chapter 2 argues persuasively for the importance of the idea of an Adamic language in seventeenth-century England.)
  Knowlson, J. (1975) *Universal Language Schemes in England and France 1600–1800*, Toronto, Ont.: University of Toronto Press. (The best survey of the topic; contains a valuable checklist of universal language schemes in the seventeenth and eighteenth centuries.)
  Leibniz, G.W. (1966) *Logical Papers*, trans. and ed. G.H.R. Parkinson, Oxford: Clarendon Press. (The fullest collection in English of Leibniz's writings on logic and language; includes selections from his 1666 essay *On the Art of Combinations*, in which appears his earliest plan for a universal language.)
* Mersenne, M. (1636) *Harmonie Universelle*, Paris; repr. Paris: Centre National de la Recherche Scientifique, 1986. (Book I, proposition 24 contains Mersenne's proposal for a 'perfect language', in which mathematical and scientific truths would be expressed by combinations of musical tones.)
  Rutherford, D. (1995) 'Philosophy and Language', in N. Jolley (ed.) *The Cambridge Companion to Leibniz*, New York: Cambridge University Press. (A comprehensive review of Leibniz's interests in language, including the idea of a universal language.)
  Salmon, V. (1988) *The Study of Language in 17th-Century England*, Amsterdam: John Benjamins. (A collection of ground-breaking essays on the projects of Dalgarno, Wilkins and their contemporaries; includes a bibliography of recent work in the area.)
  Slaughter, M.M. (1982) *Universal Languages and Scientific Taxonomy in the Seventeenth Century*, Cambridge: Cambridge University Press. (An important study of the relationship between seventeenth-century scientific thinking and the idea of a universal language.)
* Wilkins, J. (1668) *An Essay towards a Real Character, and a Philosophical Language*, London; repr. in the series *English Linguistics 1500–1800*, number 119, Menston: Scolar Press, 1968. (Wilkins' attempt at constructing a universal language, discussed in §2 above.)

DONALD RUTHERFORD

UNIVERSALISM IN ETHICS

The claim that ethical standards or principles are universal is an ancient commonplace of many ethical traditions and of contemporary political life, particularly in appeals to universal human rights. Yet it remains controversial. There are many sources of controversy. Universalism in ethics may be identified with claims about the form, scope or content of ethical principles, or with the very idea that ethical judgment appeals to principles, rather than to particular cases. Or it may be identified with various claims to identify a single fundamental universal principle, from which all other ethical principles and judgments derive. These disagreements can be clarified, and perhaps in part resolved, by distinguishing a number of different conceptions of universalism in ethics.

1   Form and scope: principles for everybody

One distinctive understanding of universalism in ethics is that ethical principles are principles *for everybody*. They prescribe obligations for everybody, define rights for everybody, list virtues for everybody. The most minimal version of ethical universalism is a claim about the form of ethical principles or standards. It is the claim that ethical principles hold for all and not merely for some, that is, for everybody without exception.

Those who hold that ethical principles are universal in form often disagree about their *scope*, that is to say about which beings comprise 'everybody'. Plato's character Meno tells Socrates that there are quite different virtues for men and women, for boys and girls, for old men and slaves (Meno 71e). On the other hand, Cicero famously asserted that 'there will not be different laws at Rome and at Athens, now and in the future, but one eternal and unchangeable law for all nations and all times' (De Republica III, 33) (see CICERO, M.T. §2); and St Paul proclaimed that 'there is neither Jew nor Greek, there is neither bond nor free, there is neither male nor female: for ye are all one in Christ Jesus' (Galatians 3:28). One very influential understanding of universalism in ethics, shared by many religions, by the natural law and liberal traditions, and by many others, is the contention that ethical principles are universal in form and cosmopolitan in scope, in that they hold for all humans.

However, any cosmopolitan view of the scope of ethical principles must note that living up to obligations, virtues and even some rights is impossible for human beings who lack mature capacities for action. Neither infants nor small children, neither the retarded nor the senile, can be held accountable for carrying out obligations, living virtuously or exercising certain rights, such as political rights. Yet humans who lack these capacities might have other rights, for example, to care and protection. Those who can suffer but not act can be moral patients but not moral agents, possessing some rights, but not the full range of obligations, virtues or rights. The scope of different sorts of principles of universal form will evidently have to vary (see MORAL AGENTS; RESPONSIBILITY).

Many think that the scope of some ethical principles is more-than-cosmopolitan. Jeremy Bentham famously declared that the criterion of moral standing was 'not, Can they *reason*? nor, Can they *talk*? but Can they *suffer*?' (1789: 412, footnote; original emphasis); Hindus and Buddhists too extend moral concern beyond humankind; some environmentalists extend concern not only to nonhuman animals, but to plants, even to species and habitats (see ANIMALS AND ETHICS; BENTHAM, J. §2; DUTY AND VIRTUE, INDIAN CONCEPTIONS OF; ENVIRONMENTAL ETHICS; MORAL STANDING §2–3).

Other advocates of principles of universal form join Meno in holding that their scope is less-than-cosmopolitan. For example, communitarians (who sometimes describe themselves as *rejecting* universal principles) advocate principles of universal form whose scope is restricted to particular communities (see COMMUNITY AND COMMUNITARIANISM); some virtue ethicists hold similar views (see VIRTUE ETHICS §5).

2   Content: formal principles or uniform requirements?

A second conception of universalism in ethics emphasizes the content as well as the form and scope of principles. Principles which hold for everybody will prescribe or recommend the same for everybody (same obligations, same rights, same virtues and so on). Advocates of universal principles see this as a merit: they see equality of requirement and entitlement as ethically important (see EQUALITY §3). For example, discussions of universal human rights emphasize not only that all humans have rights, but that they all have the same rights.

Two objections are commonly raised. The first is that principles which prescribe the same for all will be abstract and general, so provide too little guidance. The second is that they will be too demanding and specific, prescribing with senseless and heartless uniformity for differing cases and situations. On this account, universal principles are either too formal and minimal or else too uniformly demanding. Evidently the two criticisms cannot both be true of one and the same universal principle. If a principle is so abstract that it provides no practical guidance, then it will not prescribe rigid uniformity of action; conversely, if it prescribes with rigid uniformity it will not fail to guide action.

The charge that ethical principles which prescribe the same for all abstract from differences between cases is true, but not damaging. No principle of action – whether of universal or non-universal form, whether of cosmopolitan or lesser scope – can prescribe with total specificity; even very explicit principles abstract from many circumstances. It follows that principles of action can always be satisfied in varied ways. A principle such as 'Tell the truth' does not prescribe what we must say to whom or when; a principle such as 'Pay your debts' does not determine the means or manner of repayment. Principles of action, including ethical principles, *constrain* action or entitlements, rather than picking out a single, wholly determinate line of action. Abstract principles can therefore guide action yet allow for flexible interpretation or application that takes account of differences between cases. So an ethics of universal principles can readily avoid both barren formalism and doctrinaire rigorism.

3 Universalism and particularism: principles and judgment

Since universal ethical principles are always to some extent abstract or indeterminate they must be supplemented by *judgment* in selecting among possible implementations. This point is recognized, indeed stressed, by advocates of universal principles. Kant (1781/1787), for example, insisted that there cannot be complete rules for judgment, and that principles cannot entail their determinate applications, which require judgment (see KANT, I. §12).

The serious disagreement lies not between those who think that ethics needs *only* principles and those who think it needs *only* judgment of particular cases, but between those who think principles and judgment are both needed and those who believe that judgment alone will be enough. The deepest opposition to any sort of ethical universalism comes from ethical particularists who hold that unmediated apprehension of particular cases can guide ethical life. Ethical particularists seek to anchor ethical judgment in perception of and responsiveness to the particular, in attentiveness to the case at hand, in the salience of the personal relationship and its claims (see FRIENDSHIP; IMPARTIALITY §4). They usually hold that ethical life revolves around character and virtue. The most radical cast doubt on the very conception of following a rule or principle; the less radical cite the issues of §2 as evidence that an ethics of rules and duties is inadequate (see MORAL PARTICULARISM).

Both ethical particularists (who appeal only to judgment) and universalists (who argue that judgment is used in combination with principles) have found it difficult to explain how judgment works. Some particularists describe it as analogous to perceiving or attending or to the exercise of a craft skill. Some universalists see judgment as the skill of identifying acts that fall within the constraints set by a plurality of principles (see MORAL JUDGMENT).

4 Fundamental principles: 'golden rules'

Other conceptions of universalism in ethics combine views of the form, scope and sameness of content of principles with ambitious claims that a single fundamental universal principle provides the basis for all derivative ethical principles and ultimately for ethical judgment of particular cases.

Often the proposed fundamental principle is a version of a 'golden rule'. Variously formulated golden rules are found in Hindu and Confucian sacred texts, and in many other traditions, including natural law and popular ethical debate. One well known golden rule is Christian with Jewish antecedents: 'Do unto others as you would that they should do unto you' (for specific formulations see Matthew 7:12, Luke 6:31; for antecedents Tobias 4:15). Others are prohibitions rather than injunctions, such as 'Do not do unto others what you would not have them do unto you'.

These would-be foundational principles have been criticized for linking ethics too closely to agents' desires or consent. Why should willingness to be on the receiving end of like action make it permissible? If masochists are willing to suffer others' sadism, would that make sadism right? More generally, can acceptance of being on the receiving end of like action legitimate anything?

This problem can be overcome only by building additional constraints or complexities into the idea of considering what one would desire or consent to when putting oneself into another's shoes. This has been attempted in various principles, which are first cousin to golden rules, that have been influential in secular work in ethics. Most famously J.S. Mill asserted, in Utilitarianism (1861), that 'in the golden rule of Jesus of Nazareth, we read the complete spirit of the ethics of utility'. The link Mill draws between utilitarianism and golden rules arises only if agents consider not what they as individuals would want if on the receiving end, but what they if taking account of all others' desires would want if on the receiving end. Only then can a golden rule reflect everybody's desires, and so be thought of as aiming at the greatest happiness (see UTILITARIANISM; MILL, J.S. §10).

Other approaches of this sort have recently been advocated by P. Singer (1972), R.M. Hare (1975) and A. Gewirth (1987), each of whom recognizes affinities as well as differences between his proposal for the foundations of ethics and traditional golden rules. For example, Gewirth suggests that a rational golden rule would read 'Do unto others as you have a right that they do unto you', while Hare advocates a universal prescriptivism by which the fundamental criterion for ethical judgment is that agents be willing to universalize their judgments, that is extend them to all situations identical in their universal properties (see PRESCRIPTIVISM; HARE, R.M. §§1–2). There has been much discussion of the plausibility of these proposals, which generally reject the emphasis traditional golden rules give to what one would have if the particular victim reciprocated, and introduce some reference to what one would want if one's own principle were to be universally adopted or if one's desires took account of others' desires. These writers advocate a strong form of ethical universalism: not merely do they defend a single fundamental ethical principle, but they insist that it refer to the desires that all hold, or ought if rational to hold.

5 Fundamental principles: Kantian universalizability

An alternative conception of universalism in ethics rejects golden rules and seeks to anchor all ethical justification in a more formal fundamental universal principle, which does not refer to desires or consent to fix the content of ethics. The most famous and most ambitious attempt to go further is Kant's 'categorical imperative', of which the best known version runs: 'Act only on that maxim through which you can at the same time will that it should become a universal law' ([1785] 1903: 421). Kant claims to show that 'all imperatives of duty can be derived from this one imperative as their principle' (421). He insists that in such derivations no reference be made either to anyone's happiness or desires, consent or agreement, and that the categorical imperative is not a version of a golden rule (which he dismisses as trivial, 430, footnote). Kant's views have been influential: a German scholar recently commented that 'Kant succeeded with his objection almost in invalidating the golden rule and disqualifying it from future discussion in ethics' (Reiner 1983: 274).

English language philosophy has been less convinced that Kant undermined golden rule approaches. J.S. Mill was neither the first nor the last to think that Kant's claim to derive all principles of duty from the categorical imperative was complete nonsense. He wrote of Kant

> when he begins to deduce from this precept any of the actual duties of morality, he fails, almost grotesquely, to show that there would be any contradiction, any logical (not to say physical) impossibility, in the adoption by all rational beings of the most outrageously immoral rules of conduct. All he shows is that the *consequences* of their universal adoption would be such as no one would choose to incur.
>
> (1861: 207; original emphasis)

There has been widespread scepticism about Kant's supposed claim to show that 'immoral rules of conduct' are self-contradictory. However, he in fact makes the more circumspect *modal* claim that we should not act on principles which we *cannot* simultaneously 'will as universal laws'. An example of such a principle is that of false promising. Kant holds that false promisers who try (incoherently) to will false promising as a universal law thereby will the destruction of the very trust on which their own attempts to promise falsely must rely. Hence when we try to act on such principles Kant holds that

> we in fact do not will that our maxim (principle) should become a universal law – since this is impossible for us – but rather that its opposite should remain a law universally: we only take the liberty of making an *exception* to it for ourselves (or even just for this once).
>
> ([1785] 1903: 424; original emphasis)

In 'deriving' an 'actual principle of duty' from the categorical imperative, Kant takes it that agents not only seek principles of universal form and cosmopolitan scope which prescribe the same for all, but shun any principles which cannot be 'willed for all'. Kantian justifications of such principles, unlike golden rule justifications, do not appeal to either the desires, the happiness or the acceptance of those on the receiving end, nor indeed to actual or hypothetical desires of any or of all agents. The distinctive modal character of Kantian universalizability is its appeal to what *can be willed for all* (rather than to what *actually is* or *hypothetically would be willed by all*). It remains a matter of considerable controversy whether a strictly Kantian approach can be used to construct an account of specific principles of duty, virtue or entitlement, or whether it is indeed too formal and minimal to sustain these derivations.

See also: CRITICAL THEORY; INTUITIONISM IN ETHICS; THEOLOGICAL VIRTUES

References and further reading

* Bentham, J. (1789) *An Introduction to the Principles of Morals and Legislation*, ed. J.H. Burns and H.L.A. Hart, revised F. Rosen, Oxford: Clarendon Press, 1996. (Classic statement of utilitarianism.)
* Cicero, M.T. (54–51 BC) *De Republica*, trans. M. Grant, *On Government*, Harmondsworth: Penguin, 1993, books III, V and VI. (Early form of universalism about scope of moral principles.)
* Gewirth, A. (1987) 'The Golden Rule Rationalized', *Midwest Studies in Philosophy* 3: 133–44. (Modern

form of universalism, with affinities to golden rules.)

—— (1988) 'Ethical Universalism and Particularism', *Journal of Philosophy* 85: 283–301. (A universalist approach to ethical judgment.)

Hare, R.M. (1963) *Freedom and Reason*, Oxford: Clarendon Press. (Basic source on universal prescriptivism.)

* —— (1975) 'Abortion and the Golden Rule', *Philosophy and Public Affairs* 3: 201–22. (Application of universal prescriptivism to problem of abortion; includes discussion of golden rules.)

Herman, B. (1993) *The Practice of Moral Judgment*, Cambridge, MA: Harvard University Press. (Insightful discussions of difficulties raised about Kantian ethics.)

* Kant, I. (1781/1787) *Critik der Reinen Vernunft*, trans. N. Kemp Smith, *Critique of Pure Reason*, London: Macmillan, 1973. (*Locus classicus* for Kant's insistence that there cannot be complete rules for judgment.)

—— (1785) *Grundlegung zur Metaphysik der Sitten*, in *Kants gesammelte Schriften*, ed. Königlichen Preußischen Akademie der Wissenschaften, Berlin: Reimer, vol. 4, 1903; trans. H.J. Paton, *Groundwork of the Metaphysics of Morals* (originally *The Moral Law*), London: Hutchinson, 1948; repr. New York: Harper & Row, 1964. (References made to this work in the entry give the page number from the 1903 Berlin Akademie volume; these page numbers are included in the Paton translation. Classic, short, if difficult, exposition of Kant's ethics.)

McDowell, J. (1979) 'Virtue and Reason', *Monist* 62 (3): 331–50; revised version repr. as 'Non-cognitivism and Rule Following', in S. Holtzman and C. Leach (eds) *Wittgenstein: To Follow a Rule*, London: Routledge & Kegan Paul, 1981. 141–62. (An influential statement of a radical particularist position, which questions the very possibility of following rules or principles.)

* Mill, J.S. (1861) *Utilitarianism*, in J.M. Robson (ed.) *Collected Works of John Stuart Mill*, vol. 10, Essays on Ethics, Religion and Society, Toronto: University of Toronto Press, 1969. (Account of utilitarianism expanding on Bentham.)

O'Neill, O. (1987) 'Abstraction, Idealization and Ideology in Ethics', in J.D.G. Evans (ed.) *Moral Philosophy and Contemporary Problems*, Cambridge: Cambridge University Press. (What is abstraction? Is it avoidable? Is it harmful? In asking these questions, this essay is particularly relevant to §§2 and 3.)

—— (1989) *Constructions of Reason: Explorations of Kant's Practical Philosophy*, Cambridge: Cambridge University Press. (Papers on patterns of universalist

ethical reasoning that use Kant's categorical imperative.)

—— (1991) 'Kantian Ethics', in P. Singer (ed.) *A Companion to Ethics*, Oxford: Blackwell, 175–85. (Overview of Kant's position and some well-known criticisms).

* Plato (*c.*386–380 BC) *Meno*, in Protagoras and Meno, trans. W.K.C. Guthrie, Harmondsworth: Penguin, 1956. (Discusses the nature of virtue.)

Potter, N. and Timmons, M. (eds) (1985) *Morality and Universality: Essays on Ethical Universalizability*, Dordrecht: Reidel. (Useful papers on different conceptions of universality in ethics; large bibliography.)

* Reiner, H. (1983) 'The Golden Rule and the Natural Law', in *Duty and Inclination: The Fundamentals of Morality Discussed and Redefined with Special Regard to Kant and Schiller*, trans. M. Santos, The Hague: Nijhoff, 271–93. (Historical overview; useful references especially to German literature.)

* Singer, P. (1972) 'Famine, Affluence and Morality', *Philosophy and Public Affairs* 1: 229–43. (Well-known utilitarian argument to show that beneficence should have cosmopolitan scope: the affluent should help the hungry however far away they may be.)

Wattles, J. (1996) *The Golden Rule*, Oxford: Oxford University Press. (Examines the principle 'Do to others as you want others to do to you' in contexts of psychology, philosophy and religion, from Confucius, Hillel and Jesus to R.M. Hare and Paul Ricoeur.)

Wiggins, D. (1980) 'Deliberation and Practical Reason', in *Needs, Values, Truth: Essays in the Philosophy of Value*, Aristotelian Society Series, vol. 6, Oxford: Blackwell, 1987; revised edn, 1991. (A particularist reading of Aristotle on judgment.)

Williams, B. (1985) *Ethics and the Limits of Philosophy*, Cambridge, MA: Harvard University Press and London: Fontana. (Particularist criticism of aspects of ethical universalism.)

ONORA O'NEILL

UNIVERSALS

In metaphysics, the term 'universals' is applied to things of two sorts: properties (such as redness or roundness), and relations (such as kinship relations like sisterhood, or the causal relation, or spatial and temporal relations). Universals are to be understood by contrast with particulars. Few universals, if any, are truly 'universal' in the sense that they are shared by all individuals – a universal is characteristically the sort of thing which some individuals may have in common, and others may lack.

Universals have been conceived to be things which enable us intellectually to grasp a permanent, under-lying order behind the changing flux of experience. Some of the gods of ancient mythologies correspond roughly to various important underlying universals – social relations for instance, as for example if Hera is said to be the goddess of Marriage and Ares (or Mars) is said to be the god of War. Many traditions, East and West, have dealt with the underlying problem which generates theories of universals; nevertheless the term 'universals' is closely tied to the Western tradition, and the agenda has been set largely by the work of Plato and Aristotle.

The term often used in connection with Plato is not 'universals' but 'Forms' (or 'Ideas', used in the sense of ideals rather than of thoughts), the term 'universals' echoing Aristotle more than Plato. Other terms cognate with universals include not only properties and relations, but also qualities, attributes, characteristics, essences and accidents (in the sense of qualities which a thing has not of necessity but only by accident), species and genus, and natural kinds.

Various arguments have been advanced to establish the existence of universals, the most memorable of which is the 'one over many' argument. There are also various arguments against the existence of universals. There are, for instance, various vicious regress arguments which derive from Aristotle's so-called 'third man argument' against Plato. Another family of arguments trades on what is called Ockham's razor: it is argued that we can say anything we need to say, and explain everything we need to explain, without appeal to universals; and if we can, and if we are rational, then we should. Those who believe in universals are called Realists, those who do not are called Nominalists.

1   **Sources in ancient mathematics and biology**
2   **Samenesses and differences**
3   **Arguments for and against**
4   **Nominalism and Realism**
5   **Frege exhumes universals**

1   Sources in ancient mathematics and biology

Plato looked to mathematics as a model to find ideal 'forms' which can be grasped by the intellect and which we find to be imperfectly reflected in the world of the senses. Moral and political ideals too, Plato thought, are reflected only very imperfectly in the world of appearances. Aristotle's conception of universals was tailored to fit not mathematics but biology. Individual animals and plants fall into natural kinds, or species, such as pigs or cabbages. Various different species, in turn, fall under a genus.

Universals impose a taxonomy on the plurality of different individuals in the world. Regularities in the world can then be understood by appeal to the universals, or species, under which individuals fall, explaining why pigs never give birth to kittens, for instance, and in general why each living thing generates others of its kind.

Plato conceived of universals as transcendent beings, *ante rem* in Latin ('before things'): the existence of universals does not depend on the existence of individuals which instantiated them. This is a natural thought if your model of universals lies in mathematics: geometrical truths about circles, for instance, do not depend on the existence of any individuals which really are perfectly circular. Aris-totle, in contrast, held a theory of universals as immanent beings, *in rebus* ('in things'): there can be no universals unless there are individuals in which those universals are instantiated. This is a natural thought if your model of universals lies in biology: a species cannot exist, for instance, if there are no animals of that species. Thus, one of the key distinctions between Plato's transcendent and Aris-totle's immanent realism is that the Platonist allows, and Aristotle does not allow, the existence of uninstantiated universals (see ARISTOTLE §15; PLATO).

2   Samenesses and differences

When a property is shared by two individuals, there is something which is in or is had by both. But it is in a quite distinctive sense that one universal can be 'in' two distinct individuals. An individual person may be 'in' two places at once if, for instance, their hand is in the cookie jar and their foot is in the bath. But a universal is 'in' distinct individuals in a way which does not mean that there is one part of the universal in one thing and a distinct part of it in another. Thus, a universal is said to be the sort of thing which can be wholly present in distinct individuals at the same time: a person cannot be wholly present in two places at once, but justice can.

Some draw a distinction between certain special properties and relations which qualify for the label 'universals', and other properties and relations which do not. It is suggested that, whenever something is true of an individual (whenever a description can truly be predicated of an individual), then there is always a 'property' which that individual may be said to have. On this view, a 'property' is just a shadow of a predicate, whereas a genuine universal is something more. A genuine universal has to be something which is literally identical in each of its instances. Alternatively, the sorts of 'properties' which are just shadows of predicates are sometimes construed as set-theoretical constructions of various sorts, as for instance if we say that the 'property' of redness is the set of actual red things, or of actual and possible red things. In this spirit it is now standard practice in mathematics to use the term 'relations' to refer just to any set of ordered pairs. Set-theoretical constructions are not, however, universals – or at least they are not to be confused with the universals which are the subject matter of traditional debates.

3 Arguments for and against

Various arguments have been advanced to establish the existence of universals, the most memorable of which is the 'one over many' argument. Although it is memorable, there is little consensus on just how this argument works. Very roughly, it begins with an appeal to the manifest fact of recurrence, the fact that, as it says in the biblical text of *Ecclesiastes* (1: 9), 'What has been is what will be, and what has been done is what will be done; and there is nothing new under the sun'. There are many things, and yet they are all in some sense just the very same things over and over again. From this manifest fact of recurrence, the argument purports to derive the conclusion that there are universals as well as particulars.

There are also various arguments against the existence of universals. One family of such arguments derives from Aristotle's so-called 'third man argument' and is designed to demonstrate that Plato's Theory of Forms entails an unacceptable infinite regress. Roughly, Plato's problem is that he needs some relation to hold between the Form of Man and individual men before this Form can help to explain what it is that individual men have in common. So the theory would seem to call into being another Form, a third man, which is what the Form of Man has in common with individual men. This leads to an infinite regress, hence Plato's Theory of Forms is unacceptable. Of course, Aristotle had only intended to demonstrate the nonexistence of Plato's Forms, not of universals in general; but enemies of universals frequently advance related infinite-regress arguments against the existence of universals of any kind. Whatever you call the instantiation relation between particulars and universals, if you think of it as another universal then you are off on a regress, and this seems to count against any theory of universals.

Another argument against the existence of universals trades on what is called 'Ockham's razor' – the principle that you should not postulate more entities when everything you want to explain can be explained with fewer (see WILLIAM OF OCKHAM §2). It is sometimes argued that everything you can explain with universals can be explained just as well without them. Things which superficially seem to refer to universals can, it is maintained, generally be rephrased in ways which make no apparent reference to universals – reference to universals can be paraphrased away. If we can do without universals, then obviously we should; when you supplement this Ockhamist argument with allusions to the interminable and unresolvable internecine conflicts among Realists over numerous details, you have an even stronger case against the existence of universals.

4 Nominalism and Realism

During the Middle Ages in Europe, universals played a focal role in the intellectual economy: many issues revolved around what became known as the problem of universals. Famously, a commentary by BOETHIUS on Porphyry's *Isagoge*, which in turn was intended as an introduction to Aristotle's Categories, set very crisply but vividly and tantalizingly what came to be taken as a compulsory question in the Medieval pursuit of learning: whether genera and species are substances or are set in the mind alone; whether they are corporeal or incorporeal substances; and whether they are separate from the things perceived by the senses or set in them (Boethius *c.*510; Spade 1994). The initial problem for many was not one of deciding whether there are any universals, but of choosing between Plato and Aristotle and then fine-tuning further details.

Later in the Middle Ages, however, a growing number of philosophers and theologians became more and more impressed by arguments against the existence of universals. They began to adopt the position called 'Nominalism' which was opposed to all the various forms of Platonic or Aristotelian Realism. According to Nominalists like ABELARD and Ockham, the only thing which distinct individuals share in common is a common name, a label which we choose to apply to each of those individuals and not to others.

Nominalistic claims were echoed by many of the champions of the modern sciences as they emerged at the end of the Middle Ages. It was standardly said to be granted on all hands that all existing things are merely particular. Being assumed as granted on all hands, it was not up for debate, and so the problem of universals, explicitly so described, settled into the shadowy background of scientific and philosophical discussion. For example, an archaeologist of ideas might argue that, in Kant, the problem of universals is really alive and working very hard in the background, playing a role in discussions on almost every topic that arises. Nonetheless the problem of universals, under that name or any clear equivalent, is not featured on Kant's explicit agenda. Kant speaks of intuitions and concepts in ways which have some relation to the old problem of particulars and universals, but more has shifted than just the labels. Hence the problem of universals has received little attention across a great span of philosophical history, right through to twentieth-century philosophy in France and Germany (see NOMINALISM §2; REALISM AND ANTIREALISM).

5 Frege exhumes universals

In the twentieth century, the problem of universals has re-emerged under its familiar name, accompanied by more or less the same guiding illustrations used by Plato and Aristotle. This rebirth has occurred in the tradition of analytic philosophy, notably in the work of Frege, RUSSELL, WITTGENSTEIN, QUINE and ARMSTRONG.

A new twist to the theory of universals can be traced to groundbreaking work by Frege on the nature of natural numbers in his *Grundlagen der Arithmetik* (The Foundations of Arithmetic) (1884). As for Plato, so too for Frege, Russell and others in recent times, advances in mathematics have been the source of a philosophical focus on the problem of universals. Frege's analysis of natural numbers (1, 2, 3, . . .) proceeded in three very different stages (see FREGE, G. §9).

In the first stage of his analysis of numbers, Frege introduced the idea that numbering individuals essentially involves not the attribution of properties to individuals but, rather, the attribution of properties to properties. To illustrate: when asked 'How many are on the table?', Frege notes that there will be many different possible answers, as for instance (1) 'Two packs of playing cards' or (2) '104 playing cards'. The metaphysical truth-makers identified by Frege for these two sample answers are (1) that the property of being a pack of playing cards on the table is a property which has the property of having two instances, and (2) that the property of being a playing card on the table is a property which has the property of having one hundred and four instances. In general, natural numbers number individuals only via the intermediary of contributing to second-order properties, or properties of properties, namely properties of the form 'having *n* instances'. Like Kant, Frege speaks of concepts (*Begriffe*) rather than of 'universals'. Yet Frege's concepts are definitively not private mental episodes, but are thoroughly mind-independent, more like Plato's Forms than Aristotelian universals.

In the second stage of his analysis of numbers, Frege gives a very new twist to the theory of universals. He argues that the nature of universals, or concepts, is such as to make it impossible in principle ever to refer to a universal by any name or description. Thus for instance, in saying 'Socrates is wise', the universal which is instantiated by Socrates is something which is expressed by the whole arrangement of symbols into which the name 'Socrates' is embedded to yield the sentence 'Socrates is wise'. Suppose you were to try to name this universal by the name 'wisdom'. Then, compare 'Socrates is wise' with the concatenation of names – 'Socrates wisdom'. The mere name 'wisdom' clearly leaves out something which was present in the attribution of wisdom to Socrates. Hence a universal cannot be referred to by a name.

Thus, a property can only be expressed by a predicate, never by a name or by any logical device which refers to individuals. Indeed, if we wish to attribute existence to universals, we cannot do so by the use of the same sort of device (the first-order quantifier) which is used to attribute existence to individuals. Thus, for instance, from 'Socrates is wise' we may infer 'There exists something which is wise', and 'There exists something which is Socrates':

$$(\exists x)(\text{wise}(x)), \text{ and}$$
$$(\exists x)(x = \text{Socrates}).$$

Yet we may not infer that 'There exists something which Socrates possesses', or that 'There exists something which is wisdom':

$$(\exists x)(\text{has(Socrates}, x)), \text{ or}$$
$$(\exists x)(x = \text{wisdom}).$$

Frege does, however, allow us to attribute existence to universals, using logical devices called higher-order quantifiers, which he introduced in his *Begriffsschrift* (1879). That is, we can infer from 'Socrates is wise' to 'There is somehow such that: Socrates is that-how':

$$(\text{E}f)(f(\text{Socrates})).$$

But although there is somehow that Socrates is, this does not entail that there is anything which is the somehow that Socrates is: universals (concepts) can only have second-order existence, not first-order existence.

For Frege, numbering things essentially involved attribution of properties to properties. So the sorts of things being attributed are not the sorts of things which can be named. Yet, Frege argued, numbers can be named – numbers are abstract individuals, he says, objects not concepts. Hence the third stage of Frege's analysis of numbers consists in the attempt to find individuals – objects – which could be identified with the numbers. It was this stage of the analysis which resulted in the emergence of modern set theory. For every property, Frege argued, there is a corresponding individual: the extension of that universal, the set of all the things (or all the actual and possible things) which instantiate that universal. Thus, for instance, corresponding to the property of being a property which has two instances, there will be a set of sets which have two members. Modern mathematics has selected different candidates for identification with the natural numbers, but it has followed Frege hook, line and sinker with respect to the broad strategy of identifying numbers, and functions and relations, with sets.

Frege's legacy has significantly changed the agenda for any theory of universals which, like Plato's, aspires to do justice to mathematics. It leaves three courses open for exploration. One course is that charted by Quine (1953, 1960), of allowing the existence of sets but not of any other nameable things which might be called universals, nor of any of Frege's higher-order, unnameable universals. Another course is that of allowing the existence of nameable things other than sets: this is a course charted, for example, by Armstrong (1978). A third course allows also the irreducible significance of higher-order quantification (Boolos 1975; Bigelow and Pargetter 1990).

See also: ABSTRACT OBJECTS; PARTICULARS; UNIVERSALS, INDIAN THEORIES OF

References and further reading

* Armstrong, D.M. (1978) *Universals and Scientific Realism*, London: Cambridge University Press, 2 vols. (A groundbreaking resuscitation of a broadly Aristotelian realism about universals as extra 'objects' in Frege's sense.)
* Bigelow, J. and Pargetter, R. (1990) *Science and Necessity*, Cambridge: Cambridge University Press. (A defence of both a broadly Platonic realism about universals as extra 'objects' in Frege's sense, and of a realist construal of Fregean higher-order quantification.)
* Boethius, A.M.S. (c.510) *In Isagogen Porphyrii Commenta*, in S. Brandt (ed.) *Corpus Scriptorum Ecclesiasticorum Latinorum*, vol. 48, Vienna: Tempsky, 1906. (Latin source for the influential text on genera and species mentioned in §4 above. Translated in Spade 1994.)
* Boolos, G. (1975) 'On Second-Order Logic', *Journal of Philosophy* 72: 509–27. (A very impressive explanation of the virtues of higher-order logic, relevant to Frege's fundamental distinction between 'objects' and 'concepts'.)

Dooley, W.E. (1989) *Alexander of Aphrodisias: On Aristotle, Metaphysics 1*, London: Duckworth; Ithaca, NY: Cornell University Press. (Chapter 9 is especially relevant. Rich material on Plato and Aristotle, especially relevant to the third man argument outlined in §3.)
* Frege, G. (1879) *Begriffsschrift*, Halle: Louis Nebert; trans. J. van Heijenoort, in J. van Heijenoort (ed.) *From Frege to Gödel: A Source Book in Mathematical Logic, 1879–1931*, Cambridge, MA: Harvard University Press, 1967. (Difficult, but the only really epoch-making event in logic since Aristotle.)
* —— (1884) *Die Grundlagen der Arithmetik*, Breslav: W. Koebner; trans. J.L. Austin, *The Foundations of Arithmetic: A logico-mathematical enquiry into the concept of number*, 2nd revised edn, Oxford: Blackwell, 1959. (An accessible, informal and exciting introduction to Frege's epoch-making theory of natural numbers.)
Gödel, K. (1944) 'Russell's Mathematical Logic', in P.A. Schilpp (ed.) *The Philosophy of Bertrand Russell*, Cambridge: Cambridge University Press. (Rich, deep and mysterious reflections on the post-Frege revolution in mathematics.)
Lewis, D. (1983) 'New Work for a Theory of Universals', *Australasian Journal of Philosophy* 61: 343–77. (Clear exposition of a menu of options open to us in the post-Frege era.)
* Quine, W.V. (1953) *From a Logical Point of View*, Cambridge, MA: Harvard University Press; 2nd edn, New York: Harper & Row, 1961. (Contains a classic, accessible and entertaining, sceptical discussion of universals in 'On What There Is', and a hard but important piece on the relation between universals and sets in 'Logic and the Reification of Universals'.)
* —— (1960) *Word and Object*, Cambridge, MA: MIT Press. (In addition to notorious scepticism about semantics, this classic gives a landmark presentation of a sparse ontology containing only particulars and sets.)
Russell, B. (1903) *The Principles of Mathematics*, New York: Norton. (Exciting and accessible book assimilating Frege's revolution in logic, turning universals into sets and displaying some of the reasons why mathematical Platonists now believe in sets rather than in universals proper.)
—— (1912) *The Problems of Philosophy*, London: Clarendon Press. (An accessible classic, which, in addition to epistemological themes, also presents a classic, broadly Platonist vision of universals.)
* Spade, P.V. (trans. and ed.) (1994) *Five Texts on the Medieval Problem of Universals*, Indianapolis, IN: Hackett. (Great works from the heyday of the problem of universals, including those mentioned

at the beginning of §4 above; requires no formal logic, but both historically and conceptually difficult.)

JOHN BIGELOW

UNIVERSALS, INDIAN THEORIES OF

Indian philosophers postulated universals for two principal reasons: to serve as the 'eternal' meanings of words, upon which the eternality of language – in particular, the Hindu scriptures, the Veda – is based, and to account for why we conceive of things as being of certain types. However, universals were seen as problematic in various ways. How can something exist simultaneously in numerous individuals without being divided into parts? How can a universal, which is supposed to be eternal, continue to exist if all its substrata are destroyed? In what sense can a universal be said to 'exist' at all? Is a universal distinct from or identical with the individuals in which it inheres? In light of such difficulties, it is not surprising that certain other Indian philosophers – specifically Buddhist philosophers, who did not accept the doctrine of the eternality of the Veda – rejected universals and took up a nominalist stance. They held that general terms refer to mentally constructed 'exclusion classes', apohas. The use of the term 'cow', for example, is grounded not on some positive entity common to all cows but on the idea of the class of things that are different from all things that are not cows. This proposal, which originated with Dignāga in the sixth century AD, was debated vigorously until the eleventh century.

1   **Universals as the meanings of words**
2   **The Vaiśeṣika theory**
3   **Controversies**

1   Universals as the meanings of words

The question of universals first arose in Indian philosophy with regard to language. In his commentary on Pāṇini's grammar of classical Sanskrit, PATAÑJALI (second century BC) considers the thesis upon which the Hindu belief in the eternality of the Veda is grounded, that word, meaning and the connection between the two are 'eternal'. What would the meaning of a word have to be in order for it to be eternal? Presumably, not the individual thing or 'substance' (*dravya*), which is perishable, but the 'shape' or 'configuration' (*ākṛti*), which is common to many individuals. Although the *ākṛti* may be

destroyed with one individual, it will continue to exist in others ((*Vyākarana-*) *Mahābhāṣya*, 1.1.1, 1962, vol. 1: 7). Here, *ākṛti* is not yet a universal in the sense of an abstract entity that makes various individuals members of a single class, but the visible form by which the members of a class are recognized. Patañjali also notes, however, that the 'substance', in the sense of the stuff out of which a thing is made, can also be considered eternal: the shape of a lump of gold may be altered in various ways, but the gold itself will remain the same. Thus, he settles on neither *ākṛti* nor *dravya* as the exclusive meaning of a word. Depending on the context, one or the other emerges as the meaning. In particular, when Pāṇini says (*Aṣṭādhyāyī* 1.2.58) that nouns may optionally take plural endings when they refer to a class – that is, one may say either 'the Brahman' or 'Brahmans' when referring to the class of Brahmans – he implies that the meaning of the word is the *ākṛti*. On the other hand, when he says (*Aṣṭādhyāyī* 1.2.64) that the plural form of a word is really an abbreviation for the same word iterated several times, he seems to have the *dravya* – even in the sense of the concrete individual – in mind (*Mahābhāṣya* 1.1.1, 1962, vol. 1: 6).

Patañjali records the opinions of other ancient grammarians (*Mahābhāṣya* 1.2.64, vol. 1: 242–). Vājapyāyana held that a word must express the *ākṛti*, because the rules of *dharma* apply universally and not just to specific things. When the law forbids the killing of a Brahman, it means that one should not kill *any* Brahman, not just a particular Brahman! Moreover, words evoke general notions. When someone says 'cow', we do not think of a particular white or black cow; we just think 'cow' in general. Vyāḍi, on the other hand, pointed out that actions can be carried out only with reference to individuals. An injunction that one should sacrifice a certain animal means that one should sacrifice an individual animal of a certain type; one could hardly carry out the action with regard to the entire species! Also, it would seem that nouns could have number and gender only if they referred to individuals. Finally, Vyāḍi wonders how the *ākṛti* can be fully present in many individuals simultaneously. Vājapyāyana responds that it is possible in the same way that it is possible for the sun to shine in many places or for Indra to be simultaneously present at many sacrifices.

This same debate is played out in the *Mīmāṃsā-sūtra* (1.3.30–5), where the issue is decided in favour of the *ākṛti*, which is now explicitly declared by the commentators to be a universal (*sāmānya*). It is still recognized, however, that in certain contexts, such as sacrificial injunctions, words indirectly refer to individuals; for universals have individuals as their substrata (*Mīmāṃsāsūtrabhāṣya*, 1981, vol. 2: 266–7).

The teaching of the influential Bhāṭṭa school of Mīmāṃsā was that the universal is the primary meaning of a word, while the individual is the secondary or metaphorical meaning to which one resorts when an expression cannot be construed literally (for example, in a sacrificial context) (see MĪMĀṂSĀ §§2–3). In the Nyāyasūtra all three items – individual (vyakti), universal (jāti) and configuration (ākṛti) – are declared to be jointly the meaning of a word (2.2.66). The individual alone cannot be the meaning, because we never apprehend a mere individual, an individual which is not of a certain kind; the configuration alone cannot be the meaning, because things having the configuration of, say, a cow are not necessarily cows (for example, images of cows); and the universal by itself cannot be the meaning, because one does not apprehend the universal without perceiving an individual having a certain configuration. Thus, all three together comprise the meaning of a word, one becoming dominant, the others subordinate, in different circumstances. When one, for example, intends the distinctness of the referent from other things – as in the sentence 'Wash that cow' – then the vyakti becomes predominant; when one intends to include many things together – as in the sentence 'One should not kill a cow' – the jāti, or universal, becomes predominant.

2 The Vaiśeṣika theory

In the literature of the Hindu Vaiśeṣika school of natural philosophy the question of universals is approached from the standpoint of ontology. The Vaiśeṣikasūtra lists universals (sāmānya) as one of the six principal categories of things (1.1.4) (see NYĀYA-VAIŚEṢIKA §§4–5). Their existence is known from the fact that we have common notions and terms; there must be something identical existing in different individuals that causes us to conceive of them in the same way and refer to them by the same word. Universals can be arranged in hierarchical series: animality is higher than cowness, while substantiality is higher than animality. The highest universal of all, which stands at the pinnacle of every such series and falls under no other universal, is 'existence' (sattā). Universals below existence can be construed either as functions of generality or particularity (Vaiśeṣikasūtra 1.2.3). Cowness causes us to group together all cows in one class, but also separates them from other animals. Moreover, cowness functions as a particularity with respect to universals of wider scope, such as animality: it distinguishes a certain type of animal within the genus of animals.

All cows, all animals – in general, all substances, qualities and actions – are considered 'existents' (sat)

due to the fact that the universal 'existence' resides in them (Vaiśeṣikasūtra 1.2.7). Universals themselves, however, are not existents. While it can be said of a universal that it 'is' (asti) in so far as it possesses intrinsic nature (svarūpa), and while it can be known and be named, it does not exist in the same concrete sense as substances, qualities and actions: it is 'not expressible by the word artha ['thing']' (Padārtha-dharmasaṅgraha, 1971: 49; Vaiśeṣikasūtra 8.2.3). In a way similar to Aristotle's account, then, 'being' does not apply univocally to all categories in Vaiśeṣika (though it should be noted that Aristotle does not consider 'universal' a category; thus, it can also be said that Vaiśeṣika differs from Aristotle in considering 'being' to apply univocally to substances, qualities and actions) (see ARISTOTLE §7). Nor is there a universal 'universalness' that inheres in all universals; for that would lead to a 'third-man' type of regress.

Qualities are not universals in Vaiśeṣika thought. The red that occurs in a particular object is itself a particular. There is, however, a universal redness that is common to all particular occurrences of red. This contrasts with the view found in grammatical and Mīmāṃsā literature that qualities are repeatable types: it is the same quality red that occurs in all things red.

It is evident that the universals of Vaiśeṣika and Nyāya – the Hindu school devoted primarily to logic and epistemology, which adopted the metaphysics of Vaiśeṣika – resemble Aristotelian universals more than Platonic forms (see UNIVERSALS §1). They are neither substances nor causes of substances; they are neither essences nor responsible for the natures of things; nor are they ideal entities – a point that distinguishes them from Platonic and Aristotelian universals. Rather, a universal simply endows an individual thing, whose nature derives from other causes, with the capacity to give rise to a certain notion such as 'cow' or 'pot', a capacity that it shares with other individuals. Moreover, although universals are quite distinct from the individuals in which they inhere – for they are eternal and 'common', while individuals are perishable and particular – they are never cognized, nor in any clear sense exist apart from them.

Other thinkers, however, conceived of universals as being more intimately related to individual substances. The grammarian BHARTṚHARI (fifth century AD) held universals to be causally involved in the formation of substances; they activate the material causes that bring about the substances in which they inhere. He noted this phenomenon in the production of artefacts, much as Aristotle did: the artisan is guided by the universal (for Aristotle, read 'substantial form') in producing an object of a certain type, which will in turn exhibit the universal (Vākyapadīya

545

3.25–7). Ultimately for Bhartṛhari, who was a monist (Advaitin), both universals and individual substances are creative potencies (*śakti*) within Brahman, different ways in which it limits itself as it becomes the empirical world. Universal and individual, that is, are merely different aspects of the finite self-expressions of Brahman, hence they are identical (*Vākyapadīya* 3.22–3, 32–3; 1.1–4). This metaphysical doctrine can be seen as a reflection of the linguistic one that words refer to both universals and individuals.

The Mīmāṃsā philosopher Kumārila (seventh century AD) also held that the universal and the individual form a unity; for we do not cognize a universal as externally related to the individual. We do not cognize the universal 'cowness' as existing *in* the cow, rather we cognize the individual *as being* a cow (*Ślokavārttika*, 'Pratyakṣa' 141–2). The fact that individual and universal never exist apart from each other also bespeaks their identity. Furthermore, Kumārila held that one cannot make sense of the relation of 'inherence' (*samavāya*), by which Nyāya and Vaiśeṣika philosophers believed the universal and individual to be related. If one asks how *samavāya* itself is related to each of the terms it relates together, a regress ensues. Thus, according to Kumārila, who was a realist and a pluralist, the world is populated by numerous concrete entities that are both universal and particular in nature (*Ślokavārttika*, 'Ākṛti' 5–6, 59–65). A similar view was expressed by Jaina philosophers: universal and particular are neither absolutely different nor absolutely identical.

Jainas also held the distinctive doctrine of two types of universals, horizontal (*tīryaksāmānya*) and vertical (*ūrdhvatāsāmānya*). The former account for the various types of things that exist at the same time – cows, horses, and so on; the latter account for the identity of individual substances through time, that is, they enable us to recognize the various stages of a substance as the same thing.

One of the peculiarities of the Indian discussion of universals is that all those who believed in the reality of universals held them to be objects of perception; indeed, to be real and to be an object of perception were nearly the same in classical Indian philosophy. To say that universals are objects of thought would have been to say that they are mental constructs and therefore unreal. The latter view was in fact held by Buddhist philosophers (see §3). A theory of universals as real entities cognized by a process of mental abstraction was never achieved. Nyāya, Vaiśeṣika and Mīmāṃsā philosophers argued that universals are objects of perception because their cognition occurs simultaneously with sense organ–object contact. Even when encountering a thing for the first time – say, a camel – one is able to *see* that it is an entity of a certain type, different from other kinds of entities one knows. One never perceives something that is completely particular in nature and devoid of any general character.

3 Controversies

In the face of the Buddhist denial of the reality of universals, Hindu and Jaina philosophers were compelled to develop more rigorous arguments for their existence. The most common argument was simply that distinct cognitions must have distinct causes. We have, besides the cognition of something as an individual, a cognition of it as a member of a certain class. There must be some real basis for the latter, in the same way that, when we cognize something as blue, there is some real basis of the cognition other than the individual substance itself, namely the quality blue (*Nyāyavārttika* 2.2.64, 1985: 667). Nor can the cognition of an individual as possessing a general character be based on a similarity between it and other individuals. Cows are in certain ways similar to each other, but in important respects also different; and almost to the same extent that there is a similarity between cows, there is a similarity between cows and horses, yet we do not call a horse a cow! Moreover, similarity would merely give rise to the notion that various things are 'like' each other, not that they are the same thing. If universals were not real, it was also argued, inference and reasoning, which are based on the observation of general traits, would not be valid means of knowledge. The Nyāya philosopher UDAYANA (eleventh century) contended that universals must be postulated to explain the necessity and uniformity of causal relations, such as the fact that not just this bit of milk will now produce yoghurt, but any portion at any time.

One problem that universal theorists had to face was whether a universal exists wholly in an individual or only partially. If wholly, then it would only be in that individual and could not also exist in others. If only a part of the universal existed in each individual, then it would not be one thing common to all (compare Plato's *Parmenides* 131a–e). The standard response to this dilemma was simply to stress that the property of existing completely in each of a class of individuals is one of the things that distinguishes universals from other categories. As the Nyāya philosopher UDDYOTAKARA (sixth century) puts it: a universal is not a whole comprised of parts, nor a collection of many things, thus it is not really proper to put the question about whether it exists 'wholly' or 'partially' in something (*Nyāyavārttika* 2.2.64, 1985: 669).

What happens to a universal if all its individual

substrata perish? It cannot cease to exist, for it is eternal; yet it is never perceived independently of its substrata either. Nyāya-Vaiśeṣika philosophers held that during periods of cosmic dissolution (*pralaya*), when there are no individuals at all, universals continue to exist in an unmanifest state – in so far as they can be said to 'exist' at all. Otherwise, some (for example, Jayantabhaṭṭa) held that when all the individuals of a particular universal are destroyed, universals continue to inhere in other individuals. That is to say, cowness (along with every other universal) is present in all things, even non-cows, and so will still be located in individuals even when cows have died out; but it is *perceived* only in cows (*Nyāyamañjarī*, 1983, vol. 2: 36–7). In such doctrines one sees a tendency to favour the notion that universals exist only *in rebus*. There were even philosophers who held that during *pralaya* universals continue to exist by virtue of inhering in individuals in other universes! Perhaps only Bhartṛhari would have been sympathetic to the Western medieval view that universals are *ante res*, in so far as they are eternal potencies within Brahman.

Finally, there is the matter of *upādhis*, general traits that are not universals. Nyāya-Vaiśeṣika philosophers wanted to deny that such terms as 'cookness' or 'servantness' refer to real, objective universals. Being a cook or a servant is not natural to a person; one becomes a cook or servant only when one comes to perform the actions appropriate to a cook or servant. Universals, however, are supposed to inhere permanently in their substrata from the moment of origin. Similarly, several men carrying umbrellas can be grouped together conceptually, but that will not be due to the presence of a universal in them. Thus, a distinction was made between general terms that are based on real universals and general terms that are based on inauthentic, nominal properties. Buddhists used this point to their own advantage: if some general terms are based on inauthentic, nominal properties, why not all?

The Buddhist critique of universals was initiated by DIGNĀGA (sixth century) and continued by DHARMA-KĪRTI (seventh century), Śāntarakṣita (eighth century) and other thinkers until the eleventh century. An often-quoted verse of Dharmakīrti charges that the concept of universals is beset with a plethora of difficulties: when an individual arises in a particular place, the universal cannot move to where it is and unite with it, for a universal is without motion; nor could it have been present there all along, for then the empty space would have been cognized as falling under the universal. It is also absurd to think that a universal could join with an individual after it has arisen, since the individual would exist for a moment

without any universal inhering in it (*Pramāṇavārttika*, 'Svārthānumāna' 152–3). If various things were identical in nature through the presence of a universal, they would not really be diverse; if a concrete thing were both universal and particular in nature, how would it be unified (*Pramāṇavārttika*, 'Pratyakṣa' 41; 'Svārthānumāna' 176–9)? Less polemically, Dharma-kīrti points out that the fact that various things give rise to the same idea does not require the postulation of something that they all have in common; for we observe that a variety of herbs that have nothing in common have the same effect of alleviating fever (*Pramāṇavārttika*, 'Svārthānumāna' 73–4).

In reality, however, various individuals never give rise to the same *positive* idea, but only to a conception that is completely negative in content. That is to say, a particular cow may be seen as being different from all goats, all horses, all pots, all vegetables, and so on; another particular cow may be seen as being different from the same things. In so far as both cows are conceived of as being different from the same things, they are thought of as being of the same type; in themselves, however, they are quite distinct. This is the notorious *apohavāda*, 'the doctrine of exclusion', which asserts that general terms refer only to mentally constructed exclusion classes, *apohas*. The main thrust of the theory is that there is nothing at all positive to being an entity of a certain kind. Only individuals, which are inconceivable in nature, yet grasped immediately in perception (which is by definition devoid of all conceptualization), are real. The *apoha* doctrine was used by the Buddhists to question the reality of a wide range of phenomena that appear to be conceptually based, including substances, words and meanings (see NOMINALISM, BUDDHIST DOCTRINE OF).

The *apohavāda* evoked a spirited response on the part of realist thinkers, with numerous texts being devoted to the debate. The most serious objection to it, originally developed by Kumārila, is that it is unclear whether one can even recognize that a particular thing is *different* from other things without seeing positively that it and other things are of certain types. And if in attempting to identify a certain thing one's recognition of the 'other things' from which it differs were based on *apoha*, then one would have to be able to see that they exclude, among other things, the thing one is trying to identify, in which case one would already have to be able to identify something as being of a certain type in order to see that it is of a certain type (*Ślokavārttika*, 'Apohavāda' 2–, 65–6). Moreover, the *apohavāda* renders all words nearly synonymous: the only difference in meaning between the words 'cow' and 'horse' is that the former excludes horses while the latter excludes cows; otherwise, the vast number of the things each word excludes is identical (*ibid.* 53–4). In general, the realist arguments against the *apohavāda* raise an issue with which even modern nominalists must reckon, namely, while it may be possible to construct theories that make no reference to abstract entities, can one really understand the locutions of such theories without tacitly appealing to them?

The heated debate over universals was no mere intellectual exercise for Indian philosophers. The defenders of the reality of universals were concerned to preserve, at least up to a point, the validity of the distinctions of natural kinds upon which the prescriptions of scripture are based. The opponents of universals, on the other hand, sought ultimately to deny the reality of the world of ordinary experience and encourage the cultivation of a mystical awareness of an ineffable Absolute.

See also: LANGUAGE, INDIAN THEORIES OF; MEANING, INDIAN THEORIES OF; ONTOLOGY IN INDIAN PHILOSOPHY

References and further reading

* Bhartṛhari (5th century) *Vākyapadīya*, trans. K.A. Subramania, Iyer, Poona: Deccan College, 1965–74, 4 vols. (The main treatise of the grammarian school of Hindu thought.)
* Dharmakīrti (7th century) *Pramāṇavārttika*, ed. Swami Dwarikadas Shastri, Varanasi: Bauddha Bharati, 1984. (An important text of the logical-epistemological school of Yogācāra Buddhism.)
  Dravid, R.R. (1972) *The Problem of Universals in Indian Philosophy*, Delhi: Motilal Banarsidass. (A comprehensive treatment of the views of all schools.)
  Frauwallner, E. (1982) 'Beiträge zur Apohalehre' (Contributions to the Theory of *Apoha*), in *Kleine Schriften* (Smaller Writings), Wiesbaden: Franz Steiner Verlag. (Seminal articles on Buddhist nominalism.)
  Halbfass, W. (1992) *On Being and What There Is: Classical Vaiśeṣika and the History of Indian Ontology*, Albany, NY: State University of New York Press. (A penetrating study of Vaiśeṣika metaphysics.)
* Jayantabhaṭṭa (9th century) *Nyāyamañjarī*, ed. K.S. Varadacharya, Mysore: Oriental Research Institute, 1983. (A major Nyāya text of the late ninth century.)
* Kumārila (7th century) *Ślokavārttika*, ed. Swami Dwarikadas Shastri, Varanasi: Tara Publications, 1978; trans. G. Jha, Delhi: Sri Satguru Publications, 1983. (One of two principal subcom-

mentaries on Śabarasvāmin's *Mīmāṃsāsūtra-bhāṣya*.)
  Matilal, B.K. (1986) *Perception*, Oxford: Clarendon Press. (Treats a wide range of issues in Indian metaphysics and epistemology; chapter 12 is devoted to universals.)
* Patañjali (2nd century BC) *Vyākaraṇamahābhāṣya*, ed. F. Kielhorn, Poona: Bhandarkar Oriental Research Institute, 1962. (The principal commentary on Pāṇini's grammar.)
* Praśastapāda (5th century) *Praśastapādabhāṣya* (*Padārthadharmasaṅgraha*), ed. Bhāgīratha Prasāda Tripāṭhī, Varanasi: Sampurnand Sanskrit Vishvavidyalaya, 1971; trans. G. Jha, Benares: E.J. Lazarus, 1916. (The most important commentary on Pāṇini's grammar.)
* Śabarasvāmin *Mīmāṃsāsūtrabhāṣya*, in Gaṇeśaśāstri Josī (ed.) *Mīmāṃsādarśanam*, Varanasi: Ānandaśrama Sanskrit Series, 1981; trans. G. Jha, *Śābara-Bhāṣya*, The Gaekwad's Oriental Series, 66, 70, 73, Baroda: Oriental Institute, 1933-6. (The oldest extant commentary on the *Mīmāṃsāsūtra*; includes the text of the latter.)
* Uddyotakara (6th century) *Nyāyavārttika*, in Taranatha Nyaya-Tarkatirtha (ed.) *Nyāyadarśanam*, Delhi: Munshiram Manoharlal, 1985; trans. G. Jha, *The Nyāya-Sūtras of Gautama with the Bhāṣya of Vātsyāyana and the Vārttika of Uddyotakara*, Delhi: Motilal Banarsidass, 1984, 4 vols. (An important subcommentary on Vātsyāyana's commentary on the *Nyāyasūtra*; both Sanskrit edition and translation include the text of the *Nyāyasūtra*.)
* *Vaiśeṣikasūtra* (1st century AD?), trans. Nandalal Sinha, *The Vaiśeṣika Sūtras of Kaṇāda with the Commentary of Śaṅkara Miśra*, Allahabad: Sacred Books of the Hindus, 1910–11. (The foundational text of the Vaiśeṣika school.)

JOHN A. TABER

USE/MENTION DISTINCTION AND QUOTATION

Speakers 'use' the expressions they utter and 'mention' the individuals they talk about. Connected with the roles of used expressions and mentioned individuals is a way of uniting them and a characteristic mistake involving them. Usually the expression used in an utterance will not be the same as the individual mentioned, but the two can be made to converge. The means is quotation. Quotation is a special usage in which an expression is used to mention itself. A failure to distinguish between the roles of used expressions and mentioned individuals can lead to mistakes. Such mistakes are called use/mention confusions. In themselves use/mention confusions are a minor linguistic faux pas, *but under unfavourable conditions, they have the potential to cause greater problems.*

1 **Use and mention**
2 **Standard uses of quotation and quasi-quotation**
3 **Use/mention confusions**

1 Use and mention

Though philosophers since Plato have distinguished between language and the world it is used to describe, the terms 'use' and 'mention' were first applied to these categories by the philosopher and logician Willard Quine in 1940. Quine's choice of the terms was intended to encourage associations with their ordinary meanings. To *use* an expression linguistically is to use it as a tool; to employ it towards a linguistic end. The ends are performances of speech acts, such as making claims, asking questions and giving responses. In contrast, to *mention* an individual is to say something about it; to make it the topic of conversation between speaker and listener. An individual mentioned in a speech act is one whose characteristics help determine how the act is to be evaluated: whether a claim is true, a question pertinent or a response correct depends on the individuals mentioned in the act and what is said about them.

In every communicative setting, some expression is used and, in most, some individual is mentioned. For example, a speaker uttering (1) below succeeds in making a claim about Tucson, the capital city of the state of Arizona:

(1) Tucson is dry.

By using the words 'Tucson', 'is' and 'dry' in the appropriate order, the city is mentioned. To say that Tucson is mentioned is to say that it is Tucson's weather, rather than that of Rangoon or Vienna, which is relevant to the truth of the claim. Greetings, such as 'Good Morning' or 'Hello', are examples of speech acts in which no individual is mentioned; their success depends only on the circumstances and the speaker's intentions.

While thinking about the categories of expressions used and individuals mentioned, one should bear in mind that the distinction divides the roles individuals can play rather than the kinds of individuals that can play these roles. That the distinction does not separate individuals by kinds is shown by the fact that linguistic expressions can play both parts: expressions can be mentioned as well as used. By uttering (2), for

example, a speaker manages to mention the name 'Tucson' and, in fact, to say something true about it:

(2) The name of the capital city of Arizona contains six letters.

(1) should be compared with (2). The former uses the name of the city to mention the city, while the latter uses a description of the name to mention the name itself.

A detailed understanding of use and mention requires that one draw a distinction between the 'type' of an expression and 'tokens' of that type (see TYPE/TOKEN DISTINCTION). Expression tokens are concrete objects, individual marks or sounds made of raw materials: ink, perhaps; or sound waves. Types are abstract individuals and, as such, not made of anything. There is only one word 'Tucson' in the English language (so 'Tucson' is a type), of which there are several tokens in this entry.

The type/token distinction brings with it possibilities for what is used and mentioned. Both tokens and types can be used. To use a token, one has to utter it with the intention of saying something. Using a type requires the same intention, but also requires that the token have the right shape or sound. Tokens and types can also be mentioned. (2) mentions the type and (3) the token used in (1):

(3) The first word token in the first example sentence of the entry on 'Use/mention distinction and quotation' in the *Routledge Encyclopedia of Philosophy* has six letters.

2 Standard uses of quotation and quasi-quotation

Expressions of each grammatical category have what may be called standard uses. The standard use of noun phrases is to mention: 'Tucson', 'The name of the capital city of Arizona' and 'The first word token...Philosophy' from (3) above are all used in standard fashion. Expressions of most other categories have standard uses which do not involve mentioning. Articles and quantifiers ('every', 'some', 'all', 'most') do not themselves mention, but rather help determine the range of individuals that are mentioned. Conjunctions govern the manner in which the meanings of compound expressions depend on the meanings of their constituents. According to some theories, adjectives, adverbs and verbs mention relations, properties or events. According to other theories, they do not mention at all.

Along with their standard uses, expressions also have nonstandard uses. Chief among these is their use in quotation. Quotation is a way of using an expression to mention itself. It is the most general and efficient way of talking about expressions. Instead of the long-winded description in (2), a speaker wanting to mention 'Tucson' can simply quote it:

(4)   'Tucson' has six letters.

From the notational point of view, quotation is trivial. Its basic rule is simple: to quote an expression, enclose a token of it in quotation marks – the purpose of the marks being to indicate the nature of the usage. Or it can be simpler yet; one can leave out the marks when it is clear from the context that one wants to talk about an expression rather than use it in the standard way. (Passages which are indented or examples marked by numbers – as in this entry – are quoted using this method.) Quotation is generally used to mention expression types, unless there is an explicit qualification to the contrary.

Quotation is a leveller. No matter what they may standardly be used to mention, when quoted, all nouns mention expressions. It is instructive to compare (1) and (4) on this count to see how quotation can bring about a change in subject matter: (1) is about a large city, while (4), which differs only in the addition of a set of quotation marks, is about a medium-sized word. The effect of quotation on other categories of expressions is even more significant. It reduces the whole variety of standard uses to one. No matter what their standard use may be, when quoted, expressions of all categories become mentioning expressions. This effect can be seen in the example below:

(5)   'A' is an article and 'and' is a conjunction.

In this sentence, the first token of the word 'a' and the second token of the word 'and' are used to mention, while the second token of the word 'a', the first of 'and' and the only one of 'an' operate in standard fashion.

Related to regular quotation is a notation invented by Quine (1940), called 'quasi-quotation'. Quine, who has done more to encourage the correct use of quotation marks than any other writer, created quasi-quotation to help in capturing linguistic generalizations. Quasi-quotation treats an expression in two ways. Towards one part of the expression ('&' in the example below) it behaves as regular quotation. The other part or parts ('α' and 'β' in the example below) it treats as indeterminate elements that can mention any expression within a specific category. The marks of quasi-quotation are called corner quotes ('$\ulcorner$' on the left and '$\urcorner$' on the right). A full quasi-quotation consisting of the expression enclosed by two corners is itself an indeterminate that can mention any expression consisting of the quoted part and any expression mentioned by the indeterminate part. To take an example from logic, let 'α' and 'β' be indeterminates mentioning sentences and '&' be the conjunction symbol. A rule giving the extensional semantics for conjunction can be stated using quasi-quotation:

(6) $\ulcorner \alpha \,\&\, \beta \urcorner$ is true iff α is true and β is true,

where '$\ulcorner \alpha \,\&\, \beta \urcorner$' mentions an expression that is a conjunction of the sentences mentioned by 'α' and 'β'. If α is 'Cicero died' and β is 'Caesar spoke', then $\ulcorner \alpha \,\&\, \beta \urcorner$ is the result of writing α followed by '&' followed by β, namely 'Cicero died and Caesar spoke'.

3   Use/mention confusions

The distinction between use and mention can turn slippery. When it does and one loses hold of it, use/mention confusions can occur. The typical result of such a confusion is that a speaker ends up making a claim about nonlinguistic individuals that is appropriate only to expressions or making a claim about expressions that is only appropriate to nonlinguistic individuals. Where the distinction between use and mention turns most slippery is on the subject of abstract individuals. Numbers and expressions used to mention them can be especially hard to keep apart. The category of numbers includes whole numbers such as 1 and 3, ratios such as $\frac{1}{2}$ and $\frac{2}{4}$ and irrational numbers such as π. The expressions that mention them include the numerals '1' and '3', the fractions '$\frac{1}{2}$' and '$\frac{2}{4}$' and the Greek letter 'π'. Classroom presentations of ratios and fractions commonly involve use/mention confusions. Students are often told something like the following:

> Fractions consist of one number divided by another. The number to be divided, called the 'numerator', is placed on the top, while the number to divide by, called the 'denominator', is placed on the bottom, with a line between the two. So, 2 is the numerator and 3 the denominator of $\frac{2}{3}$.

However, the clever student may wonder how this could be. Since $\frac{2}{3}$ is the same quotient as $\frac{4}{6}$, the above remarks suggest that they ought to be the same fraction. Therefore 3 ought to be the denominator of both (on the grounds that the denominators of identicals are identical), but it is not. This puzzle exposes the use/mention confusion. The teacher has confused fractions with ratios. '$\frac{2}{3}$' is a fraction; $\frac{2}{3}$ a ratio. Only fractions have numerators and denominators, while it is the ratios mentioned by fractions that may be identical. The numeral '3' is the denominator of the fraction '$\frac{2}{3}$', but it is the *ratios* $\frac{2}{3}$ and $\frac{4}{6}$ which are identical. Because '$\frac{2}{3}$' is not the same fraction as '$\frac{4}{6}$', they need not, and indeed do not, have the same denominator.

The need to achieve clarity and avoid confusions such as the one above is the main reason why it is important to maintain a clear separation between use and mention. As far as errors go, the mix-up with fractions and ratios is probably mid-level. Some use/ mention confusions are of less consequence. Others pose greater problems (see MODAL OPERATORS §1). Where subtlety and precision are at a premium, as they are in logic and linguistics, use/mention confusions can severely impair the intelligibility of a discussion.

See also: DE RE/DE DICTO; LOGICAL AND MATHEMATICAL TERMS, GLOSSARY OF

References and further reading

Davidson, D. (1984) 'Quotation', in *Inquiries into Truth and Interpretation*, Oxford: Oxford University Press, 1991, 79–92. (Davidson puts forward the view that quotation marks are demonstratives, an alternative to the view advanced in §2.)

Frege, G. (1892) 'Über Sinn und Bedeutung', *Zeitschrift für Philosophie und philosophische Kritik* 100: 25–50; trans. 'On Sense and Reference', in A.P. Martinich (ed.) *The Philosophy of Language*, New York: Oxford University Press, 3rd edn, 1996. (Frege's discussion in this essay contains what may be the first application of the use/mention distinction in the context of a philosophical argument. Frege also introduces the view, stated in §2, that quotation marks are context markers and that a quoted word is used to mention itself.)

Garcia-Carpentera, M. (1994) 'Ostensive Signs: Against the Identity Theory of Quotation', *Journal of Philosophy* 91: 253–64. (Endorses Davidson's theory and defends it against criticisms.)

Geach, P. (1957) *Mental Acts*, London: Routledge & Kegan Paul, 79–82. (Clearest statement of the view, first formulated by Tarski, that quotations can be seen as descriptions.)

* Quine, W.V. (1940) *Mathematical Logic*, New York: Norton; repr. Cambridge, MA: Harvard University Press, 1951, 23–37. (A careful discussion of the use/ mention distinction, quotation and quasi-quotation.)

Russell, B.A.W. (1919) 'Descriptions', in *Introduction to Mathematical Philosophy*, London: Allen & Unwin, 167–80; repr. in A.P. Martinich (ed.) *The Philosophy of Language*, New York: Oxford University Press, 1985, 213–19; 3rd edn, 1996. (Contains numerous examples of use/mention confusions.)

Tarski, A. (1933) *Pojęcie prawdy w językach nauk dedukcyjnych*, Warsaw; trans. J.H. Woodger (1956), 'On the Concept of Truth in Formalized Languages', in *Logic, Semantics, Metamathematics*, ed. J. Corcoran, Indianapolis, IN: Hackett Publishing Company, 2nd edn, 1983, 152–278. (The classic work on the view that quotations are names.)

Washington, C. (1992) 'The Identity Theory of Quotation', *Journal of Philosophy* 91: 582–605. (Gives a detailed description and defence of Frege's view.)

COREY WASHINGTON

UTILITARIANISM

Utilitarianism is a theory about rightness, according to which the only good thing is welfare (wellbeing or 'utility'). Welfare should, in some way, be maximized, and agents are to be neutral between their own welfare, and that of other people and of other sentient beings.

The roots of utilitarianism lie in ancient thought. Traditionally, welfare has been seen as the greatest balance of pleasure over pain, a view discussed in Plato. The notion of impartiality also has its roots in Plato, as well as in Stoicism and Christianity. In the modern period, utilitarianism grew out of the Enlightenment, its two major proponents being Jeremy Bentham and John Stuart Mill.

Hedonists, believing that pleasure is the good, have long been criticized for sensualism, a charge Mill attempted to answer with a distinction between higher and lower pleasures. He contended that welfare consists in the experiencing of pleasurable mental states, suggesting, in contrast to Bentham, that the quality, not simply the amount, of a pleasure is what matters. Others have doubted this conception, and developed desire accounts, according to which welfare lies in the satisfaction of desire. Ideal theorists suggest that certain things are just good or bad for people, independently of pleasure and desire.

Utilitarianism has usually focused on actions. The most common form is act-utilitarianism, according to which what makes an action right is its maximizing total or average utility. Some, however, have argued that constantly attempting to put utilitarianism into practice could be self-defeating, in that utility would not be maximized by so doing. Many utilitarians have therefore advocated non-utilitarian decision procedures, often based on common sense morality. Some have felt the appeal of common sense moral principles in themselves, and sought to reconcile utilitarianism with them. According to rule-utilitarianism, the right action is that which is consistent with those rules which would maximize utility if all accepted them.

There have been many arguments for utilitarianism, the most common being an appeal to reflective belief or 'intuition'. One of the most interesting is Henry Sidgwick's argument, which is ultimately intuitionist, and results from sustained reflection on common sense morality. The most famous argument is Mill's 'proof'. In recent times, R.M. Hare has offered a logical argument for utilitarianism.

The main problems for utilitarianism emerge out of its conflict with common sense morality, in particular justice, and its impartial conception of practical reasoning.

1 **Introduction and history**
2 **Conceptions of utility**
3 **Types of utilitarianism**
4 **Arguments for utilitarianism**
5 **Problems for utilitarianism**

1 Introduction and history

Defining utilitarianism is difficult, partly because of its many variations and complexities, but also because the utilitarian tradition has always seen itself as a broad church. But before offering a history, we must supply a working definition. First, utilitarianism is, usually, a version of *welfarism*, the view that the only good is welfare (see WELFARE). Second, it assumes that we can compare welfare across different people's lives (see ECONOMICS AND ETHICS). Third, it is a version of consequentialism (see CONSEQUENTIALISM). Consequentialists advocate the impartial maximization of certain values, which might include, say, equality. Utilitarianism is welfarist consequentialism, in its classical form, for instance, requiring that any action produce the greatest happiness (see HAPPINESS).

The concern with welfare, its measurement and its maximization is found early, in Plato's *Protagoras*. In the process of attempting to prove that all virtues are one, Socrates advocates *hedonism*, the welfarist view that only pleasurable states of mind are valuable, and that they are valuable solely because of their pleasurableness (see PLATO §9; SOCRATES §24; HEDONISM).

The debate in the *Protagoras* is just one example of the many discussions of welfare in ancient ethics (see EUDAIMONIA). Some have seen Greek ethics as primarily egoistic, addressing the question of what each individual should do to further their own welfare (see EGOISM AND ALTRUISM §4). Utilitarianism, however, is impartial.

The Stoics, who followed Plato and Aristotle, began to develop a notion of impartiality according to which self-concern extended rationally to others, and eventually to the whole world (see STOICISM §18). This doctrine, allied to Christian conceptions of self-sacrifice, and conceptions of rationality with roots in Plato which emphasize the objective supra-individual point of view, could plausibly be said to be the source of utilitarian impartiality (see IMPARTIALITY).

In the modern period, the history of utilitarianism takes up again during the Enlightenment. The idea of impartial maximization is found in the work of the eighteenth-century Scottish philosopher Francis Hutcheson (1755) (see HUTCHESON, F. §2). The work of his contemporary, David Hume (1751), also stressed the importance to ethics of the notion of 'utility' (see HUME, D. §4.1). A little later, the so-called 'theological utilitarians', Joseph Priestley (1768) and William Paley (1785), argued that God requires us to promote the greatest happiness (see PRIESTLEY, J.; PALEY, W.). Meanwhile, in France, Claude Helvétius (1758) advocated utilitarianism as a political theory, according to which the task of governments is to produce happiness for the people. He influenced one of the most extreme of all utilitarians, William Godwin (1793) (see HELVÉTIUS, C.; GODWIN, W.).

It was Jeremy BENTHAM, however, who did most to systematize utilitarianism. Bentham's disciple, J.S. MILL, was the next great utilitarian, and he was followed by Henry SIDGWICK. G.E. Moore (1903) distanced himself from Mill's hedonism, and offered an influential 'ideal' account of the good. One of the most important recent versions of utilitarianism is that of R.M. Hare (see MOORE, G.E.; HARE, R.M.).

2 Conceptions of utility

Before you can maximize utility, you need to know what utility is. It is essential to note that the plausibility of utilitarianism as a theory of right action does not depend on any particular conception of welfare. An account of the good for a person is different from an account of right action (see RIGHT AND GOOD).

Utilitarians have held many different views of utility. The 'classical' utilitarians – primarily Bentham (1789) and Mill (1861) – were hedonists. There are many objections to hedonism. What about masochists, for example, who seem to find pain desirable? Well, perhaps pain can be pleasurable. But is there really something common – pleasure – to all the experiences that go to make up a happy life? And would it be rational to plug oneself into a machine that gave one vast numbers of pleasurable sensations? Here there may be a move towards the more eclectic view of Sidgwick (1874), that utility consists in desirable consciousness of any kind. Some philosophers, however, such as Nietzsche (1888), have suggested that a life of mere enjoyment is inauthentic.

Hedonists have been criticized for sensualism for millennia. J.S. Mill sought to answer the charge, suggesting that hedonists do not have to accept that all pleasurable experiences – drinking lemonade and reading Wordsworth – are on a par, to be valued only according to the *amount* of pleasure they contain. Bentham and others had suggested that the value of a pleasure depends mainly on its intensity and its duration, but Mill insisted that the *quality* of a pleasure – its nature – also influences its pleasurableness and hence its value. But why must the effect on value of the nature of an experience be filtered through pleasurableness? Why cannot its nature by itself add value?

Perhaps the most serious objection to any theory that welfare consists in mental states is the so-called 'experience machine'. This machine is better than the pleasure machine, and can give you the most desirable experiences you can imagine. Would it be best for you to be wired up to it throughout your life? Note that this is not the question whether it would be *right* to arrange for yourself to be wired up, leaving all your obligations in the real world unfulfilled. Even a utilitarian can argue that that would be immoral.

Some people think it makes sense to plug in, others that it would be a kind of death. If you are one of the latter, then you might consider moving to a desire theory of utility, according to which what makes life good for you is your desires' being maximally fulfilled. On the experience machine, many of your desires will remain unfulfilled. You want not just the experience of, say, bringing about world peace, but actually to bring it about. Desire theories have come to dominate contemporary thought because of economists' liking for the notion of 'revealed preferences' (see RATIONALITY, PRACTICAL). Pleasures and pains are hard to get at or measure, whereas people's preferences can be stated, and inferred objectively from their behaviour.

A simple desire theory fails immediately. I desire the glass of liquid, thinking it to be whisky. In fact it is poison, so satisfying my desire will not make me better off. What desire theorists should say here is that it is the satisfaction of intrinsic desires which counts for wellbeing. My intrinsic desire is for pleasure, the desire for the drink being merely derived.

The usual strategy adopted by desire theorists is to build constraints into the theory in response to such counterexamples: what makes me better off is not the fulfilment of my desires, but of my informed desires.

But why do desire theorists so respond to such counterexamples? It is probably because they already have a view of utility which guides them in the construction of their theories. This means that desire theories are themselves idle, which is to be expected once we realize that the fulfilment of a desire is in itself neither good nor bad for a person. What matters is whether what the person desires, and gets, is good or bad.

For reasons such as this, there is now a return to ancient *ideal* theories of utility, according to which certain things are good or bad for beings, independently in at least some cases of whether they are desired or whether they give rise to pleasurable experiences (see PERFECTIONISM). Another interesting ancient view which has recently been revived is that certain nonhedonistic goods are valuable, but only when they are combined with pleasure or desire-fulfilment (see Plato, *Philebus* 21a–22b). The nonhedonistic goods suggested include knowledge and friendship. Questions to ask of the ideal theorist include the following. What will go on your list of goods? How do you decide? How are the various items to be balanced?

3 Types of utilitarianism

Theories of right and wrong have to be about something, that is, have to have a focus. Usually, at least in recent centuries, they have focused on actions, attempting to answer the questions, 'Which actions are right?', and, 'What makes those actions right?'. The ancients also asked these questions, but were concerned also to focus on lives, characters, dispositions and virtues. Nearly all forms of utilitarianism have focused on actions, but in recent decades there has been some interest in utilitarianism as applied to motives, virtues and lives as a whole.

Utilitarianism is a form of consequentialism. But it is important to note that, since utilitarians can attach instrinsic moral importance to acts (especially, of course, the act of maximizing itself), there are problems in attempting to capture the nature of utilitarianism using the act/consequence distinction. A recent alternative has been to employ the 'agent-neutral'/'agent-relative' distinction. Agent-neutral theories give every agent the same aim (for example, that utility be maximized), whereas agent-relative theories give agents different aims (say, that *your* children be looked after). Logically, however, there is nothing to prevent a utilitarian's insisting that *your* aim should be that *you* maximize utility. Though this theory would be practically equivalent to an agent-neutral theory, its possibility suggests there may be problems with attempting to use the agent-neutral/agent-relative distinction to capture the essence of utilitarianism.

What clearly distinguishes utilitarianism from other moral theories is what it requires and why, so we should now turn to that. The commonest, and most straightforward, version of utilitarianism is *act-utilitarianism*, according to which the criterion of an action's rightness is that it maximize utility.

Act-utilitarians might offer two accounts of rightness. The objectively right action would be that which actually does maximize utility, while the subjectively right action would be that which maximizes expected utility. Agents would usually be blamed for not doing what was subjectively right.

Another distinction is between *total* and *average* forms. According to the total view, the right act is the one that produces the largest overall total of utility. The average view says that the right action is that which maximizes the average level of utility in a population. The theories are inconsistent only in cases in which the size of a population is under consideration. The most common such case occurs when one is thinking of having a child. Here, the average view has the absurd conclusion that I should not have a child, even if its life will be wonderful and there will be no detrimental effects from its existence, if its welfare will be lower than the existing average.

But the total view also runs into problems, most famously with Derek Parfit's 'repugnant conclusion' (1984), which commits the total view to the notion that if a population of people with lives barely worth living is large enough it is preferable to a smaller population with very good lives. One way out of this problem is to adopt a *person-affecting* version of utilitarianism, which restricts itself in scope to existing people. But there are problems with this view (see Parfit 1984: ch. 18). Recently, certain writers have suggested that one way to avoid the 'repugnant conclusion' would be to argue that there are *discontinuities* in value, such that once welfare drops below a certain level the loss cannot be compensated for by quantity. There is a link here with Mill's view of the relation of higher pleasures to lower.

Imagine being an act-utilitarian, brought up in an entirely act-utilitarian society. You will have to spend much time calculating the utility values of the various actions open to you. You are quite likely to make mistakes, and, being human, to cook the books in your own favour.

For these reasons, most act-utilitarians have argued that we should not attempt to put act-utilitarianism into practice wholesale, but stick by a lot of common sense morality (see COMMON-SENSE ETHICS). It will save a lot of valuable time, is based on long experience, and will keep us on the straight and narrow. Act-utilitarians who recommend sole and constant application of their theory as well as those who recommend that we never consult the theory and use common sense morality can both be called *single-level* theorists, since moral thinking will be carried on only at one level. Most utilitarians have adopted a *two-level* theory, according to which we consult utilitarianism only sometimes – in particular when the principles of ordinary morality conflict with one another.

The main problem with two-level views is their psychology. If I really accept utilitarianism, how can I abide by a common sense morality I know to be a fiction? And if I really do take that common sense morality seriously, how can I just forget it when I am supposed to think as a utilitarian? The two-level response here must be that this is indeed a messy compromise, but one made to deal with a messy reality.

Act-utilitarianism is an extremely demanding theory, since it requires you to be entirely impartial between your own interests, the interests of those you love, and the interests of all. The usual example offered is famine relief. By giving up all your time, money and energy to famine relief, you will save many lives and prevent much suffering. Utilitarians often claim at this point that there are limits to human capabilities, and utilitarianism requires us only to do what we can. But the sense of 'can' here is quite obscure, since in any ordinary sense I can give up my job and spend my life campaigning for Oxfam.

The demandingness objection seems particularly serious when taken in the context of widespread non-compliance with the demands of act-utilitarian morality. Most people do little or nothing for the developing world, and this is why the moral demands on me are so great. An argument such as this has been used to advocate *rule-utilitarianism*, according to which the right action is that which is in accord with that set of rules which, if generally or universally accepted, would maximize utility. (The version of the theory which speaks of the rules that are *obeyed* is likely to collapse into act-utilitarianism; see Lyons 1965.)

Unlike act-utilitarianism, which is a *direct* theory in that the rightness and wrongness of acts depends directly on whether they fit with the maximizing principle, rule-utilitarianism is an *indirect* theory, since rightness and wrongness depend on rules, the justification for which itself rests on the utilitarian principle.

The demandingness of act-utilitarianism has not been the main reason for adopting rule-utilitarianism. Rather, the latter theory has been thought to provide support for common sense moral principles, such as those speaking against killing or lying, which appear plausible in their own right.

Rule-utilitarianism has not received as much attention as act-utilitarianism, partly because it detaches itself from the attractiveness of maximization. According to rule-utilitarianism there may be times when the right action is to bring about less than the best possible world (such as when others are not complying). But if maximization is reasonable at the level of rules, why does it not apply straightforwardly to acts?

4 Arguments for utilitarianism

The most famous argument for utilitarianism is John Stuart Mill's 'proof' (1861). This has three stages:

1 Happiness is desirable.
2 The general happiness is desirable.
3 Nothing other than happiness is desirable.

Each stage has been subjected to much criticism, especially the first. Mill was an empiricist, who believed that matters of fact could be decided by appeal to the senses (see EMPIRICISM). In his proof, he attempted to ground evaluative claims on an analogous appeal to desires, making unfortunate rhetorical use of 'visible' and 'desirable'. The first stage suggests to the reader that if they consult their own desires, they will see that they find happiness desirable.

The second stage is little more than assertion, since Mill did not see the vastness of the difference between egoistic and universalistic hedonism (utilitarianism). In an important footnote (1861: ch. 5, para. 36), we see the assumption that lies behind the proof: the more happiness one can promote by a certain action, the stronger the reason to perform it. Egoists will deny this, but it does put the ball back in their court.

The final stage again rests on introspection, the claim being that we desire, ultimately, only pleasurable states. Thus even a desire for virtue can be seen as a desire for happiness, since what we desire is the pleasure of acting virtuously or contemplating our virtue. One suspects that introspection by Mill's opponents would have had different results.

Perhaps the most common form of utilitarianism, as of any other moral theory, is, in a weak sense, intuitionist (see INTUITIONISM IN ETHICS). To many, utilitarianism has just seemed, taken by itself, reasonable – so reasonable, indeed, that any attempt to prove it would probably rest on premises less secure than the conclusion. This view was expressed most powerfully by Henry Sidgwick (1874). Sidgwick supported his argument with a painstaking analysis of common sense morality. Sidgwick also believed that egoism was supported by intuition, so that practical reason was ultimately divided (see EGOISM AND ALTRUISM §§1, 3).

In the twentieth century, R.M. Hare wished to avoid appeal to moral intuition, which he saw as irrational. According to Hare (1981), if we are going to answer a moral question such as, 'What ought I to do?', we should first understand the logic of the words we are using. In the case of 'ought', we shall find that it has two properties: prescriptivity (it is action-guiding) and universalizability (I should be ready to assent to any moral judgment I make when it is applied to situations similar to the present one in their universal properties) (see PRESCRIPTIVISM). Hare argues that putting yourself in another's position properly – 'universalizing' – involves taking on board their preferences. Once this has been done, the only rational strategy is to maximize overall preference-satisfaction, which is equivalent to utilitarianism.

Hare's moral theory is one of the most sophisticated since Kant's, and he does indeed claim to incorporate elements of Kantianism into his theory (see KANTIAN ETHICS). Objectors have claimed, however, that, rather like Kant himself, Hare introduces 'intuitions' (that is, beliefs about morality or rationality) through the back door. For example, the logic of the word 'ought' may be said not to involve a commitment to the rationality of maximization even in one's own case.

5 Problems for utilitarianism

There are many technical problems with the various forms of utilitarianism. How are pleasure and pain to be measured? Which desires are to count? Is knowledge a good in itself? Should we take into account actual or probable effects on happiness? How do we characterize the possible world which is to guide us in our selection of rules? These are problems for the theorists themselves, and there has been a great deal said in attempts to resolve them.

More foundational, however, is a set of problems for any kind of utilitarian theory, emerging out of utilitarianism's peculiarly strict conception of impartiality. A famous utilitarian tag, from Bentham, is, 'Everybody to count for one, nobody for more than one'. This, however, as Mill implies (1861: ch. 5, para. 36), is slightly misleading. In a sense, according to utilitarianism, no one matters; all that matters is the level of utility. What are counted equally are not persons but pleasures or utilities.

This conception of impartiality has made it easy for opponents of utilitarianism to dream up examples in which utilitarianism seems to require something appalling. A famous such example requires a utilitarian sheriff to hang an innocent man, so as to prevent a riot and bring about the greatest overall happiness possible in the circumstances (see CRIME AND PUNISHMENT §2).

Utilitarians can here respond that, in practice, they believe that people should abide by common sense morality, that people should accept practical principles of rights for utilitarian reasons (see §2). But this misses the serious point in many of these objections: that it matters not just how much utility there is, but how it is shared around. Imagine, for example, a case in which you can give a bundle of resources either to someone who is well-off and rich through no fault of their own, or to someone who is poor through no fault of their own. If the utility of giving the bundle to the rich person is only slightly higher than that of giving it to the poor person, utilitarianism dictates giving it to the rich person. But many (including some consequentialists) would argue that it is reasonable to give some priority to the worse-off.

These are problems at the level of the social distribution of utility. But difficulties arise also because of the fact that human agents each have their own lives to live, and engage in their practical reasoning from their own personal point of view rather than from the imaginary point of view of an 'impartial spectator'. These problems have been stated influentially in recent years by Bernard Williams (Smart and Williams 1973), who puts them under the heading of what he calls 'integrity' (see WILLIAMS, B.A.O. §4).

In a famous example, Williams asks us to imagine the case of Jim, who is travelling in a South American jungle. He comes across a military firing squad, about to shoot twenty Indians from a nearby village where some insurrection has occurred. The captain in charge offers Jim a guest's privilege. Either Jim can choose to shoot one of the Indians himself, and the others will go free, or all twenty will be shot by the firing squad.

Williams' point here is not that utilitarianism gives the wrong answer; indeed he himself thinks that Jim should shoot. Rather, it is that utilitarianism reaches its answer too quickly, and cannot account for many of the thoughts we know that we should have ourselves in Jim's situation, such as, 'It is I who will be the killer'. Practical reasoning is not concerned only with arranging things so that the greatest utility is produced. Rather it matters to each agent what role they will be playing in the situation, and where the goods and bads occur. This point emerges even more starkly if we imagine a variation on the story about Jim, in which the captain asks Jim to commit suicide so as to set an example of courage and nobility to the local populace, on the condition that if he does so the twenty Indians will go free. The utility calculations are as clear, perhaps clearer, than in the original story. But it is only reasonable that Jim in this story should

think it relevant that it is he who is going to die. To any individual, it matters not only how much happiness there is in the world, but who gets it.

See also: ANIMALS AND ETHICS; DEONTOLOGICAL ETHICS; GOOD, THEORIES OF THE; HELP AND BENEFICENCE §2; TELEOLOGICAL ETHICS

References and further reading

* Bentham, J. (1789) *An Introduction to the Principles of Morals and Legislation*, ed. J.H. Burns and H.L.A. Hart, revised F. Rosen, Oxford: Clarendon Press, 1996. (Highly influential statement of hedonistic act-utilitarianism.)

Crisp, R. (1992) 'Utilitarianism and the life of virtue', *Philosophical Quarterly* 42: 139–60. (Discussion of two-level utilitarianism with focus on lives.)

Glover, J. (ed.) (1990) *Utilitarianism and Its Critics*, New York: Macmillan. (Contains essential readings, with helpful guidance by the editor. Good starting place; helpfully structured bibliography.)

* Godwin, W. (1793) *Enquiry Concerning Political Justice*, ed. K. Codell, Oxford: Clarendon Press, 1971. (Radical anarchist utilitarianism.)

Griffin, J. (1982) 'Modern utilitarianism', *Revue Internationale de Philosophie* 141: 331–75. (Good starting place for study of recent work on utilitarianism.)

—— (1986) *Well-Being: Its Meaning, Measurement, and Moral Importance*, Oxford: Clarendon Press. (Key discussion of different conceptions of utility. Defends ideal account with preferences entering at level of explanation of value.)

* Hare, R.M. (1981) *Moral Thinking: Its Methods, Levels and Point*, Oxford: Clarendon Press. (Sophisticated modern two-level act-utilitarian, influenced by Aristotle, Kant and Mill.)

* Helvétius, C. (1758) *De l'esprit* (On the Mind), Paris: Arthème Fayard, 1988. (Enlightenment utilitarian political theorist.)

Hooker, B. (1990) 'Rule consequentialism', *Mind* 91: 67–77. (Contains defence of rule-consequentialism – also applicable to rule-utilitarianism – on grounds of undemandingness and fairness.)

* Hume, D. (1751) *An Enquiry Concerning the Principles of Morals*, ed. L.A. Selby-Bigge, revised by P.H. Nidditch, Oxford: Clarendon Press, 3rd edn, 1975. (See esp. section 5, 'Why utility pleases', on the usefulness of the social virtues.)

* Hutcheson, F. (1755) *A System of Moral Philosophy*, in *Collected Works*, vols 5–6, Hildesheim: Georg Olms, 1969. (Important Enlightenment work, anticipating Bentham and Mill.)

* Lyons, D. (1965) *Forms and Limits of Utilitarianism*,

Oxford: Clarendon Press. (Classic discussion of act- and rule-utilitarianism.)

* Mill, J.S. (1861) *Utilitarianism*, ed. R. Crisp, Oxford: Clarendon Press, 1998. (One of the most important and widely studied works in moral philosophy. Contains argument that pleasures can be seen as higher and lower.)

Miller, H.B. and Williams, W.H. (eds) (1982) *The Limits of Utilitarianism*, Minneapolis, MN: University of Minnesota Press. (Interesting and wide-ranging collection. Contains bibliography of works on utilitarianism from 1930 to 1980.)

* Moore, G.E. (1903) *Principia Ethica*, ed. T. Baldwin, Cambridge: Cambridge University Press, revised edn, 1993. (Includes critique of Mill, and development of ideal account of the good.)

* Nietzsche, F. (1888) *Die Götzen-Dämmerung*, trans. A.M. Ludovici, *The Twilight of the Idols*, London: Allen & Unwin, 1911, 94–6. (Criticizes the life consisting solely of happiness or pleasure.)

* Paley, W. (1785) *Principles of Moral and Political Philosophy*, New York: Garland, 1978. (Theological utilitarian, whose great success is said to have spurred Bentham to publish his *Introduction to the Principles*.)

* Parfit, D. (1984) *Reasons and Persons*, Oxford: Clarendon Press. (Central modern work. Part IV contains discussion of population problems.)

* Plato (c.386–380 BC) *Protagoras*, trans. with notes by C.C.W. Taylor, Oxford: Clarendon Press, 2nd edn, 1991. (Develops early account of hedonism.)

* —— (c.360–347 BC) *Philebus*, trans. J.C.B. Gosling, *Plato: Philebus*, Oxford: Clarendon Press, 1975. (A discussion of the relative merits of pleasure and wisdom in the good life.)

* Priestley, J. (1768) *Essay on the First Principles of Government; and on the Nature of Political, Civil, and Religious Liberty*, London: Dodsley, Cadell, Johnson; repr. in P. Miller (ed.) *Political Writings*, Cambridge: Cambridge University Press, 1993. (Influential theological utilitarian.)

Railton, P. (1984) 'Alienation, consequentialism, and the demands of morality', *Philosophy and Public Affairs* 13: 134–71. (On the everyday moral thinking recommended by utilitarianism.)

Scarre, G. (1996) *Utilitarianism*, London: Routledge. (Useful introduction, including history. Contains bibliography.)

Sen, A. and Williams, B. (eds) (1982) *Utilitarianism and Beyond*, Cambridge: Cambridge University Press. (Useful collection. Introduction provides general survey, including discussion of desire theory and rights. Contains bibliography. See essays by R.M. Hare for introduction to his views, and by

T.M. Scanlon for contractualist discussion of utilitarianism.)

Sidgwick, H. (1874) *The Methods of Ethics*, London: Macmillan; 7th edn, 1907, books III and IV. (Intuitionist defence of utilitarianism embedded within perceptive discussion of common sense morality.)

* Smart, J.J. and Williams, B. (1973) *Utilitarianism For and Against*, Cambridge: Cambridge University Press. (Smart discusses the 'experience machine', Williams integrity.)

TIM CHAPPELL
ROGER CRISP

UTOPIANISM

Utopianism is the general label for a number of different ways of dreaming or thinking about, describing or attempting to create a better society. Utopianism is derived from the word utopia, coined by Thomas More. In his book Utopia *(1516) More described a society significantly better than England as it existed at the time, and the word* utopia *(good place) has come to mean a description of a fictional place, usually a society, that is better than the society in which the author lives and which functions as a criticism of the author's society. In some cases it is intended as a direction to be followed in social reform, or even, in a few instances, as a possible goal to be achieved.*

The concept of utopianism clearly reflects its origins. In Utopia *More presented a fictional debate over the nature of his creation. Was it fictional or real? Was the obvious satire aimed primarily at contemporary England or was it also aimed at the society described in the book? More important for later developments, was it naïvely unrealistic or did it present a social vision that, whether achievable or not, could serve as a goal to be aimed at? Most of what we now call utopianism derives from the last question. In the nineteenth century Robert Owen in England and Charles Fourier, Henri Saint-Simon and Étienne Cabet in France, collectively known as the utopian socialists, popularized the possibility of creating a better future through the establishment of small, experimental communities. Karl Marx, Friedrich Engels and others argued that such an approach was incapable of solving the problems of industrial society and the label 'utopian' came to mean unrealistic and naïve. Later theorists, both opposed to and supportive of utopianism, debated the desirability of depicting a better society as a way of achieving significant social change. In particular, Christian religious thinkers have been deeply divided over utopianism. Is the act of envisaging a better life on earth heretical, or is it a normal part of Christian thinking?*

Since the collapse of communism in eastern Europe and the former Soviet Union, a number of theorists have argued that utopianism has come to an end. It has not; utopias are still being written and intentional communities founded, hoping that a better life is possible.

1 **Background**
2 **Utopian socialism**
3 **Utopian social theory**
4 **The end of utopia**

1 Background

Utopianism has existed at least as long as written history. Descriptions of better societies are found on a Sumerian clay tablet, in the Old Testament and among early Greek writers. There is considerable debate over whether or not it is a universal human phenomenon, but the only culture that seems to be lacking an early utopian tradition is Japan. The term that is used to characterize the phenomenon first occurs in the title of Thomas More's book *Libellus vere aureus nec minus salutaris quam festivus de optimo reip[ublicae] statu, deq[ue] noua Insula Vtopia* (1516), now known simply as *Utopia*. The word was based on the root *topos*, meaning *place*, and the prefix *u* or *ou*, meaning *no* or *not*. Thus, strictly speaking, utopia refers simply to a nonexistent place, but More punned on an alternative prefix, *eu* or *good*. As a result the word *utopia* came to refer to a nonexistent good place. Even though some scholars prefer to retain the distinction between *utopia* and *eutopia*, common usage conflates them (Sargent 1994).

The word *utopia* was rapidly added to most European languages and was in fairly common use by the end of the sixteenth century, being employed as part of a book title as early as 1520. The utopia as a literary genre developed quickly (Hölscher 1996); more than twenty utopias were published in the sixteenth century after More's *Utopia* (Sargent 1988), and the first study of this new phenomenon was published in 1704 (Ahlefeld 1704; see Widdicombe 1992 for a discussion of early studies).

Utopia is a small but complex book in that it presages much of the later debate over the importance of utopianism. Within *Utopia* More presented arguments for and against his invention, using arguments that have a long history and still continue to be used today.

Discussion of utopianism and its role in political philosophy surfaces as early as Aristotle, who in *Politics* criticized Plato and other projectors of better

societies. ARISTOTLE (§§27–8) argued that depicting an ideal society is the wrong approach to political theorizing. He suggested that both the criticism of contemporary societies and the development of proposals for bettering them need to be based on a detailed, realistic understanding of how human beings behave and the ways that political systems are both shaped by, and can shape, that behaviour. Plato can be interpreted as doing just that, particularly in his *Laws*, which contrary to popular opinion is closer to later utopian thinking than his *Republic*. Aristotle's position, however, still forms one of the starting points for much contemporary criticism of utopianism. Today both Marxists and liberals use utopianism as a pejorative term, meaning 'unrealistic' or 'against human nature' or simply 'too idealistic'. Others have argued that utopianism is essential to any positive social change and may even be part of what makes us human (see HUMAN NATURE §1).

In the late 1920s Karl Mannheim, primarily known as the theorist of the sociology of knowledge, used the concepts utopia and ideology as the two basic mental constructs that distort political discourse. Mannheim hoped to rid the words utopia and ideology of their negative meanings and reconstitute them as means of understanding the ways that certain social groups perceive the world around them. He first developed these ideas in his *Ideology and Utopia* (1929). In 1935, in an influential encyclopedia article, he defined the two concepts succinctly:

> The term utopian, as here used, may be applied to any process of thought which receives its impetus not from the direct source of reality but from concepts, such as symbols, fantasies, dreams, ideas and the like, which in the most comprehensive sense of that term are non-existent. Viewed from the standpoint of sociology, such mental constructs may in general assume two forms: They are ideological if they serve the purpose of glossing over or stabilizing the existing social reality; utopian if they inspire collective activity which aims to change such reality to conform with their goals, which transcend reality.
>
> (Mannheim 1935)

Mannheim's definitions influenced the use of the words, although not in the way he intended. His definition reinforced the old message that to be utopian meant to be naïve and out of touch with the real world. Mannheim scholars now consider *Ideology and Utopia* to be a minor part of his work, but his definitions are still used, not always accurately, by scholars of both ideology and utopianism (see IDEOLOGY §1).

2 Utopian socialism

Historically the most important critics of utopianism after Aristotle were Karl MARX and Friedrich ENGELS. In his *Die Entwicklung des Sozialismus von der Utopie zur Wissenschaft* (*Socialism: Utopian and Scientific*), published in 1882, Engels coined the phrase 'utopian socialist' to describe Owen, Fourier, Saint-Simon and, in some editions, Cabet, whose idealistic proposals he regarded as distinctly inferior to Marx's 'scientific socialism'. Among these writers only Cabet wrote a work that a narrow definition would call a utopia – *Voyage en Icarie* (1840). Owen and Fourier described social systems based on relatively small communities, now generally called 'intentional communities' but in the past frequently called 'utopian communities'. Owen and Cabet actually participated in the development of such communities – Owen in the UK and the USA and Cabet in the USA – while followers of Fourier and Saint-Simon built them, mostly in France and the USA. Such communities are now generally thought of as examples of utopianism, and there are currently thousands of them based in at least twenty-one countries, the best-known example being the kibbutz movement in Israel.

Engels' primary target was not the building of small communities; in fact at one time he actually praised such community construction, using the example of the Rappites in Pennsylvania. What bothered the Marxists was that the utopian socialists made what Marx and his followers thought were unwarranted assumptions about human nature and about their own ability to predict and construct a better future. For all of his desire to overthrow the currently existing socio-economic system, Marx was adamant that a future constructed by people freed from domination could not be predicted. Marxists also argued that the utopian socialists were extremely naïve about the problems of constructing such a future society and the opposition that would be brought against any attempt to do so. Marxists contended that the construction of small communities was the wrong approach because they would never be allowed to succeed or, if they were, it would be because they were no threat to those in power. None of the communities built by the utopian socialists lasted very long (the seven Icarian communities founded by the followers of Cabet had a combined life span of fifty years), and none ever posed a threat. In contrast, nearing the end of the twentieth century, certain religious intentional communities have been in existence for nearly two hundred years, while fifty years is no longer uncommon and twenty-five years is almost the norm, even for secular communities; however, as before, these are not in any real sense threats to the existing order in any of the countries in which they exist (see COMMUNISM).

3 Utopian social theory

While the main line of criticism of utopianism initially developed in the context of utopian socialism and the small community, it was not that aspect of utopianism that became the focus for either its attackers or defenders, and Marxists have appeared in both ranks. Both Marxists and anti-Marxists argue that utopian thinking is naïve and unrealistic and makes assumptions about 'human nature' that will not withstand scrutiny. Marxists argue that 'human nature' is socially constructed and varies from society to society and time to time. Conservative, mostly Christian, opponents argue that sinful human nature is incapable of the improvements that they believe utopianism requires (Molnar 1967). It is true that many utopians have assumed that human nature is fundamentally 'good', usually meaning cooperative, but that contemporary society distorts that goodness; a new, better society would allow it to be expressed. However, such thinking is by no means the norm among utopians.

The modern debate around utopianism developed historically from its rejection. At the turn of the century, Edward Bellamy's novel, *Looking Backward 2000–1887* (1888), depicting a centralized socialist (he called it nationalist) utopia became the best-selling novel published up to that time and remained so until well into the twentieth century. Nationalist societies were founded in countries around the world. Bellamy effectively rekindled interest in utopianism after Engels had destroyed it. Since then, although deeply disputed, utopianism has never been ignored, even though for one fairly lengthy period it was the anti-utopians that kept it visible.

The anti-utopians generally regard utopias as blueprints of a desired perfect future society that must be achieved in all of its details. Since perfection is beyond human capabilities, the utopians, it is believed, will have to resort to force and violence to achieve utopia. Therefore, utopias are a first step that almost inevitably leads to totalitarianism (see TOTALITARIANISM). Karl POPPER is the best-known exponent of this position. In *The Open Society and Its Enemies*, he wrote: 'the Utopian approach can be saved only by the Platonic belief in one absolute and unchanging ideal, together with two further assumptions, namely (a) that there are rational methods to determine once and for all what this ideal is, and (b) what the best means of its realization are' ([1945] 1957, vol. 1: 161).

Utopians deny that utopias are the problem; the problem is with the believers. They argue that utopias are not blueprints of some future perfect society but act both as a critique of contemporary society and as a generalized goal rather than something to be realized in all its details. Utopias are seen by their defenders as expressions of the highest human aspirations.

This position is put most forcefully by the Dutch sociologist F.L. Polak in his *The Image of the Future*. He argued that our images of the future (whether utopias or dystopias) affect the actual future: 'We will view human society and culture as being magnetically *pulled* towards a future fulfilment of their own preceding and prevailing, idealistic images of the future, as well as being *pushed* from behind by their own realistic past' (1961, vol. 1: 15; original emphasis). Polak goes on to contend that 'if Western man now stops thinking and dreaming the materials of new images of the future and attempts to shut himself up in the present, out of longing for security and for fear of the future, his civilization will come to an end. He has no choice but to dream or to die, condemning the whole of Western society to die with him' (vol. 1: 53).

Ernst BLOCH (§3) has become the most influential utopian thinker of the twentieth century. Bloch has become important for utopians because he argues that there always exists unrealized potential for positive social change. In other words, there are always utopian possibilities in any given situation. For scholars of utopianism, Bloch is significant today because in his most important work, *Das Prinzip Hoffnung* (The Principle of Hope, 1959), he demonstrates the long history of utopianism and its important contribution to social improvement.

For Bloch utopia is constantly on the horizon, not yet achieved, but open to the possibility of being achieved. It is these utopian aspirations and the hope that they can be realized that make human life bearable and a better life possible. For Bloch, human beings are active participants in creating that better future; we must think and act experimentally, driven by the utopian visions that Bloch found in art, literature, music, and social theory. In this he separates himself from the more deterministic versions of Marxism while at the same time seeing Marx as one of the great utopians of the past.

Utopianism has been a particular problem for Christian theorists, with some seeing any expression of utopianism as heretical (Molnar 1967) and others seeing it as an essential aspect of Christianity (Tillich 1971).

4 The end of utopia

Recent discussion of utopianism has focused on the so-called 'end of utopia'. Proponents of this have tended to identify utopian aspirations with the communist regimes of the former Soviet Union and eastern Europe. Thus, they saw in the collapse of communism a vindication of the futility of utopianism in the face of the obdurate material of human nature. The end of utopia was predicated on the same misidentification of utopia with totalitarianism found earlier in Popper.

Just as with the 'end of ideology' debate of the 1950s – which was based on almost precisely the same arguments – utopia has not ended. In fact, it has been argued that the collapse of communism (a utopia that became a dystopia) was based on the development of a new and powerful utopia within communist countries, a utopia of freedom and materialism. Generalized, the position is that a new utopia is always needed to overcome the old dystopia. This point was made by the late Viktoriia Chalikova in *Utopiia rozhdaetsia iz utopii: cesse raznykh let* (Utopia is Born by Utopia, 1992).

Utopianism remains alive and well in all three of its forms. A constant stream of utopian novels is published in a wide variety of languages. The utopias found in these novels are more complex and self-reflective than in the earlier tradition, less certain that utopia can be both created and maintained, more aware both of the powerful forces marshalled against social betterment and the dangers inherent in the utopian enterprise, dangers pointed out by the anti-utopians. This has led one critic, Tom Moylan, to argue in his *Demand the Impossible* (1986) that a new type of utopia, the 'critical utopia', has been created. Moreover, since the beginning of the 1970s feminist novelists and theorists have produced a steady and continuing stream of feminist utopias.

There are more long-lived and well-established intentional communities currently in existence than at any time in the past, including the 1960s, when there was a great upsurge of community building. While generally little known, they are found throughout the world, with the greatest numbers in Australia, Europe and North America, and a number of ecologically based communities have recently been founded in the former Soviet Union. These communities express the desire of thousands of people to live a better life now.

Utopian theorists are also publishing more than ever before, arguing that social dreaming is both essential and potentially dangerous. Alongside Bloch and Polak, such theorists see the need to have utopian aspirations, but they are also intensely aware that there are always people ready to impose their utopia on others. None the less, the utopians argue, this does not in any way diminish the need to dream of a better life for all.

See also: SAINT-SIMON, COMTE DE

References and further reading

* Ahlefeld, H. ab (1704) *Disputatio philosophica de fictis rebuspublicis. Quam divina favente gratia, praeside Georgio Paschio, Artis rationis, Philos. In Auditorio Majori publice defendet Henricus ab Ahlefeld, Esques Holsatus* (A Philosophical Argument Concerning Fictional Republics), Kiloni: Typis Bartholdi Reutheri; trans. W. Biesterfeld, 'Ein früher Beitrag zu Begriff und Geschichte der Utopie. Heinrich von Ahlefeldts *Disputatio philosophica de fictis rebuspublicis*' (An Early Contribution to the Concept and History of Utopia), *Archiv für Begriffsgeschichte* 16 (1): 28–47, 1972. (Earliest study of utopianism.)

* Bellamy, E. (1888) *Looking Backward: 2000–1887*, ed. C. Tichi, Harmondsworth: Penguin, 1982. (The most popular utopian novel ever published.)

* Bloch, E. (1959) *Das Prinzip Hoffnung*, Frankfurt: Suhrkampf Verlag; trans. N. Plaice, S. Plaice and P. Knight, *The Principle of Hope*, Oxford: Blackwell, 1986, 3 vols. (Bloch's most important work.)

Buber, M. (1949) *Paths in Utopia*, trans. R.F.C. Hull, Boston, MA: Beacon Press. (Early work arguing for the importance of utopian goals for social change.)

* Cabet, E. (1840) *Voyage en Icarie*, Paris: Bureau au Populaire. (Utopian novel.)

* Chalikova, V.A. (1992) *Utopiia rozhdaetsia iz utopii: cesse raznykh let* (Utopia is Born by Utopia), London: Overseas Publications Interchange. (Argues that utopias are essential for overcoming regimes that have become dystopic.)

Dahrendorf, R. (1958) 'Out of Utopia: Toward a Reorientation of Sociological Analysis', *American Journal of Sociology* 64 (September): 115–27. (Anti-utopian.)

* Engels, F. (1882) *Die Entwicklung des Sozialismus von der Utopie zur Wissenschaft*, Zurich: Schweizerische Genossenschaftsdruckerei; trans. E. Aveling (1892) *Socialism: Utopian and Scientific*, New York: International Publishers, 1935. (Classic Marxist statement on utopian socialism.)

Goodwin, B. (1980) 'Utopia Defended Against the Liberals', *Political Studies* 28 (3): 384–400. (Argument for the importance of utopianism.)

* Hölscher, L. (1996) 'Utopie', *Utopian Studies* 7 (2): 1–65. (A history of the concept of utopia.)

Kateb, G. (1963) *Utopia and Its Enemies*, New York: Free Press. (Early study of utopian and anti-utopian thinkers.)

Levitas, R. (1990) *The Concept of Utopia*, Hemel Hempstead: Philip Allan, and Syracuse, NY: Syracuse University Press. (Best consideration of utopianism in recent social theory.)

* Mannheim, K. (1929) *Ideology and Utopia: An Introduction to the Sociology of Knowledge*, trans. L. Wirth and E. Shils, London: Routledge, 1936; new edn, 1991. (Classic treatise on the sociology of knowledge.)

* —— (1935) 'Utopia', in *Encyclopedia of the Social Sciences*, New York: Macmillan, vol. 15, 200–3. (Definition of the concept from Mannheim's viewpoint.)

Manuel, F.E. (ed.) (1967) *Utopias and Utopian Thought*, Boston, MA: Beacon Press. (Collection of essays on aspects of utopianism.)

Manuel, F.E. and Fritzie, P.M. (1979) *Utopian Thought in the Western World*, Cambridge, MA: Belknap Press. (Best general history of utopian thought.)

Minerva, N. (ed.) (1992) *Per una definizione dell'utopia: Metodologie e discipline a confronto. Atti del Convegno Internazionale di Bagni di Lucca 12–14 settembre 1990* (On the Definition of Utopia), Ravenna: Longo Editore. (Excellent collection on various aspects of utopian studies. Includes essays in English and French as well as Italian.)

* Molnar, T. (1967) *Utopia: The Perennial Heresy*, New York: Sheed & Ward. (Anti-utopian.)

* More, T. (1516) *Utopia*, ed. G.M. Logan and R.M. Adams, Cambridge: Cambridge University Press, 1989. (The origin of the word utopia and an early statement of communism and religious toleration.)

* Moylan, T. (1986) *Demand the Impossible: Science Fiction and the Utopian Imagination*, London: Methuen. (Exposition of the 'critical utopia'.)

* Polak, F.L. (1961) *The Image of the Future; Enlightening the Past, Orientating the Present, Forecasting the Future*, New York: Oceana Publications, 2 vols. (Strongest pro-utopian argument.)

* Popper, K.R. (1945) *The Open Society and Its Enemies*, London: Routledge & Kegan Paul, 3rd edn, 1957, 2 vols. (Strongest anti-utopian argument.)

—— (1948) 'Utopia and Violence', *Hibbert Journal* 46 (January): 109–16. (Anti-utopian.)

Saage, R. (ed.) (1992) *Hat die politische Utopie eine Zukunft?* (Does Political Utopia Have a Future?), Darmstadt: Wissenschaftliche Buchgesellschaft. (Essays on the 'end of utopia'.)

Sargent, L.T. (1982) 'Authority and Utopia: Utopianism in Political Thought', *Polity* 14 (4): 565–84. (Argument for the importance of utopianism.)

* —— (1988) *British and American Utopian Literature 1516–1985: An Annotated, Chronological Bibliography*, New York: Garland. (The most comprehensive bibliography of materials in English.)

* —— (1994) 'The Three Faces of Utopianism Revisited', *Utopian Studies* 5 (2): 1–37. (General consideration of various aspects of utopianism.)

* Tillich, P. (1971) 'The Political Meaning of Utopia', in *Political Expectation*, trans. W.J. Crout, W. Bense and J.L. Adams, New York: Harper & Row, 125–80. (Strong pro-utopian argument.)

Utopian Studies (1990–). (Best journal in the field.)

* Widdicombe, R.T. (1992) 'Early Histories of Utopian Thought (to 1950)', *Utopian Studies* 3 (1): 1–38. (Survey of early research on utopianism.)

LYMAN TOWER SARGENT

UTTERER'S INTENTION
see COMMUNICATION AND INTENTION

V

VAGUENESS

It seems obvious that there are vague ways of speaking and vague ways of thinking – saying that the weather is hot, for example. Common sense also has it that there is vagueness in the external world (although this is not the usual view in philosophy). Intuitively, clouds, for example, do not have sharp spatiotemporal boundaries. But the thesis that vagueness is real has spawned a number of deeply perplexing paradoxes and problems. There is no general agreement among philosophers about how to understand vagueness.

1   **Vagueness in language and the world**
2   **Paradoxes and problems**
3   **Theories**

1   Vagueness in language and the world

Many linguistic terms are vague. But of what exactly does their vagueness consist? Consider, for example, the term 'bald'. This term has borderline cases of application. There are people to whom the term, as it is ordinarily used, neither clearly applies nor clearly fails to apply. In this respect, the term 'bald' is different from the term 'square root', say. There are no borderline square roots, nor could there be. Let us say that a general term (a word or phrase which potentially applies to many things) is intensionally vague (that is, vague with respect to its meaning) only if its meaning permits possible borderline cases of application. Then 'bald' is intensionally vague.

Vagueness can also be found in singular terms (words or phrases that potentially apply to single things). Consider, for example, 'the friend of Amy'. Suppose Amy has a love–hate relationship with Jane, without Amy clearly having any other friends. Then, it is indeterminate whether the singular term, 'the friend of Amy', designates Jane. So, 'the friend of Amy' has a possible borderline case of designation. And this indicates that it is intensionally vague.

It is plausible to suppose that intensional vagueness in general terms is more basic than intensional vagueness in singular terms, since uncontroversial examples of vague singular terms either contain vague general terms (non-relational or relational) or are the abstract singular counterparts to those terms. In the case of 'the friend of Amy', the term 'friend of' is intensionally vague.

The vagueness so far discussed does not require vagueness in the world. But worldly vagueness can be treated in a similar way. Suppose, as we normally do, that there really is a nonlinguistic property of being red, a property expressed by the predicate 'is red'. This predicate is vague and so is the property. Just as the former has borderline cases of application, so too the latter has borderline instances (objects which are neither clearly red nor clearly not red). Moreover, even if the actual world had not contained borderline red objects, still, intuitively, that would not have shown that the property, redness, is not vague. What the vagueness of properties seems to require is that there be possible borderline instances. Consider next concrete objects, for example, Mount Everest. Some molecules are definitely inside Everest and some are definitely outside. But intuitively, some have a borderline status: there is no determinate fact of the matter about whether they are inside or outside. Everest, then, has borderline spatiotemporal parts. In this way, it is like a cloud. So Everest is a vague concrete object.

There is another way in which, according to some philosophers, objects in the world can be vague. If, for a given object, *o*, there is an object, *o′*, such that it is indefinite whether *o* is identical with *o′*, then *o*, by virtue of its entering into an indefinite identity relation, is a vague object. Here is one possible example (due to D. Parfit, cited in Broome 1984). There is a club which has a clubhouse, a membership list and a set of rules. This club is never formally disbanded, but through time its members meet less and less frequently and the clubhouse becomes run down. There are no meetings for several years. Twelve years later, however, a few of the original members get together with some new people and start to meet once more in the same building (now redecorated). The club they belong to at this later date has the same name as the earlier one.

It has been held that the claim that the first club is identical with the second one is indefinite. Moreover, this indefiniteness, it has been suggested, is not an epistemic matter, since there is no further information which would settle the issue. On this view, each club has a vague identity and is thereby a vague object.

There is at least one respect in which the proposed characterizations of vagueness are incomplete. Consider the following sequence of conditionals, each of which includes the vague term 'tall':

(1a) If a man whose height is 7 feet is tall, then a man whose height is 6 feet 11 and $\frac{99}{100}$ inches is tall.

(1b) If a man whose height is 6 feet 11 and $\frac{99}{100}$ inches is tall, then a man whose height is 6 feet 11 and $\frac{98}{100}$ inches is tall.

$\vdots$

(1n) If a man whose height is 5 feet and $\frac{1}{100}$ inches is tall, then a man whose height is 5 feet is tall.

Intuitively, there is no sharp dividing line between the true conditionals in this sequence and those that have some other value. This fact is not captured in the earlier account of intensional vagueness. But it seems to be part and parcel of our ordinary conception of the vagueness of terms such as 'tall' or 'bald'. Their vagueness is robust or resilient. And a corresponding point can be made about vague concrete objects. For example, it does not seem to be true that there is a sharp dividing line between the molecules that are inside Everest and those that have a borderline status.

2 Paradoxes and problems

The oldest puzzle of vagueness, which allegedly derives from Eubulides, is the paradox of the bald man. It goes as follows:

(2) A man with no hairs on his head is bald.

(3) For any number, n, if a man with n hairs on his head is bald then a man with $n+1$ hairs on his head is bald.

(4) Therefore, a man with ten thousand hairs on his head is bald.

The conclusion is derived from the premises via ten thousand applications of the classical logical rules of *modus ponens* and universal instantiation, so this argument is valid. Now, premise (2) is certainly true and the conclusion, (4), is certainly false, so it is inferred that premise (3) is false. Therefore, there is an n such that a man with n hairs on his head is bald and a man with $n+1$ is not. Therefore, the term 'bald' is precise, contrary to appearances. And what is true in this one case is true by parallel reasoning for any general term which is ordinarily classified as vague.

It is worth observing that the paradox of the bald man does not rely essentially on the use of a universal generalization. The same result can be generated by means of a sequence of (ten thousand) conditionals such as in (1a)–(1n), with (2) as a starting point. Since the conclusion, (4), is false, and (2) is true, then at least one of the conditionals must be false. So, given

that (2) is true and that each conditional is either true or false, there must be an adjacent pair of conditionals such that the first is true and the second false. This runs directly counter to the idea that 'bald' is vague.

If the paradox of the bald man really does demonstrate that the term 'bald' is not vague, contrary to what we all ordinarily believe, then 'bald' cannot express a vague property. So, the property of being bald cannot itself be vague. Since the paradox of the bald man can be restated so as to apply to any vague general term, one overall conclusion which has been reached is that no general terms or properties are vague. This conclusion, of course, not only threatens the thesis that there are vague abstract objects but also challenges the idea that there is any such thing as vagueness in language at all, however it is understood.

There are also sorites arguments which attack the concrete objects of common sense, on the assumption that these objects have vague boundaries. These arguments, like the paradox of the bald man, can be stated without the use of a universal generalization.

There are other problems for the view that individual concrete objects are vague. One of these is directed against vague objects, conceived of as objects having indeterminate identities (Evans 1978). Suppose that 'a' and 'b' are (precise) singular terms for vague objects and that '$a=b$' is indefinite in truth-value. Then, if we let '∇' symbolize 'indefinitely', the following is true:

(5) $\nabla(a=b)$

(5) ascribes to b the property of being indefinitely identical with a. Now surely we have

(6) $\sim\nabla(a=a)$

and hence that a lacks the property of being indefinitely identical with a. By the principle that if object o and object o' differ in a property, then they are not identical (the contrapositive of Leibniz's Law; see IDENTITY), it follows that a is not identical with b. Since, on the standard understanding of 'indefinitely', it cannot be the case both that it is indefinite whether a is identical with b and that a is not identical with b, there cannot be vague identities.

The deepest problems of vagueness, in my view, are the sorites paradoxes. And these arise whether or not there is vagueness in the nonlinguistic world.

3 Theories

It has been suggested that a proper understanding of vagueness requires the admission that truth and set membership come in degrees, rather than being 'all or nothing' (see Zadeh 1965, Goguen 1969). On this approach, real numbers in the interval from 0 to 1 are typically taken to be truth-values, with 1 being fully fledged truth and 0 being fully fledged falsity. The same numbers are assigned to the degrees to which objects belong to sets. So, for example, if Herbert is clearly bald, then the sentence

(7) Herbert is bald

is assigned the value 1, and Herbert is taken to belong to the set of bald men to degree 1. But if Herbert is a borderline case then (7) is assigned some number less than 1, say, 0.6, and the degree of Herbert's membership in the set of bald men is now taken to be 0.6 too. In general, a singular sentence 'Fa' is treated as having the truth-value n, where $0 \leq n \leq 1$, if and only if the referent of 'a' belongs to the set of Fs to degree n (see FUZZY LOGIC).

A consequence of this approach is that vague predicates do not sharply divide the world into those things to which they apply and those things to which they do not. Rather, vague predicates apply to objects to varying degrees. As a man loses hair he becomes more and more bald; so the predicate 'is bald' applies to him more and more and the assertion that he is bald increases gradually in its degree of truth.

One serious objection to this view is that it really replaces vagueness with the most refined and incredible precision. Set membership, as viewed by the degrees-of-truth theorist, comes in precise degrees, as does predicate application and truth. The result is a commitment to precise dividing lines that is not only unbelievable but also thoroughly contrary to how we think of everyday vagueness (as noted in §1).

It is often supposed by philosophers that vagueness resides in language. One popular view here is that vagueness itself is a matter of semantic indecision (for example, Lewis 1986). On this view, all external objects, properties and relations are precise. Each vague linguistic term has a meaning which can be made precise in a whole range of different permissible ways. For example, 'over 70 years of age' is one acceptable way of making precise the meaning of the term 'old'. But other equally good ways are 'over 72' and 'over 74'. The rules that govern the use of the term 'old' are not specific enough for us to be able to choose non-arbitrarily some one precise term as capturing its meaning. When the term 'old' was first introduced, no decision was made to link it exclusively with one particular precise property. Instead it was applied widely in a range of cases, thereby acquiring a vague meaning. And what is true here for 'old' is true *mutatis mutandis* for all other vague terms.

Now if it is indeed true that there are no vague properties expressed by vague predicates, but instead ranges of precise properties, then, under some ways of making precise a vague predicate, it will definitely apply to a given object (in virtue of the object having the appropriate precise property) and, under other ways, it will not. Suppose that Alfred is 67. If 'old' is sharpened to mean 'over 70' then Alfred is not old: he lacks the precise property of being over 70. But if 'old' is sharpened to mean 'over 65', then Alfred is old – this time he has the right precise property. Is it really true that Alfred is old, then? If these two ways of sharpening the term 'old' are equally acceptable – if they both express precise properties falling in the range associated with 'old' – then the natural answer is that it is neither true nor false that Alfred is old. He is a borderline case. So, there really is no definite age at which Alfred becomes old: the boundary between being old and not being old is not sharp. By contrast, if Alfred is 97 years of age, then, under any acceptable way of making 'old' precise, he will count as old. So here it is unquestionably true that Alfred is old. And if he is 21, then, no matter which acceptable precisification we choose for 'old', he will not count as old. The claim that Alfred is old is false.

The thesis that vagueness is semantic indecision thus leads straightforwardly to the following claims. Vague sentences have three possible truth-values: true, false and 'indefinite' (neither true nor false). A vague sentence is to be counted as true if it comes out true under all acceptable ways of making precise its component vague terms; as false if it comes out false in every such case; and as neither true nor false if it comes out true under some ways and false under others. These claims entail that the law of excluded middle (LEM) remains true for vague sentences. So, the semantic indecision theory of vagueness provides us with a classical conception of reality (all that there is in the world is precise), a safe haven for vagueness in the linguistic realm and a conservative attitude towards the retention of LEM.

There are grave difficulties, however. In particular, it is far from clear that the semantic indecision approach fares any better than the degrees-of-truth view with respect to sorites paradoxes and robust or resilient vagueness. Another objection concerns LEM. The objection is that

(8) Either Herbert is bald or Herbert is not bald,

to take one instance of LEM, should not be counted as true if Herbert is a borderline bald man. For if (8) is true then either Herbert is bald or he is not bald. If this is the case then the question, 'Well, which is he then?', must surely have an answer; that is, if (8) is true then precisely one of the disjuncts in (8) must be true. So 'Herbert is bald' must be either true or false. This runs contrary to the assumption that Herbert is a borderline bald man. So, (8) is not true.

One common feature of both the standard degrees-of-truth approach and the semantic indecision theory is that they employ precise metalanguages in stating the truth-conditions for vague object language sentences (a metalanguage is used to talk about the object language). It is this feature which, in my view, dooms them to failure. A central aspect of the resilient vagueness of ordinary terms is that, in sorites sequences, there simply is no determinate fact of the matter about the transition from true to some other value. Any attempt to state truth-conditions for vague discourse in precise language will inevitably fall foul of this fact.

Another possible approach, then, is to start out using a vague metalanguage, which mirrors in its vagueness the object language. One proposal along these lines is based on the three truth-values, true, false and indefinite. Just as sentences in the object language can be indefinite, so too can sentences in the metalanguage (and indeed in all the higher metalanguages). If this approach is to avoid the sorites paradoxes, it is essential that it not be true that every object language sentence is true or false or indefinite. For this would create sharp dividing lines. But neither can it be false that every such sentence is true or false or indefinite. For this would require further truth-values. Instead, it has been argued that the above generalization about object language sentences must be indefinite. This permits us to hold that the claim that there is a last true sentence, followed by a first indefinite one, in a sorites sequence is indefinite. And if this is the case then sorites arguments cannot be sound (see Tye 1990).

There are many philosophers who would reject all three of the alternative proposals sketched so far. The fourth and final approach I shall mention is the epistemic view (Sorensen 1988, Williamson 1994). According to this position, vagueness is a kind of ignorance. The nonlinguistic world is precise. Standard logic holds even for vague discourse. Every molecule is either inside or outside Everest, for example. We just do not know where the boundaries lie. Likewise, there is always a single hair, the addition of which would turn a bald man into a man who is not bald, even though we cannot say which hair this is. Our sensory and conceptual mechanisms are simply not equipped to make the necessary fine-grained discriminations. Sorites arguments, then, rest upon a false premise.

This view is pleasingly straightforward. Unfortunately, it seems counterintuitive. It denies outright the existence of robust or resilient vagueness. Moreover, it seems to misconceive borderline cases. Our ordinary concept of a borderline case is the concept of a case that is neither one thing nor the other.

'Definitely' here does not seem to mean 'known' or 'knowably'.

So, whichever way we turn, we quickly become enmeshed in difficulties. Of all the philosophical mysteries, vagueness is one of the most perplexing.

See also: LOGICAL AND MATHEMATICAL TERMS, GLOSSARY OF; MANY-VALUED LOGICS, PHILOSOPHICAL ISSUES IN

References and further reading

* Broome, J. (1984) 'Indefiniteness in Identity', *Analysis* 44: 6–12. (Discussion of whether objects can have vague identities.)
Dummett, M. (1975) 'Wang's Paradox', *Synthèse* 25: 301–24. (Vague observational predicates as logically incoherent.)
* Evans, G. (1978) 'Can There Be Vague Objects?', *Analysis* 38: 208. (An argument against the existence of vague objects.)
Fine, K. (1975) 'Vagueness, Truth, and Logic', *Synthèse* 25: 265–300. (Classic early presentation of vagueness as semantic indecision.)
* Goguen, J. (1969) 'The Logic of Inexact Concepts', *Synthèse* 19: 325–73. (An early statement of the degrees-of-truth theory.)
Horgan, T. (ed.) (1994) Spindel Conference on Vagueness, *Southern Journal of Philosophy* 33, supplement. (Good collection of new papers on vagueness.)
* Lewis, D.K. (1986) *The Plurality of Worlds*, Oxford: Blackwell. (Simple statement of the semantic indecision theory.)
* Sorensen, R. (1988) *Blindspots*, Oxford: Clarendon Press. (Vagueness as ignorance.)
* Tye, M. (1990) 'Vague Objects', *Mind* 99: 535–57. (Vagueness in both the object language and the metalanguage; defence of vagueness in the world.)
* Williamson, T. (1994) *Vagueness*, London: Routledge. (Clear defence of the view that vagueness is ignorance.)
* Zadeh, L. (1965) 'Fuzzy Sets', *Information and Control* 8: 338–53. (Early presentation of the degrees-of-truth approach.)

MICHAEL TYE

VAIHINGER, HANS (1852–1933)

Hans Vaihinger was a German philosopher and historian of philosophy. Much of his work was a response to Kant's philosophy, and he contributed to the revival of interest in Kant at the end of the nineteenth century both in his published commentaries and in founding a journal and society for the discussion of Kant's thought. He developed his own philosophy, the philosophy of 'as-if', which was derived from the Kantian notion of 'heuristic fictions'.

Vaihinger was born near Tübingen in Germany. He studied theology and philosophy, graduating from the Tübingen seminary. He taught at Strasbourg and later Halle until 1906, when he retired because of failing eyesight.

In 1881 and 1892 he published two volumes of his massive *Kommentar zu Kants Kritik der reinen Vernunft* (Commentary on Kant's Critique of Pure Reason), a detailed commentary, not only on the first seventy pages of Kant's *Critique of Pure Reason*, but also on previous commentaries. This still valuable work was never completed. However, the numerous articles that he wrote set out his views on the major sections of the *Critique* not covered in the *Kommentar*.

Vaihinger never counted himself a member of any particular school of Neo-Kantianism, but contributed to the renewal of interest in Kant. In 1897 he founded the journal *Kant-Studien* (Kant Studies). In the first issue he claimed that its purpose was to avoid partisan approaches to Kant scholarship that were prevalent in the Neo-Kantian 'school' journals and instead to provide an arena for all Kantian scholars. However, Vaihinger could be as polemical as other Neo-Kantians. In 1904 he formed the *Kant-Gesellschaft*, a society whose membership funded *Kant-Studien*.

With his retirement from teaching, Vaihinger resumed work on the philosophy of 'as-if', begun in 1876. He drew from Lange and Schopenhauer as well as Plato, Darwin and Nietzsche, but above all from Kant. It was primarily the Kantian notion of 'heuristic fictions' that led him to his philosophy of 'as-if'. In the *Critique of Pure Reason* Kant argues that although we cannot prove that the soul is a simple substance, it serves as a regulative idea: we act *as if* the soul is indivisible (see KANT, I. §8). For Vaihinger this counts as a 'fiction' and is to be distinguished from a 'hypothesis'. While we cannot always differentiate between a fiction and a hypothesis, the latter must be capable of being confirmed. Once found to be true a hypothesis loses that status. A fiction, however, can never be confirmed; its validation comes in being justified. Thus the Kantian 'fiction' that we must act as if we are free moral agents is justified by the moral actions that result from that belief. Vaihinger argued that fictions are useful in a wide range of areas. For example, the notions of the atom and the 'thing-in-itself' are important for science and metaphysics. Fictions also have consequences for religion and ethics. Reflecting his early religious training he suggested that the fiction of the 'virgin birth' is particularly 'beautiful'. And he argued that a fiction of major significance in terms of human action is to act *as if* we were morally free agents.

In 1911, Vaihinger and Raymond Schmidt founded *Annalen der Philosophie* (Annals of Philosophy) to further the philosophy of 'as-if'.

List of works

Vaihinger, H. (1876) *Hartmann, Düring, und Lange*, Iserlohn: J. Baedeker. (An early work, documenting Vaihinger's influences.)

—— (1881–92) *Kommentar zu Kants Kritik der reinen Vernunft* (Commentary on Kant's Critique of Pure Reason), Stuttgart: Union deutsche Verlagsgesellschaft; 2nd edn, 1922. (An indispensable but difficult and lengthy account of the *Critique of Pure Reason* which focuses on the first 75 pages.)

—— (1902a) *Nietzsche als Philosoph* (Nietzsche as Philosopher), Berlin: Reuther & Reichard. (An early, objective and straightforward account of Nietzsche's thought.)

—— (1902b) *Die Transcendentale Deduktion der Kategorien* (The Transcendental Deduction of the Categories), Halle: Niemeyer. (An early but disputed account of the transcendental deduction in which Vaihinger claims that it is a 'patchwork' of ideas from different stages in Kant's development.)

—— (1911) *Die Philosophie des als-ob*, Berlin: Reuther & Reichard; 10th edn, 1927; trans. C.K. Ogden, *The Philosophy of As-If*, London: Harcourt, Brace, 1924. (A lengthy and rather difficult work in which Vaihinger sets out his notion of fiction, based on his reading of Kant and Nietzsche.)

References and further reading

Del Negro, W. (1934) 'Hans Vaihingers philosophisches Werk mit Besonderer Berücksichtigung seiner Kantforschung' (Hans Vaihinger's Philosophical Work, With Special Consideration of His Kant Investigations), *Kant-Studien* 39: 316–27. (A slightly uncritical overview of Vaihinger's scholarly life.)

Handy, R. (1967) 'Hans Vaihinger', in *Encyclopedia of Philosophy*, ed. P. Edwards, New York: Macmillan, vol. 8, 221–4. (A useful overview of Vaihinger's work, with a special emphasis on his notion of 'fictions'.)

Seidel, A. (ed.) (1932) *Die Philosophie des Als Ob und das Leben* (The Philosophy of As-If and Life),

Berlin: Reuther & Reichard; repr. Aalen, Scientia, 1986. (A large collection of laudatory articles on Vaihinger's philosophy of 'as-if'.)

CHRISTOPHER, ADAIR-TOTEFF

VAISESIKA *see* NYĀYA-VAIŚEṢIKA

VALLA, LORENZO (1407–57)

Unlike most Renaissance humanists, Valla took a special interest in philosophy. However, his most influential writing was a work of grammar, Elegantiae Linguae Latinae *(The Fine Points of the Latin Language); he had no comprehensive philosophy, nor did he write mainly on philosophy. Valla considered himself to be a revolutionary overturning received opinions, bragging that through his works he was 'overturning all the wisdom of the ancients'. His preference for Quintilian over Cicero and criticism of classical authors shocked older humanists, and religious authorities were upset by his views on the Trinity and on papal authority, but Valla never sought the overthrow of classical studies – or the papacy for that matter. He sought rather to destroy the Aristotelianism then reigning in the universities. In* De Vero Falsoque Bono *(On the True and False Good) (1431), he argued for the superiority of Epicureanism over Stoic and Aristotelian ethics. In* De Libero Arbitrio *(On Free Will) (1439), he corrected Boethius' treatment of free will and predestination. In the* Dialectica *(1438–9) he set out to reform logic and philosophy because he believed Aristotle had corrupted them. Asserting that Aristotle had falsified thought because he had falsified language, Valla was determined to show how logic rightly conformed to the linguistic usage of the classical literary authors; essentially Valla had aggressively revived the ancient competition between the rhetorical and philosophical traditions. The first great humanist, Francesco Petrarca (better known in English as Petrarch), had attempted something similar in the fourteenth century, but Valla's knowledge of philosophy was greater than Petrarch's and he had access to more sources. Furthermore, Valla knew Greek and could read texts which the medieval Aristotelians knew only in Latin translation.*

1   Life and works
2   Ethics
3   Free will and determinism
4   Logic

1   Life and works

Valla was born in Rome. His family came from Piacenza, but had firmly entrenched itself in the papal bureaucracy. Valla's father, grandfather, uncles and brother-in-law all worked in the papal curia as legal and secretarial officials. His father Luca died when Valla was still a boy. His mother Caterina (Scribani) saw eight of her eleven children die young, and buried her two adult sons as well: Paolo (a friar) died in 1439, and Lorenzo on 1 August 1457. Valla never attended university, but he was fortunate enough to learn Greek. He never married but around 1450, in the space of two years, Valla had three children by a servant girl in Rome. He claimed to have done so to prove to his relatives that he was celibate by choice and not incapacity. He gave the children to his sister whose marriage had proven infertile.

In 1430, after failing to gain the position as papal secretary vacated by the death of his uncle, Valla left Rome for northern Italy. He spent time in Venice and Piacenza before becoming professor of rhetoric at the University of Pavia in early 1431. He fled Pavia, however, in the spring of 1433 because of the indignation of the law faculty at his letter attacking the ignorance of the medieval jurist Bartolo of Sassoferrato. He spent the next few years travelling about northern Italy supporting himself as a private teacher. Finally, in 1435, he joined the court of King Alfonso of Aragon, who was engaged in the conquest of the kingdom of Naples. Valla had the title of secretary, but functioned more like a scholar-in-residence. The king was generous, granting Valla temporal benefices and protection during his controversies. Valla's years in southern Italy were the most fruitful of his scholarly career. Once established in Naples (conquered by Alfonso in 1442), Valla was even able to take up teaching rhetoric again. But Valla yearned for Rome. In late 1447, after receiving favourable signs from the papal court, he returned to his native city. Pope Nicholas V (1447–55) made him a papal scribe (in Valla's case this was a sinecure) and appointed him professor of rhetoric at the University of Rome. He also generously rewarded Valla for his scholarly labours, giving him, for instance, 500 gold ducats for translating Thucydides. The next pope, Calixtus III (1455–8), made Valla a papal secretary (another sinecure) and showered him with ecclesiastical benefices, including (although Valla was not a priest) the position of canon in St John Lateran, the cathedral of Rome.

Valla provoked his first controversy in 1428 with a now lost comparison of Quintilian and Cicero, scandalizing fellow humanists by his preference for Quintilian. Valla found in Quintilian's *Training in*

Oratory a lifelong guide not only to rhetoric, but also to philosophy, logic and language. Later in life, Valla claimed that he had virtually memorized *Training in Oratory*. Indeed, an awareness of Quintilian's influence is essential for a correct understanding of Valla's work.

Valla completed his first major work, the dialogue *De Voluptate* (On Pleasure), in the early 1430s; in later redactions he changed its title to *De Vero Falsoque Bono* (On the True and False Good), but did not alter its Epicurean slant. The first versions of his other major works were finished while Valla was in the employ of King Alfonso.

To his most ambitious work, Valla gave the shorthand title *Dialectica*. Its full title changed with every redaction: first it was the *Re-tilling...* (*Repastinatio...*), then the *Refabrication...* (*Reconcinnatio...*) and finally the *Restructuring* (*Retractatio*) *of All Dialectic with the Foundations of the Whole of Philosophy*. For all of Valla's grand hopes, the *Dialectica* failed to galvanize Renaissance humanism. It experienced a moderate manuscript circulation and was printed separately only four times before entering Valla's *Opera Omnia* of 1540.

Elegantiae Linguae Latinae (The Fine Points of the Latin Language), on the other hand, was a huge success. With nearly seventy known manuscripts and more than 150 printed editions before 1600, the *Elegantiae* made Valla a major authority on the language. Treating a wide range of grammatical and lexicographical points, Valla took as his standard not the rules of the classical grammarians, but the actual usage of those whom he viewed as the very best practitioners of Latin: the *oratores* (specifically Cicero and Quintilian). With extraordinary erudition, Valla presumed not merely to teach his contemporaries correct classical Latin usage, but also to criticize the Latin of classical writers and grammarians. He conspicuously condemned the late ancient author Boethius as 'a Roman who did not know how to speak Roman'.

In 1440 Valla published his famous *Oratio* (Oration) on the Donation of Constantine, the document with which Emperor Constantine purportedly deeded the western part of the empire to the papacy. Numerous medieval jurists and political thinkers had denied its validity, and some had even denied its authenticity, but no one before Valla had effectively demonstrated (on the basis of linguistic, numismatic and historical evidence) that this was an early medieval forgery.

Valla's *Oratio* long remained subject to controversy. Of greater long-term significance, however, was another work Valla completed in these years: the *Collatio Novi Testamenti* (Collation of the New Testament) (called in its last redaction *Annotationes in Novum Testamentum*), where he compared the Greek text of the New Testament with the Vulgate Latin translation. Valla had no sense of the difficulties caused by the Greek tradition and focused narrowly on the peccadillos of the Latin translation instead. None the less, he showed how humanists could use their philological and historical expertise to compete as scriptural theologians with the dogmatic theologians of the medieval tradition. Valla's work had little impact in Italy, but once 'discovered' by ERASMUS, the *Annotationes* became an inspiration for humanist scripture scholarship in the Reformation era.

While in southern Italy, Valla also produced works typical of Renaissance humanism. He wrote a history of the deeds of King Alfonso's father, dashed off several philological opuscula, prepared a lost commentary on the pseudo-Ciceronian *Rhetorica ad Herennium*, translated Greek classics (Aesop, Homer, Xenophon, St Basil the Great and Demosthenes), wrote invectives against fellow humanists and composed dialogues. In the first, *De Libero Arbitrio* (On Free Will), Valla asked how free will related to divine foreknowledge, condemning Boethius for mishandling the issue out of an excessive affection for philosophy. In the second, *De professione religiosorum* (On the Professing of Vows by those in Religious Orders), he challenged the notion that the members of the religious orders are more religious or meritorious than lay people. *De professione religiosorum* had a minimal circulation, but its boldness had a price. In 1444 Valla was called before the Inquisition. Only royal protection saved him. Subsequently, he wrote a *Defensio quaestionum in philosophia* (Defence of Questions in Philosophy) rebutting the charges of heresy and in 1444 an *Apologia* to Pope Eugenius IV.

The *Apologia* was part of Valla's campaign to return to Rome, which succeeded in late 1447. In the last decade of his life Valla continued to revise his major works, but embarked on no new large project apart from the Latin translations of Herodotus and Thucydides undertaken at the behest of Pope Nicholas V. He also entered into a lengthy literary war with Poggio Bracciolini, a leading humanist in the papal curia. Finally, in these last years, he delivered an encomium on the mystery of the Eucharist and another on Thomas Aquinas. Valla praised Aquinas as the best of the medieval theologians, although he considered Aquinas inferior to the church fathers because they did not mix theology with 'petty dialectical syllogising and metaphysical musing' nor 'make philosophy the basis of their arguments' (*Opera Omnia*, vol. 2: 350).

2 Ethics

The notion that Valla was a neo-pagan libertine is not borne out by his life and writings. The basis of that myth is the Epicureanism of *De Vero Falsoque Bono*; ironically the dialogue was principally an exercise in Christian apologetics. Valla was neither the first nor the last Renaissance intellectual to appreciate Epicureanism. In a 'moral letter' of about 1429, the minor humanist Cosma Raimondi argued that Epicureanism answered the needs of human beings as composites of body and soul much better than Stoicism. In his youth the fifteenth-century Platonist Marsilio FICINO was also much taken with Epicureanism, and in the sixteenth century Thomas More had his Utopians base their lives on the principle that pleasure was the highest good. But no one in the Renaissance argued so extensively and forcefully for Epicurean ethics as Valla (see EPICUREANISM §§10, 11; STOICISM §16).

In denying that happiness resided in virtue, Valla took the same position towards Stoic ethics as Thomas AQUINAS (§13), and observed at the start of the *De Vero Bono* that to argue otherwise would render the Incarnation otiose. By refuting the Stoics, Valla was affirming the insufficiency of human beings to achieve happiness outside the Christian dispensation, but Valla carried the argument much further than was needed to refute Stoicism. This defence of Christianity was not an end in itself. It was rather the means by which Valla was able to attack a highly respected philosophy and specifically a highly respected Christian philosopher, Boethius, the sixth-century Roman author whom Valla seems to have considered the root of medieval philosophical evil. At the end of the *De vero bono* it becomes clear that Valla's aim was to destroy Boethius' assertion in Book 4 of *The Consolation of Philosophy* that virtue was the true path to happiness.

Similarly, Valla's appropriation of Epicureanism can be seen as another means by which to discredit philosophy. Although Valla has been criticized for presenting an inaccurate picture of Epicureanism and for relying only on Latin sources, his intention was not to explain Epicureanism, but simply to use it in his campaign against philosophers. Philosophy, as he says early in the *De vero bono*, is merely a foot-soldier in the army of Queen Oratory. This is not to say that Valla failed to value Epicureanism or Christianity, but rather that neither the exposition of Epicureanism nor the defence of Christianity were his ultimate purpose.

Valla divided the *De vero bono* into three books. In the first, he had the Stoic speaker complain that all nature conspires against virtue. Animate beings spontaneously, that is to say naturally, seek pleasure and flee the pain imposed by virtue, thus refuting by their actions the famous Stoic formula that virtue is living according to nature. Taking his cue from pseudo-Quintilian (*Major Declamations* 2.1), Valla further argued that virtue actually makes us miserable, while pleasure makes us happy. Opponents of Epicureanism had traditionally charged Epicureans with having no reason for rejecting heinous behaviour if it was pleasurable (see Cicero *On the Ends of Good and Evil* 2.27). Valla agreed: at the end of Book 1, Valla had his Epicurean speaker approve of adultery, advocate free love (what Valla called 'Platonic love'), condemn virginity and present for imitation the shameless behaviour of the Olympian gods.

Book 2 presented the other side of the argument. In it, Valla proved that the moral goodness propounded by the philosophers (*honestas philosophorum*) was fraudulent. Even in their most apparently selfless actions people always act out of self-interest. Virtue consists precisely in actions which bring about this selfish advantage (*utilitas*), and actions that are not self-serving are foolish. The moral goodness of the Stoics is nothing more than empty verbiage. At the end of Book 2, the Epicurean speaker denies the immortality of the soul and reaffirms worldly pleasure as the only valid good.

Valla began Book 3 with an attack on the Aristotelian notion of virtue as the mean between two vicious extremes, condemning the artificiality of this scheme. He denied, for example, that liberality was really the mean between avarice and miserliness because the opposite of liberality is in fact a virtue, thriftiness. Earlier, in Book 2, he had the Epicurean speaker refute Aristotle's assertion that the contemplative life was the highest and happiest form of existence. In the *Dialectica* (*Repastinatio Dialecticae* 75–7), Valla further attacked Aristotelian ethics by denying that prudence was a virtue, explaining that virtue resided exclusively in the will while prudence resided in the mind (see ARISTOTLE §22–5).

Thus Valla discredited not only Stoicism and pagan Epicureanism, but also Aristotelianism. Having proved the unacceptability of all forms of philosophic ethics, he could 'condemn and damn philosophy' (*De vero bono* 271 §7) and explain that the highest good is found not in philosophy but in religion, which teaches that resistance to vice in this life means torment and death for the sake of eternal happiness in heaven, where we will enjoy the vision of God. In short, having exposed the inanity of the philosophers, Valla changed the terms of the dialogue and moved from philosophy to theology. In the last part of the dialogue he launched into an exposition of Christian teachings on heaven and hell. In the process, he transformed Christian ethics into a form of Epicureanism, equating the delight of heaven with pleasure, the vision of God with the love of God, and love itself with pleasure (*amatio ipsa delectatio est*). That left the question of why we love God. Christianity traditionally answered that we loved God *propter se*, because of what he is. But if that were so, then the end of Christian ethics would not be pleasure, but God. Consequently, in both the *De vero bono* and the *Dialectica*, Valla insisted that we love God not as an end, but as an efficient cause, as the producer of the pleasure of heaven. Valla's Christian Epicureanism thereby ends up instrumentalizing God.

3 Free will and determinism

In *De Libero Arbitrio*, Valla once again condemned philosophy for corrupting Christian theology and attacked Boethius for leading the way. In the *Consolation of Philosophy*, Boethius had reconciled human free will and divine foreknowledge by arguing that God knows in an instantaneous 'now' what we experience as past, present and future (see BOETHIUS §5). Valla found this explanation inadequate: his own solution was to compare God's foreknowledge to an oracle who had the power to see the future without causing it. At best, this explanation is the same as Boethius'; at worst, it is tautological.

Valla's target, however, was not really Boethius' explanation of divine foreknowledge, but his confidence in having proven human free will. While denying that God has deprived us of liberty and therefore responsibility, Valla did not know how anyone could reconcile free will with the omnipotent will of God. Citing biblical passages which suggest predestination, Valla condemned philosophers who presumed to understand 'the power and will of God'. Instead, he argued that 'we stand by faith, not the probability of reasons' (*De Libero Arbitrio* 180). Thus, when he refuted astrology in the *Dialectica*, he based his argument not on human liberty, but on divine omnipotence: God's will and not the heavens controlled human destiny. He was therefore consistent in the *Dialectica* in insisting that nothing in nature happened by chance. On the subject of divine power, he rebuked Aristotle for denying that God can make not to have happened what has already happened. The past is not immutable because that would be a limitation on divine power. Without feeling any need to develop the implications of his positions, Valla denied contingency, held that God predestined everything and insisted that there was no conceivable limit to God's power (see FREE WILL).

4 Logic

The *Dialectica* was Valla's philosophical *summa*. Into it he poured his thought on logic, philosophy, and theology. It has two main themes. One is that logic is 'a matter indeed short and easy', no more than a subsection of the far more comprehensive discipline of rhetoric. The second and predominant one was that Aristotle and his followers had erred because they had departed from common linguistic usage (*consuetudo loquendi*). By common linguistic usage Valla did not mean what has been called ordinary language: he scorned the 'stupid' popular manner of speaking when it suited him to do so (*Repastinatio Dialecticae* 55), and he had little use for the vernacular. Rather Valla meant classical literary Latin. He never stopped to give a theoretical explanation of why linguistic usage is the touchstone of truth.

Valla conceived of logic in terms of the corpus of logical texts used in the twelfth century when medieval Aristotelianism first appeared (Porphyry's *Isagōgē* and Aristotle's *Categories, De Interpretatione, Prior Analytics, Posterior Analytics, Topics* and *On Sophistical Refutations*), not in terms of contemporary logic which had moved significantly beyond Aristotle in many areas. Although Valla divided the *Dialectica* into three books, he gave half of it over to the discussion of the categories in Book 1. He did not challenge the value of the categories; his purpose was simply to reduce their number. He kept substance, the first of Aristotle's ten categories, and reduced the remaining nine (the accidental categories) to just two, quality and action, expending a great deal of effort to show how the remaining seven reflected one of these other two.

Valla also reduced six transcendental terms (being, thing, something, one, true and good) to one term, 'thing' (*res*). The transcendentals had emerged among medieval Aristotelians as a set of terms which transcended the limitations of the categories and were convertible with each other. Their number was not universally agreed upon (John DUNS SCOTUS, for instance, recognized more than the six transcendentals listed by Thomas AQUINAS and treated by Valla) and they played a minimal role in logic, but they were important in metaphysics. Valla probably seized upon the transcendentals because the first of them, being (*ens*), provided him with a starting point for his destruction of medieval Aristotelianism. He denied that *ens* could be a transcendental since in classical Latin it was exclusively a participle, not a noun, and therefore resolvable into 'that thing (*res*) which is'. Hence *res*, and not the illegitimate noun *ens*, is the universal term encompassing all terms and all categories.

Valla also denied the validity of a whole group of abstract terms of medieval philosophy formed by the addition of the suffix *itas* to a noun or pronoun, such as *quiditas* (whatness) and *haecceitas* (thisness). These terms, Valla explained, were illegitimate because in Latin only adjectives can properly accept *itas*, an example being *bonitas* (goodness) which is formed from *bonus* (good). Since Valla also denied that Latin permits neuter singular adjectives to constitute entities in themselves (that is, *bonum* alone means not 'the good' but 'good thing'), he has sometimes been portrayed as a radical nominalist. In fact, he quite happily accepted the legitimacy of abstractions and universals if they were properly formed according to the rules of Latin. He simply ignored the metaphysical implications of his positions.

Similarly, he ignored the epistemological implications of his view of truth. He explicitly accepted the traditional correspondence theory of truth, that truth was the correspondence between what one asserts about a thing and what the thing itself is. Yet, in also making God the fount (*fons*) of truth, attributing truth to divine illumination, and asserting without further elaboration that falsity consists in the obstruction of this fount (*Repastinatio Dialecticae* 20), Valla left the way open for a different approach to truth based on the absolute power of God. Consistent with his view that God can make not happen what has happened, he seems also to have held that human capacity to attain truth is circumscribed by the fact that God can change truth at any time and that the only people who know truth are those whom God chooses to illumine.

The same indifference to developing the implications of his theories appears in Valla's discussion of language. Treating the category of quality, Valla characterized signification as a quality of human utterance (*Repastinatio Dialecticae* 122–4). He further explained that significant speech is a human institution: people apply 'signs' to objects. The first to have done so was Adam, who later taught these significations to posterity. Up to this point Valla hardly differed from the medieval Aristotelians, but then he suddenly dropped this line of argument and took up the relationship between 'word' and 'thing' within his scheme of categories. Though he viewed language as the touchstone of truth, Valla never bothered to develop a linguistic theory (see LANGUAGE, RENAISSANCE PHILOSOPHY OF §§2, 3).

At several points in Book 1, Valla discussed physics. Having no overarching physical theory of his own (apart from reliance on the criteria of common sense and linguistic usage), he only made small alterations to Aristotelian physical theory. He had no inkling of the use of mathematics in physics and no patience with geometric descriptions of nature, mocking, for instance, the notion that the earth could be treated as a mere point in space. On occasion he appealed to his own experience to correct Aristotle; in one example he cites his observation of modern bombards. He also challenged fundamental Aristotelian tenets, such as the principle that whatever is moved is moved by another. But these criticisms do not come together as a coherent whole and at times amount to very little. For instance, in rejecting the principle that whatever is moved is moved by another Valla merely referred the reader to Macrobius.

After the categories, Valla treated propositions (Book 2) and various forms of argumentation, especially the syllogism (Book 3). Though he rejected much that Aristotle said about modal propositions and modal syllogisms and though he banned outright Aristotle's third figure of the syllogism (see ARISTOTLE §5), Aristotelian logic survived Valla's critique essentially intact. On the subject of topics, examples and enthymemes, Valla incorporated Quintilian's discussions of them from the *Training in Oratory* (*Institutio Oratoria*). In sophistics, Valla was much concerned, using literary examples, to defeat the argument from *sorites* (that is, the argument from accumulation: with the subtraction of which grain of sand does a pile cease to be a pile?) and dilemma (see VAGUENESS §2). To defeat the latter he constructed a fictive oration in which Protagoras answers a dilemma put to him. This section alone disproves the notion that Valla was a sceptic.

The centrepiece of these pages revolves about a point of language. In Greek the marker for an indefinite proposition is *tis*, which can mean the indefinite 'some', but also the particular 'a certain'. Since Boethius, the standard translation in logic of *tis* had been *quidam*, which, Valla pointed out, means 'a certain' and not 'some'. Valla could therefore severely criticize the medieval Latin analysis of propositions and syllogisms wherever *quidam* was used as an indefinite. Furthermore, he showed that whereas Greek was limited to *tis*, Latin had many words with nuanced differences to express 'some' and 'a certain', thus proving not only the superiority of Latin (a cause close to Valla's heart), but also that correct logic rested on the correct use of language.

The *Dialectica* failed to overthrow Aristotelian logic, let alone Aristotelian philosophy, and it never really confronted contemporary logic. The vast majority of humanist logicians declined to follow Valla's prescriptions. The *Dialectica* did, however, forcibly argue for the use of a natural language in logic and in this respect Valla was clearly in the vanguard of a broad drive by humanists to simplify logic and make it more amenable to rhetoric and literary practice.

See also: Aristotelianism, Renaissance; Humanism, Renaissance; Language, Renaissance philosophy of; Logic, Renaissance

List of works

Valla, L. (1407–57) *Opera Omnia* (Complete Works), ed. E. Garin, Turin: Bottega d'Erasmo, 1962, 2 vols. (Volume 1 is a photographic reprint of the 1540 *Opera Omnia*, printed by Henricus Petri in Basle; volume 2 collects in photographic reprint opuscula published separately over four centuries.)

—— (1431) *De Vero Falsoque Bono* (On the True and False Good), ed. M. Lorch, Bari: Adriatica, 1970; English text and Latin translation in M. Lorch and A.K. Hieatt (trans and eds) *On Pleasure. De Voluptate*, New York: Abaris, 1977. (Valla's Epicurean dialogue was originally called *De Voluptate*; later redactions were retitled *De Vero Falsoque Bono*.)

—— (1438–9) *Repastinatio Dialecticae et Philosophiae* (Re-tilling of Dialectic and Philosophy), ed. G. Zippel, Padua: Antenore, 1982. (Edition of all three redactions of Valla's *Dialectica*.)

—— (1439) *De Libero Arbitrio* (On Free Will), trans. C. Trinkaus, in E. Cassirer *et al.*, *The Renaissance Philosophy of Man*, Chicago, IL, and London: University of Chicago Press, 1948, 147–82.

—— (1440) *Oratio de falso credita et ementita Constantini Donatione* (Oration on the Falsely Believed and Fabricated Donation of Constantine), ed. W. Setz, Munich: Monumenta Germaniae Historica, 1986. (Valla's exposure of the Donation of Constantine as a medieval forgery.)

—— (1440–1) *De professione religiosorum* (On the Professing of Vows by those in Religious Orders), ed. M. Cortesi, Padua: Antenore, 1986.

—— (1443) *Collatio Novi Testamenti* (Collation of the New Testament), ed. A. Perosa, Florence: Sansoni, 1970. (Comparison of the Greek text of the New Testament with the Vulgate Latin translation. Called *Annotationes in Novum Testamentum* in its last redaction.)

—— (1444a) *Elegantiae Linguae Latinae* (The Fine Points of the Latin Language), in E. Garin (ed.) *Opera Omnia*, Turin: Bottega d'Erasmo, 1962, vol. 1, 1–235. (The date of the first redaction is 1444.)

—— (1444b) *Defensio quaestionum in philosophia* (Defence of Questions in Philosophy), trans. G. Zippel, 'L'autodifesa di Lorenzo Valla per il processo dell'Inquisizione napoletana (1444)', *Italia medioevale e umanistica* 13 (1970): 59–94.

References and further reading

Besomi, O. and Regoliosi, M. (eds) (1986) *Lorenzo Valla e l'Umanesimo italiano* (Lorenzo Valla and Italian Humanism), Padua: Antenore. (Acts of a conference of leading Valla scholars.)

Camporeale, S. (1972) *Lorenzo Valla: Umanesimo e teologia* (Humanism and Theology), Florence: Istituto Nazionale di Studi sul Rinascimento. (An enthusiastic study especially emphasizing the influence of Quintilian.)

* Cicero, M.T. (mid-45 BC) *De finibus bonorum et malorum* (On the Ends of Good and Evil), trans. H. Rackham, Cambridge, MA: Harvard University Press, Loeb Classical Library, 1914. (One of Cicero's major works on ethics; presents Epicurean, Stoic and Peripatetic arguments. Referred to in §2.)

Fois, M. (1969) *Il pensiero cristiano di Lorenzo Valla nel quadro storico-culturale del suo ambiente*, Rome: Università Gregoriana. (Sound, comprehensive and containing new factual information.)

Mack, P. (1993) *Renaissance Argument: Valla and Agricola in the Traditions of Rhetoric and Dialectic*, Leiden: Brill. (The best and most thorough study to date of Valla's logic.)

Mancini, G. (1891) *Vita di Lorenzo Valla* (The Life of Lorenzo Valla), Florence: Sansoni. (The standard biography.)

Monfasani, J. (1994) *Language and Learning in Renaissance Italy: Selected Articles*, London: Variorum. (Articles on Valla's logic and philosophical thought.)

* Pseudo-Quintilian (late 4th century) *Declamationes Maiores*, trans. L.A. Sussman, *The Major Declamations Ascribed to Quintilian: A Translation*, Studien zur Klassischen Philologie 27, New York: Peter Lang, 1987. (Known to have existed by the late 4th century, the attribution of these rhetorical works to Quintilian is now subject to serious doubt. Referred to in §2.)

Sabbadini, R. (1891) *Cronologia documentata della vita del Panormita e del Valla*, in L. Barozzi and R. Sabbadini, *Studi sul Panormita e sul Valla*, Florence: Istituto di studi superiori practici e di perfezionamento. (Important biographical compendium. Available in the 1962 edition of Valla's *Opera Omnia*, vol. 2.)

Trinkaus, C. (1970) *In Our Image and Likeness*, Chicago, IL, and London: University of Chicago Press, 2 vols. (Extensive discussion of Valla's ethics and logic.)

JOHN MONFASANI

VALLABHĀCĀRYA (1479–1531)

A pivotal figure in the history of Indian philosophy and religion, Vallabhācārya was the last of the classical Vedānta philosophers, as well as the originator of a religious community which called for the worship of Krṣna through acts of devotion, in return for grace and deliverance from rebirth. He proposed a modification to Śankara's philosophy of nondualism, claiming his 'pure nondualism' better explained the relationship between the Supreme Being and the soul. For the laity, he offered a practical religious regimen called the 'path of fulfilment', through which the devotee is initiated into an individual relationship with Krṣna before proceeding to fulfil the relationship through specific personal acts of devotional worship.

Vallabhācārya (Vallabha Bhaṭṭa), born into a Tailangana Bhāradvāja Brahman family belonging to the Taittirīya branch of the Yajurveda, was an important religious leader of the later medieval period of North India. He promulgated a religious association (*sampradāya*) called *Puṣṭimārga* ('path of fulfilment'), based on the popular religious notion of selfless devotion (*bhakti*) to God, which has influenced millions and persists to the present day, especially among the mercantile communities of Gujarat, Rajasthan, Maharashtra, Harayana, western Uttar Pradesh and western Madhya Pradesh. Vallabha's life and work must be understood in the context of his times, a context influenced by popular forms of ecstatic religion and the confrontation of Islamic and Hindu thought, as well as threatened by an unstable political atmosphere.

In a sense, Vallabha was a Brahmanic or Sanskritic reaction to the challenge of being Hindu in the early sixteenth century. His birth was the culmination of a prediction that an incarnation of Viṣṇu would appear in his family after it had performed 100 soma sacrifices. His mother gave birth to a stillborn child in a forest while fleeing their home in Benares which was threatened by Muslim armies from Delhi and Jaunpur. Informed by Krṣna that the child was alive, the parents returned to find Vallabha surrounded and protected by fire. The phenomenon of fire dominates the themes of Vallabha's life. The circumstances of his birth are an obvious connection, but in addition his family were experts in the *Yajurveda*, a book of Vedic rituals and sacrifices; the basis for all Vedic rituals is fire, of which Agni is the god. For his followers, Vallabha speaks as the fire-mouth (*jvālamukha*) of Krṣna, cleansing the world of impurities. Vallabha called himself 'Vaiṣvānara' ('universal divine fire'), incarnated on earth to be a source of knowledge of the Supreme Being. Upon his death, Vallabha walked into the Ganges at Benares and disappeared in a ball of flame.

Sampradāya sources claim that an image of Krṣna, which, in 1410, had pushed its hand and arm through the ground on Mount Govardhan in Braj (the region in which Krṣna was born), suddenly erupted further at the moment of Vallabha's birth, exposing the face and uplifted arm of Krṣna as Lord Govardhananātha, the form of Krṣna which protected the people of Braj from the wrath of the rain-god Indra. It is believed that this image was a *svarūpa*, or self-manifestation, of Krṣna, and that Vallabha was the 'mouth' of the *svarūpa*. Later, Vallabha was instructed by Krṣna in a dream to proceed to Mathura, identify the half-hidden image and see to its worship. Shortly thereafter, while staying at the village of Gokul, the historic birthplace of Krṣna, Vallabha was given the *brahmasambandha* (connection to the Supreme Being) by Krṣna in a dream. The *brahmasambandha mantra*, *śrīkrṣnahṣaranam mama* ('Radiant Krṣna is my refuge'), was an act of initiation, in which Vallabha unconditionally placed himself in the grace of Krṣna while assuming responsibility for the care and worship of the *svarūpa* of Govardhananātha, later known as Śrīnāthajī.

Vallabha believed that he lived in a time when it had become impossible for the individual to achieve spiritual liberation through study or the use of ascetic practices. Five impurities (*doṣas*) inevitably prevented the soul from realizing its connection with the Supreme Being: innate impurities; impurities resulting from one's habitation; those resulting from one's time of life; those resulting from all kinds of association; and those resulting from direct contact. The notion of impurity, and its absence being an a priori condition for spiritual progress, is an ancient principle of Brahmanism; thus, it is not surprising that Vallabha placed this notion at the centre of his liberation philosophy. Initiation into the *sampradāya* through the *brahmasambandha mantra* results in the immediate cleansing of the five *doṣas* from the soul (*jīva*).

Vallabha belongs to the Vedānta school of Hindu philosophers, which includes ŚANKARA, RĀMĀNUJA, MADHVA and Nimbārka. Vallabha argued that Śankara's form of Advaita (monism) erroneously relied upon the notion of *māyā* (illusion) to explain the apparent division or difference between the Supreme Being and the soul. He insisted that no amount of self-study or ascetic austerity could clarify the relative positions of the Supreme Being and the soul. For Vallabha, the soul's ability to discern the relationship correctly is occluded by the presence of impurities accumulated through worldly associations. Only initiation by Vallabha or one of his direct descendants, through taking the *brahmasambandha* and dedicating one's body, mind and wealth to the service (*sevā*) of Kṛṣṇa, can put one in a position to receive the grace of Kṛṣṇa. Such grace, however, is not guaranteed, as it is dispensed by Kṛṣṇa, who may bestow it at any time on whomsoever he pleases. The initiated are given a particular form of Kṛṣṇa, usually drawn from his childhood, to worship as a personal *svarūpa*. Observing this 'path of fulfilment', the initiated create the conditions in which Kṛṣṇa is likely to provide grace.

As a teacher (*ācārya*), Vallabha departed from tradition by marrying and having children. He did so in response to a command from Kṛṣṇa, who insisted that only his direct descendants would be qualified to transmit the *brahmasambandha mantra*. Vallabha's second son, Viṭṭhalanātha, greatly expanded the membership of the *sampradāya*, and elaborated the service (*sevā*) stipulated by Vallabha. He in turn had seven sons, all of whom were given *svarūpas* of Kṛṣṇa. A month before his death, Vallabha took initiation into the fourth stage of life, *sannyāsa*, completing his duty as a Brahman; the lateness of this act is interpreted as a signal to his descendants not to follow the ascetic imperative.

See also: VEDĀNTA

List of works

Vallabhācārya (*c*.1479–1531) *Śrīmadbrahmasūtrānubhāyam*, ed. H. Shastri, Bombay: Trustees of Sheth Narayanadasa and Sheth Jethananda Asanamala Trust, 1942. (Commentary on the basic aphorisms of the Vedānta schools of philosophy, in which Vallabhācārya defends his interpretation of Vedānta.)

—— (*c*.1479–1531) *Śrīsubodhinī* (Giving a Good Explanation), ed. N. Kishora Sharma, Nathadvara: Vidya Vibhaga, 1928. (A commentary on parts of the *Bhāgavata Purāṇa*, a scripture that Vallabhācārya considered of fundamental importance to a correct understanding of Vedānta.)

—— (*c*.1479–1531) *Ṣoḍaśagranthaḥ: Sakārikā Rasapañcādhyāyī Veṇugopikayugala-brahmaragitasubodhinī ca*, ed. M.G. Shastri, Bombay: Mohanlalbhai Govardhanadas, 1933. (A collection of sixteen separate Sanskrit texts, detailing the main points of Vallabhācārya's philosophy.)

—— (*c*.1479–1531) *The Tattvārtha-Dīpa-Nibandha with Prakāsha* (Treatise that is a Lamp onto Reality), ed. H. Onkarji Shastri, Bombay: Trustees of Sheth Narayandas, 1943, 2 vols. (Divided into three parts, this text discusses the *Bhagavad Gītā*, the major Hindu philosophical systems and the *Bhāgavata Purāṇa*.)

—— (*c*.1479–1531) *The Tattvadīpanibandha with Prakāsha*, ed. S. Shastri, Bombay: Shridhara Shivalalji, 1905–8, 2 vols. (An older and less easily obtainable edition of the work cited above.)

References and further reading

Barz, R. (1976) *The Bhakti Sect of Vallabhācārya*, Faridabad: Thomson Press (India). (A trustworthy historical treatment of Vallabhācārya's life and work.)

Marfatia, M.I. (1967) *The Philosophy of Vallabhācārya*, Delhi: Munshiram Manoharlal. (Offers an accessible overview of Vallabhācārya's philosophical system, with detailed summaries of his key works. Abundance of Sanskrit terms may be daunting to beginners.)

Parekh, Bhai Manilal C. (1943) *Sri Vallabhācārya: Life, Teachings, and Movement*, Rajkot: Sri Bhāgavata Dharma Mission. (An accessible biographical sketch.)

Vaidya, Chimanlal M. (1959) *Shri Vallabhācārya and His Teachings*, Kapadwanj: Shri Shuddhadwaita Samsada. (A discussion of Vallabhācārya's work and his teachings.)

RICHARD J. COHEN

VALUE JUDGMENTS IN SOCIAL SCIENCE

Leading theorists in the social sciences have insisted that value judgments should be strictly separated from scientific judgments, which should be value-free. Yet these same thinkers recognize that social scientists are often committed to values in carrying out their work and may be motivated by moral goals of removing or remedying social conditions. From this perspective, scientific conclusions (one sort of fact) and moral commitments (one sort of value) are intertwined in scientific practices, and the question arises whether a social scientist qua scientist makes value judgments or only makes such judgments in a nonscientific capacity. Related questions concern the role played by moral, social, and political values in the pursuit of scientific knowledge and the impact of these values on scientific theories and methods.

1   The values question in classical social science methodology
2   The model of a value-free social science
3   Problems of motivation and selection
4   Problems of bias and partiality

5 Problems of advocacy and strength-of-evidence judgments

6 Professional codes of conduct

1 The values question in classical social science methodology

Émile DURKHEIM (§2) (founder of academic sociology in France and a pioneer of the discipline) believed that sociology, as a science, must not be contaminated by value judgments (Durkheim 1895). 'Social facts' alone have a legitimate role in sociological explanation, and the scientific explanation of a social phenomenon seeks only its efficient causes. None the less, Durkheim maintained that a scientific sociology could help determine the appropriateness of moral values and practices for societies by showing which values best promote human happiness and social solidarity. He thought a science that examines society should regard its work as incomplete unless it established a 'science' of morality (comprised of what is 'generally accepted' in a culture), and he therefore moved freely from social facts to embedded moral values and from the scientific study of morality to moral judgments. In this way, a social science delivered practical results.

Max WEBER (§2) resisted such linking of science and valuation, arguing that there must be an 'unconditional separation' between empirical facts and the evaluation of those facts (Weber 1949). He viewed facts and values as 'entirely heterogeneous'. He maintained that the social scientist must shun evaluative commitments that might bias scientific work. None the less, Weber agreed with Durkheim that moral and other values are of the highest importance in social life, and Weber recognized that facts and norms are intertwined in several ways in the 'praxis' of social science. For example, scientists choose research projects based on cultural values, and in carrying out science they dedicate themselves to values of honesty and accuracy.

Weber's recommendation of a value-free social science was immensely influential, eventually becoming the orthodox position in the social sciences and philosophy. His recommendation also promoted the view that the judgments of science are demonstrable, that value judgments are not, and that scientific judgments therefore have a superior epistemological status. However, these ideas, which grew out of early sociology, enjoyed less currency in other quarters. For example, many economists and political scientists doubted from the start that a value-free model suits their 'value-impregnated' fields (see ECONOMICS, PHILOSOPHY OF §2). Many questions persist about whether the value-free ideal is possible or desirable, and about whether social scientists can or should avoid value judgments in their work.

2 The model of a value-free social science

Weber's distinction between praxis and methodological principle illuminates this dispute: the critics of value-free science tend to point to values present in social scientists' practices and role in society, whereas proponents argue primarily from the methodological principles and ideals of science. Weber himself was not concerned about the evaluative criteria underlying and motivating scientific practice, but with the justification of scientific conclusions. He emphasized the logical independence of facts and values and the validity of scientific methods.

The central premise in the model of a value-free social science is that the truth or falsity of scientific hypotheses and the scientific methods used to determine truth or falsity are independent of value judgments. The model presupposes the defensibility of the distinction between facts and values, but is not dependent upon any particular interpretation of the nature of a fact or the nature of a value. It also does not depend on any particular view about whether value judgments are true or justifiable, though some proponents have argued that value judgments are neither rationally justifiable nor true. Nor need the model incorporate any form of scepticism about either facts or values.

The central premises commonly found in attacks on this value-free model are the following:

1 Science presupposes values such as truthfulness, knowledge, explanatory power, and criteria that distinguish good from bad theories and explanations.
2 In selecting a problem for scientific study, values drive the process of selection.
3 All scientists have evaluative viewpoints that inevitably affect how they interpret and report their findings, including how they construct the evidence and the importance they give to some evidence to the exclusion of other evidence.
4 Whenever scientists accept hypotheses, they make a value judgment that sufficient evidence supports the hypothesis; this judgment does not follow exclusively from the scientific method, because no hypothesis is ever fully verified by that method.
5 A scientist who accepts funding from institutions whose values control the funding tacitly accepts the values and priorities of those institutions.

Value-free conceptions of scientific method and explanation must resolve these problems. Proponents typically argue that the values mentioned are prescientific considerations external to the science itself; they believe that observation, explanation, and theory construction are not affected by such contextual matters. However, the intermixture of facts and values in the actual conduct of scientific research makes it difficult to establish clean lines of separation, if indeed they are separate.

3 Problems of motivation and selection

One challenge to a value-free social science comes from the moral and political motivations of scientists, for example, their desire to see protection increased for vulnerable members of society or their ambition to increase the reputation of their institution. These moral and social commitments influence the selection of research topics as well as the way the results of research are interpreted, reported, and applied. Social scientists also report their results selectively, typically in a manner that supports their hypotheses and viewpoints. What will be undertaken in studies, how it will connect to social policy, and what can be accepted as a scientific answer all depend on an evaluative framework.

From Weber to the present, defenders of value-free science have not denied that knowledge is selective, influenced by values, and motivated by social concerns. The question, from the value-free viewpoint, is whether these background or extra-scientific features of work in science are relevant to questions of methodology and whether they infect the science. Underlying motives seem to defenders of value-freedom to have no direct bearing on the science. They maintain that when scientists who are motivated to demonstrate *x* obtain results from their studies demonstrating *not-x*, they report their results accordingly, if they are good scientists. Scientific methodology, from this perspective, is consistent with moral motives and value-driven selection that play a vital role but can be set aside in scientific practice.

The proponents of value-free science acknowledge that selectivity, like standards of accuracy, is a filtering device essential to good science. But they insist that the evaluative character of selectivity does not by itself taint the data or the reporting of data. This contention moves the issues from selectivity in general, to the question of whether selection involves some form of bias or failure to be impartial.

4 Problems of bias and partiality

Rigour in the design of studies to eliminate or minimize bias is a canonical principle. In general, a bias is a deviation of a finding from the truth. Many processes in the collection, interpretation, review, and publication of data can cause bias. However, bias is often difficult to pinpoint, and the term 'bias' is used in different senses in these discussions.

One sense of bias is distortion in an alleged finding due to a limitation in the design of the study. A biased sample, for example, may cause a problem in the generalizability of findings. Unless the sampling method ensures that all members of the reference population have a chance of selection in the sample, bias may occur. For example, some early surveys of 'lesbian behaviour' were limited to small samples of lesbians encountered in bars. This sample is biased if generalized to all lesbians; it may also convey negative impressions of this diverse community of women. Similarly, an early study of gay men used a sample entirely comprised of gay men in psychiatric therapy.

Many methodologists believe that scientists rarely, if ever, eliminate all biases from their studies. These methodologists propose not the complete elimination of biases, but a reporting of them wherever they can be ascertained (the reverse of so-called 'reporting bias', which involves a selective suppression of information). They insist that risks of bias can be minimized in well-designed research, but no method can eliminate bias or ensure that it will not be present. In the ideal, social science is free of bias in this sense, but in practice it almost always falls short.

A second sense of bias is maintaining a personal point of view that distorts the answers scientists give to the questions they investigate. This use of bias refers to a lapse of impartiality or partisanship. Partiality results from a value-directed departure from accuracy, objectivity, and balance, not merely an inadvertent distortion of facts or a limitation in sample selection. Bias of this sort can be a factor in research design, critical analyses, the interpretation and publication of results, and in peer review. Again, a basic methodological principle is that protection against partiality be built into research design, but should this prove impossible, one strategy is to disclose the personal values and how they might affect study results and reports.

Partiality should be distinguished from legitimate forms of opinion and appraisal. Partiality occurs only if there is a value-directed departure from accuracy and objectivity. If, for example, a social scientist fails to notice that an accidental omission has distorted a crucial part of a study, the distortion results from error, not partiality. A bias in the second sense is present only if distorted information is causally connected to the investigator's values.

5 Problems of advocacy and strength-of-evidence judgments

Charges of bias can arise when a social scientist has adopted an advocacy role or has been employed to represent a particular institutional or special-interest point of view. For example, social scientists who have identified hazardous conditions, criminal activity, government neglect and the like, and who serve as experts on such matters sometimes become advocates who propose interventions and control measures. In practice, these recommendations often develop from patterns of empirical evidence that the advocates may or may not have generated themselves. These scientists apply causal criteria to the findings of studies and then make judgments about causes (of poverty, say) that are inextricably bonded to their recommendations.

Although appropriate to and required of social scientists in some roles, such as those of public health officials, advocacy is a threat to scientific objectivity whenever a group such as a government bureau, a labour union, industrial management, or a public interest group has sponsored the research. Social scientists who view themselves as social architects, using their own research to achieve what they consider a noble goal of eliminating all putative causes of human poverty, distress, disease and the like, are commonly viewed with scepticism by colleagues.

However, advocacy does not necessarily impugn either the underlying science or institutional and social policy recommendations based on it. Being loyal, dedicated, or even partisan is not equivalent to a loss of impartiality about scientific conclusions, although such participation does threaten impartiality. Partisan or institutionally loyal social scientists can, in principle, restrain or even completely eliminate their commitments in conducting a study and reporting its findings. Advocacy is also sometimes distanced from the conduct of research. For example, scientists may be advocates for the funding of research and for particular types of research needed to address what they consider unanswered research questions.

Related to problems of advocacy are problems of strength-of-evidence judgments that depend upon what is morally at stake. The social consequences of making a mistake in assessing evidence are very serious in some cases, minimal in others. These social consequences can and often do affect judgments about the strength of scientific evidence. Judgments that the evidence is sufficient and that a hypothesis should be accepted often depend heavily upon context consequences. For example, consider a study designed to determine whether women who receive state welfare payments can be deterred from becoming pregnant or, if they become pregnant, from giving birth to their child, by depriving them of increased financial aid assistance. The research is to evaluate a deterrent effect by examining the impact of a state-mandated, child-exclusion provision on fertility and birth rates among women. No prior evidence was sufficient to answer this question. Hypothesis acceptance in this study will almost certainly be contingent upon value judgments about what the consequences of acting on the evidence would be for both pregnant women on welfare and state officials.

The idea that degrees of scientific evidence are free of interpretation is challenged by this argument (which was first advanced by Richard Rudner 1953), because 'strength of evidence' is itself a value-impregnated notion. It seems impossible to give responsibility for judgments about strength of evidence exclusively to public officials, contractors, or employers, because it is the business only of a scientist, not someone else, to make a judgment about the strength of scientific evidence and about whether a scientific hypothesis is adequately supported.

6 Professional codes of conduct

Social science research can never be a morally neutral activity as long as it involves human research subjects. Many problems of value judgements in social science concern how these subjects may permissibly be used. The book *A Time to Speak: On Human Values and Social Research* (1968) by Herbert Kelman, combined with a number of controversial cases of abuses of subjects by social scientists, alerted scientists in the late 1960s to a variety of problems in research ethics. Careful attention was subsequently paid to the moral judgments that social scientists do and should make in carrying out their research. Problems stem from practices such as the experimental deception of subjects, the collection of data on persons in an individually identifiable form, and the use of financial incentives to obtain subjects.

Two types of value judgments merit attention in this context. The first type involves moral assessments of the protocols and the behaviour of social scientists. The second type concerns methodological evaluations of research practices (similar to those previously discussed). Methodological criteria govern how a procedure is to function in a research design in order to avoid screening out effects that could render the results ungeneralizable, or perhaps unreliable or of very limited generalizability. A procedure may satisfy criteria of methodological adequacy and be morally unjustified; or the procedure may be morally justified but methodologically inadequate. Here we encounter methodological–moral dilemmas. Sometimes methodological rigour is sacrificed to yield a moral gain, and sometimes moral rigour is sacrificed to yield a methodological gain (for example, by waiving a consent requirement for research involving deception).

Value judgments here intersect in several ways. A design adequate to achieve the objectives of a research protocol is generally considered a necessary condition of the moral justifiability of the research. Many argue both that it is irresponsible to use valuable resources to conduct methodologically flawed research and that it is morally unjustified to conduct research that presents risk to subjects if the research design is defective. Both claims presume criteria for assessing the methodological adequacy of research procedures, and in both cases the reasons for making methodological soundness a condition of moral justifiability are independent of these criteria.

The aforementioned normative rule that study bias must be avoided sometimes contingently conflicts with moral and professional obligations to protect the rights of research subjects. For example, because the validity of a study and the availability of funding to conduct it may be adversely affected by a poor response rate, potential subjects are sometimes encouraged to participate by repeated telephone calls and aggressive follow-ups. This badgering may fail to respect the decisions of subjects and violate their right to privacy. The point is that choices between alternative study populations, control groups, interviewing procedures, and approaches to minimizing the likelihood of bias will involve both ethical and methodological values.

Most professions arguably have an indigenous professional morality with precepts governing research ethics. These precepts specify responsibilities to research subjects, responsibilities to society, responsibilities to employers and funding sources, and responsibilities to professional colleagues. Particular codes developed for professional associations of social scientists are usually attempts to discover, formulate, and develop this inchoate morality rather than attempts to apply some general ethical theory. However, philosophical ethics has been explicitly used in some cases to help in developing this professional morality. Many social scientists have recognized that there are serious problems with attempts to base professional ethical standards entirely in practice standards, that often do not exist within the relevant field, group, or profession. If practice standards are deficient, ethical theory may be a valuable resource for reflection on, criticism of, and reformulation of the standards.

See also: ECONOMICS AND ETHICS; SCIENTIFIC METHOD; SOCIAL SCIENCES, PHILOSOPHY OF

References and further reading

Barnes, B. (1974) *Scientific Knowledge and Sociological Theory*, London: Routledge & Kegan Paul. (Defends a 'strong programme' for the sociology of scientific knowledge in which social interests control scientific practice, including the acceptance of scientific hypotheses.)

Beauchamp, T.L., Faden, R.R., Wallace, Jr, R.J and Walters, L. (eds) (1983) *Ethical Issues in Social Science Research*, Baltimore, MD: Johns Hopkins University Press. (An anthology of original essays by leading figures in social science methodology and moral theory.)

* Durkheim, É. (1895) *The Rules of Sociological Method*, ed. G.E.G. Catlin, trans. S.A. Solovay and John H. Mueller, Glencoe, IL.: The Free Press of Glencoe, 8th edn, 1938. (An influential and difficult work that touches only tangentially on issues of value-free science and the basis of moral norms.)

Gräfrath, B. (1991) 'Forschungsinterese, Tatsachenwissen und praktische Orientierung', *Zeitschrift für philosophische Forschung* 45: 558–70. (Interpretation and defence of Max Weber's concept of value-freedom 'Wertfreiheit'.)

Keat, R. (1989) 'Relativism, Value-Freedom, and the Sociology of Science', in *Relativism: Interpretation and Confrontation*, ed. M. Krausz, Notre Dame, IN: University of Notre Dame Press, 272–98. (Cautious, analytical study of the relationships between issues in value-freedom, value relativism, and value-free sociology of science.)

* Kelman, H. (1968) *A Time to Speak: On Human Values and Social Research*, San Francisco, CA: Jossey-Bass. (Powerful and pioneering work on ethical issues in social science research.)

Longino, H.E. (1989) *Science as Social Knowledge: Values and Objectivity in Scientific Inquiry*, Princeton, NJ: Princeton University Press. (Wide-ranging interpretation of scientific inquiry as a contextual process in which social values give shape to scientific development and claims to knowledge.)

Myrdal, G. (1958) *Value in Social Theory*, ed. P. Streeten, London: Routledge & Kegan Paul. (A comprehensive treatment by a leading spokesman for the value-impregnation of the social sciences.)

Proctor, R. (1991) *Value Free Science: Purity and Power in Modern Knowledge*, Cambridge, MA: Harvard University Press. (Detailed historical and contemporary treatment of controversies about value judgments in science, but excluding moral problems in the professions and ethics and public policy.)

* Rudner, R. (1953) 'The Scientist *Qua* Scientist Makes Value Judgements', *Philosophy of Science* 20: 1–6. (Brief and clear argument that value judgments are essentially involved in the procedures of science.)

Schumpeter, J.A. (1949) 'Science and Ideology', *American Economic Review* 39: 345–59. (Influential address on whether ideological bias is a significant factor in 'scientific economics', with an examination of Adam Smith, Marx, and Keynes.)

* Weber, M. (1949) *The Methodology of the Social Sciences*, ed. and trans. E.A. Shils and H.A. Finch, Glencoe, IL: The Free Press of Glencoe. (The most celebrated spokesman for value free science and the most influential work.)

Weed, D. (1994) 'Science, Ethics Guidelines, and Advocacy in Epidemiology', *Annals of Epidemiology* 4: 166–71. (A strong, readable defence of advocacy in social and public health research, especially for scientists in roles requiring value judgments.)

TOM L. BEAUCHAMP

VALUE, ONTOLOGICAL STATUS OF

We evaluate persons, characters, mental states, actions, inanimate objects and situations using very abstract terms such as 'good', 'unjust' and 'beautiful', and more concrete terms, such as 'courageous', 'cruel' and 'crass', drawn from fields such as aesthetics, ethics, politics and religion. Do these evaluations ascribe value properties to the entities evaluated? If so, what are these properties like? If not, what are we doing when we evaluate?

The simplest way to understand ethical discourse is by analogy with ordinary fact-stating discourse. An ethical judgment is to be understood as either true or false, being true if the situation it describes obtains, false if it does not. If ethical judgments are fact-stating, then it is natural to take evaluative vocabulary such as 'is good' and 'is courageous' as picking out properties of the entities which are evaluated.

What are these value properties like? First, we need an account of how properties are different from other kinds of entities. Then we need to decide whether values are natural or non-natural properties, where natural properties are the proper subject matter of the various sciences. G.E. Moore in *Principia Ethica* (1903) argued that goodness is a *sui generis* non-natural property. In contrast, many have tried to

conceive of value properties as natural, principally by defining evaluative vocabulary in terms of the psychological states of some subject or subjects in certain conditions. By varying the state, subject and conditions, numerous such accounts can be obtained; for example, 'is good' might mean 'is desired by the speaker here and now' or 'is something we would desire to desire.... in conditions of full imaginative acquaintance'.

Mackie (1977) thinks that our ethical discourse commits us to the existence of value properties which he calls 'objective values'. But he argues that such values would be non-natural, Moore's property of goodness vividly illustrating their 'queerness'. Our knowledge of them would be unexplained and, since ethical judgments are automatically motivating, these values would have a mysterious action-guiding force, quite unlike natural properties. Thus Mackie adopts an error theory of our evaluative discourse. There are no objective values. Since every ethical judgment commits us to such values, they are all false. His diagnosis of the error draws upon Hume's projectivism (see PROJECTIVISM). In truth, there is only the world of natural properties and our affective reactions to it, such as moral approval and disapproval. But we project such reactions back onto the world and speak as if it contained properties, such as goodness and badness, which merit the reactions.

Denying the existence of objective values need not force one to accept the error theory, for one can deny Mackie's conceptual claim that our ethical discourse says that there are objective values. Instead, one can think of this discourse as having an expressive, as opposed to a descriptive, function. Ayer's emotivism is an early version of this idea (see EMOTIVISM). It is too crude, however, because it merely says that ethical judgments serve to express our affective reactions, failing to explain how it is that ethical discourse appears so similar to genuine descriptive discourse. After all, we are happy to say that ethical judgments are true or false, we engage in ethical argument to determine the correct answers to our ethical questions, we presume to persuade others to abandon their mistaken views and we acknowledge that our current ethical opinions may be wrong. Each of these features of our ethical practice tempts us to think that there is a realm of ethical facts which constrain the practice, facts which we aim to describe with our ethical discourse.

Blackburn's quasi-realist project (1984; 1993) attempts to explain the shape of our ethical practice on the basis of its expressive function. He argues that our ethical discourse is all right as it is, for, despite the appearances, it contains no erroneous commitment to objective values. Blackburn insists that we express, rather than describe, our affective reactions when we make ethical judgments. But one should ask whether a sharp line can be drawn between expression and description and, in turn, whether there is much to choose between Blackburn's position and the view which takes values to be natural properties involving our psychological states.

Mackie and Blackburn share the conception of the natural world as the world of science, which exists independently of human sensibility. A real entity belongs to the natural world, and values are not real. But perhaps this is too restrictive. McDowell (1985) has argued that values should be compared with secondary qualities, such as redness (see SECONDARY QUALITIES). It is a conceptual truth that an object is red if and only if it would look red to appropriately receptive subjects in appropriate conditions. Thus redness is a dispositional property which is conceptually connected to human sensibility, and so cannot belong to the natural world. But, since an object can possess this disposition independently of any particular experience, we are happy to think of an object as really being red, its looking red to us in the right conditions being perception of the redness which it possesses. Analogously, McDowell urges that a value, such as goodness, is to be thought of as a dispositional property of objects which is conceptually connected to an affective reaction in the right subjects in the right conditions. Again, such a value is not part of the natural world, but it is nevertheless real, the relevant affective reactions detecting its presence. If all this is right, one can argue against Mackie that our ethical discourse only commits us to the reality of values in the weak sense that their existence is independent of any particular experience. The appropriateness of the analogy between values and secondary qualities is fiercely debated. In particular, one ought to question whether any sense can be made of a perceptual route to values, especially when our affective states are often reactions to imagined or described situations, not perceived ones.

See also: MORAL REALISM

References and further reading

Ayer, A.J. (1936) *Language, Truth and Logic*, London: Victor Gollancz. (Chapter 6 contains his emotivist theory of ethical discourse.)

* Blackburn, S. (1984) *Spreading the Word*, Oxford: Clarendon Press. (Chapters 5 and 6 introduce his distinctive combination of projectivism and quasi-realism.)

* —— (1993) *Essays in Quasi-Realism*, New York: Oxford University Press. (A collection of essays

developing his quasi-realist project; chapter 8 includes criticism of Mackie's error theory and of the analogy between values and secondary qualities.)

Darwall, S., Gibbard, A. and Railton, P. (1992) 'Toward *Fin de siècle* Ethics: Some Trends', *Philosophical Review* 101 (1): 115–89. (An excellent overview of different theories of the metaphysics of value.)

Lewis, D. (1989) 'Dispositional Theories of Value', *Proceedings of the Aristotelian Society* 63: 113–37, supplement. (Argues that it is a conceptual truth that something is a value if and only if we are disposed in conditions of fullest imaginative acquaintance to desire to desire it.)

* McDowell, J. (1985) 'Values and Secondary Qualities', in T. Honderich (ed.) *Morality and Objectivity*, London: Routledge & Kegan Paul, 110–29. (Argues that values are real by comparing them with secondary qualities.)

McGinn, C. (1983) *The Subjective View*, Oxford: Clarendon Press. (Chapter 8, sect. iii criticizes the analogy between values and secondary qualities.)

* Mackie, J.L. (1977) *Ethics: Inventing Right and Wrong*, Harmondsworth: Penguin. (Chapter 1 advances the error theory of ethical discourse.)

* Moore, G.E. (1903) *Principia Ethica*, ed. T. Baldwin, Cambridge: Cambridge University Press, revised edn, 1993. (Chapter 1 argues for goodness as a *sui generis*, non-natural property.)

Sayre-McCord, G. (ed.) (1988) *Essays on Moral Realism*, Ithaca, NY: Cornell University Press. (An excellent collection of papers both for and against the existence of ethical value, including a reprint of McDowell's paper and the relevant passages from Mackie.)

ALEX OLIVER

VALUES

The theory of value has three main traditions: subjectivism, which holds that the only valuable goods are subjective states of sentient beings; objectivism, which claims that while values must be human-related, they exist independently of us; and Neo-Kantian rationalism, which suggests that value is postulated on the basis of practical reason. Central distinctions in the theory of value are between subjective and objective values, instrumental and final values, intrinsic and extrinsic values, organic unities and the idea of an ultimate or architectonic value. There are also distinc-

tions drawn between different types of value, such as moral and aesthetic value.

The theory of value has been neglected within Anglo-American analytical philosophy. However, recent philosophy has seen a revival in value theory. The *subjectivist* school remains the dominant orthodoxy, but recent philosophy has seen the development of new forms of *objectivism* and an increasing emphasis on value theory within the *Neo-Kantian rationalist* tradition, a tradition which does tie an account of value directly to a theory of practical reasoning.

Subjectivists assert that the only valuable goods are subjective states of sentient organisms. 'Subjective' can be given a wide reading to include the essential interests of a subject; on a wide definition of subjective value even the conditions necessary for the flourishing of an organism can be included in the definition. Here, as elsewhere, 'subjective' and 'objective' accounts of the subject matter shade into each other. Thus, utilitarian theories of value have evolved from Bentham's simple hedonism, via revealed preference theories, to definitions of the valuable in terms of what is objectively good for people (see HEDONISM; PERFECTIONISM; RATIONALITY, PRACTICAL; UTILITARIANISM).

Objectivists claim greater degrees of independence between values and human interests and concerns. Moderate objectivists would concede that value is an anthropocentric category, and that their list of the good things in life must relate to human concerns. However, they would insist that these components of a good life are preferable because they are good, and not vice versa (see GOOD, THEORIES OF THE §5). Extreme objectivists argue that value is not a category distinctively attuned to human concerns but exists independently of human interests. Is biodiversity, for example, good in itself? Or is it good only relative to our interests (see ENVIRONMENTAL ETHICS §2)?

Neo-Kantian rationalists offer a third approach to the nature of value. They argue that subjective interests give rise to reasons, which are then subjected to formal tests to see if they are sufficient to bring about the ends they prescribe for an agent. If the reason passes these tests, the end is taken to be valuable. This theory views the connection between practical reasoning and value differently from its rivals; practical reasoning does not solely work out the means to pre-given ends but also establishes which ends are worthy of choice.

Something may be valued in itself, or for the contribution it makes to achieving a further state which is valuable. Jogging may be tedious, but it is instrumental in achieving health, which is finally valuable as an end in itself. This distinction between the instrumentally valuable and the finally valuable is properly located within the theory of practical reasoning, since it concerns the place of an 'end' or goal within an agent's system of practical ends. (Thus it is sometimes called the *means/ends* distinction – see PRACTICAL REASON AND ETHICS.)

It ought not to be confused with a related distinction, properly located within the theory of value, between *intrinsic* and *extrinsic* values. There are philosophically motivated arguments for collapsing these distinctions, but keeping them apart avoids begging the question against those who, for example, believe in final ends which are extrinsically valuable. It has been argued that Kant's theory of happiness, for example, sees it as an extrinsic value which is none the less our final end (see KANT, I. §11).

The idea of intrinsic value has been explained in many different ways. A central line of thought, found in G.E. Moore, is that intrinsically valuable things are the source of their own value whereas extrinsically valuable things derive their value from another source; intrinsic value is grounded on, but not reducible to, the 'natural' intrinsic properties of the object (see MOORE, G.E. §1; SUPERVENIENCE). Another proposal is to explain the grounds of intrinsic value via the idea of *organic unity*. Combinations of valuable things can form 'organic' wholes whose value is greater than the sum of the value of their component parts. The same was argued to be true of combinations of valuable with disvaluable or 'indifferent' things. For example, harming a sentient creature is bad, but taking pleasure in doing so much worse.

Many philosophers have argued that values collectively have a structure and that *higher* values can be discerned which organize the entire system of value and are therefore most worthy of choice. Examples would be Aristotle's belief that contemplation was the best and most self-sufficient good that made human life as a whole worthy of choice and the similar role Kant attaches to the good will (see ARISTOTLE §§21, 26; EUDAIMONIA).

How is *moral value* to be demarcated from other forms of value? One, admittedly controversial, criterion is to relate the nature of value to the test of convergence. If qualified experts converge in the making of a judgment, that is enough to sustain a 'thin' model of objectivity, which may perhaps offer a sufficient account of aesthetic values. There is no more to aesthetic value than being the fit object of such convergent judgment. However, in the moral case one requires the further feature that competent judges converge in judging a case to be, say, cruel in virtue of the fact that it is indeed cruel. In this latter case there is indispensable reference to the property, anthropocentric but real, which merits the response. This method of demarcation would have the advantage of explaining why it is internal to the practice of aesthetic judgment that a plurality of such judgments is inherent in the subject matter and can rationally be tolerated. However, this is not so in the moral case, where divergent judgment invites correction.

See also: ART, VALUE OF; AXIOLOGY; FACT/VALUE DISTINCTION; GOOD, THEORIES OF THE; IDEALS; LI; MORAL REALISM; VALUE, ONTOLOGICAL STATUS OF

References and further reading

Cavell, S. (1979) *The Claim of Reason*, Oxford: Oxford University Press, part III. (Reflects on the different roles of pluralism and disagreement within moral and aesthetic discourse.)

Grice, P. (1991) *The Conception of Value*, Oxford: Oxford University Press. (Another foundational work in value theory, suggestively parallel to the Korsgaard but drawing inspiration as much from Aristotle as from Kant.)

Griffin, J. (1986) *Well-Being: Its Meaning, Measurement and Moral Importance*, Oxford: Oxford University Press, esp. part I. (A comprehensive and important study of the fundamental idea of an agent's wellbeing which explains many of the different approaches to the issue.)

Korsgaard, C. (1983) 'Two Distinctions in Goodness', *Philosophical Review* 92: 27–49. (Argues against collapsing the means/ends and extrinsic/intrinsic distinctions and suggests that Kant's concept of happiness is as an extrinsic yet final end.)

—— (1986) 'Aristotle and Kant on the Source of Value', *Ethics* 96: 486–505. (Explains the idea of a 'source' of value in the context of these two foundational theories of morality in the Western tradition.)

—— (1996) *The Sources of Normativity*, Cambridge: Cambridge University Press. (A classic presentation of a Kantian 'rationalist' approach to practical reasoning and value.)

Nozick, R. (1981) *Philosophical Explanations*, Cambridge, MA: Harvard University Press, part V, chaps 1–6. (Nozick's extended discussion is the closest in recent philosophy to the classical doctrines of the Austro-German school of axiology. These chapters contain discussions of a wide range of issues in value theory, including the doctrine of organic unities.)

Wiggins, D. (1987) *Needs, Values, Truth*, Oxford: Blackwell; revised edn, 1991. (Contains many seminal papers which present the view that moral

properties are tied to our evaluative interests and thus anthropocentric, but none the less real.)

ALAN THOMAS

VALUES AND FACTS *see* FACT/VALUE DISTINCTION

VAN HELMONT, FRANCIS MERCURIUS *see* HELMONT, FRANCISCUS MERCURIUS VAN

VARDHARMANA *see* MAHĀVĪRA

VASUBANDHU (4th or 5th century AD)

An Indian Buddhist philosopher of the fourth or fifth century, Vasubandhu was a prolific author of treatises and commentaries. Best known for his synthesis of the Sarvāstivāda school of Abhidharma, he was sympathetic with the Sautrāntika school and frequently criticized Sarvāstivāda theory from that perspective. Vasubandhu eventually became an eminent exponent of the Yogācāra school. He also wrote short treatises on logic that influenced Dignāga, traditionally said to have been his disciple.

Probably the most original of Vasubandhu's philosophical works are his two short works in verse, known as the Viṃśatikākārikāvṛtti *(Twenty-Verse Treatise) and the* Triṃśikākārikāvṛtti *(Thirty-Verse Treatise). In these two works, he argues that one can never have direct awareness of external objects, but can be aware only of images within consciousness. Given that some of these images, such as those in dreams and hallucinations, are known to occur without being representations of external objects, one can never be certain whether a given image in awareness corresponds to an external object. Because one can never be sure of what is externally real but can be sure of internal experiences, he concludes, a person seeking* nirvāṇa *should focus attention on the workings of the mind rather than on the external world.*

1   Life and works
2   Contributions to Abhidharma theory
3   Contributions to Yogācāra

1 Life and works

The earliest and the most complete biography of Vasubandhu was compiled by Paramārtha (499–569), a Chinese Buddhist pilgrim monk. It is preserved in the Chinese Buddhist canon. Some information can be gathered also from Tibetan biographies by Bu ston (1290–1364) and Tāranātha (1575–1634). The Tibetan biographies, however, differ in many points from Paramārtha's work. The available data from the various sources have been collected and studied by Erich Frauwallner.

According to Buddhist tradition, Vasubandhu was born in Peshawar, now part of Pakistan. Early biographers claim that he was initially a follower of the Sarvāstivāda (also known as Vaibhāṣika) school of Buddhism, later switched his allegiance to the Sautrāntika school and finally was converted to Mahāyāna by his elder brother Asaṅga, a founder of the Yogācāra school. Modern scholars have been divided on the questions of his date and which of the many works attributed to him are really of his authorship. Frauwallner argued (1951), on the basis of discrepancies within the Chinese and Tibetan biographies concerning Vasubandhu's dates, that there were two influential Buddhist philosophers named Vasubandhu who became conflated by Paramārtha. According to this hypothesis, the earlier Vasubandhu lived in the fourth century and was the younger brother of Asaṅga; he wrote numerous extensive commentaries on Mahāyāna scriptures, especially those associated with the Yogācāra school. The later Vasubandhu, according to Frauwallner, was the author of the *Abhidharmakośa* and lived in the late fifth century: it was he who wrote several short Yogācāra treatises and short works on logic and trained Dignāga, who eventually became best known as a logician. Frauwallner's hypothesis was quickly disputed by P.S. Jaini (1958) and has since been disputed by other scholars as well. Although the issue has not been definitively settled, Frauwallner's once-influential hypothesis has become decreasingly accepted by specialists in Vasubandhu's philosophy, although it still has adherents among prominent specialists in the history of Buddhist thought. This controversy has no bearing on the discussions that follow, since all scholars on both sides of the debate agree that the texts discussed below were by the same author.

2 Contributions to Abhidharma theory

One of the most influential texts in all of Indian Buddhism is Vasubandhu's *Abhidharmakośa*. According to the author's own explanation of the title, the text is comparable to a scabbard (*kośa*) from which one extracts the sword of wisdom, which is the means by which one cuts through delusions and attains the highest reality (*abhidharma*), namely *nirvāṇa*. The central argument of the book is that all complex entities are, by the very fact that they are complex, less stable and therefore less capable of providing satisfaction than simple entities. Therefore, one seeking satisfaction should focus the attention on simple objects rather than on complex entities. Examples of simple objects are the basic building blocks of experience, namely the basic qualities such as colour and shape that are apprehended in vision, sounds that are apprehended by hearing, the various qualities apprehended by the other external senses, and the moods and emotions apprehended by the mind. Examples of complex objects are houses, chariots, people and all the various things that one tries to acquire or to influence. Another example of a complex object is that which we take to be at the centre of all experience, the self.

Much of the *Abhidharmakośa* is dedicated to showing how a world constructed only of causally related qualities can function in the absence of a substantial substratum; the world is a world of properties (*dharma*) but not of property-owning (*dharmin*) substances. The work is divided into nine chapters. The first deals with a catalogue of the *dharmas* that form the content of all experience. The second discusses sense faculties and various other faculties of living beings. The third discusses the cosmos and its various populations. The world, it is argued, derives not from a single source but from the combination of the karma of billions of sentient beings; so karma becomes the subject matter of the fourth chapter. Karma is action that arises from latent patterns of habit; these habitual tendencies are discussed in detail in chapter five. People who eliminate negative, destructive habits become noble persons, who are classified in the sixth chapter. Nobility of character is a function of correct understanding, discussed in chapter seven. Since knowledge arises through skill in meditation, meditation is the subject of the eighth chapter. The ninth chapter, which may originally have been an independent treatise, recapitulates a series of arguments against a substantial basis for our sense of personal identity and individuality.

The *Abhidharmakośa* is a text written in verse, to which the author wrote an extensive prose commentary. The verse text presents a straightforward account of cosmology and psychology as taught by the Vaibhāṣika school of Buddhism. The prose commentary, however, examines these doctrines more critically. Since the author often goes into considerable detail about various positions that Buddhist philosophers of different views presented in the past, the work is an invaluable source of information on the controversies among Buddhists and between Buddhists and non-Buddhists during the first few centuries AD. Vasubandhu often, but by no means always, sides with critics from the Sautrāntika school of Buddhism. One of the salient characteristics of this school was a tendency to regard most Buddhist theories as merely provisional or heuristic doctrines, aimed not at giving a definitive account of the inner and outer worlds but at providing a framework within which the realities of these worlds can be discovered. Because the Sautrāntika school tended to be doctrinally more fluid than the relatively rigid orthodoxy of the Vaibhāṣika school, it is often seen as a conceptual bridge leading from the more conservative schools to the Mahāyāna movement. Owing to its comprehensive nature and to its serving as a propaedeutic for Mahāyāna philosophies, the *Abhidharmakośa* became a cornerstone of the curriculum at Indian Buddhist universities such as the one at Nālandā monastery. It is still common for Tibetan scholastics to devote five to eight years of their training to a thorough study of the *Abhidharmakośa* before going on to study Mādhyamika and Yogācāra philosophy. The text was also central to Buddhist scholastics in China. All told, it was as central to medieval Buddhist education as Aquinas' *Summa theologiae* to medieval Christian scholastics in Europe.

3 Contributions to Yogācāra

The early Buddhists discussed different worlds of experience, by which was meant different ways of experiencing the world. The 'foolish masses' of unreflective people are preoccupied with pleasures of the senses, so they are said to live in the realm of desire. More reflective people see sensible objects without hankering after them as much as unreflective people, so they are said to live in the world of appearances, by which it is meant that they perceive what appears to the senses without desiring them or despising them. People who abstract their attention away from sensible objects altogether are said to live in the world of nonappearance. While all these beings may live side by side in the same physical world, their subjective experiences of the world are radically different. Taking this commonplace observation as a point of departure, Vasubandhu argues in his *Viṃśatikākārikāvṛtti* (Twenty-Verse Treatise) and *Triṃśikākārikāvṛtti* (Thirty-Verse Treatise) that every sentient being is in a sense locked within its subjective world and has no direct contact with the external physical world. That there is an external world can be known through inference only, not through direct cognition. All experience, in other words, is mediated through one's habitual ways of seeing things. What makes one person's experience of physical circumstances different from another person's experience of those same circumstances is not the circumstances themselves; rather, it is the moods, emotional tendencies, memories and associations that each person uniquely brings to the circumstances.

One of Vasubandhu's arguments for this conclusion is that beings who experience the torments of hell cannot actually be in a physical setting of the sort described in descriptions of the hells. Those reports speak of guardians and beasts that prowl environments with heat of unbearable intensity and torment the inhabitants of those regions. But reason shows that these hell-guardians cannot themselves suffer from the conditions that the victims of hell find intolerable. If the guardians suffered as much as the inmates, they would be so overcome with pain that they would not be able to perform their task of tormenting the captives. Therefore the guardians and beasts, and indeed all the other torments of hell, must be purely subjective experiences that cannot have an objective counterpart in the external world, no matter how intensely they are felt.

Vasubandhu observes that when our senses are capable of presenting us with experiences of things that are not really as they are experienced, our only recourse to correct the presentations of the senses is reason. But reason also lets us down. Reason, for example, provides us with the notion of atoms, that is, bits of matter that are tiny to the greatest possible extent. Reflection, however, shows that the concept of atoms leads to inconsistencies. If an atom is really ultimately tiny, then it cannot be made up of parts that are physically smaller than the atom itself. If the atom has no parts, then the region of space occupied by the atom can have no subregions; there can be no upper region or lower region or eastern region and so on. If that is true, then the atom can occupy no space at all. If one atom occupies no space, then several atoms added together cannot occupy any space. Therefore what reason presents to us, namely that a macroscopic object is a complex of a very large number of ultimately small component parts, cannot really be the case after all. The atom, then, is a concept to which nothing in the real world can correspond.

If neither the senses nor reason can provide reliable pictures of external reality, we have no reliable means of knowing what the objective basis of our experiences is. When one thoroughly understands that a sentient being can never be aware of anything but its own awareness, says Vasubandhu, full attention can be turned to those subjective factors that give experience its flavour. Distracted neither by the appearances of the senses nor by the conceptual categories of reason, one gives up either hankering for or dreading what experience provides and one cultivates a bare attention to experience. This bare attention becomes an experience that is 'unthinkable, healthy and stable'. This is the experience of liberation or *nirvāṇa*.

Along with texts by Asaṅga and Sthiramati, Vasubandhu's Yogācāra treatises became the textual foundation for much of scholasticism in both China and Tibet. Given the central importance of both the *Abhidharmakośa* and his Yogācāra writings, Vasubandhu had an influence on Asian Buddhism second only to that of the Buddha himself.

See also: BUDDHISM, ĀBHIDHARMIKA SCHOOLS OF; BUDDHISM, YOGĀCĀRA SCHOOL OF

List of works

Vasubandhu (4th or 5th century AD) *Abhidharmakośa*, ed. and trans. L. de la Vallée Poussin, *L'abhidharmakośa de Vasubandhu*, Paris and Louvain: Paul Geuthner, 1923–31, 6 vols; repr. Brussels: Institut belge des hautes études chinoises, 1971, 6 vols; trans. L.M. Pruden, Berkeley, CA: Asian Humanities Press, 1988. (La Vallée Poussin's is still the best translation available of this key work from Vasubandhu's phase as an Abhidharma scholar; Pruden's translation, from La Vallée Poussin's French, is to be used with great caution, but is the only one available in English.)

—— (4th or 5th century AD) *Karmasiddhiprakaraṇa*, trans. S. Anacker, 'A Discussion for the Demonstration of Action', in Anacker, S. 1984; trans. E. Lamotte, 'Le Traité de l'acte de Vasubandhu. *Karmasiddhiprakaraṇa*', *Mélanges chinois et bouddiques* 4: 151–288, 1936. (A work from Vasubandhu's Yogācāra phase in which he criticizes Sarvāstivādin views of the mechanics of ethically charged actions and their fruitions.)

—— (4th or 5th century AD) Madhyāntavibhāgaśāstra, trans. S. Anacker, 'Commentary on the Separation of the Middle from Extremes', in Anacker 1984; trans. T. Kochumuttom, 'Discrimination Between Middle and Extremes', in Kochumuttom, T.A. 1982. (An important work from the author's Yogācāra phase.)

—— (4th or 5th century AD) *Pañcaskandhakaprakaraṇa*, trans. S. Anacker, 'A Discussion of the Five Aggregates', in Anacker 1984. (An analysis of the classes of characteristics that constitute the physical body and the mentality of human beings.)

—— (4th or 5th century AD) *Trisvabhāvanirdeśa*, trans. S. Anacker, 'The Teaching of the Three Own-Beings', in Anacker 1984; trans. T. Kochumuttom, 'A Treatise on the Three Natures', in Kochumuttom 1982; trans. F. Tola and C. Cragonetti, 'The *Trisvabhāvakārikā* of Vasubandhu', *Journal of Indian Philosophy* 11: 225–66, 1983. (A seminal work in early Yogācāra theory.)

—— (4th or 5th century AD) *Triṃśikākārikāvṛtti*, trans. L. de la Vallée Poussin, along with the *Viṃśatikākārikāvṛtti* and a Chinese commentary by Xuanzang as *La Siddhi de Hsuan-tsang*, Paris, 1928–48, 3 vols; trans. S. Anacker, 'The Thirty Verses', in Anacker 1984; trans. T. Kochumuttom, 'A Treatise in Thirty Stanzas', in Kochumuttom 1982. (An important Yogācāra treatise; La Vallée Poussin's French translation is excellent and well annotated.)

—— (4th or 5th century AD) *Vādavidhi*, trans. S. Anacker, 'A Method for Argumentation', in Anacker 1984. (One of the earliest Buddhist works on debate and logic, later criticized by Dignāga, whose work on logic superseded Vasubandhu's.)

—— (4th or 5th century AD) *Viṃśatikākārikāvṛtti*, see *Triṃśikākārikāvṛtti* for French translation; trans. S. Anacker, 'The Twenty Verses and their Commentary', in Anacker 1984; trans. T. Kochumuttom, 'A Treatise in Twenty Stanzas', in Kochumuttom 1982. (Along with the *Triṃśikākārikāvṛtti*, one of the foundational texts for Yogācāra theory.)

References and further reading

Anacker, S. (1984) *Seven Works of Vasubandhu, the Buddhist Psychological Doctor*, Delhi: Motilal Banarsidass. (Contains well-annotated translations, along with good introductions, of seven key works. Also has a general introduction and short biography of Vasubandhu, with discussion of Frauwallner's hypothesis of two Vasubandhus.)

* Frauwallner, E. (1951) *On the Date of the Buddhist Master of the Law Vasubandhu*, Rome: Serie Orientale Roma. (The author's first presentation of the hypothesis that there were two prominent Buddhist authors by the same name who were conflated into one by traditional biographers.)

—— (1957) 'Vasubandhus *Vādavidhiḥ*', *Wiener Zeitschrift für die Kunde Süd- und Ostasiens* 1: 104–46. (A study in German of the *Vādavidhi*.)

—— (1961) 'Landmarks in the History of Indian Logic', *Wiener Zeitschrift für die Kunde Südasiens* 5: 125–48. (A classical study of the relative chronologies of key Indian philosophers. Further discussion of the two-Vasubandhu hypothesis.)

* Jaini, P.S. (1958) 'On the Theory of Two

Vasubandhus', *Bulletin of the School of Oriental and African Studies* 21 (1): 48–53. (Disputes Frauwallner's hypothesis.)

Kochumuttom, T.A. (1982) *A Buddhist Doctrine of Experience: A New Translation and Interpretation of the Works of Vasubandhu the Yogācārin*, Delhi: Motilal Banarsidass. (Contains studies and translations of Vasubandhu's Yogācāra writings, disputing the common claim that these texts argue for subjective idealism.)

Nagao, Gadjin (1987) 'Vasubandhu', in M. Eliade (ed.) *Encyclopedia of Religion*, New York: Macmillan, vol. 15, 191a–193b. (A study by one of the world's leading scholars of Yogācāra Buddhism.)

RICHARD P. HAYES
MAREK MEJOR

VĀTSYĀYANA (5th century)

Vātsyāyana belonged to the Nyāya school of Indian philosophy, and his Nyāyabhāṣya *is the first extant commentary on the* Nyāyasūtra, *the foundational text of that school. In it, he emphasized the distinctive epistemological and logical character of the topics he deemed appropriate for treatment by Nyāya philosophers. In so doing, he helped both to establish the authority of the Nyāya school in matters related to logical reasoning, and to demarcate the enterprise of the Nyāya school from that of the earlier, more traditional, soteriological approach of the Upaniṣads. His commentary on the* Nyāyasūtra *set the agenda for succeeding generations of Nyāya commentators and their Buddhist opponents. In particular, Vātsyāyana initiated arguments that were to become crucial in the Nyāya defence of its characteristic brand of realism.*

Little is known about Vātsyāyana, who is also known as Pakṣilasvāmin. His precise dates remain a matter of scholarly interpretation of the relevant textual materials, most particularly the dating of the *Nyāyasūtra*, but placing him between 400 and 500 AD is a good working hypothesis. Vātsyāyana's chronological place in the enduring philosophical dialogue between the Nyāya and Buddhist philosophers is, however, much clearer. He directed many of his arguments against his Buddhist predecessor, NĀGĀRJUNA, and, in turn, his work was criticized by the great Buddhist logician DIGNĀGA. The dialogue continued with UDDYOTA-KARA, who sought to repair and develop Vātsyāyana's thought in the light of Dignāga's criticisms. In this fashion, the philosophical debate between the Nyāya and Buddhist philosophers continued until the

eleventh century, with each side offering an ever more refined defence of its position; it culminated in the great philosophical wrangle between the Nyāya philosopher UDAYANA and his Buddhist opponent Jñānaśrīmitra.

At stake was the Nyāya defence of realism. Nyāya is distinctive among Indian schools of philosophy in its advocacy of a form of direct realism, in which the world is seen to be made up of everyday objects, such as pots and cows, amenable to both direct perception and to verbal expression. The possibility of forming correct judgments about the objects in the world (*prameya*) rests upon the efficacy of the four accredited instruments of knowledge (*pramāṇa*), listed in the *Nyāyasūtra* as perception, inference, comparison and verbal testimony (see NYĀYA-VAIŚEṢIKA §6). In the *Nyāyabhāṣya*, Vātsyāyana attempted to counter Nāgārjuna's devastating critique of the very notion of a *pramāṇa*, a critique which had endangered the whole epistemological enterprise of the Nyāya school. He also defended, in the face of a developing Buddhist phenomenalism, the Nyāya view of the direct perception of objects. In so doing, he helped to clarify the relationship between perception and language.

Nāgārjuna had charged that the Nyāya dependence on the four *pramāṇas* was itself in need of substantiation. How can we be sure of the reliability of the *pramāṇas* themselves? Does our certitude come from invoking a further set of *pramāṇas*, taking the first step towards an infinite regress? In the *Nyāyasūtra* itself (2.1.19) we find a hint of the problem, when it is suggested rather cryptically that the *pramāṇas* are like lamp light. Since a lamp is self-illuminating, it was suggested that a *pramāṇa* could be self-validating. Vātsyāyana rejected such an interpretation. Not only does it fail to address Nāgārjuna's doubts about the *pramāṇas*, it also contradicts the basic Nyāya view that the *pramāṇas* alone, without any additional category of self-evidence, should be the source of knowledge. In his commentary on this *sūtra*, Vātsyāyana explains that the purpose of the lamplight analogy is to demonstrate that the *pramāṇa–prameya* distinction is neither rigid nor mutually exclusive. Since a lamp can fulfil two roles, both revealing other objects with its light and itself being an object of cognition, this demonstrates how one and the same object can function as both *pramāṇa* and *prameya*. Having resisted the idea that any set of *pramāṇas* should be considered axiomatic, Vātsyāyana attempts to show how the justification for any *pramāṇa* can come from the *pramāṇas* themselves. He points out that each *pramāṇa* is a generic term, encompassing different acts of knowing of the same type. Thus if one act of perception is validated by another act of perception, this should not be seen as a *pramāṇa* validating itself. Vātsyāyana's reply to Nāgārjuna may be viewed as somewhat pragmatic. Any individual use of a *pramāṇa* can itself be the object of another cognition. This, he says, is sufficient for the pursuit of everyday business as well as liberation (*mokṣa*), and does not lead to an infinite regress.

In dealing with the individual *pramāṇas*, Vātsyāyana's dispute with the Buddhist phenomenalists over where to draw the line between perception and inference was crucial to Nyāya's realist view of the world. In the *Nyāyasūtra* (1.1.4), perception had been characterized as 'that which is not expressible' (*avyapadeśyam*). Vātsyāyana uses this *sūtra* to argue that, as with infants, the ability to perceive an object is different from the ability to name it. This distinction between the perception of an object and its linguistic characterization anticipated an important distinction later Nyāya philosophers made between qualified and nonqualified perception. Vātsyāyana, however, strongly opposed the Buddhist view, which sought to drive a wedge between perception and language by making judgments of the form 'this is a cow' inferential rather than perceptual. Nyāya asserted a close accord between language and perception with the argument that perception gives us direct access to substantial, enduring objects like cows and trees. In the course of his arguments for the direct perception of physical objects, Vātsyāyana develops the arguments given in the *Nyāyasūtra* (2.1.31–6) concerning the relationship between a whole and its parts. While accepting that we can never simultaneously perceive all the parts of a tree, Vātsyāyana rejects the assumption that we need to do so in order to see a tree as such. A tree is a unity which is more than a mere conglomeration of its component parts, and which resides in its entirety in the parts of the tree. Vātsyāyana argues that if we are to speak of 'trees' at all, we must maintain the distinction of a whole over and above its parts. Later Nyāya realists, especially Uddyotakara and Udayana, made effective use of this distinction.

See also: KNOWLEDGE, INDIAN VIEWS OF; SENSE PERCEPTION, INDIAN VIEWS OF §§3–6

List of works

Vātsyāyana (5th century) *Nyāyabhāṣya*, in G. Jha (trans.) *The Nyāya-Sūtras of Gautama with the Bhāṣya of Vātsyāyana and the Vārttika of Uddyotakara*, Delhi: Motilal Banarsidass, 4 vols, 1984. (This four-volume set gives a translation of Vātsyāyana's commentary (*bhaṣya*) on the founda-

tional text (*sūtras*) of the Nyāya system alongside a later commentary (*vārttika*) by Uddyotakara.)

References and further reading

Matilal, B.K. (1971) *Epistemology, Logic and Grammar in Indian Philosophical Analysis*, The Hague: Mouton. (A detailed account of the differences between the Nyāya and Buddhist schools, with a focus on their respective theories of language and perception. Contains references to Vātsyāyana and the role he played in the early years of this long philosophical dialogue.)

—— (1977) *A History of Indian Literature*, vol. 6, *Scientific and Technical Literature*, Wiesbaden: Otto Harrassowitz. (Part 3, fasc.2 deals with Nyāya-Vaiśeṣika. In section 8 of chapter 2, Matilal discusses Vātsyāyana's style of doing philosophy using a short translation of Vātsyāyana's commentary on the *Nyāyasūtra*.)

—— (1986) *Perception: An Essay on Classical Indian Theories of Knowledge*, Oxford: Clarendon Press. (Chapter 2 contains a good discussion of the *pramāṇas*.)

Mohanty, J.N. (1970) *Phenomenology and Ontology*, The Hague: Martinus Nijhoff. (Chapter 17 gives a good account of Vātsyāyana's arguments concerning the direct perception of physical objects.)

* *Nyāyasūtra* (*c.*400 AD) trans. G. Jha, *The Nyāya-Sūtras of Gautama with the Bhāṣya of Vātsyāyana and the Vārttika of Uddyotakara*, Delhi: Motilal Banarsidass, 4 vols, 1984. (Complete translation with detailed notes.)

Phillips, S.H. (1995) *Classical Indian Metaphysics*, La Salle, IL: Open Court. (A work more specifically about the debate between the New Nyāya, or Navya-Nyāya, school and the Advaitin philosopher Śrīharṣa. It does, however, contain several references to Vātsyāyana in a chapter about earlier Nyāya philosophers.)

Potter, K.H. (ed.) (1977) *Encyclopedia of Indian Philosophies*, vol. 2, *Nyāya Vaiśeṣika*, Delhi: Motilal Banarsidass. (A comprehensive introduction to the Nyāya–Vaiśeṣika system, containing detailed summaries of all known Nyāya–Vaiśeṣika works.)

Sastri, D.N. (1964) *The Philosophy of Nyāya-Vaiśeṣika and its Conflict with the Buddhist Dignāga School*, Delhi: Bharatiya Vidya Prakashan. (A detailed account of the defence of Nyāya realism in the face of Buddhist opposition. There are frequent references to Vātsyāyana and his role in this long philosophical dispute.)

JOY LAINE

VEDĀNTA

Indian philosophical speculation burgeoned in texts called Upaniṣads (from 800 BC), where views about a true Self (ātman) in relation to Brahman, the supreme reality, the Absolute or God, are propounded and explored. Early Upaniṣads were appended to an even older sacred literature, the Veda ('Knowledge'), and became literally Vedānta, 'the Veda's last portion'. Classical systems of philosophy inspired by Upaniṣadic ideas also came to be known as Vedānta, as well as more recent spiritual thinking. Classical Vedānta is one of the great systems of Indian philosophy, extending almost two thousand years with hundreds of authors and several important subschools. In the modern period, Vedānta in the folk sense of spiritual thought deriving from Upaniṣads is a major cultural phenomenon.

Understood broadly, Vedānta may even be said to be the philosophy of Hinduism, although in the classical period there are other schools (notably Mīmāṃsā) that purport to articulate right views and conduct for what may be called a Hindu community (the terms 'Hindu' and 'Hinduism' gained currency only after the Muslim invasion of the South Asian subcontinent, beginning rather late in classical times). Swami Vivekananda (1863–1902), the great popularizer of Hindu ideas to the West, spoke of Vedānta as an umbrella philosophy of a Divine revealed diversely in the world's religious traditions. Such inclusivism is an important theme in some classical Vedānta, but there are also virulent disputes about how Brahman should be conceived, in particular Brahman's relation to the individual.

In the twentieth century, philosophers such as Sarvepalli Radhakrishnan, K.C. Bhattacharyya and T.M.P. Mahadevan have articulated idealist worldviews largely inspired by classical and pre-classical Vedānta. The mystic philosopher Sri Aurobindo propounds a theism and evolutionary theory he calls Vedānta, and many others, including political leaders such as Gandhi and spiritual figures as well as academics, have developed or defended Vedāntic views.

1   Pre-classical Vedānta
2   The *Brahmasūtra*
3   Issues among the subschools
4   Neo-Vedānta

1   Pre-classical Vedānta

The most abstract teaching of the earliest Upaniṣads centres on questions of theological metaphysics: what is the ultimate reality, what is its nature and relation to the world, and how can it be known? The ultimate reality is called Brahman, and all Vedānta, from the pre-classical to the modern, is Brahman-centred

philosophy. Early Upaniṣads also include much psychological speculation, about a true self (*ātman*), at places declared identical with Brahman. Dimensions or layers of self-experience are identified, for example, a series of states of awareness in dream and sleep, and a series of bodies (*kośa*) ranging from the physical body to a vital 'sheath', then a mental sheath, then a 'supramental' sheath, and finally a most essential sheath said to be 'made of bliss'.

Early Upaniṣads are as much mystical treatises as philosophical texts. A mystical awareness of Brahman (*brahma-vidyā*) is the core teaching concerning human destiny, a 'supreme personal good' (*parama-puruṣārtha*). Upaniṣadic idealist speculation appears to be an attempt to explain the possibility of an exalted consciousness: Brahman as transcendent (timeless, spaceless) but also as world ground is somehow directly experienced as identical with the individual self. Even theistic passages, which suggest that Brahman is transcendent to the world and individuals as their Creator and Lord, teach the value of knowing Brahman directly through assiduous efforts of meditation and yoga (which literally means 'self-discipline').

The psychological thesis that self-awareness is nondual, that awareness is evident to itself without an intermediary or another awareness, is presented with an analogy to light: light is self-luminous; similarly, awareness is self-aware. This thesis is key to the classical Vedāntic subschool known as Advaita ('Nondualism') – as too is a causal doctrine, namely, that an effect is prefigured, or immanent, in its material cause, for example, a gold bracelet in gold (see §3). The Advaita Upaniṣadic reading stresses the sole reality of Brahman, who is nondualistically self-aware. Positions key to theistic subschools, opposed to the Advaita reading, are also adumbrated in various passages. Early Upaniṣads do not speak with a single voice.

However, views are expressed that span not only all the classical Vedāntic subschools but also the full extent of pre-classical, classical and even much modern Indian thought. For example, doctrines of karma and rebirth are veritably pan-Indian. Some Upaniṣadic teachings about moral virtues remain fairly constant through the later civilization, although different emphases emerge in different religious and ascetic traditions. Social doctrines of caste are not prominent in the earliest Upaniṣads, but there are indications that a hereditary system of social privilege and responsibility was in the process of being formed.

Another pre-classical Vedāntic text is that portion of the *Mahābhārata* (the great Indian epic) known as the *Bhagavad Gītā* (Song of God), which is probably the most popular religious work in the whole of

Indian civilization. The *Bhagavad Gītā* echoes several Upaniṣads and develops Upaniṣadic themes and theses about the self as well as about Brahman. But whereas early Upaniṣads include many passages centred on ideas dear to classical Advaita Vedānta (and there are middle and late Upaniṣads that express only the Advaita point of view), the *Bhagavad Gītā* is to be aligned for the most part with the theistic classical subschools. Brahman is God, according to the *Bhagavad Gītā*, the Creator of the universe that God indwells. God is both transcendent to and immanent in this world (see GOD, INDIAN CONCEPTIONS OF §3). The *Bhagavad Gītā* upholds mystical awareness of Brahman – along with the yoga or discipline required for such awareness – as the solution to this-worldly ethical and political crises, a view echoed in modern times by Mahatma GANDHI and other nationalist leaders. In contrast to Upaniṣadic ideas about Brahman as beyond good and evil, in the Vedāntic theism of the *Bhagavad Gītā* and other texts, God upholds *dharma*, right conduct, and in special manifestations or *avatāras* (Kṛṣṇa, Rāma and so on) is born into the world to keep the social order on track.

In this way, by the end of the Upaniṣadic period (200 BC or thereabouts) Vedānta had begun to develop along two lines: Brahman – the Supreme Being by all counts – is conceived as a personal God, the Creator and Sustainer of the universe, manifesting as the several gods and goddesses and incarnate in *avatāras*; or, alternatively, Brahman is seen as an impersonal Ground of Being in the (idealist) sense of the entire phenomenal display of this universe viewed as a dream or illusory projection of a single Self. In all cases, the notion of liberation, that is, mystical knowledge or realization of Brahman (*brahma-vidyā*), is prominent, but the term is not understood in the same way by Advaita Vedāntins and theists. Advaitins come to hold that the self (*ātman*) of everyone is in reality nothing other than Brahman, and that in the mystical knowledge of Brahman there is known only the One, the sole true Existent, whose nature is strictly beyond determination by finite beings such as us; but that it is a homogeneous Being, Consciousness and Bliss is put forth as an idea to guide mystic pursuits. Vedāntic theists, in contrast, come to hold that the individual and God are meaningfully distinct. In the 'highest knowledge', the Supreme cannot be known in precisely the fashion that God knows God, for an individual knower is not strictly identical with the Creator, although God indwells everywhere, including, to be sure, the individual self. Advaita Vedāntins come to stress meditation and study of Upaniṣads to attain the *summum bonum*, while Vedāntic theists stress love and devotion to God.

2 The *Brahmasūtra*

Classical Indian philosophy is marked by argument and self-conscious defence of positions, as well as by an acute awareness of systematic interlock among the planks of a worldview or school. Distinct worldviews, represented in the several schools of classical philosophy, had emerged by the first few centuries AD. With exceptions (principally concerning Buddhist schools), each school has an early *Ur*- or root text that lays out positions comprehensively but also in abbreviated form – in *sūtras*, 'threads' or aphorisms that are compact and easy to memorize. Examples of basic texts are the *Mīmāṃsāsūtra*, defining the school of Mīmāṃsā, the *Nyāyasūtra*, spelling out Nyāya, and so on. The apparent root text of classical Vedānta is the *Brahmasūtra*. However, although the founders of the prominent Vedāntic subschools (ŚAṄKARA, Bhāskara, RĀMĀNUJA, Nimbārka, MADHVA and VALLABHĀCĀRYA) all write commentaries on the *Brahmasūtra* – each interpreting distinctively at least some of the terse and often vague or ambiguous *sūtras* – the Upaniṣads themselves, and not the *Brahmasūtra*, are the foundational Vedāntic texts. This is unlike the situation with, for example, Nyāya, where the *Nyāyasūtra* is veritably the foundational text. The *Brahmasūtra* should be regarded, then, as the text that first establishes a Vedāntic system, but not as the definitive statement of Vedāntic positions. The fact that there are diverse Vedāntic subschools attests to the diversity of Upaniṣadic teachings and to the vibrancy of Upaniṣadic traditions of study and learning well into classical times.

The *Brahmasūtra* is also known as the *Śārīrakamīmāṃsāsūtra* (Aphorisms of (Scriptural) Exegesis Concerning the Embodied). The *Brahmasūtra* presupposes the *Mīmāṃsāsūtra* (Aphorisms of (Scriptural) Exegesis (Proper)) – that is, an interpretation of the Veda including – according to classical Exegetes (Mīmāṃsakas), Vedānta's Upaniṣads as well as the Vedas proper. Classical Vedānta is sometimes referred to as Uttara Mīmāṃsā, Later Exegesis, being focused on the later portions of scripture (Upaniṣads) and contrasting but also continuous with Pūrva Mīmāṃsā, Prior Exegesis, which is focused on the earlier portions of scripture and is the school of Mīmāṃsā proper. A principal task the *Brahmasūtra* sets for itself is to differentiate Vedānta from Mīmāṃsā. This it does by declaring Brahman to be the object of Upaniṣadic statements, whose point is to provide insight and lead to mystical knowledge, as opposed to the Mīmāṃsā understanding of scripture as a series of injunctions on right ritual, right practice and in general the right way to live. The *Brahmasūtra* adopts Mīmāṃsā's epistemology of scripture as self-certifying and authoritative within its own sphere (see KNOWLEDGE, INDIAN VIEWS OF §3; MĪMĀMSĀ). But it specifies that that sphere is distinct in the case of the Upaniṣads; it is, namely, Brahman and knowledge of Brahman. The rites and actions prescribed by scripture for the embodied soul, the human agent, according to Exegetes, are, according to Vedāntins, nullified by the superior path of knowledge, whereby the embodied will come to know Brahman and be liberated from rebirth and death and future embodiment.

The *Brahmasūtra* has less subtle quarrels with other classical schools, although regarding Sāṅkhya, scriptural interpretation remains the major issue. Early Upaniṣads do, in fact, at places resonate with Sāṅkhya's understanding of nature or *prakṛti* as prefiguring within her unmanifest form all worldly manifestations. Moreover, Sāṅkhya's hierarchical psychology of an embodied soul and its instruments or faculties, from reason to sense organs and organs of action, is rather clearly an Upaniṣadic teaching (see SĀṄKHYA). The *Brahmasūtra* is intent on integrating these views within a Brahman-centred philosophy, and disputes the contention that Sāṅkhya is expressed in the Upaniṣads. But the *Brahmasūtra* also disputes Sāṅkhya on metaphysical and other nonscriptural grounds. And Buddhist schools, Nyāya, Vaiśeṣika, Jainas and others are engaged and refuted on a wide range of philosophical issues.

For example, against the Vaiśeṣika notion of inherence (*samavāya*) as ontic glue binding a property to a property-possessor, the *Brahmasūtra* alleges that an infinite series of relators would be required to bind the inherence itself to the property and to the property-possessor. In this way, the notion is shown to be bankrupt. Against a Buddhist understanding of awareness as neither occurring in a self nor revealing external states of affairs, the *Brahmasūtra* alleges that the evidence of perception is to the contrary. The Jaina view that the soul has size is opposed on the grounds of untoward ramifications with regard to liberation. Bādarāyaṇa, the person (otherwise unknown) to whom the *Brahmasūtra* is traditionally ascribed, appears thoroughly knowledgeable about the philosophical landscape of his time (probably the first or second century AD), and the *Brahmasūtra* suggests a similar development of argument as is evinced in other early *sūtra* texts of the philosophical schools.

3 Issues among the subschools

No *Brahmasūtra* commentary has come down us that is earlier than Śaṅkara's (early eighth century), but we know that there were earlier commentaries because

Śaṅkara and others whose works are extant mention a few. After Śaṅkara, the great Advaitin, there are commentaries by Bhāskara (*c.*750), Rāmānuja (11th century), Nimbārka (*c.*1250), Madhva (1238?–1317?) and Vallabhācārya (1479–1531), authors who establish subschools rival to Advaita. Other, mostly later (original), commentaries were written as well, but these philosophers are the founders of the major classical subschools. Śaṅkara and most of the others have followers who write subcommentaries, and within Advaita a couple of these (by Padmapāda, *c.*725, and Vācaspati Miśra, *c.*950) carve out distinct interpretations that are important even from a distant perspective contemplating classical Indian philosophy as a whole. The writings of classical Vedāntins are not confined to *Brahmasūtra* commentaries and subcommentaries; there are numerous noncommentarial treatises, as well as commentaries written on various Upaniṣads and the *Bhagavad Gītā*.

In these works, the *Brahmasūtra*'s attacks on competing worldviews are extended and refined, with some shift of focus as various non-Vedāntic philosophies become prominent or decline. But increasingly – and as early as Bhāskara – internecine disputes are aired, and by the era of Madhva come to dominate Vedāntic argument. And although it would be an error to ignore differences among non-Advaitic subschools, it is Advaita that the other subschools are keen to combat. With Madhva and his followers, not only is opposition to Advaita vehement, but also an alliance with Nyāya, a pluralist worldview with its own long history and literature, has to be counted as important as any Vedāntic heritage. This contrasts sharply with the polemics of the Advaitin Śrīharṣa (*c.*1150), who devotes enormous energy to refuting Nyāya, dismantling that realist and pluralist philosophy's every position down to apparent minutiae. Thus the nature of Vedāntic unity becomes problematic, and in fact scholars rarely refer to classical philosophers merely by a 'Vedānta' tag, but at least differentiate Advaitins from the rest. The key issue that divides Advaita from its Vedāntic opponents, and that (loosely) unites the opponents as well, is one that, as noted above (§1), flows out of the Upaniṣads themselves and the *Bhagavad Gītā*: is Brahman the impersonal homogeneous Absolute of Advaita, or the God of the rival camps?

Other issues are tied closely to disputes about Brahman, in particular, controversies about the nature of the individual (*jīva*) in relation to Brahman. In fact, the most commonly employed designations of Vedāntic subschools derive from stances taken on this issue: Advaita (Nondualism: Brahman and the individual – *qua* being conscious or being a self – are identical; otherwise individuality is illusion),

Bhedābheda (the Distinctness in Nondistinctness view of Bhāskara and others: Brahman and the individual are in at least one way distinct realities and in another nondistinct), Viśiṣṭādvaita (the Qualified Nondualism view of Rāmānuja and followers: both Brahman and the individual are realities and also identical in a qualified sense), Dvaita (the Dualism view of Madhva and company: Brahman and the individual are fundamentally distinct realities), and so on.

The relation of Brahman and the individual was not considered simply a matter of abstract metaphysics; the soundness of practical disciplines, indeed, of whole ways of life, was viewed as hinging on it. Theistic Vedāntins upheld – and today Hindu theists continue to advocate – practices known as *bhakti*, 'love' or 'devotion', as the way to a mystical *summum bonum* sometimes symbolized as adulterous love-making with God. In contrast, Advaitins advocate more ascetic paths, along with intellectual pursuits – in particular, Upaniṣadic study. And the *summum bonum* is conceived as realization of Brahman where one nondualistically (and timelessly, and so on) knows only oneself.

Exegetical issues dominate the intra-Vedānta cross-fire. Advaitins, sensing a tension between Upaniṣads theistic statements and their view of Brahman's transcendence and unitary consciousness, develop exegetical strategies to reinterpret troublesome passages. Foremost among these is a view of scripture as like a wise and patient guru tailoring his teaching to his audience's capacities. Thus theistic views, and *bhakti* practices as well, are regarded as helpful for those incapable of appreciating the highest Upaniṣadic teaching, the utter truth, namely, that there is a single, undifferentiated self. (Some Advaitins make greater concessions to theism, holding that God is the inevitable conception of the Absolute from the finite human point of view. This position is often rehearsed among academic Neo-Vedāntins; see §4.)

Theistic Vedāntins, for their part, insist on a more literal reading of the Upaniṣads. Some also argue that all conveyance of meaning presupposes things as distinct. Moreover, the very act of comprehension of scriptural statements presupposes the reality of an individual cognizer. Advaitins are pushed by some of these points to assert the importance of nonliteral language, and struggle to formulate an appropriate theory of metaphor. They also admit that even a scripturally based understanding belongs to the province of illusion (*māyā*).

Concerning psychological and epistemological stances, there is less disagreement. Vedāntic theists tend to endorse the Advaita view of self-awareness as irreflexive and the Mīmāṃsā epistemology of self-certification (see EPISTEMOLOGY, INDIAN SCHOOLS OF §3). They also embrace the Upaniṣadic monism of Brahman as all-containing. But they refuse to go the subjectivist route in interpreting this doctrine, and dispute the Advaita view of worldly, finite things as an illusory projection of a single self. Instead, they see the unity of Brahman as a doctrine of material causality. With regard to the 'stuff' of the universe, a kind of Advaita is right: the world is the body of God. Even Madhva, who often seems intent on holding that in no way are God and individuals anything but distinct, says that God's body is the universe. According to Rāmānuja and other theists less radical than Madhva, Brahman has two natures: God as God is in God's self, which is God's necessary and essential nature, and God as God self-manifests in the world, as finite things that are real but contingent and inessential (see GOD, INDIAN CONCEPTIONS OF §3).

4 Neo-Vedānta

In modern India, the intellectual landscape has changed dramatically from classical times, reflecting science and influenced by Western thought. Vedānta, however, has proved surprisingly resilient, and not just within religious traditions but within universities as well. Colleges and universities were founded in India during the nineteenth century and academia has expanded enormously since then. Sanskrit, the intellectual language of the ancient and classical civilizations, has been replaced by regional vernaculars or English in most educational settings, and in higher education English predominates. Philosophy is taught by professionals who are, by and large, at least as knowledgeable about the history of Western philosophy as about ancient or classical Indian thought. Nevertheless, what has come to be called Neo-Vedānta is a major intellectual movement on the campuses. There is also a Neo-Vedānta that is more a folk or religious phenomenon. Both types of Neo-Vedānta have complex roots, reflecting in part contemporary Hinduism and healthy traditions of mysticism, in part survival of classical modes of learning, in part Western idealist philosophy and in part deepened scholarly appreciation of classical Indian thought.

Concerning the folk phenomenon, it is probable that all Indian worldviews propounding a mystic goal grew up within traditions marked by the prominence of a spiritual teacher or guru; similar traditions continue today. Within contemporary Hinduism, each guru fashions a heritage from a wealth of prior Indian religious literature (the *Bhagavad Gītā*, Upaniṣads, Purāṇas, stories of the living enlightened, and so on) and, in some cases, from literature of other traditions as well. The best-known spiritual figures, eminently articulate gurus with national and international audiences, such as Swami Vivekananda (1863–1902) and Sri AUROBINDO (1872–1950), are folk Vedāntins in the sense that, without allegiance to a school of classical thought, they draw on the *Bhagavad Gītā* and Upaniṣads and works influenced by classical Vedāntic conceptions. Both of these two great men learned Sanskrit, but, as has become increasingly common, both write in English. Vivekananda defends Vedānta as the plastic philosophy of Hinduism (see RAMAK-RISHNA MOVEMENT); Aurobindo articulates a Brahman-centred worldview which he says is attuned to science but provides a deep explanation of which science, he argues, is incapable.

With regard to the nineteenth and early twentieth centuries, there would be little point in trying to differentiate folk and academic Neo-Vedānta. Although not professional academic teachers of philosophy (a rare thing in India, and indeed the West, at that time), Vivekananda and Aurobindo were well schooled in Western modes of thought. But it is with such broadly important cultural figures as Raja Rammohun Roy (1772–1833), sometimes referred to as the father of modern India, that Vivekananda and Aurobindo have affinity, not with any contemporary professor. Indeed, although Roy was no guru or spiritual leader, he may be taken as the first to articulate in the religious arena a synthesis of Western and Indian views. Among diverse accomplishments, he translated the New Testament into Bengali after learning Greek to read the original text. In ethics, he championed Christianity, urging that Hindus could and should embrace Christian moral teachings without relinquishing their own Vedāntic theological beliefs. In 1828, he founded the Brahmo Samaj (see BRAHMO SAMAJ), a 'church' dedicated to 'the worship and adoration of the Eternal, Unsearchable and Immutable Being, who is the Author and Preserver of the universe' (Roy 1906, vol. 1: 216).

But although having wide influence, Roy, Vivekananda, Aurobindo and other important cultural figures were and are not professional philosophers. Academic Neo-Vedāntins differ markedly from nonprofessionals in ways reflective of a university setting. Sarvepalli RADHAKRISHNAN (1888–1975), the most distinguished to date of these Neo-Vedāntins – President of India (1962–7), Spaulding Professor at Oxford (1936–9), Vice-Chancellor of Benares Hindu University (1939–48), Chancellor of Delhi University (1953–62) and teacher of philosophy at three other Indian institutions – used books and papers on classical systems, heavily peppered with apt comparisons to Western thought, to develop his own views. These are stated forthrightly in *An Idealist View of Life* (1929), but with Radhakrishnan's typically care-

ful scholarship and much attention to forerunners, chiefly Western idealists, but also classical Vedāntins. K.C. Bhattacharyya (1875–1949), professor of philosophy at the University of Calcutta and the teacher of many of the most important philosophers of the next generation, supports several Advaita-like views with tightly constructed arguments and insights expressed in austere, difficult prose. T.M.P. Mahadevan (1911–92), longtime professor of philosophy at the University of Madras, authored literally hundreds of papers and a dozen or so books, principally in exposition of the views of classical Advaitins – often defending Advaita in contemporary terms. More conservative than Radhakrishnan or Bhattacharyya, Mahadevan built bridges to folk traditions by discussing such popular saints as Ramakrishna and Ramana Maharshi. The Neo-Vedānta that these three present is a deep-set movement among philosophy professionals. Several others of similar persuasions deserve mentioning, but this is not the place for a long list.

See also: AWARENESS IN INDIAN THOUGHT; BRAHMAN; HINDU PHILOSOPHY; MONISM, INDIAN

References and further reading

* Bādarāyaṇa (1st–2nd century AD) *Brahmasūtra*, trans. S. Radhakrishnan, *The Brahma Sūtra*, London: Allen & Unwin, 1960. (A translation with extracts from the commentaries of Śaṅkara, Rāmānuja, Madhva and others.)
* *Bhagavad Gītā* (200 BC – AD 200, disputed), trans. F. Edgerton, Harvard Oriental Series 38–9, Cambridge, MA: Harvard University Press, 1944, paperback repr. 1972. (Though Edgerton's interpretive essay – orginally volume 39 in the HOS – too much reflects outworn assumptions of nineteenth-century indologists, his translation is excellent, faithful and elegant. There are, however, dozens of acceptable translations into English and other modern languages.)
Bhattacharyya, K.C. (1956, 1958) *Studies in Philosophy*, ed. G. Bhattacharyya, Calcutta: Progressive Publishers, 2 vols. ('Studies in Vedantism' in volume 1 is a penetrating analysis by the astute philosopher.)
—— (1976) *Search for the Absolute in Neo-Vedanta*, ed. G.B. Burch, Honolulu, HI: University Press of Hawaii. (A collection of three Kantian reflections supporting an Advaita understanding of self; a long introduction by Burch traces influences and themes.)
Dasgupta, S. (1922–55) *A History of Indian Philosophy*, Cambridge: Cambridge University

Press, 5 vols. (Volumes 2–5 are dominated by expositions of varieties of classical Vedānta; volume 1 includes a discussion of the thought of early Upaniṣads as well as Śaṅkara's Advaita; the five volumes are probably still the premier introduction to ancient and classical Indian philosophies.)

Deutsch, E. and Buitenen, J.A.B. van (eds) (1971) *A Source Book of Advaita Vedānta*, Honolulu, HI: University Press of Hawaii. (The editors' introductions are excellent, explaining the positions and context of pre-classical Vedānta and the *Brahmasūtra*, as well as classical Advaita.)

Lacombe, O. (1937) *Absolu selon le Vedānta* (The Absolute According to Vedānta), Paris: Librairie orientaliste Paul Geuthner. (A classic study of the systems of Śaṅkara and Rāmānuja.)

Mahadevan, T.M.P. (1969) *The Philosophy of Beauty*, Bombay: Bharatiya Vidya Bhavan. (A short book that is interesting for Mahadevan's endorsement of the classical Advaita understanding of Brahman on the one hand, and of a criterion of beauty as reflection of Brahman in the terms of temporality and finitude on the other.)

Narain, K. (1962) *An Outline of Madhva Philosophy*, Allahabad: Udayana Publications. (A valuable overview of Madhva's positions, stressing Madhva's opposition to Advaita.)

Potter, K.H. (ed.) (1981) *Encyclopedia of Indian Philosophies*, vol. 3, *Advaita Vedānta*, Princeton, NJ: Princeton University Press. (Contains an excellent introduction to Advaita philosophy, as well as summaries of works in the early Advaita school.)

* Radhakrishnan, S. (1929) *An Idealist View of Life*, London: Allen & Unwin, 2nd edn, 1937. (The last chapter, entitled 'Ultimate Reality', shows the influence of classical Vedānta, as well as Western idealism.)

Raju, P.T. (1953) *Idealist Thought of India*, London: Allen & Unwin. (An excellent survey with many apt Western comparisons in the tradition of Radhakrishnan, who among other folk and academic Neo-Vedāntins is himself discussed.)

* Roy, Raja Rammohun (1906) *The English Works of Raja Rammohun Roy*, ed. J.C. Ghose, Allahabad: Panini Office, 4 vols. (A collection of some of Roy's administrative, political, religious and philosophical writing; the passage in §4 is from 'The Trustdeed of the Brahmo Samaj'.)

Srinivasachari, P.N. (1934) *The Philosophy of Bhedābheda*, Madras: Adyar Library and Research Centre. (Although focused on Bhāskara, this well-written book traces the development of much classical theistic Vedānta; comparisons with Western thought are drawn at the end.)

Thibaut, G. (trans.) (1890) *The Vedānta Sūtras of Bādarāyaṇa, with the Commentary by Śaṅkara*, New York: Dover. (An excellent, highly readable translation of Śaṅkara's principal philosophic work.)

—— (trans.) (1904) *The Vedānta Sūtras of Bādarāyaṇa, with the Commentary by Rāmānuja*, New York: Dover. (An excellent, highly readable translation of Rāmānuja's principal philosophic work.)

* Upaniṣads (800–300 BC), trans. P. Olivelle, *Upaniṣads*, Oxford: Oxford University Press, 1996. (A new translation that may well be the best; readable and accurate.)

Vallooran, A.D. (1988) *In Search of the Absolute*, Shillong: Vendrame Institute. (A critical study of the Advaita philosophy of T.M.P. Mahadevan.)

STEPHEN H. PHILLIPS

VENN, JOHN (1834–1923)

John Venn was a British symbolic logician and methodologist of science. He is known for having invented the method of Venn diagrams for judging the validity of categorical syllogisms and for advocating the 'compartmental' conception of categorical propositions which they display. He strongly defended Boole's algebraic methods in logic by giving them clear logical meanings. He provided the first systematic formulation of the frequency theory of probability, and he showed the uncertainties inherent in the use of J.S. Mill's inductive methods.

Venn was born in Drypool, Hull. A member of Gonville and Caius College, he graduated from Cambridge in 1857. He became college lecturer in moral science at Cambridge in 1862 and worked for thirty years on problems in symbolic logic and the methodology of science. He turned later to biographical and antiquarian topics related to his family and college, of which he was President from 1903 until his death.

Venn is best known as the creator of the method of Venn diagrams for testing categorical syllogisms (see LOGIC MACHINES AND DIAGRAMS §3). Two features of Venn's method are especially important. The first is that it is not limited to three classes. He was, in fact, remarkably adept at using Venn diagrams to test arguments involving four or even five class terms. The second feature is that these diagrams graphically represent Venn's analysis of categorical propositions. Venn detected three types of analysis of categorical propositions in the logical tradition: the predicational view ('all *X* are *Y*'), the class inclusional and exclusional view ('the class of *X*s is included in the class of *Y*s'), and the compartmental or existential view ('the class of things that are *X* and non-*Y* is empty'). Venn adopted the latter conception, and this is precisely what is shown by Venn diagrams. His use of the compartmental view was based on its convenience rather than its ultimate truth. While a 'complete Theory of Logic' would require that one give the '*true* account', his own goal was to find the most convenient logical methods.

Venn's most important work, *Symbolic Logic* (1881), was a spirited defence of Boole's algebraic techniques for logic in the face of the modifications which Jevons, Peirce and others had made in the preceding decades; (see BOOLE, G.; BOOLEAN ALGEBRA). Of Boole's use of inverse operations – subtraction as the inverse of class union and division as the inverse of class intersection – the latter caused most controversy. Boole had claimed that the use of division gave rise to uninterpretable formulas, but thought this acceptable as long as the end results of logical calculations were interpretable. Jevons and others, though, claimed that such a mysterious sign should be dropped from logic entirely. Venn strongly defended its retention, holding that by dropping it, 'nearly everything which is most characteristic and attractive in the system is thrown away' (1881: xxviii).

Venn's project, then, was to reinstate Boole's original techniques by allowing division. Contrary to Boole, though, he believed that the formulas which resulted from using division could be given clear logical meanings. On his view, 'x/y' stands for any class which is such that the intersection of x/y and y is identical with x. This will obtain only when all x is y (that is, $x = xy$). Furthermore, there will usually be many classes which have this characteristic. Thus 'x/y' stands for a one–many partial function of x and y. This explanation allowed Venn to give a logical explanation of many of the otherwise puzzling formulas in Boole's logic.

Venn was also concerned with the logic of science. In *The Logic of Chance* (1866), he rejected the commonly held view that probability theory deals with degrees ('gradations') of belief. He presented, instead, the first systematic formulation of the frequency theory of probability, in which probability assertions are empirical assertions about the frequency with which types of events will happen in the long run. Venn realized that the relationship between probability in this sense and other uses of the word 'probability' remained puzzling. The probability of single events seems undefined, as is the probability that an empirical frequency may give to a hypothesis

concerning a long-run frequency (see PROBABILITY THEORY AND EPISTEMOLOGY).

Venn presented a systematic analysis of scientific method in *The Principles of Empirical or Inductive Logic* (1889). While heavily influenced by Mill, he found Mill's inductive methods to be uncertain (see MILL, J.S. §5). Applying Mill's methods to scientific problems requires far more knowledge than scientists normally have. This criticism reflects the strongly empiricist, even sceptical, mode of thought which characterized Venn's work.

See also: LOGIC IN THE NINETEENTH CENTURY §3

List of works

Venn, J. (1866) *The Logic of Chance*, London: Macmillan, 3rd edn, 1888. (The first systematic formulation of the frequency theory of probability.)

—— (1881) *Symbolic Logic*, London: Macmillan, 2nd edn, 1894; repr. New York: Chelsea Publishing Company, 1971. (A survey of the symbolic logic of Venn's time and defence of Boole's original notation and methods.)

—— (1889) *The Principles of Empirical or Inductive Logic*, London: Macmillan, 2nd edn, 1907. (A systematic analysis of scientific method, based upon, yet critical of, Mill's inductive methods.)

References and further reading

Copi, I. and Cohen, C. (1994) *Introduction to Logic*, New York: Macmillan, 9th edn, 235–42, 251–61. (An introduction to Venn diagrams in a standard textbook.)

Keynes, J.M. (1921) *A Treatise on Probability*, London: Macmillan, 92–110. (An incisive critique of Venn's frequency theory.)

Passmore, J.A. (1957) *A Hundred Years of Philosophy*, London: Duckworth, 134–7. (A brief discussion of Venn's work.)

DANIEL D. MERRILL

VERIFICATION PRINCIPLE
see LOGICAL POSITIVISM; MEANING AND VERIFICATION

VERIFICATION THEORY OF MEANING *see* MEANING AND VERIFICATION

VERNIA, NICOLETTO (d. 1499)

Nicoletto Vernia was a celebrated Aristotelian philosopher during the second half of the fifteenth century. His acquaintances included such personalities as Ermolao Barbaro, Giovanni Pico della Mirandola, Pietro Pomponazzi and Agostino Nifo. His special interests were in natural philosophy and psychology, but he also revealed interests in logic. Although usually characterized as a rigid Averroist, he moved from a clear commitment to Averroes as the true interpreter of Aristotle to a preference for the Greek commentators, especially Themistius and Simplicius. Nonetheless, throughout his career he also maintained a noteworthy interest in Albert the Great. After first attempting to conciliate Albert with Averroes as much as possible, he later attempted to conciliate Albert with the Greek commentators. He was one of the first Renaissance Aristotelians to use the commentary on Aristotle's On the Soul that is attributed to Simplicius, and also to cite Plato, Plotinus and their translator and expositor, Marsilio Ficino.

1 **Life and works**
2 **Logical issues**
3 **Natural philosophy**
4 **Psychology**

1 Life and works

Nicoletto Vernia, a native of Chieti, studied at Padua with Cajetan of Thiene (Gaetano da Thiene) and Paul of Pergola. Around 1467–8 he spent a year at Pavia studying the *Calculationes* of Richard Swineshead (see OXFORD CALCULATORS), most likely with Giovanni Marliani. After his return to Padua he took the chair of Cajetan of Thiene in 1468. In his early writings he consistently states that Averroes (see IBN RUSHD) gives the true interpretation of ARISTOTLE. What is striking is that he regularly attempts to reconcile Averroes and ALBERT THE GREAT. In 1489 Pietro Barozzi, Bishop of Padua, issued a decree which forbade lecturing on the unity of the intellect according to Averroes and accused Vernia of having filled Italy with this error. Although Vernia submitted to the decree, it appears from the marginal annotations dating from 1487 and 1489 in his copies of Aristotle and John of Jandun that he already had

doubts about the philosophical viability of the doctrine of the unity of the intellect, and had begun to study the Greek commentators on Aristotle, especially ALEXANDER OF APHRODISIAS, THEMISTIUS and SIMPLICIUS (see ARISTOTLE COMMENTATORS). That interest in the Commentators, which may reflect the influence of Ermolao Barbaro and Giovanni PICO DELLA MIRANDOLA, is obvious in his posthumously published questions against the 'perverse doctrine' of the unity of the intellect (*Contra perversam Averrois opinionem*) (dated 1492, but published posthumously in 1504). In that work, Vernia uses Marsilio FICINO and reconciles Albert the Great with Themistius and Simplicius. Basing himself in particular on Simplicius, he proposes that Plato and Aristotle hold the same doctrine, and differ only in words. Throughout his life Vernia seems to have had an irascible side that on occasion led to the expression of hostility towards others.

2 Logical issues

Vernia was one of the Renaissance Aristotelians who discussed the nature of a so-called most powerful, or absolute, demonstration (*demonstratio potissima*) and the sources of its premises. Such a demonstration was considered to provide perfect causal knowledge of some effect. Vernia explains that after resolution of the information provided by sense experience into a preliminary and imperfect universal knowledge there is a movement of the intellect (*negotiatio intellectus*) that seeks the cause of the effect being studied and that establishes the premises that produce the desired demonstrative or apodictic knowledge (see ZABARELLA, J. §5).

In his treatise on the division of the sciences (1482a), Vernia states that while the dialectical syllogism concerns the probable, the probable includes necessary things as well as contingent things. Even natural philosophers, mathematicians and metaphysicians can be considered to study the probable. In his question on whether medicine is more excellent than civil law (1482b), he maintains that medicine, subalternated to natural philosophy, demonstrates and knows that it is doing so, whereas law rests on the authority of the learned and is subalternated to politics, a science lower than natural philosophy. At best law achieves the dialectical habit of mind that prepares for demonstration.

3 Natural philosophy

In a question on the subject of natural philosophy (1480), Vernia pays Thomas Aquinas great respect but argues against the view of the Angelic Doctor that mobile being (*ens mobile*), which might include angels, is the subject of natural philosophy. He takes the true interpretation of Aristotle to be that of Averroes, whom he presents as holding mobile body (*corpus mobile*) to be the subject of natural science (*scientia naturalis*). He attacked such earlier writers as John Canonicus and Antonius Andreas for not speaking in a natural fashion when they appeal to the motion of angels in order to discredit Aristotle's natural philosophy (see CAJETAN §3).

In his early *De gravibus et levibus* (On Things Heavy and Light) (before 1476), Vernia examines the problem whether heavy and light inanimate things move locally by themselves or by virtue of something else, once the factor preventing (*prohibens*) motion is removed. He argues that Averroes' position on the question is the correct reading of Aristotle. He emphatically rejects as 'theologizers' (*theologizantes*) those who maintain that the quality of heaviness (*gravitas*) moves objects as a primary and principal agent, arguing from transubstantiation in the Eucharist that the heaviness of the consecrated host moves downwards even though that heaviness is separated from the substance of the bread. In like fashion, he rejects all appeals to God's absolute power (*potentia absoluta*) when discussing questions of natural philosophy.

A particular target of his attack is the position that explains the motion of a projectile not by air pushing behind it but rather by an impetus (*impetus*) imparted to the projectile. Vernia considers this view to deviate from Aristotle and truth. In contrast, he attempts to reconcile Averroes and Albert the Great on the topic, maintaining that when two such excellent philosophers agree, no one of sound mind should doubt that this is the mind of Aristotle.

4 Psychology

In an early work that he calls the *Question on the Unity of the Intellect* but never published, Vernia discusses whether the human soul is eternal and one in number for all humans or whether it is united in existence to the human body as a true substantial form. His announced purpose is threefold: (1) to set forth the doctrine of Plato; (2) to present what Aristotle held according to his most famous Greek and Arab commentators; and (3) to examine the Latin commentators and the truth of the Catholic faith. His brief summary of Plato's doctrine of the soul is culled from Albert the Great and Calcidius' translation of *Timaeus* 41 A–D (see PLATO §§4, 13). In the second part, he presents and defends Averroes' doctrine of the unity of the intellect (namely that all human beings share one intellect) as the true interpretation of

Aristotle. In the third part he attacks Albert, Aquinas and DUNS SCOTUS for teaching that there are many intellective souls which are created by God, since Aristotle did not admit creation. To attribute to Aristotle the thesis of creation would be to hold that he maintained an infinite number of intellective souls infused in an infinite number of bodies, but this is false. Moreover, he rejects the accounts of individuation held by Aquinas and Duns Scotus, namely individuation through the soul's relation to a body and individuation through 'thisness' (*haecceitas*). He also characterizes Aquinas' and Duns Scotus' insistence that the human being cannot have a direct vision of God during this life as false according to Aristotle.

Subsequently Vernia changed his mind completely and wrote questions, dated 1492 but published posthumously in 1504, against Averroes' doctrine of the unity of the intellect. In the first part he again relies on Albert the Great when presenting Plato. But he now quotes Plato's *Timaeus* 41 A–D in the translation of Marsilio Ficino. In the second part, he rejects Averroes' doctrine of the unity of the intellect, basing himself on what he takes to be the common doctrine of the Greek commentators, namely Theophrastus, Alexander of Aphrodisias, Themistius and Simplicius. His misreading of Alexander as a proponent of the immortality of the soul is also to be found in Giovanni Pico della Mirandola, and was later strenuously attacked by his former student, Agostino Nifo.

Vernia maintained that Aristotle held the intellective soul to be multiplied according to the number of bodies. He even claims, citing Simplicius, that any disagreement between Plato and Aristotle is only verbal, since both maintain that the intellective soul was created by God from all eternity and therefore pre-exists the body. Only subsequently is the soul infused into a body as its substantial form; at death it will return to the dwelling place of a star. Vernia attributes to Aristotle Plato's doctrine that knowledge is recollection from a prior existence. Vernia's psychological thought thus evolved from a strict adherence to Averroes to a commitment to the Greek Commentators, and to an interest in Plato and Plotinus as known through the translations and comments of Ficino.

See also: ARISTOTELIANISM, RENAISSANCE; AVERROISM; NATURAL PHILOSOPHY, MEDIEVAL

List of works

Vernia, N. (before 1476) *Quaestio de gravibus et levibus* (Question on Things Heavy and Light), in

Cajetan of Thiene, *Expositio in libros Aristotelis De coelo et mundo*, ed. N. Vernia, Padua: Magister Bonus. (Vernia considers the question whether inanimate objects move locally by themselves or due to something else to be the most difficult question in physics. An impetus given to air and not to the body is the cause of the body's motion.)

—— (1480 or earlier) *Utrum anima intellectiva humano corpore unita tanquam vera forma substantialis dans ei esse specificum substantiale eterna atque unica sit in omnibus hominibus* (Whether the Intellective Soul is United to the Human Body as a True Substantial Form or is Eternal and One in All Humans). (Vernia's *Question on the Unity of the Intellect*; available in a single manuscript held at the Biblioteca Nazionale San Marco (Marciana) in Venice (see Pagallo 1964). Averroes' doctrine of the unity of the intellect is presented as the true mind of Aristotle. Albert the Great, Aquinas and Duns Scotus are criticized for attempting to prove that each human being has an individual intellective soul.)

—— (1480) *Quaestio an ens mobile sit totius naturalis philosophiae subiectum* (Question whether Mobile Being is the Subject of All Natural Philosophy), in Giles of Rome and Marsilius of Inghen, commentaries on Aristotle's *On Generation and Corruption*, ed. N. Vernia, Padua: Joannes Herbort. (Completed at Padua in 1480. Averroes' position, that mobile body is the subject of natural science, is the true interpretation of Aristotle.)

—— (1482 or earlier) *Utrum sint ponendae rationes seminales in materia respectu rerum quae ex ipsa generantur* (Whether Seminal Reasons are to be Posited in Matter with Respect to the Things Generated from It), in E.P. Mahoney, 'Nicoletto Vernia's Question on Seminal Reasons', *Franciscan Studies* 38 (1978): 299–309. (Vernia presents and then rebuts twenty arguments against seminal reasons.)

—— (1482a) *De divisione philosophiae* (On the Division of Philosophy), in W. Burley, *Expositio in libros octo de physico auditu*, ed. N. Vernia, Venice: Joannes Herbort, 1482. (Vernia shows special interest in Themistius in the translation of Ermolao Barbaro.)

—— (1482b) *Quaestio an medicina nobilior atque praestantior sit iure civili* (Question whether Medicine is More Noble and Distinguished than Civil Law), in E. Garin (ed.) *La disputa delle arti nel Quattrocento*, Florence: Vallecchi, 1947, 111–23. (Completed in 1482 and first published with the *De divisione philosophiae*. Medicine as theory or science consciously uses demonstrative reasoning and is subalternated to natural philosophy; law rests on authority and is subalternated to politics. Medicine is therefore superior.)

—— (1492) *Contra perversam Averrois opinionem de unitate intellectus et de animae felicitate quaestiones divinae* (Divine Questions Against the Perverse Opinion of Averroes on the Unity of the Intellect and the Felicity of the Soul), in Albert of Saxony, *Acutissimae quaestiones super libros de physica auscultatione*, Venice: Alexander Calcedonius and Jacobus Pentius, 1504. (Vernia now takes Averroes to have erred regarding Aristotle on the soul and intellect. The Greek commentators disagree with Averroes on the unity of the intellect. Philosophical arguments can be given for the creation of individual souls by God. Plato and Aristotle can be reconciled.)

References and further reading

Kessler, E. (1994) 'Nicoletto Vernia oder die Rettung eines Averroisten' (Nicoletto Vernia or the Deliverance of an Averroist), in F. Niewöhner and L. Sturlese (eds) *Averroismus im Mittelalter und in der Renaissance*, Zurich: Spur, 269–90. (Accepts that Vernia's abandonment of Averroes' doctrine of the unity of the intellect resulted from studying the Greek commentators and not from fear of Church authorities. Underscores influence of humanism.)

Mahoney, E.P. (1968) 'Nicoletto Vernia and Agostino Nifo on Alexander of Aphrodisias: An Unnoticed Dispute', *Rivista critica di storia della filosofia* 20: 268–96. (Examines in detail Vernia's argument that Alexander taught the immortality of the soul and Nifo's critique of this argument.)

—— (1976) 'Nicoletto Vernia on the Soul and Immortality', in E.P. Mahoney (ed.) *Philosophy and Humanism: Renaissance Essays in Honor of Paul Oskar Kristeller*, New York: Columbia University Press, Leiden: Brill, 144–63. (Examines Vernia's early treatise in favour of Averroes' doctrine of the unity of the intellect and his later work attacking that doctrine.)

—— (1983) 'Philosophy and Science in Nicoletto Vernia and Agostino Nifo', in A. Poppi (ed.) *Scienza e filosofia all'Università di Padova nel quattrocento*, Contributi alla storia dell'Università di Padova 15, Padua: Lint, 135–202. (Contains details on Vernia's various treatises, their dating and their contents. Impact of the Greek commentators delineated.)

—— (1986) 'Marsilio Ficino's Influence on Nicoletto Vernia, Agostino Nifo and Marcantonio Zimara', in G.C. Garfagnini (ed.) *Marsilio Ficino e il ritorno di Platone: Studi e documenti*, vol. 2, Florence:

Olschki, 509–31. (Shows how Vernia came to use Ficino and his translations in his late thought.)

—— (1991) 'Nicoletto Vernia's Annotations on John of Jandun's *De anima*', in B. Mojsisch and O. Pluta (eds) *Historia philosophiae medii aevi: Studien zur Geschichte der Philosophie des Mittelalters*, Amsterdam: Grüner, 573–93. (Discusses Vernia's annotations in his copies of Aristotle and Jandun's *De anima* that date from the late 1480s and reveal his rejection of the unity of the intellect and his preference for the Greek commentators.)

Nardi, B. (1958) *Saggi sull'aristotelismo padovano dal secolo XIV al XVI* (Essays on Paduan Aristotelianism from the 14th to the 16th Century), Università degli Studi di Padova: Studi sulla tradizione aristotelica nel Veneto 1, Florence: Sansoni, 95–126, 153–65, 284–7, 323–4. (Stresses the less admirable side of Vernia's personality but gives some attention to his career and his works and thought.)

Pagallo, G.F. (1964) 'Sull'autore (Nicoletto Vernia?) di un'anonima e inedita quaestio sull'anima del secolo XV [Venezia, Bibl. Naz., Lat. VI, 105 (=2656)]' (On the Author of an Anonymous and Unedited Question on the Soul of the 15th Century), in *La filosofia della natura nel medioevo: Atti del Terzo Congresso Internazionale di Filosofia Medioevale*, Milan: Società Editrice Vita e Pensiero, 670–82. (Establishes Vernia's authorship of an anonymous treatise that presents a strongly Averroist interpretation of Aristotle on the soul.)

—— (1983) 'Di un'inedita "Expositio" di Nicoletto Vernia "In posteriorum librum priorem"' (On an Unedited 'Expositio' of Nicoletto Vernia 'On the Prior Book of the *Posterior Analytics*'), in L. Olivieri (ed.) *Aristotelismo veneto e scienza moderna: Atti del 25° anno accademico del Centro per la Storia della Tradizione Aristotelica nel Veneto*, vol. 2, Padua: Antenore. (Important analysis of unpublished lectures by Vernia on Aristotle's *Posterior Analytics*. Expresses high regard for Themistius and conciliates Plato and Aristotle.)

Ragnisco, P. (1891) *Nicoletto Vernia: Studi storici sulla filosofia padovana nella 2a metà del secolo decimoquinto* (Historical Studies on Paduan Philosophy in the Second Half of the 15th Century), Atti del Reale Istituto Veneto di scienze, lettere ed arti, 7th series, vol. 2. (Only general work on Vernia, it remains a useful study.)

Vasoli, C. (1968) *Studi sulla cultura del Rinascimento* (Studies on Renaissance Culture), Manduria: Lacaita Editore, 241–56. (Discusses Vernia's conception of nature and physical science.)

EDWARD P. MAHONEY

VIA NEGATIVA *see* NEGATIVE THEOLOGY

VICES *see* VIRTUES AND VICES

VICO, GIAMBATTISTA (1668–1744)

Vico lived in a period in which the successes of the natural sciences were frequently attributed to the Cartesian method of a priori demonstration. His own first interest, however, was in the cultivation of the humanist values of wisdom and prudence, to which this method was irrelevant. Initially, therefore, he sought a methodology for these values in the techniques of persuasion and argument used in political and legal oratory. But he soon came to believe that the Cartesian method was too limited to explain even the advances in the natural sciences and developed an alternative constructivist theory of knowledge by which to establish the degree of certainty of the different sciences. Wisdom and prudence, however, came low on this scale.

Through certain historical studies in law, he became convinced that, although there were no eternal and universal standards underlying law at all times and places, the law appropriate to any specific historical age was dependent upon an underlying developmental pattern of social consciousness and institutions common to all nations except the Jews after the Fall. His New Science *(1725, 1730 and 1744) was a highly original attempt to establish this pattern, originating in a primeval mythic consciousness and concluding in a fully rational, but ultimately corrupt, consciousness. He believed that knowledge of the pattern would enable us to interpret a wide range of historical evidence to provide continuous and coherent accounts of the histories of all actual gentile nations. The primacy of consciousness in the pattern led him to claim that there must be a necessary sequence of ideas upon which institutions rested, which would provide the key to the historical interpretation of meaning in all the different gentile languages. He supported this conception by extensive comparative anthropological, linguistic and historical enquiries, resulting most famously in his interpretation of the Homeric poems. He also advanced a more developed account of his earlier theory of knowledge, in which the work of philosopher and historian were mutually necessary, to show how this conception of 'scientific history' was to be achieved.*

Vico believed that the knowledge that wisdom and prudence vary in different historical ages in accordance with an underlying pattern could provide us with a higher insight into those of our own age and enable us to avoid a collapse into barbarism which, in an over rational age in which religious belief must decline, was more or less inevitable. Unfortunately, the metaphysical status of his pattern rendered this impossible. Much of his thought was expressed in a context of theological assumptions which conflict with important aspects of his work. This has given rise to continuous controversy over his personal and theoretical commitment to these assumptions. Despite this, however, his conceptions of the historical development of societies, of the relation between ideas and institutions, of social anthropology, comparative linguistics and of the philosophical and methodological aspects of historical enquiry in general, remain profoundly fruitful.

1 Life
2 Early thought
3 Early thought (continued)
4 The *New Science*: structure and contents
5 The *New Science*: structure and contents (continued)
6 Theory of historical knowledge
7 Ultimate doubts
8 Influence

1 Life

Vico was born in Naples. His erratic early education included grammar, the Latin classics and philosophy. In 1684 he began to study for a practising career in law but he abandoned this in 1686 when he became tutor to the children of a wealthy family at Vatolla near Salerno. The years 1686–95 represent his only prolonged absence from Naples. In his *Autobiography* (1725, 1728, 1731) this is presented as a period of isolation from the lively intellectual life of Naples whereas, in fact, he remained in contact with it through membership of certain private societies and salons which had arisen to counteract the conservative influence of the Church and university. Through an intensive, self-directed course of study in the excellent library at Vatolla, he became acquainted with the thought of Plato and the Neoplatonists, the classical atomists such as Democritus and Lucretius, physicists such as Galileo and Gassendi, English thinkers such as Francis Bacon, Hobbes, Locke and Boyle and the rationalists, Descartes, Malebranche, Spinoza and Leibniz. By the end of this period he had acquired an encyclopedic, if idiosyncratic, understanding of the worlds of ancient and modern learning. The activities of the Inquisition make it difficult to be certain of his religious sentiments. Many of his friends were suspected of being atheists

and it is sometimes thought, on the evidence of a Lucretian poem written in 1692, that he may have been an atheist at this time.

In 1694 he took his doctorate in law at Salerno and in 1699 he was appointed to the poorly paid Chair of Rhetoric at the University of Naples. Married in the same year, he subsequently had eight children and was constantly beset with financial problems which forced him to augment his income by the composition of official orations and histories. In 1723 he failed to gain the prestigious Chair of Civil Law. Abandoning hope of personal advancement, he turned to the construction of the philosophy for which he is most famous, developing it progressively in the various versions of his *New Science* (1725 onwards). Much of our knowledge of his intense intellectual life is derived from the first and second parts of his *Autobiography*, written soon after the production of the first and second editions of the *New Science*. A third part, going up to his death, was later added by the Marquis of Villarosa. He remained a leading figure in Naples for the rest of his life, retiring from his Chair only three years before his death.

2 Early thought

Vico's primary aim was to show how philosophy could contribute to an understanding of the nature of wisdom and prudence in all their manifestations, personal, civil and political. This is evident from his earliest thought, expressed in *Six Inaugural Orations* given between 1699 and 1707, in which he argued that wisdom and prudence could be understood only through a study of the entire world of learning, human and divine. To justify the possibility of success he drew upon a Neoplatonic conception of the human mind as the image of God (see NEOPLATO-NISM). Just as God knows the world of his creation because he is active throughout that world, mind is the active incorporeal component in the cognitive, emotional and sensitive abilities required for the acquisition of knowledge. He supported the theological assumptions of this position by a series of Cartesian arguments: the *Cogito* and the causal and ontological proofs of God's existence (see DESCARTES, R. §§5, 6). But his conclusion, that we have been given all that the discovery of truth and virtue requires, rendered problematic why success should prove so elusive. In the sixth of his *Six Inaugural Orations* he therefore introduced a historical theory, drawn from the Bible, emphasizing our moral and intellectual corruption after the Fall. Dispersed throughout the world, the gentile nations have lost the languages, beliefs and inclinations necessary to reach the truth. What is needed, therefore, is a study of the world of human learning, ancient and modern, in order to establish the correct method to regain it. This is to be achieved by the development of wisdom, eloquence and prudence through an educational programme which respects a natural order of psychological development.

The metaphysical theory of mind played an important part in Vico's next two works. The first, *On the Study Methods of Our Time* (1709), clearly influenced by Francis BACON, was an ambitious attempt to carry out the programme of the sixth of his *Six Inaugural Orations*. Vico's conclusion is that while there have been major advances in modern geometry, mechanics and physics, not all of these have the certainty claimed for them. They have, however, been influential in a loss of interest in the methods of education required for the successful conduct of social and political life because their advance has mistakenly been attributed to the Cartesian demonstrative method (see DESCARTES, R.). But the only field of knowledge in which demonstration can produce certainty is geometry, the elements of which are human constructions. This is the first indication of Vico's constructivist theory of knowledge: that we can know fully only what we have made. Accordingly, although geometrical truths are required for the construction of physical theory, physics cannot achieve similar certainty because of its indispensable need for empirical experiment. At best it can claim verisimilitude. Demonstration is even less appropriate for the wisdom and prudence required in social and political life, because of the ineliminable influence of choice and chance. What is required here is a method for the development of sound judgment in human affairs. This existed in the classical art of topics, which was a body of categories and argumentative procedures used by lawyers to reach judgments in matters of fact and right in everyday life. But since this art is beyond the reach of the masses, who are ruled more by emotion than judgment, politicians must also master the ancient art of eloquence so that they can persuade the masses to adopt the practices recommended by the judgments reached through topics.

3 Early thought (continued)

Vico's next work, *On the Most Ancient Wisdom of the Italians Unearthed from the Origins of the Latin Language* (1710), was intended as a three-part treatise on metaphysics, physics and ethics. Only the first part was completed and published but the constructivist elements in his thought were now made quite explicit. The metaphysical thesis remains in the conception of a God who knows the metaphysical Forms on which the physical world is modelled because he creates

them. We, made in the image of God, can also know what we create. This is expressed in Vico's *verum-factum* theory: the true is convertible with the made. The true is thus relativized to the mode of mental construction. To this, however, Vico now added the Aristotelian view that knowledge is of causes, which he treated as meaning that knowledge is possible only where we are responsible for the whole construction, including its most primitive elements. Since God contains eminently the elements of everything within himself, what he knows is both true and real. As part of God's world, we cannot attain such completeness. Nevertheless, through our ability to abstract from God's creation, we can create such fictive elements as mathematical points and lines and from these construct theorems that are true but fictive. Beyond mathematics, however, the sciences become less certain as their subject matter becomes less amenable to the application of mathematically based theory. Hence, mathematics remains the most certain science, followed by mechanics and physics. Human behaviour, governed by caprice and emotion, remains the least certain of all. Here again, the art of topics is required.

This constructivist theory enabled Vico to reject his earlier Cartesian arguments. We cannot start from *Cogito* since, not knowing how mind is made, we can have certainty – that is, the mere inability to doubt – of our existence, but not full causal knowledge of our mode of existence. Nor can we demonstrate the existence of God since any such demonstration would require us to create him. Possibly realizing the difficulty which this claim created for knowledge of his metaphysical theory of the human mind, Vico left knowledge of God to faith and revelation.

The transition to his mature philosophy was occasioned by a close study of Grotius' *The Law of War and Peace* in 1717 (see GROTIUS). Grotius' purpose was to justify a system of international law by arguing philosophically and historically that it was an extension of a rationality existent universally in the natural law of nations. This gave Vico an insight into a way in which philosophy, which is concerned with the universal, could contribute to an understanding of the nature of the human world. But he advanced two general criticisms of Grotius. First, he had failed to recognize the metaphysical importance of God and the historical importance of the Fall. Second, his historical treatment of law lacked sound principles of historical interpretation, leading to anachronistic accounts of ancient law which assimilated it to that of his own civilized times. Criticism of the historical accounts of other political theorists, particularly HOBBES, PUFENDORF and SELDEN, confirmed Vico's belief that a sound method was required to show how a rational system of law could have developed historically from the Lucretian-style brutes with whom, it was generally agreed, history began (see LUCRETIUS).

His first attempt at such a system came in two large works, *On the One Beginning and One End of Universal Law* (1720) and *On the Constancy of the Jurisprudent* (1721), the second of which was divided into a philosophical and a philological or historical part. The metaphysical theory of human nature still remained, now as the basis for a deduction of the virtues of prudence, temperance and courage and, thence, the authority of law over property, liberty and wardship. The theory of the Fall was also retained to support the idea that the historical state of law (the 'certain') is never purely contingent and unjustifiable because it incorporates a partial and developing degree of rationality left within us after the Fall, the end product of which will be the full development of the concepts of truth and equity.

Vico first tried to give these claims historical support by showing that the history of Roman law could be read in this way, but he soon realized that their universal character could be demonstrated historically only by showing that they applied to the histories of all nations. His attempt to do this, however, in *On the Constancy of the Jurisprudent*, revealed to him that the law of a nation could not be treated in isolation from other fundamental aspects of its life. Hence, in the various versions of the *New Science*, he engaged in the enormous task of showing that there was a common pattern to the development of all the major facets of the histories of the nations. The one exception which he carefully allowed was Jewish history, in order to respect the Biblical account of the Fall.

4 The *New Science*: structure and contents

The *New Science* exists in three editions, written in 1725, 1730 and 1744. The *First New Science* (1725) and *Second New Science* (1730), as they are called, are structurally very different. The *Third New Science* (1744) was an attempt to incorporate into the text of the *Second New Science* many additions and improvements developed after its publication. Since it would be impossible here to treat each separately, what follows is an overview of Vico's main doctrines.

The *New Science* offers an account both of the philosophical foundations, ontological and epistemological, required for an understanding of history and partial demonstrations of certain actual histories. The central ontological claim is that all (gentile) nations share a common nature which is exhibited to a greater or lesser degree in their actual histories in so far as they are affected by different external contingencies. This nature has two fundamental features. First, it is essentially sociable, expressing itself in a holistic network of cultural and institutional creations. Second, it is essentially developmental. The seeds of justice and truth left within the gentile nations after the Fall are the causes of a development of culture and society, as we pass from an original, nonrational, mythic consciousness to a rational consciousness which is the fulfilment of human nature. Thereafter, however, civilization descends into a state of intellectual and moral depravity, the 'barbarism of reflection', from which it can be saved only by a return to something like the conditions after the Fall and a recurrence of the whole sequence. In its unactualized form this sequence is an 'ideal eternal history', tracing the career of a nation were it governed only by its internal nature. But since the actual histories of nations are affected by many contingent factors, involving physical causes such as geographical conditions, disease, famine or war, there will be no perfect exemplifications of the 'ideal eternal history'. All actual histories will nevertheless be recognizable variants of it. This conception undoubtedly owes something to the influence of Neoplatonism.

Vico gives two reasons for demonstrating that there is such a universal and necessary pattern. First, that its existence proves that there is a Providence which influences human affairs and, hence, that there is a God in whom we should believe. Second, that since it will end in a state of anarchy, an understanding of its underlying causes will enable us to avert ultimate disaster.

5 The *New Science*: structure and contents (continued)

The sequence offered involves three stages of cultural, social and political development, the 'poetic' or 'theological', the 'heroic' and the 'human' ages. The main structure of this process follows the natural order of psychological development worked out in Vico's earlier writings, now, however, taken as psychosocial principles of development. They issue in forms of a 'common sense', or sets of fundamental beliefs about the world, shared by classes within the nation or by the whole nation, which govern the culture and institutions of their age.

The poetic age is the product of the most primitive kind of human being, a brutish, egoistic creature, lacking reason but endowed with huge ideographic imaginative powers, through which is created the first primeval image of the world as a vast animate being, or God. Fear of this God and his children, who successively come into existence as imagistic ways of conceiving new social necessities, dominates every aspect of the culture and institutions of the age, giving rise to the practices of sacrifice and divination and thence to the political supremacy of the priestly classes. As mediators of the divine will, the latter acquire a semi-divine status through which they become the first kings, while law comes into existence as the means of protecting God's mediated ownership. The basis of all this, however, is our primitive capacity to create through imagination and to believe that which is created as literal truth. This is Vico's theory of myth as *vera narratio*: that what has come down to later ages as imaginative fiction was, in its origin, taken as literal truth. Accordingly, the key to understanding the poetic age depends upon taking myths as literal expressions of the way in which the physical and human world was seen and believed. These basic principles also underlie the morality, politics, geography and history of the age. Much of Vico's own account of the character of this age is dependent upon his highly original interpretation of the Homeric poems as later compilations of these original myths.

The 'heroic' age is that in which the kings, through a sequence of traceable steps, progressively lose their unique status. There are two reasons why this occurs. First, because of their corrupt nature, they abuse their powers to the extent that, in order to defend themselves against their subjects, they form political associations with other kings ('aristocratic republics') which weaken their original monarchical status. Second, their increasingly rational subjects realize the falsity of the claim to semi-divine status upon which their privileged political status depends. Thereafter, it is a question of challenging the legal conceptions which their claim to divine origin can no longer justify until, ultimately, a new form of political organization is required, resting upon new conceptions of humanity and justice.

In the 'human' age these developments reach their 'acme'. The seeds of truth in our original imperfect nature have now developed into a full understanding of the truth: that equity is the supreme and proper principle of law, that human customs should be informed by our sense of civil duty and that governments should be based upon the principle of equality under the law. The human age is not, however, in all ways superior to the earlier ages. One of Vico's fundamental principles is that imagination weakens as reason strengthens. Accordingly, although theologians and philosophers can now prove the truths of (Christian) religion, they cannot implant in the general public that degree of instinctive belief which arose when God was a product of the primeval human imagination and which once held together whole communities. Thus, the highest stage of human

rationality is also the start of a rapid period of moral corruption which will destroy the customs and institutions necessary for the maintenance of social and political order and lead to a new poetic age. Hence, the course of nations will be succeeded by a recourse such as had occurred in feudal Europe, Vico claimed, after the fall of Rome, in which he descried many parallels with the life of early Rome.

Although the 'ideal eternal history' outlines the above sequence, in his more detailed explanations of its character Vico makes extensive reference to the operation of certain 'natural' principles or 'necessities of nature'. These are largely certain psychological and psycho-social propensities which belong to us by nature. They are therefore aspects of a 'metaphysics of the human mind' which, he claims, is fundamental to his theory. They are used to explain the development of language from the gestures proper to the first poets to the articulated verbal language of the rational age, the parallel developments of ideas from the ideographic images of the poets to the abstract ideas of rational beings and the development of the institutional systems which presuppose them. The fact that the sequence from imagination to reason is itself classified as a 'natural necessity' shows that it is not correct, as is sometimes argued, to see the 'ideal eternal history', or its exemplifications, as an account of the self-development and subsequent decay of the imagination alone. Despite its undoubted importance in Vico's conception of human nature, his 'imagination' is not the self-transcending imagination of the great Romantics. Rather, it is an imagination which operates according to certain principles of human nature, some of which are most fully explained in *On the Most Ancient Wisdom of the Italians Unearthed from the Origins of the Latin Language.*

This naturalizing tendency in Vico's account of the basis of the 'ideal eternal history' raises vexed questions about the sincerity of his claim to have proved the influence of providence in history and, thereby, the existence of God. Moreover, his distinction between Jewish and gentile history requires a historical interpretation of the Old Testament which is incompatible with his claim to found the principles of true history upon a *universal* metaphysics of the human mind. Unsurprisingly therefore, he often fails to adhere to the distinction, assimilating events in the Old Testament to others in the gentile nations from which they should differ. Consequently, in the face of contemporary suspicions of heresy, he insisted that the sequence traced in the 'ideal eternal history' occurs largely through the unintended, rather than the intended, consequences of human action, thus making it possible to attribute the universally patterned nature of their outcome to the influence of Providence. Some interpreters accept this as evidence of the sincerity of his belief in the theological context in which he set his theory. But since he failed to provide any theory to give his claims about Providence explanatory force, it is difficult to believe that the suspicions he sought to allay were unfounded.

6 Theory of historical knowledge

The theory of knowledge which Vico advanced to support his theory of history is an extension of his early *verum-factum* theory: we can know only what we make or do. In his early works, where he lacked a theory of the causes of social and historical change, he had concluded that, because chance and contingency were ineliminable in the world of everyday affairs, knowledge of it was unattainable. In the *New Science*, however, where such theories are advanced, knowledge becomes possible. If human societies develop through the operation of features of human nature which we share, there seems no reason why we should not use our knowledge of them to recreate the past. Hence, Vico could advance his fundamental claim that, since the world of nations has been made by men, its principles are to be 'rediscovered within the the modifications of our own human mind'. These 'modifications' provide components of his 'metaphysics of the human mind'.

The crux of his later theory of knowledge lies in a mutually supportive relationship between philosophy and philology, the possibility of which he first saw in Grotius. Philosophy contemplates reason and issues in the true; philology is the study of what people have made and done, their particular languages, institutions and deeds, that is, the 'certain'. When correctly conceived, philosophy should seek formal and substantive principles for the interpretation and explanation of human history, while philology will reach historical truth through its consistent application of these principles. The central idea, therefore, is that philosophy should produce fundamental theories about human nature and the substantive principles which underlie human historical development, culminating in the 'ideal eternal history', in the light of which fragments of historical data can be interpreted and integrated into comprehensive and coherent accounts of the actual historical past. Philosophy does not establish its theories a priori, however, but through its success in finding a set of universal and necessary principles of which all actual histories are an expression. This conception lies behind the widespread comparative enquiries into the history of thought, languages and institutions in general, which abound in the *New Science*.

Once again, however, Vico's claims about Providence are problematic since if, as he consistently asserts, it affects the process of historical development, its workings will be unintelligible to us. The difficulty is not simply that of understanding a history in which the unintended consequences of individual human actions produce similar patterns of development in different nations. This can be explained by Vico's theory of a common sense, arising from the common nature of nations, which ultimately determines shared social decisions. If Providence is seen as nothing more than common sense, indeed, the problem disappears, but so also does the claim to have demonstrated the existence of God. If, on the other hand, Vico's insistence that Providence is something over and above common sense is genuine, as some commentators claim, there will be something at work in the historical process which is not of human construction and which we therefore cannot know. Vico's claims about Providence are therefore incompatible with his theory of knowledge. This lends support to interpretations which are sceptical of his theistic claims.

A different problem derives from Vico's vacillations about the status of the products of philosophy. In the *First New Science* he refers to them as metaphysical truths but does little to establish them. In the later versions, he describes them as hypotheses which, through confirmation, will attain the status of metaphysical truths. The suggestion here is that they originate as hypotheses and gain their entitlement to truth as a result of their interpretative and explanatory fruitfulness for the historian. In this case it might be questioned whether they are metaphysical at all. But it could equally well be argued that there is no way of establishing the truth of a wide-ranging hypothesis about reality other than by testing its capacity to inject coherence into a fundamental aspect of human experience. This seems to be what Vico finally had in mind.

7 Ultimate doubts

Vico was confident that he had produced a science which would enable us to understand the truth of human history but he became much less certain that this would enable us to diagnose the ills of our society or to remedy them. His suggestions for averting final political and social disaster – the maintenance of law by power of arms under the shield of religion, conquest by another nation or a return to conditions similar to those of the poetic age and a recurrence of the whole cycle – are so unconvincing as to seem little more than expressions of his own perplexity. Nor is this difficult to understand. For if, as he claims, imagination weakens as reason strengthens and if effective religious belief as the main social bond depends upon imagination, then, as soon as the age of reason is reached, religion and social cohesion are bound to decline and there will be no basis for the shield of religion or the other social bonds.

These doubts depend, however, upon a gratuitous inconsistency in his thought. The anarchy in which the life of a nation ends presupposes an incompatibility between imagination and reason. But Vico's general theory requires that they be able to coexist and cooperate, one for the creation of systems of belief, the other for their critical assessment. Without both, indeed, the heroic age would never be superseded. For it is only because the lower classes see the falsity of the imaginary claim to divine origin, which is the basis of the nobility's privileged legal and political status, that the latter becomes challengeable. Thus imagination and reason cannot be incompatible in the way implied by Vico's final doubts. Had he realized this he would have seen no need to postulate either the 'barbarism of reflection' or the recurrence of the life cycle of the nation.

8 Influence

The obscurity of Vico's life and thought has made the extent of his influence upon later thinkers difficult to trace. His emphasis upon the internal coherence of the culture and institutions of different historical societies based upon shared modes of thought and feeling has striking similarities with the thought of HAMANN, HERDER, HEGEL and MARX, of whom only Hegel seems almost wholly ignorant of him. His most direct influence in the nineteenth century was upon Michelet, COMTE, COLERIDGE, CROCE and SOREL. In this century he has influenced a number of writers, including BERLIN, COLLINGWOOD, GADAMER, Joyce and MACINTYRE. But there is considerable circumstantial evidence to suggest that he may have influenced many others interested in general theories of the development of civilization from Adam FERGUSON and ROUSSEAU onwards.

See also: ANTHROPOLOGY, PHILOSOPHY OF; HISTORY, PHILOSOPHY OF; JURISPRUDENCE, HISTORICAL

List of works

Vico, G. (1699–1707) *Orationes I–VI*, trans. G.A. Pinton and A.W. Shippe, *On Humanistic Education (Six Inaugural Orations, 1699–1707)*, Ithaca, NY: Cornell University Press, 1993. (With notes by G.G. Visconti.)

—— (1709) *De nostri temporis studiorum ratione*, trans. E. Gianturco, *On the Study Methods of Our*

Time, Ithaca, NY: Cornell University Press, 1990. (With notes by E. Gianturco.)

—— (1710) *De antiquissima Italorum sapientia ex linguae latinae originibus eruenda*, trans. L.M. Palmer, *On the Most Ancient Wisdom of the Italians Unearthed from the Origins of the Latin Language*, Ithaca, NY: Cornell University Press, 1988. (With notes by L.M. Palmer.)

—— (1720) *De universi iuris uno principio et fine uno* (On the One Beginning and One End of Universal Law), in F. Nicolini (ed.) *Opere di G.B. Vico*, vol. 2, Bari: Laterza, 1936.

—— (1721) *De constantia iurisprudentis* (On the Constancy of the Jurisprudent), in F. Nicolini (ed.) *Opere di G.B. Vico*, vol. 2, Bari: Laterza, 1936.

—— (1725) *Principi Di Una Scienza Nuova Intorno Alla Natura Delle Nazioni Per La Quale Si Ritruovano I Principi Di Altro Sistema Del Diritto Naturale Delle Genti* (Principles of a New Science of the Nature of Nations Leading to the Discovery of the Natural Law of the Gentes), trans. L. Pompa in *Vico: Selected Writings*, Cambridge: Cambridge University Press, 1982. (With notes by L. Pompa.)

—— (1725, 1728, 1731) *Vita di Giambattista Vico scritta da se medesimo*, trans. M.H. Fisch and T.G. Bergin, *The Autobiography of Giambattista Vico*, Ithaca, NY: Cornell University Press, 1944, 1963. (This includes an invaluable historical introduction and notes on Vico's influence, by M.H. Fisch and T.G. Bergin.)

—— (1730) *Cinque Libri Di Giambattista Vico De Principi D'Una Scienza Nuova D'Intorno Alla Comune Natura Delle Nazioni In Questa Seconda Impressione* (Five Books by Giambattista Vico on the Principles of a New Science of the Nature of Nations, Second Edition), ed. M. Sanna and F. Tessitore, Morano: Naples, 1991.

—— (1744) *Principi Di Scienza Nuova Di Giambattista Vico D'intorno Alla Commune Natura Delle Nazioni In Questa Terza Impressione*, trans. T.G. Bergin and M.H. Fisch, *The New Science of Giambattista Vico*, Ithaca, NY: Cornell University Press, 1968; repr. including the 'Practice of the New Science', Ithaca, NY: Cornell University Press, 1984. (With revisions and notes by T.G. Bergin and M.H. Fisch.)

References and further reading

Adams, H.P. (1935) *The Life and Writings of Giambattista Vico*, London: Allen & Unwin. (An excellent simple historical introduction to the development of Vico's thought.)

Bedani, G. (1989) *Vico Revisited*, Oxford: Berg. (A detailed monograph stressing the naturalistic character of Vico's doctrines and the strategies which he employed to obscure their heretical implications.)

Berlin, I. (1976) *Vico and Herder*, London: The Hogarth Press. (An influential interpretation of Vico's philosophy, emphasizing the ontological and epistemological role of a self-transcending imagination while accepting that Vico nevertheless believed in historical laws.)

Croce, B. (1911) *La Filosofia di G.B. Vico*, trans. R.G. Collingwood, *The Philosophy of Giambattista Vico*, London: Howard Latimer, 1913. (The initiator of modern Vico studies, involving a much disputed identification of Vico's 'Providence' with Hegel's concept of the cunning of reason.)

Lilla, M. (1993) *G.B. Vico: The Making of an Anti-Modern*, Cambridge, MA: Harvard University Press. (A very detailed historical account of the whole of Vico's thought, stressing its dependence upon theological and biblical doctrines.)

Nicolini, F. (1978) *Commento Storico alla Seconda Scienza Nuova* (A Historical Commentary on the Second New Science), Rome: Edizioni di Storia e Letteratura. (The most scholarly explication of the historical references in what is now known as the *Third New Science* of 1744.)

Piovani, P., Giarrizzo, G. and Tessitore, F. (eds) (1972–) *Bollettino del Centro di Studi Vichiani*, Bibliopolis: Naples. (A journal devoted largely to the historical study of Vico's life, works and influence.)

Pompa, L. (1990) *Vico: A Study of the 'New Science'*, Cambridge: Cambridge University Press, 2nd edn. (An analytic account of the main doctrines of the *New Science*, taking as primary Vico's claim to have produced a science.)

Tagliacozzo, G. (ed.) (1981) *Vico: Past and Present*, Atlantic Highlands, NJ: Humanities Press. (A collection of essays concentrating on philosophical and historical issues.)

Tagliacozzo, G., Mooney, M. and Verene, D.P. (eds) (1980) *Vico and Contemporary Thought*, London: Macmillan. (A collection of articles focusing on Vico's relevance to contemporary thought.)

Tagliacozzo, G. and Verene, D.P. (eds) (1969) *Giambattista Vico's Science of Humanity*, Baltimore, MD: Johns Hopkins University Press. (A collection of historical, comparative and philosophical articles on aspects of Vico's thought.)

—— (1983–) *New Vico Studies*, Atlantic Highlands, NJ: Humanities Press. (An English language journal, dealing with all aspects of Vico studies but with a particular focus on placing Vico's thought in the tradition of rhetoric.)

Tagliacozzo, G. and White, H.V. (eds) *Giambattista Vico: An International Symposium*, Baltimore, MD: Johns Hopkins University Press. (A wide-ranging collection of historical and philosophical articles on aspects of Vico's thought.)

Verene, D.P. (1981) *Vico's Science of Imagination*, Ithaca, NY: Cornell University Press. (A thorough discussion of Vico's concept of the imagination, arguing that it is both ontologically and epistemologically primary and that Vico did not believe in the existence of historical laws.)

—— (1991) *The New Art of Autobiography: An Essay on the Life of Giambattista Vico Written by Himself*, Oxford: Clarendon Press. (An account of Vico's *Autobiography* presenting it as his reconstruction of his life in the light of the main tenets of the *New Science*.)

LEON POMPA

VIDYARANYA *see* MĀDHAVA

VIENNA CIRCLE

The Vienna Circle was a group of about three dozen thinkers drawn from the natural and social sciences, logic and mathematics who met regularly in Vienna between the wars to discuss philosophy. The work of this group constitutes one of the most important and most influential philosophical achievements of the twentieth century, especially in the development of analytic philosophy and philosophy of science.

The Vienna Circle made its first public appearance in 1929 with the publication of its manifesto, The Scientific Conception of the World: The Vienna Circle (Carnap, Hahn and Neurath 1929). At the centre of this modernist movement was the so-called 'Schlick Circle', a discussion group organized in 1924 by the physics professor Moritz Schlick. Friedrich Waismann, Herbert Feigl, Rudolf Carnap, Hans Hahn, Philipp Frank, Otto Neurath, Viktor Kraft, Karl Menger, Kurt Gödel and Edgar Zilsel belonged to this inner circle. Their meetings in the Boltzmanngasse were also attended by Olga Taussky-Todd, Olga Hahn-Neurath, Felix Kaufmann, Rose Rand, Gustav Bergmann and Richard von Mises, and on some occasions by visitors from abroad such as Hans Reichenbach, Alfred Ayer, Ernest Nagel, Willard Van Orman Quine and Alfred Tarski. This discussion circle was pluralistic and committed to the ideals of the Enlightenment. It was unified by the aim of making philosophy scientific with the help of modern logic on the basis of scientific and everyday experience. At the periphery of the Schlick Circle, and in a more or less strong osmotic contact with it, there were loose discussion groups around Ludwig Wittgenstein, Heinrich Gomperz, Richard von Mises and Karl Popper. In addition the mathematician Karl Menger established in the years 1926–36 an international mathematical colloquium, which was attended by Kurt Gödel, John von Neumann and Alfred Tarski among others.

Thus the years 1924–36 saw the development of an interdisciplinary movement whose purpose was to transform philosophy. Its public profile was provided by the Ernst Mach Society through which members of the Vienna Circle sought to popularize their ideas in the context of programmes for national education in Vienna. The general programme of the movement was reflected in its publications, such as the journal Erkenntnis *('Knowledge', later called The Journal for Unified Science), and the* International Encyclopedia of Unified Science. *Given this story of intellectual success, the fate of the Vienna Circle was tragic. The Ernst Mach Society was suspended in 1934 for political reasons, Moritz Schlick was murdered in 1936, and around this time many members of the Vienna Circle left Austria for racial and political reasons; thus soon after Schlick's death the Circle disintegrated. As a result of the emigration of so many of its members, however, the characteristic ideas of the Vienna Circle became more and more widely known, especially in Scandinavia, Britain and North America where they contributed to the emergence of modern philosophy of science. In Germany and Austria, however, the philosophical and mathematical scene was characterized by a prolongation of the break that was caused by the emigration of the members of the Vienna Circle.*

1 **Scientific philosophy and philosophy of science**
2 **Logical positivism**
3 **Logical empiricism and the scientific conception of the world**
4 *Encyclopedia of Unified Science*

1 Scientific philosophy and philosophy of science

Proponents of 'scientific philosophy' think of philosophy not as an autonomous discipline prior to the sciences but as a critical discipline dependent upon the natural and social sciences, logic and mathematics. Changing a motto of Kant, they hold that philosophy without science is empty, science without philosophy is blind. Adoption of this scientific conception of philosophy does not, however, determine the details of one's epistemology, methodology and ontology. As far as epistemology is concerned, the Austrian tradition offers the contrasting examples of the phenomenology of Franz BRENTANO and the positivism of Ernst MACH. Similarly, there are those who

stress the unity of the natural and the social sciences and those who contrast explanation in the natural sciences with the distinctive type of understanding (*verstehen*) characteristic of human affairs. Finally, both idealist and materialist ontological positions are compatible with this understanding of philosophy. Nonetheless all proponents of scientific philosophy demand exact methods and an empirical orientation. They oppose irrational and theological systems of philosophy with an attitude that shows their commitment to the ideals of the Enlightenment and to science.

Historically, the positivism of Mach's scientific philosophy was the most important precondition for the development of the position adopted within the Vienna Circle. The term 'philosophy of science' was used to describe this position, but by this was meant a general scientific conception of philosophy as well as a commitment to providing a philosophy of the sciences. Thus within the Vienna Circle, philosophy was regarded both as a general analytic and language-oriented activity and as a discipline working on the foundations of the natural and social sciences. At the same time we find within the Vienna Circle those such as Moritz SCHLICK who defend a methodological dualism of philosophy and science, and those such as Otto NEURATH who seek to absorb philosophy altogether within a scientific conception of the world. Independent of this variety of positions, however, empiricism, an orientation towards the sciences, and an exact logical-mathematical methodology remain essential features of the Vienna Circle.

2 Logical positivism

The name 'Vienna Circle' was used in public for the first time in 1929 in the programmatic essay *The Scientific Conception of the World: The Vienna Circle* (Carnap, Hahn and Neurath 1929). It was suggested by Neurath and was supposed to have pleasant connotations similar to 'Vienna Woods' or 'Viennese Waltz'. At the same time the term should indicate the origin of this philosophical movement and its collective orientation (Frank 1949), although strictly speaking, it is anachronistic to use it for the period before 1929. In this programmatic essay the position of the 'radical' wing around Neurath, CARNAP, Hahn, Frank and others was especially prominent. This wing, institutionalized in the Ernst Mach Society, supported the idea of a unified physicalist science as represented in the programme of the *International Encyclopedia of Unified Science*. By contrast the more moderate wing of the Vienna Circle around Schlick, Waismann, Feigl and others – in fact the majority – emphasized their adherence to a dualism of science and philosophy with changing names like 'consistent empiricism', 'logical empiricism', or 'logical positivism'.

The widely used term 'logical positivism' comes in fact from Albert Blumberg's and Herbert Feigl's paper 'Logical Positivism: a New Movement in European Philosophy', published in the *Journal of Philosophy* in 1931. Blumberg and Feigl give a concise description of the new synthesis of logical and empirical factors:

> The new logical positivism retains the fundamental principle of empiricism but...feels it has attained in most essentials a unified theory of knowledge in which neither logical nor empirical factors are neglected. From the point of view of logical positivism, the Kantian synthesis concedes too much to rationalism by assuming the existence of synthetic a priori truths. Against Kant the new movement maintains as a fundamental thesis that there are no synthetic a priori propositions....it holds that factual (empirical) propositions though synthetic are a posteriori, and that logical and mathematical propositions though a priori are analytic.
>
> ...By means of the theory of knowledge thus constructed, logical positivism...shows that the propositions of metaphysics, in most senses of the term, are, strictly speaking, meaningless.
>
> (Blumberg and Feigl 1931: 282)

Blumberg and Feigl go on to describe the philosophical transformation from old to new positivism with the adoption of symbolic logic, epistemology, and research into the foundations of science. Finally, they explain, following WITTGENSTEIN, their notion of philosophy: 'The purpose of philosophy is the clarification of the meaning of propositions and the elimination of...meaningless pseudo-propositions' (Blumberg and Feigl 1931: 269). Despite its widespread currency, however, the term 'logical positivism' has the disadvantage that it associates the Vienna Circle too closely with positivism, and thus, for example, with the 'positivism dispute' that runs from Lenin to the Frankfurt School. Hence the term 'logical empiricism' is now often preferred: it takes into account the synthesis of rationalism and empiricism, and signals clearly the two most important elements in the philosophy of the Vienna Circle.

In Schlick's logical empiricism the classical philosophical positions of empiricism and rationalism were integrated with the help of modern logic and mathematics, but a distinction between philosophy and science was still admitted. Neurath's more radical 'scientific conception of the world' aimed at overcoming philosophy itself within his scheme for a unified physicalist science. This divergence in philosophical approach left room for debates within the Circle on such topics as the merits of phenomenalist and physicalist languages, coherence and correspondence theories of truth, logical syntax and semantics, verification and confirmation, and ideal and natural languages. At the same time there was a consensus concerning the merits of a logical analysis of language, a fallibilist epistemology, a scientific attitude to the world and the unity of scientific explanation and knowledge in general. After Schlick's death, however, his logical empiricist project collapsed following personal and theoretical disagreements. The project of a unified science, however, continued in the unity-of-science movement (see §4).

An important element of the logical empiricism of the Vienna Circle was the refusal to accept synthetic judgments a priori. Following Russell and Whitehead, symbolic logic and mathematics were regarded as purely analytic (because merely 'conventional') and a priori (and thus independent of any experience). Analytic truths of these kinds were contrasted with empirically true statements of the natural sciences and ordinary experience; these were synthetic judgments a posteriori. But there was no further class of synthetic a priori judgments; instead there was thought to be an important class of 'meaningless' sentences. The elements of this class, being neither analytic nor synthetic a posteriori, are 'metaphysical' in a sense which implies that they are not part of knowledge at all even though they may express some realm of experience. This anti-metaphysical position of the Vienna Circle is most prominently represented by Rudolf Carnap's 'Elimination of Metaphysics Through Logical Analysis of Language' (Carnap 1931). It prepares the logical empiricist programme for a unified reconstruction of science. But the question whether an empirical basis could be a foundation for all knowledge received strongly divergent answers from the coherence theorists around Neurath and the correspondence theorists around Schlick (Hempel 1981; 1993). The apparently strict distinction between analytic and synthetic sentences had also already been questioned (Menger 1979; 1994). Indeed, the ideal of one language of science, logic and mathematics had already been strongly relativized by the Vienna Circle itself, long before Quine put forward his classic critique (Quine 1953). Thus, contrary to its popular reputation, a heterogeneous pluralism of views was in fact characteristic of the Vienna Circle: for example in questions of ethics (Schlick 1930; Menger 1934; Kraft 1937), in regard to 'realism' versus 'positivism' (Schlick 1933; Carnap 1928; Feigl 1929; Kraft 1925), verificationism versus falsificationism (Neurath 1935), and not the least in questions of an ideological and political nature.

3 Logical empiricism and the scientific conception of the world

The relationship between Schlick's logical empiricism and Neurath's distinctive scientific conception of the world is a complex matter. Certain points are of course held in common, such as the view of philosophy as a language-oriented, analytic activity. Again, the principle of verification ('The meaning of a sentence can be given only by giving the rule of its verification.') (Schlick 1938: 341; Hempel 1950), logical atomism (following Russell) and the picture theory of language (following Wittgenstein's *Tractatus*), are constitutive features of the entire movement but are in themselves insufficient for its characterization. Kamitz (1973), mainly referring to Carnap's positions, characterizes the Vienna Circle up to about 1930 by the following principles: the formal character of mathematics (Logicism: that is, subordination of mathematics under logic which itself is purely analytic), verifiability, methodological phenomenalism (Carnap's epistemological position in *The Logical Construction of the World*), and 'scientism', which is a claim to the omnipotence of science when compared with alternative forms of knowledge in philosophy and art. For the period 1930–5 the following principles are listed: the hypothetical character of empirical claims (the criterion of verifiability is replaced by a criterion of confirmability), the conventionalist interpretation of logic, physicalism as the foundation of the unified science (a physicalist, quantitative, empirical language as unifying intersubjective language of science), and the conception of philosophy as logical syntax of the language of science. These principles reflect the growing dominance of Neurath's point of view within the Circle. In particular, the last principle restricts questions of truth to comparisons among sentences along the lines of Neurath's coherence theory in order to avoid the dualism of 'language' and 'world' suggested by the correspondence theory of truth. In line with this, Carnap and Neurath deny any absolute 'foundation of knowledge' of the kind sought by Schlick (Schlick 1934). They hold that in any empirical justification it is not single sentences that are tested, but whole systems of sentences, and science in general. This is a form of relativism that makes Neurath in particular a forerunner of recent holistic approaches in philosophy of science (see Hempel, Popper and others in Skirbekk 1977).

Although this last point of view is distinctive of Neurath, it is important to grasp that the 'scientific conception of the world' which he and others promulgated within the Circle had a much broader cultural goal. It was not simply a neo-positivist anti-metaphysical scientistic programme. Instead he looked to a unified science and a truly scientific conception of the world to make everyday life more humane and democratic. In portrayals of the Vienna Circle written after the Second World War these practical aspirations are often treated as inessential political ambitions when compared with the scientific programmes of logicism and empiricism, whereas in fact internal debates about them were emphasized and regarded as characteristic of the Vienna Circle. We find the clearest presentation of the claim to social reform that is inherent in the scientific conception of the world in the programmatic essay of the Vienna Circle of 1929:

> The endeavour is to link and harmonise the achievements of individual investigators in their various fields of science. From this aim follows the emphasis on collective efforts, and also the emphasis on what can be grasped intersubjectively; from this springs the search for a neutral system of formulae, for a symbolism freed from the slag of historical languages; and also the search for a total system of concepts. Neatness and clarity are striven for, and dark distances and unfathomable depths rejected. In science there are no 'depths'; all is on the surface. Experience forms a complex network, which cannot always be surveyed and can often be grasped only in parts. Everything is accessible to man; and man is the measure of all things...The scientific conception of the world knows no unsolvable riddle.
>
> (Carnap, Hahn and Neurath [1929: 15] 1973: 305)

This concluding paraphrase of one of Wittgenstein's claims in the *Tractatus* is the starting point for this late Enlightenment programme of science with its anti-metaphysical orientation. Traditional philosophy with its mannerisms has, in a first step, to be reduced to a critical analysis of language:

> No special 'philosophic assertions' are established, assertions are merely clarified; and at that assertions of empirical science. ...Whichever term may be used to describe such investigations, this much is certain: there is no such thing as philosophy as a basic or universal science alongside or above the various fields of the one empirical science.
>
> (Carnap, Hahn and Neurath [1929: 28] 1973: 316)

The practical impulse behind this therapeutic destruction of a philosophy of metaphysical systems and the rational subject was the desire for a unified and empirical conception of the world on the basis of simple human experience, directed against the 'Zeitgeist' of an increasing number of metaphysical movements whose rise was connected with social and economic factors. Social criticism thus becomes an accompaniment of empirical science and replaces the classical philosophical materialism of the labour movement:

> In previous times, materialism was the expression of this view; in the meantime, however, modern empiricism has shed a number of inadequacies and has taken a strong shape in the scientific conception of the world.
> (Carnap, Hahn and Neurath [1929: 29] 1973: 317)

Its closeness to real-life issues and its solidarity with the forces of progress led in the time of emerging fascism to an aggressive determination of its position on social issues:

> We witness the spirit of the scientific conception of the world penetrating in growing measure the forms of personal and public life, in education, upbringing, architecture, and the shaping of economic and social life according to rational principles. The scientific conception of the world serves life, and life receives it.
> (Carnap, Hahn and Neurath [1929: 30] 1973: 317)

Social criticism, sociology of knowledge, and philosophic-scientific collective work formed in this conception a programmatic unity in hope of comprehensive progress, which was partly put into practice. But whereas in the natural sciences, Neurath thinks, considerable progress has already been achieved, the situation in the social sciences is less clear ([1930–1: 121] 1983: 44). Neurath therefore attempts in his *Empirical Sociology* (1931) to give a 'physicalist' description of the processes of human social interaction, of the forces that make groups of people cooperate or work against each other and of their influence on the lives of the masses. And his general attitude towards long-term predictions of social sciences is manifested in his cautiously optimistic outlook on possible future developments of society and science (which can nowadays look rather utopian). In this respect it is worth mentioning that after the disintegration of the Vienna Circle (which was also a process of political neutralization) reference to the 'scientific conception of the world' was occasionally used by former members of the Vienna Circle in connection with general ideological questions. For example, Carnap (1963: 81) talks about 'scientific humanism' as a view shared by the majority of the members of the Vienna Circle. By this he means, first, that everyone determines their own life, second, that mankind has the ability to improve their

conditions of living and, third, that every liberating action presupposes knowledge about the world, knowledge that is best achieved by scientific means, so that science becomes the most important instrument for an improvement of our lives. According to Carnap, such aims require rational planning which in turn would be best achieved by some form of socialism and a world-government.

4 Encyclopedia of Unified Science

After the dissolution of the Vienna Circle, the forced emigration of most of its members, and the diffusion of the logical empiricist movement from its centres in Vienna, Prague and Budapest, the twin aims of a transformation of philosophy and the establishment of a scientific conception of the world could be envisaged only without reference to their previous cultural context and audience. But even in these difficult times Neurath and his circle still succeeded in organizing well-attended conferences of high standard ('International Congresses for the Unity of Science'), and he also managed to ensure that the unity of science movement continued in the USA (Neurath, Carnap and Morris 1970–1) (see UNITY OF SCIENCE). After 1935 Neurath devoted himself to the model of the 'encyclopedia' as a means for furthering this movement. In cooperation with Carnap, Frank and Morris, he planned an international encyclopedia of the unified science and, corresponding to it, worked on a picture language (Isotype) of visual representation. He presented this programme as a development of the ideas of the philosophers of the French Enlightenment. This vision of an unfinished Enlightenment project remains today a striking challenge for the scientific community.

See also: ANALYTICAL PHILOSOPHY; ENLIGHTENMENT, CONTINENTAL; LOGICAL POSITIVISM; MEANING AND VERIFICATION; ENCYCLOPEDISTS, EIGHTEENTH-CENTURY

List of works

Blumberg, A. and Feigl, H. (1931) 'Logical Positivism: a New Movement in European Philosophy', *Journal of Philosophy* 28: 281–96. (An important presentation of the Vienna Circle in the Anglo-American world.)

Carnap, R. (1928) *Der logische Aufbau der Welt*, Berlin and Schlachtensee: Weltkreis-Verlag; trans. R.A. George, *The Logical Structure of the World*, Berkeley, CA: University of California Press, 1967. (Central book of the phenomenalist period of the early Vienna Circle; methodological solipsism.)

—— (1931) 'Überwindung der Metaphysik durch logische Analyse der Sprache', *Erkenntnis* 2: 219–41; trans. A. Pap, 'The Elimination of Metaphysics through Logical Analysis of Language', in A.J. Ayer (ed.) *Logical Positivism*, New York: Free Press, 1959, 60–81. (Classic paper of the physicalist period of the Vienna Circle.)

—— (1963) 'Intellectual Autobiography', in P.A. Schilpp (ed.) *The Philosophy of Rudolf Carnap*, La Salle, IL: Open Court, 1–84. (One of the most important reports of the inner life of the Vienna Circle; very well balanced.)

Carnap, R., Hahn, H. and Neurath, O. (1929) *Wissenschaftliche Weltauffassung: Der Wiener Kreis*, ed. Verein Ernst Mach, Vienna: Artur Wolf Verlag; trans. P. Foulkes and M. Neurath, 'The Scientific Conception of the World: The Vienna Circle', in M. Neurath and R.S. Cohen (eds) *Empiricism and Sociology*, Dordrecht and Boston: Reidel, 1973, 299–318. (The programmatic essay of the Vienna Circle, directed to a general audience, strongly influenced by Neurath; main emphasis is on the concept of a physicalist unified science.)

Feigl, H. (1929) *Theorie und Erfahrung in der Physik* ('Theory and Experience in Physics'), Karlsruhe: G. Braun.

—— (1969) 'The Wiener Kreis in America', in D. Fleming and B. Bailyn (eds) *The Intellectual Migration: Europe and America, 1930–1960*, Cambridge, MA: Harvard University Press, 630–73. (Another important autobiographical report on the history of the Vienna Circle and its influence.)

Frank, P. (1949) *Modern Science and Its Philosophy*, Cambridge: Cambridge University Press. (Collected papers by Frank from 1907 to 1947 with an important introduction especially on the background of the Vienna Circle before the First World War.)

Hempel, C.G. (1950) 'Problems and Changes in the Empiricist Criterion of Meaning', *Revue Internationale de Philosophie* 11: 41-63 (Authentic description of the transformation of the verification principle.)

Juhos, B. (1971) 'Formen des Positivismus' ('Forms of Positivism'), *Journal for General Philosophy of Science* 2/1: 27–62. (A report of a former Vienna Circle member, with main emphasis on his own position.)

Kraft, V. (1925) *Die Grundformen der wissenschaftlichen Methoden* ('The Basic Forms of Scientific Method') *Logical Investigations*, Vienna: Sitzungsberichte der Österreichischen Akademie der Wissenschaften. Philos.-historische Klasse 203: 1–104. (Monograph on constructive realism and its hypothetico-deductive justification.)

—— (1937) *Die Grundlagen der wissenschaftlichen Wertlehre*, Vienna: Springer; trans. E.H. Schneewind as *Foundations for a Scientific Analysis of Value*, ed. H.L. Mulder and E.H. Schneewind, Dordrecht: Reidel, 1981. (A critic of phenomenologist epistemology emphasizing the constructive element in empirical knowledge, and an attempt to justify the norms of accepted morality as means to the satisfaction of universally shared needs.)

—— (1950) *Der Wiener Kreis: Der Ursprung des Neopositivismus: Ein Kapitel der jüngsten Philosophiegeschichte*, Vienna and New York: Springer; trans. A. Pap, *The Vienna Circle: The Origin of Neo-Positivism: A Chapter in the History of Recent Philosophy*, New York: Philosophical Library, 1953. (Solid, well balanced and easily accessible introduction to the main problems, topics, and results of the Vienna Circle.)

Menger, K. (1934) *Moral, Wille, Weltgestaltung: Grundlegung zur Logik der Sitten*, Vienna: Springer; trans. E. van der Schalie, *Morality, Decision, and Social Organization: Towards a Logic of Ethics*, Dordrecht: Reidel, 1974. (A representative externalist treatment of moral values.)

—— (1979) *Selected Papers in Logic and Foundations, Didactics, Economics*, Dordrecht, Boston and London: Kluwer. (Menger's collected papers with a historical-systematic part I: Papers Introducing Logical Tolerance.)

—— (1994) *Reminiscences of the Vienna Circle and the Mathematical Colloquium*, eds L. Golland, B. McGuinness and A. Sklar, Dordrecht, Boston and London: Kluwer. (Informative autobiographical account of the ideas of the logical-mathematical wing of the Vienna Circle and of Menger's Mathematical Colloquium.)

Mises, R. von (1968) *Positivism: A Study in Human Understanding*, New York: Dover. (An authentic and well-balanced introduction to the theories of the Vienna Circle, including values, arts and metaphysics.)

Neurath, O. (1930/31) 'Wege der wissenschaftlichen Weltauffassung', *Erkenntnis* 1: 106–25; trans. R.S. Cohen and M. Neurath, 'Ways of the Scientific Conception of the World', in R.S. Cohen and M. Neurath (eds) *Philosophical Papers 1913–1946*, Dordrecht and Boston: Reidel, 1983: 32–47. (An exposition of an anti-metaphysical conception of science in a social and historical context.)

—— (1931) *Empirische Soziologie: Der wissenschaftliche Gehalt der Geschichte und Nationalökonomie*, Vienna: Springer; trans. P. Foulkes and M. Neurath, 'Empirical Sociology: The Scientific Content of History and Political Economy' in M. Neurath and R.S. Cohen (eds) *Empiricism and Sociology*, Dordrecht and Boston: Reidel, 1973: 319–421. (Analysis and application of the scientific conception of the world to the social sciences.)

—— (1935) 'Pseudorationalismus der Falsifikation', *Erkenntnis* 5: 353–65; trans. R.S. Cohen and M. Neurath, 'Pseudorationalism of Falsification', in R.S. Cohen and M. Neurath (eds) *Philosophical Papers 1913–1946*, Dordrecht and Boston: Reidel, 1983: 121–31. (Fundamental criticism of Popper's Logic of Scientific Discovery as a form of pseudorationalism.)

—— (1936) 'L'encyclopédie comme "modèle"', *Revue de Synthèse* 12: 187–201; trans. R.S. Cohen and M. Neurath, 'Encyclopedia as a "model"', in R.S. Cohen and M. Neurath (eds) *Philosophical Papers 1913–1946*, Dordrecht and Boston: Reidel, 1983: 145–58.

—— (1936) *International Picture Language*, London: Kegan Paul. (Introduction to education by picture language as a supplement of the encyclopedia project.)

—— (1937) *Basic by Isotype*, London: Kegan Paul. (Visualization and illustration of C.K. Ogden's 'Basic English'.)

Neurath, O., Carnap, R. and Morris, C. (eds) (1970/1) *Foundations of the Unity of Science: Towards an International Encyclopedia of Unified Science*, Chicago and London: University of Chicago Press, 2 vols. (A collection of the 19 monographs of the encyclopedia of unified science, which started in 1938).

Schlick, M. (1930) *Fragen der Ethik*, Vienna: Springer; trans. D. Rynin, *Problems of Ethics*, New York: Dover, 1939. (A constructive positivist approach to a number of problems of traditional ethics, such as motivation, freedom and responsibility.)

—— (1933) 'Positivismus und Realismus', *Erkenntnis* 3: 1–31; trans. D. Rynin, 'Positivism and Realism', in A.J. Ayer (ed.) *Logical Positivism*, New York: Free Press, 1959: 82–107. (A defence of phenomenalist positivism against Planck's anti-positivism.)

—— (1934) 'Über das Fundament der Erkenntnis', *Erkenntnis* 4: 79–99; trans. D. Rynin, 'The Foundation of Knowledge', in A.J. Ayer (ed.) *Logical Positivism*, New York: Free Press, 1979: 209–27. (Essential text for the debate about the foundations of knowledge.)

—— (1938) *Gesammelte Aufsätze 1926–1938*, Wien: Gerold and Co. (The main articles by Schlick in German, English and French compiled by Friedrich Waismann.)

References and further reading

Dahms, H.-J. (ed.) (1985) *Philosophie, Wissenschaft,* *Aufklärung: Beiträge zur Geschichte und Wirkung des Wiener Kreises* ('Philosophy, Science, Enlightenment: Studies on the History and Influence of the Vienna Circle'), Berlin and New York: de Gruyter. (Proceedings of a conference on the development and influence of the Vienna Circle.)

—— (1994) *Positivismusstreit: Die Auseinandersetzungen der Frankfurter Schule mit dem logischen Positivismus, dem amerikanischen Pragmatismus und dem kritischen Rationalismus* ('The Positivism Dispute: The controversy between the Frankfurt School, American pragmatism and critical rationalism'), Frankfurt: Suhrkamp. (A study of the so-called positivism-dispute; impressive use of many original sources; well balanced and not ideological.)

Danneberg, L., Kamlah, A. and Schäfer, L. (eds) (1994) *Reichenbach und die Berliner Gruppe* ('Reichenbach and the Berlin Group'), Braunschweig-Wiesbaden: Vieweg. (First comprehensive documentation of the so-called Berlin Circle and the Berlin Society for Scientific Philosophy.)

Delius, H. (1970) 'Positivismus und Neopositivismus' ('Positivism and NeoPositivism'), in D.A. Diemer and I. Frenzel (eds) *Philosophie*, Frankfurt: Fischer. (Traditional survey article on positivism and neopositivism.)

Fischer, K.R. (ed.) (1995) *Das goldene Zeitalter der Österreichischen Philosophie: Ein Lesebuch* ('The Golden Age of Austrian Philosophy: A sourcebook'), Vienna: WUV Verlag. (Classic and contemporary articles on Austrian philosophy covering Brentano, Mach, Boltzmann, and the Vienna Circle.)

Fischer, K.R. and Wimmer, F.M. (eds) (1993) *Der geistige Anschluß: Philosophie und Politik an der Universität Wien 1930–1950* ('The intellectual Anschluss: Philosophy and Politics at the University of Vienna 1930–50'), Vienna: WUV Verlag. (Controversial articles and documents on the political and ideological background of the expulsion and Diaspora of the Vienna Circle.)

Geier, M. (1992) *Der Wiener Kreis mit Selbstzeugnissen und Bilddokumenten* ('The Vienna Circle with self-descriptions and photographs'), Reinbeck bei Hamburg: Rowohlt. (Illustrated introduction to the Vienna Circle.)

Giere, R.N. and A.W. Richardson (eds) (1996) *Origins of Logical Empiricism*, Minneapolis, MN and London: University of Minnesota Press. (Contributions to the cultural context, scientific philosophy, logic and mathematics, empirical knowledge of logical empiricism.)

Haller, R. (ed.) (1982) Schlick und Neurath – Ein Symposion ('Schlick and Neurath – A

Symposium'), *Grazer Philosophische Studien* 16/17, Amsterdam: Rodopi. (Collection of papers on the occasion of Neurath's and Schlick's centenary.)

—— (1993) *Neopositivismus: Eine historische Einführung in die Philosophie des Wiener Kreises* ('Neo-Positivism: A Historical Introduction to the Philosophy of the Vienna Circle'), Darmstadt: Wissenschaftliche Buchgesellschaft. (Solid, problem-oriented introduction reaching from classic empiricism/positivism to the Vienna Circle; sections on the leading figures of the Vienna Circle as well as on Einstein, Russell and Wittgenstein.)

Hanfling, O. (1981) *Logical Positivism*, Oxford: Blackwell. (A systematic survey of the themes and topics central to the Vienna Circle.)

* Hempel, C.G. (1981) 'Der Wiener Kreis und die Metamorphosen seines Empirismus', in N. Leser (ed.) *Das geistige Leben Wiens in der Zwischenkriegszeit* ('Intellectual Life in Vienna in the Interwar Years'), Vienna: ÖBV: 205–15; trans. C.J. Piller as 'The Vienna Circle and the Metamorphosis of its Empiricism', in R. Jeffrey (ed.) *Philosophical Essays: Early and Late*, Cambridge: Cambridge University Press, 1997. (Important historical account by a leading member of the Circle.)

* —— (1993) 'Empiricism in the Vienna Circle and in the Berlin Society', in F. Stadler (ed.) *Scientific Philosophy: Origins and Developments*, Dordrecht, Boston and London: Kluwer, 1–10. (A concise evaluation of logical empiricism from the point of view of contemporary philosophy of science.)

Kamitz, R. (1973) *Positivismus: Befreiung vom Dogma* ('Positivism: Liberation from Dogma'), Munich and Vienna: Langen Müller. (A systematic exposition with main emphasis on Carnap.)

* Quine, W.V.O. (1953) *From a Logical Point of View: Logico-Philosophical Essays*, Cambridge, MA: Harvard University Press. (Classic collection of papers containing the influential critique of logical positivism 'Two Dogmas of Empiricism'.)

* Skirbekk, G. (ed.) (1977) *Wahrheitstheorien: Eine Auswahl aus den Diskussionen über Wahrheit im 20. Jahrhundert* ('Theories of truth: A survey of 20th century discussions of truth'), Frankfurt: Suhrkamp. (A collection of papers on truth published between 1907 and 1973.)

Stadler, F. (1982) *Vom Positivismus zur "Wissenschaftlichen Weltauffassung": Am Beispiel der Wirkungsgeschichte von Ernst Mach in Österreich von 1895–1934* ('From Positivism to the "Scientific Conception of the World"; an example of the historical influence of Ernst Mach in Austria 1895–1934'), Vienna and Munich: Löcker.

—— (ed.) (1993) *Scientific Philosophy: Origins and Developments*, Vienna Circle Institute Yearbook 1, Dordrecht, Boston and London: Kluwer. (A contemporary look at scientific philosophy and philosophy of science by former members of the Vienna Circle and their students.)

—— (1997) *Studien zum Wiener Kreis: Ursprung, Entwicklung und Wirkung des Logischen Empirismus im Kontext* ('Studies on the Vienna Circle: Origin, Development and Influence of Logical Empiricism in Context'), Frankfurt: Suhrkamp. (Historical studies on the rise of scientific philosophy in its cultural context from the beginning of the century to the Second World War; including so far unpublished protocols of Vienna Circle meetings, an interview with Karl Popper and a bio-bibliography.)

Stadler, F. and Haller, R. (1993) *Wien–Berlin–Prag: Der Aufstieg der wissenschaftlichen Philosophie: Zentenarien Rudolf Carnap, Hans Reichenbach, Edgar Zilsel* ('Vienna–Berlin–Prague: The Rise of Scientific Philosophy: Centenary of Rudolf Carnap, Hans Reichenbach, Edgar Zilsel'), Vienna: Hölder-Pichler-Tempsky. (A collection of essays on the development of scientific philosophy, focusing on three important logical empiricists.)

Uebel, T.E. (ed.) (1991) *Rediscovering the Forgotten Vienna Circle: Austrian Studies on Otto Neurath and the Vienna Circle*, Dordrecht, Boston and London: Kluwer. (A collection of papers aiming at a new interpretation of the history of the Vienna Circle.)

—— (1992) *Overcoming Logical Positivism from Within: The Emergence of Neurath's Naturalism in the Vienna Circle's Protocol Sentence Debate*, Amsterdam and Atlanta, GA: Rodopi. (Important reconstruction and interpretation of one of the central debates in the Vienna Circle, including an attempt to justify a holistic and naturalistic approach to philosophy of science without foundationalism.)

Book series

Studien zur österreichischen Philosophie (1979–), ed. R. Haller, Amsterdam: Rodopi.

Veröffentlichungen des Instituts Wiener Kreis, ed. F. Stadler; vols 1–3, Vienna: Hölder-Pichler-Tempsky, 1991–95; vols 4–, Vienna and New York: Springer, 1996–.

Vienna Circle Collection (1973–), ed. H.L. Mulder, R.S. Cohen, B. McGuinness and R. Haller, Dordrecht, Boston, MA and London: Kluwer.

Vienna Circle Institute Yearbook (1993–), ed. F.

Stadler, Dordrecht, Boston, MA and London: Kluwer.

Translated by C. Piller

F. STADLER

VILLEY, MICHEL (1914–88)

Michel Villey was France's leading post-war philosopher of law in the 'natural law' mode. He aimed to rediscover a distinctively philosophical approach to law rooted in the history both of legal ideas and of legal institutions. Legal institutions he considered to have been uniquely a gift of Greco-Roman civilization to the world. They represent a distinctive domain of human activity, concerned with an objectively just ordering of human relationships as these affect external conduct and the possession and use of things. Villey has in common with legal positivism a belief in the differentiation of the legal, concerned with objective interpersonal relations in their 'external' concern with a distribution of things, from morality and from religion with their distinctively 'internal' and 'spiritual' concerns. In opposition to legal positivism, however, he holds that justice is a concept implicit in the legal, and discountenances positivists' tendency to reduce law to a simple aggregation of enacted statutes.

Villey poses the Aristotelian question: what is the defining end of the legal that gives it its distinctive character? His answer is: that of upholding order by settling conflicts of interest among the members of a human society. Law's particular aim is towards objective conflict-resolution in respect of the 'things', corporeal or incorporeal, in which humans take an interest. What law seeks is a just allocation or reallocation of things to persons, in the context of some concrete controversy over their rightful allocation.

This is a creative art, not a science. Guided by the equity of concrete human relations, the judge has to work out creatively the right allocation of things in issue (see JUSTICE, EQUITY AND LAW). This right resolution ('le droit', 'the right' in an objective sense) has to be guided by any relevant enacted laws. But in any seriously disputed case, rival rules of statute-law can be advanced by rival parties, and the judge must still choose. Further guidance is to be drawn from contemporary custom and from judicial precedents. These, too, are genuine parts of the law, in opposition to the ideas of merely voluntaristic positivists, who reduce law to being no more than the total body of

the statutes in force. But even when custom and precedent are brought in, they only define further the whole context in which the relations of the parties must be considered with a view to reaching the equitable resolution of their conflict, the right of the matter in an objective sense. This objective character of the right Villey regarded as the deepest element implicit in a Thomistic understanding of law. He considered it hostile to the subjectivism implicit in contemporary ideas of human rights, which in his view constituted an ideology inimical to legal order properly conceived.

Villey's version of Thomistic philosophy is an adventurous and highly contestable reading of the texts; but it constitutes an original contribution to natural law thought, and shows in an interesting way the possibility of using natural law premises to cast doubt on contemporary views of human rights.

See also: LAW, PHILOSOPHY OF; LEGAL POSITIVISM; NATURAL LAW; ROMAN LAW; THOMISM

List of works

Villey, M. (1962) *Leçons d'histoire de la philosophie du droit* (Lectures on the History of Legal Philosophy), 2nd edn, Paris: Dalloz. (An introductory work for students, relatively straightforward.)
—— (1975a) *Philosophie du droit* (Philosophy of Law), Paris: Dalloz. (A massive two-volume statement of Villey's essential positions, little changed in his later writings.)
—— (1975b) *La formation de la pensée juridique moderne* (The Formation of Modern Legal Thought), 4th edn, Paris: Montchrestien. (An account of the history of legal ideas, making clear Villey's view of the centrality of Greco-Roman practice and thought for 'law' properly so-called.)
—— (1983) *Le droit et les droits de l'homme* (Law and the Rights of Man), Paris: Presses Universitaires de France. (This work, dedicated to the Pope as well as to his own family, gives Villey's critique of the modern approach to human rights; quite an accessible text, aimed to influence public debate.)
—— (1991) 'Law in Things', in P. Amselek and N. MacCormick (eds), *Controversies About Law's Ontology*, Edinburgh: Edinburgh University Press, ch. 1. (A relatively short and witty statement of the author's view about the objectivity of right and its essential reference to 'things', in a quite wide sense; one of the regrettably few statements available in English.)

References and further reading

Freund, J. (1992) 'Michel Villey et le renouveau de la philosophie du droit' (Michel Villey and the Rebirth of Legal Philosophy), *Archives de philosophie du droit* 37: 5–14. (A useful and sympathetic short guide to the essential points of Villey's thought.)

NEIL MacCORMICK

VIOLENCE

Violence is a central concept for much discussion of moral and political life, but lots of debate employing the concept is confused by the lack of clarity about its meaning and about the moral status it should have in our development of public policy. Wide understandings of the term – for instance, structural violence – not only include too much under the name of violence, but also put an excessively negative moral loading into the concept. This is also a problem for some other definitions of violence, such as legitimist definitions, which treat violence as essentially the illegitimate use of force. It is better to confront directly the important and disturbing claim that violence is sometimes morally permissible than to settle it by definitional fiat.

1 Definitions and paradigms
2 Two theories and their difficulties
3 The restricted definition
4 More benefits of the restricted definition

1 Definitions and paradigms

In discussing violence, it helps to begin with some obvious pre-theoretical examples, such as knife attacks, savage beatings, shootings, bombings and torture. Offering such cases may be insufficient for the definitional clarification of the concept that we seek as philosophers, but these paradigms can fix our attention on at least part of what is to be made clear. If theorists claim that these are not acts of violence, then they have some explaining (or theorizing) to do.

In fact, some theorists seem to claim precisely this, while others claim that, although the above list is correct as far as it goes, there are some more surprising candidates for inclusion as paradigms. Both groups seem to suffer from a certain disdain for communicative clarity, but, more importantly still, from a tendency to overmoralize the concept. Since the idea plays a crucial role in a wide range of significant moral and political debates, it is imperative to be clear about what we mean by the term and what sort of evaluative loading it carries.

2 Two theories and their difficulties

To elaborate on this point, it is significant that, although the tendency to eliminate some of the paradigm cases and the tendency to add surprising ones usually spring from very different political motivations, both draw upon the idea that violence is inherently wrong. We can see this if we examine two theories that embody these different tendencies. Legitimists about violence instantiate the first tendency and proponents of the notion of structural violence embody the second. Legitimist definitions treat violence as the *illegitimate* use of force. Characteristically such an approach is associated with politically conservative outlooks, but this is a psychological rather than a logical connection. A major problem for these thinkers is that they have considerable difficulty explicating a theoretically helpful sense of legitimacy. Most of them employ a norm of political legitimacy (as is clear in Sidney Hook's definition of violence as 'the illegal employment of methods of physical coercion for personal or group ends' (Grundy and Weinstein 1974: 12)), but they also think of this as having some moral underpinning, and hence tend to treat violence as essentially in the category of wrongs. In a legitimate state, properly authorized employment of shooting or savage beating by police will not then count as violence since it is a politically legitimate use of force. But there are obvious problems about distinguishing its various types (*de facto, de jure,* internationally recognized though internally contested, and so on) and it is also hard to avoid the awkward consequences that the state of nature, even understood in Hobbes' extreme terms, cannot be a state of violence (since the ideas of political legitimacy or illegitimacy do not apply), and that warfare between two legitimate states cannot involve violence. In the latter case, both states will usually be engaged in the politically legitimated use of force which, by definition, cannot be violence. It is unlikely that this conceptual apparatus could help in the practical discussion of moral limits to police violence or the conduct of war (see WAR AND PEACE, PHILOSOPHY OF §§1–2, 6). If, on the other hand, in the face of the problems posed by resort to political legitimacy, moral legitimacy is invoked, then justified killing in self-defence or defence of innocent others will not involve violence and all violence will be morally illegitimate by explicit definition, which represents the serious fudging of a central question.

By contrast, the concept of structural violence, much in vogue with the political left, flaunts intuition, not by excluding what seem to be obvious candidates, but by bringing into the category of violence a wide range of things that would not, at first, be included.

This definitional proposal springs from the work of the Norwegian sociologist Johan Galtung (1969) and the basic idea is that we should use the term violence in a very wide and extended way to refer to any form of social injustice whether inflicted by individuals or by institutions or by the workings of society at large, and whether or not it involves the deliberate infliction of personal injury by episodes of physical or psychological force. Such episodes would be merely one type of violence. Advocates of this wide definitional strategy tend to argue that standard definitions of violence focus too much upon the harms intentionally inflicted by the personal employment of physical force. Since these instantiate only one type of damage that human contrivance can inflict, why not use the term violence to cover all such damage? This style of proposal faces several difficulties: it is confusing, politically unhelpful and evades a central problem about violence.

It is confusing because people do not ordinarily mean by 'violence' any and every form of social injustice, they mean such things as beating people up or torturing them with electrodes. They do not mean to refer to iniquitous taxation proposals or discriminatory housing policies. These things may lead to violence or they may need violence, or the threat of it, to sustain and implement them, but that is another matter. It may be argued that violence is a bad thing, but it is just confusing to treat every bad thing as violence. Moreover, the expansive sense of violence does not help with an agenda of social reform, because it encourages the cosy but ultimately stultifying belief that all social evils are really one and hence will yield to the one solution. The reality seems far more likely to be that the various problems we face are genuinely diverse, although related in various ways, and have their own specific features that call for detailed study with a view to solution. Better gun control legislation might well alleviate problems of violence in the USA while doing nothing to change poverty levels. Furthermore, the proponents of the concept of structural violence assume that violence is essentially morally wrong, and seek broad support for various social reforms by claiming that they will eliminate (structural) violence. But this assumption is contentious. It may be that there is something about violence which makes resort to it always, in certain ways, regrettable, while none the less, at times, it can be argued to be morally legitimate, even morally required. These issues need to be faced, not evaded.

3   The restricted definition

It is therefore preferable to operate with a concept of violence which is both narrower than that of structural violence and less morally loaded than either it or the legitimist definitions. Initial guidance is provided by such dictionary definitions as that of the *Oxford English Dictionary*: 'The exercise of physical force so as to inflict injury on or damage to persons or property'. Yet this is arguably too restrictive in excluding psychological violence since we can give some sense to the idea of damage being inflicted by psychological force. Cases of psychological pressure producing overpowering effects seem close to the paradigms given earlier, as, for example, when a parent cruelly humiliates a vulnerable child to the point of collapse or great distress. There is a tendency in the literature to slide from psychological violence to structural violence, but this embodies a confusion since it rests on the tendency to think of psychological violence as *impalpable* and then to feel that its admission endorses the even more impalpable structural violence. However, the examples which make the category of psychological violence plausible are all very palpable indeed, involving an immediacy and specificity of pressure producing overwhelming effects on the victim. The term 'verbal violence' is sometimes used merely metaphorically, but it can make literal sense in contexts where it is a species of psychological violence, and where the term 'tongue lashing' becomes strictly appropriate.

It is worth noting that a 'restricted' definition of this sort is not entirely 'descriptive' or morally neutral although it is much less morally loaded than the other definitions discussed above. It contains reference to the notions of injury or damage which are at least evaluative with respect to some notion of normal or proper functioning. In addition, these notions have complex relations to such centrally moral concepts as harm and autonomy. The conceptual structure of the definition therefore allows us insight into much that is otherwise puzzling about our attitudes to violence, and helps explain some of the appeal of the structural and legitimist outlooks as well as the nature of the distortions they produce. In particular, it helps show why many people have a strong tendency to think that violence is always wrong and that it is none the less sometimes morally right. This tendency is partly attributable to the fact that violence inherently involves the intentional infliction of injury or damage, and we have a strong tendency to equate this with the infliction of harm or wrong. At the same time, most of us recognize that the police, for instance, are sometimes justified in killing or wounding criminals to prevent violent attacks upon innocent civilians or upon the police themselves. There can be problems about the too-ready resort to violence by police, but there is nothing imaginary or fantastic about the circumstances in which such resort seems morally justifiable. In Melbourne, in December 1994, a man ran amok with a semi-automatic weapon in a suburban street, killed two perfect strangers and kept firing at police and passing motorists until a police marksman shot him dead. Such criminals are certainly injured, but they are not wronged or, in the morally significant sense, harmed.

4   More benefits of the restricted definition

Another problem that can be clarified by the restricted definition is that of violent sports that involve the consent of their participants. Some have thought that boxing, for instance, cannot be violent because the fighters mutually agree to bombard each other with punches; they are influenced by the idea that some action affecting another cannot constitute a wrong or a harm if the other consents to it. Whatever one thinks of that principle, it cannot affect the question of whether hitting someone very hard on the head with the intention of rendering him unconscious is a violent act, at least if we understand violence in the restrictive manner. Anyone so acting is clearly aiming to inflict an injury.

Moreover, the restricted definition helps elucidate two other features of violence which are otherwise puzzling; namely, the point of having such a concept and the fact that even justified violence is regrettable. On the first issue, it is clear that many of us have a distinctive fear of the intrusion into our lives of those intent upon the forceful infliction of injury upon us. We also fear the effects of natural disasters, diseases, social prejudice and injustice, indifference and accident, but our fear of violence usually has a quite particular significance because we are understandably anxious about damage that is specifically directed against us and that is aimed at immediate and dramatic impairment of our wellbeing. This combines with the fact that even justified resort to violence carries with it problems of misjudgment and escalation, as well as the possibility of disturbing psychological consequences for those who employ it, to make the use of violence regrettable even where it is not immoral.

See also: CIVIL DISOBEDIENCE

References and further reading

Arendt, H. (1970) *On Violence*, London: Penguin. (An influential discussion of the significance of violence.)

Coady, C.A.J. (1986) 'The Idea of Violence', *Journal of Applied Philosophy* 3 (1): 3–19. (A longer treatment of some of the issues explored here.)

* Galtung, J. (1969) 'Violence, Peace and Peace Research', *The Journal of Peace Research* 6 (2): 167–91, esp. 168 and 173. (A seminal exposition of the concept of structural violence and an argument for its utility.)

Garver, N. (1968) 'What Violence Is', *The Nation*, 206 (26); repr. in J. Rachels and F.A. Tillman (eds), *Philosophical Issues: A Contemporary Introduction*, New York: Harper & Row, 1972, 223–8. (A defence of a wide understanding of violence in the spirit of the 'structural' definition.)

* Grundy, K.W. and Weinstein, M.A. (1974) *The Ideologies of Violence*, Columbus, OH: Charles Merrill, 8–13. (A useful introductory discussion of some definitions of violence that bear upon those discussed here. They cite the definition by Sidney Hook mentioned in §1.)

Harris, J. (1980) *Violence and Responsibility*, London: Routledge. (Uses a very wide idea of violence to draw strong moral and political conclusions.)

Honderich, T. (1980) *Violence for Equality: Inquiries in Political Philosophy*, Harmondsworth: Penguin, esp. 96–100. (A partial defence of violence as a political tool, based upon a type of legitimist understanding of violence.)

Lee, S. (1996) 'Poverty and Violence', *Social Theory and Practice* 22 (1): 67–82. (Thoughtful article exploring the connections between violence and poverty and arguing for a 'wide' definition of violence in terms of which violence can be said to be the cause of poverty.)

Shaffer, J.A. (ed) (1971) *Violence*, New York: David McKay. (A good collection of essays, mostly on the conceptual analysis of violence.)

Wilkins, B.T. (1992) *Terrorism and Collective Responsibility*, London and New York: Routledge, esp. ch. 3 'Violence and Force'. (A good discussion of some issues to do with violence and terrorism, insisting, in particular, that violence does not always involve the violation of an actual right.)

Wolff, R.P. (1969) 'On Violence', *Journal of Philosophy* 66 (19): 601–16. (Uses a legitimist definition to devalue the moral importance of resort to violence.)

C.A.J. COADY

VIRTUE EPISTEMOLOGY

'Virtue epistemology' is the name of a class of theories that analyse fundamental epistemic concepts such as justification or knowledge in terms of properties of persons rather than properties of beliefs. Some of these theories make the basic concept constitutive of

justification or knowledge that of a reliable belief-forming process, or a reliable belief-forming faculty or, alternatively, a properly functioning faculty. Others make the fundamental concept that of an epistemic or intellectual virtue in the sense of virtue used in ethics. In all these theories, epistemic evaluation rests on some virtuous quality of the person that enables them to act in a cognitively effective and commendable way, although not all use the term 'virtue'. The early, simple forms of process reliabilism are best treated as precursors to virtue epistemology since the latter arose out of the former and has added requirements for knowledge intended to capture the idea of epistemic behaviour that is subjectively responsible as well as objectively reliable.

Proponents of virtue epistemology claim a number of advantages. It is said to bypass disputes between foundationalists and coherentists on proper cognitive structure, to avoid sceptical worries, to avoid the impasse between internalism and externalism, and to broaden the range of epistemological inquiry in a way that permits the recovering of such neglected epistemic values as understanding and wisdom.

1–2 History of virtue epistemology and its varieties
3 Advantages and disadvantages of virtue epistemology

1 History of virtue epistemology and its varieties

Virtue epistemology focuses on traits of persons or their faculties or psychological processes in the analysis of basic epistemic concepts such as justification or knowledge. It is a reaction to a style of epistemology that makes properties of individual beliefs and evidential relations between beliefs the focus of analysis. The theories in the latter category often handle epistemic evaluation on the model of deontological ethics (see DEONTOLOGICAL ETHICS). To be justified, a belief must not violate any epistemic rules or duties – it must be held for the right reason. In contrast, many forms of virtue epistemology have arisen out of reliabilism. According to reliabilist theories, what makes a true belief an instance of knowledge or, alternatively, what makes a belief justified is that it was formed by a reliable process for obtaining the truth (see RELIABILISM). Reliable processes include perception and memory whose reliability need not be cognitively accessible to the believer, and so reliabilism is a form of externalism whereas, typically, deontological theories are internalist (see INTERNALISM AND EXTERNALISM IN EPISTEMOLOGY). Reliabilism is structurally parallel to consequentialist ethics, in particular rule utilitarianism. In a reliabilist theory, the consequences (a high

proportion of true beliefs) make a belief process reliable just as in a rule-utilitarian theory the consequences (a high proportion of utility maximizing actions) make a rule a good one. A belief is epistemically justified (alternatively, warranted) by being the product of a reliable truth-producing process, just as an act is morally justified by being the product of a reliable utility-maximizing rule (see CONSEQUENTIALISM).

An advantage of reliabilism is that its requirements for knowledge are relatively easy to satisfy in ordinary circumstances, even by young children and unsophisticated adults. Hence it is often considered closer to common sense than the more rigorous deontological theories. Some theorists also think it has an advantage with respect to avoiding scepticism. For one has knowledge as long as there is no Cartesian demon and one's cognitive processes do, as a matter of fact, reliably hook up with the truth, whether or not one has an answer to the sceptical challenge (Greco 1992).

Since reliabilism shifts the focus of analysis from properties of beliefs to properties of the believer it sets the stage for a form of epistemology that makes fundamental the virtues and vices of a person. It is not uncommon, then, to classify the more recent forms of reliabilism as virtue epistemology (Kvanvig 1992; Greco 1992), and in one place Alvin Goldman classifies his later version of process reliabilism as a form of virtue epistemology (1992). Simple reliabilism, however, is only distantly related to any kind of virtue ethics. A reliable belief-forming process has little in common with the traditional notion of a virtue and, as already pointed out, reliabilism is structurally parallel to consequentialist ethics, not virtue ethics.

Act-based moral theories such as consequentialist and deontological theories make the central concept that of the right act. Similarly, reliabilist and deontologial theories in epistemology make the central concept that of a belief that is justified or, alternatively, warranted (possessing the property that converts true belief into knowledge). A virtue ethic, in contrast, makes the primary concept that of a virtue. The concept of a right act is derivative and is often less important. A moral virtue is defined neither in terms of the consequences of the acts to which it gives rise, nor in terms of the rules or principles followed by persons exhibiting the virtues. A virtue includes dispositions to have certain emotions as well as dispositions to act in certain ways, and in its Aristotelian and neo-Aristotelian forms virtuous traits are closely tied to a teleological understanding of human nature (see VIRTUE ETHICS).

Given this account of the characteristics of virtue ethics, the epistemic parallel would be one in which intellectual virtue is the fundamental concept, and the concept of a justified belief is derivative and may also be less important. A property is not an intellectual virtue simply because of its propensity to produce true beliefs, nor is it a virtue because it involves following epistemic rules or principles. The parallel with virtue ethics would be even closer if an intellectual virtue includes emotion-dispositions as well as dispositions to act cognitively in certain ways, and a neo-Aristotelian form of virtue epistemology would include a connection between epistemic goods and the good life.

While simple reliabilism is quite a distance from virtue epistemology as just described, recent theories have increasingly moved in that direction. Ernest Sosa (1980) first introduced the concept of intellectual virtue into contemporary literature as a refinement of reliabilism. Sosa proposed that the concept of an intellectual virtue can be used to bypass the dispute between foundationalists and coherentists about the logical or evidential relations needed for proper cognitive structure (see KNOWLEDGE, CONCEPT OF §4). What Sosa meant by an intellectual virtue was a reliable belief-forming faculty like eyesight or memory, and he defined such a virtue in terms of its consequences: 'An intellectual virtue is a quality bound to help maximize one's surplus of truth over error' (Sosa 1985: 227). In subsequent work, Sosa (1991) has distinguished animal knowledge from reflective knowledge. For the former it is sufficient that the belief was caused by a reliable truth-producing faculty. For the latter he adds an internalist component. The believer must have a reliable grasp of the fact that their belief is grounded in a reliable cognitive faculty. Sosa also ties the concept of an intellectual virtue to the 'inner nature' of the knowing subject. These recent moves bring Sosa's concept of an intellectual virtue closer to the traditional notion of virtue as used in ethics.

2 History of virtue epistemology and its varieties (cont.)

A version of virtue epistemology that moves even closer to virtue ethics is Alvin Plantinga's theory of warrant as proper function (1993b). Plantinga uses the term 'warrant' for that property which in sufficient quantity converts true belief into knowledge. A warranted belief, according to Plantinga, is one that is produced by properly functioning faculties in the appropriate environment according to a design plan aimed at truth. Like Sosa, Plantinga makes faculties the focus of analysis, but unlike Sosa he does not identify faculties as virtues because of their consequences. So Plantinga's theory is not modelled on consequentialist ethics, but it is not modelled on virtue ethics either. In fact, Plantinga never uses the term 'virtue' nor does he give any attention to the rich history of the concept of virtue as used in ethics. Plantinga's theory moves closer to traditional accounts of virtue, however, because what counts as properly functioning faculties is determined by a background notion of what is good or desirable for human beings with the nature that they have.

John Greco's version of virtue epistemology modifies Sosa's theory by adding an element that is intended to capture the idea of epistemically responsible as well as reliable belief. To have 'positive epistemic status', Greco says (1990, 1993), not only must a belief be the result of a reliable cognitive faculty (a virtue), but that virtue must have its basis in the believer's conforming to epistemic norms they countenance. Greco's and Sosa's additions of an internalist requirement of belief formation to the reliability condition give their versions of virtue epistemology an ethical component which is missing from simple reliabilism and Plantinga's theory.

Two of the first attempts to link epistemological inquiry with intellectual virtues in the traditional sense of virtue were made by Lorraine Code and James Montmarquet. Code (1987) gives an account of intellectual virtue that 'socializes' epistemology, stresses the place of the knowing subject in the epistemic community, and contextualizes the state of knowing within a background of states that include the non-cognitive (see FEMINIST EPISTEMOLOGY §2–3). She calls her position 'responsibilism' rather than reliabilism because of the knower's degree of choice in cognitive structuring and degree of accountability for these choices. Code does not offer a detailed account of the concept of intellectual virtue, but she is perhaps the first in contemporary epistemology to call attention to the way intellectual virtues in the sense of virtue used in ethics can be useful to the interests of epistemology.

James Montmarquet (1993) gives an extensive treatment of epistemic virtues in the classical sense of a trait for which we are responsible and which are similar to moral virtues. Montmarquet includes in his list of epistemic virtues such traits as open-mindedness; intellectual carefulness, thoroughness, and impartiality; and intellectual courage and perseverance. He maintains that epistemic virtues are the traits which people who desire the truth would desire to have, but he denies that they are reliably truth-conducive in any straightforward way. So Montmarquet's theory, like Code's, does not evolve out of reliabilism, and his principal concerns are somewhat different from those driving reliabilism.

Linda Zagzebski (1996) has developed a version of

virtue epistemology that is explicitly modelled on virtue ethics. Like Code and Montmarquet, what she means by intellectual virtues are such traits as intellectual autonomy and courage, intellectual carefulness and thoroughness, open-mindedness and fair-mindedness, but like Sosa and Greco, she regards reliability as a component of virtue. Zagzebski offers a virtue theory of ethics inclusive enough to handle the intellectual as well as the moral virtues within a single theory, proposing that moral and intellectual virtues have the same basic structure and are acquired in the same way. Both include a motivational component and a component of reliable success in bringing about the aims of the motivational component. In the case of the intellectual virtues this means that reliability in acquiring the truth is a component of intellectual virtue, but there is also a component of intellectual motivation from which the cognitive behaviour characteristic of intellectually virtuous persons arises. Zagzebski then defines the concepts of justified belief and epistemic duty in terms of intellectual virtue in the same way the concepts of right act and of moral duty can be defined in terms of moral virtue in a pure virtue ethics. In both cases the concept of virtue is more basic. She subsequently defines an 'act of virtue', the concept of an act that is praiseworthy in every way – in the act itself, in its motive, in the end it achieves, and which reaches its end because of these other praiseworthy features of the act. An act of intellectual virtue is an act that has an intellectually virtuous motive, is an act that would be characteristically performed by intellectually virtuous persons in the same circumstances, and which reaches truth because of these other features of the act. Knowledge is belief arising out of acts of intellectual virtue. This strategy captures the combination of internal responsibility and epistemic success desired by virtue epistemologists.

3 Advantages and disadvantages of virtue epistemology

When Sosa introduced the concept of intellectual virtue into the contemporary literature, he thought that the shift of focus from properties of beliefs to properties of persons should make it possible to bypass the dispute between foundationalists and coherentists over the logical and evidential relations between beliefs needed for proper epistemic structure. In addition, two possible advantages of reliabilism have already been mentioned. First, its requirements for knowledge are easier to satisfy than internalist theories and, hence, it is said to be closer to common sense than are internalist theories. Second, its requirements for knowledge do not include the

possession by the knower of an answer to the sceptical challenge. For example, they need not be able to answer the question 'But what if there is an evil demon?', even though the presence of an evil demon would deprive them of knowledge. Since having an answer to this question is usually thought to be at best difficult, and probably impossible for the average knower, it is an advantage of a theory of knowledge if its formulation permits us to ignore such worries (see SCEPTICISM).

These advantages of reliabilism may be offset by certain disadvantages, however. Consider first the requirement that reliability is a necessary condition for knowledge. Most versions of virtue epistemology have this requirement. A common objection to the reliability requirement for knowledge or justification is the so-called 'generality problem'. This is the problem that a particular belief can be described as an instance of many different belief-forming processes, some broader (believing whatever you read), some narrower (believing what you read in a particular journal), some so narrow as to apply only to a single belief (believing what you read in a certain journal on a certain subject by a certain writer). The degree of truth-conduciveness will vary greatly, depending upon the way in which the belief-forming process is described. This problem requires refinements to the theory rather than outright rejection. Ways of handling the generality problem have been suggested by Goldman (1986), Greco (1993), Sosa (1991) and Zagzebski (1996). Zagzebski suggests that the class of cases against which truth-conduciveness is to be measured should be empirically determined by the way in which people naturally generalize their belief-forming processes. So if a person who believes what they read in a reliable journal then goes on to believe whatever they read in any periodical, their belief would not count as deriving from a reliable belief-forming process, whereas it would be reliable if they do not tend to generalize their belief-forming tendency to unreliable sources.

Simple reliabilism maintains that reliability is not only necessary, but is sufficient for knowledge. Zagzebski denies that simple reliabilism ought to be considered a form of virtue epistemology, but it is worth mentioning the most serious objection to it since reflection on it was one of the motivations leading to the development of virtue epistemology. The problem is that simple reliabilism does not rule out of the category of knowledge beliefs formed by processes or faculties that are reliable by accident (Plantinga 1993a; Zagzebski 1996). This suggests that any theory that includes reliability as a requirement for knowledge should include an account of what makes a process, trait or faculty reliable in the right way. Virtue epistemologists, then, characteristically add requirements for knowledge other than reliability to eliminate this problem by showing how reliability arises out of something else – in the case of Sosa, the believer's inner nature; in the case of Plantinga, faculties whose proper function is determined by design; for Greco, the norms the believer countenances; for Zagzebski, intellectual virtues. These conditions involve activity on the part of the knower that exhibits epistemic responsibility or features praiseworthy from an internal perspective.

Requirements for knowledge in addition to reliability are seen by their adherents as improving upon simple reliabilism, but these requirements can also be perceived as detracting from one of the advantages of simple reliabilism. This is its generosity in spreading the domain of knowledge to include true beliefs formed in typical circumstances by young children and unreflective adults. But the more we add responsibility and internal awareness to the conditions for knowledge, the more we shrink the resulting class of knowing states. Can children and unreflective adults have perceptual and memory knowledge on these more demanding theories? Sosa's way of handling the problem is to distinguish animal knowledge from reflective knowledge. Zagzebski prefers not to make it a condition for knowledge that the believer actually possesses the full virtue but, rather, that the believer has virtuous intellectual motivations and acts cognitively the way virtuous persons do in the same circumstances. Given that virtuous persons formulate perceptual and memory beliefs in many circumstances with little or no reflection or investigation, it is not difficult for children to imitate their behaviour and, hence, to have knowledge in these cases. Greco's way of handling the problem (1990) is to say that while a belief has positive epistemic status only if it conforms with the norms that the believer countenances, this does not require that the believer should have cognitive access either to the norms themselves or to the fact that their beliefs conform with them.

It can be argued that virtue epistemology has the potential to deal effectively with two other problems of contemporary epistemology. First, there are the problems surrounding the concept of justification which have led to the impasse between internalism and externalism. Since justification is a property of a belief, it is very difficult to adjudicate disputes over this concept if the belief is treated as the bottom-level object of evaluation. If we focus instead on the deeper concept of an intellectual virtue and treat the justifiability of a belief as derivative, it may turn out that justifiability is only one normative property of beliefs among others and the competing intuitions of internalists and externalists require the analysis of more than one property of beliefs, all of which are based in some way on the concept of virtue. Second, focusing epistemology on belief has led to the neglect of two epistemic values that have been important for long periods in the past – understanding and wisdom. An approach focused on intellectual virtues, on the other hand, naturally leads to an account of these values, since understanding and wisdom are either virtues themselves or are very closely connected with virtues (see WISDOM).

See also: CONFUCIAN PHILOSOPHY, CHINESE; JUSTIFICATION, EPISTEMIC; NORMATIVE EPISTEMOLOGY

References and further reading

* Code, L. (1987) *Epistemic Responsibility*, Hanover, NH: University Press of New England for Brown University Press. (Perhaps the first book to apply virtues in the sense used in ethics to the concerns of epistemology. Particularly good for its examples.)
* Goldman, A.I. (1986) *Epistemology and Cognition*, Cambridge, MA: Harvard University Press. (Important example of contemporary reliabilism.)
* —— (1992) 'Epistemic Folkways and Scientific Epistemology', in *Liaisons: Philosophy Meets the Cognitive and Social Sciences*, Cambridge, MA: MIT Press. (The only paper in which Goldman explicitly associates himself with virtue epistemology.)
* Greco, J. (1990) 'Internalism and Epistemically Responsible Belief', *Synthèse* 85 (2): 245–77. (Proposes a version of virtue epistemology which combines reliability with following epistemic norms.)
* —— (1992) 'Virtue Epistemology', in J. Dancy and E. Sosa (eds) *A Companion to Epistemology*, Oxford: Blackwell. (Good summary of how some of the earlier work in virtue epistemology arose out of reliabilism.)
* —— (1993) 'Virtues and Vices of Virtue Epistemology', *Canadian Journal of Philosophy* 23 (3): 413–32. (More detailed discussion of virtue epistemology than his 1992 work.)
* Kvanvig, J. (1992) *The Intellectual Virtues and the Life of the Mind*, Lanham, MD: Rowman & Littlefield. (Focuses mostly on reliabilism and its problems. It then proposes a move away from atomistic epistemology.)
* Montmarquet, J.A. (1993) *Epistemic Virtue and Doxastic Responsibility*, Lanham, MA: Rowman & Littlefield. (Gives an account of the nature of epistemic virtue and uses it to contribute to the debate on the ethics of belief.)

* Plantinga, A. (1993a) *Warrant: The Current Debate*, New York: Oxford University Press. (Important discussion and diagnosis of contemporary theories.)

* —— (1993b) *Warrant and Proper Function*, New York: Oxford University Press. (Presents Plantinga's own influential theory of knowledge.)

* Sosa, E. (1980) 'The Raft and the Pyramid: Coherence versus Foundations in the Theory of Knowledge', in *Studies in Epistemology. Midwest Studies in Philosophy*, Notre Dame, IN: University of Notre Dame Press, vol. 5. (The paper that introduced the concept of intellectual virtue into the contemporary literature.)

* —— (1985) 'Knowledge and Intellectual Virtue', *Monist* 68 (2) April: 226–45. (Describes Sosa's important early version of virtue epistemology.)

* —— (1991) *Knowledge in Perspective*, Cambridge: Cambridge University Press. (This collection of essays is a valuable source on reliabilism and Sosa's own version of virtue epistemology.)

* Zagzebski, L. (1996) *Virtues of the Mind: An Inquiry into the Nature of Virtue and the Ethical Foundations of Knowledge*, Cambridge: Cambridge University Press. (Presents a virtue theory that is designed to handle both moral evaluation and epistemic evaluation within a single theory. It includes a theory of knowledge based on intellectual virtue.)

LINDA ZAGZEBSKI

VIRTUE ETHICS

Virtue ethics has its origin in the ancient world, particularly in the writings of Plato and Aristotle. It has been revived following an article by G.E.M. Anscombe critical of modern ethics and advocating a return to the virtues.

Some have argued that virtue ethics constitutes a third option in moral theory additional to utilitarianism and Kantianism. Utilitarians and Kantians have responded vigorously, plausibly claiming that their views already incorporate many of the theses allegedly peculiar to virtue ethics.

Virtue theory, the study of notions, such as character, related to the virtues, has led to the recultivation of barren areas. These include: What is the good life, and what part does virtue play in it? How stringent are the demands of morality? Are moral reasons independent of agents' particular concerns? Is moral rationality universal? Is morality to be captured in a set of rules, or is the sensitivity of a virtuous person central in ethics?

From virtue ethics, and the virtue theory of which it is a part, have emerged answers to these questions at once rooted in ancient views and yet distinctively modern.

1 **Aristotle and ancient virtue ethics**
2 **Modern virtue theory**
3 **The good of the agent and the demandingness of morality**
4 **Agency and motivation**
5 **Universality and tradition**
6 **Practical reason**

1 Aristotle and ancient virtue ethics

Modern virtue ethicists often claim ARISTOTLE as an ancestor. Aristotle, however, was himself working through an agenda laid down by PLATO and SOCRATES. Socrates asked the question at the heart of Greek ethics: 'How should one live?' All three of these philosophers believed that the answer to this question is, 'Virtuously' (see VIRTUES AND VICES §§1–3).

The ancient philosophical task was to show how living virtuously would be best for the virtuous person. Plato's *Republic* attempts to answer Thrasymachus' challenge that rational people will aim to get the most pleasure, honour and power for themselves. His argument is that justice, broadly construed, is to be identified with a rational ordering of one's soul. Once one sees that one identifies oneself with one's reason, one will realize that being just is in fact best for oneself. Thrasymachus, of course, might respond that he identifies himself with his desires.

Aristotle continued the same project, aiming to show that human *eudaimonia*, happiness, consists in the exercise (not the mere possession of) the virtues (see EUDAIMONIA; HAPPINESS). The linchpin of his case is his 'function' argument that human nature is perfected through virtue, a standard objection to which is that it confuses the notions of a good man and the good for man. Ultimately, Aristotle's method is similar to Plato's. Much of Nicomachean Ethics is taken up with portraits of the virtuous man intended to attract one to a life such as his.

For Aristotle, all of the 'practical' virtues will be possessed by the truly virtuous person, the man of 'practical wisdom' (Aristotle's central 'intellectual' virtue). Socrates believed that virtue was a *unity*, that it consisted in knowledge alone. Aristotle's position is one of *reciprocity*: the possession of one virtue implies the possession of all. At this point he joined Socrates and Plato in their opposition to Greek 'common sense'. This opposition to common sense is not something that characterizes modern virtue ethics.

2 Modern virtue theory

Virtue theory is that general area of philosophical inquiry concerned with or related to the virtues. It includes *virtue ethics*, a theory about how we should act or live. This distinction is a rough one, but it is important to grasp that much of modern virtue theory is by writers not themselves advocating virtue ethics.

Virtue theory has undergone a resurgence since G.E.M. Anscombe's article 'Modern Moral Philosophy' (1958) (see ANSCOMBE, G.E.M. §2). Anscombe believed that it was a mistake to seek a foundation for a morality grounded in legalistic notions such as 'obligation' or 'duty' in the context of general disbelief in the existence of a divine lawgiver as the source of such obligation (see DUTY). She recommended that philosophy of psychology should take the place of moral philosophy, until adequate accounts of such central notions as action and intention were available. Then, she suggested, philosophers might return to moral philosophy through an ethics of virtue.

What is virtue ethics? It is tempting to characterize it as a theory advocating acting virtuously, but this is insufficiently precise. Virtue ethics is usually seen as an alternative to utilitarianism or consequentialism in general (see CONSEQUENTIALISM; UTILITARIANISM). To put it roughly, utilitarianism says that we should maximize human welfare or utility. A utilitarian, however, may advocate acting virtuously for reasons of utility. Ethical theories are best understood in terms not of what acts they require, but of the reasons offered for acting in whatever way is in fact required.

Which properties of actions, then, according to virtue ethics, constitute our reason for doing them? The properties of kindness, courage and so on. It is worth noting that there is a difference between acting virtuously and doing a virtuous action. One's doing a virtuous action may be seen as doing the action a virtuous person would do in those circumstances, though one may not oneself be a virtuous person. Virtue ethics, then, concerns itself not only with isolated actions but with the character of the agent. There are reasons for doing certain things (such as kind things), and also for being a certain type of person (a kind person).

This account of virtue ethics enables us to distinguish it from its other main opponent, deontology or Kantianism (see DEONTOLOGICAL ETHICS; KANT, I. §§9–10; KANTIAN ETHICS). A Kantian, for example, might claim that my reason for telling the truth is that to do so would be in accordance with the categorical imperative. That is a property of the action of telling the truth quite different from its being honest.

3 The good of the agent and the demandingness of morality

A pure form of virtue ethics will suggest that virtuous properties – 'thick' properties as opposed to thin properties such as 'rightness' and 'goodness' – of actions constitute our only reasons for performing them. Aristotle came close to this position, but it is perhaps more plausible to interpret him as claiming that the rationality of virtue lies in its promotion of the agent's *eudaimonia*. Aristotle's view is nevertheless radical. Since my *eudaimonia* consists only in the exercise of the virtues, I have no reason to live a non-virtuous life.

More common than pure forms of virtue ethics are pluralistic views according to which there are other reason-constituting properties, some perhaps of the kind advocated by utilitarians and Kantians. The open-mindedness of virtue ethics contrasts sharply at this point with what Bernard Williams (1985) has identified as the peculiar narrowness of focus in modern ethics (see WILLIAMS, B.A.O.). Considerations other than the moral are relevant to the question of how one should live. Modern virtue ethicists can thus adopt a position on the demandingness of morality between the extremes of Aristotle and their modern opponents. For they need claim neither that self-interest is constituted entirely by being moral nor that morality completely overrides self-interest.

Much of virtue theory has been concerned to develop Williams' criticism of utilitarianism and Kantianism that through their impersonality and impartiality, utilitarianism and Kantianism violate the *integrity* of moral agents. Philippa Foot has developed these critical arguments in a direction favourable to virtue ethics. According to both the principle of utility and the Kantian categorical imperative, moral reasons, being universal, are independent of the desires of agents. Foot (1978), impressed by the rationality of fulfilling one's own desires, has argued that moral reasons do depend on the desires of the agent, so that a person who acts consistently ungenerously may be described as ungenerous, but not necessarily as having any reason to act generously, unless they have a desire which would thereby be fulfilled. Foot is here expressing a doubt similar to Anscombe's about the possibility of ungrounded 'ought' judgments.

4 Agency and motivation

Imagine that you are thanking a friend for visiting you in hospital. She replies, 'Oh, it was nothing. It was obvious that morality required me to come.' This case, taken from an influential article by Michael Stocker (1976), and related to the discussion in the previous section concerning the demandingness of morality and the pervasiveness of the moral point of view, serves to illustrate an ideal of agency which lies implicit in much modern ethical theory (see MORAL MOTIVATION; MORAL REALISM). The unattractiveness of this ideal can be avoided by utilitarians, who may argue that thinking in the way your friend did about morality is likely to be self-defeating in utilitarian terms. Even the utilitarians, however, can be charged with missing the point. What is wrong with your friend is not that moral thinking like hers fails to maximize utility. Nevertheless, the case constitutes a far more serious problem for Kantians, given Kant's insistence on the explicit testing of courses of action using the categorical imperative, and his view that the moral worth of an action lies entirely in its being done out of a sense of duty.

Modern virtue ethicists such as Lawrence Blum (1980) have endeavoured to replace this conception of moral agency with a virtue-centred ideal allowing agents to be moved directly by emotional concern for others. This ideal can once again be seen as emerging from Anscombe's attack on the notion of duty. A morality of duty is said to pay insufficient attention to the inner life: the dutiful agent is not doing, or feeling, enough (this criticism is an interesting counterpoint to the accusation that Kantianism is excessively demanding). The charge, then, is not only that modern moral theory fails to provide plausible justifying reasons for action, but that the motivational structure of what is clearly moral agency is quite different from what the theories lead us to expect. Moral agency consists at least partly in acting and feeling in ways prompted by bonds of partiality, requiring no further backing from impersonal ethical theory (see FRIENDSHIP §4).

5 Universality and tradition

We have already seen how some virtue theorists link moral reasons to motivation. This is one route to a narrowing of the scope of moral reasons. Without any motivation to do so, there is no reason, say, to maximize utility or respect the moral law. Another route is followed by writers such as Alasdair MACINTYRE who ground moral rationality in traditions.

MacIntyre's critique of modern ethical theory, outlined in *After Virtue* (1981), is the most stringent in virtue theory. He claims that present moral discussion is literal nonsense: we unreflectively use a mix of concepts left over from moribund traditions; since these traditions are incommensurable, arguments using concepts from rival traditions are irresoluble and interminable. MacIntyre does not, however, follow through the implications of this critique into a Nietzschean moral scepticism, advocating instead a return to Aristotelian virtue ethics (see NIETZSCHE, F.). The question of how he accomplishes this is an example of a puzzle about virtue theory present since Anscombe's original article: after the sustained critique of modern ethical theory by virtue theorists, is the remaining conceptual apparatus sufficiently strong to support an alternative prescriptive ethics?

The relationship between modern virtue ethicists and Aristotle is complex. Most virtue ethicists, including Foot and MacIntyre, combine an Aristotelian emphasis on the virtues with a modern scepticism about the possibility of an objective theory of the good for an individual. Likewise, MacIntyre's stress on the importance of context is quite Aristotelian, but the relativism to which this leads him would be anathema to Aristotle (see MORAL RELATIVISM). MacIntyre claims that goods are internal to practices, and not assessable from some external point of view, while Aristotle believed that teleological reflection on universal human nature enabled one to identify those practices which are good *haplōs*, 'simply good'.

The relativism of modern virtue ethics has emerged also in political theory in the debate between communitarians, such as MacIntyre, and liberals (see COMMUNITY AND COMMUNITARIANISM; LIBERALISM). Along with a predilection for virtue-centred over rule-centred ethics go preferences for the local and particular to the universal, the specific to the general, the embedded to the abstracted, the communal to the individual, the inexplicit to the explicit, the traditional to the revised, the partial to the impartial. In MacIntyre's work, the notion of goods internal to diachronic practices and grounded in traditions is tied to a criticism of a free-floating liberal self, choosing goods from some Archimedean standpoint. MacIntyre's narrative conception of a self opens another door for the readmittance of the notion of character into moral philosophy.

The most serious problem for relativism has yet to be resolved in modern virtue ethics. What are we to say of practices and ways of life constituting internally coherent traditions, yet containing undeniably evil components?

6 Practical reason

One reason for the fading of the notion of character in ethical theory is that utilitarianism and Kantianism have commonly been developed as ethics of rules to resolve dilemmas. An argument against a rule-based ethics is found in Aristotle's discussion of the legal virtue of *epieikeia*, 'equity'. Rules will always run out in hard cases, and some sensitivity is required on the part of the judge to fill the gap between the law and the world. Likewise, for Aristotle, the virtuous man possesses *phronēsis*, 'practical wisdom', a sensitivity to the morally salient features of particular situations which goes beyond an ability to apply explicit rules.

This view has been revived in virtue ethics, by among others Iris Murdoch (1970) and John McDowell, in his article, 'Virtue and Reason' (1979). McDowell argues that we cannot postulate a world as seen by both the virtuous and the unvirtuous, and then explain the moral agency of the virtuous through their possessing some special desire. Since moral rules run out, any object of desire could not be made explicit. McDowell uses Wittgenstein to support his claim that rational action does not have to be rule-governed (see WITTGENSTEIN, L. §§10–12). This has clear implications for moral education: it should consist in enabling the person to see sensitively, not (or at least not only) in inculcating rigid and absolute principles. This is one of the strands in the feminist critique of modern ethical theory, itself closely tied to virtue theory. Writers such as Carol Gilligan (1982) argue that the moral sensibility of women is less rule-governed than that of men, and this has influenced the 'ethics of care' of, for example, Nel Noddings (see FEMINIST ETHICS §1; MORAL EDUCATION §§1–2).

The emphasis in virtue ethics on non-rational factors in moral motivation sits well with the notion of moral sensitivity. And this latter notion provides another standpoint from which one might criticize the basing of morality on the categorical imperative. As we have seen, Foot claims that immorality is not necessarily irrational, since moral reasons depend on the agent's desires. Writers such as McDowell who depict practical reason as perceptual can also deny that immorality is irrational. The unvirtuous lack not any capacity of the theoretical or calculative intellect, but moral sensitivity. Unlike Foot, however, McDowell would argue that this is in fact a failure to perceive genuine reasons for action independent of the agent's motivations.

Again, in McDowell, we see the pastiche, characteristic of virtue ethics, of ancient and modern: rationality is made to depend on social practice, and yet, as Socrates thought, virtue turns out to be a kind of knowledge.

See also: CHENG; DUTY AND VIRTUE, INDIAN CONCEPTIONS OF; IMPARTIALITY; LIFE, MEANING OF; MENCIUS; MORAL JUDGMENT

References and further reading

* Anscombe, G.E.M. (1958) 'Modern Moral Philosophy', *Philosophy* 33: 1–19. (Seminal article, critical of modern ethics and advocating return to the virtues.)

* Aristotle (*c.* mid 4th century BC) *Nicomachean Ethics*, trans. with notes by T. Irwin, Indianapolis, IN: Hackett Publishing Company, 1985. (Essential reading. The 'function argument' occurs in I 7. Books II–V concern the virtues of character, while practical wisdom is the topic of VI.)

* Blum, L.A. (1980) *Friendship, Altruism and Morality*, London: Routledge & Kegan Paul. (Includes criticism of Kantian ethics, and a virtue-based alternative.)

Crisp, R. (1996) *How Should One Live? Essays on the Virtues*, Oxford: Clarendon Press. (Edited collection of commissioned papers on central issues in virtue theory.)

Crisp, R. and Slote, M. (1997) *Virtue Ethics*, Oxford: Oxford University Press. (A collection of well-known papers on the virtues, with introductory essay. Includes bibliography on various topics.)

* Foot, P. (1978) *Virtues and Vices*, Oxford: Blackwell. (A collection of important papers. Ch. 1 is on virtues and vices, while 8–11 concern moral reasons for action.)

* Gilligan, C. (1982) *In a Different Voice: Psychological Theory and Women's Development*, Cambridge, MA: Harvard University Press. (Suggests that feminine ethics may be less abstract and rule-governed than masculine ethics.)

Kant, I. (1785) *Grundlegung zur Metaphysik der Sitten*, trans. L.W. Beck, *Foundations of the Metaphysics of Morals*, Upper Saddle River, NJ: Prentice Hall, 2nd edn, 1995. (Classic defence of the categorical imperative and the centrality of moral motivation by the sense of duty rather than by inclination.)

* MacIntyre, A. (1981) *After Virtue*, London: Duckworth. (Influential critique of modern ethics, and advocacy of Thomistic virtue ethics.)

* McDowell, J. (1979) 'Virtue and Reason', *The Monist* 62: 331–50. (Important article, combining themes from Aristotle and Wittgenstein. Difficult.)

* Murdoch, I. (1970) *The Sovereignty of Good*, London: Routledge & Kegan Paul. (Profound reflections on modernity by a Platonist.)

Noddings, N. (1984) *Caring: A Feminine Approach to Ethics and Moral Education*, Berkeley, CA: University of California Press. (A version of feminist ethics, in which the virtue of caring is made central, as opposed to concern for moral obligation or duty.)

* Plato (c.380–367 BC) *Republic*, trans. R. Waterfield, Harmondsworth: Penguin, 1994. (First major expression of virtue ethics.)
* Stocker, M. (1976) 'The Schizophrenia of Modern Ethical Theory', *Journal of Philosophy* 73: 453–6. (Influential article, capturing much of the unhappiness with modern ethical theory.)
* Williams, B. (1973) 'A Critique of Utilitarianism', in J.J. Smart and B. Williams, *Utilitarianism For and Against*, Cambridge: Cambridge University Press. (A wide-ranging and suggestive series of criticisms of utilitarian ethics. Sections 3–5 concern integrity.)
* —— (1985) *Ethics and the Limits of Philosophy*, Cambridge, MA: Harvard University Press and London: Fontana. (Important discussion and critique of modern ethics.)

ROGER CRISP

VIRTUE, INDIAN CONCEPTIONS OF *see* DUTY AND VIRTUE, INDIAN CONCEPTIONS OF

VIRTUES AND VICES

The concept of a virtue can make an important contribution to a philosophical account of ethics, but virtue theory should not be seen as parallel to other 'ethical theories' in trying to provide a guide to action.

Modern accounts of the virtues typically start from Aristotle, but they need to modify his view substantially, with respect to the grounding of the virtues in human nature; the question of what virtues there are; their unity; and their psychological identity as dispositions of the agent. In particular, one must acknowledge the historical variability of what have been counted as virtues.

Aristotle saw vices as failings, but modern opinion must recognize more radical forms of viciousness or evil. It may also need to accept that the good is more intimately connected with its enemies than traditional views have allowed. Virtue theory helps in the discussion of such questions by offering greater resources of psychological realism than other approaches.

1 Virtues and theory

2 Beyond Aristotle: ground; content
3 Beyond Aristotle (continued): unity; reality
4 Vices, failings and evil
5 Links between virtue and vice

1 Virtues and theory

Ethical theories are standardly presented as falling into three basic types, centring respectively on *consequences*, *rights* and *virtues* (see CONSEQUENTIALISM; DEONTOLOGICAL ETHICS; RIGHTS; VIRTUE ETHICS). One way of understanding this division into three is in terms of what each theory sees, at the most basic level, as bearing ethical value. For the first type of theory, it is *good states of affairs*; for the second, it is *right action*; while virtue theory puts most emphasis on the idea of a *good person*, someone who could be described also as an ethically admirable person. The last is an important emphasis, and the notion of a virtue is important in ethics; but its importance cannot be caught in this way, as the focus of a theory which is supposedly parallel to these other types of theory. Consequentialist and rights theories aim to systematize our principles or rules of action in ways that will, supposedly, help us to see what to do or to recommend in particular cases. A theory of the virtues cannot claim to do this: the theory itself says that what one needs in order to do and recommend the right things are virtues, not a theory about virtues. Moreover, the thoughts of a virtuous person do not consist entirely, or even mainly, of thoughts about virtues or about paradigms of virtuous people. Indeed, they will sometimes be thoughts about rights or good consequences, and this makes it clear that thoughts about the good person cannot displace these other ethical concepts, since a good person will have to use some such concepts. 'Virtue theory' cannot be on the same level as the other types of theory.

An emphasis on virtues is important to moral philosophy for other reasons. Although it need not exclude cognitivism, it shifts attention from morality as a system of propositions or truths to its psychological (and hence, eventually, social) embodiment in individual dispositions of action, thought and emotional reaction. It draws attention to the variety of reasons for action and judgment that may play a part in ethical life, beyond the theorists' favourites, duty and utility (see MORAL MOTIVATION §§1–3; MORALITY AND IDENTITY §4; MORALITY AND EMOTIONS). Such reasons will not typically embody virtue concepts themselves, or, still less, involve reflection on the agent's own virtues. But virtue theory can help to explain how considerations such as 'she needs it', for instance, or 'he relied on what you said', can function as an agent's reasons. An approach through the virtues also leaves room for the important idea that ethically correct action may be only partly codifiable and may involve an essential appeal to judgment (see MORAL JUDGMENT §4; UNIVERSALISM IN ETHICS §3).

2 Beyond Aristotle: ground; content

The first systematic investigation of the virtues was made by Plato, in such works as *Gorgias* and the *Republic*, and it was extremely significant, for instance in setting the problem of the unity of the virtues (see §3). Plato also posed in a particularly challenging form questions about the value of virtues to their possessor. The classical account of the virtues, however, to which all modern treatments refer, is that of Aristotle (Nicomachean Ethics) (see ARISTOTLE §22–5). Just because of the power and the influence of this account, it is easy to underestimate the extent to which a modern theory needs to distance itself from Aristotle. A modern account is likely to agree with Aristotle that virtues are dispositions of character, acquired by ethical training, displayed not just in action but in patterns of emotional reaction. It will agree, too, that virtues are not rigid habits, but are flexible under the application of practical reason. But there are at least four matters on which it is likely to disagree with Aristotle, which may be labelled *ground*; *content*; *unity*; and *reality*.

Ground. Aristotle held that the virtues (for which the word in his language means only 'excellences' – see ARETĒ) had a teleological ground, in the sense that they represented the fullest development of a certain kind of natural creature, a nondefective male human being. No one now is going to agree with Aristotle that there are creatures who are biologically human beings but who are excluded from this full development by their nature as women or as 'natural slaves'. Having abandoned his views about women and slaves, modern thinkers face the harder question of how far they agree with Aristotle about the natural basis of the virtues. This in turn raises the question of how strongly Aristotle's own teleological view should be taken. On one interpretation, he had a comprehensive functional conception of the contents of the universe, with each kind of creature fitting into a discoverable overall pattern. On such a conception, substantial parts of the theory of the virtues will be discoverable by top-down systematic inquiry which will tell us what sorts of creatures human beings are, and hence what their best life will be (see PERFECTIONISM; TELEOLOGICAL ETHICS). Other interpreters give a more moderate account of Aristotle's enterprise, according to which his intentions will be honoured by a hermeneutical inquiry into what we, now, regard as the most basic and valuable aspects of human beings.

Content. What is undeniably lacking from Aristotle's thought, as from that of other ancient thinkers, is an historical dimension. Some modern virtue theorists share this weakness. Aristotle's account is in several respects different from any account of the virtues one would give now, with respect both to what it puts in and what it leaves out. He gives a particularly important place to a quality called *megalopsuchia*, 'greatness of soul', which has a lot to do with a grand social manner and which bears even less relation to a contemporary ethic than its name, in itself, might suggest. A modern person, asked for the principal virtues, might well mention kindness and fairness. Fairness bears a relation to an important Aristotelian virtue, justice, but the latter is defined to an important extent in political and civic terms, and gives a fairly restricted account of fairness as a personal characteristic. Kindness is not an Aristotelian virtue at all. Moreover, there is no account of an important modern virtue, truthfulness; what Aristotle calls the virtue of truth is (surprisingly, as it seems to us) concerned exclusively with boasting and modesty.

There has been obvious historical variation in what is seen as the content of the virtues. Aquinas, who notably developed Aristotle's account, of course modified it to accommodate Christianity, holding in particular that besides the moral virtues, there were 'theological' virtues, which have God as their immediate object (see THEOLOGICAL VIRTUES). The pagans were not in a position to display these, but so far as the moral virtues were concerned, they could be truly virtuous in the light of natural reason. However, there was still something imperfect about their virtue even at this level since, Aquinas held, the whole of ethical life is properly grounded in the virtue called charity, which has a divine origin (see CHARITY).

For Hume (1751), on the other hand, Aristotle's account and other pagan sources served to support an ethics of the virtues that was precisely designed to discredit and exclude Christianity (see HUME, D. §4). The historical variation, both in philosophical formulations and in cultural realizations of the virtues, raises wider issues of how theories of the virtues are to be understood. The conceptions of human nature and human circumstances that underlie such theories are open to wide reinterpretation in the face of changing values, and the Aristotelian presupposition that an understanding of human nature could yield a determinate account of the virtues – even if that idea is interpreted relatively unambitiously – looks unrealistic. There are of course constants in the psychology and circumstances of human beings that make certain virtues, in some version or other, ubiquitous: in every society people need (something like) courage, (something like) self-control with regard to anger and sexual desire, and some version of prudence. These platitudes, which are stressed by those who look to a substantive universal virtue theory, severely underdetermine the content of such a theory. This is shown by the very simple consideration that the constant features of human life are indeed constant, but the virtues that have been recognized at different times and by different cultures vary considerably.

3 Beyond Aristotle (continued): unity; reality

Unity. Aristotle inherited from Plato, and ultimately from Socrates, an interest in the unity of the virtues (see SOCRATES §5). Socrates seems to have held that there was basically only one virtue, which he called wisdom or knowledge. The conventional distinctions between the various virtues – justice, self-control, courage and the rest – were taken to mark only different fields of application of this power. Aristotle did think that there were separate virtues, but nevertheless his view came almost to the same thing as Socrates', since he thought that one could not have one virtue without having them all. One could not properly possess any one virtue unless one had the intellectual virtue which is called in Aristotle's language *phronēsis* (often translated as 'practical wisdom', but better rendered as 'judgment' or 'good sense'); but, Aristotle held, if one had this quality, then one had all the virtues.

It is not hard to see the general idea underlying this position. Generosity is linked to justice – someone who gives only what justice demands is not being generous. Similar points can be made about the interrelations of some other virtues. However, it is important to the theory of the virtues that they provide psychological explanations as well as normative descriptions, and from a realistic psychological point of view it is hard to deny (as many ancient Greeks other than Socrates and Aristotle agreed) that someone can have some virtues while lacking others. In particular, the so-called 'executive virtues' of courage and self-control can be present without other virtues; indeed, they themselves can surely be deployed in the interests of wicked projects. The refusal to acknowledge this may simply represent an ethical reluctance to give moral accolades to bad people.

The fact that the virtues can, to some degree, be separated from one another itself helps to give point to virtue theory. Some modern ethical theories do imply that there is basically only one moral disposition. Utilitarianism, at least in its direct form, places everything on impartial benevolence (see UTILITARIANISM; IMPARTIALITY); and though Kant himself did have a theory of the virtues, Kantianism insists on the primacy of a sense of duty (see KANT, I. §§9–11; KANTIAN ETHICS). An advantage of virtue theory is that it allows for a more complex and realistic account of ethical motivation.

Relatedly, it can acknowledge psychological connections between the ethical and other aspects of character, accepting that people's temperaments have something to do with how they conduct themselves ethically. For the same reason, virtue theory is implicitly opposed to sharp boundaries between the 'moral' and the 'nonmoral', and is likely to acknowledge that there is a spectrum of desirable characteristics, and that no firm or helpful line can be drawn round those that are specifically of moral significance. Aristotle did not even try to draw such a line: his own terminology distinguishes only between excellences of character and intellectual excellences, and one of the latter, *phronēsis*, is itself necessary to the excellences of character. Hume, who, unlike Aristotle, was surrounded by moralists who wanted to draw such a line, goes out of his way to mock the attempt to draw it, and his deliberately offensive treatment of the subject is still very instructive.

Reality. Aristotle conceived of the virtues as objective dispositional characteristics of people which they possess in at least as robust a sense as that in which a magnet possesses the power to attract metals, though people, unlike magnets, have of course acquired the dispositions – in the way appropriate to such things – by habituation (see MORAL EDUCATION). Modern scepticism, however, to some extent supported by social and cognitive psychology, questions whether we can take such a naïve view of what it is for someone to have a virtue. There are at least two different sources of doubt. One is the extent to which people's reactions depend on situation: it is claimed that they will act in ways that express a given virtue only within a rather narrow range of recognized contexts, and if the usual expectations are suspended or even, in some cases, slightly shifted, may not act in the approved style.

The other doubt concerns ascription. When we understand people's behaviour in terms of virtues and vices, or indeed other concepts of character, we are selecting in a highly interpretative way from their behaviour as we experience it, and the way in which we do this (as, indeed, we understand many other things) is in terms of stereotypes, scripts, or standard images, which may range from crude 'characters' to sophisticated and more individuated outlines constructed with the help of types drawn, often, from fiction. The available range of such images forms part of the shifting history of the virtues. At different times there have been pattern books of virtue and vice, and one of the first was the Characters written by Theophrastus, a pupil of Aristotle's (see THEOPHRASTUS; EXAMPLES IN ETHICS).

Even assuming such ideas to be correct, it is not clear exactly to what extent they have a negative impact on virtue theory. Everyone knows that virtues do not express themselves under all circumstances, and also that agents may be very rigid in their ability to understand how a situation is to be seen in terms of virtues. Again, with regard to ascription, it is very important that if it is true that we construct our interpretations of another person's character in terms of a stock of images, it is equally true that the other person does so as well. The point is not so much that there is a gap between the interpreter and the person interpreted, but rather that all of us, as interpreters of ourselves and of others, use shared materials that have a history. There are lessons in such ideas for ethics generally and for virtue theory, but they need not be entirely sceptical. The points about the situational character of the virtues and about their ascription serve to remind us that an agent's virtues depend in many different ways on their relations to society: not simply in being acquired from society and reinforced or weakened by social forces, but also in the ways in which they are constructed from socially shared materials.

4 Vices, failings and evil

Aristotle named a variety of vices, each of which was basically constituted by the absence of the restraining or shaping influence of virtue, together with the operation of some natural self-centred motive. Thus cowardice was the disposition, in the absence of courage, to give in to fear; self-indulgence and irascibility the dispositions to give in to bodily pleasure and to anger. In this range of what may be called 'failings', actions that are expressions of vices do have distinctive motives, but those are not in themselves distinctively bad motives: it is rather that natural motives are expressed in ways in which they would not be expressed by a virtuous person. There are other failings in which the agent's motivation is distinctively deplorable, because it is constituted by the exaggeration, parody or perversion of a virtue: an ostentatious disposition to distribute gifts or favours, in place of generosity, or, to take a modern example, sentimentality in place of kindness. Aristotle notices some failings of this type, but, in line with his 'doctrine of the mean', he oversimplifies their psychology under an unexamined category of 'excess'.

A peculiar case, in Aristotle's treatment, is justice. At the level of actions, at least, it might be thought that there were no distinctive motives to injustice; a person can act unjustly from a variety of motives, and indeed Aristotle mentions the possibility that a coward might treat others unjustly, by 'getting an unfair share of safety'. If this is generalized, an unjust person might be understood not as one with some characteristic motive, but rather as one who is simply insensitive to considerations of justice. However, Aristotle does introduce a distinctive motive for injustice – 'greed' or the desire to have more than others. An unjust person, then – as opposed to someone who has some other vice as a result of which he acts unjustly – is, for Aristotle, a particular greedy type, one who might roughly be recognized in modern terms as 'a crook'.

Aristotle also notices another kind of failing or deficiency, a lack of perception or feeling for others, but this is typically registered by him only as an extreme characteristic, lying off the scale of the ethical, in the form of a brutality or beastliness which virtually falls out of the category of the human. The fact that he does not have anything to say about the more domesticated forms of such a failing, very familiar to us, is a corollary to his not recognizing a virtue of kindness.

It follows from Aristotle's holistic and teleological conception of virtue as the fulfilment of the highest human capacities that vices should be basically failings, instances of a lack or an absence. This hardly leaves room for a notion of the *vicious*: the nearest that Aristotle gets to such an idea is the figure of an obsessional and unscrupulous hedonist. We possess, only too obviously, notions of viciousness deeper and more threatening than this. They point to a concept conspicuously lacking from Aristotle (though to a lesser extent, perhaps, lacking from Plato) – the concept of evil (see EVIL).

This leads decisively beyond the conception of vices as failings, even very serious failings. Among evil or vicious motivations, a basic type is cruelty, the desire to cause suffering, a disposition which, as Nietzsche pointed out, contrasts markedly with brutality: it has to share, rather than lack, the sensitivity to others' suffering that is displayed by kindness. In the most typical modes of cruelty, agents derive their pleasure from the sense of themselves bringing about the pain or frustration of others, and their cruel behaviour is directly an attempted expression of power. Rather different from this, though close to it, is maliciousness, as it might be called, a motivation in the style of envy, where the desire is merely that other people's happiness should not exist. Persons in this state of mind may be pleased if others come to grief, even though they do not bring it about themselves. Alberich, in Wagner's *Götterdämmerung*, says, 'Hagen, mein Sohn! hasse die Frohen!' – 'hate the happy'; such a hatred can have many expressions, only some of which involve the specifically active pleasures of cruelty.

Sometimes, cruelty may not only share, as it must, the perceptions that kindness uses, but model itself negatively on kindness, calculating what a kind person might want to do, in order to parody or subvert it. It then takes on the character of perversity. This style of reversal can be applied to virtues other than kindness. There is counter-justice, the disposition to frustrate the ends of justice, not simply in one's own interests, or to hurt or frustrate a particular person whom one hates or envies, but to take pleasure in the frustration of justice as such and the disappointments inflicted on those of good will. At the limit, this can constitute an almost selfless aesthetic of horribleness, one of the less obvious forms that may be taken by the satisfactions of Milton's Satan, with his resolve that evil should be his good.

5 Links between virtue and vice

Unlike the failings recognized by Aristotle, these evil motivations are more than mere negations. It is important, however, that this need not be taken as a metaphysical claim: one need not be committed to a Manichean view (or even the very various compromises with such a view that have been negotiated by orthodox Christianity), to the effect that human nature or the world itself contains some perversely destructive principle (see MANICHEISM). One might, for instance, hold, as some optimistic programmes of psychotherapy do, that vicious and cruel motivations are, indeed, perversions, produced by a failure of love or other deficiency in the individual's upbringing. This is an encouraging position, inasmuch as it holds out the hope of a world free of such motivations, but it does not think that such motivations, while they exist, are to be understood simply in terms of the lack of a shaping or restraining influence. It would accept that vicious motivations were specially and inventively active.

Other psychological and social views are less hopeful. It is not simply that they see no ground for Utopian hopes that the world could ever be freed from vicious motivations. Some of them detect deeper ways in which virtue, and more generally the good, depend on their opposites. At the most superficial level, there are contemporary versions of the point made in Mandeville's *Fable of the Bees* (1714) (see MANDEVILLE, B. §2): many benefits, including ethical benefits, have come from the development of commercial society, but there is no known way of replacing greed as a means of sustaining it. At another level, there is no doubt that valuable human achievements, for instance in the arts and sciences, have come about only because of a certain indifference to values of justice and benevolence, both at an institutional level and in the lives of those who have brought about these achievements. (Here, as so often, moralists have to face the question whether or not they are relieved that the values which they think should prevail have not always done so.)

At the deepest level, however, it is not a question simply whether nonethical values may often require the neglect or denial of morality, but whether morality itself does not require it. One of the metaphysicians' illusions, Nietzsche said (1886), is 'the belief in opposing values'. In fact, he thought, moral values will always turn out to implicate their opposites – historically (in terms of how new moral values come to exist), socially (in terms of how they sustain themselves), and psychologically (in terms of how they are learned and of how they derive their energy).

Even if we accept the force of the Nietzschean suspicions, this need not damage, but rather encourages, the project of thinking about morality in ways that give an important place to virtues and vices. A theory of virtues, handled in a truthful way, offers better hope of being psychologically realistic than other prominent pictures of the ethical life do. If, further, it extends its realism to the motivations of immorality as well, and does not treat them as mere negations of the moral dispositions, it will better understand morality itself. It will be more successful in this than other theories of morality, which usually pass over in silence the forces that oppose it, or register them simply as objects of moral disapproval, or treat them as the products of a (typically unexplained) cognitive failure.

See also: HELP AND BENEFICENCE; HUMAN NATURE; JUSTICE; MENCIUS; MORAL JUDGMENT §4; NIETZSCHE, F.; PRUDENCE; SELF-CONTROL; TRUTHFULNESS

References and further reading

Aristotle (*c.* mid 4th century BC) *Nicomachean Ethics*, trans. W.D. Ross, revised by J. Urmson, ed. and revised by J. Barnes in *The Complete Works of Aristotle*, vol. 2, Princeton, NJ: Princeton University Press, 1984. (Generally accepted as the most considered statement of his position. For secondary works, see Broadie (1991) and Sherman (1989) below.)

Baier, A.C. (1991) *A Progress of Sentiments: reflections on Hume's Treatise*, Cambridge, MA: Harvard University Press. (A thoughtful consideration of Hume's moral philosophy, useful on the relations between virtue and sentiment.)

Broadie, S. (1991) *Ethics with Aristotle*, New York: Oxford University Press. (A notably subtle and philosophically helpful commentary.)

Crisp, R. and Slote, M. (eds) (1997) *Virtue Ethics*, Oxford: Oxford University Press. (A helpful collection of papers.)

Flanagan, O. (1991) *Varieties of Moral Personality: Ethics and Psychological Realism*, Cambridge, MA: Harvard University Press. (Relates the moral psychology of various ethical positions to empirical material.)

French, P.A., Uehling, T.E. and Wettstein, H.K. (eds) (1988) *Ethical Theory: Character and Virtue*, Midwest Studies in Philosophy, vol. 13, Notre Dame, IN: University of Notre Dame Press. (A useful collection of papers on contemporary virtue theory.)

Hume, D. (1751) *An Enquiry Concerning the Principles of Morals*, in *Enquiries Concerning Human Understanding and Concerning the Principles of Morals*, ed. L.A. Selby-Bigge, revised by P.H. Nidditch, Oxford: Clarendon Press, 3rd edn, 1975. (A more compact, though also less searching, account than book III of *A Treatise on Human Nature* (1739–40). Appendix IV discusses the idea of 'moral' virtue.)

MacIntyre, A. (1981) *After Virtue*, Notre Dame, IN: University of Notre Dame Press. (An influential, negative, assessment of modern moral ideas in contrast to Aristotelian and medieval virtue theory.)

* Mandeville, B. (1714) *The Fable of the Bees: or, Private Vices, Publick Benefits*, ed. F.B. Kaye, Indianapolis, IN: Liberty Fund, 1988. (The work was first intended as a political satire, but has been seen as offering a serious case for private vices turned into public benefits.)

Nietzsche, F. (1886) *Jenseits von Gut und Böse*, trans. R.J. Hollingdale, *Beyond Good and Evil*, Harmondsworth: Penguin, 1990. (Considers, among many other things, the 'faith in opposing values'.)

—— (1887) *Zur Genealogie der Moral*, trans. C. Diethe, *On the Genealogy of Morality*, Cambridge: Cambridge University Press, 1994. (A powerfully influential study, phenomenological rather than historical, of moral values – including, importantly, the passion for truthfulness which motivates the work itself.)

Plato (*c*.395–387 BC) *Gorgias*, trans. D.J. Zeyl, Indianapolis, IN: Hackett Publishing Company, 1987. (His most dramatic and radical enquiry into scepticism about the virtues.)

—— (*c*.380–367 BC) *Republic*, trans. G.M.A. Grube, revised by C.D.C. Reeve, Indianapolis, IN: Hackett Publishing Company, 1992. (His fullest account, political as well as ethical, of the nature and value of the virtues.)

Sherman, N. (1989) *The Fabric of Character: Aristotle's Theory of Virtue*, Oxford: Clarendon Press. (A useful philosophical and interpretative discussion.)

Westberg, D. (1994) *Right Practical Reason*, Oxford: Clarendon Press. (A discussion of practical reason and virtue in Aquinas.)

BERNARD WILLIAMS

VIRTUES, THEOLOGICAL

see THEOLOGICAL VIRTUES

VISION

Vision is the most studied sense. It is our richest source of information about the external world, providing us with knowledge of the shape, size, distance, colour and luminosity of objects around us. Vision is fast, automatic and achieved without conscious effort; however, the apparent ease with which we see is deceptive. Since Kepler characterized the formation of the retinal image in the early seventeenth century, vision theorists have known that objects do not look the way they appear on the retina. The retinal image is two-dimensional, yet we see three dimensions; the size and shape of the image that an object casts on the retina varies with the distance and perspective of the observer, yet we experience objects as having constant size and shape. The primary task of a theory of vision is to explain how useful information about the external world is recovered from the changing retinal image.

Theories of vision fall roughly into two classes. Indirect *theories characterize the processes underlying visual perception in psychological terms, as, for example, inference from prior data or construction of complex percepts from basic sensory components.* Direct *theories tend to stress the richness of the information available in the retinal image, but, more importantly, they deny that visual processes can be given any correct psychological or mental characterization. Direct theorists, while not denying that the processing underlying vision may be very complex, claim that the complexity is to be explicated merely by reference to non-psychological, neural processes implemented in the brain.*

The most influential recent work in vision treats it as an information-processing task, hence as indirect. Computational models characterize visual processing as the production and decoding of a series of increasingly useful internal representations of the distal scene. These operations are described in computational accounts by precise algorithms. Computer implementations of possible strategies employed by the visual system contribute to our understanding of the problems inherent in complex visual tasks such as edge detection or shape recognition, and make possible the rigorous testing of proposed solutions.

1   **Historical background**
2   **Direct v. indirect perception**
3   **Direct theories of vision**
4–7 **Computational models of vision**

1   Historical background

The fact that the image on the retina does not correspond in an obvious manner to the way things look suggests that some processing of the stimulus occurs in visual perception. Theorists of vision have proposed various accounts of the nature of the processing responsible for our perception of size, shape and distance. *Geometric* models, popular among optic theorists in the seventeenth century, and suggested in some of René Descartes' work on vision (particularly, his Sixth Set of Replies 1641: §9), construe visual processing as a species of mathematical calculation (see MOLYNEUX PROBLEM). Geometric models can therefore be seen as precursors of modern-day computational models of vision (see §§4–7 below). According to one geometric model, the visual system computes the distance of an object in the visual field from the angles at which the light from the object strikes each eye, and the distance between the two eyes. The knowledge required for the calculation, including knowledge of the precise angles formed by the eyes when looking at an object, and knowledge of the relevant mathematical theorems, was thought to be provided by innate mechanisms, rather than acquired from experience (see INNATE KNOWLEDGE). A significant defect of geometric models is that they failed to provide an account of how the requisite knowledge is made available to the visual system, or how it is deployed in calculations that were presumed to be unconscious.

The philosopher George BERKELEY, in his influential 'Essay Towards a New Theory of Vision' (1709), questioned the psychological reality of the geometric models, arguing in effect that the information upon which the postulated calculations are based is not available to the visual system. Berkeley agreed with the geometric theorists that retinal information alone is insufficient to account for our perception of distance and size, but, consistent with his more general empiricism, he claimed that the process by which we acquire such knowledge is not a species of calculation based on innately specified information, but rather associative and learned.

According to Berkeley, our ideas of distance and size, unlike our ideas of colour, are not really *visual* ideas at all. Whereas light reflected at different wavelengths affects the retina differentially, and so gives rise to different colour sensations, light reflected from different distances does not. There is no characteristic retinal pattern associated with something's being 10 feet away. As Berkeley put it in his famous 'one point' argument, 'distance being a line directed end-wise to the eye it projects only one point in the fund of the eye, which point remains invariably the same whether the distance is larger or shorter' (1709: §2). Similarly for size: there is no characteristic retinal pattern produced by our looking at an object that is 6 cubic feet in volume. A larger object placed at a greater distance along the line of sight will have the same geometric effect on the retina. Our ideas of distance and size, Berkeley concluded, derive not from visual experience, but from movement and touch; from our tangible acquaintance with objects. We can tell the distance and size of objects by sight only because we learn to associate visual cues, including sensations caused by the convergence of the eyes and the accommodation of the lens, with ideas originally derived from our tangible sense.

Central to Berkeley's account of distance and size perception is the empiricist doctrine that there are no meaningful abstract ideas, that is, ideas not reducible to sensation (see EMPIRICISM; SENSE-DATA). He rejected the possibility that we might possess abstract spatial ideas that are shared by visual and tangible experience (see MOLYNEUX PROBLEM). Later theorists of vision who do not share Berkeley's epistemological and metaphysical assumptions have found his claim that our ideas of distance and size are derived from our sense of touch uncompelling; however, his discussion of the phenomena to be explained by a theory of vision shaped the field well into the twentieth century.

2   Direct v. indirect perception

The claim that visual perception is not direct or immediate involves more than the truism that some processing of the retinal image is necessary to account for what we see. Ideas or perceptions are thought not to be 'direct' if they are produced by *psychological* processes. While the notion of a psychological process admits of no precise definition, examples come readily to mind. Any process that occurs in consciousness, such as the association of ideas, is a psychological process, as is any process that involves learning. Mathematical calculation of distance and size based on the prior *representation* of lines and angles, whether accessible to consciousness or not, is a psychological process (see INTENTIONALITY). Since Berkeley's theory and the models of the geometric writers both posit psychological processing of the image (albeit of different sorts), they are considered indirect theories of vision.

The difference between direct and indirect accounts of perception has been characterized as a disagreement over the richness of the stimulus, with direct theorists typically arguing that the stimulus contains more information than indirect theorists have been willing to allow. For example, James J. Gibson (1904–79), a prominent direct theorist, claimed that the input to the visual system is not a series of static 'time slices' of the retinal image, but rather, the smooth transformations of the optic array as the subject moves about its environment (what Gibson (1979) called 'retinal flow'). But to characterize the fundamental difference between direct and indirect theories as a disagreement over the richness of the stimulus is to misplace the dispute. The issue that separates the two camps concerns neither the amount of information contained in the stimulus, nor even the precise character of this information, but, rather, how the information in the stimulus is accessed and used by the visual system to produce knowledge that is useful to the organism. In other words, it concerns the character of the intervening processes. Direct theorists deny that visual processes can be characterized in terms of ideas, beliefs, representations, knowledge or memories. In other words, they deny that visual processes have any true psychological description. A direct theory explicates any intervening or supplementary processing that occurs in perception in terms of neural structures and processes directly implemented in the brain. Indirect theorists, of course, do not deny that perceptual processes are implemented in neural structures, but they argue that such processes should be characterized at a distinct, psychological, level of description.

Direct theories of perception are sometimes explicitly contrasted with accounts that treat perception as a species of inference, akin to the drawing of a conclusion from premises according to a principle or rule. The nineteenth-century German physicist and physiologist Hermann von HELMHOLTZ argued that the processes underlying visual perception are of the same general sort as inductive generalization employed in scientific reasoning (see INDUCTIVE INFERENCE; INFERENCE TO THE BEST EXPLANATION). The contemporary psychologist Irvin Rock (1983) advances a view that explicitly treats much of perception as a process of hypothesis generation and testing. But the use of 'inferential' as a blanket term to refer to indirect theories of perception is somewhat misleading. The various processes that can be thought of as psychological (for example, conscious inference, unconscious calculation, habit-based association, and so on) seem too heterogeneous a collection to justify characterizing the entire class in terms of the drawing of conclusions from antecedently established premises.

3 Direct theories of vision

The 'Gestalt' movement of the early twentieth century rejected the view, prevalent since Berkeley, that complex percepts can be analysed into simple sensory components (see GESTALT PSYCHOLOGY). According to the Gestalt theorists, perception is *holistic*: perceptual wholes are not built up out of more basic sensory elements, in the way, for example, that a painting is just the combination of all the paint-covered segments of the canvas. Gestalt theorists claimed further that perception is direct – perceptual processing is not correctly described in terms of psychological or mental processes. The structure of a visual experience is to be explicated in terms of the structure of the underlying brain states, that is, in neurophysiological terms. The Gestalt psychologist Wolfgang Köhler characterized as a *physical gestalt* any dynamic system that settles into an equilibrium state of minimal energy. A soap bubble forming a perfect sphere is an example of a physical gestalt, as is, Köhler argued, the brain producing an organized percept. Köhler proposed a theory that appealed to electrical fields within the brain to account for perception (and all other mental processes). Gestalt speculative physiology was not borne out by subsequent brain research, which failed to discover evidence of Gestalt mechanisms implicated in perceptual processing.

The psychologist James J. Gibson shared with the Gestalt theorists the belief that visual perception is not mediated by processes characterizable in psychological terms. Gibson argued that indirect theorists have mischaracterized the information in the optical array. If the effective stimulus for the visual system is taken to be retinal flow (the smooth transformations of the optic array as we move about), then, according to Gibson, there are important constancies in the stimulus that indirect theorists have typically missed. There is therefore no need to posit inferences, calculations, memories, association of ideas, or any other intervening psychological process, to explain our perception of size and shape constancy. In addition to brightness and colour, properties directly picked up in the stimulus include, according to Gibson, higher-order properties that remain invariant through movement and changes in orientation. These higher-order invariants specify not only structural properties such as 'being a cube', but also what Gibson called 'affordances', which are functionally significant aspects of the distal scene, like the fact that an object is edible or could be used for cutting.

Two fundamental assumptions underlie Gibson's 'ecological optics': (1) that functionally significant aspects of the environment structure the ambient light in characteristic ways; and (2) that the organism's visual system has evolved to detect these characteristic structures in the light. Both assumptions are controversial. With respect to (2), indirect theorists have complained that Gibson provides no account of the mechanism that allegedly detects salient higher-order invariants in the optical array. His claim that the visual system 'resonates', like a tuning fork, to these properties is little more than a metaphor. But it should be noted that in claiming that perception of higher-order invariants is direct, Gibson is simply advocating that the mechanism be treated as a black box, from the point of view of psychology, because no inferences, calculations, memories or beliefs mediate the processing. (The physiological account of the mechanism's operation will no doubt be very complex.) This claim might be plausible if assumption (1) is true – if there is a physically specifiable property of the light corresponding to every affordance. But for all but the simplest organisms it seems unlikely that the light is structured in accordance with the organism's goals and purposes. More likely, the things that appear to afford eating or cutting or fleeing behaviour structure the light in all kinds of different ways. This likelihood has led indirect theorists to claim that something like categorization – specifically, the bringing of an object identified initially by its shape, colour or texture under a further concept – is at work when an organism sees an object *as* food, *as* a cutting implement, or *as* a predator.

4 Computational models of vision: general approach

The predominant theoretical approach in cognitive psychology in recent years has been computationalism, which treats human cognitive processes, including perceptual processes, as a species of information processing (see MIND, COMPUTATIONAL THEORIES OF). Computational theories of vision attempt to specify the aspects of the external world that are represented by the visual system, and to characterize the operations that derive these representations from the information contained in the retinal image.

One of the most prominent early computational vision theorists was David Marr (1945–80), a researcher in the Artificial Intelligence Laboratory at the Massachusetts Institute of Technology. While the details of Marr's specific computational model have been challenged by later theorists, his work is of continuing interest to philosophers and psychologists concerned with the foundations of the computational approach to vision.

Marr argued in his book *Vision* (1982) that an information-processing capacity can be analysed at three distinct levels of description. The 'theory of the computation' is a precise specification of the function computed by the mechanism, in other words, what the mechanism does. For example, the theory of the computation for a particular device may tell us that it adds numbers, or computes averages when given a list of numbers as input. The *algorithm* specifies the procedure or rule for computing the function, and the *implementation* level describes how the computation is carried out in neural or computer hardware. The first two levels in the hierarchy – the abstract characterization of the problem and the rule for its solution – exemplify a fundamental commitment of the computational approach: that cognitive processes can be understood in a way that is independent of the particular mechanisms that implement them in the brain.

Computational models treat the visual system as computing from the retinal image a representation of the three-dimensional structure of the distal scene. Marr's theory divides this process into three distinct stages, positing at each stage the construction of a representation that makes explicit (some of) the information contained in the image and represents it in a way that is efficient for later use. Various computational processes, some running in parallel, are defined over these representations. The algorithmic level of description characterizes the procedures the visual system uses to produce increasingly more useful representations of the scene.

Most of the processes that Marr describes are *data driven*, or 'bottom up' – they operate on information contained in the image, without supplementation by high-level information or beliefs about the world that the subject may have. These processes use information about intensity changes across the visual field, or the orientation of surfaces, not such facts as that objects of a particular shape typically make good cutting implements. Marr advocated 'squeezing every ounce of information out of the image' before positing the influx of supplementary knowledge.

Data-driven models of perception have a number of advantages over *hypothesis-driven* models which appeal to high-level knowledge very early in visual processing. Data-driven processes are generally faster – the visual system does not have to retrieve the relevant piece of specialized knowledge before processing the information in the image – and tend to be more reliable. In Marr's model, the point at which high-level information is available to the visual system marks a distinction between *early* and *late* vision. Early visual processes are said to be 'cognitively impenetrable' by the subject's beliefs about the world (see MODULARITY OF MIND). As a consequence, they cannot be influenced by learning.

Marr emphasized the importance of the 'topmost' level of description – the theory of the computation – in developing accounts of human cognitive capacities. He noted that there is no point attempting to describe how a mechanism works before knowing what it does. A crucial first step in constructing a theory of a perceptual capacity is discovering constraints on the way the world is structured that enable adapted organisms to solve perceptual problems in their normal environments. An example should make the point clear. Marr's student and co-worker Shimon Ullman (1979) has proved that three distinct orthographic views of four non-coplanar points are sufficient to determine the three-dimensional structure of a rigid body (the 'structure from motion' theorem). If a body is not rigid, much more information is required to compute its shape. In a world such as ours, where most things are relatively rigid, a visual system built (that is, adapted) to assume that the objects in its environment are rigid would be able to compute the structure of those objects more easily and quickly than a visual system that had to consider the many non-rigid interpretations consistent with the data. Accordingly, Marr posited a mechanism that given three views of four non-coplanar points as input selects the unique rigid interpretation consistent with the data.

Recall Berkeley's objection to the geometric theorists' accounts of size and distance perception. He claimed that the information required for the postulated calculations was not generally available to the visual system, nor to the organism. Such a criticism, if true, is devastating for a computational account of a cognitive capacity. Any computational theory that posits processing beyond the computing capabilities of the mechanism, or that relies on information unavailable to the mechanism, is a nonstarter as a biological model. An important lesson of Marr's work is that the theorist must attend to the structure of the organism's environment before attempting to characterize computational mechanisms, because the environment determines the nature of the computational problems that the organism's visual system needs to solve. The perceptual systems of adapted organisms can be assumed to 'exploit' very general information about the environment. Consequently, the problems they have to solve may be simpler and computationally more tractable than might initially be assumed.

5 Computational models of vision: modularity

Another characteristic feature of Marr's theory is that it treats the visual system as comprising a number of individual components or modules that can be analysed independently of the rest of the system. A 'module' is, by definition, cognitively impenetrable: its operation is not influenced by information external to it that may be available to the cognitive system as a whole, for example, information in the system's memory (see MODULARITY OF MIND). Marr posited a module responsible for computing three-dimensional structure from apparent motion, another for computing depth from disparity information available in stereo images, a third for computing shape from shading. Each of these modules is designed to exploit general environmental constraints in the manner that the 'structure from motion' module, described above, incorporates the rigidity assumption.

The various modules operate in parallel, and since they yield information about the depth of the distal scene from different input data, they may give inconsistent results. This is an advantage for the organism, because in cases where the general environmental constraints assumed by a processing module do not hold, the output of the module is subject to correction by another module operating on different data, and exploiting different environmental constraints. For example, imagine a non-rigid mass of jelly moving through space. Since the 'structure from motion' module is built to assume rigidity it will probably give an incorrect interpretation of the jelly's structure. But its output is then likely to be inconsistent with, and correctable by, the output of modules operating on shading or disparity information, which, though they exploit other environmental constraints, do not assume rigidity.

The principle of modular design has an evolutionary rationale. Modular processes are typically fast, because a time-consuming search of general memory is avoided. And assuming that the constraints governing a module's operation are generally true, the process will normally be reliable. Commitment to the principle of modular design makes the computational theorist's job easier, since modular processes can be studied and modelled without the theorist knowing how more central reasoning systems work. For all their theoretical advantages, however, modules do pose a general problem. The theorist has to explain how the outputs of various modular processes are combined in a single representation of the structure of the scene. The possibility of inconsistent results from different modules suggests that this is a non-trivial problem.

In general, then, the visual processes posited in Marr's theory have three important features. They are data-driven, adapted to exploit general environmental constraints, and modular. The visual system, according to Marr, computes a series of intermediate representations of distal information, culminating in a representation of the three-dimensional structure of the scene. The input to the system is the image on the retina, in effect, a grey-level intensity array. The initial processing of the image produces what Marr called the 'primal sketch', a representation of the way that light intensities change over the visual field. The primal sketch makes explicit precisely the information that is required for subsequent processing. Discontinuities in intensity tend to be correlated with significant features of the scene, that is, object boundaries, although it is too early at this stage to assume that all sharp intensity changes in the image indicate edges in the world. Some may be produced by changes in illumination or surface reflectance (see COLOUR AND QUALIA).

The various processing modules described above operate on aspects of the information contained in the primal sketch. The results are encoded in a representation that Marr called the '2.5-dimensional sketch'. It makes explicit the depth and surface orientation of the scene, and is the input representation for later visual processing. The visual system is assumed to be cognitively impenetrable up to the production of the 2.5-dimensional sketch, hence its operation to this point cannot be influenced by learning.

6 Computational models of vision: object recognition

Late or high-level visual processes use the representations of depth and surface orientation produced by early vision for tasks such as object recognition, locomotion and visually guided manipulation. Marr's own account of late visual processing is rather sketchy. His concrete proposals concern the computational level of description, with little or no detail supplied at the algorithmic level. In general, computational models of high-level vision are not as well developed as accounts of early visual processes. The difficulty is due in part to the fact that later processing

is hypothesis- (or goal-)driven, and hence cognitively penetrable. The input to these processes is not limited to information contained in the image. Object recognition, for example, makes use of specific knowledge about objects in the world. This knowledge is usually characterized as a catalogue of object types stored in long-term memory. It is worth noting that only at this rather late stage does the visual system do anything like identify what Gibson calls 'affordances', and in computational accounts such identification is typically treated as a process of categorization, in other words, as a psychological process (see CONCEPTS §1).

Various types of computational models of object recognition have been proposed. According to the simplest models, recognizing an object currently in view involves comparing it with previously stored views of objects and selecting the one that most resembles it. A problem with this approach is that it fails to explain our ability to recognize objects from novel views that do not straightforwardly resemble any previously stored views.

More promising are accounts that treat object recognition as associating with the current view of the object a description of the object type, perhaps in addition to previously stored views of representative examples. Here again, different approaches are possible. 'Invariant-property' accounts assume that the set of possible retinal projections of objects typically have higher-level invariant properties that are preserved across the various transformations that the object may undergo. Such proposals face the same problem as Gibson's account of higher-order invariants. For most object types it has proved impossible to find specifiable properties of the image that are common to all possible recognizable views.

The 'decomposition' approach to object recognition maintains that objects are identified on the basis of prior recognition of their component parts. An assumption of this approach is that the relevant part–whole relations are invariant and detectable in all possible views where the subject would recognize the object. The most developed proposal is Irving Biederman's 'recognition by components' theory (1990), according to which a given view of an object can be represented as an arrangement of simple primitive volumes called 'geons' (for 'geometric icons'). Geons can themselves be characterized in terms of viewpoint-invariant properties, and, proponents of the theory claim, are recognizable even in the presence of visual noise. In general, though, the decomposition approach to object recognition has proved to be fairly limited in its application. Many objects do not decompose in a natural way into easily characterizable parts; and for many of those that do the decomposition is insufficient to specify the object in question.

A third strategy, known as the 'alignment' approach, suggests that the visual system detects the presence of transformations between the current view of an object and a stored model, and can 'undo' the transformation to achieve a correspondence between the two. For example, suppose that the current view of the object differs from the model stored in memory because the object has undergone a three-dimensional rotation and moved further away from the viewer. On the current proposal, the visual system first detects the nature of the transformations, and then performs them in reverse on the current view to bring it into 'alignment' with the stored model (assuming that the object is rigid). The main problem for this approach, as for the other proposals, is its limited applicability. It is only feasible for a small range of possible transformations that an object can undergo (for example, rotation and scaling) and then only for a limited range of objects. (Imagine detecting and 'undoing' the rotation of a crumpled piece of newspaper.)

'Mixed' approaches to object recognition attempt to extend the range of applicability of the decomposition and alignment approaches by combining elements of the two, positing separate identification systems that operate in parallel. While mixed accounts appear promising, they face the additional burden of explaining how the outputs of the two recognition systems are combined.

7 Computational models of vision: problems and prospects

The most common criticism of computational models of human cognitive capacities, including accounts of our perceptual abilities, is that they are unable to approximate actual human performance. It is true that many impressive computer models fail miserably in the real world. Sometimes they fail because the information required is not available to the mechanism. As Marr emphasized, the computational theorist can try to avoid this problem by first attempting to characterize the computational problems that perceptual mechanisms, in their natural context, are required to solve, a process that involves discovering general environmental constraints that perceptual mechanisms of adapted organisms can be expected to exploit.

But the study of biological visual systems faces additional hurdles. Even if the information on which a posited process runs is in some abstract sense 'in the data', the input may be too 'noisy' for the mechanism to make use of it. Computational theorists are of course aware of this problem. Some of the processing posited by computational accounts, especially in early vision, involves the elimination of extraneous or irrelevant information in the image. (For example, the primal sketch, which represents intensity changes in the image, does not preserve the absolute values of intensity gradients at every point in the grey-level array.) Moreover, the theorist must eventually find neural hardware capable of doing the computationally characterized job, before being confident that the model is biologically feasible. Given the difficult nature of the task it is unlikely that a complete computational account of vision is just around the corner. None the less, computational theorists make an important contribution to our understanding of vision by their careful study of the nature of the problems to be solved by visual mechanisms, although the solutions they offer are properly evaluated by their performance in the real world.

An alternative style of computational model may ultimately prove better suited to explicating human vision than models, such as Marr's, that treat perceptual processing as rule-governed operations defined over representations. In 'connectionist' computational architectures information is typically represented by patterns of activation over a connected network of units or nodes. Connectionist processes are explicated at a level distinct from the neurological or implementational. Connectionist cognitive models typically appeal to representations, memory and learning, hence they qualify as indirect; although connectionist accounts of representation, memory and learning differ in significant respects from more traditional computational accounts (see CONNECTIONISM). Connectionist theorists have claimed that their models are better able to handle noisy input and 'multiple simultaneous constraints' characteristic of real-world processing situations, though traditional computationalists dispute this claim. Whether the best models of human visual processing will be connectionist remains to be seen.

See also: COLOUR AND QUALIA; CONSCIOUSNESS; MOLYNEUX PROBLEM; PERCEPTION

References and further reading

* Berkeley, G. (1709) 'An Essay Towards a New Theory of Vision', in *The Works of George Berkeley, Bishop of Cloyne*, vol. 1, ed. A.A. Luce and T.E. Jessop, Edinburgh: Thomas Nelson, 9 vols, 1948–57. (Referred to in §1.)

* Biederman, I. (1990) 'Higher-Level Vision', in D.N. Osherson *et al.* (eds) *Visual Cognition and Action: An Invitation to Cognitive Science*, vol. 2, Cam-

bridge, MA: MIT Press. (An example of the 'decomposition' approach to object recognition.)

Descartes, R. (1637) 'Optics', in *The Philosophical Writings of Descartes*, trans. J. Cottingham, R. Stoothoff and D. Murdoch, Cambridge: Cambridge University Press, 1985, vol. 1, 152–75. (Discourses 5 and 6 are particularly relevant.)

* —— (1641) 'Author's Replies to the Sixth Set of Objections', in *The Philosophical Writings of Descartes*, trans. J. Cottingham, R. Stoothoff and D. Murdoch, Cambridge: Cambridge University Press, 1984, vol. 2, esp. §9: 294–6. (Referred to in §1 – Descartes' 'intellectualist' theory of vision.)

Fodor, J.A. and Pylyshyn, Z. (1981) 'How Direct is Visual Perception?: Some Reflections on Gibson's "Ecological Approach"', *Cognition* 9: 139–96. (A critical discussion of Gibson's direct theory of perception. Includes detailed argument but no technicality.)

* Gibson, J. (1979) *The Ecological Approach to Visual Perception*, Boston, MA: Houghton Mifflin. (The most developed statement of Gibson's theory of perception.)

Helmholtz, H. von (1950) *Treatise on Physiological Optics*, ed. J. Southall, New York: Dover, 3 vols. (Influential nineteenth-century account of perceptual processing as a species of inference.)

Hinton, G.E. (1992) 'How Neural Networks Learn from Experience', *Scientific American* 267 (3): 144. (Includes a discussion of connectionist models of shape recognition.)

Horn, B. (1986) *Robot Vision*, Cambridge, MA: MIT Press. (A detailed account of work in computer vision, with exercises. Very technical.)

* Marr, D. (1982) *Vision*, New York: Freeman Press. (Somewhat technical, but includes a clear account of the rationale behind the computational approach to vision.)

* Rock, I. (1983) *The Logic of Perception*, Cambridge, MA: MIT Press. (Account of perceptual processing as a form of hypothesis formation and testing.)

Schwartz, R. (1994) *Vision: Variations on Some Berkelian Themes*, Oxford: Blackwell. (A useful discussion of historical work on the problems of vision. Also includes a chapter on Gibson's theory.)

* Ullman, S. (1979) *The Interpretation of Visual Motion*, Cambridge, MA: MIT Press. (A detailed analysis of the computations involved in visual motion perception.)

FRANCES EGAN

VITAL DU FOUR (*c*.1260–1327)

A Franciscan philosopher and theologian, Vital du Four was noted for denying the distinction between a thing's essence and its existence, for expounding an Augustinian theory of perception and for emphasizing the absolute power and contingency of God's will in creating the universe. One interpretation of his views holds that created things have no intrinsic goodness, only that which has been conferred upon them by God.

Born in Bazas, in the southwest of France, Vital du Four (or Vitalis de Furno) entered the Franciscan order, was educated in theology at Paris in 1285–91, and taught at Montpellier (1292–6) and Toulouse (1296–1307). He was appointed a cardinal in 1312, becoming Cardinal-Bishop of Albano in 1321. He died in 1327 in Avignon. A contemporary of John DUNS SCOTUS, du Four has been so overshadowed by his Franciscan colleague's philosophical accomplishments that until recently, one of du Four's major works, *De rerum principio* (On the Origin of Things), was erroneously included in Scotus' *Opera omnia*.

Du Four rejected Thomas Aquinas' thesis that, except for the case of God, there is a distinction between an individual's essence and its existence (see AQUINAS, T. §9). According to du Four, the existence of any individual (other than God) just is that individual's essence as related to the individual's efficient cause. Du Four's thesis seems to be that for Socrates to exist is for Socrates' essence – namely, to be a rational animal – to stand in a certain relation to whatever is the efficient cause of Socrates. The relation includes the notion of participation: the relevant activity of Socrates' efficient cause results in an individual, Socrates, who participates in the essence of being a rational animal.

Unlike a theory, popularly associated with Aquinas, that maintained that genuine knowledge must be only of universal, necessary truths, du Four allows knowledge to extend to contingent particulars. Knowledge of physical objects comes about through sensation, which apprehends individual things. Du Four claims, however, that sensation itself necessarily involves the simultaneous operation of the intellect, thus precluding any view that maintains that the intellect operates only after it receives the testimony of the senses. While the senses apprehend individuals, the intellect cognizes the activities of the senses along with the individuals that are the objects of those activities. Augustine's theory of 'vital attention' had maintained that sense perception is possible only when the soul actively attends to the events occurring in the body, because the inferior body cannot in itself cause changes in the superior soul (see AUGUSTINE).

Du Four's account of the intellect's activity in sense perception is reminiscent of Augustine's theory, although it is not clear that du Four subscribes to Augustine's causal principle.

In contrast to the way in which knowledge of contingent particulars is acquired, du Four introduces a theory of divine illumination (an important expression of which could also be found in Augustine's writings) to account for knowledge of necessary, universal truths. Human intellects are too inconstant to grasp such immutable truths by their own natural means. Knowledge of necessary truth is the result of the soul's union with God's light, and the acquisition of such knowledge is entirely dependent on God's will.

Du Four rejects the opinion, expressed in Plato's *Timaeus* (see PLATO §16), amplified by PSEUDO-DIONYSIUS the Areopagite and expounded afterwards by Avicenna (see IBN SINA), that creation is a necessary outcome of God's goodness. God is necessarily infinitely good, but the necessity of God's goodness has its source in God's own immutable will and not in any kind of external compulsion. No aspect of creation is sufficient to move God to create. In particular, the goodness of creatures does not enhance God's goodness, and so their goodness is accidental to God's willing to create.

As du Four puts it, creatures add nothing to God's goodness 'just as a point adds nothing to a line' (*De rerum principio* 4.1.3). He may have intended this analogy only to imply that because God is *infinitely* good intrinsically, no extrinsic good can add to God's goodness; but he may also have intended the analogy to convey the thesis that just as points have no length in themselves by which to augment the length of a line, so created beings have no goodness in themselves. On either interpretation, du Four's view stresses the contingency of God's creating: God could have refrained from creating anything, let alone this world. The second interpretation, however, adds the further thesis that the goodness of the created world is not something intrinsic to it, and suggests that if the world is properly to be regarded as good, its goodness must be conferred on it by a declaration of God's free will. Du Four's analogy may thus have influenced the voluntaristic views of WILLIAM OF OCKHAM less than a generation later.

See also: CREATION AND CONSERVATION, RELIGIOUS DOCTRINE OF; GOODNESS, PERFECT; VOLUNTARISM

List of works

Vital du Four (late 13th–early 14th century) *De rerum principio* (On the Origin of Things), ed. L. Wadding in *Joannis Duns Scoti Doctoris Subtilis, Ordinem Minorum Opera Omnia*, Paris: L. Vivès, 1891, vol. 4, 267–70. (Question 4 contains du Four's discussion of whether God created of necessity.)

—— (late 13th–early 14th century) *Quaestiones disputatae* (Disputed Questions), ed. F.M. Delorme in 'Le Cardinal Vital du Four: Huit questions disputées sur le problème de la connaissance', *Archives d'histoire doctrinal et littéraire du moyen âge*, Paris: Vrin, vol. 2, 1927: 151–337. (Contains du Four's denial of a distinction between a thing's essence and existence and his views on human knowledge.)

References and further reading

Lynch, J.E. (1972) *The Theory of Knowledge of Vital du Four*, St Bonaventure, NY: The Franciscan Institute. (Useful on du Four's theory of knowledge of particulars, along with the theories of other Franciscan thinkers.)

Mann, W.E. (1991) 'The Best of All Possible Worlds', in S. MacDonald (ed.) *Being and Goodness: The Concept of the Good in Metaphysics and Philosophical Theology*, Ithaca, NY: Cornell University Press. (Contains a brief discussion of du Four's possible voluntarism.)

WILLIAM E. MANN

VITALISM

Vitalists hold that living organisms are fundamentally different from non-living entities because they contain some non-physical element or are governed by different principles than are inanimate things. In its simplest form, vitalism holds that living entities contain some fluid, or a distinctive 'spirit'. In more sophisticated forms, the vital spirit becomes a substance infusing bodies and giving life to them; or vitalism becomes the view that there is a distinctive organization among living things. Vitalist positions can be traced back to antiquity. Aristotle's explanations of biological phenomena are sometimes thought of as vitalistic, though this is problematic. In the third century BC, the Greek anatomist Galen held that vital spirits are necessary for life. Vitalism is best understood, however, in the context of the emergence of modern science during the sixteenth and seventeenth centuries. Mechanistic explanations of natural phenomena were extended to biological systems by Descartes and his successors. Descartes maintained that animals, and the human body, are 'automata', mechanical devices differing from artificial devices only in their degree of complexity. Vitalism developed as a contrast to this mechanistic view. Over the next three centuries, numerous figures opposed the extension of Cartesian mechanism to biology, arguing that matter could not explain movement, perception, development or life. Vitalism has fallen out of favour, though it had advocates even into the twentieth century. The most notable is Hans Driesch (1867–1941), an eminent embryologist, who explained the life of an organism in terms of the presence of an entelechy, *a substantial entity controlling organic processes. Likewise, the French philosopher Henri Bergson (1874–1948) posited an* élan vital *to overcome the resistance of inert matter in the formation of living bodies.*

1   **Experimental physiology**
2   **Physiological chemistry**
3   **Developmental biology**
4   **Conclusion**

1   Experimental physiology

The role of vitalism in physiology is exemplified in the work of the French anatomist Xavier Bichat (1771–1802). Bichat analysed living systems into parts, identifying twenty-one distinct kinds of tissue, and explaining the behaviour of organisms in terms of the properties of these tissues. He characterized the different tissues in terms of their 'vital properties', as forms of 'sensibility' and 'contractility'. Bichat thought the sensibility and contractility of each tissue type constituted the limit to decomposing living matter into its parts. These vital properties preclude identifying life with any physical or chemical phenomenon because the behaviour of living tissues is irregular and contrary to forces exhibited by their inorganic constituents. Insofar as living matter maintains itself in the face of ordinary physical and chemical processes that would destroy it, Bichat thought it could not be explained in terms of those forces. He therefore allowed that there are additional fundamental forces in nature that are on a par with those Newton ascribed to all matter: 'To create the universe God endowed matter with gravity, elasticity, affinity...and furthermore one portion received as its share sensibility and contractility' (Bichat 1801, vol. 1: xxxvii). These are vital properties of living tissues.

The key to explaining the distinctive properties of living systems is showing how those properties stem from the constitution of the system. Bichat traced the properties of living systems back to their components; when this was done, the vital properties assigned to these components were opposed to their physical properties. François Magendie (1783–1855) provides a useful contrast. Many of Magendie's experiments mirrored those of Bichat, but he interpreted them as

revealing the different steps in a physiological process. Magendie's avowed goal was to abolish the vital properties known as sensibility and contractility, and to 'consider them as functions' (1809). Magendie rejected a mechanistic account of those functions, and acknowledged that many physiological phenomena remained beyond experimental reach, so that it was not possible to explain them in more basic physical terms. Because he acknowledged this distance between vital functions in living organisms and what it was possible to explain in physical terms at the time, Magendie was construed by many as a vitalist; if he is a vitalist at all, his vitalism is very different from that of Bichat.

2   Physiological chemistry

Inspired by Lavoisier's new analysis of combustion, and his demonstration with Laplace in 1780 that respiration in animals is 'slow combustion', chemists in the early nineteenth century hoped to explain many of the reactions found in living organisms. Organic compounds are apparently formed only in living organisms, and thus appear to be products of vital activity. The physiological chemists of the early nineteenth century set out to show, contrary to initial appearances, that these products *are* the results of chemical processes. Jacob Berzelius (1779–1848) argued that chemistry could account for all of the reactions occurring within living organisms, and that organic and inorganic processes differ only in complexity. 'There is', he said, 'no special force exclusively the property of living matter which may be called a vital force' (1836).

A vitalistic view of the relationship of chemistry to physiology is found in Justus Liebig's study of chemical reactions in plants and animals (1842). In animals he was particularly interested in reactions which metabolize foodstuffs, separating the constituents needed for growth. Liebig offered detailed chemical analyses of the sequence of reactions, based upon chemical analysis of the foods taken in, the products absorbed, and the waste products released. Liebig saw a need for some form of regulation of these reactions, and posited a vital force controlling them. Chemical and vital processes operate in opposite ways, and consequently both sorts of process are necessary in order to understand metabolism. Liebig's vital forces were not meant to undermine a mechanist programme; rather, they are forces comparable to other physical forces such as gravity and chemical affinity that are possessed by matter and would be exhibited under appropriate conditions. 'There is nothing to prevent us from considering the vital force as a peculiar property, which is possessed by certain material bodies, and becomes sensible when their elementary particles are combined in a certain arrangement or form' (Liebig 1842). Vital forces were invoked to explain phenomena which would otherwise lack an explanation.

Though Berzelius and Liebig were divided over what vital forces they would tolerate, they were united in the desire to explain activities in living organisms in chemical terms. They thought vital forces were necessary because some phenomena have no adequate chemical explanation. Their position is evident in the stance they took on fermentation: it is a chemical process and should be interpretable in chemical terms, whether it is occurring within living organisms or in the test tube. They viewed fermentation and putrefaction as the least challenging cases for chemists, since both processes are simply processes of decomposition and thus the result of simple chemical activity of the sort found in inorganic cases. With the development of better microscopes, Theodor Schwann (1810–82) observed in 1838 that single-celled organisms (yeasts) are involved in fermentation, setting the stage for a controversy that continued for the rest of the century. Schwann and Louis Pasteur (1822–95) argued that fermentation was an activity of whole living organisms and not reducible to ordinary chemistry. This seemed to be a vitalist position. Schwann, though, advanced a mechanistic theory of cell formation, claiming cells simply constitute special environments in which ordinary matter appears in different concentrations. This is not vitalistic. Pasteur, by contrast, fitted fermentation into a more general programme describing special reactions that only occur in living organisms. These are irreducibly vital phenomena. Pasteur demonstrated empirically in 1858 that fermentation only occurs when living cells are present and, further, that cells only carry out fermentation in the absence of oxygen, leading him to describe fermentation as 'life without air'. Finding no support for claims such as those advanced by Berzelius, Liebig, Traube and other chemists that fermentation resulted from chemical agents or catalysts within cells, Pasteur concluded that fermentation was a 'vital action'.

In addition to their apparent success in showing that fermentation only occurs in living cells, vitalists like Pasteur also appealed to their demonstration that living organisms always originate from living organisms and that there is no spontaneous generation. The idea of spontaneous generation was inspired in part by the observation of small organisms forming in putrefying matter. The controversy is rooted in the conflict between John Needham (1713–81) and Lazarro Spallanzani. Needham heated closed vessels of meat-broth, discovering that when cooled they still yielded micro-organisms. Spallanzani insisted on longer heating, and in his vessels no micro-organisms developed. In this context, Pasteur showed that heated organic matter remained sterile unless contaminated but that, if contaminated, the previously heated material sustained life. This supported the conclusion that new life-forms only emerge from existing ones and provided additional evidence for the vitalist claim that living organisms are inherently different from non-living entities.

3 Developmental biology

Perhaps the greatest challenge for a mechanist, and the context in which vitalism retained its influence most strongly, was development. Beginning with an undifferentiated and singular egg, development results in an organism with a regular and differentiated structure. The problem is to explain how this regular differentiation is possible. Descartes defended an epigenetic view of embryological development; however, Descartes could not explain how a complex living organism could result from matter and motion (see DESCARTES, R. §8). This led Nicolas MALEBRANCHE (1638–1715) to develop a theory of preformation by *emboitement*, according to which the germ cells contain, fully formed, the organism. During the seventeenth century, preformation offered a way of accommodating the view that mechanistic laws were insufficient as explanations of the construction of living organisms from unorganized matter. Pre-existence of the organism also avoided the atheistic and materialistic implications of a mechanistic epigenesis, by allowing that all organisms were preformed by the creator. Preformation was widely embraced by the beginning of the eighteenth century. Pierre-Louis Maupertuis (1698–1759), the Comte de BUFFON (1713–81) and Needham took up the defence of epigenesis in mid-century, challenging preformationism. All three expanded the range of mechanisms available to include attractive forces. Faced with the problem of explaining the emergence of organization, Maupertuis attributed intelligence and memory to the smallest living particles. On the basis of experiments performed with Needham, Buffon proposed that the development of organisms depended on 'penetrating forces' analogous to gravity and magnetic attraction. Needham concluded that there was a 'vegetative force' which was the source of all the activities of life. These are vitalistic proposals, which make sense only within a mechanistic programme.

Similar problems persisted throughout the eighteenth and nineteenth centuries. Though Berzelius was mechanistic when faced with physiology, the production of organic form seemed to defy chemical explanation. He thus suggested there was a vital force differing from inorganic elements and regulating development. Charles BONNET (1720–93), on the other side, was an enthusiastic champion of preformationism. He discovered parthenogenesis in the aphid, concluding that the female germ cell contained wholly preformed individuals, though he allowed that it need not be in exactly the form in which it exists in the adult organism. Beyond this he saw no explanation, emphasizing that the current state of physical knowledge does not allow any mechanical explanation of the formation of an animal. Bonnet embraced no vital forces, and therefore needed some primal organization.

At the end of the nineteenth century, analogous controversies resurfaced, though transformed and subject to experimental investigation. In investigating development, Wilhelm Roux (1831–1924) initiated an experimental version of *Entwicklungsmechanik* in support of internal determinants of development. He embraced a 'mosaic' theory of development, according to which the hereditary determinants are distributed in a qualitatively uneven way within the fertilized egg. As the cell divides, the daughter cells are genetically differentiated and these differences explain the differentiation of organisms. In 1888, Roux described experiments designed to test the idea of embryonic self-differentiation. At the first cleavage in the development of a frog, he destroyed one blastomere with a hot needle. In about 20 per cent of the cases, the remaining blastomere continued to develop, and it developed into half an embryo. He concluded that blastomeres develop independently, depending primarily on their internal constitution. This supported the view that development was controlled by material that was successively divided among the cells of the organism. This material, he thought, determined the growth of the organism in a fully mechanical form. In 1891, Driesch performed what seemed at first to be a very similar experiment, but with dramatically different results. Using sea urchins, he separated the blastomeres at the two-cell stage. Each blastomere developed into a smaller but complete blastula. He saw this result as inconsistent with Roux's mechanistic account and, in particular, as inconsistent with the idea that division of the cell involved a division of the 'germ' controlling development. Since the blastomeres have the ability to develop into complete organisms, there could not be the kind of internal differentiation and control Roux had observed. Driesch initially sought external epigenetic factors to explain development. He came to see development as the response of a living organism rather than a mechanically predetermined process. He did not deny that physical and chemical processes are manifested in development, but held that the timing of development requires some special explanation. Physical laws thus place constraints on possibilities, but leave the actual outcome underdetermined. The connections were not immediately made, but Driesch was eventually led to a teleological and vitalistic view of development which he thought could explain developmental patterns.

4 Conclusion

Vitalism now has no credibility. This is sometimes credited to the view that vitalism posits an unknowable factor in explaining life; and further, vitalism is often viewed as unfalsifiable, and therefore a pernicious metaphysical doctrine. Ernst Mayr, for example, says that vitalism 'virtually leaves the realm of science by falling back on an unknown and presumably unknowable factor' (1982: 52). C.G. Hempel, by contrast, insists that the fault with vitalism is not that it posits entities which cannot be observed, but that such explanations 'render all statements about entelechies inaccessible to empirical test and thus devoid of empirical meaning' because no methods of test, however indirect, are provided (1965: 257). The central problem is that vitalism offers no definite predictions. Neither complaint has much historical credibility. Many vitalists were in fact accomplished experimentalists, including most notably Pasteur and Driesch. Moreover, vitalists took great pains to subject their views to experimental test. Magendie, for example, insisted on the importance of precise quantitative laws. Vitalism, as much as mechanistic alternatives, was often deeply embedded in an empirical and experimental programme. Typically, vitalists reacted to perceived inadequacies of mechanistic explanations; in many cases they rightly recognized that the forms of mechanism, materialism or reductionism advocated by their contemporaries were undercut on empirical grounds. In the end, though, their own proposals were supplemented by empirically more adequate mechanistic accounts.

See also: ARISTOTLE; BERGSON, H.; GALEN; LIFE, ORIGIN OF

References and further reading

Allen, G. (1978) *Life Science in the Twentieth Century*, Cambridge: Cambridge University Press. (A survey of the history of biology in the first part of the twentieth century.)

* Berzelius, J.J. (1836) 'Einige Ideen über bei der Bildung organischer Verbindungen in die lebenden Naturwirksame ober bisher nicht bemerkte Kraft',

Jahres-Berkcht über die Fortschritte der Chemie 15: 237–45. (Organic and inorganic processes differ only in complexity.)

* Bichat, X. (1801) *Anatomie générale appliquée à la physiologie et à la médicine*, Paris: Brossom, Gabon et Cie. (See §1.)

Coleman, W. (1977) *Biology in the Nineteenth Century: Problems of Form, Function and Transformation*, Cambridge: Cambridge University Press. (A survey of the history of biology in the nineteenth century.)

Driesch, H. (1914) *The History and Theory of Vitalism*, London: Macmillan. (Driesch's synoptic discussion of vitalism, from its leading twentieth-century proponent.)

* Hempel, C.G. (1965) 'Studies in the Logic of Explanation', in C.G. Hempel (ed.) *Aspects of Scientific Explanation, and Other Essays in the Philosophy of Science*, New York: Free Press. (See §4.)

* Liebig, J. (1842) *Animal Chemistry or Organic Chemistry in its Application to Physiology and Pathology*, trans. W. Gregory, Cambridge: John Owen. (Liebig's statement of the central issues in physiology.)

* Magendie, F. (1809) 'Quelques Ideés Générales sur les Phénomènes Particuliers aux Corps Vivens', *Bulletin des Sciences de la Société Médicine d'émulation de Paris* 4. (Considers as functions the vital properties of sensibility and contractility. See §1.)

Maienschein, J. (1991) 'The Origins of *Entwicklungsmechanik*', in S. Gilbert (ed.) *A Conceptual History of Modern Embryology*, New York: Plenum Press, 43–61. (A good synopsis of the principal figures involved in the emergence of developmental biology from the end of the nineteenth century into the early twentieth century.)

* Mayr, E. (1982) *The Growth of Biological Thought*, Harvard, NY: Harvard University Press. (An excellent general introduction, covering the span of biological thought from early Greek thought through to the twentieth century.)

* Pasteur, L. (1858) 'Mémoire sur la Fermentation Appelée Lactique', *Annales de Chimie Ser.*, 52: 404–18; partially reprinted and translated as 'Pasteur's Memoir on Lactic Fermentation', in J.B. Conant (ed.) *Harvard Case Histories in Experimental Science*, Harvard, NY: Harvard University Press, 1970. (Pasteur's classic work.)

Roe, S. (1981) *Matter, Life and Generation: 18th Century Embryology and the Haller–Wolff Debate*, Cambridge: Cambridge University Press. (A historical examination of debates in embryology and developmental biology at the end of the eighteenth century, focusing on the disputes between Haller and Wolff.)

* Roux. W. (1888) 'Beiträge zur Entwicklungsmechanik Des Embryo', *Virchows Archiv für pathologische Anatomie und Physiologie und für klinische Medizin* 114: 113–53; trans. in B. Willier and J.M. Oppenheimer (eds) *Foundations of Experimental Embryology*, New York: Hafner, 1974, 2–37. (Roux's classic experimental work.)

WILLIAM BECHTEL
ROBERT C. RICHARDSON

VITORIA, FRANCISCO DE (*c.*1486–1546)

Francisco de Vitoria, who spent most of his working life as Prime Professor of Theology at Salamanca, Spain, was one of the most influential political theorists in sixteenth-century Catholic Europe. By profession he was a theologian, but like all theologians of the period he regarded theology as the 'mother of sciences', whose domain covered everything governed by divine or natural, rather than human, law; everything, that is, which belonged to what we would describe as jurisprudence. Vitoria's writings covered a wide variety of topics, from the possibility of magic to the acceptability of suicide. But it is on those which deal with the most contentious juridical issues of the period – the nature of civil power and of kingship, the power of the papacy and, above all, the legitimacy of the Spanish conquest of America – that his fame chiefly rests.

1 Rights and political authority
2 The Spanish conquest of America

1 Rights and political authority

It was one of Vitoria's central concerns that all rights (*iura*) were natural and the consequence of God's law not of God's grace. The contrasting claim, made first by the fourteenth-century English theologian John WYCLIF (see §4), then by the fifteenth-century Bohemian reformer Jan HUS. More recently, and far more menacingly, what Vitoria referred to as 'the modern heretics', the Lutherans, made rights, and hence the authority of secular princes, dependent upon God's grace. On this account only a godly ruler could be a just legislator. Thus, if a prince was a heretic or proved, in the eyes of those who chose to judge him, to be in a state of sin, his laws could not be binding in conscience and he might legitimately be deposed. For Vitoria it was vital that such a theory, with all that it implied for the effective right of lesser magistrates to make war upon their ordained princes, should be discredited.

All civil power, for Vitoria, is vested in the commonwealth since, if all societies are natural organisms, it follows that no individual could have held power prior to their formation. It follows too that if, as he said in *De poteste civili* (On Civil Power) (1528), 'legislative power exists in the commonwealth by Divine and Natural Law', the commonwealth may, and indeed if it is to constitute a civil society where there can be only one ruler, *must*, 'delegate its power and offices'. The person or persons to whom it delegates may, of course, be one or many. In the traditional Aristotelian division, with which Vitoria was familiar, there were three types of political rule: monarchy, aristocracy and timocracy (or democracy). Of these Vitoria, like ARISTOTLE, unsurprisingly, considers that 'the greatest and best of all forms of rule and magistracy is monarchy or kingship'. The power exercised by monarchy, apart from being the most common form of rule (or so the historical record would suggest), and hence the most natural, is also of a different order from all others. It is the power to act on behalf of the community – what we today would call the 'high executive prerogative' of the state – and for Vitoria it 'is not from the commonwealth, but from God himself'. Such power, however, is what he calls a 'capability'. It cannot be exercised by an individual monarch until he has received 'authority or executive power' from the community. For the king may be the ultimate source of law, but he is also subject to the laws he makes, and these must always be in accordance with the customs of the commonwealth for which they are intended. There is, however, some doubt as to whether he may be coerced in any way if he fails to behave like a subject. Vitoria was willing to admit the possibility of tyrannicide on the grounds that, as he said in *De iure* (On Law) (1533–4) 'even if the commonwealth has given away its authority, it nevertheless keeps its natural right to defend itself'. But, in common with all early-modern political theorists on both sides of the confessional divide, he was also reluctant to ascribe coercive, and thus potentially revolutionary powers, to any authority other than that of the established ruler, whatever his conduct might be.

This conception of power, inevitably, played a central role in Vitoria's observations on the most pressing, and certainly the most intractable, issue in contemporary political theory: the legitimation of the Spanish conquest of America.

2 The Spanish conquest of America

Vitoria composed two treatises on the subject of the Spanish conquest of America: *De Indis* (On the American Indians) (1539) and *De iure belli* (On the Law of War) (1539). Both are answers to the question: By what laws were the barbarians subjected to Spanish rule? The answer to this question, however, turned upon another: Had the Indians, in fact, enjoyed property rights (*dominium*) over their own affairs, and over the territories they occupied, before the arrival of the Spaniards?

There could be, Vitoria argued, only three possible grounds for the Castilian crown's claim that the Indians were not, as were all other men, the subject of natural rights: either that they were sinners, non-Christians, madmen (*insensati*) or simpletons (*amentes*). The first of these invoked, once again, the Lutheran supposition that rights depended not upon God's laws, but upon God's grace. Man, argued Vitoria, is a rational creature and cannot lose that characteristic through sin, any more than he can willingly renounce his natural rights. He therefore concluded 'that, although the Indians were undeniably barbarians, they undoubtedly possessed the same rights, both public and private as any Christians'. This made any a priori claim to rights of conquests, or the claim to have occupied previously unoccupied territory – the so-called 'right of discovery' – invalid.

Vitoria also rejected the widely discussed claim that the Indians might be 'slaves by nature' largely on the empirical grounds that the Indians clearly did have 'some kind of rational order in their affairs'. They lived in cities, had a recognized form of marriage, magistrates, rulers, laws, industry and commerce, 'all of which require the use of reason'.

None of these arguments could provide the Castilian crown with rights to either sovereignty or property in America. Vitoria believed, however, that the Spaniards might legitimately claim a right drawn from the 'law of nations' – the *ius gentium*. This he called 'the right of natural partnership and communication'. There was nothing new in this argument, but Vitoria's formulation of it has won him the reputation of being the 'father of international law'. The seas, shores and harbours are, he argued, necessary to man's survival as a civil being, and must, therefore, be common to all. There was also, under the legal definition given to 'communication', an implied right to trade. If it could be said that the Spaniards had originally come to America as ambassadors, travellers and traders, they had to be treated with respect and be permitted access to all those who wished to trade with them. Vitoria also argued that the laws of nations granted the Spaniards the right to preach their religion without interference (although it did not oblige the Indians to listen) and that it permitted them to wage a just war 'in defence of the innocent against tyranny'.

The Spaniards could enforce these rights if opposed because any attempt to deprive a man of his rights constitutes an injury, and the vindication of injuries provides grounds for a just war. By the terms of a just war the victor acquires the status of a judge and may, therefore, appropriate the property of the vanquished. Similarly prisoners taken in a just war may legitimately be enslaved (see WAR AND PEACE, PHILOSOPHY OF §§3, 6).

The Castilian crown could claim that its conquests had been 'just wars' only if, in fact, the Indians had 'injured' the Spaniards by denying them access to their lands, or if they had attempted to prevent them from preaching. If, however, as seemed overwhelmingly the case, they had done none of these things, then all that Vitoria was left with was the claim that, since the Spaniards were there already, any attempt to abandon the new American colonies would only result in 'a huge loss to the royal exchequer, which would be intolerable'. However, he argued, there was no evidence that the Portuguese in Africa had gained less by licit trade than the Castilians had gained in America by illicit occupation.

Vitoria's writings on power and the rights of conquest effectively set the agenda for most subsequent discussions on those subjects in Catholic Europe until the late seventeenth century. In Spain his rulings – as they came to be seen – on the legitimation of the colonization of America became something of an orthodoxy. They also provided much of the theoretical underpinning for an extensive body of ethnographical writings on the American Indians. And although it is clearly false to speak of Vitoria as the father of anything so generalized, and modern, as 'International Law', it is the case that his writings became an integral part of later attempts to introduce some regulative principle into international relations (see INTERNATIONAL RELATIONS, PHILOSOPHY OF).

List of works

Vitoria, F. de (1557) *Relectiones XII in duos tomos diuisae, quarum seriem uersa pagella indicabit, summariis suis ubique locis adietis una cum indice omnium copiosissimo,* Lyon: Jacobus Boyerius, 2 vols in one. (Contains, among others, Vitoria's writings, *De poteste civili, De potestate ecclesia prior, De potestate ecclesia posterio, De iure, De Indis* and *De iure belli.*)

—— (1933–5) *Relecciones teologicas del Maestro Fray Francisco de Vitoria* (Theological Reflections of

Francisco de Vitoria), ed. L.G. Alonso Getino, Madrid: Imprenta La Rafa. (Bilingual edition in Latin and Spanish.)

—— (1932–52) *Commentarios á la 'Secunda Secundae' de Santo Tomás* (Commentaries on the *Secunda Secundae* of Thomas Aquinas), ed. V. Béltran de Heredia, Salamanca: Universidad de Salamanca, 6 vols.

—— (1991) *Francisco de Vitoria, Political Writings,* ed. A. Pagden and J. Lawrance, Cambridge: Cambridge University Press.

References and further reading

Barbier, M. (1966) *Introduction* to *Francisco de Vitoria, Leçons sur les indiens et sur le droit de guerre,* Geneva: Droz. (Probably the best general account of Vitoria's view on the laws of war.)

Hamilton, B. (1963) *Political Thought in Sixteenth-Century Spain,* Oxford: Clarendon Press. (Although unsophisticated in many respects, this is still a useful summary of Vitoria's political thought.)

Pagden, A. (1982) *The Fall of Natural Man. The American Indian and the Origins of Comparative Ethnology,* Cambridge: Cambridge University Press. (Offers a detailed analysis of some aspects of Vitoria's writings on the American Indians.)

—— (1987) 'Dispossessing the Barbarian: The Language of Spanish Thomism and the Debate over the Property Rights of the American Indians', in *The Language of Political Theory in Early-Modern Europe,* ed. A. Pagden, Cambridge: Cambridge University Press. (An account of the role played by Vitoria and his successors in the struggle over the Castilian crown's claims to *dominium* in America.)

Skinner, Q. (1978) *The Foundations of Modern Political Thought,* vol. 2, *The Age of Reformation,* Cambridge: Cambridge University Press. (Provides the best overall account of the context for Vitoria's political writings.)

ANTHONY PAGDEN

VIVEKANANDA *see* RAMAKRISHNA MOVEMENT

VIVES, JUAN LUIS (1493–1540)

Vives, Spanish humanist and educational reformer, was an eclectic but independent thinker, blending Aristot-

elianism and Stoicism with Christianity. He wrote on philosophy and psychology, religion and social concerns, and a wide range of subjects related to education. He was known by his contemporaries both for his lively attack on scholastic logic and for his practical judgment, or common sense. Familiar with classical, Christian and contemporary literature, he believed, with the Stoics, that learning should be applied for the common good. His original contributions are associated with an empirical approach to the sciences and the observation of nature, and his interest in the practical arts and inventions.

His social concerns included international politics (in which he is always a pacifist), and the relief of the poor in cities. His most scholarly work was an edition, with commentaries, of Augustine's De civitate Dei *(The City of God) (1522), but he is best known for his pioneer work on psychology and educational reform. De anima et vita (On the Soul and Life) (1538) offers the first empirical study of the emotions and their relations with the body, based on Galen's theory of humours, and enriched with insights from Vives' lifelong observation of human nature and conduct. De disciplinis (On Instruction) (1531), the outstanding work on education in the sixteenth century, is nothing less than a programme for education from infancy to old age, with due emphasis on moral training and, in the case of the study of nature, reverence for its creator.*

1 **Life and works**
2 **Moral and political thought**
3 **Metaphysics and epistemology**
4 **Psychology and pedagogy**

1 Life and works

Vives was born in Valencia to Jewish parents who had converted to Christianity. At sixteen he was sent to the University of Paris, and spent the rest of his life in exile. His parents were burnt by the Inquisition as relapsed Jews; he kept their fate to himself. His identification with his native country remained strong, and he proudly used the cognomen Valentinus, but he never saw Spain again. He taught at Louvain and Oxford and associated with the great Northern humanists, especially with his friends Erasmus, More and the French humanist Guillaume Budé. While at Oxford he attended the court of Henry VIII and Catherine of Aragon and was tutor to their daughter, Mary. He was expelled from England for taking Catherine's side in the divorce, and returned to Bruges where he died twelve years later.

At the College of Montaigu in Paris, Vives was drilled for three years in terminist logic and medieval physics. His exasperation at the abstract, sterile

speculations, barbarous Latin and combative disputations of the scholastics prompted the book he published in Louvain in 1519, *Adversus pseudodialecticos* (Against the False Dialecticians), which established him as a prominent figure in the conflict with the scholastic dialecticians (see LOGIC, RENAISSANCE §2). When he left Paris in 1512 Vives settled among the Spanish colony in Bruges. Here, except for periods in Louvain and England, he was to spend the rest of his life, and here he married, in 1524, Margaret Valdaura of an old Valencian family.

From 1517 to 1523 Vives was at Louvain, teaching privately and at the university. At Erasmus' urging in 1520 he undertook his edition, with expansive commentaries, of Augustine's *De civitate Dei* (The City of God), which he completed in 1522 and dedicated to Henry VIII. (This is the only major work of Vives not included in the *Opera Omnia* (1555) because it was frowned upon by the church for its dedication and its warm praise of Erasmus, as well as for the heterodoxy of some of Vives' notes; it ended up on the *Index Expurgatorius*.) In 1523, at Cardinal Wolsey's invitation, he went to teach at Oxford. In preparation for his visit to England, he composed and dedicated to his compatriot, Queen Catherine of Aragon, his treatise *De Institutione Feminae Christianae* (On the Education of a Christian Woman) (1524). Vives' Spanish austerity towards women gives the book a medieval flavour – for example: 'A woman's greatest ornament is silence' (*De Institutione*: 1 xi.136). More generous is the popular little handbook of morals and manners, blending stoicism and Christianity, which he prepared for the Princess Mary and called *Introductio ad Sapientiam* (Introduction to Wisdom) (1530).

Vives spent the better part of five years in England. He was professor of Latin, Greek and rhetoric at Corpus Christi College, and left his mark on Oxford through humanistic changes and improvements in the curriculum. He complained about the climate, but enjoyed the company of the great English humanists, More, Linacre and Fisher, and began to address himself to problems of a social and political nature. It was during this period that he wrote the original and important work on poor relief which he dedicated to the city of Bruges, *De subventione Pauperum* (On Assistance to the Poor).

Vives' loyalty to Henry's Spanish queen in the matter of the divorce ended his association with the English court, and he went home to Bruges to devote the rest of his life to writing. During those dozen years of poverty and failing health, racked with gout, he produced his major works. These included *De disciplinis* (On Instruction) (1531) and *De anima et vita* (On the Soul and Life) (1538). The eight books

De artibus (On the Arts), which were published as Part III of *De disciplinis*, consisted of five books on logic (including 'De censura veri' and 'De instrumento probabilitatis') and three ('De prima philosophia') on Aristotelian physics and metaphysics from a Christian viewpoint. In this period he also produced the most popular of his books on education, *Linguae Latinae Exercitio* (Use of the Latin Language) (1539), which, in twenty-five entertaining dialogues, employs all the Latin words in current usage. A posthumous work, *De veritate fidei Christianae* (On the Verity of the Christian Faith), intended for the conversion of pagans, Moors, Jews and heretics, was published in Basle in 1543.

2 Moral and political thought

Vives was a moral philosopher of sound and perceptive judgment, admirable for his sincerity and generosity of spirit. Erasmus said of him that he had a 'wonderfully philosophic mind' (*animo mire philosophico*). He was committed to the project of harmonizing Aristotelianism with Christianity and was sympathetic to the Stoic emphasis on personal virtue, inward tranquillity and social engagement. The writers he most often cites are CICERO, SENECA, Pliny, Plutarch and Quintilian. He once said there is no better Christian than a Stoic sage, and his own maxim was 'Without complaint' (*Sine querela*).

Accordingly, he was an *homme engagé*. He agreed with the Stoics that 'having acquired our knowledge we must turn it to usefulness and employ it for the common good' (*Opera Omnia*: vol. 6, 1.423). Deeply troubled by the political turmoil in Europe, he wrote urgently to heads of state and church on behalf of international peace among Christian nations; in *De Europae dissidiis et bello Turcico* (On European Discord and the War with the Turks) (1526), Vives urged that if they must employ their armies, they should unite against the encroaching Turks. His social concern found expression in his enlightened plan for poor relief, which was adopted by numerous Flemish cities. He also wrote a tract against the Anabaptists called *De communione rerum* (On the Common Ownership of Goods) (1535).

He was a staunch Christian. Like ERASMUS, he said that if he differed from the church he would submit to it, but his personal religion tended more to ethical and spiritual values than to rite and observance, and it is significant that his ideal institutions, whether for poor relief or education, were intended to be secular. None the less his belief in God and the moral order of the universe was the foundation for all his thought, and piety was the motive and inspiration for his work.

3 Metaphysics and epistemology

Religion apart, his idea of the world and the place of people within it is essentially Aristotelian. Vives was known in his lifetime and after as a critic of ARISTOTLE because of his incisive critique of Aristotle in *De disciplinis*. In fact he had read Aristotle more deeply than most other humanists, and had found him superior to all other philosophers. Vives identifies Aristotle's faults, but the Aristotelian systematization of knowledge based on self-evident first principles forms the basis of Vives' thinking about nature, matter and the mind.

In his metaphysics ('De prima philosophia') he discusses the creation of the world and the innate tendency of all peoples to believe in God. We are sorely hampered because of the Fall, but God has left us one priceless resource – a lively intelligence which is spontaneously active. Vives sometimes identifies this with 'natural light' (*lumen naturalis*), defined as those natural gifts given to us to enable us, through reason, to behold the truth. He accepts the Stoic doctrine of anticipations and common notions in the mind before birth (such as the innate belief among all peoples of the existence of God). From these first truths we gradually infer other truths, as plants grow from seeds. The order of knowledge is: sense perception, imagination, reason (composed of intelligence, memory and will) and judgment. To Vives a trained and enlightened judgment, based on experience, was the single most important quality for learning and life. He called it *prudentia*, that is, practical judgment or common sense. This is the surest guide to conduct. It is also the quality for which Vives was known by his contemporaries.

Vives is well aware of the limits to human reason. Of the three paths we have to knowledge: the senses, faith in authority and reason based on the senses, none is infallible. Only God has perfect knowledge. Therefore Vives issues a strong caution at the beginning of the metaphysics, that we should not inquire into the intimate workings of nature. God has his own reasons for his creation and it is impious for man to seek, for example, to know about the elements, the forms of living things, and the number, magnitude, dispositions and powers of these things. Here Vives seems to be recalling with distaste the speculative natural philosophy characteristic of late scholasticism.

He is sceptical about the possibility of acquiring certain rational knowledge not only in theology but also about ordinary nature. Even here, he warns us, what knowledge we have gained can only be reckoned as probable, not as absolutely true. His scepticism did not, of course, extend to religious authority. Fundamental doctrines like the Fall were unquestioned, and in fact formed the basis for his doubts about certainty in human knowledge. In contrast with this is the optimism and confidence Vives expresses elsewhere over the progress of science and the open-endedness of learning. He declares that:

> Nature is not yet so effete and exhausted that she can bring forth, in our times, nothing comparable to those of earlier ages. She always remains equal to herself, and not rarely she comes forward stronger and more powerful than in the past.... Much is left for future generations to discover.
>
> (Preface to *De disciplinis*)

Perfect truth may be unattainable, but steady progress in knowledge can be made. By way of proof, Vives likes to point to the recent remarkable discoveries of 'our [Spanish] countrymen' beyond the ancient borders of the East and West.

4 Psychology and pedagogy

The new ingredient Vives brought to humanism was an empirical approach to the sciences. Having fled the closed scholastic world and embraced humanism and the classics, he moved a step further into the practical sphere. His original contribution lay in the importance he gave to observation and experiment in psychology, the teaching of natural history, law and medicine, and in his attitude towards the practical arts and inventions. He advocated the use of the vernacular in teaching young pupils, and in the presentation of laws, so that they could be understood by the people. His pragmatic voice is not that of the literary Erasmian humanist, but rather of the Spanish émigré in Bruges, heir to a long Jewish tradition of practical service in law and medicine, friend of merchants (he once held an export licence for his relatives), and especially of doctors and lawyers.

The last precept in Vives' handbook of morals, *The Introduction to Wisdom*, is first to know oneself, and ultimately to know God. This rule he set out to implement in his two most important works, and to this task he brought his deep learning, critical spirit, and years of experience, observation and reflection on psychology and education.

The first of the two (though published second) was *De anima et vita* (1538), a pioneer work in psychology. Some consider it Vives' masterpiece. It is an empirical study of the soul or mind and its interaction with the body. He classifies our emotions in relation to the Galenic humours (the four humours: blood, phlegm, yellow bile and black bile, which come to constitute the four classic temperaments: sanguine, phlegmatic, choleric and melancholic), describes how they are affected by internal and external circumstances (such as age, health, climate and events), and how they can be motivated and controlled by thought, judgment and will. Elsewhere Vives mentions the importance of this knowledge in politics and law, and it provides a foundation for his pedagogy (which is based on attention to individual capacities and their development).

The second, *De disciplinis* (1531), is a monumental work, divided into two parts, one critical, *De causis corruptarum artium* (The Causes of the Corruption of the Arts) and one constructive, *De tradendis disciplinis* (The Transmission of the Arts). *De causis* traces the arts, or disciplines, from their beginning in our primitive human needs, through their growth by an empirical process, to their peak and decline. Decline was brought about sometimes by external causes (such as the barbarian invasions and the destruction by Goths and Vandals which produced the Dark Ages), most often by the weakness and vices of men and the emotions that cloud our reason. For example pride, arrogance and greed have diverted the pure study of astronomy into astrology, which is firmly to be shunned. *De tradendis* is a comprehensive programme for education from infancy to old age. No detail is overlooked, from physical requirements – site of the school, exercise, diet – to the bedside manner of the physician. Much space is given to nature study, observation and experiment, backed for every subject by a selective and critical reading list ranging from the classics to contemporary sources. Higher studies follow, and professional training. Like Hippocrates, Vives links medicine with dietetics, and includes the composition of medicines, anatomy and dissection. He balances this with moral philosophy (ethics, politics, jurisprudence) and stresses the importance of historical studies. Nor does education stop there. After formal study one will turn one's interest to the arts and inventions that contribute to our daily life: food and shelter, gardening, architecture, travel, navigation. Finally, for the elderly, observing nature offers pleasant recreation, a walking exercise and sauce for the appetite.

Vives' originality as well as his sound judgment attracted many readers. Estelrich mentions nearly 500 editions of his works, 200 for the dialogues alone. In England his influence is evident in Elyot, Ascham and Milton, and he was read and quoted by the dramatist Ben Jonson. Some of his prayers found their way into the Book of Common Prayer. On the Continent his educational theories left their mark on Rabelais, Sturm and Comenius. As a critic of Aristotle he was read by Ramus and Gassendi, who also cited him for his emphasis on experiment. His scepticism about the reliability of knowledge, combined with an optimistic belief in the progress of science, appealed to Francisco Sanches and Montaigne (who also cited his edition of Augustine), as well as Gassendi. His theory of the emotions influenced Descartes' *Les passions de l'âme* (The Passions of the Soul) (1649). Finally, leaders of the Scottish school of Common Sense, Thomas Reid and Dugald Stewart, praised his theory of innate common notions, his emphasis on practical judgment, and his foresight as to the future of science. After a period of neglect he was rediscovered and read by such nineteenth- and twentieth-century scholars as Lange, Renan, Duhem, Dilthey and Cassirer.

See also: ARISTOTELIANISM, RENAISSANCE; HUMANISM, RENAISSANCE; SCEPTICISM, RENAISSANCE

List of works

Early writings and opuscula of Vives are currently being edited and translated by a group of scholars, notably J. Ijsewijn, C. Matheeusen, C. Fantazzi and E. George, and published by Leiden: Brill (1987–).

Vives, J.L. (1493–1540) *Opera Omnia* (Complete Works), ed. G. Mayans y Siscar, Valencia, 1782–90, 8 vols; facsimile edn, London: Gregg Press, 1964. (Vives' complete works; following the *Opera Omnia* of 1555, this collection does not include Vives' commentary on Augustine's *De civitate Dei*.)

—— (1493–1540) *Obras Completas* (Complete Works), ed. L. Riber, Madrid: Aguilar, 1947–8, 2 vols. (Spanish edition of Vives' works.)

—— (1519) *Adversus pseudodialecticos* (Against the False Dialecticians), Louvain; trans. and ed. R. Guerlac, Synthese Historical Library 18, Dordrecht and Boston, MA: Reidel, 1979; C. Fantazzi (trans. and ed.) *In pseudodialecticos*, Leiden: Brill, 1979. (Critical editions of Vives' attack on scholastic dialecticians. The Guerlac edition also includes Books III and V–VII of *De causis*.)

—— (1522–8) *Literae virorum eruditorum ad Franciscum Craneveldium* (Letters of Learned Men to Francis Craneveldt), ed. J. de Vocht, Louvain: Libraire universitaire, Uystpruyst, 1928. (An important biographical source, it includes letters between Vives and his friend Craneveldt.)

—— (1524) *De Institutione Feminae Christianae* (On the Education of a Christian Woman), Antwerp: Hillenius; in G. Mayans y Siscar (ed.) *Opera Omnia*, London: Gregg Press, 1964, vol. 4, 65–301.)

—— (1526) *De subventione Pauperum*, Bruges: Hubert de Crouck; in G. Mayans y Siscar (ed.) *Opera Omnia*, London: Gregg Press, 1964, vol. 4, 421–94;

trans. A. Tobriner, *A Sixteenth Century Urban Report. Translation of Vives' On Assistance to the Poor*, Chicago, IL: University of Chicago Press, 1971. (One of Vives' important works of practical social philosophy; written during his stay in England.)

—— (1526) *De Europae dissidiis et bello Turcico* (On European Discord and the War with the Turks), in G. Mayans y Siscar (ed.) *Opera Omnia*, vol. 6, London: Gregg Press, 1964. (Vives' attempt to reconcile European leaders.)

—— (1530) *Introductio ad Sapientiam*, Antwerp: Apud Martinum Caesarem; in G. Mayans y Siscar (ed.) *Opera Omnia*, London: Gregg Press, 1964, vol. 1, 1–48; trans. A. Tobriner, *Vives' Introduction to Wisdom, A Renaissance Textbook*, Chicago, IL: University of Chicago Press, 1968. (The little handbook of manners and morals written for Mary Tudor, daughter of Catherine of Aragon and Henry VIII.)

—— (1531) *De disciplinis* (On Instruction), in G. Mayans y Siscar (ed.) *Opera Omnia*, London: Gregg Press, 1964, vol. 3, 82–297; vol. 6, 1–437. (Both parts of *De disciplinis* appear in the Gregg Press facsimile edition of Vives' works. The first part of this work, *De causis corruptarum artium*, has been translated into German by Sendnes and Hidalgo Serna, and English by Guerlac; the second part, *De tradendis disciplinis*, by Watson. The third part, *De artibus*, was published posthumously in 1555.)

—— (1531) *De causis corruptarum artium* (On the Causes of the Corruption of the Arts), in G. Mayans y Siscar (ed.) *Opera Omnia*, vol. 6, London: Gregg Press, 1964; German trans. W. Sendnes and E. Hidalgo Serna, Munich: Fink, 1990; English trans. R. Guerlac *De causis*, in preparation. (The first part of Vives' *De disciplinis*; traces the history of the arts, or disciplines.)

—— (1531) *De tradendis disciplinis* (On the Transmission of the Arts), in G. Mayans y Siscar (ed.) *Opera Omnia*, vol. 6, London: Gregg Press, 1964; trans. F. Watson, *On Education, a translation of the 'De Tradendis Disciplinis'*, Cambridge: Cambridge University Press, 1913. (One of Vives' most important works on education; the second part of Vives' *De disciplinis*. The Watson translation provides a useful introduction to Vives's work.)

—— (1531) *De artibus* (On the Arts), Antwerp: Apud Michaelem Hillenium, 1555; in G. Mayans y Siscar (ed.) *Opera Omnia*, London: Gregg Press, 1964, vol. 3, 82–297. (Published after Vives' death as the third part of *De disciplinis*; includes five books on logic and three on Aristotelian physics and metaphysics, all from a Christian viewpoint.)

—— (1535) *De communione rerum* (On the Common Ownership of Goods), in G. Mayans y Siscar (ed.) *Opera Omnia*, vol. 5, London: Gregg Press, 1964. (A tract written to oppose the Anabaptists.)

—— (1538) *De anima et vita* (On the Soul and Life), trans. into Italian and ed. M. Sancipriano, Padua: Gregoriana, 1974. (Critical edition of Vives' groundbreaking work on psychology.)

—— (1539) *Linguae Latinae Exercitio* (Use of the Latin Language), in G. Mayans y Siscar (ed.) *Opera Omnia*, London: Gregg Press, 1964, vol. 1, 283–408; trans. F. Watson, *Tudor School-boy Life, the Dialogues of Juan Luis Vives*, London: Dent, 1908; repr. London: Frank Cass, 1970. (Twenty-five entertaining dialogues, demonstrating all the Latin words in current usage; most popular of Vives' books on education.)

—— (1543) *De veritate fidei Christianae* (On the Verity of the Christian Faith), Basle: Oporinus; in G. Mayans y Siscar (ed.) *Opera Omnia*, vol. 8, London: Gregg Press, 1964. (Intended for the conversion of pagans, Moors, Jews and heretics; published posthumously.)

References and further reading

Bonilla y San Martin, A. (1903) *Luis Vives y la filosofia del Rinacimiento* (Luis Vives and Renaissance Philosophy), Madrid: Imp. del Asilo de Huésfanos. (The first full-scale modern work on Vives.)

Erasmus, D. (1906–47) *Opus Epistolarum Des. Erasmi Roterodami* (Collected Letters of Desiderius Erasmus), ed. P.S. Allen, Oxford: Clarendon Press, 12 vols. (Includes correspondence with Vives.)

* Estelrich, J. (1942) *Vives, Exposition organisée à la Bibliothèque Nationale* (Exhibition Organized by the National Library), Paris: Darantière. (Referred to in §4. A detailed bibliography and evaluation of Vives' reputation throughout Europe; the exhibition was held in Paris in 1941.)

Guy, A. (1972) *Vivès, ou l'humanisme engagé* (Vives, or Committed Humanism), Paris: Seghers. (Explores Vives' practical and social concerns.)

Noreña, C.G. (1970) *Juan Luis Vives*, The Hague: Nijhoff. (A general study, but badly edited.)

—— (1989) *Vives and the Emotions*, Carbondale, IL: Southern Illinois University Press. (A useful study of Vives' *De anima et vita*.)

—— (1990) *A Vives Bibliography*, Lewiston, NY: Mellen Press. (Supplements Estelrich and brings his work up to date.)

Santamaria, J.A.F. (1990) *Juan Luis Vives. Esceptismo y Prudencia en el Renacimiento* (Scepticism and Wisdom in the Renaissance), Salamanca: Universidad de Salamanca.

RITA GUERLAC

VLASTOS, GREGORY (1907–91)

A leading figure in the study of ancient Greek philosophy, Vlastos was a pioneer in the application to ancient philosophers of the techniques of analytic philosophy. Concentrating on figures of early Greek philosophy, he made major contributions to the understanding of the Presocratics, Socrates and Plato. He saw the Presocratics as applying ethical concepts to nature which ultimately rendered nature intelligible. He distinguished between the early dialogues of Plato, which represent the philosophy of Plato's master Socrates – a philosophy the early Plato shared – and the middle dialogues in which Plato develops a transcendental metaphysics and rationalist epistemology to ground Socratic ethical concepts. Vlastos's work played a major role in bringing the history of philosophy into the mainstream of philosophical research.

1 Presocratic studies
2 Platonic studies
3 Socratic studies

1 Presocratic studies

Born in 1907 in Istanbul to a Greek father and a Scottish mother, Vlastos was brought up as a Protestant and moved to America to study for the ministry at the University of Chicago. An interest in philosophy took him to Harvard, where he completed a Ph.D. under Alfred North WHITEHEAD in 1931. Accepting a teaching position at Queen's University in Ontario, he became heavily involved in causes of economic and social reform. He published articles in Christian journals and wrote several lively and insightful defences of Whiteheadian metaphysics.

In 1938, in what was to be the turning point in his career, he went to Cambridge to study ancient philosophy with F.M. Cornford. His research culminated in a paper, 'The Disorderly Motion in the *Timaeus*' (1939), which challenged the then almost unanimous view of Plato scholars, including Cornford, that the creation of the world described in the *Timaeus* was meant figuratively rather than literally. His work began a reassessment of the *Timaeus* which has tended to vindicate his literalist reading. After serving as an officer in the Royal Canadian Air Force during the Second World War, Vlastos returned to academia, setting out on an ambitious programme of examining Greek political ideas he saw as providing the foundations of philosophical thought. In 'Equality and Justice in Early Greek Cosmologies' (1947) he explained how democratic ideals of equality before the law shaped conceptions of cosmic justice held by Presocratic philosophers. By ascribing such ideals to nature, early philosophers naturalized justice on the one hand and rendered nature intelligible on the other.

In 1948 Vlastos joined the faculty of Cornell University, where he was able to imbibe from Max Black, Norman Malcolm, and Arthur Murphy the latest techniques of analytic philosophy, which, imported from Britain and Austria, was now sweeping the USA. His 'Theology and Philosophy in Early Greek Thought' (1952), a broad survey of religion in early Greek philosophy, argues for a middle ground between the view that the Presocratics were naturalists without religion (argued by Burnet 1930) and the view that they devised theologies of their own (Jaeger 1947): rather, they assimilate divine attributes to nature, thus naturalizing religious values. On the basis of his research Vlastos was able to argue effectively against two views of Presocratic development (both propounded, at different times, by Cornford (1912; 1952)), first that philosophy developed as a scientific reaction to a religious background, and second that it never provided a scientific alternative to religion, as Hippocratic medicine did. Vlastos argued that Presocratic thought was often scientific in spirit, but that it was most indebted to social-political ideas, such as those of justice and equality, that were projected onto nature. In other studies Vlastos examined the epistemology of PAR-MENIDES, defended a traditional reading of HERA-CLITUS against a revisionist anti-flux reading by G.S. Kirk, reconstructed a consistent theory of matter for ANAXAGORAS and a naturalistic basis for ethics in DEMOCRITUS. He convincingly refuted claims that Parmenides and ZENO OF ELEA were reacting to a Pythagorean theory of point-atoms – a widely held view originated by Paul Tannery (1930) and promulgated by Cornford (1939) and J.E. Raven (1948) – by showing that there was no evidence that the alleged theory ever existed (see PRESOCRATIC PHILOSOPHY).

2 Platonic studies

Having returned to the sources of Greek philosophy, Vlastos was now ready to return to PLATO. His essay 'The Third Man Argument in the Parmenides' (1954) was a watershed event in a number of ways. In the first place it marked not only Vlastos's re-entry into Plato

studies, but his application of the tools of analytic philosophy to ancient philosophy. Second, its thesis that Plato's presentation of the argument provided a 'record of honest perplexity' satisfied no one and provoked immediate replies from leading philosophers on both sides of the Atlantic, initially from Wilfrid SELLARS and Peter Geach. But further, the ensuing controversy had the effect of bringing ancient philosophy into the mainstream of philosophical debate – whereas the history of philosophy was in danger of being marginalized by the ahistorical or anti-historical bias of analytic philosophy, particularly in the USA. Indeed, the paper came to serve as a kind of paradigm of a new style of analytic history of philosophy. In the controversy Vlastos more than held his own against clever readings of the Third Man Argument by insisting that any interpretation be grounded in the text. His hermeneutical principle was as follows: 'If history is an empirical discipline, so is the history of philosophy. And no one can practise the empirical method unless he is willing to submit even the most deeply entrenched presumptions – his own or those of others – to the arbitrament of factual data' (1973: 255).

In 1955 Vlastos accepted an appointment as Stuart Professor of Philosophy at Princeton University, where he founded a joint Ph.D. programme in classical philosophy in conjunction with the Classics Department, a programme which quickly became a model for the rigorous training of specialists in ancient philosophy. Students were attracted from around the world and graduates were sent out to the best universities to practise and teach the new methods. Vlastos also published important papers in ethics and social philosophy: 'Justice' (1957) and 'Justice and Equality' (1962), the latter of which was widely anthologized. In the 1960s he began a series of studies on Zeno of Elea which still provide the definitive exposition of that philosopher's thought. He also produced an important series of articles on Plato, many of which were collected in *Platonic Studies* (1973), ranging from discussions of slavery in Plato to technical analyses of predication. His studies combined close readings with broad-ranging scholarship and sophisticated philosophical analyses that often investigated Platonic theories in the light of modern philosophical interests. He did not, however, try to force Plato into a modern mould, but rather to indicate where he stood with respect to modern issues and how and why he differed. For instance, in studying Plato's characterization of degrees of reality, Vlastos argued that what is at stake is not degrees of existence, but degrees of cognitive reliability, linked with moral or aesthetic valuation. By attributing a higher degree of reality to Forms than sensible particulars, Plato was in part exploring the greater degree of cognitive reliability that universals have over particulars – though he should have settled for a theory positing kinds rather than degrees of reality.

One area in which his work was especially fruitful was the study of predication. His earlier paper on the Third Man Argument had laid out the premises of the argument and had focused attention on 'self-predication', that is, on claims of the form 'F-ness is F' (for example, 'Justice is just'), as the most vulnerable step of the argument, which was used against Plato to generate an infinite number of Forms, apparently using only Plato's own principles. In 1965 Vlastos realized that some of Plato's utterances of the form 'F-ness is G' could be taken as 'Pauline predications' (named by reference to St Paul's 'Charity is kind' and so on) and analysed as 'necessarily, whatever is F is G'. Subsequently he found Pauline predications in the *Protagoras* and the *Sophist*, but no evidence that Plato himself recognized the ambiguity in his own use of 'F-ness is G' expressions. In general, Vlastos held, Plato's own view of the Forms as paradigms kept him from seeing the dangers of self-predication.

3 Socratic studies

In 1975 Vlastos published *Plato's Universe*, a series of lectures which demonstrated how Plato's cosmology embodied scientific hypotheses despite its seemingly anti-scientific basis. The following year he retired from Princeton, becoming a permanent 'visiting' professor at the University of California, Berkeley, until his death in 1991, teaching classes, giving summer seminars on Socrates for postdoctoral students, and lecturing widely. He continued to publish on Plato, for instance, defending him against Karl POPPER in 'The Theory of Social Justice in the Polis in Plato's Republic' (1977), where he argued that Plato does have a genuine normative and meta-normative theory of justice. But his work increasingly focused on SOCRATES. Vlastos had always seen Plato's philosophy as developing over time. Furthermore, he had long been convinced that the philosophy of Socrates could be reconstructed from Plato's early dialogues, which represent a fictionalized but historically faithful portrait of Plato's master. Now he tried to work out to his own satisfaction the details of a coherent philosophy for this enigmatic but, for Vlastos, highly sympathetic figure.

According to Vlastos, the Socrates of Plato's early dialogues is inconsistent in a number of important ways with the Socrates of the middle dialogues. We find that other sources, such as ARISTOTLE and XENOPHON, tend to attribute to Socrates the traits we find in the Socrates of the early dialogues, for

example, that he is solely a moral philosopher and claims to have no special knowlege. It is plausible to think that the early Plato agreed with his master and only abandoned the Socratic method as he became immersed in geometry as a result of his contact with the Pythagorean philosopher-mathematician-statesman ARCHYTAS on his first voyage to Sicily. Socrates' method is not one of mathematical demonstration, but of refutation, requiring that the interlocutor express his real opinions and have them examined; in pursuing this method Socrates can be ruthless, but he never misleads or cheats his opponent. His *elenchus* or method of refutation is not merely a negative method but yields positive results, for it is based on the (well-confirmed) hypothesis that everyone who holds a false belief holds a true belief which conflicts with it, whereas Socrates' set of beliefs is self-consistent, and hence true.

Socrates' disavowal of knowledge can be understood if we make a distinction between 'certain' (demonstrative) knowledge and 'elenctic' knowledge; the latter, being the fallible result of a dialectical process, does not measure up to the former. Since Socrates' method at best yields elenctic knowledge, he is justified in disavowing certain knowledge. Socrates holds that virtue is sufficient for happiness, though he does not make the stronger claim that virtue is identical to happiness: nonmoral goods can and do contribute to happiness, but only when used in conjunction with virtue.

Vlastos succeeded in reconstructing a philosopher's Socrates who is more theoretically interesting than any previous construct, and his teaching produced a new generation of students of Socrates who are continuing a lively debate. Vlastos's greatest talent was perhaps his ability to see in ancient texts arguments and concepts that had philosophical interest for modern thinkers. No other single individual has contributed more to making ancient philosophy a part of contemporary philosophical study in the Anglo-American tradition.

See also: OWEN, G.E.L.

List of works

Vlastos, G. (1939) 'The Disorderly Motion in the Timaeus', *Classical Quarterly* 33: 71–83; also in Vlastos (1995), vol. 2, 247–64. (An argument against the prevailing orthodoxy that read the creation story of the *Timaeus* allegorically, that it should be taken literally.)

—— (1947) 'Equality and Justice in Early Greek Cosmologies', *Classical Philology* 42: 156–78; also in Vlastos (1995), vol. 1, 57–88. (Shows the influence of Greek political ideas on the early Greek conception of the cosmos.)

—— (1952) 'Theology and Philosophy in Early Greek Thought', *Philosophical Quarterly* 2: 97–123; also in Vlastos (1995), vol. 1, 3–31. (Argues against Burnet (1930) that Presocratic thinkers were not mere naturalists and against Jaeger (1947) that they were not really theologians either; rather they attributed to nature divine properties.)

—— (1953) 'Review of J.E. Raven, Pythagoreans and Eleatics', *Gnomon* 25: 29–35; also in Vlastos (1995), vol.1, 80–88. (Convincingly criticizes the view shared by Tannery (1930), Cornford (1930), and Raven (1948) that Parmenides and the Eleatics were reacting to a Pythagorean theory of 'number atomism'. It now appears that there never was such a theory. Provides the basis for Vlastos' later studies of Zeno.)

—— (1954) 'The Third Man Argument in the *Parmenides*', *Philosophical Review* 63: 319–49; also in Vlastos (1995), vol. 2, 166–90. (By applying techniques of logical analysis to the Third Man Argument against Plato's Theory of Forms, the author raises discussion of the problem to a new level. His conclusion that the argument was a 'record of honest perplexity' on the part of Plato has been rejected by most scholars. But he challenges his critics to find textual evidence to show that Plato had a reply to the argument.)

—— (1955a) 'Review of F.M. Cornford, Principium Sapientiae', *Gnomon* 27: 65–76; also in Vlastos (1995), vol. 1, 112–23. (Uses a superior understanding of scientific method to criticize his mentor's interpretation (Cornford 1952) of the Greek medical writers as scientific, the Ionian Presocratics as unscientific. Also rejects Cornford's earlier theory (1912) that philosophy had grown out of religion, in favour of a view that political ideas were decisive for the development of philosophy.)

—— (1955b) 'On Heraclitus', *American Journal of Philology* 76: 337–68; also in Vlastos (1995), vol. 1, 127–50. (Defence of a traditional reading of Heraclitus as philosopher of flux against Kirk (1952), showing the influence of earlier Ionian thought on Heraclitus.)

—— (1957) 'Justice', *Revue internationale de philosophie* 11: 324–43. (A study in moral and social philosophy arguing that agreement, contribution and need constitute 'irreducible components of the concept of justice'.)

—— (1962) 'Justice and Equality', in R. Brandt (ed.) *Social Justice*, Englewood Cliffs, NJ: Prentice Hall, 31–72. (Develops an equalitarian theory of justice based on natural rights which can accommodate

unequal distribution of some goods. Reprinted in several anthologies of essays in moral philosophy.)

—— (1973) *Platonic Studies*, Princeton, NJ: Princeton University Press. (Collects many of Vlastos's essays on Plato.)

—— (1975) *Plato's Universe*, Seattle, WA: University of Washington Press. (Lectures on Plato's cosmology and scientific method, arguing that Plato's appeal to the supernatural paradoxically produced valuable scientific theories.)

—— (1977) 'The Theory of Social Justice in the Polis in Plato's Republic', in H. North (ed.) *Interpretations of Plato*, Leiden: E.J. Brill, 1–40; also in Vlastos (1995), vol. 2, 69–103. (Arguing against Karl Popper's criticisms of Plato, this paper maintains that there is a legitimate normative and meta-normative theory of justice in the *Republic*, one based not on inequality but on impartiality.)

—— (1991) *Socrates: Ironist and Moral Philosopher*, Cambridge: Cambridge University Press. (Vlastos's major study of Socrates.)

—— (1994) *Socratic Studies*, ed. M. Burnyeat, Cambridge: Cambridge Unversity Press. (Essays on Socrates.)

—— (1995) *Studies in Ancient Philosophy*, ed. D.W. Graham, Princeton: Princeton University Press, 2 vols. (Collects those of Vlastos's major essays which do not appear in *Platonic Studies*, *Socrates: Ironist and Moral Philosopher* and *Socratic Studies*. Volume 1: studies in the Presocratics; volume 2: studies on Socrates, Plato and later figures. Contains a complete bibliography of Vlastos's work.)

References and further reading

* Burnet, J. (1930) *Early Greek Philosophy*, London: Adam & Charles Black, 4th edn. (The standard textbook on the Presocratics of its time, this work presents views on Presocratic naturalism which Vlastos (1952) criticizes.)

* Cornford, F.M. (1912) *From Religion to Philosophy*, London. (Presents a view on the origins of philosophy which Vlastos (1955a) criticizes.)

* —— (1939) *Plato and Parmenides*, London: Routledge & Kegan Paul. (Presents a view of Parmenides as reacting to Pythagorean theories which Vlastos (1953) criticizes.)

* —— (1952) *Principium Sapientiae*, Cambridge: Cambridge University Press. (Presents a view on the origins of philosophy different from Cornford (1912), which Vlastos (1955a) criticizes.)

* Jaeger, W. (1947) *Theology of the Early Greek Philosophers*, Oxford. (A treatment of the Presocratics as theologians which Vlastos (1952) criticizes.)

* Kirk, G.S. (1954) *Heraclitus: The Cosmic Fragments*, Cambridge: Cambridge University Press. (A study of Heraclitus which rejects the traditional interpretation of Heraclitus as a flux theorist. Vlastos (1955b) defends the traditional interpretation against Kirk.)

Lee, E.N., Mourelatos, A.P.D. and Rorty, R. (1976) *Exegesis and Argument*, Assen: Van Gorcum. (Festschrift containing reactions to Vlastos's work.)

* Raven, J.E. (1948) *Pythagoreans and Eleatics*, Cambridge: Cambridge University Press. (Presents a view of Parmenides and the Eleatics as reacting to Pythagorean theories which Vlastos (1953) criticizes.)

* Tannery, P. (1930) *Pour l'histoire de la science hellène*, Paris: Gauthier-Villars. (Similar to Raven, holds that Parmenides and the Eleatics reacted to Pythagorean theories.)

DANIEL W. GRAHAM

VOEGELIN, ERIC (1901–85)

Throughout his career, Voegelin was concerned with modernity; unlike his contemporaries he sought the explanation of its character and deformities (especially totalitarianism) in the restoration of 'political science' as Plato and Aristotle understood it. He therefore explored order in the individual's soul, political society, history and the universe, and its source in God. He did so by studying the representation of order in philosophy (Eastern as well as Western) and in revelation and myth. Voegelin concluded that 'gnosticism', the misinterpretation of the insights of myth, philosophy and revelation as descriptions of some future perfected society, and the wilful denial of transcendence and human limitation, represented the essence of modernity.

1 Life and works
2 Critique of contemporary social science and philosophy
3 Reality and consciousness
4 Gnosticism and political order

1 Life and works

By profession and self-description, Eric Voegelin was a political scientist, but philosopher, political theorist, theologian, mystic and intellectual historian would be equally accurate and equally misleading titles. Expelled by the Nazis from a lectureship at Vienna University, where he had studied, taken his Ph.D. and worked as Hans Kelsen's assistant, Voegelin lectured

in political science at Baton Rouge, Louisiana from 1942 until 1958. He then took up Max Weber's former chair at Munich University. In 1969 he returned to the USA as Distinguished Scholar in the Hoover Institute, Stanford, California, and remained there until his death. His intellectual power and astonishing scholarly range have been widely acknowledged. His main endeavour was to reconstitute the study of politics, a project publicly initiated in his *The New Science of Politics* (1952) and partly executed in his *Order and History* (1956–87), as well as many other books and articles.

2 Critique of contemporary social science and philosophy

Voegelin's permanent concern was with order and disorder in the soul and in society, and the nature of modernity. Originally prompted by the rise of the totalitarian movements, of which he had first-hand experience, this concern was widely shared by academics. However, Voegelin's public stance was confrontational, and his insistence that knowledge of Mesopotamian, Israelite, Greek, Roman and medieval history and philology, as well as of myth and non-Western cultures, was indispensable to the restoration of a genuine science of order won him few friends. His condemnation of positivism was comprehensive, but he regarded the 1960s and 1970s debate between positivists and their opponents as merely a theoretically more impoverished re-run of its early twentieth-century predecessor (see POSITIVISM IN THE SOCIAL SCIENCES). He interpreted both modernity and totalitarianism as 'gnosticism' (see §4). He made sweeping claims about the 'essence' of modern '-isms', 'climates of opinion', doctrines and movements, and about the mediations between these and the thought of the 'representative' thinkers he identified as their progenitors. His philosophical vocabulary is often difficult (drawing on Greek philosophy), and although bilingual and eloquent, he sometimes relies on a background of untranslatable German terms, most notably when he identifies 'the tension (*Spannung*) to the Ground (*Grund*) of divine Being (*Sein*)' as both the source and the object of the philosopher's quest (1956: 2).

3 Reality and consciousness

The questions Voegelin addresses are familiar to phenomenology and existentialism (Alfred SCHÜTZ was his lifelong friend, and he was deeply sympathetic to *L'homme révolté* of CAMUS), and were formulated in explicit critical confrontation with Kant, Hegel, Comte, Marx, Nietzsche, Weber, Husserl and Heidegger. Of contemporary philosophies, he found something to praise in every contemporary philosophy except positivism and Marxism, which (in his view) yielded virtually nothing valuable enough to compensate for their persistent 'prohibition' of fundamental questions.

At the centre of Voegelin's thinking is the metaphysical question of Leibniz, Schelling and Heidegger: Why is there something? Why not nothing? Why are things as they are? The quest for the answer is 'philosophy', which is not epistemology but the love of knowledge. Knowledge can only be knowledge of truth and reality, and reality is not merely or mainly to be found in external objects, which non-philosophical experience, ordinary language and ideologies suppose to exhaust reality. Reality is experienced in consciousness, which in its exploring never encounters anything in the universe which is not of its own 'substance'. What is encountered at the limit is a transcendent order, or structure, of being which has its Beginning or ground (*archê*) and its End (*telos*) in the Beyond, or divine. And individuals (there is no consciousness except the consciousness of individuals) apprehend reality in this ultimate sense, not as external observers, but as 'participant observers'. This reality, the 'utterly real' (*realissimum*) of myths, philosophers and mystics, the order of the universe and the 'divine ground of [all] being' that generates and sustains it and towards which it tends, is sought and found, the finding being experienced as the divine revealing itself: *theophany*.

There are three kinds of theophany: the wisdom of myth; 'philosophy' (paradigmatically Plato's); and the Revelation of the Old Testament and (paradigmatically) Christ in Paul and St John. These are equally valid explorations of the experience of reality, compact in the case of myth, differentiated in philosophy and revelation. Each such exploration is culturally specific and personal (although the experiences are available to all who do not deliberately close them off), and becomes luminous only through language symbols. Some of these explorations have been epochal, rendering previous symbolizations (for example, the intra-cosmic gods of myth) obsolete and breaking historical time into a 'before' and 'after' the irruption of the divine. But none can ever be final, or perfectly adequate, or make sense independently of the experience of reality from which it arises.

Voegelin's exploration of the nature of consciousness becomes ever more complex, since he must transcend solipsism and relativism, but rejects the privileged vantage point of the transcendental ego postulated by Kant, Fichte and Hegel; for Voegelin there is no such vantage point. And neither mystery nor the tensions inherent in the human 'In-between'

are to be abolished. Nor must the symbols whereby this experience of transcendence and order becomes luminous be broken away from their engendering experience. Conversely, philosophical exploration of reality can never be symbol-free; consciousness and symbols always emerge from reality simultaneously, and language and experience are inseparable. The history of consciousness thus becomes a tracking of the trail of symbols and doctrines to their source in experience.

4 Gnosticism and political order

The experience of reality has profound implications, not only for the order of the philosopher's or prophet's own soul, but also for their apperception of true order in society and meaning in history. Voegelin's historical work always centred on the former. As to the latter, he focused on 'derailments' and perversions of insight into order by 'gnosticism' (the essence of modernity) from antiquity onwards, culminating in totalitarianism (see TOTALITARIANISM). His two attempts at a historical account of order in society and history foundered. In the 1940s, he abandoned an already well-advanced history of political ideas, because ideas, doctrines and doctrinal disputes of any sort are merely a lifeless (or pernicious) residue, when sundered from the experience which they symbolically articulate, or pervert. In *Order and History* (1956–87), Voegelin intended to present symbolizations of experience and their representation in political order as a meaningful historical sequence. His fidelity to evidence, however, made this impossible, and he came to see the idea of a unilinear history of mankind as itself misguided. 'Mankind' is a symbol intelligible only in the context of a common relation to the divine; empirically, mankind is no more a historic unity than 'cat-kind'. He excoriated all equations of the history of mankind with the history of Western high culture, or what he called Western ecumenical imperialism. Nor, although there is meaning *in* history, is there a meaning *of* history. And any idea of a unilinear history terminating in the self-revelation (*egophany*) of a Condorcet, Hegel, Comte, Marx, Husserl or Heidegger, he saw as the height of the lust for power and a disease of the soul (see HISTORICISM).

He construed such derailments as grounded in a refusal to recognize the inevitably circumscribed and uncertain character of human existence as the divine-human 'In-between' (Plato's *metaxy*); this refusal makes man instead of God the measure of all things. Philosophers and prophets can counteract this evil only to a limited extent. The ground has already been occupied by others (individuals and societies) who

655

claim to know reality and to be able accurately to represent it by the time that they arrive. The philosophers and prophets in turn can offer only symbolizations which are inevitably couched in an object-oriented language and are thus always liable to misrepresentation, especially since philosophy and myth have no certainties or definitive answers of their own to propound; and they cannot abolish empirical reality and its disorder and injustice. In particular they cannot abolish the profound sense of injustice of the subjects of 'ethnic' orders (that is, culturally cohesive and territorially limited polities) conquered by 'ecumenical' orders (polities aiming at a more or less inclusive empire). To such individuals, 'ethnic' orders had represented the order of the universe; 'ecumenical' empires represent nothing except the triumph of naked power.

Gnosticism, whether as a pernicious potential within Christianity, or stemming from other sources, insulates itself against reality by prohibiting metaphysical questions (notably Marx's ruling out such questions as irrelevant for 'socialist man'), and by 'immanentizing' (interpreting the symbols of transcendence as descriptions of some present or future perfect mankind or society). It may remain mere speculation, or it may become a political force in times of disorientation and disorder, taking the form of political activism, 'liberation', revolution or nihilism. Voegelin sees a similar, but less resolute and destructive infidelity to reality in doctrinaire religion and progressivism of all kinds.

It would have been absurd for Voegelin to present his own insights as a doctrine, even for the sake of remaking the now vanished link between symbols and their engendering experience provided in the past by myth, religion and authority. And it may be the case that humankind finds reality or uncertainty difficult to bear, especially when it lacks a stable institutional tradition and common sense (which the UK and the USA in Voegelin's view still had). Although he was no cultural pessimist, it did not surprise Voegelin that he did not 'find many, or favourable hearers'.

List of works

Voegelin, E. (1990–) , *The Collected Works of Eric Voegelin*, series ed. P. Caringella, Baton Rouge, LA: Louisiana State University Press. (An exemplary edition which aims to present all of Voegelin's unpublished, as well as published, writings in thirty-four volumes. Volume 12, *Published Essays 1966–1985*, includes striking critiques of Hegel (as a 'magician') and Heidegger, literary interpretations and late statements of his theology and Christianity.)

Voegelin, E. (1952) *The New Science of Politics*, Chicago, IL, and London: University of Chicago Press. (The most widely known of Voegelin's writings, now superseded by later work but still a useful introduction to Voegelin's themes of representation, modernity and gnosticism. Often reprinted.)

—— (1959) *Wissenschaft, Politik und Gnosis*, Munich: Kösel; trans. W.J. Fitzpatrick, *Science, Politics and Gnosticism*, Chicago, IL: Regnery, 1968. (His most accessible, although polemical presentation in two essays, the former outlining the projected *Order and History*, the latter containing the most succinct exploration of *Gnosis* and the notorious critique of Marx; the translation includes an additional essay on 'Ersatz Religion'.)

—— (1956–87) *Order and History*, vol. I: *Israel and Revelation* (1956), vol. II: *The World of the Polis* (1957), vol. III: *Plato and Aristotle* (1957) , vol. IV: *The Ecumenic Age* (1974), vol. V: *In Search of Order* (1987), Baton Rouge, LA: Louisiana State University Press. (The finest of Voegelin's productions. Posthumous and unfinished, it does not cover the Middle Ages, Reformation or Modernity; of especial note are the preface and 'Historiogenesis' in vol. IV.)

—— (1966) *Anamnesis*, Munich: R. Piper; abridged edn, trans. and ed. G. Niemeyer, Notre Dame, IN, and London: University of Notre Dame Press, 1978. (Good translation but omits some important early writings on Husserl; includes the fullest statements of Voegelin's philosophy of consciousness.)

—— (1975) *From Enlightenment to Revolution*, trans. J.H. Hallowell, Durham, NC: Duke University Press. (The only part of Voegelin's projected history of political ideas to be published in his lifetime; a very good introduction to Voegelin's thought; incisive exegesis of Voltaire, Helvétius, Comte and Marx *inter alia*.)

—— (1989) *Autobiographical Reflections*, ed. E. Sandoz, Baton Rouge, LA: Louisiana State University Press. (Fascinating insights into Voegelin's life, times and intellect.)

References and further reading

Cooper, B. (1986) *The Political Theory of Eric Voegelin*, Lewiston, NY, and Queenston, Ont.: Edwin Mellen Press. (A circumspect account.)

Hughes, G. and Lawrence, F. (1995) 'The Challenge of Eric Voegelin', *Political Science Reviewer* 24: 398–452. (Survey of Voegelin's thought in the light of the most recently published works.)

Opitz, P.J. and Sebba, G. (eds) (1981) *The Philosophy*

of Order: Essays on History, Consciousness and Politics, Stuttgart: Klett-Cotta Verlag. (Volume commemorating Voegelin's eightieth birthday.)

Sandoz, E. (1971) 'The Foundations of Voegelin's Political Theory', *The Political Science Reviewer* 1: 30–73. (Explores Voegelin's reputation and discusses *Anamnesis*.)

—— (ed.) (1982) *Eric Voegelin's Thought A Critical Appraisal*, Durham, NC: Duke University Press. (Articles by friends and colleagues, comment by Voegelin; ample references; see particularly contributions by Sebba, Webb, Altizer and Havard.)

H.M. HÖPFL

VOLTAIRE (FRANÇOIS-MARIE AROUET) (1694–1778)

Voltaire remains the most celebrated representative of the reformers and free-thinkers whose writings define the movement of ideas in eighteenth-century France known as the Enlightenment. He was not, however, a systematic philosopher with an original, coherently argued world-view, but a philosophe *who translated, interpreted and vulgarized the work of other philosophers. His own writings on philosophical matters were deeply influenced by English empiricism and deism. His thought is marked by a pragmatic rationalism that led him, even in his early years, to view the world of speculative theorizing with a scepticism that was often expressed most effectively in his short stories. As a young man, Voltaire was particularly interested in Locke and Newton, and it was largely through his publications in the 1730s and 1740s that knowledge of Lockean epistemology and Newtonian cosmology entered France and eventually ensured the eclipse of Cartesianism.*

After his stay in England Voltaire became interested in philosophical optimism, and his thinking reflected closely Newton's view of a divinely ordered human condition, to which Alexander Pope gave powerful poetic expression in the Essay on Man *(1733–4). This was reinforced for the young Voltaire by Leibnizian optimism, which offered the view that the material world, being necessarily the perfect creation of an omnipotent and beneficent God, was the 'best of all possible worlds', that is to say the form of creation chosen by God as being that in which the optimum amount of good could be enjoyed at the cost of the least amount of evil.*

Voltaire's later dissatisfaction with optimistic theory brought with it a similar loss of faith in the notion of a meaningful order of nature, and his earlier acceptance

of the reality of human freedom of decision-taking and action was replaced after 1748 with a growing conviction that such freedom was illusory. The 1750s witness Voltaire's final abandonment of optimism and providentialism in favour of a more deterministically orientated position in which a much bleaker view of human life and destiny predominates. Pessimistic fatalism was a temporary phase in his thinking, however, and was replaced in turn by a melioristic view in which he asserted the possibilities of limited human action in the face of a hostile and godless condition.

1   Life
2   Metaphysics and ethics: the *Traité de métaphysique*
3   Cosmology: *La Métaphysique de Newton*
4   Optimism and freedom

1   Life

Voltaire (born François-Marie Arouet) was one of the most prolific and controversial writers of *ancien régime* France, and his works encapsulate the spirit and ideology of the French Enlightenment. His writings, which span a broad spectrum of genres, do not readily provide the reader with a single, coherent philosophical system or even a systematically argued world-view. In fact, Voltaire deeply mistrusted systems and system-builders, and he frequently satirized, particularly in his later years, the terminology and theories of metaphysicians such as Spinoza, Descartes, Leibniz and Wolff (see LEIBNIZ, G.W.). He wrote mostly, though not exclusively, as a *philosophe* rather than as a philosopher, that is to say, as a dissident polemicist concerned more with persuasive forms of discourse, and the effective advancement of a programme of moral and political reform, than with the pursuit of abstract speculation and analysis *per se*. Some aspects of his philosophical thinking are conducted at an arguably superficial level in the form of short, satirical tales. The term 'philosopher', in its post-nineteenth-century sense, thus sits uneasily with Voltaire. Had he known about the modern meaning of the term, he would have dissociated himself from it. He remained deeply sceptical about the mission of philosophy, and the absurdity of metaphysics is a striking leitmotif of his writings.

In 1726, as the result of a scandal, Voltaire was exiled from Paris, and decided to go to London where he stayed until 1728. His stay in England enabled him to engage with the Baconian tradition of English empiricism and to familiarize himself with the work of Locke, Hobbes, Newton, Clarke, Berkeley, Collins and others. The impact of England on his thinking resulted in 1734 in the publication of the *Lettres philosophiques*, composed originally in English as the

Letters concerning the English Nation. In 1734 he also started work on another important fruit of the English experience, the *Traité de métaphysique.* This is one of the few Voltairean treatises to contain sustained, relatively sophisticated, philosophical argument and analysis.

The controversy following the publication of the *Lettres philosophiques* forced Voltaire to flee Paris for the chateau of Mme DU CHÂTELET-LOMONT at Cirey, where he stayed for the rest of the decade working on his most ambitious scientific achievement, the *Éléments de la philosophie de Newton* (1738). After a brief stay at Frederick the Great's court at Potsdam, Voltaire settled in Geneva in 1754–5, and the following decade saw the publication of major historical, polemical and satirical works, including the anti-Leibnizian *Candide* (1759), the *Philosophie de l'histoire* (1759), the *Dictionnaire philosophique* (1764–9) and *Le Philosophe ignorant* (1766). The 1755 Lisbon earthquake proved to be a catalyst in his long debate with others and with himself on the problem of evil and predetermination, culminating in *Candide*, his most brilliant and enduring philosophical narrative.

Between his earliest writings on philosophical matters in 1734 and those works that appeared after 1755, his position changed from one of qualified deistic providentialism and belief in a logically ordered creation, whose harmony had been convincingly demonstrated by Newton's mathematical principles, to one of uncompromising rejection of providentialism and philosophical optimism. Voltaire has few claims to originality as an abstract thinker. As his commentaries in the *Lettres philosophiques* on the work of Francis BACON, LOCKE and above all NEWTON show, he excels in the art of exposition and vulgarization. As a result, he occupies a uniquely influential position as a mediator and disseminator of English and German seventeenth-century philosophy in a France that was to remain dominated by Cartesianism until well into the 1740s. Newton and Locke, in particular, enter the French consciousness through Voltaire's pen.

2 Metaphysics and ethics: the *Traité de métaphysique*

Voltaire's early adherence to rational deism was reinforced in England, although the problems of theodicy and free will had started to preoccupy him well before his exile (see DEISM). The first version of the *Traité de métaphysique* (1734) grew out of Voltaire's reactions to Locke's *Essay concerning Human Understanding* (1689), and its composition was shaped by the controversy aroused in France by the *Lettres philosophiques*. By 1736 the text had evolved

to take in the implications of Alexander Pope's *Essay on Man* (1733–4), and included chapters dealing with ethics and with man as a social being, reflecting also the influence of SHAFTESBURY, MANDEVILLE and CLARKE. The philosophical balance of the *Traité* moved between 1734 and 1736 from metaphysics to ethics. The *Traité* consists of a brief introduction dealing with doubts about the nature of man, written in the sceptical tradition as transmitted to the eighteenth century through the writings of MONTAIGNE and Le Mothe Le Vayer, followed by nine chapters. Voltaire's philosophy at this stage owes much to the theodicy of English deism and the optimism of Pope and Shaftesbury. The *Traité* also contains traces of the influence of ancient scepticism and epicureanism, the French Pyrrhonian tradition, and late seventeenth-century libertinism (see LIBERTINS).

Much of the *Traité* is anchored to Lockean problems, the second, third, fifth, sixth, seventh and ninth chapters correlating closely to Locke's programme of epistemological investigation. Voltaire follows Locke in the rejection of innate ideas (attributed to DESCARTES), and in the location of the source of ideas in the senses and the reflective processes. He does not deal with reflection *per se* except to note that thought is not, *pace* Descartes, necessarily a spiritual attribute. Voltaire fully shared Locke's view of the limitations of human understanding, and epistemological modesty was to be the organizing theme of a later wide-ranging essay, *Le Philosophe ignorant.*

Voltaire's starting-point is an awareness of the relative combined with an insistence on the practical aspects of ethics and the lessons of natural morality. Establishing a significant order of priorities, his argument moves from man to God, bypassing Christian notions of creation and original sin. God's existence is deduced empirically in the second, and longest, chapter in the treatise, although knowledge of God's existence is not seen as being either universal or necessary to man's happiness. God's existence is argued from final causes and the Locke–Clarke propositions concerning necessity. The counter-arguments denying certainty in God's existence, and affirming the reality of evil as a negation of the possibility of belief in divine benevolence and omnipotence, are also expounded, but at this stage in Voltaire's thinking they are not allowed to undermine what was essentially a deistic position.

On the question of the soul, Voltaire's view in the *Traité* was that man was composed of thinking matter. He rejected the notion of thought itself as a material compound, but in 1734 he was not prepared to discount entirely the notion of the spirituality and immortality of the soul. He was to advance that argument even more positively in the article 'Ame' in the *Dictionnaire philosophique*. In spite of a tenacious belief in the existence of the soul, often identified with thought itself as a 'principle' invested in inert matter by God, Voltaire did not allow man to occupy a special, privileged place in nature. Man was just a 'reasonable animal'. Unlike the rest of creation, however, man had a measure of free will, although freedom and the power to act freely in accordance with the dictates of reason, always remained for Voltaire severely limited features of man's condition. But on freedom depended morality, and morality provided the focus for the last two chapters of the *Traité*.

Here Voltaire addressed the question of whether man was a social being, together with the related issue of vice and virtue. Concepts of good and evil were determined by what was useful or harmful to society. Parting company with Locke, Voltaire postulated, reflecting again a measure of inconsistency in his thinking, that man possessed innate moral sentiment and an instinct for justice. The assumption of universal morality followed logically from that, and supported the notion of legality, although Voltaire accepted at the same time that specific, contingent laws could well be diverse and contradictory in different parts of the world. Vice and virtue were seen to be relative to social contexts, as was man's understanding of what was useful. However, like BAYLE, Voltaire accepted the proposition that all men concurred in the general notions of what was good or evil in those natural laws on which all men in all societies ultimately agreed. Reflecting Shaftesbury's influence, Voltaire's view of human nature was determined by the premise that man possessed latent moral qualities derived from God, and he was never able to reconcile this successfully with his Lockean rejection of innate ideas in other contexts.

Much as God had given the bees a powerful instinct to organize the communal life of the hive, so he had given man, not moral instructions on how to behave, but certain instincts conducive to social and moral life. These were in addition to the instincts of sexuality and self-preservation common to all animals, and included benevolence, compassion, honour, love of truth, pride and the passions, of which even the unattractive, such as pride and envy, had teleological purpose, and served to promote the public good. In all this, God's role in human affairs remained remote and non-interventionist. Voltaire's moral philosophy was essentially a naturalist code in which his concern was less with logical argument than with a passionate determination to define man as an ethical being whose moral conduct and decisions owed nothing to theology or faith, but a great deal to the will to action.

3 Cosmology: *La Métaphysique de Newton*

When it first appeared in 1738, the *Éléments de la philosophie de Newton* was exclusively concerned with optics and gravitational theory, that is with 'natural philosophy', rather than with philosophy as such, and there is little reference to the 'Scholium generale' with which Newton had concluded his *Principia* (1687). However, the 1741 edition of the *Éléments* contained a nine-chapter essay prefacing the commentary on Newtonian physics. This had been printed separately in 1740 as *La Métaphysique de Newton, ou Parallèle des sentiments de Newton et de Leibniz*.

Much of this work is concerned with an exposition of the problems of free will, morality and the mind-body relationship, many of which had been raised earlier in the *Traité de métaphysique*. The new ground that Voltaire now broke concerned Leibniz, and the treatise represents Voltaire's most sustained analysis of Leibnizian science and cosmology. Voltaire's long engagement with Leibnizianism was to drive much of his thinking on questions relating to theodicy and philosophical optimism between 1740 and 1755, culminating in 1756 in his first major attack on optimistic theory in the *Poème sur le désastre de Lisbonne*, reinforced three years later in his satirical demolition of Leibnizian cosmology in *Candide*. Voltaire's attention had been drawn to Leibniz through the work of Christian von WOLFF, who had systemized some of Leibniz's thoughts on logic and metaphysics, and whose merits had been commended to Voltaire by Mme Du Châtelet-Lomont and Frederick the Great. Voltaire's knowledge of Leibniz was also based on a Latin translation of the *Monadology* (1714), and he was familiar with the Leibniz–Clarke correspondence concerning space and time.

In *La Métaphysique de Newton* he resumed Newton's arguments from design as a proof of God's existence as a First Cause, outside time and space, of the contingent phenomena of the universe. Whereas in the *Traité de métaphysique* Voltaire's God had been an absent Prime Mover, in *La Métaphysique* he was more sympathetic to the providentialism that marked Newtonian assumptions of divine paternalism. Voltaire still managed to deflect the paradoxes presented by the spectacle of man's suffering and experience of evil, although in *La Métaphysique* the problem of theodicy was raised again in the context of man's freedom to act within the parameters inherent in a providentially ordered human condition. It was here that Leibniz entered the discussion with reference to sufficient reason, necessity and contingency, matters upon which Voltaire had already exchanged views with Clarke. Like Clarke, he argued that divine omnipotence would be compromised if God's will was made subject to the principle of sufficient reason. Voltaire preferred the Newtonian position in which God is seen to have made many things, the reason for whose existence is God's will alone.

Voltaire avoided determinism at this stage in his thought by preserving, by means of extended implication, the capacity for unmotivated choice arising from 'liberty of indifference'. His position on 'liberty of indifference' was not consistent or rigorously applied, however, and elsewhere – in the *Discours en vers sur l'homme* (1738–42), for example – this received less emphasis than the Lockean view that man's freedom consisted in the power to act and put conscious choices into effect, the question of motivation or absence of motivation being irrelevant. On the question of freedom, and free will in general, Voltaire's views were to change radically, and by the 1750s his position was much more deterministic.

Despite his acceptance of Newtonian arguments from design as proof of an ordered universe in *La Métaphysique*, signs of contradiction and traces of scepticism, to be more strongly articulated at a later stage, were already surfacing in Voltaire's discussion of Leibniz' arguments relating to sufficient reason and to the existence of simple substances, or monads. Leibnizian monadology underpinned the elaboration of the Great Chain of Being theory and the postulation of a cosmos of active metaphysical atoms, or monads, each following a programme of dynamic evolution established by the Creator, and each in harmony with other monads, one of their more controversial characteristics being perceptivity. This infinite multitude of monads constituted a metaphysical substratum of the world of material reality and conscious experience. Voltaire measured Leibniz' theory of monads by simplistically empirical criteria that he associated with Lockean epistemology and Newtonian mathematics. His approach reflected only a partial understanding of the *Theodicy* (1710) and the *Monadology*, and incoporated a great deal of caricatural commentary.

Voltaire objected that Leibniz' postulation of a cosmos of infinitely divisible, nonmaterial and non-spatial matter as an integral component of the material cosmos was self-contradictory. Any explanation of matter that involved the nonmaterial was fanciful, and the notion of perceptivity in all monads, including those constituting inanimate matter, was against common sense. He countered with arguments not entirely free of speculation themselves, drawn from Newtonian science, and advanced a view of matter whose atomic structure was diverse but immutable. Change was accounted for in terms of the effects of gravitational attraction, the 'active force which sets everything in the universe in motion'. Newtonian physics and cosmology did solve for Voltaire some of the philosophical problems arising from his study of Leibnizian monadology and harmony. After 1741, however, notwithstanding his deep admiration for Newton's empirical rigour, he was to have little more to say about Newton. His preoccupation with Leibnizianism, and with its broader philosophical implications, would continue, on the other hand, for many decades.

4 Optimism and freedom

Voltaire's engagement with the problem of evil arose as part of a general broadening of his philosophical interests during his stay in England. Prior to that, he might have already gained some awareness of the issues through the well-publicized debate on theodicy that had taken place between 1697 and 1716 between Archbishop King, Bayle and Leibniz. It was, however, Pope's *Essay on Man* that fired his interest initially in the philosophical issues generated by optimistic theory.

The first serious discussion of the implications of optimism had occurred in the *Traité de métaphysique* where Voltaire had been concerned almost exclusively, as was Pope, with mounting an effective defence of deism against the objections of the atheists. The central argument in this defence related to the question of human ignorance. Voltaire sought to account for evil in terms of a contingent, rather than transcendental, phenomenon, whose nature and effects were falsely determined by the partial, imperfect nature of human understanding. Evil was relative, and to ascribe to God injustice and cruelty was as meaningless as to call him blue or square. The human mind could not conceive of perfection on a cosmic scale, and thus assertions of imperfection were necessarily flawed. Any moral judgment on God's creation must therefore be suspended for lack of evidence.

While Voltaire never quite shared Pope's confidence in providence as an unambiguously benevolent force in human affairs, his early views can be aligned with Pope's 'Whatever is, is right' formulation, and this was fully reflected in his own *Discours en vers sur l'homme* (see especially Part 6). However, the problem of theodicy had been deflected rather than resolved, and after 1740 it re-emerged in Voltaire's thought as a major issue. By 1740 he was aware of Leibniz' arguments on the *Theodicy* as these related to evil, not as a contingent but as an absolute, universal phenomenon that sought to leave intact the providentialist thesis of creation as the work of a beneficent and omnipotent God. Dogmatic promulgation of Leibnizian optimism by German commentators such as Wolff and Kahle became increasingly a subject for ridicule and caustic satire in Voltaire's letters and works. Leibnizian optimism, immortalized in the figure of Candide's tutor, Dr Pangloss, soon came to exemplify for him the irrelevance of speculative metaphysics to the real world of human suffering and everyday experience.

The evolution of Voltaire's position with regard to Pope and Leibniz, and the related problems of evil, optimism and freedom, is best illustrated not in treatises but in Voltaire's short philosophical stories, and in particular in *Zadig, ou la destinée* (1748) and *Candide, ou l'optimisme*. In *Zadig* he approached the problem of evil from the standpoint of human destiny. Using dialogic format he distilled philosophical optimism into three main propositions that were not argued, or even endorsed, but asserted arbitrarily by an angelic *persona* as articles of faith: chance does not exist; man's destiny is organized in a beneficent way, immutably determined by providence; every apparent evil is part of a larger good and is impenetrable to limited human logic and understanding. While 'Whatever is, is right' still obtained in theory, by 1748 Voltaire no longer adhered fully to his earlier view that evil had no absolute reality. In *Zadig* the focus of attention is clearly on the realities of human suffering and the illogicality of the human predicament rather than on the metaphysical rationale for its existence. Man's place in the Great Chain of Being might have been allotted to him by God for an unknowable purpose, but Voltaire was now firmly of the view that while transcendental perspectives may help to explain the human condition, they contributed nothing to the alleviation of that condition, or to the resolution of the problems that it posed for individual freedom and action.

In the 1750s Voltaire's thinking was dominated by an awareness of the immediacy of evil in day-to-day human experience, and this gradually undermined his earlier sympathy for the optimistic-providentialist position. Events such as the 1755 Lisbon earthquake and the Seven Years War offered further brutal proof of the sterility of optimistic theory, and the darker tones of Voltaire's world-view emerged clearly in the *Poème sur le désastre de Lisbonne*. It was in this didactic poem that he first gave explicit expression to what had by now become his principal objection to the providentialist axiom that all was for the best in the best of all possible worlds. Such a philosophy was now nothing less than a doctrine of despair and a denial of human freedom and of human capacity for action. Philosophical optimism had nothing to offer the stricken citizens of Lisbon.

On the question of free will, Voltaire's earliest discussion of the problem is to be found in the seventh chapter of the *Traité de métaphysique*, where he had accepted that to will and to act accordingly was to be free. Freedom, however, was relative and, even at this 'optimistic' stage in his thinking, it was almost without constraints. He developed his thoughts on freedom further in 1737 in *De La Liberté*. Here he made use of the Lockean definition of freedom as being the choice of whether to act or to refrain from acting, but he now preferred to concentrate on 'power of self-motion' (Clarke's phrase) as being the only true source of freedom. By the mid-1750s Voltaire's views on freedom had evolved considerably, and in ways that mirrored his change of direction with regard to providentialism and philosophical optimism. His denial of free will, and his scepticism with regard to the notion of freedom in human decision-taking and action, was now complete, and it is set out in the fifty-six 'doubts' that constitute the *Doutes sur la liberté* (1752) (see also the articles 'Destin', 'Franc arbitre' and 'Liberté' in the *Dictionnaire philosophique*). Little trace remained of the arguments against determinism that had characterized the *Traité de métaphysique* and *De La Liberté* some two decades earlier, in which a high value had been placed on man's power of judgment and his power to act on that judgment. Men, like animals, are determined by 'instinct' and by 'ideas' that they receive but over whose reception they have no control, and man is subject to the same laws of necessity that govern the whole of nature. The deep sense of futility that was to permeate *Candide* permeates also his list of doubts (see particularly the fourteenth).

Voltaire's loss of faith in philosophical activity reached its climax in *Candide*, in which he finally turned his back on the 'métaphysico-théologo-cosmo-lonigologie' of Dr Pangloss. Candide inhabits a bleak, arbitrary and possibly godless universe in which evil is an omnipresent, crushing reality. Man might be the victim of forces beyond his control, but experience (not philosophy) taught Candide that the potential for limited, but effective, action still lay within man's grasp: 'Il faut cultiver le jardin' (We must cultivate the garden). The point of thought was action, not the construction of inconclusive speculative systems.

See also: EDUCATION, HISTORY OF PHILOSOPHY OF; EMPIRICISM; ENLIGHTENMENT, CONTINENTAL; RATIONALISM; WILL, THE

List of works

Voltaire, F.-M. A. de (1980) *Oeuvres complètes de Voltaire* (The Complete Works of Voltaire), ed. R. Pomeau, Oxford: The Voltaire Foundation. (The standard edition.)

—— (1734) *Lettres philosophiques* (Philosophical Letters), Paris: Jore; repr. G. Lanson and A.M. Rousseau (eds), Paris: Garnier, 1964. (This text was published originally in English in 1733 as the *Letters Concerning the English Nation*: see the edition by N. Cronk, Oxford: Oxford University Press, 1994.)

—— (1737) *De La Liberté* (On Freedom), in *Oeuvres complètes de Voltaire*, Oxford: The Voltaire Foundation, 1980. (This text was based on the seventh chapter of the *Traité de métaphysique*, and developed in letters to Frederick the Great in 1737–8.)

—— (1738–42) *Discours en vers sur l'homme* (Discourse in Verse on Man), Paris: Prault; in *Oeuvres complètes de Voltaire*, Oxford: The Voltaire Foundation, 1980, vol. XVII, 453–530.

—— (1738) *Éléments de la philosophie de Newton* (Elements of Newton's Philosophy), Amsterdam: Ledet and Desbordes; in *Oeuvres complètes de Voltaire*, Oxford: The Voltaire Foundation, 1980, vol. XV, 195–805.

—— (1740) *La Métaphysique de Newton ou Parallèle des sentiments de Newton et de Leibniz* (Newton's Metaphysics or Parallel between the Views of Newton and Leibniz), Amsterdam: Ledet and Desbordes; in *Oeuvres complètes de Voltaire*, Oxford: The Voltaire Foundation, 1980, vol. XV, 195–252.

—— (1748) *Zadig ou la destinée, histoire orientale* (Zadig or Fate, an Oriental Tale), Paris: Prault and Machuel; repr. H.T. Mason (ed.), Oxford: Oxford University Press, 1971. (This tale first appeared as *Memnon, histoire orientale*.)

—— (1752) *Dialogue entre un brachmane et un jésuite sur la nécessité et l'enchaînement des choses* (Dialogue between a Brahmin and a Jesuit on Necessity and the Chain of Being), Dresden: Walther; in *Oeuvres complètes de Voltaire*, Oxford: The Voltaire Foundation, 1980, vol. XV, 646–52. (This text was added to the 1752 edition of the *Éléments* as chapter 6.)

—— (1752) *Doutes sur la liberté* (Doubts on Freedom), Dresden: Walther; in *Oeuvres complètes de Voltaire*, Oxford: The Voltaire Foundation, 1980, vol. XV, 643–6. (This text was added to the 1752 edition of the *Éléments* as chapter 5.)

—— (1756) *Poèmes sur le désastre de Lisbonne, et sur la loi naturelle* (Poems on the Lisbon Disaster, and on Natural Law), Geneva: Cramer; repr. F.J. Crowley (ed.), Berkeley, CA: University of California Press, 1938.

—— (1759) *Candide, ou l'optimisme. Traduit de l'allemand de m. le docteur Ralph* (Candide or Optimism. Translated from the German by Dr Ralph), Geneva: Cramer; trans. R. Pearson, *Candide and Other Stories*, Oxford: Oxford University Press, 1990. (Also appears in *Oeuvres complètes*, vol. XLVIII.)

—— (1764–9) *Dictionnaire philosophique portatif* (Pocket Philosophical Dictionary), Geneva: Cramer; in *Oeuvres complètes de Voltaire*, Oxford: The Voltaire Foundation, 1980, vols XXXV–XXXVI.

—— (1766) *Le Philosophe ignorant* (The Ignorant Philosopher), Geneva: Cramer; in *Oeuvres complètes de Voltaire*, Oxford: The Voltaire Foundation, 1980, vol. LXII, 3–105.

—— (1784) *Traité de métaphysique* (Treatise on Metaphysics), Paris: De l'Imprimerie de Société Littéraire-Typographique; repr. H.T. Patterson (ed.), Manchester: Manchester University Press, 1957. (Also appears in *Oeuvres complètes*, vol. XIV, pages 359–503. The text was composed in 1734.)

References and further reading

Alexander, I. (1944) 'Voltaire and Metaphysics', *Philosophy* 19: 19–48. (This is a well-argued analysis of Voltaire's pantheism and materialism, concentrating particularly on empiricism and the influence of Locke. Written for specialists.)

Barber, W. (1955) *Leibniz in France. Arnauld to Voltaire*, Oxford: Clarendon. (A clearly argued general study of Leibniz's impact on France. Readers are referred particularly to pages 174–243 dealing with the linked problems of freedom and optimism. Particularly useful for studying the *Traité de métaphysique* and *De La Liberté*, and aimed mainly at specialists.)

Besterman, T. (1962) 'Voltaire and the Lisbon Earthquake, or the Death of Optimism', *Voltaire Essays and Another*, Oxford: Oxford University Press, ch. 3. (A well-written essay with a biographical focus for the general reader.)

Henry, P. (1977) 'Voltaire as Moralist', *Journal of the History of Ideas* 38: 141–6. (For specialists. Useful background for the *Traité de métaphysique*.)

James, E. (1978) 'Voltaire on the Nature of the Soul', *French Studies* 33: 20–33. (A clear exposition of the evolution of Voltaire's views on this central issue, particularly helpful for an understanding of the *Traité de métaphysique*. Mainly for specialists.)

—— (1987) 'Voltaire on Free Will', *Studies on Voltaire and the Eighteenth Century* 249: 1–18. (An informative study of the impact of the thought of Samuel

Clarke, Anthony Collins and John Locke on this central issue in Voltairean metaphysics. For the specialist.)

Kendrick, I. (1956) *The Lisbon Earthquake*, London: Methuen. (A general account of the earthquake and its intellectual impact. Readers are referred to pages 119–31 and 134–9 for information relevant to Voltaire. For the general reader.)

Niklaus, R. (1994) 'Voltaire et l'empirisme anglais', *Revue internationale de philosophie* 48: 9–24. (A detailed study of the debt owed by Voltaire to English empiricism. Particularly relevant to Hume and Locke in the context of the *Traité de métaphysique* and the *Éléments de la philosophie de Newton*. For specialists.)

Spink, J. (1960) *French Free Thought from Gassendi to Voltaire*, London: University of London Press. (A well-documented overview of the key stages in the development of sceptical traditions of thought in France. On Voltaire, see particularly pages 312–24. For the general reader.)

Wade, I. (1969) *The Intellectual Development of Voltaire*, Princeton, NJ: Princeton University Press. (A rich intellectual biography. Part IV deals with Voltaire's philosophical thought and development and has special sections on Newton, Locke, Leibniz, Spinoza and Malebranche relevant to Voltaire's position on cosmology, optimism and freedom. For the general reader.)

DAVID WILLIAMS

VOLUNTARISM

Voluntarism is a theory of action. It traces our actions less to our intellects and natural inclinations than to simple will or free choice. Applied to thinking about God's actions, voluntarism led late medieval philosophers to see the world's causal and moral orders as finally rooted in God's sheer free choice, and to take God's commands as the source of moral obligation. Medieval voluntarism helped pave the way for empiricism, Cartesian doubt about the senses, legal positivism and Reformation theology.

Our wants and our natures (including our rationality) help shape our choices and actions. Intellectualists and voluntarists offer rival views of how great a role these factors play. AQUINAS (§§12–13), a major intellectualist, held that our will is a rational appetite, a desire for items we think good for us. Its nature is to choose what we judge good for us; we can choose among actions because different acts can seem good

to us in different respects. We can err about what is good for us, or fail to will it. But we cannot knowingly reject anything that seems to us the best in the circumstances. Further, while our wills do influence our intellects, we cannot determine our intellects to accept beliefs in the face of sufficient evidence against them. So Aquinas sees our passions (which shape what seems good to us), our nature as good-seekers and our intellects as moulding our choices.

DUNS SCOTUS (§14) adds a second rational desire to Aquinas' picture. ANSELM OF CANTERBURY (§6) held that we have a will for what seems good for us and also a will for moral rectitude. Scotus generalizes Anselm's second 'will': for him, we naturally incline to what seems good for us, but also naturally love things for their objective goodness. So we can reject what seems best for us if we desire more what seems objectively best, or reject what seems objectively best if we desire more what seems best for us: our natures leave us a wider range of choice. Yet both natural will-inclinations are towards good. So we still cannot knowingly reject happiness or whatever else seems best in the circumstances both objectively and for us.

WILLIAM OF OCKHAM (§10) tends towards voluntarism. For Ockham, it is false that we can choose freely because we have intellects or rational desires: it is just a basic fact about us that we can do so. So our will is independent of reason and natural inclination. Neither restricts our choices. Ockham thinks we can knowingly reject happiness or whatever else seems in all ways best, and will evil because it is evil rather than because we think it in some way good. If we can, that an act seems best does not fully explain our doing it. For we can always reject what reason or our natures counsel.

For both intellectualists and voluntarists, God is 'absolutely' able to do whatever he is powerful enough to do, and 'ordinately' able to do just whatever he *would* do, given his character and covenants. For both, God is absolutely powerful enough to lie, but ordinately cannot do so. That God should lie is no contradiction. So God's omnipotence can effect it. But God would never actually lie. For intellectualists, this is because, as perfectly rational, God sees that lying is wrong and chooses accordingly. For voluntarists, God would not lie just because he has so chosen.

For Aquinas, all ten Commandments are necessary moral truths, which God sees and proclaims. For Scotus, necessarily, loving God is right and hating him wrong: as God is infinitely good, there can be no reason to prefer anything else to him, and so rational agents must love him above all. All other acts, though naturally good or bad (perfecting or destroying our nature), are right or wrong contingently, because God

663

commands or prohibits them. Further, God sometimes revokes his contingent commands. Yet according to Scotus, this does not make morality arbitrary. God commands or prohibits acts due to their natural goodness or badness, which reason sees. God revokes precepts only rarely, where the values a law serves are better served by exception. For Scotus, God cannot command irrationally. So where God makes moral exceptions, these are rational; reason might anticipate his doing so. Even contingent moral laws are 'natural' in the sense of being accessible to reason.

Ockham held that only acts in accord with reason can be virtuous. But reason tells us that if there is one personal God, we should do as he says, and so reason tells us that both reason and a revelation by such a God can teach us what is right. Still, while both reason and revelation can teach right and wrong, only God's command *makes* acts right or wrong. God in fact commands only acts that accord with right reason. He need not have done so. For Ockham, only a superior's command can impose an obligation, and God has no superior: so God has no obligations. Evil is acting counter to obligation. So according to Ockham, God cannot do evil. God in his absolute power can order fornication or theft. If he did so, these acts would be right. Even if God made Satan hate God, God would do no evil (as he has no obligation not to do this). Nor would Satan, as he would not control his own actions.

For Ockham, God can cause any creaturely effect unaided or block any creaturely cause. So even if a cause reliably yields an effect, the occurrence of one does not entail that of the other: causal connections are contingent. If so, a priori reasoning can tell little about real causal relations. Consequently, Ockhamist voluntarism was a prod to empiricism. Since it could in any case be God rather than a creature who produces an effect, voluntarism led too towards scepticism about created causality (see NICHOLAS OF AUTRECOURT §2). Among the effects God can produce are apparent sensations of an object. So voluntarism insisted that what we seem to sense need not really be there, thus making God a remote ancestor of Descartes' deceiving demon (see DESCARTES, R. §4). The idea that only a will's command imposes obligations helped sow the seeds of legal positivism (see LEGAL POSITIVISM §§1–2). The voluntarist claim that God need not have accepted acts consonant with our nature or in our power as meritorious was a source of the Reformers' insistence that human salvation is wholly a matter of divine grace.

See also: ASHʿARIYYA AND MUʿTAZILA §5; FREEDOM, DIVINE; OCCASIONALISM §§1–2; RELIGION AND MORALITY

References and further reading

Adams, M. (1987) *William Ockham*, Notre Dame, IN: University of Notre Dame Press. (Detailed, careful treatment of Ockham's logic, ontology, natural philosophy and philosophical theology.)

—— (1987) 'William Ockham: Voluntarist or Naturalist?', in J. Wippel (ed.) *Studies in Medieval Philosophy*, Washington, DC: Catholic University Press. (An overview, with some emphasis on ethics.)

Bourke, V. (1964) *Will in Western Thought*, New York: Sheed & Ward. (Historical survey, more broad than deep.)

Courtenay, W.J. (1984) *Covenant and Causality in Medieval Thought*, London: Variorum. (Discusses voluntarism, the absolute/ordained power distinction, causation and theology.)

Freppert, L. (1988) *The Basis of Morality According to William Ockham*, Chicago, IL: Franciscan Herald Press. (Clear and straightforward.)

Kennedy, L. (1986) *Peter of Ailly and the Harvest of Fourteenth-Century Philosophy*, Queenston, Ont.: Mellen. (Argues that a typical voluntarist's view of God's absolute power led him to scepticism.)

Oakley, F. (1964) *The Political Thought of Pierre D'Ailly*, New Haven, CT: Yale University Press. (Clear, detailed treatment of voluntarist political philosophy.)

Oberman, H. (1963) *The Harvest of Medieval Theology*, Cambridge, MA: Harvard University Press. (The absolute/ordained distinction in action in the voluntarist theology of Gabriel Biel.)

Wolter, A. (1990) *The Philosophical Theology of John Duns Scotus*, Ithaca, NY: Cornell University Press. (Collected articles of the twentieth century's preeminent Scotus scholar; several are concerned with will and ethics.)

BRIAN LEFTOW

VOLUNTARISM, JEWISH

Voluntarism with respect to humanity and divinity became a powerful current in medieval Jewish philosophy, partly in response to the Neoplatonic doctrine of eternal and necessary emanation, which seemed to rob God of the freedom to create, and partly in response to predestinarianism. Solomon ibn Gabirol and Hasdai Crescas were among the Jewish philosophers whose metaphysics gave pride of place to the divine will over intellect, like medieval Christian voluntarists. For many other Jewish thinkers, the centrality of actions sets voluntarism firmly into the context of moral responsibility rather than of metaphysics. Predestinarian arguments like those of Abner of Burgos seemed to Jewish thinkers to rob human beings of moral responsibility. Among the typical defenders of Jewish voluntarism against these arguments was Abraham Bibago.

1 **Will versus intellect**
2 **Will as freedom**
3 **Will versus necessity**

1 Will versus intellect

In Western Christianity, voluntarism has long been associated with the precedence of will over intellect in humanity and divinity. An early Jewish voluntarist in this sense, IBN GABIROL, made the will the intermediary between God and the universal matter and form that anchor his ontology. In classical Neoplatonism, intellect, not will, was the first emanation in the divine production of the world. Crescas reacted against the Aristotelianism of Maimonides, much as Duns Scotus reacted against the Aristotelianism of Aquinas, by making will, not intellect, the basis of the affinity between God and humanity (see CRESCAS, H.; MAIMONIDES, M.).

Ibn Gabirol and Crescas, however, had a limited impact on later Jewish philosophy. Ibn Gabirol did profoundly influence the Franciscan Augustinians, who knew him as Avicebrol or Avicebron and relied on him in laying the groundworks of later Christian voluntarism. His chief philosophic work, *Mekor Hayyim* (Fountain of Life), survives intact only in Latin translation, *Fons Vitae.* In Jewish thought, only traces of his approach to foregrounding God's will are found – in Kabbalah, in the work of Joseph IBN TZADDIK (d. 1149), and in the writings of the thirteenth-century philosopher-Kabbalist, Isaac ibn Latif (see KABBALAH). As for Crescas, his approach to this issue, for many later philosophers, was eclipsed by that of Maimonides.

Medieval Christian philosophers emphasized the will/intellect issue more than Jewish philosophers. Christianity is classically a religion of faith: inner states, beliefs and contemplation are foundational. Greek philosophy, especially Platonism, can place a similar emphasis on the inner life of the soul. This helps explain Augustine's affinity for Platonism. For the Greeks, however, intellect was the dominant inner faculty: as rational animals, humans differ from other beasts in their powers of rational discrimination.

Intellect is determinative for rational choice; will is the dynamic power. Socrates even spoke of knowledge as sufficient to determine choices. For St Paul and Augustine, by contrast, one might know the good and still not do it. Will rather than intellect seemed the dominant inner faculty.

In Judaism actions, not inner states, are the central goal. Religious commitment is expressed not by affirming dogmas but by fulfilling God's commandments. Ancient Judaism has no creed, and questions about the dominance of will or reason were not central at the outset. But for actions to have moral value and to merit reward or punishment, they must be freely chosen. Freedom of choice, accordingly, was upheld by most Jewish thinkers, typically alongside a strong commitment to divine omnipotence.

In the early fourteenth century, freedom became a particularly vexed doctrinal issue when Abner of Burgos, who had converted to Christianity late in life (changing his name in the process to Alfonso de Valladolid), attacked the idea of human freedom, arguing that God's omniscience and providence require all human acts to be determined. Seeking to preserve both human freedom and divine providence, Isaac Pollegar (also spelt as Pulgar) responded by proposing that, since the whole universe is one individual, God's will joins with our own in the production of free human actions, much as the soul's will joins with the nerves of the hand to move the finger. Moses Narboni also responded to Abner and defended free choice on Maimonidean lines. Over a century later, the determinism of Hasdai Crescas may still have reflected the influence of Abner.

2 Will as freedom

In Jewish philosophy voluntarism was typically a question of the nature of the will and its freedom. Aristotelians generally saw free choice in terms of rationality. But many thinkers put the emphasis on volition, especially in regard to divine freedom. Maimonides, for instance, demarcated philosophers of the Aristotelian tradition from the adherents of the Torah by the commitment of the latter to the world's creation by God's free act – which we humans can construe only in terms of our idea of will.

Abraham Bibago (d. *c.* 1489), writing two decades before the expulsion of the Jews from Spain, begins *Derekh Emunah* (The Way of the Faith), his book on divine providence and Jewish faith, with a disquisition on divine will and agency. Starting from an Aristotelian distinction, he describes voluntary agents as being conscious of their actions and being able to perform either of two contrary actions. A natural agent is unconscious of its action and can perform only one of two opposing actions essentially. Divine agency is obviously not natural: God is omniscient. Voluntary action, however, typically aims at a goal which the agent lacks, and lack, or deficiency, is impossible in God. Philosophers consequently posit a third kind of agency for God, conscious but performing only one of two opposing actions, and not in pursuit of a goal.

This doctrine harks back to Plotinus' imagery, in which the world proceeds from the One as light issues from the sun (see PLOTINUS §5). To many religious philosophers this doctrine seemed to say that God acts involuntarily. But Aristotle's conception of voluntary agency allowed the necessary agency of emanation to be called voluntary, since voluntary agency for Aristotle required only the absence of external compulsion and the presence of knowledge. With this in mind, Avicenna specified that God's agency in emanation was the sheer result of knowledge, and could therefore be called voluntary in Aristotle's sense. Will here becomes God's joy in the overflow of goodness that is in fact an inevitable consequence of that goodness. Maimonides judged such combining of necessity and will to be incoherent, but the philosophers most deeply committed to the Neoplatonic-Aristotelian synthesis continued to call necessary emanation voluntary.

Against these philosophers, Bibago argued that a God who acts by necessity would be just as deficient as a voluntary agent who has needs. Furthermore, a necessary cause must produce an effect similar to itself, as fire produces heat. Thus necessary agency does not explain how an infinite deity can produce a finite universe. Only voluntary agency, in Bibago's view, could solve this problem.

But if a voluntary agent lacks the end it intends, why would a voluntary God not be deficient? Bibago explains that ends can be either internal or external. Pursuit of an external end implies a deficiency in the pursuer. But God acts for an internal end, his own essence, and thus remains without deficiency.

3 Will versus necessity

The intellectualist necessitarianism that Bibago opposed was denounced by traditional philosophers and theologians in Christianity, Judaism and Islam. It was part of the so-called Latin Averroism condemned in 1277 by the Bishop of Paris (see AVERROISM, JEWISH; AVERROISM). The most 'Averroist' of Jewish philosophers was Isaac Albalag (fl. thirteenth century), who translated into Hebrew al-Ghazali's Maqasid al-falasifah (Intentions of the Philosophers), a summary of Avicenna's philosophy. Albalag was routinely attacked by traditional minded Jewish philosophers

of the fifteenth century. He seems to be the target of Bibago's arguments against those who considered God an agent by necessity. The Averroist fusion of necessity and freedom forms the background for Spinoza's combination of liberty and necessity and helps explain the hostility of traditional Jews towards his philosophy (see SPINOZA §4).

From a Christian perspective, perhaps because of Augustine's Platonic affinities, Neoplatonism has often been viewed as more congenial to religion than the Aristotelianism that came to dominate later medieval philosophy. For Jewish voluntarists, however, the threat to divine and human freedom seemed to come from Neoplatonic necessitarianism. The teleological perspective of Jewish voluntarism and its commitment to human freedom gave it an affinity to Aristotle, although Aristotle assigns no will to God and does not offer a theory about a faculty of free will.

The idea of a voluntary deity resonates with the biblical portrayal of God. For the voluntarists, what God and humans share, the divine image in humanity, is not simply the intellect but the spontaneity of freedom – not just an intellectual link but the possibility of personal dialogue. The spirit of Jewish voluntarism, understood in this vein, persists in the philosophy of dialogue pioneered in modern Judaism by Martin BUBER and Franz ROSENZWEIG.

See also: CRESCAS, H.; FREE WILL; IBN GABIROL, S.; NEOPLATONISM

References and further reading

* Bibago, A. (before 1489) *Derekh Emunah* (The Way of the Faith), ed. C. Fränkel-Goldschmidt, Jerusalem: Bialik Institute, 1978. (Describes voluntary agents as being conscious of their actions and being able to perform either of two contrary actions; holds that voluntary action typically aims at a goal which the agent lacks.)

Bourke, V.J. (1964) *Will in Western Thought: An Historico-Critical Survey*, New York: Sheed & Ward. (Eight different meanings of will, with introductory and concluding chapters.)

Goodman, L.E. (ed.) (1992) *Neoplatonism and Jewish Thought*, Albany, NY: State University of New York Press. (A collection of eighteen essays, including three on Ibn Gabirol and three on Maimonides, that pay attention to the divine will, as does the editor's introduction.)

Guttmann, J. (1964) *Philosophies of Judaism: The History of Jewish Philosophy from Biblical Times to Franz Rosenzweig*, trans. D.W. Silverman, New York: Holt. (An older but still excellent analysis that includes voluntaristic themes.)

Katz, S.T. (ed.) (1975) *Jewish Philosophers*, New York: Bloch. (Articles from the *Encyclopedia Judaica* on philosophers from the ancient, medieval and modern periods, with an introduction and a fourth part on Jewish thought since 1945 by the editor.)

Lazaroff, A. (1981) *The Theology of Abraham Bibago: A Defense of the Divine Will, Knowledge and Providence in Fifteenth-Century Spanish-Jewish Philosophy*, Tuscaloosa, AL: University of Alabama Press, ch. 4. (Discusses voluntaristic themes.)

Sirat, C. (1985) *A History of Jewish Philosophy in the Middle Ages*, Cambridge: Cambridge University Press. (Comprehensive and detailed survey with numerous references to the themes of free will and divine will.)

Wolfson, H. (1965) *Religious Philosophy: A Group of Essays*, New York: Atheneum. (Contains three essays dealing with the nature of the will and its freedom.)

ALLAN LAZAROFF

VON CIEZKOWSKI, AUGUST

see CIESZKOWSKI, AUGUST VON

VON HARTMANN, EDOUARD

see HARTMANN, KARL ROBERT EDUARD VON

VON HELMHOLTZ, HERMANN *see* HELMHOLTZ, HERMANN VON

VON HUMBOLDT, WILHELM

see HUMBOLDT, WILHELM VON

VON JHERING, RUDOLF

see JHERING, RUDOLF VON

VON WRIGHT, GEORG HENRIK (1916–)

G.H. von Wright is one of the most influential analytic philosophers of the twentieth century. Born in Helsinki, Finland, von Wright did his early work on logic, probability and induction under the influence of logical empiricism. In 1948–51 he served as Ludwig Wittgenstein's successor at Cambridge, but returned to his homeland and later became a member of the Academy of Finland. He did pioneering work on the new applications of logic: modal logic, deontic logic, the logic of norms and action, preference logic, tense logic, causality and determinism. In the 1970s his ideas about the explanation and understanding of human action helped to establish new links between the analytic tradition and Continental hermeneutics. Von Wright's later works, which are eloquent books and essays written originally in his two native languages (Swedish and Finnish), deal with issues of humanism and human welfare, history and future, technology and ecology.

Georg Henrik von Wright was born in Helsinki on 16 June 1916. The family, belonging to the Swedish-speaking minority in Finland, had moved from Scotland in around 1650. (Phonetically the name is pronounced as 'rigt' rather than 'rait'.) In 1934 von Wright began to study philosophy at the University of Helsinki under the supervision of Eino Kaila. Kaila, a charismatic teacher and cultural personality, was the Finnish associate to the Vienna Circle (see VIENNA CIRCLE). The young von Wright's studies in logic and philosophy of science in the spirit of logical empiricism led to his doctoral dissertation *The Logical Problem of Induction* in 1941. His main thesis is that Hume's problem is logically unsolvable: the demand for a justification of induction is self-contradictory. Von Wright later showed his expertise in probability theory and its history in a number of articles on subjective probability, randomness, paradoxes of confirmation and inductive logic. The most important of his contributions is *A Treatise on Induction and Probability* (1951), which carefully develops a system of eliminative induction in the tradition of Bacon and Mill by using the concepts of necessary and sufficient conditions.

In the spring of 1939 von Wright went to Cambridge to meet C.D. Broad, and was permitted to follow Ludwig Wittgenstein's lectures. WITTGENSTEIN made a very strong personal impression on the young Finn. The contact and friendship was renewed after the war. Regular discussions with G.E. Moore also made an impact on his philosophical views. In 1948 von Wright was invited to become Wittgenstein's

667

successor as Professor at Trinity College, Cambridge. After Wittgenstein's death in 1951 he decided to return to Helsinki, where already in 1946 he had been appointed the Swedish-language Professor of Philosophy. Together with Elizabeth Anscombe and Rush Rhees, von Wright became the executor and editor of Wittgenstein's posthumous works. The study, organization, systematization and publication of this exceptionally rich *Nachlass* was a lifelong task for him.

Von Wright's early work on philosophical logic discusses classical topics like predication, negation and entailment. The characterization of logical truth by means of the constituents of monadic predicate logic led his most renowned Finnish student Jaakko Hintikka to a general theory of distributive normal forms in 1953. In his Cambridge years von Wright became interested in the logical properties of various kinds of modalities: alethic (possible, impossible, necessary), deontic (permission, prohibition, obligation), epistemic (verified, undecided, falsified). In 1951 he published *An Essay in Modal Logic*, which studies in a syntactical way various deductive systems of modal logic. In the same year he published perhaps his most famous article, 'Deontic Logic', in *Mind*, which made him the founder of modern deontic logic. These works of philosophical logic had a profound influence on the direction of analytic philosophy – including action theory and the philosophy of law. Von Wright distinguishes technical oughts (means-ends relationships) from norms issued by a norm authority. The classical book *Norm and Action* (1963a) discusses philosophical problems concerning the existence of norms and the truth of normative statements; on these issues the author has often changed his mind. Von Wright's main work on meta-ethics and value theory is *The Varieties of Goodness* (1963b), which analyses different concepts of goodness. The two major works in 1963 established his position as a leading philosopher of his time.

In *Explanation and Understanding* (1971) von Wright turned to philosophical problems concerning the human and social sciences. He defends a manipulative view of causality, where the concept of action is primary to the concept of cause. He argues that human action cannot be explained causally by Hempel's covering law model, but has to be understood intentionally (see HEMPEL, C.G.). The basic model of intentionality is practical syllogism, which relates action by a sort of logical connection with wants and beliefs. This work, sometimes characterized as anti-positivist analytical hermeneutics, has been regarded as an important bridge between analytic philosophy and the Continental tradition. Von Wright's studies in truth, knowledge, modality, lawlikeness, causality, determinism, norms and prac-

tical inference were published in 1983–4 as three-volume *Philosophical Papers*. The preparation of a volume in the Library of Living Philosophers was started in the early 1970s, but its publication was delayed until 1989.

In 1961 von Wright inherited Kaila's position as one of the twelve members of the Academy of Finland; this research professorship is the highest honour that Finland has given its most prominent scientists. Von Wright has written eloquent essays in Swedish and Finnish on the history of ideas and the philosophy of culture. In the 1950s he explored the philosophy of history (Tolstoi, Spengler) and myths about knowledge (Genesis, Faust). In his later work on humanism and the ethics of science, he became increasingly critical of the modern scientific-technological civilization, its narrowly instrumental concept of rationality, and its myth of progress. Von Wright's public pleas for peace and human rights, a better society and a more harmonious coexistence between human beings and nature have made him the most esteemed intellectual in the Scandinavian countries.

See also: ACTION; DEONTIC LOGIC; INDUCTION, EPISTEMIC ISSUES IN; MODAL LOGIC; SCANDINAVIA, PHILOSOPHY IN

List of works

Von Wright, G.H. (1941) *The Logical Problem of Induction*, Helsinki: Societas Philosophica Fennica; 2nd revised edn, Oxford: Blackwell, 1957. (Hume's problem and its attempted solutions.)

—— (1951a) *A Treatise on Induction and Probability*, London: Routledge & Kegan Paul. (On eliminative induction.)

—— (1951b) *An Essay in Modal Logic*, Amsterdam: North Holland. (Axiomatic systems of modal logic.)

—— (1955) *Tanke och förkunnelse* (Thought and Prophecy), Helsinki: Söderströms; also publ. in Finnish as *Ajatus ja julistus*, Helsinki: Söderström, 1961. (Includes essays on Tolstoi, Dostoevsky, Spengler and Toynbee.)

—— (1957a) *Logical Studies*, London: Routledge & Kegan Paul. (Papers on logical truth, quantification, predication, negation, deontic logic and entailment.)

—— (1963a) *Norm and Action*, London: Routledge & Kegan Paul; also publ. in German as *Norm und Handlung*, Königstein: Scriptor, 1979. (The truth and existence of norms, and a theory of action.)

—— (1963b) *The Varieties of Goodness*, London: Routledge & Kegan Paul. (A meta-ethical study of different meanings of the concept of goodness.)

—— (1971) *Explanation and Understanding*, London: Routledge & Kegan Paul; also publ. in German as Erklären und Verstehen, Frankfurt: Atheneum, 1974. (Positivism and hermeneutics in history and the social sciences.)

—— (1983a) *Practical Reason: Philosophical Papers, vol. 1*, Oxford: Blackwell. (Papers on practical inference, promises, norms, truth, and logic.)

—— (1983b) *Philosophical Logic: Philosophical Papers, vol. 2*, Oxford: Blackwell. (Logical paradoxes, preference, time and change.)

—— (1984) *Truth, Knowledge, and Modality: Philosophical Papers, vol. 3*, Oxford: Blackwell. (Truth-logic, predication, determinism, laws of nature.)

—— (1993b) *The Tree of Knowledge and Other Essays*, Leiden: Brill; also publ. in German: *Erkenntnis als Lebensform*, Vienna: Böhlau, 1993. (Myths about knowledge and progress, humanism and the good.)

References and further reading

Apel, K.O. (1984) *Understanding and Explanation*, Cambridge, MA: The MIT Press. (Comments on von Wright's relation to Continental hermeneutics.)

* Hintikka, J. (ed.) (1976) *Essays on Wittgenstein in Honour of G.H. von Wright*, Amsterdam: North Holland. (Includes material on von Wright's relation to Wittgenstein.)

Manninen, J. and Tuomela, R. (eds.) (1976) *Essays on Explanation and Understanding*, Dordrecht: Reidel. (Critical essays and replies.)

Niiniluoto, I., Sintonen, M., and von Wright, G.H. (eds) (1992) *Eino Kaila and Logical Empiricism*, Helsinki: Societas Philosophica Fennica. (On von Wright's teacher.)

Schilpp, P.A. and Hahn, L.E. (eds.) (1989) *The Philosophy of Georg Henrik von Wright*, La Salle, IL: Open Court. (Includes an intellectual autobiography, 32 critical essays and replies, and a complete bibliography up to 1988.)

ILKKA NIINILUOTO

VULNERABILITY AND FINITUDE

Power has always been a central category of political thought and theory; its counterparts, powerlessness or vulnerability, and more generally finitude, have seemingly been much less discussed. Yet finitude has been a theme for many writers, particularly on metaphysical and epistemological topics, who emphasize that claims about human knowledge cannot presuppose that we command a God's-eye view of ourselves or the world; while vulnerability has been a theme in ethical and political philosophy, challenging idealized 'models of man' that take exaggerated views of human capacities and autonomy, and which overlook the mundane realities of dependence, poverty and frailty.

1 Finitude
2 Vulnerability

1 Finitude

Writing on finitude emphasizes that we can look at matters only from the vantage point of finite and fallible beings, of men rather than of angels. It criticizes some traditional metaphysical writing for taking divine omniscience and omnipotence, and other divine 'perfections', as models or standards of power, goodness and knowledge, for measuring human achievements by these yardsticks, and for concluding that human finitude is to be seen as (ineliminable) deficiency, lack or privation.

Such metaphysical writers – (PLATO, DESCARTES and other rationalists are often cited as paradigms – see RATIONALISM) assume that, finite as they are, human beings can form a conception of unlimited power and knowledge, and can understand their own limitations from that perspective. In doing so these writers take divine or infinite power, reason, goodness and knowledge as models for human performance – or rather lack of performance. Assumptions that human beings can appeal to powers of understanding and standards of perfection appropriate to an infinite being or to a transcendent vantage point have repeatedly been criticized. Yet many writers who have thought that they had successfully put aside appeals to transcendent, ideal standards have been accused by their successors of covertly reintroducing one or another variant of those very standards. For example, Kant (1781/1787) insists that he starts from the standpoint of *human* reason, but many of his critics have thought that he reinstates a God's-eye view of the world and human life, and in particular that his accounts of freedom and of ethics require him to do so (see KANT, I. §§9–11; KANTIAN ETHICS). NIETZSCHE and HEIDEGGER both criticized Kant for this failing, and both aimed to put aside any appeal to a transcendent standpoint or to the knowledge and goodness of an infinite being; both have in their turn been criticized for tacit reliance on such a standpoint.

2 Vulnerability

In one way, writing in ethics must assume the possibility of human limitations: it would be pointless to propose norms or standards unless the possibility of failure to live up to them was acknowledged. However, much writing on ethics, while allowing for human failure, has invoked idealized conceptions of human rationality, knowledge and autonomy, or alternatively of human intimacy and affections, which are not achieved by many or even by any human beings (see AUTONOMY, ETHICAL). Writing that is unrealistic in these ways can overlook the vulnerability of human lives and may then recommend action that takes too little account of others' vulnerabilities. Critics of various idealized conceptions of the human agent in ethics and political philosophy have emphasized a variety of ways in which people may be vulnerable. Some have stressed ways in which poverty limits action and capacities for action; others have pointed more generally to the fragility of human life, action and achievement; yet others have pointed to the fact that dependence on others is normal and far from being a form of moral failure may be a form of moral achievement.

There are then many ways in which writing on ethics can underestimate the significance of human vulnerability. For example, certain models of rational choice, and with them much utilitarian writing, assume idealized abilities to choose rationally, which are not in fact achievable by human beings: ordinary people may find such reasoning and the prescriptions it points to unconvincing (see UTILITARIANISM; RATIONALITY, PRACTICAL).

Some accounts of justice, in particular those favoured by libertarians, see justice as a matter only of according others like liberties (see LIBERTARIANISM). They deploy idealized views of human autonomy, by which others' needs and vulnerability are irrelevant to justice. Many other accounts of justice take some account of poverty and need (see LIBERALISM). They may, for example, argue for welfare systems that could protect people from these sources of vulnerability, or for certain sorts of equality. Yet theories of justice often say little about vulnerability that arises from subordination or dependence on others, in particular about those that can arise from quite ordinary familial or gender relationships (see FAMILY, ETHICS AND THE).

Some of these misleading idealizations have been challenged in feminist writing, in discussions of friendship, and in writing on the virtues (see FEMINIST ETHICS; FEMINIST POLITICAL PHILOSOPHY; VIRTUE ETHICS; VIRTUES AND VICES). A common criticism of all writing on justice is that it takes an idealized view of the autonomy of individuals or of citizens, forgetting that people are also linked in friendship and family, and that family relationships are often relationships of dependence, and so of power and of vulnerability. On the other hand, some of the proponents of friendship and virtue ethics, who acknowledge the moral importance of relationships and attachments, tend to take a rosy and even a falsely idealized view of the quality of close relationships, and thereby ignore the fact that vulnerabilities can be created and deepened by dependence. Feminist writers have often been more realistic about this range of vulnerabilities.

See also: FRIENDSHIP; GOD, CONCEPTS OF; HUMAN NATURE; IDEALS; LEVINAS, E.; RECOGNITION

References and further reading

Blum, L.A. (1980) *Friendship, Altruism and Morality*, London: Routledge & Kegan Paul. (Argues for the moral importance of friendship and sympathy; criticizes the 'models of man' used in moral philosophy which neglects these themes.)

Drèze, J. and Sen, A. (1990) *Hunger and Public Action*, Oxford: Clarendon Press. (Discusses the realities of poverty and hunger. Rather than assuming that basic capabilities are given, we should take action to secure them.)

Heidegger, M. (1927) *Sein und Zeit*, trans. J. Macquarrie and E. Robinson, *Being and Time*, Oxford: Blackwell, 1962. (Depicts human beings as finite, worldly, historical, oriented to care for other beings.)

—— (1943) 'The Word of Nietzsche: "God is Dead"', in W. Lovitt (trans. and ed.) *The Question of Technology and Other Essays*, New York: Harper & Row, 1977. (Heidegger on Nietzsche's writings on the 'death of God'.)

* Kant, I. (1781/1787) *Kritik der Reinen Vernunft*, trans. N. Kemp Smith, *Critique of Pure Reason*, London: Macmillan, 1973. (The limits of human reason and its incapacity to sustain metaphysical claims which assume a God's-eye view are basic themes.)

Levinas, E. (1982) *Éthique et infini*, Paris: Fayard; trans. R. Cohen, *Ethics and Infinity*, Pittsburgh, PA: Duquesne University Press, 1985. (Introductory discussion of themes such as the ethical primacy of the face-to-face relationship with the other and its relation to the infinite.)

Nietzsche, F. (1882) *Die fröhliche Wissenschaft*, trans. W. Kaufmann, *The Gay Science*, New York: Random House, 1974, esp. no. 125. (Nietzsche's most famous discussion of the 'death of God', the human realization of our lack of an infinite vantage point.)

Nussbaum, M. (1986) *The Fragility of Goodness: Luck and Ethics in Greek Tragedy and Philosophy*, Cambridge: Cambridge University Press. (Explores

Greek ethics and its awareness of the vulnerability of human life to contingency.)

O'Neill, O. (1996) *Towards Justice and Virtue: A Constructive Account of Practical Reasoning*, Cambridge: Cambridge University Press. (Argues for a conception of practical reasoning which does not presuppose a transcendent vantage point and can support linked accounts of justice and virtue which take account of human vulnerabilities.)

Pateman, C. (1988) *The Sexual Contract*, Cambridge: Polity Press. (Considers the justice of the traditional marriage contract and of the dependence it created.)

ONORA O'NEILL

VYGOTSKII, LEV SEMËNOVICH (1896–1934)

Vygotskii was a Soviet psychologist, the most comprehensive in creative reach and the most influential. Trained in literary studies and originally active as a critic, he took a post in a pedagogical institute and came thus to psychological science, with a special interest in child development. That was the period of foundational debates between rival schools of psychology, intensified in the Russian case by the Revolution of 1917 and the subsequent campaign for a Marxist school. Vygotskii became the major theorist at the central Institute of Psychology. While dying of tuberculosis he worked his intensive way through contested claims to know what mind is and how it acts. His profuse reflections on that large contest remained largely unpublished for decades, while disciples echoed his call for a 'cultural-historical' approach to a unified science of the mind, and actually worked on the mental development of children and the neuropsychology of brain damage. The concept of 'activity', which was supposed to resolve philosophical issues, served largely to evade them, while harmonizing with Marxist-Leninist slogans on 'practice'. Among Western cognitive psychologists Vygotskii acquired a tardy reputation as a pioneer who emphasized social interaction in the mental development of children. The publication of his major works in the 1970s and 1980s revealed a much broader theorist. His central theme was the obvious truth at the basis of each artistic and psychological school, the lure of an effort to unify all of them, and the present impossibility of achieving such unification within science, outside philosophical speculation.

1 Life
2 Thought

1 Life

Son of a bank officer in a provincial town of tsarist Russia, Vygotskii was given a secularized Jewish education until he entered Moscow University, where he studied language and literature. He was already publishing critical essays when he graduated in 1917, the year of the communist Revolution. Vygotskii returned to his home town, where he spent the years of civil war and economic collapse teaching in a secondary school and a pedagogical institute, adding child development and mental defect to literary art as crucial problems for claims to know what mind is and how it acts. A Marxist approach, increasingly demanded by the new government, provoked hostility among some psychologists, varied mixtures of Marxisms and psychologies among others, and an inclination in the ideological establishment to favour the reduction of mind to neural reflexes, as Pavlov and Bekhterev claimed to be doing. In 1924, at a conference devoted to the campaign for Marxism, Vygotskii's presentations struck the audience as a major event, the illumination of a way out of an impasse.

Bukharin, the Party's chief of ideology, had been commending 'reflexology', but the central Institute of Psychology had continued to set it aside as physiology, not psychology, which seeks to understand consciousness, not to explain it away. The founder of the Institute, G.I. Chelpanov, who rebuked the Party ideologists for misunderstanding both psychology and Marxism, had been replaced as director by K.N. Kornilov, who enthusiastically endorsed the Party's campaign, while continuing the kinds of research that he had learned from Chelpanov. The impending clash between the ideological establishment and the specialists in psychology was brilliantly finessed by Vygotskii. He praised Bukharin while bringing out the underlying clash between Pavlov and Marx, between the reduction of mind to conditioned reflexes and the analysis of mind as it expresses itself in 'cultural-historical' development.

He was appointed to the Institute of Psychology, where he became the most influential theorist by virtue of his astonishing breadth of knowledge, acute insight and critical appreciation for all the approaches to a contested discipline. That eclecticism, at odds with the drift in the ideological establishment towards an exclusive Marxism, was the probable reason why Vygotskii's major writings of the 1920s went unpublished. They circulated in manuscript, provoking discussion, attracting disciples in part, one supposes, by the sense of daring in his quiet dismissal of projects for a uniquely Marxist science. *Psikhologiia iskusstva (The Psychology of Art)* – awarded a doctorate in

1925, first published in 1965, heavily abridged – emphasized Marx's confession that enduring works of art did not fit within his scheme of evolving base and superstructure, and drew on 'formalist' aesthetics and on Freudian psychology, though both were disapproved of by the ideological establishment. *The Historical Meaning of the Psychological Crisis* – completed in 1927, unpublished until 1982 – used Marxism once again as an expression of the crisis more than a solution for it: each major school of psychology was founded on an obvious truth, and all together were an incoherent jumble. Marxism suggested a way to coherence only at the most abstract level of methodology, by proposing a 'cultural-historical' approach.

Condensed bits of these views were published during Vygotskii's lifetime in special studies and brief surveys, which can be confusing, for Vygotskii was conciliatory towards the ideological establishment. If it believed, for instance, that Pavlov had discovered the neural mechanism of mental activity, Vygotskii would endorse that view in some publications – such as a textbook or a celebratory survey of Soviet psychology – while elsewhere he showed that Pavlov's claim was at odds with neuroscience and with the *Gestalten* of mental activity. Such amiable segregation of viewpoints became extremely difficult after 1930, when vehement crude young men brought Stalin's 'great break' (*velikii perelom*) to higher learning as well as industry and agriculture. They required an aggressively Soviet philosophy and psychology, thoroughly hostile to 'bourgeois' or Western scholarship. Vygotskii still tried to be nice. He did not perform the odious ritual of 'self-criticism', for instance, for praising Piaget as the main source of his own work on child development. He published a translation of a major work by Piaget, prefaced by exaggerated disagreement – a common technique in the Stalin era for keeping foreign ideas before the public in spite of official disapproval.

The 'great break' brought insistence on practicality as well as exclusivity: science must prove its difference from 'bourgeois' pseudo-science by immediate service to 'the construction of socialism'. Vygotskii and his disciples responded in three ways: by emphasizing the pedagogical utility of their studies in child development, the therapeutic promise of their work in mental illness and brain damage, and most broadly the usefulness of their evolutionary vision in the 'cultural revolution', which they interpreted as a drive to modernize the primitive mentality of the masses. *Etiudy po istorii poredeniia: obez'iana, primitiv, rebënok* (*Studies in the History of Behavior: Ape, Primitive, Child*), a little survey that Vygotskii and Luria brought out in 1930, presented their version of

'the biogenetic law'. Ontogeny recapitulates phylogeny; the child's mental development repeats in brief the evolution from ape through primitive to civilized mentality. That was offered as an orienting vision for organizers of collective farms as well as teachers of lower-class children, but the establishment declared it an insufferable insult to the masses.

A field study of 1931 was especially offensive. The peasant mentality in Kazakhstan was found to be mired in 'situational thinking', ill prepared for universal rationality. Though unpublished, the study was angrily attacked in the press. Any effort at comparative analysis of different mentalities was implicitly disapproved, even one that might try, as Vygotskii and his colleagues did not, to take into account the shaping influence of class or status in the interaction of researcher and subjects. Group psychology was a field of intuitive expertise for master politicians and managers; they were not to be instructed by academics, not even psychologists preaching visions of a 'cultural-historical' Marxist discipline founded on 'the biogenetic law' of mental development.

Tuberculosis killed Vygotskii in 1934, while he and his school were being denounced as pseudo-Marxist imitators of 'bourgeois' or Western scholarship, along with all other schools of would-be Soviet psychology. Even in that time of the triumphant yahoo, Vygotskii had exceptional influence. V.N. Kolbanovskii, the militant communist who was installed as director of the Institute of Psychology with a mandate to 'Bolshevize' it, published a brief précis of Vygotskii's *Istoricheskii smysl psikhologicheskogo krizisa* (The Historical Meaning of the Psychological Crisis), expressing the hope that this landmark book would soon appear. Disappointed in that hope, Kolbanovskii managed to bring out a little collection of Vygotskii's essays called *Myshlenie i rech'* (Thinking and Speech) (1934), called *Thought and Language* in the 1962 English translation.

In Russia and abroad that text shaped understanding of Vygotskii's psychology for so long that the limitations and misperceptions built into it may be incorrigible. The dying author, with some help from Kolbanovskii, fashioned the book to appease the establishment in a time of rampant Stalinism – for instance, by omitting his arguments against any claim of a uniquely Marxist science, and by including his exaggerated criticism of Piaget. Moreover, the surviving disciples shaped the dead man's legacy to fit their own agendas, avoiding a 'cultural-historical' approach as anything but a slogan for studies of child development. The recovery of Vygotskii's actual thought became a historical project, of little interest to most specialists in psychology, who prefer to work in their separate trends and ignore the rivals. Foundational debates over the opposed assumptions of diverse trends, which preoccupied the emergent discipline in the late nineteenth and early twentieth centuries, have come to be considered pointless excursions into useless philosophy. In academic practice that is what the separation of psychology from philosophy means: studied disregard for the implicit incoherence of rival trends in psychology. The transformation of Vygotskii's legacy is an especially ironic case in point.

2 Thought

Specialists in the cognitive development of children often distinguish Vygotskii's approach from Piaget's as a contrast between exogeny and endogeny, acquisition from without versus unfolding from within (see PIAGET, J.; COGNITIVE DEVELOPMENT). That is, as most acknowledge, an oversimplified scheme, for interaction between the child and its external world, mediated by adults and other children, is essential to Piaget's approach as it is to Vygotskii's, or indeed to any analysis of action, thought and speech in their intertwined emergence, whether in phylogeny or ontogeny or both together. Piaget's landmark studies in that large field were fundamental to Vygotskii, as he repeatedly acknowledged. The correction that he offered was originally limited to the special problem of 'egocentric' speech. Very young children talk to themselves a lot, gradually ceasing by school age. Piaget interpreted this by analogy with autism; Vygotskii demurred. He argued that talking to oneself is the child's way of trying out patterns of speech – and thought and appropriate action – as learned from other people. When Piaget learned of that correction, many years later, he gratefully accepted it as 'a new hypothesis: that egocentric speech is the point of departure for the development of inner speech, which is found at a later stage of development, and that this interiorized language can serve both autistic ends and logical thinking' (1962: 7).

The important distinctiveness of Vygotskii's approach is implicit in Piaget's final phrase, his simple contrast between autism and 'logical thinking', his neglect of expressive thinking in the mind's connections with the world. Piaget came to the problem of childhood mental development from an original interest in biological science and in the standardization of intelligence tests, and wound up with a theory of evolutionary epistemology, oriented most of all towards the scientific or logical and analytical functions of thought and language. Vygotskii came to the would-be science of mind through literary studies, trying to understand aesthetic experience as a mode of cognition at odds with the scientific mode.

His first major work was a lengthy analysis of *Hamlet* that focused on the meaning of the play, as established by a cultural tradition endlessly absorbed and reshaped in the interacting minds of audiences, actors and writers, including critics as well as original authors. Set within that context Vygotskii's interpretation of *Hamlet* came down to a sense of tension between a traditional formula and a creative alteration of it. What the audience expects to see enacted on the stage – criminal outrage corrected by vengeful justice – is contradicted by what the author and actors actually present – random violence, insanity, vengeance dissolving into pointless deaths. Melodrama, a traditional formula for anxiety aroused and set to rest, is thus evoked and altered to create tragedy, an unsettling sense of life and death as a process that cannot be justified. Thus Vygotskii sets a problem for the would-be science of mind: how to explain the satisfaction that author-actors-audience jointly derive from artistic expression of a tragic meaning of life.

Vygotskii recalls the ancient explanation – catharsis – and rehearses some modern claims such as Freud's of scientific grounding for it. He criticizes Freud for a primitive understanding of 'the pleasure principle' at odds with 'the reality principle', and for other sloppinesses in mixing aesthetic understanding with claims of scientific explanation. But Vygotskii's deepest disagreement is with all contemporary schools of psychological science which rest on a dream of reducing subjective experience and cultural expression to nerve energies accumulating and discharging. Such explanatory reduction of mind to body would be irrelevant to knowledge of the mind in the sense of understanding, in this case, the meaning of *Hamlet*.

Vygotskii quotes Spinoza, confronting the fundamental anomaly as follows: 'Solely from the laws of nature considered as extended substance' one cannot 'deduce the causes of buildings, pictures, and things of that kind which are produced only by human art; nor would the human body, unless it were determined and led by the mind, be capable of building a single temple'. Since Vygotskii cannot find in modern science any way out of that dualism, *The Psychology of Art* begins and ends with Spinoza's metaphysical response: 'The objectors [to monism] cannot fix the limits of the body's power, or say what can be concluded from a consideration of its sole nature'. Intent on a monistic fusion of aesthetic understanding and psychological explanation, Vygotskii was sufficiently rigorous to acknowledge that the two types of inquiry are incoherent.

Specialists in cognitive psychology have paid scant attention to Vygotskii's emphasis on the problems that expressive thought presents for their discipline, though *Thought and Language*, the little book that most shaped their understanding of Vygotskii, comes back to such problems repeatedly. A crucial case in point is his distinction between *znachenie* and *smysl*, usually translated as 'meaning' and 'sense'. It might be less bewildering to say logical meaning versus expressive meaning, the former acknowledging the law of identity, the latter deliberately violating it. Vygotskii offers a vivid example from a conversation that Dostoevskii overheard among six drunken men, who took delight in using a one-syllable obscene word for six different meanings, expressed by changing tone and gesture. (The fact that the word is still taboo in a respectable encyclopedia is further evidence of the difference between logical and expressive meaning.)

Vygotskii liked to recall Franz Brentano's *Psychology from the Empirical Viewpoint* (1874), which boldly confronted the unscientific clutter of psycholog*ies*, and started two more schools (Gestalt and phenomenology) with its arguments for unification (see BRENTANO, F.C.; GESTALT PSYCHOLOGY; PHENOMENOLOGICAL MOVEMENT). The gap that Brentano came to acknowledge between 'genetic' and 'descriptive' psychology, and the analogous distinction that several thinkers made between 'explanation' and 'understanding' as different modes of knowing ourselves, were major influences in Vygotskii's brooding over psychology. So was William James' review of 1892, ending with confidence in the future, though now 'there is no science, ... only the hope of a science. Something definite happens when to a certain brainstate a certain "sciousness" corresponds' (see JAMES, W.). By the 1920s, among psychologists who were unwilling to put on blinkers, to ignore the fragmentation of the would-be science and its separation from expressive understanding of the mind, James' witty optimism had given way to gloomy talk of 'crisis'. Karl Bühler, most notably, was writing *Die Krise der Psychologie* about the same time that Vygotskii wrote *The Historical Meaning [smysl] of the Psychological Crisis*, which shares with other such ruminations the ironic fate of marking the end of an era by dreaming of a new one. Vygotskii's dream was unique in its special attention to Marxism as well as the 'meaning [*smysl*] of the psychological crisis' – in the sense of a crisis in 'the meaning of life' as well as the would-be science of mind.

He disapproved of claims of a supposedly distinctive Marxist psychology, arguing that they confused three different realms of discourse: the fragmented discipline called psychology, the methodology that might transform it into a genuine science, and the most general methodology of knowledge as a whole. Marxism, in his view, was relevant only in

discussion of that broadest realm. It could be transformed into concrete methodological principles for psychology only through protracted labour within the discipline, striving to overcome the war of schools. 'Our science will become Marxist to the degree that it will become true, scientific; and we will work precisely on that, its transformation into a true science, not on its agreement with Marx's theory'.

His reading of 'Marx's theory' emphasized its 'cultural-historical' vision of human development, including its insistence on a reciprocal relationship between understanding ourselves and changing ourselves, progressing thus towards authentic humanity in activity-cum-consciousness. 'Activity' in this very long-term historical usage is so much broader than in psychological studies of a child's 'activity' that the word becomes a different concept. Inattention to that difference, which marked Soviet psychologists' talk of 'activity' after Vygotskii, deprived such talk of any deeper function than soothing the ideological establishment, which glorified 'practice' in even looser, less meaningful ways.

When Vygotskii argued that the science of mind is inchoate, he recalled Trotsky's observation that 'man is himself inchoate' (*stikhiia*, elemental chaos, from Greek *stoicheia*). The socialist revolution would create a new authentic human being along with a new authentic science of psychology. When Vygotskii indulged in such talk, he was far closer than Trotsky or any other political leader of 'the Soviet experiment' to explicit utopianism, with overtones of modernist absurdity:

In the future society psychology will be in actuality the science of a new person [*chelovek*]. Without that perspective Marxism and the history of science would not be complete. But that science of the new person will still be psychology; we now hold in our hands the thread leading to it. Never mind that that psychology will resemble present-day psychology as little as – in Spinoza's words – the constellation Canis resembles the dog, a barking animal.

(1982–4: vol. 1: 436)

That image – the would-be science of mind as a dog barking at the orderly splendour of the night sky – concluded Vygotskii's *Historical Meaning of the Psychological Crisis*, projecting Spinozist faith in monism upon the incoherence of contemporary culture.

See also: PIAGET, J.

List of works

Vygotskii, L.S. (1982–4) *Sobranie sochinenii* (Collected Works), Moscow: Pedagogika, 6 vols. (The most comprehensive collection of his works. Vol. 1 contains *The Historical Meaning of the Psychological Crisis*.)

—— (1987–3) *The Collected Works*, New York: Plenum, 3 vols, trans. and ed. R.W. Rieber, A.S. Carton, J.S. Bruner and N. Minnick. (Translation of vols 2 and 5 of *Sobranie sochinenii*, with extensive notes and commentary.)

—— (1925) *Psikhologiia iskusstva; The Psychology of Art*, Cambridge, MA: MIT Press, introduction and commentary by A.N. Leontiev and V.V. Ivanov, 1971. (This is a translation of the Russian edition of 1968.)

Vygotskii, L.S. and Luria, A.R. (1930) *Etiudy po istorii poredeniia: obez'iana, primitiv, rebenok,* trans., ed., and introduced by V.I. Golod and J.E. Knox, *Studies in the History of Behavior: Ape, Primitive and Child,* Hillsdale, NJ: Lawrence Erlbaum, 1993. (Reproduces the 1930 survey with a substantial introduction.)

Vygotskii, L.S. (1934) *Myshlenie i rech'* (Thinking and Speech); trans. *Thought and Language*, Cambridge, MA: MIT Press, 1962; revised and ed. by A. Kozulin, 1986. (An expanded translation, with an illuminating introduction.)

References and further reading

Iaroshevskii, M. (1989) *Lev Vygotskii*, Moscow: Progress. (Vygostkii's achievement, by a Soviet historian of psychology.)

Joravsky, D. (1989) *Russian Psychology: A Critical History*, Oxford: Blackwell. (Vygotskii and his school within a large historical context.)

Kozulin, A. (1990) *Vygotskii's Psychology: A Biography of Ideas*, Cambridge, MA: Harvard University Press. (Vygotskii's development, by a thoughtful, well-informed psychologist.)

* Piaget, J. (1962) 'Comments', in Vygotskii, *Thought and Language*, Cambridge, MA: MIT Press, 1962. (Referred to in §2.)

Valsiner, J. (1988) *Developmental Psychology in the Soviet Union*, Bloomington, IN: Indiana University Press. (The history of the Vygotskian school.)

van der Veer, R. and Valsiner, J. (1991) *Understanding Vygotskii: A Quest for Synthesis*, Oxford: Blackwell. (The richest biography, using archives and published matter; with the most extensive bibliography of Vygotskii's writings and unpublished papers.)

Wertsch, J.V. (1985) *Vygotskii and the Social Formation of Mind*, Cambridge, MA: Harvard University Press. (The Vygotskian legacy in developmental psychology as perceived by an American admirer.)

DAVID JORAVSKY

VYSHESLAVTSEV, BORIS PETROVICH (1877–1954)

Boris Petrovich Vysheslavtsev, Russian idealist philosopher and religious thinker, was exiled from his homeland in 1922 because of his anti-Marxism (which he later elaborated in a full-fledged philosophical critique). In western Europe he became a leading figure in the Russian émigré philosophical community, lecturing and writing on questions of metaphysics, ethics, philosophical psychology and social philosophy. Vysheslavtsev was particularly noted for his study (begun in an early work on the ethics of Fichte) of the irrational as the sphere of human contact with the Absolute. Subsequently he developed this theme through the application of concepts of depth psychology to ethics and to the interpretation of Christian doctrine.

The son of a Moscow lawyer, Vysheslavtsev matriculated in 1895 in the Law Faculty of the University of Moscow, where his mentor was the eminent legal philosopher Pavel Novgorodtsev. After graduating in 1889 he worked for some years as an attorney before beginning postgraduate studies at the university. In 1908 he was sent abroad for two years to prepare himself for a professorship; he worked principally at Marburg, under the Neo-Kantians Hermann Cohen and Paul Natorp. Vysheslavtsev was awarded the doctorate by the University of Moscow and appointed to a position as docent there in 1914; three years later he was named professor in the Law Faculty. After his expulsion from Russia he went first to Berlin and in 1924 settled in Paris, where he became a professor at the Orthodox Theological Institute. During the Second World War he moved to Switzerland. He died in Geneva in October 1954.

Vysheslavtsev's first major philosophical work was his doctoral dissertation, *Ètika Fikhte* (Fichte's Ethics) (1914). Although he was initially an orthodox proponent of Fichte's transcendental idealism, in this book Vysheslavtsev presented an original interpretation of Fichte by concentrating on the role of the irrational and the concept of 'the Absolute' in the German thinker's outlook. Arguing that philosophy is confronted with a basic antinomy between what he calls 'system' (rationality) and 'infinity' (irrationality), Vysheslavtsev affirmed that beyond every rational concept there is 'the mysterious limitless' – the infinity or Absolute that cannot be dealt with conceptually but is accessible only to intuition. Vysheslavtsev attempted to describe this irrational infinity by the use of concepts in the modern philosophy of mathematics, such as Cantor's distinction between potential and actual infinities (see CANTOR §1–2). But he concluded that no form of discursive, conceptual thinking is adequate to the task; although philosophy can show us the necessity of acknowledging the Absolute, philosophy cannot analyse it as Hegel sought to do in his metaphysics of Absolute Spirit.

In his efforts to explore this elusive realm, Vysheslavtsev in later works turned towards the study of religion, believing that the quest for the Absolute is the core of the religious attitude. In *Serdtse v khristianskoi i indiiskoi mistike* (The Heart in Christian and Indian Mysticism) (1929), he examined the biblical notion of 'the heart' as a fundamental non-rational human capacity; he found that 'the heart', in addition to being a source of mystical knowledge distinct from the knowledge gained by the intellect, is the fundamental ontological principle at the root of the human self as a loving and free being. He noted that both Christian and Hindu mystics affirm such an ontological principle, although they differ in their understanding of its relation to human individuality.

In his most important philosophical work, *Ètika preobrazhennogo Èrosa* (The Ethics of Transfigured Eros) (1931), Vysheslavtsev employed concepts of depth psychology to construct an ethical theory grounded in the irrational nature of human beings and their relation to the Absolute. Ethical 'laws' or imperatives as traditionally understood are ineffectual, Vysheslavtsev believed, because they are merely addressed to consciousness and rationality and do not engage the unconscious depths of instinctual human life; indeed, drawing on the work of the French psychologists Émile Coué and Charles Baudouin, he argued that such imperatives generate subconscious resistance in accordance with what he calls 'the law of irrational opposition'. Christian ethics, in Vysheslavtsev's view, pursues the correct approach to morality by presenting not legalistic commands but beautiful images of moral virtue in the persons of Christ and the saints; these images engender deep-seated responses of admiration and love, thereby transfiguring the irrational instincts and impulses ('Eros') that resist conscious control. In the spirit of Freud and Jung (he knew their works well), Vysheslavtsev called this moral transformation of basic instincts 'sublimation', and he saw in it the key to the understanding of the Christian moral life.

Sublimation, for Vysheslavtsev, is not a purely deterministic process subject to psychologistic explanation. It occurs only if the individual will has freely chosen the path of elevating and refining Eros and has enlisted the imagination in creating the needed images of moral virtue. Sublimation takes place, furthermore, only with the aid of divine grace; the individual spirit must be inspired from on high, by its vision of the Absolute as the fullness and perfection of being. This orientation towards the Absolute makes sublimation possible, but the divine grace that flows from it must still be freely accepted in order to be morally significant in the life of the individual. Thus in Vysheslavtsev's ethics of sublimation, both free will and grace are necessary but not sufficient conditions for the moral life. In their interaction free will is itself sublimated, being raised from its primitive state of arbitrariness to the condition of moral freedom.

The two books published by Vysheslavtsev in the last years of his life reflect the heightened interest in social issues that marked his thinking from the late 1930s, when he was also active in the ecumenical movement. *Krizis industrial'noi kul'tury* (The Crisis of Industrial Culture) (1953) is a work of social philosophy in which he rejects Marxism (and socialism generally) as a socioeconomic system and elaborates an alternative he calls 'neo-liberalism', which stresses the humanization of industrial culture through the widespread application of economic democracy. In *Filosofskaia nishcheta marksizma* (The Philosophical Poverty of Marxism) (written in the mid-1940s but not published until 1952), he presented a searching and philosophically sophisticated critique of the self-styled 'dialectical and historical materialism' then prevailing in the Soviet Union.

List of works

Vysheslavtsev, B.P. (1914) *Ètika Fikhte: osnovy prava i nravstvennosti v sisteme transtsendental'noi filosofii* (Fichte's Ethics: The Foundations of Law and Morality in the System of Transcendental Philosophy), Moscow: A. Snigirov.

—— (1929) *Serdtse v khristianskoi i indiiskoi mistike* (The Heart in Christian and Indian Mysticism), Paris: YMCA-Press.

—— (1931) *Ètika preobrazhennogo Èrosa: problemy zakona i blagodati* (The Ethics of Transfigured Eros: Problems of Law and Grace), Paris: YMCA-Press; repr. together with *Vechnoe v russkoi filosofii* (see below) in a single volume, with an introduction and notes by V.V. Sapov, Moscow: Respublika, 1994.

—— (1952) *Filosofskaia nishcheta marksizma* (The Philosophical Poverty of Marxism), Frankfurt am Main: Posev. (This first edition was published under the pseudonym 'B. Petrov'; a second edition was published under Vysheslavtsev's own name in 1957.)

—— (1953) *Krizis industrial'noi kul'tury: marksizm,*

neosotsializm, neoliberalizm (The Crisis of Industrial Culture: Marxism, Neo-Socialism, Neo-Liberalism), New York, NY: Chekhov Press.

—— (1955) *Vechnoe v russkoi filosofii* (The Permanent in Russian Philosophy), New York: Chekhov Press. (A posthumous collection of essays; see 1931 title above.)

References and further reading

Kline, G.L. (1955) 'A Philosophical Critique of Soviet Marxism', in *The Review of Metaphysics* 9 (1): 90–105. (Formally a review of Vysheslavtsev's 1952 book on Marxism, this article contains much information about Vysheslavtsev's thought.)

Zenkovsky, V.V. (1948–50) *Istoriia russkoi filosofii*, Paris: YMCA-Press, 2 vols; 2nd edn 1989; trans. G.L. Kline, *A History of Russian Philosophy*, 2 vols, London: Routledge & Kegan Paul and New York: Columbia University Press, 1953, vol. 2, 814–19. (Summary of Vysheslavtsev's thought by the authoritative historian of Russian philosophy.)

—— (1955) 'B.P. Vysheslavtsev, kak filosof' (B.P. Vysheslavtsev as a Philosopher), in *Novyi zhurnal* 15: 249–61. (A more detailed treatment of Vysheslavtsev's work.)

JAMES P. SCANLAN

W

WAHL, JEAN *see* HEGELIANISM

WALLACE, ALFRED RUSSEL (1823–1913)

Co-discoverer with Charles Darwin of the theory of natural selection, Wallace travelled to the Amazon in 1848. Four years of collecting specimens there for sale in Europe revealed patterns of geographical distribution among animals. Unfortunately, much of his South American collection was lost in a fire at sea during the voyage home, which forced him to begin his collecting anew. This led to eight more years of travel (1854–62), this time in the Malay Archipelago, where he made his own momentous discovery of the theory of natural selection in 1858. An exceptionally clear thinker, he made many valuable contributions to evolutionary thought.

Wallace was a self-taught naturalist, as was his friend H.W. Bates, who accompanied him to South America. They read many of the books that DARWIN read, thus sharing to some degree the same intellectual climate despite their plebeian background. Indeed, both Wallace and Darwin read T.R. Malthus on population, and both cited him as a major factor in their independent discoveries of the agency of natural selection. Wallace also read Darwin and C. Lyell, among others, Lyell being of special interest because Wallace cast him in the role of chief opponent as he developed his own thoughts during his travels in the Malay Archipelago, as recorded in his (unpublished) 'Notebook' (see GEOLOGY, PHILOSOPHY OF §1).

It was broadly believed in the 1850s that species were permanent, while varieties were not; rather, they were thought to be produced by ordinary generation and to vary only within strict limits. Species were somehow 'created' in one or more centres of 'special creation', a term widely used, even by Wallace and Darwin, meaning to a zoologist, as Robert Owen remarked, 'a process he knows not what'. Wallace maintained that 'every species has come into existence coincident both in time and space with a pre-existing closely allied species' (1855). In his 'Note on the Theory of Permanent and Geographical Varieties'

(1858a), he asked, 'why should a special act of creation be required to call into existence an organism differing only in degree from another which has been produced by existing laws?'. And, finally, there was the famous manuscript sent to Darwin in the spring of 1858. These three papers formed the foundation of Wallace's theory of evolution by means of natural selection, his explanation of 'creation', with natural selection as the agent of change. H. SPENCER later suggested 'survival of the fittest' as an alternative term for 'natural selection', an idea accepted by both Wallace and Darwin.

Wallace's manuscript reached Darwin on 18 June 1858. In an effort to protect Darwin's priority, Lyell and J.D. Hooker worked out the immediate reading of Wallace's paper before the Linnaean Society of London on 1 July, preceded by two contributions from Darwin. These three taken together are known as the 'joint papers'. Neither author was present. Darwin always maintained that their two theories were exactly alike, when in fact they differed markedly in detail. For example, Darwin relied heavily on data from domestic animals, while Wallace based his theory largely on data from wild animals. Only the concept was the same. Furthermore, over the years various errors regarding this event have crept into the record. Wallace and Darwin continued their fruitful correspondence, initiated by Wallace in October 1856, until just a year before Darwin's death in 1882, as often as not disagreeing with one another in lively argument.

Attracted to the subject of geographical distribution during his travels in South America, Wallace became its leading authority, his work culminating in his *Geographical Distribution of Animals* in 1876: 'The present work is an attempt to collect and summarize the existing information on the Distribution of Land Animals; and to explain the more remarkable and interesting of the facts, by means of established laws of physical and organic change'. This was supplemented four years later by *Island Life*. Basic to this development was the recognition of zoological regions, Wallace supporting the scheme proposed by P.L. Sclater in 1858. The sharp division between the Asian and Australian faunas found on either side of the strait separating the Indonesian islands of Bali and Lombok was named 'Wallace's Line' in his honour by T.H. Huxley.

When it came to human beings, Wallace partially abandoned natural selection. In 1864, in the first of several papers, he tried to show how humans could have been affected by natural selection, first in regard to physical form and then to the brain (also subject to natural selection) which took over control once sufficiently advanced, while the body remained essentially unchanged. Humans could easily make a warmer coat if necessary, once the mind had been developed, while an animal would have to go through the slow process of growing one, thus changing physically under pressure of natural selection. In *Darwinism* (1889), Wallace recognized a number of human faculties – mathematical, musical, and so on, as well as knowledge of such fields as gravitation, chemical force, electricity – which he felt could not have been the results of natural selection but to belong rather to some spiritual world. This explains in part his interest in spiritualism, then a very popular but non-scientific pastime. In fact, a century later questions he raised in that connection have yet to be fully resolved. He disagreed with Darwin on the importance of sexual selection as the principal agent in human evolution, holding that sexual selection was merely a form of natural selection.

See also: EVOLUTION, THEORY OF; HUXLEY, T.H.; SPECIES; TAXONOMY

List of works

Wallace, A.R. (1855) 'On the Law Which has Regulated the Introduction of New Species', *Annals and Magazine of Natural History* 16: 184–96. (Darwin asked, 'but why does his law hold good?'.)
—— (1858a) 'Note on the Theory of Permanent and Geographical Varieties', *Zoologist* 16: 5,887–8. (An important step in the development of his theory.)
—— (1858b) 'On the Tendency of Varieties to Depart Indefinitely from the Original Type', *Journal of the Linnean Society of London (Zoology)* 3: 53–62. (Wallace's part of the 'joint papers'.)
—— (1858c) 'Charles Darwin and Alfred Russel Wallace, On the Tendency of Species to Form Varieties; and on the Perpetuation of Varieties and Species by Natural Means of Selection', *Journal of the Linnean Society of London (Zoology)* 3: 45–62. (This is the collective title of the 'joint papers'.)
—— (1864) 'The Origin of Human Races and the Antiquity of Man Deduced from the Theory of "Natural Selection"', *Journal of the Anthropological Society of London* 2: clviii–clxx. (A caveat on natural selection.)
—— (1876) *The Geographical Distribution of Animals: With a Study of the Relations of Living and Extinct Faunas as Elucidating the Past Changes of the Earth's Surface*, London: Macmillan, 2 vols. (A typical Wallace book, filled with facts and insights.)
—— (1880) *Island Life*, London: Macmillan. (A further elaboration of Wallace's contribution to geographical distribution.)
—— (1889) *Darwinism: An Exposition of the Theory of Natural Selection, with Some of Its Applications*, London: Macmillan. (A comprehensive and well-organized survey.)

References and further reading

* Beddall, B.G. (ed.) (1969) *Wallace and Bates in the Tropics: An Introduction to the Theory of Natural Selection*, London: Macmillan. (Aimed at the nonprofessional.)
* —— (1988) 'Darwin and Divergence: The Wallace Connection', *Journal of the History of Biology* 21: 1–68. (Continues an examination, begun in 1968, of circumstances surrounding the discovery of the agency of natural selection.)
* George, W. (1964) *Biologist Philosopher: A Study of the Life and Writings of Alfred Russel Wallace*, London: Abaelard-Schuman. (Contains a lengthy list of references.)
* Marchant, J. (1916) *Alfred Russel Wallace: Letters and Reminiscences*, New York and London: Harper. (The Wallace–Darwin correspondence, as well as Wallace's correspondence with others, and an extensive bibliography of his works.)
* McKinney, H. (1980) *Wallace and Natural Selection*, New Haven, CT: Yale University Press. (Interesting documents included, as well as a lengthy bibliography.)

BARBARA G. BEDDALL

WANG CHONG (AD 27–c.90)

The Han philosopher Wang Chong wrote a text called Lunheng *(Disquisitions or Discourses Weighed in the Balance), one of the most exceptional and original documents in Chinese thought, compiled as it was during a crucial transitional period. Wang's main approach can be defined as a rational scepticism, questioning accepted history, the contents of canonical texts and philosophical claims about reality. His writings on fate develop ideas such as necessity, cause and uncertainty.*

Wang Chong was born in Shangyu in the district of Kuaiji. His work, the *Lunheng* (Disquisitions or

Discourses Weighed in the Balance), composed of eighty-five chapters and more than two hundred thousand characters. Three themes pervade the text: a rational discussion on the nature of the classics (*jing*) (see CHINESE CLASSICS), his rational approach to nature and his original conception of fate (*ming*).

Wang Chong's intellectual context was the complex debate between the so-called New Text and Old Text schools, a discussion concerning the authenticity and interpretation of certain early texts. An example of his approach may be seen in Chapter 45 (On the Rain Sacrifice) of the *Lunheng*. Here, Wang asks on what do the texts base their affirmation that the rain sacrifice is necessary. In another example, in Chapter 23 (On Thunder), he asks if the destructive properties of thunderstorms actually reflect the 'anger of heaven'. He responds to the question by concluding that thunder is fire.

In questioning the ideal type of sage, the authority of the canonical texts and the practice of divination, Wang Chong adheres to the Old Text tradition, which emphasizes the creative nature of interpretation rather than a narrow scholasticism. In Chapter 14 (The Nature of Things), he states that Heaven did not create man on purpose. He makes it clear that there is no link between *ming* and virtue. One example he gives cites the careers of the favourite disciples of Confucius, Ran Boniu and Yan Hui, who were virtuous and scholarly but nevertheless died young. He believed in the injustice of Heaven, and gives many examples of the incapacity of Heaven to punish the guilty.

Wang's concept of fate is complex because it is linked with divination, cosmology and politics. He proposed three kinds of fate: natural destiny (*zhengming*), concomitant destiny (*suiming*) and adverse destiny (*zaoming*). The first refers to luck that results from original physical conditions; the second results from a combination of unpredictable coincidences; and the third signifies events that are contrary to expectations and opens up the possibility of contingency and the random factor. These approaches can be found in Chapter 3 of the *Lunheng*. This seems to be the most crucial and interesting chapter, especially as it concerns the ideas of necessity, cause and uncertainty.

The *Lunheng* is a text which belongs to the critical sources of Chinese culture, and it demonstrates that such sources are able to bring up original ideas and a new point of view concerning the Chinese world. Because of this text, we are aware that the Chinese world has many contradictory voices. There is not a static consensus in this debate, but a lively interplay of views among Chinese thinkers.

See also: CHINESE CLASSICS; TIAN

List of works

Wang Chong (AD 27–*c.*90) *Lunheng* (Disquisitions or Discourses Weighed in the Balance), ed. Huang Hui, 1938; repr. Taiwan: Shangwu yinshuguan, 1983; trans. A. Forke, *Lun-heng: Philosophical Essays of Wang Ch'ung*, Berlin, 1907; repr. New York: Paragon, 1962, 2 vols. (The standard translation of most but not all of the text.)

References and further reading

Loewe, M. (1974) *Crisis and Conflict in Han 104 BC–9 AD*, London: George Allen & Unwin. (Concerns the social and historical conflict in China prior to Wang Chong's time.)
—— (1982) *Chinese Ideas of Life and Death*, London: George Allen & Unwin. (An account of the mainstream of Chinese thought and its internal contradictions during the Han period.)
Pokora, T. (1957) 'How Many Works Were Written by Wang Ch'ung?', *Archiv Orientalni* 25. (An examination of the writings of Wang Chong.)
—— (1962) 'The Necessity of More Thorough Study of the Philosopher Wang Chong and His Predecessors', *Archiv Orientalni* 30. (An invitation to read classic Chinese texts and Wang Chong in particular, so as to better understand Chinese antiquity.)

AGNES CHALIER

WANG CHUANSHAN/WANG FU-CHIH *see* WANG FUZHI

WANG CH'UNG *see* WANG CHONG

WANG FUZHI (1619–92)

A seventeenth-century neo-Confucian and Ming loyalist, Wang Fuzhi is best known for his nationalism and his theories of historical and metaphysical change. His classical commentaries and other writings, not published until the nineteenth and twentieth centuries, present an exceptionally comprehensive and vigorously argued synthesis and critique of China's intellectual tradition. His ideas on topics such as politics, cosmology and knowledge have fascinated readers of widely differing philosophic persuasions.

Having but recently passed his first civil service examination when the Manchus invaded the Ming capital of Beijing in 1644, Wang Fuzhi (Wang Chuanshan) defied the new Qing dynasty, at first militarily and politically, then with his pen through more than forty years of relative reclusion. The secrecy of his writings accounts for their preservation until their publication in the nineteenth and twentieth centuries. It also explains his overdue recognition as one of China's best thinkers. The sense of political crisis underlying his writing attracts the interest of Chinese Marxists and non-Marxists alike.

More philosophically significant in this regard is Wang's cosmology and metaphysics, traced by him to the Song philosopher ZHANG ZAI but also historically connected to late Ming trends. Wang's work is based on the dynamic concept of *qi* (material force, literally breath) (see QI). His practical emphasis on *qi* as opposed to *li* (principle) lends itself to a materialist interpretation particularly when linked with Wang's claim that the world consists of concrete things (see LI). However, the importance of *qi* is that it is self-moving and not predetermined from without, yet so constituted that its activity necessarily tends to produce order. This, together with mentalistic descriptions of *qi*'s activity, suggests an expressive cosmology akin to Wang's view of poetic expression. His mode of thought is organicist, which is partly why it is difficult to classify in idealist–materialist terms.

Wang's epistemology and ethical psychology are shaped by an awareness of non-Confucian systems. He opposes the extreme scepticism of the Daoists and Buddhists, but a dash of Chinese empiricism, together with his belief in the ultimate unfathomability of the non-human cosmos, makes him sharply critical of tidy, predictive systems such as those offered by numerology or Western science. Mind and senses work together to produce knowledge, but the mind comes into its own in the development of a 'synthetic a priori' type of moral knowledge through a mixture of intuition and reflection (also represented as the unfolding of *qi*). This kind of knowledge is based on moral experience and leads to moral practice (see KNOWLEDGE, CONCEPT OF). Supporting Wang's ethical epistemology is an original and dynamic view of human nature as a perpetually renewed source and product of moral cultivation (see XING).

Wang's organic conception of *qi* lends originality to his philosophy of history. In place of the common Confucian nostalgia for the 'feudal' past, Wang credits the historical process with its own natural trends and rationale (*li*). He even sees the possibility

of other civilizations replacing that of the Chinese. However, this theoretic detachment does not extend to tolerance of foreign conquest in his own time. Wang Fuzhi's nationalism comes closer to racism than does normal Confucian ethnocentrism. Though passionately felt, it stands in uneasy relation to the philosophy which it ironically helped to inspire.

See also: NEO-CONFUCIAN PHILOSOPHY; QI

List of works

Wang Fuzhi (1619–92) *Chuanshan quanshu* (Complete Works of Wang Fuzhi), Changsha: Yuelu shushe, 1988–, 16 vols. (The most comprehensive edition of Wang's writings, including all extant titles. Vol. 16, consisting of miscellaneous supporting materials, has so far not been published.)

—— (1619–92) *Chuanshan yishu* (Surviving Works of Wang Fuzhi), Shanghai: Taipingyang, 1933. (Based on earlier, less complete editions, the most important of which is that edited by Zeng Guofan in 1865. Various facsimile reprints of the 1933 edition are available under title *Chuanshan quanji* (Complete Works of Wang Fuzhi) or *Chuanshan yishu quanji* (Complete Surviving Works of Wang Fuzhi).)

—— (begun 1655) *Zhouyi waizhuan* (Outer Commentary on the Book of Changes), in *Chuanshan yishu* (Surviving Works of Wang Fuzhi), Shanghai: Taipingyang, 1933. (Along with *Zhangzi Zhengmeng zhu*, provides the metaphysical and cosmological foundation for Wang Fuzhi's philosophy of change, including criticism of Daoist and Buddhist ideas.)

—— (1656) *Huangshu* (Yellow Book), in *Chuanshan yishu* (Surviving Works of Wang Fuzhi), Shanghai: Taipingyang, 1933. (A short but important text for Wang's nationalistically oriented political thought.)

—— (1655–65) *Shangshu yinyi* (Elaboration on the Meaning of the *Book of Documents*), in *Chuanshan yishu* (Surviving Works of Wang Fuzhi), Shanghai: Taipingyang, 1933. (Wide-ranging commentary on the Confucian classic, embracing metaphysics, ethics and epistemology.)

—— (c.1660?) *Shiyi (Interpretation of the Odes)*, trans. as *Jiangzhai shihua* in Wong Siu-kit, *Notes on Poetry from the Ginger Studio*, Hong Kong, 1987. (Constitutes an accessible source for Wang's theory of poetry.)

—— (after 1660–5) *Shi guangzhan* (Extended Commentary on the *Odes*), in *Chuanshan yishu* (Surviving Works of Wang Fuzhi), Shanghai: Taipingyang, 1933. (Important for Wang's theories of mind and human nature as well as of poetry.)

—— (revised 1655) *Du Sishu Daquan shuo* (Revised Commentary on *Reading the Compendium of the Four Books*) (revised 1665), in *Chuanshan yishu* (Surviving Works of Wang Fuzhi), Shanghai: Taipingyang, 1933. (An important critique of the neo-Confucian handling of the four books at the heart of its canon, this text is essential for Wang's ethical psychology.)

—— (after 1678) *Siwen lu* (Record of Thoughts and Questions), in *Chuanshan yishu* (Surviving Works of Wang Fuzhi), Shanghai: Taipingyang, 1933. (A series of significant 'jottings' on miscellaneous topics such as Chinese and Western cosmology.)

—— (after 1678) *Zhangzi Zhengmeng zhu* (Zhang Zai's *Correction of Youthful Ignorance* Annotated), in *Chuanshan yishu* (Surviving Works of Wang Fuzhi), Shanghai: Taipingyang, 1933. (In the form of a commentary on Zhang Zai, this is the mature expression of Wang's *qi*-based metaphysics.)

—— (before 1682?) *Zhuangzi jie* (Zhuangzi explained), in *Chuanshan yishu* (Surviving Works of Wang Fuzhi), Shanghai: Taipingyang, 1933. (Reckoned one of the best commentaries on the Daoist philosopher.)

—— (1682) *Emeng* (Nightmare), in *Chuanshan yishu* (Surviving Works of Wang Fuzhi), Shanghai: Taipingyang, 1933. (A late reiteration of Wang's political nationalism.)

—— (1685) *Zhouyi neizhuan* (Inner Commentary on the *Book of Changes*), in *Chuanshan yishu* (Surviving Works of Wang Fuzhi), Shanghai: Taipingyang, 1933. (More strictly focussed and esoteric than the *Waizhuan*.)

—— (1687) *Du Tongjian lun* (On reading the *Comprehensive Mirror*), in *Chuanshan yishu* (Surviving Works of Wang Fuzhi), Shanghai: Taipingyang, 1933. (An examination of Chinese imperial history as treated by the Song historian Sima Guang, this is an essential source for Wang's philosophy of history, state and society.)

—— (1690) *Xitang Yongri xulun* (Jottings from Summer Days in the Western Chamber), trans. as *Jiangzhai shihua* in Wong Siu-kit, *Notes on Poetry from the Ginger Studio*, Hong Kong, 1987. (Constitutes an accessible source for Wang's theory of poetry.)

—— (1691) *Song lun* (On the Song dynasty), in *Chuanshan yishu* (Surviving Works of Wang Fuzhi), Shanghai: Taipingyang, 1933. (A continuation of Wang's efforts to draw political lessons from history. An annotated translation of the first chapter can be found in A.H. Black, 'The Theme of the Mandate of Heaven in the Political Thought of Wang Fu-chih (1619–92)', M.Litt. thesis, University of Glasgow, 1970.)

References and further reading

Black, A.H. (1989) *Man and Nature in the Philosophical Thought of Wang Fu-chih*, Seattle, WA: University of Washington Press. (Develops expressionist interpretation of Wang's philosophy – cosmology, epistemology and theory of poetry – against Western creationist background.)

Gernet, J. (1978–90) 'Cours sur Wang Fuzhi' (Lectures on Wang Fuzhi), in *Annuaire du College de France*, Paris. (Studies by an eminent Sinologist with a particular interest in Wang's view of history.)

Jullien, F. (1989) *Procès ou Création: Une introduction à la pensée des lettrés chinois: Essai de problématique interculturelle* (Process or Creation: An Introduction to Chinese Literati Thought: Essay on an Intercultural Problematic), Paris: Éditions du Seuil. (Comparative study of Wang as a process philosopher in contrast to Western creationism. Good presentation of the relevant ideas and terminology.)

McMorran, I. (1992) *The Passionate Realist: An Introduction to the Life and Political Thought of Wang Fuzhi*, Hong Kong: Sunshine Book Company. (Substantially based on his doctoral thesis, McMorran's study forms an excellent introduction to the subject and includes a useful bibliography.)

Vierheller, E.J. (1968) *Nation und Elite im Denken von Wang Fu-chih (1619–92)* (Nation and Elitism in the Philosophy of Wang Fuzhi), Hamburg: Gesellschaft für Natur- und Völkerkunde Ostasiens. (A critical interpretation of Wang's nationalism and its motivation; reviewed at length by J.-F. Billeter in *T'oung Pao* 57, 1970.)

Yan Shoucheng (1994) 'Coherence and Contradiction in the World View of Wang Fuzhi', Ph.D. dissertation, University of Indiana. (On how to reconcile apparent contradictions in Wang's philosophy. Through detailed discussion of the main terms and concepts, the author argues effectively for Wang's role as the greatest synthesizer of Chinese intellectual tradition since Zhu Xi. Good bibliography.)

ALISON H. BLACK

WANG YANGMING (1472–1529)

Wang Yangming was an influential Confucian thinker in sixteenth-century China who, like other Confucian thinkers, emphasized social and political responsibilities and regarded cultivation of the self as the basis for fulfilling such responsibilities. While sometimes drawing on ideas and metaphors from Daoism and Chan

Buddhism, he criticized these schools for their neglect of family ties and social relations. And, in opposition to a version of Confucianism which emphasized learning, he advocated directly attending to the mind in the process of self-cultivation.

Having gone through a series of political ups and downs, Wang Yangming was acutely aware of the political degeneration and moral decay of his times. The influential teachings of ZHU XI no longer offered a solution to such problems, the study of classics emphasized by Zhu having degenerated into a tool for social advancement, resulting in habits of memorization and fragmentary studies. Wang, who in his youth studied Zhu's teachings, developed a new version of Confucian thought, the main ideas of which are contained in the *Quanxilu* (Instructions for Practical Living) a collection of conversations and letters compiled by Wang's disciples, as well as in other essays and poems.

According to Zhu Xi, the mind already knows principle (or pattern); in relation to human lives, principle constitutes the realm of the ethical (see LI). In the original state, the mind's knowledge of principle guides and is sufficient for ethical action, but such knowledge can be obscured by distortive factors of the mind often referred to as selfish desires. 'Investigation of things' and 'extension of knowledge', two steps in a self-cultivation process described in a Confucian classic, are interpreted to mean arriving at the principle in things (via the study of classics and examination of daily affairs) so as to expand one's knowledge of principle, thereby regaining the knowledge one originally has (see SELF-CULTIVATION IN CHINESE PHILOSOPHY).

While Wang also believed that everyone has 'innate knowledge' which can be obscured by selfish desires, he regarded innate knowledge not as prior knowledge of principle but as a disposition to respond to particular situations in appropriate ways without guidance from such prior knowledge. Principle is revealed in the responses of the mind when unobscured, and 'mind is principle' in the sense that principle does not exist independently of such responses. Furthermore, while such responses may involve some kind of knowing, there is a 'unity of knowledge and action' in the sense that the responses also involve motivations to act which are not explained by the knowing and which are sufficient for action (see ACTION).

Given his view that principle resides just in the responses of the mind when unobscured, Wang regarded Zhu Xi's emphasis on learning as misguided. He interpreted 'investigation of things' and 'extension of knowledge' to mean correcting what is incorrect in

the activity of the mind so as to allow innate knowledge to reach out. That is, a main task of self-cultivation is constantly to watch for and eliminate selfish desires, until the mind is purified and selfish desires no longer arise. While de-emphasizing learning, he did not totally reject it since studying the classics can help one understand one's mind, and since there are details such as institutional arrangements that innate knowledge may tell one to learn.

Other interesting ideas of Wang's include his conception of the myriad things as forming 'one body'; that different things are linked is seen from the way plants and animals nourish human beings or the way herbs cure disease. Thus, ideally, one should be sensitive to the well-being of all things. Another idea is his view that things do not exist outside of the mind, an idea sometimes interpreted as a form of idealism (see IDEALISM). It is possible, though, that 'things' in this context refers to what forms a meaningful structure, so that what is at issue is not an ontological thesis but an observation about how the mind's awareness contributes to objects forming a meaningful structure for humans (see AWARENESS IN INDIAN THOUGHT).

Another well-known idea of Wang's is his 'Four Sentence Teaching', which describes (1) what is without good and evil as the substance of the mind, (2) what is with good and evil as the movement of intent (the starting point of the mind's activity), (3) what knows good and evil as innate knowledge, and (4) what does good and eliminates evil as the investigation of things. Since principle, and correspondingly the distinction between good and evil, resides ultimately in the responses of innate knowledge ('mind is principle'), there is a sense in which innate knowledge, which Wang identified with the substance of the mind, cannot itself be described as good or evil. Furthermore, innate knowledge is without good and evil in the further sense that, when responding to situations, it is not guided by thoughts of doing good or avoiding evil ('unity of knowledge and action'). As for the second sentence, it describes how, when the mind is activated, intent arises and can point in a good or evil direction because of the distortive effects of selfish desires. The third sentence concerns how, despite such distortive effects, innate knowledge can still distinguish between good and evil, while the fourth sentence explains the investigation of things in terms of doing good and eliminating selfish desires so as to restore the original state of the mind. On this interpretation of the teaching, self-cultivation is a gradual process of persistently doing good and eliminating evil.

However, if it is innate knowledge that enables one to recognize selfish desires as problematic, then, since innate knowledge operates without guidance from a conception of good and evil, it seems that the elimination of selfish desires should also be a spontaneous process not requiring effort. That is, as soon as innate knowledge is brought to bear on things, all incorrect elements get corrected and one achieves sagehood without any need for persistent efforts to do good and eliminate evil. These two views represent a disagreement among disciples which Wang addressed by proposing that the two views capture two teachings, directed respectively to the ordinary people and to those of sharp intelligence. Subsequently, such disagreement led to divergent developments of Wang's teachings by later followers.

See also: CONFUCIAN PHILOSOPHY, CHINESE; LEGALIST PHILOSOPHY, CHINESE; NEO-CONFUCIAN PHILOSOPHY; SELF-CULTIVATION IN CHINESE PHILOSOPHY; ZHU XI

List of works

Wang Yangming (1472–1529) *Quanxilu* (Instructions for Practical Living), trans. Chan Wing-tsit, *Instructions for Practical Living and Other Neo-Confucian Writings by Wang Yang-ming*, New York: Columbia University Press, 1963. (Translation of main work containing Wang's philosophical ideas, with introduction by translator giving summary of Wang's biography and philosophy.)

—— (1503–27) Philosophical Letters, ed. and trans. J. Ching, *The Philosophical Letters of Wang Yang-ming*, Columbia, SC: University of South Carolina Press, 1972. (Translation of Wang's philosophical letters between 1503 and 1527.)

—— (1472–1529) Essays and Poems, trans. J. Ching in *To Acquire Wisdom: The Way of Wang Yang-ming*, New York: Columbia University Press. (Translation of selected essays and poems by Wang, with introduction by translator giving summary of Wang's philosophy and analysis of key terms.)

References and further reading

Chang, C. (1962) *Wang Yang-ming: Idealist Philosopher of Sixteenth-Century China*, New York: St. John's University Press. (An introduction to Wang's life and philosophy.)

Ching, J. (1976) *To Acquire Wisdom: The Way of Wang Yang-ming*, New York: Columbia University Press. (Translation of selected essays and poems by Wang, with introduction by translator giving summary of Wang's philosophy and analysis of key terms.)

Cua, A.S. (1982) *The Unity of Knowledge and Action:*
A Study in Wang Yang-ming's Moral Psychology, Honolulu, HI: University Press of Hawaii. (Explication of Wang's doctrine of the unity of knowledge and action in light of modern ethical theories, and reconstruction of Wang's moral psychology.)

Tu Wei-ming (1976) *Neo-Confucian Thought in Action: Wang Yang-ming's Youth (1472–1509)*, Los Angeles, CA: University of California Press. (Discussion of the formative years of Wang that led to his advocacy of the unity of knowledge and action.)

SHUN KWONG-LOI

WAR AND PEACE, PHILOSOPHY OF

The war/peace dichotomy is a recurrent one in human thought and the range of experience it interprets is vast. Images of war and peace permeate religion, literature and art. Wars, battles, pacts and covenants appear as outcomes and antecedents in historical narratives. Recurrent patterns of warlike and pacific behaviour invite scientific explanations in terms of underlying biological, psychological or economic processes. War and peace are also often matters of practical concern, predicaments or opportunities that call for individual or collective action. While philosophers have explored all these ways of looking at war and peace, they have paid most attention to the practical aspects of the subject, making it part of moral and political philosophy.

Practical concern with war and peace can go in either of two main directions, one focusing on war and the other on peace. Those who doubt that war can be abolished naturally worry about how it can be regulated. So long as war is possible, there will be principles for waging it. Whether such principles should limit war-making to ends like self-defence or leave the choice to the discretion of political and military leaders is a matter of continuing dispute. Nor is there agreement regarding restrictions on the conduct of war, some holding that belligerents need only avoid disproportionate damage, others that it is morally wrong to harm innocents (for example, noncombatants). In situations of emergency both limits may give way, and moralists have debated whether this relaxation of standards is defensible. Disputes over the principles governing war raise difficult questions about action, intention and the character of morality itself.

If we think that wars can be prevented, it becomes important to focus on the conditions of permanent peace. Some who do this conclude that peace depends on the conversion of individuals to an ethic of

nonviolence, others that it requires strengthening the rule of law. According to a powerful version of the latter argument, the absence of law creates a condition in which persons and communities are at liberty to invade one another: a condition that, in Hobbes's classic metaphor, is a 'state of nature' which is also a perpetual state of war. While treaties of peace may terminate particular wars, only political institutions that establish the rule of law within and between communities can provide security and guarantee peace.

1 **War and peace as ideas**
2 **Grounds for war**
3 **Conduct of war**
4 **Pacifism and nonviolence**
5 **Peace as an institution**
6 **War and peace within and between communities**

1 War and peace as ideas

War can be conceived in many ways. For some it is a metaphor for all that is violent, destructive and lawless. The realm outside the world of Islam, for example, is thought of by Muslims as 'the house of war', a realm of unbelief and strife. General Sherman's idea that 'war is hell' exploits the Christian idea of hell as a domain of radical disorder (Pandemonium) as well as of fire and torment. War can also stand for the clash of opposites from which (as Heraclitus taught) all things spring. For Clausewitz, war is a self-driven process having its own principles of order. And war may be understood as a social practice or institution that takes different forms over time or in different cultures. Understood as organized armed combat, war may be distinguished both from lawless violence and from other kinds of force and coercion (see COERCION; VIOLENCE). 'War', in short, is a kind of order as well as disorder.

Similar dichotomies mark conceptions of peace. 'Peace' can mean either a temporary suspension of hostilities (a truce) or a permanent condition of tranquillity in which war is no longer feared. Where war is identified with lawlessness, peace becomes not the mere absence of fighting but a secure condition of mutual cooperation between individuals within a community or between communities. The idea that peace depends on legal order is a recurrent theme of Western political philosophy, one stated eloquently by Thomas Hobbes in *Leviathan* (1651) (see HOBBES, T. §7).

Hobbes identifies war with the condition of humanity in the absence of civil order – a condition of nature in which each human being has a right to all things. The state of war is the opposite of the civil condition, and avoiding its inconveniences is the chief motive for seeking peace. War is the natural consequence of a disposition to fight that exists wherever there is no guarantee of peace. Peace requires assurance that one will not be forced to fight, and this is possible only in the civil condition. Peace is a state of affairs that emerges not from the kind of agreement that terminates a particular war, but from an agreement creating a permanent legal order with civil institutions to declare and administer its laws (see §5).

On this view, peace is disrupted not by the lawful use of armed force, but only by the use of force contrary to law. The postulated antithesis between war and law must be seen not only in causal terms but conceptually: not only is law needed to secure the conditions that lead to war, but 'war' *means* the abrogation of lawfulness. One cannot hold that people are obliged by law to respect one another's rights and at the same time that they are free to attack one another at will.

The premise of most political philosophy is that war is an evil to be escaped or at least regulated. But some philosophers, like MACHIAVELLI (§4) and NIETZSCHE, have considered war a good rather than an evil. It may be a field for the display of virtues like courage, virtues which are quite different from those urged by Jesus in the Sermon on the Mount, or a way of cleansing the corruption of a decadent civilization, thereby recovering the greatness of former times or developing unrealized human potentialities.

For other philosophers, war must be understood before it is judged. It calls for philosophical investigation because it is an aspect of experience, a part of reality. In one version of this approach (illustrated by J. Glenn Gray in *The Warriors* (1959)), war is understood phenomenologically by considering how it appears to those who experience it. In another, the study of war takes a scientific turn as the philosopher seeks to identify the 'causes of war' in human nature, in the character of different states or in the structure of the international system. The concept of innate human aggression, the hypothesis that 'liberal' states do not fight wars with one another and the argument that war is an inevitable consequence of a decentralized international order illustrate explanatory theories at each of these levels.

2 Grounds for war

Although the philosophical justification of war predates the modern states system, the problem of justification is most easily introduced in this setting. According to what might be called the 'political realist' point of view, there is in the international system no authority superior to that of the separate states. Force may be used by governments to uphold their own internal law, but there is no international law that it properly upholds (see INTERNATIONAL RELATIONS, PHILOSOPHY OF §2). War is an instrument of foreign policy and its use is restrained only by prudence, not justice. It follows that there can be no distinction between just and unjust wars. States may agree for prudential reasons to restrict the use of force but obligations thus incurred can be overridden by 'reasons of state'; that is, by considerations of national security. Where vital interests are at stake, states remain free to violate their agreements, acting in ways that non-realists might deem 'unjust'.

The alternative view is that one *can* distinguish lawful and unlawful uses of force between states, that is, distinguish just from unjust wars. Although this has long been a part of the tradition of Catholic natural law, this view has had many non-Catholic interpreters, from GROTIUS to Michael Walzer, and is thoroughly embedded in international law. An unjust war does not merely interrupt peace (understood as a condition of calm marked by the absence of fighting), it violates the lawful order that guarantees states their independence and territory. An unjust war is not a brute fact but a wrong, and as such it justifies the use of force by other states to resist and punish it.

Underlying the distinction between just and unjust wars is the assumption that there is a society of states comparable to the community of individuals that comprise a single state. In place of laws made and applied by sovereign authority, the laws of the international community rest on international custom and natural justice. Although the international order is more uncertain than that which prevails within a peaceful state, only if we presume such an order can we distinguish just (lawful) and unjust (unlawful) wars (see JUSTICE, INTERNATIONAL §1–2). In the same way that the rule of law in civil society protects the liberty and security of each citizen, the rule of law in international society protects the political independence and territorial integrity of each state. A state that violates these principles makes itself liable to action by other states, acting singly or together, to protect their rights and defend the principles on which international order rests. Unlike a citizen, a state may fall back on self-help because there is no superior power on which it can rely.

The idea of just war may be seen as a middle position between realist and holy war conceptions. For political realists, any war a state chooses to fight to protect its security is justified. But because security can be threatened by the mere power of other states as well as their conduct, realist reasoning can be used to rationalize aggression. For holy warriors (and their secular imitators), in contrast, it is the imperative to disseminate the faith that justifies attacking others and, often, subjugating, converting, expelling or exterminating them. If we understand war to be an instrument of human will to secure justice, a just war must be distinguished both from self-preservation and from the promotion of a religious or ideological cause.

Although it is agreed in the just-war tradition that a war must be fought for 'just cause', there is dispute about which grounds for war meet this criterion. According to AQUINAS (§13), a just war is neither a war of conquest nor a war of self-defence. It is a war in which another community is attacked for refusing to redress wrongs inflicted by its members or to restore goods or territory it has unjustly seized (Aquinas 1266–73: II, 2, q.40, a.1). The United Nations Charter, in contrast, limits the grounds for war by states to self-defence. But such a limitation, taken literally, would forbid assisting another state to resist attack. It would also forbid armed intervention within another state to end abuses by its government, for a government can mistreat its own subjects without attacking other states – a fact international law now recognizes and tries to prevent by distinguishing crimes against humanity from the crime of aggressive war. If a just war is one that redresses wrongs, the crimes of a government against its own subjects (today understood as violations of their 'human rights') may be included among these wrongs and therefore among the lawful grounds for war.

A much-debated question is whether war can justly punish, as well as resist, wrongs committed by other states. Some argue that states may resist aggression but not punish it. Punishment must be licensed by an international authority, and there is no such authority. Others reply that if states are not authorized to punish wrongdoing, it is hard to see how they can be authorized to resist it, either. Yet both might agree that waging punitive war against entire communities, long sanctioned by moralists as well as by state practice, rests on unacceptable views of collective responsibility. The practice of reprisals, however, continues to be justified by some moralists as a deterrent to further wrongdoing.

Other considerations besides 'just cause' may be offered for judging decisions to initiate a war. Aquinas, for example, argues that war cannot be justly chosen, even by those whose cause is just, unless that choice has been authorized by a ruler: 'private wars' cannot be just. This constraint does not limit the wars of sovereigns against one another, however, unless there is a higher authority to whom they are subject. Today the United Nations claims such authority. Although the Charter prohibits the unilateral use of force by states except in self-defence against armed attack, the Security Council may authorize collective military action to rectify a variety of other wrongs.

Aquinas also repeats the judgment of AUGUSTINE, that those who choose war must do so to resist wrongdoing and secure peace, not for the sake of vengeance or to gain power. In other words, the intention with which one fights, like the act of fighting itself, must meet a moral test. On one view of intention, to intend is to choose and thus to act. But we can further distinguish between intentions (what is aimed at) and motives (the state of mind or 'spirit' in which one acts). Some in the just-war tradition argue that intentions are always morally relevant, even if motives are not. For them, a war justified by the 'cause' of reversing an unjust conquest (like the Iraqi conquest of Kuwait) but one which is really intended to achieve some less defensible end (like permanently weakening Iraq) must be deemed unjust, as must one carried out in a spirit of hatred or cynicism. For political realists, in contrast, neither intentions nor motives count for much.

Because wars can occur within as well as between communities, moralists have asked whether there can be just civil wars. Under what circumstances are revolutions or wars of national liberation justified? When is it proper to overthrow a tyrant or usurper, or to resist a government when it demands the performance of immoral acts like participation in genocide or service in an unjust war? How, if at all, can terrorist acts against a regime be defended? Is morally-justified resistance to authority limited to various forms of noncooperation, including conscientious objection? Although just-war and pacifist ideas are clearly relevant to these questions, answering them also raises questions about political authority and obligation (see CIVIL DISOBEDIENCE; REVOLUTION).

3 Conduct of war

Just wars are defined not only by the ends for which they can be fought but by the means used to fight them. If war is a practice, it has rules. Of these, rules restricting the targets that can be attacked are more basic, morally speaking, than those restricting the use of particular weapons or techniques like napalm or area bombing. Some moralists argue that the rules of war are adequately summed up in the principle that the harm inflicted by military operations should be 'necessary' for and 'proportionate' to the ends sought, others insist that attacks on persons or objects not involved in fighting are wrong for reasons unrelated to these expediential considerations. Such attacks are wrong because they violate a fundamental prohibition against harming the innocent or their possessions.

This further restriction on the conduct of war is often stated as the proposition that persons who fight must not intend, either as an end or a means, the deaths of those not directly involved in the fighting. Waging war in ways that fail to discriminate between combatants and noncombatants is morally forbidden. In the classic vocabulary of natural law, those who are not engaged in fighting are 'innocent' (from Latin *nocens*, engaged in harmful activity). Innocents may not be attacked 'intentionally', although no wrong is done if they are harmed incidentally, as a foreseeable but unavoidable side-effect of permissible military action. According to the principle of 'double effect', acts that harm innocents may be justified if such harm cannot be avoided in pursuing a morally permissible end and the level of such harm is not disproportionate. One question in calculating proportionality is whether one should consider impartially the interests of everyone affected by an act, as both natural lawyers and many consequentialists argue, or should favour the interests of one's own soldiers and civilians, as political realists hold. A more difficult issue is whether the distinction between the intended and unintended effects of an act is philosophically coherent (see DOUBLE EFFECT, PRINCIPLE OF).

An even stricter position is that one is barred from intending the deaths of combatants as well as noncombatants. One may seek to thwart an attack, but in doing so one must use no more than the minimum force needed. Here, too, the double effect principle may be invoked to distinguish permissible from impermissible harm. That one can foresee the deaths of enemy soldiers whose attack one is resisting does not mean that one intends their deaths, provided that in resisting one is choosing only to repel the attack, and that the foreseen deaths are the unavoidable consequence of using the only means of resistance available.

Should moral limits on the conduct of war be ignored if the stakes are high enough? If a country is about to be overrun by a genocidal adversary, many think that the victim may use any means to defeat the conqueror. Moral constraints that hold in ordinary situations are not binding in situations of extremity. This view reverses the usual structure of just-war argument: thus, although under normal circumstances moral principles constrain consequentialist calculations, when catastrophe threatens such calculations may be substituted for reliance on moral principle. There is an escape clause in cases of authentic necessity.

Most natural law and Kantian theories of morality reject the argument from extremity. In situations of communal emergency one might justifiably waive rules based on mere custom or utility. But one may not violate the exceptionless precepts of the moral law, like those forbidding aggression or the deliberate killing of innocents. For these reflect the basic principle (sometimes called 'St Paul's principle') that evil may not be done for the sake of good. To permit such acts is to hold that a moral community can survive by measures that its own traditions condemn as immoral. In abandoning its principles, the community would be trying to preserve the lives of its members while denying the principles that define its integrity as a community. This problem does not arise for political realism, which treats all rules as merely conventional and instrumental. Realism assumes that a community can temporarily transgress its moral principles without changing its character as that community.

The argument from extremity plays an important part in the debate over nuclear deterrence. In so far as it targets civilians, and thus intentionally threatens innocents, a nuclear retaliatory strategy is not easily reconciled with ordinary moral ideas. It is sometimes argued that the deterrent is not immoral because it only threatens, but does not actually destroy, innocent lives. But if (see §2 above) intentions are themselves actions – if they involve choices and commitments, can determine the character of the chooser and can have a variety of consequences – it can be wrong to intend what it is wrong to do (the 'wrongful intentions principle'). Unless it is just a bluff, the deterrent threat expresses an intention to do wrong under certain conditions and is therefore morally objectionable. It is doubtful whether such stratagems as counterforce targeting or the mere possession of nuclear weapons can justify nuclear deterrence under ordinary moral principles. The claim that the nuclear predicament creates a (permanent) state of emergency, which therefore necessitates the deterrent threat, is yet another way of attempting such a justification.

4 Pacifism and nonviolence

Because those who condemn war do so on many grounds, there are many different kinds of 'pacifism'. Some pacifisms are personal (it is morally wrong for me to fight), others general (no-one may fight). Some object to organized war, others to killing human beings, still others to killing any living creature or to any use of force whatsoever. In each case, war is opposed as a matter of moral principle.

But the label 'pacifist' is also applied to the position of those who, like Mahatma GANDHI or Martin Luther King, Jr, urge nonviolent resistance on pragmatic as well as moral grounds. Arguing that power rests on acquiescence, its advocates contend that tyranny and aggression can be resisted without armed force (although not without a kind of nonviolent coercion). Nonviolent resistance can range from militant noncooperation (like Sorel's general strike) to the practice of 'living in truth' followed by dissidents in communist eastern Europe during the 1980s.

So-called nuclear pacifism, which objects to war involving nuclear but not conventional weapons, would seem to follow from just-war or perhaps even realist premises rather than from a principled objection to war as such. What is to be abolished is not war itself but a weapon that makes war too terrible to fight. More radical are movements that seek to abolish war by getting rid of war-causing social or political institutions (capitalism, the military–industrial complex, patriarchy) or by reforming the international order (through promoting free trade, collective security or world government).

Christian pacifism rejects war as an instrument of human purposes while recognizing it as a recurrent situation in which Christians must bear witness to their faith, serve others and search for nonviolent ways of dealing with a hostile world. Pacifism of this kind is an interpretation of the meaning of a religious faith. Like the early Christianity from which it takes its guidance, it focuses on creating a community of believers committed to living their lives together according to Christian principles. There are Christian pacifists like TOLSTOI who see government as intrinsically violent and who therefore incline to anarchism: to govern is necessarily to act evilly, like Caiaphas, for the common good. Although often branded as 'sectarian' for turning away from the world, Christian pacifism can be missionary, concerned with transforming the world.

Pacifists attempt to seize the moral high ground, charging not only realists but just-war moralists with a myopic acceptance of the existing world and lack of faith in the possibility of social transformation. They also accuse those who believe war can be justified of presuming, against the evidence, that force is more effective than nonviolent action. In so far as the issue is whether morality permits war in some circumstances, pacifists are engaged in debate with those committed to the just-war idea. But if the issue is whether morality applies to war at all, pacifists find themselves allied with just warriors against political realists and others for whom morality is circumscribed by prudence. And in invoking necessity, even realists make clear their aversion to war, thereby taking sides with the just warrior and the pacifist against those who celebrate war as a good in itself.

5   Peace as an institution

For many philosophers, peace is an aspect of legal order. But what kind of legal order? For law can be a tool of domination and oppression, a form of war by other means – as Augustine was not the first nor Foucault the last to observe. Any legal order that can establish and guarantee peace acknowledges the subjectivity (and therefore the personality, freedom and human rights) of those who belong to it. So-called 'martial law', which is really a suspension of law, is an expedient rationalized as necessary to restore legal order. It is not the foundation on which permanent peace, an ordered tranquillity, can be constructed.

It is sometimes argued that although peace based on law can be enjoyed by portions of humanity (if states can be established), such peace is not possible for the world as a whole. HEGEL argued that a world state is inconceivable because the existence of one state implies the existence of others: 'without relations with other states, the state can no more be an actual individual than an individual can be an actual person without a relationship with other persons' (1821: §331). The state therefore cannot exist alone; it needs other states to accord it recognition and give it an identity. But a state might acquire an identity in resisting other associations: pirates, terrorists or insurgents, for example. The idea of a world state is different from that of a state among states, but it does not follow that a single law-making authority for all humanity is inconceivable.

Others perceive not logical but practical difficulties: a world state would be ungovernable or likely to suppress human diversity and freedom. For KANT (§10), a world state is conceivable but would pass through despotism back to anarchy. For Hobbes, a world state is conceivable but unnecessary because adequate security can be enjoyed in much smaller associations: the state of nature that exists between sovereign states is not nearly as bad as that which exists among individuals in the absence of civil order.

Both these conclusions may seem doubtful, however. If it is the fear of war that motivates individuals to accept political authority, one can imagine circumstances in which this fear is better escaped by creating a single world state, which would abolish war between states, than by creating many states, which can only perpetuate war. This argument becomes more persuasive as war becomes more dangerous. If, in contrast, states can coexist without threatening the lives or prosperity of their members, then individuals cannot be rationally motivated to establish a world state. But this second line of argument seems to undermine the case for any state. If states can coexist in a condition of nature, why cannot individuals or voluntary associations of individuals do the same? If the state of nature is tolerable for sovereigns then, under some imaginable circumstances, it may be tolerable for others. Even though its inconveniences may be greater, it does not follow that these must be so great as to necessitate sovereignty.

Although he thinks a world state would endanger rather than secure perpetual peace, Kant (1795) insists on the moral necessity of establishing a global legal order by means of a contract among independent states, for the rule of law among states both depends upon and reinforces the rule of law within each state. If peace depends on legal order, it must be 'formally instituted' by means of a constitution, internationally as well as internally. But the order established by the international constitution is confederal rather than unitary. The crucial elements of this constitution are: (1) that every state shall have a 'republican' constitution – that is, one that makes government the common business (res publica) of the people, and ensures that it is conducted according to law; and (2) that the international order must be a federation of republican states, not a world state. The first condition means not that each state must be a democracy, for democracies can be despotic, but that each should be governed by the rule of law; for Kant, this means separating the legislative and executive powers. If there is to be an international order based on just laws, each state must conduct its internal as well as external affairs on the basis of such laws. The second condition (federation) demands that even republican states give up their liberty to make war. If states do not yield this sovereign prerogative, they remain in a state of nature. To establish permanent peace, they must renounce not only the means of war (for example, standing armies) but the right of war. The new power to which they surrender this right must be a federation of republics.

Kant's argument, then, is that to secure permanent peace, states must first agree to acknowledge one another's subjectivity by observing the rules of civilized international relations. Those that are republics must then establish a federation. If a state is not a republic, it must become one before it can join this federation. There will be a universal, permanent peace only when all states are republics and have entered the federation. This argument seems open to the objection that a federation in which states can remain sovereign would not succeed in bringing them out of the state of nature. Either the members retain their sovereignty, in which case the state of nature continues, or they do not, in which case we have a world state, not a confederation of independent states.

It is an open question whether this contradiction can be resolved (see STATE §3).

6 War and peace within and between communities

For Hobbes, the rule of law is possible within but not between political communities. For Kant, permanent peace based on the rule of law is possible at the international level, but it holds only among republics – that is, states governed according to the rule of law. War remains a real possibility in relations with other kinds of states. The world is bifurcated into two realms, each ruled by its own principles. The divided structure of international order implicit in these arguments appears in many other theories of international relations. Socrates suggests that Greeks and barbarians are natural enemies who may ravage one another in war in ways that are entirely inappropriate among Greeks (Plato: 469b–471c), a sentiment later echoed by J.S. Mill in the context of European imperialism. Muslims distinguish between the house of war and the house of Islam, Christian pacifists between the house of fear and the house of love. Liberal thinkers divide the world into a 'free world' or 'zone of peace' and a world inhabited by the enemies of freedom, states which, because of the character of their regimes, are not 'peace-loving'. In the international law theory of the former Soviet Union, the rules governing cooperation within the family of communist states differ from those regulating the coexistence of communist and non-communist states.

This multilevel conception of international order continues to be influential. John Rawls' 'law of peoples', for example, invokes the idea of a Kantian federation embracing liberal (what Kant calls 'republican') states, based on principles of non-aggression and non-intervention. However, Rawls' law permits liberal states to intervene in the internal affairs of non-liberal societies (so-called 'outlaw states') (Rawls 1993).

Implicit in all these views are actually three rather than two levels of international order. The first is a condition of war among communities forced to take each other's power into account but unwilling to grant each other recognition. The second level is a pluralist society composed of states that recognize one another's rights as states, no matter what the character of their internal regimes; its rules are those of a minimum order of coexistence based on mutual restraint but not on shared values or a common way of life. Here, although not a constant condition, war is always possible and sometimes justified. The third level is a peaceful international society of rule-of-law states in which each conducts both its internal and external affairs according to shared standards of justice.

See also: BUSHI PHILOSOPHY; INTERNATIONAL RELATIONS, PHILOSOPHY OF; SUNZI

References and further reading

Airaksinen, T. and Bertman, M.S. (eds) (1989) *Hobbes: War among Nations*, Aldershot: Avebury Press. (Considers many aspects of the Hobbesian analysis of war and peace.)

* Aquinas, T. (1266–73) *Summa theologiae* (Synopsis of Theology), selections translated in *On Law, Morality and Politics*, ed. W.P. Baumgarth and R.J. Regan, Indianapolis, IN: Hackett Publishing Company, 1988. (Includes Aquinas' brief but classic essay on war)

Barnes, J. (1982) 'The Just War', in N. Kretzmann, A. Kenny and J. Pinborg (eds) *The Cambridge History of Later Medieval Philosophy*, Cambridge: Cambridge University Press. (Provides a context for understanding Aquinas on war.)

Ceadel, M. (1987) *Thinking about War and Peace*, Oxford: Oxford University Press. (A clear introduction to a wide range of positions in twentieth-century debates about war and peace.)

Finnis, J., Boyle, J.M., Jr and Grisez, G. (1987) *Nuclear Deterrence, Morality and Realism*, Oxford: Clarendon Press. (Natural law treatment of deterrence that covers much of the literature and debate; excellent bibliography.)

Forsyth, M. (1981) *Unions of States: The Theory and Practice of Confederation*, Leicester: Leicester University Press. (Clear, comprehensive and reliable study of federalism as an approach to peace.)

* Gray, J.G. (1959) *The Warriors: Reflections on Men in Battle*, New York: Harcourt Brace. (Readable war memoir by a philosopher.)

* Hegel, G.F.W. (1821) *Elements of the Philosophy of Right*, ed. A.W. Wood, Cambridge: Cambridge University Press, 1991. (Discusses international relations and war in §§330–40.)

* Hobbes, T. (1651) *Leviathan*, ed. E. Curley, Indianapolis, IN: Hackett Publishing Company, 1994. (Presents law and war as conceptual alternatives.)

* Kant, I. (1795) *Perpetual Peace*, trans. H. Nisbet in H. Reiss (ed.) *Political Writings*, Cambridge: Cambridge University Press, 2nd edn, 1991. (Includes several essays on war, peace and international relations.)

Kenny, A. (1985) *The Logic of Deterrence*, London: Firethorn Press. (An accessible investigation of arguments for and against nuclear deterrence and nuclear disarmament.)

Lackey, D.P. (1989) *The Ethics of War and Peace*, Englewood Cliffs, NJ: Prentice Hall. (An introductory textbook covering pacifism, just-war theory and nuclear strategy, with many examples and extensive suggestions for further reading.)

Nardin, T. (ed.) (1996) *The Ethics of War and Peace: Religious and Secular Perspectives*, Princeton, NJ: Princeton University Press. (Compares natural law, realist, Jewish, Islamic, pacifist and feminist viewpoints.)

Norman, R. (1995) *Ethics, Killing and War*, Cambridge: Cambridge University Press. (Rejects the just-war theory in favour of a consequentialist ethic of war.)

Pangle, T. (1976) 'The Moral Basis of National Security: Four Historical Perspectives', in K. Knorr (ed.) *Historical Dimensions of National Security Problems*, Lawrence, KS: University Press of Kansas. (Surveys the ideas on war and peace of the major philosophers.)

* Plato (*c*.380–367 BC) *Republic*, trans. R. Waterfield, Oxford: Oxford University Press, 1994, 416d–324a. (Implies but does not develop a theory of international relations.)

* Rawls, J. (1993) 'The Law of Peoples', in S. Shute and S. Hurley (eds) *On Human Rights*, New York: Basic Books. (Extends Rawls' theory of justice to international society.)

Waltz, K.N. (1959) *Man, the State and War*, New York: Columbia University Press. (Treats philosophers as seeking causal explanations of war in the individual, the society and the international system.)

Walzer, M. (1977) *Just and Unjust Wars: A Moral Argument with Historical Illustrations*, New York: Basic Books. (The best introduction to its topic.)

Yoder, J.H. (1992) *Nevertheless: Varieties of Religious Pacifism*, revised, Scottdale, PA: Herald Press. (Discusses alternative conceptions of pacifism from an evangelical perspective.)

TERRY NARDIN

WATSUJI TETSURŌ (1890–1960)

Watsuji Tetsurō stands out as the leading thinker on ethics in twentieth century Japanese philosophy. He is regarded as a peripheral member of the 'Kyoto School' of philosophers centring around the thought of Nishida Kitarō. Like Nishida and the Kyoto School, the thought of Watsuji can be characterized by the effort to formulate a syncretic East–West philosophy developed within the framework of a Buddhist metaphysic of 'emptiness'. At the same time, Watsuji established his own highly distinctive system of ethics. He must rank as one of the most creative and profound thinkers in modern Japanese philosophy.

Watsuji was born in Himeji, Hyōgo prefecture, and entered the philosophy department at Tokyo University in 1909. From 1925 to 1934 he was a professor of ethics in the philosophy department at Kyoto University, and was a colleague of Nishida Kitarō, Tanabe Hajime, Kuki Shūzō and others associated with the 'Kyoto School' of modern Japanese philosophy (see KYOTO SCHOOL). During this period Watsuji also spent two years studying abroad in Germany under the direct tutelage of Martin HEIDEGGER. In his later years Watsuji moved to Tokyo University, where he taught from 1934 until his retirement in 1949.

The *Watsuji Tetsurō zenshū* (Complete Works of Watsuji Tetsurō) fill twenty volumes and cover a vast range of topics in philosophy, art, religion and cultural history. Whereas his earliest works focussed on Western philosophers, notably studies of Nietzsche and Kierkegaard, in his book entitled *Guzō saikō* (Revival of Idols) (1918) he announced a 'turning point', a shift from Western individualism to a social and ethical standpoint represented by Sino-Japanese modes of thought. At this point, Watsuji's interest in Asian and Japanese moral thought was influenced especially by the *samurai* ethic of group-loyalty and self-sacrifice (see BUSHI PHILOSOPHY) as developed by his teacher Nitobe Inazō, in a book entitled *Bushidō, The Soul of Japan* (1905). He was also indebted to another of his teachers, the writer Natsume Sōseki, who describes the turn from egocentrism to a Buddhistic social concept of existence in his various letters, literary essays and novels. Among Watsuji's investigations into Japanese Buddhist philosophy, art and culture, of special importance is his pioneering study of DŌGEN; his study *Shamon Dōgen* (Dōgen, The Novice) (1920–3) is regarded as the work responsible for rediscovering the significance of Dōgen as the foremost original thinker in classical Japanese Buddhist philosophy.

Watsuji is above all recognized for his ethics and moral philosophy, as developed in a three-volume work entitled *Rinrigaku* (Ethics). For Watsuji a system of ethics requires an adequate definition of the person. From this perspective, he criticizes Western liberal ethics based on individualism, egocentrism and atomism as the departure point for working out a Japanese communitarian ethics of the family system based on a social, relational and contextual model of self. According to Watsuji's philosophical anthropology, the Japanese word for 'person' (ningen) clarifies the twofold structure of the self as both individual and social in character. This social understanding of the self in turn provides the basis for a communitarian system of ethics based on the 'betweenness' (aidagara) of persons in relation. In Watsuji's ethics, this social concept of the person as an individual–society interaction implies not only a moral but also a deeply aesthetic mode of human existence as manifest through Japanese social art forms such as the tea ceremony (chanoyu) and linked verse (renga) (see AESTHETICS, JAPANESE).

Watsuji's social concept of Japanese personhood represents an original synthesis of Confucian and Buddhist ideals of the self (see CONFUCIAN PHILO-SOPHY, JAPANESE; BUDDHIST PHILOSOPHY, JAPA-NESE). He articulates a Confucian model of self as a network of familial and social relationships norma-tively governed by rites of propriety which embodies increasingly larger social groups in the process of becoming a person. At the same time, his social concept of the person is ultimately grounded in a Buddhist metaphysic of 'emptiness' (kū) whereby there is a dependent co-arising of the individual and society (see BUDDHIST CONCEPT OF EMPTINESS). There is thus a systematic character underlying Watsuji's framework in that his aesthetics and ethics are both developed in connection to his social concept of the person, which is in turn formulated in the context of a Buddhist notion of emptiness as interrelational existence.

In his most popular book, Fūdo (Climate), first published in 1934, Watsuji criticizes Heidegger's ethics as being grounded in an individualistic concept of self based on a one-sided phenomenological description of authentic human existence as a being-in-time. According to Watsuji the Japanese concept of 'person' (ningen) has a twofold structure as both an individual existence in time and a social existence in a 'climate' (fūdo) of space. Watsuji thus establishes the basis for an environmental ethics arguing that the self arises through a relationship between the in-dividual and its entire spatial climate including both human society and living nature (see SOCIETY, CONCEPT OF).

Scathing criticisms have often been levelled against the ultra-nationalism, totalitarianism and authoritar-ianism of Watsuji's socio-political framework, by both Japanese and Western scholars. Critics point out that in Watsuji's ethics of the Japanese family system and its underlying metaphysic of emptiness, the result is a totalitarian ethics wherein the individual is 'emptied' into progressively larger household groups, finally emptying into the Imperial household of the Japanese nation-family through an ideal of loyal self-sacrifice to the Emperor. Although Watsuji's philosophical anthropology starts with an effort to formulate a balanced notion of self as a twofold individual–society relation, thereby to establish a middle way between individualism and collectivism, it ends by falling into a mode of totalitarian collectivism wherein the individual is emptied into the whole of the nation through the absolute negativity of Bud-dhist emptiness. Moreover, Watsuji's ethical frame-work has been charged with falling into a dangerous form of moral relativism which defines good and evil or right and wrong in terms of the particular familial group as the frame of reference, not as universal principles which transcend the group.

See also: BUDDHIST PHILOSOPHY, JAPANESE; CONFUCIAN PHILOSOPHY, JAPANESE; ETHICS; JAPANESE PHILOSOPHY; KYOTO SCHOOL; TOTALITARIANISM

List of works

Watsuji Tetsurō (1913–49) *Watsuji Tetsurō zenshū* (Complete Works of Watsuji Tetsurō), Tokyo: Iwanami Shoten, 1961–3, 20 vols. (Edition of Watsuji's complete works.)
—— (1934) *Fūdo* (Climate), trans. G. Bownas, *A Climate*, Tokyo: Unesco, 1961. (Work on climate and nature.)
—— (1934) *Ningenaku to shite no tetsugaku* (The Significance of Ethics as the Study of Man), trans. D.A Dilworth, *Monumenta Nipponica* 26, 1971 (3–4). (Work on ethics.)
—— (1934) *Nihon no bungei to bukkyō shishō* (Japanese Literary Arts and Buddhist Philosophy), trans. Hirano Umeyo, *The Eastern Buddhist*, 4, 1971 (1): 88–115. (Article on Buddhism and literary aesthetics.)

References and further reading

Bellah, R.N. (1965) 'Japan's Cultural Identity: Some Reflections on the Work of Watsuji Tetsurō', *Journal of Asian Studies* 24 (4): 573–94. (Looks at Watsuji's importance in the study of Japanese culture.)
Dilworth, D.A. (1974) 'Watsuji Tetsurō: Cultural Phenomenologist and Ethician', *Philosophy East and West* 24 (1). (Looks at his ethical and cultural works.)
Kodera, T.J. (1987) 'The Romantic Humanism of Watsuji Tetsurō', *Dialogue and Alliance* 1 (3): 4–11. (Discussion of Watsuji's views.)
LaFleur, W.R. (1978) 'Buddhist Emptiness in the Ethics and Aesthetics of Watsuji Tetsurō', *Religious*

Studies 14 (June): 237–50. (The impact of Buddhism on Watsuji's thought.)

Nagami Isamu (1981) 'The Ontological Foundations in Tetsurō Watsuji's Philosophy: *Kū* and Human Existence', *Philosophy East and West* 31 (3): 279–96. (Looks at Watsuji's ontology.)

Odin, S. (1992) 'The Social Self in Japanese Philosophy and American Pragmatism: A Comparative Study of Watsuji Tetsurō and G.H. Mead', *Philosophy East and West* 42 (3). (Cross-cultural study of Watsuji and Mead.)

STEVE ODIN

WEAKNESS OF WILL

see AKRASIA

WEBER, MAX (1864–1920)

Max Weber, German economist, historian, sociologist, methodologist, and political thinker, is of philosophical significance for his attempted reconciliation of historical relativism with the possibility of a causal social science; his notion of a verstehende *(understanding) sociology; his formulation, use and epistemic account of the concept of 'ideal types'; his views on the rational irreconcilability of ultimate value choices, and particularly his formulation of the implications for ethical political action of the conflict between ethics of conviction and ethics of responsibility; and his sociological account of the causes and uniqueness of the western rationalization of life.*

These topics are closely related: Weber argued that the explanatory interests of the historian and social scientist vary historically and that the objects of their interest were constituted in terms of cultural points of view, and that consequently their categories are ultimately rooted in evaluations, and hence subjective. But he also argued that social science cannot dispense with causality, and that once the categories were chosen, judgments of causality were objective. The explanatory interests of the sociologist, as he defined sociology, were in understanding intentional action causally, but in terms of categories that were culturally significant, such as 'rational action'. Much of his influence flowed from his formulation of the cultural situation of the day, especially the idea that the fate of the time was to recognize that evaluations were inescapably subjective and that the world had no inherent 'meaning'. The existential implications of this novel situation for politics and learning were strikingly

formulated by him: science could not tell us how to live; politics was as a choice between warring Gods. Weber's scholarly work and his politics served as a model for Karl Jaspers, and a subject of criticism and analysis for other philosophers, such as Karl Löwith, Max Scheler, and the Frankfurt School.

1 Life
2 The methodological essays of 1903–07
3 The idea of an 'understanding' sociology
4 The conflict of values and world-view

1 Life

Weber was born in Erfurt in Thuringia 12 April 1864. His father was a businessman and prominent National Liberal politician, who served in the Prussian House of Deputies (1868–97) and the German Reichstag (1872–84). The Weber household was a meeting place for prominent academics and political figures. Weber began his university training in Heidelberg in 1882 and continued it in Berlin, Strasbourg and at Göttingen to 1886. He attended lectures on law and history, passing his bar exam in 1887. He received a Berlin doctorate in 1889 for a study of medieval trading companies: his habilitation, in 1891, was for a study of legal aspects of Roman agrarian history. While preparing for his habilitation, he participated in a study under the sponsorship of the Verein für Sozialpolitik (Social Policy Association) on the subject of agricultural labourers in the East Elbian estates. He began a legal career, but soon returned to academic life. From 1894 to 1897 he was a professor of Nationalökonomie at Freiburg; from there he was appointed to a similar position at Heidelberg. A mental breakdown in 1902 led him to relinquish his teaching duties, but he soon returned to an active role as an editor and producing scholar. His sociological works began to appear after the 1904–5 publication of *The Protestant Ethic and the Spirit of Capitalism* and included a series of works on the sociology of religion dealing primarily with the theme of the economic ethics of the world religions. It is controversial whether these works or his *Wirtschaft und Gesellschaft* (*Economy and Society*), posthumously published in 1922, represented the core of his thought.

His major 'methodological' essays (posthumously published as his *Gesammelte Aufsätze zur Wissenschaftslehre* (Collected Essays in Scientific Theory) in 1922) included part one of 'Roscher and Knies', published in 1903, '"Objectivity" in Social Science and Social Policy', in 1904, part two of 'Roscher and Knies' and 'Critical Studies in the Logic of the Cultural Sciences', in 1905 and 1906, and, in 1907,

'Critique of Stammler'. Among the other essays collected in the *Wissenschaftslehre* were 'The Meaning of "Ethical Neutrality"', published in 1918, which grew out of an earlier dispute with the Social Policy Association on the possibility of making policy without making value-choices that cannot be grounded scientifically, and a widely distributed speech, 'Science as a Calling', published in 1919. This and another speech, 'Politics as a Calling', given and published in 1919, were actively debated by the younger generation of intellectuals.

After the war Weber served as a member of the constitutional commission of the Weimar republic, became a professor of economics at Vienna in 1918 and Munich in 1919, and unsuccessfully pursued a career in politics. His early death came when his influence among intellectuals was at its peak. The 'Calling' speeches were an aggressive and telling formulation of a world-view that challenged the cultural and political optimism of the time, and remained in the Weimar era as a central reference in the long-running discussion of the 'Crisis of the Sciences'. Much of his work was published posthumously in editions that did not reflect his original intentions, but his 'methodological' writings were intended to be collected, and the collection largely follows his intentions. The major work published as *Economy and Society*, however, was unfinished, and his intentions for the texts that compose the extant edition were unclear.

Weber in his political writings and methodological writings rigorously separated factual and evaluative considerations, especially in connection with the consideration of policy means to political ends, in order to demonstrate the concealed and confused value premises of the teaching of the 'Socialists of the Chair' and the factual naïveté of 'ethical' political postures, and he promoted the idea that intellectual integrity demanded the making of explicit ultimate value choices. He believed that in a democratic age the only political leaders who could make free value choices and rise above mere interest-politics to greatness were those who had the charisma necessary to build a personal following, and he devoted his constitutional efforts to the task of creating means by which such leaders could rise.

2 The methodological essays of 1903–7

Weber's major methodological article, 'Objectivity in Social Science and Social Policy', published in 1904, brought together the key themes of his thinking as a methodologist of social science. Weber argued that the results of the cultural sciences could be valid in an objective sense, and that indeed, 'scientific truth is precisely what is *valid* for all who seek the *truth*' (1904–17: 84). Yet he also argued that the objects of explanation in social science are constituted by culture-specific and discipline-specific cognitive interests and consequently are historically relative and in this sense subjective (see EXPLANATION IN HISTORY AND SOCIAL SCIENCE; VALUE JUDGMENTS IN SOCIAL SCIENCE). He resolved the conflict between these two claims by a complex argument. The premises were epistemic: exhaustive description and hence explanation of concrete reality was impossible; all science is necessarily selective and concerned with a finite portion of reality. The natural sciences are, however, selective in a different way than the cultural sciences. The natural sciences select as important the segment that can be constructed as casual regularities, and take it to be the essence of reality. The cultural sciences, in contrast, begin with the finite segment that is significant to us as cultural beings with a specific culture, and then construct within this segment objects of explanation, which he called, following Heinrich Rickert, 'historical individuals' that are significant or meaningful to us as cultural beings. This enterprise is necessarily 'evaluative' in the sense that only as cultural beings do we regard these objects as significant, and culture is conditioned by valuative ideas. Accepting as our starting point this distinctive segment of reality has the effect of excluding the possibility of a social science that is based on principles like those of physics or chemistry operating at the level of an atomistic psychology, because a physics-like social science that reduced social life to elementary factors, if such a thing were indeed possible, would simply fail to apply to objects that are configured to be culturally significant to us, and would apply to a different or differently configured finite segment of reality.

One difficulty this line of argument poses arises over the question of whether causation itself is relative to our cultural starting point and interests, and is thus not a truth there for all who seek it? Weber's response to this question is elaborated in 'The Logic of the Cultural Sciences' (1904–17), in which he argues that historical explanation is logically equivalent to establishing legal responsibility, and applies a contemporary legal theory of probabilistic causation, the theory of 'objective possibility' and 'adequate cause', to the problem of the objectivity of causal explanation. Legal determinations of responsibility perforce employ categories that arise from a particular and distinctive interest, the juridical interest; the cultural scientist simply has different interests and different categories.

The criteria for 'adequate' causation in the theory is the existence of a significant difference between the probability of a given result if a particular set of conditions held (the background probability), and the probability of the result if these conditions absent the condition in question. If purely classificatory concepts could be employed and probabilities for the two cases empirically derived, these judgments would be 'empirical'. Thus the core of causal judgment in this theory is an objective fact. But there are two kinds of selection that are ordinarily involved in historical explanation that are not objective. Whether a difference in probabilities is significant, and hence whether a cause is 'adequate', depends on the set of conditions selected to provide the background probability. This choice cannot be made objectively, but must be made on the basis of the historian's interest. A second kind of selection occurs because 'historical individuals', the objects of the concepts of interest to historians, cannot be reduced to the sum of the ways they can be classified. So the historical analyst proceeds by constructing abstract ideal types and comparing them to other causal situations that are also known to be irreducible to the ways they can be classified. Judging the 'adequacy' of a historical causal relation is thus, in practice, largely abstract or conceptual, and unavoidably so.

Weber used these considerations to support the claim that explicitly constructed conceptual schemes were necessary in the cultural sciences, for example in economics. But he argued for a particular understanding of these constructions: as ideal types that diverged from empirical reality in its full richness. The constructed types of the cultural sciences resemble those of the natural sciences with respect to selectivity; they differ in the cognitive purposes they serve: the cultural scientist seeks conceptual clarity in relation to the particular intellectual aims of particular disciplines, each of which arises from practical purposes (see VALUE JUDGMENTS IN SOCIAL SCIENCE §§1–2). Weber also used this understanding of ideal-types critically, to argue against the taking of ideal type constructions for a deeper or essential reality. Crude Marxism, he thought, traded on this error, as did German theories of the state.

Weber's ideal types of legitimate rule (*Herrschaft*) were perhaps the most influential of his constructions. Weber distinguished between three kinds of belief in the legitimacy of orders or rulers: traditional, based on unwritten rules; rational-legal, based on written rules; and charismatic, where beliefs about the extraordinary character of a leader justified command. He showed how these beliefs were associated with particular kinds of social organization, and how particular kinds of belief, such as 'traditional' patrimonial beliefs were associated with orders that developed in history in particular ways. Charismatic

authority, which in its pure form is personal, is unstable and short-lived, though it can be combined with other forms to ground a routinized order, such as a monarchy, which retains some charismatic elements, such as the notion of royal blood. Rational-legal orders make belief in the legality of the order the basis of legitimacy. This form characteristically results in the bureaucratization of administration. Weber explicitly intended the concept of bureaucracy to be a timeless and value free ideal type rather than a historical teleological construct. But the vision of a world of men who are little cogs trying to become bigger cogs in the huge machinery of modern bureaucracies horrified him and represented the end of the practical possibility of an individual making a choice to devote his life to some higher self-chosen goal.

3 The idea of an 'understanding' sociology

Weber's essay on 'Some Categories of Interpretive Sociology' (1913) and his introduction to *Economy and Society* stipulated a definition of sociology as the science concerned with the interpretive understanding (*Verstehen*) of social action, that is, actions that take account of others, and the causal understanding of the course and consequences of actions (see SOCIAL ACTION). The intended meaning of an act for its agent is causally essential to an act. Accordingly, a sociological explanation of an action should be correct both on the level of cause and meaning. The understanding of meanings requires the application of type-concepts rather than empathy. Meanings are ascertained by comparing the course of action to an appropriate ideal type of a meaningful act, such as obedience to a command. Many of the causes bearing on social life, such as psychophysical or biological effects, are not intentional in character, and thus are not part of sociology as Weber defines it. 'Collective' concepts, such as the state, understood as real entities, are also excluded by Weber's definition, but the social phenomenon they refer to may be understood sociologically in terms of individual actions: the concepts are ideal-typifications of patterns of action that in turn result from the beliefs and expectations of individuals.

Subsequent commentators on Weber have made a great deal of his use of the notion of *Verstehen*, and have argued that a social science based on *Verstehen* or understanding must be radically unlike one based on any analogy to the natural sciences. The distinction between understanding and explanation was treated as a fundamental epistemological divide between two kinds of science. When Weber's works were imported to the Anglo-American world, especially during the 1930s, primarily to an audience of sociologists, this distinction was often stated as methodological distinction, and *Verstehen* was understood as a 'method'. Social phenomenologists, such as Alfred Schütz, attempted to provide a basis for an alternative social science in the problem of understanding and particularly in the problem of the attainment of 'adequacy' in the individual's understanding of another.

Weber's own statements about *Verstehen* are characteristically directed toward other issues. *Verstehen* entered primarily in connection with concepts used by the historical figure whose actions were being explained as well as by those employed by the historical interpreter. Since the historical interpreter often was part of a culture which employed different concepts, there is a positive task of interpreting the purposes and therefore the concepts of the agent whose actions are to be explained in terms of broader and more permanent categories of action or in terms of the concepts of the historian and his own historical audience.

The treatment of intention at the beginning of *Economy and Society* distinguishes between direct and indirect evidence of intention. This is a distinction borrowed from the law, and reflects Weber's utterly unmystical attitude to assessing an agent's purposes and motives. Weber specifically rejected appeals to historical intuition. His discussion of interpretation in the beginning of *Economy and Society* treats the attribution of motivation and intent as a practical necessity dictated by the task of the inquiry, which could ordinarily be done by examining the course of action and the information available to the agent. Assessing such things requires, to some extent, thinking through a problem from the point of view of the agent, but Weber stressed that one did not need to be Caesar in order to 'understand' Caesar, but rather to assimilate the acts of a Caesar to an already 'understood' model or ideal type of action. Models of perfect rational action are, in practice, a starting point for reconstructions of intentions in complex situations, such as the battlefield decisions of a general, for which there is no alternative.

4 The conflict of values and world-view

Weber's writings on the subject of values, value-orientations, and value conflicts were directed at specific topics, such as the ethics of advocacy in the classroom, but had a well-defined philosophical core. Weber held that there were rational grounds for the selection of means to ends, and for assessing the consistency of sets of choices of ends, but that ultimate value choices could not be rationally

justified. He also held that hidden conflicts became apparent when means and the subsidiary consequences of the use of the means to obtain given ends were considered, and that such conflicts were common.

In the sphere of politics, Weber argued, the decisive means is violence, and this inevitably produces conflicts of a particular kind. Consider the political leader who is an adherent to what Weber calls an 'ethic of uncompromising conviction' with respect to truth-telling in politics, that is, who upholds the value of truth-telling come what may. A foreseeable subsidiary effect of an instance of truth-telling might be to unleash uncontrollable passions. Weber argues that the only way an ethic of uncompromising conviction may be consistently upheld in the political sphere would be for its adherents to disclaim responsibility for such results of their actions, as do religious ethics which counsel their followers to 'do rightly and leave the results with God'. Weber contrasted such ethics with what he called 'ethics of responsibility', which hold their adherents to responsibility for the foreseeable consequences, both good and evil, of their actions. He rejected political moralists who obscured the tragic character of politics through wishful thinking, such as the belief that only good comes from good and only evil from evil.

Weber's characterization of the modern situation, and his explanation of it, are the subject of continuing controversies of interpretation. Weber posed the problem of explaining the distinctive 'rationality' of Western society, and particularly the dynamic process of continuing rationalization. The most famous portion of Weber's account of this process takes the form of an ideal-typical construction of the genetic development of the psychological effect of particular religious ideas. Weber argued that the Calvinist doctrine of predestination was a source of deep anxiety to believers, who sought signs that they were among the elect. He argued that the pastoral practice of responding to this anxiety through the idea that diligence in the pursuit of worldly callings and the living of a self-disciplined life were signs of election, channelled this psychological force in a direction that produced a new type of person. The presence of this new type – rationalistic, individualistic, self-examining, conscience-driven, and work-sanctifying – facilitated the process by which capitalist economic conduct and the rational organization of work displaced traditional modes of economic conduct. In the later stages of this development, however, the routines of capitalistic rationalization become inescapable, and these routines undermined religious belief. In response, religion became more 'other-worldly', and culture became the increasingly senseless pursuit of mutually antagonistic self-chosen ends in a world that had itself become 'disenchanted' or 'meaningless'.

Weber's Protestant ethic essay could be construed as an alternative to the Marxian account of the rise of capitalism. The idea that religious ideas were an extra-economic cause of economic development is in conflict with Marx's *Überbau* or superstructure theory of ideology. Weber greatly expanded on his insight that different religious traditions create characteristically different 'economic ethics' or modes of thinking morally about the economic world. Most of these modes precluded the development from within the society of modern capitalism of the Western kind, which Weber took to be based on the rational organization of labour. But Weber did not address Marx's history of capitalism directly until his late lectures on economic history, in which he provided an overall account of the history of capitalism that incorporates the few elements of Marx's account of the development of factory production that Weber accepted. The differences in their views of this topic are characteristic: where Marx saw the organization of work into factories simply as a means of increasing exploitation, Weber argued that production was itself rationalized, and that factory work required the new type of worker that the rationalizing discipline of Protestantism was producing.

In the Weimar era, during which Marx was taken more seriously as a thinker, interpreters such as Karl Löwith, compared the two more systematically. Weber came to be regarded as the bourgeois alternative to Marx, and former members of Weber's circle, such as Georg Lukács and Karl Jaspers, also construed Weber in this way, each for their own purposes. Jaspers made Weber into a heroic figure whose radical liberal leadership Germany had tragically failed to accept. In a work by Lukács designed to discern and root out the sources of his own ideological deviations from Communist orthodoxy, Weber was classed as a powerful exponent of irrationalism, to which dialectical materialism was the alternative. Weber later became both subject and hidden interlocutor for the critical theorists of the Frankfurt School, and as they and their successors became concerned with the problem of modernity, Weber came to be regarded as a major theorist of modernity (see FRANKFURT SCHOOL).

List of works

Weber, M. (1903–5) *Roscher und Knies: The Logical Problems of Historical Economics*, trans. G. Oakes, New York: Free Press, 1975. (Contains a useful introductory essay by G. Oakes.)

—— (1904–5) *The Protestant Ethic and the Spirit of Capitalism*, trans. and ed. T. Parsons, New York: Charles Scribner's Sons, 1958. (Presents Weber's account of the role of the Protestant theology of salvation in producing the rationalistic individuals who could bring about the capitalistic rationalization of labour.)

—— (1904–17) *The Methodology of the Social Sciences*, trans. and eds E.A. Shils and H.A. Finch, New York: Free Press, 1949. (Includes Weber's three most important methodological essays, two of which focus on causality.)

—— (1907) *Critique of Stammler*, trans. and ed. G. Oakes, New York: Free Press, 1977. (Contains a valuable introductory essay by G. Oakes.)

—— (1913) 'Some Categories of Interpretive Sociology', trans. E. Graber, *The Sociological Quarterly* 22: 151–80, 1981. (Formulates an individualist analysis of collective social phenomenon within the framework of an account of action explanation.)

—— (1916a) *The Religion of China: Confucianism and Taoism*, trans. and ed. H.H. Gerth, Glencoe, IL: Free Press, 1951. (Companion study to the *Protestant Ethic* and part of a larger project on the economic ethics of the world religions; deals with Chinese religion and capitalism, and especially with the inhibitory effects on capitalism of Confucianism.)

—— (1916b) *The Religion of India: The Sociology of Hinduism and Buddhism*, trans. and ed. H.H. Gerth and D. Martindale, Glencoe, IL: Free Press, 1958. (Similar study of Indian religion as part of same project as 1916a.)

—— (1917–18) *Ancient Judaism*, trans. and ed. H.H. Gerth and D. Martindale, Glencoe, IL: Free Press, 1952. (Part of same 1916a project, but important for other themes, such as the role of the prophets in rationalizing theodicy.)

—— (1922a) *Wirtschaft und Gesellschaft (Economy and Society)*, trans. G. Roth and C. Wittich, Berkeley, CA: University of California Press, 1978. (Detailed examination of the basic concepts of social sciences and economics, as applied to history.)

—— (1922b) *Gesammelte Aufsätze zur Wissenschaftslehre* (Collected Essays in Scientific Theory), Tübingen: Mohr, expanded edn, 1951. (This text is a collection of essays, most of which have been translated into English, but not in one place. Many of the other works cited in this entry contain parts of this text, some include other texts as well.)

—— (1923) *General Economic History*, trans. F.H. Knight, Glencoe, IL: Free Press, 1950. (Posthumously published lecture notes providing a summary of Weber's account of the origin and history of capitalism from the ancient world to modern Europe.)

—— (1984–) *Max Weber – Gesamtausgabe*, H. Baier, M.R. Lepsius, W.J. Mommsen, W. Schluchter and J. Winckelmann (eds), Tübingen: J.C.B. Mohr (Paul Siebeck). (Weber's works, presently being published in a full scholarly edition.)

—— (1994) *Weber: Political Writings*, P. Lassman and R. Speirs (eds), Cambridge: Cambridge University Press. (Includes major political writings, most of which apply themes of his scientific writing.)

References and further reading

Bruun, H.H. (1972) *Science, Values and Politics in Max Weber's Methodology*, Copenhagen: Munksgaard. (A comprehensive discussion of Weber's use of ethical terms.)

Gerth, H.H. and Mills, C.W. (1946) *From Max Weber: Essays in Sociology*, New York: Oxford University Press. (The standard translation of Weber's major essays.)

Mommsen, W. (1959) *Max Weber und die deutsche Politik, 1890–1920* (*Max Weber and German Politics, 1890–1920*), trans. M.S. Steinberg, Chicago, IL: University of Chicago Press, 1984. (Historical overview of Weber's political activities and writings.)

Oakes, G. (1988) *Weber and Rickert: Concept Formation in the Cultural Sciences*, Cambridge, MA: MIT Press. (An analysis of the relation between the Neo-Kantianism of Rickert and Weber.)

Turner, S.P. (1986) *The Search for a Methodology of Social Science: Durkheim, Weber and the Nineteenth Century Problem of Cause, Probability, and Action*, Dordrecht: Reidel. (Contains an explication of Weber's concept of probabilistic causality and its epistemic presuppositions.)

Wegener, W. (1962) *Die Quellen der Wissenschaftsauffassung. Max Weber und die Problematik der Werturteilsfreiheit der Nationalökonomie: ein wissenschaftssoziologischer Beitrag* (The Sources of Scientific Views. The Set of Problems Relating to Freeing the National Economy from Value Judgments: a Sociological Contribution), Berlin: Duncker & Humblot. (Contends, following a long tradition of German criticism, that Weber's social science is reflexively inconsistent.)

STEPHEN P. TURNER
REGIS A. FACTOR

WEIL, SIMONE (1909–43)

Simone Weil's life and work represent an unusual mixture of political activism, religious mysticism and intense speculative work on a wide range of topics, including epistemology, ethics and social theory. Much of her most important writing survives in fragmentary form, in notebooks published after her untimely death. Though Jewish by family, her attitude to Judaism was largely hostile; and despite a deep commitment in the later part of her life to Christian ideas and symbols, she consistently refused to be baptized. Her religious views are eclectic in many ways, drawing on Plato and on Hindu sources. In everything she wrote, she was preoccupied with the dehumanizing effects of economic unfreedom and the servile labour required by industrial capitalism; but this is only one instance, for her, of the experience of 'necessity' or 'gravity' that dominates material transactions. The essence of moral and spiritual action is the complete renunciation of any privileged position for an ego outside the world of 'necessity'. Such renunciation is the only escape from necessity, in fact: what she calls 'decreation' becomes our supremely creative act, since only in the ego's absence is love, or an apprehension of non-self-oriented goods, possible. Marx, Kant and the gospels are all in evidence here.

1   **Being in the world**
2   **Decreation and grace**
3   **Violence and justice**

1   Being in the world

Born in Paris in 1909, Weil studied at the Lycée Henri IV and the École Normale Supérieure. Her career as a schoolteacher was interrupted by a year of manual work in a factory and a brief and disastrous spell as a volunteer in the Spanish Civil War. Ill-health obliged her to resign from full-time work, and, after living with her parents for a time (and working on the land in Southern France after the German occupation), she joined them in emigrating to New York in 1942. By the end of that year, however, she was in London, working for the Free French. Overwork, a lung infection and the refusal to eat more than the current level of rationing in France led to a collapse in the spring of 1943. In hospital, she refused food and resisted medical help, and, because of this, her death in August 1943 was recorded as suicide. Some of the most significant of her notebooks are from the period in the South of France (1940–2) and the months in New York and London: they show very clearly the effects upon her thinking of a profound experience of religious conversion in 1938, but continue to develop themes that she had begun to explore almost a decade earlier.

Her earliest published work, from her time at the École Normale, was much influenced by her lycée teacher Alain (Émile Chartier), an eccentric and charismatic thinker who stressed the radical freedom of the will and the intimate connection of will and intelligence: mental action is an indivisible whole, a moral self-location in response to the experience of the body's life in the world. Weil's early work applies this perspective to the question of labour: work is the antithesis to the immediacy of thought, because it demands that we engage in actions we do not want to perform in order to realize the goal we *do* want. Such actions have no intrinsic relation to the mind's movement towards its goal; but the pure freedom of thought and will has to be activated in the concrete world by mediation and indirectness. Work is thus a paradigm of all she would later designate as necessity – that which imposes itself on mind. Yet without the primitive mental act meeting frustration in this way, there would be no *conceptuality* of the world as extended in time and space, no way of talking about objects or about duration (what intervenes between desire and realization).

We form concepts as we form 'strategies' for getting what we want. Our concepts are neither Platonic givens nor abstractions from sensation, but more like compact sets of instructions for negotiating obstacles. They are – as Weil's early *Lectures on Philosophy* put it – the product of 'a sort of dance', the body learning its way around in a world where realization is not contemporary with desire. And what we call 'reality' is thus neither purely given nor self-constructed but, as she says in a late fragment, 'a certain relationship to what is given'. This relationship is charged with ambiguity. At the simplest level, the body learns to interpret situations in a way that is more or less instantaneous: it 'reads' what has to be done (as promptly as we interpret marks on paper as words). But reading becomes more complex as we reflect on it, and the imagination intrudes – a faculty which for Weil is always morally shady. Imagination pulls apart the direct relationship of embodied thought to the surrounding obstacles, denying the character of these obstacles, seeking to avoid the suffering of real work, offering *ersatz* gratifications for our desires. This is specially acute in our relations to other subjects: slavery is the imposition of my (imaginative) reading of another person upon their reality (their actual relation to me). So being in the world as a moral subject, wanting the truth, wanting to live in appropriate relation to the given, requires a fierce assault on the imagination, so that we may be returned to a direct confrontation with necessity.

2 Decreation and grace

There are two implications to this programme. First, all our *specific* goals or desires are likely to be flawed, because they invite us to form images of what we want, and so to evade necessity. Second, the root of corruption in our seeing and acting is the desire not to lose control, the longing to pretend that the immediacy of thought can be translated into our negotiations with what is given. The moral and spiritual task is to purify our desire by the rigorous renunciation of the ego, its position, its 'rights', its account of its individual wants. Pure desire is absolute consent to what is given, a submission to the otherness of the world that abandons any claim to a place, over against the world, from which I can manipulate the given. In the most radical expressions of this in the late notebooks, Weil will speak of the need for the 'I' to disappear: 'To say "I" is to lie', to defend an illusory self against necessity. The residual Cartesian and Kantian elements in her earlier thought are here subjected to their most ruthless purgation – though not without leaving strong traces. Here too her religious vision comes most clearly in view. The total acceptance of the given, the 'desire' for reality, *is* the desire for God, the only proper object of desire, since God is no particular thing. The Christian narrative shows us a God who wills the universe into being, a universe that is devoid of God, in the sense that God is not identical with any object or state of affairs in it. Thus God's supreme liberty is expressed in creation as consent to an order of God-less necessity. Creation is divine renunciation; and the further narrative of the incarnation shows God becoming present in the Godless world in the only way possible – as a person without power or rights, becoming finally a dead body on the cross and a passive, mute object in the bread of the Mass. The Christian God is thus absent from the world but also, consequently, 'present' in the very character of the world as God-forsaken.

To accept the world is to love God. But the introduction of God into the discourse here has its paradoxical side. While we can deploy the theological narrative of creation and incarnation, we have no possibility of constructing a religious metaphysic in the usual sense. As soon as we conceptualize and represent God and an existing reality over against us, we lose sight of the 'real' God; and, on the basis of what is said elsewhere about reality, we should conclude that the reality of God is a particular relation between the self and what is given *in its entirety*. Weil's kinship is with the tradition, inside and outside Christianity, of regarding with suspicion any suggestion that God is a kind of object among other possible objects of experience. She is not straightforwardly aligned with those radical theologians who deny the extra-mental reality of God.

When the ego is displaced in this complete acceptance, what follows is 'grace' or 'the supernatural', a relation to persons and things devoid of private interest and desire. Only this can properly be called love. The connection between such love and any particular person or object is complex, and Weil's interpreters are not at one in analysing it. On the one hand, the sheer otherness of the world in its concrete variety is precisely what resists and checks my ego; and I begin to learn something of grace by submission to this concrete otherness, by what Weil calls 'attention'. One of her most deservedly famous essays ('Reflections on the Right Use of School Studies with a View to the Love of God', written in 1942 and published in *Attente de Dieu* (1950a)) elaborates the spiritual significance of intellectual discipline. But, on the other hand, love is not properly bestowed on any individual object in its historicity, because this would be to make it serve transient needs or projections of the ego. Only what is timeless can be loved without corruption. There is no easy resolution of this tension, which points up central difficulties in Weil's conception of the self: the self's material and historical identity is both axiomatic and the source of 'infinite error'.

3 Violence and justice

This creates some problems in her social thinking. Much of what she writes suggests that social life and cooperative labour is always 'primitively' a common sacrifice of individual desires before the given imperatives of collaboration. The struggle for social dominance is the struggle for the position of least sacrifice. She writes with great eloquence about the distortions of awareness produced by the exercise of force, both in the powerful and the powerless, and she is deeply sceptical about prevailing models of political legitimacy, resting as they do upon uneasy truces between different centres of power and interest. In her very substantial late (and unfinished) essay *L'enracinement* (1949) (The Need for Roots (1952)), designed in part as a vision for post-war France, she pleads for a society in which the impersonal instrumentalism of labour in a capitalist economy is replaced by work that can more readily be grasped as direct confrontation with necessity. This implies a radical dismantling of international capitalist structures, including colonialism, and a reorientation towards local (regional rather than national) sociopolitical units. It also means the dismantling of 'modern' political structures, such as political parties and trade unions, since

these take for granted the 'violence' of competitive interests. Justice will emerge not from bargaining but from the common reality of encounter with necessity; and this spiritual anchor for justice will be nourished by the corporate appropriation of a local past, a specific and harmonious culture. Weil did not shrink from the further implication that there could be no long-term future in such a society for religious or cultural minorities: they would be gently but firmly educated out of existence. Nothing could more clearly underline her own passionate rejection of her Jewishness, her own 'roots'. It is a final, and revealing, paradox in an *oeuvre* full of contradictions, yet so often profound in its critiques of modernity, of moral illusion and of cheap religious consolation. Only gradually has she come to attract serious philosophical study, rather than either mere abuse or hagiography; but she deserves just the unsparing 'attention' she herself so forcefully commends.

List of works

Weil, S. (1988–) *Oeuvres complètes*, Paris: Gallimard. (The collected works.)

—— (1947) *La Pesanteur et la grace*, Paris: Plon; trans. E. Crauford, *Gravity and Grace*, London: Routledge, 1952. (Selected aphorisms from the *Cahiers*, often, regrettably, quoted or discussed without reference to their context in these notebooks.)

—— (1949) *L'enracinement*, Paris: Gallimard; trans. A. Wills with a preface by T.S. Eliot, *The Need for Roots*, London: Routledge, 1952. (Written in 1943, shortly before her death, this was intended both as an examination of the causes of alienation (especially among workers) in modern society and also as a blueprint for a post-war future in which individuals might enjoy a fruitful, rooted relation with society as a whole.)

—— (1950a) *Attente de Dieu*, Paris: La Colombe; trans. E. Crauford, *Waiting on God*, London: Routledge, 1951. (A collection of essays and meditations, largely but not exclusively religious. It has been the most widely read introduction to Weil's thought.)

—— (1950b) *La Connaissance surnaturelle*, Paris: Gallimard. (Contains Weil's *Notebooks* written in New York in 1942.)

—— (1951a) *La Condition Ouvrière*, Paris: Gallimard. (A painstaking diary of the time she spent labouring in factories (Alsthom and Renault) in 1934–5, with a series of texts reflecting on the experience in political and moral terms.)

—— (1951b) *Intuitions pré-chrétiennes*, Paris: La

Colombe. (Material in Greek philosophy and its relation to Christianity.)

—— (1951c) *Lettre à un religieux*, Paris: Gallimard; trans. A. Wills, *Letter to a Priest*, London: Routledge, 1953. (A long letter addressed to a Dominican, le Pére Couturier, outlining her doubts about, and spiritual affinities with, Catholicism. Written in the autumn of 1942, ten months before her death.)

—— (1951d) *Cahiers*, Paris: Plon; trans. A. Wills, *The Notebooks of Simone Weil*, London: Routledge, 1956; also trans. R. Rees, *First and Last Notebooks*, London: Oxford University Press, 1970. (Fundamental for her developed religious metaphysics, though often very difficult for the interpreter.)

—— (1953) *La source grecque*, Paris: Gallimard. (Essays on Greek literature, also on Plato.)

—— (1955) *Oppression et liberté*, Paris: Gallimard; trans. A. Wills and J. Petrie, *Oppression and Liberty*, London: Routledge, 1958. (Contains the essay 'Reflections Concerning the Causes of Liberty and Social Oppression'. This considers the manner in which our social development has put limitations upon, rather than enhancing, human liberty.)

—— (1957) *Intimations of Christianity among the Ancient Greeks*, chapters from 1951b and 1953, trans. E. Geissbuhler, London: Routledge. (Finished reviews, and the texts of talks given in the Dominican Monastery at Marseilles. Discusses Greek philosophy as a harbinger of the Christian message.)

—— (1959) *Leçons de philosophie, Roanne 1933–4*, Paris: Plon; trans. H. Price with an introduction by R. Rees, *Lectures on Philosophy*, Cambridge: Cambridge University Press, 1978. (Provides insights into her earliest philosophical positions.)

—— (1962) *Selected Essays: 1934–1943*, trans. R. Rees, Oxford: Clarendon Press. (Mostly political essays.)

—— (1966) *Sur la Science*, Paris: Gallimard. (Early work on Descartes, and later essays on science.)

—— (1970) *Science, Necessity, and the Love of God*, trans. R. Rees, London: Oxford University Press. (Essays on science and on Plato, from the 1953 work.)

Further reading

There are several other collections and anthologies; see Bell (1993), for a good list.

Bell, R.H. (ed.) (1993) *Simone Weil's Philosophy of Culture: Readings Toward a Divine Humanity*, Cambridge: Cambridge University Press. (Essays on a wide range of aspects of Weil's thought.)

Cabaud, J. (1965) *Simone Weil: A Fellowship in Love*, New York: Harvill. (A fundamental survey of life and work together.)

McLellan, D. (1989) *Simone Weil: Utopian Pessimist*, London: Macmillan. (Oriented towards Weil's social thought.)

Petrement, S. (1976) *Simone Weil, A Life*, trans. R. Rosenthal, New York: Pantheon, and London/ Oxford: Mowbray. (The most comprehensive biography, by a former fellow student of Weil's.)

Vetö, M. (1994) *The Religious Metaphysics of Simone Weil*, Albany, NY: State University of New York Press.

Winch, P. (1989) *Simone Weil: 'The Just Balance'*, Cambridge: Cambridge University Press. (Incomparably the best philosophical study, drawing out parallels with Wittgenstein.)

R. WILLIAMS

WEINBERGER, OTA (1919–)

Weinberger is noted as a proponent of 'institutionalist positivism' in legal theory. By contrast with earlier forms of so-called 'institutionalism' in law, Weinberger advances a theory in which norms are ideal entities linked by logical relations inter se, while being at the same time social realities identifiable in terms of the effect they exercise in guiding human social behaviour. The institutions which make possible this duality of ideal entity and social reality have themselves to be understood as structured by norms. Hence, in contrast with earlier proponents of institutionalism, who denied the foundation of law in norms, Weinberger is normativist in his approach; and for the metaphysical vitalism of precursors, he substitutes a social realism.

Born in Brno, Czechoslovakia, Weinberger trained in law and philosophy in Brno under František WEYR in the 'Brno School' of the 'Pure Theory of Law' (see KELSEN, H.), developing an early interest in the logic of norms. Imprisoned in a wartime concentration camp, he was able to resume his career as a scholar after 1945 in the difficult circumstances of post-war Czechoslovakia. During the 'Prague Spring' of 1968, he was able to leave for Austria, where he became Professor in Philosophy of Law in Graz, continuing actively as professor emeritus after retirement in 1988.

While rejecting ethical cognitivism, and with it natural law, Weinberger sees his position as promising some *rapprochement* between positivism and natural law theory (see LEGAL POSITIVISM §5; NATURAL LAW §1). For he acknowledges that concerns with justice are inherent in attitudes to law. He also fully acknowledges a place for reason – for rational analysis – in practical matters, but denies that reason ever finally determines the right, this being dependent on a taking-up of practical attitudes in a non-rational or pre-rational way. Reason and justice have a critical role to play in reflection upon action. But justice is never itself a primary motive to action; rather, it sets critical constraints on conduct whose motivation is fundamentally utilitarian (see JUSTICE, EQUITY AND LAW).

Weinberger's early work was in spheres of logic which eluded even a stringent communist censorship, and already in his pre-Graz period he made significant contributions to the study of norm-logic, a field still in its infancy. He sees two spheres for this, one concerning the logical relations of established norms, the other concerning their establishment, in particular the question what logical account can be given of the way in which a power-exercising act under a norm of competence is to be understood as validly establishing a lower-order norm (see NORMS, LEGAL). In parallel to his differentiation of justice and utility, he has distinguished the logic of action from norm-logic, producing what he calls a 'formal-finalistic' or 'formal-teleological' theory of action, in which action is seen as activity guided by a processing of information. In this context, he insists upon the ultimate non-derivability of practical from theoretical information. This is his version of the non-derivability of 'ought' from 'is'. He rejects John Searle's purported derivation, reflection on which contributed greatly to development of his own conception of institutions such as promising or law-making.

See also: INSTITUTIONALISM IN LAW; LAW, PHILOSOPHY OF

List of works

Weinberger, O. with MacCormick, N. (1986) *An Institutional Theory of Law*, Dordrecht: Reidel. (A collection of essays by two authors, with a joint introductory essay, explaining the development and implications of an 'institutionalist' theory of law, and its relationship to legal positivism.)

Weinberger, O. (1991) *Law, Institution, and Legal Politics*, Dordrecht: Kluwer. (A selection of the author's most definitive papers on fundamental problems of legal theory and social philosophy, including also important essays on the logic of norms and the theory of action.)

References and further reading

Koller, P. *et al.* (1994) *Institution und Recht: Grazer Internationales Symposion zu Ehren von Ota Weinberger* (Institution and Law: an International Symposium at Graz in Honour of Ota Weinberger), Berlin: Duncker und Humblot. (This volume, which appears as Beiheft 14 of the journal *Rechtstheorie*, contains a series of tributes to and arguments with Ota Weinberger by a significant group of colleagues and friendly critics; it also contains a complete bibliography of Weinberger's vast output of writings in languages other than in English, and of the smaller body of his work, including journal articles, published in English.)

NEIL MacCORMICK

WELFARE

Notions of welfare occur widely in political philosophy and political argument. For example, utilitarianism is a social ethic that may be interpreted as giving a pre-eminent place to the idea that the welfare of society should be the overriding goal of public policy. Discussion of the ethics of redistribution focuses upon the institutions and practices of the so-called welfare state. Even those not convinced that we can validly speak of animal rights will often accept that considerations of animal welfare should play a part in legislation and morals. Moreover, the concept of welfare is clearly related to, and indeed overlaps with, concepts like 'needs' or 'interests', which are also central to public decision making and action.

Welfare can be thought of in three ways. Firstly, there is a subjective sense, in which to say that something contributes to a person's welfare is to say that it makes for the satisfaction of a preference. However, people can adapt their preferences to their circumstances, and happy slaves might be better off changing their preferences than having them satisfied. This thought leads on to the second sense of welfare as doing well according to some objective measure, like the possession of property. However, this conception can ignore subjective differences between people and fail to account for their capacity to take advantage of their objective circumstances. Hence, a third conception of welfare would make the capacity to take advantage of one's possessions an essential element of welfare. A satisfactory overall conception will have to bring these ideas together.

1   Welfare as preference
2   Objective accounts of welfare

1 Welfare as preference

A common, perhaps the predominant modern, approach to the idea of welfare is to see it as the satisfaction of individual preferences or wants. This idea derives from the Benthamite felicific calculus (Bentham 1789) as mediated through modern welfare economics and the idea of consumers' utility. In this conception, persons are regarded as having preferences over various commodities (apples versus oranges) or states of the world (a world with or without the whale), and peoples' welfare, or utility, depends upon the extent to which their most highly ranked preferences are satisfied.

The notion of preference in this conception hangs uneasily between the notion of wanting and that of choice. Preferring commodity A to commodity B can seem to be like wanting or desiring to possess A rather than B, where the want is either a mental event or a disposition. On the other hand, some accounts of preference identify the notion simply with choice, asserting that all that is involved in preferring commodity A to commodity B is that one would choose to have A rather than B, without any assumptions being made that a choice reflected any inner feelings.

Whichever of these two views of preference is chosen, the main thrust of the preference-based conception of welfare is that the welfare of a person is to be judged from their point of view. This conception is particularly suited to those political theories that stress the diversity of individuals and societies, thereby implying that it is impossible to construct generalizations of what makes life go well for people.

Despite its appeal, the preference-based conception of welfare has difficulties. Some have urged that there must be limits on the desires or wants that we can sensibly ascribe to individuals, so that we should simply find unintelligible, not just unusual, someone who said that they wanted, say, a saucer of mud, without specifying any recognizable purpose for it. From this point of view the subjectivism implicit in the preference-based conception of welfare would be bounded by an understanding of desires that it would be intelligible to ascribe to individuals.

However, even within these limits, there are problems with treating welfare as preference. Slaves and harassed tenants may find that they adapt their preferences to their lot, coming to believe that it is in the nature of things. But if, after a while, such persons find that they prefer secure bondage to previously yearned for freedom, has their welfare increased? In terms of the preference-based account it has, but to many this has seemed counterintuitive. Limiting one's wants in this way seems instead to be the model of a frustrated life.

For these sorts of reasons theorists who favour a preference approach have sought to modify its simple form to take into account not raw preferences but informed ones. If the previously resigned come to see that things could be other than they are, then their preferences may change. Taken to the limit, the thought is that it is only the preferences that persons have in the full knowledge of their circumstances and the possibilities open to them that could form the basis for a judgement about their welfare. If I know all there is to know about a commodity or a state of the world and I still choose it in preference to something else, then we might want to say that I have thereby established what makes for my welfare.

One advantage of this approach is that it seems to offer a coherent analysis of the idea of human dignity. For example, when J.S. MILL (§9) argues that it is better to be Socrates dissatisfied than a fool satisfied, because the fool knows only one side of the story but the dissatisfied knows both, he is implicitly appealing to a hypothetical choice or preference criterion, in order to make the idea of welfare consistent with some idea of human dignity.

Despite the appeal of the account, it raises a number of questions. To say that someone currently prefers A to B, in their present state of knowledge, but would prefer B to A if they were fully informed invites the question of how we might know what the hypothetical preference was. In the absence of any theory about how people choose, it is impossible to say. Moreover, if there were such a theory and if it were based on accounts of how in fact the bulk of persons do choose, it looks as though the account is merely slipping into an objectivist account of welfare reflecting views about human nature and what makes things go well for people in general (see NEEDS AND INTERESTS).

A final difficulty with the preference-based account, in either its raw or informed preference view, is the difficulty of making interpersonal comparisons of welfare. The problem here is that interpersonal comparisons seem plausible (we think we know that the prince is better off than the pauper), but it is difficult to see how such judgements could be intellectually justified (see ECONOMICS AND ETHICS; UTILITARIANISM).

Within the preference-based account these difficulties appear to be insurmountable. If the welfare of persons is simply constituted by their preferences over alternatives, what evidence could be employed to make comparisons? Ingenious attempts have been made to employ the idea of extended sympathy in this context, in which a judgement of interpersonal comparisons is made by someone saying that they would rather be person A, with all that A has, than person B, with all that B has, but it has been pointed out that this merely shows that people think they can say what they find attractive or otherwise in the position of others, not what is comparatively of value in the position of others.

2 Objective accounts of welfare

Objective accounts of welfare appeal to the thought that there are features of the circumstances, position or characteristics of persons that enable us to judge how well off they are.

There are in principle two forms of objective account of welfare; the criterial and the indexical. Criterial accounts state that welfare is made up of those things that are necessary to achieve some end state or goal, such as human flourishing or agency. To enjoy a certain level of welfare, on such accounts, is simply to be in possession of just those goods that make the achievement of the goal or end state possible. Special mention should be made in this context of Rawls' notion of 'primary goods' (Rawls 1971) (see RAWLS, J. §1). These are defined as those things it would be rational to want if one were to want anything at all. Although this seems like a subjectivist notion, it is more plausibly construed as objectivist, since the wanting is grounded in external reasons, and the criterion is normally interpreted by appeal to standard empirical evidence about what is necessary to lead a life in society.

Indexical accounts simply list goods thought to be components of welfare, such as health, possessions and good fortune. In practice these two distinct logical conceptions, the criterial and the indexical, turn out to have similar implications, since the criterion of welfare will typically end in a list of some sort. Thus, Rawls' primary goods are listed as income and wealth, opportunities and powers and the bases of self-respect, and subsequent commentators (for example, Pogge (1989)) simply cash them out as familiar lists of rights.

One appeal of the objective approach is that it seems consistent with much that is ordinarily said and thought about welfare. It seems to make sense to say that we are well off when our health is good, our careers go well, our possessions and prospects are secure, our political and civil rights protected and our personal relationships flourishing. Moreover, such an objective approach would solve the problems associated with the interpersonal comparison of welfare.

Although it might be difficult to combine the various dimensions of wellbeing into a single index, we could at least measure how well things were going for people by reference to such criteria as have been listed. Indeed, there is a branch of social science – the construction of social indicators – that is devoted to measuring the welfare of people in society by reference to such criteria.

At this point the subjectivist will object and say that just as possessions do not make for happiness, so doing well on some objective list does not make for welfare. There are a number of reasons why this might be so. Certain spiritual aspirations may mean that people have to forgo their possessions in order to discover their soul, and Brentano is said to have treated the blindness of his old age as a blessing because it meant that he concentrated on his philosophy. Moreover, how in the absence of an appeal to subjective assessment do we evaluate conflicts among goods on the list? For example, certain risky occupations involve a trade-off between income and the chance of accidents leading to ill health. How people balance the conflict between income and additional health risks seems properly a matter for their own judgement, for which the most obvious rationalization is the thought that the assessment of welfare must be done from the point of view of the person experiencing it.

Yet these anti-objectivist arguments are not without problems. Cases of giving up one's possessions to save one's soul or the example of Brentano's blindness, although revealing, may be treated as special in the sense that they give extended meaning to a concept but do not affect its central application. The argument from the trade-off of benefits may be reinterpreted to yield objectivist conclusions, if we admit that it makes sense to have an external evaluation of the choices that people make. It seems entirely plausible to think that we can know in some cases that people make the wrong choice, from the point of view of their own welfare, between income and health, and we may also be critical of social arrangements that give the poor hard choices between earning a living and avoiding an unsafe working environment. All such judgements presuppose a certain objective conception of welfare.

The appeal to diversity does have a point, however. Suppose we observe a community of persons with roughly similar material circumstances and similar educational opportunities pursuing different occupations, different lifestyles and taking different attitudes to risk. Each person may enjoy quite distinct bundles of possessions and characteristics. Yet we may judge the members of the community to have similar levels of welfare, in the sense that each person has used similar resources to different effect according to their own conception of what is good for them. This line of argument might suggest that we can reconcile objective and subjective accounts of welfare provided we take into account the ability of people to use the resources at their disposal. This thought brings us to the third conception of welfare, namely that of welfare as capabilities.

3 Welfare as capabilities

Amartya Sen has argued that to treat welfare simply as a function of the commodities that people have is misleading, since it ignores the capacity or capability that people have to use those commodities to their own advantage (Nussbaum and Sen 1993). An obvious example would be the contrast between the physically handicapped and the able-bodied. The former may need more resources to bring them up to the same standard of living as the latter. The implication of this view is that we need to take into account the ability of people to use their objectively given level of resources to achieve welfare in their own terms.

Sen suggests that we need to base our conception of welfare on capabilities, rather than commodities, in order to do justice to this insight. However, it is doubtful if this implication can be drawn. Capabilities are difficult to measure directly, and the way in which the idea has in practice been developed is in terms of social indicators of the rather conventional objectivist sort. However, the value of the idea of capabilities is that we need to take into account this dimension of welfare if we are to make adequate interpersonal comparisons.

4 Conclusion

Can we extract a coherent conception of welfare from these competing views? If we accept that human diversity means that people will find their welfare in diverse combinations of goods, then there has to be an irreducibly subjective element to our concept of welfare. One way to avoid the problems with such an account is to modify our assessment of peoples' choices and preferences not in terms of a hypothetical choice that they would make, but in terms of our knowledge of preferences generally exhibited by persons in circumstances we understand. Moreover, we should further modify this assessment by a calculation of how far people are able to take advantage of the resources at their disposal, which is in large part an empirical matter.

If we take the notion of welfare to have both these subjective and these objective elements, allowing the subjective to operate within the limits of our understanding of what in general makes life go well for people, then we are faced with the problem of how broadly we are to construe the notion of welfare. In particular, is individual freedom or autonomy a component of welfare or a distinct characteristic of humans? There is probably only a conventional, rather than essentialist, answer to this question, but if it is sensible to ask how valuable it is for people to secure their autonomy, then it would seem to be more plausible to make freedom an element of welfare rather than distinct from it. As such, the concept of welfare will always remain central to questions of political philosophy.

See also: HAPPINESS

References and further reading

Arrow, K.J. (1963) *Social Choice and Individual Values*, New Haven, CT: Yale University Press, 2nd edn. (States the idea that interpersonal comparisons in the preference view of welfare might be based on extended sympathy.)

* Bentham, J. (1789) *An Introduction to the Principles of Morals and Legislation*, ed. J. Burns and H.L.A. Hart, London: Athlone Press, 1970. (The best statement of the traditional utilitarian view.)

Doyal, L. and Gough, I. (1991) *A Theory of Human Need*, Basingstoke: Macmillan. (Provides a good foundation for the understanding of social indicators and their philosophical significance.)

Griffin, J. (1986) *Well-being*, Oxford: Clarendon Press. (A clear statement of the informed desire view of welfare.)

Hargreaves Heap, S., Hollis, M., Lyons, B., Sugden, R. and Weale, A. (1992) *The Theory of Choice*, Oxford: Blackwell. (An introduction to economic theories of welfare.)

* Nussbaum, M. and Sen, A. (1993) *The Quality of Life*, Oxford: Clarendon Press. (Contains a set of essays exploring the view of welfare as capabilities, including a review essay by Sen.)

Parfit, D. (1984) *Reasons and Persons*, Oxford: Clarendon Press. (Has a valuable appendix on various theories of welfare.)

Plant, R. (1991) *Modern Political Thought*, Oxford: Blackwell. (Has a good discussion of various approaches to welfare, including their implications for social policy.)

* Pogge, T. (1989) *Realizing Rawls*, Ithaca, NY: Cornell University Press. (Elaborates the implications of Rawls' notion of primary goods.)

* Rawls, J. (1971) *A Theory of Justice*, Cambridge, MA:

Harvard University Press. (States the idea of primary goods.)

ALBERT WEALE

WESENSSCHAU (PERCEPTION OF ESSENCE)

see PHENOMENOLOGY, EPISTEMIC
ISSUES IN

WEYL, HERMANN (1885–1955)

A leading mathematician of the twentieth century, Weyl made fundamental contributions to theoretical physics, to philosophy of mathematics, and to philosophy of science. Weyl wrote authoritative works on the theory of relativity and quantum mechanics, as well as a classic philosophical examination of mathematics and science. He was briefly a follower of Brouwer's intuitionism in philosophy of mathematics. Upon moving closer to Hilbert's finitism, he articulated a conception of mathematics and physics as related species of 'symbolic construction'.

Hermann Weyl was born on 9 November, 1885 in Elmshorn, near Hamburg, Germany. He received his doctorate in mathematics under the direction of David Hilbert at Göttingen University in 1908. From 1913 until 1930, when he returned to Göttingen as Hilbert's successor, Weyl was Professor of mathematics at the Federal Institute of Technology in Zurich. As head of the world-renowned Mathematical Institute in Göttingen when the Nazi regime came to power in 1933, Weyl's unsuccessful attempts to protect his colleagues from arbitrary dismissal prompted him to accept, later that year and at Einstein's urging, an appointment as Professor at the newly formed Institute for Advanced Study in Princeton. The recipient of many prizes and awards for his mathematical work, including the Lobachevskii prize in 1925 for his geometrical research, Weyl was elected a contributing member of the Royal Society of London in 1936. Upon his retirement from the Institute in 1951, Weyl divided his time between Princeton and Zurich where he died of a heart attack on 9 December 1955.

A mathematician of extraordinary depth and breadth, Weyl worked in nearly all parts of mathematics: analysis, geometry, number theory, algebra and mathematical logic. He also continued the Göttingen tradition of Felix Klein and David Hilbert of carrying out mathematical investigations of fundamental questions in theoretical physics. In the decade 1917–27 he was at the height of his powers, producing a succession of contributions of the highest order to mathematics and to physics. In 1918 he published *Raum-Zeit-Materie*, the first self-contained treatment of Einstein's new general theory of relativity, which Einstein termed 'a masterful symphony'. Running through five editions by 1923, the work was no mere exposition but considerably illuminated the mathematical and philosophical foundations of the theory. For example, Weyl was first to show that there is a natural geometric but non-metrical expression ('manifold with an affine connection') for the combined gravitational–inertial field, underscoring that in general relativity gravitation is but counterpart to inertia.

Still in 1918, Weyl proposed a generalization of the Riemannian geometry underlying the Einstein theory which contained an additional metrical term formally analogous to the tensor expression for the electromagnetic field. As gravitation and electromagnetism were then the only known physical forces, Weyl's geometry appeared to account for all known physical phenomena in terms of the metric of spacetime. Though his theory did not survive the advent of quantum mechanics in 1925–6, Weyl's approach considerably influenced Einstein's first attempts at a unified field theory, and its central principle, 'local gauge [scale] invariance', now reinterpreted in the context of quantum theory, remains a leading principle of the physics of elementary particles. As an outcome of his research on group representations in 1925–6, which Weyl himself viewed as his greatest mathematical achievement, he pioneered investigation of the connections between group theory and the new quantum mechanics in 1927.

Despite his then deep involvement with the theory of relativity, Weyl also published in 1918 *Das Kontinuum*, a controversial monograph on the foundations of analysis. In agreement with the diagnosis of Poincaré and Russell that the root of the crisis in the foundations of mathematics concerned the freedom in unrestricted set theory to form 'impredicative' sets or classes, Weyl sketched out an iterative method of set formation (essentially a predicative set theory) in whose terms some, but not all, of classical analysis might be reconstructed. The remainder, Weyl proclaimed, would simply have to be jettisoned as illicit extensions of mathematical thinking. Thus would be surrendered such a fundamental theorem as that every bounded set of real numbers contains a unique least upper bound. At the time predisposed toward Husserlian phenomenology, by 1920 Weyl had abandoned his own attempts to resolve the crisis in foundations and joined the Dutch mathematician Brouwer in intuitionism. Weyl proved to be a wayward disciple. While endorsing the conception of the continuum as an *open* and not a *completed* totality, Weyl differed fundamentally from Brouwer in linking the grounding of analysis (for example, the concepts of real number and function) with its applications, especially in physics.

In the late 1920s, Weyl argued that the interconnected character of justification of individual mathematical assertions, as shown in Hilbert's finitism and paralleling the epistemological situation in physics where theories as a whole confront the evidence of experience, posed 'a decisive defeat for the program of pure phenomenology' in the foundations of mathematics. In later writings, Weyl emphasized the *essentially* symbolic character of mathematics and physics. As species of 'constructive cognition', both exhibit the freedom of mental operations to idealize from the given and to introduce symbols, which may then be freely manipulated according to certain rules. In this way symbols acquire a relative independence. Agreeing with idealism that scientific objectivity is not given but is constructed in symbols, Weyl nonetheless posited an unbridgeable chasm between the objective world of symbols and the ego, the 'light of consciousness'.

See also: GENERAL RELATIVITY, PHILOSOPHICAL RESPONSES TO; HILBERT'S PROGRAMME AND FORMALISM; INTUITIONISM; PHENOMENOLOGICAL MOVEMENT

List of works

Weyl, H. (1918a) *Raum-Zeit-Materie*, Berlin: Springer; 4th edn, 1921, trans. H. Brose, *Space-Time-Matter*, London: Methuen, 1922; repr. New York: Dover, 1952. (The third and later editions present Weyl's generalization of Reimannian geometry.)
—— (1918b) *Das Kontinuum; Kritische Untersuchungen ueber die Grundlagen der Analysis*, Leipzig: Veit; trans. S. Pollard and T. Bole, *The Continuum; A Critical Examination of the Foundation of Analysis*, Kirksville, MO: Thomas Jefferson University Press, 1987; repr. New York: Dover, 1994. (A controversial monograph on the foundations of analysis.)
—— (1927) *Philosophie der Mathematik und Naturwissenschaft*, Munich and Berlin: R. Oldenbourg; repr. *Philosophy of Mathematics and Natural Science*, Princeton, NJ: Princeton University Press, 1949. (The revised and augmented edition of 1949 was based on a translation by Olaf Helmer, and included material Weyl added in

English. Chapter II 'Methodology' contains an account of 'constructive cognition'.)
—— (1928) *Gruppentheorie und Quantenmechanik*, Leipzig: S. Hirzel; trans. H.P. Robertson, *The Theory of Groups and Quantum Mechanics*, London: Methuen, 1931; repr. New York: Dover, 1950. (The 1931 translation is based on the second, 1931, German edition. Explores the connection between group theoretic symmetry principles and fundamental relationships in quantum mechanics.)
—— (1952) *Symmetry*, Princeton, NJ: Princeton University Press. (Lectures on the role of symmetry in mathematics, science and the arts.)
—— (1968) *Gesammelte Abhandlungen*, ed. K. Chandrasekharan, Berlin, Heidelberg and New York: Springer, 4 vols. (The collected scientific papers, many also of philosophical interest.)

References and further reading

Chandrasekharan, K. (ed.) (1986) *Hermann Weyl 1885–1985*, Centenary Lectures at the Eidgenössische Technische Hochschule in Zurich, Berlin, Heidelberg, and New York: Springer. (Appreciations by C.N. Yang, R. Penrose, and A. Borel of Weyl's contributions to physics, geometry and group theory.)
Deppert, W. and Hübner, K. (eds) (1988) *Exact Sciences and their Philosophical Foundations*, Proceedings of the International Hermann Weyl Congress, Kiel, 1985, Frankfurt, Bern: Peter Lang. (Papers on many aspects of Weyl's scientific and philosophical work.)
Feferman, S. (1988) 'Weyl Vindicated: "Das Kontinuum" 70 Years Later', Atti del Congresso Temi e prospettive della logica e della filosofia della scienza contemporanee, Cesena, 1987, Bologna: CLUEB, vol. I, 59–93. (A recasting, in modern terms, and a defence of the essentials of Weyl's monograph by a leading proof theorist.)
Newman, M.H.A. (1957) 'Hermann Weyl', *Biographical Memoirs of the Royal Society of London* 3: 305–28. (Obituary summarizing Weyl's scientific accomplishments.)

THOMAS A. RYCKMAN

WEYR, FRANTIŠEK (1879–1951)

František (Franz) Weyr was Professor in Legal Philosophy and Public Law in Brno, Czechoslovakia, and a main author of the Czechoslovakian Constitution

*of 1920. His influence on Czechoslovakian jurispru-
dence was exceptional. He advocated the 'Pure Theory
of Law', demanding that law be studied in a
methodologically distinct way, pure of natural-scientific
or ideological inputs. He was founder and leader of the
'Brno School' of Pure Theory (or 'Normative Theory',
in his preferred terminology). This school stands close
to the Vienna School of Hans Kelsen.*

Weyr and KELSEN were also close in political stance.
Both fought for democracy and against the Austrian
monarchy, with its elements of a police state. Weyr's
analysis of the relation between private and public law
is particularly pro-democratic in tendency; according
to him, procedures in public law no less than in
private law are themselves bound by law.

In Weyr's conception, law belongs to a legal order
which is: (1) a logically unitary system of norms
ascribed to the state; (2) a dynamic system with
hierarchical structure; (3) valid under a presupposed
basic norm; (4) subject to cognition of its content
understood as *sui generis* and studied in abstraction
from social and evaluative considerations (thus
jurisprudence as cognition differs from legal politics
as volition); (5) identifiable through attribution to the
state as their ideal subject. (Hence Weyr sharply
rejects Kelsen's sanction theory of legal norms;
NORMS, LEGAL §2.)

Weyr's philosophical background is Kantian,
grounded in the opposition of 'is' and 'ought',
cognition and volition. Thus his theory of law and of
legal processes explains cognition of them in terms of
their formal and general validity. He accepts Kant's
theory of the nature of cognition so far as it stresses
the distinction of 'is' and 'ought', but rejects Kant's
commitment to a form of natural law theory (see
LEGAL IDEALISM §2; NATURAL LAW). The dualism of
'is' and 'ought' is not only semantic, but rooted in
different rational relations in the respective fields.
Weyr is a strict positivist and value-relativist, and
founded legal methodology on the difference of
argumentations about the existence of law and about
its merit as such. The realm of jurisprudence is a
realm clearly distinct from that of nature: in law (and
morality) free action is essential, whereas nature is
governed by causality. Latterly, he tended towards
Karel Engliš' triadic view of the forms in which we
apprehend reality, namely causality, teleology and
normativity, but underlined the nearer relation
between teleology and normativity. He articulated
explicitly the problem of the specificity of norm-
logical relations, and acknowledged that the logic of
descriptive language is inapplicable to norms. He
rejected the norm-logical scepticism of Engliš and
Kelsen.

Elements of Weyr's theory that remain of importance are: the view that structure-theory is the basis of
legal theory, and that it should be linked with an
appropriate theory of legal argumentation; and the
dynamic theory of law as foundational for investigations of legal processes and legality. Weyr's and
Kelsen's teachings belong to the first phase of
analytical jurisprudence, seeking a universal structure
of all law. The present second phase looks for
differentiations of legal structures, thus transcending
the Brno and Vienna schools alike. The postulate of
strict purity of jurisprudence should be given up; what
survives is Weyr's postulate that methods of inquiry
must not be mixed up, but must match objects of
inquiry.

See also: LAW, PHILOSOPHY OF; LEGAL POSITIVISM

List of works

Weyr, F. (1908) 'Zum Problem eines einheitlichen
Rechtssystems' (On the Problem of a Unified
System of Law), *Archiv für öffentliches Recht* 23:
529–80. (An essay on the problem of the unitary
character of a legal system.)

—— (1914) 'Zum Unterschiede zwischen Öffentli-
chem und privatem Recht' (On the Difference
between Public and Private Law), *Österreichische
Zeitschrift für öffentliches Recht* 40: 439–41. (This
essay discusses the distinction between private and
public law, insisting that both are subject to the
demands of the rule of law.)

—— (1920) *Základy filosofie právní. Nauka o pozná-
vání právnickém* (Foundations of the Philosophy of
Law: the Theory of Legal Cognition), Brno: A.
Píša.

—— (1922) *Československé právo správní. Část obecná*
(Czechoslovakian Administrative Law: the General
Part), Brno: Právník.

—— (1930) *Správní řád* (The Administrative System),
Brno: Barvič a Novotný.

—— (1936) *Teorie práva* (The Theory of Law), Brno
and Prague: Orbis.

—— (1937) *Československé právo ústavní* (Czechoslovakian Constitutional Law), Prague: Melantrich.

References and further reading

Kubeš, V. and Weinberger, O. (1980) *Die Brünner
rechtstheoretische Schule* (The Brno School of Legal
Theory), Vienna: Manz Verlag. (Weyr's work is
almost inaccessible in English or even in French;
but this collection of essays in German, by Czech

authors, gives a rounded account of the work of Weyr and his school.)

OTA WEINBERGER

WHEWELL, WILLIAM (1794–1886)

William Whewell's two seminal works, History of the Inductive Science, from the Earliest to the Present Time *(1837) and* The Philosophy of the Inductive Sciences, Founded upon their History *(1840), began a new era in the philosophy of science. Equally critical of the British 'sensationalist' school, which founded all knowledge on experience, and the German Idealists, who based science on a priori ideas, Whewell undertook to survey the history of all known sciences in search of a better explanation of scientific discovery. His conclusions were as bold as his undertaking. All real knowledge, he argued, is 'antithetical', requiring mutually irreducible, ever-present, and yet inseparable empirical and conceptual components. Scientific progress is achieved not by induction, or reading-out theories from previously collected data, but by the imaginative 'superinduction' of novel hypotheses upon known but seemingly unrelated facts. He thus broke radically with traditional inductivism – and for nearly a century was all but ignored. In the* Philosophy *the antithetical structure of scientific theories and the hypothetico-deductive account of scientific discovery form the basis for novel analyses of scientific and mathematical truth and scientific methodology, critiques of rival philosophies of science, and an account of the emergence and refinement of scientific ideas.*

1 Life and works
2 Theory of science
3 Methodology

1 Life and works

Whewell was born on 25 May 1794, son of a master carpenter in Lancaster. He died on 6 March 1866, Master of Trinity College, Cambridge, and one of the most eminent and prolific individuals of the era. His works include scientific research, physics and mathematics textbooks, books on ethics and law, university education, natural theology, church architecture, scientific nomenclature, political economy and the history and philosophy of science. He wrote poetry, translated Greek and German classics and edited the works of Hugo Grotius and Isaac Barrow. He was an active member of more than a dozen learned societies,

a force in the founding and running of the British Association for the Advancement of Science, an influential Master of Trinity (1841–66), and dominant Vice Chancellor of Cambridge University during two terms of office (1842 and 1856). Whewell, however, was not just a polymath. He wrote with the explicit view not merely of encompassing the world of early Victorian learning, but of synthesizing it and rendering it a unified intellectual whole.

Drawing on the *History* that endeavoured, for the first time ever, to chart the development of all known 'inductive sciences', the *Philosophy* proposes a novel theory and methodology of science that describe the nature, structure and aims of a well-formed natural science, explain how scientific discoveries are made and propose ways of retrospectively assessing their truth. The *Philosophy*, however, deviated too sharply from the prevailing empiricism, advocated, for example, by John Herschel and John Stuart Mill, to obtain acceptance in its time (see MILL, J.S. §5; EMPIRICISM; INDUCTIVE INFERENCE §4). Only recently, especially in the light of Karl Popper's critique of inductivism, is Whewell's philosophy beginning to receive the hearing it deserves (see POPPER, K. §§2–3).

2 Theory of science

Whewell's theory of science is presented in the *Philosophy* as an argument from a theory of the sources of knowledge to a detailed description of well-developed science. Somewhat systematized, it comprises the following four theses:

(1) *The Fundamental Antithesis.* Convinced that neither the empiricists, who sought to base all knowledge on experience alone, nor the intellectualists, who based science on a priori ideas, could adequately account for the development and accomplishments of science, Whewell proposed a bold alternative: all knowledge necessarily incorporates an objective element given by the world, informed and structured by conceptions furnished by the mind (which are refined during scientific research to describe the world as it is). Even the most commonplace perception must go beyond mere sensation. To perceive requires a singling out of sensation, a retention of it by the mind, and some awareness of its relations to other sensations past and present – none of which can be given by sensation alone. All knowledge thus embraces an antithesis of irreducible opposites: things as opposed to ideas, sensation as opposed to conception, fact as opposed to theory. And yet, Whewell notes, it is a 'Fundamental Antithesis of Philosophy', one that can only be reflected upon theoretically. In practice no item of

real knowledge can be fully resolved into its primordial factual and conceptual ingredients; so Kant's conclusion is unavoidable: the purely substantial is unknowable in itself (see KANT, I. §5).

(2) *Theory of 'Induction'.* From the near-Kantian epistemology of the Fundamental Antithesis, Whewell goes on to argue for a theory of the acquisition of knowledge thus construed. He termed the process 'induction', but meant something quite different from all current uses of the word. Whewell envisaged induction as a corrective hermeneutic process of reading meaning, structure, regularity and law *into* the facts, rather than gleaning such information *from* the empirical data. If all items of real knowledge comprise facts, unconnected in themselves and 'colligated' by concepts furnished by the mind, it follows that new knowledge is obtained exactly when a new concept, suggested by the mind, is successfully 'superimposed' upon formerly known but seemingly unrelated facts. His language notwithstanding, Whewell was an outspoken anti-inductivist.

(3) *Theory of Excellent Science.* A well-formed science takes shape in the course of repeated 'inductions' of ever higher generality that yield a series of nested, hence deductively related, conceptual colligators. According to Whewell, the conceptual component of each such science is governed by a 'Fundamental Idea', such as that of space for geometry, force and matter for dynamics, or life for biology. As work progresses certain features of the science's Fundamental Idea gradually come to light and are formulated as axioms considered to be true *of* the Fundamental Idea. Ideally, a science will consist of an entire corpus of fact perfectly colligated by such a fully axiomatized conceptual scheme.

(4) *Theory of Truth.* Lastly, such a view of science inevitably yields a two-pronged theory of scientific truth. This is because the propositions comprising a scientific theory strive to attain two different, and *prima facie* independent forms of perfection: to be on the one hand well-formed theorems of a well-formed system of ideas, and at the same time perfect colligators of fact. In the role of colligator a proposition may at best be considered empirically true, while as a theorem of a well formed system of ideas, it may be considered necessarily true *of the science's Fundamental Idea* – acknowledged to the point that *within the system* one cannot distinctly intuit its negation. Whewell's contention that a proposition may thus be considered necessarily true (of a Fundamental Idea) and yet eventually prove empirically false, has baffled many of his critics. Truth within a conceptual scheme only implies that the proposition in question is conceived to be true of a Fundamental Idea (and hence must necessarily hold

each time the Idea is applied to facts). But whether or not it is also true of the facts is forever contingent upon empirical test. Whewell's notion of truth within a conceptual scheme thus defies Kant's celebrated taxonomy. Since he insisted that a truth relation (other than mere coherence and resting on more than formal definitions) obtains within pure systems of ideas (as in pure mathematics) it cannot be considered merely analytic. On the other hand, although a priori with respect to the facts, such truths cannot be considered synthetically true prior to independent empirical test.

3 Methodology

Whewell's methodology falls under three major headings corresponding to the stages preceding, during and following scientific discovery. This part of his philosophy is largely anticipated in the *History*, in which major scientific breakthroughs are broken down into 'inductive epochs', their 'preludes' and their 'sequels'.

Whewell considered discovery itself reducible to no more than an imaginative 'happy guess', a 'felicitous and inexplicable stroke of inventive talent' defying methodological prescription. Like Popper almost a century later, Whewell called upon scientists to hypothesize freely, fancifully and frequently. Bacon's condemnation of 'anticipation', and Newton's '*Hypotheses non fingo*', he urged, expressed the wrong attitude. He refused, however, to view scientific conjecture as entirely capricious. By 'decomposing' the facts in hand as far as possible into their conceptual and factual ingredients, he argued, a part of the science's conceptual scheme, at least that to which the facts in hand directly pertain, may be (re)constructed. Such (partial) knowledge of a science's conceptual history can provide discoverers with the appropriate setting and idiom for their new conjectures.

But bold speculation will lead to real knowledge, he argued further, only if firmly coupled to an 'ingenuity and skill which devises means for rapidly testing false suppositions as they offer themselves'. The 'Popperian' ring is again unmistakable: the worth of a conjecture is measured not by reports of favourable data, but by its proven resistance to falsification.

Resilience in the face of prudent testing, however persistent, Whewell observed, cannot be considered conclusive proof of the actual (empirical) truth of a hypothesis. And yet he maintained that truth lies within the reach of science. True theories distinguish themselves from merely good ones on two related accounts. First in repeatedly exhibiting what he termed 'consilience of inductions', or explanatory surprise. And second, in generating 'progressive simplification' as they are repeatedly applied to new and different kinds of phenomena. In Whewell's opinion both gravitation theory and the undulatory theory of light had proved themselves true in this manner. Both criteria are as questionable (as criteria of truth) as they are intriguing (as criteria of acceptability), and have attracted considerable attention.

See also: CONVENTIONALISM; DISCOVERY, LOGIC OF; SCIENCE, NINETEENTH CENTURY PHILOSOPHY OF §§3–6; SCIENTIFIC METHOD

List of works

Whewell, W. (1833) *Astronomy and General Physics Considered with Reference to Natural Theology* (Bridgewater Treatise), London: William Pickering. (Whewell's first major reflections on science. Contains an interesting chapter on the Inductive and Deductive 'habits'.)

—— (1835) *Thoughts on the Study of Mathematics as Part of a Liberal Education*, Cambridge: J.J. Deighton. (Mathematics presented for the first time by Whewell as governed by Fundamental Ideas of which its axioms are true.)

—— (1837) *History of the Inductive Sciences, from the Earliest to the Present Time*, London: J.W. Parker, 3 vols. (Whewell's history of science.)

—— (1840) *The Philosophy of the Inductive Sciences Founded upon their History*, London: J.W. Parker, 2 vols. (The third, enlarged edition of 1858–60 was republished by J.W. Parker, in three separate works: a conceptual history of the sciences, *The History of Scientific Ideas* (1858); a critical history of the philosophy of science, *On the Philosophy of Discovery* (1860); and Whewell's own philosophical system, dubbed *Novum Organon Renovatum* (1858).)

—— (1845) *The Elements of Morality, Including Polity*, London: J.W. Parker, 2 vols. (A system of ethics ranging from jurisprudence to international law, developed in close analogy to science and mathematics.)

—— (1849) *Of Induction, with Special Reference to Mr J. Stuart Mill's System of Logic*, London: J.W. Parker. (Whewell's systematic reply to J.S. Mill's criticism of the *Philosophy*.)

Buchdahl, G. and Laudan, L.L. (eds) (1987) *The Historical and Philosophical Works of William Whewell*, London: Frank Cass, 10 vols. (An annotated edition of all of Whewell's published work in history and philosophy of science.)

Butts, R.E. (ed.) (1968) *William Whewell's Theory of Scientific Method*, Pittsburgh, IL: University of Pittsburgh Press. (A short selection of Whewell's philosophical writings.)

Elkana, Y. (ed.) (1984) *William Whewell: Selected Writings on the History of Science*, Chicago, IL, and London: University of Chicago Press. (A selection of Whewell's philosophical and historiographical texts that bear on his history of the sciences.)

References and further reading

Blanché, R. (1935) *Le Rationalisme de Whewell* (Whewell's Rationalism), Paris: Librairie Felix Alcan. (A close study of the ultimately unreconciled Kantian and Platonist aspects of Whewell's philosophy.)

Fisch, M. (1991) *William Whewell: Philosopher of Science*, Oxford: Clarendon Press. (A detailed account of the formation of Whewell's philosophy of science from his early involvement in the reform of Cambridge mathematics, and a critical appraisal of his mature system.)

Fisch, M. and Schaffer, S. (eds) (1991) *William Whewell: A Composite Portrait*, Oxford: Clarendon Press. (A collection of 13 authoritative studies of the content and context of Whewell's life, work and impact. Contains a useful bibliography.)

Marcucci, S. (1963) *L'idealismo scientifico di William Whewell* (William Whewell's Scientific Idealism), Pisa: Instituto di filosofia. (A study of Whewell's philosophy of science that places him within the idealist school.)

Stair-Douglas, M. (1881) *The Life and Selections from the Correspondence of William Whewell D.D.*, London: Kegan Paul. (A brief biography and selection of correspondence pertaining mainly to Whewell's personal life.)

Todhunter, I. (1876) *William Whewell, D.D. Master of Trinity College Cambridge: An Account of his Writings with Selections from his Literary and Scientific Correspondence*, London: Macmillan, 2 vols. (Contains an intellectual biography structured around Whewell's published works, and a wide selection of his professional correspondence.)

MENACHEM FISCH

WHICHCOTE, B. *see* CAMBRIDGE PLATONISM

WHITE, THOMAS (1593–1676)

Thomas White's reputation has suffered unmerited decline since he was described by John Evelyn in 1651 as 'a learned priest and famous philosopher'. His works embrace theology, metaphysics, natural philosophy and political theory. The leader of a minority faction of English Catholics, known after his alias as 'Blackloists', White's overall intellectual position is determinedly antisceptical, characterized by a certainty-seeking synthesis of old and new. The traditional Aristotelianism of his own education is blended with aspects of the 'new philosophy' which he encountered in the 1640s; and in this respect White stands as an important representative of the intellectually turbulent times in which he lived.

As an English Catholic, White was educated in continental Europe. He was particularly associated with the English College at Douai, where he was ordained as a priest in 1617, and at which for some years he taught scholastic philosophy, or 'rigid Thomistry'. His ideas were extended during periods in Rome from 1625–9, in Paris in the 1640s and in London after 1655. His intellectual contacts included members of the Mersenne circle and of the embryonic Royal Society (see MERSENNE, M.). White's thought is remarkable for embracing such varied influences within an essentially Aristotelian framework.

White's antisceptical metaphysics is most clearly outlined in his debate with Joseph GLANVILL. Responding to the fashionably Pyrrhonian *Vanity of Dogmatizing* (1661), White argues in his *Sciri, sive sceptices* (1663) that a sceptical denial of the possibility of certain knowledge not only insults past and present philosophers, but also threatens the very basis of morality. Seeking some fundamental starting-point, and specifically rejecting the validity of Descartes' introspective quest for an infallible generator of knowledge, White resorts to an essentially Aristotelian, logical procedure. He thus assumes the existence of some unquestionable 'identical propositions', from which certain knowledge can be generated: in its simplest form, what is, is, and 'whilst it is, it cannot not-be'. This invincible truth provides at least one 'first step' against the sceptics.

As a second step, 'self-known propositions' are cited. For example, a number must be odd or even, on the assumption that 'even and not-even are all'; or a man must be an animal, where 'rational animal' is subsumed within the category 'animal'. From such propositions, it is then possible to proceed by syllogistic reasoning: thus, we may start with the self-known propositions that 'every man is an animal', and that 'every animal is a living creature',

and from these we may go on justifiably to conclude that what is a 'man' is a 'living creature'. Though obviously limited in scope, such examples served to demonstrate for White that at least some certain knowledge was in principle possible; and on this solid foundation, more could then be built.

The defeat of scepticism was particularly important in a theological (and related moral) context. Though denying some important Catholic orthodoxies, including the widespread belief in papal authority and conventional notions of purgatory, White retained an emphasis on 'tradition' as the rule of faith, and additionally synthesized theology with his own brand of natural philosophy, to produce a so-called 'philosophical divinity'. Catholic tradition was to be seen as perfectly compatible with a natural philosophy grounded on Aristotelian first-principles and incorporating important elements of the new science. White's approach here is well illustrated in the Theological Appendix to his *Institutionum Peripateticarum* (1646). Here the seemingly miraculous story of the Flood is shown to be in perfect conformity with the rational and empirical methods of the new science; and the two approaches are to be seen as mutually-supportive in their stand against scepticism.

White's natural philosophy is best studied in *De Mundo* (1642) and *Institutionum Peripateticarum* (1646). It is, again, particularly interesting for its synthesizing of old and new philosophies. This is evident in both cosmology and physics. With some ambiguities, Copernican cosmology can be shown to be consistent with Aristotelian philosophy and Christian theology. Thus while heliocentrism is nominally accepted, the earth is still described as 'situated in the very middle of the universe': this apparent anomaly can allegedly be justified by identifying the 'middle' not with the centre of the terrestrial globe but with the whole circumference of the earth's orbit; and that ploy is legitimated by reference to the magnitude of the universe, in terms of which that circumference is itself a mere 'point'. The earth's continuing motor (still required by an Aristotelian) is found in the wind acting on contiguous sea; and the air surrounding the earth is also assumed to move, circumventing another traditional scholastic argument. Finally, Christian scripturally-based insistence on an immobile earth can be appeased by an appeal to the relativity of motion, in terms of which 'both statements are made with absolute correctness and accuracy: that the earth has been continually moved with regard to the sun, and the sun with respect to the earth'.

White's ambivalence in cosmology is paralleled in his physics: retaining such Aristotelian premises as the impossibility of a vacuum, motion's need of a mover, and the infinite divisibility of a continuum, he subscribes none the less to a form of atomic theory, by conflating newly-revived Epicurean 'atoms' with traditional Aristotelian 'minima'. In this White may be compared to his fellow-Blackloist friend Kenelm Digby.

Blackloist political philosophy is outlined in White's *Grounds of Obedience and Government* (1655). Aiming for toleration of Catholic worship, and from the starting-point of 'salus populi', White argues essentially for a contract theory, whereby the king's power is held in trust for the people. Revolution may therefore be justified; and in practical terms Catholics should accept the *de facto* rule of Cromwell. White's outspokenness proved his downfall: following the restoration of the monarchy he was repudiated by Protestants and fellow-Catholics alike, and was all but lost to history.

See also: ARISTOTELIANISM IN THE 17TH CENTURY; DIGBY, K.; SERGEANT, J.

List of main works

White, T. (1642) *De Mundo Dialogi Tres* (Three dialogues concerning the world), Paris. (White's first comprehensive treatise on natural philosophy, which established his reputation amongst contemporaries. The work was criticized by Hobbes (see below).

—— (1646) *Institutionum Peripateticarum...pars theorica*, Lyons; trans. as *Peripateticall Institutions*, London, 1656. (Cosmological treatise apparently influenced by Kenelm Digby. Scientific matters are subordinated to religious and moral concerns, especially in a Theological Appendix.)

—— (1653) *Villicationis suae de medio animarum statu...*, Paris; trans. as *The Middle State of Souls*, London, 1659. (Notorious theological work, which includes denial of purgatory. Condemned both by Roman authorities and by the English Parliament.)

—— (1655) *The Grounds of Obedience and Government*, London: repr. facsimile Farnborough, Gregg International Publishers Ltd., 1968. (White's much condemned, allegedly pro-Cromwellian, political treatise.)

—— (1657) *Euclides Physicus*, London. (Mathematically expressed work of physics, claimed to have influenced Leibniz.)

—— (1659) *Controversy-Logicke or the method to come to truth in debates of religion*, Paris. (An apologia for Catholicism, in response to the Protestant John Biddle.)

—— (1660) *Religion and Reason*, Paris. (A theological work aiming to show the compatibility of science and reason with Christianity.)

—— (1663) *Sciri, sive sceptices et scepticorum a jure disputationis exclusio*, London; transl. as *An Exclusion of Scepticks from all Title to Dispute*, London, 1665. (White's anti-sceptical response to Joseph Glanvill's *Vanity of Dogmatizing*.)

References and further reading

Henry, J. (1982) 'Atomism and Eschatology: Catholicism and natural philosophy in the inter-regnum', *British Journal for the History of Science* 15: 211–39. (Argues for importance of 'Blackloists' in early development of 'mechanical philosophy'.)

Hobbes, T. (*c*.1642–3) *Thomas Hobbes: Thomas White's De Mundo Examined*, ed. H.W. Jones, London: Bradford University Press/Crosby Lockwood Staples, 1976. (Translation of Hobbes' critique of White's cosmology.)

Jones, G.H. (1975) 'Leibniz' Cosmology and Thomas White's *Euclides Physicus*', *Archives Internationales d'Histoire des Sciences* 25: 277–303. (Discusses White's originality, and claims his influence on Leibniz.)

Southgate, B.C. (1993) *'Covetous of Truth': The Life and Work of Thomas White, 1593–1676*, Dordrecht: Kluwer Academic Publishers. (Includes bibliography.)

Tavard, G.H. (1978) *The Seventeenth Century Tradition: A Study in Recusant Thought*, Leiden: E.J. Brill. (Includes chapter on White's theology.)

BEVERLEY SOUTHGATE

WHITEHEAD, ALFRED NORTH (1861–1947)

Whitehead made fundamental contributions to modern logic and created one of the most controversial metaphysical systems of the twentieth century. He drew out what he took to be the revolutionary consequences for philosophy of the new discoveries in mathematics, logic and physics, developing these consequences first in logic and then in the philosophy of science and speculative metaphysics. His work constantly returns to the question: what is the place of the constructions of mathematics, science and philosophy in the nature of things?

Whitehead collaborated with Bertrand Russell on Principia Mathematica *(1910–13), which argues that all pure mathematics is derivable from a small number of logical principles. He went on in his philosophy of science to describe nature in terms of overlapping series of events and to argue that scientific explanations are constructed on that basis. He finally expanded and redefined his work by developing a new kind of speculative metaphysics. Stated chiefly in* Process and Reality *(1929), his metaphysics is both an extended reflection on the character of philosophical inquiry and an account of the nature of all things as a self-constructing 'process'. On this view, reality is incomplete, a matter of the becoming of 'occasions' which are centres of activity in a multiplicity of serial processes whereby the antecedent occasions are taken up in the activities of successor occasions.*

1   **Life**
2   **Mathematics and logic**
3   **Philosophy of science**
4   **Speculative metaphysics**

1   Life

Alfred North Whitehead studied mathematics at Trinity College, Cambridge. In 1884 he became a Fellow of Trinity, where he taught mathematics, Bertrand Russell and J.M. Keynes being among his pupils. He was a liberal in politics and an advocate of women's rights. He wrote *Principia Mathematica* (1910–13) with Russell, moving to London in 1910, where he taught mathematics at University College and was active in educational reform. He became Professor of Applied Mathematics at the Imperial College of Science and Technology in 1914, thereafter writing on the philosophy of science. In 1924 he took up a chair in philosophy at Harvard, where he produced a series of works in speculative metaphysics.

Whitehead's work falls into three periods: the early period of mathematics and logic, the middle period concerned with the philosophy of science; and the late period of speculative metaphysics. Although it is a matter of debate, his philosophical development is best seen as a shifting, ever-widening analysis of the concept of construction (see CONSTRUCTIVISM §1; CONSTRUCTIVISM IN MATHEMATICS §6).

2   Mathematics and logic

Whitehead's three main early works indicate the central role played by mathematics, logic and science in shaping the themes and models which inform his philosophical thought. His first book, *A Treatise on Universal Algebra: With Applications* (1898), develops Grassmann's work in what was then the new field of abstract algebra. Although it had little influence on the subsequent development of mathematics, the

Treatise has at least three philosophically significant features.

First, it is concerned with the 'universalization' or 'generalization' of variables beyond their traditional restriction as symbols for numbers. Generalization takes the form of 'substitutive schemes', which at this stage in Whitehead's career are non-axiomatized algebraic formulae having the status of a calculus which symbolizes the operations of addition and multiplication. He holds that the construction of substitutive schemes involves some (here unspecified) relation to the empirical world and that, to be significant, such schemes must have applications or substitutions in some field. In turn, application assists in the investigation of the schemes themselves, which have heuristic value even if they are only partially interpretable at a given stage of knowledge.

Second, alongside the emphasis on empirical connection and a realist concern with the significant application of schematized structures, a strong formalist tendency is evident in the *Treatise*: while consistency is repudiated as the sole ground for existence-theorems, mathematical schemes are defined as conventional idealizations independent of perceptual content (see REALISM IN THE PHILOSOPHY OF MATHEMATICS §2). Third, however, Whitehead also emphasizes the synthetic processes of intellectual construction involved in mathematical inference. Like the mathematical intuitionists later on, he regards '2 + 3' and '3 + 2' as nonidentical (see INTUITIONISM §1); he holds that the difference of order directs different processes of thought and that equivalence is a matter of identity-in-difference.

The development of a philosophy which would coherently relate the different orientations – realist, formalist and intuitionist – evident in the treatment of construction in his mathematical writings is a central concern of Whitehead's subsequent thought.

Whitehead's Royal Society memoir On Mathematical Concepts of the Material World (1906) offers different logical schemes or models for different theories of the structure of the physical world. As later in *Process and Reality* (1929), Whitehead employs the axiomatic method in constructing a scheme and defines a scheme as a hypothesis to be assessed on the principle of Ockham's razor (see WILLIAM OF OCKHAM §2): the preferred scheme in the memoir is that which posits only one class of ultimate entities. He anticipates his later thought by criticizing the Newtonian account of nature as composed of externally related atoms each occupying a position in absolute space at an absolute time (see MECHANICS, CLASSICAL §§1, 4–5; NEWTON, I. §§3–4). His preferred scheme is constructed on the model of electromagnetic theory in terms of the flux of energy. The ultimate entities are complexes of relations: points are classes of linear relations which can be given an empirical interpretation in terms of vectors or lines of force. The emphasis is on a logic of relations as a way of uniting permanent structure and change in one schematized serial order – an issue which occupied Whitehead for the rest of his career.

Principia Mathematica (1910–13), written in collaboration with Russell, (see RUSSELL, B. §3) is best seen as an account of the logic of relations and an attempt to develop as far as possible the hypothesis of 'logicism' – the claim that all pure mathematics can be derived from an axiomatic scheme of logical concepts taken as primitive (see LOGICISM §4). The effect of the difficulties which subsequently emerged in the logicist project was to strengthen the mathematical-intuitionist tendencies in Whitehead's thought: he later treats Gödel's incompleteness theorem as indicating that mathematical logic is an instance of the finite character of all constructions (see GÖDEL'S THEOREMS §§3–5).

3 Philosophy of science

Whitehead's philosophy of science analyses the ontological status of scientific and mathematical concepts in terms of their derivation from the elements and relations of nature as disclosed in sense-experience. He abandons the Newtonian concept of 'nature at an instant' and rejects the 'bifurcation' of nature into perceived qualities and the theoretical entities of science (such as electrons), in particular Russell's phenomenalist view of theoretical entities as constructions out of atomic sense-data. The new theories of physics, the new logic of relations and Bergson's account of the fluidity of nature are seen as making possible an empiricism which is neither representationalist nor phenomenalist. Logical constructions and perceived qualities are to be analysed as features of 'one system' of multiple relations by means of a redefinition of sense-experience as the disclosure of the 'passage of nature', that is, of occurrences or events with spatiotemporal spread.

'Events' are one of the two basic constituents of nature that Whitehead holds to be disclosed in sense-experience. Taking the place of traditional concepts of substance, events are unrepeatable, relational entities which overlap or extend over one another (see SUBSTANCE §3). Their nature as spatiotemporal regions, however, expresses only some of the features of this fundamental relation of extension, for Whitehead also terms it 'process' and 'creative advance'. Events thus imply a special kind of activity pointing

towards the later, speculative account of reality as 'creativity' (see EVENTS).

'Objects' are the second basic constituent of nature disclosed in sense-experience. Objects take the place of universals: they are repeatable characters or properties which are neither Platonic forms nor nominalist resemblances but, as 'ingredients' in events, are like Aristotelian *universalia in rebus* (see ARISTOTLE §15; UNIVERSALS §1). However, objects do not act and do not stand to events in an invariable two-termed relation of predication; they are terms in a multiple relation of 'ingression'. Thus a 'sense-object' – for example, a colour which is perceived as situated in an event – involves multiple relations between the percipient event (the relevant bodily state of the observer), the event which is the situation of the object, and the conditioning events relating the percipient event to the situation. As this multiple relation is a facet of nature, the perspective relative to the percipient event is not 'outside' the world but belongs to the world in that relation, thereby dissolving the duality of 'subjectivity' and 'objectivity'. Scepticism is never an issue for Whitehead, as scepticism assumes that duality has fundamental metaphysical status (see SCEPTICISM §1). His complex account of different types of objects is replaced in his later work by an account of the relation of what he calls 'eternal objects' to the becoming of 'occasions'.

What Whitehead called his 'Method of Extensive Abstraction' is primarily an application of a constructivist logic of classes to the question of the status of such theoretical entities as instants of time and points in space. Instants and points are routes of approximation across, respectively, the durations of events and spatial volumes, which are arranged in a continuum of whole and part like a nest of Chinese boxes. As we descend in the series we progressively reach durations and volumes of ever smaller extension. Instants and points are sets or classes of the whole – part relations of the durations and volumes which enclose them.

Whitehead's attempt to unify space, time and matter in a single system of relations led him to address Einstein's theory of relativity critically. He agrees with Einstein that space and time are abstractions from spacetime events and that there is an infinite plurality of different 'time-series'. However, Whitehead's analysis of the perceptual relations between events allows him to maintain the objectivity both of the distinction between space and time for the observer and of the relative position of the observer. Further, the problems of rotation, incongruent counterparts and the application of geometries lead him to give the passage of events its own internal, uniform (homoloidal) spatial structure, independent of any relation to the objects of which they are the situations, and he treats that structure as actual. This brings him into conflict with the general theory of relativity in which spacetime varies with its (material) contents (see RELATIVITY THEORY, PHILOSOPHICAL SIGNIFICANCE OF §2).

4 Speculative metaphysics

Whitehead's speculative thought challenges the critique of metaphysics characteristic of twentieth-century Anglo-American and European philosophy. In contrast to Russell and his successors who interpret modern mathematical and logical developments in the context of a weak theory of being or existence as quantification, Whitehead sees these developments as reopening the possibility of a strong theory of being or existence as 'act' (see BEING §4; EXISTENCE §2). Like Bergson and the later Heidegger (see HEIDEGGER, M. §2), Whitehead defines the act of being in terms of finite self-actualization, independent of any metaphysically complete cause or ground; but unlike them, he regards self-actualization as rationally analysable.

There is no longer any foundationalist appeal to sense-experience in Whitehead's metaphysics (see FOUNDATIONALISM §1). The subject matter of his 'speculative scheme' is the 'empirical side' of the analysis, defined as everything of which we are conscious as historically situated beings. The construction of an axiomatized scheme of categories is a matter of 'imaginative generalization': significant features of the historical world are employed as analogues for the analysis of the nature of all things. The cogency of the categories depends upon the range of their 'substitutions' or 'applications' on the 'empirical side'. Categories and applications stand in a relation of proportional analogy (as A is to B, so C is to D).

As a 'generalized mathematics', Whitehead's speculative scheme of categories can be epitomized as universalizing the mathematical concept of series and as closely akin to the mathematical intuitionists' theory of number construction. The self-actualization of all things is interpreted as a finite series of acts of self-construction which are asymmetrical, transitive and irreflexive, constituting an iterative, infinitely proceeding multiplicity of sequences. This is the 'process' of 'actual [that is, actualizing] entities', or 'actual occasions' which constitute the 'one genus' by which the scheme aspires to describe everything. Whitehead terms the scheme 'the philosophy of organism' to indicate that it embraces biology as much as physics and constitutes a theory of the

'experience' of all things as self-constructing centres of activity (see PROCESSES §4).

Whitehead's complex analysis of the serial process of the becoming of occasions employs a variety of analogies with 'mentality', 'feeling' and the vectorial transfer of energy. Although they do not overlap, there are no 'single' occasions, for occasions are relational or serially constituted entities in two senses. First, the completion of an occasion in a series of occasions is its 'objectification' by successor occasions. Second, a successor occasion has its own internal serial structure as a self-constructing synthesis or 'concrescence'. The relation of freedom and determination simply depends on an occasion's complexity of response, allowing it to modify the extent to which it is determined by its predecessors and environment.

Whitehead's theory of eternal objects or 'pure potentials' is modelled on that of the propositional function. However, the theory does not grant the propositional function any metaphysically primitive status but explains what makes the propositional function possible. In the state of 'general potentiality' eternal objects do not form an infinite class of possibilities, but a 'matrix' of the 'multiplicity' of the endlessly nested possibilities which finite actualizations afford. As components of predecessor occasions which are objectifiable by successor occasions, eternal objects have the status of 'real potentiality'. Potentiality and actuality are defined as relations of seriality, states or stages of actualization, which stand in a strictly functional relation of satisfaction and not in any of the traditional relations of agency, resemblance or imitation.

Eternal objects of a special kind, 'the objective species', constitute the 'extensive continuum' or abstract system of part and whole relations. The key philosophical difference with Whitehead's middle-period extension is that the extensive continuum is potential, not actual, and is actualized by the becoming of occasions. Mathematical relations can thus be intuitionistically defined as equivalently ideal and real, potential and actual: that is to say, they are definable as states or stages of serial actualization.

Whitehead's scheme of categories has a number of significant applications, some of which can be summarized here.

Epistemological Realism. By serializing occasions, Whitehead would reconcile the claim that knowledge is perspectival or 'situated' with the claim that knowledge is to be defined in terms of objects distinct from and independent of the subject or concrescent occasion.

Relations. Whitehead would dissolve the opposition between F.H. Bradley and Russell on relations by interpreting the doctrines of internal and external relations in the context of his serial pluralism (see BRADLEY, F.H. §§4–5): a successor occasion is internally related to its antecedent occasions, but its antecedent occasions (as completed or 'perished') are not internally related to it. Internal and external relations are thus states or stages of seriality.

Perception. The primary mode of perception is not a matter of distinct impressions or sense-data but, under the principle of serial connection, is the direct experience of the 'causal efficacy' of the antecedent world. The other mode of perception is 'presentational immediacy', which is the presented locus or spacetime region of the percipient occasion. The two are combined in an adverbial theory of sensation.

God. Whitehead does not attempt to prove God's existence but to show that, contrary to the views of many theorists of finite self-actualization, there is nothing to prevent the redefinition of the concept of God in that context. Thus eternal objects in their state of 'general potentiality' are 'termed' God because of the ultimate, underivable character of possibilities of structure: as the final principle of determination, the concept of God is their nearest conceptual correlate. Similarly, 'real potentiality' can be said to be derived from God because the experience of potentiality from an occasion's standpoint is nothing other than the ultimacy of 'appetition' for actualization. Interpreted as God, these aspects are termed his 'primordial nature' and revise the concept of God as creator: he does not create occasions but provides them with potentiality. In his 'consequent nature' God objectifies and transforms occasions in the eternal harmony of his nature. As a nontemporal being, God is an 'actual entity', not an occasion, but his primordial and consequent natures define him as a component of serial process. This 'dipolar' nature expresses the way in which the scheme has a place for the concept of God as both first cause and redeemer (see PROCESS THEISM).

Speculative Analysis. Whitehead's general strategy is to define ideality and reality, not as fundamental metaphysical opposites, but as states or stages of the serial process of self-construction. While his universalization of the concept of finite or serial construction makes him a speculative realist, his metaphysics is also self-referentially inclusive, that is, the metaphysical scheme is an instance of finite or serial intellectual construction which as such is not subject to the law of the excluded middle (see INTUITIONISTIC LOGIC AND ANTIREALISM §1). The scheme can thus be regarded as real inasmuch as it is constructed or applied, and ideal or hypothetical inasmuch as it is finite and revisable and consequently does not exclude alternative analyses. While most readers of Whitehead interpret his speculative realism to mean that his categories are accounts of the metaphysical contents of the world, one can also regard them as conditions of the contents of the world, that is, as transcendental categories of a new kind which are neither real in the medieval sense nor ideal in the Kantian sense, but fallible, historically situated constructions, formulating the ultimate generalities which constitute the nature of things.

List of works

Whitehead, A.N. (1898) *A Treatise on Universal Algebra: With Applications*, Cambridge: Cambridge University Press. (A pioneer work in the field of abstract algebra.)

—— (1906) On Mathematical Concepts of the Material World. Philosophical Transactions of the Royal Society of London, Series A; in F.S.C. Northrop and Mason W. Gross, *Alfred North Whitehead: An Anthology*, Cambridge: Cambridge University Press, 1953, 11–82. (This book contains extensive extracts from Whitehead's main works.)

Whitehead, A.N. and Russell, B.A.W. (1910–13) *Principia Mathematica*, Cambridge: Cambridge University Press, 3 vols; 2nd edn, 1927. (One of the central works in modern logic and the philosophy of mathematics.)

Whitehead, A.N. (1911) *An Introduction to Mathematics*, London: Williams & Norgate; repr. Oxford: Oxford University Press, 1948, 1958, 1969. (A clear, elegant account of the basic elements of modern mathematics.)

—— (1917) *The Organization of Thought*, London: Williams & Norgate, and Philadelphia, PA: J.B. Lippincott. (This collection of papers, with others presented to the Aristotelian Society between 1916 and 1923, notably 'Uniformity and Contingency' (1922), is reprinted in A.H. Johnson (ed.) *Alfred North Whitehead: The Interpretation of Science*, New York: Bobbs-Merrill, 1961.)

—— (1919, 1925) *An Enquiry Concerning the Principles of Natural Knowledge*, Cambridge: Cambridge University Press. (The second edition of 1925, with additional notes, should be consulted.)

—— (1920) *The Concept of Nature*, Cambridge: Cambridge University Press, 1993. (A nontechnical analysis of the philosophy of science and nature which Whitehead sees as required by physics.)

—— (1922) *The Principle of Relativity*, Cambridge: Cambridge University Press; philosophical sections repr. in Whitehead (1906). (A critical analysis of the theory of relativity from the point of view of Whitehead's philosophy of science.)

—— (1925) *Science and the Modern World*, New York:

Macmillan, and Cambridge: Cambridge University Press, 1926; New York: The Free Press, 1967. (A critical history of the development of modern science, concentrating on the concept of organism as the basic principle of modern scientific thought.)

—— (1926) *Religion in the Making*, New York: Macmillan, and Cambridge: Cambridge University Press, 1926; New York: Meridan, 1974. (A historical and critical reflection on the nature of religion in the light of Whitehead's metaphysics. References are usually to this or the Cambridge edition.)

—— (1926) *Symbolism, Its Meaning and Effect*, Cambridge: Cambridge University Press; New York: Macmillan, 1927; London: G.P. Putnam's Sons, 1959. (A clear statement of Whitehead's theory of perception, later elaborated in *Process and Reality*.)

—— (1929) *The Aims of Education and Other Essays*, New York: Macmillan, and London: Ernest Benn, 1929; New York: The Free Press, 1967. (This work is essentially a shorter version of *The Organization of Thought*.)

—— (1929) *The Function of Reason*, Princeton, NJ: Princeton University Press, 1929. Boston, MA: Beacon Press, 1958. (A prolegomenon to *Process and Reality*, this work presents philosophy as a matter of the creation of novel concepts.)

—— (1929) *Process and Reality: An Essay in Cosmology*, New York: Macmillan, and Cambridge: Cambridge University Press; corrected edn, with comparative readings and detailed index, by D.R. Griffin and D.W. Sherburne, New York: The Free Press, 1978. (Whitehead's central work in speculative metaphysics, presented in axiomatized form with extensive applications.)

—— (1933) *Adventures of Ideas*, New York: Macmillan, and Cambridge: Cambridge University Press; New York: The Free Press, 1967. (An analysis of the concepts of civilization and history from the standpoint of Whitehead's metaphysics, this work includes a clear statement of his position and a redefinition of the 'transcendentals' of medieval philosophy.)

—— (1938) *Modes of Thought*, New York: Macmillan, and Cambridge: Cambridge University Press; New York: The Free Press, 1968. (A rich and suggestive restatement of Whitehead's metaphysics, clearly underlining his mathematical intuitionist orientation.)

—— (1947) *Essays in Science and Philosophy*, New York: The Philosophical Library. (An important collection of papers, including some of Whitehead's clearest programmatic and methodological statements, notably 'Uniformity and Contingency',

'Analysis of Meaning', 'Process and Reality' and 'Mathematics and the Good'.)

Woodbridge B.A. (ed.) (1977) *Alfred North Whitehead: A Primary-Secondary Bibliography*, Bowling Green, OH: Philosophy Documentation Center, Bowling Green State University. (A complete bibliography of Whitehead's works and the secondary literature up to 1977, totalling 1,868 entries.)

References and further reading

Braithwaite, R.B. (1926) Review of Science and the Modern World, *Mind* 35: 489–500. (A clear, critical analysis of Whitehead's metaphysics in the light of his earlier work.)

—— (1927) Contribution to 'Symposium: Is The "Fallacy of Simple Location" A Fallacy?', *Aristotelian Society* supplementary vol. 7: 224–36. (A clear, critical analysis of Whitehead's philosophy of science.)

Christian, W.A. (1959) *An Interpretation of Whitehead's Metaphysics*, New Haven, CT: Yale University Press. (A standard, detailed analysis.)

Deleuze, G. (1988) *Le Pli: Leibnix et le Baroque*, Paris: Les Éditions de Minuit; trans. T. Conley, *The Fold: Leibniz and the Baroque*, Minneapolis, MN: University of Minnesota Press, 1992; London: The Athlone Press, 1993. (The importance of Whitehead's metaphysics in the modern philosophical tradition.)

Dewey, J. (1937) 'Whitehead's Philosophy', *Philosophical Review* 46: 170–7; also in *Problems of Men*, New York: Philosophical Library, 1946, 410–18. (Whitehead's response is 'Analysis of Meaning' in Whitehead (1947): 122–31.)

Emmet, D. (1946) *The Nature of Metaphysical Thinking*, London: Macmillan; repr. New York: St Martin's Press, 1966. (The role of analogy in metaphysical thinking, with valuable analyses of Whitehead's theory of perception and use of analogy).

Fitch, F.B. (1957) 'Combinatory Logic and Whitehead's Theory of Prehensions', *Philosophy of Science* 24: 331–5. (A partly technical analysis, presenting combinatory logic as the basis of the theory of prehensions and eternal objects.)

Ford, L.S. (1984) *The Development of Whitehead's Metaphysics, 1925–1929*, Albany: State University of New York Press, 1984. (A detailed discussion of the development of Whitehead's central metaphysical concepts).

—— (ed.) (1971) *Process Studies*, California: Claremont. (A journal devoted to Whitehead and 'process' philosophies.)

Ford, L.S. and Kline, G.L. (1983) *Explorations in*

Whitehead's Philosophy, New York: Fordham University Press. (A useful collection which includes essays by Buchler, Christian, Cobb, Henry, Kline, Ford and Rorty.)

Haack, S (1979) 'Descriptive and Revisionary Metaphysics', *Philosophical Studies* 35: 361–71. (An instructive comparison of *The Concept of Nature* with P.F. Strawson's *Individuals*.)

Hampe, M. and Maassen, H. (eds) (1991) *Prozess, Gefühl und Raum-Zeit: Materialen zu Whitehead's Prozess und Realität*, vol. 1; *Die Gifford Lectures und Ihre Deutung: Materialen zu Whitehead's Prozess und Realität*, vol. 2, Frankfurt: Suhrkamp. (A valuable collection, historical and contemporary. Some of the material translated into German has not been published in English.)

Harris, E.E. (1954) *Nature, Mind and Modern Science*, New York: The Macmillan Company. (A valuable analysis and critique of Whitehead's metaphysics from a British Idealist viewpoint, with comparisons to Hegel).

Holz, H. and Wolf-Gazo, E. (eds) (1981) *Whitehead and the Idea of Process*, Proceedings of the First International Whitehead Symposium, Freiburg and Munich: Karl Alber. (A wide-ranging collection of essays by American, British and Continental philosophers.)

Kline, G.L. (ed.) (1963) *Alfred North Whitehead: Essays on His Philosophy*, Englewood Cliffs, NJ: Prentice Hall. (A useful collection which includes essays by Hall, Hartshorne, Leclerc and Rorty.)

Lawrence, N. (1956) *Whitehead's Philosophical Development: A Critical History of the Background of Process and Reality*, Berkeley, CA: University of California Press. (A useful account, which reads Whitehead's development in terms of a tension between 'realism' and 'conceptualism' – a view strongly challenged by Schmidt (1967).)

Leclerc, I. (1958) *Whitehead's Metaphysics: An Introductory Exposition*, London: Allen & Unwin; 2nd edn, 1965. (A standard introductory text to Whitehead's metaphysics.)

—— (ed.) (1961) *The Relevance of Whitehead*, New York: Humanities Press and London: Allen & Unwin. (A collection which includes indispensable essays by Leclerc on Aristotle and Whitehead, and Mays on the Royal Society Memoir of 1906.)

Lowe, V. (1962) *Understanding Whitehead*, Baltimore, MD: The Johns Hopkins University Press; 2nd edn, 1966. (The standard introductory text to Whitehead's entire *oeuvre*.)

—— (1985, 1990) *Alfred North Whitehead: The Man and His Work*, Baltimore, MD: The Johns Hopkins University Press, 2 vols. (A detailed biography of Whitehead, with analyses of his works.)

Mays, W. (1959) *The Philosophy of Whitehead*, New York: The Macmillan Company and London: Allen & Unwin. (An indispensable, nontechnical analysis of Whitehead's metaphysics, relating it to his logical and mathematical work.)

Murphy, A.W. (1927) 'Objective Relativism in Dewey and Whitehead', *Philosophical Review* 36: 121–44; also in W. Hay and M.G. Singer (eds) *Reason and the Common Good: Selected Essays of A.W. Murphy*, Englewood Cliffs, NJ: Prentice Hall Inc., 1963, 163–77. (A striking analysis of the significance and relation of the philosophies of Dewey and Whitehead.)

Nobo, J.L. (1986) *Whitehead's Metaphysics of Extension and Solidarity*, Albany, NY: State University of New York Press, 1986. (This work contains very useful analyses and clarifications of Whitehead's central concepts.)

Palter, R.M. (1960) *Whitehead's Philosophy of Science*, Chicago, IL: University of Chicago Press; 2nd edn, 1970. (A technical and detailed analysis of Whitehead's theories of extension, including an account of his relativity theory.)

Quine, W.V.O. (1941) 'Whitehead and the Rise of Modern Logic' in P.A. Schilpp (ed.) *The Philosophy of A.N. Whitehead*, The Library Of Living Philosophers, La Salle, IL: Open Court, 127–63. (An indispensable analysis, partly technical, which presents Whitehead as tending to 'platonic' realism.)

Rapp, F. and Wiehl R. (eds) (1983) *Whitehead's Metaphysics of Creativity*, Proceedings of the International Whitehead Symposium, Freiburg and Munich: Verlag Karl Alber, 1986; trans. G. Treash et al. New York: State University of New York Press, 1990. (A useful collection of essays mainly by German philosophers and theologians.)

Russell, B. (1948) 'Whitehead and Principia Mathematica', *Mind* 57, 137–8. (An account of the co-authorship of *Principia*, emphasizing Whitehead's role.)

—— (1956) *Portraits From Memory*, London: Allen & Unwin, 1956; chapter 5. (An historically important and amusing account of the influence on Russell of Whitehead's early thoughts on 'construction'.)

Schmidt, P.F. (1967) *Perception and Cosmology in A.N. Whitehead's Philosophy*, New Brunswick, NJ: Rutgers University Press, 1967. (A clear and detailed analysis of Whitehead's philosophical development.)

Wahl, J. (1932) *Vers le concret*, Paris: Vrin. (An influential analysis of Whitehead's place in twentieth-century philosophy, relating him to Heidegger and others.)

Wilson, E. (1931) *Axel's Castle*, New York: Charles Scribner's Sons. (The conceptual connections between Whitehead's thought and twentieth-century literature, Proust in particular.)

JAMES BRADLEY

WHORF, BENJAMIN LEE *see* SAPIR-WHORF HYPOTHESIS

WIENER KREIS *see* VIENNA CIRCLE

WILL, FREEDOM OF THE *see* FREE WILL

WILL, THE

As traditionally conceived, the will is the faculty of choice or decision, by which we determine which actions we shall perform. As a faculty of decision, the will is naturally seen as the point at which we exercise our freedom of action – our control of how we act. It is within our control or up to us which actions we perform only because we have a capacity to decide which actions we shall perform, and it is up to us which such decisions we take. We exercise our freedom of action through freely taken decisions about how we shall act.

From late antiquity onwards, many philosophers took this traditional conception of the will very seriously, and developed it as part of a general theory of specifically human action. Human action, on this theory, is importantly different from animal action. Not only do humans have a freedom of or control over their action which animals lack; but this freedom supposedly arises because humans can act on the basis of reason, while animal action is driven by appetite and instinct. Both this freedom and rationality involve humans possessing what animals are supposed to lack: a will or rational appetite – a genuine decision making capacity.

From the sixteenth century on, this conception of the will and its role in human action met with increasing scepticism. There was no longer a consensus that human action involved mental capacities radically unlike those found in animals. And the idea that free actions are explained by free decisions of the will came to be seen as viciously regressive: if our freedom of action has to come from a prior freedom of will, why shouldn't that freedom of will have to come from some yet further,

will-generating form of freedom – and so on ad infinitum?

Yet it is very natural to believe that we do have a decision making capacity, and that it is up to us how we exercise that capacity – that it is indeed up to us which actions we decide to perform. The will-scepticism of early modern Europe, which persists in much modern Anglophone philosophy of action, may then have involved abandoning a model of human action and human rationality that is deeply part of common sense. We need to understand this model far better before we can conclude that its abandonment by so many philosophers really was warranted.

1 The will and rational action
2 The will and the free will problem
3 The will and ethical theory
4 Scepticism about actions of the will

1 The will and rational action

Talk of an individual's will may mean simply what actions they are motivated to perform. In this sense any performer of actions, or *agent*, has a will. But talk of the will has served more specifically to pick out the motivations of those action performers who are *rational agents*.

Suppose that there are rational justifications for performing some actions rather than others – justifications which come from a practical or action-governing reason. Then a rational agent is an agent who has the capacity to come to recognize these requirements, and then apply them.

Not all agents need be rational agents. To be a rational agent, one needs, first, a practical intellect or deliberative capacity to form practical judgments about what actions are rationally justified; and second, one needs an executive capacity to apply these judgments in one's actions. Animals, in particular, have often been seen (by Aquinas, for instance) to lack practical intellect. They supposedly have no conception of a justification for action, and so act simply on the basis of appetite.

Notice that rational agents, on our definition, can act irrationally, through defective use of their deliberative and executive capacities. They might make a deliberative mistake as to what actions are justified, or (though this possibility is controversial; see AKRASIA) the defect might be purely executive, in their deliberate performance of an action despite their judgment of this action as unjustified.

Someone who does count as a rational agent can be said to possess a *rational appetite* – a capacity to become motivated to act through rational decision making, thereby forming intentions to act, decisions and intentions based in turn on their deliberations about what actions would be justified. Talk of a faculty of will has typically served to pick out this rational appetite or decision making capacity. *Intellectualists*, most famously Thomas Aquinas, see the will as tied to the practical intellect, decisions to perform a particular action occurring through a practical judgment that that action should be performed. Accordingly, any freedom of decision must derive from a freedom of the practical intellect (see VOLUNTARISM). Whereas, flourishing after Aquinas, *voluntarists* maintain that the will has a freedom independent of the practical intellect. One might even decide, irrationally, to perform an action despite judging its performance to be unjustified.

Medieval and early modern scholasticism produced highly developed theories of human agency as involving the will. Thus Aquinas saw intentional or deliberate human action as generally involving the exercise of the will: when I intentionally move my hand, that action arises out of my willing my hand to move. And Aquinas thought this because, in his view, a truly deliberate action must arise from a capacity to respond motivationally to rational requirements attendant upon action – in other words, from an exercise of the rational appetite. Animal action could not be intentional as ours is, precisely because animals lack this rational motivational capacity.

Furthermore, Aquinas conceived the exercise of the will to be itself a case of action. The *first-order* agency of ordinary actions such as deliberately raising one's hand, was to be explained in terms of a *second-order*, action-generating agency of the will. Why see the willings or decisions to act which, allegedly, explain our actions as being actions themselves? A key assumption is that action in its distinctively human, fully intentional form, consists in agents conforming to or violating requirements of practical reason. 'An act is [fully] voluntary when it is an operation of reason' (*Summa theologiae* Ia IIae, q.6 a.1). On this *practical reason-based* view of human agency, to act is to exercise our rationality, whether competently or defectively, in a distinctively practical way. And this we do, in particular, in the decisions by which we motivate ourselves to perform this action rather than that. For whether we count as conforming to or violating practical reason does indeed plausibly depend on which actions we decide to perform (see AQUINAS, T. §12).

Wherever a conception of human agency as essentially the exercise of practical rationality has remained compelling, so theorists have been inclined to characterize ordinary human actions, such as intentional hand-raisings, as involving an inherently intentional, action-motivating agency of the will. How more precisely the will is conceived then greatly depends on the accompanying conception of our practical rationality. Thus Kant, holding practical reason to be the legislation of all rational agents, conceived the will partly as *Wille*, a capacity for autonomous legislation, and partly as *Willkür*, an executive, action generating capacity that was itself exercised freely. Deliberate human agency, whether rational or irrational – whether conforming to *Wille* or not – generally involved the operation of *Willkür*.

Did the Greeks entertain analogously will-based theories of human agency? Only rational humans, according to Aristotle, can act on the basis of *prohairesis*, or a rational choice based on deliberation about how it would be good to act (see *Nichomachean Ethics*, Book III). Aquinas took Aristotle's *prohairesis* to be equivalent to his own *electio* or decision of the will; but mistakenly, since Aquinas' decision of the will was supposed to be a general feature of intentional human action, whereas for Aristotle only some such human action was prohairetic: intentional human agency could also occur without involving a distinctively rational appetite.

Stoicism did develop a more truly will-involving conception of human agency. While animal action was seen as simply driven by impulse, humans were considered to have a rational capacity for *sunkatathēsis* – a capacity for judgmental assent to, or dissent from, a given action – which capacity was believed essential to our deliberate agency. Thus humans had control over what actions they assented to. The voluntary was thought to begin then at the point where, through *sunkatathēsis*, we motivated ourselves to perform a given action (see STOICISM §12).

2 The will and the free will problem

The free will problem can arise as a strictly ethical problem about our moral responsibility for our actions: under what conditions can we genuinely deserve morally based reward or blame for what we do? (See §3.) But the free will problem can also arise as a problem, not immediately ethical, about freedom of action – about whether we possess genuine control of how we act, in the sense of possessing a freedom to act otherwise than as we actually do: is it really up to us which actions we perform?

It is nowadays sometimes assumed that, as a problem about action, the free will problem has nothing much to do with the will. But this is a mistake, as our ordinary intuition about freedom of action suggests. It is up to us which actions we perform only because we are capable of taking decisions about how we shall act, and it is up to us which actions we decide to perform. Is not that a claim about our freedom to which we naturally assent? If so, then our ordinary conception of our freedom is *psychologizing*: that is, the freedom of our first-order action is held to depend on our possession of a prior, psychological analogue of that freedom located in a second-order agency of the will.

We have seen that the idea that we have a capacity for a second-order agency of the will at all – that the decisions which explain our actions are actions themselves – comes with a practical reason-based conception of our agency: human action consists in the exercise of practical rationality. It is plausible then that our psychologizing conception of our freedom of action is likewise to be explained in terms of some connection between freedom of action and practical rationality. A widely believed condition of possessing freedom of action, after all, is that one have a capacity for practical rationality. Free agents must be able to exercise their control over their actions in a reason-applying way. Animals such as sharks or mice are not free to act otherwise than as they do, precisely because they are not plausibly rational agents. Perhaps this connection between freedom and practical rationality can explain why freedom of action should depend on a freedom of the will in particular.

One way this explanation might work is if we suppose that free agents must indeed be able to exercise their control over their actions in a reason-applying way. How then does practical reason recommend actions to us? Plausibly it does so in the form of plans, or sequences extending through time. When we deliberate about how to act, we are almost invariably deliberating between rival *plans* or sequences of action extending into the future, our performance of which as a whole depends on our continuing motivation into the future. And that is because how we act in the present generally only has value for us on the assumption that we do go on to perform further appropriate actions in the future. Saying a given word now generally only has value if we do go on to utter the other words composing our message. Stepping out of the door now only has value if we do continue walking to the supermarket thereafter. The unit of practical reason – the form in which actions have value for us, and so the form in which we deliberate about them – is the plan.

So to exercise action control in a reason-applying way, we need to exercise control over whole plans, and so over sequences of action extending into the future. Without plan control, as we just saw, we should at any given time lack control over such elementary matters as what we communicated, or where we shopped: for such depend on which plans we execute. Now such plan control can only come from some controlled doing in the present, available to us as rational deliberators, by which we can determine which future actions we shall be performing. And deciding to act looks as though it is precisely the doing required. By deciding on a given plan of action, we can ensure that we thereafter remain motivated to execute it, so that we do act as we have deliberated we should. That is why our decisions can often leave us and others knowing in advance that we shall indeed be acting as we have decided. Decision making can give us plan control, provided of course that taking a particular decision to act is indeed something that we deliberately do, so that we can have control over which actions we decide to perform. Given free will, decision control gives us a capacity for rational self-determination – for controlling our actions in the form in which they matter to us as rational agents. And that is a capacity which free agents plausibly need.

3   The will and ethical theory

Does being a morally responsible agent require any special capacity of will, beyond even that required for being a rational agent?

Thomas Nagel has claimed that there is an aspect of common sense morality which excludes luck: someone's moral goodness or conformity to moral requirements must not depend on any factors which are outside their control, or for which they are not morally responsible. Yet people's ordinary first-order actions and their consequences do seem to depend on luck. Whether, for example, a given person ever manages to help others must depend on matters for which they may well not be responsible, such as the presence of others needing help, and their own possession of the skill and resources to provide the help (see MORAL LUCK).

The only capacity for action that could ever be independent of luck seems to be the second-order action of one's will – of one's decisions to perform first-order actions. For whether or not others are around to be helped, and whether or not one could help others if one tried, one can still take an advance *decision* to help others should the need arise and should one be able to help. It is in such inner decisions of the will, then, that the moral life must be lived: moral obligations are obligations on the will; and it is solely through the agency of one's will that one can count as virtuous or morally good.

However, perhaps even the actions of the will are not really independent of luck either. What decisions I take depends on my education and upbringing, matters of luck too. The doctrine that morality excludes luck is arguably a sceptical view, that prevents morality applying to any empirical agents like us.

But there is a quite different view which also implies moral obligations on the will. *Virtue legalism* is the view that the moral life involves conformity to a moral law containing obligations; and that, in particular, we are under an obligation to be virtuous or morally good.

Now moral goodness does seem to depend, not on our ordinary first-order actions and their consequences, but on the motivation behind those actions. The morally good person is not the person who actually helps others, but rather the person who is motivated to help others if they can. One's moral goodness reflects, after all, how far one is swayed to appropriate first-order action by morally relevant considerations, such as the needs of others. It follows then, that an obligation to be morally good is an obligation to be motivated to perform certain first-order actions.

Now one very natural view is that the only proper object of obligation is action, or refraining from action. We can only be obliged, just as we can only be commanded, to do things or refrain from doing them. We cannot be under an obligation to have things simply happen to us, independently of any action or omission on our part. Suppose then that any moral obligation must be an obligation on action; then, if moral virtue lies in being motivated to perform certain first-order actions, and this moral virtue is obligatory, it follows that such motivation must itself arise from an action-motivating, second-order agency of the will.

Virtue legalism has a long history. Writers as diverse as Abelard (1136–9) and Leibniz (1706), the Stoics and Richard Cumberland (1672), teach that the moral law is distinguished from merely human laws precisely by virtue of its demanding, not simply conformity to rules governing our external behaviour, but the right disposition of will.

Recent moral philosophy has seen a revival of the view that morality presupposes an agency of the will – but this time outside virtue legalism. David Gauthier (1986) has argued that conformity to moral obligations, say to altruism, can be rationally justified in terms of self interest. While altruistic first-order actions may not be in one's interest, the disposition to perform them may be, in that holding it secures the cooperation of others. In which case self interest makes it rational to secure that cooperation by disposing oneself – through a decision of the will – to altruism. The rationality of the disposition formation qua decision to act is then supposed to imply the rationality of the altruistic action decided on, should the occasion for performing it ever arise.

Gauthier's theory reveals a tension in our ordinary thinking about rationality and the will. If taking a particular decision is itself an action, then can it not be made rational, like any action, by its expected good consequences? But these expected good consequences may arise, as in Gauthier's example, independently of performance of the action decided upon. So the thought that decisions to act are actions themselves seems to imply that the rationality of a decision to act is to be determined as Gauthier determines it – in terms of the decision's consequences, and not those of the action decided upon, and so other than by reference to a prior and independent rationality attaching to the action decided upon.

But we also think that the rationality of deciding to do A *does* depend wholly on a prior and independent rationality attaching to doing A: since the function of decisions to act is to apply reason as it concerns the actions decided upon, what makes it rational to decide to do A in particular can only be the prior rationality of doing A – in which case, of course, the rationality of deciding to do A would indeed (as Gauthier also wants to maintain) imply the rationality of doing A thereafter.

The natural idea that decisions serve to apply reason as it concerns the actions decided upon is not obviously consistent with the equally natural idea that decisions are themselves deliberate actions. This is a deep and unresolved problem in our conception of rational agency and the will.

4 Scepticism about actions of the will

Scepticism about actions of the will developed when, in the early modern period, theorists abandoned a practical reason-based theory of human action, characterizing human action instead as, hitherto, animal action had been characterized – in purely motivational terms, as a product of appetite.

Something at least analogous to human action occurs in animals. We talk of animals performing actions for purposes, such as stalking in order to catch prey. But if animals are not rational agents, their actions cannot be characterized as exercises of practical rationality. And so the same philosophers who proposed practical reason-based theories of human action, also proposed importantly different, motivation-based accounts of animal action. Animal action was merely the purposive product of appetite: it was performed simply as a believed or perceived means to desired ends, whether for its own sake or as a means to further ends. A non-rational animal's A-ing counted as its action in virtue of its being moved to A by some appetite for a given end, and a belief or perception that doing A would or might further that end.

We have here an analogue of human action, simply

because so much human action is purposive in its motivation too. It is just that this motivation in humans was supposed to come from an exercise of rationality. Whereas in animals, the appetites that motivated were supposed non-rational in origin.

Notice, however, that not all human actions are purposive. Particular decisions to act, even if actions themselves, still are not taken as means to ends. My decision to do A rather than B will characteristically be based on beliefs about what ends would be furthered by doing A rather than B – not on the basis of beliefs about what ends would be furthered by *deciding to do* A rather than B. In deliberation we consider as means to ends, not our decisions to act themselves but the actions between which we must decide. If deciding to perform a particular action counts as a deliberate action itself, that must be because the decision counts as an exercise of practical rationality, and not because of its purposiveness.

From the sixteenth century on, we find increasing numbers of theorists characterizing all action, human and animal, in terms of a purposive motivation. And the will itself was reconceived, no longer as a distinctively rational appetite peculiar to humans, but as a simple locus of action-motivating passion found in animal and human alike. In other words, all action, human and animal alike, was characterized as a product of a will to perform it. As Hobbes put it in *Leviathan* chapter 6, 'a Voluntary Act is that, which proceedeth from the Will, and no other'. Since the willing of a particular action is not plausibly purposive itself, or willed – on any view, we do not generally take particular decisions to act on the basis of having decided so to decide – the will itself ceased to appear to be a locus of agency or freedom.

What encouraged the abandonment of a practical reason-based conception of human agency? Relevant developments in early modern thought are: (a) scepticism about human practical rationality; (b) projects of reconceiving rational human action in the same terms as animal action; and (c) scepticism about practical reason itself.

(a) Thanks to Augustine, it was generally agreed by Western Christians that Adam's Fall had seriously damaged our practical rationality. Now, on many views, fallen humans still retained some capacity for practical rationality, the will remaining a rational appetite. But the Reformation popularized a radical conception of the Fall that denied the practical rationality of fallen humanity outright. John CALVIN, for example, admitted that as fallen we retained an intellect which distinguished us from the animals. We still formed rational judgments about which actions were justified. But the Fall had wholly removed our executive capacity to apply these rational judgments,

which no longer affected what actions we were motivated to perform. Human action now took the same appetite-driven form as animal action, and the human will was no longer a rational appetite or locus of free agency (see Calvin 1559 Book II, Chapter 2).

(b) Unlike Calvin, Thomas Hobbes allowed that humans could still be practically rational as animals were not. However, Hobbes also wanted to develop an economical action-explanatory theory in materialist terms, characterizing rational human action in the same terms as non-rational animal action: so not as an exercise of a distinctively human practical rationality, but as a will-motivated, purposive doing. For Hobbes, human practical rationality had done nothing to transform human action into anything different in nature from animal action. Our practical rationality came with language – reasoning, in Hobbes's view, being just the reckoning of the implications of the general terms of a language. Language on this view was simply an invented tool which served to record and express action-motivating beliefs and appetites that were themselves language-independent. As language users, reasoning beings did not have either a psychology or a capacity for agency different in kind from that found in non-reasoning beings, any more than the actions of those who enjoy the invention of another communicative tool, writing, are different in kind from the actions of those who lack that tool.

(c) A final source of support for a motivation-based account of human agency is, of course, scepticism about practical reason itself. There may seem little point in characterizing our agency as an exercise of rationality if, in fact, as Hume expressly claimed, our agency is not governed by reason at all. It is no surprise then that for David Hume, far from being a locus of rational appetition and agency, the will was simply a phenomenological marker for passion-motivated action: as he put it in the *Treatise* in 'Of liberty and necessity': 'By the *will*, I mean nothing but *the internal impression we feel and are conscious of, when we knowingly give rise to any new motion of our body, or new perception of our mind*'.

See also: ACTION; FREE WILL; INTENTION; PRACTICAL REASON AND ETHICS; VIRTUE ETHICS

References and further reading

* Abelard, P. (1136–9) *Ethics*, trans. and ed. D. Luscombe, Oxford: Clarendon Press, 1971. (Referred to in §3; states a legalism of merit or moral worth in the form of an ethics of obligations on the will.)

* Aquinas, T. (1265–74) *Summa theologiae*, ed. T.

Gilbey, with Latin and English texts and notes, London and New York: Blackfriars, 60 vols, 1962–. (Referred to in §1; Aquinas's theory of action is given in volume 17.)

* Aristotle (*c*. mid 4th century BC) *Nicomachean Ethics*, trans. and notes T. Irwin, Indianapolis, IN: Hackett Publishing Company, 1985. (Referred to in §1; *prohairesis* is characterized in books 3, 6 and 7.)

* Calvin, J. (1559) *Institutes of the Christian Religion*, trans. F.L. Battles, ed. J.T. McNeill, Philadelphia, PA: Library of Christian Classics, 1960. (Referred to in §4; Calvin's account of fallen human action and the will is given in volume 1, book II, chapter 2.)

* Cumberland, R. (1672) *A Treatise of the Laws of Nature*, selections in J.B. Schneewind (ed.) *Moral Philosophy from Montaigne to Kant*, Cambridge: Cambridge University Press, vol. 1, 1990. (Referred to in §3; chapter 8 contains a statement of virtue legalism as implying obligations on the will.)

* Gauthier, D. (1986) *Morals by Agreement*, Oxford: Oxford University Press. (Chapter 6 contains the argument for the rationality of altruistic actions from the rationality, in self interested terms, of deciding to act altruistically. This argument is referred to in §3.)

* Hobbes, T. (1651) *Leviathan*, ed. R. Tuck, Cambridge: Cambridge University Press, 1991. (Referred to in §4. Chapters 4–5 provide Hobbes's account of human rationality as language-involving. Chapter 6 his account of human and animal action as uniformly language and reason independent.)

* Hume, D. (1739–40) *Treatise of Human Nature*, ed. L.A. Selby-Bigge, revised P.H. Nidditch, Oxford: Oxford University Press, 1978. (Referred to in §4; see Book 2, Part 3, Section 3 'Of liberty and necessity' where the will is characterized merely as a phenomenological marker for subsequent action.)

Kahn, C. (1988) 'Discovering the Will', in J. Dillon and A. Long (eds) *The Question of 'Eclecticism'*, Berkeley, CA: University of California Press. (Compares conceptions of motivation and will in Aristotle, the Stoics and Aquinas.)

Kent, B. (1996) *Virtues of the Will: The Transformation of Ethics in the Late Thirteenth Century*, Washington, DC: Catholic University of America Press. (Describes the medieval conflict between intellectualist and voluntarist views of the will.)

* Leibniz, G.W. (1706) *Opinion on the Principles of Pufendorf*, in *Leibniz: Political Writings*, ed. P. Riley, Cambridge: Cambridge University Press, 1972. (Referred to in §3; in Section 3 Leibniz defends, against Pufendorf, the virtue legalistic view that natural law addresses the internal move-

ments of the soul, and not merely external behaviour.)

* Nagel, T. (1976) 'Moral Luck', in *Mortal Questions*, Cambridge: Cambridge University Press, 1979. (Referred to in §3. Nagel considers the view that morality is concerned with the will, rather than external action, because external action depends on luck, while morality excludes luck.)

Pink, T. (1996) *The Psychology of Freedom*, Cambridge: Cambridge University Press. (Expansion of the material in §§2–3. The book explains how common sense psychology conceives of decision making as a second-order, action-generating action; and how our freedom of action depends on a freedom specifically of decision-making.)

—— (1997) 'Reason and Agency', *Proceedings of the Aristotelian Society*, 263–80. (Expansion of the material in §§1 and 4. The article compares a practical reason-based conception of action, which allows for an agency of the will, with motivation-based conception, which does not.)

THOMAS PINK

WILLIAM OF AUVERGNE (*c.*1180–1249)

Active in Paris during the third and fourth decades of the thirteenth century, when universities were emerging as centres of Western European intellectual life, William played a decisive role in the early development of high medieval philosophy. His writing reveals a familiarity with Aristotle, all of whose major works except the Metaphysics *were readily available in Latin translation, and with the Islamic philosophers, most especially Avicenna but also Averroes, whose commentaries on Aristotle were just beginning to circulate. William looked back to the Neoplatonic traditions of the twelfth century, but he also looked ahead to the late-thirteenth-century Aristotelianizing that he and his contemporary, Robert Grosseteste, did so much to promote.*

Born in Aurillac, France, around 1180, William of Auvergne went to Paris to study arts and then theology, in which field he became a university master in the 1220s. In 1228 he was named bishop of Paris and ex officio the ecclesiastical overseer of the university. He died in that post in 1249. His major philosophical work is a massive and sometimes rambling collection of treatises called the *Magisterium divinale ac sapientiale* (Teachings on Divinity and Wisdom), the exact contents of which are debated but

725

which surely included the important *De universo* (On the Universe) and possibly *De anima* (On the Soul). Parts of the *Magisterium* date from the 1220s, but the finishing touches were applied in the 1230s and perhaps, in the case of *De anima*, shortly after 1240.

On the surface, William presented himself as a resolute defender of the largely Augustinian principles of Christian tradition (see AUGUSTINIANISM) against what he saw as the alternately dangerous and absurd presuppositions of the pagan philosophers, most especially Plato and Aristotle. His metaphysics was consciously anti-Platonic, for although he accepted the exemplarist notion that the world was fashioned after archetypal ideals – which he, like AUGUSTINE, interpreted as ideas in the mind of God – he resolutely opposed Plato's preoccupation with the tenuousness of material reality. His position was manifested most clearly in semantics, where he rejected the contention that the real reference of the terms of normal speech was more directly to the archetypes than to the concrete world around us. Like Aristotle, he held that simple terms referred to real essences in the actual world (see LANGUAGE, MEDIEVAL THEORIES OF). Yet William's concrete realism likewise spurned the Aristotelian notion that individuals were the instantiation of universal essences particularized by material accidents. Instead, he maintained that real essences were in themselves completely particular and fully specific, so that individuals differed not just by their material accidents but also by their own individual essential cores. The idea remained an important subcurrent in medieval thought, emerging again with particular force in the post-Aristotelian metaphysics of the fourteenth century.

In his philosophy of mind, William also claimed to be setting himself against the Greek models. His metaphysics of essence ruled out Platonic reminiscence, for knowledge was of and from essences in the actual, material world. Yet he also attacked the Aristotelian notion of an agent intellect providing the mind with the forms of objects to be known. On this point he was reading Aristotle through the eyes of Avicenna (see IBN SINA), who posited a separate agent intellect, the tenth of the celestial intelligences and immediate creator of the human mind. In contrast, William proposed an Augustine-inspired intellectual occasionalism by which the mind, naturally capable of perceiving essences directly but handicapped in the world of sin, drew from sensation the material for an almost discursive penetration beyond accidents to the essential nature. For this the mind needed no separation into active and passive functions and did not have to be made subject to material impressions from the level of sensation, but merely relied on its own dynamic capacity to grasp the

objects of intelligibility. His explanation of the procedure whereby it did so depended on the Aristotelian notion of abstraction of the universal from the particular and provided succeeding thinkers with a theoretical base from which to develop the idea at length.

For all his rhetorical anti-peripateticism, therefore, William drew extensively upon Aristotelian perspectives. However, one last aspect of his philosophy of mind provided later Neoplatonizing scholastics such as Roger BACON with reason to claim him as a defender of their view that God was the mind's agent intellect and thus its source of knowledge. In the case of knowledge of selected terms, most significantly those that entered into the first, self-evident principles of science and truth – terms such as 'true', 'good', 'whole' and 'part' – William maintained that the human intellect was indeed required to turn to God, who poured into it the formal elements of such cognition by a kind of intelligible illumination. In this restricted sense, God was the agent intellect William otherwise so vehemently opposed; and to this degree he sowed the seeds of Augustinian illuminationism of the latter part of the thirteenth century.

In epistemology, William was more completely faithful to the emergent Aristotelianism of his day (see ARISTOTELIANISM, MEDIEVAL). Knowledge of the truth was obtained by comparing a proposition to actual conditions in the external world, due account being taken for temporal determination and proper quantification. A true proposition states what actually has been, is or will be the case. He furthermore adopted the basic elements of Aristotle's apodictic theory of science, referring his readers to the classic expositions of scientific knowledge in the *Physics* and the *Posterior Analytics*. His account served along with that of GROSSETESTE as a primary conduit for the reception of such views in the Latin West. 'Science' was certain knowledge of universal conclusions demonstrated from even more certain premises, the whole structure being ultimately reducible to indemonstrable, sometimes self-evident, first principles. This foundationalist model was dominant throughout the rest of the Middle Ages.

However, it is important not to overlook an empiricist side to William's views on science. Like most Aristotelians of the thirteenth century, he thought science – or, in his case, that part of science not traceable to God's illuminated principles – was derived by induction from experience in the world. There is moreover in his works a dramatically non-Aristotelian notion of experience that harked back to Arabic and Hebrew lore on magic and the occult. The real 'experimenters' were for him natural magicians, whose ability to manipulate hidden forces in the natural world held out the promise of marvellous accomplishments. Here again was a theme of major importance for later scholastic thought, picked up with fervour by Roger Bacon and many of the so-called Perspectivists.

See also: ARISTOTELIANISM, MEDIEVAL; AUGUSTINIANISM; GROSSETESTE, R.; NATURAL PHILOSOPHY, MEDIEVAL

List of works

William of Auvergne (*c.*1220–after 1240) *Guilemus Alverni Opera omnia* (Complete Works of William of Auvergne), Orleans: Hotot, 1674; reprinted Frankfurt: Minerva, 1963, 2 vols with supplement. (Contains the treatises variously assigned to the *Magisterium*, including *De anima.*)

—— (*c.*1223) *De trinitate (On the Trinity)*, ed. B. Switalski, Toronto, Ont.: Pontifical Institute of Mediaeval Studies, 1976; trans. R.J. Teske and F.C. Wade, *The Trinity*, Milwaukee, WI: Marquette University, 1989. (Theological treatise, also important for psychology and theory of mind.)

—— (*c.*1225–*c.*1235) *De immortalitate animae* (On the Immortality of the Soul), ed. G. Bülow, *Des Dominicus Gundissalinus Schrift von der Unsterblichkeit der Seele*, Beiträge zur Geschichte der Philosophie des Mittelalters II, 3, Münster: Aschendorff, 1897; trans. R.J. Teske, *The Immortality of the Soul*, Milwaukee, WI: Marquette University, 1991. (This treatise, attributed by Bülow to Gundisalvi, is now generally held to be by William and is extant in two versions.)

—— (*c.*1225) *De bono et malo* (On Good and Evil), ed. J.R. O'Donnell, *Mediaeval Studies* 8, 1946: 245–99. (Besides ethics, contains much on theory of mind.)

—— (after 1228) *Tractatus secundus de bono et malo* (Second treatise on Good and Evil), ed. J.R. O'Donnell, *Mediaeval Studies* 16, 1954: 219–71. (Similar to the earlier treatise of the same name.)

References and further reading

Baumgartner, M. (1893) *Die Erkenntnislehre des Wilhelm von Auvergne* (The Epistemology of William of Auxerre), Münster: Aschendorff. (Still reliable despite its early date.)

Jüssen, G. (1987) 'Wilhelm von Auvergne und die Transformation der scholastischen Philosophie im 13. Jahrhundert' (William of Auvergne and the Transformation of Scholastic Philosophy in the Thirteenth Century), in J.P. Beckmann *et al.* (eds) *Philosophie im Mittelalter*, Hamburg: Meiner,

141–64. (The best overview of William's place in the history of scholasticism.)

Marrone, S.P. (1983) *William of Auvergne and Robert Grosseteste: New Ideas of Truth in the Early Thirteenth Century*, Princeton, NJ: Princeton University Press. (Emphasizes William's epistemology and relation to Aristotelian 'science'.)

Masnovo, A. (1945–6) *Da Guglielmo d'Auvergne a s. Tommaso d'Aquino* (From William of Auvergne to St Thomas Aquinas), Milan: Vita e Pensiero, 3 vols. (Pathbreaking but sometimes unreliable.)

Moody, E.A. (1975) 'William of Auvergne and his Treatise *De anima*', in *Studies in Medieval Philosophy, Science, and Logic: Collected Papers, 1933–69*, Berkeley, CA: University of California Press, 1–109. (Excellent analysis of William's psychology.)

Rohls, J. (1980) *Wilhelm von Auvergne und der mittelalterliche Aristotelismus* (William of Auvergne and Medieval Aristotelianism), Munich: Kaiser. (Places William in the context of thirteenth-century theology.)

Teske, R.J. (1994) 'William of Auvergne on the Individuation of Human Souls', *Traditio* 49: 77–93. (Locates William's arguments concerning the nature of the soul precisely in historical context.)

STEVEN P. MARRONE

WILLIAM OF AUXERRE (1140/50–1231)

William's career spans the decades at the end of the twelfth century and the beginning of the thirteenth century during which the newly recovered Aristotelian natural philosophy, metaphysics and ethics and the newly available works of great Muslim thinkers such as Avicenna and Averroes brought enormous energy and upheaval to intellectual culture. William's own views are traditional, owing their largest debts to Augustine, Boethius and Anselm. However, his major work, Summa aurea, is an influential precursor of the monumental systematic theological treatises that followed half a century later.

William of Auxerre (Guillelmus Altissiodorensis) was a master of theology at Paris. In 1231 Pope Gregory IX appointed him to a commission charged with correcting the works of Aristotle that had been proscribed at Paris in 1210, but William died a few months later and the commission seems never to have carried out its assignment. Of William's work, we possess only *Summa aurea* (The Golden Synopsis [of

Theology]) composed sometime between 1215 and 1225, and *Summa de officiis ecclesiasticis* (Synopsis of Ecclesiastical Offices), a detailed description and explanation of the offices and liturgical practices of the church.

Summa aurea is modelled generally on Peter Lombard's *Sentences* (see LOMBARD, P.) Like the *Sentences*, the *Summa* consists of four books devoted, respectively, to the unity and trinity of God, the created realm (especially human beings and humanity's fall through sin), the incarnation of the Son and the redemption and reparation of fallen humanity, and the sacraments. However, the *Summa* diverges from the *Sentences* significantly in ways that point toward future developments in medieval philosophical thought and literature.

William has broad systematic and philosophical interests reflective of and sensitive to the rapidly expanding intellectual horizons of the early thirteenth century. In the prologue to *Summa aurea*, for example, William reflects on the nature of his project and the methodology appropriate to it, raising the question of the relation between faith and what he calls 'natural reasoning'. His Augustinian position is optimistic about the usefulness of what we would characterize as broadly philosophical methods in theological inquiry: one ought not to believe only what can be established by natural reasoning or expect natural reasoning to be entirely adequate for understanding divine matters, but natural reasoning can support and confirm faith, defend it against heresy and move simple-minded people toward the true faith.

The openness to philosophical reasoning and investigation expressed in the prologue goes some way toward explaining William's willingness to depart from the narrowly doctrinal and theological interests of Lombard's *Sentences* to develop systematic philosophical foundations for the theological issues he wants to address. Whereas Lombard's treatment of God (in Book I of the *Sentences*) begins with a discussion of the mystery of God's trinity-and-unity, William takes up the doctrine of the Trinity only after independent discussion of four proofs for God's existence (in the first treatise of Book I) and arguments for God's unity, simplicity and eternality (in the second treatise).

In Book III, concern for philosophical depth and systematic procedure lead William to replace Lombard's collection of assorted matters associated with the theological virtues with an enormous systematic discussion of moral issues. William begins (in treatise 10) by raising issues prefatory to a discussion of the virtues (*quaestiones praeambulae ad virtutes*). Among these prefatory issues is one concerning the nature of the good in general: 'The fourth question prefatory to

the discussion of virtue is a question about the good. This must be dealt with prior to dealing with virtue because good is placed in the definition of virtue. Moreover, the good is the end of virtue, and the end is conceptually prior to what is directed toward the end' (Book III, treatise 10, ch. 4). William's discussion of the nature of the good is the seed from which grow the famous thirteenth-century treatises on the transcendentals by PHILIP THE CHANCELLOR, ALEXANDER OF HALES, ALBERT THE GREAT, Thomas AQUINAS and BONAVENTURE. William goes on to discuss virtue in general (treatise 11), the theological virtues (12–6), natural law (18), the political virtues (19), cardinal and other moral virtues (20–9), the gifts of the Holy Spirit (30–4) and the beatitudes (35). In all, William's treatment of these matters takes up nearly the whole of Book III (46 of its 55 treatises, 900 of the 1068 pages in the critical edition), and raises moral theory in the Middle Ages to a new level of philosophical sophistication. The immediate influence of this part of *Summa aurea* can be clearly seen in both Philip the Chancellor's *Summa de bono* and Albert the Great's *Summa de bono*.

See also: ALBERT THE GREAT; PHILIP THE CHANCELLOR

List of works

William of Auxerre (1215–25) *Summa aurea* (The Golden Synopsis), ed. J. Ribaillier, Grottaferrata: Editiones Collegii S. Bonaventurae, 1980–7. (William's broad summary of theological and philosophical doctrine, modelled on Lombard's *Sentences*.)

References and further reading

Lottin, O. (1942–60) *Psychologie et Morale aux XIIe et XIIIe siècles*, Gembloux: Duculot. (Several important studies in the first four of these six volumes discuss William's contributions to medieval thought.)

MacDonald, S. (1992) 'Goodness as Transcendental: The Early Thirteenth-Century Recovery of an Aristotelian Idea', *Topoi* 11: 173–86. (An examination of William's and Philip the Chancellor's discussions of the metaphysics of goodness.)

Ribaillier, J. (1967) 'Guillaume d'Auxerre', *Dictionnaire de Spiritualité* vol. 6, ed. Gabriel-Guzman, Paris: Beauchesne, cols. 1192–9. (A fuller account of William's life and work than that provided in the introductory material in Ribaillier's edition of *Summa aurea*.)

St. Pierre, J.A. (1966) 'The Theological Thought of William of Auxerre: An Introductory Bibliography',

Recherches de théologie ancienne et médiévale 33: 147–55. (A useful bibliographical essay.)

SCOTT MacDONALD

WILLIAM OF CHAMPEAUX (*c.*1070–*c.*1120)

William studied under Anselm of Laon and became one of a number of famous teachers of logic, rhetoric, grammar and theology in early twelfth-century France, teachers who helped to establish the schools which eventually turned into the University of Paris. He is perhaps best known for his dispute with his young pupil Peter Abelard over the reality of universals, a debate which William lost so badly that most of his students elected to be taught by Abelard instead.

William's position on the nature of universals (genera and species) was that they were real things that were determined by accidents in much the way that some amorphous material is determined by shapes accidentally accruing to it (see UNIVERSALS). Thus a highest genus, such as substance, becomes determined to its various species, such as body and spirit, by different, opposed accidents which it possesses simultaneously. Like many thinkers at this time, especially among the theologians, William accepted the Porphyrian interpretation of Aristotle's *Categories*, according to which the categories provide a 'tree-structured' classification scheme for all entities (see PORPHYRY). Actually there are ten different 'trees' corresponding to each of Aristotle's ten categories, and each successive 'branching' of each tree leads to more and more specific species of entities in the category in question. Each tree culminates in the individuals within the category, that is, the things that do not undergo any further 'branching' (see CATEGORIES §1).

William treated the mutually opposed differences, which create the species that immediately branch off from a genus, as accidents of that genus, and then went on to allow for individuating differences, which create the individuals that branch off from a final species and are mutually opposed accidents of that species. Just as one individual is distinguished from another individual of the same species only by characteristics that are accidental to that species, so each species under the same genus is distinguished by forms accidental to that genus. William's view encourages one to see each individual as ontologically constructed of successive layers of forms attaching themselves to a core that is like the highest genus under which the individual is subsumed.

ABELARD quickly pointed out that this view defied the principle that opposites cannot simultaneously belong to one and the same thing, and that it also entailed that there were really only ten distinct things in the world, the ten highest genera, or categories. In William's view, everything turns out to be either one of those highest genera without any accidents or one of them with layered accumulations of accidental forms. Naturally, few were willing to accept such consequences, and William's form of realism ceased to be a live option among medieval thinkers once Abelard's critique became known.

According to Abelard, William also held that simple categorical sentences of the form of 'Socrates is white' had two senses, a grammatical sense and a dialectical (that is, logical) sense. The former treats the sentence as identifying Socrates with some white thing, while the latter treats it as asserting that whiteness inheres in Socrates. Although, according to William, the dialectical sense is 'higher', it is in its grammatical sense that the sentence is true or false. William's realist approach to universals is again apparent in the talk of the inherence of some property.

William's realism surfaces again in connection with the doctrine of topics. The topic or *locus* on which some argument depends for its logical force is, according to him, a thing in the world the argument is talking about. For example, the argument 'Socrates is a man; therefore he is an animal' has as its *locus* the thing 'man'. The general principle behind the argument, the *maxima*, is, 'What the species is predicated of, so also is the genus', and William interprets this as multiply ambiguous. Each conditional proposition that exemplifies the *maxima*, such as, 'If Socrates is a man, Socrates is an animal', expresses one of the *maxima*'s meanings. The *maxima* is then a kind of schema for propositions rather than a proposition itself. According to Abelard, one reason William held this was that the *maxima* could prove inferences only if it were about the things those inferences concerned. Thus again realism shapes William's logical doctrines.

This controversy over universals is the result of very divergent views of how the genera, species and differences, mentioned so frequently in the Aristotelian writings, should be interpreted. Among logicians in the late eleventh and early twelfth centuries the view that universality is consequent on linguistic signification had been gaining converts, while among theologians there was a pronounced tendency to see universality as a feature ontologically independent of thought and language. Abelard represents the former interpretation, and William the latter. William went on from his disastrous confrontation with Abelard to become a teacher of theology and eventually Bishop of Chalons-sur-Marne.

See also: ABELARD, P.; ARISTOTELIANISM, MEDIEVAL; LANGUAGE, MEDIEVAL THEORIES OF; REALISM AND ANTIREALISM; UNIVERSALS

List of works

Fragments of works probably by William of Champeaux can be found in Fredborg (1976) and Green-Pedersen (1974).

William of Champeaux (*c.*1070–*c.*1120) Commentary on *Rhetorica ad Herennium*, ed. K.M. Fredborg, 'The Commentaries on Cicero's *De Inventione* and *Rhetorica ad Herennium* by William of Champeaux', *Cahiers de l'Institut du Moyen-Age Grec et Latin* XVII, 1976, 1–39. (A recently discovered text by William; for advanced scholars.)
—— (*c.*1070–*c.*1120) Commentary on Boethius' *De topicis differentiis*, in N.J. Green-Pedersen (ed.), 'William of Champeaux on Boethius' Topics according to Orleans Bibl. Mun. 266', *Cahiers de l'Institut du Moyen Age Grec et Latin* XIII, 1974: 13–30. (For specialists on the 'topics' literature.)

References and further reading

Fredborg, K.M. (ed.) (1976) 'The Commentaries on Cicero's *De Inventione* and *Rhetorica ad Herennium* by William of Champeaux', *Cahiers de l'Institut du Moyen-Age Grec et Latin* XVII: 1–39. (Some significant, recently discovered texts, evidently by William himself; for advanced scholars.)
Green-Pedersen, N.J. (ed.) (1974) 'William of Champeaux on Boethius' *Topics* according to Orleans Bibl. Mun. 266', *Cahiers de l'Institut du Moyen Age Grec et Latin* XIII: 13–30. (For specialists on the 'topics' literature.)
—— (1984) *The Tradition of the Topics in the Middle Ages; the Commentaries on Aristotle's and Boethius' Topics*, Munich: Philosophia Verlag. (See pages 165– for a discussion of William's contribution to the medieval devlopment of 'topics', that is, non-formal logical inference.)
Stump, E. (1988) 'Logic in the Early Twelfth Century', in N. Kretzmann (ed.) *Meaning and Inference in Medieval Philosophy*, Dordrecht: Kluwer, 31–55. (Discusses a treatise composed in William's school as well as other known logical works of the period.)
Tweedale, M. (1988) 'Logic (i): From the Late Eleventh Century to the Time of Abelard', in P. Dronke (ed.) *A History of Twelfth-Century Western Philosophy*, Cambridge: Cambridge University Press, 196–226. (Places William in the general context of logical and grammatical thought of his period.)
—— (1976) *Abailard on Universals*, Amsterdam: North Holland, 95–111. (An analysis of William's view of universals and Abelard's critique.)

MARTIN M. TWEEDALE

WILLIAM OF CONCHES
(*fl. c.*1130)

William of Conches – whom many historians have attached to the School of Chartres – was one of the early twelfth century's keenest commentators on Platonic texts, and wrote also on natural science. He believed in the harmony of Platonism and Christianity. He thought that the ostensibly pagan texts of Plato and his followers contained Christian truths which the interpreter needed to uncover, while Platonic (and more recent) science could help towards an understanding of the account of creation in Genesis.

Born in Normandy, William of Conches was already teaching and writing in the early 1120s and appears to have remained active until the 1150s. Where he taught is much disputed; he may have taught at Paris, but there is a little more evidence to link him with Chartres. Certainly his pupil JOHN OF SALISBURY regarded him as at least the spiritual successor of Bernard of Chartres (see CHARTRES, SCHOOL OF). Like Bernard, William was a grammar teacher as well as an enthusiast of Plato, and it is around the twelfth-century conception of grammar that William's apparently diverse interests and writings cohere. Grammar involved detailed technical study of Latin (including the theoretical questions about semantics it raised) (see LANGUAGE, MEDIEVAL THEORIES OF). William's commentary on Priscian's *Institutiones grammaticae* (Principles of Grammar), written when he was young, and revised by him as an old man, fulfilled this task, drawing extensively on the anonymous eleventh-century *Glosule* to Priscian.

The grammarian's work also included the detailed explanation of classical texts, and there was no clear distinction between literary and philosophical material. William is known to have glossed Juvenal, but he concentrated on Platonic works including Plato's own *Timaeus* (in Calcidius' translation), Boethius' *De consolatione philosophiae* (On the Consolation of Philosophy), Macrobius' commentary on Cicero's *Somnium Scipionis* (Scipio's Dream) and probably Martianus Capella. The *Timaeus* and Macrobius were regarded as important sources for natural science, so it is not unexpected that William should have developed this interest independently, in his *Philosophia* and the dialogue *Dragmaticon* (between 1144 and 1149). In these works he also made use of – and sometimes combined or developed in an original way – medical and scientific sources translated from the Arabic and Greek.

By William's time, there was already a long tradition of assimilating Platonic texts by interpreting them allegorically in explicitly Christian terms (see PLATONISM, MEDIEVAL). Indeed, at times he could simply borrow from the late ninth-century commentary on Boethius by Remigius of Auxerre. William differed from his predecessors in the thoroughness with which he applied the idea that the philosophers were using what he called *integumenta* (extended metaphors) to cloak the Christian truth. When pressed, he would admit that the pagan authors were indeed pagans and could not be trusted in everything they said, but usually he discovered a satisfactory reading.

His most daring interpretation was that which made Plato's World Soul an *integumentum* for the Holy Spirit. He shared this interpretation with ABELARD, who may even have been his source. However, there is a revealing difference between the two thinkers' approaches. The identification was controversial because it could be taken to suggest that the Holy Spirit is lower than the other two persons of the Trinity. For Abelard, this had important implications about the knowability of God and the soundness of pagan virtues, which made it impossible for him to give up this identification. By contrast, William is willing to qualify, question and finally, after Abelard's condemnation in 1141, to drop the idea altogether. For him, the identification is no more than a reading of an ancient text, convenient but dispensable.

It was when classical texts provided him with scientific, rather than theological or philosophical ideas, that William took them most seriously and elaborated them for his own use. The account of creation which he gives in the *Philosophia* and the *Dragmaticon*, and also in the glosses to the *Timaeus*, shows how all things – not merely the heavens and earth, but also birds, fishes, animal and humans – came into being through the natural interaction of the four elements (fire, air, water and earth). Only the creation of the human soul required separate divine intervention. To potential critics who objected on religious grounds to such discussions, William argued that he was merely extending the account of creation in Genesis. The Bible says certain things were made: William is explaining *how* they were made. While remaining in the Catholic faith, he says, we should always look for a reason for things and only fall back on authority as a last resort. It is not enough to say 'God made it', because although God can act directly – as he does in miracles – he does not usually do so.

See also: ABELARD, P.; CHARTRES, SCHOOL OF; NATURAL PHILOSOPHY, MEDIEVAL; PLATONISM, MEDIEVAL

List of works

William of Conches (?1120–30) Commentary on Boethius' *De consolatione philosophiae*, in C. Jourdain, 'Des commentaires inédits de la Guillaume de Conches et Nicholas Trivet sur la Consolation de la philosophie de Boèce', *Notices et extraits des manuscrits de la bibliothèque impériale* 20, 2, Paris: Imprimerie impériale, 1865. (Contains extracts from William's commentary on Boethius's *De consolatione philosophiae*.)

—— (?1120–30) *Philosophia mundi* (Natural Philosophy), ed. G. Maurach, Pretoria: University of South Africa Press, 1980. (A treatise on the universe, nature, physiology and the soul.)

—— (c.1130) *Glosae super Platonem* (Glosses on Plato), ed. E. Jeauneau, Paris: Vrin, 1965. (Commentary on *Timaeus*.)

—— (1144–9) *Dragmaticon*, ed. W. Gratarolus, *Dialogus de substantiis physicis*, Strasbourg, 1567; repr. Frankfurt: Minerva, 1967. (A version of the *Philosophia mundi* in dialogue form.)

References and further reading

Elford, E. (1988) 'William of Conches', in P. Dronke (ed.) *A History of Twelfth-Century Western Philosophy*, Cambridge: Cambridge University Press, 308–27. (Mainly on William's scientific thought.)

Gregory, T. (1955) *Anima mundi. La filosofia di Guglielmo di Conches e la Scuola di Chartres* (The World Soul: The Philosophy of William of Conches and the School of Chartres), Florence: Sansoni. (General study of William's thought and its context.)

Jeauneau, E. (1973) *Lectio philosophorum* (Reading the Philosophers), Amsterdam: Hakkert. (Includes essays on William's Priscian and Macrobius commentaries.)

JOHN MARENBON

WILLIAM OF OCKHAM (*c*.1287–1347)

William of Ockham is a major figure in late medieval thought. Many of his ideas were actively – sometimes passionately – discussed in universities all across Europe from the 1320s up to the sixteenth century and even later. Against the background of the extraordinarily creative English intellectual milieu of the early fourteenth century, in which new varieties of logical, mathematical and physical speculation were being explored, Ockham stands out as the main initiator of late scholastic nominalism, a current of thought further exemplified – with important variants – by a host of authors after him, from Adam Wodeham, John Buridan and Albert of Saxony to the school of John Mair far into the sixteenth century.

As a Franciscan friar, Ockham taught theology and Aristotelian logic and physics from approximately 1317 to 1324, probably in Oxford and London. He managed to develop in this short period an original and impressive theological and philosophical system. However, his academic career was interrupted by a summons to the Papal Court at Avignon for theological scrutiny of his teachings. Once there, he became involved in the raging quarrel between Pope John XXII and the Minister General of the Franciscan Order, Michael of Cesena, over the poverty of the church. Ockham was eventually excommunicated in 1328. Having fled to Munich, where he put himself under the protection of the Emperor Ludwig of Bavaria, he fiercely continued the antipapal struggle, devoting the rest of his life to the writing of polemical and politically-oriented treatises.

Because he never was officially awarded the title of Doctor in Theology, Ockham has been traditionally known as the venerabilis inceptor, *the 'venerable beginner', a nickname which at the same time draws attention to the seminal character of his thought. As a tribute to the rigour and strength of his arguments, he has also been called the 'Invincible Doctor'.*

The core of his thought lies in his qualified approach to the old problem of universals, inherited by the Christian world from the Greeks through Porphyry and Boethius. Ockham's stand is that only individuals exist, generality being but a matter of signification. This is what we call his nominalism. In the mature version of his theory, species and genera are identified with certain mental qualities called concepts or intentions of the mind. Ontologically, these are individuals too, like everything else: each individual mind has its own individual concepts. Their peculiarity, for Ockham, lies in their representative function: a general concept naturally signifies *many different individuals. The concept 'horse', for instance, naturally signifies all* singular horses and the concept 'white' all singular white things. They are not arbitrary or illusory for all that: specific and generic concepts, Ockham thought, are the results of purely natural processes safely grounded in the intuitive acquaintance of individual minds with real singular objects; and these concepts do cut the world at its joints. The upshot of Ockham's doctrine of universals is that it purports to validate science as objective knowledge of necessary connections, without postulating mysterious universal entities 'out there'.

Thought, in this approach, is treated as a mental language. Not only is it composed of signs, but these mental signs, natural as they are, are also said to combine with each other into propositions, true or false, just as extra-mental linguistic signs do; and in so doing, to follow rules of construction very similar to those of spoken languages. Ockham thus endowed mental discourse with grammatical categories. However, his main innovation in this respect is that he also adapted and transposed to the fine-grained analysis of mental language a relatively new theoretical apparatus that had been emerging in Europe since the twelfth century: the theory of the 'properties of terms' – the most important part of the logica modernorum, *the 'logic of the moderns' – which was originally intended for the semantical analysis of spoken languages. Ockham, in effect (along with some of his contemporaries, such as Walter Burley) promoted this new brand of semantical analysis to the rank of philosophical method* par excellence. *In a wide variety of philosophical and theological discussions, he made sustained use of the technical notions of 'signification', 'connotation' and, above all, 'supposition' (or reference) and all their cognates. His distinctive contribution to physics, for example, consists mainly in semantical analyses of problematic terms such as 'void', 'space' or 'time', in order to show how, in the end, they refer to nothing but singular substances and qualities.*

Ockham's rejection of universals also had a theological aspect: universals, if they existed, would unduly limit God's omnipotence. On the other hand, he was convinced that pure philosophical reasoning suffices anyway for decisively refuting realism regarding universals, since all its variants turn out to be ultimately self-contradictory, as he endeavoured to show by detailed criticism.

On the whole, Ockham traced a sharper dividing line than most Christian scholastics before him between theological speculation based on revealed premises and natural sciences in the Aristotelian sense, which are based on empirical evidence and self-evident principles. He wanted to maintain this clear-cut distinction in principle through all theoretical and practical knowledge, including ethics and political reasoning. In this last field, in particular, to which Ockham devoted thousands of pages in the last decades of his life, he strenuously defended the independence of secular power from ecclesiastical power, stressing whenever he could the autonomy of right reason in human affairs.

1   **Life**
2–3   **Ontology**
4–5   **Epistemology**
6–7   **Logic and philosophy of language**
8   **Physics**
9   **Natural theology**
10   **Ethics**
11   **Political thought**

1   Life

William of Ockham was born around 1287, probably in the village of Ockham in Surrey, near London. Of his youth we know next to nothing, only that he joined the Franciscan Order (perhaps as a child), that he was ordained subdeacon in London on 27 February 1306 (an appointment for which he would normally have had to be at least eighteen), and that he was licensed to hear confessions on 19 June 1318 (for which he would have had to be at least 30). He must have studied Aristotelian philosophy – and especially logic – quite thoroughly before turning to theology in Oxford around 1310. Following the normal curriculum, he would then have spent the next seven years as a theology student and have lectured for two years (probably from 1317 to 1319) on Peter Lombard's *Sentences* (see LOMBARD, P.) The commentary that resulted is Ockham's first major work. It is a huge treatise in four books, the first of which was later revised by the author for publication and is known, for that reason, as the *Ordinatio*, while the other three, jointly known as the *Reportatio*, circulated merely in the form of a detailed, authorized set of students' notes.

This early, and strikingly original, work might already have raised misgivings in certain quarters at Oxford. Whether for that reason or some other, Ockham was not immediately granted the degree of master of theology, which would have entitled him to continue teaching in the field. He was sent instead to a Franciscan convent, possibly in London, to teach logic and physics, which he did from 1320 to 1324. This turned out to be a very productive period, during which he wrote his commentaries on Porphyry's *Isagoge*, Aristotle's *Categories*, *On Interpretation* and *Sophistical Refutations*, and at least part of his commentary on Aristotle's *Physics*. He also revised his *Ordinatio*, engaged in public disputations on various matters theological and philosophical, and

wrote a few more treatises on especially delicate questions such as transsubstantiation and God's foreknowledge. In the same years he may also have begun (or even completed, according to some) his great *Summa logicae* (Summa of Logic); originally intended for beginners, it eventually became one of the major reference books for the new nominalistic semantics and logic which was to be so influential in the fourteenth and fifteenth centuries.

In the summer of 1324, Ockham left England for Avignon. Most scholars think he was summoned to the papal court there by Pope John XXII for investigation of his teachings. In the previous year a Provincial Franciscan Chapter held in Cambridge had already publicly raised questions about some of his philosophical theses that could be deemed theologically dangerous. In 1325, the Pope established an advisory commission of six renowned theologians to examine fifty-one articles extracted from Ockham's commentary on the *Sentences*. The group included the French Dominican DURANDUS OF ST POURÇAIN, otherwise known for his nominalistic sympathies, and John Lutterell, the ex-Chancellor of Oxford and one of Ockham's fiercest opponents. In 1326 the commission gave a preliminary report, which, while identifying many of Ockham's opinions as erroneous, did not condemn any as clearly heretical. Apparently this did not satisfy the Pope, and a second report was prepared, much more along Lutterell's lines. Ockham became officially suspected of heresy, especially with regard to his theory of moral merits, which was accused of Pelagianism (see PELAGIANISM), and in 1327 Pope John XXII launched a formal inquisitorial process against him.

This process was never brought to a conclusion. However, Ockham in the meantime had got involved in other sorts of troubles. It is probable that during his first years at the Franciscan convent in Avignon, he continued to work on some of his philosophical or theological treatises, such as the *Summa logicae*, the *Quodlibeta septem* (Seven Quodlibetal Questions) and the *Expositio in libros Physicorum Aristotelis* (Commentary on Aristotle's *Physics*). Towards the end of 1327 the Franciscan Minister General, Michael of Cesena, who had himself been recently summoned to Avignon by the Pope, ordered Ockham to study John XXII's bulls of 1322–4 on whether Christ and the Apostles had owned anything and on the poverty of the Franciscan Order in particular. The question was delicate. The papal court was by then scandalously opulent, and John XXII was very much aware of the challenge to it by the advocacy of poverty that had been spreading in many Franciscan quarters in the previous decades. His series of bulls on the subject had been intended to put a stop to this movement.

Comparing these with the Gospels and the writings of previous popes, Ockham boldly concluded that John XXII was himself heretical. Matters eventually got worse between Michael of Cesena and the Pope, and on the evening of 26 May 1328 five Franciscans, including Michael and William, fled from Avignon, fearing for their lives. Having narrowly escaped the Pope's soldiers, they reached Pisa by boat and joined another enemy of John XXII, the Emperor Ludwig of Bavaria. All five were immediately excommunicated.

From 1330 on, Ockham stayed at the Franciscan convent in Munich under the protection of Ludwig of Bavaria and devoted himself to the writing of political treatises. At first, the goal of Michael of Cesena's supporters was to convince the Christian community that John XXII ought to be deposed. Such was the context for Ockham's *Opus nonaginta dierum* (Work of Ninety Days), written in three months in 1332 or 1333, and for the first part of his important unfinished dialogue on the distribution of powers within and outside the church, known simply as the *Dialogus*. In December 1334, John XXII died. Political discussions were opened between Ludwig of Bavaria and the new Pope, Benedict XII, during which Ockham's literary activity was brought to a halt. However, no agreement was reached, and from 1337 to 1342 he produced an impressive number of new writings in which he defended more and more explicitly the independence of the imperial and royal powers from those of the Pope. Especially worth mentioning are the *Tractatus contra Benedictum* (Treatise Against Benedict), the *Octo quaestiones de potestate papae* (Eight Questions on the Power of the Pope) and treatises 1 and 2 (the only ones extant) of *Dialogus* III. After another hiatus at the time of Clement VI's accession to the papal throne, Ockham finally synthesized his political thought in the treatise *De Imperatorum et Pontificum potestate* (On the Power of Emperors and Popes) in 1346 or 1347. He died in April 1347, a few months before Ludwig of Bavaria. Contrary to an old legend, he had taken no steps toward submitting to the Avignon church.

2 Ontology: antirealism

The core of Ockham's philosophical system lies in the idea that only individual beings exist and that universals are nothing but signs, spoken, written or mental. This is what has been called his *nominalism*, a label that came to be associated with his thought towards the end of the fourteenth century (see NOMINALISM).

The theoretical problem it was intended to solve was provided by Porphyry's old questions about universals (see PORPHYRY): do species (such as 'horse') and genera (such as 'animal') exist by themselves outside the mind or not? Are they corporeal or incorporeal? And are they located in the individual beings or do they exist apart from them? By Ockham's time, Platonism, identified as the position according to which universals do exist outside the mind as incorporeal beings over and above the individuals that participate in them, had fallen into disrepute (see PLATONISM, MEDIEVAL). Aristotle was credited with having definitively refuted it. Most philosophers, then, would follow Thomas AQUINAS or John DUNS SCOTUS in adopting some form or other of what we today call 'moderate realism', the thesis according to which universals exist outside the mind but only within the individuals that exemplify them. But this, in the eyes of Ockham, was 'the worst error in philosophy'; and his defence of his own ontology – which he always presented as orthodox Aristotelianism – consisted largely in a detailed, ruthless criticism of the different variants of moderate realism (see ARISTOTELIANISM, MEDIEVAL).

For one thing, he deemed them all incompatible with God's omnipotence. If the universal 'horse' was a common part of each individual horse, then God could not completely destroy any single horse – Bucephalus, for example – without destroying all the others; for in order to destroy the universal 'horse' that was part of Bucephalus, God would have to destroy all the other horses as well. This overtly theological argument reveals one of Ockham's deepest philosophical intuitions: everything that exists, he insisted, should be logically independent of any other thing. This ontological atomism is what he frequently expresses by means of thought experiments involving God's omnipotence. Since God is credited with the power to do anything which is not self-contradictory – a fundamental theological principle, according to Ockham – the realm of what he can do corresponds to the whole array of logical possibilities, and he should, in particular, be able to destroy any single contingent being while keeping any of the others in existence.

However, Ockham's main accusation against the varieties of moderate realism he identified among his contemporaries is that in one way or another they all fall short of internal logical consistency. His chief weapon in ontological disputes was the principle of non-contradiction. The best example of this line of attack lies in his famous critique of Duns Scotus' 'formal distinction'. Scotus, also a Franciscan, whose work Ockham deeply respected and often discussed at great length, had held that the universal natures such as equinity or animality did have some sort of existence outside the mind, but that they were not *in reality* distinct from the individuals that exemplified them. They were merely, Scotus contended, *formally* distinct from them. By this distinction he meant that while they could not exist in reality apart from their individual exemplifications – even by God's omnipotence – there nevertheless was a 'foundation in the thing' for thinking of them as separate. Scotus, like Ockham after him, was dissatisfied with any version of moderate realism that posited the universal nature as being both internal to the individual thing and really distinct from it, because this would entail that the individual thing and the universal nature should logically be able to exist apart from one another, which leads to absurdities. On the other hand, Scotus thought that the validity of the conceptual distinction between the universal and the individual did require that they should not be wholly identical with one another: hence his idea of a formal distinction within real identity.

According to Ockham, this leads directly to contradiction. If the universal nature and the individual thing are really identical to one another, then whatever is true of one of them should also be true of the other, and thus it will be true of the same thing that it is both universal and not universal, individual and not individual. Conversely, if incompatible predicates such as universality and individuality are attributed respectively to the common nature and the individual thing, then this in itself suffices to show that they are distinct from one another *in reality*, for this is precisely the paradigmatic way of proving that two things are really distinct from one another. Scotus' formal distinction thus collapses into the real distinction he wanted to reject in the first place. It is easy to see that this argument, like many others Ockham adduces in similar contexts (against Aquinas, for example), makes a crucial use of what we nowadays call the principle of the indiscernibility of identicals: if *a* and *b* are identical to one another, then whatever is true of *a* is true of *b*; conversely, if something is true of *a* which is not true of *b*, then *a* and *b* are really distinct from one another.

To avoid an old misunderstanding, it must be stressed that Ockham's critique of the ontology of universals does not explicitly rely on the methodological principle of economy that Sir William HAMILTON, in the nineteenth century, labelled 'Ockham's razor': entities are not to be multiplied without necessity. It is true that Ockham's thought consistently shows a strong drive towards ontological economy and that he did on many occasions use the razor (which he himself formulated either as 'a plurality should never be posited without necessity' or as 'it is pointless to do with more what can be done with fewer'). However, this principle was commonly accepted before him, even by realist philosophers. It was thought of – by Ockham as well as by others – as

a mere methodological rule which, taken by itself, yielded only 'probable' conclusions. By contrast, the refutation of the external reality of universals was considered by Ockham as absolutely conclusive since it rested on the principle of non-contradiction.

3 Ontology: substance, quality, form, matter

Although Ockham's nominalism posits only individual things in the external world, it nevertheless admits of ontological differences among them. First of all, he accepted (for a time) a fundamental difference of status between extramental and mental existence. While universals were refused the former, they were granted the latter. They were thought of, in the first version of Ockham's *Ordinatio*, as enjoying a special sort of intentional existence in the mind. This was the existence appropriate to a *fictum*, a mind-made intelligible object which existed only while consciously produced by the mind as an abstract correlate for acts of intellection, and which, for the duration of its existence, could serve as a natural sign representing certain individual beings. Admittedly, there was no room for this sort of existence within the framework of Aristotle's ten categories, but Ockham at first explained away this lacuna by restricting Aristotle's taxonomy to a limited theory of predicates for extramental entities. Later on, however – probably in the early 1320s, under the incisive criticism of his confrère Walter CHATTON – Ockham realized that he could achieve an important ontological economy by letting the act of intellection itself play the role of the natural sign. Since internal acts, interpreted as actualized mental potentialities (*actus*), were commonly classified as qualities of the mind, no special ontological category was needed any longer for intramental existence. The intentional *fictum* could simply be dropped as soon as one recognized that intellectual acts themselves can serve as semantic contents without any need for internal correlates after all. This is a salient instance of Ockham's actually using the razor principle: after a period of hesitation, he finally favoured the *actus* theory over the *fictum* theory as more probable because it could do with less what the other did with more.

However, even with this simplification, ontology was not utterly stripped of categorial plurality. For one thing, Ockham always maintained a fundamental distinction between substances and qualities. Although he interpreted Aristotle's theory of the ten categories as a classification of signs rather than things, he would nevertheless acknowledge, corresponding to it, a basic duality amongst individual entities themselves. Substances, whether corporeal or spiritual, were thought of along the Aristotelian line as autonomous beings, while qualities were held to depend upon them for their own existence. Qualities, Ockham would say, 'inhere' in the individual substance which displays them. They are not essential parts of it, however, and any one of them can be removed (by natural causes or by God's omnipotence) without the substance losing its identity. Each substance, on the other hand, has many qualities, simultaneously and successively, and each one has its own: the whiteness of Bucephalus is a particular thing, numerically distinct from Bucephalus itself and from all the whitenesses of any other beings in the world as well, however similar they might be. Ockham endorses particularism with respect to qualities.

Moreover, this nominalistic ontology is further complicated by the incorporation of Aristotelian hylomorphism, the theory of matter and form. Each singular composite corporeal substance is endowed with a variety of internal parts without which it would not be itself: a certain parcel of prime matter on the one hand, and one or more substantial forms on the other hand. Each human being, for example, is a compound of a determinate piece of matter and a number of substantial forms, such as a nutritive form, a sensory form and an intellectual form. Although these *partes essentiales* are naturally incapable of existing by themselves outside the hylomorphic compound, they are nevertheless counted by Ockham as real, and therefore singular, beings. Matter is thus granted a certain actuality of its own (in opposition to AQUINAS). Forms, on the other hand, are stripped of intrinsic generality, each substance having its own.

Ockham, in summary, admits of four basic sorts of singular beings: substances, qualities, substantial forms and pieces of matter. Together they make up a still comparatively simple ontological system, of which singular substances constitute the core, qualities being attached to them as external properties, and forms and matter incorporated as internal parts.

What struck Ockham's contemporaries in this picture – and many commentators after them – was that it left out not only universals, but relations and quantities as well. These last exclusions, in fact, were a major source of Ockham's early troubles with religious authorities. The Catholic church was at the time imposing severe pressure on philosophical theories, for fear that philosophers might rule out any of its doctrines as impossible. The doctrines of the Trinity, the Incarnation and the Eucharist in particular, were commonly considered as having important implications for theories about relational connections (such as parenthood or ownership) and quantitative dimensions (such as weight, height or length). Ockham held that neither those connections nor those dimensions had any distinct existence of their

own, and this aroused suspicion. However, Ockham had not meant to say that sentences making relational or quantitative claims were neither true nor false, or arbitrarily so. Most of them, he thought, are indeed true or false independently of the human mind: it is not the intellect, for example, that brings it about that Plato is taller or heavier than Socrates. What makes such sentences true or false, Ockham strenuously tried to show, is nothing but substances and qualities themselves. What characterizes a relational or a quantitative sentence, he would typically say, is not the sort of things needed to make it true, but its terms' modes of signifying. This last point he developed indefatigably and argued for in great detail. To the semantics of quantitative language, in particular he devoted many lengthy passages in his major works, as well as the bulk of two special treatises on the Eucharist, *De corpore Christi* (On the Body of Christ) and *De quantitate* (On Quantity), which were obviously written as defences against theological attacks.

4 Epistemology: intuitive and abstractive cognition

Apart from pointing out the inconsistency and imprecision of his opponents, what Ockham had to do in order to accredit his simplified ontology was also to explain as clearly as possible how it fitted with Aristotelian science and with Christian doctrine. For this he had especially to account for the adequacy of knowledge in general. It was a respected Aristotelian adage that science had essentially to do with universals. How could it be salvaged if there are no such universals in reality? Ockham answered the challenge by providing a detailed theory of how mental universals are produced, a theory that was meant as the basis for any validation of conceptual knowledge.

The epistemological process, in this picture, always starts as a direct encounter between singular beings. When a knowing mind equipped with both sensory and intellective substantial forms is in the presence of a perceptible singular object such as a table or a horse, a causal chain naturally ensues, according to Ockham. First, there occurs an apprehension, or *intuition*, within the sensitive part of the mind. This in turn, together with the object itself, causes certain actual states, or *actus*, in the intellectual part, states which Ockham labels 'intellectual intuitions'. These are characterized by the fact that they naturally elicit within the intellect true contingent beliefs about the world, especially judgments regarding existence or non-existence. If Socrates has the right relation to Bucephalus (perceiving it from the right distance, awake, sane and so on), there naturally takes place within Socrates a simple intellectual act, his 'intuitive cognition' of Bucephalus, which in turn causes his judgments that Bucephalus exists, is white, is standing there and so on.

Such judgments, of course, even though they are singular, require the availability of certain general concepts such as those of whiteness and existence. These, in Ockham's view, are also brought about by the same concrete intuitions through an equally natural course. Every time Socrates forms an intuitive act caused by a certain individual in the world, there occur within Socrates' mind other derivative simple intellectual acts, called *abstractive* cognitions. These new acts in themselves will not induce empirical judgments of existence; and for that reason they are said to 'abstract' from existence and non-existence. However, in virtue of a certain isomorphism (*similitudo*) they have with the original external thing, they may be used by the mind to represent or stand for this very same thing in its absence, and for any others as well that resemble it sufficiently for the same isomorphism to hold. General signs are thus naturally generated, either as mind-made objects of abstractive acts (according to the *fictum* theory) or as abstractive acts themselves (according to the *actus* theory). In either case, the result is what Ockham calls the mind's concepts (*conceptus* or *intentiones*). General concepts, for him, are always causally derivative: 'every naturally acquired abstractive cognition of a thing presupposes an intuitive cognition of the same thing' (*Ordinatio*, prologue, q. 1).

Intellectual intuitions and abstractive concepts, then, are simple mental terms or signs, each naturally representing one or more singular beings in the world. Once produced, these simple terms can be combined with each other, by natural causes or by the will of their possessors, to form cognitive complexes, such as mental propositions. A mental proposition is a structured sequence of mental terms that is either true or false with respect to the singular beings that are referred to by its terms. Such a propositional complex is formed by an intellect's composite act of apprehension (*actus apprehensivus*). In the *fictum* theory, Ockham saw the mental proposition as the intentional correlate of this complex apprehensive act, but later he simply identified the two in the *actus* theory. Once the mind apprehends a proposition, it can go further and commit itself with respect to its truth or falsity; this is the act of assent, the judgment (*actus judicativus*). Mental propositions, finally, can be compounded with each other in chains of reasonings, theoretical or practical.

The detailed theory of exactly which structural features and relations with the world render a mental proposition true or false was part of logic for Ockham

(see §7 below). Supposing that this semantical part of the programme can be achieved, the general picture we have of knowledge in Ockham's final theory is that of a natural causal process, involving, apart from external objects themselves, only real qualities of the mind, and leading in stages from intuitive encounters with external singular beings to judgments and inferences involving complex propositional contents, each basic signifying unit in the process being a singular act of a singular mind. There is no longer any such thing as *the* concept 'horse', for example; only token concepts exist. Every mind forms its own single, momentary intellectual acts, which owe their generality, if any, to their signification rather than to a special mode of existence: 'Nothing is universal save by signification' (*Summa logicae* I, 14).

Such mental tokens normally will not subsist very long, but they leave traces when they disappear. We keep intellectual memories of them. Abstractive acts, Ockham contends, causally generate within the mind certain corresponding dispositions (*habitus*) to form similar acts in the future, and these cognitive dispositions are themselves identified with real qualities of the mind. Thus a general concept comes to be available to a particular mind for future use. When Socrates met Bucephalus, there naturally occurred within Socrates an intellectual intuitive cognition of Bucephalus; and then, as a causal result of this, abstractive cognitions were also produced, which turned out to be capable of simultaneously representing all beings in the world that are sufficiently similar to Bucephalus. In this way Socrates acquires the concept of a horse, the concept of a white thing and so on. Once formed, these general concepts elicit in turn mental dispositions within Socrates to produce replicas of them under appropriate circumstances, new mental tokens representing all horses or all white things, just as the original acts did.

Accordingly, sciences – organized bodies of knowledge – are described by Ockham as 'collections of intellectual *habitus*' in the mind of particular knowers. To say of someone that they have a certain science – that of grammar, for example – is to say that they have internalized, as real qualities of their mind, a certain collection of intellectual dispositions which enable them to form general propositions of grammar when required and which adequately incline them to assent with certainty to those which are true: sciences are ultimately made up of apprehensive and judicative psychological dispositions. Ockham has often been taken to task for having taught that the objects of a science, like the objects of all knowledge or belief, are mental propositions rather than things themselves; but by this he only meant that mental propositions – corresponding to complex apprehensive acts – are precisely what knowers are inclined to assent to by the sciences they have internalized. The contents of knowledge are thus seen as sequences of mental propositions, of which certain terms naturally signify certain singular beings in the world. Thought is mental discourse.

5 Epistemology: direct realism

Ockhamism has often been suspected of leading to radical scepticism in epistemology. If general concepts represent nothing but independent individual things, how can such groupings fail to be arbitrary or misleading? But radical scepticism was, in fact, very far from Ockham's intentions and spirit, and his theory of universals and knowledge has been more accurately characterized by the best commentators as 'realistic conceptualism' (Boehner 1958) or 'direct realism' (Adams 1987) (see EPISTEMOLOGY, HISTORY OF).

For one thing, as was seen in the previous section, the process of concept formation is completely natural. It is the same in every human being and leaves no room for idiosyncratic vagaries. Secondly – and most importantly – this naturally acquired stock of concepts does cut the world at its joints, according to Ockham. Species and genera, of course, are denied any outside reality as distinct beings, but Ockham readily grants that whether an individual thing is or is not of the same species or of the same genus as another is not for the human mind to decide. The conditions of being in the same genus or of the same species are not subjective or arbitrary. They are determined, on the contrary, by what the individual things are in themselves and how they in fact stand to each other. Whether something resembles Bucephalus enough to be naturally represented by the same general concepts does not, Ockham insists, depend upon the human mental apparatus at all. It simply is a rock-bottom fact of the universe. Concept formation, being a natural process, derivatively mirrors the natural distribution of causal powers among individual things, which powers depend in turn on real singular essences and qualities. In this lies the adequacy of abstractive cognition.

Different kinds of accurate, simple, general concepts are thus formed on the basis of direct experience, according to this theory. First, there are more or less general substantial concepts, such as 'horse' or 'animal', which are identified with species and genera and which are taken to represent in the mind certain groups of individual substances essentially similar to each other independently of their qualities. Second, there are concepts such as 'whiteness' or 'colour', which represent immediately percep-

tible singular qualities of substances but not substances themselves. Third, there is another sort of qualitative concepts, such as 'white' or 'coloured', which represent substances – white things or coloured things in the chosen examples – insofar as they possess certain perceptible qualities. Finally, there are some elementary relational concepts such as 'darker' or 'taller', which represent individual beings – substances or qualities – insofar as they are related to some others in certain perceptible ways. The first two groups are called 'absolute concepts', while the last two are classified among 'connotative concepts' (see §6), but all of these are simple mental terms naturally generated as causal results of empirical encounters with singular objects, without any combinatorial activity from the intellect. Together, they are held to provide an adequate basis for knowledge.

Is this empiricism? It would appear so, insofar as it holds that the formation of simple representative concepts in human minds is always triggered by direct singular experiences (of external objects or of mental states themselves). However, it must be stressed that the cognitive process described by the theory presupposes a very strong innate apparatus of rational capacities. A well-formed basic species-concept such as 'horse', for example, is automatically generated, according to Ockham, as the result of a single encounter with a horse. More general genus-concepts such as 'animal' are formed, in turn, as the results of a minimal number of encounters with individuals of different species. Moreover, certain true contingent beliefs, such as 'a horse exists' or 'this horse is larger than this dog' are naturally triggered in the mind, as has been seen, as the results of causal processes which also involve highly determinate mental machinery. Certain universal truths are even supposed to be immediately known as such by the mind once the relevant concepts are made available to it, for example, that all horses are animals. The mind, according to Ockham, is equipped from the start with a rich apparatus of cognitive capacities which enable it, under the right circumstances, to reach true scientific knowledge.

One independent reason for linking Ockhamism with scepticism has sometimes been found in its acceptance of the possibility of an intuitive or pseudo-intuitive cognition of nonexistent beings (see SCEPTICISM). However, two different theses must be distinguished in this respect, and neither of them, in Ockham's view, leads to radical scepticism. First, Ockham did admit the theoretical possibility of an intuitive cognition of nonexistent beings, realizable only, he thought, by the supernatural intervention of God. Since an intuitive act is a real quality of the mind, he reasoned, it is itself a singular being distinct from its own external object; and hence, it is not self-contradictory that it should exist without the object. If this is not self-contradictory, then God can induce in a prophet's mind, for example, a certain singular cognition of a presently nonexistent being, in virtue of which the prophet would know that this particular being – a future one, or even a merely possible one – does not presently exist, but that it will exist in the future or that it would exist under appropriate circumstances. This singular cognition would then be an adequate intuitive cognition since it would cause within the prophet's mind true existential judgments about the thing in question. Accordingly, there is no hold for scepticism here: such a supernaturally induced intuition, although abnormal, would not be misleading.

The second possibility seems more disturbing. Ockham admits, since this is not self-contradictory either, that God could directly cause in any human being the *false* belief that there is a horse in front of them while in fact there is none. Strictly speaking, this would not be an intuitive cognition (it would not cause a true judgment of existence or non-existence), but it could certainly be an undetectable source of error. Such a possibility, however, does not belong to the range of natural processes; and, although it cannot be ruled out by the theory, it can in practice be disregarded by the epistemologist who wishes to assess the scope of natural knowledge. In the normal course of things, intuitive cognition is a totally reliable starting point for science.

6 Logic and philosophy of language: levels of discourse, connotation, intentions

Once concepts are available as natural signs, mental propositions can be assembled. Their truth and falsity will depend upon the semantical properties of their component terms and their syntactical arrangements. Thought is seen as an internal discourse with a compositional structure very similar to that of spoken sentences. Ockham took the ancient idea of mental discourse (found in BOETHIUS, for example) more seriously than any other philosopher before him, and his logic systematically exploits, for the analysis of mental propositions and inferences, the theory of the properties of terms (*proprietates terminorum*) to which he had been introduced as a student. This theory was an original medieval contribution, which had been progressively developed since the twelfth century by a host of logicians such as PETER OF SPAIN and WILLIAM OF SHERWOOD, for the analysis of spoken sentences. Ockham adapted it to his nominalistic ontology on the one hand, and enlisted its rich apparatus of concepts and distinctions on the other

hand – the theory of *suppositio* in particular – in the service of a fine-grained understanding of mental computation. This is to a large extent what his logic is about (see LOGIC, MEDIEVAL).

At the very outset of *Summa logicae*, Ockham states that there are three levels of propositions: spoken, written and mental. Those of the first two groups, he says, are composed of publicly perceptible signs, visible or audible; but mental propositions are sequences of concepts – or intentions of the mind – existing only in the privacy of the intellect. Each proposition is composed of terms, and the basic semantical property in this picture is the signification (*significatio*) of the component terms. The signification of a concept is natural, as has been seen, and that of the other two sorts of terms is conventionally derived from it: spoken terms are conventionally subordinated to concepts, and written terms are conventionally subordinated to spoken ones. A spoken or written term inherits the signification of the previously existing sign to which it is subordinated. When the Latin spoken word '*equus*', for example, is conventionally subordinated to the mental concept 'horse', it thereby acquires the signification that belonged to that concept naturally; and the very same signification is afterwards transmitted in the same way to the corresponding written term. Ockham, then, refuses to say – as did BOETHIUS and AQUINAS, among others – that a spoken word signifies the underlying concept. It will instead be said to signify conventionally the individual things themselves that the concept was a natural sign of in the first place: real singular horses in the case of the spoken words 'horse', '*cheval*' or '*equus*', for example. The same will hold, *mutatis mutandis*, for the corresponding written words.

At each of the three levels, many distinctions are to be drawn among terms with respect to their signification. First, categorematic terms are distinguished from syncategorematic ones by the fact that they do have a signification of their own before being combined with others into propositions. Proper names such as 'Socrates' and common nouns or adjectives such as 'horse' or 'white' are salient examples of categorematic terms. *Syncategoremata*, on the contrary, are particles such as prepositions, logical connectives and quantifiers, which do not when taken alone direct the mind towards particular individual beings in the world. Their semantical roles are ancillary: they do not signify anything by themselves but, when combined with categorematic terms, they can affect the modes of reference of those terms and determine the truth-conditions of propositions.

Another important distinction found in mental language as well as in spoken and written discourse, according to Ockham, is between absolute and connotative terms. The former correspond to what we today call natural kind terms, such as 'horse' or 'animal'. These are characterized by the fact that they simultaneously and equally signify all the individuals they are true of, and nothing else: 'horse' signifies all horses and nothing but horses. Each connotative term, on the other hand, has at least two different groups of significates: its primary significates are the individuals the term is true of; and its secondary significates are individuals also called to mind by the term, but in an 'oblique' way. 'White', for example, is a salient case of a connotative term: it primarily signifies all white things and secondarily signifies – or connotes – their whitenesses; although it cannot be said that whitenesses are white, they are nevertheless obliquely called to mind by the term 'white'. All relational terms, Ockham insists, are connotative: 'owner' primarily signifies all owners and connotes their possessions, 'father' primarily signifies the fathers and connotes their children, and so on. This idea of connotation thus turns out to be a crucial device for the simplification of ontology. All significates, whether primary or secondary, are singular substances or qualities, and nothing else. Relations, in particular, are no longer needed among real beings. The relevant complexity, here, is located in the semantical structure of certain terms rather than in the ontology.

Finally, some terms signify nonlinguistic things, while others signify signs. When restricted to mental terms, this idea is cashed out, in Ockham's vocabulary, as a distinction between 'first and second intentions'. First intentions are mental terms, the significates of which are external beings. Aristotle's theory of the ten categories is precisely interpreted in this framework as a classification of first intentions according to their modes of signification: the category of relation, for example, is identified with the group of relational first intentions such as 'owner' or 'mother', the category of quality with that of qualitative first intentions such as 'white' or 'whiteness', and so on. Second intentions, on the other hand, are concepts signifying concepts. Philosophically, in Ockham's eyes, the most interesting instances of these are the mental terms 'species' and 'genus' themselves. 'Species' is seen as a metalinguistic concept signifying certain general terms such as 'horse' or 'dog', while 'genus' amounts to approximately the same except that it signifies terms even more general, such as 'animal' or 'flower'. This is exactly what realism about universals crucially misses: it fails to see that concepts referring *to* universals are fundamentally metalinguistic (see LANGUAGE, MEDIEVAL THEORIES OF).

7 Logic and philosophy of language: supposition and inference

Signification, then, in Ockham's logic, is a prepropositional property of categorematic terms taken in themselves. When such a term, whether spoken, written or mental, is inserted into a proposition as subject or predicate, it is said to acquire a new semantical property called *supposition*, which is derivative with respect to its signification but which, contrary to signification, can vary from one proposition to another according to contextual factors. Supposition, in modern terms, is the referential function fulfilled by the term in a given propositional context: for a term to 'supposit for' certain things, Ockham says, is just for it to stand for these things in a given proposition.

Normally a subject or predicate term supposits for its primary significates. It is then said to be taken in personal supposition (*suppositio personalis*): in 'some horses are white', for example, the subject term 'horse' personally supposits for – or refers to – all horses, whether white or not, while the predicate term 'white' personally supposits for all white things (but not for whitenesses, which are its secondary significates). Special cases can occur, however: in a sentence such as 'horse is a five-letter word', the subject term 'horse' does not stand for its primary significates – real horses – but for written tokens of the English word 'horse'. When a term thus supposits for spoken or written tokens of itself, it is said to be taken in material supposition (*suppositio materialis*). When it stands for tokens of the corresponding mental sign, such as 'horse' in 'horse is a concept', it is said to be taken in simple supposition (*suppositio simplex*). This last case is especially important in Ockham's discussion of the problem of universals, since the subject terms of sentences such as 'horse is a species' or 'animal is a genus' are typically considered by him as being taken in simple supposition, and interpreted accordingly as referring in a special way to mental tokens rather than to mysterious external entities such as equinity or animality.

Which individual beings a term refers to in a certain propositional context is thus determined in the first place by the signification of the term and by whether it is taken in personal, simple or material supposition. However, this is still incomplete. It is also determined, Ockham insists, by the tense and the modality of the main verb in the proposition, according to precise rules. A present-tense verb, in particular, is said to restrict both the subject and the predicate of the proposition to supposit for individual beings which exist at the time of utterance. A past-tense verb restricts the predicate to supposit for past individuals, but allows the subject to supposit both for past individuals and for individuals existing at the time of utterance, and so on.

In this way, propositions are linked to reality. Discourse, whether spoken, written or mental, refers to nothing but singular entities, some of which are themselves significant tokens, and it does so through the referential functions of the terms in specific contexts. Propositions considered as complex semantical units do not, according to this view, signify special entities over and above the *supposita* of their terms. Their peculiarity instead is to have truth-conditions, a detailed theory of which Ockham gives in the second part of his *Summa logicae*. For elementary statements of the form 'subject + copula + predicate', these truth-conditions are entirely formulated in terms of relations between the supposition of the subject-term and that of the predicate. For the truth of a universal affirmative proposition, for example, it is both necessary and sufficient that the predicate supposits for all the individuals the subject supposits for. Similarly, the truth of a universal negative proposition requires that the predicate have no common *supposita* with the subject, and so on. The theory gets more complicated when it reaches modal propositions, non-elementary propositions (such as conjunctions, disjunctions or conditionals) or other difficult cases such as propositions involving special verbs like 'cease' or 'begin', which fascinated logicians in the fourteenth century. However, the basis is always provided by the referential link established through supposition between the terms in the proposition and the singular beings out there in the world.

The same is true generally of Ockham's theory of inferences developed in the very long third part of *Summa logicae*. This is not formal logic in the modern sense. The validity of inferences is always made to rest in the last analysis upon the referential properties of the component terms. Syllogisms, notably, are described as special arrangements of terms, and their validity is said to depend on the connections between the purported suppositions of the major, the minor and the middle terms. The whole syllogistic theory, in Ockham's view, ultimately rests, directly or indirectly, on only two relevant connections between terms: the *dici de omni* (being said of all) and the *dici de nullo* (being said of none). The former holds when a certain term *A* supposits for everything another term *B* supposits for, and the latter when *A* supposits for none of the *supposita* of *B*. 'All horses are mammals, all mammals are animals, therefore all horses are animals', for example, is based on the transitivity of the *dici de omni*. 'No stone is an animal, all horses are animals, therefore no horse is a stone' is based on an interplay between the *dici de omni* and the *dici de*

nullo. All other syllogistic figures are reduced in one way or another to these two connections. In the same vein, nonsyllogistic inferences – which had come to be a major new field of interest in medieval logic under the heading of *consequentiae* – are also systematically analysed by Ockham as depending upon interconnections between the suppositions of terms. This is how he is led to accept the soundness of such direct inferences as 'all animals run, therefore all horses run' or 'no material body exists, therefore no white thing exists', the key to which lies not in the formal structure, but in the semantical relations between terms, and ultimately on their reference to singular beings (see LANGUAGE, MEDIEVAL THEORIES OF; LOGIC, MEDIEVAL).

8 Physics

The objects of science for Ockham, as was seen in §4, were universal mental propositions. This controversial thesis, however, did not lead him anywhere near idealism or scepticism, precisely because the supposition of terms was called upon to secure the required links between such mental propositions and real external individual beings. Natural science in particular was recognized as adequate general knowledge of sensible substances. Ockham in fact devoted several treatises to it, the most important of which are his unfinished *Expositio in libros Physicorum Aristotelis*, his *Summa philosophiae naturalis* (Synopsis of Natural Philosophy) and his *Quaestiones in libros Physicorum Aristotelis* (Questions on the Physics of Aristotle). Taken together, these three works occupy more than 2,000 pages in the Franciscan Institute edition and contain some of Ockham's most intriguing ideas.

The main goal of natural philosophy, as Ockham sees it, is to provide a theory of the general principles of change among sensible things. Following ARISTOTLE, Ockham acknowledges different types of change in nature: generation and corruption of substances, intensification and diminution of qualities, rarefaction and condensation of matter and, finally, local motion. About each one of these he has detailed – and often provocative – positions to defend. However, in the last analysis all change is accounted for in his system on the sole basis of the four kinds of beings admitted by his ontology: substances, qualities, substantial forms and prime matter. Much of his natural philosophy is accordingly devoted to showing that space, void, time, motion and the like are not distinct, absolute things. Prime matter in particular is considered as being actually extended by itself, and its spatial dimensions are not – as in Aquinas and many other medieval authors – given the status of special quantitative forms enjoying an existence of their own.

The core of the method in this peculiar variety of physics is neither empirical nor mathematical but semantical, the point being to show that general sentences which appear to be about space, void, time or motion are in fact about substances, qualities, forms and pieces of matter. Thus reinterpreted, such sentences can very well convey truths, even necessary truths, about physical reality. The crucial device for this type of reductive analysis is the idea that a single word in spoken or written language, such as 'motion' or 'time', is often an abbreviation for a complex mental expression including not only absolute categorematic terms, but also conjunctions, adverbs, verbs and, above all, connotative terms. Moreover, these abbreviative words are often to be interpreted contextually – for example, the analyst should not systematically try to replace the relevant word by one and the same definition in all its occurrences, but should instead try to reformulate, on the basis of a few rules of thumb, the whole sentences in which the problematic word occurs.

An abstract noun such as 'change' (*mutatio*), for example, does not designate a special entity of its own. Rather, its uses are derivative with respect to those of the corresponding verb 'to change' (*mutare*). The meaning of the verb in such a case provides the key for the interpretation of the various sentences in which the derivative noun occurs. The verb 'to change' in effect normally applies to something (for example, a substance) acquiring something which it did not have before (for example, a new form or a new quality) or entering into relations with new things (for example, new substances). This is what should be kept in mind when considering spoken or written sentences involving the derivative noun, such as 'every change is by an agent' (which is to be interpreted as 'everything that changes is changed by an agent') or 'change moves from the prior to the posterior' (which means that 'when something changes, it moves from a prior state to a posterior state'). The term 'motion', in the same vein, normally supposits for the things which are moved, but it may also, if the context favours it, supposit for the things that cause the others to move; or it may even in special cases receive a metalinguistic interpretation and supposit for linguistic or conceptual units such as the verb 'to move'. The word 'time', to take a last example, does not signify any special extramental entity either, but supposits, in the sentences in which it occurs, for the very same things the word 'motion' would supposit for in similar contexts, and connotes in addition a certain numbering activity of the human soul.

Sentences involving such words, then, can be

'saved' without enriching the ontology, and when they are so reinterpreted, it can be admitted that their truth or falsity is neither illusory nor subjective. Nominalism here does not preclude the objectivity, the mind-independence, or even the necessity of physical phenomena. Ockham in particular is no precursor of HUME in being suspicious about natural causality. Efficient causality in his view is a natural necessary connection holding between singular causes and singular effects in virtue of their respective intrinsic natures; and it can be safely ascertained as such in appropriate circumstances. Ockham readily grants a causal version of the principle of the uniformity of Nature: 'causes of the same kind have effects of the same kind' (*Ordinatio*, prologue, q. 1). The fact that a certain individual A is, in virtue of its intrinsic substantial forms, of the same species as another individual B necessarily implies a strong similarity between A and B with respect to their causal powers. This is true to such an extent that a single observation, in appropriate circumstances, suffices in principle to justify an induction about causal connections: if it could be safely established in a single case that a given singular plant has a certain curative power, it could be correctly concluded by induction that all plants of the same species as this one do have similar curative powers. In conformity with the Aristotelian model, natural philosophy in Ockham's view is an authentic science of necessary connections. Although the ontology is simplified with the help of sophisticated semantical analysis, traditional metaphysics is not abandoned (see NATURAL PHILOSOPHY, MEDIEVAL).

9 Natural theology

Theology, on the contrary, is not in the normal course of things properly called a science, according to Ockham, because it does not rest on the required sort of natural evidence. In his view a science, strictly speaking, is a set of cognitive *habitus* (see §4) having to do with necessary conclusions that were formerly dubitable for the agent but that became ascertained through syllogistic reasoning from self-evident general premises or well-established empirical generalizations. It is not so with theology, most of which rests on faith and revelation; the parts that can be demonstrated by natural reason alone are very thin indeed. Compared to most of his medieval predecessors, Ockham is quite sceptical with respect to a purely natural theology (see NATURAL THEOLOGY).

First, no simple and proper concept of God, he holds, is accessible to human beings in this life. The human person in this life – frequently called the 'traveller' (*viator*) by medieval theologians – is characterized precisely by the fact of having no direct intuitive cognition of God. However, intuitive cognition of something is a prerequisite condition for the formation of any proper and simple abstract cognition of that thing (see §4), and therefore neither is any such cognition naturally possible in this life with respect to God. The only simple concepts applicable to God that a human being can naturally form are general concepts that will also signify other beings in one way or another. Some will be absolute (or quidditative) concepts (see §6), such as the general concept of 'being' which, according to Ockham, univocally applies to God and to creatures. However, most will be connotative or negative terms, such as 'creator' (which connotes the creatures) or 'immortal' (which negatively signifies death). A proper concept of God, for Ockham, is naturally constructible in this life only as a composite bundle of such general quidditative, connotative and negative concepts.

In the second place, even if some general or composite concepts applicable to God can naturally be formed, this will not suffice for the 'traveller' to *know* that these concepts apply to the Supreme Being. What would have to be known in addition is at least that such a being exists. One can easily form, for instance, the concept of an immortal being, simply by negatively referring to death, but this possibility in itself does not suffice to warrant the belief that such a concept does apply to anything real.

Can the existence of God be proven by natural reason? Ockham criticizes and rejects most of the alleged proofs of his predecessors. Anselm's celebrated argument, for one, is considered by him as valid only insofar as it proves that among actually existing entities there is at least one with respect to which none is greater (see ANSELM OF CANTERBURY). This is far from enough, in Ockham's eyes, to conclude that nothing could possibly be greater, if it existed. Consequently, the argument does not establish that the greatest possible being does exist in fact. Proofs from final causality, such as Aquinas' fifth way, do not work either because, Ockham says, it cannot be demonstrated that material things that lack cognition do act according to final causes pre-established by a will (see GOD, ARGUMENTS FOR THE EXISTENCE OF).

The proofs of God's existence that Ockham considers strongest are the arguments from efficient causality. However, these are not all equally conclusive, and even in the best cases they do not prove as much as most of his predecessors would have hoped for. Ockham admits as a self-evident principle that being cannot come from non-being, and concludes accordingly that every natural thing does indeed need to have been brought into existence by some external

cause. But nothing, he adds, impedes in principle the possibility of an infinite regress in time in the series of such productive causes. Since no actual infinity would be involved, the past eternity of the material world is not philosophically impossible. What Ockham does deem impossible, on the other hand, is the existence of an actual infinity of simultaneous *conserving* causes; and this is the basis for the only relevant scientific proof he is ready to grant on this subject. Each caused thing, he believes, needs not only to be brought into existence, but also to be conserved in existence by some external cause (see CREATION AND CONSERVATION, RELIGIOUS DOCTRINE OF). Such a conserving cause must exist simultaneously with its effect as long as the effect exists, and the infinite regress in this case is consequently ruled out in principle since it would entail the existence of an actual infinity of distinct beings. This argument, then, does establish that there actually exists at any moment a first efficient conserving cause. What it does not prove, however, is that there should be only one such cause at any moment and that this cause should be identified with God: a celestial sphere or an angel could do equally well.

A fortiori, none of the other traditionally accepted characteristics of the Supreme Being can be proven by natural reason alone to be actually exemplified. In particular, it cannot be philosophically demonstrated, Ockham argues, that God is the first efficient cause of everything, that he is the final cause of something, that he is infinite or even that he knows anything. Articles of faith about God are not in general a matter for reason to settle. Rational argumentation is not ruled out of theology, of course – far from it – but its most crucial premises are accepted solely on the basis of religious faith. Some of the theological truths indeed even run counter to what natural reason by itself would favour: Ockham admits, for instance, that the doctrine of the Trinity involves the actual existence of distinct relational entities, something which, as a philosopher, he firmly rejects. In such cases, Ockham always clearly asserts the priority of the authority of the church over the pronouncements of reason and experience. Philosophy and theology nevertheless tend to be much less intertwined in his thought than they were in the thought of Aquinas or Scotus, for example.

10 Ethics

Ethics is especially interesting in this regard insofar as it simultaneously displays both the intimate interconnection and the relative independence of the philosophical and the theological outlooks. Ockham devoted no special elaborate treatise to ethics and nowhere systematically collected his views on the matter; but many scattered relevant developments in the commentary on the *Sentences*, the *Quodlibeta septem* and the collection known as the *Quaestiones variae* (Various Questions) do reveal, when considered together, an original two-sided theory of the object and foundations of moral knowledge (see ETHICS).

Taken as a whole, moral science in this view is the practical normative knowledge of what is to be done, in general or under particular circumstances. It includes two distinct and independent parts. Positive moral science, on the one hand, is knowledge about the legal obligations one is formally subject to; it subdivides in turn into knowledge about human laws and knowledge about divine laws. Non-positive moral science, on the other hand, is directive knowledge about human action (or *praxis*) insofar as it is based on natural reason and experience. The former, says Ockham, is not a demonstrative science properly speaking, since it depends on human and divine precepts which are not evidently known *per se* or empirically. The latter, which corresponds to what Aristotle discusses in his own ethical books, is indeed a proper part of demonstrative philosophy, and it is even more certain and useful, Ockham insists, than many other sciences. It rests jointly on natural experience and on a number of general principles evidently known *per se*, such as: 'what is honest should be done and what is dishonest avoided', 'benefactors deserve gratitude', 'the will should conform to the dictates of right reason', and so on.

The philosophical part of ethics will shed light, in particular, on the general criteria of what is humanly laudable or blameworthy, even for a pagan. Ockham's theses on this are characteristic. Only acts, according to him, can be morally good or virtuous; and among acts, only internal acts of the will can be rightly considered as *intrinsically* virtuous. Other sorts of acts, whether bodily or mental, are sometimes called 'virtuous', of course, but this is only 'by extrinsic denomination', exactly as a beverage is sometimes called 'healthy' not because it is itself in good health but because it has some salient causal relation with something else which is (or could be) intrinsically in good health. Ockham's ethics, like Abelard's, consistently stresses the basic moral character of intentions rather than that of outward behaviour (see ABELARD, P.). His point is that for an act to be intrinsically virtuous, some necessary conditions need to be met that can be fulfilled only by internal acts of the will. First, it has to be free of internal necessity or external compulsion; it has, in other words, to be under the direct power of the will itself. Second, it has to conform to the dictates of what he repeatedly calls

'right reason' (*recta ratio*), which is the rational and well-informed use of prudence and moral conscience.

This notion of 'right reason' is central to Ockham's philosophical ethics. The highest degree of moral virtue pagans can reach, according to him, precisely requires that they should will not merely to fulfil their moral obligations, but also that they should so will precisely in view of the fact that these obligations are dictated by right reason. Right reason, on the other hand, does not reduce to natural reason alone. It involves correct and prudential reasoning enlightened by whatever relevant true knowledge is available to the agent. In the case of the Christian believer, then, the dictates of right reason cannot be independent of the content of Christian faith. This is the exact point where non-positive moral demonstrative science yields, for Ockham, to a higher form of ethics: positive Christian moral science, as enlightened by religious faith.

This is not to say that philosophical moral science by itself is completely unreligious. Ockham explicitly holds, on the contrary, that reason suffices to demonstrate that there is at any time an actually existing *summum bonum*, and right reason, then, dictates, independently of any divine revelation, that nothing else ought to be loved more than this *summum bonum*. However, Christian revelation goes much further. It tells the believer, among other things, that this *summum bonum* is the unique God, that he is not only the highest good in fact, but also the highest possible good, that he is our creator and benefactor, that he is a personal knower and so on. Once these data from revelation are taken into account, right reason should lead the believer towards an even higher degree of moral virtue, which will correspond to Christian morality proper. It is reached when agents will to fulfil their obligations not merely because they conform to the dictates of right reason anymore, but primarily for the love of God himself and because these obligations derive from God's will. This alone is the level of perfect moral virtue.

The real ultimate foundation of ethical norms, then, turns out to be God's will and nothing else. The sole fact that God commands something to be done is what makes that thing morally good. God could at any time change his precepts and our moral obligations would then change accordingly. He could command, for example, that we should from now on steal whenever we can and it would *ipso facto* become morally good to do so. However, this is no longer demonstrative ethics; it is Christian theology based on revelation and on the indemonstrable principle of God's absolute supremacy. Even though religious faith leads him beyond philosophical ethics into what has often been called a 'divine command ethics', which ultimately plays a foundational role in his overall system, Ockham in the last analysis does not blur the distinction he had drawn between the two sorts of moral knowledge, and he never expresses serious doubts about the soundness of secular moral reasoning in the actual world.

11 Political thought

While Ockham had not ventured into political philosophy during his academic career in England, almost all the works he is taken to have written in Munich from 1330 to his death in 1347 are directly related to his conflicts with the Avignon papacy (with the possible exception of one short logical tract, the *Elementarium logicae* (Elements of Logic)). His goal at first was to expose the errors and heresies of Pope John XXII, especially about poverty within the church and about the beatific vision. This raised in effect the delicate question of papal heresy: who, in such a case, is entitled to denounce it? Who has the power to depose the Pope? Reflections on such matters progressively led Ockham to be more and more interested in political theory proper, and most of his writings after 1337 were directly devoted to it, notably the *Octo quaestiones de potestate papae*, Book III of the *Dialogus* and the *De Imperatorum et Pontificum potestate*.

In this endeavour, Ockham primarily thought of himself as a theologian. Many of his arguments against the Avignon curialists were designed for the ecclesiastical community and based on the Bible, the writings of the Church Fathers or canon law. However, he also liberally used Aristotle's *Politics* and much of his thought in this field can be seen, in fact, as being in direct continuation with his philosophical ethics of right reason: politics, after all, is but a province of human *praxis*.

Indeed, Ockham's basic political idea is that the spiritual and the temporal powers should normally be kept apart and not be allowed to overlap, except in special cases of crisis such as papal heresy or tyrannical abuse. On the whole, he found much to say in favour of the institution of papacy, but he energetically opposed the papalist doctrine of the *plenitudo potestatis* of the Pope and emphatically denied the dependence in principle of secular on ecclesiastical power. The church, he thought, should as a general rule disentangle itself from worldly politics. Consecration by the Pope, for example, was not in his view a necessary condition for the legitimacy of the Emperor.

What then is the basis for the legitimacy of secular political power? Popular consent, according to Ockham, is the normal original source of legitimacy; but

beyond this, the rightness of a certain political regime ultimately depends on how well it fulfils its functions. Government is instituted for the good of a community of individual subjects, and if a regime adequately performs this task, it is not legitimate, for the Pope or even for the majority of subjects, to try to overthrow it by force. Ockham's approach to politics is basically functional. What he thinks should be expected from a government is mainly that it should prevent and punish injustice and so preserve in this way the rights and freedom of the individual members of the community. Monarchy, for him, is usually the best regime insofar as it is, in most circumstances, best suited to such a role; but there is nothing absolute – or divinely founded – in this judgment in Ockham's eyes. A political regime is a man-made institution to be judged by its expediency in achieving the goal for which it should ideally be designed: and common welfare or public security can in principle be enhanced by different regimes in different circumstances.

Natural rights, in this perspective, are what a government is expected to protect (see RIGHTS). Ockham never gave a systematic account of these rights, but examples of them in his writings include the individual's right to the necessities of life, the collective right for a people lacking a ruler to choose one, the right to resist an unjust government, and so on. As a general rule, the rights and obligations of rulers and subjects, he thought, can be determined in particular circumstances by the normal prudential use of human right reason. Ultimately, what the political and legal institutions should be aiming at preserving is the individual freedom of the members of the community in their own private spheres.

At the same time this respect for freedom sets a limit in principle to the exercise of any political power, whether ecclesiastical or secular: 'free persons, who are not slaves', Ockham writes, 'should never, without some fault, be compelled by new laws to do things which are not necessary to the commonwealth or to their neighbour' (*Breviloquium de potestate Papae* II, 17). Political rule should be kept to the minimum which is required in any circumstances for the fulfilment of its social functions.

It has often been wondered whether Ockham's political thought is dependent on the rest of his philosophy, and on his nominalism in particular. Certainly his political theories were not deduced from nominalistic premises in ontology, theory of knowledge or philosophy of language. He never defended his political stands by arguments drawn from these fields, and his conceptions of ecclesiastical and political power are compatible with different ontological or epistemological doctrines. Moreover, probably because of the new audience he was trying to reach, he did not make much use in his political writings of the technical tools of semantical analysis which he had so extensively exploited in theology and philosophy. Nevertheless, the break between the two parts of his work is far from complete. Ockham's approach to politics and natural rights is in direct continuation with his philosophical ethics of right reason. And, more importantly, the emphasis of his later writings on personal freedom can certainly be seen as the political counterpart of the accent on singularity which was the trademark of his nominalism. Even though there is no logical connection here, both aspects of Ockham's thought harmoniously fall in line with each other in consistently stressing the primacy of individuals.

See also: ARISTOTELIANISM, MEDIEVAL; BIEL, G. §2; BURIDAN, J.; CHATTON, W.; DUNS SCOTUS, J.; EMPIRICISM; GREGORY OF RIMINI; LANGUAGE, MEDIEVAL THEORIES OF; LOGIC, MEDIEVAL; NATURAL PHILOSOPHY, MEDIEVAL §9; NOMINALISM; UNIVERSALS; WODEHAM, A.

List of works

Critical editions

William of Ockham (1317–47) *Opera Philosophica et Theologica* (Philosophical and Theological Works), eds G. Gál *et al.*, St. Bonaventure, NY: The Franciscan Institute, 1967–88, 17 vols. (Excellent critical edition of all of Ockham's non-political writings, subdivided into two series: *Opera Philosophica*, 7 vols, and *Opera Theologica*, 10 vols. A selection of basic philosophical texts can be found in English translation in P. Boehner, *Ockham: Philosophical Writings*, London: Nelson, 1957.)

—— (1332–47) *Opera Politica* (Political Works), eds H.S. Offler *et al.*, Manchester: The University Press, 1956–74, vols I–III; Oxford: Oxford University Press, 1997, vol. IV. (Still incomplete; it lacks in particular the very important *Dialogus*. A selection of political texts, most of which come from the *Dialogus*, can be found in English translation in A.S. McGrade and J. Kilcullen, *William of Ockham: A Letter to the Friars Minor and Other Writings*, Cambridge: Cambridge University Press, 1995.)

Major works

—— (1317–19) *Ordinatio. Scriptum in librum primum Sententiarum* (Commentary on the First Book of the *Sentences*), in *Opera Theologica*, St Bonaventure, NY: The Franciscan Institute, vols I–IV. (The basic work for Ockham's epistemology, ontology and theology; partly revised 1320–6.)

—— (1317–19) *Reportatio. Quaestiones in libros Sententiarum II–IV* (Questions on Books Two, Three and Four of the *Sentences*), in *Opera Theologica*, St Bonaventure, NY: The Franciscan Institute, vols V–VII. (Authorized students' notes; a useful complement to the Ordinatio.)

—— (1317–24) *Quaestiones variae (Various Questions)*, in *Opera Theologica*, St Bonaventure, NY: The Franciscan Institute, vol. VIII. (Eight developments on various points such as the language of angels, the interrelations between virtues and so on.)

—— (1319–21) *Summula philosophiae naturalis* (Synopsis of Natural Philosophy), in *Opera Philosophica*, St Bonaventure, NY: The Franciscan Institute, vol. VI. (Unfinished work: Ockham's first attempt at physics.)

—— (1320–3) *Expositio in librum Porphyrii de praedicabilibus* (Commentary on Porphyry's Treatise on the Predicables), in *Opera Philosophica*, St Bonaventure, NY: The Franciscan Institute, vol. II. (Mainly on universals.)

—— (1320–3) *Expositio in librum praedicamentorum Aristotelis* (Commentary on Aristotle's *Categories*), in *Opera Philosophica*, St Bonaventure, NY: The Franciscan Institute, vol. II. (Introduce's Ockham's nominalistic interpretation of Aristotle's ten categories.)

—— (1320–3) *Expositio in librum Perihermenias Aristotelis* (Commentary on Aristotle's *De interpretatione*), in *Opera Philosophica*, St Bonaventure, NY: The Franciscan Institute, vol. II. (Contains one of Ockham's most detailed discussions on the mental existence of concepts.)

—— (1320–3) *Tractatus de praedestinatione et de praescientia Dei respectu futurorum contingentium* (Treatise on Predestination and God's Foreknowledge of Future Contingents), in *Opera Philosophica*, St Bonaventure, NY: The Franciscan Institute, vol. II; trans. M.M. Adams and N. Kretzmann, *William of Ockham: Predestination, God's Foreknowledge, and Future Contingents*, Indianapolis, IN: Hackett, 2nd edn, 1983. (How to reconcile God's infallible knowledge with the contingency of future events.)

—— (1322–4) *Expositio super libros Elenchorum* (Commentary on Aristotle's *Sophistical Refutations*), in *Opera Philosophica*, St Bonaventure, NY: The Franciscan Institute, vol. III. (Ockham's theory of logical fallacies.)

—— (1322–4) *Tractatus de quantitate et Tractatus de corpore Christi* (Treatise on Quantity and Treatise on the Body of Christ), in *Opera Theologica*, St Bonaventure, NY: The Franciscan Institute, vol. X;

trans. B.T. Birch, *The De Sacramento Altaris of William of Ockham*, Burlington, IA: The Lutheran Literary Board, 1930. (Mainly on the semantics of quantitative language; Birch's translation should be used with caution.)

—— (1322–4) *Brevis summa libri Physicorum* (A Short Summary of the Book of Physics), in *Opera Philosophica*, St Bonaventure, NY: The Franciscan Institute, vol. VI; trans. J. Davies, *Ockham on Aristotle's Physics*, St Bonaventure, NY: The Franciscan Institute, 1989. (Ockham's shortest physical work; a useful synthesis of his views on motion.)

—— (1322–4) *Quaestiones in libros Physicorum Aristotelis* (Questions on the *Physics* of Aristotle), in *Opera Philosophica*, St Bonaventure, NY: The Franciscan Institute, vol. VI. (151 Questions on concepts, change, motion, time, place and related subjects.)

—— (1322–7) *Expositio in libros Physicorum Aristotelis* (Commentary on the *Physics* of Aristotle), in *Opera Philosophica*, St Bonaventure, NY: The Franciscan Institute, vols IV–V. (Ockham's largest and most important work on physics.)

—— (1322–7) *Quodlibeta septem* (Quodlibetal Questions), in *Opera Theologica*, St Bonaventure, NY: The Franciscan Institute, vol. IX; trans. A.J. Freddoso and F.E. Kelley, New Haven, CN: Yale University Press, 1991, 2 vols. (A set of 170 short questions giving Ockham's latest views on important philosophical and theological subjects.)

—— (1322–7) *Summa logicae* (Summa of Logic), in *Opera Philosophica*, St Bonaventure, NY: The Franciscan Institute, vol. I; Part I trans. M.J. Loux (1974) *Ockham's Theory of Terms*, Notre Dame, IN: University of Notre Dame Press; Part II trans. A.J. Freddoso and H. Schuurman (1980) *Ockham's Theory of Propositions*, Notre Dame, IN: University of Notre Dame Press. (The basic work for Ockham's semantics and logic.)

—— (1332–4) *Opus nonaginta dierum* (The Work of Ninety Days), in *Opera Politica*, Manchester: The University Press, vols I–II. (A detailed discussion of Pope John XXII's ideas on poverty.)

—— (1334–47) *Dialogus* (The Dialogue), Lyons, 1494–6; repr. London: Gregg Press, 1962. (Ockham's major political synthesis; unfinished.)

—— (1334–5) *Tractatus contra Ioannem* (Treatise Against John), in *Opera Politica*, Manchester: The University Press, vol. III. (Argues that Pope John XXII, who had just died, was a heretic despite his supposed final 'retractation'.)

—— (1337–8) *Tractatus contra Benedictum* (Treatise Against Benedict), in *Opera Politica*, Manchester: The University Press, vol. III. (A discussion on papal heresy and the nature of the church; attacks Pope Benedict XII for not having reproved the errors of his predecessor.)

—— (1338–9) *Compendium errorum Papae Ioannis XXII*, Lyons, 1495; repr. London: Gregg Press, 1962 in *Opera Politica*, Oxford: Oxford University Press, 1997, vol. IV. (Synthesizes Ockham's doctrinal critique of John XXII.)

—— (1339–40) *Breviloquium de potestate Papae* (A Short Discourse on the Power of the Pope), ed. L. Baudry, Paris: Vrin, 1937; trans. A.S. McGrade and J. Kilcullen, *William of Ockham: A Short Discourse on Tyrannical Government*, Cambridge: Cambridge University Press, 1992. (On the relations between the power of the Pope and that of the Emperor.)

—— (1340–1) *Octo quaestiones de potestate Papae*, in *Opera Politica*, Manchester: The University Press, vol. I. (On various questions concerning the alleged authority of the Pope over the Emperor.)

—— (1340–7) *Elementarium logicae* (Elements of Logic), in *Opera Philosophica*, St Bonaventure, NY: The Franciscan Institute, vol. VII. (An interesting logical treatise, but its authenticity is still doubtful.)

—— (1346–7) *De imperatorum et pontificum potestate* (On the Power of Emperors and Popes), ed. C.K. Brampton, Oxford: Clarendon Press, 1927; part ed. W. Mulder in *Archivum Franciscanum Historicum* 16, 1923: 469–92, and 17, 1924: 72–97 in *Opera Politica*, Oxford: Oxford University Press, 1997, vol. IV. (A final discussion of civil and papal powers.)

References and further reading

* Adams, M.M. (1987) *William Ockham*, Notre Dame, IN: University of Notre Dame Press, 2 vols. (The best overall book on Ockham's philosophy and theology; a must for any serious study. Leaves out the political works.)

Baudry, L. (1950) *Guillaume d'Occam. Sa vie, ses oeuvres, ses idées sociales et politiques* (William of Ockham: His Life, Works and Political Ideas), vol. I: *L'homme et les oeuvres*, Paris: Vrin. (Outdated on many points, it remains the only detailed biography available; more up-to-date biographical information is to be found in the introductions to the various volumes of the critical edition.)

Beckmann, J.P. (1992) *Ockham – Bibliographie 1900–1990*, Hamburg: Felix Meiner. (A useful tool for further research.)

* Boehner, P. (1958) *Collected Articles on Ockham*, St Bonaventure, NY: The Franciscan Institute. (A collection of essays by a leading pioneer; still an indispensable reference work in the field.)

Freppert, L. (1988) *The Basis of Morality According to William Ockham*, Chicago, IL: Franciscan Herald Press. (A clear and well-informed presentation of Ockham's ethics.)

Goddu, A. (1984) *The Physics of William of Ockham*, Leiden: Brill. (The authoritative monograph on the subject.)

McGrade, A.S. (1974) *The Political Thought of William of Ockham*, Cambridge: Cambridge University Press. (A very useful and illuminating synthesis of a large body of material.)

Moody, E.A. (1935) *The Logic of William of Ockham*, New York: Sheed & Ward. (A seminal study, and a good introduction to Ockham's semantics.)

Panaccio, C. (1992) *Les mots, les concepts et les choses. La sémantique de Guillaume d'Occam et le nominalisme d'aujourd'hui* (Words, Concepts and Things: The Semantics of William of Ockham and the Nominalism of Today), Montreal/Paris: Bellarmin/Vrin. (A philosophical discussion of Ockham's nominalism with reference to contemporary analytical philosophy.)

Pasnau, R. (1997) *Theories of Cognition in the Later Middle Ages*, Cambridge: Cambridge University Press. (An analysis of the main issues in epistemology from Aquinas through Ockham.)

Tachau, K.H. (1988) *Vision and Certitude in the Age of Ockham: Optics, Epistemology and the Foundations of Semantics 1250–1345*, Leiden: Brill. (Provides a rich intellectual context for Ockham's epistemology.)

CLAUDE PANACCIO

WILLIAM OF SHERWOOD
(*c*.1200/5–*c*.1266/75)

William of Sherwood, an English logician of the mid-thirteenth century, is most noted for his theories of supposition and syncategorematic terms. In application, these theories enable us to express the true logical form of sentences with misleading grammatical forms. William's Insolubilia *(Insolubles) deals with paradoxes of self-reference, such as 'I am now uttering a falsehood'.*

William, who was born probably in Nottinghamshire, studied at Oxford and became a master there. Roger Bacon praised him as a greater logician than ALBERT THE GREAT. His *Introductiones in logicam* (Introduction to Logic) includes five chapters on traditional logic, corresponding to Aristotle's *On Interpretation, Prior Analytics, Topics* and *Sophistical Refutations*

(see ARISTOTLE) and Porphyry's *Isagōgē* (see PORPHYRY), and it is typical of its time in its reliance on BOETHIUS for much of what it says about the traditional topics.

The most interesting chapter of *Introductiones in logicam* is the one on the 'properties of terms', a logical doctrine that originated in the twelfth century. In William's account, the first of these properties is signification, the 'presentation of the form of something to the understanding'. This is the meaning of a term taken in isolation from its context, and specified extra-linguistically. Sometimes the signification of a term has nothing to do with its use in a sentence and the term 'supposits for' itself, as in 'man is a monosyllable'; this is material supposition. A term also supposits a form in a sentential context if its use there reflects its signification, so that it supposits *for* the form itself or something subordinate to it; this is formal supposition, in which a term supposits for an 'understanding of something' or, as WILLIAM OF OCKHAM might have said, for a mental term.

'Copulation' is parallel to supposition but belongs to adjectives and depends on a signification of something not as existing, but as adjoined to what exists. A term's 'appellation' is the set of those things of which the term can be predicated truly in the present tense. In an ordinary present-tense sentence a term's supposition will not extend beyond its appellation, for its subject can only supposit for actually existing things. The form that a term signifies does not of itself provide reference, then, unless the term supposits for the form itself in simple supposition, as in 'man is a species'. Otherwise, the term depends on existing individuals for its reference, a view consistent with nominalism, permitting us to take the form supposited for in simple supposition as an 'understanding of something', or a mental term, acquired through acquaintance with individuals, which are the term's primary referents. Thus William's views contrast with those of PETER OF SPAIN, which reflect a realist stance.

Usually a term supposits for individuals (or, to be precise, concepts of individuals) falling under the form it signifies, which is personal supposition. Personal supposition is 'determinate' when a word supposits for a single unspecified individual, as in 'a man is running', and 'confused' when a word supposits for more than one thing. Confused personal supposition is 'mobile' if one is entitled to attach its predicate to each of the individuals for which the term supposits, and is otherwise 'immobile'. Rules concerning personal supposition were used to assess the validity of arguments treated nowadays with quantification theory, but supposition occurs within a natural language, and no artificial language adapted to the uses of logic had been constructed. As a result, an open-ended set of rules governing the different types of supposition was introduced to handle all sorts of special contexts in scholastic Latin.

William's *Syncategoremata* (Treatise on Syncategorematic Words) extends supposition theory to sentences containing words that produce a misleading grammatical form, sometimes by altering the supposition of associated terms or concealing the true logical subject, and sometimes by abbreviating composite statements and making them appear categorical. Such words include 'every', 'whole', 'all', 'both', 'nothing', 'but', 'only', 'necessarily', 'begins', 'unless' and many others.

Also attributed to William, though doubtfully, are the treatises *De petitionibus contrarium* (On Contrary Assumptions) and *Insolubilia* (Insolubles), and an *Obligationes* which is probably by Walter BURLEY. The *Insolubilia* deals with semantic paradoxes of self-reference. For instance, when one utters 'I am now saying a falsehood', William insists that the sentence is meaningful and rejects the general rule excluding any reference within a sentence to itself, since some self-referential sentences make perfect sense and are true. Rather, he appeals to the principle of charity and takes it that the sentence refers outside itself in this case, since it is otherwise absurd. Thus, those who utter 'I am now saying a falsehood' assert that they are saying some falsehood other than the sentence they utter, which is, of course, false (see SEMANTIC PARADOXES AND THEORIES OF TRUTH).

See also: LANGUAGE, MEDIEVAL THEORIES OF

List of works

William of Sherwood (*c.*1250?) *Introductiones in logicam* (Introduction to Logic), ed. M. Grabmann, Munich: Verlag der Bayerischen Akademie der Wissenschaften, 1937; trans. N. Kretzmann, *William of Sherwood's Introduction to Logic*, Minneapolis, MN: University of Minnesota Press, 1966; ed. C.H. Lohr with P. Kunze and B. Mussler, 'William of Sherwood, "Introductiones in logicam"', Critical Text', *Traditio* 39, 1983: 219–99; ed. and trans. H. Brands and C. Kann, *William of Sherwood. Introductiones in logicam: Einführung in die Logic*, Hamburg: Meiner, 1995. (Kretzmann's translation contains extensive analytical notes. The Lohr edition supersedes the older Grabmann edition; Brands and Kann's new German translation with full explanatory notes supersedes both earlier editions.)

—— (*c.*1250?) *Syncategoremata* (Treatise on Syncategorematic Words), ed. R. O'Donnell, *Medieval Studies* 3 (1941): 46–93; trans. N. Kretzmann, *Treatise on Syncategorematic Words*, Minneapolis, MN: University of Minnesota Press, 1968. (Kretzmann's translation contains extensive analytical notes.)

—— (*c.*1250?) *Insolubilia* (Insolubles), ed. M.L. Roure, 'Insolubilia Guillelmi Shyreswood (?)', *Archives d'histoire doctrinale et littéraire du moyen âge* 37, 1970: 248–61. (No translation of this work is currently available.)

References and further reading

Braakhuis, H.A.G. (1977) 'The Views of William of Sherwood on Some Semantical Topics and Their Relation to Those of Roger Bacon', *Vivarium* 15: 111–42. (An important article on William's semantics.)

De Libera, A. (1982) 'The Oxford and Paris traditions in Logic', in N. Kretzmann, A. Kenny and J. Pinborg (eds) *The Cambridge History of Later Medieval Philosophy*, Cambridge: Cambridge University Press. (Places William's work in the context of his time.)

JOHN LONGEWAY

WILLIAMS, BERNARD ARTHUR OWEN (1929–)

Bernard Williams has written on the philosophy of mind, especially personal identity, and political philosophy; but the larger and later part of his published work is on ethics. He is hostile to utilitarianism, and also attacks a view of morality associated in particular with Kant: people may only be properly blamed for what they do voluntarily, and what we should do is the same for all of us, and discoverable by reason. By contrast Williams holds that luck has an important role in our evaluation of ourselves and others; in the proper attribution of responsibility the voluntary is less central than the Kantian picture implies. Williams thinks shame a more important moral emotion than blame. Instead of there being an independent set of consistent moral truths, discoverable by reason, how we should live depends on the emotions and desires that we happen to have. These vary between people, and are typically plural and conflicting. Hence for Williams ethical judgment could not describe independent or real values – by contrast with the way in which he thinks that scientific judgment may describe a real independent world.

1   General

Bernard Williams studied philosophy and classics at the University of Oxford. He was later Professor of Philosophy in London, Cambridge, Oxford and Berkeley, California, as well as chairing the commission set up by the British Government in 1977 to consider the legal control of obscene material.

Williams has written about many different areas of philosophy. His books include full-length studies of Descartes and of early Greek ethical thought, and he has written extensively on the philosophy of mind. His most influential writing has been in ethics, where he wrote *Morality* (1972), a book which pretends to be introductory but is in fact much more, *Ethics and the Limits of Philosophy* (1985), a criticism of utilitarianism (the 'against' half of *Utilitarianism: For and Against* (1973a)), and many occasional papers, the most important of which are collected in *Moral Luck* (1981b).

Before turning to this ethical work two important early papers on other areas should be mentioned. His first collection, *Problems of the Self* (1973b), starts with a paper on personal identity. Williams takes an imaginary case in which twin brothers both claim to remember being the same historical figure. This shows that memory claims are not sufficient to establish personal identity (since the twins, being different from each other, cannot both be the earlier person). Hence, thinks Williams (although this would involve another argumentative step), the necessity of bodily identity for personal identity. This paper's use of duplication is the basis of much of the subsequent discussion (see PERSONAL IDENTITY).

Another influential early paper in this collection is 'The Idea of Equality'. Williams here argues that some activities have an internal object, so that, for example, the internal object of the provision of medical services is medical need. Hence it is not optional whether health care should be distributed according to health need or according to ability to pay. By solving the problem of relevance in this way, Williams solves the problem of which property to consider in distribution, and hence a central problem of making egalitarian proposals practical (see EQUALITY).

2   Morality, the peculiar institution

Williams, like other philosophers, often works by critique and contrast. The centre of his ethical position can best be brought out by considering what he takes himself to be opposing. This is a view of morality principally associated with Kant. In this view, morality imposes on all people a set of duties discoverable by reason alone. These obligations are taken to be objectively true, untouched by emotion and unconstrained by interest. The area of morality is meant to be sharply distinguishable from other practical concerns and to be particularly connected to the voluntary. For Kant, we can all equally will and are equally responsible for, and only for, what we will (see KANTIAN ETHICS).

All this Williams criticizes. He resists even the word 'morality', preferring the term 'ethics' for the study of how we should live. The voluntary he regards as too weak a notion to found obligation. He holds that our moral psychology and ethical intuitions reveal our values to be more tangled, pluralist and impure than the Kantian model allows. Kantianism is centred on obligation and blame. Instead of blame, Williams proposes the centrality of shame. He discusses the nature of shame by considering the thought of the early Greeks, which he thinks is more applicable to the actuality of our current practical thinking than Kant's idealization. For Williams, Kant is wrong on the psychological facts; on the nature of the person; and on motivation. Kant is wrong to exclude the emotions. By contrast, Williams uses emotions, particularly regret, as a tool to uncover ethical requirements (see MORALITY AND EMOTIONS; PRAISE AND BLAME).

Perhaps the topic that focuses these thoughts most fully is that of moral luck. In the Kantian model, moral evaluation of people cannot depend upon mere luck (hence the importance of intention: there may be luck whether people succeed; there is no luck about whether they try). Williams wishes to show instead that our central evaluations may depend upon luck. For example, if I drive my car carefully and through no fault of my own run over a child, I may still, according to Williams, feel what he calls 'agent-centred regret' (that is, not just regret that it happened, but also regret that I did it). I may feel it proper to try and make some sort of recompense or acknowledgement of my responsibility. Yet my intentions were impeccable; if nevertheless regret is an appropriate emotion, it is a product of pure bad luck in a way that the Kantian model would preclude.

Williams' central example is the case of Gauguin (and a picture of Gauguin is used to illustrate the cover of *Moral Luck*). Gauguin left his wife and family to go to the South Seas to paint great pictures. If he succeeds he is justified; if he doesn't he is reprehensible. Again, mere intention is not enough; proper evaluation depends upon the luck of success (see MORAL LUCK).

3   Internal and external reasons

For Kant, once I know that something is the right thing to do (which I am supposed to be able to do by pure reason alone, uninfluenced by desire), this alone supplies me with a reason for action. This Williams resists. He calls such reasons 'external' reasons, and wants to argue, by contrast, that reason can only motivate me if it is connected to some already existing motivational state of myself (such as a desire). Such reasons Williams calls 'internal' reasons, because they follow from something internal to the agent. Williams' terminology here needs care and is liable to be confusing as he uses these terms in a different manner and with opposite effect than most philosophers (for whom 'internal' is taken to mean internal not to the person, but to morality; in the standard use, a reason based on antecedent desire is hence 'external').

In Williams' terminology, all reasons (that is, all real reasons) are internal reasons. That something, for example, follows from the rationally apprehended supposed requirements of justice gives me in itself no reason to do it. I only have a reason if I also happen to want to be just. For Williams it is the same with prudence. Some philosophers, such as Sidgwick, argue that I am rationally required to regard all times to be of equal value; Williams, by contrast, argues that I only have a reason to consider the distant future as important as the near future if I happen to have a particular kind of prudential psychology. Again, what counts as a reason for me depends upon my own idiosyncratic psychological state; pure reason alone is unable to tell me what to do (see MORAL MOTIVATION).

4   Utilitarianism

Williams also attacks utilitarianism, which shares with Kantianism the claim that morality has an impartial and objective foundation. Williams attacks the idea that the plurality of values can be reduced to a single metric. He probes the question of whether utilitarians can properly think that they are utilitarians. However, his central objection is again in terms of the impossible psychology that the moral theory demands.

In utilitarianism everything is justified by the consequences. In criticism, Williams wants to show that it is important not just what happens but also who does it. He takes the example of someone having the choice of doing a terrible thing, such as killing someone, in order to prevent more deaths being caused by someone else. For utilitarianism, which just counts the number of deaths, the answer is simple. But for Williams the answer is not simple; which shows that we are also concerned with who does the killing. He puts this in terms of people's integrity: there are things which people cannot be expected to do, whatever the consequences, if they are to be able to preserve any sense of themselves as people, or agents, at all (see UTILITARIANISM).

5   Consistency and realism

In two early papers Williams attempts to show that moral judgments are much more analogous to desires than to beliefs. Where there is a conflict of beliefs, he argues, this must in itself tend to weaken at least one of the beliefs, since beliefs are aimed at truth and two contradictory beliefs cannot both be true. Yet inconsistent desires are not like this. Although they cannot both be satisfied, this has no tendency to weaken at least one of them.

Williams shows that in tragic cases someone may be under two incompatible obligations, as Agamemnon in classical Greek tragedy was under incompatible obligations to his daughter and to his fleet. Whatever he does is wrong. On a Kantian view such conflict would not be possible; and it would not be rational to feel guilt about the thing not done. Yet Williams, again using moral psychology, shows that we both do and should feel regret in this sort of case. Hence what we did was wrong; hence there were incompatible obligations.

He derives from this conclusions about moral realism. The possibility of contradictory obligations shows that they cannot be taken to be descriptions of some real, independent, moral state of affairs. Our evaluative beliefs are plural and conflicting. They are therefore not descriptions of independent values which would provide objective and impersonal reasons for action (see BERLIN, I.; MORAL PLURALISM).

So far this is similar to other twentieth-century departures from the abstract impersonal reason of the Enlightenment. However, Williams disagrees with other thinkers in making a sharp distinction between ethical and other beliefs. For him, ethics is strongly contrasted with science. Both can be called kinds of knowledge, in that there can be agreement of belief about them. However, for Williams, this does not survive reflection in ethics, whereas in science it can. Scientific knowledge converges and can also explain how our scientific beliefs are caused by a real, independent world. Moral beliefs cannot in the same way survive explication of their causes.

An idea which Williams originally discussed in his book about Descartes, and which can be used to underline this distinction, is that of the 'absolute conception' of reality. Our knowledge and belief is perspectival, or from a particular position. Yet we have also the idea of things being true absolutely; that is, not from any particular position. This applies, thinks Williams, in science; at least as a regulative ideal. Things are just true; even if we do not know them. However, in ethics, it is all from a position. It is not just that it is psychologically impossible to think of ourselves being motivated by supposed moral truths which are true for all peoples and for all times; it is not just that our variable ideas show that we have no knowledge of any such truths; it is also that there are no such truths to be known.

See also: MORALITY AND IDENTITY §4

List of works

Williams, B.A.O. (1972) *Morality*, Harmondsworth: Penguin; repr. Cambridge: Cambridge University Press, 1976. (Simple, introductory account, with useful treatments of subjectivism and amoralism.)

Smart, J.J.C. and Williams, B.A.O. (1973a) *Utilitarianism: For and Against*, Cambridge: Cambridge University Press. (Smart proposes and then Williams disposes of utilitarianism; fairly easily accessible; discussed in §4.)

Williams, B.A.O. (1973b) *Problems of the Self*, Cambridge: Cambridge University Press. (A selection of early papers, up to 1972; which contains the two papers discussed in §1 and the two discussed in §5.)

——(1978) *Descartes: The Project of Pure Enquiry*, Harmondsworth: Penguin. (Critical study of Descartes; moderately hard in places; the 'absolute conception' discussed in §5 appears on page 245 and elsewhere.)

—— (1981a) *Obscenity and Film Censorship*, Cambridge: Cambridge University Press. (Abridgement of the report mentioned in §1.)

—— (1981b) *Moral Luck*, Cambridge: Cambridge University Press. (Papers of 1973–80; collecting the most important of Williams' papers on ethics, including the papers 'Moral Luck' and 'Internal and External Reasons' discussed in §§2 and 3.)

—— (1985) *Ethics and the Limits of Philosophy*, London: Fontana. (Fairly accessible central account of ethical position, including contrast between ethics and science discussed in §5.)

—— (1993) *Shame and Necessity*, Berkeley, CA: University of California Press. (Sather Classical lectures; on early Greek ethical thought and its

modern resonances; fairly accessible; and says more on shame and on the voluntary.)

—— (1995) *Making Sense of Humanity and Other Philosophical Papers*, Cambridge: Cambridge University Press. (Papers from 1982–93; contains the discussion of Sidgwick mentioned in §3.)

References and further reading

Altham, J.E.J. and Harrison, R. (eds) (1995) *World, Mind, and Ethics: Essays on the Ethical Philosophy of Bernard Williams*, Cambridge: Cambridge University Press. (Critical essays of varying difficulty.)

ROSS HARRISON

WINDELBAND, WILHELM
see NEO-KANTIANISM

WISDOM

In ancient times, wisdom was thought of as the type of knowledge needed to discern the good and live the good life. Philosophy takes its name from it (philosophía *means love of wisdom). But wisdom is little evident as a subject of contemporary philosophical discussion. It is interesting to ask how the concept of wisdom has come to vanish almost entirely from the philosophical map.*

1   Classical views of wisdom
2   Later conceptions of wisdom

1   Classical views of wisdom

Among the classical Greeks, wisdom (*sophia*) was one of the principal four virtues or human excellences (*aretai*), along with justice, moderation and courage, and was the primary focus of all epistemological discussion. In Plato's early dialogues, we find Socrates portrayed as a man on a mission given him by the god of Delphi (Apollo). Socrates tells the story (in Plato's *Apology*) that his friend Chairephon approached the oracle and asked if anyone was wiser than Socrates. The oracle answered 'no'. When Chairephon reported this encounter to Socrates, the latter found it deeply puzzling, for he regarded himself as not at all wise. In seeking to unravel the riddle of the oracle, Socrates questioned others who had the reputation for wisdom, and learned that he was indeed the wisest of men, for he alone recognized that he lacked wisdom. The mission of Socrates on behalf of the god, therefore, was to examine anyone willing to submit to his questioning, to see if they were wise and, if not, to 'assist the god' (*Apology* 23B) by showing that they are not. The pursuit of wisdom, then, and the exposure of the pretence of wisdom, was at the heart of Socratic philosophizing.

If Plato's early dialogues tell us anything about the historical Socrates, they show that, for him, wisdom would provide its possessor not only with all the other virtues (through Socrates' commitment to the 'unity of the virtues'), but also with infallible judgment in one's pursuit of a good or happy (*eudaimōn*) life. Some scholars even suppose that Socrates regarded the possession of wisdom as both necessary and sufficient to having a good or happy life, but this is controversial and seems to yield the result that no one could have a good or happy life, despite the fact that at least Socrates himself seems to have had one. Plato's early-period Socrates also recognizes minor and particularized forms of wisdom (each true craftsman would be wise in his craft, for example – see *Apology* 22C–D), but seems to regard these as philosophically insignificant, except as providing small-scale models for the really important form, which one could use in pursuit of a good and happy life. Wisdom, for Socrates, invariably requires the possession of knowledge, and not just any knowledge, but that which provides the basis for infallibly good judgment in decisions pertinent to how one should live. Wisdom, then, is the possession of such knowledge plus the disposition and skill to use this knowledge in the right ways.

In later works, Plato increasingly neglects the specific, craft-related wisdoms, coming eventually to identify wisdom only with the kind of knowledge that permits one to be infallible in judging the good. In the *Republic*, for example, Plato envisages a class of philosophical rulers who, through extensive training in mathematics and dialectic, will come to know the Form of the Good. This knowledge, we are told, will give the philosopher-rulers the fully actualized power to make infallible judgments in the state, seeing clearly, as it were, which institutions and political decisions were most just.

Aristotle is critical of Plato's theory of Forms in general, and of Plato's conception of the Good in particular. Aristotle's conception of the 'Four Causes' (*aitiai*) and his views about the categories of being require that there is a specific good for each thing – Plato's idea that there must be one Good for all things seems to Aristotle to be an absurdity (*Nicomachean Ethics* I.6; *Eudemian Ethics* I.8). Accordingly, Aristotle cannot see wisdom as requiring some vision of

the Good. Aristotle accepts the infallibilism inherent in the Socratic and Platonic accounts, but divides wisdom into two sorts: theoretical and practical. Theoretical wisdom (*sophia*) is *nous* (the ability to grasp first principles) plus *epistēmē* (scientific knowledge or understanding – see *Nicomachean Ethics* VI.7), which involves knowledge of the 'causes' – the 'why' of things (*Metaphysics* A.1–2). In so far as there can be different sciences with different first principles, there can be different examples of theoretical wisdom – one for each science. Practical wisdom (*phronêsis*), for Aristotle, is knowledge of means and ends. Some have criticized this view as being insufficiently attentive to which ends are, and which could not be, the right ends for a wise person. This criticism, however, is controversial, and depends upon the degree to which Aristotle thought the study of ends could itself be scientific.

2 Later conceptions of wisdom

After Aristotle, wisdom begins to lose its place of primacy within philosophical discourse, no doubt partly due to Sceptical attacks, and partly due (later) to Christianity. The Sceptics rarely discussed wisdom. They appear to have accepted something like the Aristotelian account of theoretical wisdom, but then cast doubt on our ability to grasp first principles by arguing that even the most rudimentary and particular forms of knowledge – such as grasping some particular fact – are problematical. Sceptical practical wisdom, such as it was, became something like the ability to withhold assent from any particular proposition, thus avoiding dogmatism and achieving quietude (*ataraxia*). The connection with knowledge was thus either broken (for practical wisdom) or required a vast and difficult defence of knowledge (for theoretical wisdom) before philosophy could even return to wisdom as a subject of study. To a substantial degree, contemporary philosophy, and its preoccupations with justification and information, continues to focus its energies on the areas problematized by the ancient Sceptics.

Early Church Fathers, on the other hand, were generally suspicious of what the Greeks had identified as wisdom. They generally agreed that wisdom at best subserved Christian faith (see, for example, Augustine's *City of God* 8.8); at worst they simply identified it with useless and deceitful book-learning and arrogant intellectual presumption, perhaps following St Paul's warning against philosophy in *Collossians* 2: 2–8 (see, for examples, Justin Martyr *Dialogue with Trypho* 2.4–5, 7.1; Tertullian *Apology* 46.5–8). Subsequent epistemological disputes within religious contexts have also largely failed to revive wisdom as an object of rational pursuit, instead attending mainly to the degree to which various religious claims can or cannot be justified.

Wisdom can be found among medieval conceptions of the virtues, but it no longer held the central place it had been afforded by the Greeks. By the time we reach the early modern period, we find wisdom mentioned only rarely, and then only at the periphery of greater works (as in the preface to the French edition of Descartes' *Principles of Philosophy*), or in revivals of ancient Greek points of view (as in the neo-Sceptical work, *De la sagesse* by Pierre Charron). From this period on, wisdom is mentioned only in passing, or simply passed by altogether by philosophers.

Given its disappearance from our discussions, none of the claims by the early Greeks has been sufficiently well scrutinized by philosophers. It is interesting, for example, that the development of fallibilism in epistemology has not served to liberate wisdom from its early association with infallibility, which was guaranteed to make wisdom seem an impossible achievement for human beings (see FALLIBILISM). On the other hand, the early connection between wisdom and some notion of a good life seems exactly right, but contemporary philosophy is deeply divided over what makes a life good. Perhaps as the criteria for human knowledge relax and conceptions of the good life (or good lives) become clearer, philosophy will find that it can return to the study of wisdom.

See also: ARETĒ; EUDAIMONIA; NIRVĀNA; NOUS; VIRTUE EPISTEMOLOGY; ZHI

References and further reading

* Aristotle (*c.* mid 4th century BC) *Eudemian Ethics*, ed. J. Barnes in *The Complete Works of Aristotle*, vol. 2, 1922–81, Princeton, NJ: Princeton University Press, 1984. (Scholars have disputed whether this or the *Nicomachean Ethics* was written first. This work seems to be more interested in practical wisdom.)

* —— (*c.* mid 4th century BC) *Metaphysics*, ed. J. Barnes in *The Complete Works of Aristotle*, vol. 2, 1552–728, Princeton, NJ: Princeton University Press, 1984. (In a certain sense, this is Aristotle's attempt to define and describe philosophy, and hence what the 'love of wisdom' consists in, in its purest sense. In many ways the *Metaphysics* is at the centre of nearly all the rest of Aristotle's philosophy. Definitely not for beginners.)

* —— (*c.* mid 4th century BC) *Nicomachean Ethics*, ed. J. Barnes in *The Complete Works of Aristotle*, vol. 2, 1729–867, Princeton, NJ: Princeton University Press, 1984. (Compared to the *Eudemian Ethics*,

this work is more interested in theoretical wisdom, especially in Book X.)

* Augustine (413–27) *City of God*, trans. D.S. Wiesen, Loeb Classical Library, vol. 3, Cambridge, MA: Harvard University Press, 1968. (One of Augustine's three major works – his most detailed review and critique of ancient Greek 'wisdom' may be found here.)

Blanshard, B. (1967) 'Wisdom', in P. Edwards (ed.) *The Encyclopedia of Philosophy*, vol. 7, New York and London: Macmillan, 322–4. (Discussion of the classical accounts of wisdom.)

* Charron, P. (1601/1604) *De la sagesse* (On wisdom), ed. B. de Negroni, Paris: Fayard, 1986. (A neo-sceptical work, which was influential in the development of libertinism and fideism in the 17th century. The main argument is that human beings can discover truth only by revelation.)

* Descartes, R. (1647) *Principles of Philosophy* (Preface to the French edition), trans. J. Cottingham in *The Philosophical Writings of Descartes*, vol. 1, 179–90, Cambridge: Cambridge University Press, 1985. (Descartes' penultimate work. The topic of wisdom appears only in the preface to the French edition, and the connection of this topic to Descartes' other epistemological preoccupations is only barely made.)

* Justin Martyr (*c.* 150) *Dialogue with Trypho*, in J.C.M. Van Winden, *An Early Christian Philosopher*, Leiden: E.J. Brill, 1971, 7–15. (Belittles the 'wisdom' of all the philosophical schools of his day, except that of the Platonists, claiming that the end of Plato's philosophy was to 'look upon God'.)

Kekes, J. (1983) 'Wisdom', *American Philosophical Quarterly* 20(3): 277–86. (One of the few discussions of wisdom in contemporary philosophy.)

* Plato (*c.* 395–387 BC) *Apology*, trans. H.N. Fowler, Loeb Classical Library, Cambridge, MA: Harvard University Press, 1914. (Plato's version of Socrates' three speeches at his trial: the defence proper, the counter-penalty proposal, and some final words to his jurors after his condemnation. Plato's Socrates describes himself as wisest among men only because he alone recognizes that he wholly lacks wisdom.)

* —— (*c.* 380–367 BC) *Republic*, trans. P. Shorey, Loeb Classical Library, Cambridge, MA: Harvard University Press, 1914. (According to Plato, political troubles can only be brought to an end in the cities 'if philosophers become rulers or rulers become philosophers'. Books V–VII give Plato's account of the kind of knowledge that makes philosophers wise as a power (dunamis) to be developed through rigorous education.)

Sternberg, R.J. (ed.) (1990) *Wisdom. Its Nature,*

Origins, and Development, Cambridge: Cambridge University Press. (Collection of essays on wisdom by psychologists.)

* Tertullian (*c.*197) *Apology*, trans. T.R. Glover in *Tertullian: Apology, De Spectaculis; Minucius Felix*, Loeb Classical Library, Cambridge, MA: Harvard University Press, 1931. (Disparages earlier Greek philosophers, even to the point of accusing Socrates of having been influenced by the devil.)

NICHOLAS D. SMITH

WITHERSPOON, JOHN
(1723–94)

John Witherspoon, Scottish-American clergyman, political leader and educator, was born at Gifford, East Lothian, educated at Edinburgh University and ordained Presbyterian minister. In his mid-forties he went to America as president of the College of New Jersey, later Princeton University. He held political office for New Jersey and played a major role in organizing the Presbyterian Church in America and improving the College at Princeton. Witherspoon was representative of eighteenth-century Scottish and American Calvinists who tried to reconcile their orthodox theological doctrines with the Enlightenment's philosophical currents of empiricism, scepticism, and utilitarianism by harmonizing reason and revelation. Although Witherspoon was a philosophical eclectic, Francis Hutcheson's moral sense philosophy was the major source of his utilitarian ethics and republican politics. Witherspoon was not an original thinker, but his popularization of Scottish common sense and moral sense philosophy through his forceful personality and effective teaching laid the foundation for its dominance of nineteenth-century American academic philosophy.

John Witherspoon was born at Gifford, East Lothian, Scotland on 5 February 1723 and died at Princeton, New Jersey, United States of America on 15 November 1794. A man of action but also of reflection, Witherspoon combined a strong interest in philosophical and theological questions with clerical, educational, and political activism. In Scotland (1723–68), he was a notable parish minister, theologian, and ecclesiastical politician in the Church of Scotland. Witherspoon gained fame in America (1768–94) as a cleric, educator, philosopher, and national leader in Church and state as president of the College of New Jersey, later Princeton University.

Witherspoon wrote numerous works on a wide variety of subjects, most notably moral philosophy, rhetoric, and theology. His divinity lectures, sermons and theological treatises stressed the practical ethics of orthodox Calvinist dogma: God's sovereignty; the individual's sinful nature; God's justification of the sinful through Christ; scriptural authority; and regeneration (see CALVIN, J.).

Witherspoon's introduction to philosophy began as an Edinburgh University student with the epistemological empiricism of John LOCKE and the logic and moral philosophy of Johann Gottlieb Heineccius. He continued to read widely in philosophy during his Scottish years, but he only wrote two brief works on philosophy of religion. His 1739 university graduation thesis on the immortality of the mind relied on traditional philosophical and theological arguments, while his 'Remarks on an Essay on Human Liberty' (1753) attempted to refute Kames' position on the freedom of the will (see HOME, H. (LORD KAMES)) using a naive version of Thomas Reid's common sense realism (see REID, T.; COMMON SENSE SCHOOL). Both works attempted to reconcile the conflicting claims of reason and revelation in defence of Calvinism against the attacks of philosophical sceptics.

Witherspoon's Scottish intellectual background provided the basis for his outstanding American career as churchman, educator, philosopher and politician. As Princeton's president (1768–94), Witherspoon stressed the unity of learning and piety in its curriculum. Required to teach philosophy for the first time, Witherspoon's most important contribution was his course on moral philosophy. His *Lectures on Moral Philosophy* (1768) derived from a wide variety of modern philosophers, but their eclectic nature caused him to make numerous philosophical errors. They were based primarily on Scottish thought, especially Hutcheson's moral sense philosophy, interpreted in the context of Witherspoon's Calvinism (see HUTCHESON, F.; MORAL SENSE THEORIES). Although the organization and subjects of the *Lectures* closely followed Hutcheson's works, they did not simply mimic Hutcheson's ideas, for on critical points Witherspoon's arguments expanded on and took different positions from Hutcheson's.

Throughout his nine brief lectures on ethics Witherspoon's epistemology rested on his claim that reason and revelation combined to provide the foundations of human knowledge. But like Hutcheson, he was also a social Newtonian who conceived of moral philosophy an as empirical science of human beings and society, based on reason and independent of revelation. Ethics was 'that branch of Science which treats the principles and laws of Duty or Morals' (Witherspoon 1768: 269). Individuals acquired their knowledge of the world through external and internal senses. Witherspoon attacked Berkeley's idealism, which he found at Princeton (see BERKELEY, G.) and replaced it with Reid's realism. In his faculty psychology he agreed with Hutcheson that the operations of the affections or passions were more important mental processes than the understanding or the will, but added religious affections to Hutcheson's incomplete catalogue of feelings.

The critical faculty was the moral sense, because it allowed persons to judge actions as evil or good. Joseph Butler's concept of conscience influenced both Hutcheson and Witherspoon, although Witherspoon mistakenly equated the moral sense 'with what, in scripture and common language, we call conscience' (1768: 281) (see BUTLER, J. §3; CONSCIENCE). Contrary to Hutcheson, Witherspoon followed Reid in arguing that reason played a critical role in aiding the moral sense to discover moral truth. The moral sense provided the philosophical linkage between Witherspoon's epistemological, psychological and moral ideas and his theological doctrines. Since it originated in God, it bound all persons to the creator in a moral relationship. Thus, the moral sense harmonized reason and revelation. Witherspoon adopted Hutcheson's utilitarian position 'that benevolence or public affection is virtue, and that a regard to the good of the whole is the standard of virtue' (1768: 285). As to the obligation of virtue, he favoured duty over interest, because the moral sense intimates 'that it is duty independent of happiness' (1768: 291). Benevolence was the central virtue in motivating persons to the duties they owed God, their fellow human beings, and themselves. Witherspoon's discussion of rights emphasized the inalienable rights of intellectual, political, and religious liberty as well as self-preservation.

Witherspoon's political thought, explicated in three short lectures on politics, domestic society and civil society, was a logical extension of his ethics as a science of society. His republican political ideas, like his ethics, were eclectic, generally followed Hutcheson's, and sought always to harmonize his philosophical and theological ideas. A political realist unlike Hutcheson, Witherspoon argued that civil society originated both in Locke's social contract and in Calvin's religious covenant. He thought that a wide distribution of property was necessary for the public good; that a republic was the best form of government; and that the right of revolution was fundamental. The value and advantage of civil liberty was not that it caused virtuous behaviour or insured individual freedom, but rather that it was useful. Witherspoon elaborated his republicanism in pamphlets, sermons, speeches and other works during the American Revolution. His moral philosophy and theology led him to conclude that the Revolution resulted in the moral regeneration of the American people and the creation of a virtuous, Christian republic.

See also: AMERICAN PHILOSOPHY IN THE 18TH AND 19TH CENTURIES; RIGHTS; UTILITARIANISM

List of works

Witherspoon, J. (1800–1) *The Works of the Rev. John Witherspoon*, Philadelphia, PA: Woodward. (This first edition contains all of Witherspoon's major works, and several, but not all, of his minor writings.)
—— (1753) 'Remarks on an Essay on Human Liberty', *Scots Magazine* XV: 165–70. (Witherspoon's attempt to refute Kames' scepticism.)
—— (1768) *Lectures on Moral Philosophy*, in *The Works of the Rev. John Witherspoon*, Philadelphia, PA: Woodward, vol. 3. (Not published until 1800.)
—— (1982) *An Annotated Edition of Lectures on Moral Philosophy by John Witherspoon*, ed. J. Scott, Newark, DE: University of Delaware Press. (The most recent and accessible edition of the *Lectures* with excellent annotations, bibliography and introduction.)

References and further reading

Collins, V. (1925) *President Witherspoon: A Biography*, Princeton, NJ: Princeton University Press, 2 vols. (The standard biography, portraying Witherspoon in great detail as a man of action.)
Fechner, R. (1982) 'The Godly and Virtuous Republic of John Witherspoon', in H. Craven (ed.) *Ideas in America's Cultures: From Republic To Mass Society*, Ames, IA: Iowa State University Press, 7–25. (A succinct summary of the relationship between Witherspoon's moral philosophy and theology relative to his political ideas.)
—— (1974) *The Moral Philosophy of John Witherspoon and the Scottish–American Enlightenment*, unpublished Ph.D. dissertation, University of Iowa, Ann Arbor, MI: Xerox–University of Michigan Microfilms, order no. 75–13, 747. (The fullest exposition of Witherspoon's moral philosophy in its Scottish and American cultural, intellectual and religious contexts.)
Flower, E. and Murphey, M.G. (1977) 'Philosophy in Academia Revisited – Mainly Princeton', *A History Of Philosophy In America*, New York: Putnam, vol. 1, 203–73. (A sophisticated analysis of the place of Scottish philosophy in the history of American philosophy with special focus on Witherspoon's role, 226–38.)
Landsman, N. (1990) 'Witherspoon and the Problem

of Provincial Identity in Scottish Evangelical Culture', in R. Sher and J. Smitten (eds) *Scotland and America in the Age of Enlightenment*, Edinburgh: Edinburgh University Press, 29–45. (A subtle discussion of Witherspoon as a Scottish and American provincial in the wider cultural and religious world of eighteenth-century Britain.)

Meyer, D. (1976) *The Democratic Enlightenment*, New York: Putnam, 182–209. (A sensitive characterization of Witherspoon as a public intellectual in the American Enlightenment through his role as an educator.)

Noll, M. (1989) *Princeton and the Republic, 1768–1822*, Princeton, NJ: Princeton University Press, 16–58. (A skilful weaving together of several strands of Witherspoon's thought in its academic and religious contexts.)

Sloan, D. (1971) *The Scottish Enlightenment and the American College Ideal*, New York: Columbia University Teachers College Press, 101–45. (A thoughtful study of Witherspoon's role in the transmission of the Scottish Enlightenment to American Presbyterianism and to Princeton.)

R.J. FECHNER

WITTGENSTEIN, LUDWIG JOSEF JOHANN (1889–1951)

Ludwig Wittgenstein was born in Vienna on 26 April 1889 and died in Cambridge on 29 April 1951. He spent his childhood and youth in Austria and Germany, studied with Russell in Cambridge from 1911 to 1914 and worked again in Cambridge (with some interruptions) from 1929 to 1947.

His first book, the Tractatus Logico-Philosophicus, *was published in 1921. It presents a logical atomist picture of reality and language. The world consists of a vast number of independent facts, each of which is in turn composed of some combination of simple objects. Each object has a distinctive logical shape which fits it to combine only with certain other objects. These objects are named by the basic elements of language. Each name has the same logical shape, and so the same sort of possibilities of combination, as the object it names. An elementary sentence is a combination of names and if it is true it will be a picture of the isomorphic fact formed by the combination of the named objects. Ordinary sentences, however, are misleading in their surface form and need to be analysed before we can see the real complexity implicit in them.*

Other important ideas in the Tractatus *are that these deep truths about the nature of reality and representa-tion cannot properly be* said *but can only be* shown. *Indeed Wittgenstein claimed that pointing to this distinction was central to his book. And he embraced the paradoxical conclusion that most of the* Tractatus *itself is, strictly, nonsense. He also held that other important things can also be shown but not said, for example, about there being a certain truth in solipsism and about the nature of value. The book is brief and written in a simple and elegant way. It has inspired writers and musicians as well as being a significant influence on logical positivism.*

After the Tractatus *Wittgenstein abandoned philosophy until 1929, and when he returned to it he came to think that parts of his earlier thought had been radically mistaken. His later ideas are worked out most fully in the* Philosophical Investigations, *published in 1953.*

One central change is from presenting language as a fixed and timeless framework to presenting it as an aspect of vulnerable and changeable human life. Wittgenstein came to think that the idea that words name simple objects was incoherent, and instead introduced the idea of 'language games'. We teach language to children by training them in practices in which words and actions are interwoven. To understand a word is to know how to use it in the course of the projects of everyday life. We find our ways of classifying things and interacting with them so natural that it may seem to us that they are necessary and that in adopting them we are recognizing the one and only possible conceptual scheme. But if we reflect we discover that we can at least begin to describe alternatives which might be appropriate if certain very general facts about the world were different or if we had different interests.

A further aspect of the change in Wittgenstein's views is the abandonment of solipsism. On the later view there are many selves, aware of and co-operating with each other in their shared world. Wittgenstein explores extensively the nature of our psychological concepts in order to undermine that picture of 'inner' and 'outer' which makes it so difficult for us to get a satisfactory solution to the so-called 'mind–body problem'.

Although there are striking contrasts between the earlier and later views, and Wittgenstein is rightly famous for having developed two markedly different philosophical outlooks, there are also continuities. One of them is Wittgenstein's belief that traditional philosophical puzzles often arise from deeply gripping but misleading pictures of the workings of language. Another is his conviction that philosophical insight is not to be gained by constructing quasi-scientific theories of puzzling phenomena. Rather it is to be achieved, if at all, by seeking to be intellectually honest and so to neutralize the sources of confusion.

757

1 Life

Wittgenstein was the eighth and last child of a wealthy Austrian industrialist. From 1903–8 he was educated on the assumption that he would be an engineer and in 1908 he came to Manchester to study aeronautics. He continued with this for three years, but at the same time developed his interest in philosophy. He was particularly engaged with logic and the foundations of mathematics, in connection with which he read FREGE (§§6–10) and RUSSELL (§§4–11). In October 1911 he gave up engineering and, on Frege's advice, came to Cambridge to study with Russell. In the 1914–18 war he served in the Austro-Hungarian army and during this time completed the *Tractatus Logico-Philosophicus* (1922).

For a time Wittgenstein thought that the *Tractatus* said everything which could be said in philosophy, and so he turned to other things. From 1920 to 1926 he was a schoolteacher in Austria, though this was not a success, since he was severe and demanded too much of his pupils. In 1926–8 he helped to design a house for his sister. In 1927 he resumed philosophical discussion with some members of the Vienna Circle, and in 1929 he returned to Cambridge, lecturing there from 1930 to 1936. From 1936 to 1938 he visited Norway and Ireland, returning to Cambridge in 1938 and being appointed professor there in 1939. He held the chair until 1947, although from 1941 to 1944 he was given leave of absence to work first at Guy's Hospital, London, then at the Royal Victoria Infirmary, Newcastle. After resigning his chair in 1947 he lived in various places, Ireland chief among them, and also visited America.

Wittgenstein impressed those who met him with the power of both his intellect and personality. He had an intense concern for truth and integrity which exerted great attraction, but which also made him difficult to deal with, since he was liable to accuse others of superficiality or dishonesty. He greatly disliked what he perceived as the artificiality and pretentiousness of academic life. His later ideas became known in the 1930s and 1940s through the circulation of copies of *The Blue and Brown Books* (1958) and reports of his lectures, and they acquired considerable influence.

2 Works and method of writing

Throughout his life Wittgenstein wrote down his thoughts in notebooks, returning to the same topics many times, trying to get the most direct and compelling formulation of the ideas. He then made selections and arrangements from these remarks, followed by yet further selection, reworking and rearrangement. The *Tractatus* was the only book published during his lifetime. In 1930 he assembled what we now know as the *Philosophical Remarks*, a work still having much of the outlook of the *Tractatus* and also showing considerable sympathies with verificationism, and in 1932–4 he wrote the *Philosophical Grammar*, in which some central themes of the later philosophy are foreshadowed. But he was not satisfied with either of these, and from 1936 onwards worked on various versions of what we now know as the *Philosophical Investigations* (1953), which he hoped would provide a definitive presentation of his thought. The earlier half of the volume is the part of his work with which he was most nearly satisfied, but he was never fully content with any of it, and in 1949 he abandoned the project of completing it.

The other books we have under his name are all early or intermediate versions of material, left in his papers and edited and published after his death. The *Notebooks* are preliminary versions of ideas which later became the *Tractatus*. The *Blue and Brown Books* were prepared so as to help his students in 1932 and 1933. *Remarks on the Foundations of Mathematics* (1956) contain ideas he worked on from 1937 to 1944 and which he intended at that time to form the second part of the *Investigations* (rather than the psychological topics we now have). From 1944 onwards he worked mainly on philosophical psychology: *Zettel* (1967), *Remarks on the Philosophy of Psychology I and II* (1980) and *Last Writings on Philosophical Psychology I and II* (1982) are from these years. From 1950 to 1951 we also have *On Certainty* (1969) and *Remarks on Colour* (1977). Another source for his views is records of his conversations and lectures taken by friends and pupils.

3 The picture theory of meaning

The *Tractatus* consists of nearly eighty printed pages of numbered remarks. The numbers do not run consecutively but are designed to indicate the relative importance and role of the remarks. There are seven major sentences and each of them (except 7) has subordinate and clarificatory remarks following it, labelled '2.2', '5.4' and so on, down as far as such numbers as '4.0312'.

The topics that preoccupied Wittgenstein when he arrived in Cambridge included the nature of logical truth and Russell's Theory of Types. On both of these matters Russell held that we need an account of very general features of the world and of the kinds of things in it. But Wittgenstein soon came to think that the route to insight was through the contemplation of the nature and presuppositions of individual meaningful sentences such as 'Socrates is wise' and that this contemplation showed Russell's approach to be misguided.

The central fact about such individual sentences is that each says one thing – that Socrates is wise, for example – but is essentially such that it may be either true or false. A false sentence is both out of touch with the world, inasmuch as it is false, but also in touch with the world, inasmuch as it succeeds in specifying a way that things might be. Wittgenstein holds that all this is possible only because the sentence is complex and has components which represent elements of reality, which exist whether the sentence is true or false and are (potentially) constituents of states of affairs. So, in rough illustration, 'Socrates' represents Socrates and 'is wise' represents wisdom. The truth or falsity of the sentence then depends on whether these elements are or are not assembled into a fact.

Not all sequences of sentence components are acceptable. A mere list of names (for example, 'Socrates Plato') does not hang together as a sentence. And although it looks as if we may apply a predicate to itself (as in '"is in English" is in English' or '"is wise" is wise') it seems important to disallow such sequences as truth-evaluable sentences, on pain of falling into Russell's paradox. Russell's account of these matters is that elements of reality come divided into different types – individuals, properties and so on – and that a sentence is to be allowed as meaningful, and so truth-evaluable, only if the elements picked out by the components are of suitably related types.

Wittgenstein maintains, against this, that we do not need rules to bar sentences which would lead to paradox, because when we properly understand the nature of our language we see that we cannot formulate the supposed sentences in the first place.

We think we can only because we have misidentified that component in 'Socrates is wise' whose presence in the sentence attributes wisdom to Socrates. This component is not the phrase 'is wise' but the property which the word 'Socrates' has when the words 'is wise' are written to the right of it. To see why this is plausible, consider the fact that there could be a language in which properties are attributed to people by writing their names in different colours. If, for example, we could claim that Socrates is wise only by writing 'Socrates' in red letters then we could never formulate any analogue to '"is wise" is wise' because we could not take the redness of 'Socrates' and make it red. And although we have given a linguistic role to 'Plato' (as representing Plato) we have not given any role to the property of a name which it acquires when we write 'Plato' to the right of it. That is why a mere list of names does not hang together to make a statement.

Wittgenstein generalizes this idea to claim that the formal properties of any element of the world, that is, the properties which fix its potential for combining into facts with other elements, must be mirrored in the formal properties of the linguistic component which represents it. So the kind of item we call a sentence, and which we often wrongly think to be a complex object, is really a fact. In a sentence certain linguistic components are put together experimentally in a structure which mirrors the formal structure of some possible state of affairs (see THEORY OF TYPES §1).

4 Negation and tautology

This account does away with the need for a theory of types and Wittgenstein holds that the ideas invoked by Russell to explain the nature of logical truth are similarly unnecessary. His view was that logical truths, such as that all sentences of the form 'p or not p' are true, should be explained by pointing to relations holding between some very abstract kind of logical items – negation, disjunction and the like.

Wittgenstein maintains that the negation sign is not a component of a sentence and so does not represent any element of a possible fact (in the quasi-technical sense of 'component', 'element' and 'represent' introduced above). Rather it is the visible mark of an operation one can perform on a meaningful sentence to produce another sentence. The role of the second sentence is to deny that things are as they would need to be to make the first sentence true.

To see the force of this, we must look again at the account of truth given above. What makes a negative sentence true is not the presence of some 'not-ness' in a fact but rather the absence of that (the combination of elements) which would have made the unnegated sentence true. This is similarly the case with the other so-called logical constants. Thus 'or' does not stand for a possible element in a fact but is a sign by which one can correctly link two sentences if the components of either are so combined as to yield a truth.

Logical tautologies thus do not reveal the nature of special logical objects. Such sentences as 'It is raining or it is not raining' do not say anything. But their possibility is a corollary of the existence of a language adequate to say the kind of thing which can be said. So contemplating them can draw our attention to the logical structure of the world (see LOGICAL CONSTANTS; LOGICAL FORM; LOGICAL LAWS).

5 Simples

The ideas outlined in the last two sections are already present in the sets of notes which Wittgenstein wrote in late-1913 and 1914. But the *Tractatus* in its complete form incorporated several further important ideas. One of these, perhaps adopted from Frege, is the view that sense must be determinate, that is, that every meaningful sentence must be either true or false in every possible state of affairs. But Wittgenstein differs from Frege in thinking that ordinary language, although misleading in surface form, is in order, and so already fulfils this condition of determinacy.

Determinacy entails that there must be 'objects', that is, utterly simple, eternal and unalterable elements, out of which all facts are composed. Moreover the links between our language system and reality must be set in place at this basic level. Suppose that language–world links were set up so as to connect a basic linguistic component with some element of reality which was not basic. The existence of this element would be contingent and would depend upon some simpler elements being suitably combined in a fact. A sentence containing this imagined basic component is clearly not true in a world where the simpler elements are not suitably combined. But it is equally unhappy to say that it is false, because the component itself does not specify what the simpler elements are or that they must be combined, and so it is no part of its meaning that their failure to be combined is relevant to its falsehood. To insist on the undefinability of this imagined basic element of language is to insist that it has meaning only through its connection with the item it represents. So in a world lacking that item it has no meaning, and sentences containing it are neither true nor false. But this, given the assumption of determinacy of sense, is a *reductio ad absurdum* of the idea that meaning can be conferred in this imagined way.

We may have an apparently basic sentence compo-

nent which is linked to a contingently existing item (for example 'Socrates' as a name of Socrates). But this is only possible because a definition of that component can be given in our language system. The link between Socrates and his name is thus not a basic point of attachment between language and the world (contrary to the impression given in our earlier rough and ready example). It is a consequence of these ideas that there must be a complete analysis of every sentence of our language into a truth-functional combination of elementary propositions, the components of which are simple signs representing objects.

But what are these simple objects? Wittgenstein, like Russell but unlike Frege, does not allow for any contrast between sense and reference within the meaning possessed by names of simples. This puts one demand on simples: they cannot be items with distinguishable aspects, that is, items which can be conceived of in several logically distinct ways. If they were, then there would also be the possibility of one name for a simple as conceived one way and another non-synonymous name for it as conceived another way – contrary to the denial of the sense–reference distinction. So a simple is the kind of thing which, if apprehended in such a way that it can be named, is apprehended exactly as it is in its entirety.

In so far as Wittgenstein drops any hints, it is that simples are phenomenally presented items, such as points in the sensory field and the properties they have, for example, shades of experienced colour. But he cannot give this answer officially because to do so would clash with another of the themes brought to prominence in the later development of the *Tractatus*. This is the claim that all necessity is logical necessity, and hence would be revealed as tautological in a complete analysis (see §7 below). A corollary of this is that all atomic facts are independent of each other and no elementary sentence can entail or be the contrary of any other. Such things as colours cannot then be 'objects' because attribution of different colours to one thing, as in 'a is red' and 'a is green', produces sentences which are contraries.

The topics so far discussed are treated primarily in the remarks following the main sentences numbered 2, 3 and 4. The remarks following 5 and 6 deal mainly with implications of this atomist conception for certain issues in logic (generality and identity for example) and for the nature of science, mathematics and statements of probability. On the last mentioned subject, Wittgenstein's brief remarks are one important source for the approach later developed by Rudolf Carnap (see CARNAP, R. §5; LOGICAL ATOMISM §1).

6 Thought, self and value

Wittgenstein writes, 'There is no such thing as the subject that thinks or entertains ideas' (5.631). His grounds for this are similar to those of Hume, namely that a unified, conscious self cannot be an element in any encountered fact. Hence no such item can be among those objects represented in thought. So reports of the form 'A believes that p', which seem to mention such a subject, are really of the form '"p" says that p'. They report the existence of a sentential complex, the components of which are correlated with the elements of the potential fact that p. There are then no selves in the world but, at best, bundles of sentence-like items.

But Wittgenstein also says 'What the solipsist means is quite correct; only it cannot be said but makes itself manifest' (5.62), and 'The subject does not belong to the world: rather, it is a limit of the world' (5.632). One interpretation connects these remarks with the idea of projection – he speaks of using a propositional sign as a projection of a possible situation by thinking out its sense. The picture suggested is that of a subject who is the origin of the lines of projection which link representing items with what they represent and whose existence is thus presupposed by their meaningfulness. 'The world is *my* world: this is manifest in the fact that the limits of *language* (of that language which alone I understand) mean the limit of *my* world' (5.62). So perhaps Wittgenstein's idea is that the existence of a unique self (me) at the limit of the world is shown by the existence of representations which are meaningful to me.

Wittgenstein also offers, in the closing pages of the *Tractatus*, a number of gnomic remarks about value, death and the mystical, among them that no value exists in the world, that ethics cannot be put into words, that the will as a subject of ethical attributes cannot alter facts but only the limits of the world, that at death the world does not alter but comes to an end, that feeling the world as a limited whole is the mystical and that the solution of the problem of life is seen in the vanishing of the problem. These claims are to some extent intelligibly grounded in ideas concerning the self and what can be said. But they also represent a leap of development beyond those, a leap which comes in part from Wittgenstein's experiences in the First World War and the religious convictions to which his always intense and serious outlook then led him.

7 Saying and showing

Wittgenstein thought that by reading the *Tractatus* one might come to grasp certain things about the nature of meaning, reality and value, among them the kinds of things outlined above. But he also held that these things could not be *said* but only *shown*, and the attempt to say them ends up producing nonsense. Most of the *Tractatus* itself is thus nonsense. This claim is highly paradoxical and may seem to be unnecessary and grandiose mysticism, especially when viewed as part of the same package as the difficult remarks about the will and solipsism. But this is unfair. In many of its applications, the claim is well motivated, given the picture theory of meaning.

Most of the linguistic manoeuvres which Wittgenstein condemns as nonsensical are attempts to say things which are both necessary but also substantive – that is, not mere tautologies. Thus they include moves to assign elements of reality or language to their logical types ('Socrates is a particular'), related attempts to describe the logical forms of sentences or facts and also efforts to list the simples. (Claims about what is valuable could also have this status of seeming to be both substantial and necessary.) But if the picture theory of meaning holds in complete generality there cannot be such statable necessary truths. To say, for example, that object b is F we require that there be a linguistic representative of b ('b') and one of F-ness (the property of having 'F' to the right) which can be combined or not, just as b and F-ness can be combined or not. There must be complexity and there must therefore be the possibility of dissociation as well as association. But if b and F-ness necessarily go together (for example, Socrates must be a particular) then b cannot be dissociated from F-ness and it is a confusion to imagine that its being F is a fact with a composite structure. Hence it is also a confusion to imagine that it is something of the kind which can be said, on the account of saying which is offered by the picture theory.

8 Transition

In the *Tractatus* Wittgenstein took a lofty tone about simple objects; he had proved that they existed and it was of no importance that we cannot say what they are. But in the first years of his return to philosophy in 1927–31 one thing which occupied his attention was the detailed workings of various parts of our language, notably those involved in talking of shape, length and colour and other observable properties of items around us. His aim in considering them was to fill in that earlier gap by giving an account of the fundamental features of both language and the world.

He soon became convinced that the idea of independent elementary propositions was indefensible. For example, the incompatibility of 'a is red' and 'a is green' cannot be explained (contrary to what he had urged in the *Tractatus*) by analysing the two propositions and showing that one contains some elementary proposition which contradicts an elementary proposition in the analysis of the other. Rather the whole collection of colour judgments come as one set, as the marks along the edge of a ruler come as a set. To measure an object we hold a ruler with its marks against the object, that is, in effect we hold up a whole set of possible judgments of length, and we read off which is correct; to see that one judgment is correct is to see at the same time that all the others are incorrect. Something similar holds for colour and for many other concepts, except that in these cases the 'ruler' is not physically present. The differences between concepts have to do with the logical shapes of their 'rulers' and with the different methods by which they are compared to reality.

Other topics which occupied Wittgenstein at this time were those of psychological phenomena and the use of the word 'I'. And he also worked extensively on the nature of mathematics. Ideas in common with those of the logical positivists are apparent in some of the writings of this time. Indeed the slogan known as the verification principle – 'the meaning of a proposition is its method of verification' – may have originated with Wittgenstein. But he found it impossible to accept this as a clear statement which could provide one of the starting points for elaborating a philosophical system. He was aware of further puzzles and was temperamentally incapable of putting them on one side for the purpose of building an intellectual construct which might be based on misapprehension and which failed to address questions which still perplexed him (see LOGICAL POSITIVISM §§3–4; VIENNA CIRCLE §2).

9 Dismantling the *Tractatus* picture

Paragraphs 1–242 of the *Philosophical Investigations* (roughly the first third of the book) are generally agreed to provide the most focused presentation of some of the central ideas of Wittgenstein's later outlook, in the context of which his views on philosophy of mind, mathematics and epistemology can helpfully be seen. We may divide the paragraphs into three groups: §§1–88 raise a variety of interrelated difficulties for the outlook of the *Tractatus*, §§89–142 discuss the nature of logic, philosophy and truth, and §§143–242 contain the so-called rule-following considerations.

The first group has two main targets: first, the idea that most words have meaning in virtue of naming something and, second, the idea that meaning requires determinacy and so exactness. Against the former Wittgenstein points out that different words function in different ways. To understand 'five', for example, a person needs to be able to count and behave appropriately on the result of a counting; to understand a colour term might, by contrast, involve knowing how to compare the specimen to be judged with a sheet of samples. To teach language one must train a person to produce and respond to words in the context of everyday activities such as fetching things, measuring, building, buying and selling. We can throw light on meaning by reflecting on simple 'language games', involving such integration of speech and action. To say that every word names something is like saying that every tool in the tool box modifies something. We can describe things this way if we insist: 'The saw modifies the shape of the board; the ruler modifies our knowledge of a thing's length'. But such assimilation may lead us to overlook important variety rather than representing a useful insight. To get someone to understand a word it is not enough to bring them face-to-face with the supposed referent while repeating the word. In order to profit from the confrontation, the learner must know what kind of word is being taught (for a number, shape, colour, and so on). And this in turn involves already being at home with the everyday activities into which remarks using the word are woven. 'For a large class of cases – though not for all – in which we employ the word "meaning" it can be defined thus: the meaning of a word is its use in the language' (1953: §43).

On the second topic Wittgenstein remarks that drawing a contrast between 'simple' and 'complex' depends upon context and interest. Items which might be seen as complex in one context could be taken as simple in another and vice versa. So the related notion of exactness is also context-relative. A word does not become unusable and hence meaningless because its use is not everywhere bounded by rules. That we can imagine circumstances in which a given description would seem inappropriately vague or in which we would not know whether to say that it was true or false is no criticism of its current use and hence no argument that it does not have meaning. Hence the idea that every meaningful sentence must have some underlying analysis in terms of simples is mistaken.

Each sort of word is at home in its own language game. But there are not always clear-cut relations of subordination or dependence between different language games. There are many predicates (for example, 'intention', 'thought', 'statement', 'number', 'game') which clearly do not name simples, because they have interesting richness and apply to complex items. But it is not the case that such predicates must have an analysis in terms of 'simpler' predicates. Search for such an analysis may reveal instead a 'family resemblance'.

Persons who recognizably belong to the same family may have various resemblances, of build, features, colour of eyes, gait, temperament and so on, which 'form a complicated network of similarities, overlapping and criss-crossing' (1953: §66), without one set of such resemblances being necessary and sufficient for having the appearance of a member of that family.

On the basis of this survey of the actual workings of language, Wittgenstein then concludes that the *Tractatus* picture of a detailed crystalline structure present in both world and language is an illusion.

But perhaps the considerations outlined require only minor tinkering with the *Tractatus* picture? We might say: 'Certainly linguistic representations of states of affairs are put to various uses, in commands, jokes, stories etc., as well as in straight reports; also what degree of exactness we need is fixed by context; hence we should accept that for many practical purposes vague remarks are adequate. But none of this shows that we must discard the *Tractatus* picture of a fully determinate world, structured by simples; nor does it show that the idea of constructing a complete and exhaustive description of it need be abandoned. All it shows is that our everyday language mirrors the world less accurately than an imaginable ideal scientific language.' That such a reading is inadequate is shown by considering the remarks on rule-following found in paragraphs 143–242.

10 Rule-following

By 'rule' Wittgenstein does not mean an abstract standard according to which some act may be judged right or wrong. Rather he means a concrete item, such as a noise, mark or gesture, which is presented to a person and by attending to which they direct their behaviour, the link between rule and response being learned and conventional. An enormous number of human activities can be seen as instances of rule-following. The activities include imitating the gestures and noises which others make, copying shapes, converting marks into noises as in reading music, chanting the number sounds in sequence, and so on. More generally, both nonverbal behaviour in response to verbal instruction (fetching a book when told to do so) and also producing linguistic reports (where the world itself is the guide and the utterance is the response) may be described as rule-following. Rule-following is thus at the heart of linguistic competence. If we further accept that coming to use a rich and expressive language is an indispensable part of coming to grasp complex concepts and to make reflective judgments, then rule-following is also at the heart of our lives as thinking creatures.

It is generally agreed that Wittgenstein has telling negative points to make about one attractive but misleading picture of rule-following. On this picture, to understand a rule, for example, to grasp what is meant by 'Add two', it is necessary and sufficient to have a certain sort of item, an image, feeling or formula, occur in the mind when the instruction is heard. For example, having a mental image of two blocks appearing at the end of a line of blocks is the sort of thing which might be imagined to constitute understanding 'Add two'. This image is supposed to do two things. First, it helps bring about that the person goes on to produce a particular response, for example, saying 'Eight' if the previously given number was six; second, it sets a standard by which that response can be judged correct or incorrect.

But the picture will not do. A person might have such an image while responding to 'Add two' as if it meant 'Multiply by two'. Moreover the person's behaviour (the regular patterns of action, what seems to be regarded as a mistake, and so on) could show that for them, 'Add two' actually means 'Multiply by two'. So images guarantee neither subsequent behaviour nor the appropriateness of a particular standard of assessment.

What the case makes us see is that an image, feeling or formula is merely another rule-like object (that is, a potential vehicle of meaning) rather than the meaning itself. An item is not automatically a self-interpreting sign, that is, one which fixes and enforces a certain reading of itself, simply in virtue of existing in the mind rather than in the outer public world. So images and the like are not sufficient for understanding; but neither are they necessary, since in many cases they do not occur. Typically when someone responds to everyday and familiar language they just act unhesitatingly and spontaneously, without consulting any inner item.

To teach someone to follow a rule, for example, to understand 'Add two', we put them through a finite amount of training, primarily by working through examples of adding two. These examples may appear to be another resource for pinning down meaning. But being only finite in number, they are bound to have more than one feature in common. Thus they do not themselves determine a unique interpretation for the sign we associate with them. A learner might exhibit a future bizarre divergence from what is expected, for instance by saying that adding two to 1000 yields 1004. And if this occurred it would suggest that they had all along been struck by some feature other than the one intended.

The central point here is that, for there to be meaning, the rule-followers must have fixed on one rather than another of the various similarities between the teaching examples and have associated it with the rule, that is, with the mark or sign to which they respond. 'The use of the word "rule" and the use of the word "same" are interwoven' (1953: §224). But neither the examples nor the rule itself determine which similarity this is; and imagined inner surrogates, in which we would like to see the relevant resemblance encapsulated, turn out to be equally inefficacious.

These reflections do not just undermine one picture of the psychology of understanding. They are also relevant to the metaphysics of the *Tractatus*. If the world consisted of intrinsically articulated facts as envisaged in the *Tractatus*, then there would exist items, namely the simple objects, which would fix the one and only absolute standard of similarity. If there is a simple which is a common element in two separate facts then there is a basic real resemblance between those facts; if not, not. Every other real resemblance which can be meaningfully labelled, for example, by the predicates of everyday language or science, must be founded in simples. A putative linguistic expression which is not tied to some definite combination of simples is, on the *Tractatus* view, an expression without meaning which is merely randomly applied. Further, as we saw earlier, a simple is the kind of thing which, when apprehended, must be apprehended as it is. So representing a simple, whether by a direct cognition of it or by having in mind something which encapsulates its nature, is to be aware of a self-interpreting item, something which dictates what is to count as 'the same'. But this sort of confrontation is what the rule-following considerations suggest to be unintelligible.

Thus the discussions of §§143–242 can be seen as interweaving with and reinforcing those of §§1–88. The whole undermines not only the idea of closeness of fit between a *Tractatus* world and everyday language, but the underlying conception of that world itself, namely as already determinately articulated into facts by simples which we can apprehend (see MEANING AND RULE-FOLLOWING §§1–2).

11 The later picture of meaning

The *Tractatus* view offers us a world articulated of its own nature into value-free facts which are the subject matter of the natural sciences together with a mind confronting that world and attempting to mirror it in its thoughts. It also tells us that there is only one self and that it is an item at the limit of the world which cannot act responsibly in the world.

However attractive the first element here, everyone would agree that there is something seriously wrong with the solipsism of the second. So one essential move in amendment is to make the self responsibly active, to bring it in from the limit and to locate it firmly in the world, together with other selves. We may do this while leaving in place the idea of the world as the totality of value-free facts. Then the self which appears in the world must be some subset of such facts. This yields an extremely powerful and attractive overall picture. But it also generates many philosophical puzzles, those to do, for example, with giving naturalistic accounts of consciousness, free will, rationality and so on.

This overall picture cannot be Wittgenstein's, however, if §10 is right in its reading of the rule-following considerations. The idea of an independently articulated world is not acceptable to him. We cannot understand our concepts by pointing to simples in the world which force them on us. To understand meaning we must look to use, at how our actions and concepts are interwoven. The fact that makes a sentence true is grasped through seeing when the sentence is correctly used, and that in turn is grasped only by seeing the full shape of the language games in which it is used. For a concept to be truly applicable to the world, and so for its corresponding property to have instances, is not for it to pick out some simple which is among the timelessly given building-blocks of all worlds. Rather it is for the life of which use of that concept is a part to be liveable in this world. Wittgenstein thus moves from a bold and simple form of the correspondence theory of truth in the *Tractatus* to a redundancy theory in the *Investigations*.

The self need not, on this view, be an assemblage of value-free facts. It is rather a locus of abilities, a person who can be trained to follow rules, to use and respond to language, in the way normal humans can. And since concepts are aspects of our way of life rather than items forced on us by the world, understanding what it is to have a particular concept involves 'assembling reminders' about how it works for us and how our various activities and ways of talking build together into our way of life.

If it is correct to conceive of understanding as an ability, then the exercise of this ability in everyday situations will often be just some confident, spontaneous action or utterance, which the subject will not be able to justify by pointing to something, other than the situation or words responded to, which guided them.

'How am I able to obey a rule?' – if this is not a question about causes, then it is about the justification for my following the rule in the way I do. If I have exhausted the justification I have reached bedrock and my spade is turned. Then I am inclined to say: 'This is simply what I do'.

(1953: §217)

But this need not worry us. 'To use a word without justification does not mean to use it without right' (1953: §289). The fact is that we do find such confident and unhesitating responses in ourselves. Also we (usually) agree with others; and where we do not we (usually) agree on how to settle the dispute. So we have no reason to doubt that in general we do indeed mean what we take ourselves to mean.

Indeed we can put things more strongly than this. It is not just that it is sensible, practically speaking, for me to make a leap of faith and decide to carry on as if I and others mean what it seems we mean. We have no more choice about this than we do about taking 'Eight' to be the right response to 'Add two to six'. The language game of ascribing meanings to the remarks of ourselves and others is as central and indispensable to a recognizably human life as anything in our linguistic repertoire. Moreover the rich and complex social world in which we find ourselves sustains our practice of so doing. So we and our meanings are just as much part of the world as the stars, rocks and trees around us. And since we are no longer committed to the idea of one totality of facts, those of value-free natural science, this recognition does not now produce cramps or pressures to reductive manoeuvres (see PRIVATE STATES AND LANGUAGE §4).

12 Alternative readings

The account of §§9–11 presents Wittgenstein as inviting us to abandon the idea of our meanings and judgments being securely moored to something outside us which imposes itself on us and keeps us in line. We are to become aware of our involvement in and responsibility for our own judgments and the way of life of which they are part. We are also to acknowledge that we cannot prove the unique correctness of our way of life and its associated concepts. (The arguments of the *Investigations* against the position of the *Tractatus* thus have much in common with themes explored by other late-nineteenth-century and twentieth-century thinkers, such as Nietzsche, William JAMES, Heidegger, Quine and DERRIDA (see NIETZSCHE, F. §6; HEIDEGGER, M. §§2–4; QUINE, W.V. §5).) But, the reading given in §11 implicitly suggests, this need not lead us to scepticism about the notions of meaning, fact, objectivity or truth.

This interpretation, although not idiosyncratic, is by no means generally accepted. There are a large number of differing construals of Wittgenstein's overall intention, many of which have in common that they present the consequences of abandoning the *Tractatus* view as more radical and/or more deflationary, than is suggested in §11.

One interpretation stresses a contrast between the *Tractatus* and the later writings which is different from any highlighted earlier. It takes the rule-following considerations to show that we cannot make sense of grasp of meaning which fixes truth conditions independent of our ability to verify that they obtain. The later Wittgenstein is thought to insist (as against his earlier self) that all meaning be explicated by appeal to assertibility conditions rather than such possibly verification-transcendent truth conditions and he is recruited onto the antirealist side of the debate in the dispute between realism and antirealism.

Another much discussed view is presented by Saul KRIPKE. If there were facts about meaning, he argues, they would have to be constituted by something about past behaviour or present occurrences in the mind. So §§143–242 can be read as showing that there are no facts about meaning. Our practice of labelling remarks 'correct' or 'incorrect' and ascribing 'meanings' to them has a role in our social life. But such linguistic moves do not have truth conditions. Instead they have only appropriateness conditions. We are licensed to make them when others in our community keep in step with us in certain ways in their patterns of utterance.

Yet a third interpretation takes it that Wittgenstein espouses relativism. One response to the idea that there are no simples is to take it that the world is a featureless mush or unknowable something. Any apparent structure in it is then imposed by us. Hence the familiar physical and social world we experience is a creation of ours. But there are several possible but incompatible ways of imposing structure, one of which we are physiologically and/or socially caused to adopt. So no judgment can claim to be 'true' in a non-relative sense; at best it can be 'true for us'.

One interesting issue in assessing this view is what status Wittgenstein intended for the sketched alternative ways of responding to language teaching. Certainly they need enough feasibility to dislodge the idea of the one and only enforced way of dividing up the world. On the other hand it is not clear that he takes us to be entitled to assert that there are conceptual schemes which are both incompatible with ours and also fully possible.

Many other readings are also possible, detecting in his writings elements of pragmatism, behaviourism and even deconstructionism (see BEHAVIOURISM, ANALYTIC; DECONSTRUCTION; PRAGMATISM §2; REALISM AND ANTIREALISM §4; RELATIVISM).

13 Philosophy of mind

The *Tractatus* picture of the relation of language to its subject matter is especially attractive in the case of

765

psychological notions. A sensation such as pain is easily conceived as a phenomenon which impresses its nature and identity conditions on one who has it, independent of external circumstances or bodily behaviour. The private language argument (§§243–71) examines this idea in the light of the earlier discussion of meaning. One aim is to show that our actual use of terms for sensations does not and could not conform to the pattern suggested.

The rule-following considerations suggest that no standard for what is to count as 'the same' can be fixed merely by uttering a word to oneself while being vividly aware of what one experiences. For one kind of item rather than another to come into focus out of the indefinite variety potentially presented in an experience, that experience must be embedded in one kind of life rather than another. Relatedly, for a word to have meaning there must be some extended practice in which its use has a point. This is as true of sensation words as of any others. We teach and use them in a complex setting of physical circumstances and expressive bodily behaviour. This setting, says Wittgenstein, is not externally and contingently linked to sensation but is an integral part of the sort of life in which the general category 'sensation' makes sense and in which particular sensations can be individuated.

Wittgenstein considers many other topics in philosophical psychology, among them intention, expectation, calculating in the head, belief, dreaming and aspect perception. A constant theme is the need to counter the attraction of the model of name and object, which (together with such things as the special authority which each person has to pronounce on their own psychological states) leads us to conceive of the 'inner' as a special mysterious realm, distinct from the 'outer' or physical. He offers such general remarks as 'An "inner process" stands in need of outward criteria' (1953: §580). He also returns repeatedly to the idea that authoritative first-person psychological claims should be seen as expressions or avowals of those states which we are inclined to insist that they describe. These sorts of moves have led to the idea that he denies the existence of the 'inner' and is really a behaviourist.

He was aware of the risk of this reading:

'But you will surely admit that there is a difference between pain-behaviour accompanied by pain and pain-behaviour without any pain?' – Admit it? What greater difference could there be? – 'And yet you again and again reach the conclusion that the sensation itself is a *nothing*.' Not at all. It is not a *something*, but not a *nothing* either!

(1953: §304)

Thoughts and experiences are, on his view, necessarily linked to expressive behaviour. 'Only of a living human being and what resembles (behaves like) a living human being can one say: it has sensations; it sees; is blind; hears; is deaf; is conscious or unconscious' (1953: §281). But this does not mean that any reduction of the mental to the behavioural is possible or that the psychological is not real. To see Wittgenstein's view sympathetically it is important to keep in mind the upshot of §§1–242. There is no a priori guarantee of some privileged set of classifications (for instance, those of natural science) in terms of which all others must be explained. To understand any phenomenon we must get a clear view of the language games in which terms for it are used; and the logical shapes of these may be very different from those which are initially suggested by the pictures which grip us (see PRIVATE LANGUAGE ARGUMENT §§1–3).

14 Philosophy of mathematics

Platonism in mathematics involves two claims, that there is a realm of necessary facts independent of human thought and that these facts may outrun our ability to get access to them by proofs. Platonism is attractive because it accounts for several striking features of mathematical experience: first that proofs are compelling and yet may have conclusions which are surprising, and second that we seem to be able to understand some mathematical propositions without having any guarantee that proofs of them exist.

Wittgenstein never accepted Platonism because he always took the view that making substantive statements is one thing, while articulating the rules for making them is another. So-called necessary truths clearly do present rules of language, inasmuch as accepting them commits one to allowing and disallowing certain linguistic moves. Wittgenstein holds that it is therefore a muddle to think that such formulations describe some particularly hard and immovable states of affairs. Thus in the *Tractatus* mathematical propositions are treated together with tautologies as sets of signs which say nothing, but show the logic of the world.

Nevertheless the *Tractatus* view has some kind of affinity with at least the first claim in Platonism, inasmuch as the rules of our language are taken to reflect some logical structure independent of us. But when Wittgenstein comes to see linguistic rules as features internal to our practices, the resulting picture is unwelcoming even to this. There is now no such thing as 'the logic of the world', whether to be shown or said. Instead, in *Remarks on the Foundations of Mathematics*, he explores ideas of the following kinds.

At a given time we have linguistic practices directed

by certain rules. Someone may now produce a proof of a formula which if accepted would be a new rule – for example, '$14 + 3 = 17$'. It is natural to think that to accept this is to unpack what we were already committed to by our understanding of '17', '+', and so on. But the rule-following considerations unsettle this assumption because they undermine the idea of an intellectual confrontation with an abstract item which forces awareness of its nature upon us and they also bring to our attention the element of spontaneity in any new application of a given term. Rather to accept the proof and its outcome is to change our practices of applying signs like '17', because it is to adopt a new criterion for judging that seventeen things are present, namely that there are two groups of fourteen and three. Hence to accept the proof is to alter our concepts. What makes mathematics possible is that we nearly all agree in our reaction to proofs, and in finding them compelling. But to seek to explain this by pointing to Platonic structures is to fall back into incoherent mythology.

My own view is that it is persistent uneasiness with the first claim in Platonism which primarily motivates Wittgenstein's reflections on mathematics. But those who see him as an antirealist will put more stress on hostility to the second claim (the idea of verification transcendence) and certainly some of Wittgenstein's remarks (for example, his suspicion of the application of the law of excluded middle to mathematical propositions) have affinities with ideas in intuitionistic logic. A third reading will bring out the conventionalist-sounding elements, on which we choose what linguistic rules to adopt on pragmatic grounds.

In addition to reflections on the nature and use of elementary arithmetical claims, Wittgenstein also applies his ideas to some more complex constructs in mathematical logic, such as the Frege–Russell project of deriving mathematics from logic, Cantor's diagonal argument to the non-denumerability of the real numbers, consistency proofs and Gödel's theorem. His general line here is not that there is anything wrong with the mathematics but that the results have been misconstrued, because they have been interpreted against a mistaken background Platonism. Some mathematical logicians claim that Wittgenstein has not understood properly what he is discussing. His views on consistency and Gödel in particular have aroused annoyance (see ANTIREALISM IN THE PHILOSOPHY OF MATHEMATICS §2; INTUITIONISM; REALISM IN THE PHILOSOPHY OF MATHEMATICS §2).

15 Ethics, aesthetics and philosophy of religion

In the *Tractatus* Wittgenstein consigns ethics to the realm of the unsayable, and he takes the same line in his 'Lecture on Ethics' ([1929] 1993). Here he says that ethics (which he links to aesthetics and religion) arises from a tendency in the human mind to try to express in words something – roughly the existence and nature of absolute value – which seems to manifest itself to us in certain experiences. (He gives as an instance the experience of finding the existence of the world miraculous.) It is essential to this impulse that it seeks to go beyond the world and significant language; so it is bound to issue in utterances which are nonsensical. Nevertheless, he says, he has the greatest respect for this impulse and would not for his life ridicule it.

This position resembles the emotivism associated with logical positivism in distinguishing ethical utterances sharply from those of science (that is, those which are capable of rational assessment, and can be true or false). But it also differs from it in being, in spirit, an ethical realism, albeit of a mystical kind.

In his later writing he rethought his views on meaning, mathematics and the mind but did not return to any sustained discussion of ethics or aesthetics (although there are scattered remarks, particularly on the aesthetics of music, in *Culture and Value* (1980)). One interpretation of the later outlook, however, provides a hospitable setting for an ethical realism of a less mysterious kind, one which allows for the statement and rational discussion of truth-evaluable ethical claims. Philosophers of meta-ethics taking themselves to be working within a Wittgensteinian outlook have urged that our inclination to insist on a dichotomy between fact and value, or between cognition and feeling, should be resisted, as the outcome of the grip on us of some misapplied picture. Moreover Wittgenstein's emphasis on attention to the actual workings of language could encourage a distinctive approach to first order ethical questions (see WITTGENSTEINIAN ETHICS §2). But he himself never developed this, nor does he engage with issues in political philosophy.

The later outlook enjoins us to study each distinctive area of language as far as possible without preconceptions. If we do this for religious language, Wittgenstein holds, we shall see that religion is not a kind of science and hence is not open to criticism on the grounds that, as science, it is unconvincing (see, for example, 'Remarks on Frazer's *Golden Bough*' ([1931] 1993)). Some take it that this implies that no religious utterance can be properly subject to any criticism other than that coming from inside the same religious community or tradition.

16 Epistemology

One familiar traditional philosophical problem is that of scepticism, that is, whether we can rightly claim to know such things as that physical objects exist independent of our perception, that the world was not created five minutes ago and so forth.

Wittgenstein's most extended discussion of these issues is in *On Certainty* (1969). He starts from the kinds of examples invoked by G.E. Moore in his attempt to combat scepticism, such as 'Here is a hand' and 'The Earth has existed for a long time before my birth' (see MOORE, G.E. §§3–4). Moore is wrong, Wittgenstein thinks, in taking it that we are plainly entitled to assert that we know these things. But Moore is right in thinking that the claims form an interesting class. It is impossible to conduct life and thought without taking some things entirely for granted, and the propositions Moore identifies are the articulated forms of things which play this role for us. They help to define our world picture and underpin the procedures by which other claims (ones that are in fact doubted and tested) can be assessed. But they cannot themselves be assessed because there is nothing relatively more certain by which we can get leverage on them. Someone who seems to doubt them is thought mad and, from a first-person point of view, when I imagine doubting such things I contemplate a situation in which I would no longer know how to reason about anything. There are close links between these themes and the idea that the workability of any language game presupposes certain very general facts of nature.

The relevance of this for the traditional question of scepticism is that it is, in its form, misconceived. The central use of 'know' is in connection with propositions where testing is possible. Hence one who uses it in connection with the propositions which help define our worldview (as is in fact done only in philosophy and not in ordinary life) has extended the word to a situation where procedures do not exist for assessing either the first-order claim or the claim to knowledge of it. This is not to say that the word 'know' is unintelligibly and wrongly used in the philosophical debate. We can sympathize with the sceptical impulse, which springs from awareness of the fact that our language games are not based on grounds which compel us to them or guarantee their continued success. But we can also sympathize with the anti-sceptical position which insists that acceptance of these central propositions underpins our being able to do any thinking at all, so that claims to doubt them are empty (see SCEPTICISM).

17 Wittgenstein's conception of philosophy

In two central respects Wittgenstein stands squarely within the main historical tradition of philosophy, first in the nature of the issues which excited and intrigued him intellectually – meaning, the self, consciousness, necessity – and second (going back to the roots of the tradition) in his being a 'lover of wisdom', that is, one who is seriously concerned about having a right stance to the world both intellectually and practically and who is committed to the use of the intellect (among other things) in helping to achieve this.

But he differs from many philosophers in his conviction that a great number of traditional philosophical problems are the result of some deep kind of muddle, and in his belief that the answers given and the way they are debated hinder rather than help us in achieving wisdom. This conviction gripped him from very early on and philosophical thought therefore presented itself to him as a tormentingly difficult struggle to be honest and to free himself from misleading preconceptions.

So the word 'philosophy' has, in all his writings, two uses. On one it describes a body of confused utterances and arguments, arising largely from misunderstanding of the workings of language, and on the other it describes an activity of helping people to get free of the muddles. Another important continuity is his insistence that there cannot be philosophical theories and that the helpful activity of philosophy ought only to consist of making uncontentious statements, of describing and assembling reminders. In the context of the picture theory of meaning, this is comprehensible (see §7). But it is less clear that it is required by the later view.

In part Wittgenstein is here stressing that we cannot have the kind of explanation of our concepts which the *Tractatus* picture seemed to promise. Our form of life cannot be grounded but only described and lived. In part he is questioning the impulse to look for quasi-scientific theories of the nature of philosophically puzzling phenomena. But these two interrelated points do not obviously add up to a complete embargo on anything which could be called 'philosophical theory'. It is in the spirit of the later philosophy to point out that there are many different kinds of things which can be called 'theories'. Everyone engaged in reflection on the topics Wittgenstein considers (including Wittgenstein himself) finds it natural to articulate in words the states they arrive at and to engage with these words and those of others in the mode of further comment and assessment.

We become aware here, and at many other places, of the open-ended and unfinished nature of Wittgenstein's reflections. His writings have aroused great devotion because of the honesty and depth which many find in them. But it is important not to treat them with superstitious reverence. Rather they should be read in the spirit in which he intended, namely as an invitation to explore with as much integrity as possible one's own perplexities and what would resolve them.

See also: CRITERIA

List of works

Wittgenstein, L.J.J. (1922) *Tractatus Logico-Philosophicus*, trans. C.K. Ogden and F.P. Ramsey, London: Routledge; trans. D.F. Pears and B.F. McGuinness, London: Routledge, 1961. (The major work of Wittgenstein's early period and the only book published during his lifetime. The first English translation was revised and approved by Wittgenstein himself, though the later version is now standard. The German version was published in 1921 in *Annalen der Naturphilosophie*.)

—— (1953) *Philosophical Investigations*, ed. G.E.M. Anscombe and R. Rhees, trans. G.E.M. Anscombe, Oxford: Blackwell. (The most polished and worked over of all Wittgenstein's later work; it contains the presentation of his ideas on meaning and philosophical psychology with which he was most nearly satisfied.)

—— (1956) *Remarks on the Foundations of Mathematics*, ed. G.H. von Wright, R. Rhees and G.E.M. Anscombe, trans. G.E.M. Anscombe, Oxford: Blackwell, 3rd edn, 1978. (Selections from Wittgenstein's notebooks and manuscripts from 1937 to 1944. The third edition contains a larger selection of material than the first edition.)

—— (1958) *The Blue and Brown Books*, Oxford: Blackwell. (These were dictated to his pupils in 1933–5 and are among the few works composed by Wittgenstein in English. A good way of approaching his later thought.)

—— (1961) *Notebooks 1914–16*, ed. G.H. von Wright and G.E.M. Anscombe, trans. G.E.M. Anscombe, Oxford: Blackwell. (Helpful for understanding the *Tractatus*, since it contains what is left of the preliminary writings of that period.)

—— (1967) *Zettel*, ed. G.E.M. Anscombe and G.H. von Wright, trans. G.E.M. Anscombe, Oxford: Blackwell. (A selection, made by Wittgenstein himself, of remarks that he wrote mainly between 1945 and 1948.)

—— (1969) *On Certainty*, ed. G.E.M. Anscombe and G.H. von Wright, trans. D. Paul and G.E.M. Anscombe, Oxford: Blackwell. (A collection of all the material on knowledge and certainty from the last year and a half of Wittgenstein's life, where he treated the topics at length at several points in his notebooks.)

—— (1974) *Philosophical Grammar*, ed. R. Rhees, trans. A. Kenny, Oxford: Blackwell. (Written in 1931–4, this deals extensively with logic and mathematics, as well as topics such as language and meaning.)

—— (1975) *Philosophical Remarks*, ed. R. Rhees, trans. R. Hargreaves and R. White, Oxford: Blackwell. (Written in 1929–30 and interesting in that it shows the kinds of reflection on the *Tractatus* which drove Wittgenstein from his earlier to his later outlook.)

—— (1977a) *Remarks on Colour*, ed. G.E.M. Anscombe, trans. L.L. McAlister and M. Schättle, Oxford: Blackwell. (All the material on this topic from the writings of 1950–1, in which Wittgenstein worked on it extensively.)

—— (1977b) *Vermischte Bemerkungen*, Suhrkamp Verlag: Frankfurt am Main; trans. P. Winch, ed. G.H. von Wright and H. Nyman, *Culture and Value*, Oxford: Blackwell, 1980. (Wittgenstein's notebooks and typescripts often contain remarks on topics which are not directly philosophical. This collection assembles all of them from 1914 to 1951.)

—— (1980) *Remarks on the Philosophy of Psychology*, vols 1 and 2, ed. G.E.M. Anscombe and G.H. von Wright, trans. G.E.M. Anscombe, Oxford: Blackwell. (Selections made by Wittgenstein in 1947 and 1948 from material written in 1946–8. Contains much of interest on the topics treated in Part II of the *Philosophical Investigations*.)

—— (1982; 1992) *Last Writings on the Philosophy of Psychology*, ed. G.E.M. Anscombe, G.H. von Wright and H. Nyman, trans. C.G. Luckhardt and M.A.E. Aue, Oxford: Blackwell, 2 vols. (Writings from 1948–9, from which selections were made by Wittgenstein for Part II of the *Philosophical Investigations*.)

—— (1993) *Philosophical Occasions*, ed. J.C. Klagge and A. Nordmann, Indianapolis, IN: Hackett. (Usefully anthologizes several short pieces, including the 'Lecture on Ethics' (1929) and 'Remarks on Frazer's *Golden Bough*' (1931).)

References and further reading

Anscombe, G.E.M. (1959) *An Introduction to Wittgenstein's Tractatus*, London: Hutchinson. (A stimulating, although in parts quite difficult, discussion of many of the central ideas of the *Tractatus*.)
Baker, G.P. and Hacker, P.M.S. (1980, 1988, 1990) *An Analytical Commentary on the Philosophical Inves-*

tigations, Oxford: Blackwell, 3 vols. (An immensely detailed commentary, informed by extensive knowledge of the Wittgenstein papers. The third volume is by P.M.S. Hacker alone.)

Budd, M. (1989) *Wittgenstein's Philosophy of Psychology*, London: Routledge. (A clear survey of Wittgenstein's views on a variety of psychological topics.)

Canfield, J.V. (ed.) (1986–8) *The Philosophy of Wittgenstein*, New York and London: Garland Publishing Company, 15 vols. (A useful collection of articles on all aspects of Wittgenstein's philosophy.)

Carruthers, P. (1990) *The Metaphysics of the Tractatus*, Cambridge: Cambridge University Press. (Contains extensive consideration of determinacy of sense and the related topic of simple objects.)

Cavell, S. (1979) *The Claim of Reason*, Oxford: Oxford University Press. (Subtle and stimulating book on Wittgenstein's later philosophy. The elaborate style takes some getting used to.)

Fogelin, R.J. (1987) *Wittgenstein*, London: Routledge, 2nd edn. (A good general book, particularly helpful as an introduction to Wittgenstein's treatment of logic and mathematics. Also contains a helpful bibliography.)

Hacker, P.M.S. (1986) *Insight and Illusion*, Oxford: Oxford University Press, 2nd edn. (Another good general book, particularly strong on Wittgenstein's treatment of the self.)

Heal, J. (1989) *Fact and Meaning*, Oxford: Blackwell. (Further discussion of the themes of §§9–12.)

Johnston, P. (1993) *Wittgenstein: Rethinking the Inner*, London: Routledge. (A reading of Wittgenstein's later views on mind.)

Kenny, A. (1973) *Wittgenstein*, London: Allen Lane. (The best general introduction.)

* Kripke, S. (1982) *Wittgenstein on Rules and Private Language*, Oxford: Blackwell. (An exceptionally clear and gripping exploration of the idea that the rule-following considerations lead to scepticism about meaning.)

McDowell, J. (1984) 'Wittgenstein on Following a Rule', *Synthèse* 58: 325–63. (In part a criticism of Kripke (1982), in part an interesting exposition of Wittgenstein.)

McGinn, M. (1989) *Sense and Certainty: A Dissolution of Scepticism*, Oxford: Blackwell. (A clear account of Wittgenstein's views on knowledge and certainty, expanding on the points in §16 above.)

McGuinness, B. (1988) *Wittgenstein: A Life, Young Ludwig 1889–1921*, London: Duckworth. (Biographical study, containing much on Wittgenstein's intellectual background which is not in Monk's book and culminating on a chapter on the *Tractatus*.)

Monk, R. (1990) *Ludwig Wittgenstein*, London: Jonathan Cape. (A full and illuminating biography.)

Pears, D. (1987) *The False Prison*, Oxford: Oxford University Press. (A two-volume study containing much interesting discussion of the transition period and the private language argument.)

Wright, C. (1980) *Wittgenstein on the Foundations of Mathematics*, London: Duckworth. (Extended exploration of the idea that Wittgenstein should be seen as an antirealist or as a conventionalist.)

JANE HEAL

WITTGENSTEINIAN ETHICS

Although the strict 'fact-value distinction' of Wittgenstein's early period has shaped much subsequent work on ethics, his most profound influence on the subject stems from the later Philosophical Investigations *and associated writings. Of particular significance have been, first, the concept of a 'language game', and second, the discussion of following a rule. The vision of morality itself as a language game – a complex of speech and action ordered in a way that makes sense to the participants – has seemed to diminish the urgency of traditional questions about the 'foundations' of ethics, and has promoted acceptance of moral experience and consciousness as natural (human) phenomena. More recently there has been a growing interest in how Wittgenstein's general reflections on rule-governed practices might apply to the specific case of moral understanding.*

1 **The early Wittgenstein**
2 **Describing language games**
3 **Rule-following and ethics**

1 The early Wittgenstein

WITTGENSTEIN once told a friend that, although he was not a religious man, he could not help seeing every problem from a religious point of view (Rhees (ed.) 1984: 79). Given the austerity of much of his philosophical subject matter, the statement is a curious one. However, it is a useful reminder that throughout his career he was in search not just of intellectual insight but of a correct attitude to life. This is already apparent in the first phase of his work.

The main ethical theme of Wittgenstein's *Tractatus Logico-Philosophicus* (1921), and the subject of his 'Lecture on Ethics' (1929), is the inexpressibility of (absolute) value. He bases this idea on a distinction between the world as a whole, or the 'totality of facts', and the particular facts that obtain within the world. Whereas the latter can be represented linguistically, anything we may say about the former will be 'nonsense' (even if it is the special kind of nonsense exemplified by all the propositions of the Tractatus). But since any given fact might have been otherwise, and is thus a mere accident, Wittgenstein holds that the entire domain of fact – and hence of what can be put into words at all – is, from an absolute standpoint, devoid of value. Ethics therefore – along with aesthetics – has to do not with particular facts but with the totality, or rather with the way in which the totality presents itself to us; and this in turn depends on the quality of our will – not the empirical 'will' recognized by psychology, but one whose good or bad exercise makes the world 'wax and wane as a whole'.

Wittgenstein mentions in the 'Lecture' some states of mind that seem to possess this transfigurative power: 'wondering at the existence of the world', 'feeling absolutely safe' and 'feeling guilty'. However, he stresses that one can speak only for oneself about such experiences and that language can in any case do no more than gesture towards what is important in them. We rely here on (apparent) allegory or simile of a kind that is essentially unconvertible into literal factual statement.

These views reflect Wittgenstein's desire to safeguard the private, spiritual nature of ethics and not to let it be demeaned by philosophical 'chatter'. Even at a more practical level, though, he sees little scope for discursive argument about moral questions. An individual may or may not 'have an ethics'; if so, then they will have a basis (be it Christian, Nietzschean, or whatever) for their life choices; but the question whether one *ought* to be a Christian or a Nietzschean is senseless, since there is no suitably authoritative standard by which to settle it.

2 Describing language games

One offshoot of this conception of value was the 'noncognitivist' theory of ethics, which classifies the functions of language under the two main headings of description and expression (see ANALYTIC ETHICS). Wittgenstein himself, by contrast, moved during the 1930s towards an appreciation of the indefinite variety of 'language games' or types of rule-governed linguistic activity. In *Philosophische Untersuchungen (Philosophical Investigations)* (1953), our main source for his later thought, he sees language-use as part of our 'natural history' – one of those elements in human life that are given rather than chosen, and so 'have to be accepted'. This does not mean that 'good', in the

ethically interesting sense, can after all be analysed ('naturalistically') in terms of a value-free notion of human welfare (see NATURALISM IN ETHICS). What it means is that the proper aim of moral philosophy (like that of philosophy in general) is not justification but a certain kind of clarity, and that its proper method is one of reflection on what we might do or say in various concretely imagined contexts – not of trying to formulate universal normative principles that would validate our behaviour.

This approach was seen by its exponents in the 1950s and 60s partly as a check on the pretensions of 'theory', but it also yielded illuminating discussions of familiar moral practices, which could now be accorded the same respect as the 'alien' anthropological phenomena conjured up in some of Wittgenstein's thought experiments. A practice, it was argued, generates its own characteristic patterns of reasoning, and theorists are wrong to suppose that the behaviour internal to it admits of any better explanation than can be gathered from the participants themselves. Thus if someone (presumably a child) does not understand punishment, what we actually provide is help in seeing how the concept of punishment relates to others within the same region of social experience, such as wrongdoing, responsibility, forgiveness, making amends. And this is all the 'explanation' needed.

The view that philosophy should limit itself to 'describing language games' without passing judgment on them may seem to lead in the direction of relativism, a tendency already discernible at the end of §1 (see MORAL RELATIVISM). It should be remembered, though, that Wittgenstein officially holds 'ordinary' (as opposed to philosophical) language to be in perfect order as it is, so that if our (ordinary) ethical language game happens to incorporate activities of critical observation and reflection, there would seem to be no (philosophical) reason why we should renounce these. Such activities might well go against Wittgenstein's own anti-modern, even primitivist taste; but in keeping with the nonjudgmental attitude, he states no principle by reference to which they could be condemned. (Relatedly, one might ask about the 'we' that figures in this section: who exactly counts as being located outside 'our' moral practices, and so beyond the reach of 'our' judgment? (see MORAL AGENTS; UNIVERSALISM IN ETHICS §1).)

3 Rule-following and ethics

During the 1970s and 80s Wittgenstein studies took a new turn, the effect of which was felt in ethics. Partly in response to Saul Kripke's reappraisal of the 'rule-following considerations', attention began to focus less on the specificity of particular language games and more on the idea of a rule-governed practice as such – the genus that includes all 'games' involving conventional signs (see MEANING AND RULE-FOLLOWING §3). Above all, how should we understand Wittgenstein's account of the way a rule or order can 'reach into the future' and determine in advance what will and will not comply with it?

Because of the prominence it gives to the notion of criteria and to communal standards of correctness, Wittgenstein's later philosophy has often been regarded as 'anti-realist'. However, the rule-following considerations can be interpreted in a way that challenges this view and gives more weight to Wittgenstein's own metaphysical 'quietism' – his disavowal of any substantive philosophical position. This different interpretation is unfavourable, in particular, to theories that refuse to take at face value the ostensibly factual character of certain regions of discourse. For example, it is opposed to the neo-Humean view that evaluative judgment cannot be genuinely factual because it involves a projection of our subjective attitudes onto the world (see PROJECTIVISM).

In the spirit of Wittgenstein's remark that 'words are also deeds' (1953: part I, 546), and of the link he sets up in *Philosophische Untersuchungen* between linguistic understanding and socialization, the 'quietist' reading gives a central place to the ethical in reconstructing his overall account of rules. Wittgenstein notes that interpretation, explanation or justification necessarily 'comes to an end', giving way – if successful – to a moment when we see the point (or grasp the message) without the mediation of any further signs. The possibility of such immediate, tacit understanding is ultimately due to our common nature as members of an animal species, but the human species is distinguished from others by the fact that it exploits this natural 'likemindedness' in order to transmit to successive generations the various culturally distinct forms of likemindedness realized in particular languages. The work of socialization carried on within human cultures maintains in existence an array of shared sensibilities – the 'feel' speakers have for what a rule-governed practice requires in this or that particular case – and it is these sensibilities that support all our resources of normative judgment, whether about overtly ethical 'right' and 'wrong' or about right and wrong ways of describing things, right and wrong conclusions to draw from given premises, and so on.

References and further reading

Johnston, P. (1989) *Wittgenstein and Moral Philosophy*, London: Routledge. (Monograph providing useful orientation and guide to sources.)

Lovibond, S. (1983) *Realism and Imagination in Ethics*, Oxford: Blackwell. (Examines the relation of the later Wittgenstein to a possible 'moral realism' emerging from truth-conditional semantics.)

McDowell, J. (1979) 'Virtue and Reason', *Monist* 62: 331–50. (Connects Aristotle's ethics with Wittgenstein's rule-following considerations.)

—— (1981) 'Non-cognitivism and rule-following', in S. Holtzman and C. Leich (eds) *Wittgenstein: To Follow a Rule*, London: Routledge & Kegan Paul. (A Wittgensteinian critique of noncognitivist theories of ethics.)

—— (1992) 'Meaning and Intentionality in Wittgenstein's Later Philosophy', *Midwest Studies in Philosophy* 17: 40–52. (Defends a reading of Wittgenstein as 'quietist' – one who disavows any substantive philosophical position.)

Phillips, D.Z. and Mounce, H.O. (1969) *Moral Practices*, London: Routledge & Kegan Paul. (Wittgensteinian argument for the ineliminable diversity of moral life.)

Pitkin, H.F. (1972) *Wittgenstein and Justice*, Berkeley, CA: University of California Press. (Extended discussion of the significance of the later Wittgenstein for political theory.)

Rhees, R. (ed.) (1984) *Recollections of Wittgenstein*, Oxford: Oxford University Press. (For insight into Wittgenstein's personality and moral concerns.)

* Wittgenstein, L. (1921) *Tractatus Logico-Philosophicus*, trans. D.F. Pears and B.F. McGuinness, London: Routledge & Kegan Paul, 1961. (The only philosophical work by Wittgenstein published during his lifetime, and the source for his 'early' view of logic and language; sections 6.4 onwards relate to ethics.)

* —— (1929) 'Lecture on Ethics', first published posthumously in 1965 as 'Wittgenstein's Lecture on Ethics', in *Philosophical Review* 74: 3–26. (Short statement influenced by the general philosophical position of the Tractatus; with valuable background material by F. Waismann and R. Rhees.)

* —— (1953) *Philosophische Untersuchungen*, trans. G.E.M. Anscombe, ed. G.E.M. Anscombe and R. Rhees, Philosophical Investigations, Oxford: Blackwell; 3rd edn, 1967. (Little explicitly on ethics; should be studied as a whole.)

—— (1961) *Notebooks 1914–1916*, ed. G.E.M. Anscombe and G.H. von Wright, trans. G.E.M. Anscombe, Oxford: Blackwell; 2nd edn, 1979. (Contains interesting pre-Tractarian material on ethics and the will.)

—— (1980) *Vermischte Bermerkungen*, trans. P. Winch, ed. G.H. von Wright and H. Nyman,

Culture and Value, Oxford: Blackwell. (Collected remarks, mainly from the 1930s and 40s.)

SABINA LOVIBOND

WODEHAM, ADAM
(*c.*1298–1358)

An English Franciscan theologian, Wodeham was preoccupied with logical and semantic questions. He lectured for about a decade on Peter Lombard's Sentences, *first at London, then at Norwich and finally at Oxford. His lectures emphasized the dependence of the created world on God and the contingency of nature and salvation.*

John Duns Scotus and William of Ockham exerted the most important influences on Wodeham. He regarded Scotus as a vigorous thinker and respected him enough to accept his opinion in case of doubt. Proud to have learned logic from Ockham, Wodeham devoted considerable time to defending Ockham's views from Walter Chatton, whom he saw as someone whose errors in logic arose from malice as well as ignorance. However, despite Wodeham's reservations about Chatton, he was considerably influenced by him. Similarly, Wodeham modified his own opinion about sensory illusions in response to Peter Aureol, whom he saw as skilled and prudent but often mistaken, sometimes as a result of faulty logic.

1 Psychology
2 Epistemology
3 Semantics
4 Logic
5 Metaphysics
6 Natural philosophy
7 Influence

1 Psychology

Appealing to experience, Wodeham denied the distinction between the sensory and intellective souls; a single soul suffices to explain all the cognitive acts we perform. On this point, Wodeham opposed both DUNS SCOTUS (who proposed formally distinct sensory and intellective souls) and Ockham (who proposed souls that were really distinct). Against Ockham's opinion that sensory and intellective souls must be distinct since contraries could not coexist in the same subject, Wodeham argued that sensory inclination and intellectual appetite in regard to the same external object were only virtually, not formally, contraries. The same soul apprehends sensible parti-

culars and universals. These acts are sensations when they are partially caused by external objects; intellections, when they abstract from singulars (*Lectura secunda* I, 9–33).

A similar predilection for reductionism reveals itself in Wodeham's discussion of enjoyment. He claims that all appetitive acts are cognitive acts, since we cannot will or desire an object without apprehending it; but cognition does not necessitate volition. Like Ockham, Wodeham holds that clear knowledge of God without enjoyment is possible, at least at first. Conversely, loving God necessarily includes the implied judgment that God is lovable. This leads Wodeham to conclude that acts of volition can be described as true or false. Rejoicing about being a Franciscan, for example, includes the correct apprehension of a practical truth as well as the act of enjoyment (*Lectura secunda* I, 253–85).

2 Epistemology

Scepticism is a problem for Wodeham, who sees Ockham's response to it as inadequate. For Ockham, intuitive cognition, the basis of all other cognition, is reliable by definition. By contrast, Wodeham holds that whether or not the object of intuition exists, intuition will always incline us to believe that its object exists. He was among the first to recognize that sceptical consequences could be drawn from the long list of sensory illusions adduced by Peter Aureol against Scotus' account of intuitive cognition. In response, Wodeham defined three degrees of certainty. The greatest degree, which compels the intellect, is not available regarding contingent propositions, since the intellect is aware of the possibility of deception. The least degree of certainty is compatible with error. It is in this degree that I may be certain of a mistaken proposition – as for example, when I judge that a straight stick half submerged in water is bent.

Despite his preoccupation with possible natural and supernatural obstructions in the perceptual process and the concessions he made to them, Wodeham remained a reliabilist, maintaining that cognition is reliably though not infallibly caused by its object. His basic reply to the sensory illusions adduced by Aureol was that although illusions will continue to incline us to make false judgments, reason and experience enable us to correct our judgments and to avoid being systematically misled by illusions (*Lectura secunda* I, 65–111, 163–79) (see EPISTEMOLOGY, HISTORY OF).

3 Semantics

In semantics, Wodeham's most important contribution was the concept of the *complexe significabile* (complexly signifiable) (see LANGUAGE, MEDIEVAL THEORIES OF). Wodeham developed his views as a compromise between Chatton and Ockham on the question of the object of scientific knowledge. What is the object of our assent when we assert that man is a rational animal? Is it an external object in the real world (Chatton's *res*) or a mental object (Ockham's *complexum*)? Are we assenting to man considered as a rational animal, or to the complex mental entity that-man-is-a-rational-animal? Wodeham argues against both solutions. If Chatton is right, then there is no difference between a Catholic who asserts that Christ was incarnate and a heretic who asserts that Christ will be incarnate. Both assent to Christ as incarnate; the difference between their creeds can only be expressed by the tense of the verbs which connect Christ and incarnation. If Ockham is right, then sciences of real things deal only with mental objects and not with the external world; the objects of the 'real' sciences do not differ from the objects of logic and semantics. Such considerations lead Wodeham to postulate a third way: the true object of assent is what is complexly signifiable by a phrase, such as that-man-is-a-rational-animal, the *complexe significabile* (Nuchelmans 1980).

The *complexe significabile* itself is neither something in the external world nor a mental object. It is neither a substance nor an accident and thus is not included in any Aristotelian category. It is not something, but neither is it nothing. Rather, the question 'What is it?' is ill-formed; it makes no more sense than the question 'Is a people a man or a nonman?' When we assent to a *complexe significabile*, we are not assenting to some thing; instead we are affirming that something is the case (*Lectura secunda* I, 180–208).

4 Logic

A terminist logician and a conceptualist, Wodeham employs three different kinds of supposition: personal, simple and material. Personal supposition is reference to things in the external world, simple supposition to concepts, and material supposition to written or spoken words (see LANGUAGE, MEDIEVAL THEORIES OF; LOGIC, MEDIEVAL).

Wodeham's analysis of the distinction between abstract and concrete predication was indebted to but different from that of Ockham. In defining concrete predication, Wodeham aims to avoid generating nonsense expressions. Thus for Wodeham the nominal definition of the term *albus* is 'having whiteness', not 'body having whiteness'. Eliminating the bearer from the definition of concrete terms prevents the generation of the nonsense-sentence 'Socrates is a body having whiteness body', which would otherwise result from replacing 'white' with its definition in the sentence 'Socrates is a white body' (*Lectura secunda* II, 244).

Wodeham's denial that the bearer is signified *per se* in concrete predication is reminiscent of Anselm's distinction between *per se* and *per aliud* predication (see ANSELM OF CANTERBURY). For Wodeham as for Anselm, reference is signification only in a secondary sense. What we think of when we hear a term is not necessarily the objects to which it refers (its *supposita* or *appellata*). There is no difference between the *per se* signification of abstract and concrete terms; and in the case of substance terms, supposition and signification coincide. Thus both 'man' and 'humanity' signify and supposit for a substance composed of body and soul. The sentence 'A man is a humanity' is false only in the case of Jesus, who has a divine as well as a human nature and hence cannot be identified with his humanity (Spade 1988).

Wodeham relies on his theory of *per se* predication in dealing with problems of Trinitarian theology. The chief problem was the apparent conflict between the Aristotelian principle of non-contradiction and the truths of the faith. Thus Aristotelian logic seems to require that if 'the Father is not the Son' and 'the Father is the deity', then 'the deity is not the Son'. Confronting this problem, Wodeham rejects *ad hoc* theological modifications of logic; such approaches, he says, deserve the ridicule of heathens. Wodeham also criticizes the solutions of Ockham and Scotus. His own solution is to treat identity as a special case of predication; identity is not necessarily a symmetrical relationship (see IDENTITY). Following Scotus, Wodeham distinguishes between identifying or formal predication and denominative predication. Unlike denominative predication, where the subject and predicate have the same supposition, in formal predication the predicate has broader supposition than the subject. Thus deity can be formally predicated of the Father, but the converse is not true (*Lectura Oxoniensis* I d.33; Gelber 1974).

5 Metaphysics

Wodeham was a conceptualist who identified universals with mental acts, and hence maintained that only individuals exist (*Lectura secunda* I, 21). In this respect, as in his emphasis on ontological parsimony, Wodeham followed Ockham (see NOMINALISM; UNIVERSALS).

Considering proofs for God's existence, Wodeham analyses fourteenth-century Franciscan theories of causality. He defends Ockham's challenge to Scotus' inference: 'since the universe of essentially ordered effects is caused, the universe must be caused'. Exploiting his understanding of the logic of infinity, Wodeham argues that Chatton's defence of Scotus' theory of essentially ordered causes and effects is absurd. Chatton errs by inferring categorematic conclusions from premises which are true only if understood syncategorematically (*Lectura secunda* II, 117–21; Adams 1993).

6 Natural philosophy

In opposing the atomism or indivisibilism of his day, Wodeham repeatedly applied his understanding of the logic of infinity, continuity and infinitesimal change (see NATURAL PHILOSOPHY, MEDIEVAL). Like Ockham he believed that limits of place, time and motion – such as points, lines, surfaces, temporal instants and mutations (instants of change) – had no independent ontological status. Indeed, Wodeham says he anticipated Ockham's arguments for non-entitism, the claim that terms such as 'point' are non-referring (*Tractatus de indivisibilibus* q.2 a.1 n.20).

Wodeham presents many arguments against indivisibilism. Some depend on the distinction between the categorematic (perfectively actualized) and syncategorematic (processively actualized) meaning of the phrase 'infinitely divide'. Others, based on an analysis of the compounded and divided senses, claim that strictly speaking not the continuum, but its parts are divided. Most instructive in his view were arguments relying on the impossibility of indivisibles in contact with one another.

Wodeham accepted Ockham's claim that the infinity of parts in a continuum exists not just potentially but actually. Acceptance of this claim led Wodeham to argue for the possibility of unequal infinities (*Tractatus de indivisibilibus* q.5).

7 Influence

Although Ockham died in 1347, less than forty years after Scotus, Wodeham saw Scotus as an 'ancient' author and Ockham as a modern contemporary. Respectful but seldom vitally concerned with his views, Wodeham calls Thomas AQUINAS the *Doctor communis* (Universal Doctor). Many subsequent authors, even in the fifteenth century, saw the history of philosophical theology in the same way (Courtenay 1978). Wodeham's view of the history of thought was based less on the dating of authors than on the extent to which their theology was characterized by explicit appeals to logical arguments. The continued currency of his views is a measure of his influence.

Huge crowds flocked to Wodeham's lectures in the 1330s, and John MAJOR held that Wodeham would be reputed a greater philosopher than Ockham were it not for Ockham's political writings. However, almost nothing by or about Wodeham was published in the four centuries between 1512 and 1976. Despite a spate of recent publications on Wodeham, comparatively little is or can be known about his views until a critical edition of his most important work is prepared.

See also: CHATTON, W.; LANGUAGE, MEDIEVAL THEORIES OF; NATURAL PHILOSOPHY, MEDIEVAL; WILLIAM OF OCKHAM

List of works

Wodeham's most significant works were three sets of theology lectures based on Peter Lombard's *Sentences*. His first lectures, delivered in London, have not been independently preserved, though portions are included in his second lectures. His second lectures (*Lectura secunda*), intended for a Franciscan audience in Norwich, were first published in 1990. The final lectures, written for a larger Oxford audience, are his most influential work but still await publication. In the Renaissance, John Major chose to print Henry Totting von Oyta's abbreviation of the Oxford lectures, rather than the work itself. Lost works by Wodeham include two Bible commentaries (on the *Canticum Canticorum* and on *Ecclesiasticus*), a set of *Determinationes* and a treatise against Richard of Wetherset, defending the right of friars to hear confessions.

Wodeham, Adam (after 1323, before 1331) *Tractatus de indivisibilibus*, ed. R. Wood, Dordrecht: Kluwer, 1988. (Wodeham's longest sustained discussion of issues in natural philosophy, which quotes frequently from Ockham's *Physics*. Also printed here is Wodeham's *Quaestione de divsione et compositione continua*, dated 1322–31.)

—— (before 1333) *Lectura Oxoniensis*, ed. J. Major, *Abbreviatio Henrici Totting de Oyta, seu Adam goddam super quattuor libros sententiarum*, Paris: P. le Preux, 1512. (This Renaissance edition prints Henry Totting von Oyta's abbreviation of the Oxford lectures, not the work itself. In addition to the bulk of *Lectura Oxoniensis*, this volume also includes Major's life of Wodeham.)

—— (before 1339) *Lectura secunda*, ed. R. Wood and G. Gál, St Bonaventure, NY: St Bonaventure University, 1990. (Though limited to the first book of the *Sentences*, these three volumes include more than 1260 pages of exposition. The introduction discusses Wodeham's life and influence and summarizes some of his views. There is a bibliography in Vol. III.)

References and further reading

* Adams, M.M. (1993) 'Review of Wodeham's *Lectura secunda*', *Philosophical Review* 102: 588–94. (An able summary of about 800 pages of text.)

Adams, M.M. and Wood, R. (1981) 'Is to Will It as Bad as to Do It?', *Franciscan Studies* 41: 5–60. (Compares Wodeham with Scotus and Ockham on the morality of external acts.)

* Courtenay, W. (1975) 'Ockhamism among the Augustinians: the Case of Adam Wodeham', *Scientia augustiniana*, ed. C. Mayer and W. Eckermann, *Cassiciacum* 30: 267–75. (Illustrates Wodeham's influence.)

—— (1978) *Adam Wodeham*, Leiden: Brill. (The most complete introduction to Wodeham's life and times.)

Gál, G. (1977) 'Adam Wodeham's Question on the *Complexe Significabile*', *Franciscan Studies* 37: 66–102. (Shows that Wodeham, not Gregory of Rimini, should be credited with the view that the immediate object of an act of scientific knowledge is the *complexe significabile*.)

* Gelber, H.G. (1974) 'Logic and the Trinity: A Clash of Values in Scholastic Thought, 1300–1335', Ph.D. dissertation, University of Wisconsin. (See especially 235–64 and 615–28, where extended excerpts from Wodeham's *Lectura Oxoniensis* I d.33 are printed and discussed.)

Grassi, O. (1986) *Intuizione e Significato: Adam Wodeham e il problema della conoscenza nel XIV secolo* (Intuition and its Significate: Adam Wodeham and the Problem of Knowledge in the Fourteenth Century), Milan: Editoriale Jaca. (Epistemological study comparing Aureol, Ockham, Chatton and Wodeham; based on texts from Wodeham's *Lectura Oxoniensis* as well as the *Lectura secunda*.)

Kretzmann, N. (1984) 'Adam Wodeham's Anti-Aristotelian Anti-Atomism', *History of Philosophy Quarterly* 1: 381–98. (Characterizes Wodeham as a macro-indivisibilist.)

Maierù, A. (1984) 'Logique et Théologie Trinitaire: Pierre d'Ailly' (Logic and Trinitarian Theology: Pierre d'Ailly), in A. Kaluz and P. Vignaux (eds) *Preuve et Raisons. l'Université de Paris*, Paris: Vrin, 253–68. (A study of Pierre d'Ailly's response to Wodeham and Gregory of Rimini in the field of Trinitarian theology.)

McGrade, A.S. (1987) 'Enjoyment after Ockham: Philosophy, Psychology and the Love of God', in A. Hudson and M. Wilks (eds) *From Ockham to Wyclif*, Oxford: Blackwell, 63–88. (Wodeham on fruition.)

* Nuchelmans, G. (1980) 'Adam Wodeham on the Meaning of Declarative Sentences', *Historiographia Linguistica* 7: 177–86. (Insightful analysis suggesting that Wodeham's theory is more coherent than that of Rimini.)

Reina, M.E. (1986) 'Cognizione intuitiva ed esperienza interiore in Adamo Wodeham' (Intuitive Cognition and Internal Experience in Adam Wodeham), *Rivista di storia della filosofia* 41: 19–49, 211–44. (A detailed analysis of Wodeham's views on the soul and introspective cognition.)

* Spade, P.V. (1988) 'Anselm and the Background to Adam Wodeham's Theory of Abstract and Concrete Terms', *Rivista di storia della filosofia* 43: 261–71. (Clear and concise.)

Tachau, K. (1988) *Vision and Certitude in the Age of Ockham*, Leiden: Brill, 275–99. (Wodeham viewed as an influential interpreter of Peter Aureol.)

Wood, R. (1982) 'Adam Wodeham on Sensory Illusions', *Traditio* 38: 214–52. (Discusses Wodeham's refutation of Peter Aureol and Walter Chatton on the topic of sensory illusions.)

—— (1989) 'Epistemology and Omnipotence', in S. Chodorow and J. Sweeney (eds) *Popes, Teachers and Canon Law in the Middle Ages*, Ithaca, NY: Cornell University Press, 160–78. (Establishes Wodeham's influence on John of Mirecourt, and compares Wodeham's views on certainty and intuitive cognition of nonexistents with his contemporaries.)

Zupko, J. (1994) 'Nominalism Meets Indivisibilism', *Medieval Philosophy and Theology* 3: 158–85. (Summarizes Wodeham's discussion of contiguity and explores his influence on Buridan.)

REGA WOOD

WOLFF, CHRISTIAN (1679–1754)

Christian Wolff was a rationalistic school philosopher in the German Enlightenment. During the period between the death of Leibniz (1714) and the publication of Kant's critical writings (1780s), Wolff was perhaps the most influential philosopher in Germany.

There are many reasons for this, including Wolff's voluminous writings in both German and Latin in nearly every field of philosophy known to his time, their unvarying employment of a strict rationalistic method to establish their conclusions, the attention directed to Wolff and his views as a result of bitter controversies with some theological colleagues, his banishment from

Prussia by King Frederick Wilhelm I in 1723 and triumphant return from Hesse–Cassel in 1740 after Frederick the Great assumed the throne, and his active teaching at the Universities of Halle and Marburg for nearly 50 years. Through his work as a university professor, his prolific writings, and the rigour and comprehensiveness of his philosophy, Wolff influenced a very large group of followers, educators and other writers. Even after his influence had begun to wane, Kant still referred to 'the celebrated Wolff' and spoke of 'the strict method of the celebrated Wolff, the greatest of all dogmatic philosophers'.

Wolff thought of philosophy as that discipline which provides reasons to explain why things exist or occur and why they are even possible. Thus, he included within philosophy a much broader range of subjects than might now be recognized as 'philosophical'. Indeed, for Wolff all human knowledge consists of only three disciplines: history, mathematics and philosophy.

The reasons provided by Wolff's philosophy were to be established through unfailing adherence to a strict demonstrative method. Like Descartes, Wolff first discovered this method in mathematics, but he concluded that both mathematical and philosophical methods had their ultimate origins in a 'natural logic' prescribed to the human mind by God. In fact, the heart of Wolff's philosophical method is a deductive logic making use of syllogistic arguments.

For Wolff, the immediate objective of philosophical method is to achieve certitude by establishing an order of truths within each discipline and a system within human knowledge as a whole. The ultimate goal is to establish a reliable foundation for the conduct of human affairs and the enlargement of knowledge.

Wolff applied his philosophical method unfailingly in each of the three principal parts of philosophy: metaphysics – knowledge of those things which are possible through being in general, the world in general, human souls, and God; physics – knowledge of those things which are possible through bodies; and practical philosophy – knowledge of those things which are concerned with human actions. Wolff's philosophical system also includes logic, an art of discovery (to guide the investigation of hidden truth and the production of new insights), some experiential disciplines (for example, empirical psychology) and several bodies of philosophical knowledge that were not well developed in Wolff's time concerning law, medicine, and both the practical and liberal arts.

1   Life and works

Christian Wolff was born in Breslau, where he received his early education. He studied at the University of Jena and received a master's degree in 1703 at the University of Leipzig. In these settings, Wolff became familiar with Lutheran, Calvinist and Roman Catholic viewpoints in theology; Aristotelian, Scholastic and Cartesian school traditions in philosophy; and the emerging empirical methods of Newtonian science. The most important single influence on Wolff's thought was Leibniz. But Wolff resisted characterizations of himself as merely a follower or systematizer of Leibniz's thought. This unflattering stereotype first arose during Wolff's lifetime and is commonly heard today.

Leibniz provided a letter of recommendation which helped Wolff obtain his first teaching position as Professor of Mathematics and the Natural Sciences at the new University of Halle in 1706 where he taught and wrote about the subjects indicated, only gradually taking an interest in selected philosophical topics.

In 1713, Wolff published his *Vernünftige Gedanken von den Kräften des menschlichen Verstandes* (Rational Thoughts on the Powers of the Human Understanding; referred to as the *German Logic*), an introductory handbook on logic. This became the most popular of all of Wolff's writings, appearing in fourteen different editions during his lifetime. It was his only major philosophical work published during Leibniz's lifetime.

During the early 1720s, Wolff published a series of philosophical works in German. These included books on metaphysics (1720), ethics (1720), politics (1721), physics (1723), teleology (1724), and physiology (1725), many of which later appeared in numerous reprintings or new editions.

The titles of all of Wolff's central philosophical writings in German begin with the common phrase, 'Rational Thoughts on...'. For example, the *German Metaphysics* (published in twelve editions during Wolff's lifetime) bears the ambitious title, 'Rational Thoughts on God, the World, and the Human Soul, and All Things in General', indicating both the methodic rigour which the author prized and the ambitious scope of the work.

Together with a volume of annotations on the metaphysics (1724) and another (1726) offering a review and defence of all of Wolff's previous writings on the various parts of philosophy ('Weltweisheit'), these German publications contributed significantly to the establishment of the German language as a vehicle for scientific communication (Blackall 1959). In addition, during Wolff's lifetime Latin remained in wide use by scholars and other vernacular languages (for example, French) were far more advanced in their development than German.

Unfortunately, Wolff's writings and lectures entangled him in bitter quarrels with critics led by Pietist members of the theology faculty at Halle, such as Joachim Lange, and Johann Franz Budde at Jena (see PIETISM). The issues had to do with the proper roles of reason and faith in human life, along with charges that Wolff's views implied a fatalistic and necessitarian view of the world, human beings and God. For example, it seemed heretical to Wolff's opponents for him to have said in a public lecture in 1721 that the pagan Chinese could develop a satisfactory ethical philosophy on the basis of reason alone without the assistance of the Christian revelation. Similarly, Wolff's acceptance of the Leibnizian doctrine of pre-established harmony and his emphasis on God's intellect as the controlling framework for divine freedom and power seemed to his critics to lead directly to a deterministic universe.

When Wolff did not give in to his critics and could not otherwise be bested, his opponents appealed to external authority. Without holding a hearing on the charges against him, King Frederick William I issued an order on 8 November 1723 that removed Wolff from his professorship and banned him from Prussia within forty-eight hours on pain of death.

Wolff was able to take up a teaching post previously offered to him at the University of Marburg in Hesse-Cassel. Official censure and exile only heightened his popularity. Nevertheless, Wolff decided to write no more in German and to turn to the wider intellectual world by composing a new series of philosophical publications in Latin, the dominant scientific language of the time. That series occupied the rest of his life.

Wolff's Latin works expanded and restated in a more thoroughgoing and systematic way his views on philosophy and other subjects. They began with a *Preliminary Discourse on Philosophy in General* (1728). Most of Wolff's Latin writings share a common subtitle, *methodo scientifica pertractata* ('treated according to the scientific method'). Thus, the Latin ontology volume is entitled, *Philosophia prima, sive Ontologia, methodo scientifica pertractata, qua omnis cognitionis humanae principia continentur* (First Philosophy, or Ontology, Treated According to the Scientific Method, in Which Are Contained All of the Principles of Human Knowledge; referred to henceforth as the *Latin Ontology*).

Wolff's Latin works include treatises on logic (1728), ontology (1729), general cosmology (1731), empirical (1732) and rational (1734) psychology, natural theology (2 vols, 1736–7), practical philosophy (2 vols, 1738–9), natural law (8 vols, 1740–8), international law (1749), ethics (5 vols, 1750–3) and economics (2 vols, 1754–5). In 1740, Wolff was recalled to the University of Halle where he became Chancellor in 1743. After a period of fame and influence, he died on 9 April 1754, the author of some seventy volumes of published work in mathematics and philosophy.

Wolff's distinctive contributions involve his description of the scope of human knowledge (comprising history, philosophy and mathematics), his definition of philosophy and its goals, his systematic description of the parts of philosophy, his views on philosophical method and some of his central metaphysical doctrines.

2 Human knowledge: history, mathematics and philosophy

Wolff divided all human knowledge into three basic types: (1) history or 'knowledge of those things which are and occur either in the material world or in immaterial substances'; (2) philosophy or 'knowledge of the reason of things which are or occur'; and (3) mathematics or 'knowledge of the quantity of things' (*Preliminary Discourse* §§3, 6 and 14). This division is intended to organize human knowledge by finding the proper place for each division and identifying its role in the schema of human understanding.

According to Wolff, philosophy originates in experience or historical knowledge. Some historical facts are common to all, requiring only human attention and some acumen. Other facts 'do not spontaneously present themselves to one who is attentive' (*Preliminary Discourse* §20). Such facts are hidden and must be sought out by observation, investigation, and experiments. Mathematics assists the search for such facts, as well as their philosophical explanation, by perfecting the evidence, guiding reason and confirming demonstrations.

3 Philosophy: definition and goals

Wolff defined philosophy more precisely as 'the science of the possibles in so far as they can be' (*Preliminary Discourse* §29; École 1978). A key element here is the meaning of the term 'science'. 'By science here I mean the habit of demonstrating propositions, that is, the habit of inferring conclusions by legitimate sequence from certain and immutable principles' (*Preliminary Discourse* §30). Scientific knowledge is characterized by its method and order, that is, certain and immutable principles, methodic inferences, and orderly conclusions.

Wolff's proximate goal in philosophy and the trait which is most typical of his writings was demonstration, the 'showing forth' of conclusions distinguished by their certitude. Thus, he wrote that 'nothing is more important than certitude' (*Preliminary Discourse* §28). In fact, however, Wolff pursued certitude as the foundation upon which philosophy can best serve human interests and needs. Thus, he observed that 'the fruit of philosophy...[is] its usefulness in knowledge and in life' (*Preliminary Discourse* §116; compare Corr 1970).

4 The parts of philosophy

Wolff's mature description of the parts of philosophy appears in Table 1 (compare Blackwell 1961b). The basic division is between those parts of philosophy that deal with things and those concerned with human actions. Within that, philosophical discussions of things are divided into metaphysics and physics, while practical philosophy is divided into ethics, economics and politics, together with some mention of philosophy of the arts and with an important role for logic or the philosophy of human cognition.

According to Wolff, 'the beings which we know by examining ourselves before we philosophize are God, human souls and bodies' (*Preliminary Discourse* §55). Natural theology is 'the science of those things which are known to be possible through God'; psychology is 'the science of those things which are possible through human souls' (*Preliminary Discourse* §§57–8). In addition, ontology or first philosophy is 'the science of being in general, or in so far as it is being', and general cosmology is 'the science of the world in general' or of that which is common to the existing world and to any other possible world (*Preliminary Discourse* §§73 and 78).

Together, natural theology and psychology make up 'pneumatics' or 'the science of spirits'; along with ontology and general cosmology, these four bodies of philosophical knowledge constitute 'metaphysics' (*Preliminary Discourse* §79).

Physics is 'the science of those things which are possible through bodies' (*Preliminary Discourse* §59). It includes general physics (the science of those things which are common to all bodies or to many diverse kinds of bodies), together with specific physical sciences of particular kinds of bodies.

Practical philosophy is 'the science of directing the appetitive faculty in choosing good and avoiding evil' (*Preliminary Discourse* §62). Its components address free human actions in different situations: ethics examines free actions in the natural state or when humans act as individuals; economics studies free actions within smaller societies distinct from the state; and politics explores free actions in a civil society or state. Practical philosophy also includes a general science or basic theory about good and evil actions (the law of nature or *jus naturae*), and a body of knowledge about the general theory and practice of practical philosophy (universal practical philosophy). Wolff acknowledged that these last two sciences (presumably, along with *jus gentium* or international law which he developed later) could in principle be treated as subordinate parts of ethics, economics, and politics, but he preferred to keep them separate for the sake of clarity and demonstrative rigour.

Within his discussion of human action, Wolff admitted the possibility of philosophical knowledge about the arts, whether these are the practical arts like wood cutting, agriculture, or civil architecture, bodies of knowledge like law and medicine, or the liberal arts like grammar, rhetoric and poetry. Nevertheless, he acknowledged that philosophers had not previously given much attention to the reasons behind these types of human arts.

Logic is 'the science of directing the cognitive faculty in the knowing of truth' and avoiding error (*Preliminary Discourse* §61). Because logic guides all of philosophy, Wolff recommended that it be given first place among philosophical disciplines. However, to demonstrate its own rules, logic must follow ontology and psychology from which its principles are derived. In addition to logic, Wolff also commended a new body of knowledge called the 'art of discovery' (*ars inveniendi*) (*Preliminary Discourse* §74) intended to guide the investigation of hidden truth by following the example of algebra and the analytic arts of the mathematicians (Corr 1972).

Wolff believed 'there are many philosophical disciplines which still lie hidden' (*Preliminary Discourse* §86). His review of the parts of philosophy was intended to organize those bodies of philosophical knowledge known to his time and to show that the various parts of philosophy must be 'ordered in such a way that those parts should come first which provide principles for the other parts' (*Preliminary Discourse* §87; see Table 1).

Wolff chose the method of learning over the method of demonstration by beginning with logic because of its importance in leading to a knowledge of all other parts of philosophy. Also, Wolff believed that logic could easily explain the ontological and psychological principles which it needed.

Similarly, because 'the principles of philosophy must be derived from experience' (*Preliminary Discourse* §34), Wolff acknowledged the importance

Table 1. Wolff's division of philosophy

Of things			Of human actions	
Metaphysics (being in general) (spirits) (the world in general)		Ontology (being in general)	Cognitive philosophy	Logic (directing the cognitive faculty in knowing truth and avoiding error
		General cosmology (the world in general)		Ars inveniendi (art of investigating or discovering hidden truth)
	Pneumatics (spirits)	Psychology (human souls)	Practical philosophy (directing the appetitive faculty in choosing good and avoiding evil)	Jus naturae or Law of nature (knowledge of good and evil actions)
		Natural theology (God)		Universal practical philosophy (general theory and practice of practical philosophy)
Physics (bodies)	General physics (general affections of all bodies or of many diverse species)			Ethics (directing man's free actions in the natural state or individual morality)
	Cosmology (world as such)			Economics (directing free actions in smaller societies distinct from the state)
	Meteorology (atmospheric phenomena)			Politics (directing free actions in a civil society or state)
	Oryctology (minerals)		Philosophical knowledge of the arts	(reasons explaining the arts and works of art, whether medicine or law, practical arts such as wood cutting, agriculture, or civil architecture [technology], or the liberal arts (grammar, rhetoric, poetry))
	Hydrology (fluids) Phytology (plants or vegetables) Physiology (animated bodies) Teleology (final cause of natural things)			

of observations and experiments in philosophy. In addition, he hoped to develop an art of discovery, and he distinguished between empirical and rational psychology (*Preliminary Discourse* §§111–12; see Blackwell 1961a; Corr 1975b). All of this was intended to contribute to 'a marriage of reason and experience' (*Latin Logic* §1232) within philosophy in particular and human knowledge in general.

Nevertheless, it is the requirements of demonstration that govern Wolff's analysis of the parts of philosophy. Accordingly, metaphysics must precede physics and practical philosophy, and within each of these three primary philosophical disciplines the order of their subordinate parts should be that given in Table 1. Furthermore, demonstrative method is the most notable feature in each part of Wolff's philosophy.

5 Philosophical method

'Philosophical method is the order which the philosopher ought to use in treating dogmas' (*Preliminary Discourse* §115). Furthermore, 'the supreme law of philosophical method is that those things must come first through which later things are understood and established' (*Preliminary Discourse* §133). In other words, method involves a certain kind of ordering of dogmas or propositions. It proceeds from accurate definitions and precise terminology to establish certain and immutable principles, legitimate deductions, and demonstrated conclusions. Initial conclusions become the bases for further inferences and deductions, all of which yields certitude and utility.

Like some contemporaries, Wolff believed that philosophical and mathematical method are fundamentally identical because they derive from a common source, the notion of certitude. Thus, he observed that 'philosophy does not borrow its method from mathematics; rather, both philosophy and mathematics derive their methods from true logic' (*Preliminary Discourse* §139). In his *Eigene Lebensbeschreibung* (Autobiography) (pp. 121–2, 143), Wolff wrote that he had studied mathematics in order to discover the key to its success and to apply this discovery to the improvement of philosophy, theology, and the art of discovery. This reflects Wolff's commitment to a 'natural logic' or set of 'rules prescribed by God to the understanding and the natural ability to act accordingly' (*German Logic*, ch. 16 §3; compare *Latin Logic* §6; also Corr 1970).

Unlike others, Wolff found in the categorical syllogism what he understood to be the basic principles and the best expression of true logic and philosophical method. 'By these syllogisms everything is found out that can be discovered by human understanding, and everything is proven to others that they want to be convinced of, although neither in discovering nor in demonstrating do we always have the form of the syllogisms distinctly before our eyes' (*German Logic*, ch. 4 §20; compare *Latin Logic* §50). Thus, 'a syllogism is a speech in which reasoning or discourse is distinctly stated' (*Latin Logic* §332).

Whenever certitude cannot be established, a principle of tried usefulness can be admitted into philosophy as a probability or hypothesis, that is, 'an assumption which cannot yet be demonstrated, but which provides a reason' (*Preliminary Discourse* §126). This recognizes that, 'probability, in so far as it is clearly distinguished from certitude, is not to be eliminated from philosophy' (*Preliminary Discourse* §132).

6 Selected metaphysical doctrines

As noted above, Wolff defined philosophy as 'the science of the possibles in so far as they can be' (*Preliminary Discourse* §29). Accordingly, natural theology is the science of that which is possible through God, physics the science of that which is possible through bodies, and so forth.

This means that philosophy must provide scientific or demonstrative explanations as to why anything is or is not intrinsically possible (that is, not inherently self-contradictory). Further, philosophy must also explain why any possible being actually does or does not exist. Wolff defined existence as the 'fulfilment of possibility' (*German Metaphysics* §14) or the 'complement of possibility' (*Latin Ontology* §174; Van Peursen 1987).

Within Wolff's system, 'ontology or first philosophy is defined as the science of being in general, or in so far as it is being' (*Latin Ontology* §1; École 1990). Ontology is rooted in two central axioms which apply equally to the orders of being and of knowing (there is no separate, explicit discussion of theory of knowledge within Wolff's philosophy; see Gracia 1994). These fundamental axioms are the principle of contradiction and the principle of sufficient reason. The first and most basic is the principle of contradiction: 'it cannot happen that the same thing is and is not' (*Latin Ontology* §28). The principle of sufficient reason ('nothing exists without a sufficient why it is able to be rather than is not'), is explicitly subordinated to and deduced from the principle of contradiction (*Latin Ontology* §70). Following these two fundamental principles, every philosophical explanation must demonstrate two things about the subject matter in question: (1) that it is not impossible, that is, not inherently self-contradictory; and (2) that there is a sufficient reason why it actually exists or occurs.

'Being' is defined by Wolff as 'that which is able to exist, that is, to which existence is not repugnant' (*Latin Ontology* §134). The structure of being depends on three principal components: (1) 'essentialia' or ultimate factors within a being characterized by their lack of mutual determination and contradiction; (2) 'attributes' or constant factors which depend on 'essentialia' to explain their possibility and actuality; and (3) 'modes' or variable elements which must be compatible with its 'essentialia', but whose actual presence depends on external factors such as circumstances and other agents (*Latin Ontology* §§143, 146 and 148).

Both Wolff's ontology and general cosmology are notable for not including the Leibnizian doctrine of monads (see LEIBNIZ, G.W. §§4–5). Wolff described the world and the bodies within it as complex or compound entities constituted by the interconnection of simpler entities (*General Cosmology* §§48 and 119). Ultimately, the most fundamental of these simple substances or 'elements' are indivisible, physical points or 'atoms of nature' (*General Cosmology* §187) which are imperceptible and simple. They lack extension or figure, but are not characterized by a spiritual force or the perceptual activity of Leibniz's monads.

As noted above, Wolff divided psychology into 'empirical' and 'rational' parts (Blackwell 1961a; Corr 1975b). This division respects the need to incorporate observation and experience within philosophy, although the way in which the two parts of psychology are implemented reflects Wolff's search for demonstrative conclusions. Thus, empirical psychology organizes the facts of our psychological experience through an extended review of human cognitive and appetitive operations, and an attempt to define the basic vocabulary of psychology. It also offers a pivotal argument for the existence of the human soul:

> Whatever being is actually conscious of itself and of other things outside itself, that being exists. But we are actually conscious of ourselves and of other things outside ourselves. Therefore we exist.
>
> (*Empirical Psychology* §16)

On this basis, rational psychology provides a definition of the essence of the human soul: 'The essence of the soul consists in the force of representing the universe limited materially by the placement of the organic body in the universe and formally by the constitution of the sensory organs' (*Rational Psychology* §66).

Wolff's psychology accepted a classic dualism between soul and body (*Rational Psychology* §§530–642). Ideally, empirical psychology would dis-close the simultaneous occurrence of mental and bodily actions, while rational psychology would systematically explain their interdependence. However, Wolff conceded that he had not been able to find any reason in the nature of the soul from which the necessity of its 'commerce' or interaction with the body could be deductively demonstrated. As a result, he resorted to a hypothetical explanation. Among possible candidates for this, both direct physical influx or interaction and occasionalism were rejected as unlikely (see OCCASIONALISM), while Leibniz's theory of pre-established harmony (see LEIBNIZ, G.W. §6) was accepted as the most likely account (*Rational Psychology* §639). However, in Wolff's view pre-established harmony was not without its own difficulties and was admitted only as a probable explanation limited to the relationship between the human soul and body.

Natural theology is 'the science of those things which are possible through God' (*Natural Theology* I §1). By contrast with a supernatural or revealed theology originating in a divine revelation or sacred scripture, natural theology proceeds 'solely by the light of nature' (*Natural Theology* I §1n). Nevertheless, for Wolff 'there is no more sublime philosophy than that which clearly demonstrates the highest perfections of the supreme divinity and how all things are in it, from it, and through it, and which completely roots out the profane thoughts of men concerning God and religion' (*Natural Theology*, dedication to Part I).

Wolff divided natural theology into two major parts: Part I contains an a posteriori demonstration of the existence and attributes of God drawn from the characteristics of the visible world; Part II treats the same subjects from an a priori standpoint based on the notion of a most perfect being and the nature of the human soul (Bissinger 1970; Corr 1973). The a posteriori argument for the existence of God is complex (compare, *Natural Theology* I §§24 onwards): the human soul exists or we exist; there must be a sufficient reason why this is so; that reason must be contained either in ourselves or in some other being different from us; in either case, the reason must lie in a necessary being if it is to be truly sufficient; therefore, a necessary being exists; a necessary being is an *ens a se* (being in itself) or one which contains the sufficient reason of its existence in its own essence, that is, an '*ens a se* exists therefore, because it is possible' (*Natural Theology* I §34); neither the visible world, its elements, or the human soul can be *ens a se*; therefore, God exists; 'God' being defined nominally as 'the *ens a se* in which is contained the sufficient reason of the existence of this visible world and of our souls' (*Natural Theology* I §67).

Wolff noted that an *ens a se* (in contrast to an *ens ab alio* or being from another) is possible because its essential constituents involve no contradiction; it exists because it possesses these particular essential determinations. The fact that its essential constituents explain both its possibility and its actual existence is the special 'privilege' of an *ens a se*. 'And thus it is that existence is not inferred from possibility in general, nor is existence determined from possibility considered in general or in itself' (*Natural Theology* I §34n).

Wolff's a priori proof for the existence of God was based on the notion of an *ens perfectissimum* or 'most perfect being' understood as that being 'to which belong all compossible realities in the absolutely highest degree' (*Natural Theology* II §6). The *ens perfectissimum*, nominally defined as God, contains in the highest degree all of the real or ontological components of the essence of a being which are both possible in themselves and in relation to each other. On this basis, the a priori demonstration of God's existence is this:

> God contains all compossible realities in the absolutely highest degree. But He is possible. Wherefore, since the possible can exist, existence can belong to it. Consequently, since existence is a reality, and since realities are compossible which can belong to a being, existence is in the class of compossible realities. Moreover, necessary existence is the absolutely highest degree. Therefore, necessary existence belongs to God or, what is the same, God necessarily exists.
>
> (*Natural Theology* II §21)

In other words, 'God exists through His essence or His existence is essential' (*Natural Theology* II §27).

The principal attributes of God are intellect, power, and will. The divine intellect explains the intrinsic possibility of the world (its lack of internal self-contradiction), the divine power explains its extrinsic possibility (or compatibility with the nexus of other existents that together constitute a particular universe), and the divine will accounts for its actual existence (by providing the sufficient reason for or final determination of that existence). In addition, 'God wills whatever He represents to Himself as the best, both in itself and in relation to Himself' (*Natural Theology* I §390). Thus, the visible universe is the best of all possible worlds. But Wolff believed God may bring other possible worlds – one or all of them – into actual existence along with the best one. Therefore, Wolff maintained that the existence of any world is only a contingent fact. God acts reasonably, but the divine creative act is not coerced or necessitated by the objective, existential dynamism of a world of possible essences.

7 Practical philosophy

Wolff wrote extensively on various areas of practical philosophy, but that portion of his philosophy has had less influence than his views on method and metaphysics. Contrary to radical fideists, Wolff argued for a moral philosophy based on the concept of perfection (*German Ethics* §2). The good is that which makes us and our condition more perfect; the bad is that which makes us and our condition more imperfect. These notions arise from the structure of being and can be known by human beings through natural reason even without the assistance of Christian revelation. In short, neither the good nor our knowledge of the good are directly dependent upon God's will or influence.

Perfection involves self improvement, both in internal and external conditions, as well as the improvement of other human beings and the promotion of God's honour. In striving for this extended concept of perfection, human beings are acting according to a natural moral law, one which applies to individuals, small communities, nation states, and the international human community. The idea of perfection is the fundamental motivating force in the practical sphere. Thus, intellect or reason directs the will in the search for an objective moral good. And education or the formation of clear and distinct ideas associated with perfection is the chief spur to moral living. Here is the ultimate outcome of Wolff's conviction that clear and certain ideas are the best foundation for both the advancement of theoretical knowledge and practical living.

8 An assessment

Christian Wolff is not a first-rank, original thinker. He was important in particular as an organizer and systematizer of philosophical thought during the eighteenth century. Wolff's thought emphasized clarity, rigour and comprehensiveness. In the history of German philosophy, Wolff was the first major systematic thinker. His philosophical system helped to define important philosophical terms and advance the cause of the German language as a tool for scholarly work.

Leibniz was the single most important influence on Wolff's thought. But Wolff did not like to be regarded merely as someone who gave a new and more orderly presentation to the views of his great predecessor (*Autobiography*: 142–3). In fact, there were important limitations in what the two men knew of each other's writings and Wolff departed from Leibniz's views on several key points (Corr 1975a). In addition, Wolff drew upon other sources as well (Corr 1983). And

Wolff helped to make room for the emerging sciences of his day, even though his own deductive methodology in philosophy was not wholly compatible with the methods of those sciences.

Through his lengthy teaching career, extensive writings, and many followers, Wolff was extremely influential in shaping German philosophical thought for a period of fifty years and more during the middle of the eighteenth century. Against the Pietists who became his opponents, Wolff spoke on behalf of what he regarded as the legitimate claims of natural human reason, as well as the compatibility of faith and reason (École 1983). In defending his own views, he composed extended refutations of atheism, deism, fatalism, naturalism and Spinozism (Morrison 1993). In reaction to censure from his theological critics and political opponents, Wolff also wrote eloquently on behalf of the freedom to philosophize (*Preliminary Discourse* §§151–71), arguing that 'if one is to use philosophical method in developing philosophy, then the yoke of philosophical servitude cannot be imposed' (§153). Praised by Kant for the rigour of his thought, Wolff helped to frame many of the issues addressed by his great successor.

See also: ENLIGHTENMENT, CONTINENTAL; RATIONALISM

List of works

Wolff, C. (1964–) *Christian Wolff's Gesammelte Werke* (Collected Works), Hildesheim and New York: Georg Olms. (Wolff's collected works are being reprinted in three series: German writings; Latin writings; and a supplementary series of materials and documents relevant to Wolff's life, works and thought. This very large publishing project is now almost complete. It consists of a total of 109 separate volumes: 29 German, 41 Latin and 39 supplementary.)

German series

The principal works of philosophical importance in the German series are given here.

Wolff, C. (1713) *Vernünfftige Gedancken von den Kräfften des menschlichen Verstandes und ihrem richtigen Gebrauche in Erkänntnis der Wahrheit*, trans. as *Logic, or Rational Thoughts on the Powers of the Human Understanding, with Their Use and Application in the Knowledge and Search of Truth*, London: L. Hawes, W. Clarke & R. Collins, 1770. (Referred to as the *German Logic*; translated anonymously into English.)

—— (1720) *Vernünfftige Gedancken von Gott, der Welt und der Seele des Menschen, auch allen Dingen überhaupt* (Rational Thoughts on God, the World and the Human Soul, and All Things in General). (Referred to as the *German Metaphysics*.)

—— (1720) *Vernünfftige Gedancken von der Menschen Thun und Lassen, zu Beförderung ihrer Glückseligkeit, den Liebhabern der Wahrheit mitgetheilet* (Rational Thoughts on Human Conduct). (Referred to as the *German Ethics*.)

—— (1721) *Vernünfftige Gedancken von dem gesellschaftlichen Leben der Menschen und insonderheit dem gemeinen Wesen zu Beförderung der Glückseligkeit des menschlichen Geschlechts* (Rational Thoughts on the Social Life of Humans and Especially the Commonwealth for the Promotion of the Happiness of the Human Race). (Referred to as the *German Politics*.)

—— (1723) *Vernünfftige Gedancken von den Wirkungen der Natur, den Liebhabern der Wahrheit mitgetheilet* (Rational Thoughts on the Operations of Nature. (Referred to as the *German Physics*.)

—— (1724) *Vernünfftige Gedancken von den Absichten der natürlichen Dinge, den Liebhabern der Wahrheit mitgetheilet* (Rational Thoughts on the Purposes of Natural Things). (Referred to as the *German Teleology*.)

—— (1724) *Anmerckungen über die vernünfftige Gedancken von Gott, der Welt und der Seele des Menschen, auch allen Dingen überhaupt, zu besserem Verstande und bequemeren Gebrauche derselben* (Annotations to the *Rational Thoughts on God, the World and the Human Soul*).

—— (1725) *Vernünfftige Gedancken von dem Gebrauche der Theile in Menschen, Thieren und Pflantzen, den Liebhabern der Wahrheit mitgetheilet* (Rational Thoughts on the Use of Parts in Humans, Animals and Plants). (Referred to as the *German Physiology*.)

—— (1726) *Ausführliche Nachricht von seinen eigenen Schrifften die er in deutscher Sprache von den verschiedenen Theilen der Welt-Weiszheit herausgegeben, auf Verlangen ans Licht gestellet* (Detailed Account of His Own Works Which He Published in the German Language on the Different Parts of Philosophy).

—— (c.1740) *Christian Wolff's eigene Lebensbeschreibung* (Autobiography).

Latin series

The principal works of philosophical importance in the Latin series.

Wolff, C. (1718) *Ratio praelectionum Wolffianarum in*

mathesin et philosophiam universam (Plan of the Wolffian Lectures in Mathematics and Universal Philosophy).

—— (1728) *Discursus praeliminaris de philosophia in genere*, trans. R.J. Blackwell, *Preliminary Discourse on Philosophy in General*, Indianapolis, IN: Bobbs-Merrill, 1963. (Originally published together with the *Philosophia rationalis sive Logica*.)

—— (1728) *Philosophia rationalis sive Logica, methodo scientifica pertractata et ad usum scientiarum atque vitae aptata* (Rational Philosophy or Logic, Treated According to the Scientific Method). (Referred to as the *Latin Logic*.)

—— (1729) *Philosophia prima, sive Ontologia, methodo scientifica pertractata, qua omnis cognitionis humanae principia continentur* (First Philosophy, or Ontology, Treated According to the Scientific Method). (Referred to as the *Latin Ontology*.)

—— (1731) *Cosmologia generalis, methodo scientifica pertractata, qua ad solidam, inprimis Dei atque naturae, cognitionem via sternitur* (General Cosmology, Treated According to the Scientific Method). (Referred to as the *General Cosmology*.)

—— (1732) *Psychologia empirica, methodo scientifica pertractata, qua ea, quae de anima humana indubia experientiae fide constant, continentur et ad solidam universae philosophiae practicae ac theologiae naturalis tractationem via sternitur* (Empirical Psychology, Treated According to the Scientific Method). (Referred to as the *Empirical Psychology*.)

—— (1734) *Psychologia rationalis, methodo scientifica pertractata, qua ea, quae de anima humana indubia experientiae fide innotescunt, per essentiam et naturam animae explicantur, et ad intimiorem naturae ejusque autoris cognitionem profutura proponuntur* (Rational Psychology, Treated According to the Scientific Method). (Referred to as the *Rational Psychology*.)

—— (1736) *Theologia naturalis, methodo scientifica pertractata. Pars Prior, integrum Systema complectens, qua existentia et attributa Dei a posteriori demonstrantur* (Natural Theology, Treated According to the Scientific Method. First Part of the Complete System, in Which the Existence and Attributes of God are Demonstrated a posteriori). (The first part of the *Natural Theology*.)

—— (1737) *Theologia naturalis, methodo scientifica pertractata. Pars Posterior, qua existentia et attributa Dei ex notione entis perfectissimi et natura animae demonstrantur, et Atheismi, Deismi, Fatalismi, Naturalismi, Spinosismi, aliorumque de Deo errorum fundamenta subvertuntur* (Natural Theology, Treated According to the Scientific Method. Second Part, in Which the Existence and Attributes of God are Demonstrated from the Notion of a Most Perfect Being and the Nature of the Soul, and the Foundations of Atheism, Deism, Fatalism, Naturalism, Spinozism and Other Errors Concerning God are Overthrown). (The second part of the *Natural Theology*.)

—— (1738–9) *Philosophia practica universalis, methodo scientifica pertractata. Partes I–II* (Universal Practical Philosophy, Treated According to the Scientific Method).

—— (1740–8) *Jus Naturae, methodo scientifica pertractatum. Partes I–VIII* (Natural Law, Treated According to the Scientific Method).

—— (1749) *Jus Gentium, methodo scientifica pertractatum, in quo jus gentium naturale ab eo, quod voluntarii, pactitii et consuetudinarii est, accurate distinguitur* (Law Binding the World at Large, Treated According to the Scientific Method).

—— (1750) *Institutiones juris naturae et gentium, in quibus ex ipsa hominis natura continuo nexu omnes obligationes et jura omnia deducuntur* (Precepts of Natural Law and Law Binding the World at Large).

—— (1750–3) *Philosophia moralis sive Ethica, methodo scientifica pertractata. Partes I–V* (Moral Philosophy or Ethics, Treated According to the Scientific Method).

—— (1754–5) *Oeconomica, methodo scientifica pertractata. Partes I–II* (Economics, Treated According to the Scientific Method).

Supplementary series

The supplementary series (39 separate volumes) contains: contemporaneous works on the history and influence of Wolff's philosophy; some textbooks and other titles by Wolff's students or followers (including Baumeister, Baumgarten, Frobesius, Gottsched, Stiebritz and Thümmig) who sought to popularize various aspects of Wolff's thought; tracts by some of Wolff's critics (such as Lange); and selected secondary works by modern writers (for example, Campo, École and Thomann) on Wolff's thought.

References and further reading

* Bissinger, A. (1970) *Die Struktur der Gotteserkenntnis: Studien zur Philosophie Christian Wolffs* (The Structure of the Recognition of God: Studies to accompany the philosophy of Christian Wolff), Bonn: H. Bouvier & Co. (A careful study of Wolff's natural theology.)

* Blackall, E.A. (1959) *The Emergence of German as a Literary Language 1700–1775*, Cambridge: Cambridge University Press.

* Blackwell, R.J. (1961a) 'Christian Wolff's Doctrine of the Soul', *Journal of the History of Ideas* 22 (3): 339–54. (On Wolff's psychology.)

* —— (1961b) 'The Structure of Wolffian Philosophy', *The Modern Schoolman* 38 (3): 203–18. (A helpful schematic exposition and analysis by the translator of Wolff's *Preliminary Discourse on Philosophy in General*.)

* Corr, C.A. (1970) 'Certitude and Utility in the Philosophy of Christian Wolff', *The Southwestern Journal of Philosophy* 1 (1): 133–42. (Discussion of the basic goals of Wolff's philosophy.)

* —— (1972) 'Christian Wolff's Treatment of Scientific Discovery', *Journal of the History of Philosophy* 10 (3): 323–34. (Exploration of Wolff's undeveloped notion of an *ars inveniendi* or art of discovery.)

* —— (1973) 'The Existence of God, Natural Theology, and Christian Wolff', *International Journal for Philosophy of Religion* 4 (2): 105–18.

* —— (1975a) 'Christian Wolff and Leibniz', *Journal of the History of Ideas* 36 (2): 241–62. (Detailed examination of direct testimony, circumstantial data and doctrinal comparisons bearing on the links between Wolff and Leibniz; questions the stereotype of Wolff as little more than a systematizer and vulgarizer of his predecessor's thought.)

* —— (1975b) 'Christian Wolff's Distinction Between Empirical and Rational Psychology', *Studia Leibnitiana*, Supplementum 14: 195–215.

* —— (1983) 'Cartesian Themes in Christian Wolff's German Metaphysics Volumes', in *Christian Wolff (1679–1754)*, ed. W. Schneiders, Hamburg: Felix Meiner, 113–20.

* École, J. (1978) 'La conception wolffienne de la philosophie d'après le Discursus praeliminaris de philosophia in genere' (The Wolffian Conception of Philosophy according to the *Preliminary Discourse on Philosophy in General*), *Filosofia Oggi* 4 (4): 403–28. (Thorough review of Wolff's conception of philosophy as set forth in the *Preliminary Discourse on Philosophy in General*.)

* —— (1983) 'Les rapports de la raison et de la foi selon Christian Wolff' (The Relationship between Reason and Faith according to Christian Wolff), *Studia Leibnitiana* 15 (2): 205–14. (Knowledgeable reflection on the relationship between reason and faith in Wolff's philosophy.)

* —— (1990) *La métaphysique de Christian Wolff*, Hildesheim: Georg Olms; in C. Wolff, *Gesammelte Werke*, vol. 3, 12.1–12.2. (Definitive study of its subject; clearly superior to the only earlier book-length treatment (Campo's *Cristiano Wolff e il razionalismo precritico*, 2 vols, 1939; reprinted in *Gesammelte Werke*, vol. 3, section 9). Ecole also has an extensive series of articles published between 1961–80 in journals such as *Giornale di Metafisica*, *Les études philosophiques*, *Filosofia Oggi*, *Archives de Philosophie* and *Studia Leibnitiana*, many of which arose from editorial work for the Latin philosophical texts in Wolff's *Gesammelte Werke*.)

Gerlach, H.-M., Schenk, G. and Thaler, B. (eds) (1980) *Christian Wolff als Philosoph der Aufklärung in Deutschland* (Christian Wolff as Philosopher of the Enlightenment in Germany), Halle: Wissenschaftliche Beiträge der Martin-Luther-Universität Halle-Wittenberg. (Proceedings of a colloquium held at Halle in 1979 on the 300th anniversary of Wolff's birth; contains some two dozen contributions.)

* Gracia, J.J.E. (1994) 'Christian Wolff on Individuation', in *Individuation and Identity in Early Modern Philosophy: Descartes to Kant*, ed. K.F. Barber and J.J.E. Gracia, Albany, NY: State University of New York Press, 219–43. (An expanded version of a 1993 article by the same title in *History of Philosophy Quarterly* 10 (2): 147–64 examining Wolff's views on individuation as an example of a conjunction of metaphysical and epistemological issues that the author believes is characteristic of modern philosophy.)

* Morrison, J.C. (1993) 'Christian Wolff's Criticisms of Spinoza', *Journal of the History of Philosophy* 31 (3): 405–20. (Addresses issues at the heart of Wolff's philosophy and his disputes with theologians. Can usefully be compared with an earlier article by École from 1983: 'La critique wolffienne du Spinozism' (Interpretations in his philosophy and its influence, with a bibliography of literature on Wolff), *Archives de Philosophie* 46 (4): 553–67.)

Schneiders, W. (ed.) (1983) *Christian Wolff (1679–1754): Interpretationen zu seiner Philosophie und deren Wirkung, mit einer Bibliographie der Wolff-Literatur* (trans?), Hamburg: Felix Meiner. (Proceedings of a colloquium held at Wolfenbuttel on November 21–3, 1979; contains twenty articles and a good bibliography of secondary literature published between 1800–1982.)

* Van Peursen, C.A. (1987) 'Christian Wolff's Philosophy of Contingent Reality', *Journal of the History of Philosophy* 25 (1): 69–82. (Sensitive and thoughtful re-examination of this important issue in Wolff's thought.)

CHARLES A. CORR

WOLLASTON, WILLIAM (1660–1724)

William Wollaston, a popular eighteenth-century English moral philosopher, is often grouped with Samuel Clarke as a staunch defender of the kind of moral rationalism that David Hume later opposed. Wollaston's project, as he describes it, is to find a rule to distinguish right actions from wrong. He complains that previous philosophers have either overlooked this task or proposed rules which are imprecise, incomplete or misleading. The rule he proposes is fidelity to truth. Actions, he argues, express propositions and so may be true or false. Moral actions express truths and immoral actions express falsehoods. He thinks this rule explains other widely held views about morality, for example, that we should live in accordance with nature, right reason or the will of God. His most remembered (and most misunderstood) claim is that an evildoer 'lives a lie'.

Wollaston was born at Coton-Clanford, England. He received an MA from Sidney Sussex College, Cambridge, in 1681, and was then assistant master in Birmingham Grammar School. In his late twenties he came into a large inheritance, married an heiress and retired to a life of study. His *The Religion of Nature Delineated* was first published privately in 1722.

More than a decade before *The Religion of Nature Delineated* appeared, Samuel CLARKE had argued that right actions are 'fit' or appropriate to the real nature and relations of things. Evildoers, Clarke insists, by opposing the nature and reason of things, 'endeavour (as much in them lies) to make things be what they are not and cannot be' (1706: 613). This is as absurd as attempting to alter a mathematical truth. Wollaston constructs his whole moral theory around this idea. But, unlike Clarke, for whom the basic moral notions are fitness and unfitness, Wollaston seeks to reduce moral notions to truth and falsehood. True propositions 'express things as they are'; actions in general express propositions and so may be true or false. Whatever can be understood has meaning and, since actions can be understood, they have meaning. Actions, as Wollaston conceives of them, are simply our thoughts translated into deeds. Since we represent things with our actions, what we represent may be true or false. Immoral actions deny things to be what they are and so express falsehoods. If I take your property, I falsely declare it is mine. If I am ungrateful, I falsely declare I never received favours from you. The evildoer 'lives a lie' because his conduct, as Wollaston puts it, breathes untruths. As moral creatures, our aim should be to mirror truth,

representing the way things are in our conduct. But Wollaston thinks that the reality we should strive to represent is our ordinary, everyday natural and social world, not a metaphysically independent moral order, as Clarke had maintained.

Wollaston thinks that the Stoic formula – follow nature – is correct if interpreted as enjoining us to treat things as being what they are and so according to truth (see STOICISM §15). He also argues that 'the way to happiness, and the practice of reason' are the same as 'a careful observation of truth'. Our nature is such that we aim at our own happiness. Not only is happiness our natural good, but we also have a duty to strive for our own and other people's happiness. Anticipating Jeremy BENTHAM, Wollaston defines happiness as the 'true quantity of pleasure': pleasures and pains may be measured in terms of their intensity and duration, and we are happy when the sum total of pleasures exceeds the sum total of pains. He argues that just as happiness cannot be achieved by anything that interferes with morality (truth), so the practice of truth (acting morally) cannot make a person unhappy. Morality and happiness are congruent – if not in this world, then in the afterlife.

Wollaston thinks his theory explains what we mean when we say that morality is a matter of following right reason. He characterizes reason as the power to survey and compare ideas and to make inferences from these. We discover truth by means of reason or, more precisely, right reason. So when our actions are in accord with right reason, they express truths. Immoral actions are contrary to reason because they assert falsehoods. The reports of our senses are true and may be acted upon as long as there is no reason against them. It is the nature of reason to command, Wollaston says; it enjoins, forbids or permits, and as rational creatures it should govern us. True happiness can be achieved only by pursuing means consistent with our rational nature; false pleasures are inconsistent with or destructive of it.

Wollaston concludes that the 'truest' definition of morality is 'the pursuit of happiness by the practice of truth and reason'. And when we act morally, he argues, we obey God's will. In rejecting the way things are, the evildoer is implicitly rebelling against God's will. The truths we should aim to mirror in our actions are God's truths. They are natural, however, because we are able to grasp them by reason unaided by divine revelation. So there is, Wollaston says, such a thing as natural religion (see NATURAL THEOLOGY).

Wollaston's attempt to reduce moral categories to truth and falsehood was criticized by subsequent philosophers, starting with David Hume (1739/40) and continuing today with John Mackie (1980) and Joel Feinberg (1977) (see HUME, D.). The problem these philosophers found with Wollaston's idea that immoral actions express falsehoods is that as a criterion of wrong actions it is circular. It is wrong for me to take your property, Wollaston says, because I falsely declare it to be mine, not yours. But if we ask why this is what my action means, the answer is that the fact that it is yours *means* that I should not steal it. In every case, the truth that is supposedly denied by a wrong action already has moral or normative content.

In the latter part of *The Religion*, Wollaston details our specific duties to God, others and ourselves. Anticipating PRICE and KANT, he thinks many duties command us to respect our own and other people's rational nature. He argues against attempts to persuade others without giving them reasons. To do so is to attempt to treat others as if they did not have reason.

List of works

Wollaston, W. (1691) *On the Design of Part of the Book of Ecclesiastes, or the Unreasonableness of Men's Restless Contention for the Present Enjoyments, Represented in an English Poem*, printed privately. (Contains Wollaston's poem in heroic couplets inspired by chapters 1–4 of the Ecclesiastes, plus a paraphrase of these chapters, with notes on the paraphrase.)

—— (1722) *The Religion of Nature Delineated*, printed privately; repr. London: Samuel Palmer, 1724. The 'Life of Wollaston' is prefixed to the 6th edn, London, 1738. 10 more editions by 1750. (Wollaston's philosophically important work; argues that as moral creatures we should aim to mirror truth, representing the way things are in our conduct.)

References and further reading

* Clarke, S. (1706) *A Discourse concerning the Unchangeable Obligations of Natural Religion, and the Truth and Certainty of the Christian Revelation*, in The Works of Samuel Clarke, vol. 2, New York: Garland, 1978. (Clarke defends a rationalist view of ethics. He argues that we come to see that actions are fit or unfit by rationally grasping the eternal and necessary relations holding between actions and situations. He also claims that reason by itself both obliges and motivates us to do what is fit.)
* Feinberg, J. (1977) 'Wollaston and his Critics', *Journal of the History of Ideas* 38: 345–52. (A defence of Wollaston against his critics and their misinterpretations, although he agrees to some extent with Hume's main objections.)
* Hume, D. (1739/40) *A Treatise of Human Nature*, ed.

L.A. Selby-Bigge, Oxford: Clarendon Press, 1960, esp. book 3, part I, section 1, 461–3, and footnote. (Hume opposes Wollaston's moral theory, although at points he misinterprets it.)
Joynton, O. (1984) 'The Problem of Circularity in Wollaston's Moral Philosophy', *Journal of the History of Philosophy* 22: 435–43. (A recent attempt to defend Wollaston from the charge that his criterion of right action is circular or empty.)
* Mackie, J.L. (1980) *Hume's Moral Theory*, London: Routledge & Kegan Paul, ch. 2. (Contains a brief but clear explanation of Wollaston's moral theory.)
Tweyman, S. (1976) 'Truth, Happiness and Obligation: The Moral Philosophy of William Wollaston', *Philosophy* 51: 35–46. (A sympathetic explanation of Wollaston's moral theory.)

CHARLOTTE BROWN

WOLLSTONECRAFT, MARY (1759–97)

Wollstonecraft used the rationalist and egalitarian ideas of late eighteenth-century radical liberalism to attack the subjugation of women and to display its roots in the social construction of gender. Her political philosophy draws on Rousseau's philosophical anthropology, rational religion, and an original moral psychology which integrates reason and feeling in the production of virtue. Relations between men and women are corrupted by artificial gender distinctions, just as political relations are corrupted by artificial distinctions of rank, wealth and power. Conventional, artificial morality distinguishes between male and female virtue; true virtue is gender-neutral, consists in the imitation of God, and depends on the unimpeded development of natural faculties common to both sexes, including both reason and passion. Political justice and private virtue are interdependent: neither can advance without an advance in the other.

1 Life and influences
2 Wollstonecraft and philosophy
3 Political philosophy
4 Moral philosophy
5 Moral psychology

1 Life and influences

Mary Wollstonecraft was born into a declining middle-class family. Her father became a heavy drinker who beat his wife, and possibly his daughter too. Wollstonecraft had little formal education and early sought independence as a lady's companion, a schoolkeeper, and a governess, before rejecting such conventionally female occupations for the usually male one of translator and reviewer for *The Analytical Review*, a periodical founded by the dissenting publisher Joseph Johnson. She achieved fame with two political tracts: *A Vindication of the Rights of Men* (1790), attacking Edmund Burke's *Reflections on the Revolution in France* (1790) and *A Vindication of the Rights of Woman* (1792), her most substantial work (see BURKE, E.). She also published educational works, a novel, an account of the French Revolution, and a travel book; a second novel was unfinished at her death. All the work published in her lifetime was written for money, the two *Vindications* extremely rapidly, without revision. While living in France to study the Revolution of 1789 at first hand she had an illegitimate daughter; after return to London and rejection by the child's father she made two attempts at suicide. She then resumed her journalistic career and formed a liaison with the political philosopher William GODWIN, whom she married on becoming pregnant with a second daughter (later to become Mary Shelley). She died of complications following childbirth. Wollstonecraft seems to have been influenced chiefly by the eighteenth-century culture of sensibility, the educational theories of LOCKE and Catherine Macaulay, the dissenting, 'enlightened', politically radical circles round Joseph Johnson and Richard PRICE, who lived near the school she kept in Newington Green, and by wide and miscellaneous reading, particularly of ROUSSEAU and Burke, opposition to whom formed her understanding of her own experience.

2 Wollstonecraft and philosophy

Wollstonecraft was not a systematic political philosopher aiming primarily at theoretical rigour, but something more like a *philosophe* as defined in Diderot's *Encyclopedie* (see DIDEROT, D. §1) For the *philosophe*, reasoning consisted in speculative generalization from experience, applied to the social issues of the day with an eye to practical improvement. Wollstonecraft combined ideas drawn from a variety of Enlightenment philosophies, from contemporary science, and from prevailing political, cultural and social movements into an explanation and evaluation of the current condition of women, of the state of society, and of her personal and professional experience within it. Her object was a rational programme of reform; her political works use philosophy only incidentally, to support political polemic.

Though this political polemic uses the language of liberalism, its philosophical foundations are, first, a speculative anthropology which distinguishes between natural and artificial human attributes, assigns most of human development to environmental influences, and expects progressive human improvement in morality and civilization; and second, a moral philosophy and psychology inspired by personal experience, current theories of the nervous system, and the suggestions of rational religion about the purpose of human life. This philosophical moral psychology achieved only fragmentary expression in Wollstonecraft's political works, but its outlines are fairly clear from her educational, fictional and travel writings.

3 Political philosophy

For Wollstonecraft, human beings were created to perfect their nature as rational and moral beings (see PERFECTIONISM). Natural humanity is not unsocialized humanity, as in Rousseau, but humanity freely developing its capacity for self-improvement, which includes the capacity for socialization. The function of society is further improvement of humankind. Social and political arrangements which thwart or fail to recognize this corrupt human nature.

Eighteenth-century society and politics are corrupted by artificial distinctions of rank (such as the aristocracy), the products of historical accident, which impede the development of all ranks towards human perfection; relations between the sexes are similarly corrupted by artificial distinctions of character and capability, such as the association of reason and moral strength with men, and feeling or sensibility and moral weakness with women. These artificial distinctions impede the development of both sexes towards full flowering of their human faculties.

Such corrupted environmental influences produce social injustice, along with vice in the aristocracy and brutish insensibility in the poor; the best hope of virtue lies with the middle classes. But even among these, artificial rank and gender distinctions are maintained by factitious interests such as social snobbery, male interest in the reduction of women to docile sexual objects, and female enjoyment of the opportunity this affords for sexual tyranny over men.

Thus the effect of artificial distinctions on social relations and public and private morality is, in the public sphere, political tyranny, social enmity, and a distorted conventional morality assigning different virtues to the two sexes; in the private sphere, domestic tyranny and the degradation of both male and female nature, to the detriment of physical health, moral development and parenthood.

The remedy is the abolition of artificial distinctions through political and social reform and the education of potential future citizens of both sexes into a radically revised, gender-neutral morality, based on religious but rationally derived principles. This new morality will redescribe conventionally gendered and sexualized virtues such as courage and modesty in forms applicable to both sexes, enabling women to become independent moral agents and rational wives and mothers.

Moral re-education, however, will be effective only in a context of gradual institutional, cultural and political evolution towards a republican meritocracy. Political revolution without moral evolution is dangerous (though it may sometimes be necessary as the lesser evil), since individual and social moral development are interdependent; private virtue will be difficult and therefore rare unless supported by the appropriate social and political structures, which will in turn be unstable without private virtue. For instance, the destructive passions aroused by oppression are likely to wreak havoc if released from social and political control before development of the capacity for rational management of the passions in the oppressed. Hence the later excesses of the initially benign and rational French Revolution of 1789.

4 Moral philosophy

The purpose of human life is perfection of human faculties in the imitation of God, who is moral perfection; however human perfection can be achieved only beyond the grave. In this life imitation of God consists in virtue, that is, acting autonomously from moral principle derived by reason from the attributes of God. Moral principles are not specified, but the supreme principle seems to be universal benevolence, conjoined with or entailing a principle of justice; God's benevolence can be inferred from the convenient arrangements for his creatures manifested in nature. Benevolence prompted by sympathy for particular cases is a juvenile precursor, perhaps a precondition, of rational, adult morality motivated by principled universal benevolence.

5 Moral psychology

Moral development towards principled action depends on adequate development of the appropriate faculties, namely imagination, passion and reason, whose joint function is to reveal the true end of human life. Human beings come into the world endowed with appetite and the capacity to develop these higher faculties, though capacities vary with sensibility and development may be impeded by mistaken upbringing. Appetite, whose function is to preserve the body, proposes merely sensual, achievable objects of desire; imagination proposes ideal objects which make possible desire for something beyond the physically attainable. Such desires spring from the passions (fear, anger, love and so on), whose function is to elevate the mind. Sensibility (nervous sensitivity) is, or is linked to, capacity for imagination and passion.

Reason is developed by reflecting on efforts, especially frustrated efforts, to satisfy the passions and appetites. The reason which recognizes the function of the appetites, and tempers their satisfaction accordingly, is prudence; temperately satisfied appetite is earthly or animal happiness. The reason which recognizes the function of the passions, whose natural outcome is discontent, identifies the true end of human life, namely moral perfection or likeness to God; it produces virtue by transforming passionate desire into desire for perfection as the only object which can satisfy it. Attainment of perfection is true human happiness, which is impossible in this life.

Since the development of virtue depends on reason's interaction with the appetites and passions, virtue is not served by premature or inappropriate attempts to curb or stifle these. Rather, social conventions and education which restrict the activities and aspirations of women prevent the development of both reason and virtue, thereby justifying and reinforcing conventional gender roles. Conventional female education, by encouraging attention to sensory attractions, and instilling outward propriety instead of virtue, discourages development of the higher functions of imagination and passion, thus depriving an already weakened reason of opportunities to acquire knowledge of the true end of human life, and hence adult virtue.

See also: FEMINISM; FEMINIST ETHICS; MORALITY AND EMOTIONS

List of works

Wollstonecraft, M. (1989) *The Works of Mary Wollstonecraft*, ed. J. Todd and M. Butler, London: William Pickering, 7 vols. (Contains all of Wollstonecraft's works, which are listed individually below.)

—— (1787) *Thoughts on the Education of Daughters: with Reflections on Female Conduct, in the More Important Duties of Life*, in The Works of Mary Wollstonecraft, London: William Pickering, vol. 4, 1989. (Wollestonecraft's first published work; a handbook on female education probably based on her own practical experience.)

——(1788) *Mary: a Fiction, in The Works of Mary Wollstonecraft*, London: William Pickering, vol. 1, 1989. (A novel of ideas written to show 'that a genius will educate itself'; illustrates Wollstone-craft's early view of the course of ideal moral development, of the disadvantages of marriage for women, and of what would constitute an acceptable female social role.)

—— (1788) *Original Stories from Real Life: With Conversations Calculated to Regulate the Affections and Form the Mind to Truth and Goodness*, in The Works of Mary Wollstonecraft, London: William Pickering, vol. 4, 1989. (A children's storybook carefully designed to promote moral development; the most detailed working-out of Wollstonecraft's views on moral education.)

—— (1790) *A Vindication of the Rights of Men, in a Letter to the Right Honourable Edmund Burke*, in The Works of Mary Wollstonecraft, London: William Pickering, vol. 5, 1989. (An impassioned defence, by appeal to a rationalist as opposed to a sentimentalist moral philosophy, of Price's welcome of the French Revolution against Burke's attack; lays the foundation for Wollstonecraft's feminist politics.)

—— (1792) *A Vindication of the Rights of Woman with Strictures on Moral and Political Subjects*, in The Works of Mary Wollstonecraft, London: William Pickering, vol. 5, 1989. (Attacks conventional female education, morality and gender role as presented by various contemporary authors of educational and conduct books, principally by Rousseau in Émile.)

—— (1794) *An Historical and Moral View of the Origin and Progress of the French Revolution; and the Effect it has produced within Europe*, in The Works of Mary Wollstonecraft, London: William Pickering, vol. 6, 1989. (Wollstonecraft's reaction to the increasing violence of the French Revolution; historically derivative but useful for signs of development in her political thought.)

—— (1796) *Letters Written During a Short Residence in Sweden, Norway, and Denmark*, in The Works of Mary Wollstonecraft, London: William Pickering, vol. 6, 1989. (Provide probably the most accessible introduction to Wollstonecraft's thought; they suggest a movement away from rationalism towards a greater interest in imagination and sensibility under the impact of personal experience.)

—— (1798) *The Wrongs of Woman, or Maria*, in W. Godwin (ed.) Posthumous Works of the Author of A Vindication of the Rights of Woman, in The Works of Mary Wollstonecraft, London: William Pickering, vol. 1, 1989. (Unfinished; her first engagement with the wrongs of lower-class women; suggests that her earlier political and moral ideas, particularly on sensibility, were in a state of constant flux.)

—— (1979) *Collected Letters of Mary Wollstonecraft*, ed. R. Wardle. Ithaca, NY: Cornell University Press. (Useful for following the development of Wollstonecraft's self-conception; also one of the few sources of knowledge of what she read.)

References and further reading

Barker-Benfield, G.J. (1992) *The Culture of Sensibility: Sex and Society in Eighteenth-Century Britain*, Chicago, IL and London: University of Chicago Press. (A sociocultural study of a key concept in Wollstonecraft's moral psychology.)

Blair, H. (1783) *Lectures on Rhetoric and Belles-Lettres*, London: A. Strahan, T. Cadell, W. Creech, 1787. (A handbook of style summarizing Enlightened sentimentalist views on discourse; described by Wollstonecraft as 'an intellectual feast' (Letters: 138).)

Burke, E. (1757) *A Philosophical Enquiry into the Origin of our Ideas of the Sublime and Beautiful*, ed. J. Boulton, London: Routledge & Kegan Paul, 1958. (Burke's gendered aesthetic theory, partly an influence on Wollstonecraft and partly her target.)

* —— (1790) *Reflections on the Revolution in France*, ed. C.C. O'Brien, Harmondsworth: Penguin, 1968. (A furious response to Richard Price's A Discourse on the Love of our Country (1790, 3rd edn); defends British political traditions and correctly predicts some of the disastrous developments which followed. Criticized in Wollstonecraft's first Vindication.)

Coole, D.H. (1988) *Women in Political Theory*, Sussex: Wheatsheaf Books, Boulder, CO: Lynne Rienner Publishers, ch. 5. (Places Wollstonecraft as a political theorist; good on the relationship with Rousseau.)

Khin Zaw, S. (1994) '"Appealing to the Head *and* Heart": Wollstonecraft and Burke on Taste, Morals and Human Nature', in G. Perry and M. Rossington (eds) *Femininity and Masculinity in Eighteenth Century Art and Culture*, Manchester and New York: Manchester University Press. (Analyses Wollstonecraft's philosophical debt to Burke in her Rights of Men.)

Locke, J. (1693) *Thoughts on Education, in The Educational Writings of John Locke*, ed. J.L. Axtell, Cambridge: Cambridge University Press, 1968.

Macaulay, C. (1790) *Letters on Education, with Observations on Religious and Metaphysical Subjects*, London. (Conduct literature grounded in contemporary philosophy; generously credited in Wollstonecraft's second Vindication.)

Rousseau, J-J. (1762a) *Du Contrat social*, trans. and ed. D.A. Cress, with introduction by P. Gay, On the

Social Contract, Indianapolis, IN: Hackett Publishing Company, 1987. (Prime source of French Revolutionary political theory.)

—— (1762b) *Émile: ou, de l'éducation*, trans. A. Bloom, Emile: or, On Education, Harmondsworth: Penguin, 1991. (Rousseau's theory of gendered education; praised and attacked by Wollstonecraft in her second Vindication.)

Sapiro, V. (1992) *A Vindication of Political Virtue: the Political Theory of Mary Wollstonecraft*, Chicago, IL and London: University of Chicago Press. (The first book-length study of Wollstonecraft's philosophy; generally reliable.)

SUSAN KHIN ZAW

WÔNCH'ŪK (613–96)

Wônch'ūk, a Korean monk-scholar, was head of the Ximing Monastery in Tang China. Neglected by history, research has now recovered this prolific writer, whose commentaries on Yogācāra texts influenced later Buddhist scholars in China and also in Tibet, notably Tsong kha pa.

The *Prajñāpāramitā-sūtras* and the *Samdhinirmocana-sūtra* are scriptures of Mādhyamika and Yogācāra Buddhism respectively. Xuanzang (596–664) introduced Yogācāra to China after having studied at Nālandā University, the bastion of Yogācāra in India. Returning to China with voluminous Sanskrit manuscripts, he presided over the Imperial translation project at Changan.

Wônch'ūk, Xuanzang's colleague and critic, wrote an extensive commentary on the *Samdhinirmocana-sūtra*, 'Explication of the Underlying Meaning' which is extant today. One of the main points at issue is that while Mādhyamika declares that 'dependently co-originated things' do not have an unchanging intrinsic nature at all, Yogācāra insists on some real basis for these occurrences. Citing the theory of 'three natures' (*svabhāvatraya*), Xuanzang's disciple Ji (632–82) simply asserts the superiority of the *Samdhinirmocana-sūtra* over the *Prajñāpāramitā-sūtras*' 'two truths' (*satya dvaya*) theory. Wônch'ūk, however, unfolds a more careful investigation by claiming that Mādhyamika and Yogācāra are not competitors, but are in fact complementary schools. The *Prajñāpāramitā-sūtras*, for example, also contain the 'three natures' theory.

Wônch'ūk had an influence on Tibetan Buddhism as well. In the ninth century, Chos grub was ordered by a Tibetan king to translate Wônch'ūk's commentary on the *Samdhinirmocana-sūtra* into Tibetan. Later, TSONG KHA PA (1357–1419) followed Wônch'ūk's methodology in his magnum opus *Drang nges legs bshad snying po* (The Essence of True Eloquence). Here he quotes Wônch'ūk's commentary on the *Samdhinirmocana-sūtra* extensively.

Yogācāra provides a religio-psychological analysis of the structure of mental activity by charting the path between consciousness and the dynamic unconscious, that is, between *manas* and *ālaya-vijñāna* (seventh and eighth consciousness) (see BUDDHISM, YOGĀCĀRA SCHOOL OF). Paramārtha (499–569) had posited the ninth consciousness as pure cognition. Wônch'ūk refutes this view in detail in his commentary on the *Samdhinirmocana-sūtra*. Tsong kha pa in turn uses the same argument critically in his work, *Yid dang kun Gzhi*.

Ji forced Xuanzang to make a selective translation entitled *Ren weishi lun* (Treatise on the Proof of Representation Only), gleaned from the Indian commentaries of the *Trim'sikā* (Thirty Verses). Although Wônch'ūk, along with the other disciples, was excluded from this project, he wrote his own commentary on this work, expressing many views divergent from those of Ji. Some pages of this lost work can be recovered from the rebuttals of Wônch'ūk's commentaries made by Ji's disciples.

While Ji became the systematizer of the Faxiang or Yuishiki Hossō school in Japan, Wônch'ūk's fate was bleak. Even so, he was revered 'as a living Buddha' by the Empress Wu, who refused the request of a Silla king to send him home. But in the *Biographies of the Eminent Monks of the Song*, Wônch'ūk is described as being of obscure origin and of clever but dubious character. The truth is suggested by the following eulogy by his country man, Ch'oe:

Which ever translation of a *sūtra* it might be, he always

presided over that endeavour:

What ever commentary it might be, he always had something

unique to say:

Whenever he sought seclusion, he always attained inspiration:

To whomever he gave lectures on the Dharma,

he always reached everyone.

See also: BUDDHISM, MĀDHYAMIKA: INDIA AND TIBET; BUDDHISM, YOGĀCĀRA SCHOOL OF; BUDDHIST PHILOSOPHY, CHINESE; TSONG KHA PA

References and further reading

Iida Shotaro (1986) 'Who best can turn the Dharma-cakra? A controversy between Wônch'ûk and Kuei-chi', *Journal of Indian and Buddhist Studies* 34 (2): 11–18. (On Wônch'ûk 's thought.)

Lancaster, L.R. and Yu, C.S. (eds) (1991) *Assimilation of Buddhism in Korea*, Berkeley, CA: Asian Huma-nities Press. (On the arrival of Buddhism in Korea.)

Paul, D.V. (1984) *Philosophy of Mind in Sixth-century China: Paramārtha's 'Evolution of Consciousness'*, Stanford, CA: Stanford University Press. (Looks at the background of Korean Buddhism.)

Thurman, R.A.F. (1984) *Tsong Khapa's Speech of Gold in the Essence of True Eloquences: Reason and Enlightenment in the Central Philosophy of Tibet*, Princeton, NJ: Princeton University Press. (Transla-tion with an introduction.)

SHOTARO IIDA

WÔNHYO (617–86)

Wônhyo is one of the most important figures in Korean Buddhism, and a significant influence on the develop-ment of East Asian Buddhism in general. His lifework was the reconciliation of ideological conflicts among the various Buddhist schools. His goal was to create an all-inclusive, non-sectarian Buddhist doctrine. To do this he utilized the all-embracing, systematic metaphysics of the Hwaôm school of Buddhism, deriving both a guiding theoretical principle – hwajaeng or 'the harmonization of all disputes' – and a powerful dialectical method for the examination of Buddhist doctrinal conflicts.

Born in the Korean village of Puljich'on, not far from present-day Kyôngju, Wônhyo became a Buddhist monk at an early age and was a prolific writer, composing over one hundred books in 240 rolls. However, only twenty-three of these works survive, complete or in fragments. The most well-known of these are *Shimmun hwajaengnon* (The Treatise on the Harmonization of all Disputes in Ten Chapters), *Daesûng kishillonso* (The Commentaries on the Awakening of Faith in the Mahāyāna), *Kûmgang sammaegyông* (The Treatise on the *Vajrasamādhi-sūtra*) and *Yôlban'gyông jong'yo* (The Essentials on the Nirvāna-sūtra).

Wônhyo's dialectical method is based on the interrelation of two pairs of concepts, 'doctrine' (*chong*) and 'essence' (*yo*), as well as what he called the 'opening' (*kae*) and 'sealing' (*hap*) of Buddhist truth. Using these four key terms, he was able to place the various Buddhist ideologies of his day within a larger conceptual structure, demonstrating how points of conflict on the level of doctrine could be reconciled on the level of essence.

To Wônhyo, the term 'doctrine' referred to the expression of Buddhism's essentially ineffable, unitary truth through the differing conceptual vocabularies of the various Buddhist schools. When this unitary truth was 'opened' through philosophical discourse it became doctrine, accessible to the intellect for study and contemplation. Yet this 'opening of the one into the many', as Wônhyo termed it, was also the source of conflict and disagreement, for doctrinal truth was inherently self-limiting, defined by its own means of expression and therefore partial and biased.

In contrast, Wônhyo used the term 'essence' to refer back to the ineffable truth underlying all Buddhist ideology. He believed that doctrinal truth could be 'sealed' – that is, converted back to its unitary essence – beyond the scope of language or reason and therefore free of the limited perspective imposed by doctrine. He called this return to essence 'the sealing of the many into the one', and through it he sought to reconcile the various schools of Buddhist thought into a single, syncretic vision: *t'ong pulgyo*, 'the Buddhism of total interpenetration'.

The search for *t'ong pulgyo* has continued among Buddhist thinkers ever since, but Wônhyo's influence remains indelible. By combining the concepts of doctrine and essence with those of opening and sealing, he created a powerful interpretive tool for the examination of Buddhist texts, one that allowed him to apply the principle of *hwajaeng*, or 'harmoniza-tion', to a wide variety of theoretical conflicts. In so doing, he created the conceptual framework within which all subsequent discussion of *t'ong pulgyo* has taken place, up to and including the present day.

See also: BUDDHIST PHILOSOPHY, KOREAN

List of works

Wônhyo (617–86) Collected works, in *Han'guk pulgyo chônsô* (The Collected works of Korean Buddhism), Seoul: Dongguk University Press, 1979, vol. 1, 480–843. (Contains all the extant works of Wônhyo, a total of twenty-three texts in Sino-Korean.)

—— (617–86) *Shimmun hwajaengnon* (The Treatise on the Harmonization of all Disputes in Ten Chap-ters), in *Han'guk pulgyo chônsô*, Seoul: Dongguk University Press, 1979, vol. 1, 838–40. (The most well-known of Wônhyo's works, the theme of which is the harmonization of all scholastic disputes among different schools and texts. Only a few fragments remain.)

—— (617–86) *Daesûng kishillonso* (The Commentaries on the *Awakening of Faith in the Mahāyāna*), in *Han'guk pulgyo chônsô*, Seoul: Dongguk University Press, 1979, vol. 1, 698–732. (Wŏnhyo's philosophical introduction to the *Awakening of Faith* along with a running commentary to the text.)

—— (617–86) *Kûmgang sammaegyông* (The Treatise on the *Vajrasamādhi-sūtra*), in *Han'guk pulgyo chônsô*, Seoul: Dongguk University Press, 1979, vol. 1, 604–77. (Wŏnhyo's philosophical introduction to the text and a running commentary. The relationship between original enlightenment and and initial enlightenment is seriously discussed. The text is seen to have directly influenced Chan Buddhism in East Asia.)

—— (617–86) *Yôlban'gyông jong'yo* (The Essentials on the Nirvāna-sutra), in *Han'guk pulgyo chônsô*, Seoul: Dongguk University Press, 1979, vol. 1, 524–47. (Comments on the *sutra* with comprehensive overall analysis; there is an extensive discussion of the meaning of *nirvāna*.)

References and further reading

Koh Ikchim (1989) *Han'guk Kodae Pulkyo sasangsa* (A History of Buddhist Thought Before the Koryo Dynasty), Seoul: Dongguk University Press. (A collection of essays discussing pre-Koryo Dynasty Buddhist philosophy.)

Kim Young-tae (1986) *Introduction to the Buddhist History of Korea*, Seoul: Kyôngsô wôn. (A chronological history of Korean Buddhism.)

Lee, P.H. (ed.) (1993) *Sourcebook of Korean Civilization*, vol. 1, *From Early Times to the Sixteenth Century*, New York: Columbia University Press. (Contains selected English translations of important Korean texts reflecting the culture and civilization of Korea, including excerpts from Wŏnhyo on pages 145–59.)

Park Chong-hong (1976) 'Wŏnhyo ûi chôrhak sasang', in *Han'guk sasang sa* (A History of Korean Thought), edited by the Han'guk sasang yôn'guhoe (Association for the Study of Korean Thought), Seoul: Ilshinsa, 59–88. (A philosophical approach to the logical structure of Wŏnhyo's soteriological system.)

Park Sung Bae (1983) *Buddhist Faith and Sudden Enlightenment*, Albany, NY: State University of New York Press. (A thematic approach to the relationship between patriarchal faith and sudden enlightenment in the actual practice of Buddhist meditation.)

—— (forthcoming) *Wŏnhyo's Commentary on the 'Treatise on the Awakening of Mahāyāna Faith'*, Albany, NY: State University of New York Press. (A

translation and exegesis of Wŏnhyo's commentaries on the *Awakening of Faith in the Mahāyāna*.)

SUNG BAE PARK

WORK, PHILOSOPHY OF

Unlike play, work is activity that has to involve significant expenditure of effort and be directed toward some goal beyond enjoyment. The term 'work' is also used to signify an individual's occupation, the means whereby they gain their livelihood. In modern market economies individuals contract to work for other individuals on specified terms. Beyond noting this formal freedom to choose how one shall work, critics of market economies have maintained that one's occupation should be a realm of substantive freedom, in which work is freely chosen self-expression. Against this unalienated labour norm, others have held that the freedom of self-expression is one good among others that work can provide, such as lucrative pay, friendly social contact and the satisfaction of the self-support norm, and that none of these various work-related goods necessarily should have priority over others. Some philosophers place responsibility on society for providing opportunities for good work for all members of society; others hold that the responsibility for the quality of one's occupational life appropriately falls on each individual alone. Finally, some theorists of work emphasize that performance of hard work renders one deserving of property ownership (John Locke) or enhances one's spiritual development (Mahatma Gandhi).

1 Work versus play; work versus leisure
2 Work as occupation
3 Other perspectives

1 Work versus play; work versus leisure

Work is effort directed at some goal other than enjoyment taken in the experience of putting forth the effort. In contrast, play is effort that is not aimed at any goal beyond the enjoyable experience of that very effort. Work and play seem to differ further in that a threshold level of effort must be put forth before an activity is properly called work, whereas play either involves a much lower threshold of effort or none at all. Tying my shoelaces is not typically work, even though the activity is goal-directed, because the effort involved is too slight. Effortlessly twiddling my shoelaces for fun qualifies as play even though hardly any effort is expended. Another example would be a spontaneous expression of joy by dancing a jig or of sorrow by singing a sad song. These expressive activities are not aimed at enjoyment, rather at expression of emotion, hence they do not qualify as play. But if effortless or close to effortless, they do not qualify as work either. Another example of an activity that is neither work nor play is lying on a beach in order to get a suntan. Again the effort constraint seems to be operative. Of course, if sunbathing can be described as involving expenditure of effort, say, because one's body is becoming hot or one is bored and one must actively overcome the desire to leave the beach by an effort of will, then in these circumstances sunbathing can be characterized as work.

In the Book of Genesis, God punishes Adam for sin by condemning him to unpleasant labour for his daily bread: 'By the sweat of your brow shall you live'. In order to meet their basic needs many, perhaps most, people throughout history have had to work in ways that are onerous and unpleasant, recalling Adam's curse. But work can give intrinsic satisfaction without ceasing to be work. Of persons engaged in work one can ask: (1) would they prefer to gain the goal they are seeking without working for it (if that is possible)?; and (2) would they wish to engage in the work activity for its enjoyment even if the goal they are seeking could be attained without the effort of work? An affirmative answer to the second question indicates that the work has the quality of a fusion of work and play. A negative answer to the first question indicates working is partly valued for its own sake, not just as a means to a further goal.

Work in the sense of goal-directed activity is opposed to play. In another sense of the term, work refers to what persons do in order to gain their livelihood. Time spent at work in this sense – work as occupation – is distinct from time spent at leisure – the free time in which individuals may do as they please and which is not spent at one's occupation. A day in the life of an individual may be divided into time spent at one's occupation, time spent in nightly rest, time spent in nonoccupational necessary drudgery such as household chores, and leisure or free time. This division is not exhaustive, however, because hours spent at childrearing do not comfortably fit into any of the categories just listed.

2 Work as occupation

With the rise of market economies work as occupation has become organized primarily by means of voluntary contracts among individuals who are not deemed to be under prior social obligation to engage in economic cooperation. Owners and managers of economic firms hire individuals to work as employees on specified terms. The tendency of market economies has been to generate greatly increased specialization of economic function and task segmentation compared to earlier modes of economic organization. In the late eighteenth century Adam SMITH analysed this process of division of labour and its economic consequences. He described a pin factory in which the making of pins was broken down into many small separate tasks, each small task performed over and over by an individual worker. This division of labour increases the productivity of labour; more is produced with less human labour input. Smith expressed the concern that repeated performance of a small boring task would ultimately dull the mental faculties of the workers.

Towards the middle of the nineteenth century Karl MARX (§4) propounded an ideal of unalienated labour and criticized the capitalist market economy of the day for subjecting ordinary workers, the bulk of the population, to grim lives that revolve around alienated labour. A capitalist market economy is one in which owners of capital establish firms that hire propertyless workers to produce goods for sale. In Marx's conception there are four aspects to alienated labour. One can be alienated from one's own activity of working, from the product one creates, from one's fellow human beings at work, and from one's true human nature. According to Marx, the worker in a capitalist factory is the epitome of an alienated labourer. A paradigm example of unalienated labour would be that of a creative artist, one who enjoys the freedom to produce art in one's own way and exercises this freedom in ways that are satisfying, controls the disposition of the art works so created, produces in such a way as to establish community with those directly affected by these economic transactions, and is motivated to create art by the desire to serve the human community (ALIENATION §§3–5).

The unalienated labour ideal raises many questions. One is whether fulfilment at work should be made available to all members of society as a matter of justice, or is better seen as a prize for which all may compete but which only especially meritorious individuals will win. If the norm of reducing alienated labour is deployed to criticize the institutions of society, the question arises how one should measure the progress of society in this respect. (For simplicity, this discussion assumes the possibility of precise measurement.) One might rate society by the average level of unalienated labour among those in the workforce, or one might rate society by the level of unalienated labour enjoyed by the member of society who is worst off in this respect, or by some other standard. In societies as we know them, access to desirable conditions of work is unevenly distributed between men and women and between members of favoured and disfavoured racial, ethnic and religious groups. There are the questions of how to characterize the good of desirable working conditions and what would count as a fair distribution of this good.

Jobs can evidently score higher or lower on the different dimensions of the unalienated labour norm, and one may wonder which dimensions are ethically more significant. If my occupation consists of menial work such as licking stamps for a worthy cause to which I am dedicated, my work life may be on the whole very meaningful, even if the work activity itself is unsatisfying. Alternatively, an individual's occupation might consist of challenging and interesting tasks performed for an enterprise that manufactures shoddy products of little true social utility. If one's workplace is a cooperative owned and managed by its workers, employment provides the opportunity for democratic participation in policy formation. A job that is regimented and unpleasant might provide high pay, which gives the jobholder freedom to carry out any of a wide variety of richly fulfilling plans of life. Jobs provide varied packages of benefits and burdens.

Work as occupation can provide benefits other than those that figure in the unalienated labour ideal. Lucrative pay, mentioned above, is one. Where most people subscribe to the social norm that each able-bodied adult should be self-supporting, supporting oneself by holding a job, even an undesirable job, earns the respect of other people and bolsters one's own self-esteem. There is a flip side to the coin of social recognition through jobholding, however. Since jobs vary greatly in prestige, holding an unprestigious job confers low status that can erode the jobholder's self-esteem. Another potential benefit from jobholding is that a regular job gives structure to one's life and organizes one's daily schedule. No doubt fully autonomous individuals could give a sensible shape to their lives without this external prop, but many of us are less than fully autonomous, and benefit from some degree of imposed order. Also, most jobs provide regular social contacts with workmates and perhaps with customers of one's firm. These contacts can be pleasant or abrasive, but usually there is at least the opportunity for friendly human interchange, and sometimes opportunities develop for deeper bonds of solidarity, friendship and mutual aid.

Regarding work as occupation, philosophers have argued for opposed views of the obligation of society. One is that the responsibility for each individual's work life belongs to that person alone; there is no positive obligation of society to ensure good work for all. A second view is that opportunities for decent employment should be made available to all able-bodied adults. A third view is that the obligation of society is to provide each individual, so far as is feasible, freedom from the necessity to work by guaranteeing a basic minimum income to all individuals whether or not they participate in the workforce. The contrast between the second and third views reflects disagreement as to whether the necessity of working is a benefit or a burden and disagreement as to the validity of the social norm that each able-bodied adult is obligated to work for one's own livelihood.

3 Other perspectives

Philosophers have espoused perspectives on work different in kind from any of the views canvassed to this point. The seventeenth-century English philosopher John LOCKE emphasizes work as conferring entitlement to ownership of natural resources, particularly land, under appropriate conditions. According to Locke, an individual acquires ownership of nonscarce unowned land by labouring on it with the intent to establish ownership, and one sustains the right of ownership by continuing to work the land productively or by arranging for its productive use. Hard work renders an individual deserving of good fortune. Locke maintains that a more complex version of this story still holds true when land and other natural resources become scarce. The twentieth-century leader of the movement for the emancipation of India from colonial rule, Mahatma GANDHI, similarly holds that hard work for one's livelihood is a moral obligation and that working hard renders one deserving and morally virtuous. But in contrast to Locke, Gandhi upholds a norm of voluntary poverty and asceticism and recommends the discipline of hard work for its enhancement of the spiritual growth of the worker. In this spirit Gandhi urges the Indian people, and by implication all of us, to eschew modern industrial civilization and to earn our livelihood by hard work at pre-industrial, traditional forms of craft work.

References and further reading

Arneson, R.J. (1990) 'Is Work Special? Justice and the Distribution of Employment', *American Political Science Review* 84 (4): 1127–47. (Argues that society ought to provide opportunities for decent employment to all its members.)

Elster, J. (1988) 'Is There (or Should There Be) a Right to Work?', in Amy Gutmann (ed.) *Democracy and the Welfare State*, Princeton, NJ: Princeton University Press. (Argues against the claim that there should be a right to work in the sense of a right on the part of each individual in society to guaranteed employment opportunities.)

Gandhi, M. (1966) *An Autobiography: The Story of My Experiments with Truth*, trans. M. Desai, Boston, MA: Beacon Press. (Outlines Gandhi's ascetic philosophy and celebrates pre-industrial craft work.)

Locke, J. (1690) *Two Treatises of Government*, ed. P. Laslett, Cambridge: Cambridge University Press, 1960. (The chapter 'Of Property' in the *Second Treatise* is the classical statement of a liberal view of the connection between work and entitlement to property ownership in the context of a defence of the market economy.)

Marx, K. (1844) 'Economic and Philosophic Manuscripts of 1844', in Robert Tucker (ed.) *The Marx–Engels Reader*, New York: W.W. Norton & Co. (Outlines the ideal of unalienated labour and criticizes capitalist market economies for subjecting workers to alienated labour.)

Nozick, R. (1974) *Anarchy, State, and Utopia*, New York: Basic Books. (Expresses a libertarian view that repudiates any positive obligations on the part of society to provide desirable work opportunities for members of society.)

Parijs, P. van (1995) *Real Freedom for All*, Oxford: Oxford University Press. (Argues that so far as is feasible, society is obligated to guarantee freedom from the necessity of working to all its members.)

Walzer, M. (1983) *Spheres of Justice: A Defense of Pluralism and Equality*, New York: Basic Books. (Chapter 6 considers how society ought to distribute hard – in the sense of oppressive – work.)

RICHARD ARNESON

WRIGHT, G. VON *see* VON WRIGHT, GEORG HENRIK

WRÓBLEWSKI, JERZY (1926–90)

Jerzy Wróblewski was a leading representative of analytical legal theory in Poland in the second half of the twentieth century. Leon Petrażycki and the school of logical thought of Lwów and Warsaw provided his background inspiration. His approach to legal theory and legal science belongs, in philosophical terms, to minimalism, relativism and moderate reconstructivism.

Born in Vilnius, Wróblewski became involved as a partisan in guerrilla warfare during the German occupation of Poland, 1939–45, and was able to complete his education, taking a doctorate at the Jagiellonian University of Cracow, only after the defeat of Germany and the restoration of government in Poland. Immediately on graduation, he moved to Lódz to take up the chair in the theory of state and law there, remaining at that university (and serving a term as its Rector in the troubled years around 1980) until his death.

Wróblewski subdivides the tasks of legal theory into seven problem areas: the theory of the legal norm, the theory of interpretation of law, the theory of legal system, the theory of legal interpretation, the theory of the application of law, the theory of lawmaking, and the methodology of legal sciences. Norms he considered in linguistic terms, as part of natural language, giving a pragmatic analysis in terms of the speech acts from which they originate and through which they are interpreted and applied (see NORMS, LEGAL). His theory of legal system was Kelsenian in background, though he rejected transcendental reasoning and disputed the conception of legal order as purely dynamic, involving no possibility of logical derivation of conclusions from normative statements.

His most distinctive work was on the application of law, understood as the process of implementation of a legal norm by a state organ. His approach is marked by a painstaking and detailed analysis. He proposed what he called a 'decisional', as opposed to an informational or a functional, model of law-application. He analysed the problem of truth in judicial factfinding on the basis of evidence, paying special attention to the variety of evidentiary facts presented to courts. In relation to the application of law, he disputed a narrow positivism that treats enacted law as sufficient in itself to control decision-making, and he argued for the necessity of referring to evaluations and values in this process; relevant sets of values he called the 'ideology of application of the law'.

His interest in the rationality of legal processes extended to a concern with rationality in law-making and in the application of principles of legislative policy, using an instrumental conception of rationality based on the relationship between means and ends. As for methodology, he differentiated onedimensional from multi-dimensional models of legal science. The former treat law exclusively as norm or as psychological fact or as social fact; the latter (favoured by Wróblewski) treat law as an ontologically and epistemologically complex phenomenon, and therefore approach the study of law using a variety of methods, techniques and conceptual apparatus derived from different social and mental sciences.

See also: KELSEN, H.; LAW, PHILOSOPHY OF; LEGAL REASONING AND INTERPRETATION; PETRAŻYCKI, L.

List of works

Wróblewski, J. (1992) *The Judicial Application of Law*, ed. Z. Bankowski and N. MacCormick, Dordrecht, Boston, MA, and London: Kluwer. (This is Wróblewski's major work available in English, giving the main elements of the points discussed above, and exhibiting the author's logical as well as analytical proclivities. It contains a substantial bibliography of Wróblewski's main works, in the various languages in which he was competent.)

References and further reading

MacCormick, D.N. and Summers, R.S. (1991) *Interpreting Statutes: A Comparative Study*, Aldershot: Dartmouth. (This is a collection of papers by several authors on interpretation of statutes in a number of legal systems. Wróblewski contributed the chapter on interpretation in Poland, and had a decisive hand in helping to establish a common framework and methodology for the comparative study of interpretation. See in particular chapter 2, which he co-authored but chiefly inspired.)

MAREK ZIRK-SADOWSKI

WU FORMS *see* CONFUCIAN PHILOSOPHY, CHINESE

WUNDT, WILHELM (1832–1920)

The German philosopher, psychologist and physician Wilhelm Wundt founded the world's first psychological laboratory in Leipzig in 1879 – at a time when psychology was still generally regarded as a theoretical and institutional part of philosophy. This event typified his life's work and its reception in many respects. On the one hand Wundt tried to develop psychology as an independent science by defining its subject matter and methodology; on the other, he wanted to integrate psychology into the context of philosophy, cultural theory and history. With both attempts he acquired world fame and at the same time became a most controversial figure. Systematizing his approach, Wundt worked on a great amount of material in very different disciplines. He has been called the last philosophical 'polyhistor' in the tradition of Leibniz and Hegel, as well as the first modern scientist in psychology.

1 Life
2 Philosophy, psychology and science
3 *Völkerpsychologie*

1 Life

Wundt was born in 1832 in Neckarau, near Mannheim, and died in 1920 in Gro boten, near Leipzig. He studied medicine at the universities of Tübingen, Heidelberg and Berlin, and began his academic career as a research assistant of Johannes Müller and Emil du Bois-Reymond in Berlin. From 1857 to 1864 he was *Privatdozent* at the Physiological Institute in Heidelberg directed by Hermann von Helmholtz. Rejecting Helmholtz's materialism, Wundt's own physiological studies shifted to the theory of sense perception, which he conceived of as a deeply philosophical question. Furthermore, he began to lecture on anthropology, ethnography and natural history. During these Heidelberg years, Wundt changed from physiologist to psychologist, yet always orientated himself within a philosophical framework. After a professorship in inductive philosophy at Zürich, in 1875 he accepted a professorship in Leipzig, where he founded his famous *Institut für Experimentelle Psychologie*. Beginning as a purely private institute, it later became the point of departure for many international students who returned home to establish similar institutions. Wundt taught at Leipzig until his death, continuously developing and changing his system in a spirit of encyclopedic scholarship. Over the last twenty years of his life he worked out his *Völkerpsychologie*. As an old man he became the rector of Leipzig University and was accorded tremendous national and international recognition.

2 Philosophy, psychology and science

With Wundt, the psychological zeitgeist shifted from philosophy to science, yet, even as a scientist, Wundt never left philosophical ground. Beside his seminal studies in physiological psychology, he lectured and wrote on logic, ethics, epistemology and other traditional philosophical topics, drawing especially on LEIBNIZ and HEGEL, but also on Mill's methodology (see MILL, J.S.). It has often been overlooked that for Wundt himself 'experimental psychology' was only a particular way to tackle traditional philosophical issues – and to engender new ones. If he was himself an experimenter at heart, as Robinson notes, then he was surely the 'first philosophical psychologist spawned by experimental science' (1982: 129).

Although his *Physiological Psychology* was taken above all as a programme for experimental research, it also represented an attempt to resolve the mind–body problem. Investigating both physiological and mental phenomena, Wundt's basic intention was twofold: he wanted to overcome the traditional Cartesian dualism of *res extensa* and *res cogitans* without falling into materialistic monism. As he saw it, psychology studies particular events which cannot be reduced to a class of mere bodily events. Both physical and psychical processes exist 'side by side' but must conform to their own epistemological principles. Rather, historically and systematically, psychology draws upon these different approaches; its subject matter emerges at the point of contact of distinct epistemic spheres. Thus, Wundt's idea of psychophysical parallelism was a heuristic principle, not an objective law. The main distinction was not between mind and body, but between reasons and causes, that is, between forms of explanation adequate for different categories of events.

In calling the new discipline of this border region 'experimental psychology', Wundt wanted to place a major emphasis on the methodological characteristics by which he distinguished his approach from the traditional science of mind, which was based above all on introspection. Rejecting any idea of the mind as a separate spiritual or mental substance, Wundt believed it to be the totality of conscious experiences (and its partly unconscious emergence) at a given moment. He called this the 'actuality' of the mind.

Experiences, ideas and thoughts are active events – neither simple reactions nor things or impressions appearing in and disappearing from consciousness (as associationists and structuralists claimed). Will is the fundamental principle of mental activities. But there is no will without emotion. Inextricably interwoven, both intention and feeling organize the meaningful syntheses of all psychological events. Thus, Wundt called his conception of the mind 'voluntaristic', underlining the peculiar human quality of actively creating meanings.

Wundt designated the idea of a conscious focus of attention, which synthesizes the elements of experience and thought into larger units (*Gesamtvorstellungen*), the 'principle of creative resultants or synthesis'. This is closely linked to another key concept in Wundt's system: the concept of 'apperception'. Deriving from Leibniz and Kant, 'apperception' referred to the active synthesizing function of consciousness. Hence, it represented a central feature of higher mental activities, as it is responsible for all conscious constructions or wholes, such as thought, language, reasoning and judgment.

In adapting the methods of empirical, experimental and historical sciences to the questions of philosophy, Wundt wanted to create an integrated discipline of the mind. This was the content of his 'Heidelberg programme' of psychology which he only partly realized in the second half of his life in Leipzig (Graumann 1980). This programme consisted of: (1) the experimental study of human consciousness or mind; (2) the evolutionary history of mind; (3) comparative psychology (particularly dedicated to the analysis of ontogenetic and phylogenetic development).

Wundt's theory of the mind was a universal developmental theory. To understand the strong historic-genetical dimension of this conception (which for many decades had been widely ignored), one must take into account the influence of the two cultures Wundt wanted to fuse together: for the philosopher Wundt, the emphasis on cultural-historical development was a typical legacy of most German nineteenth-century philosophy since Hegel, Herder and the Enlightenment; for the physiologist and physician, the crucial event of those years – as it was for all life scientists – was the publication of Darwin's *Origin of Species* in 1859.

3   *Völkerpsychologie*

Wundt considered experimental psychology only as an elementary approach to the study of the mind. He rejected the idea that higher mental processes could be represented by a kind of mechanics of the mind parallel to physical mechanics. Physical causality (as investigated, for example, in the psychophysics of Gustav FECHNER (§2)) is only a quite limited aspect of human psychology which, as a whole, is characterized by a qualitatively different causality: 'psychical causality'.

To understand fully the psychological causality of the mind, it is not enough to examine the isolated consciousness of an individual, because in reality this is always embedded in a cultural web. These cultural mediations between the individual and the world determine the characteristics of the human mind. Therefore, we must expand the merely analytical framework of the individual mind and conceive of it as the product of a multilayered development. Ontogeny, natural history and social history are interwoven processes which demand multidisciplinary study. Wundt called this study of cultural development '*Völkerpsychologie*'. (The translation 'folk psychology' is misleading; better would be 'cultural psychology' or 'historical psychology' – in fact, Wundt also used both these terms.)

Völkerpsychologie is the comparative study of the products of social life in different historical periods and cultures. Wundt focused on language, custom, ritual, institutions and collective representations such as myth, art and religion. The great importance given to language as the central mediation between the individual mind and a culturally meaningful context was reflected in his psycholinguistic theory.

Like the 'Heidelberg programme' of Wundt's early years, the cultural-historical programme of the Leipzig *Völkerpsychologie* must be seen against the background of the tradition of philosophy of mind in German Idealism (see GERMAN IDEALISM). Wundt's thought was a Hegelian variant, as was the conception of *Geisteswissenschaften* of his contemporary Wilhelm DILTHEY; while a few years later, Ernst CASSIRER presented a Kantian variant in his *Philosophie der symbolischen Formen*.

Wundt believed that in order to complete individual psychology, the methodological spectrum had to be broadened. Like history, anthropology or psychopathology, *Völkerpsychologie* is based on the ability to immerse oneself in an alien state of mind and various stages of the cultural evolution of human thought. In the ten volumes of *Völkerpsychologie*, Wundt outlined an initial methodology of 'participant observation' which he thought essential to all cultural psychology.

While many elements of *Völkerpsychologie* were developed in disciplines such as sociology, anthropology and cultural history, Wundt's approach did not play a major role in mainstream psychology or philosophy of mind. In the behaviourist movement especially, it was completely discarded. Only since the 1970s has a new orientation in philosophy and psychology towards the mind yielded a growing interest in the cultural and historical mediations of mental development and thus in Wundt's work (see Bruner 1990; Jahoda 1992).

See also: DUALISM; INTROSPECTION, PSYCHOLOGY OF; PSYCHOLOGY, THEORIES OF §2

List of works

Wundt, W. (1862) *Beiträge zur Theorie der Sinneswahrnehmung* (Contributions to the Theory of Sense Perception), Leipzig and Heidelberg: Winter. (An exposition of Wundt's starting point: experimental analysis of the elementary psychological (not physiological) processes of perception.)

—— (1863–) *Vorlesung über die Menschen- und Thierseele*, Leipzig: Voß; trans. J.E. Creighton and E.B. Titchener, *Lectures on Human and Animal Psychology*, New York: Macmillan, 1894. (Wundt's first systematic treatment of the traditional philosophical field of 'mind', 'soul' and 'thought' from the point of view of an experimental and quantitative psychology.)

—— (1874) *Grundzüge der physiologischen Psychologie*, Leipzig: Engelmann, 6th edn, 3 vols, 1908–11; Part 1 of 5th edn, trans. E.B. Titchener, *Principles of Physiological Psychology*, New York: Macmillan, 1904. (A systematic account of the new scientific (that is, psychological) psychology, which deals with all areas of psychological life from the nervous system to thought, affect and intention, to anomalies of the mind. Volume 3 includes the exposition of a specific epistemology of psychology.)

—— (1880–3) *Logik. Eine Untersuchung der Prinzipien der Erkenntnis und der Methoden der wissenschaftlichen Forschung* (Logic: An Investigation of the Principles of Knowledge and on the Methods of Scientific Research), Stuttgart: Enke, 2 vols; 4th and 5th edn, Leipzig: Engelmann, 1919–24, 3 vols. (Wundt's systematic account of methodology, epistemology and philosophy of science.)

—— (ed.) (1883–1902) *Philosophische Studien*, 20 vols. (A periodical to which Wundt also contributed numerous articles.)

—— (1886) *Ethik. Eine Untersuchung der Tatsachen und Gesetze des sittlichen Lebens*, Stuttgart: Enke; 5th edn, 1923–4, 3 vols; trans. E.B. Titchener, J.H. Gulliver and M.F. Washburn, *Ethics: An Investigation of the Facts and Laws of the Moral Life*, New York: Macmillan, 1897. (An empirical and scientific analysis of 'moral life'; for Wundt the basis of all moral philosophy and metaphysics.)

—— (1889) *System der Philosophie* (System of Philosophy), Leipzig: Engelmann; 4th edn, 1919, 2 vols. (Wundt's systematic treatment of metaphysics on an empirical basis; at the same time it is shown that science always presupposes philosophical thought.)

—— (1896) *Grundriß der Psychologie*, Leipzig: Engelmann; 15th edn, 1922; trans. C.H. Judd, *Outlines of Psychology*, Leipzig: Engelmann; 3rd revised edn, 1907. (One of Wundt's most published and read works, summarizing his view of scientific psychology and its relevance to philosophy.)

—— (1901) *Einleitung in die Philosophie* (An Introduction to Philosophy), Leipzig: Kröner; 9th edn, 1922. (A historical presentation of philosophy and its development from Greek antiquity to the twentieth century, based on a series of lecture courses.)

—— (1900–4) *Völkerpsychologie. Eine Untersuchung der Entwicklungsgesetze von Sprache, Mythus und*

Sitte (Folk Psychology: An Investigation of the Laws of Development of Language, Myth and Custom), Leipzig: Engelmann, 2 vols; 3rd edn, Stuttgart, Kröner, 10 vols, 1911–20. (The monumental attempt to develop an all-encompassing cultural-historical psychology focusing on language (volumes 1 and 2), myth and religion (volumes 4 to 6), society (volumes 7 and 8), law (volume 9) and history of culture (volume 10).)

—— (1911) *Einführung in die Psychologie*, Leipzig: Voigtländer; trans. R. Pinter, *An Introduction to Psychology*, London, 1912. (A brief introduction to the psychology of —— (1914) *Leibniz*, Leipzig: Kröner. (Wundt's only monographic work on a philosopher, emphasizing his importance for the modern conception of scientific psychology and philosophy.)

—— (1912) *Elemente der Völkerpsychologie. Grundlinien einer psychologischen Entwicklungsgeschichte der Menschheit*, Leipzig: Kröner; trans. E.L. Schaub, *Elements of Folk Psychology: Outlines of a Psychological History of Mankind*, London, 1916. (A synthesis of the major themes of *Völkerpsychologie*.)

—— (1920) *Erlebtes und Erkanntes*. Stuttgart: Kröner. (Wundt's autobiography: the attempt to describe his life as a 'resultant' of cultural history.)

—— (1927) *Wilhelm Wundts Werke. Ein Verzeichnis seiner sämtlichen Schriften*, Munich: Beck. (A bibliography of Wundt's publications.)

References and further reading

Beuchelt, E. (1974) *Ideengeschichte der Völkerpsychologie* (A History of 'Völkerpsychologie'), Meisenheim am Glan: Hain. (The history of *Völkerpsychologie* before and after Wundt, in Germany, France, Britain and North America.)

Boring, E.G. (1957) *A History of Experimental Psychology*, New York: Appleton Century Crofts, 2nd edn, 318–47. (Boring, a student of Titchener, highlighted the significance of Wundt as an experimental scientist but dismissed the philosophical and cultural-historical aspects of his work. This was for a long time the dominant reading of Wundt.)

Bringmann, W.G. and Scherer, E. (eds) (1980) *Psychological Research, Wundt Centennial Issue* 42 (1–2). (The articles of these volumes offer a rather differentiated overview of many aspects of Wundt's life and work, pointing out its impact especially on American philosophy and psychology, for instance on William James.)

Bringmann, W.G. and Tweney, R.D. (eds) (1980)

Wundt Studies, Toronto: Hogrefe. (A selection of essays on Wundt's life and work.)

Bringmann, W.G. and Ungerer, G.A. (1980) 'An archival journey in search of Wilhelm Wundt', in J. Brozek and L.J. Pongratz (eds) *Historiography of Modern Psychology*, Toronto: Hogrefe, 201–40. (An overview of the numerous primary sources by and about Wundt in archives and libraries, and of major research projects on Wundt.)

* Bruner, J.S. (1990) *Acts of Meaning*, Cambridge, MA, and London: Harvard University Press. (Bruner argues that the study of human nature must be based on cultural psychology: developing the Wundtian approach after cognitive revolution and linguistic turn.)

Diamond, S. (1980) 'Wundt before Leipzig', in R.W. Rieber (ed.) *Wilhelm Wundt and the Making of a Scientific Psychology*, New York and London: Plenum, 3–70. (Diamond sketches the first forty years of Wundt's life as a period of scientific and philosophical formation; at the end of this period the appearance of *Physiological Psychology* suddenly made Wundt the most prominent figure in an emerging science.)

* Graumann, C.F. (1980) 'Experiments, statistics, history: Wundt's first programme of psychology', in W.G. Bringmann and R.D. Tweney (eds) *Wundt Studies*, Toronto: Hogrefe. (An account of the 'Heidelberg programme' of psychology developed in Wundt's seventeen years in Heidelberg. This program included the attempt to systematically unite the two disparate branches of the study of the mind – experimental individual psychology and non-experimental *Völkerpsychologie* – in an evolutionary and historical perspective.)

* Jahoda, G. (1992) *Crossroads between Culture and Mind: Continuities and Change in Theories of Human Nature*, New York and London: Harvester Wheatsheaf. (Outlines the history of cultural psychology, focusing on Enlightenment, German Idealism and – against this background – Wundt's conception of mind, *Kultur* and *Völkerpsychologie*.)

* Robinson, D.N. (1982) *Toward a Science of Human Nature. Essays on the Psychologies of Mill, Hegel, Wundt, and James*, New York: Columbia University Press. (Robinson locates Wundt along the intellectual coordinates of nineteenth-century philosophy. He presents the philosophical psychologist Wundt as a psychological philosopher who developed his system – 'a kind of applied Hegelian psychology' – at a time when the tensions between *Geisteswissenschaften* (humanities) and *Naturwissenschaften* (sciences) centred on problems of psychology.)

Wundt, E. (1927) *Wilhelm Wundts Werke. Ein*

Verzeichnis seiner sämtlichen Schriften, München: Beck. (A complete catalogue of Wundt's writings.)

JENS BROCKMEIER

WYCLIF, JOHN (*c.*1330–84)

John Wyclif was a logician, theologian and religious reformer. A Yorkshireman educated at Oxford, he was first prominent as a logician; he developed some technical notions of the Oxford Calculators, but reacted against their logic of terms to embrace with fervour the idea of the real existence of universal ideas. He expounded his view as a theologian, rejecting the notion of the annihilation of substance (including the euchar- istic elements) and treating time as merely contingent. The proper understanding of universals became his touchstone of moral progress; treating scripture as a universal idea, he measured the value of human institutions, including the Church and its temporal property, by their conformity with its absolute truth. These views, though temporarily favoured by King Edward III, were condemned by Pope Gregory XI in 1377 and by the English ecclesiastical hierarchy in 1382, forcing him into retirement but leaving him the inspirer of a clandestine group of scholarly reformers, the Lollards.

1 Life
2 Contribution to logic
3 Philosophical ideas
4 Scripture and human dominion
5 Influence

1 Life

John Wyclif was born to a Richmondshire (Yorkshire) family about 1330 and ordained in 1351. He made his reputation as a logician and natural philosopher at Oxford. Though his earliest logical works and *De actibus animae* (The Actions of the Soul) were unremarkable, his distinctive ideas emerged from theological study, in the several tracts of his *Summa de ente* (Summa on Being) and especially in *De universalibus* (On Universals), where he developed his distinctive theory of universals in logical terms, though not without theological opposition. Seeing the Bible as one such eternal idea in the mind of God and therefore an unchanging moral yardstick, he contrasted the ephemeral institutions of the Church with the absolute values instilled by scripture in the individual conscience, in *De civili dominio* (On Civil Dominion) and *De ecclesia* (On the Church). These

opinions made him numerous ecclesiastical enemies, while gaining him the temporary patronage of government and the lasting loyalty of a group of scholars. He went on to dismiss the doctrine of transubstantiation on logical grounds, an unorthodox view which forced him to leave Oxford for his Leicestershire living. In retirement, he produced a mass of repetitive controversial pamphlets and summaries. He inspired the Lollard scholars and preachers who supported him in translating the scriptures into English and in disseminating his ideas throughout England.

2 Contribution to logic

Wyclif's philosophical ideas were those of an accom- plished logician inspired by a Platonizing religious vision. His contribution to logic is primarily found in the tracts published as *De logica* (On Logic), written for theologians with a defective logical training. He expounded the logic of the Oxford Calculators, of whom Thomas BRADWARDINE, William HEYTESBURY and Richard Billingham were the most influential (see OXFORD CALCULATORS). Billingham in particular, whose lectures Wyclif may have attended in the 1350s, provided the basis for Wyclif's ideas of possible proofs of propositions. Wyclif proposed a fourfold division of proof: a priori, a posteriori, proof by reduction and proof *ab aequo*, that is, by definition and exposition or resolution of terms. This division was adopted and refined by later Oxford logicians (see LOGIC, MEDIE- VAL).

Wyclif also made a contribution to the under- standing of insoluble propositions which approached the modern notion of semantic groundedness. Furthermore, he rejected the nearly unanimous view of contemporary logicians that there were real *continua*, such as time, maintaining instead that these consisted of discrete instants, points and so on (see NATURAL PHILOSOPHY, MEDIEVAL). He saw such abstract concepts, or universals, as real entities, indestructible ideas in the mind of God, rejecting the linguistic thinking of contemporary logicians, whom he came to dismiss in later works as 'sign- doctors' (see LANGUAGE, MEDIEVAL THEORIES OF).

3 Philosophical ideas

Wyclif took a distinct view in his most important philosophical work, *De universalibus*, on the real existence of universals, to which his approach was again that of a logician. He set out his view primarily as an analysis of predication: how could Socrates *be* a man, and how could man *be* a species? Predication involved the notions of identity and distinction;

besides the traditional 'essential' distinctions of genus and species, he posited the 'real' distinction of entities with the same essence, like the persons of the Trinity, and the 'formal' distinction between the matter and substantial form of an individual, such as between God the Father and the divine nature. An individual 'participated' in a number of universals, being the end of a chain of inherence. The predication of a universal could presuppose a real and not merely a linguistic relation: as smoke signifies fire, and fire is thus predicated of smoke, so a real universal could be predicated of an individual (see UNIVERSALS).

It followed that if a real universal outside the accidents of time and space inhered in all substances, no substance could be destructible: God 'could not annihilate a creature without annihilating the whole created universe' (*De universalibus* 307), as such destruction would include the destruction of eternal intelligible being, a universal in which it inhered. Creatures subject to change and confined in place and time, being also ideas, must equally exist outside time, in the state Wyclif called *duratio*. Wyclif resolved the question of what distinguished two individuals in which the same universal inhered by positing a distinction in their different positions in time.

Wyclif's understanding of real universals seemed to him to resolve in an original way a great question of the schools, the relation of human free will (which he acknowledged like his contemporaries) to the perfection of divine foreknowledge. Though all human actions follow upon the will of God, still the unchanging will of God as to future contingent events may be determined by human volition at any moment. Since God's will is outside time, operating at once in the past and the future, events now may constitute causes determining God's will from the beginning of time. Human merit, therefore, may temporally, but not in principle, be prior to divine grace; grace must be necessary and eternal as it proceeded from God, and only contingent as it inhered in essences (see ETERNITY; FREE WILL; GRACE).

Some further, unorthodox theological consequences of real universals were more difficult to adopt, and Wyclif hesitated before embracing them. One clear consequence of his belief that substances could not be annihilated touched the eucharist. The doctrine of transubstantiation required that the elements, bread and wine, were annihilated and replaced by the body of Christ. Eventually, after attempting to reconcile orthodox doctrine with real universals, Wyclif rejected transubstantiation, maintaining that the sacramental elements remained in the consecrated host. This was a principal reason for the condemnation of his theology.

His view of universals, albeit couched in contemporary logical language, was at root a religious conviction formed under the Platonizing influence of Robert GROSSETESTE. Wyclif considered a proper understanding of universals the firm ground of moral progress, a prophylactic against moral relativism. Awareness of this marked a quantum leap (*gradus percipuus*) up the ladder of wisdom: 'error about universals is the cause of all the sin that reigns in the world' (*De universalibus* 175–7). His convictions gave him the strength to pursue their moral and political implications.

4 Scripture and human dominion

From about 1374, while Wyclif worked out what he saw as the moral and practical consequences of his ideas, he propagated them in countless lectures, pamphlets and sermons, and gathered disciples who carried out a scheme for an English text of the scriptures. He had already identified the Bible as a real universal. Faced with the problem of a corrupt text, he explained that 'intellection in the mind is more truly scripture than lines on a membrane' (*De veritate sacrae scripturae* (1377–8), i. 189). Scripture was a moral absolute, but operated internally as a guide, allowing for no earthly authority to interpret it.

On this basis, he approached the currently discussed question of divine and human dominion. The latter was merely contingent and relative, depending on its conformity with God's will in each individual case; there was no independent right of dominion on the part of ecclesiastical or secular authorities. Lordship was merely stewardship, and depended upon the state of grace of its wielder. Wyclif strongly emphasized the implications for the temporal possessions of the clergy; the consequences for civil government were only gradually recognized. His subjective political philosophy thus attracted some superficial support from the English government, but was explicitly condemned by successive church authorities. Together with his views on transubstantiation, it ensured his removal from Oxford and confinement to his role as the inspirer of a body of evangelizers.

5 Influence

As the inspirer of the Wycliffite English bible and of a programme of disendowment and purification of devotion, Wyclif had great influence in England, in Bohemia through the Hussite reformers (see HUS, J.) and throughout Protestant Europe in the sixteenth century. His logic circulated with that of other Oxford logicians in fifteenth-century Italy, as a set of texts for instruction. His more general philosophical works were much read in England up to the mid-fifteenth century, and played a subordinate role in the corpus of his writings copied in Bohemia; but they were forgotten in the general disfavour which the logic of the schools attracted after 1500, and when Wyclif's works began to be republished in the late nineteenth century, their importance and originality was not recognized. Substantial sections are still unpublished, including the important tract *De tempore*. However the significance of their contents was appreciated by several scholars, beginning with M.H. Dziewicki and S. Harrison Thomson (1931), who each edited some of his philosophical works, and by J.A. Robson (1961), Anthony Kenny (1985, 1986) and Paul V. Spade (1975), who all noted original features of his thought. Further study and editions of the remaining philosophical works are still required.

See also: LANGUAGE, MEDIEVAL THEORIES OF; TRINITY; UNIVERSALS

List of works

Wyclif, John (1368–9) *De actibus animae* (On The Actions of the Soul), ed. M.H. Dziewicki, London: Trubner, for the Wyclif Society, 1902. (The only surviving account of Wyclif's earliest philosophical thought.)

—— (1368–9) *De ente praedicamentali* (On Categorial Being), ed. R. Beer, London: Trubner, for the Wyclif Society, 1901. (Develop's Wyclif's views of quality and quantity.)

—— (1368–9) *Summa insolubilium* (Summary of Insoluble Propositions), ed. P.V. Spade and G.A. Wilson, Binghamton, NY: Medieval and Renaissance Texts and Studies, 1986. (Contains the fullest discussion of Wyclif's logic of insolubles.)

—— (1371–2) *Summa de ente libri primi tractatus primus et secundus* (Summary on Being, Book I, Tracts 1 and 2), ed. S.H. Harrison Thomson, Oxford, 1930. (Wyclif's first ideas on universals.)

—— (1371–3) *Tractatus de logica* (On Logic), ed. M.H. Dziewicki, London: Trubner, for the Wyclif Society, 1893. (An extended treatment of Wyclif's logic for the use of theologians.)

—— (1371–4) *De ente* (On Being), ed. M.H. Dziewicki, London: C.K. Paul, for the Wyclif Society, 1909. (Further development of Wyclif's ideas on being and universals.)

—— (1371–4) *De trinitate* (On The Trinity), ed. A. du Pont Breck, Boulder, CO: University of Colorado Press, 1962. (Wyclif's idea of God in the light of his theory of universals.)

—— (1374) *Tractatus de universalibus* (Treatise on Universals), ed. I.J. Mueller, Oxford: Clarendon

Press, 1985; trans. A. Kenny, *On Universals*, Oxford: Clarendon Press, 1985. (Wyclif's final and full ideas on universals.)

—— (1375–7) *De civili dominio* (On Civil Dominion), ed. R.L. Poole and J. Loserth, London: Trubner, for the Wyclif Society, 1885–1904. (Wyclif's theory of dominion and his answer to his critics.)

—— (1377–8) *De veritate sacrae scripturae* (The Truth of Holy Scripture), ed. R. Buddensieg, London: Trubner, for the Wyclif Society, 1905–7. (Wyclif's application of his idea of universals to scripture.)

—— (1378) *De ecclesia* (On The Church), ed. J. Loserth, London: Trubner, for the Wyclif Society, 1886. (Wyclif's theory of the visible and invisible church.)

—— (1380–3) *De eucharistia* (On The Eucharist), ed. J. Loserth, London: Trubner, for the Wyclif Society, 1892. (Wyclif's final views on transubstantiation.)

References and further reading

Ashworth, E.J. and Spade, P.V. (1992) 'Logic in Late Mediaeval Oxford', in J.I. Catto and T.A.R. Evans (eds) *The History of the University of Oxford*, Oxford: Clarendon Press, vol. 2, 35–64. (Discusses Wyclif's logic in historical context.)

Catto, J.I. (1992) 'Wyclif and Wycliffism in Oxford, 1356–1430', in J.I. Catto and T.A.R. Evans (eds) *The History of the University of Oxford*, Oxford: Clarendon Press, vol. 2, 175–261. (A comprehensive survey of Wyclif's and his academic contemporaries' ideas and activities.)

Hudson, A. (1988) *The Premature Reformation*, Oxford: Clarendon Press. (A full study of Wycliffite popular thought and its influence.)

* Kenny, A. (1985) *Wyclif*, Oxford: Clarendon Press. (An admirably clear exposition of Wyclif's philosophy.)

* —— (ed.) (1986) *Wyclif in his Times*, Oxford: Clarendon Press. (Contains excellent essays on Wyclif's thought and influence by Anne Hudson, Maurice Keen, Anthony Kenny, Norman Kretzmann and Gordon Leff.)

Mallard, W. (1961) 'John Wyclif and the Tradition of Biblical Authority', *Church History* 30: 50–60. (A clear summary of Wyclif's view on scripture.)

* Robson, J.A. (1961) *Wyclif and the Oxford Schools*, Cambridge: Cambridge University Press. (The best description and analysis in context of Wyclif's philosophy.)

Stalder, R. (1962) 'Le concept de l'église selon le "de Ecclesia" de Wiclif' (The Concept of the Church in Wyclif's *De ecclesia*), *Bijdragen. Tijdschrift voor Filosofie en Theologie* 22: 38–81, 287–302. (The best exposition of Wyclif's notion of church authority.)

* Spade, P.V. (1975) *The Mediaeval Liar*, Toronto, Ont.: Pontifical Institute of Mediaeval Studies. (Discusses the literature, including that of Wyclif, on insoluble propositions.)

* Thomson, S.H. (1931) 'The Philosophical Basis of Wyclif's Theology', *Journal of Religion* 11: 86–116. (The pioneering essay on Wyclif's philosophical ideas.)

Thomson, W.R. (1983) *The Latin Writings of John Wyclyf: an Annotated Catalog*, Toronto: Pontifical Institute of Medieval Studies. (A full bibliography of Wyclif's Latin works.)

Workman, H.B. (1926) *John Wyclif*, Oxford: Clarendon Press, 2 vols. (The most modern biography and a comprehensive study.)

JEREMY CATTO

X

XENOCRATES (396–314 BC)

The Greek philosopher Xenocrates was the third head of the Platonic Academy. Like his predecessor Speusippus, he further developed Plato's philosophy, but along more orthodox lines. Indeed, Xenocrates contributed much to the formalization of Plato's philosophy into dogma. Starting from a metaphysical system of Monad and Dyad, the former being a self-contemplating intellect on the Aristotelian model and the latter a material principle, he systematically derived the rest of creation, postulating first the generation of number, and then soul, defined as 'self-moving number'. He is notable for a tendency towards triadic divisions of the universe, and a developed theory of daemons. He was probably responsible for the first definitive edition of Plato's works.

1 Life and works
2 Metaphysics and cosmology
3 Ethics and logic

1 Life and works

Xenocrates was a native of Chalcedon, on the Bosporus. He succeeded to the headship of the Platonic Academy in 339 BC, on the death of SPEUSIPPUS (see ACADEMY). He had been a member of the Academy since early youth, and had accompanied Plato to Sicily, presumably on Plato's second or third visit (see PLATO §1). He continued in the headship to his death, when he was succeeded by Polemo.

Xenocrates is credited with being the first to distinguish formally between the three branches of philosophy that comprise physics (including metaphysics), ethics (including politics) and logic (fr. 1 Heinze, fr. 82 Isnardi Parente; Xenocrates' fragments appear in two separate editions, cited below as 'H' and 'IP', respectively) – although Aristotle does seem to make the distinction in *Topics* I 14. Seventy-six works of his are listed by the biographer Diogenes Laertius, covering all of these fields, the most important being *On Nature* in six volumes, *On Wisdom* (*sophia*) also in six books, *On Being, On Fate, On Virtue, On Forms, On the Gods, On the Soul, On the Good, Solution of Logical Problems* (ten volumes) and *On Genera and Species*. He also wrote on Pythagoreans and on numbers, which indicates a continuation of Speusippus' interest in these areas. All of his works have perished, apart from a short extract from his *Life of Plato* (fr. 53 H, frs 264–6 IP), attributing to Plato a doctrine of five (instead of the usual four) elements, on the basis of an interpretation of the *Timaeus*.

2 Metaphysics and cosmology

As first principles, like Plato and Speusippus, Xenocrates postulated a pair, which he seems to have termed Monad and Dyad (fr. 15 H, fr. 213 IP), the latter a principle of multiplicity and unlimitedness (fr. 68 H, fr. 188 IP). Xenocrates also identifies his second principle as matter (fr. 28 H, fr. 101 IP). What we seem to have here is a 'female' principle manifesting itself sequentially at various levels of reality, rather like that of Speusippus. As regards the Monad, however, Xenocrates differs significantly from Speusippus in declaring it to be an intellect, or *nous* (fr. 16 H, fr. 214 IP) – possibly in reaction to Aristotle's criticisms of Speusippus. At any rate, the essentially Aristotelian concept of a self-contemplating divine intellect is that which is dominant in all subsequent 'official' Platonism up to Plotinus.

Another point of difference between Xenocrates and his predecessors seems, if we accept the view of Theophrastus (*Metaphysics* 6a23–), to have been the comprehensiveness of his attempt to derive the totality of existence from his first principles. The doxographic report in fragment 15 H (fr. 213 IP) tends to confirm this, although it contains problems: it is not even clear whether Xenocrates intends his Monad to be transcendent or immanent, while the Dyad, unless the text is to be amended, is presented as identical with the world-soul, which it should not be, since we learn from Plutarch (*On the Creation of Soul* 1012d–e) that for Xenocrates the world-soul is the product of Monad and Dyad.

Xenocrates first derived number from the Monad and Dyad, then point, line, plane and solid from number – or perhaps from the first four numbers, the Pythagorean *tetraktys* (see PYTHAGOREANISM §2). This involved him in the troublesome doctrine of indivisible lines (and planes and solids), which is criticized in the pseudo-Aristotelian work *On Indivisible Lines* (frs 41–9 H, frs 123–47 IP) (see ATOMISM, ANCIENT).

As regards the Platonic theory of Forms, Xeno-crates is reported as going the opposite way to Speusippus, abandoning the 'mathematicals' while Speusippus dismissed the Platonic ideal numbers, but this is doubtless an oversimplification. Aristotle asserts that Xenocrates postulated only Forms, which he identified with numbers (fr. 34 H, frs 103–12 IP). Although mathematical entities, the Forms are still causes of sensible particulars. Xenocrates is on record (fr. 30 H, fr. 94 IP) as defining a Form as 'the paradigmatic cause of regular natural phenomena', a definition intended to rule out forms of artificial objects and things contrary to nature (*ta para physin*). This became the standard definition in later Platonism. As to the location of the Forms, since the Monad is an intellect, and an intellect must think, it seems not unreasonable to trace the later Platonic doctrine of the Forms as the thoughts of god back to Xenocrates, but we have no evidence on this point (see PLATONISM, EARLY AND MIDDLE (§3) for a more detailed discussion of Form-numbers).

Soul he defined as 'a self-moving number' (fr. 60 H, frs. 176–87 IP). We learn from Plutarch's *On the Creation of Soul* that Xenocrates gave a description of the formation of the soul that was simply a development of the creation of number (and thus of Forms) (fr. 68 H, fr. 188 IP). Basing himself on Plato's account of the soul's components in *Timaeus*, he takes the 'indivisible substance' as the Monad and the 'divisible substance' as the Dyad. Their mixture results in number, but not yet soul. It lacks 'motion', the defining characteristic of soul. This is supplied by the elements of sameness and otherness, the former representing stability, the latter motion and change.

A notable feature of Xenocrates' physics is his triadic division of reality into intelligible, sensible and 'opinable' realms, this last comprising the heavens, the contents of which are visible, but their nature only cognizable by reasoning (fr. 5 H, fr. 83 IP). A rather different, and more peculiar, triadic division is reported by Plutarch (fr. 56 H, fr. 61 IP), involving different degrees of 'density', combined with various of the four elements.

Xenocrates had a developed doctrine of daemons (see PLATONISM, EARLY AND MIDDLE §7), about which we learn much, again, from Plutarch (fr. 23 H, frs 222–3 IP). Again, mathematics is involved, since daemons are declared analogous to isosceles triangles, intermediate between the equilateral triangles of the gods and the scalene triangles proper to humanity. He postulated evil daemons as well as good, as an explanation for all the nasty aspects of religion such as ritual obscenity and human sacrifice (fr. 25 H, frs 229–30 IP).

3 Ethics and logic

On ethics Xenocrates wrote a good deal, but not much that is distinctive survives. He defined happiness (see EUDAIMONIA) as 'the possession of the excellence (*arēte*) proper to us, and of the power subservient to it' (fr. 77 H, fr. 232 IP). He agreed with Aristotle about the necessity of a modicum of bodily and external goods (this constituting the 'power' of the definition). He anticipated the Stoics by identifying the first principles of happiness as 'the primary natural instincts' (*ta prōta kata physin*) (frs 78–9 H, frs 233–4 IP) (see STOICISM §15–17).

In logic, he still maintained the Platonic system of 'division', together with the basic categories of absolute and relative (fr. 12 H, fr. 95 IP), rejecting the Aristotelian ten categories (see ARISTOTLE §7). In epistemology he recognized three levels of cognition, corresponding to the three levels of the universe (fr. 5 H, fr. 83 IP).

References and further reading
Cherniss, H. (1945) *The Riddle of the Early Academy*, Berkeley and Los Angeles, CA: University of California Press. (A useful discussion of Form-numbers, especially in chapter 2.)

Dillon, J. (1977) *The Middle Platonists*, London: Duckworth. (See pages 22–39 for an introductory account of Xenocrates.)

Krämer, H.-J. (1967) *Der Ursprung der Geistmetaphysik* (The Origin of the Metaphysic of Mind), Amsterdam: Grüner. (Pages 21–191 deal with Xenocrates, with a useful presentation of the evidence, although on a rather speculative level.)

* Xenocrates (396–314 BC) Fragments, in R. Heinze, *Xenokrates*, Leipzig: Teubner, 1892; repr. Hildesheim: Olms, 1965; M. Isnardi Parente, *Senocrate – Ermodoro: frammenti*, Naples: Bibliopolis, 1982. (Two collections of fragments with commentary, the latter including an Italian translation; textual references to fragments from these texts are H and IP, respectively.)

J.M. DILLON

XENOPHANES
(*c*.570–*c*.478 BC)

Xenophanes was a philosophically minded poet who lived in various cities of ancient Greece. He is best remembered for an early comment on the limits of knowledge, a critique of anthropomorphism in religion and an advance towards monotheism. The surviving fragments of his poems span a wide range of topics, from proper behaviour at symposia and the measures of personal excellence to the nature of the divine, the forces that rule nature and how much can be discovered by mortals concerning matters in either realm. Both Plato and Aristotle characterized him as the founder of Eleatic philosophy, a view echoed in the pseudo-Aristotelian treatise, On Melissus, Xenophanes and Gorgias, *and in ancient doxographical summaries. But in many of his poems Xenophanes speaks as a civic counsellor and inquirer into nature in the tradition of the philosopher-scientists of Miletus. While his one, unmoving, whole and eternal divinity bears some resemblance to Parmenides' 'being', in other teachings he anticipates the views of Heraclitus and Empedocles. His comments on divine perfection, the limited utility of the victorious athlete and the need to restrict poetic expression all foreshadow views expressed by Plato in the* Republic.

1 **Life and writings**
2 **Social criticism**
3 **Religious views**
4 **Natural science**
5 **Theory of knowledge**

1 Life and writings

Xenophanes is reported to have been the son of Dexios (or Dexinos or Orthomenes) of Colophon. In fragment 8 he claims to have lived in Colophon for twenty-five years before leaving to spend the next sixty-seven as a travelling bard 'tossing about the Greek land'. If we tie his departure from Colophon to the conquest of Ionia by Harpagus the Mede (in 546/5 BC) and accept the report of the historian Timaeus that Xenophanes lived in the reign of Hieron of Syracuse (478–467 BC), we may date his life to the years 570–478 BC.

Ancient reports of his contacts with other philosophers are few and inconclusive, but the reference in fragment 7 to a puppy which possessed the soul of a friend shows some awareness of Pythagorean teachings (see PYTHAGOREANISM §3) and the remarks about earth, sun, sea, waters and rainbow in fragments 27–32 display an interest in matters investigated by the Milesians. Herodotus (I 74) reports Xenophanes' 'admiration' or 'wonder' (or perhaps 'amazement') regarding Thales' successful prediction of a solar eclipse (see THALES §1); Heraclitus' fragment 40 disparages him as a (mere) polymath; and Empedocles' fragment 39 challenges the view of the earth's 'unlimited' depths expressed in Xenophanes' fragment 28.

Xenophanes wrote in verse, a fact which reflects both his chosen profession and an age that drew no sharp distinction between poet, sage and teacher. Most of his poems eschew complex argument in favour of simple and emphatic dissent (the Greek words *de* and *alla* – both meaning 'but' – appear often), but fragments 2, 15, 30, 34 and 38 employ hypothetical suppositions or 'thought experiments' to establish unnoticed contrasts and connections, and the different aspects of his teachings can be placed within a coherent overall scheme. He is the first Greek philosopher for whom an appreciable body of work has survived, but his difficult terminology and phrasing, along with the conflicting ancient testimonia, have spawned radically different interpretations of his teachings and sharply divergent appraisals of his importance as a thinker.

2 Social criticism

The material contained in five fragments (1, 5, 8, 22 and 45) appears to have been composed for performance at symposia; seven others (2, 3, 4, 6, 7, 20 and 21) mention individuals or issues suitable for discussion in such a setting. Although often considered of little philosophical interest, these verses establish Xenophanes in a role subsequently assumed by Heraclitus and Socrates – the philosopher as civic gadfly.

The detailed description of a wholesome banquet scene with which fragment 1 opens prepares the way for a concluding injunction to a parallel purity in speech and conduct, particularly in the songs sung on such festive occasions. Xenophanes' disapproval of the old stories of divine warfare and factional strife reflects the concern for the wellbeing of the city evident in his criticisms of the honours lavished on athletes (fr. 2), the luxurious lifestyle of the citizens of old Colophon (fr. 3), the stories told about the gods by Homer and Hesiod (frs 11–12) and Homer's exalted status as the educator of Greece (fr. 10). His description of himself as a travelling counsellor (frs 8 and 45), a reference to the Lydians as the inventors of coinage (fr. 4), a preferred method of wine-mixing (fr. 5) and a listing of topics suitable for discussion at symposia (fr. 22) reflect similar concerns.

Since Xenophanes lived before the time of the SOPHISTS he had nothing to say on the many questions their sceptical and relativist views generated. Nevertheless, a number of his teachings – that the divine is incapable of immoral conduct, that wealth and luxury pose a threat to the survival of the city, that a civic good outweighs any individual good, and that the songs sung by poets must be censored for the sake of the city's welfare – survive in the work of Plato and Aristotle.

3 Religious views

Since 'greatness' for a Greek god typically meant 'greatness in power and honour' (Homer, *Iliad* II 412 and *Odyssey* V 4), Xenophanes' assertion that 'one god is greatest among gods and men' (fr. 23) helps to explain a number of his remarks about god's powers and perfections: god's capacity to shake 'all things' simply by thinking (fr. 25); the 'whole' character of god's thinking and perceiving (fr. 24); the degree of seemliness appropriate to god (fr. 26); various denials of divine births, bodies and voices (frs 14 and 23); the call to honour the gods (fr. 1); and the repudiation of the poets' tales (frs 1, 11 and 12). While the 'one greatest god' of Xenophanes embodies some qualities popularly ascribed to Zeus, his unchanging and isolated form of existence (according to frs 25 and 26) rules out many other popular beliefs – for example, that a god might reside in pine branches (fr. 17), that gods intimate their intentions to mortals (fr. 18, A52); and that the sun, sea, earth, moon and rainbow are themselves gods or goddesses (frs 30–32, A39, 41–6).

Xenophanes' repeated use of the plural 'gods' has sparked debate concerning the depth of his monotheism. Fragment 23 speaks merely of one *greatest* god, and it was the immoral conduct of Homer's and Hesiod's gods that prompted Xenophanes' criticism, not their plurality. We may also reasonably doubt 'whether a convinced monotheist in an unreceptive polytheistic society would cloud the issue by a mention of plural gods which is at best ambiguous in the very context in which he is stating his revolutionary view' (Stokes 1971: 76).

Fragment 16 asserts that 'Ethiopians [say that their gods are] snub-nosed and black/Thracians [that theirs are] blue-eyed and red-haired' (similarly, fr. 15: '...if horses or oxen or lions had hands...horses would draw the figures of the gods as similar to horses and the oxen as similar to oxen...'). It is not clear whether these famous remarks were meant to refute all anthropomorphic conceptions of the gods, or merely to explain how the gods came to have the qualities popularly ascribed to them (that is, rightly or wrongly, people always assume that the gods are like themselves). Fragment 34 concedes that even unintelligent opinion occasionally enshrines the truth (see §5) and, since a different bodily feature is mentioned in each case, fragment 16 does not actually point to inconsistencies in popular views of the gods.

Later doxographical summaries report that Xenophanes identified god with the entire (spherical) physical universe, but many scholars consider the doxographers' accounts to have been inspired mainly by Plato's and Aristotle's loose identifications of Xenophanes as the founder of Eleatic thought, and the practice of crediting the putative founder of a school with discoveries made by his followers.

4 Natural science

The seriousness of Xenophanes' interest in natural science has been generally discounted, in part as a consequence of the bizarre character of some of the views ascribed to him and also (as in the case of Aristotle) because his real interests were assumed to lie elsewhere. But neither of these lines of thinking can withstand scrutiny.

Fragment 29 gives earth and water as his dualist response to the 'basic substance' question raised by the Milesians. Fragments 27–33 and testimonia A1, 32, 33 and 36–48 all address standard Ionian scientific topics. Fragment 18 asserts in part that 'as mortals search they discover (a) better', and A33 (from Hippolytus) reports that Xenophanes based his theory of periodic flooding on the discovery of fossilized sea creatures at inland locations. The view of all atmospheric and celestial phenomena as essentially 'cloud' (see A38–41 and 43–6) fits nicely with the description of 'great sea' in fragment 30 as the source of all winds, clouds and waters, together with the view of fragment 27 that 'all things come from and return to (the) earth'. The breadth of Xenophanes' scientific interests, his evident appreciation of the value of inquiry and observation, and the internal coherence of his explanations make it unlikely that he pursued scientific inquiry merely to acquire a weapon to wield against popular religion.

To charge Xenophanes with a belief in the earth's 'infinite' depth (fr. 28), 'infinite' worlds (A1), and the sun's 'infinite' travels (A 41a) we would have to translate *apeiron* by 'infinite' rather than the more plausible 'indefinite'. His eccentric view that the sun cannot shine without someone present to observe it (A41a) has been plausibly reinterpreted as the argument that since the sun is generated from rising moist vapours it cannot continue to exist in arid (hence unpopulated) regions. While Xenophanes' scientific understanding was deficient in a number of respects, he remains a central figure in the Ionian scientific revolution.

5 Theory of knowledge

Xenophanes' brief remarks about human knowledge were the subject of competing interpretations as early as the fourth century BC. Although sometimes regarded as an early statement of philosophical scepticism, they are best understood in the light of a traditional poetic contrast between the narrow scope of human experience and the synoptic view enjoyed by the gods (Homer, *Iliad* II 484–7; Semonides, fr. 1; Archilochus, fr. 70). Fragment 37 speaks in this vein when it links what mortals think to what they have experienced: 'If god had not made yellow honey, they would think that figs were much sweeter'. Fragment 36, '... however many they have made evident for mortals to look upon', suggests that what we can experience is neither unlimited nor entirely within our control. Fragment 35, 'let these be accepted, of course, as like the realities, but...', presents a similarly divided outlook: one should accept these (perhaps what Xenophanes presents as his account of the nature of all things) as true, but... (that is, certain knowledge exceeds our grasp).

In fragment 34 Xenophanes denies that anyone has known or ever will know 'the clear and certain truth (*to saphes*) about the gods and what I say about all things', adding (in yet another 'thought experiment') that 'even if one were to say precisely what is brought to pass, he himself would still not know'. Since other ancient writers linked the possession of knowledge of *to saphes* with direct observation (Herodotus, II 44; Thucydides, I 22.4; Alcmaeon, fr. 1), Xenophanes' argument can be analysed as a combination of a common view of the requirements for knowledge with the recognition that no account of the nature of the divine or the forces controlling the cosmos (including his own novel proposals on both topics) could possibly be confirmed on the basis of direct observation.

References and further reading

Barnes, J. (1979) *The Presocratic Philosophers*, London: Routledge & Kegan Paul, 2 vols. (Includes an idiosyncratic but philosophically stimulating account of Xenophanes' views and supporting arguments.)

Classen, C.J. (1989) 'Xenophanes and the Tradition of Epic Poetry', in K.J. Boudouris (ed.) *Ionian Philosophy*, Athens: International Centre for Greek Philosophy and Culture, 91–103. (An informative study of Xenophanes' diction and poetic style.)

Fränkel, H. (1925) 'Xenophanesstudien', *Hermes* 60: 174–92; repr. in *Wege und Formen frühgriechischen Denkens*, Munich: C.H. Beck Verlag, 3rd edn, 1968; a portion has been translated into English by M.R. Cosgrove, 'Xenophanes' Empiricism and his Critique of Knowledge', in A.P.D. Mourelatos (ed.) *The Pre-Socratics*, Garden City, NY: Doubleday, 1974. (An important study of Xenophanes' views on knowledge.)

Guthrie, W.K.C. (1962–78) *A History of Greek Philosophy*, Cambridge: Cambridge University Press, 6 vols. (Includes the most detailed and comprehensive English-language history of early Greek thought; Xenophanes is discussed in volume 1 pages 360–402.)

Heitsch, E. (1983) *Xenophanes: Die Fragmente*, Munich and Zurich: Artemis Verlag. (A full-length study of Xenophanes; contains Greek texts of the fragments with translations and commentary in German.)

Kirk, G.S., Raven, J.E. and Schofield, M. (1983) *The Presocratic Philosophers*, Cambridge: Cambridge University Press, 2nd edn. (A valuable survey of Presocratic philosophy; selected fragments appear in Greek with English translations; Xenophanes is discussed in chapter 5 pages 163–80.)

Lesher, J. H. (1992) *Xenophanes of Colophon: Fragments*, Toronto, Ont.: University of Toronto Press. (A full-length study of Xenophanes in English; contains Greek texts of fragments with English translations, notes and commentaries, translations of ancient testimonia and essays on various aspects of Xenophanes' philosophy.)

* Stokes, M.C. (1971) *One and Many in Presocratic Philosophy*, Washington, DC: Center for Hellenic Studies. (Contains a lucid discussion of the doxographers' accounts of Xenophanes' theological views.)

* Xenophanes (*c*.570–*c*.478 BC) Fragments, in H. Diels and W. Kranz (eds) *Die Fragmente der Vorsokratiker* (Fragments of the Presocratics), Berlin: Weidemann, 6th edn, 1952, vol. 1, 126–38. (The standard collection of the ancient sources, both fragments and testimonia, the latter designated by 'A'; includes Greek texts with translations in German.)

J.H. LESHER

XENOPHON (*c*.427–355/50 BC)

The Greek historian and philosophical writer Xenophon was a companion of Socrates, and is second in importance only to Plato as a source for our knowledge of him. He was also a penetrating and influential political thinker in his own right. He left Athens to embark on a spectacular military career in 401 BC, two years before Socrates' execution, and his military experiences had a deep impact on his thought and writings. An important historian and an innovator in literary forms, Xenophon limited his philosophical interests to political and ethical themes. Two questions are especially prominent: (1) What are the psychological roots of human virtue, and how can it be taught?

(2) What are the limits of and the prospects for human attainment of self-sufficiency? He develops these themes most fully in two major works that present two competing models of the best human being. His Memoirs *(usually referred to by the Latin title* Memorabilia*) presents the model of the philosophical life, mainly by recounting conversations between Socrates and a wide variety of human types. His* The Education of Cyrus *(often referred to by its Latin title* Cyropaedia*) presents the model of the political life, mainly by giving a fictionalized account of the rise to power of Cyrus the Great, founder of the Persian empire. Generally speaking, Xenophon seems in these works less willing than Plato and Aristotle to privilege the claims of philosophy over the claims of politics, and less optimistic about the power of reason to produce happiness. His works were highly esteemed by the Romans, as well as by such moral thinkers as Machiavelli, Montaigne and Rousseau.*

1 Life
2 Philosophical writings
3 Virtue and education
4 Self-sufficiency and the divine

1 Life

Born in Athens, Xenophon was in his youth a companion of SOCRATES. While still a young man he became an accomplished military leader, then in later life a distinguished prose author. He wrote two major historical works. The *Hellenica* covers political and military events from the late 400s down to the 360s. The autobiographical *Anabasis* is a pseudonymous account of his own greatest military success. It tells the story of how, although Socrates warned him of trouble ahead, Xenophon left Athens in 401 to join a Greek mercenary force hired by Cyrus, the younger brother of the king of Persia, for a campaign to take over the throne. (This Cyrus must not be confused with Cyrus the Great, founder of the Persian empire.) When Cyrus and the Greek generals were defeated and killed, the still youthful and inexperienced Xenophon was elected to take over leadership of the desperate Greek remnant, trapped in the middle of Asia Minor. He proved a brilliant commander, and saved the mercenaries by leading them to the Black Sea, where they met up with a Spartan force. His account of this expedition shows him a great tactician and skilful rhetorician. For obscure reasons, perhaps involving his Spartan connections, Xenophon was banished from Athens in the 390s, and subsequently served with distinction under the Spartan king Agesilaus. He did not return to Athens until the

banishment was lifted shortly before his death in the later 350s.

Xenophon's thought and writings were deeply influenced by his military experiences. He was also a devotee of the vigorous outdoor entertainments of Greek gentlemen, and wrote influential practical treatises on hunting and horsemanship. Perhaps because of these influences and interests, scholarly opinion in the twentieth century tended to cast him as rather conventional and simple, lacking in the gifts of intellect and imagination necessary for original philosophical thought, or for a real appreciation of Socrates. But Xenophon was clearly a very brilliant and charismatic young man, in talents if not in tastes a rival of Alcibiades, to judge from their achievements. His moral wisdom was esteemed by the Romans (Cicero recommended Xenophon to his brother as the best writer on effective political leadership), as well as by moral thinkers such as MONTAIGNE and ROUSSEAU, who shared his lack of interest in more theoretical areas of philosophy. His intellectual interests and achievements are perhaps best compared to those of MACHIAVELLI, who made much use of Xenophon. Both excel at thoughtful observation rather than theory construction, and both are model writers of clear, vivid and discreet prose, which often leaves their readers to draw out the lessons left implicit in their presentations of conversations and events.

2 Philosophical writings

After Socrates' execution in 399 BC, a number of his companions began to write reflections and remembrances about him, usually in the form of dialogues, and the style and approach of these 'Socratic discourses' defined them as a literary genre (see SOCRATES §§1–2, 7; SOCRATIC DIALOGUES). The genre came to include works in the dialogue style with protagonists other than Socrates, such as Cyrus the Great. Plato was of course far the greatest of the writers in this genre, but Xenophon was an honourable second. This is the literary context within which Xenophon wrote his most directly philosophical works.

Many scholars in the nineteenth and twentieth centuries have tried to locate the true, historical Socrates by comparing and contrasting the Socratic dialogues of Plato and Xenophon. This search has reached no certain results. Some scholars have claimed that because Xenophon was a historian he is likely to be a better witness than Plato; others declare that because Plato was a 'real' philosopher he could appreciate Socrates with a depth allegedly unavailable to the soldierly Xenophon. Neither position takes into account the peculiar nature of the genre of 'Socratic discourses', best summarized by Arnaldo Momigliano: '[B]iography acquired a new meaning when the Socratics moved to that zone between truth and fiction which is so bewildering to the professional historian. We shall not understand what biography was in the fourth century if we do not recognize that it came to occupy an ambiguous position between fact and the imagination.... With a man like Plato, and even with a smaller but by no means simpler man like Xenophon, this is a consciously chosen ambiguity' (1993: 46).

Xenophon constructed his Socratic writings with a view to thinking about the moral and political issues raised by Socrates' way of life. He emphasizes primarily what furthers his own thinking, not what gives a full or historical portrait of Socrates. Where he differs from Plato, the difference is more likely to reflect their different estimates of Socrates' significance than their different recollections of the historical Socrates. Both bend historical fact to the service of moral analysis.

Xenophon wrote six works in this genre of Socratic discourses. His *Apology of Socrates to the Jury* and *Symposium* appear to be responses to Plato's works of the same titles. The *Oeconomicus* is in part a response to the comic attack on Socrates in Aristophanes' *Clouds*. The *Hiero* is a conversation about political power between Hiero the tyrant and Simonides the poet. His two major philosophical works, the *Memorabilia* and *Cyropaedia*, focus on two philosophical issues: (1) What are the psychological roots of human virtue, and how can it be taught? (2) What are the limits of and the prospects for human attainment of self-sufficiency? Generally speaking, Xenophon seems in these works less willing than Plato and Aristotle to privilege the claims of philosophy over the claims of politics, and less optimistic about the power of reason to produce happiness.

3 Virtue and education

Xenophon presents both Socrates and Cyrus the Great as educators, and has much to say about their influence on others. His Socrates is presented in the *Memorabilia* primarily through the educational effect he has on his companions, while the *Cyropaedia* is as much about the education that Cyrus *gives* to those he commands as it is about the education he *receives* in his youth. In these works, Xenophon presents no general theory or scheme of education comparable to, for example, Plato's in the *Republic* (see PLATO §14). Instead, he emphasizes the many ways in which moral formation must accommodate the particular aspirations and even prejudices and vices of those to be educated. Through the contrast between Socrates and Cyrus as educators, Xenophon reveals a stark choice between two competing possibilities for human virtue (see ARETĒ), but without clearly privileging one possibility over the other. He seems more interested in exploring the ambiguities of virtue than in making a case for one type over the other.

Xenophon's Socrates influences others partly through precepts he teaches in conversation, partly simply through the force of his own example. The moral advice and example he imparts amount to commentary on the two great maxims inscribed over the portico of the oracle of Apollo at Delphi: 'Know thyself' and 'Nothing in excess'. In conversation, Xenophon's Socrates is a master of refutation (elenchus), like Plato's Socrates (see SOCRATES §§3–4). These conversations often demonstrate to Socrates' interlocutors that they are ignorant of what they must know to live up to their own aspirations. But Xenophon's Socrates is more willing than Plato's to offer explicit moral advice, at least to receptive young men whose pride has been humbled by refutation, and quicker to drop the pose of being a mere questioner who has no knowledge of his own. He teaches his companions to consider how much knowledge they must really have to prosecute successfully the projects they want to undertake, especially when these projects involve political power. The knowledge required turns out in part to be quite practical, such as how to guarantee Athens' grain supply or the productivity of the silver mines. But it also requires answers to more philosophical questions, such as whether a young man will benefit from wielding great power rather than being destroyed by it. Xenophon has his Socrates show how ambition often would be made less rash if forced to acknowledge such considerations. In addition, Socrates exhorts his companions and inspires them through his own example to an ascetic control over passion and desire. He presents his own ascetic way of life as the foundation of his freedom, and Xenophon makes this freedom the heart of people's fascination with Socrates. Indeed, Xenophon's portrait seems to give Socrates' freedom precedence over his wisdom, probably in conscious competition with Plato's portrait.

Xenophon's Cyrus is also a paragon of knowledge and self-control, but his example and his exhortations have an essentially different emphasis from those of Xenophon's Socrates. In general, Socrates improved the virtue of his companions by deflating their ambitions and reining in their desires. Cyrus instead convinces his followers that virtue is an indispensable means if they are to reach the ends of glory and wealth that they seek. The crucial moment in Cyrus' rise to power, as Xenophon presents it, comes when he convinces his Persian troops to pursue virtue, not for its own sake, but for the rewards that come from it. For this sort of education in virtue to take hold, it is absolutely necessary that the 'students' have vigorous desires for wealth and passions for power; such a psychological endowment is the fertile ground out of which Cyrus grows virtue, whether his own or other people's. Xenophon shows that this view of virtue creates a difficult dilemma for the leader: the very desires and passions that make talented people virtuous and therefore manageable by the effective leader also motivate them to become rivals for power. Cyrus is a master at using others' talents without undermining his own position of authority. The importance of this theme in the *Cyropaedia* explains why Xenophon's Cyrus is such an important point of reference in Machiavelli's *Prince* (see MACHIAVELLI, N.).

This tension between Socrates and Cyrus as moral educators reveals an ambiguity about the nature and preconditions of virtue that is also prominent in two of Xenophon's smaller contributions to the genre of 'Socratic discourses'. His *Oeconomicus* shows Socrates trying to convince the young and rather irresponsible Critobulus to take more care of his family's wealth. This treatise on the household was a popular classic with the Romans, but it might seem odd that it should also be a vehicle for exploring political themes about virtue. In the conversation with Critobulus Socrates makes explicit the connection between the themes: he claims that there is in principle no difference between governing a city and governing a household, a claim also found in Plato's *Statesman* (see PLATO §16). Most of the dialogue is taken up with Socrates' account of the teaching about household management of a gentleman farmer named Ischomachus. A critical component of household management as Ischomachus understands it is knowing how to motivate one's wife, servants and slaves to promote one's own good. In effect, Ischomachus looks for the same psychological endowment in these domestic subordinates that Cyrus sought in good soldiers: strong desire mixed with prudent calculation. Xenophon presents a politically more provocative version of essentially this same view of leadership and moral education in his *Hiero*, a dialogue between Hiero the tyrant and Simonides the poet about the costs and benefits of tyranny. Hiero complains that the best men in his city are exactly the ones most irked by subjection to his rule, and especially by the presence of his personal bodyguard of mercenaries. Simonides suggests that the tyrant can make himself more acceptable to these best men if he deploys the mercenaries to aid his subjects in controlling their own slaves. In other words, appeal not just to their desire for wealth or glory, but directly to their own interests in despotism. This will make the mercenary bodyguard palatable to the best men, even although it is the guarantee of their own subjection.

4 Self-sufficiency and the divine

Xenophon also considers Socrates and Cyrus in themselves rather than in their influence on others. This allows him to compare the highest achievement possible within the ways of life of philosophy and politics. For Xenophon, this comparison focuses on the extent to which the two ways of life achieve self-sufficiency (*autarkeia*). He conceives of self-sufficiency as a defining attribute of the divine, so that it is no mere figure of speech to say that Xenophon's two heroes represent two different paths to apotheosis. Here again, Xenophon is engaged in an examination that also engaged Plato and Aristotle, as well as the tragedians and Herodotus. And here too Xenophon refuses simply to subject the aspirations of the political life to a philosophical critique. Instead, he brings out the limitations of *either* political power *or* philosophy for living up to the aspiration to self-sufficiency. To a large extent, Xenophon opposes the position of ARISTOTLE (§26), who said that humans should not merely think human thoughts, but should try to be as divine as possible.

Xenophon's Socrates seems to believe that both paths to divinization, the philosophical and the political, are impious and based on a failure to acknowledge divine constraints on human ambition. He rejects outright the claims of natural philosophers that the study of the cosmos is humanity's highest accomplishment. He denies that they in fact have the knowledge of divine things they claim, and defends the Delphic view that 'Know thyself' takes precedence over any other investigation. To political ambition his response is more complicated. He fascinates his politically ambitious young companions because they see in him an image of the self-sufficient control over happiness to which they aspire. They are not sure how he does it, but they think that spending time with him will surely let them in on the secret. Socrates lets them believe this, and the tempting and teasing that result are at the core of Socrates' claim that his life is filled with *erōs* (love). Ambitious young men conceive an erotic passion for Socrates because they see him as the means to the knowledge, especially the self-knowledge, required by their political projects. Xenophon exposes the vanity of this passion by showing that, while in a sense Socrates does have the divinizing wisdom such men seek, it cannot be communicated or exchanged. Socrates' secure possession of the knowledge of what makes humans happy is ultimately supernatural: his wisdom is grounded in his 'divine sign', which is his unique prophetic endowment. This 'divine sign', a voice that occasionally gave Socrates advice and which is also reported by Plato, is crucial to Xenophon's understanding of how Socrates chastened the political ambitions of his companions. Socrates forced them to acknowledge that their own lack of this supernatural wisdom was an insuperable limitation to their pursuit of self-sufficient control over their own political success.

On this issue, too, Cyrus is the vehicle Xenophon employs to explore a less uncompromising view of the potentialities of the political life. His Cyrus does not have Socrates' sure access to divine guidance about which choices will prove beneficial or harmful. But he has the best 'political' approximation to the 'supernatural' divine sign of Socrates: he knows how to be his own diviner, so that he will never be at the mercy of anyone else's interpretation of sacrifices, omens or other signs of the divine purpose. Besides the useful information this pious dependence on divination provides to Cyrus, it is also a powerful rhetorical tool, for people are happy to follow a leader who seems to operate with divine favour. (The *Anabasis* shows that Xenophon was fond of such rhetoric himself.) Cyrus can then achieve a sort of self-sufficient control within politics that avoids the demands of knowledge that Socrates impressed upon his interlocutors. Thus Cyrus shows the farthest extreme of merely human control over success, a control whose limitations are brought into focus by comparison to Socrates.

List of works

Xenophon (*c*.390 BC) *Anabasis*, trans. C.L. Brownson, Loeb Classical Library, Cambridge, MA: Harvard University Press and London: Heinemann, 1922. (Parallel Greek text and English translation.)

—— (*c*.385 BC) *Apology of Socrates to the Jury*, trans. O.J. Todd, Loeb Classical Library, Cambridge, MA: Harvard University Press and London: Heinemann, 1923. (Parallel Greek text and English translation.)

—— (*c*.370s BC) *Symposium*, trans. O.J. Todd, Loeb Classical Library, Cambridge, MA: Harvard University Press and London: Heinemann, 1923. (Parallel Greek text and English translation.)

—— (perhaps *c*.370 BC) *Hiero*, trans. E.C. Marchant, Loeb Classical Library, Cambridge, MA: Harvard University Press and London: Heinemann, 1925. (Parallel Greek text and English translation.)

—— (*c*. 360s BC) *Memorabilia*, trans. E.C. Marchant, Loeb Classical Library, Cambridge, MA: Harvard University Press and London: Heinemann, 1923. (Parallel Greek text and English translation.)

—— (*c*. 360s BC) *Oeconomicus*, trans. E.C. Marchant, Loeb Classical Library, Cambridge, MA: Harvard University Press and London: Heinemann, 1923. (Parallel Greek text and English translation.)

—— (*c*.361 BC) *Cyropaedia*, trans. W. Miller, Loeb Classical Library, Cambridge, MA: Harvard University Press and London: Heinemann, 1914. (Parallel Greek text and English translation.)

—— (*c*.358 BC) *Hellenica*, trans. C.L. Brownson, Loeb Classical Library, Cambridge, MA: Harvard University Press and London: Heinemann, 1918. (Parallel Greek text and English translation.)

References and further reading

Anderson, J.K. (1974) *Xenophon*, London: Duckworth. (A useful account of Xenophon's life and times, with a typical twentieth-century prejudice against him as a serious thinker.)

Gera, D.L. (1993) *Xenophon's Cyropaedia*, Oxford: Oxford University Press. (A detailed study of the literary context and accomplishment of the *Cyropaedia*.)

Joel, K. (1893–1901) *Der Echte und der Xenophontische Sokrates*, Berlin: Gaertner. (In German, a massively documented argument against the historicity of Xenophon's portrait of Socrates.)

* Momigliano, A. (1993) *The Development of Greek Biography*, Cambridge, MA: Harvard University Press, 1971. (A short but pithy discussion of the literary genres within which Xenophon worked; chapter 3 is especially relevant.)

Morrison, D. (1987) 'On Professor Vlastos' Xenophon', *Ancient Philosophy* 7: 922. (A useful corrective to Gregory Vlastos' influential and dismissive attitude to Xenophon's Socratic writings.)

—— (1988) *Bibliography of Editions, Translations, and Commentaries on Xenophon's Socratic Writings 1600–Present*, Pittsburgh, PA: Mathesis Publications. (An excellent reference tool with a full listing of scholarly work on Xenophon's Socratic writings.)

Strauss, L. (1991) *On Tyranny*, New York: Free Press. (This seminal work contains Strauss' close and provocative analysis of the *Hiero*, followed by a brilliant exchange between Alexandre Kojève and Strauss over the contemporary relevance of Xenophon's thought; also contains a translation of *Hiero* more careful than the 1925 Loeb edition.)

Tatum, J. (1989) *Xenophon's Imperial Fiction*, Princeton, NJ: Princeton University Press. (A stimulating literary examination of the *Cyropaedia*.)

Vander Waerdt, P.A. (ed.) (1994) *The Socratic Move-

ment, Ithaca, NY: Cornell University Press. (A collection of essays on Socrates' influence, the following of which are especially relevant: P.A. Vander Waerdt's Introduction and D. Clay for the issues on Xenophon's literary and philosophical context discussed in §2 of this entry; D.R. Morrison and J.A. Stevens on the themes of §3 on virtue and education; and D.K. O'Connor and T.L. Pangle on the themes of §4 on Socrates and Cyrus as exemplars of self-sufficiency.)

Vlastos, G. (1971) 'The Paradox of Socrates', in *The Philosophy of Socrates*, Garden City, NY: Anchor Books, 1–21. (Vlastos' widely influential dismissal of Xenophon's Socratic writings occurs in pages 1–3, which are the focus of the rebuttal in Morrison (1987).)

DAVID K. O'CONNOR

XIN (HEART-AND-MIND)

In the West, questions of the distinguishability of mind and matter and of rationality and emotion or sentiment are central issues within the philosophy of mind. Neither of these topics is of much interest, however, to the mainstream of Chinese thought. On the one hand, the notion of qi, *the vital energizing field that constitutes all natural processes, renders discussions of the relevance of any psychophysical dualism moot. On the other hand,* xin, *normally translated as 'heart-and-mind', preludes the assumption of distinctions between thinking and feeling, or idea and affect. Xin is often translated simply as 'heart', but since it is the seat of thinking and judgment, the notion of mind must be included in its characterization if the term is to be properly understood. Indeed, what we often think of as 'will' or 'intention' is likewise included in the notion of* xin.

In the classical period, the heart (*xin*) as the seat of thinking is considered to be an organ similar to the other sensing organs, but with the advantage of being able to think: 'Organs such as those of hearing and of sight, being unable to think, can be misled by external things.... But the heart does think. Only by thinking will the answer be found' (*Mengzi* 6A15). Such a characterization is not, of course, unique to the Chinese; the classical Hebrews also believed the heart to be a seat of thought and action.

The interpenetration of idea, intention and affect expressed in the notion of *xin* entails the conclusion that thinking is never a dispassionate speculative enterprise but involves normative judgments which assess the relative merit of the sensations, inclinations and appetites that interpenetrate our experience of the world and ourselves. Since appetites and ideas are always clothed with emotion, they are to be understood, more often than not, as dispositions to act. (We have here some basis for understanding what is often thought to be the paternalistic desire of Chinese governments, from the classical period to the present, to protect the people from the 'disruptive' consequences of ideas.)

Another implication of the unity of feeling and thinking is the practical orientation of most of Chinese thought. If ideas are dispositions to act, what might be thought of as theories are little more than wholesale practical recommendations. Thus it is most difficult in Chinese cultures to find contexts within which the separation of theoretical and practical activities would prevail. When, for example, Confucius said, 'at fifteen my heart-and-mind was set upon learning' (*Analects* 2.4), he was indicating his commitment to an ethical regimen aimed at self-realization. Thinking and learning are, within the Chinese tradition, oriented to the practical ends of the moral life (see SELF-CULTIVATION IN CHINESE PHILOSOPHY). As Mencius observes: 'For a person to realize fully one's heart-and-mind is to realize fully one's nature and character' (*Mencius* 7A1).

Western people are accustomed to think of efforts aimed at moral perfection (see PERFECTIONISM) as involving a struggle between reason and passion, or between what we believe we ought to do and an obstreperous will that frustrates the enactment of that belief, or in the words of St Paul: 'The good that I would do I do not do, and the evil that I would not do, that I do.' In the Chinese tradition there is little such internal conflict involved in ethical development. The unpartitioned self characterized by *xin* means that it is unlikely that we should find Hamlets or St Pauls prominent among the Chinese.

If, however, the conflict associated with self-realization is not between heart and mind, what are the dynamics of moral development? If the problematic of unrealized selfhood does not entail the self divided against itself, what is the source and nature of the disturbance that the moral discipline is meant to overcome? If it is not located primarily within the soul, it can only be a disturbance in the relationships which constitute the self in its interactions with external things. 'The stillness of the sage is not a matter of his saying: "It is good to be still!" and thus he is still. He is still because none of the myriad things are able to agitate his heart and mind' (*Zhuangzi* 13).

It is precisely *not* through an internal struggle of reason against the passions, but through mirroring the things of the world as they are in their relatedness to us, that we reach a state in which 'none of the myriad things is able to agitate' our hearts-and-minds. In other words, we defer to the integrity of those things which contextualize us, thus establishing a frictionless relationship with them.

See also: CHINESE PHILOSOPHY; CONFUCIAN PHILOSOPHY, CHINESE; INTENTION; MENCIUS; SELF-CULTIVATION IN CHINESE PHILOSOPHY; SELF-REALIZATION; ZHUANGZI

References and further reading

* *Analects* (c. 4th–2nd century BC?), trans. D.C. Lau, *Confucius: The Analects*, Harmondsworth: Penguin Classics, 1979. (An authoritative translation.)
* *Mengzi* (c. 2nd century BC–2nd century AD?), trans. D.C. Lau, Harmondsworth: Penguin Classics, 1970. (An authoritative translation.)
* *Zhuangzi* (c. 4th century BC?), trans. A.C. Graham, *Chuang-tzu: The Seven Inner Chapters and Other Writings From the Book 'Chuang-tzu'*, London: Allen & Unwin, 1981. (The most philosophically sensitive translation.)

DAVID L. HALL
ROGER T. AMES

XIN (TRUSTWORTHINESS)

The earliest and basic sense of xin *is 'being true to one's word'. While one's words can be* xin *(that is, worthy of trust), in most cases* xin *indicates an excellence of character; it is thought to be the central virtue governing the relationship between friends. Since* xin *is primarily a virtue, its exercise involves practical reasoning and not a mechanical adherence to one's promises.* Xin *later was added to an original list of four cardinal Confucian virtues, though its status as a distinct disposition remained controversial. Buddhist thinkers broadened the sense of the term to include religious faith. This innovation in turn influenced certain neo-Confucian thinkers who then talked about the need to* xin *(have faith in) one's innate moral faculty.*

The basic sense of being trustworthy and reliable is well-attested in some of the earliest appearances of the character *xin*. In the *Zuozhuan* (Zuo Annals), a true and reliable worshipper is described as *xin* (Duke Zhuang, 10th year), as is a son who can be counted on to uphold and maintain his father's orders (Duke Xi, 7th year). In both cases, *xin* is used to describe someone who can be trusted to fulfil and not overstep their proper religious and ethical obligations.

In a variety of early texts, *xin* is linked with another character to form the pair *zhong xin* (loyalty and trustworthiness). These two virtues are seen as cognates: those who are *zhong* (loyal) steadfastly maintain their obligations, which makes them *xin* (trustworthy). Again, however, they are not 'loyal' and 'trustworthy' in a blind or mechanistic fashion. Their allegiance is to the moral way.

During the Han dynasty, *xin* was added to the four cardinal virtues of humanity, righteousness, propriety and wisdom (see ZHI; CONFUCIAN PHILOSOPHY, CHINESE §§5–6) first put forth by Mencius (*Mengzi* 2A6). This addition posed a problem for later Confucian philosophers, as the virtue *xin*, unlike the other four, was not associated with a corresponding nascent tendency of the human heart–mind. CHENG YI accounted for this asymmetry by regarding *xin* as a kind of meta-virtue which supervenes upon and emerges from the original four. ZHU XI believed that it was the ground or necessary constituent of the other virtues.

Xin was used as a verb to mean 'to believe or trust' (for example, in the *Daodejing* 49) and hence could mean faith in the sense of mental assent. However, since indigenous Chinese religion and ethics were strongly naturalistic, there was little room for a notion of 'faith' in the sense of *fiducia*. However, with the arrival of Buddhism (see BUDDHIST PHILOSOPHY, CHINESE), it came to mean 'belief' or 'faith'; in this latter, voluntaristic sense, in a teaching, text, order or deity. This is clearly its meaning in the title of Buddhist works such as the *Dasheng qixinlun* (The Awakening of Faith in Mahāyāna) (see AWAKENING OF FAITH IN MAHĀYĀNA).

This sense of *xin* as the attitude or spiritual virtue which provides one with the motivation to remain true to what is right and good is seen in later Confucian thinkers such as WANG YANGMING. Wang believed that all people are endowed with a complete and perfect moral faculty called *liangzhi* (pure knowing) which, given full rein, had the power to eliminate all misguided tendencies and steer one unerringly to what is right and good. The challenge was to generate a full and active commitment to follow one's *liangzhi*, a task which Wang once described as 'creating something out of nothing'. His advice to simply *xin* (have faith in) *liangzhi* is similar to the kind of religious faith familiar in Christian thinkers such as Luther.

See also: AWAKENING OF FAITH IN MAHĀYĀNA; NEO-CONFUCIAN PHILOSOPHY; CONFUCIUS; DAXUE; TRUST; WANG YANGMING

References and further reading

* *Zuozhuan* (Zuo Annals), trans. J. Legge, *The Ch'un Ts'ew with the Tso Chuen*, in *The Chinese Classics*, vol. 5, Hong Kong: Hong Kong University Press, 1970. (A translation of the *Zuozhuan*.)

PHILIP J. IVANHOE

XING

Xing is conventionally translated as 'nature' or 'human nature'. Some read xing *as meaning a heavenly endowed tendency, directionality, or potentiality of growth in the individual. On this essentialistic reading,* xing *is an innate and unchanging 'given', a defining condition of all human beings. Others have given a historicist interpretation of* xing, *reading it as an achievement concept rather than as a given. In this view,* xing *is derived from, and is a refinement on,* sheng, *denoting the entire process of birth, growth and ultimate demise that constitutes the life of a living creature.*

There is some controversy in the published literature on the meaning of *xing*, conventionally translated as 'nature', or 'human nature'. On one side, there are those who read *xing* as a heavenly endowed tendency, directionality, or potentiality of growth in the individual, and see it as similar to the Greek *phuo* (to grow) and the Latin *nascor* (to be born) (see HUMAN NATURE; ESSENTIALISM). On the other side, there are those who have an historicist interpretation of *xing*, reading it as an achievement concept rather than as a given. A.C. Graham (1990) takes issue with the simple identification of the classical Chinese concept of *xing* with the familiar conception of 'nature' as something 'inborn and innate', those qualities which a thing has to start with. His claim is that the dynamic thrust of *xing* has not been adequately noticed.

As a corrective on his own earlier work, Graham argues that early Chinese thinkers who discuss *xing* seldom seem to be thinking of fixed qualities going back to a thing's origin, but rather to the process of its maturation within a specific context. *Xing* thus understood covers the career of a person's existence, denoting the entire process of becoming human. Strictly speaking, a person is not a sort of *being* but first and foremost a *doing* or *making* and, only derivatively and retrospectively, something done.

If we were going to speculate on why terms such as *xing* tend generally to be more dynamic in meaning than their Western equivalents (which indeed seems to be the case), we might want to reflect on the implications of cosmogonic speculation, a signal feature of the Western tradition that is made important in this analysis by its absence in classical Chinese cosmology. Where something within a single-ordered *kosmos* is shaped and invested by an external originative principle, the most fully creative act lies in the creator's endowment of a given potential: the creature's subsequent actualization of that potential is derivative. Where a phenomenon is initiated by, and dependent upon, some externally derived or 'given' creative principle for the 'nature' of its existence and, put another way, where it is other than self-generative (*ziran*), the creative contribution of that phenomenon tends to be diminished. In the absence of cosmogonic beginning, on the other hand, the power of creativity and the responsibility for creative product reside more broadly in the phenomena themselves in their ongoing interactive processes of becoming (see TIAN; DAO).

The difference between the 'nature' of a thing in a cosmogonic tradition and its *xing* in a non-cosmogonic cosmology is suggested by the kinds of questions that each culture's philosophers ask. Cosmogonic concern generates metaphysical questions, a search for essential principles. How did the cosmos begin? What are its first principles? What are the fundamental elements from out of which it was constructed? What is the origin of the existence and growth of natural phenomena? The search is for the One behind the many.

Genealogical cosmology, on the other hand, will generate primarily historical and rhetorical questions: who and what are our historical antecedents that have given us our present definition? What are their achievements that we can appropriate to enculturate ourselves? How can we further cultivate ourselves so as to contribute to the appropriated tradition as it is embodied in our contemporary exemplars? How can we turn this historical and cultural interdependence to maximum benefit? The thinker's role in the non-cosmogonic tradition, then, will not be as much to discover an answer as to create a model of humanity that is persuasive, and that evokes emulation.

A related implication of this distinction between a cosmogonic and non-cosmogonic worldview is that in the absence of some overarching *archē* (beginning) as an explanation of the creative process, and under conditions which are thus 'anarchic' in the philosophic sense of this term (see ARCHĒ), although *xing* might indeed refer to 'kinds', genus and species as categories would be dependent upon generalizations made by analogy among *sui generis* phenomena. Difference is prior to identified similarities. Certain things to which *xing* is applied – water and rocks, for example – are not over their respective careers marked by growth and cultivation, and hence it makes little

817

sense to speak of them in terms of starting conditions and mature state. The *xing* of such things remains relatively constant. However, the human being – that phenomenon most given to cultivation and refinement – is a different case.

While the human *xing* might include certain generalizable conditions that define it at birth, in its more important aspects it seems to refer to what is existentially achieved. In defining the human *xing*, the relatively constant and uninteresting tendencies which constrain the creative project of personal development are outweighed by the massive transformative process that occurs between the 'stirring' or 'germination' of the initial fundament and the full-blown creative achievement. What is 'innate' in the *xing* of persons is simply the propensity for growth, cultivation and refinement. *Xing*, then, denotes a human capacity for radical changeability that is qualitatively productive.

Further, *xing* is realized *in situ*. It is a dynamic process conditioned by its particular context. Stated more explicitly, the human *xing* is a creative process that can only be understood situationally as the outcome of specific interdependent relationships. It at once refers to the continuing existence of a particular thing itself, and also to that in one thing which continues the life and culture of other things.

See also: ARCHĒ; CHINESE PHILOSOPHY; COSMOLOGY; DAO; DE; HUMAN NATURE; TIAN

References and further reading

Ames, R.T. (1991) 'The Mencian Concept of *Ren xing*: Does It Mean "Human Nature?"' in H. Rosemont, Jr (ed.) *Chinese Texts and Philosophical Contexts*, LaSalle, IL: Open Court. (A further development of A.C. Graham's analysis.)

Bloom, I. (1994) 'Mencian Arguments on Human Nature (*jen-hsing*)', *Philosophy East and West* 44 (1): 19–53. (A summary statement of the innatist position.)

* Graham, A.C. (1990) 'The Background of the Mencian Theory of Human Nature', in A.C. Graham (ed.) *Studies in Chinese Philosophy and Philosophical Literature*, Albany, NY: State University of New York Press. (A rejection of the innatist position.)

DAVID L. HALL
ROGER T. AMES

XUN KUANG *see* XUNZI

XUN QING *see* XUNZI

XUNZI (*fl.* 298–238 BC)

Xunzi is one of the most brilliant Confucian thinkers of ancient China. His works display wide-ranging interest in such topics as the relation between morality and human nature, the ideal of the good human life, the nature of ethical discourse and argumentation, the ethical uses of history, moral education and personal cultivation. Because of the comprehensive and systematic character of his philosophical concerns, Xunzi is sometimes compared to Aristotle. Noteworthy is his emphasis on li, or rules of proper conduct, and the holistic character of dao, the Confucian ideal of the good human life. He criticized other philosophers not because of their mistakes, but because of their preoccupation with one aspect of dao to the exclusion of others.

Xunzi (Hsün Tzu) is also known as Xun Kuang and Xun Qing. His fundamental doctrines are contained in the *Xunzi*. Like his predecessors, CONFUCIUS and MENCIUS, Xunzi focuses on developing a conception of a well-ordered society governed by an enlightened, virtuous and sagely ruler, a ruler who cares for people's welfare and moral character based on the cultivation of *ren* (benevolence), *li* (propriety) and *yi* (rightness, righteousness). The enlightened ruler is one who is good at organizing the people in society in accordance with *ren*, *li* and *yi*.

The *li*, as formal prescriptions or rules of proper conduct, are especially emphasized by Xunzi. While they represent an inherited ethical tradition, they do not always provide adequate guidance in the perplexing, exigent situations of human life. As markers of *dao* (the Way), 'the *li* provide models, but no explanations' (*Xunzi* 1, in Watson 1963: 20); basically they provide general guidelines delimiting the boundary of proper behaviour and individual responsibility. Perhaps even more important, the *li* 'provide for satisfaction of people's pursuit' of their individual desires or interest (*Xunzi* 19). In this respect, the *li* may be compared to the laws of contracts or of wills, enabling the agents to fulfil their desires effectively. Of course the key question, whether the existing *li* in fact perform their proper functions, depends on whether they satisfy the requirements of *yi* (that is, whether they are the right sort of rules) and the extent to which they ennoble human character in terms of *ren* (benevolence) and cultural refinement (*wen*) (Cua 1989) (see CONFUCIAN PHILOSOPHY, CHINESE).

For Xunzi, the regulative or delimiting function of

li is important in ensuring a good, stable social and political order. The necessity of the *li* is due to the problematic motivational structure of human nature. This is the force of his rather misleading remark that 'the human's nature is evil; his goodness is the product of conscious activity' (*Xunzi* 23, in Watson 1963: 157). In terms of its inborn motivational structure, consisting of feelings and desires, every human is a self-seeking animal actuated by fondness for personal gain. In the absence of regulative rules, this propensity may be viewed as bad or evil because it tends to lead to conflict and disorder in society. What is good is that which is 'upright, reasonable and orderly' and what is bad is 'that which is partial, irresponsible and chaotic' (*Xunzi* 23, in Watson 1963: 162). In addition, scarcity of resources to satisfy everyone's desires will lead to competition which requires *li*-regulation as well as a sense of *yi* (rightness).

In this light, inborn human nature is value-neutral, not intrinsically bad or evil but requiring regulation and moulding. This nature provides the basic materials for ethical transformation as does clay for the making of pottery. Indeed, in respect to human nature, the sage and ordinary humans are alike. Every man can become a sage: 'What makes the sage emperor Yu a Yu was the fact that he practised *ren* and *yi* and complied with proper rules and standards of conduct.' Moreover, the rationales of *ren*, *yi* and proper rules and standards can be known and practised by ordinary persons, because they possess the capability of obtaining such knowledge and acting accordingly. It must be admitted that not every person can actually become a sage, for they are not willing to make the effort, especially in moral learning (*Xunzi* 23).

Xunzi's essay 'Encouraging Learning' presents a sketch of his conception of moral learning as a continuing process that ceases only with death. Principally, the learning is devoted to acquiring knowledge of various classics such as the *Shijing* (Book of Songs), the *Shujing* (Book of Documents), the *Lijing* (Classic of Rites) and the *Spring and Autumn Annals*, as well as the established musical text. While recitation is stressed, Xunzi calls attention to understanding and insight concerning the concrete significance of these works in human life. Initially, learning to be an ethical person depends on teachers of exemplary ethical character, but this learning continues throughout one's life. The proximate objective is to become a scholar-official; the ultimate objective is to become a sage. Notably, the classics provide an introduction to what Xunzi considers as the best Ru or Confucian tradition. Xunzi's own writings attest to the importance of acquiring historical knowledge (Cua 1985b). Special stress is given to four different functions of the ethical uses of history in discourse: pedagogical, rhetorical, elucidative and justificatory uses (see HISTORY, PHILOSOPHY OF).

These uses of history provide a better guidance than religious beliefs and superstition about *tian* (Heaven) as dispensing fortunes and misfortunes (see TIAN). *Tian* is a natural order of regularities, not an order governed by a supreme, personal being. The proper attitude toward strange events or phenomena is wonder and awe (*Xunzi* 17). Practices such as prayer and divination are based on superstitious beliefs. However, the *li* or rites of mourning and sacrifices are ethically acceptable and, in fact, to be encouraged. Their significance lies in their function of satisfying human yearnings and providing an avenue for the proper expression of reverence, honour and affection for the dead. Moreover, these rites contribute to the Confucian conception of cultural refinement (*wen*) (*Xunzi* 19). Moral learning culminates in the attainment of completeness and purity, that is, a state of ethical integrity (*Xunzi* I) (see MORAL DEVELOPMENT).

Xunzi frequently uses the word *dao* to express his ideal of the good human life as a whole. The significance of *dao* as a generic term lies in a practical understanding of *ren*, *li* and *yi*. However, knowing *dao* requires clarity of mind (*ming*). When a clear mind is guided by reason, it will be free from all sorts of factors that obscure (*bi*) the clarity of vision. One must be especially watchful of the contextual significance of such distinctions as between desires and aversions, immediate and distant consequences, the past and the present. Failure to weigh the relevance of one item of the distinction is liable to blind the agent to consideration of the significance of the other item. Basically, distinctions are relative to the purpose and context of discourse; they are not exclusive disjunctions or absolute dichotomies. Since distinctions in general are the products of the mind's intellectual function at the service of cognition and action, their utility in a particular situation is also relative to purpose and context. Even in cases where the utility of the distinction is not in question, the agent must render a reasoned judgement concerning the significance of each item in the distinction. Obscuration (*bi*) of the mind arises when the mind exclusively attends to the significance of one item without proper regard for that of the other (see PERCEPTION, EPISTEMIC ISSUES IN).

Even philosophers are susceptible to *bi*. MOZI, for example, exaggerates the importance of utility without understanding the importance of culture or the beauty of forms; ZHUANGZI is preoccupied with *tian* (Heaven) without regard for humanity. In general,

819

ordinary people as well as philosophers tend to see only 'one corner' of *dao* and thus fail to appreciate its holistic character. Only an enlightened sage 'confronts all things and weighs them impartially on a balance' (*Xunzi* 21; Cua 1993).

Today, Xunzi is widely acknowledged to be one of the greatest Chinese philosophers. Apart from his critical and coherent exposition of ancient Confucianism, he is also distinguished for his insights into the nature of ethical knowledge and argumentation (Cua 1985a).

See also: CONFUCIAN PHILOSOPHY, CHINESE; DAO; ETHICS; LAW AND RITUAL IN CHINESE PHILOSOPHY; MORAL DEVELOPMENT; SELF-CULTIVATION IN CHINESE PHILOSOPHY

List of works

Xunzi (*c.*298–238 BC) *Xunzi*, ed. Li Disheng, *Xunzi chishi*, Taibei: Xuesheng, 1979; trans. B. Watson, *Hsün Tzu [Xunzi]: Basic Writings*, New York: Columbia University Press, 1963; trans. H.H. Dubs, *The Works of Hsüntze [Xunzi]*, Taibei: Chengwen, 1966; ed. and trans. J. Knoblock, *Xunzi: A Translation and Study of the Complete Works*, 3 vols, Stanford, CA: Stanford University Press, 1988, 1990, 1994. (Li is a good modern Chinese annotated edition. The Knoblock edition contains long, valuable introductions in volumes 1 and 2, and extensive bibliographies in volumes 1 and 3.)

References and further reading

Chan Wing-tsit. and Fu, C. (1978) *Guide to Chinese Philosophy*, Boston, MA: C.K. Hall. (A contemporary bibliography.)

* Cua, A.S. (1985a) *Ethical Argumentation: A Study in Hsün Tzu's [Xunzi's] Moral Epistemology*, Honolulu, HI: University of Hawaii Press. (A Xunzi-based philosophical study of Confucian ethical argumentation with emphasis on the character of the participants, standards of competence, uses of definition and diagnosis of erroneous ethical beliefs.)

* —— (1985b) 'Ethical Uses of the Past in Early Confucianism: The Case of Hsün Tzu [Xunzi]', *Philosophy East and West* 35: 133–56. (A study of Xunzi's uses of the historical appeal from the point of view of Confucian discourse, focusing its pedagogical, rhetorical, elucidative and evaluative functions.)

* —— (1989) 'The Concept of *Li* in Confucian Moral Theory', in R.E. Allinson (ed.) *Understanding the Chinese Mind: The Philosophical Roots*, Hong Kong: Oxford University Press. (A study of three basic functions of *li* and their ethical roots.)

* —— (1993) 'The Possibility of Ethical Knowledge: Reflections on a Theme in the *Hsün Tzu [Xunzi]*', in H. Lenk and G. Paul (eds) *Epistemological Issues in Ancient Chinese Philosophy*, Albany, NY: State University of New York Press. (A study of possibility of knowing dao and the problem of cognitive blindness.)

Dubs, H.H. (1927) *Hsüntze [Xunzi]: The Moulder of Ancient Confucianism*, London: Arthur Probsthain. (The first comprehensive English study of Xunzi.)

A.S. CUA

Y

YANG *see* YIN-YANG

YANG CHU *see* YANGZHU

YANG HSIUNG *see* YANG XIONG

YANG XIONG (53 BC–AD 18)

Master Yang Xiong, the first Confucian classicist and the greatest of the pre-Song metaphysicians, is best known for two major philosophical works, the Taixuanjing *(Canon of Supreme Mystery) and the* Fayan *(Model Sayings). Both works explore the interaction between significant cosmic and social patterns by explicit reference to earlier canonical traditions.*

Master Yang came to Changan (modern Xian), then the capital of the Western Han dynasty, in his early thirties. As the foremost poet of his age, Yang Xiong was in effect appointed poet laureate to the court in 10 BC. In middle age, after the death of his beloved son, Yang experienced a sense of profound revulsion for his earlier poetic efforts. Condemning court poetry as inherently frivolous, if not immoral, Yang turned to composing works of philosophy.

His first such work was the *Taixuanjing* (Canon of Supreme Mystery), which like its prototype, the *Yijing* (Book of Changes), correlates the significant patterns of the universe with different combinations of solid and broken lines accompanied by brief texts and ten autocommentaries. However, the *Taixuanjing* adjusts the structure and imagery of the *Yijing* to better address Han preoccupations with correlative thinking, fate and time. As the first grand synthesis of Chinese thought, skilfully weaving together elements of early Confucianism, classical Daoism, *yin–yang* Five Phases theory (see YIN–YANG), alchemy, and astrology into an organic whole, the *Taixuanjing* came to occupy a place in Chinese intellectual history roughly comparable to that of the *Summa theologiae* of Thomas AQUINAS in the West. Its most important contribution is its account of individual human destiny, which is said to result from the interplay of

four major factors: time (meaning 'present opportunity'), virtue (or 'character'), tools (including training) and position (societal and physical). Of these four factors, only virtue is completely subject to human control, so Yang identifies adherence to the Good as defined in the Confucian 'Way' as the single most reliable method of improving individual fate. In the course of outlining this theory of fate, the *Taixuanjing* pinpoints the logical fallacies inherent in various philosophical positions that competed with Confucianism for general approval during Yang's time.

Following a draft of the *Taixuanjing* before 2 BC, there came at least four lengthy philosophical poems whose style parodies the prose-poems of Yang's youth. Two of these *fu* are dedicated to the defence of his provocative masterwork, the *Taixuanjing*. Around AD 12, Yang finished the *Fayan* (Model Sayings), which adopts both the format and style of the Confucian *Analects* to provide a relatively straightforward catechism for the would-be sage (see CONFUCIUS). The *Fayan* evaluates the conflicting goals of immortality, fame, power and scholarship to disentangle prevailing notions that confused the 'good life' with ideas of the Good. As its main theme is the need to immerse oneself in the model of the former sages, the *Fayan*, like the *Analects*, devotes considerable attention to the reassessment of historical figures whose conduct or writings were considered worthy of emulation (see HISTORY, CHINESE THEORIES OF).

When Yang died, he left unfinished a third remarkable work on significant pattern, the *Fangyan* (Regional Expressions). As the first Chinese dialect dictionary, the *Fangyan* is far more than a sourcebook of philological glosses culled from disparate sources; it is a synchronical word list that focuses on rare expressions in an attempt to trace linguistic boundaries and connections. In a surviving letter, Yang justified the enormous task of compiling this text in fairly standard Confucian terms: Since regional cultures evolve from complex factors, the wise ruler must have such texts at his disposal so that government policies may be suitably adjusted to varying locales.

Thanks to the volume and quality of his output, Yang's stature as Confucian master remained unchallenged until the Song period. At that time a few prominent neo-Confucian thinkers (including ZHU XI), in an effort to disengage themselves from certain pre-Song moral constructs, objected to Yang's considerable influence and denounced his character, cosmological vision and eclecticism. Nonetheless, as most Chinese philosophical works dating to the first millennium have been lost, the *Taixuanjing* and *Fayan*, two undisputed classics, together provide one of the best keys to understanding early Confucian ideology in its formative stage.

See also: CONFUCIUS; CONFUCIAN PHILOSOPHY, CHINESE; DAOIST PHILOSOPHY; YIJING; YIN–YANG; ZHU XI

List of works

Yang Xiong (*c.* 4 BC) *Taixuanjing* (Canon of Supreme Mystery), trans. M. Nylan, Albany, NY: State University of New York Press, 1993; ed. Zheng Wangeng, *Taixuan jiaoshi* (Collated Explications for the Supreme Mystery), Beijing: Teacher's Normal University, 1989. (An inquiry into the relation of fate and virtue. Zheng is the best annotated edition of the classic text, with notes in modern Chinese.)

—— (*c.* AD 12) *Fayan* (Model Sayings), trans. E. von Zach, *Yang Hsiung's Fa yen: Worte strenger Ermahnung*, in Sinologische Beiträge 4, Batavia: Drukkerji Lux, 1939; B. Belpaire, *Le catechisme philosophique de Yang-Hiong-tsé*, Brussels, Éditions de L'Occident, 1960. (Analecta devoted to historical figures and philosophical concepts.)

—— (before AD 18) *Fangyan* (Regional Expressions), in P.L.-M. Serruys, *The Chinese Dialects of Han Time According to Fang Yen*, Berkeley, CA: University of California Press, 1959. (There are several editions of this work, all of which coincide.)

References and further reading

Knechtges, D. (1981) *The Han shu Biography of Yang Xiong (53 B.C.–A.D. 18)*, Tempe, AZ: Arizona State University. (Translates Yang's *Hanshu* biography, based on his autobiography.)

Mitarai Masaru (1957) 'Yō Yū to Taigen' (Yang Hsiung and the Supreme Mystery), *Shinagaku kenkyū* 18: 22–32. (Emphasizes the originality of the *Tai xuan jing*.)

Suzuki Yoshijirō (1964) *Taigen no kenkyū* (Research on the Supreme Mystery), Tokyo: Meitokusha. (Explains the *Tai xuan jing* in light of Han cosmological theories.)

MICHAEL NYLAN

YANGZHU (5th–4th century BC)

Yangzhu, detested by the Confucians, is important in the Chinese tradition for initiating the explicit discussion of human nature. He focuses on the thesis that human nature has no inherent ethical or mystical qualities; instead, there is simply an innate tendency to live a long life, a tendency that must be carefully nurtured by a rational regulation of sense stimulation and by the avoidance of any of the entanglements incumbent in a life of working for the good of human society.

Yangzhu is commonly dated to a generation or two before MENCIUS, who said of him that he was so egotistical he would not even pull out one hair to benefit human society. There are no extant writings of Yangzhu; we know of his ideas through the writings of his followers included in five essays in the *Lushi chunqiu* (Lu's Spring and Autumn Annals) in the third century BC, and in four chapters from the *Zhuangzi* that are dated to about 205 BC (see LUSHI CHUNQIU; ZHUANGZI). There is no evidence of his intellectual lineage continuing after this time.

Yangzhu is known for initiating in Chinese thought the explicit discussion of human nature (see XING), and also for three related teachings: 'keeping one's nature intact', 'protecting one's genuineness' and 'not letting the body be tied by external things'. For Yang, human nature at its most basic level consists in the spontaneous tendency for humans to live a long life if undisturbed by external things, since the various 'physiological' systems of *qi* that constitute the human organism tend to function harmoniously provided they are unimpaired and sufficiently nourished by the proper degree of sensory stimulation (see QI).

A related aspect of human nature is the desire of the various sense faculties for their objects. It is this that helps to maintain the health and development of the organism, enabling it to realize its inherent tendency for longevity. However the senses, themselves, need to be regulated and limited to only a suitable amount of stimulation; there is a naturally suitable degree of sense-stimulation which is conducive to health and development. This degree must be rationally determined by the Sage; the senses on their own cannot do this. Excessive stimulation, say the Yangists, reduces the individual's finite supply of the refined form of *qi* called *jing* (vital essence) needed to maintain health and vitality.

Yangist political philosophy is meagre, but straightforward. One should not seek after fame, wealth and power, all of which are far beyond essential needs. One should never do anything to impair one's inherent tendency to live a long and satisfied life.

Only when a person knows this do they understand 'the essentials of our nature and destiny' and are then fit to rule over others.

Yangzhu's challenge to the social interpretation of human nature of the Confucians consisted in the primacy he placed on the maintenance of the individual. In his advocacy of personal cultivation over social concern, he initiated an individualistic counteractive to the often overwhelming pressure toward social conformity in China that was later continued by Daoist and Buddhist thought. However unlike these later schools, there was absolutely nothing mystical in the teachings of Yang and his followers, even though some think them related to the early Daoists.

See also: CONFUCIAN PHILOSOPHY, CHINESE; DAOIST PHILOSOPHY; SELF-CULTIVATION IN CHINESE PHILOSOPHY; QI

References and further reading

Fung Yu-lan (1952) *A History of Chinese Philosophy*, trans. D. Bodde, Princeton, NJ: Princeton University Press, 132–43. (Presents a detailed but rather difficult analysis of the ideas of Yangzhu, valuable for its discussion of possible links between him and early Daoists.)

Graham, A.C. (1967) 'The Background of the Mencian Theory of Human Nature', *Tsing Hua Journal of Chinese Studies* 6 (1–2): 215–74; repr. in A.C. Graham, *Studies in Chinese Philosophy and Philosophical Literature*, Albany, NY: State University of New York Press, 1986, 7–66. (Contains a useful summary of Yangzhu's ideas on human nature as an important part of the intellectual context for Mencius' development of the concept.)

—— (1981) *Chuang Tzu: The Inner Chapters*, London: George Allen & Unwin. (Provides the authoritative English translation of the Yangist essays in the *Zhuangzi*.)

—— (1989) *Disputers of the Tao: Philosophical Argumentation in Ancient China*, LaSalle, IL: Open Court, 53–64. (This is the best introduction available to Yangzhu's thought.)

Knoblock, J. and Riegel, J. (trans.) (1997) *The Almanac of Lü Buwei*, Stanford, CA: Stanford University Press. (Translation of the *Lushi chunqiu*.)

H.D. ROTH

YI *see* CONFUCIAN PHILOSOPHY, CHINESE; CONFUCIUS

YI HWANG (1501–70)

Yi Hwang, also known by his honorific name T'oegye, is one of the two most honoured thinkers of the Korean neo-Confucian tradition. His fully balanced and integral grasp of the complex philosophical neo-Confucian synthesis spun by Zhu Xi during China's Song dynasty marks the tradition's arrival at full maturity in Korea. His 'Four–Seven Debate' with Ki Taesûng established a distinctive problematic that strongly oriented Korean neo-Confucian thought towards exacting investigation of critical issues regarding the juncture of metaphysics and their all-important application in describing the inner life of the human heart-and-mind.

Yi Hwang, also known by his honorific name T'oegye, was born of a relatively modest aristocratic lineage in the village of Ongyeri, near Andong in Kyongsan province, about 200 kilometres southwest of Seoul. He took the civil service examinations, and served in government for a number of years, but his true longing was for a life of quiet study, reflection, and self-cultivation. He retired from office in his late forties to pursue his dream, and the following two decades were a period of tremendous productivity in spite of frequent recalls to office as his fame as a scholar and teacher grew.

Neo-Confucianism was adopted as the official orthodoxy at the foundation of the Chosôn dynasty in 1392. It was a rich synthesis, containing a metaphysical system of Daoist proportions and a meditative cultivation of consciousness reminiscent of Buddhist practice which Zhu Xi and other early neo-Confucians had woven about the core of traditional Confucian concerns for government and proper social ethics (see NEO-CONFUCIAN PHILOSOPHY). It provided wide scope for varied and uneven development. During the first century of the Chosôn dynasty, activists in government focused on institutional reform while, far from the capital, scholars in the countryside concentrated on the more meditative features of neo-Confucian learning and self-cultivation. The differing orientations crystallized into bloody clashes and purges by the end of the fourteenth century as young men steeped in moral rigorism began to move from the countryside into government.

Yi Hwang's comprehensive grasp of Zhu Xi's

thought clarified the balance between activity and quietism, government and retired self-cultivation, and by the end of his life it was his disciples who were moving into high government positions. A year before his death he crystallized and presented to the king his understanding of the way in which metaphysics and psychological structures inform ascetical theory and eventuate in the conduct of daily life. This work, the *Sônghak sipdo* (Ten Diagrams on Sage Learning), became one of the most famous and influential works of Korean neo-Confucianism. After Yi Hwang, it was no longer possible to deny the legitimacy of intensive, almost monastic devotion to study and meditative self-cultivation when the situation permitted, nor to ignore the expectation that the proper fruition of such formation should be the proper conduct of government and the ordering of society.

On the level of philosophical theory, Yi Hwang left a lasting imprint on Korean neo-Confucianism, for his 'Four–Seven debate', carried on in correspondence with a younger scholar, Ki Taesûng (1527–72), established the problematic for Korean thinkers for centuries. In particular, it centred Korean neo-Confucian reflection on questions relating to the interface of metaphysics and psychological theory. For Yi Hwang and other neo-Confucians committed to self-cultivation, this was a topic of intense concern: in the framework of neo-Confucian thought, a proper, metaphysically-grounded understanding of the structure and functioning of the psyche explains human perfection and imperfection; it is thus the foundation for any theory behind the practice of spiritual cultivation.

The Four–Seven Debate centred on an issue directly related to one of the most important advances of neo-Confucian thought, its explanation of a cause within human beings that could disrupt our natural responsiveness to situations and cause us to err. This was accomplished by the elaboration of a dualistic monism. The single *dao* or *li* (in Korean, *to* and *i*), both formative and normative, runs through all things, constituting the diverse nature of each one without losing its ultimate unity. The diversity is accomplished by pairing it with a complement, *qi* (in Korean, *ki*), a vital, active, concretizing and hence particularizing component. The unity of *i*, the substance of mind as well as the nature of all things in existence, supported the possibility of cultivating a condition of perfect responsive interrelation with all things, a Confucian sagehood equivalent to Buddhist enlightenment. *Ki*, on the other hand, provided an explanation for imperfection: its various degrees of turbidity or purity accounted not only for the differentiation of *i* into various levels of nature, but also distorted to varying degrees the otherwise perfect

responsiveness of the human mind to its surroundings (see QI).

The Four–Seven Debate took up the question of the role of this dualism in the issuance of the feelings (see CONFUCIAN PHILOSOPHY, KOREAN). Spontaneously good responses, such as compassion or the tendency to save a child from danger, seem different from feelings such as anger or desire, which may or may not be appropriate and always need watching. Since the nature (*i*) is normative and *ki* the explanation of disruption, an easy conclusion might be that the reliable feelings (the 'four') arise from *i* while the questionable ones (the 'seven') are rooted in *ki*. This, however, is an extremely dualistic interpretation that ignores the necessary and constant interdependence of *li* and *ki*. Good ethics becomes bad metaphysics. Emphasizing the interdependence, on the other hand, puts all our responsive feelings on exactly the same footing. Neo-Confucian cultivation, and especially meditative practice, set great store on somehow establishing a quiet contact with our purely good deep nature and nurturing the sound tendencies stemming from it. Yi Hwang conceived an approach that recognized interdependence but carved out a distinction between the two sorts of feelings, though this could not settle the question, for there were those who wanted such consistent interdependence that no such variation was satisfactory. Yi Hwang's theory, entirely within the framework of Zhu Xi's thought, was a sophisticated alternative to the radical cleavage that arose in China between the schools of ZHU XI and WANG YANGMING in connection with similar issues.

See also: CONFUCIAN PHILOSOPHY, KOREAN; NEO-CONFUCIAN PHILOSOPHY; YI YULGOK

List of works

Yi Hwang [T'oegye] (1501–70) *T'oegye Chônsô* (The Complete Works of Yi Hwang), Seoul: Sônggyun'gwan Taehakkyo Taedong Munhwa Yônguwôn, 1958. (Photo reprint.)

—— (1501–70) *Chu Sô Chôryo* (The Essentials of Zhu Xi's Letters), in Abe Yoshio (ed.) *Ilbon kakp'an Yi Toegye chônjip* (Japanese edition of the works of Yi T'oegye), Seoul: Taeil Chongp'ansa, 1975, 2 vols. (Yi Hwang's comments on Zhu Xi.)

—— (1569) *Sônghak sipdo* (Ten Diagrams on Sage Learning), ed. and trans. M.C. Kalton, *To Become a Sage: The Ten Diagrams on Sage Learning by Yi T'oegye*, New York: Columbia University Press, 1988. (A translation of the *Sônghak sipdo*, his most famous work. Includes a long introduction dealing with Yi Hwang's life, times and work.)

References and further reading

de Bary, W.T. and Haboush, J.K. (eds) (1985) *The Rise of Neo-Confucianism in Korea*, New York: Columbia University Press. (This conference volume includes three chapters dealing with various aspects of Yi Hwang's thought.)

Kalton, M.C. (ed. and trans.) (1994) *The Four–Seven Debate: An Annotated Translation of the Most Famous Controversy in Korean Neo-Confucian Thought*, New York: State University of New York Press. (A translation of the debate correspondence between Yi Hwang and Ki Taesûng, and between Yi Yulgok and Sông Hon as well. Includes a long introduction dealing with the background, content and significance of the debate.)

Lee, P.H. *et al.* (eds) (1993) *Sources of Korean Tradition*, New York: Columbia University Press. (Includes translations from a variety of Yi Hwang's works.)

Yun Sasoon (1991) *Critical Issues in Neo-Confucian Thought: The Philosophy of Yi T'oegye*, trans. M.C. Kalton, Seoul: Korea University Press. (A sophisticated analysis of Yi Hwang's philosophy by one of Korea's leading experts on neo-Confucianism.)

MICHAEL C. KALTON

YI I *see* YI YULGOK

YI KAN (1677–1727)

Yi Kan was a major Korean neo-Confucian thinker. He is best remembered as a major protagonist in the Horak controversy where he opposed Han Wônjin, championing the position of the school of Yi Yulgok against Han's novel tri-level theory of nature.

The Horak controversy originated when HAN WÔNJIN stated that even in the state of meditative quiescence, *ki* (in Chinese, *qi*) or 'material force' is present. Neo-Confucian metaphysics is a dualistic monism in which the single *dao* or pattern running through all things is concretized and individualized in real beings only through *ki*. The patterning element, known as *i* (in Chinese, *li*) and often translated as 'principle', also constitutes the innermost nature of all things; its presence as the substance of the human heart-and-mind accounts for our innate potential to respond appropriately to all things and situations (see LI; QI).

Yi objected strongly to Han's proposition. Meta-physically, it seems the obvious consequence of the interdependence of *i* and *ki*, a theme especially emphasized in the school of YI YULGOK, to which both Han and Yi Kan belonged. However, in addition to individuation, imperfection or turbidity in *ki* also is a distorting element that accounts for our often imperfect response to things. Han's observation seemed to imply that a quiet criminal is still just a criminal. But in the ascetical life the meditative practice of 'quiet-sitting' was commonly held to obviate the distortion of *ki* and nurture the responsiveness of the heart-and-mind in direct union with its pure, unsullied inner nature. Yi accused Han of violating the authoritative tradition regarding the pure 'original nature' and its role in spiritual cultivation.

Metaphysical theory might favour Han's position, but its implications were intolerable, especially insofar as the major rationale for neo-Confucian metaphysics is to serve as a framework for ascetical theory. In defending conventional ascetical theory and practice, Yi Kan was forced into an unconventional metaphysical position: to make the pure nature accessible without denying the ever-present *ki*, he was forced to introduce the notion that the *ki* of the heart-and-mind is naturally pure; it is only the *ki* that constitutes our physical bodies that is subject to turbidity. In quieting the body and returning to pure objectless consciousness, we enter a level in which *ki* offers no distortion to the nature, which is also the substance or ground of the heart-and-mind. Instead of a dualism of *li* and *ki*, we thus end with a dualism of *ki*. This illustrates the difficulty of accommodating realistically the moral tensions of spiritual practice in the consistently monistic interpretation of ZHU XI as advocated in Yulgok's school.

In the closely related aspect of the controversy regarding whether the normative nature of all creatures is the same or differentiated according to species, Yi Kan championed the more conventional position against Han's novel tri-level theory of the nature. According to Yi, *i* is normative precisely as considered apart from any (distorting) limitation from *ki*, but *ki* is likewise the source of all differentiation. Hence there is only the unitary *i* of 'the single origin,' and the multitude of concrete individuals, each with their unique *ki* constitution.

See also: CONFUCIAN PHILOSOPHY, KOREAN; NEO-CONFUCIAN PHILOSOPHY; HAN WÔNJIN

List of works

Yi Kan (1677–1727) *Woeam Yugo* (The Writings of Yi Kan), Seoul: Cho Yongsung, 1976, photo reprint. (Contains the collected writings of Yi Kan.)

References and further readings

There is at present no further information on Yi in western languages.

MICHAEL C. KALTON

YI YULGOK (1536–84)

Yulgok was one of the foremost neo-Confucian scholars in Korea during the Yi (Chosôn) dynasty. He is considered one of two pillars, along with Yi T'oegye, of the Korean neo-Confucian tradition. Yulgok, an active statesman and educator as well as scholar, not only compiled the theories of previous Confucian scholars of China and Korea but, more importantly, developed his own interpretations of them.

Yi Yulgok (real name Yi I; Yulgok was the village to which he retired) was known as a non-dualistic thinker in interpreting the relationship between *i* and *ki*, or 'principle' and 'material force', 'the mind of *dao*' and the 'human mind', 'the four beginnings' and 'the seven feelings'. Yulgok was neither a dualist nor a monist. For example, while he rejected the division between 'principle' and 'material force' on an ontological level, he made a clear distinction between these two concepts on a phenomenological level.

Yulgok's family was intellectually very distinguished: his father came from a long line of Confucian scholar-officials, and his mother, Sin Saimdang, was famous for her intellectual and artistic brilliance. She took Yulgok's education personally in hand and became his first teacher. Yulgok himself was a prodigy. He underwent a long series of civil service examinations, taking the first at the age of thirteen and the last when he was twenty-nine. These examinations opened opportunities to various important functions in the government, and Yulgok performed brilliantly, reaching the very highest official ranks. One examination essay written at the age of twenty-three, *Ch'ôndo ch'aek* (A Treatise on the Way of Heaven), offered a compelling theory of the unity of heaven and humanity, and it became so important among Confucian scholars of the time that it was eventually carried as far as Ming dynasty China.

Yulgok passed his last civil service examination in 1565. In 1570, he wrote *Tongho mundap* (Questions and Answers at Eastern Lake), dedicated to the new king Sônjo, with the purpose of instructing him in methods for realizing the ideal Confucian state. An imaginary dialogue between host and guest, cast in a question and answer format, it discusses ways to deal with disordered government, explains 'the way of the ruler' as opposed to 'the way of the subject', and juxtaposes 'the way of the king' with that of the despot. It stresses the importance of the moral cultivation of the ruler himself as a necessary first step towards good government in general. *Tongho mundap* reflects Yulgok's strong social and political concerns, and his horror of the petty political factionalism he encountered at court.

In 1571, while serving as the governor of Ch'ôngju, Yulgok wrote *Sôwôn hyangyak* (Community Treaty of Sôwôn), a manual on local self-government aimed at teaching local people how to govern themselves. The following year he resigned from the governorship due to illness and retired. At this time he started his famous debate with the Confucian thinker Sông Hon (Ugye) on the interconnected concepts of *i* (principle) and *ki* (material force); 'the four beginnings' and 'the seven feelings'. Yulgok argued that 'the four beginnings' do not contain 'the seven feelings' (or emotions) but the seven feelings (or emotions) do contain the four beginnings. Throughout this debate Yulgok maintained a non-dualistic way of understanding the nature of the relationship between *i* and *ki*; *tosim* (the mind of *dao*) and *insim* (the human mind); and the four beginnings and the seven feelings.

Over the next four years Yulgok also wrote a number of works, addressing issues from practical government to the individual moral cultivation. He compiled *Sônghak chibyo* (A Compendium of Sagely Learning), selections from the Four Books and the Five Classics – central works of the Confucian canon – grouped around the two themes of moral self-cultivation and proper governance of the people. The choice of selections and their presentation were uniquely Yulgok's own, based on his by then mature grasp of the Confucian and neo-Confucian traditions.

In 1582, Yulgok finished his famous book, *Kyôngmong yogyôl* (A Key to Annihilating Ignorance), a work which had an enormous and long-lasting influence on Confucian education in Korea. An introduction delineating all the basic elements of Confucian learning and sagely discipline, it was widely used as a textbook for both beginning and advanced students in the Confucian schools. *Yukcho-kye* (The Memorials of Six Articles), his last work, was a practical treatise on defence policy, outlining methods for strengthening the kingdom's defences. This work became a central work on the subject, commonly referred to by Yulgok's own slogan, 'nourish and train hundreds of thousands of soldiers'. It was while serving as Defence Minister that Yulgok died of illness in 1584.

As mirrored in his life, Yulgok's thought was divided and moved in two directions. First, there was the study of 'human nature and principle' (*sôngnihak*; in Chinese, *xinglixue*); second, there were the practical considerations of good government. In attempting to relate these two areas of concern – individual self-cultivation and sociopolitical application of the Confucian ideal – Yulgok had to confront on a practical level many of the most pressing political issues of his time: the sixteenth-century Yi dynasty was plagued by countless problems ranging from economics to defence. Yulgok tried to establish a Confucian state by realizing the Confucian social and political ideals through moral self-cultivation.

See also: CONFUCIAN PHILOSOPHY, KOREAN; LI; QI; SELF-CULTIVATION IN CHINESE PHILOSOPHY; YI HWANG

List of works

Yi I [Yi Yulgok] (1564–84) *Yulgok chônsô* (The Complete Works of Yi Yulgok), Seoul: Sônggyun'gwan Taehakkyo Taedong Munhwa Yôn'guwon, 1958, 2 vols. (Collection of Yulgok's original writings in Chinese.)

—— (1564) *Ch'ôndo ch'aek* (A Treatise on the Way of Heaven), in Yulgok chônsô, Seoul: Sônggyun'gwan Taehakkyo Taedong Munhwa Yôn'guwon, 1958, 14: 54a–60b. (This is a concise and yet broad treatise on neo-Confucian metaphysics, cosmology, ethics and political thought, written for a civil service examination when Yulgok was twenty-two.)

—— (1570) *Tongho mundap* (Questions and Answers at Eastern Lake), in Yulgok chônsô, Seoul: Sônggyun'gwan Taehakkyo Taedong Munhwa Yôn'guwon, 1958, 15: 2a–33b. (A major political writing on the way of righteous government, written while Yulgok was minister of justice. It deals with the Confucian idea of sagely and kingly government and how to reform government administration.)

—— (1571) *Sôwôn hyangyak* (Community Treaty of Sôwôn), in Yulgok chônsô, Seoul: Sônggyun'gwan Taehakkyo Taedong Munhwa Yôn'guwon, 1958, 16: 2a–7a. (A systematic political and social guideline for local community and government addressing social order, Confucian moral norm and mutual cooperation for the community.)

—— (1572) *Sônghak chibyo* (A Compendium of Sagely Learning), in Yulgok chônsô, Seoul: Sônggyun'gwan Taehakkyo Taedong Munhwa Yôn'guwon, 1958, 20: 1a–38b. (Yulgok's unique way of summarizing and interpreting Cheng–Zhu neo-Confucian thought. It also includes the moral and practical aspects of government administration, and Yulgok's concern for practical learning.)

—— (1582) *Kyôngmong yogyôl* (A Key to Annihilating Ignorance), in Yulgok chônsô, Seoul: Sônggyun'gwan Taehakkyo Taedong Munhwa Yôn'guwon, 1958, 27: 3a–21b. (Deals with various themes of Confucian way in practice, including not only Confucian learning and self-cultivation but also practical guidelines for Confucian family regulation, human relationships and rituals.)

—— (1583) *Yukchokye* (The Manifestation of Six Articles), in Yulgok chônsô, Seoul: Sônggyun'gwan Taehakkyo Taedong Munhwa Yôn'guwon, 1958, 8: 18a–23b. (Six specific reform proposals for economy, government, defence policy, nourishing people and army, education, society and people; written while Yulgok was defence minister and submitted to the king.)

References and further readings

Chung, E.Y.J. (1995) *The Korean Neo-Confucianism of Yi T'oegye and Ti Yulgok*, Albany, NY: State University of New York Press. (A comparative study of Yi T'oegye (Yi Hwang) and Yi Yulgok; a very good introduction to Korean Confucianism.)

Hyun Sang-yun (1971) *Chosôn yuhaksa* (History of Korean Confucianism), Seoul: Minjungsokwan. (A comprehensive view of Korean Confucianism, written in Korean.)

Kalton, M.C., Kim Oaksook, Park Sung-Bae, Ro Youngchan, Tu Wei-ming and Yamashita, S. (eds) (1994) *The Four–Seven Debate: An Annotated Translation of the Most Famous Controversy in Korean Neo-Confucian Thought*, Albany, NY: State University of New York Press. (A most thorough and comprehensive discussion on the issues regarding the Four Beginnings and the Seven Feelings among the Korean neo-Confucian scholars, including Yulgok.)

Kim Kyung Tak (1960) *Yulgok eui Yôn'gu* (The Study of Yulgok), Korean Studies Series 7, Seoul: The Korean Research Center. (An in-depth study of Yulgok's neo-Confucian philosophy. This book has an English summary at the back.)

Lee, P., Baker, D., Ch'oe Yongho, Kang, H.H. and Kim Han-kyo (eds) (1992) *Sources of Korean Tradition*, New York: Columbia University Press. (For a general understanding of Korean cultural and intellectual understanding including Korean Confucianism, this book is a good resource.)

Pae Chong-ho (1974) *Han'guk yuhaksa* (History of Korean Confucianism), Seoul: Yonsei Taehakkyo Ch'ulp'anbu. (Korean neo-Confucian thought is well discussed in this book, including a comparison between the two most significant Korean neo-Confucian thinkers, Yi T'oegye and Yi Yulgok.)

Pak Chong-hong (1976) *Han'guk sasangsa* (History of

Korean Thought), Seoul: Somun-dang. (Although this book is a history of Korean philosophy, it includes an in-depth investigation of Yulgok's thinking.)

Ro Young-chan (1989) *The Korean Neo-Confucianism of Yi Yulgok*, Albany, NY: State University of New York Press. (An interpretation of Yulgok's non-dualistic way of thinking in his cosmology, ontology and anthropology.)

Son In Soo (1976) *Yulgok eui Kyoyuksasag* (Yulgok's Philosophy of Education), Seoul: Pakyoungsa. (A good summary introduction to Yulgok's idea of education.)

Yi Byung Do (1973) *Yulgok eui Saengae wa Sasang* (Life and Thought of Yulgok), Seoul: Seomoon Dang. (A good survey of Yulgok's life and thought.)

Yi Joon Ho (1973) *Yulgok eui Sasang* (Yulgok's Thought), Seoul: Hyunamsa. (Yulgok's political, philosophical and educational thought are well discussed.)

YOUNG-CHAN RO

YIJING

The Yijing *(Book of Changes) or* Zhouyi *(Changes of the Zhou) was originally a divination manual, which later gradually acquired the status of a book of wisdom. It consists of sixty-four hexagrams (*gua*) and related texts. By the time the* Yijing *became a coherent text in the ninth century* BC, *hexagram divination had changed from a means of consulting and influencing gods and spirits to a method of penetrating moments of the cosmic order to learn the shape and flow of the* dao *and determine one's own place in it. By doing so, one avoids wrong decisions, failure and misfortune and achieves their contrary. Tradition has it that the* Yijing *can only be successfully approached through humility, honesty and an open mind. Through interaction with it, one gains ever increasing self-knowledge and sensitivity to one's relations to others and to one's situation in life. 'Good fortune', 'happiness' and 'success' are but by-products of such self-knowledge and sensitivity.*

1   **Organization of the** *Yijing*
2   **History of the text**
3   **The commentary tradition**
4   **The hexagram as discourse**

1   Organization of the *Yijing*

The *Yijing* (Book of Changes) consists of sixty-four hexagrams (*gua*) and related texts. The hexagrams are formed by combinations of two trigrams and result in six solid or unbroken (yang +) and/or broken (yin –) lines (*yao*), arranged one above the other in vertical sequence. The combinations are determined by the numerical manipulation of divining sticks, originally yarrow stalks (*achillea millefolium*), or later, by the casting of coins. Each hexagram is accompanied by a hexagram name (*guaming*), a hexagram statement (*guaci*) or 'judgment' (*tuan*), and line statements (*yaoci*) for each of the six lines. The line statements have a sequential organization related to the judgment; each states a specific instance of the judgment, which in complete line statements (many are fragmentary) is followed by an injunction – that one should take some action or refrain from it – and a final determination – 'misfortune', 'good fortune' and so on.

The hexagrams, hexagram statements or judgments and the line statements are the oldest parts of the *Yijing*. Whereas the hexagrams themselves may be much older, the names and statements probably date from the ninth century BC and constitute the first layer in a three-layered text. The second layer consists of another two parts: commentaries on the hexagram statements or judgments called *tuanzhuan* (commentary on the judgments) and commentaries on the abstract meanings or 'images' (*xiang*) of the judgments and the line statements called *xiangzhuan* (commentary on the images). The judgments have 'great images' (*daxiang*) – the abstract meanings of whole hexagrams – and the line statements have 'little images' (*xiaoxiang*) – the abstract meanings of individual lines. These commentaries seem to date from the sixth or fifth century BC and are the first of the exegetical materials in the *Yijing* traditionally attributed to CONFUCIUS.

The traditional format of the *Yijing* divides the *tuanzhuan* and the *xiangzhuan* each into two sections. They thus form the first four of the so-called 'Ten Wings' (*shiyi*) of the exegetical material included in the classic. Although all of the 'Ten Wings' are attributed to Confucius, individual 'wings' actually date from different periods, with some earlier and others from as late as the third century BC. However, except for the commentaries on the judgments and the commentaries on the images, which do seem the direct product of Confucius' school if not of Confucius himself, the rest of the 'Ten Wings' consists of later materials, which probably contain reworking of earlier texts. These constitute the third layer of the *Yijing* and include two fragments of an apparently lost commentary on the hexagrams as a whole called the *Wenyan* (Commentary on the Words of the Text), but only those parts attached to the first two hexagrams –

qian (pure *yang*) and *kun* (pure *yin*) – survived into the period of textual redaction (early Han era, in the third century BC). The *Wenyan* seems to be a borderline text that contains elements of both the second and third layers. It constitutes the fifth of the 'Ten Wings' and deals with the philosophical and ethical implications of the judgments, line statements and images, all given a Confucian slant.

The sixth and seventh 'wings' are formed by the two sections of the so-called *Xicizhuan* (Commentary on the Appended Phrases) or *Dazhuan* (Great Commentary). This commentary contains two kinds of material; one deals with the nature and meaning of the *Yijing* in general, and the other is concerned with the meaning of the judgments and line statements of individual hexagrams. The *Xicizhuan* seems to consist of fragments of two different texts, one a general essay or group of essays and the other a collection of specific remarks on individual hexagrams. The eighth of the 'Ten Wings,' *Shuogua* (Explaining the Trigrams) consists of remarks on the nature and meaning of the eight trigrams (*bagua*), the permutations of which form the sixty-four hexagrams. Much here is couched in terms of *yin–yang* dualism and the theory of the *wuxing* (five elements), and so dates probably from the early Han era (third century BC) (see YIN–YANG). It is among the latest of the exegetical materials included. The ninth 'wing' is the *Xugua* (Providing the Sequence of the Hexagrams), a collection of remarks on each of the hexagrams which attempts to justify their order in terms of etymological and pseudo-rational considerations. This also seems to be quite late material. The tenth 'wing', the *Zagua* (Hexagrams in Irregular Order), is a collection of brief remarks on the meanings of individual hexagrams, often in terms of contrasting pairs; this is another late addition to the text.

2 History of the text

Traditionally, the hexagrams are thought to have been developed by King Wen of the Zhou in the twelfth century BC, out of the eight trigrams invented by the legendary cultural hero and sage Fu Xi in remotest antiquity. King Wen is also supposed to have composed the hexagram statements or judgements. The line statements are attributed to the Duke of Zhou (d. 1094 BC). However, the assertion that historically identifiable sages are responsible for the origins of the hexagrams and the composition of the first layer of the material is most unlikely. Recent advances in archaeology, paleography and textual studies, which compare the earliest textual layer of the *Yijing* with roughly contemporary inscriptions on bone, shell, metal, stone and other ancient writings

that exhibit similar syntax and vocabulary have thoroughly discredited the myth of its sagely authorship. Modern scholarship has also discovered that the original meaning of the judgments and line statements is radically different from what the earliest layer of exegesis took it to be, and often bears little relation to the values of Confucian morality and ethics. Either the writers of the *tuanzhuan* and the *xiangzhuan* were ignorant of this original meaning – being concerned largely with the mechanics of divination and (often) its amoral consequences – or they knowingly suppressed it in order to replace it with a Confucian (or proto-Confucian) reading. However, with this first layer of exegesis the collection of texts, which eventually developed into the *Yijing*, was given a Confucian slant that shaped all subsequent interpretation right up to modern times.

3 The commentary tradition

Although many commentaries on the *Yijing* were written during the Han period (206 BC– AD 220), these were mostly prognostication recipes based on numerological correspondences between the cosmic, natural and human realms (including calendrical considerations) – a so-called *xiangshu* (image and number) approach in which interpreters identified the trigrams and hexagrams with certain standardized images (symbols with fixed meanings). Wang Bi (226–49) broke completely with this and may be said to have written the first philosophical commentary on the *Yijing*; that is, apart from those sections of the work which are themselves commentaries. His *Zhouyizhu* (Commentary on the Changes of the Zhou), a synthesis of Confucian, Legalist and Daoist views with Confucian views predominant, was extremely influential during the pre-Tang and Tang eras (fourth to tenth centuries AD) and was canonized in the *Zhouyi zhengyi* (Correct Meaning of the Changes of the Zhou) of Kong Yingda (574–648) as the orthodox interpretation of the *Yijing*. Although the commentaries of the later neo-Confucians largely eclipsed Wang's interpretation, much of his commentary was incorporated into the official neo-Confucian orthodox view of the *Yijing*, and what they rejected also helped to shape that view.

A comparison of Wang's commentary with those of CHENG YI (1033–1107) and ZHU XI (1130–1200), the most important of neo-Confucian interpretations, reveals how carefully Cheng and Zhu read Wang's remarks and, whether they agreed with him or not (disagreements mostly involve rejection of elements of Legalism and Daoism perceived in Wang's thought), how his arguments tended to shape theirs. Cheng's *Yichuan Yizhuan* (Yichuan's Commentary on the

Yijing), a commentary of textual interpretation (*yili*), explains the work in terms of how the interplay of *yin* and *yang* defines the moral ideals and behaviour of the noble man (*junzi*). Zhu's *Zhouyi benyi* (Original Meaning of the Changes of the Zhou) attempts a reform of the *xiangshu* (image and number) approach combined with neo-Confucian moral interpretation (*yili*): here the *Yijing* is interpreted both as a manual of divination and a book of moral wisdom. Many other commentaries on the *Yijing* were written throughout traditional times, and not only Confucian/neo-Confucian but also Daoist and even Buddhist versions exist. Nevertheless, the most important commentaries were those noted above by Wang Bi, Cheng Yi and Zhu Xi, and most modern annotated editions and translations in Chinese, Japanese, English and other Western languages are based on one or more of these commentaries.

4   The hexagram as discourse

Although later neo-Confucians often disagreed with Wang Bi, they agreed with his general approach to the meaning of whole hexagrams, individual lines and line positions, and the interaction of lines and positions: each hexagram is a unified entity whose 'controlling principle' is expressed in its name and amplified in the hexagram judgement. The controlling principle usually resides in the ruler of the hexagram, one line that is sovereign over all the others. Change occurs because of the interaction between the innate tendency of things and their counter-tendencies to behave in ways opposed to their natures. 'Things' include individual human beings, and the lines of a hexagram represent different kinds of people in different positions and different situations. The action and interaction of lines occur as if people were involved in a particular set of circumstances. Some lines respond to each other and resonate together, signifying harmonious relationships, and some lines repel and clash, signifying opposition and divergence of interests. This resonance or clash produces movement and change, the understanding of which leads to insight into the innate tendencies of things – 'how things are going' – and adjusting one's behaviour accordingly leads to success. Certain hexagrams signify moments of either obstruction or facility and are indicators that one should either refrain from action or engage in it. *Yin* lines are soft and weak; *yang* lines are hard and strong.

The positions of a hexagram are calculated from bottom to top. The odd number places – first (bottom), third and fifth – are strong *yang* positions; the even number places – second, fourth and sixth (top) – are weak *yin* positions. *Yin* and *yang* lines form resonating pairs, and *yin* and *yin* or *yang* and *yang* lines form discordant pairs: the unlike attract and the like repel. Proper resonate relationships can take place between lines of the lower and upper trigrams: one with four, two with five, three with six, but each must pair with its opposite, *yin* with *yang* or *yang* with *yin*. Secondary harmonious relationships can also occur between contiguous lines when '*yang* rides atop *yin*' or '*yin* carries *yang*' but never the reverse, for this is an unnatural, discordant relationship – as when a superior supports or 'carries' his subordinate.

These sixty-four combinations of *yin* and *yang* lines and *yin* and *yang* positions schematically represent all major kinds of situations found in life. One must know how to cast the hexagrams and how to understand the texts of the *Yijing*, for if one can determine which situation prevails at any given moment, what one's place is in that moment and situation and how one relates to the other participants, 'change will yield its all'. As first (bottom) and sixth (top) lines are at the beginning and end points of hexagrams respectively (and thus signify the beginning and ending of situations), they are at the junctures of what precedes and what follows a given situation, and so 'neither of these positions has a constant status'. The other four line positions are either *yang* and 'noble' (three and five) or *yin* and 'humble' (two and four). *Yang* lines 'should' be in *yang* positions and *yin* lines 'should' be in *yin* positions, for this results in hexagrams that generally indicate facility and harmony. Lines 'out of position' (*yin* in *yang* positions, *yang* in *yin* positions) result in hexagrams that generally indicate obstruction and disharmony.

A special role is assigned to the middle positions in the trigrams, positions two and five. These middle positions indicate 'centrality' and 'the mean' (*zhong*), the territory of proper and balanced behaviour and action. The middle position in the lower trigram is a *yin* position (two), and the one in the upper trigram is a *yang* position (five), so very often, regardless of other considerations, the line in the fifth position – whether *yin* or *yang* – is the ruler of the hexagram as a whole, for it is the 'most noble' place, the 'exalted position'.

This approach to the *Yijing* assumes that the casting of hexagrams is an absolutely sure and accurate method of determining the character of moments of time. This is true of all traditional commentators on the *Yijing*: the way that the yarrow stalks or coins fall is indicative of the shape of that particular moment. Everything that occurs in a given moment is interrelated, and all such events share in the same basic character.

See also: CHINESE CLASSICS; CONFUCIAN PHILOSOPHY, CHINESE; DAOIST PHILOSOPHY; NEO-CONFUCIAN PHILOSOPHY; YIN–YANG

References and further reading

* Kong Yingda (574–648) *Zhouyi zhengyi* (Correct Meaning of the Changes of the Zhou), in Ruan Yuan (ed.) *Shisanjing zhushu* (Commentaries and Subcommentaries on the Thirteen Classics), 1815 woodblock edn; repr. Taibei: Yiwen yinshuguan, 1955. (This edition contains texts of the *Changes*, with the entire commentaries of Wang Bi and Kong Yingda.)

Li Guangdi (ed.) (1715) *Zhouyi zhezhong* (Equitable Judgments on Interpretations of the Changes of the Zhou), woodblock edn; in Yan Lingfeng (ed.) *Yijing jicheng* (Collectanea of Works on the *Book of Changes*), Taibei: Chengwen, 1975. (Contains texts of the *Yijing*, with the entire commentaries of Cheng Yi and Zhu Xi as well as excerpts from other significant commentaries.)

Smith, K., Bol, P.K., Adler, J.A. and Wyatt, D.J. (1990) *Sung Dynasty Uses of the I Ching*, Princeton, NJ: Princeton University Press. (Collection of essays on the history, interpretation and role of the *Yijing* in Song era (960–1279) intellectual life, the formative period of neo-Confucianism.)

* Wang Bi (226–49) *Zhouyizhu* (Commentary on the Changes of the Zhou), in vols 1– 2 of Lou Yulie (ed.) *Wang Bi ji jiaoshi* (Critical Edition of the Works of Wang Bi with Explanatory Notes), Beijing: Zhonghua shuju, 1980. (The best edition of Wang Bi's commentary, with annotations in modern Chinese.)

* * *Yijing* (*c*.9th–2nd century BC), trans. R.J. Lynn, *The Classic of Changes: A New Translation of the I Ching as Interpreted by Wang Bi*, New York: Columbia University Press, 1994. (An integral translation of the *Yijing* along with the commentary by Wang Bi. Where Wang's interpretation differs significantly from the later readings of Cheng Yi and Zhu Xi, references to and translated excerpts from their commentaries are provided for purposes of comparison.)

RICHARD JOHN LYNN

YIN *see* YIN–YANG

YIN–YANG

Yin and yang *always describe the relationships that obtain among unique particulars. Originally these terms designated the shady side and the sunny side of a hill, and gradually came to suggest the way in which one thing 'overshadows' another in some particular aspect of their relationship. Any comparison between two or more unique particulars on any given topic is necessarily hierarchical: one side is* yang *and the other is* yin. *The nature of the opposition captured in this pairing expresses the mutuality, interdependence, hierarchical relationship, diversity and creative efficacy of the dynamic relationships that are immanent in and give value to the world. The full range of difference in the world is deemed explicable through this pairing.*

Yin and *yang* are elements of a correlative pairing which are pragmatically useful in sorting out 'this' and 'that', and are not, as often claimed, dualistic principles of light and dark, male and female, action and passivity where light and dark both exclude each other and logically entail each other and, in their complementarity, constitute a totality. Rather, *yin* and *yang* are first and foremost a vocabulary of qualitative contrasts which have application to specific situations and enable us to make specific distinctions.

To bring this observation to bear on our understanding of *yin* and *yang*, we must start with the relationship that obtains between any two particular things or events. For example, in a given relationship, 'this' older woman might by virtue of her wisdom be regarded as *yang* in contrast to 'that' younger woman who is *yin*. However, if we were to focus on their fecundity or physical strength, the correlation would likely be the opposite. Important here is the primacy of the particular and the fluidity of the relationship. Although things in this world – that is, particular things – are resolutely hierarchical, no one thing excels in all respects, making this same hierarchy the basis for their complementarity.

In the classical Chinese world, things of the same 'kind' are not defined in terms of their essences as natural kinds but by virtue of their affinity or 'kinship' resemblances that associate them, their 'family resemblances'. Important here is the primacy of particular difference and the absence of any assumed sameness or strict identity. Things are deemed to have resemblances based upon analogous roles or functions. Thus one thing, by virtue of its relationships, evokes many. The suggestiveness of each phenomenon in calling up other similar phenomena is comparable to the multivalence of poetic images. Describing a particular phenomenon does not require the discovery of some underlying determinative and originative principle – a basis for making 'many' one – but a mapping out and an unravelling of the phenomenon's multiple correlations and of the relationships and conditions that make up its context. *Yin* and *yang* define the tension between multiple perspectives on phenomena, and they enable us to interpret and bring coherence to our circumstances by allowing us to discern the patterns in relationships within particular contexts. They provide a vocabulary for sorting out the relationships that obtain among things as they come together and constitute themselves in unique compositions.

Thus, *yin* and *yang* as correlatives are not universal principles that define some essential feature of phenomena, but are explanatory categories that register a creative tension in specific differences and thus make the immediate concrete things of the world intelligible. It is only through a process of generalization that feminine and male gender traits are construed as predominantly *yin* and *yang* respectively, and vocabulary such as vaginal orifice (*yinmen*) and virility (*yangdao*) emerges to essentialize the *yin* and *yang* contrast.

The *yin–yang* vocabulary is functional. In order to evaluate the propensity of a situation and manipulate it in advance, we must make distinctions. This is where the vocabulary of *yin* and *yang* comes into play. We begin from the assumed uniqueness of each situation and the uniqueness of the components that constitute it. The *yin–yang* contrast provides a line, enabling us to divide a continuous situation into distinct yet interdependent particulars. *Yin* is a becoming-*yang*; *yang* is a becoming-*yin*. We must come to know the particular conditions that govern a situation so that we can manipulate them to advantage. This requires that one translate the situation into the *yin–yang* vocabulary of complementary opposites: strong–weak, fast–slow, many–few, regular–irregular and so on. *Yin–yang* is a vocabulary that enables us to discriminate among the many factors which together constitute the force of circumstances, and that allows us to control this force through the strategic adjustments. Once we have arrived at an understanding of the circumstances, we must identify those critical factors which will enable us to turn the configuration of an unfolding situation into an opportunity.

See also: CATEGORIES §4; CHINESE PHILOSOPHY; DAO; DE; PARTICULARS; QI; YOU–WU

References and further reading

Graham, A.C. (1989) *Disputers of the Tao: Philosophical Argument in Ancient China*, LaSalle, IL: Open Court. (A survey of ancient Chinese thought.)

Hall, D.L. and Ames, R.T. (1995) *Anticipating China: Thinking Through the Narratives of Chinese and Western Culture*, Albany, NY: State University of New York Press. (A comparative study of the uncommon assumptions that ground the Chinese and Western philosophical traditions.)

ROGER T. AMES

YOGĀCĀRA SCHOOL OF BUDDHISM *see* BUDDHISM, YOGĀCĀRA SCHOOL OF

YONG AND TI *see* TI AND YONG

YORUBA EPISTEMOLOGY

*The Yoruba of west Africa have articulated systematic criteria that are used to assign varying degrees of epistemic certainty to experience. What one views with one's own eyes and experiences at first-hand (*ìmò*) are judged as reliable ways of knowing the truth, providing there is conscious comprehension of what one is perceiving. Only propositions describing such experiences are regarded as true, or* òótó. *Less reliable is information received via books, other people, the media and the oral tradition. If such comparatively secondhand information, or* ìgbàgbó, *can be experimentally tested and accordingly verified, it has the potential to become* ìmò. *If verification cannot be attested, discussion, analysis and good judgment are essential tools for distinguishing the more reliable information from the less reliable.*

The semantic distinction the Yoruba make between *ìmò* and *ìgbàgbó* serves as a basis for comparison with that between knowledge and belief in traditional Western epistemological theory (see BELIEF AND KNOWLEDGE §1). Although the Yoruba affirm the epistemic importance of all sensory perception, they single out visual perception, or *ìrírin*, as clearer and more reliable. When conjoined with cognitive comprehension, or *èrí okòn* (literally meaning 'the witnessing of the mind', connoting the conscious processes that arise from both the act of seeing and the sense that one understands what one sees), the two satisfactory conditions for *ìmò*, or knowledge, have been achieved. Experience that satisfies these conditions and propositions that relate such experience, are characterized as being true, or *òótó*. The emphasis placed upon propositions being true because they accurately report experience indicates elements of a correspondence theory of truth (see TRUTH, CORRESPONDENCE THEORY OF §1).

Ìgbàgbó encompasses all the events and information which do not constitute first-hand experience. This applies to most of what one is taught in the course of a formal education, what one learns from books, the media, other people and, of particular interest in the case of the Yoruba, from the oral tradition. *Ìgbàgbó* is the conflation of 'agree' and 'accept', or *gbà*, and 'hear' and 'understand', or *gbó*. The independent application of negation to its component parts produces four distinct logical possibilities, each of which may be said to correspond to a likely speaker–hearer relationship. These four levels of communication are identified by the Yoruba in the following concrete terms:

(1) *Hearing and agreeing* (p.q): where a hearer, H, understands and accepts as credible what is being reported and therefore, in principle, has no objection to incorporating it into their own store of information. This is optimum communication.
(2) *Hearing and not-agreeing* (p.~q): H understands what is being offered but declines to accept it as authoritative or correct. Disagreements or lies are offered as standard examples.
(3) *Not-hearing and not-agreeing* (~p.~q): failure to communicate. H does not understand what is being said and therefore cannot agree.
(4) *Not-hearing and agreeing* (~p.q): in effect, to agree with what one does not understand. Either a case of error or H is described as a fool.

When *ìmò* and *ìgbàgbó* are challenged and an argument or *àríyàn jiyàn* results, the tactics recommended for resolving the dispute are complex and interwoven. Often the disputants do not share the same (relevant) first-hand experiences. This may be corrected by a process of verification so long as it is possible to test the claim empirically and thereby enable people to see the results for themselves: counterclaims about the effectiveness of a certain medicine, for example, can be checked by testing the treatment. When such testing is impossible, there is no way in which the *ìmò* of one person can become the *ìmò* of another. In such a case, the only recourse is to a process of justification. The parties concerned should each explain (*àlàyè*) their own position by giving a full account of relevant first- or second-hand experiences. Any witnesses whose experiences may be relevant should also be called in the hope that their testimony will help decide which account, if any, should be favoured. Such things as the moral

character, or *ìwà*, of each participant must be considered, as this might affect the reliability of information.

The aim in this extensive process of justification and evaluation is to lead the various parties to reflect upon and perhaps modify their respective positions, so that agreement may be reached on an accurate account of events, or *papò*, meaning literally 'the word has come together'. Of course it is recognized that, even if the parties concerned supply full explanations, their moral characters are found to be intact and the testimonies of witnesses are adjudged satisfactory, the dispute may remain unsettled and the argument may continue. In such cases the only realistic alternative is to begin again in the hope that further discussion and reflection may achieve a resolution.

The system that emerges from these criteria is three-tiered. *Imò* is the sole category of experience or propositions permitted to be regarded as both certain and true (*òótó*). *Ìgbàgbó*, which in principle is open to empirical testing, verification and thereby transformation into *ìmò*, is the next most reliable category. *Ìgbàgbó* that can never be verified and can only be evaluated on the basis of explanation, discussion and reflection is the least certain.

Prevalent paradigms describe African traditional thought systems as insignificantly critical or reflective (particularly of the oral traditions, which are said to be the locus of knowledge in such societies), and only marginally empirical because of their emphasis on magic, superstition and secrecy. This account of the ways in which the Yoruba employ and explain key epistemological terms in their language demonstrates that they are more critically- and empirically-minded than had been supposed (see EPISTEMIC RELATIVISM §1). The oral tradition, the wealth of knowledge passed down through one's forbears, has not been regarded as an authoritative system of truths. As *ìgbàgbó*, the status of its truth is hypothetical and conditional on being tested or proven practically effective. When proof cannot be obtained, critical discussion and reflection are vital.

References and further reading

Abimbola, W. and Hallen, B. (1993) 'Secrecy and Objectivity in the Methodology and Literature of *Ifá* Divination', in M.H. Nooter (ed.) *Secrecy: African Art that Conceals and Reveals*, New York, NY: Museum for African Art. (The instrumental functions of secrecy in an African system of divination.)

Appiah, K.A. (1982) 'Old Gods, New Worlds: Some Recent Work in the Philosophy of African Traditional Religion', in *In My Father's House: Africa in the Philosophy of Culture*, London: Methuen; 2nd edn, Oxford: Oxford University Press, 1992. (Incisive discussion and analysis of various characteristics said to distinguish 'traditional' from 'modern' societies, particularly with respect to the formulation and criticism of theoretical explanations.)

Hallen, B. and Sodipo, J.O. (1986) *Knowledge, Belief and Witchcraft: Analytic Experiments in African Philosophy*, London: Ethnographica. (Chapter two expands on Yoruba epistemology and draws comparisons with English-language epistemological equivalents.)

Wiredu, K. (1996) 'The Concept of Truth in the Akan Language', *Cultural Universals and Particulars: an African Perspective*, Bloomington and Indianapolis: Indiana University Press. (Analysis of epistemological variations between the Akan language of Ghana and English. Further evidence of the epistemological sophistication of traditional African systems of thought.)

BARRY HALLEN

YOU–WU

In the Western metaphysical tradition, 'being' has most generally been thought to denote either a common property of things or a container which relates things by placing them within its own structure. Metaphysical notions of being are generally associated with the concept of ground. By contrast, the Chinese existential verb you *(being) overlaps with the sense of 'having' rather than the copula, and therefore* you *(to be) means 'to be present' or 'to be around' while* wu *(not to be) means 'not to be present' or 'not to be around'. This means that* wu *does not indicate strict opposition or contradiction, but absence. Thus, the* you–wu *distinction suggests mere contrast in the sense of either the presence or absence of* x, *rather than an assertion of the existence or nonexistence of* x.

Not a little misunderstanding of classical Chinese thought has been occasioned by the fact that uses of *you* (being) and *wu* (not-being) often seem to echo the speculative understandings of classical Western metaphysics. Thus the Daoist sentiment, often rendered in English as 'Not-being is superior to being,' has given rise to a host of mystical and speculative reflections inspired by the Parmenidean or Heideggerian projects (see PARMENIDES; HEIDEGGER, M.). In fact, a better translation is simply, 'Nothing is superior to something'. However, even this might suggest presence and absence in some absolute sense. For the Western thinker, an even more accurate translation would be 'Not-having is superior to having': or as a contemporary Chinese Marxist translation reads, 'Not-owning is superior to owning'.

It may be said that the proper understanding of 'being' in the Chinese tradition, more than any other philosophical concept, depends upon the ability to suspend predispositions deriving from Western philosophical sources. For, without recourse to the senses of being associated with Western speculative philosophies (see BEING), and in the absence as well of the sophisticated logical apparatus employed by the nominalistic traditions in contemporary thought, the interpretative contexts familiar to Western trained thinkers are simply not relevant. Thus the Chinese discussions of the *you–wu* relation must not be thought to be 'metaphysical', if we mean by metaphysics anything like a universal science of principles or of being-itself. Nor may we be allowed to interpret 'being' and 'not-being' by recourse to logical operators associated with modal or truth-functional logics (see MODAL LOGIC).

Thus when the Chinese discuss cosmological issues of the sort that require an understanding of kinds of existing things, or the basic categories that make up the world as we know it, we must proceed with caution. While it is true that Chinese thinkers, particularly the Daoists, ask about things, they do not ask about 'categories' or 'kinds' in any manner that would suggest that things have 'logical essences' or constitute 'natural kinds' (see ESSENTIALISM).

The principal reason Chinese thinkers are not apt to ask after the *logos* of the cosmos is that they lack an operative sense of cosmos or 'world' as a coherent whole. Their sense of *logos* – *li* (pattern) – is a radically situated notion (see LI). In fact, the Chinese understanding of 'cosmos' as 'the ten thousand things' means that, strictly speaking, they have no concept of cosmos at all insofar as that notion entails either a coherent, single-ordered world or a congeries of entities with essential features or essential modes of connectedness. The Chinese are therefore primarily 'acosmotic' thinkers.

In the absence of a sense of being as the ground of things, the act of understanding and articulating the sense of things – *daoli* (the grasp of the patternings (*li*) of *dao* (the ways of things)) – cannot have ontological reference (see DAO). The closest to our typical understanding of 'reason' or 'reasoning' is to be found in 'seeking the *li*'. *Wulixue* in modern Chinese is 'the investigation of the patterns of things and events', what we term 'physics'. 'Psychology' is *xinlixue*, 'the investigation of the patterns of the heart–mind'. In general, to be *heli*, to be in accord with *li*, is to be reasonable or rational (see LI; CONFUCIAN PHILOSOPHY, CHINESE).

The translation of *li* as 'principle' has created some confusion in the minds of Western interpreters of Chinese, many of whom just assume that *li* must, at some level, be transcendent. But *li*, as a 'making sense of things', cannot be understood as a process of seeking principles as determining sources of order, or of discovering essential categories inclusive of particular things. It is, rather, an activity which constructs categories (*lei*) analogically, then traces, again by analogical means, correlated details which manifest patterns of relationships immanent within things and events. This sort of reasoning depends upon non-inferential access to enlarged and deepened patternings. Inclusion or exclusion of items within a 'category' are never associated with notions of logical 'type' or 'class'. The sortings are analogical, not logical. This understanding of 'reason' and 'reasoning' is one more implication of the fact that the Chinese never asked 'the question of being'.

See also: BEING; CHINESE PHILOSOPHY; CONFUCIAN PHILOSOPHY, CHINESE; DAO; DAOIST PHILOSOPHY; EXISTENCE; LI

References and further reading

Daodejing (*c.*350–250 BC?), trans. D.C. Lau, *Tao te Ching*, Harmondsworth: Penguin, 1963. (The being–nonbeing relation, expressed through the *yin–yang* pairing, is a principal theme of the *Daodejing*.)

Graham, A.C. (1989) *Disputers of the Tao: Philosophical Argument in Ancient China*, LaSalle, IL: Open Court, 1989. (See especially Parts II: 3, III: 1 and Appendix 2.)

—— (1990) 'Being in Western Philosophy Compared with Shih/Fei and Yu/Wu in Chinese Philosophy' in A.C. Graham (ed.) *Studies in Chinese Philosophy and Philosophical Literature*, Albany, NY: State University of New York Press. (Graham's discussions in this essay and the work immediately cited above, constitute the most nuanced comparative treatment of the senses of 'being' and 'nonbeing' in Chinese and Western traditions.)

Hall, D.L. and Ames, R.T. (1995) *Anticipating China: Thinking Through the Narratives of Chinese and Western Culture*, Albany, NY: State University of New York Press. (A comparative study of the uncommon assumptions that ground the Chinese and Western philosophical traditions.)

DAVID L. HALL
ROGER T. AMES

YUGOSLAVIA, PHILOSOPHY IN *see* SOUTH SLAVS, PHILOSOPHY OF

Z

ZABARELLA, JACOPO (1533–89)

Jacopo Zabarella was a professor of philosophy at the University of Padua. His work shows conclusively not only that it was possible to philosophize creatively within the limits of the Aristotelian tradition but also that this was still being done towards the end of the Renaissance period. Zabarella's aim was not to overthrow Aristotle's doctrines, but to expound them as clearly as possible. He produced an extensive body of work on the nature of logic, arguing that it was neither an art nor a science, but rather an instrumental intellectual discipline which arose from the philosopher's practice of philosophizing or forming secondary notions. He also worked extensively on scientific method. He gives an account of order as disposing what we come to know through method, and he divides method into the method of composition, which moves from cause to effect, and the method of resolution, which moves from effect to cause. He also discussed regressus *(a method for uniting composition and resolution) and thought that it would enable the scientist to discover new causal relations at the same time as proving conclusions with absolute necessity. Zabarella's work was instrumental in a renewal of natural philosophy, methodology and the theory of knowledge; and it had a major impact on seventeenth-century philosophy textbooks, especially in the Protestant countries of northern Europe.*

1 Life
2 The nature of logic
3 Arts and sciences
4 Method
5 The method of *regressus*
6 Natural philosophy

1 Life

Count Jacopo (or Giacomo) Zabarella seems never to have left his native city, Padua. He enjoyed a thorough education, receiving his doctorate in philosophy and the liberal arts in 1553, and began his teaching career in 1564 when he obtained the first chair of logic. In 1568 he obtained the second extraordinary chair of natural philosophy, and was promoted to the first

extraordinary chair of natural philosophy in 1577. Finally, in 1585, Zabarella obtained the second ordinary chair of natural philosophy, which he held until his death. Padua was a leading university, and Zabarella was taught by some of the best teachers there: Francesco Robortello in the humanities, Bernardino Tomitano in logic, Marcantonio Genua in physics and metaphysics, and Pietro Catena in mathematics. His academic career was exemplary for a Paduan professor of philosophy, with two exceptions. First, the statutes of the university prevented him, as a native Paduan, from obtaining the first ordinary chair in natural philosophy; second, he never took a degree in medicine, perhaps through his own choice. His publications reflect his teaching in the Aristotelian tradition. From 1578 to 1584, he published on logical problems, including a commentary on the *Posterior Analytics*. In 1590 he published a volume of questions in the contemporary Aristotelian manner, which contained 30 books and followed the traditional order of Aristotle's works on nature. These were supplemented by commentaries on the *Physics*, *On Generation and Corruption*, *On Meteors* and *On the Soul*.

2 The nature of logic

Zabarella's introductory treatise on the nature of logic, *De natura logicae* (On the Nature of Logic), is basic to his teaching in logic (see LOGIC, RENAISSANCE §1). He defines logic as being neither a science nor an art, but, in keeping with the traditional meaning of the word 'organon', just an instrument of the arts and sciences. Logic does not have a real subject of its own, but deals with concepts, which stand for real beings. In this it is comparable to grammar. The difference between grammar and logic is that grammar is concerned with the perfect verbal expression of concepts, and hence is a linguistic discipline (*disciplina sermocinalis*), while logic invents second notions (*notiones secundae*, often called second intentions), that are able to create order among concepts, and serve to recognize the truth and distinguish it from falsehood in every instance. Logic is thus a rational discipline (*disciplina rationalis*). It is not itself philosophy, but springs from philosophy and is devoted to philosophical ends.

Zabarella followed Averroes in dividing logic into

two parts: universal logic, which is common to all subjects; and particular logic, which is specific to particular subjects. The first three books of Aristotle's Organon, the *Categories*, *De Interpretatione* and the *Prior Analytics*, constitute universal logic. Aristotle's *Posterior Analytics*, *Topics* and *Sophistical Refutations* are said to deal with particular logic, in that they deal respectively with the demonstrative syllogism, the dialectical syllogism and the sophistical syllogism (see ARISTOTLE §1). Following the Neoplatonic commentators SIMPLICIUS and AMMONIUS, Zabarella included Aristotle's *Rhetoric* and *Poetics* in logic. The former is included because it teaches the use of the rhetorical syllogism or enthymeme, and rhetorical induction or example; the latter because it also teaches the use of example, not to persuasive ends, but for imitation. It has been argued that Zabarella here paved the way for modern aesthetics.

3 Arts and sciences

Since logic, viewed as the universal instrument for distinguishing between the true and the false, differs according to the objects to which it is applied and the ends for which it is used, its nature depends on the realm of possible objects and ends. Rhetoric and poetics are special cases because they deal not with knowledge but with the political disciplines (*disciplinae civiles*) in so far as they are concerned with the good of the people. Sophistical syllogistic is another special case, because it is directed towards deception and prefers to use falsehoods as its material. Dialectic and demonstration, however, are directed towards the expression of truth. Dialectic is aimed at the production of opinion, and deals with probable and contingent material; demonstration is dedicated to the acquisition of truth, and so is exclusively occupied with necessary, true objects. As a result the sciences in the proper sense of that term, as pertaining to demonstrative knowledge, are limited to those disciplines that deal with the necessary and eternal or with what can be deduced from necessary principles. These disciplines are the contemplative sciences, metaphysics, mathematics and physics. The necessity involved is both ontological, with respect to the objects known, and cognitive, with respect to the knowing subjects.

All the other so-called arts and sciences deal with contingent objects, that is, with objects which depend on our volition and are therefore either actions, as in the case of the moral disciplines, or artificial beings generated by our productive faculties, as in the case of the arts in the proper sense of that term. The arts as arts are unable to generate true knowledge rather than mere opinion, except where inferences from the desired ends to the necessary means are concerned.

Given this distinction, Zabarella presents the contemplative sciences as being the only defenders of true knowledge. However, by describing the arts in terms of their specifically productive character, he secures for them the autonomy of modern technical disciplines. The use made of Zabarella's discussion in the textbooks of seventeenth-century Protestant countries prove this seemingly traditional Aristotelian division to have been fruitful.

4 Method

The instrument for acquiring knowledge in the broadest sense is method. Since knowledge can be acquired either through teaching or through invention, Zabarella distinguished between two kinds of method: *ordo doctrinae*, which is the order of teaching, and *methodus* in the narrow sense, which is the method of finding new knowledge. Both involve leading the way from something known to something hitherto unknown. *Methodus* does this by the inference of new items of knowledge; *ordo* does it by the disposition of items already known to the teacher. Neither procedure is governed by the nature of the objects known, but by the nature of human knowledge. *Methodus* starts with what is better known to us, which can be the cause for further cognition, rather than with the better known in itself, which can be the cause of a known object. *Ordo* starts with what is either necessary or useful for teaching and learning. In the contemplative sciences, which aim at perfect knowledge, *ordo* follows the so-called way of composition (*compositio*) from general principles to particular beings; in moral philosophy and the arts, which aim at action or production, *ordo* follows the so-called way of resolution (*resolutio*) from the desired end to its first principles. The bitterly polemical reaction of Zabarella's contemporaries, especially his colleague Francesco Piccolomini, to this grounding of method and order on cognitive rather than ontological principles, shows how revolutionary his approach seemed at the time.

5 The method of *regressus*

Although, given their concern with perfect knowledge, the contemplative sciences cannot do without the deductive procedures of composition, they also depend on the inductive procedures of resolution, at least in the case of physics, where the particular beings or effects are better known to us.

The so-called method of *regressus* is a model for combining both procedures that is found in the

Aristotelian tradition from Averroes on, and was revived during the Italian Renaissance. According to this method, the natural philosopher should first infer from the known effect the existence of the cause of the effect. This is the so-called *demonstratio quia* or demonstration of the fact. Then in a second step, in the so-called *demonstratio propter quid* or demonstration of the reasoned fact, the natural philosopher should infer from the cause to the effect, which is now known through its cause, and hence in a scientific manner. The crucial problem with this procedure is how to avoid mere circular reasoning, or rather, how to make sure that the cause, whose existence is demonstrated in the first step, is indeed the cause of that effect. From the beginning of the sixteenth century, it had become clear that it was necessary to introduce a third, intermediary step, which involved some kind of *negotiatio intellectus* or intellectual operation. How the intellect did this was a matter of dispute.

Zabarella himself solves the problem of the *negotiatio intellectus*, which he calls a mental examination (*examen mentale*) in terms of his psychology of knowledge. Since for him the task of this intermediary step is to make distinct the confused knowledge of the cause that was acquired through the first step, he refers to his work on the agent mind in which he develops an account of the transformation of confused into distinct knowledge through the analysis of a given whole in terms of its parts. He presents this process as the specific ability of the human mind. Thus once more method as a means for acquiring knowledge is based on the cognitive structure of the knowing subject rather than on the ontological structure of the object of knowledge. This foreshadows the substitution of epistemology for metaphysics in much modern philosophy.

6 Natural philosophy

Natural philosophy, which deals with corporeal beings that have an inner principle of movement, differs from metaphysics (which contemplates being as being) and from mathematics (which deals with abstracted beings), both with respect to the object considered (*res considerata*) and with respect to the way of considering (*modus considerandi*). As a result, it is autonomous and independent of both the other contemplative sciences. It has to know and teach the very essence of natural beings. First, it has to deal with their basic principles, such as matter and motion, which are not natural beings themselves. They are discussed in Aristotle's *Physics*. Second, it has to deal with the accidents of natural beings understood through their causes. These are the subject of Aristotle's other writings on nature, from *On the Heavens* to *On the Soul*. Generally speaking, Zabarella saw natural philosophy as developed by Aristotle as complete according to the scope of its subject matter as well as in its manner of consideration. His main emphasis is therefore on teaching, for invention is only needed in the rare case of a gap in the Aristotelian corpus (see NATURAL PHILOSOPHY, MEDIEVAL).

In spite of its empirical basis, Zabarella's natural philosophy is not concerned with anything akin to experiment. Indeed, if experiments were to be developed, they would find their place in the productive arts rather than in natural philosophy. Nor was he concerned with the role of mathematics in scientific procedure. However, attempts have been made to link him with Galileo. For instance, Randall (1961), following Cassirer, referred to the Renaissance discussion of *regressus* up to Zabarella as a preparation for Galileo's new method of natural science. This hypothesis has been widely debated but remains problematic.

See also: ARISTOTELIANISM, RENAISSANCE; LOGIC, RENAISSANCE

List of works

Zabarella, J. (before 1578) *De natura logicae* (On the Nature of Logic), in J. Zabarella, *Opera Logica*, Hildesheim: Olms, 1966, 1–102. (Zabarella's fundamental work on logic.)

—— (1582) *In duos Aristotelis libros Posteriores Analyticos commentarii* (Commentary on the Two Books of Aristotle's *Posterior Analytics*), Venice. (Exposition of Aristotle's theory of science.)

—— (1585) 'Una "oratio" programmatica di G. Zabarella' (A Programmatical Lecture by Jacopo Zabarella), ed. M. Dal Pra, *Rivista critica di storia della filosofia* 21 (1966): 286–91. (Inaugural lecture on the relation between logic and philosophy.)

—— (1597) *Opera logica* (Logical Works), Cologne: Lazarus Zetznerus; repr. Hildesheim: Olms, 1966. (The basic collection of Zabarella's writings on logic, method and theory of science. Contains editions from 1578, 1580, 1582 and 1584.)

—— (1602) *Commentarii in Aristotelis libros Physicorum, In libros De generatione et corruptione, In Meteora* (Commentary on Aristotle's *Physics*, *On Generation and Corruption* and *On Meteors*), Frankfurt: Lazarus Zetznerus. (Expositions of the three most general Aristotelian writings on nature.)

—— (1606) *In tres libros Aristotelis De anima commentarii* (Commentary on Aristotle's Three Books *On the Soul*), Frankfurt: Lazarus Zetznerus;

repr. Frankfurt: Minerva, 1966. (Exposition of Aristotle's psychology, including his theory of knowledge.)

—— (1607) *De rebus naturalibus* (On Natural Things), Frankfurt: Lazarus Zetznerus; repr. Frankfurt: Minerva 1966. (The basic collection of his treatises in natural philosophy.)

References and further reading

Edwards, W.F. (1960) 'The logic of Jacopo Zabarella (1533–1589)', unpublished dissertation, Columbia University, NY. (Logic and methodology presented from Randall's point of view; vast biography and bibliography.)

—— (1969) 'Jacopo Zabarella: A Renaissance Aristotelian's View of Rhetoric and Poetry and their Relation to Philosophy', in *Arts libéraux et philosophie au moyen âge*, Paris and Montreal, Que.: Vrin. (On the view that rhetoric and poetics are parts of logic.)

Kessler, E. (1988) 'The intellective soul', in C.B. Schmitt *et al.* (eds) *The Cambridge History of Renaissance Philosophy*, Cambridge: Cambridge University Press, 485–534. (Zabarella's psychology in the context of the Renaissance.)

Lohr, C.H. (1988) *Latin Aristotle Commentaries II: Renaissance Authors*, Florence: Olschki, 497–503. (Bibliography including Zabarella's unpublished works and works available only in Renaissance editions.)

Mikkeli, H. (1992) *An Aristotelian Response to Renaissance Humanism. Jacopo Zabarella on the Nature of Arts and Sciences*, Studia Historica 41, Helsinki: Societas Historica Finlandiae. (Basic exposition of Zabarella's conception of the arts and the sciences; good bibliography.)

* Randall, J.H. (1961) *The School of Padua and the Emergence of Modern Science*, Padua: Antenore. (Randall's revolutionary hypothesis about the significance of the discussion of *regressus*. Referred to in §6.)

Schmitt, C.B. (1969) 'Experience and Experiment: A Comparison of Zabarella's View with Galileo's in *De motu*', *Studies in the Renaissance* 16: 80–138. (Explains why Zabarella is unacquainted with experiments in the modern sense.)

Wallace, W.A. (1988) 'Randall Redivivus: Galileo and the Paduan Aristotelians', *Journal of the History of Ideas* 49: 133–49. (Defence of Randall's hypothesis supported by new documents.)

ECKHARD KESSLER

ZEAMI (1363–1443)

Zeami was one of the leading innovators in the art of Nō, *at a time when Zen Buddhism dominated the Japanese intellectual and cultural order. He practised Zen Buddhism (Sōtō branch), and found in Zen teachings the epistemology that gave* Nō *its aesthetic foundations. While his* Nō *treatises are buttressed by his observation of the nature and the workings of the mind, they also reveal Shintō sensibility in their view that the origin of entertainment is sacred.*

Nō (or *noh*) is a theatrical entertainment which mixes singing and dance movements by actors (the main actor usually wears a mask), accompanied by a chorus and musicians. Zeami (real name Kanze Motokiyo) became the head of the Kanze-za, a prominent *Nō* troupe. He composed or reworked at least sixty *Nō* plays, directed and choreographed them, trained his sons as *Nō* actors and playwrights, wrote *Nō* treatises for them, toured with his troupe and entered *Nō* competitions on various occasions.

A passage in the treatise *Kakyō* (A Mirror Held to the Flower) illustrates how Zeami gave his attention to the mental and psychological aspects of *Nō* performance. He discusses several essential practices for the *Nō* actor. For instance, in order to move the audience, he advises that an actor first enunciate his line and then follow with a physical movement. It is more effective for an actor to sing, 'I cry', and then move his arm to cover his face to express that gesture, than it is for him to cover his face and then sing 'I cry'. Zeami explains that in the latter case the actor's words would have no lingering effect. He holds that this slight staggering of the auditory and visual inputs is crucial in creating an artistic effect.

Zeami places at the foundation of his art the same development of mental awareness that is sought in Zen Buddhism (see BUDDHIST PHILOSOPHY, JAPANESE). In *Kakyō*, he notes that to achieve a graceful appearance, the actor must see what is at his right, left and in front of him with his physical eyes, but he must also train himself to see himself from behind with his mind. Zeami terms this ability to see what the physical eyes cannot see *riken no ken* (seeing separate [from an ego-bound mode of] seeing). The cultivation of this mental capacity, which transcends our ego-centred perspective, requires of the actor a conscious training of his mind. Zeami does not say outright that a *Nō* actor must go through meditation practice as a Zen monk, but he seems to maintain that the mental practice involved in *Nō* training and Zen practice is one and the same. Through his assiduous practice and training, the *Nō* actor will eventually have to attain awakening (*satori*), just as a Zen monk must, and he then must further incorporate his awakening into his performance. Zeami warns his sons that expert spectators also see into the accomplishment of the actor and his performance with their *riken no ken*. Thus, it is essential for the actor to develop his *riken no ken* to take account of even the critical eyes of the spectators.

Because of the homogeneity of the mindset required of the *Nō* actor and Zen practitioner, the aesthetic hierarchy of *Nō*, at least at the time of Zeami, was heavily informed by Zen taste. Accordingly, what Zeami terms the higher sort of plays or performances do not consist of surface beauty that merely please eyes and ears. Rather, they comprise plays and performances that possess an ethereal beauty like that of the heavenly maiden, or which can be compared to 'white plum blossoms' or the 'icy quality' of 'snow piled up in a silver container'. According to Zeami, this sort of beauty is pure, beyond any conscious manipulation of mere technique, and evokes deep emotional resonance in the minds of the audience (see the *Kakyō*, *Kyūi* (Notes on the Nine Levels) and *Shūgyoku tokka* (Finding Gems and Gaining the Flower)).

Zeami could not neglect Zen partly because the Shogun Yoshimochi (reigned 1408–28) patronized it. However, Shintō sensibility was also inherently present in his formation of *Nō* as a distinct genre of art. For instance, Zeami ascribes one of the origins of *Nō* to the Shintō account of the 'incident of the heavenly rock cave', in which the Sun Goddess Amaterasu hid herself inside a rock cave and the entire world became dark. Ama no Uzume, a goddess, performed a shamanic dance in a trance and aroused the other deities present. The uproarious noise these deities made brought Amaterasu out of the cave; the world became bright again, and the gods' faces (*omo*) shone 'white' (*shiro*) in the bright light. In the *Fūshi kaden* (Teachings on Style and the Flower) Zeami subscribes to this traditional etymology of the word *omoshiro* (delightful or interesting).

We find in Zeami's treatises penetrating psychological insights, an applied Zen epistemology and vibrant religious sensibility. All of these contributed to his articulation of the art of *Nō* as a path of self-awakening and a god-inspired entertainment that gives pleasure to the people.

See also: AESTHETICS, JAPANESE; BUDDHIST PHILOSOPHY, JAPANESE; SHINTŌ

List of works

Zeami (1400–33) *Zeami-shū* (Works of Zeami), ed. Konishi J., Tokyo: Chikuma Shobō, 1970; ed.

Omote A. and Katō S., *Zeami. Zenchiku*, Nihon Shisō Taikei 24, Tokyo: Iwanami Shoten, 1974. (Konishi contains the original text and translation into modern Japanese; helpful. Omote and Kato contains the original texts of Zeami's and Zenchiku's *Nō* treatises with extensive notes.)

—— (1400–6) *Fūshi kaden* (Teachings on Style and the Flower), ed. and trans. J.T. Rimer and Yamazaki Masakazu, *On the Art of the Nō Drama: The Major Treatises of Zeami*, Princeton, NJ: Princeton University Press, 1984. (Zeami's earliest and most complete work. As well as instructions for actors, the last part of the work contains Zeami's own philosophy of the art of *Nō* performance.)

—— (1420) *Shikadō* (The True Path to the Flower) ed. and trans. J.T. Rimer and M. Yamazaki, *On the Art of the Nō Drama: The Major Treatises of Zeami*, Princeton, NJ: Princeton University Press, 1984. (An instruction on how to achieve the 'free rank' of the art of performance, going beyond the ordinary level; the importance of mental attitude is introduced.)

—— (*c.*1420) *Yūgaku shūdō fūken* (Disciplines for the Joy of Art), trans. Izutsu Toshihiko and Izutsu Toyo, *The Theory of Beauty in the Classical Aesthetics of Japan*, The Hague: Martinus Nijhoff, 1981; ed. and trans. J.T. Rimer and M. Yamazaki, *On the Art of the Nō Drama: The Major Treatises of Zeami*, Princeton, NJ: Princeton University Press, 1984. (An instruction on how to raise a young actor into a mature actor.)

—— (1423) *Nōsakusho* (also known as *Sandō*, The Three Elements for Composing a Play), ed. and trans. J.T. Rimer and M. Yamazaki, *On the Art of the Nō Drama: The Major Treatises of Zeami*, Princeton, NJ: Princeton University Press, 1984. (An instruction by Zeami to his son on how to write good *Nō* plays.)

—— (1424) *Kakyō* (A Mirror Held to the Flower), trans. M. Nearman, '*Kakyō*, Zeami's Fundamental Principles of Acting', *Monumenta Nipponica* 1982, 37 (3): 333–74 and 37 (4): 459–96; ed. and trans. J.T. Rimer and M. Yamazaki, *On the Art of the Nō Drama: The Major Treatises of Zeami*, Princeton, NJ: Princeton University Press, 1984. (Zeami's secrets of how to perform well, contains the gist of his understanding that leads to successful *Nō* performance; very important work.)

—— (*c.*1424) *Ongyoku kowadashi kuden* (The Art of Singing and Articulation), ed. Konishi J., Tokyo: Chikuma Shobō, 1970. (Instructions on how to use the voice in performance.)

—— (1428) *Kyūi* (Notes on the Nine Levels); trans. Izutsu Toshihiko and Izutsu Toyo, *The Theory of Beauty in the Classical Aesthetics of Japan*, The

Hague: Martinus Nijhoff, 1981; ed. and trans. J.T. Rimer and M. Yamazaki, *On the Art of the Nō Drama: The Major Treatises of Zeami*, Princeton, NJ: Princeton University Press, 1984. (Divides *Nō* plays into nine levels and describes how actors learn to play different levels as they reach different degrees of accomplishment.)

—— (1428) *Shūgyoku tokka* (Finding Gems and Gaining the Flower), trans. Izutsu Toshihiko and Izutsu Toyo, *The Theory of Beauty in the Classical Aesthetics of Japan*, The Hague: Martinus Nijhoff, 1981; ed. and trans. J.T. Rimer and M. Yamazaki, *On the Art of the Nō Drama: The Major Treatises of Zeami*, Princeton, NJ: Princeton University Press, 1984. (An instruction handed down to his son-in-law, containing a summary of Zeami's secret of successful performance.)

—— (1430) *Shūdōsho* (Learning the Way), ed. and trans. J.T. Rimer and M. Yamazaki, *On the Art of the Nō Drama: The Major Treatises of Zeami*, Princeton, NJ: Princeton University Press, 1984. (An instruction to the members of the Kanze troop, regarding the responsibilities of each.)

—— (1430) *Sarugaku dangi* (An Account of Zeami's Reflection on Art), ed. and trans. J.T. Rimer and M. Yamazaki, *On the Art of the Nō Drama: The Major Treatises of Zeami*, Princeton, NJ: Princeton University Press, 1984. (A record of Zeami's words and comments, recorded and handed down by his second son, Kanze Motoyoshi.)

—— (1433) *Kyakuraika* (The Flower of Returning to the Beginning), ed. Konishi J. Tokyo: Chikuma Shobō, 1970. (Written for his son, this short work intimates but does not spell out the highest stage in the art of *Nō* performance.)

References and further reading

Keene, D. (1966) *Nō: The Classical Theatre of Japan*, Tokyo: Kodansha International. (Includes a comprehensive 'List of Nō Plays Currently Performed'.)

—— (ed.) (1970) *Twenty Plays of the Nō Theatre*, New York: Columbia University Press. (An English translation of some often played *Nō* texts.)

Izutsu, T. and Izutsu, T. (1981) *The Theory of Beauty in the Classical Aesthetics of Japan*, The Hague: Martinus Nijhoff. (Includes a discussion of the metaphysical background of the theory of *Nō*, and English translations of *Kyūi*, *Yūgaku shūdō fūken* and *Shūgyoku tokka*.)

Hare, T.B. (1986) *Zeami's Style*, Stanford, CA: Stanford University Press. (A fine and detailed study of Zeami's life and works in English, well-supported by the wealth of Japanese scholarship on the history and performance of *Nō*.)

Kōsai, T. (1962) *Zeami Shinkō* (New Thoughts About Zeami), Tokyo: Wanya Shoten, 3–8. (Articles in this work cover subjects such as Zeami's possible affiliation with the Sōtō branch of Zen Buddhism, his affiliation with the Fuganji Temple and his knowledge of Zen literature.)

Nose, A. (1930) *Zeami Jūrokubushū Hyōshaku* (Exposition of Sixteen Works by Zeami), Tokyo: Iwanami Shoten. (A classic study of Zeami's *Nō* treatises with detailed commentaries.)

Rimer, J.T. and Yamazaki, M. (ed. and trans.) (1984) *On the Art of the Nō Drama: The Major Treatises of Zeami*, Princeton, NJ: Princeton University Press. (English translation of eight treatises written by Zeami plus the *Sarugaku dangi*. The volume includes a helpful glossary of important persons mentioned in the text and a list of plays and entertainments mentioned in the text.)

Sanari, K. (ed.) (1964) *Yōkyoku Taikan* (Compendium of *Nō* Plays), Tokyo: Meiji Shoin, 5 vols. (A total of 235 *Nō* plays are compiled; essential for the study of *Nō* plays.)

Smethurst, M. (1989) *The Artistry of Aeschylus and Zeami: A Comparative Study of Greek Tragedy and Nō*, Princeton, NJ: Princeton University Press. (An eye-opening application of Zeami's dramaturgy to reconstructing Aeschylus's works.)

Yasuda, K. (1989) *Masterworks of the Nō Theater*, Bloomington, IN: Indiana University Press. (Detailed English translation of 17 *Nō* plays, each accompanied by an informative introduction.)

Yusa, M. (1987) '*Riken no Ken*, Zeami's Theory of Acting and Theatrical Appreciation', *Monumenta Nipponica* 42 (3): 331–45. (A closer study of Zeami's theory of *riken no ken* reveals its affinity with the teaching of 'the original mind' and 'awakening' espoused in Zen Buddhism.)

MICHIKO YUSA

ZEN *see* BUDDHIST PHILOSOPHY, JAPANESE; BUDDHIST PHILOSOPHY, CHINESE

ZENO OF CITIUM (334–262 BC)

Zeno of Citium, a Greek philosopher from Cyprus, founded the Stoic school in Athens c.300 BC. His background and training lay in various branches of the Socratic tradition, including the Platonic Academy, but especially Cynicism. His controversial Republic was a utopian treatise, founded on the abolition of most civic norms and institutions. He laid the main foundations of Stoic doctrine in all areas except perhaps logic.

Zeno was born at Citium, a town in Cyprus of mixed Greek and Phoenician culture. His father, a merchant, used to bring copies of Socratic dialogues back from his visits to Athens. It was perhaps these that inspired Zeno, at the age of 22, to move to Athens and study philosophy in the milieu in which SOCRATES himself had lived.

Zeno chose a series of teachers representing different branches of the Socratic tradition, starting with the Cynic Crates. Cynic ethics (see CYNICS) remained a dominant influence on his thought. Polemo, the head of the Platonic Academy, (see PLATONISM, EARLY AND MIDDLE §§1, 8) and the Megarian philosopher Stilpo (see MEGARIAN SCHOOL) were among his other teachers, and both will have supplied a primarily ethical orientation as well, although with some input of metaphysics. Stilpo's most celebrated doctrine was the self-sufficiency of the wise. Finally DIODORUS CRONUS, whose classes he attended along with the future logician Philo, represented the dialectical side of the Socratic tradition, offering Zeno a training in logic as well as in the study of sophisms (see PHILO THE DIALECTICIAN).

In time – around the turn of the century – Zeno formed his own philosophical group, at first known as Zenonians but eventually dubbed 'Stoics' after the Painted Stoa in which they used to congregate. Zeno remained in Athens until his death in 262 BC, and the school he had founded became the dominant school of the Hellenistic age.

Zeno was more an inspirational than a systematic philosophical writer, and later generations took on the task of formalizing and developing his philosophy. The most provocative of his twenty-seven recorded works – reported also to be his first – was a utopian political tract, the *Republic*, whose title echoes those of like-named works not just by Plato but also by the Cynic DIOGENES OF SINOPE. Its exact character is disputed. Some fragments suggest a cosmopolitan theme, anticipating and no doubt inspiring the later Stoic conception of the cosmic city (see STOICISM §18). But many others make it clear that its main proposals were for the radical reform of a single political community. In characteristically Cynic fashion, most civic institutions – temples, law courts, coinage, differential dress for the sexes, conventional education, marriage, and so on – were to be abolished. The city was to be a community of the wise, united by concord and, it seems, a sublimated form of erotic love. Some later Stoics found this work so deeply

embarrassing that they branded it, or parts of it, as spurious. However CHRYSIPPUS, his second successor, wholeheartedly defended its proposals and tenets.

Despite the controversy surrounding his *Republic*, Zeno undoubtedly established, often against tough opposition, the main canonical positions of Stoic ethics, epistemology and physics. His most distinctive ethical innovation was the insistence that moral indifferents like wealth and poverty could be placed in a natural ranking order of preferability. In developing it he faced resistance on the one side from his former Platonist teacher Polemo, who insisted that such a ranking must be a moral one, in terms of relative goodness, on the other from his colleague ARISTON OF CHIOS (§2) who denied that any differentiation between 'indifferents' was possible. His epistemological thesis that certainty can be attained through the senses was persistently challenged by the New Academy (see ARCESILAUS §2) and adjusted to meet the criticisms. He approved of dialectic mainly as a defence against the sophistries of others, and is not known to have made any major contribution of his own to Stoic logic.

In some areas it was less his doctrines than his daring style of argument that forced later Stoics to rally to his defence. The flavour can be glimpsed from two of his more controversial syllogisms. 'It would be reasonable to honour the gods; it would not be reasonable to honour the non-existent; therefore the gods exist.' 'Voice comes through the windpipe; if it were coming from the brain, it would not come through the windpipe; where speech comes from is where voice also comes from; but speech comes from the mind; therefore the mind is not in the brain.' (This latter argument obliged Chrysippus and other Stoics to fight a rearguard action against the latest anatomical discoveries.)

See also: CLEANTHES

References and further reading

Arnim, H. von (1903–5) *Stoicorum Veterum Fragmenta* (Fragments of the Early Stoics), Leipzig: Teubner, with vol. 4, indexes, by M. Adler, 1924, vol. 1, 3–72. (The standard collection of early Stoic fragments, in Greek and Latin, commonly abbreviated as *SVF*; Zeno is in volume 1, pages 1–72.)

Baldry, H.C. (1959) 'Zero's Ideal State', *Journal of Hellenic Studies* 79: 3–15. (Reconstruction of Zeno's *Republic*.)

Erskine, A. (1990) *The Hellenistic Stoa*, London: Duckworth. (A challenging reinterpretation of Stoic political thought and practice, including Zeno's *Republic*.)

Graeser, A. (1975) *Zenon von Kitium: Positionen und Probleme* (Zeno of Citium: Positions and Problems), Berlin: de Gruyter. (Too important to ignore, but a very difficult read, made even harder by the ubiquitous misprints.)

Schofield, M. (1983) 'The syllogisms of Zeno of Citium', *Phronesis* 28: 31–58. (Explains Zeno's philosophical style and the problems it created for later generations of Stoics.)

—— (1991) *The Stoic Idea of the City*, Cambridge: Cambridge University Press. (Outstanding reconstruction of Zeno's *Republic* and its place in Stoic political thought.)

* Zeno of Citium (334–262 BC) Fragments, in A.C. Pearson (ed.) *The Fragments of Zeno and Cleanthes*, Cambridge: Cambridge University Press, 1891. (Still useful, but mainly for specialists.)

DAVID SEDLEY

ZENO OF ELEA (*fl. c.*450 BC)

The Greek philosopher Zeno of Elea was celebrated for his paradoxes. Aristotle called him the 'founder of dialectic'. He wrote in order to defend the Eleatic metaphysics of his fellow citizen and friend Parmenides, according to whom reality is single, changeless and homogeneous. Zeno's strength was the production of intriguing arguments which seem to show that apparently straightforward features of the world – most notably plurality and motion – are riddled with contradiction. At the very least he succeeded in establishing that hard thought is required to make sense of plurality and motion. His paradoxes stimulated the atomists, Aristotle and numerous philosophers since to reflect on unity, infinity, continuity and the structure of space and time. Although Zeno wrote a book full of arguments, very few of his actual words have survived. Secondary reports (some from Plato and Aristotle) probably preserve accurately the essence of Zeno's arguments. Even so, we know only a fraction of the total.

According to Plato the arguments in Zeno's book were of this form: if there are many things, then the same things are both F and not-F; since the same things cannot be both F and not-F, there cannot be many things. Two instances of this form have been preserved: if there were many things, then the same things would be both limited and unlimited; and the same things would be both large (that is, of infinite size) and small (that is, of no size). Quite how the components of these arguments work is not clear. Things are limited (in number), Zeno says, because they are just so many, rather than more or less, while they are unlimited (in number) because any two of them must have a third between them, which separates them and makes them two. Things are of infinite size because anything that exists must have some size: yet anything that has size is divisible into parts which themselves have some size, so that each and every thing will contain an infinite number of extended parts. On the other hand, each thing has no size: for if there are to be many things there have to be some things which are single, unitary things, and these will have no size since anything with size would be a collection of parts.

Zeno's arguments concerning motion have a different form. Aristotle reports four arguments. According to the Dichotomy, motion is impossible because in order to cover any distance it is necessary first to cover half the distance, then half the remainder, and so on without limit. The Achilles is a variant of this: the speedy Achilles will never overtake a tortoise once he has allowed it a head start because Achilles has an endless series of tasks to perform, and each time Achilles sets off to catch up with the tortoise it will turn out that, by the time Achilles arrives at where the tortoise was when he set off, the tortoise has moved on slightly. Another argument, the Arrow, purports to show that an arrow apparently in motion is in fact stationary at each instant of its 'flight', since at each instant it occupies a region of space equal in size to itself. The Moving Rows describes three rows (or streams) of equal-sized bodies, one stationary and the other two moving at equal speeds in opposite directions. If each body is one metre long, then the time taken for a body to cover two metres equals the time taken for it to cover four metres (since a moving body will pass two stationary bodies while passing four bodies moving in the opposite direction), and that might be thought impossible.

Zeno's arguments must be resolvable, since the world obviously does contain a plurality of things in motion. There is little agreement, however, on how they should be resolved. Some points can be identified which may have misled Zeno. It is not true, for example, that the sum of an infinite collection of parts, each of which has size, must itself be of an infinite size (it will be false if the parts are of proportionally decreasing size); and something in motion will pass stationary bodies and moving bodies at different velocities. In many other cases, however, there is no general agreement as to the fallacy, if any exists, of Zeno's argument.

1   Life and works

Information about Zeno's life is scarce. PLATO (§15), in his *Parmenides*, reports a visit to Athens by Zeno, in the company of Parmenides, usually dated around 450 *bc*. Zeno was then in his late thirties, a younger contemporary of Parmenides who was then in his mid-sixties. He had associated with Parmenides for some time. By the time of this visit Zeno had already produced a book, the reputation of which preceded him to Athens. Diogenes Laertius writes about Zeno's courage and his political activities, detailing some unreliable stories about his heroic death at the hands of a tyrant.

Reliable information about Zeno's writings is equally paltry. Some of his arguments have been saved verbatim (mainly those concerning plurality); others have survived only via brief reports (mainly those concerning motion). In most cases, the arguments are baldly stated, and some effort is required to reveal their strength and structure.

2   The arguments against plurality

There is no universal agreement on what Zeno hoped to achieve with his arguments. The orthodox view, stemming from Plato, is that Zeno's purpose was to defend Parmenides' monism, which denied the reality of both plurality and motion. Zeno defended Parmenides by attacking those opponents who mocked his position. This view of Zeno has two consequences. First, Zeno's arguments are *ad hominem*: so, while Zeno's opponents should be committed to any assumptions they involve, those assumptions need not be endorsed by Zeno himself. Second, the Parmenidean position should, ideally, be immune to the destructive force of Zeno's arguments.

Monism, the view that only one thing exists, is not very plausible. An intuitively more attractive position is pluralism:

(1)   The world contains more than one thing.

Pluralists differ from one another as regards *which* things the world contains. We do not know which pluralists Zeno was attacking. Some have argued for a philosophically sophisticated target – for example, Pythagoreans – but this is now widely rejected. A more appealing denial of monism is an unsophisticated pluralism. 'Simple pluralism' is the common-sense view which holds both (1) and

(2)   These things are ordinary objects such as horses, human beings, oaks, ...

According to the sixth-century philosopher Philoponus, Zeno's target was simple pluralism:

> Those who introduce plurality put their confidence in its self-evidence; for there exist horses and people and a variety of individual things, and the aggregation of these produces plurality. This self-evidence therefore Zeno tried to overthrow...
> (*On Aristotle's Physics* 42.18–21 in Lee 1936: §8)

Zeno's challenge to simple pluralism is successful, in that he forces anti-Parmenideans to go beyond common sense. Post-Zenonian atomism (see ATOMISM, ANCIENT; DEMOCRITUS §§2–3), for example, conjoins (1) not with (2) but with

(3)   These things are indivisible masses of atomic stuff moving in empty space.

Aristotelian pluralism retains (2), but only by working out a far more sophisticated understanding of what constitutes a unity than is provided by common sense (see ARISTOTLE §§11–14)).

Several of Zeno's arguments rely on a pluralist's accepting that any magnitude can be divided infinitely many times. However, Parmenides' One would not be vulnerable to these arguments, because the only premise concerning infinite divisibility that the arguments require is

(ID)   If anything at all is divisible, then whatever is extended is divisible.

Since PARMENIDES (§5) held that there is nothing which is divisible, the conditional (ID) would pose no threat for him. Simple pluralists, by contrast, think that the whole is divisible – that is what makes them pluralists. (ID) relies on the thought that there is something objectionably arbitrary in a world which is a homogeneous and continuous mass of existing things being divisible, but only up to a certain point: being divisible just this far (into horses and oaks, . . .) but no further (not, for example, into horse bits and oak bits). Subsequent pluralists could nevertheless evade Zeno's arguments by denying (ID), as the atomists did; Democritus denied the homogeneity of the world, by introducing two quite distinct types of real entity – atoms and void. In such a case (ID) is no longer plausible, since an explanation can be provided of why the world should be divisible into atoms and no further (see DEMOCRITUS §2).

It should be noted, however, that Plato's interpretation of Zeno as supporting Parmenides is not mandatory. Eudemus, the pupil of Aristotle, read him as attacking not only pluralities but also Parmenides'

One, and this alternative view of Zeno as a nihilist, rather than a monist, gained some currency (Seneca, *Letters* 88.44–5).

3 The 'limited and unlimited' argument

The 'limited and unlimited' argument is fragment 3. It is preserved by Simplicius, and appears to be a direct quotation from Zeno.

[(A)]   If there are many things, it is necessary that they are just as many as they are, and neither more nor less than that. But if they are as many as they are they will be limited.

[(B)]   If there are many things, the things that are are unlimited; for there are always others between the things that are, and again others between those. And thus the things that are are unlimited.

(A) is a strong argument, granted a false, although very appealing, assumption. Suppose

(A1)   There are many things [call them the totality T].

Then

(A2)   It is necessary that they are just as many as they are [T contains exactly as many items as T]

(A3)   and neither more [T does not contain as many items as T^+, which contains everything T contains, along with some extra items] nor less [T does not contain as many items as T^-, which contains almost everything T contains, apart from some items].

So

(A4)   If they are as many as they are they will be limited [the content of T is limited to just so many items, in contrast to the number in T^+ or the number in T^-].

This argument requires the assumption

(A5)   If T^* contains everything that T contains, along with some extra items, then T^* contains more items than T and T contains fewer items than T^*.

(A5) is extremely appealing: for it can seem that T^* *must* contain more items than T, just because it is T with some extra items added. But (A5) is false. It claims that if T is a subset of T^* then T and T^* do not contain the same number of items, and that is not unrestrictedly true: it is false if T and T^* each contain infinitely many things (see INFINITY §6).

The other half of Zeno's argument, (B), shows in contrast that (A4) fails for any totality of units comprising the simple pluralists' world. (B) provides a method for adding extra items to any specification of T, and so expanding it into a totality T^+, which according to (A5) contains more items than T.

The method Zeno provides for expanding T into T^+ is this: *there are always others between the things that are, and again others between those.* Suppose T is specified as this horse, that human being, the oak over there.... (B) concentrates attention on the claim that this horse and that human being, for example, are distinct units. A simple intuition lies behind including this horse and that human being within T: namely, that they are distinct units because there is something else between them – for example, this saddle. But an obvious question then arises: what makes this saddle and this horse distinct units? Zeno envisages two possible answers. First, that they too are distinct because there is something else between them – for example, this horse blanket. Second, that they are distinct even though they are in contact. If the simple pluralist offers the first answer, a method of expanding any specification of T follows immediately (since the next question to arise will be: what makes this saddle and this horse blanket distinct items?). If the second answer is offered, another expansion method suggests itself. If this horse and this saddle can be distinct units, even though they are in contact, then why not say, by parity of reasoning, that this leftmost horse chunk and that rightmost horse chunk are distinct units? In either case (A4) fails to hold: any specification of T can be expanded into a totality containing extra members.

It is necessary to go beyond the resources of simple pluralism to respond to this argument. Zeno assumes that his opponents view the world as a homogeneous and continuous mass of existing things. In the absence of absolutely basic differences between things, the only way to pick out units will be by their relations to one another – for example, by their being spatially discrete. (B) is a cogent argument against that position. One response would deny the assumption of homogeneity. Democritus was able to identify units because his world contained atomic stuff and void as two fundamentally different types of entity. Any two atoms are distinct because they are separated from one another by void, while an atom and the void surrounding it are distinct because they are intrinsically different. But to resist Zeno's argument by making that move is to abandon simple pluralism. Democritus' world is not a plurality of horses and human beings, but of atoms. A deeper response would involve a more sophisticated view of units and pluralities: for example, the Aristotelian ontology of substantial unities rehabilitates entities like this horse and that human being and picks them out as units in terms of their functional organization (see ARISTOTLE §13).

4 The 'large and small' argument

The 'large and small' argument can be found in fragments 1 and 2, which consist of material quoted by Simplicius in his commentary on Aristotle's *Physics* (he reports Zeno's 'limited and unlimited' argument in the same pages). Simplicius reports three different sub-arguments, contributing to a single Zenonian argument: that if there is a plurality, the same things will be 'large' (of infinite magnitude) and 'small' (of no magnitude).

According to Simplicius (in fr. 2.17–18), Zeno argued that the units of a plurality would have *no* magnitude by means of the following argument:

[(C)]   It has no magnitude since each of the many is the same as itself and one.

Argument (C) requires three premises, including (ID) (see above):

(C1)   If there is a plurality there must be units *which are not themselves pluralities.*

(C2)   Whatever is divisible is *ipso facto* a plurality.

According to the simple pluralist there is a plurality. So given (C1) there must be non-plural units. But those units cannot have magnitude. For according to (ID), if they had magnitude, they would be divisible, in which case according to (C2) they would themselves be pluralities, contrary to (C1). So (ID), (C1) and (C2) imply that any unit (anything that is *the same as itself and one*) will have no magnitude. Argument (C) is valid. The way to evade the argument is to deny one of its premises. The atomists deny (ID), while denial of either (C1) or (C2) augurs a more sophisticated understanding of the relation between unity and plurality.

Before giving Zeno's argument for the conclusion that the units of a plurality must have unlimited magnitude, Simplicius (fr. 2.8–14) reports a Zenonian argument that what has no magnitude does not exist:

[(D)]   For if it were added to something else that exists, it would make it no larger; for if it were of no magnitude, but were added, the thing it was added to could not increase in magnitude. And thus what was added would in fact be nothing. If when it is taken away the other thing is no smaller, and again when it is added will not increase, it is clear that what was added was nothing nor again what was taken away.

Adding what has no magnitude (for example, a point) to something would not increase its magnitude, and so would be tantamount to adding nothing. Zeno concludes that what has no magnitude would *be* nothing, and so would not exist. It seems, however, that Zeno's argument will inevitably be question-begging. Imagine adding an electric charge to a metal sphere: the sphere's *magnitude* will not be increased, but adding an electric charge is not tantamount to adding nothing, since the addition may greatly affect the sphere's behaviour. Zeno's conclusion would follow from the assumption that the only significant differences are differences in magnitude: but that assumption is worryingly close to the conclusion Zeno wants to establish by argument (D), namely:

(D1)   Whatever exists has magnitude.

Still Zeno's endorsement of (D1) would be consistent with his defending Parmenides, according to whom what exists is apparently spherical in shape (see PARMENIDES §8). What is more interesting than the argument for (D1), however, is the way in which Zeno uses argument (D) in order to show that the units of a plurality will be of unlimited magnitude.

Fragment 1 gives the argument for this conclusion, which Simplicius puts in Zeno's own words.

For having first proved [(D) above] that if what is had no magnitude it would not even exist, [Zeno] goes on

[(E)]   But if it exists, it is necessary for each to have some magnitude and thickness, and for the one part of it to be away from the other. And the same argument holds about the part out in front; for that too will have magnitude and a part of it will be out in front. Indeed it is the same thing to say this once and to go on saying it always; for no such part of it will be last, nor will there not be one part related to another.

Thus if there are many things, it is necessary that they are both small and large: so small as not to have magnitude [the conclusion of argument (C)], so large as to be unlimited [the conclusion of argument (E)].

In argument (E) Zeno relies on the earlier argument (D), and the claim (ID) that if anything is divisible, then whatever is extended is divisible.

Each unit of a plurality must have some magnitude: Zeno argued in (D) that what has no magnitude does not exist, so units without magnitude would not exist and could not compose a plurality. But according to (ID) any product of division which has magnitude is divisible, and the products of that further division would have magnitude (since according to argument (D) they would not exist otherwise). This line of argument can be repeated endlessly. Zeno draws two related conclusions in argument (E), deriving the second from the first:

(E1) Any unit will contain an unlimited *number* of parts.

(E2) Any unit will be of an unlimited *size*.

Argument (E) can be blocked at different stages. First (E1) might be denied, on the ground that divisions can be carried on indefinitely but cannot be completed. (ID) entitles Zeno to argue that

(4) Given any finite N a magnitude admits of more than N divisions and contains more than N (non-overlapping) parts.

But (4) is not equivalent to, and does not entail

(5) A magnitude admits of an infinite number of divisions, and contains an infinite number of (non-overlapping) parts.

and it is (5) that is required for (E1).

An alternative response would be to allow that (E1) is true, although harmless, and to deny (E2). This response involves a distinction between two types of division (and part). A 'partial' division (P-division) of a magnitude would be a division into halves, followed by a division of one of those halves into two quarters, followed by a division of one of those quarters into two eighths, ... At any stage only some of the possible divisions of equal-sized parts are made; the products of a completed P-division would include some P-parts that could be further divided. A 'total' division (T-division) would be a division into halves, followed by a division of both halves into four quarters, followed by a division of all those quarters into eight eighths, ... At any stage all possible divisions of equal sized parts are made; if a T-division could be completed, all the divisions that could have been made would have been made. At any stage of a division the T-parts produced will be of equal size, whereas the P-parts will be of different size.

Zeno probably gets from (E1) to (E2) via an assumption about addition (ADD):

> The sum of an infinite number of parts, each having a positive magnitude, is an infinite magnitude.

But (ADD) is not unrestrictedly true. In particular, it would be false of an infinite number of P-parts whose magnitudes decreased in a regular progression. Replacing (ADD) with (ADD′)

> The sum of an infinite number of parts, each having an *equal* positive magnitude is an infinite magnitude.

gives something which is unrestrictedly true, but (ADD′) will not license the move from (E1) to (E2) if the parts to which (E1) refers are P-parts, since P-parts are not of equal magnitude.

The orthodoxy is that Zeno's argument (E) does introduce P-parts. However, it is easy enough to reformulate Zeno's argument in terms of T-divisions and T-parts (Simplicius, *On Aristotle's Physics* 139.26–140.6 in Lee 1936: §2). There are two ways of responding to argument (E), if it is thus reformulated, although neither of these appealed to ancient thinkers.

First, it could be claimed that even if a P-division could be completed, a T-division could *not* be. The completability of a T-division cannot be inferred from the completability of a P-division, since there would be more T-parts produced by a completed T-division than there are P-parts produced by a completed P-division: there would be a denumerable infinity ($\aleph_0$) of P-parts, but a super-denumerable infinity($2^{\aleph_0}$) of T-parts (since at the first (pre-division) stage there would be 1 P-part and 1 T-part, at the second stage 2 P-parts and 2 T-parts, at the third stage 3 P-parts and 4 T-parts... at the nth stage n P-parts and 2^{n-1} T-parts). A proof that not all infinities are of the same size awaited the work of Georg Cantor in the nineteenth century (see CANTOR'S THEOREM; CONTINUUM HYPOTHESIS, THE §2; INFINITY §1).

An alternative response would be to allow that a T-division can be completed, and accept that the T-parts that result have equal, although *zero* magnitude, but to deny that it follows that the original magnitude composed of those T-parts would have no magnitude. None of those in the ancient world who considered Zenonian arguments in terms of T-divisions found this solution attractive, and the exposition by its modern champions requires sophisticated mathematical resources.

5 The Dichotomy

We now move from Zeno's arguments against plurality to those concerning motion. The Dichotomy is probably the best known of these. It is reported by Aristotle (*Physics* 239b11–13).

(F) [The Dichotomy] asserts the non-existence of motion on the ground that that which is in locomotion must arrive at the half-way stage before it reaches the goal.

Zeno's aim is to redescribe motion in such a way that it can be shown to be impossible. It is impossible to complete an arbitrary journey from A to B – to start at A, move to B, and then stop, for

847

(F1)   A journey from A to B is a series of sub-journeys with no last member: from A to $\frac{1}{2}$AB, from $\frac{1}{2}$AB to $\frac{3}{4}$AB, ...

and

(F2)   It is impossible to complete a series of sub-journeys with no last member.

It would equally be possible to specify instead a series of sub-journeys with no *first* member, from A to $\frac{1}{2}$AB, preceded by A to $\frac{1}{4}$AB, ..., and allege a corresponding impossibility.

The form of argument is valid: if doing X is doing Y, and doing Y is impossible, then doing X is impossible. Zeno needs to establish both that some re-description of a journey from A to B, such as (F1) provides, is acceptable; and that a journey so re-described is impossible, as (F2) alleges. There are, correspondingly, two main strategies for avoiding Zeno's conclusion: rejection of (F1), and rejection of (F2).

A particularly brusque rejection of (F1) is the view that there are minimal distances (d) which do not admit of further division, so that there is a last sub-journey, from $B-d$ to B (and a first, from A to $A+d$). Although there is little evidence of spatial atomism among Presocratics, a thorough-going spatial atomism is found later in DIODORUS CRONUS (§2). Plato's successor XENOCRATES (§2) may also have adopted this position. But the costs of this strategy are high: for example, as Aristotle pointed out, the mathematical consequences are severe (all lines, for instance, will be commeasurable).

If a denial of (F1) is not feasible, there are further alternatives. One is a straightforward acceptance of (F1) and denial of (F2). Another is to distinguish different readings of (F1) and (F2), and deny that there is any single reading on which both are true together.

An example of the first strategy is Aristotle's claim that the distance between A and B and the time available to cover it are infinite in the same way, since both are divisible into smaller intervals without limit (*Physics* 233a24–31). This disposes of an intuition which may lie behind (F2); a runner would have insufficient time in which to complete a series of sub-journeys with no last member. But that response will not apply to the following variant of the Dichotomy (*Physics* 263a11–23): passage of an arbitrary time interval $t_1 - t_2$ is impossible, since

(F1′)   A time interval $t_1 - t_2$ is a series of sub-intervals with no last member: from t_1 to $\frac{1}{2}(t_1 - t_2)$, from $\frac{1}{2}(t_1 - t_2)$ to $\frac{3}{4}(t_1 - t_2)$, ...

(F2′)   Passage of a series of sub-intervals with no last member is impossible.

Aristotle's preferred response to the Dichotomy is an instance of the second strategy. He distinguishes between *actual* and *potential* sub-intervals (*Physics* 263a28–b8). An actual interval is an interval made actual by being marked out in some way from its surroundings – for example, by a runner starting and stopping, or by a division being made, at its termini. Intervals which could be, but are not, made actual are merely potential. Actual sub-journeys are journeys over actual sub-intervals. With Aristotle's distinction to appeal to, the premises of the Dichotomy can be taken in two ways: either as

(F1a)   A journey from A to B is a series of actual sub-journeys with no last member.

(F2a)   It is impossible to complete a series of actual sub-journeys with no last member.

or as

(F1b)   A journey from A to B is a series of potential sub-journeys with no last member.

(F2b)   It is impossible to complete a series of potential sub-journeys with no last member.

Aristotle's view is that Zeno fails to establish his conclusion because with neither (F1a)/(F2a) nor (F1b)/(F2b) do we have a pair of jointly true premises. (F1b) is a true anti-atomist claim: there is no sub-journey across an interval within AB that *has* to be the last, and there is no sub-journey that *could not* be broken into two further discrete sub-journeys. But (F2b) is false: there is no difficulty in completing a series of sub-journeys that is endless only in the sense that it contains no member that *has* to be the last.

On the other hand, according to Aristotle, (F2a) is true. It would be impossible, he claims, to complete a journey by marking off each of an endless series of sub-journeys: a runner stopping for $\frac{1}{2}$ minute after covering the first half of AB in $\frac{1}{2}$ minute, for $\frac{1}{4}$ minute after covering the next quarter in $\frac{1}{4}$ minute, ... and for $(\frac{1}{2})^n$ minutes after covering the next $(\frac{1}{2})^n$ in $(\frac{1}{2})^n$ minutes would *not* cover AB in a staccato fashion in 2 minutes. Such cases have generated considerable discussion. But reaching agreement about these cases, and hence about (F2a), is less urgent if Aristotle's claim that (F1a) is false is both defensible and important: for in that case someone running from A to B does not have to complete a series of actual sub-journeys with no last member, and so would not be trying to do what (F2a) alleges cannot be done.

However, concentrating further on (F1a) would not be a good strategy for dealing with the Dichotomy. For Zeno's problem persists so long as there is *some* series which would have to be completed in order to get from A to B, but which cannot be completed.

Suppose Zeno allows that (F1a) is false. Still, consider a series of points at which AB could be divided: $\frac{1}{2}$AB, $\frac{3}{4}$AB, ... To get from A to B a runner will have to be next to each of those points in turn, although the runner will not stop at each point; and, given any one of those points, there is some other point the runner has to be next to before arriving at B. Here, Zeno will say, we have a series that cannot be completed because it has no last member.

Another distinction is now relevant. There are two series of points that Zeno might have in mind: either the (half-open) series

(S) $\quad \frac{1}{2}AB, \frac{3}{4}AB, \ldots, \frac{2^n-1}{2^n}AB, \ldots$

(that is, B not included)

(S′) $\quad \frac{1}{2}AB, \frac{3}{4}AB, \ldots, \frac{2^n-1}{2^n}AB, \ldots, B$

(that is, B included).

Zeno alleges that it is impossible for a runner to start at A, move to B and then stop. The task which Zeno alleges to be impossible might be

(TS)   Being adjacent to each member of (S), not being adjacent to any point not in (S), and then after that resting.

It is indeed impossible to complete task (TS): where would a runner who completed that task be? Furthermore, the reason it is impossible to complete (TS) is that the series (S) is a series with no last member. So if moving from A to B and then resting were a matter of completing (TS), motion from A to B would be impossible. But travelling from A to B and then resting is not a matter of performing task (TS) and doing nothing else. It is rather a matter of completing the task

(TS′)   Being adjacent to each member of S′, not being adjacent to any point not in S′, and then resting.

and nothing Zeno has said shows that it is impossible to complete (TS′). For the series (S′) does have a last member (namely B), and that is just where a runner who finishes (TS′) will be. Of course Zeno may now try to introduce some other series with no last member that would, although impossible, have to be traversed in order to complete the task (TS′): for example, how can a runner complete (TS′) and get to B, since there is no last point at which the runner has to arrive just before arriving at B? But that question assumes that completing (TS′) would require com-

pleting TS and then doing one more thing (arriving at B), and that is a false assumption.

It is plain that Zeno has a strategy for keeping the Dichotomy argument going: he can look for another series which would have to be traversed in order to get from A to B, but which cannot be traversed. Neither the series of actual sub-journeys, nor the series of potential sub-journeys, nor the series of points between A and B provides him with such a series. But Zeno's strategy is open-ended, and two consequences follow from that. First, there is unlikely to be a single resolution of the Dichotomy argument: given different choices of series, it will sometimes be relevant to deny that the series chosen cannot be traversed, and sometimes to deny that it has to be traversed. Second, given the ingenuity of philosophers, there are likely to be ever more subtle redescriptions of a journey from A to B which call for ever more subtle responses.

6   The Achilles

Zeno's Achilles argument is very closely related to that of the Dichotomy. According to Aristotle (*Physics* 239b14–16),

[(G)]   The second [argument concerning motion] is the so-called Achilles, and it amounts to this, that in a race the quickest runner can never overtake the slowest, since the pursuer must first reach the point where the pursued started, so that the slower must always hold a lead.

Suppose Achilles is running faster than the tortoise. Then as their runs proceed, the distance between the two will decrease, at a rate determined by their relative velocities. Let the distance between them initially be AB, and suppose their relative velocities are such that after $\frac{1}{2}$ minute it has shrunk to $\frac{1}{2}$AB, after a further $\frac{1}{4}$ minute to $\frac{1}{4}$AB, ... and so on. Achilles' task is to complete an infinite series of lead-narrowings ($\frac{1}{2}$AB, $\frac{1}{4}$AB, ... This series of lead-narrowings will sum to a total distance no more than AB, and thus it is plain that as long as Achilles can traverse a distance AB in a finite time then he can close the distance between himself and the tortoise in a finite time. That is to say that as long as the Dichotomy can be resolved, the Achilles can be resolved. The resolutions will be parallel.

7   The Arrow

Aristotle (*Physics* 239b5–9, 239b30–3) reports the Arrow along with a summary response.

[(H)] Zeno argues fallaciously; for if, he says, everything always rests when it is against what is equal, and what is in locomotion is always in the now, the arrow in locomotion is motionless. But this is false, for time is not composed of indivisible 'nows', no more than is any other magnitude.

The third [argument concerning motion] is the one just mentioned, that the arrow in locomotion is at rest. This follows from assuming that time is composed of 'nows'; for if that is not granted, the conclusion will not follow.

The argument as Aristotle sets it out requires expansion:

(H1) Everything always rests when it occupies a space equal to itself.

(H2) What is moving is always in the now.

(H3) What is in the now occupies a space equal to itself.

Therefore

(H4) What is moving always occupies a space equal to itself [from (H2) and (H3)].

Therefore

(H5) What is moving is always at rest [from (H4) and (H1)].

(H6) Time is composed of indivisible nows.

Therefore

(H7) The 'flying arrow' does not move.

(H1) and (H2) are from Aristotle's text. (H1) glosses the Aristotelian expression 'is against what is equal'. (H3) is required to get from (H1) and (H2) to (H4). (H6) is included because it is mentioned by Aristotle. Some have suggested that the Aristotelian report gives only a fragment of a wider Zenonian argument; whether or not that is so, (H1)–(H7) present the core of the problem. The orthodoxy is that the phrase 'the now' in (H2) and (H3) is an Aristotelian way of talking about unextended temporal instants (or possibly indivisible temporal atoms); according to a less common interpretation the argument raises problems concerning the present.

One main line of approach, endorsed by Aristotle among others, is denial of (H1). Another is to deny an appropriate interpretation of (H3). Rejection of (H6) is also recommended by Aristotle: however, while (H6) may well be false, its relevance to Zeno's argument is disputed. (H2) seems unassailable.

Aristotle denies (H1) on the grounds that 'being at rest' and 'being in motion' are defined only over temporal periods, and nothing can move or be at rest at an unextended instant of time: to be at rest is to occupy the same space for some period of time (*Physics* 239a23–b4). In that case (H1) is false since it admits of counter-instances: any object considered at an *instant* will occupy a space equal to itself at that instant, but will not be at rest at that instant. However, Zeno would accommodate this point by amending (H1) to

(H1′) Nothing moves when it occupies a space equal to itself.

and (H5) correspondingly to

(H5′) What is moving never moves.

(H1′) should be unobjectionable to Aristotle, yet (H5′) still seems dangerous.

Another way of denying (H1) would be to introduce definitions of instantaneous motion (and instantaneous rest), and consequently to reject both (H1) and (H1′). Zeno has a response. Someone who tries in this way to deny (H1) and (H1′) has two options.

(6) To define motion at an instant derivatively from *motion over a period*: A is moving at an instant t as long as A is moving over a period containing t; A is moving over a period as long as A covers a distance during that period.

(7) To define motion at an instant derivatively from *location at other instants*: A is moving at an instant t as long as A occupies other places at all other instants within some period containing t.

Rejecting (H1) and (H1′) on the basis of (6) begs the question against Zeno: it is to say that an arrow is flying at t because t occurs within a period in which it is flying, and Zeno will not be impressed by such a blunt rejection of the Parmenidean world view. On the other hand, (7) allows the possibility of a quasi-Parmenidean view on which temporal process is replaced by a series of static distributions of objects to places (see TENSE AND TEMPORAL LOGIC); furthermore, if instants were replaced by temporal atoms, (7) would lend support to the view of DIODORUS CRONUS §2, who was widely regarded in antiquity as denying the existence of motion.

An alternative line is to challenge (H3). If read as a claim about the *present*, (H3) relies for its appeal on the assumption that the present is an unextended instant separating past and future. That assumption could be denied, and replaced with an account of the present as a period of indeterminate extension – although Zeno could reasonably demand some independent support for such a revisionary view of the present. Still, if an instantaneous present is rejected, (H3) would no longer be guaranteed. Zeno's Arrow argument would be no more persuasive than the following: no object can have a size; for every object is, for some place, located *here*; any extended place can be split into part *there* and part *there*; so *here* must be extensionless; so any object located *here* must be extensionless. That argument rests on the false assumption that 'here' must be an extensionless location.

Aristotle has another response to Zeno's argument, which is to reject (H6). Some commentators doubt the relevance of (H6) to Zeno's argument; and (H6) embodies something which Aristotle is keen to emphasize independently of his concern with Zeno's arguments. Aristotle's point is that motion and rest are characteristics which apply irreducibly over periods of time. In much the same way, colour is a feature of extended surfaces which cannot be reduced to features of extensionless points: it would not be legitimate to argue that, since no body is coloured at an extensionless point, there are no coloured bodies.

8 The Moving Rows

Aristotle's report of the Moving Rows is condensed, and a diagram, such as is provided by Alexander of Aphrodisias, is useful (Aristotle, *Physics* 239b33–240a1).

[(J)] The fourth [argument about motion] is the one about equal bodies which move in opposite directions past equal bodies in a stadium at equal speed, the one row from the end of the stadium and the other from the middle – in which he thinks it follows that half the time is equal to double.

Figure 1	$A1$	$A2$	$A3$	$A4$
$B4$	$B3$	$B2$	$B1$	
		$C1$	$C2$	$C3$ $C4$

Figure 2	$A1$	$A2$	$A3$	$A4$
	$B4$	$B3$	$B2$	$B1$
	$C1$	$C2$	$C3$	$C4$

The *A*s, *B*s and *C*s are of the same size; the *A*s are stationary, and the *B*s and *C*s are moving at equal speeds in opposite directions. The two examples above show how the positions of the bodies change over the time taken for $B1$ to go past two of the *A*s. Neither the significance of the conclusion, that 'half the time is equal to double', nor Zeno's route to that conclusion are altogether clear. Suppose Zeno assumed that

(J1) A body moving at a certain velocity will take the

same time to pass two bodies of the same size, even if one is stationary and one moving.

He could then argue in this way. Suppose the time it takes $B1$ to move from its position in the first example to its position in the second example is t. In the second example $B1$ has arrived at $C4$, and so

(J2) The time it takes $B1$ to move from its starting position to $C4$ is t.

But it is equally true that t is the time taken for $B1$ to get from its starting position to $A2$; then by assumption (J1) it will take $B1$ the same time (t) to get from its starting position to $C2$ (since $C1$ and $C2$ are together equal in size to $A1$ and $A2$); and therefore it will take $B1$ twice as long to get to $C4$ (since $C3$ and $C4$ together represent an extra distance to be covered which is equal in size to $C1$ and $C2$, and $B1$ continues at a constant speed); therefore

(J3) The time it takes $B1$ to move from its starting position to $C4$ is $2t$.

(J2) and (J3) together entail

(J4) $t = 2t$

If Aristotle's diagnosis is based on an accurate presentation of Zeno's argument, then Zeno's argument is weak. For (J1) is plainly false, and in the absence of (J1) no contradiction threatens: $B1$ passes twice as many *C*s as *A*s in a given period of time, but this is because the *C*s but not the *A*s are moving relative to $B1$. Some have found a better argument for Zeno by supposing that the bodies in question are atomic, moving in an atomically structured time. It is not likely, though, that Zeno had such a target in mind; and it is of course possible that Zeno offered the occasional weak argument. It is also possible that Zeno sought to direct attention to the relativity of velocity and motion, and by doing so to impugn their status: a similar suspicion of what is relative is found slightly later in the atomist Democritus, who downgraded sensible properties such as sweet, bitter, hot and cold because they depended as much on the perceiver as on what is perceived (see DEMOCRITUS §3).

9 Two other arguments

Zeno's reputation is founded on his arguments concerning plurality and motion. However, there are ancient reports (of doubtful reliability) which identify two further arguments as Zenonian. Aristotle twice mentions a Zenonian argument against the existence of place (*Physics* 209a23–5, 210b22–4, Lee §38), resting on the thought that if place exists it would itself have to be in a place. Another Zenonian argument mentioned by Aristotle poses this problem (250a19–24; expanded by Simplicius, *On Aristotle's Physics* 1108.18–28, Lee §38, who identifies Protagoras as its target): how can smooth variations give rise to radical and discontinuous differences? When a large mass of corn hits the ground it makes a noise, so that a fraction of that mass (for example, one ten-thousandth of a single grain) should make a fraction of the noise – but in fact it makes no noise at all. The second of these arguments in particular raises large issues, which cannot be adequately considered here.

References and further reading

Allen, R.E. and Furley, D.J. (eds) (1975) *Studies in Presocratic Philosophy*, vol. 2, London: Routledge & Kegan Paul. (Contains important papers by Fränkel, Owen and Vlastos on a wide range of Zeno's arguments.)

* Aristotle (*c.* mid 4th century BC) *Physics*, ed. W.D. Ross, Oxford: Oxford University Press, 1949; trans. in J. Barnes (ed.) *The Complete Works of Aristotle*, Princeton: Princeton University Press, 1985. (Much of book VI is concerned with Zenonian issues.)

Barnes, J. (1979) *The Presocratic Philosophers*, London: Routledge, (Chapters 12 and 13 contain provocative discussions of all Zeno's arguments, including fuller accounts of the two arguments mentioned in §9 above.)

—— (1987) *Early Greek Philosophy*, Harmondsworth: Penguin. (Chapter 11 translates Plato's account of Zeno, and the passages relevant to all Zeno's extant arguments, along with their original contexts.)

Cajori, F. (1915) 'The History of Zeno's Arguments on Motion' *American Mathematical Monthly* 22: 1–6, 77–82, 109–15, 143–9, 179–86, 215–20, 253–8, 292–7. (An account of the influence of Zeno's arguments up to Russell and Bergson in the twentieth century.)

Grünbaum, A. (1968) *Modern Science and Zeno's Paradoxes*, London: Allen & Unwin. (Concentrates on the problems Zeno raises for modern mathematical physics; the book requires some mathematical ability.)

Guthrie, W.K.C. (1962–78) *A History of Greek Philosophy*, Cambridge: Cambridge University Press, 6 vols. (Volume 2 chapter 1B provides a clear and detailed English-language survey of work on Zeno.)

Kirk, G.S., Raven, J.E. and Schofield, M. (1983) *The Presocratic Philosophers*, Cambridge: Cambridge University Press, 2nd edn. (Chapter 11 provides the Greek text, with English translation, of Zeno's arguments against plurality and motion, with

accompanying exposition; the translations in this entry mainly follow Kirk, Raven and Schofield.)

Lear, J. (1981) 'A Note on Zeno's Arrow', *Phronesis*, 26: 91–104. (Avoids the Arrow argument by denying that the present is unextended; also discusses the appropriate way to respond to 'sceptical' puzzles such as Zeno's.)

* Lee, H.D.P. (1936) *Zeno of Elea*, Cambridge: Cambridge University Press. (Greek text and English translation of the majority of fragments and passages relevant to Zeno's arguments; Lee's comments have now been somewhat superseded.)

Moore, A.W. (1990) *The Infinite*, London: Routledge. (A relatively non-technical account of mathematical and philosophical problems concerning infinity; chapter 1 on early Greek thought, and chapters 8 and 10 on Cantor and transfinite mathematics, are particularly useful.)

Owen, G.E.L (1957) 'Zeno and the Mathematicians', *Proceedings of the Aristotelian Society* 58: 199–222; repr. in R.E. Allen and D.J. Furley (eds) *Studies in Presocratic Philosophy*, vol. 2, London: Routledge & Kegan Paul, 1975; repr. in W.C. Salmon, *Zeno's Paradoxes*, Indianapolis, IN: Bobbs-Merrill, 1970; repr. in G.E.L. Owen, *Logic, Science and Dialectic*, Cambridge: Cambridge University Press, 1986. (Offers an account of Zeno's arguments as an organized whole; includes a lengthy discussion of the Arrow.)

* Plato (*c.*380–367 BC) *Parmenides*, trans. F.M. Cornford, *Plato and Parmenides*, London: Routledge & Kegan Paul, 1939; trans. M.L. Gill and P. Ryan, *Plato: Parmenides*, Indianapolis, IN: Hackett, 1996. (Presents Zeno in conversation with Socrates.)

Sainsbury, M. (1988) *Paradoxes*, Cambridge: Cambridge University Press. (Chapter 1 is a philosophically lively discussion of a selection of Zeno's arguments; and includes a number of footnoted questions, designed to draw the reader into the problems Zeno raises.)

Salmon, W.C. (1970) *Zeno's Paradoxes*, Indianapolis, IN: Bobbs-Merrill. (A collection of previously published papers, mostly concerning the arguments about motion; includes influential papers by Black, Thomson and Benacerraf on the possibility of completing infinite series of tasks in staccato fashion.)

* Simplicius (AD 538–or after) *On Aristotle's Physics 6*, trans. D. Konstan, London: Duckworth, 1989. (Contains commentary on Aristotle's report and discussion of Zeno's arguments against motion.)

Sorabji, R. (1983) *Time, Creation and the Continuum*, London: Duckworth. (Chapter 21 concerns Zeno's arguments; chapters 22–5 trace out the development of atomist accounts of time, space and motion.)

Stokes, M.C. (1971) *One and Many in Presocratic Philosophy*, Washington, DC: Center for Hellenic Studies. (Relates Zeno to other Presocratic philosophers, including Parmenides, Melissus and Democritus.)

Vlastos, G. (1971) 'A Zenonian Argument against Plurality', in *Essays in Ancient Greek Philosophy*, ed. J.P. Anton and G.L. Kustas, Albany, NY: State University of New York Press. (Reconstruction and discussion of the 'large and small' argument in Zeno's fragments 1 and 2.)

White, M.J. (1992) *The Continuous and the Discrete: Ancient Physical Theories from a Contemporary Perspective*, Oxford: Clarendon Press. (An extended account of the conflict between different ancient accounts of time and space, with some reference to the problems raised by Zeno's arguments.)

* Zeno of Elea (*fl. c.*450 BC) Fragments, in H. Diels and W. Kranz (eds) *Die Fragmente der Vorsokratiker* (Fragments of the Presocratics), Berlin: Weidemann, 6th edn, 1952, vol. 1, 247–58. (The standard collection of the ancient sources; includes Greek texts with translations in German.)

STEPHEN MAKIN

ZERMELO, ERNST (1871–1953)

The German mathematician Ernst Zermelo is today best known for his axiomatization of set theory (1908), presented in the spirit of Hilbert's early axiomatic programme. Originally working in the calculus of variations and mathematical physics, Zermelo concentrated on set theory after proving that every set can be well-ordered (1904). His proof, based on the axiom of choice, provoked a lively controversy. In the 1930s Zermelo worked on infinitary logic, trying to overcome Gödel's incompleteness results.

1 Life
2 Work

1 Life

Ernst Zermelo studied mathematics, physics and philosophy at the universities of Berlin, Halle and Freiburg. In 1894 he obtained his doctorate from Berlin with a dissertation taking a Weierstrassian approach to the calculus of variations (see ANALYSIS, PHILOSOPHICAL ISSUES IN). He became an assistant to Max Planck, but in 1897 he went to the University of Göttingen where he finished his *Habilitation* thesis on hydrodynamics in 1899. He began to teach as a *Privatdozent* at Göttingen and was made a titular professor in 1905. In 1910 he accepted a chair of mathematics at the University of Zurich, but resigned in 1916 because of poor health. After 1921 he lived in retirement in Freiburg, where he became honorary professor of mathematics in 1926. After National Socialistic students had denounced him, he resigned to avoid being dismissed. Following the war he was reinstated but, then almost blind, was never again able to teach.

2 Work

After working in the calculus of variations, thermodynamics and statistical mechanics, Zermelo published his first paper on set theory, concerning the addition of transfinite cardinals (see SET THEORY §3), in 1902. His later work on set theory can be seen as a contribution to the lively discussion of Cantor's continuum hypothesis. Cantor had conjectured that every infinite subset of the continuum is either denumerable or has the power of the continuum (1878: 257; see CONTINUUM HYPOTHESIS). In 1900, in his seminal Paris lecture, 'Mathematische Probleme', Hilbert had emphasized the importance of proving Cantor's 'remarkable assertion' that every set could be well-ordered, and that this fact could be used to prove the continuum hypothesis. In 1904 Zermelo succeeded in proving the well-ordering theorem using a construction of sets by transfinite recursion justified by appeal to what would later be called the 'axiom of choice' (see AXIOM OF CHOICE). This proof, together with the axiom of choice, was rejected by many mathematicians working in foundations. Zermelo responded to his critics with a new proof, retaining the axiom of choice and emphasizing the purely formal character of the well-ordering, which has nothing to do with 'spatiotemporal arrangements' (1908a: 107). He accompanied his proof by a polemical discussion of objections, arguing that his critics also used infinite numbers of arbitrary choices and that he was by no means the first to use the axiom.

Zermelo shifted his emphasis to set theory both because of the heavy reactions to his former proof and also because of the fact that set theory began to move into the focus of foundational research in Göttingen. The sensation caused by the publication of the set-theoretical paradoxes by Bertrand Russell in 1903 led to a revision of David Hilbert's early axiomatic programme (see PARADOXES OF SET AND PROPERTY; HILBERT'S PROGRAMME AND FORMALISM). Although Zermelo had independently found a similar paradox in 1899 or 1900, it was only with Russell's publications that it became evident that Hilbert's programme, which centred on the problem of proving the consistency of arithmetic, had to take into account the consistency of logic itself; and that set theory was necessary for an axiomatization of arithmetic. In this vein Zermelo began working on a new axiomatization of set theory by 1905 (see Moore 1982: 152–7), though, unable to find a consistency proof for it, he delayed publication until 1908. In the published version (1908b: 262–7) Zermelo stated seven axioms: the axiom of choice, the power set axiom and the axioms of extensionality, elementary sets, separation, union and infinity (see SET THEORY §1; SET THEORY, DIFFERENT SYSTEMS OF). He mentioned the lack of a consistency proof for this set of axioms, but remarked that it was not subject to Russell's paradox since from his axiom of separation (if a propositional function $\mathfrak{E}(x)$ is definite for a set M, then there is a subset $M_\mathfrak{E}$ containing precisely those elements x of M for which $\mathfrak{E}(x)$ is true) it follows that a universal set cannot be derived.

Zermelo's axiomatization underwent several revisions, the most important of which was the addition of the axiom of replacement, formulated by Dmitry Mirimanoff (1917), Thoralf Skolem (1923) and Abraham Fraenkel (1922), and adopted by Zermelo in Fraenkel's version. Skolem gave the first first-order exposition of Zermelo's set theory, which grew into the Zermelo–Fraenkel set theory (ZF) of today.

Subsequent work was spawned by Zermelo's opposition to the 'Skolemist' interpretation of the Löwenheim–Skolem theorem, according to which 'every mathematical theory, even set theory, can be realized in a denumerable model' (Zermelo 1931: 85; original emphasis). In 1929 Zermelo gave a second-order axiomatization of the property of definiteness which was presupposed by the axiom of separation and which was the feature of his set theory at which most of the criticism had been directed. In response to his critics (among them especially Thoralf Skolem), Zermelo created in 1930 a new (supplemented) version of ZF – ZF' – which was formed by dropping the axiom of infinity and reclassifying the axiom of choice as a principle of the background logic. He also introduced the axiom of foundation, which prohibits infinitely descending chains of membership (1930: 31). This led to the introduction of well-founded sets which were used to define a cumulative type hierarchy, consisting of layers (indexed by ordinals) which are sets made up of objects from previous layers. At the annual meeting of the Deutsche Mathematiker-Vereinigung at Bad Elster on 15 September 1931, Zermelo used this hierarchy to propose a new infinitary mathematical logic without any quantifiers

(see Moore 1980: 124–8). He claimed, contrary to what was suggested by Gödel's then just recently announced work, that this logic would decide every proposition. These ideas did not find the audience that Zermelo had hoped for, although there are several similarities to today's systems of set theory (see Lavine 1994).

See also: INFINITARY LOGICS; LOGICAL AND MATHEMATICAL TERMS, GLOSSARY OF; LÖWENHEIM–SKOLEM THEOREMS AND NONSTANDARD MODELS; SET THEORY; SET THEORY, DIFFERENT SYSTEMS OF

List of works

Zermelo, E. (1894) *Untersuchungen zur Variationsrechnung* (Investigations on the Calculus of Variations), Berlin: Diss. (Zermelo's doctoral dissertation on the calculus of variations.)

—— (1897) 'Hydrodynamische Untersuchungen über die Wirbelbewegungen in einer Kugelfläche' (Hydrodynamic Investigations into the Spin of a Spherical Surface), *Zeitschrift für Mathematik und Physik* 47: 201–37, 1902. (Zermelo's *Habilitation* thesis, published several years after its submission.)

—— (1902) 'Über die Addition transfiniter Cardinalzahlen' (On the Addition of Transfinite Cardinals), *Nachrichten von der königlichen Gesellschaft der Wissenschaften zu Göttingen, mathematisch-physikalische Klasse aus dem Jahre 1901*: 34–8. (Zermelo's first paper on set theory.)

—— (1904) 'Beweis, daß jede Menge wohlgeordnet werden kann', *Mathematische Annalen* 59: 514–16; trans. S. Bauer-Mengelberg, 'Proof that Every Set can be Well-Ordered', in van Heijenoort (1967), 139–41. (Includes the heavily debated proof of the well-ordering theorem.)

—— (1908a) 'Neuer Beweis für die Möglichkeit einer Wohlordnung', *Mathematische Annalen* 65: 107–28; trans. S. Bauer-Mengelberg, 'A New Proof of the Possibility of a Well-Ordering', in van Heijenoort (1967), 183–98. (Zermelo's reply to his critics, and a new proof of the well-ordering theorem.)

—— (1908b) 'Untersuchungen über die Grundlagen der Mengenlehre. I', *Mathematische Annalen* 65: 261–81; trans. S. Bauer-Mengelberg, 'Investigations in the Foundations of Set Theory I', in van Heijenoort (1967), 200–15. (The first axiomatization of set theory.)

—— (1929) 'Über den Begriff der Definitheit in der Axiomatik' (On the Notion of Definiteness in Axiomatics), *Fundamenta Mathematicae* 14: 339–44. (Second-order axiomatization of the property of definiteness.)

—— (1930) 'Über Grenzzahlen und Mengenbereiche. Neue Untersuchungen über die Grundlagen der Mengenlehre', *Fundamenta Mathematicae* 16: 29–47; trans. M. Hallett, 'On Boundary Numbers and Domains of Sets: New Investigations in the Foundations of Set Theory', in W. Ewald (ed.) *From Kant to Hilbert: A Source Book in the Foundations of Mathematics*, Oxford: Clarendon Press, 1996, vol. 2, 1,219–33. (Revised version of the axiomatization of set theory.)

—— (1931) 'Über Stufen der Quantifikation und die Logik des Unendlichen' (On Levels of Quantification and the Logic of the Infinite), *Jahresbericht der Deutschen Mathematiker-Vereinigung* 40 (2nd section): 85–8. (The introduction of an infinitary logic without quantifiers.)

—— (ed.) (1932) G. Cantor, *Gesammelte Abhandlungen mathematischen und philosophischen Inhalts* (Collected Papers with Mathematical and Philosophical Contents), Berlin: Springer, 1980. (Still the edition of choice of Cantor's works.)

—— (1935) 'Grundlagen einer allgemeinen Theorie der mathematischen Satzsysteme (erste Mitteilung)' (Foundations of a General Theory of Systems of Mathematical Sentences (First Communication)), *Fundamenta Mathematicae* 25: 136–46. (Elaboration of the 1931 paper.)

References and further reading

* Cantor, G. (1878) 'Ein Beitrag zur Mannigfaltigkeitslehre' (A Contribution to the Doctrine of Manifolds), *Journal für die reine und angewandte Mathematik* 84: 242–58; repr. in *Gesammelte Abhandlungen mathematischen und philosophischen Inhalts*, ed. E. Zermelo, Berlin: Springer, 1932, 118–33. (Includes Cantor's continuum hypothesis.)
* Fraenkel, A. (1922) 'Zu den Grundlagen der Cantor–Zermeloschen Mengenlehre' (On the Foundations of Cantor–Zermelo Set Theory), *Mathematische Annalen* 86: 230–7. (Revision of Zermelo's axiomatization of set theory.)
  Heijenoort, J. van (ed.) (1967) *From Frege to Gödel: A Source Book in Mathematical Logic, 1879–1931*, Cambridge, MA: Harvard University Press. (Important omnibus version with key texts in the history of logic and foundations of mathematics.)
* Hilbert, D. (1900) 'Mathematische Probleme. Vortrag, gehalten auf dem internationalen Mathematiker-Kongress zu Paris 1900', *Nachrichten von der königlichen Gesellschaft der Wissenschaften zu Göttingen, mathematisch-physikalische Klasse*: 253–97; trans. M.W. Newson, 'Mathematical Problems', *Bulletin of the American Mathematical Society* 8: 437–79, 1902. (Seminal lecture which influenced the direction of mathematical research in several branches.)
—— (1905) 'Über die Grundlagen der Logik und der Arithmetik', in A. Krazer (ed.) *Verhandlungen des dritten internationalen Mathematiker-Kongresses in Heidelberg vom 8. bis 13. August 1904*, Leipzig: Teubner, 174–85; trans. B. Woodward, 'On the Foundations of Logic and Arithmetic', in van Heijenoort (1967), 130–8. (Hilbert's first step towards an axiomatization of arithmetic as a reaction to the publication of Russell's paradox.)
* Lavine, S. (1994) *Understanding the Infinite*, Cambridge, MA, and London: Harvard University Press, 134–41. (An account of Zermelo's late second-order set theories.)
* Mirimanoff, D. (1917) 'Les antinomies de Russell et de Burali-Forti et le problème fondamental de la théorie des ensembles' (The Antinomies of Russell and Burali-Forti and the Foundational Problem of Set Theory), *L'Enseignement mathématique* 19: 37–52. (Revision of Zermelo's axiomatization of set theory.)
* Moore, G.H. (1980) 'Beyond First-Order Logic: The Historical Interplay Between Mathematical Logic and Axiomatic Set Theory', *History and Philosophy of Logic* 1: 95–137. (A nontechnical historical overview of the relations between mathematical logic and set theory.)
* —— (1982) *Zermelo's Axiom of Choice: Its Origins, Development, and Influence*, Studies in the History of Mathematics and Physical Sciences, 8, New York, Heidelberg and Berlin: Springer. (Despite its title, a full account of Zermelo's writings on set theory, their historical context and their influences in contemporary set theory.)
  Peckhaus, V. (1990) '"Ich habe mich wohl gehütet, alle Patronen auf einmal zu verschießen". Ernst Zermelo in Göttingen' ("I Made Sure Not To Use Up All My Bullets At Once". Ernst Zermelo in Göttingen), *History and Philosophy of Logic* 11: 19–58. (Focuses on Zermelo's collaboration with Hilbert during his time at Göttingen.)
* Skolem, T. (1923) 'Einige Bemerkungen zur axiomatischen Begründung der Mengenlehre', in *Matematikerkongressen i Helsingfors den 4–7 Juli 1922, Den femte skandinaviska matematikerkongressen, Redogörelse*, Helsinki: Akademiska Bokhandeln, 217–32; repr. in *Selected Works in Logic*, ed. J.E. Fenstad, Oslo, Bergen and Tromsö: Universitetsforlaget, 1970, 137–52; trans. S. Bauer-Mengelberg, 'Some Remarks on Axiomatized Set Theory', in van Heijenoort (1967), 291–301. (First first-order exposition of Zermelo's set theory.)

VOLKER PECKHAUS

ZHANG ZAI (1020–77)

Zhang Zai was a seminal neo-Confucian cosmologist and ethical thinker. Like Zhou Dunyi and Shao Yong, he was inspired by the Yijing *(Book of Changes) and its commentaries; unlike them, he worked out a conception based solely on the concept of* qi *(cosmic vapour). He espoused an ethical vision, global in spirit, that greatly enhanced the moral significance of Confucianism.*

Zhang Zai was born in Changan, China, and grew up in an age of intellectual ferment. He studied Buddhism, Daoism and even military strategy before embarking on a serious study of the Confucian classics and joining the ranks of the neo-Confucians. He focused his learning on the *Zhongyong* (Doctrine of the Mean) and the *Yijing* (Book of Changes) (see ZHONGYONG; YIJING). Later, when he lectured on the *Yijing* in the capital, his students included such luminaries as the historian Sima Guang and the philosopher brothers CHENG HAO and CHENG YI. Zhang held occasional government positions but, since he opposed the reforms of Wang Anshi (1021–86), he balanced his government service with teaching at home. He died of illness while travelling home from the capital.

In 1070, Zhang had an uncanny dream in which he envisaged the formation of the cosmos. He articulated this vision in the book *Zhengmeng* (Correcting Youthful Ignorance), an attempt to explain the cosmos and man, and even such fundamental terms as the supreme polarity (*taiji*) and the Way (*dao*), in terms of *qi* states, permutations and processes. To many interpreters, this approach resembles reductive materialism, but *qi* in the Chinese view is a fluid proto-material which gives rise to phenomena of all sorts, mental and spiritual as well as physical (see QI). Hence, unlike reductive materialism, there is no attempt to deny any realms of phenomena such as the mental. However, because Zhang's *qi*-based theory did not seem to provide an adequate account of order in the cosmos and the constancy of human values, it was long overshadowed by the *li* (pattern) based thought of the Cheng brothers and ZHU XI (see LI). Centuries later, WANG FUZHI, believing that the Cheng–Zhu idea of *li* was arbitrary and inflexible and thus lent itself to rigid conservatism, strongly advocated a revival of Zhang Zai's teachings. Chinese scholars today tend to praise Zhang's thought as anti-metaphysical and proto-scientific.

Cheng Yi accused Zhang's book of a false objectivism that diluted the Confucian moral message, which Cheng deemed purely a matter of subjective intuition. On his part, Zhang postulated *qi* as the common substance to ground a universal morality of sympathy and benevolence. Whatever the merits of this idea, he wrote the noblest and most compelling moral tract to come out of the neo-Confucian movement, the *Ximing* (Western Inscription), which reads, in part:

> Heaven is my father and Earth is my mother, and even such a small creature as I find an intimate place in their midst.
> Therefore that which fills the universe I regard as my body and that which directs the universe I consider as my nature.
> All people are my brothers and sisters, and all things are my companions.
> …Wealth, honour, blessings, and benefits are meant for the enrichment of my life, while poverty, humble station, and sorrow are meant to help my fulfillment.
> In life I follow and serve [Heaven and Earth]. In death I will be at peace.
>
> (*Ximing* in Chan (1963): 497–8)

See also: NEO-CONFUCIAN PHILOSOPHY; QI; ZHU XI

List of works

Zhang Zai (1020–77) *Ximing* (The Western Inscription), trans. Chan Wing-tsit, *A Source Book in Chinese Philosophy*, Princeton, NJ: Princeton University Press, 1963. (This inspiring poetic tract placed Confucian ethics in cosmological perspective. Moreover, it broadened the scope of Confucian 'benevolence' to all of mankind.)

—— (1020–77) *Zhengmeng* (Correcting Youthful Ignorance), trans. Chan Wing-tsit, *A Source Book in Chinese Philosophy*, Princeton, NJ: Princeton University Press, 1963. (This work sets forth a philosophy of nature, humanity and ethics, based on the concept of *qi*. Notably, this book contains a serious attempt to solve the problem of evil in Confucianism.)

References and further reading

Kasoff, I. (1984) *The Thought of Chang Tsai (1020–1070)*, Cambridge: Cambridge University Press. (Systematic overview of Zhang's philosophy; clear and accessible.)

Huang, S. (1968) 'Chang Tsai's Concept of *Ch'i*', *Philosophy East and West* 18 (3): 247–59. (Analytic account of Zhang's fundamental cosmological concept; somewhat technical.)

—— (1971) 'The Moral Point of View of Chang Tsai', *Philosophy East and West* 21 (2): 141–56. (Study of the implications of Zhang's *Ximing* (Western Inscription); clear, but somewhat technical.)

Tang, C. (1956) 'Chang Tsai's Theory of Mind and Its Metaphysical Basis', *Philosophy East and West* 6 (2): 113–36. (Sophisticated analysis of Zhang's moral psychology; rather difficult, but rewarding.)

KIRILL OLE THOMPSON

ZHENG XUAN (AD 127–200)

Zheng Xuan, perhaps the most influential commentator on the Confucian classics, is widely credited with constructing both a compelling unitary vision of Chinese civilization and a hierarchy of written authorities which upheld the supremacy of the five Confucian classics as infallible guides to morality and history. Inevitably, scholars (including Zheng's many critics) have 'read' early Chinese society through the filter of Zheng's surviving commentaries, which ultimately superseded earlier divergent scholastic traditions.

Of the nearly sixty texts attributed to Zheng, only four complete works remain: commentaries on each of the three Rites Classics – the *Liji* (Book of Rites), *Zhouli* (Rites of Zhou) and *Yili* (Ceremony and Rites) – and a subcommentary appended to the Mao *Shijing* (Book of Songs). Judging from these works, Zheng Xuan's genius lay in his ability to embody a great deal of information in succinct comments; in imitation of the heroic sages of antiquity, Zheng aimed to 'raise a single principle that applies to a myriad cases...so as to minimize [the need for independent] thought'. Thus, Zheng's commentaries frequently include general statements recapitulating the main principles that underpin the entire Confucian tradition, which he tied to philological explanations based on archaic or regional pronunciations (complementing the *Shuowen* dictionary's emphasis on the visual components of Chinese characters). Zheng's commentaries also relate material from different classical authorities, so that puzzling passages may be solved by 'internal evidence' provided by the sages; in addition, Han customs, popular expressions and even artefacts are described whenever they shed light on ancient practices. As a result, Zheng's annotations go far beyond the standard pre-Han commentarial format (which usually presented glosses in the form '*X* means *Y*'), without lapsing into the prolixity of many Han scholarly explications.

Collected fragments of early polemical texts offer tantalizing clues about three famous disputes (with Xu Shen, He Xiu and Wang Su) involving Zheng and his disciples. Often misinterpreted, these disputes did not centre on either the authenticity of the apocryphal (*wei*) texts or allegiances to New Script/Old Script (*jinwen/guwen*) 'schools'. As Zheng cited the apocrypha only when other early sources corroborate their accounts, his reliance on the apocrypha was quite conservative by contemporary standards. Further, after twenty years devoted to the study of both Old and New Script texts, Zheng was determined to find common ground in competing theories about the classics. Basically, Zheng deplored the literalist approach of Xu and He, which would require the rejection of parts of the sacred canon. Zheng further objected to He's elevation of the *Gongyangzhuan* (Gongyang Commentary) to the *Chunqiu* (Spring and Autumn Annals) to virtual canonical status (see CHINESE CLASSICS); in Zheng's view, none of the three major commentaries to the *Chunqiu* could rival the 'subtle message' (*weiyan*) of Confucius' own masterwork. A third dispute, continued over centuries by the disciples of Zheng and Wang Su, was apparently prompted by Zheng's failure to preserve *jiafa* (discrete scholastic lines) and by Wang's pronounced royalist sentiments. The very virulence of the attacks launched against Zheng only attests to his seminal influence on classical studies.

Although Zheng established the basic conventions for critical scholarship in China, modern scholarship discounts his famous 'proofs' for the single, divine origin for the classics and their apocrypha, and also questions Zheng's dating of important works, including the *Zhouli* (Rites of Zhou). Such empirical errors clearly stem from Zheng's fervent desire to reconcile contradictory passages. Zheng's attempts to shore up the political system of late Han dynasty certainly coloured his commentaries; hence his continual reiteration of ritual's function in preserving the *status quo* and his rejection of the usual ethical dimensions of key status terms (such as 'ruler' and 'gentleman'). However, researchers readily acknowledge Zheng's remarkable erudition with regard to scribal errors, loan characters, dialect pronunciations, script variants, authorial mood and literary context. The ease with which Zheng moves between different disciplines and interpretations confirms his place as a *tongru* (polymath), though it surely also signals a loss of faith in the earlier formulations of Confucian orthodoxy.

See also: CHINESE CLASSICS; CHINESE PHILOSOPHY; CONFUCIUS

List of works

Zheng Xuan (AD 127–200) *Bowujingyiyi* (Contra Variant Interpretations of the Five Classics), in

Wenjingtang congshu, compiled by Sun Fengyi in *Baibucongshujicheng*, Taibei: Yiwen yinshuguan, 1968. (The most important polemic on the classics by Zheng, now in fragments.)

References and further reading

Chang, S. (1984) *Zheng Xuan congshu* (Collected Writings on Zheng's Scholarship), Jinan: Qilushushe. (Covers all aspects of Zheng's work, with particular emphasis on his distinctive style in writing commentaries.)

Kramers, R.P. (1949) *K'ung tzu chia yü: The School Sayings of Confucius*, Leiden: Brill, 77–98. (Outlines the major controversy between Zheng Xuan and Wang Su.)

Ozawa, B. (1970) *Kandai Ekigaku no kenkyū* (Research on *Yijing* Studies in the Han), Tokyo: Meitoku Publishers. (Limits his discussion to Zheng's theories on the *Yijing* (Book of Changes).)

Wang, L. (1983) *Zheng Kangcheng nianpu* (Chronology of Zheng Xuan), Jinan: Qilushushe. (The standard chronological biography (*nianpu*) of Zheng.)

MICHAEL NYLAN

ZHI

In classical Chinese philosophy, zhi, conventionally translated as 'knowing', is not so much a knowing 'what', which provides some understanding of the natural world, as it is a knowing 'how' to be adept in relationships, and 'how', in optimizing the possibilities that these relations provide, to develop trust in their viability. The cluster of terms that define knowing are thus programmatic and exhortative, encouraging the quality of the roles and associations that define us. Propositions may be true, but it is more important that husbands and friends be so.

If the major concern in the Chinese tradition is for *how* rather than *what* – finding a way (*dao*) rather than seeking the Truth – this can only mean that most of the theoretical and practical correlates of the search for truth will themselves be absent, with the consequence that the shape of the Chinese cultural sensibility may be expected to be radically distinct from that of Western culture. Rather than a vocabulary of truth and falsity, right and wrong, good and evil – terms that speak to the 'whatness' of things – we find pervasively the language of harmony and disorder, genuineness and hypocrisy, trust and dis-simulation, adeptness and ineptness; terms which reflect the priority of the continuity that obtains among things, and the quality of that continuity. That is, 'how well' do things hang together?

In contrast to Western philosophy that began from the decontextualizing metaphysical sensibilities of the classical Greeks, the Chinese tradition is resolutely historicist. Reason is a series of historical instances of reasonableness; culture is a specific historical pattern of human flourishing; logic is the internal coherence of this particular human narrative; knowledge, always local and site-specific, is knowing how to make one's way smoothly and without obstruction. In fact, the performative and perlocutionary entailments of 'knowing' often make 'realizing', in the sense of 'making real', a better translation of this term. Truth is proximate: it is the capacity to foster productive relationships that begin with the maintenance of one's own integrity and extend to the enhancement of one's own natural, social and cultural contexts.

Truth-seekers want finally to get to the bottom line, to establish facts, principles and theories which characterize the way things are. Truth-seekers see a world divided into the way things appear and the way they truly are, and continually try to come up with propositions – true sentences – that describe the reality of things in an accurate manner.

Way-seekers have dramatically different interests. They accept that they live in a human world and seek those forms of action which promote harmonious social existence. For the Way-seekers, truth is most importantly a quality of persons rather than of propositions. Truth as 'way' refers to the genuineness and integrity of a fully functioning person – a *true* human being. To 'know' the way is to walk it, and to become wise in doing so.

See also: CHINESE PHILOSOPHY; DAO; DAOIST PHILOSOPHY; KNOWLEDGE, CONCEPT OF; TRUTH, CORRESPONDENCE THEORY OF

References and further reading

Graham, A.C. (1989) *Disputers of the Tao: Philosophical Argument in Ancient China*, LaSalle, IL: Open Court. (A survey of ancient Chinese thought.)

Hall, D.L. and Ames, R.T. (1995) *Anticipating China: Thinking Through the Narratives of Chinese and Western Culture*, Albany, NY: State University of New York Press. (A comparative study of the uncommon assumptions that ground the Chinese and Western traditions.)

DAVID L. HALL
ROGER T. AMES

ZHI DUN (AD 314–66)

Buddhist monk and specialist on the Zhuangzi, *Zhi Dun was active in the* xuanxue *or 'learning of the mysterious' salons of the Eastern Jin regime in southeastern China. For him, the sage described by the* Zhuangzi *and Buddhist texts alike was a great man who knows the ways of heaven triumphantly and responds to beings in perfect freedom. Zhi Dun was also known for his interpretation of emptiness and his expansion of the concept of li ('order' or 'pattern') into an underlying metaphysical principle.*

Zhi Dun is the primary representative of a new social development in Chinese history, when numbers of men sought purely spiritual learning in monasteries apart from the secular realm, and when the religion became widely accepted at the highest levels of Chinese society, among both men and women. He was ordained in AD 338 after studying the Perfection of Wisdom (*prajñā pāramitā*) so popular at the time, and died after spending several years teaching at the imperial court. At some point he wrote a commentary on the 'Free and Easy Wandering' chapter of the *Zhuangzi*, now lost. A homely man known for his waspish tongue and trenchant characterizations of people, he was friendly with some of the most prominent men of his day, including the Daoists Wang Xizhi (a famous calligrapher) and Sun Chuo. Xi Chao, a layman whose summary of Buddhist doctrine survives, was his student. Zhi Dun was a devotee of Amitābha, the Buddha of the Pure Land, and wrote a commentary on a scripture devoted to meditation on breathing.

The most significant element in Zhi Dun's thought was his understanding of the sage or perfect man, which he described on the basis of both the *Zhuangzi* and Buddhist texts (see ZHUANGZI). He disagreed with the contemporary interpretation of the *Zhuangzi* which held that everyone should follow one's own nature and be happy, which was too amoral and deterministic for his Buddhist inclinations. Instead, the sage was a supramundane embodiment of truth, able to respond to the myriad demands of sentient beings without moving himself. Just as the myriad sounds of the world would cause a bell to reverberate, so would the sage resonate according to the needs of beings, yet the various words and teachings spoken by the sage would not be identical to his own inner wisdom. Implicit in this concept of the sage is the sense that there is an absolute (*tathatā*, but often rendered as *li*) underlying all things (see LI). Zhi Dun was one of the earliest figures to explain Buddhism in terms of being and nonbeing (*you* and *wu*) (see YOU-WU).

Zhi Dun's understanding of emptiness is described as 'form as such'; known only through very sketchy fragments, it apparently refers to the existence of form through a plethora of co-dependent causes. He denied that there was any permanent substrate underlying form, and he realized that form was both equivalent to and different from emptiness. (Here form represents *se*, or *rūpa* in Sanskrit, the first of the five *skandhas* or constituents of the human being; it thus stands as part for the whole of conditioned phenomena.) Based on the scanty evidence extant, Zhi Dun's theory of emptiness seems to contradict his redefinition of *li* as a metaphysical substrate underlying phenomena.

See also: BUDDHIST PHILOSOPHY, CHINESE; BUDDHIST CONCEPT OF EMPTINESS; LI; ZHUANGZI

References and further reading

Zürcher, E. (1959) *The Buddhist Conquest of China: The Spread and Adaptation of Buddhism in Early Medieval China*, Leiden: Brill. (The best treatment of the earliest phase of Chinese Buddhism in any language.)

JOHN R. McRAE

ZHIYI (538–97)

The Chinese Buddhist monk Zhiyi is revered as the chief architect of the Tiantai school of Buddhism, one of the most distinctive and influential systems of Mahāyāna Buddhist thought and practice to take shape on East Asian soil. His systematization of the Tiantai teachings marked the emergence of the first major indigenous articulation of Buddhist thought and practice in China. This is considered an important watershed in the development of the East Asian Buddhist tradition, for it effectively brought to a close some five centuries of Chinese dependence on Indian Buddhist traditions of exegesis and opened the way to creation of the distinctive forms of scriptural hermeneutics and motifs of religious life that we regard as representative of East Asian Buddhism today.

Historically, Zhiyi's religious career spans the key transition between the last years of the strife-torn North–South Dynasties Period (317–581) and the lengthy era of political unification ushered in by the Sui (589–618) and Tang dynasties (620–906). Zhiyi himself is often credited with producing a synthesis of different regional currents of medieval Buddhism that is the religious analogue to the reintegration achieved by the Tang ruling house in the social and cultural spheres.

Born of a well-to-do family distantly connected with the Liang ruling house, Zhiyi's life was abruptly shattered at the age of 17 with the death of his parents and the sack of his home city, Jiangling, at the hands of the Western Wei army. Deeply shaken, he resolved shortly thereafter to become a Buddhist monk. Over the next few years he wandered through Hubei and Henan in search of a suitable teacher, eventually settling down with Nanyue Huisi (515–77), the spirited master of meditation who would later be listed as Zhiyi's predecessor in the Tiantai patriarchal lineage. Under Huisi's guidance, Zhiyi achieved his first major spiritual awakening and was exposed to the rudimentary system of doctrinal classification around which he would fashion his own mature scheme of Tiantai thought and practice.

In 568, at his teacher's urging, Zhiyi proceeded to the southern capital of Jinling to begin his own teaching career. He was received with enthusiasm and over the next seven or eight years acquired a large following among the aristocracy and Buddhist clergy of the capital, including members of the Chen ruling house. However, despite his growing popularity, Zhiyi became increasingly troubled by the limitations that such a bustling environment placed on his ability to train disciples and pursue his own religious practice. This led him in 575 to leave the capital and retire with a small group of students to the isolation of Mount Tiantai in central Zhejiang province. The decade of quiet religious pursuit that followed is regarded as a turning point in Zhiyi's spiritual and intellectual development, marked above all by the maturation of the distinctive system of doctrine and practice that we identify with Tiantai.

Between 585 and his death in 597, Zhiyi again threw himself into the bustling life of court and capital. During this period he enjoyed not only the support of the last Chen ruler but, when the Chen fell to the Sui in 581, also gained the enthusiastic patronage of prince Yang Guang, the man who would ultimately succeed the first Sui emperor, Wen (or Yang Jian), as the ill-fated Emperor Yang. Through the influence of Yang Guang and the Sui court, Zhiyi built Yuquan Monastery in Hubei and laid plans for the expansion of monastic facilities on Mount Tiantai (the construction of the famous Guoqing Monastery, realized several years after Zhiyi's death). With the death of Yang Guang and the collapse of the Sui in 617, Tiantai access to imperial patronage was severed. Nevertheless, over the two centuries that followed the Guoqing and Yuquan communities continued to function as vibrant centres of Tiantai learning. Their traditions influenced not only the formation of Tang Buddhism at large but also found their way to Korea and Japan, giving rise to the powerful Chôntae and Tendai orders in those two countries (see BUDDHIST PHILOSOPHY, JAPANESE; BUDDHIST PHILOSOPHY, KOREAN).

Despite the significance that we attribute to Zhiyi as *de facto* founder of the Tiantai tradition, it would be misleading to say that he intentionally set out to create a new Buddhist school. Like Confucius many centuries before him, Zhiyi thought of himself more as a reclaimer of the old than a creator of the new. Throughout Zhiyi's writings one finds a deep sense of anxiety over the petty rivalries and clerical malaise that he perceived among his Buddhist compatriots. As one who believed profoundly in the inherent unity of the Buddha's enlightened vision and received word, his synthesis was nothing short of an effort to rescue the 'true Dharma' or 'true intent of the Buddha' from the fragmentation and moral ossification that he saw around him. Against this backdrop, Zhiyi develops a distinctive vision of the Buddha as master of both the transcendent and mundane worlds, whose special genius lies not so much in his grasp of the ineffable reality of enlightenment as in the compassion and pedagogical skill to reach out and guide beings effectively to this end. Zhiyi defines the Tiantai religious path as a twofold discipline involving the seamless integration of meditative experience (*guan*) with comprehensive study of received scriptural tradition (*jiao*). To serve these ends, he developed detailed schemes for meditative practice as well as classification of scripture and its contents (see BUDDHIST PHILOSOPHY, CHINESE).

Tiantai tradition credits Zhiyi with a prodigious literary output – over fifty works in nearly two hundred fascicles, according to the most fanciful count. However, critical research has significantly reduced this number. Of the works that we may safely connect with Zhiyi, only a handful were written by the man himself; the majority were taken down and edited from his lectures by various disciples, notably his attendant Guanding (561–632). Three treatises in particular have been singled out by later tradition as offering the definitive statement of Tiantai teaching: the *Fahua xuanyi* (Profound Meaning of the *Lotus Sutra*), *Fahua wenju* (Words and Phrases of the *Lotus Sutra*), and *Mohe zhiguan* (Great Calming and Contemplation). The first two are synthetic and interlinear commentaries to the *Lotus Sutra*, the scripture hailed by Tiantai tradition as the culmination of the Buddha's career, in which the Buddha professed with the greatest clarity and finality the harmonious unity of his *dharma* (see BUDDHA). The *Mohe zhiguan* is a work of meditation dedicated to the 'perfect and sudden' contemplation. Although no explicit connection with the *Lotus Sutra* is developed in this text, Tiantai tradition regards it as the practical counterpart to the sublime doctrinal vision spelled out in the two *Lotus* commentaries. All three treatises bear the mark of Guanding's editorial hand. Among contemporary scholars there has developed considerable debate as to how much of their final form is the work of Zhiyi or of Guanding.

See also: BUDDHIST PHILOSOPHY, CHINESE; BUDDHIST PHILOSOPHY, JAPANESE; BUDDHIST PHILOSOPHY, KOREAN

List of works

Zhiyi (538–97) *Fahua xuanyi* (Profound Meaning of the *Lotus Sutra*), ed. Takakusu Junjirō and Watanabe Kaigyoku, Taishō daizōkyō 1716, vol. 33, Tokyo: Taishō issaikyō kankōkai, 1924–35. (One of Zhiyi's two commentaries on the *Lotus Sutra*.)
—— (538–97) *Fahua wenju* (Words and Phrases of the *Lotus Sutra*), ed. Takakusu Junjirō and Watanabe Kaigyoku, Taishō daizōkyō 1718, vol. 34, Tokyo: Taishō issaikyō kankōkai, 1924–35. (One of Zhiyi's two commentaries on the *Lotus Sutra*.)
—— (538–97) *Mohe zhiguan* (Great Calming and Contemplation), ed. Takakusu Junjirō and Watanabe Kaigyoku, Taishō daizōkyō 1716, vol. 33, Tokyo: Taishō issaikyō kankōkai, 1924–35; ed. and trans. N. Donner and D. Stevenson, *The Great Calming and Contemplation: A Study and Annotated Translation of the First Chapter of Chi-i's Mo-ho chih-kuan*, Kuroda Institute Classics in East Asian Buddhism, Honolulu, HI: University of Hawaii Press, 1993. (A work of meditation dedicated to 'perfect and sudden' contemplation.)

References and further reading

Chappell, D. (ed.) (1983) *T'ien-t'ai Buddhism: An Outline of the Fourfold Teaching*, Tokyo: Daiichi-shobō.
Hurvitz, L. (1962) 'Chih-i (538–597): An Introduction to the Life and Ideas of a Chinese Monk', *Mélanges Chinoises et Bouddhiques* 12: 1–372.
Swanson, P. (1989) *Foundations of T'ien-t'ai Philosophy*, Berkeley, CA: Asian Humanities Press.
Weinstein, S. (1973) 'Imperial Patronage in the Formation of T'ang Buddhism', in A. Wright and D. Twitchett (eds) *Perspectives on the T'ang*, New Haven, CN: Yale University Press.

DANIEL B. STEVENSON

ZHONGYONG

The Zhongyong *(Doctrine of the Mean) has traditionally been ascribed to Zisi, the grandson of Confucius and the indirect teacher of Mencius. Although this ascription has been challenged by modern critical scholarship since the turn of the twentieth century, recent archaeological finds indicate that the traditional view is not without textual base. If the* Zhongyong *actually predated the* Mengzi, *it seems that a significant portion of the* Liji *(Book of Rites), of which the* Daxue *(Great Learning) and* Zhongyong *are chapters, contains documents of the fifth century BC. This fact alone merits a fundamental restructuring of classical Confucian chronology and reinterpretation of the Mencian line of the Confucian tradition.*

The Chinese title of the essay is composed of the characters 'centrality' (*zhong*) and 'normality' or 'commonality' (*yong*). *Zhongyong* (Doctrine of the Mean), suggesting the basic moral idea of moderation, balance and suitability, conveys a profoundly meaningful notion of humanity as both an anthropological and cosmological ideal. Centrality and commonality in the *Zhongyong* connotes that ordinary human virtues such as filial piety, honesty, reciprocity, and benevolence, if thoroughly comprehended and fully embodied in our action, can help us to understand not only ourselves but also nature and Heaven. This faith in the improvability of the human condition through self-effort and in the human capacity to know and realize the truth and reality of Heaven through self-knowledge leads to the theory and practice that philosophy as a way of life addresses the ontological issues of who we are, what we know, how we should act and what we can hope (see SELF-CULTIVATION IN CHINESE PHILOSOPHY).

Intent on relating what is most essential in humanity to the underlying reality of the cosmos, the *Zhongyong* is organized around three integrated visions: the profound person, the fiduciary community and moral metaphysics. Since human nature is endowed by the decree of Heaven, there is a wellspring of creativity inherent in the structure of human existence here and now. If we allow that wellspring to flow naturally, we will find the most authentic way of learning to be human. Indeed, the ultimate concern of education is none other than the cultivation of the human way. Implicit in this seemingly optimistic vision of self-realization are four inseparable dimensions of human flourishing: self, community, nature and Heaven. Learning to be human entails the fruitful interplay between self and community (family, society, nation and the world), the dynamic equilibrium between the human species and nature and the creative fidelity between the human heart-and-mind and the way of Heaven (see TIAN; XIN). This requires constant attention to even the minute details in our daily living and ceaseless effort in elevating our levels of consciousness and self-reflexivity.

Profound people optimize their capacity to realize the full potential inherent in human nature. Such a project of self-realization, if shared as a joint venture for mutual exhortation, will form a discourse fellowship which may serve as a standard of inspiration for the creation of a fiduciary community. A community, based upon mutual trust of its members for the sake of completing the human project as co-creator of the cosmic process, is a 'holy rite' in which the sanctity of the earth, the sacredness of the body and the beatitude of the family enable a concrete living person to become not only a moral agent but also an anthropocosmic presence:

> Only those who thoroughly embody sincerity can fully realize their own nature. If they can fully realize their own nature, they can fully realize human nature. If they can fully realize human nature, they can fully realize the nature of all things. If they can fully realize the nature of all things, they can participate in the transforming and nourishing processes of Heaven and Earth. If they can participate in the transforming processes of Heaven and Earth, they can form a trinity with Heaven and Earth.
>
> (*Zhongyong* XXII)

See also: CONFUCIAN PHILOSOPHY, CHINESE; CHINESE PHILOSOPHY; SELF-CULTIVATION IN CHINESE PHILOSOPHY; TIAN

References and further reading

Chan Wing-tsit (1963) *A Source Book in Chinese Philosophy*, Princeton, NJ: Princeton University Press. (A translation and commentary on this text translated as *The Doctrine of the Mean*.)

Schwartz, B.I. (1985) *The World of Thought in Ancient China*, Cambridge, MA: Harvard University Press. (A discussion of several of the central concepts in the *Zhongyong*.)

Tu Wei-ming (1989) *Centrality and Commonality: An Essay on Confucian Religiousness*, Albany, NY: State University of New York Press. (A monograph dedicated to an analysis and exegesis of the *Zhongyong*, which uses the standard Chan (1963) translation.)

TU WEI-MING

ZHOU DUNYI (1017–73)

*Zhou Dunyi was the father of Chinese neo-Confucianism. His oracular presentation of the notions of supreme polarity (*taiji*), yin and yang, and the five phases to explain the formation of the cosmos and sagehood became enshrined by Zhu Xi as the authoritative neo-Confucian view.*

Born in Daozhou, China, Zhou served with distinction in a series of official posts from about 1040 to 1072 but is famed for his love for nature and his secluded cottage near a waterfall on Lu Mountain. There he wrote two visionary tracts on metaphysics, sagehood and ethics. His contemporaries SHAO YONG and ZHANG ZAI pursued similar themes, but lacked Zhou's clear synthetic vision and subtle articulation. CHENG HAO and CHENG YI, who went on to develop neo-Confucianism into an intellectual movement, studied under Zhou but later concealed his formative influence.

Zhou's synoptic essay *Taiji tushuo* (Explanation of the Diagram of the Supreme Polarity) presents a dynamic conception of reality. It begins with an account of the formation of the cosmos in levels from elementary forces to complex phenomena, and ends with an account of the sage as a reflection of the cosmos. The text opens with an intriguing dialectical proposition that even now arouses discussion and debate: 'Free from any polarity (*wuji*), and yet the supreme polarity (*taiji*)!' Taking *wuji* as the Daoist 'utmost of non-being', LU XIANGSHAN (1139–93) saw this proposition as an illicit attempt to bifurcate basic reality into two distinct categories. His contemporary ZHU XI countered that *wuji* here does not refer to a positive concept. It simply indicates that *taiji* (supreme polarity) is not a discrete, locatable entity; it is the primal pattern of change, that which describes the intercourse between *yin* and *yang* and thus pervades reality. Next, the *Taiji tushuo* goes on to describe how *yin–yang* intercourse gives rise to the five phases – earth, wood, fire, water, metal – which in turn engender 'heaven, earth and the myriad things', the empirical world (see YIN–YANG).

Humanity reflects this fecund cosmos, but most consummately in the person of the sage, 'whose virtue matches that of heaven and earth, whose brilliance matches that of the sun and moon, whose order matches that of the four seasons, and whose fortunes match those of the gods'. In the *Tongshu* (Penetrating the Book of Changes), Zhou describes sagehood, self-cultivation and related concepts. The distinguishing virtue of sagehood is cheng (sincerity, authenticity). The sage authentically manifests the creative virtues of the cosmos. Through this sincerity, he abides by the mean and acts according to the cardinal virtues adumbrated by CONFUCIUS. The sage is thus one who acts in an upright manner yet spontaneously and without deliberation. Those who aspire to this sphere must, above all, cultivate a pure, tranquil mind (see CONFUCIAN PHILOSOPHY, CHINESE).

Dedicated to this view, Zhou impressed others with his distinctive manner. The poet Huang Tingjian (1045–1105) lauded Zhou as 'a man of lofty character, fresh and vigorous as a breeze in the sunlight.... Modest in striving for renown yet ardent in seeking self-realization, he is indifferent to worldly success yet steadfast in friendship' (*Songshi* (History of the Song Dynasty) 427: 3).

See also: NEO-CONFUCIAN PHILOSOPHY; SELF-CULTIVATION IN CHINESE PHILOSOPHY; ZHU XI

List of works

Zhou Dunyi (1017–73) *Taiji tushuo* (Diagram Explaining the Supreme Ultimate), trans. Wing-tsit Chan, *A Source Book in Chinese Philosophy*, Princeton, NJ: Princeton University Press, 1963, 463–80. (This essay is a rather oracular presentation of Zhou's metaphysics and ethics; thus, the supporting notes and discussion are required reading.)

—— (1017–73) *Tongshu* (Penetrating the Book of Changes), Princeton, NJ: Princeton University Press, 1963, 463–80. (This essay is a rather oracular presentation of Zhou's metaphysics and ethics; thus, the supporting notes and discussions are required reading.)

References and further reading

Chan Wing-tsit (ed. and trans.) (1966) *Reflections on Things at Hand: the Neo-Confucian anthology compiled by Chu Hsi and Lu Tsu-ch'ien*, New York: Columbia University Press. (Presents passages from Zhou's works with commentaries by traditional scholars; abstruse and technical yet interesting.)

Fung Yu-lan (1953) 'Chou Tun-i', trans. D. Bodde in *A History of Chinese Philosophy*, Princeton, NJ: Princeton University Press, 434–50. (Systematic overview of Zhou's metaphysics and ethics; somewhat technical, but generally understandable.)

Needham, J. (1956) 'The "Supreme Pole"', *Science and Civilisation in China*, vol. 2, *History of Scientific Thought*, Cambridge: Cambridge University Press, 460–72. (Influential attempt to understand Zhou's thought according to the philosophy of organism; abstruse yet lucid and fascinating.)

Huang, S. (1974) 'The Concept of *T'ai-chi* (Supreme Ultimate) in Sung Neo-Confucianism', *Journal of Chinese Philosophy* 1 (3): 275–94. (Review of various Song Chinese understandings of Zhou's guiding concept of *taiji*; technical.)

KIRILL OLE THOMPSON

ZHU XI (1130–1200)

The Chinese neo-Confucian philosopher Zhu Xi was a consummate scholar and classicist as well as a superb critical and synthetic thinker. He fused the ideas of the seminal eleventh-century thinkers Shao Yong, Zhou Tunyi, Zhang Zai, Cheng Hao and Cheng Yi into a grand philosophical synthesis. In addition, by effectively editing and annotating the essential classical Confucian texts – the Analects *of Confucius – the* Mengzi *of Mencius, the* Daxue *(Great Learning) and the* Zhongyong *(Doctrine of the Mean) – as the Four Books, Zhu worked out a lasting renewal of the Confucian project.*

Zhu Xi was born in Youqi in Fujian province, China. He was a precocious child who at five asked what lay beyond heaven and at eight grasped the significance of the *Xiaojing* (Book of Filial Piety). Reared in the company of scholars, Zhu obtained the *jinshi* degree (presented scholar degree, the highest level qualifying degree in the examination system) at nineteen. He nurtured an eclectic interest in Daoism and Chan Buddhism until becoming a student of Li Tong (1093–1163) in 1160. Li persuaded him of the superiority of Confucianism, to which he devoted himself for the rest of his life. He held various prefectural administrative posts but, disapproving of court policy, preferred temple guardianships, sinecures that gave him leisure to read, write and teach. He thus became a highly productive scholar who made lasting contributions to classical studies, historiography and literary criticism as well as to philosophy. He also was a master prose stylist and poet.

As a renowned master, Zhu taught the classics and neo-Confucianism. His teachings are preserved in the *Zhuzi yulei* (Classified Dialogues of Master Zhu). An assiduous teacher and scholar, Zhu continued to work right up to his death. He set rigorous new standards for textual criticism and philosophic thought; his idealistic spirit and productive life remain an inspiration to this day in East Asia.

Zhu Xi created an impressive metaphysical synthesis that has been compared broadly to the systems of such cardinal Western thinkers as PLATO, ARISTOTLE, Thomas AQUINAS and A.N. WHITEHEAD. Zhu developed Zhou Dunyi's dynamic conception of reality, as depicted in the *Taiji tu* (Diagram of the Supreme Polarity) (see ZHOU DUNYI), in order to conceive the Cheng brothers' concept of li (pattern) and Zhang Zai's notion of qi (cosmic vapour) as organically integrated (see CHENG HAO; CHENG YI; ZHANG ZAI). In Zhou's treatise *Taiji tushuo* (Diagram Explaining the Supreme Ultimate), Zhu found a viable account of the formation of the cosmos in levels: from the original unformed *qi* and the supreme polarity (*taiji*), to *yin*, *yang* and the five phases – earth, wood, fire, water and metal – down to 'heaven, earth and the myriad things', the empirical world. Zhu blended this conception with ideas from the *Yijing* (Book of Changes) and its commentaries (see YIJING) to set forth a comprehensive philosophy of cosmic creativity and to ground the Confucian notions of human nature, self-cultivation and self-realization. Zhu's penchant for thinking in polarities, however, has stirred critics to regard him as a dualist.

On the basis of this complex conception of reality, Zhu set forth a sophisticated theory of human nature that accounts for the possibility of evil as well as of sagehood. In this view, whereas people are fundamentally good – that is, sensitive and well-disposed – how one manifests this original nature will be conditioned by one's specific *qi* make-up, one's personality and intelligence, and level of attainment. The differences in people's disposition, character and aptitude for self-realization are regarded as due to variations in their *qi*-endowments.

Not registering the complexity of human nature and the wide variation of individual differences, the preceding generations of neo-Confucian scholars had advocated straightforward methods of self-cultivation to purify the mind and elicit the original nature; they understood this to constitute self-realization (see XING; SELF-CULTIVATION IN CHINESE PHILOSOPHY). Zhu's teacher Li Tong had advocated a form of meditation called 'quiet-sitting', the efficacy of which Zhu doubted from the outset. Later Zhu held discussions with Zhang Shi, a disciple of Hu Hong, who advocated introspection in action. At first, Zhu accepted this approach, but he soon found that introspection in action is not viable, for such introspection cannot inform action in the desired way; it in fact impedes effective action.

Zhu Xi's solution was a two-pronged approach to cultivation: to nurture a sense of reverence (*jing*) while investigating things to explore their patterns (*li*). Reverence purifies the mind, attunes one to the promptings of the original nature and impels one to act with appropriateness. At the same time, by grasping the patterns which constitute the world and upright interpersonal relations, one learns more about appropriate conduct. The mind which is imbued with reverence and comprehends these patterns will develop into a good will.

In later years, Zhu regarded this conception of cultivation as insufficiently motivational. He then argued that, like Confucius, one must at the outset establish the resolve to realize the Confucian ideals (see CONFUCIAN PHILOSOPHY, CHINESE). Zhu believed that such resolve lends an overriding purpose to one's cultivation effort and thus preserves one's motivation. This was a theme which WANG YANG-MING developed effectively some three centuries later.

In *Renshuo* (A Treatise on Humanity), Zhu articulates the classical Confucian ideal of humanity (*ren*) in cosmic and human perspective. At the same time, he effectively criticizes competing accounts of *ren* on logical and semantic grounds. Zhu associates *ren* with cosmic creativity; at root, *ren* is the impulse of 'heaven and earth' to produce things. It is manifested in the cycle of seasons and the fecundity of nature. This impulse is instilled in all creatures, but in man it is sublimated into the virtue of *ren*, which when fully realized involves being diligent and responsible to others. Zhu similarly correlated the four stages of production in nature – origination, growth, flourishing and firmness – mentioned in the *Yijing* with the four cardinal virtues enunciated by CONFUCIUS – humanity, appropriateness, ritual action and wisdom – in order to portray the realized person as a vital participant in cosmic creativity as well as a positive catalyst for the well-being and self-realization of others. On this basis, Zhu went on to formulate the authoritative definition of *ren* for the tradition as 'the character of mind' and 'the pattern of love'. *Ren* thus grounds the fundamental disposition of mind as commiserative and describes the core of moral self-realization as love for others, appropriately manifested.

See also: CHENG HAO; CHENG YI; CONFUCIAN PHILOSOPHY, CHINESE; LI; NEO-CONFUCIAN PHILOSOPHY; QI; SELF-CULTIVATION IN CHINESE PHILOSOPHY; ZHANG ZAI; ZHOU DUNYI

List of works

Zhu Xi (1130–1200) *Zhuzi yulei* (Classified Dialogues of Master Zhu), trans. J.P. Bruce, *The Philosophy of Human Nature*, London, 1922. (Compendium of Zhu's moral psychology drawn from the *Zhuzi quanshu* ('Complete' works of Master Zhu), abstruse. Translated selections can be found in Chan 1963, 1966; Gardner 1986, 1990; Wittenborn 1991.)

References and further reading

Chan Wing-tsit (1963) 'The Great Synthesis in Chu Hsi', in *A Source Book in Chinese Philosophy*, Princeton, NJ: Princeton University Press, 605–53. (Detailed overview of Zhu's thought drawn primarily from *Zhuzi quanshu*; clear and thoroughly annotated.)

—— (1966) *Reflections on Things at Hand: The Neo-Confucian Anthology Compiled by Chu Hsi and Lu Tsu-ch'ien*, New York: Columbia University Press. (Zhu's comprehensive compendium of seminal neo-Confucian pronouncements; clear and well-annotated.)

—— (ed.) (1986) *Chu Hsi and Neo-Confucianism*, Honolulu, HI: University of Hawaii Press. (Anthology of essays by prominent Zhu Xi scholars; contains Zhu's biography and authoritative articles on all aspects of Zhu's thought and scholarship.)

—— (1987) *Chu Hsi: Life and Thought*, Hong Kong: Hong Kong University Press. (General essays; clear and accessible.)

—— (1989) *Chu Hsi: New Studies*, Honolulu, HI: University of Hawaii Press. (Detailed studies of arcane issues in Zhu Xi scholarship; for the specialist.)

Fung Yu-lan (1953) 'Chu Hsi', trans. D. Bodde in *A History of Chinese Philosophy*, Princeton, NJ: Princeton University Press, 533–71. (Pioneering English presentation of Zhu's thought; technical but clearly presented.)

Gardner, D. (1986) *Chu Hsi and the Ta-hsueh: Neo-Confucian Reflection on the Confucian Canon*, Cambridge, MA: Harvard University Press. (Contains Zhu's commentary on the *Daxue* (Great Learning), a classical cultivation text; commentary with supporting essays.)

—— (1990) *Learning to Be a Sage: Selections from the Conversations of Master Chu, Arranged Topically*, Berkeley, CA: University of California Press. (Zhu's discussions on learning as a method of self-cultivation; clear and accessible.)

Needham, J. (1956a) 'The Neo-Confucians', in *Science and Civilisation in China*, vol. 2, *History of Scientific Thought*, Cambridge: Cambridge University Press, 455–84. (Innovative organismic account of Zhu's thought; lucid and fascinating.)

—— (1956b) 'Chu Hsi, Leibniz, and the Philosophy of Organism', in *Science and Civilisation in China*, vol. 2, *History of Scientific Thought*, Cambridge: Cambridge University Press, 455–84. (Innovative organismic account of Zhu's thought; lucid and fascinating.)

Schirokauer, C. (1962) 'Chu Hsi's Political Career: A Study in Ambivalence', in A. Wright and D. Twitchett (eds) *Confucian Personalities*, Stanford, CA: Stanford University Press, 162–88. (Detailed account of Zhu's official career; quite readable and engaging.)

Thompson, K. (1988) '*Li* and *Yi* as Immanent: Chu Hsi's Thought in Practical Perspective', *Philosophy East and West* 38 (1): 30–46. (Reinterpretation of Zhu's ontology and ethical theory; lucid and informative.)

Wittenborn, A. (1991) *Further Reflections at Hand: A Reader. Chu Hsi*, New York: University Press of America. (A comprehensive compendium of Zhu's philosophic pronouncements; clear translation with detailed commentary.)

KIRILL OLE THOMPSON

ZHUANGZI

The Zhuangzi is a Daoist text usually associated with 'Master Zhuang' (fourth century BC), also known as Zhuang Zhou. Scholarly consensus regards the thirty-three chapters of this text to be composite, containing passages that offer different and sometimes even contradictory interpretations of basic Daoist tenets. The opening seven 'inner chapters' are traditionally thought to be from the hand of Master Zhuang himself, while the remaining 'outer' and 'miscellaneous' chapters are taken to be later elaborations and commentary by members of what retrospectively can be called a Master Zhuang school, or better, lineage. As a philosophical text, the Zhuangzi is for the most part addressed to the project of personal realization, and only derivatively concerned about social and political order. As one of the finest pieces of literature in the classical Chinese corpus, the Zhuangzi is itself an object lesson in marshalling every trope and literary device available to provide rhetorically charged flashes of insight into the most creative way to live one's life in the world.

The consummate human being in *Zhuangzi* is called the 'Authentic Person' (*zhenren*), and consummate 'ethical' concerns have to do with the contributions one is able to make to the *ethos* or total character of one's world. Thus, 'ethics' in a Daoist sense would involve not simply moral judgments, but the total character of the person as it is constructed in their social and natural environments (see DAOIST PHILOSOPHY). This total character is the changing lineaments of habit and disposition that include not only what might be deemed 'good' or 'moral' but the full complement of the qualities which constitute the personal, social and natural fabric of one's existence.

Having said this, it must be clear that any 'ethical' judgments in the narrow sense are going to be derived from aesthetic sensibilities – the intensity, integrity and appropriateness that one detail has for its environing elements as interpreted from some particular perspective. Thus, no clear direction into ethics, social, political, and environmental philosophy, exists in this tradition.

To the extent that Daoism is normative and prescriptive (and it certainly is), it is so not by articulating rules to follow or asserting the existence of some underlying moral principles, but by describing the conduct of an achieved human being – the Authentic Person – as a recommended object of emulation. The model for this human ideal, in turn, is the orderly, elegant and harmonious processes of nature. Throughout the philosophical Daoist corpus, there is a 'grand' analogy established in the shared vocabulary used to describe the conduct of the achieved human being on the one hand, and the productive harmony achieved in the mutual accommodations of natural phenomena on the other.

Among the *Zhuangzi*'s central concerns is human creativity. To be fully integrative, inchoate individuals must overcome any sense of discreteness and disjunction with their environments to contribute personally to the emerging pattern and regularity of the world around them. This creativity can be compromised, however, where one attempts to express one's unique particularity in a 'dis-integrative' way that fails to accommodate the mutuality and interdependence of other things. This diminution in creative possibilities can be brought about either by interpreting one's environs reductionistically through one's own fixed conceptual structures and values, thereby impoverishing context in service to oneself, or by allowing oneself to be shaped wholly by context without contributing one's own uniqueness, thereby abnegating oneself in service to context.

The choice of 'authentic' rather than 'true' or 'real' as a translation for '*zhen*' in *zhenren* is calculated. With the same root as 'author', 'authentic' captures the primacy given to the creative contribution of the particular person in authoring the world. It further registers this contribution as what is most fundamentally 'real' and 'true'. It is because of the primacy of the 'authorship' of the 'authentic person' in creating human order that the *Zhuangzi* insists: 'there must be the Authentic Person before there can be authentic knowledge'. To 'know' a world is to 'realize' it in the sense of making it real. This claim made at the beginning of *Zhuangzi* 6 means that 'knowing' is not simply a cognitive exercise, the grasping of some pre-existing reality. Rather, 'knowing' is also performative: one must participate actively in the 'realization'

of one's world through one's own 'self-disclosure' (*ziran*). 'Knowing' for the Daoist, in addition to being cognitive, is profoundly experiential and collaborative.

In translating (*ziran*) as 'self-disclosure', we must bear in mind that 'self' is always 'in context'. For the Daoist, like the classical Chinese tradition broadly, there is a priority of situation over agency, and a priority of change over form. The particular self is thus neither discrete nor superordinate, but is always continuous with its ever changing world. It is sponsored by, and ultimately reflects in itself, the full consequence of existence. 'Self' is an individuated focus (*de*) in the ongoing field of the social, natural and cultural processes (*dao*) that articulate our world.

The Authentic Person's activity, characterized as *wuwei* (non-assertive action) is defined by flexibility, efficacy and non-contentiousness. One collaborates with one's social and natural environments, serving as frictionless ground for their self-disclosure, and they reciprocally for one's own. Because one develops a sense of identity and continuity with the process as a whole, one is calm and imperturbable. This sense of continuity enables one to exist beyond the plethora of disintegrative dualisms – self and other, creator and creature, life and death, reality and appearance – and to overcome death not by escaping to some more 'real' existence, but by coming to realize and to celebrate the mutually entailing identity of oneself and one's world.

Early Daoism has had an incalculable influence on the development of Chinese philosophy and culture. Second in influence only to the Confucian school, the classical Daoist philosophers in many ways have been construed as both a critique on and a complement to the more conservative, regulatory precepts of their Confucian rivals. When Buddhism entered China in the second century AD, Buddhist adepts appropriated many of the ideas and vocabularies of indigenous Daoism as a sympathetic language through which to express a fundamentally foreign system of thought. In so doing, they made Buddhist ideas more palatable to the Chinese audience, but at the same time, they also set Buddhism on a course of irrevocable Sinicization.

See also: CHINESE PHILOSOPHY; DAO; DAODEJING; DAOIST PHILOSOPHY; DE; HUAINANZI; QI; YIN–YANG; YOU–WU

References and further readings

Hall, D.L. and Ames, R.T. (1997) *Thinking from the Han: Self, Truth, and Transcendence in China and the West*, Albany, NY: State University of New York Press. (An interpretative study of some of the presuppositions underlying the Daoist world view.)

Jullien, F. (1995) *The Propensity of Things: Toward a History of Efficacy in China*, New York: Zone Books. (An examination of the way in which underlying assumptions have influenced the evolution of Chinese culture broadly).

LaFargue, M. (1994) *Tao and Method*, Albany, NY: State University of New York Press. (A primer on how to read the Daoist texts.)

Roth, H.D. (1991) 'Who Compiled the *Chuang Tzu*?', in H. Rosemont (ed.) *Chinese Text and Philosophical Contexts: Essays Dedicated to Angus C. Graham*, La Salle, IL: Open Court. (A textual study of the *Zhuangzi* that continues the earlier work of A.C. Graham in sorting the text into different philosophical strata.)

Wu Kuang-ming (1990) *The Butterfly as Companion: Meditations on the First Three Chapters of the Chuang Tzu*, Albany, NY: State University of New York Press. (A detailed analysis and exegesis of the first three chapters.)

Zhuangzi (*c.*4th century BC?), trans. B. Watson, *The Complete Works of Chuang Tzu*, New York: Columbia University Press, 1968; trans. A.C. Graham, *Chuang-tzu: The Inner Chapters*, London: George Allen & Unwin, 1981. (Watson is the standard translation of the *Zhuangzi* which takes advantage of the Japanese translation by Fukunaga Mitsuji. Graham is a philosophically sophisticated translation of about 85 per cent of the original text.)

ROGER T. AMES

ZI MOZI *see* MOZI

ZIONISM

Zionism, the idea of Jewish nationality in its modern form, emerged towards the end of the nineteenth century, several decades after nationalism had taken hold among most European peoples. The term denotes the ideology as well as the movement(s) whose goal is re-establishment of the Jewish people as a nation in its homeland in Palestine. Unlike many other movements of national liberation, Zionism seeks not the removal of a colonial regime but the return of a people to its land. The most ancient roots of this aspiration were religious, but many forms of modern Zionism shed the messianic and eschatological elements of the two-thousand-year-old hope in favour of more immediate political and social aims that were often philosophically shaped.

1 Moses Hess
2 Hibbat-Zion
3 Land and language
4 Socialist Zionism
5 Martin Buber

1 Moses Hess

The most important philosophical forerunner of Zionism was Moses Hess (1812–75). Against the background of the unification of Italy in 1859, Hess saw the quest of the Jewish people for renewed nationhood as 'the last national problem'. Philosophically, his vision was shaped by Hegelian philosophy (see HEGELIANISM), an enthusiastic response to the philosophy of SPINOZA, and the Fichtean idea of *Bestimmung*, destiny, an idea that conveyed at once a sense of mission and of objective historical laws setting the parameters of that mission's fulfilment. The historic mission of the Jewish people was to spread the idea of universal human harmony throughout the world and so to contribute to the global struggle for social and national liberation. But that ancient mission could be achieved only if the people of Israel could re-establish its own state.

Hess's metaphysical conceptualization of Israel's mission among the nations did not diminish the concreteness of his attention to the anomalies of diaspora Jewish life. His prescriptions for renewal and normalization in the historic Jewish homeland anticipated many of the ideas proclaimed half a century later by the labour Zionist movement. A friend and co-worker of the young Karl MARX, Hess was a pioneer both of socialism and of Zionism, and particularly of socialist Zionism. His *Rom und Jerusalem* (Rome and Jerusalem) (1862) evoked no positive responses when first published. Only some thirty years later, with the founding of the Zionist organization, was the book retrieved from oblivion and made integral to Zionist ideology. Although unsystematic and often favouring intuition and sentiment over rigorous argument as a guide to its speculation, the work endures as a monument and anchor of philosophical Zionism.

2 Hibbat-Zion

Zionist ideas were spread through eastern Europe by the Hibbat-Zion movement, which drew its inspiration from Jewish tradition. Religious longing for 'the Land' joined with disappointment in the fruits of the emancipation promised by Enlightenment rhetoric. These emotions far outweighed any philosophical deliberations in the rise of Zionism as a popular ideology. But Leopold Pinsker and Ahad Ha'am did give a philosophical bent to Hibbat-Zion.

Pinsker (1821–91) began his celebrated pamphlet *Auto-Emancipation* (1882) with an analysis of anti-Semitism. Like Hess, he argued that the Jewish people is a distinct ethnicity that cannot be assimilated – not that Jews will not integrate into the societies in which they live but that in the long run they are not tolerated, not allowed to do so. Hatred towards Jews, 'Judophobia', Pinsker argued, was the chief cause of Jewish separateness (see ANTI-SEMITISM), and the perennial isolation of Jews as outsiders can be overcome only when Jews become once again a proper nation with a state of their own, regaining their own homeland and the chance to live in peace and dignity like any other nation. Among his chief goads in writing *Auto-Emancipation*, Pinsker confesses, were Spinoza's parallel but more negatively couched remarks at the end of the third chapter of the *Tractatus Theologico-politicus*.

Theodor Herzl, the founder of political Zionism, devoted his *Der Judenstaat* (The Jewish State) (1896) to elaborating Pinsker's thesis that 'the Jewish problem' could be solved only if the Jews were no longer a national anomaly. Yet Herzl's role as a visionary statesman and powerful journalist did not make him a philosopher.

AHAD HA'AM (Asher Ginzberg, 1856–1927) is a thinker of a different stamp. Although no systematic philosopher, he was deeply influenced by nineteenth-century evolutionist ideas, especially those of Herbert SPENCER. His outlook never became the main road of Zionist thinking, but it had a powerful impact on Zionist theory. Jewish particularity, he argued, is grounded in a spontaneous sentiment of national belonging. The sentiment, akin to family ties, needs no theoretical justification or argument. For such feelings are prior to consciousness itself. A nation's 'will to live' is a resultant of every individual's will to live. But the Jewish situation engenders problems of special complexity – most portentously, that of assimilation. A 'spiritual centre' in Palestine, Ahad Ha'am argued, would constitute an effective barrier against assimilation: here Judaism could be preserved, and the identity of the Jews of the diaspora would be assured by the ideas radiating from this centre. Tragically, however, Ahad Ha'am neglected the underlying problem of anti-Semitism and its pressures towards assimilation, isolation and, in the extreme, annihilation of the Jews.

3 Land and language

Jacob Klatzkin (1882–1948), whose intellectual work dealt mainly with medieval Jewish philosophy and

Spinoza, also elaborated a philosophical Jewish nationalism. He castigated the tendency of Reform Jews to transform Judaism into a merely spiritual idea. This 'trying to be a Jew without being Jewish' (*Jude-Sein ohne Jüdisch-Sein*) only paves the way to assimilation. But Orthodoxy is equally flawed. Where the reformers seemed to reduce Judaism to a spiritual mission, Orthodoxy reduced Jewishness to mere norms of practice – just another subjective criterion of Jewishness. If Jewishness is to be a durable fact, Klatzkin argued, it cannot be a matter of religion or morality. For to be a Jew no longer entails a particular religious or spiritual commitment. Rather, the subjective historical will to belong to the Jewish people finds its objective expression in the fact of national belonging. The spiritual influence of Judaism on other religions and on Western culture was undeniable, and Klatzkin did not deny the distinctive spirit of Judaism and of Jewish ethics and values. But he bitterly opposed efforts to make these the national paradigms or foci. Jewish nationalism must be rooted in the objective ground of land and language. The very survival of the Jewish people demanded that the Jewish people abandon its inveterate intellectualizing and spiritualizing and resume national life in its own homeland, with its own language.

Klatzkin's arguments were fraught with conceptual shortcomings. His thesis that 'only forms can serve as national criteria', for example, led him to define 'land' and 'language' as national forms, denying them material content! But even such philosophically dubious moves do not diminish the importance of his recognition that the will to settle on one's own land and speak one's own language is vital to Jewish peoplehood. Nor did Klatzkin underrate such external factors as hatred directed against Jews as such, the persecution and discrimination that Ahad Ha'am had underrated. A mere spiritual centre in Palestine would not be enough. Only a national home would resolve the Jewish question.

The inference was clear: the modern definition of a Jew is secular. Only those whose homeland is Palestine and whose language is Hebrew (or who aspire to achieve this) can be Jews. Klatzkin's arbitrary definition of Jewishness in effect excludes all Jews who continue to live outside Israel and do not intend to settle there. It was perhaps his exclusion of the bulk of diaspora Jewry that in the end marginalized Klatzkin as a Zionist thinker and led to his playing only a minor role in the unfolding of Zionist thought.

4 Socialist Zionism

Among the Zionist thinkers who deserve philosophical attention, Nahman Syrkin (1868–1924) developed an early synthesis of socialism and Zionism, and Ber Norochov (1881–1917) went further in the same direction. Borochov grounded his reflections in a distinctive version of the Marxist idea of class struggle. Without a country of their own, he reasoned, Jews remain a powerless minority, confined to 'unproductive' and peripheral pursuits, petty and secondary trades. Barred from heavy industry, 'the axle of the historical wheel', they cannot become true proletarians and so lack a 'strategic base' for carrying forward the class struggle. Jewish 'proletarization' will occur only when the 'inverted pyramid' of Jewish economic life is returned to its broad base; and only in their own country will Jewish workers be able to struggle successfully against the bourgeoisie and win their way to a healthy and independent economic life. Socialism and Zionism are thus necessarily intertwined. Borochov, accordingly, unlike many a Marxist and bourgeois Jewish thinker, condemned assimilation: not only will it never succeed but even its pursuit is a dangerous illusion, since it turns Jews away from the struggle for national emancipation. Efforts to emigrate from Europe to other countries such as those of North and South America, similarly, will only perpetuate the anomaly of the diaspora. What Jews must do is return to their own country, Palestine. Many of Borochov's Marxist notions about Jewish nationhood now require critical re-examination. But his thinking had a powerful impact on labour Zionism and endures in the recognition that labour must be the foundation of the restored Jewish nation.

Among the non-Marxist socialist Zionists, A.D. Gordon, Berl Katznelson and their disciples were especially important. For them Zionism begins in a voluntary act of the individual, affirming the dignity of physical labour and of ties to the soil. These rather agrarian thinkers aspired to create a new Jew to replace the dispossessed Jews of the diaspora. J.H. Brenner and others, influenced by Nietzsche, similarly denounced what they saw as a diaspora mentality and demanded a radical break with the Jewish spiritual heritage. But here, as with Klatzkin, the exclusionary tendency in the end proved more limiting to the influence of its authors than to the scope and appeal of the Zionist idea.

5   Martin Buber

Finally, Martin BUBER played an important role in shaping Zionist consciousness among young Jews in western Europe, especially through his famous *Drei Reden über das Judentum* (Three Addresses on Judaism) (1909–11). In time his Zionist thought was overshadowed by his studies of Hasidism and the Bible and above all by his dialogical philosophy and social thinking. But Buber's Zionism carried forward some of the utopian socialist ideas developed by A.D. Gordon and the anarchist G. Landauer. It grew into what he called Hebrew Humanism, which found the differentia of Zionism from other national movements in its idealism. In keeping with his philosophical vision and with the universalism that he drew from the wellsprings of Jewish moral thought, Buber was among the first and most important Zionist theorists seriously to address the issue of Jewish–Arab relations. His philosophical humanism led him to insist that Jews and Arabs should live together in peace and harmony in a common homeland. But at the time of their enunciation these claims were not taken up by most Zionists as integral to the Zionist programme.

The foregoing examples of philosophical Zionism, exemplified in the writings of its 'founding fathers' are hardly a comprehensive listing. Many other philosophers have engaged in theoretical exploration of the promise and problems of Zionism – among them, J. Kaufmann, J. Klausner, F. Weltsch, M. Brod, N. Rotenstreich, Y. LEIBOWITZ, M.M. KAPLAN, A.J. HESCHEL, A. Neher and E. LEVINAS. Still other names would need to be mentioned if one were to address the politically divergent views within Zionism, such as Zionist Revisionism. But despite the importance and originality of the living exponents of Zionist thinking, they all belong to a generation for whom Zionism is a *fait accompli*, a living reality, whose theorists, perforce, must now regard not only its 'roots' but – to continue the metaphor – the cultivation of its varied and multi-coloured 'flowers'.

On the theoretico-philosophical plane, a controversy has arisen recently concerning whether contemporary Judaism and the State of Israel belong already to a post-Zionist era, characterized by coexistence between the State of Israel and diaspora Judaism. The majority of the present-day immigrants to Israel (mainly from Russia and Ethiopia) do not migrate out of Zionist conviction but for pragmatic reasons – to exchange their adverse living conditions for better ones. This, however, reaffirms the Zionist idea that a Jewish homeland is the solution to their existential problems in the diaspora.

See also: ANTI-SEMITISM; BUBER, M.; HA'AM, AHAD; JEWISH PHILOSOPHY, CONTEMPORARY; LEIBOWITZ, Y.; NATION AND NATIONALISM; POLITICAL PHILOSOPHY, HISTORY OF

References and further reading

Avineri, S. (1981) *The Making of Modern Zionism*, London: Weidenfeld & Nicolson. (A historical survey of the unfolding of Zionist theory.)

* Buber, M. (1909–11) *Drei Reden über das Judentum* (Three Addresses on Judaism), Frankfurt: Rütten & Löning; trans. E. Jospe, 'Three Addresses on Judaism', in N. Glatzer (ed.) *On Judaism*, New York: Schocken, 1967. (On Judaism and Jews, Judaism and humanity, and the renewal of Judaism by Zionism.)

Borochow, B. (1937) *Nationalism and the Class Struggle*, selections ed. M. Cohen, New Brunswick, NJ: Transaction Books. (A Marxian view of Zionism as the solution to the 'Jewish Problem'.)

Cohen, I. (1946) *The Zionist Movement*, New York: The Zionist Organization of America. (History and issues of Zionism, with a supplementary chapter on the Zionist movement in America.)

Halpern, B. (1969) *The Idea of the Jewish State*, Cambridge, MA: Harvard University Press. (Historical survey.)

Heller, J. (1949) *The Zionist Idea*, New York: Harper & Row. (Ideological analysis and survey.)

Hertzberg, A. (ed.) (1970) *The Zionist Idea*, Westport, CT: Greenwood Press. (Anthology about the intellectual history of the Zionist movement.)

* Herzl, T. (1896) *Der Judenstaat. Versuch einer modernen Loesung der juedischen Frage* (The Jewish State: Attempt at a Modern Solution to the Jewish Question), New York: American Zionist Emergency Council, 1946. (Proposes the creation of a Jewish state in Palestine (or Argentina) as a prerequisite for organized migration and settlement, in order to solve the Jewish question.)

* Hess, M. (1862) *Rom und Jerusalem: Die letzte Nationalitätenfrage (Rome and Jerusalem: The Last Questions of Nationality)*, Cologne, Vienna: R. Löwit, 1918; trans. M.J. Bloom, *Rome and Jerusalem*, New York: Philosophical Library, 1958. (Protozionist classic.)

Klatzkin, J. (1921) *Krisis und Entscheidung im Judentum* (Crisis and Decision for Jewry), Berlin: Jüdischer Verlag. (An analysis of Jewish existence and nationality, of diaspora versus Palestine as a national centre.)

* Pinsker, L. (1882) '"Autoemancipation": Mahnruf an seine Stammesgenossen von einem russischen Juden'; *Auto-Emancipation*, London: Federation of Zionist Youth, 1936. (An analysis of the psychological and social roots of antisemitism and call for the establishment of a Jewish homeland as a national centre.)

Sokolow, N. (1919) *History of Zionism*, London: Longman, Green, 2 vols. (Traces the origins of the Zionist movement.)

Z. LEVY

ZONGMI (780–841)

Zongmi was a Chinese Buddhist Chan (Zen) and Huayan scholar, traditionally reckoned as the fifth 'patriarch' both in the Heze line of Southern Chan and in the Huayan scholastic tradition. He is important for his revision of Huayan doctrine, his commentaries to the Yuanjuejing *(Scripture of Perfect Enlightenment), his accounts of Chan teachings and his contribution to the theory of the essential unity of the three teachings of Buddhism, Confucianism and Daoism.*

Zongmi (more fully, Guifeng Zongmi) was born into a family of local prominence in a town in the southwestern province of Sichuan. As a youth he received a traditional education in the Confucian classics; he became interested in Buddhism as an adolescent, but continued his Confucian studies at a local academy in preparation for the imperial examinations that would open the door to an official career. In 804, however, he met the Chan master Daoyuan and was so impressed that he abandoned his worldly ambitions to become the latter's disciple. Later, while still a novice monk, he experienced his first awakening after reading a few pages of the *Yuanjuejing* (Scripture of Perfect Enlightenment). Zongmi continued his Chan study under Daoyuan, receiving full ordination in 807.

In 810, Zongmi was introduced to the commentary and subcommentary to the *Avatamsaka Sūtra* written by the eminent Huayan scholar Chengguan (738–839). These works so impressed him that in 812 he became a disciple of Chengguan and studied intensively with him for two years in the imperial capital of Changan. He subsequently embarked on an extensive reading of the Buddhist canon. In 816 he left the capital to continue his research at various temples on Mount Zhongnan, where he spent much of the remainder of his life. This period of prolonged study bore fruit in a series of definitive commentaries and subcommentaries to the *Yuanjuejing* completed during 823 and 824.

In 828 Zongmi was invited to court, where he was honoured with a purple robe and the title of 'Great Worthy'. He returned to Mount Zhongnan a year or two later, where he carried on an active correspondence with a number of the leading scholar-officials he had met in Changan. He also wrote two major works on Chan, *Chanyuan zhuquanji duxu* (Preface to the Collected Writings on the Source of Chan) and *Zhonghua chuanxindi chanmen shizi chengxi tu* (Chart of the Master Disciple Succession within the Chan School That Transmits the Mind Ground in China). His scholarly activity came to an abrupt end in 835, when he became implicated in an abortive attempt to oust the eunuchs from power at court. Afterwards he withdrew from public life, and nothing further is known about him until his death in 841.

Zongmi's work can be seen as the culmination of a number of themes important in the evolution of the medieval Chinese Buddhist scholastic enterprise. By simplifying the doctrinal complexities of earlier scholasticism, it achieved a greater coherence and systematic unity. Philosophically, it illustrates the tendency within Chinese Buddhism to de-emphasize the teaching of emptiness, which undermines ontological speculation (see BUDDHIST CONCEPT OF EMPTINESS), by elaborating the ontological implications within the Indian Buddhist doctrine of the *tathāgatagarbha* (the potentiality for Buddhahood inherent in all sentient beings, more popularly referred to as Buddha-nature) (see BUDDHIST PHILOSOPHY, CHINESE).

In the context of the Huayan tradition, Zongmi's systematic classification of Buddhist teachings marks a significant revision of the tradition from its classical formulation by FAZANG (643–712). Most significantly, Zongmi omitted the Perfect Teaching, which Fazang had ranked highest in his fivefold scheme, and, in its stead he raised to pre-eminence the teaching that Fazang had merely ranked third. The teaching that was displaced had elaborated the unimpeded interrelation of all phenomena, and was precisely that which Fazang had taken to express the most profound insight of the Buddha, which was revealed exclusively in the *Avatamsaka Sūtra* and was therefore the basis of the Huayan tradition's claim to represent the most exalted teaching of Buddhism. Textually, Zongmi's rearrangement of Buddhist teachings signals his displacement of the *Avatamsaka Sūtra* in favour of the *Yuanjuejing* as the ultimate basis of Huayan thought; doctrinally, it reveals his emphasis on the *tathāgatagarbha* as the most fundamental teaching of the Buddha.

The revision that Zongmi made in Huayan doctrinal classification can be understood as part of his effort to provide an ontological basis for Buddhist practice. His revalorization of Huayan thought in turn points back to his involvement with, and reaction to, various developments that had taken place within Chan. The iconoclastic rhetoric of the radical movements that had gained currency within Chinese Chan during the later part of the Tang

dynasty (618–907) could easily be misinterpreted in antinomian ways that denied the need for spiritual cultivation and moral discipline. Having grown up and received his early Chan training in Sichuan, an area in which the most extreme of these movements flourished in the late eighth and early ninth centuries, Zongmi was particularly sensitive to such ethical dangers. Zongmi's concern with the ethical implications of Chan teachings, moreover, reflects the lasting influence of his early study of the Confucian classics.

The importance of Confucianism for Zongmi can be seen in his attempt to develop a syncretic framework in which Confucian moral teachings could be integrated within Buddhism. He thus claimed that the differences among the three teachings of Buddhism, Confucianism and Daoism were a matter of expedients, being a function of the particular historical circumstances in which they were taught and having nothing to do with level of understanding attained by each of the three sages (Buddha, Confucius and Laozi). Zongmi's writings demonstrate his life-long effort to justify the values that he had learned as a youth in terms of the discrepant claims of the religion to which he had converted as an adult.

See also: BUDDHIST PHILOSOPHY, CHINESE; CONFUCIAN PHILOSOPHY, CHINESE; FAZANG

List of works

Zongmi (780–841) *Chanyuan zhuquanji duxu* (Preface to the Collected Writings on the Source of Chan), ed. and trans. J.L. Broughton, 'Kuei-feng Tsung-mi: The Convergence of Ch'an and the Teachings', Ph.D. dissertation, Columbia University, 1975. (The thesis contains an annotated translation of Zongmi's *Chanyuan zhuquanji duxu*.)
—— (780–841) *Zhonghua chuanxindi chanmen shizi chengxi tu* (Chart of the Master Disciple Succession within the Chan School That Transmits the Mind Ground in China).
—— (780–841) *Yuanrenlun* (Inquiry into the Origin of Humanity), ed. and trans. P.N. Gregory, *Inquiry into the Origin of Humanity: An Annotated Translation of Tsung-mi's Yüan jen lun with a Modern Commentary*, Honolulu, HI: University of Hawaii Press, 1995. (Uses a translation and commentary to Zongmi's *Yuanrenlun* as a means of presenting medieval Chinese Buddhist thought to the nonspecialist.)

References and further reading

Gregory, P.N. (1991) *Tsung-mi and the Sinification of Buddhism*, Princeton, NJ: Princeton University

Press. (The most comprehensive treatment of Zongmi's life and thought within the context of Chinese Buddhism and Chinese intellectual history.)

Jan Yün-hua (1972) 'Tsung-mi: His Analysis of Ch'an Buddhism', *T'oung Pao* 58: 1–54. (Good introduction to Zongmi's life and understanding of Chan.)

PETER N. GREGORY

ZOROASTRIANISM

Zarathushtra, better known to the Classical and modern world in the Greek form of his name 'Zoroaster', revealed his vision of truth, wisdom and justice in the verse texts known as the Gāthās *(c.1200–1000 BC) and is revered by Zoroastrians as their holy prophet. The religion is correctly described as* mazdāyasna, *'the worship of Ahura ('Lord') Mazdā, creator of the world and source of all goodness. Since the Avestan word* mazdā *means 'wise, wisdom', Zoroastrians see their prophet as the original* philoso-phos, *'lover of wisdom'. Zarathushtra's message is primarily ethical and rationalistic. Zoroastrianism teaches a life based on (1) the avoidance of evil, through rigorous discrimination between good and evil, and (2) the service of wisdom through the cherishing of seven ideals. These latter are personified as seven immortal, beneficent spirits: Ahura Mazdā himself, conceived as the creative 'holy' spirit; Sublime Truth; Virtuous Power; Good Purpose/Mind; Beneficent Piety; Wholeness/Health and, finally, Immortality. Evil originates neither from God nor from his creatures, but from a wholly other source, personified as Angra Mainyu, the 'Hostile Spirit', whose existence is ritually and doctrinally rejected as being pretended and parasitic. Real existence is solely the domain of Ahura Mazdā and his creation; Angra Mainyu and his demons are actually states of negativity, denial or, as the religion puts it, 'the Lie'. Thus the charge that the religion is ontologically dualistic is no more true than it is of other systems which conceive of good and evil as being in fundamental opposition. Equally, the allegation that its theology is ditheistic or polytheistic is a misunderstanding of the Zoroastrian theological and ritual tradition. The influence which this religion has exerted on classical philosophy and the thought and practice of Judaism, Christianity and Islam is being reappraised by scholars in modern times.*

1   **Prophet and community**
2   **Cosmology and doctrine**
3   **Moral and physical purification**

1   Prophet and community

The Iranian prophet Zarathushtra founded one of the world's oldest and most enduring religions many centuries before Jesus of Nazareth and several millennia before Nietzsche's usurpation of the name (see NIETZSCHE, F. §10). Zoroastrianism was the religion of pre-Islamic Iran and survives to this day in one of the world's smallest and most widely dispersed communities, the Iranian Zardushtis and their Indian 'Parsi' co-religionists. In the classical world and in pre-modern Europe, the figure of Zoroaster has been associated, in esoteric and popular circles, with a mysterious and arcane wisdom, but the actual religious tradition which bears his name is generally unknown, or underestimated as to its historical importance.

Zoroastrianism was the principal religion of the Iranians under the Achaemenian, Parthian and Sasanian empires for a thousand years from the sixth century BC, and as the state church of the Sasanian kings in their long wars against Rome it clashed directly with Christianity. It was disestablished by the Islamic conquest of Iran in the mid-seventh century AD, and since then Zoroastrians have lived as a dispossessed religious minority in their homeland. As a result of religious persecution, a number of them migrated to northwest India in the tenth century AD and established the Parsi ('Persian') community. Their descendants flourished in the Indian milieu, first as agriculturalists, then as traders, merchants and entrepreneurs in the colonial and postcolonial periods. Zoroastrianism is an ethnic religion which generally does not accept converts; in modern times the problems of the community's demographic decline have worsened as a result of inter-marriage, secularization and emigration to Western countries from India, Pakistan and post-revolutionary Iran. The total number of Zoroastrians worldwide is reckoned to be less than 120,000.

Zarathushtra's revelation is preserved in the *Gāthās*, a small body of very ancient hymns dated by scholars as originating from the latter part of the second millennium BC and written in a northeastern Iranian language, Gāthic Avestan. The *Gāthās* are the oldest stratum of a larger scriptural canon, known collectively as the *Avesta*, which were originally transmitted orally and subsequently written down in Avestan (a language related closely to Sanskrit). As a result of the destruction of the priesthood and their lore at the hands of Alexander the Great (forever cursed by the tradition) and the later Muslim conquerors, only one fifth of the original *Avesta* survives. The *Avesta* was from ancient times accompanied by an exegetical body of texts known as the

Zand. This *Zand* is extant now only in a later, Middle Persian language, Pahlavi, written down in its present form in the Sasanian and early Islamic periods (4th–10th centuries AD). Taken on their own, without the evidence of these later books, the *Gāthās* are difficult to interpret because of their prehistoric context and archaic symbolism: the study of the *Gāthās* continues to divide modern scholars, with regard to dating, geography and the precise nature of Zarathushtra's teachings. However, the Zoroastrian tradition as preserved in the Avestan and Pahlavi texts gives a clearer picture of the prophet and his mission. Zarathushtra refers to himself as a priest of his ancestral religion, skilled in its ritual and teachings. Dissatisfied, however, he went in search of a nobler doctrine to deliver the world from the tyranny of oppressors and, after years spent wandering, at the age of thirty he received the first of many visions from Ahura Mazdā. His prophetic mission lasted the rest of his life, receiving and delivering the divine message to those who would listen until, as tradition says, he was killed by an assassin in his old age.

2 Cosmology and doctrine

According to Zoroastrian doctrine, before all existence there were two spirits, one good, creative of life, and beneficent; the other one evil, inimical to life, and malevolent. The two spirits are eternally opposed to one another. Ahura Mazdā is identified in the tradition with the spirit of goodness, called Spenta Mainyu, translated as 'Holy or Beneficent Spirit'; he created first the spiritual then the physical worlds as a means of combating and finally annihilating Angra Mainyu, the 'Hostile Spirit'. The physical world was originally perfect when created, but was invaded and is now afflicted by the Hostile Spirit. Zarathushtra urges those who will listen to choose goodness and smite evil by aligning themselves with Ahura Mazdā and his spiritual helpers, the *amesha spentas*, 'blessed immortals' and *yazatas* '[beings] worthy of worship'. Human beings have a soul, embodied in this physical world, which is part of an eternal nature that remains in the spiritual world. The human soul records a person's acts of virtue and wickedness which will be respectively rewarded and atoned for in a spiritual state after one life in the physical state. The religion advocates purity in thought, word and deed, as Angra Mainyu and his demons benefit from all acts of wickedness and defilement of Ahura Mazdā's creation. Human life is therefore a constant struggle for both goodness and purity. Towards the end of human history a *saoshyant*, 'one who brings benefit', will come to champion the victory of the righteous over the forces of evil. Time will end, there will be a

resurrection of all the dead and a last judgment of all souls. A new, spiritually and physically perfect world will be made here on earth, and evil will be banished for eternity from the universe. There will be a return to the pristine perfection of the original creation, but with the fullness of physical and spiritual multiplicity of forms unafflicted by evil in a state called *Frashokereti* ('Renovation'). The religion is thus based on a vision which is primarily soteriological and eschatological, promising deliverance from imperfection, through human effort aligned with the divine will. There is also a sophisticated philosophical theology which reflects on Zoroastrian salvation history, cosmology and ethics, contained in some of the Pahlavi books, notably the *Dēnkard*, based upon older Avestan material which is now lost.

3 Moral and physical purification

Zarathushtra's vision became embedded in a sacramental liturgical tradition which is a continuation and elaboration of the pre-Zoroastrian cult. Scholars believe that in remote antiquity an Indo-Iranian civilization of Central Asia comprised one great cultural and linguistic group, living a semi-nomadic pastoral existence on the inner Asian steppes. Their common religious tradition would have been formed in the fourth to third millennia BC, and thus when, around 1800 BC, the Indians and Iranians separated and began to move to what are now their respective homelands, they took with them the basis of what became the related religious cultures of Brahmanism and Zoroastrianism (see HINDU PHILOSOPHY). Over time they articulated their religious cult and beliefs in distinctive ways, but both share a fundamental regard for the world as *alive with divinity*, needing maintenance, through spiritual and physical acts, which refresh and reconsecrate the elements and of the cosmos as a whole. The central religious act was the rite called *yasna* in Avestan, *yajña* in Vedic Sanskrit, literally 'act of worship', performed in order to re-enact the primordial cosmic sacrifice by which the universe was begun. In Zoroastrianism, although it is an elaborate ceremony, it is essentially an act of reconsecration of the elements of the world: metal, water, earth, plant, animal, human and fire.

The common basis of the Indian and Iranian religious traditions is also exemplified by the cognate words of Vedic Sanskrit *ṛta* and Zoroastrian Avestan *asha*, both of which mean 'order, law, truth', the highest principle in the universe. *Asha* also means spiritual and moral righteousness: the righteous man is called *ashavan*, as distinct from the *dregvant*, the one who adheres to evil (Avestan *drug*). Zarathushtra's message is a transformation of the old Indo-

Iranian religion, which emphasizes as paramount the *human* (as opposed to superhuman) ethical responsibility for the maintenance of the world through the fight against the forces of disorder. The beliefs and practices of Zoroastrianism all aim at achieving a harmony of the human world with that of nature, physical, spiritual and divine. The Blessed Immortals named in the *Gāthās* were associated with the elements of the physical world, not as merely symbolic correspondences but as the potent invisible realities which protect and inhabit the elements of the physical world. The living world of plants and animals, and the rest of the natural world, is felt to be alive with divinity, not in a pantheistic sense of a 'nature-cult', but because the physical and spiritual realms of existence are thought to be mutually sustained and protected. This is the basis of the moral and physical code of purity in Zoroastrianism. Fire, for example, is revered not in itself but as the manifestation of the Blessed Immortal Asha Vahishta 'Best Righteousness/ Law', and has the epithet 'truth-strong fire'. The dubbing of Zoroastrians as 'Fire-worshippers' is an old and obvious misunderstanding of the religion.

Zoroastrians understand purity as both moral and physical: physical purity is an essential requirement for any religious or moral action. Although the physical world is vulnerable to pollution, it must be emphasized that it is not intrinsically polluted or inferior to the spiritual state. The traditional daily regime of purification for the laity and particularly the priesthood might be thought strenuous by non-Zoroastrians, but this is seen as enhancing the state of persons in physicality, not diminishing their condition of embodiment. As far as is known there have never been any tendencies towards the ascetic practices of self-mortification found in other religions. Little has been said in this entry of the complex ritual and liturgy of the traditional practice of priesthood and laity. Modernist tendencies in the contemporary community question the value of the traditional forms of practice, while conservative elements adhere to them as unchangeable. Underlying all forms of Zoroastrianism, however, is the belief that the example of Zarathushtra and his *spenta daēna* ('virtuous conception') of humanity express a true human potentiality to reflect the divine nature.

See also: ILLUMINATION; NEOPLATONISM; RELIGION, PHILOSOPHY OF

References and further reading

There is no complete English translation of the Avestan and Pahlavi scriptures. However, Boyce (1984: 161–5) provides a bibliography of sources.

Boyce, M. (1975–) *A History of Zoroastrianism*, Leiden: Brill. (The most authoritative scholarly treatment of the subject to date. Volumes 1, 2 and 3 have been published.)

—— (1977) *A Persian Stronghold of Zoroastrianism*, Oxford: Universities of America Press, 1989. (Ethnographic study of Zoroastrians in pre-revolutionary Iran.)

—— (1979) *Zoroastrians, their Beliefs and Practices*, London: Routledge & Kegan Paul; 3rd revised repr. 1988. (Succinct account of the religion.)

—— (1984) *Textual Sources for the Study of Zoroastrianism*, Manchester: Manchester University Press. (New, reliable translations of major texts.)

* de Menasce, J. (1973) *Le troisième livre du Dēnkart*, Paris: Travaux de l'Institut d'Etudes Iraniennes de l'Université de Paris III, 5, Bibliothèque des Oeuvres Classiques Persanes, 4. (The only European translation of this important philosophical text.)

* Insler, S.H. (1975) *The Gāthās of Zarathustra*, Acta Iranica 8, Leiden: Brill. (Scholarly translation of the oldest Zoroastrian scripture.)

Kulke, E. (1974) *The Parsis in India, A Minority as Agent of Social Change*, Munich: Verlag. (On Parsis in the modern world.)

Williams, A.V. (1989) 'The Body and the Boundaries of Zoroastrian Spirituality', *Religion* 19: 227–39. (On purity and pollution in the scheme of cosmology.)

—— (1990) *The Pahlavi Rivāyat Accompanying the Dādestān ī Dēnīg*, Copenhagen: Royal Danish Academy of Sciences and Letters, 2 vols. (Representative miscellany of ninth-century Pahlavi religious genres.)

—— (1997) 'Later Zoroastrianism', in I. Mahalingam and B. Carr (eds) *Companion Encyclopedia of Asian Philosophy*, London, Routledge, 24–45. (On the philosophy and theology of the Pahlavi books.)

ALAN WILLIAMS